The Motion Picture Guide

★ ★ ★ ★ ★ ★ ★ ★ ★ ★ ★ ★ ★ ★ ★ ★ ★ ★ ★

1999 Annual

THE MOTION PICTURE GUIDE

★ ★ ★ ★ ★ ★ ★ ★ ★ ★ ★ ★ ★ ★ ★ ★ ★ ★ ★

1999 ANNUAL (THE FILMS OF 1998)

Editor : Edmond Grant
Associate Editor : Ken Fox

CineBooks

Published by CineBooks, a division of News America Publishing Group Incorporated,
620 Avenue of the Americas, 6th Floor, New York, NY 10011

First Edition
Printed in the United States
1 2 3 4 5 6 7 8 9 10

Library of Congress Catalog Number 8571145

ISBN: 0-933997-00-0 THE MOTION PICTURE GUIDE (10 Vols.)
ISBN: 0-933997-11-6 THE MOTION PICTURE GUIDE INDEX (2 Vols.)
ISBN: 0-933997-41-8 THE MOTION PICTURE GUIDE 1998 ANNUAL (THE FILMS OF 1997)
ISBN: 0-933997-43-4 THE MOTION PICTURE GUIDE 1999 ANNUAL (THE FILMS OF 1998)

TABLE OF CONTENTS

FOREWORD

The 1999 *Motion Picture Guide Annual*, covering films released during 1998, is the fourteenth supplement to the original, twelve-volume *Motion Picture Guide*. As the number of films released in America grows each and every year, so does the MPG annual; this edition contains 700 titles, more than any past volume in the series. We pride ourselves on being the only reference guide to cover the broad spectrum of films available to American viewers. We include both theatrical and home-video features, offering entertaining and enlightening in-depth reviews of everything from Hollywood blockbusters to no-budget independent efforts, high-profile foreign imports to Hong Kong action movies and Japanese anime, "adult" melodramas to wholesome family fare, experimental features to the bumper crop of straight-to-video and made-for-cable fare. We'd like to acknowledge our fine staff of expert reviewers for doing such excellent work, and single out Associate Editor Ken Fox for his invaluable technical contribution to the preparation of the book and his uncanny eye for detail. Editorial Assistant Melanie Asofsky provided valuable help in dealing with the raw mass of credits which makes up so much of the book. Angelo Virgona, Brandon Trenz, and M. Faust deserve special thanks for their excellent work in helping us maintain a consistent tone and format throughout the book. Joe Frazzetta and Stephen Pell produced an obituary section loaded with fascinating details about the year's departed and, as always, we salute Noel Harrington for his patience and expertise in turning our data into a book. We hope you enjoy the fruits of their labors and welcome your comments, which should be sent to us at the address on the copyright page.

Edmond Grant
Editor

Michelle Diliberto
Business Manager

The Year in Review

Is the auteur theory still relevant? The notion that a film is the product of a single, focused imagination (usually that of the director), so central to American film criticism over the past four decades, seems increasingly archaic in a movie marketplace dominated by corporate financing and filmmaking by committee, where it is expected that the costs of marketing and promotion may be as high as the actual costs of the film's production. The hundreds of movies released in the US in 1998 include an incredible amount of near-anonymous product, flowing through multiplex screens and video store shelves and seldom leaving a mark. There's no room for directorial identity in corporate cash engines like GODZILLA, ARMAGEDDON, or DEEP IMPACT. Visionary film artists in other countries who alienate the movie-going public are still able to trade on their critical cachet to find funds for yet another project. But in Hollywood, which values only the art of the deal, it is remarkable when a director is able to preserve his or her vision through to the final edit.

Nevertheless, a small handful of challenging, intelligent, and visually innovative films were able to battle their way onto the few screens allocated across the country for "art-house" releases. The obstacles confronting truly independent filmmakers were particularly evident in the case of Paul Schrader's AFFLICTION, one of the year's most powerful and disturbing films. Schrader's decision to focus on the emotional meltdown of a middle-aged character stood in stark contrast to the sort of character studies produced by the major studios. Despite a cast of well-known stars (two of whom—Nick Nolte and James Coburn—received Oscar nominations for their performances, Coburn taking home the award), it had substantial difficulty finding a distributor. Similar troubles befell the year's most daring American film, Todd Solondz's HAPPINESS, a wildly uneven but compelling dark comedy that included a half-comic, half-tragic look at child molestation, the likes of which had never been seen before in an American production with recognizable stars. Funded by October Films, it was distributed by the production company Good Machine when October's parent company Universal, objecting to its content, refused to finance its release. Subversion from the inside came from Warren Beatty, a well-connected soul in the Hollywood community, with BULWORTH, an acidic political satire that harkened back to the incisive political thrillers and comedies made in Hollywood in the 1970s; the screenplay could have used some fine tuning, but the film's anti-establishment posture made it a wholly unique mainstream Hollywood production.

While other films by seasoned off-mainstream auteurs certainly had their flaws—John Sayles's lyrical and pointed MEN WITH GUNS ran on too long, Hal Hartley's brittle-yet-engaging HENRY FOOL contained oddly discordant "gross-out" sequences, and Woody Allen's ambitious, Altman-like media satire CELEBRITY featured a cloying impression of Allen by Kenneth Branagh—they were nevertheless the works their creators intended them to be. Even the calculated and abrasive BUFFALO '66, the debut feature by character actor Vincent Gallo, got to the public exactly as Gallo desired.

Other auteurs managed to work in or around the Hollywood system in 1998. With OUT OF SIGHT, noted independent director Steven Soderbergh fashioned a wonderfully intelligent, sexy crime movie while essentially working as a mere gun-for-hire. Similarly, when cult horror director Sam Raimi was hired to replace John Boorman on A SIMPLE PLAN, he proved himself a far more versatile and mature artist than previously indicated, with a somber yet suspenseful rendering of a TREASURE OF SIERRA MADRE-like parable. One of 1998's most widely acclaimed films, THE TRUMAN SHOW was an auteurist work with two authors, director Peter Weir and scripter Andrew Niccol. The film harkened back to Weir's best work, as it depicts a man ill at ease with his environment; Niccol's well-balanced script explored both the comic and tragic aspects of the hero's situation, while indicting the media's relation to the common man. Although Hollywood's deep pockets have continued to fund amazing technical advances in what can be created on screen, it takes more than money to find a use for visual technique. The year's most visually striking American films, FEAR AND LOATHING IN LAS VEGAS and VELVET GOLDMINE were both fever-dreams set in the early 1970s. Terry Gilliam's adaptation of Hunter Thompson was the kind of all-out psychedelic odyssey that hasn't been seen since the Age of Aquarius (Oliver Stone aside), while Todd Haynes's vision of glam rock's heyday was fueled not by drugs, but by sexual curiosity. Though each went astray as they proceeded, both films were absorbing sensory experiences, reflecting the singular visions of their creators.

But the most resonant and rewarding works by dyed-in-the-wool visionary filmmakers to appear on American screens in 1998 came from Asia and Europe. Topping the list was Italian comedian Roberto Benigni, whose carefully composed comic fable about a supremely unfunny moment in world history, LIFE IS BEAUTIFUL, placed him firmly in the lineage of Keaton, Chaplin, Tati, and Woody Allen. With LIVE FLESH, Pedro Almodovar proved that his is a truly versatile talent; the taut, absorbing film dispelled once and for all any notion that he only is adept at handling broadly satirical situations. Danish filmmaker Thomas Vinterberg supplied a less apocalyptic, but equally hard-hitting piece of social commentary with his film THE CELEBRATION. Actor Gary Oldman made an impressive debut as a writer-director with the hard-hitting, harshly realistic drama NIL BY MOUTH. Takeshi Kitano, a major celebrity in his home country of Japan, finally achieved a degree of notoriety on these shores with his spare and hardhitting SONATINE and his exquisite FIREWORKS. Hong Kong trendsetter Wong Kar-wai offered up a touching meditation on love and loneliness in his stylish FALLEN ANGELS. And Neil Jordan, whose work inevitably suffers when he leaves home, returned to Ireland to create the disturbing and unforgettable character study THE BUTCHER BOY. Jordan is hardly the only world-class filmmaker to suffer this problem: foreign directors who did subpar work in Hollywood this year include Barbet Schroder (DESPERATE MEASURES), Volker Schlondorff (PALMETTO), and Vincent Ward (WHAT DREAMS MAY COME). Even Jackie Chan was forced to relinquish the creative control that has made him a top box-office attraction everywhere but America in order to score his first bona fide American hit, the wan RUSH HOUR. Of course, a sure auteurist hand is no guarantee of quality. Adrian Lyne's LOLITA was more notable for the terror it struck in controversy-shy American distributors than for its content, reducing taboo subject matter to a teensploitation film with a literary pedigree. Similarly, PSYCHO, YOU'VE GOT MAIL, and CITY OF ANGELS were woefully formulaic and pointless remakes that may have been the brainchildren of separate individuals, but possessed the unmistakably calculated flavor of corporate filmmaking.

Though the year's best films clearly were the products of singular imaginations, Hollywood had its mind set on what it felt was grander game. With the concept of "high art" inextricably tied to the notion of period pieces, the film which stood head and shoulders above the rest in terms of popularity was SHAKESPEARE IN LOVE, a good-natured entertainment that offered viewers a sugar-coated vision of the Bard's life, work, and milieu. Other big-budget period pieces—THE MAN IN THE IRON MASK, LES MISERABLES, COUSIN BETTE, FIRELIGHT, and DANGEROUS BEAUTY—fared poorly with both audiences and critics.

A more recent slice of world history was presented in a fictionalized form in two of the year's most critically acclaimed releases. THE THIN RED LINE, Terrence Malick's cerebral and visceral meditation on war, and Steven Spielberg's SAVING PRIVATE RYAN were prematurely touted as a resuscitation of the dormant war-movie genre. Both films had several things in common: they were lengthy, impassioned accounts of specific episodes in WWII, which featured long battle set-pieces and boasted large ensemble casts peopled with "name" performers. But the two filmmakers approached their material in entirely different ways: Malick's first film in two decades (after what is surely the longest layoff of any non-blacklisted American director) went for a philosophical approach to the dilemma of war, while Spielberg indulged in the kind of flag-waving simplicity found in war movies of the 1930s and '40s. At least Malick's attempt to touch both the mind and the senses reflected a vital cinematic sensibility; Spielberg made a blunt grab for the viewer's emotions—as a puppet master, his strings are always far too apparent.

The same simplistic attitude that characterized the year's historical dramas was strongly evident in Hollywood's latest depictions of the lives of African-Americans. Unfortunately, if a black artist is not of the same social strata as Oprah Winfrey—the prime mover behind Jonathan Demme's adaptation of Toni Morrison's *Beloved*—or Maya Angelou—who made her directorial debut with DOWN IN THE DELTA—the likelihood of getting a decent budget for a three-dimensional depiction of black characters is highly unlikely. There were a few exceptions to this rule, but for every HAV PLENTY, there were several BELLYs and I GOT THE HOOK UPs.

Similarly, in the world of comedy, for every RUSHMORE, there was another Adam Sandler or Eddie Murphy vehicle. Wes Anderson's RUSHMORE was the year's most stylish comic creation, offering an earnestly demented portrait of a singleminded teenage nerd. THE OPPOSITE OF SEX was equally unsentimental in its depiction of a willful teen; the film's memorably sarcastic dialogue and a winning lead turn by the ubiquitous Christina Ricci made the movie into a "sleeper" hit. While farces from noted comic filmmakers flopped at the box office (the Coen Bros. funny but uneven BIG LEBOWSKI, John Waters's overly congenial PECKER, Jim Abrahams's gag-addled JANE AUSTEN'S MAFIA!), the Farrelly Bros. had a major hit with THERE'S SOMETHING ABOUT MARY, the most leisurely paced bad-taste comedy in movie history. Of course, what can one expect comedically from a year in which pot humor came back into style (HOMEGROWN, HALF BAKED), and the stupidly racist KRIPPENDORF'S TRIBE and a sequel to THE ODD COUPLE actually saw the light of day?

It doesn't help that Hollywood is once again in a cycle of targeting younger viewers, inevitably lowering the overall quality of its product. The success of SCREAM and SCREAM 2 opened the floodgates not only to a wave of similar teen-oriented horror films (I STILL KNOW WHAT YOU DID LAST SUMMER, DISTURBING BEHAVIOR, URBAN LEGEND, THE FACULTY), but to a tidal wave of teen relationship movies that dwarves even the John Hughes swell of the mid-1980s, a wave that seemed to be approaching its crest in the early months of 1999.

Some interesting phenomena occurred in the nearly auteurless world of home video releases. Younger viewers who had been hooked by recent big-screen animated films (themselves a growing field, as other studios seek to cash in on what has traditionally been a Disney niche) were reharvested with such direct-to-video sequels (all reviewed in the following pages) as LION KING II: SIMBA'S PRIDE, POCAHONTAS II: JOURNEY TO A NEW WORLD, THE BRAVE LITTLE TOASTER GOES TO MARS, and FERN-GULLY 2: THE MAGICAL RESCUE; on the live-action side of things, name performers picked up quick paychecks in CASPER MEETS WENDY and DENNIS THE MENACE STRIKES AGAIN. Video store shelves also offered proof that the indie/art house boom, so heavily hyped in the mid-1990s, was over. More and more lower-budgeted features went the "Cable Premiere" route before being released on video, indicating the low esteem in which their distributors hold them. Films featuring name performers, which might have been expected to appear in at least a few theaters, instead arrived on video with little fanfare (THE NIGHT AND THE MOMENT, MUSIC FROM ANOTHER ROOM) and, in some cases, with misleadingly generic titles (SUMMER FLING, ROYAL DECEIT).

It seems that a filmmaker with a clear vision has only two choices: be amenable to change and inordinate compromise in order to woo Hollywood money, or do it yourself, with help from private investors and foreign production companies. In 1998, a seminal work by Orson Welles, a master filmmaker who tried both approaches, was rereleased. The "director's cut" of TOUCH OF EVIL proved that Welles's flamboyant modernism was far ahead of its time, retaining a power and enthusiasm that puts current-day multiplex fare to shame. Welles also made the news when CITIZEN KANE (1941) ranked at the top of the highly contested "100 Greatest American Movies" poll conducted by the American Film Institute. KANE may still be universally acknowledged as the most influential and important American film of all time, but its creator wound up a veritable joke in the film capital, acting in awful movies and appearing on even worse TV series in order to raise funds to make a film in his native land. More now than ever, in the Hollywood of craftsmen like James Cameron and businessmen like George Lucas, Welles would inevitably still be getting the short end of the stick. Of course, one can only speculate about what he might have come up with in the straight-to-video "Cable Premiere" arena, but chances are that he'd simply be competing for the same few art-house screens, while still traveling overseas to look for completion funds....

Edmond Grant
New York City
April 1999

Country(ies) of Origin & Release Year — Title — Production Co(s). ~ Distributor — Running Time — Star Rating — Color (c) or Black & White (bw) — Also Known As

LIFE IS BEAUTIFUL ★★★★

(Italy, 1997) 114m Melampo Cinematografica ~ Miramax c

(LA VITA E BELLA)

Cast & Characters

Roberto Benigni *(Guido Orefice)*; Nicoletta Braschi *(Dora)*; Giorgio Cantarini *(Giosue)*; Giustino Durano *(Uncle)*; Sergio Bustric *(Ferruccio Orefice)*; Marisa Paredes *(Dora's Mother)*; Horst Buchholz *(Dr. Lessing)*; Lydia Alfonsi *(Guicciardini)*; Giuliana Lojodice *(Didactic Principal)*

Synopsis & Critical Appraisal

Comic filmmaker Roberto Benigni makes a risky comedic gambit pay off in this gentle-hearted "fable" about the Holocaust in Italy. Though the film makes a swift, somewhat jarring transformation from broad farce to tearjerking sentiment about midway through, Benigni's unique charm as a performer and his talent as an old-fashioned storyteller carry the film through to a touching conclusion. The film won the Grand Prize at the 1998 Cannes Film Festival and three Oscars, including Best Foreign Film and Best Actor (Benigni).

In 1939 in the town of Arezzo, drifter Guido (Roberto Benigni) finds work as a waiter through his uncle (Giustino Durano)...

Benigni's triumph in LIFE IS BEAUTIFUL is twofold: first, he successfully sustains his endearing screen persona against the backdrop of an unspeakable historic nightmare; second, he is able to give the victims of this nightmare a human face, by setting up a very odd allegory about the act of sacrifice. (Violence, adult situations.)— E.G.

Reviewer — Content Advisory

Production Credits

d, Roberto Benigni; p, Gianluigi Braschi, Elda Ferri; exec p, Mario Cotone; w, Roberto Benigni, Vincenzo Cerami; ph, Tonino Delli Colli; ed, Simona Paggi; m, Nicola Piovani; prod d, Danilo Donati; set d, Danilo Donati; sound, Tullio Morganti (mixer); cos, Danilo Donati; makeup, Walter Cossu, Enrico Jacoponi

Academy Award Results

AA Best Actor: Roberto Benigni; *AA Best Foreign Language Film; AA Best Original Dramatic Score:* Nicola Piovani; *AAN Best Picture; AAN Best Director:* Roberto Benigni; *AAN Best Original Screenplay:* Vincenzo Cerami, Roberto Benigni; *AAN Best Film Editing:* Simona Paggi

Genre(s) — Parental Recommendation — MPAA Rating

Comedy/Drama (PR: C MPAA: PG-13)

INFORMATION KEY

Titles
All entries are arranged alphabetically by title, with articles (A, AN, THE) appearing after the main title.

International Productions
When a film has been produced by a country or countries other than the US, these are noted in parentheses on the first line following the title.

Production Companies/Distributor
The film's production company or companies are listed first, with a tilde (~) separating them from the distributor.

Production Credits
The credits for the creative and technical personnel of a film include: d (director); p (producer); exp (exec. producer); asp (assoc. producer); cop (co-producer); w (writer); ph (cinematographer); ed (editor); m (music composer); md (music director); prod d (production designer); art d (art director); set d (set decorator); anim (animation); chor (choreography); sound; fx (special effects); casting; cos (costumes); makeup; stunts; tech (technical adviser).

Academy Award Results
Academy Award information is preceded by *AA,* for a winner, or *AAN,* for a nominee, followed by the category and the name of the recipient, where appropriate.

Genres
Each film is classified by up to three genres drawn from the following list: Action, Adventure, Animated, Biography, Children's, Comedy, Crime, Dance, Disaster, Docudrama, Documentary, Drama, Erotic, Fantasy, Historical, Horror, Martial Arts, Musical, Mystery, Opera, Political, Prison, Religious, Romance, Science Fiction, Sports, Spy, Thriller, War, Western.

Parental Recommendations
The parental recommendation (PR) provides parents with an indication of the film's suitability for children. The recommendations are as follows: AA – good for children; A – acceptable for children; C – cautionary, some scenes may be objectionable for children; O – objectionable for children.

Film Reviews

A

A OSTRA E O VENTO
(SEE: OYSTER AND THE WIND, THE)

A TOUTE VITESSE
(SEE: FULL SPEED)

ABERRATION ★½
(Australia/U.K., 1998) 93m Grundy Films; Victor Film Co. ~ Artisan Entertainment c

Pamela Gidley *(Amy Harding)*; Simon Bossell *(Marshall Clarke)*; Valery Nikolaev *(Uri Romanov)*; Helen Moulder *(Mrs. Miller)*; Norman Forsey *(Mr. Peterson)*

After coming up with a decent creature concept, the makers of this chiller erred by not giving their monsters enough characters to terrorize.

Amy Harding (Pamela Gidley) arrives at her parents' remote cabin and finds slimy material on the premises. She rents exterminating equipment at a general store owned by Mrs. Miller (Helen Moulder), where she meets biologist Marshall Clarke (Simon Bossell), who is investigating ecological abnormalities. Marshall and Amy's concerns prove to have the same source: a strain of mutated lizards that devour Amy's cat and terrorize her and Marshall at the cabin. They kill one of the reptiles and Marshall dissects it, finding that they can develop immunities to weapons used against them. As a blizzard begins, the pair discovers the corpse of Amy's neighbor Mr. Peterson (Norman Forsey), and crash their car. Amy and Marshall return to the cabin, where Amy's vicious ex-boyfriend Uri (Valery Nikolaev) arrives. He reveals that Amy's real name is Alex, that the two once pulled cons together and that Amy has stolen a large sum of money from him. Uri is soon killed by the lizards, and the duo escapes in his car. When it breaks down in the snow, the creatures attack Amy, and Marshall sets the car and the lizards on fire, then carries Amy to Mrs. Miller's store. There, the last of the beasts kills Mrs. Miller before it is dispatched by Marshall and Amy.

The reptilian villains crawl along a lot faster than this movie, which spends too much of its first act following Amy around her cabin and not enough of it developing her character. While the arrival of the lizards and then Marshall promise to perk up interest, the creatures aren't convincing enough to be sufficiently scary and the ostensible hero proves to be as annoying as he is effective. Focusing on only two people battling the creepy terrors could have worked if the right atmosphere and character intrigue were developed, but Tim Boxell's direction is pedestrian and the script half-baked.

By the time Uri finally shows up at the hour mark, his arrival feels less like a satisfying narrative twist than an act of storytelling desperation. His demise is a gruesome highlight, though, and in fact, the infrequent splattery demises of humans and lizards provide the film's only excitement. Like such past horror titles as STRANGE BEHAVIOR (1981), THE FRIGHTENERS (1996), and the Stephen King miniseries THE TOMMYKNOCKERS (1994), this movie uses New Zealand locations to stand in for the American Midwest. *(Graphic violence, profanity.)*—M.G.

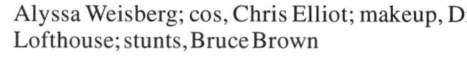

d, Tim Boxell; p, Chris Brown, Tim Sanders; exec p, Alasdair Waddell, Ian Ousey; co-p, Scott Lew; w, Darrin Oura, Scott Lew; ph, Allen Guilford; ed, John Gilbert; m, Plan9, David Donaldson, Janet Roddick, Steve Roche; prod d, Grant Major; art d, Joe Bleakley; sound, Ray Beentjes, Mike Hopkins; fx, David Riley, Daniel Perry, Suzanne Morphett, Kevin Chisnall, Clint Ingram, George Port; casting, Mary Vernieu, Alyssa Weisberg; cos, Chris Elliot; makeup, Di Lofthouse; stunts, Bruce Brown

Horror/Science Fiction (PR: O MPAA: R)

ACCORDING TO PEREIRA
(SEE: PEREIRA DECLARES)

ACT OF WAR ★½
(Canada/Czech Republic, 1998) 105m North American Pictures; Antibes Productions ~ York Home Video c

Jack Scalia *(Jack Gracy)*; Douglas H. Arthurs *(Sergei Constantine)*; Ingrid Torrance *(Katherina Mirova)*; Jan Nemejovsky *(President Mirovich)*; Milan Gargula *(Vassily Krutov)*; David Nykl *(George Willmont)*; Katerina Kornova *(Alexa)*; Terry Barclay *(Commander Kelly)*; Shannon McCormick *(Branford)*; Nancy Bishop *(Johnson)*; Richard Haas *(Ambassador Pierce)*; Christopher Clarke *(Willie)*; Michael Rogers *(General Thomas)*; Vitezslav Bouchner *(General Mitchell)*; Martin Hub *(Max)*; Ljubo Tomanovic *(Ljubo)*; Dusan Hyska *(Technician #2)*; Pavel Cajzl *(Gate Guard #1)*; Ranger Brooklyn *(Gary E. Beach)*; Peter Drozda *(Yuri)*; Chris Binney *(H.Q. Operative)*; Petr Kosata *(Shoe Shine Rebel)*; Leos Stransky *(Bed Rebel)*; Pavel Myslik *(Escaping Technician)*

This direct-to-video tale of terrorists, nuclear missiles, and a lone renegade who singlehandedly saves the day tries hard to be DIE HARD (1988) but falls far short of the mark.

Commandos storm a missile silo in the Soviet Republic of Bazrakhistan, killing everyone. The takeover is detected by Jack Gracy (Jack Scalia), a recently dismissed US secret agent who still possesses a missile tracer unit. Gracy crashes a party at the presidential palace and warns the American ambassador that there has been a breach. His information is discredited and he is turned away.

Jack's departure from the palace is prevented by his former lover, Katherina (Ingrid Torrance), the president's daughter, who leads him to her bedroom. Jack and Katherina rekindle their passion as the president (Jan Nemejovsky) gives a speech to the assembled dignitaries below. Meanwhile, rebel forces surround the palace and Krutov (Milan Gargula), the vice premier, announces a coup. The president and his guests, including Katherina, are held hostage.

Jack is preparing to leave Katherina's bedroom when he hears shots and discovers that the palace is under siege. He discovers that the terrorists plan to launch a nuclear missile at America and steal $50 million in US aid. When his calls to US intelligence are refused, Jack must stop the terrorists himself. He outsmarts and overpowers the commandos, steals the launch access disc, and averts the nuclear attack on America. But the US has launched cruise missiles toward the palace, and Jack and the hostages escape with only seconds to spare.

The production's biggest asset is Scalia, who adroitly plays the handsome hero. His commanding presence and easy charm make ACT OF WAR almost watchable. Douglas H. Arthurs is suitably sinister as Sergei, the mastermind of the terrorist operation. The supporting cast is competent, with the exception of David Nykl, who is miscast as Willmont, Gracy's greedy replacement. The character is supposed to be less effective than Gracy, but Nykl's ineffectual Willmont could never have been hired to head an international security force.

ACT OF WAR pales in comparison to DIE HARD, the 1988 blockbuster it flagrantly mimics. The formulaic script offers fleeting moments of originality, but the predictable turn of events quickly diminishes any real sense of suspense. Least plausible of the scenes are those in which members of the White House cabinet bicker over what action to take. The actors are saddled with insipid dialogue and none display military bearing. The cat-and-mouse relationship between Jack and Sergei lacks the intelligence and chemistry of DIE HARD's Bruce Willis-Alan Rickman pairing. The action and gunplay are standard fare. ACT OF WAR's one true note of authenticity lies in its scenery; the film was shot on location in the Czech Republic. *(Violence, sexual situations, profanity.)*—B.R.

d, Robert Lee; p, Lloyd A. Simandl; exec p, Lloyd A. Simandl, Michelle Gahagan; w, Pavel Jech, Michael Bafaro, Christopher Donaldson; ph, David Pelletier; ed, David Whelan; m, Peter Allen; set d, Ladislav Balous; sound, Rene Mikan (mixer); casting, Tom McSweeney, Susan Taylor Brouse; cos, Eva Stanek; makeup, Adela Rob; stunts, Peter Drozda

Action/Adventure (PR: C MPAA: NR)

ADVENTURES OF MOWGLI ★★

(Russia/U.S., 1996) 92m Cyrillic Films; Films by Jove Inc. ~ TSC Releasing c

VOICES OF: Charlton Heston *(Narrator)*; Dana Delany *(Bagheera)*; Sam Elliott *(Kaa)*; Ian James Corlett, billed as Ian Corlett *(Mowgli)*; Scott McNeil *(Shere Khan)*; Cam Lane *(Baloo)*; Alec Willows *(Tabaqui)*; Cathy Weseluck *(Young Mowgli)*; David Kaye *(Akela)*; Pauline Newstone *(White Cobra)*; Venus Terzo *(Mother Wolf)*; Jon Byrnes *(Father Wolf)*; Don Brown *(Chil)*; Lalainia Lindbjerg *(Gita)*; Harry Kalensky *(Wolves)*; Christopher Gaze *(Red Dogs)*

Dubbed into English, this Russian-produced cartoon uses nonstop action to make its episodic approach palatable to squirming kiddies. Based on Rudyard Kipling's classic, ADVENTURES OF MOWGLI lacks the allure of a Disney animated feature, but compensates with a softer visual style and subtle vocal performances.

Inadvertently abandoned by his human parents during a wild animal attack, infant Mowgli is adopted by a wolf family. At the council session determining Mowgli's fate, his cause is championed by the panther Bagheera (voice of Dana Delany) and the bear Baloo (voice of Cam Lane). Over the objections of the tiger Shere Khan (voice of Scott McNeil) and his querulous jackal pal, Tabaqui (voice of Alec Willows), who hunger for humans and regard Mowgli as a tasty tidbit, Mowgli is welcomed into the jungle family.

Sponsored by Bagheera and Baloo, the boy Mowgli (voice of Ian Corlett) hunts with his brother wolves and cements his bond with the other creatures by rescuing a baby elephant. While thwarting a band of mischievous monkeys, Mowgli is befriended by the python Kaa (voice of Sam Elliott), who becomes another advisor. When Shere Khan stages a coup against the dominance of the Wolf Leader, Bagheera advises Mowgli to obtain the "Red Flower" (fire) from the human village. This flaming weapon defeats Shere Khan, but peace is threatened by an outside attack from hordes of red dogs. Cleverly derailing this invasion by sidetracking the dogs with angry bees, Mowgli preserves the sanctity of his jungle. As a man, Mowgli becomes homesick for his own kind and eventually leaves to raise a family of his own.

Intended less as a salute to Kipling than a cash-in on the popularity of THE LION KING (1994), ADVENTURES OF MOWGLI skips lightly through the wilds, but suffers from the monotony of its color palette (too bleached out to sustain interest) and from a blandly cheery score (consisting of the composer's upbeat trunk ditties). Tykes will be spellbound by this modest retelling of Kipling's celebration of the brotherhood of man and beast. Older children, however, may pine for splashier production values. Parents could do worse than this simply stated jaunt through *The Jungle Book*, but kids are still likely to prefer the jivey jazz of Disney's livelier THE JUNGLE BOOK (1967) *(Violence.)*— R.P.

d, R. Davidov; p, Jack Silberman, Cordell Wynne; exec p, Rebecca Nunberg, Yury Avrutin; co-p, Oleg Vidov, Joan Bornstein; w, L. Belokurov (based on *The Jungle Book* by Rudyard Kipling), David Longworth, Cordell Wynne, Harry Kalensky, Allan Stanleigh (English adaptation); m, Tom Keenlyside, John Mitchell; art d, P. Repkin, A. Vinokurov; sound, Ernie Sheesley; casting, Elizabeth Carol Savenkoff

Animated/Children's (PR: AA MPAA: NR)

AFFLICTION ★★★★

(U.S., 1998) 114m Kingsgate Films ~ Lions Gate Films c

Nick Nolte *(Wade Whitehouse)*; Sissy Spacek *(Margie Fogg)*; James Coburn *(Glen Whitehouse)*; Willem Dafoe *(Rolfe Whitehouse)*; Mary Beth Hurt *(Lillian)*; Jim True *(Jack Hewitt)*; Marian Seldes *(Alma Pittman)*; Holmes Osborne *(Gordon LaRiviere)*; Brigid Tierney *(Jill)*; Sean McCann *(Evan Twombley)*; Wayne Robson *(Nick Wickham)*; Steve Adams *(Mel Gordon)*

A quietly powerful work, AFFLICTION details the disintegration of a troubled man obsessed with a murder mystery.

Wade Whitehouse (Nick Nolte), a middle-aged native of a small New Hampshire town called Lawford, gets by with two odd jobs: functioning as the town's police officer and working for a local businessman, Gordon LaRiviere (Holmes Osborne). Since his bitter divorce from Lillian (Mary Beth Hurt), Wade feels he must find the money to sue for custody in order to see his daughter, Jill (Brigid Tierney), more often. Wade even proposes marriage to his current girlfriend, Margie (Sissy Spacek), a waitress, merely as a way to strengthen his court fight.

One day, Wade hears that a wealthy visiting businessman, Twombley (Sean McCann), has accidentally shot himself in the woods while hunting with Wade's friend and fellow officer, Jack (Jim True). When Wade sees blood on Jack's sleeve, he suspects a conspiracy is afoot. He sets out to prove that LaRiviere and Mel Gordon (Steve Adams), Twombley's rich son-in-law, hired Jack to kill the wealthy businessman so that Twombley could not interfere with their secret plans to buy up all the real estate in Lawford and turn it into a ski resort.

But Wade runs into roadblocks throughout his investigation, during which he must also contend with his messy personal life. While trying to care for his cruel, alcoholic father, Pop Whitehouse (James Coburn), after the death of his mother, Wade alienates Margie by forcing her to see his family problems up close. Meanwhile, Wade's custody suit further estranges him from Jill, and, after airing his suspicions about Gordon and LaRiviere, Wade loses his job and is replaced by Jack, his former friend.

Nevertheless, Wade tries to solve the murder and mend his frayed relationships. But he accidentally hits Jill during an outing, and Margie, who witnesses the blow, leaves him for good. Angry and alone, Wade finally confronts his father about his abusive behavior, and ends up killing him in a fight. He sets his farmhouse on fire to cover up the crime, but he also kills Jack before escaping the town as a fugitive. Just before his disappearance from Lawford, Wade learns that Twombley's murder really was an accident and that his suspicions were unwarranted.

AFFLICTION cuts through the slick veneer of contemporary filmmaking styles to produce the kind of raw, character-driven portraits that were produced in greater quantities in 1970s American cinema. Not surprisingly, AFFLICTION has been made by many of the veterans of that era, including writer-director Paul Schrader, production designer Anne Pritchard, star (and co-producer) Nick Nolte, and a supporting cast that includes Sissy Spacek, Mary Beth Hurt, and James Coburn, whose work here garnered him the Oscar for Best Supporting Actor.

Schrader masterfully adapts the Russell Banks novel of a broken man who realizes all too late he is on a dangerous downward spiral. With deliberate pacing but a moody atmosphere, AFFLICTION builds slowly but surely to a shattering climax and conclusion that illustrates the far-ranging effects of child abuse and family dysfunction. With his bottled rage always close to the surface, Nolte gives one of his best performances (which is saying a lot, given his body of work thus far) as Wade, the small-town-loser-turned-paranoid-sleuth (a part similar in certain, surface ways to Sylvester Stallone's small-town lawman in COPLAND); Coburn matches Nolte as the monstrous, alcoholic Pop, the cause for so much of Wade's pain (brilliantly symbolized in the story by a lingering toothache); Spacek and Hurt have much less to do, but deliver effective moments playing the very different women in Wade's life; only Willem Dafoe is not as well cast as Wade's younger brother (also the narrator), but his performance is solid.

AFFLICTION boasts excellent technique, including Paul Sarossy's cinematography, which perfectly captures the chilly (and often chilling) small-town milieu (Sarossy also photographed Atom Egoyan's THE SWEET HEREAFTER, which was based on another Russell Banks' novel). Anne Pritchard's designs for the sepia-toned flashbacks to Wade's violent childhood convincingly evoke a supposedly more innocent era. Michael Brook's muted, mournful score also deserves mention.

AFFLICTION tells a sad story in a compelling way and may remind viewers of a time when filmmaking didn't always seem computer-generated and prepackaged. *(Violence, adult situations, extreme profanity.)*—E.M.

d, Paul Schrader; p, Linda Reisman; exec p, Nick Nolte, Barr Potter; co-p, Eric Berg, Frank K. Isaac ; w, Paul Schrader (based on the novel by Russell Banks); ph, Paul Sarossy; ed, Jay Rabinowitz; m, Michael Brook; prod d, Anne Pritchard; casting, Ellen Chenoweth, Kathleen Chopin; cos, Francois Laplante

AAN Best Actor: Nick Nolte; *AA Best Supporting Actor:* James Coburn

Drama **(PR: C MPAA: R)**

AFIRMA PEREIRA
(SEE: PEREIRA DECLARES)

AIR BUD: GOLDEN RECEIVER ★★½
(U.S./Canada, 1998) 90m Golden Receiver Productions; Keystone Pictures ~ Dimension c

Kevin Zegers *(Josh Framm)*; Cynthia Stevenson *(Jackie Framm)*; Gregory Harrison *(Patrick Sullivan)*; Nora Dunn *(Natalya)*; Perry Anzilotti *(Popov)*; Robert Costanzo *(Coach Fanelli)*; Shayn Solberg *(Tom)*; Tim Conway *(Fred Davis)*; Dick Martin *(Phil Phil)*; Suzanna Ristic *(Principal Salter)*; Alyson MacLaren *(Andrea Framm)*; Tyler Thompson *(Oliver)*; Rhys Williams *(Goose)*; Shahari Khaderni *(Juan)*; Jason Anderson *(Weeble)*; Myles Ferguson *(J.D.)*; Cory Fry *(Cole Powers)*; Jeff Gulka *(Pudge)*; Marcus Tucker *(Giants Quarterback)*; Jay Brazeau *(Official)*; Frank C. Turner *(Official)*; Mark Brandon *(Richard)*; Jaida Hay *(Tammy)*; Richard Martin *(Guy in Stands)*; Doreen Esary *(Receptionist)*; Julio Caravetta *(Giants Coach)*; David Lewis *(Herb)*; Monica Marko *(Lady with Broom)*; Scott Ateah *(Official)*; Ritch Renaud *(Photographer)*; Barry MacDonald *(Sportcaster)*; Simon Isherwood *(Rams Coach)*; John Keelan *(Ice Cream Boy)*; Warren Moon; Joey Galloway; Blue Edwards; Pete Chilcutt; George Lynch; Sam Mack; Lee Mayberry; Ivano Newbill *(Pro Basketball Players)*

The basketball-dunking canine hero of 1997's surprise hit AIR BUD tackles the football field and his owner's growing pains in this painless sequel.

Still hurting from the death of his father, Josh Framm (Kevin Zegers) feels betrayed when his mother Jackie (Cynthia Stevenson) starts dating. And though he otherwise likes her beau, veterinarian Patrick Sullivan (Gregory Harrison), Josh can't bear the thought of someone else trying to take his father's place. Discovering that he has a good arm for throwing a football, he goes out for the school team simply as an excuse to be away from home. Coach Fanelli (Robert Costanzo) gives him a spot as back-up quarterback, and promotes him when the team's star quarterback is injured during the first game. Josh's insecurities are mitigated when his dog Buddy follows him to the field and, proving as adept with a football as he is with a basketball, catches a pass and scores a touchdown.

Taking Fanelli at his word that kids' sports are supposed to be about fun, Josh makes Buddy a team uniform and brings him to practice. Because Fanelli is about to lose his job for not having won a game in longer than anyone can remember, he agrees to let him play, and Buddy leads the team all the way to the state finals.

When he sees Patrick proposing to Jackie, Josh runs away from home, but is retrieved by Fanelli, who suggests that it is no dishonor to the memory of his father to let another good man into their family's life. Buddy almost misses the state championship, having been kidnapped by a villainous pair (Nora Dunn, Perry Anzilotti) who are assembling performing animals for a Russian circus. But after he escapes, he joins the game in time to even up the score. Buddy is sidelined after a rough tackle, but Josh and friend Tom (Shayn Solberg) win the championship with a last-second 60-yard pass.

Just once, it would be nice to see a children's film that preached about how winning isn't everything, a morality tale that had the courage of its convictions and let the hero(es) *lose* the big game, while having fun merely playing. AIR BUD: GOLDEN RECEIVER, unfortunately, goes the regular route: it treats the other kids on the team as mere undifferentiated extras; the only one who seems to be having any fun here is star Buddy.

Like its predecessor, this AIR BUD is designed to show off the talents of its canine star, and matters of plot are strictly secondary. (For that matter, it's not even the same dog. Because the original Buddy had died—sorry, kids—he was replaced here by a team of six Golden Retrievers, each with a different specialty.) Still, despite the slimness of the script, there are pleasing performances by the stars, particularly Robert Costanzo's coach. And there's nice cameo bit by Tim Conway and Dick Martin (whose son was the film's director) as a pair of announcers. AIR BUD moves quickly, and won't tax the patience of young viewers, at the same time offering enough droll slapstick to keep parents from nodding off.—M.F.

d, Richard Martin; p, Robert Vince; exec p, Michael Strange, Anne Vince, William Vince; assoc p, Ian Fodie; w, Paul Tamasy, Aaron Mendelsohn (based on the character created by Kevin DiCicco); ph, Mike Southon; ed, Bruce Lange, Melinda Seabrook; m, Brahm Wenger; prod d, Rex Raglan; art d, Eric Norlin; set d, Grant Pearse; sound, Kevin Sands; casting, Abra Edelman, Elisa Goodman; cos, Patricia Hargreaves; makeup, Jo Ann Fowler; stunts, Scott Ateah

Children's/Sports/Comedy **(PR: A MPAA: PG)**

ALARMIST, THE ★★
(U.S., 1998) 93m Bandeira Entertainment; Key Entertainment ~ Lions Gate Films c

David Arquette *(Tommy Hudler)*; Stanley Tucci *(Heinrich Grigoris)*; Kate Capshaw *(Gale Ancona)*; Mary McCormack *(Sally)*; Ryan Reynolds *(Howard Ancona)*; Tricia Vessey *(April)*; Ruth Miller *(Mrs. Fielding)*; Hoke Howell *(Mr. Fielding)*; Michael Learned *(Beth Hudler)*; Lewis Arquette *(Bruce Hudler)*; Richmond Arquette *(Andrew Hudler)*; Gabriel Dell Jr. *(Skippy Hudler)*; Valerie Long *(Doris)*; Kim Tobin *(Bambi)*; Colin Campbell *(Waiter)*; Eric Zivot *(Shelly)*; Vincent J. Bilancio *(Assistant Director)*; Clea DuVall *(Suzy)*; David Brisbin *(Detective Flinkman)*; Bradley J. Gorman *(Grigoris Employee)*; Dennis Cockrum *(Vendor)*; Matt Malloy *(Morgue Technician)*; Alex Nepomniaschy *(Installer)*

THE ALARMIST is a well-produced but confused little comedy-drama about the troubles that befall an alarm system salesman.

Heinrich Grigoris (Stanley Tucci) hires Tommy Hudler (David Arquette) as a salesman for his alarm system company. On his first attempt, Tommy makes a sale to a recent widow, Gale (Kate Capshaw), who lives with her teenage son, Howard (Ryan Reynolds). Although Gale is considerably older than Tommy, they begin an affair. In short time, Tommy becomes a top salesman and is chosen to star in the company's television commercial.

Late one night, Heinrich and Tommy go to a customer's house, where Heinrich kicks a door open. An alarm goes off and the two flee. The following day, the grateful homeowner calls Heinrich to explain that the alarm system prevented a burglary, and that his neighbors are also interested in having alarms installed. After the call, Heinrich tells Tommy that this is how he generates business, and also explains that he sometimes disables a system to burglarize a house. Tommy is shocked at Heinrich's revelations, and later hints at them to Gale, who advises him to quit.

That weekend, Tommy brings Gale to meet his parents (Lewis Arquette and Michael Learned). Tommy's parents are uncomfortable with the couple's age difference, so Gale leaves. When he returns from his visit, Tommy tries and fails repeatedly to contact Gale. Later, he hears from police that Gale and Howard have been slain, probably by a burglar. Tommy suspects Heinrich and confronts him, but Heinrich denies any knowledge of the crime. Unpersuaded, Tommy quits Heinrich's business. Soon after, he kidnaps Heinrich, drives him to a deserted quarry and is about to kill him when he gets word that the case has been solved, and that the confessed killer is in custody. As the two drive back, Tommy apologizes to Heinrich. Heinrich accepts and offers to rehire Tommy. Having reconciled, the two pull over for lunch.

Although intermittently entertaining, THE ALARMIST is very uneven, so much so that it's difficult to tell exactly what writer-director Evan Dunsky meant the film to be. Is it supposed to be a satire on American business ethos? An absurdist comedy about a regular guy who gets caught up in a paranoiac nightmare? A May-December romance with a gender switch? THE ALARMIST undergoes several seismic shifts in tone as it proceeds, continually undermining its dramatic, comic, and romantic intentions. The film develops several intriguing narrative strands, but its indecisive character prevents any of them from being satisfactorily sustained. And although THE ALARMIST is brightened by a few individual scenes, its overall lack of consistency renders it a jumble.

Yet THE ALARMIST is modestly entertaining, thanks principally to its cast. David Arquette puts his patented low-watt nice guy turn to good use here; his Tommy is a likely and likable patsy. Capshaw is bright, warm, and quietly amusing as Gale. Tucci, as expected, enhances every scene he's in. He embellishes and enriches the contradictions of a contradictory character—a man who's grossly unethical in his work but who adheres fiercely to his own personal code of ethics—and makes Heinrich believably slimy yet charming, scary yet pathetic. Tucci is a truly gifted performer, and he's the best thing in this movie.

Dunsky deserves credit for his fine handling of the performers, and he also merits credit for putting together a good-looking film. Although a thematic mess, THE ALARMIST is technically proficient, nicely photographed, edited, and scored.

THE ALARMIST is also noteworthy as an Arquette family mini-reunion. Besides David, the film features his father Lewis (as Tommy's father) and brother Richmond (as Tommy's brother). Moviegoers who just can't get enough of the Arquette acting clan should take note. *(Violence, sexual situations, extreme profanity.)*—D.C.

d, Evan Dunsky; p, Dan Stone, Lisa Zimble; exec p, Thomas Augsberger, Matthias Emeke, Beau Flynn, Stephan Simchowitz; assoc p, Keith Reddin; co-p, Jonathan King; w, Evan Dunsky (based on the play *Life During Wartime* by Keith Reddin); ph, Alex Nepomniaschy; ed, Norman Buckley; m, Christophe Beck; prod d, Amy B. Ancona; art d, Rachel Kamerman; sound, Anthony Ortiz; casting, Concetta DiMatteo, Carolyn Long; cos, Denise Wingate

Comedy/Crime/Drama **(PR: C MPAA: R)**

ALFRED HITCHCOCK: MASTER OF SUSPENSE ★★★
(U.S., 1973) 58m American Cinematheque; City Center of Music and Drama; Director's Guild of America ~ Fox Lorber Home Video c
(AKA: MEN WHO MADE THE MOVIES: ALFRED HITCHCOCK)

Alfred Hitchcock; Cliff Robertson *(Narrator)*

ALFRED HITCHCOCK: MASTER OF SUSPENSE (originally produced for PBS-TV in 1973 as part of the MEN WHO MADE THE MOVIES series) is an entertaining survey of Hitchcock's career that's most valuable for the fascinating, in-depth interviews it contains with the Master himself.

As excerpts from a number of Hitchcock films unspool—including PSYCHO (1960), NORTH BY NORTHWEST (1959), FRENZY (1972), THE LODGER (1926), SABOTEUR (1942), SHADOW OF A DOUBT (1943), NOTORIOUS (1946), THE BIRDS (1963), and TORN CURTAIN (1966)—Hitchcock comments on his cinematic style and his films' themes.

The MEN WHO MADE THE MOVIES series, which was written, produced, and directed by *Time* magazine critic Richard Schickel, was one of the first mainstream television attempts to offer the general American public an auteurist view of movies, analyzing films not just as entertainment, but also as art and largely as the vision of the director. The great thing about the series was that since it was made in the early 1970s, all of the great directors being profiled were still alive (the other episodes covered Frank Capra, George Cukor, Howard Hawks, Vincente Minnelli, Raoul Walsh, William Wellman, and King Vidor), enabling them to record for posterity their thoughts about their own work. In ALFRED HITCHCOCK: MASTER OF SUSPENSE, Schickel's spare commentary (spoken by Cliff Robertson) touches upon all the usual topics (Catholic guilt, fear of police, psychological anxiety, the "McGuffin," etc.) with intelligence, if not much depth, but thankfully lets Hitchcock and the films clips speak for themselves. Though there are only clips from nine of Hitchcock's films, the excerpts are well chosen and run fairly long, allowing Hitchcock to elucidate on his philosophy of creating "pure cinema" through strictly visual means and how he manipulates audiences.

Many of Hitchcock's comments are basically reiterations of his famous stories in the Francois Truffaut book and other interviews, but it's fascinating to watch the great director, dressed like an undertaker in his immaculate Universal Studio office, reveal his various fears and phobias. The film is also invaluable as one of the few examples of Hitchcock speaking about his art in serious terms, eschewing his usual jocular evasion and self-deprecation. Though he claims that content is secondary to the style of his films, his observations contradict this, as he calls his early English films "more instinctive and less calculated for audiences" than his American films, talks about his use of such locations as the Statue of Liberty and Mount Rushmore as "symbols of order thrown into disorder," and discusses the changing nature of evil, from the picturesque apple-pie small town setting of SHADOW OF A DOUBT to the modern-day brutality of serial killers and rapists as depicted in FRENZY. Most interesting is hearing Hitchcock explain his cinematic techniques and his belief that "the whole art of cinema is its ability to appeal to all audiences in any language." Detailing his theories about the importance of montage and the use of his patented subjective POV shot (with a clip from PSYCHO showing alternating close-ups of Vera Miles's face and tracking shots of what she's looking at), he states that this is an essential component of creating emotion and transferring the menace from the mind of the character on the screen into the mind of the audience. The documentary may be somewhat old-fashioned and simplistic in its approach, but it stands as an important testimonial by one of the greatest of all filmmakers. *(Violence.)*—M.S.

d, Richard Schickel; p, Richard Schickel; assoc p, Gene Stavis; w, Richard Schickel; ph, John A. Morrill; ed, Mirra Bank; sound, Peter Pilafian

Documentary (PR: C MPAA: NR)

ALL DOGS CHRISTMAS CAROL, AN ★

(U.S., 1998) 73m Metro-Goldwyn-Mayer Animation ~ MGM Home Entertainment c

VOICES OF: Steven Weber *(Charlie/Ghost of Christmas Future)*; Dom DeLuise *(Itchy/Ghost of Christmas Past)*; Sheena Easton *(Sasha/Ghost of Christmas Present)*; Ernest Borgnine *(Carface)*; Charles Nelson Reilly *(Killer)*; Bebe Neuwirth; Taylor Emerson *(Timmy)*

AN ALL DOGS CHRISTMAS CAROL is a cheaply produced made-for-video cartoon that's a dreadful bit of humbuggery. The film is about as much fun as finding a lump of coal in your stocking on Christmas Day.

A wicked witch dog named Belladonna (voice of Bebe Neuwirth) has her evil dog assistants, Carface (voice of Ernest Borgnine) and Killer (voice of Charles Nelson Reilly), use a special dog whistle to put all of the town's dogs under her spell. After Carface steals some money that has been collected for an operation for a lame puppy named Timmy (voice of Taylor Emerson), a brave dog named Charlie (voice of Steven Weber) and his pal Itchy (voice of Dom DeLuise) unsuccessfully try to get it back, and they learn that Belladonna is plotting to stop Christmas by building a gigantic dog whistle to be used on Christmas Eve to make all the dogs steal presents from their masters. Charlie and Itchy decide to imitate Dickens's "A Christmas Carol" to frighten Carface, and they, along with Charlie's girlfriend Sasha (voice of Sheena Easton) pretend to be ghosts. The ploy works, and when Belladonna tries to use the dog whistle on Christmas Eve, Carface stops her. Belladonna's cousin, an angel dog named Anabella (voice of Bebe Neuwirth), destroys Belladonna. Christmas is saved and Carface dresses as Santa Claus to deliver presents to all of the dogs.

AN ALL DOGS CHRISTMAS CAROL not only besmirches the memory of Dickens's immortal tale, which has already been subjected to far too many feeble variations, but also makes the very mediocre original ALL DOGS GO TO HEAVEN (1989) look like a classic Disney cartoon feature from the 1930s or '40s. Indeed, the animation (and that's a dubious term in this case) is so crude, coarse, and unimaginative that it makes contemporary Saturday morning cartoons look like the work of artistic geniuses by comparison, while the most rudimentary CD-ROMs are possessed of more fluid motion and sophisticated design. The movement is so slow and jerky that the script even has to justify it at one point, when Sasha says to the gimpy Timmy, "I hope I'm walking slow enough for you." Instead of wasting funds on the requisite group of annoying and superfluous songs, the producers should have given more money to the Taiwanese animation company that actually did most of the artwork. About the only entertainment value the film has to offer—at least for anyone over the age of three—is the chance to hear the gravelly-voiced Ernest Borgnine warble a couple of tunes, including a charming little holiday ditty about how, when Carface was a pup, he was kicked out of his master's house for going wee-wee all over the Christmas tree, which is duly presented in a touching and colorful flashback.— M.S.

d, Paul Sabella; p, Paul Sabella, Jonathan Dern; assoc p, Cary Silver; co-p, Jymn Magon; w, Jymn Magon; m, Mark Watters

Animated/Children's (PR: AA MPAA: G)

ALL THE RAGE ★

(U.S., 1998) 105m Pink Plot Productions ~ Jour de Fete Films c

John-Michael Lander *(Christopher Bedford)*; David Vincent *(Stewart)*; Jay Corcoran *(Larry)*; Paul Outlaw *(Dave)*; Merle Perkins *(Susan)*; Jeff Miller *(John)*; Peter Bubriski *(Tom)*; Alan Natale *(Kenny)*

ALL THE RAGE is writer-director Roland Tec's adaptation of his own one-act play *A Better Boy.* While Tec's subject—a gay yuppie's breakdown under the weight of his own complacency—is original and compelling, his treatment of it is dramatically weak and cinematically negligible.

Although Christopher (John-Michael Lander), a young lawyer, enjoys his affluence, he's lonely and "tired of meeting Mr. Wrong." At a party one night, he meets Stewart (David Vincent), and is attracted to him despite Stewart's sloppy appearance and the fact that he has a low-paying job. The two begin to date and become lovers. In short time, however, Christopher begins to find fault with Stewart, put off by his poor eating habits and lack of exercise. Christopher becomes friendly with Stewart's roommate, Kenny (Alan Natale), who assists Christopher with his work out. Late one night, while sleeping at Stewart's, Christopher gets out of bed and locates Kenny. The two head to the roof of the building and begin to make out but are interrupted, and Christopher quietly returns to bed with the sleeping Stewart.

The next day, Christopher tries repeatedly to call Stewart, but Stewart, who has learned what has happened, refuses to return the calls. Having lost Stewart, Christopher cruises bars and picks up a man, John (Jeff Miller), whom he brings back to his apartment for sex. Afterwards, John tells Christopher that the two had met and had sex several years earlier, and he excoriates and threatens Christopher for having forgotten him. Afraid at first, Christopher becomes angry and strikes John. As John cowers, Christopher rants that he forgets men like John because they are meaningless to him, that he's superior to other people, and, almost raving, screams, "I'm a winner" repeatedly, until his fury is finally spent.

The best thing that ALL THE RAGE has to offer is its punning title, which refers to both the lead character's compulsive competitiveness and the aggression that this compulsion builds up inside him. That's about it for entertainment or enlightenment, for the film that follows the title credit is a thoroughly flat, lifeless affair. Its plot is serviceable if standard, but Tec's direction is flaccid, and the film plods along without ever developing momentum. The emotional catharsis that closes ALL THE RAGE is intended to be explosive, but since the drama never builds, it completely lacks force.

As a scenarist, Tec fails to give his characters dimension. The main characters are types—Christopher is a shallow yuppie, Stewart is a soft and sensitive intellectual—and the secondary characters function merely as sounding boards for the leads. Tec's shortcomings as a scenarist are also painfully apparent in his use of "video diary" segments which that the film, in which Christopher is shown videotaping himself and speaking his true feelings in a way that he cannot to anyone else. These bits are clearly meant to provide a better understanding of the principal character, but their inclusion is so clumsily handled that rather than granting greater insight into Christopher, they betray Tec's inability to have his characters express themselves in a less direct, more subtle manner.

The problems don't end with Tec's directing and writing. The performances are uniformly wooden and the cinematography is unimaginative, failing to make any appreciable use of the story's Boston setting. Even the scoring (also by Tec) is poor, the selection of background music being obvious and obtrusive. Like its main character, ALL THE RAGE is rather superficial, but in stark contrast to him, it's completely enervated. *(Violence, nudity, sexual situations, adult situations, profanity.)*—D.C.

d, Roland Tec; p, Roland Tec; co-p, Catherine Burns; w, Roland Tec; ph, Gretchen Widmer; ed, John Altschuler; m, Roland Tec; prod d, Louis Ashman; sound, Doug Snyder; casting, Kevin Fennessy; cos, Sarah Pfeiffer

Comedy/Drama **(PR: O MPAA: NR)**

ALMOST HEROES ★½

(U.S., 1998) 90m Di Novi Pictures; Turner Pictures ~ Warner Bros. c

Chris Farley *(Bartholomew Hunt)*; Matthew Perry *(Leslie Edwards)*; Eugene Levy *(Guy Fontenot)*; Kevin Dunn *(Hidalgo)*; Bokeem Woodbine *(Jonah)*; Lisa Barbuscia *(Shaquinna)*; Steven Porter *(Higgins)*; David Packer *(Bidwell)*; Hamilton Camp *(Pratt)*; Lewis Arquette *(Merchant)*; Patrick Crenshaw *(Jackson)*; Christian Clemenson *(Father Girard)*; Harry Shearer *(Narrator)*; Frank Sotonoma Salsedo *(Old Indian)*; Barry Del Sherman *(Sergeant)*; Robert Tittor *(Priest)*; Franklin Cover *(Nicholas Burr)*; Jonathan Joss *(Best Twig)*; George Aguilar *(Chief Two Roads)*; Gregory Norman Cruz *(Iowa Indian)*; Don Lake *(Elias)*; Brent Hinkley *(Trapper)*; John Farley *(Bartender)*; Tim DeKay *(New Bartender)*; Keith Sellon-Wright *(Merriweather Lewis)*; Scott Williamson *(William Clark)*; David Barrera *(Ferdinand)*; Jay Lacopo *(Hector)*; Billy Daydoge *(Strong Like Mountain)*; T. Dan Hopkins *(Running Puma)*; Axel Lindgren *(Salmon Brave)*; Scott Anderson *(Conquistador #2)*

The cinematic swan song of Chris Farley, ALMOST HEROES is a mediocre comedy that relies on crude humor and the over-the-top antics of its corpulent star.

In 1804, Lewis and Clark depart to chart new western territory. Tracker Bartholomew Hunt (Chris Farley) is about to be hanged for drunken and disorderly conduct. Leslie Edwards (Matthew Perry) arrives with a stay of execution, just as Hunt is set to swing. Edwards informs the tracker that his services are needed for an expedition; Edwards hopes to beat Lewis and Clark to the Pacific.

The duo acquire the services of translator Guy Fontenot (Eugene Levy), who is accompanied by Shaquinna (Lisa Barbuscia), a beautiful Native American woman. Their crew is completed by a motely assortment of misfits, including the daft Pratt (Hamilton Camp), the bagpipe-playing Higgins (Steven M. Porter), and the dismemberment-prone Bidwell (David Packer). As their journey progresses, they reach the last charted outpost of the American territories. There they encounter the vain conquistador Hidalgo (Kevin Dunn). The Spaniard enlists Fontenot in his search for great treasures. Edwards and Shaquinna are about to be conscripted as well when Hunt arrives and challenges Hidalgo to a drinking duel. The tracker drinks the entire regiment of conquistadors under the table, and the team resumes their quest.

While crossing the Rockies, Edwards is taken ill. Shaquinna needs the egg of a bald eagle to cure him. Hunt sets out and returns with such an item—after breaking down and eating the first two eggs he procured. With Edwards cured, the expedition continues. Traveling downriver, they pass Lewis and Clark, but they encounter turbulent rapids and are flung over a waterfall. The bedraggled crew are then attacked by Hidalgo's band, including Fontenot. Edwards and Hunt manage to escape, and, with the help of some geriatric Indian ninjas, the duo rescue their companions and defeat the conquistadors.

The expedition races to the Pacific, only to find that Lewis and Clark are close to reaching the ocean. Hunt descends a cliff, but he is attacked by the eagle whose nest he violated. The bird carries him off, dropping him into the ocean; he swims to the shore, plants the American flag, and the expedition team find that they have beaten Lewis and Clark to the coast. Edwards proposes that the team continue their explorations.

ALMOST HEROES is essentially another Chris Farley/David Spade buddy movie, with Matthew Perry substituting for Spade. The pivot of the film's comedy is the clash between Farley's boisterous Hunt and Perry's effete, wise-cracking Edwards. While this formula proved successful with the Farley/Spade film TOMMY BOY (1995), the charm had evaporated by the time of BLACK SHEEP (1996), that picture's milquetoast clone. HEROES director Christopher Guest makes full use of Farley's one trademark routine, as the bloated comedian is given ample opportunity to indulge in apoplectic, crimson-faced screaming fits. Though amusing when he was a mere cast member on "Saturday Night Live," these antics are seldom humorous in this film.

Yet the blame cannot be placed entirely on the star's broad shoulders; the film also engages in puerile humor based on the rather tired subjects of scatology, sexual abnormality, and other garden-variety gross-outs. For instance, the hapless Bidwell is routinely disfigured, losing both an ear and a foot along the journey. The trio of screenwriters it took to turn out this mush was most likely angling for Monty Python-esque grotesquery, but what ultimately reaches the screen is a watered-down Hollywood version of that brash style of comedy. ALMOST HEROES is, above all, a movie that *thinks* it's offbeat and peculiar.

This lackluster quality is surprising given the presence of talents such as Levy, Dunn, and Guest, whose WAITING FOR GUFFMAN (1996) was pithy, intelligent, and pointedly hilarious. Perry dutifully delivers his lines in the style of his "Chandler Bing" character on TV's "Friends," but most of the time he seems embarrassed by the proceedings (he does get to kiss the luscious Barbuscia, which probably kept him from bolting the production outright).

On the plus side, ALMOST HEROES is not unwatchable and does provide two or three humorous, if crude, moments. Still, as Chris Farley's final screen appearance, ALMOST HEROES is anticlimactic; the film also chalked up another cinematic failure for Perry (following the disappointing FOOLS RUSH IN). For die-hard Farley fans, the movie may be essential viewing, but for the majority of viewers, it's strictly a "wait until cable" affair. *(Violence, nudity, profanity.)*—D.G.

d, Christopher Guest; p, Denise Di Novi; co-p, Mary Kane; w, Mark Nutter, Tom Wolfe, Boyd Hale; ph, Adam Kimmel, Kenneth MacMillan; ed, Ronald Roose; m, Jeffery C.J. Vanston; prod d, Joseph T. Garrity; art d, Patrick Tagliaferro; set d, Linda Allen; ch, Adam Shankman; sound, Mark Weingarten (mixer); fx, Tommy Bellissimo, Charles Belardinelli; casting, Mary Gail Artz, Barbara Cohen; cos, Durinda Wood; makeup, Angela Moos, Kate Shorter; stunts, Max Kleven

Historical/Comedy/Adventure (PR: C MPAA: PG-13)

ALMOST PARTNERS ★★
(U.S., 1987) 53m Wonderworks ~ BWE c

Paul Sorvino *(Jack Welder)*; Royana Black *(Molly McCue)*; Mary Wickes *(Aggie Greyson)*; Jayce Bartok *(Leon Jones)*; Roy Brocksmith *(Pierre La Rue)*; Bill Fagerbakke *(Willard)*; Ray Xifo *(Milo)*; Peter Bergman *(Dan Trigger)*; Richard Portnow *(Nicky)*; Joe Amodei *(Starvos)*; Mark Margolis *(Kristopholous)*; Doris Belack *(Anna McCue)*; P.J. Benjamin *(Slick)*; Joseph Leon *(Hallery)*; Rik Colitti *(Cabbie)*; Lorraine Serabain *(Gypsy)*; Steven Keyes *(Amazon Woman #1)*; Brick Hartney *(Amazon Woman #2)*; Russell Giesenshlag *(Amazon Woman #3)*; Joe Cirillo *(Forensics Expert)*; Elizabeth Brown *(Margo Clevitch)*

Originally aired as an episode of the PBS children's series "Wonderworks," the pleasant but unmemorable ALMOST PARTNERS was released as a feature on home video in 1998.

Fascinated with mysteries, 14-year-old Molly McCue (Royana Black) imagines herself as the partner of a detective featured in a famous mystery novel. When Molly's grandmother (Mary Wickes) is robbed of the urn holding her late husband's ashes, Molly is on the case. At her grandmother's apartment, she meets police detective Jack Welder (Paul Sorvino). He dismisses Molly's theory that three men committed the crime. Dismayed by Welder's reaction, Molly and her pal Leon (Jayce Bartok) head to the La Rue funeral home in disguise. Molly deduces that the shady Pierre La Rue (Roy Brocksmith) and his henchmen are involved in the theft. When she goes to Welder, he explains the crooks have called to ransom the urn. She follows Welder to the drop, but they attempt to run her down. Back at the station, Molly realizes that the urn holding her grandfather's ashes is actually the Ming-Lung Urn—a $3 million artifact that had been stolen. She and Welder team up, and their investigation leads them back to La Rue. They correctly deduce that La Rue planned to sell the urn to big-time criminal Kristopholous (Mark Margolis), but decided to keep it out of sight—by using it as an urn for Molly's grandfather—until he could get $300,000 out of Kristopholous. Racing to stop the sale, Molly manages to hide within the coffin in which the urn is stored while Welder follows the crooks. Before the sale can take place, Welder takes La Rue into custody amidst a volley of gunfire.

Filmed in 1987, ALMOST PARTNERS is an amusing mystery intended for young viewers. The production values are on the level of most television fare, but the cast is populated by a roster of seasoned character actors, including Paul Sorvino, Mary Wickes, Roy Brocksmith (THE ROAD TO WELLVILLE), and Richard Portnow (PRIVATE PARTS). They support perky lead Royana Black quite well, and add a note of interest for adult viewers. Director Alan Kingsberg does a capable job, but aside from the views of picturesque NYC locations, the film has little visual flair. The locations actually serve to brighten up certain scenes: one of the film's more inspired moments has the characters' detective work being punctuated by the prominent Sony video screen in Times Square, which lights up with the words "New York's Finest Detectives." *(Violence.)*—P.L.

d, Alan Kingsberg; p, Gary Weiner; exec p, Charles S. Morris; assoc p, Sidney Palmer; w, Alan Kingsberg, Gary Weiner; ph, Peter B. Fernberger; ed, Gary Karr; m, Paul Chihara; prod d, Ray Recht; sound, Douglas Tourtelot; casting, Pat McCorkle; cos, Barbara Shulman Breslin; makeup, Meredith Soupious; stunts, Frank Ferrara

Children's/Mystery (PR: AA MPAA: NR)

ALONE
(SEE: HORTON FOOTE'S ALONE)

ALONE IN THE WOODS ★
(U.S., 1997) 81m Royal Oaks Entertainment; Concorde Productions ~ New Horizons Home Video c

Brady Bluhm *(Justin Rogers)*; Chick Vennera *(Perry)*; Matthias Hues *(Kurt)*; Laraine Newman *(Sherry Rogers)*; Dan McVicar *(Danny Rogers)*; Sarah Bibb *(Kate Rogers)*; Krystee Clark *(Chelsea Stuart)*; Jim Doughan *(Tracker)*; Willie Garson *(Lyle)*; Blake Clark *(Sarge)*; Pamela Putch *(Ethel)*; Stephen Bradbury *(Stu Stuart)*

Not taken too seriously by anyone on or offscreen, this kiddie movie comes courtesy of the home-video company founded by budget-minded producer Roger Corman.

Justin Rogers (Brady Bluhm), a 10-year-old serial prankster, unwillingly accompanies his family to a wilderness park for Thanksgiving weekend. At a rest stop, Justin accidentally gets into the wrong vehicle, an identical van being driven by goofy criminals Perry (Chick Vennera) and Kurt (Matthias Hues). By the time the boy realizes his mistake, he's at their cabin. Justin spies on Perry and Kurt as they leave, then arrive later with a hostage. She's Chelsea Stuart (Krystee Clark), a toy tycoon's teen daughter being held for a $1 million ransom. Justin locates his family, who have been pestering local hayseed cops with their alert for a missing boy. But the Rogers believe Justin's kidnap tale is just another prank. Alone, Justin goes back and frees Chelsea. To hunt them down Perry summons his old friend "the Tracker" (Jim Doughan), who indeed leads the kidnappers right to the young fugitives. By then, however, the Rogers family has realized that Justin was telling the truth. They lead a small posse of bumbling lawmen to rescue the kids and arrest the bad guys. Chelsea's wealthy father joins the Rogers for a Thanksgiving celebration.

It's been posited that the folks at New Horizons purge themselves after grinding out much lewd and violent dreck for the direct-to-video market by making harmless children's features, almost as a form of therapy. To judge from ALONE IN THE WOODS a whole lot of purging went on. Producers Andrew Stevens and Ashok Amritraj, responsible for much sinfully dumb horror, action, and "erotic thrillers," leave behind the world of makeup gore and augmented breasts for what amounts to an anemic blend of "The Ransom of Red Chief" and the HOME ALONE series (actually, it's much less violent than John Hughes's comedy blockbusters). ALONE IN THE WOODS is one of those comedies that assumes a guy with his foot stuck in a bucket is hilarious—the adjective "lame" would seem most apt, and the only honest laugh comes from a black-and-white flashback to the Tracker's youth. Bluhm looks too bright for this stuff,

Vennera and Hues try to generate a spark of energy in their bickering byplay, and nobody for a moment pretends the material has any realism, suspense or thrills, although there is that cliched moral about a businessman dad (Chelsea's) learning to spend quality time with his offspring. That's all well and good for sleaze-weary actors and filmmakers, but viewers can spend quality time elsewhere than ALONE IN THE WOODS.—C.C.

d, John Putch; p, Andrew Stevens, Ashok Amritraj; assoc p, Tripp Reed; w, J. Riley Lagesen; ph, Frank E. Johnson; ed, Vanick Moradian; m, David Lawrence; prod d, Billy Jett; sound, Brian S. Tracey; casting, Hannah Burks, Noble Henry; cos, Bonnie Stauch; makeup, Shauna G.

Children's/Comedy **(PR: A MPAA: PG)**

ALWAYS OUTNUMBERED ★★★½

(U.S., 1998) 108m Palomar Pictures ~ HBO c/bw

Laurence Fishburne *(Socrates Fortlow)*; Bill Cobbs *(Right Burke)*; Daniel Williams *(Darryl)*; Natalie Cole *(Iula Browne)*; Bill Nunn *(Howard M'Shalla)*; Bridgid Coulter *(Corina M'Shalla)*; Laurie Metcalf *(Mrs. Grimes)*; Kevin Carroll *(Petis)*; Jamaal Carter *(Phillip)*; Bill Duke *(Blackbird Wills)*; Cicely Tyson *(Luvia)*; Isaiah Washington *(Wilfred/Willie)*

This HBO production is based on acclaimed mystery author Walter Mosley's book *Always Outnumbered, Always Outgunned,* a series of short stories featuring Socrates Fortlow, an ex-con just trying to keep his head above water in south central Los Angeles. A fine screenplay by Mosley and a terrific performance by star Laurence Fishburne make it a film that's not to be missed.

Socrates Fortlow (Laurence Fishburne)—or "Socko" as his friends call him—is an ex-convict living one step above homelessness. He tries to apply for a job in a white neighborhood, but the manager (Laurie Metcalf) repeatedly refuses to accept his application because he doesn't have a phone. One morning he discovers a boy, Darryl (Daniel Williams), stealing food; after fixing him a meal, Socrates sees a familiar look in the boy's eye, and the boy reluctantly admits that he saw a violent teen, Phillip (Jamaal Carter), kill another boy. Socrates anonymously informs the dead boy's mother, then encourages the boy to stand up to Phillip.

Socrates, it seems, has a knack for helping people out: he helps a friend, Howard (Bill Nunn), ashamed because he cannot find a job that suits his computer skills, to reconcile with his beautiful wife, Corina (Bridgid Coulter); he organizes a gang of neighbors to shake down a vicious crack head who has been mugging old ladies and run him out of town; and, when things become too dangerous for Darryl, he asks Howard and Corina to take the boy with them as they move to Venice, where Howard has found a job. Finally, he helps his best friend, Right Burke (Bill Cobbs), an old man just diagnosed with terminal stomach cancer, by buying street painkillers from a local dealer (Bill Duke). To show thanks, Burke takes Socrates out for a night on the town, during which he reveals he's going to take all the painkillers at once, killing himself. Knowing there's nothing else that can be done, Socrates leaves his dying friend at a bus stop and heads home.

ALWAYS OUTNUMBERED, ALWAYS OUTGUNNED succeeds due to the happy marriage of star and screenwriter, Laurence Fishburne and Walter Mosley (who also serve as the film's executive producers). As created by Mosley, Socrates Fortlow is a gem of character: strong, wise, and almost classically flawed (not unlike Ezekiel Rawlins in 1995's DEVIL IN A BLUE DRESS, based on a Mosley novel). Brought up on the street and raised in prison, Socrates is well aware that the world is a harsh place, and that the real challenge is in getting by with your self-respect intact. Fishburne seizes the role of Socrates and soars, depicting the fear and agonizing frustration that comes with trying to keep it together on the street: it's almost painful watching him return to the supermarket again and again just to apply for a job as a bagger, only to be lied to and tossed out by the manager.

But ALWAYS OUTNUMBERED, ALWAYS OUTGUNNED also features a dynamite supporting cast. In addition to the always reliable Bill Nunn and Bill Cobbs, there are small roles by Bill Duke, Natalie Cole (as the proprietor of a local diner), and Cicely Tyson (as Burke's distrustful landlady). Daniel Williams, too, holds his own as young Darryl, a boy growing up in a world of guns and indiscriminate murder. To see these characters strive to maintain their dignity amidst their poverty is a rare and wonderful thing. *(Violence, sexual situations, profanity.)*—B.T.

d, Michael Apted; p, Anne-Marie MacKay, Jonathan Ker; exec p, Laurence Fishburne, Walter Mosley; co-p, Jeffrey Downer; w, Walter Mosley (from the book by Mosley); ph, John Bailey; ed, Rick Shaine; m, Michael Franti; prod d, Keith Brian Burns; casting, Linda Lowry, John Brace

Drama **(PR: C MPAA: R)**

AMERICAN DRAGONS

(SEE: DOUBLE EDGE)

AMERICAN HISTORY X ★★★★

(U.S., 1998) 118m The Turman/Morrissey Co.; The Steve Tisch Co.; New Line ~ New Line c/bw

Edward Norton *(Derek Vinyard)*; Edward Furlong *(Danny Vinyard)*; Fairuza Balk *(Stacey)*; Stacy Keach *(Cameron Alexander)*; Avery Brooks *(Bob Sweeney)*; Beverly D'Angelo *(Doris Vinyard)*; Jennifer Lien *(Davin)*; Ethan Suplee *(Seth)*; Elliott Gould *(Murray)*; Joe Cortese *(Rasmussen)*; William Russ *(Dennis)*; Guy Torry *(Lamont)*; Jason Bose-Smith *(Little Henry)*; Antonio David Lyons *(Lawrence)*; Alex Sol *(Mitch McCormick)*; Keram Malicki-Sanchez *(Chris)*; Giuseppe Andrews *(Jason)*; Michelle Christine White *(Lizzy)*; Jonathan Fowler Jr. *(Jerome)*; Chris Masterson *(Daryl Dawson)*; Nicholas R. Oleson *(Huge Aryan)*; Jordan Marder *(Curtis)*; Paul LeMat *(McMahon)*; Tommy L. Bellissimo *(Cop #2)*; Cherish Lee *(Kammi)*; Sam Vlahos *(Dr. Aguilar)*; Tara Blanchard *(Ally)*; Anne Lambton *(Cassandra)*; Steve Wolford *(Reporter)*; Richard Noyce *(Desk Sergeant)*; Danso Gordon *(Buddy #1)*; Jim Norton *(Randy)*; David Basulto *(Guard)*; Alexis Rose Coen *(Young Ally)*; Kiant Elam *(Lawrence's Partner)*; Paul Hopkins *(Student)*; Keith Odett *(Random Skinhead)*; Paul Short *(Stocky Buddy)*; Nigel Miguel *(Basketball Player)*

First-time director Tony Kaye's assured handling of a difficult subject, complemented by the magnetic performance of star Edward Norton, makes AMERICAN HISTORY X an absorbing, challenging message drama.

The publicly expressed Nazi beliefs of LA high schooler Danny Vinyard (Edward Furlong) enrage his history teacher Murray (Elliott Gould). Brought before school principal Bob Sweeney (Avery Brooks), Danny is asked to participate in an experimental class called "American History X." Danny will be the only student and his only assignment is to write a paper explaining the circustances behind his older brother's imprisonment for the murder of a black man three years earlier. Danny idolizes his skinhead brother, Derek (Edward Norton), who's being released that day. Derek has changed, however, and becomes alarmed when he returns home to find Danny running with his old cronies: his trashy girlfriend (Fairuza Balk), the obese Seth (Ethan Suplee), and white power guru Cameron Alexander (Stacy Keach). Derek protects his family from the white supremacists, kicking Seth out of the house, beating Alexander when he pleads with Derek to reclaim his status, and making plans to find a job so the Vinyards can move away to a safer neighborhood.

Meanwhile, Danny writes his paper, revealing the family's story: his fireman father (William Russ) was shot by a black gang member, an event which sent grief-stricken Derek down the path of race hate. His stature as a white power leader grows after he confronts minorities on the local basketball court, harasses a shop owner employing illegal immigrants, and later castigates his widowed mother's boyfriend (history teacher Murray) with an anti-Semitic diatribe. Derek's rein of terror ends in the slaying of two blacks trying to steal his truck. Danny witnesses Derek's actions.

Sentenced to three years, Derek becomes disillusioned by drug trafficking between his white power brethren and the black community in prison. When he's beaten and raped in a prison shower by his comrades, Derek breaks away from the skinheads.

Back in the present, Derek walks Danny to school but is stopped by the LAPD. Alexander's been assaulted and his followers are threatening revenge; the police ask Derek to defuse the tension. Reluctantly, Derek agrees, while Danny continues on to school. Confronted in the lavatory by a black classmate he once threatened, Danny is shot and dies. As Derek arrives and cradles his brother's body, Danny's voice recites a passage from his "American History X" essay, a quote from Abraham Lincoln's inaugural address to the nation that "we must not be enemies."

British director Kaye battled with the producing-releasing company that funded AMERICAN HISTORY X, New Line, over the right to a final cut. He claimed he was wholly dissatisfied with the version of the film that was released to theaters (asking at one point to have his name struck from the film's credits and the moniker "Humpty Dumpty" substituted). Whether his protests were the valid effort of an artist to retain creative control of his vision or an example of his own "hype art" ballyhoo (the phrase Kaye has given to his own confrontational style of dealing with the art world and the press), the finalized version of the film is indeed superb. Save for the bloated sequence depicting Derek's homecoming, AMERICAN HISTORY X is consistently engrossing. The flashbacks revealing the Vinyards' history is cleverly arranged in chronologically reverse order; the film moves simultaneously backward and forward after Danny begins writing his assignment. Murder-mystery style, this allows Kaye to strip away Derek's defense mechanisms much like the layers of an onion. As his character becomes younger in the flashbacks, a stark contrast is established between Derek as a naive boy and his later incarnation as a muscular, demonic murderer. The third act, in which a teenage Derek falls under the influence of his racist father, while Danny moves forward toward his death, is heartbreaking.

Norton's extraordinary performance (which earned him an Oscar nomination) is the film's most important asset. In the slow-motion interlude in which Derek is arrested in the street following his grisly slaying of the car thieves, a symphony of rage, pain, defiance, and fear move across the actor's face. This dramatic instant, and the insanely sadistic murder preceding it, constitute a brutal one-two punch.

AMERICAN HISTORY X is an intelligent, emotionally draining examination of race hatred. Revealing Derek's monstrosities in the film's first act, Kaye then audaciously sets about transforming him back into a human being, daringly attempting to elicit sympathy for him. AMERICAN HISTORY X doesn't flinch in its depiction of Derek's crimes, nor does it stoop to emotional manipulation in its efforts to redeem him. That the film gets viewers to pity Derek Vinyard is a testament to Kaye's inventive camerawork, inspired writing from scripter David McKenna, and an impeccably nuanced performance by Norton. *(Graphic violence, extensive nudity, sexual situations, adult situations, substance abuse, extreme profanity.)*—K.W.

d, Tony Kaye; p, John Morrissey; exec p, Steve Tisch, Lawrence Turman, Kearie Peak, Bill Carraro; co-p, David McKenna, Jon Hess; w, David McKenna; ph, Tony Kaye; ed, Gary Greenberg, Alan Heim; m, Anne Dudley; prod d, Jon Gary Steele; art d, Dan Olexiewicz, James Kyler Black; set d, Tessa Posnansky; sound, Steve Nelson (mixer), Frederick Howard (design); fx, Tom Bellissimo; casting, Valerie McCaffrey; cos, Douglas Hall; makeup, Christina Smith, John E. Jackson, Matthew W. Mungle (effects); stunts, Ernie Orsatti, Noon Orsatti, Denney Pierce, Paul Short

AAN Best Actor: Edward Norton

Drama **(PR: O MPAA: R)**

AN ALAN SMITHEE FILM
(SEE: BURN HOLLYWOOD BURN)

ANOTHER DAY IN PARADISE ★★★
(U.S., 1998) 101m Chinese Bookie Pictures; Larry Clark Film ~ Trimark c

James Woods *(Mel)*; Melanie Griffith *(Sid)*; Vincent Kartheiser *(Bobbie)*; Natasha Gregson Wagner *(Rosie)*; James Otis *(Reverend)*; Branden Williams *(Danny)*; Brent Briscoe *(Clem)*; Peter Sarsgaard *(Ty)*; Paul Hipp *(Richard Johnson)*; Kim Flowers *(Bonnie Johnson)*; John Gatins *(Phil)*; Ryan Donahue *(Barry)*; Christopher Doyle *(Conan)*; Dick Hancock *(Breather)*; Pamela Gordon *(Waitress)*; Jay Leggett *(Security Guard)*; Michael Jeffrey Woods *(Big Man)*; Karen Lee Sheperd *(Big Man's Wife)*; Mitchell Orr Jr. *(Big Man's Boy)*; Leo Fitzpatrick *(Guard at Reverend's Gate)*; Simon Williams *(Maitre d')*; Steven Gererd Connell *(Gas Station Attendant)*; Clarence Carter *(Himself)*; Band Members: Roosevelt Bitten; Greg Dalton; Donald Hayes; Ishma Israel; Maurice James; Eddie Lott; Will Miller; Darryl Richards; Isaac Smith

A homage to the art-gangster film, the harsh ANOTHER DAY IN PARADISE tells the story of a lowly band of outlaws. The film generally succeeds as a narrative, but lacks any original elements.

In the 1970s Midwest, Mel (James Woods), a professional thief, helps save the life of a petty burglar, Bobbie (Vincent Kartheiser), after Bobby is bludgeoned by a guard during an attempted robbery. Mel takes a liking to Bobbie, and, despite the failure of the break-in, enlists him as a partner for his next heist. Mel also invites Bobbie's girlfriend, Rosie (Natasha Gregson Wagner), to join him and his moll, Sid (Melanie Griffith), in their upcoming road trip.

At first, the four become a makeshift family on the road, enjoying each other's company during shopping trips and nightclub hopping. Sid even grows maternal when she learns that Rosie is pregnant with Bobbie's baby. But life quickly turns grim during an attempted drug deal when some redneck customers think they are being outfoxed and start beating and shooting at the foursome. Though they escape, Mel is badly hit, Bobbie is severely bruised, and Rosie loses her baby. Sid drives them to the Reverend (James Otis), an odd, gun-happy ex-preacher, who nurses the invalids back to health.

After his recuperation, an angry and increasingly deranged Mel tries once more to score big. He gets a tip about some valuable jewels in a store, which he plans to rob, but on the night of the theft, Mel, Sid, and Bobbie find the store safe empty. Later, Bobbie returns to the hotel where they are staying and finds Rosie dead from a drug overdose. The next morning, Mel, Sid, and a numb Bobby head over to the home of the store owners, the Johnsons (Paul Hipp, Kim Flowers), to get the jewels from them directly. Mel goes berserk and kills the Johnsons after the robbery. Now on the lam for murder, Mel plans to kill Bobbie, because he is afraid Rosie's corpse might be linked to them. At a rest stop, however, Sid gives Bobbie some of their loot and secretly arranges for him to escape from Mel. When Mel finds out, he tries to track Bobbie down, but fails; instead, he drives off, furious at Sid for her act of charity.

Larry Clark's follow-up to KIDS (1995) features the same sort of realistic, cinema verite edginess that made his debut feature hard to ignore—and controversial in its depiction of underage sex. There's sex here, too, and some of it feels gratuitous, as does Clark's almost pornographic coverage of the thin nude body of his young protagonist (sensitively played by Vincent Kartheiser). As was the case with KIDS, and Clark's celebrated coffee table photo essay-books, ANOTHER DAY IN PARADISE has the creepy resonance of a Calvin Klein underwear ad.

But aside from this, the film (based on ex-con Eddie Little's novel), builds solidly as a story about social outcasts who form an unlikely family unit, but whose dysfunction proves their downfall. Clark and screenwriters Stephen Chin and Christopher Landon clearly pay their respects to both Arthur Penn's BONNIE AND CLYDE (1967) and Robert Altman's THIEVES LIKE US (1974), two films that also encourage identification with violent antiheroes and heroines. ANOTHER DAY IN PARADISE works just as well as a modern social tragedy, although it follows so many other imitations of those landmark revisionist gangster films (GUNCRAZY, KALIFORNIA), it may not seem so raw or shocking, even with many scenes of extreme, bloody violence, and drug use.

The usually annoying James Woods (who also coproduced with Clark and Chin) fits perfectly into his role (the actor's expletive-filled logorrhea is used appropriately for once), and Melanie Griffith reminds viewers she was once more than a kewpie-doll Hollywood type (Clark effectively uses uncompromising close-ups to accentuate Griffith's role as a faded, desperate beauty). Natasha Gregson Wagner seems slightly mature for Rosie, but she plays the role with tender perception, and James Otis adds a note of comic horror in his role as the Reverend. Technically, the film is first-rate, with Clark intermingling naturalism with some interesting photographic effects to mimic the hallucinatory haze of the characters. Only Griffith's collagen-filled lips distract from Clark's seemingly realistic reproduction of the 1970s Midwest, with its period rock and rhythm-and-blues soundtrack (including "Me & Mrs. Jones," "That's How It Feels," and the perfect finale, "One More Cup of Coffee"). Though familiar in many respects, ANOTHER DAY IN PARADISE raises its unpleasantness to art-form level. *(Graphic violence, nudity, sexual situations, adult situations, substance abuse, extreme profanity.)*—E.M.

d, Larry Clark; p, Stephen Chin, Larry Clark, James Woods; co-p, Scott Shiffman; w, Christopher Landon, Stephen Chin (based on the book by Eddie Little); ph, Eric Edwards; ed, Luis Colina; prod d, Aaron Osborne; art d, Erin Cochran; set d, Michelle Munoz; sound, Arthur Rochester; fx, Darryl Pritchett; casting, John Papsidera; cos, Kathryn Morrison; makeup, Elisa beth Deitrich Fry; stunts, Steven Lambert

Drama/Crime/Action **(PR: O MPAA: R)**

ANTZ ★★½

(U.S., 1998) 83m Pacific Data Images; DreamWorks Pictures ~ DreamWorks SKG c

VOICES OF: Woody Allen *(Z-4195)*; Dan Aykroyd *(Chip)*; Anne Bancroft *(Queen)*; Jane Curtin *(Muffy)*; Danny Glover *(Barbatus)*; Gene Hackman *(General Mandible)*; Jennifer Lopez *(Azteca)*; John Mahoney *(Drunk Scout)*; Paul Mazursky *(Psychologist)*; Grant Shaud *(Foreman)*; Sylvester Stallone *(Weaver)*; Sharon Stone *(Princess Bala)*; Christopher Walken *(Cutter)*; Jim Cummings; Jerry Sroka; April Winchell *(Additional Voices)*

The second feature to be fully computer-generated (following 1995's TOY STORY), ANTZ represents the initial foray by DreamWorks SKG (Spielberg-Katzenberg-Geffen) into the Disney-dominated animation field; the film beat Disney's own CGI insect movie, A BUG'S LIFE, out of the gate by opening a few weeks earlier in 1998. Technically impressive and humorously voiced by an all-star cast, the film is nevertheless disappointing for its dumbed-down plot and the pandering way in which it injects gratuitous violence and commercial product plugs.

A worker ant named Z (voice of Woody Allen) becomes dissatisfied with his job digging a giant tunnel in the ant colony under the tyrannical control of Gen. Mandible (voice of Gene Hackman). After work, Z meets a drunk who tells him about an above-ground paradise called Insectopia. Looking for some excitement, Princess Bala (voice of Sharon Stone), who's unhappily engaged to Mandible, goes slumming in the workers' bar and dances with Z, who immediately falls in love with her, but she then leaves him. Hoping to see Bala again, Z convinces a soldier friend of his named Weaver (voice of Sylvester Stallone) to switch places with him, but Z is unaware that Mandible has declared war against the termites, and he's shipped out to the front lines.

On the battlefield, the termites are wiped out, but so are all of the ants, except for Z, who inadvertently survives. He's hailed as a hero upon his return, but Mandible tries to arrest him when he learns that he danced with Bala. Z takes Bala hostage and goes above-ground with her, where he finds Insectopia: a picnic area stocked with food-filled trash cans. Initially hostile toward Z, Bala gradually falls for him, especially after he saves her life several times. After Bala is captured and taken back to Mandible, Z returns to the underground colony and learns that Mandible intends to overthrow the queen (voice of Anne Bancroft) and kill all of the worker ants, but Z frees Bala and with help from Weaver and the other workers, they defeat Mandible.

The very idea of Woody Allen as a neurotic ant is hilarious, and his vocal contribution emerges as the best thing about ANTZ, spicing up the proceedings with typically droll putdowns, angst-ridden narration, and even some Bob Hope-style romantic growls. First seen on a couch kvetching to a psychologist about his upbringing as "the middle child in a family of 5 million," and complaining that he wants more out of life than to lift 10 times his body weight, the nebbishy-intellectual character of Z is straight out of an early Woody Allen movie (he reportedly reworked his dialogue to match his usual screen persona). It's just a shame that they didn't let Allen write the whole script, since he undoubtedly could have come up with something a little more imaginative than what's here. Depicting the insect society in anthropomorphic terms and giving the ants human characteristics is amusing in the early scenes, but the novelty quickly wears off as the plot develops into a standard royalty-commoner romance featuring an ultra-bitchy and obnoxious princess, and a military coup subplot with much "Indiana Jones"-like underground cave skullduggery. Much funnier and more inventive are the above-ground sequences which deal with the bugs' hazardous interaction with human society (dazzlingly rendered images involving a flame-igniting magnifying glass, a fly-swatter, and a piece of gum stuck to a gigantic stomping sneaker), as well as the satire of the insect class-system, as when Bala and Z run into a hilariously snooty pair of WASP-y wasps, and later a group of slacker bugs.

As for the computer animation, there's no denying that it's often visually striking, featuring exceptional detail and depth, but curiously, the ants don't really look that much like ants, and they're not black, but rather have been given a p.c. light brown color, along with a grainy texture that makes them look like wood. And for all of the CGI's mathematical, geometrical, and rhythmic perfection, there is something missing—call it heart or soul or the human touch—as reflected in the ants' giant, coldly robotic looking eyes. What's not missing, unfortunately, are blatant and extended plugs for Pepsi products (the company is one of DreamWorks's business partners), as well as typically Spielbergian excess in the fright and violence department (such as the gory STARSHIP TROOPERS-like termite battle), while Gen. Mandible's fascist rants seem a bit extreme for a kid's movie. Indeed, despite the film's purported pro-individualist message, there's something vaguely demagogic about the whole enterprise, in which every element has been calculated for maximum populist appeal. *(Profanity, violence.)*—M.S.

d, Eric Darnell, Tim Johnson; p, Brad Lewis, Aron Warner, Patty Wooton; exec p, Penney Finkelman Cox, Sandra Rabins, Carl Rosendahl; w, Todd Alcott, Chris Weitz, Paul Weitz; ed, Stan Webb; m, Harry Gregson-Williams, John Powell; prod d, John Bell; art d, Kendal Cronkhite; set d, Don Weinger; anim, Rex Grignon, Raman Hui; fx, Ken Bielenberg; casting, Leslee Feldman

Animated/Children's/Fantasy (PR: A MPAA: PG)

APPARITION

(SEE: PHOTOGRAPHING FAIRIES)

APT PUPIL ★★★½

(U.S., 1998) 111m Bad Hat Harry Productions; Phoenix Pictures ~ TriStar c

Ian McKellen *(Kurt Dussander)*; Brad Renfro *(Todd Bowden)*; Bruce Davison *(Richard Bowden)*; Elias Koteas *(Archie)*; David Schwimmer *(Edward French)*; Joshua Jackson *(Joey)*; Mickey Cottrell *(Sociology Teacher)*; Michael Reid MacKay *(Nightmare Victim)*; Ann Dowd *(Monica Bowden)*; James Karen *(Victor Bowden)*; Marjorie Lovett *(Anges Bowden)*; David Cooley *(Gym Teacher)*; Blake Anthony Tibbetts *(Teammate)*; Heather McComb *(Becky Trask)*; Katherine Malone *(Student)*; Grace Sinden *(Secretary)*; Anthony Moore *(Umpire)*; Kevin Spirtas *(Paramedic)*; Michael Byrne *(Ben Kramer)*; Danna Dennis *(Nurse)*; Jan Triska *(Isaac Weiskopf)*; Joe Morton *(Dan Richler)*; Michael Artura *(Detective Getty)*; Donna Marie Brown *(Mother)*; Mark Flythe *(Darren)*; Warren Wilson *(Newscaster)*; Jill Harris *(Reporter)*; Norbert D. Singer *(Hospital Administrator #1)*; Mildred Singer *(Hospital Administrator #2)*; Mary Ottoman *(Doctor)*

For the followup to his 1995 hit THE USUAL SUSPECTS, director Bryan Singer adapted one of novelist Stephen King's darker, nonsupernatural works, the tale of a young boy's obsession with a former Nazi. The result is a mesmerizing, if sometimes discomforting, examination into the nature of evil.

Todd Bowden (Brad Renfro) seems like a typical bright high school kid, but he's really a closet WWII freak with a keen interest in Nazis. One day he spots a familiar-looking old man (Ian McKellen) on a bus; by studying war books and surreptitiously collecting the man's fingerprints, Todd determines he is former Nazi concentration camp officer Kurt Dussander, in hiding from governments that wish to prosecute Nazis for war crimes. Todd threatens to expose Dussander unless he tells him all the grisly details of the concentration camps, the ones that history books are afraid to include. Fearing the wrath of the Nazi hunters, Dussander has no choice but to comply.

As Dussander spins his terrible tales, the Nazi inside him is reawakened, as evidenced by his attempt to cook a stray cat alive in his oven; meanwhile, the old man's stories haunt Todd to the point of his having disturbing visions, and his grades fall sharply. Posing as Todd's grandfather, Dussander meets with Todd's counselor (David Schwimmer) and negotiates a deal that will keep the boy from being expelled—a deal that finally gives Dussander some leverage against Todd, creating a tense and distrustful partnership. Things come to a head when Dussander attempts to murder a homeless man (Elias Koteas) and, in the process, suffers a heart attack. He summons Todd to finish off the wounded man and call an ambulance. While in the hospital, Dussander is recognized by another patient, a former concentration camp victim, who alerts the authorities. When Todd is questioned during the ensuing investigation, he denies any knowledge of Dussander's past. Only the counselor suspects anything different, but Todd silences him by threatening to manufacture a story that he is a pedophile. By the time Dussander dies in his hospital bed, Todd has blossomed into a full-blown sociopath.

Many viewers and critics were put off by the very dark territory through which APT PUPIL travels, and the film earned criticism (largely unfounded) for reducing the horror of the Holocaust to a plot point. That APT PUPIL is at times difficult to watch is undeniable, but only because director Singer and his cast do such a fine job of plumbing the depths of the human soul. Along with his regular editor-composer, John Ottman (whose contributions in both capacities cannot be overstated), Singer proves expert at crafting scenes of dark suspense that build to an explosively satisfying conclusion. (That woefully overused label "Hitchcockian" fits Singer nicely.) That the audience is often left squirming is far from accidental, and is evidence of a director in complete control.

Those viewers put off by APT PUPIL's dark subject matter missed fine performances by Brad Renfro and Ian McKellen. Renfro in particular is chilling as the all-American boy next door who would rather read about the atrocities of war than make out with a girl. McKellen's performance is masterful in the way it builds momentum: as an old man hiding from his past, Dussander seems fragile and perpetually exhausted; once the old spark is reignited, however, he is possessed of (or by) an inner strength that allows him to turn the tables on his young persecutor. The relationship between these two characters is the engine that drives APT PUPIL, and it is by turns fascinating and repulsive.

APT PUPIL's release was delayed by almost a year by a lawsuit in which several underage extras in a shower scene claimed they were filmed nude without their permission. Though in retrospect it appears the whole thing was likely an unfortunate misunderstanding, the film was stuck in court for months, during which time the shower scene was reshot with older extras (though the producers claimed the reshoot was not done in response to the film's legal troubles). *(Violence, profanity, adult situations.)*—B.T.

d, Bryan Singer; p, Jane Hamsher, Don Murphy, Bryan Singer; exec p, Tim Harbert; assoc p, John Ottman, Jay Shapiro; co-p, Thomas DeSanto; w, Brandon Boyce (from the novella by Stephen King); ph, Newton Thomas Sigel; ed, John Ottman; m, John Ottman; prod d, Richard Hoover; art d, Kathleen M. McKernin; set d, Jennifer Herwitt; sound, Geoffrey Lucius Patterson (mixer); casting, Francine Maisler, Kathryn Eisenstein; cos, Louise Mingenbach; makeup, Joni Meers Powell; stunts, Gary Jensen, Ben Jensen, Dustin Courtney

Thriller/Drama **(PR: C MPAA: R)**

ARGUING THE WORLD ★★★

(U.S., 1998) 107m Riverside Film Productions; Thirteen/WNET ~ First Run Features c/bw

Daniel Bell; Irving Howe; Nathan Glazer; Irving Kristol; Alan Rosenberg *(Narrator)*

Four New York intellectuals look back over their lives in ARGUING THE WORLD, an informative if prosaic documentary about the differences among leading political and social thinkers of the 20th century.

During their days as young radicals in City College in the 1930s, Irving Howe, Daniel Bell, Nathan Glazer, and Irving Kristol argued that ideas could change the world, especially *their* ideas. These men were soon considered the leaders of the Second Generation of New York's Jewish intellectual society, which had formed a decade earlier with such stalwarts as Lionel and Diana Trilling, Meyer Shapiro, and Hannah Arendt. The preoccupying issue for this new generation was the future of Marxism around the world. College cafeteria debates pitted the "card-carrying" Communists—the Stalinists—against those disillusioned with Stalin's mandate for the Soviet Union—the Trotskyites (which included Howe, Bell, Glazer, and Kristol).

WWII and the Stalin-Hitler pact forced the two groups together temporarily, as part of the Socialist (and countrywide) effort to defeat Fascism. The four scholars' personal lives also changed: Irving Howe became a soldier in the War; Irving Kristol become wealthy; all became famous beyond their circle by writing provocatively about politics in such prestigious journals as *The New Leader*, *Commentary*, *Dissent*, and *The Public Interest*.

After the War and during the Cold War with the Soviet Union, ideological shifts occurred. Irving Howe remained an unreconstructed Leftist, but Irving Kristol became rabidly anti- Communist, to the point of implicitly condoning the congressional witch-hunts of the 1950s; Bell and Glazer also became more conservative and conformist, although supposedly remaining civil libertarian in their outlook. The four men had never been great friends to begin with; now they were more at odds than ever. In the 1960s, Howe and the college radicals of the day (e.g., Tom Hayden, Vickie Goldberg) accused the Old Guard of selling out their ideals. Even Howe himself was critiqued with his contemporaries as an "armchair intellectual liberal."

By the 1970s and '80s, Kristol actively supported the candidacy of ultraconservative Ronald Reagan, Glazer castigated liberal social policy, and all four continued writing and lecturing. Before his death in 1993, Irving Howe maintained his lack of sentiment for both the past and the rifts among his colleagues. His memorial service brought together many former friends and radical thinkers, but not Bell, Glazer, or Kristol.

ARGUING THE WORLD covers a lot of personal and political ground about the four celebrated philosophers and the times in which they lived. Joseph Dorman's documentary bolsters the history lesson with some interesting insights into the lives of the men, how their Jewish backgrounds affected their beliefs, and how their thoughts changed over the years. Mostly, the film dutifully familiarizes viewers with facts about the American political scene from the Depression to the 1990s.

Not surprisingly, ARGUING THE WORLD, as a film, reflects the staidness, not the radicalism, of its subject matter. It might be asking too much to expect Dorman (who produced, wrote, and directed) to have created more than another "talking head," PBS-style documentary, but any film about nonconformity could benefit from *some* artistic envelope-pushing. For example, there are no visual metaphors for any philosophy discussed and very few uses of the medium to explicate the ideas.

Even within its own style, however, ARGUING THE WORLD misses the mark at times: after setting up a new "debate" between Kristol and Bell by crosscutting their recent interviews, Dorman goofs on the eye-line matching, diminishing the effectiveness of the moment. While Dorman places his subjects within needed social, cultural, and historical context, and includes interviews with individuals other than the four, he also tends to glorify the stuffy quartet too much. When the "armchair intellectual" attack is mentioned, the labeling seems justified, but the film generally favors the four men (even the supercilious neoconservative Kristol) over their ideological descendants and adversaries.

Still, the information itself is useful and some of the participants (particularly Irving Howe) display an engaging wit that compensates for the dryness of the approach to the subject matter. ARGUING THE WORLD may not inspire great thinking itself, but it allows viewers to understand a large and significant chunk of increasingly distant history.—E.M.

d, Joseph Dorman; p, Joseph Dorman; exec p, Arnold Labaton; assoc p, Gail Segal; w, Joseph Dorman; ph, Peter Brownscombe, Barrin Bonet, Wayne De La Roche, Boyd Estus; ed, Jonathan Oppenheim; m, Adam Guettel; sound, Beo Morales, Quentin Chiapeta, Carrie Guinta

Documentary **(PR: A MPAA: NR)**

ARMAGEDDON ★★½

(U.S., 1998) 150m Touchstone ~ Buena Vista c

Bruce Willis *(Harry S. Stamper)*; Billy Bob Thornton *(Dan Truman)*; Ben Affleck *(A.J. Frost)*; Liv Tyler *(Grace Stamper)*; Keith David *(General Kimsey)*; Chris Ellis *(Walter Clark)*; Jason Isaacs *(Ronald Quincy)*; Will Patton *(Charles "Chick" Chapple)*; Steve Buscemi *(Rockhound)*; Ken Campbell *(Max Lennert)*; William Fichtner *(Colonel William Sharp)*; Jessica Steen *(Co-Pilot Jennifer Watts)*; Grayson McCouch *(Gruber)*; Owen Wilson *(Oscar Choi)*; Clark Brolly *(Freddy Noonan)*; Michael Clarke Duncan *(Jayotis "Bear" Kurleenbear)*; Peter Stormare *(Lev Andropov)*; Marshall Teague *(Colonel Davis)*; Anthony Guidera *(Co-Pilot Tucker)*; Greg Collins *(Lt. Halsey)*; J. Patrick McCormack *(General Boffer)*; Michael Kaplan *(NASA Tech #5)*; Ian Quinn *(Astronaut Pete Shelby)*; Christopher Worret *(Operator #1)*; Adam C. Smith *(Operator #2)*; John Mahon *(Karl)*; Grace Zabriskie *(Dottie)*; K.C. Leomiti *(Samoan)*; Eddie Griffin *(Little Guy)*; Mark Boone Jr. *(New York Guy)*; Deborah Nishimura *(Client #1)*; Albert Wong *(Client #2)*; Jim Ishida *(Client #3)*; Stanley Anderson *(President)*; James Harper *(Admiral Kelso)*; Ellen Cleghorne *(Helga the Nurse)*; Udo Kier *(Psychologist)*; John Aylward *(Dr. Banks)*; Mark Curry *(Stu the Cabbie)*; Seiko Matsuda *(Asian Tourist—Female)*; Harry Humphries *(Chuck Jr.)*; Dyllan Christopher *(Tommy)*; Judith Hoag *(Denise)*; Sage Allen *(Max's Mom)*; Lawrence Tierney *(Hollis Vernon "Grap" Stamper)*; Judith Drake *(Grap's Nurse)*; Steven Ford *(Nuke Tech)*; Christian Clemenson *(Droning Guy)*; Duke Valenti *(Roughneck #1)*; Michael "Bear" Taliferro *(Roughneck #2)*; Billy Devlin *(Roughneck #3)*; Frank Van Keeken; Kathleen Matthews *(Newscaster #2)*; J.C. Hayward *(Newscaster #3)*; Andrew Glassman *(Newscaster #4)*; Shawnee Smith *(Redhead)*; Dwight Hicks *(FBI Agent #1)*; Odile Broulard *(Geo Tech #1)*; Vic Manni *(Loanshark)*; Jim Maniaci *(Biker Customer)*; Layla Roberts *(Molly Mounds)*; Joe Allen *(Kennedy Launch)*; Bodhi

Pine Elfman, billed as Bodhi Elfman *(Math Guy)*; Alexander Johnson *(Newscaster)*; Kathy Neff *(Reporter #1)*; Victor Vinson *(Sector Director)*; Joseph Patrick Kelly *(Marine #1)*; Peter White *(Secretary of Defense)*; Rudy Mettia *(G-Man)*; Frederick Weller; Googy Gress; H. Richard Greene; Peter Murnik; Andrew Heckler; Jeff Austin; Matt Malloy; Brian Brophy; Brian Hayes Currie; Andy Milder *(NASA Techs)*; Patrick Richwood *(Dr. Nerd)*; Brian Mulligan *(Dr. Nerd)*; Greg Warmouth *(KSC News Reporter)*; John H. Johnson *(Pad Director)*; Charles Stewart *(Vacuum Chamber Tech)*; Scarlet Forge *(Young Grace)*; John Frazier *(Priest)*; Frankie *(Little Richard)*; Charlton Heston *(Narrator)*

One can never say that Hollywood is bereft of ideas: two something-big-is-about-to-hit-the-Earth-and-kill-us-all thrillers came out within a few weeks of each other in the summer of 1998. While the first of the two, DEEP IMPACT, had a serious case of the warm fuzzies, ARMAGEDDON is a jacked-up, in-your-face spectacle which has its sights set on being bigger, badder, faster, and louder than anything that came before it.

A meteor shower destroys several New York City landmarks. NASA subsequently learns of an asteroid the size of Texas that is set to hit Earth and extinguish all life on the planet in a mere 18 days. The only hope to avoid this calamity is to send an astronaut to the asteroid; there, the astronaut will dig an 800-foot hole, and drop a nuclear bomb into the asteroid's center. NASA director Dan Truman (Billy Bob Thornton) recruits Harry Stamper (Bruce Willis), the world's best deep-core oil driller, and his roughnecks—a ragtag bunch of kooks and reprobates—for the job. Stamper's #2 man is the headstrong A.J. (Ben Affleck), who's been pursuing a forbidden romance with Stamper's headstrong daughter, Grace (Liv Tyler). While Stamper and his men undergo some hasty astronaut training, Truman tries to keep the global threat a secret. In the meantime, another meteor shower wipes out Paris, and word gets out. Two space shuttles, with separate teams led by Stamper and A.J., are launched, but disaster plagues the mission. When the shuttles dock at the rickety *Mir* space station for refueling, an oil leak leads to an explosion, which almost kills the astronauts. Then, A.J.'s shuttle crashes on the asteroid, killing most of the crew. A.J. sets out in the mobile driller to find the other team, which has landed far off-target on a deep crust of iron, making drilling nearly impossible.

After learning of the problems experienced by the drilling crews, governmental powers back on Earth decide that the drillers are expendable, and make plans to explode the nuclear bomb by remote control, but Truman, who believes in Stamper, intervenes and allows the crews to continue their mission. Back on the asteroid, Stamper's drill wears out and all looks lost, until A.J. shows up with his equipment to finish the job. Once the preparatory work is included, the question remains as to whom in the drilling crews will accept the fatal task of staying behind to detonate the bomb. The survivors draw straws and A.J. loses, but at the last moment Stamper takes his place and gives the young man's engagement to Grace his blessing. With only seconds to spare, Stamper blows the big rock into halves that skim past the Earth. The survivors return and are welcomed as heroes by the public. A.J. and Grace wed.

Ever since the end of the Cold War, Hollywood has struggled to find a villain that would inspire the appropriate amount of indignation and jingoistic fervor in American audiences. In 1996, INDEPENDENCE DAY demonstrated that a grave threat to life, liberty, and the pursuit of a bull market could come from outer space. ARMAGEDDON (fittingly released on the 4th of July weekend) offers a wicked-looking asteroid. Despite the rock's inanimate status, it represents a threat to the red, white, and blue, and thus hero Bruce Willis has a clear reason for turning ballistic.

Director Michael Bay fashions the movie as a sadistic assault on the senses. A veteran of commercials and music videos, Bay is the kind of filmmaker who never opts for a simple straightforward view of the action when a swooshing camera movement or an obliquely-angled shot is possible. Bay's movies (BAD BOYS, THE ROCK) have proven that he is less concerned with narrative than he is with presenting totemic images in a rapid-fire fashion, fueled by a special kind of mindless momentum. To offer a simple instance of the way in which Bay avoids any kind of narrative consistency, one need only point to a scene early on in which Stamper finds Grace in A.J.'s bed, and then chases the young man around an oil-drilling platform with a shotgun, as if he were a moonshining hillbilly chasing off a revenuer. The scene is played for comedy, like much of the film's first half. Once the astronauts reach their destination, however, the viewer is supposed to take the characters seriously and care about their dilemmas. By that point, one assumes, Bay is hoping that the film's hyperkinetic editing will have wiped clean the viewer's memory of the film's coy comic moments.

Despite its inconsistent tone, the film does have enough slam-bang action to please viewers in search of a full-out, no-brain action movie. Add to this the welcome reunion of FARGO kidnappers Steve Buscemi and Peter Stormare, cast here as an always-horny super-genius and a crazy cosmonaut, and you've got a film that offers plenty of manufactured thrills and a few chuckles, as long as the viewer is willing to forget about logic, and remain comfortably numb. *(Profanity, violence.)*—P.R.

d, Michael Bay; p, Jerry Bruckheimer, Gale Anne Hurd, Michael Bay; exec p, Jonathan Hensleigh, Jim Van Wyck, Chad Oman; assoc p, Barry Waldman, Pat Sandston, Kenny Bates; w, J.J. Abrams, Jonathan Hensleigh (adapted by Tony Gilroy and Shane Salerno from a story by Jonathan Hensleigh and Robert Pool); ph, John Schwartzman; ed, Mark Goldblatt, Chris Lebenzon, Glen Scantlebury; m, Trevor Rabin; prod d, Michael White; art d, Geoff Hubbard; set d, Rick Simpson; sound, Keith A. Wester (mixer), Kevin O'Connell, Greg P. Russell, George Watters II; fx, Pat McClung, Richard R. Hoover, John Frazier, Dream Quest Images, Richard Stutsman; casting, Bonnie Timmerman; cos, Michael Kaplan, Magali Guidasci; makeup, Edouard F. Henriques III, Rick Stratton, Fred Blau; stunts, Kenny Bates

AAN Best Original Song: "I Don't Want to Miss a Thing"; Diane Warren; *AAN Best Sound:* Kevin O'Connell, Greg P. Russell, Keith A. Wester; *AAN Best Sound Effects Editing:* George Watters II; *AAN Best Visual Effects:* Richard R. Hoover, Pat McClung, John Frazier

Science Fiction/Action/Adventure (PR: C MPAA: PG-13)

ARMOUR OF GOD ★★★½

(Hong Kong, 1986) 94m Golden Harvest ~ Tai Seng c

(AKA: ARMOR OF GOD, THE; OPERATION CONDOR: THE ARMOUR OF GOD; OPERATION CONDOR 2: THE ARMOUR OF THE GODS; LONG XIONG HU DI)

Jackie Chan *(Jackie)*; Alan Tam *(Alan)*; Rosamund Kwan *(Laura)*; Lola Forner *(May)*; Bozidar Smiljanic *(Bannon)*; Ken Boyle *(Grand Wizard)*; John Ladalski *(Chief Lama)*; Robert O'Brien *(Witch Doctor)*; Boris Gregoric *(Man at Auction)*; Marcia Chisholm; Alicia Shonte; Vivian Wickliffe; Stephanie Evans; William Williams; Linda Denley *(Fighters)*; Kenny Bee; Bennett Pang; Anthony Chan; Danny Yip; Clarence Fok; Carina Lau *(Singers)*

Originally titled ARMOUR OF GOD, Jackie Chan's expensive, thrill-ride version of the INDIANA JONES series was so popular in Asia that it led to a tenuously related sequel, OPERATION

CONDOR. After the latter saw release in America, the earlier film underwent a title change to make *it* appear to be the sequel, and went straight to US video in 1998 as OPERATION CONDOR: THE ARMOUR OF GOD (with an entirely different title on the video box art, OPERATION CONDOR 2: THE ARMOUR OF THE GODS!).

Stealing an ancient sword from an African tribe, adventurer Jackie (Jackie Chan), known as the Asian Hawk, uses martial arts and grand stuntwork to effect his escape. After auctioning the sword, he is approached by his old friend, pop-singer Alan (Alan Tam), to help rescue Alan's girlfriend Laura (Rosamund Kwan), the girl that came between them when they all played in a band together. Demanded as ransom is the legendary Armour of God, of which the sword is part. Borrowing the Armour from a wealthy Count—on condition that they take his daughter May (Lola Forner) along on the adventure—they tangle with the kidnappers, a group of monks who live in a mountain monastery. Sneaking inside the stronghold, they easily rescue Laura, unaware that she has been drugged and programmed to retrieve the Armour.

And so she does, bringing a drugged Alan with her. Jackie breaks back into the monastery and rescues them both, along the way fighting battalions of monks and a group of wickedly acrobatic leather-clad women. In the end, he rather inadvertently dynamites the monastery, escaping by diving off the mountain onto a hot-air balloon piloted by Alan, Laura, and May.

In 1982, Eric Tsang had directed pop singer Sam Hui in the first of the immensely popular ACES GO PLACES films—a globe-hopping, stunt-filled, action comedy series featuring a suave, international rogue/jewel thief and his inept comic rival. For ARMOUR OF GOD, Tsang was enlisted as director and traveled to Yugoslavia along with numerous of Hong Kong's filmmaking elite. Shooting stopped when on the second take of a minor stunt, Chan fell from a tree and cracked open his skull, necessitating emergency surgery. (The accident and its aftermath are shown under the closing credits.) When filmmaking resumed, Chan was director.

Playing a pop singer was hardly a stretch for Alan Tam, who is one in real life; several of his songs (one a duet with Chan) and footage from an actual concert are interpolated into the film. With filming taking place in France and Austria, they naturally turned to Lola Forner, who had previously appeared with Chan in WHEELS ON MEALS (1983) and was, according to Chan, "the only European actress we knew." Her character disappears completely about two-thirds of the way through, when the serious fighting is about to start. Not long after, with Jackie entering the fortress for the second time, the film hits escape velocity, moving straight from one phenomenal set piece to another, with no room between to catch your breath. The opening scene, recognizable as Eric Tsang's original footage by Chan's uncommonly short haircut, is another gem of wild, sustained action. *(Violence, nudity.)*—A.B.

d, Jackie Chan, Eric Tsang; p, Leonard Ho; exec p, Raymond Chow, Chan Pui Wah, Edward Tang; co-p, Chua Lam; w, Edward Tang, Roy Szeto, billed as Szeto Chuck Hon, Ken Lowe, John Sheppard (based on an original story by Barry Wong); ph, Peter Ngor, Robert Thompson, Arthur Wong, Joseph Cheung; ed, Peter Cheung; m, Michael Lai; art d, William Cheung, Eddie Ma, Jonathan Cheung; fx, Steve Courtley, Brian Cox; cos, Shirley Chan; stunts, Jackie Chan's Stuntmen Club, Lau Kar Wing, Yuen Chun Yeung

Adventure/Comedy **(PR: C MPAA: R)**

ARTEMISIA ★★★

(Italy/Germany/France, 1997) 102m 3 Emme Cinematografica; Dania Film; Schlemmer Film; Premiere Heure; France 3 Cinema ~ Miramax Zoe c

Valentina Cervi *(Artemisia Gentileschi)*; Michel Serrault *(Orazio Gentileschi)*; Miki Manojlovic *(Agostino Tassi)*; Luca Zingaretti *(Cosimo Quorli)*; Emmannuelle Devos *(Costanza)*; Frederic Pierrot *(Roberto)*; Maurice Garrel *(The Judge)*; Brigitte Catillon *(Tuzia)*; Yahn Tregouet *(Fulvio)*; Jacques Nolot *(The Lawyer)*; Silvia De Santis *(Marisa)*; Renato Carpentieri *(Nicolo)*; Dominique Reymond *(Tassi's Sister)*; Liliane Rovere *(The Rich Merchant's Wife)*; Alain Ollivier *(The Duke)*; Patrick Lancelot *(The Acadamy Director)*; Rinaldo Rocco; Enrico Salimbeni *(Academy Students)*; Catherine Zago *(The Mother Superior)*; Lorenzo Lavia *(Orazio's Assistant)*; Sami Bouajila; Edoardo Ruiz; Aaron De Luca *(Tassi's Assistants)*; Guido Roncalli *(The Duke's Servant)*; Pierre Bechir *(The Rich Merchant's Son)*; Massimo Pittarello *(The Torturer)*

The little-known story of "the first female painter in art history" is eloquently told in ARTEMISIA, a distinctive though flawed biographical film.

In 1610 Italy, 17-year-old Artemisia Gentileschi (Valentina Cervi) studies painting under the guidance of her father, Orazio (Michel Serrault), a respected artist in the Florentine master's studio tradition. Orazio tries but fails to get his daughter admitted into the nearby painting Academy, which refuses her because of her gender. Orazio still supports Artemisia, although even he is upset by her desire to sketch and paint nude men. In the meantime, a young man she finds on a beach becomes her prime model.

Eventually, Orazio and the renowned artist Agostino Tassi (Miki Manojlovic) receive an important commission to paint religious frescoes in a local church. During the partnership, Artemisia asks Agostino to teach her his bold, unusual painting techniques. Initially, he refuses, but eventually he becomes enthralled by the talented, headstrong woman, particularly after she shows him her sketches. Gradually, the old master and the young student fall in love, and they spend most of their lesson time together having sex. Agostino even allows Artemisia to sketch him nude.

When Orazio hears about the romance, he investigates and finds the two together. Horrified, he accuses Agostino of betrayal and corruption, despite Artemisia's impassioned defense. Matters become more serious, however, when Orazio asks the church to arrest Agostino for raping his daughter. During the five-month trial, Artemisia refuses to condemn her lover, and the prosecution shifts to determine whether *she* had seduced *him*. Artemisia's nude sketches and her painting of herself as Judith (titled "Judith Beheading Holofernes") is used as proof of her wickedness, which is confirmed by a test of her virginity. The church officials try to force Artemisia to confess her sin by nearly breaking her hands, but Agostino, unable to watch the torture, confesses to raping her instead. He is jailed and she is freed. Immediately after the trial, she leaves her father and considers painting again once her hands heal. She never sees Agostino again, but she does reunite with her father 10 years later in England, after creating many fine works.

Artful but never ostentatious, ARTEMISIA treats the true story with a respectfully cool elan. The pictorial beauty never overwhelms the subject or the story, which is engrossing enough without sweeping flourishes. Artemisia Gentileschi indeed deserves greater recognition, despite the fact that both Miramax and writer-director Agnes Merlet ignore several other women artists (including Sofonisba Anguissola, Lavinia Fontana, and, earlier, several Greek painters) by calling Artemisia "the first female painter in art history." Still, Merlet's own use of chiaroscuro and skillful framing mirrors the Baroque era painter's best work (shown mainly in a climactic scene patterned after the similar "artist's epiphany" montage in LUST FOR LIFE, the 1956 van Gogh story). The most enjoyable parts of the film show Artemisia forging ahead against all odds (Valentina Cervi's refreshing performance recalls Judy Davis's work in MY BRILLIANT CAREER, 1979, another real-life story about a spunky heroine). Other highlights reveal the process of Artemisia's technique, in painting and sketching.

Unfortunately, Merlet's emphasis on Artemisia's romance with Agostino detracts somewhat from the feminist power of her tale. It's true that Artemisia's art and love intertwined early in her life with the lengthy scandal-trial, an important sequence, but the romanticized view of her passion here (for an overbearing and not very charismatic older married man) seems more like the stuff of a PBS adaptation of Bronte rather than an art biography with a modern sensibility. (It's also an insult to the historic record that the film portrays Agostino heroically stopping Artemisia's torture by confessing, something that never happened.)

At least ARTEMISIA presents both the art and amour in a sensible way, unlike the more greatly romanticized CAMILLE CLAUDEL (1988), the story of the eponymous sculptor. For those seeking a postmodern take on the art biography—and a film set in the same period as ARTEMISIA—Derek Jarman's CARAVAGGIO (1986) fits the frame a bit better. *(Violence, nudity, sexual situations, adult situations, profanity.)*—E.M.

d, Agnes Merlet; p, Patrice Haddad; exec p, Lilian Saly, Daniel Wuhrmann, Patricia Allard, Conchita Airoldi, Dino Di Dionisio; co-p, Christophe Meyer-Wiel, Leo Pescarolo; w, Agnes Merlet, Christine Mille, Patrick Amos; ph, Benoit Delhomme; ed, Guy Lecorne; m, Krishna Levy; prod d, Antonello Geleng; sound, Francois Waledisch, Jean-Pierre Laforce; casting, Bruno Levy; cos, Dominique Borg

Biography/Drama **(PR: C MPAA: R)**

ASYLUM ★★½

(U.S., 1997) 92m Westwind Productions ~ Norstar Entertainment c

Robert Patrick *(Nicholas Tordone)*; Malcolm McDowell *(Sullivan Rane/The Surgeon)*; Henry Gibson *(Dr. Edward Bellcheck)*; Jason Schombing *(Tommy)*; Peter Brown *(Dr. Frank Myers)*; Sarah Douglas *(Dr. Emily Hill)*; Kevin Anthony Cole *(Simmons)*; Deborah Worthing *(Amanda)*; Tom Billet *(Dearborn)*; Debra Wilson *(Belinda)*; Adam Gierasch *(Ronald Briggs)*; John Huffman *(Dr. Carl Bradley)*; Joseph Ashton *(Young Nick Tordone)*; Gary Roledar *(Michael Tordone)*; Rebecca Rothstein *(Hospital Receptionist)*; Alan Charof *(Dominick)*; Karl Bury *(Jake)*; Tom Poster *(Acting Instructor)*; Tyrone Douglas *(Hospital Orderly)*; Lawrence Crowley *(Subway Cop)*; Loren Lazerine *(Alucard)*; Irwin Keyes *(Screaming Patient)*; David Kirkwood *(Jigsaw)*; Sam Manning *(Marlboro Man)*; Kathryn Kates *(Nurse Taylor)*; Lewis Hanneman *(Night Rider)*

Writer-director James Seale exhibits a fondness for nonstop plot twists that makes ASYLUM a lively rehash of slasher pic cliches. Unfortunately, this movie clumsily circles the perimeter of camp, and muddies its potential as an intricate mystery.

Having witnessed the suicide of his father many years ago, traumatized private eye Nick Tordone (Robert Patrick) has been in therapy with Dr. Frank Myers (Peter Brown) since childhood. When Myers's sudden death at Fallbrook State Mental Hospital is ruled a suicide, a suspicious Nick goes undercover as a charity patient.

Run by eccentric genius Dr. Bellcheck (Henry Gibson), Fallbrook has been beset by a rash of patient disappearances. The murderer may be Sullivan Rane (Malcolm McDowell), a recently escaped serial killer. Nick surreptitiously gathers info from two patients—Tommy (Jason Schombing), who fancies himself a comic book hero, and "The Surgeon," actually the missing lunatic Rane in disguise. Nick soon discovers that Myers's death is similar to that of the vanished-presumed dead patients; he also finds air vents that provide easy access for a killer and an abandoned building that is off limits to the general population.

When the Surgeon admits he is Rane, Nick mistakenly presumes he is the patient-snuffer. But Rane is killed by an unseen assassin as Nick pursues him through the air vents. Inside the abandoned building, Nick is overpowered by Dr. Bellcheck's henchman Simmons (Kevin Anthony Cole). It is Dr. Bellcheck who has been "kidnapping" his own patients to use as guinea pigs for a suicide-inducing drug; he killed Dr. Myers when he became suspicious about the disappearances. (Bellcheck had been using cannibalistic Rane to dispose of the corpses). After Bellcheck shoots the now-expendable Simmons, Nick kicks Bellcheck into needles containing a lethal dose of his own drug.

While the subject of an investigator posing as a madman has been handled with more finesse, particularly in the harrowing SHOCK CORRIDOR (1963, whose star Peter Breck appears here as Dr. Myers), ASYLUM is nevertheless a fairly effective retread of the feigned-madness motif. Gruesome, but reasonably suspenseful, ASYLUM scarily travels those madhouse vents where deranged Bellcheck spirits away his helpless patients.

ASYLUM would be easier to recommend had it stuck to chills. Instead, it falls victim to tiresome SNAKE PIT stereotypes. And it wastes time with tired comic relief provided by lovable loony Tommy, whose crimefighting alter ego, Captain Destructo, becomes Nick's sleuthing partner. ASYLUM also spends too much energy developing Rane as a red herring. (Horror buffs will deduce the identity of the real killer from Henry Gibson's special billing.) As hard as it labors to mislead the audience, ASYLUM won't fool anyone. *(Graphic violence, extreme profanity, sexual situations, adult situations.)*—R.P.

d, James Seale; p, James Seale, William Webb; exec p, Richard Lowry; assoc p, Deverin Karol; w, James Seale; ph, David Rakoczy; ed, Mark Manos; m, Alan Williams; prod d, David Blass; art d, Christopher Lewis; set d, Beth Ann Lundin; sound, Darryl Patterson; fx, John Hartigan; casting, Dean Fronk; cos, Charmian Schreiner; makeup, Jennifer Montgomery; stunts, Kurt Bryant

Horror/Mystery **(PR: O MPAA: R)**

ATOMIC DOG ★½

(U.S., 1998) 86m Wilshire Court Productions ~ Showtime/Viacom c

Daniel Hugh Kelly *(Mr. Yates)*; Cindy Pickett *(Mrs. Yates)*; Isabella Hofmann *(Janice Rifkin)*; Micah Gardner *(Josh Yates)*; Katie Stuart *(Heather Yates)*; Deryl Hayes *(Dr. Herb Boyle)*; Scott Olynek *(Dwayne Compton)*; Ryan Northcott *(Hank)*; Matt Clarke *(Second Boy)*; Hal Kerbes *(Dr. Art Matoyan)*; J.C. Roberts *(Smitty)*; Andy Curtis *(Cop)*; Carrie Schiffler *(Office Manager)*; Paul Cowling *(Biohazard Worker)*

Camp fanatics may enjoy the cheesy nature of ATOMIC DOG's premise, but this mutant tale-wagger can't hold a candle to such classics of the possessed canine subgenre as DEVIL DOG, THE HOUND OF HELL (1978). Free of gore, this mild sci-fi is recommended for families of dog-fancying, anti-nuke activists.

Mr. and Mrs. Yates (Daniel Hugh Kelly, Cindy Pickett) move their family to an idyllic community near the Devils' Canyon Nuclear Power Plant. Unlike his pre-teen sister Heather (Katie Stuart), rebellious adolescent Josh (Micah Gardner) hates suburbia. He toys with joining a delinquent gang headed by Dwayne Compton (Scott Olynek), who dares his buddies to trespass at the nuke plant, not realizing its guard dog has been exposed to a radiation leak. After a frightened Josh heads home with his pooch Trixie, the Atomic Dog chases Dwayne, who falls to his death down a gully.

Trixie's scent has been picked up by the amorous Atomic Dog. Lured away and impregnated, Trixie later dies while delivering puppies Scamp and Lobo. Proud papa Atomic Dog begins communicating mentally with his son Lobo. When Atomic Dog kills a veterinarian (Deryl Hayer), he lets Lobo take the blame. With the help of neighbor Janice Rifkin (Isabella Hofmann), an animal biologist, a chastened Josh sets out to prove Lobo's innocence in the killing. But Josh is forced to shoot Lobo when, on orders from his father, the pup attacks Dr. Rifkin. Unable to control Scamp as he could Lobo, Atomic Dog adopts Heather, encouraging her to follow him to the plant. When the Yates try to reclaim their daughter, Atomic Dog tries to kill Josh and Mr. Yates by pulling the cord on overhead pipes. But when Heather gets in the way, Atomic Dog sacrifices his own life to push her to safety.

By the time the titular pooch has redeemed himself by turning heroic, the jaws of most viewers will be sore from dropping in disbelief. Who were ATOMIC DOG's producers trying to appeal to with this loopy script about a mutant mutt with Kreskinesque powers? To get to the nuggets of bad movie fun, however, you have to sift through tedious scientific explanations and pabulum about parental-child trust. Had the screenplay paralleled Atomic Dog's brainwashing parenting with Mr. Yates's dissipating control over his kids, this might have been a deliberate howler instead of what it is, an inadvertent dog. *(Violence.)*—R.P.

d, Brian Trenchard-Smith; p, Mark H. Ovitz; co-p, Ted Bauman; w, Miguel Tejada-Flores; ph, David Lewis; ed, Stephen Myers; m, Peter Bernstein; prod d, Roy Allan Amaral; set d, Linda Williams; sound, George Tarrant (mixer); fx, Robert Sheridan; casting, Penny Musarra; cos, Christine Thomson; makeup, Al Magallon; stunts, Kirk Jarrett

Science Fiction/Action (PR: C MPAA: PG-13)

AVENGERS, THE ★½

(U.S., 1998) 91m Jerry Weintraub Productions; Warner Bros. ~ Warner Bros. c

Ralph Fiennes *(John Steed)*; Uma Thurman *(Doctor Emma Peel)*; Sean Connery *(Sir August De Wynter)*; Fiona Shaw *(Father)*; Jim Broadbent *(Mother)*; Eddie Izzard *(Bailey)*; Eileen Atkins *(Alice)*; John Wood *(Tribshaw)*; Carmen Ejogo *(Brenda)*; Keeley Hawes *(Tamara)*; Shaun Ryder *(Donavan)*; Nicholas Woodeson *(Doctor Darling)*; Patrick Macnee *(Voice of Invisible Jones)*; Michael Godley *(Butler)*; Richard Lumsden *(Boodle's Porter)*; Daniel Crowder *(Messenger)*; Nadim Sawalha *(World Council of Ministers)*; Christopher Godwin *(World Council of Ministers)*; David Webber *(World Council of Ministers)*

Proving that a big budget and big-name stars can't compensate for the lack of witty scripting and charming characterizations, this feature-film update of the 1960s spy TV show bungles every chance to reinvent a classic.

British Ministry superior, "Mother" (Jim Broadbent), calls on his best secret agent, John Steed (Ralph Fiennes), to investigate recent odd fluctuations in the weather. Mother suspects the extreme swings in temperature have been masterminded by former Ministry official, Sir August De Wynter (Sean Connery), a rich eccentric, so he teams Steed up with Mrs. Emma Peel (Uma Thurman), a doctor in meteorological science.

Steed and Mrs. Peel visit De Wynter at his mansion, where, outside, Steed becomes caught in a snowstorm while, inside, Peel interrogates the clever owner. During their conversation, Peel realizes that De Wynter has an obsession with her, which is confirmed by Steed when Peel's cloned evil twin takes a shot at him on the grounds. Fortunately, the real Mrs. Peel rescues Steed and takes him back to her apartment, where she nurses him back to health.

Steed and Peel's investigation confirm Mother's theory that De Wynter has created technology to affect weather conditions as a way to blackmail world leaders into ceding him greater wealth. What Mother and the Avengers do not realize is that "Father" (Fiona Shaw), the Ministry's second-in-command, has been secretly aiding De Wynter.

On their way back to De Wynter's mansion, Steed and Peel are attacked by huge electronic insects, but they survive the onslaught and sneak onto the premises. Soon, they are separated, however, and, while Steed fights with De Wynter's henchmen, De Wynter tries seducing an unconscious Mrs. Peel. This time, Steed saves Peel, and brings her back to *his* apartment.

Finally, the Avengers learn about Father's traitorous role, and Mrs. Peel foils her balloon escape out of London just as De Wynter begins freezing the city. Back at De Wynter's mansion, Peel dismantles the device that is causing havoc in the weather, while Steed swashbuckles with De Wynter, killing him with his sword. The Avengers narrowly prevent a cyclone from hitting the city, and Mother later celebrates his victory, sipping champagne with his favorite superagents.

Unsure whether to recall the beloved past or create a novel present, THE AVENGERS invites the snickering criticism that it is cashing in on the trend to adapt small-screen successes for the large screen. In truth, there have been many attempts to make an AVENGERS feature, and the idea has always been sound, but this sorry effort points out a huge irony—that not only was the original TV series so much better made, but it was also so much more cinematic.

The screenplay is the main defect of the new film. Although patterned after the black-and-white Diana Rigg episode, "A Surfeit of H20," the story becomes muddled and confusing, particularly with the poorly explained presence of the evil Emma Peel doppelganger. More surprisingly, the dialogue completely lacks wit, so the suggestive banter between Steed and Mrs. Peel sounds puerile. A subtler, more serious flaw is that the film loses much of Mrs. Peel's point of view. Thus, whereas the original show championed the first capable, independent action heroine, the new incarnation turns her into just another sidekick, without the same fighting skills or sharp intelligence.

As portrayed by the overrated Uma Thurman, Mrs. Peel also loses her classiness. While Ralph Fiennes plays Steed with a look of wistful resignation, Thurman turns Mrs. Peel into a vain dilettante (with fake British accent). Both TV and film versions use Mrs. Peel as a sex object (in tight leather catsuits), but at least Diana Rigg and the TV writers rounded out her role (additionally, Rigg was far sexier in said catsuits). The other actors—including Eileen Atkins as an elderly agent—give more lively performances than the leads, although Sean Connery, in a rare villain role, merely shouts his lines.

Fans of the TV show looking for homages will appreciate the surreal production design, even if most of the film takes on the cold-plastic look of the BATMAN movies; and the few snatches of Laurie Johnson's famous theme music make Joel McNeely's new score all the more nondescript. It is sadly symbolic that Patrick Macnee, the original Steed, plays an invisible, unheralded agent in a cameo here. Comparisons to the TV series may be unfair, but even those who have never heard of THE AVENGERS will find the film barely passable in the action-spy genre; as the Avengers' boss declares early on: "Yes, it's bad!" From bad to worse. *(Violence.)*— E.M.

d, Jeremiah Chechik; p, Jerry Weintraub; exec p, Susan Ekins; w, Don Macpherson (based on characters from the British television series); ph, Roger Pratt; ed, Mick Audsley; m, Joel McNeely; prod d, Stuart Craig; art d, Michael Lamont, Andrew Ackland-Snow, Mark Harris; set d, Stephanie McMillan; sound, Clive Winter; fx, Joss Williams, Nick Davis; casting, Susie Figgis; cos, Anthony Powell; makeup, Daniel Parker; stunts, Mark Boyle

Adventure/Spy/Fantasy (PR: C MPAA: PG-13)

AYN RAND: A SENSE OF LIFE ★★

(U.S., 1998) 145m A G Media; Copasetic ~ Strand Releasing c

Sharon Gless *(Narrator)*; Dr. Michael S. Berliner; Dr. Harry Binswanger; Sylvia Bokor; Daniel E. Greene; Cynthia Peikoff; Dr. Leonard Peikoff; Al Ramrus; Dr. John Ridpath; Mike Wallace; Phil Donahue; Janne Peters *(Kay Gonda—cast of "Ideal")*; Peter Sands *(Dietrich von Esterhazy—cast of "Ideal")*

AYN RAND: A SENSE OF LIFE is a 145-minute deification of the noted atheistic rationalist. Its Academy Award nomination for Best Documentary further proves that, when it comes to nonfiction, Oscar doesn't have a clue.

The author of two perennial best-selling novels—*The Fountainhead* (1943) and *Atlas Shrugged* (1957)—Ayn Rand tirelessly promoted a philosophy centered on the "virtue of selfishness." Rand's rabid materialist philosophy embraces laissez-faire capitalism, reviles all forms of spiritualism, and brands altruism as "evil." An alternately sensible and repugnant philosophy that often neglects the realities of human nature, Rand's extremist views are ripe for a debate that filmmaker (and apparent Rand disciple) Michael Paxton refuses to offer.

The interview subjects are unwavering Randians like Leonard Peikoff, identified as "Ayn Rand's intellectual heir." Peikoff has said that he doesn't have "the slightest interest in supporting those who disseminate falsehoods about Ayn Rand." He gave Paxton access to the Ayn Rand Institute's files under strict conditions, including a proviso that Paxton couldn't interview longtime Rand collaborator and extra-marital lover Nathaniel Branden. The absence of this key figure robs the film of much validity, and contributes to its lopsided portrait of its subject.

Branden helped codify Rand's ideas into the philosophy of Objectivism and founded an institute to propagate his mentor's creed. Twenty-five years her junior, Branden carried on an affair with Rand with the knowing consent of their respective spouses. In 1968, Branden opted for a younger lover, and the doyenne of rationalism excommunicated him from the movement, even though he still wholeheartedly supported her ideas. The rift persisted until Rand's death in 1982.

As a result of Peikoff's stipulation, the film makes only a cursory mention of Branden, and it doesn't make any reference to Rand's most illustrious follower: Federal Reserve chairman Alan Greenspan (perhaps Greenspan had a falling out with the ultra-orthodox Peikoff as well). The film effuses endlessly about the great romance between Rand and her uninteresting, pretty-boy cuckold, Frank O'Connor. This sanitizing spin on the reality of Rand's relationships is unfortunately typical of filmmaker Paxton's approach.

Narrator Sharon Gless laments that when Rand was unable to gain full artistic control of her plays during the 1930s, she grew frustrated with the producers whom she felt were butchering her work. It appeared as if the same sort of difficulty was going to arise when Warner Bros. set about filming Rand's adaptation of her novel *The Fountainhead.* But, like a "bull dog," Rand pulled off the unprecedented, retaining control over the studio movie and its director, King Vidor. Despite Vidor's objections, not a word of the long-winded, philosophical speech that the hero (played by Gary Cooper) delivers at the climax was deleted. The documentary glosses over the fact that THE FOUNTAINHEAD (1949), with its cardboard characters and ideological diatribes, was a critical failure.

Throughout the film, Paxton repeatedly takes Rand's colossal self-image at face value, with nary a word of contradiction. As a university student in Russia, Rand denounced the works of Plato and told her exasperated professor, "My views are not yet part of the history of philosophy. But they will be." She maintained this level of juvenile hubris throughout her life. Entertaining clips from television interviews conducted by Phil Donahue and Tom Snyder show that the elderly Rand grew even more full of herself later in life. But Paxton clearly intends for the viewer to bow, not snicker. Thus, AYN RAND: A SENSE OF LIFE will be appreciated only by the most uncritical Rand adherents. Others should skip this slavish portrait, read Rand's overwritten tomes, and judge for themselves.—T.Y.

d, Michael Paxton; p, Michael Paxton; assoc p, Jeff Britting; w, Michael Paxton; ph, Alik Sakharov; ed, Lauren Schaffer, Christopher Earl; m, Jeff Britting; sound, Michael M. Moore (mixer); makeup, David Alan-Dittmar

AAN Best Documentary Feature

Documentary/Biography (PR: C MPAA: NR)

AYNEH

(SEE: MIRROR, THE)

B

BABE: PIG IN THE CITY ★★

(Australia, 1998) 95m Kennedy/Miller Productions; Universal ~ Universal C

Magda Szubanski *(Mrs. Hoggett)*; James Cromwell *(Farmer Hoggett)*; Mary Stein *(The Landlady)*; Mickey Rooney *(Fugly Floom)*; VOICES OF: E.G. Daily *(Babe)*; Danny Mann *(Ferdinand)*; Glenne Headly *(Zootie)*; Steven Wright *(Bob)*; James Cosmo *(Thelonius)*; Nathan Kress *(Easy/Tough Pup)*; Myles Jeffrey *(Easy)*; Stanley Ralph Ross *(The Pitbull and The Doberman)*; Russi Taylor *(The Pink Poodle)*; Adam Goldberg *(Flealick)*; Eddie Barth *(Nigel and Alan)*; Bill Capizzi *(The Sniffer Dog)*; Miriam Margolyes *(Fly)*; Hugo Weaving *(Rex)*; Roscoe Lee Browne *(The Narrator)*; OTHER CAST: Paul Livingston *(Hot Headed Chef)*; Babs McMillan *(Matriarch)*; Matthew Parkinson *(Nervous Waiter)*; Julie Godfrey *(Suspicious Neighbor)*; Kim Story *(Judge)*; Richard Carter *(Detective)*; Simon Westaway *(Detective)*; Margaret Christiansen *(Haughty Woman)*; Janet Foye *(Mrs. Hoggett's Friend)*; Pamela Hawken *(Mrs. Hoggett's Friend)*; Basil Clarke *(Doctor)*; Cecilia Yates *(Flight Attendant)*; Damian Monk *(Customs Guards)*; Terrell Dixon *(Customs Guards)*; Gabby Millgate *(Female Officer)*; Anthony Phelan *(Security Guard)*; Van Epperson *(Night Cleaner)*; Mark Gerber *(Motorcycle Cop)*; Ken Radley *(Motorcycle Cop)*; John Samaha *(Van Cop)*; Paul Moxey *(Tough Guy)*; Gareth Clydesdale *(Tough Guy)*; Ken Johnson *(Court Stenographer)*; Jennifer Kent *(Lab Lady)*; Richard Huggett *(Cop)*; Ric Herbert; Felix Williamson; David Allsberry; Michael Boxer; Steve Martin; Hubert Wells *(Raiders)*; John Walton *(Padded Raider)*; Gandhi MacIntyre *(Lab Technician)*; Christian Manon *(Lab Technician)*; Sacha Horler *(Night Nurse)*; John Upton *(Sick Boy)*; Peter Callan *(Hospital Doctor)*; Dean Nottle *(Doctor in Tails)*; Paul Maybury *(Hospital Orderly)*; Saskia Campbell *(Woman in Billowing Gown)*; Kristoffer Greaves *(Chef)*; Dominic Condon *(Kitchen Hand)*; Elizabeth Allen *(Lady Zammitt)*; OTHER VOICES: Katie Leigh *(Kitten)*; Evelyn Krape *(Old Ewe and Alley Cats)*; Charles Barlett *(Cow)*; Michael Edward-Stevens *(Horse)*; Al Mancini *(Feisty Fish)*; Larry Moss *(Feisty Fish)*; Jim Cummings *(Pelican)*; Danny Mann *(Tug)*; Russi Taylor *(Choir Cat)*; Lisa Baily; Blayn Barbosa; Victor Brandt; Jeannie Elias; Pippa Grandison; J.D. Hall; Mark Hammond; Eandy Kamenoff; Scotty Leavenworth; Julie Oppenheimer; Deborah Packer; Roger Rose; Carly Schroeder; Joseph Sicari; Aaron Spann; Drew Lexi Thomas; Naomi Watts; Barbara Harris; The Looping Group

Fans of the original BABE (1995) will be aggrieved by this unnecessarily dark and over-produced follow-up. A work of unfettered imagination but no heart, BABE: PIG IN THE CITY replaces the uncomplicated sweetness of its predecessor with a cynical bemusement.

When Farmer Hoggett (James Cromwell) falls down a well, his injuries prevent him from tending to his farm. Threatened with foreclosure, Hoggett's overworked wife Esme (Magda Szubanski) accepts a lucrative county fair appearance for her prize-winning pig, Babe (voice of E.G. Daily).

Mrs. Hoggett and Babe take an out-of-state plane ride to the show. But when Mrs. Hoggett seems to be identified by a drug-sniffing dog (who is actually simply yapping to impress Babe), she is subjected to a strip search, causing them to miss both the fair and the plane home, which doesn't leave for another day. Hoggett finds lodging for both herself and Babe in an animal boarding house run by a spinster landlady (Mary Stein) and her uncle, clown Fugly Floom (Mickey Rooney). Needing money for the Hoggetts, Babe is persuaded to join Uncle Fugly's seedy act by Bob (voice of Steven Wright) and Zootie (voice of Glenne Headly), two monkeys living at the boarding house. While Babe is away performing, a disraught Mrs. Hoggett can't find him; she winds up getting arrested for causing a disturbance. When gullible Babe learns he won't be paid for his performance, he beats a hasty retreat, precipitating a miniature cannon explosion that causes a fire. Uncle Fugly is hospitalized and his hungry animals are forced to fend for themselves.

Bob and Zootie use Babe as a decoy while they try to steal jellybeans from a store guarded by a Doberman and a pit bull. Babe is chased by the pit bull, who tumbles over a river bridge and nearly drowns before Babe extricates him. The grateful dog appoints Babe the urban animals' unofficial leader.

While the landlady is visiting Uncle Fugly in the hospital, city pound officials round up most of her animal boarders, due to a tip from an animal-hating neighbor. They are taken to an institution where experimentation and death await. While a hospital benefit takes place next door, Babe frees the animal prisoners. Released from jail, Mrs. Hoggett finally retrieves Babe from the hosptial. Happily reunited with her animal borders, the landlady decides she's tired of big-city life, and decides to sell the boarding house. She shares the proceeds from the sale with the Hoggetts, who provide a home for all of Babe's city buddies.

What made BABE so enchanting was its creation of an insular fairy-tale world, where talking animals seemed like natural phenomena. One appreciates the filmmakers' ambition to test Babe's mettle in a more challenging environment, but in so doing they lose all sense of Babe's stubborn innocence. Writer-director George Miller (of "Mad Max" fame) foolishly tries to transform children's whimsy into an adult fable on the order of *Animal Farm.*

PIG IN THE CITY deserves credit for its eye-popping backdrop, a devilishly clever amalgam of several major cities. But in turning up the decibel level and escalating the violence of this grotesque Gotham, Miller neglected to provide Babe with amusing sounding boards like the idiosyncratic farm animals from the first film. The homeless pooches Babe befriends here are interchangeable, while a streetwalking poodle that comports itself like Blanche Dubois spouts dialogue that will go right over the heads of moppets. For whom was this movie made? Among the travails Babe undergoes are an incredibly detailed representation of Farmer Hoggett's accident, a scary children's hospital ward fire, and near-death at the jaws of a pit bull.

Because Babe still disarms us with his good-natured resilience, the film isn't a total bust. Blessedly, the singing mice stop the show with their rendition of Edith Piaf's "Non, Je Ne Regrette Rien." On the debit side, one must consider the film's brutalization of actress Magda Szubanski, who is treated as a fat lady joke. Perhaps turning this dimpled darling of a comedienne into a mere buffoon fits the tone of a movie that's too busy, too loud, too out of touch with its audience. BABE: PIG IN THE CITY is a prankish exercise in spectacular art direction and jarring mean-spiritedness. *(Violence, adult situations.)*— R.P.

d, George Miller; p, George Miller, Bill Miller, Doug Mitchell; exec p, Barbara Gibbs; assoc p, Colin Gibson, P.J. Voeten, Catherine Barber, Guy Norris; w, George Miller, Judy Miller, Mark Lamprell (based on the characters created by Dick King-Smith); ph, Andrew Lesnie; ed, Jay Friedkin, Margaret Sixel; m, Nigel Westlake; prod d, Roger Ford; art d, Colin Gibson; set d, Kerrie Brown; anim, Neal Scanlon; sound, Ben Osmo (recordist); fx, Tom Davies; casting, Alison Barrett, Nikki Barrett; cos, Norma Moricaeu; makeup, Lesley Vanderwalt; stunts, Guy Norris

AAN Best Original Song: "That'll Do"; Randy Newman

Fantasy **(PR: C MPAA: G)**

BAD MANNERS ★★★
(U.S., 1998) 90m Davis Entertainment Classics; Skyline Entertainmnet Partners; Wavecrest ~ Phaedra Cinema c

David Strathairn *(Wes Westlund)*; Bonnie Bedelia *(Nancy Westlund)*; Saul Rubinek *(Matt Carroll)*; Caroleen Feeney *(Kim Matthews)*; Julie Harris *(Professor Harper)*; Robin Pooley *(First Musicologist)*; Daniel Koch *(Musicologist)*; Steve Bruce *(Coffeehouse Troubadour)*

Two couples confront their inner demons in BAD MANNERS, a chamber piece with some insightful moments but also some synthetic drama.

Matt (Saul Rubinek), a musicologist, and Kim (Caroleen Feeney), a computer scientist and Matt's assistant, spend a few days with Wes (David Strathairn) and Nancy (Bonnie Bedelia) Westlund, two married fellow teachers, when Matt is invited to lecture at Harvard—and publish an article—about the work of a Vietnamese electronic composer, Min Schumann. But Wes eyes Matt (and his mathematical theories about Schumann) suspiciously, since 20 years earlier, he was Nancy's boyfriend. Recently rejected for tenure, Wes also takes offense at Matt's promising career and Kim's invasive questions about Nancy and his childless status.

The problems start in earnest for the foursome when Wes believes that the young, carefree Kim has stolen $50 from his wallet. The hosts' decision to take back what they believe is their money sets in motion a series of encounters, where each person speaks in cryptic language about their suspicions. As the tense house visit continues, everyone begins doubting each other, not only about the money, but also about their sexual fidelity and academic professionalism.

On the morning of Matt's meeting with the Harvard journal editor, Prof. Harper (Julie Harris), Matt accuses Wes and Kim of having had sex the night before, although they both deny it. During Matt's meeting, the Professor rejects his article and scoffs at the main finding that a fragment of "A Mighty Fortress Is Our God" lies hidden in the text of Schumann's work. Hurt in his career aspirations, Matt returns to the house and now accuses Kim of having faked her research, which had prompted the discredited interpretation.

Ultimately, Matt and Kim break up, and they leave the house separately. Wes and Nancy, however, seem to get closer together after the harrowing stay, but Nancy also exhibits a newfound sexual freedom, as she pursues young male students on campus. Meanwhile, a house cleaner finds Wes's original missing $50 dollar bill stuck in the Westlund couch.

BAD MANNERS immediately evokes memories of WHO'S AFRAID OF VIRGINIA WOOLF?, the Edward Albee play and 1966 Mike Nichols film, also about two academic couples (one middle-aged and childless, the other younger with a promising future) engaging in damaging psycho-sexual war games. This update succeeds much better than Tom Noonan's similar Albee revision, THE WIFE (1994), and contains a new set of interesting characters whose intellectual savvy allows the simple set-up (i.e., the stolen money) to evolve into a plausible excuse for philosophical debate amidst the vicious, soul-scaring clashes. The actors limn the parts well, with Strathairn and Bedelia delivering their best work in some time.

But unlike Nichols's noirish adaptation of VIRGINIA WOOLF, BAD MANNERS stays in a theatrical mode without much cinematic interest (Nichols turned the insular setting into an asset on screen). Director Jonathan Kaufer (SOUP FOR ONE, 1982) does little stylistically with David Gilman's 1993 play, *Ghost in the Machine*, and up-close on the screen the original's flaws creep through, particularly the inexplicable reason why the house guests stay with their hosts after so many nasty accusations and confrontations.

Still, BAD MANNERS develops as a sophisticated foray into several sharp but unstable minds and as a thoughtful treatise about differing interpretations of language and the often fine line between trust and truth. It's thought-provoking, however aesthetically unimaginative. *(Nudity, sexual situations, adult situations, extreme profanity.)*—E.M.

d, Jonathan Kaufer; p, J. Todd Harris, Alan Kaplan, Stephen Nemeth; exec p, John Davis; assoc p, Ronnie Reade, Tom Traub; co-p, Ed Cathell III, M. Cevin Cathell; w, David Gilman (based on his play *Ghost in the Machine*); ph, Denis Maloney; ed, Robin Katz; m, Ira Newborn; prod d, Sharon Lomofsky; set d, Susan Ogu; sound, Ben Patrick (mixer); casting, Sheila Jaffe, Georgianne Walken; cos, Katherine Jane Bryant; makeup, Kelly Macneal, Rebecca Turner

Drama **(PR: C MPAA: R)**

BARNEY'S GREAT ADVENTURE—THE MOVIE ★★½
(U.S., 1998) 75m Lyrick Studios; Bloster Productions; Ben Myron Productions; Lyons Partnership; PolyGram ~ PolyGram c

George Hearn *(Grandpa Greenfield)*; Shirley Douglas *(Grandma Greenfield)*; Trevor Morgan *(Cody Newton)*; Diana Rice *(Abby Newton)*; Kyla Pratt *(Marcella Walker)*; Alan Fawcett *(David—Dad)*; Jane Wheeler *(Christine—Mom)*; Bob West *(Voice of Barney)*; Renee Madeleine Le Guerrier *(Miss Goldfinch)*

Barney the purple dinosaur, the popular PBS TV star and merchandising phenomenon, makes his big-screen debut in BARNEY'S GREAT ADVENTURE, a modest little kidpic that's a sure-fire hit for the under-10 set and is short enough (not to mention being less treacly than the TV series) to be a relatively painless experience for their parents.

Nine-year-old Cody (Trevor Morgan) is upset about having to stay with his grandparents (Shirley Douglas, George Hearn) on their farm for a week, although his sister Abby (Diana Rice) and her friend Marcella (Kyla Pratt) are both excited about it. When Cody takes Abby's Barney doll and hides it in the bathtub, Abby and Marcella use their imaginations to bring it to life, and the six-foot-tall Barney (voice of Bob West) magically materializes. That night, Barney shows Cody a shooting star in the sky and when Cody wishes for a real adventure, the star crashes in the barn and a burst of white light produces a giant colored egg. Barney and the kids take the egg to a neighbor, the eccentric bird doctor Miss Goldfinch (Renee Madeleine Le Guerrier), who tells them it's a magic "Dreammaker" egg and that it will hatch in a few days.

When the egg is accidentally put on a truck and driven away, the kids, along with Barney and his two little dinosaur friends B.J. and Baby Bop, follow it into town and embark on a long chase that takes them through a parade, into a snobby French restaurant, inside a circus, and up to a hot-air-balloon race. Cody finally believes in Barney and uses his power of imagination to turn a log into a plane, and they fly into the sky and retrieve the egg from a balloon. When it hatches, a tiny, white furry animal called Twinkin comes out and gives Abby a vision of her dream about becoming a jockey and winning a championship horse race.

Love him or hate him, there's no denying the quasi-mystical effect that Barney seems to have on toddlers or the cultural impact of the Barney franchise itself, and while it became quite fashionable in the mid-1990s to Barney-bash, the effort seems to be a little wasted, since he's such a benign and innocuous presence, and a gentle alternative to the majority of modern kids' shows, which are filled with sarcasm and nonstop fantasy violence. The film's creators have cleverly taken the Barney-haters into account by making the cynical Cody a stand-in for all the naysayers who flee the room every time Barney breaks into a song. They have also designed the film to be interactive, as Barney and the other dinosaurs turn to the audience at several points to implore them to help find something or sing along with them. By the end of the movie, Cody is a true believer who has jettisoned his shades and jaded attitude and joins in with everyone else for the inevitable "I Love You, You Love Me. . . " hug-filled finale.

Ironically, however, Barney's philosophy about the power of the imagination is practically ignored by the filmmakers themselves, who seem to have used as little of it as possible in assembling the movie. It certainly could have used some more action-fantasy elements, and several fewer insipid musical numbers, which even try the patience of children, replete with dances that resemble elementary-school productions of Busby Berkeley musicals (although one number does allow Barney to don a white tux and parlez a little French!). The only sequences that capture a truly childlike sense of fantasy and wide-eyed wonder are the scenes at Miss Goldfinch's giant toy-like house, which is filled with birds and books, and the convincing special effects where the log plane chases the hot air balloons. BARNEYS GREAT ADVENTURE is not much of an adventure and it's far from great, but its intended target audience isn't likely to mind its aesthetic deficiencies.—M.S.

d, Steve Gomer; p, Sheryl Leach, Dennis DeShazer; exec p, Ben Myron; co-p, Jim Rowley; w, Steven White (from a story by Stephen White, Sheryl Leach, and Dennis DeShazer); ph, Sandi Sissel; ed, Richard Halsey; m, John Herman, Van Dyke Parks; prod d, Vincent Jefferds; art d, Colin Niemi; set d, Diane Lamothe; sound, Donald Cohen (mixer); casting, Ronna Kress; cos, Francesca Chamberland

Children's/Fantasy/Adventure (PR: AA MPAA: G)

BARRIERS ★

(U.S., 1998) 85m AB Film Productions c

Annie Golden *(Phil)*; Jamaul Roots *(Tori Addison)*; Geoff Garcy *(Snake)*; Derrick Robberts *(Keith)*; Julie Henry *(Tori's Mom)*; Sedley Bloomfield *(Geoff Addison, Tori's Dad)*; Quentin Crisp *(Raymond, the Deli Owner)*

A very low-budget independent production, BARRIERS is an amateurish drama about the friendship of two New York City black youths with disparate backgrounds.

Tori (Jamaul Roots), a Manhattan prep school student, is losing a schoolyard fight when a passing boy comes to his aid. Tori befriends the boy, nicknamed Snake (Geoff Garcy), not caring that he comes from a poor neighborhood. The two begin spending their days together and greatly enjoy each other's company, but when Snake's older brother, Keith (Derrick Robberts), learns of the friendship, he coerces Snake into agreeing to steal something valuable from Tori's home when the opportunity arises.

Since both of Tori's parents work, Tori's mother (Julie Henry) hires a young woman, Phil (Annie Golden), to watch him after school. One afternoon, Phil reluctantly agrees to let Tori have Snake over, although she knows Tori's parents would object. The boys have fun playing, but while momentarily alone, Snake finds and pockets a credit card receipt, which he later gives to Keith.

A few days afterwards, Tori's father (Sedley Bloomfield) finds a large, unexplained expense on his credit card bill. Phil tells Tori that she suspects Snake, but Tori denies Snake's involvement. Phil also passes her suspicions to Tori's father, who fires her in anger. The firing upsets Tori, who had become close to Phil, and strains the relationship between him and his father.

Days later, Tori encounters Snake outside a store, which he is helping Keith to rob. The attempt goes awry, Keith is shot and the two boys flee to nearby Central Park. There, Snake admits that he stole the receipt, but Tori vows to remain his friend anyway. An armed and wounded Keith finds the pair and attempts to shoot Tori, but accidentally kills his brother. Later, at Phil's, Tori blames himself for Snake's death, although Phil assures him that it wasn't his fault. Tori's parents arrive, and before they take their son home, Tori and Phil pledge friendship to one another.

Overly earnest and underdeveloped, BARRIERS has little to recommend it. Perhaps one's expectations shouldn't be too high for a feature that cost $135,000, but BARRIERS is inept even in consideration of its budgetary limitations. Director Alan Baxter and writer-producer Charles Ricciardi have set out to analyze how class difference serves as an artificial and often insurmountable obstacle to normal human interaction, but they've done so in a crude, obvious manner. The characters they've created are stereotypes (e.g., Tori's rich parents are insensitive snobs, Snake's older brother is shady) and the story line they've composed is predictable and cliched.

Baxter employs extensive location shooting, in such New York neighborhoods as Harlem and the Upper West Side, to demonstrate how geographic distance reinforces class divisions. It's an interesting concept, but BARRIERS has been so clumsily assembled that the locales and the distances between them are never clearly established. Much of the problem lies in the editing, which is rife with continuity errors. The film has other technical shortcomings: the cinematography is adequate, but the soundtrack is tinny, occasionally out of sync, and has been so poorly mixed that the background music sometimes drowns out the dialogue.

The performances are about at the level of the rest of the production, amateurish and unconvincing. Derrick Robberts does manage to bring some vibrancy to his role, but Annie Golden, ironically one of the few recognizable cast members, actually comes off worse than her lesser known costars in an embarrassingly flat attempt at comic relief. Roots and Garcy are fairly good individually but have absolutely no chemistry between them, a fault that renders the film's key relationship lifeless.

BARRIERS does, however, boast what has to be the year's most indelible bit of casting: Quentin Crisp as a gun-toting deli clerk. Crisp's oddball presence is as welcome here as it is inexplicable. *(Violence, sexual situations, extreme profanity.)*—D.C.

d, Alan Baxter; p, Charles Ricciardi; w, Charles Ricciardi; ph, David Sharples; ed, Thomas R. Rondinella; m, Jong Hwa Hong; sound, Jong Hwa Hong

Drama (PR: C MPAA: R)

BASEKETBALL ★★½

(U.S., 1998) 98m Zucker Brothers Pictures; Universal ~ Universal c

Trey Parker *(Joseph "Coop" Cooper)*; Matt Stone *(Doug Remer)*; Robert Vaughn *(Baxter Cain)*; Ernest Borgnine *(Theodore Denslow)*; Dian Bachar *(Kenny "Squeak" Scolari)*; Yasmine Bleeth *(Jenna Reed)*; Jenny McCarthy *(Yvette Denslow)*; Bob Costas *(Himself)*; Al Michaels *(Himself)*; Trevor Einhorn *(Little Joey)*; Kareem Abdul-Jabbar *(Himself)*; Shawn David Berchlin *(Beers Reserve Player)*; Jim Boensch *(Rollerblading Referee)*; Stephan Desjardins *(Cast-Roller Ref)*; Julie Dolan *(Beers Mas-*

cot); Isabella Popa *(Dream Foundation Kid)*; C.B. Spencer *(Beers Ball Girl)*; Robert Stack; Steve Garvey; Dale Earnhart; Alma Avery; Nancy Ann Bates; Kelli Camarina; Brooke Morales *(Beers Cheerleaders)*

Directed, coscripted, and coproduced by David Zucker of AIRPLANE! (1980) and the NAKED GUN comedies, BASEKETBALL stars Trey Parker and Matt Stone—the *enfants terribles* co-creators of the raunchy, animated TV sensation "South Park"—as smart-asses who invent a new sport combining the laziest aspects of baseball and basketball.

"Coop" (Trey Parker) and Remer (Matt Stone) are a pair of slacker losers who, for their own amusement, invent a game they call BASEketball. In BASEketball, players shoot free throws from varying distances to score singles, doubles, and home runs. The opposing team plays defense by trying to "psych-out" the shooter with insults or distracting behavior. BASEketball becomes very popular in Coop and Remer's hometown of Milwaukee, and billionaire Theodore Denslow (Ernest Borgnine) approaches the boys about starting a professional league.

Within a few years, BASEketball is a nationwide sensation. Coop, Remer, and their diminutive pal "Squeak" (Dian Bachar) comprise the Milwaukee Beers. Denslow passes away and bequeaths the Beers to Coop on the condition that they win the next league championship, otherwise the team will revert to Denslow's gold-digging widow, Yvette (Jenny McCarthy). Baxter Cain (Robert Vaughn), greedy owner of the Beers' perennial rivals, the Dallas Felons, wants to change the league rules to allow lucrative endorsement deals, a move Coop steadfastly opposes.

Coop and Remer begin vying for the affections of Jenna Reed (Yasmine Bleeth), and Cain exploits this wedge in their friendship to convince Remer that Coop is keeping him down. Coop reluctantly agrees to allow endorsement deals and Remer quickly turns into a self-promoting egomaniac. When the Beers face the Felons in the championship, the divisiveness between Coop and Remer threatens to cost them the game. During the seventh inning stretch show, Squeak reminds them of the bond of friendship that led them to invent BASEketball, and the Beers mount a comeback. Taking the Beers' final shot, Coop scores a home run to win the game, keep the team, foil Cain's plans, and secure Jenna's love.

Perhaps taking a cue from the game itself, BASEKETBALL is a low-energy affair that bats in the .300 range. A lot of gags are thrown up on screen, but the film's pace is sluggish nonetheless. Sequences involving Coop and his biggest fan, a dying little boy named Joey (Trevor Einhorn), provide some of the best laughs, and culminate in a hospital scene that possesses a manic energy which would have benefited the rest of the movie. Another comic highlight has Robert Stack doing an absurd "Unsolved Mysteries" story about Coop. The psych-outs, which should be gutbusters, are only mildly amusing, though Remer spraying milk from his nipples is an unfortunately indelible image. Surprisingly, considering Zucker's past efforts, BASEKETBALL doesn't directly parody sports movies or their cliches.

The contention that the American moviegoing public has an insatiable appetite for "dumb" comedies that revel in juvenilia and toilet humor ("made for, and by, idiots") got tested during the summer of 1998 as three comedies with a Zucker-Abrahams-Zucker pedigree (BASEKETBALL, the mob parody MAFIA!, and the Leslie Nielsen comedy WRONGFULLY ACCUSED) were released within a month of each other. All three were beaten at the box office by the hit THERE'S SOMETHING ABOUT MARY from the Farrelly Brothers, bearers of the new gold standard in over-the-top, gross-out humor. Parker and Stone have an easy camaraderie and regular-guy charm, but the duo's much-hyped presence in BASEKETBALL was neutralized by the film's R-rating, which kept much of "South Park's" young audience away. Curiously though, for a movie with almost exclusive appeal to a young male demographic, BASEKETBALL is surprisingly free of raunchy or graphic sex jokes, despite the presence of bosomy sex symbols Bleeth and McCarthy. *(Extreme profanity, adult situations.)*—P.R.

d, David Zucker; p, David Zucker, Robert LoCash, Gil Netter; co-p, Jeff Wright; w, David Zucker, Robert LoCash, Jeffrey Wright, Lewis Friedman; ph, Steve Mason; ed, Jeffrey Reiner; m, Ira Newborn; prod d, Steven Jordan; art d, Bill Hiney; set d, John Jefferies, Anne D. McCulley; sound, Hank Garfield (mixer), Harry Snodgrass (design); fx, David Kelsey, Jesse Silver; casting, Junie Lowry-Johnson, Ron Surma; cos, Catherine Adair; makeup, Jackie Dobbie; stunts, John Ashker

Sports/Comedy (PR: C MPAA: R)

BATMAN & MR. FREEZE: SUBZERO ★★★
(U.S., 1998) 67m Warner Bros. ~ Warner Home Video c

VOICES OF: Kevin Conroy *(Batman/Bruce Wayne)*; Michael Ansara *(Mr. Freeze)*; Loren Lester *(Robin/Dick Grayson)*; Efrem Zimbalist Jr. *(Alfred)*; George Dzundza *(Dr. Gregory Belson)*; Robert Costanzo *(Det. Bullock)*; Bob Hastings *(Commissioner Gordon)*; Mary Kay Bergman *(Batgirl/Barbara Gordon)*; Marilu Henner *(Veronica Vreeland)*; Dean Jones *(Dean Arbagast)*

The first ever direct-to-video feature-length production from Warner Bros. Animation, BATMAN & MR. FREEZE: SUBZERO is a very tolerable cartoon that's more enjoyable—and far less campy—than Joel Schumacher's first two live-action BATMAN movies.

Mr. Freeze (voice of Michael Ansara), a former scientist whose experiments with cryogenic technology have transformed him into a super-criminal, comes to Gotham City to try to revive his late wife Nora whom he has kept frozen for the past 15 years. In Gotham, Freeze coerces a doctor into helping him with the operation, but when no dead organ donors are found, Freeze kidnaps Barbara Gordon, aka Batgirl (voice of Mary Kay Bergman), who's the daughter of Police Commisioner Gordon (voice of Bob Hastings). Barbara's boyfriend Dick Grayson, aka Robin (voice of Loren Lester), gives chase on a motorcycle but loses them. Bruce Wayne, aka Batman (voice of Kevin Conroy), discovers that Barbara has been kidnapped because her rare blood type matches that of Freeze's wife.

Using the Batwing airplane, Batman and Robin track Freeze down to an abandoned oil derrick in the middle of the ocean and rescue Barbara, but a fuel tank catches on fire and the entire derrick explodes. Batman, Robin, and Barbara get onto the Batwing, but Batman goes back to save Freeze, who has sacrificed himself so that his wife could be taken away by Batman. Freeze is unable to hold onto a rope and falls into the sea. Two weeks later, workers at a US weather station in the Arctic are watching a TV news report about Nora being successfully revived after an operation financed by the Bruce Wayne Foundation. A deformed Mr. Freeze watches the TV report through a window and then disappears into the snowy night with his two polar bear companions.

Fast moving and highly stylized, BATMAN & MR. FREEZE: SUBZERO follows along the lines of the 1990s BATMAN animated TV series, but features a more elaborate production, consisting of an excellent blend of old-fashioned hand-drawings and computerized digital animation. Unlike too many modern cartoons, the computer effects are used judiciously and for action scenes only. The opening underwater submarine scene, the exciting motorcycle chase which turns into a huge multicar pileup, the fireball finale, and shots of the various Bat-vehicles firing up and roaring out of the Batcave are all significantly enhanced by the mixture of traditional animation and computer technology, helping to create a striking 3-D look. The whole film has a sleekly angular look that combines elements of film noir with art deco, in keeping with the visual design of the original cartoon. The characters all have more depth than those in Joel Schumacher's BATMAN films; this is exemplified by the complexity of the relationship between Batman and Mr. Freeze, who's depicted as a tragic figure whose love for his wife drives him to evil. Though clearly aimed at kids, there's also plenty to keep adult viewers entertained, not the least of which are the amusingly curvaceous drawings of several dishy dames and the exaggerated muscularity of Batman and Robin.*(Violence.)*—M.S.

d, Boyd Kirkland; p, Boyd Kirkland, Randy Rogel; assoc p, Haven Alexander; w, Boyd Kirkland, Randy Rogel (based on the cartoon characters created by Bob Kane); ed, Al Breitsenbach; m, Michael McCuistion; casting, Andrea Romano

Animated/Action (PR: AA MPAA: NR)

BATMAN/SUPERMAN MOVIE, THE ★★★

(U.S., 1998) 61m Warner Bros. ~ Warner Home Video c

VOICE CAST: Tim Daly *(Superman/Clark Kent)*; Kevin Conroy *(Batman/Bruce Wayne)*; Dana Delany *(Lois Lane)*; Clancy Brown *(Lex Luthor)*; Mark Hamill *(The Joker)*; Arleen Sorkin *(Harley Quinn)*; Lisa Edelstein *(Mercy Graves)*; Bob Hastings *(Commissioner Gordon)*; Efrem Zimbalist Jr. *(Alfred)*; Joseph Bologna *(Dan Turpin)*; Robert Costanzo *(Detective Bullock)*; George Dzundza *(Perry White)*; Lauren Tam *(Angela Chen)*

Batman and Superman join forces when the Joker teams up with Lex Luthor to destroy them in THE BATMAN/SUPERMAN MOVIE, a hip and stylish made-for-video cartoon.

After discovering that the Joker (voice of Mark Hamill) has stolen a statuette made of kryptonite, Batman (voice of Kevin Conroy) follows the archcriminal from Gotham to Metropolis. In Metropolis, Batman's alter-ego, industrialist Bruce Wayne, meets reporter Lois Lane (voice of Dana Delany) and begins wining and dining her, much to the chagrin of Superman (voice of Tim Daly) and his alter-ego Clark Kent. Superman discovers Batman's true identity, and the rivalry between the two men spills over when they don their costumes, resulting in a fistfight. Later, the Joker coerces Lex Luthor (voice of Clancy Brown) into a scheme to destroy Batman and Superman and they kidnap Lois and bring her to Luthor's LexCorp, where he manufactures robotic military weapons. When Superman comes to rescue her, the Joker subdues him with kryptonite, but Batman arrives and restores Superman's powers by pouring acid on the deadly substance. After they repel an attack of gigantic robotic spiders, during which, Batman's mask comes off and Lois sees that he's really Wayne, the Joker tries to kill them by blowing up LexCorp, but they escape and the Joker is trapped inside during the explosion. Wayne then says goodbye to Lois and warns Kent to treat her right.

Although the narrative suffers from being formatted for eventual airing as a multi-part episode on the Cartoon Network TV series (the credits even bear the episode title "World's Finest"), the artwork in BATMAN/SUPERMAN is exceptionally well done. Drawn in the series's best neo-noir style, which imitates the look of the vintage 1940s Fleischer Bros. "Superman" cartoons, the visuals feature a striking use of forced perspective and the illusion of deep focus. Scenes of Superman and Batman soaring through the night skies of Metropolis have a sense of grace and velocity that's rare in contemporary animation, and the plethora of colorful explosions and psychedelic "lighting" schemes are imaginatively rendered. The nonstop action should delight kids, particularly the very cool robotic spiders, which are obviously modeled on Phil Tippett's creations for the ROBOCOP movies, but there's nothing childish about the movie's sensibility. In some ways, the depiction of the characters remind one of Russ Myer's formula for his movies: "Square jaws and big bosoms." The ridiculously muscular, ruggedly handsome Wayne and Kent are virtually identical cliches of he-man beefcake, possessing sharp granite-like features and huge upper torsos, while the brassy and aggressive Lois practically throws herself at Wayne and is seen in a variety of tight dresses and clinging nighties. The jealousy and clash of egos between the Man of Steel and the Caped Crusader is also amusing, prompting Lois to accuse Batman of "suffering from propulsion envy." Like its recent made-for-video predecessor, BATMAN & MR. FREEZE: SUBZERO (1998), this is another comic-strip adventure that's superior to its bigscreen, live-action cousins.*(Violence.)*—M.S.

d, Toshihiko Masuda; p, Alan Burnett, Paul Dini, Bruce W. Timm; assoc p, Haven Alexander; w, Alan Burnett, Paul Dini, Stan Berkowitz, Rich Fogel, Steve Gerber (based on a story by Alan Burnett and Paul Dini); ed, Joe Gall; m, Michael McCuistion; art d, Glen Murakami

Animated/Children's/Action (PR: A MPAA: NR)

BATTLE OF CHILE: THE STRUGGLE OF AN UNARMED PEOPLE—PART 2: THE COUP D'ETAT, THE ★★★★½

(Venezuela, 1976) 91m Equipo Tercer Ano; Cuban Film Institute ~ First Run Features/Icarus Films bw

(LA BATALLA DE CHILE: LA LUCHA DE UN PUEBLO SIN ARMAS—EL GOPE DE ESTADO)

The revival in 1998 of the second part of THE BATTLE OF CHILE in the US marked the 25th anniversary of the bloody right-wing coup that ended Salvador Allende's democratically elected Marxist government. Patricio Guzman's chilling 1978 documentary merits its landmark status.

The first part of THE BATTLE OF CHILE records the events that led up to the coup. PART 2: THE COUP D'ETAT begins with the earliest coup attempt itself, an attack on Allende's palace and the shooting in the streets by rightist soldiers in June 1973. But Allende's forces and a worker's march temporarily halt the onslaught. Allende then issues an order for martial law, but the Chilean congress denies his request. Meanwhile, right-wing officers search and interrogate workers in factories who have been sympathetic to Allende.

Back in the government, the left-wing parties (the Christian Democrats and the Socialists) differ on a solution: peaceful protest vs. armed conflict. As talks stall, the fascist right kills an Allende commander, allowing a takeover of the navy, and the antigovernment forces (led by General Pinochet) also begin killing the factory workers. A transportation strike is supported by both the Chilean fascists and the US government, which views the left as a Communist threat, however democratically elected. Allende appoints a joint civilian-military cabinet to end the strike, but his attempt fails, so the people discover their own means of transportation.

Finally, on September 11, 1973, with the support of the US, the Chilean Air Force bombs the presidential palace. Allende, however, makes his last address via radio to the people, stating he would rather die than resign. Soon enough, he is killed and General Pinochet takes over, with tanks in the streets to keep order.

Cinema verite fully flowered with THE BATTLE OF CHILE, an amazing chronicle of history. From the very first scene in THE

COUP D'ETAT, where an Argentine cameraman records his own death (as the rightist forces shoot at him), the film plunges the viewer deeply and irreversibly into the grim, tragic action. Patricio Guzman pieced together his documentary from the surreptitious filming by several cinematographers stationed around Chile during the tumultuous period (Guzman's main cinematographer, Jorge Muller-Silva, "disappeared," along with thousands of civilians, at the time of the coup). It is just as miraculous that Guzman was able to complete the film (given the conditions) as it was that he was able to get the footage out of the country (a long, fascinating story worthy of a documentary itself). To date, post-Pinochet Chile still refuses a release of the film.

Despite the dark swirl of violence and the many characters involved in the different factions, the black-and-white BATTLE OF CHILE clearly and concisely tells its story with a matter-of-fact tone (set by the English-speaking female narrator) that undercuts the argument that the film is propagandistic (it may be sympathetic to the left, but it also seems much more honest and accurate than any of the opposition material, including the slanted contemporary US newscasts seen in the film). From the workers' marches to the factory protests to the government debates to the final, savage bombing attack, THE BATTLE OF CHILE records history as it happens and brings a new awareness to the kind of events too often rewritten or forgotten by establishment chroniclers. *(Graphic violence, adult situations, profanity.)*—E.M.

d, Patricio Guzman; p, Chris Marker; ph, Jorge Muller; ed, Pedro Chaskel; sound, Bernardo Menz

Documentary **(PR: C MPAA: NR)**

BEAUTY INSPECTORS
(SEE: BEAUTY INVESTIGATOR)

BEAUTY INVESTIGATOR ★★
(Hong Kong, 1992) 87m Golden Sun Film Co; New Treasure Film Co ~ Tai Seng c
(AKA: BEAUTY INSPECTORS)

Moon Lee *(Ellen Li)*; Yukari Oshima, billed as Cynthia Luster *(Tanaka)*; Kim Je Kee *(Grace)*; Melvin Wong *(Inspector Wong)*; Tsui Zen Aie *(Bill Tam)*; Peter Chow *(David Chune)*; Sophia Crawford *(Lisa)*; Yang Chun *(Boss)*; Chen So Aie *(Ah B)*; Chung Fat *(Ah Fat)*; Wu Yue Zhu *(Ah Chai)*; Tai Boa *(Undercover)*

Another in a long line of fighting femme Hong Kong crime thrillers, BEAUTY INVESTIGATOR concerns two undercover female cops who stumble upon a gang war between HK triads and Japanese Yakuza. A contrived plot is enhanced by the presence of three authentic female fighting stars. This 1992 film received its first official US release on home video in 1998.

Two Hong Kong cops, Ellen (Moon Lee) and Grace (Kim Je Kee), are assigned to go undercover at a nightclub to track down a sex killer who has murdered three nightclub hostesses. They pick up information implicating the club owner, Bill Tam (Tsui Zen Aie), in a series of gangland murders performed by Tanaka (Yukari Oshima), a professional hit woman imported from Japan. Tam has angered both the Hong Kong mob and the Japanese Yakuza by stealing a shipment of arms and killing the Yakuza seller. The sex killer turns out to be David Chune (Peter Chow), the club manager, who is killed by Tanaka before Ellen can arrest him. The two cops then fail to stop the assassination of a Hong Kong triad boss (Yang Chun) by Tanaka. The girls' commander, Inspector Wong (Melvin Wong) reprimands them and orders them off the case.

Grace performs surveillance of Tam on her own and is caught and beaten badly. Ellen wants revenge and, learning of a meeting between Bill and the Japanese Yakuza, invades the meeting and tries to kill them all. Her unlikely ally is Tanaka, who is actually an undercover agent. The final fight, at a sprawling industrial site, includes a battle between Tanaka and Tam's mistress/bodyguard, Lisa (Sophia Crawford). Ellen and Tanaka finally defeat and apprehend Bill Tam.

A haphazardly scripted low-budget HK crime thriller, BEAUTY INVESTIGATOR (aka BEAUTY INSPECTORS) boasts three of the top HK fighting female stars—Moon Lee, Yukari Oshima (billed here as Cynthia Luster), and Sophia Crawford. Lee is quite attractive, particularly in her undercover role as club hostess. She displays a wider range of emotions here than in most of her films, ranging from comedic squabbling with her partner to dramatic histrionics as she gets drunk, ponders her fate, and protests the violence done to her partner. She's also in superb butt-kicking form as she squares off against Yukari in two memorable encounters, while Yukari squares off against English fighting star Crawford in a final battle at a spectacular industrial site. While it may not have been the best showcase for these ladies, it still offers plenty of pleasures for the undiscriminating HK fan.

The film never probes the ethical questions raised by Tanaka's actually killing several gangsters in cold blood (including a sick triad boss en route to the hospital) while posing as a hitwoman. The revelation near the end that she's a cop seems like a last-minute script change. *(Violence.)*—B.C.

d, Lee Jua Nan; p, Ng Ming Toi, William Lan; co-p, Tsui Cheng Aie; w, Chung Jei Zang; ph, Kwan Zhe Ching; ed, Paul Fang; m, Michael Fung; cos, Jenny Lee; stunts, Wu Yue Zhu

Crime/Thriller **(PR: C MPAA: NR)**

BELLY ★★½
(U.S., 1998) 95m Artisan Entertainment; The Shootin Gallery; Street Life Productions ~ Artisan Entertainment c

Nasir Jones, billed as Nas *(Sincere)*; Earl Simmons, billed as DMX *(Tommy "Buns" Bundy)*; Clifford Smith, billed as Method Man *(Shameek)*; Taral Hicks *(Kisha)*; Tyrin Turner *(Big)*; Tionne Watkins, billed as T-Boz *(Tionne)*; Hassan Johnson *(Mark)*; Oli Grant, billed as Power *(Knowledge)*; Kurt Loder *(Himself)*; Louie Rankin *(Lennox)*; Stanley Drayton *(Wise)*; Benjamin Chavis, billed as Minister Benjamin F. Muhammed *(Rev. Saviour)*; Jay Black *(Black)*; Lavita Raynor *(Kionna)*; Frank Vincent *(Roger)*; James Parris *(Lakid)*; Eric Keith McNeil *(Shorty)*; Xavier Simmons *(Young Tommy)*; Monica Michaels *(Club Manager)*; Jennifer "Nen" Gatien; Anthony "Az" Cruz *(Born)*; David Edwards; Jeffrey Kaufman; Brant Spencer; Adam C. Vignola *(Federal Agents)*; John "B.J." Bryant *(Thug #1)*; Prince "Blunt" Graham *(Thug #2)*; Wondosas "Kilo" Martin *(Thug #3)*; Shaun Morrison *(Housekeeper)*; Micaal Stevens *(Killer)*; Michael Woodhouse *(Older Barber)*; Tyrone Lewis *(Younger Barber)*; Carmen Yannuzzi Jr. *(Guard)*; Crystal N. Johnson *(Knowledge's Cop Girlfriend)*; James Gresham *(Speaker)*; Michael Manning *(Teacher)*

Nas and DMX head a host of rap stars who make the jump to acting in BELLY. While highly derivative of the host of "gangsta" movies that preceded it, BELLY is distinguished by the inventive and energetic visual style of video director Harold "Hype" Williams.

Long-time friends Sincere (Nasir Jones, aka Nas) and Tommy "Buns" Bundy (Earl Simmons, aka DMX) are small-time hoods who make a decent living robbing New York City nightclubs. But Tommy knows the real money is in drugs, so he contacts Jamaican drug king Lennox, known as "Ox" (Louie Rankin) to get him in on the action. Sincere, meanwhile, has a wife and child, and wants no part of Tommy's business. Tommy and his gang end up in Omaha serving as Ox's main dealer, a move that irks a local dealer. While Ox calls upon Tommy to go to Jamaica to help him eliminate a rival, Rico gives the FBI the location of Tommy's gang. By the time Tommy returns from Jamaica, the feds are closing in fast.

Tommy goes back to New York to get help from Sincere; though he has been reading the spiritual works of "the Minister," and no longer deals in crime, Sincere helps his old friend. Tommy gets back on the road, now with two wild kids as his gang. When one of them shoots the other over an argument in a restaurant, Tommy has had enough, and he gives himself up. The police offer Tommy a deal: no jail time if he assassinates the Minister whose ideas they oppose. In order to get close to the Minister, Tommy must join his religion; but, by the time the assassination is to occur (on New Year's Eve, 1999), he has learned enough to question his life of violence. When he actually meets the Minister (Minister Benjamin F. Muhammed), he cannot pull the trigger, and renounces his evil ways. As the Millennium arrives, both men have embraced new lives.

Aficionados of the "gangsta" genre won't find much new material in BELLY: those who aim to profit from their life of crime typically end up in jail or dead, while those who choose instead to set down their guns are rewarded. Nor is it new for a rap star (or even several, as is the case here) to turn movie star—with music videos becoming more and more cinematic every day, such a transition seems natural. If anything sets BELLY apart from the crowd, it's the assured direction of Hype Williams. Unlike many music video directors who try their hand at feature films (the many directors to come out of Propaganda Films, for example), Williams's movie, while stylish, is free of the hyper-fast cuts and overexposed film stock that have become de rigueur in music videos. Instead, Williams succeeds in translating his video-making experience to the big screen without simply making a really long video.

While DMX and Nas receive top billing (with the former garnering the lion's share of screen time), BELLY's numerous subplots make it a virtual ensemble piece. Everyone involved contributes admirably, particularly considering the number of first-time actors participating; at no time do we feel we're watching musicians turned actors. Even if the ending, in which both main characters are morally redeemed, is a bit sunny when compared to the preceding events, it is to the actors' credit that we accept it anyway. *(Extreme violence, extreme profanity, substance abuse, sexual situations.)*—B.T.

d, Hype Williams; p, Hype Williams, Bob Salerno, Ron Rotholz, Larry Meistrich; exec p, James Bigwood; w, Hype Williams; ph, Malik Sayeed; ed, David Leonard; m, Stephen Cullo; prod d, Regan Jackson; art d, Nicholas Lundy; set d, Carol Silverman; sound, Tod Maitland; fx, Drew Jiritano; casting, Winsome Sinclair; cos, June Ambrose; stunts, Julius LeFlore

Crime/Drama **(PR: O MPAA: R)**

BELOVED ★★½

(U.S., 1998) 174m Harpo Films; Clinica Estetico; Touchstone Pictures ~ Buena Vista c

Oprah Winfrey *(Sethe)*; Danny Glover *(Paul D)*; Thandie Newton *(Beloved)*; Kimberly Elise *(Denver)*; Beah Richards *(Baby Suggs)*; Lisa Gay Hamilton *(Younger Sethe)*; Albert Hall *(Stamp Paid)*; Irma P. Hall *(Ella)*; Carol Jean Lewis *(Janey Wagon)*; Kessia Kordelle *(Amy Denver)*; Jude Ciccolella *(Schoolteacher)*; Anthony Chisholm *(Langhorne)*; Dorothy Love Coates *(M. Lucille Williams)*; Jane White *(Lady Jones)*; Yada Beener *(Denver Aged 9)*; Emil Pinnock *(Howard Aged 14)*; Calen Johnson *(Buglar Aged 13)*; George E. Ray *(Reverend Pike)*; Wes Bentley *(Schoolteacher's Nephew)*; Dashiell Eaves *(Schoolteacher's Nephew)*; Tyler Hinson *(Baby Beloved)*; Brian Hooks *(Young Paul D)*; Angie Utt *(Mrs. Garner)*; Hill Harper *(Halle)*; Jim Roche *(String Show Barker)*; Vertamae Grosvenor *(Grace)*; Ramona Castle; Brooklyn James; Nora Marlowe *(Carnival Kids)*; Frederick Strother *(African Savage)*; Lillian Smith *(Lemonade Server)*; Aliya Robinson *(Denver's Carnival Friend)*; Joe Toutebon *(Frenchie)*; Brittany Hawkins *(Young Girl Sethe)*; Alerte Belance *(Nan)*; Ayoka Dorsey *(Sethe's Mother)*; Ashleigh Watson *(Baby Denver)*; Dajon Matthews *(Howard Aged 5)*; Norris Wiggins Jr. *(Buglar Aged 4)*; Harry Northup *(Sheriff)*; Tracey Walter *(Slave Catcher)*; Terel Gibson *(Buglar Aged 21)*; Damani Baker *(Howard Aged 22)*; Robert Castle *(Mr. Sawyer)*; Paul Lazar *(General Store Proprietor)*; Leigh Smiley *(General Store Helper)*; Jiggs Walker *(Good Samaritan)*; Dan Olmstead *(Policeman)*; Charles Glenn *(Helpful Gentleman)*; Jason Robards *(Mr. Bodwin)*; Anthony S. Calypso *(Denver's Boyfriend)*; THE THIRTY WOMEN: Ysaye M. Barnwell; Trazana M. Beverly; Cecelia Ann Birt; Grace Blake; Jordan Cael; Nitanju Bolade Casel; Edwidge Danticat; Yanick Etienne; Jacqueline Celestin Fils-Aime; Denise Gassant; Frances Gray; Thelma Houston; Louise Johnson; Aisha Kahlil; Carol Lynn Maillard; Dianne McIntyre; Gaynielle Neville; Madeline Preston; Matt Rochester; Millicent Sparks; Lisa Summerour; Ophelia M. Turner; Karen Lorraine Vicks; Willa Ward; Pauletta Washington

It took Oprah Winfrey nearly a decade to realize her dream of filming Toni Morrison's novel *Beloved*; the end result is a painstakingly crafted ghost story. Despite Morrison's publicized approval of director Jonathan Demme's screen translation, this self-defeatingly meticulous film interprets the metaphoric representation of slavery in far too literal a fashion.

Ohio, 1873. Former slave Sethe (Oprah Winfrey) lives with her two frightened sons and her sullen daughter Denver (Kimberly Elise) in a house beset by a vindictive poltergeist. Because the road leading her away from slavery at Sweet Home plantation was so arduous, Sethe refuses to budge from this hard-earned, imperfect haven, without considering the psychological toll on her sons, who run away, or on Denver, who's too shell-shocked to venture from the homestead. Respite arrives in the form of old friend Paul D (Danny Glover), who shares Sethe's abhorrence of plantation life. Despite the resentment of both Denver and the mean-spirited ghost, Paul D resolves to build a life with Sethe. Sensing the fresh start Paul D offers, the supernatural world retaliates by manifesting the house's unseen oppressor as a physical entity called Beloved (Thandie Newton). Although Beloved is actually the ghost of an abused slave-girl, Sethe irrationally comes to regard the wild-eyed creature as her own long-dead baby, magically restored to life. Denver welcomes Beloved as a companion, but skeptical Paul D suspects a darker purpose in Beloved's curiosity about Sethe's past and estranges himself from Sethe.

It is revealed that Sethe suffered horrific abuses at Sweet Home. Fleeing the plantation during the last stages of pregnancy, battered Sethe gave birth in a canoe and was rescued by a former slave, who escorted her by boat to the farm of her mother-in-law Baby Suggs (Beah Richards). Sethe basked in life as a free woman for a month until she was located by the plantation master. Rather than let her children return to Sweet Home, Sethe attempted to kill them—and, in the case of her baby daughter, succeeded. Since that infanticide, Sethe has been bedeviled by an accusatory entity, a tangible reminder of her unforgivable sin. This confession hastens Paul D's departure, a farewell for which Beloved sets the stage by seducing him.

As Sethe runs through her life savings by heaping luxuries on Beloved and Denver, Denver realizes that the pernicious apparition is not a reanimated version of her dead sister. As Sethe deteriorates, painfully shy Denver has no recourse but to uproot herself from fears instilled in her by her mother and seek employment in town. When the town's religious women are apprised of Denver's plight, they congregate at Sethe's house of pain and pray until Beloved is exorcised. Drawn back, Paul D nurses the shattered Sethe, who remains figuratively shackled to her slave past.

Toni Morrison's acclaimed novel used the device of supernatural entities to embody the heritage of slavery. On the printed page, *Beloved* worked as both an African-American *Turn of the Screw* and a scorching examination of the aftershocks of human bondage on successive generations. Somehow, this highly touted cinematic translation makes Morrison's "magic realism" too realistic a proposition. In addition to securing expert performances (including one flawless one by Kimberly Elise), Demme is adept at stage managing the symbolic interaction of ghost and haunted humans. A master at saturating his mise-en-scene with dread, Demme knows how to raise the hackles (e.g., the scene in which Beloved is reborn in mourning clothes, a gurgling swamp sprite unable to inhale enough oxygen). Yet Demme's images are horrific without being resonant. As the subtext of terror plays out conventionally, Demme's BELOVED lacks one essential ingredient of the novel: an air of mystery.

BELOVED fails its audience by summoning up the despair of slavery without providing any emotional release. One waits in vain, not for a happy ending, but a joint discovery by the audience and Sethe that one of the repercussions of her sin may not be forgiveness but self-understanding. Reacting to BELOVED as a glimpse into American history's heart of darkness, we shudder at the ectoplasmic chill emanating from Beloved, but we never share the overwhelming pain that dims the light in Sethe's eyes. Lusting after the kind of greatness that wins Academy Awards, BELOVED betrays its own promise to provide something more trenchant than "big themes" superimposed over Morrison's poignantly direct scenario. *(Graphic violence, nudity, profanity, sexual situations.)*—R.P.

d, Jonathan Demme; p, Oprah Winfrey, Jonathan Demme, Edward Saxon, Kate Forte, Gary Goetzman; exec p, Ron Bozman; assoc p, Steve Shareshian; w, Akosua Busia, Richard LaGravenese, Adam Brooks (based on the novel by Toni Morrison); ph, Tak Fujimoto; ed, Carol Littleton, Andy Keir; m, Rachel Portman; prod d, Kristi Zea; art d, Tim Galvin; set d, Karen O'Hara; ch, Dianne McIntyre; sound, Willie D. Burton (mixer); fx, Tom Ward, John Ottesen; casting, Howard Feuer; cos, Colleen Atwood; makeup, Carl Fullerton (special effects makeup), Neal Martz (special effects makeup); stunts, Tony Brubaker

AAN Best Costume Design: Colleen Atwood

Historical/Drama **(PR: C MPAA: R)**

BELOW UTOPIA
(SEE: BODY COUNT)

BEST MAN, THE ★★★½
(Italy, 1998) 100m FilmAuro; Duea Film ~ October Films c
(IL TESTIMONE DELLO SPOSO)

Diego Abatantuono *(Angelo Beliossi)*; Ines Sastre *(Francesca Babini)*; Dario Cantarelli *(Edgardo Osti)*; Cinia Mascoli *(Peppina Campeggi)*; Valeria D'Obici *(Olimpia Campeggi Babini)*; Toni Santagata *(Manlio Lobianco)*; Nini Salerno *(Sauro Ghinassi)*; Mario Erpichini *(Sisto Babini)*; Ugo Conti *(Marziano Beliossi)*

In THE BEST MAN, writer-director Pupi Avati (STORY OF BOYS AND GIRLS) invests an outwardly slight story about an arranged marriage that's set on the eve of the 20th century with considerable warmth and symbolic resonance, creating a captivating and gentle romantic comedy of manners.

In a small town in northern Italy on December 31, 1899, the Babini family prepares for the wedding of daughter Francesca (Ines Sastre), whose arranged marriage to wealthy businessman Edgardo Osti (Dario Cantarelli) is to be held that day. Francesca, however, is not in love with the elderly Edgardo, and objects to the union, but is coerced into going through with it by her parents. At the church, Francesca falls instantly in love with Edgardo's best man Angelo (Diego Abatantuono), a handsome millionaire who has just returned to his hometown from the US, and with whom Edgardo hopes to become partners. During the ceremony, she recites her wedding vows while staring at Angelo instead of Edgar. At the wedding party, Francesca makes a scene and announces that she's in love with Angelo, and Edgardo threatens to sue her family when Francesca refuses to join him in a connubial "nap."

Francesca later makes up with Edgardo, but is unable to control her feelings for Angelo. Finally, she kisses him passionately, then tells him that she is "married" to him. That night, Edgardo lures Angelo away from Francesca by having Angelo's long-lost ex-lover come to the house. Angelo says goodbye to the hysterical Francesca, but she tells him that she'll be married to him forever. Her marriage to Edgardo is annulled and the scandalized Francesca goes to live at a country church and becomes a schoolteacher. One day, a car pulls up to the church and Francesca goes outside with her class of young boys. When Angelo steps out of the car and walks toward Francesca, her students ask who he is; he replies, "Her husband" and they embrace each other.

THE BEST MAN may be short on plot, but it's long on charm and possesses a kind of magical glow in its bittersweet reflections on the rituals of a vanished world. With the soft, golden light of its cinematography and a lushly romantic score, it's a lovingly detailed recreation of the past as it collides with the present, and its observation of the small town's social and religious customs is wise and witty. The large ensemble cast of characters—eccentric aunts, uncles, cousins, and friends—is highly amusing, and the stunningly beautiful Ines Sastre is a real find as Francesca. The specter of the encroaching 20th century and the promise it holds for the characters—no more wars, scientific cures for every ill, trips to the moon for everyone—hovers symbolically throughout the story, and culminates with a lovely touch: a slide show of the New World which Angelo presents to the astonished guests on a giant projector which he's brought from America.

The entire film is a series of tiny and seemingly inconsequential incidents, which altogether add up to an evocative portrait of families and traditions: the village's preparations for the nuptials, Francesca's bridesmaids reading her a romance novel, the cooking of food and cleaning of the house, seamstresses carrying the wedding dress across the countryside, Francesca dappling herself with holy water to ward off evil spirits, a blindfolded virgin putting undergarments on the bride, the bride's three cousins—all priests—performing the ceremony, the formal presentation (and ultimate return) of the wedding gifts, the leisurely party that stretches into the night, a drunken guest trying to molest a maid, a religious spinster aunt breaking down as she recalls a long ago date with Edgardo, a boy counting down thousands of seconds until midnight to himself. The happy ending may be a bit improbable, but there's no doubt it's immensely satisfying, and like the entire film, is utterly captivating in its sincerity and simplicity. *(Sexual situations.)*—M.S.

d, Pupi Avati; p, Aurelio De Laurentiis, Antonio Avati; w, Pupi Avati; ph, Pasquale Rachini; ed, Amedeo Salfa; m, Riz Ortolani; prod d, Alberto Cottignoli, Steno Tonelli; sound, Raffael De Luca (design); cos, Vittoria Guaita

Romance/Comedy/Drama **(PR: C MPAA: PG)**

BEST OF THE BEST: WITHOUT WARNING ★★½
(U.S., 1998) 90m Picture Securities Ltd. ~ Buena Vista Home Entertainment c

Phillip Rhee *(Tommy Lee)*; Ernie Hudson *(Detective Gresko)*; Tobin Bell *(Lukass Stava)*; Thure Riefenstein *(Yuri Stava)*; Jessica Collins *(Karlina)*; Chris Lemmon *(Detective Jarvis)*; Paul Gleason *(Father G.)*; Jessica Huang *(Stephanie)*; Jill Ritchie *(Mickey)*; Art La Fleur *(Big Joolie)*; Sven Ole Thorson *(Boris)*; Garnett Warren *(Viktor)*; David Shark Fralick, billed as David Fralick *(Oleg)*; Monte Perlin *(Sergei)*; Marco Verdier *(Cop)*; Terrance Stone *(Cop)*; Michael Colton *(Rookie)*

The BEST OF THE BEST series continues with this predictable but high-octane fourth entry. Making an impressive directorial debut, leading man Phillip Rhee keeps a firm grip on the story line while satisfying viewers' appetites for death-defying stunts.

Seizing control of LA's traffic control center, murderous Russian mobsters Yuri Stava (Thure Riefenstein) and Karlina (Jessica Collins) instigate an automotive logjam that enables their coconspirators to hijack a truck containing a government currency disc and Treasury Department printing paper. But the counterfeiting gang, headed by Yuri's brother Lukass (Tobin Bell), is foiled by a snitch named Mickey (Jill Ritchie), who appropriates the computer disc for the LA district attorney. While LAPD partners Detective Gresko (Ernie Hudson) and Detective Jarvis (Chris Lemmon) investigate the heist, the Stava gang pursues Mickey to her dad's convenience store, where she slips the disc into the pocket of martial arts instructor Tommy Lee (Phillip Rhee). Before she is killed by the gang, Mickey informs Tommy that the gang is being helped by a crooked cop.

When he discovers the disc, Tommy hands it over to Jarvis, who turns out to be the bad cop. Tommy is forced to kill him in self-defense. Keeping a step ahead of vengeful Detective Gresko, Tommy leaves his daughter Stephanie (Jessica Huang) at a church for safekeeping. Tommy is captured by Karlina, posing as Mickey's DA connection. Although Tommy escapes, Yuri forces him to trade the disc for Stephanie at the church. Tommy tracks Lukass and Yuri to the airport. Having learned about his ex-partner's crooked dealings, Detective Gresko drives to Tommy's rescue, only to be wounded by the Stava Brothers. As the Stavas attempt to fly away, Tommy tosses a bomb into the cargo hold of their plane, which explodes in midair.

BEST OF THE BEST: WITHOUT WARNING pumps new vitality into a series that had been showing signs of atrophy. The supple Phillip Rhee may lack onscreen charisma, but he proves dynamic behind the camera. The self-defense segments are cleverly staged, and the intricate action sequences are adroitly mapped out and executed. Particularly impressive is a chase through a tunnel in which Rhee rides his motorbike under a careening truck. If the script development sometimes seems musty, director Rhee blows the cobwebs off its formula plotting. When he decides to retire from kickboxing, Rhee is assured of a career in the more strenuous arena of film directing. *(Graphic violence, extreme profanity, nudity.)*—R.P.

d, Phillip Rhee; p, Phillip Rhee, Peter E. Strauss; exec p, Frank Guistra; co-p, Steve Rundell, Blondel Aldoo, Jed Daly; w, Phillip Rhee, Fred Vicarel; ph, Michael Margulies; ed, Bert Lovitt; m, David Grant; prod d, Douglas Dick; set d, Karen A. Gresti; sound, Daniel D. Monahan; fx, Tassilo Baur; casting, James F. Tarzia, Annelise Collins; cos, Amy Rhee; makeup, Kathleen Sandoval; stunts, Phillip Rhee

Crime/Martial Arts **(PR: C MPAA: R)**

BEYOND SILENCE ★★★
(Germany, 1998) 109m Claussen + Wobke Filmproduktion GmbH; Buena Vista International ~ Miramax c

Sylvie Testud *(Lara)*; Tatjana Trieb *(8-Year-Old Lara)*; Howie Seago *(Martin)*; Emmanuelle Laborit *(Kai)*; Sybille Canonica *(Clarissa)*; Matthias Habich *(Gregor)*; Alexandra Bloz *(Marie)*; Hansa Czypionka *(Tom)*; Doris Schade *(Lilli)*; Horst Sachtlenben *(Robert)*

An Academy Award nominee for Best Foreign Language Film, BEYOND SILENCE is a heartfelt but unexceptional film about a young woman struggling to reconcile her love of her parents, who are deaf, with her desire to be a musician.

At the age of eight, Lara (Tatjana Trieb) is an expert at translating for her parents, both of whom were born deaf. Martin (Howie Seago) and Kai (Emmanuelle Laborit) are particularly forced to rely on their daughter because German society at the time does little to help the hearing impaired. Although Lara does not feel oppressed by her duties (occasionally turning her prerogative of translation into a personal advantage), her free-spirited aunt Clarissa (Sibylle Canonica) tries to broaden her horizons by giving her a clarinet—the first one Clarissa played as a girl. Clarissa and Martin's unresolved sibling tensions, going back to childhood, are exacerbated by Lara's infatuation with music, which represents to Martin a world that has always spurned him and his wife.

Ten years later, Lara (Sylvie Testud) is given a chance to study music in Berlin. Clarissa offers to tutor her for the summer in preparation, an offer seen by Martin as an attempt to steal his daughter. Lara goes anyway, leaving her younger sister Marie (Alexandra Bloz) to care for their parents. In Berlin, Lara meets and falls in love with Tom (Hansa Czypionka), a teacher for the deaf who is also the child of deaf parents. The rift between Lara and her father deepens when Kai is killed by a car while riding a bicycle, something Lara encouraged her to do. Nor is it helped when Martin sees Lara making love to Tom. Lara returns to Berlin, where she sees the downside of her revered aunt's flighty lifestyle. Lara and Martin are reunited when he comes to watch her school audition, promising that he will try to understand this thing that means so much to her.

Writer-director Caroline Link was working as an au pair in the United States when she became interested in the use of sign language at LA's Deaf West Theater. Several years of research showed her the separate and particular culture of the hearing impaired. But while BEYOND SILENCE seems authoritatively to depict the experience of living with deaf parents, deafness is not the film's major subject. It functions instead as a metaphor for the gaps that exist between members of a family, particularly parents and children. And while BEYOND SILENCE is adequate-to-good as a family drama, it's hardly unexplored territory. One can't help wishing that, having done the research, Link had concentrated more on the aspect of living without hearing, something known to fewer of us than the pains of growing up. There are enough little touches—Martin asking his daughter how snow sounds, Lara translating a TV movie for her mother and therefore (because she must face Kai in order to sign) being unable to watch it herself—to suggest how much better a film this could have been. In Germany, the film prompted governmental reform in the recognition of sign language as a means though which the deaf can communicate with others, as opposed to the previously preferred policy of forcing them to learn to speak (no matter how poorly) and lip-read. *(Nudity, sexual situations, adult situations.)*—M.F.

d, Caroline Link; p, Thomas Wobke, Jakob Claussen, Luggi Waldleitner; w, Caroline Link, Beth Serlin; ph, Gernot Roll; ed, Patricia Rommel; m, Niki Reiser; prod d, Susann Bieling; casting, Risa Kes

AAN Best Foreign Language Film

Drama **(PR: C MPAA: R)**

BEYOND, THE ★★★½

(Italy, 1981) 88m Fulvia Film srl ~ Rolling Thunder c
(AKA: SEVEN DOORS OF DEATH; L'ALDILA)

David Warbeck *(Dr. John McCabe)*; Catriona MacColl, billed as Katherine MacColl *(Liza Merril)*; Cinzia Monreale, billed as Sarah Keller *(Emily)*; Antoine Saint John *(Schweick)*; Veronica Lazar *(Martha)*; Anthony Flees *(Larry)*; Giovanni de Nava *(Joe the Plumber)*; Pier Luigi Conti, billed as Al Cliver *(Doctor Harris)*; Michele Mirabella *(Martin)*; Giampaolo Saccarola *(Arthur)*; Maria Pia Marsala *(Jill)*; Laura De Marchi *(Maryanne)*; Lucio Fulci *(Town Clerk)*

Released uncut in the US for the first time in 1998, this 1981 Italian production marks the highpoint of horror specialist Lucio Fulci's career.

In 1927 Louisiana, a painter and practitioner of witchcraft named Schweik (Giovanni de Nava) is murdered by an angry mob. Decades later, the hotel in which he practiced is inherited by Liza Merril (Catriona MacColl), who sets about restoring it. A worker suffers a bad fall after seeing an apparition in one of the rooms, and a plumber, Joe (Anthony Flees), is killed in the basement. Liza is befriended by local doctor John McCabe (David Warbeck) and visited by a blind woman, Emily (Cinzia Monreale), who warns her about evil forces within the hotel. At the morgue, Joe's wife is killed by spilled acid and his daughter Jill is blinded and possessed by the evil spirits. Liza has her architect friend Martin look into the hotel's history, and he is killed by tarantulas.

John initially scoffs at Liza's stories of the bizarre occurrences, but soon the hotel's caretaker, Martha (Veronica Lazar), and her son, Arthur (Giampaolo Saccarola), also suffer horrible deaths. Investigating the house where Liza claims she spoke to Emily (who supposedly died decades before), John finds an ancient book revealing that the hotel was built over one of the seven gates to hell. Confronted by the undead Schweike, who wants her to return to the netherworld, Emily is killed by her seeing-eye dog. Assailed by violent forces, John and Liza flee to the local hospital, where they encounter John's terrorized associate, Dr. Harris (Pier Luigi Conti), and the possessed Jill. A group of zombies attacks, Harris is killed, John shoots Jill, and he and Liza run into the hospital's basement. They find themselves back in the hotel's cellar—and ultimately in a hellish landscape.

The plot of THE BEYOND is a melange of borrowed ideas, the acting ranges from acceptable to abysmal, and the dialogue is often hackneyed. Yet the film evokes powerful chills nonetheless, especially in its uncut form. The movie originally played American theaters in an edited version titled 7 DOORS OF DEATH, released in 1983 with a different score by Aquarius Releasing. The '98 bookings of the complete film were done under the sponsorship of a number of Fulci fans, including Quentin Tarantino, film editor Bob Murawski, and Sage Stallone, Sylvester's son. THE BEYOND bears out their enthusiasm for the director (who died in 1996), demonstrating his facility for intense, atmospheric horror.

While THE BEYOND is as explicitly gory as much of its early '80s Italian ilk, Fulci choreographs the bloodshed into some memorably macabre images, as in the scene where the terrified Jill backs away from her mother's corpse as a tide of blood and acid washes across the floor towards her. Sergio Salvati's cinematography expertly creates an aura of menace, and Giannetto De Rossi's makeup effects are grotesquely convincing—and even when they're not, as in the spider attack, Fulci makes the scene intriguingly discomfiting through the use of unpleasant sound effects. In particular, the finale that propels John and Liza from the hotel to the hospital and back, confronting them with a parade of grotesqueries along the way, is heart-poundingly effective. Rougher and in certain ways less convincing than many 1990s horror films, THE BEYOND still delivers more memorable imagery and sharper thrills than its bigger-budgeted successors. *(Graphic violence, adult situations, profanity.)*—M.G.

d, Lucio Fulci; p, Fabrizio De Angelis; w, Lucio Fulci, Giorgio Mariuzzo, Dardano Sacchetti; ph, Sergio Salvati; ed, Vincenzo Tomassi; m, Fabio Frizzi; prod d, Massimo Lentini; fx, Germano Natali; cos, Massimo Lentini; makeup, Giannetto De Rossi, Maurizio Trani

Horror **(PR: O MPAA: NR)**

BIG HIT, THE ★★

(U.S., 1998) 93m Amen Ra Films; Zide-Perry Films; Lion Rock Productions; TriStar Pictures ~ TriStar c

Mark Wahlberg *(Melvin Smiley)*; Lou Diamond Phillips *(Cisco)*; Christina Applegate *(Pam Shulman)*; Avery Brooks *(Paris)*; Bokeem Woodbine *(Crunch)*; Antonio Sabato Jr. *(Vince)*; Lainie Kazan *(Jeanne Shulman)*; Elliott Gould *(Morton Shulman)*; Sab Shimono *(Jiro Nishi)*; Lela Rochon *(Chantel)*; China Chow *(Keiko Nishi)*; Robin Dunne *(Gump—the Stutterer)*; Danny Smith *(Pimply Faced Kid/Video Store Clerk)*; Joshua Peace *(Lance)*; David Usher *(Sergio)*; Hardee T. Lineham *(Accountant)*; Gerry Mendicino *(Slave Trader)*; Robert Vernon Eaton; John Stoneham Sr. *(Pimps)*; Nicola Jones *(Blond)*; Alexa Gilmour *(Aly—Keiko's Friend)*; John Stoker *(Sid Mussberger—the Neighbor)*; Cotton Mather *(Moe)*; Derek Peels *(Windbush)*; Tig Fong *(Kaya)*; Danny Lima *(Aaron the Limo Driver)*; Morgan Freeman *(Boy in Hotel Lobby)*; Giovahann White *(Paris's Son)*; Bobby Hannah *(Paris's Driver)*

An action comedy about a hit man with a heart of gold who becomes involved in a misbegotten kidnap caper, THE BIG HIT marks the Hollywood debut of Hong Kong director Che-Kirk Wong. Despite engaging performances by leading man Mark Wahlberg and newcomer China Chow, the mixture of farcical comedy and wholesale slaughter never quite gels.

After completing a successful raid on the hotel headquarters of a rival crime lord, Melvin Smiley (Mark Wahlberg), a hit man for crime boss Paris (Avery Brooks), is approached by his partner Cisco (Lou Diamond Phillips) to participate in a freelance kidnap caper. In need of money to appease his mistress Chantel's (Lela Rochon) creditors, Melvin agrees and joins Cisco, Gump (Robin Dunne), and Crunch (Bokeem Woodbine) in the kidnapping of Keiko Nishi (China Chow), the teenaged daughter of Japanese industrialist Jiro Nishi (Sab Shimono).

Cisco orders Mel to stash Keiko at the house Mel keeps for Chantel. Mel returns to his own home to find his fiancee Pam Shulman (Christina Applegate) expecting a visit from her parents (Elliott Gould and Lainie Kazan). Having siphoned off sufficient funds from Mel, Chantel decides to flee with her other boyfriend, Sergio (David Usher). She deposits the bound-and-gagged Keiko on Mel's doorstep, leading to a comedy of errors as Mel must keep Keiko's presence a secret from Pam and her parents while thwarting Keiko's persistent efforts to escape. While the Shulmans go to temple, Mel bonds with Keiko during the course of his disastrous efforts to cook a kosher meal for his future in-laws.

Cisco demands $1 million in ransom from Mr. Nishi. Recently bankrupted, Nishi calls his close friend Paris, who happens to be Keiko's godfather. An enraged Paris calls in Cisco and orders him to find the kidnappers, retrieve Keiko, and kill the culprits. Cisco gets Gump, in Paris's presence, to identify Mel as the mastermind and then kills Gump and speeds to Mel's house with his henchmen.

Mel's dinner with the Shulmans is interrupted by the arrival of Cisco and his thugs. After a gun battle in his house, Mel escapes in his sports car with Keiko. A series of chases and shootouts ensue, but Cisco finally catches up to Mel at a video store, where Mel has stopped to return a long-overdue video rental. Mel's car is pushed over a ravine by Cisco's car, precipitating more chases and shootouts. Mel and Cisco have their final battle inside the video store, where Mel has to dodge Cisco's twirling twin knives. The battle ends with Mel stabbing Cisco with one of the knives and Cisco being killed by an explosive tossed by Mel. Mel is left for dead in the rubble and Keiko is reunited with her father. Days later, Keiko is met after school by Mel, who had miraculously survived the explosion, and goes away with him on Cisco's luxurious sailboat.

Kirk Wong (billed here as Che-Kirk Wong) was known in Hong Kong for his compact, intense thrillers, ORGANIZED CRIME AND TRIAD BUREAU (1993), ROCK & ROLL COP (1994), and the subdued Jackie Chan vehicle CRIME STORY (1993). Here Wong suffers the fate of other Hong Kong directors in the US (Tsui Hark, Ringo Lam, Stanley Tong) and is forced to work with a subpar script and a group of disparate talents. Sadly, the farcical elements, similar to those in GROSSE POINT BLANK (1997) and 8 HEADS IN A DUFFEL BAG (1997), could have been quite funny if handled with a lighter touch and separated from the mind-numbing scenes of high-octane violence. Had the main character, Melvin, been an ordinary guy rather than a high-tech killer, the comic moments would have been funnier and the violent outbursts would have garnered audience identification for the protagonist. As it stands, Melvin's nonchalant acceptance of the carnage around him, including Cisco's cold-blooded murder of Keiko's friendly chauffeur, serves to distance an otherwise likeable character from the audience.

The film's blatant attempts to pitch to a young, urban male demographic involve most of the leading male characters talking in exaggerated homeboy slang; this is particularly true of Lou Diamond Phillips, whose imitation of a black "gangsta" rapper gets more ludicrous in each scene. Furthermore, the employment of blatant Jewish stereotypes in the characterizations of the Shulman family would be offensive if the rest of the characters weren't equally silly. The film's use of nondescript Toronto locations undermine any credibility the film might have hoped to earn from its use of street language. *(Violence, profanity.)*—B.C.

d, Che-Kirk Wong; p, Warren Zide, Wesley Snipes; exec p, John Woo, Terence Chang, John Eckert; co-p, Craig Perry, Victor McGauley, Roger Garcia; w, Ben Ramsey; ph, Danny Nowak; ed, Robin Russell, Pietro Scalia; m, Graeme Revell; prod d, Taavo Soodor; art d, Andrew Stearn, Craig Lathrop; set d, Enrico Campana; sound, Douglas Ganton (mixer), Sandy Gendler (design); fx, Kaz Kobielski; casting, Roger Mussenden; cos, Margaret M. Mohr; makeup, Donald J. Mowat; stunts, John Stoneham Stoneham, Lau Chi-Ho

Crime/Action/Comedy **(PR: C MPAA: R)**

BIG LEBOWSKI, THE ★★½

(U.S., 1998) 117m Bitter Creek Productions; Working Title Films; PolyGram ~ Gramercy Pictures c

Jeff Bridges *(Jeff Lebowski—the Dude)*; John Goodman *(Walter Sobchak)*; Julianne Moore *(Maude Lebowski)*; Steve Buscemi *(Donny)*; David Huddleston *(The Big Lebowski)*; John Turturro *(Jesus Quintana)*; Peter Stormare *(Uli—Nihilist)*; Sam Elliott *(The Stranger)*; David Thewlis *(Knox Harrington)*; Ben Gazzara *(Jackie Treehorn)*; Jimmie Dale Gilmore *(Smokey)*; Philip Seymour Hoffman *(Brandt)*; Tara Reid *(Bunny Lebowski)*; Flea *(Kiefer—Nihilist)*; Torsten Voges *(Franz—Nihilist)*; Philip Moon; Mark Pellegrino *(Treehorn Thugs)*; Jack Kehler *(Dude's Landlord)*; James G. Hoosier *(Quintana's Partner)*; Carlos Leon; Terrance Burton *(Maude's Thugs)*; Richard Gant *(Older Cop)*; Christian Clemenson *(Younger Cop)*; Dom Irrera *(Tony the Chauffeur)*; Gerard L'Heureux *(Lebowski's Chauffeur)*; Lu Elrod *(Coffee Shop Waitress)*; Michael Gomez *(Auto Circus Cop)*; Peter Siragusa *(Gary the Bartender)*; Marshall Manesh *(Doctor)*; Mary Bugin *(Arthur Digby Sellers)*; Jesse Flanagan *(Little Larry Sellers)*; Irene Olga Lopez *(Pilar)*; Luis Colina *(Corvette Owner)*; Leon Russom *(Malibu Police Chief)*; Ajgie Kirkland *(Cab Driver)*; Jon Polito *(Private Snoop)*; Aimee Mann *(Nihilist Woman)*; Jerry Haleva *(Saddam)*; Jennifer Lamb *(Pancake Waitress)*; Warren David Keith *(Funeral Director)*

The third and least resonant of Joel and Ethan Coen's kidnapping movies (the other two were RAISING ARIZONA and FARGO), THE BIG LEBOWSKI virtually disdains its Raymond-Chandlerish plot (in contrast to the concurrent PALMETTO, which developed a remarkably similar premise too predictably) in favor of comedy, eccentric characterization, and expressionistic parody. A bowling-buddy-movie that recalls POCKET MONEY (1972), a better film about the comic misadventures of two clueless comrades, the picture rates as minor Coen brothers, but has a few compensations.

Jeff "The Dude" Lebowski (Jeff Bridges), an ex-hippie-activist, lives in a rundown corner of LA where, apart from bowling with his pals, he does as little as he possibly can. Upon returning home one day, he is greeted by two thugs on a debt-collecting assignment. When they realize that The Dude is the wrong Jeff Lebowski, they urinate on his rug and leave.

The Dude calls on the other Jeff Lebowski (David Huddleston), a high-powered, middle-aged millionaire, to get a new rug, and is hired to deliver a large ransom to a kidnapping ring that claims to have snatched the older Lebowski's giddy young wife, Bunny (Tara Reid). The Dude recruits his friend Walter (John Goodman), a Vietnam War vet with a take-no-prisoners attitude, to help him make the drop.

Everything that can go wrong does go wrong: the avaricious Walter substitutes a dummy suitcase for the briefcase containing the ransom; the Dude's car is stolen, and with it the ransom money; Lebowski angrily shows the Dude a severed toe which the abductors have sent him; and the Dude finds himself being threatened and roughed up from all sides. He is hit by the kidnappers, by Bunny's creditors—even by Maude (Julianne Moore), Lebowski's eccentric daughter, who first punches him out, then beds him down in the hope of conceiving a child.

The Dude concludes that the "real" ransom briefcase was itself a phony, and that Lebowski had wanted all along to be rid of his profligate wife. When he revisits Lebowski's mansion to proffer this theory, the Dude notices Bunny in residence, toes intact.

Later, in a parking lot, the Dude, Walter, and Donny (Steve Buscemi), the third member of their bowling team, are confrronted by three toughs who demand the (probably nonexistent) ransom money. Walter easily vanquishes them, but in the excitement, Donny has a heart attack and dies. After he and Walter scatter their buddy's ashes, the Dude returns with relief to his uneventful life of bowling and B.S.-ing.

The plot of THE BIG LEBOWSKI is nothing more than a frayed clothesline for the Coens' dazzling visuals. FARGO (1996), their preceding film, had managed to instill plenty of laughs into a similar kidnapping scenario without snubbing the genre's requisite elements of suspense, danger, and dread. The film put its characters' lives and reputations on the line and, as a result, its klutzy kidnappers—like those in Martin Scorsese's superb THE KING OF COMEDY (1982)—were not merely funny but also disquieting. In THE BIG LEBOWSKI, nothing much is at stake and nothing much lingers in the memory after the end credits.

THE BIG LEBOWSKI has its virtues, but on the whole the film is more valuable for its sidebars than for its story line. Under the opening credits, a lovely ode to bowling captures the artificial beauty of bowling alleys—among mankind's most flawless artifacts—in all their immaculately clean splendor. Two imaginative dream sequences make sport of Busby Berkeley-like visual conceits and phallic symbolism. (The Coens understand that Freud cannot be successfully invoked in the cinema except irreverently.)

Several of the performances are oustandlingly comic, chief among them the hilariously intense turns of John Goodman, David Huddleston, and, best of all, John Turturro (as mega-bowler Jesus Quintana), who postures, preens, and all but pirouettes his way to the ultimate send-up of supermacho arrogance. Sam Elliott, an invaluably anachronistic actor, makes an affable appearance as an old-time cowboy who functions as mock narrator and benevolent presence. (Older audience members will relate when he asks The Dude, "Do you have to use so many cuss words?")

As THE BIG LEBOWSKI is totally untouched by a love interest (notwithstanding the cold-blooded quickie Maude grants The Dude) or heroics, Jeff Bridges' considerable skills as a leading man are wasted. The film would have benefited if Steve Buscemi, a wonderful comedian, had been promoted from the thankless role of Donny ("Shut the fuck up, Donny" is Walter's invariable response to his conversational input) to that of The Dude.

If one chalks up BARTON FINK (1991) and THE HUDSUCKER PROXY (1993) as honorable failures, THE BIG LEBOWSKI is clearly the weakest of the Coen Brothers' first seven pictures. The Berkeley spoof, which was photographed in an airplane hangar, makes one long to see the Coens try their hand at a lavish and artificial musical in the grand manner ("Gold Diggers of 2001"?) *(Violence, nudity, extreme profanity.)*—D.T.

d, Joel Coen; p, Ethan Coen; exec p, Tim Bevan, Eric Fellner; co-p, John Cameron; w, Joel Coen, Ethan Coen, billed as Roderick Jaynes; ph, Roger Deakins; ed, Roderick Jaynes, Tricia Cooke; m, Carter Burwell; prod d, Rick Heinrichs; art d, John Dexter; set d, Chris Spellman; sound, Allan Byer (mixer); fx, Janek Sirrs, Janet Yale, The Computer Film Company; casting, John Lyons; cos, Mary Zophres; makeup, Jean Black

Comedy/Mystery **(PR: C MPAA: R)**

BIG ONE, THE ★★★½

(U.K., 1998) 96m Dog Eat Dog Films; BBC Films ~ Miramax c

Michael Moore; Garrison Keillor; Studs Terkel; Rick Nielson; Phil Knight

Documentary filmmaker Michael Moore's debut, ROGER AND ME, received many critical accolades in 1989. However, apart from a short follow-up entitled PETS OR MEAT (1992), Moore hadn't visited the documentary arena since, concentrating instead on the television series "TV Nation" and the feature-length comedy CANADIAN BACON (1994). With THE BIG ONE, Moore reenters the world of nonfiction film, and though it lacks the emotional punch of ROGER AND ME, the film is one of the most entertaining documentaries in a long time.

While on a 50-city tour to promote his bestselling book, *Downsize This! Random Threats From an Unarmed American,* Michael Moore decides to assemble a small film crew to document his travels and the experiences he has meeting people across the nation. When Moore is not giving lectures and appearing at book signings, he is doing the kind of thing that made him famous—namely, harassing CEOs of corporations that lay off workers in times of economic prosperity. Moore visits Payday candy bars in Centralia, Illinois, which is closing down; Johnson Controls in Milwaukee, Wisconsin, which is moving to Mexico; the office of Wisconsin governor Tommy Thompson, bringing with him a group of "welfare mothers" who want to prove they'd rather work than live on the dole; and Pillsbury in Minneapolis, Minnesota, and Procter & Gamble in Cincinnati, Ohio, both downsizing despite posting record profits. In each case, Moore doesn't get past the front lobby, and more often than not is escorted off the property by the police.

During his tour, Moore also encounters a number of colorful personalities, including a group of Borders Books employees who are trying to unionize, an ex-con who booked flights for TWA while in prison, and Cheap Trick guitarist Rick Nielson. It is not until he reaches Portland, Oregon, that Moore finally gets to meet an actual CEO: Phil Knight of Nike. Perhaps in an attempt to defuse Moore's attentions, Knight invites Moore to visit; not surprisingly, Moore goes for the throat, interrogating Knight about Nike's use of 14-year-old Indonesian labor to manufacture its shoes—at a cost of pennies an hour. When Knight claims American workers would not want to work in a shoe factory, Moore goes back to his hometown of Flint, Michigan, to assemble a group of unemployed workers who beg Knight to open at least one factory in the United States and give them a job. Not surprisingly, Knight refuses.

Though billed as a documentary, THE BIG ONE plays like a mixture of travelogue and stand-up comedy. Moore peppers the film with numerous "bits" from his book-signing appearances—his theory that political hopeful Steve Forbes is actually an alien, for example. These bits are entertaining, certainly, but detract from the overall impact of the film. Misapplied, too, is Moore's standard man-of-the-people shtick. He may still dress like a slob, but Moore has come a long way from the streets of Flint; after success on both the big- and small-screens, his "regular guy" act feels a bit disingenuous at times.

This is not to say that THE BIG ONE is not a fine documentary and an entertaining film. As he did in ROGER AND ME and "TV Nation," Moore displays a keen eye for the absurdly funny in everyday life, as well as for the bewilderingly greedy actions in corporate America. Despite his somewhat unfair modus operandi of barging in unannounced, cameras rolling, into corporate offices, Moore doesn't have to work all that hard to show that, eight years after ROGER AND ME, profitable companies are still in the business of laying off large numbers of workers. *(Profanity.)*—B.T.

d, Michael Moore; p, Kathleen Glynn; exec p, David Mortimer, Jeremy Gibson; w, Michael Moore; ph, Brian Danitz, Chris Smith; ed, Meg Reticker; m, World Famous Blue Jays; sound, Sarah Price

Documentary/Comedy **(PR: C MPAA: PG-13)**

BILLBOARD DAD ★★
(U.S., 1998) 90m Dualstar Productions ~ Tapestry Films c

Mary Kate Olsen *(Tess Taylor)*; Ashley Olsen *(Emily Taylor)*; Tom Amandes *(Maxwell Tyler)*; Jessica Tuck *(Brooke Anders)*; Carl Banks *(Nigel)*; Ellen Ratner *(Debbie)*; Sam Selatta *(Ryan)*; Rafael Rojas III *(Cody)*; Troian Bellisario *(Kristen)*; Angelique Parry *(Julianne)*; Bailey Luetgert *(Brad)*; Vincent Bowman *(Buzz Cut)*; Debra Christofferson *(Autumn)*; Lisa Montgomery *(Enola Rubenstein)*; Twink Caplan *(Chelsea)*; Diana Morgan *(Katherine Buxbaum)*; Kevin Fry *(Mail Carrier)*; Erin Sadiello *(Pretty Young Model)*; Toran Caudell *(Surfer)*; Matthew Carey *(Surfer)*; Mitch Gibney *(Waiter)*; Helene Cardona *(Henriette)*; Guy Dill *(Counterfeit Artist)*; Amy Enuke *(Skinny Model)*; Liberty Bradford *(Flower Seller)*; Gary Miller *(Rich Man)*; Adrienne Meltzer *(Rich Woman)*; Lisa Amsterdam; Lisa Kushell; Teresa Ganzel; Patrice Mozes *(Max's Dates)*

BILLBOARD DAD has a tailor-made script that allows nearly-pubescent child stars Mary Kate and Ashley Olsen to demonstrate a tad more acting skill and presence than they had as moppets. The problem is that they're still driving the same sitcom-esque vehicle: twin buttinskis playing Cupid for their single dad.

Sports-loving Tess Tyler (Mary Kate Olsen) and her brainy twin Emily (Ashley Olsen), won't be truly content as long as their dad Max (Tom Amandes) keeps mourning for his late wife. A successful sculptor, Max is managed by conniving agent Nigel (Carl Banks), who doesn't want Max's depressing (but profitably trendy) style to change.

Knowing their lonely dad needs prodding, the twins paint a singles' ad on an LA billboard; as the billboard garners attention, Max is inundated with marriage offers. During a date with Debbie (Ellen Ratner), Max instead becomes attracted to her friend Brooke Anders (Jessica Tuck), a single mom with an unruly son, Ryan (Sam Selatta).

Distraught over Max's declining productivity while he courts Brooke, Nigel doctors a taped phone conversation in order to persuade the eavesdropping twins that Brooke is a gold digger. He also lets Brooke misinterpret Max's innocent relationship with a nubile model. After Brooke and Max split up, Ryan overhears Nigel plotting to sell mass-market copies of Max's sculptures. Tess and Emily secretly record Nigel's admission of guilt, and publicly discredit him at Max's exhibition. Max and Brooke patch up their differences, and loner Ryan and the twins become friends.

Intended as wholesome family fare, BILLBOARD DAD is a tapioca pudding filled with a few lumps, including an excess of practical jokes perpetrated by the twin terrors, horrendous acting by Tom Amandes as the wussy father and Carl Banks as the flamboyant art-parasite, and an air of familiarity that chokes the merriment like a thick smog. To their credit, the Olsen girls slam across the hoary gags and syrupy sentiment for their fans. But the Olsen-phobic will be less likely to enjoy the adventures of these Miss Fix-Its as they meddle in adult matters and presume to know what's best for everyone else.—R.P.

d, Alan Metter; p, Neil Steinberg; exec p, Robert L. Levy, Peter Abrams; co-p, Andy Cohen; w, Maria Jacquemetton; ph, Mauro Fiore; ed, Sharyn L. Ross; m, David Michael Frank; prod d, Martina Buckley; art d, Ivana Letica; sound, Jon Ailetcher; fx, Hyper Image; casting, Melissa Skoff; cos, Judy B. Swartz; makeup, Sandy Williams; stunts, Marty Pistone

Comedy/Children's **(PR: AA MPAA: PG)**

BILLY'S HOLLYWOOD SCREEN KISS ★★½
(U.S., 1998) 92m Revolutionary Eye ~ Trimark c

Sean P. Hayes *(Billy)*; Brad Rowe *(Gabriel)*; Meredith Scott Lynn *(Georgiana—"George")*; Richard Ganoung *(Perry)*; Paul Bartel *(Rex Webster)*; Matthew Ashford *(Whitey)*; Christopher Bradley *(Andrew)*; Carmine Giovinazzo *(Gundy)*; Armando Valdes-Kennedy *(Fernando)*; Holly Woodlawn; Robbie Cain

A cheery valentine to gay romance, BILLY'S HOLLYWOOD SCREEN KISS is a pleasant but ultimately vacuous addition to the growing legion of queer-positive independent films.

Billy (Sean P. Hayes) is a struggling Los Angeles photographer with an unfortunate penchant for unavailable men. Billy's best friends George (Meredith Scott Lynn) and Perry (Richard Ganoung), who has an unrequited love for Billy, constantly warn him about his penchant for pursuing the unobtainable, but Billy, ever the romantic, still believes Mr. Right can be found. When he meets the gorgeous Gabriel (Brad Rowe), a struggling musician and waiter at the local cafe, Billy is immediately smitten. He gets the idea that Gabriel would be a perfect model for his latest project—re-creating famous Hollywood kiss scenes in photographs, with men filling in for the female leads.

Perry thinks it's a good idea, and decides to financially sponsor Billy's photography project. Billy finally gets the courage to ask Gabriel about the project when he meets him at a party. Gabriel is intrigued by the idea. As the two hit it off, Billy discovers that the seemingly straight Gabriel has broken up with his girlfriend and now finds himself confused about his sexuality. This puts Billy into a tailspin: he becomes determined to not only help Gabriel through his identity crisis, but also to make Gabriel his lover. Billy takes Gabriel to an art opening featuring the works of Rex Webster (Paul Bartel), a famous photographer who wants Gabriel to pose in underwear ads to be shot on Catalina Island.

After a successful photography session in which Gabriel takes the Burt Lancaster role in a re-creation of the beach scene from FROM HERE TO ETERNITY (1953), Billy invites Gabriel over. After some drinking, the two men somehow wind up in Billy's bed, and Billy makes his move, but Gabriel backs off. When Billy finds out that Gabriel has accepted the job offer in Catalina on a whim, he takes a ferry to the set where he hopes to confront Gabriel about his feelings. But when Billy and Gabriel finally have a chance to talk, another male model beckons Gabriel back to the party, and Billy realizes that Gabriel is indeed gay but interested in someone else. Dejected, Billy heads back in LA, where he prepares an exhibit of his kiss photographs. Not only is Billy a smashing success, he also hits it off with a very attractive male admirer (Robbie Cain).

As is customary of late in gay cinema, the characters in BILLY'S HOLLYWOOD SCREEN KISS are uniformly attractive, yet never seem to be able to find the right romantic partner. In fact, the entire movie rests on the premise of the "tyranny of looks" in the gay community. Everyone lusts after Gabriel, but he, with his nonchalance towards the attention of others, is about as three-dimensional as one of Billy's polaroid snapshots—a fact that doesn't seem to matter to all the men who swoon over him. It's as if writer-director Tommy O'Haver, who demonstrates a great technical facility in the film, is trying to imply that gay men only come in two categories: the swooners and the swoonies. The film is thus, despite its light-hearted air, a somewhat disturbing commentary on contemporary gay relationships.

That said, the film does indeed have its virtues. O'Haver's script is quite witty at times, and includes some delightfully elaborate musical fantasies, which are far more entertaining than the embarrassing numbers included in the 1995 film JEFFREY (1995). In a particularly charming sequence, Billy daydreams about dancing with Gabriel in formal attire while a chorus of drag queens behind them lip-synch Petula Clark's "This Is My Song." O'Haver also makes clever use of polaroid snapshots in one scene to accompany Billy's sad recollections about how he obtained his first camera when he was a boy.

O'Haver's central coup, however, lies in his casting decisions. As Billy, Sean P. Hayes (a regular on the NBC sitcom "Will and Grace") is exceedingly charming, and injects such charisma into his character that we almost forget what an obsessive dope he is. As Gabriel, Brad Rowe gives a surprisingly compelling performance, despite the character's rather obvious limitations. Most touching of all, however, is the sensitive turn by Richard Ganoung, who beautifully articulates Perry's unrequited passion for Billy in a heartbreaking speech his character delivers near the film's end. This understated declaration of affection makes one wonder why Billy, for all his smarts, is too stupid to notice Perry's affection for him. The potential for a relationship between the two characters conjures up images of a possible starting point for "Billy's Hollywood Screen Kiss, Part 2." *(Strong language, sexual situations, profanity.)*—D.O.

d, Tommy O'Haver; p, David Moseley; assoc p, Marcus Hu; co-p, Meredith Scott Lynn, Irene Turner; w, Tommy O'Haver (based on his short film "Catalina"); ph, Mark Mervis; ed, Jeff Betancourt; m, Alan Ari Lazar; prod d, Franco-Giacomo Carbone; sound, Jeff Bennett; cos, Julia Bartholomew

Romance/Comedy **(PR: O MPAA: NR)**

BLACK DOG ★★

(U.S., 1998) 90m Universal; Mutual Film Company; Prelude Pictures; Raffaella Productions; Neufeld/Rehme Productions ~ Universal c

Patrick Swayze *(Jack Crews)*; Randy Travis *(Earl)*; Meat Loaf *(Red)*; Gabriel Casseus *(Sonny)*; Brian Vincent *(Wes)*; Brenda Strong *(Melanie)*; Graham Beckel *(Cutler)*; Stephen Tobolowsky *(Agent McClaren)*; Charles Dutton *(Agent Ford)*; Rusty De Wees *(Junior)*; Cyril O'Reilly *(Vince)*; Erin Broderick *(Tracy)*; Lorraine Toussaint *(Avery)*; Hester Hargett *(FBI Tech)*; Stuart Greer; Whitt Brantley *(Troopers)*; Mark Steven Robison *(Chicken Truck Driver)*; Elizabeth Jaye Moore *(Linda)*

Patrick Swayze and a bunch of guys with redneck twangs drive around in trucks, crashing into each other on a regular basis, in BLACK DOG, a film that would have been helped (though not enough) by the presence of Burt Reynolds, who used to have a monopoly on this sort of thing.

Jack Crews (Patrick Swayze) has been working as a mechanic in a New Jersey truckyard ever since getting out of prison. He served two years for vehicular homicide after falling asleep at the wheel of his truck caused him to hit and kill a man. Having lost his license, he rejects an offer by his boss Cutler (Graham Beckel) to make a no-questions-asked run from Atlanta to New Jersey for $10,000. But when he finds out that his mortgage is $9,000 overdue, he accepts the job rather than risk having to move his wife and daughter back to urban Newark.

In Atlanta, Jack picks up his load from Cutler's partner Red (Meatloaf). His co-driver is Earl (Randy Travis); they will be followed in a support car by Wes (Brian Vincent) and Sonny (Gabriel Casseus). Before they've been on the road long, they are attacked by two men working for Red, who is planning to double-cross Cutler and hijack this load. After wiping the attackers out with some fancy driving, Jack discovers he is hauling a truck full of illegal arms. He calls Cutler, who threatens to cause trouble with Jack's parole officer if he doesn't get the guns to New Jersey. Despite changing their course, they are again attacked by Red's men. After escaping, they find that Wes has been tipping Red off. Jack tries to quit the run, only to find that Cutler is holding his family hostage. In another altercation with Red's men, Sonny is shot; before dying, he reveals to Jack that this is part of an FBI/ATF operation to bring down Cutler. Jack arranges to trade his cargo for his family in New Jersey, where Cutler is arrested by the FBI (after being tipped off by Jack). The grateful feds promise to take care of Jack's mortgage and license, and he is free to start a new life—after one more encounter with a vengeful Red, who dies in a truck crash while trying to kill Jack.

The assistant stunt coordinator for BLACK DOG was named Dickey Beer, which probably tells you all you need to know about this diesel opus. At barely 83 minutes before credits, it would seem as though most anything having to do with character development was jettisoned before this was rolled into theaters. What's left is a lot of character tics (Red is fond of quoting the Bible to his own ends; Earl is a wannabe singer who can't sing), and plot suggestions (Jack's marital problems) that don't go anywhere. What appears to be bad makeup detracts severely from Swayze's ability to look as macho as this role requires. It's clear that all involved with this film decided to put all their apples into the spectacle of 16-wheelers colliding at high speed: if that's your idea of a good time, give it an extra half star. *(Violence, adult situations, profanity.)* —M.F.

d, Kevin Hooks; p, Raffaella De Laurentiis, Peter Saphier, Mark W. Koch; exec p, Mace Neufeld, Robert Rehme, Gary Levinsohn, Mark Gordon; assoc p, Jim Wedaa; co-p, Hester Hargett, Susan Solomon; w, William Mickelberry, Dan Vining; ph, Buzz Feitshans IV; ed, Debra Neil-Fisher, Sabrina Plisco-Morris; m, George S. Clinton; prod d, Victoria Paul; art d, Ken Hardy, Randall Richards; set d, Diana L. Stoughton; sound, Mary Ellis (mixer); fx, Kit West, Trevor Neighbour; casting, Elisabeth Rudolph; cos, Peggy Stamper; makeup, Lynn Barber; stunts, Vic Armstrong

Action/Drama **(PR: C MPAA: PG-13)**

BLACK LIGHT ★½

(Canada, 1998) 91m Edge Entertainment; IMF Film Associates ~ Peachtree Entertainment c

Michael Ironside *(Frank Schumann)*; Tahnee Welch *(Sharon Avery)*; Currie Graham *(Larry Avery)*; Anne Marie Loder *(Detective Howard)*; Walter Mills *(Inspector Randwick)*; Lori Hallier *(Dr. Anna Godard)*; Billy Morton *(Killer)*; Jane Redlyon *(Mrs. Atwood)*; Kirk Jarrett *(Edwin Bosisto)*; Chris Hails *(Forensic Technician)*; Stephanie Knight Thomas *(TV Journalist)*; Melanie Peterson *(Detective #1)*; Alphonse Gaudet *(1st Park Officer)*; Dwayne Brenna *(Tower Park Officer)*; Robert Benz *(Rick)*

BLACK LIGHT, a Canadian direct-to-video thriller, is a convoluted concoction of murder and paranormal phenomena. The film features Tahnee Welch as a blind clairvoyant who leads police to a serial killer only to become his next target.

Clairvoyant since childhood, Sharon Avery (Tahnee Welch) uses her gift to help police track a serial killer who is preying on young children. After a car accident robs her of her eyesight and her psychic abilities, Sharon is despondent. She tries to drown herself, but the trauma brings about another vision of a child in peril. Sharon warns Inspector Frank Schumann (Michael Ironside), who initially dismisses her insights. But when a victim turns up matching the description Sharon gave police, Schumann brings her on the case. Sharon's resentful husband Larry (Currie Graham) leaves her. More determined than ever to catch the killer, she sets herself up as bait by going on the local news and taunting him. When the police apprehend their prime suspect, Sharon is believed to be safe. Meanwhile, Larry digitally enhances an electronic image of the killer transmitted by Sharon's brainwaves during laser therapy on her eyes. When the image sharpens, he realizes that the police nabbed the wrong guy. Schumann, who has developed feelings for Sharon, discovers that the killer is still on the loose when he receives a phone call saying that the arrested suspect had an alibi. It's too late, though, the killer strangles Schumann, murders Larry, and tries to drown Sharon in a pool, who frees herself and shoots her stalker. Sharon is reunited with Schumann, who survived his attack.

BLACK LIGHT attempts to put a twist on the woman-in-jeopardy theme by endowing its blind heroine with a unique (and convenient) ability to psychically "see" perilous situations as they occur. But the device is so preposterously employed that each successive development tops the last for sheer absurdity. In Sharon's final showdown with the killer, she uses her psychic vision to locate Schumann's gun, which has fallen into the pool. She surfaces with the gun and aims it at the killer, who is struggling with Schumann. Though Sharon previously stated that her visions were seen through the killer's eyes, she sees him from her own perspective, clearly enough to distinguish him from Schumann and fire a bull's-eye shot to his chest.

Welch plays the central role with a determined seriousness, but she can't overcome the implausibility of her character's actions—such as intentionally luring the deranged killer to her home. Sure, she's strong, independent, and psychically gifted. But she's also blind, alone, and supposedly unable to control when her visions will occur. The thin script makes no attempt to carve out an identity for the killer, who is billed simply as "killer." What the film lacks in dramatic tension is not made up for with sexual tension. The only hint of eroticism is a brief poolside clinch between Welch and Ironside, and though Welch goes into the pool twice, she does so fully clothed. *(Violence, sexual situations.)*—B.R.

d, Michael Storey; p, Leanne Arnott, Torin Stefanson; exec p, David Doerksen, Antony I. Ginnane, Ann Lyons; co-p, Crawford Hawkins, Michael J. LeGresley; w, Vincent Monton; ph, Michael Storey; ed, Torin Stefanson; m, Kenneth Richard Harrison; prod d, Hugh Shankland; art d, Carmen Milenkoyic; set d, Kim Wall; fx, Jay Robertson; casting, Stephanie Gorin, Marion Mills; cos, Brenda Shenher; makeup, Tracey George; stunts, Kirk Jarrett

Thriller **(PR: C MPAA: NR)**

BLACK THUNDER ★★

(U.S., 1998) 85m Concorde Productions ~ New Horizons Home Video c

Michael Dudikoff *(Vince Connors)*; Richard Norton *(Tom Ratcher)*; Michael Cavanaugh *(Barnes)*; Nancy Valen *(Mela)*; Gary Hudson *(Rick Jannick)*; Robert Miranda *(Rojar)*; Rob Madrid *(Stone)*; Frederic Forrest *(Admiral Pendelton)*

BLACK THUNDER updates the old Cold War thriller formula by replacing the Soviets with Arabs, but it's really the same jingoistic stuff, and not terribly well done.

During a test of the Nova, an Air Force stealth jet nicknamed "Black Thunder," a Libyan agent posing as a pilot steals the "invisible" plane and apparently kills the American flyer, Tom Ratcher (Richard Norton). The Air Force calls upon Vince Connors (Michael Dudikoff), a top gun trained by Tom, to travel over the Atlantic and retrieve Black Thunder. On his mission, Vince reluctantly pairs with Rick Jannick (Gary Hudson), a daredevil Vince considers a mere skydiver. Vince and Rick know they have only 24 hours before the US President will order carpet bombing of Libya.

Once in Libya, Vince and Rick land their supersonic SR-71 and fight on the ground against Libyan soldiers while searching for the jet. During the scramble, Rick is caught and taken prisoner by Stone (Rob Madrid), the leader of the terrorist group that stole the plane, and Vince hides out in the home of a sympathetic dissident, Mela (Nancy Valen). With Mela's help, Vince tries to rescue Rick from the army base and steal back Black Thunder. However, Rick is injured in a shootout, but before he dies, he blows up the entire base, with Stone in it.

Just as he makes his getaway, Vince learns that the American traitor behind the original theft was none other than Tom, his beloved teacher; in the air, Tom chases down Vince in order to steal the plane again, or at least make a deal with his former student. But Vince, feeling betrayed, kills Tom with a missile and brings Black Thunder back safely to Edwards Air Force Base in California. His commander offers him a medal for averting the all-out war, but Vince says the honors should really go to Rick, who died for his country.

Quoting TOP GUN (1986) and FIREFOX (1982), BLACK THUNDER takes nostalgic delight in reviving the sort of high-flying heroics that characterized Cold War spy thrillers. The film also lifts the spy-mask gambit from the "Mission: Impossible" 1960s TV series and its subsequent movie version. The reactionary ideology is the same, but BLACK THUNDER ranks at least a grade below those films in terms of quality—from the woeful performance by Rob Madrid as the lead terrorist to the backlight reflections on the pilots' helmets, BLACK THUNDER is a botched job.

One might wonder why Roger Corman would want to executive produce a film with so little redeeming artistic value (an argument can usually be made for his other cheesy genre outings, however low-budget), or what attracted Frederic Forrest to make a bland, meaningless cameo (as an admiral) in such an effort. Still, even today's best action flicks turn Arabs into bad guys, make the female leads shed their clothes, and contain technical glitches (just look at James Cameron's TRUE LIES), so perhaps it's unfair to pick on a little straight-to-video release like BLACK THUNDER.*(Violence, nudity, sexual situations, adult situations, extreme profanity.)*—E.M.

d, Rick Jacobson; p, Ashok Amritraj, Andrew Stevens; w, William C. Martell; ph, Michael Wojciechowski; ed, Michael Kuge; m, Michael Clark; prod d, Nava; cos, Marissa Borsetto

Action/Adventure **(PR: O MPAA: R)**

BLACKJACK ★★

(Canada, 1998) 112m Alliance Communications ~ Dimension c

(AKA: JOHN WOO'S BLACKJACK)

Dolph Lundgren *(Jack Devlin)*; Kate Vernon *(Dr. Rachel Stein)*; Phillip MacKenzie *(Rory)*; Kam Heskin *(Cinder James)*; Fred Williamson *(Hastings)*; Padraigin Murphy *(Casey)*; Tony De Santis *(Detective Trini)*; Albert Shultz; Andrew Jackson; Janet Bailey; Saul Rubinek *(Thomas)*; Peter Keleghan *(Bobby Stern)*; Slavko Hochevar *(Hairy)*; Michael Bodner *(Eyeball)*; Glyn Thomas *(Prototel Bodyguard)*; Peter Virgile *(Richard)*; Laurence Walsh *(Dorothy)*; Frank Crudele *(Murphy the Doorman)*; Ted Simonett *(Mark Smoot)*; George King *(Witehead)*; Sharon Bernbaum *(Nurse)*; Cherilee Taylor *(Motel Clerk)*; Nicu Branzea *(Ghide Sinno)*; Antonella LaCaprara *(MC)*; Michelle Moffett *(Policewoman)*; Robert Lee *(Doctor)*

Innovative Hong Kong action director John Woo helmed this feature-length TV pilot about a tough bodyguard and his dangerous lifestyle. Though it boasts several rousing action sequences, the film is sabotaged by lackluster acting, thin characterization, and a derivative story line.

When the daughter of casino owner Bobby Stern (Peter Keleghan) is threatened by a mobster who wants a piece of his lucrative business, he calls on his old friend Jack Devlin (Dolph Lundgren), a US Marshall turned professional bodyguard. Taking Stern's nine-year-old daughter Casey (Padraigin Murphy) under his wing, "Uncle Jack" fends off an attack of her home, but in the process, is temporarily blinded by a "white-light grenade" and now freezes up at the sight of the color white. When Casey's father is later murdered by the mob, she moves in with Devlin. Devlin's next assignment involves guarding supermodel Cinder James (Kam Heskin) from an obsessed killer (Phillip MacKenzie). After initially turning down the job, he changes his mind after his buddy, US Marshall Hastings (Fred Williamson) is almost murdered while in her company. Soon, Devlin earns Cinder's confidence as he saves her from yet another murder attempt, this time by hitmen on motorcycles.

Realizing that Cinder has something to hide, Devlin interrogates her until she finally admits that the assassin pursuing her is actually her ex-husband, who's enraged by her success as a model. Aided by the comely Dr. Rachel Stein (Kate Vernon), Devlin discovers that Cinder's insurance-hungry manager is in league with her ex. Despite Devlin's presense, Cinder is kidnapped by her stalker in the middle of a high-profile fashion show. Rushing to her aid, Devlin locates the hideout, kills her stalker, and in the process, cracks through his own phobia of the color white.

The sophomore teaming of John Woo and Canada's Alliance Communications Corporation (their first effort was a TV pilot remake of Woo's 1991 Hong Kong film ONCE A THIEF) is a mixed bag of good and very bad moments. While the script often feels like a rushed compilation of generic plot twists, BLACKJACK is expertly filmed, thanks to Woo's innate ability to spin straw into gold. Packed with gunplay, pyrotechnics, and slo-mo action sequences-several of which border on the ludicrous (e.g., Devlin taking out hitmen while bouncing off a trampoline)—the film's primary deficiencies lie in its convoluted script. Devlin's phobia of the color white is a pathetic Achilles heel, while Casey's sudden appearance in his household turns the film into a crime-fighting version of "Family Affair."

Lundgren is mildly likable as Devlin, bringing a welcome touch of humanity to his traditionally steely presence. Unfortunately, the rest of the cast prove forgettable, or at worst, openly irritating (as is the case with child actress Padraigin Murphy). Meanwhile, fans of blaxploitation superstar Fred Williamson will be disappointed by his brief, nearly pointless appearance. Boasting some very unconvincing Canadian locations (standing in for NYC), this actioner sprinkles on a few arresting sequences, but more often than not, takes the quick-and-easy route. It will thus undoubtedly disappoint fans of Woo's big-screen, high-octane masterworks. *(Violence, profanity.)*—S.P.

d, John Woo; p, John Ryan; exec p, John Woo, Terence Chang, Christopher Godsick, Peter Lance; assoc p, David Wu; w, Peter Lance; ph, Bill Wong; ed, Ron Wisman; prod d, Karen Bromley; art d, Edward S. Bonutto; set d, Megan Less; cos, Suzette Daigle; makeup, Micki Erbe, Meribeth Soloman

Action/Crime **(PR: C MPAA: R)**

BLADE ★★★½

(U.S., 1998) 110m Amen Ra Films; Imaginary Forces; New Line ~ New Line c

Wesley Snipes *(Blade)*; Stephen Dorff *(Deacon Frost)*; Kris Kristofferson *(Abraham Whistler)*; Kevin Patrick Walls *(Krieger)*; N'Bushe Wright *(Karen)*; Donal Logue *(Quinn)*; Arly Jover *(Mercury)*; Udo Kier *(Dragonetti)*; Traci Lords *(Racquel)*; Eric Edwards *(Pearl)*; Tim Guinee *(Curtis Webb)*; Sanaa Lathan *(Vanessa)*; Donna Wong *(Nurse)*; Carmen Thomas *(Senior Resident)*; Shannon Lee *(Resident)*; Kenneth Johnson *(Heatseeking Dennis)*; Clint Curtis *(Creepy Morgue Guy)*; Judson Scott *(Pallantine)*; Sidney Liufau *(Japanese Doorman)*; Keith Leon Williams *(Kam)*; Andray Johnson *(Paramedic)*; Stephen R. Peluso *(Paramedic)*; Marcus Aurelius *(Pragmatic Policeman)*; John Enos III *(Blood Club Bouncer)*; Eboni Adams *(Martial Arts Kid)*; Lyle Conway *(Reichardt)*; Freeman White III *(Menacing Stud)*; D.V. De Vincentis *(Vampire Underling)*; Marcus Salgado *(Frost's Goon)*; Esau McKnight Jr. *(Frost's Goon)*; Erl *(Von Esper)*; Matt Schulze *(Crease)*; Lennox Brown *(Pleading Goon)*; Yvette Ocampo *(Party Girl)*; Irena Stepic *(Slavic Vampire Lord)*; Jenya Lano *(Russian Woman)*; Levani *(Russian Vampire)*

In what might be the best adaptation of a comic series yet, Wesley Snipes portrays Blade, a half-human vampire hunter. Hip visuals and jaw-dropping action sequences set this film head and shoulders above standard stake-pounder fare.

Vampires walk among us. Politically and financially powerful, they have struck treaties with humanity that keep the peace between the races. Those treaties are threatened by two men: Deacon Frost (Stephen Dorff), a maverick vampire who seeks to rule humanity; and Blade (Wesley Snipes), a half-human, half-vampire vigilante who hunts the creatures of the night that fed on his pregnant mother, transforming him in the womb. Blade possesses the vampire's heightened speed, strength, and senses, but is able to endure sunlight, earning the title "Daywalker" among vampires. He keeps his thirst for blood in check with the help of a serum developed by fellow vampire hunter Abraham Whistler (Kris Kristofferson). Into this war comes Karen (N'Bushe Wright), a victim of a vampire bite who is rescued by Blade and given the serum to halt her transformation into a bloodsucker. Once cured, Karen, a hematologist, creates a cure for vampirism along with a poison lethal to vampires.

Meanwhile, Frost is climbing the ranks of the vampire hierarchy. He uncovers an ancient text that describes the ritual for summoning the Blood God—a ritual that requires, as its centerpiece, the blood of the Daywalker. By killing Whistler and kidnapping Karen, Frost lures Blade to vampire central, where he is taken captive. He is placed in a device that lets his blood, channeling it into the Blood God ritual. Karen finds the weakened Blade and revives him with her own blood, but by this time Frost has been transformed into the Blood God, a kind of super-vampire. Blade and Frost go head-to-head, and Blade finishes him off with Karen's poison. Though Karen offers him the cure, Blade elects to keep his vampiric powers in order to continue the extermination of all vampires.

There seems to be an unwritten rule in Hollywood that says "when in doubt, make a vampire movie"—despite the fact that nine out of ten of them are just plain bad. BLADE is the first good vampire movie in a long, long time (containing more original touches than the more conventional INTERVIEW WITH THE VAMPIRE and Coppola's BRAM STOKER'S DRACULA). Director Stephen Norrington (1994's DEATH MACHINE) draws upon his special effects background and the increasing influence of Hong Kong action flicks to create a unique look, using fast-motion photography and strobing film stock to evoke the hyper-kinetic world of the vampire. Starting with the opening scene, in which an underground dance club is transformed into a literal blood orgy, BLADE goes from zero to sixty and doesn't look back.

Proving himself with each film to be one of the most versatile actors around, Wesley Snipes turns in the kind of performance that could earn him the action A-list status that he attempted with films like PASSENGER 57 (1992) and DEMOLITION MAN (1993). In keeping with the kung fu vibe, Snipes plays Blade as raw energy held in check—restrained, but *this* close to gonzo. On the other side of the stake is Stephen Dorff, who manages yet again to play an annoying punk, though this time it works, largely due to the balancing presence of Udo Kier as the well-manicured leader of the vampire council.

Fans of the CROW movies might experience a feeling of deja vu while watching BLADE, and with good reason: it was written by David S. Goya, who co-penned THE CROW: CITY OF ANGELS (1996) and THE CROW director Alex Proyas's DARK CITY (1998). While BLADE is a marked improvement on both those films, it's really the marriage of Goya's script with Norrington's visuals that sets it apart from the pack. *(Extreme violence, profanity.)*—B.T.

d, Stephen Norrington; p, Peter Frankfurt, Wesley Snipes, Robert Engelman; exec p, Stan Lee, Avi Arad, Joseph Calamari; co-p, Andrew J. Horne, Jon Divens; w, David S. Goyer (based on characters created for Marvel Comics by Marv Wolfman and Gene Colan); ph, Theo Van De Sande; ed, Paul Rubell; m, Mark Isham; prod d, Kirk M. Petruccelli; art d, Barry Chusid; set d, Greg Grande; sound, Lee Orloff (mixer); fx, Lou Carlucci; casting, Rachel Abrams, Jory Weitz; cos, Sanja Milkovic Hays; makeup, Greg Cannom, Deborah LaMia Denaver, Stephen Abrums, Fred Blau; stunts, Jeff Ward

Horror/Action **(PR: C MPAA: R)**

BLEEDERS ★★½
(U.S./Canada, 1998) 92m Fries/Shultz Film Group; Kingsborough Greenlight Pictures ~ A-Pix Entertainment c

Rutger Hauer *(Dr. Marlowe)*; Roy Dupuis *(John Strauss)*; Kristin Lehman *(Kathleen Strauss)*; Jackie Burroughs *(Lexie Krongold)*; John Dunn-Hill *(Hank Gordon)*; Joanna Noyes *(Byrde Gordon)*; Felicia Shulman *(Yolanda)*; Janine Theriault *(Alice)*; Michelle Brunet *(Ramona)*; David Deveau *(Ben)*; Spencer Evans *(Squeakie)*; Lisa Bronwyn Moore *(Toot)*; Carmen Ferlan *(Mrs. Shea)*; John Harold Cail *(Ferryman)*; Leni Parker *(Baby Laura)*; Gillian Ferrabee *(Eva Van Daam/Her Twin Brother/John's Twin Sister)*; Pascal Gruselle *(Vermeer)*; Robert Baril; Andre Dandurand; Denis LaPalme; Matthieu Parent; Gary Jewell *(The Van Daams)*; Christopher Heyerdahl *(Narrator)*

Filmed in 1996 as HEMOGLOBIN (a title retained in the end credits), this Canadian-filmed chiller is stronger on atmosphere than it is on narrative.

In the 1600s, aristocratic Eva Van Daam (Gillian Ferrabee) begins an incestuous affair with her twin brother, siring a family that shut itself up in a mansion on a remote island. In the present, John Strauss (Roy Dupuis), suffering from a blood disease, arrives at the island—where he was born—with his wife Kathleen (Kristin Lehman). The couple seek help from local doctor Marlowe (Rutger Hauer). Meanwhile, bodies have been disappearing from coffins in the island's cemetery. The Strausses take a room at the hotel/funeral parlor owned by Byrde Gordon (Joanna Noyes), and Dr. Marlowe tells Kathleen that John's condition suggests he's related to the Van Daams. At the Van Daam cemetery, Alice (Janine Theriault), Byrde's daughter, is attacked and dragged off by a humanoid creature.

The Strausses visit Lexie (Jackie Burroughs), nurse to the last known member of the Van Daams, who reveals that John is descended from them, but was born normal. The remaining family now lives in tunnels beneath the island, where they have mutated and are feeding off corpses—and now humans. One of them kills Lexie and another drags off a little girl, and as night falls and a storm blows up, Marlowe and the townspeople seek refuge in a lighthouse. Giving in to the hunger for flesh, John eats a preserved fetus that gives him strength. As the islanders fight off the attacking creatures, Kathleen is dragged into the tunnels. Marlowe rescues her, and John distracts the creatures while they escape. A cave-in then entombs John with the rest of his "family."

While it ultimately falls short of its ambitions, BLEEDERS does have a number of things going for it. The screenplay, cowritten by two of the people responsible for 1979's ALIEN, is based on an intriguing premise (albeit one borrowed somewhat from H.P. Lovecraft's story "The Lurking Fear"). The scenes in the fishing town benefit from evocative location photography and set up a persuasive sense of community—one consisting largely of women, as the men are mostly out fishing. Director Peter Svatek plays the action for straight, gruesome chills without attempted humor or gimmickry.

Somehow, though, the elements don't quite add up. While the movie has its share of effective sequences (particularly the attack on Alice), it doesn't sustain sufficient tension overall. Perhaps it's because the stunted monsters, while intriguingly designed by Adrien Morot, don't elicit a true sense of menace, or because the story development is rather cut-and-dried. Whatever the case, BLEEDERS is a nice try (and a well-acted one) that doesn't quite live up to its promise. *(Graphic violence, extensive nudity, sexual situations, profanity.)*—M.G.

d, Peter Svatek; p, Pieter Kroonenburg, Julie Allan; exec p, John Buchanan, Gary Howsam, Ed Elbert; w, Charles Adair, Dan O'Bannon, Ronald Shusett; ph, Barry Gravelle; ed, Heidi Haines; m, Alan Reeves; prod d, Michel Proulx; art d, Isabelle Guay; set d, Ginette Pare; sound, Louis Marion; fx, Adrien Morot; casting, Elite Productions, Rosina Bucci, Vera Miller, Nadia Rona; cos, Claire Nadon; makeup, Henri Khouzam; stunts, Dave McKeown

Horror **(PR: O MPAA: R)**

BLOODSTORM: SUBSPECIES IV
(SEE: SUBSPECIES IV: BLOODSTORM)

BLUES BROTHERS 2000 ★★
(U.S., 1998) 124m House of Blues Productions; Universal ~ Universal c

Dan Aykroyd *(Elwood Blues)*; John Goodman *(Mighty Mack McTeer)*; Joe Morton *(Cabel Chamberlain)*; J. Evan Bonifant *(Buster)*; Steve Cropper *(Steve "The Colonel" Cropper—Lead Guitar)*; Donald Dunn *(Donald "Duck" Dunn—Bass Guitar)*; Murphy Dunne *(Murph—Keyboards)*; Willie Hall *(Willie "Too Big" Hall—Drums)*; Lou Marini *("Blue Lou" Marini)*; Tom Malone *("Bones" Malone)*; Alan Rubin *("Mr. Fabulous")*; Aretha Franklin *(Mrs. Murphy)*; James Brown *(Reverend Cleophus James)*; B.B. King *(Malvern Gasperon/Member of the Louisiana Gator Boys Band)*; Nia Peeples *(Lt. Elizondo)*; Kathleen Freeman *(Mother Mary Stigmata)*; Sam Moore *(Reverend Morris)*; Wilson Pickett *(Mr. Pickett)*; Frank Oz *(Prison Warden)*; Eddie Floyd *(Ed)*; Jonny Lang *(Ed's Love Exchange Janitor)*; Steve Lawrence *(Maury Sline)*; Junior Wells; Lonnie Brooks *(Themselves)*; John Popper; Bobby Sheehan; Brendan Hill; Chan Kinchla *(Motel Band)*; Jeff Morris *(Bob)*; Shannon Johnson *(Matara)*; Erykah Badu *(Queen Mousette)*; Darrell Hammond *(Robertson)*; Sharon Riley; Faith Chorale *(Tent Revival Choir)*; Prakash John; Fred Keeler; Shiraz Tayyeb; John T. Davis *(Tent Revival Band)*; Jeff Baxter; Gary U.S. Bonds; Eric Clapton; Clarence Clemons; Jacques de Johnette; Bo Diddley; Jon Faddis; Isaac Hayes; Dr. John; Tommy McDonnell; Charlie Musselwhite; Billy Preston; Lou Rawls; Joshua Redman; Koko Taylor; Travis Tritt; Jimmie Vaughan; Willie Weeks; Steve Winwood; Grover Washington Jr. *(Louisiana Gator Boys Band)*; Paul Shaffer *(Marco)*; Walter Levine *(Same Guard)*; Tom Davis *(Prison*

Clerk); Gloria Slade *(Police Receptionist)*; Jennifer Irwin *(Nun #1)*; Leon Pendarvis; Steve Potts; Birch "Crimson Slide" Johnson; Demo Cates *(Stripster Band)*; Michael Bondar *(Russian Thug #1)*; Slavko Hochevar *(Russian Thug #2)*; Igor Syyouk *(Tstetsevkaya)*; Victor Pedtrchenko *(Ivan)*; Wally High *(Russian Thug #3)*; Richard Kruk *(Russian Thug #4)*; John Lyons *(Russian Thug #5)*; Matt Murphy *(Matt "Guitar" Murphy)*; Esther Ridgeway; Gloria Ridgeway; Gracie Ridgeway *(Mrs. Murphy's Friends)*; George Sperdakos *(Priest)*; Jillian Hart *(Phone Operator)*; Liz Gordon *(Nun #2)*; Susan Davy; Soo Garay *(Indiana State Troopers)*; Howard Hoover *(FBI)*; Chris Marshall *(Skinhead)*; Nicholas Rice *(County Fair Announcer)*; Max Landis *(Ghostrider)*; Sandi Ross *(Church Woman)*; Danny Ray *(Deacon)*; Candide Franklin *(Ton Tons Macoutes)*; Patrick Patterson *(Sheriff)*

A sequel to THE BLUES BROTHERS (1980) was hardly necessary, especially after the death of John Belushi. Nevertheless, here it is.

Released from prison, Elwood Blues (Dan Aykroyd) learns of the death of his brother Jake. Returning to Chicago, he attempts to connect with some kind of family. He visits the orphanage where he was raised, where the Mother Superior (Kathleen Freeman) tells him that his now-deceased father-figure Curtis had an illegitimate son. After being asked to look after a young orphan named Buster (J. Evan Bonifant) for the afternoon, Elwood seeks out the son, Cabel (Joe Morton), a commander in the Illinois State Police who wants nothing to do with Elwood.

Elwood puts the Blues Brothers Band back together, with new lead singer Mighty Mack McTeer (John Goodman). In tracking down his bandmates, Elwood runs afoul of the state police (who are seeking him for absconding with Buster), the Russian mafia, a white supremacist group, and his guitar player's wife (Aretha Franklin). The band hits the road, one step ahead of their adversaries, stopping to masquerade as a bluegrass band at a county fair. Led by Cabel, the police catch up with Elwood at a tent revival meeting. The sermon by Rev. Cleophus James (James Brown) brings Cabel in touch with his roots, and he joins the band.

The band heads to the Louisiana bayou for a battle-of-the-bands competition overseen by Queen Moussette (Erykah Badu), who quickly gets rid of the menacing Russians and white supremacists with her magical powers. Though they lose to a blues all-star group led by B.B. King and Eric Clapton, Elwood forms a brotherly bond with Mack, Cabel, and especially Buster. Never having returned Buster to the orphanage, Elwood faces kidnapping charges, but he and his newfound "partner" in hell-raising escape from the concert hall, with dozens of police cars following.

Trying to revive the Blues Brothers without John Belushi is like reuniting the Beatles without John Lennon. There is a gaping hole that even the combined talents of Goodman, Morton, and Bonifant cannot fill. If star Aykroyd and director John Landis were so intent on a sequel, they should have at least concocted an original script. Instead, BLUES BROTHERS 2000 is filled with replays of scenes from its predecessor: Aretha Franklin's scene, the show where the band attempts to play bluegrass, the religious revival, the wanton destruction of police cars—even the catchphrase "The Lord works in mysterious ways" echoes the original's "We're on a mission from God." In the amount of time that the sequel took to get made (Aykroyd shopped the script around for years and at one time considered a role for James Belushi), more effort could have been put into the script. Instead, there is an attitude that, if something worked once, it will work again. That is most apparent in Landis's direction, which is never more than workmanlike and is always looking for ways to mimic the first film.

Aykroyd lacks the force of personality with which Belushi carried the original BLUES BROTHERS. Among the supporting cast, Bonifant shines as a tough kid redeemed by music and friendship. Goodman's low-key performance is a refreshing contrast to most of the cast's over-the top grandstanding, though in the ersatz Belushi role he never gets to dominate—Aykroyd even butts into Goodman's only song. Morton, always a fine actor, gets to do little but a prolonged slow burn through most of the movie. He seems as liberated as his character when he finally gets to do something. The music is what carries the film, especially the final scene; with the conspicuous absences of Ray Charles and John Lee Hooker (both of whom appeared in THE BLUES BROTHERS), just about every performer of note in the world of blues and soul music provides a cameo appearance. *(Profanity.)*—K.Fr.

d, John Landis; p, Dan Aykroyd, John Landis, Leslie Belzberg; assoc p, Grace Gilroy; w, Dan Aykroyd, John Landis (based on "The Blues Brothers" by Dan Aykroyd and John Landis); ph, David Herrington; ed, Dale Beldin; m, Paul Shaffer; prod d, Bill Brodie; art d, Dan Yarhi; set d, Steve Shewchuk, Clive Thomasson; ch, Barry Lather; sound, Glen Gauthier; fx, Martin Malivoire, Kaz Kobielski, Ted Ross, Walter Hart; casting, Ross Clydesdale, Joanna Colbert; cos, Deborah Nadoolman; makeup, Patricia Green; stunts, Rick Avery

Comedy/Musical **(PR: A MPAA: PG-13)**

BODY COUNT ★★

(U.S., 1998) 89m Subutopian Films ~ CineTel Films c
(AKA: BELOW UTOPIA)

Alyssa Milano *(Susanne Barrison)*; Justin Theroux *(Daniel)*; Ice T *(Jim)*; Tiny Lister, billed as Tommy "Tiny" Lister *(Tiny)*; Jeanette O'Connor *(Aunt Estelle)*; Nicholas Walker *(Justin)*; Eric Saiet *(Cousin Allen)*; Marta Kristen *(Marilyn)*; Ron Harper *(Jack)*; Robert Pine *(Wilson)*; Richard Danielson *(Cole)*

Unhappy families, goes the adage, are unhappy in a thousand different ways. Viewers can easily find a thousand different ways to be unhappy with BODY COUNT, as the sordid mix of domestic discord and action makes this straight-to-video item qualify as DIE HARD in a dysfunctional household.

Susanne Barrison (Alyssa Milano) accompanies fiance Daniel (Justin Theroux) to his wealthy family's fancy estate for a New Years reunion. It's an uncomfortable situation; patriarch Jack (Ron Harper) views English-teacher Daniel and his boozy brother Justin (Nicholas Walker) as wastrels, failing to carry on the family art dealership. Jack mourns his more industrious, favorite son John, recently killed while rock climbing, and threatens to disown Daniel if he doesn't become a businessman. Susanne and Daniel are making love in a basement studio when the mansion is crashed by a trio of gunmen, who cut phone lines, pitilessly shoot down servants and bluebloods alike, and start loading their truck with the estate's valuable paintings. From their hiding places Susanne and Daniel overhear thug Jim (Ice T) mentioning that the whole massacre and robbery was a contract job, commissioned by Justin. When one of the home invaders finds Susanne, Daniel kills the man, then the other two. Jim is particularly caught off guard, since he knew Daniel as "Justin," the client paying him to murder and loot. Daniel has engineered the foul scheme to rid himself of his troublesome relatives, cash in their fortune, and eliminate his accomplices, with Susanne as a witness who can pin it all on Justin. Susanne realizes the truth—partially because Daniel flips out, rants about murder as an art form, and confesses to having killed John in the first place. Susanne shoots him dead and drives off with fellow survivor Justin.

Though directed with a noirish gloss by B-grade thriller specialist Kurt Voss (HORSEPLAYER), BODY COUNT fatally fails to convince on either side of its agenda. The monied, moody, art-mongering family are painted with a bit too broad a brush to be believable, and there's heavy-handed symbolism in Daniel's incomplete basement mural of Sodom and Gommorah that prefigures the clan's apocalyptic end. Then the plot becomes a vest-pocket DIE HARD (1988), with endless scenes of the protagonists creeping around wide-eyed in the shadows. The initial sense of claustrophobic terror is mitigated by typical action cliches, as Susanne's crotch kicks disable towering assailants, and Daniel's complicity is a terribly foregone conclusion. The plot seems to set up some sort of racial dichotomy, comparing the aristocrat's silent, docile, and nameless black servants with the aggressive, colorful marauders Ice T and Tom "Tiny" Lister, but nothing much develops.

It may be germane that rapper-actor Ice T fronted a band also named Body Count. Turning to another sort of body, actress Milano earned notoriety as a wholesome juvenile performer (TV's "Who's the Boss?") who graduated to very sexy adult roles. She stays relatively demure here, in addition to executive-producing. *(Violence, adult situations, profanity, sexual situations, substance abuse.)*—C.C.

d, Kurt Voss; p, Paul Hertzeberg, Lisa Hansen, Catalaine Knell; exec p, Alyssa Milano, Steven Roffer; w, David Diamond, Richard Shepard; ph, Denis Maloney; ed, John Rosenberg; m, Joseph Williams; prod d, Cecil Gentry; set d, Jeff Sibille; casting, Phaedra Harris; cos, Anita Cabada; makeup, Elzbieta Barozewska; stunts, Gary Paul

Thriller **(PR: O MPAA: R)**

BODY COUNT ★½

(U.S., 1998) 84m PolyGram; Island Pictures; Main Line Pictures ~ Polygram Video c

David Caruso *(Hobbs)*; Linda Fiorentino *(Natalie)*; John Leguizamo *(Chino)*; Ving Rhames *(Pike)*; Donnie Wahlberg *(Booker)*; Forest Whitaker *(Crane)*; Michael Corrigan *(Security Officer #1)*; Michael Hunter *(Security Officer #2)*; Matt Giehl *(Security Officer #3)*; Richard Fullerton *(Officer Forrest)*; Deacon Dawson *(Proprietor)*; Rebbeca Koon *(Wife)*; Juliet Poe *(Convenience Store Woman #1)*; Mary Lucy Bivens *(Convenience Store Woman #2)*; James Spruill *(Special Agent Bradley)*; Terry Loughlin *(SWAT Commander Rollins)*; Bill Robinson *(Prison Guard)*; Virginia Ernsberger *(Motel Clerk)*

BODY COUNT is a derivative straight-to-video heist movie that's as generic and undistinguished as its oft-used title, and is only notable for how it wastes an above-average cast, which includes David Caruso, Linda Fiorentino, Ving Rhames, and Forest Whitaker.

Five thieves flee a Boston art museum with $15 million worth of stolen paintings, but their leader Crane (Forest Whitaker) is killed during the getaway. Pike (Ving Rhames) takes charge and leads his cohorts—cool wheelman Hobbs (David Caruso), trigger-happy Chino (John Leguizamo), and Booker (Donnie Wahlberg)—to Miami to meet Crane's contact. During their car trip, they think back to the robbery. The journey is also fraught with constant arguments and violence: Booker is killed in a fight with Hobbs; Chino shoots a nosy traffic cop, and threatens to kill Hobbs for insulting him.

Later, Chino picks up a girl named Natalie (Linda Fiorentino), whose car has broken down, and she informs Hobbs that she overhead Chino plotting to kill him. Hobbs pulls a gun on Chino, who shoots Hobbs in the arm, and finishes him off at a hotel that night. Chino then comes on to Natalie, who knocks him out with a lamp. The hotel manager hears the struggle and calls the police. Natalie and Pike escape, but Chino is caught and gunned down. Natalie then forces Pike out of the car at gunpoint and drives away with the paintings, but she's caught by a police roadblock. Pike gets away and discovers a painting in the sleeve of his jacket which Chino had hidden there.

Two minutes and two-dozen variations of the F-word into BODY COUNT, it's painfully obvious that the film is going to be yet another in the seemingly interminable string of Tarantino wannabe crime films. It's got a fractured flashback structure, one-name hipster criminals whose "offbeat" conversations encompass everything from explicit descriptions of the power of women's private parts to pretentious talk about a belief in God, and gory violence that's meant to be funny (Chino being stabbed by an old lady while trying to rob a gas station, to the "hilarious" accompaniment of a Christmas song). But what it's missing is any credibility or sense of style whatsoever, and whether one admires Tarantino or not, at least he steals from the best (particularly—and most often—THE KILLING), while his many imitators only aspire to copy him. To be fair, however, the film does steal from another source besides Tarantino: several key plot elements (including bickering criminals stuck in a car following a heist, and a female pickup) are lifted directly from Mario Bava's recently discovered RABID DOGS (1974), which the filmmakers apparently believed would never see the light of day. The talented cast is reduced to being a group of unconvincing poseurs, and when not doing indulgent improvisations—including Leguizamo's entire manic-riff performance, which he treats like a one-man stage show—they give the impression of a group of embarrassed actors who know they're superior to their material. *(Graphic violence, extreme profanity, sexual situations.)*—M.S.

d, Robert Patton-Spruill; p, Mark Burg, Doug McHenry, George Jackson; exec p, Carl Mazzocone; w, Theodore Witcher; ph, Charles Mills; ed, Richard Nord; m, Curt Sobel; prod d, Tim Eckel; sound, Barney Cabral, Kelly Cabral; fx, Lorenzo Hall; casting, Paige Johnston, Mitzi Corrigan; cos, Pauline White; makeup, Anita Gibson

Crime/Drama **(PR: O MPAA: R)**

BODYGUARD FROM BEIJING ★★★

(Hong Kong, 1994) 94m Eastern Production Ltd. ~ World Video c

Jet Li *(Hui Ching-yang)*; Christy Chung *(Michelle Yeung)*; Kent Cheng, billed as Ken Cheng *(Sgt. Leung Kam-po)*; Ngai Sing *(Wang Wen-jun)*; Leung Wing-chung; Ng Wai-kwok; William Chu; Corey Yuen *(Passersby in Mall)*

Like Hollywood, Hong Kong is crazy for sequels and remakes. Their version of Kevin Costner's THE BODYGUARD (1992), is, predictably, an exercise in excess. It's also grand hyperbolic fun. The film received its first official US release on home video in 1998.

Mainland Chinese security agent Hui Ching-yang (Jet Li) is assigned to Hong Kong to protect Michelle Yeung (Christy Chung), the last surviving witness to a murder. Strict and unyielding, Hui dismisses all but two of Michelle's squadron of local bodyguards, and tightens security, to her chagrin. When she finally convinces him to take her shopping, they are assaulted by dozens of hitmen.

After Hui lays waste to the killers and whisks Michelle home, she finds herself falling for him. But even as the duty-bound Hui spurns her advances, Wang Wen-jun (Ngai Sing), brother of one of the fallen killers, lays siege to the house with scores of gunmen, who are subsequently slain by Hui. Following a protracted battle, Hui takes a bullet protecting Michelle, but manages to kill Wang with a knife.

The original BODYGUARD had one insurmountable problem from the very inception—the casting of Kevin Costner as the indomitable title character. Jet Li on the other hand is entirely believable as he dispatches Michelle's original bodyguards in a lightning-fast showcase of martial skills. The film dispenses with many of the silly contrivances of Lawrence Kasdan's original script, substituting even sillier contrivances of its own, starting with the very first scene, in which Hui protects a government official by mowing down countless assassins. This is then shown to be a "mock raid," a practice to test Hui's abilities. If it's only a practice however, why was everybody bursting with bloody wounds? It's a cinematic cheat of course, but the sequence does adequately inform the viewer of the suspension of disbelief necessary to swallow the fairly dopey plot to follow, with its total disregard for logic and/or continuity. For the climax, not only does Michelle outrun a bullet seen speeding toward Hui in slow motion, but Hui *outruns her outrunning the bullet*, tossing her from harm's way. Nonetheless, the final battle in the sealed house, with gas mains opened precluding gunfire and making the combatants literally fight for breath, is an extended treasure-trove of witty if implausible gimmickry. Making extensive use of wirework for conspicuously impossible feats, the inventive choreography by director Corey Yuen (who has a one-line cameo in the shopping scene) was nominated for a Hong Kong Film Award as best action design of the year.

Made in 1994, the film's political agenda deserves mention. Hong Kong cops, still in the employ of the British government, are depicted as lazy, gluttonous, hedonistic consumers and inveterate gamblers. Michelle, an "ABC" (American-Born Chinese), is self-indulgent and petty. Mainland Chinese (including both Hui and the main villain, Wang), are by contrast stern, capable, disciplined, single-minded, and loyal unto death. Michelle's wealthy boyfriend shows up for the end and attempts to buy off Wang, but is told his money means nothing; it's a matter of honor between the Mainlanders. Veteran bad guy Ngai Sing makes an excellent foil for Li, possessing acrobatic fighting skills along with an intense and vicious demeanor. Li and Ngai's characters seem to have killed one another at film's end, but a quick fade brings us to a brief coda wherein the other principals race to say goodbye to the bodyguard at the border. They don't quite make it, and Li's absence from the scene (he is shown in an unrelated shot as the credits roll) suggests the ending was a last-minute addition, after he had already left the production. *(Graphic violence.)*—A.B.

d, Corey Yuen, billed as Yuen Kwai; p, Jet Li; w, Gordon Chan, Chan Kin Chang

Action/Crime/Martial Arts (PR: C MPAA: NR)

BOLD AFFAIR, A

(SEE: INTERLOCKED: THRILLED TO DEATH)

BONE DADDY ★½

(U.S., 1998) 91m The Kushner-Locke Company; Chesler/Perlmutter Productions ~ Artisan Entertainment c

Rutger Hauer *(William Palmer)*; Barbara Williams *(Sharon Hewlett)*; R.H. Thomson *(Marshall Stone)*; Joseph Kell *(Peter Palmer)*; Robin Gammell *(Cobb)*; Blu Mankuma *(Trent)*; Mimi Kuzyk *(Kim)*; Wayne Best *(Rodman)*; Daniel Kash *(Rocky)*; Peter Keleghan *(Tarnower)*; Kirsten Bishop *(Leslie)*; Michael Caruana *(Hurwitz)*; Dean McDermott *(Mort Jr.)*; Diego Matamoros *(Baxter)*; Kyra Azzopardi *(Cindy)*; Marc Donato *(Mark)*; Christopher Kelk *(Dr. Franz)*; Panou Mowling *(Bellman)*; Sandi Ross *(Housekeeper)*; Terri Hawles *(Anchorwoman)*; Kelly King *(Reporter #1)*; Johnie Chase *(Reporter #2)*; Lesley Kelly *(Reporter #3)*; Yank Azman *(McDougall)*

A thriller about a serial killer that's severly lacking in thrills, this Canadian-shot movie debuted on cable before making its way to video.

Former chief medical examiner William Palmer (Rutger Hauer) has written a best-selling fictional book based on a case he once worked on: a serial killer who called himself "Bone Daddy" and was never caught. Rocky (Daniel Kash), Palmer's agent, is kidnapped by Bone Daddy. At a party celebrating the appointment of Palmer's son Peter (Joseph Kell)—with whom Palmer has a strained relationship—to assistant chief medical examiner, a package arrives containing one of Rocky's bones. It is determined that Rocky was alive when the bone was removed, and detective Sharon Hewlett (Barbara Williams) is assigned to the case, with Palmer consulting. They first investigate an old suspect, Palmer's former rival Dr. Franz (Christopher Kelk), but he proves to be an invalid.

Palmer receives a threatening phone call from Bone Daddy, and Rocky's body turns up outside Sharon's house. Further evidence seems to implicate Peter, who is nowhere to be found. Comparing the stitching on Rocky's body to other cadavers in the morgue, Palmer realizes that the killer is current Medical Examiner Marshall Stone (R.H. Thomson). Palmer and Sharon arrive at Stone's house to find Peter held captive, and Palmer appears to lay Stone low after a fight. Stone revives, stabs Sharon and attacks Palmer, but Sharon recovers and shoots him dead.

By this point in the serial killer stakes, a movie of this type requires the character depth of SILENCE OF THE LAMBS (1991) or a specific vision a la SEVEN (1995) to stand out. Neither is the case here, as the movie marks time with arguments between Palmer and his son, arguments between Sharon and her chief, Palmer ruminating over whether he's responsible for resurrecting Bone Daddy by writing his book, and the investigation of suspects who are all too obviously red herrings. None of this is very compelling, thanks in part to what may be the most listless, uninspired performance of Hauer's career.

Along the way, this manages to be a serial-killer film in which there's only one victim, and Rocky's introduction as a foul-mouthed lout doesn't generate much in the way of sympathy for him. The convincingly grisly makeup effects do elicit a few shivers—certainly more than Mario Azzopardi's direction, which relies too much on such worn-out conventions as a woman who, with a psycho killer on the loose, goes outside her house at night to check on her cat while lightning flashes and thunder booms. *(Graphic violence, nudity, extreme profanity.)*—M.G.

d, Mario Azzopardi; p, Lewis B. Chesler, Jean Desormeaux; exec p, David M. Perlmutter, Donald Kushner; w, Tom Szollosi; ph, Danny Nowak; ed, Dean Balser; m, Christophe Beck; prod d, Jeff Ginn; art d, Brandt Gordon; set d, Brendan Smith; sound, Greg Chapman; fx, Laird McMurray; casting, Hank McGann, Lisa Parasyn; cos, Margaret Mohr; makeup, Suzanne Benoit, David Scott (effects), Matthew DeWilde (effects); stunts, Anton Tyukodi

Thriller/Crime (PR: O MPAA: R)

BOOGIE BOY ★★★

(U.S., 1998) 104m Road Dog Pictures ~ Sterling Home Entertainment c

Mark Dacascos *(Jesse)*; Emily Lloyd *(Hester)*; Jaimz Woolvert *(Larry)*; Frederic Forrest *(Edsel Dundee)*; Traci Lords *(Shonda)*; Joan Jett *(Jerk)*; Scott Sowers *(Bulldog)*; Karen Lee Sheperd *(Marlene)*; Robert Bauer *(Breeze)*; John Hawkes *(T-Bone)*; Ben

Browder *(Freddy)*; James Lew *(Jason)*; Jonathan Scarfe *(Leland)*; John Koyama *(Lawrence)*; Linnea Quigley *(Gretchen)*; Thommy Price; Sean Koos; Tony Bruno *(The Rocket Brutes)*; Brett R. Goetsch *(Roadie)*; Ethan Jensen *(Dave)*; Phil Culotta *(Mike)*; Rich Turner *(Bartender)*; Michael Pena *(Drug Dealer)*

A young ex-con's attempt to start a new life is jeopardized by his drug-addicted former cellmate in BOOGIE BOY, a passable crime drama that could have used a little more plot and a lot less attitude.

Freed after serving time for stealing a motorcycle, Jesse (Mark Dacascos) meets his prison friend Larry (Jaimz Woolvert) in LA. He takes Jesse to the house where he lives with a group of other drug addicts and dealers. Jesse is offered a tryout as drummer with a rising rock band. But when he reluctantly agrees to act as muscle on a drug deal that Larry has set up with two yuppies, a fight erupts and the prospective buyers are killed. Knowing there will be repercussions, he and Larry head for the desert on Jesse's motorcycle.

Sick from prolonged drug abuse, Larry forces Jesse to stop at an abandoned motel occupied by Edsel (Frederic Forrest) and his wife Hester (Emily Lloyd). Jesse is as anxious to get to Detroit for his audition as he is to get away from LA, and so grows increasingly annoyed with Larry's drug use. He is also puzzled by Hester, who comes on to him and complains that Edsel will kill her if she tries to leave.

Larry secretly calls his house to arrange for more drugs, not knowing that his roommates have been killed by the yuppies' vengeful older brothers Freddy (Ben Browder) and Jason (James Lew). Edsel reveals that Hester is a former hooker who married him only to get his stash of money. Freddy and Jason arrive while Jesse is out of sight, and offer not to kill Larry if he tells them where Jesse is. He gives up his friend, leading to a shootout in which Edsel, Freddy and Jason are killed. Disgusted with them both, Jesse leaves Hester and Larry a bag with the money, drugs, and a gun. As he rides away, he hears a gunshot.

For a Quentin Tarantino wannabe crime drama aimed squarely at trendy twentysomethings, BOOGIE BOY isn't bad, though it is rather desperate about trying to make that Tarantino connection. (The video box boasts that this is "From the Academy Award winning writer of PULP FICTION," though you have to read the credits carefully to see that that line refers to Roger Avery, who is only one of this film's executive producers.) Anyone who takes this too seriously will only get annoyed at the relentless attitudinizing from characters who embody every youth cliche current at the time the film was shot. And the script comes down unnecessarily hard on characters who are gay and female (with the exception of Joan Jett, essentially playing herself). But despite the limitations of the script and the obviousness of the direction, there are more than a few good performances in a story that at least maintains your interest all the way through. *(Violence, sexual situations, adult situations, substance abuse, profanity.)*—M.F.

d, Craig Hammann; p, Brandon Mendelson; exec p, Roger Avery, Cathryn Jaymes, Ash R. Shah; assoc p, James Lew, Jacque Allen; co-p, Todd King; w, Craig Hammann; ph, Adam Kane; ed, Glenn Garland; m, Tim Truman; prod d, Thomas P. Wilkins; set d, Tim Colohan; sound, Peter V. Meiselmann; fx, Mike Tristano, Randall D. Buenaflor; casting, Hank McCann; cos, Roseanne Fiedler; makeup, Kenneth Beck; stunts, James Lew

Action/Crime/Drama **(PR: O MPAA: R)**

BORROWERS, THE ★★½

(U.K., 1997) 83m Working Title; PolyGram ~ PolyGram c

John Goodman *(Ocious P. Potter)*; Jim Broadbent *(Pod Clock)*; Celia Imrie *(Homily Clock)*; Mark Williams *(Exterminator Jeff)*; Bradley Pierce *(Pete Lender)*; Hugh Laurie *(Officer Steady)*; Ruby Wax *(Town Hall Clerk)*; Aden Gillett *(Joe Lender)*; Doon Mackichan *(Victoria Lender)*; Flora Newbigin *(Arietty Clock)*; Tom Felton *(Peagreen Clock)*; Raymond Pickard *(Spiller)*; Andrew Dunford *(Dustbunny)*; Bob Goody *(Minty)*; Patrick Monkton *(Swag)*; George Yiasoumi *(Wrigley—the Chauffeur)*; Dick Ward *(Milkman)*; Alex Winter *(TV Gangster)*; Michael Hewitt *(TV Sergeant)*; Simon Hewitt; David Freeman *(TV Constables)*

Based on Mary Norton's popular series of children's books about a race of tiny people known as "Borrowers," this unabashedly commercial venture should have taken a tip from its title and borrowed more from its source material.

The Clocks—Pod (Jim Broadbent), Homily (Celia Imire), and their children, Arrietty (Flora Newbigen) and Peagreen (Tom Felton)—are Borrowers, little people who live under the floorboards and survive by surreptitiously poaching food and supplies from the Lender family, the normal-sized folks who live upstairs. All is well until the Lenders are evicted by Ocious P. Potter (John Goodman), their late Aunt Agatha's greedy attorney, who plans to raze the Lender home and replace it with a "Pottersville."

On moving day, young Pete Lender (Bradley Pierce) sees to it that the Clocks, whom he has befriended, are provided with space in the van. En route to their new lodgings, Arrietty and Peagreen fall out of the vehicle and return to the old house to consult a map. There, they are interrupted by Potter, who has come to find and destroy Aunt Agatha's hidden will, which he knows bequeaths the house to the Lenders. The two young Clocks flee with the precious document, but in the process, Peagreen falls into an empty milk bottle and is transported to a dairy plant, pursued by Potter. In the nick of time, Spiller (Raymond Pickard), a Borrower boy Arrietty has just met, saves her brother from the clutches of Potter and the jaws of the plant's rebottling machinery.

The frustrated Potter moves on to City Hall to obtain a demolition permit. There, he finds himself trapped in a supply room, surrounded by an army of hundreds of Borrowers. After the will is produced, the Clocks and the Lenders return to their home, and Potter is led off by the police.

Not bad on its own limited terms, THE BORROWERS will be a disappointment to devotees of the Norton series. To an even greater extent than Terry Jones's concurrent adaptation of another gentle and genteel classic of English juvenilia, THE WIND IN THE WILLOWS (1997), THE BORROWERS downplays mood, characterization, period evocation, and interesting plotting in favor of noisy action and broad physical comedy. About all that's left of Norton's Borrowers tales is the premise. The special effects are impressive, but the movie's relentless pacing, dark lighting, and aggressive editing prevent the viewer from savoring them. The discerning child is advised to curl up instead with a copy of *The Brownies: Their Book* or *Stuart Little.*

This was the second of two versions of THE BORROWERS made by Working Title Films. The previous adaptation, a 199-minute movie made for British TV, was truer to the Victorian spirit of the original stories. One wonders how Norton, had she lived to see THE BORROWERS of 1998, would have reacted to the running gag about the flatulent dog. (Violence.)—D.T.

d, Peter Hewitt; p, Tim Bevan, Eric Fellner, Rachel Talalay; exec p, Walt DeFaria; co-p, Debra Hayward, Liza Chasin; w, Gavin Scott, John Kamps (based on the novels of Mary Norton); ph, John Fenner, Trevor Brooker; ed, David Freeman; m, Harry Gregson-Williams; prod d, Gemma Jackson; art d, Jim Morahan; set d, Careen Hertzog; sound, David Stephenson (mixer); fx,

Digby Milner, Lyn Nicholson, Peter Chiang, Tim Field; casting, Nina Gold; cos, Marie France; makeup, Joan Hills; stunts, Jim Dowdall

Children's/Adventure/Fantasy (PR: AA MPAA: PG)

BOYS IN LOVE 2 ★★½

(U.S., 1998) 97m Body and Soul Productions ("Boot Camp"); Ambrosia Entertainment ("SPF 2000"); Willing Suspension Films ("SPF 2000"); Zee Films ("Twilight of the Gods") ~ First Run Features c/bw

"Boot Camp": Matthew Solari *(Novice)*; John Cantwell *(Master)*; Alex Benjamin *(Bartender)*; Doug Bradford *(Master with Whip)*; Tyne Firmin *(Slave on Leash)*; David Kibbe *(Slave in Shackles)*; Sam Lipton *(Master with Leash)*; "Karen Black Like Me": Ira Rosenburg *(Emil)*; Anita Gillette *(Mother)*; "SPF 2000": Joseph Paolini *(Kip)*; Kelvin Walker *(Pucci/Suroh's Body)*; Peter Gingerich *(J.J.)*; Colleen O'Neill *(Gretchen)*; Phillip de Leon *(Suroh's Body)*; Jonathan Ceniceroz *(Suroh's Body)*; Peter Perrone *(Suroh's Voice)*; "Twilight of the Gods": Greg Mayor *(Toa)*; Marton Csokas *(Soldier)*; Joel Lund; Adam Cohen; Craig Jenkins; Nick Abbs; Gregan Songhurst *(Renegades)*; John Maunsell; Tony Kingi; Wayne Pivac *(Warriors)*; "Dirty Baby Does Fire Island": Rosy Ngo *(Voice of Deer)*; Men of Fire Island *(Themselves)*; "My Body": Joel Moffett *(Charlie)*; Mitchell Sternard *(The Body)*; Kim Strauss *(Dr. Lockerman)*; Donna Peroni *(Mrs. Sparky)*; Sheila A. Grenham *(Tina)*; Jeremy D. Lawrence *(Heart Patient)*; Michael Nissman *(Mr. Sparky)*; Mark Eric Howell *(The Butcher)*; Lee Everett *(911 Operator)*; Tia Texada *(Hospital Receptionist)*; Kalena Coleman *(Nurse #1)*; Robyn Rice *(Nurse #2)*; Brianna Shebby *(Little Indian)*; Danielle Shebby *(Little Indian)*

BOYS IN LOVE 2 is a mixed bag of seven short films about gay men that ranges from the sublime to the ridiculous.

In "Achilles," animated clay figures, modeled after Greek statues, offer a decidedly different take on the mythological hero's life. Achilles and his friend Patroclus are lovers who engage in a passionate affair during the Trojan War. When Achilles is humiliated by King Agamemnon, he abandons both the war and Patroclus. With Achilles gone, Patroclus, in disguise, takes Achilles' place in combat and is killed by Hector, the Trojan leader. When a grief-stricken Achilles learns of the murder, he returns to the war and kills Hector in revenge. In retaliation, Hector's brother Parris shoots Achilles in his most vulnerable spot—his heel. In death, both lovers are reunited as heroes.

In "Twilight of the Gods," Toa (Greg Mayor), a young Maori warrior becomes involved with a European soldier (Marton Csokas) who's been wounded and left for dead in the jungle. As Toa nurses him back to health, he succumbs to the overt sexual advances of the blond, muscular soldier. But their love affair is brief—when a group of marauding soldiers kills Toa, his horrified lover discovers the bloodied body hanging upside down.

In "Boot Camp," a young "novice" (Matthew Solari) cruises a leather-clad "master" (John Cantwell) in an S&M bar. But instead of engaging in sex, the men break into song and dance, to the delight of the other patrons, who join in as chorus boys.

In "Karen Black Like Me," Emil (Ira Rosenberg), a repressed gay man, receives a package containing a giant dildo, which comes to life and stalks Emil around his apartment. After a fierce struggle, Emil throws the creature into the microwave where its spirit is again unleashed, this time into Emil, who's transformed into a gay stud.

In "My Body," the closeted Charlie (Joel Moffett, who also directed) wakes up from a one-night stand to discover that he's in bed with a mannequin that resembles him. Suffering from a permanent erection, Charlie takes the mannequin with him to the hospital, seeking emergency treatment for his problem. The doctor in charge diagnoses him with a new gay disease which causes repression of homosexual desire, and recommends a treatment called "reintegration." But once Charlie sees how brutal the treatment will be, he realizes he is happily gay.

In "SPF 2000," two buddies (Peter Gingerich, Kelvin Walker) cruise a hunky guy by a lake. Suddenly, an alien comes out of the water, holds them captive and experiments with an earthling ritual he's been observing: rubbing suntan lotion on his victims.

In "Dirty Baby Does Fire Island," a bewildered baby doll washes up on a Fire Island beach and secretly observes some private moments between men, who are bodybuilding; making love, and taking drugs.

In the visually striking "Twilight of the Gods," director Stewart Main beautifully articulates the connection between men of different cultures by shooting the film in stark black and white and replacing dialogue with the unspoken—seductive eye contact, which visualizes the tension between longing and the forbidden. "Boot Camp," also shot in black and white and without dialogue, hilariously satirizes gay desire by exaggerating gay stereotypes: macho leather men and campy devotees of Hollywood musicals. Viewers who are unfamiliar with Karen Black's star turn in the "Amelia" episode of the made-for-television movie TRILOGY OF TERROR (1975) won't appreciate the almost scene-by-scene and word-for-word parody of "Karen Black Like Me." But fans looking for the ultimate salute to Ms. Black will be sorely disappointed by the film's strained attempts at sustaining laughs.

In "My Body," "SPF 2000," and "Dirty Baby," clever techniques outweigh the storytelling. In "My Body," director Moffett (who also stars) uses classic slapstick antics to make some simplistic observations about the suppression of sexual identity. In the execrable "SPF 2000," the characters speak out of synch in director Patrick McGuinn's evocation of badly-dubbed foreign films. And while the stop-action motion in "Dirty Baby" is intermittingly witty, it soon wears on the viewer's nerves.

Passionately narrated by Derek Jacobi, "Achilles" is a gorgeously romantic work; it's not too often that clay figures make such charismatic leading men. Director Barry Purvis, an Academy Award-nominated animator, is not, however, a sophisticated craftsman; the animation is at times quite awkward. But that awkwardness communicates the uncertainty of new romance and confusion of forbidden sexuality. In blatantly eroticizing the relationship, Purvis also recognizes that gay culture, whether in history books or in mythology, has been all but whitewashed through the centuries. At last we have an Achilles who is a hero and a gay man for the ages. *(Violence, sexual situations, nudity, profanity.)*—D.O.

d, John Matthews ("Boot Camp"), David Briggs ("Karen Black Like Me"), Patrick McGuinn ("SPF 2000"), Stewart Main ("Twilight of the Gods"), Todd Downing ("Dirty Baby Does Fire Island"), Matthias Visser ("My Body"), Joel Moffett ("My Body"), Barry Purvis ("Achilles"); p, Melinda Hsu ("Boot Camp"), David Briggs ("Karen Black Like Me"), Patrick McGuinn ("SPF 2000"), Michele Fantl ("Twilight of the Gods"), Matthias Visser ("My Body"); w, John Matthews ("Boot Camp"), David Briggs ("Karen Black Like Me"), Patrick McGuinn ("SPF 2000"), Stewart Main ("Twilight of the Gods"), Todd Downing ("Dirty Baby Does Fire Island"), Joel Moffett ("My Body"); ph, Kate Phelan ("Boot Camp"), Amy Gissen ("SPF 2000"), Todd Downing ("Dirty Baby Does Fire Island"), Andrew Thomas ("My Body"); ed, John Matthews ("Boot Camp"), David Briggs ("Karen Black Like Me"), Patrick McGuinn ("SPF 2000"), Todd Downing ("Dirty Baby Does Fire

Island"), Mark Catalena ("My Body"); m, Jeffrey Hoffman ("Boot Camp"); prod d,

Comedy/Romance/Drama **(PR: O MPAA: NR)**

BOYS WILL BE BOYS ★½
(U.S., 1998) 90m Crystal Sky Communications ~ Unapix c

James Williams *(Matt Clauswell)*; Drew Winget *(Robbie Clauswell)*; Julie Hagerty *(Emily Clauswell)*; Randy Travis *(Lloyd Clauswell)*; Mickey Rooney *(Wellington)*; Michael DeLuise *(Skip LaRue)*; Catherine Oxenberg *(Patsy "B.B" Parker)*; Jon Voight *(Lt. Palladino)*; Charles Nelson Reilly *(Mr. Rudnick)*; Ruth Buzzi *(Mrs. Rudnick)*; Carol Arthur *(Blanche)*; Dom DeLuise *(Chef)*; Glenndon Chatman *(Einstein)*; Steven Hartman *(Bugsy)*; Brian Wagner *(Eddie)*; Skylar Shuster *(Samantha)*; Eileen Saki *(Barbecue Chef)*; Hari Ozioi *(French Boy)*; Lloyd Batista *(Man in Hallway)*; Christopher Reinders *(Waiter)*; Erik Troy *(Cop #1)*; Bill Troy *(Cop #2)*; Bob Markwood *(Magician)*; Cindy Lee Duck *(Newscaster)*; Bonnie Paul *(Lead Singer)*; Rick Shae *(Guitarist)*; Bob Fergo *(Keyboard/Violinist)*; Keith Barrows *(Bassist)*; Miles Robinson *(Drummer)*

Infantile gags and elements cribbed from the HOME ALONE series form the basis for BOYS WILL BE BOYS, a highly derivative straight-to-video screwball comedy directed by beloved actor Dom DeLuise. Be forewarned: This film could induce terminal boredom.

Police Lt. Palladino (Jon Voight) interrogates eight-year-old Robbie Clauswell (Drew Winget) and his 12-year-old brother Matt (James Williams) about the burglar they claim entered their house. The suspect, Skip LaRue (Michael DeLuise), claims the boys attacked him. The boys tell their side of the story: the previous Saturday, their father Lloyd (Randy Travis) and mother Emily (Julie Hagerty) were planning to attend a barbecue at the home of Lloyd's boss, Mr. Wellington (Mickey Rooney). The boys ask their father if they can spend the time without a babysitter, as they promise to take care of each other. Brotherly love soon disappears, however, and the boys manage to wreck the house with the help of some friends.

LaRue, who also works for Wellington and wants a promotion that's coming up at work; follows a plan dreamt up by his girlfriend Patsy (Catherine Oxenberg), and steals $50,000 from the company. He plants the money in Lloyd's house in order to frame him for the crime. When the boys realize that LaRue is in their house, they splatter him with an all-out assault of eggs, silly string, and fly paper. Lloyd, realizing he doesn't spend enough time with his boys, tells Wellington he doesn't want the promotion, but happily, Wellington gives it to him anyway. The now-battered LaRue is arrested, the boys quickly clean the house, and upon their parents' arrival home, they are praised as heroes.

As a director (FATSO, HOT STUFF), Dom DeLuise shows none of the comic flair that marks his work as an actor. BOYS is merely a rehash of HOME ALONE (1990), with two bratty kids and one bumbling crook taking the place of two crooks and one Macaulay Culkin. In fact, the plot includes another, even less involving, element: the brothers declaring war on each other with the help of their friends Einstein, Bugsy, and Eddie. Initially, they begin with name-calling ("water weenie" and "duncehead" being two choice examples), but their antics soon turn violent, with water balloons and a remote-controlled lawn mower as the weapons of choice. Perhaps this stuff looked funnier on the story boards; on film, it's simply tiresome.

The performances are hokey, but obviously reflective of the contrived nature of the script. Julie Hagerty, who displayed comic ability in AIRPLANE! (1980), is fine in a thankless role, but country music singer Randy Travis proves to be a complete stiff. The other "name" cast members, including Jon Voight, Michael DeLuise (Dom's son), Catherine Oxenberg, Charles Nelson Reilly and Mickey Rooney, provide marquee value and little else. Director DeLuise cameos as an angry chef. *(Violence.)—P.L.*

d, Dom DeLuise; p, Steven Paul; exec p, Hank Paul, Robert Baruc, Pablo Dammicco; w, Gregory Poppen, Mark Dubas; ph, Leonard Schway; ed, Heidi Charfe; m, Kristopher Carter; prod d, Deren P. Abram; art d, Matthew Geer; sound, Eric Enroth; fx, Bill Troy; casting, Dorothy Koster; cos, Anna Marie Brooks; makeup, Peter Christopher; stunts, Michael R. Long

Comedy/Children's **(PR: A MPAA: PG)**

BRAM STOKER'S LEGEND OF THE MUMMY
(SEE: BRAM STOKER'S THE MUMMY)

BRAM STOKER'S SHADOWBUILDER ★★★
(U.S., 1998) 101m Imperial Entertainment; Hammerhead Productions; Applecreek Communications ~ Sterling Home Entertainment c
(AKA: SHADOWBUILDER)

Michael Rooker *(Father Jacob Vassey)*; Leslie Hope *(Jenny Hatcher)*; Shawn Alex Thompson *(Sheriff Sam Logan)*; Kevin Zegers *(Chris Hatcher)*; Andrew Jackson *(Shadowbuilder)*; Tony Todd *(Evert Covey)*; Hardee Lineham *(Nestor Tibbot)*; Catherine Bruhier *(Maggie MacKinnon)*; Gordon M. Woolvert *(Larry Eggers)*; James B. Douglas *(Doc Cole)*; Richard McMillan *(Father Finler)*; Charlotte Sullivan *(Jazz)*; Andrew Sardella *(Paul)*; David Calderisi *(Bishop Gallo)*; Lawrence Bayne *(Quinlan)*; Eric Murphy *(Vic Lambert)*; Paul Soles *(Mr. Butterman)*; Billie Mae Richards *(Mrs. Butterman)*; Nicole Stoffman *(Kelly)*; Toby Proctor *(Harvey Price)*; Tara Crooks *(Lizzie)*; Steven Jay Blum *(Shadowbuilder Voice)*

A small gem of a horror film—which unfortunately failed to achieve theatrical release and debuted on video—this adaptation of a short story by the *Dracula* author ably balances drama and special effects.

Father Jacob Vassey (Michael Rooker) invades a satanic ceremony in which Victor Lambert (Eric Murphy) offers up a photo of his son Chris. Vassey kills the satanists, but not before they have raised a demon called the Shadowbuilder (Andrew Jackson). Following clues at the site, Vassey travels to the town of Grand River, where Chris (Kevin Zegers) lives with his young aunt, Jenny (Leslie Hope), who is having an affair with sheriff Sam Logan (Shawn Alex Thompson). The Shadowbuilder arrives and kills Sam's deputy Larry (Gordon M. Woolvert), Doc Cole (James B. Douglas) and Father Finler (Richard McMillan). Vassey tells Jenny that Chris is in danger, and explains to Sam that the Shadowbuilder is after the boy, who was "born pure"; the demon, which can be repelled by light, needs to sacrifice Chris during a coming solar eclipse to open a door to his world.

The Shadowbuilder's presence begins compelling the townspeople to violence, and it incarnates as a ferocious dog that chases Chris and Jenny to the compound of eccentric Covey (Tony Todd), whose multiple-light setup dispels the hound. Vassey, Jenny, Sam, Chris, and Covey hole up at Jenny's place, but with the help of possessed locals, the Shadowbuilder invades the house and spirits Chris to a church. When the eclipse begins and the Shadowbuilder prepares to sacrifice Chris, Vassey interrupts and blocks its scythe. As the sun emerges and strikes the Shadowbuilder, Sam uses the scythe to deliver a destroying blow to the demon. While the basic premise and a few details of SHADOWBUILDER are familiar, the movie has been put together with commendable skill. The imaginative direction by special effects artist Jamie Dixon is well-attuned to both character and scares, and he's abetted by Michael Stokes' smart script. It's refreshing, for example, to see an authority figure (in this case, Sam) become a fast believer in the unreal events, and to have a character (Chris) describe a symbolic dream instead of having it presented for cheap shock effect. Especially clever is the heroes' use of household weapons from flashlights to Polaroid cameras to combat the light-sensitive fiend, and the CGI effects depicting its victims collapsing into ashes are startlingly good.

The filmmakers wisely incarnate the evil in the identifiable form of the dog for several scenes; the characters' reactions to the threat are refreshingly smart and believable for a genre film. And there's a wealth of nicely chilly details, like the Shadowbuilder reciting the Book of Genesis in reverse during its ritual and children pulling apart their dolls as its virulent influence begins to spread. As the pistol-packing priest, Rooker makes a compelling central figure; while the backstory of his having slaughtered an evil African warlord and his men wasn't really necessary, the idea of a man of the cloth functioning as a religious "cleaner" is a subversively entertaining one. *(Graphic violence, extensive nudity, extreme profanity.)*—M.G.

d, Jamie Dixon; p, Andy Emilio; exec p, Ash R. Shah, Dan Chuba; assoc p, Ian Hall; w, Michael Stokes (based on the short story by Bram Stoker); ph, David Pelletier; ed, Craig Nisker; m, Eckart Seeber; prod d, Ian Hall; art d, Brent McGillivray; set d, Grid Jurek; sound, Henry Embry, Patrick M. Griffith; fx, Hammerhead Productions, Thad Beier, Paul L. Jones, Mark Rice; casting, Maria Armstrong, Penny Perry Davis; cos, Nancy McHugh; makeup, Catherine Davies Irvine, Francois Dagenais (effects); stunts, John Stoneham Stoneham

Horror **(PR: O MPAA: R)**

BRAM STOKER'S THE MUMMY ★★
(U.S., 1998) 100m Goldbar Entertainment ~ Unapix c
(AKA: BRAM STOKER'S LEGEND OF THE MUMMY)

Louis Gossett Jr. *(John Corbeck)*; Amy Locane *(Margaret Trelawny)*; Eric Lutes *(Robert Wyatt)*; Mark Lindsay-Chapman *(Daw)*; Richard Karn *(Brice Renard)*; Lloyd Bochner *(Abel Trelawny)*; Victoria Tennant *(Mary)*; Aubrey Morris *(Dr. Winchester)*; Mary Jo Catlett *(Mrs. Grant)*; Julian Stone *(Jimmy)*; Laura Otis *(Lily)*; Portia Doubleday *(Young Margaret)*; Rachel Naples *(Queen Tera)*; Donald Monat *(Hutchins)*; Kelly Perine *(Keene)*; Kahlil Sabbagh *(Bedouin Guide)*; Stayce Allison *(Woman)*; Cher Summers *(Operator)*; Tico Wells *(Young Corbeck)*; John Rixy Moore *(Young Trelawny)*

BRAM STOKER'S THE MUMMY unearths a story familiar from classic Universal and Hammer horror movies; unfortunately, this straight-to-video rendition of the tale has few chills, and pales in comparison to the originals.

In 1947, a little boy witnesses a bizarre death in an ancient Egyptian tomb. In present day California, Egyptologist Abel Trelawny (Lloyd Bochner) falls into a coma after he speaks the words that will awaken a mummy. His daughter Margaret (Amy Locane) enlists the aid of her former lover Robert (Eric Lutes) to help him. Robert discovers that the Mummy is the cursed Queen Tera. After several strange occurrences, the mummy appears in Trelawny's basement and Margaret begins having odd dreams about the powerful Egyptian queen. Robert finds Abel's partner John Corbeck (Louis Gossett Jr.) who explains the ancient formula to resurrect Tera's mummy. When he sees Margaret possessed by Tera's spirit, it comes to him that Tera wants to live through the young woman when seven stars align. Claiming it will cure Abel, Corbeck prepares for the ceremony. Tera is unwrapped to reveal perfect skin and seven-fingered hands. Robert attempts to halt the resurrection, but Corbeck, consumed by his thirst for power, stops him. Queen Tera awakens and kills Corbeck. Her spirit then enters Margaret's body through the vehicle of a little girl.

Afterwards, Abel is healthy and Robert and Margaret take off for a vacation. They make love, and Robert is shocked to find a seven-fingered scratch down his back.

Reworking elements from mummy movies past, director-writer-executive producer Jeffrey Obrow (DEAN R. KOONTZ' SERVANTS OF TWILIGHT) does a capable job on a low budget, but his screenplay is alternately confusing and predictable. The film's special effects and Egyptian set generally cut-rate, but there is one effectively frightening dream sequence in which the mummy tears off "Home Improvement" star Richard Karn's fingers. The acting is undistinguished, despite the presence of familiar faces like Amy Locane (SCHOOL TIES), Lloyd Bochner (THE NAKED GUN 2-1/2: THE SMELL OF FEAR) and Aubrey Morris (A CLOCKWORK ORANGE). Louis Gossett Jr. contributes a particularly hammy turn as the nutty Corbeck; adorned in an Egyptian headdress, he dramatically intones lines like, "Tonight, it will be my destiny to bring her back! Tonight, I hold the power!" Karloff's legacy remains unchallenged. *(Extreme profanity, violence, sexual situations.)*—P.L.

d, Jeffrey Obrow; p, Harel Goldstein, Bill Barnett; exec p, Robert Baruc, Jeffrey Obrow; co-p, Tad Driscoll; w, Jeffrey Obrow (from a story by Jeffrey Obrow, Lars Hauglie, and John Penney, based on the novel *The Jewel of Seven Stars* by Bram Stoker), Bram Stoker; ph, Antonio Soriano; ed, Gary Meyers; m, Rick Cox; prod d, Ken Larson; art d, Amy Perry; sound, Jon Ailetcher (mixer); casting, Rosemary Welden; cos, Caroline Marx; makeup, Sandy Williams, Chad Washam (effects), Chris Fording (effects); stunts, Eddie Perez

Horror **(PR: O MPAA: R)**

BRANDON TEENA STORY, THE ★★★★
(U.S., 1998) 90m Bless Bless Productions ~
Zeitgeist Films c

Fascinating but sickening, THE BRANDON TEENA STORY details the events leading up to the murder of a young woman whose only "offense" to society was in pretending to be a man. This deeply-felt documentary covers both the crime story and its larger social implications with intelligence and care.

THE BRANDON TEENA STORY retraces the path of Brandon Teena, an attractive but mannish-looking Nebraskan who transposed her name from Teena Brandon as a teenager when she decided she preferred being male. The film begins with her family, friends, and girlfriends fondly remembering her charm and good manners.

Trouble began for Brandon, however, when she started forging checks and shoplifting gifts for her girlfriends. She left her home in 1993 at the age of 20 to live in Falls City, an lower-middle class community with a history of domestic violence. In the new town, Brandon met and started dating Lana Tisdel, who was unaware of Brandon's actual gender. During this time, Brandon also began hormone therapy for a future sex-change operation.

But just as life was turning around for Brandon, two of Lana's friends, Thomas Nissen and John Lotter, learned of Brandon's gender and decided to punish her for the deception, first by telling Lana, then by beating and raping Brandon on Christmas Eve. When Brandon later told the police about the crime, the detectives interrogated Brandon more harshly than either of her rapists. But once the news got out about the event, Tom and John were teased by the townspeople for enjoying sex with a freak.

Eventually, Brandon sought refuge from the publicity by staying with a friend, Lisa Lambert, in a small farmhouse in the nearby town of Humbolt. On New Year's Eve, Tom and John tracked Brandon down to the dwelling and assassinated Brandon, Lisa, and another visiting friend, Philip Devine. They left only Lisa's baby unharmed. In 1995, Tom and John were tried and convicted of the murders, although Tom got a plea agreement while John got the death sentence. Brandon's mother, JoAnn, approved of the verdict, but her wrongful death suit against the sheriff of Falls City was dismissed.

If Brandon Teena had never existed, she would have made an extraordinary literary invention, and her short life story is the stuff of great pulp fiction. Sadly, of course, Brandon Teena *did* exist, and her soul seems to rise from the grave in THE BRANDON TEENA STORY, a haunting documentary (filmed in 1996) and just the first of three films to tell Brandon Teena's tragic tale (the other two are feature docudramas).

In a reflective and non exploitative way, directors Susan Muska and Greta Olafsdottir investigate their subject and uncover a mesh of themes, in particular how ignorance about sex and gender feeds prejudice and how poverty can influence violent behavior (the verite documentaries PARADISE LOST: THE CHILD MURDERS AT ROBIN HOOD HILLS and LICENSED TO KILL address some of these same issues in similar ways). Muska and Olafsdottir (who also coproduced, photographed, and edited) drive home their points with simple but effective techniques, crosscutting interviews with Brandon's friends, her killers, a detective, etc. Elsewhere, the filmmakers use more poetic license. In a climactic sequence, the camera tracks through the empty farmhouse where the killings had occurred while photos of the shooting victims are superimposed and the impassioned pleas of the trial prosecutor fill the soundtrack. Also, the plaintive vocalizing of Lorrie Morgan, Dinah Washington, April Stevens, and the Brown Brothers punctuate key moments in Brandon's dispiriting journey. In the end, Brandon's own sad, gravelly voice, recorded during the jailhouse interview after her rape, makes knowledge of the crimes against her all the more frightening to comprehend. THE BRANDON TEENA STORY is not easy to sit through, but it is well worth the effort. *(Sexual situations, adult situations, extreme profanity.)*—E.M.

d, Susan Muska, Greta Olafsdottir; p, Susan Muska, Greta Olafsdottir; exec p, Jane Dekrone; w, Susan Muska, Greta Olafsdottir; ph, Susan Muska, Greta Olafsdottir; ed, Susan Muska, Greta Olafsdottir

Documentary **(PR: C MPAA: NR)**

BRAT

(SEE: BROTHER)

BRAVE LITTLE TOASTER GOES TO MARS, THE ★★½

(U.S., 1998) 72m Hyperion Studio; Kushner-Locke Productions ~ Walt Disney Home Video c

VOICES OF: Thurl Ravenscroft *(Kirby)*; Deanna Oliver *(Toaster)*; Eric Lloyd *(Blanky)*; Tim Stack *(Lampy)*; Roger Kabler *(Radio)*; Randy Midler *(Ratso)*; Fyvush Finkel *(Hearing Aid)*; Stephen Tobolowsky *(Calculator)*; Farrah Fawcett *(Spout)*; Redmond O'Neal *(Squirt)*; Wayne Knight *(Microwave)*; Jessica Tuck *(Chris)*; Chris Young *(Rob)*; Russ Taylor *(Robbie)*; Brian Doyle-Murray *(Wittgenstein the Supercomputer)*; Carol Channing *(Fanny)*; DeForest Kelley *(Viking 1)*; Kath Soucie *(Tinselina)*; Alan King *(Supreme Commander)*

Those adorably anthropomorphic household appliances are back for more misadventures in THE BRAVE LITTLE TOASTER GOES TO MARS, a cute, but lightweight, straight-to-video animated sequel to the more accomplished THE BRAVE LITTLE TOASTER (1987).

Toaster (voice of Deanna Oliver), Radio (voice of Roger Kabler), Blanky (voice of Eric Lloyd), Lampy (voice of Tim Stack), and Kirby the vacuum cleaner (voice of Thurl Ravenscroft), make a vow to protect their master's new baby, Robbie (voice of Russ Taylor). However, an old Hearing Aid (voice of Fyvush Finkel) which was left in a drawer by the house's previous owner, receives messages from outer space and is about to be beamed up to Mars when Robbie crawls in the way of the beam and is accidentally transported to the red planet. Using plans from a Wittgenstein the Supercomputer (voice of Brian Doyle-Murray), the appliances utilize a Microwave Oven (voice of Wayne Knight), some microwave popcorn, a Calculator (voice of Stephen Tobolowsky), and Fanny the fan (voice of Carol Channing) to fly to Mars.

On Mars, the appliances find Robbie but encounter an army of refrigerators and other militant appliances that rebelled against their manufacturer and fled to Mars, and have built a missile to destroy Earth. Toaster challenges the appliances's Supreme Commander (voice of Alan King) to an election and defeats it, then deactivates the missile. They all head back to Earth, along with Tinselina, a Christmas Tree Angel (voice of Kath Soucie) that sacrifices its organic hair and dress to use as fuel so that they can fly back. Robbie is returned to his crib before his parents wake up, and when he learns how to walk, he rescues Tinselina from a trash can and his parents put it on top of their tree.

THE BRAVE LITTLE TOASTER was a charmingly old-fashioned and nicely animated fable about growing up and leaving behind childhood possessions and memories, and the visually identical sequel is entertaining enough for kids, but lacks the thematic poignancy that made the original such a pleasant surprise. The additional characters are amusing, particularly the Yiddish-accented hearing aid and the wisecracking microwave, but there are simply too many of them, including a "cameo" by Farrah Fawcett as, yup, a talking faucet. There are a number of clever touches designed to appeal to adults, such as the voyage to Mars where the appliances encounter lost balloons floating in space who sing about their past lives (a hippie balloon from the Woodstock concert, a cowgirl from a Buffalo Bill Wild West shows, etc.), but the silly new songs can't compare to those of Van Dyke Parks's in the original. The story, based on a novella by noted sci-fi author Thomas M. Disch, is also quite complicated for a kid's cartoon, exhibiting signs of suppressed intellectual elements struggling to break through, as in the bizarre subplot involving Albert Einstein, who is revealed to have been Hearing Aid's former owner, and his Unified Field Theory! Additionally, whether Disney realizes it or not, there is an obvious capitalism vs. communism subtext, manifested in the commander's speeches to his "oppressed" workers, whom he tells "you have no master but yourselves."—M.S.

d, Robert Ramirez; p, Donald Kushner, Tom Wilhite; exec p, Willard Carroll, Peter Locke; co-p, Kurt Albrecht; w, Willard Carroll (based on the novella by Thomas M. Disch and characters created by Jerry Rees and Joe Ranft); ed, Julie Lau; m, Alexander Janko; art d, Dave Dunnet; casting, Brian Charanne, Mary Hidalgo

Animated/Children's **(PR: AA MPAA: G)**

BREAK, THE ★★½

(U.K./Germany/Japan/Ireland, 1997) 96m CSL Films; Samson Films; Channel Four Films; Road Movies; NFD International; Zephyr Films; Dritte Film; Pony Canyon ~ Castle Hill c

Stephen Rea *(Sean Dowd)*; Alfred Molina *(Tulio)*; Rosana Pastor *(Monica)*; Brendan Gleeson *(Richard)*; Maria Doyle Kennedy *(Roisin)*; Jorge Sanz *(Paco)*; Pruitt Taylor Vince *(Scott)*; Sean McGinley *(Tommy Breen)*; Frankie McCafferty *(Danny)*; Paul Ronan *(Liam)*; Richard Dormer *(Joe)*; Roy Haybeard *(Food Lorry Driver)*; Toby Bradford *(Charlie)*; Robert Taylor *(Prison Officer—Visiting Room)*; B.J. Hogg *(Albert)*; Seamus Ball *(First Prison Officer—Tallylodge)*; James Duran *(Gate Prison Officer)*; Dierdre O'Kane *(Breen's Girlfriend)*; Catriona Hinds *(Richard's Wife)*; Paul Giamatti *(Hotel Clerk)*; Brian Vincent *(Lorenzo Bauch)*; Caroline Seymour *(Junkie)*; Ciaran O'Reilly *(Passer-by)*; Jerry Grayson *(Restaurant Manager)*; Ken Solarino *(Subway Man)*; Myra Carter *(Neighbor)*; Sheik Mahmud-Bey *(Knifeman)*; Esteban Fernandez *(Ramon)*; Luis Argueta *(Ramon's Bodyguard)*; George Bass *(Ramon's Driver)*; Graeme Malcolm *(Lattimer)*; Richard Council *(FBI Agent No. 1)*; John Rothman *(FBI Agent No. 2)*; Ndehru Roberts *(Kid Gun Dealer)*; Coati Mundi *(Pepe)*; Alba Oms *(Stall Owner)*; Barry Snider *(Eamonn)*; Mario Mendoza *(Mustachioed Man)*; Teresa Yenque *(Indian Woman)*

An IRA terrorist escapes from prison but discovers that he can't escape his destiny in THE BREAK, a minor film that strikes a minor chord in its first scene, and never modulates it.

After breaking out of a Belfast prison, Sean Dowd (Stephen Rea), a member of the Irish Republican Army, attempts to break with his past by leaving his girlfriend (Maria Doyle Kennedy) and illegally emigrating to New York City, where he takes a job as a dishwasher and boards at a seedy hotel. When a violent domestic altercation erupts down the hall, Sean plays the good Samaritan and is knifed for his trouble. Badly wounded, he is taken in and nursed back to health by Tulio (Alfred Molina), a Guatemalan coworker, and his sister, Monica (Rosana Pastor).

After becoming involved with Monica, Sean discovers that she and Tulio are planning to assassinate Ramon (Esteban Fernandez), a powerful Guatemalan politico who murdered their father and is currently in New York. Seeing that his friends are hopeless amateurs when it comes to terrorism and unable to convince them to drop their vendetta, Sean takes over the operation.

The assassination plot is a success, but when Sean, accompanied by Monica, arrives at a local Irish bar to receive aid in fleeing the area, the FBI, which has long had its eye on him, is waiting. Realizing his number is up, Sean refuses to surrender, suicidally draws his gun, and is shot to death. When Monica, who is not under suspicion, asks an FBI agent to explain what is going on, she is told that it's "some Irish thing."

THE BREAK tells its grim, horizontal story with considerable efficiency and lucidity. Appropriately dreary are its washed-out color photography, which appears to wish it were black-and-white, and drab locations: the movie succeeds in making New York look even crummier than it actually is, and Ireland is no longer the Emerald Isle.

THE BREAK's alternate title was the awkward "A Further Gesture," but it might as well have been "Dead Man Walking." Stephen Rea, one of the '90s' most unpretentious and empathetic actors, plays the dour Sean Dowd as if Dowd knows all along he's a goner. (Actors portraying doomed figures should, perhaps, be given mock scripts with happy endings.)

In a standard specimen of this genre, the protagonist's anomie would be cured by the loving new woman in his life, here named Monica, before his tragic destiny closes in on him. By muting this renaissance—Dowd is almost as glum *with* Monica as *without* her—THE BREAK avoids emotional cliche but doesn't replace it with much of anything, not even irony. ODD MAN OUT (1946), the film to beat about an IRA man on the lam, benefited from its unabashed embrace of high melodrama and soared into greatness. *(Violence, nudity, sexual situations, extreme profanity.)*—D.T.

d, Robert Dornheim; p, Chris Curling; exec p, David Aukin, Ulrich Felsberg, Rod Stoneman, Michiyo Yoshizaki; assoc p, Laurie Borg; co-p, David Collins, Bonnie Timmermann; w, Ronan Bennett (from an idea by Stephen Rea); ph, Andrzej Sekula; ed, Masahiro Hirakubo; m, Harald Kloser, Shaun Davey; prod d, Kalina Ivanov, Tom McCullagh; art d, Anna Rackard; set d, Diane Lederman; sound, Simon Willis (mixer), Brian Miksis (mixer); fx, Gerry Johnston, J.C. Brotherhood, Eddie Drohan II; casting, Ros Hubbard, John Hubbard; cos, Stephanie Maslansky, Maggie Donnelly; makeup, Morag Ross; stunts, Patrick Condren, Manny Siverio

Thriller/Drama/Action **(PR: C MPAA: R)**

BREAKOUT ★★

(Canada, 1998) 86m Breakout Inc. ~ S. Entertainment c

J. Evan Bonifant *(Joe Hadley)*; Robert Carradine *(Zack Hadley)*; James Hong *(Larry Hwang)*; Chris Chinchilla *(Stewart)*; Breanne Grant *(Maggie)*; Jerome Silvano *(Derrek)*; Holly Gagnier *(Lynn Hadley)*; Richard Anderson *(American Businessman)*; Ralph George *(Faisul)*; Mike Peng *(Luis)*; Michaela Arroyaye *(Princess)*; Paul Arno *(Detective Kovacs)*; Bob Denison *(Sergeant)*; Sara Mininni *(Reporter)*; Ben Hackman *(5 Year Old Boy)*; Dan Berardi *(Bully)*; Scott MacKinnon *(Bully)*

Sweet-tempered and easily dismissed, BREAKOUT is assembly line fare about a lad's trust in his father, an inventor. Dispensing good clean inanity, it offers kiddie kickboxing, lummox villains, and homilies about teamwork.

Gizmo-fancying Joe Hadley (J. Evan Bonifant) admires his father, Zack (Robert Carradine), an engineer involved in a top-secret project for investor Larry Hwang (James Hong). Already concerned about industrial theft, Zack grows short-tempered at Joe's efforts to peek in his basement workshop.

Unbeknownst to Zack, Larry is a point man for an oil conglomerate determined to thwart Zack's breakthrough, a super battery for powering electric cars. Meanwhile, Joe makes the schoolyard acquaintance of two foster kids, Maggie (Breanne Grant) and Derrek (Jerome Silvano), who teach him self-defense and the spirit of cooperation. To stymie Zack's progress, Larry hires Stewart (Chris Chinchilla) and his two rogues to kidnap Joe (and friends) in order to force Zack to cease his experimentation. Having proved themselves troublesome by beating up their kidnappers, the young friends are released by Stewart and his buddies, who are relieved when Zack agrees to abandon his project.

Playing upon Zack's financial woes, Larry offers to "temporarily" buy the patent to his battery. When Joe and his pals scientifically retrace their steps to the kidnappers' hangout, they discover Larry's involvement. Joe convinces his dad not to cede his inventor's rights, but Larry threatens to blow up the entire Hadley family. In the interim, Maggie and Derrek alert the police, and they arrest Larry's gang. Ultimately, Zack perfects his super battery and becomes Maggie and Derrek's new foster father.

It's all so neatly resolved. Calumny is banished; orphans are adopted; the lesson of working together is instilled in the young target audience. This eco-friendly escapade hits its intended marks in a formulaic fashion. As a mild diversion for attention-deficit tykes, it's serviceable without ever being outstanding. Once again, a little child shall lead them (thus, one precocious David outsmarts the shrewdest legal and illegal efforts of a petroleum Goliath). Still, grade-schoolers will cheer as their onscreen peers knock about bad guys with martial artistry. *(Violence.)*— R.P.

d, John Bradshaw; p, Nicolas Stiliadis; assoc p, Michael Jannetta, Alice O'Neil; co-p, Paco Alvarez; w, Naomi Jantzen; ph, Edgar Egger; ed, Nick Rotundo; m, Gary Koftinoff; prod d, Michael Close; art d, Robin Rhodes; set d, Kevin Perkins; sound, Peter Clements; fx, Brock Jolliffe, Rudy Rivas; casting, Gloria Mann; cos, Stephanie Garrison; makeup, Charlene Cordoba, Tali Kalb; stunts, Paul Rapivski, Darren McGuire, Plato Fountidakis

Children's/Action (PR: A MPAA: NR)

BREAST MEN ★★★½

(U.S., 1998) 95m Gary Lucchesi Productions ~ HBO c

David Schwimmer *(Dr. Christopher Saunders/Kevin Saunders)*; Chris Cooper *(Dr. William Larson)*; Emily Procter *(Laura Pierson)*; Matt Frewer *(Gerald Kraemica)*; Terry O'Quinn *(Hersch Lawyer)*; Kathleen Wilhoite *(Tammi-Jean)*; John Stockwell *(Robert Renaud)*; Lisa Marie *(Vanessa)*; Louise Fletcher *(Mrs. Saunders)*; Michael Cavanaugh *(Harry)*; Michael Chieffo *(Dave)*; Pat Cronin *(Committee Head)*; Amanda Foreman *(Lola)*; Lyle Lovett *(Research Scientist)*; Julie McCullough *(1970's Head Receptionist)*; Rena Riffel *(Swimming Pool Girl)*; Raphael Sbarge *(Larson's Lawyer)*; David Wells *(Lewis)*; Colleen Werthmann *(1900's Receptionist)*; Eve Plumb *(Mocher)*; Xander Berkeley *(Male Interviewer)*

An amusing medical chronicle, BREAST MEN artificially enhances the real-life story of the creation of the breast implant with bountiful results. The film was made for HBO, and subsequently was released on home video.

After several different breast-augmentation processes have failed, plastic surgeon Dr. Kevin Saunders (David Schwimmer) invents a successful saline-filled breast implant. His mentor, Dr. William Larson (Chris Cooper), laughs at the idea and reminds Saunders of past failures in this somewhat dubious area of plastic surgery. Larson, however, changes his mind when he begins to dwell on the lack of respect that plastic surgeons receive from the medical community; he feels that Saunders's discovery might lend the profession a certain amount of prestige. He has Saunders's saline mold sent to a technical lab. There, it is streamlined and filled with silicone rather than saline. After being laughed at by the medical board, Larson and Saunders then find a woman to experiment on to prove their point. The operation is a success. They open a clinic, which is floundering until Saunders advertises it, against Larson's wishes. Suddenly, business booms. Later, Saunders operates on former schoolmate Laura Pierson (Emily Procter), whom he marries and hires as his nurse.

Saunders tires of Larson claiming all the credit for his creation, and so they split. Saunders's business is dying until he meets strip-club owner, Gerald Kraemica (Matt Frewer), who sends his dancers over for breast enhancements. Saunders then falls into a fast life of drugs, girls, and money, which culminates in divorce. Several years later, a TV news special discloses that some women are suffering leakage and other problems as a result of having had breast implants. The resulting lawsuits produce a scare that results in the loss of Saunders's company. Larson has similar financial troubles, and eventually suffers a fatal heart attack. Years later, Saunders is running a small plastic surgery business when Laura appears, asking to have her painful implants removed. This gives him the impetus to start a new company—one which removes old silicone implants and replaces them with safer saline ones. The business is a big success, but soon after, Saunders is killed in an auto wreck.

Coming from a male-chauvinist perspective that seems to say that women have little confidence about themselves unless they've got balloon-like breasts, BREAST MEN is really intended for mammary-fixated males. To underscore this point of view, the film features interstitial testimonials from women who are unhappy because they have small or sagging breasts; during these segments, the camera is focused squarely on the women's chests so as not to expose their identities. This sophmoric bit of humor stands out like a sore thumb; the filmmakers otherwise keep their leering humor in check, and at the service of the plot. Director Lawrence O'Neil keeps the proceedings moving at a brisk pace, while John Stockwell's solid script smoothly links together the different time periods depicted. Schwimmer merely duplicates his schlemiel-like "Ross" persona from the TV series "Friends" for the primary section of the film—a standout sequence has him soliciting prospective breast-implant patients on the street. Despite this seeming typecasting, Schwimmer aptly handles the character's later, rather swift transformation from loser to drug-addled playboy. The rest of the cast performs admirably, though none stand out. *(Extreme profanity, violence, substance abuse, nudity, sexual situations.)*—P.L.

d, Lawrence O'Neil; p, Guy Riedel; exec p, Gary Lucchesi; co-p, Robert McMinn; w, John Stockwell; ph, Robert Stevens; ed, Michael Jablow; m, Dennis McCarthy; prod d, Jane Ann Stewart; sound, Ken King; fx, Gordon Smith; casting, Penny Perry; cos, Melinda Eshelman; makeup, Ashlee Peterson

Drama/Comedy (PR: O MPAA: R)

BRIDE OF CHUCKY ★★★

(U.S., 1998) 88m David Kirschner Productions; Universal ~ Universal c

Jennifer Tilly *(Tiffany)*; Brad Dourif *(Voice of Chucky)*; Katherine Heigl *(Jade)*; Nick Stabile *(Jesse)*; Alexis Arquette *(Damien)*; Gordon Michael Woolvett *(David)*; John Ritter *(Chief Warren Kincaid)*; Lawrence Dane *(Lt. Preston)*; Michael Johnson *(Norton)*; James Gallanders *(Russ)*; Janet Kidder *(Diane)*; Vincent Corazza *(Bailey)*; Kathy Najimy *(Motel Maid)*; Park Bench *(Stoner)*; Emily Weedon *(Girl at One-Stop)*; Ben Bass *(Lt. Ellis)*; Roger McKeen *(Justice of the Peace)*; Sandi Stahlbrand *(Reporter)*

After a seven-year hiatus, the CHILD'S PLAY franchise reemerged with what stands as the best sequel in the series.

White-trash queen Tiffany (Jennifer Tilly) bribes a cop to retrieve the remains of Chucky, the doll possessed by the spirit of serial killer Charles Lee Ray, her old lover. She invokes a spell to reanimate Chucky (voice of Brad Dourif), but after killing off her Goth boyfriend Damien (Alexis Arquette), Chucky electrocutes Tiffany in her bath, and transfers her spirit to a bride doll. Anxious to travel to Hackensack, New Jersey, where Ray has been buried with an amulet that can allow them both to regain human stature, the duo leaves a note for Tiffany's young trailer-park neighbor, Jesse (Nick Stabile), offering him money to transport the dolls there.

Jesse is more than willing to make the trip, as he is having a love affair with teenager Jade (Katherine Heigl), to the extreme disapproval of her police chief uncle, Warren (John Ritter). Just before the couple leaves with the dolls, Chucky and Tiffany kill Warren; Chucky later kills his pursuing deputy. Not realizing they are now wanted by the law, Jesse and Jade get married at a Niagara Falls honeymoon hotel, where the dolls bump off another couple. Jesse's friend David (Gordon Michael Woolvett) arrives to inform the newlyweds of the police pursuit; he also finds Warren's body in their van, and is obliterated by a truck as he attempts to flee.

Their villainy exposed, Chucky and Tiffany commandeer a motor home and order Jesse to continue to drive to Jersey. He and Jade are able to turn the dolls against each other and burn Tiffany in a microwave, but Chucky once again gets the upper hand. At the cemetery, Chucky retrieves the amulet and is about to perform the ritual when the enraged, disfigured Tiffany attacks him. She loses the fight, and as pursuing Lt. Preston (Lawrence Dane) arrives, Jesse shoots Chucky to death. Later, Preston is examining Tiffany's "corpse" when a baby Chucky squirms out of her body and leaps at his face. . .

With the possibilities of the malevolent Chucky acting solo exhausted by the end of CHILD'S PLAY 3 (1991), providing him with a mate to both bicker and kill with injects some fresh blood into the concept. And the producers did two very positive things with this entry: hiring Hong Kong favorite Ronny Yu (THE BRIDE WITH WHITE HAIR, THE PHANTOM LOVER) to direct, and Tilly to play the human Tiffany and supply the voice for her incarnation as a doll. While eschewing some of the flamboyance of his HK work, Yu (working with his longtime cinematographer Peter Pau) suffuses BRIDE OF CHUCKY with atmospheric visuals that compensate for some slack spots in the film's pacing.

Tilly is a hoot in both incarnations, while the black wit of the dolls' dialogue (courtesy of the franchise's longtime writer, Don Mancini) distinguishes the film. A mid-film sex scene between the doll couple, shot in overripe Zalman King style, is a particular highlight and a triumph of twisted humor (Tiffany: "Did you bring a rubber?" Chucky: "Come on, baby, I'm *all* rubber!"). Of immeasurable assist is Kevin Yagher's puppet effects work, which completely (and refreshingly) eschews computer-generated images to make Chucky and Tiffany completely believable, reactive characters.

Certainly, they're more engaging than the human couple they travel with. Stabile and Heigl both look exceptionally good, but neither one is an especially compelling actor, nor is there much about their characters to sustain interest, even when each (rather implausibly) starts to suspect the other of the string of murders. This leaves something of a hole at the center of the movie that's left to be filled by the endlessly entertaining dolls and amusing supporting turns by Arquette and Ritter. In addition, Yu and Mancini score extra points by giving this movie something not many '90s horror films possess: a genuinely surprising and startling "shocker" ending. *(Graphic violence, sexual situations, extreme profanity.)*—M.G.

d, Ronny Yu; p, David Kirschner, Grace Gilroy; exec p, Corey Sienega, Don Mancini; co-p, Laura Moskowitz; w, Don Mancini (based on characters created by Don Mancini); ph, Peter Pau; ed, David Wu, Randolph K. Bricker; m, Graeme Revell; prod d, Alicia Keywan; art d, James McAteer; set d, Carole Lavoie, Mike Harris; sound, Owen Langevin (mixer); fx, Colin Chilvers; casting, Joanna Colbert, Ross Clydesdale; cos, Lynne Mackay; makeup, Patricia Green; stunts, John Stoneham Stoneham

Horror/Comedy **(PR: O MPAA: R)**

BRIGHT SHINING LIE, A ★★½

(U.S., 1998) 130m HBO Pictures; Bleeker Street Films ~ HBO Home Video c

Bill Paxton *(Lieutenant Colonel John Paul Vann)*; Amy Madigan *(Mary Jane Vann)*; Eric Bogosian *(Doug Elders)*; Kurtwood Smith *(General William Westmoreland)*; Vivan Wu *(Lee)*; Donal Logue *(Steven Burnett)*; Robert John Burke *(Captain Frank Drummond)*; Harve Presnell *(General Paul Harkins)*; Les J. N. Mau *(General Chin)*; Pichariva Narakbunchai; Ed Lauter *(General Fred Weyand)*; James Rebhorn *(American Ambassador to Vietnam)*; Jon Marsh *(British Reporter)*; David Warshofsky *(Pike)*; Kay Tong Lim *(Colonel Huynh Van Cao)*; Xuyen Dangers *(School Teacher)*; John Lafayette *(Major Jones)*; Richard Libertini *(Marriage Counselor)*

Working without his usual collaborator, director Jim Sheridan, Irish screenwriter Terry George (IN THE NAME OF THE FATHER, THE BOXER) directed this made-for-HBO feature about a significant, but heretofore unheralded, figure from the Vietnam war era. The film unfortunately errs by going in too many directions at once. Subsequent to its premiere on HBO, the film was released on home video.

In 1962, John Paul Vann (Bill Paxton) is a US Army officer who requests assignment as an official observer in Vietnam. While there, he witnesses the haphazard manner in which the South Vietnamese army conducts the campaign against Communist forces in the North. Vann attempts to convince military brass that winning the hearts and minds of the Vietnamese is the only way to victory, but his pleas fall on deaf ears. Vann resigns.

In his personal life, Vann cheats on his wife Mary Jane (Amy Madigan). Professionally, he works at a desk job, but he soon wants to journey back to Vietnam. He joins a civilian aid program, under the command of General Weyand (Ed Lauter), and assumes the role of US "civilian advisor" to the South Vietnamese army. Vann and partner Doug Elders (Eric Bogosian) quickly learn that providing aid to South Vietnamese villages means bribing their South Vietnamese allies. When Vann refuses to go along, his Asian staff members are butchered and his village home is base bombed.

Weyand expands Vann's role to that of military advisor—in this way, Vann soon becomes a "commanding general" in charge of ten divisions of South Vietnamese troops (although still technically a civilian). As his stature grows, Vann becomes obsessed with beating North Vietnam's brilliant General Jiapp, causing friends like Elders and reporter Steven Burnett (Donal Logue) to feel that Vann has "sold out" his idealistic stance. After a hollow ceremony in which Vann is honored for engineering an attack on Jiapp's forces that in truth went horribly wrong, Vann is killed in a helicopter crash.

Those familiar with Paxton only from his recent nice-guy turns in films like TWISTER (1996) and A SIMPLE PLAN (1998), will be surprised by his nuanced performance here as the hyper-macho Vann, a career military man who can no more stay away from battle than he can stay faithful to his wife. Other standout performances include Bogosian as the civilian advisor and Vivian Wu as the schoolteacher with whom Vann has an affair. Amy Madigan has little to do but fret in the role of Vann's long-suffering wife.

Though George does seem at times to almost evade the actual subject of the conflict in Vietnam, detailing instead Vann's bumpy career and troubled marriage, the film's strength is its choice of subject: Vann had a bird's-eye-view of the conflict in Vietnam, and in fact has been heralded in recent years as a strategist who proposed policies (including the "hearts and minds" factor) that many believe might have won the war—or at least have ended it sooner.

George, however, does bow to cliches at various points in the proceedings: at one point, Vann drunkenly walks past a brothel where a Vietnamese hooker greets him with, "I really, really like you, GI." Been there, done that in a dozen other movies, most notably PLATOON (1986) and FULL METAL JACKET (1987).

In attempting to make A BRIGHT SHINING LIE the last word on Vietnam (Vann witnesses several seminal events at which he wasn't present in real life), George denies himself the opportunity to create a wholly original war film, one that gets inside the head of one man who was important in waging it. *(Graphic violence, adult situations, profanity.)*—K.W.

d, Terry George; p, Greg Ricketson; exec p, Lois Bonfiglio; assoc p, James B. Bigwood; w, Terry George (based on the book *A Bright Shining Lie: John Paul Vann and America in Vietnam* by Neil Sheehan); ph, Jack Conroy; ed, Nicholas Beauman; m, Gary Chang; prod d, Graham "Grace" Walker; art d, Tom Nursey, Kuladee Suchartanun; set d, Adam Slater, Caroline Usher; sound, Gary Wilkins (mixer); fx, Kevin Chisnall; casting, Dianne Crittenden; cos, Joan Bergin; makeup, Gigs Coker; stunts, Richard Boue

Drama/Historical/War/Political (PR: O MPAA: R)

BROADWAY DAMAGE ★½

(U.S., 1998) 110m Broadway Damage LP; Village Art Pictures ~ Jour de Fete Films c

Mara Hobel *(Cynthia)*; Michael Shawn Lucas *(Marc)*; Hugh Panaro *(David)*; Aaron Williams *(Robert)*; Gary Janetti *(Zola)*; Gerry McIntyre *(Jerry)*; Tyagi Schwartz *(Carl)*; Alan Filderman *(Casting Director)*; James Lecesne *(Cruise Ship Actor)*; Barbara Winters Pinto *(Temp Agent)*; Benim Foster *(The Super)*; Jean Loup *(Punk)*; Jonathan Walker *(Chuck)*; Richard Davidson *(The John)*; Michael Jefferson *(Drag Queen)*; Steven Halsey *(Waiter Guy)*; Lucille Patton; Shirl Bernheim *(Tourists)*; Kit Rachlin; Lovette George; Kimberly Jajuan *(Back-up Singers)*; Jose Rodriguez *(Security Guard)*; Robert La Croix *(Hair-in-Face)*; Tom O'Neill *(FBI Agent)*; Jay Hostetler *(Chester)*; Howard Kaye *("Peter Duquett")*; James Brosnan *("Jeremy")*

BROADWAY DAMAGE is a very slight entertainment about a trio of young hopefuls in New York.

Marc (Michael Shawn Lucas) and Cynthia (Mara Hobel) take an apartment in Greenwich Village and with the assistance of their friend Robert (Aaron Williams), fix it up nicely. All three seek success in New York, Marc as an actor, Robert as a composer, and Cynthia as personal assistant to magazine editor Tina Brown.

One morning, Marc meets David (Hugh Panaro), also an aspiring composer. They spend the day together, and then make love, but afterward David tells Marc that he's already in a relationship. Robert, unable to find romance, is advised by Cynthia to act on his attraction to Marc. Cynthia, all the while, relentlessly pursues Tina Brown and attempts to contact her continually.

David breaks with his lover and moves in with Marc and Cynthia. One night, Marc goes to visit David at his job, but is told he has quit. Marc returns home to find a sobbing Cynthia, upset because her father has ceased sending her money. Later, the two are visited by David's former lover (Jonathan Walker), who warns them that David is taking advantage of them. When David returns the next morning, he tells a skeptical Marc that he'd spent the night composing music for a film. A few days later, Marc and Robert learn from a magazine ad that David is a prostitute. With Cynthia, they throw David's possessions out of the apartment. That evening, Robert allows Marc and Cynthia to hear a love song he has composed with Marc in mind.

Unable to pay her share of the rent, Cynthia moves to her parents' house on Long Island. Soon after, she invites her two friends to visit, and they are surprised to learn that her parents own a mansion. During their stay, Marc and Robert become lovers, and Cynthia receives news that Tina Brown, impressed with Cynthia's persistence, has hired her.

BROADWAY DAMAGE is a contemporary rendering of traditional Hollywood movies about "making it big in the big city" (the 1955 version of MY SISTER EILEEN comes to mind). Despite the fashionable inclusions of sex and four-letter words, the film is insistently good-natured as it follows the fresh young protagonists on their quests for fame and fortune. The Greenwich Village they inhabit bears no resemblance to any real New York neighborhood; it's a magical place where dreams come true, and romance is as nearby as the apartment across the alley.

Yet for all its presumed charm, BROADWAY DAMAGE is mostly leaden, done in by slack direction, a cliched script, and undistinguished performances. The direction by Victor Mignatti (his debut) is capable but lacks energy. His pacing is slow and at its length, the film seems protracted. The script (also by Mignatti) depends too heavily on formulaic plot turns and such lines of dialogue as, "life should be more like a Broadway musical." While all the characterizations are stereotypical, the character of Cynthia is particularly problematic. Unlike Marc and Robert, who are intended to be boyishly charming, Cynthia is portrayed as slovenly, petulant, and spoiled. In stark contrast to Marc and Robert, her romantic needs are never addressed and her sexual behavior is presented as ridiculous. The character is obviously meant to provide comic relief, but as many of the gags are based on her gender, the whole conception of the character comes across as misogynist.

To its credit, BROADWAY DAMAGE looks and sounds good. Cinematographer Michael Mayers, who's credits include SPANKING THE MONKEY (1994), really does make Greenwich Village look like a wonderland, and production designer Dina Goldman has put together a dream of a New York apartment. The film's other technical aspects are similarly of a high professional caliber.

The idea that carries BROADWAY DAMAGE is that in the cynical, competitive environment of New York's entertainment industry, optimism and an upbeat sensibility can still win out. It's not the notion that's square and outdated here. It's the ineptitude that has never been in vogue. *(Sexual situations, extreme profanity.)*—D.C.

d, Victor Mignatti; p, David Topel; assoc p, Bruce Lang, Keith Lewis, Paul Scoles; w, Victor Mignatti; ph, Michael Mayers; ed, Victor Mignatti; m, Elliot Sokolov, Cindy Soltoff, Gabriel Zenone, Ken Dahl; prod d, Dina Goldman; art d, Rich Devine; sound, Theresa Radka (recordist); casting, Alan Filderman; cos, Jill Kliber; makeup, Kelvin Trahan; stunts, Aaron Williams

Romance/Comedy/Drama (PR: C MPAA: NR)

BROTHER ★★★

(Russia, 1997) 96m STW Film Company; Roskomkino ~ Kino International c
(AKA: BRAT)

Sergei Bodrov Jr. *(Danila Bragov)*; Victor Soukhoroukov *(Viktor Bragov)*; Svetlana Pismichenko *(Sveta)*; Maria Zhukova *(Kat)*; Yuri Kuznetsov *(The German)*; Viatcheslav Boutoussov *(Boutoussov)*

Perceptive and well-made, BROTHER tells the tale of a discharged Russian soldier who falls into a life of crime.

Danila (Sergei Bodrov Jr.) return home after completing his military service. His mother encourages him to emulate his older brother, Viktor (Victor Suhorukov), a supposedly successful businessman living in St. Petersburg. Danila travels to see Viktor, befriending odd characters along the way, including "the German" (Yury Kuznetsov), a disgruntled street hustler, and Kat (Maria Zhukova), a pretty young drug dealer.

Finally, the brothers reunite, but Danila quickly discovers that Viktor is part of a Mafia-style gang. Viktor prods Danila to join him defeat a rival gang by shooting their leader, "the Chechen." After finding a place to live, Danila agrees to perform the assassination: he dresses in a disguise, spots "the Chechen" at an open market, and kills him with one shot. During his escape from two henchmen, Danila takes refuge in a trolley car operated by Sveta (Svetlana Pismichenko). Later, while being interrogated by the gang, Sveta covers for Danila.

Danila falls for Sveta, despite her marriage to an abusive husband, Pavel. Danila begin a serious affair, but Danila still sees Kat for drugs and partying. Viktor, meanwhile, calls on Danila again to help two fellow gang members steal back some money that was stolen by the rival gang. Danila and the two thugs wrest a suitcase of money from one of the other gang members, but the plan nearly backfires, and Danila is forced to kill and bury his two partners. Later, the rival gang members avenge the death of their leader by raping Sveta and viciously attacking Viktor. The gang also forces Viktor to entice Danila to come to his apartment, where they plan to kill him, but Danila senses a trap, and comes prepared with a shotgun. Danila kills the gang members, takes the suitcase of money, and even forgives his brother for his role in all the violence and mayhem. Back at Sveta's apartment, Danila shoots Pavel in the leg when he sees him beating Sveta. Danila then asks Sveta to run away with him, but she detests the violence, and tells him to leave. Sadly, he also says goodbye to Kat and "the German." With the blood money in hand, Danila hitches a ride to Moscow where he plans to start a new life.

Cynical but sincere, BROTHER artfully captures life in post-Glasnost, post-Soviet Russia. Writer-director Alexei Balabanov tells a caustic yet cautionary gangster tale without glorifying the violence or excusing the characters. Danila is played by the charismatic young actor, Sergei Bodrov Jr. (star of his father's 1996 film PRISONER OF THE MOUNTAINS), but he remains a troubled and troubling antihero, a man all-too-easily willing to use violence as a means to an end. Unlike the typical Hollywood gloss on such protagonists, BROTHER's approach cryptically indicts both the military and the Westernized culture as influences on Danila's disaffected (though seemingly numb) mindset.

On a purely literal level, Balabanov's story lacks dimension and originality (at times, the film resembles classic gangster pictures); also, Sveta's role is not properly developed in order to help viewers understand her loyalty to her abusive husband but not Danila. Still, Balabanov's use of controlled composition (favoring warm, autumnal hues) and reflexive humor (with running gags about Danila's choice in rock music and his hatred for film directors) sets BROTHER apart from the more conventional forays of its type. Also, the sad but hopeful conclusion turns a merely violent exercise into a learning experience. BROTHER is understated but should not be overlooked. *(Violence, nudity, sexual situations, adult situations, substance abuse, extreme profanity.)*—E.M.

d, Alexei Balabanov; p, Alexei Balabanov; w, Alexei Balabanov; ph, Serguei Astakhov; ed, Marina Lipartiya; m, Viatcheslav Boutoussov; prod d, Vladimir Kartakov

Crime/Drama **(PR: C MPAA: NR)**

BRYLCREEM BOYS, THE ★★★

(U.K., 1997) 105m Rough Magic Films; Freewheel Productions; Ealing Studios Productions ~ Ciby Sales c

Bill Campbell *(Myles Keogh)*; Jean Butler *(Mattie Guerin)*; Gabriel Byrne *(Commandant O'Brien)*; Angus MacFadyen *(Rudolph von Stegenbeck)*; Joe McGann *(Captain Deegan)*; William McNamara *(Sam Gunn)*; Hal Fowler *(Bunty Winthrop)*; J. Anders Jillebo *(Sten Larsen)*; B.J. Hogg *(Sean)*; Colom Doherty *(Seamus)*; John Gordon Sinclair *(Richard Lewis)*; Oliver Tobias *(Hans Jorg Wolff)*; Hugh Vyvyan *(Henshaw)*; Marc Sinden *(Senior Allied Officer White)*; Tim Haynes *(Sergeant Walsh)*; Peter Woodward *(Ernst Stossel)*; Christopher Ryan *(Colin Parker)*; Rupert Wickham *(Preuss)*; Magnus McLeod *(Olenski)*; Matthew Penry-Davey *(Bauer)*; Alan Barry *(Mr. Guerin)*; Aine Ni Mhuiri *(Nonie)*; Jerome Pradon *(Ricard)*; Marek Vasut *(Krach)*; Matthew Idiens *(Festner)*; Clifford Hadyn-Tovey *(Horse Owner)*; David Artus *(Scarred Flier)*; Alister McLeod *(Sergeant Marshall)*; Anthony Madigan *(Policeman)*; Conor Breen *(1st Guard)*; Simon Buttimore *(Man with Cart)*; Jack O'Dwyer *(Michael)*; James Ryan *(Boy at Races)*; Michael Perberdy *(Vet)*; Neils Bruno Schmidt *(Schmidt)*; Illiam Jones *(Young Boy)*; Donal Lunny; Sharon Shannon; Nollaig Casey *(Musicians)*; Brendan Galway; Stephen Byrne; Lorcan Murphy; Kevin McCormack *(Irish Dancers)*

Time was, any new war epic inevitably claimed to be "The Last Great Untold Story of WWII!!!" Affable, peculiar, and a bit contrived, THE BRYLCREEM BOYS could well live up to that billing.

September, 1941. A dogfight ends with both Royal Air Force squadron leader Myles Keogh (Bill Campbell) and German pilot Rudolph von Stegenbeck (Angus MacFadyen) parachuting into the Republic of Ireland. The Irish government maintains its diplomatic neutrality by imprisoning any soldier, Allied or Axis, who arrives uninvited, and so both are sent to the same compound and held with other stranded British and German soldiers and sailors. Irish Commandant O'Brien (Gabriel Byrne) runs the place humanely and with a sense of irony, having once been held here as a prisoner of the British during Ireland's struggle for independence.

During the day the prisoners, nicknamed "the Brylcreem Boys" for their slicked-back hairstyles, can leave the camp on an honors system. Both Keogh and von Stegenbeck want to escape and rejoin the war, but their respective governments have ordered all POWs to remain where they are, hoping to curry favor with the Irish government. Myles' discontent is fueled when he becomes the lover of local lass Mattie Guerin (Jean Butler), who is also seeing von Stegenbeck. Keogh's cocky American roommate Sam Gunn (William McNamara), escapes to London. When he is returned, his bitter account of London under siege by the Nazis stirs a riot between the Allied and German factions. Energized, the British decide to escape en masse on New Year's Eve. During the breakout, however, Keogh chances to rescue von Stegenbeck from a murder plot by some fellow Germans, and the commotion alerts the Irish guards. But their guns are loaded only with blanks. O'Brien lets Keogh, von Stegenbeck, and the others get away, knowing most will be rounded up in the next few days. An exception is Keogh, who rejoins the RAF and is killed in action months later. Von Stegenbeck is recaptured, spends the remainder of the war at the Irish camp, and later marries Mattie Guerin, becoming stepfather to her child—by Keogh.

Even though it turns into a sort of vest-pocket edition of THE GREAT ESCAPE (1963) in the end, THE BRYLCREEM BOYS is less a rousing action spectacle than a look at a very real time, place, and political stance that turns the standard celluloid POW yarn on its head. Unlike post-Vietnam era war films that emphasize the gruesome carnage, THE BRYLCREEM BOYS coasts along on Ireland's eccentric, self-serving (and, in flashes, marvelously enlightened and sensible) nonpartisan role in WWII. Director/co-writer Terence Ryan seems to downplay the potential for overt humor that, say, classic British Ealing comedies would have brought out nicely (the image of His Majesty's military under the Irish boot would surely be verboten for the English cinema of yesteryear).

The script fall back on too many stolid, cliched characters, like von Stegenbeck—the standard "good German," an honor-bound, aristocratic Prussian who listens aghast to news of the Nazi atrocities. Then there's token Yankee Sam Gunn, a small-time Hollywood actor who only enlisted in the RAF (before America's entry in the war) as a publicity stunt. By comparison the love story with fiery colleen Mattie goes down rather easily. Actress/dancer Jean Butler came to prominence in the phenomenally popular stage show "Riverdance," and here both performs and choreographs an energetic pub jig. *(Violence, adult situations, sexual situations, profanity.)*—C.C.

d, Terence Ryan; p, Alan Latham, Bernie Stampfer, Terence Ryan, Paul Madigan; exec p, Kristi Prenn, Mohammed Yusef; assoc p, Stephen Margolis, Jo Gilbert, Pat Ferns, Sara Giles; co-p, Gabriel Byrne, Jamie Brown; w, Terence Ryan, Jamie Brown, Susan Morrall; ph, Gerry Lively; ed, Emma E. Hickox; m, Richard Hartley; prod d, Steve Hardie; art d, Shane Kenny; set d, Peta Button; ch, Jean Butler; sound, Barry Reed (mixer); fx, Alan Wibley, Jim Francis; casting, Donald Paul Pemrick, Jo Gilbert; cos, David Murphy; makeup, Sandra Exelby; stunts, Tony Smart

War/Prison/Drama (PR: C MPAA: PG-13)

BUDBRINGEREN
(SEE: JUNK MAIL)

BUFFALO '66 ★★★★
(Canada/U.S., 1998) 101m Cinepix Film; Muse Productions; Lions Gate Films ~ Lions Gate Films c

Vincent Gallo *(Billy Brown)*; Anjelica Huston *(Janet "Jan" Brown)*; Christina Ricci *(Layla)*; Ben Gazzara *(Jimmy Brown)*; Rosanna Arquette *(Wendy Balsam)*; Mickey Rourke *(Bookie)*; Kevin Corrigan *(Goon)*; Jan-Michael Vincent *(Sonny)*; Kevin Pollak *(TV Sportscaster)*; Alex Karras *(TV Sportscaster)*; John Sansone *(Little Billy Brown)*; Manny Fried *(The Donut Clerk)*; John Rummel *(Don Shanks)*; Bob Wahl *(Scott Woods)*; Penny Wolfgang *(Judge Penny M. Wolfgang)*; Anthony Mydcarz *(The Motel Clerk)*; Michael Maciejewski *(The Guy in the Bathroom)*; Jack Claxton *(The Denny's Host)*; Dominic Telesco *(The Prison Guard)*; Carl Marchi *(The Cafe Owner)*; Kim Krah *(The Denny's Waitress)*; Julius DiGennaro *(The Info Booth Clerk)*; Terry Braunstein *(The Tap Dance Teacher)*; Jack Hunter *(The Gas Station Clerk)*; Norma Gelose *(The Bus Station Woman)*; Jamie King *(The Tap Dance Kids)*; Janel King *(The Tap Dance Kids)*; The Beautiful Scott Woods Sexxotic Dancers: Ghennifer Dennis; Erin Markle; Valeria Hildebrandt; Michelle McCluskey; Terese Lenandowski; Kim Bradway; Dana Thompson; Karen Sitter; Michelle Koninick; Amy Jakabowski; Tara Thompson

The directorial debut of actor Vincent Gallo, BUFFALO '66 is the kind of independent film that truly defines the genre. Alternately funny and touching, this story of a humiliated loser returning home after a spell in prison is an utterly unique vision.

Billy Brown (Vincent Gallo) is released from prison after five years. It's a long wait for the bus to take him home to nearby Buffalo, NY, and by the time it arrives he desperately needs to urinate. His search for a public toilet in downtown Buffalo takes him into a building where a tap-dance class is in progress. He borrows a quarter from one of the students, Layla (Christina Ricci), to call his parents. Having told them that he has been working for the government to cover up his incarceration, he says that he is in town for the day with his wife and would like to come and see them. Billy then kidnaps Layla and demands that she pose as his wife, "Wendy." Not terribly afraid of the unarmed Billy, Layla agrees.

Billy's parents Jan (Anjelica Houston) and Jimmy (Ben Gazzara) warmly welcome "Wendy," who gamely praises her "husband" to the skies. They react less well to their son, however; Jimmy is openly hostile, while the football-obsessed Jan has never gotten over the fact that she missed seeing the local team at a playoff game when she was giving birth to Billy.

Before they leave, Billy calls his only friend, dimwitted Goon (Kevin Corrigan.) We learn that Billy went to prison after confessing to a crime he didn't commit, as part of a deal with a bookie (Mickey Rourke) to whom he owed $10,000 after betting on the Buffalo football team. Billy blames his loss, and the ruin of his life, on the team's place-kicker Scott Woods for missing a climactic field goal, and swears he will kill him. Goon tells him that Woods now owns a strip bar, where he can be found late each night.

To kill time, Billy take Layla bowling, and then to a diner. There they run into the real Wendy (Rosanna Arquette), whom Billy had a crush on all through school but who never gave him a second look. They leave and go to a motel room, where Layla tries to make clear to Billy that she likes him, but can't break through his self-loathing. Without telling her what he is up to, Billy goes to Woods's club armed with a pistol to kill him. But after fantasizing about the murder, he decides not to go through with it, realizing that he has been blessed with a pretty girl who likes him. He buys Layla a hot chocolate and goes back to their room.

Gallo, an idiosyncratic actor best known for Calvin Klein ads and supporting roles in films like THE FUNERAL (1996) and PALOOKAVILLE (1996), reportedly controlled every single aspect of the production of BUFFALO '66. The film steadfastly proceeds as Gallo wants it to, depending on the viewer to catch onto its peculiar design rather than playing to preconceived notions. Unshaven, greasy, and cadaverously skinny, Billy Brown is anything but sympathetic, and seems potentially dangerous until we realize how empty his threats are. Trying to get Layla to make him look good in front of his parents, he both threatens to kill her and childishly promises that if she does good he'll be her best friend. This is obviously a character whose emotional growth stopped at about the age of 12.

It isn't until we meet Billy's parents, played as monsters of indifference by Ben Gazzara and Anjelica Houston, that the film's unreality becomes clear: this is life seen through the eyes of a self-pitying loser, a vision taken to extremes. The neat trick that Gallo performs is to balance pity with humor, leavening each element with a stiff dose of the other.

Shot entirely in Gallo's hometown of Buffalo, NY, BUFFALO '66 doesn't so much escape its low budget (less than $2 million) as work its way around it. The editing, compositions, and photography (Gallo shot the film on a special reversal stock, developed for news photography, to get the particular look he wanted) all give the film a grainy, immediate look. So does the music, mixing an original score by Gallo with subtly chosen progressive rock from the 1970s. And Christina Ricci, in her first adult role, strikes a special chemistry with her costar, making it plausible that there is something worth caring about in the world's biggest loser. *(Violence, adult situations, profanity.)*—M.F.

d, Vincent Gallo; p, Chris Hanley; exec p, Michael Paseornek, Jeff Sackman, John Dunning, Andre Link; assoc p, Lauren Buckley, Janet Gallo, Timothy Peternel; co-p, Jordan Gertner, Gerry Gershman, Deborah Brock; w, Vincent Gallo (from his screen story); ph, Lance Acord; ed, Curtiss Clayton; m, Vincent Gallo; prod d, Gideon Ponte; art d, James Chinlund; set d, Jeanne

Develle; sound, Brian Miksis (mixer); fx, Paul Murphy; cos, Beatrix Pasztor; makeup, Gucci Westman

Drama/Comedy **(PR: C MPAA: R)**

BUG'S LIFE, A ★★★
(U.S., 1998) 94m PIXAR Animation Studios; Walt Disney ~ Buena Vista c

VOICES OF: Dave Foley *(Flik)*; Kevin Spacey *(Hopper)*; Julia Louis-Dreyfus *(Pricess Atta)*; Hayden Panettiere *(Dot)*; Phyllis Diller *(Queen)*; Richard Kind *(Molt)*; David Hyde Pierce *(Slim)*; Joe Ranft *(Heimlich)*; Denis Leary *(Francis)*; Jonathan Harris *(Manny)*; Madeline Kahn *(Gypsy)*; Bonnie Hunt *(Rosie)*; Michael McShane *(Tuck & Roll)*; John Ratzenberger *(P.T. Flea)*; Brad Garrett *(Dim)*; Roddy McDowall *(Mr. Soil)*; Edie McClurg *(Dr. Flora)*; Alex Rocco *(Thorny)*; David Ossman *(Cornelius)*

1998's second computer-animated insect movie, Disney's A BUG'S LIFE is similar in many ways to DreamWorks's earlier ANTZ, but it's geared more for kids, and is much more visually accomplished, having been made by the team responsible for the first computer-animated feature, TOY STORY (1995), which surpasses its original achievement by "filming" this one in widescreen.

A colony of ants gather food as an offering to a marauding gang of grasshoppers led by Hopper (voice of Kevin Spacey), but when one of the ants, Flik (voice of Dave Foley), accidentally knocks over the food, Hopper demands that they double their offering when he returns at the end of the season. The Queen (voice of Phyllis Diller) sends Flik away from ant island and into the city to find some tough bugs to help defend the colony, but he returns with a band of inept flea circus performers whom he mistakes for warriors. When Flik learns who they really are, he keeps the truth from the other ants, but after a bird attacks the ant colony, Flik is inspired to create a mechanical bird to scare off the grasshoppers. When the flea circus owner arrives to reclaim his performers, the angry Queen banishes Flik from the colony.

Hopper and his gang arrive to collect their food, but there isn't nearly enough and they take the Queen hostage. Her daughter Dot (voice of Hayden Panettiere) flies after Flik and brings him back, along with the circus performers. While the performers entertain Hopper with a show, Flik and some ants sneak into the mechanical bird and attack the grasshoppers, but the bird crashes and falls apart. Hopper beats up Flik, but Flik convinces the other ants that they're not an inferior, subservient species, and they successfully repel the grasshoppers, whom they vastly outnumber. Hopper tries to get away, but a real bird comes along and feeds him to its babies.

Although comparisons to ANTZ are inevitable, A BUG'S LIFE was in preparation long before the former was even a glint in the eye of DreamWorks's Jeffrey Katzenberg, who seems intent on sabotaging his former employer, Disney, with preemptive strikes against their biggest movies (e.g., DEEP IMPACT vs. ARMAGEDDON). While both movies concern ant colonies that are roused into rebellion against their mechanical existence by a nebbishy misfit, ANTZ had a much darker and monotonous sensibility—visually, as much of the film took place in a depressing METROPOLIS-like underground colony, and thematically, as the story involved a genocide plot by a maniacal general to kill off the worker ants. BUG'S LIFE has its share of scares (particularly Kevin Spacey's menacing Hopper), but being a Disney movie, they're all fairly mild, and the film's overall tone is broadly comical. The computer-animation is not only richer, more detailed, and more colorful than in ANTZ, but a good portion of the story refreshingly takes place above-ground, resulting in a variety of different types of bugs (unlike ANTZ) and a dazzling array of settings.

With the expanded horizons and larger canvas, the use of widescreen occasionally results in the same kind of suspension of disbelief as in the great Disney animated classics; not so that one thinks he or she is looking at real life, but rather, an artistic representation of it, such as in the beautifully "photographed" shots of the blue and purple-streaked night sky. The depiction of the city as a kind of Times Square consisting of tin cans and used food cartons, in which derelict bugs hold signs reading "Kids pulled off my wings," is very amusing, as is a Mexican-style cantina inside an old sombrero, featuring a band playing "La Cucaracha." During the flea circus performance, the screen bursts into a kaleidoscope of rapid movement and brilliant hues, and the performers—including an insecure male ladybug, a hammy praying mantis, a gentle black widow spider, a caterpillar with a humorous German accent, a sloth-like rhino beetle, and a gorgeous Gypsy moth—have all been given distinctive personalities and are exquisitely rendered. Although the story is formulaic (what kids movies aren't?) and a bit long, about the only real advantage that ANTZ had was the voice of Woody Allen as the protagonist, as Dave Foley is too bland in the similar role here. The rest of the voice cast is excellent, however, including the inimitable Jonathan Harris (Dr. Smith from "Lost in Space"), and Roddy McDowall, in his final role, while a gag reel of "outtakes" during the end-credits is a hilarious touch, even if most people won't see it.—M.S.

d, John Lasseter, Andrew Stanton; p, Kevin Reher, Darla K. Anderson; exec p, Steven Jobs, Edwin Catmull; w, Andrew Stanton, Donald McEnery, Bob Shaw; ph, Sharon Calahan; ed, Lee Unkrich; m, Randy Newman; prod d, William Cone; art d, Tia W. Kratter, Bob Pauley; anim, Glenn McQueen, Rich Quade, Ewan Johnson; sound, Gary Rydstrom; casting, Ruth Lambert, Mary Hidalgo

AAN Best Original Musical or Comedy Score: Randy Newman

Animated/Children's **(PR: A MPAA: G)**

BULLET ON A WIRE ★★★
(U.S., 1998) 84m Provisional bw

Jeff Strong *(Raymond)*; Lara Phillips *(Tanya)*; Paula Killen *(Norma)*; David Yow *(Ed—Tanya's Boyfriend)*; Rex Benson; Robert Maffia; Richard Kern *(Bartender)*

A small triumph of persistence over poverty, BULLET ON A WIRE is an ambitious if somewhat amateurish drama about the tragic consequences of a mean-spirited prank.

Raymond (Jeff Strong), a middle-aged ex-convict, is distraught when he fails to pick up a woman in a bar. For consolation, he visits his unmarried sister Norma (Paula Killen) at the hospital where she works, but when Norma tells Raymond that she is too busy with patients to talk with him, he becomes jealous. Without Norma's knowledge, he takes a patient's file from her desk and secretly calls a phone number he finds in it. When a woman answers, he advises her that her daughter is HIV-positive and pregnant, and hangs up.

The daughter, Tanya (Lara Phillips), is confronted by her furious parents as she arrives home later that day. When her stepfather assaults her during the ensuing argument, Tanya retrieves a gun from her bedroom and shoots him dead. She is charged with his killing and imprisoned.

As news of the killing spreads, Norma deduces that Raymond made the phone call. She castigates him for his action but declines to turn him over to the police, although she warns him that the call is being investigated. Raymond visits Tanya in prison but does not admit what he has done, merely identifying himself as Norma's brother. The two engage in small talk and become friendly. Tanya's raffish boyfriend, Ed (David Yow), also visits Tanya, and tries to get her to sell her sensational story to a tabloid television show. Although initially angered by Ed's callousness, Tanya eventually agrees to meet with the show's representatives. When Raymond visits Tanya a second time, he tells her that he made the call. A shaken Tanya orders him to leave and not come back. Sometime later, Tanya is visited by Norma, who is startled when Tanya tells her of Raymond's visits. As the women talk, Tanya says that she has grown to like Raymond, and wishes they could have met under normal circumstances.

Raymond returns to the same bar he left on the day he made the call. This time, he talks with confidence to a woman he meets, and continues to talk with her until a pair of police detectives arrive and take him away.

Shot in a week on a budget of less than $25,000, BULLET ON A WIRE is aptly described as primitive. In its ambition and confidence, however, this 16mm black-and-white feature recalls such other budgetless debut features as FEAR AND DESIRE (1953) and THE UNBELIEVEABLE TRUTH (1990). And while Chicago filmmaker Jim Sikora may not necessarily hold the promise of a Stanley Kubrick or even a Hal Hartley, the intelligent determination he demonstrates here more than makes up for a lack of resources.

Sikora wisely avoids doing anything too fancy, and BULLET ON A WIRE is quite effective within its means. The film's structure is relatively simple. Sikora disposes of the story's more active elements in the film's first half-hour, and then shifts towards its true dramatic intent, a study of how these characters come to relate to one another in light of an adverse circumstance. Sikora and co-scenarist Joe Carducci manage to achieve a certain poignancy through their depictions of people who in one way or another have reached a dead end: Raymond, through his criminal past and inability to relate to women; Tonya, through her crime and association with men like Ed; Norma, through her job and solitude. These three-dimensional characterizations serve as an interesting counterpoint to the film's unglamorous look.

While the film's low budget is very evident, in its often murky cinematography, tinny soundtrack, and amateurish acting, BULLET ON A WIRE does have some surprisingly assured touches, including a mise-en-scene that frequently accentuates the characters' feelings of isolation, and several fluid tracking shots that are used to good menacing effect. It also makes terrific use of Chicago locations, imbuing them with a bleak noirish tone. Yet it is Sikora's faith in both his ability and his subject matter (obvious in his admirably straightforward treatment of potentially lurid material) that makes this film work. Lacking an adequate budget, and the actors and technical support that such funding would bring, Sikora has nonetheless put together a thoughtful and compelling feature. *(Violence, extreme profanity.)*—D.C.

d, Jim Sikora; p, Jim Sikora; w, Joe Carducci, Jim Sikora (from a story by Jim Sikora); ph, John Terendy; ed, Chris Taylor; m, The Denison-Kimball Trio

Crime/Drama **(PR: C MPAA: NR)**

BULWORTH ★★★★

(U.S., 1998) 108m 20th Century Fox ~ 20th Century Fox c

Warren Beatty *(Sen. Jay Billington Bulworth)*; Halle Berry *(Nina)*; Oliver Platt *(Murphy)*; Don Cheadle *(L.D.)*; Paul Sorvino *(Graham Crockett)*; Jack Warden *(Davers)*; Christine Baranski *(Constance Bulworth)*; Joshua Malina *(Bill Feldman)*; Richard Sarafian *(Vinnie)*; Isaiah Washington *(Darnell)*; Amiri Baraka *(Rastaman)*; Sean Astin *(Gary)*; Laurie Metcalf *(Mimi)*; Wendell Pierce *(Fred)*; Michele Morgan *(Cheryl)*; Ariyan Johnson *(Tanya)*; Larry King *(Himself)*; Nora Dunn *(Missy Berliner)*; Kimberly Deauna Adams *(Denisha)*; Vinny Argiro *(Debate Director)*; Kirk Baltz *(Debate Producer)*; Ernie Banks *(Leroy)*; Adilah Barnes *(Mrs. Brown)*; Graham Beckel *(Man With Dark Glasses)*; Brandon N. Bowlin *(Bouncer 2)*; Mongo Brownlee *(Henchman 3)*; Thomas Jefferson Byrd *(Uncle Rafeeq)*; J. Kenneth Campbell *(Anthony)*; Scott Michael Campbell *(Head Valet)*; Jann Carl *(Herself)*; Kerry Cantanese *(Video Reporter 4)*; Dave Allen Clark *(Himself)*; Terry Cooley *(Henchman 2)*; Kevin Cooney *(Reverend Wilberfore)*; Christopher Curry *(Journalist)*; Stanley DeSantis *(Manny Liebowitz)*; Michael Clarke Duncan *(Bouncer)*; Jerry Dunphy *(Himself)*; Chris Mulkey *(Cop 2)*; Lou Myers *(Uncle Tyrone)*; Shawna Hagler *(Technical Director)*; Jonathan Roger Neal *(Little Gangsta)*; Ron Ostrow *(Staff Member)*; Norman Parker *(Irwin Tannenbaum)*; James Pickens Jr. *(Uncle David)*; Kenneth Randle *(Little Gangsta)*; Tony Tomas Randle *(Little Gangsta)*; Arthur Reggie III *(Little Gangsta)*; Adrian Ricard *(Aunt Alice)*; Ava Rivera *(Video Reporter 3)*; Robert Scheer *(Journalist)*; Sam Shamshak *(Fundraiser Guest)*; Sarah Silverman *(2nd American Politics Assistant)*; Brooke Skulski *(Reporter)*; Be-Be Smith *(Aunt Harriet)*; Roberto Soto *(Reporter)*; Florence Stanley *(Dobish)*; Quinn Sullivan *(Fundraiser Server)*; JoAnn D. Thomas *(Rapper)*; Robin Thomas *(Reporter in Hallway)*; Sheryl Underwood *(Woman at Frankie's)*; Gary H. Walton *(Bouncer 4)*; Andrew Warne *(Video Reporter)*; Lee Weaver *(Man in Church 2)*; Kenn Whitaker *(Henchman 1)*; Jermaine Williams *(Paul Robeson)*; John Witherspoon *(Reverend Morris)*; Sumiko Telljohn *(Lady at Banquet)*; George Hamilton *(Himself)*; John McLaughlin *(Voice of TV Commentator)*; William Baldwin; Paul Mazursky

Warren Beatty makes a triumphant return to the spirit of his 1970s political films (THE PARALLAX VIEW, SHAMPOO, MCCABE AND MRS. MILLER), as director, star, and cowriter of BULWORTH, an audacious black comedy that caustically dissects the body politic and is arguably the most radical attack on American institutions ever seen in a Hollywood movie.

On the eve of the 1996 California primary, Democratic Sen. Jay Bulworth (Warren Beatty) is depressed and hasn't eaten or slept for three days. A former crusading liberal who once fought for minorities, Bulworth now spouts conservative rhetoric and has sold out to special-interest groups who contribute money for his campaign. In exchange for tying up a health-care bill, insurance industry lobbyist Graham Crockett (Paul Sorvino) agrees to sell Bulworth a $10 million life insurance policy, after which, Bulworth takes out a hit on himself. Bulworth then gets drunk and goes to a black church in South Central LA, where he shocks his coke-snorting campaign manager Murphy (Oliver Platt) by tossing aside his prepared speech, hurling racial insults at the audience, and admitting that politicians don't care about them. In the crowd is the beautiful Nina (Halle Berry), who follows Bulworth to his next stop, a posh Hollywood fund-raiser, where he insults the crowd with anti-Semitic comments and trashes their lousy movies.

Bulworth invites Nina to ride in his limo and they spend the night dancing and getting high at an after-hours nightclub. The next day, Bulworth delivers a diatribe in the form of a "rap" about corrupt business practices and campaign finance reform during an insurance company fund-raiser, which enrages Crockett. Suddenly feeling reinvigorated, Bulworth frantically tries to call off the hit, but the word doesn't get through. After a TV debate in which Bulworth dresses as a rapper and delivers a profanity-laced diatribe against the media, Nina takes him back to her house and reveals that she was hired to help arrange the hit, but has changed her mind. While walking through Nina's impoverished neighborhood, Bulworth saves some gun-toting, drug-selling kids from the cops and clashes with the local pusher (Don Cheadle). Bulworth then passes out at Nina's house and sleeps for two days. When he awakens, he learns that he has been overwhelmingly reelected, but after addressing the throngs of reporters gathered outside, he's gunned down by Crockett.

While it would be easy to dismiss BULWORTH as the self-aggrandizing, guilt-ridden rantings of a disillusioned white liberal (not to mention an interracial sexual fantasy), the simple fact that a mainstream American movie was made at all which explicitly extols socialism, while directly accusing the US government, big business, and the media of being greedy, corrupt, and evil, and systematically involved in a conspiracy to destroy minorities and the working class, is amazing. That it was released by Rupert Murdoch's Fox studio is even more astounding, especially since Murdoch reportedly (and quite understandably) despises the movie. Whether or not one agrees with its message, it's irrefutable that Beatty argues his risky thesis logically and imaginatively, with irreverent humor worthy of a latter-day Preston Sturges. The rapper outfit which Bulworth wears and his heroics among the black community have come under fire, but the movie is an equal opportunity offender and its intentionally anti-PC stance is refreshing and exhilarating, featuring some of the most blistering language heard in a movie in ages.

It also has the courage to deal with rap music as an outgrowth of the social and economic conditions of the ghettos in which most rappers are raised and argues that the real obscenity in America is not their lyrics but the injustice of a country in which corporations get rich by moving factories abroad, thereby destroying inner-city, blue-collar families. Despite the anarchic comedy, the film is really a despairing lament for the betrayal of the revolutionary 1960s, as indicated by the shots of pictures in Bulworth's office of him with Martin Luther King, Bobby Kennedy, and others, as he rehearses his conservative rote speech about "standing on the doorstep of the new millennium." Indeed, the whole film seems to be a throwback to the kind of social satire that Michael Ritchie or Robert Altman made in the '70s, but Beatty does a more than creditable job as director, and just as Bulworth becomes liberated by telling the truth, Beatty gives a fantastically exuberant and inventive comic performance, his best in decades. BULWORTH is not perfect, but it has more intelligence and more balls than any Hollywood film in years, and actually has the nerve to challenge an audience's complacency and ask it to think, something that is definitely considered to be obscene in today's market. *(Extreme profanity, violence, sexual situations.)*—M.S.

d, Warren Beatty; p, Warren Beatty, Pieter Jan Brugge, Lauren Shuler Donner; co-p, Frank Capra III, Vickie Thomas; w, Warren Beatty, Jeremy Pikser; ph, Vittorio Storaro; ed, Robert C. Jones, Billy Weber; m, Ennio Morricone; prod d, Dean Tavoularis; art d, William F. O'Brien; set d, Marvin March; sound, Tommy Causey (mixer); fx, Pacific Title Digital; cos, Milena Canonero

AAN Best Original Screenplay: Warren Beatty, Jeremy Pikser

Political/Comedy **(PR: C MPAA: R)**

BURN HOLLYWOOD BURN ★★

(U.S., 1998) 115m Alan Smithee Productions; Ben Myron Productions; Cinergi; Hollywood Pictures ~ Buena Vista c (AKA: AN ALAN SMITHEE FILM)

Ryan O'Neal *(James Edmunds)*; Coolio *(Dion Brothers)*; Chuck D *(Leon Brothers)*; Richard Jeni *(Jerry Glover)*; Eric Idle *(Alan Smithee)*; Sylvester Stallone; Whoopi Goldberg; Jackie Chan *(Themselves)*; Leslie Stefanson *(Michelle Rafferty)*; Sandra Bernhard *(Ann Glover)*; Harvey Weinstein *(Sam Rizzo)*; Cheri Lunghi *(Myrna Smithee)*; Gavin Palone *(Gary Samuels)*; MC Lite *(Sister Il Lumumba)*; Marcello Thedford *(Stagger Lee)*; Nicole Nagel *(Aloe Vera)*; Stephen Tobolowsky *(Bill Bardo)*; Erik King *(Wayne Jackson)*; Jim Piddock *(Attendant #1)*; Naomi Campbell *(Attendant #2)*; Marianne Muellerleile *(Sheila Caslin)*; Suli McCullough *(S.L.A.)*; Dina Spybey *(Allessandra)*; Robert Littman *(Cousin Andrew)*; Doug Walker *(Photographer)*; Robin Chivers; Robin Dugger *(Bonnie N' Clyde)*; Leslie Segar *(Big Lez)*; Duane Davis *(Black Policeman)*; Hideo Kimura; Earl Kim Shiroma *(Japanese Businessmen)*; Jesse Rambis *(Lakers Fan)*; Christopher Kelley *(British Bartender)*; Robert Evans; Robert Shapiro; Linnell Shapiro; Grant Shapiro; Brent Shapiro; Shane Black; Jeremy Baka; Mario Machado; Lisa Canning; Gary Franklin; John Corcoran; Joe Eszterhas; Naomi Eszterhas; Larry King; Peter Bart; Dominick Dunne; Billy Bob Thornton; Billy Barty; Norman Jewison; Victor Drai; Stanley Ralph Ross; Alan Smith *(Themselves)*

For those who don't know, "Alan Smithee" is the designated pseudonym used by directors who wish to remove their name from a film they feel is. . . well, not what they had hoped for. Scripter Joe Eszterhas (BASIC INSTINCT, SHOWGIRLS) used this inside joke as a springboard for BURN HOLLYWOOD BURN, a snotty diatribe against Hollywood insiders disguised as a faux-documentary about a director unfortunately saddled with the name Alan Smithee.

To direct "Trio," the mega-budget action movie starring Sylvester Stallone, Whoopi Goldberg, and Jackie Chan (who play themselves), producers James Edmunds (Ryan O'Neal) and Jerry Glover (Richard Jeni) hire editor Alan Smithee (Eric Idle)—not because of his talent, but because they believe he will do as he's told whenever they tug on his leash. Their plan works until the film reaches the editing room; upset by the loss of creative control in the film's cutting, Smithee steals the master print just days before its scheduled release. Unable to take his name off the credits—after all, his name *is* Alan Smithee—Smithee goes on the run, sending producers Edmunds and Glover scrambling after their $200 million investment.

After wandering the Hollywood Hills for a few days, Smithee eventually falls in with "gangsta" filmmakers the Brothers brothers (Chuck D. and Coolio). Sympathizing with Smithee, the brothers offer to negotiate with the studio on his behalf. They browbeat Edmunds and Glover into giving Smithee final cut, a right typically reserved for directors like Spielberg and Kubrick; however, the agreement is a fake, a ruse designed to lead the police back to Smithee. Smithee escapes the trap and burns the master before suffering a nervous breakdown. Desperate to recoup their losses, Edmunds and Glover devise a new film: the life of maverick director Alan Smithee, to be directed by Alan Smithee.

It seems somewhat hypocritical that writer Joe Eszterhas should harbor so much contempt for an industry that has made him very, very rich, but that is apparently the case. His depiction of Hollywood—and of producers specifically—is shallow, mean-spirited, and not particularly funny: everybody drives a black German luxury car, hangs out at tanning salons and Lakers games, and solicits oral sex from aspiring actresses. Eszterhas's agenda is abetted by a raft of cameos by high-profile Hollywood players, including lawyer Robert Shapiro, producer Robert Evans, screenwriters Billy Bob Thornton and Shane Black, and columnist Dominick Dunne; unfortunately, their appearances are often deflated by onscreen markers that categorize them as "scumbag," "hyena," or in the case of almost every woman interviewed, "feminist" (not a complimentary term in the Ezsterhas dictionary).

BURN HOLLYWOOD BURN achieves a few real moments of humor when big stars like Sylvester Stallone and Jackie Chan spoof their own larger-than-life public images by portraying themselves as self-centered egotists who, for example, will gladly hack a perfectly good script to ensure that their character doesn't die. ("I never die," explains Chan, "and even if I did die, I would be reincarnated.") Eszterhas does, however, aim a few good-natured barbs at his own work: at one point, a character describes the butchered "Trio" as "worse than SHOWGIRLS." Still, these self-deprecating moments are rare in comparison to the many unnecessarily nasty jabs at the film industry—an industry that we already knew was pretty shallow to begin with. In a transparently self-promotional move that must have seemed terribly clever at the time, director Arthur Hiller declared that the final cut of BURN HOLLYWOOD BURN was not consistent with his vision, and had his name replaced with, you guessed it, Alan Smithee, making this a true "Alan Smithee film." Perhaps not coincidentally, the Directors Guild of America announced shortly after the film's release that they were retiring the Alan Smithee pseudonym, claiming it had become so well-known that it no longer protected the director's anonymity. *(Extreme profanity, sexual situations.)*—B.T.

d, Arthur Hiller, billed as Alan Smithee; p, Ben Myron; exec p, Andrew G. Vajna; assoc p, Michael Sloan; co-p, Fred Caruso; w, Joe Eszterhas; ph, Reynaldo Villalobos; ed, L. James Langlois, Marcus Manton; m, Chuck D, Gary G-Wiz; prod d, David L. Snyder; art d, Melanie J. Baker; set d, Claudette Didul; sound, Felipe Borrero (mixer); fx, Joshua Hakian; casting, Nancy Foy; cos, Laura Cunningham; makeup, Ashlee Peterson; stunts, Mark De Alessandro

Comedy (PR: O MPAA: R)

BUSTER & CHAUNCEY'S SILENT NIGHT ★½

(U.S., 1998) 50m Project X Productions ~ Columbia TriStar c

VOICES OF: Phil Hartman *(Chauncey)*; Tom Arnold; Judy Blazer; Townsend Coleman; Jim Cummings; Gregg Edelman; Marie Osmond *(Queen)*; Harry Goz; Earl Hammond; Lea Michele; Paul Kandel

A brief running time is the virtue of this trite Christmas cartoon, "inspired by the true story of the hymn Silent Night, and the men who created it in 1818," as the credits allege.

The Queen is coming to the Austrian village of Oberndorf for Christmas, luring two mouse minstrels. Blustery Buster looks forward to the food and profits that they can make from the pretty tune written by his guileless partner Chauncey (voice of Phil Hartman). The pair move into the local church, but the Burgomeister's ferocious cat has been terrorizing all the rodents, and Chauncey survives a chase only through the protection of animal-lover Christina, an orphan waif given shelter by kindly Father Joseph Mohr and choirmaster Franz Gruber. But the cat-and-mouse antics have left the church organ damaged and unplayable on the holiest of nights. Moreover, Christina is framed for theft by a husband-and-wife team of con artists masquerading as the Queen and her "Uncle Otto," who have been looting Oberndorf's treasures as the proud Burgomeister shows them around. Chauncey can't abandon the girl who saved him, and sets off alone to free Christina, kidnapped by the villains. Selfish Buster mourns the estrangement by grinding out on his concertina the melody Chauncey had written. Father Joseph hears and adapts the haunting tune for guitar, adding his own lyrics. While Chauncey frees Christina from her bonds, Buster, who's had a change of heart, baits the dreaded cat on a chase that overturns the thieves' getaway-wagon, spilling their loot in public. The real Queen (voice of Marie Osmond) promises to convey Christina safely to her relatives in Vienna, and at Christmas Eve services Father Joseph and Franz Gruber present the simple, heavenly hymn—"Silent Night." Buster and Chauncey set off together, vowing to spread the song throughout the land.

The true source of "Silent Night" went unknown for decades, until an elderly Franz Gruber, then based in Salzburg, revealed that he and the late Mohr had composed the piece for folk guitar, after discovering that the Oberndorf church organ was made useless by vermin gnawing the bellows. More than one storyteller has romanticized the immortal carol's origin, and in 1988 there was a live-action TV special called SILENT MOUSE which posited that the mice themselves had written it. The whimsical notion is taken to extremes of mediocrity in BUSTER & CHAUNCEY'S SILENT NIGHT, a generally flavorless holiday treat (widely distributed direct-to-video) in which all characterizations feel instantly secondhand. Designs and animation (farmed out to Far East cartoon studios) rate well below "Tom & Jerry," and the role of sweetly innocent Chauncey made a melancholy coda to the life of Phil Hartman, a comedian and voice-over artist shot by his wife in a bizarre murder-suicide earlier in 1998. Small children, the target audience, may care little about either of those drawbacks, but even they should notice how the cartoon's raison d'etre, the creation of "Silent Night" (reverently performed by Marie Osmond at the end) is reduced to a mere subplot in a limp mouse tale. Among scattered new songs, only Christina's lament "Things That I've Collected" (music by Stephen Flaherty, lyrics by Lynn Ahrens) has anything remotely resembling staying power.—C.C.

d, Buzz Potamkin; p, Lee Dannecher, Buzz Pontamkin, William R. Kowalchuk; w, George Tameel, Rob Loos; m, John Van Eps; sound, Michael Ruschak

Animated/Children's/Musical (PR: AA MPAA: G)

BUTCHER BOY, THE ★★★½

(Ireland, 1997) 106m Butcher Boy Film Productions; Geffen Pictures ~ Warner Bros. c

Stephen Rea *(Benny Brady—"Da")*; Fiona Shaw *(Mrs. Nugent)*; Eamonn Owens *(Francie Brady)*; Alan Boyle *(Joe Purcell)*; Niall Buggy *(Father Dom)*; Brendan Gleeson *(Father Bubbles)*; Peter Gowen *(Leddy)*; Stuart Graham *(Priest at College)*; Ian Hart *(Uncle Alo)*; Tom Hickey *(Gardener)*; Sean Hughes *(Psychiatrist 1)*; John Kavanagh *(Dr. Boyd)*; Rosaleen Linehan *(Mrs. Canning)*; Pat McGrath *(Farmer on Tractor)*; Sean McGinley *(Sergeant)*; Gerard McSorley *(Psychiatrist 2)*; Gina Moxley *(Mary)*; Sinead O'Connor *(Our Lady/Colleen)*; Ardal O'Hanlon *(Mr. Purcell)*; Milo O'Shea *(Father Sullivan)*; Aisling O'Sullivan *(Annie Brady—"Ma")*; Anita Reeves *(Mrs. Coyle)*; Andrew Fullerton *(Philip Nugent)*; Annie O'Neill *(Mrs. McGlone)*; Joe Pilkington *(Charlie McGlone)*; Jer O'Leary *(Dublin Man)*; Pat Leavy *(Dublin Cafe Woman)*; Janet Moran *(Dublin Shopkeeper)*; Paraic Breathnach *(Man on Lorry)*; John Olohan *(Mr. Nugent)*; Mikel Murfi *(Buttsy)*; Brendan Conroy *(Devlin)*; Gregg Fitzgerald; John Finnegan; Gavin Kelty; Eoin Chaney *(Bogmen)*; Ciaran Owens *(Boy at Fountain)*; Shane O'Connor *(Boy at Fountain)*; Paolo Tullio *(Mr. Caffolla)*; Siobhan McElvaney *(Girl at Shooting Gallery)*; Aine McEneaney *(Girl at Shooting Gallery)*; Pat McCabe *(Jimmy-the-Skite)*; Tony Rohr *(Bogman in Mental Hospital)*; Birdy Sweeney *(Man in Well)*; Marie Mullen *(Mrs. Thompson)*; Macdara O'Fatharta; Ronan Wilmot *(Policeman)*; Vinnie McCabe *(Detective)*; Dermot Healy *(Bogman in Hospital)*

After directing big-scale projects like INTERVIEW WITH THE VAMPIRE (1994) and MICHAEL COLLINS (1996), filmmaker Neil Jordan returned to his forte—psychodrama with a touch of menace—in this chilling, blackly humorous adaptation of Patrick McCabe's novel.

Francie Brady (Eamonn Owens) is a 12-year-old boy with an active imagination in early-'60s Ireland. His fantasies allow him to escape his troubled household, where his father (Stephen Rea) is an abusive alcoholic and his mother (Aisling O'Sullivan) is mentally ill. He spends most of his time playing with his best friend, Joe (Alan Boyle), and tormenting busybody neighbor Mrs. Nugent (Fiona Shaw) and her son Philip (Andrew Fullerton). Mrs. Brady suffers a breakdown and is sent to the hospital, and when she is beaten by Mr. Brady upon her return, Francie runs away. After a brief stay in Dublin, he returns home, only to find that his mother has killed herself and that everyone blames him for upsetting her. In a rage, he breaks into the Nugents' house and vandalizes it, to the extent of defecating on the floor. Caught in the act, Francie is sent to a reform school, where he is put to work cutting peat and given electroshock therapy. He begins having visions of the Virgin Mary (Sinead O'Connor), who comforts and advises him. A priest (Milo O'Shea) at the school sexually abuses him. When he is released, Francie returns home to find that his father is dying and that Joe and Philip have become friends. Taking a job at a slaughterhouse, Francie has increasingly disturbed hallucinations, and after his father passes on, the unhinged boy murders Mrs. Nugent, hacking up her body and burying her in a pile of rotting vegetables. He is eventually caught and sent to an asylum. Many years later, as an adult (also played by Rea), he is released, and has one last vision of the Virgin Mary before heading back into the world.

THE BUTCHER BOY is an almost unclassifiable film: though shocking and occasionally quite gory, it's not really a horror film; though funny, it's definitely not a comedy; though filled with gravely serious incidents, it's hardly a drama. What it most assuredly is is a transfixing character study of a disturbed young boy. Francie's violent world is molded by all that he absorbs: western TV series, comic books, the Christian lessons he's been taught in school, and the news reports he sees about the atomic bomb. Jordan (who coscripted with novelist McCabe) structures the narrative as an ever-descending spiral, in which every attempt to "cure" Francie only contributes to his mania, and in which violence begets more violence. (After Francie terrorizes Philip, he is set upon by a couple of toughs in retaliation. This only leads him to strike back even harder.)

Throughout, Jordan effortlessly intertwines fantasy and reality with the help of Adrian Biddle's evocative cinematography and Elliot Goldenthal's remarkable score (which mixes different musical styles into a cohesive, pitch-perfect whole). The whole package wouldn't work, however, without the right young actor in the lead, and in first-timer Owens, Jordan has discovered a performer of remarkable, unaffected skill. With frightening realism, Owens brings to life a boy who is at the same time charming, arrogant, troubled, and capable of both great heartache and great violence. He is ably supported by a largely unfamiliar but skilled cast of performers, with young Boyle matching him beat for beat, and Rea (appearing here in his sixth film by Jordan) and O'Sullivan most convincing as Francie's troubled folks. Much was made well in advance of the film's release of the casting of singer Sinead O'Connor—infamous for her anti-Vatican stances—as the Virgin Mary, but as so often happens, the brouhaha was blown all out of proportion; neither the character nor O'Connor's portrayal is blatantly sacrilegious (although pious Christians will still have a hard time with the Virgin's rather worldly air).

The one false note in the film is its ending, which Jordan altered from McCabe's original. Soft and inconclusive, the finale doesn't provide the proper payoff for the events that proceeded it. But for this one small quibble, THE BUTCHER BOY stands as a compelling and commendably small-scale achievement from a filmmaker whose work is always interesting. *(Graphic violence, sexual situations, extreme profanity.)*—M.G.

d, Neil Jordan; p, Redmond Morris, Stephen Woolley; exec p, Neil Jordan; w, Neil Jordan, Patrick McCabe (based on the novel by Patrick McCabe); ph, Adrian Biddle; ed, Tony Lawson; m, Elliot Goldenthal; prod d, Anthony Pratt; art d, Anna Rackard; set d, Josie MacAvin; sound, Kieran Horgan (recording), Brendan Deasy (recording); fx, Joss Williams, Steve Lloyd; casting, Susie Figgis; cos, Sandy Powell; makeup, Morag Ross; stunts, Pat Condren

Drama **(PR: O MPAA: R)**

C

CALL TO REMEMBER, A ★★★

(U.S., 1997) 101m Great Falls Productions ~ UTE Inc. c

Blythe Danner *(Paula Tobias)*; Joe Mantegna *(David Tobias)*; David Lascher *(Jake Tobias)*; Kevin Zegers *(Ben Tobias)*; Joe Spano *(Dr. Green)*; Rita Zohar *(Renya Weiss)*; Blu Mankuma *(Hank Mc Tier)*; Ingrid Kavelaars *(Amy Miller)*; Kevin McNulty *(Michael Bratten)*; Christian Tessier *(Mike Banks)*; Ben Eberhard *(Ross Glazer)*; Neil Dennis *(George Hicks)*; Bill Switzer *(Sandy Halper)*; L. Harvey Gold *(Al Weiss)*; Dave Hurtubise *(Morris Halper)*; Charles Siegel *(Jack Samuelson)*; Rosie Frier-Dryden *(Fredia Weiss)*; Irene Miscisco *(Maria Halper)*; French Tickner *(Banker Parker)*; Tamlyn Keenan *(Little Girl)*

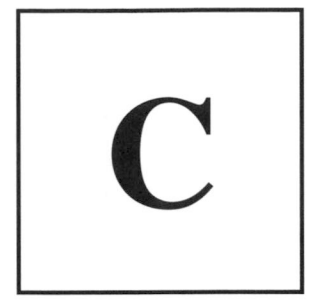

Intelligently modulating its emotional intensity, A CALL TO REMEMBER is a dignified made-for-cable drama about the burden placed on the second-generation children of Holocaust victims. Although script and direction tend toward the prosaic, this story of loss moves the audience due to exceptional performances by Blythe Danner and Joe Mantegna as concentration camp survivors.

For Paula (Blythe Danner) and David Tobias (Joe Mantegna), the good life in 1960s America comprises hard work and building a secure future for their sons, preteen Ben (Kevin Zegers) and high schooler Jake (David Lascher). Mr. and Mrs. Tobias alienate their boys by refusing to discuss their WWII experiences and expecting Ben and Jake to be perfect, as their duty to all the children lost to genocide, whose numbers include Paula and Ben's children from previous marriages.

Ben yearns to play baseball, instead of burying himself in Yeshiva studies. Openly defiant, Jake withstands Paula's efforts to have a psychiatrist declare him unfit for the draft, despite his own reservations about military service in Viet Nam. The Tobias family's crossed purposes intersect when Paula learns that her 27-year-old son Alec, presumed dead, has been located through a European refugee group. With her hopes raised stratospherically, Paula travels to New York City, only to learn the organization made a mistake. Despondent, she returns to find Jake in the process of moving out. Half-heartedly attempting suicide by inhaling pesticides, Paula plunges into a deep guilt about her dead children. Ultimately, David is able to reach his estranged children by sharing with them his grief about his deceased wife and kids. Recovering from a nervous breakdown, Paula accepts Jake's independence and shakes off her melancholy long enough to attend Ben's bar mitzvah. By allowing their sons to follow their own dreams, Paula and David put their unimaginable pain into a less damaging perspective.

This straightforward drama is stacked with the virtues of the well-made teleplay, the kind of cogent drama once popular on television staples like "Playhouse 90." Dramatically, the rising curve of crises spirals a bit too tidily to its ultimate conclusion, but the characters' journey of self-discovery is nonetheless rewarding. Some Holocaust-themed dramas like Showtime's RESCUERS offerings cannot shake off a self-congratulatory Hollywood patina. Conversely, A CALL TO REMEMBER is spare and provocative. Few dramas have addressed the gulf that exists among foreign-born parents, who've endured suffering that cuts them off from their assimilated children. Perceptively peering down that generational chasm, this melodrama forces viewers to think for themselves. In the process, it offers two virtuoso performances by stars Joe Mantegna and Blythe Danner, whose moving, but unsentimental, portrayals make A CALL TO REMEMBER must-see viewing. *(Extreme profanity, adult situations, nudity.)*—R.P.

d, Jack Bender; p, John V. Stuckmeyer; exec p, Jack Bender, Alan Jacob; w, Max Eisenberg; ph, David Geddes; ed, Mark Melnick; prod d, Richard T. Sawyer; set d, Cynthia Lewis; sound, Michael McGee; casting, Abra Edelman, Elisa Goodman; cos, Trish Keating; makeup, Victoria Down; stunts, Tony Lazarowich

Drama (PR: C MPAA: R)

CANI ARRIBBIATI

(SEE: RABID DOGS)

CAN'T HARDLY WAIT ★★★

(U.S., 1998) 96m Zide Entertainment; Topping/Thomas Productions ~ Columbia TriStar c

Jennifer Love Hewitt *(Amanda Beckett)*; Ethan Embry *(Preston Meyers)*; Peter Facinelli *(Mike Dexter)*; Summer Phoenix *(Uncredited)*; Lauren Ambrose *(Denise Fleming)*; Seth Green *(Kenny Fisher)*; Jenna Elfman *(Angel)*; Jerry O'Connell *(Trip McNeeley)*; Melissa Joan Hart *(Yearbook Girl)*; Charlie Korsmo *(William Lichter)*; Michelle Brookhurst *(Girl Whose Party It Is)*; Alexander Martin *(Exchange Student)*; Erik Palladino *(Cousin Ron)*; Channon Roe *(Jack #1)*; Sean Patrick Thomas *(Jack #2)*; Freddy Rodriguez *(Jack #3)*; Joel Michaely *(X-Phile #1)*; Jay Paulson *(X-Phile #2)*; Brian Hall *(Reak Homeboy)*; Branden Williams *(Homeboy #1)*; Bobby Jacoby *(Homeboy #2)*; Johnny Zander *(Guitar Player)*; Donald Faison *(Drummer)*; Alaa Khaled *(Bass Player)*; Jamie Pressly *(Girlfriend #1)*; Tamala Jones *(Girlfriend #2)*; Jennifer Lyons *(Girlfriend #3)*; Seth Peterson *(Keg Guy)*; Angela Vacco *(Beer Drinker)*; Nick Paulos *(Beer Drinker)*; Chris Owen *(Klepto Kid)*; Vicellous Shannon *(Reddi Whip Kid)*; Monica McSwain *(Groupie)*; Marisol Nichols *(Groupie)*; Liz Stauber *(Gossipy Girl)*; Nicole Bilderback *(Ready to Have Sex Girl)*; Jason Segel *(Watermelon Guy)*; Paige Moss *(Ashley)*; Clea Duvall *(Jana)*; Leslie Grossman *(Ready to Have Sex Girl's Friend)*; Ali MacLean *(Language Lab Girl)*; Brian Klugman *(Stoner Guy)*; Meadow Sisto *(Hippie Girl)*; Eric Balfour *(Hippie Boy)*; Selma Blair *(Girl Mike Hits on #1)*; Jennifer Paz *(Girl Mike Hits on #2)*; Sara Rue *(Earth Girl)*; Nils Larson *(Skinny Boy)*; Steve Monroe *(Headbanger)*; Eric Brice Scott *(Hockey Guy)*; Chris Wiehl *(Horny Guy)*; John Patrick White *(Tassel Guy)*; Jamie Donnelly *(Teacher)*; Reni Santoni *(Cop)*; Rob Roy Fitzgerald *(Cop)*; Corrinn Reilly *(Cop)*; Amber Benson *(Stoned Girl)*; Breckin Meyer *(Lead Singer in the Band)*

Following the ups and downs of six disparate high school seniors through the course of a raucous graduation night party, CAN'T HARDLY WAIT is a candy-coated piece of teen comedy fluff with a wisp of honest romance at its center.

Members of the Huntington Hills High senior class converge on a parent-free house for a wild graduation party. Eager to graduate to dating college women, jock Mike Dexter (Peter Facinelli) has impetuously dumped prom queen Amanda Beckett (Jennifer Love Hewitt). Preston Meyers (Ethan Embry) fell in love with Amanda at first sight freshman year, and now has poured his heart into a letter that he plans to give her at the party. Preston's best friend Denise Fleming (Lauren Ambrose), a sardonic outsider, reluctantly accompanies him to the party to provide moral support. Clownish Kenny Fisher (Seth Green) comes armed with two dozen condoms and a copy of the *Kama Sutra* in anticipation of losing his virginity. Brainy nerd William

Lichter (Charlie Korsmo) attends the party with a devious plot to exact vengeance on Mike for years of bullying.

Former grade school buddies Denise and Kenny get locked in a bathroom together all night; they fight, reconnect, and have sex. William abandons his plans when he gets drunk and becomes the life of the party, even attracting girls. Preston chickens out and discards the letter as the result of a partygoer's mention of a past embarrassment to him; he leaves the party. But a meeting with a stripper dressed as an angel (Jenna Elfman) convinces him to return. Meanwhile, Mike's meeting with a former-BMOC gone to seed (Jerry O'Connell) convinces him to try and get Amanda back, but she refuses him after finding Preston's letter. When Preston finally approaches Amanda, she doesn't connect him to the love letter, and tells him to get lost. William ends up consoling Mike, and when the police raid the party looking for drunken minors, the two are arrested. Mike lies to the police, saying he's responsible for getting William drunk, thus protecting him from the wrath of his parents.

The next morning, Preston is leaving to attend a writer's workshop in Boston. After looking in a yearbook to discover her suitor's identity, Amanda seeks Preston out at the train station. They kiss and live happily ever after.

After SCREAM (1996) revived the moribund teen slasher flick, it was only a matter of time before the return of that other 1980s genre staple, the John Hughes teen romantic comedy. In various quantities, CAN'T HARDLY WAIT borrows from SIXTEEN CANDLES (1984), THE BREAKFAST CLUB (1985), WEIRD SCIENCE (1985), and PRETTY IN PINK (1986), but with none of the social criticism. The movie also owes a major debt to the capper of the genre, Cameron Crowe's SAY ANYTHING (1989). Significantly, CAN'T HARDLY WAIT *doesn't* take a cue from the Hughes-penned SOME KIND OF WONDERFUL (1987); otherwise, Preston would have realized Denise was his true love, which actually might have been a more satisfying conclusion. With CAN'T HARDLY WAIT, the cowriting and codirecting team of Deborah Kaplan and Harry Elfont has created an entertaining journey through contemporary high school subcultures. They place more emphasis on the comedy than the romance, allowing Ambrose, Green, and Korsmo (who has the film's highlight, wildly performing Guns N Roses's "Paradise City") to steal the movie from Embry and Hewitt, who while top billed is given little to do other than to pose and look beautiful, which she does very well. *(Extreme profanity.)*—P.R.

d, Harry Elfont, Deborah Kaplan; p, Jenno Topping, Betty Thomas, Warren Zide; assoc p, Richard Graves; co-p, Karen Koch; w, Harry Elfont, Deborah Kaplan; ph, Lloyd Ahern; ed, Michael Jablow; m, David Kitay, Matthew Sweet; prod d, Marcia Hinds-Johnson; art d, Bo Johnson; set d, Jan Bergstrom; sound, David Kirschner (mixer); fx, Lou Carlucci; casting, Mary Vernieu, Anne McCarthy; cos, Mark Bridges; makeup, John Damiani; stunts, Clay Boss

Romance/Comedy **(PR: C MPAA: PG-13)**

CAN'T YOU HEAR THE WIND HOWL?: THE LIFE AND MUSIC OF ROBERT JOHNSON ★★½

(U.S., 1997) 76m Sweet Home Pictures ~ WinStar Home Entertainment c

Danny Glover *(Narrator)*; Keb' Mo' *(Robert Johnson)*; Johnny Shines; Honeyboy Edwards; Robert Jr. Lockwood; Henry Townsend; Robert Cray; John Hammond; Keith Richards; Eric Clapton; Jim O'Neal; R.L. Windum; Willie Mason; Israel "Wink" Clark; Son House; Don Law Jr.; Smokey Montgomery; Willie Mae Powell

A slick but shallow biography of blues legend Robert Johnson, who died at age 27 with a mere eleven 78s of his darkly compelling songs issued during his lifetime. A transitional artist between Delta-style blues and the more sophisticated urban style, he traveled extensively and spread his musical influence widely, although his personal life remained shadowy and mysterious for decades.

Born to a broken family, raised in itinerant labor camps in the deep South, Johnson discovered early that he would rather make music than hoe fields. Initially dismissed as untalented by elder bluesmen like Son House, he eventually surprised everyone by exhibiting a pure musical genius. Through local talent scout H.C. Speir, he hooked up with a label that recorded him in two sessions in Texas, spawning the regional hit "Terraplane Blues." A vagabond and womanizer, he was eventually fed a glass of poisoned whisky by a man he cuckolded.

With only two photographs of Johnson publicly available (a studio portrait from 1935 and a photo-booth snapshot from the early 1930s), the film offers stock period footage mixed with scenes of Keb' Mo' playing Johnson in black-and-white vignettes, including an encounter with the devil and several music-video-styled songs. Among those interviewed are frequent Johnson traveling companion Johnny Shines, and Robert Jr. Lockwood. Only four years younger than Johnson, Lockwood became known as his "stepson" when Johnson took up with Lockwood's mom, Esther; Robert Jr. subsequently switched from playing organ to guitar, becoming the only person known to receive lessons from the fiercely self-protective Johnson. Along with Honeyboy Edwards, who accompanied Johnson on that fatal night, and with brief accolades from the likes of Eric Clapton, Keith Richards, and Robert Cray, the film's resources are unassailable, yet it manages to fudge such important issues as Johnson's roots and influences. His style, however personal, however interpretive, was a skilled assimilation and outgrowth of numerous well-documented predecessors. His technique of playing the guitar "like a piano" is alluded to, without description of what that means (walking bass lines, likely borrowed from boogie-woogie pianists). Instead, a Son House anecdote depicts an untalented Johnson disappearing for half a year and returning a virtuoso; narrator Danny Glover offhandedly attributes this metamorphosis to a brief tutelage by Ike Zinnerman, a local guitarist whose name none of the interviewees even recognize.

Born out of wedlock, Johnson was raised by a man variously called Dodds and Spencer, adopting his real father's name of Johnson in his teens and using it for his recordings. But his acquaintances all knew him as Robert (or R.L.) Spencer, contributing to the difficulties encountered later by scholars trying to research his life, and the mystery that surrounded him for decades. Once the past was unlocked however, the reminiscences from cohorts started to pour forth, often contradicting one another. (He was friendly/he was aloof; he was poisoned/he was stabbed.) Overall, the film offers a simplified portrait of an individual who is universally agreed to have been a complicated and driven man.—A.B.

d, Peter W. Meyer; p, Peter W. Meyer; exec p, Thom Havens, Philip Nick; assoc p, Yolonda Williams; co-p, Constance Meyer, Philip C. Pfeiffer; w, Jean Compton, Peter W. Meyer; ph, Phillip Thomas; ed, Peter W. Meyer; m, Robert Johnson, Michael Haines, Keb' Mo'; set d, Jack Marty, Jeff Wallace; casting, Rody Kent, Yolanda Williams, Lynn Ambrose; cos, Lisa Albertson, Janet Swain

Documentary/Musical **(PR: C MPAA: NR)**

CAPTIVE ★★

(U.S./Canada, 1998) 93m Blackwatch Communications ~ Blackwatch Releasing c

Erika Eleniak *(Samantha/Sam)*; Michael Ironside *(Detective Briscoe)*; Catherine Colvey *(Dr. Kossim)*; Stewart Bick *(Joel Hoffman)*; Adrienne Ironside *(Lissy)*; Jack Langedijk *(Sal Hoffman)*; Noel Burton *(Dr. Hagan)*; Laurel Paetz *(Nurse Boland)*; Michel Perron *(Jarvik)*; Don Jordan *(Police Officer)*; Larry Day *(Bailey)*; Jane Wheeler *(Female Administrator)*; Donette McKay *(Nurse Ziller)*; Jeannie Walker *(Cleaning Lady)*; Gillian Ferrabee *(Wedding Guest)*; Gouchy Boy *(Orderly)*; Steve Adams *(Security Guard)*; Alain Goulem *(Nurse Lasky)*; Jean Marc Bisson *(Security Guard for Elite Bldg.)*

While the unimaginatively produced CAPTIVE offers one climactic plot twist for the gullible, experienced armchair detectives will simply be bored by this tale of a widow targeted for her inheritance.

New bride Sam Hoffman's (Erika Eleniak) honeymoon ends when her millionaire hubby Sal Hoffman (Jack Langedijk) is shot to death while retrieving plane tickets she had left at the office. Distraught, she cuts her wrists but is rescued by the cleaning lady. While Detective Briscoe (Michael Ironside) shuffles theories about the Hoffman homicide, Sam's brother-in-law Joel (Stewart Bick) persuades her to enroll voluntarily in a sanitarium run by Joel's lover Dr. Kossim (Catherine Colvey). Joel's display of concern masks his and Dr. Kossim's plan to kill her, making it look like suicide, so that they can grab the Hoffman millions she inherited. Sam defends her roommate Lissy (Adrienne Ironside) from sexual molestation by an orderly, an action that nets her a longer stay at the sanitarium. When Sam escapes with the help of an official pass stolen by Lissy, Dr. Kossim stabs Joel for trying to renege on their deal and frames Sam. Recaptured and returned to the institution, Sam encounters a homicidal Dr. Kossim. Sam is saved from Kossim by Lissy, who pushes murderous Dr. Kossim out the window. Deducing that Joel and Kossim hatched their plan after Sal's demise, Detective Briscoe realizes that it was Sam who murdered her own husband. She pays Briscoe off so that she can enjoy life with the vast fortune she has inherited.

Unimpressively photographed, CAPTIVE lacks the essential escapist sheen that might have redeemed its styleless hokum. Most of this movie's sneaky script is transparent from the get-go. First of all, Sam's request that Sal pick up the tickets "she forgot" seems like an obvious ploy from someone whose character has been established as well-organized. Couple this hard-to-swallow point with the film's repeated depiction of Sal's shooting from the killer's point of view, and the viewer wonders why we never are shown the murderer's face. Strenuously led down the wrong sanitarium corridors, the viewer feels more manipulated than surprised when Sam turns out to be unworthy of rescue. *(Violence, profanity, sexual situations.)*—R.P.

d, Rodney Gibbons; p, Holly A. Simpson, Stephen Maynard; exec p, William R. Mariani, Antony I. Ginnane, Peter C. Emerson; co-p, Michael Doherty; w, Bruno Philip; ed, Michael Doherty; m, Dave Findlay; prod d, Csaba Kertz; sound, Philippe Espantoso; fx, Cineffects; casting, Chelsea McIsaac; cos, Nicole Pelletier; makeup, Michele Bergeron; stunts, Dave McKeown

Crime/Mystery **(PR: C MPAA: NR)**

CARLA'S SONG ★★½

(U.K./Germany/Spain, 1996) 127m Channel Four Films; Parallax Pictures; Road Movies Dritte Produktionen; Tornasol Films ~ Shadow Distribution c

Robert Carlyle *(George)*; Oyanka Cabezas *(Carla)*; Scott Glenn *(Bradley)*; Salvador Espinosa *(Rafael)*; Louise Goodall *(Maureen)*; Richard Loza *(Antonio)*; Gary Lewis *(Sammy)*; Pamela Turner *(Eileen)*; Subash Sing Pall *(Victor)*; Stewart Preston *(McGurk)*; Margaret McAdam *(George's Mother)*; Greg Friel *(Keyboard Player)*; Ann-Marie Timoney *(Warden)*; Andy Townsley *(Taxi Driver)*; Alicia Devine *(Hospital Sister)*; John Paul Leach *(Doctor)*; Norma Rivera *(Norma)*; Jose Meneses *(Harry)*; Rosa Amelia Lopez *(Carla's Mother)*; Josefa Calderon de Calero; Azucena Figueroa; Tomasa Garcia; Alcides Gonzales; Manuela Guevara; Karla Obando; Santos Olivas; Alison Paula Rizo; Elba Aurora Talavera; Luis Talavera *(Carla's Family)*; Jimmy Jose Arguello; Jose Alberto Avendano; Ana Victoria Borge; Junior Escobar; Alma Blanco Medina; Tatiana Miranda; Ramon Monterrey; Santiago Neira; Belkis Ramirez; Maria Jose Silva *(Brigadistas)*; Amy Bank; Belinda Forbes; Mark Forget; Tom Lee; Micky McKay; Ruth Pacheco; Richard Senghas; Anita Setright; Laura Tredway *(Witnesses for Peace)*; Marcelino Cruz; Alberto Flores; Roberto Flores; Narciso Gonzalez; Claire Hemphill; Felipe Hernandez; Ford Kiernan; Ramon Lozano; Thomas McTaggart

The politics are correct in CARLA'S SONG, but the romantic story about a Scottish bus driver and a Nicaraguan woman lacks the depth of filmmaker Ken Loach's better films.

In 1987 Glasgow, George (Robert Carlyle) drives a doubledecker to support his family, a wife and two teenage children, but he is clearly dissatisfied with his lot. One day, he meets a passenger, Carla (Oyanka Cabezas), a beautiful dark-skinned woman who lacks the sufficient fare. George gallantly puts his job in jeopardy by allowing Carla to flee from a hostile ticket-taker. Carla later finds George to thank him, but she refuses his offer of a date.

George is intrigued by Carla, particularly after he spots her one night dancing on the sidewalk as a way to earn money. He follows Carla to her hostel room, but she still refuses his advances. Their loud exchange gets Carla thrown out of the hostel, but George makes it up to Carla by letting her stay at a friend's apartment. Carla finally warms up to George and tells him about her dreams of freeing her native country, Nicaragua, from the grip of the right-wing Contras. She also tells George about her former lover, Antonio, who has been missing back home, and she now accepts George's romantic advances.

George finally tells his wife and children about Carla and plans to leave them for her. Meanwhile, Carla attempts suicide over her troubles back home, but George gets her to a hospital in time to save her life. As George nurses Carla back to health, he learns more about the political struggles in her native land. After he is fired from his job over the recent incident involving Carla, George takes Carla back to Nicaragua.

On the way to where her family lives, Carla and George meet up with Bradley (Scott Glenn), an American ex-CIA agent who is working with the left-wing Sandinistas to defeat the US-backed Contras. Bradley helps Carla by directing her to people who have recently seen Antonio, including Raphael (Salvador Espinosa), a teacher and friend who lives in San Cristobel, near Carla's family home. The night Carla reunites with her family, the Contras attack the village, killing many innocent civilians. The frightening event causes George to consider leaving Carla and the country, but before he makes a final decision, Bradley tells him how Carla was scarred and Antonio brutally hurt in an earlier onslaught.

George then learns that Carla believes he has already left her and that she has moved on to Esperanza, where she continues looking for Antonio. George follows her and arrives in time to see her reunite with Antonio. George now fully realizes that Carla belongs in Nicaragua—and with Antonio. He leaves to return to Scotland, but he first says farewell to Bradley.

CARLA'S SONG has the classic elements of a star-crossed lovers tale. Though only the churlish Bradley objects to the union (and even he changes his mind), George and Carla literally and figuratively represent different worlds, so perhaps their romance is doomed from the start. In another way, CARLA'S SONG looks like a more realistic version of slick Hollywood films like Sydney Pollack's HAVANA (1990), in which courageous women light the fighting fire within apolitical heroes.

Yet CARLA'S SONG fails as both a romance and a political tract because of several flaws. Despite the film's compassion for its characters, screenwriter Paul Laverty and director Ken Loach never fully develop them (Laverty and Loach create a far richer love story in MY NAME IS JOE, 1999). Carla remains a mystery much of the time, George seems like a two-dimensional version of the working-class antihero in *Look Back in Anger*, and Bradley represents a dramatist's tool—functioning to further the plot and explain character motivation when necessary. The worst scene finds Bradley angrily telling George about the crimes of the CIA against the Nicaraguans. Whatever devastating political truth this scene holds is severely undercut by the forced and phony way it's presented.

For a director as skilled and politically aware as Loach (see HIDDEN AGENDA, 1990), CARLA'S SONG is peculiarly simplistic and uninvolving at times. Somehow, he makes the war in Nicaragua in the 1980s more remote than the Spanish Civil War in the 1930s (the subject of his much better LAND AND FREEDOM). Still, there are some effective moments, notably the early encounters between George and Carla, the attack on Carla's village, and the reunion scene between Carla and Antonio (filmed in longshot, from George's lump-in-the-throat point-of-view). Sadly, there are not enough great parts to make the whole worthwhile, however well-meant. *(Violence, nudity, sexual situations, adult situations, extreme profanity.)*—E.M.

d, Ken Loach; p, Sally Hibbin; co-p, Ulrich Felsberg, Gerardo Herrero; w, Paul Laverty; ph, Barry Ackroyd; ed, Jonathan Morris; m, George Fenton; prod d, Martin Johnson; art d, Llorenc Miquel, Fergus Clegg; sound, Ray Beckett (recordist); fx, Reyes Abades; casting, Jean Bacharach, Wendy Ettinger, Florence Jaugey; cos, Daphne Dare, Lena Mossum; makeup, Chris Blundell

Romance/War/Drama (PR: C MPAA: NR)

CARNE TREMULA
(SEE: LIVE FLESH)

CASPER MEETS WENDY ★★
(U.S., 1998) 95m Saban Entertainment; 20th Century Fox; Harvey Entertainment ~ 20th Century Fox c

Hilary Duff *(Wendy)*; Jeremy Foley *(Voice of Casper)*; Cathy Moriarty *(Geri)*; Shelley Duvall *(Gabby)*; Teri Garr *(Fanny)*; George Hamilton *(Desmond Spellman)*; Jess Harnell *(Voice of Fatso)*; James Ward *(Voice of Stretch)*; Bill Farmer *(Voice of Stinky)*; Pauly Shore *(The Oracle)*; Richard Moll *(Jules)*; Vincent Schiavelli *(Vincent)*; Blake Foster *(Josh Jackson)*; Michael James MacDonald *(Spike)*; Travis McKenna *(Phil)*; Patrick Richwood *(Vinne)*; Rodger Holston; Logan Robbins; Alan Thicke; Casper Van Dien; Billy Burnette; Maria Ford; Rodman Flender; Jim Jackman; Sheila Travis; Rick Dean; Ben Stein

Following in the wake of CASPER: A SPIRITED BEGINNING (1997), this second straight-to-video sequel to CASPER (1995) has a fine cast and some amusing gags, but the franchise is beginning to wear thin.

Wendy (Hilary Duff) is a child witch who lives with her three playful aunts (Cathy Moriarty, Shelley Duvall, Teri Garr). Meanwhile, a warlock, Desmond Spellman (George Hamilton) is told by his soothsayer mirror (Pauly Shore) that Wendy will be his downfall. Spellman's hunt for the girl sends all four witches to hide out at Sunnybride, a vacation resort where they can remain undetected by Spellman's witch-finding radar, as long as they refrain from using magic. By chance, Casper's friends, the Ghostly Trio, also arrive at Sunnybride to unwind after a season of scaring people. Casper, accompanying the Trio, accidentally runs into Wendy, and it's not exactly friendship at first sight: ghosts traditionally antagonize witches, and vice-versa. But the young pair soon realize they are both misunderstood misfits, and Casper vows to protect Wendy. The pair then decide to convince the Ghostly Trio that witches aren't so bad after all by matching up the three aunts and the three ghosts (possessing the bodies of male partygoers) at a Sunnybride dance. The supernatural sextet get along splendidly—until the Trio and the witches recognize each others' true nature. Wendy has to use magic to halt the ghosts' attack, sending them back to their suite to sulk and rage at Casper for tricking them.

In the meantime, Spellman has now pinpointed Wendy's position. He corners the witches, who prove no match for him, and conjures up "the Mystic Abyss," an endless portal in which he hurls Wendy. Casper flies in with a rope and catches hold of his friend, but all still seems lost until a hideous monster materializes and frightens Spellman into toppling into the Abyss. The apparition is actually the shape-shifting Ghostly Trio, who had a change of heart about helping the witches. Together they pull Casper and Wendy to safety.

Bringing Wendy and her aunts (characters from the Harvey Comics stable, home of Casper and friends) into this predictable plot line at least enriches the tiresome shtick that has been Casper's stock-in-trade ever since the childlike spook was created by cartoonist Joe Oriolo in the 1940s. Unfortunately, as Wendy newcomer Hilary Duff has to wear an embarrassing costume that resembles red long johns—for the proper comparison, imagine if Casper were an actor under a white sheet instead of a slick display of computer-animation effects.

George Hamilton plays his villainous part like a poor man's Vincent Price, while Duvall, Garr, and especially Cathy Moriarty put some gusto into their supporting roles, although Bette Midler, Kathy Najimy, and Sarah Jessica Parker played much the same parts in Disney's HOCUS POCUS (1993). Moriarty portrayed a completely different character in the original CASPER, and a handful of actors from other entries in the series do guest shots. In this respect it seems as if the filmmakers recognize that Casper's cinematic repertoire is limited and use the character as a sort of ectoplasmic springboard for a looser, Zucker Bros.-like gagfest. The lamest element is Spellman's two goons (Richard Moll, Vincent Schiavelli), who function as walking quotations from both MEN IN BLACK (1997) and PULP FICTION (1994). On the other hand, a reappearance of the flying cow from TWISTER (1996) and a throwaway line about the "witches' protection program" may bring a smile from jaded older viewers who feel that Casper has just about worn out his welcome. Younger viewers will more easily fall under his prankish spell. *(Violence.)*—C.C.

d, Sean McNamara; p, Mike Elliott; exec p, Haim Saban, Lance H. Robbins, Jeffrey A. Montgomery; assoc p, Nathan Rolmensz; co-p, Rob Kerchner, Amy Goldbert; w, Jymn Magon, Rob Kerchner (based on the comic book series *Casper, the Friendly Ghost* by Joseph Oriolo); ph, Christian Sebaldt; ed, John Gilbert; m, Udi Harpaz; prod d, Nava; art d, Dawn Ferry; set d, Danielle Berman; anim, Kent Butterworth; sound, Robert Rutledge; fx, Ray McIntyre Jr.; casting, Julie Ashton-Barson; cos, Tami Mor, Rina Ramon, Ryck Schmidt; makeup, John Buechler, Yolanda Holston; stunts, Patrick Statham

Children's/Comedy/Fantasy (PR: A MPAA: PG)

CATHERINE'S GROVE ★★½

(U.S., 1997) 91m DiTocco Productions ~ PM Entertainment c
(AKA: CROSSOVER)

Jeff Fahey *(Jack Doyle)*; Maria Conchita Alonso *(Charley)*; Jeffrey Donovan *(Thomas Mason)*; Michael Madsen *(Uncle Joseph)*; Priscilla Barnes *(Sally Willows)*; Andy Fiscella *(Nick Pirelli)*; Mario Sanchez *(Ernesto)*; Charlotte Walker *(Club Girl)*; Kirk Murray *(Vinnie)*; John Fionte *(Davy)*; Bill Childers *(Club Owner)*; Robyn DiTocco *(Club Owner's Girlfriend)*; Marc Macaulay *(William Mason)*; Melissa Bickerton *(Mary Mason)*; Nick Corirossi *(Young Thomas)*; Kaitlin Riley *(Young Catherine)*; Nikki Adams *(Carlina)*; David Caprita *(Bartender)*; Antoni Carone *(Detective Olsen)*; Tony Jones *(Capt. Ridges)*; Alfie Wise *(Burt)*; Robert Gwaltney *(Pawn Shop Owner)*; Dan Kelley *(Conrad)*; Kim Ostrenko *(Pamela)*; Avis-Marie Barnes *(Malatasta)*; James Hong *(Dr. Lee)*; Micah Espinoza *(Joe's Girlfriend)*

Despite being haunted by the ghosts of dozens of other direct-to-video serial killer flicks, CATHERINE'S GROVE is a moderately engrossing foray into perversity. Astute mystery buffs will anticipate the screenplay's curve balls, but the movie redeems itself with believable psychological underpinnings and some supple acting.

In South Florida, hedonism on the the alternative bar scene is dampened by a series of hammer slayings. Busy with the homicide investigation, Detective Nick Pirelli (Andy Fiscella) turns over a missing person case to his partner Jack Doyle (Jeff Fahey), who moonlights as a private investigator. Doyle and Charley (Maria Conchita Alonso), his girlfriend and PI partner, search for Catherine, the missing sister of Thomas Mason (Jeffrey Donovan).

It is revealed that Thomas maintains a close bond with Catherine and has suffered abuse at the hands of his father (Marc Macaulay). Doyle's queries lead him to Thomas's overbearing Uncle Joseph (Michael Madsen), who controls his nephew's estate, and Sally Willows (Priscilla Barnes), a glamorous party girl who had a crush on Catherine. Doyle mistakenly suspects that Thomas killed his sister to gain her share of the estate; Charley, on the other hand, responds to Thomas's sensitivity and believes him innocent.

Uncle Joseph tells Doyle that Catherine actually died years ago as a child, in a fall from Thomas's treehouse. Since then, cross-dressing Thomas has occasionally assumed his sister's identity. Having embarked on a murder spree against female impersonators, crazy Thomas has planted evidence to frame Sally, because she wanted him to become Catherine permanently. During Doyle's interrogation of an unnerved Sally, she brandishes a weapon, so Pirelli is forced to shoot her. Having fooled Charley and Doyle, Thomas retires to his family estate, where he murders Uncle Joseph and assumes his identity.

With its documentary-like footage of Florida's swinging bar scene and its cynical happy ending for a madman, CATHERINE'S GROVE offers thrill-seekers a walk on the wild side. Its principal debit stems from tedious squabbling scenes between laid-back Jeff Fahey and spitfire Maria Conchita Alonso. Also, although the split personality gimmick fuels the plot, the audience will quickly realize why pretty boy Thomas is so clean-shaven. At least its flashbacks cogently further character development; in most direct-to-video movies, they merely enhance the atmosphere or pad the running time. If the leads are only serviceable, the shrewdly cast supporting players expertly suggest ripples of madness in their methods. Structurally an old-fashioned detective story, this weird thriller draws energy from its twisted story line and forces the viewer to pivot in the stiletto heels of a transvestite who despises his own kind. *(Graphic violence, nudity, extreme profanity, substance abuse, sexual situations.)*—R.P.

d, Rick King; p, Tony DiTocco; exec p, Robyn DiTocco, Eddy Shah, Liam Walker ; assoc p, Harmon Zaslow; co-p, James Hong, Barry Hickey; w, Tony DiTocco; ph, Bart Tau; ed, Daniel Loewenthal; m, Harry Manfredini; prod d, Robert Butcher; sound, Vince Nuccio; casting, Aaron Griffith; cos, Leslie Herman; makeup, Linda Arrigoni, Carol Raskin; stunts, John Zimmerman

Thriller **(PR: C MPAA: R)**

CAUGHT UP ★★★½

(U.S., 1998) 95m Heller Highwater Productions; LIVE Film/Mediaworks ~ LIVE Entertainment c

Bokeem Woodbine *(Daryl Allen)*; Cynda Williams *(Vanessa/Trish)*; Joseph Lindsey *(Billy Grimm)*; Clifton Powell *(Herbert/Frank Lowden)*; Basil Wallace *(Ahmad)*; Tony Todd *(Jake)*; Snoop Doggy Dogg *(Kool Kat Daddy)*; LL Cool J *(Roger)*; Damon Saleem *(Trip)*; Jeffrey Combs *(Security Guard)*; Shedric Hunter Jr. *(Jerome)*; Jeris Poindexter *(Larry)*; Doug Kruse *(Freeway Cop)*; Darin Scott *(TV Field Reporter)*; Marcus Johnson *(Strap)*; Jerry Boyd *(Mayor Skrote)*; Michael Clarke Duncan *(BB)*; Courtney McLean *(Bob)*; Jason Carmichael *(Rob)*; Mather Zickel *(Rocker)*; George Anthony Baker *(Young Brotha)*; Tracy James *(Young Sista)*

Writer-director Darin Scott provides a fresh update on some noir themes in CAUGHT UP, with Bokeem Woodbine as an ex-con tempted away from the straight and narrow path by beautiful Cynda Williams.

Fresh out of prison for a drug conviction, Darryl Allen (Bokeem Woodbine) lands right back in after a friend involves him unknowingly in a bank robbery that leaves a security guard badly wounded. By the time Darryl is released five years later, his girlfriend Trish has remarried and moved away with their young son. He meets Vanessa (Cynda Williams), a woman who could be Trish's twin. They become lovers after he saves them from an attack by a mysterious gunman. Vanessa gets him a job as a limo driver with her shady friend Billy Grimm (Joseph Lindsey). Darryl angrily quits when he discovers a corpse in the trunk of a car he is delivering, but is forced to go back as a spy for cop Frank Lowden (Clifton Powell), who is investigating Billy's clients.

After they are attacked again by a gunman, Darryl demands Vanessa come clean with him. Having earlier told him it may have something to do with a former lover, she now admits to having stolen a valuable diamond from him. Later that night, Vanessa is murdered and Darryl is made to look like the killer.

Darryl gets a gun and confronts Billy, but is forced to hide when Billy is visited by Ahmad (Basil Wallace), the Jamaican tough from whom Vanessa was hiding. Ahmad tells Billy that Vanessa aided him in a robbery of $2 million worth of diamonds, which she absconded with afterwards. He assumes that Darryl now has the jewels, and kills Billy while torturing him for information. Darryl gets away and, on a hunch, digs up Vanessa's grave. A tattoo reveals that the dead woman is really Trish. He finds and confronts Vanessa, but is subdued by her partner—Lowden, who has summoned a fence who will buy the diamonds. Ahmad and his gang also arrive and, in a shootout, everyone is killed except Darryl. Escaping with the fence's cash, Darryl is accosted again by the gunman, who reveals himself to be the security guard (Jeffrey Combs) who was emasculated in the bank robbery that landed Darryl in jail. He shoots Darryl and then commits suicide. Darryl survives thanks to a bulletproof vest he was wearing and uses the money to open a club, his longtime dream.

Though aimed primarily at what marketing types like to call the "urban" audience (the film's publicity made more mention than was warranted of brief appearances by hip hop stars Snoop Doggy Dogg and L. L. Cool J), CAUGHT UP will be enjoyed by any fan of the crime thrillers of the 1940s and '50s. Filmmaker Darin Scott has previously demonstrated a keen facility with different film genres as the writer and/or producer of films like TALES FROM THE HOOD (1995), FEAR OF A BLACK HAT (1995) and THE OFFSPRING (1987). For this, his directorial debut, he takes an obvious familiarity with classic noir situations to fashion a thriller that is neither homage nor parody, but something fresher. It's a pleasure to see a movie like this pay so much attention to its story and not sink into "gangsta" cliches. Scott carefully paces his revelations of the true depths of his femme fatale, who initially seems as wholesome as can be. And he has assembled an excellent cast, with strong performances by Woodbine and Williams and effective support from Clifton Powell and Basil Wallace. All that keeps this from being a small classic is a script that could have used one more polish, and Scott's tendency to let his gruesome sense of humor run on a bit too long (the finale, with Jeffrey Combs showing Woodbine his scars, will have most audiences squirming in their seats). *(Graphic violence, nudity, sexual situations, adult situations, substance abuse, profanity.)*—M.F.

d, Darin Scott; p, Peter Heller; co-p, Elaine Dysinger; w, Darin Scott; ph, Tom Callaway; ed, Charles Bornstein; m, Marc Bonilla; prod d, Terrence Foster; set d, Melanie Paizis; casting, Tony Lee; cos, Tracey White; stunts, Julius Le Flore

Crime/Drama/Thriller (PR: O MPAA: R)

CELEBRATION, THE ★★★★

(Denmark, 1998) 105m Nimbus Film APS ~ October Films C
(FESTEN)

Ulrich Thomsen *(Christian)*; Henning Moritzen *(Helge)*; Thomas Bo Larsen *(Michael)*; Paprika Steen *(Helene)*; Birthe Neumann *(Elsa)*; Trine Dyrholm *(Pia)*; Helle Dolleris *(Mette)*; Bjarne Henriksen *(Kim)*; Gbatokai Dakinah *(Gbatokai)*; Therese Glahn *(Michelle)*; Klaus Bondam *(Master of Ceremonies)*; Lasse Lunderskov *(Uncle)*; Lars Brygmann *(Receptionist)*; Lene Laub Oksen *(Sister)*; Linda Laursen *(Birthe)*; John Boas *(Grandad)*; Erna Boas *(Grandma)*; Thomas Vinterberg *(Taxi Driver)*; Guests/Waiters: Bent Henningsen; Poul Kajbaek; Vibeke Dalset; Janne Thomsen; Anette Jakobsen; Poul Peterson; Gulli Sejrsen; Vibeke Kaiser; John Johnsen; Dan Ellertsen; Soren Sogreni; Annette Jakobsen; Kate Goldschmidt; Jens Norring; Bent Kaiser; Maria Myrgard; Peter Krag; Stig Poul Hansen; In the Kitchen: Kaj Rasmussen; Robert Strandgard; Gry Worre Hallberg; Rene; Children: Christine Louise Jorgensen; Dorte Olofsen; Kasper Olofsen; Emilian Sejersen; Susanne Funck; Rosmarie Jorgensen; Lasse Jacobsen; Sigrid Aalbaek; Mikkel Jacobsen

Winner of the Special Jury Prize at the Cannes Film Festival, THE CELEBRATION brings a rigorously experimental style to bear on what would otherwise be a soap opera-ish story of a family gathering disrupted by the revelation of dark secrets.

The extended Klingenfeldt family gathers at the hotel it owns for a formal dinner marking the 60th birthday of patriarch Helge (Henning Moritzen). Eldest son Christian (Ulrich Thomsen), who runs a successful restaurant in Paris, arrives at the same time as his younger, wilder brother Michael (Thomas Bo Larsen). Michael has come with his wife and children, even though he has not been invited back to family gatherings since his poor behavior at the last one. Also attending the birthday celebration is daughter Helene (Paprika Steen), who insists on staying in the room where her sister Linda, Christian's twin, recently killed herself. At dinner, during a speech, Christian reveals that Helge raped him and Linda regularly when they were children. After an uncomfortable silence, the guests carry on by ignoring Christian's remarks, and he goes to leave. But he is talked into remaining by his old friend Kim (Bjarne Henriksen), now the hotel's chef, who is delighted to see these wounds being aired. He arranges to have the staff collect and hide everyone's car keys so that no one can leave.

After Helge denies his son's accusations and Christian says he must be mistaken, he returns to dinner—and accuses his father of causing Linda's suicide. The party is thrown into more consternation by the arrival of Helene's date Gbatokai (Gbatokai Dakinah), who is black. Mother Elsa (Birthe Neumann) makes a speech implying that Christian has a habit of making things up; he responds by reminding her of the time she saw her husband abusing them. Michael and others throw Christian out; when he sneaks back in, they take him to the forest and tie him to a tree. Back at dinner, Michael leads the guests in singing a racist song to insult Gbatokai. Helene finds a letter Linda left in her room and reads it to the party: it verifies Christian's accusations. Helge loses his temper, berating his children for being talentless and saying he used them for the only thing they were good for. Michael, who is drunk, gives his father a beating. At breakfast the next morning, Helge speaks to his family for what he knows will be the last time, saying that although he regrets what he did to them, they will always remain his children.

In 1995, Thomas Vinterberg, along with Lars von Trier and two other Danish filmmakers, formed a group called Dogme 95. Declaring itself opposed to "the auteur concept, makeup, illusions, and dramaturgical predictability," the group aimed to make films in which the inner lives of the characters would justify the plot. To this end, it drew up a "Vow of Chastity," ten rules by which they agreed to abide. These included promises to shoot only on location, using such props as can be found there; to shoot with handheld cameras in color 35mm film, with no special lighting, post-dubbed sound or music; and to abstain from genre films, opting instead for films that "[take] place here and now." Furthermore, the director vows "to refrain from personal taste. I am no loner as artist. . . My supreme goal is to force the truth out of my characters and settings. I swear to do so by all the means available and at the cost of any good taste and any aesthetic considerations." As such, the director will not be credited.

Just how seriously the world is supposed to take Dogme 95 remains to be seen, but its purist ideals are effectively argued for in THE CELEBRATION. Vinterberg seems to be using the vows as a game, to see how much he can do with how little, and it's an impressive bit of showing off. The movie was shot with a palm-sized video camera (with the result later transferred to film stock) to provide maximal mobility. While largely unknown in the United States, the cast is excellent, and this mode of shooting (while occasionally jittery) allows Vinterberg to capture their reactions optimally. He also made the most of the restriction against special lighting (shooting nighttime scenes only by candlelight) and against music: silence, he demonstrates, can be so much more effective than an orchestra.

Certainly, THE CELEBRATION is a bit of a stunt, with content appearing less important than style. Vinterberg seems to be trying to emulate Luis Bunuel's dissections of the upper middle class (THE EXTERMINATING ANGEL, THE DISCREET CHARM OF THE BOURGEOISIE), and the film's best moments are worthy of that model. Still, it's a moody piece that manages to avoid descending into either farce or sentimentality. The young Vinterberg is obviously a talent to watch, whether he remains true to his Dogme or not. *(Violence, sexual situations, adult situations, profanity.)*—M.F.

d, Thomas Vinterberg; p, Birgitte Hald; exec p, Birgitte Hald, Bo Ehrhardt; w, Thomas Vinterberg, Mogens Rukov; ph, Anthony Dod Mantle; ed, Valdis Oskarsdottir; sound, Morten Holm (designer)

Drama/Comedy **(PR: O MPAA: R)**

CELEBRITY ★★★½

(U.S., 1998) 113m Sweetland Productions; Jean Doumanian Productions ~ Miramax bw

Hank Azaria *(David)*; Kenneth Branagh *(Lee Simon)*; Judy Davis *(Robin Simon)*; Leonardo DiCaprio *(Brandon Darrow)*; Melanie Griffith *(Nicole Olivier)*; Famke Janssen *(Bonnie)*; Michael Lerner *(Dr. Lupus)*; Joe Mantegna *(Tony Gardella)*; Bebe Neuwirth *(Hooker)*; Winona Ryder *(Nola)*; Charlize Theron *(Supermodel)*; Issac Mizrahi *(Bruce Bishop)*; Gretchen Mol *(Vicky)*; Donald Trump *(Himself)*; Mary Jo Buttafuoco *(Herself)*; Joey Buttafuoco *(Himself)*; Irina Pantaeva; Mark Vanderloo; Frederique Van Der Wal *(Friends of Supermodel)*; Donna Hanover *("Manhattan Moods" Anchor Woman)*; Anthony Mason *(Himself)*; Karen Duffy *(TV Reporter at Premiere)*; Jeffrey Wright *(Off-Off Broadway Director)*; Kate Burton *(Robin's Friend Cheryl)*; Greg Mottola *(Director)*; Dylan Baker *(Priest at Catholic Retreat)*; Andre Gregory *(John Papadakis)*; Patti D'Arbanville *(Iris)*; Allison Janney *(Evelyn Issacs)*; Aida Turturro *(Psychic)*; Jeff Mazzola *(Assistant Director)*; Dick Mingalone *(Camera Operator)*; Vladimir Bibic *(Director of Photography)*; Francisco Quidjada *(Erno Deluca)*; Aleska Palladino *(Production Assistant)*; Dan Moran *(Jackhammer Operator)*; Pete Castelotti *(Sound Recordist)*; A. Lee Morris *(Second Assistant Cameraperson)*; Douglas McGrath *(Bill Gaines)*; Maurice Sonnenberg *(Dalton Freed)*; Craig Ulmschneider *(Production Assistant Daniel)*; Mina Bern *(Elderly Homeowner)*; Janet Marlow *(Singing Nun)*; Tommie Baxter *(Second Nun)*; Kathleen Doyle; Arthur Berwick; Jodi Long *(Father Gladen's Fans)*; John Carter *(Father Gladen)*; Monique Fowler *(Robin's Friend Jan)*; Marylouise Burke; Peter Boyden; Peter McRobbie; Maureen McNamara *(Father Gladen's Fans on Porch)*; Mary Catherine Wright *(Pious Diner)*; J.K. Simmons *(Souvenir Hawker)*; Melinda Eng *(Fashion Designer)*; Alma Cuervo *(Bruce Bishop's Admirer)*; Roshumba Williams *(Bruce Bishop's Admirer)*; Polly Adams *(Exercise Tape Fan)*; Brian McConnachie *(Exercise Tape Fan)*; Richard Mawe; Ted Neustadt; Bruce Jay Friedman; Erica Jong; Ned Eisenberg; Clebet Ford *(Elaine's Book Party Guests)*

Woody Allen's CELEBRITY is a caustic satire about the ubiquity of the modern media state that's also an entertaining homage to Fellini's LA DOLCE VITA (1960), with an Americanized Kenneth Branagh playing the Marcello Mastroianni role of a writer adrift in a sea of personal and professional dissolution.

While roaming through Manhattan, entertainment journalist Lee Simon (Kenneth Branagh), engages in various amorous adventures, including receiving oral sex from a movie star (Melanie Griffith) and having a wild night on the town with a supermodel (Charlize Theron), who teases him so much that he crashes his car into a store window before he can sleep with her. Lee's ex-wife, Robin (Judy Davis), is so devastated by being recently dumped by the unfaithful Lee that she goes to a Catholic retreat and considers getting plastic surgery. While at the doctor's office, she meets TV producer Tony Gardella (Joe Mantegna) and begins dating him. Lee runs into Tony and Robin at a movie premiere, and she angrily attacks him for having cheated on her. When Lee goes to meet teen movie idol Brandon Darrow (Leonardo DiCaprio) to try to sell him a screenplay, he arrives as Brandon is beating up his girlfriend (Gretchen Mol).

Lee accompanies Brandon to Atlantic City where they indulge in a cocaine-fueled orgy, but Lee is only interested in discussing his script and Brandon eventually kicks him out. Back in New York, Lee gets involved with a book editor named Bonnie (Famke Janssen) who helps him complete his long-unfinished novel, but he dumps her for an aspiring actress named Nola (Winona Ryder); Bonnie retaliates by throwing the only copy of his novel into a river. Lee and Nola date for awhile, but they soon break up over her infidelity. Robin, meanwhile, becomes a glamorous TV reporter working for Tony, whom she eventually marries. At another movie premiere, Lee runs into Tony and Robin again, but she's now happy and pregnant, while Lee is alone and miserable.

CELEBRITY was vilified by many in the press for being mean-spirited, but if anything it doesn't go far enough in its attack on the vapidity of celebrities and the idiocy of a culture that's obsessed with them. The celebrities are portrayed as vacuous, but affable, and there's the rub; for despite its title (and a funny, foul-mouthed, hotel room-trashing 10-minute cameo by Leonardo DiCaprio), the film isn't a juicy gossip-fest about movie stars. Its real subject—and target—is the public and the media itself. Woody Allen zeroes in on the so-called entertainment media, and possibly his depiction of this sector as a bunch of sycophantic whores may hit just a little too close to home for the "reporters" who have become glorified publicists and whose stock-in-trade is sarcasm (making their protestations of Woody's nastiness more than a little hypocritical). The film's humor is undeniably—and refreshingly—biting, as in the scene where a group of rabbis, racists, and assorted freaks amiably commiserate in a green room before a TV show ("Did the skinheads eat all the bagels already?" asks a rabbi), or in a classic bit where a hooker chokes on a banana while teaching Robin how to perform oral sex. But there is also an underlying ruefulness to the film, enhanced by the stark black and white photography by the great Sven Nykvist, which at once creates an aura of glamour and gloom that recalls many of the famous images from LA DOLCE VITA.

CELEBRITY is also the first Allen movie in which he hasn't appeared since BULLETS OVER BROADWAY (1994), and consequently his direction is more accomplished than in his recent films. In particular, his handling of the restaurant scene where Lee runs into Nola while they're both with other dates is exceptionally well done, as the camera subtly circles the table, catching glimpses of the two of them peeking at each other while the soundtrack weaves in snippets of their halting conversation with the small talk of the others. Allen also elicits fully-rounded performances from his entire cast, with the women faring especially well, particularly Winona Ryder, Charlize Theron, Famke Janssen, and Judy Davis. Branagh came under fire for doing an outright Woody imitation, but it's a superb imitation and is entirely appropriate for his alter-ego role. Although it's become recently fashionable to attack Allen's post-Mia films on the grounds of (self-righteous) morality, CELEBRITY is one of his most moral films, and it ends on a sad and sobering note, as Lee realizes that he's screwed up his life because of his immaturity and chronic infidelity. Woody may mercilessly ridicule others, but he always saves his best shots for himself. *(Profanity, sexual situations.)*—M.S.

d, Woody Allen; p, Jean Doumanian; exec p, J.E. Beaucaire; co-p, Richard Brick; w, Woody Allen; ph, Sven Nykvist; ed, Susan E. Morse; prod d, Santo Loquasto; art d, Tom Warren; set d, Susan Kaufman; sound, Les Lazarowitz (mixer); fx, Russel Berg; casting, Juliet Taylor, Laura Rosenthal; cos, Suzy Benzinger; makeup, Rosemarie Zurlo, Helen M. Gallagher

Comedy/Drama **(PR: O MPAA: R)**

CENTRAL DO BRASIL
(SEE: CENTRAL STATION)

CENTRAL STATION ★★★
(Brazil, 1998) 115m Arthur Cohn; MACT Productions; Videofilms; Riofilme; Canal Plus ~ Sony Pictures Classics c
(CENTRAL DO BRASIL)

Fernanda Montenegro *(Dora)*; Marilia Pera *(Irene)*; Vinicius de Oliveira *(Josue)*; Soia Lira *(Ana)*; Othon Bastos *(Bastos)*; Otavio Augusto *(Pedrao)*; Stela Freitas *(Yolanda)*; Matheus Nachtergaele *(Isaias)*; Caio Junqueira *(Moises)*; Socorro Nobre; Manoel Gomes; Roberto Andrade; Sheyla Kenia; Malcon Soares; Maria Fernandes; Maria Marlene; Christano Camargo; Jorseba-Sebastiao Oliveira *(Dora's Clients)*

Humanistic neo-realism is alive and well in CENTRAL STATION, an unabashedly sentimental, but well-made and heartfelt, Brazilian road movie about a young boy who is cared for by a lonely and cynical old woman after his mother is killed.

A crabby 67-year-old woman named Dora (Fernanda Montenegro) works in Rio de Janeiro's train station, where she writes letters for the poor and illiterate, but rarely sends them. After writing a letter for a woman named Ana (Soia Lira) to the errant father of her 9-year-old son Josue (Vinicius de Oliveira), Ana is hit by a bus and killed. The destitute Josue sleeps in the railway station and Dora reluctantly takes him home with her. For $1,000, she gives him to a couple who supposedly place orphans with wealthy European and American families, but when she finds out that the children are actually being sold and killed for their organs, she rescues Josue. He asks her to take him to see his father Jesus, whom he has never met and believes is a successful carpenter, but whom Dora knows is really a drunkard. Nevertheless, Dora agrees and they travel to northern Brazil by bus.

After Dora unsuccessfully tries to ditch Josue at one point, they hitch a ride with a kindly evangelical trucker, who, however, leaves them stranded after Dora comes on to him. They then join a caravan of Christian worshippers on a pilgrimage and wind up in the middle of a massive religious ceremony. Josue comes up with the idea of having Dora write letters to the saints from all of the worshippers, and they earn enough money to continue on to their destination. When they get there, they learn that Jesus is gone, but they encounter Jesus's two older sons from his first marriage, who warmly welcome Josue into their home. They give Dora a letter from their father to Josue's mother which was never sent and ask her to read it for them. It says that he has gone away to earn some money and will come to Rio to find her. During the night, Dora sneaks out of the house and rides away in a bus, and while Josue chases after her, she writes him a letter saying that he'll be better off with his stepbrothers.

CENTRAL STATION is an old-fashioned arthouse tearjerker in the tradition of Vittorio De Sica (MIRACLE IN MILAN, SHOESHINE BOY)—with whom one of this film's producers, Arthur Cohn, worked several times. The film also betrays the influence of Truffaut and Fellini, in whose work harsh subject matter (poverty, child abuse, old age) is treated in a realistic, yet ultimately romanticized, manner. The concept of an adorable, hard-boiled urchin who warms the cockles of an old grouch's heart is so ancient that it could have been made (and frequently was) with Shirley Temple, but director Walter Salles, a former documentarian, captures the sights and sounds of Brazil, from the teeming cities to the undeveloped rural villages, with a vivid authenticity, and also touches on political, cultural, and religious issues. However, he seems so intent on proving that he can direct a fiction film in a stylized and artful manner that there is a mannered meticulousness to the film which seems at odds with the gritty story.

Everything seems so pre-planned and tightly controlled, from the painterly widescreen compositions and perfectly timed edits which match camera movements that end one scene to ones that begin another, to the shamelessly melodramatic piano and violin score which practically rips the tears from one's ducts, that it proves to be counterproductive to the attempt at achieving pathos. Still, the film is undeniably moving and there are a number of fine vignettes along the episodic, picareque road trip, particularly Dora's unexpected romantic yearnings for the religious trucker, and the pilgrimage scene (although one is never sure whether Salles is being ironic or not in the recurring theme of religious zealots). Fernanda Montenegro, one of Brazil's top veteran actresses, is excellent at conveying Dora's emotional transformation, and young Vinicius de Oliveira, a nonprofessional who was discovered by Salles while working as a shoeshine boy (echoes of De Sica), and won the part over 1,500 others, is thankfully free of cloying cuteness. It's a skillful and touching little film, yet seems a little too calculated in every respect, in order to appeal to the elderly Oscar committee members who vote for Best Foreign Film—the film, in fact, was not only nominated in that category, but Montenegro was also singled out for a Best Actress nomination. *(Profanity, adult situations.)*—M.S.

d, Walter Salles; p, Arthur Cohn, Martine de Clermont-Tonnerre; exec p, Elisa Tolomelli, Lillian Birnbaum, Donald Ranvaud; assoc p, Paulo Brito; w, Joao Emanuel Carneiro, Marcos Bernstein (based on an original idea by Walter Salles); ph, Walter Carvalho; ed, Isabelle Rathery, Felipe Lacerda; m, Antonio Pinto, Jaques Morelembaum; prod d, Cassio Amarante, Carla Caffe; set d, Monica Costa; sound, Jean-Claude Brisson, Francois Groult, Bruno Tarriere, Mark A. Van Der Willigen (recorder); casting, Sergio Machado; cos, Cristina Camargo; makeup, Antoine Garabedian

AAN Best Actress: Fernanda Montenegro; *AAN Best Foreign Language Film*

Drama **(PR: C MPAA: R)**

CHAIRMAN OF THE BOARD ★
(U.S., 1998) 95m 101st Street Films; Trimark Pictures ~ Trimark c

Carrot Top *(Edison)*; Courtney Thorne-Smith *(Natalie)*; Jack Warden *(Armand McMillan)*; Larry Miller *(Bradford McMillan)*; Mystro Clark *(Ty)*; Raquel Welch *(Ms. Grace Kosik)*; Jack Plotnick *(Zak)*; M. Emmet Walsh *(Freemont)*; Estelle Harris *(Ms. Krabavitch)*; Cindy Margolis; Little Richard; Taylor Negron; Butterbean

A craven attempt to ape the successful style and tone of the charming "Pee-Wee Herman" movies, the soulless comedy CHAIRMAN OF THE BOARD is a laugh-free flop. Prop comic Carrot Top (real name Scott Thompson) stars in his film debut as a dim-witted surfer-cum-inventor who inherits a Fortune 500 company.

Edison (Carrot Top) is a pale, frizzy-haired Southern Californian who lives only to surf with his roommate "buds" Ty (Mystro Clark) and Zak (Jack Plotnick) and to invent bizarre gadgets that fail to sell. Edison's landlady, Ms. Krabavitch (Estelle Harris), who uses words like "dingleberry," is less than charmed with the beach bums' inability to pay rent and threatens to evict them.

Forced to seek employment, Edison cannot hold even a position that requires him simply to dress as a giant chicken at a fast-food joint. The situation becomes dire, but then he fortuitously stops to help a senior citizen having car trouble and learns that the old man, one Armand McMillan (Jack Warden), is the CEO of a Fortune 500 company. After the two kindred spirits share an afternoon surfing and Edison reveals to McMillan his notebook of hapless inventions, McMillan dies on cue and leaves his entire $23 million stake in his own company to the wacky kid.

Enraged, McMillan's unctuous nephew Bradford (Larry Miller), who expected the company to become his, hatches a scheme to wrest the firm away from Edison with the help of corporate raider Grace Kosik (Raquel Welch). On Edison's side is the aging board of directors, headed by Freemont (M. Emmett Walsh) and Edison's new romantic interest, virtuous production head Natalie (Courtney Thorne-Smith).

Predictably, Edison's hare-brained schemes, like "Luau Wednesdays" and a TV dinner that contains an actual small-screen TV, make millions and the company's stock value triples. Success gone to his head, Edison sports power suits and ignores old pals. Sensing his opportunity, Bradford forces Edison out with a media tip-off that a new product is a health hazard. Humility restored, Edison rallies his troops and proves Bradford a liar, winning back not his old job, but a more appropriate position in research and development.

Director Alex Zamm and his editors do a workmanlike job of approximating Carrot Top's customary manic pace in CHAIRMAN OF THE BOARD. The film is also impressively cartoonish in a visual sense, but fine technical considerations can't keep the dead-weight material afloat. To say that the level of the film's humor is low-brow would be an insult to low-brows. Fart and burp jokes abound, and incredibly, Zamm isn't above injecting the gaseous noises even where they are not indicated by the action in a scene. The script's shortcomings are many: telegraphed plot twists, unmotivated character business, just plain unfunny dialogue, a score that sounds like Danny Elfman lite. By far, Zamm's worst transgression is that the film plays like it's targeted at very young kids, but contains too much sexual innuendo and salty language for what seems to be its target audience.

Carrot Top stays true to his stand-up persona and does his best to sell the shoddy material, but he's no actor. Worse, the star gets little support from two costars, Thorne-Smith and the briefly appearing Warden, who make literally no effort to find Carrot Top's antics amusing, even while the camera is rolling.

Only Miller (THE NUTTY PROFESSOR, FOR RICHER OR POORER), who has proven adept at oily, Snidely Whiplash-type villains, sidesteps a phoned-in performance and rises above the flat character and dialogue with which he must work to fashion a reasonably amusing antagonist with clever asides that seem improvised. He's the one "A" pupil in a classroom of dullards. *(Sexual situations, profanity.)*—K.W.

d, Alex Zamm; p, Peter M. Lenkov, Rupert Harvey; exec p, Mark Amin; co-p, Phillip B. Goldfine; w, Al Septien, Turi Meyer, Alex Zamm (from the story by Turi Meyer, and Al Septien); ph, David Lewis; ed, Jim Hill; m, Chris Hajian; prod d, Aaron Osborne

Comedy **(PR: C MPAA: PG-13)**

CHAMBERMAID ON THE TITANIC, THE ★★★½

(France/Italy/Spain, 1997) 96m UGC/YM; La Sept; France 2 Cinema; Rodeo Drive; Erato Films; Mate Production; Tornasol Films; Westdeutscher Rundfunk ~ Samuel Goldwyn Company c

(AKA: CHAMBERMAID, THE; LA FEMME DE CHAMBRE DU TITANIC)

Olivier Martinez *(Horty)*; Romane Bohringer *(Zoe)*; Aitana Sanchez-Gijon *(Marie)*; Didier Bezace *(Simeon)*; Aldo Maccione *(Zeppe)*; Jean-Marie Juan *(Pascal)*; Arno Chevrier *(Al)*; Marianne Groves *(Bathilde)*; Didier Benureau *(Simeon's Secretary)*; Alberto Cassadie *(Giovanni)*; Giorgio Gobbi *(Manu)*; Yves Verhoeven *(Gaspard)*; Vincenzo de Caro *(Lacroix)*; Salvador Madrid *(Leon)*; Barbara Lerici *(Blanche)*; Stefania Orsola Garello *(Mimi)*; Maurizio Solda *(Lou)*; Jim Adhi Limas *(Chinese Photographer)*

Bigas Luna's THE CHAMBERMAID ON THE TITANIC is the kinky director's most "normal" and accessible film, but one which is still of a piece with his other quirky films, employing typically surreal humor and eroticism in a passionate tale of obsessive love.

Horty (Olivier Martinez), an impoverished French foundry worker, wins a company athletic competition, for which the prize is a trip to England to witness the launch of the Titanic. However, Horty's lecherous boss Simeon (Didier Bezace) only gives Horty a ticket and hotel accommodations for one person, since he has designs on Horty's wife Zoe (Romane Bohringer). When Horty arrives at his hotel, a woman named Marie (Aitana Sanchez-Gijon) comes to his room and explains that she's a chambermaid on the Titanic, but has no place to stay for the night and asks if she can sleep in his room. Horty agrees and Marie invites him into bed with her, but they don't have sex. The next morning, Horty watches Marie get on the Titanic and buys a picture of her which a photographer has just snapped. Back in France, Horty receives a promotion and hears rumors that he got it because of Zoe's "kindness" to Simeon in his absence. Zoe denies it, but out of revenge, Horty tells his coworkers that he did sleep with Marie and regales them with nightly barroom tales of their wild night of passion.

Horty is devastated when he learns that the Titanic has sunk, and he's fired after smashing up Simeon's car. Although Zoe knows that Horty's stories about Marie are not true, she allows him to continue telling them because his nightly performances at the bar have become so popular that the owner pays him, but she gradually realizes that Horty is really in love with Marie. A traveling actor named Zeppe (Aldo Maccione) visits the bar and invites Horty to take his act on the road with him. With Zoe dressed as Marie, the act becomes so successful that it eventually plays in theaters. One night, Horty is shocked to see Marie sitting in the audience, and chases her outside. Zoe follows and finds Marie's husband, who tells her that Marie is a prostitute who came to Horty's hotel room only to steal his wallet, and that they now want their share of Horty's act. Zoe pays him off, but when Horty returns to the stage he tells the audience that he's an impostor who's made everything up, then says that he has just murdered Marie after discovering her true identity. The audience gives him a standing ovation and he later admits to Zoe that he didn't really kill Marie.

THE CHAMBERMAID OF THE TITANIC is a beautifully crafted period piece in the classical style that seems quite restrained from a director who specializes in outrageous sex farces (e.g., JAMON JAMON and 1994's astonishing and still unreleased in America THE TIT AND THE MOON, about a young boy's obsession with finding the perfect maternal mammary). Luna treats the fantastic story like a delirious and melodramatic dream, filled with romantic violin music, gorgeously composed widescreen images, rhapsodic, Vincente Minnelli-ish crane shots, multiple-exposure montages, and ultra-slow dissolves, the likes of which haven't been seen since the heyday of Josef von Sternberg. Of course, there's also plenty of eroticism and an intoxicating aura of sensuality, but it's mostly of the suggestive kind, as in the fantasy flashbacks depicting Horty's imaginary rendezvous with Marie: extreme close-ups of lips sucking fingers, champagne spraying all over Marie's voluptuous body, making love under a table in the Titanic's dining room.

With Marie representing the longing for fantasy, romance, and escape from one's mundane life, the metaphorical story deals poetically with memory, myth, storytelling, and *l'amour fou*. The story is completely unpredictable, and just as Horty's barroom tales start to become stale, the film takes a delightful detour into the picaresque when he joins Zeppe's traveling theater. The stage productions are wonderfully imaginative, with Zoe dressed as Marie and drowning in a cardboard sea and Horty getting struck in the heart by cupid's arrow, while the reappearance of Marie creates an emotionally satisfying and poignant ending. As Horty burns a giant photo of Marie to rid himself of her memory, she rides away with her husband and it's apparent that she has switched places with Horty and is now the one who's consumed by an obsessive and irrational love, fantasizing the two of them rolling in the surf and embracing in slow-motion. *(Profanity, sexual situations.)*—M.S.

d, Bigas Luna; p, Yves Marmion, Daniel Toscan du Plantier; assoc p, Mate Cantero, Stephane Sorlat, Martin Wiebel; w, Bigas Luna, Cuca Canals, Jean-Louis Benoit (from the novel by Didier Decoin); ph, Patrick Blossier; ed, Kenout Peltier; m, Alberto Iglesias; prod d, Walter Caprara, Bruno Cesari, Gualtro Caprara; sound, Jean-Paul Mugel, Laurent Quaglio, Christian Fontaine; cos, Franca Squarciapino

Romance/Historical/Drama **(PR: C MPAA: NR)**

CHAMBERMAID, THE

(SEE: CHAMBERMAID ON THE TITANIC, THE)

CHARACTER ★★★

(Netherlands, 1997) 124m First Floor Features; Kladaradatsch; NPS Television ~ Sony Pictures Classics c (KARAKTER; CHARAKTER)

Fedja van Huet *(Jacob Katadreuffe)*; Jan Decleir *(Dreverhaven)*; Betty Schuurman *(Joba Katadreuffe)*; Victor Low *(De Gankelaar)*; Tamar van den Dop *(Lorna Te George)*; Hans Kesting *(Jan Maan)*; Lou Landre *(Retenstein)*; Bernhard Droog *(Stroomkoning)*; Frans Vorstman *(De Bree)*; Fred Goessens *(Schuwagt)*

An imposing and ironic period drama about a bitter power struggle between father and son, CHARACTER won an Oscar for Best Foreign Language Film in 1998. Although its plot and characters were not entirely deserving of the lavish and skilled treatment they were accorded, this Dutch movie was superior to most of the decade's other Oscar-winning imports.

On the day of his admittance to the bar, Jacob Katadreuffe (Fedja van Huet) visits the offices of Dreverhaven (Jan Decleir), a prosperous and powerful bailiff, to break all ties with him. A heated confrontation ensues. Later that day, after being arrested for Dreverhaven's killing, Katadreuffe tells the examining officer this story: Dreverhaven has a one-time sexual encounter with Joba Katadreuffe (Betty Schuurman), his servant. Subsequently, the woman informs him she is pregnant, refuses his numerous proposals of marriage, and moves out. Jacob is born and grows up poor and illegitimate. Dreverhaven refuses to acknowledge their kinship.

When he has grown to manhood, Jacob Katadreuffe takes out a loan, buys a cigar store, goes bankrupt, and lands a position as a clerk in a law firm, where he advances rapidly. There, he learns that he is in debt to Dreverhaven, who presides over the bank that loaned him the capital to open his store. Over the next few years, Katadreuffe and Dreverhaven battle each other in court, but eventually the young man pays off his debts to his father. Meanwhile, he falls in love with a coworker (Tamar van den Dop), but his single-minded ambition prevents him from pursuing her, and she weds another.

Katadreuffe's final meeting with his father ends in a fierce and bloody fight, but the young man testifies that when he left the scene Dreverhaven was alive. The police realize that their suspect is telling the truth. When they ask him how he thinks Dreverhaven died, the young man speculates suicide. Freed by the authorities, Katadreuffe is given a letter from Dreverhaven in which the bailiff has bequeathed his extensive estate to his illegitimate son. The letter is signed "Father."

Expertly mounted, CHARACTER is as ambitious as its protagonist (though its ambitions, like his, are somewhat misplaced). The movie's limber, blue-tinged cinematography and refreshing, dynamic editing infuse it with movement and impetus, and its thematic richness and imposing urban locations lend it stature and weight.

Given this impressive framework, the film's characters are fairly disappointing. The boy is an antiheroic careerist; the girl is an also-ran; the mother is a sphinx; the father, an almost otherworldly figure who has been abstracted nearly to the point of allegory, is a golem. Jan Decleir, in the latter role, gives the picture's most potent performance.

Only twice does the film attempt to get inside the mind of this mysterious monster, and both forays are interesting ones. On one occasion, the audience is allowed to share a nightmare of Dreverhaven's, in which he dreams he is standing naked and defiant before an angry mob of his poor tenants. (When the dream later comes true, he will be fully clothed but less defiant.) And in a climactic scene that reprises father and son's final confrontation, subtle changes this time around in camera placement and line readings reveal that Dreverhaven considers himself to be his son's savior rather than his curse.

CHARACTER was released in the Netherlands in spring, 1997, and reached US audiences a year later. Based on a classic 1938 Dutch novel of the same name, it was described by several American critics as "Dickensian." When asked if the film had indeed been inspired by Dickens, its talented director, Mike van Diem, replied: "Not on a conscious level. But I'm happy to take it as a compliment." *(Graphic violence.)*— D.T.

d, Mike van Diem; p, Laurens Geels; w, Mike van Diem, Laurens Geels, Ruud van Megen (based on the novel by Ferdinand Bordewijk); ph, Rogier Stoffers; ed, Jessica DeKoning; m, Het Paleis van Boem; art d, Jelier & Schief; sound, Alek Goosse (mixer), Peter Warnier (design); casting, Jeannette Snik; cos, Jany Temime; makeup, Kathy Kuhne

AA Best Foreign Language Film

Drama/Crime **(PR: C MPAA: R)**

CHARLIE HOBOKEN ★★

(U.S., 1998) 85m Cause and Effect ~ Northern Arts Entertainment c

Austin Pendleton *(Harry Cedars)*; Ken Garito *(Charlie Hoboken)*; Tovah Feldshuh *(Angie Cedars)*; Anita Gillette *(Stepmother)*; Jennifer Esposito *(Girlfriend #1)*; George Morfogen *(Father)*; Veanne Cox *(Girlfriend #2)*; Amanda Peet *(Girlfriend #3)*; Jonathan Staci Kim *(Ping)*; Joel Friedman *(Barber)*; David Eigenberg *(Mario)*; Rocko Sisto *(Cook)*; Paula Newsome *(Office Manager)*; Kevin Bone *(Funeral Attendant/Waiter)*; Tara Hauptman; Mark Jupiter *(Opening Couple)*; Thomas F. Mazziotti *(Boss's Son)*; Ebony Jo-Ann; Nora Carreras; Alicia Jacobson; Laura Nieves *(Secretaries)*; Ian Rose *(Hit #1—Shrink)*; Robert Fisher *(Hit #2—Businessman)*; Pat Carucci *(Cleaning Woman)*; Cletus Polk Jr.; Samy Sheraf Moustafa *(Diner Patrons)*; Nicholas Cordasco; Marty Deruiter; Phyllis J.

Esposito; Thomas Gilbert; Kimberly Hirsch; Charlie Laplaca; Frank Littrigio; Andrew Masi; Debbie Masi; Rita Masi; Vera Masi; Joe Mennicucci; Gerald O'Connor; Nicholas Palma; Carol Piscitelli; James Spiegel; Karol Turner; Carmen Ventola *(Party Guests)*

Coming off as more of a slick writing exercise than a coherent motion picture, CHARLIE HOBOKEN is a highly theatrical affair, an indie crime comedy that offers up ample amounts of stylized banter spoken by a group of rigidly defined, very chatty characters.

Charlie Hoboken (Ken Garito) is the son of a New Jersey insurance agent who works in his father's office by day, while spending his evenings as a hitman. Charlie is a well-groomed young man with upwardly mobile aspirations; his partner in crime, veteran hitman Harry Cedars (Austin Pendleton) is a down-to-earth sort who approaches his job in a straightforward, no-frills manner. Charlie's notion that the pair require a "higher class" of target eventually begins making the rather staid Harry restless. Harry's wife Angie (Tovah Feldshuh) tries to quell his doubts while she voices her own regrets about not having had a child.

Charlie's dream of moving up in the underworld seems to be coming true when, during a surprise birthday party thrown for Harry by a group of hitmen, he encounters the son (Thomas F. Mazziotti) of the "big boss" and the two status-conscious young men hit it off. After the party, Charlie and Harry have a serious talk solidifying the father-son bond that has grown between them. Despite this connection, a subsequent hit takes longer than expected and Harry decides that their close relationship is impeding their work. Harry recruits another young man, a wide-eyed novice, to be his partner in an out-of-town job.

Charlie soon reads Harry's obituary and attends his wake, where Angie reveals to Charlie that Harry died because the brakes in his car didn't work. When kneeling before Harry's casket and praying, Charlie reveals that he rigged the brakes. Harry gets the upper hand, however: he sits up in his casket and points a gun at Charlie, reminding him of his repeated warning that the simpler and more direct a killing is, the safer it is. It is revealed subsequently that Harry staged his "death" and the wake as a prank upon discovering that Charlie had tampered with his brakes; this in an effort to scare the young insurance agent back to his true calling. Charlie commits to his day-job at his father's office, and a life with his patient girlfriend (Jennifer Esposito).

First-time filmmaker Thomas F. Mazziotti appears to be a frustrated playwright. His debut feature, CHARLIE HOBOKEN, is composed of a succession of two-person scenes in which his characters make declarations about their behavior and motivations, and give their fellows endless amounts of advice. Mazziotti fashions a world in which a hitman uses the word "octagenarian" when describing a target, two lovers argue over what part of speech they each represent (Charlie tells his girlfriend that he "was raised a strict verb. Nouns like love were never in my vocabulary, or my father's."), and a one-night stand is hastily concluded when a woman Charlie picks up in a bar finds out he's not a Democrat. Quirky, to be sure, but unfortunately not amusing or perceptive. Mazziotti's tendency to have his characters speak in a declarative style puts him in an artistic terrain midway between playwright Herb Gardner and independent filmmaker Hal Hartley—however, Mazziotti's writing lacks the emotional depth of the former and the eccentric wit of the latter.

Given that the film functions primarily as an actor's showcase, Mazziotti (who, like his protagonist, is a NJ insurance agent's son) was lucky to have secured the services of a trio of noted NY theater actors. The casting of nerdy Austin Pendleton as a veteran hitman is clearly one of the film's central comedic conceits. Pendleton, a consummate professional, does bring a welcome note of humanity to the character; he also copes rather well with the idiosyncratic dialogue. Tovah Feldshuh delivers a nuanced comic turn, and supplies the film's most affecting sequence as the childless Angie explains to Harry why she carries around storebought photos of other people's children. Anita Gillette effectively plays the only true villain of the piece, Charlie's reserved and greedy stepmother. Garito's lead performance hits just the right note of creepy self-assuredness and pseudo-intellectualism; the problem is that, as written, Charlie works best as an antihero, but both Mazziotti and Garito clearly envisioned him as a sympathetic character.

While the film as a whole is far more theatrical than it is cinematic, one plot detail does linger in the memory: the fact that Charlie lives in an abandoned church, his bedroom situated squarely on the altar. The fact that this plot point is never developed or exploited to any degree only serves to point up Mazziotti's neophyte status. *(Strong language, nudity, adult situations.)*—E.G.

d, Thomas F. Mazziotti; p, Linda Crean; w, Thomas F. Mazziotti; ph, Mike Slovis; ed, Thomas R. Rondinella; m, Peter C. Lopez; prod d, Dina Goldman; sound, Franklin Gonzalez (mixer); casting, Lina Todd Casting; cos, Loren Bevans; makeup, Karen Weinberg

Comedy/Crime **(PR: C MPAA: NR)**

CHICAGO CAB ★★★

(U.S., 1998) 97m Child's Will Production; New Crime Production; GFT Entertainment ~ Castle Hill c

Gillian Anderson *(Southside Girl)*; John Cusack *(Scary Man)*; Paul Dillon *(Cab Driver)*; Moira Harris *(Religious Mother)*; Michael Ironside *(Al)*; Laurie Metcalf *(Female Ad Exec)*; Julianne Moore *(Distraught Woman)*; Kevin J. O'Connor *(Southside Guy)*; Tim Reinhard *(Geek)*; Tim Gamble *(Religious Father)*; Olivia Trevino *(4-Year-Old Girl)*; Rana Khan *(Pakistani)*; Darryl Theirse *(X-Hat)*; Shanesia Davis-Williams *(Lawyer)*; Laura Kellogg Sandberg *(Bug-Eyed Woman)*; Phillip Van Lear *(Father-To-Be)*; Ora Jones *(Pregnant Woman)*; Michael Shannon *(Crack Head)*; Shulie Cowen *(Stoner Girl)*; Andrew Rothenberg *(Homer)*; Tracy Letts *(Sports Fan)*; Carol Hall *(Mega Shopper)*; Hubert Taczanowski *(Immigrant)*; Vince Green *(Young Urban Man)*; Laura Whyte *(Mom)*; Matt Roth *(Male Ad Exec)*; John C. Reilly *(Steve)*; Tara Chocol *(Receptionist)*; Ron Dean *(Old Snack Trucker)*; Don Julien *(Nail Biter)*; Marc Nelson *(Fat Guy)*; Holly Wantuch *(Dog Lady)*; Sunni Ali Powell *(Ganja Man)*; Troy West *(Story Man)*; John Morhlrein *(One-Handed Man)*; April Grace *(Shalita)*; Harry J. Lennix *(Pissed-Off Boyfriend)*; Mary Ann Thebus *(Old Drunk Woman)*; Loren Lazerine *(Obnoxious Guy #1)*; Jeff Still *(Obnoxious Guy #2)*; Reggie Hayes *(Architect)*

Adapted by Will Kern from his popular play *Hellcab*, the episodic CHICAGO CAB follows with wit and sympathy the fortunes of an urban taxi driver over the course of a long and particularly trying workday.

At six a.m. on a cold morning a few days before Christmas, a cab driver (Paul Dillon) begins his 16-hour shift. Over the course of the day he encounters a succession of bickering couples, older women on the make, eccentric and abusive fares of every class and description.

His most personally challenging experience occurs when he picks up a lovey-dovey couple: a businessman (John C. Reilly) and a receptionist (Tara Chacol). After the woman is dropped off at her office, the businessman makes humiliating and ugly remarks about his sexual relationship with her. Disgusted by the man's crude attitude and touched by the receptionist's sweet personality, the cabbie later returns to her workplace, where he tells her what her escort has said and warns her to be wary of him. The cabbie has an even more depressing experience after dark, when he picks up a woman who has just been raped (Julianne Moore). Deeply disturbed by her plight and his inability to ease her pain, the cabbie is seized by a wave of misery and hopelessness, but is somewhat comforted by his next fare, a kindly architect (Reggie Hayes), as the day ends.

Although few of CHICAGO CAB's series of backseat minidramas and comedies are particularly novel, almost all of them are effective and engaging. In the movie's most original, poetic, and filmic interlude, the cabbie takes on a sinister fare (John Cusack), identified in the credits as "Scary Man," who cryptically directs the uneasy driver down mean, decreasingly populated city streets in the dead of night. The encounter turns out to be benign when the fare tips the cabbie generously and warmly wishes him a merry Christmas, but one feels that the incident has pushed the cabbie a few days closer to an inevitable nervous breakdown. This haunting episode also illustrates CHICAGO CAB's keen sensitivity to the loneliness of Christmastime. Though a former cab driver himself, Kern was wise to make his central character a permanent member of the working class rather than an aspiring writer or actor moonlighting as a taxi temp. Paul Dillon has the perfect face—a denuded face straight out of Beckett—for the role. He looks like Bill Irwin with ulcers and, when the hood of his jacket is up, like Anders Ek's bilious monk in THE SEVENTH SEAL (1956).

The movies ought to give us more day-in-the-life films like CHICAGO CAB, which provides refreshing counterbalance to the traditional three-act scenarios we're accustomed to, as well as welcome respite from the ubiquity of New York, which filmmakers seem to think is the only city in the country. *(Sexual situations, extreme profanity.)*—D.T.

d, Mary Cybulski, John Tintori; p, Paul Dillon, Suzanne De Walt; exec p, Gary Howsam, Kathy Morgan, Charles Weber, John Cusak, D.V. Divincentis, Steve Pink; co-p, Jamie Gordon; w, Will Kern (based on his play *Hellcab*); ph, Hubert Taczanowski; ed, John Tintori, Mary Cybulski; m, Page Hamilton; prod d, Maria Nay; set d, Scott Troha; sound, Joe Yario (mixer); casting, John Papsidera; cos, Carolyn Greco; makeup, Jamie Weiss

Drama/Comedy **(PR: C MPAA: R)**

CHILDREN OF THE CORN V: FIELD OF TERROR ★★

(U.S., 1998) 83m Dimension Films; Blue Rider Pictures ~ Dimension Home Video c

Stacy Galina *(Alison)*; Alexis Arquette *(Greg)*; Adam Wylie *(Ezekiel)*; Greg Vaughan *(Tyrus)*; Eva Mendez *(Kir)*; Ahmet Zappa *(Laszlo)*; Angela Jones *(Charlotte)*; Fred Williamson *(Sheriff Skaggs)*; David Carradine *(Lucas Enright)*; Dave Buzzotta *(Jacob)*; Olivia Burnette *(Lilly)*; Aaron Jackson *(Zane)*; Matthew Tait *(Jared)*; Kane Hodder *(Bartender)*; Jennifer Badger *(Judith)*; Hiro Kada *(Caleb)*; Frank Lloyd *(Deputy Earl)*; Gary Bullock *(Farmer)*; Season Hubley *(Lilly's Mother)*; Edward Edwards *(Lilly's Father)*; Sicily *(Chloe)*; Diva Zappa *(Drill Girl)*; Christopher Stinson *(Evil Corn Kid)*; Danny Goldring *(Mr. O'Brien)*; Deborah Strang *(Mrs. O'Brien)*

Originally subtitled FIELD OF SCREAMS, this is a well-intentioned but ultimately ineffective attempt to take the CHILDREN OF THE CORN franchise in a more dramatic direction.

A young quartet—Alison (Stacy Galina), Greg (Alexis Arquette), Tyrus (Greg Vaughan), and Kir (Eva Mendez)—drive to a rural area with the cremated remains of Kurt, Kir's recently deceased boyfriend. Little do they know that a murderous cult of local children, headed by Ezekiel (Adam Wylie), has murdered Laszlo (Ahmet Zappa) and Charlotte (Angela Jones), two more of Kurt's pals who had preceded them there. The group crash their car, are briefly confronted by Ezekiel and his followers, and find their way into town, where they learn that the kids are in thrall to mysterious Lucas Enright (David Carradine) and a deity called "He Who Walks Behind the Rows." Alison realizes that this is the cult her brother Jacob joined years before.

Alison insists on staying to find Jacob, and the others reluctantly agree. Alison tracks Jacob (Dave Buzzotta) down and learns that, like all the kids, he must sacrifice himself to He Who Walks on his 18th birthday—the next day. But instead of leaping into the burning silo housing the evil spirit, Jacob flees, and Kir, still anguished by Kurt's death, jumps in in his place. Jacob is captured and stabbed by Ezekiel's minions, and when local sheriff Skaggs (Fred Williamson) confronts Lucas, the latter becomes a demonic creature, kills Skaggs and then expires himself. Alison, Greg, and Tyrus discover the dying Jacob; Greg and Tyrus are slain by the children, but Alison manages to pitch Ezekiel into the burning silo before extinguishing the demonic flame with fertilizer. Later, she adopts the baby Jacob had with one of the cult girls—an infant whose eyes glow with evil.

FIELD OF TERROR's story is notably busier than that of the previous CHILDREN films, and it's to writer-director Ethan Wiley's credit that he has attempted to reimagine the basics of this seemingly pointless series. As opposed to the rural fanatics of past installments, the children here are mostly troubled youth who have fled abusive homes and unhappy lives to follow Lucas and Ezekiel—an updated touch that gives the story more resonance. Unfortunately, Wiley's development of his premise is shaky, and he seems to have felt compelled to throw in generic horror set pieces at the expense of a more realistic approach.

Too much of the film is simply implausible, from the fact that Alison would just happen to stumble upon the cult that long ago seduced her brother to Kir's apparently sudden decision to kill herself. Some of Wiley's dialogue is equally unbelievable, and there are a number of ill-timed humorous moments reminiscent of his previous feature, HOUSE II: THE SECOND STORY (1987). If nothing else, FIELD OF TERROR does suggest that the CHILDREN movies might still have possibilities, but it hardly makes one anxious to see future installments of the series. *(Graphic violence, sexual situations, adult situations, profanity.)*—M.G.

d, Ethan Wiley; p, Jeff Geoffray, Walter Josten; exec p, Jeffrey Kurz; assoc p, Alex Epstein; w, Ethan Wiley (based on the short story "Children of the Corn" by Stephen King); ph, David Lewis; ed, Peter Devaney Flanagan; m, Paul Rabjohns; prod d, Deborah Raymond, Dorian Vernacchio; set d, Neil O'Sullivan; fx, James "Wayne" Beauchamp, Netter Digital Entertainment Inc., Jason Netter; casting, Ed Mitchell, Robyn Ray; cos, Hollywood Raggs, Malou McCartney; makeup, Deborah Wolski McNulty, Adam Brandy, SOTA FX (effects), Roy Knyrim (effects), Jerry Macaluso (effects); stunts, Kane Hodder

Horror **(PR: O MPAA: R)**

CHILE, OBSTINATE MEMORY ★★★½

(Canada/France, 1997) 58m Les Films d'Ici; National Film Board of Canada; La Sept Arte ~ First Run/Icarus Films c

Patricio Guzman

Documentarian Patricio Guzman looks back at the impact of Chile's 1973 government coup in CHILE, OBSTINATE MEMORY, a short, bittersweet essay on memory, both collective and individual.

Guzman returns to Chile in 1996, more than two decades after he recorded the events of the right-wing takeover in the landmark film, THE BATTLE OF CHILE (1976). He travels with friends and crew members who had not been back to their native country since fleeing from Gen. Pinochet's massacre in 1973. Guzman interviews many people about their recollections, showing them (for the first time) a print of THE BATTLE OF CHILE, which has never been released in the country.

A debate emerges from the various participants over the relevance of the coup and its impact on their lives. A group of grade school students argue that Chile has actually benefitted from Pinochet's post-1973 dictatorship, while the student's teacher laments her earlier support of the coup. Several artists and professionals (a painter, a filmmaker, a doctor) remember the sad losses in their community. Another teacher, who was caught on film in the original BATTLE OF CHILE, warns against obsessing over the past.

Guzman also talks to relatives close to the film's makers, including his own uncle, Ignacio, who had hid the reels of CHILE from the military junta and shipped it out of the country; Guzman then visits with the father of his former cameraman, Jorge Muller, who had "disappeared" (and was presumably assassinated) during the coup. Next, Guzman calls on the widow of the Salvador Allende, the late president of Chile who was killed in the bombing raid on the presidential palace. Mrs. Allende remembers her husband with sad fondness. In the final section, a group of college students see the film for the first time and are moved to tears by the loss; they also regret the lies they have been told over the years.

Evoking the spirit of Marcel Ophuls's SORROW AND THE PITY (1970), Patricio Guzman's CHILE, OBSTINATE MEMORY looks not only at historical events, but the way history gets rewritten by subsequent generations. Guzman's THE BATTLE OF CHILE brilliantly documented how right-wing fascists took over the Chilean government in 1973, while CHILE, OBSTINATE MEMORY reflects, with both anger and sadness, at how the coup now seems like a distant incident for some, and a life-altering milestone for others (particularly those who lived through it).

Guzman's gutsy return visit yields some vivid moments, including the separate debates with the students, young and old, and the responses to the secret screenings of THE BATTLE OF CHILE by the coup survivors. But Guzman's short (58-minute) foray feels unfinished. The interviews and stops at notable locations (e.g., Santiago's soccer stadium where many Chileans were once tortured and killed) are not ordered in a dramatically suspenseful or cathartic way, leaving viewers somewhat befuddled by the variety of opinions about Chile's repressed history. Ironically, in spite the confusion and chaos surrounding the coup, the original THE BATTLE OF CHILE succeeded, in part, because of the clear and linear storytelling techniques not utilized here.

Moreover, Guzman does not go far enough in personalizing the return to his homeland, turning much of the visit into a "talking head" documentary with little of his own presence (his courage and grief are unquestioned, but they do not come through). Finally, any appreciation of CHILE, OBSTINATE MEMORY depends on knowledge of the actual historical events under examination.

Though lacking the power of Ophuls's best work, CHILE, OBSTINATE MEMORY makes a game attempt at understanding and remembering a significant part of a country's tragic history. *(Adult situations.)*—E.M.

d, Patricio Guzman; p, Yves Jeanneau, Eric Michel; assoc p, Fernando Acuna, Ricardo Larrain; ph, Eric Pittard; ed, Helene Girard; m, Robert M. Legage; sound, Boris Herrera

Documentary **(PR: A MPAA: NR)**

CHINESE BOX, THE ★★★

(Japan/France/U.S., 1997) 99m WW Productions; Canal Plus; NDF International; Pony Canyon ~ Trimark c

Jeremy Irons *(John)*; Gong Li *(Vivian)*; Maggie Cheung *(Jean)*; Michael Hui *(Chang)*; Ruben Blades *(Jim)*; Jared Harris *(William)*; Chaplin Chang *(Homeless Man)*; Noel Rands *(John's Friend at New Year's Party)*; Emma Lucia *(Amanda Everheart)*; Ken Bennett *(Rick)*; Russell Cawthorne *(New Year's Party MC)*; Emotion Cheung *(William Wong)*; Harvey Stockwin *(Weeks)*; Jonathan Midgley *(Jonathan)*; Bruce Walker *(Bruce)*; Angelica Lofgren *(Baby-Lin)*; Dr. Julian Chang *(Dr. Chang)*; Jian Rui Chao *(Businessman #1)*; Wai Sing *(Businessman #2)*; Lo Hung *(Businessman #3)*; Shirley Hung *(Girlfriend #1)*; Michelle Yeung *(Girlfriend #2)*; Alex Ng, billed as Alex Ng Hong Ling *(Drunk Karaoke Singer)*; Chiu Wah Lee *(Minibus Passenger)*; Maria Cordero *(Mamasan)*; Pao Fung *(Godfather)*; Hui Fan *(Godfather's Wife)*; Lam Man Cheung *(Wedding Photographer)*; Lee Siu Kai *(Gangster #1)*; Leung Chi On *(Gangster #2)*; Tse Yuen Fat *(Gangster #3)*; Roderick Lee *(Manhattan Club Bouncer)*; Hui Li; Maria St. Lynne *(Black Moon Hostesses)*; Josephine Ho *(Lilly)*; Gloria Wu *(News Reporter)*

Rich in character, detail, and metaphorical resonance, THE CHINESE BOX lacks for nothing save a cohesive storyline.

It is shortly before the return of Hong Kong to China. John (Jeremy Irons), a British financial reporter, is desperately in love with Chinese expatriate Vivian (Gong Li), who in turn is wholly devoted to upwardly-mobile Chang (Michael Hui). When John discovers he is dying of leukemia, he quits his job and begins a quest to document and understand impenetrable Hong Kong, fixating on a scarred young street hustler, Jean (Maggie Cheung). She videotapes her life story for him, but it turns out to be a lie; when he tracks down her real past and confronts her with the British lover who apparently abandoned her and ruined her life, the man brushes Jean off and breaks her heart again.

Meanwhile Vivian finally realizes that Chang will never marry her due to her sordid past, and she offers to leave with John. When he spurns her, she seduces him in the guise of a prostitute named Jenny. Later she discovers that he is dying and the two become lovers, until John reluctantly deserts her. He resigns himself to death and she finds the strength to start over, just as the British leave Hong Kong.

Born in the territory, educated both there and in the US, co-writer-director Wayne Wang worked in HK television alongside the leading lights of the local new wave before establishing his filmmaking career in the states. In 1990 he turned his lens on his homeland with the dark, partially-improvised LIFE IS CHEAP. . . BUT TOILET PAPER IS EXPENSIVE. CHINESE BOX marks his return to an examination of the Hong Kong psyche, once again working from an incomplete script. Shot in sequence in pseudodocumentary fashion, its intent was in part to capture the unfolding drama of the handover. Unfortunately for the film, no particular drama unfolded. Instead we're offered a narrative bloated with symbolism (a dog running on a treadmill; an eviscerated fish with its exposed heart still beating) and a collection of characters (or characteristics), each representing part of the HK experience. Facets of a whole, their synergism is apparent in their very names: John, Jean, Jenny. Baffled, hungry, by turns regretful and resentful, Jeremy Irons is superb as the allegorical representative of the dying British presence. Gong Li is less successful as Vivian, the sophisticated butterfly who is tellingly depicted in one sequence imitating Marlene Dietrich in A FOREIGN AFFAIR (1948). Not fluent in English, Gong learned her lines phonetically, and consequently gives a somewhat stiff performance. On the other hand, she's thoroughly luminous as Jenny, Vivian's Hyde-like persona. Reverting to her prior incarnation as a Mainland immigrant hustling for a living, with broken English and little telling gestures she seduces the aptly-named John—as well as the camera.

Maggie Cheung is so captivating as the disfigured Jean—discarded by her British lover, leading her to adopt a mercenary lifestyle while she pines for his return—that she throws the entire movie off-kilter. Themes of loyalty and betrayal among the races weave throughout the script, and Jean's story embodies both in what seems at first like a digression but comes to dominate the center of the film. Director Wang has stated that he was torn between Jean's story and Vivian's, at times leaning toward making the film about one or the other. In opting for both, he weakens the dramatic structure. After what he called a "more indulgent and quite abstract" version of the film played the Venice Film Festival, Wang cut it by ten minutes, restored some scissored scenes (including the reunion of Jean and her erstwhile love) and added voiceovers in an attempt to smooth it out for American release.

As individual puzzle pieces, the assorted narrative fragments are intriguing and certainly beautiful to look at. The electric atmosphere of Hong Kong is well depicted, with some of its outstanding landmarks and local actors appearing, led by Cantonese cinema's renaissance man of the 1970s, Michael Hui, as John's rival for Vivian's affections. Graeme Revell's score, an award winner at Venice, is truly exceptional, with gorgeously evocative vocals by Dadawa. Unfortunately the component parts never quite coalesce into a whole, instead swimming around one another as a disjunctive collection of subplots. In attempting to be at once a love story, a documentary on the handover and an examination of the native psyche, the film's greatest fault is its overarching ambition. *(Violence, sexual situations, profanity.)*—A.B.

d, Wayne Wang; p, Wayne Wang, Lydia Dean Pilcher, Jean-Louis Piel; exec p, Michiyo Yoshizaki, Akinori Inaba, Jean Labadie, Reinhard Brundig; assoc p, Francey Grace; co-p, Heidi Levitt, Jessinta Liu; w, Jean-Claude Carriere, Larry Gross (from a story by Jean-Claude Carriere, Paul Theroux, and Wayne Wang); ph, Vilko Filac; ed, Christopher Tellefsen, Misako Shimizu; m, Graeme Revell; prod d, Chris Wong; sound, Drew Kunin (mixer); casting, Heidi Levitt; cos, Shirley Chan; makeup, Isabel Harkins, Lo Shui Lin

Romance/Drama **(PR: C MPAA: R)**

CHOSEN ONE: LEGEND OF THE RAVEN, THE ★½

(U.S., 1998) 88m Discovery Entertainment ~ Troma c

Carmen Electra *(McKenna/The Raven)*; Shauna Sand, billed as Shauna Sand Lamas *(Emma)*; Tim Bagley *(Ricky Dean)*; Dave Oliver *(Henry)*; Debra Xavier *(Nora)*; Michael Stadvec *(Cole)*; Charles Santore *(Dougie)*; Conrad Bachmann *(Carl)*; Frank Salsedo *(Papi)*; Lawrence Lanoff *(Serial Killer Bob)*; Leslie C. Meenen *(Tammy)*; Michael Lathom *(John)*; Priscilla Yagher *(Betz)*; Billy Fox *(Bartender)*

One would think a movie starring a "Baywatch" babe and a *Playboy* Playmate, co-produced by another Playmate and released by Troma would have its own singular charms; however, THE CHOSEN ONE is neither as sexy or as intentionally silly as that combination suggests.

In the battle between the forces of darkness and light, only the Sacred Crescent, a magic talisman, will allow good to prevail. In a rural valley, the Crescent's keeper, Emma Braveknight (Shauna Sand), is murdered by a thug named Cole (Michael Stadvec). Emma's sister McKenna (Carmen Electra) comes home for the burial. She reunites with her old boyfriend, local sheriff Henry (Dave Oliver), and is summoned by Emma's spirit to a ritual where she is made keeper of the Crescent. Nora (Debra Xavier), Henry's girlfriend who's angered by his return to McKenna, goes back to Cole, her old flame, and Cole and his boys beat Henry up. Encouraged by Emma's ghost, McKenna heals Henry with her touch. She goes after Cole, and Nora shoots her, only to be shot dead herself by Cole.

McKenna awakens with paranormal "powers of the raven." Nora also revives, transformed by evil forces. After some resistance, McKenna gives in to her destiny, dons a silver and metal outfit and sets out as a crimefighter. Nora kills Cole's goons, and McKenna and Henry set out to find her. Nora recruits a couple of small-time crooks to help her, and one of them shoots Henry when he and McKenna confront Nora. McKenna magically transports herself and Nora to an urban setting, where she kills Nora after a prolonged fight. She then returns to the valley and revives Henry.

A STAR WARS-style opening title crawl (complete with the heading "Episode One: Renewed Hope") hints that these filmmakers have the right comedic spirit—a suggestion that's quickly dashed once the film itself begins. With no development given to the notion of the apocalyptic battle between good and evil mentioned at the outset, this is really just a rural crime melodrama with a few mystical gimmicks thrown in; the mix of good ol' boy cliches and cheapjack fantasy proves a very awkward one indeed. A lighter touch behind the camera might have helped, but Lawrence Lanoff's direction is straight-faced and flat-footed, and none of the actors seem capable of giving the material the ironic tone that it deserves. Certainly, Electra and Sand—the abovementioned former "Baywatch" cast member and *Playboy* Playmate—appear to have been hired on the basis of their looks, not their dramatic or comedic gifts (the other *Playboy* alumna involved in the production, India Allen, wisely chose to remain offscreen).

In an attempt to give the mundane proceedings something of a mythic air, many scenes are accompanied by narration that explains things that are already self-evident—the narrator's comments include insights like "Although she is beautiful, McKenna burns with an unpredictable fire." One doesn't know whether to chuckle appreciatively or simply yawn and turn the whole thing off. *(Violence, extensive nudity, sexual situations, profanity.)*—M.G.

d, Lawrence Lanoff; p, India Allen, James Velasquez; exec p, Hoke M. Rose, Lawrence Lanoff; assoc p, Corey Kiefer; co-p, Freshman Production Services; w, Sam Rappaport, Khara Bromiley; ph, Robert New; ed, Thomas Teltser, India Allen; m, Keith Arem; sound, Todd Bozung, Warren Woods; casting, Dave Oliver; cos, Elisabetta Rogiani; makeup, Dewey Cook; stunts, Tony Snegoff

Action/Fantasy **(PR: O MPAA: NR)**

CITY OF ANGELS ★★

(U.S., 1998) 152m Atlas Entertainment; New Regency ~ Warner Bros. c

Nicolas Cage *(Seth)*; Meg Ryan *(Dr. Maggie Rice)*; Dennis Franz *(Nathaniel Messinger)*; Andre Braugher *(Cassiel)*; Colm Feore *(Jordan)*; Robin Bartlett *(Anne)*; Joanna Merlin *(Teresa)*; Sarah Dampf *(Susan)*; Rhonda Dotson *(Susan's Mother)*; Nigel Gibbs *(Doctor)*; John Putch *(Man in Car)*; Lauri Johnson *(Woman in*

Car); Christian Aubert *(Foreign Visitor in Car)*; Jay Patterson *(Air Traffic Controller)*; Shishir Kurup *(Anaesthesiologist)*; Brian Markinson *(Surgical Fellow)*; Hector Velasquez *(Scrub Nurse)*; Marlene Kanter *(Circulating Nurse)*; Bernard White *(Circulating Nurse)*; Dan Desmond *(Mr. Balford)*; Deirdre O'Connell *(Mrs. Balford)*; Kim Murphy *(Balford's Daughter)*; Chad Lindberg *(Balfords' Son)*; Alexander Folk *(Convenience Store Clerk)*; Rainbow Borden *(Hold-Up Man)*; Harper Roisman *(Old Man in Library)*; Sid Hillman *(Librarian)*; Wanda-Lee Evans *(Nurse in Messinger's Room)*; Wanda Christine *(Station Nurse)*; E.J. Callahan *(Waiter at Johnnie's)*; Tudi Roche *(Messinger's Daughter)*; David Moreland *(Husband Frank)*; Kristina Malota *(Hannah)*; Stan Davis *(Construction Foreman)*; Mik Scriba *(Construction Worker)*; Nick Offerman *(Construction Worker)*; Kieu-Chinh *(Asian Woman)*; Geoffrey A. Thorne *(Big Orderly)*; Peter Spellos *(Mac Truck Driver)*; Jim Kline *(Store Clerk)*; Cherene Snow *(Woman Sewing)*; Theodore Borders

In FACE/OFF (1997), Nicolas Cage took over John Travolta's face and personality. In this Hollywood-ized remake of Wim Wenders's WINGS OF DESIRE (1987), Cage takes over one of Travolta's hit movie roles—that of a sexy angel (remember 1996's MICHAEL?). Unfortunately, the new film never takes flight, despite some quality production design.

In contemporary Los Angeles, Seth (Nicolas Cage), an angel, and Cassiel (Andre Braugher), his coworker, spend their days escorting dying souls to the hereafter. During one mission, Seth becomes mesmerized by cardiothoracic surgeon Maggie (Meg Ryan), who fights to save the life of the man he is trying to take to the afterlife. When he sees her crying over the loss of her patient, Seth seeks to reassure Maggie about her professional skill and confess his love for her, but by becoming visible he knows he has broken a rule among his fellow angels. Maggie is confused but also charmed by this handsome stranger, who enters her life posing as a hospital visitor.

Nevertheless, the love-at-first-sight chemistry between Maggie and Seth creates several problems. Maggie begins to question her relationship with Jordan (Colm Feore), a straightlaced surgeon with whom she is engaged, while Seth, who is jealous of Jordan, yearns to feel like a real human being. As it happens, Maggie's newest heart patient, the rambunctious Mr. Messinger (Dennis Franz), recognizes Seth as an angel because he himself was an angel before he "fell" to Earth and became mortal. Messinger suggests Seth follow his example, but also promises to keep Seth's secret between them. During a date one night, though, Maggie accidentally discovers the truth about Seth's identity. At first horrified by the challenge to her secular materialism and rationality, Maggie eventually falls in love all over again with Seth. Still, Maggie decides to leave Seth and marry Jordan when she realizes that she and Seth could never have a true earthly relationship. Just as she learns from Messinger that Seth has the ability to become human, Seth takes the "fall to Earth" plunge—in order to head off Maggie's wedding. Seth and Maggie reunite as mortals and spend a beautiful night and day together, enjoying a fully physical relationship. But, during their stay at a Lake Tahoe vacation house, Maggie rides her bike into a truck on the road and dies. Seth experiences great pain at his loss, but also knows that his brief time with Maggie was worth his transformation from angel to mortal. Watched by his former angel friends from shoreside, Seth plunges into the ocean to celebrate his rebirth and renewal.

Like Wenders's quirky 1987 romantic fantasy, CITY OF ANGELS juggles fantasy, philosophy, romantic drama, and comic relief with a fair degree of skill. But the big problem with Dana Stevens's rewrite of the German art house hit is that there are inconsistencies in the development of the main angel character. For example, Seth—in angel mode—experiences some human emotions but not others and instinctively knows some things but not others. (Note these contradictions are inherent in nearly all angel movies, from HERE COMES MR. JORDAN, to the 1996 remake of THE PREACHER'S WIFE). In CITY OF ANGELS, one may also question why 90 percent of the other angel characters are young white men (all dressed in chic LA black). CITY OF ANGELS is further hampered by the casting of Ryan and Cage, not the most exciting of movie stars: in her Shirley Temple curls, Ryan effects a perky pose, even as a top-flight surgeon, as in the ghastly moment where she sings the Band-Aid brand jingle ("I am stuck on Band-Aid brand. . . ") while performing an operation; Cage, who has been overrated throughout his career, merely looks and acts like a somnambulistic stalker through much of the film. To their credit, however, Ryan and Cage handle the most difficult dramatic scenes without committing huge gaffes, and they are ably supported by Dennis Franz, Andre Braugher, Colm Feore, and Robin Bartlett.

Surprisingly, the most distinguished aspect of CITY OF ANGELS is its visual style. Lilly Kilvert's sleek production design, John Nelson's surreal special effects, and John Seale's smooth Panavision camerawork actually rival some of Wenders's work in the German original—no small feat for a contemporary Hollywood movie. Credit, perhaps, should also go to director Brad Silberling, but with only this and CASPER (1995) on his resume so far, it's hard to determine how much recognition he should really get for the virtues of this somewhat less-than-heavenly outing. *(Violence, nudity, sexual situations, adult situations, profanity.)*—E.M.

d, Brad Silberling; p, Dawn Steel, Charles Roven; exec p, Robert Cavallo, Arnon Milchan, Charles Newirth; co-p, Kelley Smith-Wait, Douglas Segal; w, Dana Stevens (based on the screenplay "Der Himmel uber Berlin [Heaven Over Berlin]" by Wim Wenders, Peter Handke, and Richard Reitinger); ph, John Seale; ed, Lynzee Klingman; m, Gabriel Yared; prod d, Lily Kilvert; art d, John Warnke; set d, Gretchen Rau; sound, David MacMillan (mixer); fx, David Blitstein, John Nelson, Sony Pictures Imageworks; casting, David Rubin; cos, Shay Cunliffe; makeup, Hallie D'Amore; stunts, Doug Coleman

Romance/Fantasy/Drama (PR: C MPAA: PG-13)

CIVIL ACTION, A ★★★

(U.S., 1998) 113m Wildwood Enterprises; Touchstone Pictures ~ Buena Vista c

John Travolta *(Jan Schlichtmann)*; Robert Duvall *(Jerome Facher)*; Tony Shalhoub *(Kevin Conway)*; William H. Macy *(James Gordon)*; Zeljko Ivanek *(Bill Crowley)*; Bruce Norris *(William Cheeseman)*; John Lithgow *(Judge Skinner)*; Kathleen Quinlan *(Anne Anderson)*; Peter Jacobson *(Neil Jacobs)*; Mary Mara *(Kathy Boyer)*; James Gandolfini *(Al Love)*; Stephen Fry *(Pinder)*; Dan Hedaya *(John Riley)*; David Thornton *(Richard Aufiero)*; Sydney Pollack *(Al Eustis)*; Ned Eisenberg *(Uncle Pete)*; Margot Rose *(Donna Robbins)*; Daniel Von Bargen *(Mr. Granger)*; Caroline Carrigan *(Evelyn Love)*; Paul Desmond *(Shalline)*; Michael P. Byrne *(Barbas)*; Tracy Miller *(Grace Worker)*; Paul Hewitt *(Grace Worker)*; Clayton Landey *(Grace Worker)*; Paul Ben-Victor *(Pasqueriella)*; Elizabeth Burnette *(Lauren Aufiero)*; Alan Wilder *(Insurance Lawyer)*; Gregg Joseph Monk *(Insurance Lawyer)*; Harout Beshlian *(Insurance Lawyer)*; John Pais *(Law Clerk)*; Haskell Vaughn Anderson III *(Courtroom #7 Clerk)*; Kaiulani Lee *(Mrs. Granger)*; Howie Carr *(Radio Talk Show Host)*; Denise Dowse *(Judge)*; Pearline Fergerson *(Court Clerk)*; Scott Weintraub *(PI Lawyers)*; Robert Cicchini *(PI Lawyers)*; Christopher Stevenson *(Insurance Plain-*

tiff); Kevin Fry *(Waiter)*; Brian Turk *(Mover)*; Rikki Klieman *(T.V. Reporter)*; David Barrett *(Teenager on Property)*; Ryan Janis *(Teenager on Property)*; Rob McElhenney *(Teenager on Property)*; Mike Biase *(Market Clerk)*; Richard Calnan *(Woburn Traffic Cop)*; Gene Wolande *(Hotel Clerk)*; Sam Travolta *(Grace Attorney)*; Gregg Shawzin; Juli Donald; Sayda Alan; Catherine Leahan *(Reporters)*; Bruce Holman *(Federal Marshall)*; John La Fayette; Charles Levin; Byron Jennings; Jay Patterson *(Geologists)*; Charlie Stavola *(Detective)*

Based on a true story, A CIVIL ACTION is a zestful but flawed drama about an attorney who battles two large corporations charged with polluting a small community's water supply.

Eight children in a small Boston suburb have died of leukemia, and its residents ask Jan Schlichtmann (John Travolta), a personal injury lawyer, to represent them in a lawsuit charging that the illnesses resulted from tainted drinking water. Schlichtmann is reluctant to get involved until he learns that the defendants will be wealthy corporations, Beatrice Foods and W. R. Grace. He sets about gathering evidence, hiring a research team to test the water supply and its surrounding lands, and interrogating townspeople. Having amassed evidence, Schlichtmann meets with the Beatrice lawyer, Jerome Facher (Robert Duvall), and the Grace lawyer, William Cheeseman (Bruce Norris), and offers to settle for several hundred million dollars. Facher and Cheeseman categorically reject the offer, forcing the matter to trial.

The case places great financial strain on Schlichtmann's law firm, and his partners advise him to settle or drop the suit, but Schlichtmann is confident that he can win in court. During the trial, however, the judge (John Lithgow) orders the jury to decide on the validity of the suit after Schlichtmann has presented the research team's evidence but before he has called any of the townspeople as witnesses. The jury determines that the case may continue against Grace, but not Beatrice. Having suffered a major setback, Schlichtmann meets with a Grace representative (Sydney Pollack), and accepts an $8 million settlement, which greatly disappoints the plaintiffs.

Left bankrupt by the case, Schlichtmann is deserted by his partners and opens a small storefront practice. He persists in his investigation, though, and in time comes across conclusive evidence. Unable to afford an appeal himself, Schlichtmann sends the evidence to the Environmental Protection Agency, which launches an investigation that eventually implicates both Grace and Beatrice in toxic waste dumping.

Writer-director Steven Zallian is best known for scripting SCHINDLER'S LIST (1993), but it should be kept in mind that he also penned the screenplays to AWAKENINGS (1990) and JACK THE BEAR (1993). That—and the fact that this environmentally conscious David and Goliath story was coproduced by Robert Redford—should be enough to make one approach A CIVIL ACTION with considerable trepidation. A CIVIL ACTION, however, is not an unpleasant surprise, and if it stumbles dramatically, it gets by on quick pacing, solid production values, and a terrific cast.

Although A CIVIL ACTION is about litigation, Zallian refreshingly keeps the drama out of the courtroom and concentrates instead on how an attorney builds his case, how he sizes up the competition, and how he works out his strategy for winning. Much of what makes these sequences interesting are Schlichtmann's lawyerly motivations. At the film's outset, at least, he is driven by avarice and a prideful desire to show that he can match wits the big guys. (He justifies taking the case to his partners by saying, "I like the theatrical value of several dead kids"). But Zallian is unable to resist ennobling the character, and over the course of the story Schlichtmann changes from a high-priced ambulance-chaser into a standard movie hero—a crusader who sacrifices himself on behalf of little people. This shift in characterization is inexplicable (except as Zallian's effort to make Schlichtmann sympathetic), unconvincing, and robs the film of its most compelling element.

Travolta, however, is unfaltering, bringing great force and energy to his role. Employing the same bluster and pseudo-sincerity that made his performance in PRIMARY COLORS (1998) so enjoyable, Travolta rises above Zallian's pandering to sympathy. His performance never becomes self-congratulatory, even if the film does.

None of the characters besides Travolta's are fully developed, but the performers shine nonetheless. Robert Duvall's character, for example, is supposed to be an eccentric, masterful lawyer, but since the film includes no demonstration of his brilliance, he comes across merely as dithering. Duvall gives a great, classical character performance all the same, and is electrifying every time he's on screen. Kathleen Quinlan (as the most outspoken of the plaintiffs), William H. Macy (as Travolta's law partner), and John Lithgow are all as sturdy as ever, even if they don't have much to do. The film is very well made, the cinematography proving that Conrad Hall is a master of capturing rainy days (a moment here recalls the "raining window" shot from IN COLD BLOOD (1967), also photographed by Hall).

While A CIVIL ACTION never sinks to the level of turgid earnestness that ruined the similarly themed Q & A (1990)—and while it boldly (for a Hollywood film) names real-life corporate bad guys—its high-minded intentions almost do it in. The film is worth seeing, however, for its intelligent look into legal wrangling, its good craftsmanship, and mostly for a cast that transcends the film's dramatic shortcomings. *(Profanity.)*—D.C.

d, Steven Zallian; p, Robert Redford, Rachel Pfeffer, Scott Rudin; exec p, Steven Zallian, David Wisnievitz; assoc p, David McGiffert, Henry J. Golas; w, Steven Zallian (based on the book by Jonathan Harr); ph, Conrad L. Hall; ed, Wayne Wahrman; m, Danny Elfman; prod d, David Gropman; art d, David J. Bomba; set d, Tracey A. Doyle; sound, David MacMillan; fx, Guy Clayton; casting, Avy Kaufman; cos, Shay Cunliffe; makeup, Whitney L. James; stunts, Mark Riccardi

AAN Best Supporting Actor: Robert Duvall; *AAN Best Cinematography:* Conrad L. Hall

Drama **(PR: C MPAA: PG-13)**

CLASSIFIED X ★★★

(France/U.S., 1997) 52m Le Sept Arte; Les Films d'Ici; Ecounter Voir; Yeah Inc. ~ Fox Lorber Home Video c/bw

Melvin Van Peebles

Hosted by maverick filmmaker Melvin Van Peebles, CLASSIFIED X is an analytical history of the representation of blacks in American motion pictures. Part lecture, part self-tribute, this French-financed documentary is rambling but informative, and, thanks to Van Peebles, never less than entertaining. While Van Peebles's 1971 film SWEET SWEETBACK'S BAAD ASSSS SONG was a breakthrough in American cinema in its portrayal of African-Americans, its creator rejects the notion that "it didn't owe anything to the past." He explains that the film was a reaction to the fallacious, demeaning depiction of blacks that had marked American cinema up through that time.

Racist images have appeared in American films since their inception. For the first half-century of American filmmaking, blacks were presented as grotesque stereotypes, sometimes by white actors in black face. Such post-War movies as PINKY (1949) and INTRUDER IN THE DUST (1949) addressed bigotry in America, but even in these films, blacks were secondary, with white characters representing the forces of tolerance.

A respite for black moviegoers was provided by a parallel film industry that produced movies featuring all-black casts, for exhibition in segregated theaters. These films were popular with black audiences but also reflected the racism of the broader culture in that, within them, light skin tone connoted superiority.

As a concession to the civil rights movement, Hollywood produced such works as GUESS WHO'S COMING TO DINNER (1967). By the late 1960s, Hollywood studios finally began to hire black filmmakers, including Van Peebles, Ossie Davis, and Gordon Parks, but gave them poor scripts and low budgets. Tired of token support, Van Peebles decided "to kick Hollywood's ass" and made SWEETBACK. Dismissed by the mainstream media and slapped with an X rating, SWEETBACK was nonetheless a huge hit with black audiences, and Hollywood parlayed its success into the blaxploitation cycle.

Although the 1990s witnessed the rise of a few black filmmakers, many others have trouble with the distribution and exhibition of their work. So, Van Peebles concludes, segregation may have been outlawed in 1954, "but filmwise, we're still waiting."

CLASSIFIED X is as much a performance piece as it is a history. Throughout the film, Van Peebles, decked out in shabby street clothes, stands in front of cheesy rear-projected images of grimy New York waterfront scenery as he delivers a jaundiced chronicle of the debasement of African-Americans through cinema. Van Peebles's wry depiction of himself—as a down-and-out but scrappy outsider—coupled with his defiant, sarcastic delivery (of commentary he scripted) makes CLASSIFIED X enjoyable in spite of its grim subject matter, and satisfying in spite of its shortcomings.

As a history, CLASSIFIED X is rather sloppy and incomplete. Clips used to illustrate Van Peebles's commentary are rarely identified by title, and the groupings of them are chronologically inaccurate. Segments from BLACK LIKE ME (1964), for example, are included in the sequence addressing social problem movies of the immediate post-War period. The film also mentions but shortchanges both Ossie Davis and Gordon Parks, citing none of Davis's works by title and referring to Parks's SHAFT (1971) solely as an example of how mainstream studios exploited SWEETBACK's appeal to black audiences.

Yet CLASSIFIED X does offer ample and potent filmic evidence to support its contention, demonstrating how blacks have been, and continue to be, horrendously under and misrepresented in American cinema. Van Peebles's first-person take on the matter—his comments on how his lifelong love of movies conflicted with his feelings of shame and anger as a black viewer—give the piece the immediacy of personal experience. CLASSIFIED X may not be great scholarship, but it still provides a worthwhile and insightful lesson. *(Profanity.)*—D.C.

d, Mark Daniels; p, Yves Jeanneau, Christine Le Goff; assoc p, Judy Aley; w, Melvin Van Peebles; ph, Mark Daniels; ed, Catherine Mabilat, Janice Jones; prod d, Patrick Durand; art d, Valerie Saradjian, Patrick Schmitt; sound, Norbert Gilbert (mixer)

Documentary **(PR: A MPAA: NR)**

CLAY PIGEONS ★★½
(U.S./U.K., 1998) 104m Scott Free; InterMedia Film Equities; Millennium Mediaworks ~ Gramercy Pictures c

Vince Vaughn *(Lester Long)*; Janeane Garofalo *(FBI Agent Dale Shelby)*; Joaquin Phoenix *(Clay Bidwell)*; Georgina Cates *(Amanda)*; Scott Wilson *(Sheriff Mooney)*; Gregory Sporleder *(Earl)*; Vince Vieluf *(Deputy Barney)*; Wayne Brennan *(Minister)*; Joseph D. Reitman *(Glen)*; Nikki Arlyn *(Gloria)*; Jeff Olson *(Mark)*; Monica Moench *(Kimberly)*; Kevin Rahm *(Bystander at Amanda's)*; Jesse Bennett *(Dr. Jaffe)*; Phil Morris *(Agent Reynard)*; Zane Parker *(Dr. Buckley)*; Ryan Mouritsen *(Pizza Delivery Kid)*; Kari Peterson *(Dolores)*; Duane Stephens *(Bartender)*; Steve Anderson *(Old Man Waiter)*

Merging the sensibilities of Quentin Tarantino and "Seinfeld," CLAY PIGEONS is a bloody, black comedy about unlikable characters doing despicable things. Though the film does feature enjoyable performances, it begs the question: What's so funny about a brutal serial killer?

Rural Montana. Clay Bidwell (Joaquin Phoenix) and his best friend Earl (Gregory Sporleder) are target shooting, when Earl confronts his buddy about the affair Clay is having with his wife. Earl shoots and kills himself, setting it up to look like Clay murdered him. Clay loads Earl's body in his pickup, and pushes it into a gorge. The ensuing explosion destroys all evidence of the shooting, and Sheriff Mooney (Scott Wilson) believes the crash was an alcohol-related accident.

Clay confesses the truth to Earl's trampy widow, Amanda (Georgina Cates). Less than distraught, she wants to pick up where she left off with Clay, but he won't have anything to do with her. When Clay instead goes out with Gloria (Nikki Arlyn), a local waitress, jealous Amanda shoots and kills her. Clay covers up this crime by dumping Gloria's body in the lake.

Drowning his worries at the local bar, Clay makes a new friend in Lester Long (Vince Vaughn), a trucker who dresses like a dime-store cowboy. Lester takes Clay fishing with him, and they discover a corpse in the lake. Clay and Lester discuss the possibility of going to the police to report the body; thinking the body is Gloria, Clay tells Lester that he will take all responsibility in reporting it. When Sheriff Mooney extricates the body, however, it turns out not to be Gloria. Lester picks up Amanda at a bar, and brutally murders her after a sexual tryst. Amanda's slaying brings FBI Agent Dale Shelby (Janeane Garofalo) onto the scene. She's investigating a string of stabbing murders, and all the evidence points to Clay.

Lester visits Clay in jail to tell him that he can clear Clay's name—by committing another murder. Clay breaks out of jail to stop him. They meet up at the lake and Clay helps the intended victim escape. When Lester reveals to Clay that Amanda told him about Earl's death and the circumstances leading up to it, a fearful Clay helps him evade capture by Shelby. Clay decides to leave town, but at a diner meets Lester again; however, this was a trap to deliver Lester into Sheriff Mooney's waiting arms.

CLAY PIGEONS is the product of two movie first-timers, director David Dobkin and writer Matt Healy, backed by big-shot directors Ridley and Tony Scott in producing roles. The movie is a series of murders, cover-ups, and betrayals that doesn't make enough sense (and goes on a bit too long) to be completely enjoyable. Aspiring to be a kind of noir farce along the lines of FARGO (1996), CLAY PIGEONS lacks that film's heart; it's little more than an empty genre exercise.

The major problem is that Clay, our conduit into the story, is such an unsympathetic and rather uninteresting character; the 23-year-old Phoenix seems miscast in the role. And the film never satisfactorily reconciles the clownish and brutal sides of Lester. Hints at what might have been come whenever the wonderful Garofalo is onscreen (which isn't enough). There's a terrific scene when she meets Lester the Rhinestone Cowboy at a bar, without knowing his true identity, and the two cross verbal swords. Here is when a better movie suggests itself: a black comic variation of THE SILENCE OF THE LAMBS (1991) in which his creepily amusing serial killer is tracked by her smart and sardonic FBI agent. *(Profanity, graphic violence, sexual situations, nudity.)*—P.R.

d, David Dobkin; p, Ridley Scott, Chris Zarpas; exec p, Tony Scott, Guy East, Nigel Sinclair; assoc p, Hilarie Roope Benz; co-p, Chris Dorr, Carrie Morrow, Audrey Kelly; w, Matt Healy; ph, Eric Edwards; ed, Stan Salfas; m, John Lurie; prod d, Clark Hunter; art d, Max Biscoe; set d, Tracy Kirshbaum; sound, Robert Eber (mixer); fx, David Wayne, Ultimate Effects; casting, Risa Bramon Garcia, Randi Hiller; cos, Laura Goldsmith; makeup, Gina Monaci, Kate Morgan Biscoe (effects); stunts, Edward Conna

Crime/Thriller/Comedy **(PR: C MPAA: R)**

CLOCKMAKER ★★½

(U.S., 1998) 90m Kushner-Locke Co. ~ Amazing Fantasy Entertainment c

Anthony Medwetz *(Henry)*; Zachary McLemore *(Devon)*; Katie Johnson *(Mary Beth)*; Perrino Mascarino *(Markham)*; Daisy Nystul *(Bricktop Betty)*; Eugen Cristea *(Brogram)*; Tom Gulager *(Bankwell)*; Florin Chiriac *(Time Agent Leader)*; Petre Moraru *(Time Agent)*; Christian Motiu *(Time Agent)*; Laura Jianu *(Sgt. Grillo)*; Marius Galea; Christopher Landry; Carmen Papa *(Vagrancy Cops)*; Serban Celea *(Guard)*; Mihai Niculescu *(Attendant)*; Doru Bobesiu *(Worker)*; Tomi Cristin *(Neighbor)*; Constantin Barbulescu *(Vagrant Man)*; Aristita Diamandi *(Vagrant Woman)*; Rudi Rosefeld *(Drunk)*; Marian Vasile *(Customer)*; Billy Floyd *(Big Brother)*

This time-travel movie is perfect for precocious tots who list Stephen Hawking in essays about the people they most admire. Although perkily executed, the screenplay sometimes babbles on about the mysteries of time in complex pronouncements that may perplex children and adults.

Nerdy Henry (Anthony Medwetz), tomboyish Mary Beth (Katie Johnson), and mischievous Devon (Zachary McLemore) can't quell their curiosity about eccentric neighbor Mr. Markham (Perrino Mascarino), a clock collector. When they sneak into his apartment, they discover that he is in fact the Guardian of Time.

One day, noisy Devon enters a paneled box inside Mr. Markham's apartment which serves as a time portal; once there, he disappears into a vortex and upsets the delicate balance of Past, Present, and Future. Looking for their friend, Mary Beth and Henry enter the paneled box, and then find themselves in an altered version of their own present, which has been transformed into a bleak police state. Meanwhile, Devon has traveled back to the 19th century, with Henry's 20th-century technical manual that has whetted the financial appetite of entrepreneur Mr. Brogram (Eugen Cristea) and his staff inventor Mr. Bankwell (Tom Gulager), who have found information in the book which could help them invent time machines before mankind can deal with their ramifications.

After Mr. Markham rescues Henry and Mary Beth from Vagrancy Police in the twisted present, he sends them to 1880 to reappropriate Henry's technical guide. Unfortunately, the children are trailed by militaristic time-traveling agents, who don't want the current, fascistic status quo (caused by the kids' meddling) to be erased. Following clues left by Devon, the kids arrive at a cell in Brogram's warehouse, rescue Devon, and grab the technical manual. Stealing one of the agents' vehicles, the children arrive back in their old neighborhood in the 20th century, which has been restored to its original manifestation. Subsequently, Mr. Markham smooths out the remaining wrinkles in time caused by Devon, Henry, and Mary Beth.

Although CLOCKMAKER sports ragged plot development as it nears its climax, it provides enough fanciful plot twists to keep older children alert. Devil-may-care, this adventure overcomes limitations in logic by keeping its plot spinning in constant motion. If its game attitude can't quite compensate for mediocre acting and repetitive cliffhangers, the film zips from 1880 to 1998 with sufficient directorial relish. It may not always make sense, but small fry won't have time to stare grumpily at their wristwatches. *(Violence.)*—R.P.

d, Christopher Remy; p, Christopher Landry, Vlad Panescu; exec p, Donald Kushner, Peter Locke; co-p, Dana Scanlan; w, Benjamin Carr; ph, Gabriel Kosuth; ed, Phillip Linson; m, Jim Fox; prod d, Radu Corciova; art d, Viorel Ghenea; set d, Ica Varna; sound, Tiberiu Borcoman; fx, Adriana Ionica; casting, Perry Bullington, Bob MacDonald; cos, Ioana Corciova; makeup, Mihai Stanescu; stunts, Daniel Tomescu

Children's/Science Fiction **(PR: AA MPAA: PG)**

CLOCKWATCHERS ★★★★

(U.K., 1998) 110m Goldcrest Films International; John Flock Productions ~ BMG Independents c

Toni Collette *(Iris)*; Parker Posey *(Margaret)*; Lisa Kudrow *(Paula)*; Alanna Ubach *(Jane)*; Helen Fitzgerald *(Cleo)*; Stanley DeSantis *(Art)*; Jamie Kennedy *(Eddie)*; David James Elliott *(MacNamee)*; Debra Jo Rupp *(Barbara)*; Kevin Cooney *(Mr. Kilmer)*; Bob Balaban *(Milton Lasky)*; Paul Dooley *(Bud Chapman)*; Scott Mosenson *(Jack Shoberg)*; Irene Olga Lopez *(Coffee Lady)*; Joshua Malina *(Receptionist)*; O-Lan Jones *(Madame Debbie)*; Joe Chrest *(Detective)*; Patrice Pitman Quinn *(Woman in Office)*; Michelle Arthur *(Dianne the Shoe Lady)*; Athena Ulbach *(Jane's Sister)*; Lynn Tufeld *(Woman Missing in Search)*; Jennifer Balgobin *(Attractive Woman)*; Chuck Borden *(Guard)*; Gregg Daniel *(Policeman)*; Tim Hutchinson *(Businessman)*; Sully Diaz *(Waitress)*; Jim Wise *(Man in Bar)*; Wendy Pitts *(Saleslady)*; Patti Yasotake *(Theater Woman)*; Steve Rodriguez *(Lobby Guard)*; Constance Forshind *(Flight Attendant)*; Jaime Gomez *(Derrick)*; Bridget Sienna *(Woman with Cop)*; Terri Hoyos *(Female Executive)*; Brodie Nelson *(Copy Repairman)*

CLOCKWATCHERS explores the corporate world from the point of view of "temps," the temporary workers who receive few of the perks of the full-time office staff. This peculiar, often daring film succeeds both as social satire and humanistic drama.

In a major city, a shy young woman, Iris (Toni Collette), applies for a temporary job at the Global Credit Company. She is hired and immediately makes friends with three other, very different "temps": Margaret (Parker Posey), who wants to secure a permanent job; Paula (Lisa Kudrow), who aspires to become a famous actress; and Jane (Alanna Ubach), who plans to quit after her impending marriage. Without the support of any other workers, the four women bond together and become "clockwatchers," waiting for check-out time each night.

One day the restless foursome are perturbed to find that another young woman, Cleo (Helen Fitzgerald), has been brought in as a permanent worker. Their resentment builds when office items begin to mysteriously disappear and suspicion falls on them; they, in turn, believe that the mousy Cleo is the culprit. Meanwhile, outside the office, Iris's father (Paul Dooley) urges Iris to apply for a permanent job elsewhere; Paula worries that she might be pregnant; and Iris and Margaret discover that Jane's fiance is cheating on her. At work, more objects disappear, and the head of Global Credit begins a crackdown on the workers by installing cameras and forcing the temps to work in open spaces.

Eventually, the suspicious atmosphere takes its toll on the friendships. While Margaret still asserts that Cleo is the thief, Iris begins believing that Margaret herself may be guilty. The day after Iris, Jane, and Paula fail to support Margaret in a one-day work strike, Margaret is fired. Just as Margaret angrily leaves the office, Iris realizes that Margaret is innocent—but stops short of jumping to her defense.

Soon after the incident, Iris discovers that Cleo was indeed responsible and makes her aware how much damage she has inflicted. Later, Jane gets married and leaves her job as planned; Paula, whose pregnancy was a false alarm, transfers to another part of the company; and Iris gets the recommendation needed to move on to a full-time job elsewhere. She regrets the loss of her friendships, but she feels more confident about the future.

Though promoted as "Mary Tyler Moore meets Franz Kafka," CLOCKWATCHERS could also be described as a loose remake of THE BEST OF EVERYTHING (1959), the glossy Hollywood melodrama about secretaries working in a publishing company, and LES BONNES FEMMES (1960), the trenchant *nouvelle vague* thriller about four bored young women juggling unpleasant jobs and even less appealing men. First-time director-writer Jill Sprecher and coscripter Karen Sprecher (her sister) smartly apply touches about the nature of office work today—the sexual politics, the social hierarchies, the hard economic realities.

CLOCKWATCHERS begins as razor-sharp satire before cleverly and surreptitiously becoming a heartrending drama about the odd but endearing characters. It is a testament to the Sprechers that the transition is made without compromising their attack on corporate business practices. Sprecher gives the film a decidedly modernist art look, from the askew camera angles to the Hopper-esque color and shading, which heightens the menacing sense of place, a crucial element.

It is also a tribute to the actors that the characters move beyond the sort of caricatures appropriate for sketch comedy. Parker Posey is particularly strong playing a woman whose transgressive acts most upset the conventional types around her (the scene where she turns a breath freshener into a blowtorch is a highlight). Collette, Kudrow, and Ubach are also surprisingly touching, and several supporting players stand out, including Jamie Kennedy as the goofy office mail carrier and Debra Jo Rupp as the perky (but iron-willed) office manager.

Only two minor flaws prevent CLOCKWATCHERS from having a more awesome final impact: the superfluous revelation of Cleo as the office thief (leaving the mystery unsolved would have been more in line with the modernist motifs); and the relatively "upbeat" ending to Iris's story, which indicates that by happily moving on to another company, this intelligent character hasn't learned quite enough about her experience, despite her gains in confidence and strength. This conclusion tilts CLOCKWATCHERS closer to NINE TO FIVE (1980) than Chabrol's female group-portrait LES BONNES FEMMES (which ends tragically), but, overall, CLOCKWATCHERS is a superior, thought-provoking film. *(Extreme profanity.)—E.M.*

d, Jill Sprecher; p, Gina Resnick; exec p, John Flock; co-p, Karen Sprecher; w, Jill Sprecher, Karen Sprecher; ph, Jim Denault; ed, Steven Mirrione; m, Mader; prod d, Pamela Marcotte; set d, Greta Grigorian; sound, Christopher M. Taylor (mixer); casting, Jeanne McCarthy; cos, Edi Giguere; makeup, Jason Rail

Comedy/Drama **(PR: C MPAA: PG-13)**

CLUB VAMPIRE ★½

(U.S., 1998) 77m Concorde Productions ~
New Horizons Home Video c

John Savage *(Zero)*; Starr Andreeff *(Corri)*; Diana Frank *(Laura)*; Michael J. Anderson *(Kiddo)*; Marriam Parris *(Aiko)*; Ross Malinger *(Max)*; Victoria Chapman *(Melanie)*; Sarah Shackleton *(Punk Girl)*; Tony Ervolino *(Suave Man)*; Jordan Black *(Gang Member #1)*; Gil Espinoza *(Gang Member #2)*; Donald Sager *(Man)*; Anna K. McKown *(Ragamuffin Girl)*

This Roger Corman production can't decide whether it's a serious bloodsucker drama or a burlesque send-up of the genre.

Zero (John Savage), a member of a small vampire "family," has his eye on a stripper named Corri (Starr Andreeff), but Laura (Diana Frank), another of the bloodsuckers, bites Corri and mingles their blood. This causes Corri to begin a vampiric transformation, to the consternation of her son Max (Ross Malinger). Aiko (Marriam Parris), the leader of the ghoulish group who doesn't want any new converts, sends Zero out to kill Corri. Instead, he spirits her away from her house, having fallen for her and desiring to break away from his evil brethren.

Zero procures a punk girl (Sarah Shackleton) for Corri to feed on and explains the vampire lifestyle to her. They go to the strip club, and after they make love, Zero sets out to fetch Max. He interrupts the other vampires as they're attacking the boy, and they decapitate Zero and bring Max back to the club. Corri is tied up to await the rising sun, but Zero's head grows back on and he returns just as Max has helped Corri escape her bonds. Zero kills the bad vampires, and he, Corri and Max then set off to relocate in Nepal.

CLUB VAMPIRE was written and directed by Andy Ruben, who previously collaborated on the vampire/stripper romance DANCE OF THE DAMNED (1988) and the murder mystery STRIPPED TO KILL (1987) with his then-wife, director Katt Shea Ruben. Unlike his former spouse, however, Ruben has no real feeling for the strip-club milieu, which seems to be included here simply as an excuse to show topless women. For the rest, he ham-handedly alternates the attempted drama of Corri's vampiric conversion with wild overacting by Savage (who occasionally seems to be doing a Jimmy Durante or Danny DeVito impression) and the rest of the bloodsucker crew. ("We mustn't draw attention to ourselves," says Aiko, as her group camps it up like a road company of *The Rocky Horror Show*.)

So unconcerned with character that it barely bothers to introduce any of these people by name, CLUB VAMPIRE descends into a melange of distortion and double-exposure shots, cheap gimmickry (the vampires appear and disappear through the magic of stop-the-camera tricks), and a truly awful music and song score. Only a few legitimately amusing moments shine through, as when the formerly vegetarian Corri looks through her fridge and complains, "I don't want to graze, I want to eat!" *(Graphic violence, extensive nudity, sexual situations, profanity.)*—M.G.

d, Andy Ruben; p, Darin Spillman; exec p, Roger Corman; co-p, Frances Doel, Marta M. Mobley; w, Andy Ruben; ph, Steve Gainer; ed, Dan Holland; m, Michael Elliott; prod d, Mark Harper; art d, Christopher Larsen; set d, Melissa Blanchard; sound, Buck Robinson, John Halaby; fx, Robert Hall, Almost Human; casting, Jan Glaser; cos, Jayme Bohn; makeup, Erin M. Braus; stunts, Cassimore Magda

Horror **(PR: O MPAA: R)**

COLONY, THE ★½

(U.S., 1998) 94m MA & PA Pictures; Sci-Fi Channel ~
Trimark Home Video c

Isabella Hofmann *(Harper)*; Michael Weatherly *(Kevin)*; Jeff Kober *(Desmond)*; James Avery *(Fred)*; Clare Salstrom *(Laura)*; John Prosky *(Alpha)*; Eric Allan Kramer *(Bravo)*; Cristi Conaway *(Charley)*; Robert Amico *(Homeless Man)*; David Jean-Thomas *(Cop 1)*; David Campbell *(Cop 2)*; Michelle Davisan *(Ailene)*; Nonie Muso *(Girl)*; James Sebastian *(Man)*

Threadbare production values mar this space invaders flick that seems to have borrowed its sets and costumes from a high school production of "Return to the Forbidden Planet." Cheapness aside, this made-for-cable bilge about body-snatching devolves its style from thriller to action pic to camp mockery sans rhyme or reason.

Guided by chief researcher Harper (Isabella Hofmann), space aliens kidnap Earthlings to probe our weaknesses and pave the way for colonization. Harper's vanguard, consisting of Alpha (John Prosky), Bravo (Eric Allan Kramer), and Charley (Cristi Conaway), kidnap Desmond (Jeff Kober), Fred (James Avery), Laura (Clare Salstrom), and Kevin (Michael Weatherly). While Fred's brain is examined, Desmond and Laura are injected with experimental drugs.

Temporarily escaping, the earthlings discover that their human-looking captors house their alien shells in tubes. Recaptured, Kevin impresses Harper by risking his well-being to save a weakened Laura from being crushed under a metal plate. Preferring coexistence to colonization, Harper confides in her Earth prisoners that her shipmates must recharge themselves in their original bodies.

During a showdown, Kevin fries Charlie on electric cables, Harper wounds Bravo with a ray gun, Desmond destroys the spacemen's shells, and Bravo is finally killed by Desmond. Thwarting Alpha's mutinous plans, Harper lies to her superiors that Earth is unfit for their purposes. Then, she transplants her essence into Laura's deteriorating body. After she primes the spaceship for explosion, Harper and the earthlings transport themselves to terra firma.

Too much technical hocus pocus and too much metaphysical mumbo jumbo (about man's capacity for emotion) clutter up this arthritic sci-fi hobbled by degenerative script disease. Expository dialogue replays itself, as repetitive alien dogma about human genocide clogs the script's development. There's enough material here for a half hour of episodic TV. On the plus side, some of the space-fiends vs. earth-men bouts have the satisfying crunch of a World Wrestling Federation match. On that juvenile level, THE COLONY muscles its way to a conclusion, without ever frightening us with the sangfroid of these lab technicians from outer space. *(Graphic violence, nudity, profanity.)*—R.P.

d, Peter Geiger; p, Thom Colwell; exec p, Jana Sue Memel, Philip B. Goldfine; w, Richard Kletter, Peter Geiger; ph, Zoltan David; ed, Mallory Gottlieb; m, Paul Rabjohns; prod d, C.J. Stawn, Candi Guterres, Miq Strawn; art d, Steven Schalk; sound, Michael E. Fowler, Rick Waddell; fx, Carmen Gonzalez Jr., Dale Newkirk; casting, Mary Margaret, Karen Margiotta; cos, Brigitte Mann; makeup, Dalia Saydah-Dokter; stunts, Scott McEllroy, Daniel McBride

Science Fiction **(PR: C MPAA: R)**

COMEDY'S DIRTIEST DOZEN ★★½

(U.S., 1988) 90m International Harmony Productions ~ Island Visual Arts c

Ben Creed *(Host)*; Tim Allen; John Fox; Joey Gaynor; Bill Hicks; Stephanie Hodge; Monty Hoffman; Jackie "the Jokeman" Martling; Otto Peterson; Steven Pearl; Chris Rock; Larry Scavano; Thea Vidale

A dozen openly raunchy standup comedians do abridged versions of their acts in this extremely minimalist performance film. First released on a limited basis theatrically in 1988, the film reached a wide audience in 1998, when it was released on home video. The chief selling point: early views of comedians who were later to develop cult status or achieve fame (albeit in a much more sterilized form) on television.

The comedians, in order of appearance, are: Monty Hoffman, who does jokes about his weight and former drug use; 21-year-old Chris Rock, who does the requisite sex jokes, but takes a more surreal tack (as in a bit where he uses Aunt Jemima as masturbation fodder) and speaks about Jesse Jackson's presidential bid; deadpan comic Larry Scavano follows with very timely (now very dated) routines about Oliver North, Madonna, the homeless, and safe sex; Stephanie Hodge, later a sitcom star, comments on her smoking and drinking habits; John Fox, who does conventionally "dirty" material about sex, hotel rooms, and pornography; Thea Vidale (another standup who also graduated to a sitcom a few years later) discusses being married and gives the women in the audience tips on how to treat their men; future TV (and movie) star Tim Allen does his "All Men Are Pigs" shtick, covering such lovely subjects as belching, flatulence, excretion, testicles, erections, and (for equal time) menstruation; ventriloquist Otto Peterson tries to keep his dirty-mouthed dummy George in check; Joey Gaynor does musical impressions of Sinatra, Springsteen, Ray Charles, and Joe Cocker; Bill Hicks supplies the film's most off-beat set with meditations on the media's condemnation of drug use, the indestructability of Ronald Reagan, and a view of Dick Clark as the anti-Christ; Steven Pearl holds forth on living in New York, Arnold Schwarzenegger, and the TV show "Star Search"; writer-performer for the Howard Stern radio show Jackie "the Jokeman" Martling closes things off with a barrage of cheap one-liners ("Didja hear about the guy who couldn't come? We had to get him."), punctuating his groaners with his own, Ed Wynn-like laughter.

Besides being a time capsule of a very empty period in American history, COMEDY'S DIRTIEST DOZEN is useful as a survey of comic poses. They're all here: the topical commentator, the overweight gagster, the streetwise black man, the bawdy dame, the deadpan observationalist, the piggish bad-boy, and the one-line joke machine.

An exercise in simple point-and-shoot moviemaking, the film does offer an interesting glimpse at what made an urban audience laugh in the late 1980s, and a few of the comedians do distinguish themselves. For instance, "family hour" star Tim Allen is the most pointlessly filthy of the whole crew (Fox and Vidale each run a close second). Peterson scores a few solid laughs using the oldest gimmick in the world (as when his dummy notes that he was given a microphone—"stupid [asses] think I'm real"). Though he's the youngest act on stage, Rock shows the most maturity, seriously addressing political and social issues while also slinging curses. And Bill Hicks's incisive, venomous observations give a sobering indication of what the world of comedy lost when Hicks died of pancreatic cancer at the young age of 32 in 1994. *(Extreme profanity.)*—E.G.

d, Leonard Wong; p, Stuart S. Shapiro; exec p, Martin Schwartz; assoc p, John Dofrin; co-p, Richard Baker; ph, Mark Benjamin; ed, Patricia Edick; m, Steve Trecasse; prod d, Mark Friedberg

Documentary/Comedy **(PR: C MPAA: NR)**

COMRADES, ALMOST A LOVE STORY ★★★★

(Hong Kong, 1996) 116m United Filmmakers Organization; Golden Harvest ~ Golden Harvest c
(TIAN MIMI)

Leon Lai *(Li Xiaojun)*; Maggie Cheung *(Li Qiao)*; Kristy Yeung, billed as Yang Kung-Yu *(Fang Xiaoting)*; Eric Tsang, billed as Tsang Chi-Wai *(Pau)*; Irene Tsu *(Aunt Rosie)*; Christopher Doyle *(Jeremy)*; Ting Yu *(George)*; Michelle Gabriel *(Prostitute)*; Joseph Cheung *(Restaurant Owner)*; Ting Chow-hin; Katherine Li

The big winner at the 1996 Hong Kong Film Awards, COMRADES, ALMOST A LOVE STORY tells a witty and poignant love story of two immigrants to Hong Kong from Mainland China. Stylishly directed and beautifully acted, this is Hong Kong cinema at its best.

In March 1986, Li Xiaojun (Leon Lai) arrives in Hong Kong from northern China. He seeks out his Aunt Rosie (Irene Tsu), who runs a brothel and gives him a place to stay. Handicapped by his difficulty with Cantonese, he meets another mainlander, Li Qiao (Maggie Cheung), who is eager to run a business of her own. Although Xiaojun writes regularly to his sweetheart Xiaoting (Kristy Yeung) in China, he gradually develops a romantic relationship with Qiao. When a failed business venture lands her in debt, Qiao is forced to take a job as a masseuse. There she attracts the interest of Au Pau (Eric Tsang), a local gangster.

Xiaojun eventually marries Xiaoting when she comes to Hong Kong, while Qiao marries Au Pau, who backs her assorted businesses. But when Xiaojun and Qiao resume their affair, Xiaoting leaves her husband for good. Qiao's attempt to break off with Au Pau finds her instead joining the gangster as he flees to Taiwan to escape the Hong Kong police.

Aunt Rosie dies, and with nothing to hold him in Hong Kong, Xiaojun heads for New York City to start a new life. Unbeknownst to him, Qiao is also in New York with Au Pau, who is still on the run. After Au Pau is mugged and murdered by a gang of young thugs, Qiao is deported. As she is being driven to the airport by immigration agents, she spots Xiaojun riding his delivery bike and bolts out of the car. She chases Xiaojun, but loses him in Times Square.

In 1995, Qiao is still in New York, working as a tour guide. Hearing that pop star Teresa Teng has died, she watches the news reports on TV sets playing in Chinatown windows. There she finally finds Xiaojun, watching the same reports.

Young Hong Kong director Peter Chan (HE'S A WOMAN, SHE'S A MAN) represents a new "new wave" of Hong Kong directors who have opted to remain and revitalize the country's cinema while top names like John Woo and Tsui Hark have moved on to Hollywood. Chan directs this film with self-confidence, style, and conviction, alternating fast, airy montages with long takes giving the actors room to play off each other and develop their characters.

Maggie Cheung, enjoying a broader international appeal after her appearance in the arthouse hit IRMA VEP (1997), proves her range in a role that's as far from her action roles in THE HEROIC TRIO and DRAGON INN (both 1992) as it is from her ditzy girlfriend roles in Jackie Chan's POLICE STORY films. As a lonely but ambitious young woman torn between her love for the "hick" from northern China and her desire to run her own business, Cheung balances a number of conflicting emotions. Indeed her character surprises us when she runs away with the short, dumpy Au Pau, most likely out of loyalty because of his financial support of her shops.

Although his role is somewhat less developed, pop singer Leon Lai is remarkably effective as a naive young man swept up by the passions of a stronger woman. His performance is a real surprise for fans who know him only from films like WICKED CITY (1992) and SWORD OF MANY LOVES (1992).

New York buffs will enjoy seeing Maggie Cheung running through Times Square late in the film. Movie buffs will treasure the subplot involving Aunt Rosie (played by one-time Hollywood actress Irene Tsu) and her shrine to William Holden. And Hong Kong pop culture buffs will treasure the Teresa Teng thread which runs throughout the film. *(Sexual situations.)*—B.C.

d, Peter Chan; p, Raymond Chow, Eric Tsang; exec p, Peter Chan, Claudie Chung; assoc p, Jojo Hui, Chan Wai-yee; w, Ivy Ho, On Sai; ph, Jingle Ma; ed, Chan Ki-hop, Kwong Chi-leung; m, Chiu Tsang-hei; art d, Yee Chung-man; cos, Dora Ng

Romance/Drama (PR: C MPAA: NR)

CON, THE ★★★

(U.S., 1998) 92m Mi Saamy Productions; Wilshire Court Productions ~ Paramount Home Video c

Rebecca De Mornay *(Barbara/Nancy)*; William H. Macy *(Bobby Sommerdinger)*; Frances Sternhagen *(Aunt Hattie)*; Mike Nussbaum *(Harry)*; Don Harvey *(TJ)*; Gina Mastogiacomo *(Patrice)*; Angela Paton *(Aunt Lyla)*; Tony Frank *(Edgar Wallace)*; Matthew Hill *(Conroy Gill)*; Steve Shearer *(Joe Harnin)*; Lee Stringer *(Earl Wainwright)*; Benny Bennett *(Sheriff Gill)*; Marge Kotilsky *(Glenna)*; Lionel Mark Smith *(Charlie Hayes)*; Brady Coleman *(Baptist Minister)*; Bonnie Gallup *(Landlady)*; Alex Allen Morris *(Scary Fellow)*; Mary Bernadette McCann *(Donna)*; Melanie Haynes *(Clinic Nurse)*; John S. Davies *(Lawyer)*; Nik Hagler *(Airboat Owner)*; Grayson "Jim" Helms *(Pilot)*; Blue Deckert *(Card Player)*; Kathy Lamkin *(Woman #1)*; Linda Longserre *(Woman #2)*; Cynthia Dorn *(Waitress)*; James Hansen Prince *(Mortuary Attendant)*; Big Skinny Brown *(Used Car Salesman)*; Jimmy Ray Pickens; Marti Wills *(Rowdies)*; Christine Tolson *(Vera)*; Paul Menzel *(Business Man)*; Abbi Hutcherson *(Girl in Choir)*; Jackson Earl Burns *(Thug)*

The life of a hard-bitten con artist is turned around when she tries to bilk a small-town mechanic out of a fortune he will soon inherit in THE CON, a likable if unmemorable made-for-cable romantic comedy.

In desperate need of $125,000 to pay back a mob loan, Detroit con artist Barbara (Rebecca De Mornay) appeals to former partner and mentor Harry (Mike Nussbaum). He tells her about a Mississippi mechanic, Bobby Sommerdinger (William H. Macy), who doesn't realize that he is about to inherit $2 million from the father he never knew, now on his death bed. Barbara moves to Bobby's town and, more by accident than design, gets a job teaching the fifth grade. She meets Bobby, a withdrawn middle-aged man wary of her attempts to get to know him; he, meanwhile, assumes his aunts put her up to it. But he eventually warms to her, and she gets him into bed and to the altar. What Barbara doesn't know is that Bobby learned about the inheritance several days before the wedding; surmising her motives, he marries her anyway. After their honeymoon, Bobby tells her about the inheritance, but says that they won't have the money for awhile because of lawsuits. Learning that this isn't true, and with the mob breathing down her neck, Barbara leaves town. But her conscience and her unsuspected feelings for Bobby force her back to confess and to warn him. He sees her shot and apparently killed by gunmen. After her funeral, Bobby sells his garage and leaves town—along with Barbara: the two of them faked her death so that they could start a new life together.

THE CON was cowritten by star William H. Macy, known for his frequent collaborations with playwright/filmmaker David Mamet. While it's unfair to expect Macy to have soaked up Mamet's singular style, con artists are so dear to Mamet's oeuvre that the expectation is perhaps inevitable. By that standard, THE CON is a bit of a letdown. It's a thoroughly nice, even wholesome movie whose few touches of violence (most of which take place offscreen) seem out of place. At times it seems to be heading for the direction of DOC HOLLYWOOD (1991) or Bill Forsythe's delightful LOCAL HERO (1982) by turning the city slicker/country rube genre on its ear, but that never quite happens either, despite some scenes of slick Barbara being taken by surprise by small-town life. Mostly THE CON is a pleasant comedy of the type in which cable television seems to specialize:

mildly sentimental and inoffensively adult, with sturdy characters that give actors something to do but don't overly tax them. *(Violence, sexual situations, adult situations, profanity.)* —M.F.

d, Steven Schachter; p, Bob Roe; assoc p, Jeff Henry; w, William H. Macy, Steven Schachter; ph, Peter Stein; ed, Cari Coughlin; m, Peter Manning Robinson; prod d, Alfred Sole; set d, Jeff Hartmann; sound, Tim Hines (mixer); fx, Dan Lester; casting, Penny Musarra, Dan Shaner; cos, Denise Martinez; makeup, Cheri Medcalf; stunts, Russell Towery

Romance/Comedy **(PR: C MPAA: PG-13)**

COURTING COURTNEY ★★½
(U.S., 1998) 87m Toasted Films ~
Broken Twig Productions c

Dana Gould *(Nick Hastings)*; Eliza Coyle *(Courtney Baxter)*; Sean Masterson *(Al Kennedy)*; Taylor Negron *(Dr. Phelps)*; Kathy Griffin *(Ona Miller)*; Ryan Stiles *(Chad Gross)*; Adam Eastwood *(Andrew Baker)*; Ana Gasteyer *(Rosemary Colletti)*; Ian Gomez *(Hank)*; Chris Hardwick *(Tim)*; Ann Mattingly *(Mrs. Baker)*; Al Shuerman *(Mr. Baker)*; Doug McKeon *(Barney)*; Ted Michaels *(Lance)*; Philip Pavel *(Waiter)*; John Rogers *(Aaron)*; Jane Morris *(Ms. Opremchek)*; Sarah Taylor *(Karen Mulligan)*; Sarah Noonan *(Rita)*; Nestor Ruiz *(Juan)*; COURTNEY'S GROUP: Julia Sweeney; Dawn DeNoon; Lance August; Stephanie Grodell; COURTNEY'S STUDENTS: Michael Pitts; Brandie Tinin; Peter Wiest

A humorous exploration of dating angst in the 1990s, COURTING COURTNEY is a pleasant but uninspired comedy that would have benefited from snappier dialogue.

Filmmaker Nick Hastings (Dana Gould) secures the permission of his best friend Courtney Baker (Eliza Coyle) to chronicle her romantic travails as she approaches her 30th birthday. Suppressing his own long-standing crush on her, Nick films Courtney in tandem with assorted heartbreakers like her non-committal lover Al (Sean Masterson), dating service candidates like bilious Barney (Doug McKeon), and Dr. Phelps (Taylor Negron), the lecherous moderator of her women's group.

Along the cinema-verite way to finding Courtney the perfect mate, Nick experiences his share of dating disasters. Courtney is devastated when Al unexpectedly dumps her to marry someone else. Love takes an unexpected corkscrew turn after Nick and Courtney drown their sorrows in booze and end up in bed together.

With their platonic friendship bollixed up, Courtney runs for cover; Nick becomes angry when she refuses to take his feelings for her seriously. By the time Nick swallows his pride and throws a surprise birthday party for Courtney, she has reconsidered her stance. Instead of filming others courting Courtney, Nick finally becomes her leading man.

Sunny cameos by comedians Kathy Griffin, Ryan Stiles, and Julia Sweeney can't compensate for COURTING COURTNEY's essential lightness of being. Though this happy-go-lucky fable sails by agreeably enough, director-writer Paul Tarantino is no Albert Brooks or Woody Allen. He sticks to easy targets and doesn't milk them for any subsidiary irony; you've experienced every pithy observation in similar, but funnier, romantic comedies. Nor is this satire on 90s dating sensibilities helped by the nondescript leads; in terms of white-bread blandness, Courtney and Nick are perfect for each other. Cute and cuddly, COURTING COURTNEY covers the battle of the sexes with unsurprising exactitude. *(Profanity, sexual situations, substance abuse.)*—R.P.

d, Paul Tarantino; p, Paul Tarantino, Hadeel Reda, Serge Rodnunsky; exec p, Chiqui Schatz, Jesse Dizon; w, Paul Tarantino; ph, Larry Sher, Serge Rodnunsky, Thom Otzel, William MacDonald; ed, Agita Fanucci; m, Daniel Gold; prod d, Larry Sher; art d, Ellen Guthrie; sound, Robert B. Fisher; casting, Stacey Pianico; makeup, Richard Reed

Romance/Comedy **(PR: C MPAA: NR)**

COUSIN BETTE ★★
(U.S./U.K./France, 1998) 108m Omnibus/20th Century
Fox; Sarah Radclyffe Productions; Septieme Productions ~
Fox Searchlight c

Jessica Lange *(Bette)*; Elisabeth Shue *(Jenny Cadine)*; Bob Hoskins *(Mayor Crevel)*; Hugh Laurie *(Hector Hulot)*; Aden Young *(Wenceslas)*; Kelly Macdonald *(Hortense Hulot)*; Geraldine Chaplin *(Adeline Hulot)*; Toby Stephens *(Victorin)*; John Benfield *(Dr. Bianchon)*; Paul Bandey *(Priest)*; Laura Fraser *(Mariette)*; Janie Hargreaves *(Celestine)*; Gillian Martell *(Portress)*; John Sessions *(Musical Director)*; Henrik Wagner *(Baritone)*; John Quentin *(Elderly Aristocrat)*; Jefferson Mays *(Stidmann)*; Tim Barlow *(De Forzheim)*; Heathcote Williams *(Nucingen)*; Philip Jackson *(De Wissembourg)*; Toby Jones; Kenneth Jay *(Gentlemen in Cafe des Artistes)*; Simon McBurney *(Vauvinet)*; Geoffrey Carey *(Duelmaster)*; Dermot Keaney *(Chief Gendarme)*

Celebrated theater director Des McAnuff (*Tommy*) makes a disappointing film directing debut with COUSIN BETTE, a handsomely appointed, but very crude and superficial adaptation of Honore de Balzac's satirical novel about moral and social decay in 1840s France.

Bette (Jessica Lange), the poor, spinster relative of a noble family headed by Baron Hector Hulot (Hugh Laurie), is asked by Hector to be his housekeeper following the death of his wife (Geraldine Chaplin), who was Bette's cousin. Bette, who has always felt ignored by her family in favor of her sister, is insulted by the offer, and embarks on a scheme to wreak vengeance upon her relatives. She befriends Hector's mistress, the music hall star Jenny Cadine (Elisabeth Shue) and convinces her to dump Hector for his friend Cesar Crevel (Bob Hoskins), the richest man in Paris. Bette then encourages a duel between Hector and Crevel, which results in Hector being shot in the leg. After rescuing a struggling Russian sculptor named Wenceslas (Aden Young) from suicide, Bette falls madly in love with the much younger man and helps him become successful. She then enlists him to seduce and abandon Hector's love-starved daughter Hortense (Kelly Macdonald), but is horrified when Wenceslas and Hortense fall in love and get married.

Hector gives Wenceslas a large commission to do a sculpture for the military, but seven months later, Hector's profligate ways have nearly bankrupted his household and he orders the lazy Wenceslas—who has failed to complete the statue in time—to repay his commission. Wenceslas, however, has already spent it on wine and women and Hortense is forced to get a loan from Crevel to cover the commission, but Bette intercepts the money and then successfully breaks up Hortense's marriage by fixing Wenceslas up with Jenny. Bette then arranges for Hector and Hortense to catch Jenny and Wenceslas having sex and this causes Hector to suffer a stroke. When Bette lies to Hortense and tells her that Jenny was the one who intercepted the loan from Crevel, Hortense tries to shoot Jenny but inadvertently kills Wenceslas and she's imprisoned. Six months later, as the peasants begin to riot in the streets, Jenny continues her career on the stage, and Bette raises Hortense's baby, whom she calls "little Wenceslas."

For all of its bawdy post-modern humor and intentional campiness, COUSIN BETTE comes off like an old-fashioned melodramatic "woman's picture" a la Bette Davis, only without the flair or conviction. Like so many contemporary period pieces, it forsakes substance and verisimilitude for cheap laughs and ironic distancing, and makes the trendy mistake of ridiculing all of its characters without first making the viewer care about them, which renders the entire story ineffectual. Balzac's wit and sociological satire is sacrificed for the usual blatant attempts to appeal to modern audiences by throwing in gratuitous nudity and "risque" sexual shenanigans (Crevel hiding under Jenny's dress and performing cunnilingus on her; Jenny and Wenceslas having wild sex while covered in pudding; Jenny's revealing costumes and the tacky final freeze-frame of a group of bare-assed "nuns" on stage), while the legitimately dramatic aspects of the story, such as the romantic betrayals and the duel at dawn, are treated in a crass and jokey manner (where are you, Max Ophuls?).

Another major flaw is the cold and unappealing performance of the constantly frowning Jessica Lange, who seems to believe that allowing herself to look dowdy in a black wig and minimal makeup automatically equates with "serious" acting. As played and written, Bette is a totally unsympathetic character and the script never really establishes that she has sufficient cause to be so vengeful, which merely makes her seem cruel and vindictive. The overall mocking tone of the film also undercuts its later attempts at seriousness and results in unintentional laughter, as when Bette finds out that Wenceslas is leaving her for Hortense and she starts screaming and fainting with a hilariously hysterical zeal unseen since the heyday of Joan Crawford. COUSIN BETTE proves once again that when filmmakers treat their characters as idiots, it's hard to ask the audience to be interested in their fate. *(Profanity, violence, nudity, sexual situations.)*—M.S.

d, Des McAnuff; p, Sarah Radclyffe; exec p, Lynn Siefert, Susan Tarr, Rob Scheidlinger; assoc p, Neris Thomas; co-p, Philippe Guez; w, Lynn Siefert, Susan Tarr (based on the novel by Honore de Balzac); ph, Andrzej Sekula; ed, Tariq Anwar, Barry Alexander Brown; m, Simon Boswell; prod d, Hugo Luczyc-Wyhowski; art d, Didier Naert, Richard Bridgland, Bertrand Clercq-Roques; set d, Robert LeCorre; sound, Drew Kunin (mixer); fx, Graham Longhurst, The Film Factory at VTR; casting, Mary Margiotta, Llora Reich, Nathalie Charon; cos, Gabriella Pescucci; makeup, Jenny Shircore

Comedy/Drama/Historical **(PR: O MPAA: R)**

CRACKING UP ★

(U.S., 1998) 92m Foolish Mortal Films ~ Phaedra Cinema c

Matt Mitler *(Danny Gold)*; Todd Alcott *(Himself)*; Chuck Montgomery *(M.C.)*; Kimberly Flynn *(Kimberly Lane)*; Simon Prebble *(Christopher MacAwber)*; Carolyn McDermott *(Carolyn Davis)*; The Posterboys *(Themselves)*; Toby Huss *(Himself)*; Camryn Manheim *(Nurse Manheim)*; Debra Wilson *(Herself)*; John Augustine *(Wealthy Couple)*; Sherry Anderson *(Wealthy Couple)*; David Wells *(Allan)*; Kevin Brown *(Dack)*; Jason Brill *(Jake)*; Debra K. Lynn *(Hazel)*

CRACKING UP is a dark comedy that traces a manic stand-up comedian's self-destructive downfall. Produced, directed, edited, and co-scripted by Matt Mitler, this independent production is as imbecilic and it is self-indulgent. Comic Danny Gold (Matt Mitler) is the topliner at a small Manhattan comedy club, where his more popular routines include a parody of Marlon Brando in ON THE WATERFRONT (1954) and an impersonation of Robert De Niro mimicking Henny Youngman. A talent manager who enjoys Danny's work offers to represent him and gets him the lead part in a television commercial. Meanwhile, Danny falls in love with Carolyn (Carolyn McDermott), whom he meets one night when she comes to see him perform.

Danny's work in the commercial results in more offers, but his rise in the entertainment industry is accompanied by drug abuse and increasingly outrageous behavior. He wins a recurring role on a network television series but loses it through his unwillingness to obey the director. He also loses an opportunity for a cable television program by offending the show's producers.

One afternoon, Danny is shot while visiting a drug den and lands in the hospital. He recuperates, but upon release finds that no one will hire him. After a while, his luck changes and he gets an offer to perform at an upscale benefit. Just before he goes on, however, Danny smokes crack, and during his performance he collapses. The audience, thinking it is all part of an act, howls with laughter as Danny lays on the stage.

Anyone interested in seeing CRACKING UP should be grateful to Matt Mitler for having the decency to place the film's sole inspired moment at its very beginning, a neat comedy bit in which Mitler repeats Brando's ON THE WATERFRONT (1954) dialogue in Pee Wee Herman's voice. From then on, this smug, stupid, and ugly-looking feature is a complete waste of time. Obviously his own greatest fan, Mitler expends no effort to make his screen ego understandable, agreeable, or even particularly amusing. As the star, he gives a broad, screaming performance that is probably supposed to be irresistibly manic and irreverent, but comes across as obnoxious. As director, Mitler has encouraged all the other actors to either overact as idiotically as he does or stay out of his way. As co-scenarist (with Theodore P. LoRusso), Mitler fails to give the story any shape, and the film lurches incongruously from scene to scene. To his credit, Mitler does periodically gets in a few good jibes at pretentious New York performances artists—but is there an easier target?

Oddly, Mitler's character is usually shown performing in front of silent, appalled crowds, as if Mitler were perversely aware of how unfunny he is and persisted in performing anyway. The man needs a lesson in empathy. *(Extensive nudity, sexual situations, substance abuse, profanity.)* —D.C.

d, Matt Mitler; p, Matt Mitler; exec p, Lili Mitler; assoc p, Bill Otterson, David Beal, Betsy Howie; co-p, Robert Prichard, Jennifer Prichard, Michael K. Faust; w, Matt Mitler, Theodore P. LoRusso; ph, Mark Traver; ed, Matt Mitler; m, Arthur Rosen; art d, Shawn Sullivan, Ben Dulong; sound, Rob Taz (mixer); cos, Carol Bryce; makeup, Jonathon Sobel

Comedy/Drama **(PR: C MPAA: NR)**

CROSSING FIELDS ★★½

(U.S., 1998) 101m Sterling Pictures c

Reedy Gibbs *(Carol Bradley)*; Gwynyth Walsh *(Jessica Watson)*; William James Jones *(James Carver)*; J.K. Simmons *(Guy Bradley)*; Meadow Sisto *(Denise Bradley)*; Gary Sandy

A competent, conventional little film, CROSSING FIELDS presents a view of small-town American life from the perspective of a middle-aged woman.

Carol Bradley (Reedy Gibbs) enjoys her quiet life in the small Midwestern community of Ashton, where she lives with her husband Guy (J.K. Simmons) and teenaged daughter Denise (Meadow Sisto). The family shares its large home with several boarders, among them James (William James Jones), a 19-year-old African-American.

Despite her contentment, Carol has problems. Denise is becoming rebellious and Carol's best friend Jessica (Gwynyth Walsh) is going through a divorce. One day, Jessica informs

Carol that she may lose her farm, which her family has owned for generations, to her husband as a result of the divorce. Carol tries to help Jessica with the matter, but to no avail. Later that day, Carol is shocked when she finds Denise in bed with James, neither of whom demonstrates any shame at being caught. Carol orders James to leave her house, but soon calms down and allows him to remain. A few nights afterwards, Denise sneaks out, even though Carol has grounded her. When Carol finds out she demands to know Denise's whereabouts from James, who takes her to a club where Denise performs as a singer. Carol's anger changes to admiration as she watches her daughter perform.

Days later, Carol discovers that Jessica is having sex with James, whom she has hired to work on her farm. Carol upbraids Jessica for seducing the young man, but Jessica chastises Carol in return for being judgmental, and Carol apologizes. The following Sunday, Jessica surprises the local church congregation by showing up and reconciling with her husband. Afterwards, Carol visits Jessica at her home to support her in her decision, but Jessica reveals to Carol that she has gotten back with her husband solely to retain her farm, then tearfully repeats, "It will mellow, it will."

Although similarly awash in suburban turmoil, CROSSING FIELDS is the antithesis of PEYTON PLACE (1957), which is not to say that it's any more true to life. While its adult population engages in adulterous affairs and the kids occasionally smoke pot, Ashton remains a place of down-home family values, where problems are met with patience and understanding, and mother and father always know best. Carol, the center of CROSSING FIELDS, is a woman of traditional views—a churchgoer who always has a pitcher of iced tea at the ready—yet she's boundlessly accepting of those who don't share her views. She's morally opposed to drug use and extramarital sex, but is happily tolerant of people who indulge in either. Her surname is Bradley, and although she finally breaks down and puffs a joint before the film's end, she may as well be named Carol Brady.

Not that CROSSING FIELDS is entirely saccharine. It touches lightly upon such topics as race relations and Christian moralizing. More trenchantly, the film looks at the destructive double standard that holds women more accountable than men for their sexual behavior. But while writer-director James Rosenow's treatment of these issues is fair-minded and rational; his direction, if capable, is resolutely pedestrian. Saddled with an approach that's as conservative as an Ashton inhabitant, CROSSING FIELDS is too contrived to be convincing. The cast is uniformly professional and pleasant, although, Walsh is a stand out as a woman who smilingly introduces herself to strangers as "the town slut." The technical aspects of the film are fine, if serviceable.

Rosenow probably intended his debut feature to be more thought-provoking than it is. It ends on a sour note, and to some extent questions, though never really challenges, the values to which its characters cling. With an unimaginative presentation that undermines any serious purpose, however, CROSSING FIELDS is best taken as a light entertainment. *(Nudity, sexual situations, profanity.)*—D.C.

d, James Rosenow; p, James Rosenow, David Hannah; w, James Rosenow; ph, Dejan Georgevich; ed, Angelo Corrao; m, Walter Thompson; prod d, Kathleen Harding; set d, Christian Breiding, Casi Nields, Fred Isch, Brian Cruey; sound, Gautam Choudury (mixer); casting, D. Lynn Meyers; cos, Kelley Marie Corwin; makeup, Jeni Lee Dinkel

Drama **(PR: C MPAA: NR)**

CROSSOVER
(SEE: CATHERINE'S GROVE)

CRUISE, THE ★★★½
(U.S., 1998) 76m Charter Films ~ Artisan Entertainment c/bw

Timothy "Speed" Levitch

Culled from more than 100 hours of footage, THE CRUISE is a fascinating documentary portrait of Timothy "Speed" Levitch, Manhattan tour bus guide, borderline wacko, and deep thinker. To call this one of the great films about New York City might mislead viewers about its modest charms, but Bennett Miller's film is certain to become a cult favorite of Gothamophiles.

Possessed of the kind of nasal voice that only emanates from New Yorkers, Levitch is virtually the only speaking character in THE CRUISE. Miller combines footage of him at work on a Gray Line tour bus, providing his idiosyncratic and erudite spiels on the history and meaning of Manhattan to tourists who often look like this isn't at all what they were expecting, with scenes of Levitch walking the city streets, talking more about his life, the city's life, and the points where they intersect. His love/hate relationship to the city, the film's main theme, is introduced at the beginning as he sings George Gershwin's "But Not For Me" to his tour group. At one point, he talks about how he and Manhattan almost got divorced the previous winter—"I don't know why it was so mad at me"—but things got better.

At work, Levitch particularly seems to enjoy talking to his passengers about Greenwich Village. He seems able to point out in which building every famous author who passed through New York lived, and usually has an anecdote about their bad habits. (He shares with them poet Dylan Thomas's last words: "I've just had my 16th martini.") He waxes rhapsodic about the terra cotta carvings on skyscrapers. He rails about the mediocrity exemplified by the grid system in which Manhattan's streets are arranged. And he reminds us that Central Park was designed by Transcendentalists as a place to commune with nature: they would have been appalled, he says, to see people exercising there.

Although some viewers will be annoyed at the film's failure to delve deeper into Levitch's life, Miller purposely avoided psychoanalyzing Levitch on film, preferring that audiences simply enjoy his commentaries. Still, part of what is so fascinating about him are the clues he provides toward the sources and nature of his dysfunctions. An unpublished writer, he has no fixed address and crashes at friends' apartments. He is from an upper-class Jewish background, and was regarded as a disappointment by his grandparents for not choosing a more materialistic lifestyle. When he rattles off a list of people he holds grudges against, it's an unusually personal moment, even if we don't know why he hates these people. (An exception: the other participants in what was supposed to be an orgy, but which turned into a double date with him as the fifth wheel.) Whatever Levitch's troubles, he expresses them in a fascinating, seemingly endless flurry of thoughts about the nature of man and civilization (including a particularly good poem that he reads on the subject). Yet he is never self-aggrandizing, and claims that his verbal displays are intended primarily as an on-the-job tool "to be able to seduce women from around the world."

Miller wisely chose to shoot THE CRUISE in black and white, so as not to tie Manhattan to any particular era and to help us look at it afresh, guided through Levitch's perspective. And he succeeds in making Manhattan look like what it is, a place that can be as frightening as it is fascinating. *(Profanity.)*—M.F.

d, Bennett Miller; p, Bennett Miller; exec p, David Cohen, J.B. Miller, Theodore Miller, David Yamner; assoc p, Kevin McLeod;

ph, Bennett Miller; ed, Michael Levine; m, Marty Beller; sound, David Novack (mixer)

Documentary **(PR: C MPAA: NR)**

CUBE ★★★

(Canada, 1998) 92m Cube Libre;
The Feature Film Project ~ Trimark c

Maurice Dean Wint *(Quentin)*; David Hewlett *(Worth)*; Nicole de Boer *(Leaven)*; Nicky Guadagni *(Holloway)*; Wayne Robson *(Rennes)*; Andrew Miller *(Kazan)*; Julian Richings *(Alderson)*

Strikingly designed and expertly directed, CUBE overcomes an uneven script to deliver real tension with modest means.

In a large square room with intricately patterned walls, a man (Julian Richings) awakens and attempts to escape, only to be sliced into pieces by a booby trap. In another, similar chamber, six more people find themselves trapped: cop Quentin (Maurice Dean Wint), teenager Leaven (Nicole de Boer), doctor Holloway (Nicky Guadagni), architectural designer Worth (David Hewlett), professional thief Rennes (Wayne Robson), and autistic Kazan (Andrew Miller). They soon realize that the room is one of many shifting, interlocking chambers connected by sliding doors, and attempt to find a way out. Rennes, an escape expert, leads the way, but falls victim to another deadly trap. Leaven, a math expert, deduces from numeric codes on each doorway which ones are safe to pass through. As they travel from room to room, tensions rise between Holloway and the hot-headed Quentin, and Worth reveals that he was part of the team that designed the structure, but has no knowledge of its purpose.

The group reaches one of the exterior walls, and Holloway attempts to scale it; Quentin, unbeknownst to the others, lets her fall to her death. Realizing that one room must connect to a bridge to the outside world, the remaining quartet presses on, with Kazan's gift for mathematics helping to determine the way. Quentin becomes too aggressive and must be subdued before Leaven, Kazan, and Worth arrive in the bridge room—the same one they started in. As they prepare to cross over, Quentin appears, kills Leaven and mortally wounds Worth, who lives long enough to hold Quentin back as he attempts to follow Kazan to the other side. Quentin is killed as the room shifts; Kazan passes to the outside as the dying Worth is left behind.

One of two math-themed independent thrillers, along with PI, to open in 1998, CUBE is a slicker, more rigorously composed film than Darren Aronofsky's grungy but flamboyant debut. Director and cowriter Vincenzo Natali, also making his first feature, opens with a bang, jolting the audience with one of the most original and convincing gore scenes in splatter history before following his six characters in search of an exit. While this isn't a fresh idea (TV's "The Twilight Zone," among others, has explored it), Natali uses it as the foundation for a stylistic tour de force, wringing a surprising amount of tension from what is essentially a group of people moving through the same set over and over. Varying the colors of the walls, backing the action with ominous sound effects, and making excellent use of space, Natali convinces the viewer that the characters really are trapped in an endless structure.

The script provides enough incident (often violent) to keep things from becoming redundant, and cranks up individual set pieces—particularly the quintet creeping through a room containing a sound-activated death trap—to nail-biting intensity. The characterizations, though, aren't quite as sure-handed all around. Hewlett and de Boer are convincing as, respectively, a conscience-stricken man who may literally be the architect of his own downfall, and an intially panicky girl who comes to trust her abilities. Less persuasive is Wint, whose performance and dialogue as the increasingly crazed policeman are too over-the-top, and whose running battle with the humanistic Holloway is obvious and one-dimensional. In the end, the characters are more compelling as a group struggling through an impossible situation than they are as individuals.

Yet even if it remains a triumph of style over substance, CUBE proves Natali to be a filmmaker capable of doing a lot with a little. What he needs is a script that has the same depth as his technical abilities. *(Graphic violence, extreme profanity.)*—M.G.

d, Vincenzo Natali; p, Mehra Meh, Betty Orr; exec p, Colin Brunton; w, Vincenzo Natali, Andre Bijelic, Graeme Manson; ph, Derek Rogers; ed, John Sanders; m, Mark Korven; prod d, Jasna Stefanovic; art d, Diana Mangus; sound, Steve McNamee (recordist); casting, Deidre Bowen; cos, Wendy May Moore; makeup, Louise Mackintosh, Ray Mackintosh, Russell Cate; stunts, John Stoneham Stoneham

Science Fiction/Thriller/Horror **(PR: O MPAA: R)**

CURSE OF THE PUPPET MASTER ★½

(U.S., 1998) 78m Full Moon Pictures ~ Full Moon c

George Peck *(Dr. Magrew)*; Emily Harrison *(Jane)*; Josh Green *(Robert)*; Michael Guerin *(Joey)*; Robert Donavan *(Sheriff Garvey)*; Marc Newberger *(Art)*; Michael Sollenberger *(Station Owner)*; Jason-Shane Scott *(Deputy Waybern)*; Scott Boyer *(Larry)*; Jason Dean *(Booher)*; William Knight *(Medical Examiner)*; Pat Thomas *(Shipping Agent)*; Ariauna Albright *(Operator's Voice)*; J.R. Bookwalter *(Tommy Berke's Voice)*

Following up 1994's fifth and so-called FINAL CHAPTER in the PUPPET MASTER series, this abbreviated adventure offers the viewer little more than borrowed story ideas and special effects.

Dr. Magrew (George Peck), the latest owner of Andre Toulon's living puppets, hires a slow-witted young man named Robert (Josh Green) to be his latest assistant. Impressed by Robert's wood-carving prowess, Magrew assigns him to sculpt the pieces for a new puppet, while the doctor's daughter Jane (Emily Harrison), begins to fall for him. During a confrontation with local bully Joey (Michael Guerin), Robert almost strangles him, and Magrew tells Robert that he is "a creature of violence" inside.

Joey comes calling at Magrew's place with revenge in mind. The Pinhead puppet fights him off, but it is badly damaged as a result. While Robert is busy fixing it, Magrew takes the other puppets out to kill Joey. Magrew tells Jane not to get too attached to Robert, who soon falls ill. After Magrew sends Jane on an errand, Sheriff Garvey (Robert Donavan) and his deputy arrive to investigate Joey's death, only to fall victim to the puppets. Magrew straps Robert down and transfers his soul into the new puppet, only for the other dolls to rebel and attack him. Jane arrives back just in time to see the Robert puppet delivering the coup de grace to her father.

If this entry in the PUPPET MASTER series is cursed with anything, it's a predictable script (whose basic plot is purloined from the 1973 snake thriller SSSSSSSS, of all things) that's distinctly lacking in horrific material. For the first 45 of its 78 minutes, more time is devoted to scenes of Robert carving than to scenes of the puppets in action; when the latter does occur, a good deal of it is composed of stock footage that doesn't match the rest of the film. In the midst of all this, Dr. Magrew's particular alchemic plot remains conveniently (and completely) unexplained.

Director "Victoria Sloan" (a pseudonym of busy genre/erotic filmmaker David DeCoteau) manages some atmospheric images in the midst of the hokum, and the cast is OK, even if they're forced to say things like "The brain's the most overrated organ there is." Still, while watching these unknown actors go through their paces, one looks back with even more fondness on William Hickey and Paul Le Mat's turns in the original PUPPET MASTER (1989). *(Graphic violence, sexual situations, extreme profanity.)*—M.G.

d, David DeCoteau, billed as Victoria Sloan; p, Kirk Edward Hansen; exec p, Charles Band; assoc p, Gordon Gustafson; w, Benjamin Carr; ph, Howard Wexler; ed, J.R. Bookwalter; m, Richard Band; prod d, Allison Shavitz; art d, Dani Michaeli; sound, Vik Marsh; fx, Mark Rappaport Creature Effects, Digital Armageddon, Matthew Jason Walsh; casting, Robert MacDonald, Perry Bullington; cos, Judi Jensen; makeup, Mark Williams, Heidi Gratsky

Horror **(PR: O MPAA: R)**

D

DAD SAVAGE ★½

(U.K., 1998) 104m PolyGram Filmed Entertainment; Sweet Child Films ~ PolyGram Video c

Patrick Stewart *(Dad Savage)*; Kevin Kidd *(H)*; Helen McCrory *(Chris)*; Joe McMadden *(Bob)*; Marc Warren *(Vic)*; Jake Wood *(Sav)*

Tarantino-mania may finally be subsiding in the US, but it's alive and well abroad, as evidenced by the British thriller DAD SAVAGE (which went straight to video in the States), an insufferably arch heist-and-bloody-aftermath-multiple-flashback movie starring a ludicrously miscast Patrick Stewart as an English "cowboy" and tulip-growing gangster.

A jeep carrying Dad Savage (Patrick Stewart) and H (Kevin McKidd) crashes through the wall of a deserted farmhouse and lands in the cellar. Of the three people inside the house—Bob (Joe McMadden), Vic (Marc Warren), and Chris (Helen McCrory)—only Bob is seriously injured. Accusing the three of killing his son Sav (Jake Wood), Dad pulls a rifle on them and orders them to talk. A flashback reveals that sometime earlier, Bob and Vic had been hired to work on Dad's tulip farm. H, who is Dad's assistant, inadvertently tells Bob and Vic about a stash of money that Dad keeps hidden in the woods. Bob and Vic decide to steal the money and abduct and torture Sav until he reveals where it's buried. Bob and Vic dig up a money bag, but they're unaware it's a decoy. Sav manages to grab a gun and fires some shots at Bob and Vic, who flee into the night. H comes along and sees Sav digging up the real money bag and forces Sav at gunpoint to give him the bag, but during a struggle, H's gun goes off and kills Sav. Hearing the shots, Dad goes into the woods to investigate and sees that his bags have been dug up. He picks up H and they follow Chris to the farmhouse where he crashes his jeep into the wall. Back to the present, Dad kills Bob and Vic, but the ceiling collapses and crushes him to death. H dies of injuries received in the crash and Chris escapes.

DAD SAVAGE might not be the absolute nadir of the self-consciously hip post-Tarantino crime movies, but it's certainly in there pitching. Making her feature debut, television director Betsan Morris Evans evidently wants to be the British Kathryn Bigelow; that is, a woman who can be as rough and tough as the big boys, making nasty, testosterone-filled movies with lots of gore, four-letter words, and empty stylization. Following the US indie blueprint, Morris and writer Steve Williams include the requisite torture scene, monosyllabic nicknames, "quirky" characters (such as a British criminal/tulip farmer who loves country-western music), and most importantly, a fractured structure employing pointless flashbacks in an attempt to provide suspense and depth that isn't in the script. It's hard to gauge the quality of the performances since all of the characters are so venal and vile, and all they do is scream obscenities in thick and incomprehensible accents. Stewart has the meatiest role, but his character is a cipher whose "criminal" activities are never even specified, although the scene where he line-dances to a Patsy Cline song while wearing a black cowboy outfit has to be seen to be believed. *(Graphic violence, extreme profanity.)*—M.S.

d, Betsan Morris Evans; p, Gwynneth Lloyd, Robert Jones; w, Steve Williams; ph, Gavin Finney; ed, Guy Bensley; m, Simon Boswell; prod d, Michael Carlin; sound, George Richards; fx, Tom Harris; casting, Susie Pariss, Paddy Stone; cos, Rachael Fleming; makeup, David Myers

Crime/Thriller **(PR: O MPAA: R)**

DANCE WITH ME ★★½

(U.S., 1998) 126m Weissman/Egawa; Mandalay Entertainment; Cinewa ~ Columbia c

Vanessa L. Williams *(Ruby)*; Chayanne *(Rafael)*; Kris Kristofferson *(John Burnett)*; Joan Plowright *(Bea)*; Jane Krakowski *(Patricia)*; Beth Grant *(Lovejoy)*; Harry Groener *(Michael)*; William Marquez *(Stefano)*; Scott Paetty *(Steve)*; Rick Valenzuela *(Julian)*; Chaz Oswill *(Peter)*; Liz Curtis *(Kim)*; Bill Applebaum *(Don Harrington)*; Angelo Pagan *(Cuban Mailman)*; Victor Marcel *(Fernando)*; Ana Sofia Pomales *(Fernando's Daughter)*; Nelson Marquez *(Fiance)*; Mike Gomez *(Bartender)*; Charles Venturi *(Waiter)*; Maurice Schwartzman *(Man in Dance Club)*; Janette Valenzuela *(Woman in Dance Club)*; Jim Mapp *(Fisherman on Pier)*; Robert Pike Daniel *(Emcee)*; Tony Meredith; Melanie Lapatin; Jean Marc Genereux; France Mousseau; James Kunitz; Janna Kunitz; Giacomo Steccaglia; Melissa Dexter; Eric Thomas Robinson; Maria Torres O'Connor *(Professional Latin Finalists)*; Thomas A. Slater *(Theater Arts Dancer)*; Carol Bentley *(Theater Arts Dancer)*; Jose Mesa Benjamin; Harry Bowens; Juan Carlois Cienfuegos; Leila Flores; Alicia Gomez; Raul Gomez; Monica Gonzalez; Rudy Gonzalez; Ana Hernandez; Joel Hernandez; Erika Landin; Alyra Lennox; Rojelio Moreno; Anne Noelle; Piper Orr; Jacqueline Rios; Chantal Sagouspe; Marissa Soratorio; Albert Torres; Francisco Vazquez; Joby Vazquez; Luis Vazquez; Roberto Villacorta *(Salsa Club Dancers)*

DANCE WITH ME is an unusually wholesome story about a group of Houston hopefuls preparing to compete in the annual World Open Dance Championship, held in Las Vegas. The movie's musical interludes are colorful and high-spirited but the various personal dramas that bridge them lack conviction.

Following the death of his mother, Rafael (Chayanne) moves from Cuba to Houston to take a menial job in a dance studio owned by John Burnett (Kris Kristofferson), one of his mother's old friends and professional dancing partners. Among the studio's staff members is Ruby (Vanessa L. Williams), a former champion ballroom dancer who lives with her small son (Chaz Oswill), a product of her relationship with ex-lover/dance partner Julian (Rick Valenzuela). Ruby and Rafael go dancing a couple of times, but romance fails to develop, partly because their dancing styles clash; she's all technique and he's all soul.

Meanwhile, the staff and clientele of Burnett's studio ready themselves for the upcoming world championships in Las Vegas. During this period John's advancing age causes him to be replaced in the competition by Rafael, and Ruby drops her current partner (Harry Groener) to resume her professional relationship with Julian. When suspicions are raised that John is Rafael's father, John denies parentage and announces that he intends to close the studio for good. Rafael decides to return to Cuba after the championships.

Finally, the date of the championship has arrived. John, realizing he is indeed Rafael's father, unexpectedly shows up at the competition and reconciles with his son. After Ruby and Julian win the grand prize, everybody reverses his/her plans and happily returns to the Houston studio, where Ruby and Rafael appear to be on the verge of falling in love.

The peak moments of DANCE WITH ME are provided by the dances themselves—samba, cha cha, rhumba, tango, salsa, swing, country two-step, merengue, fox-trot, et al.—performed to a wealth of very catchy Latin music. Particularly dazzling is the final round of the Las Vegas contest, in which six couples compete simultaneously for the grand prize. (Despite camerawork that is, naturally, biased, several of the runner-up couples, all of whom are portrayed by pro dancers, appear to be at least as talented as winners Ruby and Julian.) The interim material detailing the relationships between Ruby and Rafael, and Rafael and John is comparatively tepid and routine.

Former Miss America Vanessa Williams and Puerto Rican pop idol Chayanne demonstrate that their citation by a national magazine as two of the world's most beautiful people was not unwarranted. Unfortunately, the talented Joan Plowright's apparent bewilderment by her underwritten role (a woman who has discovered the pleasures of dancing late in life) is allowed to carry over into the psyche of the character herself. Her whimsically gauche pas de deux with Rafael regrettably recalls Victor Moore and Helen Broderick's ghastly parody of Fred Astaire and Ginger Roger's immortal "Pick Yourself Up" number in SWING TIME (1936).

DANCE WITH ME would have benefited from a little more directorial ambition and some of the evocative abstract quality of SKATETOWN U.S.A. (1979), another film about performers in formal competition. Also, its plot might have been more novel and interesting if it had stressed the professional rather than the personal conflicts of its personae. The movie's most impressive achievement is its successful revival of the almost lost art of providing entertainment for both adults and children without boring the former or traumatizing the latter. *(Profanity.)*—D.T.

d, Randa Haines; p, Randa Haines, Lauren C. Weissman, Shinya Egawa; exec p, Ted Zachary; assoc p, Aldric La'Auli Porter, Allan Wertheim; w, Daryl Matthews; ph, Fred Murphy; ed, Lisa Fruchtman; m, Michael Convertino; prod d, Waldemar Kalinowski; art d, Barry M. Kingston; set d, Florence Fellman; ch, Daryl Matthews, Liz Curtis; sound, David Ronne (mixer); casting, Lora Kennedy; cos, Joe I. Tompkins; makeup, Rick Sharp

Romance/Dance **(PR: C MPAA: PG)**

DANCER, TEXAS POP. 81 ★★★½

(U.S., 1998) 95m HSX Films/Hollywood Stock Exchange; Caribou Pictures; Chase Productions ~ Columbia TriStar c

Breckin Meyer *(Keller Coleman)*; Ethan Embry *(Squirrel)*; Peter Facinelli *(Terrell Lee Lusk)*; Eddie Mills *(John Hemphill)*; Ashley Johnson *(Josie)*; Patricia Wettig *(Mrs. Lusk)*; Alexandra Holden *(Vivien)*; Michael O'Neil *(Mr. Lusk)*; Eddie Jones *(Earl)*; Wayne Tippit *(Keller's Grandfather)*; Keith Szarabajka *(Squirrel's Father)*; Shawn Weatherly *(Sue Ann)*; Michael Crabtree *(Mr. Hemphill)*; LaShawn McIvor *(Mrs. Hemphill)*; Joe Stevens *(Leon)*; Tommy G. Kendrick *(Rusty)*; Steven Bland *(Wayne)*; Craig Carter *(Guy)*; Tennessee *(Old Fart Rancher)*; Mary Ann Luedecke *(Betty Sue)*; Bill Brooks *(Reverend)*; Felipe De Ortega y Gasca *(Principal)*; Kessia Kordelle *(Jean)*; Kendra Payne *(Loretta)*; Jack Vaden *(Harvey)*; Lynn Carter *(Another Rancher)*; Jon Bergholz *(Bus Driver)*; Lucy Jacobson *(Flora)*; Lisa Billing *(Sandra)*; Emilie B. Severin *(Mrs. Caldwell)*; Leigh Eaton *(Mrs. Hufheinz)*; Billie Craddock *(Mrs. Garcia)*

The population of Dancer, Texas, is on the verge of dropping to 77, as four young men ponder abandoning their tiny hometown for the big city in this sweet, funny, and charming film from first-time writer-director Tim McCanlies.

Best friends Keller (Breckin Meyer), Terrell Lee (Peter Facinelli), John (Eddie Mills), and "Squirrel" (Ethan Embry) have vowed to take the first bus to LA after they graduate from high school in Dancer. An orphan and obsessive organizer, Keller plans for the trip. But after the Saturday ceremony for the five-member senior class, Terrell Lee's overbearing mother (Patricia Wettig) tells him that he will stay home to work in the family oil business. His news prompts John and Squirrel to admit their second thoughts about leaving.

On Sunday, Terrell Lee spends the day checking drilling rigs with his easy-going father (Michael O'Neil), who reveals that the business is badly in debt and may go under. John goes horseback riding on his family's cattle ranch with his younger sister Josie (Ashley Johnson), who tries to convince him that their taciturn father (Michael Crabtree) really wants John to stay, even though he'll never come out and say so. Squirrel's heretofore awful home situation—he lives in a lopsided trailer with a drunken bum of a father (Keith Szarabajka)—brightens when his dad's new girlfriend (Shawn Weatherly) provides some desperately needed maternal attention. Keller seeks solace and counsel from the fifth graduate, Vivien (Alexandra Holden), who shares her hopes for the future; and he gets an earful of LA horror stories from a variety of concerned townspeople. That night, Keller informs his crusty grandfather (Wayne Tippit) that he's decided to stay, but the old man insists he go.

Most of Dancer has wagered on how many, if any, of the boys will leave, and Monday morning they're all at the bus stop to see the bets settled. Keller gets on the bus, alone, but as it starts to pull away, Terrell Lee races up and joins him for the journey west.

At the outset of DANCER, TEXAS, the audience is set up to identify with Keller, and view getting out of the town as not just a reasonable desire, but an unquestionable one. The movie opens with the four friends lounging in the middle of the main road, discussing their California dreams while practically daring a car to come along and disrupt the boredom. McCanlies then spends the next 90 minutes turning that mindset on its head, so that by the end, leaving Dancer behind becomes a bittersweet occasion. A portrait of the town emerges that debunks all of Keller's (and our) prejudices. What seemed dull and claustrophobic is revealed to be wholesome and familial.

In sharp contrast to Hollywood's usual condescending treatment of small-town folk as caricatured yokels, McCanlies's lovingly crafted script is filled with rich and fondly drawn characters. The film balances both subtle and broad humor with touching sentiment that is never false or bathetic. A very funny comic subplot pits nerdy Squirrel in a bumbling effort to steal a girlfriend from local lady-killer Terrell Lee, who's selfishly dating two of the town's three teenage girls. (Embry and Facinelli play similar roles in the teen comedy CAN'T HARDLY WAIT, also released in 1998.)

While DANCER isn't in the league of THE LAST PICTURE SHOW (1971), its attention to family and futures, and especially the shining scenes between Keller and Vivien, make it like a less wistful, and dustier, version of Thornton Wilder's *Our Town*.—P.R.

d, Tim McCanlies; p, Chase Foster, Peter White, Dana Shaffer; exec p, Michael Burns, Leanna Creel; co-p, Tina Brawner, Jeff Rice; w, Tim McCanlies; ph, Andrew Dintenfass; ed, Rob Kobrin; m, Steve Dorff; prod d, Dawn Snyder; art d, Jeff Adams; set d, Beau Petersen; sound, Wayne Bell (mixer); casting, Laurel Smith, Michael Testa; cos, Susan Matheson; makeup, Dara Jaramillo

Drama/Comedy **(PR: A MPAA: PG)**

DANCING ABOUT ARCHITECTURE

(SEE: PLAYING BY HEART)

DANCING AT LUGHNASA ★★★

(Ireland/U.K., 1998) 92m Ferndale; Channel Four; Noel Pearson; Capitol Films; Sony Pictures Classics ~ Sony Pictures Classics c

Meryl Streep *(Kate Mundy)*; Michael Gambon *(Father Jack Mundy)*; Catherine McCormack *(Christina Mundy)*; Kathy Burke *(Maggie Mundy)*; Sophie Thompson *(Rose Mundy)*; Brid Brennan *(Agnes Mundy)*; Rhys Ifans *(Gerry Evans)*; Darrell Johnston *(Michael Mundy)*; Lorcan Cranitch *(Danny Bradley)*; Peter Gowen *(Austin Morgan)*; Dawn Bradfield *(Sophie McLoughlin)*; Marie Mullen *(Vera McLoughlin)*; John Kavanagh *(Father Carlin)*; Kate O'Toole *(Chemist)*; Gerard McSorley *(Narrator)*

A serviceable but somewhat prosaic film version of Brian Friel's very fine autobiographical play, DANCING AT LUGHNASA records the struggles of five Irish sisters to keep their family together and make ends meet.

In a small Donegal farmhouse live the five unmarried Mundy sisters: Kate (Meryl Streep), a 40-year-old schoolteacher; 38-year-old Maggie (Kathy Burke), a housekeeper; 35-year-old Agnes (Brid Brennan) and 32-year-old Rose (Sophie Thompson), who knit gloves at home; and 26-year-old Chris (Catherine McCormack), whose seven-year-old son, Michael (Darrell Johnston) lives with them. Rejoining the family, after 25 years of missionary work in Africa, is older brother Jack (Michael Gambon), a Catholic priest who is failing in mind and body and appears to have "gone native." It is the summer of 1936 and the village is celebrating Lughnasa, an annual harvest festival left over from Pagan times.

One day Gerry Evans (Rhys Ifans), Michael's footloose father, arrives for a brief stopover on his way to Spain to join the fight against Franco. During his stay he will resume his romance with Chris and make friends with his son but it seems unlikely that he will ever settle down with and support them.

One afternoon the family is panicked by the disappearance of the simpleminded Rose. That evening Father Jack finds her at a Lughnasa celebration—in the company of Danny Bradley (Lorcan Cranitch), a married man whose wife abandoned him. Frightened by the wildness of the festivities, Rose is escorted home by her brother.

The summer ends dreadfully: Kate loses her job and a new knitwear factory terminates the livelihoods of Agnes and Rose. The ultimate fates of the five Mundy sisters will be hard, cruel, and even tragic, but the grown-up Michael (voice of Gerard McSorley) is comforted by fond memories of that long-ago summer when love, laughter, and hope were still alive.

In adapting Friel's play for the screen, the filmmakers have done some rearranging here, some opening up there—much of it unnecessary but little of it seriously damaging. In the play, the boy Michael is not seen—he is an invisible presence whose lines are spoken by the adult Michael, who stands at the side of the stage. The filmmakers wisely chose to incarnate little Michael but, not so wisely, demoted big Michael to a voice-over. Even less well advised was the decision to move the preview of the Mundy sisters' bleak future to the end of the narrative. By positioning this information somewhat before the end of the play, Friel invested the final segment with the wrenching poignancy of foreknowledge, an asset the filmmakers have sacrificed to the conventions of linear narrative.

In a theater, *Dancing at Lughnasa* has the kind of magic that does not translate easily to cinema, a medium with a distinct and special magic of its own—it's a piece whose ephemeral delicacy may be as resistant to successful film adaptation as a William Saroyan play. Still well above the average as screen fare goes, DANCING AT LUGHNASA might well have been more effective in the hands of a less literal director. (And, just this once, the decision to go with bright, crystal-clear photography may have been counterproductive.) An audacious and risky but potentially more inspired choice of director would have been Terence Davies, whose first two features, DISTANT VOICES, STILL LIVES (1998) and THE LONG DAY CLOSES (1992), memorably mapped similar narrative and thematic territory. Friel's lovely play tells us, among other things, that dancing is better than not dancing—a message that is worth spreading. Sustained by a talented cast headed by Meryl Streep, whose acknowledged gift for shifting ethnicity extends, amazingly, beyond her voice to her face, the movie version of DANCING AT LUGHNASA succeeds in introducing several of the play's many virtues to a wide audience. *(Profanity.)*—D.T.

d, Pat O'Connor; p, Noel Pearson; exec p, Jane Barclay, Sharon Harel; w, Frank McGuinness (based on the play by Brian Friel); ph, Kenneth MacMillan; ed, Humphrey Dixon; m, Bill Whelan; prod d, Mark Geraghty; art d, Conor Devlin, Clodagh Conroy; set d, Coldagh Conroy; ch, David Bolger; sound, Kieran Horgan (mixer); casting, Mary Selway; cos, Joan Bergin; makeup, Clare Lambe; stunts, Martin Grace

Drama/Comedy (PR: C MPAA: PG)

DANGEROUS BEAUTY ★½

(U.S., 1998) 114m Regency Enterprises;
Arnon Milchan/Bedford Falls ~ Warner Bros. c

Catherine McCormack *(Veronica Franco)*; Rufus Sewell *(Marco Venier)*; Oliver Platt *(Maffio)*; Moira Kelly *(Beatrice)*; Fred Ward *(Domenico Venier)*; Naomi Watts *(Giuila De Lezze)*; Jacqueline Bisset *(Paola Franco)*; Jeroen Krabbe *(Pietro Venier)*; Joanna Cassidy *(Laura Venier)*; Melina Kanakaredes *(Livia)*; Daniel LaPaine *(Serafino Franco)*; Justine Miceli *(Elena Franco)*; Jake Weber *(King Henry)*; Simon Dutton *(Minister Ramberti)*; Grant Russell *(Francesco Martenengo)*; Peter Eyre *(The Doge)*; Carla Cassola *(Caterina)*; Gianny Musy *(Joseph)*; Michael Culkin *(Bishop De La Torre)*; Ralph Riach *(Lorenzo Gritti)*; Charlotte Randle *(Francesca)*; Alberto Rossatti *(Andrea Tron)*; Anna Sozzani *(Marina)*; Luis Moltena *(Giacomo Baballi)*; Tim McMullan; Richard O'Callaghan *(Zealots)*; Lenore Lohman; Maud Bonanni; Gaia Zoppi *(Venetian Wives)*; Robert Corbiletto *(Tailor)*; Annelie Harryson *(Fanatic Woman)*; David Gant *(Bolognetti)*; Daniele Ciampi *(Naked Workman)*; Elena Mita; Federico Mita *(Elena's Children)*; Francesca Lucidi; Simona Nobili; Lena Guthorsen; Valentina Ardeatini; Tiziana Della Spina; Anna Maria Minati; Ilaria De Vincenzis; Cristina Rinaldi; Garmy Sall; Anna Maria Malipiero; Flaminia Fegarotti; Federica Federici; Angela Camuso; Patrizia Leonet; Elide Marigliani; Natascia Pastorello; Barbara Di Dio; Fulvia Lorenzetti; Olfa Ben Romdane; Laura Tedesco; Emy Kay *(Courtesans)*

Catherine McCormack stars as a liberated 16th-century Venetian courtesan in DANGEROUS BEAUTY, a crass and laughably anachronistic period piece that purports to be a story of feminist empowerment and sexual freedom, but comes off like a Playboy Channel "ribald tale" crossed with a Harlequin romance novel.

In 1583 Venice, beautiful but impoverished Veronica Franco (Catherine McCormack) falls in love with Marco Venier (Rufus Sewell), a nobleman's son. Though he also loves her, his father (Jeroen Krabbe) forbids him to marry her because she is below his station. Veronica's mother Paola (Jacqueline Bisset), a former courtesan, tells her that to get revenge she should also become a courtesan. Veronica agrees, and after training by her mother, has her first sexual encounter with a man, which she thoroughly enjoys. Marco becomes insanely jealous and sends gifts to Veronica, but she refuses to see him, and also spurns the advances of Marco's cousin, a debauched poet named Maffio (Oliver Platt). Marco's father forces him into an arranged marriage with a frigid aristocratic woman, but he continues to pursue Veronica, who has become Venice's richest and most popular courtesan, as well as a successful poetess.

While Veronica is reading from her recently published book of poems, the drunken Maffio insults her and the two engage in a duel of poetry which turns into a violent swordfight. Marco comes to her rescue and the two of them finally sleep together. He convinces her to be his exclusive lover, but when the Turks attack Cyprus, she is forced to sleep with the visiting King of France (Jake Weber) in order to gain his military assistance, and Marco angrily goes off to war. When Marco returns, he finds that Venice has been ravaged by the plague and that religious fanatics are blaming the courtesans. The Holy Inquisition comes to Venice and Veronica is accused of being a witch and put on trial, where she is persecuted by the vengeful Maffio, who has become a Monsignor. Veronica refuses to confess to heresy, and denounces her accusers. As she is about to be sentenced to death, Marco claims to be her "accomplice" and he inspires all of her other lovers to stand up in her defense, including numerous government officials, which forces the court to set her free.

When a movie sits on the shelf for months and goes through numerous title changes ("Venice," "The Courtesan," "The Honest Courtesan"), it usually signifies a major disaster, and DANGEROUS BEAUTY certainly proves to be no exception. Based on a real-life character, and dealing with such issues as women's roles in society and sexual hypocrisy, a Lubitsch, Ophuls, Visconti, or Sirk could have made a masterpiece out of the story, but director Marshall Herskovitz ("thirtysomething") displays neither a feel for the period nor affinity with the material and turns it into a tacky historical travesty. He's more interested in getting cheap laughs and pandering to modern audiences with vulgar colloquialisms ("What's biting your ass tonight, fair cousin?," constant use of such terms as "prick" and "fuck," Veronica shocking some prim aristocratic wives by swallowing a whole banana) than in creating honest emotion, and the story stops every few minutes for some slow-motion vaseline-on-the-lens coupling montages.

The sudden switch from frothy sex farce to impassioned courtroom histrionics is risible, and during the ludicrous "I am Spartacus"-style finale where all of Veronica's lovers gallantly stand up for her in court, one almost expects to see them high-fiving each other. Also straining credulity is the film's polyglot cast and jarring mixture of British and American accents, with Oliver Platt and Fred Ward being notably miscast. The film's only saving grace is Catherine McCormack's sensuous and intelligent performance as Veronica, even if her transition from naive, inexperienced virgin to sophisticated courtesan (in one easy montage) is a little too facile. But even she can't overcome the film's most offensive aspect, which is how it spuriously presents Veronica as some kind of Renaissance feminist heroine, but in actuality, merely wants to titillate with some softcore bodice-ripping. *(Nudity, sexual situations, profanity, violence.)*—M.S.

d, Marshall Herskovitz; p, Marshall Herskovitz, Edward Zwick, Arnon Milchan, Sarah Caplan; exec p, Michael Nathanson, Stephen Randall; assoc p, Debra Michael Petro; co-p, Paolo Lucidi; w, Jeannine Dominy (based on the biography *The Honest Courtesan* by Margaret Rosenthal); ph, Bojan Bazelli; ed, Steven Rosenblum, Arthur Coburn; m, George Fenton; prod d, Norman Garwood; art d, Keith Pain; set d, Ian Whittaker; sound, David Stephenson (mixer); fx, Massimo Nespoli, Robert Stromberg, Illusion Arts; casting, Mindy Marin, Wendy Kurtzman, Mary Selway; cos, Gabriella Pescucci; makeup, Fabrizio Sforza; stunts, Neno Zamperla, William Hobbs (fights)

Historical/Romance/Drama **(PR: O MPAA: R)**

DARK CITY ★★★½

(U.S., 1998) 103m Mystery Clock Productions ~ New Line c

Rufus Sewell *(John Murdoch)*; Kiefer Sutherland *(Dr. Schreber)*; Jennifer Connelly *(Emma Murdoch)*; Richard O'Brien *(Mr. Hand)*; Ian Richardson *(Mr. Book)*; William Hurt *(Inspector Frank Bumstead)*; Bruce Spence *(Mr. Wall)*; Colin Friels *(Walenski)*; John Bluthal *(Karl Harris)*; Mitchell Butel *(Husselbeck)*; Melissa George *(May)*; Frank Gallacher *(Stromboli)*; Ritchie Singer *(Hotel Manager/Vendor)*; Justin Monjo *(Taxi Driver)*; Nicholas Bell *(Mr. Rain)*; Satya Gumbert *(Mr. Sleep)*; Noah Gumbert *(Mr. Sleep Filming Double)*; Frederick Miragliotta *(Mr. Quick)*; Peter Sommerfeld; Timothy Jones; Jeanette Cronin *(Strangers)*; Paul Livingston; Michael Lake *(Assistant Strangers)*; David Wenham *(Schreber's Assistant)*; Alan Cinis; Bill Highfield *(Automat Cops)*; Terry Bader *(Mr. Goodwin)*; Rosemary Traynor *(Mrs. Goodwin)*; Edward Grant II *(Hotel Manager)*; Maureen O'Shaughnessy *(Kate Walenski)*; Deobie Oparei *(Train Passenger)*; Marcus Johnson *(Station Master)*; Doug Scroope *(Desk Sergeant)*; Cinzia Coassin *(Waitress)*; Tyson McCarthy *(Murdoch—Age 10)*; Luke Styles *(Murdoch—Teenager)*; Anthony Kierann *(Murdoch's Father)*; Laura Keneally *(Murdoch's Mother)*; Natalie Bollard *(Naked Woman)*; Eliot Paton *(Matthew Goodwin)*; Naomi van der Velden *(Jane Goodwin)*; Peter Callan *(Taxi Driver)*; Mark Hedges *(Emma's Lover)*; Darren Gilshenan *(Fingerprint Cop)*; Ray Rizzo *(Policeman)*; Bill Rutherford *(Police Officer)*; Marin Mimica *(Hotel Lobby Cop)*; Tony Mosley; Glenford O. Richards; Stanley Steer; Greg Tell *(Four Piece Band)*; William Upjohn *(Forensics Cop)*

DARK CITY is a rarity in contemporary science fiction/fantasy cinema: a film built on ideas rather than spectacle and boasting striking visuals that are integral to its theme, and not merely gratuitous eye candy.

John Murdoch (Rufus Sewell) wakes up in a hotel room in the company of a woman's dead body. He is telephoned by Dr. Schreber (Kiefer Sutherland), who tells him to flee. Outside, the world is one of perpetual night, and John, who only remembers flashes of his past, is pursued by Mr. Hand (Richard O'Brien) and his gang of Strangers—corpses reanimated by alien beings, who have created the city to experiment on the nature of humanity. John fights them off using telekinetic powers. Inspector Bumstead (William Hurt), investigating the murder, interviews John's estranged wife, Emma (Jennifer Connelly). John later finds Emma, and is plagued by memories of a childhood spent in a place called Shell Beach. Midnight comes, and everyone but John freezes. He witnesses the Strangers "tuning" the city: reshaping buildings and altering the lives of the residents. Schreber tells John that John has been injected with the memories of a murderer to see if he will behave accordingly. Mr. Hand is injected with the same memories in order to track John, but John eludes the Strangers, and he and Bumstead apprehend Schreber and force him to help them find Shell Beach. They arrive at a wall that John and Bumstead break through, only to find that the entire city is a structure built in space. The Strangers arrive; one of them grapples with Bumstead, and both are sucked into the void.

John is brought to the Strangers' underworld and prepared for a new experiment. Dr. Schreber turns the tables by injecting John with manufactured memories in which he is trained in psychic abilities, which John uses to destroy the Strangers' lair. Creating an ocean around the city and bringing out the sun, John tells Mr. Hand that humanity resides in the heart, not the mind, and is reunited with Emma—in the new identity of Anna—at Shell Beach.

For his first film since the box-office hit THE CROW (1994), director Alex Proyas came up with a fantasy that's even more visually striking (Proyas also supplied the original story). While DARK CITY lacks some of the earlier film's emotional power (intensified by the death of star Brandon Lee), it contains much stronger ideas. This lack of emotion is, in fact, one of the linchpins of the film's story line; the characters are denied emotional depth, as most of them are only just beginning to deal with the feelings with which they have been programmed. The theme is whether memories determine both identity and action; the idea of creatures that experiment on this aspect of humanity is an intriguing variation on ideas previously explored in works such as Philip K. Dick's short story "We Can Remember It For You Wholesale" (filmed as 1990's TOTAL RECALL).

Many critics commented on the fact that DARK CITY seemed to have been inspired by the Dick-derived BLADE RUNNER (1982). While both are set in finely detailed, palpably gloomy environments, Proyas's vision has a fully retro quality to it, while Ridley Scott put a futuristic cast on his noir-ish environment. DARK CITY's evocative production design (devised by George Liddle and Patrick Tatopolous) provides the perfect setting for this evocation of the noir cycle and its wrongfully accused protagonists who work to extricate themselves from a web of intrigue. (The old-fashioned approach also involves a refreshing lack of profanity for a '90s thriller.) As Murdoch, Sewell is a compellingly haunted presence, while Connelly and Hurt effectively incarnate variations on the classic torch singer/femme fatale and driven detective archetypes. More eccentric, and doing their best work in years, are Sutherland (here channeling the spirit of Peter Lorre), and O'Brien, whose character's oft-repeated command "Sleep. . . now" becomes a chilling mantra.

And while the actors and story line never play second fiddle to the special effects, Proyas clearly spent a great deal of time developing the film's stylish visuals. The Strangers' lair and costumes appear to have been painstakingly crafted, and the "tuning" of the city, in which the buildings twist and shift into new configurations, is a breathtaking effect. Yet the prevailing atmosphere of menace doesn't preclude moments of humor; in one of the best scenes, the Strangers transform a poor couple living in a tiny apartment into a pair of socialites who reside in a lavish townhouse. *(Graphic violence, nudity, sexual situations.)*—M.G.

d, Alex Proyas; p, Andrew Mason, Alex Proyas; exec p, Michael De Luca, Brian Witten; w, Alex Proyas, Lem Dobbs, David S. Goyer (from a story by Alex Proyas); ph, Dariusz Wolski; ed, Dov Hoenig; m, Trevor Jones; prod d, George Liddle, Patrick Tatopolous; art d, Michelle McGahey, Richard Hobbs; sound, David Lee (recordist), Gareth Vanderhope (design); fx, Tad Pride, Tom Davies, Mara Bryan, Arthur Windus, Andrew Mason, Bruce Hunt; casting, Valerie McCaffrey, Shauna Wolifson, Vanessa Pereira; cos, Liz Keogh; makeup, Lesley Vanderwalt; stunts, Glenn Boswell

Science Fiction/Thriller/Fantasy (PR: C MPAA: R)

DARK WATERS
(SEE: DEAD WATERS)

DAVID SEARCHING ★★½

(U.S., 1998) 101m Backpain Productions ~ L4Ltd Productions/Jour de Fete c

Anthony Rapp *(David)*; Camryn Manheim *(Gwen)*; Julie Halston *(Julie)*; Joseph Fuqua *(Walter)*; David Courier *(Michael)*; Michael Rupert *(Beau)*; Craig Chester *(Mercedes Guy)*; Leslie L. Smith *(Hotel Key Guy)*; Christopher Cook *(Stoner Share)*; Chris Duva *(Bungee Share)*; Susan Bruce *(Cat Lady)*; Jennie Moreau *(Librarian)*; Stephen Spinella *(Humus Guy)*; Juio Monge *(Homeboy)*; John Cameron Mitchell *(Man with Fruit)*; David Pevsner *(Scott)*; David Drake *(Mark)*; Alicia Hurst *(Usher)*; Kathleen Chalfant *(Grandmother)*; Melinda Wade *(Pamphlet Girl)*; Shane Bruce *(Rambles Trick)*; Richard Munroe *(Club 82 Doorman)*; Fabio Sottili *(Club 82 Trick #1)*; Brad Romaker *(Club 82 Trick #2)*; Brenda Cummings *(Nurse Brenda)*; Lee Alexander *(Danny)*; Anthony Meindl *(Diner Waiter)*; Joe Santarelli *(Gwen's Customer)*; Jaime D. Martinez *(Taxes Truth)*; LaChanze *(God Truth)*

The ideal friendship of a straight woman and a gay man is the focus of this likable but forgettable film about one man's search for love, life, and lust in New York City.

David (Anthony Rapp) is an attractive and likable twentysomething who dreams of being a documentary filmmaker. One day, he advertises for a roommate to share his small apartment. After interviewing a series of disastrous candidates, David picks Gwen (Camryn Manheim) a vivacious older woman who's going through a painful divorce. The two grow especially close and slowly begin to open up to each other. One day, they discover a dark-haired gentleman nonchalantly passed out on their couch. Walter (Joseph Fuqua), a charming roque with a taste for the odd colloquialism, explains that his girlfriend threw him out and he has come back to his old apartment—namely, David's—to crash. Despite the odd circumstances of their meeting, Gwen and Walter immediately hit it off and begin a turbulent and passionate affair, much to the dismay of lonely David.

David continues to search for Mr. Right through meaningless dates with a series of oddballs. Although his agent, Beau (Michael Rupert), pushes him to keep a meeting with PBS executives about a potential film project, David, feeling discouraged and aimless, doesn't show up. During a train ride home, he meets comedian Julie Halston (Herself) and the two strike up a close friendship. She encourages him to pursue his dreams, although he misinterprets her advice about standing up for himself with the PBS executives and chooses to miss the meeting entirely, thus resulting in the loss of the deal. David, distressed over his life, wanders through Central Park, where he spots an attractive man having sex with another man near a tunnel. Later, he visits an all-night sex club, where he spots the same attractive man, Michael (David Courier). David strikes up a conversation with him, and the two wind up having a passionate affair. David immediately falls for him, but Gwen warns him to tread lightly. One night, David spots Michael near the sex club and, unaware that Michael lives in the same neighborhood, angrily slaps him and runs home. Michael goes after him to explain and winds up following him back to the apartment. Before he can open his mouth, however, Walter, thinking he's protecting his friend, punches Michael.

David runs out of the apartment and goes over to Julie's house where he meets her lover, who is dying of AIDS. This encounter makes him realize that he truly values his relationship with Michael; he goes to find him in order to make up. Gwen in the meantime, rejects Walter's invitation to move in together, and tells him that she just wanted him for sex. With his relationship finally on a stable level, David starts filming his dream documentary. He interviews a number of people, inquiring what they hold to be "an absolute truth."

With her voluptuous Rubenesque figure and bon vivant personality, Camryn Manheim gives the standout performance in DAVID SEARCHING. Manheim, an Emmy winner for the TV series "The Practice," is terrific as Gwen, a prototypical New York woman whose aggression masks a very hurt inner child. As David, Rapp is less successful, but he nevertheless proves imminently likeable. Writer-director Leslie L. Smith (who has a small cameo as one of David's dates from hell) paces the film well, even within the confined space of David's tiny apartment, which serves as a perfect visual metaphor for David's inner turmoil, and the routine lifestyle he's dying to escape.

Smith, however, relies too often on annoying cinematic cliches. For instance, the title "David Searching" is literally acted out for some of the movie's running time—in seemingly endless musical montages, our hero walks through New York streets, strolls through Central Park, and even saunters through a sex club as he keeps. . . searching. These interludes accomplish nothing but slowing down an already uneven film; one wishes that Smith would have availed himself of the editing equipment that's prominently displayed in David's apartment. *(Sexual situations, profanity.)*—D.O.

d, Leslie L. Smith; p, Leslie L. Smith, John P. Scholz; w, Leslie L. Smith; ph, John P. Scholz; ed, Toni Blye; art d, Tina Parise; sound, Pratash "Derek" Somaru, Todd Siwinsky; makeup, Madronica Clarke

Romance/Drama/Comedy (PR: O MPAA: NR)

DAY AT THE BEACH ★★★

(U.S., 1998) 93m Mad Jack Productions ~ Arrow Releasing c

Nick Veronis *(Jimmy Hughes)*; Jane Adams *(Marie)*; Patrick Fitzgerald *(John)*; Paul Gleason *(Det. Johnson)*; Neal Jones *(Chuck)*; Catherine Kellner *(Amy)*; Robert Maisonett *(Herman)*; Marie Masters *(Seductress)*; Alec Murphy *(Crazy Car Owner)*; Joseph Ragno *(Antonio Gintolini)*; Ed Setrakian *(Augie)*; Martin Shakar *(Det. O'Leary)*; Elizabeth Stearns *(Real Estate Woman)*

A competent and fairly diverting film, DAY AT THE BEACH chronicles the misadventures of a group of young New Yorkers who spend some time in the Hamptons.

Jimmy Hughes (Nick Veronis), who works by day in a pasta factory, longs to be a filmmaker. One day, Jimmy and his friends, Chuck (Neal Jones) and John (Patrick Fitzgerald), are shooting a film when a prop John tosses kills a passerby. They flee the scene, but John later finds a newspaper article about the incident. Jimmy advises him not to worry, since it was an accident. Jimmy is later picked up by police inspectors, but they question him only about possible criminal activity at the factory. Jimmy claims to know nothing, and is released.

On a whim, the friends drive to the Hamptons, with Jimmy's girlfriend Amy (Catherine Kellner), John's wife Marie (Jane Adams) and their infant son. While there, Jimmy learns that the factory's former owner, Antonio (Joseph Ragno), has a house in the area. After he witnesses Antonio leaving it, he induces his friends into staying there, claiming that Antonio has lent him its use. The group spends the day enjoying the luxurious residence, but when Antonio returns unexpectedly, they realize that Jimmy has lied. Jimmy ties up Antonio and the group tries to leave, but when their car won't start, they are forced to spend the night. That evening, while sneaking around, Jimmy finds a suitcase filled with cash under Antonio's car.

That night, Jimmy, Chuck, and Amy walk to a local bar, while John and his family remain at Antonio's. Three men arrive at the house, kill Antonio, and search the house for the suitcase. Unable to find it, they stuff Antonio's corpse into the trunk of their car and leave. Jimmy and Amy return to the ransacked house, and find John and his family hiding in nearby bushes.

The next morning, the car is repaired and the group leaves. They return to New York, and Jimmy and John go to Jimmy's apartment. Jimmy reveals the money he has found, saying that he will use it to finance a film, but John leaves in disgust.

A bare-bones independent production, DAY AT THE BEACH is a dedicated if somewhat derivative work from first-time filmmaker Nick Veronis. As a novice, Veronis strikes a few false notes. Perhaps aspiring to follow in the footsteps of such stylists as Martin Scorsese and Quentin Tanantino, he at times indulges in overused devices like thumping rock songs on the soundtrack to set a scene's mood, or slow-motion photography to stress an action. When Veronis dabbles in such filmatic cliches, DAY AT THE BEACH is sophomoric and even grating.

Fortunately, Veronis often finds his own filmmaking voice, and when he does, the film feels less forced, more assured, and much more enjoyable. DAY AT THE BEACH works best when it is least stylish, when it breaks away from its overheated plot to concentrate on how its characters hang out and waste time. In these sequences, Jimmy and his friends idly philosophize, joke around, or quietly express their feelings for one another. The film becomes very engaging at these moments because the characters feel alive and authentic, not like one-dimensional figures in a formula piece. Veronis has the sense to let these scenes endure, and he has the confidence not to worry about them detracting from the plot's momentum. Much of his confidence, no doubt, is inspired by his cast. DAY AT THE BEACH features a fine group of young actors, each of whom gives a natural, easygoing performance that is in tune with the film's better scenes. And although he plays the film's lead, Veronis generously (and wisely) allows his fellow players ample time in front of the camera.

There are enough well-played scenes interspersed throughout DAY AT THE BEACH to leave a favorable impression. Veronis may become a quality filmmaker if he quits aping trendy directors and develops his own evident talent. *(Violence, sexual situations, extreme profanity.)*—D.C.

d, Nick Veronis; p, Nick Veronis; exec p, Sophie Marr, Michael Feldman; assoc p, Melissa Lintinger; w, Nick Veronis; ph, Nils Kenaston; ed, Mark Juergens; m, Tony Saracene; prod d, Petra Barchi, Charlotte Bourke; sound, Frederik Edwards, Harvey Edwards; makeup, Alec Murphy; stunts, Roy Farfel

Crime/Comedy/Drama (PR: C MPAA: NR)

DAY OF THE BEAST, THE ★★★★

(Spain/Italy, 1995) 104m Iberoamericana; Sogetel; Canal Plus Spain; MG Film ~ Trimark c (EL DIA DE LA BESTIA)

Alex Angulo *(The Priest)*; Armando de Razza *(Professor Cavan)*; Santiago Segura *(Jose Maria)*; Terele Pavez *(Rosario)*; Nathalie Sesena *(Mina)*; Maria Grazia Cucinotta *(Susana)*; Gianni Ippoliti *(TV Producer)*; Saturnino Garcia *(Old Priest)*; Jaime Blanch; David Pinilla; Antonio Dechent; Ignacio Carreno *(Toyotas)*

Billed as "a comedy of Satanic action" in its native Spain (where it was released in 1995), Alex de la Iglesia's second film works equally well as a supernatural chiller.

Father Angel Berriartua (Alex Angulo), a theology professor, has deduced from religious texts the day of Satan's appearance on Earth and the birth of the Antichrist: Christmas Eve. After a fellow priest to whom he reveals this secret is crushed under a huge crucifix, Angel decides he must become a sinner in order to meet the devil and head off his arrival. Seeking "satanic" music, he meets a heavy metal musician named Jose Maria (Santiago Segura), who takes him to stay at the rooming house run by his mother Rosario (Terele Pavez). On Christmas Eve in Madrid, the duo track down Ennio Lombardi, a.k.a. "Professor Cavan" (Armando De Razza), who hosts a TV occult show but is really a charlatan. At Cavan's apartment, they tie him up, along with his girlfriend Susana (Maria Grazia Cucinotta), and force Cavan to reveal how Satan can be raised. Their ritual proves successful, and the devil appears as a bipedal black goat to threaten them.

Forced to escape the apartment by climbing out a high window, the trio become separated. In the ensuing action, Angel begins to doubt his faith, while Cavan is transformed into a believer. The trio manage to reunite, and realize that since Catholic churches are built in cruciform shape, the devil will rise at a structure resembling his own sign. Working from signature markings on satanic literature, they find their way to a pair of diagonal towers on the outskirts of the city. There, they discover a homeless trio resembling the Holy Family, along with a group of fascist killers who have been terrorizing Madrid. They prove to be Satan's minions, and the devil himself soon reappears. Jose Maria is killed, as are the homeless family, but Angel and Cavan are able to defeat the evil forces. Yet they end up destitute, their heroism unacknowledged.

Following his international cult favorite ACCION MUTANTE (a 1994 political-horror satire which remains unreleased in the US), de la Iglesia's sophomore effort is better in every way, retaining his offbeat, aggressive style while applying it to a more consistent and interesting story line. He gets off to a perversely inspired start, as Angel roams the streets of Madrid, pushing mimes down stairs and stealing from accident victims. Wisely, de la Iglesia doesn't dwell on this darkly amusing material, as its episodic nature might stand in the way of the very linear saga that's about to unfold: the efforts of the priest, the heavy metal freak, and the fraudulent TV star to prevent Satan's return.

All three leads invest their off-the-wall characters with humanity and, commendably, play the roles completely straight-faced. Angulo makes his priest's quest thoroughly plausible and persuasively human, while de Razza's transition from huckster to hero is equally convincing. Segura is terrific as the metalhead who finds himself embroiled in a Satanic web; he subsequently directed, wrote, and starred in TORRENTE, EL BRAZO TONTO DE LA LEY ("Torrente, the Dumb Arm of the Law"), an equally outrageous 1998 comedy that was an enormous hit at the box office in Spain.

There's plenty of dark humor throughout the film, but de la Iglesia incorporates a number of straight horror scenes that work equally well. Satan's first appearance before the trio is especially chilling, and serves notice that de la Iglesia takes the supernatural seriously. He also orchestrates a number of striking big-scale set pieces, with spectacular special effects that belie a budget lower than that of many American independent films. A major success in Spain (where it swept the Goyas, that country's equivalent of the Oscars), DAY OF THE BEAST finally received its official US release in December of 1998. *(Graphic violence, extensive nudity, extreme profanity.)*—M.G.

d, Alex de la Iglesia; p, Teresa Font; exec p, Andres Vicente Gomez; assoc p, Fernando De Garcillan; w, Alex de la Iglesia, Jorge Guerricaechevarria; ph, Flavio Martinez Labiano; ed, Teresa Font; m, Battista Lena; art d, Jose Luis Arrizabalaga, Biaffra; sound, Miguel Rejas, Jose Antonio Bermudez; fx, Reyes Abades; cos, Estibaliz Markiegui; makeup, Jose Antonio Sanchez (special effects)

Horror/Comedy **(PR: O MPAA: R)**

DE JURK

(SEE: DRESS, THE)

DEAD END ★★

(Canada, 1998) 93m Allegro Films ~ Libra Pictures c/bw

Eric Roberts *(Henry Smovinsky)*; Jacob Tierney *(Adam Compton)*; Eliza Roberts *(Maggie Furness)*; Frank Schorpion *(Dennis)*; Lynne Adams *(Sally)*; Serge Houde *(Capt. Balfour)*; Jack Langedijk *(Lt. Lido)*; Don Jordan *(Mookie)*; David Siscoe *(Kowalchuk)*; Jayne Heitmeyer *(Kate Compton)*; Andrew Campbell *(Pimp)*; Kwasi Songhui; Larry Day; Michel Parron; Norris Dominigue; Andy Bradshaw

Despite the sleazy milieu, the cast of this cop thriller attempts an air of gravity as the characters unravel a tale containing dark hints of matricide and molestation.

In Scranton, Pennsylvania, policeman Henry Smovinsky (Eric Roberts) gets the news that his ex-wife Kate (Jayne Heitmeyer) has died from a fall off her Philadelphia balcony. Bachelor Henry must bond with son Adam (Jacob Tierney), a hostile, black-clad, nose-pierced teenager whom Henry hasn't seen formally in years. Things get even worse when Philadelphia police detective Maggie Furness (Eliza Roberts) shows up. Her investigation points toward Adam as the prime suspect in Kate's plunge. The boy flees his father's custody. Meanwhile, a witness puts Henry himself at the crime scene. He admits to Maggie that he spontaneously checked in on Kate and Adam days prior to the tragedy, but the ex-husband claims ignorance of Kate's profession as a high-class prostitute well-connected with local authorities. But Adam knew, and when Hank catches up with his fugitive son, the boy reveals that he felt he had driven his mother to suicide, by berating her in front of an unknown john.

Now Henry is able to put all the pieces together: the killer was a policeman client, and Adam is to take the rap for the cop. Henry's false story that Adam clearly saw the assailant succeeds in flushing out the guilty party. It's Dennis (Frank Schorpion), one of Henry's best friends from the Scranton force, who accidentally threw Kate to her doom in a fit of passion. Dennis plays cat-and-mouse with an unarmed Henry and Adam atop Kate's high-rise, until father, son, and Maggie eliminate the villain in spectacular fashion.

Spectacular it is, too. Like something out of a TERMINATOR movie, party-guy Frank gets electrocuted, shot, and splashed on the distant pavement—all at once. By contrast the base drama of DEAD END is strong, with a solid paternal turn from the extremely variable Eric Roberts (STAR 80, BEST OF THE BEST), who's well-matched against newcomer Tierney. The juvenile lead is neither too hard nor too sympathetic as the unprepared cop's ornery offspring, who may or may not be guilty of slaying his own mother, and Tierney keeps up that thespian balancing act until serving as a hapless quarry in the disappointingly routine action finale.

Too much of DEAD END seems to take place in a B-movie atmosphere all too familiar to viewers of straight-to-video noir; glamorous strip clubs, friendly and attractive hookers, and lady police detectives who look like they just walked in off the fashion-model runway (actress Eliza Roberts is Eric's real-life wife). When a genuinely queasy moment comes along in Karl Schiffman's script (like runaway Adam's near-seduction by a middle-aged chickenhawk), it's truly jarring, but more so for how ineffective the rest of the movie is. On the whodunit level, the movie overplays a red herring in the form of a nasty Philly lawman (Jack Langedijk), then reveals the true culprit as an absurdly peripheral character from very early on. *(Adult situations, violence, nudity, sexual situations, profanity, substance abuse.)* —C.C.

d, Doug Jackson; p, Stefan Wodoslawsky, Tom Berry; exec p, William Webb, Richard O. Lowry, Robert Baruc, Mary M. Bradley; co-p, Elissa McBride; w, Karl Schiffman; ph, Georges Archambault; ed, Claude Palardy; m, Milan Kymlicka; art d, Csaba Andras Kertesz; fx, Ryal Cosgrove; casting, Andrea Kenyon, Myriam Vezina; cos, Suzana Fischer; makeup, Byron Callaghan

Thriller/Drama **(PR: O MPAA: R)**

DEAD MAN ON CAMPUS ★½
(U.S., 1998) 89m Pacific Western;
MTV Films; Paramount ~ Paramount c

Tom Everett Scott *(Josh)*; Mark Paul Gosselaar *(Cooper)*; Poppy Montgomery *(Rachel)*; Lochlyn Munro *(Cliff)*; Randy Pearlstein *(Buckley)*; Corey Page *(Matt)*; Alyson Hannigan *(Lucy)*; Mari Marrow; Dave Ruby *(Zeke)*; Mark Carpezza *(Hank)*; Jeff T *(Jerry)*; Jason Segel *(Kyle)*; Linda Cardellini *(Kelly)*; Aeryk Egan *(Pickle)*

College campuses are breeding grounds for urban legends. One of the most commonly spread stories involves the fact that if one's roommate commits suicide, one is assured straight-A's for that semester in order to be compensated for the resulting trauma. In DEAD MAN ON CAMPUS, two hopeless freshmen test this legend; the result could have been an intriguing black comedy, but the film proves to be just another lame adolescent comedy that desperately tries to be outrageous without having the guts to be either truly original or truly tasteless.

Josh (Tom Everett Scott) and Cooper (Mark-Paul Gosselaar) are roommates at prestigious Daleman College. Josh was a straight-A high school student whose hard work earned him a full academic scholarship. Cooper is a drugged-out slacker whose rich father paid his way into the school. Josh starts out the semester with the best of intentions, but soon gets dragged into Cooper's way of life, and before long, both students are facing straight Fs. Cooper's father visits him and threatens him with entry-level work in the family toilet business if he doesn't pass the semester, and Josh discovers that if he can't keep a B+ average, he'll lose his scholarship and have to drop out.

Desperate for a solution, they hit upon the widely circulated legend that the roommates of a suicide victim will get straight As. They immediately start looking for a new, unstable roommate in order to test this theory. First is Cliff (Lochlyn Munro), a psychotic alcoholic so uncontrollable that he was thrown out of Daleman's most unruly fraternity. Though Cliff helps Josh and Cooper alienate their friends and almost get arrested, it soon appears that the best they can hope from him is an accidental death. They move ahead to choice number two, Buckley (Randy Pearlstein), a paranoid computer nerd who is convinced that the big computer corporations are out to get him. Josh and Cooper feed his fantasies, but he decides that they're in cahoots with the computer companies and leaves. Finally, Matt (Corey Page) moves into the room. He is a death-obsessed British singer who leads a gloomy campus rock band. Unfortunately, Cooper soon discovers that Matt's self-destructive image is just a pose he uses to attract women and help his band achieve fame. He's actually a cheerful guy who sings showtunes and was a high school cheerleader nicknamed "Mr. Happy."

Though none of the roommates work out, Josh and Cooper soon discover their reclusive friend Pickle (Aeryk Egan) attempting to overdose. Cooper rejoices, but Josh doesn't have the heart to let Pickle die, and calls an ambulance. As a last resort, Josh climbs a campus bridge and threatens to jump. Cooper talks him down and discovers that Josh was just tricking him. Due to Josh's "suicidal nature," Daleman allows him to keep his scholarship and have another semester to work his grade point average up, and because Cooper is the "hero" who saved Josh's life, he too is allowed to stay.

DEAD MAN ON CAMPUS took more than a year to be completed (never a good sign), and the final product is almost completely devoid of spirit and originality. The fact that the film was an MTV production, no doubt accounts for the terrible musical soundtrack, full of trendy remakes of classic older tunes. As for the cast, Tom Everett Scott shows none of the charm that made him so appealing in THAT THING YOU DO (1996), and the other performers are essentially miscast, especially Munro, who looks more like a preppie than a psychotic. It takes almost the entire film before the first decent joke appears (Matt's secretly cheery personality leads to a number of amusing scenes); in the process, DEAD MAN ON CAMPUS becomes a depressing waste of the audience's time.

This is disappointing, given that the urban legend that drives the film could have opened up a number of possibilities. It seems logical that the roommates would consider actually *murdering* one of their intended suicides to speed things up, or that they would even think about killing each other just to fulfill the legend. Audiences left wondering about the potential direction of the story line will obviously be doing so because the film itself contains lackluster characters and meager plotting. Perhaps Josh and Cooper should have just had their roommates sit through this tedious film. *(Nudity, sexual situations, adult situations, substance abuse, profanity.)*—A.M.

d, Alan Cohn; p, Gale Anne Hurd; exec p, Van Toffler, David Gale; co-p, Maggie Malina; w, Michael Traeger, Mike White (based on the story by Adam Larson Broder and Anthony Abrams); ph, John Thomas; ed, Debra Chiate; m, Mark Mothersbaugh; prod d, Carol Winstead Wood; set d, Jan K. Bergstrom; sound, Willie Burton (mixer); casting, Deborah Aquila; cos, Kathleen Detoro

Comedy **(PR: O MPAA: R)**

DEAD WATERS ★★★
(U.K./Russia, 1998) 94m ~ York Home Video c
(AKA: DARK WATERS)

Louise Salter *(Elizabeth)*; Venera Simmons *(Sarah)*; Maria Kapnist *(Mother Superior)*; Lubov Snegur *(Mother Superior's Assistant)*; Alvina Skarga *(Old Blind Woman)*; Valeriy Bassel *(Fisherman)*; Sergey Rubens; Georgiy Drozd; Anna Rose Phipps *(Theresa)*; Pavel Sokolov *(Boat Owner)*; Tanya Dobrovolskaya *(Elizabeth as a Child)*; Valeriy Kopaev *(Priest)*; Ludmila Marufova *(Nun)*; Kristina Spivak *(Sarah as a Child)*; Nadezhda Trimasova *(Crucified Nun)*

Striking location photography and dark, stylish visuals make this imported shocker (filmed in 1994 as DARK WATERS) a stand out.

Twenty years after horrible deaths occurred at a convent on a remote Russian island, a young woman named Elizabeth (Louise Salter) travels there, spurred by a letter from her sister, Theresa (Anne Rose Phipps). Before Elizabeth reaches the convent, Theresa is murdered when she sees the nuns performing an occult ritual. Elizabeth arrives, befriends young nun Sarah (Venera Simmons), and learns of the order's special practices. After finding strange drawings and references to "The Beast" in the convent library, Elizabeth sees some of the nuns carrying Theresa's body through the catacombs. She confides in Sarah, who tells her that the next boat to the mainland doesn't leave for another week.

Elizabeth is assailed by nightmares of herself and Theresa as young girls taking part in a bloody sacrifice. During their waking hours, the pair are attacked by other nuns. Elizabeth soon sees the boat leave and realizes that Sarah lied to her. Elizabeth discovers a letter from Theresa stating that an amulet of the Beast must not be put back together. Suspicious of Sarah, Elizabeth tries to get answers from an old nun (Alvina Skarga), who is set afire before she can reveal her secrets. While looking over a fragment of the amulet, Sarah is murdered—but is resurrected and confronts Elizabeth, revealing that she is really her sister, and wants to finish the ritual they began 20 years before. Elizabeth complies at first and the Beast is raised, but she then rebels and shatters the amulet. The building collapses and the Beast is destroyed; Elizabeth survives, but has been stricken blind.

While the title presumably refers to the ocean surrounding the island, first-time director Mariano Baino puts much emphasis on water in the film, shooting many scenes in dripping underground chambers or exteriors besieged by the pouring rain. The grimly beautiful locations (near Russia's Black Sea) and authentically ancient interiors add a lot to the movie's atmosphere.

While Baino's work contains echoes of the work of Italian horror-masters like Mario Bava and Dario Argento, his storytelling approcach is less elliptical than theirs was. He also displays a skill for delivering genuinely creepy visuals. And while the final revelation incorporates the usual splatter and monster effects, Baino utlizes them in an understated manner. Lead actress Salter does a good job of incarnating Elizabeth as a heroine who is neither a shrinking violet nor foolishly brave; in addition, Baino has found some very evocative local faces to populate the supporting roles. Alex Howe's photography and Igor Clark's organ-heavy score also serve to make DEAD WATERS a genuinely chilling experience. *(Graphic violence, nudity, profanity.)*— M.G.

d, Mariano Baino; p, Victor Zuev; exec p, Svetlana Polyarush, Igor Trimasov; assoc p, Andrew M. Bark, Nigel Dali; w, Mariano Baino, Andrew M. Bark; ph, Alex Howe; ed, Mariano Baino, Rick Littler; m, Igor Clark; set d, Nadezhda Lubarskaya, Tanya Tokareva; sound, Josef Goldman, Alexander Hasin; fx, Richard Field, David Mundin; casting, Marilyn Baino, Ekaterina Kondratyeva; cos, Antonina Petrova; makeup, Ludmila Kubalskaya

Horror **(PR: O MPAA: NR)**

DEAR JESSE ★★★

(U.S., 1998) 82m Bang! Inc./CineBLAST! ~ Cowboy Booking International c

Tim Kirkman; Jesse Helms; Dr. Jerry McGee; Myron Williams; Shane Webster; Mike Nelson; Mandy Carter; Karen Brown; Angela Brady; Andrew George; Gene Price; Jaki Shelton Greene; James McAfee; Lee Smith; Hal Crowther; Allan Gurganus; Patsy Clarke; Eloise Vaughn; Rose Vaughn Williams; Dr. H. Mitch Simpson; Jerry Kirkman

Nonstop vitriol could have been the order of the day in this chronicle of a gay filmmaker's attempts to elicit opinions from North Carolina residents about Senator Jesse Helms, a leading homophobe. To his credit, though, first-time documentarian Tim Kirkman refuses to demonize Helms the same way Helms demonizes homosexuals. Despite amateurish production values and a rambling structure (in which Kirkman at times "addresses" his subject directly), DEAR JESSE admirably criticizes the multiterm demagogue without ever losing a sense of humanity.

Like the Senator, the filmmaker was born a Southern Baptist in the small town of Monroe; Kirkman sarcastically notes that both he and Helms have another link—they're both obsessed with homosexual men. The outspoken Helms has a long history of battling legislation that protects homosexual rights or sanctions same-sex marriages. Thus, it comes as no surprise that Helms refused Kirkman's request for an interview. The filmmaker instead utilizes a few choice video clips of Helms. In one typical sound bite, the senator states that "If they [homosexuals] would stop what they're doing, there wouldn't be one more case of AIDS in this country." Helms also is seen putting forth the notion that AIDS victims get what they deserve. Instead of debunking such ludicrous statements, Kirkman wisely lets them stand on their own.

Various North Carolinians (writers, students, clerics, and politicians) take Helms to task on his antigay views—as well as for his racism, his protobacco stance, and his opposition to government funding of the arts. Carrboro Mayor Mike Nelson, the first openly gay politician to hold office in North Carolina, wishes Helms would use his talent for playing on people's emotions in the service of a good cause. African-American poetess Jaki Shelton Greene recounts her family's ritual of watching Helms deliver his nightly television spots, which included condescending remarks about Martin Luther King. The message was clear to Greene: know thy enemy. Kirkman wisely doesn't stick to a simple elaboration of the facts about Helms; instead he attempts to tackle the million-dollar question: if Helms's hateful, narrow-minded point of view is so distasteful to so many people, how does he consistently get reelected?

Kirkman attempts to spotlight the more positive aspects of Helms's life and career: his adoption of a cerebral palsy victim; his patent honesty, and exemplary service to his constituents. Conservative journalist Gene Price describes the Senator as a gentle man, who eschews all forms of political spin, and makes it very clear where he stands on the issues. Gay novelist Allan Gurganus comes up with three types of people who vote for Helms: the cynics who secretly embrace Helms's exclusionary message; the ignorant poor who fail to see that, while Helms pays lip service to them, he really supports big business; and the apathetic masses who are more comfortable voting for the familiar name.

In addition to underscoring Helms's bad and good points, Kirkman weaves in his own saga of coming out as a homosexual, moving from North Carolina to New York, and dealing with his ex-lover's suicide. This first-person approach to the documentary form appears to borrow heavily from filmmaker Ross McElwee, who in SHERMAN'S MARCH (1986) also shared his (heterosexual) romantic travails while speaking about his Southern heritage. Though not as editorially deft as McElwee and certainly not as funny as one of his other evident influences, Michael Moore (ROGER AND ME), Kirkman wins the viewer over with his honesty and forthrightness. Though his own story registers as mostly mundane, his reflections on Helms are quite provocative and solidly grounded in ideas and not emotion.

Kirkman's filmic letter to the Senator closes with a statement that nicely captures the film's evenhanded tone: "To some I seem evil, dangerous, and immoral. And to some you seem evil, dangerous, and immoral. Am I? Are you?" *(Profanity.)*—T.Y.

d, Tim Kirkman; p, Mary Beth Mann; exec p, Gill Holland; w, Tim Kirkman; ph, Norwood Cheek, Ashley McKinney; ed, Joe Klotz; m, John Crooke; sound, Tony Losardo, Dave Sherwin, Ben Turney, Joe Caterini (mixer)

Documentary/Political **(PR: C MPAA: NR)**

DECAMPITATED ★½

(U.S., 1998) 92m Sneaky Pig Pictures ~ Troma c

Amy Gordon *(Candice Crinkle)*; Mike Hart *(Garret Clutch'cavage)*; Steve Ladden *(Toby Tumblenick/Miles Double)*; Bethany Lavoo *(Paige Turner)*; Thomas Martwick *(Roger Rogers)*; Christine Paterson *(April Showers)*; Jonathan Scott *(Vince Austin)*; Ryan Lowery *(Jake the Transvestite)*; Wayne Larsen *(Miles DeCamp)*; Chad Drummond; Amanda Hite; Shane Redher; Rees Garner; Jon Tucker *(Stoners)*; Angela Scott *(Screamer Girl)*; Joel Beck *(Screamer Guy)*; Carolyn C. Miller *(Chainsaw Matriarch)*; Matt Cunningham *(Hillbilly/Miles Double)*; Jack D'Amore *(Tattoo Artist)*; Karla Keifer *(Travel Agent Vamp)*; Brian Walters *(Miles Double)*

As often happens with Troma releases, this is a case of a great title and a not-so-great movie.

After visiting a weird travel agent (Wayne Larsen), a group of young people head out for a cabin in the Colorado woods. They get into an accident on the way, and while the rest set up camping equipment, Vince (Jonathan Scott) heads out to find the cabin. He comes upon the dwelling of a transvestite, Jake (Ryan Lowery), who takes him captive. Garret (Mike Hart) tells the others the local legend of psycho killer Miles DeCamp, and later that night, Toby (Steve Ladden) has his throat slit. He's patched up with duct tape, but the next day, the murderer attacks April (Christine Paterson), hacking off her arm, and impales Roger (Thomas Martwick).

The survivors find their way to Jake's house, where Jake is shot with an arrow. The friends flee to the cabin, along the way encountering April, who has sewn her arm back on. Then Roger, who is also still alive, turns up. The next morning, Toby is decapitated, and the killer proves to be Miles, who is also the travel agent. He bumps off the rest of the group, and is about to kill Vince when he is shot by Jake—who has survived his wounds, and still wants Vince for himself.

Although it was only distributed and not produced by the Troma company, DECAMPITATED contains the hallmarks of their movies: overstated performances, a man in drag, and comically exaggerated gore (in the opening scene, the killer pursues a girl who has to continually hack off her own limbs when they get caught in bear traps). But it all adds up to little more than the occasional chuckle. After SCREAM (1996) single-handedly resurrected the slasher genre, the time was ripe for a new spoof of the form, yet this one is no more successful as a parody than were such lame '80s outings as STUDENT BODIES (1981).

The movie doesn't tackle enough of the specific conventions of the genre, and too many of the sight gags and punchlines simply aren't funny enough. It doesn't help that the actors practically shout a lot of the dialogue, and that some of the jokes (the killer skipping about the woods and doing his dirty work to the tune of big band music) are more odd than amusing. *(Graphic violence, sexual situations, profanity.)*—M.G.

d, D. Matt Cunningham; p, D. Matt Cunningham, Carolyn Miller, Ryan Lowery, Brian Walters; exec p, Bret Wortley; assoc p, Steve Ladden, Eric Lewis, Marilin Miller, Jonathan Scott, Victor E. Miller, Philip A. Ladden; co-p, Erik Scott Gardner, Michael Berkowitz; w, Brian Walters, Ryan Lowery, Carolyn Miller, D. Matt Cunningham; ph, Ken Carmack; ed, Michael Berkowitz; m, Jon Rossner, Cindy Levin; sound, Bret Wortley, Barak Grass; fx, Michael A. Pellegrini; cos, Steve Lowery; makeup, Betty Gardner, Brian Walters (effects), Matt Cunningham (effects), Gilbert Eckholm

Horror **(PR: O MPAA: NR)**

DECEIVER ★★½

(U.S., 1998) 102m MDP Worldwide; Polygraph Inc. ~ MGM/UA c

Chris Penn *(Braxton)*; Ellen Burstyn *(Mook)*; Tim Roth *(James Walter Wayland)*; Renee Zellweger *(Elizabeth)*; Michael Rooker *(Officer Kennesaw)*; Rosanna Arquette *(Mrs. Kennesaw)*; Don Winston *(Warren)*; Michael Parks *(Dr. Banyard)*; Mark Damon *(Wayand's Father)*; J.C. Quinn *(Priest)*; Jody Wilhelm *(Mrs. Wayland)*; Ocie Pouncie *(Boogie)*; Bob Hungerford *(Jebby)*; Genevieve Butler *(Mary Kennesaw)*; Chelsea Butler *(Chelsea Kennesaw)*; David Alan Pickelsimer II *(Billy Kennesaw)*; Paul Smith *(Wayland's Girlfriend's Father)*; George Nannerello *(Laughing Officer)*; Michael Flippo *(Police Officer)*; James Middleton *(Police Officer #2)*; Karina Logue *(Sorority Girl)*; Ashley Rogers *(Woman in Park)*

A psychological whodunnit that hinges on the malleability of truth through the machinations of its cagey protagonist, DECEIVER isn't as clever as it thinks it is, with an unnecessarily complicated plot that contains far too many loose ends.

Police polygraph expert Edward Kennesaw (Michael Rooker) and officer Phillip Braxton (Chris Penn) give a lie-detector test to James Wayland (Tim Roth), who maintains his innocence in the mutilation murder of a prostitute named Elizabeth (Renee Zellweger). Afterward, Braxton tells Kennesaw that he's a compulsive gambler who owes his bookie, Mook (Ellen Burstyn), $20,000.

The cops test Wayland again, but he has secretly swallowed some pills. Wayland claims he was drunk on absinthe, a hallucinogenic liquor, when he met Elizabeth. Abruptly, Wayland accuses Kennesaw of cheating on his wife. Kennesaw deduces that Wayland has drugged himself to beat the polygraph, but Wayland says he took medication to control temporal-lobe epilepsy, which a psychiatrist says can trigger outbursts of violence that a sufferer wouldn't remember.

The next day, Wayland is interrogated again and denies knowing Elizabeth—but remembers meeting her in a peep-show booth. Wayland offers Braxton $10,000 to let him go. Wayland secretly meets Mook, who happens to be his supplier of absinthe and pills.

Back with the cops, Wayland plays a videotape he retrieved from Elizabeth's apartment that shows Kennesaw beating Elizabeth. Wayland turns the tables and convinces Kennesaw to submit to a polygraph test. Wayland asks Kennesaw if he killed Elizabeth; he denies it. But when Wayland asks if Kennesaw killed his own wife, the machine reacts. Braxton says Mrs. Kennesaw is alive, but Wayland says Kennesaw is confused about who his wife is. Kennesaw pulls his gun and forces Wayland to explain how he knows everything. But first Wayland surreptitiously takes the pills.

Wayland says Elizabeth told him that Kennesaw was one of the customers she videotaped. Wayland found Elizabeth's body after Kennesaw killed her. To shield himself from suspicion by making the killing look like the work of a lunatic, Wayland cut the body in half. Suddenly, Wayland suffers a TLE fit and hits his head. Kennesaw pockets the videotape as EMTs place the apparently dead Wayland in a body bag—but the EMTs are Mook's men. Toting an envelope containing $10,000, Braxton quits the force. Kennesaw returns to his wife. One year later, Wayland is seen walking in a park very much alive.

A poor-man's THE USUAL SUSPECTS (1995), DECEIVER is less affecting because viewers know that Wayland's narration is probably composed of lies, thus dulling the shock value. The saving grace is that we don't know why or how much he's fibbing. That Wayland is simply holding back information instead of constructing an intricate web of deceit is unsatisfying, and the "surprise" explanation that Kennesaw is the killer lacks impact. Also, Wayland is clearly so much smarter than the cops that there's little question of his slipping up. It's also unclear whether Kennesaw was trying to frame Wayland specifically or merely using a convenient stranger as a patsy. Braxton's gambling problem is a time-consuming red herring.

Codirectors and screenwriters identical twins Joshua and Jonas Pate (THE GRAVE, 1995) are workmanlike. They keep the talking heads from becoming monotonous, and during Wayland's final revelation, the camera motion effectively suggests a world unhinged. But overall, the photography is far too murky and the storytelling self-consciously labyrinthine.

Roth is in top form, crafting an enigmatic, brilliant manipulator who toys with his targets. His Wayland has a Princeton-honed 155 IQ but an underdeveloped morality. Zellweger makes the most of her limited screen time as the world-weary hooker. For his part, Rooker goes over the top with sweaty intensity.

DECEIVER'S working title was "Liar," and while prevarication isn't really its focus, there's a decent amount of misdirection for mystery fans. *(Violence, profanity, sexual situations.)*—J.Di.

d, Jonas Pate, Joshua Pate; p, Peter Glatzer, Jonas Pate, Joshua Pate; exec p, Mark Damon; co-p, Don Winston; w, Jonas Pate, Joshua Pate; ph, Bill Butler; ed, Dan Lebental; m, Harry Gregson-Williams; prod d, John Kretschmer; set d, Chuck Potter; sound, Peter Bentley (mixer); fx, Ray Bivins; casting, Laurel Smith; cos, Dana Allyson; makeup, Sara Seidman; stunts, Cal Johnson

Crime/Thriller **(PR: O MPAA: R)**

DECLINE OF WESTERN CIVILIZATION PART III, THE ★★★

(U.S., 1998) 86m Spheeris Films Inc. c/bw

Final Conflict; Litmus Green; Naked Aggression; The Resistance; Squid; Filth; Spinner; Why Me?; Spoon; Darius; Little Tommy the Queer; Troll; Hamburger; Sage; Pinwheel; Stephen Chambers; Keith Morris; Flea; Rick Wilder; Sgt. Gary Fredo

After a number of overtly commercial projects (THE BEVERLY HILLBILLIES, THE LITTLE RASCALS, and the 1998 release SENSELESS), director Penelope Spheeris returns to her roots as a documentarian with this third entry in her series of films about LA youths' rock-and-roll lifestyles. Unlike the previous two films, however, there's no ironic aspect to the title of this DECLINE; the downbeat film focuses not on the bands that produce the music, but the aimless lives of the homeless "gutterpunks" who reside on LA's streets. The film received a limited theatrical release in 1998.

Journeying into the nucleus of LA's punk scene, Spheeris discovers a new generation of young punks who live on the streets, and weren't even born when their spiked-hair musical heroes of the 1970s were at their peak of outrageousness (they in fact weren't even born when Spheeris's first DECLINE came out, back in 1980). These self-described misfits (with names such as Squid, Spoon, Filth, and Why Me?) discuss their run-ins with racist skinheads, harassment by cops, their abusive families, and how to find a squat. Spheeris also includes interviews with survivors of the '70s scene, such as Circle Jerks' Keith Morris, Rick Wilder of the Mau Maus, and Red Hot Chili Peppers' bassist Flea (costar of Spheeris's 1984 fiction film SUBURBIA), who articulately explains how the current LA punk scene is more physically violent and less grounded in art and music.

These portraits are interspersed with onstage performances by ragtag bands like Final Conflict, Litmus Green, Naked Aggression, and The Resistance. Interviewed at home, the members of Naked Aggression discuss their day jobs, as well as the way in which independent record labels are just as likely to rip off a band as big-name companies. The Resistance also invites Spheeris's crew to visit the home of the lead singer's mom, which is a pack-rat paradise of clothes and junk.

The gutterpunks who are interviewed blithely admit to earning their cash by robbing, panhandling, and "photospanging" (posing for tourist photos). They're seen begging for loose change, swearing at people who ignore them, and (being self-confessed alcoholics) spending any money that they do receive on beer. Most of the youths are homeless, with the exception of wheelchair-bound Darius who has enough cash (thanks to his disability checks) to rent an apartment, which he has turned into a party pad filled at all hours with unconscious, hungover kids who brag about the fact that they won't be be alive in another five years. The film ends with a visit to a recently burnt-out squat, and an epilogue that informs us that one of Spheeris's main interviewees, Squid, was later knifed to death by girlfriend Spoon.

Filmed from July 1996 through August 1997, the third DECLINE starts out as a simple recycling of the themes found in her seminal 1980 documentary, but Spheeris soon takes a radical departure and abandons her interviews with musicians for a closer look at the streetwise fans and their reckless lifestyle. Lacking the cutting-edge music of the first DECLINE, or the brash humor of the second film (which focused on the LA heavy-metal scene), DECLINE 3 relies on a far less interesting group of interview subjects. The gutterpunks have attitude to spare, but it becomes apparent as they speak that they have only a minimum of functioning brain cells. Nevertheless, Spheeris succeeds in creating a touching portrait, although the depressing nature of their dead-end, emotionally numb lives offers little hope for a cheerful resolution. This becomes painfully apparent in one scene in which a punk admits to selling his dog in order to get drunk for a night. As for the film's musical performances, the selected bands are a pale imitation of their late-1970s precursors.

Descending into the maudlin in the film's final moments, Spheeris truly does evidence a concern for her subjects (she promised that all profits will go toward homeless and abused children). One can easily assume that the very real nature of the subjects' lives also offered her a refreshing break from her work as a major-studio gun-for-hire (as with the aptly titled SENSELESS). In the final analysis, Spheeris is able to dredge some brutal truths from these punks, while making an attempt to find a way to justify their largely inert lifestyle. Her effort to find glimmers of humanity in the gutterpunk scene is clearly noble, but after seeing the film, one still comes away with the notion that if these kids were actually offered some charity, they'd spit in the good Samaritan's face, and happily return to their dumpster-diving lifestyle. *(Violence, adult situations, substance abuse, profanity.)*—S.P.

d, Penelope Spheeris; p, Scott Wilder; co-p, Ross Albert; ph, Jamie Thompson; ed, Ann Trulove; m, Phil Suchomel; sound, David Ronne, David Barr Yaffe, Exra Dweck

Documentary **(PR: C MPAA: R)**

DEE SNIDER'S STRANGELAND ★★

(U.S., 1998) 88m Shooting Gallery ~ Raucus Releasing c

Dee Snider *(Captain Howdy/Carleton Hendricks)*; Kevin Gage *(Detective Mike Gage)*; Elizabeth Pena *(Toni Gage)*; Brett Harrelson *(Detective Steve Christian)*; Amy Smart *(Angela)*; Robert Englund *(Jackson Roth)*; Linda Cardellini *(Genevieve Gage)*; Amal Rhoe *(Tiana Moore)*; Brett Pirozzi; Krsztoff; R.H. Bear; Alexander Jaymz; Fort LaCourt; Bob Abuse; Sin-D *(BiLE)*

Dee Snider, former frontman of the rock group Twisted Sister, makes his debut as a writer-producer-star in this disturbing but uneven shocker. Snider proves quite menacing as the villain, a child-torturing deviant, but is let down by his director and co-stars.

Teenaged Genevieve Gage (Linda Cardellini) and a friend are on an Internet chat line when they are invited to a party by someone calling himself Captain Howdy. They end up imprisoned in the home of Howdy, whose real name is Carleton Hendricks (Dee Snider), a tattooed fetishist who tortures his victims with body piercing. Investigating his daughter's disappearance, detective Mike Gage (Kevin Gage) is taunted over the phone by Hendricks, but is ultimately able to track the villain down and rescue his daughter. Hendricks is found not guilty by reason of insanity and committed to a psychiatric hospital, where his twisted impulses are repressed with medicine. After four years, Hendricks is released to much public protest. At first, Hendricks remains peaceful, until a group of local rednecks led by Jackson Roth (Robert Englund) break into his house—an act Gage, whose daughter is still plagued by nightmares, witnesses but does nothing to stop. The mob drags Hendricks to a hilltop and attempts to lynch him; Hendricks survives but his mind snaps, and he re-adopts his Howdy persona. He kidnaps and tortures Roth and some of his other enemies, then abducts Genevieve again. Gage succeeds in reclaiming his daughter, then confronts Hendricks in a deserted church, where he hangs the madman from a chain and sets him on fire.

Snider's STRANGELAND script was based on a pair of early-'80s Twisted Sister songs, "Captain Howdy" and "Street Justice," about a child killer who is let off on a technicality and burned by a mob of angry parents (a plot quite similar to the backstory of NIGHTMARE ON ELM STREET, so it's only fitting that erstwhile Freddy Robert Englund makes an appearance here). In expanding the premise into a film, Snider has worked up a creepy screen persona for himself, a tribal fetishist who believes that he's taking his victims to a higher state of being through his "body modification." His appearance, festooned with tattoos, studs and spikes, is arresting, and his performance is enthusiastically deranged.

Unfortunately, nothing else about STRANGELAND is nearly as inspired. Feature newcomer John Pieplow (who replaced makeup effects artist Tom Savini at the helm) directs without any sense of pacing or menace, as if he believed he was crafting an intimate drama instead of a horror film. A more commanding presence in the heroic lead role might have helped, but Gage's performance is so wooden that one can't help suspecting that he was only hired because he bears the same last name as his character. The result is that the movie's approach to such themes as social aberration and capital punishment amounts to little more than lip service, and the attempts at irony (Roth is presented as being just as deranged as Hendricks) fall flat.

Michael Burnett's special makeup work creates a few queasy moments (though it's not explained why the recovered Genevieve and the reformed Hendricks bear no piercing scars), and it's amusing to see Snider as the "normal" Hendricks with combed-back hair and a Mr. Rogers cardigan. But one ultimately feels less sympathy for his character than for Snider himself, and what his project might have been in more capable hands. *(Graphic violence, extensive nudity, sexual situations, substance abuse, extreme profanity.)*— M.G.

d, John Pieplow; p, David L. Bushell, Dee Snider; exec p, Larry Meistrich, Joseph DiMartino; assoc p, The Krachman Brothers; w, Dee Snider; ph, Goran Pavicevic; ed, Jeff Kushner; m, Anton Sanko; prod d, Debbie Devilla; art d, Charlie Kulsziski; set d, Lydia Marks; sound, Gabriel Kitinski; casting, Lee Ann Groff; cos, Jillian Ann Kreiner; makeup, Michael Burnett

Horror/Crime **(PR: O MPAA: R)**

DEEP IMPACT ★★

(U.S., 1998) 105m Zanuck/Brown; Manhattan Project; DreamWorks/Amblin; Paramount ~ Paramount c

Robert Duvall *(Spurgeon Tanner)*; Tea Leoni *(Jenny Lerner)*; Elijah Wood *(Leo Biederman)*; Morgan Freeman *(President Beck)*; Leelee Sobieski *(Sarah Hotchner)*; Vanessa Redgrave *(Robin Lerner)*; Maximilian Schell *(Jordan Lerner)*; James Cromwell *(Alan Rittenhouse)*; Mary McCormack *(Andrea Baker)*; Blair Underwood *(Mark Simon)*; Jon Favreau *(Gus Partenza)*; Ron Eldard *(Oren Monash)*; Dougray Scott *(Eric Vennekor)*; Laura Innes *(Beth Stanley)*; Bruce Weitz *(Stuart Caley)*; Rya Kihlstedt *(Chloe)*; Betsy Brantley *(Ellen Biederman)*; Alexander Baluev *(Boris Tulchinsky)*; Richard Schiff *(Don Biederman)*; Gary Werntz *(Chuck Hotchner)*; O'Neal Compton *(Morton Entrekin)*; Caitlin Fein; Amanda Fein *(Caitlin Stanley)*; Joseph Urla *(Ira Moskatel)*; Una Damon *(Marianne Duclos)*; Mark Moses *(Tim Urbanska)*; Derek de Lint *(Theo Van Sertema)*; Charles Dumas *(Jeff Worth)*; Suzy Nakamura *(Jenny's Assistant)*; Alimi Ballard *(Bobby Rhue)*; Charles Martin Smith *(Marcus Wolf)*; Katie Hagan *(Jane Biederman)*; Denise Crosby *(Vicky Hotchner)*; Frank Whiteman *(Priest)*; Jason Dohring *(Harold)*; Jasmine Harrison *(Kid)*; Rahi Azizi *(Student)*; Hannah Werntz *(Holly Rittenhouse)*; Tucker Smallwood *(Ivan Bronsky)*; Merrin Dungey *(Sheila Bradley)*; Kimberly Huie *(Wendy Mogel)*; William Fair *(Grey Man)*; Francis X. McCarthy *(General Scott)*; Ellen Bry *(Stofsky)*; Lisa Ann Grant *(Reporter)*; Leslie Dilley *(Waiter)*; Concetta Tomei *(Patricia Ruiz)*; Mike O'Malley *(Mike Perry)*; Kurtwood Smith *(Otis Hefter)*; Gerry Griffin *(NASA Official)*; Charlie Hartsock *(David Baker)*; Jennifer Jostyn *(Mariette Monash)*; Don Handfield *(Dwight Tanner)*; Jason Frasca *(Steve Tanner)*; Cynthia Ettinger *(Pretty Woman)*; Benjamin Stralka *(Little Boy)*; Stephanie Patton *(Brittany Baker)*; Michael Winters *(NASA Guy)*; John Ducey *(Young Lieutenant)*; Christopher Darga *(Section Leader)*; Joshua Colwell *(CAPCOM)*; Cornelius Lewis *(Bus Sergeant)*; Kevin La Rosa *(Pilot)*

Released a few before 1998's other "cosmic collision" film, ARMAGEDDON, DEEP IMPACT is clearly modeled on INDEPENDENCE DAY (1996): the film is a special effects fest with a broad social canvas awash in patriotic red, white, and blue.

After Leo Beiderman (Elijah Wood) glimpses a heretofore unknown comet through his backyard telescope, astronomer Marcus Wolf (Charles Smith) makes a further, startling discovery: Comet Wolf-Beiderman is heading directly for Earth. Unfortunately, Wolf suffers a collision of his own (on the road, with a semi) before he can spread the news.

Several months later, TV reporter Jenny Lerner (Tea Leoni) gets word of a scandal in the White House—apparently, the President had an affair with someone known only as "Ellie." Pursuing the identity of "Ellie", Jenny finds herself abducted by the FBI and led into the presence of President Beck himself (Morgan Freeman). "Ellie," it turns out, is actually the acronym "ELE," for "Extinction Level Event." Jenny has stumbled upon the government's secret plan to deal with the approaching comet.

At the President's request, Jenny withholds the story until he can call a news conference, there he announces the launch of a joint US-Russian space mission to intercept and divert Wolf-Beiderman from its course with Earth. Veteran shuttle pilot and moonwalker Spurgeon Tanner (Robert Duvall) will be in command of the spacecraft, christened "Messiah," and its crew of six.

Months later, the *Messiah* reaches the seven mile-wide comet and lands a crew on it. Four astronauts (Blair Underwood, Jon Favreau, Ron Eldard, and Alexander Baluev) insert several nuclear warheads deep in the surface. The nukes are then detonated by remote control. Moments later, the President informs the public that the warheads have only succeeded in splitting the comet into two unequal pieces. The second fragment is still big enough to destroy all life on Earth. The *Messiah* itself was apparently lost after the detonations. The government then institutes its back-up plan: one million Americans, chosen by a national lottery, will be placed in a network of limestone caves in Missouri, where they will wait out the destruction following the comet's impact.

As the underground ark is filled the first, smaller fragment lands off the Atlantic seaboard, causing a tidal wave that devastates the entire East Coast. As the world waits for the second, final blow, mission controllers at Houston are surprised to hear a message from the *Messiah*. The spacecraft has managed to limp back to Earth with heavy damage.

Spurgen convinces the rest of the crew to crash their vessel into the comet. After tearful goodbyes to their families, they fly the spacecraft into a deep cleft in Wolf-Beiderman's surface and detonate their leftover nukes. The gambit works—the comet is destroyed. Some time later, the President pays tribute to the crew's sacrifice as he stands in front of the half-built new Capitol.

The producers of DEEP IMPACT must have thought they'd had a macabre bit of good luck when, in early 1998, an American astronomer really did announce the possibility of an asteroid impact on earth early in the 21st century. The prediction of a near collision was later revised by other astronomers to a "distant encounter." The whole episode demonstrates the absurdity of DEEP IMPACT'S "X Files"-inspired conspiracy premise: if the comet is visible, and any schoolkid with a telescope and any university astronomer with a calculator can see it, there's no possibility of keeping an imminent collision secret for very long.

It's hard to keep the focus on both a cosmic and a local scale without trivializing one or both. Morgan Freeman is given little to do here except look severe and dignified; he seems less a character than an expositional special effect. The effortlessly authentic Duvall fares better: when he is on the screen, DEEP IMPACT is a moderately involving sci-fi adventure. The rest of the drama, including Wood's doomed May-May romance with his classmate Sarah (Leelee Sobieski) and Jenny's troubled relationship with her parents (Vanessa Redgrave and Maximilian Schell) feels overly schematic and gratuitous. One wonders all these stories couldn't have been integrated into the *Messiah* subplot. This might have prevented the script from wandering in different directions.

Director Mimi Leder (1997's THE PEACEMAKER) and writers Bruce Joel Rubin and Michael Tolkin (who has done interesting work before, with VAMPIRE'S KISS and THE RAPTURE) do have a hint of a high-minded theme: the problem/miracle of how each generation "saves the world" by passing it on to the next. The idea is half-worked-out in Spurgen's strained relationship with the younger astronauts, and in the struggles of each family that is saved or doomed by the ark lottery. But who has time for that when there's tidal waves and crashing skyscrapers to visualize? *(Adult situations, profanity.)*—N.N.

d, Mimi Leder; p, David Brown, Richard D. Zanuck; exec p, Steven Spielberg, Joan Bradshaw, Walter F. Parkes; assoc p, D. Scott Easton; w, Michael Tolkin, Bruce Joel Rubin (from the novel *The Hammer of God,* by Arthur C. Clarke, and *When Worlds Collide,* by Edwin Balmer and Philip Wylie); ph, Dietrich Lohmann; ed, David Rosenbloom; m, James Horner; prod d, Leslie Dilley; art d, Gary Kosko, Tom Valentine, Dennis Bradford, Andrew Neskoromny; set d, Peg Cummings; sound, Mark Hopkins McNabb (mixer), John Paul Fasal (design); fx, Scott Farrar, Michael Lantieri, Industrial Light & Magic; casting, Allison Jones; cos, Ruth Myers; makeup, John M. Elliott Jr.; stunts, M. James Arnett, Charles Croughwell

Disaster/Adventure/Drama (PR: C MPAA: PG-13)

DEEP RISING ★★½

(U.S., 1998) 106m Hollywood Pictures; Laurence Mark Productions; Cinergi Productions; Calamari Pictures ~ Buena Vista c

Treat Williams *(John J. Finnegan)*; Famke Janssen *(Trillian)*; Anthony Heald *(Simon Canton)*; Kevin J. O'Connor *(Pantucci)*; Wes Studi *(Hanover)*; Derrick O'Connor *(Captain)*; Jason Flemyng *(Mulligan)*; Cliff Curtis *(Mamooli)*; Clifton Powell *(Mason)*; Trevor Goddard *(T. Ray Jones)*; Djimon Hounsou *(Vivo Rashoon)*; Una Damon *(Leila)*; Clint Curtis *(Billy Cook)*; Warren T. Takeuchi *(Radar Man)*; Linden Banks *(Communications Officer)*; Jack Anker *(Corpse)*; Anne-Simone *(Video Vault Woman)*; Leanne Adachi *(Toilet Lady)*; Melanie Carr *(Dealer)*; Colin McCarlie *(Sonar Man)*; Jim May *(Mystery Man)*; Jana Sommers; Marti Baldecchi *(Party Girls)*

Entertaining, big-budgeted schlock, DEEP RISING (originally titled "Tentacle") delivers efficient no-brain thrills.

John Finnegan (Treat Williams) pilots his boat through the stormy South China Sea. He has been hired by mercenaries, led by Hanover (Wes Studi), for an undisclosed mission—one whose true nature comes to light when Finnegan's mechanic, Pantucci (Kevin J. O'Connor), discovers that the mercenaries have brought warheads with them. Their destination: the *Argonautica*, the world's most modern cruise liner on its maiden voyage. When they arrive at the ship, they find it deserted, save for piles of skeletons. A few survivors turn up, including the captain (Derrick O'Connor), the ship's builder, Simon Canton (Anthony Heald), and thief Trillian (Famke Janssen), who had been caught stealing and imprisoned below decks. They reveal that the *Argonautica* has been infested by fanged, tentacle-like creatures that engulf and slowly digest their victims.

It transpires that Canton had hired the mercenaries to evacuate the passengers and blow up the ship so that he could collect the insurance. Now the small group is at the mercy of the creatures, which pick them off one by one. Canton attempts to escape at the expense of the others, and Finnegan is ultimately confronted by the one gigantic monster that has invaded the ship; the "creatures" are actually its tentacles. Finnegan rigs his boat with explosives. Thinking he's getting away, Canton jumps aboard, only to be blown up with the *Argonautica* and the monster. Finnegan and Trillian make it to a nearby island on a jet-ski, and Pantucci washes ashore as well. As they celebrate their survival, a huge *land-based* creature approaches. . .

Essentially a cross between THE POSEIDON ADVENTURE (1972) and ALIENS (1986), DEEP RISING isn't as good as either, but it's far from being a complete waste of time. Writer/director Stephen Sommers (a veteran of numerous live-action kids' films for Disney) actually does his best work in the first half of the picture, before the creature even appears. A chillingly suspenseful atmosphere is created on the supposedly empty liner, and there's some fun tough-talk among the macho characters. When the monster shows up, however, the proceedings become terribly repetitive; there are only so many ways, after all, that one can film people fleeing through flooded corridors and rooms, mouthing trite variations on "What the hell's going on now?" before they're snatched up by the monster's tentacles. In addition, only a select few of the characters are truly sympathetic, and it's clear that they are the ones most likely to survive.

Still, the movie maintains an energetic pace, and Sommers's over-the-top approach (augmented by an amusingly overwrought score from old pro Jerry Goldsmith) doesn't curdle into camp. As for the "money scenes"—those involving the monster's attacks—Rob Bottin's designs are grotesque enough, and the computer effects that bring them to life are colorful enough, to sufficiently gross out the audience. However, Sommers also drops the ball in this regard, by supplying the horrific highlight so early on in the film; nothing that follows quite surpasses the sequence in which a tentacle is shot apart and disgorges a half-digested victim who staggers toward the others before collapsing. The climactic scenes of shipboard destruction do pack a small punch, but they won't give the makers of TITANIC (1997) any sleepless nights. No doubt Sommers and his associates would have preferred that their movie had come out first. It could have—DEEP RISING was actually made in 1996, but took two years to find a theatrical release. *(Graphic violence, extreme profanity.)*—M.G.

d, Stephen Sommers; p, Laurence Mark, John Baldecchi; exec p, Barry Bernardi; assoc p, Howard Ellis; w, Stephen Sommers; ph, Howard Atherton; ed, Bob Ducsay, John Wright; m, Jerry Goldsmith; prod d, Holger Gross; art d, Kevin Ishioka, Sandy Cochrane; set d, Rose Marie McSherry, Ann Marie Corbett; sound, Rob Young, Frank Griffiths, Leslie Shatz (design); fx, Rob Bottin, Mike Shea, Jim May, Dream Quest Images; casting, Mary Goldberg; cos, Joseph Porro; makeup, Rosalina Da Silva, Stephen Dupuis (effects); stunts, Gary Combs

Horror/Thriller **(PR: O MPAA: R)**

DEFENDERS: PAYBACK, THE ★★
(U.S., 1997) 95m Stan Rogow Productions ~ Showtime/Viacom c

E.G. Marshall *(Lawrence Preston)*; Beau Bridges *(Don Preston)*; Martha Plimpton *(M.J. Preston)*; John Larroquette *(Michael Lane)*; Roma Maffia *(Mrs. Bishop)*; Rachael Leigh Cook *(Tracey Lane)*; Clea DuVall *(Jessie Lane)*; Nicholas Kilbertus *(Jack Bishop)*; Yaphet Kotto *(Judge Williams)*; Mimi Kuzyk *(Camille Preston)*; Christopher Redman *(Steven Preston)*; Chloe Brown *(Kelly Preston)*; Bradie Whetham *(Danny Bishop)*; Joe Pinque *(Mitchell)*; Kristine Fairlie *(Chris)*; Tyler Kyte *(Hockey Kid)*; David Blacker *(Construction Worker)*; Jack Duffy *(Mr. Sanders)*; Alan Mozes *(Schuman)*; Sharon Lawrence *(Judge Bach)*; Corinne Conley *(Judge Turner)*; Tony Desantis *(Mr. Kuhlman)*; Karen Robinson *(Ms. Clarkson)*; Kyra Harper *(Ms. Reynolds)*; Daniel Kash *(Frankie Mirano)*; Kim Roberts *(Psych Receptionist)*; Tony Nappo *(Officer Perez)*; Robert McClure *(Bridge Man)*; Bob Zidel *(Court Clerk)*; Emily Fleming *(8-Year-Old Jessie)*; Sean McCann *(John Broderick)*; Mark Blum *(Jackson)*

In the 1960s, "The Defenders" was a cutting-edge television series with Emmy Award caliber credits. This retro-rehash, made for Showtime, also handles controversial material, but in a less electrifying, provocative manner than the original.

Distraught Michael Lane (John Larroquette) walks up to Jack Bishop (Nicholas Kilbertus), the man who served time for raping Lane's then-nine-year-old daughter Tracey, and calmly shoots him to death. Lane's vigilante justice garners the attention of lawyer Lawrence Preston (E.G. Marshall), who engages his granddaughter M.J. (Martha Plimpton) and persuades his son Don (Beau Bridges) to come out of retirement.

At loggerheads over ethics, M.J. and her Uncle Don lay the legal groundwork for a client who refuses to plead insanity. While visiting the adult Tracey Lane (Rachael Leigh Cook), who is still traumatized by her experience, M.J. learns her client has a second, estranged daughter Jessie (Clea DuVall), whom Lane has ignored in his lifelong quest to avenge Tracey. Setbacks for the Preston firm include the judge's ruling out of a manslaughter defense and the insistence of Mrs. Bishop (Roma Maffia) that her late husband had been rehabilitated. During the trial, Don plays to the jury's sympathies while comparing Mrs. Bishop's burning desire for a conviction with Lane's own eye-for-an eye action. When the jurors are hopelessly deadlocked, the D.A. declines to retry for first degree murder, and Lane winds up with a 7-year plea bargain stretch.

A meaningful exploration of the gray areas of the law, THE DEFENDERS: PAYBACK bogs down in a debate it fails to illuminate. The controversy over victims' rights should have been examined in a torrent of cascading emotions, not talked to death. This movie could take a tip from current legal series such as "The Practice" and "Law and Order," which explore thought-provoking issues without sacrificing the satisfactions of melodrama. The authoritative Marshall links this tepid courtroom drama to the ground-breaking TV program that inspired it. But while it's good to see him in his signature role, he's just a figurehead in a film that resembles a tabloid news segment that doesn't know when to end. *(Violence, extreme profanity, adult situations, sexual situations.)*—R.P.

d, Andy Wolk; p, Beau Bridges, Sy Fisher; exec p, Stan Rogow; w, Peter Wolk, Andy Wolk (based on an episode of "The Defenders" by Reginald Rose); ph, John Newby; ed, Lauren Schaffer; m, Mark Isham; prod d, Anthony Cowley; art d, Ken Watkins; set d, Megan Less; sound, Chaim Gilad; fx, Brock Jolliffe; casting, Jason La Padura; cos, Suzette Daigle; makeup, Mary Sue Heron; stunts, Shelly Cook

Drama **(PR: C MPAA: R)**

DEJA VU ★★½
(U.S./U.K., 1998) 116m Jagtoria Film; Rainbow Film Company; Revere Entertainment ~ Rainbow Releasing c

Victoria Foyt *(Dana Howard)*; Stephen Dillane *(Sean)*; Vanessa Redgrave *(Skelly)*; Michael Brandon *(Alex)*; Glynis Barber *(Claire)*; Noel Harrison *(John Stoner)*; Anna Massey *(Fern Stoner)*; Vernon Dobtcheff *(Konstantine)*; Graydon Gould *(Dana's Father)*; Aviva Marks *(Woman in Cafe)*; Rachel Kempson *(Skelly's Mother)*; Wael Jolani *(Jerusalem Shopkeeper)*; Karen Loevy *(Young Couple in Cafe)*; David Rubin *(Young Couple in Cafe)*; Amnon Meskin *(Tel Aviv Cab Driver)*; Sabrina Jaglom *(Child on Beach)*; Simon Orson Jaglom *(Child on Beach)*; Vladimir Bershevitz *(Street Musician Violin)*; Simon Goshmir *(Street Musician Cello)*; Alexander Shtempel *(Street Musician Trumpet)*; Carl Duering *(Jewellery Shop Owner)*; Lily Martin *(Lady Jeweller)*; Thomas Poncelet *(Eurostar Conductor)*; Maureen Rimmer *(Eurostar Humming Lady)*; Barbara Hicks *(Housekeeper)*; Cathryn Harrison *(Fern's Masseuse)*; David Gant *(Antique Shop Owner)*; Jeremy Stoner *(Street Musician)*; Earl Cameron *(Doctor)*

Improvisatory acting and romantic moonshine make strange bedfellows in the fragile DEJA VU.

Dana Howard (Victoria Foyt) visits Jerusalem, on a buying trip for a business she and longtime fiance Alex (Michael Brandon) plan to open back in America. Suddenly Dana is joined by an aged Frenchwoman (Aviva Marks) at a cafe. The lady tells a painful tale of long ago finding her "soulmate," an American soldier who was unable to surmount obstacles between them and went home to his girlfriend. Sorrowfully, the woman departs, leaving Dana with the engagement pin that was her prized possession of lost love. Dana fails to find the woman again and even changes her itinerary to locate the Paris artisan whose workshop crafted the pin. While there, Dana glimpses a mystery man staring at her outside the store window.

Dana proceeds on to England, and in Dover finds Sean (Stephen Dillane), an artist who's the image of the man in Paris. Dana and Sean are crazy about each other from the first, but she breaks off their incipient affair to rendezvous with Alex at a London bed-and-breakfast inn—where things get awkward for the heroine when Sean shows up, hired for design work, with his wife Claire (Glynis Barber) in tow. Dana and Sean try to stifle their passion, but Skelly (Vanessa Redgrave), flighty sister of the B&B owners, fuels their ardor with her musings about true love, coincidence, and destiny. Finally, Dana and Sean announce their feelings for each other. Sean and Claire tearfully break up, but Dana's father's sudden illness sends her back to the United States, where she decides to marry the patient Alex anyway.

Before the wedding Mr. Howard (Graydon Gould) tells his daughter he too had a secret, thwarted love he remembers every day. Then he produces a pin, matching the one from Jerusalem. At once Dana flies to Dover and embraces Sean. In her beloved's studio Dana sees a portrait that finally identifies her father's lover, the Frenchwoman with whom she spoke. It's Sean's mother, who died years ago.

The viewer is tipped off well in advance as to the nature of the surprise ending, since Dana learns that nobody in the cafe saw the old woman but herself, a rather heavy-handed touch. Cowriter and director Henry Jaglom may perhaps be forgiven for losing his objectivity, as he claimed this was a scenerio he'd been working on since 1974, here finally completed with the assistance of his second wife and leading lady Victoria Foyt. Jaglom's work has been consistently, indulgently autobiographical. His ALWAYS (1985) grew straight out of his divorce from actress Patrice Townsend, and it's easy to see DEJA VU as a cinematic mash note from Foyt/Jaglom to Jaglom/Foyt, although the movie is not without its ancillary rewards.

The unconventionally attractive Foyt and her onscreen amour Dillane are an offbeat pair, rather like the supporting character players who normally cede the spotlight to a couple of pretty faces in more conventional Hollywood concoctions, and their freshness makes up for the general contrivance. Jaglom also had several quaint notions in the casting. The venerable Vanessa Redgrave for the first time performs onscreen with her own real-life mother, octogenerian actress Rachel Kempson, in a subplot about whether Skelly will ever settle down and care for her own weakening parent (it looks like a segment that wandered over from a Mike Leigh movie). Mummy Kempson's other adult children are played by Noel Harrison (son of Rex) and Anna Massey (daughter of Raymond). Meanwhile, the abandoned Alex and Claire are portrayed by transatlantic actors Brandon and Barber, married in real life. More than that, Jaglom resists making either ex-spouse a caricature or bringing them together as a second set of "soulmates."

Throughout, the director's loose, seemingly improvisational way with dialogue and staging tone down the sillier fantasy elements in the premise; Jaglom claimed in interviews, however, that never before had he followed a script so closely. That script includes Dillane's soliloquy about *soudade*, a Portuguese notion of nostalgic melancholy. Viewers may experience *deja vu* because *soudade* was also discussed and defined at length in Manoel de Oliveira's feature VOYAGE TO THE BEGINNING OF THE WORLD, also released commercially in the US in 1998. *(Profanity, adult situations, substance abuse.)*—C.C.

d, Henry Jaglom; p, John Goldstone; co-p, Judith Wolinsky; w, Henry Jaglom, Victoria Foyt; ph, Hanania Baer; ed, Henry Jaglom; m, Gaili Schoen; prod d, Helen Scott; art d, Helen Scott; sound, Tim Fraser; casting, Irene Lamb; cos, Rhona Russell

Romance/Drama **(PR: C MPAA: NR)**

DENNIS THE MENACE STRIKES AGAIN! ★★
(U.S., 1998) 75m Outlaw Productions ~
Warner Home Video c

Justin Cooper *(Dennis Mitchell)*; Don Rickles *(Mr. Wilson)*; George Kennedy *(Grandpa)*; Brian Doyle-Murray *(Professor)*; Carrot Top *(Sylvester)*; Betty White *(Mrs. Wilson)*; Dwier Brown *(George Mitchell)*; Heidi Swedberg *(Alice Mitchell)*; Jacqueline Steiger *(Margaret)*; Alexa Vega *(Gina)*; Danny Turner *(Joey)*; Keith Reece *(Gunther)*; George Wendt *(Cop)*

DENNIS THE MENACE STRIKES AGAIN!, an innocuous direct-to-video sequel to the 1993 big-screen adaptation of Hank Ketcham's comic strip, has only limited appeal even for kids under the age of eight, but possesses considerable camp value in the personages of Don Rickles as Mr. Wilson, and—as the press release notes—"Academy Award Winner" George Kennedy as Dennis's Grandpa.

Mischievous seven-year-old Dennis Mitchell (Justin Cooper) surprises his cantankerous elderly neighbor Mr. Wilson (Don Rickles) with a birthday gift of a frog in his bath. Dennis then learns that his young-at-heart Grandpa (George Kennedy) is moving in with him. Unexpectedly, Mr. Wilson becomes jealous and begins a rivalry with Grandpa, but always loses their competitions. Feeling old and rundown, Mr. Wilson falls prey to a pair of con men—Professor (Brian Doyle-Murray) and his sidekick Sylvester (Carrot Top)—who try to swindle him into buying a series of miracle youth cures, but Dennis thwarts them at every turn.

After Dennis destroys most of the neighborhood by substituting cotton candy mix for soap in a car-washing machine, Mr. Wilson puts his house up for sale. Posing as termite inspectors, the two con men swindle Mr. Wilson into paying them for unnecessary repairs to his house. During the repairs, Dennis's dog chases a cat into the house and Mr. Wilson is knocked through a window and hangs onto the ledge. When the police arrive, the con men try to escape, but Dennis stops them with a slingshot, and they're arrested. Mr. Wilson decides not to sell his house after all and Grandpa takes Dennis on a camping trip to the Grand Canyon, where Dennis accidentally pushes their RV into the canyon.

For anyone whose idea of fun is the chance to see the paunchy and aged Don Rickles and George Kennedy in swimsuits or having a wild hip-hop contest to the accompaniment of "Play That Funky Music White Boy," then DENNIS THE MENACE STRIKES AGAIN! is cinematic nirvana. Unfortunately, for its supposed target audience of kids, the film wastes too much time on the old geezers to the detriment of the story's ostensible protagonist—Dennis—which is a shame since the scenes involving the rascally tyke and his young friends are cute. The scenes in which Dennis plays in his "Boys Only" clubhouse with Gunther, Joey, and Gina (who's allowed in because she's a tomboy who likes bugs), while the bespectacled Margaret, dressed as a ballerina, tries to get in, are genuinely funny and come the closest to capturing the spirit of the original comic strip. The rest is pure sitcom nonsense set in a timeless suburban never-neverland, filmed in typically exaggerated wide-angle cartoon style and filled with digital effects (bugs, snakes, etc.), along with the feeble de rigueur addition of HOME ALONE—like bumbling crooks, and a sentimental finale, replete with slow-motion hugs and kisses between Dennis and Mr. Wilson, with a shameless Don Rickles shoving his mug right into the camera lens and an inexplicable, albeit uncredited, appearance by George Wendt as a cop.—M.S.

d, Charles T. Kanganis; p, Jeffrey Silver, Bobby Newmyer; exec p, Ernest Chambers; assoc p, Susan E. Novick; co-p, Cleve Lansberg; w, Tim McCanlies (based on a story by Jeff Schecter and Tim McCanlies and characters by Hank Ketcham); ph, Christopher Faloona; ed, Jeffrey Reiner; m, Graeme Revell; prod d, Joseph T. Garrity; sound, Ed Novick; fx, Martin Bresin; casting, Hill/Howard-Field; cos, Karen Patch; makeup, Janeen Schreyer

Children's/Comedy **(PR: AA MPAA: G)**

DER UNHOLD
(SEE: OGRE, THE)

DESPERATE MEASURES ★★
(U.S., 1998) 100m Eaglepoint/Schroeder/Hoffman;
Mandalay Entertainment ~ TriStar c

Michael Keaton *(Peter McCabe)*; Andy Garcia *(Frank Connor)*; Marcia Gay Harden *(Dr. Samantha Hawkins)*; Brian Cox *(Capt. Jeremiah Cassidy)*; Joseph Cross *(Matthew Connor)*; Erik King

(Nate Oliver); Efrain Figueroa *(Vargus)*; Janel Maloney *(Sarah Davis)*; Richard Riehle *(Ed Fayne)*; Tracey Walter *(Medical Inmate)*; Peter Weireter *(SWAT Team Commander)*; Keith Diamond *(Wilson)*; Steve Park *(Dr. Gosha)*; Steven Schub *(SWAT in Airduct)*; Neal Matarazzo *(Cell Guard)*; Dennis Cockrum *(Pelican Bay Head Guard)*; Charles Noland *(Cigarette Guard)*; Randy Thompson *(Library Guard)*; Michael Shamus Wiles *(Tough Inmate)*; Darren Pearce; Eric Tignini *(Convoy Guards)*; Billy Kane *(Laser Technician)*; Christine Ashe *(Young ER Nurse)*; Donna M. Duffy *(ER Nurse)*; Troy Robinson *(Cop Escorting Frank)*; Robert Baier *(Security Booth Guard)*; David Flick *(SWAT Sharpshooter in Street)*; Joe Drago *(Doctor at Walkway)*; Josh Kemble *(SWAT Sniper on Roof)*; Scott Colomby *(Patrol Cop)*; Howard Meehan *(Policeman on Street)*; Tim Kelleher *(Helicopter Shooter)*; Cliff Fleming; Dirk Vahle; Craig Hosking *(SWAT Helicopter Pilots)*; Jack Gill; Scott Waugh; Danny Rogers *(Motorcyclists)*; John Meier *(Cop Shot in ER)*; Norm Howell *(Burnt Cop 1)*; John Rottger *(Burnt Cop 2)*; Donna Keegan *(Burning Nurse)*

DESPERATE MEASURES once again proves that overheated direction can't save a bad script. Stylized visuals fail to enliven a farfetched story about a father who will do anything to get an imprisoned killer to give his son a bone marrow transplant.

Frustrated by bureaucratic roadblocks, San Francisco police officer Frank Connor (Andy Garcia) breaks into the FBI's computers to find a potential bone marrow donor for his terminally ill son, Matt (Joseph Cross). There's only one hitch: Peter McCabe (Michael Keaton), a homicidal sociopath, is indicated as the best potential donor. Connor visits McCabe in prison and tries to convince him to undergo the transplant. He agrees to the operation, secretly planning to use this as an opportunity to escape. Before the operation begins, McCabe breaks loose and wreaks havoc in the hospital, trying to make it to a little-known tunnel. Desperate, Connor secretly works to prevent his fellow officers from killing McCabe.

McCabe's relentless desire to escape leads to massive damage and casualties. Captain Cassidy (Brian Cox), Connor's superior, realizes that Connor's obsession with saving his son is getting in the way of his catching the fugitive. The renegade cop's only ally is his son's doctor, Samantha Hawkins (Marcia Gay Harden). Connor redeems himself when he saves a group of Cassidy's men from being blown up by McCabe. But he still focuses on catching the villain without killing him. McCabe finally eludes the army of hunters, makes it out of the hospital, and steals a car. He is pursued by Connor, who traps McCabe on a bridge, shoots him, and brings him back.

The operation is a success. As a recovering McCabe lies chained to a bed, he overcomes his guard with a concealed gun and resumes his escape plans.

Writer David Klass should have realized that the premise of his script for DESPERATE MEASURES was downright silly long before he pumped out his hundred-plus pages of screenplay. An audience has to suspend a lot of disbelief to accept that the only compatible donor in the whole country for a San Francisco cop's son is a San Francisco serial killer. Nor does it help that the object of all this effort is played by diminutive Joseph Cross as a flawless, precocious child who deals with death better than most adults would. DESPERATE MEASURES also seems inordinately pleased with itself for using what is actually a rather worn thematic device, a thriller staple, the good guy/bad guy doppelganger motif, in which the tactics and attitudes of the seemingly polar opposites are strikingly similar. Director Barbet Schroeder visited this terrain before in another one of his lesser efforts, SINGLE WHITE FEMALE (1992). Utilizing numerous off-kilter angles and giving everything a steely blue veneer, Schroeder does infuse the silliness with a little visual panache. He also pushes the always earnest Andy Garcia to escalate continually the protagonist's monomaniacal quest. But the performance, like the character, is too focused on only one thing, is too one-dimensional. Michael Keaton gives his character a bit more spice, mixing a bizarre intellectualism with an unlikely tomfoolery. But in the end, any discerning viewer will be left with only two words: "Yeah, right." *(Violence, profanity.)*—T.Y.

d, Barbet Schroeder; p, Barbet Schroeder, Susan Hoffman, Lee M. Rich, Gary Foster; exec p, Jeffrey Chernov; co-p, Josie Rosen; w, David Klass; ph, Luciano Tovoli; ed, Lee Percy; m, Trevor Jones; prod d, Geoffrey Kirkland; art d, Sandy Getzler; set d, Jennifer Williams; sound, Steve Nelson (mixer); fx, Paul Lombardi, Kelly Kerby, Jim Rygiel, Michael Sweeney, Boss Film Studios; casting, Howard Feuer; cos, Gary Jones; makeup, Rick Sharp, K.N.B. Effects (effects)

Action/Crime/Thriller (PR: C MPAA: R)

DESTINY ★★★★

(Egypt/France, 1997) 135m Misr International Films; Ognon Pictures; France 2 Cinema ~ Leisure Time Features c

Nour El Cherif *(Averroes)*; Laila Eloui *(The Gypsy Woman)*; Mahmoud Hemeida *(Al Mansour, The Caliph)*; Safia El Emary *(Averroes' Wife)*; Mohamed Mounir *(The Bard)*; Khaled El Nabaoui *(Nasser, The Crown Prince)*; Seif Abdel Rahman *(The Caliph's Brother)*; Abdallah Mahmoud *(Borhan)*; Ahmed Fouad Selim *(Cheikh Riad)*; Magdi Idris *(Emir of the Sect)*; Ahmed Moukhtar *(Bard)*; Cherifa Maher *(Manuella's Mother)*; Rayek Azzab *(El Razi)*; Hassan El Adl *(Gaafar)*; Hani Salama *(Abdalla)*

Written and directed by Egypt's most acclaimed filmmaker, Youssef Chahine, DESTINY is a full-bodied if slightly overextended entertainment that also serves as a call for tolerance.

In 12th century Andalusia, High Judge and scholar Averroes (Nour El Cherif) receives threats from a fundamentalist sect for teaching that the Koran is an interpretive text. He tries to warn the Caliph (Mahmoud Hemeida) about the spreading fundamentalism, but the Caliph dismisses his concern.

One night, several sect members attempt to kill the poet Marwan (Mohamed Mounir), whose poetry they consider blasphemous. The attackers are caught and convicted, but against the Caliph's orders, Averroes sentences them to a prison term rather than death, reasoning that they were not sane when they committed the crime. The sect leader, Cheik Riad (Magdi Idris), is upset by the sentence, as he hoped the assailants would be considered martyrs if executed. Soon after the sentencing, the sect members are found hanged in their cells.

A short time later, Averroes's house is mysteriously set afire. Although most of his library is destroyed, his family and students work to recopy Averroes's writings, and are able to restore much of it. Meanwhile, the Caliph's son, Abdallah (Hani Salama) is invited into Riad's sect, and almost joins, when he is kidnapped and brought to his brother Nasser (Khaled El Nabaoui), who tries to turn Abdallah away from fundamentalism. Abdallah is resistant at first, but reconciles with Nasser after learning that Riad has had Marwan slain.

When a Christian army threatens to invade Andalusia, the Caliph, aware of Riad's inspirational power, enlists his assistance in rallying the Andalusion people to his military cause. Riad does so by successfully appealing to the people's religious pride. Now allied with Riad, the Caliph accedes to Riad's demand that Averroes's books be confiscated and burned. At a ceremonial book burning, Averroes receives the reassuring news that copies of his works have been successfully transported to Egypt, after which he sarcastically throws one of his own books into the fire.

A superimposed graphic at DESTINY's close reads, "Ideas have wings. No one can stop their flight," under which the signature "Youssef Chahine" appears as if being written onto the screen. The pronouncement underscores the essentially optimistic tone of the film, in spite of the misfortune it charts, and the added signature is an acknowledgment of the filmmaker's unfaltering faith in the communicative value of his medium. DESTINY is most definitely a message movie, a term that has a pejorative ring; but Chahine, 70 when he directed this, his 33rd feature, has far too much experience to produce a feature-length lecture, no matter how meaningful the lesson. Filmed in Syria and Lebanon, DESTINY is a fast-paced, richly detailed costume drama, replete with passionate romance, battling brothers, political intrigue, and vital covert missions. It even has a couple of elaborately staged musical numbers thrown in for good measure. Chahine plays up the more lively aspects of the story in order to get the maximum entertainment value from them. His aim is not to balance the film's serious intent with fanciful elements, rather, he seems to be saying that adventure, romance, music, and the love of these are essential to combating the intellectual sterility in which fundamentalism thrives. Thus, viewing DESTINY as robust fun is not to misunderstand its purpose, but to understand it precisely.

The plot of DESTINY is a bit too busy, which makes it difficult to follow at times, but on the whole, Chahine tells a complicated story with the confidence of a storyteller who takes pride and pleasure in engaging his audience. He also makes an important, urgent point—one that is as timely and relevant to Western filmgoers as it is to Chahine's countrymen—but he never sacrifices style for the sake of instruction. DESTINY is intelligent fun and the work of a master filmmaker. *(Violence.)*—D.C.

d, Youssef Chahine; p, Humbert Balsan, Gabriel Khoury; w, Youssef Chahine, Khaled Youssef; ph, Mohsen Nasr; ed, Rachida Abdel Salam; m, Kamal El Tawil, Yohia El Mougy; prod d, Hamed Hemdane; ch, Walid Aouni; sound, Gasser Khorched; cos, Nahed Nasrallah

Historical/Musical/Drama (PR: A MPAA: NR)

DESTINY OF MARTY FINE, THE ★★
(U.S., 1996) 85m One-Two Productions ~ Plaza Entertainment bw

Alan Gelfant *(Marty Fine)*; Catherine Keener *(Lena)*; Norman Fell *(Daryl)*; James LeGros *(Grill)*; Katherine Lanasa *(Amy Fine)*; Michael Ironside *(Capelli)*; Mark Ruffalo *(Brett)*; Sarabeth Tucek *(Kelly)*; David Darmstaedter, billed as David Darmstaeder *(Juvie)*; Willie Garson *(Jack)*; Kristina Loggia *(Alice)*; Al Almeida *(Jose)*; John Diehl *(Deke)*; Glenn Plummer *(Mike)*; Sandra Seacat *(Woman on Bench)*; Michele M. Miller; Frank Medrano; Rene Assa; Timothy McNeil; Shony Alex Brown

A fatalistic film noir about a washed-up boxer, THE DESTINY OF MARTY FINE just throws the same punch, many times over.

Marty Fine (Alan Gelfant) is an ex-boxer of Russian-Jewish descent, whose life is on the ropes. He begs for seed money from mob boss Capelli (Michael Ironside) to start his own pugilistic training camp; no sooner has he managed to interest the icy crook than Capelli gets rubbed out by assassins connected with gangster Daryl (Norman Fell). Rather than eliminate Marty as a witness, Daryl tries to convince the boxer to yield to his "destiny" and turn hit man. He sends Marty to plug a small-time hoodlum who owes him. Marty can't go through with the murder, and instead he wanders around old haunts, usually mooching and always getting the cold shoulder, from his girlfriend Lena (Catherine Keener), his neurotic car repairman Grill (James LeGros), his old gym pals, even his taxi-dancer sister Amy (Katherine Lanasa). After enounters with nouveau riche Russian mafioso, philosophical barflies and a maternal bag lady, Marty ends up enjoying a free meal at the restaurant where Lena works. On his way to ask Daryl for clemency, Marty finds him dining amicably with the hoodlum Marty was ordered to kill. This time, when the target heads for the restroom, Marty finishes the job.

THE DESTINY OF MARTY FINE looks great thanks to Melinda Sue Gordon's clean black-and-white cinematography, and takes place in a timeless version of pulp-fiction LA, full of rinky-dink saloons and Spanish-colonial houses. The hardboiled story that director Michael Hacker chalk-outlines here, however, is strictly small-time, a series of repetitive and dramatically stagnant vignettes in which the pathetically self-deluded hero gets slapped down again and again as he goes scrounging for handouts. Character relations and motivations are cloudy, to say the least, and it doesn't help that lead Alan Gelfant (NEXT STOP, WONDERLAND), gamely onscreen for virtually the whole movie, looks too young for the pug he's supposed to be playing, a guy with 23 years of ring experience (or thereabouts; punch-drunk Marty can no longer keep the figures straight in his head). Despite Gelfant's efforts, the movie starts feeling like a thespian exercise, Brando's "I coulda been a contender!" speech from ON THE WATERFRONT (1954) attenuated to feature length. A number of seasoned character actors put in memorable but one-shot appearances that don't add up to much in this downbeat little requiem for a lightweight. *(Violence, profanity, substance abuse.)*—C.C.

d, Michael Hacker; p, Jeffery Miller; assoc p, Jeffrey S. Tuttle; co-p, Mark Ruffalo; w, Mark Ruffalo, Michael Hacker; ph, Melinda Sue Gordon; ed, Gabriella Christiani, Lee Garvin, Tammis Chandler, Barbara Boguski; m, Dave Stringer, Greg Ellis, Shony Alex Brown; prod d, Jo-Ann Chorney; art d, Martin Charles; set d, Isabelle Stamper; sound, Rick Norman; casting, Shana Landsburg; cos, Grania Preston; makeup, Julie Rott

Drama/Crime (PR: C MPAA: NR)

DETONATOR ★
(U.S., 1998) 84m Califilm ~ New Horizons Home Video c

Scott Baio *(Zack Ramses)*; Shannon Bruce *(Jaime Angeline)*; Don Stroud *(Whip O'Leary)*; Charlene Tilton *(Gail Davis)*; Emile Levisette *(Max Jones)*; Rick Dean *(Vince Pepper)*

Scott Baio (yep, the star of "Joanie Loves Chachi") stars in this straight-to-video nightmare about a professional assassin who specializes in blowing his victims to pieces with bombs. Bad acting, bad script, bad movie.

Corrupt and violently psychotic cop "Whip" O'Leary (Don Stroud) is making a bid to become the city's principal drug dealer, but first he must eliminate the competition. He does so by hiring hit man Zack Ramses (Scott Baio), a former green beret and explosives expert, to blow them up. During one hit, Zack very nearly kills a young girl, Jaime (Shannon Bruce), a violation of his "no kids" rule. He rescues Jaime and, pretending to be a simple good samaritan, allows her to stay at his apartment until she finds a place to live. But when O'Leary discovers Jaime has a videotape that could incriminate him, he sends his crew of crooked cops after her.

At home in his artist's studio, Zack is developing an affection for young Jaime, despite his cold exterior. Jaime, too, is warming up to Zack, until she discovers his true profession. She flees his apartment, only to be spotted by O'Leary's men. Though Jaime escapes, O'Leary shakes down Zack's agent, Gail (Charlene Tilton) for the hit man's whereabouts, then captures both Gale and Jaime in order to draw out Zack and the videotape. Zack meets O'Leary, offering to exchange the girls for the tape; O'Leary, of course, would rather have both. A firefight ensues, during which Gail and Jaime escape and all but Zack and O'Leary are killed. Zack then reveals that he has wired himself with explosives, and for the coup de grace blows them both to kingdom come.

You know a movie is in trouble when the best acting job is turned in by Scott Baio. DETONATOR features a host of performances that fall well below even the straight-to-video market's already unambitious expectations. The most grievous display is by Don Stroud, playing the requisite over-the-top villain role. His portrayal of Whip O'Leary (so named because he once beat a dog to death with a belt), with his Mike Hammer fedora and one squinty eye, is comically bad, growling out every line like a drill sergeant. In comparison, Baio looks ready for the Royal Shakespeare Company.

The acting isn't the only problem here. Ripped off from Luc Besson's THE PROFESSIONAL (1994), writer-director Garrett Clancy's script is ridiculous, beginning with its bomb-assassin hero. Wouldn't plastic explosives put a bit of a crimp in the assassin's stealthy style? And wouldn't a rash of suspicious bombings attract some attention in the law enforcement community? Not to mention Zack's laughable modus operandi: placing the explosives, then walking a few feet away to set them off by remote control. No, with this material to work with, even good actors would have had a tough go of it—though they might have had the decency to look embarrassed while trying. *(Violence, profanity, substance abuse.)*—B.T.

d, Garrett Clancy; p, Mike Elliott; exec p, Darin Spillman, Roger Corman; co-p, Marta M. Mobley; w, Garrett Clancy; ph, Mike Mickens, Christopher Landy; ed, Folmer Wiesinger; m, Paul Di Franco; prod d, Nava; fx, Greg Landerer; casting, Jan Glaser

Action **(PR: C MPAA: R)**

DETOUR ★½

(U.S., 1992) 91m Film Works Studio ~ Englewood Entertainment c/bw

Tom Neal Jr. *(Al)*; Lea Lavish *(Vera)*; Erin McGrane *(Sue)*; Brad Bittiker *(Lance)*; Duke Howze *(Charlie Haskell)*; Susanna Foster *(Evvie)*

The original DETOUR (1945) was a model of style on a budget, a minimalist noir masterpiece; the remake of DETOUR (1992) is a model of an utter lack of style on a budget, a well-intentioned but abysmal homage. The film played limited theatrical engagements, and was subsequently released on home video in 1998.

In 1942 Hollywood, a hitchhiker, Al (Tom Neal Jr.), stops at a roadside diner and recalls how his life became nightmarish. He was a pianist in a New York nightclub in love with a singer, Sue (Erin McGrane). When Sue leaves Al to pursue stardom in Hollywood, Al grows bitter and gets fired from his job. He decides to follow Sue, unaware that she has become a struggling waitress in Los Angeles.

Al hitchhikes his way to California, getting picked up along the way by a bookie named Charlie Haskell (Duke Howze). Meanwhile, Sue ends a bad date with a cowboy named Lance (Brad Bittiker), hoping never to see him again. Al takes over the wheel from Haskell and discovers during the rainy night ride that his driving companion has died. Fearing the police will blame him for murder, Al decides to hide Haskell's body on the road, steal his money and identification, and ride off in the car.

Al then picks up a woman at a rest stop, Vera (Lea Lavish), but she happens to be someone who knew the real Haskell. Nevertheless, she promises to help Al rather than blackmail him. Back in Hollywood, Sue reads that Lance has had an accident, but plans to star on Broadway after his recovery. She immediately goes to visit the actor and propose marriage to him, as a way to hitch her wagon to his star. Then she leaves him as soon as she discovers he is no longer wanted for the Broadway show.

Al and Vera, meanwhile, arrive in Hollywood, and take a room in a hotel as man and wife. They go to a car dealer to sell Haskell's car, but Vera stops the deal when she reads in the paper that Haskell's father is a wealthy dying man. Al resists Vera's idea for him to pose as Haskell in order to inherit the money, but Vera threatens to turn him to the police if he doesn't cooperate. After a drunken tussle, Al accidentally kills Vera as she tries phoning the police. He then runs away from the scene. Later, he learns that the police are chasing after Haskell, but he keeps on running, never meeting up with Sue.

The 1945 DETOUR marked the grungy peak of wartime melodramas that came to be known as film noir after WWII. The "Poverty Row" quickie was shot by Edgar G. Ulmer, an Austrian-born director who learned light-and-shadow expressionistic film techniques from Max Reinhardt and F.W. Murnau. Martin Goldsmith's screenplay anticipated postwar preoccupations with irony, fate, and existential angst. The female lead (Ann Savage) gave a striking, even scary performance, way ahead of its time. Not surprisingly, the ultra-low-budget picture became a "sleeper" in its day and cult favorite ever since.

Clearly, independent producer-director Wade Williams reveres the first version (he even purchased and now distributes the best-quality public domain print). In his 1992 remake, Williams follows the original script and story closely and even casts Tom Neal Jr. in the part that made his father, the original Al, semi-famous. Regrettably, Williams lacks the skills of Ulmer and offers nothing new in the way of contemporary insight into the old material.

The pacing is slow and sluggish. The use of color ruins many of the scenes that made the first version so perfectly grim. The technical gaffes include echoing soundstage dialogue. The actors look uncomfortable and amateurish aping 1940s styles, although Lea Lavish progressively grows into her role as Vera, throwing off sarcastic lines to Neal's Al like, "I'll bet you're in big demand now that all the men are overseas." This time, even the two story lines—Al's and Sue's—don't work in the same way (as ironic counterpoint in 1945); here, it's like watching two different movies in one package. In this DETOUR remake, that's two too many. *(Violence, sexual situations, adult situations.)*—E.M.

d, Wade Williams; p, Wade Williams, Ben Mossman, Brian Mossman; w, Roger Hull, Wade Williams (based on the story and screenplay by Martin Goldsmith); ph, Jeff Richardson; ed, Herbert L. Strock; m, Bill Crain

Crime/Thriller/Drama **(PR: C MPAA: NR)**

DIARY OF A SERIAL KILLER ★★

(U.S., 1998) 92m Goldbar International; Unapix Entertainment; Kandice King Productions ~ A-Pix Entertainment c

Gary Busey *(Nelson Keece)*; Arnold Vorsloo *(Stefan)*; Michael Madsen *(Det. Haynes)*; Julia Campbell *(Juliette)*; Reno Wilson *(Det. Laroue)*; David Michaels *(Eric/Erica)*; Marcy Kaplan *(Lori)*; Patricia Skeriotis *(Maria)*; Jazzmun *(Dancer)*; Erica Yohn *(Mrs. Morris)*; William Frankfurter *(Officer Joe)*; Brien Blakely *(Station Cop)*; Jeff N. Strong *(Desk Sergeant)*; Mario Robert *(Tough Guy)*; Wendy Schumacher *(Bookstore Cashier)*; Elisa Leonetti *(Wendy)*; Danny Kovacs *(Policeman)*; Dawn Landon *(Hot Dog Vendor)*; Michael Gabriel *(Juliette's Family at Park)*; Shawn McConnell *(Juliette's Family at Park)*

An above-average cast (for a direct-to-video movie) can't do much with the subpar script of DIARY OF A SERIAL KILLER, in which writer Gary Busey unwillingly gains the confidence of killer Arnold Vosloo and uses him as the basis for a magazine article.

A new "girl" at an LA drag bar is actually journalist Nelson Keece (Gary Busey), researching an article called "Through the Eyes of a Transvestite." His live-in girlfriend Juliette (Julia Campbell) is worried about his insistence on empathizing with his subjects, but the nearly broke Keece is desperate to sell another article. On the street, recognizing a man (Arnold Vosloo) he saw at the club, he follows him and tape records him murdering a young woman. Reece tries to report it to the police, but is followed and stopped by the murderer, Stefan. When he finds out what Keece does, he agrees to be the subject of an article by him. Keece makes other attempts to go to the police, but is stymied by either Stefan's presence or bureaucratic snags at the police station. He tells Stefan that he expects him to refrain from killing during their collaboration, but Stefan breaks his promise and stabs a woman in a library. He takes Keece to a transvestite prostitute he plans to kill, but Keece is able to foil him. For revenge, Stefan decides to make Juliette (who has separated from the troubled Keece) his next victim. Keece stops him in time and, seizing Stefan's knife during a struggle, stabs him to death. Dying, Stefan says he wanted Keece to know how it felt to kill someone before writing about it.

Aside from a good cast and competent production, there's really nothing to recommend DIARY OF A SERIAL KILLER to the thrill seeker. Despite the title, the script does next to nothing to get into the mind of a murderer. And its depiction of writer Keece is confusing: it's never clear whether he really wants to do Stefan's story, or if he's just biding his time until he can turn him in, or if he is conflicted. Costar Michael Madsen is wasted in a supporting role as a detective obsessed with the notion that this recent string of killings may be the work of whoever killed his daughter, just as the subplot in which the police come to suspect Reece of the murders is ultimately insignificant. It seems likely from some of what is in here that the original script was altered at some stage: it almost certainly was an improvement over what made it to the screen. *(Violence, sexual situations, adult situations, profanity.)*—M.F.

d, Alan Jacobs; p, Kandice King; exec p, Harel Goldstein, Bill Barnett, Robert Baruc; assoc p, Richard Filon; co-p, Lance King; w, Jennifer Badham-Stewart; ph, Keith L. Smith; ed, Christopher Koefoed; m, Steve Edwards; prod d, Ladislav Wilheim; set d, Darla Hitchcock; sound, Matthew Nicolay; fx, Kevin McCarthy; casting, Rick Pagano, Debi Manwiller; cos, Maurizio Bizzarri; makeup, Cynthia Bornia, Margaux Lancaster; stunts, Jeff Jensen

Thriller **(PR: O MPAA: R)**

DIDN'T DO IT FOR LOVE ★★★

(Germany, 1997) 80m Filmgalerie 451 ~ First Run Features c

Eva Norvind; Jan Baracz; Rene Cardona Jr.; Jose-Luis Cuevas; Nicholas Echevarria; Juan Ferrara; Jose Flores; Juan-Jose Gurrola; Franz Harland; Georg Kajanus; Johanne Kajanus; Micheline Kinery; Nadine Markova; Ronald Moglia; Gerard O'Neal; Luz Maria Rojas; Liisa Simola; Veronica Vera; Alice Vernstad; Paul Vernstad; Esther Maria Wiig

DIDN'T DO IT FOR LOVE is a profile of Norwegian-born dominatrix Eva Norvind, who turned her lifelong study of dominance and submission into a lucrative business. Fascinating and quirky, the film puts the spotlight on a lifestyle that's usually relegated to the realm of farce.

German filmmaker Monika Treut follows Eva's life from 1960s Mexico, where she worked as a B-movie sexpot, to 1990s New York, and her new career as a businesswoman who just happens to be a dominatrix. Through interviews with family, friends, and associates, Eva's life unfolds into a series of vivid tableaux. Raised with a healthy attitude toward sex, Eva journeys to Mexico as a teenager. There she quickly establishes herself in the movie business, where she becomes an instant sensation in the rather staid country. Though her movies are made on tiny budgets, her exotic Nordic looks and curvaceous figure ensure her a certain level of popularity amongst movie fans. She later takes up prostitution when a smitten politician offers to pay for her services, and soon gives birth to a daughter out of wedlock when another official approaches her about bearing a child for him. In an interview, Eva asks her elderly mother, Johanne, how she viewed this incident. Johanne notes that the politician was a "gentleman" because he insisted on paying for the sex through an assistant rather than in person. This one exchange speaks volumes, as it addresses Eva's complex relationship with her liberal-minded mother; unfortunately, Treut doesn't pursue this angle fully enough, with the exception of a comment Eva makes, concerning her astonishment and regret that her mother wasn't stricter.

Treut saves the second half of the film for Eva's career as a dominatrix. She reinvents herself in New York in the 1980s, and in 1987 opens up a highly successful business catering to upper-class clients. Eva is seen talking to a client about his desire to engage in infantilism; she has to inform him that she may not be able to persuade one of her employees to watch him urinate in a giant adult diaper. Eva isn't just the boss in this enterprise—she's also shown with a female client, whom she whips, ties up, and fondles with a sharp knife. Watching Eva concentrate on her trusting client is almost voyeuristic, but it's certainly not difficult to see the erotic component in the behavior; however, Treut's emotional detachment from the subject is most evident in these scenes; she takes as nonchalant an approach to s&m as Eva does.

The openly gay Treut is the perfect filmmaker to find substance in Eva's life and work. In fiction films such as SEDUCTION: THE CRUEL WOMAN (1985) and VIRGIN MACHINE (1988), Treut cast a nonjudmental eye on sexual subversives, focusing on stories about domination and submission, and sexually aggressive women. Here, Treut very effectively explores Eva's evolving persona, juxtaposing clips from her 1960s movies—which show her as a pouty, blond sexpot—with views of her in the present-day as a dark-haired, no-nonsense businesswoman quickly hurrying down Manhattan streets. This contrast gives DIDN'T DO IT FOR LOVE its substance, as Treut doesn't choose to exploit the lurid elements of Eva's work; she instead delves into her refusal to acknowledge society's restricted view of what women should and should not do. She ultimately reveals that this uncompromising stance has come at a high price for Eva; among other factors, her daughter, now living with a man and a child of her own, barely speaks to her because of her profession. She also appears to have sacrificed open communication with her peers and loved ones; in interviews, her friends and family complain that they often cannot get a word in edgewise. She is also seen arguing with her current boyfriend, who harangues her about her refusal to commit to a full-time relationship.

Still, curiously enough, it is indicated that Eva seems to have found a sort of inner peace, at least in regard to her own sexuality; this, Treut implies, is a reward in and of itself. *(Adult situations, sexual situations, profanity, extensive nudity.)*—D.O.

d, Monica Treut; p, Irene von Alberti; w, Monika Treut; ph, Ekkehart Pollack, Christopher Landerer; ed, Eric Marciano, Jeff

Lunger; m, Georg Kajanus, Tom Judson; sound, Andreas Pietsch-Lindenberg

Documentary **(PR: O MPAA: NR)**

DIE SALZMANNER VON TIBET
(SEE: SALTMEN OF TIBET, THE)

DIE SIEBTELBAUERN
(SEE: INHERITORS, THE)

DIGGING TO CHINA ★★½
(U.S., 1998) 99m Ministry of Film; Davis Entertainment Classics; Moonstone Entertainment ~ Legacy Releasing c

Kevin Bacon *(Ricky Schroth)*; Mary Stuart Masterson *(Gwen Frankovitz)*; Cathy Moriarty *(Mrs. Frankovitz)*; Evan Rachel Wood *(Harriet Frankovitz)*; Marian Seldes *(Leah Schroth)*; Amanda Minikus *(Sonia)*; Nicole Burdette *(Miss Mosher)*; Robert Putney *(Eric)*; Annie Jaynes *(Young Harriet)*; Joanne Pankow *(Nurse)*; Gareth Williams *(Tow Truck Driver)*; Alan Mruvka *(Tow Truck Driver #2)*; J.C. Quinn *(Minister)*; Keith Harris *(Flirting Man)*; Nicole Namer *(Girl in Classroom)*

Intermittently touching but generally depressing, DIGGING TO CHINA is a sensitive domestic drama about the traumas and disappointments faced by a 10-year-old girl living in rural Pennsylvania.

A bright child with a vivid imagination and a penchant for fantasizing, Harriet Frankovitz (Evan Rachel Wood) lives with her mother (Cathy Moriarty), who drinks too much, and sister Gwen (Mary Stuart Masterson), who is 15 years older. One day the Frankovitz family motel acquires two new customers, Leah Schroth (Marian Seldes) and her 30-year-old retarded son, Ricky (Kevin Bacon), who is about to be institutionalized.

Harriet and Ricky quickly become friends and playmates, but a major crisis occurs in the girl's life when her mother is killed while driving drunk, and Gwen informs her that they are not sisters but mother and daughter and that Mrs. Frankovitz was actually Harriet's grandmother. Harriet spurns Gwen's attempts to mother her and ignores her admonitions to avoid Ricky, whom Gwen fears might molest the little girl.

Desperately unwilling to be placed in a home, Ricky runs away from the motel and is immediately joined by Harriet. The two runaways camp out in the woods for a while but when Ricky gets the flu they are forced to return to the motel.

About to be taken to the institution, the frightened and unhappy Ricky shares an intense farewell embrace with Harriet but the moment is misinterpreted by Gwen who initiates a violent scuffle with the young man. After Ricky is arrested, cleared, and returned to the motel by the police, the day he dreads arrives. As the Schroths are leaving, Gwen apologizes to Leah for misjudging Ricky's intentions, and Ricky, who is angry at Harriet, forgives his friend. Subsequently, Harriet sheds her resentment of Gwen and the two embark on a healthy mother-daughter relationship.

The plight of Harriet, a child whose search for adventure and escape is constantly thwarted by life, could serve as a metaphor for the frustration of moviegoers of the 1990s, whose search for adventure and escape was thwarted by glum films like DIGGING TO CHINA. Although the movie elicits its share of tears, too many of them are the product of the automatic pity engendered by depictions of adult retardation. Because so much screen time is allotted to the relationship between Harriet and Ricky, Gwen, and her far more interesting relationship with Harriet, are shortchanged. Midway, the film robs Gwen even of her parade of buff boyfriends, whose sexuality represents for her—as surely as dreams of UFOs and astronauts do for Harriet—an avenue of temporary respite from her dull workaday life. ("My sister Gwen should have been a nurse," says Harriet. "She was always making some guy feel better.")

Evan Rachel Wood looks like everyone's idea of Alice in Wonderland—indeed the first time we meet Harriet she is stuck in a rabbit hole. Sweet-seeming and picture-pretty, the precociously talented Wood has not been ideally cast as Harriet, whose social status as an outsider and an oddball would have been better expressed through a preadolescent version of someone like Laura Dern. Kevin Bacon's interpretation of the retarded Ricky is bold and affecting but rather overdrawn—recalling at times Ed Grimley, the gonzo character created by comedian Martin Short.

Slated at one time to be directed by Geena Davis, DIGGING TO CHINA turned out to mark the directorial debut of another actor, Timothy Hutton. *(Violence, adult situations.)*—D.T.

d, Timothy Hutton; p, J. Todd Harris, John A. Davis, Alan Mruvka, Marilyn Vance; exec p, David T. Friendly, Stephen Nemeth, Ernst "Etchie" Stroh; w, Karen Janszen; ph, Jorgen Persson; ed, Dana Congdon, Alain Jakubowicz; m, Cynthia Miller; prod d, Robert DeVico; casting, Wendy Kurtzman; cos, Mary Zophres; stunts, Bobby Munford

Drama/Comedy **(PR: C MPAA: PG)**

DIRTY LAUNDRY ★
(U.S., 1998) 97m Hollywood Productions; Rogue Features ~ Hollywood Productions c

Jay Thomas *(Joey Greene)*; Tess Harper *(Beth Greene)*; Tresa Hughes *(Betty Greene)*; Michael Marcus *(Max Greene)*; Stanley Earl Harrison *(Lowell Bower)*; Erin Underwood *(Chloe Greene)*; John Driver *(Dr. Stoller)*; Michael Mulheren *(Nick)*; Antoinette La Vecchia *(Cathy)*; Staurt Burney *(Dale Gordon)*; Dana Chaifetz *(Amy)*; Ray Xifo *(Jerry)*; Luba Mason *(Ingrid)*

DIRTY LAUNDRY is a lame, unfunny comedy about midlife crisis as experienced by a middle class suburbanite.

Joey Greene (Jay Thomas), who runs a small dry-cleaning business, is having marital difficulties with his wife, Beth (Tess Harper). He secretly solicits the services of a prostitute while Beth begins an affair with Lowell (Stanley Earl Harrison), a married, African-American chiropractor. When Joey leaves town on business, Beth invites Lowell to stay with her. Joey returns unexpectedly and is about to expel Lowell from his house when Joey's parents, Max (Michael Marcus) and Betty (Tresa Hughes) drop by. Unaware of the situation, Max and Betty insist that Lowell stay for lunch. During the meal, Joey explains Lowell's presence by claiming that he is a friend visiting from out of town. When Betty, who grows fond of Lowell, invites him to stay with her, Joey thwarts the offer by declaring that Lowell is already staying with him, inadvertently making Lowell a resident of his house. A short time later, Beth learns that she's pregnant, and is not sure if the father is Joey or Lowell. Joey, meanwhile, visits a dating service, but is unable to find a suitable mate. Soon after, Betty dies. At the burial service, Max comments that for all the annoyance Betty caused him, he loved her deeply. Beth tells Lowell that she may be pregnant by him, but he assures her that she cannot be since his sperm count is too low. He also tells her that he has chosen to return to his wife. Joey decides to sell his failing business and prepares to meet with an interested buyer. Beth learns of his intent and rushes to stop him. She reaches Joey in time, tells him to keep his business, and informs him that he is going to be a father. Five months later, Beth, with Joey's assistance, gives birth to a black baby.

DIRTY LAUNDRY is barely more than a sitcom, augmented with four-letter words and raunchy jokes, but without the benefit of a laugh track, commercial breaks, and a remote with an on/off switch. Scenarist Michael Normand, who codirected with Robert Sherwin, has taken a ripe idea for a comedy—a complacent middle American is confronted with the worst doubts and fears—and then fails to approach it with any originality, falling back instead on tired shtick to relate Joey's problem. A sample of Normand's "comic" dialogue—analyst to Joey: "Were you breast fed as a baby?" Joey: "My mother didn't want that kind of relationship." Even this stale material might have been passably amusing if Normand and Sherwin had directed the film with any verve or wit, but DIRTY LAUNDRY plods along at a deadly slow pace, killing any comic potential. The plot is poorly laid out and surprisingly complicated for a film that says so little. In addition, DIRTY LAUNDRY is technically weak, with dim cinematography and slack editing.

Jay Thomas is a spirited comedian when he's got good material, as he's shown through his recurring television roles on "Cheers" and "Murphy Brown," but here his performance is benign, when it isn't downright grating. Harper exudes warmth and earns sympathy as the needy Beth, but even she seems to succumb to the enervation that pervades the whole film. The quality of Harrison's performance is difficult to gauge, as his undefined character exists solely to touch off the crisis between Joey and Beth.

DIRTY LAUNDRY does have one virtue. It offers perhaps the most thorough look into the workings of a dry-cleaning business that has ever been committed to film. *(Nudity, sexual situations, profanity.)*—D.C.

d, Michael Normand, Robert Sherwin; p, Robert Sherwin, Robert E. DiMilia; exec p, Buddy Rashbaum; w, Michael Normand; ph, John Newby; ed, Andrew Morreale; m, James Legg; prod d, John Paino; art d, Jim Donahue; sound, Dave Powers; cos, Suzanne Schwarzer, Danielle Hollywood

Comedy **(PR: C MPAA: R)**

DIRTY WORK ★½

(U.S., 1998) 82m Robert Simonds/Brad Grey Productions; MGM Pictures ~ MGM/UA c

Norm Macdonald *(Mitch Weaver/Writer)*; Artie Lange *(Sam McKenna)*; Jack Warden *(Pops)*; Christopher McDonald *(Travis Cole)*; Chevy Chase *(Dr. Farthing)*; Traylor Howard *(Kathy)*; Don Rickles *(Hamilton)*; Bradley Reid *(Mitch—At 8 Years Old)*; Matthew Steinberg *(Mitch—At 16 Years Old)*; Joseph Sicilia *(Sam—At 8 Years Old)*; Austin John Pool *(Sam—At 16 Years Old)*; Gerry Mendicino *(Manetti)*; A. Frank Ruffo *(Aldo)*; Hrant Alianak *(Kirkpatrick)*; Michael Vollans *(Derek—At 10 Years Old)*; Grant Nickalls *(Jason)*; Deboraha Hinderstein *(Charlene)*; Scott Gibson *(Frat Guy)*; Laura Stone *(Veronica)*; Polly Shannon *(Toni-Ann)*; Rummy Bishop *(Homeless Guy at Apartment)*; James Carroll *(Middle-Aged Guy)*; Henry Chan *(Doctor at Fat Clinic)*; David Koechner *(Anton Phillips)*; Paul O'Sullivan *(A.D.)*; Uni Park *(Saigon Whore)*; Boyd Banks *(Creepy Harry)*; B.J. McQueen *(Big Wet Man)*; Tony Meyler *(Lobby Henchman)*; Shane Daly *(Door Henchman)*; James Binkley *(Unaffected Henchman)*; Jim Downey *(Martin/Homeless Guy)*; Fred Wolf; Wilfrid Bray *(Homeless Guys)*; Jessica Booker *(Mrs. Murphy)*; Johnie Case; Conrad Bergschneider *(Policemen)*; Kay Hawtrey *(Gladys)*; Lloyd White *(Ron)*; Dini Petty *(Dini Petty)*; Mike Anscombe *(Mike Anscombe)*; Howard Jerome *(Foreman)*; Arturo Gil *(Midget Paul)*; Rebecca Romijn *(Bearded Lady)*; Joslyn Wenn *(Jenkins' Fantasy Girl)*; Robbie Rox; Chris Gillett *(Suit Guy)*; Kevin Farley; Sanjay Talwar *(Theater Workers)*; Trevor Bain *(Henchman Jenkins)*; Gord Martineau *(Gord Martineau)*; George Sperdakos *(Opera Critic)*; Eleanor Davies *(Opera Critic's Date)*; Laura Pudwell *(Opera Lady)*; Emilio Roman *(Baritone Errante)*; George Chuvalo *(Ring Announcer)*; Gary Coleman *(Gary Coleman)*; Ken Norton *(Ken Norton)*; Christine Oddy *(Aunt Jenny)*; Robert Shipman *(Crossing Guard)*; Richard Sali *(Ed)*; Silvio Oliviero; MIF *(Low Lifes)*; Cliff Saunders *(Thief)*; Bess Motta; Arlaine Wright *(Aerobics Instructors)*

Just as every kid on a Little League team gets to play, every cast member of "Saturday Night Live" seems to have been guaranteed the chance to star in a feature film. DIRTY WORK, starring former "SNL"-er Norm Macdonald as an inveterate loser who opens a revenge-for-hire business, isn't even as good as most of this wretched sub-genre.

All their lives, best friends Mitch Weaver (Norm Macdonald) and Sam McKenna (Artie Lange) have used elaborate practical jokes to strike back against bullies and abusive authority figures. After Sam's father, Pops (Jack Warden), suffers a heart attack, Dr. Farthing (Chevy Chase) offers to save the dirty old man with a transplant for $50,000, the amount Farthing owes his bookies.

Mitch hits on the idea of opening a revenge-for-hire service. On behalf of his new love interest, Kathy (Traylor Howard), Mitch uses some strategically placed "dead" hookers to ruin the business of a sleazy car salesman. They help a circus midget who has a vendetta against the bearded lady, and use rotten fish to help a man tormented by noisy neighbors. Mitch and Sam run afoul of millionaire Travis Cole (Christopher McDonald), who hires them to trash a building he owns, claiming its tenants are drug dealers and hookers he wants to evict. In fact, the tenants are old people, including Kathy's grandmother; the duo still fulfill their job, and afterward, Cole refuses to pay up. Making matters worse is Pops' revelation that Mitch is his illegitimate son.

With everything seeming hopeless, Mitch discovers that he accidentally recorded Cole confessing to wrongdoing on the mini tape recorder he always carries. With the help of Sam and Kathy, joined by some hookers, Mitch turns a Cole-sponsored benefit opera into a fiasco, extorts the needed $50,000 from Cole, and then exposes the wealthy crook to the media.

For a movie that promises nothing more than laughs, DIRTY WORK doesn't deliver very many of them. On stage, Macdonald's absurdist bent, withering wit, and self-deprecating goofiness make for a hilarious mix. But while DIRTY WORK possesses all those elements, it manages only to induce smirks. Macdonald's natural audience is the male Howard Stern fan, which helps explain why the movie is so fixated on jokes about homosexuals and whores and endless use of the word "ass." But with a PG-13 rating, DIRTY WORK just isn't raunchy enough to work even on that level. The revenge schemes are clever and amusing, but there aren't enough of them. The movie wastes time and energy adding perfunctory romantic and heroic touches to Macdonald's character.

DIRTY WORK features a number of guest stars in cameos and small roles, including a painfully unfunny turn from Don Rickles. In his final screen appearance, an uncredited Chris Farley's mostly improvised scenes yield less than stellar results.

DIRTY WORK receive a lot of media attention after Macdonald was abruptly fired from his high-profile position on "Saturday Night Live" by NBC President Don Ohlmeyer, who didn't see the humor in the comedian's jokes about his friend O.J. Simpson. NBC's reported refusal to run advertisements for DIRTY WORK was viewed by a deluded few as an act akin to the Hearst newspapers' boycott of CITIZEN KANE (1941). *(Profanity.)*—P.R.

d, Bob Saget; p, Robert Simonds; exec p, Brad Grey, Ray Reo; assoc p, Julia Dray, Rita Smith; co-p, Martin Walters, Richard Stenta; w, Frank Sebastiano, Norm Macdonald, Fred Wolf; ph, Arthur Albert; ed, George Folsey Jr.; m, Richard Gibbs; prod d,

Gregory Keen; art d, Gordon Lebredt; set d, Jaro Dick; sound, Bruce Carwardine (recordist); fx, Martin Malivoire; casting, Roger Mussenden; cos, Beth Pasternak; makeup, Leslie Sebert, Caligari Studio (effects); stunts, Branko Racki

Comedy **(PR: C MPAA: PG-13)**

DISAPPEARANCE OF KEVIN JOHNSON, THE ★½
(U.K./U.S., 1996) 106m Makani Kai Productions; Wobblyscope Productions ~ Bedford Communications c

Francis Megahy *(Documentarian/Off-Camera)*; John Hillard *(Ricky Ryan)*; Rick Peters *(Willis Stevens)*; Michael Brandon *(Jeff Littman)*; Richard Neil *(Larry Hillman)*; Guy Siner *(Fred Barrett)*; Alexander Folk *(Police Detective)*; Bridget Baiss *(Gayle Hamilton)*; Keely Sims *(Leela Kerr)*; Ian Ogilvy *(Gary)*; Heather Stevens *(Rhonda)*; Hector Elias *(Roman Garcia)*; Michael Laskin *(Bill Rackman)*; Richard Beymer *(Chad Leary)*; Tom Omundson *(Nick Ferretti)*; Stoney Jackson *(Julian)*; Kari Wuhrer *(Kristi Wilson)*; John Solari *(Capt. Hammond)*; Charlotte Brosnon *(Amy)*; Brett Baker *(Grant)*; Michael Cooke *(Judd Ramberg)*; Connie Blankenship *(Lisa)*; Katherine Lanasa *(Cathy)*; Madison Clarke *(Kiki)*; Valerie Rae Miller *(Rudi)*; Scott Coffey *(Video Engineer)*; Carl Sundstrom *(Security Guard)*; Rachhael Harris *(Waitress)*; Jayson Kalani *(Waiter)*; Eric DaRae *(Apartment Manager)*; Frederika Kesten *(Fitness Trainer)*

Dull and unnecessary, THE DISAPPEARANCE OF KEVIN JOHNSON is an interminable mockumentary featuring toothless satire and tepid movie star cameos.

An unseen British documentarian investigates the case of globe- trotting entrepreneur Kevin Johnson, who vanished just as his film proposal was green-lighted for production. Although Johnson's movie star acquaintances Pierce Brosnan, Dudley Moore, and James Coburn sing the praises of their bon vivant friend, the documentarian's interviews suggest that the saga of Kevin Johnson is a combination of toadying and confidence games, raised to an art form.

Johnson began by bribing travel agent Fred Barrett (Guy Siner) to seat him next to Hollywood's power elite on airplanes. Charming his way onto Tinseltown's A-list party circuit, Johnson began pitching movie projects like a veteran hack. How then did Johnson wind up in a luxury car that was dredged up from San Pedro Bay? Johnson's drug-abusing major domo, Ricky Ryan (John Hillard), reveals that Johnson's entre into moviedom's inner circle arose through his talent as a procurer for film execs. Pimpdom and blackmail pressured powerful moguls like Larry Hillman (Richard Neil) into financing Johnson's movie proposal.

Piecing together testimony from super agent Jeff Littman (Michael Brandon), ousted studio chief Willis Stevens (Rick Peters), and an assortment of LA flotsam and jetsam, the documentarian deduces that Johnson never intended to become a Hollywood power-broker; he only wanted to pocket the up-front money from the production deal and skip town (faking his death to leave a cold trail). Unlike the other movie-struck souls questioned in this documentary, Johnson never had any illusions about heeding the siren call of Hollywood.

Writer-director Francis Megahy clearly had visions of Robert Altman's THE PLAYER (1992) dancing in his head. However, THE DISAPPEARANCE OF KEVIN JOHNSON isn't a riddle wrapped in a wry enigma or a mean-spirited comedy ensconced in Altmanesque observations about cupidity. It's a retread of Hollywood cliches cocooned in a tabloid journalism send-up: "Hard Copy" Meets THE BAD AND THE BEAUTIFUL. Within the limits of pricking the air of Big Studio windbags, this limp mockumentary is surprisingly tame and laughless. The stars seen in cameos as themselves appear uncomfortable, and the snide vignettes spotlighting Hollywood has-beens and never-wases are flaccid and shallow. In the end, we're presented with the solution to a mystery we don't care about. *(Extreme profanity, adult situations, substance abuse.)*—R.P.

d, Francis Megahy; p, Scott Wolf; exec p, Darren Sakurai; w, Francis Megahy; ph, John C. Newby; ed, Hudson LeGrand; m, John Coda; art d, Sandy Grass; sound, Stephen Halbert (mixer); casting, Johanna Ray; cos, Marcelle McKay; makeup, Ann Marie Luddy, Wendy Robin

Comedy **(PR: C MPAA: R)**

DISENCHANTED, THE ★★★½
(France, 1990) 78m Cinea-La Sept Cinema; CNC; Sofica Sofinergie 2 ~ First Run Feature c
(AKA: LA DESENCHANTEE)

Judith Godreche *(Beth)*; Marcel Bozonnet *(Alphonse)*; Yvan Desny *(The Uncle)*; Therese Liotard *(Beth's Mother)*; Malcolm Conrath *(The Other)*; Thomas Salsman *(Remi)*; Hai Truhong *(Chang)*; Francis Mage *(Edouard)*; Marion Perry *(The Professor of French)*; Stephane Auberghen *(Edouard's Mother)*

A Parisian teenager comes of age in THE DISENCHANTED, a tender character study from writer-director Benoit Jacquot (SEVENTH HEAVEN). Though not as boldly original as Jacquot's later piece, A SINGLE GIRL, THE DISENCHANTED works in its own moving way.

When not attending classes, pretty 17-year-old Beth (Judith Godreche) takes care of her sickly mother (Therese Liotard) and younger brother, Remi (Thomas Salsman), in their cluttered Paris apartment. Beth's romantic life takes a sour turn one day when her handsome but immature boyfriend, known as "The Other" and "Whatsisname" (Malcolm Conrath), dares Beth to prove her love by sleeping with the ugliest man she can find. Insulted by the suggestion, Beth runs out on Whatsisname, but later, in anger, takes him up on the challenge. At a nightclub Beth picks up Edouard (Francis Mage), a rich but nerdy teenager. At Edouard's mother's home, her "seduction" fails miserably, and she ends up leaving unsullied.

Eventually, Beth breaks up with Whatsisname, who reacts angrily. A witness to their argument, Alphonse (Marcel Bozonnet), a writer, helps Beth defend herself when Whatsisname becomes violent. After the incident, Alphonse offers his business card in case Beth should ever want to visit him. Beth spends the rest of the day plotting revenge on Whatsisname by enlisting her artist-friend, Chang (Hai Truhong), to spraypaint an obscenity next to his picture on his apartment wall. After they commit their deed, Beth and Chang run from Whatsisname, who catches them in the act. Beth finds refuge at Alphonse's apartment, where she spends the night discussing philosophy, admiring his knife collection, and reciting Rimbaud, her favorite poet.

The next day, Beth returns home, where her mother asks her to pick up a check from "Sugardad" (Yvan Desny), the older doctor who cares for and supports her mother. Implicit in her mother's request is the demand for her to sleep with "Sugardad" or "Uncle." Reluctantly, Beth visits this "Uncle" at his spacious apartment, takes his check, and has sex with him. Finally, upon her return home, Beth hands the check over to her mother, then announces that she plans to leave the family after she is finished with her school exams. Beth contemplates the different paths she could take before running through the busy Paris streets.

Though released in the US in 1998, THE DISENCHANTED was made in 1990, five years prior to Jacquot's more winning A SINGLE GIRL (1995). The latter movie used a more concentrated "real-time" technique to great advantage and also benefitted from a delightful performance by Virginie Ledoyen in its title role. But THE DISENCHANTED offers many reawards, too; however, it is much less assured in its presentation.

Like A SINGLE GIRL, THE DISENCHANTED focuses on a young French woman experiencing difficult life choices. But both films also subtly reveal a social malaise by surrounding their protagonists with disillusioned, world-weary characters from various economic spectrums. In the moodier, more depressing THE DISENCHANTED, these misanthropes include Beth's family, her bedridden mother and streetwise kid brother, and the men in her life, her violent boyfriend, the sadsack writer Alphonse, and the corrupt "Sugardad." Even her one seemingly innocent friend, Chang, cynically pokes fun at Asian stereotypes while serving her lunch one afternoon. Beth herself struggles against the negative forces while striving to find her own identity.

Quietly, sometimes elliptically, THE DISENCHANTED echoes the disturbing, sensual poetry of Rimbaud that Beth likes to recite. It is to Jacquot's credit that no sex is shown and that the ending is left somewhat open to interpretation. But in leaving out certain details (particularly as regards the mother-daughter relationship), the film also risks losing viewer empathy and understanding. Still, THE DISENCHANTED compares agreeably with the work of Jacquot's contemporary, Olivier Assayas (IRMA VEP), and also recalls the achievements of the French New Wave directors at their most thoughtful and least indulgent. *(Violence, nudity, sexual situations, profanity.)*—E.M.

d, Benoit Jacquot; p, Philippe Carcassonne; exec p, Sylvie Blum; w, Benoit Jacquot; ph, Caroline Champetier; ed, Dominique Auvray; m, Jorge Arriagada; sound, Michel Vionnet; casting, Marie-Christine Lafosse

Drama **(PR: C MPAA: NR)**

DISTURBING BEHAVIOR ★★

(U.S., 1998) 83m Beacon Communications; MGM ~ MGM/UA C

James Marsden *(Steve Clark)*; Katie Holmes *(Rachel Wagner)*; Nick Stahl *(Gavin Strick)*; Bruce Greenwood *(Dr. Caldicott)*; William Sadler *(Dorian Newberry)*; Steve Railsback *(Officer Cox)*; Tobias Mehler *(Andy Effkin)*; Chris Owens *(Officer Kramer)*; Katharine Isabelle *(Lindsay Clark)*; Terry David Mulligan *(Nathan Clark)*; Susan Hogan *(Cynthia Clark)*; Robert Moloney *(Ferry Guy)*; Derek Hamilton *(Trent Whalen)*; Ethan Embry *(Allen Clark)*; Dan Zukovic *(Mr. Rooney)*; Tygh Runyan *(Dickie Atkinson)*; P.J. Prinsloo *(Robby Stewart)*; Michelle Skalnik *(Randi Sklar)*; Lalainia Lindbjerg *(Kathy)*; Brendan Fehr; Chad E. Donella *(U.V.)*; Garry Chalk *(Coach)*; Crystal Cass *(Lorna Longley)*; Fiona Scott *(Fiona-Blue Ribbon)*; David Paetkau *(Tom Cox)*; Erin Tougas *(Shannon)*; Ryan Taylor *(Ryan-Blue Ribbon)*; Jay Brazeau *(Principal Weathers)*; Sarah-Jane Redmond *(Miss Perkins)*; Carly Pope *(Abbey)*; John B. Destry *(Middle-Aged Man)*; A.J. Buckley *(Chug Roman)*; Glynis Davis *(Coupon Lady)*; Cynde Harmon *(Mrs. Atkinson)*; Larry Musser *(Coroner)*; Andre Danyliu *(Roscoe)*; Gillian Barber *(Judy Effkin)*; Stephen James *(Lang)*; Peter Lacroix *(Mr. Strick)*; Lynda Boyd *(Mrs. Lucille Strick)*; Daniella Evangelista *(Daniella-Blue Ribbon)*; Sean Smith *(School Bus Boy)*; Zuzana Marlow *(Shannon's Mom)*; Tamsin Kelsey *(Detrice)*; Suzy Joaquim *(Female Doctor)*; Fulvio Cecere *(Anesthesiologist)*; Bob Wilde *(Shadow Man)*; Judith Maxie *(Shadow Woman)*; Doug Abrahams *(Security Guard)*; Christopher R. Sumpton *(Screaming Man)*; Jarred Blancard *(Flossing Man)*; Kate Braidwood *(Make-up Girl)*; Stephen Holmes *(Toothbrush Boy)*; Mark Avis; Julie Patzwald *(Betty Caldicott)*; Stephen E. Miller *(Frankie)*; Marcia Rose Shestack *(Reporter)*; Robert Lewis *(Moderator)*; Dee Jay Jackson *(Assistant Principal)*; Kendall Saunders *(Disrespectful Student)*; Sean Amsing *(Damon)*

The concept of a teenage variation on THE STEPFORD WIVES (1975) is a good one, but it gets short shrift in this underdeveloped thriller.

Teenager Steve Clark (James Marsden) moves to the small town of Cradle Bay with his family following the suicide of his brother. At the high school, he makes the acquaintance of rebellious outcasts Gavin (Nick Stahl) and Rachel (Katie Holmes), and is advised of the rigidly divided social structure. At the top of the heap are the Blue Ribbons, a group of perfectly behaved, well-dressed students who nonetheless brook no opposition. Gavin and Rachel are suspicious of the Blue Ribbons, as is the school's apparently retarded janitor, Dorian Newberry (William Sadler). Gavin takes Steve to spy on a meeting in which Dr. Caldicott (Bruce Greenwood) tries to persuade local parents to enter their misbehaving kids into the Blue Ribbon program, which will cure them of antisocial tendencies.

Gavin becomes the next inductee and turns up at school completely transformed into a do-gooding Blue Ribbon; when Steve presses him for an explanation, he is beaten up by Gavin's new friends. Investigating further, Steve and Rachel discover that Caldicott once worked at a nearby mental institution and go to check it out; there they discover Caldicott's daughter, a lobotomized zombie. Returning to Cradle Bay, the two are apprehended and Rachel is prepared for a cranial implant that will transform her into the next Blue Ribbon. Steve rescues her, and the couple flee with the Blue Ribbons in pursuit. Newberry arrives and, with the aid of a sonic device, lures the transformed teens over a cliff to their deaths. Steve is confronted by Caldicott, and knocks the evil doctor over the edge as well. Gavin, however, has survived, and turns up as a substitute teacher at another school. . . .

The film's promise is reflected by its title: What's more disturbing, teen rebellion or good behavior that's forcibly programmed into young people? But writer Scott Rosenberg fritters away the possibilities of his premise in favor of numerous genre conventions. The trouble starts early, when Gavin speaks in a sort of teenage vernacular—which has everything to do with how adults think teenagers talk and not how they really converse—and shows Steve around the school's cafeteria, where the groups are carefully segregated, right down to the nerds sitting with their computer gear. This is all presented with a straight face by director David Nutter, as are such cliched tropes as the retarded janitor who knows more than he seems to and the asylum that's really a Gothic snake pit.

Cliches like these get in the way of the main story line, which maintains a minor level of tension but feels underdeveloped. (In fairness to the filmmakers, a lot of the characterization and shading that might have given the movie more depth appears to have been hacked out to achieve the tightest running time possible—despite the fact that the successful SCREAM films each ran about two hours.) The film is strongest in individual scenes, like a creepily funny moment when a sexy blonde Blue Ribbon tries to seduce Steve, only for her hormonal surge to cause her to mentally short-circuit.

Nutter, a veteran of TV's "The X Files," wisely brought several of his collaborators from the series on board, including cinematographer John S. Bartley, who supplies the moody visuals, and composer Mark Snow, whose nerve-jangling score numbers among the movie's strongest assets. The teen cast is certainly capable, though they don't have enough of a chance to make an impression. Like the film's intriguing premise, they fall victim to Nutter's emphasis on cheap thrills over narrative and character complexity. *(Violence, nudity, sexual situations, profanity.)*—M.G.

d, David Nutter; p, Jon Shestack, Armyan Bernstein; exec p, Doc Erickson; assoc p, Max Wong; co-p, Scott Rosenberg; w, Scott Rosenberg; ph, John S. Bartley; ed, Randy Jon Morgan; m, Mark Snow; prod d, Nelson Coates; art d, Eric Fraser; set d, Louise Roper; sound, Rob Young (mixer); fx, Dean Lockwood; casting, Coreen Mayrs, Lisa Beach; cos, Trish Keating; makeup, Louise Love; stunts, J.J. Makaro, Dave Hospes

Horror/Thriller/Science Fiction (PR: C MPAA: R)

DIVORCE IRANIAN STYLE ★★★★

(U.K., 1998) 80m Twentieth Century Vixen ~ Women Make Movies c

A fascinating documentary, DIVORCE IRANIAN STYLE records the difficulties several women encounter while trying to obtain a divorce in modern-day Iran.

Set mainly in a Tehran divorce court presided over by a male judge, DIVORCE IRANIAN STYLE begins with the judge urging a couple not to divorce despite the man's excessively jealous behavior (for Iranian women, the husband's insanity, impotence, or inability to provide financially are the only grounds for divorce; for men, divorce is granted upon request).

The film then concentrates on three women and their situations. One older woman tells the court how she is practically a prisoner in her own home and that her husband mistreats her young sons. The judge tells her to make herself more attractive in order to tempt her husband back. The couple then agrees to a temporary reconciliation. Ziba, on the other hand, is a teenager who feels deceived by her much-older husband (who had lied about his age when they married) and insists on a divorce in order to go back to school. But the judge informs Ziba that she was not underage when *she* married and sees no recourse for her; Ziba plans to continue her fight against her husband and the system.

Finally, Maryann is young woman who had successfully divorced her first husband and remarried, giving up her two children in the process. But now Maryann regrets her decision about her children and fights in the court to retain custody of her younger child, whom she says her ex-husband has been neglecting. Maryann pleads in court to no avail, however; her husband gets to keep their daughter.

Part "Divorce Court," part Frederick Wiseman-style documentary, DIVORCE IRANIAN STYLE pulls back the curtain to reveal both the numbingly bureaucratic legal system of Iran (which is surprisingly Western!) *and* the feisty, proto-feminist way the Moslem women fight to be heard in the strict, patriarchal society. Through these dramatic scenes, DIVORCE IRANIAN STYLE revises stereotypes about both Iran and its women, and codirectors Kim Longinotto and Ziba Mir-Hosseini gain an impressively up close and personal view of the protagonists. Maryann is not even entirely sympathetic when she lies about how her ex-husband tore her court order, but her plight is understandable and her motivations are fully explored.

Longinotto and Mir-Hosseini insert telling interstitial moments between the court cases: an unproductive arbitration meeting between Ziba and her ex-husband's uncles; a shot of a poster of the late Ayatollah Khomeini looming over the court building where armed guards stand; and a mock divorce trial put on by Paniz, the four-year-old daughter of the court secretary, who climbs into the absent judge's seat and rules in favor of the imaginary woman in her case. This last scene, both amusing and sad, signals a kind of hope for the future of Iran and its repressive, sexist laws. DIVORCE IRANIAN STYLE, however, never pulls its punches: it's also a tough critique of patriarchy in general. *(Adult situations, profanity.)*—E.M.

d, Kim Longinotto, Ziba Mir-Hosseni; ph, Kim Longinotto; ed, Barrie Vince; sound, Christine Felce

Documentary (PR: C MPAA: NR)

DR. DOLITTLE ★★½

(U.S., 1998) 95m Davis Entertainment; Joseph M. Singer Productions; Topping/Thomas Productions; 20th Century Fox ~ 20th Century Fox C

Eddie Murphy *(Dr. John Dolittle)*; Ossie Davis *(Archer Dolittle)*; Oliver Platt *(Dr. Mark Weller)*; Peter Boyle *(Calloway)*; Richard Schiff *(Dr. Gene Reiss)*; Kristen Wilson *(Lisa Dolittle)*; Jeffrey Tambor *(Doctor Fish)*; Kyla Pratt *(Maya)*; Raven-Symone *(Charisse Dolittle)*; Steven Gilborn *(Doctor Litvack)*; Erik Todd Dellums *(Jeremy)*; June Christopher *(Diane)*; Cherie Franklin *(Mrs. Parkus)*; Mark Adair-Rios *(Intern)*; Don Calfa *(Patient at Hammersmith)*; Arnold F. Turner *(Animal Control Officer)*; Kay Yamamoto *(Receptionist)*; Kellye Nakahara-Wallett *(Beagle Woman)*; Beth Grant *(Woman)*; Yule Caise *(Vet's Assistant)*; Brian Kwan *(Busboy)*; L. Peter Callender *(Policeman)*; Charles A. Branklyn *(Security Guard)*; Cliff McLaughlin *(Mounted Policeman)*; Richard Penn *(Principal)*; John LaFayette *(Reverend)*; Raymond Matthew Mason *(3 Year Old Dolittle)*; Dari Gerard Smith *(5 Year Old Dolittle)*; Karl T. Wright *(Reporter)*; Stan Sellers *(Cop)*; Ming Lo *(Cop)*; VOICES OF: Norm Macdonald *(Lucky)*; Albert Brooks *(Tiger)*; Chris Rock *(Rodney)*; Reni Santoni *(Rat I)*; John Leguizamo *(Rat II)*; Julie Kavner *(Female Pigeon)*; Garry Shandling *(Male Pigeon)*; Ellen DeGeneres *(Prologue Dog)*; Brian Doyle-Murray *(Old Beagle)*; Phil Proctor *(Drunk Monkey)*; Jenna Elfman *(Owl)*; Gilbert Gottfried *(Compulsive Dog)*; Phyllis Katz *(Goat)*; Douglas Shamburger *(Pound Dog)*; Jeff Doucette *(Possum)*; Archie Hahn *(Heavy Woman's Dog)*; Tom Towles *(German Shepard)*; Eddie Frierson *(Skunk)*; Paul Reubens *(Racoon)*; Royce D. Applegate *("I Love You" Dog)*; James F. Dean *(Orangutan)*; Chad Einbinder *(Bettleheim the Cat)*; Jonathan Lipnicki *(Baby Tiger)*; Hamilton Camp *(Pig)*; Kerrigan Mahan *(Penguin)*

The story of the eponymous man of medicine who converses with animals has been completely reworked into a vehicle for the rejuvenated Eddie Murphy. As such, it's a flimsy comedy that endures solely on Murphy's appeal.

Although he enjoyed talking with animals as a boy, the adult John Dolittle (Eddie Murphy) has little time for such diversions, too busy with his medical practice even to devote much time to his wife Lisa (Kristen Wilson) and daughters Charisse (Raven-Symone) and Maya (Kyla Pratt). While driving home from his clinic one night, he accidentally hits a dog (voice of Norm Macdonald). The dog is unhurt but startles Dolittle when he appears to mutter an insult.

The next day, Dolittle has several experiences in which animals seem to speak to him. Afraid that he's losing his mind, he has a colleague examine him, but tests show nothing. Later, Dolittle sees the dog from the previous night being taken to the pound for extermination. He saves it, and the dog, which he names Lucky, expresses thanks. In short time, Dolittle accepts that he can talk with animals, and is soon beset with an assortment of animals seeking medical care, which he provides. Dolittle enjoys his gift, but his wife and colleagues, afraid that he's delusional, commit him to a mental institution. Dolittle renounces his ability and is released.

Soon after, Dolittle begins preparation for an important press conference at which the acquisition of his facility by a health care corporation will be announced. On the night of the conference, Dolittle is persuaded by Lucky to treat an ailing tiger, Jacob (voice of Albert Brooks). Stealing Jacob from a circus, Dolittle precedes to the clinic, where the press conference is in progress. At the facility, Dolittle secretly prepares an operation, but is called into the conference before he can begin. As Dolittle is about to speak, Jacob wanders in and frightens the crowd. Dolittle restores calm, explains the situation, and performs a life-saving operation on the tiger. Impressed, the head of the health care corporation (Peter Boyle) announces his purchase intentions to attending press, but Dolittle rebuffs him, stating that the facility is not for sale. Having retained the clinic, Dolittle begins a renewed life with his family and animal friends.

Why would a movie studio spend more than $70 million to remake one of its greatest embarrassments, a big budget fiasco that crippled it three decades earlier? The answer is, simply, that 20th Century Fox has not remade DR. DOLITTLE at all. Aside from its premise (and the jaunty Louis Armstrong version of "Talk to the Animals" that closes the film), this contemporized DR. DOLITTLE bears no resemblance to either the 1967 Rex Harrison musical or the Hugh Lofting tales on which it was based. This DR. DOLITTLE owes its existence to the ongoing transformation of Eddie Murphy. Gone is the foul-mouthed, swaggering hipster of "Saturday Night Live" and the BEVERLY HILLS COP films. The new, commercially resuscitated Murphy continues along the route he took with THE NUTTY PROFESSOR (1997), presenting himself as a toned-down comedian who creates family-oriented entertainment (albeit laden with childish vulgarity).

Certainly, little else matters in this production. As filmmaking, DR. DOLITTLE is shoddy. The talking animal effects are embarrassingly transparent, and the film seems to have been constructed around carelessly shot animal footage, resulting in choppy editing and mismatched shots. Director Betty Thomas does nothing with a terrific supporting cast, as Ossie Davis, Oliver Platt, and Peter Boyle are wasted in undeveloped, inconsequential roles. The actors who supply animal voices fare somewhat better, but given the talent involved—Albert Brooks, Julie Kavner, Chris Rock, John Leguizamo, among others—the results are marginal.

The success or failure of DR. DOLITTLE, however, rests ultimately with Eddie Murphy. As in THE NUTTY PROFESSOR, Murphy demonstrates that he's comfortable and confident with his new image. As the square, stodgy doctor—the antithesis of the sort of role that brought him world wide fame—Murphy is lively and engaging, exuding charm even through a deluge of scatological jokes. That he manages to enliven such scant material is a testament to his professionalism. For Murphy's legion of fans, this apparently is enough. Everyone else can continue to hope that the new Eddie Murphy will find a project that is truly deserving of his rich talent. *(Profanity.)*—D.C.

d, Betty Thomas; p, John Davis, David T. Friendly, Joseph M. Singer; exec p, Jenno Topping, Sue Baden-Powell; assoc p, Steph Lady; co-p, Paul Neesan; w, Nat Mauldin, Larry Levin (based on the stories by Hugh Lofting); ph, Russell Boyd; ed, Peter Teschner; m, Richard Gibbs; prod d, William Elliott; art d, Greg Papalia; set d, K.C. Fox; sound, David Kirschner (mixer); fx, Burt Dalton; casting, Nancy Foy; cos, Sharen Davis; makeup, Ann Pala; stunts, Ernie Orsatti

Children's/Comedy/Fantasy (PR: A MPAA: PG-13)

DOGBOYS, THE

(SEE: TRACKED)

DOGWATCH ★★½

(U.S., 1998) 99m NuImage ~ Real Entertainment c

Sam Elliott *(Charlie Falon)*; Esai Morales *(Michael Monroe)*; Paul Sorvino *(Delgotti)*; Dan Lauria *(Halloway)*; Richard Gilliland *(Orlanski)*; Jessica Steen *(Janet)*; Mimi Craven *(Sally)*; Richard Zavaglia *(Wasserman)*; Robert Cicchini *(Mink)*; Perry Moore *(Jerome Jackson)*; Ben Brown *(L.A. Cop)*; Mike Burstyn *(Sam Levinson)*; Eric Steinberg *(Bench)*; Keith MacKechnie *(Wally)*; Susan Barnes *(Grace)*; Conni Marie Brazleton *(Mrs. Johnson)*; Dennis Dun *(Lee)*; John Ganun *(Dice)*; Mike Watson *(Winch)*; Tony Campisi *(Priest)*; Sean Johnson *(Evidence Room Clerk)*; Kristin Miller *(Naomi)*; Brenda Ferrell *(Monica)*; Keith Forster *(Cop #1)*; John Patrick Blair *(Cop Driver)*; Sharon Webster *(Lab Techician)*; Jerry Carlton *(Mechanic)*; Wayne Doba *(Owner)*; Conrad Ricketts *(Man in Window)*; Liz Francis Rolfe *(Neighbor)*

As a bitter cop railing against a corrupt world, Sam Elliott works hard but can't make this straight-to-video feature anything more than a bargain-basement BAD LIEUTENANT (1992).

Charlie Falon (Sam Elliott) works the homicide beat in San Francisco with his friend and partner Sam Levinson (Mike Burstyn). Sam is stabbed to death outside a strip bar where Charlie is visiting his sometime girlfriend Sally (Mimi Craven). Charlie leaves the bar a moment after Winch (Mike Watson), a snitch the two cops employed, arrives and finds the body. Jumping to the wrong conclusion, Charlie beats Winch to death, then dumps his body at the docks.

Capt. Delgotti (Paul Sorvino) assigns Charlie and new partner Mike Monroe (Esai Morales) to investigate Winch's murder, while Dets. Halloway (Dan Lauria) and Orlanski (Richard Gilliland) are charged to search for Sam's killer. Despite Charlie's efforts to put him off, Mike starts picking at loose ends. So does Charlie, who is appalled to learn that his partner was dealing drugs behind his back. Delgotti reveals that Sam was under investigation by Winch, who was actually an undercover cop—the man Charlie beat to death was not only innocent but a fellow officer. The real murderers are Orlanski and Halloway, who are running a ring to sell confiscated drugs. They kill an ex-con and his family after setting him up to make it look like he killed Sam. They then administer a fatal overdose to potential witness Sally, who had been getting her drugs from Sam. Their sloppiness tips Charlie off, just as Mike is piecing together that Charlie killed Winch. Orlanski and Halloway offer to cut Charlie in, which he refuses, leading to a gunfight. Charlie is fatally wounded just as Mike arrives to take out the bad cops.

DOGWATCH (the title is never explained; hopefully the film's creators weren't trying to emulate 1992's RESERVOIR DOGS) would like to be a cynical cop movie, but will only seem that way to viewers who don't otherwise watch anything that doesn't star John Wayne. Progressing from tirades against the Japanese, Elliott spends most of the film grousing through his soupstrainer mustache about the death of the good old days, when men made more money than women, women stayed home and cooked (unlike his new partner's spouse, who orders in sushi), and 90 percent of police work was style. You almost feel sorry for him as he tries to deliver dialogue like, "The only broad I ever had was this job." The other big victim in this minefield of cliches is Sorvino, who at least gets to play the *fun* stereotype of the opera-singing police captain. Better off is Morales as a young cop trying to make good but confronted with the partner from hell. Decent production values, including an inappropriate but enjoyable jazz score by Clint Eastwood mainstay Lennie Niehaus, would have made this a more enjoyable film if only it hadn't taken itself so seriously. *(Graphic violence, nudity, adult situations, profanity.)*—M.F.

d, John Langley; p, Elie Cohn; exec p, Avi Lerner, Danny Dimbort, Trevor Short, Malcom Barbour, Boaz Davidson; assoc p, Susan Carney; co-p, Joanna Lancaster, Douglas Waterman; w, Martin Zurla (based on the story by Zurla, Dan Lauria); ph,

Robert Yeoman; ed, Russell Livingstone; m, Lennie Niehaus; prod d, Jerry Fleming; sound, Jon Ailetcher (mixer); fx, Larry Fioritto; casting, Laurel Smith; cos, Bonnie Stauch; makeup, Ashley Scott; stunts, R.L. Tolbert

Crime/Action **(PR: O MPAA: R)**

DON KING: ONLY IN AMERICA ★★★½
(U.S., 1997) 116m Thomas Carter Company Production ~ HBO Home Video c

Ving Rhames *(Don King)*; Vondie Curtis Hall *(Lloyd Price)*; Jeremy Piven *(Hank Schwartz)*; Darius McCrary *(Muhammad Ali)*; Keith David *(Herbert Muhammad)*; Gabriel Casseus *(Jeremiah Shabazz)*; Loretta Devine *(Connie Harper)*; Brent Jennings *(Dick Sadler)*; Lahmard Tate *(Carl King)*; Danny Johnson *(Larry Holmes)*; Bernie Mac *(Bendini Brown)*; Donzaleigh Abernathy *(Henrietta King)*; Lou Rawls *(Harold Logan)*; Teddy Atlas *(Richie Giachetti)*; Jarrod Bunch *(George Foreman)*; Ron Leibman *(Harry Shondor)*; Don Elbaum *(Himself)*; Sarah Scott Davis *(Diane Holmes)*; Michael Gilio *(Tony Panzarella)*; Ken Lerner *(Bob Arum)*; Simon Templeman *(Keith Bradshaw)*; Jennifer Griffin *(Notary Public)*; Brad Garrett *(Assassin)*; Fofo Lukata *(Mobulu)*; Kurt Andon *(Lou)*; Ntare Mwine *(Emissary)*; Loni-Kaye Harkless *(Mrs. Jackson)*; David Kirkwood *(Mr. Jackson)*; Robby Robinson *(Sam Garrett)*; Tanisher Sornson *(Felisher)*; James Black *(Ernie Shavers)*; Detective Bob Tonne *(Himself)*; K.J. Penthouse *(Charles Wepner)*; Jim A. Douglass *(Autograph Seeker)*; Michael Bowen *(Boxing Spectator)*; Michael Blanks *(Buster Douglas)*; Israel Cole *(Joe Frazier)*; Clifford Couser *(Mike Tyson)*; Everton Davis *(Evander Hollyfield)*; King Ikpitan *(Tony Tucker)*; Kevin Grevioux *(Leon Spinks)*; Carlos Monroe *(James "Bonecrusher" Smith)*; Denorvell "Dee" Collier *(Pinklon Thomas)*; Alan Woolf *(Scram)*; Cara De Lizia *(Teen Girl #1)*; Amanda Fuller *(Teen Girl #2)*; Jennifer Crystal *(Hank's Secretary)*; Robert Fraade *(Businessman)*; Leilani Marie *(Stripper)*; Adetoro Makinde *(African Woman)*; Bob Minor *(Bad Ass #1)*; Big Daddy Wayne *(Bad Ass #2)*; Marco Verdier *(Bad Ass #3)*; Jack Newfield *(Reporter in Zaire)*; Felice Perry *(Detective John)*; Gwen McGee *(Screaming Woman)*; Keana Hall *(Woman in Bed)*; Josh Dempsey *(Foreman's Sparring Partner)*; Pat Connolly *(Ref)*; Ron Hall *(Stunt Soldier)*; Eugene Collier *(Stunt Prisoner)*; Kurek Ashley *(Sideman)*; Mark Thompson *(Reporter #2)*; James Keane *(Reporter #3)*; Tijani Abba *(Soldier)*; Jin-Jin Reeves *(Backup Singer #1)*; Sandra Chriss *(Backup Singer #2)*; Rudy Costa *(Sax Player)*; Chris Gregory *(Boxing Announcer #1)*; Larry Michael *(Boxing Announcer #2)*

As fast-moving as a flurry of overhand punches, DON KING ONLY IN AMERICA provides an insider's look at the business of boxing through the perspective of the sport's most notorious promoter. The film was made for HBO and subsequently released to home video.

In Cleveland, 1954, Don King (Ving Rhames) kills a burglar in his house. In 1966, King, who now runs a small numbers racket, consorts with the mob and hangs out with singer and good friend Lloyd Price (Vondie Curtis Hall). King finds he needs instant cash after a run-in with a gangster to whom he owes protection money. King finds and beats to death a man who is late paying him back a debt; he subsequently serves six years in prison for the murder. In prison, he considers a career as a boxing promoter. Upon his release, King puts together a successful charity match, convincing heavyweight champ Muhammad Ali (Darius McCrary) to participate. King then partners with satellite-feed entrepreneur Hank Schwartz (Jeremy Piven). Together, they innovate the "pay-per-view" concept, and make a killing on a fight between George Foreman (Jarrod Bunch) and Joe Frazier (Israel Cole). Sensing that Ali could be his meal ticket, King steals him away from a rival promoter and arranges for him to fight Foreman in Africa, naming the confrontation "the Rumble in the Jungle." The fight is a tremendous success financially. After King encounters difficulties promoting another Ali fight, he shifts his focus and begins promoting the rookies with the help of his son Carl (Lahmard Tate). He eventually owns a piece of most of the American title-belt holders, including Larry Holmes (Danny Johnson), who winds up beating Ali, which ends the champ's career and sends King to the top of the boxing world. Holmes reveals his hatred for King, whom he accuses of stealing most of the fighter's hard-earned money. Years pass, and King moves on to represent Mike Tyson (Clifford Couser), reaping rewards from his illustrious ring career.

Boxing fans will find few surprises here, but it should be noted that the filmmakers do take an unusually harsh view of their subject (unusual for a cable-feature), painting him as a first-rate con artist who essentially bled his fighters dry. The film does, however, occasionally attempt to convey King's charisma, attempting to explain how he was so easily able to convince, cajole, and deceive so many people. In this regard, Rhames is the whole show. He captures the cartoonlike essence of the flamboyant, shock-haired King familiar to fight fans in a frame device seen throughout the film, but also impresses as the younger King, who had less confidence, less money, and more of a conscience.

Kario Salem's script and director John Herzfeld's stylish visuals keep the film moving along at a fast clip; of particular note are the fight scenes, which are superbly choreographed and edited. The inclusion of a segment dealing with the notorious Tyson-Holyfield bout (which ended with Tyson biting off a part of Holyfield's ear) skews the film's focus for a short while, but does nothing to blunt the film's overall power. *(Violence, extreme profanity.)*—P.L.

d, John Herzfeld; p, David Blocker; exec p, Thomas Carter; assoc p, James T. Feitag, David Gaines; w, Kario Salem (based on the book by Jack Newfield); ph, Bill Butler; ed, Steven Cohen; m, Anthony Marinelli; prod d, Mayne Berke; art d, John Chichester; sound, Richard Lightstone; fx, Larry Fioritto; casting, Robi Reed-Humes; cos, April Ferry; makeup, John E. Jackson; stunts, Charles Picerni

Biography/Drama **(PR: C MPAA: R)**

DONG GONG, XI DONG
(SEE: EAST PALACE, WEST PALACE)

DOUBLE EDGE ★½
(U.S./Japan, 1998) 95m Orion Pictures; Daewoo Corporation ~ Orion Home Video c
(AKA: AMERICAN DRAGONS)

Michael Biehn *(Det. Tony Luca)*; Joong-Hoon Park *(Inspector Kim)*; Don Stark *(Rocco)*; Byron Mann *(Shadow)*; Cary-Hiroyuki Tagawa *(Mitsuyama)*; Benjamin Ratner *(Angelo)*; Lorena Gale *(Capt. Talman)*; Hiro Kanagawa *(Nakai)*; Brad Loree *(Mike)*; Dean Choe *(Sato)*; Chris Franco *(Pozzo)*; James Crescenzo *(Fiorino)*; Roger R. Cross *(Dion Edwards)*; Kevan Ohtsji; Warren Takeuchi; Fulvio Cecere; Michael Hirano; Crystal Cass; Yuka Kobayashi; Nadia Capone; Ron Daprocida

Ace production values and Asian exoticism can't make a single moment of DOUBLE EDGE original or fresh.

Driven New York City cop Tony Luca (Michael Biehn) tries to bust renegade mobster Rocco (Don Stark). But Luca's one-man undercover sting goes bad, leaving an innocent bystander shot dead and Rocco at large. As punishment Luca is taken off the case and assigned instead to the sword-slaughter of several prominent *yakuza* in Little Tokyo. Luca finds an origami paper lotus-flower at the bloody homicide scene and posts the clue on an international police internet. Response comes in the shape of Inspector Kim (Joong-Hoon Park) of Seoul, South Korea. Kim's family had been murdered by the same coldly-efficient assassin, "Shadow" (Byron Mann), six years ago when Kim got too close to the dreaded Black Lotus Society of Far East criminals. Now Kim arrives in the US to help Luca stop a Black Lotus invasion of New York's underworld, but Luca doesn't want "Charlie Chan" interfering. They fight; they make up. Meanwhile, successive murders of Mafia and *yakuza* chieftains threaten to set the Italian and Japanese crime families against each other. Luca and Kim abduct respective *capos* in both gangs and force them to hear the truth: the Shadow and the treacherous Rocco are both behind the hits, trying to stir up a multicultural mob war so a third faction, the Black Lotus, can move in and take over. The two heroes confront the two bad guys at a Buddhist monastery in Little Tokyo and kill Rocco and the Shadow in simultaneous showdowns. After a friendly farewell to Luca at the airport, Inspector Kim is followed on board his plane by another Black Lotus man.

Released directly to home-video in the US, DOUBLE EDGE is a slick, shiny package with nothing inside but the hollow rattle of mismatched buddy-cop cliches that were already due for retirement from the force back when the success of 48 HRS. (1982) made them standard police procedure in many ensuing Hollywood actioners. The mixed Japanese and American film-making team seems to think it can get away with serving left-overs, thanks to the heavy ethnic flavoring and visual dynamism clearly inspired by the acrobatics and high melodrama of Hong Kong gangster movies (especially those of John Woo). But all the artful slow motion and cold, saturated colors don't make any of the ethnic stereotypes more palatable. Italian-Americans are all greasy, knuckle-dragging animals, Asians are politely inscrutable, and driven, maverick cops constantly buck the system and get chewed out by their superiors. Surprising only in its absence is the usual visit to a strip club or oriental massage parlor (in between gunfights, shakedowns, and racial insults, Luca is a good Catholic boy, and he and Kim pray to each others' gods in a mawkish moment). The final scene, possibly implying impending doom for the likable Kim, ends the narrative on a sour note. *(Graphic violence, extreme profanity, substance abuse, adult situations.)*—C.C.

d, Ralph Hemecker; p, Brad Krevoy, Steven Stabler, R.J. Murillo; exec p, Jo-Ho Jung, Jennifer Muhn, Jeffrey D. Ivers; assoc p, Chris Murphy, Bradley Thomas, Michael Bernstein, Joseph Kluge; w, Eric Saltzgaber, Keith W. Strandberg; ph, Ernest Holzman; ed, Alan Shefland; m, Joel Goldsmith, Alex Wilkinson; prod d, Maya Ishiura; art d, Andrew Wilson; set d, Grant Pearse; sound, James Kusan; casting, Sue Brouse; cos, Cynthia Ann Summers; makeup, Dana Michelle Hamel, J.J. Benjamin; stunts, Marc Akerstream

Action/Crime/Thriller (PR: O MPAA: R)

DOWN IN THE DELTA ★★½

(U.S., 1998) 111m Amen Ra Films; Chris Rose Productions; Showtime ~ Miramax c

Alfre Woodard *(Loretta)*; Al Freeman Jr. *(Earl)*; Mary Alice *(Rosa Lynn)*; Esther Rolle *(Annie)*; Loretta Devine *(Zenia)*; Wesley Snipes *(Will)*; Mpho Koaho *(Thomas)*; Kulani Hassen *(Tracy)*; Anne Marie Johnson *(Monica)*; Justin Lord *(Dr. Rainey)*; Richard Yearwood *(Marco)*; Sandra Caldwell *(Volunteer)*; Colleen Williams *(Tourist Woman)*; Richard Blackburn *(Tourist Man)*; Philip Akin *(Manager)*; Mary Fallick *(Drug Addict)*; Sandi Ross *(Pawn Broker)*; Barbara Barnes Hopkins *(Prim Woman)*; Marium Carvell *(Prim Sister)*; Quancetia Hamilton *(Gina)*; Kim Roberts *(Isabelle)*; DeFoy Glenn *(Reverend Floyd)*; Jeff Jones *(Man in Congregation)*; Michelyn Emelle *(Dozing Woman)*; Johnie Chase *(Grinning Man)*; Andrea Lewis *(Cassandra)*; Nigel Shawn-Williams *(Carl)*; Bernard Browne *(Diner 1)*; Alison Sealy-Smith *(Diner 2)*; Eugene Clarke *(Citizen 1)*; Chris Benson *(Citizen 2)*; Carol Anderson *(Jesse's Wife)*; Neville Edwards *(Slave Man)*; Yanna McIntosh *(Slave Woman)*; Troy Seivwright-Adams *(Collin)*; Kevin Duhaney *(Justin)*; Joel Gordon *(Jesse 1865—17 Years Old)*; Phil Jarrett *(Jesse 1890—42 Years Old)*; Clinton Green *(Soloist in Church)*

Call it BELOVED lite. DOWN IN THE DELTA tells the story of the ways in which the legacy of slavery impacts the lives of a modern African-American family.

Loretta (Alfre Woodard) lives in a small Chicago apartment with her two children, a precocious son (Mpho Koaho) and autistic daughter (Kulani Hassen), and her mother, Rosa Lynn (Mary Alice). Since her husband has left her, Loretta would rather smoke crack than find a job, so the strong-willed Rosa Lynn decides to jolt Loretta into being more responsible. She pawns the family heirloom, "Nathan," a sterling silver candelabra, and uses the money to send Loretta and the children down to Mississippi to stay with her brother Earl (Al Freeman Jr.). Since Uncle Earl covets Nathan, Loretta promises to earn enough money working for him at his chicken restaurant in order to get the heirloom out of hock.

While staying with Earl, Loretta slowly becomes aware of the difficulties in other people's lives. Earl cares for his wife, Annie (Esther Rolle), who suffers from Alzheimer's, while Annie's nurse, Zenia (Loretta Devine), is also a single mother struggling to raise two children. Loretta also reunites with her cousin, Will (Wesley Snipes), and together they organize a protest against the closing of a local chicken plant, which would severely affect Earl's business. They even contemplate turning Earl's restaurant into a chain. Meanwhile, Annie fractures a hip and lands in the hospital, but Tracy, Loretta's daughter, learns how the speak and gives everyone renewed hope. Having grown close to Earl over the visit, Loretta decides to return to Chicago, pay for Nathan at the pawn shop, and try to wrest Nathan from her mother in order to give it to Earl. But Rosa Lynn finally tells Loretta the significance of the candelabra: she explains how her great-great-great-great-great grandfather Jesse, a Civil War soldier, stole it from the slave owners who had purchased his father, named Nathan, at auction. In telling the story, Rosa Lynn realizes Nathan should remain in its ancestral home. She travels down to the Delta with Loretta to give Earl the heirloom, and he, in turn, gives it to Loretta, who puts it on the mantle. Loretta than tells her son the story behind Nathan.

Anyone who has read the books and poetry of Maya Angelou could predict that her debut as a filmmaker, DOWN IN THE DELTA, would be a heartfelt though overly earnest, even prosaic effort. Given the fact that so few features are directed by African-American women, one can applaud the noble effort made here. Angelou and screenwriter Myron Goble clearly wish to make a prescriptive morality tale out of the city mice-meets-country mice scenario. Balancing the light EGG AND I (1947) moments with the dark "Roots" (1977) theme becomes a challenging feat that the director and writer pull off for the most part (it's also refreshing *not* to see the usual romantic subplot).

Sadly, the filmmakers get overly ambitious, cramming too many contemporary issues, including jobs, guns, drugs, and illness, into the slender package. Also, Angelou's technique is often rough, affecting the performances. In one early scene, for example, Loretta and the children react to gunfire outside their apartment by taking cover while Rosa Lynn doesn't even blink. The likable Alfre Woodard gives an odd performance, full of distracting tics, that are a function of her character's having been on drugs. However, her double-takes and delayed reactions in some scenes, such as when she hears Tracy speak for the first time, seem like a peculiar remnant of the coy Doris Day school of comedy.

The most distressing aspect of DOWN IN THE DELTA remains its emphasis on the passage of Nathan from both women to both men (symbolized by the final placement at Earl's mantle). This plot element suggests an affirmation of patriarchal values. Even Jonathan Demme's BELOVED, a higher-profile 1998 feature with an African-American cast and a much higher budget, contained a more nuanced perspective. But this simpler, more modest work at least attempts an earnest exploration of struggle in the face of a challenging heritage. *(Substance abuse, profanity.)*—E.M.

d, Maya Angelou; p, Reuben Cannon, Bob Christiansen, Victor McGauley, Rick Rosenberg, Wesley Snipes; co-p, Terri Farnsworth, Myron Goble, Alfre Woodard; w, Myron Goble; ph, William Wages; ed, Nancy Richardson; m, Stanley Clarke; prod d, Lindsey Hermer-Bell; art d, Robert Sher; set d, Megan Less; sound, Tom Hidderley (mixer); casting, Reuben Cannon; cos, Maxyne Baker; makeup, Lynda McCormack; stunts, Wayne Downer

Drama **(PR: A MPAA: PG-13)**

DRAGON BALL Z THE MOVIE: DEAD ZONE ★★½

(Japan, 1990) 42m Toei Animation Co., Ltd.; Pioneer Entertainment Funimation Productions; Ocean Studios (English Language Version) ~ Pioneer Entertainment c

English Voice Cast: Lisa Ann Beley; Don Brown; Paul Dobson; Doc Harris; Saffron Henderson; Peter Kelamis; Terry Klassen; Lalainia Lindbjerg; Scott McNeil; Ward Perry; Dave Ward; Alec Willows

DEAD ZONE is one of several "Dragon Ball Z" short theatrical features based on the long-running Japanese animated comic fantasy TV series (which appeared on the Cartoon Network in the late 1990s), and the first to be released on video in the US.

The pastoral bliss enjoyed on earth by alien superhero Goku, his wife Chi-Chi, and son Gohan, is interrupted by the emergence of a band of aliens, led by Garlic Jr., who abduct Gohan to gain possession of the magical dragon ball adorning the boy's hat. With the dragon balls now in his possession, Garlic Jr. is able to ask the Eternal Dragon to grant him his wish for immortality.

Goku invades Garlic Jr.'s palace, joined by his sidekick Krillin and sometime opponent Piccolo. A massive destructive battle ensues. Only when Gohan joins in with his own unleashed powers is the team powerful enough to defeat Garlic Jr. and trap him in his own creation, the Dead Zone.

"Dragon Ball Z" and its predecessor, "Dragon Ball," were popular animated series which ran on Japanese television from 1986-1996 and which spun off a host of short theatrical features, beginning in 1990. All were based on a long-running *manga* (comic book) series by Akira Toyama. In 1996, "Dragon Ball Z" came to US television in an English-dubbed version, with the casual nudity and off-color humor cleaned up.

The series offers a motley crew of bizarre characters who traverse a fantasy earth and other planets in battle with each other and various alien interlopers. The goal of the characters in the first series was to locate and retrieve the seven dragon balls. This aspect of the narrative drew on the famed Chinese literary texts, *Journey to the West* (the story of the Monkey King) and *The Water Margin*, both of which have been adapted by more high-minded Chinese and Japanese filmmakers and animators.

DEAD ZONE has plenty of action to satisfy the series' adolescent (and younger) fans, but offers little focus on the characters. Of this lively group, only Gohan has funny moments; when he eats a piece of forbidden fruit in Garlic's palace (in a scene deliberately recalling the antics of the Monkey King), he behaves as if stoned and, when his rescuers arrive, proceeds to urinate on Krillin's bald head. *(Violence.)*—B.C.

d, Daisuke Nishio; p, Kozo Morishita, Hiroe Tsukamoto (English Language Version); exec p, Hideki Goto (English Language Version); w, Takao Koyama (based on the original story by Akira Toriyama from the comic book "Weekly Shonen Jump"); ph, Motoaki Ikegami; m, Shunsuke Kikuchi; art d, Yuji Ikeda; anim, Minoru Maeda; sound, Kenji Ninomiya

Animated/Fantasy/Martial Arts **(PR: A MPAA: NR)**

DRAGON BALL Z THE MOVIE: THE TREE OF MIGHT ★★½

(Japan, 1990) 61m Toei Animation Co Ltd.; Fuji Television; Pioneer Entertainment; Funimation Productions Inc; Ocean Studios (English Language Version) ~ Pioneer Entertainment c

English Voice Cast: Don Brown; Ted Cole; Paul Dobson; Saffron Henderson; Peter Kelamis; Terry Klassen; Lalainia Lindbjerg; Scott McNeil; Doug Parker; Ward Perry; Laara Sadiq; Alvin Sanders; Matt Smith; Cathy Weseluck

The second "Dragon Ball Z" movie to be released in the US in the wake of the success of the Japanese animated series on US television, THE TREE OF MIGHT pits Goku and his super-powered entourage against an alien attack on earth.

Aliens led by Master Turles of the Saiyan race come to earth to plant the seed for the Tree of Might, which then grows rapidly, destroying cities and forests in its wake. The tree is designed to soak up the nutrients of earth in order to produce the fruit that will give Turles and his cohorts enough power to rule the universe.

Goku, a Saiyan who has moved to earth and raised a family, leads his entourage of super-powered warriors, including Piccolo, Krillin, and his son Gohan, in battle with the aliens. After an initial defeat, Goku calls on the power of the earth and all living things to summon up enough energy to create a "super spirit bomb," which enables him to send Turles hurling into space and destroy the Tree of Might, restoring life to planet earth.

The second of three "Dragon Ball Z" movie spinoffs released on video in the US in 1998, this one boasts enough action, martial arts, and spectacle to vastly entertain its adolescent (and younger) male audience. Others may need a score card since the film relies heavily on audience knowledge of the extensive back story, particularly Goku's alien origin. *(Violence.)*—B.C.

d, Daisuke Nishio; p, Kozo Morishita, Kenji Shimizu, Weekly Shonen Jump, Hiroe Tsukamoto (English Language Version); exec p, Hideki Goto (English Language Version); w, Takao Koyama (based on the story by Akira Toriyama from the comic book "Weekly Shonen Jump"); ph, Motoaki Ikegami; ed, Shinichi Fukumitsu; m, Shunsuke Kikuchi; art d, Yuji Ikeda; anim, Minoru Maeda; sound, Kenji Ninomiya

Animated/Fantasy **(PR: A MPAA: NR)**

DRAGON BALL Z THE MOVIE: THE WORLD'S STRONGEST ★★½

(Japan, 1990) 60m Toei Animation Co. Ltd.; Fuji Television; Weekly Shonen Jump; Pioneer Entertainment; Funimation Productions Inc.; Ocean Studios (English Language Version) ~ Pioneer Entertainment c

English Voice Cast: Lisa Ann Beley; Don Brown; Paul Dobson; Doc Harris; Saffron Henderson; Peter Kelamis; Terry Klassen; Lalainia Lindbjerg; Scott McNeil; Ward Perry; Dave Ward; Alec Willows

THE WORLD'S STRONGEST, the third "Dragon Ball Z" movie released on home video in the US in 1998, continues the adventures of alien Goku, the strongest fighter in the world, and his motley entourage. This time they're engaged in battle with a mad scientist seeking to put his brain in Goku's body.

An expert in bio-technology experiments who currently exists only in the form of a brain, Dr. Wheelo wants to put his brain into the body of the strongest fighter in the world. To achieve that end, Wheelo's cohort, Dr. Kochin, engineers the kidnapping of Master Roshi, the one-time strongest man in the world and teacher of Goku. Goku goes to the thawed-out headquarters of Dr. Wheelo and seeks to rescue Master Roshi. Upon seeing Goku in action, Wheelo now wants Goku's body rather than that of the elderly Roshi.

Goku is soon joined by his sidekick Krillin, his son Gohan, and, eventually, his sometime opponent Piccolo. Dr. Wheelo emerges from his lab housed in a monstrous mechanical body which proves too much for the combined protagonists. Goku takes him on and uses up his power to blast Wheelo into space. Wheelo sends one last burst of energy to destroy the earth. Goku calls on the power and energy of earth to summon up one last "super spirit bomb" to ward off Wheelo's blast and send the mad doctor into oblivion.

Spun off from the wildly popular Japanese animated TV series (and comic book), this one is even louder than the other "Dragon Ball Z" films in current release, filled as it is with massive explosions, colossal blasts of energy, and super-powered "spirit bombs"—more than enough to please its adolescent (and younger) audience with its video-game like images. To get a better sense of the characters and the epic saga that spawned them, viewers are advised to check out the television series (airing on American TV on the Cartoon Network), and the US comic book, which translates the original Japanese *manga* that spawned the series. *(Violence.)*—B.C.

d, Daisuke Nishio; p, Kozo Morishita, Hiroe Tsukamoto (English Language Version); exec p, Hideki Goto (English Language Version); w, Takao Koyama (based on the story by Akira Toriyama from the comic book "Weekly Shonen Jump"); ph, Motoaki Ikegami; ed, Shinichi Fukumitsu; m, Shunsuke Kikuchi; art d, Yuji Ikeda; anim, Minoru Maeda; sound, Kenji Ninomiya

Animated/Fantasy **(PR: A MPAA: NR)**

DRAGONS FOREVER ★★★½

(Hong Kong, 1988) 93m Golden Harvest ~ Tai Seng c

Jackie Chan *(Jackie Lung)*; Sammo Hung *(Wang Fei-hsiung)*; Yuen Biao *(Tung Tak-Biao)*; Deannie Yip *(Miss Yip)*; Pauline Yeung *(Wen Mei-Ling)*; Yuen Wah *(Mr. Hua)*; Crystal Kwok *(Mary)*; Roy Chaio; James Tien *(Fung)*; Billy Chow; Benny Urquidez; Lee Ka Ding; Philip Ko, billed as Ko Fei; Dick Wei; David Lam, billed as Lam Wei; Chung Fat; Feng Ko An; Benny Lai *(Thugs)*; Wong Yu Wan *(Prostitute)*; Fung Shui-fan *(Psychiatrist)*; Shing Fui-on *(Defendant Mao Shih-Cheng)*; Tai Po *(Informer on Boat)*; Lo Lieh *(Gang Boss)*

The last film to date from the spectacular team of childhood-classmates-turned-Hong-Kong movie stars Jackie Chan, Sammo Hung and Yuen Biao is a nonstop festival of fists, kicks, and comedy. It is in fact the only film in which the "three brothers" engage in free-for-all brawling with one another, in a series of quick, hysterical interludes. Who cares if the plot is made of Swiss cheese? The film received its first official US release on home video in 1998.

When Miss Yip (Deannie Yip), owner of a fish-farm, sues chemical plant owner Mr. Hua (Yuen Wah) for polluting the environment, shady defense lawyer Jackie Lung (Jackie Chan) is hired to fend her off. He enlists his criminal friends Tung Tak-Biao (Yuen Biao) and Wang Fei-hsiung (Sammo Hung) to help, but the two get off to a bad start and fight constantly. Meanwhile, Jackie falls for Miss Yip's lawyer-cousin, Wen Mei-Ling (Pauline Yeung), and Wang falls for Miss Yip herself. After the two men are revealed as frauds to their paramours, they switch allegiances to help the women. Wang is captured taking pictures inside Hua's factory—which turns out to be a front for a narcotics racket—and Jackie, after quitting the defense team, comes to Wang's rescue with Tung.

Director Hung's timing is flawless, both in the marvelously paced fight scenes, which boast a hugely inventive use of physical space and props, and in the comedy, often the low point of Hong Kong action hybrids. Never mind that it all fits together clumsily and sometimes doesn't even make sense. At one point the three antiheroes coincidentally meet Hua at a bar; suddenly a gang of thugs attack. Hua shrugs it off as one of his many enemies. But then we meet a whole new character, a gang boss who actually hired the thugs to kill Jackie. The thugs then return for a remarkable battle royale on an empty cruise ship that Jackie has hired for lunch (!), then disappear entirely from the story, along with their mysterious boss. Bad exposition, but terrific fun.

DRAGONS FOREVER was a troubled production from the start. Chan was already a major star, and his friends Hung and Yuen Baio were resentful of working in his shadow. In addition, filming was rushed to meet the all-important Chinese New Year opening date. The main nemesis is played by the acrobatic Yuen Wah, a graduate of the same Peking Opera school attended by the film's lead trio; Yuen's character is a virtual reprise of his effete villain from Hung's EASTERN CONDORS (1987). As in WHEELS ON MEALS (1983), martial-arts master Benny Urquidez was enlisted for a final-reel appearance to provide the film with a rollicking climactic fight (he takes on Chan).

Given all the film had going against it, one would expect a monumental failure, and indeed it got a lukewarm reception when it was released in Hong Kong in 1988, failing miserably in Japan, normally a hot territory for Chan. The most likely contributing factor in its poor box-office reception was the surprising depiction of the three leads as fairly smarmy outlaws. In the west, however, it was received as a genuine action classic. *(Violence, substance abuse.)*—A.B.

d, Sammo Hung, Corey Yuen, billed as Yuen Kwai; p, Jackie Chan, Corey Yuen, Leonard K.C. Ho; exec p, Leonard Ho, Raymond Chow; assoc p, Barney Wu; w, Roy Szeto, billed as Szeto Cheuk Hon (based on the original story by Leung Yiu-Ming and Gordan Chan); ph, Jimmy Leung, Joseph Cheung; ed, Peter Cheung, Joseph Chang; m, James Wong; prod d, Oliver Wong; art d, Horce Ma; set d, Butt Yiu Kwong; cos, Ingrid Kwan; makeup, Law Lai Kuen, Poon Men Wah; stunts, Jackie Chan's Stuntmen Club, Sammo Hung's Stuntmen Team

Action/Martial Arts **(PR: C MPAA: NR)**

DREAM FOR AN INSOMNIAC ★½

(U.S., 1998) 88m Tritone Productions ~
Avalanche Releasing c/bw

Ione Skye *(Frankie)*; Jennifer Aniston *(Allison)*; MacKenzie Astin *(David Schrader)*; Michael Landes *(Rob)*; Robert Kelker-Kelly *(Trent)*; Seymour Cassel *(Uncle Leo)*; Sean San Jose

Blackman *(Juice)*; Michael Sterk *(B.J.)*; Leslie Stevens *(Molly)*; David "Puck" Rainey *(Delivery Man)*

Though they do the best they can with what they're given, the cast of DREAM FOR AN INSOMNIAC can't save this cliched tale of Gen-X love in a San Francisco coffee shop.

Mere days before aspiring actress Frankie (Ione Skye) is set to leave San Francisco for Los Angeles, she meets the man of her dreams, David (MacKenzie Astin), a struggling writer who shares Frankie's penchant for quoting philosophers. When David takes a job at the family coffee house, run by Frankie's uncle Leo (Seymour Cassel) and cousin Rob (Michael Landes), she is determined to win him. A chronic insomniac, Frankie offers to let David try to help her sleep if he'll let her help him conquer his writer's block. While David's attempted lullabye—reading Frankie a bedtime story—fails, it only endears him to her more. . . that is, until she meets David's longtime girlfriend, Molly (Leslie Stevens). Discouraged but not defeated, Frankie decides on the eve of her departure to take David out for a night designed to both surmount his writer's block and win his love. However, they are arrested while spraypainting a wall, and are taken to the police station. There Frankie professes her love to David, and though he feels the same he cannot leave Molly.

So Frankie and her friend Allison (Jennifer Aniston) leave together for LA. It's not long, however, before David realizes that while he is comfortable with Molly he does not feel the same burning passion he felt with Frankie. David dumps Molly in front of the coffee shop and heads to LA; after he and Frankie make love, she is finally able to sleep.

Though blessed with an above-average cast, DREAM FOR AN INSOMNIAC is a mess of trite Gen-X movie conventions—the struggling actresses, the barrage of pop culture references—impeding an already limp romance. More so than in the usual romantic comedy, it's clear from the start that Frankie and David will end up together. They're perfect for each other—far too perfect, in fact. Nobody in the world is as perfectly paired as these two. When David's ill-matched girlfriend is introduced (how did these two ever get together in the first place?), we know she's toast. That it takes nearly 90 minutes for the characters to figure this out is almost insulting.

DREAM FOR AN INSOMNIAC poses some interesting questions, though. How does a struggling actress working part-time at a coffee shop afford an apartment in San Francisco, for example? And how does her apparently unemployed friend, Allison, afford a Mercedes convertible? What is MTV "Real World" annoyance David "Puck" Rainey doing on screen? (He makes a walk-on appearance as a delivery boy with one line.) And how did writer-director Tiffanie DeBartolo manage to get veteran cinematographer Guillermo Navarro (DESPERADO, THE LONG KISS GOODNIGHT, JACKIE BROWN) to shoot this vanity project? Alas, some questions were not meant to be answered. *(Sexual situations, adult situations, profanity.)*—B.T.

d, Tiffanie DeBartolo; exec p, Christopher Lloyd, Rita J. Rokisky, John Hackett; assoc p, Charles Kirkwood; w, Tiffanie DeBartolo; ph, Guillermo Navarro; ed, Tom Fries; m, John Laraio; prod d, Gary New; casting, Melissa Skoff; cos, Charles E. Winston

Romance/Comedy **(PR: C MPAA: R)**

DRESS, THE ★★½

(Netherlands, 1996) 98m Graniet Film ~ Attitude Films c (DE JURK)

Henri Garcin *(Van Tilt)*; Ariane Schluter *(Johanna)*; Alex van Warmerdam *(De Smet)*; Ricky Koole *(Chantalle)*; Rijk de Gooyer *(Martin)*; Elisabeth Hoijtink *(Stella)*; Eric van Donk *(Herman)*; Olga Zuiderhoek *(Marie)*; Khaldoun Elmecky *(Cremer)*; Rudolf Lucieer *(De Vet)*; Annet Malherbe *(Woman With Gun)*

A simple cotton summer frock jinxes the entire personae of THE DRESS, an offbeat Dutch film that is structured like a comic fable but ultimately emerges as an exploration of the themes of aging, death, loneliness, alienation, art, and sexual longing. After winning awards at the 1996 Venice and Netherlands Film Festivals, it received a 1998 release in the US.

It may look like a dumb little dress but it's a menace to everyone who crosses its path. Cremer (Khaldoun Elmecky), who designed the pattern, loses his lover. Van Tilt (Henri Garcin), a consultant involved in the garment's manufacture, loses his wife and his job. Sixty-one-year-old Stella (Elisabeth Hoijtink), who buys the dress in an attempt to recapture her youth, loses her life itself. A housemaid named Johanna (Ariane Schluter), the dress's next owner, is stalked by De Smet (Alex van Warmerdam), a railway employee who has become infatuated with her—then she narrowly escapes being raped by a bus driver.

Owner number three, a teenager named Chantalle (Ricky Koole), is home alone when she is confronted by De Smet, who forces her to strip and share her bed with him in platonic embrace. The next day, the dress is stolen and donned by Marie (Olga Zuiderhoek), a depressed homeless woman. Before dying of exposure, she is comforted by Van Tilt, who has hit the skids himself.

When Marie's life ends, so does the life of the unlucky frock—or does it? The deadly dress makes a final appearance reproduced on a canvas painted by Johanna's boyfriend (Eric van Donk). When De Smet spots the painting in a museum, he slashes it with a knife. As the guards are carrying him off, he shouts, "I'm normal! I'm normal!"

Normality is not a charge likely to be leveled at THE DRESS, an unclassifiable exercise in dark comedy that doesn't even attempt to be conventionally funny after its midway point. Many of the signposts of low comedy are here—the illicit lover hiding under the bed, adults squabbling and scrapping like children, men literally chasing women, lots of gun-waving but no bloodshed, even a funny foreigner or two—but the comic spirit is missing. Things begin facetiously enough with a collection of mutually hostile characters who would not seem out of place in Lars von Trier's loopy TV miniseries THE KINGDOM, but Stella's poignant death in the arms of her loving husband more or less puts a damper on the fun and games.

THE DRESS's most amusing and articulate scene is its very first, in which a classy, no-nonsense stewardess tells her sleepy, sad-sack boyfriend exactly why she is moving out on him as she is doing so. Another droll scene, a small gem of miscommunication, involves two men, a gardener and a householder, conversing over a threshold, and the latter's blind, off-camera wife.

THE DRESS is clearly not a failed comedy—its two painful death scenes signal that writer-director Alex van Warmerdam had something weightier in mind—but neither does it fully succeed as drama, satire, or Bergmanesque fable.

The dress in this movie may throw the characters into a frenzy, but it doesn t erase memories of other notable articles of clothing in cinema history, which include the title chapeau in the Rene Clair classic AN ITALIAN STRAW HAT (1927), the gadabout coat in Julien Duvivier's TALES OF MANHATTAN (1942), and the title garment in Jack Clayton's superb short "The Bespoke Overcoat" (1956). *(Violence, extensive nudity, sexual situations, profanity.)*—D.T.

d, Alex van Warmerdam; p, Marc van Warmerdam, Ton Schippers, Alex van Warmerdam; exec p, Patricia McMahon; w, Alex van Warmerdam; ph, Marc Felperlaan; ed, Rene Wiegmans; m,

Vincent van Warmerdam; art d, Jelier & Schief; sound, Ben Zijlstra; casting, Annet Malherbe; cos, Leonie Polak; makeup, Kathy Kuhne

Comedy/Drama **(PR: C MPAA: NR)**

DUMME STERBEN NICHT AUS
(SEE: PALMETTO)

DUOLUO TIANSHI
(SEE: FALLEN ANGELS)

E

E NO NAKA NO BOKU NO MURA
(SEE: VILLAGE OF DREAMS)

EAST PALACE, WEST PALACE ★★★½
(China/France/Netherlands, 1996) 91m
Amazon Entertainment; Quelqu'un d'Autre ~ Strand Releasing c
(DONG GONG, XI DONG)

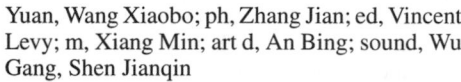

Si Han *(A-Lan)*; Hu Jun *(Xiao Shi)*

Independently made in Mainland China, this provocative work from 1996 is the first exploration of the country's contemporary gay subculture. Literate and insightful, the film boasts fine acting, naturalistic cinematography, and a superbly atmospheric musical score mixing traditional Chinese instrumentation with spare modern dissonance.

Scorned and excoriated by the general populace, homosexuals in urban China cruise for companionship in the city's parks at night, only to be rousted and harassed by the local police. Policeman Xiao Shi (Hu Jun) takes particular notice of young A-Lan (Si Han) and, after rounding him up in several different sweeps of the park, takes him into custody for interrogation. In the course of a single night, A-Lan spills out a history of loneliness and abuse—a confused mix of confession and come-on. A clearly conflicted Xiao Shi is both fascinated and repelled, becoming crueler and angrier as A-Lan seems to revel in his own victimization. Ultimately A-Lan expresses his love for Xiao Shi and the policeman forces him to don woman's clothing; the two share a brief, brutal embrace before Xiao Shi beats and humiliates the youth, then walks away as dawn breaks.

Director-cowriter Zhang Yuan invests the plot with a richness of ideas and little revelations, allowing for multiple readings. The true story unfolds slowly, in layers, with the measured pacing of a two-character play. A-Lan, who admits at one point to being a writer, paid to spin complicated heterosexual love stories with no bearing on his reality, reveals himself through confession, and we see moments from his life in flashback, opening up the film from the claustrophobic confines of a single room. But as the tale progresses, A-Lan's seemingly straightforward reminiscences begin to drift into fabrication and fantasy, while the visages of his partners and tormenters all look exactly like Xiao Shi. Submissive and masochistic by nature, A-Lan is infatuated with the policeman, drawn to the power he wields. When Xiao Shi at one point tries to remove a set of handcuffs from A-Lan's wrists, the youth backs away, offering captivity as seduction. And indeed Xiao Shi is entranced by the youth, even as he denies his own attraction. Their disturbing relationship, fraught with psychological and emotional S&M, works sublimely as a character study of two unsettled individuals—and as an allegory of political repression and intolerance.

Zhang Yuan has circumvented the familiar oppression dogging China's more famous fifth generation directors (Chen Kaige, Zhang Yimou) by making his films independently without state approval or funding—arguably an even more dangerous and difficult route. One of a clutch of social-realist directors concerned with the marginalized members of Chinese society, Zhang earlier directed the gritty, realistic BEIJING BASTARDS (1993) starring Mainland rock stars Cui Jian and Dou Wei as struggling musicians, and the documentary THE SQUARE (1994) about Tiananmen. The title of EAST PALACE, WEST PALACE, his fifth film, alludes to the public restrooms in the parks alongside the Forbidden City in Beijing. *(Violence, nudity, sexual situations, adult situations, profanity.)*—A.B.

d, Zhang Yuan; p, Zhang Yuan, Christophe Jung, Christophe Menager; exec p, Willy Tsao; assoc p, Zhang Yukang; w, Zhang Yuan, Wang Xiaobo; ph, Zhang Jian; ed, Vincent Levy; m, Xiang Min; art d, An Bing; sound, Wu Gang, Shen Jianqin

Drama **(PR: C MPAA: NR)**

EBENEZER ★★
(U.S./Canada, 1998) 94m Nomadic Pictures ~ Plaza Entertainment c

Jack Palance *(Ebenezer)*; Rick Schroder *(Sam Benson)*; Amy Locane *(Erica)*; Albert Shultz *(Bob Cratchitt)*; Darryl Shuttleworth *(Fred)*; Michelle Thrush *(Ghost of Xmas Past)*; Richard Comar *(Ghost of Xmas Present)*; Morris Chapdelaine *(Ghost of Xmas Future)*; Richard Halliday *(Jacob Marlowe)*; Susan Coyne *(Clara Cratchitt)*; Joshua Silberg *(Tiny Tim)*; Zoe Rose Hesse *(Cratchitt's Daughter)*; Jeffrey Derwent *(Cratchitt's Son)*; Jocelyn Loewen *(Rebecca Gordon)*; J.C. Roberts *(Benjamin Gordon)*; Kyle Collins *(Ebenezer Age 9, 12)*; Aaron Pearl *(Ebenezer Age 17, 18, 25)*; James Dugan *(Fezziwig)*; Linden Banks *(Simon Scrooge)*; Heather Lee MacCallum *(Mary Scrooge)*; Billy Morton *(Cowboy)*; Brenda Shuttleworth *(Bess)*; Hal Kerbes *(Minister)*; Daniel Libman *(Mr. Hoffman)*; Darcy Dunlop *(Martha)*

EBENEZER, a Wild West version of Dickens's classic *A Christmas Carol,* fails to cast a seasonal spell, mostly because of Jack Palance's cartoonishly virile, one-note interpretation of Scrooge.

Hard-drinking penny-pincher Ebenezer (Jack Palance) cheats cowpoke Sam Benson (Rick Schroder) out of the deed to his homestead in a rigged poker game. Sam can now no longer afford to wed Erica (Amy Locane), the impoverished daughter of Ebenezer's late partner, Jacob Marlowe (Richard Halliday).

Castigated by Jacob Marlowe's ghost, Ebenezer initially believes he's dreaming, as three more ghosts visit him over the course of an evening to reawaken his conscience. The Spirit of Christmas Past (Michelle Thrush) reviews the basis of Ebenezer's mendacity, beginning with his father's financial ruin. Working for kindly storekeeper Mr. Fezziwig (James Dugan), young adult Ebenezer steals a bank deposit to finance panning for gold out West, marries rancher's daughter Rebecca Gordon (Jocelyn Loewen), and greedily sells off his father-in-law's ranch.

The Ghost of Christmas Present (Richard Comar) forces Ebenezer to witness the destitution of Scrooge's former employee Bob Cratchitt (Albert Shultz), whose sickly son Tiny Tim (Joshua Silberg) is expected to die soon. After Sam Benson challenges Ebenezer to a showdown, the Ghost of Christmas Future (Morris Chapdelaine) previews how that gunfight will end in Sam's death. Having seen the repercussions of his actions, Ebenezer makes amends for his penurious ways by returning Sam's land and by giving Erica the saloon he stole from her father. Infused with Christmas charity, he becomes benefactor to the Cratchitt clan.

Aside from the novelty value of Scrooge waving a six-shooter, EBENEZER doesn't have much innate validity. Audiences may initially be intrigued at seeing frontier variations of situations and characters from the beloved Christmas fable. But Palance and the filmmakers give too much forcefulness to Ebenezer, who should be a dried-out human being; because Palance can't tone down his incessant vitality, his inevitable redemption doesn't have any resonance.

Nor do scripter Donald Martin and director Ken Jubenvill capitalize on the film's western trappings, thus making EBENEZER a feeble western in addition to being a feeble Yuletide tale. Inadvertently, this curiosity piece proves the durability of Charles Dickens's *A Christmas Carol* by showing how that classic's impeccable construction can endure even a rather unimaginative sagebrush refurbishment. *(Violence, profanity, substance abuse.)*—R.P.

d, Ken Jubenvill; p, Michael Frislev, Douglas Berquist; exec p, Cindy Lamb, Barbara Ligeti; co-p, Chad Oakes; w, Donald Martin (based on the story "A Christmas Carol" by Charles Dickens); ph, Henry Lebo; ed, Paul Mortimer; m, Bruce Leitl; prod d, Rick Roberts; art d, Tracey Baryski; set d, Penny Chalmers; sound, George Tarrant (mixer); fx, Maurice Routley; cos, Joanne Hansen; makeup, Byron Callaghan, Don Olson; stunts, Tom Eirickson

Western/Drama **(PR: A MPAA: PG)**

EDEN ★½

(U.S., 1998) 106m Eden Street Films; Water Street Pictures ~ Legacy Releasing c

Joanna Going *(Helen Kunen)*; Dylan Walsh *(Bill Kunen)*; Sean Patrick Flanery *(Dave Edgerton)*; Sean Christensen *(Rick)*; Edward O'Blenis Jr. *(Sonny)*; Stephen Lennstrom *(Johnny)*; Annie Michele Price *(Amy)*; David Estrem *(Dean Shays)*; J. Zachary Lenihan *(Isherwood)*; John Aylward *(Dr. Bryson)*; Anne Christianson *(Milly)*; Marjorie Nelson *(Ruth)*; Kevin O'Morris *(Reverend Alden)*; John Billingsley *(Lee)*; Wally Dalton *(Red Fleischer)*; Dennis Troutman *(Parker)*; Bonnie Root *(Lucy Small)*; Tony Doupe *(Officer Stanley)*; Maggie Heffernan *(Janet)*; Anna Faris *(Dithy)*; Caroline Smith *(Nurse)*; Morty Gudelsky *(Teacher)*

Although sensitive in its portrayal of a woman bound by societal constraints, EDEN is too pedestrian a film to stir up much interest in its protagonist's dilemma.

The setting is the prestigious Mt. Eden Academy in the mid-1960s. Helen Kunen (Joanna Going) is a dutiful wife to Bill (Dylan Walsh), an economics teacher at the school. Though Helen is afflicted with multiple sclerosis, she keeps a tidy house and takes proper care of the couple's two small children.

Over a period of nights, Helen begins having out-of-body experiences while sleeping. In a short time, she comes to prefer sleeping to being awake because of the sensation of freedom the experiences give her. She also develops a strong interest in Dave (Sean Patrick Flanery), a nonconformist student who struggles with his studies despite his obvious intelligence. Helen starts to assist Dave with his schoolwork, and the two develop a close friendship.

Helen changes as her experiences become more elaborate. Miraculously, her sclerosis disappears and she's able to walk without a brace. She also becomes less inhibited, but when she reveals to Bill her desire to teach at the academy, he demurs, telling her that she has enough responsibility taking care of a family. Her sclerosis soon reappears, and she begins to deteriorate physically and psychologically.

Dave, meanwhile, has become a successful student. He also remains the lone defender of Helen on campus when everyone else thinks she's losing her sanity. On the advice of her doctor, Helen is hospitalized. She remains stable for a time, but eventually lapses into a coma. While in the coma, she has her most intense out-of-body experiences yet, in which she finds herself traveling over the earth.

When it seems that she will never recover, Bill turns off her respirator at the hospital and returns home. That night, Bill waits to be arrested, but as the police arrive he receives a phone call from the hospital informing him that Helen is alive and out of the coma. In the months that follow, Helen takes a position teaching at the school, and becomes closer than ever to her family.

Writer-director Howard Goldberg has come up with an intriguing dramatic concept: situating an intelligent, reflective woman within a male-dominated setting at the dawn of the counterculture era. It's impossible not to sympathize with Helen, whose intellectual frustration seems especially acute in academic surroundings. Goldberg's realization of his concept, however, is plodding and excessively literal. EDEN is overly dependent on long dialogue exchanges to advance its narrative, and the film employs simplistic symbolism—Helen's leg brace, for example—for dramatic clarification.

Goldberg also relies on stereotyping to define his characters. Aside from Helen, none of the people in EDEN seem authentic. Bill, in his unwillingness to see Helen as anything more than a wife and mother, is a caricature of a chauvinistic male. Bill's foil, Dave, is no less one-dimensional for his understanding of Helen. Dave's rebellious nature is denoted through a Bob Dylan poster he hangs on his wall, and such lines of dialogue as "I'm interested in the soul of my work." The performances of the three leads are no more than serviceable, but it's difficult to see how even the most energetic actor could bring any of these characters to life.

EDEN's prosaic quality extends to its look. The film features static camera work, washed out cinematography, and slack editing. Even the sequences of Helen's out-of-body experiences are surprisingly unimaginative, somewhat imitative of the "space tears" sequence in 2001: A SPACE ODYSSEY (1968), but completely lacking that film's sense of astonishment.

EDEN is particularly disappointing in light of its clever concept, and its compassion for a woman who yearns to find meaningful intellectual expression at a time when such opportunities were severely limited for women. It's ironic that a film about desire should itself be so sedate. *(Sexual situations, profanity.)*—D.C.

d, Howard Goldberg; p, Harvey Kahn, Chip Duncan; exec p, Robert William Landaas; co-p, Todd Hoffman; w, Howard Goldberg; ph, Hubert Taczanowski; ed, Steve Nevius; m, Brad Fiedel; art d, Philip J. Meyer; set d, Rachel Thomson; sound, Douglas Tourtelot (mixer); fx, Gene Warren Jr., Leslie Huntley; casting, Ellie Kanner, Heidi Walker; cos, Elizabeth Kaye; makeup, Rebecca Lynne

Drama **(PR: C MPAA: R)**

EEL, THE ★★★½

(Japan, 1997) 117m Eisei Gekijo Company; Groove Corporation; KSS; Imamura Productions ~ New Yorker Films c
(UNAGI)

Koji Yakusho *(Takuro Yamashita)*; Misa Shimizu *(Keiko Hattori)*; Fujio Tsuneta *(Jiro Nakajima)*; Mitsuko Baisho *(Misako Nakajima)*; Akira Emoto *(Tamotsu Takasaki)*; Sho Aikawa *(Yuji Nozawa)*; Ken Kobayashi *(Masaki Saito)*; Sabu Kawahara *(Seitaro Misato)*; Etsuko Ichihara *(Fumie Hattori)*; Tomoro Taguchi *(Eiji Dojima)*; Sansho Shinsui *(The Doctor - Citizen's Hospital)*; Shoichi Ozawa *(The Doctor - Maternity Hospital)*; Makoto Sato *(Jukichi Takada)*; Teresa Saponangelo; Miho Shimizu

Veteran director Shohei Imamura's first film in eight years and a prize-winner at Cannes in 1997, THE EEL is a simple, unpredictable story of a man's attempt to reestablish himself in society after serving a prison sentence for the murder of his wife.

After eight years in prison for killing his wife when he found her with another man, former office worker Yamashita (Koji Yakusho) is released in the custody of Reverend Nakajima (Fujio Tsuneta), a Buddhist priest who sets him up in business with a barber shop in a remote fishing village. Yamashita brings with him his only confidante—the pet eel he adopted in prison.

Despite his standoffish attitude, Yamashita gradually makes friends with some of the locals. One day he discovers Keiko (Misa Shimizu), who looks like his dead wife, unconscious following a suicide attempt. She is taken in by the priest and his wife (Mitsuko Baisho), who persuade the reluctant Yamashita to hire her as his assistant. Keiko's good looks and friendly behavior draw customers to the barbershop.

Despite her obvious attraction to him, Yamashita avoids a romance with Keiko. Like him, she has a past: She is pregnant by Dojima (Tomoro Taguchi), a married man who has been borrowing money from Keiko's mentally unstable mother (Etsuko Ichihara) in order to prop up his failing business.

After Keiko retrieves her mother's bank book from Dojima's office, he and his henchmen angrily confront her and Yamashita at the barbershop. After a free-for-all fight, the police arrive and arrest Yamashita for violating his parole. Keiko's right to protect her mother's finances is upheld, but Yamashita must return to jail for a year. Yamashita returns his eel to the river. Keiko declares that she and the baby will wait for him.

One of the most important directors of post-war Japanese film, Shohei Imamura has always sought to push back the boundaries of on screen realism in such darkly funny, sometimes savage critiques of post-war Japanese society as PIGS AND BATTLESHIPS (1961), VENGEANCE IS MINE (1979), and BLACK RAIN (1989). Winner of the Palme d'Or at Cannes in 1997, THE EEL is gentler than his earlier works, despite the scenes of extramarital sex and graphic murder in the opening. The story unfolds at a deliberate pace, charting Yamashita's gradual readjustment to society, in beautifully photographed, carefully crafted sequences intended to establish the remote setting and eccentric characters who inhabit the picturesque seacoast town. Those characters are the source of much near-absurdist humor in a film that, as is often the case with Imamura, seems determined not to stay on the same path for too long. American viewers may be puzzled by some of the quirks of Japanese relationships, particularly the indirect manner in which two people in love express their feelings. That aside, THE EEL is a rewarding human drama that's a testament to both Imamura's skill as a storyteller and his cast's ability to elicit sympathy for their characters without resorting to the usual maudlin tricks of the trade. *(Violence, nudity, sexual situations.)*—B.C.

d, Shohei Imamura; p, Hisa Iino; exec p, Kazuyoshi Okuyama; w, Shohei Imamura, Daisuke Tengen, Motofumi Tomikawa (based on the novel *Sparkles in the Darkness* by Akira); ph, Shigeru Komatsubara; ed, Hajime Okayasu; m, Shinichiro Ikebe; prod d, Hisao Inagaki; sound, Kenichi Benitanai

Drama **(PR: C MPAA: NR)**

EIGHTEENTH ANGEL, THE ★★

(U.S., 1998) 88m Rysher Entertainment ~ Rysher Entertainment c

Christopher McDonald *(Hugh Stanton)*; Rachael Leigh Cook *(Lucy Stanton)*; Stanley Tucci *(Todd Stanton)*; Wendy Crewson *(Norah Stanton)*; Maximilian Schell *(Father Simeon)*; Cosimo Fusco *(Florian)*; Venantino Venantini *(Clockmaker)*; Ted Rusoff *(Benedetti)*; Francesca De Sapio *(Gabriella)*; Branislav Tesanovic *(Damiano)*; Enrica Maria Modugno *(Maria Elena)*; Federico Pacifici *(Dark-Eyed Cleric)*; John Crowther *(Mangram)*; Vanessa Crane *(Museum Guide)*; Linda Cerabolini *(Mila Pagano)*; Orso Maria Guerrini; Linda Gucciardo; Fabrizio Vitale *(Customs Agent)*; Rossano Rubicondi *(Model)*; Barbara Birardi *(Model)*; Ennio Coltorti *(Dr. Rinieri)*; Stefano Viali *(Pena)*; Urbano Barberini *(Monk)*; Leonardo Treviglio *(Monk)*; Jim McMullan *(Priest in News Footage)*; Chris Myers *(News Reporter)*; Marino Mase *(Local Doctor)*; Francesca Fanti *(Doctor)*

Writer David Seltzer (THE OMEN) returns to the theme of an underaged Antichrist in THE EIGHTEENTH ANGEL, a bland, brooding horror effort that would have trouble scaring up yawns, much less screams. The film premiered on pay-cable prior to a release on home video.

The Etruscans, a religious order steeped in modern science and led by the devilish Fr. Simeon (Maximilian Schell), prepare for the return of Lucifer as predicted by a 500-year-old astronomical clock. In Boston, Etruscan expert Norah Stanton (Wendy Crewson) meets Simeon and mysteriously commits suicide. Several weeks later, her grieving husband Hugh (Christopher McDonald) and 15-year-old daughter Lucy (Rachael Leigh Cook) travel to Italy so that Lucy can take a modeling job secretly arranged by Simeon. They stay in a chalet near Simeon's monastery.

Within the monastery, controversial geneticist Dr. Benedetti (Ted Rusoff) has created human bodies that have life, but no soul. Simeon reveals he is using the "blanks" as part of the ritual to welcome Lucifer. At the same time, mysterious accidents claim the lives of several children—whom Simeon has dubbed "angels"—whose facial skin is removed and grafted onto the blanks, one of whom Lucifer will inhabit. Hugh begins to connect his wife's death to Simeon and confronts him. Realizing that Lucy is in danger, he races to save her, but she is strangled by the reins of two horses. At the hospital, her brain-dead body is stolen. Hugh races to the monastery where he discovers Lucy among the blanks. He kills two of Simeon's protectors, starts a fire in the process, and races off with Lucy in his arms. Declared dead, Lucy suddenly comes back to life and reveals that she is really an evil blank.

THE OMEN (1976) was an effective terror-tale because of its use of a six-year-old child as the emobodiment of evil. THE EIGHTEENTH ANGEL takes the more common approach of having a pretty teenager stalked by older men. The result is a chaotic mix of unmemorable characters and blunted suspense, despite the presence of an ominous musical score and initially striking visual effects (which soon grow threadbare). Worse yet, the confusing nature of the plot seems to indicate that the film was severely edited.

Seltzer's inventive premise—concerning a Satanic religious order which combines modern science and the supernatural to make the antichrist human—is never fully explored. For instance, it is never entirely clear which bodies in the hospital are blanks and which are the real children. Latter parts of the story pick up the pace, but the ending is a big letdown in which the conflict between Fr. Simeon and Hugh merely fizzles out.

Performances are adequate, with a wild-looking Maximilian Schell hamming it up in the bad-guy role, while McDonald often overdoes his pseudo-heroic role, never really appearing likable or sympathetic. Stanley Tucci, whose small role as Hugh's brother disappears at the end, might have been a better choice to play the father. Cook possesses exceptional beauty and shows great promise, but her talents aren't properly displayed in this role. Special effects are minimal, but the Italian locations do much to provide a menacing atmosphere. *(Violence.)*—P.L.

d, William Bindley; p, William Hart, Douglas Curtis; exec p, Jim Burke, David Seltzer; assoc p, David Turchi; w, David Seltzer; ph, Thomas E. Ackerman; ed, William Hoy; m, Starr Parodi, Jeff Eden Fair; prod d, Stefano Maria Ortolani; art d, Alessandro Alberti; sound, Andrea Petrucci; fx, Germano Natali, Richard Jones; casting, Mary Gail Artz, Barbara Cohen; cos, Ornella Campanale; makeup, Kurtzman, Nicotero and Berger EFX

Group, Inc. (special makeup effects), Luigi Rocchetti; stunts, Artie Malesci, Angelo Ragusa

Horror **(PR: O MPAA: R)**

EL CALLEJON DE LOS MILAGROS

(SEE: MIDAQ ALLEY)

EL CHE: INVESTIGATING A LEGEND ★½

(France/Spain, 1997) 96m Cineteve; Igeldo Komunikazioa ~ White Star c/bw

Ian Marshall *(Narrator)*; Fernando; Oscar Valdovinos; Benigno; Zobeida; Carmen Cordoba; Victor Bordon; Depestre; Fidel Castro; Hildita; Jeannette Habel; Nestor Lavergne; Manolo Perez; Pablo Rivalta; Loyola; Regis Debray; Papito Serguera; Humberto Vasquez; Prado; Nino de Guzman; Juila Cortez

Released directly to American home video in 1998, EL CHE: INVESTIGATING A LEGEND is a French-Spanish coproduction on the life and work of the Latin American revolutionary Ernesto Guevara, comprised of archival film and photos, and interviews with people who knew him. Superficial and poorly made, this documentary sheds little new light on its subject.

In the early 1950s, Ernesto Guevara, son of a privileged Argentine family, left medical school and toured South America by motorcycle. The trip gave Guevara a sense of identity as a Latin American and politicized him through encounters with impoverished and exploited workers. After completing his studies, Guevara went to Mexico City where he met another young man who sought revolutionary change: Fidel Castro. Guevara, now a committed Marxist, joined Castro in his effort to overthrow the corrupt Cuban government. Immediately after the 1959 Cuban revolution, Castro declared Guevara a citizen of Cuba, and Guevara became Castro's chief assistant in setting up the new Cuban state. Policies they adopted aliened the United States but gained the support of the Soviet Union, just as Guevara's fierce dedication and principled approach to revolutionary change won him the support of Cuba's people.

Speaking at an Algerian conference in 1965, however, Guevara criticized Soviet trade policies with Third World countries. His comments damaged his relationship with Castro, and soon after Guevara quietly left Cuba. After spending a short time in the Congo in a failed effort to assist a rebellion there, Guevara went to Bolivia and endeavored to establish a revolutionary army that would sweep through Latin America. In October 1967, the Bolivian military, with American assistance, crushed Guevara's small guerrilla band, and Guevara himself was executed.

EL CHE: INVESTIGATING A LEGEND fails to do justice to its intriguing subject. Director Maurice Dugowson, primarily a fiction film director, takes a by-the-numbers approach to documentary filmmaking, relating Guevara's story by stringing together found imagery, intercutting it with interviews, and overlaying it all with guiding narration. The archival material is EL CHE's best element. The film is abundant in images of Guevara throughout his life, from black-and-white home movies of his boyhood to Bolivian military footage of his shattered corpse. Unfortunately, Dugowson uses portentous, unnecessary voice-over narration to supplement the imagery, such as (when referring to an early meeting between Guevara and Castro), "the pitfalls of power will give their relationship Shakespearean dimensions." Randomly selected library music on the soundtrack is another distraction. (Newsreel footage of Batista's Cuba is accompanied by an instrumental of "Brazil.") The interviews are also problematic. The relationship of many of the interviewees (some of whom are identified exclusively by first name) to Guevara is only tenuously established, and comments are more often anecdotal than informational.

As biography, EL CHE is clumsy. References to Guevara's personal life—his failed first marriage, his lifelong battle with asthma—seem dropped in arbitrarily. Finally, this film never makes clear why Guevara was so ardently embraced by American and European youth after his death. Those interested in researching Guevara are advised to look elsewhere, for EL CHE: INVESTIGATING A LEGEND is hardly worth investigating.—D.C.

d, Maurice Dugowson; p, Fabienne Servan Schreiber, Angel Amigo; exec p, Veronique Rabuteau; w, Maurice Dugowson, Pierre Kalfon (based on the book *CHE: Ernesto Guevara, une legende du siecle* by Kalfon); ph, Federico Ribes, Ricardo Aronovich, Francois Catonne; ed, Joseph Licide; m, Jorge Arriagada; sound, Philippe Sorlin (mixer), Pablo Sanz (recordist), Eric Munch (recordist), Jean-Yves Munch (recordist), Richard Zolfo (recordist)

Documentary **(PR: C MPAA: NR)**

EL DIA DE LA BESTIA

(SEE: DAY OF THE BEAST, THE)

ELIA KAZAN: A DIRECTOR'S JOURNEY ★★★

(U.S., 1995) 75m Lorac Productions ~ Castle Hill c

Elia Kazan; Eli Wallach *(Narrator)*

ELIA KAZAN: A DIRECTOR'S JOURNEY is an entertaining portrait of the great stage and screen director that takes a purely hagiographic approach but features valuable and revealing interview footage with Kazan (shot in 1994) commenting on his films and the legendary performers he's worked with.

Narrator Eli Wallach introduces stills, film clips, and interviews with Kazan to chronicle his career, beginning with his work as an actor and director in the 1930s with the left-wing Group Theatre, through his landmark Broadway productions of *Death of a Salesman* and *A Streetcar Named Desire* in the '40s, and focusing heavily on his feature film career, which includes such classics as ON THE WATERFRONT (1954), the prescient media satire A FACE IN THE CROWD (1957), and the controversial erotic black comedy BABY DOLL (1956). The film also deals with Kazan, who was a former Communist turned staunch anti-Stalinist, testifying before the House Un-American Activities Committee in the early 1950s and naming former Party associates. In 1963, Kazan makes AMERICA, AMERICA, based on his novel about his family's emigration from Turkey to the US, and then only makes three more films after that, but has since written seven novels and an autobiography.

ELIA KAZAN: A DIRECTOR'S JOURNEY was produced by Castle Hill Productions founder Julian Schlossberg, who befriended Kazan in the '80s and acquired the distribution rights to the three films that Kazan owned (BABY DOLL, A FACE IN THE CROWD, and AMERICA, AMERICA). The documentary makes no attempt at objective criticism; rather, it is obviously a loving tribute to Kazan, who was unquestionably a dominant creative force in the American theater of the '40s and '50s, and arguably the most important film director of the 1950s, but whose reputation has suffered because of his "naming names" to HUAC. The film doesn't gloss over this issue, but it definitely puts a positive spin on it, claiming that Kazan was "forced to testify" and that he only gave the committee the names of party members which they already knew. Furthermore, Kazan's vigorous defense of his actions at the time (and still unapologetic stance today) only added fuel to the fire. Because of this, it's now considered to be politically incorrect to praise Kazan, and as Wallach states, "in some quarters, he's never been forgiven"—in

1996, he was denied a Life Achievement award by the LA film critics purely on political grounds (although he was presented with an honorary award for career achievement at the 1999 Oscars).

While it may be impossible for some to separate their feelings about Kazan as a person from his directorial brilliance, his importance as a director cannot be minimized, both in terms of dealing with the post-war era's social issues and most importantly, his profound influence on modern acting styles, manifested in the seminal performances of Marlon Brando and James Dean (though curiously, no mention at all is made in the film about Kazan's cofounding of the Actors Studio or his relationship with fellow Method acting guru Lee Strasberg). Writer-director Richard Schickel takes a reverent and highly selective approach to Kazan's films, but Kazan's own comments and observations about his work are quite candid, revealing how he would utilize psychological tricks and exploit actors' personal problems to elicit such uniquely emotional performances (e.g., getting young Peggy Ann Garner to cry by making her think that her fighter pilot father might be killed during WWII, or encouraging the real-life hate between Dean and Raymond Massey on the set of EAST OF EDEN by letting Dean improvise, which drove Massey crazy).

In the final analysis, Kazan comes off as intelligently combative as ever and certainly won't win over any of his enemies, but when a short list of the artistic giants of the 20th-Century is written, his name will have to be near the top. *(Profanity.)*—M.S.

d, Richard Schickel; p, Julian Schlossberg; assoc p, Doug Freeman; w, Richard Schickel; ph, Edward Maritz; ed, Bryan McKenzie; m, Doug Freeman; set d, Becky Patsch

Documentary **(PR: C MPAA: NR)**

ELIZABETH ★★★

(U.K., 1998) 124m PolyGram; Channel Four Films; Working Title Films ~ Gramercy Pictures c

Cate Blanchett *(Elizabeth I)*; Geoffrey Rush *(Sir Francis Walsingham)*; Christopher Eccleston *(Duke of Norfolk)*; Joseph Fiennes *(Robert Dudley, Earl of Leicester)*; Richard Attenborough *(Sir William Cecil)*; Jamie Foreman *(Earl of Sussex)*; James Frain *(Alvaro de la Quadra)*; Emily Mortimer *(Kat Ashley)*; Kelly Macdonald *(Isabel Knollys)*; Edward Hardwicke *(Earl of Arundel)*; Fanny Ardant *(Mary of Guise)*; Kathy Burke *(Queen Mary Tudor)*; Vincent Cassel *(Duc d'Anjou)*; Daniel Craig *(John Ballard)*; Terence Rigby *(Bishop Gardiner)*; Amanda Ryan *(Lettice Howard)*; Eric Cantona *(Monsieur de Foix)*; Wayne Sleep *(Dance Tutor)*; Angus Deayton *(Waad, Chancellor of the Exchequer)*; Kenny Doughty *(Sir Thomas Elyot)*; Liz Giles *(Female Martyr)*; Rod Culbertson *(Master Ridley)*; Paul Fox *(Male Martyr)*; Peter Stockbridge *(Palace Chamberlain)*; George Yiasoumi *(King Phillip II of Spain)*; Valerie Gale *(Mary's Dwarf)*; Sally Grey; Kate Loustau; Elika Gibbs; Sarah Owen; Lily Allen *(Ladies in Waiting)*; Joe White *(Master of the Tower)*; Matt Andrews *(Norfolk's Man)*; Liam Foley *(Norfolk's Man)*; Ben Frain *(Young French Man)*; Lewis Jones *(Priest)*; Michael Beint *(Bishop Carlisle)*; Hayley Burroughs *(Elizabeth's Dwarf)*; Joseph O'Connor *(Earl of Derby)*; Brendan O'Hea *(Lord William Howard)*; Edward Highmore *(Lord Harewood)*; Daniel Moynihan *(First Bishop)*; Jeremy Hawk *(Second Bishop)*; James Rowe *(Bishop in Cellar)*; Donald Pelmear *(Third Bishop)*; Tim Bevan *(Handsome Man)*; Charles Cartmell *(Dudley's Man)*; Edward Purver *(Dudley's Man)*; Vladimir Vega *(Vatican Cardinal)*; Alfie Allen *(Arundel's Son)*; Daisy Bevan *(Arundel's Daughter)*; Jennifer Lewicki *(Arundel's Nursemaid)*; Viviane Horne *(Arundel's Wife)*; Nick Smallman *(Walsingham's Man)*

No British femme personified the concept of "girl power" quite like Elizabeth I. Due largely to ravishing production design and the lead performance of gifted actress Cate Blanchett, Indian director Shekhar Kapur (1995's THE BANDIT QUEEN) makes vivid life of textbook history in ELIZABETH.

England in the 16th century. The kingdom is split between Catholic and Protestant factions; more powerful neighbors Spain and France see imperial opportunities in the reign of Henry VIII's unhinged daughter Mary (Kathy Burke). When she isn't burning Protestants at the stake, "Bloody" Mary frets over sedition at court, particularly on the part of her Protestant half-sister Elizabeth I (Cate Blanchett). But despite the drastic advice of her advisor, the Earl of Norfolk (Christopher Eccleston), Mary can't bring herself to execute her sibling. Instead, she dies, leaving the bewildered and callow Elizabeth as her successor.

Though she has a surplus of pundits and would-be friends, Elizabeth must survive an assault of questionable advice, including Norfolk's hawkish insistence on a dangerous attack on a French garrison entrenched in Scotland. Her minister, Sir William Cecil (Richard Attenborough), can only foresee England's doom if she fails to find a more powerful husband. The attack leads to a disastrous defeat by the forces of Mary of Guise (Fanny Ardant); Elizabeth's natural caution rightly makes her suspect the motives of her main French suitor, the fey and kinky Duke of Anjou (Vincent Cassel).

To Europe's surprise, however, the young queen painfully but steadily grows into her new job. She correctly perceives the mixed motives of her loving but ambitious paramour, Robert Dudley (Joseph Fiennes), and finds not love but a true ally in Sir Francis Walsingham (Geoffrey Rush). With Walsingham's help, she uncovers a plot between Norfolk, Dudley, and the Pope (Sir John Gielgud) to assassinate her and restore Catholic power. Norfolk subsequently loses his head. With rising confidence, Elizabeth reinvents herself on the beloved but untouchable model of the Virgin Mary. "See, Sir William," she tells Cecil after forcibly retiring him, "I am married after all—to England." She goes on to rule another half-century.

Screenwriter Michael Hirst only partly avoids a common pitfall in this genre: the temptation to portray events and conflicts solely because of their biographical or historical importance, instead of the natural demands of character or plot. When ELIZABETH stays close to its heroine, it largely avoids the schematic, one-thing-after-another logic of other, less successful historical dramas. Toward the last third of the film, however, the Queen seems to become a supporting player in her own increasingly bloody biography. This was scarcely a problem in Kapur's intensely focused BANDIT QUEEN.

The film's virtues are overwhelmingly visual. Cinematographer Remi Adefarasin and production designer John Myhre look to the painterly tradition of Velazquez to create intricate interiors that brim with coarse opulence. The costumes by Alexandra Byrne match the rich standard of many less incisive, couture-and-croissant portrayals of history, yet give an impression that their wearers are a very odd tribe indeed. While some critics observed that director Kapur brings an Indian visual sensibility to Olde Blighty, it's probably more accurate to say that he is in touch with a tradition of monarchial vulgarity once common to Europe and India which is left out of most filmic recreations. The actors are uniformly excellent. Eccleston and Rush deliver fairly one-note performances but look perfect in their roles, the former achieving the lean solemnity of a figure by El Greco. Cate Blanchett (who was nominated for a Best Actress Oscar for her work) is likewise a remarkable presence, finding the ideal balance between the otherworldliness of Tilda Swinton (ORLANDO) and the earthy appeal of Kate Winslet. Hardly rising to a bravura pitch, she manages the tricky task of making a compelling character of someone who was, like her kingdom, largely a work-in-progress. *(Graphic violence, nudity, sexual situations.)* —N.N.

d, Shekhar Kapur; p, Alison Owen, Eric Fellner, Tim Bevan; co-p, Debra Hayward, Liza Chasin; w, Michael Hurst; ph, Remi Adefarasin; ed, Jill Bilcock; m, David Hirschfelder; prod d, John Myhre; art d, Lucy Richardson; set d, Peter Howitt; ch, Sue Lefton; sound, David Stephenson (recordist); fx, George Gibbs; casting, Vanessa Pereira, Simone Ireland; cos, Alexandra Byrne; makeup, Jenny Shircore; stunts, Terry Forrestal

AA Best Makeup: Jenny Shircore; *AAN Best Picture; AAN Best Actress:* Cate Blanchett; *AAN Best Art Direction:* John Myhre, Peter Howitt; *AAN Best Cinematography:* Remi Adefarasin; *AAN Best Costume Design:* Alexandra Byrne; *AAN Best Original Dramatic Score:* David Hirschfelder

Biography/Historical (PR: C MPAA: R)

ELMORE LEONARD'S GOLD COAST ★★½

(U.S., 1997) 109m Paramount Television ~ Viacom c

Marg Helgenberger *(Karen DiCilia)*; David Caruso *(Maguire)*; Jeff Kober *(Roland Crowe)*; Richard Bradford *(Frank DiCilia)*; Barry Primus *(Ed Grossi)*; Wanda De Jesus *(Vivian)*; Melissa Raven *(Marta Diaz)*; Rafael Baez *(Jesus)*; Sherry Stowe *(Real Estate Agent)*; Frederick Weller *(Arnold Rapp)*; Agustin Fernandez *(Lionel)*; Jim Coleman *(Andre Patterson)*; David Andrew Nash *(Grover Patterson)*; Timothy Britten Parker *(Marshall Fine)*; Guillermo Diaz *(Barry)*; Mark Brown *(Kenny)*; Paul Kiernan *(Brad Allen)*; Val Avery *(Jimmy Capp)*; Jeannie Blaylock *(Newscaster)*; Jose Ramirez *(Luis)*; Diana Cruz *(Epifania Cruz)*

Capturing the idiosyncratic flavor of Elmore Leonard's prose, the snappily acted GOLD COAST is a criminal caper that exhibits a firmer handle on its underworld verisimilitude than it does in oiling its suspense mechanism. Unfortunately, by the time every dog has had its day, the film has run out of steam and left its audience clamoring for less. The film, which was produced by Showtime, made its home video debut in 1998.

Even though the death of Florida Mafioso Frank DiCilia (Richard Bradford) came in the arms of another woman, he arranged to keep his widow Karen (Marg Helgenberger) faithful after he was gone. Frank's wiseguy attorney Ed Grossi (Barry Primus) tightly rations Karen's inheritance and hires enforcer Roland Crowe (Jeff Kober) to keep away any fortune hunters who might woo Karen for her money.

Karen's salvation comes in the unlikely form of ex-dolphin trainer Maguire (David Caruso), who shows up to collect payment for a country club heist commissioned by Frank before his death. Instantly smitten with Karen, Maguire agrees to prevent the intimidating Roland from extorting money from Karen. Entrapping and bumping off Grossi in order to obtain control of the DiCilia fortune, Roland also tries to kill Ed's girlfriend/business associate Vivian (Wanda De Jesus) before planting Ed's body in the car trunk of a dope dealer.

After Roland sexually harasses Karen's maid Marta (Melissa Raven), Maguire concocts a scheme in which Marta's brother Jesus (Rafael Baez) will shoot Roland in defense of his sister; Maguire sets his snare by leaking false info about Vivian hiding out at Karen's mansion. In an unforeseen turn of events, Marta panics, and Karen gives her the night off without telling Maguire. Roland comes gunning for Vivian. Instead of finding Vivian at the DiCilia house as he expected, Roland finds himself face-to-face with Maguire, whom he then attacks. Maguire distracts him and saves himself. Karen shoots Roland and pleads self-defense. She rewards Maguire and keeps him out of the homicide investigation, but then abandons him, having never intended to share the DiCilia millions with anyone.

Atmospheric and sneakily plotted, GOLD COAST zips by at a fast clip until all the doublecrosses start backing up like bad plumbing. Elmore Leonard's complicatedly shifting reversals of fortune, which make his novels so compelling, on film eclipse everything else, including the key character relationships. But before the climax grows unwieldy, GOLD COAST offers plenty of ancillary pleasures, including the escalation of Roland's sadistic methods, which begin with tossing a college student off a balcony and culminate in sexually humiliating Marta.

GOLD COAST also succeeds as a boy-beds-girl fable in which a Mafia widow seeks to reattain her innocence in the arms of a reformed thief. As the unlikely lovers, David Caruso and Marg Helgenberger play beautifully off each other, though Helgenberger's performance is hampered by too many scenes that have her in hysterics. Intended to mislead viewers about how tough Karen really is, they have the opposite effect of alerting us that Karen is not above acting weak in order to gain an advantage. But despite its longeurs and strenuous attempts to throw viewers off the trail of an obvious outcome, ELMORE LEONARD'S GOLD COAST is breezy crime-does-pay escapism about a cockeyed world where using people is a favorite pastime. *(Violence, nudity, extreme profanity, sexual situations.)*—R.P.

d, Peter Weller; exec p, Richard Maynard, Jana Sue Memel, Peter Weller; assoc p, Frank "Cat" Ballou; w, Harley Peyton, based on *Gold Coast* by Elmore Leonard; ph, Jacek Laskus; ed, Dean Goodhill; m, Peter Harris; prod d, Maria Caso; art d, Allen Terry; set d, Damon Medlen; sound, Peter Devlin; fx, Ray Bivins; casting, Mary Margiotta, Karen Margiotta; cos, Jacqueline Saint Anne; makeup, Diane Maurno; stunts, Kinnie Gibson

Crime/Action (PR: C MPAA: R)

ELVIS MEETS NIXON ★★★½

(U.S., 1997) 102m Showtime Networks Inc. ~
Avalanche Home Entertainment c

Rick Peters *(Elvis Presley)*; Bob Gunton *(Richard Nixon)*; Alyson Court *(Priscilla)*; Denny Doherty *(Vernon)*; Jackie Burroughs *(Dodger)*; Curtis Armstrong *(Farley Hall)*; Richard Beymer *(Bob Haldeman)*; Gabriel Hogan *(Bobby Bishop)*; Robbi Jay Thuet *(Elvis' Daughter)*; Chistopher Kennedy *(Larry Opper)*; Dan Redican *(Tom Fitzgerald)*; Glenn Hall *(Egil "Bud" Krogh)*; Dick Cavett *(Narrator)*; Edwin Newman; Wayne Newton; Graham Nash; Alexander Butterfield; Tony Curtis

Politics and music purists might find ELVIS MEETS NIXON to be sugar-coated and implausible, but director Allan Arkush's 1997 made-for-cable film works best when viewed strictly as a light comedy.

It's December 1970 and Elvis Presley (Rick Peters) is bored. His hangers-on, the "Memphis Mafia," want some time off from sucking-up duty for the holidays; his father Vernon (Dennis Doherty) and wife Priscilla (Alyson Court) want to curtail his spending habits by putting him on an allowance. Defiant, Elvis leaves Graceland, going out in public without an escort for the first time since the age of 21. The law-and-order junkie intends to fly to Washington DC, meet with government officials and add the badge of Federal agent to the collection of honorary sheriff's titles he's accumulated. The King's journey is circuitous, however, taking him on a picaresque tour through the nation's capital, where he essentially holds up a donut shop at gunpoint, then to San Francisco, where he interacts with hippies and war protestors and realizes that his records are now ensconced in the "oldies" bins.

Ultimately, Elvis makes his way back to DC, gets his Fed title and a bizarre photo opportunity with President Richard Nixon (Bob Gunton). As culturally out of touch as Elvis, Nixon believes that the meeting will "let the kids know that it's groovy to like me!"

While the events of the film are based on reality (the Presley-Nixon meeting and photo really happened—the filmmakers claimed in interviews that the donut-shop incident also did!), Arkush openly exaggerates. The director has fun with ongoing jokes like Elvis's claim to be traveling "incognito" (he uses phony names, but wears a sparkling purple jumpsuit with a cape throughout his trip). Arkush also uses cutaways to documentary-style talking-head interviews with celebrities like Dick Cavett and Tony Curtis, who comment on the action and move the story along, Greek chorus-style. Cavett is particularly humorous in a timeline epilogue that tracks the astonishing simultaneous peaks and valleys of Presley's and Nixon's careers.

Peters is a standout. While the actor looks and sounds enough like the genuine article, he deftly inhabits his role with just the right mixture of bravado and naivete to sell the film's take on the star. Gunton goes for a literal interpretation of Nixon's whacked-out speech impediments and physical tics, which at times sends the Nixon scenes a little over the top tonally, but this is The King's story and Arkush never strays far from his side.

Not intended as a psychedelic period piece nor as a reverent biopic, ELVIS MEETS NIXON is an amusing, and quite odd, addition to the canon of movies about the Elvis phenomenon. *(Profanity, substance abuse.)*—K.W.

d, Allan Arkush; p, Alan Rosen; exec p, Robert O'Connor; w, Alan Rosen; ph, Michael Storey; ed, Neil Mandelberg; m, Larry Brown; prod d, Harold Thrasher; casting, Beth Klein, Susan Forrest; cos, Kei Yano

Comedy **(PR: C MPAA: PG-13)**

EMPEROR'S SHADOW, THE ★★★½

(Hong Kong/China, 1996) 123m Ocean Film Co. Ltd.; Xi'an Film Studio ~ Fox Lorber c

(QIN SONG)

Jiang Wen *(Ying Zheng)*; Ge You *(Gao Jianli)*; Xu Qing *(Ying Yueyang)*; Ge Qingxiang; Di Guoqiang; Wang Ning; Shu Yaoxuan; Li Meng; Yuan Yuan

THE EMPEROR'S SHADOW is Zhou Xiaowen's epic narrative of a forbidden romance, set against the bloody occurrences that brought about the formation of the Chinese Empire in the third century BC. Massively scaled, this period melodrama succeeds in being simultaneously lavish and intimate.

As a boy, Ying Zheng of the Qin state is captured by Yan warriors, and awaits execution. A boy musician, Gao, implores Ying to listen to his music, to keep his mind off his impending doom. Ying's life is spared, however, and he is returned to his homeland. Twenty-six years later, Ying (Jiang Wen) is king of Qin, and on a military campaign to conquer neighboring states and unite China into a single empire. He decides to invade the Yan lands first, in hope of finding Gao (Ge You), and have him compose a national anthem that will stir "the hearts and minds" of the people.

The Qin army routs Yan and Gao is captured, but as he is being brought to Ying, he insults Ying's crippled daughter, Yueyang (Xu Qing), and is branded on the forehead for the offense. Furious at being branded, Gao rebuffs Ying's request and goes on a hunger strike. He is near death when Yueyang coaxes him out of the fast by pledging her devotion. The two then make love, after which Yueyang gains the use of her legs.

Ying is enraged when he learns of the affair, for he has promised Yueyang to his general's son. He forgives Gao, but orders him to compose an anthem, and still insists that Yueyang honor the marriage commitment. Both Gao and Yueyang are resistant, but Gao capitulates when Ying begins slaughtering Yan prisoners. One night, Yueyang comes to Gao and they again make love. This time, they are severely punished. Gao is blinded and Yueyang is branded and forced into the arranged marriage. His conquests completed, Ying sets a date for his coronation. Before being crowned, however, he learns that Yueyang has committed suicide. At the ceremony, Gao attempts to assassinate Ying but is himself killed. As Gao dies, the anthem he composed begins, and Ying proclaims himself the first emperor of China.

Reportedly the most expensive film ever produced in China, THE EMPEROR'S SHADOW is a superior historical epic, one that properly balances size and storytelling. As spectacle, THE EMPEROR'S SHADOW is sensational. The film is filled with sweeping panoramic images of hauntingly barren Chinese landscapes, and the massive crowds of armies that move within them. The large-scale action has been beautifully choreographed and filmed, and is quite captivating. As good as this material is, however, Zhao doesn't present it as an end in itself. Instead, it brackets and emphasizes the film's' dramatic core.

The drama of THE EMPEROR'S SHADOW would be eclipsed by the spectacle were it not for the exquisite screenplay by Lu Wei (the great Chinese scenarist who wrote 1994's TO LIVE and 1993's FAREWELL MY CONCUBINE) and Zhao's intelligent realization of it. The tensions between the three main characters—nationalistic, romantic, filial—are thoroughly and thoughtfully developed, and Lu enriches his script with touches of wry humor. More incisively, he recognizes and highlights the irony of a ruthless tyrant whose zeal for conquest is matched only by his fanatical appreciation of fine music. Zhao handles all of the story's fine detail with deft assurance, and incorporates the spectacle into the narrative so that it complements, rather than competes with, the central drama.

The performances of the three leads are outstanding. Jiang Wen and Ge You, two of China's premiere actors, are excellent, and even filmgoers familiar with their work may be amazed by the range that they display here. Xu Qing is equally good, and Zhao demonstrates, as he did with ERMO (1994), that he is a fine director of actresses. Zhao Jiping's score, although similar to the lovely music he prepared for FAREWELL, MY CONCUBINE and RAISE THE RED LANTERN (1991), is splendid.

THE EMPEROR'S SHADOW isn't perfect. It assumes a knowledge of Chinese history on the part of its audience. It also lacks the larger sense of history—of why the events it dramatizes should resonate with contemporary audiences—that distinguishes such masterworks as FAREWELL MY CONCUBINE or THE LAST EMPEROR (1987). But THE EMPEROR'S SHADOW is a film of many superior qualities. It is lush, engrossing, and terrifically entertaining. *(Violence, nudity, sexual situations, profanity.)*—D.C.

d, Zhou Xiaowen; p, Jimmy Tan, Chen Kunming, Zhang Pimin, Tong Gang, Hu Yuesheng, Cai Huansong; exec p, Ah Gui, Chen Mila; w, Lu Wei; ph, Lu Gengxin; ed, Zhong Furong; m, Zhao Jiping; art d, Cao Jiuping, Duo Guoxiang, Zhang Daqian; sound, Hong Yi

Historical/Drama **(PR: C MPAA: NR)**

ENCOUNTER OF THE SPOOKY KIND ★★½

(Hong Kong, 1980) 98m Golden Harvest ~ Media Asia Distribution Ltd. c

(AKA: SPOOKY ENCOUNTERS)

Sammo Hung, billed as Samo Hung *(Daring Cheung)*; Chung Fat *(Tsui)*; Chan Lung *(Master Chin)*; Wong Har *(Master Tan)*; Lam Ching Ying *(Superintendent)*; Cheung Ti-Hong *(Master Lau)*; Leung Suet Mai *(Cheung's Wife)*; Wu Ma *(Fa Kau)*; To Siu Ming *(Ah Tu)*

A groundbreaking blend of horror, kung fu, and comedy, Sammo Hung's ENCOUNTER OF THE SPOOKY KIND tells the story of a cuckolded husband faced with supernatural attacks. The popular 1980 comedy received its first official US release on home video in 1998.

Master Tan (Wong Har), is having an affair with the wife (Leung Suet Mai) of his employee, "Daring" Cheung (Sammo Hung), who has a reputation for spending nights in haunted temples. When Cheung finds evidence of the affair, Tan decides to have him killed through supernatural means by hiring Master Chin (Chan Lung), a warlock, to cast spells. Chin's stooge, Fa Kau (Wu Ma), tricks Cheung into accepting a dare: Cheung will stay in a haunted temple for two nights. During this time, Master Chin uses his sorcery to revive and manipulate a corpse buried in the temple. Cheung is aided beforehand by Chin's scrupulous brother, Tsui (Chung Fat), who tells him how to survive the night in the temple.

Tan and Chin then contrive to have Cheung framed for the faked murder of his wife and arrested and sentenced to hang by a corrupt superintendent (Lam Ching Ying). Cheung breaks free and flees into the countryside, where he again meets Tsui who gives him the magical training he'll need to join Tsui in launching a counterattack against Chin at his compound. The two sorcerers, Chin and Tsui, battle it out and Cheung takes on the guise of ancient mythical heroes, including the Monkey King, and fights Chin's surrogates, including Tan. The sorcerers wind up killing each other and Cheung's wife emerges from hiding. In response to her false show of affection, the enraged Cheung smacks her.

SPOOKY ENCOUNTERS (the onscreen title of the '98 video release), aka ENCOUNTER OF THE SPOOKY KIND, was an early directorial effort from Sammo Hung, who also stars. Hung (who made his US television debut as star of the CBS series, "Martial Law," in 1998), a longtime partner of Jackie Chan, is a portly kung fu star whose agility and acrobatic skills belie his size. There is a great deal of Chinese supernatural lore on display here, and its clever fusion with martial arts helped pave the way for later, similarly themed works such as Tsui Hark's ZU: WARRIORS OF THE MAGIC MOUNTAIN (1983), Ricky Lau's MR. VAMPIRE (1985), and Hark's A CHINESE GHOST STORY (1987). American audiences seeking to familiarize themselves with Hung's ouevre may wish to begin with such western-friendlier fare as the all-star action comedy MILLIONAIRE'S EXPRESS (1986) and the Vietnam war thriller EASTERN CONDORS (1987).

Though the corpse scenes are pretty gruesome, with heavily made-up decaying bodies in sight, the film does offer exciting special effects and several good fight scenes. *(Violence, sexual situations.)*—B.C.

d, Sammo Hung, billed as Samo Hung; p, Raymond Chow; w, Sammo Hung, Wong Ying; ph, Lee Yao-Tang; ed, Chang Yao-Chung; set d, Mak Woo; cos, Chu Sheng Hsi; stunts, Yuen Biao, Lam Ching Ying, Chan Hui-Ngai

Comedy/Fantasy/Horror **(PR: C MPAA: NR)**

ENEMY ★½

(U.S., 1995) 91m Bullet Hole Productions ~ Maverick Entertainment c

Chole Hopson *(Laura Nemaco)*; Richard Lasky *(Morgan)*; William Moore *(Hadid)*; Veryl Jones *(Daniel Justin)*; Chari Kay *("Boss")*; Robert Ruckstuhl *(Lee)*; Barry Saxon *(White Censor)*; Jonathan Franklin *(Black Censor)*; Morris Everett III; Anthony Washington; Thom Tyler *(Scavengers)*; Tracey Brown; Skjalg Molvaer; Charles T. Hopson

The Ohio filmmakers behind ENEMY deserve credit for trying to tackle an incendiary topic—open racial warfare on American soil. It's a tall order, and the 16mm production staggers under the weight of its own big ideas about prejudice, propaganda, and the media.

Daniel Justin (Veryl Jones), a popular black American presidental frontrunner, is slain in mid-speech by masked gunmen. The incident triggers a virtual second Civil War. As United Nations troops patrol at a distance, all-black and all-white militias tear each other to pieces. Television reporter Laura Nemaco (Chloe Hopson) accompanies a white brigade into battle, armed only with her remote-uplink camera. Straightaway, a firefight kills almost all the bloodthirsty Caucasians and belligerent blacks. Survivor Laura is discovered first by Hadid (William Moore), a black guerilla who speaks in Biblical aphorisms and is offended to learn Laura is actually a light-skinned black. Laura's camera catches Hadid being bushwacked by Morgan (Richard Lasky), a leftover white warrior who later grants Laura terse interviews about his hatred for blacks.

Back at the studio, bureaucratic censors representing both black and white interests squabble over the news transmissions of Hadid vs. Morgan. Everyone is stunned when Hadid, on the verge of bashing his enemy with a steel pipe, spares Morgan's life instead. This inspires a temporary cease-fire, but general hostilities soon resume. Laura discovers Morgan was actually a Daniel Justin supporter who personally witnessed the assassination—and believes the shooters were militant and power-hungry African-Americans who opposed Justin's conciliatory tone. When Morgan confronts Hadid a second time, now with a gun, the angry white male refuses to fire. The gesture, widely broadcast despite the censors, ends the race war for good.

Reducing a momentous war down to just two combatants is a familiar movie gimmick (perhaps done to best effect in John Boorman's 1968 WWII drama HELL IN THE PACIFIC) that not only saves money but invites a lot of pretentious allegory. Both of these aspects are in abundant evidence in ENEMY. Shot with some visual panache on a shoestring budget in the industrial valley of Cleveland, Ohio, and neighboring Lorain, ENEMY avoids any costly crowd shots, and the sets for the offices of Laura's "World News Network'" are laughably skimpy. What really hurts, however, are the awkward dialogue exchanges that make this ultimate societal nightmare seem more like a moralizing community-theatre play. For example, Morgan's monosyllabic explanation for his antipathy toward blacks: "Because they're different." While it's commendable that the regional filmmakers (producer-actor Lasky was a former Cleveland Police Officer) didn't go for straight action-exploitation—when Chloe takes a long, lyrical shower in the ruins, she modestly keeps her bra and panties on. But their ambitions far outstrip their ability to depict a powder-keg premise that even most Hollywood schlockmeisters wouldn't have dared confront head-on.

Despite the simplification, one notion that hits home is a comparison between the script's fictional American race war and the ethnic skirmishes in Eastern Europe that dominated the evening news in the 1990s. "Let them kill each other off, just like Yugoslavia," says one character. "Then we'll take the survivors out." Completed in 1995, ENEMY had to wait until 1998 for a low-level video distributor to give it a nationwide relase. *(Violence, adult situations, profanity.)*—C.C.

d, Bruce Pattison; p, Richard Lasky; exec p, Rick Trend, Don Trend; w, Bruce Pattison, Richard Lasky; ph, William Johns; ed, Skjolg Molvaer; m, David Drotis, Andrew Stolz; sound, Tracey Wright; fx, William Johns; cos, P.J. McDonald; makeup, Dan Crumloff, Mike "Boots" Taylor

Action/Political/Thriller **(PR: C MPAA: R)**

ENEMY OF THE STATE ★★★½

(U.S., 1998) 128m Scott Free; Jerry Bruckheimer Films; Touchstone Pictures ~ Buena Vista c

Will Smith *(Robert Clayton Dean)*; Gene Hackman *(Brill)*; Jon Voight *(Thomas Brian Reynolds)*; Lisa Bonet *(Rachel Banks)*; Regina King *(Carla Dean)*; Stuart Wilson *(Congressman Albert)*; Laura Cayouette *(Christa Hawkins)*; Loren Dean *(Hicks)*; Barry Pepper *(Pratt)*; Ian Hart *(Bingham)*; Jake Busey *(Krug)*; Scott Caan *(Jones)*; Jason Lee *(Zavitz)*; Gabriel Byrne *("Brill")*; James LeGros *(Jerry Miller)*; Dan Butler *(Shaffer)*; Jason Robards Jr. *(Senator Hammersly)*; Jack Black *(Fielder)*; Seth Green; Jamie Kennedy *(Jamie)*; Tom Sizemore *(Pintero)*; Philip Baker Hall; Bodhi Pine Elfman *(Van)*; Jacob Chambers *(Davis)*; Alexandra Balahoutis *(Martha)*; Anna Gunn *(Emily Reynolds)*; Jascha Washington *(Eric Dean)*; Rebecca Silva *(Marie the Nanny)*; Bobby Borriello *(Dylan)*; Carl Mergenthaler *(Mike—Law Firm)*; Mattias Kraemer *(Gas Station Cashier)*; Lillo Brancato *(Young Worker)*; John Capodice *(Older Worker #1)*; Vic Manni *(Vic—Old Mobster)*; T.R. Richards *(Cook)*; Ivana Milavich *(Ruby's Sales Clerk)*; Patsy Grady Abrams *(Accident Bystander)*; Beatriz Mayoral *(Reynold's Nanny)*; Kasey Lynn Quinn *(Reynold's Daughter)*; Elizabeth Berman *(Ruthie)*; Donna Scott *(Jenny)*; Allison Sie *(Hotel Desk Clerk)*; Mike Andolini *(Sal)*; Arthur Nascarella *(Frankie)*; Grant Heslov *(Lenny)*; John Cenatiempo *(Young Mobster #1)*; Joyce Flick Wendl *(Waitress)*; Frank Medrano *(Bartender)*; Dennis S. Fahey *(Cop with Ambulance)*; Albert Wong *(Mr. Wu)*; Christopher B. Lawrence *(Paramedic)*; John Haynes Walker *(Fireman #1)*; Joseph Patrick Kelly *(Fireman #2)*; Lennox Brown *(Tunnel Maintenance Worker)*; Martin Bosworth *(Bike Messenger)*; Nancy Yee *(Mrs. Wu)*; Troy Anthony Cephers *(ANA Hotel Security)*; Carlos Gomez *(FBI Agent)*; Arnie Alpert *(Robert Gersicoff)*; Greg Collins *(FBI Supervisor)*; Doug Roberts *(Hijacked Car Driver)*; Larry King *(Himself)*; Warren Olney *(TV Anchor #1)*; Penny Griego *(TV Anchor #2)*; Rhonda Overby *(Field Reporter #1)*; Eric Keung *(Mambo Kitchen Worker #1)*; David Han *(Mambo Kitchen Worker #2)*; Mandy Kriss *(Reporter #1)*; Noel Werking *(Reporter #2)*; Sam De Crispino *(Reporter #3)*; Wayne A. Larrivey *(Doorman)*; Mandy Kriss *(Field Reporter #1)*; Lille Shaw Hamer *(Field Reporter #2)*; Brenna McDonough *(Field Reporter #3)*; Callison Slater *(Child #1)*; Colin Brodie *(Child #2)*; Daniel Cano *(Hallway Lawyer)*; Joy Ehrlich *(Mom in Diner)*; Eric Olson *(Aide #1)*; Thomas Troy *(Aide #2)*; Adam Karkowsky *(Aide #3)*; Steve Uhrig *(Electronic Store Employee)*; Robyn Killian *(Model #1)*; Laura Eizenia *(Model #2)*; Angelica Pamintuan *(Model #3)*; Vene Arcoraci *(Model #4)*; Charlie Curtis *(Model #5)*; Raichle Watt *(Becky)*; Michael J. Walker *(Union Official)*; Jacklilynn Ward *(Pintero's Sister)*; Jason Welch *(Pintero's Kid #1)*; Joshua Ward *(Pintero's Kid #2)*; Pete Suton *(Dean House Cop)*; Thomas M. Quinn *(Tunnel Technician)*; Robert O'Rourke *(FBI Observer #1)*; John Allendorfer *(FBI Observer #2)*; Henry Sandler *(FBI Observer #3)*; Chris Holt *(Himself)*

As if there weren't enough paranoia already, in this pre-millennial age of cyber-snooping, electronic surveillance in banks, stores, public parks (and who knows where else), and proposed DNA "fingerprinting," now director Tony Scott serves up ENEMY OF THE STATE, a taut techno-thriller in which the government not only *can* invade our private lives, but does so on a regular basis, and requires little provocation to turn our secrets against us.

It is in the interest of the National Security Agency that a bill pass allowing the government to secretly monitor the public via video and audio taps. In order to prevent a Senator (Jason Robards) from casting his influential vote against the bill, NSA official Thomas Brian Reynolds (Jon Voight) kills the Senator before he can vote, making it look like an accident. However, the murder is caught on videotape by a naturalist's camera; on the run from NSA agents desperate to retrieve the tape, the naturalist (Jason Lee) manages to secret a copy of the video into a shopping bag belonging to attorney Robert Dean (Will Smith). Though he still doesn't know he has the video, Dean becomes the victim of a comprehensive character assassination, orchestrated by the NSA to pre-discredit him as a witness should he ever release the video.

Using a barrage of high-tech surveillance equipment, the NSA monitors Dean's activity, using recordings and misrepresented photographs to implicate him in mob activity and an extramarital affair with an ex-girlfriend, private investigator, Rachel Banks (Lisa Bonet). With his life collapsing around him, Dean seeks the help of Rachel's uber-paranoid contact, Brill (Gene Hackman), a former NSA man who now does freelance surveillance. They locate the murder video and, employing many of the same gizmos as the NSA, Brill and Dean implicate Reynolds in the bugging of a congressman's hotel room; now with leverage of their own, they bargain with the NSA—the video for the restoration of Dean's life. Knowing the NSA won't play fair, Brill and Dean lure the agents into a FBI-monitored mob den. A miscommunication leads to a firefight, and both the mob and NSA guys are gunned down, with the FBI rushing in to rescue Dean. Using the NSA's stash of recordings, Dean clears his name, while Brill slips silently into anonymity.

ENEMY OF THE STATE is a blue-blooded descendant of Francis Ford Coppola's terrific suspense thriller, THE CONVERSATION (1974); in fact, one scene, in which multiple NSA agents record Dean and Rachel talking in a park, is almost a literal recreation of the key scene in Coppola's film. The casting of Gene Hackman as the crusty ex-agent Brill is therefore almost a prerequisite for the film's success, as Brill is the natural evolution of THE CONVERSATION's Harry Caul, right down to his wire-cage headquarters. Without Brill, ENEMY OF THE STATE would just be *The Net, Part 2*.

But ENEMY OF THE STATE goes farther than THE CONVERSATION, assuming that people's credit card transactions and cellular phone conversations are already free for the taking, as long as you have the right hardware. With all its hidden cameras, micro-transmitters, and satellite trackers, ENEMY OF THE STATE could easily start to sound like a Radio Shack catalog read aloud. Writer David Marconi does an excellent job of conveying the raft of high-tech gadgets without getting bogged down (after all, most people already assume the government is sticking its nose in their business). Director Tony Scott relies instead on the tried-and-true chase formula, running Dean all over the city until (in a perfectly timed entrance) he meets Brill, giving him the chance to do some chasing of his own.

In addition to first-rate performances by Hackman and Will Smith, ENEMY OF THE STATE is benefitted by a host of character actors and big-name cameos, including Jake Busey and Jack Black, and uncredited roles by Jason Robards, Tom Sizemore, and "Buffy the Vampire Slayer"'s Seth Green. *(Violence, profanity.)*—B.T.

d, Tony Scott; p, Jerry Bruckheimer; exec p, Chad Oman, James W. Skotchdopole, Andrew Davis; w, David Marconi; ph, Dan

Mindel; ed, Chris Lebenzon; m, Trevor Rabin, Harry Gregson-Williams; prod d, Benjamin Fernandez; art d, James J. Murakami, Jennifer A. Davis, Donald B. Woodruff; set d, Garrett Lewis; sound, Bill Kaplan (mixer); fx, The Mill; casting, Victoria Thomas; cos, Marlene Stewart; makeup, Ellen Wong; stunts, Charles Picerni Picerni

Action/Thriller **(PR: C MPAA: R)**

ERNEST IN THE ARMY ★★

(U.S., 1998) 85m ACTIVE Entertainment ~ Investec Bank Ltd c

Jim Varney *(Ernest P. Worrell)*; Hayley Tyson *(Cindy Swanson)*; David Muller *(Colonel Gullet)*; Jeffrey Pillars *(General Rodney Allen)*; Christo Davids *(Ben Ali)*; Duke Ernsberger *(Barnes)*; Ivan Lucas *(Sheik Omar Tufuti)*; Peter Butler *(Ali Tenbu)*; Farouk Valley Omar *(Kibee)*; Amanda Wilson *(Pretty Woman)*; Tony Hawes *(Mr. Beetleman)*; Gavin Barfield *(News Anchor)*; David Trengrove *(Blostrand)*; Jeff Shapiro *(Comrade Blatz)*; Gordon Van Rooyen *(Ambassador)*; Zeno Rossouw *(Local Boy)*; Robert Foster *(Chuck)*; Josh Cherry *(Corporal Davis)*

The wacky misadventures of America's favorite goof-off, Ernest P. Worrell, continue with this professionally polished but comedically uninspired entry. Although the Army seems like an ideal arena for Ernest's exploits, the film founders on heavy-handed narration, plodding direction, and overly familiar slapstick gags.

Hoping to serve his country and score with women, Ernest P. Worrell (Jim Varney) joins the Army Reserves. While Ernest plays weekend soldier in America, Sheik Omar Tufuti (Ivan Lucas), ruler of Arizia, threatens his neighbors in the Middle East and world peace with a recently built plutonium bomb. To defuse this volatile situation, the United Nations Security Council sanctions an invasion to be headed by Colonel Gullet (David Muller), who harbors a secret agenda.

Surprisingly, Ernest's reserve unit is selected by Colonel Gullet to serve as a support team for the American troops. Concerned with his own publicity, the reserve unit's leader, General Rodney Allen (Jeffrey Pillars) welcomes the upcoming invasion as a photo-opportunity. Also tagging along on the mission is TV newscaster Cindy Swanson (Hayley Tyson).

Secretly in league with Sheik Tufuti, Colonel Gullet facilitates the kidnapping of Cindy for the Sheik's propaganda purposes. Befriended by a desert urchin named Ben Ali (Christo Davids), Ernest tracks Cindy to the Sheik's tent and rescues her. As Ernest and Cindy flee, the Sheik doublecrosses Colonel Gullet and ties him to the plutonium bomb. With Ben Ali's assistance, Ernest and Cindy hijack the vehicle transporting the P-bomb rocket. Fending off Tufuti's brigade while navigating a mine field, Ernest neutralizes the bomb's timer; the rocket-bomb then detonates with a sputter. The Mideast stalemate ends with General Allen declaring Ernest an American hero.

Technically, ERNEST IN THE ARMY stands head and shoulders above previous Ernest endeavors. But the comedic heart of the film's creative personnel beats weakly in this run-of-the mill product. Too many plot elements (e.g., Tufuti's megalomaniacal antics, General Allen's hogging the spotlight, Colonel Gullet's spyjinks) don't directly involve Ernest. For an Ernest flick to succeed on its own limited terms, the Ernest character must be featured front and center.

Non-fans may be relieved that there is less of Jim Varney's patented mugging, but then, non-fans aren't likely to watch this in the first place. This showcase for buffoonery is hobbled by an unimaginative attempt to parody military adventure films; its few potentially funny moments are misdirected or miscalculated. A few slapstick nuggets involving Ernest's basic training are all that save this series entry for enthusiasts. *(Violence.)*—R.P.

d, John Cherry; p, John Cherry, Kenneth Badish; assoc p, Ken Holloway; w, Jeffrey Pillars, Joseph Dattore; ph, James Robb; ed, Craig Bassett, Virgilo da Silva; m, Mark Adler; prod d, Chris August; art d, Josh Cherry; set d, Neil Swanepoll; sound, Mark Phillips; fx, Max Poolman; casting, Anna Feyder; cos, Yvonne de Necker; stunts, Cecil Carter

Comedy/Action **(PR: AA MPAA: PG)**

ESCAPE, THE ★½

(Canada, 1994) 92m TPA; Pacific Motion Pictures ~ MGM/UA Home Video c

Patrick Dempsey *(Charles Jacob Clayton)*; Brigitte Bako *(Sarah)*; Colm Feore *(Hickman)*; Vincent Gale *(Newby)*; W. Morgan Sheppard *(Duncan Long)*; Nathaniel Deveaux *(Moses)*; Gouchy Boy *(Pooch)*; John Aylward *(Sherriff)*; Jason Gray-Stanford; J.B. Bivens; Alfred E. Humphreys; Zook Matthews

Bearing a 1994 copyright, this rainsoaked misfit seeped onto home video four years later, after premiering on The Movie Channel.

At a prison work detail in Louisiana, one convict has had enough of sadistic chief guard Hickman (Colm Feore). The prisoner runs, and Hickman happily shoots him dead, but in the confusion a second man, Charles Clayton (Patrick Dempsey), sees his chance and bolts as well, killing a guard to hijack the prison bus. Hickman initiates a dragnet, but Clayton hops a train and winds up in part of the Mississippi delta pounded by torrential rains. The fugitive shelters in a vacant cabin and rescues nubile cellist Sarah (Brigitte Bako) after her car goes into the adjacent river. When Clayton forcibly restrains Sarah from signaling an evacuation helicopter, the girl figures out her savior is a shady type, but she doesn't realize his true nature, until he speaks about his humble origins as the bastard son of a footloose jazzman, and his plan to open a nightclub devoted to spoken-word performances.

Back in prison, Clayton's literary side is commemorated by respectful inmates in a lifer poetry-writing program, presided over by volunteer scholar Duncan Long (W. Morgan Sheppard). Finally Clayton tells the whole truth to Sarah, including the crime that put him away—murdering two drug thugs who turned on him in a dope deal. Still, Sarah makes blissful love to the convict, but in the morning he steals away as she sleeps. Troopers corner Clayton at a dam, and a sympathetic sheriff brings Sarah to talk her lover into a peaceful surrender. But vengeful Hickman descends via helicopter, spouting Clayton's poetry while gunning for the escapee. A wounded Clayton takes a suicidal plunge into the reservoir. Dying, he envisions Sarah in his nightclub, "The Cage."

After a breathless opening and situations that strongly echo THE FUGITIVE (1993), THE ESCAPE can be granted some minor points for not going the predictable, derivative action-adventure route. Alas, what it does mutate into is an unworkable melodrama of jazz, jail, poetry, passion, and precipitation in profusion, the latter all the better to show off ingenue Bako as the ideal foul-weather fantasy date, wetted to the skin in skimpy clothing. It's a bit of a surprise to learn that Dempsey's character is indeed guilty of something (99 per cent of Hollywood convicts having been framed, of course, and the worse their sentences the more innocent they are), but the way the script canonizes its hard-timer hero as a genius poet, cellblock Gandhi and, ultimately, romantic martyr seems more than a little patronizing and heavy-handed. A dearth of Louisiana accents confirms THE ESCAPE's origins, shot entirely in British Columbia. The film acknowledges the cooperation of the State of California Prison Writing Program, and the script borrows lockup verses from Breeze Todd Allan Drange, Ef Jackson, John Thomas, and John Clare. *(Violence, nudity, sexual situations, adult situations, extreme profanity, substance abuse.)*— C.C.

d, Stuart Gilliard; p, Tom Rowe, George Horie; exec p, Frank Mancusco Jr., Michael Sheehy; w, Scott Busby; ph, Tobias Schliessler; ed, Rick Martin; m, Loek Dikker; prod d, Michael Joy; art d, Bob Bottieri; sound, Jacqueline Cristianini; fx, John Gajdecki; casting, Mary Jo Slater, Steve Brooksbank; stunts, Danny Virtue

Romance/Prison/Thriller (PR: O MPAA: NR)

EVER AFTER ★★½

(U.S., 1998) 121m 20th Century Fox ~ 20th Century Fox c

Drew Barrymore *(Danielle)*; Anjelica Huston *(Baroness Rodmilla)*; Dougray Scott *(Prince Henry)*; Jeanne Moreau *(Grande Dame)*; Jeroen Krabbe *(Auguste)*; Patrick Godfrey *(Leonardo da Vinci)*; Megan Dodds *(Marguerite)*; Melanie Lynskey *(Jacqueline)*; Timothy West *(King Francis)*; Judy Parfitt *(Queen Marie)*; Richard O'Brien *(Pierre Le Pieu)*; Lee Ingley *(Gustave)*; Kate Lansbury *(Paulette)*; Matyelok Gibbs *(Louise)*; Walter Sparrow *(Maurice)*; Anna Maguire *(Young Danielle)*; Peter Gunn *(Captain Laurent)*; Joerg Stadler *(Wilhelm Grimm)*; Andrew Henderson *(Jacob Grimm)*; Toby Jones *(Royal Page)*; Virginia Garcia *(Princess Gertrude)*; Al Hunter Ashton *(Cargomaster)*; Mark Lewis *(Gypsy Leader)*; Howard Attfield *(Jeweller)*; Ricki Cuttell *(Young Gustave)*; Ricardo Cruz *(Cracked Skull)*; John Walters *(Butler)*; Elizabeth Earl *(Young Marguerite)*; Alex Pooley *(Young Jacqueline)*; Janet Henfrey *(Celeste)*; Ursula Jones *(Isabella)*; Amanda Walker *(Old Noblewoman)*; Rupam Maxwell *(Marquis de Limonges)*; Tony Doyle *(Driver of Royal Carriage)*; Christian Marc *(King of Spain)*; Elvira Stevenson *(Queen of Spain)*; Erick Awanzino *(Short Bald Man)*; Susan Field *(Laundry Supervisor)*; Francois Velter *(Choirman)*; Dominic Rold *(Choirman)*; Jean-Pierre Mazieres *(Cardinal)*

Feminism replaces fantasy in EVER AFTER, a version of "Cinderella" pitched rather tenuously between juvenile and adult entertainment. Shot in and around a series of extraordinary medieval chateaus in rural France, the film is lavish and often likable but overly talky and unconscionably long.

A queen (Jeanne Moreau) tells the Grimm brothers (Joerg Stadler and Andrew Henderson) the *true* story of Cinderella, her great-great-grandmother: Soon after acquiring a stepmother (Anjelica Huston), little Danielle (Anna Maguire) is orphaned by the death of her father (Jeroen Krabbe). Ten years later, Danielle (Drew Barrymore) has become virtually a handservant to her stepmother, Rodmilla, and two stepsisters, nasty Marguerite (Megan Dodds) and flighty Jacqueline (Melanie Lynskey). When Danielle encounters Henry (Dougray Scott), the Crown Prince of France, playing hooky from his official duties, he bribes her to keep mum. She uses the money to infiltrate the royal court and buy back the old family servant (Walter Sparrow) that her selfish stepmother has sold. There she reencounters Henry, who thinks she is a countess.

Smitten with the beautiful young "countess," the prince rendezvouses with her on several occasions. Meanwhile, he promises his parents, King Francis (Timothy West) and Queen Marie (Judy Parfitt), that he will choose a bride at a forthcoming masked ball. Rodmilla, who wants the prince to pick Marguerite as his betrothed, surmises Danielle's imposture and tells the Queen that the girl is engaged. When this lie is relayed to Henry, he becomes very angry. At the ball, Danielle discloses to the Prince that although she is not engaged, she is not a countess.

Still angry at Danielle, the Prince agrees to an arranged marriage with Princess Gertrude of Spain (Virginia Garcia) but backs out at the last minute and rides forth to rescue Danielle, his true beloved, from Le Pieu (Richard O'Brien), a lecherous merchant who has purchased her from Rodmilla. When Henry arrives, he discovers that the spunky girl has already engineered her own escape. Danielle and the Prince marry and live happily ever after. Jacqueline finds a mate, while Rodmilla and Marguerite are sentenced to a lifetime of servitude.

Photographed "in the middle of Nowhere, France," according to Drew Barrymore, EVER AFTER boasts scenic wide-screen exteriors and lush interiors that do full justice to the classic tale of Cinderella. But in the process of revising the story to conform to 1998 notions of romance, femininity, and realism, much of the original tale's magic has been lost. Parents are herein advised not to take their children to see this defantasized Cinderella unless they are prepared to explain why, after everyone has waited 90 minutes for the night of the masked ball to arrive, it arrives minus the fairy godmother and miraculous transformations. (EVER AFTER does retain the unexpendable glass slipper, but only as a meaningless memento; its original narrative function has been jettisoned.) If, however, EVER AFTER was meant as a "Cinderella" for grownups, it should have been scarier and steamier. As is, it's unlikely to fully gratify viewers of any age. Director Andy Tennant said he decided to make "a very different" version of "Cinderella" because "I did not want my daughters growing up believing you have to marry a rich guy with a big house in order to live happily ever after." If so, why does his movie end with its heroine marrying a rich guy with a big house and living happily ever after?

In the process of demythologizing "Cinderella" the filmmakers have also, unfortunately, deglamorized Barrymore, whose fresh, natural beauty deserved more enhancement than EVER AFTER's cinematography and makeup departments were willing to give her. Blessed, like her contemporary Sandra Bullock, with a very endearing personality mix of warmth, mischievousness, and sexiness, Barrymore can be wonderful playing American girls but is a bit outside her power zone here. EVER AFTER is rational, reassuring, progressive, healthy, and benign—everything a fairy tale shouldn't be. It is also sweet, engaging, and enjoyable—unless you're expecting "Cinderella." *(Violence.)*—D.T.

d, Andy Tennant; p, Mireille Soria, Tracey Trench; assoc p, Melissa Cobb; co-p, Kevin Reidy, Timothy M. Bourne; w, Susannah Grant, Andy Tennant, Rick Parks; ph, Andrew Dunn; ed, Roger Bondelli; m, George Fenton; prod d, Michael Howells; art d, Martyn John, Damien LaFranchi, Stephen Dobric; set d, Judy Farr; sound, Simon Kaye (mixer); fx, Alan Senior, John Clark; casting, Priscilla John, Lucinda Syson; cos, Jenny Beavan; makeup, Belinda Hodson; stunts, Graeme Crowther

Romance/Historical (PR: A MPAA: PG-13)

FACE DOWN ★★½

(U.S., 1997) 107m Eberhardt; Weisberg Productions ~ Showtime c

Joe Mantegna *(Bob Signorelli)*; Kelli Maroney *(Merre Lake)*; Peter Riegert *(Lt. Coop)*; Cameron Thor *(Curtis Lowell)*; Adam Ant *(Derek Fry)*; J.K. Simmons *(Herb Aames)*; Kent Staines *(Jacob)*; Shannon Lawson *(Emily Jones)*; Diana Reis *(Connie)*; Eugene Clark *(Capt. McGuinness)*; Richard Sali *(Artie)*; Gary McMillan *(Gary Ritter)*; Jesse Mainprize *(Dr. Pilch)*; Steve Cumyn *(Charles)*; Alex Karzis *(Parker Frager)*; Phillip Jarrett *(Albert)*; Darlene Mignacio *(Brooke Aames)*; Trish Lindstrom *(Girl)*; Alan Peterson *(Transit Cop)*; Shane Daly *(Vince)*; Mark Lutz *(Dupree)*; Chrisopher Crumb *(Blind Man)*; Becky Cheng *(Chinese Girl)*; Scott Wickware *(Randy)*; Beatriz Pizano *(Esperanza)*; David Mason *(Porno Partner)*; Michael Kazarian *(2nd Porno Guy)*

FACE DOWN is an entertaining made-for-cable mystery with vibrant characterizations, flavorful Manhattan backgrounds, and snappy dialogue. On the downside, the gears of its plot grind rather loudly, wasting too much energy trying to mislead the audience.

Ex-cop Bob Signorelli (Joe Mantegna) lost not only his job but the respect of his former partner Lt. Coop (Peter Riegert) when he bungled a robbery/hostage situation. Now working as a private investigator, he similarly annoys his new partner Herb Aames (J.K. Simmons) by falling for beautiful but schizophrenic Merre Lake (Kelli Maroney). A receptionist for art gallery owner Derek Fry (Adam Ant), she is a suspect in the murder of sleazy lawyer Cascio, to whom Fry owed money. Signorelli's investigation leads him to believe that Cascio could have been killed by a crooked cop hired by Fry. Replacing Signorelli on the investigation into Merre's activities, P.I. Aames meets with Merre, and is mistakenly shot to death by the same person who killed Cascio. Hounded by Coop and his ambitious new partner Curtis Lowell (Cameron Thor), Signorelli is linked by the police to the fugitive Merre who guiltily fled the Aames murder scene. Meanwhile, an internal affairs investigation targets the officers at Signorelli's old precinct. Signorelli locates Merre at a dive and forces her back on her schizophrenia medication at his apartment. After comparing her new prescription with capsules found at Merre's home, Signorelli discovers her pills had been tampered with. Fry's assistant Jacob (Kent Staines) admits handing over Merre's medicine bottle to Fry, thus suggesting that Fry has indeed been framing Merre for the murders committed by his crooked-cop assassin.

After Signorelli becomes a suspect in the murder of Jacob, whose body is found in his car, Signorelli receives vital info from his detective agency secretary, whose computer links Fry to Coop's precinct through phone records. While fleeing from Signorelli, Fry is hit by a car. Teaming up with Coop, Signorelli is too late to prevent the kidnapping of Merre by Fry's accomplice—Lowell. Bent cop Lowell tries to kill Merre on the subway tracks while making it look like suicide. When Coop shoots Lowell down, gunfire short circuits the subway car before it can hit perennially victimized Merre.

Strands of illogic aside, FACE DOWN is a moderately intriguing mystery. If only it didn't sweat and strain while trying not to tip its hand about Curtis Lowell's guilt. A lot of time is also wasted in setting up Merre's illness as a link in her possible crime involvement. A slicker screenwriter might have intertwined these schools of red herrings with a little more finesse. Another faux pas is the regrettable treatment of Merre, whose character is cavalierly written as a blonde bimbo who turns into a femme fatale under controlled medication.

F

The filmmakers seem to want to have their cheesecake and eat it too, all at the expense of a vulnerable heroine. Luckily, Kelli Maroney weathers these tricky transformations with a combination of acting chutzpah and sheer beauty. As the seedy gumshoe redeemed by the love of a split personality, Joe Mantegna matches Maroney's acting bravado. With less exploitative handling of the leading lady and nimbler clue placement, FACE DOWN might have been first-rate, instead of a merely above-average puzzler. *(Graphic violence, extreme profanity, sexual situations, substance abuse.)*—R.P.

d, Thom Eberhardt; p, Roni Weisberg; w, Thom Eberhardt; ph, John Holosko; ed, Carl Graham; m, Gunther Schuller, Joe Lovano; prod d, Anthony Greco; art d, Rob Gray; set d, Megan Less; sound, Stuart French; fx, Brock Jolliffe; casting, Beth Klein; cos, Vicki Graef; makeup, Lynda McCormack; stunts, Shane Cardwell

Crime/Mystery (PR: C MPAA: R)

FACE THE EVIL ★★

(U.S., 1998) 92m Norstar Entertainment Inc; Peter R. Simpson Production ~ A-Pix Entertainment c

Lance Henriksen *(Dangler)*; Shannon Tweed *(Sharon)*; Bruce Payne *(Jack)*; Jayne Heitmeyer *(Bobbi)*; Jeffrey Max Nicholls *(Steven Ivory)*; Joseph Griffin *(Reggie)*; David Keeley *(Ritter)*; Kevin Jubinville *(Falco)*; Sky Gilbert *(Beagle)*; Fiona Highet *(Lisette)*; Barbara Chilcott *(Mrs. Holman)*; Falconer Abraham *(Jervis)*; Hamish McEwan *(Binsey)*; Sophie Simmons *(Little Girl Rose)*; Thomas Chang *(Kidnapper)*; Simon Kim *(Asian Fighter #1)*; James Kim *(Asian Fighter #2)*

Shannon Tweed moves away from her softcore roots for this straightforward, straight-to-video actioner that is designed as a female twist on DIE HARD (1988).

Actress Sharon (Shannon Tweed) is shooting a movie with her director Jack (Bruce Payne) and costar Steven (Jeffrey Max Nicholls) at the art gallery managed by her sister Bobbi (Jayne Heitmeyer). A major heist involving the gallery's security chief Ritter (David Keeley) causes the building to be locked down while the production crew is still in it. Bobbi realizes the only way out is with her security card, which she left on her desk. Sharon runs off to retrieve it; she is distracted, and Ritter discovers it in the meantime. Meanwhile, Eric Dane (Lance Henriksen), an art impresario who has imported a valuable statue from Germany for gallery owner Mrs. Holman (Barbara Chilcott), reveals himself to be Eric Dangler, the son of a Nazi who has imported a deadly nerve gas inside the statue. Realizing her sister and film pals are hostages, Sharon overpowers one of the villains and takes his gun. While revealing his plan to sell the nerve gas to the highest bidder, Dangler shoots and kills Steven. Sharon takes out a female thug, but is discovered by the other goons, setting off a shoot-out.

By the time the shooting has stopped, Jack and Bobbi have managed to secure the room. Dangler and his accomplice Falco (Kevin Jubinville) set a timed nerve gas cannister, only to realize that they don't have the security card needed to escape. Bobbi obtains the correct security card after beating and killing Ritter. Falco finds Sharon and Bobbi, but they manage to beat him unconscious. Sharon finds the cannister and they trick Dangler, who has been holding Jack hostage, into grabbing the wrong security card. Sharon tosses the nerve gas in with him, while

Bobbi locks him in a glass room, and Sharon, Bobbi, and Jack watch as he's reduced to a quivering, bloody mass.

In one of her rare non-erotic roles, Shannon Tweed keeps her clothes on, but still manages to give a good show. What has always set Tweed's erotic films apart from dozens of other straight-to-tape sex schlockers is that she shows some ability to act. Unfortunately, this kind of action film really doesn't give her much of a script or plot to stretch with. While her toned body makes her a believable action star, her martial-arts moves look phony. The supporting performers, particularly Lance Henriksen, make the film mindlessly entertaining and even suspenseful despite the familiarity of the story. Director Paul Lynch (PROM NIGHT) keeps things moving along smoothly, but Richard Beattie's script is weak and derivative. Tech credits are fine, particularly the special makeup effects by Francois Dagenais. *(Extreme profanity, violence.)*—P.L.

d, Paul Lynch; p, Peter R. Simpson; co-p, Ilana Frank; w, Richard Beattie (based on the story by Michael Stokes); ph, Barry Gravelle; ed, Nick Rotundo; m, Paul J. Zaza; prod d, Sandra Kybartas; art d, Armando Scrignuoli; sound, Ervin Copestake; fx, Francois Dagenais; casting, Pam Rack, Rosina Bucci; cos, Nancy McHugh; makeup, Paul Raymond; stunts, Alison Reid

Action/Thriller **(PR: O MPAA: R)**

FACULTY, THE ★★

(U.S., 1998) 110m Alienated Productions; Los Hoolligans; Dimension ~ Dimension c

Jordana Brewster *(Delilah)*; Clea DuVall *(Stokely)*; Laura Harris *(Marybeth)*; Josh Hartnett *(Zeke)*; Shawn Hatosy *(Stan)*; Salma Hayek *(Nurse Harper)*; Famke Janssen *(Miss Burke)*; Piper Laurie *(Mrs. Olson)*; Chris McDonald *(Casey's Dad)*; Bebe Neuwirth *(Principal Drake)*; Robert Patrick *(Coach Willis)*; Usher Raymond *(Gabe)*; Jon Stewart *(Mr. Furlong)*; Daniel Von Bargen *(Mr. Tate)*; Elijah Wood *(Casey)*; Summer Phoenix *(F*%# You Girl)*; Jon Abrahams *(F*%# You Boy)*; Susan Willis *(Mrs. Brummel)*; Pete Janssen *(Meat)*; Christina Rodriguez *(Tatoo Girl)*; Danny Masterson *(F*%# Up #1)*; Wiley Wiggins *(F*%# Up #2)*; Harry Knowles *(Mr. Knowles)*; Donna Casey *(Tina)*; Louis Black *(Mr. Lewis)*; Eric Jungmann *(Freshman #1)*; Chris Viteychuk *(Freshman #2)*; Jim Johnston *(P.E. Teacher)*; Libby Villari *(Casey's Mom)*; Duane Martin *(Officer #1)*; Katherine Willis *(Officer #2)*; Mike Lutz *(Hornet Mascot)*; Doug Aarniokoski *(Brun Coach)*

Another too-hip retread of conventional genre films from the pen of SCREAM (1996) scribe Kevin Williamson. . . sort of. THE FACULTY tries to do for INVASION OF THE BODY SNATCHERS (1956) what SCREAM did for slasher movies: ape, honor, and satirize them all at the same time. Unfortunately, THE FACULTY's script is not nearly as good as SCREAM, resulting in a tired and annoying ripoff of much better films.

Both the teachers and students of Herrington High School are too preoccupied with their own problems to notice some strange events, including the disappearance of the principal, Ms. Drake (Bebe Neuwirth). It isn't until resident geek Casey (Elijah Wood) discovers the carcass of a shrimplike creature on the football field that his science teacher, Mr. Furlong (Jon Stewart), gets interested. When the creature is placed in water, it not only springs back to life, but replicates a second animal. In short time, the faculty of Herrington High begin acting very strange, calling the school's most influential students into private meetings from which they emerge subtly changed.

Suspecting something is wrong, Casey gathers a group of his classmates: Delilah (Jordana Brewster), the pretty snob; Stokely (Clea DuVall), the outcast; Stan (Shawn Hatosy), the football star; Zeke (Josh Hartnett), the genius drug dealer; and Marybeth (Laura Harris), the new kid. Together they determine that an alien species has taken over the faculty, and seeks to take over the world one person at a time. Of course nobody believes them, except the now-inhabited faculty who are hunting them.

Basing their plan on their knowledge of science-fiction films, the kids surmise that if they kill the original alien—the "queen bee"—then the others will revert back to their normal selves. Figuring it must be Ms. Drake, they administer to their principal a dose of Zeke's homemade dope, called scat, to which aliens exhibit a deadly intolerance. But they have guessed wrong: the aliens are still alive and well. As the kids get picked off one by one, Casey eventually discovers that new kid Marybeth is actually the queen. After a chase through the pool and gym, Casey stabs the alien with a dose of scat, killing it and returning the town back to normal.

The producers of THE FACULTY obviously hoped to get a lot of mileage out of writer Kevin Williamson's name—after all, his previous films (SCREAM, I KNOW WHAT YOU DID LAST SUMMER, SCREAM 2) had resuscitated the comatose horror genre. But THE FACULTY is not really a Kevin Williamson project: beginning with a script by David Wechter (1980's MIDNIGHT MADNESS, 1985's MALIBU BIKINI SHOP) and Bruce Kimmel (1981's THE CREATURE WASN'T NICE) that had been sitting on a shelf for years, Williamson produced a few early drafts before handing the script over to George Huang (1994's SWIMMING WITH SHARKS) to finish. That Williamson received sole screenwriting credit says more about the marketing of films than his actual contribution to the final script.

Huang manages to do a pretty good Williamson impression, populating the film with hip, good-looking high school kids who possess a near encyclopedic command of pop-culture trivia, particularly films. Like SCREAM, the kids base their survival strategy on famous films, especially INVASION OF THE BODY SNATCHERS. But unlike SCREAM's pastiche of horror conventions, THE FACULTY steals heavily—and shamefully—from two films in particular: BODY SNATCHERS and John Carpenter's THE THING (1982). In fact, two scenes from THE THING seem to have been spliced into THE FACULTY, one in which the paranoid kids must prove to each other they're not aliens, and another in which a severed head becomes gruesomely ambulatory.

THE FACULTY's one saving grace is the creative (and at times brilliant) casting of the faculty members themselves. Instead of getting big-name actors to play the beleaguered kids (as in the SCREAM and I KNOW WHAT YOU DID LAST SUMMER films), THE FACULTY features such familiar faces as Robert Patrick (the T-1000 in 1991's TERMINATOR 2), Piper Laurie, Bebe Neuwirth, Famke Janssen (1995's GOLDENEYE), comedian Jon Stewart, Salma Hayek, and Daniel von Bargen (George Costanza's boss on "Seinfeld") as the borderline incompetent teaching staff who actually seem to benefit from their alien infestation. But the originality ends there, giving way to unfunny wisecracks and an endless series of jump-and-go-boo chase scenes that not even the energetic visual style of director Robert Rodriguez (EL MARIACHI, DESPERADO, FROM DUSK TIL DAWN) can save. *(Violence, extensive nudity, substance abuse, profanity.)*—B.T.

d, Robert Rodriguez; p, Elizabeth Avellan; exec p, Bob Weinstein, Harvey Weinstein; assoc p, Tamee Smith-Zimmerman; w, Kevin Williamson (based on a story by David Wechter and Bruce Kimmel); ph, Enrique Chediak; ed, Robert Rodriguez; m, Marco Beltrami; prod d, Cary White; art d, Ed Vega; set d, Jeanette Scott; sound, Steven Nelson (mixer); fx, John McLeod; casting, Mary Vernieu, Anne McCarthy; cos, Michael T. Boyd; makeup,

Ermahn Ospina, Robert Kurtzman (special effects), Gregory Nicotero (special effects), Howard Berger (special effects); stunts, Bobby Brown

Horror/Science Fiction/Thriller (PR: O MPAA: R)

FALANDO DE ANJOS
(SEE: TALK OF ANGELS)

FALLEN ★★½
(U.S., 1998) 107m Turner Pictures; Atlas Entertainment ~ Warner Bros. c

Denzel Washington *(John Hobbes)*; Embeth Davidtz *(Gretta Milano)*; John Goodman *(Jonesy)*; Donald Sutherland *(Lieutenant Stanton)*; James Gandolfini *(Lou)*; Elias Koteas *(Reese)*; Gabriel Casseus *(Art)*; Michael J. Pagan *(Sam)*; Robert Joy *(Charles)*; Frank Medrano *(Charles' Killer)*; Ronn Munro *(Mini Golf Owner)*; Cynthia Hayden *(Society Woman)*; Ray Xifo *(Society Man)*; Tony Michael Donnelly *(Toby)*; Tara Carnes *(Teenage Girl)*; Reno Wilson *(Mike)*; Wendy Cutler *(Denise)*; Aida Tuturro *(Tiffany)*; Jeff Tanner *(Lawrence)*; Jerry Walsh *(Fat Man)*; Bob Rumnock *(Schoolteacher)*; Ellen Sheppard *(Nun on Bus)*; Christian Aubert *(Professor Louders)*; Bill Clark *(Detective Bill Clark)*; Allelon Ruggiero *(Executioner)*; Jill Holden *(Gracie)*; Drucie McDaniel *(Vendor)*; John Raphael Russell *(Distinguished Gentleman)*; Lynn Wanlass *(Complaining Woman)*; John Descano *(Cab Driver)*; Cress Williams *(Detective Joe)*; Rick Warner *(Governor)*; Jim Grimshaw *(Warden)*; Brandon Zitin *(Muscle Builder)*; Rozwill Young; Michael Shamus Wiles; Frank Davis *(Prison Guards)*; Barry "Shabaka" Henley *(Uniformed Cop)*; Mike Cicchetti *(Moustache Man)*; William C. Jeffreys III *(Transit Cop)*; Ben Siegler *(Priest)*; Jason Winston George *(College Kid)*; Anika Hawkins *(Girlfriend)*; Stan King *(Japanese Businessman)*; Thomas J. McCarthy *(Witness)*; Sheila Bader *(Witness)*; Elleanor Jean Hendley; Michael Aron; Byron Scott *(Reporters)*; Pat Ciarrocchi; Steve Highsmith; Kent Manahan *(Anchors)*

A serious-minded excursion into the supernatural, FALLEN is well-acted but never really gets off the ground.

Philadelphia detective John Hobbes (Denzel Washington) attends the execution of Edgar Reese (Elias Koteas), a serial killer he apprehended. Reese makes cryptic pronouncements before his death, and shortly thereafter Hobbes and his partner Jonesy (John Goodman) investigate a murder in which the m.o. is the same as Reese's. Hobbes also begins receiving phone calls like those Reese once made to him, and one of Reese's last statements leads Hobbes to look into a detective named Milano who shot himself after a series of identical murders. Hobbes drives to a cabin in the woods where Milano committed suicide and finds occult books and the name "Azazel" written on a wall.

More murders duplicating Reese's methods occur. Hobbes talks to Milano's daughter Gretta (Embeth Davidtz), who tells him that Reese, like her father, was possessed by Azazel, a demon that can transfer from host to host through touch. By possessing people on the street, Azazel terrorizes Gretta and taunts Hobbes, ultimately invading his police station. Lt. Stanton (Donald Sutherland) begins to suspect Hobbes of the murder spree, and ultimately Hobbes's own brother, Art (Gabriel Casseus), becomes one of the victims.

Having learned that the demon will expire if it is without a host too long, Hobbes attempts to lure Azazel to Milano's cabin. Jonesy and Stanton follow, the former possessed by Azazel. Jonesy kills Stanton; Hobbes swallows poison and then shoots Jonesy, intending to leave Azazel without anyone to inhabit. But the demon transfers into a cat and heads back toward civilization.

The presence here of Washington, Goodman, and Sutherland suggests a classier treatment of supernatural themes than usual, and all three, along with Davidtz, do indeed lend this material a welcome gravity. Throughout, director Gregory Hoblit and scripter Nicholas Kazan attempt to render a serious thriller with theological underpinnings, and while their ambition shows, FALLEN doesn't build up enough suspense to satisfy as a thriller. There's nothing wrong with a supernatural film aiming for a high degree of realism, but FALLEN only maintains a moderate level of dramatic interest.

Given that Hoblit broke out with his edgy, cinematic work on TV shows like "Hill Street Blues," it's surprising that his direction here, as in his previous feature PRIMAL FEAR (1996), is rather staid and conventional. There are the occasional distorted-color point-of-view shots (from the perspective of the demon) that have become de rigueur for this kind of film, but for the most part, Hoblit seems more comfortable depicting police-station camaraderie than the more horrific elements of the plot. He does mount one exciting sequence, however, in which Hobbes is tormented on the street by Azazel as the demon hops from one human host to another.

The alternately warm and chilly photography by Newton Thomas Sigel is a strong asset, as is the unnerving music by Chinese composer Tan Dun, which is augmented by the effective use of the Rolling Stones' "Time is on My Side," sung by Reese and the other possessees. Unfortunately, the film takes a more obvious road when "Sympathy for the Devil" is played over the end credits. And at the climax, the implausibility of Hobbes not having considered that Azazel could enter a non-human host is compounded by the unlikely presence of the stray cat in the middle of nowhere. This quick "ironic" close undercuts what could have been a satisfyingly downbeat ending. *(Graphic violence, nudity, profanity.)*—M.G.

d, Gregory Hoblit; p, Charles Roven, Dawn Steel; exec p, Elon Dershowitz, Nicholas Kazan, Robert Cavallo, Ted Kurdyla; assoc p, Richard Suckle, Patricia Graf; w, Nicholas Kazan; ph, Newton Thomas Sigel; ed, Lawrence Jordan; m, Tan Dun; prod d, Terence Marsh; art d, William Cruse ; set d, Michael Seirton; ch, Russell Clark; sound, Jay Meagher (mixer); fx, Jim Fredburg; casting, David Rubin; cos, Colleen Atwood; makeup, Edna M. Sheen; stunts, Phil Neilson, Ernie Orsatti

Horror/Thriller/Crime (PR: O MPAA: R)

FALLEN ANGELS ★★★★
(Hong Kong, 1995) 96m Jet Tone ~ Kino International c
(DUOLUO TIANSHI)

Leon Lai *(Wong Chi-ming—the Killer)*; Michelle Reis *(The Agent)*; Karen Mok *(Baby)*; Takeshi Kaneshiro *(He Zhiwu)*; Charlie Young *(Charlie)*; Toru Saito *(Sato—the Manager)*; Chen Man Lei *(Father)*; Kong To-hoi *(Ah-Hoi)*; Chan Fai-hung *(Man Forced to Eat Ice Cream)*; Kwan Lee-na *(Woman Pressed to Buy Vegetables)*; Wu-yuk Ho *(Man Forced to Have His Clothes Washed)*

Filmmaker Wong Kar-wai followed up his brilliant meditation on lost love, CHUNGKING EXPRESS (1994), with this similarly stylish and surprisingly touching account of events in the lives of three solitary nighthawks who can't seem to find the emotional connections they long for.

Wong Chi-ming (Leon Lai) is an assassin who has a "partner," nicknamed the Agent (Michelle Reis), who transmits his instructions, scouts out the locations of his jobs, and maintains an apartment that serves as a way station for him before and after his jobs. Wong and the Agent have never met in person, but she is romantically obsessed with him. Wong also works as a collector of debts. After he is injured in a butcher shop shootout on one of these assignments, he decides to quit all of his criminal activities. He informs his partner of his decision, finally makes an appointment to meet her in a local bar—and then doesn't show up.

The Agent lives in the Chunking Mansion, a transient hotel run by an elderly Taiwanese (Chen Man Lei). His son, He Zhiwu (Takeshi Kaneshiro) is a delinquent who makes his living breaking into stores after they have closed for the evening and selling their wares to the unsuspecting souls who wander by. Late one night, Zhiwu encounters Charlie (Charlie Young), who's distraught over the fact that her boyfriend is to marry a rival of hers. He helps Charlie search the city for the rival, and slowly becomes infatuated with her. Zhiwn invites her to a soccer match, but is disappointed when she continues to speak about her ex; when Zhiwu asks her out again, she stands him up, making him realize he can't compete with the memory of her former lover.

In the meantime, a hooker named "Baby" (Karen Mok) has become infatuated with Wong. She can't seem to make headway with him, but senses that he has unresolved feelings for his partner, so she sets up a meeting between the two. At this meeting, the Agent asks Wong to do her "one last favor." After the meeting, he rejects Baby outright and walks out of her life. He soon performs the "favor," which is in fact another hit, and is killed in a shootout.

Zhiwu, meanwhile, has taken a legitimate job, and now works as a waiter in a Japanese restaurant. Inspired by his boss's practice of sending videotaped messages home to his family in Japan, Zhiwu begins taping his father in candid moments around the house. A short time later, when his father dies, he is left with only his memories, in the form of the cherished videotape.

While tending a snack counter, Zhiwu sees Charlie, who is now a stewardess, waiting for her new boyfriend. A few nights later, he makes the acquaintance of the Agent in a restaurant, and offers her a ride home on his motorcycle. The two relish the companionship and warmth of the experience.

Though FALLEN ANGELS is more haphazardly constructed than the exquisite CHUNGKING EXPRESS, its conclusions are more profound and its persuasive air of melancholy establishes a more immediate connection between Wong's kinetic, expressive visuals and the characters' inner state.

FALLEN ANGELS reexplores Wong's favorite themes: the obstacles that people put in their own paths in order to prevent contentment; the breakdown in communications between lovers; the pain that is an inextricable part of romantic obsession; the unequal degree of devotion in every couple; and, most importantly, the aspect of timing in any romantic connection. "We rub shoulders with people every day," proclaims Zhiwu, "strangers who may even become friends or confidants."

And while the narrative may appear to have taken a tangential turn every so often, Wong is a master at sustaining a mood—here, the characters' isolation and lack of fulfillment causes them to meld with the city's landscape—becoming figures in windows and doorways, framed against those classic symbols of loneliness, a bar and a TV set. Once again, cinematographer Christopher Doyle (Wong's regular collaborator) does an exemplary job of creating memorable visuals—some of them so resonant that Wong keeps them on screen for minutes at a time, choreographing them with the film's soundtrack (which incorporates reggae, Cantonese pop, '80s "new wave," and the trippy musical ponderings of Laurie Anderson). Wong engages in three John Woo-like "bullet ballet" shootouts, but even these scenes are presented with a degree of alienation, as his favorite editing technique of step-printing (a form of slow-motion) fragments the action to the extent that Wong Chi-ming appears to drift through his assignments as he does through his romantic encounters.

Michelle Reis and Canto-pop star Leon Lai are highly photogenic, and supply just the right amount of tortured cool for their characters; Kaneshiro, however, steals the film as he participates in its two emotional extremes—absurdist humor (his attempts to force passersby to buy "his" goods) and doleful mourning (dealing with his father's death). The sequence where he speaks about the loss of his father stands as the most emotionally effective moment in Wong's oeuvre to date, indicating his growth as an artist, and demonstrating that his is not merely a visual talent. Though his visual bravura may obscure the serious intent of his story lines, he is in fact capable of fashioning three-dimensional characters whose emotional dead ends are remarkably familiar. Their stories, in short, are our own. *(Sexual situations, profanity.)*—E.G.

d, Wong Kar-wai, billed as Wang Jiawei; p, Wong Kar-wai, Jeff Lau; exec p, Chan Ye-cheng; assoc p, Norman Law; w, Wong Kar-wai; ph, Christopher Doyle; ed, William Chang, Wong Ming Lam; m, Frankie Chan, Roel A. Garcia; prod d, William Chang; sound, Leung Chi-tat; stunts, Poon Kin-kwun

Drama/Crime/Comedy **(PR: C MPAA: R)**

FALLING FIRE ★★

(U.S./Canada, 1998) 84m Producers Network Associates ~ New Horizons Home Video c

Michael Pare *(Daryl Boden)*; Heidi Von Palleske *(Marylin Boden)*; Mackenzie Gray *(Joe Schneider)*; Zerha Leverman *(Rene Lessard)*; Cedric Turner *(Cyril Jackson)*; Christian Vidosa *(Lopez)*; Morris Durante *(Jimmy Rice)*; Jacklyn Francis *(Nikki Bardini)*; Michaela Matthieu *(Chris Martel)*; Geoffrey Pounsett *(Marty Anderson)*; Tim Ward *(Dr. Hanan)*; Christopher Wall *(Mr.Ames)*; Herbie Terry *(Adam Boden)*

Michael Pare plays a spaceship officer trying to stop a killer—and save Earth from an asteroid while he's at it—in FALLING FIRE, a lackluster sci-fi video release that originally aired as an entry in Showtime's "Roger Corman Presents" series.

In the future, Daryl Boden (Michael Pare) is the First Officer on a space shuttle that's staging a series of explosions to destroy a massive asteroid heading for Earth. Boden suspects sabotage when some of his crew members begin to die one by one as a result of several freak accidents and he eventually discovers that one of the crew, Rene (Zerha Leverman), is behind the treachery and has programmed the ship's computer to alter the course of the asteroid so that it will crash into Earth. Meanwhile, Boden's estranged wife Marilyn (Heidi Von Palleske), is a government agent on Earth tracking a gang of eco-terrorists led by Lopez (Christian Vidosa). When Lopez is captured, Marilyn interrogates him, but his gang breaks him out and he takes Marilyn hostage to his headquarters, where he monitors the action on the shuttle via a satellite link and reveals that Rene is working for him. After Boden kills Rene, Marilyn manages to shoot Lopez and communicate with Boden through the satellite. Boden is unable to override the ship's computer, but he successfully changes the trajectory of the asteroid by crashing into it with the ship, and he saves Earth from destruction.

Made in Canada, FALLING FIRE is as generic and derivative as its title, featuring lots of Canadian actors sitting in semifuturistic sets filled with multicolored computer control panels and spitting out lines like, "We have atmospheric rebound, sir" and "Instituting reactor diagnostic now, sir" with utter seriousness. Always one to copy a trend with a quickie knock-off that actually beats its bigger-budgeted brethren to the market, Corman's obvious inspirations here are 1998's two blockbuster asteroid movies, DEEP IMPACT and ARMAGEDDON, but the film actually tries to copy the look of 2001: A SPACE ODYSSEY (1968), with such familiar visuals as a videophone transmission from Boden's son, a monitor showing a surveillance camera's POV in the ship (a la HAL), and images of the tiny astronauts floating through the vastness of space while repairing the ship. The special effects are uninspired, but competent in a low-tech way, utilizing miniature models to a great extent, but the story jumps from scene to scene and location to location without establishing a clear narrative line or even explaining what the characters are supposed to be doing, until the film is almost over. Yet, as always, one has to give Corman his due for inventing some ingenious ways to insert the requisite gratuitous nudity: a flashback of Boden in bed with his wife, holographic images of strippers created by the ship's engineer, and a zero-gravity sex scene aboard the space shuttle that just might be the first of its kind since Jane Fonda's famous striptease in BARBARELLA (1968). *(Violence, profanity, nudity, sexual situations.)*—M.S.

d, Daniel D'Or; p, G. Philip Jackson; exec p, Roger Corman, David A. Steinberg, Maryann Ridini; w, Peter I. Horton, Daniel D'Or, G. Philip Jackson (based Peter I. Horton); ph, Jonathan Freeman; ed, Anthony Coleman; m, Donald Quan; prod d, James Plaxton; fx, Ron Craig; casting, Lewis Baumander; cos, Debra Hanson; makeup, Catherine Davies Irvine

Science Fiction **(PR: O MPAA: R)**

FARM: ANGOLA, U.S.A., THE ★★★★

(U.S., 1998) 93m Gabriel Films; Firecracker Films ~ Seventh Art Releasing c

George Crawford; Vincent Simmons; Eugene "Bishop" Tannehill; Logan "Bones" Theriot; John Brown; Ashanti Witherspoon; Wilbert Rideau; Burl Cain; Bernard Addison *(Narrator)*

Several inmates are profiled in THE FARM: ANGOLA, U.S.A., a terse, eye-opening documentary about incarceration in America.

The prisoners of THE FARM: ANGOLA, U.S.A. spend their days at the Louisiana State Penitentiary at Angola, a former slave plantation named for the African origin of its laborers. Of the 5000 mostly African-American convicts who make up its population, 85 percent will die on the Farm.

The film focuses on six inmates with different backgrounds. George Crawford, a young man, enters the prison facing a life sentence for murder; his mother later visits him and cries during their meeting. Vincent Simmons, already incarcerated for 20 years, fights to prove his innocence during a clemency hearing where the board dismisses his claims in less than a minute. Eugene "Bishop" Tannehill conducts Bible readings while waiting endlessly for a pardon from the state's governor.

Logan "Bones" Theriot, dying of cancer, prepares for his death behind bars. John Brown, facing execution, pleads for life at his final clemency hearing, but fails to convince the board. Ashanti Witherspoon, incarcerated for 25 years for armed robbery, leads other inmates as a model of rehabilitation, but struggles against the odds to obtain parole.

The two other characters profiled include Wilbert Rideau, THE FARM's codirector and the inmate editor of the award-winning *Anglolite*, the nation's only uncensored, inmate-produced magazine; and Warden Burl Cain, the proud "master" of the Farm who complains about how outsiders perceive the inmates. Cain talks candidly about the poor chances for parole for most of the inmates, and he oversees them as they mount sandbags to prevent a massive flood during a storm; later, Cain surveys the damage.

Finally, John Brown is executed; Ashanti Witherspoon fails to get a hearing for parole; the "Bishop" still awaits the Governor's signature; a Superior Court rejects Vincent Simmons's application for appeal; George Crawford's family plans on raising money for trial transcripts necessary for his appeal; and the family and inmate friends of "Bones" attend his funeral on the prison grounds.

In THE FARM: ANGOLA, U.S.A. filmmakers Jonathan Stack and Liz Garbus mix traditional "talking head" interviews with the men and a straightforward cinema-verite technique to capture their daily routines. The results superbly demonstrate the individualism and humanity of the prisoners, and by doing so, eschew stereotypes and demonizing imagery. The most heart-wrenching moment occurs in Vincent Simmons's clemency board meeting, which contrasts Simmons's quiet dignity with the board's arrogant bureaucracy. Stack and Garbus don't attempt to advocate for the innocence of the prisoners, although in this particular case, Simmons seems to be both innocent and getting an unfair hearing.

The filmmakers' main concern is that the prisoners be treated as human beings, which does not appear to be the case in their current circumstances. Thus, most vignettes de-emphasize the melodramatic in favor of low-key compassion, such as in the affecting but surreal Christmas night sequence in which the prison's radio d.j. plays jingles while the prisoners are visited by a clown. Thankfully, too, the deaths (John Brown's execution and the demise of "Bones") are kept off-screen.

The main drawback to THE FARM, however minor, comes from the filmmakers' interpolation of a dramatic climax—the flood sequence—to give the film a more traditional structure. There are also some arty shots early in the piece, and the "Bishop's" revival meeting runs a bit long, but, overall, THE FARM: ANGOLA, U.S.A. is a wise, sad, and forceful record of justice (and injustice) in America. *(Adult situations, profanity.)*—E.M.

d, Jonathan Stack, Liz Garbus, Wilbert Rideau (co-director); p, Liz Garbus, Jonathan Stack; exec p, Gayle Gilman; ph, Samuel Henriques, Bob Perrin; ed, Mona Davis, Mary Manhardt; m, Curtis Lundy; sound, Ken Delbert

AAN Best Documentary Feature

Documentary **(PR: C MPAA: NR)**

FATAL PURSUIT ★

(U.S., 1998) 103m HOD Films ~ American Home Entertainment c

L.P. Brown III *(Deghy)*; Shannon Whirry *(Jill)*; Malcolm McDowall *(Bechtel)*; Charles Napier *(Herbert)*; Larry Manetti *(Gersi)*; Robert Z'Dar *(Franco)*; Lydie Denier *(Giselle)*; Larry Linville *(Shelby)*; Michael Ensign *(Pinkrose)*; Obba Babatunde *(Trinidad)*; Joe Estevez *(Morier)*; Jay Hastings *(Ortiz)*; Tommy Bull *(Girard)*; Robert Axelrod *(Billy)*; William Buzick *(Natas)*; Sheri Brummond *(Secretary)*; Phillip Jenkinsen *(Lyman)*; Tawnya Foskett *(Mrs. Lyman)*; Lenny Rose *(Dr. Dufoe)*; Irena Olasin *(Tina)*; Paul O'Linde *(Rene)*; Tony Pandolfo *(Thibault)*

Completed in 1994 but largely unseen until its home video release in 1998, FATAL PURSUIT is a substandard erotic thriller marred by bad acting and worse dialogue.

Jill Winters (Shannon Whirry), a British insurance investigator, is sent to New Orleans on assignment, where she is paired with local private eye Deghy (L.P. Brown III). Their mission is to recover a multimillion dollar stash of diamonds stolen in a bloody desert heist. Jill and Deghy clash instantly due to their contrasting natures—she is straitlaced and proper, while he is rough-hewn and randy. But their working relationship draws them closer together and before long, they become lovers.

Their investigation is impeded by police detective Gersi (Larry Manetti), who is covering up evidence because he's accepting bribes from the mastermind of the robbery, Bechtel (Malcolm McDowell). Deghy blackmails a con, Shelby (Larry Linville), into turning over evidence that implicates Bechtel. He then breaks into Bechtel's safe and retrieves the diamonds. But when he tries to collect his finder's fee from the insurance company, he learns that due to the death of the gems' rightful owner, the policy cannot be collected upon. Deghy decides to steal the diamonds for himself. Bechtel and Gersi are apprehended, while Deghy and Jill abscond to a cozy cabin with the loot.

FATAL PURSUIT was filmed on location in New Orleans (where the story is set) and features a lively Cajun score. The upbeat music underscores the campiness of the dialogue. The complicated plot doesn't hold up to scrutiny. Many clues are revealed in throwaway lines and some plot elements are never explained. The script features too many incidental characters to keep track of. But the disposition of the diamonds is just the flimsy premise around which the film contrives abundant opportunities to show Whirry being disrobed, either intentionally or accidentally. The action scenes are adequate, but one too-perfectly choreographed barroom brawl comes off more like a hoedown. The cast doesn't seem to be in agreement on how to treat their material. Brown, McDowell, and Whirry ham it up, while Manetti and Obba Babatunde (as Jill's supervisor) play it straight and serious. *(Violence, extensive nudity, sexual situations, adult situations, profanity.)*—B.R.

d, Eric Louzil; p, L.P. Brown III, Eric Louzil, Vester Mapp; exec p, Wayne M. Pecht, C. Martin Dixon; assoc p, Harmon Kaslow, Jay Hastings, Darren Miller; w, Chuck Conaway; ph, Ron Chapman; ed, Jim E. Nownes, Jeff Bradley; m, John L. Rodby; prod d, James F. Claytor Sr.; sound, Randy Lawson; casting, Joey Paul; cos, Devon Patterson; makeup, Erinn Graeser; stunts, Phil O'Dell

Thriller/Erotic (PR: O MPAA: R)

FEAR AND LOATHING IN LAS VEGAS ★★★½

(U.S., 1998) 128m Rhino Films ~ Universal c

Johnny Depp *(Raoul Duke)*; Benicio Del Toro *(Dr. Gonzo)*; Tobey Maguire *(Hitchiker)*; Ellen Barkin *(Waitress at North Star Cafe)*; Gary Busey *(Highway Patrolman)*; Christina Ricci *(Lucy)*; Mark Harmon *(Magazine Reporter at Mint 400)*; Cameron Diaz *(Blonde TV Reporter)*; Katherine Helmond *(Desk Clerk at Mint Hotel)*; Michael Jeter *(Speaker at D.A. Drug Convention)*; Penn Jillette *(Barker at Bazooko Circus)*; Craig Bierko *(Lacerda)*; Lyle Lovett *(Road Person)*; Flea *(Musician in Matrix Club Men's Room)*; Laraine Newman *(Frog-Eyed Woman)*; Harry Dean Stanton *(Judge)*; Tim Thomerson *(Hoodlum)*; Michael Lee Gogin *(Uniformed Dwarf)*; Larry Cedar *(Car Rental Agent, Los Angeles)*; Brian Lebaron *(Parking Attendant)*; Michael Warwick *(Bell Boy)*; Tyde Kierney *(Reporter)*; Richard Riehle *(Dune Buggy Driver)*; Ransom Gates *(Dune Buggy Passenger)*; Frank Romano *(Dune Buggy Passenger)*; Gil Boccaccio *(Desert Room Doorman)*; Gary Bruno *(Desert Room Doorman)*; Richard Portnow *(Wine Coloured Tuxedo)*; Debbie Reynolds *(Voice of Debbie Reynolds)*; Steve Schirripa *(Goon)*; Verne J. Troya *(Wee Waiter)*; Will Blount *(The Black Guy)*; Ben Yeager *(Barker, the Clown)*; Christopher Callen *(Bazooka Circus Waitress)*; Ben Van Der Veen *(TV Crew Man)*; Alex Craig Mann *(Stockbroker)*; Gregory Itzin *(Clerk at Mint Hotel)*; Troy Evans *(Police Chief)*; Gale Baker *(Police Chief's Wife)*; Chris Meloni *(Clerk at Flamingo Hotel)*; Chris Hendrie *(Executive Director)*; Larry Brandenburg *(Cop in Black)*; Donald Morrow *(Voice of Film Narrator)*; Jenette Goldstein *(Maid)*; Stephen Bridgewater *(Human Cannonball)*; Buck Holland *(Shopper)*; Mary Gillis *(Shopper)*; Jennifer Elise Cox *(Shopper)*; Robert Allen *(Car Rental Agent, Las Vegas)*; David Brisbin *(Man in Car)*; James O'Sullivan *(TV Newsman)*; Milt Tarver *(TV Newsman)*; Kathryn Alexander; Mia Babalis; Kristin Draudt; Kim Flowers; Nan Friedman; Judith Lieff; Tane McClure; Diana Mehoudar; Geoffrey B. Nimmer *(Lizard Performers)*; Marlene Bologna; Chobi Gyorgy; Karen E. Castoldi; Lisa S. Hoyle; Joseph S. Griffo *(Trapeze Artists)*

Received with horror and derision upon its first printing, Hunter S. Thompson's semi-fictional account of drug-drenched excess in the casino-capital was long considered "unfilmable," until director Terry Gilliam delivered this adaption, awash in hallucinogenic imagery and exaggerated characterization. One of the most subversive major studio releases of all time, it stands as a nearly perfect evocation of both Thompson's uniquely hyperactive stream-of-consciousness writing style and the confused times in which his "gonzo" experimentation flourished.

The year is 1971. Outlaw journalist Raoul Duke (Johnny Depp) is assigned to cover the Mint 400 desert motorcycle race. Samoan attorney/pal Dr. Gonzo (Benicio Del Toro) joins him on a drive to Las Vegas, armed with a convertible full of illicit drugs. Dealing with phantom bats and a hitchhiker (Tobey Maguire) who doesn't take to their craziness, the pair drop acid and soon deteriorate into a dumb bestial state, with Duke unable to maintain his sanity as he sees giant lizards occupying their hotel's bar. Coming to his senses the next day, Duke attempts to take in the absurd race, but ultimately follows his own extreme agenda, accompanied by Gonzo and his rather large cache of drugs. After being booted out of Debbie Reynolds's nightclub act, the two snort raw ether and are turned loose in the terrifying, bigtop-themed casino, the Bazooko Circus. But back in their hotel suite, events get weirder, when Gonzo takes far too much acid, becomes dangerously violent, and orders Duke to electrocute him in the bathtub during the climax of the song "White Rabbit." With their hotel room trashed in only two days, Duke runs out on his hotel bill, only to learn that Dr. Gonzo has scheduled him to cover a Las Vegas-based District Attorney's antidrug conference.

Pulling into another, unsuspecting hotel, Duke meets Gonzo and his latest pick-up, a Barbra Streisand-obsessed teenager named Lucy (Christina Ricci), who's been fed a headful of acid. Under Duke's recommendation, they ditch her; and as Duke's paranoia reaches a breaking point, he takes a massive dose of "adrenochrome" (culled from adrenaline glands of living human bodies), which sends him into a hideous, hallucinatory frenzy. Coming to, in a hotel suite that's been turned into a foul cesspool, Duke experiences grim flashbacks and realizes that their joyride might've gone too far—-particularly when Gonzo pulls a knife on a waitress (Ellen Barkin) after sexually harassing her. Racing to the airport so Gonzo can catch his flight, they bid adieu. Duke takes US Interstate 15 back home.

Director Terry Gilliam has always been acclaimed primarily for his visual prowess, and FEAR AND LOATHING is unquestionably one of his wildest, riskiest creations. Successfully translating Thompson's cult novel to the screen, he not only captures the author's one-of-a-kind voice, but coats the proceedings in extreme, drug-drenched imagery. Beginning as "a classic affirmation of everything right and true in the national character," Duke's odyssey soon degenerates into a kinetic assault on the senses (underscored by a surprisingly sentimental attachment to, and mourning for, the optimism that characterized the 1960s). There's also no shortage of dark, surreal humor, sparked by the pair's confrontation with authority figures and tourists.

Though littered with star cameos, the screen belongs to the unrepentantly-deranged Depp and Del Toro. As Duke (Thompson's fictional alter-ego), Depp perfectly captures the author's speech patterns, body language, and growing paranoia.

Depp even accompanied Thompson on a book-signing tour before starting the film, in order to make his interpretation all the more accurate (he also wore Thompson's actual clothing for much of the filming). Thompson himself can be spotted in a 1965 flashback sequence, as an aging doppelganger. For his part, Del Toro packed on a frightening girth to play Gonzo (based on Chicano activist Oscar Acosta), bringing an often lethal, decidedly incoherent edge to the road trip. Together, they make a potent, morally bankrupt combo, particularly when their characters' more savage shadings take root.

Not surprisingly, the film was condemned for its surface matter (the Disney-owned ABC-TV network refused to run commercials for the movie), which includes rampant destruction of property, partaking in highly dangerous drugs, and copious vomiting. At the heart of the film's unique vision is outstandingly deranged cinematography by Nicola Pecorini (supplying a Fellini-on-peyote view of Duke's universe) and colorfully tacky production design by Alex McDowell, which actually manages to transcend the over-the-top gaudiness of the real Las Vegas.

Staying remarkably faithful to his source material, Gilliam might not paint a pretty picture in FEAR AND LOATHING, but the film does boast an uncommonly wicked brand of satire, and also offers up a spectacularly conceived vision of unpredictable dementia and its soggy aftereffects. *(Violence, adult situations, substance abuse, extreme profanity.)*—S.P.

d, Terry Gilliam; p, Laila Nablusi, Patrick Cassavetti, Steve Nemeth; exec p, Harold Bronson, Richard Foos; co-p, Elliot Lewis Rosenblatt; w, Terry Gilliam, Tod Davies, Alex Cox, Tony Grisoni (from the book by Hunter S. Thompson); ph, Nicola Pecorini; ed, Leslie Walker; prod d, Alex McDowell; art d, Gary Diamond, Chris Gorak; set d, Nancy Haigh; sound, Jay Meagher (mixer); fx, Steve Galich, Illusion Arts; casting, Margery Simkin; cos, Julie Weiss

Comedy/Drama (PR: O MPAA: R)

FERNGULLY 2: THE MAGICAL RESCUE ★★½

(Australia/U.S., 1998) 73m Fai Films; Rosen Harper Entertainment; Wild Brain, Inc. ~ CBS Fox Video c

Voices of: James Baker *(Root)*; Kermit Beachwood *(Batty Koda)*; Erik Bergmann *(Stump, Captain)*; Connie Champagne *(Budgie)*; Holly Conner *(Nugget, Bandy, Mrs. K)*; Laura Erlich *(Crysta)*; Harry Joseph *(Boss)*; Gary Martin *(Mac, Goanna)*; Digory Oaks *(Pips)*; Westin Peace *(Mr. Chuckles)*; David Rasner *(Boof, Slasher)*; Phil Robinson *(Father)*; J.F. Rochstar *(Twig)*; K.T. Vogt *(Bark, Wal)*; Jamie Baker

It's back to the rainforest for some more enlightened eco-adventures with the cuddly cartoon critters in FERNGULLY II: THE MAGICAL RESCUE, an above-average made-for-video sequel to the politically-correct 1992 animated hit.

The peaceful world of the rainforest is shattered when two poachers arrive and capture three baby animals who are under the care of Crysta (voice of Laura Erlich), a sylvan sprite. One of the poachers later starts a fire in the rainforest and they flee with the babies. Pips (voice of Digory Oaks), another sprite, decides to go into the town and rescue the babies, and he's accompanied by a bat named Batty Koda (voice of Kermit Beachwood) and a group of insects called The Beetle Boys. In town, they stop at a carnival and befriend a young girl named Budgie (voice of Connie Champagne), and her grandfather Mr. Chuckles (voice of Westin Peace), a performing clown. Batty discovers that the poachers are hiding out in a house near there, but he's caught by them while trying to free the animals. Pips and Budgie then free all of the animals while the poachers are transporting them on a truck. Crysta arrives in town and helps to capture the poachers, and then she and Pips return to the rainforest with all of the animals.

Although FERNGULLY II: THE MAGICAL RESCUE lacks the superior artwork and celebrity voice-cast of its predecessor (including a manic Robin Williams as Batty), it has the same worthy ecological message and is perfectly pleasant entertainment for kids, especially younger viewers who'll enjoy its plethora of exotic rainforest creatures, including kangaroos, wombats, iguanas, tropical birds, and all kinds of bugs (even if some of them could only be found in a rainforest as imagined by Australian animators). The animation may not be the most sophisticated in the world, but it's more than adequate and always nice to look at, bursting with bright colors and lushly verdant, three-dimensional backgrounds in the rainforest. The action scenes (a fire, a rollercoaster ride, a car chase on the highway, the final rescue) with the flying creatures contain lots of fast motion which is always convincing without resorting to a heavily computerized look. The bouncy songs are kept to a minimum and are well integrated into the story, including an amusing gospel-like number where the caged Batty implores his fellow captives not to give up hope.

The thematic elements are not only about conservation, the environment, and pollution, but also of a vegetarian nature, as the animals discuss being eaten, worn, and experimented on, by humans. Indeed, the indictment of humanity as being representative of all that is evil and corrupt in the world is remarkably strong, even extending to the humans' culture in a kind of MAN WHO FELL TO EARTH-like subplot when Pips and the others go into town and are temporarily seduced by junk food and MTV. The only good humans are the young Budgie and her childlike Grandpa, while the Aussie-accented poachers are among the vilest of villains.—M.S.

d, Phil Robinson; p, Jeffrey Kahan, Brian Rosen, Richard Harper; exec p, Jeff Fino; assoc p, Maryann T. McClure, Holly Harold, Alex Engle; w, Richard Tulloch (based on the *FernGully* stories by Diana Young); ed, Michael Cavanaugh; m, Nerida Tyson-Chew

Animated/Children's (PR: AA MPAA: G)

FESTEN

(SEE: CELEBRATION, THE)

54 ★½

(U.S., 1998) 89m Redeemable Features; Miramax; Dollface; FilmColony ~ Miramax c

Mike Myers *(Steve Rubell)*; Neve Campbell *(Julie Black)*; Ryan Phillippe *(Shane O'Shea)*; Salma Hayek *(Anita)*; Sela Ward *(Billie Auster)*; Breckin Meyer *(Greg Randazzo)*; Sherry Stringfield *(Viv)*; Ellen Albertini Dow *(Disco Dottie)*; Cameron Mathison *(Atlanta)*; Noam Jenkins *(Romeo)*; Jay Goede *(Buck)*; Patick Taylor *(Tarzan)*; Heather Matarazzo *(Grace O'Shea)*; Skipp Sudduth *(Harlan O'Shea)*; Aemilia Robinson; Daniel LaPaine *(Marc the Doorman)*; Erika Alexander *(Ciel)*; Thelma Houston *(Herself)*; Mary Griffin *(Disco Star)*; Don Carrier *(Julian)*; Domenick Lombardozzi; Mark Ruffalo *(Ricko)*; Bruno Miguel *(Boyd)*; Jason Andrews *(Anthony)*; Laura Catalano *(Rochelle)*; Kohl Sudduth *(Rhett)*; Lorri Bagley *(Patti)*; Lauren Hutton *(Liz Vangelder)*; James Binkley *(Rubbell's Bodyguard)*; Arthur Nascarella *(IRS Agent)*; John Himes *(IRS Agent)*; Louis Negin *(Truman Capote)*; Lena Vajakas *(Conrows)*; Barbara Radecki *(TV Host)*; Ron Jeremy *(Ron)*; Sean Sullivan *(Andy Warhol)*; Vieslav Krystyan *(Photographer)*; Nick Holt *(Alpine Inn Waitress)*; David Blacker *(Bouncer)*; Bruce MacVittie *(Music Producer)*; Emmanuel Mark *(Talent Manager)*; Kabriel Lilly

(Little Girl); Michael York *(Ambassador)*; Morgan Freeman *(Angelic Boy)*; Lina Felice *(Nicaraguan Woman)*; Elio Fiorucci *(Himself)*; Drake Alonso Thorens *(Man on Horseback)*; Justin Tensun *(Blond Busboy)*; Jason Fruitman *(Busboy #1)*; Andy Grote *(54 Waiter)*; Jordan Paige *(Young Shane)*; Georgina Kess *(Shane's Mom)*; Mario Bosco *(Mario)*; Coati Mundi Hernandez *(DJ)*; Victor Sutherland *(DJ)*; Janine Longley; Michael Henderson; Chris Ingram *(Kissing Trio)*; Cindy Crawford; Sheryl Crow; Donald Trump; Georgina Grenville; Cecilia Thomson; Ling; Frederique Van Der Wal; Heidi Klum; Victor Brown; Veronica Webb; Michel Van Der Wal; Sophie Rousseau *(VIP Patrons)*; Art Garfunkel; Peter Bogdanovich; Lorna Luft; Valerie Perrine; Beverly Johnson; John Johnson; Bruce Jay Friedman; Andrea Bocaletti *(Elaine's Patrons)*; Ultra Nate; Amber; Jocelyn Enriquez *(Stars on 54)*

Purportedly providing a glimpse inside Studio 54, the reknowned late-1970s nightclub, this drama focuses less on the life of the club's notorious owner, Steve Rubell, than on a fictitious young man who is drawn in by the "scene" inside the club. Severely reedited by its studio, the resulting film has about as much depth and daring as the disco tunes on its soundtrack.

The year is 1979, and 19-year-old Shane O'Shea (Ryan Phillippe) is bored with his drab life in Jersey City, so he heads into Manhattan to check out the celebrated Studio 54. Picked out of the crowd waiting to enter the club by the owner, Steve Rubell (Mike Myers), Shane enters a paradise of bright lights, casual sex, and "the beautiful people." Instantly entranced, he gets a job as a busboy at the club and moves in with fellow-busboy Greg (Breckin Meyer) and his wife Anita (Salma Hayek), a wannabe disco-queen. At the club, Shane keeps an eye on soap opera starlet Julie Black (Neve Campbell), on whom he has a crush. While indulging in the pervasive drug scene at the club, Shane moves up to bartending, and is soon escorted into 54's back rooms, where celebrities can overindulge in private. In the meantime, Rubell is siphoning cash from the club's registers, and soon has the IRS looking into 54's cooked books.

Returning to New Jersey for Christmas, Shane is turned away by his resentful father, but then runs into Julie, who's also visiting family for the holidays. Letting down their guard, they become friends. On New Year's Eve, a jealous Shane spots Julie with another man, while Anita gets her big chance to sing on the club's stage. But in the middle of her performance, elderly club-regular Disco Dottie (Ellen Albertini Dow) collapses on the dance floor. This event disturbs Shane, but there's more to come—the IRS raids the club and arrests Rubell. Leaving 54, Julie offers him a ride, and the two decide to remain friends.

Later, after Rubell is released from jail, an older and wiser Shane attends his welcome home party, realizing that an era is now over.

One can see that this project, as conceived, had all of the elements necessary to explore a defining moment in 1970s pop culture. There's the mythos of the era's most notable hot spot, the supposedly drug- and sex-drenched Studio 54; a group of colorful characters in search of their 15 minutes of fame; and a plethora of the mechanically processed tunes that kept folks on their feet during this period—all this centered around a SATURDAY NIGHT FEVER-styled lug, who is given a shot at overnight stardom. Unfortunately, while Mark Christopher's direction has a certain visual flair, few of the characters possess charisma enough to sustain the viewer's interest, and the story line is painfully obvious at times.

The central problem with the film is its cardboard cast of characters. Ryan Phillippe looks the part of Shane, but his well-cared-for hair and pecs supply the better part of his performance. This is compounded by his annoyingly naive voice-over, which conveniently spoon-feeds information to the viewer at every turn. The only salvageable moments in 54 belong to Mike Myers, who appears to have immersed himself in the role of the hedonistic Rubell. It's unfortunate that the film doesn't give him the opportunity to follow through with his portrayal, with the exception of a few gloriously debauched scenes (at one point, he lies sprawled on a bed full of money, propositions a busboy, and then casually vomits onto his cash).

It's most unfortunate, however, that Miramax took the movie out of Christopher's hands. His original cut clocked in at over two hours long, and supplied some darker shadings for the characers. In the original, Rubell was sleazier and more manipulative, and Shane was a truly driven man—-given to sleeping with both men and women, stealing from Rubell, and even seducing the married Anita. Alas, an upbeat ending and unchallenging sexuality are deemed necessary for the marketplace, and so the film was cut down to a "releasable" 89-minute running time. The homogenized mentality that led to this revision is exactly what causes 54 to fail so dismally. *(Nudity, sexual situations, substance abuse, profanity.)*—S.P.

d, Mark Christopher; p, Ira Deutchman, Dolly Hall, Richard N. Gladstein; exec p, Bob Weinstein, Harvey Weinstein, Bobby Cohen, Don Carmody; assoc p, Jonathan King; w, Mark Christopher; ph, Alexander Gruszynski; ed, Lee Percy; m, Marco Beltrami; prod d, Kevin Thompson; art d, Tamara Deverell; set d, Karin Wiesel; ch, Lori Eastside; sound, David Lee (mixer); fx, Michael Kavanagh; casting, Billy Hopkins, Suzanne Smith, Kerry Barden; cos, Ellen Lutter; makeup, Patricia Green; stunts, Shane Cardwell

Drama **(PR: O MPAA: R)**

FIRELIGHT ★★

(U.S./U.K., 1997) 103m Wind Dancer Productions; Carnival Films; Hollywood Pictures ~ Miramax c

Sophie Marceau *(Elisabeth Laurier)*; Stephen Dillane *(Charles Goodwin)*; Dominique Belcourt *(Louisa)*; Kevin Anderson *(John Taylor)*; Lia Williams *(Constance)*; Joss Ackland *(Lord Clare)*; Sally Dexter *(Molly Holland)*; Emma Amos *(Ellen)*; Maggie McCarthy *(Mrs. Jago)*; Wolf Kahler *(Sussman)*; Annabel Giles *(Amy)*; John Flanagan *(Robert Ames)*; Thomas Fisher *(Davey)*; Valerie Minifie *(Hannah)*; Diana Payan *(Mrs. Madment)*; John Hodgkinson *(Carlo)*; Anthony Dutton *(Dodds)*; Hugh Walters *(Dr. Geddes)*; Peter Needham *(Rector)*; Melissa Knatchbull *(Mrs. Hurst)*; Frank Rozelaar-Green *(Dancemaster)*; Trevor St. John-Hacker *(Fashionable Guest)*; Katharine Levy *(French Maid)*; Valerie Sarruf *(French Patronne)*

Sophie Marceau pouts her way through her role as a buxom Swiss governess who's hired to bear a child for, and then falls in love with, a 19th-century British aristocrat with an invalid wife, in FIRELIGHT, an old-fashioned gothic soap opera gussied up with a few (but not enough) torrid sex scenes and some perfunctory and pretentious politically-correct nods to feminism and questions of morality.

In 1838, wealthy British landowner Charles Godwin (Stephen Dillane), whose wife has been comatose for three years due to a riding accident, hires impoverished Swiss governess Elisabeth Laurier (Sophie Marceau) to bear a child for him, which she only agrees to do for the money in order to keep her father out of debtors's prison. They meet in a French hotel for three days to conceive, during which their business-like lovemaking becomes more and more passionate. Nine months later, Elisabeth gives birth to a baby girl, which is immediately taken away and given to Charles. Seven years go by, during which Elisabeth realizes that she cannot keep her promise of never trying to contact her daughter. She finds Charles's estate, and while he's away, she's hired as his child's governess by his wife's sister Constance (Lia Williams), who's secretly in love with Charles, and does not know who Elisabeth really is.

When Charles returns, he orders Elisabeth to leave, but allows her to stay for one month until she can find another situation on the condition that she not reveal her true identity. The daughter, Louisa (Dominique Belcourt), is a spoiled brat who has forced one governess after another to quit, but Elisabeth talks Charles into letting her discipline the child and gradually gets through to her and teaches her how to read. Charles tries to maintain his distance from Elisabeth, but they eventually succumb to their desire. Later, Charles is forced to sell his estate to pay off the debts incurred by his profligate father (Joss Ackland). Also, Charles eventually decides to put his wife out of her misery; she dies after he leaves her window open during a blizzard. After the funeral, Louisa learns that Elisabeth is her real mother, and with Charles, they move out of the estate to start a new life together.

Freely borrowing elements from such antediluvian mother-love warhorses as MADAME X (remade several times after first being adapted to the screen in 1915), STELLA DALLAS (1937), several 1940s Bette Davis weepies, and any number of "upstairs-downstairs" Victorian-era novels, FIRELIGHT is sort of like *Jane Eyre* with nudity, and has everything that fans of what used to be called "women's pictures" could ask for, including an unwed mother who has to give up her child, a young girl who is unaware of her governess's secret identity, and a nobly suffering husband with an invalid wife (repressed desire and steamy late-night trysts are simply part of the package). It has everything, that is, except for cinematic spark or any sense of vitality, and though handsomely appointed, it's as somber and humorless as a Sunday School sermon. The only times the film comes to life are in the all-too-brief scenes featuring Joss Ackland as Charles's robustly decadent father. The splendid veteran character actor delivers an exuberant performance, in marked contrast to the rest of the cast, including the beautiful, but sullen, Sophie Marceau and the cold-fish Stephen Dillane, who treat the hokey material as if it were profound and deliver their lines with a gravity and solemnity usually reserved for the Bible.

Making his feature directorial debut, writer William Nicholson (SHADOWLANDS, NELL) doesn't display much visual imagination, relying on attractive, if gloomy, widescreen cinematography for some pretty images, but it all adds up to the type of movie that Hitchcock once described as "photographs of people talking." Nicholson's wordy script tries to camouflage the fact that the story is merely about lust by throwing in an overly-symbolic subplot about genetic sheep breeding (maladroitly mirroring Elisabeth's surrogate mother status), some anachronistic profanities, and giving Elisabeth pseudo-feminist attitudes (e.g., telling Louisa she'll be a "prisoner" if she doesn't learn to read). Yet it conveniently glosses over the morality of euthanasia in order to facilitate the predestined happy ending, where the erst-while-terror Louisa learns that Elisabeth is her mother and tearfully hugs her while plaintively crying "Mama" over and over. This kind of tearjerker can be quite enjoyable if it's handled with gusto and conviction (a la Douglas Sirk or King Vidor), but it certainly can't support spurious aspirations to seriousness, and the result here is often yawn-inducing. *(Nudity, sexual situations, profanity.)*—M.S.

d, William Nicholson; p, Brian Eastman; exec p, Carmen Finestra, David McFadzean, Matt Williams, Susan Cartsonis, Rick Leed; assoc p, Ted Morley; w, William Nicholson; ph, Nic Morris; ed, Chris Wimble; m, Christopher Gunning; prod d, Rob Harris; art d, Peter Wenham; set d, Caroline Smith; ch, Jane Gibson; sound, Sandy MacRae (mixer); casting, John Hubbard, Ros Hubbard; cos, Andrea Galer; makeup, Suzan Broad; stunts, Tony Smart

Historical/Drama/Romance **(PR: C MPAA: R)**

FIRESTORM ★★

(U.S., 1998) 90m Loeb/Weisman; 20th Century Fox ~ 20th Century Fox c

Howie Long *(Jesse Graves)*; Scott Glenn *(Wynt Perkins)*; Suzy Amis *(Jennifer)*; William Forsythe *(Shaye)*; Christiane Hirt *(Monica)*; Garwin Sanford *(Pete)*; Sebastian Spence *(Cowboy)*; Michael Greyeyes *(Andy)*; Barry Pepper *(Packer)*; Vladimir Kulich *(Karge)*; Tom McBeath *(Loomis)*; Benjamin Ratner *(Wilkins)*; Jonathon Young *(Sherman)*; Chilton Crane *(Tina's Mom)*; Robyn Driscoll *(Tina's Dad)*; Alexandria Mitchell *(Tina)*; Terry Kelly *(Lawyer)*; David Fredericks *(Guard)*; Gavin Buhr *(Childs)*; Danny Wattley *(Moody)*; Derek Hamilton *(Dwyer)*; Adrian Dorval *(Belcher)*; Jon Cuthbert *(Davis)*; Sean Campbell *(Deputy)*; Deryl Hayes *(Sheriff Garrett)*

After scoring in a small role in BROKEN ARROW (1996), former football star turned TV sports commentator Howie Long makes an unimpressive bid to become a full-fledged action hero in FIRESTORM, a routine programmer about smoke jumpers (firefighters who parachute into blazing forests) that offers just enough stunts and widescreen pyrotechnics to provide 90 minutes of mindless entertainment.

Jesse (Howie Long) is appointed to be the chief of a group of smoke jumpers after the former chief Wynt (Scott Glenn) is forced to retire following a leg injury. When someone starts a small fire in the woods near the Wyoming State Penitentiary, prison work crews are used to help put out the fire, among whom is a vicious killer named Shaye (William Forsythe). The fire is actually part of an elaborate escape plan by Shaye, who kills the prison guards and poses as a firefighter, along with some other convicts, in order to recover millions of dollars from a robbery which he had buried in the forest. Meanwhile, an ornithologist named Jennifer (Suzy Amis) who's been collecting rare bird eggs, gets trapped in the fire and is taken hostage by Shaye and his gang. When Jesse parachutes into the forest and encounters Shaye, one of the prisoners tries to kill him, but he manages to escape on a motorcycle and rescues Jennifer.

Shaye and the remaining members of his gang chase after them, and Jesse is shot in the arm by Shaye, who abducts Jennifer again. After the other smoke jumpers learn about Shaye and the prison break, Wynt parachutes into the forest and finds Jesse at the boat docks, waiting for Shaye to arrive. Wynt reveals to Jesse that he was the person who had set the fire because he needed the money, but that he was told it was for a land development deal, not part of any prison break. Wynt then confronts Shaye and sacrifices himself so that Jesse can get away. Shaye shoots Wynt, then flees in a speedboat, but Jesse hits him with an ax. Just then, a firestorm sweeps through the area, and Jesse and Jennifer take cover beneath the overturned boat. Shaye suddenly reappears and shoots a hole in the boat, but Jesse pushes his head into the hole and he's burned to death. After the firestorm subsides, it begins to rain, and Jennifer sees that her bird eggs have hatched.

FIRESTORM joins the small, undistinguished list of movies about forest fires (RED SKIES OF MONTANA, THE FOREST RANGERS) and intrepid firefighters (THE HELLFIGHTERS, BACKDRAFT), and like its predecessors, the predictable story and cliched characters are somewhat offset by the film's pictorial values. The sheer photogenic quality of fire and the visceral spectacle of watching things burn is captured with convincing realism by Dean Semler, making his directorial debut after an impressive career as a cinematographer (THE ROAD WAR-

RIOR, DANCES WITH WOLVES). The formulaic script, which was originally written as a USC master's thesis project, adheres to the proscribed film school script structure paradigm, including the introduction of the main characters via an action prologue (in this case, a shamelessly sappy forest fire rescue with Jesse saving a little girl and her pooch); and the all-important placement of plot-point #1 at exactly the 20 minute mark (Shaye and his lawyer planning the forest fire diversion to enable him to escape). As for logical plotting and credibility, don't worry about it; with all of the fast-paced action nobody will ever stop and question little things like how ridiculously easy it is for Shaye to kill all the prison guards and escape; or how it's possible for Jesse to escape from a burning cabin by riding a motorcycle off of its roof!

With his square-jaw, chiseled visage, and ultra-muscular physique, Howie Long looks and acts like a cartoon character, which is quite appropriate for a film that's about as simplistic as a comic book. And although he's generally as wooden as one of the film's numerous burning trees, his performance is on a par with such robotic action superstars as Arnold Schwarzenegger and Steven Seagal. Wisely, the script plays up his physical attributes and keeps his dialogue to a minimum, proving that even a crazed neo-Nazi like Shaye (William Forsythe at his hammiest), is no match for an even more Aryan-looking hero with blue-eyes and a blond buzz-cut, not to mention a damsel-in-distress ornithologist who carries rare bird eggs with her through a raging inferno, and has a mean right-hook. *(Profanity, graphic violence.)*—M.S.

d, Dean Semler; p, Thomas M. Hammel, Matthew Weisman, Joseph Loeb III; exec p, Louise Rosner; co-p, Douglas C. Metzger; w, Chris Soth; ph, Stephen F. Windon; ed, Jack Hofstra; m, J. Peter Robinson; prod d, Richard Paris, Linda Del Rosario; set d, Dominique Fauquet-Lemaitre; sound, David Husby (mixer), Frank Gaeta (design); fx, Chris Corbould, John "DJ" Desjardin, VIFX; casting, Allison Gordon Kohler; cos, Bruce Finlayson, Carla Hetland; makeup, Lisa Love; stunts, Glenn Wilder

Action/Crime **(PR: C MPAA: R)**

FIREWORKS ★★★★½

(Japan, 1997) 103m Office Kitano ~ Milestone Film c
(AKA: HANA-BI)

Takeshi Kitano, billed as Beat Takeshi *(Yoshitaka Nishi)*; Ren Osugi *(Horibe)*; Kayoko Kishimoto *(Miyuki—Nishi's Wife)*; Susumu Terajima *(Nakamura)*; Hakuryu *(Tojo—Sadistic Yakuza Hitman)*; Tetsu Watanabe *(Tezuka—Junkyard Owner)*; Yasuei Yakushiji *(The Criminal)*; Taro Itsumi *(Kudoh—the Detective)*; Kenichi Yajima *(Doctor)*; Makoto Ashikawa *(Tanaka)*; Yuko Daike *(Tanaka's Widow)*

Ostensibly a crime drama, FIREWORKS is actually a sad and beautiful study of one man's efforts to set things right in his life. Filmmaker-star Takeshi Kitano (SONATINE) offers a perfect fusion of form and content, as his exquisitely spartan visual style lends deeper resonance to the film's touching, elliptical story line. The film won the Golden Lion at the 1997 Venice Film Festival.

When seasoned police detective Nishi (Takeshi Kitano) takes a break from a stakeout to visit his leukemia-afflicted wife, Miyuki (Kayoko Kishimoto), he is unable to prevent the shooting of his longtime partner and friend Horibe (Ren Osugi) by the *yakuza* (gangster) they've been investigating. Nishi later takes part in another attempt to capture the same *yakuza* in an underground mall. In this case, a violent shootout ends with Nishi killing the *yakuza,* but not before the hot-tempered mobster disposes of a young police detective, Tanaka (Makoto Ashikawa).

Disturbed by these events, Nishi quits the police force. He pays a visit to Horibe, who is now wheelchair-bound and deeply depressed; he speaks with Nishi about acquiring a hobby, possibly painting. Nishi also visits Tanaka's widow (Yuko Daike), who is devastated by the loss of her husband, and needs money to make ends meet. Nishi's central concern, however, is Miyuki, who has been released from the hospital, but has been diagnosed as terminal. He is turned down by a *yakuza* loan shark (to whom he is already deeply in debt) when he asks to borrow more money. He is somehow able to scrape together the money to send Horibe a full set of painting supplies (including a beret).

Nishi then quietly hits upon an idea. Dressed in a phony police uniform, he matter-of-factly robs a bank. With the money from the heist, he is able to take Miyuki on a long-desired sight-seeing trip to Mt. Fuji. While there, he buoys her spirits and takes her mind off her condition. While the couple are on vacation, packets of money arrive in the mail: first to Tanaka's widow, then to the loan shark (thus cancelling Nishi's debt), and finally to Horibe. Horibe is subsequently questioned by Nakamura (Susumu Terajima), one of Nishi's friends on the force, and a rookie cop, Kudoh (Taro Itsumi), who believe that Nishi might have committed the bank robbery. While staying in a hotel, Nishi is menaced by representatives of the *yakuza* loan shark, who has also figured out that he is the culprit. The *yakuza* demand the money, but are summarily disposed of by Nishi.

Days later, Nakamura and Kudoh track Nishi down to a beach where he and Miyuki are watching a girl fly a kite. They call him over and indicate that they will have to arrest him for the bank job, but he asks them to wait for a moment. He returns to Miyuki's side, and the two share a blissful interlude, concluded by Miyuki's thanking him for the trip. As Nakamura and Kudoh sit by watching the couple and the young girl, two shots resound on the beach.

At the point that American audiences were discovering the work of Takeshi Kitano (performing name: "Beat" Takeshi) for the first time—thanks to the official US releases in 1998 of both FIREWORKS and SONATINE—this multitalented performer had already been enshrined as a pop-culture phenomenon in his native Japan, having published over 50 books, worked as a regular in literally dozens of TV series (in every category from variety to talk to drama), and appeared in approximately 20 films (five of which he directed, scripted, and edited).

Kitano has evidenced a fiercely original style in all of his films to date; the understated, heartbreaking plot line and sublimely austere visual style he employs in FIREWORKS attest to his quick maturation as a cinema stylist. To Western eyes, Kitano's bold yet uncommonly spare visual approach may seem like the unholy union of Yasujiro Ozu and Robert Aldrich—the intimate moments in the film call to mind the rigorous pictorial quality found in the former's work, while the sudden outbursts of violence are executed in the jarringly elliptical manner of the latter's classic film noir KISS ME DEADLY (1955).

He also uses silence to sketch the attitudes of, and relationships between, his characters. The comfortable, familiar affection that Nishi and Miyuki share is communicated largely through their nonverbal interactions—playing board games at home, sitting together in her quiet hospital room, and traveling together around the Japanese countryside in the film's closing segment. Careful use is also made of a very evocative musical score by Joe Hisaishi, which punctuates and reinforces the nobility of Nishi's charitable acts.

Having developed a sort of stock company in his first six films, Kitano reintroduces a number of familar faces here, but gives the plum role to noted television actress Kayoko Kishimoto, who is incredibly moving as Miyuki. For his part, Kitano—a specialist in deadpan depictions of volatile cops and crooks—sports an especially mask-like visage here, as a real-life motorcycle accident in 1994 paralyzed the right side of his face. During his convalescence after this accident, he began painting as a hobby and, in fact, the strikingly odd images of animals and insects with flowers for body parts created in the film by Horibe are actually Kitano's own efforts. In spite of the paralysis, however, Kitano succeeds in giving a detailed and quite touching performance as Nishi. The character's self-effacing sense of humor (his attempts to lift Miyuki's spirits invariably end in calamities, which lead the couple to break into laughter) is the decisive factor that turns the film from a crime saga into a character study.

The beauty of the film's central love story may be blunted for some by the dour nature of the film's conclusion (it can be assumed that Nishi has taken both his own life and that of Miyuki). Kitano does still leave the viewer with a redemptive sense of hope: besides the fact that Nishi has effectively accomplished all of his honorable goals, his encouragement of Horibe's painting brings about a rebirth of the handicapped policeman, allowing him to deal with his depression. This is most eloquently communicated in a scene in which he sits outside a flower shop, dazzled and inspired to action by the colors and shapes he sees within. *(Violence, adult situations, profanity.)*—E.G.

d, Takeshi Kitano; p, Masayuki Mori, Yasushi Tsuge, Takio Yoshida; co-p, Hiroshi Ishikawa, Kazuhiro Furukawa; w, Takeshi Kitano; ph, Hideo Yamamoto; ed, Takeshi Kitano, Yoshinori Ota; m, Joe Hisaishi; art d, Norihiro Isoda; set d, Tatsuo Ozeki; sound, Senji Horiuchi; casting, Takefumi Yoshikawa; makeup, Michiyo Miyauchi, Tomoo Haraguchi (effects)

Crime/Thriller/Drama (PR: C MPAA: NR)

FIRST LOVE, LAST RITES ★★★½

(U.S., 1998) 93m Forensic Films; Toast Films; Alliance Independent Films ~ Strand Releasing c

Giovanni Ribisi *(Joey)*; Natasha Gregson Wagner *(Sissel)*; Robert John Burke *(Henry)*; Donal Logue; Eli Marienthal *(Adrian)*; Jeanetta Arnette *(Sissel's Mother)*

FIRST LOVE, LAST RITES follows a young couple, both in love for the first time, as they discover that passion can't always stay at its initial heights. Debuting director Jesse Peretz emphasizes visuals over dialogue or story with results that are as likely to entrance viewers as to bore them to tears.

It's the beginning of summer in a small town on the Louisiana bayou. Joey (Giovanni Ribisi), a recent high school graduate, was here on vacation when he met local girl Sissel (Natasha Gregson Wagner). Distraught by her parents marital problems, Sissel lives by herself in a one-room apartment in a small building on flood stilts. She and Joey spend all their time here, making obsessive love, listening to 45s and sometimes playing with Sissel's young brother Adrian (Eli Marienthal).

Joey has a meeting with Sissel's father Henry (Robert John Burke), an umemployed schemer who asks the boy uncomfortable questions about his relationship with Sissel. He enlists Joey in a venture to capture and market eels, which annoys Sissel. (When Henry pays a visit to their room, she stays away.) As Joey spends all of his time making eel traps, Sissel takes a job she hates at a sugar factory and lets the room become messy. The eel farming goes poorly, which disappoints Joey more than Henry, who starts looking for another get-rich scheme. Joey and Sissel have irrational arguments. A rat which had been trapped in their walls gets into the room, and Joey beats it to death. Summer ends, and Sissel notes that "It's finally cooling down a little."

Based on a short story by British writer Ian McEwan (whose work has also been adapted for the films THE COMFORT OF STRANGERS and THE GOOD SON), FIRST LOVE, LAST RITES often resembles a David Lynch film stripped of the outrageous elements. Perhaps it is no coincidence that leads Ribisi and Wagner previously appeared in Lynch's LOST HIGHWAY (1996). Director Peretz, formerly the bassist for The Lemonheads (drummer David Ryan wrote the screenplay), comes to this feature after working in music videos, and while he avoids the rapid editing and shock effects for which that medium is known, he does tend to get lost in visual sheen at the expense of story and characterization. Although the early parts of the film feature heavy doses of sex, beginning with an opening reminiscent of BETTY BLUE (1985), the effect is merely reportorial: coming in a bit past their initial passion, we see a young man and woman getting to know each other's bodies in a post-erotic way.

The film is endlessly analyzable—what does that rat scratching in the wall throughout the movie symbolize? Or the eels?—where it should be felt. And the songs, created for the movie by the band Shudder to Think in conjunction with such alternative music stars as Matt Johnson, Billy Corgan, and Liz Phair, are clever recreations of older styles that tend to call attention to themselves more than augment the film. Still, the failures of FIRST LOVE, LAST RITES (not including the awful title, which is McEwan's) represent an ambitiousness that marks Peretz as a director to watch in the future. *(Graphic violence, extensive nudity, sexual situations, adult situations, profanity.)* —M.F.

d, Jesse Peretz; p, Robin O'Hara, Scott Macaulay, Herbert Beigel; exec p, Amanda Temple, Jeffrey Levy-Hinte; w, Jesse Peretz, David Ryan (based on the short story by Ian McEwan); ph, Tom Richmond; ed, James Lyons; m, Nathan Larson, Craig Wedron; prod d, Dan Estabrook; sound, Steve Borne

Drama (PR: O MPAA: NR)

FIXER, THE ★★

(U.S., 1998) 106m Barnstorm Films ~ Showtime c

Jon Voight *(Jack Killoran)*; Brenda Bakke *(C.J. Killoran)*; J.J. Johnston *(Angelo)*; Miguel Sandoval *(Mayor Melendez)*; Jack Wallace *(Judge Wolinski)*; Barbara Gordon *(Dede Scharber)*; Karl Pruner *(David Corliss)*; Brent Jennings *(Monsignor Njogu)*

Jon Voight sleepwalks his way through this would-be thriller about a corrupt lawyer in Chicago's political inner circle. Made for the Showtime Network, THE FIXER was released on home video in 1998.

In Chicago, the main power players are the mayor's office, the courts, the mob, and the press; working with these powers is the "fixer," the man who makes illicit deals which clear up problems encountered by the town's leading citizens. The current fixer is Jack Killoran (Jon Voight), a second-generation lawyer who inherited the fixer position from his father. Killoran has no problem greasing palms in order to get a new airport and stadium built; however, his conscience troubles him when he has to cover up the murder of a prostitute by a high-powered politico (Karl Pruner). After suffering an accident which nearly leaves him paralyzed, Killoran decides to get out of the fixer business.

That is more easily said than done: the airport deal is still pending, as is the murder cover-up. The heads of the four powers meet to discuss the situation, and decide Killoran must be "convinced" to finish his duties. Knowing his days may be numbered, Killoran approaches the FBI, but they cannot pursue an investigation despite the hours of videotape evidence Killoran has collected as an insurance policy. Meanwhile, the mob sends a pair of goons to shake Killoran down at his home; after beating him and threatening to harm his son, Killoran agrees to stay in business, and brokers both the airport deal and the murder cover-up. By then it is too late, though—the powers have decided that Killoran is too great a risk. They take him out to kill him, but are interrupted by the FBI, who have decided to take down the corrupt powers after all. Though Killoran must do some jail time for his years of corruption, he does so with a clear conscience.

THE FIXER's core concept—that big cities like Chicago operate on a system of corruption, blackmail, and bribery—shouldn't come as a surprise to most viewers. Still, writer-director Charles Robert Carner (who wrote 1985's legendarily bad GYMKATA) could have put a little more effort into supporting his premise. Instead, he assembles an "inner circle" made up of the most cliched characters imaginable, like the mob boss who hangs out in the "social club" and the judge who accepts rumpled envelopes full of twenties during his lunch break. With such one-dimensional characters, even the most plausible premise becomes suspect. The fate of THE FIXER therefore resides in the hands of its star and executive producer, Jon Voight. Since his reemergence in 1996's MISSION: IMPOSSIBLE, Voight has revived his career by playing high-powered men in suits (JOHN GRISHAM'S THE RAINMAKER, ENEMY OF THE STATE) and skuzzy whackos (ANACONDA, U-TURN). THE FIXER falls into the first category, with Voight expending little more effort than that required to fill out the suit: as a corrupt lawyer he is unimposing; as a rolling-eyed paraplegic he is almost comical; and as a repentant he is unconvincing. Without its star carrying his weight, THE FIXER gets real boring real fast. *(Violence, profanity, extensive nudity, sexual situations.)*—B.T.

d, Charles Robert Carner; p, Charles Robert Carner, Helen Bartlett, Tony Bill; exec p, Jon Voight; w, Charles Robert Carner; ph, Michael Goi; ed, Marc Leif; m, Lennie Niehaus

Crime/Drama (PR: C MPAA: NR)

FLINTSTONES: I YABBA-DABBA DOO!, THE ★★

(U.S., 1998) 92m H-B Production Co. ~ Warner Home Video c

VOICES OF: Joseph Barbera; Michael Bell; Charlie Brill; Greg Burson; Ruth Buzzi; Randy Crenshaw; Henry Gorden; June Foray; Joan Gerber; William Hanna; Pat Harrington; Jerry Houser; Nick Jameson; Kip King; Don Messick; Brian Mitchell; Howie Morris; Megan Mullally; Alan Oppenheimer; Darryl Phinnessee; Henry Polic II; Dan Reed; Roger Rose; Ronnie Schell; John Stephenson; Russi Taylor; Jean Vander Pyl; Janet Waldo; B.J. Ward; Frank Welker

Those modern Stone Age familes, the Flintstones and the Rubbles, finally become in-laws when Pebbles and Bamm Bamm tie the knot and say I YABBA-DABBA DOO!, in this tolerable, but overlong, animated feature based on the venerable 1960s cartoon series.

After losing his nest egg on a football game bet, Fred Flintstone has a fight with his best friend Barney Rubble and then finds out that his daughter Pebbles is engaged to Barney's son Bamm Bamm. Unable to admit to his wife Wilma that he's broke, Fred tries in vain to get a bank loan and is fired from his job at the rock quarry after arguing with his boss Mr. Slate over a raise. As the wedding bills begin to pile up, Fred loses some more money on a real estate scam and is forced to pawn his beloved bowling ball. He tries to sabotage the nuptials and temporarily succeeds in breaking up Pebbles and Bamm Bamm, but the two lovebirds eventually get back together.

Fed up with all the problems, Pebbles and Bamm Bamm decide to elope to Rock Vegas, and Fred and Barney chase after them. In Rock Vegas, Fred and Barney run afoul of a gang of robbers pulling jobs at wedding chapels and are responsible for their arrest, but they don't get a reward. However, Barney learns that he has won a large sum of money from a roulette bet which he placed when they first arrived and then forgot about. He splits the winnings with Fred, and with Pebbles and Bamm Bamm in tow, they return to Bedrock for a lavish wedding ceremony, but the two friends start to fight again after Barney gives the newlyweds the rest of the money.

There is something oddly comforting about the continued popularity of the Flintstones, perhaps a reassuring sign that there is still a market for old-fashioned, low-tech animation, bad puns involving endless variations of words using "rock" and "stone," and sight gags where animals are put into service as household appliances and mechanical devices. I YABBA-DABBA DOO!—which was actually made in 1993 for the Cartoon Network cable channel, but released on video in 1998—adds a Romeo-and-Juliet plot to the prehistoric "Honeymooners" premise, and has been predictably updated for '90s audiences, replete with "Jurassic" references and jokes about video stores, rollerblades, preschools, Elvis impersonators, and a TV show called "Bedrock Hills 90000." Even though Pebbles and Bamm Bamm are now grown up, their parents all inexplicably look exactly the same as they did in the '60s, although the new actors doing their voices are somewhat jarring. Though needlessly padded in order to fill up a two-hour timeslot on commercial TV, it's a moderately amusing cartoon for kids, and has a few bizarre elements (Barney in drag as a stripper who pops out of a cake at Bamm Bamm's bachelor party) and in-jokes (Hanna and Barbera making "cameos" as guests at the wedding) to keep adults awake.—M.S.

d, William H. Hanna; p, Iwao Takamoto; exec p, William Hanna, Joseph Barbera, Mark Young; w, Rich Fogel, Mark Seidenberg; ed, Pat Foley, Gil Iverson, Tim Iverson; m, John Debney; prod d, Iwao Takamoto; sound, Ed Collins

Animated/Children's (PR: AA MPAA: NR)

FORGOTTEN LIGHT ★★½

(Czech Republic, 1996) 101m Fama 92 Studio; Czech Television; Bonton Film-Alfa ~ Czech Telexport c
(AKA: FORGOTTEN LIGHT: PASSION IN LOVE AND LIFE; ZAPOMENUTE SVETLO)

Boleslav Polivka *(Parish Priest Holy)*; Veronika Zilkova *(Marjanka)*; Antonin Kinsky *(Count Kinsky)*; Petr Kavan *(Francek)*; Jiri Pecha *(Klima)*; Simona Pekova *(Olina Klimova)*; Jaromira Milova *(Betina)*; Sona Valentova *(Dr. Prokopova)*; Jiri Labus *(Parish Priest Kubista)*; Richard Metznarowski *(Chapter Vicar Farane)*; Miroslav Knoz *(Archbishop)*; Ivo Kubecka *(Novak)*; Hana Frejkova *(Novacka)*; Vaclav Legner *(Mladek)*; Zita Kabatova *(Tante)*; Jiri Samek *(Vacek)*; Milan Riehs *(Clerical Secretary)*

Set in 1987 Communist Czechoslovakia, FORGOTTEN LIGHT is a respectable, though somewhat slackly constructed, story of a priest's battle to save his church. Based loosely on the personal experiences of Catholic priest Jakub Demi, this subdued movie boasts a strong lead performance by Boleslav Polivka as the beleaguered clergyman.

Father Holy (Boleslav Polivka) used to preside over three small churches in rural Czechoslovakia; now he's down to one. After a torrential storm floods his last house of worship, Holy needs to raise funds to repair the building. Unfortunately, the state intervenes and condemns the 200-year-old structure. Holy questions the decision: "Has God outlived his function? Is this for some committee to decide?"

The mechanic-turned-priest, heads to a watering hole and rallies the locals to support a rebuilding effort. A new roof is coming along nicely, when a policeman halts the action, due to the lack of an official permit. When the policeman's dog attacks

Holy, the policeman reluctantly shoots it, and then blames Holy for the death of his rabid companion. Soon after, with the policeman's urging, the state takes away Holy's keys to the church.

Meanwhile, the priest attends to Marjanka (Veronika Zilkova), a married mother of two, who's dying of cancer. Holy does everything he can to make Marjanka's last days tolerable. Though his love is obvious, his motives remain pure and he never compromises his vows.

In an attempt to regain his church, Holy meets with Comrade Secretary Vacek (Jiri Sanek), a bureaucrat with a penchant for shooting deer from inside his jeep. Vacek has little patience for piety. He provokes the mild-mannered priest into slapping him, then strips away Holy's license as a priest and vows to have Holy shoveling manure. A spark of hope comes from one of Holy's parishioners, who has a great aunt with an inside track to a powerful vicar. The vicar offers the desperate priest his church back, but only if he agrees to work with the secret police. Holy speaks out against the vicar's hypocrisy, and is thrown in jail. After he's released, Marjanka dies. At this low point, the faithful man is finally rewarded—a cache of jewels is found inside one of his church's statues. In the end, Holy is back preaching to his small congregation inside his broken-down church.

Organized religion's struggle against the atheist mandates of Communism makes for compelling subject matter, but writer Milena Jelinek and director Vladimir Michalek invest their tale with too much earnestness and not enough verve. The intensity of Holy's quest to save his church is continually undermined by an unrelated subplot—his relationship with the terminal Marjanka. The film remains tasteful in its treatment of the age-old story of a priest battling to maintain his celibacy; it's too bad that it also cleanses the topic of its inherent dramatic tension. Since Holy's chastity is never in doubt, little interest is created. Thus, the scenes with Marjanka serve less to enrich our view of the lead character, and more to break the film's momentum.

Ably assisted by cinematographer Martin Duba, Michalek paints an inviting picture of the Czech countryside: a misty landscape of rolling verdant hills dotted with farmhouses. Though here again the film avoids a cliche—the dreary gray cities usually associated with old Soviet bloc countries—it does so at the expense of the action. It becomes less and less clear as the film continues whether the viewer should be charmed by the beauty of the changing seasons in this idyllic setting or horrified by the protagonist's struggle.

However, just when the story has hit its most prolonged lull, Michalek and Jelinek delivers a quick, intense jolt, in the scene in which Holy confronts the insidious Vacek. Here it becomes apparent that underneath the priest's beatific demeanor boils the frustration of an individual being ground under by a morally bankrupt system. The viewer feels extreme satisfaction when Holy finally erupts.

Playing a character with such an incredibly sacrosanct name is an incredible challenge, but Polivka proves that he's more than up to the task. He does a fine job lending a human face to a character who could easily have been little more than a mouthpiece for the filmmakers' concerns. But even Polivka can't do enough to breathe life into a film that's frequently too holy for its own good. *(Adult situations.)*— T.Y.

d, Vladimir Michalek; p, Alice Nemanska, Ivana Kacirkova; exec p, Jana Tomsova; w, Milena Jelinek (based on the novel by Jakub Deml); ph, Martin Duba; ed, Ivana Kacirkova; m, Radim Hladik, Michal Dvorak; sound, Radim Hladik Jr. (recordist); cos, Petra Jachymova

Drama/Religious **(PR: C MPAA: NR)**

FORMER CHILD STAR ★★½

(U.S., 1998) 81m House of Scooter Productions ~ House of Scooter Productions c

Dianna Damir *(Kimmy Archer)*; Eric Pederson *(David Miller)*; Michael Waite *(Dickie Pallasch)*; John Sheraton III *(Arthur Miler)*; Karen Davis *(Dr. Nichols)*; John Patrick Pierce *(Dougie Field)*; Steve Ryfle *(Marmoset Man)*; Elisa Surmont *(Mrs. Hunter)*; Rodney Allen Rippy *(Himself)*; Norman Dale; Joal Ryan; Rick Felkins

The cheeky, low-budget satire FORMER CHILD STAR takes its premise from the archetypal tabloid story of a has-been Hollywood child actor in chronic trouble with the law.

Kimmy Archer (Dianna Damir) was the adored star of "Cubby's World," a TV show about a tot and her talking cat. But that was in the 1970s, and now Kimmy is grown up, washed up, and working in a succession of burger joints. When a crusading insurance agent (writer-director Joal Ryan in cameo) exposes Kimmy as a potential child-star time bomb waiting to go off, the boss summarily fires her. Given a gun by a friendly postman, Kimmy decides to go with the flow and commit robbery. Fortunately her hostage is David Miller (Eric Pedersen), an understanding teacher with a secret crush on Cubby/Kimmy. He tries to straighten out Kimmy's life, taking her into his home and enrolling her in a therapy group made up exclusively of insanely neurotic former child stars. Kimmy's budding romance with David ends when he accidentally calls her "Cubby" during lovemaking. The Freudian slip repulses Kimmy into the arms of someone she thinks understands her better: Dickie Pallasch (Michael Waite), another former child star, but with a truly maniacal streak and a vision of himself and Kimmy as natural-born-former-child-star-killers on an outlaw rampage. Kimmy doesn't share this notion of destiny, so Dickie takes her hostage during a therapy-group performance of *Oedipus Rex*. Dickie's siege ends thanks to the sudden entrance of Marmoset Man (Steve Ryfle), a defunct TV superhero perpetually trying to crash the sessions. Kimmy feels ready to face the real world independent of David or Dickie.

"Embrace adulthood" is the message of FORMER CHILD STAR, such as it is. Unfolding competently despite cheap production values (we never do get to see "Cubby's World" and the younger version of Kimmy), the feature is pretty much a knowing Hollywood skit that filmmaker Ryan stretches as far as it can go. Funny moments include the writer-director herself hawking a cautionary pamphlet entitled "So You've Hired a Former Child Star" and keeping track of at-large has-beens on a wall map of LA. Of the largely obscure cast, Dianna Damir is winsome as the luckless heroine. This was her debut—one could think of a few former child starlets who would have, well, killed for a comeback even on this small scale. Afterwards, real-life former child star Rodney Allen Rippy (who enjoyed a crime-free maturity) is interviewed for his opinion on the movie. He seems more bemused than amused. Indeed, while Ryan's sitcom-like approach to the material is apt enough, this is overall a good-natured goof in which the sight of a pistol brandished onscreen comes with awareness that the weapon will never really be fired, and certainly won't hurt anybody. One yearns for the (slightly) edgier tone of the early "National Lampoon" features. Ryan, a then-29-year-old writer/performer for a Los Angeles cable-TV comedy troupe, undertook distribution of FORMER CHILD STAR herself, showing it at a variety of film festivals, comedy clubs, and coffeehouses. Meanwhile the glossy romantic comedy 'TIL THERE WAS YOU (1997), with a lot more money, did a lot less with the character of a dysfunctional former child star, there played by Sarah Jessica Parker. *(Substance abuse, adult situations.)*—C.C.

d, Joal Ryan; p, Joal Ryan, Eric Somers; w, Joal Ryan; ph, Joseph Oxman; m, The Breakfast Patties

Comedy **(PR: C MPAA: NR)**

FREE TIBET ★★

(U.S., 1998) 90m Milarepa Fund; Mammoth Pictures ~ Shooting Gallery c/bw

A Tribe Called Quest; Beastie Boys; Beck; Bjork; Chaksam-Pa; Cibo Matto; De La Soul; Foo Fighters; Fugees; Buddy Guy; The Venerable Palden Gyatso; Richie Havens; John Lee Hooker; Sean Lennon; Biz Markie; Tim Meadows; Yoko Ono; Pavement; Rage Against the Machine; Red Hot Chili Peppers; Sonic Youth; The Smashing Pumpkins; Anna Sui; Professor Robert Thurman; Tibetan Nuns Project; Dalai Lama

A diverting but lightweight, MTV-style concert film, FREE TIBET documents the first annual Tibetan Freedom Concert, an event organized by Beastie Boys' band member Adam Yauch and staged in San Francisco's Golden Gate Park over two days in June 1996.

Making her feature film debut, Sarah Pirozek—a director of hip-hop music videos—caters here to short attention spans by quickly cutting between easily digestible bites chronicling Chinese human rights violations in Tibet and all-too-abbreviated performance clips from various artists. Old-time guitar master Buddy Guy just starts to convince us of his pain in "Damn Right I Got the Blues" when the filmmakers cut away, mid-riff, to a short lesson about the nonviolent tradition of Tibetan culture. A cursory plea to boycott Chinese products jumps to the Red Hot Chili Peppers doing half of their hit "Give It Away." Trying to both educate and entertain, this jumpy effort does no more than a bit of each.

Pirozek makes use of familiar stock footage to sum up the Tibetan tragedy: the 40 years of oppression under Chinese rule, the resulting 1.2 million deaths, the destruction of sacred monasteries during the Cultural Revolution, the thousands of displaced refugees, and the Dalai Lama's establishment of an exile government in Northern India. It's a fair introduction to the cause, but presents no new perspective on the issues. Then again, knowing the demographic Pirozek is appealing to, one can't expect the film to break any exciting ground on the human rights front. Also, the notion that rocker and recent convert to Buddhism Yauch could mobilize today's youth to buck the biggest country in the world seems more than a bit futile (inevitably, the youths attending the concert and this film simply came to hear the music). Yet such earnest enthusiasm can't help but instill hope in the hearts of those concerned with the issues. Though he's no scholar, it would be unfair to question Yauch's sincerity. The message of doing something rather than nothing is well taken. This grounded ethos is best expressed by James Iha of the Smashing Pumpkins: "It's hard to raise awareness with a bunch of screaming kids, but I guess its the best dumb rock stars could do."

Though the musical acts don't mesh perfectly, as they come from different genres and backgrounds (alternative rock, hardcore, hip hop, the blues, and even Tibetan chanting), there are memorable highlights strewn throughout the film. One hardhitting, nonmusical moment is supplied by Palden Gyatso, an aged Tibetan monk, who describes his 33 years of imprisonment at the hands of Chinese officials—how he had to eat grass, vomit, and excrement to survive. The monk then holds up electric cattle prods, used for torture, and adds that he holds no hatred towards his oppressors (compassion being the central tenant of Tibetan Buddhism). In a completely different way, but almost as compelling, alternative musician Beck hypnotizes the audience with his brooding "One Foot in the Grave." Another musical highlight is delivered by the jerky, ethereal Bjork, who sings one of her signature tunes, "Hyper-Ballad." Both songs are presented intact, marking them as exceptions that buck Pirozek's usual, impatient style. Though she and editor Paula Heredia leave a lot to be desired in terms of film technique, they do contribute one juxtaposition of note by matching a shot of fraternity boys lugging coolers and shouting "Free Tibet" as if they're at the homecoming game with an image of reverent Tibetan refugees lining up before their godhead, the Dalai Lama. Additional examples of such symmetry between East and West would have served to make FREE TIBET that much more resonant a film. *(Profanity.)* —T.Y.

d, Sarah Pirozek; exec p, Jay Faires, Adam Yauch; ph, Evan Bernard, Roman Coppola, Spike Jonze; ed, Paula Heredia

Documentary **(PR: C MPAA: NR)**

FRENCH EXIT ★★

(U.S., 1998) 88m Daylight Productions ~ Cineville c

Madchen Amick *(Zina Hart)*; Jonathan Silverman *(Davis Lake)*; Molly Hagan *(Alice Wetherby)*; Kurt Fuller *(Sam Stubin)*; Vince Grant *(Charles)*; Beth Broderick *(Andie Ross)*; Craig Vincent *(Frank)*; Steven Brill *(Ben)*; Cecilia Peck *(Airline Ticket Agent)*; Charles Finch *(TV Host)*; Rebecca Broussard *(Bimbette)*; Kevin Williams *(Studio Guard)*; Alexandra Styron *(Receptionist)*; Andrea Fair *(Megan)*; Nicole Nagel *(German Bombshell)*; Timothy Leary *(Herbal Ecstasy Guy)*; Victoria Duffy *(Herbal Ecstasy Girl)*; Drew Hammond *(Anthony)*; Michael Alan Lerner *(Alice's Stud)*; Gil Kastner *(Cell Phone Exec)*; Charles Wessler *(Party Producer)*

A romantic comedy that lacks most of what the genre requires—witty dialogue, sparkling direction, star power—FRENCH EXIT is at least tolerable for its fetching musical score and sporadic insight into Hollywood egos running amok.

After meeting in a minor auto accident, established Hollywood screenwriter Davis Lake (Jonathan Silverman) and ambitious neophyte Zina Hart (Madchen Amick) find themselves in competition for a plum assignment, scripting a remake of MUTINY ON THE BOUNTY for A-list producer Sam Stubin (Kurt Fuller). Egged on by her roommate Alice Wetherby (Molly Hagen), who is Davis's ex-flame, Zina crashes Davis's power-lunch with Stubin. Because Stubin is infatuated with her, Zina becomes the front-runner for the job. Despite their career competition, Zina and Davis gradually become romantically involved.

When a children's film he wrote flops, a depressed Davis winds up in bed with Alice. Zina discovers Davis's infidelity, gets drunk, and decides to sleep with Stubin. An irate Davis breaks them up in the nick of time. Unable to reconcile his differences with Zina, Davis decides to move to Manhattan. Changing his mind at LAX, Davis bumps his car into one driven by Zina, who has followed him to the terminal, and they resign themselves to a committed relationship.

A romantic comedy works on nuances. The writer-director must strike a universal note in relating how Cupid initially misfires his arrow. And the screenplay demands engaging repartee—wit is the major weapon in the comic battle of the sexes. On both counts, FRENCH EXIT comes up short. How do the filmmakers expect us to care about two immature yuppies who are supposed to be talented writers, yet cannot even insult each other with any panache? All the viewer gets is slamming doors, gibes against Lotus Land, and the sinking sensation that the film's screenwriters spent their formative years nestled in the hermetically sealed world of a film/TV studio; they appear to have no knowledge of anything else, including how nonindustry types behave. Because the characters have no interior lives, they become mouthpieces for this comedy's creative personnel, who are sadly unaware of their own limitations as observers of human nature. *(Extreme profanity, sexual situations, substance abuse.)*—R.P.

d, Daphna Kastner; p, Zachary Matz; exec p, Michael Alan Lerner, Christopher Genkel, Carl-Jan Colpaert; assoc p, Edward Oleschack; co-p, Frederic Bouin, Robert Strauss; w, Michael Alan Lerner, Daphna Kastner; ph, Geza Sinkovics; ed, Claudia Finkel; m, Alex Wurman; prod d, Jean-Philippe Carp; art d, Matthew Carey; set d, Susanna Bernstein; sound, Clifford Gynn (mixer); casting, Abra Edelman, Elisa Goodman; cos, Tanya Gil; makeup, Suzanne Diaz, Denise Fischer

Comedy/Romance (PR: C MPAA: R)

FRIEND OF THE DECEASED, A ★★★★

(Ukraine/France, 1997) 100m Compagnie des Films; Compagnie Est-Ouest; National Dovzhenko Film Studio; Kazakhstan Aimanov Film Factory ~ Sony Pictures Classics c
(PRYATYEL PAKOYNIKA)

Alexandre Lazarev *(Anatoli)*; Tatiana Krivitska *(Lena/Vika—the Prostitute)*; Eugen Pachin *(Dima—Anatoli's Friend)*; Constantin Kostychin *(Kostia—the Contract Killer)*; Elena Korikova *(Marina—Kostia's Wife)*; Angelika Nevolina *(Katia—Anatoli's Wife)*; Sergiy Romanyuk *(Ivan—Anatoli's Contract Killer)*

In this plaintive near-masterpiece, director Vyacheslav Krishtofovich (ADAM'S RIB) uses the travails of one ordinary man to dramatize the issues that confronted the Ukraine following the dissolution of the Soviet Union.

The marriage of unemployed translator Anatoli (Alexandre Lazarev) and his cheating wife, Katia (Angelika Nevolina), is over. Depressed, he encounters an old friend, Dima (Eugen Pachin), who manages a liquor store. As they drink, he shares his woes. Dima says a friend, Kostia (Constantin Kostychin), is a contract killer. Anatoli orders a hit on his wife's lover, but when fulfilling the instructions given him by the hitman, he impulsively puts a picture of himself and the times he frequents his local cafe in a post office box—thus making himself the target of the hit. Next day at the usual time, Anatoli goes to the cafe but is forced to leave when the owner closes early. Having cheated death, he goes out on the town and beds a prostitute, Lena (Tatiana Krivitska). Later, the cafe owner tells him a man has been looking for him. Anatoli tells Dima to cancel the contract, but Dima says it's impossible.

Anatoli goes to the country to hire another contract killer, Ivan (Sergiy Romanyuk), who agrees to kill Kostia. To flush him out, Anatoli sits in the cafe while Ivan watches. On the second night, Kostia turns up and Ivan kills him. The next day, Anatoli sees Lena but she denies knowing him; her escort accosts him. Lena later apologizes, saying that the man is her intended husband.

Anatoli visits Kostia's widow, Marina (Elena Korikova), and offers her money. He learns Dima's liquor store was firebombed but Dima was unharmed. Marina invites Anatoli to dinner and tries to seduce him. Feeling guilty, he leaves. He meets his wife but it's clear they will not reconcile. Lena is beaten by her new husband, who wants to sell her. Anatoli gives her money and offers to have the man killed, using Kostia's modus operandi. In the post office box that Kostia used, he finds another envelope containing details for a hit. He warns the intended victim, a businessman. He then goes to Marina's apartment and gives her money. It is clear they will make a life together.

The film's opening shot of Kiev's domes and onion spires might well be a nostalgic reference to the old worlds of feudalism, imperialism, and communism. Against this historical backdrop, Krishtofovich presents a carefully crafted film that conveys the change to a new economic system and a new way of life through a myriad of details: Katia, armed with a cellular phone, offering Anatoli cash; her boyfriend's suitcase-laden red sports car; Dima's black market emporium; a bogus divorce proceeding; Lena's involvement with a mobster. The film contains no throwaway incidents or details. Each character's situation is reflective of the emergent society and the dog-eat-dog ethos of capitalism. Most, like Ivan and Dima, stradde the old and the new, but everyone is trying to find a way to survive. Krishtofovich thus exhibits a keen eye for moral turpitude and the lack of any serious rule of law.

The key is his feckless protagonist Anatoli, wonderfully limned by Alexandre Lazarev. He's a handsome Everyman who, once turned into a cynic, springs into action (though his initial air of melancholy never truly dissipates). The film's deadpan style accentuates the absurdity of his situation; the sight of this character sitting in the cafe awaiting death, virtually penniless and dressed in his best suit, is both comical and wrenchingly poignant. Krishtofovich's humanist vision and love for the Ukrainian people is apparent in the film's finale and in touching sequences like the one in which Dima registers his sadness upon hearing of Kostia's death.

The story line—in which a depressed man sets up a hit on himself and then attempts to cancel it—suits its setting perfectly, but film fans will recognize it as a familiar premise which has been used many times in both the suspense and comedic genres, from William Castle's THE WHISTLER (1944) to Warren Beatty's 1998 political satire BULWORTH.

A FRIEND OF THE DECEASED has a near-retro look, as if the Ukraine's absorption of Western pop culture had only reached the level of the 1970s. The pace is slow (perhaps too slow for audiences accustomed to fast-paced action) and the story unfolds meticulously, perhaps in an attempt to reflect the contrast beween the unhurried tempo of the old system with the hustle and bustle of the new. But whether or not Krishtofovich's implied thesis about the dehumanizing effects of capitalism is accurate, it serves as a fine springboard for an engrossing character study marked by its attention to detail and humor. *(Nudity, sexual situations.)*—J.M.

d, Vyacheslav Krishtofovich; p, Mykola Machenko, Pierre Rival; exec p, Jacky Ouaknine; w, Andrei Kourkov; ph, Vilen Kaluta; ed, Eleonora Sumovska; m, Vladimir Gronski; prod d, Roman Adamovich; sound, Gueorgui Stremovski; cos, Lyudmila Serdinova; makeup, Alla Melnik

Drama/Crime (PR: C MPAA: R)

FROM A FAR COUNTRY ★★

(U.K./Italy/Poland, 1998) 118m ITC; Trans World Film; RAI; Film Polski ~ BWE c

Sam Neill *(Marian)*; Christopher Cazenove *(Tadek)*; Lisa Harrow *(Wanda)*; Warren Clarke *(Wladek)*; Maurice Denham *(Sapieha)*; Jonathan Blake *(Jozef)*; Emma Relph *(Magda)*; Carol Gillies *(Wladek's Wife)*; Anne Dyson *(Wladek's Mother)*; John Franklyn-Robbins *(Curate)*; James Coyle *(Interrogator)*; Cezary Morawski *(Karol Wojtyla)*; Timothy Morand *(Worker)*; John Welsh *(Priest)*; Kathleen Byron *(Tadek's Mother)*; Zbigniew Zapasiewicz *(Professor)*; Philip Lathan *(Chaplin)*; Georgine Anderson *(Middle Aged Woman)*; David Sibley *(Chairman)*; Kazimierz Borowiec *(Wladek's Father)*; Phillip Trewinnard *(Investigating Official)*; Simon Dutton *(Assistant)*; Geoffrey Russell *(Curate)*; Matthew Long *(Official)*; Martin Milman *(2nd Security Officer)*; Rupert Frazer *(1st Security Officer)*; Andrej

Lapicki *(German Officer)*; Jerzy Suhr *(Engineer)*; Andrzej Zarnecki *(Wojtyla's Father)*; Tadeusz Bradecki *(Young Man)*; Marek Konrat *(Middleman)*; Daniel Olbrychski *(Captain)*; Maja Komorowska *(Nun)*; Jerzy Nowak *(University Professor)*; Tareusz Nudziak *(Auschwitz Prisoner)*; Liliana Glabczyncka *(Nun)*; Edward Lubaszenko *(Priest)*; Frank Finley *(Voice of Karol Wojtyla)*; Michael Jayston *(Narrator)*

Made as a hybrid production to be aired in the US in 1981 as a longer telefilm, and released in Europe theatrically in an abridged version—this supposed biography of the first Polish leader of the Roman Catholic church actually reduces its central figure to the sidelines, offering instead a perfunctory (and, at least in this version, confusing) history of 20th century Poland as experienced through the lives of several characters. The abridged version of the film was released on home video in 1998.

1939. After studying Polish literature in college, an unseen Karol Wojtyla becomes involved in a theater group that also includes Wanda (Lisa Harrow) and her brother Marian (Sam Neill) who, like Karol, works as a manual laborer for the occupying Nazis in order to avoid conscription into the German army. Marian's friend Tadek (Christopher Cazenove) becomes so disgusted by their job—removing bodies from the Jewish ghetto—that he joins the resistance movement. He is captured and imprisoned, along with Marian, who was arrested under suspicion of having helped Tadek. 1945. After the war, both Marian and Karol study for the priesthood. Marian works in Poland's massive repatriation effort.

1948. The Communist government begins to build Nova Huta, an all-socialist city. Marian is questioned for links to possible anti-Communist movements during the war; when he won't talk, he is arrested. Tadek becomes a successful writer in favor with the government. He tries but is unable to have Marian released. As Stalinism reaches its peak, Tadek falls into disfavor, but wins the heart of Wanda. 1956. After the death of Stalin, the Church continues to guide Poland through the kind of crises that befell Hungary. Karol rises in the church hierarchy. The site of a proposed church in Nova Huta sparks a controversy that lasts for the next two decades.

1968. Karol is now a cardinal. Student protests against the government increase, and over the coming decade they are joined by workers and intellectuals and backed by the church. Tadek's newest book is published by an illegal underground press. Factories and other work places begin to become centers of political unrest and organization. 1978. Karol Wojtyla is elected Pope.

The oddest thing about FROM A FAR COUNTRY is that its ostensible subject is never seen, except as a young boy and in documentary footage that concludes the film. It's like a Catholic version of MOHAMMED, MESSENGER OF GOD (1977), the film about the origins of the Moslem religion that never shows the prophet Mohammed—except that Catholics have no such prohibition against depicting what is only a man, not a diety. But what hurts most it is the fact that so much material has been removed for the home-video version (ironically, the film ends at the same time that political events left unresolved in the film were coming to a head). FROM A FAR COUNTRY appears to be a better than adequate production (it was filmed on location in Poland) made by a reputable Polish director—Krzysztof Zanussi—in collaboration with the brilliant cinematographer Slawomir Idziak, who shot many of Krzysztof Kieslowski's best films. Characters listed in the credits have been excised entirely, and too much of what remains consists of people talking about events we haven't seen. On the basis of what's left, the full version still probably wouldn't rank with 1900 (1977) or HEIMAT (1983), two other films that paint broad canvasses of 20th century sociopolitical history. But it must certainly be better than this exasperating mess. *(Violence, adult situations.)*—M.F.

d, Krzysztof Zanussi; p, Giacomo Pezzali, Vincenzo Labella; exec p, Lord Grade; w, Andrej Kijowski, Jan Josef Szczepanski, Krzysztof Zanussi, David Butler; ph, Slawomir Idziak; ed, Anthony Gibbs, Bill Blunden, Peter Honess; m, Wojciech Kilar; art d, Janusz Sosnowski; casting, Irene Lamb; cos, Ania Biedrzycka Sheppard

Docudrama/Historical/Drama (PR: C MPAA: NR)

FROZEN ★★★

(China/Netherlands/Hong Kong, 1997) 95m Shu Kei's Creative Workshop; Another Film Company; Hubert Bals Foundation ~ International Film Circuit c
(JIDU HANLENG)

Jia Hongshen *(Qi Lei)*; Ma Xiaoqing *(Shao Yun)*; Bai Yu *(Sister)*; Li Geng *(Sister's Husband)*; Bai Yefu *(Bald Guy)*; Wei Ye *(Long-Haired Guy)*; Zhang Yongning *(Lau Ling)*; Qu Lixin *(Doctor)*; Liu Jie *(Dao Shi)*

Bleak and slow-moving but possessing a jarring last act, FROZEN was made in China in defiance of a mandate against unauthorized independent filmmaking. Consequently it underwent postproduction in the Netherlands and was released with a gimmick worthy of William Castle: the director is said to be a familiar Chinese filmmaker protecting himself with the pseudonym Wu Ming, which translates as "no name."

Disillusioned and disaffected young artist Qi Lei (Jia Hongshen) announces an upcoming performance piece to culminate in his suicide. Family and friends try to talk him out of it, all except Lau Ling (Zhang Yongning), an art critic who urges him on. After Qi and his girlfriend (who is Lau's former lover) visit a soothsayer offering oblique encouragement, Qi is buried in ice and eventually rushed to the hospital where his sister, a doctor, pronounces him dead.

The girlfriend, Shao Yun (Ma Xiaoqing), mourns his death, not knowing that it was faked, part of the performance, orchestrated with Lau's help. Hiding out in the home of the soothsayer (a confederate of Lau's), Qi suffers further despondency and sneaks back into town to discover Lau trying to woo a guilt-ridden Shao Yun. Qi slips away unseen and three months later his body is discovered, his wrists slit.

The director "Wu Ming" went to art school in Beijing and graduated just after the Tiananmen massacre, when all students suddenly became suspect in the eyes of the state. Like several other "sixth generation" directors, he flouted the apprentice system and began making films outside the official network, dealing with contemporary reality in radical terms. FROZEN was filmed in 1994 (it was completed and released in 1997 and made it to the US in 1998), when performance art had become a popular—albeit illegal—form of self-assertion and symbolic protest among the avant garde in China. The story was purportedly based on an actual occurrence that clearly struck a chord with an aspiring director aching for a means of self-expression while constrained by a political bureaucracy restricting unsanctioned filmmaking.

The title FROZEN reflects both the nature of the state and the cold and detached feel of the film itself. Desperately downbeat, it allows only brief moments of ironic humor to surface, as when one of Qi's buddies accompanies him to a psychiatric hospital to be checked out; the eccentric buddy is instead mistaken for the one in need of help and gets dragged off. Languidly, inexorably, the film creeps toward Qi's final performance, with his clique of artist friends depicted as alienated and obsessive (one lengthy "performance" consists of two artists eating bars of soap until they retch), Qi himself as self-destructive and despairing. Thus the twist of his faked death comes as a jolt, followed by the completely left-field possibility that Lau Ling masterminded the whole thing to clear a path back to his ex-girlfriend Shao Yun. After the long, painstaking setup depicting art in China, perhaps more than anywhere else on the globe, as truly *dangerous*, it's a shock to wind up with an ending out of James M. Cain. *(Adult situations, profanity.)*—A.B.

d, Wu Ming; p, Shu Kei, Xu Wei; exec p, Pang Ming; co-p, Fong Xin, Zhu Bing; w, Pang Ming, Wu Ming; ph, Yang Shu; ed, Qing Qing; m, Roeland Dol; art d, Li Yanxiu; sound, Zhai Lixin, Wu Jiang; makeup, Guo Junxia

Drama **(PR: C MPAA: NR)**

FULL SPEED ★★½

(France, 1996) 85m Magouric; Telema; France 2 Cinema; Rhone Alpes Cinema ~ Strand Releasing C
(A TOUTE VITESSE)

Elodie Bouchez *(Julie)*; Stephane Rideau *(Jimmy)*; Pascal Cervo *(Quentin)*; Meziane Bardadi *(Samir)*; Romain Auger *(Rick)*; Salim Kechiouche *(Jamel)*; Mohammed Dib *(Karim)*; Frederic Fargier; Patrice Thomas; Youcef Ninach; Missoum Laimene; Laurent Diomande; Ryad Benkouider *(Jimmy's Gang)*; Paul Morel *(Quentin's Father)*; Bernard Villeneuve *(Journalist)*

FULL SPEED is a sincere, well-made, but overwrought coming-of-age film about four youths in provincial France.

Though still a teenager, Quentin (Pascal Cervo) is already a successful novelist. He passes his free time partying with his rugged friend Jimmy (Stephane Rideau) and girlfriend Julie (Elodie Bouchez). At one party, he meets Samir (Meziane Bardadi), an Algerian contemporary whose lover, Rick, had been murdered two years earlier. Quentin and Samir are attracted to each other and consider a homosexual affair. Quentin also wants to write about the killing of Rick, and asks Samir for assistance in preparing a book. Julie, feeling ignored by Quentin all the while, begins an affair with Jimmy.

A party that Julie has arranged for Quentin is attended by the four. Quentin has changed his mind about a homosexual relationship and is made uncomfortable by Samir's presence. Samir accuses Quentin of being a cowardly conformist and the two fight. Julie and Jimmy break it up, but Samir leaves in disgust, declaring that he will no longer help Quentin with his writing.

Sometime later, Samir is attacked by skinheads. Jimmy is nearby and comes to Samir's aid, but is brutally beaten himself. Quentin, meanwhile, has interested a publisher in his book, and leaves for Paris to write. In his absence, Julie and Samir become close friends, Julie approvingly acknowledging to Samir that she's aware of the homosexual quality of his relationship with Quentin.

When Quentin returns, he fails to contact his friends, which hurts them all. Jimmy, still ailing from the beating, shows up at Julie's house one evening with a nosebleed that he cannot stop. Julie rushes him to a hospital, but he dies before they arrive. Samir avenges Jimmy's death by shooting one of his attackers, then casually turns himself over to the police. Quentin, arriving late to Jimmy's funeral, encounters a grieving Julie. He tries to reconcile with her but she rejects him, telling him that he has "ruined everything," then walks away.

Writer-director Gael Morel's debut feature succeeds in evoking a teenager's view of the world, in which adults figure marginally and brooding emotion is utmost. Morel clearly sympathizes with and respects his characters, treating their adolescent anguish with all due gravity. Morel's own youth (he was 23 at the time he made the film) is no doubt a factor in his insight into young minds, as is his association with fellow French director Andre Techine. (Morel played the lead in Techine's similar but superior 1995 film WILD REEDS; several of that film's supporting cast appear in this film as well.) FULL SPEED, however, is a victim of its own earnestness. Morel is so caught up in his characters' emotional grapplings and so intent on impressing us with his empathy that he fails to develop his film dramatically. Consequently, FULL SPEED works well in conveying how its youths feel, but falters in telling what they do. Morel has created some finely etched characters, but leaves them adrift in a narrative that relies too heavily on melodramatic convention and cliche to carry it along.

Yet, Morel displays an undeniable talent as director. His handling of the young cast is assured, which results in four fine lead performances. Cervo—in a performance that is highly reminiscent of Morel's in WILD REEDS—is especially good as the bright but self-involved Quentin. The actor skillfully strikes within his character just the right balance of naivete and cunning. Bouchez brings a warm and sexy charm to her role as the deeply emotional Julie. Technically the film is accomplished, and boasts some splendid cinematography from Jeanne Lapoirie. FULL SPEED qualifies as a creditable if ultimately sophomoric effort. *(Violence, nudity, sexual situations, profanity.)*—D.C.

d, Gael Morel; p, Laurent Benegui; assoc p, Charles Gassot; w, Gael Morel, Catherine Corsini; ph, Jeanne Lapoirie; ed, Catherine Schwartz; set d, Frederique Hurpeau; sound, Ludovic Henault; casting, Jacques Grant; cos, Brigitte Faur; makeup, Catherine Bruchon; stunts, Philippe Guegan

Drama **(PR: C MPAA: NR)**

FULL TILT BOOGIE ★½

(U.S., 1998) 111m L. Driver Productions; Miramax ~ Dimension c

Robert Rodriguez; Lawrence Bender; George Clooney; Juliette Lewis; Quentin Tarantino; Harvey Keitel; Michael Parks; Tim "Stuffy" Soronen; Rick Stribling; Amy Cohen; Ken Bondy; Victoria Lucai; Celia Montiel; Jason Jake

Sarah Kelly's FULL TILT BOOGIE is a behind-the-scenes documentary about the making of Robert Rodriguez's crime thriller-meets-vampire gore-fest FROM DUSK TILL DAWN (1996). It's really little more than a video yearbook for the film's crew.

Kelly interviews behind-the-camera personnel, ranging from the assistant directors down to the craft service guy, about what their jobs are and how they got into the business. Amy and Victoria, the personal assistants to star George Clooney and costar/coscripter Quentin Tarantino, complain about running errands and doing menial tasks for the stars. Victoria has to drive two hours to retrieve a special coffee mug for Tarantino. Amy is sent out to find a glass sculpture of a raised middle finger, which Clooney presents to costar Juliette Lewis at a party. The crew holds a "best butt on the set" contest. Because FROM DUSK TILL DAWN is using a nonunion crew, IATSE (the union for film crews) has threatened to send picketers to disrupt the production. DUSK executive producer Lawrence Bender explains that strict union rules would inhibit Rodriguez's freewheeling directorial style. Kelly and her crew travel to Miami to track down a union spokesman at an IATSE convention, but he declines to be interviewed on camera.

The DUSK production moves to the desert outside Barstow, CA, for exterior shooting. Seventeen-hour days, 120 degree heat, dust storms, and lousy food are the norm. At night, cast and crew party hard in local bars and poolside at the motel. When the last shot is in the can, everyone is happy and relieved.

FULL TILT BOOGIE opens with a staged bit of comedy that finds Clooney and Tarantino on their way to the set, strutting to the Bee Gee's "Stayin' Alive," and (*a la* THIS IS SPINAL TAP) getting lost in a maze of hallways. If only the rest of the movie were half as entertaining.

Director Kelly, who worked on the crew of PULP FICTION (1994) and was invited by Tarantino to shoot this documentary, offers no real insights into the filmmaking process. Creative talents with big egos come together, artistic temperaments and financial concerns create tension, people blow off steam by drinking a lot of beer. Robert Rodriguez is glimpsed most often on camera strumming his guitar between takes. He never discusses his approach to directing, or the dynamics of his collaboration with Tarantino. And for a film so dependent on makeup and special effects, little of this movie magic is explained.

Though labor issues are very real within the film industry, the difficulty with IATSE is used as a red herring here, and the trip to Miami is pointless grandstanding. Kelly never explores, or even explains, what's at stake from each side's point of view in the union versus nonunion question. Yet, ironically, labor is at the heart of whatever point FULL TILT BOOGIE is supposed to have. Kelly seemingly wanted to find out why "the little people" on the crew remain in grueling, workaday positions in the film industry—positions that have the same amount of show business glamour as cleaning up after the elephants in the circus parade. *(Profanity, violence.)* —P.R.

d, Sarah Kelly; p, Rana Joy Glickman; assoc p, Mark Friedman; ph, Christopher Gallo; ed, Lauren Zuckerman; m, Cary Berger, Dominic Kelly; sound, Ken Ahern

Documentary **(PR: C MPAA: R)**

FUNNY GAMES ★★★½
(Austria, 1997) 103m Wega Film Productions ~ Attitude Films c

Susanne Lothar *(Anna Schober)*; Ulrich Muhe *(Georg Schober)*; Frank Giering *(Peter)*; Arno Frisch *(Paul)*; Stefan Clapczynski *(Georgie Schober)*; Doris Kunstmann *(Gerda)*; Christoph Bantzer *(Fred)*; Wolfgang Gluck *(Robert)*; Susanne Meneghel *(Gerda's Sister)*; Monika von Zallinger II *(Eva)*

The line between real and reel violence is slashed apart in this eminently disturbing psycho-thriller. German filmmaker Michael Haneke adds an extra level to the carnage on screen by having a murderous character directly address the viewing audience, thereby indicting the spectator as voyeur-accomplices to his activities.

The Schober family—father Georg (Ulrich Muhe), mother Anna (Susanne Lothar), young son Georgie (Stefan Clapczynski), and their dog Rolfi—travel to a house on a lake for a vacation. On the way, they see their neighbors, the Berlingers, talking to a pair of young men. A short time later, one of the men, Peter (Frank Giering), comes to the Schobers' door and asks to borrow some eggs for the Berlingers. He is soon joined by his friend, Paul (Arno Frisch), and their increasingly belligerent attitude unnerves Anna. Georg arrives and orders the duo out, and Peter responds by kneecapping him with a golf club.

Thus begins a series of sadistic psychological "games" Peter and Paul play with the Schobers: Anna is manipulated into discovering the dead Rolfi, Georgie is threatened with death, and Paul bets the family they won't survive till morning. At various moments as the action continues, Paul turns to the viewer to comment on the proceedings, and at one point explains to Georg that the "games" cannot end yet because FUNNY GAMES hasn't yet approached feature length.

Georgie manages to escape to the Berlingers' house, only to find all the occupants dead and to be recaptured by Paul. The boy is shot by Peter, who leaves with Paul. Anna flees the house, seeking help, only to be found and brought back by the demented duo. As Paul is about to shoot Georg, Anna grabs his shotgun away and blasts Peter. The furious Paul grabs a VCR remote control, rewinds the scene, and this time successfully shoots Georg. Early the next morning, Peter and Paul take a bound-and-gagged Anna out on the lake in the Schobers' boat and push her over the side. Later that day, Paul goes to another house on the lake and asks to borrow some eggs. . .

While far more violent and visceral, FUNNY GAMES recalls another European thriller, THE VANISHING (1988), in the way it slowly but surely ratchets up its tension. Haneke begins with deceptively bucolic settings and scenes, then gradually leads the audience into darker and darker territory, with the survival possibilities of the characters (both good and evil) always in doubt. This is not for weak hearts, and Haneke's uncompromising approach borders on the sadistic, but this is one of those movies (like 1990's HENRY: PORTRAIT OF A SERIAL KILLER) whose craft justifies its uncompromisingly horrific approach.

Haneke isn't quite as successful in his attempts at black, self-reflexive satire. Attempting to implicate the audience in the horrors he depicts, the director breaks the fourth wall by having Paul acknowledge that he's in a movie from time to time, a gambit that doesn't quite jibe with the otherwise cruelly realistic approach. More effective is the character's literal reversal of Anna's tables-turning shooting of Paul, a moment that chillingly subverts a would-be catharsis and plays havoc with the audience's expectations. Right down to its almost off-handedly callous ending, FUNNY GAMES puts viewers through an emotional wringer, thus qualifying as one of the more legitimately disturbing films of the 1990s. *(Graphic violence, adult situations, profanity.)*—M.G.

d, Michael Haneke; p, Veit Heiduschka; w, Michael Haneke; ph, Jurgen Jurges; ed, Andreas Prochaska; prod d, Christoph Kanter; sound, Walter Amann; cos, Lisy Christl

Thriller/Horror **(PR: O MPAA: NR)**

FUTURE FEAR ★★½
(Canada/U.S., 1998) 84m Producers Network Associates Inc. ~ New Horizons Home Video c

Jeff Wincott *(Dr. John Denniel)*; Maria Ford *(Lt. Anna Pontine)*; Stacy Keach *(General Wallace)*; Shawn Thompson *(Robert)*; Kristie Ropiejko *(Yvette)*; Michael Seater *(Young Denniel)*; Danielle Dasilva *(Young Anna)*; Robert Tinkler *(Young Wallace)*; Stephanie Jones *(Denniel's Mother)*; Michael Berger *(Denniel's Father)*; Matt Hummel; Joseph Clark; Robert Harrison O'Carroll; Plato Fountidakis *(Soldiers)*; Jules Delorme *(Viral Man #1)*; Glen Cullen *(Viral Man #2)*; Ken Mate *(Doctor)*; Michael Krek *(Technician)*

Wisecracking Jeff Wincott races to save humanity from a virus unleashed by evil general Stacy Keach in FUTURE FEAR, a typical bargain-basement release from Roger Corman's New Horizons.

2018 AD. Geneticist Dr. John Denniel (Jeff Wincott) is enlisted by Lt. Anna Pontaine (Maria Ford) to help study an extraterrestrial virus being gathered by a space probe. Although Denniel has hated the military since his father was killed as a result of a still-classified experiment 30 years ago, he agrees. He and Anna become lovers and marry, and Anna becomes pregnant. The probe crashes in Africa, unleashing a plague that kills billions of people. Denniel comes up with the idea of breeding human eggs with genetic information from animals resistant to the virus, producing embryos from which they can harvest a vaccine. But Anna, who suffered a miscarriage that she blames on Denniel, develops a mother fixation on the test-tube embryos and wants to bring them to term, even though to do so will mean the lives of millions of people. Pursued by Anna, Denniel flies the embryos to a secure lab where he has secretly built an acceleration unit to speed up their development.

At the nearly abandoned lab, Denniel learns that the probe was purposely crashed by General Wallace (Stacy Keach), who wants to purify the Earth for a new Aryan race. Anna is Wallace's assistant, and both have been using Denniel to breed the new race. After various battles with Anna, Denniel gets the embryos to the acceleration unit—only to be met by Wallace, who has been monitoring his progress. Wallace admits that he killed Denniel's father when he sabotaged an earlier version of Wallace's genocidal plan. Realizing that she has been emotionally manipulated by Wallace for his fascistic plans, Anna helps turn the tables in a fight that leaves all dead but Denniel, who races to manufacture his vaccine to inoculate what is left of humanity.

Although FUTURE FEAR was only released, not produced by Corman's company, in has all the hallmarks of a New Horizons production. This tale of the eminent destruction of the human race is presented by a handful of characters in a few indoor locations, with the turmoil of the outside world represented by riot footage from what appears to be a Philippine film. It's the classic Corman formula of making do with the least possible resources, though there are moments when the makers of FUTURE FEAR seem to be trying to turn this to their advantage. On the other hand, the script's infatuation with the works of Lewis Carroll, while ambitious, is never sufficiently developed: the presence of an Alice-like little girl and her pet white rabbit is merely mystifying. At least Wincott, who resembles a beefed-up version of Jim "Ernest" Varney, makes for a fun hero and gets some humorous zinger lines; Ford, on the other hand, makes the mistake of taking her part seriously, which can be even funnier. *(Violence, nudity, sexual situations, adult situations, profanity.)*—M.F.

d, Lewis Baumander; p, Daniel D'Or, G. Philip Jackson; exec p, Roger Corman, Maryann Ridini, David A. Steinberg; co-p, Demerise J. Lafleur, Christopher Rutherford; w, Jules Delorme, Glen Cullen, Lewis Baumander, G. Philip Jackson; ph, Graeme Mears; ed, David Ransley; m, Donald Quan; prod d, James Plaxton; art d, Julie Fox; set d, Richard Armstrong; sound, Jack Buchanan; fx, Ron Craig; cos, Maxyne Baker; makeup, Catherine Davies Irvine; stunts, Dwayne McLean

Science Fiction/Action/Thriller (PR: O MPAA: R)

G

GADJO DILO ★★★

(France, 1997) 97m Princes Film; Celluloid Dreams ~ Lions Gate Films c

Romain Duris *(Stephane)*; Rona Hartner *(Sabina)*; Isidor Serban *(Izidor)*; Ovidiu Balan *(Sami)*; Dan Astileanu *(Dimitru)*; Florin Moldovan *(Adrjani)*; Mandra Ramcu *(Mandra)*; Aurica Ursan *(Aurica)*; Angela Serban *(Angela)*; Calman Kantor *(Radu)*; Valentin Teodosiu *(Mayor's Secretary)*; Vasile Serban *(Vasile)*; Ioan Serban *(Ioan)*; Gheorghe Gherebenec *(Gheorghe)*; Petre Nicolea *(Grocer)*; Adrian Simionescu *(Child Prodigy)*; Lunitia Paun *(The Bride)*; Jean Paun *(Father of the Bride)*; Petre Costescu *(Father of the Groom)*; The Radu Family

The third in filmmaker Tony Gatlif's loose trilogy of films about gypsy life (after THE PRINCES, 1982, and LATCHO DROM, 1993), GADJO DILO favors local color over plot in its tale of a young Parisian who becomes part of a gypsy village.

Stephene (Romain Duris) wanders through rural Romania, hoping to find the gypsy singer who made a recording that his late father loved. Looking for a place to spend the night in one village, he encounters Izidor (Isidor Serban), a drunken old gypsy musician who takes a liking to him. Claiming to recognize the singer on Stephene's tape, he engages the young man in his drinking, and takes him home to his village to sleep. The next morning, Stephene is treated with suspicion by the other villagers, who accuse him of all the crimes with which gypsies are stereotyped, until Izidor rescues him. Encouraging him to stay and learn more about their ways (including their language, which Stephene doesn't speak), Izidor treats him as a surrogate for his own son, Adrjani, who has been jailed by the Romanians.

While continuing his search for the singer, Stephene accompanies Izidor and other musicians to a traditional wedding party, and befriends Sabina (Rona Hartner), a gypsy dancer whose status as a divorcee frees her from many of the social constraints put upon gypsy women. They travel to Bucharest, where Izidor tries unsuccessfully to pick up two young women in a bar. Back at the village, everyone is overjoyed that Adrjani (Florin Moldovan) has been released from jail, and Stephene and Sabina make love in the woods. But when Adrjani picks a fight with Rumanians at a bar, a riot ensues in which Adrjani is killed and the gypsy village burned down. Stephene burns the musical recordings and notes he has made before leaving with Sabina.

"Gadjo dilo" is a phrase from the gypsy language meaning "crazy outsider," and Stephene is initially regarded as such by the gypsy villagers with a sense of irony; it is gypsies themselves who are so often considered by others to be crazy outsiders. Filmmaker Gatlif, who is of gypsy heritage, obviously has a feel for these people, and the best parts of GADJO DILO work in documentary fashion, presenting gypsy life and culture. (A high point is the wedding scene, in which the bride's father ritually refuses to give over his daughter until he is bribed with drink and dowry money.) But Gatlif's casual filming style sometimes works against the film. Filming in a real gypsy village with a cast made up predominantly of real gypsies, it's difficult to know where we should draw the line between fact and fiction, or even if we should. And a real documentary would present more factual detail about the recent and current history of these people, instead of resorting to a melodramatic ending.

While the leading characters are somewhat cliched, the gusto with which they are played compensates. Isidor Serban easily steals the film as the Zorba-ish old man, always dancing, singing, complaining, and scolding with equal fire. Nearly as good is Rona Hartner, though her lusty profanities may be too vivid for the ears of some viewers. *(Violence, nudity, sexual situations, adult situations, extreme profanity.)* —M.F.

d, Tony Gatlif; p, Doru Mitran; exec p, Gut Marignane; w, Tony Gatlif, Kits Hilaire, Jacques Maigre; ph, Eric Guichard; ed, Monique Dartonne; m, Tony Gatlif; art d, Brigitte Brassart; sound, Nicolas Naegelen; casting, Marie de Laubier; cos, Michaela Ularu; makeup, LeanaMocanu

Drama/Comedy **(PR: C MPAA: NR)**

GENEALOGIES D'UN CRIME

(SEE: GENEALOGIES OF A CRIME)

GENEALOGIES OF A CRIME ★★

(France, 1997) 113m Gemini Films; Canal Plus; Centre National de la Cinematographie ~ Strand Releasing c (GENEALOGIES D'UN CRIME)

Catherine Deneuve *(Jeanne/Solange)*; Michel Piccoli *(Georges Didier)*; Melvil Poupaud *(Rene)*; Andrzej Seweryn *(Christian)*; Bernadette LaFont *(Esther)*; Monique Melinand *(Louise)*; Hubert Saint Macary *(Verret)*; Jean-Yves Gautier *(Mathieu)*; Mathieu Amalric *(Yves)*; Camila Mora *(Soledad)*; Patrick Modiano *(Bob)*; Jean Badin *(L'avocat)*

GENEALOGIES OF A CRIME is a highbrow jigsaw puzzle of a movie about free will, destiny, and psychology that tries to be whimsical, but settles for being intentionally abstruse, centering on an enjoyable dual-role performance by Catherine Deneuve as both a psychiatrist who is murdered by her nephew/patient and the lawyer who defends the nephew.

At a police station, a French lawyer named Solange (Catherine Deneuve) confesses to murder. She recounts her tale, starting at the point which she agreed to defend a young man named Rene (Melvil Poupaud) accused of murdering his Aunt Jeanne, a psychiatrist who was a member of controversial group called "The Franco-Belgian Psychoanalytical Society." The group's eccentric leader Georges (Michel Piccoli) tells Solange that he saw Rene murder Jeanne and warns her not to take the case, as does her mother Louise (Monique Melinand) who is one of Georges's patients, but she does.

After Rene tells Solange he's innocent, she reads Jeanne's diaries, and Rene and Jeanne (Deneuve) are depicted at various points in their relationship: the orphaned Rene moves in with Jeanne when he is nine; he kills cats and steals money and jewels from her; she soon comes to believe that he has homicidal tendencies and subjects him to her radical treatments, including role-reversal games and kinky group therapy sessions. When Rene is 19, Jeanne is killed during one of the group sessions and Georges claims to have witnessed Rene doing it. Meanwhile, Solange's mother recalls incidents when Solange used to throw cats out of the window when she was a little girl, and becomes worried that she will become a murderess. Georges lures Solange to one of the group therapy session and locks her in a room where they restage the murder for her, but Rene tells her that he was knocked out during the original session and Jeanne was dead when he awoke.

Solange becomes convinced that Rene is innocent and she gets him acquitted by casting doubt on Georges and his group's dangerous psychiatric methods. To protest the decision, Georges and his group come to a celebration party at Solange's law offices and commit mass suicide by pouring poison into their drinks.

Three days later, Rene moves in with Solange and becomes her lover, but begins to steal money from her and eventually admits that he really did kill Jeanne. When he shows up one night with a couple of friends, including a girl who warns Solange that she is in danger, Solange has a vision of herself as a little girl holding a cat and a knife. She takes the knife and stabs Rene 40 times, and kills his two friends as well. Back to the present, Solange's lawyer tells her he will plead insanity for her and she calmly goes back to her jail cell.

GENEALOGIES OF A CRIME uses its purported thriller and mystery elements as a mere pretext for some facetious philosophizing about predetermination and to play mind games with traditional notions of storytelling and cinematic conventions, but ends up being little more than a sometimes amusing, and more often exasperating, intellectual tease. It's elegantly made, but for all of its visual tricks and narrative conceits (deliberate out-of-focus shots, constant use of one-way mirrors, flashbacks-within-flashbacks, a trial that lasts 30 seconds and consists solely of a court artist's sketches, allusions to nursery rhymes and the concept of stories as "diseases," the use of doubles and surrogate characters, Deneuve playing two roles in a variety of wigs and costumes), the film remains curiously flat and uninvolving.

The casting of Deneuve and Michel Piccoli brings to mind Luis Bunuel's masterpiece BELLE DE JOUR (1967), and director/co-writer Raul Ruiz seems to be aiming for a similarly seamless mix of "reality" and "fantasy" and a kind of Bunuelian deadpan absurdism. But whereas Bunuel had the finesse to subvert the rules of storytelling while keeping everything crystal clear and employing a light and playful touch, Ruiz's style is confusing, cold, and distanced, creating an academic tone that's at odds with the pseudo-surrealist events. The cast, however, is excellent, with a still fabulous-looking Deneuve very good in the dual role, and the great Piccoli perfect as the hilariously nutty Georges, deftly capturing the delicate balance of humor and madness that the film strives for but misses. *(Profanity, sexual situations, violence.)* —M.S.

d, Raul Ruiz; exec p, Paulo Branco; assoc p, Madragoa Filmes; w, Raul Ruiz, Pascal Bonitzer; ph, Stefan Ivanov; ed, Valeria Sarmiento; m, Jorge Arriagada; prod d, Luc Chalon, Solange Zeitoun; set d, Gilles Dunn; sound, Henri Maikoff; cos, Elizabeth Tavernier; makeup, Cedric Gerard

Thriller **(PR: C MPAA: NR)**

GENERAL, THE ★★★

(Ireland/U.K., 1998) 129m Merlin Films; J&M Entertainment ~ Sony Pictures Classics bw

Brendan Gleeson *(Martin Cahill)*; Adrian Dunbar *(Noel Curley)*; Sean McGinley *(Gary)*; Maria Doyle Kennedy *(Frances)*; Angeline Ball *(Tina)*; Jon Voight *(Inspector Ned Kenny)*; Eanna McLiam *(Jimmy)*; Tom Murphy *(Wille Byrne)*; Paul Hickey *(Anthony)*; Tommy O'Neill *(Paddy)*; John O'Toole *(Shea)*; Ciaran Fitzgerald *(Tommy)*; Ned Dennehy *(Gay)*; Vinnie Murphy *(Harry)*; Roxanna Williams *(Orla)*; Eamonn Owens *(Young Martin Cahill)*; Colleen O'Neill *(Patricia)*; Maebh Gorby *(Sylvie)*; Pat Laffan *(Higgins)*; Frank Melia *(Lawless)*; Ronan Wilmot *(James Donovan)*; Lynn Cahill *(Arcade Woman)*; David Wilmot *(Assassin)*; Stephen Brennan *(Arthur Ryan)*; Don Wicherley *(Henry Mackie)*; Kevin Flood *(Judge)*; Pat Kinevane *(Desk Guard)*; Barry McGovern *(IRA Leader)*; Pat Leavy *(Mrs. Duggan)*; Neile Conroy *(Maeve)*; Peter Hugo Daly *(Beavis)*; Aoife Moriarity *(Young Frances)*; Brendan Coyle *(UVF Leader)*; Jim Sheridan *(CPAD Leader)*; Gavin Kelty *(Young Hood #1)*; Owen O'Neill *(Revenue Man)*; David Carey *(Revenue Man)*; Niamh Lineham *(Reporter)*; Jason Byrne *(Reporter)*; Ann Doyle *(TV Newsreader)*; Daragh Kelly *(Young Detective)*; Des O'Malley *(Himself)*

Among the best of the many 1998 films set and shot in Ireland, THE GENERAL is the more or less true story of Martin Cahill, one of the most cunning and colorful gangsters in modern Irish history. Probably John Boorman's most accomplished movie since DELIVERANCE (1972), it won him the Best Director Prize at the Cannes Film Festival.

On August 18, 1994, Martin Cahill (Brendan Glesson) is killed by as assassin. Just before he is shot, his life flashes before his eyes:

A poor boy growing up in Dublin, Martin (Eamonn Owens) begins his crime career as a petty thief. Years later he is an ex-con who lives in an open and surprisingly unstrained relationship with his wife, Frances (Maria Doyle Kennedy), their children, and Frances's sister Tina (Angeline Ball), who will also bear him a child. Ned Kenny (Jon Voight), a local policeman, urges Cahill to change his thieving ways before it is too late, but to no avail. Kenny will go on to devote the greater part of his career to bringing Cahill to justice.

Brilliant, brazen, and brutal when he feels the need, Cahill and the gang he commands like a general steal $60,000,000 over the course of the next 20 years. His biggest coup is the heist of a collection of invaluable paintings, including the world's only privately owned Vermeer. Although regarded with veiled admiration by many of his fellow Dubliners, he is despised by the city's police and politicians. He also incurs the wrath of the Irish Republican Army when he refuses to cut them in on his plunder and especially when he fences one of his hot canvases to Irish Loyalists.

After the Dublin Police Department institutes an aggressive policy designed to get Cahill at any cost, things begins to go bad for the master crook; one of his right-hand men (Adrian Dunbar) goes straight and tells the police where the hidden paintings are—or so believes the increasingly paranoid Cahill; another cohort (Sean McGinley) becomes a potential informer when he is charged with raping his own daughter. One morning Cahill arises to find that the army of police surveillants who customarily surround his house have mysteriously disappeared. After entering his car, he is shot and killed by an IRA gunman.

Boorman directed his three masterworks early in his career: POINT BLANK in 1967, HELL IN THE PACIFIC in 1968, and DELIVERANCE in 1972. Although he never lost his great pictorial flair, nothing he has made since then has matched the richness, originality, and vision of those three films. Still, THE GENERAL (along with the Dutch film CHARACTER) is one of the most cinematically imposing and assured pictures of the year, and a vast improvement on the deadly BEYOND RANGOON (1995), Boorman's previous film.

THE GENERAL benefits enormously from having been shot in black-and-white, "something of a lost art," according to Boorman, who said that "Eastman and Fuji color films are too saturated. They prettify. They vulgarize. And particularly, they romanticize poverty." The movie is to be commended also for bringing an unusually high degree of artistic shape to a bastard genre: the (supposedly) true story, as adulterated by the input of screenwriters and actors. Its uncommon success in this area is due not only to Boorman's great filmmaking sophistication but also to his readiness to fudge history. Boorman called THE GENERAL "a fiction based on fact. The frameworks would be built of incidents that occurred. Beyond that I would rely on the truth of the imagination."

Brendan Gleeson is first-rate as Cahill, a classic Irish mocker whose rough manner disguises a delicate mind. Perhaps Cahill's most impressive accomplishment, if you can believe what you see on the screen, was not his audacious criminal career but his gift for domestic engineering. It must have taken a kind of genius to persuade two sisters to love him, bear him children, and continue to love each other.

Although clearly an incorrigible criminal and sociopath, Gleeson's Cahill can be perceived also as an iconoclastic rebel who refuses to settle for the crushing and mean existence that would have been his lot as an honest man. And though THE GENERAL reaches the unoriginal conclusion that crime doesn't pay, it also implies, a bit subversively, that in some cases at least, neither does the alternative. *(Violence, adult situations, extreme profanity.)*—D.T.

d, John Boorman; p, John Boorman; exec p, Kieran Corrigan; w, John Boorman; ph, Seamus Deasy; ed, Ron Davis; m, Richie Buckley; prod d, Derek Wallace; sound, Brendan Deasy (recordist); fx, Team FX; casting, Jina Jay; cos, Maeve Paterson; makeup, Maire O'Sullivan

Crime/Biography **(PR: O MPAA: R)**

GENERAL CHAOS: UNCENSORED ANIMATION ★★

(U.S./Germany/U.K., 1998) 90m ~ Manga Entertainment c

VOICES OF: "Performance Art: Starring Chainsaw Bob": Chris Hardwick; Fred Tattasciore; Ed Shively; "American Flatulators": Jeff Beith; Buddy Smith; Chris Stewart

A dazzling array of animation techniques is on display in this compilation of short films. The films concentrate on sex, violence, and scatalogical humor, making them high on shock value, but low on intelligence. Twenty-one short films, created by American and British independent animators (and one German), many of them students, make full use of an array of animation media, from 3-D models and cel animation to computer graphics and a combination of cartoon characters and live actors. Highlights include:

"Quest," a short showing a clay sandman digging for water and falling through a succession of different landscapes, including sand, paper, rock, metal, and industrial buildings; "Donor Party," a macabre look at a gathering of surgery victims at a mansion party, done with computerized recreations of 19th century-style lithographs; "Oh Julie," animation with doll figures in which a man and woman, both seedy and aging, embark on a one-night-stand by donning supplemental body parts; "Zerox and Mylar," a traditional cat-and-mouse cartoon done in clay animation; "Junky" combines an actor playing a sadistic parrot owner with an animated parrot model who pleads persistently for a cracker; "Attack of the Hungry Hungry Nipples" uses traditional cartoon cel animation to depict the tale of a poor abused young boy, Jean-Jean, who is mistreated by an invading pair of nipples until he enlists the aid of "the Evil Cat"; "Expresso Depresso" focuses on a trendy coffee bar and a fatal combination of pretentious patrons and an indignant overworked waitress; "Body Directions" involves the animation of cutout figures emerging from the crevices of the body of the animator's girlfriend; and "Mutilator" is a seriously executed take on the post-apocalyptic superhero genre as the title character slaughters murderous mutants in a future wasteland.

The entire program is interspersed with short gag pieces by Bill Plympton under the heading "Sex and Violence," including "Confused Sense of Priorities" in which a man interrupts a passionate sexual encounter in order to floss his teeth.

As in so many of these collections, the technique and craft far outweigh the level of humor or the depth of thought. Much of the humor consists of sophomoric, frat-boy hijinks designed to titillate and shock. The biggest laugh-getters are the Plympton shorts and the traditional gag cartoons, "Zerox and Mylar" and "Attack of the Hungry Hungry Nipples," which is memorable for its trademark line "You suck something!" voiced by the nipples. The Academy Award-winning "Quest" seems to have been tacked on at the beginning to give a little class to the proceedings.

Most of the pieces are thankfully quite short, making this less of a chore to sit through than similar collections, such as TOO OUTRAGEOUS ANIMATION (1995). It's also packaged well, with the Plympton shorts perking things up at regular intervals and the better pieces spaced apart. The production dates range from 1982 to 1997, and the lengths of the pieces from one to 12 minutes. *(Violence, nudity, sexual situations, profanity.)*—B.C.

d, Jeff Sturgis ("American Flatulators"), Walter Santucci ("Attack of the Hungry Hungry Nipples"), Keith Alcorn ("Beat the Meatles"), Karl Staven ("Body Directions"), Laurence Arcadias ("Donor Party"), David Donar ("Espresso Depresso"), Tony Nittoli ("Junky"), Stefan Eling ("Killing Heinz"), Joel Brinkerhoff ("Zerox and Myler"), Mr. Lawrence ("Looks Can Kill"), Vince Collins ("Malice in Wonderland"), Frances Lea ("Oh Julie!"), Brandon McKinney ("Performance Art: Starring Chainsaw Bob"), Kathryn Travers ("Sunny Havens: A.K.A.—Meat!!!"), Brad Schiff ("No More Mr. Nice Guy"), Eric Fogel ("Mutilator"), Bill Plympton ("Sex and Violence"), Mike Booth ("The Saint Inspector"), Amanda Enright ("Misfit"), Emily Skinner ("The Perfect Man"), Tyron Montgomery ("Quest"), Thomas Stillman ("Quest"); exec p, Marvin Gleicher; co-p, Jerry Park ("Looks Can Kill"); m, Gerald Stockton ("Beat the Meatles"), Stefan Eling ("Killing Heinz"), Jamie Goltont ("Oh Julie!"), The Insects ("The Saint Inspector"); anim, Walter Santucci ("Attack of the Hungry Hungry Nipples"), Paul Claerhout ("Beat the Meatles"), Karl Staven ("Body Directions"), David Donar ("Espresso Depresso"), Stefan Eling ("Killing Heinz"), Joel Brinkerhoff ("Zerox and Myler"), Laurence Arcadias ("Donor Party"), Burt Klein ("Looks Can Kill"), Vince Collins ("Malice in Wonderland"), Jayne Bevitt ("Oh Julie!"), Brandon McKinney ("Performance Art: Starring Chainsaw Bob"), Kathryn Travers ("Sunny Havens—A.K.A. Meat!!!"), Brad Schiff ("No More Mr. Nice Guy"), Eric Fogel ("Mutilator"), Jeff Sturgis ("American Flatulators"), Bill Plympton ("Sex and Violence"), Mike Booth ("The Saint Inspector"), Lee Wilton ("The Saint Inspector"), Tony Nittoli ("Junky"), Amanda Enright ("Misfit"), Emily Skinner ("The Perfect Man"), Tyron Montgomery ("Quest"), Thomas Stillman ("Quest")

Animated **(PR: O MPAA: NR)**

GEORGE WALLACE ★★★½

(U.S., 1998) 178m TNT Original ~ Warner Bros. c/bw

Gary Sinise *(George Wallace)*; Mare Winningham *(Lurleen Wallace)*; Angelina Jolie *(Cornelia Wallace)*; Joe Don Baker *(Big Jim Folsom)*; Clarence Williams III *(Archie)*; Mark Valley *(Robert Kennedy)*; Don Blakey *(Loosh)*; Cliff De Young *(Dr. Jeff McKinney)*; Bobby Kirby *(James Hood)*; Ketema Nelson *(Vivian Malone)*; Steve Harris *(Neal)*; Mel Jackson *(Eddie)*; Frank Jones *(Jamison)*; Tiffany Salerno *(Velma)*; Ron Perkins; Skipp Sudduth; Tracy Fraim; Mark Rolston; William Sanderson; Terry Kinney

Anchored by a brilliant lead performance from Gary Sinise, GEORGE WALLACE chronicles the political career of one of America's most notorious statesmen, the Alabama governor who qualified as one of the greatest enemies of the American Civil Rights movement. This made-for-cable miniseries was released on home video in 1998.

In 1955, George Wallace (Gary Sinise) is a judge who is being groomed by Governor "Big Jim" Folsom (Joe Don Baker) to succeed him. When it comes time to campaign for that office four years later, though, Wallace is defeated when he denounces the Ku Klux Klan. Vowing never again to lose touch with his constituency, Wallace becomes a zealous proponent for segregation, a platform that carries him to the governor's office in 1963. In order to retain his seat, Wallace opposes the Civil Rights movement in all its forms. When two black students attempt to enroll in the all-white University of Alabama, Wallace stands in the doorway to bar them, and must be removed by the National Guard. Wallace prepares for a presidential bid; however, he soon finds that crowds in the North do not share his views on racial segregation. Back in Alabama, Martin Luther King organizes a march from Selma to Montgomery, the state's capital. Wanting to hold onto his office, Wallace first appeals to the Alabama Legislature to amend the state's constitution to allow him to succeed himself; when that fails, he convinces his wife, Lurleen (Mare Winningham), to run for governor. For a few months it appears as though Wallace may continue the fight through Lurleen, but the campaign comes to an end when Lurleen, suffering from cancer, collapses. Wallace retires from politics to be by her side, and remains there after her death.

Several years later, Wallace meets Cornelia Folsom (Angelina Jolie), the niece of Big Jim, and the two quickly marry. Feeling rejuvenated, Wallace once again enters the political world, regaining the governor's office and setting his sights on the presidency. While on the campaign trail in 1972, Wallace is shot five times by a would-be assassin, an attack that leaves him paralyzed from the waist down. Still he continues his presidential campaign, until a chilly reception to a pro-segregation speech at the Democratic National Convention reveals that he has once again lost touch with the people. Two years later, his marriage falling apart, Wallace begins to realize the error of his ways. One night he goes to Martin Luther King's former church, the birthplace of the Civil Rights movement, and asks forgiveness for his years of fighting on the wrong side.

The centerpiece of GEORGE WALLACE is the performance by its star, Gary Sinise, who captures the complexity of the man who stood against Martin Luther King. As the consummate "man of the people," Sinise effectively conveys the bafflement Wallace felt when his reluctance to embrace the Klan separated him from his constituents; and, years later, that same disbelief when his pro-segregation platform began to crumble beneath him, leaving him high and dry. Sinise's performance is perfectly complemented by Mare Winningham and Angelina Jolie as his two wives, one loyal to the point of self-destruction, the other too ambitious for her crippled husband to keep up with.

The only sour note among the performances (if there is one) comes from Clarence Williams III as Archie, a prison trustee who works as a servant in the Governor's mansion from the days of Big Jim Folsom to the end of Wallace's term. As explained at the end of the film, Archie is not a real person, but a construct intended to illuminate a particular point of view. As such, his presence feels a bit forced, and the frequent shots of Archie's horrified or seething reaction to Wallace's statements are unnecessarily unsubtle.

In addition to fine performances, GEORGE WALLACE offers viewers some distinctive visual techniques, care of veteran director John Frankenheimer (THE MANCHURIAN CANDIDATE). Frankenheimer frequently switches to a grainy, black-and-white documentary style to recreate key scenes, such as Wallace's stand at the doors of the University of Alabama. These pieces help to underscore the film's comparison of the hard-line public Wallace with the often self-doubting private man.

GEORGE WALLACE was nominated for a number of awards, garnering Emmys for Gary Sinise, Mare Winningham, and director John Frankenheimer. *(Profanity, sexual situations, adult situations, violence.)*—B.T.

d, John Frankenheimer; p, John Frankenheimer, Julian Krainin; exec p, Mark Carliner; co-p, Ethel Winant; w, Paul Monash, Marshall Frady (based on the book *Wallace* by Frady); ph, Alan Caso; ed, Tony Gibbs; m, Gary Chang; prod d, Michael Hanan; casting, Iris Grossman; cos, May Routh

Biography/Political/Drama (PR: C MPAA: NR)

GIA ★★★½

(U.S., 1998) 120m Marvin Worth Production; Citadel Entertainment; Khan Power Pics; HBO Pictures ~ HBO Home Video c

Angelina Jolie *(Gia Carangi)*; Elizabeth Mitchell *(Linda)*; Eric Michael Cole *(T.J.)*; Kylie Travis *(Stephanie)*; Louis Giambalvo *(Joe Carangi)*; John Considine *(Bruce Cooper)*; Scott Cohen *(Mike Mansfield)*; Edmond Genest *(Francesco)*; Mercedes Ruehl *(Kathleen Carangi)*; Faye Dunaway *(Wilhelmina Cooper)*; Holly Baker *(Emergency Room Nurse)*; Joe Basile *(Disco Doorman Tony)*; Rick Batalla *(Hispanic Stylist Phillipe)*; Lombardo Boyar *(Hood #2)*; Julio Dolce Vita *(Hood #3)*; Brian Donovan *(Junkie at Shooting Gallery)*; Alexander Enberg *(Chris Von Wagenheim)*; Vylette Jezel Fagerholm *(Blonde Girl in Philadelphia)*; Guido Foehrweisser *(German Makeup Artist)*; Scott Genkinger *(Philadelphia Photographer)*; Judy Gillet *(Beverly)*; Johnny Green *(Gia's Brother, Joey)*; Cee-Cee Harshaw *(Winter)*; Meleney Humphrey *(Booker #1)*; Tim Hutchinson *(TV Interviewer)*; Michelle Jonas *(Vogue Assistant #1)*; Mila Kunis *(Gia, Age 11)*; Steve Carson *(Drug Dealer in Alley)*; Drinda La Lumia *(Booker #3)*; Shelby Leverington *(Woman at Funeral)*; Allison Mackie *(Red Dress Designer)*; Norman Merrill *(Doctor in AIDS Ward)*; Tricia O'Neil *(Vogue Editor)*; Sam Pancake *(Francesco Stylist #1)*; Adina Porter *(Girl at Group Therapy)*; Joan Pringle *(Therapist at Rehab)*; Michael E. Rodgers *(Red Dress Photographer)*; Holly Sampson *(Amy)*; Paul Sandman *(Vogue Assistant #2)*; Antony Sandoval *(John Casablancas)*; John-Clay Scott *(Policeman)*; Phillip Simon *(Fashion Store Manager)*; Alexis Smart *(Jenny)*; Nick Spano *(Michael, Gia's Brother)*

Playwright Michael Cristofer (*The Shadow Box*) turned filmmaker with this sizzling made-for-cable biopic that takes an unflattering look at the fashion industry.

After arriving in New York City from Philadelphia, Gia Carangi (Angelina Jolie) is discovered by a photographer while she is shopping. During her first photo shoot, she models both clothed and nude, and becomes friendly with photographer's assistant Linda (Elizabeth Mitchell). They have a tryst at Gia's apartment, but Linda leaves feeling troubled about the experience. Gia's career skyrockets as a result of her renegade attitude and look, but she quickly develops a dependency on cocaine. After visting her mother in Philadelphia, Gia attempts to resume her relationship with Linda, who rejects her. Gia's mother begins regularly visiting Gia in her New York apartment, but an argument between the two sends her mother back to Philadelphia. Her career spiralling downward, Gia switches from cocaine to heroin. Suffering from withdrawal pains during a major photo shoot, Gia bolts off in a costly gown to score drugs. She shoots up in an alley.

Realizing her problem, she makes up with Linda, who helps her dry out. Gia returns to modeling—and to using heroin, causing a reckless-driving incident. A subsequent argument severs her relationship with Linda once more. After her falling-out with Linda, she appeals to her mother, who refuses to let her return home. Finally, she successfully beats her addiction, but then becomes ill and is informed she has contracted AIDS. She has a friendly reunion with Linda, during which Gia doesn't reveal her illness. After leaving Linda's apartment she attempts to purchase a suicidal amount of heroin, which results in her being robbed and beaten. Later, her mother bids her farewell in the hospital; Gia eventually expires of AIDS-related illnesses.

The tragic, true-life story of Gia Carangi contains so many highs and lows (mostly the latter) that it was merely a matter of time before it served as the source material for a movie. This small-screen production does justice to the cautionary tale of her rise and fall in fashion circles, emphasizing a lifestyle of sex, drugs, and indulgence that seemingly had to end in death.

Cristofer, who has worked as an actor and writer in both theater and film, directs the film in a taut, no-nonsense style, complemented by Rodrigo Garcia's stylish camerawork. On the performance level, Angelina Jolie turns in a star-making performance as Gia, playing the part with a conviction that reinforces the dead-end trajectory of the young supermodel's life. And while the well-choreographed sexual interludes between Jolie and Mitchell may lead one to believe that the film is glamorizing Gia's experiences, Cristofer is careful to underscore the character's perenially depressed state, and the fact that her drug use stemmed essentially from a neediness that engulfed everyone with whom she interacted. Indeed, the film poses some difficult questions about the underside of glamour, and makes a very strong argument against the "heroin chic" phenomenon. *(Sexual situations, violence, extreme profanity, extensive nudity, substance abuse.)*—P.L.

d, Michael Cristofer; p, James D. Brubaker; exec p, Marvin Worth, Ilene Kahn Power, David Ginsburg; assoc p, Tina L. Fortenberry, Richard Licata; w, Jay McInerney, Michael Cristofer; ph, Rodrigo Garcia; ed, Eric Sears; m, Terence Blanchard; prod d, David J. Bomba; art d, John R. Jensen; sound, Patrick Mitchell; fx, Bruno Van Zeebroeck; casting, Junie Lowery Johnson, Libby Goldstein; cos, Robert Turturice; makeup, Nena Smarz; stunts, Jake Crawford

Drama **(PR: O MPAA: R)**

GINGERBREAD MAN, THE ★★

(U.S., 1998) 115m Island Pictures;
Enchanter Entertainment ~ PolyGram c

Kenneth Branagh *(Rick Magruder)*; Embeth Davidtz *(Mallory Doss)*; Robert Downey Jr. *(Clyde Pell)*; Daryl Hannah *(Lois Harlan)*; Robert Duvall *(Dixon Doss)*; Tom Berenger *(Pete Randle)*; Famke Janssen *(Leeanne)*; Jesse James *(Jeff)*; Mae Whitman *(Libby)*; Troy Beyer *(Konnie Dugan)*; Julia R. Perce *(Cassandra)*; Danny Darst *(Sheriff Hope)*; Sonny Seiler *(Phillip Dunson)*; Walter Hartridge *(Edmund Hess)*; Vernon E. Jordan Jr. *(Larry Benjamin)*; Lori Beth Sikes *(Betty)*; Rosemary Newcott *(Dr. Bernice Sampson)*; Wilbur T. Fitzgerald *(Judge Russo)*; David Hirsberg *(Tom Cherry)*; Paul Carden *(Judge Cooper)*; Michelle Benjamin-Cooper *(Principal)*; Christine Seabrook *(Secretary)*; Bob Minor *(Mr. Pitney)*; Myrna White *(Tax Clerk)*; Jim Grimshaw *(Desk Cop)*; Stuart Greer *(Detective Hal)*; Nita Hardy *(Policewoman)*; Ferguson Reid *(Detective Black)*; Benjamin T. Gay *(Court Clerk)*; Mark Bednarz; Bill Cunningham; Chip Tootle *(Effingham County Sheriffs)*; Sonny Shroyer; Mike Pniewski; Jay S. Pearson *(Chatham County Sheriffs)*; L.H. Smith *(Storm Evacuee)*; Wren Arthur *(Barfly Robin)*; Angela Costrini *(Barfly Wren)*; Gregory H. Alpert *(Barfly Clark)*; Lydia Marlene *(Tattooed Bartender)*; Bill Crabb *(Huey)*; Jin Hi Soucy; Richie Dye; Chad Darnell *(Huey's Patrons)*; Natalie Hendrix; Gregg Jarrett; Doug Weathers *(Television Anchorpersons)*; Jeremy Cooper; Beth Eckard; Brad Huffines; Patrick Prokop *(Television Weathercasters)*; Mike Manhattan; David Jordan; George Lyndel Brannen; Gregory F. Pallone; Alice Stewart; Vanessa Young *(Television Field Reporters)*; Alyson E. Beasley; Angela Beasley *(Puppeteers)*; Scott Troughton *(Dredge Worker)*; Grace Tootle *(Gas Station Attendant)*; Shane James *(Ricky Butch Banks)*; Herb Kelsey; William L. Thorp IV *(Doss Gang Members)*

In a decided misfire, master director Robert Altman—working from an original screen story by bestselling novelist John Grisham—serves up a compendium of suspense-thriller cliches executed in a lukewarm, workmanlike manner. The effectively menacing moments found in the film's first two-thirds are cancelled out by the presence of a major red herring and a "surprise" conclusion that's evident from the beginning.

A party is held at the office of Savannah, Georgia, lawyer Rick Magruder (Kenneth Branagh) to celebrate his victory in a recent case. Working as a waitress at the party is catering employee Mallory Doss (Embeth Davidtz) who needs a lift home after her car is stolen. The gallant—and always on-the-make—Magruder offers her a ride, and the two wind up sleeping together. Mallory soon turns to Magruder for help, asking him to protect her from her father, abusive hillbilly evangelical Dixon Doss (Robert Duvall). Magruder employs a private detective, Clyde Pell, (Robert Downey Jr.) to guard her; he also has the eccentric Doss committed to a mental hospital, but Doss soon breaks out.

When he receives threats against the lives of his children, Magruder assumes that Doss is responsible, and moves his kids from their school to a local motel for safety. When Magruder leaves the motel room to call Mallory, the children are abducted.

Mallory leads him to a possible hiding place, Doss's backwoods compound. There Magruder and Doss have an armed standoff, and the lawyer kills the hillbilly. Pell arrives and tells Magruder that the children are safe—having been deposited at the police station by their abductor. Magruder is arrested for the killing of Doss and is set to stand trial.

Doss's will is discovered and Mallory is named as the heir to Doss's land, which contains a rare and valuable form of timber. Pell informs Magruder that Mallory and her husband, Pete (Tom Berenger), are still legally married—thus qualifying Pete for a half interest in the timber land. Magruder goes to visit Pete on the boat where he works. There, he discovers Pell's dead body; he then confronts Pete and the two fight. The fight is interrupted by Mallory, who kills Pete (her collaborator in deceiving Magruder) with a flare gun; she then turns the flare gun on Magruder, not realizing that it is no longer loaded. Magruder locks her in the cabin of the boat.

A short time later, the verdict is in: Magruder will get five years probation, loss of his license, and community service for Doss's death; Mallory will serve time for her scheming and the killing of Pete.

Robert Altman reportedly chose to direct THE GINGERBREAD MAN because he'd yet to tackle a thriller in the classic Hitchcock fashion. His decision was faulty for several reasons. Firstly, many of his films contain suspenseful sequences, and two in particular—the dreamlike IMAGES (1972) and his psychotic character study THAT COLD DAY IN THE PARK (1969)—could easily be categorized as thrillers.

More importantly, Altman's modernist filmmaking style (a mixture of roving camerawork, overlapping dialogue, and frequently "busy" sequences in which several characters are gathered in a single space) is the utter antithesis of classical thriller direction (read: Hitchcock), in which the only way to craft a suspenseful sequence is to conceal visual information, thus metaphorically leading the viewer along by the nose. Altman's "open" approach flys in the face of such calculation.

Still, Altman does his best to deliver some chills and succeeds at certain points, especially in the sequence where Magruder searches the backwoods for Doss's cabin in order to find his missing children. Aided by the very talented Chinese cinematographer Gu Changwei (FAREWELL, MY CONCUBINE), Altman situates the menace in nature—the trees, overcast sky, and the dark roadway are the source of Magruder's (and our) edgy feeling. However, even this gripping sequence is diminished by cliche—in this case, the fact that Magruder's search is taking place on "a dark and stormy night," and the entire segment revolves around the oldest suspense gambit in the book, bar none: children in peril.

Altman's usually brilliant instinct for casting is blunted here, due to the wholly mainstream nature of the project. As ever, Robert Duvall is impeccable in a character part; once Doss is killed, all intrigue drains right out of the story line. Branagh holds his own as the noble but flawed hero, but one's attention is drawn away by Robert Downey Jr., who pretty much documented his real-life late '90s meltdown from drug abuse in a number of 1998 releases (US MARSHALS, TWO GIRLS AND A GUY); here, his character is perenially stoned drunk, and Downey's performance is needlessly spot-on. Much was made in the press about Altman's battles with his distributor Polygram; what was eventually released was said to be Altman's final cut. As it stands, it's the least Altman-like work to bear his name since the major-studio astronaut saga COUNTDOWN (1968). *(Nudity, violence, sexual situations, substance abuse, profanity.)*—E.G.

d, Robert Altman; p, Jeremy Tannenbaum; exec p, Mark Burg, Todd Baker, Glen A. Tobias; assoc p, David Levy; w, Al Hayes (based on an original story by John Grisham); ph, Gu Changwei; ed, Geraldine Peroni; m, Mark Isham; prod d, Stephen Altman; art d, Jack Ballance; set d, Brian Kasch; sound, John Pritchett (mixer), Randle Akerson (design), Richard King (design); fx, Tom Kittle; casting, Mary Jo Slater; cos, Dona Granata; makeup, Deborah Larsen; stunts, Greg Walker

Thriller/Crime **(PR: C MPAA: R)**

GIRL GETS MOE, THE
(SEE: LOVE TO KILL)

GIRLS IN PRISON ★★★
(U.S., 1994) 83m Showtime Networks; Spelling Films ~ Buena Vista Home Video c

Missy Crider *(Aggie)*; Ione Skye *(Carol)*; Anne Heche *(Jennifer)*; Nicolette Scorsese *(Suzy)*; Bahni Turpin *(Melba)*; Jon Polito *(Boss Johnson)*; Nestor Serrano *(Benito Borcelino)*; Miguel Sandoval *(Lucky)*; Richmond Arquette *(Detective Campion)*; Raymond O'Connor *(Mickey Maven)*; Tom Towles *(Norman Stoneface)*; William Boyett *(Shainmark)*; Angie Ray McKinney *(Miranda)*; Harvey Chao *(Lum Fong)*; Ralph Meyering Jr. *(Jim Jeffrey)*; Diane McGee *(Mrs. Felton)*; Letitia Hicks *(Receptionist)*; J. Patrick McCormack *(Gordon Madison)*; William G. Clark *(Actor Playing McCarthy)*; David Paul Needles *(MCarthy on Newsreel)*; Tamara Clatterbuck *(Actress on Newsreel)*; Martin Charles Warner *(Coroner's Physician)*; Richard Saxton *(Newscaster)*; Rick Cicetti *(Cop)*; Mil Nicholson *(Warden)*

Originally produced for Showtime's uneven series of remakes of 1950s AIP B features (titled "Rebel Highway"), this densely plotted women's prison picture is something different—a tongue-in-cheek melodrama that spoofs the babes-behind-bars subgenre, action-movie cliches, and various '50s phenomena including the McCarthy witchhunts. Compulsively watchable trash, the film may have been directed by John McNaughton, but its over-the-top tendencies bear the clear imprint of its coscripter, legendary filmmaker Sam Fuller.

In the 1950s, three girls become friendly while serving time in prison. They are: Melba (Bahni Turpin), who murdered a Red-baiting TV commentator for exploiting a photo of her soldier brother's corpse on his show; Carol (Ione Skye), a playwright, who was made so disraught by the failure of her anti-McCarthy play and her actor-father's having fallen into a coma, that she impulsively killed a barroom loudmouth; and country singer-songwriter Aggie (Missy Crider), accused but innocent of having murdered a record company executive, Boss Johnson (Jon Polito), who got physical with her. The three young women form a clique with a fourth member, the impressionable Suzy (Nicolette Scorsese).

When a riot breaks out in the prison yard, Melba and Carol protect Aggie from a "hitgirl," and warn her that there is a contract out on her life. On the outside, Aggie's song "Endless Sleep" has been turned into a hit, after having been taken from Johnson's office by the scheming Benito Borcelino (Nestor Serrano) and Johnson's associates Jennifer (Anne Heche) and Miranda (Angie Ray McKinney). Melba's restaurant-owner friend, Lum Fong (Harvey Chao) recruits a private detective, Lucky (Miguel Sandoval) to investigate Aggie's case. Little does Lucky (or anyone else) know that Suzy is in fact the next designated "hitgirl"—Borcelino (who is, in fact, Suzy's boyfriend) asks her to kill Aggie as a favor to him. After a strip-tease performance for the prison inmates, a riot breaks out and Suzy is unmasked; she kills herself in shame.

When Lucky roughs up Borcelino, he finds out who is behind the frame-up of Aggie: Jennifer, who not only killed Johnson, but is also a full-blown sociopath. At the same instant, Jennifer is getting herself arrested and placed in the same prison as Aggie. In a move to protect Aggie and flush out a possible "hitgirl," the prison authorities decide to hold a potato-sack race in the prison yard. As the race becomes a shambles, Jennifer tries to kill Aggie, but is instead forced by the young country singer to confess, and thus vindicate Aggie of the killing of Boss Johnson, in full view of the prison populace.

"Hitgirls"? A newscaster bludgeoned to death on live TV in the 1950s? An experimental play in which a character condemns McCarthy to his face—performed while the Senator was still in ascendence? A striptease show in a women's prison? A potato sack race? GIRLS IN PRISON is an incredibly imaginative, and at points downright bizarre, concoction that has nothing to do with its namesake, a 1956 potboiler about teens in trouble. Fuller's presence as a coscripter—he wrote the screenplay along with his actress wife Christa Lang—is curious, given the low-profile nature of his contribution to this made-for-cable project (this was the last Fuller screenplay filmed during his lifetime). Fuller's involvement is also unusual for the very fact that the film is first and foremost a campfest. No matter how absurd the occurrences are in Fuller's work as a filmmaker (SHOCK CORRIDOR, THE NAKED KISS) he rarely, if ever, played them for intentional laughs.

Perhaps this emphasis on humor is more Lang's contribution than Fuller's, but it can be said for director McNaughton that he does deliver the requisite prison-picture brutality at several points—in fact, the movie more often resembles '80s fare like THE CONCRETE JUNGLE (1982) and THE NAKED CAGE (1986) more than it does a seminal 1950s entry in the genre like WOMEN'S PRISON (1955). McNaughton also makes impressive use of a gaudy color scheme and faux-noir lighting patterns (nearly every set contains a shadow cast by venetian blinds or prison bars).

The performers give their roles the proper level of cartoonish intensity, with Missy Crider qualifying as a properly simpering lead, and Anne Heche stealing the show as the psychotic villainess. Her sincere approach to such an outrageously overwrought role (recalling her work in the equally insane WILD SIDE) is one of the film's closest ties to the Fuller tradition. *(Profanity, violence.)*— E.G.

d, John McNaughton; p, Lou Arkoff, Debra Hill, Willie Kutner, David Giler; assoc p, Amy Grauman Danziger; co-p, Llewellyn Wells; w, Samuel Fuller, Christa Lang; ph, Jean De Segonzac; ed, Larry Bock; m, Hummie Mann; prod d, Deborah Raymond , Dorian Vernacchio; set d, Nancy S. Fallace; sound, Mark Deren; fx, Bellisimo/Bejardinelli FX Inc.; casting, Julie Alter; cos, Susan Bertram; makeup, Carlos David Armador; stunts, Chris Howell

Prison **(PR: C MPAA: R)**

GO NOW ★★½

(U.K., 1995) 88m Revolution Films; BBC Films ~ Gramercy Pictures c

Robert Carlyle *(Nick Cameron)*; Juliet Aubrey *(Karen Walker)*; James Nesbitt *(Tony)*; Sophie Okonedo *(Paula)*; Berwick Kaler *(Sammy)*; Darren Tighe *(Dell)*; Sean Mackenzie *(George)*; John Brobbey *(Geoff)*; Sara Stockbridge *(Bridget)*; Sean Rocks *(Charlie)*; Tom Watson *(Bill Cameron)*; Barbara Rafferty *(Madge Cameron)*; Tony Curran *(Chris Cameron)*; Erin McMahon *(Julie Cameron)*; Dave Schneider *(Doctor #1)*; Jenny Jules *(Doctor #2)*; Anna Godsiff *(Nurse)*; Susie Fugle *(Scan Doctor)*; Roger McKern *(Patient)*; James Trehearne *(Male Nurse)*; Cal McGregor *(Man in Wheelchair)*; Tricky *(Himself)*

A modest 1995 British film about a vigorous young man who contracts multiple sclerosis, GO NOW probably owed its 1998 US release to the increased visibility accrued by its male star and its director in the years between. Viewers' reactions to the movie are likely to be evenly split between "I loved it!" and "Who needs it?" depending on their degrees of tolerance to pain and suffering.

Nick (Robert Carlyle), a young Scotsman living in Bristol, England, spends his time at his plasterer's job and having fun with his mates on an amateur soccer team. He meets Karen (Juliet Aubrey), they embark on a romance, and she agrees to move in with him.

When Nick begins to suffer from numbness and blurred vision, Karen suspects multiple sclerosis. As his condition worsens, he becomes unable to walk without canes and experiences problems with continence and potency. Resisting the urgings of his girlfriend and his family to move back to Scotland, he fears that Karen has taken to sleeping with her boss (Sean Rocks), a suspicion that comes true. Things get so bad that eventually, Nick—crippled, bitter, in deep physical and emotional pain—exhorts Karen to leave him, but she refuses. Resolved to face the future together, the couple wed.

GO NOW begins with a joke told by Nick's friend, Tony (James Nesbitt), that is raunchy, sick, and very funny. Much of the first half of the movie is devoted to this kind of adolescent sexual badinage and, after a while, it gets a little wearing, particularly when the director joins the personae in the fun. Periodically, he halts the narrative to make way for a series of black-and-white freeze frames over which are superimposed such puerile legends as "Nick Makes a Last Desperate Effort to Stop Wanking" and, over a shot of Tony dropping trou, "Tony Gives the Ref a Bit of Cheek."

Then, disease sets in, and things sober up quickly. Unfortunately, all of the problems and conflicts introduced in the second act—Nick's impotence and Karen's resultant sexual straying, the dilemma of whether or not to move back to Glasgow, etc.—are allowed to go totally unresolved. Is there a missing sequence somewhere?

Outstanding among GO NOW's performers is Juliet Aubrey, a young woman with an easy, unneurotic acting style and the sort of stark, basic beauty that is only enhanced by pouring rain. Carlyle is also impressive, but his thick Scottish accent may make many viewers regret that they did not bring along interpreters. Carlyle's brogue is an instance of authenticity undercutting art.

Cowriter Paul Henry Powell was himself a victim of MS. The success of TRAINSPOTTING (1996) and THE FULL MONTY (1997), both of which starred Carlyle—along with critical enthusiasm for director Michael Winterbottom's WELCOME TO SARAJEVO (1997)—may have been responsible for GO NOW ultimately finding a US distributor. *(Nudity, sexual situations, adult situations, extreme profanity.)*—D.T.

d, Michael Winterbottom; p, Andrew Eaton; exec p, David M. Thompson; assoc p, Sheila Fraser Milne; co-p, Roxy Spencer; w, Paul Henry Powell, Jimmy McGovern; ph, Daf Hobson; ed, Trevor Waite; m, Alastair Gavin; prod d, Hayden Pearce; art d, Frazer Pearce; sound, Martin Trevis; fx, Mark Turner; casting, Simone Ireland; cos, Rachael Fleming; makeup, Amanda Warburton; stunts, Roy Alon

Romance/Drama **(PR: O MPAA: NR)**

GODS AND MONSTERS ★★½

(U.S., 1998) 105m Regent Entertainment ~ Lions Gate Films c/bw

Ian McKellen *(James Whale)*; Brendan Fraser *(Clayton Boone)*; Lynn Redgrave *(Hanna)*; Lolita Davidovich *(Betty)*; Kevin J. O'Connor *(Harry)*; David Dukes *(David Lewis)*; Brandon Kleyla *(Young Whale)*; Pamela Salem *(Sarah Whale)*; Michael O'Hagan *(William Whale)*; Jack Plotnick *(Edmund Kay)*; Sarah Ann Morris *(Daisy)*; Mark Kiely *(Dwight)*; David Millbern *(Dr. Payne)*; John Gatins *(Kid Saylor)*; Amir Aboulela *(Young Karloff)*; Rosalind Ayres *(Elsa Lanchester)*; James Lecesne *(Jack Pierce)*; Matt McKenzie *(Colin Clive)*; Martin Ferrero *(George Cukor)*; Cornelia Hayes O'Herlihy *(Princess Margaret)*; Jack Betts *(Elder Karloff)*; Jesse H. Long *(Assistant Director)*; Owen Masterson *(Camera Assistant)*; Lisa Vastine *(Librarian)*; Kent George *(Whale at 25)*; Todd Babcock *(Leonard Barnett)*; David Fabrizio *(Photographer)*; Jesse James *(Michael Boone)*; Lisa Darr *(Dana Boone)*; Paul Michael Sandberg *(Sound Man)*; Judson Mills *(Young Man)*; Arthur Dignam *(Ernest Thesinger)*

GODS AND MONSTERS profiles the last year in the life of James Whale, the director of FRANKENSTEIN (1931). Despite rich possibilities, however, the docudrama, which appeared at the 1998 New York Film Festival, takes too tentative and conventional an approach to the mysterious and controversial filmmaker's life.

In 1957, British-born James Whale lives a quiet life in the Hollywood Hills, reproducing great works of art on canvas. Whale's days as a Hollywood director exists only as a distant memory. His friend, David Lewis (David Dukes), and his maid, Hanna (Lynn Redgrave), worry about his ill health; Hanna becomes particularly alarmed when her employer suffers from a serious fainting spell after an interview with a young reporter who quizzes Whale on his openly gay lifestyle. But Whale choses to ignore the dire physical signs, and prefers instead to ogle his handsome new gardener, Clayton Boone (Brendan Fraser).

Whale seduces the unsuspecting Clayton by asking him to pose for a picture. Eventually, a friendship forms and the men learn about one another's background, trading stories of Clayton's experience in the Korean War and Whale's experience in WWI—and his status as a director most famous for his horror films. Clayton is bothered, however, when he learns from Hanna that Whale is gay. Whale assures Clayton he is not interested in him sexually, but he teases the young man provocatively, nonetheless, forcing Clayton to walk out angrily.

Later, Clayton returns, wanting to renew their platonic friendship. Whale agrees to behave himself around his attractive friend, although he passes Clayton off as his lover during a rare public appearance—a party for Princess Margaret hosted by rival director George Cukor. That night, back at Whale's house, a rainstorm forces Clayton to stay over. Moved by Whale's artistic eloquence, he suggests Whale paint him in the nude. But the session becomes violent when Whale tries to molest Clayton and Clayton responds by beating Whale. Later that night, the men forgive each other for the incident, but the next morning Hanna finds Whale drowned in the pool, an apparent suicide.

Years later, a married Clayton watches FRANKENSTEIN on television with his son and explains to him how he knew the great director. After putting his son to bed, Clayton mimics the Frankenstein Monster walking in the rain, his tribute to an old friend.

Two biographies of the underappreciated Whale were published in the late 1990s. GODS AND MONSTERS is based not on the similarly titled *James Whale: A New World of Gods and Monsters* by James Curtis, but on *Father of Frankenstein* by Christopher Bram. As these books and GODS AND MONSTERS make clear, Whale made many more worthy and interesting films than just FRANKENSTEIN (1931) and THE BRIDE OF FRANKENSTEIN (1935), but, much to his irritation and (sometimes) amusement, he was best remembered for those two horror classics. While the Curtis book surveys an entire career, which also included work on THE OLD DARK HOUSE (1932), THE INVISIBLE MAN (1933), and SHOWBOAT (1936), the Bram book and GODS AND MONSTERS focus on Whale's lengthy "retirement" and suicide. A la SUNSET BOULEVARD, this partly speculative account discovers drama and an odd sort of unrequited romance in the relationship between Whale and Clayton, which is utilized as a metaphor for Whale's love-hate for his famous "Monster" (Clayton often resembles him, particularly in some fanciful dream sequences). The film also comments on the decaying Old Hollywood (depicted mainly in the party set-piece).

Yet GODS AND MONSTERS misses a great opportunity to better illuminate Whale's full oeuvre and create a really superior story out of his last hurrah. Unfortunately, the film highlights the FRANKENSTEIN pictures more than anything else Whale ever made (they are discussed, clips are aired on TV, and recreated in flashback "on-the-set" scenes). Also, the "romance" between Whale and Clayton fails to be touching, perhaps because of Brendan Fraser's stolidity and Ian McKellen's theatrical archness (compare the latter performance to John Hurt's masterful work in a similar role in LOVE AND DEATH ON LONG ISLAND); McKellen was nonetheless nominated for a Best Actor Oscar. Regarding Whale's sexuality, writer-director Bill Condon—who won an Oscar for Best Adapted Screenplay—often turns his hero into a stereotypical tragic loner while never really figuring out what factor sex played in short-circuiting Whale's career. Finally, the legendary mystery over Whale's demise is treated bluntly and anticlimactically. With its Merchant-Ivory look and feel, perhaps GODS AND MONSTERS would have benefited from direction more akin to the Whale approach—stylish, expressionistic, and consistently creative. *(Violence, nudity, sexual situations, adult situations, extreme profanity.)*—E.M.

d, Bill Condon; p, Paul Colichman, Gregg Fienberg, Mark R. Harris; exec p, Clive Barker, Stephen P. Jarchow ; w, Bill Condon (based on the novel *Father of Frankenstein* by Christopher Bram); ph, Stephen M. Katz; ed, Virginia Katz; m, Carter Burwell; prod d, Richard Sherman; set d, James Samson; sound, Shawn Holden (mixer); fx, Ultimate Effects; casting, Valorie Massalas; cos, Bruce Finlayson; makeup, Tarra Day; stunts, Chuck Borden

AA Best Adapted Screenplay: Bill Condon; *AAN Best Actor:* Ian McKellen; *AAN Best Supporting Actress:* Lynn Redgrave

Drama/Fantasy **(PR: C MPAA: R)**

GODSON, THE ★

(U.S., 1998) 100m Three Spear; Defiant Films ~ Sterling Home Entertainment c

Kevin McDonald, billed as Kevin Hamilton McDonald *("Guppy" Calzone)*; Rodney Dangerfield *(The Rodfather)*; Dom DeLuise *(The Oddfather)*; Fabiana Udenio *(Don Na)*; Lou Ferrigno *(Bugsy)*; Paul Greenberg *(Frito Calzone)*; Bob Hoge *(Sunny Calzone)*; Carol Arthur *(Mama Calzone)*; Barbara Crampton *(Goldy)*; Irwin Keyes *(Tracy Dick)*; Eileen Kenney *(FBI Agent Hoover)*; Dom Irrera *(Himself)*; Carlos Alazraqui *(Tony Montana)*; Bobbie Brown *(Sunny's Babe)*; Perry Stephens *(Father O'Connell)*; Jerry Lamert *(The Professor)*; Keith Coogan *(Clumsy Student)*; Henry Carbo *(Vinnie the Tailor)*; Alicia Hoge *(Phone Sex Lady)*; Gregory Allen Webb *(Transvestite Dancer)*; John LaMotta *(Club Maitre D')*; Sonya Eddy *(Bank Clerk)*; Jerry Douglas *(Freddie Green)*; Jerry Ray *(Waiter at Party)*; Craig Barnett *(President Clinton)*; Gina Angela Ritchie *(Sexy Sue)*; D. Paul Abram *(Billy Bob)*; Jay Lacopo *(Studio Executive)*; Debra Christofferson *(Screenwriter)*; Lisa London *(Busty Secretary)*; Don Pardo *(Himself)*; Joey Buttafuoco *(Himself)*

A long nap with the fishes would be preferable to viewing this painfully unfunny Mafia send-up. You know a movie is really bad when the highlight is a cameo appearance by Joey Buttafuoco.

The Oddfather (Dom DeLuise) is ready to step down as Don of the Calzone crime family. Heir apparent Sunny (Bob Hoge) survives a hit, but gets knocked unconscious and is mistakenly buried alive. Because #2 son Frito (Paul Greenberg), a postal worker, has gone insane, the Oddfather names his youngest son "Guppy" (Kevin McDonald), a prissy weirdo, the new mob chieftain. After graduating from Mafia University, Guppy meets The Rodfather (Rodney Dangerfield), Don of a rival *famiglia*, and his beautiful daughter Don Na (Fabiana Udenio). As part of his plan to ruin the Calzones, The Rodfather has Don Na date Guppy, but when she really falls in love with Guppy, The Rodfather imprisons her.

Guppy desperately needs to raise funds to save his bankrupt family, but after such moneymaking schemes as starting a 1-800 phone sex line and robbing a sperm bank go awry, he decides to throw a $20,000-a-plate fund-raising dinner. After clawing out of his grave, Sunny shows up at the party, as does Don Na, who has escaped from her father's dungeon. The Rodfather, Frito, and other guests all attempt to murder Guppy. When the bloodshed subsides, Guppy announces his plan to take the Calzones out of the crime business and buy a movie studio with the money he's raised. Against The Rodfather's wishes Don Na marries Guppy.

Beneath the lowly level of even 1998's other gangland parody, JANE AUSTEN'S MAFIA!, THE GODSON aspires to the Mel Brooks school of comedy. Writer-director Bob Hoge (who plays Sunny) certainly tries hard. Along with predictable nods to THE GODFATHER (1972), SCARFACE (1983), and GOODFELLAS (1990), there are pop culture references on subjects ranging from "Charlie's Angels" to SLING BLADE (1996), as well as topical jokes on Mike Tyson's ear- biting and Bill Clinton's womanizing. There are also pure Brooks's moments, like when the movie stops to let a producer and writer discuss the script's developments and Guppy hawks GODSON action figures. The problem is, none of it is funny.

This cinematic train wreck is about par for the course for DeLuise (who would have thought he could do worse than 1994's SILENCE OF THE HAMS?); it would toll the death knell for the movie career of Dangerfield, except he barely has one to speak of anyway. As for Kevin McDonald, who was hilarious as a member of the "Kids in the Hall" troupe, he should just be very embarrassed. *(Violence, sexual situations.)*—P.R.

d, Bob Hoge; p, Jeff Ritchie, Kevin Flint; exec p, George Marinos, Lynn Mooney, Morris Ruskin, Mary Skinner; w, Bob Hoge; ph, Tom Lappin; ed, Tracy Curtis; m, Boris Elkis; prod d, Deren P. Abram; art d, Flip Filippelli; set d, Jon Joseph Glover; sound, Matthew Nicolay; cos, Mandi Line, Lisa Rae Sandoval; makeup, Laura Markert; stunts, Gary Paul, Terrance James

Comedy/Crime **(PR: C MPAA: PG-13)**

GODZILLA ★★

(U.S., 1998) 139m Centropolis Entertainment; Fried Films; Independent Pictures; Woods Entertainment ~ TriStar c

Matthew Broderick *(Dr. Niko Tatopoulos)*; Jean Reno *(Philippe Roache)*; Hank Azaria *(Victor "Animal" Palotti)*; Maria Pitillo *(Audrey Timmonds)*; Arabella Field *(Lucy Palotti)*; Kevin Dunn *(Colonel Hicks)*; Doug Savant *(Sergeant O'Neal)*; Harry Shearer *(Charles Caiman)*; Michael Lerner *(Mayor Ebert)*; Vicki Lewis *(Dr. Elsie Chapman)*; Malcolm Danare *(Dr. Mendel Craven)*; Lorry Goldman *(Gene—Mayor's Aide)*; Christian Aubert *(Jean-Luc)*; Philippe Bergeron *(Jean-Claude)*; Frank Bruynbroek *(Jean-Pierre)*; Francois Giroday *(Jean-Philippe)*; Nicholas J. Giangiulio *(Ed)*; Robert Lesser *(Murray)*; Ralph Manza *(Old Fisherman)*; Greg Callahan *(Governor)*; Chris Ellis *(General Anderson)*; Nancy Cartwright *(Caiman's Secretary)*; Richard E. Gant *(Admiral Phelps)*; Jack Moore *(Leonard)*; Steve Giannelli *(Jules)*; Brian Farabaugh *(Arthur)*; Stephen Xavier Lee *(Lt. Anderson)*; Bodhi Pine Elfman, billed as Bodhi Elfman *(Freddie)*; Rich Battista *(Jimmy)*; Lloyd Kino *(Japanese Tanker Cook)*; Toshi Toda *(Japanese Tanker Captain)*; Clyde Kusatsu *(Japanese Tanker Skipper)*; Masaya Kato *(Japanese Tanker Crew Member)*; Glenn Morshower *(Kyle Terrington)*; Lola Pashalinski *(Pharmacist)*; Rob Fukuzaki *(WIDF Co-Anchor)*; Dale Harimoto *(WKXI Anchor)*; Gary Cruz *(WFKK Anchor)*; Derek Webster *(Utah Captain)*; Stuart Fratkin *(Utah Ensign)*; Frank Cilberg; Jason Edwards Jones; Roger McIntyre; David Pressman *(Anchorage Captain)*; Robert Faltisco; Chris Maleki; Scott Lusby *(Anchorage Ensigns)*; Alex Dodd *(Anchorage Sailor)*; Terence Winter; Kirk Geiger; Pat Mastroianni; Eric Saiet; Burt Bulos; Robert Floyd; Seth Peterson *(Apache Pilots)*; Jamison Yang; Nathan Anderson; Mark Munafo; Dwight Schmidt *(F-18 Pilots)*; Dwayne Swingler *(Raven Pilot #2)*; Lawton Paseka *(Officer)*; Greg Collins *(Soldier on Bridge)*; James Black; Thomas Giuseppe Giantonelli; Paul Ware *(Soldiers)*; Monte Russell *(Soldier on Plane)*; Christopher Carruthers; Daniel Pearce *(Radio Technicians)*; Mark Fite *(Radio Operator)*; Craig A. Castaldo *(Radio Man)*; Eric Paskel *(Rodgers)*; Lee Weaver; Leonard Termo *(Homeless Guys)*; Joshua Taylor *(Spotter)*; Al Sapienza *(Taxi Cab Driver)*; Stoney Westmoreland *(Tunnel Guard)*; Gary Warner *(Gun Technician)*; Ed Wheeler *(New York Cop)*; Bill Hoag *(New Jersey Cop)*; Joseph Badalucco Jr. *(Forklift Driver)*; Jonathan Dienst *(Field Reporter)*; Benjamin V. Baird; Madeline McFadden; Julian M. Phillips; Raymond Ramos *(Reporters)*

Summer 1998's state of the art special-effects showcase, GODZILLA was also the year's most notable flop: while its massive advertising drew crowds to its opening weekend, the film—produced by the team who made INDEPENDENCE DAY (1996)—failed to attract the kind of repeat business necessary to push ticket sales well into the desired nine-figure region. The special effects may be spectacular, but special effects aren't enough to get an audience involved.

Dr. Niko Tatopoulos (Matthew Broderick), an expert in the effects of nuclear radiation on animals, is retrieved from studying worms in Chernobyl. The government sends him to Panama, where the only clue to massive destruction is a series of giant footprints. On a similar path are a team of French investigators led by Philippe Roche (Jean Reno). Niko's surmise—that the damage is the result of a giant lizard much larger than any known dinosaur—is proven true when the beast attacks Manhattan. After wreaking havoc, it seems to disappear, and the Army arrives to evacuate the city. Niko's guess that it has disappeared into the subway tunnels proves correct. As mountains of fish are gathered to lure the monster (dubbed "Godzilla" by a TV reporter), Niko encounters his ex-lover Audrey Timmonds (Maria Pitillo), now a fledgling journalist looking for a big break.

The army's heat-seeking missiles are unable to fix on the cold-blooded Godzilla, and do more damage to buildings than the monster, which disappears again. Niko analyzes a sample of Godzilla's blood and discovers that it is pregnant. When Audrey steals Niko's notes and they turn up on TV, he is removed from the team—only to be picked up by Philippe, who reveals that he and his men are with the French Secret Service, "cleaning up" the mistakes caused by his country's nuclear testing. As the American military launches what appears to be a successful effort to kill Godzilla, Niko and the French team follow the monster's trail to Madison Square Garden, where several hundred eggs are just beginning to hatch into 10-foot baby Godzillas. Trapped inside, they use the Garden's television facilities to contact the Army, then manage to escape the building just before it is bombed. Niko and the others encounter the still-living adult Godzilla, which they lure to the Brooklyn Bridge. As the monster becomes entangled in the bridge's suspension cables, it is destroyed by the army's missiles. But at Madison Square Garden, an undamaged egg begins to hatch.

Never mind what it's called, this just isn't a Godzilla movie. An American adaptation of the Japanese series was at best doomed to be like a McDonald's MacSushi sandwich—just not the real thing. The irony is that Godzilla is budget-proof; fans enjoy the original movies because of, not in spite of, their low budgets and hokey special effects. They had what this movie wholly lacks—personality. This Godzilla, which looks nothing like its predecessor (it resembles an iguana, walking semi-erect, with stegosaurus-like spinal plates the only nod to the original design) is simply a lumbering black hole.

Expensive special effects like these create another problem: the more realistic the monster appears, the more we become aware of the film's unreal aspects. How does a monster this big manage to sneak up on people? How does it manage to walk around Manhattan without the sidewalks collapsing under its weight? What is it even doing in Manhattan? (It's a long commute from Panama.) As in INDEPENDENCE DAY, the filmmakers are either unable or unwilling to generate any sense of fear, suspense, or tension—buildings crumble, but there's no sense that there were people in them who might have been hurt. You look but never become involved. Instead, the script undercuts the mood every few minutes with various running jokes, the dumbest of which concerns New York Mayor Ebert bickering with his assistant Gene. (If you don't get it right off, they keep hitting you over the head until you do.) And a large chunk of the film is devoted to a surprisingly blatant rip-off of JURASSIC PARK (1993), with the baby Godzillas standing in for Spielberg's murderous velociraptors. Seldom has a final set-up for a sequel been less needed. *(Violence, adult situations, profanity.)*—M.F.

d, Roland Emmerich; p, Dean Devlin; exec p, William Fay, Roland Emmerich, Ute Emmerich; co-p, Peter Winther, Kelly Van Horn; w, Roland Emmerich, Dean Devlin (from a story by Ted Elliott, Terry Rossio, Dean Devlin, and Roland Emmerich; based on the character created by Toho Co.); ph, Ueli Steiger; ed, Peter Amundson, David J. Siegel; m, David Arnold; prod d, Oliver Scholl; art d, William Ladd Skinner; set d, Victor Zolfo; sound, Jose Antonio Garcia (mixer), SOUNDELUX (design); fx, Patrick Tatopoulos, Volker Engel, Patrick Ellis, Centropolis Effects; casting, April Webster; cos, Joseph Porro; makeup, Zoltan; stunts, R.A. Rondell

Science Fiction/Adventure/Thriller (PR: C MPAA: PG-13)

GODZILLA AND MOTHRA: THE BATTLE FOR EARTH ★★★½

(Japan, 1992) 102m Toho ~ Columbia Tri-Star c

Tetsuya Bessho *(Takuya Fujita)*; Megumi Odaka *(Miki Saegusa)*; Satomi Kobayashi *(Masako Tezuka)*; Akira Takarada *(Joji Minamino)*; Keiko Imamura; Sayaka Osawa *(Cosmos)*; Takehiro Murata *(Kenji Ando)*; Makoto Otake *(Takeshi Tomokane)*; Kenpachiro Satsuma *(Godzilla)*; "Hurricane Ryu" Hariken *(Battra)*

Following the success of 1991's GODZILLA VS. KING GHIDORAH, Toho continued to revive its giant monsters with GODZILLA AND MOTHRA, the most popular film of the newer series. The winged giant and the two tiny princesses who guide it are faced not only with Godzilla but with Battra, a deadly antithesis of Mothra.

Takuya (Tetsuya Bessho), an Indiana Jones-ish adventurer, is jailed in Thailand after stealing artifacts from an ancient temple. Representatives of the Marutomo Corporation, including his estranged wife Masako (Satomi Kobayashi), offer to bail him out in exchange for heading an expedition to Infant Island. There they discover a giant egg and two tiny women (Keiko Imamura, Sayaka Osawa). They are the Cosmos, remnants of an ancient civilization that was destroyed when the Earth rebelled against the attempts by scientists to control the planet by creating a monster, Battra. Now, man's meddling with the ecology has led to the revival of Battra, which (in a larval state) is headed toward Japan. Under orders from Marutomo, Takuya loads the egg and the Cosmos on a boat back to Japan. When the ship is attacked by Godzilla, the egg hatches into Mothra. Also in a larval state, it is attacked by both Godzilla and Battra before retreating back to Infant Island.

Looking to save face after losing the egg, company representative Andoh (Takehiro Murata) brings the Cosmos to CEO Tomokame (Makoto Otake), a ruthless businessman who refuses to take responsibility for despoiling the ecology. Takuya and Masako reconcile, and their daughter tries to shame her father out of his thieving ways.

Mothra comes to Japan, destroying everything in its path while searching for the Cosmos. Takuya steals the Cosmos back in order to return them to Mothra. But instead of leaving, it spins a cocoon in order to transform into its winged state. It emerges to battle Godzilla again, joined by Battra (also now in its winged form). The two giant insects defeat Godzilla and carry him off to the deepest ocean, but in the process Battra is mortally wounded. Translated for human observers by the Cosmos, Battra reveals that it was revived to destroy a huge meteor that is headed toward Earth. Mothra agrees to take on that responsibility and, with the Cosmos, heads off for outer space.

A plot description doesn't really convey the poetic, fairy tale-like aspect of a film in which Godzilla seems a bit out of place. Mothra remains the most beautiful of Toho's giant creatures, especially with improved special effects that make its flight look plausibly realistic. (That can't be said for the larval Mothra, which never looks very real, although it is always strikingly dramatic.) Of course, a giant monster movie can't be built around an effete insect, so Mothra is also given the usual accoutrements of 1990s monsters, including unexplained destructo-beams that shoot out of its head, the ability to secrete a powder that neutralizes Godzilla's radioactive capabilities, and the complementary ability to deflect Godzilla's destructo-beam. (Much of this is not mentioned in the English dubbing, though to be fair it isn't that much clearer in the Japanese version.) Battra is an equally striking creation, more like a bat (appropriate to its name) than an insect. The new Mothra went on to its own series of films, while Godzilla returned in GODZILLA VS. MECHAGODZILLA II (1993). *(Violence.)* —M.F.

d, Takao Okawara; p, Shogo Tomiyama; exec p, Tomoyuki Tanaka; w, Kazuki Omori; m, Akira Ifukube; fx, Koichi Kawakita

Science Fiction (PR: A MPAA: NR)

GODZILLA VS. KING GHIDORAH ★★★½

(Japan, 1991) 100m Toho ~ Columbia TriStar c

Anna Nakagawa *(Emmy Kano)*; Isao Toyohara *(Kenichiro Terasawa)*; Megumi Odaka *(Miki Saegusa)*; Chuck Wilson *(Chuck Wilson)*; Yoshio Tsuchiya *(Businessman Yasuaki Shindo)*; Katsuhiko Sasaki *(Prof. Mazaki)*; Kenji Sahara *(Minister of Defense Takayuuki Segawa)*; Richard Berger *(Grenchiko)*; Kent Gilbert *(Ship Commander)*; Kiwako Harada *(Chiaki Moriyuma)*; Shoji Kobayashi *(Yuzo Tsuchiashi)*; Tokuma Nishioka *(Takehito Fujio)*; Kenpachiro Satsuma *(Godzilla)*; Robert Scottfield *(Android M-11)*; Koichi Ueda *(Ikehata)*; So Yamamura *(Prime Minister)*

Toho Studios' series of new Godzilla films, tentatively launched with GODZILLA 1985 (1984) and GODZILLA VS. BIOLLANTE (1989), kicked into high gear with GODZILLA VS. KING GHIDORAH, which blithely invents a whole new backstory for everyone's favorite giant monster (as well as for popular foe King Ghidorah, aka Ghidrah). Like all movies about time travel, the plot—in which visitors from the future attempt to alter the past in order to take over Japan's history—doesn't stand up to logical scrutiny, but it's twisty and fast-paced enough to compel your interest.

Delving into the history of Yasuaki Shindo (Yoshio Tsuchiya), a rich businessman who has created a theme park devoted to monsters, writer Terasawa (Isao Toyohara) discovers that, as a soldier on the island of Lagos in WWII, Shindo and his garrison were saved from enemy attack by a dinosaur. Terasawa theorizes that this prehistoric remnant was exposed to the atomic testing on nearby Bikini and mutated into Godzilla. His theory is proven correct when Japan is visited by three people from the year 2204, Emmy (Anna Nakagawa), Wilson (Chuck Wilson), and Grenchiko (Richard Berger). They plan to prevent the annihilation of Japan in an upcoming attack by Godzilla. Travelling to 1944, they transport the dinosaur to an underwater site far from the upcoming nuclear tests. They also leave behind three Dorats, winged pets genetically engineered to be responsive to their human masters. Returning to 1992, Godzilla has been erased from history; but Japan is now under attack by King Ghidorah, a three-headed dragon produced when the Dorats were exposed to nuclear radiation. Wilson's true goal is to use Ghidorah to take over Japan, the future's leading superpower. Horrified at his plans, Emmy joins forces with Terasawa and the others. Meanwhile, exposure to a sunken Russian nuclear sub has created Godzilla anew, bigger and more powerful than ever. He heads toward Tokyo and battles with Ghidorah. Wilson and Grenchiko are killed when Emmy transports their ship into the middle of the monster fight. Godzilla kills Ghidorah, and then turns his attention to Tokyo. Shindo, who has considered Godzilla a savior since the Lagos experience, is killed when he refuses to flee from Godzilla's rampage. Emmy and the others concoct a desperate plan: returning to the future, she retrieves Ghidorah's corpse and mechanically revives it as Mecha-King Ghidorah, in which she returns to 1992 to stop Godzilla. She and the robot creature overcome Godzilla, and she deposits both her creation and the defeated Godzilla at the bottom of the ocean. Before returning to her own time, she reveals to Terasawa that he is her ancestor.

The first of five popular films that went unreleased in the US until the American GODZILLA (1998) sparked a renewed interest in all things Godzillan, GODZILLA VS. KING GHIDORAH will come as a surprise to viewers who have only seen the earlier Toho films. With a substantially larger budget and more sophisticated special effects, this ain't your Dad's Godzilla. Liquidating and recreating Godzilla served a particular purpose: the monster needed to be bigger so as not to be dwarfed by a Tokyo that looms much higher than it did in 1954. While Godzilla himself is impressively lean and mean, the most notable beneficiary of the improved effects is the three-headed King Ghidorah, which for the first time *doesn't* look like a spastic marionette. Of course, the monsters are still played largely by men in rubber suits, and American viewers accustomed to computer-generated effects are still likely to turn up their noses. But GODZILLA VS. KING GHIDORAH and its successors (beginning with 1992's GODZILLA VS. MOTHRA) make up in imagination what they may lack in verisimilitude. A little suspension of disbelief is an investment that is rewarded handsomely here.

On the downside, the English dubbing, while technically proficient, is too often laughably written ("Take that, you dinosaur!" smirks one American naval officer, jokingly named "Major Spielberg.") Too many of the dubbing actors mispronounce "nuclear." Emmy's android sidekick M-11 borrows a little too much from TERMINATOR 2 (1991). And the script's view of nuclear waste as a well-known growth hormone is a bit much to take. The film was also subjected to (sight unseen) criticism in the US in 1991 when it was accused of being anti-American for showing a dinosaur killing American soldiers. *(Violence, profanity.)*—M.F.

d, Kazuki Omori; p, Shogo Tomiyama; exec p, Tomoyuki Tanaka; w, Kazuki Omori; ph, Yoshinori Sekiguchi; ed, Michiko Ikeda; m, Akira Ifukube; fx, Koichi Kawakita

Science Fiction **(PR: A MPAA: NR)**

GOLGO 13: QUEEN BEE ★★★

(Japan, 1998) 57m Saito Production; Shogakukan; Goodhill Vision; BMG Japan; Filmlink International ~ Urban Vision Entertainment c

ENGLISH VOICE CAST: John DiMaggio *(Golgo 13/Duke Togo/Informant)*; Denise Poirier *(Sonia/Queen Bee/Joanna)*; Carlos Ferro *(Thomas Waltham)*; Dwight Shultz *(Robert Hardy)*; Joe Lala *(Don Roccini/Gomez)*; John Hostetter *(General Gordon)*; Michael Sorich *(Bernard)*; Julia DeMita *(Nursemaid)*

A stylish and engrossing Japanese animated action thriller, GOLGO 13: QUEEN BEE follows a running battle between a high-tech hit man and a sexy female rebel leader against the background of the 2000 American presidential race. Robert Hardy (voice of Dwight Shultz), the likely Democratic candidate for President of the US in the year 2000, is getting cryptic notes from Queen Bee, the female leader of the Comnero Liberation Army. His running mate, Thomas Waltham (voice of Carlos Ferro), hires Duke Togo, aka Golgo 13 (voice of John DiMaggio), a highly paid international hit man, to kill the woman. Queen Bee, known to her friends as Sonia (voice of Denise Poirier), arrives in America and offers herself to Duke and tries to hire him to kill Hardy. He refuses, sticking to his strict policy of "one job at a time."

Sonia is actually Joanna, the illegitimate daughter of Hardy, abandoned by him as a child. Waltham, desperate to silence Sonia, has his military adviser, General Gordon (voice of John Hostetter) send a covert action team into the Central American jungle to wipe out the village outpost of the Comnero Liberation Army. With Duke's reluctant help, Sonia escapes with her many children, each of them fathered by different men who have gone off and died for the cause.

At the Democratic Convention, accepting the nomination, Hardy breaks down on the platform, pulls out a gun and declares his love for his lost daughter Joanna and apologizes to her. He then shoots himself. At her father's grave, Sonia has her final confrontation with Duke. As she dies from his gunshot, she declares that she's wired the necessary sum to his Swiss bank account. He knows what to do and goes on to kill both Waltham and General Gordon.

A 1998 made-for-video production, GOLGO 13: QUEEN BEE is only the second animated film based on the popular, long-running comic book character of the title, a stoic, rock-hard, top-dollar hit man who has no trouble attracting gorgeous women to him. The previous film, THE PROFESSIONAL: GOLGO 13 (1983), was a theatrical release (released in the US in 1993) by the same director. The new film tells a suspenseful, well-wrought story with numerous twists and turns packed into its 57-minute running time and underscored by a poignant back story of a family torn apart by political ambitions and a little girl who acts out her bitterness in the international political arena. The animation succeeds in creating a modern-day noir look, with lots of close-ups, shadows, oblique angles, dramatic compositions, and quick cuts to suggest larger actions.

One of the rare anime to focus on American institutions, the film boasts a spectacular look at the 2000 Democratic Convention with echoes of THE MANCHURIAN CANDIDATE (1962). Its general view of American politics is pretty grim and the unlicensed American attack on a Central American village is particularly harrowing (although topically out-of-date). *(Extreme violence, nudity, sexual situations.)*—B.C.

d, Osamu Dezaki, Jack Fletcher (English Version); p, Hitoshi Yoshimura, Taka Nagasawa, Kara Redmon (English Version), Sandy Yamamoto (English Version); exec p, Mataichiro Yamamoto; assoc p, Yuji Suzuki, Yaem Aoki; w, Akihiro Tago, Matt Aichir (based on novel by Takao Saito), R.D. Makepeace (English Version); ph, Hirokata Takahashi, Hajime Noguchi; ed, Seiji Morita; m, Fujimaru Yoshino; art d, Mieko Ichihara; anim, Akio Sugino, Hiroshi Uchida; sound, Chiaki Yamada

Animated/Thriller **(PR: O MPAA: NR)**

GONIN ★★★½

(Japan, 1995) 109m Bunkasha Publishing; Image Factory; First Production Company; Kanox Company; Team Okuyama; Shochiku Company; Leo Films ~ Phaedra Cinema c

Koichi Sato *(Bandai)*; Naoto Takenaka *(Ogiwara)*; Takeshi Kitano *(Kyoya)*; Jinpachi Nezu *(Hizu)*; Masahiro Motoki *(Mitsuya)*; Kippei Shiina *(Jimmy)*; Megumi Yokoyama *(Nammy)*;

Kazuya Kimura *(Kazuma)*; Shingo Tsurumi *(Hisamatsu)*; Toshiyuki Nagashima *(Ogoshi)*

Bleak and bracing, bristling with exciting, atmospheric set-pieces, this sterling crime thriller was a popular hit in Japan in 1995 and was subsequently released in the US in 1998.

Disco owner Bandai (Koichi Sato), hard-hit by the downturn in the Japanese economy, owes big money to the local mob. Repeatedly humiliated by the *yakuza*, he plots to rob them with a motley assortment of cronies, including gay hustler Mitsuya (Masahiro Motoki) and down-on-his-luck ex-cop Hizu (Jinpachi Nezu). The crime doesn't go quite as planned, but the robbers manage to escape with the cash, only to be hunted down one at a time by a pair of brutal hitmen (Takeshi Kitano, Shingo Tsurumi). Bandai and two of his fellow robbers are killed, along with Hizu's family; in revenge Hizu and Mitsuya stage an assault on the *yakuza* headquarters. Everyone is killed except Mitsuya and one of the hitmen, who meet again on a bus out of town, where they kill one another.

The title GONIN translates as "Five," referring to the team of misfit robbers. Writer-director Takashi Ishii structures his tale like a conventional heist picture (setup/robbery/pursuit and fatalistic denoument), but steers it into wholly new genre territory with inventive plot twists—and by exploding the homoerotic subtexts of similar male-dominated hardboiled pictures. Bandai is clearly the focus of the film, but he is killed about two-thirds of the way through (planting a kiss on Mitsuya as he dies), belying viewer expectations. In his grief, Mitsuya contemplates suicide but decides instead to avenge Bandai against his killers, one of whom, Kyoya, was earlier seen beating and raping his partner for a perceived slight. Kyoya is played by veteran *yakuza* tough-guy Takeshi Kitano (SONATINE, FIREWORKS), in his first role following a near-fatal motorcycle accident. In fact the eye-patch he wears throughout the film is a result of the accident, although Ishii weaves it into the story, opening the film with Bandai dreaming about having his eye cut out by Mitsuya, setting up the parallel between homosexual robbers and homosexual pursuers.

Also among the five are wigged-out salaryman Ogiwara (played by Naoto Takenaka from SHALL WE DANCE?) who refuses to see his family and admit that he's been fired from his job. Following the heist he triumphantly returns home with the cash, unaware that the killers are on his tail. In a truly tense and eerie sequence, we gradually become aware that his family is dead, and discover further that it is the disturbed salaryman himself who killed them. Ishii's use of detail and manipulation of sound (a fly buzzing in Ogiwara's charnel-house apartment; a sudden silence in a formerly busy restaurant, denoting the arrival of the hitmen) is masterly, his sense of composition and pacing superb. Born Hideki Ishii, he adopted the name Takashi in 1970 when he began producing *ero gekiga* (erotic, adults-only graphic novels). After seeing a number of his stories adapted to film (the TENSHI NO HARAWATA or "Entrails of the Angel" series beginning in 1978, MERMAID LEGEND in 1984) he began directing his own scripts, debuting with the 1988 entry in the TENSHI NO HARAWATA series and progressing to thoughtful and stylish psychothrillers like A NIGHT IN NUDE (1993). He has since directed GONIN 2, a similar crime story featuring five women. *(Graphic violence, sexual situations, substance abuse, extreme profanity.)*—A.B.

d, Takashi Ishii; p, Kanji Miura, Taketo Niitsu, Katsuhide Motoki; exec p, Kazuyoshi Okuyama; w, Takashi Ishii; ph, Yasushi Sasakibara; ed, Akimasa Kawashima, Keiichi Hasegawa, Katsumi Yamaura; m, Goro Yasukawa; art d, Teru Yamazaki; sound, Mineharu Kitamura

Crime **(PR: C MPAA: NR)**

GOVERNESS, THE ★★★½

(U.K., 1998) 114m Parallax Pictures; Pandora Cinema; BBC Films ~ Sony Pictures Classics c

Minnie Driver *(Rosina da Silva/Mary Blackchurch)*; Tom Wilkinson *(Mr. Charles Cavendish)*; Harriet Walter *(Mrs. Cavendish)*; Jonathan Rhys Meyers *(Henry Cavendish)*; Florence Hoath *(Clementina Cavendish)*; Bruce Myers *(Rosina's Father—Papa)*; Arlene Cockburn *(Lily Milk)*; Emma Bird *(Rebecca)*; Adam Levy *(Benjamin)*; The Countess Koulinskyi *(Aunt Sofka)*; Diana Brooks *(Rosina's Mother)*; Raymond Brody *(Litnoff)*; Olga *(Leonora)*; Cyril Shaps *(Doctor)*; Kendal Cramer *(Young Rosina)*; Ralph Riach *(Mr. Hewlett)*; Joe Bromley *(Prostitute)*; Stephen Robbins *(Rabbi)*

Minnie Driver is ideally cast in the title role of this accessible period drama. The film boldy superimposes a modern sense of sexuality and a strong feminist message on historical realities.

A Jewish quarter of London in the 1840s. When the patriarch of a Sephardic family is murdered leaving large debts, his eldest daughter—the strong-willed Rosina (Minnie Driver)—refuses an arranged marriage, instead deciding to earn money by posing as a Christian nanny. Calling herself Mary Blackchurch, she takes a position with the Cavendish family on a remote Scottish island.

The dreary household is run by the desiccated Mrs. Cavendish (Harriet Walter). Rosina's charge is Clementina (Florence Hoath). Miserable, Rosina writes to her sister and dreams of her dead father. In one wing of the house, Mr. Cavendish (Tom Wilkinson) is preoccupied with cutting-edge research in photography, specifically perfecting a process of fixation that prevents images of photographed objects from fading. Cavendish asks the well-educated Rosina to assist, and their scientific collaboration evolves into a passionate sexual affair. While Rosina conducts a secret seder meal in her room, salt water spills on a print and she discovers that sodium is the key to the fixation process—a breakthrough that fuels both sides of their relationship. Rosina urges Cavendish to photograph people in addition to natural objects; they take portraits of one another, some in revealing poses.

Young Henry Cavendish (Jonathan Rhys Meyers) arrives, having been sent down from Oxford, and quickly becomes infatuated with Rosina. Rummaging through her belongings, he discovers her true identity. As Cavendish and Rosina prepare for the arrival of an eminent scientist to review their work, the relationship deteriorates. When she takes a picture of him in the nude, he is incensed and seeks to end the affair. Not knowing why she is upset, Henry tries to console her. Henry tells his father he loves Rosina and is enraged when told they are lovers. When the scientist arrives, Cavendish calls Rosina to the lab but treats her as a mere assistant. Devastated, she displays naked pictures of herself and Cavendish throughout the lab and shows one to Mrs. Cavendish. Rosina leaves for London. Henry collapses weeping and naked in the ocean.

Rosina returns to find her neighborhood ravaged by cholera, the family home dilapidated, and her mother dead. Having taken some essentials from the lab, she opens her own photography studio. After some time has passed, Cavendish shows up and has his portrait taken, leaving without any serious communication. Patronized by the Jewish population, her business thrives. Rosina makes a self-portrait and declares: "I hardly ever think of Scotland."

Once viewers can accept the improbability of Rosina's ruse, they can begin to identify with the characters in writer-director Sandra Goldbacher's literate and sensuous film. Ashley Rowe's cinematography accentuates the stark beauty of the seaside locale as well as the sexual goings-on taking place indoors. His chiaroscuro lighting effects, plus the Pre-Raphaelite look of the actors (especially Driver and Rhys Meyers) give the film a visual coherence that sporadically clashes with its modern ideas and verbiage.

The initial themes of religion and cultural identity rapidly give way to sexual politics and gender relations. Photography, and related metaphors like mirrors, fixation, and mimesis, are the perfect trope, directly addressing the concerns of feminist film theory regarding the voyeuristic nature of spectatorship. Goldbacher also plays with the traditional dichotomy of male reason versus feminine emotion. In his mind, Cavendish is engaged in a strictly scientific pursuit (echoing Victorian narratives such as *Frankenstein* and *Dr. Jekyll and Mr. Hyde*) while Rosina appreciates the artistic potential of the medium. As his conventional misogyny is revealed, Rosina turns the tables. It is okay for him to penetrate her, to objectify her with the lens, but he cannot accept it when the roles are reversed; he is afraid of losing his sanity, i.e., his masculinity. Goldbacher captures minute power shifts between the two lovers that are echoed in Rosina's scenes with Henry. Her eventual success using the photographic method she helped devise, especially contrasted with the childlike behavior of both male Cavendishes, is an unequivocal endorsement of her feminine strength and vision.

Driver is one with the tailor-made role, while Wilkinson's rather muted performance is the only subtle note in the picture, and Rhys Meyers dazzles as the sallow youth. THE GOVERNESS can be criticized as overwrought and schematic—in short, of indulging in the hysteria women were accused of in the 19th century—yet because Rosina overcomes this stereotype so forcefully in the course of the film, Goldbacher's handsome movie should be given every benefit of the doubt. *(Nudity, sexual situations.)*— J.M.

d, Sandra Goldbacher; p, Sarah Curtis; exec p, Sally Hibbin; w, Sandra Goldbacher; ph, Ashley Rowe; ed, Isabel Lorente; m, Edward Shearmur; prod d, Sarah Greenwood; art d, Philip Robinson; set d, Katie Spencer; sound, Danny Hambrook (recordist); fx, Chris Reynolds; casting, Michelle Guish; cos, Caroline Harris; makeup, Veronica Brebner; stunts, Nick Powell

Drama **(PR: C MPAA: R)**

GREAT EXPECTATIONS ★★½

(U.S., 1998) 111m Knickerbocker Films;
20th Century Fox ~ 20th Century Fox c

Ethan Hawke *(Finnegan Bell)*; Gwyneth Paltrow *(Estella)*; Anne Bancroft *(Ms. Nora Dinsmoor)*; Robert De Niro *(Prisoner/Lustig)*; Chris Cooper *("Uncle" Joe)*; Hank Azaria *(Walter Plane)*; Josh Mostel *(Jerry Ragno)*; Kim Dickens *(Maggie Bell)*; Nell Campbell *(Erica Thrall)*; Gabriel Mick *(Owen)*; Jeremy James Kissner *(Finnegan—Age 10)*; Raquel Beaudene *(Estella—Age 10)*; Stephen Spinella *(Carter Macleish)*; Marla Sucharetza *(Ruth Shepard)*; Isabelle Anderson *(Lois Pope)*; Peter Jacobson *(Man on Phone)*; Drena De Niro *(Marcy)*; Lance Reddick *(Anton Le Farge)*; Craig Braun *(Mr. Barrow)*; Kim Snyder *(Mrs. Barrow)*; Nicholas Wolfert *(Security Guard)*; Gerry Bamman *(Ted Rabinowitz)*; Dorin Seymour *(Senator Elwood)*; Clem Caserta *(Hitman #1)*; Frank Pietrangolare *(Hitman #2)*; Dennis Paladino *(Hitman #3)*; Clem Caserta Jr. *(Hitman #4)*; Marc Macaulay *(Cop on Boat)*; Ana Susana Gerardino *(Clemma)*; Francis Dumaurier *(Waiter)*; Pedro Barquin *(Lover)*; Kendall Williamson *(7-Year-Old Girl)*; Shobha Jain *(Singing Indian Woman)*; Aditi Jain *(Singing Indian Girl)*; Margo Peace *(Anchor Woman)*; Kimmy Suzuki *(Waitress)*; John P. Casey *(Doorman)*; Adusah Boakye *(Taxi Driver)*; Dyan Kane *(Gallery Waitress)*; Anne Ok *(Gallery Receptionist)*; Alva Chinn; G.B. Thomas; Albert Zihenni; Fritz Michel; Lisa Herth; Nino Pepicelli; Wills Robbins; Jewel Turner; Jim Taylor McNickle; Martin Alvin; William Rothlein *(Gallery Guests)*

Ethan Hawke and Gwyneth Paltrow star in GREAT EXPECTATIONS, a very loose update of the Dickens classic, as modernized for the MTV generation. Visually stylized in the same fairy tale manner as director Alfonso Cuaron's THE LITTLE PRINCESS (1995), the script unfortunately has no more substance than a perfume commercial, and manages to turn one of the great narratives of the English language into a mushy tale of raging teen hormones.

Budding 10-year-old artist Finn Bell (Jeremy James Kissner) lives in Florida with his sister (Kim Dickens) and her handyman boyfriend Joe (Chris Cooper). While fishing one day, Finn is accosted by an escaped convict named Lustig (Robert De Niro) who coerces the boy into helping him, then disappears. When Joe is hired to work at the mansion of wealthy eccentric Ms. Dinsmoor (Anne Bancroft), Finn accompanies him and meets Dinsmoor's beautiful young niece Estella (Raquel Beaudene), who has been trained by Dinsmoor to toy with the opposite sex in revenge for Dinsmoor's fiance leaving her at the altar. Finn falls in love with Estella, even though she continually teases him, and he becomes a regular visitor to Dinsmoor's house, spending his time dancing with Estella and making sketches of her. Now in their late teens, Finn (Ethan Hawke) and Estella (Gwyneth Paltrow) continue their tentative relationship, but when she leaves for Europe without telling him, he angrily rejects his artistic endeavors.

When a mysterious lawyer (Josh Mostel) visits Finn and offers him a one-man art show in New York, Finn suspects that Dinsmoor is behind it, especially when she informs him that Estella is in New York. In Manhattan, Finn runs into Estella, and they finally make love after he does a nude portrait of her, but is shocked when she tells him that she is engaged to a wealthy businessman named Walter (Hank Azaria). Estella leaves for her honeymoon on the night of Finn's gallery opening, and when he drunkenly goes to her house, he finds Dinsmoor, who admits that she had originally encouraged him to go to New York in order to force Walter to propose to Estella. When Finn goes home, he encounters an old man who turns out to be Lustig. He tells Finn that he's on the run from some mobsters and also reveals that he is actually Finn's benefactor. Finn helps him onto the subway, but a man attacks Lustig and stabs him to death. Finn returns home to Florida, and when he visits Dinsmoor's mansion, he sees the now-divorced Estella, who's with her young daughter, and she apologizes for breaking his heart.

Having discovered that the classic works of such authors as Dickens and Shakespeare are in the public domain, 20th Century Fox is apparently unable to resist using famous titles but updating the stories in a blatant attempt to attract the short-attention-span teeny-bopper crowd, a la 1996's ludicrously MTV-ized WILLIAM SHAKESPEARE'S ROMEO & JULIET. While there is nothing inherently wrong with this trend, the problem with GREAT EXPECTATIONS is that the sensibility of the script (by Mitch Glazer, whose previous hatchet job on Dickens was SCROOGED) is closer to John Hughes than to Dickens, with a cinematic style that has an annoying music-video tendency (replete with jump cuts, titled angles, and a soundtrack consisting of The Grateful Dead and Iggy Pop). The story's themes—ambition, desire, fate, fortune, and the mysteries of love—remain as valid as ever, but take a back seat to the emphasis on the steamy histrionics of its two protagonists, looking like they both stepped out of a Calvin Klein commercial, but conspicuously lacking any romantic chemistry.

Ethan Hawke fails to communicate Finn's artistic passion, while Gwyneth Paltrow coldly pouts her way through the role of Estella, lacking the necessary sense of mystery and the physical requirements to be convincing as a devastatingly seductive heartbreaker. Robert De Niro and Anne Bancroft ham it up in what are basically extended cameos, with Bancroft's Miss Havisham-surrogate coming off less like a tragic figure than a campy drag queen. As in THE LITTLE PRINCESS, director Cuaron's sensitivity to the emotional and fantasy worlds of children is impressive, and the best parts of the film are the early scenes with young Finn and Estella, where the luminous widescreen cinematography creates some magical imagery. His treatment of their adult characters is mannered and superficial, however, and in the end, the film only makes one want to go back and read Dickens's book, or at least rewatch David Lean's masterly 1946 film version. *(Profanity, sexual situations, nudity.)* —M.S.

d, Alfonso Cuaron; p, Art Linson; exec p, Deborah Lee; co-p, John Linson; w, Mitch Glazer (based on the novel by Charles Dickens); ph, Emmanuel Lubezki; ed, Steven Weisberg; m, Patrick Doyle; prod d, Tony Burrough; art d, John Kasarda; set d, Susan Bode; sound, Tom Nelson (mixer), Doug Martines (recordist), Richard Beggs (design); fx, Steve Kirshoff, Rich Thorne, Digital Filmworks, Inc.; casting, Jill Greenberg; cos, Judianna Makovsky; makeup, Cecelia M. Verardi, Manlio Rocchetti (effects)

Romance/Drama **(PR: C MPAA: R)**

GUN, A CAR, AND A BLONDE, A ★★

(U.S., 1996) 107m Avalanche Home Entertainment ~ Showcase Entertainment c/bw

Jim Metzler *(Richard/Rick Stone)*; Kay Lenz *(Peep/Madge)*; Billy Bob Thornton *(Syd/Monk)*; Andrea Thompson *(The Blonde/Jade Norfleet)*; Victor Love *(Bobby/The Black Chinaman)*; Norma Maldonado *(Adele/Bunny)*; Paula Marshall *(Deborah/Girl in Photograph);* Paul Parducci *(Bear/Petrovich);* Time Winters *(Ed/Catalina Eddie);* Vann Johnson *(The Singer);* John Ritter *(Duncan/The Bartender)*

Mixing film noir with flights of fantasy, this ineffectual straight-to-video release concerns a handicapped man who escapes his painful existence by imagining himself as a 1950s private eye.

Paralyzed from the waist down as a result of spinal cancer, Richard (Jim Metzler) is in the care of his annoying sister Peep (Kay Lenz). Richard spends his days getting drunk, staring at a pretty blonde neighbor (Andrea Thompson), and watching old crime movies on TV. A friend, new-age adherent Duncan (John Ritter), urges him to escape his pain by "objectifying" himself into an imaginary world. Following this advice, Richard leaves his wheelchair behind as '50s-era gumshoe Rick Stone.

Sultry widow Jade Norfleet (Thompson) visits Stone's office, seeking help after being attacked. Meanwhile, back in the real world, Richard becomes aggravated with Peep and her boyfriend Syd (Billy Bob Thornton), questions his life, and reverts further into his fictional story. There he obtains information about the attack on Jade from low-life sources, makes love to Jade, and discovers that her sister Madge (Lenz) and seedy cop Monk (Thornton) were responsible for Jade's assault. Stone is kidnapped, but in the nick of time, Jade rescues Stone, Monk is shot, and before dying, murders Jade. Back in the real world, Richard kicks out Peep and Syd, and discovers a renewed interest in life. But when he has a sudden attack and passes away, Richard awakens as fantasy-hero Rick Stone, with Jade alive and at his side.

Although boasting a playful concept and earnest performances, A GUN, A CAR, A BLONDE rates as lackluster, since neither the real-life drama nor the "low-rent flatfoot" mystery are enticing enough on their own merits. Thus, the film's success rests solely on the transitions made from one story line to another, a device that gets old rather quickly. The detective sequences are played in a suprisingly straight manner—although the dialogue is so trite they come across as more of a sendup.

While Metzler is effective as the paralyzed protagonist, he makes a bland hero in the detective story line, seeming less hard-boiled than simply lethargic. Despite being billed third in the credits, Thornton (who earlier co-starred with Metzler in ONE FALSE MOVE) is given little to do, playing the type of thug that Elisha Cook Jr. used to essay on a regular basis. Only Ritter brings a modicum of humor and warmth to the proceedings.

Hampered by minimal production values, the film stands as a well-intentioned but utterly muddled mix of hackneyed drama and homogenized pulp fiction. *(Violence, extensive nudity, substance abuse, profanity.)*—S.P.

d, Stephani Ames; p, Tom Epperson, Gary M. Bettman; exec p, David R. Miller; assoc p, Robert B. Steuer, Jim Metzler, Vince Flaherty; co-p, Stefani Ames, Peter Zinner; w, Tom Epperson, Stephani Ames; ph, Carlos Gaviria; ed, Peter Zinner; m, Harry Manfredini; art d, Sharon Winkler; sound, David Waelder; cos, Deborah Waknin; makeup, Pamela Roth

Crime/Drama/Fantasy **(PR: O MPAA: R)**

H

HALF BAKED ★★
(U.S., 1998) 85m Robert Simonds Productions ~ Universal c

Dave Chappelle *(Thurgood/Sir Smoka Lot)*; Jim Breuer *(Brian)*; Guillermo Diaz *(Scarface)*; Harland Williams *(Kenny)*; Rachel True *(Mary Jane)*; Clarence Williams III *(Samson Simpson)*; Tommy Chong *(Squirrel Master)*; Laura Silverman *(Jan)*; Steven Wright *(The Guy)*; Snoop Doggy Dogg; Willie Nelson; Dave Garcia; Jon Stewart; Janeane Garofalo; Stephen Baldwin; R.D. Reid; Gregg Rogell; Kevin Brennan; Alice Poon; Rick Demas; David Bluestein; Angela Featherstone

HALF BAKED begs the question: how entertaining today is a movie about potsmoking when viewed without weed in hand? The answer: not very.

In New York, four roommates, Thurgood (Dave Chappelle), Brian (Jim Breuer), Scarface (Guillermo Diaz), and Kenny (Harland Williams) plan a typical evening of potsmoking and partying. On his way out to pick up some food for the party, Kenny accidentally kills a police officer's horse, an act which immediately puts him to jail, without even a trial!

In order to bail Kenny out, his three friends plan for Thurgood to steal a potent form of "medicinal" marijuana from the science lab where he works as a porter. With large quantities of the drug in their possession, the three friends set up shop in the apartment, selling "joints" around town at premium prices. Meanwhile, in jail, Kenny fends off the advances of lecherous prisoners and waits for the bail to come through. After a visit to reassure Kenny of his progress, Thurgood meets and falls for Mary Jane (Rachel True); in order to secure a date with her, however, Thurgood promises the wary young woman that he does not use or deal with drugs. Soon after their first date, Mary Jane finds out about the business and angrily drops Thurgood. The drug sales face another threat when drug lord Samson Simpson (Clarence Williams III) discovers how successful the men are at their home-operated enterprise. In retaliation, Simpson kills Thurgood's pet dog and sends a warning to them to get out of the drug business. Scared but determined, Thurgood, Scarface, and Brian visit Simpson in order to cut a deal and split their profits. Simpson agrees to the arrangement, but the friends are arrested when they stage their latest heist at the science lab. As a way to avoid prison and finally get Kenny out of jail, the friends allow themselves to be wired, which helps the police catch Simpson, a much bigger dealer. The plan almost fails, however, when the police accidentally get "high" from some marijuana, but the ghost of Jerry Garcia, the musician and drug guru, helps the friends to kill Simpson. Finally, all four friends are reunited, while Thurgood promises Mary Jane he will give up drugs so that they may date again.

Naturally, HALF-BAKED's premise is just an excuse for a loosely assembled series of pot gags, prison-rape jokes, and riffs on other movies. Star and co-writer Dave Chappelle comes up with the best bits, including a spoof of a rich, spoiled rap artist ("Sir Smoka Lot"), and co-star Breuer (as the most fully "baked" buddy) nails a celebrated Tom Cruise moment from JERRY MAGUIRE (1996).

Otherwise, the references to DEAD PRESIDENTS (1995), MISSION IMPOSSIBLE (1996), PSYCHO (1960), BATMAN (1989), even CHASING AMY (1997), waft by without much impression, and, sadly, Chappelle's romance subplot becomes increasingly and unforgivably conventional (does director Tamra Davis believe members of her own gender lack a sense of humor?). Worst of all, though, several promising unbilled cameos—by Steven Wright, Jon Stewart, Snoop Doggy Dog, Willie Nelson, Janeane Garofalo, Stephen Baldwin, and others—are distinctly unfunny.

Chappelle and Breuer ("Goat Boy" on "Saturday Night Live") are likable young comics with presence, and it is somewhat courageous these days to make a drug-friendly Hollywood movie, but in the comedy department, Cheech and Chong have nothing to worry about: HALF BAKED barely gets off the couch. *(Violence, nudity, adult situations, substance abuse, extreme profanity.)*—E.M.

d, Tamra Davis; p, Robert Simonds; assoc p, Julia Dray, Rita Smith; co-p, Ira Shuman; w, Neil Brennan, Dave Chappelle; ph, Steven Bernstein; ed, Don Zimmerman; m, Alf Clausen; prod d, Perry Andelin Blake; art d, Paul Austerberry; set d, Gord Sim; sound, Owen Langevin; casting, Joanna Colbert, Tina Gerussi; cos, Vicki Graef

Comedy **(PR: C MPAA: R)**

HALLELUJAH! ★★★
(U.S., 1998) 90m Aubin Pictures ~ Artistic License Films c
(AKA: HALLELUJAH! RON ATHEY: A STORY OF DELIVERANCE)

Ron Athey; Vaginal Creme Davis; Julie Tolentino Wood; Darryl Carlton; James Stone; Sweet P.; Myers Rifkin; Cathy Opie; Cross; Alex Binnie; Julie Fowells; Brian Murphy; Katia Esperanza; Mario Kovac; Russell McEwan; Theresa Saso

HALLELUJAH! is a documentary on the life and work of the highly controversial and openly gay performance artist Ron Athey. Obviously the work of a sympathetic and supportive filmmaker, this is a well-made, straightforward, and uncritical portrait.

In an interview, Athey talks of his childhood, of how his family trained him to be a Pentecostal minister, and how he abandoned religion at age 15. Although he now disavows religious faith, his religious upbringing is strongly evident in his theater work. He talks about how being HIV-positive and having lost many friends to AIDS informs his work as well. Athey's career as a performance artist began to take shape in the Los Angeles post-punk club scene of the early 1990s, a scene in which body piercing and tattooing were common. Athey's performances at one such club led to his first formal show, titled "Martyrs and Saints," which dealt with AIDS and loss. Its success led to other, increasingly controversial shows, which featured Athey and his fellow performers appearing in various stages of nudity, piercing themselves and bleeding. Sex, torture, death, and religion were prominent subjects in these works.

Athey came to national attention in 1994 when he was at the heart of a controversy involving National Endowment of the Arts funding of his theater pieces. Political conservatives demanded that the NEA cease funding such artists or have its own funding discontinued. As a result of the controversy, Athey stopped performing in the United States and began to perform in Europe and Latin America. His performances in Mexico City and Zagreb, Croatia, no less explicit than his American works, are very well received by appreciative audiences. HALLELUJAH! has been largely structured around a single interview with Athey, the interview footage interacting with lengthy, well-photographed excerpts of Athey's stage work. His own best explicator, Athey provides cogent autobiographical information and lucid, articulate descriptions of his career and individual theatrical creations. Coming across as intelligent and acutely self-aware, Athey is earnest and forthright in explaining and defending both his lifestyle and his work.

Director Catherine Saalfield—whose previous credits include the acclaimed gay-themed documentaries AMONG GOOD CHRISTIAN PEOPLES (1991) and SACRED LIES, CIVIL TRUTHS (1993)—takes Athey's word and worth as a given, never questioning his importance as an artist or evaluating his contribution to the current culture scene. While she interviews others besides Athey, the speakers—mostly colleagues, or curators who have shown his work—are all ardent supporters, not one of them offering a dissenting view.

The uncritical tone of HALLELUJAH! can be frustrating in a documentary, as it usually signifies intellectual laxity or compromise (Chris Hegedus and D.A. Pennebaker's THE WAR ROOM is a good example of the latter). But offering a critique of Athey or his work seems besides Saalfield's point. Saalfield understands that since Athey is best known through the NEA controversy, he is as much a political figure as a cultural one, and it is a political rather than a cultural stance that she takes with this film. Thus, she lays out who Athey is—an outspoken, irreligious gay man who confronts his audience with his illness—and serves up an ample amount of graphic performance footage, in which Athey appropriates religious theater to explore spiritual and sexual ecstasy and pain, to make clear why his attackers were so unsettled by Athey, and why well-meaning liberals were unprepared or unwilling to defend him.

As far as his artistic worth is concerned, while Saalfield obviously admires Athey, she also seems genuinely interested in letting the film's audience decide his value on its own, contenting herself with affirming his right to do what he does. HALLELUJAH! isn't likely to change anyone's mind about Athey, and will certainly leave some viewers revolted, but it makes plainly evident what the so-called "culture wars" are all about. *(Violence, extensive nudity, sexual situations, adult situations, profanity.)*—D.C.

d, Catherine Gund Saalfield; p, Catherine Gund Saalfield; assoc p, Cat Crosby, Sarah Perry; ph, Catherine Gund Saalfield; ed, Aljernon Tunsil; sound, Margaret Crimmons, Paul Hsu, Dog Bark Sound

Documentary **(PR: O MPAA: NR)**

HALLELUJAH! RON ATHEY: A STORY OF DELIVERANCE
(SEE: HALLELUJAH!)

HALLOWEEN H20: TWENTY YEARS LATER ★★★
(U.S., 1998) 87m Nightfall; Moustapha Akkad ~ Dimension c

Jamie Lee Curtis *(Laurie Strode/Keri Tate)*; Adam Arkin *(Will)*; Josh Hartnett *(John)*; Michelle Williams *(Molly)*; Adam Hann-Byrd *(Charlie)*; Jodi Lyn O'Keefe *(Sarah)*; Janet Leigh *(Norma)*; LL Cool J *(Ronny)*; Joseph Gordon Levitt *(Jimmy)*; Nancy Stephens *(Marion)*; Branden Williams *(Tony)*; Larisa Miller *(Claudia)*; Emmalee Thompson *(Casey)*; Matt Winston *(Matt)*; Beau Billingslea *(Fitz)*; David Blanchard *(Waiter)*; John Cassini *(Cop #1)*; Jody Wood *(Cop #2)*; Lisa Gay Hamilton *(Shirl)*; Chris Durand *(Michael)*; Tom Kane *(Voice Over)*

Thanks in large part to the return of star Jamie Lee Curtis, this seventh installment in the long-running horror series is an entertaining homage to John Carpenter's original.

Twenty years after terrorizing his sister, Laurie Strode, Michael Myers (Chris Durand) is still on the loose. He murders Marion Wittington (Nancy Stephens), former nurse of his late doctor Sam Loomis, and steals her file on Laurie. Having faked her death years ago, Laurie (Jamie Lee Curtis) has changed her name to Keri Tate and is headmistress at a boarding school where John (Josh Hartnett), her teenage son from a marriage that went bad, is a student. With Halloween approaching, Laurie has become skittish about the possibility of Michael returning, and her guidance counselor boyfriend, Will Brennan (Adam Arkin), tries to calm her frayed nerves.

On Halloween day, the students leave the school for a camping trip, but unbeknownst to Laurie, John stays behind with his girlfriend Molly (Michelle Williams) and their friends Charlie (Adam Hann-Byrd) and Sarah (Jodi Lyn O'Keefe) for a private party. Michael arrives and murders Charlie and Sarah; the fleeing John and Molly are rescued by Laurie and Will. As they try to escape, Will accidentally shoots security guard Ronny (LL Cool J) before Michael kills him; Laurie sends John and Molly off to safety before turning back to confront Michael. A lengthy battle ends with Laurie stabbing her brother and pitching him out a window. When the paramedics arrive, Laurie steals the coroner's van containing Michael's "body," and when he revives, she crashes the van, then decapitates Michael with an ax.

The awkwardly titled HALLOWEEN: H20 dispenses with the mythology built up in the previous three films (in fact, it ignores their story lines entirely)—and that's one of its strong points. All the belabored, ridiculous backstory about Michael's ties to ancient druids only helped kill any sense of fear about him; even here, where he's once again an unexplained, almost supernatural force, Michael has lost some of his creepy mystery. Indeed, the other characters talk so much about him, it almost seems like they'd be disappointed if he *didn't* show up.

But if this HALLOWEEN lacks the original's scare power, it has clearly been made by people who respect it, and have crafted an entertaining homage. Director Steve Miner (a slasher sequel veteran, having helmed the second and third FRIDAY THE 13TH movies) and cinematographer Daryn Okada ably emulate the first film's shadowy widescreen visuals, and the movie is packed with in-references that generally convey affection rather than a film-geek mentality. Particularly amusing are the return of Stephens' Marion, the encore of "Mr. Sandman" (the intro song from HALLOWEEN II), and the casting of Janet Leigh—the mother of Curtis *and* cinematic slasher heroine—who is seen at one point getting into her car from PSYCHO (1960).

It's the presence of Curtis herself that truly elevates this movie. The actress (who conceived the plot with executive producer and SCREAM scripter Kevin Williamson, who also made uncredited contributions to the final script) clearly relishes the idea of exploring where Laurie has wound up after all these years. Whether in conflict with John or finally standing her ground against her brother, Curtis possesses the fiery intelligence that has made Laurie one of the horror genre's most memorable heroines; the character also has a realistic air of vulnerability—a necessity for any potential victim in a slasher movie. Without Curtis, HALLOWEEN: H20 might well have been just another formulaic sequel; with her, this rather thinly plotted film develops a fun sense of nostalgia—and closure. *(Graphic violence, sexual situations, profanity.)*—M.G.

d, Steve Miner; p, Paul Freeman; exec p, Moustapha Akkad; assoc p, Malek Akkad; w, Robert Zappia, Matt Greenberg (based on characters created by Debra Hill and John Carpenter); ph, Daryn Okada; ed, Patrick Lusser; m, John Ottman, John Carpenter; prod d, John Willet; art d, Dawn Snyder; set d, Beau Petersen; sound, Jim Tanenbaum (mixer); fx, John Hartigan; casting, Ross Brown, Christine Sheaks; cos, Deborah Everton; makeup, Tania McComas; stunts, Donna Keegan

Horror **(PR: C MPAA: R)**

HAMAM: IL BAGNO TURCO
(SEE: STEAM: THE TURKISH BATH)

HANA-BI
(SEE: FIREWORKS)

HANDS ON A HARDBODY ★★★½

(U.S., 1997) 97m j k livin productions; S.R. Bindler; Kevin Morris ~ Legacy Releasing c

Russell Welsh; Kerri Parker; Kelli Mangrum; Greg Cox; Norma Valverde; Janis Curtis; J.D. Drew; Blake Long; Benny Perkins; Ronald McCowan

Documenting an unusual and amusing slice of Americana, HANDS ON A HARDBODY is half satire and half celebration of the contestants participating in a standing marathon. As one former champion explains, "It's not just a contest... it's a human drama thing."

"Hands on a Hardbody" is a contest held annually since 1992 at a Nissan dealership in Longview, TX, in which the entrants place their hands on a new pickup truck and stand there until they drop. The last person standing wins the vehicle. Contestants are required to keep one hand on the truck at all times (no leaning allowed), and get periodic short restroom breaks.

The 1995 contest begins on a Tuesday with 23 entrants. Spectators handicap the contestants based on their choice of footwear, their dietary choices on the breaks, and their general demeanor. Previous winner Benny Perkins and Kelli, a young woman with a fiery determination, are pegged as early favorites.

Seventeen people are left as Day Two begins. Feet and legs start getting numb as contestants become punchy from lack of sleep. It becomes clear the contest is not just about stamina, but sanity as well. Norma, a devout Christian who listens to religious music on her Walkman, starts to impress onlookers.

Day Three is particularly hot, and the near-100 degree heat takes its toll on the 10 remaining standers. Frayed nerves and fits of uncontrollable laughter become common. By Friday, only Benny, Kelli, Norma, and taciturn J.D. (the eldest entrant) remain.

After 68 hours, Kelli simply wanders off in a daze. Soon after, Benny limps off due to severe leg pains. During the 78th hour, Norma is so overcome by her music that she starts absentmindedly clapping along. The winner is J.D., who presents the prize to his wife as a gift.

At first it seems silly, and seems designed to appear so, but the competition depicted in HANDS ON A HARDBODY is as real and engaging as the coverage of any "legitimate" sporting event. Unfortunately, dark horse J.D.'s win (attributed to the patience he's developed as a hunter) is somewhat anticlimactic.

Interspersed with coverage of the contest are snippets from interviews with the entrants, filmed in advance of the event. The contestants discuss the practical and spiritual requirements of owning a pickup truck in Texas, and their "training regimens" in preparation for the contest. Norma's supporters include 200 families praying on her behalf. Previous winner Benny, whose participation rankles the ambitious Kelli, is like a malaprop-prone Zen warrior. He likens this "big dog's hunt" to the battling of the Immortals in the movie HIGHLANDER (1986), and the thrill of victory to the rush one gets killing a deer.

Filmmaker S.R. Bindler noted in interviews that over the grueling course of the contest, camaraderie developed amongst the contestants, as did empathy between the filmmakers and their subjects. The film's technical crew didn't anticipate the rigors of the marathon shoot, and reportedly they became punchy too. It was questionable editorial judgment on Bindler's part not to include more of the moments when the artificial wall of objectivity came down, and the "bonding of the exhausted" occurred.

As it stands, however, the film does offer a fascinating document of the dogged determination and single-mindedness that reigns in such contests. The inevitable comparison to the marathon dance-contest held in THEY SHOOT HORSES, DON'T THEY? (1969) finds these characters somewhat lacking—seeing as this event is not taking place during an economic depression, and the participants are competing merely for a luxury, instead of money to live on—but Bindler takes great care to make their goal seem worthwhile and, at points, even mildy heroic.—P.R.

d, S.R. Bindler; p, Kevin Morris, Chapin John Wilson, S.R. Bindler; exec p, Matthew McConaughey; assoc p, Julia Wall; ph, Michael Nickels, Chapin John Wilson, S.R. Bindler; ed, S.R. Bindler; m, Neil Kassanoff; sound, Lev Vertov

Documentary **(PR: A MPAA: PG)**

HANGING GARDEN, THE ★★★★

(Canada, 1998) 91m Triptych Media; Galafilm; Emotion Pictures ~ MGM/UA c

Chris Leavins *(Sweet William)*; Troy Veinotte *(Teenage Sweet William)*; Kerry Fox *(Rosemary)*; Sarah Polley *(Teenage Rosemary)*; Seana McKenna *(Iris)*; Peter MacNeill *(Whiskey Mac)*; Joel Keller *(Fletcher)*; Joan Orenstein *(Grace)*; Jocelyn Cunningham *(Laurel)*; Christine Dunsworth *(Violet)*; Heather Rankin *(Black-Eyed Susan)*; Ashley MacIsaac *(Basil—Fiddler)*; Martha Irving *(Dusty Miller)*; Renee Penney *(Grace the Nun)*; Ian Parsons *(Little Sweet William)*; Mark Austin *(Preacher)*; Jim Faraday *(Mr. MacDougal)*; Annabelle Raine Dexter *(Bud)*; Tom Chamber; Michael Weir *(Police Officers)*; Shendi *(Old Peat)*; Lucy *(Young Peat)*

Writer-director Thom Fitzgerald's memory-piece is an astonishing debut film, a black domestic comedy that simultaneously provokes tears and laughter. Blasphemous and riveting, this caustic chronicle of a black sheep's homecoming raises the concept of the dysfunctional family to the nth power.

After living nearly a decade as an openly gay man in the big city, Sweet William (Chris Leavins) revisits Nova Scotia for the wedding of his sister Rosemary (Kerry Fox). William grew up verbally and physically abused by his alcoholic father Whiskey Mac (Peter MacNeill), who cared more for his garden than his family. Back home he experiences disturbing memories of his life as an affection-starved boy (Ian Parsons), who found solace in food, and as an obese teen (Troy Venoitte), who attempted suicide.

William is fearful of encountering not only his father and mother, Iris (Seana McKenna), but also Rosemary's bisexual bridegroom Fletcher (Joel S. Keller). As teens, William and Fletcher were caught having sex by William's grandmother, who's now ravaged by Alzheimer's disease. At the ceremony, William meets Violet (Christine Dunworth), a young child whom he is told is an unexpected by-product of his parents' loveless marriage. While William takes refuge in food, his mother seizes his return as her final chance at abdicating familial duty, and walks out after the wedding reception. William remembers his troubled adolescence: his mother was so disturbed by his homosexuality that she hired a neighbor lady to "straighten him out." The experience was so traumatic that William attempted to hang himself in the garden. Now he finds that there is a remnant of his former miserable existence: Violet is his daughter, the result of his only heterosexual intercourse. William decides that he and his male lover will take custody of Violet. Whiskey Mac is left alone in the house with his precious garden, but his emotionally damaged children have learned how to love despite his heritage of repression.

Rocketing off from the establishing shots of the wedding-from-hell, THE HANGING GARDEN reopens old wounds while humorously and bitterly explaining how this family is capable of inflicting new injuries. Hilariously depressing, the wedding functions as a microcosm of family discord, sets up the major players, and prepares the audience for the film's unusual tone, melancholy suffused through mordant wit.

Writer-director Thom Fitzgerald's most daring cinematic device is the infusion of the characters of young William and adolescent William into the narrative, with both characters placed within the same time- and film-frame as adult William; at key points, adult William confronts his younger selves. At first shocked by the reappearance of these discarded identities, William comes to embrace his ghosts, even as they haunt him. Because Fitzgerald is, as yet, a more astute writer than filmmaker, these juxtapositions are sometimes jarring, although they're never awkward enough to destroy the cumulative power of William's cascading insight into his past.

Constantly jolting viewers, Fitzgerald's passion play is filled with imaginative visual touches. Nothing is sacred in this freewheeling dramedy, which bashes organized religion, alcoholic parenting, and heterosexual brainwashing. That the ensemble performances linger in the memory is a testament to Fitzgerald's ability to help his actors draw dignity from undignified behavior. The film achieves a vital sense of transcendence at the climax, as we share in William's realization that he is not a prisoner of his father's emotionally barren methods. THE HANGING GARDEN is a triumphant celebration of learning how to cultivate love in rocky soil. *(Violence, extreme profanity, nudity, adult situations, substance abuse.)*—R.P.

d, Thom Fitzgerald; p, Louise Garfield, Arnie Gelbart, Thom Fitzgerald; assoc p, Mark Hammond; w, Thom Fitzgerald; ph, Daniel Jobin; ed, Susan Shanks; m, John Roby; prod d, Taavo Soodor; art d, Darlene Shields; sound, Peter Harper; casting, Marsha Chesley, John Dunsworth; cos, James A. Worthen

Drama/Comedy **(PR: C MPAA: R)**

HAPPINESS ★★★★

(U.S., 1998) 139m Good Machine; Killer Films; Livingstone Pictures ~ Good Machine c

Jane Adams *(Joy Jordan)*; Lara Flynn Boyle *(Helen Jordan)*; Cynthia Stevenson *(Trish Maplewood)*; Dylan Baker *(Bill Maplewood)*; Philip Seymour Hoffman *(Allen)*; Ben Gazzara *(Lenny Jordan)*; Louise Lasser *(Mona Jordan)*; Jared Harris *(Vlad)*; Elizabeth Ashley *(Diane Freed)*; Camryn Manheim *(Kristina)*; Jon Lovitz *(Andy Kornbluth)*; Marla Maples *(Ann Chambeau)*; Rufus Read *(Billy Maplewood)*; Anne Bobby *(Rhonda)*; Dan Moran *(Joe Grasso)*; Evan Silverberg *(Johnny Grasso)*; Molly Shannon *(Nancy)*; Justin Elvin *(Timmy Maplewood)*; Lila Glantzman-Leib *(Chloe Maplewood)*; Gerry Becker *(Psychiatrist)*; Arthur Nascarella *(Detective Berman)*; Ann Harada *(Kay)*; Doug McGrath *(Tom)*; Dr. Eric Marcus *(Courteous Waiter)*; Eytan Mirsky *(Angry Picketer)*; Lisa Louise Langford *(Radical Picketer)*; Socorro Santiago *(Crying Teacher)*; Allison Furman *(Consoling Teacher)*; Wai Ching Ho *(Student #1)*; Bina Sharif *(Student #2)*; Tsepo Mokone *(Student #3)*; Hope Pomerance *(Hysterical Woman)*; Matt Malloy *(Doctor)*; Dan Tedlie *(Don)*; Marina Gaizidorskaia *(Zhenia)*; Johann Carlo *(Betty Grasso)*; Joe Lisi *(Police Detective)*; Jose Rabelo *(Pedro)*; Diane Tylor *(Janet)*; Olga Stepanova *(Zhenia's Mother)*

A dark comedy with a difference, HAPPINESS mixes irony and empathy in its depiction of a middle-class American family warped by repressed sexual desires; the film was a hit at Cannes and The New York Film Festival in 1998.

The Jordans of New Jersey live busy but unhappy lives that are removed from one another. Thirty-year-old Joy (Jane Adams) hopes to fulfill her dream of a career in music, but works in a sales office in the meantime; her love-life also leaves much to be desired. Trish (Cynthia Stevenson), Joy's sister, seems much more content, with her husband, Bill (Dylan Baker), and three children, Billy (Rufus Read), Timmy (Justin Elvin), and Chloe (Lila Glantzman-Lieb). But Trish feels inferior to her more attractive sister, Helen (Lara Flynn Boyle), a successful writer. Secretly, Helen expresses *her* frustrations by courting an anonymous stalker who has been making obscene phone calls to her apartment. Meanwhile, the sisters' parents, Lenny (Ben Gazarra) and Mona (Louise Lasser), live in retirement in a Florida condominium, and argue all day about splitting up over Diane (Elizabeth Ashley), a vixenish neighbor.

Trouble brews constantly for the family. Joy leaves her sales job for a teaching position, but is harassed by striking teachers on her first day. When she becomes involved with one of her students, Vlad (Jared Harris), a Russian emigre cab driver, Joy does not know that he is married and a former thief. Trish, meanwhile, remains unaware that Bill, a psychoanalyst, is a pederast who has just started acting on a compulsion to seduce friends of Billy. He has also recently offered to teach Billy how to masturbate.

Helen finally meets her mysterious caller, a meek neighbor, Allen (Philip Seymour Hoffman), but she is disappointed and rejects him immediately. Allen, meanwhile, begins dating Kristina (Camryn Manheim), another lonely neighbor, who confesses to him that she recently murdered their apartment doorman after he had raped her. Back at the Maplewood home, the police close in on Bill, armed with evidence of his crimes against the neighborhood youngsters. Trish leaves her husband, taking the children and fleeing to Florida, where Lenny and Mona have decided to stay together in misery. Joy bids adieu to Vlad, paying him to get back the items he has stolen from her, and she joins her sisters in Florida for a Thanksgiving dinner during which Billy finally learns how to masturbate.

Predictably, there's little sunlight in HAPPINESS, unless you count the artificial rays that shine on Trish's spotless, Martha Stewart-styled kitchen. Todd Solondz's brutally funny comedy depicts characters who never seem to realize that happiness is an emotion, not a state of being, and their pursuit of some kind of spiritual nirvana (mainly through sex) leads most of them into depression and ennui. Yet, for all the pathos (and even bathos), Solondz finds unexpected empathy for most of his characters, including Dr. Maplewood, whose attempt to rape a child becomes inept but hilarious bedroom farce. Somehow, HAPPINESS pushes the envelope more than almost any other mainstream movie in recent memory and succeeds without nauseating the viewer (only Sam Fuller's NAKED KISS [1964] shocked further by revealing its romantic hero as a child molester).

Unlike the similarly chilling farce YOUR FRIENDS AND NEIGHBORS (1998), where the lives of several unhappy characters also intertwine, HAPPINESS is more concerned with showing the roots of dysfunction and the affects of social alienation; ultimately, the film is less misanthropic than NEIGHBORS. Expanding upon his winning first feature, WELCOME TO THE DOLLHOUSE (1996), Solondz develops multiple points of view and a deliberate pace that draws in the viewer. He also gets brave, dimensional portrayals that encourage identification, even in the midst of repulsive acts. Dylan Baker is superb as the child-molesting therapist; the way his calm demeanor belies his troubled brow speaks volumes. Also distinguishing himself,

Philip Seymour Hoffman gives Allen, a potential caricature, a scary, compelling complexity. Of the sisters, Cynthia Stevenson turns the perfectionist Trish into a joyfully wicked creation, Lara Flynn Boyle is sharply and surprisingly funny, and Jane Adams makes Joy, the most put-upon but also the most likeable character, a pleasure to watch (her fragile style is reminiscent of a young Julie Hagerty). All the older actors lend zesty cameos, and even Marla Maples is well utilized in a cameo as a real estate agent.

The few defects in HAPPINESS include some weakly handled extra players and the rather over-the-top subplot about Kristina (which registers as just one of too many tabloid topics in the film by the time of her gruesome revelation). But Todd Solondz knows better than anyone that nothing is perfect, including his fine film, which is probably as close to perfection as he'll get. *(Violence, nudity, sexual situations, adult situations, substance abuse, extreme profanity.)*—E.M.

d, Todd Solondz; p, Ted Hope, Christine Vachon; exec p, James Schamus, David Linde; w, Todd Solondz; ph, Maryse Alberti; ed, Alan Oxman; m, Robbie Kondor; prod d, Therese Deprez; art d, John Bruce; set d, Nick Evans; sound, Neil Danziger (mixer), Damien Vople; fx, Drew Jiritano; casting, Ann Goulder; cos, Kathryn Nixon; makeup, Nicki Ledermann

Comedy/Drama **(PR: O MPAA: R)**

HARD CORE LOGO ★★★★

(Canada, 1996) 96m Terminal Pictures; Shadow Shows ~ Rolling Thunder c/bw

Hugh Dillon *(Joe Dick)*; Callum Keith Rennie *(Billy Tallent)*; Bernie Coulson *(Pipefitter)*; John Pyper-Ferguson *(John Oxenberger)*; Julian Richings *(Bucky Haight)*; Art Bergmann *(Himself)*; Jennifer Bishop *(Tracy/Louise/Bongo Player)*; Morgan Brayton *(Victoria)*; Dan Fazzio *(Flash Bastard)*; Claudia Ferri *(John Oxenberger's Girlfriend)*; Benita Ha *(Pipefitter's Girlfriend)*; Samaya Jardey *(Naomi)*; Mike Kopsa *(Mary's Husband)*; Corrine Koslo *(Laura Cromartie)*; Megan Leitch *(Mary the Fan)*; Alexa Mardon *(Little Billie)*; Bruce McDonald *(Documentary Filmmaker)*; Pete Mills *(Flash Bastard)*; Terry David Mulligan *(Mulligan)*; Danny Novak *(Documentary Cameraman)*; Dean Paras *(Terry the D.J.)*; Nicole Parker *(Journalist)*; Xantha Radley *(Joanne/Thelma)*; Joey Ramone *(Joey Ramone)*; Daniel Salerno *(Satan)*; Jochen A. Schliessler *(Documentary Sound Recordist)*; Tony Tucker *(Bongo Player)*

Following a once-infamous Canadian punk band during their strained reunion tour, this mock-documentary captures the lower depths of the rock world, warts and all. Although the film is entirely fictional, this character-driven group portrait is one of the most authentic and observant films ever made about life on the road and the tenuous relationships between musicians.

Formed in 1978, the punk band Hard Core Logo made seven records, played over 1,000 shows, and broke up in 1991. Despite personal differences, the four band members—Joe Dick (Hugh Dillon), Billy Tallent (Callum Keith Rennie), John Oxenberger (John Pyper-Ferguson), and Pipefitter (Bernie Coulson)—reunite for a 1995 "Rock Against Guns" benefit concert, organized by Joe, for punk legend Bucky Haight, who was recently shot and had his legs amputated. Joe even recruits indie filmmaker Bruce McDonald (Himself) to cover the gig. The band's raucous appearance is so successful that Joe sets up a five-city tour across Western Canada.

Guitarist Billy—once Joe's best friend—is waiting to learn if he's the newest member of the popular LA band Jenifur, but after some coercing, agrees to the mini-tour. McDonald brings his camera along for the ride. In the process, the reasons for Hard Core Logo's original disintegration become apparent: Joe's unwillingness to go "corporate" clashes with Billy's desire to succeed in the music world. Packed into a run-down van, the band stop first in Calgary and Regina, as each member begins to feel the stress. Oxenberger loses his medication and freaks out, Billy learns that he's lost his gig with Jenifur, the group's cash is stolen, and the Winnipeg venue is shuttered when they arrive. The band makes a visit to the secluded home of Bucky Haight (Julian Richings), discovering that their punk idol is in fact uninjured. It seems Joe made up the entire story and used the benefit money to fund their reunion tour. After a night of experimentation with LSD, Bucky tells Joe how upset he is at being used, and asks him never to come by again. The band's final stop is Edmonton, where Billy learns he has indeed been hired as Jenifur's new guitarist. Joe is crushed when he's told that Billy is ditching the group. On stage, Joe attacks Billy and smashes his prized guitar. Afterward, on-camera, Joe shoots himself in the head.

Director Bruce McDonald (ROADKILL, HIGHWAY 61) caps off his rock 'n' roll, road-movie trilogy with this inventive, unexpectedly introspective faux-documentary. And while comparisons to THIS IS SPINAL TAP (1984) seem obvious, this film is an entirely different type of creation, since the laughs arise out of one's understanding of the caustic lifestyle of a touring band—there's rarely a moment when uninformed viewers would realize the fictional agenda. Based on the similarly titled book by Michael Turner, the film finds McDonald working overtime at establishing his characters, supplying them with nuances that rarely turn up outside of the most intuitive music documentaries. Expertly capturing the highs and extreme lows of life on the road, the film registers as far more than a simple riff on a single idea, as it explores the tense, loving, and often manipulative relationships between bandmates.

Hugh Dillon and Callum Keith Rennie are both excellent as once-close-pals Dick and Tallent. In particular, Dillon (who's also the lead singer of the real-life band Headstones) is self-destruction incarnate—struggling to hang onto a best friend, despite his scorn of Billy's "money trip." The film also gets high marks for its believable music, which pegs the band as having been just good enough to maintain a cult following, but no more. Danny Nowak's skillfully raw photography perfectly captures the cold, desolate locations the band travels to, while an additional level of versimilitude is supplied by the appearances of such real-life rockers as Joey Ramone, Canadian musicians D.O.A., Art Bergmann, and the Modernettes.

HARD CORE LOGO succeeds as well as it does thanks to McDonald's understanding of the thin line that exists between satire and painful accuracy. Skillfully mixing introspective interviews with the characters, hard-driving on-stage antics, and confrontations thought to be off-camera, he uncovers the heart of this bogus band, and gives them a depth and crude poignancy that real-life musicians would be lucky to have achieved. *(Violence, substance abuse, extreme profanity.)* —S.P.

d, Bruce McDonald; p, Christine Haebler, Brian Dennis; w, Noel S. Baker (based on the book by Michael Turner); ph, Danny Nowak; ed, Reginald Harkema; m, Schaun Tozer; prod d, David Willson; sound, Bill "Otis" Sheppard (designer)

Comedy/Drama/Musical **(PR: C MPAA: R)**

HARD RAIN ★★

(U.S., 1998) 93m Mark Gordon/Gary Levinsohn; Mutual Film Company; Paramount ~ Paramount c

Morgan Freeman *(Jim)*; Christian Slater *(Tom)*; Randy Quaid *(Sheriff)*; Minnie Driver *(Karen)*; Edward Asner *(Charlie)*; Michael Goorjian *(Kenny)*; Dann Florek *(Mr. Mehlor)*; Ricky Harris *(Ray)*; Mark Rolston *(Wayne)*; Peter Murnik *(Phil)*; Wayne Duvall *(Hank)*; Richard Dysart *(Henry)*; Betty White *(Doreen)*; Ray Baker *(Mayor)*; Lisa Fuhrman *(Mayor's Wife)*; Jay Patterson *(Mr. Wellman)*; Michael Monks *(Father on Local News)*; Mackenzie Bryce *(Baby on Local News)*

Greed, murder, romance, betrayal, and a monstrous flood are all combined to soggy effect in HARD RAIN, a movie that features a better cast than it deserves (the cast, in turn, seem to be enduring worse on-set conditions than they deserve). Viewers must don hip-boots to wade through the script's plethora of cliches.

A ceaseless downpour has raised floodwaters, threatening a small Indiana town. The Sheriff (Randy Quaid) and his deputies are evacuating the citizenry. Armored-car drivers Tom (Christian Slater) and his Uncle Charlie (Edward Asner) are moving $3 million from the local banks to higher ground. After their truck stalls in a flooded roadway, they are intercepted by armed robbers, who shoot and kill Charlie. Tom runs for his life, with the money in tow, and hides the sacks of cash in the cemetery. The criminals, led by Jim (Morgan Freeman), steal a speedboat and jet-skis, and follow Tom.

Tom seeks refuge in a church and gets hit on the head by Karen (Minnie Driver), who—believing he's a looter—subsequently delivers him to the police. The Sheriff doubts Tom's story, but agrees to check out the cemetery. Karen agrees to evacuate, but obstinately returns to finish sandbagging the church. When another floodgate on the nearby dam is opened, the water starts rising fast. Karen returns to rescue Tom, who's drowning in a jail cell. Karen and Tom are then spotted and pursued by Jim and his gang. On the run, they cross paths with Doreen (Betty White) and Harry (Richard Dysart), a loony old couple who refused to evacuate their home.

Jim takes Doreen and Harry hostage, thus compelling Tom to lead him to the money, but when they arrive at the cemetery, the loot is gone. Karen comes to the rescue again and frees Doreen and Harry. The Sheriff and his boys arrive on the scene. They have the $3 million and plan to keep it. Deputy Wayne (Mark Rolston) takes Karen back to her house to rape and kill her. Meanwhile, newly allied Tom and Jim make a stand in the church, where after a protracted battle, Jim gets shot.

The dam breaks, and a tidal wave hits the town. Tom escapes the Sheriff long enough to go rescue Karen, who managed to kill Wayne with a penknife, but is still handcuffed to a banister. When the Sheriff finally has Tom and Karen cornered, Jim pops up and kills the lawman. As the National Guard arrive on the scene, Jim escapes with a sack of cash and Tom's blessing.

Cliched characterizations, corny dialogue, predictable plotting, and *a lot* of water. These are the hallmarks of HARD RAIN; they also could be used to describe TITANIC (1997). And in the first month of 1998, one of these films was going completely unnoticed by moviegoers, while the other was setting new box-office records. (You figure out which is which.) Working as the cinematographer on James Cameron's underwater epic, THE ABYSS (1989), HARD RAIN director Mikael Salomon learned a tough lesson in filming under adversely wet conditions; he apparently didn't learn enough about the peculiar alchemy of movie storytelling from Cameron, though.

In a concerted effort to make HARD RAIN "not just another disaster movie," Salomon positions the flood as a mere backdrop for the action. (In fact, the movie's original title, "The Flood," was dropped for just that reason.) Except for their being soaking wet, the characters barely acknowledge the real and very imminent dangers of the rising water—it's almost as if the leads in THE POSEIDON ADVENTURE (or TITANIC, for that matter) ignored the fact that they were on a sinking ship.

HARD RAIN scripter Graham Yost's previous efforts, SPEED (1994) and BROKEN ARROW (1996), certainly tested viewers' credulity; likewise the action here. The fact that the characters are incarnated by a cast of first-rate actors (especially the terrific Freeman) is the one and only factor that allows HARD RAIN to stay afloat. *(Violence, profanity.)*—P.R.

d, Mikael Salomon; p, Mark Gordon, Gary Levinsohn, Ian Bryce; exec p, Allison Lyon Segan; co-p, Christian Slater; w, Graham Yost; ph, Peter Menzies Jr.; ed, Paul Hirsch; m, Christopher Young; prod d, J. Michael Riva; art d, David Klassen, Richard Mays; set d, Ron Reiss; sound, Lee Orloff (mixer); fx, Ed Jones, John Frazier, Jim Schwalm; casting, Risa Bramon Garcia, Randi Hiller; cos, Kathleen Detoro; makeup, Mike Hancock, Sharon Ilson ; stunts, Jeff Habberstad

Crime/Action/Disaster (PR: C MPAA: R)

HAV PLENTY ★★½

(U.S., 1998) 92m Wanderlust Pictures; Edmonds Entertainment; e2 Filmworks ~ Miramax c

Christopher Scott Cherot *(Lee Plenty)*; Chenoa Maxwell *(Havilland Savage)*; Tammi Katherine Jones *(Caroline Gooden)*; Robinne Lee *(Leigh Darling)*; Hill Harper *(Michael Simmons)*; Reginald James *(Felix Darling)*; Kim Harris *(Bobby Montgomery)*; Betty Vaughn *(Grandma Moore)*; Margie St. Juste *(Alexandria Beaumont)*; Chuck Baron *(Mr. Savage)*; Michele Turner *(Sylvia Savage)*; P.G. Reese *(Evelyn)*; Wanda Candelario *(Girl in Gas Station)*; Robyn M. Green; Courtney Berlin; Jennifer Gaglia; Julio Yurnet; Diane Barone; Arnold Bayley *(Dream Extras)*; Anthony Beneri; Emir Radoncic; Mandy Zagon; Isaac B. Marten *(Brunch Extras)*; Melissa Brooks; Juana Cullen; Marco Materassi; Celia Didier; Vincent Nolasco *(Hav's Co-Workers)*; Nia Long *(Trudy)*; Shemar Moore *(Chris)*; Lauryn Hill *(Debra)*; Chilli *(Kris)*; Mekhi Phifer *(Harold)*; Leslie "Big Lez" Segar *(Jane)*; Christopher Batyr *(Emcee)*; Shontonette Crawford; Reginald Bruce; Alaina Irizarry *(Spectators)*; Keith Hudson *(Festival Participant)*; Tracey E. Edmonds *(Amy Madison)*; Kenneth "Babyface" Edmonds *(Lloyd Banks)*; Bridget D. Davis; Shara P. Fleming; Patrik Ian Polk *(Caprice Films Entourage)*

The story of a latent romance between two mismatched people, a materialistic young woman and a laid-back young man, HAV PLENTY was welcome as one of the few black independent films of its time to focus on African-Americans well above the underclass level.

Lee Plenty (Christopher Scott Cherot), a well-educated but penniless writer who lives in his car in New York City, is apartment-sitting for Havilland Savage (Chenoa Maxwell), a successful and ambitious career woman who is visiting her prosperous family in Washington, DC. When Hav learns that Lee has no New Year's Eve plans, she invites him down to Washington.

During the course of the weekend, Lee deflects the advances of both Hav's friend Caroline (Tammi Katherine Jones) and sister Leigh (Robinne Lee), who has been considering leaving her husband, Felix (Reginald James). After Felix socks Lee for messing with his wife, Leigh confesses to her husband that she, not Lee, was to blame and that she has decided to move to New York to become her sister's personal assistant.

Angry with her womanizing fiance, Michael (Hill Harper), a rising pop singer, Hav begins necking with Lee one night, but their total lack of sympathy with each other's values prevents the encounter from escalating and they agree to remain just friends.

Leigh realizes she loves her husband and decides to stay with him.

Back in New York, Michael begs Hav's forgiveness and Lee sends her a love letter to which she fails to respond. During the course of the following year, Lee writes and directs *Tru Love*, an autobiographical movie dramatizing the events that occurred over the New Year's holiday. He assures the audience at a festival screening that he has no intention of sweetening *Tru Love*'s inconclusive ending to score a distribution deal. After the screening, Hav, who was in the audience, tells him she's a changed woman and that she loves him. Approached by an important distributor, Lee readily agrees to reshoot the end of his film, comforting himself with the thought that he has won the girl of his dreams and the deal of his life—and he only had to sell out a little bit.

HAV PLENTY was written, directed, edited, and coproduced by young Christopher Scott Cherot on a very low budget and tight shooting schedule. When both of the picture's lead players dropped out at the 11th hour, Cherot promoted Chenoa Maxwell from the supporting cast to the role of Hav and took on the portrayal of the passive, hard-to-get hero himself. His gamble paid off; he proved himself to be a photogenic, winning screen presence. He also showed himself also to be a dexterous editor—another hat he had never worn before.

Cherot's final scramble was an ingenious one. When Miramax, the movie's distributor, reportedly required him to come up with a more commercial conclusion to HAV PLENTY, he agreed but saved some face by incorporating this agreement into the movie itself, lending it a wry, sly, and self-mocking twist. Perhaps he realized that Miramax was right; fashioning a romantic comedy without a happy ending is not honesty, it's perversity. If a filmmaker as uncompromising as John Cassavetes could find it in his heart to bring MINNIE AND MOSKOWITZ (1971) together, why shouldn't Hav and Lee wind up in each other's arms?

Cherot's debut film has value also as a corrective to the overall social portrayal of African-Americans on the screen. Black Americans are disproportionally poor, and thus filmmakers have doted on this aspect of their lives (perhaps engaging in a sort of reverse-racism). Therefore, it is gratifying to see a movie like HAV PLENTY that draws its characters from the millions of underrepresented black Americans who are *not* fighting it out in the projects. *(Extreme profanity.)*—D.T.

d, Christopher Scott Cherot; p, Christopher Scott Cherot, Robyn M. Greene; exec p, Kenneth "Babyface" Edmonds, Tracey E. Edmonds, Bridget D. Davis, S.J. Cherot; co-p, Dana Offenbach; w, Christopher Scott Cherot; ph, Kerwin Devonish; ed, Christopher Scott Cherot; m, Wendy Melvoin, Lisa Coleman; sound, Damian Canelos (mixer); makeup, Christina G. Miller

Romance/Comedy **(PR: C MPAA: R)**

HE GOT GAME ★★½

(U.S., 1998) 131m 40 Acres and a Mule Filmworks; Touchstone Pictures ~ Buena Vista c

Denzel Washington *(Jake Shuttlesworth)*; Ray Allen *(Jesus Shuttlesworth)*; Milla Jovovich *(Dakota Burns)*; Hill Harper *(Coleman "Booger" Sykes)*; Bill Nunn *(Uncle Bubba)*; Jim Brown *(Spivey)*; Thomas Jefferson Byrd *(Sweetness)*; Rosario Dawson *(Lala Bonilla)*; Zelda Harris *(Mary Shuttlesworth)*; Lonette McKee *(Martha Shuttlesworth)*; Roger Guenveur Smith *(Big Time Willie)*; Ned Beatty *(Warden Wyatt)*; Joseph Lyle Taylor *(Crudup)*; Michele Shay *(Aunt Sally)*; John Turturro *(Coach Billy Sunday)*; Arthur J. Nascarella *(Coach Cincotta)*; Travis Best *(Sip)*; Walter McCarty *(Mance)*; John Wallace *(Lonnie)*; Rick Fox *(Chick Deagan)*; Al Palagonia *(Dom Pagnotti)*; Leonard Roberts *(D'Andre Mackey)*; Saul Stein *(Prison Guard Books)*; Ron Cephas Jones *(Prison Guard Burwell)*; Jade Yorker *(Jesus Shuttlesworth—Age 12)*; Shortee Red *(Booger—Age 12)*; Quinn Harris *(Mary Shuttlesworth—Age 6)*; Coach Dean Smith; Coach Lute Olson; Coach John Chaney; Coach John Thompson; Coach Roy Williams; Coach Nolan Richardson; Coach Denny Crum; Coach Tom Davis; Coach Clem Haskins; Coach George Karl; Coach Jim Boeheim; Coach Rick Pitino; Coach Robert "Bobby" Cremins; Dick Vitale; Bill Walton; Shaquille O'Neal; Reggie Miller; Charles Barkley; Scottie Pippen; Michael Jordan; Robin Roberts *(Themselves)*; Gus Johnson *(PSAL Announcer)*; Stuart Scott *(TV Announcer)*; Ray Clay *(Tech U Announcer)*; J.C. MacKenzie *(Doctor Cone)*; Coati Mundi *(Clerk in Motel)*; Avery Glymph *(Sneaker Clerk)*; Ciara A. Shields *(Mary's Friend)*; Lin Que Ayoung; Angela Meryl; Dionne D. Phillips; Gary Frith; Jamie Hector; Harry Philippe; Kelli-Lin McMillan; Lamar Tookes *("I Love You" Leeches)*; Mark Breland *(Man with Gat)*; Heather Hunter *(Female in Sex Montage)*; Christopher Wynkoop *(The John)*; Alonzo Scales *(Goose)*; Lori Rom *(June)*; Kim Director *(Lynn)*; Felicia Finley *(Molly)*; Tiffany Jones *(Buffy)*; Jill Kelly *(Suzie)*; Jennifer Esposito *(Ms. Janus)*; Tony Paige *(Correction Officer)*

Denzel Washington gives a great performance in HE GOT GAME, an uneven basketball drama about a family divided.

Convicted in his wife's accidental death and serving time in Attica, Jake Shuttlesworth (Denzel Washington) gets a time-limited chance to reduce his jail sentence if he can persuade his son, a star high school basketball player named Jesus (Ray Allen), to attend the Governor's college of choice. While carefully monitored by two undercover parole officers, Jake sets himself up in an apartment located near his daughter, Mary (Zelda Harris), and son's home in Coney Island, New York. He ingratiates his way back into Mary's life, but has a more difficult time with Jesus, who holds a grudge against his father for the death of his mother.

Jesus also resents Jake's suggestion to attend the State school, and resists the pressure to attend other schools by his greedy Uncle Bubba (Bill Nunn), his seemingly loyal coach, Cincotta (Arthur J. Nascarella), countless school officials, and even his cheating girlfriend, Lala (Rosario Dawson). In the meantime, Jake recognizes the resentment he had left behind in the outside world, and tries to reconnect to people by helping an abused prostitute and neighbor, Dakota (Milla Jovovich). As Jesus visits various schools, and tries to maintain his integrity in the face of lucrative offers, Jake's days become numbered in securing a deal with his recalcitrant son. Finally, Jake makes an offer Jesus can't refuse: if Jake can win a basketball match against Jesus, then he will determine where Jesus goes to school; if he loses, then he will leave Jesus alone. Jesus wins the *mano a mano* game, however, and Jake is carted back to jail. Behind bars, however, Jake learns that Jesus has chosen the State school anyway, too late to reduce his father's jail sentence, but in time to still make him proud.

Like so many Spike Lee films, HE GOT GAME displays a range of filmmaking quality. Laced with references to the Bible (the self-consciously named Jesus) and Greek myths (the more subtle evocation of Icarus and Daedalus), the father-son drama represents the strongest part of Spike Lee's screenplay. Otherwise, the narrative barely expands upon recent films, including BLUE CHIPS and HOOP DREAMS (both 1994), that also dealt with the harsh realities and racial undercurrents of the basketball business (though some of the hustling to sign Jesus is both amusing and telling). Meanwhile, director Lee excels in several formalist sequences: the great opening basketball-playing montage, the climactic confrontation, and other smaller set pieces (two different love-making scenes are beautifully designed, lit, and shot by Malik Hassan Sayeed). Best of all, Washington delivers one of his most winning performances in a very difficult role—a complex, angry, but charming antihero.

Lee's misjudgments abound, however. The stately Aaron Copland music (including "Rodeo: 'Hoe-Down'" and "Fanfare for the Common Man") becomes pretentious and overused, particularly during the simple dialogue scenes. The romance between Jake and Dakota, though affecting, is not well integrated into the main story. All the other female characters are also either abused or predatory, typical nasty Lee stereotypes. The conclusion too neatly and optimistically wraps up the downbeat situation. The anticonsumer message flies in the face of Lee's own off-screen commercial enterprises. And, finally, Lee never quite allows nonbasketball fans into the game itself (a frustration particularly in the scoring during the climactic game), although his love for the sport is evident in his filmmaking style and use of real-life stars and coaches (including lead Allen, an NBA star, who is very convincing here). Ultimately, HE GOT GAME gets it together, but the careless streaks keep it from being a slam dunk. *(Violence, nudity, sexual situations, adult situations, extreme profanity.)*—E.M.

d, Spike Lee; p, Jon Kilik, Spike Lee; w, Spike Lee; ph, Malik Hassan Sayeed; ed, Barry Alexander Brown; m, Public Enemy; prod d, Wynn Thomas; art d, David Stein; set d, Carolyn Cartwright; sound, Allan Byer (mixer), Matthew Price (mixer); fx, Randall Balsmeyer; casting, Aisha Coley; cos, Sandra Hernandez; makeup, Anita Gibson; stunts, Jeff Ward, Manny Siverio

Drama/Sports **(PR: C MPAA: R)**

HEALING BY KILLING ★★★★½

(Israel, 1998) 90m New Israel Foundation for Cinema and Television ~ New Yorker Films c/bw
(RIPUI B'HAREG)

Robert Jay Lifton; Dr. Hans Munch; Dr. Elise Huber

HEALING BY KILLING details the incremental steps Nazi doctors took toward the Final Solution of the Holocaust. This superior documentary explores an infamous part of history, providing current-day viewers with important information and insight.

Tracing the work of several German doctors and psychiatrists in Europe from the mid-1930s, HEALING BY KILLING illustrates how these professionals, despite their allegiance to the Hippocratic oath, enmeshed themselves in Nazi experiments with euthanasia. The film focuses on the lives of two doctors, in particular: Dr. Irmfried Eberl, a hygiene specialist, and Prof. Carl Clauberg, a renowned gynecologist.

By first using gas chambers in 1939 as a "mercy killing" machine for the mentally ill and retarded, Eberl convinced himself and his colleagues that sterilizations and executions occurred for a greater good. Fearing a public backlash after almost 100,000 people were killed, Adolf Hitler officially stopped the operation, but privately, Eberl moved to Poland where he began a mass campaign of death-camp killings. Eventually, in 1942, Eberl became the first commander of the Treblinka death camp, but a dispute over some misdirected funds led to his dismissal. Under the supervision of Dr. Josef Mengele, Dr. Clauberg took over the experimentations, sterilizing 1000 women a day when not directing other victims to their deaths in the camp. After WWII, officials caught and jailed Clauberg for his crimes, although the medical community did not immediately bar him. In 1957, on the verge of targeting other Nazi officials, Clauberg died in prison under mysterious circumstances. Eberl was also imprisoned and eventually committed suicide.

Though HEALING BY KILLING could be perceived as simply one more documentary about the Holocaust, it stands out strongly as a compact, unemotional, but deeply meaningful review of the tragic events. Through well-selected and edited interviews and carefully researched archival materials, director Nitzan Aviram gives a context to the period, which makes it no less sorrowful but somewhat more lucid than usual. At least the development of what Hannah Arendt called "the banality of evil" becomes understandable as the underachieving Dr. Eberl charts his course for success within the hierarchy of Nazi power. In a vital and resonant way, HEALING BY KILLING reveals how the bureaucracy and institutionalization of the killings allowed so many doctors, scientists, and health care professionals to evade and deny responsibility.

The simplicity of Aviram's filmmaking only lends power to the story. Thankfully, the film eschews footage of the death-camp victims in favor of chillingly quiet contemporary footage of the empty camp sites and operating rooms (a possible reference to Alain Resnais's chilling NIGHT AND FOG), a few important photographs, and the wide-ranging interviews—with Robert Jay Lifton, the author of the book, "Nazi Doctors," on which the film is based, experts and historians on euthanasia, Mengele's still photographer, several camp experiment survivors, young German medical students, and even a doctor (Dr. Munch) who participated in the horrors (it is galling to hear Munch preach about responsibility near the end of the film, but Aviram wisely counters this statement with a final word from one of the sterilization victims).

Interestingly, Aviram comes from Israel and the film was cosponsored by the Museum of Jewish Heritage, but, except for Lifton, there are no Jews interviewed, and the film emphasizes both the Jews *and* gentiles killed in the Holocaust. HEALING BY KILLING, thus, represents a courageous, intelligent effort without a hidden political agenda. *(Adult situations.)*—E.M.

d, Nitzan Aviram; p, Nitzan Aviram; w, Nitzan Aviram (inspired by the book *Nazi Doctors* by Robert Jay Lifton); ph, Yoram Millo; ed, Naomi Press-Aviram; m, Oded Zehavi; sound, Uri Buzaglo (recordist)

Documentary **(PR: C MPAA: NR)**

HEAVEN'S BURNING ★★

(Australia/Japan, 1997) 104m Duo Art Productions; Amuse Cinema; South Australian Film Corp; Beyond Films ~ Trimark Home Video c
(AKA: YOU DON'T KNOW WHAT LOVE IS)

Russell Crowe *(Colin O'Brien)*; Youki Kudoh *(Midori Takada)*; Kenji Isomura *(Yukio Takada)*; Ray Barrett *(Cam O'Brien)*; Robert Mammone *(Mahood)*; Petru Gheorghiu *(Boorjan)*; Anthony Phelan *(Detective Bishop)*; Matthew Dyktynksi *(Detective Moffat)*; Colin Hay *(Jonah)*; Susan Prior *(Sharon)*; Norman Kaye *(Store Owner)*; Kate Fitzpatrick *(Gloria)*; Mark Hembrow *(Truck Driver)*

A road movie about a young couple on the run, HEAVEN'S BURNING has enough attractive players, stunt-powered confrontations, and whirling camera movements to ensure that it will never get dull. But neither is it vital nor original. Action junkies will get just enough sex and mayhem to avoid genre-withdrawal symptoms.

The Australian honeymoon quickly ends for visiting Japanese executive Yukio (Kenji Isomura) when his unloving bride Midori (Youki Kudoh) fakes her own kidnapping after having second thoughts about settling for a marriage of convenience. Having been left in the lurch by a married boyfriend, Midori nonetheless imprudently abandons and disgraces the status-conscious Yukio.

Meanwhile, a down-and-out Aussie mechanic named Colin (Russell Crowe) reluctantly becomes a bank heist driver for his Afghani immigrant pal Mahood (Robert Mammone) and Mahood's father Boorjan (Petru Gheorgiu). During the disastrous holdup, which leaves one robber dead, the stickup crew takes a customer hostage; it is the luckless Midori. After eluding the cops, Mahood's gang decides to execute Midori; while defending her, Colin fatally wounds Mahood's brother.

On the lam from the Mahood gang, Colin and Midori are also trailed by dishonored Yukio (who has spotted Midori on the evening news). The vengeful Afghanis locate Colin through credit card receipts. Mahood and Boorjan torture Colin, nailing his hand to a dresser in his motel room, but he breaks free and shoots them dead.

After recuperating from his wounds at the sheep ranch of his father Cam (Ray Barrett), Colin takes Midori to an ocean resort. The unrelenting Yukio continues his pursuit, slaughtering Cam and anyone else who has aided the fugitive couple. At the resort, Yukio shoots Colin; Midori shoots and kills Yukio, but not before he wounds her as well. After a subsequent police chase, the couple's car catches fire. Colin dies, and Midori shoots herself in the head before the car explodes.

Ever since Quentin Tarantino beat Hollywood's crimescape to a pulp with PULP FICTION (1995), brash young filmmakers have set their sights on his territory. Punctuated by scenes of sadistic torture, car explosions, HEAVEN'S BURNING is neither a top- nor bottom-drawer entry in that wannabe arena.

Although magnetic star Russell Crowe dominates the dark scenario, his character's judgment is so questionable, one loses patience with him. The other principals (runaway bride Midori, the vengeful Mahood gang, hubby/spree-killer Yukio) register as little more than comic book sidekicks for an anti-hero who embraces a criminal lifestyle far too easily. The self-absorption of the film's characters is only memorable for the glee with which they attack each other; the audience only stays awake due to the director's skill in conveying appetites for brutality. In HEAVEN'S BURNING, the audience becomes a cheering section at a marathon sporting event of Getting Even. *(Graphic violence, extreme profanity, nudity, sexual situations.)*— R.P.

d, Craig Lahiff; p, Al Clark, Helen Leake; exec p, Craig Lahiff, Georgina Pope; w, Louis Nowra; ph, Brian Breheny; ed, John Scott; prod d, Vicki Niehus; art d, Tony Cronin; sound, Tovlo Lember (mixer); fx, Peter Stubbs; casting, Anna Lennon-Smith; cos, Annie Marshall

Action **(PR: C MPAA: R)**

HENRY FOOL ★★★★

(U.S., 1998) 141m True Fiction Pictures; Shooting Gallery; Henry Films ~ Sony Pictures Classics c

Thomas Jay Ryan *(Henry Fool)*; James Urbaniak *(Simon Grim)*; Parker Posey *(Fay)*; Kevin Corrigan *(Warren)*; Miho Nikaido *(Gnoc Deng)*; Maria Porter *(Mary)*; Chuck Montgomery *(Angus James)*; Nicholas Hope *(Father Hawkes)*; James Saito *(Mr. Deng)*; Liam Aiken *(Ned)*; Gene Ruffini *(Officer Bunuel)*; Diana Ruppe *(Amy)*; Veanne Cox *(Laura)*; Jan Leslie Harding *(Vicky)*; Chaylee Worrall *(Pearl—age 7)*; Christy Romano *(Pearl—age 14)*; Melanie Vesey *(Go-Go Dancer #1)*; Denise Morgan *(Go-Go Dancer #2)*; Jill Morely *(Afternoon Table Dancer)*; Paul Boocock *(Steve)*; David Latham *(Barry)*; Marissa Chibas *(Newspaper Reporter)*; Julie Anderson *(Woman Outside Store)*; Reggie Harris *(Anchorman)*; Don Creech *(Owen Feer)*; Camille Paglia *(Herself)*; Maraya Chase *(TV Reporter)*; Shoshana Ami *(Young Woman in Library)*; Karen DiConcetto *(Girl in Library #1)*; Tiffany Sampson *(Girl in Library #2)*; Rachel Miner *(Girl in Library #3)*; Paul Lazar *(Doctor)*; Gretchen Krich *(Nurse)*; Valorie Hubbard *(Patty the Bartender)*; Dave Simonds *(Bill)*; Fay Ann Lee *(Lawyer)*; Paul Greco *(Concierge)*; Blake Willett *(Cop #1)*; Raymond Cassar *(Cop #2)*; Katreen Hardt *(Airline Ticket Clerk)*; Rebecca Nelson *(Flight Attendant Lucy)*; Paul Albe *(Angry Customer)*; Vivian Bang; Brandon Boey; Claire Ritchie; Herbie Duarte; Toy Connor *(Teenagers at World of Donuts)*

Quirky independent Hal Hartley continues to develop his distinctive cinematic vision with this fable of America in the 1990s. HENRY FOOL mixes elements from the legends of Faust and Kasper Hauser in the story of a dissolute would-be writer who inspires a meek garbageman to become a writer.

Simon Grim (James Urbaniak) works collecting garbage in Queens, New York, where he lives a dreary existence with his hypochondriacal mother Mary (Maria Porter) and slutty sister Fay (Parker Posey). Into the Grims' basement apartment moves Henry Fool (Thomas Jay Ryan), a gross lout who tells Simon he is a writer working on a memoir that he describes in grandiose but vague terms. Henry, who has recently been paroled after serving time for statutory rape, never actually seems to write, but spends plenty of time drinking, looking for sex, and spinning tales of his bohemian life. He's the opposite of Simon, who is quiet to the point of catatonia and the perpetual target of neighborhood bully Warren (Kevin Corrigan).

Simon decides to try his hand at writing and, in one exhausting night, fills a notebook Henry gave him with the beginning of an epic poem. Excerpts from it move people in surprising ways, both positive and negative. Local students spark a controversy by printing Simon's work in the high school newspaper. In the meantime, Warren becomes a campaign worker for a right-wing politician, while Henry is distracted from his attempts to seduce Fay by the sexual availability of mother Mary.

Unable to get his work published, Simon asks Henry to recommend him to Angus James (Chuck Montgomery), a publisher he claims to know. (Actually, Henry was a janitor in James's offices.) The business-minded James reads Simon's poem but rejects it. Mary reads one of Simon's notebooks and later kills herself. Fay gets pregnant by Henry and the two get married. Simon's poem is posted on the Internet, where it causes a national ruckus. Sensing a salable controversy, James agrees to publish it, even though he openly hates it. Simon demands that he publish Henry's work as well, but backs down after he reads it.

Years later, Simon is a respected author, while Henry has taken his old job as a garbageman. He and Fay are the parents of a young son, Ned (Liam Aiken). Henry learns that Warren, who is now married, is abusing both his wife and stepdaughter. He confronts him, leading to a fight in which Warren is accidentally killed. Simon helps Henry flee the country by giving him his passport and plane ticket to Stockholm, where Simon is to be awarded the Nobel Prize.

Hartley describes HENRY FOOL in the film's press notes as "A story about the culture we live in. . . a new modern myth. . . My aspiration. . . was to create a broad but meaningful sketch of our culture and some of its current preoccupations, to leave a fossil of a particular time and place in America." Fans of Hartley's previous films, from THE UNBELIEVABLE TRUTH (1989) through FLIRT (1995), should rest assured that this isn't as much of a change as it may sound. HENRY FOOL may be concerned with issues of art and commerce, mass communications, and politics, but it situates them in Hartley's usual context: a generic slice of suburbia in which the locals either delight in justifying their deadend existences or are straining to escape. Henry and Simon are archetypal Hartley characters: one determined to fashion an identity for himself, the other fleeing the identity he already has (placed on him by family, an institution

Hartley does not seem to hold in high regard). The nature of identity also torments Simon's sister Fay, who reassures herself about her fading sexual attractiveness by sleeping with everyone she can, and bullying Warren, who reinvents himself after hearing the empty promises of a right-wing politician, only to sink deeper into his worst traits when the politician fails to be elected.

Of course, HENRY FOOL is also, like all of Hartley's film, dryly funny: he continues to write the wittiest dialogue of any contemporary American screenwriter. But underneath the usual deadpan ironies is a layer of pain not found in his previous films. The continual abuse that has left Simon so withdrawn ("I'm not retarded," he feels compelled to tell Henry when they meet. "People think that—well, you know—because") clues us in to the nature of the work he eventually writes—a work that we (wisely) are never directly exposed to. And Henry's determination to become a great writer primarily by acting like one is ultimately as pathetic as it is ridiculous. Both characters are splendidly brought to life by Thomas Jay Ryan and James Urbaniak, leading a cast of performers who, for the most part, are newcomers to Hartley's acting troupe. Hartley's work remains something of an acquired taste, but more than ever it is one worth acquiring. *(Violence, nudity, sexual situations, adult situations, profanity.)*—M.F.

d, Hal Hartley; p, Hal Hartley; exec p, Larry Meistrich, Daniel J. Victor, Keith Abell; assoc p, Jerome Brownstein, Thierry Cagianut; w, Hal Hartley; ph, Michael Spiller; ed, Steve Hamilton; m, Hal Hartley, Jim Coleman, Ryful, Bill Dobrow, Lydia Kavanagh, Hub Moore; prod d, Steve Rosenzweig; set d, Melissa P. Lohman; sound, Daniel McIntosh (mixer); casting, Chelsea Fuhrer; cos, Jocelyn Joson; makeup, Claus Lulla

Comedy/Drama **(PR: C MPAA: R)**

HENRY: PORTRAIT OF A SERIAL KILLER PART 2 ★★½

(U.S., 1998) 85m H-2 Productions; MPI Media Group; Maljack Films ~ Margin Films c

Neil Giuntoli *(Henry)*; Rich Komenich *(Kai)*; Kate Walsh *(Cricket)*; Carri Levinson *(Louisa)*; Daniel Allar *(Rooter)*; Penelope Milford *(Woman in Woods)*; Mike Houlihan *(Bartender)*; James Otis *(Homeless Shelter Man #1)*; Rich Baker *(Homeless Shelter Man #2)*; Bill Pirman Jr. *(Construction Worker)*; Larry Calicchio *(Obnoxious Boy #1)*; Sam Saletta *(Obnoxious Boy #2)*; Don Rimgale *(Father of Boys)*; Kathleen Perkins *(Mother of Boys)*; Miles Stroth *(Car Salesman)*; Marlon "Furry" Newson *(Gene)*; Marco Santucci *(Casey)*; Rich Wilke *(Vagrant)*; Kevin Hurley *(Lester)*; Kevin Sorenson *(Gas Station Mechanic)*; Leslie Zang *(Liquor Store Girl #1)*; Kam Heskin *(Liquor Store Girl #2)*; Richard Henzel *(Man Tied to Bed)*; Fran Smith *(Woman on Couch)*

While wholly unnecessary, this follow-up to the critically praised 1990 thriller does a decent job of honoring its predecessor.

Serial killer Henry (Neil Giuntoli) murders a woman (Penelope Milford) in the woods. A drifter, he lands a job working for Rooter (Daniel Allar) delivering portable toilets, and is befriended by co-worker Kai (Rich Komenich). Invited by Kai to stay with him for the time being, Henry meets Kai's wife, Cricket (Kate Walsh), and her emotionally fragile niece, Louisa (Carri Levinson). Kai soon reveals to Henry that he's been making extra money by pulling arson-for-hire jobs for Rooter, and invites Henry to join him. Henry is a more than willing participant, and when the duo discover a couple of junkies at the scene of one of their crimes, he shoots one and hands the gun to Kai, who briefly hestitates before killing the other.

Henry is soon up to his murderous ways again, bringing Kai along for a series of random slaughters. Though unaware of the pair's activities, Cricket has become distrustful of Henry, while Louisa has developed an attraction to him. She tries to seduce Henry, but he rebuffs her. That night he kills Rooter after a drug-fueled party. When Henry, Kai and Cricket return home, the distraught Louisa shoots herself in front of them, and the furious Henry shoots both Kai and Cricket. Placing their bodies in the cellar, Henry sets the house on fire and drives away.

Writer-director Chuck Parello (who served as publicist on the original film) doesn't break much new ground with this sequel, but he does demonstrate a respect for the mechanics of the first film's story line. The structure of both films is similar, with the early section devoted to white-trash melodrama rather than chills. Here, black-humored touches are included that play off memories of the original ("You got a woman stashed somewhere?" Kai asks Henry, by way of inquiring about his love life). While Giuntoli brings an effective, low-key menace to the role of Henry, he makes the character more obviously disturbed than did Michael Rooker, the original HENRY. The movie's real acting discovery is Komenich as Kai; big and burly, with a deep, gravely voice, he has a genuinely imposing presence, and his volatile relationship with Cricket carries the threat of violence even before he turns murderous.

Parello avoids modeling his script in any way on the life of real-life serial killer Henry Lee Lucas (the inspiration for the first film); given that he chose to fabricate all-new characters and situations, it's a shame that he wasn't a little more daring in his storytelling. It would have been a nice jolt, for example, to have Kai turn the tables on Henry, kill him off, and assume his serial-killing mantle; as it stands, the climactic scenes, while viscerally effective, assume fait accompli status. Despite this major drawback, Parello does a creditable job of preserving the first film's downbeat, uneasy spirit; in this regard, he is helped along by cinematographer Michael Kohnhorst's gritty-looking but still polished imagery. Unlike many genre-movie sequels, this one seems to have been motivated more by its predecessor's artistic success than by the money that it made. *(Graphic violence, sexual situations, substance abuse, extreme profanity.)*—M.G.

d, Chuck Parello; p, Chuck Parello, Thomas J. Bush; exec p, Waleed B. Ali, Malik B. Ali; w, Chuck Parello; ph, Michael Kohnhorst; ed, Tom Keefe; m, Robert F. McNaughton; prod d, Rick Paul; art d, Angela Howard; sound, Jake Collins (mixer); fx, Don Parsons; casting, Suzanne Gardner; cos, Patricia L. Hart; makeup, Art Anthony; stunts, Jim Fierro

Horror/Thriller **(PR: O MPAA: R)**

HERCULES AND XENA THE ANIMATED MOVIE: THE BATTLE FOR MOUNT OLYMPUS ★½

(U.S., 1997) 80m Renaissance Pictures; Universal Cartoon Studios ~ Universal Home Video c

VOICES OF: Kevin Sorbo *(Hercules)*; Lucy Lawless *(Xena)*; Michael Hurst *(Iolas)*; Renee O'Connor *(Gabrielle)*; Alexandra Tydings *(Aphrodite)*; Kevin Smith *(Ares)*; Josephine Davidson *(Alcmene/Artemis)*; Joy Watson *(Hera)*; Peter Rowley *(Zeus)*; David Mackie *(Porphyrion)*; Alison Wall *(Tethys/Mnemosyne)*; Ted Raimi *(Crius)*

Hoping that the audience for cartoons about Greek gods has not already been satiated by Disney's HERCULES (1997), the folks who produce the live-action TV series "Hercules: The Legendary Journeys" and "Xena: Warrior Princess" have repackaged their characters in an action-packed and occasionally charming, but very poorly animated, straight-to-video feature-length film.

Hercules (voice of Kevin Sorbo) is the legendary half-man, half-god whose mission is to avenge all wrongs, including those committed by his cruel, impetuous godly relations—namely, his father Zeus (voice of Peter Rowley), and his half-siblings Ares (voice of Kevin Smith), Artemis (voice of Josephine Davidson), and Aphrodite (voice of Alexandra Tydings). Hercules and his sidekick Iolas (voice of Michael Hurst) believe they've witnessed a kidnapping when they see Zeus taking Hercules's mortal mother Alcmene (also voiced by Davidson) aboard his chariot to return to Mount Olympus. Zeus's wife Hera (Joy Watson), is angered, and causes an earthquake that frees the Titans—four giants who once ruled the world but lost control to Zeus.

Aphrodite asks Hercules for help, but he is loathe to do any favors for the gods. Ares fails to interest Xena (voice of Lucy Lawless), a pal of Hercules and former warmonger turned do-gooder, in their plight, but Xena is forced to help the gods when Artemis changes Xena's sidekick Gabrielle (voice of Renee O'Connor) into a huge bird of prey and refuses to change her back until the Titans are defeated. Hera intends to rule the world with the Titans as her army, but her plan is foiled when the Titans, interested only in absolute power, dispose of her. While each Titan wreaks havoc on his or her particular milieu—earth, air, fire, and water—Hercules, Xena, and Iolas fight them bravely. Xena realizes that Gabrielle's presence as a bird could come in handy; they succeed in snatching the Titans in her talons and dropping them into the huge crevice left by the earthquake. The gods are grateful for their help, and Artemis returns Gabrielle to human form. Hercules, however, must face the fact that his beloved mother never required rescuing from his estranged father Zeus. Rather than a kidnapping, Hercules had witnessed only the makings of a romantic tryst between his parents. Against Hercules's wishes, Alcmene has chosen to leave her earthly home and join Zeus on Mount Olympus.

HERCULES AND XENA: THE BATTLE FOR MOUNT OLYMPUS will qualify only as a must-see for die-hard fans of the two syndicated series, who will be pleased that the story remains true to the characters (especially as regards the warm friendship between Xena and Gabrielle), albeit in a watered down form suitable for children. The title song (sung by amphibian characters, blessed with feline ears) explains the conflict between the Titans and the family of Zeus so that those unfamiliar with Greek mythology can make sense of the story. While this song and others that appear in the film are not unpleasant, they are largely forgettable.

The film's worst problem is the mediocre nature of the animation. Clearly, little effort was put into developing interesting backgrounds, or any illusion of three-dimensional space. The excessive angularity of the characters (Hercules being the most extreme example) renders them stiff and unexpressive. These flaws may matter little to fans rooting on their favorite heroes, but is likely to turn off viewers who aren't "Hercules" or "Xena" cultists. *(Violence.)*—C.Ch.

d, Lynne Naylor; p, Lynne Naylor; exec p, Sam Raimi, Robert Tapert; w, John Loy; ed, Scott Jeffries; m, Joseph LoDuca, Michelle Browman, Amanda McBroom; art d, Scott Morse, Christina Long, Lynne Naylor; anim, Chris Reccardi, Mike Kim, Stephan Destefano, Charlie Bean, Carey Yost, Scott Morse; sound, Jason Schmid

Animated/Children's/Adventure (PR: A MPAA: PG)

HEROES SHED NO TEARS ★★★

(Hong Kong, 1986) 81m Paragon Films ~ Golden Harvest c

(YINGXIONG WULEI)

Eddy Ko *(Chan Chung/Kirk)*; Lam Ching Ying *(Colonel)*; Chen Yue Sang; Lau Chau Sang; Lee Hoi Suk; Jang Doo Hee; Kum Ho Kon; Phillip Loffredo; Cecile Le Bailly; Ma Ying Chun; Choke Thachalom; Samrit Sripitakulvikai; Naetdao Sakaoduen; Anchana Thumaraksa; Sureeporn Worapinrat; Yeung Tsui Kuen; Pan Yun Cheung; Chow Kam Kong

Made in the early 1980s, John Woo's first contemporary action film is an entertaining bloodbath about mercenary warfare in the Golden Triangle. Dusted off and recut for theatrical release after A BETTER TOMORROW (1986) made him a household name in Hong Kong, the film received its first official US release on home video in 1998.

A band of mercenaries led by Chan Chung (Eddy Ko) is hired to bring druglord Samton back to Thailand. Seizing him in a violent confrontation, they proceed to rescue Chan's young son Keung and girlfriend Julie from Samton's men. Later witnessing a double murder, they attack the soldiers responsible and rescue a French woman from being shot by the Colonel (Lam Ching-Ying).

Having lost an eye in the confrontation, the Colonel forces a tribe of natives to track down and ambush the mercenaries. Chan's men win the fight, but young Keung flees and is trapped in a burning field by the Colonel. Burying himself to escape the flames, Keung is soon reunited with the mercenaries, who pause to rest in the hut of Chan's old army buddy Louis and his three wives.

When the Colonel, now allied with Samton's men, assaults the hut, the surviving mercenaries flee, leaving behind a wounded Chan to be tortured by the Colonel. Keung blows up the hut to rescue his father, and reunited with Louis they discover the others under siege from Samton's men. Louis sacrifices himself and his wives in the ensuing battle and both sides are gradually wiped out—leaving the Colonel to kill Julie and be killed by Chan in a hand-to-hand duel.

Woo would return to the concept of an episodic trek through Asian warzones with his 1990 masterpiece A BULLET IN THE HEAD, but by then he'd know enough to make the story character-driven. Here he offers only thumbnail sketches of characterization, dropped into some inspired set-pieces but without any emotional resonance. Two of Chan's men are given short expository sequences to flesh out their motivation for becoming mercenaries, but both are simple comic asides that only serve to break the mood and narrative flow. The Colonel is actually the most interesting of the bunch, obsessed with revenge and mainlining local drugs as painkillers, killing his own men when they question his motives, striding through a barrage of explosions without so much as a flinch—an obvious nod to Robert Duvall in APOCALYPSE NOW (1979).

In other cinematic references, the natives springing from the earth and the swamp are heavily reminiscent of Japanese swordplay films, and the child burying himself in a flaming field is a direct lift from LONE WOLF AND CUB, although Woo claims never to have seen the series, averring that—despite the credits—he didn't actually script HEROES SHED NO TEARS. Whoever did write it, the difference between the various available translations of the film is best summed up when a mercenary eating a steak asks his buddy where it came from and gags on the repugnant response. In the tamer subtitled version for mallgoers: "I've been carrying it around in my bag for about the last three weeks." In the darker, more cynical subtitled translation for cinema purists: "Sliced it off the ass of that soldier I just killed." And in the original Cantonese import, shown theatrically throughout Asia: "From the corpse of a black soldier. . . " *(Graphic violence, nudity, sexual situations, extreme profanity.)*—A.B.

d, John Woo; p, Peter Chan; exec p, Raymond Chow; w, John Woo; ph, Naragawa Kenichi; ed, Peter Cheung; m, Chung Siu Fung; prod d, Fung Yuen Chi; fx, Saraburi Effects Team; cos, Patrick Leung, Duangporn Haernathorn; stunts, Chen Yue Sang

Action **(PR: C MPAA: NR)**

HIGH ART ★★★½

(U.S., 1998) 101m High Art Pictures ~ October Films c

Ally Sheedy *(Lucy Berliner)*; Radha Mitchell *(Syd)*; Patricia Clarkson *(Greta)*; Gabriel Mann *(James—Syd's Boyfriend)*; Bill Sage *(Arnie)*; David Thornton *(Harry—Syd's Boss)*; Anh Duong *(Dominique—"Frame" Editor)*; Tammy Grimes *(Vera—Lucy's Mother)*; Helen Mendes *(White Hawk)*; Cindra Feuer *(Delia)*; Anthony Ruivivar *(Xander)*; Elaine Tse *(Zoe)*; Rudolf Martin *(Dieter)*; Laura Ekstrand *(Waitress)*; Charis Michelson *(Debby)*

After more than a decade of appearing in forgettable cable productions and straight-to-video features, Ally Sheedy jump-starts her career with a complex lead performance in this moody and erotic lesbian love story that also serves as a cautionary tale about the hazards of heroin abuse.

Lucy Berliner (Ally Sheedy) is a celebrated photographer whose career ended abruptly a decade ago. Since then, she's been living in Manhattan with her heroin-addicted girlfriend, Greta (Patricia Clarkson), who constantly laments about her former career as part of director Rainer Werner Fassbinder's acting troupe. In the apartment below Lucy, Syd (Radha Mitchell) lives with her bland boyfriend James (Gabriel Mann) and works as an assistant editor for *Frame,* a photography magazine. Noticing a leak from her ceiling one evening, Syd investigates the apartment upstairs and is introduced to Lucy. Syd is immediately drawn to the ambiguous Lucy, who's hosting a heroin party with a bunch of strung-out friends. As Syd tries to fix the leak, she notices an astonishing array of photographs taken by Lucy many years ago. Seeing a chance to help Lucy, Syd persuades her bosses to give Lucy a cover story in the magazine. Lucy reluctantly agrees, but only if Syd will edit the piece. Syd accepts, seeing it as a way to thumb her nose at her standoffish bosses—and to spend more time with Lucy.

However, Lucy's preoccupation with Greta's drug addiction, and her growing feelings for Syd, cause her to procrastinate on the project. Deciding that she needs a change of scenery, Lucy takes Syd along to her mother's house in upstate New York where she can concentrate. There, Syd and Lucy slowly and awkwardly make love for the first time. Sensing Syd's fear, Lucy asks her what's wrong—and Syd admits that she's in love with Lucy. The next morning, Lucy takes some sensuously erotic pictures of Syd languishing in bed after their night of passion.

Back in Manhattan their deadline looms. Lucy hastily hands in some old pictures, which are rejected by the editors. Syd, realizing that the pictures Lucy took of her were meant for the assignment, hands them in; they are immediately approved. Meanwhile, Lucy finally decides to separate from Greta, but Greta, in desperation, begs her to do one more hit of heroin. When Syd comes to the office the next morning, she discovers that Lucy's photograph of her has made the cover of the magazine—and that Lucy has died of an overdose.

With gorgeously subtle cinematography by Tami Reiker, carefully modulated acting, and a trendy industrial soundtrack by the group Shudder to Think, HIGH ART is a triumph of melancholy chic. First-time writer-director Lisa Cholodenko demonstrates a knack for visualizing the unspoken throughout: an ominous sense of doom pervades the underlit scenes set in Lucy's apartment, and even the more ordinary interludes—a walk towards a locked car, a bath taken alone at night register as unsettling, seemingly alluding to something more profound. When Syd first steps into Lucy's apartment and squints at the dim decadence around her, it's like she's transported into another dimension, one full of drug-trances and illicit passion. Cholodenko's character development is so sly that we're never quite sure what Lucy's feelings towards Syd really are—she could potentially be experiencing the first true love of her life, or merely exploiting a talented individual in order to move her editorial career up a notch. In the process, Cholodenko even gets in a few stabs at the pretentions of the New York art world and the shiftless hangers-on who claim to be working "in the arts."

It's hard to believe that Cholodenko was, as she claimed in interviews, "unfamiliar" with Sheedy's work (where was she in the 1980s?); regardless, she elicits a performace from Sheedy that rates far above any acting work she has done thus far; in fact, it's astonishing that this is the same young woman who played the sullen misfit in THE BREAKFAST CLUB (1985). With her new, strikingly gaunt looks, Sheedy seems to have completely reinvented herself into a more mature and appealing actress. In HIGH ART, she's not only the center attraction, but she also gets to deliver some of the best lines of dialogue ("I haven't been deconstructed in a long time," she says in response to Syd's admiration for her pictures). Mitchell and Clarkson are equally compelling as Syd and the tragic, very jaded Greta—two influential figures in Lucy's life who sit at opposite ends of the spectrum. The assumption at the film's end, however, is that the wholesome Syd is the one who indirectly caused Lucy's death by attempting to remove her from her milieu and clean her up; by having her emerge into the spotlight once more, she has signed her death warrant, just as surely as Greta does when she asks her to share the lethal hit of heroin.

While HIGH ART does try to make some lofty, sometimes outright pretentious connections between lust, casual drug use, and careerism, the movie is a stark reminder that the power of love can't necessarily triumph over substance abuse. *(Profanity, sexual situations, nudity.)*—D.O.

d, Lisa Cholodenko; p, Dolly Hall, Jeff Levy-Hinte, Susan A. Stover; assoc p, Lori E. Seid; w, Lisa Cholodenko; ph, Tami Reiker; ed, Amy E. Duddleston; m, Shudder To Think; prod d, Bernhard Blythe; art d, Caryn Marcus; sound, Noah Timan (mixer), Jonah Lawrence (design); casting, Billy Hopkins, Suzanne Smith, Kerry Barden; cos, Victoria Farrell; makeup, Mia Thoen

Drama **(PR: C MPAA: R)**

HIJACKING HOLLYWOOD ★★★

(U.S., 1998) 91m Broken Twig Productions ~ Broken Twig Productions c

Henry Thomas *(Kevin Conroy)*; Scott Thomas *(Russell Burnside)*; Mark Metcalf *(Michael Lawrence)*; Neil Mandt *(Tad)*; Nicole Gian *(Sarah)*; Helen Duffy *(Mother)*; Paul Hewitt *(Harvey)*; Art La Fleur *(Eddie)*; Shirley Brener *(Ginger)*; J.F. Pryor *(Shaft)*; Steve Van Wormer *(Tony)*; Mark Holton *(Officer 1)*; Loren Lazerine *(Officer 2)*; Hedy Popson *(Sandy)*; Noella Akwri *(Receptionist)*; Bobbie Knoral *(Airport PA)*; Joe Watson *(Bicycler)*; Randy West *(Porno Guy)*; Michael Mandt *(Porno Guy)*; Kenna Kalonne *(Beach Girl)*; Chris Morris *(Camera Operator)*

An abused Hollywood production assistant who wants to direct discovers the easy way to fame and fortune in HIJACKING HOLLYWOOD. As a filmland satire, it's no THE PLAYER (1992) or THE LOVED ONE (1965), but the film does have some amusing moments.

Film school graduate Kevin Conroy (Henry Thomas) moves from Detroit to Hollywood to work as a production assistant on a new movie by blockbuster producer Michael Lawrence (Mark Metcalf), his aunt's ex-husband. Needing a place to live, he answers an ad and moves in with Tad (Neil Mandt), an amiable sort who is determined to work in movies even though he has no particular talents. Kevin is put to work under production coordinator Russell Burnside (Scott Thompson), who enjoys running him ragged.

Part of Kevin's job is to pick up the day's filming, shipped to LA from location in Hawaii, at the airport and take it to the lab to be developed. The lack of security at the airport gives him an idea: on the day that Lawrence completes a special effects sequence costing $18 million, Kevin and Tad will steal the film and, disguising their identities, extort $150,000 from Lawrence, which they will then use to film Kevin's script, "Three Days in a Salt Mine." Worried only that the studio will find out about it, Lawrence easily diverts the cash from his budget. But when he discovers who is behind the scheme, he threatens Kevin and Tad at gunpoint. Tad reveals that he still has some of the film. He demands that Lawrence get them a production deal with the studio and executive produce their film if he wants to avoid embarrassment. Admiring Tad's brass, he agrees, and Kevin gets to make his film—with Russell as a PA.

The central notion underlying HIJACKING HOLLYWOOD—the irony of giving poorly-paid production assistants the weighty responsibility of caring for the transportation of film that represents literally millions of dollars—is a great basis for a Hollywood satire. But filmmaker Neil Mandt fails to do much with it. Instead, he fills out the film with details of Kevin's job as a production assistant (which doesn't really look as demanding or humiliating as that job probably can be) and a pointless subplot involving Kevin with Lawrence's sexpot wife. Mark Metcalf and Scott Thompson are appropriately obnoxious as Hollywood players, and there are lines of dialogue that film buffs will enjoy ("You got one chance in this business to get it right," Russell tells Kevin. "Unless you're John Landis.") But overall, HIJACKING HOLLYWOOD is merely likable, seldom memorable. Filmed in 1996, it was released on home video in 1998. *(Nudity, sexual situations, adult situations, extreme profanity.)*—M.F.

d, Neil Mandt; p, Neil Mandt; exec p, Ann Mandt; assoc p, Maura Mandt, Michael Mandt, David Houston; w, Neil Mandt, Jim Rossow; ph, Anton Floquet; ed, Charlie Webber; m, Eric Lundmark; prod d, Todd Cherniawsky; art d, Linda Louise Sheets; set d, Ruth O'Neill; sound, Lawrence Freed; cos, Michele Michel; makeup, Saundra Jourdan

Comedy **(PR: C MPAA: R)**

HILARY AND JACKIE ★★★½

(U.K., 1998) 124m Oxford Films; Film Four ~ October Films c

Emily Watson *(Jacqueline du Pre)*; Rachel Griffiths *(Hilary du Pre)*; David Morrissey *(Kiffer Finzi)*; James Frain *(Daniel Barenboim)*; Charles Dance *(Derek du Pre)*; Celia Imrie *(Iris du Pre)*; Rupert Penry-Jones *(Piers du Pre)*; Bill Paterson *(Jackie's Cello Teacher)*; Keeley Flanders *(Young Hilary)*; Auriol Evans *(Young Jackie)*; Nyree Dawn Porter *(Dame Margot Fonteyn)*; Vernon Dobtcheff *(Professor Bentley)*

Based on a true story, HILARY AND JACKIE chronicles the tragic life of British cellist Jacqueline du Pre and her disturbing relationship with her sister Hilary. Despite its shaky structure, this film boasts two strong lead performances and an interesting take on sibling rivalry.

As a child, Hilary (Keely Flanders) demonstrates such tremendous talent on the flute that she's invited to perform on the BBC. Jackie (Auriol Evans), in an attempt to get out of her older sister's shadow, obsesses over mastering the cello. Eventually both are lauded for their music, but while Jackie enjoys the spotlight, Hilary shrinks from it.

As adults, it is Jackie (Emily Watson) who blossoms into a virtuoso and Hilary (Rachel Griffiths), who, feeling overshadowed, quits playing her instrument. At first they celebrate Jackie's success, getting drunk together after her smashing professional debut as a soloist. Soon after, Jackie goes on a triumphant, though lonely, tour of Europe, while Hilary falls in love with the charming Kiffer Finzi (David Morrissey). Jackie returns and discovers her sister is getting married. Jealous and unable to break up the impending union, she uses her musical prowess to lure her own man, renowned Israeli conductor Daniel Barenboim (James Frain). Jackie, lacking identity outside of music, marries Barenboim, converts to Judaism, and even starts affecting a similar accent to her husband. The couple receives raves around the globe for their combined talents, but Jackie, unsatisfied, remains jealous of her sister.

Hilary and Kiffer, living a simpler life in the country, escape from their children for a few minutes and are about to make passionate love when they're interrupted by a surprise visit from Jackie. That night, Jackie announces that she wants to sleep with Kiffer. Hilary refuses. A naked Jackie, streaked with blood, complains that she isn't loved. Hilary relents. Kiffer sleeps with Jackie. With the sisters' relationship poisoned, the cellist goes back to the touring life.

Jackie becomes clumsier, more disconnected from her body, and starts to struggle with her playing. She is diagnosed with multiple sclerosis. First she loses the ability to play, then walk, and finally is unable to even dial a telephone. Daniel abandons his wife for a prestigious job and a mistress in Paris. Jackie is deprived of speech and is sliding towards death when Hilary finally visits, and reminds Jackie of their closeness as young girls. At 42, Jackie dies.

In its best moments, HILARY AND JACKIE explores the way in which a person's relationship with a sibling can define one's own sense of identity. Hilary clearly needs to give to Jackie as much as Jackie needs to take from Hilary. Scripter Frank Cottrell Boyce strengthens this bond by subtly playing down the position of the women's parents, thereby making their relationship the only one that truly matters. The film's strong sense of this connection doubtlessly comes from its source, the memoir written by the real Hilary (cowritten with her brother Piers, whose role in the family is marginalized in the movie). Long after Jackie's death, a large part of Hilary's life still seems to revolve around their relationship.

Emily Watson, who made her mark playing a deeply disturbed character in Lars Von Trier's 1996 BREAKING THE WAVES, once again proves adept at depicting a person who lives on the edge of her emotions. Her performance is highly energetic and quite impressive, but detached and difficult to respond to in a sympathetic fashion. Rachel Griffiths (from MURIEL'S WEDDING, COSI, and the 1998 comedy MY BEST FRIEND'S WEDDING) gives the viewer someone to connect with in the less flashy role of Hilary; her performance serves to balance the movie's emotional extremes.

The film duplicates the classic structure of RASHOMON (1950), in which the viewer is confronted with different characters' perspective on the same scene. Thus, certain sequences here are duplicated in their entirety, as we see both Jackie and Hilary's point of view. This kind of structural gamesmanship is artistically intriguing, but ultimately proves distracting and detracts from the viewer's involvement.

Ultimately, however, the film's virtues outweigh its deficits. The psychology behind the sisters' codependent relationship is believably sketched, Watson and Griffiths (both Oscar nominees, Watson for Best Actress and Griffiths for Best Supporting Actress) do exemplary jobs of bringing their characters to life, and the visual style of director Anand Tucker (making his feature debut) and cinematographer David Johnson (who worked on the Laurence Fishburne OTHELLO) is both picturesque and moving. *(Sexual situations, nudity, profanity.)*—T.Y.

d, Anand Tucker; p, Andrew Paterson, Nicholas Kent; exec p, Guy East, Nigel Sinclair, Ruth Jackson; w, Frank Cottrell Boyce (based on the book *A Genius in the Family* by Hilary and Piers du Pre); ph, David Johnson; ed, Martin Walsh; m, Barrington Pheloung; prod d, Alice Normington; sound, David Crozier; casting, Simone Ireland, Vanessa Pereira; cos, Sandy Powell

AAN Best Actress: Emily Watson; *AAN Best Supporting Actress:* Rachel Griffiths

Drama **(PR: C MPAA: R)**

HI-LIFE ★★★

(U.S., 1998) 100m Gun for Hire Films; Silverman ~ Lions Gate Films c

Campbell Scott *(Ray)*; Eric Stoltz *(Jimmy)*; Daryl Hannah *(Maggie)*; Charles Durning *(Fatty)*; Katrin Cartlidge *(April)*; Moira Kelly *(Susan)*; Peter Riegert *(Minor)*; Anne DeSalvo *(Sherry)*; Saundra Santiago *(Elena)*; Kathleen Widdoes *(Frankie)*; Bruce MacVittie *(Cluck)*; Tegan West *(Phil)*; Carlo Alban *(Ricky)*; Dean Cameron *(Santa)*; Tucker Smith *(Adrien)*

HI-LIFE is an extended anecdote about a dozen friends and acquaintances who spend one of the nights before Christmas roaming the streets of Manhattan at cross-purposes. Although the film is charming and amusing, its dialogue and performances only intermittently live up to its nifty premise and dazzlingly intricate structure.

Jimmy (Eric Stoltz), a struggling young actor, is under heavy pressure to pay Fatty (Charles Durning), a full-time bartender and part-time bookie, the $900 he owes him. Jimmy turns to his girlfriend, Susan (Moira Kelly), for help, telling her he needs the dough to finance an abortion for his sister Maggie (Daryl Hannah). Susan, in turn, solicits the help of brother Ray (Campbell Scott), a bartender, but because Ray is carrying a torch for Maggie, Susan tells him the money is for her own abortion. Ray spends the rest of the evening calling in debts, accompanied by April (Katrin Cartlidge), a customer who is sweet on him.

Anxious to get his money, Fatty instructs his friend Minor (Peter Riegert) to stick with Jimmy wherever he goes. In order to obtain the money, Minor persuades his girlfriend's teenaged son (Carlo Alban) to mug him and Jimmy, but the stratagem backfires when Jimmy accidentally shoots Minor in the arm. Meanwhile, Ray gets the cash he's seeking from Maggie's current boyfriend (Tucker Smith).

Eventually, everyone converges at Fatty's Hi-Life Bar and Grille. Ray, who still think his sister is pregnant, threatens Jimmy; Minor is informed by his girlfriend (Saundra Santiago) that he is soon to become a father; and Fatty is bullied by his wife (Anne DeSalvo) into canceling Jimmy's debt. After the true facts are revealed, Jimmy snatches a car and embarks for LA to change his luck while Ray and April pair off for the night.

Too often movies like HI-LIFE are dismissed as trivial or damned with faint praise. In truth, HI-LIFE, like some of the films of Robert Altman and many of the films of Eric Rohmer, is a rare and welcome attempt to do one of the things the cinema does best: following a large, loosely connected group of individuals on their separate ways over the course of a short period. A valiant effort, HI-LIFE needed a bit more inspiration in just about every department, however, to register as truly first-rate.

Despite rich, velvety urban-nocturnal photography throughout, the movie never really comes alive until its spirited final scene, when the convoluted crisscrossing stops, everybody ends up at the Hi-Life, and all the plot intricacies and intrigues are sorted out, sort of. The performances are generally little more than serviceable, although Eric Stoltz's air of breezy irresponsibility, in tandem with his exceptional handsomeness, is hard to resist.

Minor HI-LIFE highlights include the refreshingly persuasive case Ray makes for why men are entitled to an opinion on the abortion issue, and a bit in which two of Fatty's stooges (Bruce MacVittie and Tegan West) plot to flush Jimmy out with a bogus report of actors' auditions for the sequel to SCHINDLER'S LIST (1993). ("They're baaack! This time it's personal.") Following the end credits, a choir of street carolers face the camera and sing "We Wish You a Merry Christmas" at length—a nice finishing touch for a likable film. Writer-director Roger Hedden was a regular at the Manhattan saloon after which HI-LIFE is named. "Making a movie about a bar is the best way to justify spending so much time there," he said. "Otherwise, they think you're just a drunk." *(Adult situations, profanity.)*—D.T.

d, Roger Hedden; p, Erica Spellman-Silverman; exec p, Michael Paseornek, Jeff Sackman, Steven C. Beer; w, Roger Hedden; ph, John Thomas; ed, Tom McArdle; m, David Lawrence; prod d, Sharon Lomofsky; casting, Deborah Brown; cos, Isis Mussenden

Comedy/Drama **(PR: C MPAA: R)**

HI-LO COUNTRY, THE ★★½

(U.S., 1998) 114m PolyGram; Martin Scorsese; Working Title; Cappa/De Fina Productions ~ Gramercy Pictures c

Woody Harrelson *(Big Boy Matson)*; Billy Crudup *(Pete Calder)*; Patricia Arquette *(Mona)*; Cole Hauser *(Little Boy)*; James Gammon *(Hoover Young)*; Penelope Cruz *(Josepha O'Neil)*; Sam Elliott *(Jim Ed Love)*; Enrique Castillo *(Levi Gomez)*; John Diehl *(Les Birk)*; Darren Burrows *(Billy Harte)*; Jacob Vargas *(Delfino Mondragon)*; Robert Knott *(Jack Couffer)*; Sandy Baron *(Henchman)*; Craig Carter *(Art Logan)*; Walter C. Hall *(Auctioneer)*; Will Cascio *(Chickie Cobain)*; Richard Purdy *(Bartender)*; Keith Walters *(Man on Horse)*; Lane Smith *(Steve Shaw)*; Sarge McGraw *(Nick the Bartender)*; Rosaleen Linehan *(Mrs. Matson)*; Rose Maddox *(Grandmother)*; Bob Tallman *(Rodeo Announcer)*; Buff Douthitt *(Rodeo Wrangler #1)*; H.P. Evetts *(Rodeo Wrangler #2)*; Kate Williamson *(Mrs. Young)*; Katy Jurado *(Meesa)*; Don Pope *(Sheriff Fitts)*; Leslie Cook *(Choreographer/Dancer)*; Monica Sundown *(Singer at Sano Dance)*; Amanda Cordova *(Singer at Sano Dance)*; Gaye Grant; Leon Rausch; Chris O'Connell; Marty Stuart; Donald R. Walser *(Singers at Rodeo Dance)*

Woody Harrelson and Billy Crudup star as best friends in post-WWII New Mexico in THE HI-LO COUNTRY, an absorbing, but emotionally unsatisfying adaptation of Max Evans's 1961 novel that was almost filmed several times by Sam Peckinpah (most intriguingly with Steve McQueen and Lee Marvin), and suffers by the unavoidable comparisons to what his version would have been like.

As he sits in front of a church waiting to kill someone, Pete Calder (Billy Crudup) begins narrating the story of what has brought him there: After his Army duty during WWII, Pete returns to his cattle ranch in Hi-Lo, New Mexico, and waits for the return from the War of his hellraising best friend Big Boy Matson (Woody Harrelson). Pete learns that during his absence, a rancher named Jim Ed Love (Sam Elliott) has become Hi-Lo's biggest cattle baron and has forced out many of the area's smaller ranchers. Pete becomes romantically involved with two women: Mona (Patricia Arquette), the unhappy wife of Love's foreman, Les Birk (John Diehl), and the Latina Josepha (Penelope Cruz). Pete falls for Mona, but is heartbroken when Big Boy returns and reveals that Mona is his girlfriend. After learning that his younger brother Little Boy (Cole Hauser) is working for Love, Big Boy spends his time humiliating Little Boy and antagonizing Love and his crew as much as possible, including spurning a job offer from Love and hooking up with Pete and independent rancher Hoover (James Gammon) on a cattle drive.

Pete learns that the cuckolded Birk is gunning for Big Boy and warns him to stop seeing Mona, but Big Boy provokes a fight with Birk instead and runs away for the weekend with Mona. Pete tries to stay away from Mona, but when Big Boy passes out after getting drunk one night, Pete makes love to her. Later, Big Boy and Mona announce that she has left her husband and has made plans to marry him. She also reveals that she's pregnant, but Big Boy is shot to death by Little Boy after he goes home to see his mother (Rosaleen Linehan) and beats up Little Boy for not repairing her house. Back in the present, Pete loads his gun as Little Boy (pretending he's not the guilty party) and the other mourners emerge from the church, but at the cemetery, Big Boy's mother begs Pete not to kill Little Boy, and he relents. Mona comes to the grave and tells Pete that Big Boy knew about the two of them having sex, but that he wanted to name their child Pete if it was a boy. Pete then drives off to California to find Josepha.

Despite being well crafted and intelligent, THE HI-LO COUNTRY seems like pseudo-Larry McMurtry, recalling the film versions of THE LAST PICTURE SHOW (1971) and HUD (1963) in its bittersweet, anti-nostalgic evocation of the modern American west as the sun begins to set on the good old days of the real western, leaving in its wake the anachronistic cowboys who can't adjust to the changing times. Although Stephen Frears's films can be wildly inconsistent, ranging from the good (MY BEAUTIFUL LANDRETTE, THE GRIFTERS, DANGEROUS LIAISONS) to the bad (SAMMY AND ROSIE GET LAID, MARY REILLY) to the indifferent (HERO), his direction is always sensitive, yet his British attributes of unfailingly good taste and restraint are antithetical to the demands of THE HI-LO COUNTRY. The film desperately needs an adrenaline shot of Peckinpah's lyrical violence, maniacal energy, and out-of-control emotions, yet it continually underplays everything to a fault, starting with Pete's droning narration.

The widescreen images of the spectacular landscapes, featuring panoramic shots of riders silhouetted against the dusky sky, are pretty, but lack the intrinsic muscularity of Ford or Peckinpah's visuals, and along with the attractive young cast that's stylishly attired in colorful flannels, the result looks regrettably like a Ralph Lauren "Chaps" commercial. The film's other main flaws are that it's virtually plotless, with the narrative consisting mostly of well-observed drunken barroom brawls, poker games, sexual shenanigans, and cattle drives, while the supporting cast, especially the superb Sam Elliott, is more credible than the leading players. Woody Harrelson hams it up, whooping and hollering as a crazed cowboy, but at least he's lively, while Billy Crudup is hopelessly passive as the laconic Pete, and Patricia Arquette fails to exhibit the kind of sex appeal and charisma which would supposedly inspire men to kill for her. Perhaps it's unfair to compare the film to a hypothetical Peckinpah version, but it's impossible not to fantasize about what might have been. *(Violence, profanity, sexual situations.)*—M.S.

d, Stephen Frears; p, Martin Scorsese, Barbara De Fina, Tim Bevan, Eric Fellner; exec p, Rudd Simmons; co-p, Liza Chasin; w, Walon Green (based on the novel by Max Evans); ph, Oliver Stapleton; ed, Masahiro Hirakubo; m, Carter Burwell; prod d, Patricia Norris; art d, Russell J. Smith; set d, Leslie Morales; sound, Drew Kunin (recordist); fx, Dieter Sturm; casting, Victoria Thomas; cos, Patricia Norris; makeup, Bridget Bergman; stunts, Shawn Howell, Tim Trella

Drama/Western **(PR: C MPAA: R)**

HIT & RUN
(SEE: HOT BLOODED)

HIT ME ★★½
(U.S., 1998) 125m Ice Cream Dimension Company; Slough Pond Company ~ Castle Hill c

Elias Koteas *(Sonny)*; Laure Marsac *(Monique)*; Jay Leggett *(Leroy)*; Bruce Ramsay *(Del)*; Kevin J. O'Connor *(Cougar)*; Philip Baker Hall *(Lenny Ish)*; J.C. Quinn *(Bascomb)*; Haing S. Ngor *(Billy)*; William H. Macy *(The Cop)*

A story about a violent hotel robbery, HIT ME is loosely based on *A Swell-Looking Babe*, a crime melodrama by the legendary pulp novelist Jim Thompson. In attempting to avoid the cliches of "hard-boiled" fiction, HIT ME emerges less as an innovation than as an oddity.

Sonny (Elias Koteas), the sole support of his demented brother Leroy (Jay Leggett), is a bellhop. One night he saves hotel guest Monique (Laure Marsac) from suicide. On a subsequent night she seduces him, then screams for help. Sonny is rescued from the difficult situation by two fellow employees, Del (Bruce Ramsay) and Cougar (Kevin J. O'Connor), who kidnap Monique and enlist the bellhop in a plan to rob a poker game conducted on the hotel premises by a man named Lenny Ish (Philip Baker Hall). Monique surfaces and contacts Sonny to tell him that Del and Cougar paid her to scream rape so that Sonny would be forced to take part in the robbery. He pledges to take her away to start a new life with her after the heist.

The big night arrives. In the course of the robbery, Cougar shoots two innocent desk clerks (Haing S. Ngor and J.C. Quinn), and Sonny is forced to finish off one of them. Sonny goes home with Monique and all $750,000 of the stolen cash. When the time comes to divide the loot, he discovers that Del and Cougar have been playing him for a sucker and intend to cut him out of the split. A shoot-out ensues and Sonny and Monique kill Del and Cougar. When the couple returns home, Ish and his bodyguard are waiting for them. After his man beats up Sonny, Ish, who was in on the robbery, takes the money but allows Sonny and Monique to live. Her dreams of a new life shattered, Monique walks out, leaving Sonny alone with Leroy.

The participation in HIT ME of one of America's most brilliant writers, Denis Johnson (*Angels*, *Jesus' Son*), augured a project of major potential, but HIT ME's screenplay, unfortunately, does not represent Johnson at his best. In *A Swell-Looking Babe*, the main character makes love to his mother (almost) and kills his father (in a way). In his adaptation, Johnson has removed the oedipal element by replacing mom and pop, to the story's detriment, with an idiot kid brother.

Thompson's characters induce mixed feelings of revulsion and pity; HIT ME's fragile couple elicit only pity. The protagonist has been reduced from a compellingly twisted and self-deluded egoist, a Thompson specialty, to a dime-a-dozen loser—and Thompson's "swell-looking babe," though still swell looking, has become closer to a crybaby than a true babe.

Elias Koteas's audacious but misguided performance as Sonny seems at times to be inspired by Jerry Lewis in THE BELLBOY (1960)—supplemented with echoes of Huntz Hall and The Three Stooges—whereas Warren Oates in BRING ME THE HEAD OF ALFREDO GARCIA (1974), or Dan Duryea in just about anything, would have been a more appropriate model.

HIT ME qualifies as a good try, but the definitive American adaptation of Jim Thompson's powerful pulp fiction still remains to be made (the 1979 French film SERIE NOIRE came closest to evoking the low-rent atmosphere, troubled characters, and doomed existential feel of Thompson's work). *(Graphic violence, sexual situations, extreme profanity.)*—D.T.

d, Steven Shainberg; p, Steven Shainberg, Gregory Goodman; exec p, Steven Shainberg, Gregory Goodman; w, Denis Johnson (based on the novel *A Swell-Looking Babe* by Jim Thompson); ph, Mark J. Gordon; ed, Donn Aron; m, Peter Manning Robinson; prod d, Amy Danger; art d, Joaquin Grey; sound, Steve Tibbo; casting, Mali Finn; cos, Karyn Wagner

Crime/Drama **(PR: C MPAA: R)**

HOLLYWOOD CONFIDENTIAL ★★

(U.S., 1996) 92m Yerkovich Productions ~ Paramount c/bw

Edward James Olmos *(Stan Navarro)*; Anthony Yerkovich *(Jack Hansen)*; Ricky Aiello *(Joey DiRosa)*; Charlize Theron *(Sally Bowen)*; J. Downing *(Barry Bliss)*; Brent Huff *(Larry Brent)*; Sarah Lassez *(Heather Norland)*; Kristen Dalton *(Dee Dee Powers)*; Thomas Patti *(Bartender)*; Angela Alvarado *(Teresa)*; Christine Harnos *(Shelly)*; Richard T. Jones *(Dexter)*; Brendan Kelly *(Mike Mooney)*; Thomas Jane *(V Phree)*; Evelina Fernandez *(Kate)*; Valerie Rae Miller *(CC)*; Amanda Pays *(Jaon Travers)*; Billy Marti *(Tommy)*; William James Olmos *(Teddy)*; Patrick Dollaghan *(Striver)*; Kaylan Romero *(Stan Jr.)*; Brendan Chao *(Bobby)*; Warren Reno *(Actor)*; Madison Clark *(Actress)*; Billy Kane *(Security Guard)*; Anthony Hickox *(Waiter)*; Ivana Milicevic *(Waitress)*

A contemporary detective saga, HOLLYWOOD CONFIDENTIAL is a feature-length pilot for a never-realized syndicated series that offers pasteurized sleaze.

Having renounced the LAPD over its failure to prevent a battered wife from becoming a fatality, ex-cop Stan Navarro (Edward James Olmos) runs a state-of-the art detective agency. His large staff of specialists includes Joey DiRosa (Ricky Aiello), who is currently scrutinizing the background of acting coach/movie producer Dee Dee Powers (Kristen Dalton), surveillance expert Jack Hansen (Anthony Yerkovich), and Sally Bowen (Charlize Theron), who goes undercover to nab a bartender (Thomas Patti) suspected of skimming at a trendy nightclub.

Though he accepts many seamy cases, Stan bristles at being pressured by studio executive Barry Bliss (J. Downing) into representing movie director Larry Brent (Brent Huff). But because he doesn't want to offend a steady customer, Stan agrees to dig up dirt on starlet Heather Norland (Sarah Lassez) to prevent her from going public about her affair with (and pregnancy by) the married Brent.

Sally is viciously beaten when the bartender she is investigating catches on to her. Lacking sufficient evidence to prosecute, Hansen and a fellow detective turn vigilante and return the beating. Stricken with remorse after Heather tries to kill herself, Stan publicly humiliates Brent at an awards dinner and forces him to pay college tuition and child support to Heather. Stan's detectives plan to let their consciences be their guides when considering future cases.

As HOLLYWOOD CONFIDENTIAL zigs and zags through assorted sordid files, the viewer feels no connection to any of the paper-thin characters investigating or being investigated. Indeed, one story line (the Dee Dee Powers stakeout) doesn't even receive a proper conclusion, beyond some suggestions of lesbian impropriety. Clumsily setting up further episodes that were never made, this pilot introduces too many payrolled employees and is interrupted too often by flashbacks to Stan's LAPD tenure. Another liability is the sporadic narration by star-producer-screenwriter Anthony Yerkovich (renowned as a "Miami Vice" co-creator). His florid descriptions of soulless Los Angeles are inadvertently hilarious, like something inspired by Fred Astaire's Mickey Spillane patter in the "Girl Hunt" ballet from THE BANDWAGON (1954). With its sleek production sheen and attractive cast, HOLLYWOOD CONFIDENTIAL had some promise as a weekly dip into the Hollywood cesspool. But instead of titillating viewers with juicy tidbits about blackmail and sexual trysts, it offers only sanitized sleuthing and perfunctory storytelling methods. *(Violence, profanity, substance abuse.)*—R.P.

d, Reynaldo Villalobos; p, James Hebert; exec p, Anthony Yerkovich; assoc p, Skip Schoolnik; w, Anthony Yerkovich; ph, Reynaldo Villalobos; ed, Skip Schoolnik; m, Marc Bonilla; prod d, Jeffrey Howard; set d, Leslie Morales; sound, Tim Cooney (mixer); casting, Johanna Ray, Elaine Huzzar; cos, Cynthia Hamilton; makeup, Gloria Ponce; stunts, Buck McDancer

Crime/Drama **(PR: C MPAA: R)**

HOLY MAN ★★

(U.S., 1998) 114m Caravan; Touchstone; Roger Birnbaum Productions ~ Buena Vista c

Eddie Murphy *(G)*; Jeff Goldblum *(Ricky Hayman)*; Kelly Preston *(Kate Newell)*; Robert Loggia *(McBainbridge)*; Jon Cryer *(Barry)*; Eric McCormack *(Scott Hawkes)*; Sam Kitchin *(Director)*; Robert Small *(Assistant Director)*; Marc Macaulay *(Cameraman/Brutus)*; Mary Stout *(Laundry Lady #1)*; Edie McClurg *(Laundry Lady #2)*; Kim Staunton *(Grace)*; Morgan Fairchild *(Herself)*; Betty White *(Herself)*; Florence Henderson *(Herself)*; James Brown *(Himself)*; Soupy Sales *(Himself)*; Dan Marino *(Himself)*; Willard Scott *(Himself)*; Nino Cerruti *(Himself)*; Kim Alexis *(Amber, Keratin Girl)*; Veronica Webb *(Diandre, Keratin Girl)*; Barbara Hubbard Barron *(Sunbather #1)*; Cristina Wilcox *(Sunbather #2)*; Clarence Reynolds *(TV Host)*; Mal Jones; Jody Wilson *(Elderly Couple)*; Pamela West *(Fresca, the Foot Model)*; Tim Powell *(Doctor Simon)*; Lori Viveros Herek *(Nurse #1)*; Angel Schmiedt *(Nurse #2)*; Whitney Dupree *(Laurie)*; Jennifer Bini Taylor *(Hot Tub Girl)*; Robert Walker *(Farmer)*; Elodia Riovega *(Housekeeper)*; Avrohom Horovitz *(Rabbi)*; Al Kamaar *(Moslem Theologian)*; Dan Fitzgerald *(Priest)*; Mark Brown *(Grass Mat Salesman)*; Mike Benitez *(Bullet Proof Vest Man)*; Deborah Magdalena *(Control Booth Technician)*; Adriana Catano *(TV Hostess #1)*; Andrea Lively *(TV Hostess #2)*; Lee Bryant *(Money "Meg")*; Nick Santa Maria *(Sword Salesman)*; Aaron Elbaz *(Glue-Gun Boy)*; Scotty Gallin *(Jock Salesman #1)*; John Bosa *(Jock Salesman #2)*; Jeffrey Wetzel *(Stage Manager)*; Erin Morrissey *(Host #1)*; Daryl Meyer *(Host #2)*; Ronda Pierson *(Host #3)*; Brett Rice *(Detective #1)*; John Archie *(Detective #2)*; Armando Ramos *(Grace's Little Boy)*; Nancy Duerr *(Reporter #1)*; Tonya Oliver *(Reporter #2)*; Fred Workman *(Reporter #3)*; Jacqueline Chernov *(Reporter #4)*; Roger Reid *(Reporter #5)*; Peter Paul DeLeo *(Stagehand)*; Errol Smith *(GBSN Staffer)*; Dave Corey *(Announcer)*; Alan Oliney *(G's Stunt Double)*; Mike Christopher *(Ricky's Stunt Double)*; Alejandro Acosta Fox *(Flamenco Guitarist)*; Maria Alejandra Carpio

(Flamenco Dancer); Laurie Wallace *(Facial Mist Girl)*; Willie Gault *(Nordic Track Guy)*; Amanda Lynn *(Nordic Track Girl)*; Charlie Haugk *(Party Girl)*; Margaret Muldoon *(Attractive Party Guest)*; Mark Massar *(Set Dresser)*; Toy Van Lierop *(G Makeup Artist)*; Dana Hawkins *(Hair Chat Girl #1)*; Denise Heinrich *(Hair Chat Girl #2)*; Antoni Cornacchione *(Chain Saw Host)*; Marc C. Geschwind *(GBSN Electrician)*; A.J. Alexander O. Parhm *(UPS Guy)*; Alan Jordan *(Marksman #1)*; Mike Kirton *(Marksman #2)*

While it may be a little too obvious and facile to call HOLY MAN a holy mess, that is the kindest thing that one can say about this abysmal fable about a mysterious guru (Eddie Murphy) who becomes a home shopping channel host, although it does achieve something truly rare even in these days of debased standards: it's an alleged "comedy" without a single, solitary laugh.

Ricky Hayman (Jeff Goldblum), a struggling programmer for the Good Buy Home Shopping Network is told by his boss McBainbridge (Robert Loggia) to boost his sales within two weeks or he'll be fired, and McBainbridge brings in media analyst Kate Newell (Kelly Preston) to help the network. While driving together, Kate and Ricky have a flat tire and encounter a strange bald man dressed in pajamas who offers to help and tells them his name is "G" (Eddie Murphy), then faints. Ricky and Kate take G to the hospital and they're told he has a heart murmur. Later, G shows up at the TV studio and Ricky reluctantly puts him up at his house. After G cures designer Nino Cerruti (himself) of his fear of flying during a cocktail party, Ricky gets Cerruti's account for the network, and he offers G his own show.

G accepts, but on his first show, he throws away his script and preaches antimaterialism and pro-spiritualism to the viewers. Ricky is fired, but rehired after the ratings and sales go way up. Ricky becomes romantically involved with Kate, and G becomes a huge star, despite the efforts of a scheming producer (Eric McCormack) who tries to take over the network with a smear campaign against G But Kate begins to worry about the overworked G's health and happiness and she breaks up with Ricky after overhearing him plotting to trick G into signing a longterm contract. G signs the contract anyway and Ricky is given a huge promotion and salary increase, but right before G is to debut on his new primetime show, Ricky comes clean and tells him to quit. Ricky goes live on the air and apologizes for exploiting G and begs Kate to forgive him. She drives to the station and tells Ricky she loves him, and the two of them bid a tearful farewell to G, who continues on his mystical journey.

Somewhere buried deep inside HOLY MAN is a worthy, albeit not particularly original, germ of an idea about how the media makes people lose touch with their souls and encourages them to pursue meaningless materialism at the expense of human contact and what's really important in life. But after the undoubted multiple rewrites mandated by a committee of studio executives, marketing experts, test screenings, demographic samplings, and stars's egos, the final result emerges as a shrill, mushy, and derivative piece of blatant Hollywood commercialism that ironically resembles what it purports to abhor. It desperately aspires to the kind of biting satire displayed in such films as NETWORK (1976), A FACE IN THE CROWD (1957), and BEING THERE (1979), but the spoofing of infomercials is not exactly daring stuff, while the actual level of humor is illustrated by such cutting-edge dialogue as "I have to go stinky" and the abundance of pathetic double-entendres uttered by the "hilarious" parade of shopping channel hosts playing themselves (Betty White hawking sex perfume called "Clam"; Florence Henderson repeating the phrase "suck it" while selling a storage bag called "Suck 'n' Seal"; a stain remover called "Blue Balls," and several other kneeslapping bon mots).

Disney's house hack Stephen Herek (THE MIGHTY DUCKS, 101 DALMATIANS) directs with a sledgehammer touch, giving the film the inappropriately dark and sinister look of a mystery thriller, along with a strident tone and a frenetic pace that's exacerbated by an incessantly "funny" Latin music score that futilely tries to punch home laughs that never materialize. The performances are all fairly embarrassing, with Jeff Goldblum muttering incomprehensibly to himself at 100 miles-per-hour most of the time and Eddie Murphy kissing the ground and wearing a phony beatific smile that seems more like the result of a lobotomy than spiritual enlightenment. By the time the shamelessly corny and contrived ending rolls around, the response that one is most likely to have is a depressing realization that one has just wasted two hours of life on a film that spuriously urges people to stop wasting their lives. *(Profanity, sexual situations.)*—M.S.

d, Stephen Herek; p, Stephen Herek, Roger Birnbaum; exec p, Jeffrey Chernov, Jonathan Glickman; co-p, Rebecca Rudd, Ray Murphy; w, Tom Schulman; ph, Adrian Biddle; ed, Trudy Ship; m, Alan Silvestri; prod d, Andrew McAlpine; art d, James Tocci; set d, Chris Spellman; sound, Peter J. Devlin (mixer); fx, Kevin Harris; casting, Amanda Mackey Johnson, Cathy Sandrich; cos, Aggie Guerard Rodgers; makeup, Joe Campayno; stunts, Alan Oliney

Comedy/Drama **(PR: C MPAA: PG)**

HOMBRES ARMADOS

(SEE: MEN WITH GUNS)

HOME BEFORE DARK ★★

(U.S., 1998) 110m Hazelwood Films; Scout Productions c

Stephanie Castellarin *(Nora)*; Brian Delate *(Martin)*; Katharine Ross *(Rose)*; Patricia Kalember *(Dolores)*; Helen Lloyd Breed *(Concilia)*

An 11-year-old does everything she can to hold her troubled family together in writer-director Maureen Foley's clunky, overwrought debut feature. The heartfelt story line is undermined by uneven acting and awkward plotting.

In 1963 rural Massachusetts, the calm life of Nora (Stephanie Castellarin) is disrupted by family troubles. Her clinically-depressed mother, Dolores (Patricia Kalember), is haunted by a truck accident that killed three of her children before Nora was born. Martin (Brian Delate), Nora's beleaguered father, tries to earn a living and raise his daughter and three-year-old twins, a boy and a girl, with little help from his wife. The family's shaky structure collapses when Dolores, who treasures an encounter she had with JFK many years ago, tries to kill herself when the President is assassinated. When her mother is committed, Nora is sent to live with her prim-and-proper Aunt Rose (Katharine Ross).

The embittered Rose tries to make Nora into the daughter she never had. She attempts to alienate Nora from her mother and frowns on Nora's attempts to write fictional stories about Dolores's first set of children. Nora despises her aunt and schemes to get back with her father and the twins, who are now living with relatives in Boston. Nora discovers that Rose is cheating on her husband, and threatens to expose the affair. Rose surrenders and the willful girl is sent back to live with her father and the twins.

Saddled with the added expense of a baby-sitter, Martin falls behind on his bills. He's also disturbed by the fact that, though the doctors are willing to release her, Dolores refuses to come home and cope with life. Nora bears the brunt of her father's frustration. In response, the 11-year-old rids the house of all reminders of her deceased siblings in an attempt to make it a healthier place for her mother, if and when she returns.

When Martin explodes at Nora for throwing out family mementos, Nora runs away. She boards a bus, and makes her way to the mental hospital. Dolores, inspired by her daughter's pluck, decides to move back home.

If there is indeed any truth behind the cruel maxim "Those who can't do, teach" HOME BEFORE DARK, written and directed by Harvard screenwriting teacher Maureen Foley, certainly adds fuel to the fire. The verdict, based on her first feature is a definite. . . maybe. Foley gets marked down a grade for violating a few screenwriting commandments, for instance, thou shalt not create stereotypical side characters—like the twins' shrill, impatient babysitter or Nora's catty, disloyal school chum. And thou shalt not suddenly wrap a tale of a troubled family story up with a perfectly neat, hard to believe, ending. It's one thing to reunite this dysfunctional family, but quite another to leave them in a cozy "goodnight, John Boy" mood.

Foley does show promise, though, in her sketching of Nora, who comes across as a three-dimensional, flesh-and-blood girl pulled straight out of 1963. While the budding young writer primarily acts in a loving manner to her family, she can also be vindictive, as with Rose, or simply fed up with the way in which she's been prematurely pushed into adulthood. At certain moments in the film, the subtle power of a detail or a nuance of behavior leads one to sense that Foley is somehow drawing on autobiographical inspiration. It's too bad she often short-circuits her own creation with amateurish direction. The crucial scene in which Nora discovers her mother after a suicide attempt is staged in a very awkward fashion—not only does the blood look fake, but it's difficult to follow the action. At another point, when Rose offers her niece a Coke, the stiffness of the acting becomes readily apparent. You can almost hear the director advising the actors to "Act tense."

Newcomer Stephanie Castellarin is likable, but lacks the dynamism needed to carry the entire film. Coming out of her self-imposed semi-retirement, Katharine Ross does a solid job as the remote Rose. Unfortunately, though, Foley does little to help Patricia Kalember inject a note of empathy, or even consistency, into the pivotal character of Dolores. *(Adult situations.)*—T.Y.

d, Maureen Foley; p, Michael Williams, Dorothy Aufiero, David Collins, Maureen Foley; exec p, Robert Laubacher; w, Maureen Foley; ph, Brian Heller, Mark Petersson; ed, James Rutenbeck; m, Jeanine Cowen; prod d, Kathleen Rosen; art d, Sophie Carlhian; sound, G. John Carrett; casting, Susan Willett; cos, Susan Ander

Drama **(PR: C MPAA: NR)**

HOME FRIES ★★½

(U.S., 1998) 93m Baltimore/Spring Creek; Mark Johnson Pictures; Kasdan Pictures ~ Warner Bros. c

Drew Barrymore *(Sally Jackson)*; Jake Busey *(Angus Montier)*; Catherine O'Hara *(Mrs. Lever)*; Shelley Duvall *(Mrs. Jackson)*; Luke Wilson *(Dorian Montier)*; Kim Robillard *(Billy)*; Daryl "Chill" Mitchell *(Roy)*; Lanny Flaherty *(Red)*; Chris Ellis *(Henry Lever)*; Blue Deckert *(Sheriff)*; Mark Walters *(Deputy)*; Tommy Shane Steiner *(Soldier in Jeep)*; Therese Merritt *(Mrs. Vaughn)*; Jill Parker-Jones *(Lamaze Instructor)*; Morgana Shaw *(Lucy Garland)*; Robert Graham *(Reverend)*; Zeke Mills *(Tobacco Warehouse Supervisor)*; John Hawkes *(Randy)*; Brady Coleman *(Doctor)*; Jean Donatto *(Nurse #1)*; Mona Lee Fultz *(Nurse #2)*; Marco Perella *(Good Ol' Boy in Pickup)*; Meason Wiley *(Photo Lab Employee)*; Zachary Moore *(Benny)*

Definitive proof that black humor only works in the hands of skilled professionals, HOME FRIES is a dark comedy that loses its way early on—veering from creepy satire to soppy romance to irrational pulse-pounding action drama. A skilled cast does their best, but the changes in tone are so radical that the film can never regain its initial momentum.

Riding home from a brief meeting with his pregnant mistress Sally Jackson (Drew Barrymore), tobacco company executive Henry Lever suffers a fatal coronary when his car is halted by a hovering Army helicopter, armed and ready to fire at him.

The perpetrators of this crime are Henry's two stepsons, Dorian (Luke Wilson) and Angus (Jake Busey), who are Army National Guard members and did the deed at the request of their domineering mother, Mrs. Lever (Catherine O'Hara). Mrs. Lever is glad that Henry is dead, but informs her sons that she had only wanted them to scare the daylights out of him (as payback for his infidelity), not kill him.

Angus has one major concern: the headset-wearing workers at the Burgermatic, a local fast-food joint, might have heard his and Dorian's voices when they were speaking over the helicopter's radio. Angus persuades Dorian to take a job at the Burgermatic to ferret out information. While working there, Dorian becomes infatuated with a coworker, Sally, not realizing her connection to Henry. Sally (who is equally unaware of Dorian's identity) is determined to speak to Henry's wife to apologize to her. Mrs. Lever, in the meantime, has become obsessed with finding out the identity of Henry's mistress; she convinces Angus that the woman must be killed.

Dorian informs Sally about his relation to Henry when she visits the Lever household; shocked, she breaks off their relationship. Angus, meanwhile, has uncovered pictures of Sally and Henry together, and goes on a rampage. While Mrs. Lever is visiting the Jacksons in a feigned attempt to make amends with Sally, Dorian rushes over to warn the family about Angus. They don't believe him—until Angus begins buzzing the house in a helicopter. Dorian escapes in a truck with Mrs. Lever and Sally, who is going into labor. Angus forces the truck to a stop and then is faced with a quandry: should he shoot Sally or his mother, whom Dorian attempts to convince him is the true villain? Angus chooses to simply fly away without shooting anyone. Dorian strands Mrs. Lever in the middle of the road, racing Sally to the hospital. After she gives birth, he talks to the newborn about its tangled family heritage; Sally indicates that they can start again.

Watching HOME FRIES, one wonders exactly what audience the film was intended for. Those viewers who enjoy the dark tone of the film's first section are going to be alienated by the film's gradual slide into hearts-and-flowers territory, while those teenage viewers expecting a youthful romance are sure to dislike the nastier machinations of the plot. It also follows that both audiences will be turned off by the film's brainless third act, in which a classically-styled "race against time" eventually reveals the sympathetic side of Angus—to anyone who's still interested.

It's to the credit of the cast that we care about these simple-minded souls at all. Luke Wilson (BOTTLE ROCKET) is a serviceable enough male lead as the naive Dorian (although he frequently speaks in a Christian Slater-like nasal tone that reeks of Jack Nicholson). Drew Barrymore provides the film's main appeal—her radiant cheerfulness as Sally deflects attention away from the fact that Sally is a pretty naive person herself, and instead injects a note of self-suffiency into the character.

As Angus, Jake Busey is actually a fairly menacing figure—although whether because of his acting skill or his incredible resemblance to his toothy father Gary is open to question. Shelly Duvall has little to do as Sally's mother, while the incredibly versatile Catherine O'Hara does plenty, but all in the one-note "mother from hell" style dictated by the script.

The fact that Vince Gilligan wrote HOME FRIES as a fledgling scripter back in 1989, before his success as a producer/writer of "The X-Files," explains a lot about the off-kilter manner in which the story line proceeds. One is less certain why Dean Parisot, the director of the very amusing Oscar-winning short "The Appointments of Dennis Jennings," thought this would be the best vehicle for his big-screen debut. Producers Barry Levinson and Lawrence Kasdan obviously agreed with his decision—but all involved should've faced up to the fact that the script needed a rewrite, and that even Ms. Barrymore's effervescent charm can't sustain a film that's neither fish nor fowl. *(Violence, profanity.)*— E.G.

d, Dean Parisot; p, Barry Levinson, Mark Johnson, Lawrene Gordon, Charles Newirth; exec p, Raul Lassally; assoc p, Susann Jones; w, Vince Gilligan; ph, Jerzy Zielinski; ed, Nicholas C. Smith; m, Rachel Portman; prod d, Barry Robison; art d, Phil Dagort; set d, Suzette Sheets; sound, Jennifer Murphy; fx, David Blitstein, Randy Cabral, Brian McCarty, Jack Sander; casting, Jill Greenburg Sands, Debra Zane; cos, Jill O'Hanneson; makeup, Kimberly Greene, Matthew W. Mungle; stunts, Greg Elam

Comedy/Romance/Thriller (PR: C MPAA: PG-13)

HOMEGROWN ★★

(U.S., 1998) 95m Rollercoaster Films; Underdog Films; Lakeshore Entertainment ~ Columbia TriStar c

Billy Bob Thornton *(Jack)*; Hank Azaria *(Carter)*; Kelly Lynch *(Lucy)*; Ryan Phillippe *(Harlan)*; John Lithgow *(Malcolm/Robert)*; Jon Bon Jovi *(Danny)*; Jamie Lee Curtis *(Sierra Kahan)*; Judge Reinhold *(Policeman)*; Jon Tenney *(Pilot)*; Matt Ross *(Ben Hickson)*; Matt Clark *(Sheriff)*; Ted Danson *(Gianni)*; Kleoka Renee Sands *(Girl—Age 4)*; Leigh French *(Waitress)*; Christopher Dalton *(Old Farmer)*; Tiffany Paulsen *(Heather)*; Jeanette H. Wilson *(White Haired Woman)*; Matthew Winter *(Shine Kahan)*; Jake Gyllenhaal *(Jake/Blue Kahan)*; Michelle Bonilla *(Nurse)*; Maggie Gyllenhaal *(Christina)*; Ramsay Midwood *(Bill)*; Milo Plasil *(Mafia Enforcer)*; Daniel Alonso *(Thug Holding Dog)*; Tom Burke *(Straight Man)*; Seamus McNally Jr. *(Hippie)*; Joe McCrackin *(Cowboy)*; Paul Prendergast *(Man—Age 25)*

HOMEGROWN is a regrettable time capsule experience that might have been made in the late 1960s and shelved for decades. It's a retro pothead comedy that gussies up an outmoded counterculture sensibility with au courant violence.

Paranoid marijuana maven Malcolm (John Lithgow) toys with a Mafia alliance despite the simmering resistance of underlings. Meanwhile, his Northern California dope farmers Jack (Billy Bob Thornton), Carter (Hank Azaria), and Harlan (Ryan Phillippe) harvest his cash crop. When he copters down to buy their dope, Malcolm is murdered by his Mafia-phobic pilot (Jon Tenney). Improvising a slapdash plan, Jack, Carter, and Harlan bury Malcolm, decide that Jack will masquerade as Malcolm over the phone, and lie to their dope-packager Lucy (Kelly Lynch) about Malcolm's demise.

Before they can unload the crop on drug wholesaler Danny (Jon Bon Jovi), Lucy catches on and demands a percentage of the scam. Bribing cops proves easy, but the dope-peddling trio find themselves squeezed between Malcolm's mob-hating pilot and gangster capo Gianni (Ted Danson). Although Jack survives capture and threats from Gianni, the pilot kidnaps Jack and his associates and vows to bury them in Malcolm's grave if they cooperate with Gianni. Lying convincingly to Malcolm's twin brother (John Lithgow) when he comes looking for his missing sibling, Jack continues his Malcolm impersonation with Danny. When Danny spots Harlan at the secret meeting, he believes Jack has betrayed him. As Danny scurries from the rendezvous, policemen arrive, confiscate the marijuana crop, and ignite it in front of the failed entrepreneurs.

HOMEGROWN literally ends in a puff of smoke, as the potheads get high while their ticket to the big time burns. Unfortunately, there's little humor for the audience to inhale. Staggering cloddishly along a line between goofball merriment and graphically depicted peril, HOMEGROWN wants to put viewers off balance, but instead merely puts them off. Were the film's creators engineering a distancing shock of recognition shared by audience and protagonists alike? Are we supposed to believe that Jack and his cohorts are too dimwitted to be unaware of the dangers in their business? Or is this trivial pursuit supposed to be about the corruption of the once laid-back marijuana trade? Scenes like the one in which the heroes are forced to lie in Malcolm's dug-up grave are too nasty for this screwed-up paean to aging flower children. *(Graphic violence, extreme profanity, extensive nudity, sexual situations, substance abuse.)*—R.P.

d, Stephen Gyllenhaal; p, Jason Clark; exec p, Thomas B. Rosenberg, Sigurjon "Joni" Sighvatsson, Ted Tannebaum, Naomi Foner; assoc p, Howell Caldwell; w, Nicholas Kazan, Stephen Gyllenhaal (from a story by Jonah Raskin and Stephen Gyllenhaal); ph, Greg Gardiner; ed, Michael Jablow; m, Trevor Rabin; prod d, Richard Sherman; set d, Maurin Scarlata; sound, Albee Gordon (mixer); fx, Wayne Beauchamp; casting, Linda Lowry, John Brace; cos, Joseph Porro; makeup, Julie Purcell; stunts, Jake Crawford

Crime/Drama/Comedy (PR: C MPAA: R)

HONEY SWEET

(SEE: COMRADES, ALMOST A LOVE STORY)

HONG KONG 1941 ★★★½

(Hong Kong, 1984) 100m Boho Films Co. Ltd.; D&B Films Co. Ltd. ~ Tai Seng c

Chow Yun-Fat *(Yip Kim Fay)*; Cecilia Yip *(Ah Nam)*; Alex Man *(Wong Hak Keung)*; Shih Kien *(Ha Chung Sun)*; Paul Chun *(Sergeant Wing)*; Ku Feng *(Shui)*; Wu Ma *(Chairman Liu Yan-Mau)*; Leong Po-Chin

A flawed but entertaining film about a Chinese love triangle interrupted by the Japanese invasion. Lead actor Chow Yun-Fat won his first major international recognition when he was voted best actor at Taiwan's Golden Horse Awards and the Asia Pacific Film Festival. This well-regarded 1984 production was officially released in the US on home video in 1998.

Young vagabond Yip Kim Fay (Chow Yun-Fat), ever anxious to leave Hong Kong, befriends laborer Wong Hak Keung (Alex Man). After trouble breaks out at their workplace, they plan to skip town with Keung's girlfriend, Nam (Cecilia Yip). But the war changes everything, and only Fay makes the boat; seeing his friends still on the dock, he jumps off and joins them.

The invasion leads to chaos, with Nam raped by Police Sergeant Wing (Paul Chun), who is subsequently killed by Keung. While Fay courts the Japanese, Keung heads into the country to make some black market cash, getting captured by local mercenary Chairman Liu Yan-Mau (Wu Ma). Fay shows up and maims Keung to gain Liu's confidence, then kills Liu and the pair escape. While Keung recovers, Fay and Nam share a brief embrace, after which Fay resolves to join the resistance. But a Japanese officer arrives to make Nam his own; a fight ensues, with Nam killing the officer. The three then flee on a junk that is intercepted by the Japanese, and Fay sacrifices himself to blow up the enemy boat.

HONG KONG 1941 is packed with period detail, lending a palpable feeling of desperation: A man tries to sell his granddaughter for potatoes; parents cut their daughter's hair and make her unattractive to save her from Japanese attention; children collect horse dung to pick undigested rice kernels from it; and Nam finds a photo of Japanese bayoneting a baby—an image that later motivates her to kill the Japanese officer.

The character of Nam is perhaps the film's biggest flaw. Childish and impetuous and prone to sudden crippling headaches, she doesn't seem to justify the attention given to her by the male leads. Fay, on the other hand, is so nobly self-sacrificing and desperate for friendship that he seems to be an inveterate masochist. When assisting the Japanese, he reveals himself as a double agent to a fleeing resistor, handing over his gun and asking to be hit. The next shot, of Fay removing a white bandage with a red bloodstain from his head (resembling a Japanese kamikaze bandana), is indicative of the film's ironic symbolism. In a similar vein, another sequence has a Japanese officer singing "London Bridge is Falling Down" while playing with local children for a staged documentary.

The film was released in Hong Kong in 1984, the year the Joint Declaration was signed, setting 1997 as the date for Hong Kong's return to China. Unsurprisingly, there is a decided air of allegory about the proceedings, of anxiety regarding the handing over from British rule to another mistress. Wounded British soldiers are seen stumbling toward Stanley Prison, street signs being changed from English names to Japanese. Director Leong Po-Chih, born and schooled in London, worked for the BBC and then HK television before embarking on a film career exhibiting a fascination for the bicultural identity of Hong Kong. Referring to himself as a "banana" Chinese (yellow on the outside, white on the inside), he co-directed a 1997 HK/UK television documentary on the handover to China. *(Graphic violence, sexual situations, substance abuse, profanity.)*—A.B.

d, Leong Po-Chih; p, John Shum, billed as John Sham; exec p, Dickson Poon, Sammo Hung; w, John Chan, billed as Chan Goon-Jung; ph, Lai Shui-Ming; art d, Hai Jung-Man

Drama/Historical/Romance (PR: C MPAA: NR)

HOPE FLOATS ★½

(U.S., 1998) 112m Lynda Obst Productions;
Fortis Films ~ 20th Century Fox c

Sandra Bullock *(Birdee Pruitt)*; Harry Connick Jr. *(Justin Matisse)*; Gena Rowlands *(Ramona Calvert)*; Mae Whitman *(Bernice Pruitt)*; Cameron Finley *(Travis)*; Michael Pare *(Bill Pruitt)*; Kathy Najimy *(Toni Post)*; Bill Cobbs *(Nurse)*; Connie Ray *(Bobbi-Claire)*; Mona Lee Fultz *(Teacher)*; Sydney Berry *(Orange Julia)*; Rachel Lena Snow *(Big Dolores)*; Christina Stojanovich *(Kristen)*; Allisa Alban *(Debbie Reissen)*; Dee Hennigan *(Dot)*; Martha Long *(Waitress)*; Norman Bennett *(Mr. Davis)*; James N. Harrell *(Harry Calvert)*; Chris Drewy *(P.E. Teacher)*; Meason Wiley *(Young Man at Dance)*; Tisa Hibbs *(Suzy)*; Art Michael Tamez *(Bartender)*; Jeanette Sieh *(Volleyball Captain)*; Tara Price *(Young Birdee)*; Richard Nance *(Priest)*; Rosanna Arquette *(Connie—uncredited)*

A former high school beauty queen moves back home to rebound from a failed marriage in HOPE FLOATS. It's the equivalent of romantic Novocain, with pretty pictures and wan platitudes dulling any real emotions that might have emerged from the morass of drivel.

Birdee Pruitt (Sandra Bullock) is lured to appear on a daytime-TV talk show, where her best friend Connie (Rosanna Arquette) confesses that she and Birdee's husband Bill (Michael Pare) have been having an affair. With her 9-year-old daughter Bernice (Mae Whitman) in tow, Birdee flees Chicago for her childhood home in Smithville, Texas, and the arms of her eccentric mother Ramona (Gena Rowlands).

Despite Ramona's urgings for her to return to her vivacious high school ways (she was twice voted "Queen of Corn"), Birdee stays in bed and wallows in her depression, ignoring her daughter's pain over the separation. Ramona tries to fix Birdee up with hunky local handyman Justin Matisse (Harry Connick Jr.), whose adolescent crush on Birdee never waned, but she rebukes him. When she ventures out to find a job, former classmates rub her nose in her nationally broadcast humiliation, and Birdee ends up working at a one-hour photo developing shop.

Still expecting to reconcile with Bill, Birdee accepts Justin's company, but resists his charms. Eventually though, she succumbs to those as well. Bernice resents the relationship as a betrayal of her father. After Ramona's unexpected death, Bill comes to the funeral and asks Birdee for a divorce. When Bernice demands to return to Chicago with her father, he tells her that he and Connie don't want her. Birdee and Bernice start their lives afresh with Justin.

HOPE FLOATS begins with a bang, after which it limps along like a dog with a sore leg, whimpering for sympathy. The plot is shamelessly predictable. Is there any doubt Birdee will fall for Justin? Of course not. Her need to be reassured that he is an architect, and not a mere handyman, before taking the plunge is pathetic. Also pathetic is seeing Gena Rowlands reduced to playing a kooky knock-off of TERMS OF ENDEARMENT's Aurora Greenway, only to die as a plot device.

HOPE FLOATS returns Sandra Bullock to the romantic stomping grounds of her first starring vehicle, WHILE YOU WERE SLEEPING (1995), and the milieu suits her. Her presence alone puts the audience squarely in this character's corner, even when she's drunk and a lousy parent. But Birdee never develops enough for us to invest in her. What happened to turn her from a young firecracker into this wet pack of matches? Bill's affair doesn't seem like enough of a reason when Birdee admits awareness and acceptance of his past infidelities. Director Forest Whitaker pads HOPE FLOATS with hokey scenes of cute business rather than getting down to the business of developing the main character. You find yourself siding with those former classmates who are grinning like Cheshire cats at the sight of this Birdee brought down to earth. *(Adult situations, substance abuse.)*— P.R.

d, Forest Whitaker; p, Lynda Obst; exec p, Sandra Bullock, Mary McLaglen; assoc p, Elizabeth Joan Hooper; w, Steven Rogers; ph, Caleb Deschanel; ed, Richard Chew; m, Dave Grusin; prod d, Larry Fulton; art d, Christa Munro; set d, Douglas A. Mowat; sound, Felipe Borrero (mixer); fx, Randy E. Moore, Margaret Johnson, Rich Thorne, Sharon Holly; casting, Ronnie Yeskel; cos, Susie DeSanto; makeup, Christina Smith; stunts, Kiante Elam, Danny Castle

Romance/Drama (PR: A MPAA: PG-13)

HORSE WHISPERER, THE ★★½

(U.S., 1998) 164m Wildwood Enterprises;
Touchstone Pictures; Hollywood Pictures; Double Divide ~
Buena Vista c

Robert Redford *(Tom Booker)*; Kristin Scott Thomas *(Annie MacLean)*; Sam Neill *(Robert MacLean)*; Dianne Wiest *(Diane Booker)*; Scarlett Johansson *(Grace MacLean)*; Chris Cooper *(Frank Booker)*; Cherry Jones *(Liz Hammond)*; Catherine Bosworth *(Judith)*; Don Edwards *(Smokey)*; Ty Hillman *(Joe Booker)*; Austin Schwarz *(Twin #1)*; Dustin Schwarz *(Twin #2)*; Jeanette Nolan *(Ellen Booker)*; Steve Frye *(Hank)*; Jessalyn

Gilsig *(Lucy)*; William "Buddy" Byrd *(Lester Petersen)*; John Hogarty *(Local Tracker)*; Mike La Londe *(Park Ranger)*; C.J. Byrnes *(Doctor)*; Kathy Baldwin Keenan *(Nurse)*; Allison Moorer *(Barn Dance Vocalist)*; George Sack Jr. *(Truck Driver)*; Kelley Sweeney *(Nurse #2)*; Stephen Pearlman *(David Gottschalk—Voiceover)*; Joelle Carter *(Officer Worker #1)*; Sunny Chae *(Office Worker #2)*; Anne Joyce *(Office Worker #3)*; Tara Sobeck *(Schoolgirl #1)*; Kristy Ann Servidio *(Schoolgirl #2)*; Marie Engle *(Neighbor)*; Curt Pate *(Handsome Cowboy)*; Steven Brian Conard *(Ranch Hand)*; Tammy Pate *(Roper)*; Cliff Fleming; Dirk Vahle *(Pilots)*

Based on the bestseller by Nicholas Evans, THE HORSE WHISPERER puts Robert Redford both behind and in front of the camera for the first time to tell the story of physical and spiritual healing in Montana. Though absolutely gorgeous to look at, THE HORSE WHISPERER's unlikable characters hobble this would-be romance before it can get out of the gate.

When New York fashion magazine editor Annie MacLean (Kristin Scott Thomas) describes a page layout as "perfect and boring," she could be describing her home life: married to a kind, handsome man, Robert (Sam Neill), for whom she feels no passion, and with a bright, beautiful daughter, Grace (Scarlett Johansson), whose life Annie is too busy to be a part of. This perfect scene is shattered when Grace and a friend are hit by a truck while horseback riding on a snowy road. Grace is badly injured, losing a leg, and her friend is killed; also badly injured is Grace's horse, Pilgrim, whom Annie cannot bear to have put down. Even after its physical recuperation, Pilgrim is wild and nearly unapproachable, even by Grace, sending the girl into a deep depression.

Determined to give Grace back some of her old life, Annie calls Tom Booker (Robert Redford), a Montana rancher whose keen rapport with horses has earned him the title of "horse whisperer." When Tom refuses Annie's offer to come to New York to help Pilgrim, Annie takes Pilgrim—and Grace—to Montana. Seeing that Pilgrim's healing will take some time, Tom's brother Frank (Chris Cooper) offers to let them stay in an empty house on their property and earn their keep by helping out on the ranch. Though clearly out of place at first, mother and daughter eventually get into the swing of farm life; what's more, romance seems to be growing between Annie and Tom. Just as they admit their feelings to one another, husband Robert pays a surprise visit, just in time to see the completion of Pilgrim's remarkable recovery. Robert and Grace head back to New York, and despite the burning love for Tom that she will never feel for her husband, Annie ultimately joins them.

"Perfect and boring," unfortunately, could also describe THE HORSE WHISPERER itself. Though beautifully filmed (by Robert Richardson, veteran cinematographer of many of Oliver Stone's films) and well acted, THE HORSE WHISPERER feels empty, without any real emotional weight. One problem is that we just can't buy Annie's dissatisfaction with her life—after all, she's successful, has a gorgeous apartment in Manhattan, a great husband and daughter. . . so what's the problem? The doomed romance that develops between her and Tom therefore cannot elicit much sympathy from the audience—quite the contrary, Annie comes off as kind of a bitch for betraying her husband. Good tearjerkers are not made of this.

When it was published, *The Horse Whisperer* drew comparisons to the last big weepy novel, *The Bridges of Madison County* (and rightly so—it duplicated the latter's formula exactly). It's appropriate then that THE HORSE WHISPERER features a near-legendary director/star, Robert Redford, just as Clint Eastwood's THE BRIDGES OF MADISON COUNTRY (1995) did. Redford turns in his trademark performance, one whose very repetition carries with it a certain comfortable familiarity—the onscreen equivalent of broken-in blue jeans—and the flinty Kristen Scott Thomas is appropriately cast as the uptight Annie. The real standout performance, though, comes from Scarlett Johansson, an old soul who portrays young Grace with impeccable poise. In all, however, THE HORSE WHISPERER probably serves best as a video postcard, an infomercial for the Montana Board of Tourism. *(Violence, adult situations.)*—B.T.

d, Robert Redford; p, Robert Redford, Patrick Markey; exec p, Rachel Pfeffer; assoc p, Karen Tenkhoff; co-p, Joseph Reidy; w, Eric Roth, Richard LaGravenese (based on the novel by Nicholas Evans); ph, Robert Richardson; ed, Tom Rolf, Freeman Davies Jr., Hank Corwin; m, Thomas Newman; prod d, Jon Hutman; art d, W. Steven Graham; set d, Hilton Rosemarin, Gretchen Rau; sound, Tod A. Maitland (mixer), Gary Rydstrom (design), Steve Boeddeker (design); fx, Neil Trifunovich, Peter Donen, Peter Crosman; casting, Ellen Chenoweth, Gretchen Rennell; cos, Judy L. Ruskin; makeup, Gary Liddiard; stunts, Gary Combs

AAN Best Original Song: "A Soft Place to Fall"; Allison Moorer, Gwil Owen

Romance/Drama **(PR: C MPAA: PG-13)**

HORTON FOOTE'S ALONE ★★★
(U.S., 1997) 107m Brandman Productions ~ Hallmark Entertainment c
(AKA: ALONE)

Hume Cronyn *(John Webb)*; Chris Cooper *(Gus Jr.)*; Frederic Forrest *(Carl)*; James Earl Jones *(Grey)*; Joanna Miles *(Jaclyn)*; Roxanne Hart *(Grace Ann)*; Starletta Dupois *(Lois)*; Ed Begley Jr. *(Gerald)*; Shelley Duvall *(Estelle)*; Hallie Foote *(Agnes)*; Piper Laurie *(Lillie Dawson)*; Rex Linn *(Travis Floyd)*; David Selby *(Paul)*; Beatrice Winde *(Sarah Davis)*; Devon Abner *(Gilbert Jackson)*; Priscilla Pointer *(Susan Hight)*; Bob Symonds *(Jack Hight)*; Matthew Howard *(Gus III)*; Sarah Rayne *(Little Agnes)*; Azura Skye *(Jocelyn)*; Betty Murphy *(Ann)*; Sean Barnes *(Joe Davis)*; Chris Ufland *(Hector)*; Lisa Robin Kelly *(Mary Louise)*

The subject of grief is tellingly addressed in the spare drama, HORTON FOOTE'S ALONE, which touches viewers, thanks to that bastion of seamless acting, Hume Cronyn. If other aspects of ALONE don't approach Cronyn's level, the film deserves kudos for showing how the tapestry of an entire family can unravel with the removal of a single member. The film, which was produced by Showtime, made its home video debut in 1998.

Widowed farmer John Webb (Hume Cronyn) has been depressed since the death of Bessie, his wife of 30 years. He musters the energy to keep his yearly harvest going without the help of daughters Jaclyn (Joanna Miles) and Grace Ann (Roxanne Hart), who have made urban-centric lives for their own families in Houston. Now, Webb learns that his overseer and best friend Grey (James Earl Jones) has been pressured to move in with his children in Houston. Isolated on his farm, stoic Webb is lonely until he is visited by his nephews, Carl (Frederic Forrest) and Gus Jr. (Chris Cooper). The two inherited 50 percent of the mineral rights to Webb's land from their father, and have been promised big money from an oil company if they can get Webb to agree to sell his share. At the same time, Webb's financially strapped daughter Jaclyn moves back home with her husband Paul (David Selby). Webb gives Paul a job, but Paul is unsuited to farm life. Jaclyn's family returns to Houston, and Gus Jr. and Carl leave when Webb's land fails to produce the oil gusher they had anticipated. Readjusting to loneliness, Webb welcomes the return of Grey. In his company and that of Bessie's former housekeeper Lois (Starletta Dupois), Webb shares memories of Bessie that begin as a comfort but end up a reminder of devastating loss.

If you've seen one Horton Foote teleplay about an embattled Texas clan, you've seen them all. Usually, the protagonist is a solitary widower or widow beset on all sides by ungrateful kin-folk. Foote always concentrates his considerable craft on the heroic central figure, while fashioning the dragon offspring as caricatures. Because the basic domestic crises enveloping that hero ring true, ALONE impresses viewers with gentle reflections on the inescapable solitude of the elderly. In the leading role, Hume Cronyn masterfully unveils his portrait of a decent man, whose well-intentioned daughters can't fit him into their distant lives. He is ably supported by James Earl Jones and Starletta Dupois. Although the rest of the talented cast offers stereotypical renderings of selfishness, Cronyn manages to massage the film's episodic confrontations into potent drama. As he sings a few bars of his wife's favorite hymn at the fade-out, Cronyn breaks the audience's heart. *(Profanity, adult situations.)* —R.P.

d, Michael Lindsay-Hogg; p, Steven Brandman; exec p, Michael Brandman; co-p, Matthew David Hensley; w, Horton Foote; ph, Jeffrey Jur; ed, Norman Buckley; m, David Shire; prod d, Vaughan Edwards; set d, Sam Gross; sound, Mark Weingarten (mixer); fx, John Hartigan; casting, Juel Bestrop; cos, Betty Pecha Madden; makeup, Deborah Larsen

Drama **(PR: A MPAA: NR)**

HOSTILE INTENT ★★½

(U.S./Canada, 1998) 89m Le Monde Entertainment; Alliance ~ Cabin Fever Entertainment c

Rob Lowe *(Mike Cleary)*; Sofia Shinas *(Gina)*; James Kidnie *(Adams)*; John Savage *(John "Bear" Barrington)*; Saul Rubinek *(Kendall)*; Louis Del Grande *(Soames)*; Ronn Sarosiak *(Gordon)*; Rino Romano *(Press)*; Christopher Kennedy *(Witt)*; Gerry Quigley *(Bill Dunnel)*; Jody Racicot *(Rawlins)*; Simon Reynolds *(Crowther)*; Patrick Chilvers *(Martino)*; Marlon Brand *(Wexler)*; Sean Sullivan *(Charlie)*; Kevin Rushton *(Sidley)*; Randy Butcher *(Buckner)*; Chris Adams *(Sherwood)*; Damir Andrei *(Fischer)*; Jonathan Potts *(ATF Agent)*

Bullets trump paint guns when computer hackers are stalked by murderous federal agents in HOSTILE INTENT, a straight-to-video production that ranks with ENEMY OF THE STATE (1998) in terms of anti-government paranoia.

Computer specialist Mike Cleary (Rob Lowe) has spent two years and gone deep into debt to perfect a crack-proof information shield, which he hopes will counter a new chip designed to give the government access into everyone's computers. His development team likes to relax on weekends in the woods playing wargames, and Mike decides to join them when the competition will be headed by Gordon (Ronn Sarosiak), his former employer, who sold a system Mike developed to the government.

As the game progresses, members of both teams are killed, shot with real guns. Dunnel (Gerry Quigley), one of Mike's workers, reveals that he has been getting money from federal agents who want the program, not realizing that they would kill to get it. The survivors join with local survivalist Bear (John Savage) to escape the feds, led by Adams (James Kidnie), who continue to pick them off. Mike uses his portable computer equipment to scramble the feds' satellite surveillance of them, and to trick them into killing a few of their own. Mike and Bear escape into the latter's underground bunker, where Mike plants his program on the Internet so that anyone can get it for free. Adams is killed in a final explosion, and Mike and Bear hit the road, fugitives from the government.

HOSTILE INTENT might have had more impact had it spent less time on action and more with the issues of the government's steadily growing surveillance capabilities. Instead, it starts on the assumption that viewers have a rabid suspicion and hatred of the government, which is (at least at this level) rather a lot to assume. That element aside, this is perfunctory fare, with most of the film devoted to members of the two teams being stalked and killed by unseen government killers, as if the country were being run by a coalition of Jason Vorhees and Michael Meyers. There's too little of ace hacker Mike turning the tables, and too much that will go over the heads of the non-computer literate, who will be left with little to ponder aside from why costar John Savage always looks so irate. *(Violence, profanity.)*—M.F.

d, Jonathan Heap; p, Julian Grant; exec p, Louis B. Chester, David M. Perlmutter, John Fremes, Gigi Pritzker, Deborah Del Prete; w, Manny Coto; ph, Gerald R. Goozee; ed, Paul Day; m, Christophe Beck; prod d, John Gillespie; set d, Rick Gilbert; sound, John Megill (mixer); fx, Brock Jolliffe; casting, Hank McCann, Marjorie Lecker; cos, Judith England; makeup, Traci Loader; stunts, John Stoneham Stoneham

Action/Adventure/Science Fiction **(PR: C MPAA: R)**

HOSTILE WATERS ★★★½

(U.S./U.K./Germany/France, 1997) 92m HBO NYC Productions; BBC; World Productions; Inivision Productions Ltd.; UFA Filmproduktion GMBH; UFA Babelsberg GMBH; Flach Film ~ HBO Home Video c

Rutger Hauer *(Britanov)*; Martin Sheen *(Aurora Skipper)*; Max von Sydow *(Admiral Chernavin)*; Colm Feore *(Pshenishny)*; Rob Campbell *(Sergei Preminin)*; Harris Yulin *(Admiral Quinn)*; Regina Taylor *(Lieutenant Alex Curtis)*; John Rothman *(Aurora Executive Officer)*; Michael Attwell *(Kuzmenko)*; Dominic Monaghan *(Sasha)*; Peter Guinness *(Vladminirov)*; James E. Kerr *(Aznabaev)*; Alexis Denisof *(John Baker)*; Seamus McQuade *(Helmsman)*; Paul Birchard *(Torpedo Chief)*; Oliver Marlo *(Doctor)*; Mark Drewry *(Petrachkov)*; Denzil Kilvington *(Volnigbirov)*; Garry Cooper *(Gennady)*; Frank Baker *(Pumps)*; Richard Graham *(Belikov)*; Philip Martin Brown *(Cook)*; Joachim Paul Assbock *(Tigran Gasparian)*; E. Alexander Wachholz *(Martinov)*; David King *(Admiral 2nd Class)*; Todd Boyce *(Larry Brock)*; Michael J. Shannon *(Admiral)*; Lawrence Elman *(Officer)*; Norbert Tefelski *(Admiral/Engineer)*; J.J. Gordon *(Officer 4)*; Erik Hansen *(Naval Marshall)*; Rainer Sellien *(Technician)*; Eckbert Matschie *(Helmsman)*; Sanja Spengler *(Britanov's Wife)*

A gripping dramatization of actual events, HOSTILE WATERS recreates the October 1986 collision of Russian and American submarines off the coast of Bermuda—an incident the US government maintains never occurred. Based on extensive interviews with survivors, eyewitnesses, and military officials, this made-for-cable thriller aired on HBO in 1997 and was released to home video in 1998.

Eight days before the Reagan-Gorbachev peace summit in Reykjavik is scheduled to take place, a Russian K-219 nuclear submarine furtively patrolling the western Atlantic detects the presence of an American sub in its wake. Captain Britanov (Rutger Hauer) orders a 360-degree turn to evade the enemy vessel. In the turbulence caused by the maneuver, the USS Aurora loses its sonar signal and the two vessels collide. The collision causes a gas explosion on the Soviet sub and a fire breaks out which could cause a nuclear meltdown large enough to decimate the entire eastern seaboard of the US. The beleaguered Soviet sub surfaces in western waters—an unprecedented occurrence that stuns the Aurora skipper (Martin Sheen). Realizing that the Russian sub is in trouble yet suspicious of its every move, the Aurora skipper and his crew are poised to attack—an action that would start an all-out war.

Britanov submerges his sub with its missile hatches open in order to take on enough water to extinguish the fire. The risky strategy works, but moments later the sub's reactor alarm sounds, signaling imminent nuclear meltdown. The crisis is averted in part by the heroic efforts of a young crewman (Rob Campbell) who loses his life shutting down the reactors. The rest of the crew is rescued, and the sub sinks without deploying its missiles. Though a hero to his men, Britanov is dismissed from the Soviet Navy. Fearful that public announcement of the incident might impede the peace talks, the White House suppresses the information.

Treading similar waters as THE HUNT FOR RED OCTOBER (1990) and CRIMSON TIDE (1995), HOSTILE WATERS is a riveting, tightly scripted submarine adventure. The tension is made more palpable by the real-life implications of the event—though it is unclear to what extent dramatic liberties have been taken in adapting the story to the screen. An alarming postscript to the film notes that 51 nuclear warheads and 7 nuclear reactors have been lost at sea.

Hauer gives a powerful performance as the courageous yet compassionate Soviet captain. Sheen is equally commendable as the American skipper (his character isn't named because commanders of US nuclear subs are never identified by name), but his job is largely to react—the real action takes place on the Soviet sub and Hauer is the driving force of the drama. The underseas action is punctuated by cutaways to strategy sessions in Washington and the Kremlin. The military officials on land—Harris Yulin as an American admiral and Max von Sydow as his Kremlin counterpart—are effective. The production values are strong, particularly the imposing submarine interiors. *(Profanity.)*—B.R.

d, David Drury; p, Tony Garnett; exec p, Konstantin Thoeren, David M. Thompson, William Cran, Stephanie Tepper; assoc p, Carla Thoeren; w, Troy Kennedy Martin (based on research by Peter Huchthausen, William Cran and Tom Mangold); ph, Alec Curtis; ed, Ian Farr; m, David Ferguson; prod d, Jon Bunker; art d, Udo Scharnowski, Ian Reade Hill; set d, Bernard Heinrich; sound, Derek Norman; fx, Karl-Heinz Bochnig; casting, Mary Colquhoun, Sarah Bird; cos, Anne Hoffman; makeup, Martina Raschke, Jens Bartram

Drama/Political/Thriller **(PR: C MPAA: PG)**

HOT BLOODED ★

(U.S., 1998) 86m S Entertainment ~ F.C.P. Media Ventures c
(AKA: HIT & RUN; RED BLOODED AMERICAN GIRL II)

Kari Wuhrer, billed as Kari Salin *(Miya)*; Kristoffer Ryan Winters *(Trent)*; Burt Young *(Roy)*; David Keith *(Mr. Colbert)*; Elaine Martin *(Mrs. Colbert)*; Nicholas Pasco *(Trooper Vukelich)*; Roland Rothchild *(Trooper Whitman)*; Art MacDonald *(Buster)*; Philip Riccio *(Jimmy)*; Anne Scanlon *(Emily)*; Clinton Walker *(Pez)*

A nerd picks up a hitchhiking hooker who takes him on a wild ride full of hot sex and bloody murder in HOT BLOODED, a 1998 straight-to-video thriller that subsequently aired on cable under the equally generic title HIT & RUN.

At a highway truck stop, prostitute Miya (Kari Salin) propositions a truck driver, Roy (Burt Young), who she then recognizes as her father. Not as put off as she is by the idea, he tries to rape her. She escapes by hopping into a car driven by Trent (Kristoffer Ryan Winters), a nebbish on his way home from college for Thanksgiving. While escaping, they hit another trucker.

Trent and Miya stop for the night at a motel, and Miya treats Trent to a demonstration of her skills. When the motel's owner tries to force Miya to service him at gunpoint, she disarms him and escapes into the night. The next morning, state troopers question Trent about the hit and run at the truck stop, but let him go. Miya calls Trent on his cell phone, and persuades him to take her on the road with him.

Roy catches up with them and forces them off the road. When he again tries to rape her at gunpoint, Trent intervenes, and Miya shoots and kills Roy. Back on the road, Miya encourages Trent to stand up to his overbearing parents and take control of his life. After a roll in the hay in a barn, Trent invites her to meet his parents. To freak them out, they stop and buy some fetish wear, and get Trent tattooed and pierced.

The state troopers catch up with the couple, but Miya shoots one of them, and she and Trent escape. When they arrive at his parents' home, the police are waiting in force. Miya holds a gun on Trent's dad (David Keith), but Trent gets it away from her by promising to kill his parents himself. Instead, Trent shoots Miya.

HOT BLOODED surfaced on video and cable in 1998, but was filmed in 1995 under the title RED BLOODED AMERICAN GIRL II. Aside from director David Blyth, it has nothing in common with the 1990 vampire flick RED BLOODED AMERICAN GIRL, alhough had any of the characters in HOT BLOODED turned out to be vampires, it could only have helped this ludicrous thriller. Such a turn of events would have been no less preposterous than the many other head-scratchers here, such as: Why do the troopers let Trent go when he is *so* obviously their suspect in the hit and run? How do those same troopers then determine that Miya is responsible for killing Roy? How does Roy track Miya and Trent down? And why does Trent drive for three days to make a seven-hour trip? Oh, right, to fill the time between the sex scenes. *(Violence, sexual situations, nudity, profanity.)*—P.R.

d, David Blyth; p, Nicolas Stiliadis; co-p, Paco Alvarez; w, Nicolas Stiliadis; ed, Nick Rotundo; m, Paul J. Zaza; prod d, Michael Close; art d, Alexx Kovacs; set d, Yasmin Zeitler; sound, Urmas Rosin; cos, Sharmon Luchuck; makeup, Charlene Cordoba; stunts, Tony Cordiero

Thriller/Drama/Crime **(PR: C MPAA: R)**

HOW STELLA GOT HER GROOVE BACK ★★

(U.S., 1998) 121m Deborah Schindler Productions; 20th Century Fox ~ 20th Century Fox c

Angela Bassett *(Stella)*; Whoopi Goldberg *(Delilah)*; Taye Diggs *(Winston Shakespeare)*; Regina King *(Vanessa)*; Suzzanne Douglas *(Angela)*; Michael J. Pagan *(Quincy)*; Sicily *(Chantel)*; Richard Lawson *(Jack)*; Barry "Shabaka" Henley *(Buddy)*; Lee Weaver *(Nate)*; Glynn Turman *(Doctor Shakespeare)*; Phyllis Yvonne Stickney *(Mrs. Shakespeare)*; Lou Myers *(Uncle Ollie)*; James Pickens Jr. *(Walter)*; Carl Lumbly *(Judge Boyle)*; Denise Hunt *(Ms. Thang)*; Lisa Hanna *(Abby)*; Philip Casnoff *(Kennedy)*; D'Army Bailey *(Minister)*; Art Metrano *(Doctor Steinberg)*; Phina Oruche *(Leslie)*; Tenny Miller *(Kitchen Worker)*; Andrew Palmer *(Buffet Server)*; Harold Dawkins *(The Upbeaters Band)*; Kenneth Buckford *(The Upbeaters Band)*; Simon Street *(The Upbeaters Band)*; Craig Blake *(Winston's friend)*; Elisabeth Granli *(Girl in Jamaica Commercial)*; Steve Danton *(Man in Commercial)*; Elly McGuire *(Stella's Friend)*; Selma McPherson *(Friend at Party)*; Fern Ward *(Friend at Party)*

The passionate, turbulent romance between a 40-year-old female California stock broker and a 20-year-old Jamaican man is the provocative premise of HOW STELLA GOT HER GROOVE

BACK. Yet in spite of this promisingly sexy scenario, the film fails in almost every way to stoke the flames of sensuality.

A broker, Stella (Angela Bassett), lives a busy, luxurious but ultimately lonely life in San Francisco with her young son, Quincy (Michael J. Pagan). Since her divorce, Stella has yearned for romance, but never finds anyone who meets her needs. When Quincy leaves to stay with his Dad for two weeks, Stella takes a vacation to Jamaica with her best friend, Delilah (Whoopi Goldberg), where she immediately meets Winston Shakespeare (Taye Diggs), a handsome man half her age.

Despite the age difference, Stella warms to Winston's charms and the two begin a passionate romance. But just as soon as the relationship gets serious, Winston takes an assistant chef's job that keeps him from seeing Stella towards the end of her trip. Stella leaves the island feeling saddened and betrayed. Upon her return to San Francisco, Stella gets teased about her affair by her nosy sisters, Vanessa (Regina King) and Angela (Suzzanne Douglas), and she is further disheartened when she finds herself downsized out of her job.

Life turns around for Stella when Winston calls her from Jamaica and she agrees to return to see him, taking Quincy and her niece, Chantel (Sicily), with her. Upon her arrival, Stella and Winston resume their affair, but their romance is again cut short when Winston's wealthy mother accuses Stella of "cradle-snatching" and Stella learns from a doctor that Delilah is gravely ill in Manhattan. Stella quickly leaves the island with the children to be with her friend. Sadly, Delilah dies, but Stella receives comfort from Winston who shows up at the funeral.

Stella and Winston then travel back to San Francisco, where Winston takes up residence with her. But conflicts emerge between the couple as Stella tries to establish a furniture craft business and Winston becomes demanding about their future marriage. When Stella refuses to accept his marriage offer, Winston plans a return to Jamaica, where he considers going to medical school. On his way to the airport, however, Winston is stopped by Stella, who finally welcomes his marriage proposal and suggests he attend medical school in San Francisco.

Like the similar WAITING TO EXHALE (1995), HOW STELLA GOT HER GROOVE BACK was adapted by Terry McMillan and Ron Bass from a McMillan novel, and the result is another welcome portrait of a confident African-American woman. Likewise, the film's older woman-younger man relationship is a refreshing change, making STELLA an antidote to other 1998 releases concerning older men involved with younger women (SIX DAYS, SEVEN NIGHTS, A PERFECT MURDER, LOLITA, etc.).

So it's all the more disappointing that HOW STELLA GOT HER GROOVE BACK never goes beyond the level of being a picture-postcard fantasy romance. The first half-hour looks like a travelogue for Jamaican sightseeing, with vulgar sex jokes and reverse sexism dotting the affair between vacationing Stella and the handsome Winston. Once the story line turns dramatic, the promise of conflict between the couple and the disapproving outside world dissipates into a series of homey "feel good" scenes. Though patterned after classic romantic melodramas, STELLA lacks the artful irony and economy of Douglas Sirk's ALL THAT HEAVEN ALLOWS (1955), a much better film about the romance of an older woman and younger man. (Rainer Werner Fassbinder's 1974 reworking of the Sirk film, ALI, FEAR EATS THE SOUL, also explores the topic in a most in-depth and moving way.)

While Bassett gives a strictly tense, humorless performance, the actors playing her friends and family go for ribald caricatures. Whoopi Goldberg and Regina King are particularly over-the-top in ugly stereotypes of predatory, upwardly mobile females. Diggs, meanwhile, possesses some quiet dignity, but simply lacks depth in the male lead. With an ensemble of attractive leading players and a non-stop R & B soundtrack, HOW STELLA GOT HER GROOVE looks and sounds good, but it winds up teasing and pandering to an audience that deserves much better. *(Nudity, sexual situations, profanity.)*—E.M.

d, Kevin Rodney Sullivan; p, Deborah Schindler; exec p, Terry McMillan, Ron Bass, Jennifer Ogden; w, Terry McMillan, Ron Bass (based on the novel by Terry McMillan); ph, Jeffrey Jur; ed, George Bowers; m, Michel Colombier; prod d, Chester Kaczenski; art d, Marc Dabe; sound, Alvin Susumu Tokunow (mixer); fx, John Hartigan; casting, Francine Maisler; cos, Ruth E. Carter

Romance/Drama/Comedy (PR: C MPAA: R)

HUMAN BOMB ★★

(U.S., 1996) 93m Light & Edge; Griffin Productions; Tele-Munchen Group ~ Showtime/Viacom c

Patsy Kensit *(Marcia Weller)*; Jurgen Prochnow *(Gerhardt)*; Robert Spitz *(Ned Lud)*; Dorian Healy *(Jon Stedman)*; James Gaddas *(Franck)*; Kate Harper *(Mrs. Macky)*; Bob Sherman *(Bob Macky)*; Nicholas Day *(Secretary Eicher)*; Richard Moore *(Stensen)*; Kim Fenton *(Doctor)*; Martin Ronan *(Journalist 1)*; Alisa Bosschaert *(Journalist 2)*; Anthony Naylor *(Herr Dietrich)*; Amanda Drewry *(Jeanne)*; Chris Armstrong *(Engineer)*; Paul Humpoletz *(Hans)*; Martin Ontrup *(Passport Officer)*; Elizabeth Richmond *(Girl 1)*; Carle Harris *(Girl 2)*; Peter Cant *(Boy 1)*; Justin Cirdler *(Boy 2)*

Inspired by the true story of a German hostage crisis in which a teacher shepherded her gradeschoolers to safety, HUMAN BOMB is a listless thriller ripped from yesterday's headlines. The film premiered on the Movie Channel and was subsequently released on home video in 1998.

Recently widowed American schoolteacher Marcia Weller (Patsy Kensit) opts for a fresh start in Germany with her mother Mrs. Macky (Kate Harper) and her stepfather Mr. Macky (Bob Sherman), a business tycoon. Terrorist Ned Lud (Robert Spitz), who was planning to kidnap Macky, shifts his focus to Marcia, because her new charges are the pampered offspring of Europe's social elite. Wired with explosives set to detonate in the event of his death, Lud invades Marcia's classroom, demanding a ransom of 50 million marks. He uses her as a go-between in dealing with the authorities led by Capt. Gerhardt (Jurgen Prochnow).

Pressured by politicians currying favor with the childrens' parents, Gerhardt stalls Lud. Marcia calms her frightened pupils and cleverly scores concessions from their captor. Furious when the government refuses to meet the full amount demanded, Gerhardt manages to position his snipers and to install a mini-video camera through the wall of the classroom. Marcia discovers that Lud's activated timebomb has a five-second delay. The sacks of money are delivered to Lud, who plans to spot-check every bag. When he temporarily removes his finger from the device trigger, the assault team rushes into the room. Startled, Lud drops his device; Marcia grabs it and re-stops the mechanism; Lud is arrested.

Time codes flash across the bottom of the screen to lend HUMAN BOMB a sense of urgency, but this sluggish film seems to unspool over decades rather than a day or two. Prosaically scripted and flatly directed, this yawn-inducer is competently produced and acted but never heats up its thriller dynamics past a low boil. Instead of causing the audience to shiver as the terrorist badgers his captives, the film only manages to elicit our admiration for Marcia's cool-headed profile in courage. Kensit believably underplays her heroine's resourcefulness and keeps the viewer in Marcia's cornered corner. Wallpapered with the usual criticism about governmental intransigence in terrorist situations, HUMAN BOMB runs its course sans surprises but with lots of flaccid crosscutting and missed suspense opportunities. *(Violence.)*—R.P.

d, Anthony Page; p, Matthew Bird; exec p, Michael Deakin, Adam Clapham, James Dowaliby, Rikolt Von Gagern; assoc p, John Paul Chapple; w, Lionel Chetwynd; ph, Remi Adefarasin; ed, Christopher Blunden; m, John Powell; prod d, Chris Robillard; art d, David Bowes; set d, Dave Rogers; sound, Ronald Bailey; casting, Beth Charkam; cos, Sheena Napier; makeup, Suzanne Jansen; stunts, Andrew Bradford

Thriller/Political **(PR: A MPAA: PG-13)**

HUNTED, THE ★★

(U.S./Canada, 1998) 96m Wildshire Court Productions ~ Showtime/Viacom c

Madchen Amick *(Samantha "Sam" Clark)*; Harry Hamlin *(Doc Kovac)*; Hannes Jaenicke *(Jan Kroeger)*; Enuka Okuma *(Tracy)*; Robert Moloney *(Dorse)*; Peter Lacroix *(Ranger McNulty)*; Fulvio Cecere *(Detective Cuneo)*; Peter Bryant *(Uniformed Officer)*; Andy Thompson *(Fielder)*; Terence Kelly *(Griffin)*; Garvin Cross *(Harry)*; Sean Campbell *(Jogger)*

1998 saw the home-video release of two movies starring Madchen Amick with nearly identical plotlines. WOUNDED (a 1996 cable premiere) and THE HUNTED both involve the former "Twin Peaks" star in mediocre reworkings of the oft-copied plot line of the action-adventure classic THE MOST DANGEROUS GAME (1932). At least THE HUNTED gives her a leaner script and a more magnetic leading man than WOUNDED. Hunted or wounded, Amick runs for her life with lithesome appeal.

Workaholic insurance investigator Samantha "Sam" Clark (Madchen Amick) cancels a vacation with her artist boyfriend Jan (Hannes Jaenicke) to trek through the Pacific Northwest on a case involving Harry Augerman, a missing businessman who absconded with a $12 million company payroll. Despite the warnings of a forest ranger, Sam races off to the wilderness and wrecks her ATV. She stumbles into the cabin of hermit Doc Kovac (Harry Hamlin), who tends her injuries and agrees to take her to the site where Augerman crashed his plane.

There, Sam sees Augerman's corpse hanging on an Indian totem pole like a trophy. He was killed by Doc, a lunatic sportsman. Planning to hunt her down just as he did Augerman, Doc offers Sam a head start and a gun. As she runs for her life, Doc wounds her with an arrow to her shoulder. Allowing him to believe she's dead, Sam later doubles back to his cabin, retrieves the Augerman cash, awaits Doc's return, locks him in the cabin, sets it ablaze and shoots him through the closed, burning door.

Surviving nonetheless, Doc tracks Sam back to the city, where he torments her and Jan. After cornering them at the museum where Jan work, Doc pursues them to a lighthouse. Sam shoots Doc, who retaliates by wounding Jan with a knife. Finally, Sam fatally blows away Doc, who plunges into the sea.

Whipping up synthetic suspense, THE HUNTED quickly forgoes the sexual sparks that sizzle when Doc tends to wounded Sam. Uninterested in exploring character layering or psychological underpinnings, the picture soon settles into its true purpose: a sadistic aerobics work-out over hill, dale, and concrete jungle. There have certainly been worse variations of this oft-adapted story, but this sprint-for-your-life thriller is scripted with marginal dexterity and directed in lazy short-hand technique. Attractive actors, a couple of jolts, and the thrill of the chase result in serviceable escapism that's all about escaping. *(Graphic violence, profanity, adult situations)*—R.P.

d, Stuart Cooper; assoc p, Martin Ganz, Doris Kirch; w, David Ives, Bennett Cohen; ph, Curtis Peterson; ed, Robert A. Ferretti; prod d, Doug Higgins; set d, Leslie Beale; sound, Ralph Parker (mixer); fx, Michael Blacklock, Jim Fisher; casting, Penny Musarra; cos, Terri Bardon; makeup, Fern Levin, Tibor Farkas (special makeup effects); stunts, Marc Akerstream

Action/Thriller **(PR: C MPAA: R)**

HURLYBURLY ★★★

(U.S., 1998) 122m Storm Entertainment ~ Fine Line c

Sean Penn *(Eddie)*; Kevin Spacey *(Mickey)*; Robin Wright Penn *(Darlene)*; Chazz Palminteri *(Phil)*; Garry Shandling *(Artie)*; Anna Paquin *(Donna)*; Meg Ryan *(Bonnie)*

Adapted from David Rabe's acclaimed eponymous play, HURLYBURLY is about a group of friends who are becoming increasingly addled by drugs and muddled by equivocal modern values. Discreetly opened up for the screen, the movie, like the play, is at its liveliest and most intriguing in its first act. Sean Penn's performance won him the Best Actor award at the 1998 Venice Film Festival.

Eddie (Sean Penn) and Mickey (Kevin Spacey) are motion picture casting directors who work together and share a posh condo in the Hollywood Hills. Eddie, who is becoming heavily dependent on drugs, is divorced and Mickey is temporarily separated from his wife. Their violent friend Phil (Chazz Palminteri), an untalented would-be actor, also is experiencing problems in his marriage. Eddie is mad at Mickey for horning in on his relationship with Darlene (Robin Wright Penn), a photographer. Eventually, Mickey steps aside, allowing Eddie and Darlene to pick up where they left off.

One day Artie (Garry Shandling), another crony, arrives with Donna (Anna Paquin), a 15-year-old runaway whom he donates to his friends as a kind of sexual house gift. Eddie immediately takes her to bed, but Phil's brutal behavior toward the girl impels her to seek haven elsewhere.

A year later, Phil's wife, who has just given birth, is divorcing him. To cheer him up, Eddie and Mickey summon Bonnie (Meg Ryan), a good-time gal who once fellated a client of theirs while her six-year-old daughter looked on. Phil shows his gratitude by pushing Bonnie out of her own car while it is moving.

Several days later Eddie throws a jealous tantrum when Darlene reminisces about a pair of her old boyfriends and the abortion that ensued. That night he is staggered by the news that Phil has committed suicide. After the funeral, Donna returns unexpectedly and tries to comfort Eddie, who has now become almost completely devastated by drugs and despair.

Much of the play's outrageously convoluted dialogue—the kind of twisted rhetoric Darlene refers to as "semantic insanity"—has been left intact. Perhaps too much. In adapting his award-winning play for the screen, David Rabe tightened it some but might well have tightened it even further—there's a significant risk that the destructive Eddie will wear out his welcome with many viewers before they have been sufficiently primed to share his pain. Countering this danger to a great extent is Sean Penn's sympathetic, at times audaciously childlike performance. Less flamboyant but almost as impressive is Kevin Spacey, a Gold Medalist in the art of swimming with the sharks.

Director Anthony Drazan has done a good job with a reported budget of only $4,000,000. Car phones proliferated in the 14 years between the premieres of the stage and screen versions of HURLYBURLY, and Drazan cleverly capitalized on the trend by opening up on Eddie and Mickey's argument about Darlene, and extending it over the course of an entire morning and several locations. (At one point the cars of the two bickerers almost collide in midargument.) Another deft directorial touch was the shooting of a conversation between two cocaine snorters through the glass top of a coffee table.

The filmmakers' most unfortunate idea was the decision to pepper the movie with apocalyptic montages of TV reports of pervasive bad news. Not only has this device become a tired cliche, it tends to undermine one of Mickey's most perceptive appraisals of his tortured housemate: "I mean, Eddie, it's not the time that's dark, it's just you."

A key work in the men-behaving-badly genre (before he hit on *Hurlyburly*, Rabe labeled it "Guy's Play"), the vehicle, like CARNAL KNOWLEDGE (1971) before it, has been branded as misogynistic by those who choose to mistake critiques of misogyny for celebrations of it. *(Violence, sexual situations, adult situations, substance abuse, extreme profanity.)*—D.T.

d, Anthony Drazan; p, Anthony Drazan, Richard N. Gladstein, David S. Hamburger; exec p, H. Michael Heuser, Frederick Zollo, Nicholas Paleologos, Carl Colpaert; w, David Rabe (based on his play); ph, Gu Changwei; ed, Dylan Tichenor; m, David Baerwald, Steve Lindsey; prod d, Michael Haller; cos, Mary Claire Hannan

Drama/Comedy **(PR: O MPAA: R)**

HURRICANE STREETS ★★½

(U.S., 1998) 88m (giv'en) Productions ~ MGM/UA c

Brendan Sexton III *(Marcus)*; David Roland Frank *(Chip)*; Antoine McLean *(Harold)*; Carlo Alban *(Benny)*; Mtume Gant *(Louis)*; Jose Zuniga *(Kramer)*; Lynn Cohen *(Lucy)*; Edie Falco *(Joanna)*; Heather Matarazzo *(Ashley)*; David Moscow *(Shane)*; Damian Corrente *(Justin)*; Shawn Elliott *(Paco)*; Isidra Vega *(Melena)*; Adrian Grenier *(Punk)*; Andrew Ko *(Little Kid)*; Terry Alexander *(Duane)*; Socorro Santiago *(Gloria)*; Jin S. Kim *(Lee)*; Preston B. Handy *(Detective #1)*; Terry Sturiano *(Detective #2)*; Anna Basoli *(Social Worker)*; Richard Petrocelli *(Hank)*; Leslie Body *(Police Man)*; L.M. Kit Carson *(Mack)*; Jared Harris

The feature debut of writer-director Morgan J. Freeman, HURRICANE STREETS is a well-intentioned but conventional study of kids growing up on New York City's mean streets.

Marcus (Brendan Sexton III), just turning 15, is spending the summer hanging out on the street and in a clubhouse with his friends Louis (Mtume Gant), Benny (Carlo Alban), Chip (David Roland Frank), and Harold (Antoine McLean). He lives with his grandmother Lucy (Lynn Cohen), since his father is dead and his mother Joanna (Edie Falco) is in jail for smuggling illegals into New Mexico. While keeping a stash of money in an abandoned building, Marcus is awaiting a promised ticket from his uncle to come to New Mexico. He meets a girl named Melena (Isidra Vega), but the relationship is disapproved of by her father Paco (Shawn Elliott). The ticket shows up—though Lucy figures out that her sympathetic boyfriend Mack (L.M. Kit Carson) has actually sent it—and Marcus asks Melena to come with him.

The police come after Mack on an old charge, and Marcus is arrested for dealing stolen goods outside an elementary school. The police tell him that his mother is actually in jail for murder, and when Marcus goes to visit her, she reveals that she killed his abusive father. Marcus finds Mack wounded at the clubhouse and gives him the ticket to New Mexico. Louis and Chip want to rob an apartment that Louis's uncle Duane (Terry Alexander) is housesitting, and Marcus resists. After a confrontation with Paco, however, he resolves to run away with Melena, and joins his friends for the robbery, where they retrieve money and a gun. Paco finds the clubhouse just before the boys return to it, and while he's hiding in a closet, Harold accidentally shoots him. The boys dispose of the body and Marcus goes for his money stash, only to find that Chip has stolen it. Harold confesses to the shooting, and he and Chip are arrested; Marcus tries to sell the gun to Duane, and when Duane resists, Marcus robs him instead. He meets Melena at Penn Station, and they board a train leaving the city together.

The best thing about HURRICANE STREETS is Sexton's lead performance. Freeman and Sexton first encountered each other when the former worked as second assistant director on the 1996 film WELCOME TO THE DOLLHOUSE, which featured Sexton in the cast. (DOLLHOUSE star, Heather Matarazzo, appears briefly here). In the opening scenes, Sexton sets up the character perfectly—his every gesture carrying the inference that Marcus is a street thug—yet as the film goes on, the young actor begins to evoke the boy's more human, sensitive side. Would that the film's script were even halfway as compelling as Sexton's performance; instead, Freeman offers up a story line that rehashes themes presented in past urban dramas, and a supporting cast of characters that is purely one-dimensional. Marcus confronts the usual pressures, makes the usual mistakes, and finds the usual forces (both inside and outside his circle of friends) conspiring to lead his life down the wrong path.

Freeman's direction is vibrant, though, and the supporting performances have enough of a degree of reality to keep these conventions from becoming tiresome. The young ensemble is effectively naturalistic and Vega is most likable as Melena. There are also some well-observed details, like the automated voicemail message informing Paco that Melena has been skipping summer school. There just aren't enough surprises to distinguish the film, and towards the end, when the pace should be quickening, Freeman unfortunately resorts to coincidence and illogic. It seems as if he has no distance from the characters, liking them so much that he can't allow real tragedy to befall them, thus blunting the drama. The result is a movie with muted impact, particularly in the inconclusive final scene; the movie's last shot echoes that of THE GRADUATE (1967), but bears little of its quiet power. *(Violence, adult situations, substance abuse, extreme profanity.)*—M.G.

d, Morgan J. Freeman; p, Galt Niederhoffer, Gil Holland, Morgan J. Freeman; exec p, L.M. Kit Carson, Cynthia Hargrave; co-p, Nadia Leonelli; w, Morgan J. Freeman; ph, Enrique Chediak; ed, Sabine Hoffman; m, Theodore Shapiro; prod d, Petra Barchi; art d, Iliana Sakas; sound, Robert Taz Larrea (recordist); fx, Rakus Khan, Robert Yoho, East Coast Effects; casting, Susan Shopmaker; cos, Nancy Brous; makeup, Callie French

Drama **(PR: O MPAA: R)**

HUSH ★

(U.S., 1998) 100m Red Wagon Productions; TriStar Pictures ~ TriStar c

Jessica Lange *(Martha)*; Gwyneth Paltrow *(Helen)*; Johnathon Schaech *(Jackson)*; Hal Holbrook *(Dr. Hill)*; Nina Foch *(Alice Baring)*; Debi Mazar *(Lisa)*; Richard Lineback *(Hal Bentall)*; Kaiulani Lee *(Sister O'Shaughnessy)*; David Thornton *(Gavin)*; Richard Kohn *(Clayton Richards)*; Faith Potts *(Georgina Richards)*; Tom Story *(Priest)*; Jolene Carroll *(Church Warden)*; Jacob Press *(Usher)*; Joe Inscoe *(Doctor)*; Catherine Shaffner *(Nurse)*; Lenny Steinline *(Paramedic)*; Rick Gray *(Banker)*; Tom Holmes *(Auctioneer)*; Owen Valentine *(Official)*; Ricardo Miguel Young; Woody Robertson Jr. *(Policemen)*; Charles Thomas Baxter *(Racing Enthusiast)*; Jayne Hess *(Nursing Home Nun)*; Sarah Elspas; Rebecca Elspas; Jacob Elspas *(Helen's Baby)*

It's Jessica Lange as the mother-in-law from Hell vs. Gwyneth Paltrow as the daughter-in-law from Dullsville, in HUSH. The movie's no-brain plot and sheen of class combine to keep the melodrama from being either very interesting or much fun, though ardent fans of bone structure will want to check out the leading trio's fabulous cheekbones.

Jackson Baring (Johnathon Schaech) and his girlfriend Helen (Gwyeth Paltrow) make a Christmas visit to his old Kentucky home, an estate and horse farm called Kilronan. Jackson's widowed mother Martha (Jessica Lange) overbearingly dotes on her son, and sweetly disdains Helen. Martha pressures Jackson to stay and help run Kilronan, which has fallen on hard financial times, but despite her entreaties, Jackson and Helen return to New York. Soon after, Helen discovers she's pregnant.

In the spring, Jackson and Helen marry at Kilronan. Helen meets Jackson's paternal grandmother, Alice (Nina Foch), who warns her to beware of Martha's duplicity. Back in New York, Helen is attacked by a masked robber, prompting the newlyweds to relocate to Kilronan for the duration of the pregnancy. Jackson reveals that he owns Kilronan, having inherited it from his late father. He also tells Helen how he, as a child, was responsible for his father's death, having accidentally pushed him down the stairs.

As the months pass, Jackson makes Kilronan profitable. Martha subtly sows seeds of discontent between Jackson and Helen, while spreading misinformation about Helen's frail health around town. On a weekend when Jackson is away for a derby, Helen discovers a nursery Martha has secretly prepared, and finds her necklace, stolen during the attack in NY, in a dresser drawer. She tries to escape, but Martha retrieves her, and drugs her to induce the pregnancy. She prepares to let Helen bleed to death after labor, but Jackson returns home unexpectedly and interrupts his mother's gruesome plan.

When Helen is back on her feet, she confronts Martha with the truth she's learned from Alice about how Jackson's father was killed. Helen's evidence triggers Jackson's repressed memory that his mother murdered his father. He announces his intention to sell Kilronan and put Martha out on the street.

HUSH would like to be a gut-wrenching Southern Gothic in the mold of HUSH. . . HUSH, SWEET CHARLOTTE (1964), but the only suspense is how long it will take Helen to realize what's going on . . . and it takes way too long. That mother Martha is a few mints shy of a julep is obvious from the opening scenes, her spoken devotion to Catholicism being Hollywood shorthand for mental instability. The trail of clues she leaves behind as she plots against Helen are as clandestine as the trail of road apples left behind a horse.

The story is premised on the completely absurd notion that Martha could keep the truth about her husband's "accidental" demise hushed up. The plot is further hobbled by compounding absurdities (wouldn't Granny Alice find an opportunity over the course of 20-odd years to take her grandson aside and set him straight?), until the movie is put out of our misery by the leadenly anti-climactic denouement.

Pouring on a honey-sweet drawl, Lange seems to be doing little more than a riff on Blanche DuBois in her portrayal of the malevolent mama. Both the role and the movie could desperately have used a little Bette Davis arch to liven up the proceedings. *(Violence, sexual situations, profanity.)*—P.R.

d, Jonathan Darby; p, Douglas Wick; co-p, Ginny Nugent; w, Jonathan Darby, Jane Rusconi (from a story by Jonathan Darby); ph, Andrew Dunn; ed, Dan Rae, Lynzee Klingman, Robert Leighton; m, Christopher Young; prod d, Thomas A. Walsh, Michael Johnston; art d, James F. Truesdale; set d, Michael Seirton; sound, Jay Meagher (mixer); fx, David P. Kelsey; casting, Heidi Levitt, Billy Hopkins; cos, Ann Roth; makeup, Vivian Baker, Alterian Studios Inc. (effects); stunts, Glory Fioramonti

Thriller/Drama **(PR: C MPAA: PG-13)**

I GOT THE HOOK UP ★

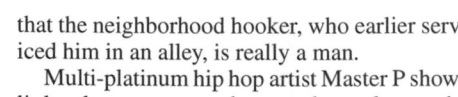

(U.S., 1998) 90m No Limit Films; Priority Films; Shooting Star Pictures; Master P Films ~ Dimension c

I

Master P *(Black)*; A.J. Johnson *(Blue)*; Gretchen Palmer *(Sweet Lorraine)*; Tiny Lister, billed as Tommy Lister Jr. *(T-Lay)*; Helen Martin *(Grandmother)*; John Witherspoon *(Mr. Mim)*; Anthony Boswell *(Little Brother)*; Mia X *(Lola Mae)*; Frantz Turner *(Dalton)*; Richard Keats *(Jim Brady)*; Joe Estevez *(Lamar Hunt)*; William Knight *(Agent In Charge)*; Mack Morris *(Andrew)*; Corey Miller *(T-Lay Boy #1)*; Edward Smith *(T-Lay Boy #2)*; Michael L. Taylor *(T-Lay Boy #3)*; Pablo Marz *(Hispanic Man)*; Tangie Ambrose *(Nasty Mouth Carla)*; Harrison White *(Tootsie Pop)*; Howard Mungo *(Mr. Tucker)*; Laura Hayes *(Mrs. Tucker)*; Richard Balin *(Communications Trucker)*; Ella Mae Evans *(Customer #1)*; Kourtney Locke *(Little Girl)*; John Wesley *(Minister)*; Lawrence Williams *(Family Member #1)*; Vercy Carter *(Family Member #2)*; Izetta Karp *(Ms. Rose)*; Paula Bellamy Franklin *(Old Lady #1)*; Dollie Butler *(Old Lady #2)*; Tommy Chunn *(Dooley)*; Leland Ellis *(Man)*; Sacha Kemp *(Woman)*; Judy Jean Berns *(Customer #2)*; Duffy Rich *(Policeman #1)*; Andrew Shack *(Policeman #2)*; Cindy L. Sorensen *(Martha)*; Dana Woods *(Big Daddy)*; Will Gill Jr. *(Black Lamar)*; Jerry Dixon *(Black Jim)*; Ice Cube *(Gun Runner)*; Fiend *(Roscoe)*; Daniel Garcia *(Lorraine's Lover)*; David Garcia; Eric Vidal *(DJs)*; Michael D. Harris *(Homeless Man)*; Sheryl Underwood *(Bad Mouth Bessie)*; Maryam Beigi; Shantele Blackmon; Stacia Gardner; Ursula Houstin; Lori Morrissen; Dora Riestra; Shayna Ryan; Tina White *(Topless Performers)*; Snoop Doggy Dog; Daryl Anderson; T. David Binns; Joshua Chew; Rico Crowder; Rasheed H. Hogan; Lawrence Johnson; Desmond Mapp; Greg Mapp; Billy Moore; Bobby J. Sardie Jr.; David Weiner *(Bar Patrons)*

A couple of inner-city hustlers attempt an elaborate cellular phone scam in this feeble attempt at streetwise comedy. The more interesting scam is how this film reached theaters in the first place.

Deep in the 'hood of South Central Los Angeles, straight man Black (Master P) and his wacky, sawed-off sidekick Blue (A.J. Johnson) sell fenced goods from the back of their van. Their defective wares, along with an adamant "all sales final" policy, leads to a continual stream of irate customers. Spotting a lost, white delivery man, Black claims to be the sought after Mr. Goldstein, then he fraudulently signs for a large shipment of cellular phones. His lustful girlfriend Lorraine (Gretchen Palmer), who happens to work for a cellular phone company, provides illegal technical support. Soon everyone in sight, including Blue's reefer smoking grandmother (Helen Martin), totes a Black and Blue phone and the boys rake in the profits.

The bubble bursts when the clogged airwaves cause repeatedly crossed connections and widespread dissatisfaction. The situation goes from bad to worse—a mob boss, using a Black and Blue phone, inadvertently broadcasts the location of a $70,000 payoff over the radio. The boss's enforcer T-Lay (Tommy Lister Jr.) pursues the conning duo. But he's not the only one. FBI agents are also on the trail, as is Dalton (Franz Turner), a stiff little bureaucrat from the cellular company where Lorraine worked before she was fired for her involvement in the scam.

Black and Blue defeat T-Lay by slipping one of his stooges a laced joint and rolling the enforcer himself down a hill in a Porta-John. The two FBI agents are uncovered as African-Americans posing as Caucasians (they didn't want to wait for affirmative action), and Dalton is humiliated when he finds out that the neighborhood hooker, who earlier serviced him in an alley, is really a man.

Multi-platinum hip hop artist Master P shows little talent as an actor here, and even less as the cowriter of this juvenile collection of obvious, badly executed gags. Master P and his collaborators, Leroy Douglas and Carrie Mungo, stitch together repetitive, profane street lingo, a childishly conceived, hard to believe premise (the cellular phone scam), and broad, ill-timed attempts at comedy. They get little support from first-time director Michael Martin, who has a knack for placing the camera in the most serviceable, uninteresting places.

Ridiculous things happen with no rhyme or reason; the conventional rules of comedy (set-up and payoff) are ignored—as when Blue demonstrates farcical talent in kung fu-fighting in a set-to with T-Lay and his crew. Blue's fighting skill hasn't been mentioned before, and is never seen again—even when the character would have a need for it (instead, later potential opportunities for a fight scene are avoided). With a seeming need to plaster his name all over this mess, Master P gets third billing as the film's executive producer. He also contributes a couple of songs. Besides himself, he packs the soundtrack with fellow rappers Bone Thugs-N-Harmony, Jay-Z, Mystikal, Sikk the Shocker, C-Murder and Sons of Funk—many from his own No Limit record label. If selling CDs was P's only real goal, he and director Michael Martin should have simply cranked out a series of music videos. Schlock goes down easier in three-minute doses. *(Extreme profanity, violence, nudity.)*—T.Y.

d, Michael Martin; p, Jonathan Heuer; exec p, Master P; assoc p, Leroy Douglas; co-p, Andrew Shack; w, Master P, Leroy Douglas, Carrie Mungo; ph, Antonio Calvache; ed, T. David Binns; m, Toomy Coster, Brad Fairman, Beats By Da Pound, Master P; prod d, Michael Pearce; set d, Jennifer Fraser; sound, Rick Maclane, Carlos Isais (recordist); fx, SPFX; casting, Stevie "Black" Lockett, Megalarge Casting; cos, Jhane Isaacs; makeup, Gloria Elias, Marc Linn (effects), Total Fabrication (effects); stunts, Julius LeFlore

Comedy **(PR: O MPAA: R)**

I LOVE YOU, DON'T TOUCH ME! ★★½

(U.S., 1998) 86m Goldwyn Entertainment; Westie Films; Big Hair Productions ~ MGM/UA c

Marla Schaffel *(Katie)*; Mitchell Whitfield *(Ben)*; Meredith Scott Lynn *(Janet)*; Michael Harris *(Richard Webber)*; Darryl Theirse *(Jones)*; Nancy Sorel *(Elizabeth)*; Wally Kurth *(David Barclay)*; Jack McGee *(Lou Candela)*; Julie Ariola *(Mom)*; Victor Raider-Wexler *(Dad)*; Sara Van Horn *(Analyst)*; Debbie Munroe *(Margo)*; Tim deZarn *(Vagrant)*; Janine Venable *(Deirdre)*; George P. Saunders *(Ted)*; Michael Candela *(Audition Man)*; Ramesh Pandey *(Bob Yager)*; Jackie Debatin *(Jenny)*; Nell Balaban *(Nina)*; Julie Davis *(Lisa)*; Michael Dell *(Asshole #1)*; Mathew R. Eyraud *(Asshole #2)*; Tom Hodges *(Asshole #3)*; Mitchell Rose *(Asshole #4)*; Geoffrey Infeld *(Club Sin Hunk #1)*; Mark St. James *(Club Sin Hunk #2)*; Shannon McLeod *(Ben's Dream Date)*; Melanie Wachsman *(Naked Blonde)*; Julia Bruglio *(Naked Woman in Shower)*; Andrew Camp *(Clark's Lover)*

First-time writer-director Julie Davis crafts a few amusing moments in this bitchy-on-the-outside, mellow-on-the-inside meditation on the imperfect nature of love. Betraying its severe budgetary limitations, the film is a likable though forgettable debut effort.

Katie (Marla Schaffel) catches her boyfriend cheating on her. When the naked young man runs after her to explain, he gets run over by a car. Four years later, Katie still hasn't gotten over the shock of the event, to the extent that she hasn't had another relationship. Describing her life as a "romantic holocaust," she maintains a close relationship with the ever-sensitive Ben (Mitchell Whitfield), who repeatedly expresses his love for her. Instead of reciprocating his feelings, Katie fixes Ben up with a series of losers. When she introduces him to one of her fellow office temps, Janet (Meredith Scott Lynn), a skeptic with a penchant for jumping from bed to bed, the two hit it off. Katie, a 25-year-old virgin who's scared to fall in love, is so sickened by the couple's happiness that she lambastes Janet for her sluttiness and severs her friendship with Ben.

Driving along the highway frustrated, the unfulfilled office worker rear-ends a Ferrari. Uninsured, she accepts a lunch invitation from the debonair driver, Richard (Michael Harris), a womanizer almost twice her age. Full of come-ons, he informs her that "there are no accidents, just cosmic conveniences." Katie, an aspiring singer, is reluctantly turned on by this wealthy composer. After losing her virginity and falling in love with Richard, Katie catches the cad bedding another woman.

Heartbroken, she apologizes to Janet, who has since broken up with Ben. Janet convinces Katie to join her at a pickup joint so they can find partners for meaningless sex. Katie tries, but can't go through with the plan; what she wants is love. Mending things with Ben, she finally returns his love.

Ten minutes into I LOVE YOU, DON'T TOUCH ME!, when Ben presents Katie with a love poem, it becomes obvious that she'll eventually see the light, and the two will wind up falling into a clinch before the final fade. Such predictability is endemic to even the best romantic comedies, from IT HAPPENED ONE NIGHT (1934) to WHEN HARRY MET SALLY. . . (1989). The challenge is to make the journey so diverting that no amount of telegraphing will ruin the inevitable union. In that respect, the movie comes up short.

Katie's sour disposition does, however, provide some comic fodder. It's certainly provokes a chuckle when she describes a woman's discussion group as something out of a Henry Jaglom film, or when she wonders aloud during a supposed moment of abandon how a man can put his tongue between her legs without even knowing her name. But the bulk of I LOVE YOU feels stale, particularly when the characters theorize on the ways in which men aren't built to remain monogamous. Most importantly, Katie and Ben simply aren't charismatic enough characters; the viewer doesn't connect to them enough to care whether they will embrace at the end. Without this connection, there isn't any urgency, and the film just fizzles out as it proceeds.

In addition, the film never transcends its shoestring status. The camera seems to have been placed before the actors with little thought given to framing, and there are several unfocused shots (*not* apparently intended as an artistic statement). The actors are all competent, but nothing more. Marla Schaffel plays Katie throughout with too much of a kvetchy snarl, and Michael Harris's effete, intelligent bearing immediately qualifies the actor as the poor man's Jeremy Irons.

At one point in the film, Katie announces that she simply wants to find a nice Jewish man with a big penis and a big wallet. Her friend says she should settle for one out of three. If first-time filmmaker Julie Davis were judged on three criteria—engaging characters, memorable dialogue, and competent visuals—she would just miss on the first two, and lose out entirely on the third. *(Sexual situations, nudity, profanity.)*—T.Y.

d, Julie Davis; p, Julie Davis, Scott Chosed; exec p, Jennifer Chaiken; assoc p, Matthew R. Eyraud, Meredith Cruse, Michael Hirshenson, Jonathan Blinderman; co-p, Christopher Keenan; w, Julie Davis; ph, Mark Allan Putnam; ed, Julie Davis; m, Jane Ford; prod d, Carol Strober; set d, Caroline Halili; sound, Lee Howell (mixer); casting, Karen Church; cos, Wendy Greiner; makeup, Brandi Robertson; stunts, Ignacio Alvarez

Romance/Comedy **(PR: C MPAA: R)**

I MARRIED A STRANGE PERSON! ★★½

(U.S., 1998) 73m PlympCorp Productions; Italoons ~ Lions Gate Films c

VOICES OF: Charis Michelson; Tom Larson; Richard Spore; Toni Rossi *(Kerry)*; J.B. Adams; John Russo; Max Brandt; Ruth Ray; Chris Cooke; Etta Valeska

The most prominent independent American animator of his time, Bill Plympton fails to bring sufficient variety or any sense of proportion to I MARRIED A STRANGE PERSON, a shamelessly but cheerfully uncouth tale about a young man whose life is changed when he suddenly acquires unlimited power. After two fornicating ducks collide with his satellite TV dish, Grant Boyer sprouts an unsightly lobe on the back of his neck, a growth that gives him the ability to make his fantasies come true instantly—including transforming his new bride Kerry into a series of other women in bed.

When he sees Grant on television demonstrating his miraculous powers, Larson Giles, a broadcasting executive in quest of 100-percent ratings, resolves to appropriate the young man's mysterious gift. After being abducted by Giles's right-hand man, Colonel Ferguson, Grant escapes and is recaptured. During this period, the precious lobe is snatched and self-implanted in turn by Giles, Ferguson, and Solly Jim, a washed-up comedian. All hell ultimately breaks loose as the two villains and their awesome private army pursue Grant and Kerry, who has come to her husband's rescue. After a spectacular battle, the lobe winds up in the stomach of a dog, who uses it to conjure a batch of mammoth bones.

Animated by the tireless Plympton without the help of in-betweeners or computers, I MARRIED A STRANGE PERSON indicated that he should stick to the short format, in which he excels. Creating an animated feature film for adults is almost a lost cause from the outset most grown-ups need to see real people after a while. Plympton seems to have sensed that in order to hold audience attention a full-length cartoon must alter its graphics often, but I MARRIED A STRANGE PERSON's stylistic changes are neither frequent nor radical enough to sustain interest over the long haul. The movie's most successful interludes (as was the case with Plympton's first feature, the 1992 film THE TUNE) are those that could qualify as self-sufficient shorts: a pair of amusing songs ("How'd You Get So Cute?" and "Would You Love Me If. . . ") in which wickedly scurrilous lyrics are mismated to sprightly, innocuous tunes—and highlights from a wacky self-help videotape entitled "How to Make Love to a Woman" (previewed in 1997's compilation film MONDO PLYMPTON).

As a scan of the above synopsis will verify, the film's pseudo-sci-fi plot line is willfully, overwhelmingly stupid. What it required was a writer like Harvey Kurtzman or Mel Brooks to render it with *inspired* stupidity.

The picture opens with a Pablo Picasso quote attacking tastefulness, a statement he might have retracted if he were alive to see I MARRIED A STRANGE PERSON. What follows is over an hour of outrageous sight gags: a woman's mouth is invaded by a platoon of beetles; another woman experiences a literal "fat attack"; a couple of army tanks engage in sexual intercourse; ad nauseam. Despite his worst intentions, however, a certain irresponsible goodheartedness prevents Plympton's work from being truly shocking and it is this benign quality that renders the resolute tastelessness of I MARRIED A STRANGE PERSON essentially toothless. Some adult viewers, consequently, may find the film's scattershot grossness simultaneously too much and not enough. The dudes in ninth grade, on the other hand, will probably eat the movie up—if they can get in to see it. *(Graphic violence, extensive nudity, sexual situations, profanity.)*—D.T.

d, Bill Plympton; p, Bill Plympton; co-p, John Holderried; w, Bill Plympton; ph, John Donnelly; ed, Anthony Arcidi; m, Maureen McElheron; prod d, Signe Baumane; anim, Bill Plympton, Greg Pair, Graham Blyth; sound, David Rovin

Animated/Comedy **(PR: O MPAA: NR)**

I STILL KNOW WHAT YOU DID LAST SUMMER ★★
(U.S., 1998) 96m Original Film; Mandalay Entertainment; Neal H. Moritz Productions ~ Columbia c

Jennifer Love Hewitt *(Julie James)*; Freddie Prinze Jr. *(Ray Bronson)*; Brandy, billed as Brandy Norwood *(Karla Wilson)*; Mekhi Phifer *(Tyrell)*; Muse Watson *(Benjamin Willis/Fisherman)*; Bill Cobbs *(Estes)*; Matthew Settle *(Will Benson)*; Jeffrey Combs *(Mr. Brooks)*; Jennifer Esposito *(Nancy)*; John Hawkes *(Dave)*; Ellerine Harding, billed as Ellerine *(Olga)*; Ben Brown *(Darick the Dockhand)*; Red West *(Paulsen)*; Michael P. Byrne *(Thurston)*; Michael Bryan French *(Doctor)*; Dee Ann Helsel *(Nurse)*; John Harrington *(Todd)*; Mark Boone Jr. *(Pawn Shop Owner)*; Dan Priest *(Professor)*; Sylvia Short *(Old Woman)*

The unimaginatively-titled sequel to 1997's horror hit I KNOW WHAT YOU DID LAST SUMMER is frustratingly contrived and conventional until an exciting conclusion.

A year after apparently killing vengeful fisherman Ben Willis, Julie James (Jennifer Love Hewitt), now attending a New England college, is still suffering nightmares. Her relationship with boyfriend Ray (Freddie Prinze Jr.), who has remained back home, has become strained. Julie's roommate Karla (Brandy) wins four tickets for a Bahamas vacation, and she invites her boyfriend Tyrell (Mekhi Phifer) and Julie, who calls Ray to ask him along. He turns her down, but then changes his mind and heads for the college, only to be waylaid by Willis (Muse Watson) and hospitalized. When Ray doesn't show, Karla asks Will Benson (Matthew Settle), a student who's romantically interested in Julie, to join them on the trip.

The four arrive at the remote Tower Bay resort, only to find that it's the last weekend of operation before the place closes down for hurricane season. Julie begins seeing increasingly frightening signs that Willis is alive and has followed them there. Everyone discounts her claims, and Willis starts killing off the resort's staff, along with local ganja dealer Titus (Jack Black) and finally manager Brooks (Jeffrey Combs). As a storm blows up, Julie's friends finally become convinced of the danger, and Willis kills Tyrell and renders Karla unconscious, whereupon Will reveals that he's actually the fisherman's son and arranged the whole trip. All the while, Ray has been struggling to make it to Tower Bay, and arrives as Willis and Will are about to kill Julie. He contrives Will's death before being laid low by Willis, whom Julie then shoots down. She and Ray are reunited with the wounded Karla. Some time later, Julie is living happily with Ray, but Willis shows up again to attack her. . .

Before it devolved into standard stalker fare, the original I KNOW was a better-than-average teen chiller that focused on its characters' guilt over covering up a violent incident, and the way that guilt informed their actions when the past came back to haunt them. I STILL KNOW attempts a similar resonance, as Julie is still troubled about prior events, imagining Willis is stalking her when he's not really there. This is a promising starting point, but its effectiveness is quickly blunted when it becomes clear that Willis really is still around.

While the idea of turning a tropical paradise into rain-swept terror grounds is a good one (and Vernon Layton's cinematography creates a foreboding atmosphere), scripter Trey Callaway and director Danny Cannon's attempts to build tension are pedestrian at best. At least half a dozen times, a character walks slowly towards a door from which strange sounds have issued, while John Frizzell's music swells to the point where one knows exactly when the jump is going to occur. Cannon does pull it together in the rousing last half hour, staging some vivid mayhem that has a charge the rest of the film lacks. Then, unfortunately, he and Callaway spoil it all with a ridiculous "it's still not over" ending.

Not helping matters are the movie's many implausibilities: How does Willis know that Ray changes his mind about coming to see Julie, and exactly where to wait for him? Why does Will adopt a name (Benson = Ben's son) that gives away his identity? And, most important: If Will is already attending Julie's college, why do he and his father go to all the trouble to arrange the Bahamas trip in the first place? *(Graphic violence, sexual situations, substance abuse, extreme profanity.)*—M.G.

d, Danny Cannon; p, Neal H. Moritz, Erik Feig, Stokely Chaffin, William S. Beasley; w, Trey Callaway (based on the characters created by Lois Duncan); ph, Vernon Layton; ed, Peck Prior; m, John Frizzell; prod d, Doug Kraner; art d, Charles Butcher, Scott Ritenour; set d, Jan Bergstrom; sound, David Ronne (mixer); fx, John Milinac; casting, Jackie Burch; cos, Dan Lester; makeup, Bonita DeHaven; stunts, Freddie Hice

Horror **(PR: C MPAA: R)**

I THINK I DO ★★★
(U.S., 1998) 92m Sauce Entertainment; Danger Filmworks; House of Pain ~ Strand Releasing c

Alexis Arquette *(Bob)*; Maddie Corman *(Beth)*; Guillermo Diaz *(Eric)*; Marianne Hagan *(Sarah)*; Jamie Harrold *(Matt)*; Christian Maelen *(Brendan)*; Lauren Velez *(Carol)*; Tuc Watkins *(Sterling Scott)*; Patricia Mauceri *(Mrs. Gonzalez)*; Marni Nixon *(Aunt Alice)*; Elizabeth Rodriguez *(Celia)*; Dechen Thurman *(Photographer)*

I THINK I DO is a fun, fast-paced, gay variation on WHEN HARRY MET SALLY. . . (1989). Writer-director Brian Sloan has fashioned a surprisingly good screwball comedy about the absurdities of contemporary romance, without a trace of the "coming-out blues" plot line that seems to be de rigueur in gay films of late.

Five years after graduating college, best buddies Bob (Alexis Arquette) and Brendan (Christian Maelen), along with pals Sarah (Marianne Hagan) and Beth (Maddie Corman), are reunited for the wedding of their friends Carol (Lauren Velez) and Matt (Jamie Harrold) in Washington, D.C. Bob has always had an unrequited crush on Brendan, who's always claimed to be heterosexual. But this time, Bob brings along his hunky boyfriend Sterling (Tuc Watkins), a leading man on a soap opera for which Bob writes in New York. When he spots Brendan arriving, Bob's feelings are immediately rekindled. Most confusing, though, is that Brendan seems to be reciprocating. His flirtation is almost too much for Bob to take.

Confused and unsure, Bob tries to avoid Brendan's charms, but a hotel mix-up forces the two of them to share sleeping quarters. After a night of passionate sex, Bob suffers from morning-after guilt—and is horrified to discover that he is sporting a huge hickey. Desperate to hide the evidence from Sterling, Bob wears a neck brace, claiming he had an accident. After a series of mishaps, Sterling and the other guests soon figure out what has happened. Bob tries desperately to comfort his enraged boyfriend, but Sterling dumps him. Dejected and alone, Bob heads home and runs into Brendan at the train station, where they discuss a possible future together.

After a series of forgettable roles in indie films, Alexis Arquette (brother of Rosanna, Patricia, et al.) seems to have found his niche in screwball farce. He's not given much to do here, other than to react to the wacky goings-on, but his double takes and boyish cluelessness are engaging. In fact, the whole cast seems to have fun chewing up the scenery. Lauren Velez ("New York Undercover"), who played a loud Latina archetype in Darnell Martin's highly overrated I LIKE IT LIKE THAT (1994), is more appealing here as Carol. Sloan commendably doesn't play up her character's ethnic background for comic relief; the fact that she's a Hispanic woman isn't an issue. Sloan also depicts the gay protagonists as regular guys having a tough time in their private lives, not as stereotypical comedic stick-figures (Maelen in particular distinguishes himself with a suave, sexy presence). Sloan's sense of respect for the characters and their need for human contact lends I THINK I DO an extra, humane dimension.

His grasp of pacing and storytelling is evident as well (although he could have left the ubiquitous "I Think I Love You" by the Partridge Family off the soundtrack without damaging the playful spirit of the film). Sloan seems to know exactly where to situate a pratfall or a sight-gag for maximum effect without compromising the integrity of the characters or their romantic dilemmas. Even two subplots—one involving Carol's sister's pursuit of Brendan's pothead friend Eric (Guillermo Diaz) and the other centering around man-hungry Beth's flirtation with the wedding photographer—are goofily diverting. Most importantly, everyone lives happily ever after! *(Adult situations, profanity.)*—D.O.

d, Brian Sloan; p, Lane Janger; exec p, Daryl Roth, Marcus Hu, Jon Gerrans, Robert Miller; w, Brian Sloan; ph, Milton Kam; ed, Francois Keraudren; prod d, Debbie Devilla; sound, Robert Taz Larrea; casting, Stephanie Corsalini; cos, Kevin Donaldson, Victoria Farrell

Romance/Comedy **(PR: C MPAA: R)**

I WENT DOWN ★★½

(U.K., 1998) 107m Treasure Films; BBC Films; Shooting Gallery ~ TSG Pictures c

Brendan Gleeson *(Bunny Kelly)*; Peter McDonald *(Git Hynes)*; Tony Doyle *(Tom French)*; Peter Caffrey *(Frank Grogan)*; Antoine Byrne *(Sabrina Bradley)*; David Wilmot *(Anto)*; Michael McElhatton *(Johnner Doyle)*; Joe Gallagher *(Steo Gannon)*; Liam Regan *(Little Boy at Teresa's)*; Kevin Hely *(Petrol Station Attendant)*; Eamonn Hunt *(Cork Barman)*; Frank O'Sullivan *(Cork Man No. 1)*; Jason Byrne *(Cork Man No. 2)*; Eamon A. Kelly *(Cork Man No. 3)*; Carly Baker *(Caroline)*; Carmel Callan *(Teresa)*; Margaret Callan *(Caroline's Mum)*; Denis Conway *(Garda)*; Donal O'Kelly *(The Friendly Face)*; Amelia Crowley *(Receptionist)*; Conor McPherson *(Loser in Nightclub)*; Rachel Brady *(Git's Girlfriend)*; Anne Kent *(Bunny's Girlfriend)*; Johnny Murphy *(Sonny Mulligan)*; Don Wycherley *(Young Frank)*; John Bergin *(Young Tom)*

A character comedy with a wafer-thin crime-caper plot line, I WENT DOWN relates the adventures of two guys forced by a gangster to do an unsavory errand. A film festival favorite, this likable movie broke Ireland's all-time box-office record for domestic independent productions.

Git Hynes (Peter McDonald) is visited in prison by girlfriend Sabrina (Antoine Byrne), who tells him she is keeping company with his pal Anto (David Wilmot). Released three months later, young Git saves Anto from a bad beating by thugs and, as recompense, is required by the thugs' boss, Tom French (Tony Doyle), to locate and bring back to Dublin an old crime cohort named Frank Grogan. Git will be accompanied on his mission by Bunny Kelly (Brendan Gleeson), a small-time criminal.

Git and Bunny drive to Cork, where they find and snatch Grogan (Peter Caffrey), who claims that French is after him for sleeping with his wife. After checking into a hotel, the two abductors go downstairs to the bar, where Bunny confesses that French has blackmail power over him; the partners then pick up a pair of women and spend the night with them. Git tells his bedmate (Rachel Brady) that his sickly father was the actual perpetrator of the crime for which Git did time.

Grogan escapes, is recaptured, and is delivered by Git to a middleman (Donal O'Kelly), who is about to execute both men when Bunny arrives to rescue them. Then French, his two emissaries, and their hostage rendezvous in the woods. After valuable counterfeiting plates and a large cache of bills are dug up, French and Grogan are killed in a shootout.

Bunny delivers a money envelope to Sabrina on behalf of Git. Now free of French and in the chips, the two new buddies embark for America.

Although there is nothing arty about this modest, straightforward, and unpretentious film, I WENT DOWN could be described as an "art-house comedy" in that it's more droll than hilarious, subtle rather than sentimental, keyed to character rather than to action. Quite well done, it would have been even better with female characters who are less peripheral—it might have been fun, for example, to meet the sexy but unseen Mrs. French, whom Grogan describes as "a smashing little broad. . . Do anything to you—do anything." As things stand, the picture's lone lasses are Sabrina, whose sole narrative function is to periodically attempt to return Git's ring, and Git's nameless pickup, who shares with him a brief interlude of sex and pillow talk before exiting the story as abruptly as she entered it.

Viewers who haven't been victimized by over-hype will find that I WENT DOWN goes down easily. The picture is enhanced by Cian de Buitlear's crisp cinematography and Dario Marinelli's jangling music, an invigorating rock-and-roll score in the "Green Onions" and "Mashed Potatoes" tradition. Best gag: Tied to his hotel bed for the evening, the luckless Grogan fumbles and drops the TV remote control, just after it lights on a talking-heads special devoted to algebra.

I WENT DOWN's creators were proud of their film's eschewal of Irish-movie cliches. As recited by producer Robert Walpole, these include: "(1) a crippling guilt complex, (2) a long-suffering Irish mother, (3) a brute of an Irish father, (4) a loveless marriage, (5) a horse, (6) an Irish guy and a foreign woman who is dying for sex with him, (7) a barroom brawl" and "(8) the Troubles, of course." *(Violence, nudity, sexual situations, extreme profanity.)*—D.T.

d, Paddy Breathnach; p, Robert Walpole; exec p, Mark Shivas, David Collins, Rod Stoneman; w, Conor McPherson; ph, Cian de Buitlear; ed, Emer Reynolds; m, Dario Marinelli; prod d, Zoe MacLeod; art d, Tom McCullagh; sound, Simon J. Willis (recordist); fx, Maurice Foley; casting, Deirdre O'Kane, Fiona McGarry; cos, Kathy Strachan; makeup, Debbie Boylan; stunts, Phillippe Zone

Comedy/Crime/Drama **(PR: C MPAA: R)**

IL TESTIMONE DELLO SPOSO
(SEE: BEST MAN, THE)

I'LL BE HOME FOR CHRISTMAS ★½
(U.S., 1998) 86m Mandeville Films; Walt Disney Pictures; Leo Productions; Buena Vista ~ Buena Vista c

Jonathan Taylor Thomas *(Jake Wilkinson)*; Jessica Biel *(Allie)*; Adam LaVorgna *(Eddie)*; Gary Cole *(Jake's Father)*; Eve Gordon *(Carolyn)*; Lauren Maltby *(Tracey)*; Andrew Lauer *(Nolan)*; Sean O'Bryan *(Max)*; Lesley Boone *(Marjorie)*; Amzie Strickland *("Tom Tom Girl" Mary)*; Natalie Barish *("Tom Tom Girl" Darlene)*; Mark De La Cruz *(Esteban)*; Kathleen Freeman *("Tom Tom Girl" Gloria)*; Jack Kenny *(Gabby)*; Celia Kushner *("Tom Tom Girl" Mama)*; Blair Slater *(Ian)*; P.J. Prinsloo *(The Brandt-Man)*; James Sherry *(The Murph-Man)*; Kevin Hansen *(The Ken-Man)*; Alexandria Mitchell *(Little Girl in Hospital)*; Eric Pospisil *(Little Boy at Bus Station)*; Cathy Weseluck *(Wendy Richards)*; Peter Kelamis *(Clyde)*; Betty Linde *(Older Lady on the Bus)*; Awaovieyi Agie *(Service Man)*; Brendan Beiser *(Bellhop)*; Graeme Kingston *(Pizza Eating Santa)*; Ian Robison *(Mayor Wilson)*; Ernie Jackson *(Kenyan Santa)*; Kurte Max Runte *(Taxi Driver)*; Nicole Oliver *(Ticket Agent)*; Tasha Simms *(Parade Manager)*; Dimitry Chepovetsky *(Angel)*; Dolores Drake *(Fraulein Maid)*; Chris Willes *(Race Official #1)*; Nick Misura *(Groundskeeper)*

I'LL BE HOME FOR CHRISTMAS combines two formulas that have permeated the market for young people's movies in the past few years: the college road-trip scenario and the rich-kid-learns-about-responsibility story line. The film attempts to teach a lesson about the true spirit of Christmas and importance of family, but proceeds in such an unrealistic, farcical way that even the youngest kids in the audience will remain unconvinced.

Jake (Jonathan Taylor Thomas) is a spoiled rich boy from suburban New York who is disturbed that his father (Gary Cole) has remarried after his mother's death. Jake attends college in California, where he spends more time conning people than studying. Unfortunately, one of his scams—involving an attempt to aid students intent on cheating on an exam—goes awry, and the disgruntled victims, led by Jake's rival Eddie (Adam LaVorgna), knock Jake out, dress him in a Santa Claus suit, take him to the desert, and leave him there.

This unexpected turn of events leaves Jake in dire straits, since his father, desperately trying to get Jake to come home for the holiday, has offered his prize Porsche to Jake if he can be home by 6:00 on Christmas Eve. Jake had planned to fly home with his girlfriend Allie (Jessica Biel), but when he can't find his way back to the dorm in time she accepts a ride from Eddie. Desperate to find his way home, Jake begins a series of hitchhiking escapades, and then manages to scrape up money for a bus ticket. When Jake's bus stops for gas, he sees a local news report and discovers that Allie and Eddie are only a few towns away. He cons the bus driver into stopping at their hotel, but Jake's sweet-talk doesn't work. Allie discovers that Jake cares more about the Porsche than her. She steals Jake's place on the bus, leaving him to ride with Eddie, who promptly dumps him by the side of the road.

Jake stumbles upon a five-kilometer foot race for people dressed in Santa costumes. He wins the race and its $1000 prize, but he learns that the winner traditionally donates the money to the poor. Feeling guilty, he gives the money back. As a last resort, he sneaks into the baggage crate of an airplane, and makes it home just in time. He makes up with Allie, then arrives at his house at 5:59. He waits until 6:01 to walk in. His dad offers him the Porsche anyway, but Jake, after three days spent on the road, has learned the value of responsibility and the need for close relationships. He will return home every Christmas and they can share the car then.

I'LL BE HOME FOR CHRISTMAS asks us to accept that a selfish and conniving person like Jake can be reborn as a generous and loving soul after only three days of mildly adverse experiences. The filmmakers seem so intent on moving the plot along that several absurd and impossible-to-explain events are thrown into the mix. Even if the viewer can accept the fact that a big Christmas Eve parade would proceed for some reason through a sparsely-populated suburban side street, it's unlikely that anyone could accept Jake running into Eddie and Allie purely by accident three times during a 3000-mile trip. It's also hard to believe that Jake would return the money he wins from the Santa Claus Race, when he is completely stranded, and even a small portion of the money could have paid for a bus ticket home.

"Home Improvement" star Jonathan Taylor Thomas lacks the charm required for the part of a con artist. The other young cast members prove uniformly awful, and the normally entertaining Gary Cole (who did well with the cartoonlike caring-dad role in the latter-day BRADY BUNCH movies) merely goes through the motions.

The filmmakers compensate for the film's plethora of inconsistencies by supplying plenty of crass jokes about binge eating, dog flatulence, and vomit. It thus came as no surprise that this solidly seasonal film was released somewhat prematurely, in early November of 1998, so that it could die a quick death in theaters before the Christmas season had truly kicked into gear. *(Profanity.)*—A.M.

d, Arlene Sanford; p, Tracey Trench, David Hoberman; exec p, Robin French; co-p, Justis Greene; w, Harris Goldberg, Tom Nursall (based on story by Michael Allin); ph, Hiro Narita; ed, Anita Brandt-Burgoyne; m, John Debney; prod d, Cynthia Charette; art d, Alexander Cochrane; set d, Lin MacDonald; sound, Rob Young; fx, William H. Orr; casting, Roger Mussenden, Karen Church; cos, Maya Mani; makeup, Sandy Cooper, Connie Parker

Comedy **(PR: A MPAA: PG)**

ILLTOWN ★★½
(U.S., 1998) 97m Shooting Gallery ~ Shooting Gallery c

Michael Rapaport *(Dante)*; Lili Taylor *(Micky)*; Adam Trese *(Gabriel)*; Kevin Corrigan *(Francis—"Cisco")*; Angela Featherstone *(Lilly)*; Tony Danza *(D'Avalon)*; Isaac Hayes *(George)*; Paul Schulze *(Lucas)*; Saul Stein *(Gunther)*

Dishonor among thieves. Nick Gomez shifts stylistic gears with ILLTOWN (the title appears onscreen in all lower-cased letters), a hallucinogenic take on the same bad boy-gangster territory he explored in a more realistic fashion in LAWS OF GRAVITY (1992) and NEW JERSEY DRIVE (1995). This time out, Gomez embroiders his tale of a drug dealer confronting his past with a dream-like quality; the drama, unfortunately, winds up taking a back seat to the artistic aspirations.

In Miami, Dante (Michael Rapaport), his girlfriend, Micky (Lili Taylor), and his partner, Cisco (Kevin Corrigan), specialize in dealing drugs to the city's youth. The news that Dante's ex-partner, Gabriel (Adam Trese), has been released from jail, comes as a bad omen to Dante, since it was Dante who had helped the police catch Gabriel during a frame-up years earlier.

Though Gabriel talks of "saving" Dante, he secretly seeks revenge. Micky, meanwhile, urges Dante to leave Miami with her deaf younger brother. Dante, instead, tries to preempt Gabriel's plans by aligning himself with a mob boss, D'Avalon (Tony Danza). But by lethally "spiking" Dante's drug supply and hiring some young thugs to kill a cop on Dante's trail, Gabriel implicates Dante in a serious offense. D'Avalon tries to help Dante, but fails to stop Gabriel from killing Cisco. Dante and Gabriel then meet for a bloody shootout that ends in their deaths.

ILLTOWN may develop a cult following, thanks to Nick Gomez's stylized approach to the gangster melodrama, but this experiment-gone-wrong may make some viewers wonder if its always wise to reformalize conventions. The impressionistic set designs, languid pacing, and minimal narrative set the film apart from the classics (LITTLE CAESAR, SCARFACE, WHITE HEAT) as well as Gomez's earlier successes, though not always to the most substantial effect.

Perhaps ILLTOWN would have been more gripping if it had made better sense of Dante's back story and motivations. The *in medias res* approach fails to draw the viewer in, despite the many flashbacks. It would seem hard to make such a basic story so complicated and confusing, but Gomez does this by mixing the oblique with the obvious. He also fails to update the central woman's role—the moll—and turns the bloody gunplay into the same boys-will-be-boys cliche one finds in most action pictures.

On the plus side, Gomez has assembled an excellent cast. It's hard not to be drawn in by these actors, even when they are underused (like leads Taylor and Rapaport) or misused (like comic actor Corrigan looking uncomfortable in a straight "heavy" role). Even television's Tony Danza turns in a fine job, although his role as a gay gangster is just another stereotype that needs updating. While it is admirable that Gomez tried something different, it appears that his third—not second—film is the one where he fell into his "sophomore slump." *(Graphic violence, adult situations, substance abuse, extreme profanity.)*—E.M.

d, Nick Gomez; p, David L. Bushell; exec p, Larry Meistrich, Donald C. Carter; co-p, Burtt Harris; w, Nick Gomez; ph, Jim Denault; ed, Tracy Granger; m, Brian Keane; prod d, Susan Bolles; sound, Jeff Kushner (design); casting, Walken & Jaffe Casting; cos, Sara Slotnick

Crime/Drama **(PR: O MPAA: R)**

IMPOSTORS, THE ★★★½

(U.S., 1998) 102m LowTide Productions; First Cold Press Productions; Fox Searchlight ~ Fox Searchlight c

Stanley Tucci *(Arthur)*; Oliver Platt *(Maurice)*; Lili Taylor *(Lily)*; Alfred Molina *(Jeremy Burtom)*; Campbell Scott *(Meistrich)*; Hope Davis *(Emily)*; Steve Buscemi *(Happy Franks)*; Billy Connolly *(Sparks)*; Isabella Rossellini *(Queen—Veiled Woman)*; Dana Ivey *(Mrs. Essendine)*; Matt McGrath *(Marco)*; Allison Janney *(Maxine—Maxi)*; Richard Jenkins *(Johnny—Frenchman)*; Teagle F. Bougere *(Shiek)*; Elizabeth Bracco *(Pancetta Leaky)*; Tony Shalhoub *(First Mate)*; Allan Corduner *(Captain)*; Michael Emerson *(Burtom's Assistant)*; Walker Jones *(Maitre d')*; Jessica Walling *(Attractive Woman)*; David Lipman *(Baker)*; E. Katherine Kerr *(Gertrude)*; George Guidall *(Claudius)*; William Hill *(Bernardo)*; Jack O'Connell *(Stage Manager)*; Matt Malloy *(Mike—Laertes)*; Ted Blumberg *(Francisco)*; Arden Myrin *(Stewardess with Luggage)*; Christopher Pomeroy *(Steward)*; Sarah McCord *(Stewardess with the Queen)*; Lewis J. Stadlen *(Bandleader)*; Phyllis Somerville *(Woman at Bar)*; Amy Hohn *(Woman with Captain)*; Michael Higgins *(Older Man)*; Ken Costigan *(Bartender)*; Woody Allen *(Producer—uncredited)*

Much less polished than his directorial debut, BIG NIGHT (1996), Stanley Tucci's THE IMPOSTORS is an energetically silly farce with a lot of funny sequences but not enough plot to shape them into a satisfying whole.

Manhattan in the 1930s. Arthur (Stanley Tucci) and Maurice (Oliver Platt) are fiercely dedicated but unemployed actors. A scheme to con a baker out of pastries leaves them still hungry but with a pair of tickets to see a new production of *Hamlet* starring master thespian Jeremy Burtom (Alfred Molina). Arthur and Maurice consider Burtom an overrated ham, an opinion they loudly express in a bar after the play, not knowing that Burtom and his retinue are listening. When the resultant brawl gets out of hand, their flight from the police leads them to hide on the dock of a cruise ship. Trapped after the ship sails, they attempt to masquerade as porters, all the while hiding from Burtom, who is a passenger. As they dash from stateroom to stateroom, Arthur and Maurice become acquainted with many of the crew and passengers. These include head stewardess Lily (Lili Taylor), who tries to help them out of their dilemma; her boyfriend Marco (Matt McGrath), the ship's callow detective; Nazi-ish head steward Meistrich (Campbell Scott), who wants Lily for his own; Sparks (Billy Connolly), an avidly homosexual tennis player; Happy Franks (Steve Buscemi), a depressed singer; the equally unhappy socialite Emily (Hope Davis) and her mother Mrs. Essendine (Dana Ivey); a wealthy sheik (Teagle F. Bougere); con artists Johnny (Richard Jenkins) and Maxi (Allison Janney), who plan to rob and kill Mrs. Essendine and the Sheik; a deposed Queen (Isabella Rossellini); and the ship's First Mate (Tony Shalhoub), who, as Arthur and Maurice learn, is really an enemy agent planning to assassinate the Queen by blowing up the ship and everyone on it.

Arthur and Maurice attend the Captain's Ball disguised as man and wife and manage to foil the First Mate's bombs. Maxi and Johnny are exposed, while romance blossoms for Lily and Marco, Happy and Emily, the Queen and the Captain, and the Shiek and Mrs. Essendine.

According to the production notes for THE IMPOSTORS, director Tucci instituted an award called the "Jambon d'Or" (Golden Ham), which he presented at the end of each day's shooting to the most deserving performer. That it was a much sought-after award will come to the surprise of no one; THE IMPOSTORS was obviously the kind of film that everyone involved enjoyed making. Ironically, the film's problem is that it's too top-heavy with talent: there are so many funny performers and characters that the film would need to be four hours long to do them all justice. One wishes Tucci had simply concentrated on himself and co-star Oliver Platt, who make a sublime comic team. (One quibble: in the finale, it would have been better to have put Tucci rather than Platt in drag.) And the film's production doesn't entirely overcome a modest budget, concocting a shipboard set that never looks like real for a moment (though Tucci turns that to his advantage with an end-credit sequence that has the entire cast dancing off the set and backstage). Such problems notwithstanding, there are many comic highlights, including Steve Buscemi singing (surprisingly well) sad songs to an audience expecting dance music; the libidinous gleam in Billy Connolly's eyes as he discusses Grecian wrestling; and an uncredited Woody Allen as a playwright considering hiring Arthur and Maurice. *(Violence, sexual situations, adult situations.)*—M.F.

d, Stanley Tucci; p, Stanley Tucci, Beth Alexander; exec p, Jonathan Filley; w, Stanley Tucci; ph, Ken Kelsch; ed, Suzy Elmiger; m, Gary DeMichele; prod d, Andrew Jackness; art d, Chris Shriver; set d, Catherine Davis; sound, William Sarokin (mixer); casting, Ellen Lewis; cos, Juliet Polcsa

Comedy **(PR: C MPAA: R)**

IN GOD'S HANDS ★★

(U.S., 1998) 96m Triumph Films ~ TriStar c

Patrick Shane Dorian *(Shane)*; Matt George *(Mickey)*; Mathew Stephen "Matty" Liu *(Keoni)*; Shaun Thompson *(Wyatt)*; Maylin Pultar *(Serena)*; Bret Michaels *(Philips)*; Brion James *(Captain)*; Brian L. Keaulana *(Brian)*; Darrick Doerner *(Darrick)*; Peter Cabrinha; Mike Stewart

There's a great surfing documentary hiding inside IN GOD'S HANDS, Zalman King's gloriously photographed, but dramatically incoherent and amateurishly acted paean to "riding the big one," that's filled with some hilarious half-baked philosophy as well.

Three surfing buddies travel the world looking for the ultimate wave: aging former champion Mickey (Matt George) from Montana, Hawaiian teenage neophyte Keoni (Matty Liu), and Shane (Patrick Shane Dorian), a California prodigy who refuses to taint the purity of the sport by competing for money. While training in East Africa, Mickey gets involved with a local chieftain's daughter and the three are tossed into jail, but escape with the aid of a mysterious journalist named Wyatt (Shaun Thompson), who follows them on their journey. Traveling by steamer, the trio goes to Madagascar and Shane has a fling with the daughter (Maylin Pultar) of the ship's captain (Brion James). In Bali, they run into another group of surfers, including big-wave surfing legend Darrick Doerner (Himself), who uses a jet ski to tow himself into the largest and fastest waves. After Keoni recovers from a bout of malaria, the three continue on to Hawaii, where they take turns riding the huge waves, but Mickey refuses to use the assistance of a jet ski and is killed after paddling into a massive wave. Keoni returns home to his mother, but Shane goes to Mexico and starts to surf again.

Taking a break from his customary erotic escapades, softcore auteur Zalman King turns his leering, orange-filtered lens on tanned and toned male bodies with the same fetishized delirium he usually lavishes on nubile female flesh. The film is basically a feature-length travelogue in a quasi-docudrama framework, shot and edited in the non-linear style of a fashion commercial or music video, replete with slow-motion, smoke effects, saturated colors, and a blaring techno-pop score. The so-called narrative is impossible to follow, as virtually every scene with dialogue lasts no more than a minute or two and is constantly interrupted with flashcuts and montages of maps and waves, but the story is merely a peg on which to hang some superb surfing footage featuring riders gliding atop and inside of massive 50-footers. Being a true sensualist, King emphasizes the mesmerizing physical beauty of the sun, the surf, and the exotic locales, but after the 30th or 40th killer wave, the sense of awe begins to diminish, leaving one with way too much time to ponder the absurd romantic subplots (such as Mickey's tryst with a Nubian princess) and the risible New Age psychobabble ("We build temples to adrenaline") uttered by Wyatt, the pretentious combination Greek chorus/omnipotent narrator/deus ex machina.

Secretly following the surfers everywhere with a camera, a tape recorder, and a typewriter, and passing out black pearls to the authorities to smooth their way, he, and the film, treat the act of standing on a piece of fiberglass in the water as some kind of deeply spiritual and mythological experience. The three leads are all accomplished professional surfers, but nonprofessional actors unfortunately, resulting in some unintentional hilarity during the plethora of late-night beach barbecues where they look at each other soulfully and deliver such pithy philosophy as "You're gonna burn out, man." "Yeah, people burn out." With all due respect, more depth was exhibited by Sandra Dee back when she told James Darren: "Hang ten, Moondoggie." *(Profanity, violence, sexual situations.)*—M.S.

d, Zalman King; p, Tom Stern; exec p, Zalman King, Aladdin Pojhan, David Saunders; co-p, Nicolas Stern, Matt George, Chris Bongirne; w, Zalman King, Matt George; ph, John Aronson; ed, James Gavin Bedford, Joe Shugart; m, Paradise; prod d, Marc Greville-Mason, Paul Holt; art d, Jacqueline R. Masson; set d, P.J. Boston; sound, Adam Grete, Paul N. Martin; casting, Cathy Henderson-Martin, Dori Zuckerman; cos, Jolie Anna Andreatta

Sports/Adventure/Drama (PR: C MPAA: PG-13)

IN HIS FATHER'S SHOES ★★½

(U.S./Canada, 1997) 105m Temple Street Productions ~ Showtime/Hallmark c

Robert Ri'chard *(Clay Crosby)*; Louis Gossett Jr. *(Frank Crosby/Richard Crosby)*; Barbara Eve Harris *(Janice Crosby)*; Rachael Crawford *(Celeste Crosby)*; Djanet Sears *(Virginia Crosby)*; Shadia Simmons *(Maggie Crosby)*; Dylan Provencher *(Peter)*; Kevin Duhaney *(Bruce)*; Dan Petronijevic *(Dennis Beck)*; A.J. Cook *(Lisa Palmineri)*; Fiona Reid *(Gypsy)*; R.D. Reid *(Dorfman)*; Dan Warry-Smith; Mary Long; Naomi Lee Allen; Christine Brubaker; Eric Fink; Timm Zemanek; David Roemmele; Joel Keller; Kenner Ames

Agreeable performances and a low-key narrative keep this gimmicky family fantasy's feet firmly planted on earth. This Showtime-financed film won a 1997 Daytime Emmy Award for Outstanding Children's Special.

Frank Crosby (Louis Gossett Jr.) and his 15-year-old son Clay (Robert Ri'chard) go to a funky junk shop, at which Frank impulsively buys a pair of gaudy wingtip shoes from a mystic gyspy lady (Fiona Reid). Clay has a loving relationship with his ailing dad, and wonders why Frank never talks to his own parents. That painful matter remains unresolved, for Frank subsequently dies of the cancer that his wife (Barbara Eve Harris) had long treated with herbal medicine. Clay is inconsolable, until he happens to slip on the untouched wingtip shoes, and is instantly teleported to his father's high school in 1962. Clay has become Frank Crosby, and witnesses how his father's father, Richard (Gossett again), a stern WWII vet, ran the household like a drill sergeant, repressing overt displays of affection and approval for his kids—traits that eventually led to both Frank and his aspiring-actress sister Celeste (Rachael Crawford) breaking with the old man. Young Frank/Clay also suffers typical bully mishaps at his (racially integrated) high school, but he learns that simply by slipping off the shoes he can safely return to his own era.

Clay repeatedly goes back to 1962, trying to retrieve valuable, collectible baseball cards (he can't), but more determined to find an old postcard Frank had described with his last dying breath as the key to their whole family. Meanwhile in the present, Clay pays a long-deferred visit to his grandparents, whom he regards in a new light thanks to his flashbacks. When pressed, Richard Crosby declares that despite his hardshelled exterior he always loved Frank and Celeste, and regrets he wasn't able to make peace with them. Clay also locates the postcard; bearing a Leyte Gulf address, it's Richard's wartime love letter to his bride, revealing the grandfather's gentler side. Clay gives the postcard back to the old guy, and subsequently Richard telephones Celeste for the first time in years. At the gypsy shop, Clay is granted a final, magical vision of his proud dad.

An inveterate punster would doubtlessly dub this movie "Black to the Future," for its resemblance to the 1985 Robert Zemeckis time-warp hit in which Michael J. Fox got to behold his own parents' teen travails. Despite some rather unnecessary special effects, however, IN HIS FATHER'S SHOES takes a much less larkish approach. Even though he draws astonished stares in 1962 with his anarchronistic hip-hop dance moves, and mentions of other phenomena that haven't yet taken place, Clay apparently can't alter the course of events. What remains, ultimately, is a warmhearted, low-impact primer in parenting, about a nice kid healing his divided family and better appreciating the man who raised him, geared to a modern African-American audience.

Robert Ri'chard, who won a Daytime Emmy for Outstanding Performance in a Children's Program, is adequately likeable as the young hero. Gossett, an Oscar-winning actor too often wasted in action movies, is okay playing two generations, even though Richard Crosby doesn't quite seem the ogre the script wants to make him. The movie soft-pedals depictions of American racism ingrained in the time period. The nostalgic 1962 school-age milieu shows remarkably little ethnic intimidation. What name-calling there is mostly comes from Richard Crosby, who offends Clay/Frank through the politically incorrect terms "negroes" and "colored boys," and disparages Martin Luther King's followers as troublemakers.—C.C.

d, Vic Sarin; p, Dan Redler, Patrick Whitley; exec p, Louis Gossett Jr., Hilliard Elkins; w, Gary Gelt; ph, Michael Storey; ed, Bill Goddard; m, John Welsman; prod d, John Dondertman; art d, Gordon Lebredt; set d, Doug McCullough; sound, Stuart French; fx, Jonathan Gibson; casting, Tina Gerussi; makeup, Lynda McCormack; stunts, Shane Cardwell

Children's/Fantasy/Drama (PR: A MPAA: PG)

IN THE LINE OF DUTY
(SEE: ROYAL WARRIORS)

INCOGNITO ★½

(U.S., 1997) 107m James G. Robinson; Morgan Creek ~ Warner Bros. c

Jason Patric *(Harry Donovan)*; Irene Jacob *(Marieke Van Den Broeck)*; Thomas Lockyer *(Alistar Davies)*; Ian Richardson *(Turley—Prosecutor)*; Simon Chandler *(Iain III)*; Pip Torrens *(White—Defense)*; Michael Cochrane *(Detective Inspector Deeks)*; Rod Steiger *(Milton A. Donovan)*; Togo Igawa *(Thomas Agachi)*; Joseph Blatchley *(Professor Scheerding)*; Paul Brennen *(Detective Sargeant Steed)*; Olivier Pierre *(Lecuyer)*; Peter Gale *(Andrew Westerbrook)*; David Marrick *(Richard Bright)*; Dudley Sutton *(Offul)*; Adam Fogerty *(Ugo)*; Ricardo Montez *(Juan Del Campo)*; Antonio Elliot *(Grandson)*; Jonathan Newth *(Judge)*; Bryan Matheson *(Concierge)*; Lex van Delden; Hugo Bower; Walter van Dyke *(Dutch Experts)*; Frank Nendels *(Chemist)*; John Tordoff *(Pub Owner)*; Jean-Luc Caron *(Cafe Intellectual)*; Maja Ottesen *(Artist's Model)*; Danielle Allan *(Museum Attendant)*; Anna Korwin *(Museum Official)*; David Sibley *(Pawn Shop Owner)*; Michael Dimitri *(Landlord)*; John Paul Morgan *(Train Porter)*; Stephen Webber *(Iain III's Solicitor)*; Keith Anderson *(Court Translator)*; Heike Willmann *(Saleswoman in Gallery)*; Miriam Karlin *(Saleswoman in Paint Shop)*; Jon Cartwright *(Auctioneer)*; Andrew Forbes *(Newscaster)*; Nora Connolly *(Barmaid)*

Despite a cast headed by Jason Patric and Irene Jacob, major studio backing, and direction by John Badham, who usually is at least able to deliver mindlessly diverting commercial entertainment, INCOGNITO is a laughably cliched and incredibly hoary Euro-thriller about art forgery that was barely released theatrically before being consigned to video-bins.

Art forger Harry Donovan (Jason Patric) is offered $500,000 by British gallery owners Davies (Thomas Lockyer), Iain III, known as "Ill" (Simon Chandler), and Agachi (Togo Igawa) to create a Rembrandt forgery. Donovan agrees, against the advice of his ailing artist father (Rod Steiger), who urges his son to become a serious painter. Donovan flies to Europe to study Rembrandt's work, and he meets art student Marieke Van Den Broeck (Irene Jacob), with whom he has a one-night fling. After creating the forgery, Donovan delivers the painting to Davies, who takes it to a farm in Spain and pays off its owner (Ricardo Montez) to "discover" it in his barn. A group of experts authenticate the painting, but when Marieke—who is actually the world's foremost Rembrandt authority—doubts its authenticity, Davies panics and refuses to pay Donovan. A struggle ensues and Donovan flees with the painting.

Davies kills Agachi, then reports that Donovan stole the painting and shot Agachi. Donovan takes Marieke hostage and goes on the run, but after unsuccessfully trying to sell the painting, he's caught by the police. During his trial, Donovan claims that the painting is not a stolen Rembrandt but his own forgery. To prove it, he starts to restage his forgery in court, but stops after learning that his father has died. However, Donovan is freed after Ill testifies that Davies really killed Agachi. Ill takes possession of the painting and auctions it off, but the Spanish government claims the rights to the painting and the farmer gets $10 million, which he splits with Donovan. Donovan then joins Marieke in Paris, where he gives her one of his own paintings.

Beginning with a pre-flashback prologue of TV news footage depicting Donovan being chased and arrested, which is unaccountably shot in slow-motion black-and-white (those British newscasts sure are arty), INCOGNITO is one miscalculation and implausibility after another. The narrative is a disjointed mess, with Donovan's abundant voice-overs trying to smooth over the illogic, while half the film seems to consist of montages accompanied by a generic rock score, e.g., Donovan gathering illicit materials to produce the forgery and sensuously painting while barechested as the camera does a rhapsodic 360-degree circle; and then another one when Donovan restages his forgery in court, replete with dissolves to, yes, a ticking clock to show the hours going by, as Donovan hears his dead father's voice in his head, pleading with him to "develop a style of your own." The plot has so many absurd coincidences and holes that it's not even worth detailing them all; most egregious, however, is the fact that Marieke turns out to be the top Rembrandt authority and just happens to be at the train station when Donovan flees there so he can abduct her.

As the story plods improbably from one touristy location to another (Big Ben, the Eiffel Tower, Dutch windmills, et al), Donovan insults Marieke's pony-tail-wearing Eurotrash friends with such witticisms as "I'm never offended by flatulence, I just move away from the smell," and when he and Marieke go on the lam, they alternate between heavy petting and screaming at each other using the tritest dialogue imaginable: When she calls him a fraud, he replies "When are you going to realize that all this art crap is a fraud. Art was my dog's name." Dressed in black leather and a beret, the permanently sullen and bestubbled Jason Patric exhibits a singular lack of leading-man charisma, and as in U.S. MARSHALS (1998), Irene Jacob is reduced to mere window-dressing, while the gushy Rod Steiger appears in three brief scenes (two of them on the phone) and cries in each one. Badham's direction is as slick and superficial as ever, but it's amazing that he didn't see the irony in how his attempt to copy Hitchcock (right down to having Donovan and Marieke handcuffed together on the train; and lifting the screaming lady-train whistle segue from THE 39 STEPS) is identical to Donovan's imitative and artistically anonymous character, who's chided for playing it safe and not taking creative risks. *(Profanity, violence, nudity, sexual situations.)*—M.S.

d, John Badham; p, James G. Robinson; exec p, Gary Barber, Bill Todman Jr.; assoc p, Cammie Crier; co-p, William P. Cartlidge;

w, Jordan Katz; ph, Denis Crossan; ed, Frank Morriss; m, John Ottman; prod d, James Leonard; art d, Mark Raggett, Su Whitaker; set d, Jill Quertier; sound, David Crozier (recordist); fx, David Harris; casting, Noel Davis; cos, Louise Stjernsward; makeup, Lynda Armstrong, Dave Elsey (effects); stunts, Mark Boyle, Eddie Stacey

Thriller **(PR: O MPAA: R)**

INDISCREET ★½

(U.S., 1998) 101m Magic Hour Pictures ~ MRG Entertainment c

Luke Perry *(Michael Nash)*; Gloria Reuben *(Eve Dodd)*; Peter Coyote *(Detective Roos)*; Vladimir Nemirovsky *(Sean)*; Adam Baldwin *(Jeremy)*; James Read *(Zacariah Dodd)*; Lisa Edelstein *(Beth Sussman)*; Laura Rogen *(Kate Johnson)*; Kirk Baily *(Larry Neal)*; Jo De Winter *(Nurse)*; John Lafayette *(Gary)*; Walker Brandt *(Secretary)*; Richard Rosenberg *(Older Man)*; Gabriella Hall *(Younger Woman)*; Julio Oscar Mechoso *(Detective Burns)*

Contemporary film noir comes a cropper in this misguided mystery clamoring after the style of BODY HEAT (1981). It takes more than a saxophone to create atmosphere; what this film lacks is a sinuous screenplay whose curves aren't obvious a mile away.

Ex-cop and recovering alcoholic Michael Nash (Luke Perry) makes a living snapping incriminating photos for lawyer Beth Sussman (Lisa Edelstein). Zachariah Dodd (James Read), a powerful, feared attorney at Beth's firm, requests Jimmy's aid in proving the infidelity of his wife Eve (Gloria Reuben). Dodd has many enemies, including an attorney named Jeremy (Adam Baldwin) whom he passed over for partnership.

While Michael is secretly photographing Eve at the ocean, she attempts suicide by washing down pills with a brand of exclusive wine. Michael rescues her from the surf. Neglecting his girlfriend Kate (Laura Rogen), Michael foolhardily falls for unhappy Eve. One night, a frazzled Eve hands Michael the gun with which she claims she just killed control freak Dodd. Although Michael utilizes his ex-cop skills to cover up Eve's involvement, Detective Roos (Peter Coyote) senses a conspiracy between Eve and a secret lover to share Dodd's $75 million estate.

Tipped off by his precinct informant (and AA buddy) Sean (Vladimir Nemirovsky), Michael learns that Eve's first husband also died under mysterious circumstances; Michael has been set up to take the fall for Dodd's murder. Scanning his surveillance photographs of Eve, Michael spots the brand of wine that Eve attempted suicide with. Once Michael recalls that Jeremy shares Eve's taste in wine, he realizes that Jeremy is Eve's inamorata. Although Michael nearly gets shot by Eve as he confronts the celebrating lovers, the police arrive to apprehend Eve and Jeremy.

The interminable INDISCREET doesn't leave a single femme fatale cliche unturned. Filled with stale plot twists, this neo-noir grinds to a halt every time some new Eve deception comes into play. Although some of the supporting roles are intriguingly conceived and energetically played—including Linda Edelstein as the aggressive lawyer and James Read as the unscrupulous power broker—the leads siphon off our interest in the mystery due to their juiceless portrayals of generic roles. This moody clinker strikes too many wrong notes while seeking that lost chord of classic Hollywood Film Noir. *(Graphic violence, nudity, sexual situations, substance abuse.)*—R.P.

d, Mark Bienstock; p, Mark Bienstock, Rich Goldberg; exec p, Luke Perry, Marc Greenberg; assoc p, Lindsay Chag; w, Vladimir Nemirovsky; ph, Sead Mutarevic; ed, Ivan Ladizinsky; m, Steven M. Stern; prod d, Elina Katsioula; art d, Scott H. Campbell; set d, Sandra Grass; sound, Peter Meiselmann; cos, Tammy Surber; makeup, Merc Archeneaux; stunts, Kurt Bryant

Crime/Mystery **(PR: C MPAA: R)**

INFORMANT, THE ★★

(U.S., 1998) 106m Leon Falk Productions ~ Showtime/Viacom c

Anthony Brophy *(Gingy McAnally)*; Cary Elwes *(Lt. David Ferris)*; Timothy Dalton *(D.C.C. Rennie)*; Sean McGinley *(Frankie Conroy)*; Maria Lennon *(Roisin McAnally)*; John Kavanagh *(IRA Chief)*; Frankie Cafferty *(Dalton)*; Stuart Graham *(Detective Astely)*; Gary Lydon *(Detective McDonough)*; Sean Kearns *(Detective Prentice)*; B.J. Hogg *(Constable Gross)*; Ciaran Fitzgerald *(Gerard McAnally)*; Virginia Cole *(Roisin's Ma)*; James Gaddas *(British I.O.)*; Ian Gelder *(British C.O.)*; Brian Mallon *(Reilly)*; Paul Hickey *(Father Francis)*; Tim Loane *(Ollie)*; Paul McParland *(Liam)*; Simone Bendix *(Samantha)*; Des Braiden *(Murdered Judge)*; Robert Cavanah *(Lt.Lauter)*; Pat Kinevane *(IRA Back-Up)*; Ian Fitzgibbon *(Joey McGillivary)*; Joe Rea *(Fergus)*; Conor Bradford *(Newscaster)*; Ben Palmer *(Judge's Driver)*; Kevin Reynolds *(Screaming Detective)*; Barry McGovern *(Courtroom Judge)*; Gerry Walsh *(Court Clerk)*; Tara O'Neile *(R.U.C. Policewoman)*; Luke Hayden *(R.U.C. Escort)*; Gavin O'Connor *(R.U.C. Escort)*

Unlike film classics involving Ireland's tragic political squeeze-play, from THE INFORMER (1935) through IN THE NAME OF THE FATHER (1993), THE INFORMANT (1998) lacks poetry, suspense, or illuminating discourse. It's just a made-for-cable action movie with a better pedigree than most.

1983. After five years in a British jail, burnt-out Irish patriot Gingy McAnally (Anthony Brophy) reluctantly agrees when the IRA coerces him into assassinating a judge. He is quickly apprehended, and becomes a political pawn for investigating officer Rennie (Timothy Dalton), who despises extremists and uses torture to break down Gingy.

When Gingy unexpectedly bonds with a sympathetic Brit soldier, Lt. David Ferris (Cary Elwes), wily Rennie persuades the decent Ferris to cultivate Gingy's trust. Realizing that the IRA has once again let him take the fall, Gingy accepts an immunity deal that infuriates his loyalist wife Roisin (Maria Lennon). Irish radicals locate the heavily guarded safehouse where Gingy is hiding and bomb it, though they fail to injure him. Gingy's rebel superior, Frankie Conroy (Sean McGinley) rapes Roisin, threatens her children, and bullies her into giving him the name of Gingy's British supporter, Ferris. Before Gingy can testify, the IRA kills Ferris in another bombing. Ferris's murder is a final blow to Gingy's resolve, and it is unsure whether he will testify against the IRA or not.

Hopelessness is the operative word for THE INFORMANT, as ideology exacts a high price on both sides of the Catholic/Protestant enmity. While engrossing as a political melodrama, it loses focus by trying to encompass too many subgenres at once. It lacks vitality as a prison thriller, with Rennie acting like Inspector Javert as he interrogates a broken suspect. It only builds a modicum of suspense as a perilous cat-and-mouse game instigated by the IRA. Additionally, all the dilemmas are spelled out for us so that audiences may choose to retreat from a bleak foregone conclusion. The film's coda suggests that whether or not Gingy chooses to name names, his life is already shattered—an insight viewers got in the first three minutes of the film. *(Graphic violence, extreme profanity, sexual situations, substance abuse.)*—R.P.

d, Jim McBride; p, Leon Falk; exec p, Steven-Charles Jaffe, Nicholas Meyer; co-p, Morgan O'Sullivan, Ted Adams Swanson; w, Nicolas Meyer (based on the novel *Field of Blood* by Gerald Seymour); ph, Affonso Beato; ed, Eva Gardos; m, The Pogues, Shane Magowan; prod d, Mark Geraghty; art d, Conor Devlin; sound, Trevor O'Connor (mixer); fx, Maurice Foley; casting, John Hubbard, Ros Hubbard; cos, Joan Bergin; makeup, Jennifer Hegarty; stunts, Patrick Condren

Drama/Political **(PR: C MPAA: R)**

INHERITORS, THE ★★½

(Austria, 1998) 93m DOR Film; ORF; Bayericher Rundfunk ~ Stratosphere Entertainment c
(AKA: ONE-SEVENTH FARMERS, THE; DIE SIEBTELBAUERN)

Simon Schwarz *(Lukas)*; Sophie Rois *(Emmy)*; Lars Rudolph *(Severin)*; Julia Gschnitzer *(Old Nane)*; Ulrich Wildgruber *(Danninger)*; Elisabeth Orth *(Rosalind)*; Tilo Pruckner *(Foreman)*; Susanne Silverio *(Lisbeth)*; Kirstin Schwab *(Liesl)*; Dietmar Nigsch *(Sepp)*; Werner Prinz *(Policeman)*; Gertraud Maibock *(Gertrud)*; Christoph Gusenbauer *(Stable Boy)*; Eddie Fischnaller *(Florian)*

A Marxist parable about a group of peasants who inherit the farm they work on, this Austrian film is an impressively mounted but disappointingly programmatic entry in the good-workers-versus-bad-owners genre of leftist narrative.

When Hillinger, a mean and sadistic farmer, is found dead, a mysterious old woman named Rosalind (Elisabeth Orth) is arrested for murder. The whole town is shocked when the old farmer's perverse will bequeaths his entire estate to his ten employees, among them a happy-go-lucky youth named Lukas (Simon Schwarz), his friend Severin (Lars Rudolph), and the farm's foreman (Tilo Pruckner). When the foreman attempts to sell the farm to local landowners, he and two other legatees are banished by the other seven.

Somehow the new communards manage to pay their inflated taxes and pay off their three former partners. Then their barn is torched by a gang of men led by the foreman, who, after giving Lukas a savage beating, is killed by the youth. Danninger (Ulrich Wildgruber), the area's most powerful and ruthless landowner, offers a reward for Lukas's apprehension.

As he is about to flee to America, Lukas is told that he is the product of Hillinger's rape of Rosalind. Pursued by bounty hunters, he visits his mother in jail, slays her guard, and attempts to set her free, but Rosalind, who is unable to accept her child by Hillinger, refuses his help and dies alone that night. The next day the communal farmers are raped and tortured by the foreman and his gang. When Lukas arrives on the scene, he is killed. The defeated communards abandon their farm, but before leaving the territory, Severin murders Danninger.

THE INHERITORS' doctrinaire script is quite unworthy of the film's dynamic direction and rich yet rigorous cinematography. By humanizing and sexualizing what once would have been squeaky-clean protagonists, Marxist movies like THE INHERITORS have taken the first step in undermining the simplistic moralism of socialist drama, but they are still reluctant to render their villains the same courtesy: THE INHERITORS' baddies are as inhumanly, hissably evil as the basest curs, cads, and bounders of Victorian melodrama—and the film's top fat cat is literally obese.

This black-and-white approach to drama robs the movie of the necessary subtlety required to engage the sympathies of sophisticated viewers—and that's a shame, because the presence of several arresting faces in the cast, Peter Von Heller's robustly-colored visuals, and Eric Satie's bracing piano music should have added up to something more provocative and memorable.

According to its writer-director Stefan Ruzowitsky, THE INHERITORS was an attempt at a modern version of a *heimatfilm*, a venerable Austrian genre comprising kitschy tales of agrarian life. The movie won the Best Actor Award for Simon Schwarz at the 1998 Saarbrueken Film Festival and the Best Picture Award at the 1998 Rotterdam Film Festival. *(Violence, nudity, sexual situation, adult situations, profanity.)*—D.T.

d, Stefan Ruzowitzky; p, Danny Krausz , Kurt Stocker; w, Stefan Ruzowitzky; ph, Peter Von Haller; ed, Britta Burkert-Nahler; art d, Isi Wimmer; sound, Heinz Ebner; casting, Barbara Vogel; cos, Nicole Fischnaller; makeup, Helga Klein, Georgie Schillinger

Drama **(PR: O MPAA: R)**

INNOCENT SLEEP, THE ★★

(U.K., 1995) 97m Timedial Films ~ Trident Releasing c

Annabella Sciorra *(Billie Hayman)*; Rupert Graves *(Alan Terry)*; Michael Gambon *(Matheson)*; Franco Nero *(Cavani)*; John Hannah *(James)*; Graham Crowden *(George)*; Oliver Cotton *(Lusano)*; Tony Bluto *(Thorn)*; Paul Brightwell *(Pelham)*; Campbell Morrison *(Mac)*; Hilary Crowson *(Sheila Terry)*; Kieran Smith *(Newspaper Vendor)*; Sean Gilder *(Police Constable)*; Brian Lipson *(Police Sergeant)*; Dermot Kerrigan *(Willie)*; Dermot Keaney *(Driver)*; Alex Richardson *(Thug)*; Chris Jury *(News Photographer)*; Laura Berkeley *(Glamorous Blonde)*; Hugh Walters *(Lewis)*; Crispin Redman *(Simon CID)*; Katie Carr *(Alice)*; Chris Armstrong *(CID Man)*; Lehla Eldridge *(Morgue Attendant)*; Straun Rodger *(Peter Samson)*; Stephen Yardley *(Drago)*; Ken Ratcliffe *(Stephens)*; Carmen DeVenere *(Cavani's Aid)*; Paul Gregory *(Newsreader)*; Robert James *(Hopkin)*; Susan Gilmore *(New Programme Presenter)*; Peter Cartwright *(Gerald Philips)*; Julian Rivett *(Bike Courier)*; Patrick Duggan *(Landlord)*; Hilary Waters; Riz Abbasi; Martin Biltcliffe; James Peck *(Journalists)*; Peter Howell *(Sir Frank)*; Ben DeSaumserez *(Assassin)*

A mystery-thriller that's never thrilling and doesn't even bother to solve its paltry mystery, the veddy British THE INNOCENT SLEEP is a cliched and soporific yarn about an innocent man who knows too much and is chased around foggy London town by both cops and crooks.

While spending the night near London's Tower Bridge, homeless derelict Alan Terry (Rupert Graves) witnesses a murder being committed by a group of men. Alan is discovered and chased by the men, but gets away; however his wallet and ID are found by the killers. When the murder is reported as a suicide the next day, Alan goes to the police, but is shocked when he recognizes one of the killers at the station—a cop named Matheson (Michael Gambon), although Alan mistakenly thinks his name is Stephens. Alan's elderly alcoholic friend George (Graham Crowden), a former journalist, arranges a meeting with tabloid reporter Billie (Annabella Sciorra), to whom Alan tells his story. Skeptical at first, Billie believes Alan after her investigation uncovers evidence that the murder victim was an associate of a powerful Italian banker named Cavani (Franco Nero), who's suspected of having underworld ties.

Meanwhile, Matheson tracks down Alan and sets fire to the vagrants' "cardboard city" in an attempt to flush him out, but only succeeds in killing George. Alan moves in with Billie, but when he discovers a tape that shows she had previously double-crossed an informant, he decides to call the police for help. Believing that Stephens is the killer cop, however, Alan unwittingly talks to Matheson and sets up a meeting with him at Tower Bridge. Billie finds out about the meeting and rushes to the scene just as Matheson is about to kill Alan, but Matheson himself is shot and killed by one of Cavani's henchmen. Later, Billie is told by her editor that he's been ordered by people in "high places" to kill the story.

Filmed in 1995 and barely released in 1997 in the US, THE INNOCENT SLEEP vainly tries to pump up a formulaic and dated type of British thriller by injecting bloody violence, four-letter words, and social conscience (concern for the homeless), but only succeeds at being an anachronistic version of the scores of British mystery "quota quickies" of yore. Similarly, like the English B movies of the '40s and '50s, wherein faded American stars such as Pat O'Brien, George Raft, and Wayne Morris crossed the Atlantic for some quick cash, here, Annabella Sciorra goes slumming as the requisite Yank, depicted in typically stereotyped, foul-mouthed, chain-smoking fashion. The film's style consists of such genre staples as a profusion of gloomy fog, portentous low-angle titled shots of the bad guys (coolly mouthing such threats as "I don't tolerate mistakes"), and a bombastic, operatic score (including a choir singing over shots of the "cardboard city") that tries to create suspense and dramatic urgency where none exists. Still, the film would be a watchable, minor thriller if the plot made any sense, or more specifically, if the filmmakers had even bothered to solve the "mystery" of the first murder and explain exactly who, and what, Cavani is. Instead, the entire plot hinges on the improbable and contrived misunderstanding of Alan mistaking Matheson for another cop, and culminates in a predictable nick-of-time rescue before wrapping up with a shamelessly equivocal and murky finale that lets the screenwriter off the hook by suggesting the usual corrupt government-big business conspiracy theories. *(Violence, profanity.)*—M.S.

d, Scott Michell; p, Scott Michell, Matthew Vaughn; exec p, Rod Michell; w, Ray Villis, Derek Trigg; ph, Alan Dunlop; ed, Derek Trigg; m, Mark Ayres; prod d, Eve Mavrakis; casting, Simone Ireland; cos, Stephanie Collie

Thriller/Mystery **(PR: O MPAA: R)**

INSIDE/OUT ★★★½

(U.S./France, 1997) 115m Parallel Pictures; The Baltimore Film Factory ~ Cinema Parallel bw

Tom Gilroy *(David Shepard)*; Berangere Allaux *(Monica)*; Frederic Perriot *(Jean Hammett)*; Stefania Rocca *(Grace Patterson)*; Mikkel Gaup *(Eric Johnson)*; Steven Watkins *(Roger Freeman)*; David Roland Frank *(Young Orderly)*; Brian Hemingson *(Police Man)*; Jim Czarnecki *(Red Neck Patient)*; Johanna Cox *(Nurse Peterson)*; Courtney Wilkenson *(Nurse Wilson)*; David Beaudoin *(Dylan Johnson)*; Edgar Davis *(Running Man)*; Dominic Valentine *(Escaping Man)*; Branch Warfield *(Doctor Ridgley)*; Eareckson Mary Tregenza *(Harpist)*

Simultaneously bleak and alluring, INSIDE/OUT is independent filmmaker Rob Tregenza's French-produced narrative of random occurrences in a mental institution.

Jean (Frederic Pierrot) is a patient in a remote mental hospital, from which he continually attempts to escape. On and off the hospital grounds, Jean regularly encounters a sadistic local law officer (Mikkel Gaup), with whom he fights. Monica (Berangere Allaux), another patient at the hospital, is romantically attracted to Jean, and jealous of the attention that Grace (Stefania Rocca), an organist in the institution's chapel, gives to him. Meanwhile, Roger (Steven Watkins), also a patient, receives a visit from his parents. Although the three are silent for the duration of the visit, Roger breaks down and cries when his parents leave.

One day, Monica sneaks from her ward into Jean's. She finds him asleep, undresses, climbs into his bed, and lies with him until a nurse comes and takes her away. A dance party is arranged for the inmates, who are upset by the loud music until a harpist (Eareckson Mary Tregenza) plays a quiet piece that lulls them all. An Episcopal priest (Tom Gilroy) who heads the chapel carries on an affair with Grace, but she abruptly ends the relationship. Later, Grace teaches Monica how to play the organ. Monica overcomes her jealousy and befriends Grace.

Jean finds Monica in an abandoned house with both the law officer and a hospital orderly (David Roland Frank), and he shoots the officer dead. Later, Grace finds Jean painting images on a wall in the sanitarium, and assists him. When they finish, Jean makes sexual advances, but Grace breaks free of him and runs away. Jean finds Monica crouching in the corner of an empty room and embraces her. Elsewhere, Grace entertains herself by playing the organ, while Roger blows a trumpet on the hospital grounds.

As its title suggests, INSIDE/OUT is a film of opposites. Abstruse to the point of bafflement, it is nonetheless involving and, at times, entrancing. The tone is predominantly melancholic, and writer-director Tregenza (who also served as the cinematographer and editor) imbues the film with a drab, wintry feel, filling it with images of decay and emptiness. Yet INSIDE/OUT is also seductive, both in its beautiful, wide-screen cinematography and in its otherworldliness. The locale and time period are unspecified (although it appears to be a small American town in the 1950s), and the film is virtually nonverbal. Motivations go unexplained—the law officer's antipathy toward Jean, for example—but rather than provoking frustration or confusion these absences make INSIDE/OUT literally dreamlike, filled with events that are unaccountable yet somehow acceptable. Tregenza is a true stylist. While his film might not, as he has boasted, evoke "the entire history of cinema," it does successfully incorporate seemingly antithetical filmmaking approaches. INSIDE/OUT alternates fluid, all-encompassing tracking shots with long static takes. It is starkly realistic in its harsh visuals, yet includes touches of fantasy. The film may be described as impressionistic, since events are simply recorded without being interpreted, but it occasionally moves into expressionism (mostly through the soundtrack) to emphasize a particular character's state of mind. Tregenza manages to keep these oppositions balanced, through an assured command of the medium and with a rich appreciation of the affect of form on narrative.

Such a film might have come across as pretentious or deadly dull if Tregenza and his cast (who, given the lack of dialogue, communicate more though gesture and facial expression than through words), had not addressed their material with the discipline, conviction, and intelligence that they display here. INSIDE/OUT may be less grand than Tregenza envisioned, but even at its most ponderous, it is an eminently interesting film. *(Violence, nudity, profanity.)*—D.C.

d, Rob Tregenza; p, J.K. Earekcson, Tom Garvin; assoc p, J.C. Davidson, Robert Sutton; co-p, Gill Holland; w, Rob Tregenza; ph, Rob Tregenza; ed, Rob Tregenza; m, Earekcson Mary Tregenza; sound, Francois Musy (mixer); cos, Paula Stonestreet

Drama **(PR: C MPAA: NR)**

INSOMNIA ★★★½

(Norway, 1998) 97m Norsk Film/Nordic Screen ~ First Run Features c

Stellan Skarsgard *(Jonas Engstrom)*; Sverre Anker Ousdal *(Erik Vik)*; Bjorn Floberg *(Jon Holt)*; Gisken Armand *(Hilde Hagen)*; Maria Bonnevie *(Ane)*; Kristian Figenschow *(Arne Zakariassen)*; Thor Michael Aamodt *(Tom Engen)*; Bjorn Moan *(Eilert)*; Marianne O. Ulrichsen *(Froya)*; Frode Rasmussen *(Chief of Police)*; Guri Johnson *(Mia Nikolaisen)*; Maria Mathiesen *(Tanja Lorentzen)*

When is a film noir not noir? When it takes place up near the arctic circle, a region of perpetual, pale daylight and the setting for Erik Skjoldbjaerg's notable feature debut, an eerie rumination on guilt and deception.

A sensational criminal case hits northern Norway. Tanja Lorentzen (Maria Mathiesen), a 17-year-old schoolgirl with no family and a somewhat wanton reputation, turns up lifeless in a beach shack, her body carefully washed of all clues. Locals summon a homicide specialist from neighboring Sweden. Jonas Engstrom (Stellan Skarsgard) is a detective famed for relentlessly solving cases—and tainted by rumors of a sex scandal in his past. Engstrom floats a false story in the media about Tanja's backpack remaining at the crime scene, in order to trap the secretive killer. Sure enough, police spy someone entering the hovel to look for the backpack. Chasing the fleeing shape, Engstrom fires blindly in the fog, fatally wounding his longtime partner Erik Vik (Sverre Anker Ousdal). Tanja's elusive killer is blamed for the tragedy, an impression Engstrom has no intention of correcting. He alters ballistics evidence from his gun to throw off the investigation of Hilde Hagen (Gisken Armand), a Norwegian detective assigned to Vik's shooting.

Meanwhile, there's still the Lorentzen case, and even as his conscience consumes him, Engstrom obsessively pursues the dead girl's friends and live-in lover. He determines that Tanja spent her last hours in a sexual dalliance with novelist Jon Holt (Bjorn Floberg). Holt is indeed the mystery figure from the shack—thus he knows that Engstrom really shot Vik. The sleazy writer and the unstable cop play cat-and-mouse with each other, until a shoreline chase in which Holt hits his head, and Engstrom watches him drown. Engstrom is hailed as a hero, despite the autopsy verdict that Tanja died of an accidental aneurism, not in a murder. Only Hagen realizes the whole truth about Engstrom, but cannot prove his misdeeds as the detective drives away.

The title refers to Jonas Engstrom's inability to sleep soundly, troubled as he is by the dull glare of the region's 24-hour sun (he must tack up a blanket over his hotel window to create artificial twilight), then later by the crushing guilt over the unspeakable—but, apparently, not unprecedented wrongs he has committed. Skarsgard commands an equal measure of sympathy and revulsion in the difficult role of a repressed, tormented antihero whose flailing and desperate attempts to point the finger of suspicion at (relative) innocents in the Lorentzen affair are misinterpreted, by all but the baneful Hilde, as dynamic police work. If there's a hollow note in the screenplay, it's the Jan Holt character, apparently just a randy intellectual who happened to be in the wrong place with the wrong girl at the wrong time, and whose own agenda is never clear as he toys with the quietly imploding Engstrom, then conveniently meets his own grim end.

Erik Skjoldbjaerg, a native of the Arctic-north territory portrayed onscreen, stated that he intended INSOMNIA as a "reversed film noir, with light, not darkness, as its dramatic force," and cinematographer Erling Thurmann-Andersen renders that light in all its shades, from Tanja's death in stark, high-grain images, to a mist-shrouded beach, a dismal coastal town perpetually puddled with rainwater, and, ultimately, Engstrom's tortured eyes glowing demonically behind his windshield as the picture fades to black. But INSOMNIA's psychological depth, not technical tricks or cheap scare tactics, is what should keep viewers up well past their bedtimes. *(Adult situations, sexual situations, nudity, violence, substance abuse.)*—C.C.

d, Erik Skjoldbjaerg; p, Anne Frilseth; exec p, Petter J. Borgli, Tomas Backstrom, Tom Remlov; w, Erik Skjoldbjaerg, Nikolaj Frobenius; ph, Erling Thurmann-Andersen; ed, Hakon Overas; m, Geir Jenssen; prod d, Eli Bo; sound, Kari Nytro, Randall Meyers (design); cos, Runa Fonne; makeup, Veslemoy Fosse Ree

Crime/Thriller **(PR: C MPAA: NR)**

INTERLOCKED: THRILLED TO DEATH ★★

(U.S., 1998) 94m Royal Oaks Entertainment ~ Unapix c
(AKA: BOLD AFFAIR, A)

Jeff Trachta *(Michael Anderson)*; Schae Harrison *(Eva/"Roxanne")*; Sandra Ferguson *(Emily Anderson)*; Howard Mungo *(Detective Taylor)*; Peter Fogel *(Archie)*; Kristine Mejia *(Heather)*; Bruce Kirby *(Walter Stevenson)*; Maitland Ward *(Eleanor)*; Dana Lee *(Kenji)*; George Alvarez *(Sly)*; John Rubinow *(Doctor)*; Caroline Cornell *(Epidural Nurse)*; Mark Conley *(Police Officer #1)*; Randal James Jeffrey *(Police Officer #2)*; Deva Nichole *(Hooker)*; Franklin Vallette *(Pizza Guy)*; Louhan Lowe *(Receptionist)*; Amy "Blue" Finnegan *(Young Nurse)*; Danica Ivancevic *(Lamaze Teacher)*

Soap stars populate the cast of this FATAL ATTRACTION clone, which went the straight-to-video route in 1998.

Eva (Schae Harrison) is an Internet temptress who approaches her victims by e-mail, and seduces them into meeting her. One of her conquests, a gentleman named Sly (George Alvarez), is put off by her after they have sex, and storms out of her life. When she begins working as a computer programmer in an advertising agency, however, she begins flirting with another target: executive Michael Anderson (Jeff Trachta), who is trying to land a big account while caring for his pregnant wife Emily (Sandra Ferguson). After an argument with Emily, Michael heads to work. He is e-mailed by Eva, who calls herself "Roxanne." She reveals her attraction to him, and they correspond, getting more and more intimate. In the meantime, Michael's co-worker Heather (Kristine Mejia) lands the account he has been pursuing, but when her car is mysteriously vandalized, she is unable to make her presentation to the client, and Michael and his partner Archie (Peter Fogel) win the account.

After receiving a watch from "Roxanne," Michael breaks off their steamy relationship, and he and Emily make up. This sends Eva into a frenzy. She hacks into Michael's computer, ruining his finances and deleting his work files. As a result of her sabotage, he loses the account, and Emily discovers evidence of his online affair. Soon after, Eva breaks into their house and stabs Emily in the shoulder. After conducting some research, Heather and Archie discover that "Roxanne" is Eva. They call Michael to warn him, but Eva taps into the call and kills the pair, pinning the blame on Michael. He is arrested and calls home, only to discover that Eva is now posing as a friend of Emily's. Michael convinces a policeman, Detective Taylor (Howard Mungo), to send a unit to the house, where they discover that Emily is about to give birth. In the delivery room, Eva tries to harm Emily by changing information on her chart. After Taylor tells Michael of Emily's situation, Michael breaks out of police custody. He saves Emily, and battles Eva. Taylor sees Eva about to kill Michael and trains his gun on her, but she stabs herself to death first.

More than a decade after FATAL ATTRACTION (1987) first surprised audiences, the world of low-budget film continues to crank out imitation after imitation of that influential (and rather elementary) thriller. The only innovation here is the use of e-mail for terror (and lovemaking) purposes.

Daytime soap stars Jeff Trachta, Schae Harrison, Sandra Ferguson, George Alvarez, and Maitland Ward (all cast members of "The Bold and the Beautiful") do their best to lend some liveliness to the film's melodramatic tangles, giving credible performances under the circumstances. What they are not able to enliven are the sex scenes, which come across like, naturally enough, torrid scenes from a daytime soap. Director Rick Jacobson, a veteran of several straight-to-video movies, struggles mightily to draw suspense out of the predictable scenario, and is successful in the final third, during which Michael and Eva engage in a furious fight that qualifies as the film's highlight. Their weapons of choice? Syringes, alcohol, scalpels, and electrodes(!).

Though not quite on the level of the straight-to-video "classic" BODY CHEMISTRY (1990), this is a serviceable variant on the "mistress from hell" thriller subgenre. *(Violence, sexual situations, nudity, profanity.)*—P.L.

d, Rick Jacobson; p, Androush Fatassian, Don Key; exec p, Robert Baruc; co-p, Jeff Trachta; w, Al Sophianopoulos; ph, Jesse Weathington; ed, Jeffrey Schwartz; m, Don Zelig; prod d, Tom Salvitti; set d, Nancy Lowry; sound, Lee Alexander, Gerald Beg; casting, Joey Paul; cos, Lia Niskanen; makeup, Megan Johnson; stunts, Patrick Statham

Erotic/Thriller **(PR: O MPAA: R)**

INVADER, THE ★½

(U.S., 1998) 97m Spectator Films; Promark Entertainment Group ~ LIVE Entertainment c

Sean Young *(Annie Nielsen)*; Ben Cross *(Renn)*; Daniel Baldwin *(Jack Logan)*; Nick Mancuso *(Willard)*; Lynda Boyd *(Gail)*; Tim Henry *(Older Cop)*; Ken Tremblett *(Davidson)*; Robert Andre *(McNeil)*; Craig Brunanski *(Gessner)*; Joe Maffi *(Bartender)*; Alan Franz *(Rookie Cop)*; Howard Storey *(Hunter #1)*; Patrick Stevenson *(Hunter #2)*; Linda Ko *(Doctor)*; Stephen Dimoupolous *(Motel Clerk)*; Kyle Hogg *(Classroom Boy)*; Alexa Mardon *(Classroom Girl)*; Mark Baur *(Portsmith Cop)*; Jim Filipone *(Helicopter Cop)*; J.M. Landry *(The Man)*

STARMAN (1983) meets THE TERMINATOR (1984) in this terminally uneventful straight-to-video title.

The alien Renn (Ben Cross) crash-lands his ship in Washington state, while a pursuing extraterrestrial craft is struck down by lightning. Renn tracks down infertile schoolteacher Annie Nielsen (Sean Young). Annie is estranged from her cop boyfriend, Jack Logan (Daniel Baldwin), because she's not interested in adopting children. At a nightclub, Renn passionately kisses Annie and departs; after collapsing the next day, Annie learns that she is over two months pregnant. That night, Renn kidnaps her, and Jack sets out in pursuit. The enemy alien, calling himself Willard (Nick Mancuso), joins Jack's team, claiming to be a bounty hunter and that Renn is a wanted criminal.

Renn explains to Annie that he is among the last of a persecuted alien race, and that the baby she is carrying is necessary to propagate his kind. They begin to develop feelings for each other. Willard eventually shows his true colors, shoots several cops and attempts to kill Jack. On a tram to a mountaintop, Renn delivers Annie's baby; at the summit, he is attacked and mortally wounded by Willard before he electrocutes his enemy. As Jack arrives, Renn informs Annie that she can now have children, then dies, and his people arrive to spirit his body and the baby back into space.

The problem with THE INVADER is not so much that it is derivative, but that it does so little with its borrowed parts. One waits in vain through its overlong running time for a truly imaginative twist or character quirk, and is ultimately left to wonder what led these good actors to take on such colorless parts. Each of the lead characters has only one distinctive trait: Annie is very vulnerable, Renn is very earnest, Jack is very determined, and Willard is very, very bad. Much of the film is concerned with little more than these people following each other through the forest, into a small town and back into the woods, interrupted by a rare affecting moment (as when Renn uses an alien device to allow Annie to see her rapidly developing baby).

This is all a shame, as writer-director Mark Rosman made a stylish debut with THE HOUSE ON SORORITY ROW (1982) and was able to goose some excitement into the formulaic EVOLVER (1996). This time, his work is distinguished only by its predictability, and despite the copious stunt credits at the end, the action is routine and underwhelming. *(Violence, sexual situations, profanity.)*—M.G.

d, Mark Rosman; p, Lisa Richardson; exec p, David Newlon, Jon Kramer; co-p, Lawrence McDonald; w, Mark Rosman; ph, Gregory Middleton; ed, Joseph Gutowski; m, Todd Hayen; prod d, Eric Norlin; art d, Walter Ockley; set d, Michael Webb; sound, Mark Schroeder, Paul Ratajczak; fx, Stargate Films, Inc., Sam Nicholson, Dan Schmidt, Michael Huitron, Al Benjamin; casting, Elisa Goodman, Abra Edelman, Lindsay Walker; cos, Barb Nixon; makeup, Dana Hamel, Rudy Beltramello (effects), Jarmen Janeza Benjamin (effects); stunts, Marc Akerstream, Rick Pearce

Science Fiction **(PR: O MPAA: NR)**

INVISIBLE DAD ★

(U.S., 1998) 90m Royal Oaks Entertainment ~ Sacis Entertainment/Unapix c

William Meyers *(Doug Baily)*; Daran Norris *(Andrew Baily)*; Mary Elizabeth McGlynn *(Sandy Collier)*; Steve Scionti *(Duncan Gilbert)*; Robert Donovan *(J. Emerson Rivington/Gerald Rivington)*; Ross Hagen *(Stillwell)*; Charles Dierkop *(Mr. Weiderman)*; Nicholas Dunn *(Jimmy)*; Karen Black *(Courtney Witmer)*; Shayna Ryan *(Shari Vail)*; Mark Kadlec *(Artie)*; Vicki Skinner *(Mrs. Wiederman)*; Hoke Howell; Carl Lamb; John Maynard; Tony Lorea; Gary Graver; G. Gordon Baer; John Murgo; Roberto Correa; Steve Latshaw; Joe Haggerty; Claire Polan; Bob Vincent; Kim Read

The cluttered, banal children's comedy INVISIBLE DAD is hard to watch, for reasons unrelated to its title.

Teen electronics buff Doug Baily (William Meyers) is new in town, the latest of many moves for his widowed, workaholic dad Andrew (Daran Norris), an architect now creating a shopping mall. Their house previously belonged to an eccentric inventor, and neglected Doug finds his ultimate achievement, a computerized gizmo that makes wishes come true. Doug wishes for harmless things, like finishing his homework or teleporting a bikinied girl from the TV into the living room. But when Andrew finds the machine he demands Doug destroy it, declaring that Bailys earn solely through honest labor. "I wish my dad would just disappear," mutters Doug before smashing the device. Sure enough, the wish turns Andrew transparent, perhaps permanently.

The Invisible Dad adapts as best he can, doing his renderings at home and wearing head-to-foot clothing (including a beekeeper's mesh hat) when he ventures outside. Doug meanwhile tries to repair the machine, with the eventual aid of an African explorer (Robert Donovan), the twin brother of its original inventor. Invisibility comes in handy for Andrew when an office rival steals his blueprints and tries to give the mall contract to corrupt builders in exchange for kickbacks. Andrew exposes the perfidy, just as his son manages to wish him visible again. The machine is taken to remote Africa for safekeeping, and Andrew Baily decides to share more quality time with Doug.

Prolific cheapie director Fred Olen Ray (who at one point was directing ten features per year) previously devised a formula kiddie film called INVISIBLE MOM (1998) for direct-to-cable and home-video markets. In INVISIBLE DAD, Ray manages to conjure a follow-up that resists being a remake or sequel. One hopes mainstream filmmakers, allegedly far more upmarket than Fred Olen Ray, would set similar goals, in an era in which Hollywood eats its own waste products with further blockbuster sequels and overhyped adaptations of comic books and TV shows. That mild appreciation aside, INVISIBLE DAD is pretty bad. All actors apparently learned the dramatic arts from a whoopee cushion, and both script and character continuity leave a lot to be desired (blowhard Andrew tolerates being invisible better than he can handle Doug not finishing household chores). Goonish subplots come and go, like the one about a neighborhood paranoiac (Charles Dierkop) who believes the Bailys are aliens, providing unwelcome comic relief from the comic relief.

Juvenile lead William Meyers plays what amounts to the straight man in all these sandbox antics, but even he can't wring much out of the canned moral about a driven single parent needing to spend time with his kid. That cliche has gotten so old one can only ponder what sort of nightmarish upbringings drive successive generations of screenwriters to revive it. Special effects are unimpressive, and in-joke fans should be similarly unenthused that Doug "invents" a videogame called Amazing Mouse Maze, which itself was a plot detail from producer/actor Andrew Stevens's R-rated thriller THE CORPORATION (1997). *(Substance abuse.)* —C.C.

d, Fred Olen Ray; p, Andrew Stevens, Ashok Amritraj; exec p, Pablo Dammicco, Stefano Dammicco, Robert Baruc; w, Steve Latshaw; ph, Gary Graver; ed, Vanick Moradian; m, Jeffrey Walton; art d, Yvette Taylor; sound, Lee Alexander, Bill Montei; fx, John Crawford; cos, Bonnie Stauch; makeup, Rhonda Rae; stunts, Bobby Bragg

Children's/Science Fiction/Comedy (PR: A MPAA: NR)

INVISIBLE MOM ★★

(U.S., 1997) 82m Royal Oaks Entertainment; Concorde Productions ~ New Horizons Home Video c

Dee Wallace Stone *(Laura Griffin)*; Barry Livingston *(Karl Griffin)*; Trenton Knight *(Josh Griffin)*; Russ Tamblyn *(Dr. Woorter)*; Christopher Stone *(Colonel Cutter)*; Phillip Van Dyke *(Skeeter)*; Stella Stevens *(Mrs. Pringle)*; Joey Andrews *(Johnny Thomas)*; Brinke Stevens *(Dr. Price)*; John Ashley *(Mr. Pringle)*; Vanessa Koman; Fred Olen Ray; Beth Ulrich; Tripp Reed; William C. Martell; Pamela Phillips

Colorless is the word that best describes this low-budget children's effort.

Mild-mannered inventor Karl Griffin (Barry Livingston) finds all his fanciful, altruistic experiments co-opted by overbearing boss Dr. Woorter (Russ Tamblyn), who declares that anything Griffin develops is the sole property of the science lab where they work. When Karl attempts an invisibility serum, he takes the research home, away from Woorter's greedy gaze. Karl erases the family dog Cosmo from sight, and announces his success to wife Laura (Dee Wallace Stone) and son Josh (Trenton Knight).

Josh has been grounded for messing up the house (actually the fault of the invisible Cosmo), and sees the serum as a way to sneak out and have some fun with his buddies. He pours the chemical into a soda bottle, but Mrs. Griffin drinks the stuff instead. Indeed, the serum does work on humans, a theory that Karl did not want to test until he had an antidote. Now, while Laura gets accustomed to invisibility, her husband must use the lab's computers to formulate a cure. All this is closely monitored by Woorter, who waits until Karl brews a counteractive serum. Then Woorter has Griffin arrested for the possible murder of his disappeared wife, and puts Josh in an orphanage. The clever villain even anticipates Laura attempting a rescue. He traps and cages the Invisible Mom as his proof when he presents the serum to the US military as a way to create undetectable soldiers. Laura escapes, however, and infiltrates the inquest into her husband's sanity. Unseen, Laura pranks and pokes main accuser Woorter until he looks like a lunatic instead. Vindicated, Karl is immediately rewarded with Woorter's job. At the fadeout the happily reunited Griffins face a fresh challenge: Cosmo has lapped up Karl's new growth serum.

Harmless but bland, INVISIBLE MOM may well have been an installment in Disney's downtrending "Wayne Szalinski" series that kicked off with HONEY, I SHRUNK THE KIDS (1989), but for the low-budget scale and painfully threadbare special effects. Props hung on wires and a novelty-shop invisible-dog collar don't come close to James Whale's original THE INVISIBLE MAN (1933), even though this movie affectionately quotes from the Claude Rains classic. Plotting is predictable, from the entrance of a standard-issue school bully to the lame closing gag.

Still, veteran actress Dee Wallace Stone maintains her dignity in the title role, playing it surprisingly straight. Russ Tamblyn, whose roller-coaster career ranged from dancing in WEST SIDE STORY (1961) to bottomed-out freak parts in the likes of DRACULA VS. FRANKENSTEIN (1971), also does nicely as the smug, suave bad guy. Executive producer Andrew Stevens's own mom, actress Stella Stevens, has a (visible) supporting part as a nosy neighbor, and prolific cheapie director Fred Olen Ray does a cute bit as an unflappable cabbie. Also in the cast is actor Christopher Stone, Dee Wallace's husband and frequent co-star, as a military man whose mild double-entendres are the only remote excuse for the PG rating. Christopher Stone died in 1995 of a heart attack, well before this film was released to cable-TV and home-video markets. —C.C.

d, Fred Olen Ray; p, Fred Olen Ray; exec p, Andrew Stevens, Ashok Amritaj; w, William C. Martell; ph, Gary Graver; ed, Peter Miller; m, Jeffrey Walton; prod d, Helen Harwell; art d, Lori Kussin; sound, David Waelder; fx, Mark Rappaport, Jason Ryan; makeup, Heidi Grotsky, Pamela Phillips

Children's/Science Fiction/Comedy (PR: A MPAA: PG)

IRIS AND ROSE

(SEE: UNDER THE SKIN)

J

JACK FROST ★

(U.S., 1998) 96m Canton Company; Big Kids Entertainment; Warner Bros. ~ Warner Bros. c

Michael Keaton *(Jack Frost)*; Kelly Preston *(Gabby Frost)*; Joseph Cross *(Charlie Frost)*; Mark Addy *(Mac MacArthur)*; Andy Lawrence *(Tuck Gronic)*; Eli Marienthal *(Spencer)*; Will Rothhaar *(Dennis)*; Mika Boorem *(Natalie)*; Benjamin Brock *(Alexander)*; Taylor Handley *(Rory Buck)*; Joe Rokicki *(Mitch)*; Cameron Ferre *(Pudge)*; Ahmet Zappa *(Snowplow Driver)*; Paul F. Tompkins *(Audience Member)*; Henry Rollins *(Sid Gronic)*; Dweezil Zappa *(John Kaplan)*; Steve Giannelli *(Referee)*; Jay Johnston *(TV Weatherman)*; Jeff Cesario *(Radio Announcer)*; Scott Thomson *(Dennis's Dad)*; Jimmy Michaels *(Devil's Goalie)*; Ajai Sanders *(Interviewer)*; John Ennis *(Truck Driver)*; Wayne Federman *(Dave, Policeman)*; Golden Henning *(Bank Customer)*; Pat Crawford Brown *(Scorekeeper)*; Mr. Chips *(Chester the Dog)*; Denise Cheshire *(In Suit Performer)*; Bruce Lanoil *(In Suit Performer)*; The Jack Frost Band: Trevor Rabin *(Trevor, Lead Guitar)*; Lili Haydn *(Lili, Violin)*; Louis Molino III *(Lou, Drummer)*; Scott Colomby *(Scott, Bass)*

A boy's dead father comes back to life as a snowman in JACK FROST, a treacly, holiday-themed fantasy that possesses all the warmth of a snowball down the pants.

Jack Frost (Michael Keaton) leads a Colorado rock-n-blues band, a job that too often keeps him away from his wife Gabby (Kelly Preston) and their 11-year-old son Charlie (Joseph Cross). At Christmastime, Jack gives his favorite harmonica to Charlie, telling the boy that it's magical, so that he will always be able to hear when Charlie plays it, no matter where he might be.

After a recording session keeps Jack away from Charlie's big hockey game, he promises Gabby and Charlie a holiday vacation at their Rocky Mountain cabin. But Jack disappoints yet again when his band is invited to play at a Christmas Day party for record company executives. On his way to the gig, Jack has a change of heart and heads home, but he is killed in an accident on a snowy mountain road.

One year later, Charlie builds a snowman, and dresses it with his dad's old scarf and hat. He blows on the magic harmonica and the snowman comes to life, inhabited by the spirit of his father. After calming Charlie down, Frost the Snowman makes up for lost time and missed opportunities by becoming Charlie's constant companion (though they keep his existence a secret from Gabby). Frost helps Charlie defeat the school bully in a snowball fight, and teaches Charlie his special hockey shot.

On an unseasonably warm Christmas Eve, Frost avoids melting long enough to see Charlie score the winning goal in the year's big game. After, Charlie races to get Frost to the safety of the mountain cold. They go to their family's cabin, but the next morning Frost breaks the news that it's time for him to leave. He tells Charlie not to despair because he will always be present in the boy's heart. Gabby arrives just in time to see that the magic was real, and say good-bye to her husband.

It's a good gamble: Make a "family" (i.e., kids) movie with some Christmas themes and if it's halfway decent, you've got a profitable video seller for years to come. For the creators of JACK FROST, though, that roll of the dice came up snake eyes. A labored effort that will bore even its youthful target audience, this E.T.-wannabe is woefully devoid of creative ideas, or even an approximation of honest emotion. A child's parent returns from beyond the grave, and the most important thing the script can have them do is win the big hockey game? Some of the slapstick comedy is mildly amusing (very mildly), but JACK FROST's attempts to tug at the heartstrings are as clumsy and chilly as a novice ice-skater. Worst of all, the Snowman itself (a product of the Jim Henson Creature Shop) is not particularly lovable: in fact, it's downright creepy.—P.R.

d, Troy Miller; p, Mark Canton, Irving Azoff; exec p, Matthew Baer, Richard Goldsmith, Jeffrey Barry, Michael Tadross; w, Mark Steven Johnson, Steve Bloom, Jonathan Roberts, Jeff Cesario (based on the story by Johnson); ph, Laszlo Kovacs; ed, Lawrence Jordan; m, Trevor Rabin; prod d, Mayne Berke; art d, Gary Diamond; set d, Ronald R. Reiss; sound, Thomas Brandau; casting, Marci Liroff; cos, Sarah Edwards

Children's/Fantasy (PR: A MPAA: PG)

JACK HIGGINS' MIDNIGHT MAN ★★

(U.S./Canada, 1996) 104m Telescene Pictures; Carousel Productions; Visionview Productions ~ Showtime/Viacom c

Rob Lowe *(Sean Dillon)*; Hannes Jaenicke *(Engel)*; Kenneth Cranham *(Sir Charles Ferguson)*; Deborah Moore *(Hannah Bernstein)*; Daphne Cheung *(Su Yin)*; Michael Sarrazin *(Tayi)*; Ben Gaule *(Mirov)*; Ellen Cohen *(Myra)*; James Duggan *(Danny Farmer)*; Samantha Giles *(Mary Farmer)*; Aaron Shirley *(Dovotny)*; John Warnaby *(Nigel)*; Laura Marine *(Tania)*; Jay Simon *(Billy)*; Simon Kelly *(Jack Harvey)*; Ron Berglas *(Harvey Flood)*; Fernard Monast *(Touissant)*; Bunny Reed *(Korchov)*; Herve Sogne *(Jacob Joubert)*; Steven Lander *(Pierre Joubert)*; Oengus MacNamara *(Frank Doyle)*; Stefan Gryff *(Antov)*; Pete Smythe *(Leon)*; Peter Riemens *(Sir Charles' Driver)*; Enrich Redman *(Ilya)*; Vito Grossman *(Mordechi)*; David Buckley *(Diplomat)*; Cirian O'Hai *(Francis)*; Brendan Morgan *(Jeweller)*

Rob Lowe stars as soldier of fortune Sean Dillon in this first of four films adapted from the novels of Jack Higgins. The film premiered on The Movie Channel and made its home-video debut in 1998.

British Secret Service officials Sir Charles Ferguson (Kenneth Cranham) and Hannah Bernstein (Deborah Moore) pressure former mercenary Sean Dillon (Rob Lowe) to unmask elusive assassin Engel (Hannes Jaenicke), but Dillon is reluctant to capture the man who once saved his life. Discovering that Engel's target is Sir Charles, Dillon employs a remote-controlled auto and dummies to dupe Engel into thinking he has car-bombed his nemesis.

When Engel heatedly confronts Dillon about the ruse, Dillon's worried girlfriend pulls a gun on the high-strung assassin, who opens fire in self-defense; the Dillon-Engel friendship is finita. Through snitches, Dillon learns that Engel is in the market for a deadly high-powered rifle. To obtain the weapon, Engel prevails upon old IRA weapons master Danny Farmer (James Duggan) to create one for him. He coldly romances Danny's crippled daughter Mary (Samantha Giles) to cinch the deal, but winds up falling for her. Dillon informs the IRA that Engel is planning to let them take the fall for an upcoming hit with Danny's traceable rifle. After the IRA wipes out foolhardy Danny, the police prevent Engel from assassinating his targets, Prince William and Prince Henry. Informed of Engel's role in her father's death, Mary tips off the Secret Service. At an airport rendezvous, Engel makes sure Mary is safe before he commits suicide with his revolver.

Despite a surfeit of the usual Jack Higgins's claptrap (too many triple crosses, extraneous dastards, stop-and-go suspense development), MIDNIGHT MAN benefits from exploring the human side of its international hit men. Even after botching his strike against the Royal Family, Engel never loses his cool; it's his affection for Mary that brings him down. Engel's surprising vulnerability is neatly juxtaposed with loner Dillon's own doomed relationship. Jaenicke's charismatic turn as the callous trigger-man is outstanding. Aside from those virtues, though, MIDNIGHT MAN pours out formulaic spyjinks mired in a formula that should be varied by source author Jack Higgins. *(Graphic violence, extreme profanity, sexual situations.)*—R.P.

d, Lawrence Gordon-Clark; p, Jim Reeve; exec p, Romain Schroeder, David Elstein, Paul Painter, Jim Howell; co-p, Robin Spry; w, Jurgen Wolff (based the novel *Eye of the Storm* by Jack Higgins); ph, Ken Westbury; ed, Tim Ritson; m, Leon Aronson; prod d, James Helps; art d, Simon Bowles; set d, Daisy Bodley; sound, Viktor Dekker (mixer); fx, Harry Wiessenhaan; casting, Elite Agency; cos, Deborah Alexander; makeup, Marie Jose-Lopez, Lesley Lamont-Fisher; stunts, Rick Wiessenhaan

Spy/Action **(PR: C MPAA: R)**

JACK HIGGINS' ON DANGEROUS GROUND ★★

(U.S./U.K., 1996) 97m Visionview Productions; Carousel Productions; Telescene Productions ~ Paramount Home Video c

Rob Lowe *(Sean Dillon)*; Kenneth Cranham *(Sir Charles Ferguson)*; Deborah Moore *(Hannah Bernstein)*; Jurgen Prochnow *(Carl Morgan)*; Ingeborg Dapkunaite *(Asta)*; Daphne Cheung *(Su Yin)*; Claude Blanchard *(Don Giovanni)*; Yvonne Antrobus *(Lady Campbell)*; Richard Rees *(Yuan Tao)*; Christopher Greet *(Chiao Lin)*; Burnell Tucker *(US President)*; Jason Hetherington *(Major Ian Campbell)*; Richard Orr *(Michael Ahern)*; Maria Connolly *(Norah Bell)*; Hi Ching *(Lee Ho Ching)*; Sam Mancuso *(Marco)*; Peter Gilmore *(Murdoch)*; Gilbert Martin *(Angus)*; Adrian Cairns *(Professor Bellamy)*; Dudi Appleton *(Billy Quigley)*; Robert James *(Jack Tanner)*; Peter Harlowe *(Mountbatten)*; Nadio Fortuna *(Ponti)*; Tony Xu *(Mao Tse Tung)*; John Warnaby *(Nigel)*; Joseph Alessi *(Volonti)*; Avi Nassa *(Halabi)*; Richard Ridings *(Borga)*; Patrick Logan *(Young Tanner)*; Lawrence Elman *(Dr. Tony Jackson)*; Janice Kerman *(Maggie Turner)*; David Howey *(Roland)*; Christopher Whitehouse *(Driscoll)*

Pity poor super spy Sean Dillon, who just wants to come in from the cold! As in the other three entries in this series, which premiered on cable, adapted from Jack Higgins's novels, anti-hero Dillon is cajoled out of retirement; no wonder that, as Dillon, Rob Lowe looks so tired and primed for redundancy. The film premiered on Showtime in 1996, and made its debut on home video in 1998.

British secret service chief Sir Charles Ferguson (Kenneth Cranham) and his second-in-command Hannah Bernstein (Deborah Moore) inveigle former mercenary Sean Dillon (Rob Lowe) into protecting the visiting US president from Irish terrorists at a peace conference. However, the terrorists actual target is the Chinese Minister Chiao Lin (Christopher Greet). In the process of thwarting the assassination, Dillon gets stabbed. While Dillon recuperates, he is informed by Hong Kong businessman Yuan Tao (Richard Rees), a British ally, that the assassination attempt was plotted by Mafiosi hoping to seesaw financial leverage after China's takeover of Hong Kong.

It is revealed that, in the past, Lord Mountbatten once signed an extension of British sovereignty in Hong Kong with then-rebel leader Mao Tse Tung; that a WWII document guarded by Major Ian Campbell disappeared in a plane crash over the late Campbell's estate. Now, Hong Kong crimelords Don Giovanni (Claude Blanchard) and his nephew Carl Morgan (Jurgen Prochnow) covet the Chungking document.

Persuaded by Sir Charles to work for Her Majesty and Yuan Tao, Dillon curries the favor of Morgan's stepdaughter Asta (Ingeborg Dapkunaite). All the principals converge for a weekend at the estate of Lady Campbell (Yvonne Antrobus), the late Major's daughter. After Dillon dives into the Campbell's loch and retrieves the Chungking document, traitorous Asta seizes it at gunpoint. At a subsequent Mafia rendezvous with Communist representative Lee Ho Chiang (Hi Ching), Lee, Don Giovanni, and Morgan are gunned down by Dillon and the police. After Dillon retrieves the document during the melee, Asta escapes to London but gets stabbed by Sir Charles before she can kill Dillon. At the airport, as Sir Charles hands over the Chungking document to Yuan Tao, the historic covenant gets sucked up into a plane engine.

That climactic bit of irony suggests cynical bemusement, but will irk viewers who sit through 96 minutes of confusing intrigue only to have the scriptwriter wimp out on grounds of historical accuracy. One tires of author Jack Higgins's penchant for inventing fictitious documents (e.g., the Windsor Protocol, which figured in the next two films in this made-for-cable series, JACK HIGGINS' THUNDER POINT and JACK HIGGINS' THE WINDSOR PROTOCOL). ON DANGEROUS GROUND also suffers from script-overload upfront; the IRA assaults should have been tightened. Ultimately, Higgins's historical revisionism is too facile; this Sean Dillon action workout bandies about big ideas and lets them do the work of an out-of-shape, underdeveloped narrative. *(Graphic violence, profanity, adult situations.)*—R.P.

d, Lawrence Gordon-Clark; p, Jim Reeve; exec p, David Elstein, Paul Painter, Jim Howell, Robin Spry, Romain Schroeder; w, Christopher Wicking (based on the book by Jack Higgins); ph, Ken Westbury; ed, Tim Ritson; m, Leon Aronson; prod d, James Helps; art d, Simon Bowles; set d, Daisy Bodley; sound, Nic Le Messurier (mixer); fx, Harry Wiessenhaan; casting, Jennifer Joffrey; cos, Deborah Alexander; makeup, Lesley Lamont-Fisher, Marie Jose Lopez; stunts, Rick Wiessenhaan

Spy/Action **(PR: C MPAA: R)**

JACK HIGGINS' THE WINDSOR PROTOCOL ★★½

(U.K./Canada, 1998) 96m Telescene Pictures ~ Showtime c

Kyle MacLachlan *(Sean Dillon)*; Alan Thicke *(Senator Joplin Hardy)*; John Colicos *(Heinzer, Greenfield)*; Lisa Bronwyn Moore *(Lenny)*; Chris Wiggins *(Sir Charles Ferguson)*; Macha Grenon *(Catherine)*; Sonia Benerza *(Altina Morales)*; Janine Theriault *(Burundi)*; David Siscoe *(FBI Agent)*; Alan Fawcett; Vlasta Vrana; Ken Pogue; Eugene Clark; James Bradford; Lorne Brass; Serge Houde; Tom Rack; Colin Fox; Arron Tager

In this sequel to JACK HIGGINS' THUNDER POINT, which premiered on The Movie Channel, mercenary Sean Dillon counterchecks international power brokers who are infiltrating the White House under the aegis of the Windsor Protocol, a list of Nazi sympathizers and dormant bank accounts.

At an economics summit in Montreal, phony eco-terrorists snatch a busload of prominent politicians. The hijacking is a ploy to terminate a too-talkative British ambassador with links to the Neo-Nazi movement. By the time special agent Sean Dillon (Kyle MacLachlan) infiltrates the kidnappers' headquarters, the British ambassador has been killed by a terrorist following orders from Senator Joplin Hardy (Alan Thicke), one of the kidnapped dignitaries. Pretending to be a hero, Hardy camouflages his guilt by shooting his own terrorist.

Already suspecting a hidden purpose behind the kidnapping, Dillon is briefed by British Intelligence chief Sir Charles Ferguson (Chris Wiggins), who coordinates Dillon's US mission with field operative Lenny (Lisa Bronwyn Moore), who works out of her uncle's Washington tailor shop. Meanwhile, Sir Charles supports Dillon's mission by masquerading as a Nazi-sympathizing Swiss banker, but he doesn't fool the Nazi ringleader Mr. Greenfield, AKA Heinzer (John Colicos). After arranging the incapacitation of the standing Vice President, Heinzer backs Senator Hardy as the replacement and orders the near-fatal ambush of Sir Charles.

Staking out Heinzer's headquarters at a stationery store, Dillon kills the store manager but gets overpowered by Heinzer, who ties him up in the basement. As Lenny creates a distraction upstairs, Dillon breaks his bonds. When Dillon catches and overpowers Heinzer, Heinzer winds up choosing self-immolation in the basement over arrest. From a safe distance, Dillon detonates a bomb planted in the car of Hardy's fiancee Catherine (Macha Grenon), leading her to publicly discredit Senator Hardy at his press conference.

JACK HIGGINS' THE WINDSOR PROTOCOL takes advantage of the expository groundwork laid out by its prequel, THUNDER POINT. Instead of a far-flung game of global tag, this spy adventure is more of a compact game of hide-and-seek. Because there are fewer peripheral bad guys, the screenplay concentrates on energizing the major no-goodniks, thus allowing John Colicos to flesh out his reprehensible anti-Semite, and permitting a cast-against-type Alan Thicke to show the unphotogenic ambition beneath the facade of a handsome public figure. Although plot incidents could have been reorganized and tightened, these second Holocaust scare tactics present an unlikely scenario with often nightmarish conviction. *(Graphic violence, extreme profanity, nudity, adult situations.)*—R.P.

d, George Mihalka; p, Jim Reeve, Robert Wertheimer; exec p, Paul Painter, Jim Howell, Robin Spry; assoc p, Stephen Zoller; w, David Preston, Stephen Zoller (based on the book by Jack Higgins); ph, Peter Benison; ed, Simon Webb, David McLeod; m, Stanislas Syrewicz; prod d, Tony Hall; art d, Jean Bourret; sound, Jo Caron, Greg Shine; casting, Elite Casting; cos, Paul Andre Guerin; makeup, Colleen Quinton; stunts, Minor Mustain

Action/Political/Spy **(PR: C MPAA: R)**

JACK HIGGINS' THUNDER POINT ★★

(U.S., 1998) 96m Telescene Communications; Visionview ~ Showtime c

Kyle MacLachlan *(Sean Dillon)*; Pascale Bussieres *(Jenny)*; Kenneth Welsh *(Armstrong)*; David Hemblen *(Sir Francis)*; Michael Sarrazin *(Crawford)*; Cedric Smith *(Henry Baker)*; Gillian Ferrabee *(Angela)*; Chris Wiggins *(Charles Ferguson)*; John Colicos *(Heinzer)*; Deano Clavet *(Junior)*; Gerard Parker *(Prime Minister)*; Mike Scherer *(Mike)*; Daniel Giverin *(London Policeman)*; Linda Singer *(Linda Singer)*

Kyle MacLachlan takes over from Rob Lowe as mercenary Sean Dillon in this third in a series of four Jack Higgins's adaptations. This espionage adventure, which premiered on The Movie Channel, is fancifully embroidered with leftover nightmares about the Third Reich, but standard in all other respects.

Treasure hunter Henry Baker (Cedric Smith) hits the jackpot when a Caribbean dive nets him the Windsor Protocol, Hitler's long-lost directive for a Nazi resurgence. (Allegedly signed by the Duke of Windsor, the document also contains information about dormant bank accounts, and 1990s swastika-loving politicians hope to use the money to resurrect Hitler's dreams.) Baker is murdered by neo-Nazis who then terrorize his ward Jenny (Pascale Bussieres), believing she can lead them to where Baker hid the Protocol.

At the behest of British Intelligence, Sir Francis (David Hemblen) hires mercenary Sean Dillon (Kyle MacLachlan) to protects Jenny and to find the document. What Dillon doesn't realize is that Sir Francis is a Nazi sympathizer. Without knowing where it is, Jenny agrees to sell the Windsor Protocol to the British government. Subsequently, fascist industrialist Armstrong (Kenneth Welsh) orders his thugs to ply Jenny with truth serum. When that fails, they torture and murder her friend and Baker's former pilot, Crawford (Michael Sarrazin).

Mistakenly believing that Dillon's go-between dealings with Armstrong are a betrayal, Jenny gives Dillon the slip and hides out with her pal Angela (Gillian Ferrabee), who's nearly murdered by an Armstrong henchman. Reunited with Dillon, Jenny discovers a note in a necklace given her by Baker which leads her to the hiding place of the Protocol (in a relative's crypt). She gives the document to the treacherous Sir Francis. At the climax, Armstrong orders the execution of Sir Francis for being too wishy-washy, and Dillon infiltrates Armstrong's estate and assassinates his hired killers. Dillon shoots Armstrong to death—but not until he has faxed the Windsor Protocol's contents to a Hitler loyalist in Washington, DC.

What a doomsday coda! By the time THUNDER POINT sputters to its conclusion, we are so saturated in gratuitous violence (e.g., gouging out Crawford's eyes), we don't care about the chances of a second coming of Hitler. The nonstop assault on our sensibilities is more to be feared than anything the Fuhrer-fixated villains might later do. Given the gloating fondness for brutality in evidence, one would think the film's perpetrators had unearthed the Marquis De Sade's Protocol. Unlike a campy diversion like THE BOYS FROM BRAZIL (1978), THUNDER POINT is grim and humorless. The thrill sequences are competently staged, but the direction has no brio and the cast performs by rote. The story was continued in a sequel, JACK HIGGINS' THE WINDSOR PROTOCOL (1998). *(Graphic violence, extreme profanity, nudity, adult situations.)*—R.P.

d, George Mihalka; p, Jim Reeve, Robert Wertheimer; exec p, Paul Painter, Jim Howell, Robin Spry; assoc p, Stephen Zoller; w, Morrie Ruvinsky (based on the novel by Jack Higgins); ph, Peter Benison; ed, David R. McLeod; m, Stanislas Syrewicz; prod d, Tony Hall; art d, Jean Bourret; sound, Gabor Vadnay; fx, Cineffects; casting, Elite Casting; cos, Paul Andre-Guerin; makeup, Colleen Quinton; stunts, Minor Mustain

Action/Spy **(PR: C MPAA: R)**

JACK LONDON'S THE CALL OF THE WILD: DOG OF THE YUKON ★★½

(Canada/U.S., 1996) 93m Wild Dog Films; Blue Rider Pictures; Erratic Entertainment ~ Hallmark Entertainment c

Rutger Hauer *(John Thornton)*; Luc Morissette *(Perrault)*; Burke Lawrence *(Charles)*; Bronwen Booth *(Mercedes)*; Charles Powell *(Kal)*; Robert-Pierre Cote *(Francoise)*; Lynne Adams *(Maggie)*; John Dunn Hill *(Hans)*; Jack Langdijk *(Pete)*; John Novak *(Matthewson)*; Steve Adams *(Kerns)*; Richard Dreyfuss *(Narrator)*

The umpteenth dramatization of Jack London's primordial sled-dog novel has some intriguing casting choices, but doesn't do much to lead the pack.

During the Gold Rush of the late 1800s, miners clamor for big, resilient dogs to tackle the Arctic snows. So it is that Buck, a pet on an idyllic Sacramento estate, is literally dognapped, clubbed into snarling obediance, taken up North and sold to Yukon mail-carrier Perrault (Luc Morissette). While in the care of this firm but fair master, Buck adapts to the brutality of the frontier, finally killing another dog for leadership of the sled team. Perrault sells Buck to Charles (Burke Lawrence) and Mercedes (Bronwen Booth), a gold-hungry pair of tenderfeet from Milwaukee who foolishly drive their dogs past the point of exhaustion as they work toward the fabled ore fields. Charles almost shoots Buck, but the animal is saved and sheltered by John Thornton (Rutger Hauer), a veteran prospector wintering in the area. Thornton gains the dog's trust, love, and devotion, even though Buck feels an urge to run feral and free in the wilderness.

When Buck wins a sled-pulling contest, Thornton has the money to look for a legendary lost mine deep in Indian territory. Thornton indeed strikes it rich, but he's fatally wounded by hostile natives. Buck kills the marauders, and, after brooding over his slain master, heeds "the call" and joins the resident wolves. For years afterwards, Indians tell of a mighty "ghost dog" and his progeny prowling the valley.

The genius of Jack London's novel is how persuasively it takes readers into the canine mind; almost the whole story takes place from Buck's simple, unsentimentalized point of view. Screen adaptations must contend with human characters who barely register as three-dimensional personalities. Rather than filling out the narrative with contrived anthropocentric scenes and subplots, the filmmakers here simply have actor Richard Dreyfuss reciting lengthy passages of London's prose—an effective device, but one upon which director Svatek relies overmuch. The gold-crazed Homo Sapiens in the cast are generally flat, Hauer most disappointingly so (fans might recall that Ridley Scott metaphorically compared the Dutch actor to a wolf in 1982's BLADE RUNNER). Buck himself is played by three different dogs, all rather shaggy and unhandsome St. Bernard-shepherd mixes, which itself is far more faithful to the original novel than the Rin Tin Tin lookalikes commonly cast in Yukon features.

One wonders what Jack London would say about the prominent, politically- correct opening disclaimer assuring viewers that all animal performers were monitored and pampered, all the savagery was simulated, and absolutely none of the performing cast of critters was harmed. *(Violence, profanity.)*—C.C.

d, Peter Svatek; p, Pieter Kroonenburg, Julie Allan; exec p, John Buchanan, Gary Howsam, Jeff Geoffray, Walter Josten; w, Graham Ludlow (based on the novel by Jack London); ph, Sylvain Brault; ed, Denis Papillon; m, Alan Reeves; prod d, Michael Devine; art d, Michael Devine; set d, Louise Pilon; sound, Louis Marion; fx, Pierre Rivard; casting, Vera Miller, Nadia Rona, Rosina Bucci; cos, Claire Nadon; stunts, Jerome Tiberghien

Adventure **(PR: A MPAA: PG)**

JAMES ELLROY: DEMON DOG OF AMERICAN CRIME FICTION ★★

(Austria, 1993) 90m Osterreichischer Rundfunk Fernsehen; Fischer Film ~ First Run Features c

James Ellroy; Bill Moseley; Phil Tinter *(Narration)*

Fans of crime fiction will love JAMES ELLROY: DEMON DOG OF AMERICAN FICTION; others won't be interested much by this documentary-essay about the life and work of Ellroy, one of America's top scribes of the genre.

Ellroy is the author of several best-selling murder mysteries set in Los Angeles, including *White Jazz, Black Dahlia,* and *L.A. Confidential,* which was turned into a popular movie in 1997. In JAMES ELLROY: DEMON DOG OF AMERICAN FICTION, Ellroy tours his old haunts in LA, discusses his writing, and tries to come to terms with his private obsessions.

During the car ride through the city streets, Ellroy shows the viewer the different enclaves, including the Mexican, Korean, and black sections of town. He passes by a hotel where he used to live when he was a young alcoholic thief—after being kicked out of high school and the army. He happens upon the spot where the Black Dahlia, the movie starlet, was slain in 1947, and he discusses his nearly primal interest in the case. Later, he revisits the area where his mother was also killed in a similarly brutal fashion when he was a young boy in the 1950s.

At his home, Ellroy talks about his work, his life as a golf caddie before he became a writer, his inspirations, other writers he enjoys reading (Chandler, Wambaugh, et al.), how Alcoholics Anonymous saved his life, and his new life with his second wife. At a signing for *White Jazz* at a local bookshop, Ellroy basks in the adulation of the crowd. Looking at LA from the Hollywood Hills, Ellroy ponders its power and mystique and wonders if he will ever fully understand it.

The Austrian filmmakers that shot JAMES ELLROY: DEMON DOG OF AMERICAN CRIME FICTION clearly embrace their subject, but they fail to convey their enthusiasm in an effective way. The 1993 documentary (completed many years before the filming of L.A. CONFIDENTIAL), rambles through Ellroy's life the same way Ellroy roams the street scenes. Quite unlike Ellroy's work, structure is a minor consideration, and pieces of his life remain totally unexamined (his two marriages, for example). Most problematically, James Ellroy himself does not cut a very dashing figure on screen. His writing style may possess flair and originality, but in front of the camera, Ellroy speaks in a stoic monotone, looks awkwardly away from the camera (when direct address would be more appropriate), and dresses in bright Hawaiian t-shirts that undercut his dark sensibility.

Ellroy isn't entirely dull, and he comes up with some pithy, writerly quotes: speaking about his research on the Black Dahlia, he says "some dim reptile part of me could capitalize on her death"; about his goals, he remembers, "I wanted to be Tolstoy, I wanted to be Dostoyevsky, I wanted to be Balzac. I wanted to be all these guys, who, frankly, I've never really read. I wanted to give people crime fiction on an epic transcendental scale." There are also some intriguing—if salacious and gruesome—stories from the files, and Ellroy's struggle to come to terms with his own demons almost emerges as touching.

Yet, the only truly memorable and cinematically satisfying touches in the film are the candid night shots of prostitutes and street people around the Sunset Strip. These brief, wordless sequences, the only ones not featuring Ellroy incidentally, speak eloquent volumes about LA's culture, atmosphere, and very mystique that so beguiles the author. Too bad nothing else in JAMES ELLROY: DEMON DOG OF AMERICAN CRIME FICTION rises to this level of these moments. *(Graphic violence, nudity, adult situations, substance abuse, extreme profanity.)*—E.M.

d, Reinhard Jud; p, Markus Fischer; w, Reinhard Jud, Wolfgang Lehner; ph, Wolfgang Lehner; ed, Karina Ressler; m, Deedee Neidhart, Sam Auinger; sound, Sam Auinger (design)

Documentary/Biography **(PR: C MPAA: NR)**

JANE AUSTEN'S MAFIA! ★½

(U.S., 1998) 86m Tapestry Films; Touchstone ~ Buena Vista c
(AKA: MAFIA!)

Jay Mohr *(Anthony Cortino)*; Billy Burke *(Joey Cortino)*; Christina Applegate *(Diane)*; Pamela Gidley *(Pepper Gianini)*; Olympia Dukakis *(Sophia)*; Lloyd Bridges *(Vincenzo Cortino)*; Jason Fuchs *(Young Vincenzo)*; Joe Viterelli *(Clamato)*; Tony LoBianco *(Marzoni)*; Blake Hammond *(Fatso Pauli Orsatti)*; Phil Suriano *(Frankie Totino)*; Vincent Pastore *(Gorgoni)*; Marisol Nichols *(Carla)*; Carol Ann Susi *(Clamato's Wife)*; Gregory Sierra *(Bonifacio)*; Vera Lockwood *(Rosa Cortino)*; Martin

Charles Warner *(Jimmy Big Features)*; Joseph Jumbo Rufo *(Willy Denunzio)*; Tyler Daniel Wenz *(Toddler)*; Jason Davis *(Geno)*; T.J. Cannata *(The Boy Diane)*; Louis Mandylor *(Middle-Aged Vincenzo)*; Georgia Simon *(Middle-Aged Rosa)*; Joey Dente *(Middle-Age Clamato)*; Sebastian Aza *(Young Joey)*; Seth Adkins *(Tiny Anthony)*; Andreas Katsulas *(Narducci)*; Joseph R. Sicari *(Rizzo)*; Allyson Call *(Jenny)*; Monica Mikala *(Young Rosa)*; Anthony Jesse Cruz *(Young Clamato)*; James Costa *(Immigration Thug)*; Mark Goldstein *(Clerk)*; Stefan Lysenko *(Ruffo)*; Sofia Milos *(Young Sophia)*; Anthony Crivello *(Luigi Cortino)*; Saverio Carubia *(Villager)*; Bill Livingston *(Guess The Number Croupier)*; Gerald Emerick *(Guess The Number Player)*; Frankie Como *(Waiter)*; Brian Tahash *(Bodyguard)*; Richard Abraham *(Evil Priest)*; Frank Birney *(Wedding Priest)*; Don Bovingloh *(Funeral Priest)*; Henry Harris *(Nonchalant Guy)*; Karen Leigh Hopkins *(Nurse)*; Dan Klein *(Judas)*; Pat Harvey *(Newscaster)*; Jerry Haleva *(Saddam Hussein)*; Mr. Oh *(Korean Soldier)*; Trinity Dance Troupe *(Irish Dancers)*; Jack Bernstein *(ATM Man with Double Chin)*

A ponderous parody overloaded with references to films as diverse as SHOWGIRLS (1995) and IL POSTINO (1994), JANE AUSTEN'S MAFIA! uses criminally dull humor to spoof the dormant gangster genre, and may only succeed in rubbing out the career of creator Jim Abrahams, who has long worn out the style of parody he helped create in the classic AIRPLANE! (1980).

Mobster Anthony Cortino (Jay Mohr) recounts his history and that of his father, Mafia patriarch Don Vincenzo (Lloyd Bridges). Young Vincenzo fled Sicily in 1901 after witnessing a Mafia drug deal and the murder of his father by a one-thumbed man. In 1966, he is the patriarch of a Mafia family that includes hot-headed moron son Joey (Billy Burke) and Anthony, who is in love with Diane (Christina Applegate). At Joey's wedding, Anthony meets the powerful crime boss Don Marzoni (Tony LoBianco) and his girl, stripper Pepper Gianini (Pamela Gidley). Vincenzo survives an assassination attempt by rival Gorgoni (Vincent Pastore). When Anthony offers to make the revenge hit, Diane walks out on him.

After icing Gorgoni, Anthony flees to Las Vegas, where he falls under the spell of Pepper. Anthony is entrusted by Don Marzoni to run the Peppermill Casino, but he's so distracted by Pepper that business suffers—exactly as Marzoni planned. Don Vincenzo turns control of the family over to Anthony, who discovers Pepper is having an affair with his brother Joey. After he storms out, Anthony is blown up by a car bomb. Don Vincenzo finally dies tending his garden. At his funeral, a badly burned Anthony notices that Don Marzoni has only one thumb.

Back in 1967, Anthony is reunited with Diane, who is now President of the United States. During their wedding ceremony, Anthony has his enemies, including Pepper and Marzoni, rubbed out. He banishes Joey to Fargo, North Dakota, for helping arrange the hit on their father. When President Diane confronts Anthony about rumors of his family business, he denies everything.

So unfunny it should be a crime, JANE AUSTEN'S MAFIA! seems to operate on the premise that references to other well-known movies are intrinsically funny. Director Abrahams employs his usual Tommy-gun approach to humor: Fire enough rounds and you're bound to hit something. But so what if he can invoke THE GODFATHER, PART II (1974) and FORREST GUMP (1994) in the same scene if the gags aren't funny? NATIONAL LAMPOON'S VEGAS VACATION (1997) already used the kiddie-games-in-the-casino joke. And how many times have we seen "the shooting victim who won't die"? Abrahams is firing blanks.

Of the performers, only Applegate, a splendid comic actress, makes a positive impression. As he demonstrated in the cast of "Saturday Night Live," Mohr is a gifted voice mimic, but he lacks charisma as an actor; his performance is so laid-back he makes Kevin Costner look like Robin Williams. Aping Sharon Stone in CASINO (1995) and Elizabeth Berkley in SHOWGIRLS, Gidley takes part in the movie's best gag, a pool sex scene that skewers both JAWS (1975) and SHOWGIRLS. Sadly, the late Bridges seems to be in a perpetual daze. His clumsy Vincenzo is just a rehash of his bumbling character in HOT SHOTS! (1991), making this a disappointing coda to a wonderful career. This labored parody raises the question: In the age of the Farrelly brothers (THERE'S SOMETHING ABOUT MARY) and *South Park*, is Abrahams still relevant? In 1998 he's still making O.J. Simpson and Menendez brothers jokes. On the other hand, he has a sexy character named "Pepper" but no Spice Girls gags.

Although the film retains its original title JANE AUSTEN'S MAFIA! on the screen, it was advertised simply as MAFIA! after studio marketing gurus discovered audiences were confused by the sly non sequitur. *(Violence, profanity, substance abuse, sexual situations.)*—J.Di.

d, Jim Abrahams; p, Bill Badalato; exec p, Peter Abrams, Robert Levy; assoc p, Jack Bernstein, Jennifer Gibgot; co-p, Greg Norberg, Michael McManus; w, Jim Abrahams, Greg Norberg, Michael McManus; ph, Peter Letarte; ed, Terry Stokes; m, Gianni Frizzelli; prod d, William Elliott; art d, Greg Papalia; set d, Jerie Kelter; sound, David Ronne (mixer); fx, Bruno Van Zeebroeck, Sam Nicholson; casting, Jackie Burch; cos, Mary Malin; makeup, Jasen Sica, Vera Yurtchuk; stunts, Ernie Orsatti

Comedy/Crime (PR: C MPAA: PG-13)

JERUSALEM ★★★

(Sweden/Denmark/Finland/Norway/Iceland, 1996) 166m
SVT Drama; Svensk Filmindustri; Metronome Film;
Danish Broadcasting Corp; YLE; Marko Rohr Productions;
Schibstedt Film; Norsk Rikskringkasting;
Rikisutvarpid-Sjonvarp ~ First Look Pictures c

Maria Bonnevie *(Gertrud)*; Ulf Friberg *(Ingmar)*; Lena Endre *(Barbro)*; Max von Sydow *(The Vicar)*; Olympia Dukakis *(Mrs. Gordon)*; Pernilla August *(Karin)*; Reine Brynolfsson *(Tim)*; Jan Mybrand *(Gabriel)*; Sven-Bertil Taube *(Hellgum)*; Bjorn Granath *(Storm)*; Viveka Seldahl *(Stina)*; Mona Malm *(Eva Gunnarsdotter)*; Hans Alfredson *(Mats Hok)*; Annika Borg *(Gunhild)*; Johan Rabaeus *(Eljas)*; Sven Wollter *(Big Ingmar)*; Mats Dahlbeck *(Hans Berger)*; Anders Nystrom *(Sven Persson)*; Claes Esphagen *(Forest Administrator)*; Fredrik Ohlsson *(Lawyer)*

A 1996 Swedish feature released directly to American home video in 1998, JERUSALEM is a high quality, late 19th century-set drama about a small Swedish community caught in the grip of religious fervor.

Though still a boy, Ingmar is left the family farm when his father dies. His older sister Karin (Pernilla August), whose irresponsible husband covets the inheritance, places her brother in the protective care of the local minister, Reverend Storm (Bjorn Granath). She agrees to manage the farm until Ingmar is old enough to do so himself.

As a young man, Ingmar (Ulf Friberg) fails in love with Gertrud (Maria Bonnevie), Storm's daughter. At the same time, a mysterious minister, Hellgum (Sven-Bertl Taube), arrives in town. A harsh, fervent preacher, Hellgum upsets many townspeople but wins over several others, among them Karin and Gertrud. Ingmar is shocked when he learns that Karin has given his farm to Hellgum, who establishes a religious commune on it.

One day, Hellgum tells his assembly that God has called him to Jerusalem to join a larger sect, and promptly sells the farm. Unable to purchase it himself, Ingmar agrees to marry the buyer's daughter, Barbro (Lena Endre), in hope of regaining control of the land, even though it means losing Gertrud. Gertrud, meanwhile, accompanies Hellgum to Palestine, where she and other followers move in with the sect. Over time, Gertrud comes to hate the sect's ascetic ways, although her faith remains strong.

When her father dies, Barbro offers to give Ingmar the farm and also proposes divorce, knowing that he still loves Gertrud. Ingmar agrees and goes to Jerusalem to find and bring back Gertrud. Gertrud resists Ingmar's beseeching, but eventually is persuaded to return with him. Upon arrival in Sweden, however, Ingmar discovers that Barbro has borne him a son in his absence. For Barbro's sake, Gertrud renounces any love for Ingmar. Quickly embracing his responsibility as a father, Ingmar takes his son to a church, has him baptized, and names him Ingmar.

JERUSALEM is an elaborate and intelligent adaptation of Nobel prize-winning author Selma Lagerlof's 1903 novel, itself based on a true story. Perhaps in deference to his source, writer-director Bille August has structured the film like a novel. Individual sequences are as fully developed and self-contained as chapters in a book, but are most meaningful when considered as part of an overarching narrative scheme. The film's pace is deliberate and steady, August directing with great attention to characterization and plot development. The resulting work delivers the narrative satisfaction of well-written literature.

The overall production contributes to a sense of grandness. The production design by Anna Asp is exact, carefully inclusive of such small but atmospheric details as the kind of decorations that would grace a small community wedding. The great cinematographer Jorgen Persson (August's regular director of photography) captures the simultaneously enchanting and forbidding qualifies of both the cold Swedish countryside and the arid desert city (the Jerusalem sequences were actually shot in Morocco).

Yet for all its quality, JERUSALEM is never emotionally engaging. August has given the film a lovely, minutely crafted texture, but he never gets below the surface, and while JERUSALEM is great to watch it is not particularly engrossing. The characters are vividly drawn and their motivations and actions are clear, but August's approach to the material is so removed that they remain distant, their problems unmoving. The austerity that defined August's PELLE THE CONQUEROR (1988) was appropriate to depicting the harsh lives of its protagonists, but is here misplaced in what is essentially a story of unfulfilled passion.

At the very least, however, JERUSALEM is a prime example of movie craftsmanship; and as a cautionary tale of the divisiveness of sectarianism, it is as timely today as when Lagerlog first wrote it. *(Violence, nudity, sexual situations.)*—D.C.

d, Bille August; p, Ingrid Dahlberg; exec p, Agneta Jansson; co-p, Mads Egmont Christensen; w, Billie August (based on the novel by Selma Lagerlof); ph, Jorgen Persson; ed, Janus Billeskov-Jansen; m, Stefan Nilsson; prod d, Anna Asp; sound, Paul Jyrala (mixer), Olli Paranen, Patrick Boullenger; casting, Renate Fryklund; cos, Ann Margret Fyregard; makeup, Horst Stadlinger, Lotta Ulfung

Drama **(PR: C MPAA: PG-13)**

JIDU HANLENG
(SEE: FROZEN)

JOEY ★★

(Australia, 1997) 96m Village Roadshow; Pacific Film & TV Commission ~ MGM/UA Home Video c

Jamie Croft *(Billy MacGregor)*; Alex McKenna *(Linda Cross)*; Rebecca Gibney *(Penny McGregor)*; Ed Begley Jr. *(Ambassador Ted Ross)*; Ruth Cracknell *(Sylvia)*; Harold Hopkins *(Kanga Catcher)*; Tony Briggs *(Mick)*; Errol O'Neill *(Old Man Dixon)*; Martin Jacobs *(Constable Walker)*

JOEY is another innocuous family film from Down Under in which adorable animals are hunted by crazed poachers and need to be rescued by wide-eyed young kids, who teach adults a thing or two in the process.

Young Billy MacGregor (Jamie Croft) lives on a farm in Australia with his widowed mom Penny (Rebecca Gibney), where he plays with a group of kangaroos, especially a baby called Joey. Unfortunately, the kangaroos congregate on the farm of Billy's animal-hating neighbor Dixon (Errol O'Neill), and he brings in a hunter known as the Kanga Catcher (Harold Hopkins) to remove the roos, which are drugged and taken to Sydney.

Joey escapes and is rescued by Billy, and the two of them venture into the city to find Joey's parents. Eventually, Billy hooks up with a young girl named Linda (Alex McKenna), the daughter of the new US ambassador Ted Ross (Ed Begley Jr.), who's also looking for some kangaroos. They discover that the kangaroos have been taken to an abandoned park called Kangaroo Kingdom, where the Kanga Catcher is organizing illegal human-kangaroo boxing matches. Billy and Linda go to her father for help, but he doesn't believe them and accuses Billy of kidnapping Linda. The kids run away and meet a rich old lady named Sylvia (Ruth Cracknell) who runs an animal rescue service.

Along with a TV reporter friend of Sylvia's, they all sneak into Kangaroo Kingdom during a fight and Billy uses a remote-controlled car with a built-in hidden camera to broadcast video of the illegal match on television. The Kanga Catcher is arrested and Joey is reunited with his parents. Back on Billy's farm, Linda and Billy play with the kangaroos while Linda's father gets friendly with Billy's mother.

JOEY contains all the ingredients of the modern family film, including a kindly single parent who's oblivious to her child's misadventures, cuddly animals endangered by caricatured villains, and a journey into the big, bad city, which is contrasted with the wholesome and idealized countryside. Thankfully, the film has refrained from the popular practice of putting human voices into the mouths of the animals, and kids will get a kick out of the well-shot footage of the kangaroos, as well as an amusing slapstick sequence where Billy's dog chases Joey through the kitchen and destroys an apple pie, a blender, and a dishwasher.

However, the filmmakers seem confused as to what age group they're trying to appeal to and have gone overboard with the depiction of the menacing city, replete with street gangs and threatening characters on every corner, as well as an excessively frightening portrayal of the Kanga Catcher and the boxing matches. Dressed in a long black-leather coat and hat, and brandishing a whip and a rifle, Kanga is always filmed from below and looks like a killer from a Spaghetti Western, while the vicious gladiator-like boxer who fights the kangaroos appears to have been left over from one of the old "Mad Max" movies. Tilted camera angles and distorted lenses, along with a hyperactive score and aggressive sound effects only add to the cartoonish exaggeration, which tends to swamp the film's worthy animal-rights message; but unfortunately, that style seems to be de rigueur for today's so-called family films, which emphasize noise and frenzied action over warmth and gentleness. *(Violence.)* —M.S.

d, Ian Barry; p, Michael Lake; exec p, Alex Waislitz, Heloise Waislitz, Greg Coote, Robyn Burke; assoc p, Maxwell Grant, Stuart Beattie; w, Stuart Beattie; ph, David Burr; ed, Lee Smith; m, Roger Mason; prod d, Peta Lawson; sound, John Schiefelbein; fx, John Cox; casting, Maura Fay; cos, Marion Boyce

Children's/Drama **(PR: A MPAA: PG)**

JOHN CARPENTER'S VAMPIRES ★★½

(U.S., 1998) 107m Spooky Tooth Productions; Storm King Productions; Largo Entertainment ~ Columbia TriStar c
(AKA: VAMPIRES)

James Woods *(Jack Crow)*; Sheryl Lee *(Katrina)*; Daniel Baldwin *(Montoya)*; Maximilian Schell *(Cardinal Alba)*; Thomas Ian Griffith *(Valek)*; Tim Guinee *(Father Adam Guiteau)*; Mark Boone Jr. *(Catlin)*; Gregory Sierra *(Father Giovanni)*; Cary-Hiroyuki Tagawa *(David Deyo)*; Tommy Rosales *(Ortega)*; Henry Kingi *(Anthony)*; David Rowden *(Bambi)*; Clarke Coleman *(Davis)*; Mark Silvertsen *(Highway Patrolman)*; John Furlong *(Father Molina)*; Angelina Calderon Torres *(Cleaning Lady)*; Jimmy Ortega *(Male Vampire #1)*; Gilbert Rosales *(Male Vampire #2)*; Danielle Burgio *(Woman Vampire #1)*; Laura Cordova *(Girl Vampire #2)*; Troy Robinson *(Male Master #1)*; Anita Hart *(Female Master #2)*; John Casino *(Male Master #3)*; Chad Stahelski *(Male Master #4)*; Steve Blalock *(Male Master #5)*; Marjean Holden *(Female Master #6)*; Cris Thomas Palomino *(Female Master #7)*; Julia McFerrin *(First Hooker)*; Lori Dillen *(Second Hooker)*; Jake Walker *(County Sheriff)*; Michael Huddleston *(Motel Owner)*; Todd Anderson *(Deputy Sheriff)*; Steven Hartley *(Clerk)*; Dennis E. Garber *(Limousine Driver)*; Robert L. Bush *(TV News Anchor)*; Frank Darabont *(Man With Buick)*; HOOKERS: Mona Garcia; Candice Kirkiles; Neva Lucero; Helen Moreno; Janice Richmond; Juanita Romano; Ann Romero; Elisa Valdez; April Winters

Packed with good ideas into which it never quite manages to sink its fangs, JOHN CARPENTER'S VAMPIRES makes excellent use of bleeding-edge gore effects, but lurches through an unfocused story line and curiously lifeless action sequences.

Jack Crow (James Woods) heads a crew of high-tech vampire hunters commissioned by the Vatican to wipe out the scourge of the undead. Their attack on a vampire nest in New Mexico fails to net the "master" vampire Valek (Thomas Ian Griffith), who gains revenge later that night by slaughtering everyone except Crow, his assistant Montoya (Daniel Baldwin), and Katrina (Sheryl Lee), a prostitute Valek already has bitten.

Fleeing, Crow realizes that Valek must have been tipped off. He tells Montoya to keep Katrina alive until she transforms so they can use her telepathic link to track the Master. Meanwhile, Crow reports to his superior, Cardinal Alba (Maximilian Schell), who explains that Valek was once a Catholic priest possessed by a demon, who in 1311 became the first Vampire Master. Alba assigns neophyte priest Father Adam (Tim Guinee) to aid Crow. Growing sympathetic to Katrina as she slowly changes into a vampire, Montoya is bitten by her. He hides the wound when Crow and Adam return. The priest explains that Valek is on the verge of capturing the long-lost Black Cross, used in Valek's long ago failed exorcism, which would allow vampires to walk in sunlight.

Led by Katrina's visions of her master, Crow, Montoya and Adam invade the deserted southwestern jail in which Valek and his minions are hiding. Crow is captured and Adam hides while Montoya and Katrina flee. Katrina completes her transformation into a vampire, and bites Montoya, killing him.

The ceremony to give Valek the full powers of the Black Cross is conducted by Cardinal Alba, who fears death and plans to join Valek in immortality. Adam disrupts the ceremony and he, Montoya, and Crow battle Valek to the vampire's ultimate destruction. Still sworn to destroy all vampires, Crow gives Montoya and Katrina a two-day head start.

While the needless plot complications (why is Adam reluctant to share information that could save his own life?) bog down the pace, the biggest problem with this film is the miscasting of Woods as Crow. With a physically unimposing figure, he awkwardly snarls Crow's one-liners with an intensity that makes it seem like he's trying to exterminate his fellow actors from the scene. One imagines Carpenter alter-ego Kurt Russell (ESCAPE FROM NEW YORK) cruising through this part with the perfect laconic attitude. As Montoya, Baldwin is sturdy—if stiff. Lee soldiers through yet another titillating part that ignores her acting chops in favor of her bare butt.

The special makeup effects by Robert Kurtzman, Gregory Nicotero, and Howard Berger's KNB Effects are state-of-the-art and extremely realistic. But despite the abattoir decor, the action sequences lack in energy: the vampires snarl and allow themselves to be ever-so-slowly dragged into the sunlight while the vampire killers stand and watch. There's a lot of screaming and howling, but not a lot going on. The movie uses lazy dissolves instead of punchy quick-cutting, which contributes to the lethargic pace. The screenplay, by John Steakley (based on his own novel, *Vampire$*) and Don Jakoby, is packed with flat, Carpenteresque dialogue, and wanders from its central focus too often. JOHN CARPENTER'S VAMPIRES may be Carpenter's best film in years, but it doesn't live up to its potential, and falls far short of the slick action standard set by the similar-yet-superior BLADE (1998). *(Graphic violence, adult situations, profanity, nudity.)*—J.Di.

d, John Carpenter; p, Sandy King; exec p, Barr Potter; co-p, Don Jakoby; w, Don Jakoby (based on the novel *Vampire$* by John Steakley); ph, Gary B. Kibbe; ed, Edward A. Warschilka; m, John Carpenter; prod d, Thomas A. Walsh; art d, Kim Hix; set d, David Schlesinger; sound, Hank Garfield (mixer); fx, Darrell D. Pritchett; casting, Reuben Cannon, Eddie Dunlop; cos, Robin Michel Bush; makeup, Gregory Nicotero, Robert Kurtzman, Howard Berger; stunts, Jeff Imada

Horror/Action/Thriller **(PR: O MPAA: R)**

JOHN WOO'S BLACKJACK

(SEE: BLACKJACK)

JOHNNY MYSTO BOY WIZARD ★★½

(U.S., 1998) 87m The Kusher-Locke Company; Full Moon Entertainment ~ Paramount c

Toran Caudell *(Johnny Mysto)*; Russ Tamblyn *(Blackmoor/Sid Berkowitz)*; Michael Ansara *(Malfeasor)*; Amber Tamblyn *(Sprout)*; Ian Ambercrombie *(Merlin)*; Patrick Crawford Brown *(Margaret Lattimer)*; Jack Donner *(King Arthur)*; Magda Catone *(Rose)*; Sarah Hazeltine *(Andrea)*; Eric Countryman *(Bunko)*; Catalina Mustata *(Guinevere)*; Patrick Renna *(Glenn)*; Cezara Dafinescu; Razvan Ionescu; Stefan Velniciuc; Claudiu Romila; Dan Victor; Theodor Danetti; Dan Moraru; Traian Zecheru; Gheorghe Danila; Doru Ana; Petre Moraru; Manuela Ciucur; Gabriel Mican; Igor Harnoff; Hazvan Castian; Margaret Tate; Ady Kuchok; Madalina Constantinescu

This middling children's fantasy went the straight-to-video route in 1998.

The medieval land of Merlin the Magician (Ian Abercrombie) is attacked by invaders. The wizard sends a mystic summons through time and space. In the present, an adolescent amateur magician dubbed Johnny Mysto (Toran Caudell) bumbles badly on his suburban backyard stage, so along with buddy Glenn (Patrick Renna) he seeks advice from TV illusionist "Blackmoor" (Russ Tamblyn). Blackmoor is an irascible has-been actually named Sid Berkowitz; sorry at disappointing the boys, he gives them a "magic" ring mailed to him by a well-wisher.

Back home, Johnny is amazed to discover he can perform genuine feats of sorcery with the ring on—but cannot retrieve his sister Andrea (Sarah Hazeltine) after making the little girl disappear in front of neighborhood kids. Accompanied by a shaken Blackmoor, Johnny and Glenn determine that the ring was passed down in a neighboring family for more than a thousand years, from Merlin himself. Only through Merlin can Johnny recover Andrea.

Johnny and Blackmoor teleport to Arthurian England, conquered by a ghoulish usurper named Malfeasor (Michael Ansara), who has imprisoned King Arthur (Jack Donner) and tricked Merlin out of his mighty ring. Johnny's presence now means that *two* mighty rings are present, but their opposing power cancels each other out, and Johnny fights the fiend. Fortunately, Blackmoor finds the sword Excalibur, and it tips the balance to destroy Malfeasor. A grateful Arthur knights Blackmoor, and Merlin returns the heroes to their own era, where Johnny makes Andrea reappear, just in time for their parents' return from a trip.

There's something innocent and appealing about the way in which JOHNNY MYSTO begins, focusing as it does on juvenile characters and their preoccupation with feats of legerdemain. But the hex of a slow pace and low budget keep the pot merely simmering instead of bubbling over with entertainment. The mythic Camelot (actually a castle near Bucharest) looks bleak, underpopulated, and uninviting, and both Merlin and Arthur lack any sense of grandeur.

Child-star-turned-B-cult-actor Tamblyn (TOM THUMB, SATAN'S SADISTS, INVISIBLE MOM), on the other hand, is most aptly cast as a Blackstone-type prestidigitator who's seen better days. Tamblyn's daughter Amber, eagerly spouting Olde English, takes a supporting role as Merlin's apprentice. For his part, Ansara tries hard to bring life into the film, but winds up looking like a hammier version of "Death" from THE SEVENTH SEAL (1957). The barrage of computer-generated special effects in the finale perk the proceedings up a bit, but as it stands, JOHNNY MYSTO is mostly forgettable kiddie fare. *(Violence, substance abuse.)*—C.C.

d, Jeff Burr; p, Mark Headley, Vlad Paunescu; exec p, Peter Locke, Donald Kushner; assoc p, Melanie Weiner; w, Benjamin Carr; ph, Viorel Sergovici; ed, Carol Oblath; m, Joseph Williams; prod d, Vali Calinescu; art d, Viorel Ghenea; set d, Ica Varna; sound, Dragos Stanomir; fx, Al Magliochetti; casting, Bob MacDonald, Perry Bullington; cos, Oana Paunescu; makeup, Mihai Stanescu, Dana Busoiu; stunts, Doru Dumitrescu

Children's/Fantasy/Adventure (PR: A MPAA: PG)

JOHNNY SKIDMARKS ★★★½

(U.S., 1998) 97m Cinepix Film Properties ~ Lions Gate Films c

Peter Gallagher *(Johnny Skidmarks)*; Frances McDormand *(Alice)*; John Lithgow *(Larry Skovik)*; John Kapelos *(Walter Lippinscott)*; Jack Black *(Jerry)*; Geoffrey Lower *(Woody Washawski)*; Charlie Spradling *(Lorraine)*; Bill Robertson *(Earl)*; Michael Weathered *(Ernie)*; Lee Arenberg *(Louie)*; David Doty *(Brooks Brothers)*; Marvin Moskowitz *(Lammings)*; Michael Beach *(Mike)*; Bill Lee Brown *(Coroner)*; Rick Hoffman *(Bartender)*; Pat Crawford Brown *(Mrs. Stanky)*; Jordan Taylor *(Officer Espinoza)*; Peter McKernan *(Helicopter Pilot)*; Vanessa Verdugo *(Waitress)*; Phillip Bruns *(Old Coot)*; William B. Ward Jr. *(State Senator)*

A bracing, thinking man's thriller, this neo-noir deals with a morally barren crime photographer who specializes in vehicular homicide and blackmail until he is forced to empathize with those he has abused. The film premiered on HBO and was subsequently released on home video in 1998.

Freelance photographer Johnny Skidmarks (Peter Gallagher) shoots car crashes for police detectives Larry Skovik (John Lithgow) and Woody Washawski (Geoffrey Lower). Off the job, he is also part of a blackmail ring masterminded by Walter Lippinscott (John Kapelos). Along with Walter's driver Earl (Bill Robertson) and Lorraine (Charlie Spradling), a hooker, Johnny sets up and photographs cheating husbands at motel trysts; Walter uses the photos to extort money or favors for Mafia associates.

Johnny finds Lorraine and Earl's corpses in death sites he is photographing. Worried, he uncharacteristically opens up about his past to Alice (Frances McDormand), a night owl who has begun frequenting the all-night greasy spoon where Johnny hangs out. Johnny continues confiding in this self-proclaimed lush until he spots a photo of her father, who bears an uncanny resemblance to one of Walter's long-forgotten marks. Johnny mistakenly suspects Alice of being behind the killings of his associates, and stops confiding in her.

After Walter and his attorney are killed, Johnny tells Detective Skovik about the blackmail racket. Suspecting either contumelious Washawski or mysterious Alice, Johnny fesses up about his profitable part-time gig. Shockingly, the hearty Skovik is Johnny's tormentor. The toupeed cop lost his wife and his honor in the aftermath of being snapped by Johnny, who didn't even recognize Skovik without his hairpiece. Skovik admits this to Johnny, and then savagely beats him up. Although Johnny flees, Skovik follows him by car to Alice's apartment where Johnny is turned away. Skovik knocks him unconscious and transports him to an abandoned building. By the time, Washawski stumbles upon a candid photo of Skovik in Johnny's mementos, Skovik is preparing to reeducate cold-hearted Johnny with sledge hammers, etc. Before the first blow, Washawski pumps Skovik full of lead. Transformed by his injuries and his comprehension of the suffering he blindly caused others, Johnny renews his relationship with Alice.

In most crime dramas, survival is the key issue, but here, Johnny has made an art out of "just getting by." This dark-hearted film addresses the high cost of survival, when its price is paid by the people you victimize. Benefiting from tart dialogue, the screenplay explores Johnny's conscious decision to shut down his emotions, before tracing the reawakening of his dormant humanity, via his encounters with those who have been victimized by his actions.

As the defensive loner Johnny, Peter Gallagher has his best role in years and draws the audience into the character's flawed perspective. John Lithgow registers like a witch-hunter from Salem in a bone-chilling performance, while the superb supporting cast rises to his level in more narrowly conceived roles. The film sputters a bit at the climax as Johnny keeps escaping Skovik's clutches, and Frances McDormand's shadowy role could be more fully integrated into the story line. Aside from these slipping cogs, this movie's suspense mechanism grinds away full blast. Daring the audience to ponder a conundrum about personal responsibility, JOHNNY SKIDMARKS pays big dividends to crime buffs willing to invest their intelligence in a philosophical thriller. *(Graphic violence, extreme profanity, extensive nudity, substance abuse, adult situations.)*— R.P.

d, John Raffo; p, Karen Severin, Karen Weaver, Michael Pascornek; exec p, Jeff Sackman, Andre Link, John Dunning; assoc p, William Preston Robertson; co-p, Frank Hildebrand; w, William Preston Robertson, John Raffo; ph, Bernd Heinl; ed, Sean Albertson; m, Brian Langsbard; prod d, Jerry Fleming; art d, Rami Rivera Frankl; set d, Betty Berberian; sound, Steuart P. Pearce (mixer), Patrick Mitchell (mixer), Ed White (mixer); fx, Ken Tarallo, Vincent Montefusco; casting, Ferne Cassel; cos, Bonnie Stauch; makeup, Suzanne Rodier, Gary Perticone, Todd Masters (special effects); stunts, Randy File

Thriller/Crime (PR: C MPAA: R)

JOURNEY TO THE BEGINNING OF THE WORLD
(SEE: VOYAGE TO THE BEGINNING OF THE WORLD)

JUNGLE BOOK: MOWGLI'S STORY, THE ★★½
(U.S., 1998) 76m Disney Enterprises ~
Walt Disney Home Video c

Brandon Baker *(Mowgli)*; Ryan Taylor *(Young Mowgli)*; Rajan Patal *(Indian Soldier)*; VOICES OF: Eartha Kitt *(Bagheera)*; Brian Doyle-Murray *(Baloo)*; Kathy Najimy *(Chil)*; Marty Ingels *(Hathi)*; Stephen Tobolowsky *(Tabaqui)*; Sherman Howard *(Shere Khan)*; Clancy Brown *(Akela)*; Peri Gilbin *(Raksha)*; Wallace Shawn *(Tarzan the Chimp)*; Ashley Peldon *(L'il Raksha)*; Fred Savage *(Narrator)*; Nancy Cartwright *(Skunk.Macaws/Others)*; Frank Welker *(Porcupine/Baboon/Jungle Noises/Others)*

Disney continues to pillage Rudyard Kipling's venerable yarn about the boy raised by wolves in the jungles of India for THE JUNGLE BOOK: MOWGLI'S STORY, a live-action made-for-video adventure that will amuse its target audience of younger children with its rambunctious scenes of a real boy interacting with real animals who speak with wisecracking celebrity voices.

While on safari with his parents, a small boy named Mowgli (Brandon Baker) is abandoned in the jungle when the evil tiger Shere Khan (voice of Sherman Howard) and his hyena sidekick Tabaqui (voice of Stephen Tobolowsky) attack their encampment. Shere Kahn is driven off by a gunshot wound, and Mowgli runs into the forest where he is adopted by a loving pack of wolves headed by the wise Akela (voice of Clancy Brown) and his mate Raksha (voice of Peri Gilpin).

As Mowgli grows into a strong boy, he's taught the ways of the wild by a collection of friendly animals, including Bagheera the panther (voice of Eartha Kitt), Baloo the bear (voice of Brian Doyle-Murray), and Hathi the elephant (voice of Marty Ingels). When Akela and Raksha refuse to turn Mowgli over to Shere Khan, the tiger has some monkeys lure the boy to a party, where he is locked up in a cabin. Shere Khan then tries to kill Mowgli, but he's thwarted by Raksha, who sacrifices her life to save Mowgli, and Baloo and Bagheera rescue him. When Mowgli learns that Shere Khan has killed his "mother" Raksha, he runs away, but returns to face down Shere Khan and defeats the animal by scaring it with a fire started with the matches he had found in the cabin. He then banishes the tiger from the jungle and goes to live in the "man village."

THE JUNGLE BOOK: MOWGLI'S STORY follows the basic plot of Kipling's story fairly closely, and Disney's 1967 cartoon version even more so. It is competently made (even if the Indian jungles look a lot like pristine Southern California theme parks), with some well-trained animals and amusing voice-overs, but it has been specifically designed for tots and preteens, with a plethora of music, dancing, and slapstick jungle comedy. When the animals aren't singing Curtis Mayfield's "Monkey Time," their dialogue seems to consist entirely of bad puns and modern colloquialisms ("Show me the honey," "Don't get your fur in a bunch," "You da' man cub") and the general level of humor is exemplified by a vulture named Chil, who's constantly being told to "chill, Chil," as well as the scene where the baby wolf suggests giving the man cub foundling the name of "poo-poo, pee-pee."

While there's certainly nothing wrong with aiming the film squarely at very young kids with silly and innocent fun (more so-called children's films should do the same), somebody at Disney was asleep at the wheel when they allowed the incredibly imprudent use of matches (and the enticing description of fire as the "red flower") by Mowgli as a sanctioned way to combat Shere Khan.—M.S.

d, Nick Marck; p, Mark H. Ovitz; exec p, Barry Bernardi; co-p, Nick Marck; w, Jose Rivera, Jim Herzfeld (based on the novel by Rudyard Kipling); ph, Ronn Schmidt; ed, Alan Baumgarten; m, Robert Folk; prod d, Thomas A. Walsh; sound, Phillip Seretti; fx, Van Ling (visual effects); cos, Tom Bronson

Children's/Adventure (PR: A MPAA: G)

JUNK FOOD ★★½
(Japan, 1998) 88m Junk Food Connection; Omiya Visual Image Production; Stance Company; Transformer c

Miyuki Ijima *(Miyuki)*; Shizuko Yamamoto *(Woman)*; Arata Furuta *(Yokoyama)*; Yoshiyuki *(Hide)*; Onimaru *(Ryo)*; MIA *(Myan)*; Ali Ahmed *(Cawl)*; Mariarna *(Esther Moreno)*; Kanji Tuda *(Sato)*; Choudry Ikram Ul Haq *(Sarym)*; Tatsutoshi Kawamura *(Shu)*; Akifumi Yamaguchi *(Boss)*; Keigo Naruse *(Murdered Man)*; Yoichi Okamura *(Miyuki's Husband)*; Mika Kumagai *(Shop Girl)*; Rumi Otori *(Shop Manager)*; Yuta Todo *(Kiku)*; Yoko Kobayasi *(Mami)*; KENTA.S *(Kenta)*; Kansai Horitatsu *(Horitatsu)*; Nobutaka Kuwabara *(Hide's Friend)*

Japanese culture takes a beating in JUNK FOOD, a harsh, uncompromising, but ultimately unexceptional tour through the squalor of a supposedly law-abiding nation.

In modern Tokyo, citizens with different backgrounds go about their day. Toshiko (Shizuko Yamamoto), an elderly blind woman, gets ready in the morning for a trip to the grocery store. Miyuki (Miyuki Ijima), a married office worker and drug-addict, kills her lover (Keigo Naruse) during a heroin fix, and rushes off to her job. In need of another fix, Miyuki blackmails her boss (Akifumi Yamaguchi) into giving her money, then searches the streets for a dealer; the paranoid dealer she finds beats her before giving her the drugs. She goes home that night to her husband (Yoichi Okamura) where she eats dinner without discussing her eventful day.

Hide (Yoshiyuki) arrives from Kyoto to attend the funeral of a friend. He meets a prostitute, Myan (MIA), in the red light district, and they spend the night together roaming the city. Elsewhere, a Mexican professional wrestler, Mariarna (Esther Moreno), finishes her bouts and goes to her hotel to pack for home. In another part of the city, a Pakistani immigrant, Cawl (Ali Ahmed), feels abused by his Japanese girlfriend and kills her in a moment of rage. He enlists a fellow Pakistani to help him out of his bind, but the businessman's greed leads Cawl to kill him, too.

Meanwhile, Ryo (Onimaru), the leader of a street gang, is pressured into helping Sato (Kanji Tuda), who claims that his girlfriend was abducted along with his car. Ryo and his gang search for the car, but a fight breaks out between the two men's gangs—leading to bloodshed. As it turns out, Sato had lied about his car in order to get back at his cheating girlfriend. When Ryo finds out about the deception, he beats Sato nearly to death. Hide, Myan, Cawl and Ryo all end up meeting at a Latin nightclub that same night. They leave together to throw the ashes of Hide's friend into the sea. During the ceremony, Hide tells his new companions that his friend had been dead on a Tokyo train for a full day without anyone noticing. As dawn breaks, the foursome go their separate ways, Mariarna leaves for Mexico, and Toshiko wakes up to start a new day.

Writer-director Masashi Yamamoto is known for debunking the myths of a harmonious Japanese culture in films like CARNIVAL IN THE NIGHT (1982) and ROBINSON'S GARDEN (1987). JUNK FOOD continues this kind of expose cinema but lacks the requisite bite, mainly because it's been done before—not only by Yamamoto, but by Oshima (CRUEL STORY OF YOUTH), Imamura (VENGEANCE IS MINE), and Murakami (TOKYO DECADENCE). In fact, the supposedly startling revelation of a violent, debased Japanese subculture has become a bit cliche.

There are worthy aspects to this particular project, first and foremost Yamamoto's attempt to link several disconnected stories and characters, although the general tenor of the film owes a lot to the character studies of Hong Kong innovator Wong Kar-wai (CHUNGKING EXPRESS), particularly in the way in which Miyuki's story is set off on its own (a la the separate narratives in CHUNGKING), while the other plot strands are interwoven (in the manner of Wong's FALLEN ANGELS). Also, Yamamoto's intelligent use of point of view techniques serve to better engage the viewer in the characters' activities. The highlights come early, in Miyuki's bizarre "typical" day of office work, drug addiction, family life, and murder: Yamamoto employs jump cuts in order to mimic Miyuki's "high," and, later, slow-motion in order to capture her quiet desperation while searching for her fix. There are also a few awkward camera moves and some shadows of the camera itself, but this first section evokes the squalid subject matter in an elegant, empathetic way (much like TOKYO DECADENCE).

Unfortunately, Miyuki is one of the few characters to which the circular narrative never returns, yet she remains the most interesting and the one given the greatest focus. The rest of JUNK FOOD suffers by comparison, particularly in the over-the-top but weakly acted story about Cawl, the Pakistani immigrant, and the undeveloped "story" (a blurb, really) about Mariarna, the Mexican wrestler. If anything, less might have meant more, both in terms of the number of characters depicted and the amount of violence. Sadly, Yamamoto never finds connections beyond the superficial and his technique lacks consistency (a visible microphone in one shot is followed by a brilliant bit where a gang member swings a bat close to the camera lens). JUNK FOOD contains praiseworthy passages, but also serious flaws and a lack of originality. *(Graphic violence, nudity, sexual situations, adult situations, substance abuse, extreme profanity.)*—E.M.

d, Masashi Yamamoto; p, Toshihiro Isomi; exec p, Koich Omiya, Kazunao Sakaguchi, Eisuke Ishige; w, Masashi Yamamoto; ph, Hiroshi Ito; ed, Syuichi Kakesu; m, DJ Krush, Ko Machida; set d, China Hayashi; sound, Osamu Takizawa (design); cos, Teruaki Hoshi; makeup, Teruaki Hoshi

Drama **(PR: O MPAA: NR)**

JUNK MAIL ★★½

(Norway/Denmark, 1997) 81m Moviemakers; Filmselskabet Atlas; Norsk Film ~ Lions Gate Films c (BUDBRINGEREN)

Robert Skjaerstad *(Roy Amundsen)*; Andrine Saether *(Line Groberg)*; Per Egil Aske *(Georg Rheinhardsen)*; Eli Anne Linnestad *(Betsy)*; Trond Hovik *(Saether)*; Henriette Steenstrup *(Gina)*; Trond Fausa Aurvag *(Espen)*; Adne Olav Sekkelsten *(Per)*; Bjorn Sundquist *(Stein)*; Karl Sundby *(Rune)*; Rolf Arly Lund *(Postmaster)*; Geir Morstad *(Einar Karlsen)*; Rolf Dolven *(Security Guard)*; Helge Sveen *(Secondhand Bookseller)*; Geir Johnsen; Henrik Hole; Harald Kolaas *(Junkies)*; Marit Syversen *(Woman at Dry Cleaners)*; Henning Syverud; John Ivar Bye; Runar Johannessen *(Post Office Colleagues)*; Bentine Holm *(Nurse)*; Jan Zaborowski *(Pole)*; Suzanne Paalgaard; Lars Frogner *(Couple in Cafe)*

A 1996 Norwegian movie that had a 1998 US release, JUNK MAIL is a deadpan comedy grafted onto a standard, crime-intrigue story line, supplemented with intimations of a romance waiting to happen. It was the recipient of several film festival citations, the most prestigious of which was first-place honors at Cannes's International Critics Week.

When Roy (Robert Skjaerstad), an Oslo mailman, finds the house keys of Line (Andrine Saether), an attractive, hearing-impaired blonde on his route, he duplicates them and is soon in the habit of surreptitiously hanging around her place while she is out working in a dry-cleaning service. Incoming phone messages from a man named Georg (Per Egil Aske) reveal to Roy that Georg and Line are the undetected perpetrators of a recent, highly publicized robbery.

One day, Line comes home unexpectedly and attempts suicide. Roy, who has been hiding under the bed, pulls the unconscious young woman's body out of her tub, calls for an ambulance, and leaves. While Line is in the hospital, Roy, using Georg's name, picks up a blowzy babe called Betsy (Eli Anne Linnestad) and takes her to Line's flat, but the tryst ends in a fight.

When Georg finds out that Roy is on to him, he goes after the mailman but, in the process, is himself ambushed by Betsy, bent on revenge, accompanied by two thugs. Betsy's friends beat up Georg, thinking he is Roy, and when the real Roy shows up, they pursue him and Line who unexpectedly appears at the scene. Georg is killed in the ensuing car chase, but Roy and Line get away. Line puts two and two together, surmises that Roy has been snooping around her apartment, slaps him, and angrily walks away—in spite of his avowal that he was the one who saved her life. The infatuated postman follows her, just a few paces behind.

A slight misplacement of emphasis stops JUNK MAIL from being a competely satisfactory film. Despite its refreshing brevity (81 minutes), the movie takes a good while to get rolling and, not long after it does, it ends. Too much of the first half-hour is devoted to establishing Roy's credentials as a civil service slacker (he dumps junk mail in a train tunnel and is not above reading personal letter before delivering them) and domestic slob (he sponge-bathes with dishwashing liquid and eats out of the can). A tightening of JUNK MAIL's opening reels would have bought more time to spend with Line, a character many viewers would wish to know better. Indeed, Line's only big scene in the film's first half finds her comatose and totally nude. Talk about "thankless"; one can imagine Andrine Saether saying to herself, "I put in years at drama school and the Norwegian National Theater for *this?*"

Conscious and clothed—in a bargain-basement wardrobe that is as charming as it is poignant—Line displays an attractive, unpretentious, and, for the movies, unusual Everywoman quality, which Saether makes even more appealing by overlaying it with the slightly distracted air of the hard-of-hearing. One would like to see more of the unsmiling dry-cleaner and her nonrelationship with the hapless mailman.

JUNK MAIL's latent romance and oblique plot are mimicked by its offbeat humor. A little too subtle in its comedy, the movie could have used a few more blatantly funny bits like the one in which an almost psychotically sheepish co-worker of Roy's sings a karaoke rendition of "Born to Be Wild" in a style better suited to "I'm a Lonely Little Petunia in an Onion Patch." *(Violence, extensive nudity, sexual situations, profanity.)*—D.T.

d, Pal Sletaune; p, Dag Nordahl, Peter Boe; co-p, Tom Remlov, Anders Berggren; w, Pal Sletaune, Jonny Halberg; ph, Kjell Vassdal; ed, Pal Gengenbach; m, Joachim Holbek; art d, Karl Juliusson; set d, Vidar Thune; sound, Berndt Frithiof (mixer), Ragnar Samuelson, Sturla Einarson; fx, Pal Morten Hverven; casting, Liv Sandvik, Kjersti Paulsen, Eva Isaksen; cos, Bente Winther-Larsen; makeup, Eva Rygh; stunts, Wolfgang Wedde

Crime/Comedy **(PR: C MPAA: NR)**

KAMISORI HANXO JIGOKUZEME
(SEE: RAZOR: THE SNARE, THE)

KARAKTER
(SEE: CHARACTER)

K

KICK BOXER'S TEARS ★★
(Hong Kong, 1992) 89m Jia's Motion Picture Co ~ Tai Seng c

Moon Lee *(Joan Lee)*; Yukari Oshima, billed as Cynthia Luster *(Mrs. Wong)*; Wilson Lam *(Tommy)*; Mark Cheng *(Alan)*; Jimmy Lee *(Joey Wong)*; Billy Chow *(Billy Chow)*; Ken Lo *(Michael Lee)*; Gabriel Wong Yat-San, billed as Wong Yat-San *(Sammy)*; Sui Tak Fu; Li Chi Leih

A routine tale of a woman out to avenge her brother's death in the ring, KICK BOXER'S TEARS boasts a handful of good fight scenes featuring Moon Lee and Yukari Oshima (billed here as Cynthia Luster), two favorite fighting femmes of Hong Kong action cinema. The 1992 film received its first official US release on home video in 1998.

Joan Lee (Moon Lee), a Chinese doctor, comes to Hong Kong to see her brother, Michael Lee (Ken Lo), a kickboxer who runs a gym with his partners Sammy (Gabriel Wong Yat-San) and Alan (Mark Cheng). When Michael is killed in the ring after a bout with Billy Chow (Billy Chow), Joan approaches Joey Wong (Jimmy Lee), Chow's manager, and demands an underground grudge match. She fights Chow and, learning of his tactic of putting chili powder on his gloves to blind his opponents (as was done with Michael), she becomes enraged and beats Chow, breaking his spine.

Joey's wife, Mrs. Wong (Yukari Oshima), the cousin and secret lover of Billy, demands a fight to the death with Joan. Her thugs kidnap the drunken Alan to coerce Joan into participating. Fighting on a stone arena in an abandoned ruin outside of the city, Joan wins the bout when one of her kicks sends Mrs. Wong into a wall, impaling her on a jutting spike. Joan, her friend Tommy (Wilson Lam), and Sammy get into a pitched battle with Joey Wong and his men in an abandoned house. They manage to kill Joey and most of his henchmen although Sammy and Tommy are seriously wounded in the effort.

Patterned roughly along the lines of the old Warner Bros. boxing melodramas of the 1930s, KICK BOXER'S TEARS offers a bare minimum of story line in order to keep viewers waiting for Moon Lee's handful of fight scenes, including two bouts with her frequent costar Yukari Oshima (ANGEL, ANGEL FORCE, BEAUTY INVESTIGATOR). The film also includes one lengthy kickboxing match between Billy Chow, another genre favorite, and Ken Lo (billed here as Lu Wai Kwon), Jackie Chan's real-life bodyguard and occasional onscreen opponent (DRUNKEN MASTER 2). *(Violence)*—B.C.

d, Shun Tai Wai; p, Lo Chia Po; w, Szeto On, John Tsang, Dick Lee; ed, Cheng Keung; art d, Ronald Chu, Fu Fai; stunts, Sui Tak Fu

Crime/Martial Arts **(PR: C MPAA: NR)**

KID IN ALADDIN'S PALACE, A ★★½
(U.S., 1998) 89m Trimark Pictures ~ Tapestry Films c

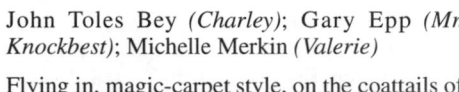

Thomas Ian Nicholas *(Calvin)*; Rhona Mitra *(Scheherazade)*; Nicholas Irons *(Ali Baba)*; James Faulkner *(Luxor)*; Taylor Negron *(Genie)*; Aharon Ipale *(Aladdin)*; Diana Kent *(Jasmine)*; Roger Ennals *(Koos Koos)*; David Kirsch *(Bob)*; Gordon Winter *(Hussesis)*; Neil Conrish *(Rishad)*; Jonathan Kaplan *(Elliot)*; John Toles Bey *(Charley)*; Gary Epp *(Mr. Knockbest)*; Michelle Merkin *(Valerie)*

Flying in, magic-carpet style, on the coattails of the theatrical feature A KID IN KING ARTHUR'S COURT (1995), this undistinguished straight-to-video sequel repeats the fish-out-of-water formula found in that film by placing its cheery-faced protagonist (the returning Thomas Ian Nicholas) in an "Arabian Nights" context.

In eighth-century Baghdad, the evil Luxor (James Faulkner) casts a spell over his brother Aladdin (Aharon Ipale). In this way, Luxor hopes to be free to find the key to the Cave of Wonders, the exotic place where Aladdin has hidden a magical lamp that contains an all-powerful genie (Taylor Negron). According to legend, the only other force that can free the genie is a nebulous entity known as "the Great Deliverer." Since the genie is imprisoned by space and not by time, he lunges forward to the 20th century, materializing in a dingy pizza joint. There he finds Calvin (Thomas Ian Nicholas), the eatery's cloddish delivery boy. The genie tells the callow youth that he, Calvin, is "the Great Deliverer" who is destined to free the genie from his prison in the cave. Suddenly, Calvin is whisked back to the eighth century where he becomes the comrade of Ali Baba (Nicholas Irons). The youth's forceful and unexpected arrival unwittingly saves the legendary thief from Luxor's merciless sword.

Calvin soon meets Aladdin's daughter Scheherazade (Rhona Mitra), who joins him and Ali Baba on a sand-filled trek. After the trio remove the lamp from the cave, Luxor takes possession of it. Several skirmishes later, our heroes regain possesion of it, and free Aladdin from the spell. With Luxor defeated, the trio is able to liberate the genie and celebrate their victory.

Despite its witty script, lavish production values, inspiring music, and a spate of special effects, A KID IN ALADDIN'S PALACE is strictly kid's stuff. The bulk of the movie's humor is derived from obvious verbal and visual anachronisms, such as an in-the-desert sequence in which Calvin sees a mirage—instead of a body of water, the youngster sees a Burger King.

The genie character registers as the film's strong point. His amusing hipster attitude finds him addressing Calvin's feeling of inadequacy with an offhanded philosophy. ("Stop the insecurity thing. It's very annoying.") Standup comic Taylor Negron's flamboyant performance makes the character particularly memorable. Overall, this KID sees plenty of action, but the movie's message about good triumphing over evil is telegraphed soon enough to tire out even the most ardent six-year-old viewer.—M.K.

d, Robert L. Levy; p, Robert L. Levy, Peter Abrams, J.P. Guerin, Natan Zahavi; exec p, Mark Amin; assoc p, Nick Zuvk; co-p, Jonathon Komack Martin; w, Michael Part (based on characters created by Michael Part and Robert L. Levy); ph, Walter Psfister; ed, Sherwood Jones; m, David Michael Frank; prod d, Ladislav Wilheim; art d, Roger Kelton; set d, Mohsen Rais, Ferid Habaschi; sound, David Bach (effects); fx, Franco Galimo; casting, Ros Hubbard, John Hubbard; cos, Anissa Bediri; makeup, Fatima Jaziri

Fantasy/Adventure **(PR: A MPAA: G)**

KIKI'S DELIVERY SERVICE ★★★★
(Japan, 1989) 103m Studio Ghibli; Tokuma Publishing Co.; Yamato Transport Co.; Nippon Television Network ~ Buena Vista Home Video c

ENGLISH VOICE CAST: Kirsten Dunst *(Kiki)*; Phil Hartman *(Jiji the Cat)*; Janeane Garofalo *(Ursula)*; Matthew Lawrence

(Tombo); Debbie Reynolds *(Madame)*; Tress McNeille *(Osono)*; Edie McClurg *(Barsa)*; Kath Soucie *(Mom)*; ADDITIONAL VOICES: Jeff Bennett; Pamela Segall; Debi Derryberry; June Angela; Corey Burton; Lewis Arquette; Fay Dewitt; Susan Hickman; Sherry Lynn; Matt Miller; Scott Menville; Eddie Frierson; John DeMita; Julia Demita

One of the most celebrated Japanese family films in recent memory, KIKI'S DELIVERY SERVICE is an animated feature which tells the story of a 13-year-old girl who attempts to make good during a year as resident witch of a large city. Considered by many fans to be the finest work from Japanese animator Hayao Miyazaki, the long-awaited US home video release of the feature benefits from superior English dubbing utilizing celebrity voices.

Kiki (voice of Kirsten Dunst), a 13-year-old witch-in-training, leaves her family and country town to settle for a year in a large city, as dictated by witch custom. Flying off on her broomstick with her wise-cracking black cat, Jiji (voice of Phil Hartman), she decides on a large, unnamed Northern European metropolis. After some difficulty finding a place to stay, she performs a good deed for a baker, Osono (voice of Tess McNeille), and is given an attic room until she can get settled on her own. She sets herself up as a delivery girl, performing errands around the city on her trusty broomstick. In the course of one of her errands, Kiki meets a young artist, Ursula (voice of Janeane Garofalo), who lives in a cabin in the woods outside the city.

A local boy, Tombo (voice of Matthew Lawrence) develops a crush on Kiki; she initially rebuffs him, but gradually warms up to him. He shows her his propeller-powered bicycle, a flying-machine-in-progress. Soon after, however, Kiki finds herself losing her powers. She is visited by Ursula, who takes her out to the cabin for a day so Kiki can recuperate and recover her powers. Ursula describes her own crisis of confidence when she was Kiki's age and insists that Kiki relax and allow her powers to return of their own accord.

Upon her return to the city, Kiki visits her aged customer, Madame (voice of Debbie Reynolds), and sees on Madame's TV that a huge dirigible visiting the city has gone out of control. It begins to fly away with one person still clinging to the line—Tombo. Kiki runs to the site of the catastrophe, commandeers a janitor's broom, and after several halting attempts manages to fly up and rescue Tombo in the nick of time. Tombo goes on to complete his own flying machine, while Kiki writes to her parents that all is going well.

Produced in 1989, KIKI'S DELIVERY SERVICE has long had a glowing reputation among anime buffs, although it was never officially distributed in the US until its release in 1998 on home video. It's the first release from the Disney Corporation's deal with Tokuma Shoten, a publishing company with the rights to the works of Studio Ghibli, the animation studio operated by Hayao Miyazaki, Japan's preeminent animator.

KIKI'S benefits from extremely detailed production design, particularly in the illustrations of Kiki's adopted city, which registers as a beautiful if slightly romanticized embellishment of a European metropolis from another era (period details from different decades—extending from the 1930s to the 1950s—are featured in the city). The animation is particularly fluid, especially in the scenes where Kiki flies over the city and along its streets. The action is underscored by the lyrical music of composer Joe Hisaishi, whose piano solos are featured on the soundtrack. The only complaint about the soundtrack is the substitution of two new English-language songs for the delightful original Japanese-language opening and closing songs.

Deliberately eschewing the fast pace, strenuous action, frenzied special effects and wall-to-wall songs of the standard Disney animated feature, the film allows the audience to get to know the character of Kiki and feel the emotional highs and lows she undergoes in the course of her year in training. This rite-of-passage theme is found in most other Miyazaki films, including MY NEIGHBOR TOTORO (1988, released in the US in 1993), as well as his most recent film, PRINCESS MONONOKE (1997), Japan's biggest boxoffice hit at the time of its release.—B.C.

d, Hayao Miyazaki; p, Hayao Miyazaki; exec p, Yasuyoshi Tokuma, Mikihiko Tsuzuki, Morihasa Takagi, Jane Schonberger (English version); assoc p, Toshio Suzuki; w, Hayao Miyazaki (based on the novel by Eiko); ed, Takeshi Seyama; m, Joe Hisaishi, Paul Chihara (English version), Sydney Forest (English version); art d, Hiroshi Ono; anim, Shinji Otsuke, Katsuya Kondo, Yoshifumi Kondo; sound, Shuji Inoue, Ernie Sheesley (English version); casting, Jack Fletcher (English version)

Animated/Children's/Fantasy (PR: AA MPAA: G)

KILLER ANGELS ★★½

(Hong Kong, 1989) 85m Jia's Motion Picture Co. ~ Tai Seng c

Moon Lee *(Yolie)*; Gordon Liu, billed as Lau Kar Fai *(Michael)*; Leung Kar Yan *(Don Chu)*; Lau Jia Hui *(Jackie Chan)*; Futumi Nabeki; Shing Fui-On; Tai Chi Wai; Ng Man Tat *(Ted)*; Chan Lau; Lau Shiu Kwan; Yuen Hung; Yuen Lai King; Chai Chun; Yueng Lam; Eric Tsang; Chu Din Mo; On Kam See; Leung Mui Chung; Shu Chu; Kam Bun; Wong Chung Yu; Kang Lung Shing; Kam To; Poon Sam; On On

Hong Kong female action star Moon Lee plays a kung fu-fighting, expert-shooting policewoman who shields a government witness, romances a hit man, and breaks up a criminal gang in KILLER ANGELS, a spinoff of Lee's popular ANGEL films of the late 1980s (themselves a variant of the "Charlie's Angels" TV series). The 1989 film received its first official US release on home video in 1998.

A former gang member returns from Los Angeles to Hong Kong to present to the Justice Department, in exchange for immunity, a list of members of the Shadow gang operating in Hong Kong. The gang member, Jackie Chan (Lau Jia Hui), is placed under the protection of the Blue Angels, an all-female special operations unit of the HKPD. The Angels' mission is to identify the head of the Southeast Asian Shadows. Chan and his list are to be used as bait to apprehend the Shadow gang leaders Don Chu (Leung Kar Yan) and Chico. The leading Blue Angel, Yolie (Moon Lee), goes undercover by working as a singer-dancer at Don Chu's night club, where she is drawn to Michael (Gordon Liu), Chu's bodyguard/hit man.

Don Chu is informed by his LA contacts that Jackie has no list, so Jackie is killed when he goes to meet Chico. The Angels capture Chico, but he is shot and killed by a sniper—Michael—before he can reveal anything. Yolie and the Angels launch a raid on the house where Chu keeps female slaves for sale to buyers from the Middle East. In the ensuing shootout, Chu is apprehended, and Michael takes a bullet meant for Yolie and dies.

Made in the midst of the ANGEL series starring Moon Lee (1988-90), KILLER ANGELS (1989) boasts four fighting females and a virtual nonstop series of action set pieces involving shoot-outs, car chases, motorcycle stunts, explosions, and kung-fu fights. Unfortunately the final cast list omits the character names, making identification of Moon Lee's three femme costars difficult. Gordon Liu, a popular 1970s Shaw Brothers kung-fu star (THE MASTER KILLER), plays a hit man who kills dozens of people with his long-barreled automatic pistol, but never once participates in the kung-fu set-tos. Also on hand as stock bad guys are familiar Hong Kong players Shing Fui On and Ng Man Tat.

The plot is contrived, but the action scenes generally make some dramatic sense and the characters' relationships are more intricate than usual for this kind of film. Camp fans should be warned, however, that the English-dubbed version of the film deletes Moon Lee's celebrated disco song-and-dance number. *(Violence.)*—B.C.

d, Loo Chun Kok; p, Lo Kar Po, billed as Lo Chia Po, Chang Chung Lung, billed as Chang Tsung Lung; ed, Cheung Keung; m, Sammy Lam; art d, Bill Chan; stunts, Chiu Fat, Yuen Yan

Crime/Thriller **(PR: C MPAA: NR)**

KILLER CONDOM, THE ★★½

(Germany/Switzerland, 1997) 107m German Film Board; Ascot Film ~ Troma c
(KONDOM DES GRAUENS)

Udo Samel *(Luigi Mackeroni)*; Peter Lohmeyer *(Sam O'Connery)*; Iris Berben *(Dr. Riffelson)*; Marc Richter *(Billy)*; Leonard Lansink *(Babette)*; Henning Schluter *(Robinson)*; Gerd Wameling; Ralf Wolter *(Professor Smirnoff)*; Meret Becker; Otto Sander; Monika Hansen; Hella von Sinnen; Adrian Altaras; Ron Williams; Evelyn Kunnecke; Inga Busch; Georg-Martin Bode *(Dick McGouvern)*; Lillemor Malau

This 1996 German production has the right idea and the right spirit, though it ultimately can't, er, keep it up.

In Manhattan's seedy Hotel Quickie, a college professor attempting to seduce a female student has his penis bloodily severed. Several similar incidents are blamed on vicious prostitutes, and police detective Luigi Mackeroni (Udo Samel) is assigned to investigate. During a visit to the hotel, Mackeroni goes for a tryst with young hustler Billy (Marc Richter), only to have one of his testicles bitten off by a fanged creature resembling a condom. Despite the disbelief of his partner Sam (Peter Lohmeyer) and other police, Mackeroni sets out to trap one of the vicious rubbers, and succeeds in catching and killing one with the help of cop-turned-transsexual singer Babette (Leonard Lansink).

Examining the creature, a coroner tells Mackeroni that it is an organic hybrid. The deadly condoms begin to spread across the city, emasculating presidential candidate Dick McGouvern (Georg-Martin Bode) and biting off the nose of an unfortunate woman. This victim tells Mackeroni that she has seen one of the creatures during her hospital stay, and he tracks them to the basement. There, he finds that Dr. Riffelson (Iris Berben) has created the killer rubbers with the help of abducted scientist Prof. Smirnoff (Ralf Wolter) as part of her campaign to rid New York City of perversion. She has captured and intends to sacrifice Billy, Babette and several others to the condoms, but Mackeroni turns the tables and it is she who falls victim. His case solved, Mackeroni is reunited with Billy.

While THE KILLER CONDOM is everything one might expect from a movie with that title—and one released in the US by Troma, which sent a subtitled version to theaters and a dubbed one to cable—it's a slicker production than one might imagine. Technically polished, with a bright-yet-scuzzy look and proficient makeup effects by Jorg Buttgereit (director of the notorious NEKROMANTIK movies), it is highlighted by Samel's amusingly deadpan performance. Looking like Germany's answer to Bob Hoskins, Samel (whose character's name is more literally spelled "Macaroni" in the subtitles) tackles the role with just the right amount of gusto, tossing off dialogue about killer condoms as if he spoke about them every day.

He's a solid anchor in a film that frequently threatens to split off in too many different directions. Particularly distracting is the subplot involving Babette, who pines for Mackeroni and spends too much screen time trying to seduce him. Director Martin Walz, who wrote the script with Ralf Konig, upon whose comics the movie is based, also lets a number of individual scenes go on too long, and while his pro-gay approach demonstrates a welcome progressiveness in the exploitation genre, it also becomes overstated at times.

To his credit, though, Walz doesn't underline or unduly force the comic moments. With some judicious trimming, the film's bizarre vision would be more than the sum of its frequently amusing parts; still, it's hard not to get a kick out of a New York-set film in which all the characters (including the American values-spouting politician) speak German. *(Graphic violence, nudity, sexual situations, extreme profanity.)*—M.G.

d, Martin Walz; p, Ralph S. Dietrich, Harald Reichebner; exec p, Michael Stricker; w, Ralf Konig, Martin Walz (based on the comic book by Konig); ph, Alexander Honisch; ed, Simone Klier; set d, H.R. Giger; fx, Jorg Buttgereit; cos, Anja Niehaus

Horror/Comedy **(PR: O MPAA: NR)**

KILLING TIME ★

(U.K., 1998) 88m Pilgrim Films; Metrodome Films ~ Avalanche Releasing c

Craig Fairbrass *(Bryant)*; Nigel Leach *(Jacob Reilly)*; Kendra Torgan *(Maria—the Assassin)*; Peter Harding *(Madison)*; Neil Armstrong *(John)*; Ian McLaughlin *(George)*; Stephen D. Thirkeld *(Charlie)*; Rick Warden *(Smithy)*; Phil Dixon *(Frank)*

KILLING TIME is a crime thriller about a female assassin's effort to carry out a contract hit. Lacking the ingenuity to overcome the constraints of an obviously low budget, director Bharat Nalluri turns in a crude, shoddily constructed film.

An assassin, Maria (Kendra Torgan), arrives by plane from Italy. She checks into a hotel and then proceeds to a gangster's lair, where she guns down all but one of its inhabitants. She obtains valuable information from him about the arrival of a train later that day, then shoots him dead.

Later, police inspectors Madison (Peter Harding) and Bryant (Craig Fairbrass) arrive at the scene and survey the carnage. Madison determines that a woman is responsible, and is suspicious when Bryant agrees too readily. Pressured by Madison, Bryant admits that he has hired Maria to kill crime boss Jacob Reilly (Nigel Leach) in retaliation for Reilly's murder of Bryant's former police partner. Bryant further admits that he cannot afford to pay Maria, and so has hired a group of men to kill her after she has finished the job.

Late in the afternoon, the awaited train arrives at its station. Reilly disembarks and is confronted by the police inspectors and the assassin. A shoot-out ensues and Madison is seriously wounded. Maria threatens to kill Reilly to fulfill the contract, and also Bryant for his treachery. Bryant pleads on behalf of Madison, telling Maria to forget the hit but to take a satchel of money that Reilly holds as payment. She continues to threaten Bryant, but finally shoots Reilly. Having completed the hit, she takes the satchel of money and spares Bryant his life.

KILLING TIME closes with Godard's statement that, "all you need to make a film is a girl and a gun." This quotation betrays this film's sentiment, but the work fails to live up to its aspirations. KILLING TIME tries to be a stylish and clever genre piece, but its ineptitude renders it merely amateurish. The film's title is an obvious play on words, referring both to the graphic slaughter that makes up the film's more dramatic moments and to the hours that the characters pass as they await the arrival of Reilly's train. The concept of waiting—of how characters "kill time"—is an intriguing and challenging one, especially in the crime genre. But KILLING TIME is so flaccid and lethargically paced that it becomes tedious in its attempt to portray tedium.

The film is also weak technically, with poor visual and sound quality. The cast is generally good; Fairbrass and Harding manage to generate some playful chemistry as the bickering police duo. But Kendra Torgan proves a wholly colorless actress, whose transparent Italian accent is indicative of her overall performance. KILLING TIME, more often than not, is a waste of time. *(Graphic violence, nudity, sexual situations, adult situations, profanity.)*—D.C.

d, Bharat Nalluri; p, Richard Johns; exec p, Paul Brooks; assoc p, Alan Martin; w, Neil Marshall, Fleur Costello, Caspar Berry; ph, Sam McCurdy; ed, Neil Marshall; m, Christopher Slaski; prod d, Ronald Gow

Crime/Thriller (PR: C MPAA: NR)

KINGDOM OF SHADOWS ★★★½

(U.S., 1998) 70m Kino on Video ~ Kino on Video c

Rod Steiger *(Narrator)*

A stellar compendium of clips from early horror films, KINGDOM OF SHADOWS is weighted down by narration so overwrought it verges on self-parody.

Using a broad definition of horror, the chronology of the genre begins with several sensationalistic turn-of-the-century depictions of faked executions and violent accidents. A discussion of cinema's perennial fascination with religious persecution and torture segues into a segment on the portrayal of the medical profession and its practitioners in early fear films: as reckless experimenters, body snatchers, mad scientists. With new, popular acceptance of the precepts of psychiatry, terrors of the mind begin to show up onscreen, spreading to include sleepwalkers, hypnotists and the ultimate somnambulists, zombies. Other topics addressed include carnivals and related traveling entertainments as settings for dark tales, the preponderance of sexually charged images and innuendo in early horror cinema, and the profound twin influences of German Expressionism and Edgar Allan Poe. The documentary argues that after Carl Dreyer's masterful VAMPYR in 1932 and the accession of sound film, horror largely lost its imagination and symbolic power, prefering simply to recycle old staples from the silent era.

KINGDOM is a well thought-out presentation with cogent points to make. Unfortunately writer Bret Wood, clearly an acolyte of Poe, adopts a hysterically melodramatic style that never allows a simple phrase to suffice when he can concoct a baroque one, engorged with gothic menace and dripping with Stygian grotesquerie. Narrator Rod Steiger compounds the problem with a menacing voice-over recalling nothing so much as the "Count Floyd" character from the television comedy series "SCTV."

This drawback notwithstanding, there's still one excellent reason to watch the documentary: the clips themselves. Including scenes from numerous classics (PHANTOM OF THE OPERA, THE CABINET OF DOCTOR CALIGARI, THE GOLEM) and equally impressive forgotten titles (WITCHCRAFT THROUGH THE AGES, LEAVES FROM SATAN'S BOOK), the film gives a superbly organized tour through the astonishing diversity of early horror. The roots of cinematic expressionism are aptly displayed, along with the breathtaking experimentalism of the silent filmmakers. Wood has a valid argument when he states that later filmmakers, given more sophisticated equipment and greater technical expertise, often became less creative and audacious with their imagery. Similarly, he points out that film noir borrowed heavily from the conventions established by these aggressively talented pioneers. Directors from Murnau to DeMille, Griffith to Leni to Lang, are well represented in the marvelous collection of clips. Too bad writer Wood's words didn't get as skillful an edit as his images. *(Violence, nudity.)*—A.B.

d, Bret Wood; exec p, Dan Clark; w, Bret Wood; ed, John Kuhn, Dustin Adair; m, Joseph Turrin

Documentary/Horror (PR: C MPAA: NR)

KINGDOM, PART 2, THE ★★★

(Denmark, 1997) 295m Zentropa Entertainments; Danish Broadcasting Corporation; Liberator Productions; RAI Cinema Fiction; Sveriges Television; Norsk Rikskringkasting; La Sept/ARTE ~ October Films c
(RIGET II)

Ernst-Hugo Jaregard *(Stig G. Helmer)*; Kirsten Rolffes *(Mrs. Sigrid Drusse)*; Holger Juul Hansen *(Dr. Einar Moesgaard)*; Soren Pilmark *(Jorgen Krogshoj—"Krogen")*; Ghita Norby *(Rigmor Mortensen)*; Jens Okking *(Harly Drusse—"Bulder")*; Birthe Neumann *(Miss Svendsen)*; Otto Brandenburg *(Hansen)*; Erik Wedersoe *(Ole)*; Baard Owe *(Prof. Palle Bondo)*; Birgitte Raaberg *(Judith Bang Petersen)*; Henning Jensen *(Bob)*; John Hahn-Petersen *(Nivesen)*; Peter Mygind *(Mogens Moesgaard—"Mogge")*; Vita Jensen *(Dishwasher 1)*; Morten Rotne Leffers *(Dishwasher 2)*; Solbjorg Hojfeldt *(Camilla)*; Udo Kier *(Little Brother/Aage Kruger)*; Soren Elung Jensen *(Man in Top Hat)*; Paul Huttel *(Dr. Steenbaek)*; Holger Perfort *(Professor Ulrich)*; Klaus Wegener *(Doctor—Casualty)*; Michelle Bjorn-Andersen *(Pediatrician)*; Timm Mehrens *(Doctor—Operating Theater)*; Louise Fribo *(Susanne Jeppesen—Sanne)*; Tine Miehe-Renard *(Night Nurse)*; Julie Wieth *(Pediatric Nurse)*; Annette Ketscher *(Nurse—Casualty)*; Birthe Tove *(Nurse 1)*; Lise Schroder *(Nurse 2)*; Dorrit Stender-Petersen *(Assisting Nurse)*; Ole Boisen *(Christian)*; Thomas Stender *(Student)*; Cecilie Brask *(Young Woman in Therapy)*; Claus Nissen *(Madsen)*; Thomas Bo Larsen *(Falcon)*; Steen Svarre *(Man in Overalls)*; Laura Christensen *(Mona)*; Mette Munk Plum *(Mona's Mother)*; Michael Philip Simpson *(Man from Haiti)*; Fash Shodeinde *(Philip Marco)*; Kim Jansson *(Detective Jensen)*; Claus Flygare *(Detective Nielsen)*; Nis Bank-Mikkelsen *(Hospital Pastor)*; Britta Lillesoe *(Woman in Bed)*; Henrik Fiig *(Car Crash Victim)*; Birger Jensen *(Janitor)*; Peter Hartmann *(Removal Man)*; Lars Lunoe *(Minister of Health)*; Jens Jorn Spottag *(Attorney Bisgaard)*; Helle Virkner *(Emma)*; Annevig Shelde Ebbe *(Mary)*; Torben Zeller *(Crematorium Functionary)*; Jannie Faurschou *(Orthopedist)*; Stellan Skarsgard *(Swedish Lawyer)*; Klaus Pagh *(Bailiff)*; Vera Gebuhr *(Gerda)*; Mette Hald *(Cross Girl)*; Bjarne G. Nielsen *(Hospital Pastor—New)*; Anders Hove *(Celebrant)*; Ingolf David *(Death)*; Philip Zanden *(Jonsson from Lund)*; Ruth Junker *(Voice of Dishwasher 1)*; Peter Gilsfort *(Voice of Dishwasher 2)*; Evald Krog *(Voice of "Little Brother")*; Ulrik Cold *(Narrator)*

The much-anticipated second set of episodes of filmmaker Lars Von Trier's TV miniseries THE KINGDOM continues the strange tale of evil doings in a contemporary Danish hospital. Von Trier's epic comedy-cum-medical thriller is highly entertaining, although the novelty of the show's concept (mixing the supernatural, soap opera-like characters and romantic interactions, and odd, surreal touches) fades a bit this time around.

The inhabitants of a Copenhagen hospital called "The Kingdom" are affected in random ways by the ghosts that are said to be haunting the building. Consultant neurosurgeon Stig Helmer (Ernst-Hugo Jaregard) has returned from Haiti with a potion to kill his nemesis, Dr. Krogen (Soren Pilmark); Helmer's attempts to poison Krogen fail miserably at first. Mrs. Drusse (Kirsten Rolffes), the medium who unearthed the ghost of a litle girl named Mary, is severely injured on her way out of the hospital, requiring her to stay longer. Professor Moesgaard (Holger Juul Hansen) is burdened by his administrative duties and seeks the help of Ole (Erik Wedersoe), the unorthodox psychiatrist he had been assigned to dismiss. Professor Bondo (Baard Owe), who has had a cancerous liver implanted into his own body in order to continue his experimental research, will die unless a donor is found. Mogge (Peter Mygind) and a fellow medical student, Christian (Ole Boisen), are caught in a love triangle with Sanne (Louise Fribo), another student. And a doctor, Judith (Birgitte Raaberg), has given birth to a baby conceived with Kruger (Udo Kier), the late, ghostlike father of little Mary; the baby (also played by Kier) not only resembles Kruger, it grows at a superhuman rate.

Eventually, Dr. Krogen succumbs to Helmer's poisonous brew, but Helmer tries to get an antidote when he realizes the administration and police are looking into his affairs, including his botched operation of a brain-damaged girl named Mona (Laura Christensen). Taking the advice of a Swedish attorney (Stellan Skarsgard), Helmer flees the law, and Rigmor (Ghita Norby), the consultant anaesthetist who knows his secrets, blackmails Helmer into marrying her. Meanwhile, Mrs. Drusse, recovered from surgery, and her son, Bulder (Jens Okking), a hospital porter, search throughout the hospital for an evil spirit. And as Judith's baby, "Little Brother," keeps growing and growing, Kruger's spirit forces Judith to choose either killing their baby for the greater good of humankind or sustaining his life and, thus, by extension, Kruger's dark forces.

Judith finally kills her baby, much to her heartache. Sanne chooses Mogge over Christian, but all three find themselves trapped in an ambulance driven by Death itself! Helmer averts the authorities successfully, but Dr. Krogen resurfaces to get revenge for his attempted murder. Mrs. Drusse confesses that she is Dr. Bondo's mother, and encourages Bulder, Bondo's unknown half-brother, to donate part of his liver; it becomes questionable whether Bondo will survive the surgery. By happenstance, Mrs. Drusse also discovers that the beautiful nurse, Camilla (Solbjorg Hojfeldt), harbors the evil spirits she has been seeking to release from the Kingdom; but Mrs. Drusse gets stuck in an elevator heading for the underworld before she can do anything about it.

THE KINGDOM, PART 2 is the compilation of the fifth through eighth episodes of the popular Danish television series packaged for the international film market. As with most soap operas, it is not necessary that one has seen the earlier episodes, although in this case it enhances the viewer's enjoyment (for example, a discussion about Mogge having stolen a patient's head will make little or no sense to a viewer who hasn't seen the original KINGDOM). On the other hand, a few cliffhangers from the end of Part 1 are resolved at the beginning in a perfunctory manner, but, as could be expected, Part 2 also ends with more cliffhangers (Von Trier intially announced that the series would be comprised of 12 episodes). For the patient movie-goer who has waited 279 minutes, another cliffhanger ending is frustrating indeed. The only other drawback (common to both KINGDOM feature-compilations) is the way that von Trier's intentionally jarring camerawork (seemingly intended as a parody of the fast-paced, hand-held visuals used on such night-time dramas as "ER") and oblique perspectives (conceived for the small screen) look when blown up for 35mm projection.

Still, THE KINGDOM, PART 2 succeeds as a riotous black comedy, with clever writing (by Lars von Trier and Niels Vorsel), direction (by von Tier and Morten Arnfred), and performances (especially Ernt-Hugo Jaregard as the arrogant Stig Helmer).

The slight thematic problems of Part 1 resurface here, including the use of a pair of Down Syndrome teenagers (Vita Jensen, Morten Rotne Leffers) working in the hospital's kitchen as mystical conduits to the spirits haunting the hospital. And Part 2 further intensifies the association between black characters and voodoo practices, another stereotype. In a new twist, Part 2 introduces a philosophical element vis-a-vis the subplot about Judith's baby. In fact, Judith's dilemma about whether or not to kill "Little Brother" recalls the plot dynamics of von Trier's much more serious BREAKING THE WAVES (1996). As odd and initially amusing it is to see renowned actor Udo Kier playing an oversized baby (with his voice-dubbed by Evaid Krog), this subplot eventually turns morose and weighs the film down. However, in spite of its difficulties, THE KINGDOM, PART 2 will keep fans and newcomers quite happy—if a little bit spooked. *(Violence, nudity, adult situations, profanity.)*—E.M.

d, Lars Von Trier, Morten Arnfred; p, Vibeke Windelov, Svend Abrahamsen; assoc p, Peter Aalbaek Jensen, Marianne Slot; w, Lars von Trier, Niels Vorsel; ph, Eric Kress; ed, Molly Malene Stensgaard, Pernille Bech Christensen; m, Joachim Holbek; art d, Jette Lehmann, Hans Christian Lindholm; sound, Peter Christian Hansen (recordist), Hans Moller (design); fx, Annette Rolfshoj, Lars Kolding Andersen; cos, Annelise Bailey; makeup, Birthe Lyngso, Jeanet Keil, Kim Olsson (effects), Lis Olsson (effects); stunts, Hans-Peter Ludvigsen

Horror/Drama/Comedy (PR: C MPAA: NR)

KISSING A FOOL ★½

(U.S., 1998) 93m RL Entertainment; Mendillo/Form Productions ~ Universal c

David Schwimmer *(Max Abbitt)*; Jason Lee *(Jay Murphy)*; Mili Avital *(Samantha "Sam" Andrews)*; Bonnie Hunt *(Linda)*; Vanessa Angel *(Natasha)*; Kari Wuhrer *(Dara)*; Frank Medrano *(Cliff Randal)*; Bitty Schram *(Vicki Pelam)*; Judy Greer *(Andrea)*; Ron Beattie *(Priest)*; Doug Ellin *(Bartender/Springer Guest)*; Tag Mendillo *(Wedding Guest at Bar/Springer Guest)*; Justine Bentley *(Beautiful Woman at Bar)*; Liza Cruzat *(Dara's Friend)*; Jessica Mills *(Dara's Friend #2)*; Sammy Sosa; Jerry Springer *(Themselves)*; Mike Squire *(Spanish Man in Bed)*; Marco Siviero *(French Man in Bed)*; Steve Seagren *(Heckler)*; Philip R. Smith *(Fan on the Street)*; Jayson Fate *(Rudolpho)*; Ross Bon *(Blue Kings Lead Singer)*; Antimo Fiore *(Tony)*

KISSING A FOOL is a virtually laughless big-screen sitcom for those who want their movies to look and sound exactly like television and who find the prospect of David Schwimmer saying the F-word innumerable times to be hilarious. For everyone else, the contrived plot—about a compulsive womanizer who enlists his best friend to test his fiancee's fidelity—and 93 minutes of Schwimmer's perpetual hangdog expression prove to be a deadly combination.

While hosting a wedding at her home, book publisher Linda (Bonnie Hunt) relates to some guests the story of how she fixed up the bride and the groom: Max (David Schwimmer) and Jay (Jason Lee) are best friends, but while Max is a swinging bachelor who works as a sports reporter for a Chicago TV station, Jay is a sensitive writer looking for true love. While working on his first novel, Jay is assigned by Linda to work with an attractive editor named Sam (Mili Avital). Since Jay is unable to get over being recently dumped by his girlfriend, he fixes Sam up with Max and the two of them fall instantly in love. Max moves in with Sam and they're engaged two weeks later, but when Max realizes that he'll never be able to sleep with another woman again, he begins to have doubts about Sam's faithfulness as well.

To test Sam's fidelity, Max asks Jay to try to seduce her; if she doesn't respond, he'll go through with the wedding. Jay refuses to go along, but when Linda pushes the deadline up on his book, he and Sam are forced to spend long hours working together and they become close friends. When Max goes to Detroit on business, Jay and Sam get drunk and almost sleep together. When Max returns, Jay tells him what happened, and he finds out that Max cheated on Sam while he was away. They both go to see Sam and Jay tells her he loves her, but the truth about Max's test comes out, and she angrily storms out. Jay moves to New York and Sam and Max break up. Months later, after Jay's book comes out and is a huge success, Max engineers a meeting between Sam and Jay. As Linda finishes her story, it's revealed that Sam and Jay are the ones getting married and Max is the best man.

The only real difference between KISSING A FOOL and a typical sitcom episode is its length, the crude language (self-consciously trying to imitate the profanely witty dialogue of Kevin Smith's movies), and the lack of a laugh track, which this film desperately needs. All of the sitcom cliches have been dutifully assembled, including the stereotyped "opposites-attract" premise (Sam is a book editor who hates sports; Max is a sports reporter who hates to read! Zany romantic hijinks ensue!), attractive young characters with glamorous jobs and fabulous apartments who rarely seem to work, and glib wisecracks substituting for recognizably human conversation. Besides starring, Schwimmer was also one of the executive producers and the whole film has the feel of a vanity project designed to give him a hip, hard-edged image. Unfortunately, he's completely unconvincing as an irresistible stud (the scene where he announces his engagement on TV and a group of girls in a bar scream in shock and disappointment is particularly laughable), and his relentless mugging and immature character is charmless and strident, typified by his annoying TV catchphrase of "Whaddup Chicago!," repeated ad nauseam with countless variations by him and everyone he meets.

The script is so anemic and poorly structured that the "test" plot doesn't even kick in until the movie is half over, and the final act—where Max suddenly turns into a nice guy and gets Sam and Jay together—is a rush of inexplicable events and incidents that make no sense. The writers apparently came up with their "surprise" ending first, and then couldn't figure out how to make it seem plausible, so it's just presented without any explanation. Obviously aware of the thinness of the material, cowriter and director Doug Ellin (PHAT BEACH) desperately tries to jazz up every scene with pointless inserts and other visual interpolations (subjective flashbacks, fantasies, etc. a la ANNIE HALL) so that we "see" what each character is describing, but this only prolongs the already sluggish pace. All in all, KISSING A FOOL proves that as a screen presence, Schwimmer is smaller than life, and definitely shouldn't give up his day job. *(Extreme profanity, sexual situations.)*—M.S.

d, Doug Ellin; p, Stephen Tag Mendillo, billed as Tag Mendillo, Andrew Form, Rick Lashbrook; exec p, David Schwimmer, Stephen Levinson; assoc p, Mark S. Hoerr, Warren Kohler, Liza Moore, James Frey; w, James Frey, Doug Ellin (from a story by James Frey); ph, Thomas A. Del Ruth; ed, David Finfer; m, Joseph Vitarelli; prod d, Charles Breen; set d, Tricia Schneider; sound, David Obermeyer (mixer); casting, Ferne Cassel, Brody Tenner Paskal; cos, Susan Kaufmann; makeup, Denise Wynbrandt

Romance/Comedy **(PR: C MPAA: R)**

KNOCK OFF ★★

(U.S., 1998) 90m Film Workshop; Val D'Oro Entertainment; Knock Films; A.V.V. and MDP Worldwide ~ Columbia c

Jean-Claude Van Damme *(Marcus Ray)*; Rob Schneider *(Tommy Hendricks)*; Lela Rochon *(Karen Leigh)*; Paul Sorvino *(Harry Johansson)*; Carmen Lee *(Ling Ho)*; Wyman Wong *(Eddie Wang)*; Glen Chin *(Skinny)*; Michael Wong, billed as Michael Fitzgerald Wong *(Han)*; Moses Chan *(Officer Fong)*; Raymond Leslie Nichols *(Karl)*; Jeff Wolfe, billed as Jeff Joseph Wolfe *(Skaar)*; Michael Miller *(Tickler)*; Steve Brettingham *(Hawkeye)*; Mark Haughton *(Bear)*; Peter Nelson *(Biff)*; Kim Marfee Penn *(Chip)*; Thomas Hudak *(Kyle)*; Steve Nation *(Kip)*; Rosa Librizzi *(Budda CIA)*; Noel Rands *(Racemaster)*; Dennis Chan *(Choy/Eddie Kid)*; William Chow *(Papa Wang)*; Stuart Kavanagh *(Colonel Carrington)*; Noorie Razack *(Fruit Market Old Man)*; Heung Hoi *(Fruit Market Accountant)*; Cheung Simon *(Supermarket Kid)*; Leslie Cheung *(Young Worker—Skinny Freight)*; Matt Grant *(Tarzan)*; Nyree Hansen *(Jane)*; Kent Osborne *(Pachy)*; Lynne Francis *(V-Six Secretary)*; Cordelia Choy *(Mel)*; Leon C. Somera Jr. *(Eddie's Ringer)*; Mathew Tang; Wong Yui Sang; Chan Man Cheong; Leung Yiu Hay; Roks Chik; Tse Wai Yin; Irene Luk *(Han's Assistants)*; Kerrie Jordan; Bethany Wetjen; Dominique; Eniko Mayer; Anika Yuen; Anu Kattoor; Hanna Josesina Chaplain; Karin Holm; Amena Lee Schlaikjer; Helen Praetorius; Leta Chung; Belinka Polakova; Sinna Ping; Simone Lee; Irena Budayova; Marilka Aling *(V-Six Models/Cheerleaders)*; Nina Mackenzie; Maria Butler; Trudy Jane Mansfield *(V-Six Office Girls)*; Denis Couprie; William Chan; Duane Davis *(Skinny Bodyguards)*; Brad Warren; Tony Trimble; John Whitney; Max G.; Michael Lambert; David Fiddes; Jason Todd Hancock; David Saunders; Ian Bruton; Phillip Duffy; Stuart Lee Markham; Jude Poyer; Jake Sear Jacob; Peter Kramer *(Russian Mafia)*; Pascale Harris; Robert Baynton Eke; Alex Mazija *(CIA Staff)*; Martyn A. Minns; Ian Clarke; Cesar Liesa; Kevin Butler; Melanie Page; Phil John Greatches; Ted Johan Michaels; Albert Dedem *(Rickshaw Racers)*; Garry Beckhurst; Steve Syson; Ian Tang; David Rolls; Leon C. Somera Jr.; Paolo Mario Moscardini; Barry Wensueen; Aaron Richardson; Au Man Leong; Yiu Shiu Chung *(Rickshaw Passengers)*

Jean-Claude Van Damme stars in his fourth action thriller helmed by a Hong Kong director and his second consecutive film for HK legend Tsui Hark. A convoluted tale of industrial sabotage and joint Russian/CIA-sponsored terrorism, KNOCK OFF performs the remarkable, if unenviable, feat of making DOUBLE TEAM (1997), the previous Van Damme-Hark collaboration, look positively entertaining by comparison.

Marcus Ray (Jean-Claude Van Damme) and Tommy Hendricks (Rob Schneider), partners in the Hong Kong division of V-Six Jeans, find themselves the victims of a "knock-off" operation, in which cheap, shoddy imitations are substituted for their product at the shipping point. The company's vice president, Karen Leigh (Lela Rochon), arrives in Hong Kong to investigate and joins with Hong Kong Police Lieutenant Han (Michael Wong) to put pressure on Ray and Tommy. Implicated in the scandal is Ray's longtime buddy Eddie Wang (Wyman Wong), who leased the factory to V-Six, and local shipping magnate Skinny (Glen Chin). An attempt is made on Eddie's life and Eddie goes into hiding.

Ray soon learns that Tommy is actually an undercover CIA agent working for Harry Johansson (Paul Sorvino), who informs Ray that the Russians are behind the knock-offs and have planted tiny explosive microchips in thousands of electronic products, toys, and items of clothing set to be shipped to the US. Eddie is killed in an explosion at his warehouse hideout but not before he implicates Skinny as the liaison to the Russians. Ray apprehends Skinny, who is killed in an explosion at Johansson's office. Examination of the surveillance tape from Eddie's hideout reveals Karen as the possible saboteur/killer. A confrontation with Karen reveals that she too is a CIA agent and has been sent to HK to locate a "mole" in the division. Karen and Tommy are abducted by the Russians and taken aboard a ship set to sail to the US with a shipment of the jeans equipped with explosive microchips in their pants buttons. Johansson is seen talking to the Russians, and is thus revealed to be a double agent.

As ceremonies begin to mark that day's (June 30, 1997) handover of Hong Kong to mainland China, Ray and Lieutenant Han head out alone to stop the ship. An extended battle aboard the ship culminates in Karen tossing several chips at Johansson before she dives to safety. Johansson, in the meantime, has pressed the detonator, unaware of Karen's last act. He is blown to bits, while Karen, Ray, Tommy and Han escape.

DOUBLE TEAM, Van Damme's previous Hark-directed vehicle, at least had colorful supporting turns by the likes of Mickey Rourke, basketball star Dennis Rodman, and British actor Paul Freeman, along with moments of genuine suspense. KNOCK OFF suffers from a lackluster cast and an unnecessarily complicated script (by action specialist Steven E. De Souza) that makes ham-handed use of the 1998 ceremonial handover of Hong Kong to mainland China (an event much better treated in the film CHINESE BOX).

Although there are lots of action scenes, most of them involve acrobatic stunts—thus making this the first Van Damme vehicle to de-emphasize his martial arts skills. The Russian mobsters are an undifferentiated mass, as are the rogue CIA agents, led by a tired-looking Paul Sorvino. The only Hong Kong players on hand are Carman Lee and Michael Wong (billed Michael Fitzgerald Wong), in somewhat minor roles as Hong Kong cops.

Hark's direction relies here on all sorts of gimmicky traveling shots (a bullet leaving the barrel of a gun) and unnecessary computer effects (a wild camera trip through wires and computer circuitry from one end of a phone surveillance call to the other). He is clearly going through the motions in KNOCK OFF, repressing the stylistic flair that distinguished his Hong Kong work, including such modern HK classics as PEKING OPERA BLUES (1986), ONCE UPON A TIME IN CHINA (1991), and GREEN SNAKE (1994). Although KNOCK OFF is a coproduction of Columbia and Hark's own Hong Kong company, Film Workshop, Hark seems to have treated the film as just an assignment-for-hire rather than a sincere attempt to fuse two distinct cinematic cultures. *(Violence, profanity.)*—B.C.

d, Tsui Hark; p, Nansun Shi; assoc p, Peter Nelson, Richard G. Murphy; co-p, Raymond Fung; w, Steven E. De Souza; ph, Arthur Wong; ed, Mak Chi-Sin; m, Ron Mael, Russell Mael; prod d, James Leung, Bill Lui; sound, Gary Wilkins (mixer); fx, Fred Cramer; casting, Illana Diamant, Lauris Freeman; cos, Ben Luk, William Fung, Mable Kwan

Action/Crime **(PR: C MPAA: R)**

KONDOM DES GRAUEN
(SEE: KILLER CONDOM, THE)

KRAA! THE SEA MONSTER ★
(U.S., 1998) 69m Monster Island Entertainment ~ Amazing Fantasy Entertainment c

R.L. McMurray *(Bobby Macek)*; Teal Merchande *(Alma James)*; Robert Garcia *(Bridger)*; Robert J. Ferrelli *(Monroe)*; J.W. Perra *(Mogyar)*; Jeff Rector *(Team Leader)*; Jeffery Meyer *(Team Member)*; Colton Scott *(Captain Ruric)*; Alison Lohman *(Patrolman Curtis)*; Anthony Furlong *(Patrolman Garth)*; Candida Tolentino *(Lt. Able)*; Michael Guerin *(Lord Doom)*; Jerry Lentz *(Voice of Doom)*; Jon Simanton *(Chamberlain)*; Leon W. Grant *(Wheeler)*; David Wall *(Landerson)*; Deborah Hatch *(Scientist)*; Jon Fedele *(Kraa)*

From the makers of ZARKORR! THE INVADER (1996) comes another resolutely underwhelming giant-monster "epic."

On the "cold planet" Proyas, the evil Lord Doom orders the towering monster Kraa sent to Earth, "the warm planet," as part of his plan for conquest. Elsewhere in space, the youthful Planet Patrol detects the "unauthorized transport" of Kraa. Their base is hit by Doom's crippling pulse cannon, and they are forced to contact a turtle-like alien agent named Mogyar, who arrives on Earth and befriends biker (and science-wiz) Bobby Macek (R.L. McMurray) and diner owner Alma James (Teal Merchande). Mogyar explains his mission, and that only a lab in Naples has the necessary equipment to stop Kraa. Government operatives led by Bridger (Robert Garcia) show up and take Alma, Bobby and Mogyar to a hidden base for interrogation.

As Kraa approaches the base, it is evacuated, and Mogyar helps Alma and Bobby escape. The trio learns that the Naples lab has been destroyed, and Bobby, using codes overheard by Mogyar, contacts the Harvest Point nuclear facility, posing as Bridger. They commandeer the base and, despite the interruption by Bridger and his men, create an energy weapon to attack Kraa. The Planet Patrol reroutes the beam off Kraa and up to their base, which is restored to full power and helps blast Kraa into vapor. The Patrol members then travel to Proyas and place Doom under interstellar arrest.

KRAA! not only borrows from many giant-monster fantasy classics, but also shoehorns in a "Mighty Morphin Power Rangers" ripoff (in the form of the "Planet Patrol") in a baldfaced attempt to pander to the youth market. However, even children aren't naive enough to cotton to this cheap-looking melange of rubber monster mayhem, needlessly cluttered plotting, poorly staged fight scenes, and cheap comedy (as when the Italian-accented Mogyar spouts lines like "Let's-a get outta here!"). To make matters worse, the intrigue surrounding the Planet Patrol's attempts to repair their base rates as little more than a distraction from the central plotline. Given that Michael S. Deak, billed as "miniature F/X director," shot all the monster footage, and a closing title reveals that Dave Parker helmed all the Planet Patrol and Lord Doom scenes, this may be the first movie in which the director credited up front was only responsible for about a third of the actual feature. *(Violence.)*— M.G.

d, Aaron Osborne; p, Kirk Edward Hansen; exec p, Charles Band; co-p, Steve Sechrist, Rob Martin; w, Benjamin Carr; ph, Joe Caramico Maxwell; ed, Poppy Das, Gregory Sanders; m, Carl Dante; prod d, Erin Cochran; art d, Ron Strathum; set d, Foster Vick; sound, John Halaby; fx, Michael S. Deak, Total Fabrication, Mark Williams, Mark Rappaport, Creature F/X, Al Magliochetti; casting, Bob MacDonald, Perry Bullington; cos, Heather Priest; makeup, Lois Anne O'Malley; stunts, Kim Koscki

Science Fiction **(PR: A MPAA: PG)**

KRIPPENDORF'S TRIBE ★½
(U.S., 1998) 94m Touchstone; Morra-Brezner-Steinberg-Tenenbaum Entertainment; Dreyfuss/James Productions; Hollywood Pictures ~ Buena Vista c

Richard Dreyfuss *(James Krippendorf)*; Jenna Elfman *(Veronica Micelli)*; Natasha Lyonne *(Shelly Krippendorf)*; Gregory Smith *(Mickey Krippendorf)*; Carl Michael Lindner *(Edmund Krippendorf)*; Stephen Root *(Gerald Adams)*; Elaine Stritch *(Irene Hard-*

ing); Tom Poston *(Gordon Harding)*; David Ogden Stiers *(Henry Spivey)*; Lily Tomlin *(Ruth Allen)*; Doris Belack *(President Porter)*; Julio Oscar Mechoso *(Simon Alonso)*; Siobhan Fallon *(Lori Hayward)*; Susan Ruttan *(Mrs. O'Brien)*; Barbara Williams *(Jennifer Krippendorf)*; Zakes Mokae *(Sulukim)*; Jacob Handy; Zachary Handy *(Young Edmund)*; Amzie Strickland *(Gladys Schmades)*; Phil Leeds *(Dr. Harvey)*; Frances Bay *(Edith Proxmire)*; Sandy Martin *(Nurse)*; Lance Kinsey *(Principal Reese)*; Mila Kunis *(Abbey Tournquist)*; Robin Karfo *(Mrs. Tournquist)*; Tim Halligan *(Mr. Tournquist)*; Peter Tilden *(Larry Swift)*; Shashawnee Hall *(Mabu)*; Timothy Wells *(Ruth's Guide)*; Kari Leigh Floyd *(Party Guest)*; Michael Steve Jones *(Alcove Man)*; Ian Busch *(Flagpole Boy)*; Grace Lee *(College Student #1)*; Todd Cattell *(College Student #2)*; Chris Duque *(Outpost Man)*; Valerie Reid *(Divorced Woman)*; Rachel Winfree *(Lecture Woman #1)*; Suanne Spoke *(Lecture Woman #2)*; Catherine Paolone *(Lecture Woman #3)*; Bill Rosier *(TV Store Customer #1)*; Robb Derringer *(TV Store Customer #2)*; Laura Cayouette *(TV Studio Woman)*; China Brezner *(Elevator Teen)*; Bruce Jarchow *(Andrews)*; Wendy Worthington *(Secretary)*

Continually veering between the offensive and the saccharine, KRIPPENDORF'S TRIBE tries to go both ways and as a result gets nowhere. This weary farce about a anthropologist who gets back in touch with his kids by involving them in a scheme to fake evidence of a "lost" New Guinea tribe is a product of the Disney factory (via its Touchstone subsidiary) at its most mechanical.

Since the death of his wife two years ago, grieving Prof. James Krippendorf (Richard Dreyfuss) has been ignoring his faculty duties and living off of a Proxmire Foundation grant. As a single father, he is barely able to cope with his children Shelly (Natasha Lyonne), Mickey (Gregory Smith), and Edmund (Carl Michael Lindner). Veronica Micelli (Jenna Elfman), a gregarious but conniving former student who is now a faculty colleague, shows up at his door to tell him that his Proxmire lecture is due—tonight. Having done nothing to locate the "undiscovered" tribe that is the subject of his grant, he instead extemporizes a talk about the "Shelmikedmu," a fictitious tribe named after his kids and characterized by details of his own chaotic family life. Goaded by suspicious colleague Ruth Allen (Lily Tomlin), Veronica speaks for James in saying that he has plenty of film footage of the tribe. James is forced to fake these scenes in his backyard, using himself and his kids dressed in native garb.

Veronica continues to insinuate herself into the project and arranges a sale of the footage to a cable network, which turns it into a series. Forced to continue the escalating ruse, James concocts a tribal mating ritual by inviting Veronica to his house, seducing her while both are wearing "Shelmikedmu" outfits, and filming their lovemaking. The fictional tribe attains nationwide popularity, and James is forced to pose as a native chief on a TV talk show and at a posh dinner party. By the time Veronica discovers the ruse, she is so deeply involved that she must join it, taking turns posing as "the chief." James finally gives up when Ruth faxes a letter from New Guinea saying that they don't exist. But a university meeting to discuss his punishment is ended by another fax from Ruth saying she has found the tribe after all. (What she has actually found are impostors, arranged by daughter Shelly with the participation of friends the family made on a previous trip to New Guinea.)

From beginning to end, the idiotically plotted KRIPPENDORF'S TRIBE skirts an outrageous racism as a middle-class white family does everything but shout "Ooga booga!" in attempting to portray a native tribe; in the film's nadir, the score accompanies their cavortings with the song "Boogie Fever." (The fact that a scholarly community falls for this ruse is a worthy source of satire; if only that had occurred to scripter Charlie Peters, previously responsible for such leaden comedies as MY FATHER THE HERO and PASSED AWAY). Ironically, it would have been better had KRIPPENDORF'S TRIBE been *more* offensive; at least then it would have been doing so blatantly, rather than working such elements into what it supposed to be a family comedy.

Richard Dreyfuss acts throughout with the air of a man under contractual obligation; called on to appear grieving or frantic, he merely looks annoyed. Co-star Jenna Elfman is engaging, but her character is so poorly written that it is impossible to develop any perspective on her. One can only hope that this asinine film doesn't do too much to hurt the career of director Todd Holland, of HBO's brilliant "The Larry Sanders Show." *(Sexual situations, adult situations, profanity.)*—M.F.

d, Todd Holland; p, Larry Brezner; exec p, Whitney Green, Ross Canter; w, Charlie Peters (based on the novel by Frank Parkin); ph, Dean Cundey; ed, Jon Poll; m, Bruce Broughton; prod d, Scott Chambliss; art d, Bill Rea; set d, Karen Manthey; sound, James E. Webb; fx, J.D. Streett; casting, Jackie Burch; cos, Isis Mussenden; makeup, Ben Nye Jr., David L. Anderson (effects)

Comedy **(PR: C MPAA: PG-13)**

KRISTIN LAVRANSDATTER ★★★½

(Norway/Germany/Sweden, 1998) 144m Norsk Film; Lavaransdatter Film; Telemunchen Film; Fernseh; Northern Lights; NRK Drama ~ Home Vision Cinema c

Elisabeth Matheson *(Kristin Lavransdatter)*; Bjorn Skagestad *(Erlend Nikulausson)*; Sverre Anker Ousdal *(Lavrans)*; Henny Moan *(Ragnfrid)*; Rut Tellefsen *(Lady Ashild)*; Jorgen Langhelle *(Simon Darre)*; Erland Josephson *(Brother Edvin)*; Lena Endre *(Eline Ormsdatter)*

A lush, sweeping, and passionate epic in the David Lean mold, KRISTIN LAVRANSDATTER is the impressive second film to come from actress-turned-filmmaker Liv Ullmann.

In the 14th-century Norwegian town of Gudbrandsdalen, Kristin Lavransdatter (Elisabeth Matheson) lives with her kind and attentive parents. Her father, Lavrans (Sverre Anker Ousdal), is a landowner and her mother, Ragnfrid (Henny Moan), remains devoted to Lavrans despite some compromises she made before they married. Lavrans places his hopes upon Kristin, since her sister is handicapped and her three brothers were killed in war. When she turns 18, Lavrans arranges for her to marry Simon Darre (Jorgen Langhelle), the son of a fellow landowner. Kristin is horrified at the notion of a loveless marriage and persuades her family to let her stay in a convent in Oslo before she marries, so she can carefully make a decision. While socializing in town, Kristin spots dashing knight Erlend Nikulausson (Bjorn Skagestad) staring at her. Soon, they meet formally and fall deeply in love. Kristin decides to defy her father and marry Erlend. But Erlend, it turns out, has been living for ten years with a married woman, Eline Ormsdatter (Lena Endre), with whom he has had children.

When she returns home, Kristin decides to tell Simon and her parents about her plans to marry Erlend. Simon takes the news badly, while Lavrans is devastated by his daughter's desire for Erlend, whom he considers an unscrupulous man. Ragnfrid, angered by Lavrans's harsh judgment of Kristin's actions, confesses to Lavrans that she too slept with another man before she married him—and that one of their sons might have belonged to her lover. Lavrans is stunned, but he forgives Ragnfrid and decides that his daughter must follow her heart. Kristin makes plans for their wedding, but the ceremony is plagued by tragedy when a fire guts the entire church. Still, the participants gather together in the ruins of the church and become husband and wife.

Edited down from its original Norwegian running time of three hours, KRISTIN LAVRANSDATTER received a home-video release in the US in 1998 after limited theatrical releases around the country. Even in its edited state, KRISTIN remains a masterfully conceived and executed fable about the moral consequences of an all-consuming passion. Based on the first book of Sigrid Undset's three-volume novel, the film has the look of a centuries-old picture postcard, with Sven Nykvist's unapologetically lush cinematography showcasing the wonders of the Norwegian landscape. Ullmann frequently makes metaphorical use of the scenery, giving it the status of a character in the film—as in the sequence where Kristin must cross a rock-filled path on a journey to meet Erlend for a forbidden tryst at the beach.

Ullmann has been clearly influenced as a filmmaker by her mentor Ingmar Bergman. This influence becomes most apparent in KRISTIN when the characters' actions seem guided by an unseen and judgmental God (the sort of uncaring deity that rules over Bergman's world). The Bergman connection is also made in the scene in which Erlend feeds Kristin some freshly picked berries; here, one is reminded of the moment in THE SEVENTH SEAL (1957) in which a young couple traveling the countryside offers some strawberries to a weary knight (Max von Sydow) in medieval Scandinavia.

The film also boasts a number of fine performances, particularly from Matheson, who bears a striking resemblance to the young Ullmann. Skagestad does a finely nuanced turn as Erlend, making it uncertain whether the character's intentions are honorable or if he's just a cad. Bergman regular Erland Josephson puts in a brief appearance, playing a man of the cloth who tries in vain to counsel Kristin about her romantic and sexual dilemmas. The film's most unaffected performance, however, comes from Henny Moan; during the sequence in which Ragnfrid confesses her love for the man she slept with long ago, Moan's face conveys the pain of lost love and the acceptance of compromise. Ullmann sets the scene in the dark, cramped confines of the couple's modest cabin—a comfortable, homey setting for a harsh, shattering revelation. The scene is one that would make Bergman proud. *(Adult themes, violence.)*—D.O.

d, Liv Ullmann; p, Goran Lindstrom; exec p, Esben Hoilund Carlsen; w, Liv Ullmann (based on the novel by Sigrid Undset); ph, Sven Nykvist; ed, Michal Leszcylowski; m, Ketil Hvoslef; prod d, Karl Juliusson; sound, Owe Swensson; cos, Inger Pehrsson

Drama **(PR: C MPAA: NR)**

KRZYSZTOF KIESLOWSKI: I'M SO-SO ★★★

(Denmark, 1995) 56m Kulturmode Film; Statens Filmcentral; Danish TV 1 ~ First Run Features c/bw

Krzysztof Kieslowski; Krzysztof Wierzbicki

"*Not* knowing is my business," says Krzysztof Kieslowski in KRZYSZTOF KIESLOWSKI: I'M SO-SO. . ., a wistful documentary profile of the late Polish director. With a revealing interview and clips from his work, the film pays proper homage.

The film begins with interviews of several people who know of Kieslowski, including a graphologist, an analyst, a clairvoyant, a doctor, and a priest. Then the director, Krzysztof Wierzbicki, Kieslowski's most frequent cinematographer, questions Kieslowski himself about his life and work in a series of segments alternating between black-and-white and color, shot at Mazury Lakeland in Poland.

Kieslowski discusses his abusive childhood, the early death of his father, his entering the famous Lodz film school, and some of his early film experiments. He rails against Communism in Poland after WWII and tells how the political atmosphere affected some of his early work. Fragments are shown from TALKING HEADS (1980), THE CALM (1976), CAMERA BUFF (1979), BLIND CHANCE (1981), DECALOGUE I (1988), and THREE COLORS: RED (1994). At the end, Kieslowski looks forward to making other films.

The limited release of KRZYSZTOF KIESLOWSKI: I'M SO-SO. . . coincides with growing public and critical interest in Kieslowski's canon, a group of formally vibrant, socially aware films. Though still best known for his last production, the artful trilogy, THREE COLORS: BLUE, WHITE, RED (1993-94), Kieslowski may have contributed more to the form with his earlier, smaller works, which this documentary excerpts generously.

In fact, it's a wonder why the portrait shows so little from Kieslowski's late, better-known pictures (just THE DECALOGUE I, not parts II-X, his updating of The Ten Commandments, and THREE COLORS: RED, but not BLUE or WHITE, and nothing from THE DOUBLE LIFE OF VERONIQUE, 1991); very possibly the filmmakers had problems obtaining the rights to show clips from these films—whatever the reason, their absence is felt. But viewers will benefit from seeing the little-screened TALKING HEADS and THE CALM, both of which document the lives of striking Polish workers; CAMERA BUFF, about how an amateur cameraman destroys his life by using his camera once too often; and BLIND CHANCE, about how fate influences the lives of several working-class people.

As the title suggests, KRZYSZTOF KIESLOWSKI: I'M SO-SO. . . delves into the heart and mind of a melancholy man, and, like Kieslowski's own films, this documentary takes on a romantically humanistic tone. An added layer of sorrow comes from the knowledge that the subject died of a heart attack in March 1996, less than a year after the film was completed (in May 1995). The last shot of Kieslowski on a barge at sunset makes a perfect finale. The only problem with the production is that stylistic flourishes gloss over and sentimentalize the harsh undercurrents, existential philosophizing, and even some biographical details (for example, what did Kieslowski think of his Lodz school comrades, like Roman Polanski?). Still, Kieslowski would probably be proud of this sincere tribute from his friends and coworkers.—E.M.

d, Krzysztof Wierzbicki; p, Karen Hjort; w, Krzysztof Wierzbicki; ph, Jacek Petrycki; ed, Milenia Fiedler; m, Zbigniew Preisner; prod d, Andrzej Gorz; sound, Michal Zarnecki

Documentary **(PR: C MPAA: NR)**

KURT AND COURTNEY ★★½

(U.K., 1998) 95m Strength Ltd. ~ Roxie Releasing c

Kurt Cobain; Courtney Love; Hank Harrison; El Duce; Dylan Carlson; Tom Grant; Alan Bowman; The Dwarves

Intrepid low-budget documentarian Nick Broomfield (HEIDI FLEISS HOLLYWOOD MADAM) investigates the death of grunge icon Kurt Cobain, asking the question: Did the heroin-addicted singer-songwriter really kill himself?

About 25 percent of Broomfield's study concentrates on Cobain's sweet-natured demeanor and the ways in which he demonstrated that he couldn't handle fame and fortune; 74 percent vilifies his widow, rocker Courtney Love, who is seen as mercenary and social-climbing by nature; the final one percent concludes that though she didn't kill Cobain, Love probably did drive him to his bleak finale. Though even Broomfield might have to admit that KURT AND COURTNEY is little more than a journalistic joke, relying on crackpot, marginal sources, the film does supply plenty of sordid fun.

Having already exhibited a strong taste for chronicling society's bottom-feeders (demonstrated to good advantage in his

AILEEN WUORNOS: THE SELLING OF A SERIAL KILLER), here Broomfield interviews one ranting, self-involved misfit after another. Most memorable is Love's estranged father, Hank Harrison, whose puffy face and rounded features resembles what Love used to look like before she began altering herself with plastic surgery. After plugging his book on Kurt Cobain, Harrison describes his daughter's history of violence, whoring, drugs, and her succeed-at-all-costs philosophy of life. He quotes a poem she wrote as a teenager: "Destroy everyone in my way; destroy every lousy lay. . . " Though his words are consistently damning, it's hard not to see Harrison as a ruthless, not to mention jealous, opportunist trying to horn in on Love's success—like father, like daughter.

Harrison is just one in a series of interview subjects who alternately fear and loathe Courtney Love, the leader of the band Hole who turned actress with a well-received supporting turn in THE PEOPLE VS. LARRY FLYNT (1996). Broomfield couldn't, or didn't want to find one Love supporter. The most direct attack against her comes from an incredibly cartoonish source: El Duce, leader of the misogynist hardcore band the Mentors. Broomfield captures the bald, big-bellied "shock rocker" ambling in front of his ramshackle house brandishing a fly swatter. His claim? Love offered him $50,000 grand to kill Kurt. The credibility of this loon suffers when he offers to provide more dirt to Broomfield in exchange for a beer. Broomfield notes that soon after the interview, El Duce was run over by a train. Was this part of Love's conspiracy? Or was it, more likely, the case of a crazy drunk tempting death once too often?

KURT AND COURTNEY is as much about Broomfield as it is about his two subjects. The filmmaker often steps into the shot, and (as he has frequently done in his films) he gives his pursuit of the story as much attention as the story itself. One sequence shows this self-styled guerilla filmmaker discovering that one of his main financial backers, Showtime (owned by Viacom, which also owns MTV), is pulling out of the project, due to pressure from Love. Broomfield also maintained that Love's intimidation tactics extended to the film's soundtrack—he was legally locked out of using any Cobain concert footage or Nirvana songs on the soundtrack. Suffice it to say, Love also refused to be interviewed for the film.

The film's highlight comes when the filmmaker trails the uncooperative Love to an ACLU awards dinner, where she's slated to speak. He notes that he can't stomach the idea that a woman who has a history of threatening and even beating up reporters who write unflattering things about her has the gall to publicly support free speech. After Love finishes her speech, Broomfield commandeers the podium and asks her publically if she ever threatened journalists. Before he can follow up on this unanswered question, the director is kicked out. While a documentarian being shut up at a civil liberties gathering drips with delightful irony, the scene is partly undermined by shaky, almost unwatchable, camera work.

When one gets past Broomfield's vanity, the thinness of the material, and the technical ineptitude (often past the bounds of acceptable guerilla filmmaking), KURT AND COURTNEY still succeeds in satisfying one's appetite for sleaze while presenting an interesting (albeit often confused) message about the power of celebrity and the price of fame. *(Extreme profanity.)*—T.Y.

d, Nick Broomfield; p, Tine Van Den Brande, Michael D'Acosta; exec p, Nick Frazer; ph, Joan Churchill, Alex Vendor; ed, Mark Atkins; m, David Bergeaud

Documentary **(PR: C MPAA: NR)**

KYOSHIRO NEMURI: FULL MOON-CUT

(SEE: SLEEPY EYES OF DEATH: FULL CIRCLE KILLING)

L

L'ALDILA
(SEE: BEYOND, THE)

LA BATALLA DE CHILE: LA LUCHA DE UN PUEBLO SIN ARMAS—EL GOPE DE ESTADO
(SEE: BATTLE OF CHILE, THE)

LA DESENCHANTEE
(SEE: DISENCHANTED, THE)

LA FEMME DE CHAMBRE DU TITANIC
(SEE: CHAMBERMAID ON THE TITANIC, THE)

LA SEPARATION ★★★

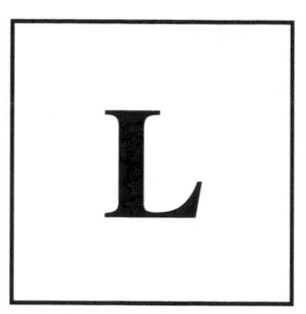

(France, 1994) 88m C.M.V. Productions; Le Studio Canal; France 2 Cinema; D.A. Films; Renn Productions ~ Phaedra Cinema c
(AKA: SEPARATION, THE)

Isabelle Huppert *(Anne)*; Daniel Auteuil *(Pierre)*; Jerome Deschamps *(Victor)*; Karin Viard *(Claire)*; Laurence Lerel *(Laurence)*; Louis Vincent *(Loulou)*; Nina Morato *(Marie)*; Jean-Jacques Vanier *(Speaker at Party)*; Christian Benedetti *(Lawyer)*; Frederic Gelard *(Estate Agent)*; Gerard Jumel *(Man at Party)*; Estelle Larrivaz *(Girl at Party)*; Claudine Challier *(Loulou's Grandmother)*

The small-scale French drama LA SEPARATION looks closely at a professional married couple's break-up. Though realistically executed, the imbalance in point-of-view diminishes the film's overall impact.

Pierre (Daniel Auteuil) and Anne (Isabelle Huppert) have been married for several years, and have a two-year-old son named Louis (Louis Vincent), nicknamed LouLou. But Pierre, a commercial artist, and Anne, a business executive, find a void developing in their relationship. Their petty disagreements often turn into all-out fights, even around their best friends, Claire (Karin Viard) and Victor (Jerome Deschamps).

One night after a party, Anne tells Pierre that she is in love with another man. Oddly, Pierre accepts the news calmly, hoping that Anne's happiness with her lover will spill over into their souring relationship. Yet, as Anne continues her affair, Pierre becomes increasingly jealous and cruel. Still, Anne insists on living in the same apartment, because she does not want to leave LouLou.

Finally, Anne announces she wants a divorce and takes LouLou to her mother's. Pierre responds by attacking Anne violently, then getting a divorce lawyer. Anne and Pierre reunite briefly at a bar to discuss who will keep the apartment. After some reminiscing, Pierre agrees to move out. Later, a desolate Pierre walks the streets, feeling lost.

Here is yet another variation on Bergman's seminal SCENES FROM A MARRIAGE (1974), although, in many ways, Robert Benton's KRAMER VS. KRAMER (1979) seems to be the greater inspiration (even the apartment set looks the same). Like KRAMER, this disintegration-of-a-marriage drama follows the husband's point-of-view, from the opening shots as he videotapes LouLou drooling in his crib to the closing moments where he wanders the boulevards of the city. The problem with this narrow focus is that it leaves many questions unanswered about the wife's behavior (we never even see "the other man"), and almost turns her into a stereotypical shrew. Pierre's violent outburst becomes all the more disturbing, since the viewer has been mainly encouraged to empathize with him all along. Fortunately, LA SEPARATION overcomes some of this major dramatic weakness through the accomplished work of the filmmakers. Director Christian Vincent (LA DISCRETE) adapts co-writer Dan Franck's novel with a skillful naturalism, allowing minute details to add to the sense of doom about the relationship. Vincent also integrates a level of ironic and suspenseful reflexivity by showing Pierre and Anne at the cinematheque watching Rossellini's EUROPA '51 (a.k.a. THE GREATEST LOVE, 1952), in which a married couple (Ingrid Bergman, Alexander Knox) discover that their son has committed suicide.

On a technical level, Denis Lenoir's cinematography sharply emphasizes the tight, restricted spaces, neither glamorizing the characters nor the Paris setting. Best of all, Huppert and Auteuil invest each of their scenes with an honest emotional intensity. With so many gaps in her character's prehistory and development, Huppert deserves particular commendation for her nuanced work, making Anne a much more dimensional person than what must have appeared on paper. Clearly, LA SEPARATION never meant to flesh out all the details of this marriage (in the tradition of Bergman's film), yet a few more key scenes might have turned this drama into a powerhouse. *(Violence, extreme profanity.)*—E.M.

d, Christian Vincent; p, Claude Berri; exec p, Pierre Grunstein; w, Christian Vincent, Dan Franck (based on the novel by Dan Franck); ph, Denis Lenoir; ed, Francois Ceppi; prod d, Christian Vallerin; art d, Christian Vallerin; sound, Calude Bertrand; cos, Sylvie Gautrelet; makeup, Thi-Loan N'Guyen

Drama **(PR: C MPAA: NR)**

LA TREGUA
(SEE: TRUCE, THE)

LA VIE DE JESUS
(SEE: LIFE OF JESUS, THE)

LA VITA E BELLA
(SEE: LIFE IS BEAUTIFUL)

LAND GIRLS, THE ★★½

(U.K./France, 1998) 111m West Eleven Films; Greenpoint Films; InterMedia Film Equities; Skreba-Creon Films; Arena Films; Camera One ~ Gramercy Pictures c

Catherine McCormack *(Stella)*; Rachel Weisz *(Ag)*; Anna Friel *(Prue)*; Steven Mackintosh *(Joe Lawrence)*; Tom Georgeson *(Mr. Lawrence)*; Maureen O'Brien *(Mrs. Lawrence)*; Gerald Down *(Ratty)*; Lucy Akhurst *(Janet)*; Paul Bettany *(Philip)*; Nick Mollo *(Barry)*; Michael Mantas *(Desmond)*; Nicholas Le Prevost *(Agricultural Officer)*; Celia Bannerman *(District Commissioner)*; Ann Bell *(Philip's Mother)*; Nigel Planer *(Gerald)*; Edmund Moriarty *(Harry)*; Shirley Newberry *(WAAF at Dance)*; Kate Lock *(Lady in Charge)*; Esther Hall *(Mavis)*; Charlie Higson *(Subaltern)*; Russell Barr *(Jamie—the Scottish Airman)*; John Gill *(Doctor)*; Arnold Brown *(C.O.)*; Crispin Layfield *(German Pilot)*; Grace Leland *(Baby Barry)*; Reverend Alan Bennett *(Reverend Alan Bennett)*; Martha Mackintosh; Felix Davis; Jacob Leland *(Children at Christening)*; Jack O'Hampton *(Jack the Dog)*

THE LAND GIRLS, the story of three young Britons who joined the Women's Land Army during WWII, is a well acted and nicely mounted, but talky and slow moving, period piece that turns into an old-fashioned romantic tearjerker despite a revisionist feminist approach.

England, 1941: with Britain at war with Germany, male farm workers have to leave the land and join the armed forces. Women from all walks of life volunteer to take their places on the farms and call themselves The Women's Land Army. Three of these young women—Stella (Catherine McCormack), Ag (Rachel Weisz), and Prue (Anna Friel)—go to work on a farm in rural Dorset owned by Mr. Lawrence (Tom Georgeson) and his wife (Maureen O'Brien), and become close friends, despite the differences in their classes and backgrounds. The bold Prue immediately seduces Lawrence's handsome young son Joe (Steven Mackintosh), even though he's engaged. At a local dance, Prue meets a British pilot named Barry (Nick Mollo) and Ag falls for a Canadian flier named Desmond (Michael Mantas), but is afraid to have sex with him because she's a virgin.

At Prue's recommendation, Ag asks Joe to deflower her, and he gladly complies, but finds himself falling in love with Stella, who's engaged to a cold British naval officer named Philip (Paul Bettany). When Stella leaves the farm to visit Philip, she realizes that she's really in love with Joe. Prue eventually marries Barry, but he's killed in combat, and Stella plans on breaking up with Philip, but can't bring herself to do it after she learns that he's been badly wounded. After the War, the three women meet up at the baptism of Prue's baby. Prue is married to a wealthy man who's much older than she, and Ag is married to Desmond, who now works for the Canadian consulate in Egypt. Stella tells them that Philip is divorcing her, but when she sees Joe with his wife and kids, she lies and says she's happy. Privately, they admit their still-existing affection for each other but then go their separate ways.

The main appeal of THE LAND GIRLS lies in its convincing atmosphere of camaraderie and sisterhood between the disparate Stella, Ag, and Prue. Each character is given a distinctive personality—Stella is reserved and serious, Ag prim and proper, and Prue earthy and funny—which are all developed with sufficient detail and believability and vivaciously brought to life by Catherine McCormack, Rachel Weisz, and Anna Friel, so that they never become stereotypes. In fact, all of the characters, even minor ones, are bestowed with a degree of individuality and sympathy, such as the crotchety Mr. Johnson, who gradually reveals a warm and soft side. The film is also handsomely crafted, evocatively recreating another time and another place (the nightly air raids; a performance of "Lambeth Walk" at the dance interrupted by the announcement of the bombing of Pearl Harbor; a German plane suddenly crashing into the farm), featuring lovely widescreen photography of the English countryside, and first-rate art direction and costumes (those Land Girl uniforms of vests, ties, tweed jackets, and jodhpurs sure are cute).

Unfortunately, where the film fails is its lack of a compelling dramatic spark (several scenes consist of nothing but plowing the fields and uneventful family dinners), and its wildly inconsistent tone, which wavers between light comedy and sappy melodrama. The early scenes on the farm are amusing, with some humorous softcore titillation (phallic symbolism where Joe teaches the girls how to milk cows; Ag and Prue "having a go" with Joe, which is like a reversal of the old sex joke about the traveling salesman and the farmers' daughters), and lots of "randy" talk of "fornication," "buggering," and "getting your knickers off." Later, however, the story becomes a dated romantic soap opera, with lots of typically British stiff-upper-lip suffering and stifled emotions, along with a not-so-subtle message about "holding on to what you want" and "making hay while the sun shines." The reunion epilogue, which strains for a kind of SPLENDOR IN THE GRASS-like lost-love poignancy and regret, fails to move simply because Stella and Joe's supposedly intense passion for each other was never convincingly conveyed, and it's hard to believe that she could have left him so easily in the first place if she really loved him that much, especially since the film offers nothing more persuasive to explain her reasons than the same old spurious sentiments about noble sacrifice. *(Profanity, sexual situations, violence.)*—M.S.

d, David Leland; p, Simon Relph; exec p, Ruth Jackson; assoc p, Andrew Warren; w, David Leland, Keith Dewhurst (based on the novel *Land Girls* by Angela Huth); ph, Henry Braham; ed, Nick Moore; m, Brian Lock; prod d, Caroline Amies; art d, Frank Walsh; sound, Stuart Wilson (recordist); casting, Jeremy Zimmerman; cos, Shuna Harwood; makeup, Jenny Shircore; stunts, Nick Powell

Romance/War/Drama **(PR: C MPAA: R)**

LAND OF THE FREE ★

(U.S., 1998) 96m PM Entertainment; Independent Creative Artists Pictures ~ PM Entertainment c

Jeff Speakman *(Frank Jennings)*; William Shatner *(Aidan Carvell)*; Lisa Darr *(Annie Jennings)*; Larry Cedar *(Green)*; Cody Dorkin *(Randy Jennings)*; Chris Lemmon *(Thorton)*; John Furey *(Luckenbill)*; Charlie Robinson *(McCuster)*; Robert Torti *(Fitzpatrick)*; Candice Azzara *(Waitress)*; Arthur Hiller *(Judge)*; Bobby Bragg; Tony Blassfield; Danny Breen; Chris Byrne; Alisa Cristensen; Rance Howard; Bernie Kopell; Signy Coleman

Car crashes and creepy campaign contributions make strange bedfellows in this clunky thriller.

Maverick adman-turned-populist Aidan Carvell (William Shatner) looks like the next senator from California, thanks to his patriotic stump speeches and bestselling manifesto *Land of the Free*. During one appearance an assassin tries to shoot Carvell but is taken out by his campaign manager Frank Jennings (Jeff Speakman), an upright ex-Navy man. However, FBI agents pull Jennings aside and inform him that the attempted murder might have been staged, and that Carvell's campaign funds have come from homegrown anti-government "militia" terrorists. Reluctantly, Jennings breaks into Carvell's computer and passes on incriminating files to the feds, barely escaping Carvell's "Free America" thugs in the process.

Four months later the government's trial against a smug, still-popular Carvell is about to begin, with Frank Jennings the star witness. Although supposedly in a federal protection program, Jennings finds himself fingered by a turncoat agent. He, his wife (Lisa Darr) and son (Cody Dorkin) go on the run, hunted by goons, and only after an apocalyptic car/bus chase does the hero survive to testify. Then, due to a corrupt judge, the evidence is thrown out and Carvell exonerated. Jennings knows that the former defendant will not forgive or forget him, so he girds himself for a one-man assault on Carvell's residence. He blows up the villain's house, bodyguards, and helicopter, and after a furious fistfight, drowns Carvell in a small pond. A subsequent sham FBI inquest returns a verdict of accidental death and keeps Jennings's name out of it.

LAND OF THE FREE staggered out from under the auspices of PM Entertainment, a straight-to-video outfit which grinds out dozens of lowbrow action pictures, commonly concerning the antics of kickboxers vs. druglords. While a political thriller seems an ambitious goal for such producers, the end result here is no improvement whatsoever. Cars careen and explode on cue into fireballs, martial-arts mayhem reigns, and the commando family man with the biggest guns and bombs wins, regardless of real-world logic or police procedure. SEVEN DAYS IN MAY (1964) this is not.

There's a sideshow attraction in the doughty shape of ever-stolid movie and TV hero William Shatner as a master bad guy (patterned, it would seem, after real-life, third-party political gadabout H. Ross Perot). Indeed Shatner's broad delivery makes him a credible office-seeker when Carvell gladhands before media cameras. But his one-note pomposity continues unvaried, whether the ill-conceived Carvell gloats over his militia minions or gets pummeled bloody by B-level action star Speakman (THE PERFECT WEAPON) in the ludicrous finale. The cast contains other offbeat, offnote cameos by the likes of director Arthur Hiller (THE HOSPITAL) as the judge and Bernie Kopell ("The Love Boat") as a TV newsman. *(Violence, profanity, nudity, sexual situations.)*—C.C.

d, Jerry Jameson; p, Ronald Jacobs; exec p, Richard Pepin, Joseph Merhi; assoc p, Jeff Albert; co-p, John Kelly; w, Maria James, Terry Cunningham (based on the story by Ronald Jacobs and Jerry Jameson); ph, Ken Blakey; ed, Stephen Adrianson; m, Stephen Cohn; set d, Heather Foley, Ande Brittan; sound, Mike Hall; casting, Mike Fenton; cos, Amber Lynn Garcia; stunts, Cole McKay

Political/Action/Thriller **(PR: O MPAA: R)**

LANDLADY, THE ★½

(U.S., 1998) 98m Image Organization ~
Trimark Home Video c

Talia Shire *(Melanie Leroy)*; Jack Coleman *(Patrick Forman)*; Bruce Weitz *(Pepper McAllen)*; Melissa Behr *(Liz Reese)*; Bette Ford *(Justine Welch)*; Dee Freeman *(Jenny Hagen)*; Nathan Le Grand *(Ralston Leroy)*; Luisa Leschin *(Mrs. Inez)*; Laura Pursell *(Louanne)*; Susie Singer *(Venice)*; Clement von Franckenstein *(Lawrence Gerard)*; David Parker *(Detective Troyer)*; Courtney Gains *(Tyson Johns)*; Christopher Kriesa *(Ralphie)*

A gothic horror tale that can't decide between camp amusement or gory pandering, THE LANDLADY stars Talia Shire as a psycho who is supposed to be attacking her victims with relish but, in Shire's potrayal, more suggests a wallflower half-heartedly trying to become a lady wrestler.

Self-righteous Melanie Leroy (Talia Shire) abhors the infidelity of her husband Ralston (Nathan Le Grand) because it blemishes her idealization of marital bliss. After killing Ralston by feeding him shellfish to which he is fatally allergic, Melanie moves into an apartment building she has inherited. She sets her sights on one of the tenants, handsome social worker Patrick Forman (Jack Coleman). Melanie installs surveillance equipment (replete with a two-way mirror) to give her a bird's eye view of Patrick's pad. She also kills building manager Justine Welch (Bette Ford) for asking too many questions about Ralston's demise.

Continuing her pursuit of Patrick, Melanie forces his girlfriend Liz Reese, (Melissa Behr), at gunpoint to overdose on medication. When a tenant, a hooker named Venice (Susie Singer), spies Melanie's two-way mirror set-up, Melanie bashes in her skull with a lamp, frames one of Venice's johns, and shoots him, too.

When Patrick wants to simply remain friends with Melanie, Melanie knocks him unconscious and ties him up. When building super Pepper McAllen (Bruce Weitz) and inquisitive tenant Lawrence Gerard (Clement von Franckenstein) stumble onto Melanie's string of homicides, she is forced to kill them. When Patrick's client, Jenny Hagen (Dee Freeman), comes looking for her missing case worker, Melanie tries to smother her with a dry cleaning bag and then stabs her with a letter opener. Having freed himself, Patrick tackles his amorous landlady; in the scuffle, he shoots Melanie with her own pistol.

This flick is more remarkable for the number of killing methods on display than it is for any discernible variety in its writing or acting. Talia Shire is handicapped by a screenplay that rips off the modern classic THE STEPFATHER (1987) without deciding whether to build up the body count for frissons or laughter. While talented thesps like Bruce Weitz and Bette Ford give it the old college try, Shire does no more than nibble at the scenery. Hampered by its tentative black comedy tone, THE LANDLADY contributes to the decline of the "Crazy Old Broad" horror subgenre, popularized by WHAT EVER HAPPENED TO BABY JANE? (1962). *(Graphic violence, profanity, sexual situations, substance abuse.)*—R.P.

d, Rob Malenfant; p, Pierre David; assoc p, Frank Rehwaldt, Talia Shire; co-p, Noel Zanitsch, Clark Peterson, Ken Sanders; w, Frank Rehwaldt, George Saunders; ph, Darko Suvak; ed, Julian Semilian; m, Eric Lundmark; prod d, Aaron Osborne; art d, Eric Cochran; set d, Christopher H. Davis; sound, Alan Samuels (mixer); casting, Aaron Griffith; cos, Nanette Acosta; makeup, Cynthia Bornia; stunts, Kurt Bryant, Thomas Dewer

Horror **(PR: C MPAA: R)**

LAST ASSASSINS ★½

(U.S., 1996) 90m Silverline Pictures ~
A-Pix Entertainment c

Lance Henriksen *(Roger McBride)*; Nancy Allen *(Anna Bishop)*; Scott Lincoln *(Brock Daniels)*; Dean Scofield *(Mitch Stevens)*; Ashley Buccille *(Carrie Bishop)*; Floyd Red Crow Westerman *(Indian Bob)*; Zahn McClarnon *(Indian Louis)*; Shashawnee Hall *(Hayes)*; Ron Bryon *(Norton)*; Philip Lehl *(Hallman)*; Jim Menza *(Russell)*; Mary Deese *(Angel Martinez)*; Oliver Darrow *(Himself)*; Steve Merrick *(Storm Troop Leader)*; Kiran Gonsalves *(Assassin)*; Bob Anderson *(Assassin)*; Carol Crane *(Anna's Mother)*

LAST ASSASSINS is a generic title for a generic film, originally titled DUSTING CLIFF 7 about a spy who rebels against the meglomaniacal plans of her boss.

Anna Bishop (Nancy Allen) has been raised to work as a professional assassin by shadowy government operative Roger McBride (Lance Henriksen). Having learned that McBride's agenda is his own and not that of the United States, she has split with him. Because she has top-secret papers stolen from the Joint Chiefs of Staff which McBride needs, he kills her mother and kidnaps her young daughter Carrie (Ashley Buccille) to force her to return them. They agree to meet in 36 hours at a location in the desert of the Southwest for the exchange.

Anna arrives early to try to secure a strategic advantage, assuming that McBride and his men will try to kill her. She is helped by Mitch Stevens (Dean Scofield), a charter pilot familiar with the area: he says his father was killed by chemical contamination there. Examining an abandoned government building and the papers McBride wants, she determines that she is at a storage site for both dangerous chemicals and nuclear fuel. McBride plans to arm his own fleet of nuclear warheads to restore order to a world he feels has grown lawless. With explosives she finds there, Anna rigs the site so that everything will be irretrievably buried. In a showdown, Anna, aided by Mitch and his Native American friends Bob (Floyd Red Crow Westerman) and Louis (Zahn McClarnon), saves Carrie, bests McBride and his men, and seals off the dangerous materials forever.

If the above plot synopsis reads like a rough story sketch, well, that's how LAST ASSASSINS plays. Only a few action set pieces justify this film's existence—one in the beginning, as Anna is chased by two other assassins; another at the end, as the various forces chase each other through the underground tunnels of the abandoned desert installation. It's not that either sequence is all that exciting, but at least there's something cinematic happening. The rest of the film barely even rises to the level of a first draft. There's a little talk about Anna's life as a "La Femme Nikita" type, a little conversational bonding between Anna and Mitch, and some nonsensical Native American mysticism that even Oliver Stone would wince at. None of this does anything besides kill time in the most obvious way. The closest thing LAST ASSASSINS dredges up in the way of entertainment is Henriksen's depiction of a mad would-be dictator, but that's hardly an excuse to sit through the film. *(Violence, profanity.)*—M.F.

d, William H. Molina; p, Leman Getiner, Axel Munch; exec p, Guenter Heinlein; assoc p, Amila Giducos; w, Jim Menza, Charles Philip Moore, Justin J. Stanley, William H. Molina; ph, William H. Molina; ed, Daniel Lowenthal; m, David Wurst, Eric Wurst; prod d, W. Brooke Wheeler; art d, Chuck Outrow; set d, Keith Cuba; sound, Matthew Nicolay (mixer); fx, Wayne Beauchamp, Gary Bentley; casting, Laura Schiff; cos, Gulbin Yavuz; makeup, Margaux Lancaster; stunts, Phil O'Dell

Action/Drama **(PR: C MPAA: R)**

LAST BIG THING, THE ★★

(U.S., 1996) 98m Byronic Pose Productions ~ Stratosphere Entertainment c

Dan Zukovic *(Simon Geist)*; Susan Heimbinder *(Darla)*; Mark Ruffalo *(Brent)*; Pamela Dickerson *(Tedra)*; Andrew Falk *(Chris)*; Sibel Ergener *(Magda)*; James Lorinz *(Comic)*; Yul Vasquez *(1st Interviewer)*; Thomas Prisco *(2nd Interviewer)*; Louis Mustillo *(Video Producer)*; Steven Kay *(Video D.P.)*; Blaine Capatch *(Band Leader)*; Mitch Mayer *(Band Member)*; Will Huston *(Band Member)*; Yevo *(Band Member)*; Carl Lamb *(Bennett Hames)*; Maria Von Hartz *(Woman in Video Store)*; Ron Zwang *(Man in Video Store)*; Mitch Seyfer *(Neighbor Watering Lawn)*; Rick Askew *(Man in Parking Lot)*

It has become a cliche for a first-time writer-director to make a low budget, no-star movie about the shallow artistic wasteland that is Los Angeles. At first, Dan Zukovic's THE LAST BIG THING appears to be just another of these petty diatribes. Those who stick with it, though, will discover a clever twist that makes THE LAST BIG THING an original film, if not necessarily a great one.

Eccentric LA denizen Simon Geist (Dan Zukovic) hates just about everything about Los Angeles. With the help of his nutty sort-of-girlfriend, Darla (Susan Heimbinder), he vents his contempt by interviewing models, actors, musicians, and stand-up comedians for a fictional magazine called "The Next Big Thing," using the subjects' hunger for exposure as an opportunity to publicly ridicule them. When he meets model Tedra (Pamela Dickerson), an intelligent, well-spoken young woman, he is caught offguard and becomes attracted to her. Explaining to a horrified Darla that he is infiltrating the enemy culture, Simon agrees to direct a music video for some of Tedra's friends.

While Simon's away, Darla is visited by Brent (Mark Ruffalo), an actor Simon "interviewed" for the magazine. Brent knows the interview was bogus, but is intrigued by Simon's attempt to deflate the LA ego. For a while, the four of them—Simon, Darla, Tedra, and Brent—continue the attack on cheesy comedians and other typical Hollywood types. Then Simon is approached by two men who wish to interview him for a magazine, "The Next Big Thing," inspired by Simon's anti-culture philosophy. Simon gladly accepts his appointment as spokesman for the end of the millennium—not the next big thing, but the *last* big thing—until the interviewers hand him a sheaf of his old reviews and head shots that reveal him for what he is: a failed actor, model, musician, and comedian. With Simon's anticultural posturing exposed as the whining of a sore loser, Brent and Tedra leave together, while Darla finally emerges from Simon's shadow to create her own underground 'zine, "Geist Has Fallen."

Playwright Dan Zukovic took something of a risk in THE LAST BIG THING, exposing one of the dark secrets of the independent film industry: that much of the anti-Hollywood sentiment espoused by the so-called "indie" crowd is based largely on jealousy, and that these iconoclasts would jump at the chance to trade in their black turtlenecks for BMWs. It is only by creating a character like the odiously eccentric Simon Geist (insert *zeitgeist* joke here), someone so far off the scale as to be beyond comparison to the real media underground, that Zukovic may escape evisceration by his peers. Maybe.

As original as Zukovic's film is (and portraying models and pretty-boy actors as intelligent is pretty daring these days), THE LAST BIG THING suffers from many of the same problems as other independent films: a glaring lack of budget, actors of dubious skill, and somewhat sophomoric writing. The best part of THE LAST BIG THING is the portrayal of Darla by Susan Heimbinder. Though she is at first almost annoyingly enamored of Simon Geist, Darla is the first to sense that he is not all that he projects; as this realization dawns on her, she grows on us, so that by the end of the film, when she sets out to find success on her own terms, we are behind her one hundred percent. *(Profanity.)*—B.T.

d, Dan Zukovic; p, Vladmir Perlovich, Anthony Rubenstein; exec p, David Barnett, Philip Starr; assoc p, Joe Curio, Tony Raugust; w, Dan Zukovic; ph, M. David Mullen; ed, Markus Lofstrom; m, Cole Coonce; prod d, Martina Buckley; art d, Giolliosa Fuller; sound, Lee Howell (mixer); casting, Ann Maney; cos, Tami Stover; makeup, Karen Scherer

Comedy/Drama **(PR: C MPAA: R)**

LAST BREATH ★★

(U.S., 1988) 90m Overseas Filmgroup; Felder Pompus Entertainment ~ A-Pix Entertainment c

Luke Perry *(Marty Devoe)*; Francie Swift *(Chrystie Devoe)*; Gia Carides *(Gale Pullman)*; Gary Barsaraba *(John)*; Jack Gilpin *(Dr. Stevens)*; Lisa Gay Hamilton *(Dr. Quinlan)*; David Margulies *(Abe Gross)*; Matt McGrath *(Todd Rusk)*; Hillary B. Smith *(Edie Weinreb)*; Nathaniel Kalin *(Dr. Peck)*; Margaret Devine *(Hope)*; Karen Shallo *(Group Therapy Leader)*; Maureen Shannon *(Kitty Hughes)*; Alyson Hildreth *(Laura Burden)*; Monique Fowler *(Joyce Burden)*; Bill McIntyre *(Jack MacLaughlin)*; Gerta Grunin *(Blood Bank Director)*; Jonathan Baltzer *(Mr. Denny)*; Marjorie Johnson *(Ms. Grimes)*; Jeremy Gold *(Mr. Lawrence)*; Pamela Holden Stewart *(Mrs. Novack)*; Jennifer Gareis *(Elevator Woman)*; Summer Mahoney *(Student)*; Lisa Louise Langford *(Intensive Care Nurse)*; Bill Hogue *(911 Operator)*; Joel Posner *(Emergency Room Physician)*; Edward James Hyland *(Neurosurgeon)*; Diane Kagan *(Gale's Mother)*; Dean Winters *(Chrystie's Lover)*; Mark Jupiter *(Man in Car)*; Delanie Yates *(Woman in Car)*

LAST BREATH squanders its intriguingly bizarre premise about a misguided romantic who decides to commit a heinous crime to save his wife's life. "Beverly Hills 90210" star Luke Perry tried for a bit of a stretch with this thriller, but theatrical distributors weren't having any—the film went the straight-to-video route in 1998.

Children's book illustrator Chrystie DeVoe (Francie Swift) has cystic fibrosis and desperately needs new lungs, but she has a rare blood type, and a potential transplant falls through. Her husband, Marty (Luke Perry) looks into the possibilities—both ethical and unethical—of finding a donor, but what he finds out isn't encouraging. He takes a volunteer job with a blood bank and begins calling past donors with the correct blood type, eventually meeting a young woman named Gale (Gia Carides). They begin an affair, and Chrystie's editor, Edie (Hillary B. Smith) soon sees the couple together. Though Marty denies Chrystie's suspicions, she takes to spying on him herself, and learns the truth.

After another argument, Chrystie begins to suspect what Marty's up to. Meanwhile, he has recorded Gale reading poetry and alters it to sound like a cry for help. Chrystie's condition worsens, and she tries to warn Gale, but can't bring herself to speak to the young woman. Chrystie soon collapses and winds up in the hospital. Marty then puts his plan into action, breaking into Gale's apartment, playing her "call for help" to 911 just before she enters, and bludgeoning her when she comes in. Gale dies, and Chrystie receives her lungs—but her knowledge of where they came from has destroyed her faith in Marty, and it is she who then takes a lover.

LAST BREATH was promoted as a thriller for its release on home video, but the script by director P.J. Posner and his brother Josh contains very few possibilities for suspense. It's clear early on what Marty's plot is, and Chrystie has it figured out by the halfway point, so one waits in vain for new plot twists to emerge. Viewers will eventually become aware that the film is simply about the way in which the Devoes deal with Marty's immoral solution to Chrystie's illness. Yet Marty seems to have as few qualms about bedding Gale as he does about killing her, which not only robs his character of necessary texture but quells the chance to identify with him.

Perry is good, given the severe limitations of his role, and Swift is appealing and sympathetic as his terminally ill wife. It is she who enacts the film's one effective moment of moral doubt, when Chrystie reconsiders telling Gale about Marty's plan—stopping at the moment that she imagines her own death. LAST BREATH could have used more disturbing and effective moments like this. *(Violence, extensive nudity, sexual situations, profanity.)*—M.G.

d, P.J. Posner; p, P.J. Posner, William H. Watkins, Alexa L. Fogel; exec p, Geoffrey J. Felder; assoc p, Robert J. Epstein, Nathaniel Khan; co-p, Bruna Papandrea, Joel Posner; w, P.J. Posner, Joel Posner; ph, Oliver Bokelberg; ed, David Zieff; m, Michael Kessler; prod d, Daniel Goldfield; art d, Tom Manion; set d, Steve Beatrice; sound, Steve Borne, Jeffrey Parsons; fx, Drew Jiritano; casting, Alexa L. Fogel, Kathleen Chopin; cos, Rhonda Roper; makeup, Direct Effects (effects), Tim Considine (effects), Rob Benevides (effects), Evelyn Weyhe (effects), Sabine Roller (effects)

Drama/Thriller **(PR: O MPAA: R)**

LAST DAYS OF DISCO, THE ★★★½

(U.S., 1998) 112m Westerly Films; Castle Rock ~ Gramercy Pictures c

Chloe Sevigny *(Alice Kinnon)*; Kate Beckinsale *(Charlotte Pingress)*; Chris Eigeman *(Des McGrath)*; MacKenzie Astin *(Jimmy Steinway)*; Matt Keeslar *(Josh Neff)*; Matthew Ross, billed as Matthew Rose *(Dan Powers)*; Tara Subkoff *(Holly)*; Burr Steers *(Van)*; David Thornton *(Bernie Rafferty)*; Jaid Barrymore *(Francesca—"Tiger Lady")*; Michael Weatherly *(Hap)*; Robert Sean Leonard *(Tom Platt)*; Jennifer Beals *(Nina Moritz)*; Taylor Nichols *(Charlie/Ted Boynton)*; Sonsee Ahray *(Diana)*; Edoardo Ballerini *(Victor)*; Scott Beehner *(Adam)*; Zachary Taylor *(Backdoorman)*; Neil Butterfield *(Rick)*; James Murtaugh *(Marshall)*; John C. Havens *(Steve)*; Amanda Harker *(Model 1)*; Brandi Seymour *(Model 2)*; Leslie Lyles *(Sally)*; Cate Smit *(Helen)*; Kathleen Chalfant *(Zenia)*; Jan Austell *(Bob)*; Robin Miles *(Josephine)*; Carolyn Farina *(Audrey Rouget)*; Bryan Leder *(Fred)*; Dylan Hundley *(Sally Flower)*; Debbon Ayer *(Betty)*; Mark McKinney *(Rex)*; Linda Pierce *(Real Estate Lady)*; Carlos Jacott *(Dog Walker)*; Sharon Scruggs *(Justine Prashker)*; Ajay Mehta *(Pharmacist)*; Norma Quarles *(Anti-Disco Rally Reporter)*; George Plimpton; Anthony Haden-Guest; Kimball Chen; Desiree Von La Valette; Ivy Supersonic & The Groovy Girls; Bunny Beekman; Inmaculada de Habsburgo; Redman Maxfield; Jack Staub; Elizabeth Strong Cuevas; Isabelle Townsend *(Clubgoers)*

In 1990 writer-director Whit Stillman came out of nowhere with METROPOLITAN, one of the richest and most precise social comedies ever made in America. It was followed in 1994 by the less impressive but quite likable BARCELONA. THE LAST DAYS OF DISCO was the third and, according to Stillman, final installment in what he called his "Doomed-Bourgeois-in-Love-series." DISCO sets Stillman's young innocents adrift in the early 1980s—a time of drugs, unemployment, one-night stands, and herpes.

Alice (Chloe Sevigny) and Charlotte (Kate Beckinsale) are recent graduates of Hampshire College. Together they work in a New York publishing house, find a railroad apartment on Manhattan's Upper East Side, which they share with a third roommate (Tara Subkoff), and frequent their favorite discotheque. There they hobnob with several Harvard men: Des (Chris Eigeman), the manager of the club; Jimmy (MacKenzie Astin), a junior advertising executive; Tom (Robert Sean Leonard), a corporate lawyer; and Josh (Matt Keeslar), an assistant district attorney. Jealous of her friend, whose virginal air men seem to prefer to her own worldlier manner, Kate encourages Alice to act sexier. Alice takes her advice, goes home with Tom one evening, and spends the night with him. After discovering a large cache of cash in the disco's basement, Des tells his friend Jimmy about it and eventually word gets back to Josh at the DA's office.

Several months elapse, Jimmy is fired for his failure to get clients admitted to the disco. (Some of the "clients" he *has* gotten into the club are, unbeknownst to Jimmy, undercover IRS agents.) When Alice tell Tom that he has infected her with herpes and gonorrhea, he informs her that he and his ex-girlfriend are getting back together. Des, who is competing with Josh for the affections of Alice, apprises her of his rival's history of mental instability. Jimmy, who is also attracted to Alice, breaks off a relationship he has formed with Kate, who immediately collapses and is taken to the hospital. One night the disco is raided by government agents, and Josh arrests Bernie (David Thornton), the club owner, for tax evasion.

Eventually, Kate, Des, and Josh all lose their jobs, while Alice is promoted. Josh sadly announces the death of the disco craze but predicts it will someday make a comeback. As Kate and Des appear to be on the verge of pairing off, Alice and Josh happily embark on a true romance.

A man who loves both disco music and hymns, Stillman, the American Eric Rohmer, is invaluable as probably the only filmmaker of his generation to treat young American bluebloods with respect and sardonic affection rather than contempt and veiled envy. And Stillman's characters deserve the respect he allots them. Despite their general solipsism, frequent tactlessness, habitual backbiting, and occasional treachery, Stillman's post-preppies are among the last movie Americans to believe in the importance of common everyday decency and dignity, and to aspire to do the right thing, even when they are incapable of it.

When adman Jimmy unwittingly embarrasses his boss at the disco, he is abject—not just for careerist reasons but also because his boss is a "nice guy" who doesn't need to be embarrassed. And at the end of a manuscript reader's report she is typing at work,

Kate recommends a "very kind decline." Almost alone among his cinema peers, Stillman is a champion of good manners as a function of sensitivity, as opposed to sensitivity as an excuse for bad manners, the more fashionable point of view.

Equally refreshing is Des's monologue on anti-yuppieism, the anti-Semitism of the left and the left out. Baffled and hurt by "Yuppie Scum" graffiti, Des (splendidly played by Stillman standby Chris Eigemen with his customary mix of sincerity and deviousness)—in attempting to validate simultaneously yuppies and deny being one—furnishes THE LAST DAYS OF DISCO with one of its high points. Another is a hilariously serious debate about the underlying meanings of LADY AND THE TRAMP (1955), an interlude almost as good as the deliciously perverse review one of the BARCELONA boys gave THE GRADUATE (1967).

At one point, Tom tells Alice that his initial impression of her as "a vision of loveliness. . . virtue and sanity" was mistaken. He was right the first time, of course, Alice is all of the above and Chloe Sevigny (KIDS, TREES LOUNGE) nails it down. Her performance is the kind that doesn't win awards, and perhaps shouldn't, but she is nonetheless perfect. Even stills from the movie reveal in Sevigny's face the attractive blend of modesty, vulnerability, intelligence, and innate elegance that make her Alice such a sympathetic and subtly enchanting presence. *(Violence, nudity, sexual situations, adult situations, profanity.)*—D.T.

d, Whit Stillman; p, Whit Stillman; exec p, John Sloss; co-p, Edmon Roch, Cecilia Kate Roque; w, Whit Stillman; ph, John Thomas; ed, Andrew Hafitz, Jay Pires; m, Mark Suozzo; prod d, Ginger Tougas; art d, Molly Mikula; set d, Lisa Nilsson; sound, Scott Breindel (mixer); fx, Todd Wolfeil; casting, Billy Hopkins, Suzanne Smith, Kerry Barden; cos, Sarah Edwards; makeup, Fern Buchner; stunts, Peter Bucossi

Drama/Comedy **(PR: C MPAA: R)**

LAST LIVES ★½

(U.S., 1997) 99m CEG Productions ~ Promark Entertainment c

C. Thomas Howell *(Aaron)*; Jennifer Rubin *(Adrienne)*; Billy Wirth *(Malakai)*; Judge Reinhold *(Merkhan)*; Robert Pentz *(Khafar)*; David Lenthall *(Denza)*; J.C. Quinn *(Lt. Denny Park)*; Richard Fullerton *(Roma)*; Rick Wagner *(Dad)*; Talmadge Ragan *(Tess)*; Michael Monks *(Dave)*; Ray Bouchard *(Service Station Attendant)*; George Gaffney *(Sgt. Wilson)*; David Hugghins *(Motorcycle Cop)*; Keith Harris *(Police Officer)*; Dan Duling *(Body Bag Officer)*; David Cutting *(Aaron Jr.)*; David Hagar *(County Sheriff)*

Another blow against the integrity of serious sci-fi is struck by this immobilized scenario about unwanted visitors from a parallel dimension. Repeating dream sequences when all else fails, LAST LIVES is mired in expository sloth and directorial impersonality. The film premiered on the Sci-Fi Channel and was subsequently released on home video in 1998.

On the eve of her wedding to Aaron (C. Thomas Howell), Adrienne (Jennifer Rubin) is troubled by nightmarish visions of an oddly attired suitor (Billy Wirth). Invading Adrienne's thoughts telepathically, Malakai is actually a lovestruck jailbird from an alternate universe; Adrienne is the equivalent of the wife he lost in his world.

Political prisoner Malakai submits to painful dimension-travel experiments conducted by jailer Merkhan (Judge Reinhold). Obsessed with Adrienne, Malakai seizes control of Merkhan's transport apparatus and journeys to our world with two fellow inmates, who interrupt Adrienne's wedding by murdering the best man, gassing the attendees, knocking out the groom, and kidnapping Adrienne.

Tracking the convicts, Merkhan arrives and enlists Aaron in his quest. He gives him life-bands, energy-restoring devices that will counteract lethal attacks by Malakai's thugs. Using the life-bands, Aaron revives himself at a gas station massacre (where Merkhan perishes) and a deadly police roadblock, before trailing his errant bride to an abandoned resort. There, Aaron allows himself to be electrocuted and blown up, in order to eliminate Malakai's enforcers. Reanimating himself with the life-bands, Aaron battles Malakai as the confused police follow the trail of carnage to the resort. The police gun down all three, and Aaron uses the last life-bands to resurrect Adrienne and himself.

The idiocy flies fast and furious in this two-different-worlds odyssey, a time-travel flick in mufti. As telepathic insurgent Malakai transplants himself sideways into our world, LAST LIVES fails to entertain as a thought-provoking sci-fi puzzler, a forbidden romance, or a cheating-death thriller. Recommended only for inveterate action junkies, this badly acted miasma represents missed opportunities for all its creative personnel. *(Graphic violence, nudity, adult situations, sexual situations.)*—R.P.

d, Worth Keeter; p, Steve Beswick; exec p, Jon Kramer, Conny Lernhag; co-p, Gary Magder; w, Dan Duling; ph, Kent Wakeford; ed, Bob Murawski; m, Greg Edmonson; prod d, David Rawlins, C. Daniel Hall; art d, Travis Riley; set d, Jackie Fenney; sound, Austin McKinney; fx, Greg Hull; casting, Henderson/Zuckerman; cos, Gloria Glynn; makeup, Starr Jones; stunts, Chris Nielsen, Gary Paul

Science Fiction **(PR: C MPAA: R)**

LAST OF THE HIGH KINGS

(SEE: SUMMER FLING)

LAST SEDUCTION II, THE ★

(U.S., 1998) 96m Polygram Entertainment ~ Specific Films c

Joan Severance *(Bridget Gregory)*; Con O'Neill *(Troy Fenton)*; Beth Goddard *(Murphy)*; Dean Williamson *(Earl McLoughlin)*; Rocky Taylor *(Gabriel)*; Josef Pilato *(Marvin Dishman)*; David Gilliam *(Mr. Swale)*; Quque Neant *(Taxi Driver)*; Tara Shaw *(Hotel Manager)*; Phil Harris *(Jimmy)*; Perry Benson *(Samuel Burgess)*; Liz Daniels *(Rosa)*; Fison Burgess *(Cecile)*; Simon Fisher *(Ramon)*; Helena Boobleswang *(Ellie)*; Nicola Damassa *(Angela)*; Gillian Elisa *(Barbara)*; Caroline Trowbridge *(Maria)*; Dave Atkins *(Jose Guzman)*; Nicholas Caunter *(Simon Laurie)*; Terry Arnold *(Barman)*; Lloyd Carlton *(Chip Douglas)*; Juan Cuso *(Cab Driver)*; Simon Gregor *(Perez)*; Alex Brendemuhl *(Check-In Clerk)*

Fans of THE LAST SEDUCTION (1994) will find little to enjoy in this crude, direct-to-video sequel. Saddled with an entirely new, sub-par cast, this low-rent tale of manipulation and money lacks the original's subtlety, intelligence, and sly humor.

Residing in Spain, sexy schemer Bridget Gregory (Joan Severance) is enjoying the benefits of her previous scam—even as the obsessed father of her last, now-convicted, conquest hires an equally-alluring female detective, Murphy (Beth Goddard), to track her down. In Barcelona, Bridget meets cold-hearted thug Troy Fenton (Con O'Neill), who runs a telephone-sex service; Troy invites Bridget to stay with him. Alone in his office, she secretly alters the company's computerized billing program so that the clients will be overbilled, with the surplus cash going straight into her personal bank account.

Murphy uses her feminine wiles to persuade a travel agent to provide information about Bridget's whereabouts. Once in Barcelona, she purchases a handgun, threatens Bridget over the phone, and challenges her to meet in person. After emptying her now-hefty bank account, Bridget goes to Murphy's hotel room, with local thug Gabriel (Rocky Taylor) as her muscle. After he beats the detective unconscious, Bridget cold-bloodedly shoots Gabriel, and leaves behind Troy's business card in order to frame him for the killing. When Murphy comes to, she attempts to flee the country, only to be detained because Bridget had planted the murder weapon in her luggage. Bridget, in the meantime, has made a successful getaway and is busy enjoying her ill-gotten gains in London.

Sequels to hit films are invariably disappointing; in this instance, however, the artistic chasm between the original and the knockoff is gargantuan. The plot of this European-lensed atrocity is not only wholly unrelated to that of John Dahl's sexy "sleeper," but it also contains no implicit appeal of its own: it's an artless, unimaginative yarn that provides no insight into its cardboard characters. In the lead role, Joan Severance delivers little more than a flat impression of her predecessor, Linda Fiorentino, in every aspect including hairstyle and fashion sense. Alas, when it comes to acting, she's no match for her sultry model; she cuts a fine figure in the collection of black lingerie chosen for her character, but without the depth and wit exhibited by Fiorentino's character, Bridget is merely a garden-variety man-hating femme fatale. And while the male characters in Dahl's film were mildly sympathetic hormonal patsies, here they are immoral, drug-abusing scum who ultimately deserve their fates. The acting is uniformly mediocre, and though the plot requires that the viewer buy into Bridget's deceitful allure, Severance's dull vamping wouldn't fool a boatload of sailors on shore leave.

The first LAST SEDUCTION was a well-crafted latter-day film noir; the followup—one hopes this truly *will* be the last seduction—is merely late-night, pay-cable filler at its most inane. *(Violence, nudity, sexual situations, substance abuse, profanity.)*—S.P.

d, Terry Marcel; p, Clare Wise, David Ball; exec p, Michael Hamlyn; w, David Cummings; ph, Geza Sinkovics; ed, Belinda Cottrell; m, Jon Mellor; prod d, Hayden Pearce; art d, Frazer Pearce; set d, Tom Pearce; sound, Alan Jones (recordist); fx, Richard Reeves; cos, Leila Ransley; makeup, Sallie Adams; stunts, Rocky Taylor

Crime/Drama/Erotic **(PR: O MPAA: R)**

LAVENDER LIMELIGHT: LESBIANS IN FILM ★★★

(U.S., 1997) 57m Arcadia Productions ~ First Run Features c

Jennie Livingston; Rose Troche; Monika Treut; Maria Maggenti; Su Friedrich; Heather Lyn MacDonald; Cheryl Dunye

LAVENDER LIMELIGHT: LESBIANS IN FILM features interviews with seven prominent women directors who offer refreshing and amusing insights into the world of independent filmmaking.

Filmmaker Marc Mauceri gives his subjects the floor, adding very little extemporaneous footage or expository narration. His interview subjects—Jennie Livingston, Rose Troche, Monika Treut, Maria Maggenti, Su Friedrich, Heather Lyn MacDonald, and Cheryl Dunye—discuss their varying backgrounds, and the tenuous and often amusing way they came into independent filmmaking. Other topics covered include the blessings and burdens of being known as a "lesbian filmmaker"; how a lesbian identity can emerge in one's work; and the temptation of the mainstream film world (on that latter count, it is the understanding amongst these women that working with a bigger budget is tempting, but having a lasting impact with one's work is more important).

Two of the subjects speak about the ways in which their debut features afforded them a new understanding of themselves. Speaking eloquently about the making of her acclaimed documentary about drag culture, PARIS IS BURNING (1990), Livingston candidly reveals how she became fascinated by the sight of men "vogueing" in Washington Square Park in New York. The experience of watching these men "deconstructing the very fabric of how we construct our identities" served as a vehicle for her to come to terms with her own sexual identity. Troche had an even more emotionally direct experience in the making of her film GO FISH (1994). She and her collaborator Guinevere Turner had been lovers, but broke up during the shooting of the film and yet continued to get on well. She notes here that somehow the desire to get the movie finished on such a low budget allowed the couple to keep their "demons at bay."

Other notable insights imparted in the film include the reflections of German maverick Monica Treut (DIDN'T DO IT FOR LOVE) who speaks about the validity of the documentary mode, and the 1990s "trend" in lesbian independents. Maria Maggenti (THE INCREDIBLY TRUE ADVENTURE OF TWO GIRLS IN LOVE) speaks about the huge responsibility that comes with addressing the needs of the gay community in the context of a feature film. Cheryl Dunye (THE WATERMELON WOMAN) expresses interest in the future of lesbian cinema, after the "magical moment in the mid-90s" ends.

Mauceri clearly doesn't intend LAVENDER LIMELIGHT to be an all-encompassing survey of lesbian filmmaking; he simply lets the camera run, thus allowing a greater intimacy between each interview subject and the viewer. This produces some genuinely charming moments, as when Livingston enthusiastically recalls writing a letter to Werner Herzog and receiving a suitably eccentric response; as communicated by Mauceri, her joy over this event is positively contagious.

One wishes, though, that Mauceri had expanded his focus to cover filmmakers whose work prefigured the 1990s vogue in lesbian filmmaking. A brief prologue mentioning the work of true pioneers like Dorothy Arnzer (DANCE, GIRL, DANCE) and the inclusion of interviews with more recent (but now unfortunately forgotten) trailblazers like Donna Deitch (whose DESERT HEARTS garnered much attention in 1985) might've been able to lend a valuable sense of perspective to the words of the relative newcomers who are interviewed here. *(Adult situations.)*—D.O.

d, Marc Mauceri; p, Marc Mauceri, Becky Neiman, Carol A. Ross; exec p, Seymour Wishman; ph, Mike Harlow; ed, Carol A. Ross; sound, Mike Harlow

Documentary **(PR: C MPAA: NR)**

LAWN DOGS ★★½

(U.K., 1997) 101m Toledo Pictures; Duncan Kenworthy Productions ~ Strand Releasing c

Sam Rockwell *(Trent Burns)*; Mischa Barton *(Devon Stockard)*; Christopher McDonald *(Morton Stockard)*; Kathleen Quinlan *(Clare Stockard)*; Bruce McGill *(Nash)*; David Barry Gray *(Brett)*; Eric Mabius *(Sean)*; Tom Aldredge *(Jake—Trent's Father)*; Beth Grant *(Beth—Trent's Mother)*; Miles Meehan *(Billy)*; Angie Harmon *(Pam)*; Jose Orlando Araque *(Mailman)*

At times lyrical and poetic, British director John Duigan's offbeat drama LAWN DOGS is unequal to the sum of its parts. Scripted by Kentucky playwright Naomi Wallace, the film is populated by vivid characters and contains a few delightfully eccentric, dream-like sequences, but in the final analysis seems to have no point, except to illustrate the sexual and class hypocrisies of suburban America.

The family of 10-year-old Devon Stockard (Mischa Barton) has just moved to Camelot Gardens, a gated, upper-middle class suburban development in Louisville, Kentucky. Her father, Morton (Christopher McDonald) is a politician, while her mother, Clare (Kathleen Quinlan) is a homemaker having an affair with a college student neighbor, Brett (David Barry Gray). Having parents and neighbors that are models of all-American conformity, Devon compares herself to a little girl living behind walls that protect her from the mysterious forest outside, the lair of the evil fairy tale witch Baba Yaga.

Riding his lawnmower through this insular world is 21-year-old Trent Burns (Sam Rockwell), a groundskeeper who keeps everyone's vast, treeless acres trimmed. Trent is a self-described "country bumpkin" whose chief responsibility, second only to lawn maintenance, is staying invisible to the snobby residents, according to community cop Nash (Bruce McGill). Trent's small acts of rebellion include diving nude from a one-lane bridge while traffic backs up behind him and running over anything that gets in his mower's way, including kids' toys.

Recognizing a kindred spirit, Devon visits Trent's backwoods trailer and the two strike up an unlikely friendship, though both are status-conscious and keep their relationship secret. Devon decorates a tree next to Trent's home with ribbons and sleeps over one night, telling her parents that she's at a girlfriend's house.

Hearing rumors about Trent and Pam, Brett and his friend Sean (Eric Mabius) harass Trent, though secretly, Sean finds Trent attractive. When a neighborhood boy steals compact discs from their car, Brett and Sean suspect Trent. Retaliating, they pour sugar into the tank of his lawnmower, ending his career.

Returning from a visit to his parents with Devon, Trent accidentally hits Sean's dog with his pickup truck and is forced to kill it. Fond of the dog, Devon is furious with Trent and tells her parents that Trent has "touched" her (in fact, Trent and Devon compared scars). Morton, Nash and Sean beat Trent, but Devon stops them by shooting Sean with her father's pistol. Knowing Trent will be framed for the shooting, Devon urges him to flee, giving him gifts inspired by the Baba Yaga tale: a comb and towel that she claims have magical properties. Driving out of town, Trent drops the gifts onto the road. River waters and a forest arise to block any pursuers.

In its first half, LAWN DOGS seems to be delivering a message about class. Each character except Trent and Devon is shown to be a phony or liar in some sexual way, as with Clare's affair or Sean's menacing Trent when Brett is around, but coming on to him in private. It seems that Wallace and Duigan are making a statement about the sexual hypocrisy of the American class system. That message, if intended, never gels. Perhaps the problem is that class divisions aren't sharply drawn in the States, that sexual "slumming" isn't the taboo in America it is in Duigan's homeland of England. More effective is the sly sexual tension between Trent and Devon. Devon spies on Trent when he's in the midst of a tryst with a neighborhood college girl (Angie Harmon) and when Devon prepares to show Trent her surgical scar (she's had heart surgery), he reacts as if she wants to show him her breasts. Though Devon laughs at him, there is a low-level electricity between the friends. Performers Barton and Rockwell seem fully clued in to this subtle reality and the actors have fun with the innocent attraction.

Even better are the magical realist properties of LAWN DOGS. Devon, on a whim, climbs out onto the roof of her house and takes off her nightie, which flies away like a kite as she howls at the moon. Later, the rising waters and forest effects precede a slow fade to black and white that closes the film. Those scenes illustrate Devon's child's eye-view of the world better than any others in the film. Unfortunately, there just aren't enough such inspired moments to make LAWN DOGS memorable.

LAWN DOGS was one of two films by Duigan to be released in the US in 1998; the Jon Bon Jovi starrer, THE LEADING MAN, was the other. *(Nudity, sexual situations, profanity.)*—K.W.

d, John Duigan; p, Duncan Kenworthy; exec p, Ron Daniels; co-p, David Rubin; w, Naomi Wallace; ph, Elliot Davis; ed, Humphrey Dixon; m, Trevor Jones; prod d, John Myhre; set d, James Edward Ferrell Jr.; sound, Michael Barosky (mixer); fx, Peter Kunz; casting, Ronna Kress; cos, John Dunn; makeup, Patricia Schenkel Regan; stunts, Peter Bucossi, John Copeman

Drama **(PR: O MPAA: NR)**

LE SEPTIEME CIEL

(SEE: SEVENTH HEAVEN)

LEADING MAN, THE ★★½

(U.K., 1997) 100m J&M Entertainment; Northern Arts Entertainment ~ BMG c

Jon Bon Jovi *(Robin Grange)*; Anna Galiena *(Elena Webb)*; Lambert Wilson *(Felix Webb)*; Thandie Newton *(Hilary Rule)*; Barry Humphries *(Humphrey Beal)*; Patricia Hodge *(Delvene)*; Diana Quick *(Susan)*; David Warner *(Tod)*; Harriet Walters *(Liz Flett)*; Laura Austin-Little *(Miranda Webb)*; Camilla Ohlsson *(Jessie Webb)*; Daniel Worters *(Danny Webb)*; Tam Dean Burn *(Henry)*; Claire Cox *(Serena)*; Kevin McKidd *(Ant)*; Victoria Smurfitt *(Annabel)*; Harry Jones *(Doorman)*; Sheridan Morley *(TV Interviewer)*; Geoffrey Freshwater *(Attendant)*; Michael Gunn *(Technician)*; Elizabeth Spender *(Anne)*; Roz Freeman-Atwood *(Caro)*; Nicole Kidman *(Academy Awards Presenter)*; Robert McDonald *(Michael)*; Andrew Lucre *(Rob)*; Neve McIntosh *(Cashier)*; Ginny Holder *(Georgina)*; James Haggie *(Jessie's Friend)*; Simon Elliot *(Toby)*; Anna Rose *(Andrea)*; David Smidman *(George)*; Georgia Reece *(Lotte)*

Boasting an intricately plotted script full of dark twists and turns and a surprisingly solid lead performance by rock star Jon Bon Jovi, THE LEADING MAN still manages to wear out its welcome as it drags onward toward a predictable and downbeat finale.

Referred to as "England's greatest living playwright," Felix Webb (Lambert Wilson) is in the process of casting his latest London play, "The Frontline." Most key roles have been filled, including an assassin to be portrayed by American movie star Robin Grange (Jon Bon Jovi), who's seeking the legitimacy that only theater can bring. Left open is a part perfect for a young ingenue, so Webb throws his weight behind the casting of Hilary (Thandie Newton), a pretty young actress with zero stage experience but some presence. At Webb's insistence, Hilary is hired.

When Webb later enjoys a romantic rendezvous with Hilary, it becomes clear that he has been engaged in an adulterous affair with her. Webb's wife Elena (Anna Galiena) is miserably aware of her husband's philandering and takes to cutting up his ties and shearing off tufts of his hair while he sleeps.

Grange, a wily sort who manipulates his fellow cast members in order to stay in their good graces, sizes up the truth and makes Webb an odd offer. He will engage Elena in a clandestine love affair, for which Webb must pay all expenses, getting the writer's wife off his back and allowing him to proceed with his affair unfettered. At wit's end, Webb reluctantly agrees after Elena suffers a nervous breakdown in front of their children.

A meeting at a cast party is arranged and the affair begins, neglected Elena blooming under Grange's studly attentions. Grange discovers that Elena is herself a talented playwright hiding in her husband's shadow, and arranges for a respected troupe to read her work.

However, Grange is also attempting to seduce Hilary, who is tiring of Webb's romantic vacillating. Though Hilary remains faithful, Webb is overwhelmed with suspicion. On the night of his premiere, Webb attempts to murder Grange by replacing a prop gun's blanks with real ammunition, but the new bullets also turn out to be fakes. At the after-party, Grange announces he will star in Webb's new movie, blackmailing the writer.

Months later, Grange, Elena on his arm, wins an Oscar for his work in Webb's film, while Webb obsessively types away on his new work, ignoring an unhappy Hilary as callously as he once ignored Elena.

Director John Duigan's tale is flawed in several respects that have little to do with the director's obvious stylistic talents (seen to good advantage in THE YEAR MY VOICE BROKE and SIRENS). THE LEADING MAN uses the dark, burnished tones, compositional flair, and satisfying transitions of a good American cop drama to excellent effect. Two of the film's actors also produce top-shelf results: Bon Jovi is a fine surprise in his first starring motion picture role, while Galiena is radiant as Elena. While not exactly breaking any new ground with his sly, mellow portrayal of a handsome cad, Bon Jovi delivers an engaging performance, made all the more notable for the degree to which Grange turns out to be a cipher. Galiena shines in her scenes, as she sketches Elena moving through stages of grief, rage, lust, love, and eventually, acceptance.

The film's pacing sags, especially when the proceedings slows to a crawl in the second act and never really pick up again, until literally the penultimate sequence. But the film's real problem is its script, written by Duigan's sister, theater critic Virginia Duigan. Tangents that seem integral to the plot—like Webb's financial support to Grange in the seduction of his wife and another actor's affection for Hilary—are simply dropped. The characters motivations also seem quite hazy—for instance, Grange's reason for making his initial offer never does become clear. By obscuring the character's intentions, are the Duigans trying to imply that Grange's purpose in offering to seduce Elena is too complex to be easily explained? Is it that Grange's goals change when he learns of Elena's hidden writing talents?

That Grange and Elena are still a couple in the film's final scenes seems to imply a point, but Duigan doesn't provide very much aid to his audience to help them discover what that point might be. *(Sexual situations, nudity, profanity, violence.)*—K.W.

d, John Duigan; p, Bertil Ohlsson, Paul Raphael; exec p, Julia Palau, Michael Ryan; w, Virginia Duigan; ph, Jean-Francois Robin; ed, Humphrey Dixon; m, Edward Shearmur; prod d, Caroline Hanania; art d, Andrew Munro; set d, Trisha Edwards; sound, Colin Nicolson (recordist); casting, Jina Jayawardena; cos, Rachael Fleming; makeup, Robert McCann, Graham Johnston; stunts, Peter Brayham

Romance/Drama/Comedy **(PR: O MPAA: R)**

LENA'S DREAMS ★★★½

(U.S., 1997) 85m Olympia Pictures; Lena's Film ~ Olympia Pictures c

Marlene Forte *(Lena)*; Gary Perez *(Mike)*; Susan Peirez *(Suze)*; Jeremiah Birkett *(Johnny)*; David Zayas *(Jorge)*; Judy Reyes *(Maritsa)*; Kal Adwoa *(Angela)*; Pat Lucenti *(Casting Director)*; Christine Clementon-Smith; Al D. Rodriguez *(Reader)*; Suzette G. Powell *(Melissa)*; Don Braden *(Street Musician)*; Ronald Guttman *(Bob)*

A very low-budget effort that chronicles the difficulties faced by a struggling New York actress, LENA'S DREAMS offers some genuine and often profound truths about the creative process. It also serves as a fine showcase for its lead, versatile actress Marlene Forte.

At 25 Lena (Marlene Forte) claimed she would quit acting if she didn't make it by the time she was 30. Two years past the deadline the determined actress still hustles from audition to audition, and still has to wait tables to pay the rent. As a Cuban-American, she rarely gets to compete for anything but the hot-blooded Latina temptresses, though she may be better suited for more cultured roles. On her 32nd birthday, Lena finally reaches her breaking point and, after she is given the wrong information about an audition, tells her opportunistic manager Jorge (David Zayas) that she's fed up with his incompetence and the whole acting profession. She subsequently quits her restaurant job and breaks up with her longtime boyfriend Mike (Gary Perez), a struggling actor and director, who recently decided to give up his creative aspirations and join the nine-to-five world, opting for a regular paycheck, health insurance, and a stable family life with Lena by his side.

Lena, confused and desperate, visits her old acting chum Suze (Susan Peirez), who gave up the craft years ago. Though ensconced in suburban comfort, the Long Island housewife details her own depressing life, including an impending divorce and a stalled career as a lawyer. The two women return to Manhattan, where Mike, intent on winning Lena back, throws a birthday party for her. Lena's sour mood poisons the festivities. When Jorge arrives with the news that Lena has been offered a plum role in the musical "Castro" with Andy Garcia, she scoffs at having snared the plum role and kicks her manager out. Everyone insists that Lena should take the part. Unable to cope, she retreats to the rooftop; Mike follows. Lena hurls numerous insults at Mike, then finally relents when he makes a final stand to save their relationship. After they make love, Lena decides to stick with acting and take the role.

Cowritten and codirected by the husband-and-wife team of Heather Johnston and Gordon Eriksen, LENA'S DREAMS refuses to resort to treacly cliches about following one's dreams. Lena, in fact, continues to act because she can't help herself. The film is a study of addiction, as Lena searches for her next fix, attending cattle calls, dealing with unctuous agents, and attempting to cope with the attendant rejection; her moments of creative exultation are all too fleeting. In Johnston and Eriksen's vision, even success isn't enough to raise one's spirits: at one point in her frantic day, Lena meets an old teacher (Kai Adwoa), who's now a sitcom star. Instead of enjoying her success, the woman drinks heavily and bemoans the emptiness of the material. Even when Lena decides to take the "Castro" role, she does so knowing full well that it could die in previews and send her back to waitressing.

Cinematographer Armando Basulto utilizes handheld cameras and 16mm stock to create a gritty visual style that perfectly reflects the film's world-view. Long takes are the rule; several scenes are presented without a single edit. This allows the actors to work through their characters' emotions and create their own transitions. It's fun to watch Marlene Forte transform herself, during the space of one audition, from a profane, volatile Latin spitfire to a well-bred governess. Forte's own well-honed acting skills allow us to see that Lena is actually a talented performer, worthy of the many roles for which she's been rejected.

Forte offers a tour-de-force turn in the painfully uncomfortable climactic rooftop scene. The raw nature and improvisational feel of the sequence bring to mind the stronger moments in a number of John Cassavetes' films (A WOMAN UNDER THE INFLUENCE, OPENING NIGHT). Though LENA'S DREAMS doesn't attain the sublime heights of vintage Cassavetes, it does tread in the same territory, and explores the same emotional conflicts with a similar degree of raw honesty. *(Sexual situations, profanity.)*— T.Y.

d, Heather Johnston, Gordon Eriksen; p, Chip Garner; co-p, Marlene Forte, Armando Basulto, Ignacio Quiles; w, Heather Johnston, Gordon Eriksen; ph, Armando Basulto; ed, Steve Silkensen; m, Don Branden; art d, Robert Nassau; sound, Noah Vivekananad; cos, Jennifer L. Eriksen, Karen Graff; makeup, Ronnie Sibblies

Drama **(PR: C MPAA: NR)**

LENNY BRUCE: SWEAR TO TELL THE TRUTH ★★★½
(U.S., 1998) 94m Whyaduck Productions;
HBO Documentary Films c/bw

Robert De Niro *(Narrator)*; Sally Marr; Honey Bruce; Kitty Bruce; Martin Garbus; Paul Krassner; Nat Hentoff; Steve Allen; Maynard Sloate; JoJo D'Amore; John Dolan; Howard Solomon; Richard Kuh; Jackie Gayle; Lotus Weinstock

LENNY BRUCE: SWEAR TO TELL THE TRUTH offers an absorbing and sympathetic portrait of the standup comic who has been enshrined as a martyr to the cause of free speech. Filmmaker Robert Wiede deftly weaves together newspaper articles, family photos, newsreels, home movies, some rare TV appearances, and interviews with those who knew Lenny Bruce best, thus supplying ample evidence that he was not only an incisive and innovative performer, but also a handy target for those who opposed the ideas he espoused on stage.

Narrator Robert De Niro effects a somber tone as he tracks Bruce's life. He was born Leonard Alfred Schneider in 1925, and was brought up by his mother, comedian Sally Marr. He began as an impressionist, doing imitations of movie stars; a fresh-faced Lenny is seen performing this type of material on "Arthur Godfrey's Talent Scouts" and "Broadway Open House" (playing straight man to a very young Buddy Hackett in the latter clip). He continued as a standup, eventually marrying singer-turned-stripper Honey Harlowe. The two developed a "double act" and maintained a strained domesticity when daughter Kitty was born in 1955. Drugs and their separate infidelities broke up their marriage just as Lenny's star was on the rise. Working as an m.c. in strip clubs, he developed a new style of comedy in which he combined a "hip" sensibility (the routines were directed to the clubs' musicians, not the patrons) and the freedom to speak about taboo subject matter. He also made his personal life the subject of many of his routines (as in a plaintive song about divorce, "All Alone," he's seen performing on "The Steve Allen Show").

His mocking onstage dissections of religious and sexual mores caused critics to label him a "sick comic," but as his bad reputation grew, so did his audience. The tide turned in September 1961 when he was first arrested on a narcotics charge. Bruce was a steady user (he did, however, take care to obtain prescriptions for the pharmaceuticals he took) and a pattern developed that remained in place for the remainder of his life: Bruce was hounded by police in whatever cities he played, getting repeatedly busted on drug charges and more significantly for onstage "obscenity." Although he was acquitted of the latter charges in several cities, his reputation as a performer was damaged by the arrests and club owners were hesitant to employ him, in fear that their licenses would be revoked. In 1963-64, Bruce had severe difficulties getting bookings and thus he increased both his drug use and his obsession with clearing his name through legal channels. He pored over law books in his off-hours, read from the transcripts of his trials on stage, and decided to represent himself in what proved to be his single most notorious legal wrangle: an obscenity charge stemming from an April 1964 performance in New York City. A pariah on the nightclub circuit, Bruce withdrew to his house in California, where he planned legal strategies and continued to take drugs; he died of an overdose in August 1966.

Wiede has De Niro grimly observe that the authorities who doggedly pursued Bruce had the last laugh, as his corpse was left where it had been discovered, naked on the bathroom floor, while the police allowed newspaper and newsreel cameramen to file in and photograph it for a full hour. Heady stuff indeed. Wiede is a clearly biased biographer, but his focus on both Bruce's comedy and his insurmountable legal difficulties does much to correct the damage done by the purportedly "definitive" Albert Goldman book *Ladies and Gentlemen, Lenny Bruce!!* which focused primarily on Bruce's character defects and his enormous intake of drugs.

Wiede labored for a dozen years on the film, and his devotion pays off: though Sally Marr had spoken frequently in public about her son's life, Wiede elicits interesting comments from Honey Bruce, the various legal figures who helped and hindered Lenny, and fellow comedians (Bruce comrade Jackie Gayle offers up the most accurate assessment of the situation when he notes that there were literally dozens of comedians who were far filthier than Lenny was—but none of them chose to tackle organized religion and suburban hypocrisy).

Wiede wisely mixes footage from a number of incredibly rare but not consistently funny TV appearances Bruce made (the Allen clips seen here are featured virtually intact in Fred Baker's 1972 documentary LENNY BRUCE WITHOUT TEARS) with some of his strongest material—which was preserved on LPs released after his death. SWEAR does surprisingly skip over several events in Bruce's personal life—including an auto accident that nearly killed Honey and him (detailed in both the Bob Fosse film LENNY and Bruce's own autobiography). Wiede does, however, a top-notch job of fostering Bruce's legacy by detailing the factors that caused a mediocre burlesque comic to develop into one of the most important pundits of his day. *(Profanity, adult situations.)*—E.G.

d, Robert B. Weide; p, Robert B. Weide; exec p, Sheila Nevins; w, Robert B. Weide; ed, Robert B. Weide, Geof Bartz

AAN Best Documentary Feature

Documentary **(PR: O MPAA: NR)**

LES MISERABLES ★★★½
(U.S., 1998) 129m Mandalay Entertainment; Sarah Radclyffe Productions/James Gorman Productions ~ Columbia c

Liam Neeson *(Valjean)*; Geoffrey Rush *(Javert)*; Uma Thurman *(Fantine)*; Claire Danes *(Cosette)*; Hans Matheson *(Marius)*; Reine Brynolfsson *(Captain Beauvais)*; Peter Vaughan *(Bishop)*; Christopher Adamson *(Bertin)*; Tim Barlow *(Lafitte)*; Timothy Bateson *(Banker)*; Veronika Bendova *(Azelma)*; David Birkin *(Courfeyrac)*; Patsy Byrne *(Toussaint)*; Kathleen Byron *(Mother Superior)*; Vaclav Chalupa *(Andre)*; Ian Cregg *(Feuilly)*; Ben Crompton *(Grantier)*; Zdenek David *(Peasant)*; Paola Dionisotti *(Forewoman)*; Edna Dore *(Old Woman)*; Louis Hammond *(Letter Reader)*; Gillian Hanna *(Mme. Thenardier)*; Janet Henfrey *(Mme. Gilot)*; Shane Hervey *(Gavroche)*; Zdenek Hess *(Foreman)*; Gerard Horan *(Digne Gendarme)*; Kelly Hunter *(Mme. Victurien)*; Lennie James *(Enjolras)*; Toby Jones *(Doorkeeper)*; Jon Kenny *(Thenardier)*; Pavel Koci *(Coachdriver)*; Sylvie

Koblizkova *(Eponine)*; Jan Kuzelka *(Furniture Dealer)*; Peter Mackriel *(Doctor)*; Margery Mason *(Nursing Nun)*; Shannon McCormick *(Redheaded Gendarme)*; John McGlynn *(Carnot)*; Philip McGough *(Judge)*; David McKay *(Informer)*; Mimi Newman *(Cosette—aged 8)*; Alex Norton *(General)*; Ralph Nossek *(Clerk)*; Frank O'Sullivan *(Brevet)*; Zoja Oubramova *(Old Woman)*; Jiri Patocka *(Old Man)*; Petr Penkava *(Beggar Child)*; Julian Rhind-Tutt *(Bamatabois)*; Milan Riehs *(Priest)*; James Saxon *(Chabouillet)*; Petr Strnad *(Young Homeless Boy)*; John Surman *(Stonemason)*; Miroslav Taborksy *(Gendarme)*; Terry Taplin *(Prosecutor)*; Richard Toth *(Gendarme)*; Edward Tudor Pole *(Landlord)*; Zdenek Vencl *(Messenger)*; Tony Vogel *(Lombard)*; Pavel Vokoun *(Sergeant)*; Jan Unger *(Officer)*; Joshua Wren *(Old Homeless Boy)*; Libor Zidek *(Wig Maker)*

Victor Hugo's timeless novel about Jean Valjean, the petty thief who is persecuted by the merciless Inspector Javert, is brought to the screen yet again in this handsome production. Liam Neeson and Geoffrey Rush are excellent in the lead roles, but some instances of less felicitous supporting casting and a weak third act keep this adaptation from being a classic.

France, 1815. After 19 years at hard labor for stealing bread, Jean Valjean (Liam Neeson) is released from prison, a broken and suspicious man. His soul is restored by the example of a clergyman who refuses to press charges after Valjean beats and robs him, offering instead to give him more as a start to a new life.

Nine years later, Valjean lives under an assumed name in Vigau, where he has become a wealthy and respected factory owner and the town's mayor. Vigau receives a new police inspector, Javert (Geoffrey Rush), an ambitious fanatic obsessed with the letter of the law. He recognizes the mayor as Valjean and determines to expose him. Valjean interferes when Javert unjustly arrests Fantine (Uma Thurman), a sickly prostitute. Learning that she was fired from his factory for being an illegitimate mother, Valjean takes her in and tries to nurse her back to health. He is forced to reveal his true identity when another man is accused of being him. Fleeing because he is still wanted for parole, Valjean promises the dying Fantine that he will raise her daughter Cosette. They journey to Paris and find sanctuary in a convent where the caretaker is a man whose life Valjean once saved.

Ten years later, they leave the convent when Cosette (Claire Danes) wants to see the real world. As Valjean uses his fortune to tend to the poor, Cosette falls in love with Marius (Hans Matheson), a student revolutionary. Marius is being investigated by Javert, now Chief Inspector of Paris; his trail leads Javert to Valjean. Valjean makes plans for them to escape to England during the coming uprising. He braves the embattled streets to find Marius, and saves Javert from revolutionaries who are planning to kill him. After the uprising is quelled, Javert captures Valjean, but instead of taking him to prison, he releases him and kills himself. Valjean is at last a free man.

The strength of this, approximately the 20th film of *Les Miserables,* is largely in the casting. With his strong physique and sorrowful eyes, Liam Neeson was born to play Jean Valjean, and gives an excellent performance. The same can be said for Geoffrey Rush, who evokes Javert's obsession without making him any less horrifying. And Uma Thurman takes to death by consumption as if she were a veteran of silent melodramas.

At the same time, the biggest flaw here is also the casting. As Cosette and Marius, Claire Danes and Hans Matheson make you remember why these roles were once referred to as "juveniles": both are awfully callow, and simply don't seem worth the sacrifice Valjean is prepared to make for them. It doesn't help that their parts were apparently reworked to get some youth appeal into the film, but their puppy-love romance brings the film to a halt at the worst possible time.

LES MISERABLES also sags in its final section in its depiction of the failed uprising of 1830. For one thing, the otherwise admirable script by novelist Rafael Yglesias provides far too little historical context for audiences who may not be familiar with the actual event. And director Bille August's staging of the street riots is wan; instead of providing an explosive finale, they fade into the background behind the main characters. Still, this is the first English-language film helmed by August that begins to approach the level of the excellent work he has done in his native Sweden (PELLE THE CONQUEROR, THE BEST INTENTIONS). Good use of European locations and a suitably rousing score by Basil Poledouris contribute to a film that isn't as good as it might have been, but still makes for engrossing viewing. *(Violence, adult situations.)*—M.F.

d, Bille August; p, Sarah Radclyffe, James Gorman; co-p, Caroline Hewitt; w, Rafael Yglesias (based on the novel by Victor Hugo); ph, Jorgen Persson; ed, Janus Billeskov-Jansen; m, Basil Poledouris; prod d, Anna Asp; art d, Peter Grant; sound, David John (mixer); fx, Terry Glass, Jaroslav Stolba; casting, Leonora Davis; cos, Gabriella Pescucci; makeup, Morag Ross; stunts, Gareth Milne

Historical/Drama (PR: C MPAA: PG-13)

LETHAL WEAPON 4 ★★½

(U.S., 1998) 123m Silver Pictures; Shuler Donner/Donner Productions; Warner Bros. ~ Warner Bros. c

Mel Gibson *(Det. Martin Riggs)*; Danny Glover *(Det. Roger Murtaugh)*; Joe Pesci *(Leo Getz)*; Rene Russo *(Lorna Cole)*; Chris Rock *(Lee Butters)*; Jet Li *(Wah Sing Ku)*; Steve Kahan *(Capt. Ed Murphy)*; Kim Chan *(Uncle Benny)*; Darlene Love *(Trish Murtaugh)*; Traci Wolfe *(Rianne)*; Eddy Ko *(Hong)*; Steven Lam *(Ping)*; Jack Kehler *(State Dept. Official)*; Calvin Jung *(Det. Ng)*; Damon Hines *(Nick Murtaugh)*; Ebonie Smith *(Carrie Murtaugh)*; Mary Ellen Trainor *(Stephanie Woods)*; Michael Chow *(Benny's Assistant)*; Tony Keyes *(Ng's Partner)*; Richard Riehle *(INS Agent)*; Phil Chong *(Yee)*; Roger Yuan *(Chu)*; Jeff Imada *(Thug)*; Simon Rhee *(Thug)*; Zu-Wu Qian *(Uncle Chung)*; Danny Arroyo *(Gomez)*; Raymond Ma *(Doctor Cheng)*; Jennie Lew Tugend *(Cheng's Receptionist)*; Elizabeth Sung *(Hong's Wife)*; Jessica Jann *(Little Girl)*; Dan Wynands *(Human Tank)*; Paul Tuerpe *(Helicopter Co-Pilot)*; James Lew *(Freighter Captain)*; Conan Hutch Lee; James Wing Woo; Raymond May; Francois Chau *(Four Fathers)*; Stephen Liska; Robin Link; Roland Kickinger; Benjamin King; John Harms; Al Sapienza; Darren Peel; Jamie Donovan; Shawn Michaels; Paul Bollen *(Detectives)*; Jeanne Chin *(Ping's Mother)*; Ray Chang *(Ping's Father)*; Ryan C. Benson; Daniel Getzoff; Theodore Toure Johnson Jr. *(Construction Workers)*; Dana Lee *(General)*; George Kee Cheung *(Fan)*; Edward J. Rosen; Jay Fiondella; J. Matthew Jordan; Lisa Rhianna Smith *(Murtaugh's Neighbors)*; Marian Collier *(Maternity Worker)*; Cece Neber Labao *(Maternity Worker)*; Barret Swatek; Kerry Kletter; Joyce Ingalls; Joan Frasco *(Nurses)*; Glenn Tannous *(Patrolman)*; Larkin Campbell *(Patrolman)*; Doug Weaver *(Police Officer)*; Glenn Friedman *(Police Officer)*; Brittany Gamble; James Oliver; Rick Hoffman *(Police Officers at Port)*; Sarah Sullivan *(News Reporter)*; Tim Cooney *(News Cameraman)*; Bill Henderson *(Angry Patient)*; Philip Tan *(Waiter)*; Judith Woodbury *(Question Lady)*; Jey Wada *(Master Printer)*; Wallace Gudgell *(ATF Officer)*; Gary Hand *(Coroner's Assistant)*; Nancy Rosenfield *(Candy Striper)*; Kenneth Jackson *(Hospital Employee)*; Nancy Hopewell *(Patient with IV)*; Christina Orchid *(News Crew)*; Bruce Orchid *(News*

Crew); Richard M. Sieker *(Motorcycle Officer)*; Jen Wei Chang *(Bicycle Guy)*; James W. Gavin *(Helicopter Pilot)*; Craig Hosking *(Helicopter Pilot)*

With the preceding LETHAL WEAPON films having exhausted virtually everything of interest about the relationship between Los Angeles cops Martin Riggs and Roger Murtaugh, the fourth film in the series barely even tries to offer anything of substance amid the wisecracks, shootouts, and explosions. It's not so much a sequel as an episode, for fans of the series only.

During a stressful confrontation with a man armed with a flamethrower, Riggs (Mel Gibson) and Murtaugh (Danny Glover) learn from each other that both are facing pregnancies—of Riggs's girlfriend Lorna Cole (Rene Russo) and Murtaugh's daughter Rianne (Traci Wolfe). Nine months later, as both women are about to give birth, the overly protective Murtaugh is the only person who doesn't know that his daughter is secretly married to junior detective Lee Butters (Chris Rock); thanks to a prank by Riggs, he thinks that Butters's attempts to get to know him better stem from a homosexual attraction. Riggs, still feeling guilt for the death of his first wife, dodges the issue of marriage to Lorna. While night-fishing on the boat of their friend Leo Getz (Joe Pesci), the pair intercept a boat filled with illegal Asian immigrants. Touched by their plight, Murtaugh secretly brings one of the immigrant families home with him.

Because the city's insurance problems require that they be kept off the street, where they're prone to cause a lot of expensive damage, Sgts. Riggs and Murtaugh are promoted to captains. Joined by Butters, they investigate the immigrant smuggling operation, gaining the ire of Triad member Wah Sing Ku (Jet Li). Following leads from Murtaugh's "houseguests," he and Riggs learn that Wah is behind a counterfeiting operation with which he plans to buy the freedom of the four leaders of the Hong Kong Triads, who have been smuggled out of a Chinese prison. Riggs and Murtaugh disrupt the exchange at a dockside warehouse; in the ensuing battle, Wah is killed. Murtaugh accepts Butters into his family, while Riggs, touched by Leo's declaration of friendship, decides to marry Lorna; they complete their vows in the hospital seconds before she gives birth. With the city's insurance crisis averted, Riggs and Murtaugh are "busted" back to sergeants.

The original LETHAL WEAPON was a buddy-cop movie built around the tension between a veteran cop looking to stay alive until retirement and his younger partner, prone to Viet Nam flashbacks and so suicidally depressed at his wife's death that he doesn't care about his own safety. The title originally referred to this aspect of Riggs's character; now it's simply vague hyperbole, which is appropriate. LETHAL WEAPON 4 coasts entirely on audience familiarity with these characters and their appetite for broad gags and big explosions. The holes in the plot are too large and too numerous to list here. For that matter, this collection of random, disposable incidents barely deserves to be called a plot. Remove any of the various story elements—the multiple pregnancies, Riggs's suspicion that his partner may be on the take, Murtaugh and Riggs's promotions, Leo's fledgling detective career—and the only difference it would make to the rest of the film would be to shorten it.

Glover overacts and Gibson's puns aren't nearly as funny as he seems to think, but the pair still manages to get by on charm. Everyone else in the cast is underused. The entire point of Rene Russo's character is lost by taking this tough policewoman and rendering her literally barefoot and pregnant. Chinese action star Jet Li's American debut suffers the usual problem of martial arts stars in mainstream films: in a climax that requires him to battle nonmartial artists Gibson and Glover, the film must minimize his skills to make the others look plausible. The production is blandly professional, with the exception of the irritating musical score, which consists primarily of unfocused improvisations by Eric Clapton and David Sanborn. As emphasized at great length in the end-credit sequence (which is designed to present a scrapbook of photos from the film's production), everyone involved in the production of LETHAL WEAPON 4 (most of whom worked on other films in the series) seem to have enjoyed each other's company. Maybe that explains why the film looks like a vacation rather than something into which any effort was put. *(Violence, adult situations, profanity.)*—M.F.

d, Richard Donner; p, Joel Silver, Richard Donner; exec p, Jim Van Wyck, Steve Perry; assoc p, Ilyse Reutlinger, Spencer Franklin, Jennifer Gwartz; co-p, J. Mills Goodloe, Dan Cracchiolo; w, Channing Gibson (from a story by Jonathan Lemkin, Alfred Gough, and Miles Millar; based on characters created by Shane Black); ph, Andrzej Bartkowiak; ed, Frank J. Urioste, Dallas Puett; m, Michael Kamen, Eric Clapton, David Sanborn; prod d, J. Michael Riva; art d, Richard Mays; set d, Lauri Gaffin; sound, Tim Cooney (mixer); fx, Matt Sweeney; casting, Marion Dougherty; cos, Ha Nguyen; makeup, Gary Liddiard, Robert Scribner; stunts, Conrad E. Palmisano, Mic Rodgers

Crime/Comedy/Action (PR: C MPAA: R)

LET'S KILL ALL THE LAWYERS

(U.S., 1997) 103m Lighten Up Films; Dakota Jas ~ Barrister Films c

Rick Frederick *(Foster Merkul)*; James Vezina *(Junior Rawley)*; Michelle DeVuono *(Satori Bunko)*; Lee Gusta *(Pops)*; Cheryl Roy *(Larissa)*; Joanne Long *(Penelope)*; Ron Senkowski *(Crazy Mikey)*; Brian C. Manoogian *(Dude Who Delivers Blank Paper)*; Marina Seeman *(Moms)*; Scott J. Shumaker *(Little Foster)*; Deborah Nymshack *(Divorcee)*; Lisa Bernhardt; Sandra Seebree Daniels; John Hollingsworth; Gerald L.A. Smith; Jacqueline Beaumont; Steve Dixon; Mark Kanzawa; Marty Smith; Carol Teegardin *(Burnt Out Retreat Lawyers)*; Tony Dobrowolski *(Lawyer Whose Wife Once Moaned)*; Marie Boyle *(More Red Tape Than a Mummy on the Rag Lawyer)*; Joanne Newman *(Anal Retentive Mother Lawyer)*; "Roman Era" Sequence: Richard Moll *(The Centurian)*; Dick Butkus *(The Turnkey)*; Lewis Arquette *(Antinus)*; Harry Hankin *(Timonus)*; Hamilton Camp *(Marcus)*; Jack Thibeaux *(Junius)*; Felton Perry *(Cyrus)*; David Christensen *(Christ)*; Kevin O'Kane *(Escaping Prisoner)*

An ultra-low budget, sloppy plot construction, and wooden acting give one the impression that LET'S KILL ALL THE LAWYERS is little more than an overblown student film. The film's plot—what there is of it—concerns an idealistic young lawyer who attempts to cope with the lack of integrity he discovers in legal circles.

In 33 AD, a lawyer in prison (at the same time that Jesus Christ is awaiting the verdict of his trial) is taunted about his profession by his fellow inmates.

In the present day, Foster Merkul (Rick Frederick) is an intern at the upscale law firm of super shyster Junior Rawley (James Vezina). An ambulance chaser who's built a successful firm through unscrupulous acts like disguising himself as a priest and consoling the families of plane crash victims while they're still in shock at the airport, Rawley is irredeemable. The daydreaming Foster imagines that he will be able to change Rawley and make him more compassionate; in the meantime, however, one of Foster's fantasies has appeared in human form: Satori (Michelle DeVuono), a beautiful avenger who is stalking, mating with, and then murdering unscrupulous lawyers in the area by luring them back to a mansion she lives in, where she kills them with a remote-control-operated gun concealed inside a painting of Abraham Lincoln.

Tired of Foster's philosophizing, Junior fires him. The same day, Foster learns that he's been accepted to all the schools to which he applied, and later, he meets Satori in person for the first time. He begins working in the garden outside her mansion; she, in turn, runs a New Age encounter group for disillusioned lawyers. She soon focuses her attention on Junior, whom she beds down in an effort to get close enough for a murder attempt. While Junior is tied down, she shoots at him; the projectile bounces off his beloved, expensive briefcase and kills her instead. Foster bursts in too late and considers killing Junior, but instead allows his former boss to free himself from his bond. After Foster leaves to bury Satori, Junior accidentally kills himself using her remote control gun.

LET'S KILL ALL THE LAWYERS is amateurishly executed, with director Senkowski forgetting such basic tenets of filmmaking as establishing shots, thus making it often difficult to follow the action and story. Compounding the problem are frequent senseless cutaways to mock commercials for "1-800" TV lawyers or vignettes that depict outrageous phone conversations conducted by various attorneys (not to mention the nonsensical Mel Brooks/LIFE OF BRIAN-like opening prologue). The result is a mess that leaves many unanswered questions: it's never clear, for instance, why others can see Satori and interact with her if she's only a figment of Foster's imagination.

The writing is also jejune. Foster's jarringly serious voice-overs (totally out of place in a broad comedy) periodically describe his inner turmoil over the ethical problems he's encountering, but any viewer of "L.A. Law" has already seen and heard it all before—delivered in a far more eloquent fashion. A former lawyer himself, Senkowski does seem to have something urgent to say about the legal profession, it's just never clear exactly what that something is—or why he chose to express it in a broadly comedic manner. Neither entertaining nor enlightening, LET'S KILL ALL THE LAWYERS does not hail the arrival of a major new talent. *(Violence, nudity, sexual situations, profanity.)*—K.W.

d, Ron Senkowski; p, Shannon Hamed; exec p, Shannon Hamed, Ron Senkowski, James A. Courtney, Brian C. Manoogian; assoc p, Shannon Rain Berritt, David Monforton, Tom Tucker, Fritz Gronow ("Roman Era" Sequence); co-p, Ron Senkowski; w, Ron Senkowski; ph, Lon Stratton; ed, Christa Kindt; m, Martin Liebman; art d, Tom Chaney; sound, Al Rizzo, Joseph Productions (design); cos, Scarlett Jade

Comedy **(PR: C MPAA: R)**

LET'S TALK ABOUT SEX ★

(U.S., 1998) 82m Manga Entertainment ~ Fine Line c

Troy Beyer *(Jazz)*; Paget Brewster *(Michelle)*; Randi Ingerman *(Lena)*; Joseph C. Phillips *(Michael)*; Michaline Babich *(Morgan)*; Tina Nguyen *(Drew)*

The trailers for LET'S TALK ABOUT SEX promised a lively, provocative, and above all, honest look into female sexuality. Forget it. This dreadful concoction exploits the topic it purports to explore in order to enlivening a plot line centering around three bratty Miamians who suffer their way through romantic difficulties.

Eager to have her own local television show, Jazz (Troy Beyer) enlists the assistance of her roommates, Michelle (Paget Brewster) and Lena (Randi Ingerman), in creating a sample program. Wanting to focus on "dating and mating in the '90s," Jazz plans to conduct a series of spontaneous interviews with women about relationships and sex.

On their first day of shooting, Jazz and her friends talk with women, both straight and gay, about their sexual interests. That night, a former boyfriend visits Lena and although she is initially reluctant, she has sex with him, after which he promises to call her. The next day, the three friends tape more interviews, asking women to discuss what they dislike in men and sex. That evening, Lena is distraught when her former boyfriend fails to call, but she's comforted by Jazz and Michelle. The following day, the trio tape women who talk about—and in some cases demonstrate—unique sexual skills. When one of the interviewees talks about domination, however, Michelle halts the taping. Asked why by Jazz and Lena, the usually tough Michelle admits that she's upset by the subject because she indulges in it herself, to prevent others from controlling her.

When all interviewing is completed, Jazz edits the material onto a single tape and gives it to Michelle to drop off at the television station. A mix-up ensues and the tape is destroyed before Michelle can deliver it. Having lost her only copy of the program and missed the station's submission deadline, Jazz is devastated. Supported by her friends, however, she endeavors to start again. She also calls and asks for a date with her former boyfriend, Michael (John C. Phillips), of whom Lena and Michelle think highly. When Michael picks her up for the date, he proposes marriage, and Jazz accepts.

The production notes for LET'S TALK ABOUT SEX describe it as a "hybrid of documentary and feature film," and trumpet the fact that first-time director Troy Beyer (co-scenarist of the 1997 comedy B.A.P.S.) shot "guerrilla-style" street interviews with women in order to get "the real deal" on their feelings about sex. In fact, LET'S TALK ABOUT SEX is virtually devoid of interviews. The "interviews" Beyer has conducted (several of which have obviously been scripted) have been chopped into sound bites and sprinkled carelessly into the film, and serve as such to spice up a dull, cliche-ridden story.

Even as narrative, LET'S TALK ABOUT SEX is a complete failure. The story line is insipid when it isn't preposterous. When the videomaking trio learn, for example, that the program into which they have put so much effort has been destroyed (what happened to the video masters?), they show their dismay by. . . cleaning their apartment. The script is just as absurd, with such inane lines of dialogue as, "I'm so convinced that the reason girls like to shop is that clothes give us confidence." The performances are sub-soap opera, and for a film that is supposed to articulate a feminine perspective, LET'S TALK ABOUT SEX is alarmingly sexist, filled with innumerable shots of bikini-bound breasts and buttocks, and showing contempt for older woman (i.e., anyone over the age of 30). The idea of relating documentary material to fiction is an intriguing one (as evinced by such films as MEDIUM COOL and ROUTE ONE/USA) and, given the subject matter, may have made for an enticingly risky film, if Beyer had even a grain of imagination. Next time around, she'd be better off keeping her opinions to herself, and letting others handle the talking. *(Nudity, sexual situations, adult situations, extreme profanity.)*—D.C.

d, Troy Beyer; p, Deborah Ridpath; exec p, Susan Ainsworth; co-p, Sara King; w, Troy Beyer; ph, Kelly Evans; ed, Bill Henry; m, Michael Carpenter; prod d, Joe Warson; casting, Mary Jo Slater, Ellen Jacoby; cos, Timothy Biel

Documentary/Drama **(PR: O MPAA: R)**

LETTER FROM DEATH ROW, A ★½

(U.S., 1998) 93m Showcase Entertainment ~ Michaels Entertainment Group c

Martin Sheen *(Michael Raine's Father)*; Bret Michaels *(Michael Raine)*; Kristi Gibson *(Kristi Richards)*; Lorelei Shellist *(Jessica Foster)*; Simon Elsworth *(Officer Windell)*; Rob Wilds *(Prison Warden)*; Tommy Smith *(Danker)*; Bill Pankey *(Redford)*; Drew Boe *(Lucifer T. Powers)*; Tim Hubbard *(Spencer)*; Tim Northern *(Tyrone)*; Phil Valentine *(Donald Bateman)*; Swan Burrus *(Governor of Tennessee)*; Susan Davis *(Governor's Wife Linda)*; Billy Wirtz *(B.J. Hawkins)*; Charlie Sheen *(Cop #1)*; Antonio Lewis *(Cop #2)*; Judge John Jones *(Judge)*; Lisa Foster *(TV Anchor Woman)*; Susan Welch *(Amber)*; Mike Donegan *(Announcer)*; Dave Chandler *(Strip Club Manager)*; K.C. Carlson *(Governor's Guard)*; Carl Johanson *(Club Bouncer)*; Evante Brookshire *(911 Officer)*; Ken Jackson *(Courtroom Judge)*

Bret Michaels, best known as the lead singer for heavy metal band Poison, financed, scripted, codirected, and stars in this psychological profile of a convict on death row. In a clear bid to prove that there's indeed life after rock stardom, Michaels simply succeeds in coming up with another hackneyed straight-to-video drama.

A stripper named Kristi (Kristi Gibson) is attacked in her home by a masked rapist; the culprit is actually her boyfriend, Michael Raine (Bret Michaels), and the "rape" is actually a sex-game played by the couple. The event is captured by a video camera, however, and when Kristi is killed by another intruder a few moments later, the tape is used as evidence to convict Raine on a murder charge. He's sentenced to death in the Tennessee State Prison. While on Death Row, Raine is visited by the Governor's assistant Jessica Foster (Lorelei Shellist), to whom he tells his story.

After his head is shaved by the sadistic warden, Raine begins to snap from the pressure. Meanwhile, inmate-priest Lucifer T. Powers (Drew Boe), confides that after the Governor confessed to him about having an affair with a hooker, Powers was framed with a murder charge. Explaining matters once and for all, Raine gets a letter from his lawyer, who is suffering a bout of conscience. It seems the lawyer was in on the fact that Raine's murder charge was set up by the Governor's office; the violently jealous Jessica was in fact responsible for Kristi's murder (since Kristi was the Governor's hooker). With Jessica arrested, Raine is released from jail. . . but in the end, all that has happened (after the killing of Kristi and the imprisonment of Raines) is shown to have been the product of a faceless scriptwriter who's been controlling Raine's destiny. A babbling wreck, Raine is led to the electric chair.

Aside from Michaels's evident ambition to break out of the rock-star mold and the film's effective Nashville prison backdrop, there is very, very little to distinguish A LETTER FROM DEATH ROW. What starts as a hallucinogenic look at crime and punishment (think NATURAL BORN KILLERS on a shoestring budget) quickly degenerates into a cliche-ridden experiment in suspense, including elements familiar from the prison subgenre (mistreatment by guards and an escape attempt) and other erotically tinged thrillers (the unmasking of a spurned woman as the puppet master). Unfocused and illogical, the film attempts to redeem itself with a last-minute plot twist—but even that's been hinted at from the beginning, as the faceless scriptwriter—who may or may not be Michaels himself—is seen (from oblique angles) reading along with the story line throughout the film.

Michaels's pal Charlie Sheen makes a cameo appearance (and after completion, bought 40 percent of the movie), while his father Martin shows up for a two-minute sequence as Raine's blue-collar father. The remainder of the performances are all either amateurish or overwrought (no surprise given that Michaels once stated that his favorite actresses included Jami Gertz and Brigitte Nielsen). Michaels himself is serviceable in the lead, and while he may be bald for most of the movie, clearly wants viewers to remember his stint as a *Playgirl* cover-boy (August 1993) since he wastes no opportunity to show off his buff body.

It should be noted that, given Michaels's subsequent real-life troubles concerning a publically-marketed home-video of him and ex-girlfriend Pamela Lee Anderson having sex, that the early sequences of DEATH ROW obviously didn't require much of a stretch of Michaels's imagination. *(Violence, nudity, sexual situations, adult situations, extreme profanity.)*—S.P.

d, Bret Michaels, Marvin Barker; p, Ann Gillis; exec p, Bret Michaels ; w, Bret Michaels; ph, W.S. Pivetta, Scott Spears; ed, Bret Michaels, Marvin Baker, Shane Stanley; m, Bret Michaels; prod d, Michael Davis; stunts, Kevin Kowboy Kirten

Crime/Drama/Fantasy (PR: O MPAA: NR)

LEWIS & CLARK & GEORGE ★

(U.S., 1998) 85m Davis Entertainment Classics; Dark Matter Productions ~ BMG c

Rose McGowan *(George)*; Salvator Zuereb *(Lewis)*; Dan Gunther *(Clark)*; Art La Fleur *(Fred)*; Aki Aleong *(Chang)*; James Brolin *(Rev. Red)*; Paul Bartel *(Cop)*; Brian Taylor *(George's Boyfriend)*; Jerry Gardner *(Yo-Yo Man)*; Richard Butterfield *(Pick-up Cowboy)*; Sally Jackson *(Waitress)*; Suzanne Mari *(Nefertiti)*; Tamara Clatterbuck *(Blonde Hooker)*; E.E. Bell *(Mailman)*; Paula Sorge *(Tammee)*; Nathan Perkins *(J.R.)*; Destiny Esposito *(Gun Girl)*; Stephanie Bacon *(Woman Cop)*; Corinne Michaels; Delana Michaels; Linda Mitchell; Dave Bennett; Dick T. Chen *(New York Tourists)*; Ruben Moreno *(Puerto Old Man)*; Patrick Jones *(Roadblock Cop)*; C.E. Mitchell *(Roadblock Cop)*; Embry Hale *(Mine Guide)*; J. Todd Harris *(Banker)*; Forrest Maldin *(Banker)*

LEWIS & CLARK & GEORGE ranks at the bottom of the "disaffected but cool twentysomethings hit the road for a crime 'n' sex spree" subgenre that has flourished in the 1990s.

After escaping from a Southwestern prison, illiterate lug Lewis (Salvator Zuereb) and computer hacker Clark (Dan Gunther) head for New Mexico, where a now-dead fellow convict hid a map to a Mexican gold mine. Elsewhere, George (Rose McGowan) hits the road after running out on her boyfriend and Fred (Art La Fleur), who gave them $10,000 for drugs they never delivered. Distraught at Lewis's penchant for shooting people who annoy him, Clark sets out on his own. He gets a ride from George, who is driving a stolen car and is accompanied by a deadly snake. Not knowing that her interest is primarily in the gold (about which she heard him and Lewis arguing), Clark falls for George when she takes him to bed. Lewis enjoys his own dalliance with trashy trailer park Mom Tammee (Paula Sorge) before catching up with Clark and George at the map site.

Putting aside their differences, they head for the mine in Mexico. Their trail is picked up by Fred, who thinks George has his money. He kidnaps her from the Mexican motel where the trio spent the night. George escapes after her snake bites Fred, and returns to a confrontation in which the suspicions of all three boil over. A shootout leaves George as the only survivor. She finds the mine and sells it for a fortune. But as she drives away, she notices police taking note of the license of the stolen car she is still driving, just as she notices the snake she thought missing is still in the car, poised to strike her.

Obviously influenced by Gregg Araki's THE DOOM GENERATION(1995), which also costarred McGowan, LEWIS & CLARK & GEORGE is a particularly irritating example of the "Indie" film, a marketing gimmick that has nothing to do with independent filmaking. Like other purveyors of the form, writer-director Rod McCall loads up on every element thought to appeal to youthful viewers: pointless violence, anti-social attitudes, and "retro" music performed by anonymous musicians who have perfected the art of smirking audibly. (A mark of the film's desperate trendsucking is that all of the leads smoke cigars, ostentatiously.) The video box trumpets the film's appearance at the Sundance Film Festival and drops references to "Tarantino" (no first name needed) and Hong Kong cinema. McCall certainly tries to ape those touchstones, but the strain is obvious. Pointless jumpcuts and off-kilter camera angles are no substitute for style, and a sequence in which McGowan mimes to a recording of "Where the Boys Are" seems interminable. Costars Zuereb and Gunther (who coproduced) are at least lively on occasion, but "indie queen" McGowan's performance is limited to a perpetual pout; she's enough to make you think kind thoughts about last year's model, Parker Posey. *(Violence, nudity, sexual situations, adult situations, profanity.)*—M.F.

d, Rod McCall; p, Dan Gunther, J. Todd Davis; exec p, John Davis; co-p, Ed Cathell III; w, Rod McCall; ph, Michael Mayers; ed, Ed Marx; m, Ben Vaughn; prod d, John Huke; casting, Cathy Henderson-Martin, Dori Zuckerman; cos, Kari Perkins; makeup, Leah Rial

Crime/Thriller/Comedy (PR: C MPAA: R)

LIFE IS BEAUTIFUL ★★★★

(Italy, 1997) 114m Melampo Cinematografica ~ Miramax c

(LA VITA E BELLA)

Roberto Benigni *(Guido Orefice)*; Nicoletta Braschi *(Dora)*; Giorgio Cantarini *(Giosue)*; Giustino Durano *(Uncle)*; Sergio Bustric *(Ferruccio Orefice)*; Marisa Paredes *(Dora's Mother)*; Horst Buchholz *(Dr. Lessing)*; Lydia Alfonsi *(Guicciardini)*; Giuliana Lojodice *(Didactic Principal)*; Amerigo Fontani *(Rodolfo)*; Pietro De Silva *(Bartolomeo)*; Francesco Guzzo *(Vittorino)*; Raffaella Lebboroni *(Elena)*; Andrea Nardi *(Upholsterer)*; Franco Mescolini *(School Inspector)*; Giovanna Villa *(City Hall Secretary)*; Hannes Hellmann *(German Corporal)*; Nino Prester *(Bruno)*; Richard Sammel *(German Lieutenant)*; Giancarlo Cosentino *(Ernesto the Waiter)*; Carlotta Mangione *(Elenora)*; Gina Rovere *(Dora's Governess)*; Francesca Messinese *(Woman at the Opera)*; Gil Baroni *(Prefect)*; Claudio Alfonsi *(Rodolfo's Friend)*; Massimo Salvianti *(Policeman in Bookstore)*; Alessandra Grassi *(Teacher)*

Comic filmmaker Roberto Benigni makes a risky comedic gambit pay off in this gentle-hearted "fable" about the Holocaust in Italy. Though the film makes a swift, somewhat jarring transformation from broad farce to tearjerking sentiment about midway through, Benigni's unique charm as a performer and his talent as an old-fashioned storyteller carry the film through to a touching conclusion. The film won the Grand Prize at the 1998 Cannes Film Festival and three Oscars, including Best Foreign Film and Best Actor (Benigni).

In 1939 in the town of Arezzo, drifter Guido (Roberto Benigni) finds work as a waiter through his uncle (Giustino Durano). Guido is entranced by schoolteacher Dora (Nicoletta Braschi) who, unfortunately, is the fiancee of pompous town official Rodolfo (Amerigo Fontani). Guido's infatuation with Dora leads him to shanghai her after she exits an opera she's attended with Rodolfo. The two hit it off, but Dora's marriage is still impending. Guido gets work as a waiter at a party being held to celebrate the engagement. As the evening continues, Dora grows restless and asks Guido to "take me away." This he does, riding her off on his uncle's horse—which has been painted with anti-Semitic slogans by local Fascist hoods.

Time passes. Dora and Guido are happily married and have a son, Giosue (Giorgio Cantarini). By this point, Jews in Arezzo (including Guido and his uncle) are regularly interrogated by the authorities, and anti-Semitic signs and graffiti appear around the town square. On Giosue's birthday, Dora returns home to find that Guido, his uncle, and Giosue have been rounded up and placed on a cattle car. She demands a place on the same train (although she is not Jewish), and the entire family is confined in the same concentration camp.

Guido hits upon a way to answer Giosue's questions about the camp: he informs the boy that the entire experience is an elaborate contest, a game in which the people with the most points accumulated will win first prize, a tank. After Guido's uncle is killed in "the showers," Guido tells Giosue that a key component of the game now requires the boy to hide in the barracks all day long, so he won't be discovered by the guards. In the meantime, Guido gets an occasional message across to Dora, who's imprisoned on the women's side of the camp.

Guido eventually takes a big risk, encouraging Giosue to briefly play with the children of the German officers and later join them for a meal, at which he, Guido, will be present as a waiter. Both father and son escape punishment. As the war comes to a close, Guido helps Giosue to escape the final purge by telling him about the final phase of the game—in which Giosue must hide silently in a storage bin until everyone has gone away. While making a last-minute search for Dora, Guido is shot by a German soldier, but the boy survives, coming out of hiding only when the camp is completely deserted. American forces arrive, and a soldier gives the boy a ride in a tank, causing Giosue to believe that the game has been won. Giosue later reunites with his mother on the road leading out of the camp. The adult Giosue reminisces about the precious "gift" his father's imagination gave him.

Giosue's voice-over narration declares at the beginning of the film that this is "a simple story but not an easy one to tell." For those doubtful about the film's verisimilitude, it has been documented that some families during the Holocaust were all interned in the same concentration camp, and that some inmates were indeed able to conceal children from the guards' sight. This historical reality shores up some of the situations dreamt up by Benigni and coscripter Vincenzo Cerami, but as for the "ease" with which the story is told, that has everything to do with Benigni's sublime skill as a comedian, actor, and filmmaker. The specter of Chaplin hangs over the film, for not only does Benigni's bittersweet treatment of Jewish persecution bring to mind THE GREAT DICTATOR (1940), but the father-son sequences echo THE KID (1921). Any comparison to Chaplin is naturally a daunting one, but Benigni acquits himself quite nicely, striking just the right balance of comic heroism and vulnerability.

The film's only drawback is its narrative structure. As it stands, the transition from comedy (Arezzo) to drama (the concentration camp) is a sharp one. Benigni defended this sudden shift in the film's tone by noting that many people in the camps had lived their lives in a manner similar to Guido—ignoring the oppressive political climate of their homeland until the moment they were herded onto cattle cars. Even so, it still must be noted that Benigni doesn't properly set up the game-playing aspect of the father-son relationship. (One brief conversation, in which Guido smooths over Giosue's questions about an anti-Semitic sign, is the only lead-in to this key element of the plot.)

Any qualms about narrative progression disappear, however, once the film's second half gets underway, and one begins to realize that Guido is not cruelly deceiving his child as much as he is saving the boy's life. Benigni's acting skills come to the fore in incredibly dicey scenes like the one in which Giosue questions Guido about the inmates being turned into buttons and soap.

Guido's response is to mock the very notion, thereby offering a comment on the impossible-to-believe nature of the Nazis' very real atrocities.

Benigni is not the only one doing exemplary work here: Nicoletta Braschi, his real-life wife, exhibits a beguiling, uncommonly sympathetic presence (with a face that's as openly emotive as Benigni's). Cantarini is thankfully only so precocious as Giosue, and Horst Buchholz is memorable in his tortured turn as a doctor who encounters Guido in the camp after having been regularly served by him as a waiter. Cinematographer Tonino Delli Colli (who has collaborated with Pasolini, Fellini, Leone, and Wertmuller) also does impressive work, especially in one darkly lyrical instant in which Guido wanders through the camp in a fog, happening upon a mountain of naked corpses.

Benigni's triumph in LIFE IS BEAUTIFUL is twofold: first, he successfully sustains his endearing screen persona against the backdrop of an unspeakable historic nightmare; second, he is able to give the victims of this nightmare a human face, by setting up a very odd allegory about the act of sacrifice. *(Violence, adult situations.)*— E.G.

d, Roberto Benigni; p, Gianluigi Braschi, Elda Ferri; exec p, Mario Cotone; w, Roberto Benigni, Vincenzo Cerami; ph, Tonino Delli Colli; ed, Simona Paggi; m, Nicola Piovani; prod d, Danilo Donati; set d, Danilo Donati; sound, Tullio Morganti (mixer); cos, Danilo Donati; makeup, Walter Cossu, Enrico Jacoponi

AA Best Actor: Roberto Benigni; *AA Best Foreign Language Film; AA Best Original Dramatic Score:* Nicola Piovani; *AAN Best Picture; AAN Best Director:* Roberto Benigni; *AAN Best Original Screenplay:* Vincenzo Cerami, Roberto Benigni; *AAN Best Film Editing:* Simona Paggi

Comedy/Drama **(PR: C MPAA: PG-13)**

LIFE OF JESUS, THE ★★

(France, 1997) 96m 3B Productions/CCRAV/Norfilms; Tadrart Films ~ Fox Lorber c

(LA VIE DE JESUS)

David Douche *(Freddy)*; Genevieve Cottreel *(Yvette, Freddy's Mother)*; Marjorie Cottreel *(Marie)*; Kader Chaatouf *(Kader)*; Sebastien Delbaere *(Gege)*; Sebastien Bailleul *(Quinquin)*; Samuel Boidin *(Michou)*; Steve Smagghe *(Robert)*; Rene Gilleron *(Rene)*; Mme Chaatouf *(Kader's Mother)*; M Chaatouf *(Kader's Father)*; Daniel Tanchon *(Gege's Father)*; Sophie Ruckebusch *(Majorette)*; Jean-Claude Lefebvre *(Inspector)*; Gerard Wallyn *(Majorette's Father)*; Jean-Benoit Gros *(Pierrot)*; Suzanne Bertelot *(Nurse)*; Melinda Deseure *(Majorettes' Leader)*; Jean-Paul Potteuw *(Harmonies' Leader)*; Les Majorettes de Bailleul *(Themselves)*; L'Harmonie de Bailleul *(Themselves)*; Bernard Fillebeen *(Michou's Father)*; Francis Desure *(Policeman with Freddy)*; Alain Lenancker *(Policeman with Freddy)*; Helene Blaevoet *(Marie's Colleague)*; Marie-Josee van Overbeke *(Quinquin's Mother)*; Nadir Ghilmoinou *(Kader's Friend)*

A group of aimless teens in a small village in northern France ride motorcycles, have sex, get drunk, and beat up foreigners in THE LIFE OF JESUS, which aims to be a sort of modern parable about racism and redemption, but comes off more like a Euro-trash version of KIDS (1995) and, like its title, is ultimately pretentious and devoid of real meaning.

Freddy (David Douche), a 20-year-old epileptic, lives in Flanders with his mother (Genevieve Cottreel), the owner of a cafe. Unemployed and unambitious, Freddy spends his days racing his beloved motorcycle with a group of wayward friends and having frequent, animalistic sex with his girlfriend Marie (Marjorie Cottreel), who works as a supermarket cashier. Their routine is interrupted only by the AIDS death of the brother of one of his buddies, and the arrival in town of an Arab family at whom they hurl racial epithets and whose teenage son Kader (Kader Chaatouf) tries to pursue Marie. Marie continually rejects Kader, but Freddy becomes insanely jealous anyway and threatens to beat Kader up. After Freddy and his friends molest a girl in the town's marching band, however, Marie gets fed up with Freddy and becomes friendly with Kader. A short time later, Freddy and his friends catch Kader and viciously attack him, with Freddy kicking him in the head repeatedly. Kader dies and Freddy is arrested, but escapes from the police station while being interrogated. He hides out in a grassy field and begins to cry while staring up at the clouds.

THE LIFE OF JESUS is tedious, obscure, and extremely unpleasant, despite its garnering some surprisingly good reviews from critics seemingly trying to flatter themselves for their open-mindedness and appreciation of foreign esoterica. The film also somehow won France's prestigious Prix Jean Vigo, a move that would probably horrify the great Vigo, whose lyrical films are filled with all the compassionate poetry that this lacks. Succumbing to anomie while purporting to depict it, the film never transcends the emptiness and ugliness of its lowlife characters (unlike, say, Bunuel's brilliant LOS OLVIDADOS), and instead of producing an emotional catharsis or any kind of moral edification, it leaves one feeling as benumbed and alienated as its protagonists. It may not be necessary for characters to be likable, but they at least have to be interesting, and it's hard to be interested in the fate of a bunch of loutish skinheads whose every action and conversation is based on narcissism, hate, and ridiculing others.

Likewise, the complete lack of a plot would also be acceptable if the level of observation was at all perceptive or insightful, but the best that debuting writer-director Bruno Dumont (reportedly a former philosophy teacher) can offer is the cliched use of constant cutaways to the TV in Freddy's mom's cafe, showing one disaster after another (famine, disease, war, ecology, et al.), with the net result being that the film merely seems like an arthouse version of a juvenile delinquency exploitation pic about "crazy young speed demons going too fast on the road to nowhere in a world spinning out of control." Dumont's style, alternating panoramic long shots and long takes with inexpressive close-ups, and invariably ending scenes with slow "artistic" fade-outs, confuses dispassion with seriousness, and makes sitting through the episodic film something of a chore.

Technically, the film is well made, highlighted by its expansive widescreen cinematography. The acting is acceptable, considering that the entire cast is made up of amateurs that Dumont found in the town in which he was filming, although professionals may have been able to provide the characters with some spark of humanity with which to engender audience sympathy. A measure of the movie's spurious "brutal honesty" is the fact that the "shockingly realistic" sex scenes between Marie and Freddy, featuring full penetration shots which are literally pornographic, are revealed in the final credits to have been filmed with body doubles. *(Graphic violence, extreme profanity, extensive nudity, sexual situations.)*—M.S.

d, Bruno Dumont; p, Jean Brehat, Rachid Bouchareb; w, Bruno Dumont; ph, Philippe Van Leeuw; ed, Guy Lecorne, Yves Dechamps; m, Richard Cuvillier; art d, Frederique Suchet; sound, Thierry Sabatier; cos, Nathalie Raoul, Isabelle Sanchez; makeup, Ferouz Zaafour

Drama **(PR: O MPAA: NR)**

LIKE IT IS ★★

(U.K., 1998) 90m Deep In You; Fulcrum Productions; Channel Four ~ First Run Features c

Steve Bell *(Craig)*; Ian Rose *(Matt)*; Roger Daltrey *(Kelvin)*; Dani Behr *(Paula)*; Jude Alderson *(Gloria)*; Emile Charles *(Aylon)*; Christopher Hargreaves *(Tony—Craig's Brother)*; Paul Broughton *(Minto)*; P.J. Nicholas *(Jamie)*; Sean Simpson *(Jack)*; Charlie Caine *(Terry—DJ)*; Stephen Burke *(Luke)*; Dickon Tolson *(Dirty Dave)*; Chris Ross *(Andy)*; Tony Van Silva *(Fight Loser)*; Suzy King *(Amy)*; Ursula Lea *(Sonya)*; Suzanne Hall *(Train Girl)*

The feature debut of British filmmaker Paul Oremland, LIKE IT IS is a passable but fairly routine independent production about a troubled romance between two young men who work within the London club scene.

One night, in the resort city of Blackpool, Matt (Ian Rose) finds Craig (Steve Bell), a bare-knuckles fighter, hanging around outside a popular nightclub. They return to Craig's apartment to engage in sex, but Craig finds that he cannot go through with it. Days later, Craig shows up at Matt's London flat, which he shares with a club singer, Paula (Dani Behr), and Matt agrees to let Craig live with him. In time, Craig becomes comfortable with his homosexuality, and he and Matt become lovers.

Kelvin (Roger Daltrey), a record company executive, enlists Matt's assistance in promoting a band. Kelvin also gives Craig a job as a chauffeur, which Craig accepts, although it will keep him away from Matt for days at a time. Matt's promotional efforts are successful, and Kelvin offers to let him manage a club he's soon opening, although he first wants Matt to handle the preparations for a band's appearance on a music awards show. Craig, meanwhile, sleeps with one of the band members, at Kelvin's prompting.

On the night of the awards show, Matt confronts Craig backstage concerning the latter's infidelity. Craig apologizes and Matt forgives him. As Matt gets back to work, however, Kelvin tells Craig that his services are no longer needed. Dejected, and exasperated by Matt's unsettled lifestyle, Craig returns to Blackpool, where he resumes fighting for money. When Matt later learns of Craig's predicament, he walks out on his job at Kelvin's club and heads to Blackpool. With the assistance of Craig's older brother, Tony (Christopher Hargreaves), Matt finds Craig outside a warehouse, brutally beaten from a fight. Although he's barely conscious, Craig agrees with Matt that the two should "give it another go," before they climb into Tony's car and head for a hospital.

LIKE IT IS strains to present itself as a sharp, knowing insider's view of the contemporary London music scene. Director Oremland and scenarist Robert Gray endeavor to offer a rarified look into how the music industry operates. They populate their film with the people who move within it, people who are aggressively hedonistic and opportunistic, who take what they want without asking, and who dabble heedlessly in sex and drugs. Perhaps the filmmakers intend to startle the audience with the brazenness and apparent amorality of their characters. At its core, however, LIKE IT IS is quite traditional, telling a familiar story about urban vice transformed by rustic virtue, as a jaded city boy learns what really matters in life through his relationship with an unworldly bumpkin. As such, the film fails to provide a fresh or even particularly interesting perspective on its well-worn theme, merely glossing it over with strobe lights and a "techno" soundtrack. Nor is LIKE IT IS especially good filmmaking. Oremland has the characters racing around England, darting in and out of interchangeable clubs, and the film is so poorly edited that it becomes difficult at times to keep track of the action. The soundtrack is often muddy so that the actors, speaking in thick regional accents, are nearly unintelligible (the slang-laden dialogue doesn't help). The film is well acted, though, with strong performances from British television veterans Ian Rose and Dani Behr, and a warm, unassuming turn from Steve Bell (a former amateur boxer making his film debut). Roger Daltrey makes the best of his cardboard character, lively and amusing as the slimy music executive.

To its credit, the film provides an almost documentary glance at contemporary British trends, and it's commendably nonjudgmental about its characters' unconventional behavior. As storytelling, however, LIKE IT IS fails to distinguish itself from the way it's always been. *(Violence, nudity, sexual situations, substance abuse, extreme profanity.)*—D.C.

d, Paul Oremland; p, Tracey Gardiner; exec p, Christopher Hird; assoc p, Michael Jessey, Guy Holmes; w, Robert Gray (from a story by Robert Gray, Paul Oremland, and Kevin Sampson); ph, Alistair Cameron; ed, Jan Langford; m, Don McGlashan; prod d, Tim Sykes; art d, Louise Bedford; sound, John Avery (recordist); casting, Abi Cohen, Georgina Baker; cos, Sarah Bowern; makeup, Michele Baylis; stunts, Rod Woodruff

Romance/Drama **(PR: O MPAA: NR)**

LION KING II: SIMBA'S PRIDE, THE ★★½

(U.S., 1998) 81m Walt Disney Enterprises ~ Buena Vista Home Entertainment c

VOICES OF: Matthew Broderick *(Simba)*; Neve Campbell *(Kiara)*; Andy Dick *(Nuka)*; Robert Guillaume *(Rafiki)*; James Earl Jones *(Mufasa)*; Moira Kelly *(Nala)*; Nathan Lane *(Timon)*; Jason Marsden *(Kovu)*; Suzanne Pleshette *(Zira)*; Ernie Sabella *(Pumbaa)*

Although of a slightly higher quality than Disney's previous made-for-video animated sequels, THE LION KING II: SIMBA'S PRIDE comes nowhere near the level of its big-screen predecessor (which is the fourth-highest grossing film of all-time worldwide), either musically or artistically.

Kiara (voice of Neve Campbell), the daughter of Simba the Lion King (voice of Matthew Broderick) and his mate Nala (voice of Moira Kelly), is a free-spirit who is always wandering off in the African Pride Lands. Escaping her bumbling babysitters Timon (voice of Nathan Lane) and Pumbaa (voice of Ernie Sabella), Kiara runs off to the forbidden Outlands. There, she befriends Kovu (voice of Jason Marsden), who's the son of Zira (voice of Suzanne Pleshette), an outcast lioness who was a friend of the late Scar, and who has been exiled by Simba. As Kovu grows, Zira plots to use his friendship with Kiara to destroy Simba, but Kovu's obedience to his vengeful mother begins to wane as he and Kiara fall in love. The betrayed Zira ambushes Simba and makes it look like Kovu set him up, but Simba escapes and exiles Kovu. Kiara runs after Kovu and brings him back, just in time to help break up an impending battle between Zira's and Simba's forces. When Zira's warriors turn on her, she tries to kill Kiara, but falls into a river and is killed, and Simba welcomes Kovu into his family.

After several substandard made-for-video animated sequels, Disney had a chance to finally get one right with a worthy follow-up to their 1994 classic, but they blew it by taking the cheap route once again, as THE LION KING II: SIMBA'S PRIDE is just another undistinguished and formulaic marketing "product." Produced by Disney's television animation units in Australia and Canada, the artwork competently imitates the lush look of the original, but is rarely inspired and has a cut-rate appearance, as evidenced by the skimpy backgrounds and limited action. Aside from the poignant story about parent-child bonding, one of the reasons that THE LION KING was so good was because its Oscar-winning score was not only perfectly integrated into the story, but the superb songs by Elton John and Tim Rice could also stand on their own. By contrast, the new songs shoehorned here are totally unmemorable and all too obviously designed to sound like the original hits, notably the precredit "He Lives in You," which copies the "Circle of Life," and the jaunty "Upendi," which echoes the classic "Hakuna Matata." While the original story could be described as BAMBI-meets-*Hamlet*, this one borrows from the Bard's *Romeo and Juliet* for its cliched young-lovers-from-feuding-families plot, along with a simplistic "hate destroys" and "can't we all just get along" message. Though most of the original characters and their voices are back, they all sound bored, apart from the zesty addition of Suzanne Pleshette as the scheming Zira. The overall result is OK for kids, who will enjoy the low humor provided by the comical meerkat Timon and the flatulent warthog Pumbaa, but it could have been so much better.—M.S.

d, Darrell Rooney, Rob LaDuca; p, Jeannine Roussel; w, Flip Kobler, Cindy Marcus; ed, Peter N. Lonsdale; m, Nick Glennie-Smith; art d, Fred Warter; sound, David E. Stone

Animated/Children's/Musical (PR: AA MPAA: NR)

LITTLE BIGFOOT 2: THE JOURNEY HOME ★

(U.S., 1998) 94m PM Entertainment ~ PM Entertainment c

Stephen Furst *(Derby Ferris)*; Taran Noah Smith *(Brian Ferris)*; Melody Clarke *(Shelly Ferris)*; Michael Fishman *(Mike Holliday)*; Joseph S. Griffo *(Little Bigfoot)*; Steve Eastin *(Cavendish)*; Tom Bosley *(Ranger Tasker)*; Erika Page *(Aiyana Stillwater)*; Mark Stephen Brien *(Mingen)*; Chuck Borden *(Leonard)*; Kelly Hirano *(Owen)*; Tim Baker; Art Camacho; Nick Finch; Steve Nave; Daniella Sando; Joe Murphy; Kevin LaRosa; Larry Finch

A little bigfoot goes a long way in this unwanted, unwarranted sequel.

Meanie tycoon Cavendish (Steve Eastin) systematically destroys Indian artifacts he finds on his property in scenic Sasquatch Valley so the government won't repossess the land as sacred tribal ground; he also hunts the legendary hairy humanoids known as "Bigfoots"' roaming the forest. The searchers tranquilize a female creature, but her body falls off a cliff and disappears, leaving a "Little Bigfoot" (Joseph Griffo) unprotected. Meanwhile, a city family stops on adjacent parkland, led by dithery divorced insurance man Derby Ferris (Stephen Furst) spending quality time with son Brian (Taran Noah Smith) and daughter Shelly (Melody Clarke). Though Cavendish tries to spook the group with warnings of a "rabid" beast on the loose, when tiny Shelly meets Little Bigfoot in the forest, the girl immediately befriends the teddy-bear-like creature, and the children promise to protect L.B. against its pursuers. They hide the Sasquatch cub in their camper, and finally introduce Mr. Ferris to Little Bigfoot. The notion of saving the innocent creature turns dad from a wimp to a man of action, and he decoys hunters away while the youngsters take Little Bigfoot back to his woods. But hired Indian tracker Mingen (Mark Stephen Brien) is not so easily fooled, and he leads Cavendish to Little Bigfoot. Because Sasquatches are sacred animals, once Cavendish fires a knockout dart into the critter a native curse strikes him with pain, and he surrenders to lawmen ready to arrest him for his archaeological misdeeds. Wounded Little Bigfoot, tended by the kids and a repentant Mingen, recovers and reunites with his tribe.

Like its predecessors (a loose series from the same production company that kicked off with BIGFOOT: THE UNFORGETTABLE ENCOUNTER in 1995), this went straight to video and cable markets. And like those forebears, this movie isn't very good. As the workaholic father too busy to bond with his offspring, Stephen Furst takes an overused cliche way over the top, and his whiny, effeminate characterization is grating beyond belief, while juvenile performers trade zingers and bathroom humor like wizened sitcom vets. One exception is appealing newcomer Melody Clarke, but her nonstop animal-rights dialogue, while in lockstep with the movie's tiresome eco-themes, makes her a little spooky, like a VILLAGE OF THE DAMNED waif gone militant-vegatarian. The rest of LITTLE BIGFOOT 2 offers few compensations. Art Camacho's direction avoids the the bombastic faux Steven Spielberg style of his LITTLE BIGFOOT (1996), but the one-note chase plot even more slavishly follows the template of Spielberg's E.T. THE EXTRATERRESTRIAL (1982), not to mention HARRY AND THE HENDERSONS (1987). No number of closeups of Little Bigfoot's animatronic, ping-pong-ball eyes can make this third-hand material fresh. As before, the feature carries a closing-credit dedication to "the Supreme Being." Divine intervention does come to mind, if only as the one agency able to save the poor viewer from lousy sequels.—C.C.

d, Art Camacho; p, Raymond Khoury; w, Richard Preston Jr.; ph, Jeffrey A. Cook; ed, Howard Flaer; m, Jim Halfpenny; art d, Adriano Karasek; sound, Lee Archer; fx, John Criswell, Larry Finch; casting, Mark Sikes; cos, Dana Lynne Loats; makeup, Reala Martine; stunts, Chuck Borden

Children's/Fantasy/Adventure (PR: A MPAA: PG)

LITTLE BOY BLUE ★½

(U.S., 1998) 103m Jazz Pictures ~ Castle Hill c

Ryan Phillippe *(Jimmy West/Danny Knight)*; Nastassja Kinski *(Kate West)*; John Savage *(Ray West)*; Shirley Knight *(Doris Knight)*; Tyrin Turner *(Nate Carr)*; Jenny Lewis *(Traci Connor)*; Devon Michael *(Mark West)*; Adam Burke *(Mikey West)*; Brent Jennings *(Tom)*; John Doman *(Andy Berg)*; Kaitlin Hopkins *(Young Doris)*; Dennis Letts *(Sgt. Phillips)*; Jerry Cotton *(Det. Fleaharty)*; Michael Boston *(Leo Dalt)*; Gail Cronauer *(Motel Clerk)*; Carine Chalfoun *(Paramedic)*

Like a dramatic re-creation of the story behind the most twisted episode of "The Jerry Springer Show" ever, LITTLE BOY BLUE is a lurid tale of incest, murder, deception, and kidnapping—all within one family.

In rural Starlight, Texas, sadistic Ray West (John Savage) rules his family's trailer home like a white-trash kingdom of terror. Son Jimmy (Ryan Phillippe), a high school pitching ace, has a chance to escape to college with his moneyed girlfriend Traci (Jenny Lewis), but feels compelled to stay and protect his two younger brothers from their father's abuse.

A man named Berg (John Doman) comes to the roadhouse bar managed by Ray and wife Kate (Nastassja Kinski). When he starts asking questions about the old VW van that sits rusting on the West's property, Ray kills him, staging it to look like an accident. Returning home, Ray forces Jimmy to have sex with Kate at gunpoint while he watches. This forced incest, which has been going on for years, provides Ray's only sexual thrills since he suffered injuries to his genitalia in Vietnam. A few nights later, Ray catches Jimmy and Kate in bed together voluntarily. In a rage, Ray reveals to Jimmy that his brothers are really his sons. Soon after, Jimmy disappears. Both Traci and Jimmy's friend Nate Carr (Tyrin Turner), a rookie cop, suspect Ray of foul play but have no proof.

A mysterious woman named Doris (Shirley Knight) arrives in Starlight. Almost 20 years ago, she and her husband picked up a hitchhiking soldier in their VW van; he returned the favor by killing her husband and kidnapping their baby son. Berg had been a private investigator in her employ. Doris happens into the bar, recognizes Ray, and follows him home. She kills Ray and Kate, and then is killed by Carr. Searching the crime scene the next morning, Carr finds Jimmy, clinging to life in a tomb where Ray had buried him alive.

With spare and moody atmospherics, and strong performances from Savage and Phillippe, LITTLE BOY BLUE is never uninteresting, but it is a mystery that isn't very mysterious. Thoughtful viewers will figure out the first major plot twist (Jimmy's fatherhood) well before its revelation. By the time Doris shows up to fill in the rest of the puzzle, our attention is focused on the ineptitude of the local law enforcement. Ray has a dead body, a missing boy, other accusations surrounding him, and these guys don't see grounds to do any investigating?

The big unanswered mystery in LITTLE BOY BLUE involves Kinski's character, Kate. How did she come to be with Ray, and why has she stayed with him all these years? (He's crazy, not charismatic.) How come neither she nor Jimmy has ever sought help from any outsiders or the authorities? At the very least wouldn't she have confessed to Jimmy that she really isn't his mother? Without the answers to some basic questions about its characters, sick as they may be, LITTLE BOY BLUE is just a contrivance of freakish circumstances—all rhyme and no reason. *(Adult situations, sexual situations, profanity, violence.)*—P.R.

d, Antonio Tibaldi; p, Amadeo Ursini; exec p, Virginia Giritlian; w, Michael Boston; ph, Ron Hagen; ed, Antonio Tibaldi, Tobin Taylor; m, Stewart Copeland; prod d, John A. Frick; set d, Gabriella Villareal; sound, Jennifer Murphy; casting, Michelle Guillermin; cos, April Ferry; stunts, Walter Strait

Drama/Crime/Mystery (PR: O MPAA: R)

LITTLE DIETER NEEDS TO FLY ★★★

(Germany/U.K., 1997) 80m Werner Herzog Filmproduktion; ZDF Enterprises; BBC Films c

Dieter Dengler; Werner Herzog *(Narrator)*

In LITTLE DIETER NEEDS TO FLY, Werner Herzog comes up with another documentary that tests the boundaries of the form. Though the film itself is flawed in many ways, its remarkable story of a German-born POW from the Vietnam war makes for compelling viewing.

LITTLE DIETER is Dieter Dengler, who, at an early age in Germany's Black Forest region during WWII, became fascinated with Allied planes. As a young adult, Dengler moved to the US, enlisted in the Navy, learned how to fly, and in 1966 was sent to Southeast Asia where, on his first mission, he was shot down over Laos. As a prisoner of war, Dengler was tortured by his captors before escaping six months later.

The film emphasizes Dengler's ordeal as a prisoner by taking him back to the Vietnam jungle and having him relate and relive some of his experiences. He remembers how he was marched around for weeks and physically abused with knives and bamboo shoots. He also remembers seeing his seven fellow prisoners eating rats for food and using nails to drain pus from their teeth.

Dengler's escape with the other prisoners to Thailand was minutely planned, but not entirely successful: all of his friends died in the brutal jungle terrain and Dengler himself only barely survived. During his transportation back on a aircraft carrier to the US, Dengler suffered from what would become a lifelong struggle with post-traumatic stress syndrome (huge open-air windows adorn his San Francisco home today). Towards the end of the film, Dengler reunites with Colonel Deatrick, the man who found him in Thailand.

As with LA SOUFRIERE (1977), LESSONS OF DARKNESS (1992), and his several other great documentaries, Werner Herzog, who is better known for his fiction films, blurs the line in LITTLE DIETER NEEDS TO FLY between the two seemingly antithetical kinds of filmmaking. For one thing, the story of Dieter Dengler defies reality by its very odd and unlikely plot turns, and Dengler himself is a curiosity, much like the heroes of Herzog's story films (e.g., in THE MYSTERY OF KASPAR HAUSER, 1975, and FITZCARRALDO, 1982). At one point, for example, Herzog (as bemused narrator) realizes that the war experience "was the fun part of his life." More crucially, Herzog plays with classical documentary techniques at times by creating artful passages, including a memorable dance by some jellyfish in an aquarium, a thoughtful moment at a bridge during "magic hour" (as Dengler recalls the brutal killing of one of his friends), and the extraordinary closing shot of an airfield of planes—Dengler's idea of heaven! He also uses ironic distance in his narration to undercut the foolish attitude of an army training film.

But Herzog errs with some of his other artistic impositions. His decision to bring Dengler back to the jungle to "maybe chase the demons away" might have worked better if he hadn't actually tied up the ex-prisoner and had him led around, this time by a group of silent young Laotians who don't seem to fully understand the socio-political implications of their participation. One funny but awkward moment during this sequence finds Dengler telling one native—who misses a cue—that "it's only a movie—don't worry about it."

Herzog also fails to delve enough into interesting areas of Dengler's life, including his family background (his father was a Nazi, but his grandfather was anti-Nazi) and his life since the escape (there is only a bare mention of his having a fiancee in 1965). Finally, as with some of his better films (AGUIRRE, THE WRATH OF GOD), Herzog opens himself up to criticism by reveling too much in the beauty of horror and spectacle in the repeated shots of the bombing of the Vietcong jungles.

In spite of these drawbacks, however, LITTLE DIETER NEEDS TO FLY tells an unforgettable tale and appropriately questions the nature of human warfare. *(Adult situations, profanity.)*— E.M.

d, Werner Herzog; p, Werner Herzog; exec p, Lucki Stipetic; ph, Peter Zeitlinger; ed, Rainer Standke, Glen Scantlebury, Joe Bini; sound, Ekkehart Baumung

War/Documentary (PR: C MPAA: NR)

LITTLE GHOST ★

(U.S., 1998) 90m The Kushner-Locke Company ~ Paramount c

Jameson Baltes *(Kevin)*; Kristina Wayborn, billed as Kristine Wayborn *(Christine)*; Trishalee Hardy *(Sofia Klemenko)*; James Fitzpatrick *(Tony)*; Laura Bruneau *(Joanna)*; Luc Leestemaker *(Pavel)*; Sally Kirkland *(Mother Klemenko)*; Rudy Rosenfeld *(Butler)*; Donald MacKenzie *(Baron)*; Theodor Danetti; Claudia Soare; Bogdan Voda; Razvan Popa; Florin Chiriac

"Haunting" is the last adjective one would use to describe LITTLE GHOST, a low-budget family flick shot in Romania for the straight-to-video market.

Glamorous former TV actress Christine (Kristina Wayborn) arrives in the country of Solvania to open a lavish health resort inside the historic Castle Klemenko, which has been acquired by her boyfriend/business manager Tony (James Fitzpatrick). Christine is accompanied by her neglected, fatherless son Kevin (Jameson Baltes). Kevin doesn't like Tony, and with good reason; the boyfriend is carrying on an affair with Christine's greedy personal secretary and "spiritual advisor" Joanna (Laura Bruneau). When Tony's decorating schemes start ruining the look of the castle, the guardian ghost of the house, the three-centuries-dead Sofia Klemenko (Trishalee Hardy), appears. Sofia is just an 11-year-old, and so her doll-like appearance doesn't scare Kevin when she materializes in his room. Recognizing that they have a common goal, Kevin and Sofia cooperate to harass Tony and steer Christine instead toward the castle's caretaker Pavel (Luc Leestemaker).

On the day of the spa's grand opening, Kevin manages to raise the formidable ghost of Sofia's mother (Sally Kirkland) who wrecks the party; she then turns on poor Sofie, accusing her of failing to guard the estate. Kevin saves his little ghost friend from oblivion by upbraiding Mother Klemenko for her centuries of absence. Christine, meanwhile, sees the light about Tony and Joanna; she takes Kevin's scolding to heart, and becomes a better mother to her son as they continue to live in the castle.

Drawing inspiration from sources like the cartoon series *Casper, the Friendly Ghost* and the *The Canterville Ghost,* LITTLE GHOST actually has very little going for it, except the picturesque Old World setting and the blonde beauty of onetime Bond girl (OCTOPUSSY) Wayborn. Her character, however, is only one of a cast of vapid characters, acting out for the umpteenth time the modern morality play about career-crazed parents who neglect their children. Watching the sneaky Tony get hit with flying objects is no funnier or more wonderous the fifth time around than it is the first, and director (and former actress) Linda Shayne belabors things by having the whole tale narrated in childlike tones by a grown-up Kevin, in an adult voiceover (uncredited) that keeps reiterating the obvious. The child performers call to mind participants in a school pageant. Most of the ghostly special effects are saved for the finale, and they're way too brief for a supernaturally themed movie. The film's first sequence does include some interesting computer-generated specters, an attention-getting device obviously intended to keep viewers hooked. What follows quickly puts a stop to that.—C.C.

d, Linda Shayne; p, Vlad Paunescu, Peter Yuval; exec p, Peter Locke, Donald Kushner; assoc p, Melanie Weiner, Roberto Bernacchi; w, Timothy Michaels, James W. McLaughlin; ph, Dan Alexandru; ed, Carol Oblath; m, Cynthia Miller; prod d, Cristian Niculescu; art d, Doina Popa, Viorel Ghenea; set d, Ica Varna; sound, Tibi Borcoman, William Smith; fx, Jor Van Kline; casting, Bob MacDonald, Perry Bullington; cos, Oana Paunescu; makeup, Mihai Stanescu, Dana Busoiu; stunts, Doru Dumitrescu

Children's/Comedy/Fantasy (PR: A MPAA: G)

LITTLE MEN

(SEE: LOUISA MAY ALCOTT'S LITTLE MEN)

LITTLE VOICE ★★★½

(U.K., 1998) 99m Scala Productions ~ Miramax c

Brenda Blethyn *(Mari Hoff)*; Jane Horrocks *(LV)*; Ewan McGregor *(Billy)*; Philip Jackson *(George)*; Annette Badland *(Sadie)*; Michael Caine *(Ray Say)*; Jim Broadbent *(Mr. Boo)*; Adam Forgerty *(The Bouncer)*; James Welh *(The Bouncer)*; Karen Gregory *(Stripper)*; Fred Feast *(Arthur)*; Graham Turner *(LV's Dad)*; George Olivier *(Pawnbroker)*; Virgil Tracy *(Loan Advisor)*; Dick Van Winkle *(Money Lender)*; Howard Grace *(Talent Scout)*; Alex Norton *(Bunnie Morris)*; Melodie Scales *(George's Girlfriend)*; Kitty Roberts *(Brenda Bailey)*; Fred Gaunt *(Wild Trigger Smith)*; Alita Petrof *(Elaine)*; Jonathan Clark *(Fireman)*; Take Fat: Sean Hadland; Roger Neville; Paul Swan; Carl Wittaker; Mr. Boo's Band: George Bradley; Geoffrey Emmerson; Barry Gomersalt; Angela Harrison; Jean Hotton; David Kemp; Aiden Lawrence; Michael Lynskey; Peter Marshall; Peter Minns; Christine Quick; Len Rangely; Bob Scott; Melanie Simpson; Doug Stewart; Peter Thompson; Stan Wright

A funny and affecting fable about a pathologically shy young woman with a gift for mimicry, LITTLE VOICE was based on a hit London play of 1992.

LV ("Little Voice") Hoff (Jane Horrock) lives with her widowed mother, Mari (Brenda Blethyn), in an industrial town on the coast of northern England. Mari's overbearing and unloving personality has turned her daughter into a recluse who rarely speaks or leaves her room, where she spends her time listening to Shirley Bassey, Billie Holiday, Marilyn Monroe, and other mainstays of her beloved dad's old record collection.

Mari's newest squeeze is Ray Say (Michael Caine), a two-bit talent agent who is perennially down on his luck. One night Ray overhears LV mimicking the singing voice of Judy Garland with extraordinary fidelity and feeling. After convincing Mari that LV is their ticket to fortune and fame, he tries to persuade LV to become a professional performer. The reclusive girl resists at first but is quickly bullied into making her show business debut at Mr. Boo's, a local nightclub. Immobilized by stage fright, she is a total flop.

LV reluctantly agrees to try again "just once." This time, inspired by the ghost of her father (Graham Turner) in the audience, she is a smash hit. On the second night of her engagement she refuses to leave her room. Frustrated and desperate, Ray turns on Mari and cruelly scorns and spurns her before being tongue-lashed himself by LV. His last chance at success gone, he bitterly prepares to face his creditors.

That night, the Hoff home catches on fire. LV is rescued by Billy (Ewan McGregor), the young telephone repairman who recently befriended her. After going back to her burnt-out house just long enough to confront and tell off her mother for the first time in her life, LV returns to Billy to embark on a new life of freedom, maturity, and self-sufficiency.

The adaptors of the play *The Rise and Fall of Little Voice* admirably resisted the temptation to succumb to the property's potential for maudlinism, preciousness, and whimsey. The movie's pace is brisk and its tone is coolly dispassionate, except on those brief occasions when LV is visited by the ghost of her father. By turning the original stage Billy into a keeper of pigeons, LITTLE VOICE's makers risked opening the door to heavy-handed doses of bird and cage symbolism, but even these tired tropes are rendered with a light touch.

Adaptor-director Mark Herman admitted to toning down playwright Jim Cartwright's playfully poetic language but wisely allowed a measure of Mari Hoff's idiosyncratic way with words to survive the transition from stage to screen. Confronted with the never-ending torrent of delightfully loopy locutions that pour out of her garbage-mouth, one is tempted to speculate that Mari's mother may have whiled away her pregnancy reading Dylan Thomas and James Joyce (although it's highly unlikely that Mari herself ever has). Portrayed with funny and ferocious abandon by Brenda Blethyn, Mari embodies all the earthiness of the English working-class woman, amplified and demonized by grotesque selfishness and desperation. Michael Caine's Ray Say joins Alfie of ALFIE (1966) and Mortwell of MONA LISA (1986) in Caine's most memorable portrait gallery of ethically challenged Cockneys.

All of LV's vocal impersonations were performed by Jane Horrocks herself. Fully as important to the authenticity of the film was the method used to capture these turns: Horrocks performed them live on camera rather than recording the numbers first then lip-synching them on set. Nevertheless, it was inevitable that some immediacy would be lost when the play reached the screen, and outstanding as Horrocks's impersonations are, her portrayal of LV ultimately impresses one more than her talent for mimicry. Horrocks's refreshingly dry, quirky, and unsentimental approach to the role recalls, in a more understated way, her hilariously eccentric performance in the Mike Leigh masterpiece LIFE IS SWEET (1991), another bittersweet comedy involving a neurotic girl who keeps to her room too much and doesn't relate well with her mother. *(Nudity, profanity.)*—D.T.

d, Mark Herman; p, Elizabeth Karlsen; exec p, Nik Powell, Stephen Woolley; co-p, Laurie Borg; w, Mark Herman (based on the play *The Rise and Fall of Little Voice* by Jim Cartwright); ph, Andy Collins; ed, Michael Ellis; m, John Altman; prod d, Don Taylor; art d, Jo Graysmark (supervising), Paul Westacott (construction); set d, John Bush; sound, Peter Lindsay; fx, Bob Hollow; casting, Priscilla John; cos, Lindy Hemming; makeup, Peter King; stunts, Lee Sheward

AAN Best Supporting Actress: Brenda Blethyn

Drama/Comedy **(PR: C MPAA: R)**

LIVE FLESH ★★★½

(Spain/France, 1997) 101m CiBy 2000; France 3; El Deseo S.A.; Goldwyn Films ~ MGM/Goldwyn c (CARNE TREMULA)

Javier Bardem *(David)*; Francesca Neri *(Elena)*; Liberto Rabal *(Victor Plaza)*; Angela Molina *(Clara)*; Jose Sancho *(Sancho)*; Pilar Bardem; Penelope Cruz; Alex Angulo

Using a tricky Ruth Rendell novel as his basis, director Pedro Almodovar returns to form with LIVE FLESH, his best film in some time. The story of an ex-con's new lease on life contains many memorably melodramatic moments.

At Christmastime in 1970, a young prostitute gives birth on a bus to a baby boy. In 1990, that boy has grown up to be the handsome Victor (Liberto Rabal), whose crush on a drug addict named Elena (Francesca Neri), causes a life-altering incident. When Victor shows up at Elena's apartment uninvited, Elena furiously tries to throw him out. Their loud fight attracts the attention of two police officers, David (Javier Bardem) and Sancho (Jose Sancho), who come to the scene. In a struggle, David is accidently shot and Victor goes to prison for the crime.

While serving a four-year sentence, Victor one day sees David on television as a star wheelchair basketball player and Elena cheering him on from the sidelines. Elena, who is now a brunette and free from drugs, has married David, and despite her husband's injury, she enjoys a happy sex life. Upon his release from prison, Victor vows to break up the union. Yet, before he meets up with Elena again, he begins an affair with Clara (Angela Molina), who happens to be the sex-starved wife of Sancho, David's ex-partner.

Victor finally meets Elena again by obtaining a job in the kindergarten where she teaches. David is outraged when he hears that Elena has consented to keep Victor on at the school. Elena swears her love for David, but, slowly, she develops an attraction to Victor. Her defenses come down completely after Victor explains that Sancho had forced Victor to shoot David in the shootout because he suspected David was having an affair with Clara. Eventually, Victor and Elena make love one night, sparking jealousy all around, and causing David, Elena, Clara, and Sancho to descend upon Victor's apartment the following day. In a struggle similar to the one that occurred four years earlier, guns are drawn and, this time, Sancho is killed. Later, David and Elena reconcile, while Victor, who is now married, begins a new life teaching in another day school. Victor's son is born into a society that is both freer and happier than the one he was born into in 1970.

After a series of disappointments, including the controversial KIKA (1993), LIVE FLESH reminds us of the incredible talent that Almodovar exhibited in his earlier films (WHAT HAVE I DONE TO DESERVE THIS?, MATADOR). True, there are his trademark politically incorrect moments, including Clara's declaration to Victor that "the greatest pleasure for a woman is pleasing her man," and David's bitter reflection, "Like all cripples, I've got an ugly temper." But LIVE FLESH demonstrates that Almodovar's best work is composed of more than shock value and a colorful design sense. For the most part, Almodovar invests all his characters with strength, humor, pathos, and enough dramatic dimension to make the odd twists and turns of Rendell's plot seem almost plausible. Moreover, LIVE FLESH (a great title, even if it has little relation to the plot), frames the story with socio-political critique, by implying that the dark days of Franco's regime set the tragicomedy in motion. The film ends with Victor's liberating pronouncement vis-a-vis the Spanish people: "we stopped being scared."

As with nearly all Almodovar films, the visuals provide a sensual delight, although LIVE FLESH is pointedly more baroque (and Bunuel-esque) than usual. The lengthy prologue features startling imagery of Victor's mother giving birth on the bus in the desolate Madrid streets, and the closing shot of the same streets teeming with people years later makes the film's political point succinctly. Elsewhere, Affonso Beato's cinematography elegantly surveys the richly designed interiors *and* exteriors. And as with the better Almodovar films, the acting ensemble displays the flair of a great repertory company—no one hits a false note. Whether or not a British mystery writer was the inspiration, LIVE FLESH marks a high point of inventive filmmaking in an up-and-down director's career. *(Violence, nudity, sexual situations, adult situations, substance abuse, extreme profanity.)*—E.M.

d, Pedro Almodovar; exec p, Agustin Almodovar; w, Pedro Almodovar (based on the novel by Ruth Rendell); ph, Affonso Beato; ed, Jose Salcedo; m, Alberto Iglesias; art d, Antxon Gomez; sound, Bernardo Menz, J.A. Bermudez (mixer); fx, Molina; casting, Datrina Bayonas; cos, Jose M. De Cossio; makeup, Juan Pedro Hernandez

Drama **(PR: C MPAA: R)**

LIVERS AIN'T CHEAP

(SEE: REAL THING, THE)

LIVING IN PERIL ★½

(U.S., 1998) 92m Green Communications; Emerald Entertainment; Talaat Captan Productions ~ New Line Home Video c

Rob Lowe *(Walter Woods)*; James Belushi *(Harrison/Oliver)*; Dean Stockwell *(William)*; Dana Wheeler-Nicholson *(Linda Woods)*; Alex Meneses *(Catherine Langtry)*; Richard Moll *(Fritz)*; Tony Longo *(Truck Driver)*; Patrick Ersgard *(Dieter Krankbaum)*; Earl Boen *(Fingerprint Technician)*; Earl Billings *(Detective)*; Richard Partlow *(Detective Barnes)*; Elise Rothberg *(Jane)*; Stan Yale *(Bearded Man)*; Brian Cousins *(Kevin)*; Ray Baker *(Martin Campbell)*; Peter Spellos *(Jack Robinson)*; Jonathan Frazer *(Officer Coursen)*; Joe Jokubeit *(Catherine's Client)*; Carrie Robinson *(Operator)*; Pamela Brull *(Detective Siccarelli)*

Rob Lowe stars as an architect who's being terrorized by a not-so-mysterious culprit in LIVING IN PERIL, a truly dumb thriller that was made in 1996, but justifiably dumped directly to home video in 1998.

Seattle-based architect Walter Woods (Rob Lowe) goes to Los Angeles for a month to design a home for Beverly Hills millionaire, Mr. Harrison (James Belushi), leaving behind his pregnant wife Linda (Dana Wheeler-Nicholson), who's nervous about recent threats from her violent ex-husband. Following an altercation with a reckless truck driver (Tony Longo) who tries to run him off the road, Walter gets the man fired. Walter then gets a temporary apartment, but is beset by a series of mysterious incidents: his blueprints are inexplicably ruined, he wakes up one morning with his bed crawling with rats, and a masked intruder breaks into his room and breaks his toe. Walter suspects that the fired truck driver is behind it all and calls the police, but they have no evidence and the man has an alibi.

After a woman (Alex Meneses) who lives across the hall from Walter turns up dead in his bed, he gets an anonymous phone call from someone threatening to pin the murder on him. Walter buys a gun to protect himself and when he returns, sees the truck driver in his hallway and knocks him unconscious. Harrison then arrives and reveals that he's really Linda's ex-husband, Oliver, and has been the one terrorizing Walter. A fight ensues and the two men wind up on the roof, where Oliver gets his tie sucked into the air conditioner and is strangled to death. Linda then comes to LA and drives Walter back home.

Despite the professional sheen of moody cinematography, decent production values, and an aggressively Bernard Herrmann-esque string score that promises thrills which are never delivered, LIVING IN PERIL is undone by idiotic plotting, an obvious villain, and the irritating stupidity of its lead character. The plot is riddled with holes and lapses in logic (such as how it's possible that Walter is unaware of what Linda's ex-husband looks like, considering the severity of her problems with him), and there are preposterous "clues" (such as a detailed detour involving "rat urine"). The story is flaccid because of the superfluous and heavy-handed red-herrings, including the truck driver and a loony apartment manager played by the incomparably scuzzy Dean "I'll take any role" Stockwell. There is virtually no suspense once Belushi's character is introduced, as it takes about two minutes to figure out that he's really Linda's ex-husband, and it doesn't help that the hammy, stogie-chomping Belushi is less-than-convincingly cast as a millionaire businessman. Rob Lowe wears a constant expression of uncomprehending befuddlement and the dunce-like Walter's increasingly incredulous actions are extremely exasperating. A decade ago, Lowe co-starred with Belushi in ABOUT LAST NIGHT (1986), but now they're both lucky just to play the leads in a bad vidpic like this. *(Violence, profanity, sexual situations.)*—M.S.

d, Jack Ersgard; p, Talaat Captan, Brad Southwick; exec p, Jerry Ang, Marion Oberauner, Juan C. Collas; assoc p, Daryl De Quetteville; w, Patrick Ersgard, Jesper Ersgard, Jack Ersgard; ph, Ross Berryman; ed, Chris Peppe; m, Randy Miller; prod d, Narbeh Nazarian; sound, Bruce Nazarian; fx, Steve Newquist; casting, Donald Paul Pemrick, Dean E. Fronk; cos, Mark Bridges; makeup, Jeanne Van Phue

Thriller **(PR: O MPAA: R)**

LIVING OUT LOUD ★★★
(U.S., 1998) 100m Jersey Films; New Line ~ New Line c

Holly Hunter *(Judith)*; Danny DeVito *(Pat Francato)*; Queen Latifah *(Liz Bailey)*; Martin Donovan *(Bob Nelson)*; Richard Schiff *(Philly)*; Elias Koteas *(The Kisser)*; Suzanne Shepherd *(Mary)*; Mariangela Pino *(Donna)*; Eddie Cibrian *(The Masseur)*; Clark Anderson *(Gary)*; Ellen McElduff *(Crying Woman)*; Ivan Kronenfeld *(Angry Boyfriend)*; Fil Formicola *(Santi's Man)*; Nick Sandow *(Santi's Man)*; Jenette Goldstein *(Fanny, Pat's Wife)*; Lin Shaye *(Lisa's Nurse)*; John F. Donohue *(Sid)*; Fred Scialla *(Johnny)*; Anthony Russell *(Mo)*; Sy Sher *(Lou)*; Sal Jenco *(Len)*; Gina Philips *(Lisa)*; Kate McGregor-Stewart *(Female Diner)*; Mitch Greenburg *(Anchorman Voice-Over)*; Tamlyn Tomita *(Bob's Wife)*; Henry Woronicz *(Fifth Avenue Parent)*; Taylor Leigh *(Fifth Avenue Parent)*; Matthew McKane *(Andy)*; Robin McDonald *(Heckled Singer)*; Yolanda Snowball *(Jasper's Waitress)*; Deborah Geffner *(Woman with Makeup)*; Rachael Leigh Cook *(Teenage Judith)*; Christian Hill *(Teenage Lover)*; Ed Fry *(Formal Dress Man)*; Judith Regan *(Formal Dress Woman)*; Sean Dooley *(Late Teenager)*; Terry Rhoads *(Across Hall Man)*; Susan Reno *(Across Hall Woman)*; Claudia Shear *(Drunken Fan)*; Mike G. Moyer *(Jeweler)*; Sybil Azur *(Confessional Dancer #1)*; Carmit Bachar *(Confessional Dancer #2)*; Monique Chambers *(Confessional Dancer #3)*; Donielle Artese *(Confessional Dancer #4)*; Aisha Dubone *(Confessional Dancer #5)*; Shawnette Heard *(Confessional Dancer #6)*; Tanika Ray *(Confessional Dancer #7)*; Laurie Sposit *(Confessional Dancer #8)*; Adrian Young *(Confessional Dancer #9)*; Roger Nehls; Mary Schmidtberger *(Married Couple in Lawyer's Office)*; Lou Richards *(Judith's Lawyer)*; Tom Howard *(Bob's Lawyer)*; Michael Clair Miller *(Couple's Lawyer)*; Willie Garson *(Man in Elevator)*; Ellen Buckley *(Pat & Judith's Waitress)*; Laura Salvato *(Neo-Natal AIDS Volunteer)*; Hattie Winston *(Hospital Nurse)*; Mario Piccirillo *(Cousin Louie)*; Carole Ruggier *(Italian Girlfriend)*; JASPER'S HOUSE BAND: Mervyn Warren *(Piano)*; Reggie Hamilton *(Bass)*; Peter Michael Escovedo *(Drums)*; Mark Schulz *(Guitar)*; Michael James *(Guitar, Vocals)*; Gerald Albright *(Alto Saxophone)*; Plas Johnson *(Baritone Saxophone)*; Justo Almario *(Tenor Saxophone)*; Vincent Trombetta Jr. *(Tenor Saxophone)*

Acclaimed screenwriter Richard LaGravenese (THE FISHER KING, THE BRIDGES OF MADISON COUNTY) makes his directorial debut with this tale of two New Yorkers who inspire each other to become open to life and love. Inspired by two short stories by Anton Chekov ("The Kiss" and "Misery"), LIVING OUT LOUD is a basketfull of interesting ideas and tender moments that never quite congeal.

Recently divorced after 16 years of marriage to Dr. Bob Nelson (Martin Donovan), Judith Nelson (Holly Hunter) is a childless woman in her 40s with an apartment on Fifth Avenue and no life outside of her new job as a private nurse. Her major pastimes are talking to herself and entertaining dramatic suicide fantasies. Pat Francato (Danny DeVito) is divorced, grieving over the death of his daughter, and forced to live with his more successful brother while he dreams up get-rich schemes. He is working as an elevator operator in Judith's building. One night at Jasper's, a jazz club she likes to frequent, Judith is passionately kissed by a stranger (Elias Koteas) who has mistaken her for someone else. They talk, discover that they have similar lives, and agree to meet at the club the following week. With this wedge driven into her emotional armor, she notices Pat when she returns home, leading to a conversation which the two continue in her apartment. Over the week the two grow closer; Pat tells her his idea to open an importing business, she talks about wanting to go back to medical school (which she quit to support her ex-husband).

When her date never shows at Jasper's the next week, Judith gets drunk and has to be calmed down by Liz Bailey (Queen Latifah), a jazz singer she admires. The two become friends, and Judith's world opens up a little more. After spending the night at an after-hours dance club with Liz, Judith goes to a meeting with Bob regarding the sale of their country house. She loses her temper and he threatens to put her in jail unless she gives up her share of the house. At dinner with Pat, who is proceeding with his import idea, she politely rejects his romantic overtures.

Several months later Judith is living downtown, back in school and working in a neo-natal AIDS ward. At Jasper's, she sees Pat with a date, happily singing at amateur night.

Richard LaGravenese made a name for himself with a series of intelligent scripts that explore adult romanticism while avoiding mawkish sentimentality. He has also demonstrated a fanciful streak, whether whimsical as in THE FISHER KING (1991), or darker as in his adaptation of Toni Morrison's BELOVED (1998). LIVING OUT LOUD displays both of those traits, but suggests that LaGravenese is for the time being still better employed as a writer than a director. His film doesn't lack visual imagination, but it is unleashed primarily in discrete segments, most notably a fantasy sequence in which Judith leads the dance at a bar filled with music video-type women. (A similar idea was better integrated by director Terry Gilliam in THE FISHER KING.) The talky scenes are less striking, as characters simply sit and yak for long periods of time (the traditional vice of writers who get to film their own scripts). The conversations have plenty of nice ideas, like Pat's comment that things you never noticed about yourself show up in your kids. But while LIVING OUT LOUD takes us into its leading characters, it doesn't really do much with them once we get there, as if the back story didn't leave any room for the plot. In a supporting role as the singer, Queen Latifah commands a disproportionate part of the movie simply by being more visually striking than the other characters. Danny DeVito (who also coproduced) gives the best performance, while Holly Hunter occasionally seems unable to meet the impossible demands the script makes of her character—demands which, to be fair, would tax any actress. *(Nudity, adult situations, profanity.)*—M.F.

d, Richard LaGravenese; p, Danny DeVito, Michael Shamberg, Stacey Sher; co-p, Eric McLeod; w, Richard LaGravenese (based on "The Kiss" and "Misery" by Anton Chekov); ph, John Bailey; ed, John Gregory, Lynzee Klingman; m, George Fenton; prod d, Nelson Coates; art d, Joseph Hodges; set d, Linda Lee Sutton; ch, Frank Gatson Jr.; sound, Petur Hliddal (mixer); fx, John Ziegler; casting, Margery Simkin; cos, Jeffrey Kurland; makeup, Valli O'Reilly; stunts, Steve Davison

Comedy/Drama/Romance **(PR: C MPAA: R)**

LOLIDA 2000 ★★

(U.S., 1998) 83m Surrender Cinema ~
Amazing Fantasy Entertainment c
(AKA: LOLITA 2000; O-LITA 2000)

Jacqueline Lovell *(Lolita)*; David Squires *(Jake)*; Skylar Nicholas *(Kealy)*; Robert John *(Derrick)*; Heather James *(Casey)*; Eric Acsell *(Tom)*; Gabriella Hall *(Sherri)*; Taylore St. Clair *(Jolene)*; William Briganti *(Billy Ray)*; Everett J. Rodd *(Shemp)*; John C. Babcock *(Lefty)*; Rick *(Hank)*; Michael Feichtner *(Fighter #1)*; Bobby Young *(Fighter #2)*; J.N. Italiano-Zaza *(Maya)*; Lisa Sutton *(Juno)*; Trisha Berdot *(Bren)*; Ronnie Tarr *(Guard #1)*; Roxanne Miller *(Guard #2)*; Frederick Aronzon *(Guard #3)*; Kurt Schwoebel *(Doctor Conrad)*; Darko Malesh *(Sasha)*; Caroline Alexander *(Madeline)*; Lynne Barnes *(Doctor)*; Kelly Ashton *(Nude Model)*; Steve De Falco *(Orderly)*; Isabella Dumaurier *(Mina)*

Adrian Lyne should have taken some pointers from this straight-to-video softcore title that is everything that Lyne's movie isn't: short, humorous, and titillating. Of course, in true erotic-movie fashion, the film's title belies the fact that the plot has *nothing* whatsoever to do with the Nabokov novel or its two filmed adaptations.

Lolita (Jacqueline Lovell) is a member of a future society where pornography and video have been banned. Opposed to the government policy of deleting these "stories," Lolita broadcasts them on taped transmissions that are sent out via satellite.

In the first story, art student Sherri (Gabriella Hall) suffers from intense dreams. Under hypnosis, she recalls being abducted by aliens, who simply wish to study humans having sex. She winds up having sex with a fellow human prisoner, in order to satisfy the curiosity of her alien captors. Story two is set on a penal colony on another planet. Casey (Heather James) is an Earth girl caged within the prison. She works out a deal to escape with a male inmate, with whom she has sex. The male inmate chooses to stay in the prison. Later, she has sex with the female warden, whom she manages to lock up. She escapes through an air duct—but it only takes her to another place inside the prison. In the third story, truck driver Jake (David Squires) stops at a diner where he has sex with waitress Kealy (Skylar Nicholas) in the restroom. Upon exiting, he is transported to 1955 and learns from an old man that he's stuck in a "time slip." After Jake watches the diner customers have sex, he goes back in the restroom. It takes him to a violent future where he views two females fighting and then having sex. Another trip in the restroom takes him to prehistoric times where he has sex with two cave girls.

Pirate broadcaster Lolita returns, vowing to continue transmission of the forbidden "stories."

No pretentious images here, or cries of pedophilia. Rather, LOLIDA 2000 is a fast-paced, arousal-inducing, 83-minute foray into sex. Plot be damned, writer-director Sybil Richards simply goes for the money shots. The sex scenes are plentiful, graphic, nicely choreographed, and backed by an amusing musical score (including doo-wop for the 1955 scene). The main problem is that the sex scenes are too similar. Fortunately, the women are all attractive, and Gabriella Hall is not only gorgeous, but actually manages to do a little acting in her story.

The film was released on home video as one of three softcore, pay-cable-friendly erotic reworkings of classic tales; the other two titles were THE EXOTIC HOUSE OF WAX and THE EXOTIC TIME MACHINE (both 1998). In each case, the original source material was ignored, and the filmmakers let their (limited) imaginations run free.

The film was initially called LOLITA 2000 in press releases; when it arrived on tape it had its official title, LOLIDA 2000 (presumably to avoid confusion with the Irons film—a confusion the producers presumably intended to create in the first place), but when aired subsequently on pay-cable channels, it was called O-LITA 2000. *(Violence, extensive nudity, sexual situations, adult situations, profanity.)*—P.L.

d, Sybil Richards; p, Pat Siciliano; exec p, David De Falco, Michael Feichtner; w, Sybil Richards (based on the story by Lucas Riley); ph, Andrea Rossotto; ed, Rebecca Pellegrino; m, Carl Dante; prod d, Roger Ambrose; sound, Robert "Frog" Mathews; casting, Pat Siciliano, Keely Rene; cos, Roxanne Miller; makeup, Shutchai "Tym" Buacharern

Erotic **(PR: O MPAA: NR)**

LOLITA ★★

(U.S./France, 1997) 137m Lolita Productions;
Chargeurs Productions ~ Samuel Goldwyn Company c

Jeremy Irons *(Humbert Humbert)*; Melanie Griffith *(Charlotte Haze)*; Frank Langella *(Clare Quilty)*; Dominique Swain *(Lolita Haze)*; Suzanne Shepherd *(Miss Pratt)*; Keith Reddin *(Reverend*

Rigger); Erin J. Dean *(Mona)*; Joan Glover *(Miss LeBone)*; Pat P. Perkins *(Louise)*; Ed Grady *(Doctor Melnick)*; Michael Goodwin *(Mr. Beale)*; Angela Paton *(Mrs. Holmes)*; Ben Silverstone *(Young Humbert Humbert)*; Emma Griffiths-Malin *(Annabel Leigh)*; Ronald Pickup *(Young Humbert's Father)*; Michael Culkin *(Mr. Leigh)*; Annabelle Apsion *(Mrs. Leigh)*; Don Brady *(Frank McCoo)*; Trip Hamilton *(Doctor Blue)*; Michael Dolan *(Dick)*; Hallee Hirsh *(Little Girl Bunny Suit)*; Scot Brian Higgs *(Policeman at Accident)*; Mert Hatfield *(Policeman at Accident)*; Chris Jarman *(Policeman)*; Hudson Lee Long *(Elderly Clerk)*; Jim Grimshaw *(Policeman)*; Lenore Banks *(Nurse at Hospital)*; Dorothy Deavers *(Receptionist)*; Donnie Boswell Sr. *(Taxi Driver)*; Judy Duggan *(Solo Singer/Piano Player)*; Margaret Hammonds *(Nurse)*; Paula Davis *(Motel Clerk)*; Tim Gallin *(Hospital Orderly)*

After years of sitting on the shelf, Adrian Lyne's embattled LOLITA finally debuted in 1998 with a whimper on Showtime (before receiving a limited theatrical release), which seems appropriate considering that it ultimately feels like an extended episode of the cable channel's "Red Shoe Diaries" series and like most "serious" cable movies, is pretentious, superficial, and utterly humorless.

While in France in 1921, 14-year-old Humbert Humbert (Ben Silverstone) falls madly in love with a young girl who suddenly dies, leaving Humbert devastated and forever obsessed with pubescent girls. In 1947, Humbert (Jeremy Irons) moves to America to teach at a small New England college and takes a room at the house of the widowed Charlotte (Melanie Griffith). Humbert becomes fixated on Charlotte's precocious 12-year-old daughter Lolita (Dominique Swain) and marries Charlotte just to be near her. Charlotte learns about Humbert's love for Lolita by reading his diary, but she's immediately hit by a car and killed after running out of the house. After Humbert picks up Lolita from summer camp, they drive across the Midwest, stopping at a number of motels along the way, and finally make love. At one of the motels, they meet a writer named Clare Quilty (Frank Langella), who takes an inordinate interest in their activitites.

When Lolita begins prep school, she performs in a school play that was written by Quilty, and the insanely jealous Humbert comes to believe that she is cheating on him. While on another driving trip, Humbert sees that a car is following them, and later, Lolita is stricken with a virus and has to stay in the hospital. The next day, Humbert learns that Lolita has already been checked out by her "uncle," and he frantically searches for her to no avail. Three years later, Humbert receives a letter from Lolita, who tells him she's married, pregnant, and destitute. When he goes to see her, he gives her $4,000 and asks her to come away with him, but she refuses. She reveals that it was Quilty whom she ran off with and that he's a degenerate pedophile. Humbert tracks Quilty down and kills him and is then arrested.

A post-script states that Humbert died in prison and Lolita died giving birth.

After all the ridiculous media furor and controversy, all that matters is the quality of the film, and the salient issue is not whether a work of art glorifies perversion or immorality, but whether it's an artistic achievement. In this regard, LOLITA is an irrefutable failure. Whether or not it is more faithful to the letter of Nabokov's novel than Stanley Kubrick's highly entertaining 1962 black comedy version is irrelevant, since Lyne and his writer are no longer constrained by the Draconian production code, and they have almost completely ignored the novel's (and Kubrick's) biting satire of mid-century, middle-class American mores. Instead, Lyne makes the fatal mistake of treating the material as if it were a poignant tragedy about Humbert, pouring on somber narration about his "poisonous wound" and a faux-lyrical, recycled score by Ennio Morricone, and flooding every image with smoke and streams of blue light in the same slick fashion-commercial style he has previously lavished on such penetrating social studies as FLASHDANCE (1983), 9 1/2 WEEKS (1986), and INDECENT PROPOSAL (1993).

The film is not so much directed as art directed, with more detail and attention paid to the period sets, costumes, cars, and music, than to a grasp of the material or a cohesive mise en scene (alternating between hazy softcore images straight out of a David Hamilton photo book, frenetic handheld shots, and distorted nightmares). And Lyne's lurid visuals belie his ostensibly high-minded approach, resulting in endlessly vulgar tease shots: Humbert's first vision of Lolita, stretched out on the grass in a clingy wet dress as a pair of sprinklers strategically placed next to her backside squirt water in slow-motion; Lolita suggestively removing her retainer; Lolita rubbing Humbert's crotch with her bare foot; Lolita with a milk mustache; Lolita sucking on a banana; Lolita doing anything, period. Despite good performances by Jeremy Irons and Dominique Swain, the only time the film achieves the pathos it strains for is the ending where Humbert hears a group of children at play and realizes he's stolen Lolita's youth and innocence, yet Lyne once again undermines the impact by resorting to a cheap final shot of the young Lolita's head on a pillow and a post-credits shot of her flipping an apple in the air, both in leering slow-motion, naturally. *(Profanity, nudity, violence, sexual situations.)*—M.S.

d, Adrian Lyne; p, Mario Kassar, Joel B. Michaels; w, Stephen Schiff, Harold Pinter, James Dearden (based on the novel by Vladimir Nabokov); ph, Howard Atherton; ed, Julie Monroe, David Brenner; m, Ennio Morricone; prod d, Jon Hutman; art d, W. Steven Graham; set d, Debra Schutt, Steve Parenti; sound, Franco Patrignani (engineer), Fabio Venturi (engineer), Charles Wilborn (mixer); fx, Jeffrey A. Okun, Joseph Mercurio; casting, Tracy Kilpatrick, Ellen Chenoweth; cos, Judianna Makovsky; makeup, Richard Dean; stunts, Danny Aiello Aiello

Romance/Drama **(PR: O MPAA: R)**

LOLITA 2000

(SEE: LOLIDA 2000)

LOS LOCOS ★★½

(U.S., 1997) 99m Volcanic Films; PolyGram Films; Propaganda Films; Van Peebles Films ~ PolyGram Video c
(AKA: LOS LOCOS: POSSE RIDES AGAIN)

Mario Van Peebles *(Chance)*; Rene Auberjonois *(Presidente)*; Tom Dorfmeister *(Baby Brother)*; Paul Lazar *(Beck)*; Rusty Schwimmer *(Sister Drexel)*; Danny Trejo *(Batista Manuel)*; Melora Walters *(Allison)*; Eric Winzenried *(Spackman)*; Jean Speegle Howard *(Mother Superior)*; Jim Cody Williams *(Wyatt)*; Reno Wilson *(Deacon)*; Brian "Skinny B" Lewis *(Thomas)*; Marc Miles *(Spit)*; Mike Traylor *(Rat)*; Sam Hernandez *(Ortiz Batista)*; Frank Soto *(Indian)*; Lisa Vitello *(Clara)*; Marcia Charity Raymon *(L'il Ethyl)*; Robert May *(Jimmy)*; Sam Taylor *(Guitar Player)*; Joe Culp *(Captain Parish)*; Ted Parks *(One Eye)*; Joe Faust *(Sheriff)*; Terey Summers *(Shopkeeper)*; James Espenoza *(Bandro)*

Mario Van Peebles wrote, produced, and stars in this western feature that attempts to forge a new frontier in the genre, but gets corralled by its own bland plot. The film premiered in 1997 on The Movie Channel and was subsequently released on home video in 1998, with promotional materials dubbing it LOS LOCOS POSSE to create a tie between it and Van Peebles's 1993 theatrical feature POSSE.

In the Old West, cowboy Chance (Mario Van Peebles) is found tarred and feathered by an ill-tempered nun, Sister Drexel (Rusty Schwimmer), who is traveling with a band of mentally ill people whom she's transporting to a new mission. Believing him to be a fugitive, the group's aged Mother Superior (Jean Speegle Howard) tells him he will be freed if he leads the group to a mission across the desert. But after she dies, Sister Drexel keeps Chance in shackles and forces him to navigate their path. Meanwhile, in the desert, Mexican bandits, led by Batista Manuel (Danny Trejo), conduct a violent search for a whore named Allison (Melora Walters), who castrated Batista. Allison is now amongst the troupe traveling with Drexel.

Chance grudgingly leads the group until he manages an escape from Sister Drexel with Presidente (Rene Auberjonois), a idiot-savant member of the group who has an uncanny knack for winning card games. Chance and Presidente go on to win a fortune at a gambling den, but soon find themselves back under Drexel's thumb when she engages a squad of rangers to capture them. As the trip continues, they are attacked by two of Batista's men, who kill Drexel before Chance kills them. He tries to leave the group, but feels responsible for their safety. When they arrive at the mission, they find it in ruins and are forced to go to the nearby town of Dead Man's Creek. The town is abandoned and the group discovers that Batista and his men are coming. In the ensuing gun battle, Presidente and Chance are wounded, but still manage to kill Batista's men. With Batista holding a gun on Allison, Chance staggers out in the street and kills him.

LOS LOCOS is such a scattered affair that one wonders if the result would have been different had Van Peebles chosen to direct it (as he did with POSSE). Though generally entertaining, the film moves from scene to scene without really progressing. It introduces unnecessary characters like Chance's ex-girlfriend Clara and his nemesis Deacon, only to then drop them. Some comical plot threads—Allison wants to become pregnant with Chance's child, Chance wants to get Presidente laid—dissipate the film's focus energy. And while Chance is the primary character, we learn virtually nothing about him.

Despite the evident problems with Van Peebles's script, director Jean-Marc Vallee captures the look and feel of the classic western. The cast does its best, with Rene Auberjonois and Tom Dorfmeister particularly good as two of the main "locos." Van Peebles contributes a solid lead, but he could have been far more effective had his character been more adequately explored. *(Profanity, violence, nudity.)*—P.L.

d, Jean-Marc Vallee; p, Mario Van Peebles, John Vohlers; exec p, Alan Poul; w, Mario Van Peebles; ph, Pierre Gill; ed, Jean-Marc Vallee; m, Lesley Barber; prod d, Greta Grigorian; set d, Mia Boccella; sound, Christopher M. Taylor; fx, Thomas C. Ford; casting, Christine Sheaks; cos, Thomas S. Dawson; makeup, Tina Dyer; stunts, Terrance James

Western **(PR: O MPAA: R)**

LOS LOCOS: POSSE RIDES AGAIN
(SEE: LOS LOCOS)

LOST IN SPACE ★★
(U.S., 1998) 90m Space Dog Productions; Neufeld/Rehme Productions; Prelude Pictures; Irwin Allen Productions ~ New Line c

Gary Oldman *(Dr. Zachary Smith/Spider Smith)*; William Hurt *(Professor John Robinson)*; Matt LeBlanc *(Major Don West)*; Mimi Rogers *(Maureen Robinson)*; Heather Graham *(Judy Robinson)*; Lacey Chabert *(Penny Robinson)*; Jack Johnson *(Will Robinson)*; Jared Harris *(Older Will Robinson)*; Lennie James *(Jeb Walker)*; Edward Fox *(Business Man)*; Mark Goddard *(The General)*; June Lockhart *(The Principal)*; Marta Kristen *(Reporter No. 1)*; Angela Cartwright *(Reporter No. 2)*; Adam Sims *(Lab Technician)*; John Sharian *(Noah Freeman)*; Abigail Canton *(Annie Tech)*; Richard Saperstein *(Attack Pilot)*; Dick Tufeld *(Voice of Robot)*; Gary Hecker *(Voice of Blawp)*; William Todd Jones *(Spider Smith—Shadow)*

This big-budget adaptation of the 1960s TV series has kid appeal, but won't hold the interest of baby-boomer parents. The premise—a star-trekking family gets lost in space—is sound for a movie, but more concern was paid to marketing and sequel possibilities than to developing an involving narrative.

The year: 2058. Planet Earth is dying. Professor John Robinson (William Hurt), a brilliant astrophysicist but a dunce as a dad, has volunteered his family for an experimental journey to the nearest habitable planet, Alpha Prime. The rest of the Robinson clan consists of: mother and biochemist Maureen (Mimi Rogers); daughter Judy (Heather Graham), a no-nonsense physician; rebellious adolescent daughter Penny (Lacey Chabert); and young son Will (Jack Johnson), a robotics genius who dabbles with time travel experiments. Gung-ho Major Don West (Matt LeBlanc) is selected to pilot the Robinson's spaceship, the *Jupiter 2*, on its planned ten-year voyage.

Saboteur Dr. Zachary Smith (Gary Oldman) gets stranded aboard the *Jupiter 2* after reprogramming the Robot (voiced by Dick Tufeld) to destroy the ship. Will is able to gain control of the Robot and West saves the ship, but in so doing, it is flung into an unexplored section of the galaxy. Traveling into the future via a time bubble, they find a ship that had been sent to rescue them. It is infested with giant spiders that attack them, wounding Dr. Smith. Under Will's control, the Robot fights off the creatures. West blows up the infested ship, causing an explosion that crashes the *Jupiter 2* on a nearby (inhabitable) planet.

Searching for supplies, Prof. Robinson and West enter another time bubble, where they encounter a now 30-year-old Will (Jared Harris), a new Robot, and a Smith who, as a result of his wound, has mutated into a human/spider monster. Adult Will has constructed a time machine to return him to the Earth of 2058, so he can stop the mission. Young Will and the human Smith also enter the bubble, and this Will convinces the Robot to help fight the spider Smith. Major West, young Will, and Dr. Smith escape and rejoin the Robinson women on the *Jupiter 2*. Old Will sacrifices himself to save his father by sending him, via the time machine, back aboard the ship, which takes off just as the machine causes the planet to explode.

Originally intended to focus on the Robinson family's heroics, the cheap and cheesy "Lost in Space" TV show found its popularity playing up the comic relationship between Dr. Smith and the Robot. Peculiarly dark and ominous (and occasionally perverse. . . what's with the quasi-fetishistic, black rubber body suits?), LOST IN SPACE, the movie, just isn't much fun.

In the misbegotten name of dramatic seriousness, an unhealthy dose of familial dysfunction has been slathered over the narrative, and each actor is provided with a spotlight scene in which they can emote. This gives the movie an undirected, herky-jerky momentum. By virtue of its premise and the fact that the cast was all signed up for two potential sequels, the movie features an unsatisfying conclusion: everyone remains lost in space so they can have further, contractually obligated adventures. As such, the narrative is just a strung-together series of little episodes.

Though lots of money was obviously spent on the special effects, the result is little more than eye candy, effects for their own sake. Penny's pet space monkey, a completely computer-generated effect (and an expensive one) is less important to the film than it is as an opportunity for toy merchandising. Visually, all of the major action sequences are shot from the first-person perspective used in CD-ROM games. So, for instance, the (actually pointless) dogfight that opens the film is just a rapidly edited together jumble of shots with no coherent vantage point. As such, it's rather emblematic of the story to follow. *(Violence.)*—P.R.

d, Stephen Hopkins; p, Mark W. Koch, Akiva Goldsman, Stephen Hopkins, Carla Fry; exec p, Mace Neufeld, Robert Rehme, Richard Saperstein, Michael De Luca; assoc p, Chris Carreras; co-p, Tim Hampton, Kris Wiseman; w, Akiva Goldsman (based on the television series created by Irwin Allen); ph, Peter Levy; ed, Ray Lovejoy; m, Bruce Broughton; prod d, Norman Garwood; art d, Keith Pain; set d, Anna Pinnock; sound, Simon Kaye (mixer); fx, Nick Allder, Camilla Gittens, Angus Bickerton, Jim Henson's Creature Shop, Cinesite; casting, Mike Fenton, Allison Cowitt, Mary Selway; cos, Robert Bell, Gilly Hebden, Vin Burnham; makeup, Yvonne Coppard; stunts, Greg Powell

Science Fiction/Adventure/Action (PR: A MPAA: PG-13)

LOST WORLD, THE ★★

(U.S., 1998) 96m Fries Film Group;
Shostak-Rossmen Productions ~ Trimark Home Video c

Patrick Bergin *(George Challenger)*; David Nerman *(John Roxton)*; Jayne Heitmeyer *(Amanda White)*; Julian Casey *(Malone)*; Michael Sinelnikoff *(Professor Summerlee)*; Russell Yuen *(Myar)*; Gregoriane Minot Payeur *(Djena)*

THE LOST WORLD is a low-budget alternative to Steven Spielberg's 1997 blockbuster sequel to JURASSIC PARK. Though based on different source material—in this case a story by Sir Arthur Conan Doyle—we can be sure this straight-to-video wonder won't keep Mr. Spielberg from sleeping at night.

In 1934 London, a zoologist, George Challenger (Patrick Bergin), seeks to prove to a museum committee that live dinosaurs exist in the mountains of Northern Mongolia. The museum offers him reward money if he can bring back an example, and they send Professor Summerlee (Michael Sinelnikoff) on the expedition as a witness. The others who join Challenger include Malone (Julian Casey), a reporter, John Roxton (David Nerman), a mercenary hunter, and Amanda White (Jayne Heitmeyer), an anthropologist and the daughter of a late colleague.

In Mongolia, the group is helped with the arduous trek to the mountain by Myar (Russell Yuen) and Djena (Gregoriane Minot Payeur), brother and sister guides. Once they arrive at their destination, Amanda is immediately kidnapped by Neanderthal tribesmen. The travelers rescue her, but as they try to escape the area in a balloon, they are attacked by flying pterodactyls, an incident that proves the existence of dinosaurs. The skeptical Professor is finally impressed, but Myar is killed, the balloon busts, and the others crash and take refuge in a cave.

Later, Roxton attempts to flee the mountain with a baby dinosaur, as reward bounty, and leave the others behind, but Challenger stops him. Roxton is then attacked and apparently killed by another dinosaur. Subsequently, as the others try to figure out how to repair their balloon in order to escape, the Professor and Djena are killed by dinosaurs. Challenger and Amanda try but fail to save Malone from yet another attack. They return to London and keep their findings a secret, telling the museum that the dinosaurs do not exist. Meanwhile, Malone turns up alive on the mountain, living as one with nature.

The producers of THE LOST WORLD clearly hope to confuse at least a few video store customers looking for the Spielberg title (the box art design is very similar). But this humdrum sci-fi adventure owes itself more to Spielberg's INDIANA JONES series than the director's JURASSIC PARK sequel: the opening sequence pays direct tribute to RAIDERS OF THE LOST ARK (1981), femme lead Jayne Heitmeyer resembles Alison Doody of INDIANA JONES AND THE LAST CRUSADE (1989), and even the production design resembles the dusty brown look of the three Harrison Ford films.

But, alas, this LOST WORLD makes the special effects of the earlier screen versions of Conan Doyle's tale, made in 1925, 1960, and 1993, seem state-of-the-art next to the slapdash, cut-and-paste computer graphic work here. The dinosaur attacks include one violent killing, but are not particularly scary (and the tribesmen look like rejects from *Cats*). The performers don't offer much charisma, and lead Patrick Bergin seems to be settling into a sad late Errol Flynn-style career phase—looking jowly and walking through his roles. Who the film really needs is Mel Brooks (or at least George of the Jungle).

But at least this LOST WORLD doesn't include an expected, banal romance between the leads and the running time is mercifully short, unlike the 1998 sci-fi bomb, GODZILLA. *(Graphic violence, adult situations.)*—E.M.

d, Bob Keen; p, Danny Rossner, Murray Shostak; w, Leo St. Pierre, Jean Lafleur (based on the novel by Sir Arthur Conan Doyle); ph, Barry Gravelle; ed, Isabelle Levesque; m, Milan Kymlicka; prod d, Sylvain Gringas; fx, Image Animation, Big Bang Animation; cos, Nicole Pelletier

Science Fiction/Adventure (PR: C MPAA: R)

LOU REED: ROCK AND ROLL HEART ★★½

(U.S., 1998) 73m American Masters;
Thirteen Productions; WNET ~ Fox Lorber c/bw

Lou Reed; James Atlas; John Cale; Maureen Tucker; Jonas Mekas; Kirk Varnedoe; Ronnie Cutrone; Billy Name; Mary Woronov; Waldemar Januszczak; Thurston Moore; Patti Smith; Gerard Malanga; Philip Glass; David Byrne; Holly Woodlawn; Jim Carroll; David Bowie; Penn Jillette; Bob Ezrin; Mark Leyner; Bon Ludwig; Fernando Saunders; Laurie Anderson; Lee Ranaldo; David Fricke; Joe Dallasandro; Lisa Robinson; Suzanne Vega; John Rockwell; Nan Goldin; David Stewart; Mike Rathke; Tony Smith

An expanded version of a 1997 documentary that aired as part of the PBS series "American Masters" and subsequently received limited theatrical release, LOU REED: ROCK AND ROLL HEART is an overly respectful portrait that avoids or ignores too many elements of the career of one of popular music's most influential figures.

While ROCK AND ROLL HEART features some footage of singer/composer/guitarist Reed taken by his friend Timothy Greenfield-Sanders, it's fairly minor stuff. Most of the film consists of interviews with people who either knew or were influenced by Reed and archival footage, though the scarcity of such footage causes Greenfield-Sanders to overemphasize those documented areas of Reed's career at the expense of other areas for which no footage exists.

In its favor, the film does dig up some rare film, including some of Reed with one of his high school bands, and seldom-heard songs like "The Ostrich," which Reed wrote and performed when he was working as a staff songwriter for Pickwick Records in the early 1960s. That was where he met John Cale, with whom he founded the Velvet Underground, a band which was widely ignored when it was together but which had as much influence on young musicians in the 1970s and '80s as The Beatles did in the '60s. (Philip Glass, David Byrne, Jim Carroll, David Bowie, Patti Smith, and Sonic Youth's Thurston Moore and Lee Ranaldo are among the musicians who discuss Reed's importance.)

Andy Warhol took the Velvet Underground under his wing, which had the effect of introducing Reed to the avant garde of Manhattan in the 1960s. The era is discussed by Warhol associates Gerard Malanga, Mary Woronov, Joe Dallasandro, Billy Name, and Holly Woodlawn (that rarity, a gracefully aging drag queen).

Skipping past the breakup of the Velvets, Reed's brief retirement from music and his first solo album, the film visits his most memorable albums of the 1970s—*Transformer, Berlin, Rock and Roll Animal,* and *Metal Machine Music,* the latter 64 minutes of guitar feedback which is alternately described as serious music and as unlistenable noise recorded and released out of sheer antipathy to the marketplace. Most of Reed's work of the late 1970s and '80s is also passed over so that the film can concentrate on the most recent decade, beginning with the death of Andy Warhol and the subsequent *Songs For Drella,* a song-suite memorializing Andy Warhol, which reunited Reed with Cale. Honing his craft rather than fading into repetition or self-parody as do many musicians of his age, Reed is shown to be at the top of his powers, continuing to write songs about particularly adult subjects while branching out into theater.

ROCK AND ROLL HEART is interesting more for the people interviewed about Reed than for anything it has to say about Reed himself. Where else could you get to see Jonas Mekas, Penn Jillette, producer Bob Ezrin, and writer Mark Leyner all in the same film? Additionally, a clip of longtime Reed fan Vaclav Havel presenting the reunited Velvet Underground in Prague will come as a surprise to many. Still, the documentary misses or avoids far too much about its subject to be taken as definitive. There's no mention of the electroshock treatments Reed was subjected to as a teenager (his parents thought it would cure his homosexual leanings). Nor, for that matter, are Reed's heavy drug use and ambiguously gay persona of the 1970s mentioned. What comes across is that a lot of well-known people think highly of Reed; it is left to the viewer not already familiar with his work to go to Reed's body of work and discover why. *(Profanity.)*—M.F.

d, Timothy Greenfield-Sanders; p, Timothy Hacker, Timothy Greenfield-Sanders, Tamar Hacker; exec p, Susan Lacy; assoc p, Karen Bernstein; co-p, Karen Bernstein; ph, Timothy Greenfield-Sanders, Frank DeMarco, John Chimpeles, Cees Samson; ed, Jed Parker, Kate Schmitz; sound, Joseph Keppler, Gerald Prezeau, Rudolph Prezeau, Zoe Sarnat, Jan Schoen, Carla Van Der Meijs; makeup, Alexis Kelley, Ashana Morgan, Bahram Rasizadeh, Lia Van de Donk

Documentary **(PR: C MPAA: NR)**

LOUISA MAY ALCOTT'S LITTLE MEN ★★½

(U.S./Canada, 1998) 98m Allegro Films; Brainstorm Media; Image Organization ~ Legacy Releasing c
(AKA: LITTLE MEN)

Mariel Hemingway *(Jo Bhaer)*; Chris Sarandon *(Professor Fritz Bhaer)*; Ben Cook *(Dan)*; Michael Caloz *(Nat Blake)*; Michael Yarmoush *(Emil)*; Ricky Mabe *(Tommy Bangs)*; Gabrielle Boni *(Nan Harding)*; Julia Garland *(Daisy Brooke)*; B.J. McLellan *(Jack Ford)*; Tyler Hynes *(Demi Brooke)*; Mathew Mackay *(Franz)*; Serge Houde *(John Brooke)*; Emma Campbell *(Meg Brooke)*; Kathleen Fee *(Molly/Narrator)*; James Bradford *(Silas Blake)*; David Deveau *(Stuffy Cole)*; Justin Bradley *(Dolly Pettinghill)*; Mickey Toft *(Teddy Bhaer)*; Frank Fontaine *(Man in Market)*; Bill Corday *(Vendor)*; Richard Azimov *(Newspaper Boy)*; Mark Camacho *(Police Sergeant)*; Michael Azeff *(Boy at Xmas Party)*

LOUISA MAY ALCOTT'S LITTLE MEN relies on the considerable vigor of its youthful cast to carry this moralistic tale, a sequel to the classic LITTLE WOMEN, of how goodness is found in everyone, even the rowdiest little boys.

The year is 1871. Jo March (Mariel Hemingway) now runs the Plumfield School for Boys with her husband Fritz Bhaer (Chris Sarandon). A new boy, Nat Blake (Michael Caloz) is saved from his hand-to-mouth existence living on the streets of Boston, and is deposited at Plumfield by Jo's kindly brother-in-law John Brooke (Serge Houde), who has married Meg March (Emma Campbell). Nat desperately wants to fit into his strange and uptight new environs, where the Bhaers even regulate fun, in the form of a weekly pillow fight that lasts exactly 15 minutes.

Though Nat is gradually cured of lying and other supposed remnants of his streetwise ways by stern schoolmaster Fritz, he is still not fully accepted by the other boys. So he is delighted when Dan (Ben Cook), a pal from Boston, shows up. As soon as the Brookes agree to pay Dan's tuition, he sets about introducing the other boys to the manly arts of boxing, card-playing, drinking, and smoking. Each violation of the Bhaer's rules jeopardizes his future at Plumfield. Jo insists that his goodness will prevail with just a little more kindness and patience, but Fritz runs out of the latter and banishes the boy. Dan returns to Plumfield for another chance. Jack (B.J. McLellan), a boy who never liked the street urchins, steals money and tries to frame Dan, but circumstantial evidence points to Nat. Jack's plan gone awry, his guilty conscience gets the better of him and he confesses. Both Nat and Dan are absolved, and welcomed once again into the family circle. Christmas spirits are dampened by the death of the boys' benefactor John Brooke, but Meg remains to watch over them.

Structured around a series of moral lessons, LOUISA MAY ALCOTT'S LITTLE MEN teeters at the brink of the truly heartwarming, veering into the implausibly saccharine more often than necessary. The boys are an interesting bunch; the weak link is the character of Jo. Hemingway need not shoulder the blame, despite the fact that her lanky good looks have never made up for her deadpan delivery. The script provides little for Jo to do but embroider compulsively, tend to the boys' wounds, and speak platitudes in the shadow of her husband, played by Sarandon as downright cold. When the school takes on a new female student, Jo is gleeful that tomboyish Nan (Gabrielle Boni) reminds her of herself at that age, but sadly Jo retains none of her own youthful, free-spirited nature.

Like the 1940 adaptation of this story, LITTLE MEN pales in comparison to the screen adaptations of LITTLE WOMEN, particularly the 1933 and 1994 versions. However, for true Alcott fans, especially those who won't mind if Jo has settled down more than a bit, for parents seeking holiday fare for the kids that deemphasizes consumerism—or in need of a point of departure for discussing honesty, a relative's death, even the expense of education—LITTLE MEN may hold enough of its own charms. *(Violence.)*— C.Ch.

d, Rodney Gibbons; p, Pierre David, Franco Battista; exec p, Meyer Shwarzstein, Tom Berry; assoc p, Elissa McBride; w, Mark Evan Schwartz (based on the novel by Louisa May Alcott); ph, Georges Archambault; ed, Andre Corriveau; m, Milan Kymlicka; prod d, Donna Noonan; set d, Mario Hervieux; sound, Donald Cohen (recordist), Simon Goulet (recordist); fx, Ryal Cosgrove, Cineffects Inc.; casting, Karen Margiotta, Mary Margiotta; cos, Janet Campbell; makeup, Patricia Morgan; stunts, Michael Scherer

Children's/Drama **(PR: A MPAA: PG)**

LOVE AND DEATH ON LONG ISLAND ★★★½
(U.K./Canada, 1998) 93m Skyline/Imagex ~
CFP Distribution c

John Hurt *(Giles De'Ath)*; Jason Priestley *(Ronnie Bostock)*; Fiona Loewi *(Audrey)*; Sheila Hancock *(Mrs. Barker)*; Maury Chaykin *(Irving Buckmuller)*; Gawn Grainger *(Henry)*; Elizabeth Quinn *(Mrs. Reed)*; Linda Busby *(Mrs. Abbott)*; Bill Leadbitter *(Eldridge)*; Ann Reid *(Maureen)*; Danny Webb *(Video Assistant)*; Andrew Barrow *(Harry)*; Dean Gatiss *(Rob)*; Robert McKewley *(Video Salesman)*; Tusse Silberg *(Abigail's Mother)*; Rebecca Michael *(Abigail)*; Jean Ainslie *(Ticket Seller 1)*; Nigel Makin *(Ticket Seller 2)*; Jonathan Stratt *(Taxi Driver)*; Magnus Magnusson *(Quiz Master)*; Shaun Seymour *(Quiz Show Contestant)*; Harvey Atkin *(Lou)*; Marguerite McNeil *(Irv's Customer 1)*; Andrew Smith *(Irv's Customer 2)*; Jocelyn Cunningham *(Realtor)*; Jeffrey Hirschfield *(Policeman)*; Tommy Hurst *(Mailman)*; Lex Gigeroff *(Cab Driver 1)*; Michael Pellerin *(Cab Driver 2)*; Cecil Wright *(Cab Driver 3)*; Charlie Rhindress *(Fax Assistant)*; Benita Ha *(Weather Reporter)*; Vincent Corazza *(Corey)*; Geoffrey Herod *(Brad)*; Ryan Rogerson *(Tommy)*; Bruce Fillmore *(Big Guy)*; Nancy Marshall *(Corey's Mother)*; Elizabeth Murphy *(The Stomper)*; Jennie Raymond *(Molly)*; Charles Jannasch *(Rusty)*; Shaun D. Richardson *(Pete)*; Mary Allison Putnam *(Girl on Bed)*; Gabriel Hogan *(Jake)*; Jeremy Akerman *(Father Bryson)*; Christine Jeffers *(Sitcom Mother)*; Morrissey Dunn *(Sitcom Father)*; Swayzee *(Strider)*; Ouzo *(Mrs. Reed's Dog)*

John Hurt gives a tour de force performance as a middle-aged writer smitten with a teen idol in LOVE AND DEATH ON LONG ISLAND, a surprisingly low-key updating of the Thomas Mann classic, *Death in Venice*. The film lacks overwhelming impact, but contains many fine nuances.

In modern-day London, the wealthy and reclusive widower, Giles De'Ath (John Hurt), prepares to write his latest study of Rimbaud's poems. Giles's knowledge of nineteen-century poetry is profound, but his experience with twentieth-century culture is wanting. On the recommendation of his publisher, Giles ventures one night to a local movie theater to see the latest film adaptation of a literary work, E.M. Forster's *Eternal Moment*. But Giles accidentally stumbles into the wrong theatre, and witnesses instead a screening of "Hot Pants College 2," a silly American teen comedy. Giles gets ready to bolt out of his seat when he notices teenage heartthrob Ronnie Bostock (Jason Priestly) in one of the roles on screen. Mesmerized by Ronnie, Giles stays through the entire picture.

Giles becomes so obsessed by the handsome Ronnie that he begins making a secret scrapbook of "Bostockian" clippings from magazines. He also rents and watches all the available videos in which Ronnie appears. Finally, after studying every aspect of Ronnie's life, Giles decides to travel to America to meet Ronnie in person. He books passage overseas and eventually settles in a motel in the Long Island town where Ronnie lives.

Giles's search for Ronnie leads nowhere until he accidentally bumps into Audrey (Fiona Loewi), Ronnie's fiancee, in a supermarket. Using his guile, Giles poses as an author who would be in a position to help Ronnie's blossoming career and talks his way into an introduction. When the two men finally meet, Giles further uses his quick wit to convince Ronnie that he has a future as a major star of artistically worthy productions. They then spend the next few days together at Ronnie's house happily discussing and planning for Ronnie's breakthrough role.

But trouble looms when Fiona begins to suspect that Giles's real motivation in meeting Ronnie is to steal him away. Thus, Fiona presses Ronnie to accept a recent offer to move to Hollywood, where they plan to get married. In response, Giles hastily confesses his love to Ronnie and asks him to come with him back to England. Shocked and also saddened by the proposition, Ronnie declines the offer. Just before leaving town alone, however, Giles faxes Ronnie a long love letter that emphasizes Giles' true belief in Ronnie's talent and also his regret over what might have been. Finally, Giles returns to England, while Ronnie, having absorbed the letter, integrates Giles's idea of reading a Walt Whitman poem during a moving graveside scene in his latest teen movie production.

The idea of revising and modernizing *Death in Venice* is a great one with many possibilities. Most of LOVE AND DEATH ON LONG ISLAND matches and preserves the wit and wisdom of Gilbert Adair's cult novel, which, of course, greatly alters Mann's original but nicely preserves the same spirit. Thankfully both book and film avoid becoming a camp spectacle, the result of much of Luchino Visconti's 1971 adaptation of DEATH IN VENICE.

In his first feature, Richard Kwietniowski writes and directs with sharp attention to detail, from the romantic leitmotif (composed by Richard Grassby-Lewis) to the flowery, old-style title sequence. Best of all, the spoofs of both "low-brow" and "high-brow" cultures permeate almost every scene: somehow, Kwietniowski effectively skewers both the stuffy, elitist attitude of Giles and the foolish, artless quality of the pop culture he is just beginning to discover. Even American "junk" food seems funnier than ever through Giles's eyes.

Perhaps little of Kwietniowski's efforts would work as well without John Hurt's superbly subtle yet daring and demanding performance (arguably the actor's best). Sadly, by comparison, Jason Priestly, while adequate, proves no match for Hurt, as he lacks that extra something that would explain Giles's obsession with his character (although, thanks to Hurt, the viewer willingly suspends disbelief). The other supporting actors fare better, particularly newcomer Fiona Loewi as the suspicious fiancee, Sheila Hancock as Giles's snoopy housekeeper, and Maury Chaykin as a friendly diner owner. Unfortunately, despite its evident virtues, the film just misses becoming an instant classic. Whether it's the casting of Priestly, the overly tidy and anticlimactic ending, or the fact that the film has a resolutely light and airy approach to its protagonist's tortured fixation, LOVE AND DEATH ON LONG ISLAND ends up being alternately moving and funny, but never as perfect as it might have been. *(Violence, nudity, sexual situations, adult situations, profanity.)*—E.M.

d, Richard Kwietniowski; p, Steve Clark-Hall, Christopher Zimmer; assoc p, Brian Donovan; w, Richard Kwietniowski (from the novel by Gilbert Adair); ph, Oliver Curtis; ed, Susan Shipton; m, The Insects, Richard Grassby-Lewis; prod d, David McHenry; casting, Kate Day, Jon Comerford; cos, Andrea Galer; makeup, Tory Wright

Drama/Comedy **(PR: C MPAA: R)**

LOVE IS THE DEVIL: STUDY FOR A PORTRAIT OF FRANCIS BACON ★★★½
(U.K., 1998) 90m BBC Films; British Film Institute; BBC Films; Premiere Heure; Uplink; Arts Council of England; Partners in Crime; State ~ Strand Releasing c

Derek Jacobi *(Francis Bacon)*; Daniel Craig *(George Dyer)*; Tilda Swinton *(Muriel Belcher)*; Anne Lambton *(Isabel Rawsthorne)*; Adrian Scarborough *(Daniel Farson)*; Karl Johnson *(John Deakin)*; Annabel Brooks *(Henrietta Moraes)*; Richard Newbold *(Blonde Billy)*; Ariel De Ravenel *(French Official)*; Tallulah *(Ian Board)*; Andy Linden *(Ken Bidwell)*; David Kennedy *(Joe Furneval)*; Gary Hume *(Volker Dix)*; Damian Dibben *(Brighten Rent Boy)*; Anthony Cotton *(Brighton*

Rent Boy); Anthony Riding *(London Rent Boy)*; Christian Martin *(Bell-Hop)*; Ray Olley *(Boxing Referee)*; Wesley Morgan *(Boxer)*; Nigel Travis *(Boxer)*; Eddie Kerr *(Tailor)*; George Clarke *(Wrestler)*; David Windle *(Wrestler)*; William Hoyland *(Police Sergeant)*; Mark Umbers *(P.C. Denham)*; Hamish Bowles *(David Hockney)*; Victoria Bartlett; William Dunbar; Julia Fodor; Christopher Gibbs; Gordon John; Pat John; Stella McCartney; Stuart Richman; Jerry Stafford; PARISIAN ART WORLD: Jibby Beane; Gentuca Bini; James Birch; Tim Burke; Liz Clarke; Jemima Cotter; Fiona Dealey; John Dunbar; Victoria Fernandez; Natalie Gibson; Caroline Hardy; Charlie Hayward; Miles Johnson; Kate St. Johnston; Ulla Larson; Alistair Mathieson; Chiara Menage; James Mitchell; Gregor Muir; Lorcan O'Neill; John Spiteri; Francesco Vezzoli; Thalia Valeta; Marjorie Walker; Gillian Young; COLONY ROOM CLUB: Maira Bjornson; Judy Blame; John Byrne; Les Child; Jake Dodds; Daniel Farson; Sandy Fawkes; David Harrison; Malcom Key; Phillipe Krutchey; Steven Linard; Alan McDonald; Norman Rosenthal; Thomasina Smith; Yolanda Sonnabend; Annie Symons; David Symons; Sue Tilley; Virginia Wetherell; Winford; Michael Wojas; RESTAURANT: Bowdler Roger; Duggie Fields; Pam Hogg; Ben Martin; Amanda Menage; William Middleton; Christina Moore; Elspeth Thompson; Tu Tu Mortimore; Nick Mortimore; Piers Feltham; Baillie Walsh; Ben Gibson; Sam Jilkes; Alan Percy; CASINO: Suzie Bick; Lucy Ferry; Simon Goldberg; David Harvey; Rifat Ozbek; Anita Pallenberg; Jimmy Trindy; Andy Walsh; FRENCH HOUSE PUB: Gaby Agis; Melanie Arnold; Matt Cogger; Angus Fairhurst; Georgie Hopton; Marco Jackson; Sarah Lucas; Jean Mortimore; Lance Patterson; Johnnie Shand Kydd; Josephine Soughan; BRIGHTON PUB: Dave Berry; Sam Chapman; Andrew Coltrane; Daniele Minns; Tracey Emin; Caron Geary; Sam Hawkins; Darren King; Donald McInnes; Martin Meister; Gillian Wearing; Johnathan Williams; Steven Zivanovic; April; Sheena

LOVE IS THE DEVIL explores the relationship between artists and their muses through the story of gay British painter Francis Bacon. Boldly artistic in its own right, the film nevertheless leaves a bitter aftertaste.

At the Grand Palais in Paris, middle-aged Francis Bacon (Derek Jacobi) is celebrated as the "greatest living painter," while back at his hotel, his young lover of the last seven years, George Dyer (Daniel Craig), overdoses on pills and alcohol. Francis recalls how the relationship started. Back in 1964, in his Soho studio, George literally drops in one night, ready to burgle Francis's house. Francis instead seduces George into bed, and their affair begins.

But while the men seem truly in love, problems quickly arise between them. George, as model and muse, enjoys his time alone with Francis, but feels competition from Francis's drunken but more sophisticated artist friends, including Muriel Belcher (Tilda Swinton) and John Deakin (Karl Johnson). Also, Francis starts tiring of George sexually and seeks out other young men, and George begins a downward spiral of drunken binges. Though Francis agrees—out of pity—to take George to his latest show in America, George nearly commits suicide during the visit.

Back in England, Francis's confidante, Isabel Rawsthorne (Anne Lambton), encourages Francis to get help for George, whom she realizes Francis still loves. But Francis rejects the idea. Finally, on their last trip, during the Grand Palais show in France, George falls completely apart and kills himself.

This sad chapter late in the life of Francis Bacon will hardly endear people to the already controversial artist, who comes across as a revoltingly egotistical creature. Yet, LOVE IS THE DEVIL is hardly meant to be hagiography; the artist's unrepentant arrogance is treated matter-of-factly, a symptom of his misanthropy. More meaningfully, writer-director John Maybury uses Bacon as a springboard to examine the artistic mind and the creative process, teasing out how love, sex, and psychosis play their respective roles.

It is also taken for granted that Bacon was a great artist, working in an unrealistic representative mode during a period of "pure" abstraction. But for legal reasons, no actual Bacon works are ever shown in the film. (One may miss seeing *Three Studies for a Crucifixion* or his *Pope* series.) Instead, Maybury, with his avant-garde background, brilliantly creates a look that mimics Bacon's grotesque style, with wide-angle distorting lenses, soft focus, dark, rich colors, skewed lighting, and (though the entire film functions like a nightmare) fanciful, disturbing dream sequences. As an objet d'art itself, LOVE IS THE DEVIL works brilliantly, both as a tribute to Bacon's distinctive techniques and as a filmmaker's aesthetic experiment.

It is as a biography that LOVE IS THE DEVIL becomes more problematic. In the tradition of other famous artist biopics (e.g., SURVIVING PICASSO, 1996), Maybury suggests excusing the protagonist's bad behavior in light of his talent and tends to make Bacon a tortured soul who, as Isabelle's character states, cared much more deeply than his public bons mots would indicate. Fortunately, Maybury allows George's downfall to represent the destructive results of Bacon's stinging words and deeds. Daniel Craig's portrayal matches Derek Jacobi's, neurosis for neurosis, in a weird S&M tango. No matter how one ends up judging the romantic relationship or Bacon's own legacy, LOVE IS THE DEVIL is both oppressive and depressing. But at least it's much better made than most films of its ilk. *(Violence, extensive nudity, sexual situations, adult situations, substance abuse, extreme profanity.)*—E.M.

d, John Maybury; p, Chiara Menage; exec p, Ben Gibson, Frances-Anne Solomon; w, John Maybury; ph, John Mathieson; ed, Daniel Goddard; m, Ryuichi Sakamoto; prod d, Alan MacDonald; art d, Christina Moore; sound, Ken Lee (recordist); fx, Alan Church, Simon Giles; casting, Anne Laure Combris; cos, Annie Symons; makeup, Jaquetta Levon; stunts, Rod Woodruff, Glen Marks

Biography/Drama **(PR: O MPAA: R)**

LOVE LETTER

(SEE: WHEN I CLOSE MY EYES)

LOVE TO KILL ★½

(U.S., 1997) 102m Goldbar Entertainment ~ A-Pix Entertainment c
(AKA: GIRL GETS MOE, THE)

Tony Danza *(Moe)*; Elizabeth Barondes *(Monica)*; James Russo *(Brannigan)*; Louise Fletcher *(Gloria)*; Rustam Branaman *(Franco)*; Amy Locane *(Beth)*; Michael Madsen *(Donnelly)*; Brian Brophy *(Harry)*; Richmond Arquette *(Lizard)*; David Ripley *(Smith)*; Glen Chin *(Chang)*; Daniel Meyer *(Ned)*; Christine Harnos *(Dotty)*; John Solari *(Ralph)*; Elan Frank *(Duck)*; David Keeps *(Jim)*; Ray Mancini *(Zito)*; John Del Regno *(Jack)*; Emily Procter *(Tammy)*; Todd Bridges *(Dr. Glick)*; Michael Goldman *(Walter)*; Moon Zappa *(Hostess Jillian)*; Freddy Deane *(Officer Biffin)*; Joe Pecararo *(Joe)*; Scott Rogers; Phil Lodwick; Hubie Kerns; Al Goto *(Blackie)*; James Lew *(Brez)*; Chris Doyle *(O'Mallroy)*

The dimwitted LOVE TO KILL falls flat in its attempts at black comedy and romance. The film premiered under the title THE GIRL GETS MOE on HBO, before it was released on home video.

Illegal arms dealer Moe (Tony Danza) considers quitting the business after he falls in love with Monica (Elizabeth Barondes), a gun enthusiast living with her sister Beth (Amy Locane) and their cancer-stricken mother (Louise Fletcher). After a gun deal turns into a messy shoot-out, Moe and his partner Franco (Rustam Branaman) enjoy a double date with Monica and Beth. The evening culminates in erotic escapades at Moe's house until Beth, romping around with a nearly naked Franco, slips and breaks her neck. Franco panics and hides the body, which Moe finds the following morning. Afraid of losing Monica, he agrees to hide it. Monica witnesses them stashing the cadaver and calls the cops, believing she's witnessed a murder. She reaches Detective Brannagin (James Russo), a dirty cop who tips off Moe.

Meanwhile, Moe and Franco attempt a huge gun deal they can retire on, but it results in another shoot-out. In Monica's apartment, Brannagin tries to prevent her from leaving, but she realizes he's covering for Moe and scalds him with boiling water to get away. She drives her truck through Moe's living room and, amidst the subsequent gunplay by Moe's confederates, accidentally kills Franco. At the coroner's office, she learns that Beth's death was indeed accidental. Brannagin, angry at Moe's amused reaction to his scarred face, is blown up trying to plant a bomb in Moe's house. Monica returns to Moe's and the pair argue and point guns at each other until her neighbor Harry (Brian Brophy) arrives and shoots Moe in the shoulder. Later, in handcuffs, the pair reconcile and promise to get married upon their release from jail.

Director James Bruce and actor/co-screenwriter Rustam Branaman, who collaborated on HEADLESS BODY IN TOPLESS BAR (1996), reteam for this feeble comedy. Lacking a cohesive plot, LOVE TO KILL never sustains much interest or momentum; the result is a boring, unfunny waste of time. Things become even more convoluted with the introduction of several unnecessary (and lengthy) scenes and subplots that stall any progress in the story. These include Beth and Monica's sick mother, a "death-brokering" scheme that a supporting character (played by Michael Madsen) tries to lure Moe into, and a car-chase scene towards the end that could have been removed completely. Performances never rise above ordinary, with Danza giving the same one-note, lovable-lug performance he's been delivering since his start on the TV series "Taxi," while Madsen does his stock bad-guy impression, with one fresh twist added—he likes to pick through the pockets of dead people. Costars Branaman, Elizabeth Barondes, James Russo, Louise Fletcher, and Amy Locane are well-cast, but play poorly-written characters. Minor celebs Moon Zappa and Todd Bridges ("Diff'rent Strokes") are amusing in brief cameos. The technical side of the film is adequate, but the art direction and sets are uninspired and reflective of the film's low budget. *(Extreme profanity, violence, sexual situations.)* —P.L.

d, James Bruce; p, Harel Goldstein, Bill Barnett; exec p, Daniel Suh, Linda Brown, Jon Laolagi; w, Rustam Branaman, Monica Clemens; ph, Keith Smith; ed, Gary Meyers; m, Barry Coffing; prod d, Ladislav Wilheim; art d, Cherie Day Ledwith; sound, Adam Joseph; fx, Kevin McCarthy; casting, Rosemary Welden; cos, Susan Bertram; makeup, Mira Tal; stunts, Bob Bralver

Comedy **(PR: O MPAA: R)**

LOVE WALKED IN ★★

(Argentina/U.S., 1998) 90m Apostle Pictures; JEMPSA ~ Triumph Releasing c

Denis Leary *(Jack Morrisey)*; Aitana Sanchez-Gijon *(Vicky Rivas)*; Terence Stamp *(Fred Moore)*; Gene Canfield *(Joey)*; Michael Badalucco *(Eddie Bianco)*; Marj Dusay *(Mrs. Moore)*; Danny Nucci *(Cousin Matt)*; Neal Huff *(Howard)*; Moira Kelly *(Vera)*; Rocco Sisto *(Jim Zamsky)*; J.K. Simmons *(Mr. Shulman)*

Film noir never seemed dreary until LOVE WALKED IN, a barely passable updating of old-style Hollywood thrillers. The absence of any original elements makes this low-rent LADY FROM SHANGHAI barely worth wading through.

In the Northern California seaside Blue Cat Club, Jack Morrisey (Denis Leary) plays piano for his sexy singer wife, Vicky (Aitana Sanchez-Gijon). Jack's old friend, Eddie (Michael Badalucco), arrives in town and suggests a way to make them all rich. Eddie, a private detective, has been hired to find out if the wealthy patron of the club, Fred Moore (Terence Stamp), is cheating on his wife (Marj Dusay). When Eddie realizes that Fred is actually faithful, he suggests to Jack that Vicky seduce Fred while they document the encounter and later use the photographs as blackmail.

At first Jack rejects the idea; later, however, he reconsiders the financial benefits of Eddie's plan and talks a reluctant Vicky into going along with it. Initially, Vicky has trouble alluring Fred during a visit to his estate because Fred, although enamored by Vicky, needs to stay with his wife, Mrs. Moore, who holds his pursestrings. But just when Jack and Eddie think that their plan is going nowhere, Vicky, feeling alienated by Jack's scheming, seduces Fred for real over a secret lunch. Eddie happens to capture their kissing on film, and shows Jack the photo. Jack breaks with Eddie. Eddie then tries to get money for the photo from Mrs. Moore, but he is killed in a car accident instead.

Later, Jack pretends he doesn't know about the lunch, and tells Vicky they should complete their con without Eddie. Jack's new plan is to have Vicky lure Fred into the master bedroom of the Moore home during an upcoming party. Outside the bedroom window, Jack arranges to be ready to photograph the lovemaking. But on the night of the party, the jealous Jack takes along a revolver instead of a camera; despite his feelings of betrayal, however, Jack cannot bring himself to shoot either his wife or his rival. In the end, Vicky leaves Jack for Fred, who in turn leaves his wife. Fred and Vicky give Jack ten thousand dollars for his troubles, but Jack returns the money to Vicky at the club where she still sings. Embittered by his experience, Jack walks away alone.

With this film and BLISS (1997), Terence Stamp seemingly has attempted to start a third act to his career by playing sexy, distinguished, though slightly creepy older men involved in twisted love triangles. Stamp is too good an actor, however, to waste his time appearing in this film, which amounts to little more than a rehash of film noir cliches. Based on a novel by Jose Pablo Feinmann, all the elements are present for a worthy homage to the noir cycle, including the bitter tone and ironic plot twists, but the scripting by Juan Jose Campanella, Lynn Geller, and Larry Golin, and the direction by Campanella (the director of the unpleasant 1991 indie BOY WHO CRIED BITCH) keep the plot strictly by-the-numbers. With Jack's nasty (and not very well-motivated) manipulation of his beloved Vicky, the plot becomes painfully similar to the sexist and degrading big-scale Hollywood melodrama, INDECENT PROPOSAL (1993).

Little of the scripters' embroidery works either—from Denis Leary's all-too-familiar monologue-rants in the club to the uninspired vamp songs (blandly dubbed in for Sanchez-Gijon by Deanna Kirk) to some very confusing and unnecessary scenes visualizing the parallel love story in a novel Jack is writing. Sanchez-Gijon (THE MASK OF ZORRO) and Stamp are charismatic performers and make their scenes somewhat intriguing, but most of LOVE WALKED IN should have been left in the shadows. *(Graphic violence, nudity, sexual situations, extreme profanity.)*—E.M.

d, Juan Jose Campanella; p, Ricardo Freixa; exec p, Jorge Estrada Mora; w, Lynn Geller, Larry Golin, Juan Jose Campanella (based on a novel by Jose Pablo Feinmann); ph, Daniel Shulman; ed, Darren Kloomok; m, Wendy Blackstone; prod d, Michael Shaw; sound, Peter Schneider; casting, Pat MacCorkle; cos, David Carl Robinson

Crime/Thriller **(PR: C MPAA: R)**

LOVELIFE ★½

(U.S., 1997) 96m Storm Entertainment; Skyline Entertainment; Dogsmile Entertainmnet; D.V. Entertainmnet ~ Trimark Home Video c

Sherilyn Fenn *(Molly)*; Matthew Letscher *(Danny)*; Carla Gugino *(Amy)*; Jon Tenney *(Alan)*; Saffron Burrows *(Zoey)*; Bruce Davison *(Bruce)*; Peter Krause *(Tim)*; Tushka Bergen *(Helene—The Blonde at the Party)*; Robert Arce *(Guy Buying Porn at the Newstand)*; Laura Cayouette *(Woman in the Window)*; Koji Kataoka *(Chinese Restaurant Owner)*; Michael Maguire *(Suit Salesman)*; Tom Jourden *(Rick)*; Claudia Gold *(Candy)*; George "Butch" Hammett *(First Guy at the Party)*; Gil Cates Jr. *(Brad—The Second Guy at the Party)*

The up-and-down love lives of six collegians are chronicled in LOVELIFE, a direct-to-video release that benefits from the talents of its ensemble cast, but suffers from a very pedestrian plot.

Danny (Matthew Letscher), Amy (Carla Gugino), and Zoey (Saffron Burrows) are all graduate students at an unidentified university. One of their professors is Alan (Jon Tenney), a narcissistic ass who's worshipped by his bartender girlfriend, Molly (Sherilyn Fenn). Danny is dating Zoey, who's visiting from Britain on a fellowship. He wants to fix Amy up with his friend Tim (Peter Krause), a reclusive oddball, but she resists because she is secretly in love with Danny.

Zoey begins an affair with Alan. After a time, she dumps Danny, and he quits school. Bruce (Bruce Davison), a divorced professor with an unprofessional interest in Molly, convinces her to take his script writing class. Amy confesses her feelings to Danny, who is still hung up on Zoey. Alan confesses his affair to Molly, prompting her to move out and land on Bruce's doorstep. Amy and Tim run into each other at a restaurant and subsequently start dating. When Danny learns that Zoey is now with Alan, he decides to pursue Amy, but it's too late. Because she isn't a doormat like Molly, Zoey and Alan fight constantly and soon break up. Molly jumps at the chance to get back with Alan, and leaves Bruce.

Several months pass. Zoey returns to Europe. Molly comes to her senses, leaves Alan, and moves back in with Bruce. Danny returns to school and renews his friendship with Amy, and since she and Tim have broken up, romance between Amy and Danny is now a definite possibility.

Written and directed by Jon Harmon Feldman, LOVELIFE is a pleasant enough little feature, but one without anything especially compelling to recommend it. With seven characters busy playing romantic tag, none are too well developed. Unfortunately, most of LOVELIFE's "young adults" appear to be thirtysomethings making their confusion about life and immaturity about love a little pathetic, and a little less enjoyable to watch than Feldman probably intended. The characters come across simply as talkative, overeducated, white individuals who actually have very little to say—making one think of the similarly directionless feature KICKING AND SCREAMING (1995). Both that film and LOVELIFE are decidedly inferior attempts to traffic in the territory staked out by Whit Stillman's METROPOLITAN (1990).

Feldman did succeed in attracting good talents to the project. Sherilyn Fenn is known from the television series "Twin Peaks," Carla Gugino and Matthew Letscher scored high profile supporting roles in 1998 releases (SNAKE EYES and THE MASK OF ZORRO, respectively), and Bruce Davison was nominated for an Oscar for LONGTIME COMPANION (1990). *(Profanity.)*—P.R.

d, John Harmon Feldman; p, Todd Hoffman; exec p, H. Michael Heuser, Gary Abramson, Dave Fleming; assoc p, Fuller French; co-p, Elan Sassoon, Jason Goldberg; w, John Harmon Feldman; ph, Anthony Jannelli; ed, Samuel Craven; m, Adam Fields; prod d, Nanci B. Roberts; set d, Tiffany Cowsill; sound, D.J. Ritchie; casting, Bruce H. Newburg; cos, Danielle King

Romance/Comedy **(PR: C MPAA: R)**

LOVER GIRL ★★

(U.S., 1997) 87m Dream Entertainment; Peninsula Films ~ Bedford Entertainment c

Sandra Bernhard *(Marci)*; Tara Subkoff *(Jake)*; Loretta Devine *(Coco)*; Susan Barnes *(Jean)*; Kristy Swanson *(Darlene)*; Tim Griffin *(Wright)*; Renee Humphrey *(Teddy)*; Sahara Lotti *(Bambi)*; Larry Termo *(Mr. Johnny)*; Robert Romanus *(Mr. Hairdresser)*; William Utay *(Mr. Smith)*; Eric Siegel *(Disgruntled John)*; Kurt Bryant *(Hank)*; Cullen Chambers *(Ed)*

The topic of teen prostitution gets light treatment in LOVER GIRL, a moderately enjoyable but ultimately forgettable effort from first-time feature filmmakers Lisa Addario and Joe Syracuse. The film traveled the festival circuit in 1997 and was released to home video in 1998.

Abandoned by her mother, 16-year-old Jake (Tara Subkoff) shows up on the doorstep of her older sister, Darlene (Kristy Swanson), who turns her away. Broke and alone, Jake sleeps outside until Marci (Sandra Bernhard), Darlene's neighbor and the manager of a nearby massage parlor, reluctantly takes her in. Jake quickly surmises that Marci and her staff—Coco (Loretta Devine), Teddy (Renee Humphrey), and Bambi (Sahara Lotti)—do more than just shiatsu their clients. She wants to learn the trade, but Marci won't allow it because she's underage. But after Jake takes a client on the sly and pulls in more money than the other girls, Marci senses Jake's potential to become the cathouse's cash cow. She lets Jake work—provided she hides when the owner, Jean (Susan Barnes), comes around.

Jake quickly bonds with Marci and the girls, who share an apartment and pool their earnings. It's the closest thing she has ever had to family. When Darlene sees the money her little sister is raking in, she wants in on the action. She gets hired at the spa, where she butts heads with Marci and exposes Jake's secret employment. The high times are over, and none too soon for Jake, who has decided that she isn't cut out for the business. Marci, who has developed maternal affection for Jake, perhaps as a surrogate for the daughter she gave up for adoption years ago, pledges to take care of her.

Addario and Syracuse conceived the idea for their script after moving into a neighborhood rife with massage parlors. To research the project, Syracuse toiled with a company called "Wet, Hot and Wild," which receives an acknowledgment in the closing credits. But rather than exposing pseudo-massage parlors, this film strives to defend them, and to challenge the stereotypical image of sex workers. The women in LOVER GIRL are independent, forward-thinking businesswomen who found the path to female empowerment while letting their fingers do the walking.

Surprisingly absent from the film—considering the subject matter—are nudity and gratuitous sex. The script is deliberately vague about just how far Jake goes with her clients, and the girls are never seen in less than bras and panties. Also absent is any moralizing. Though Jake expresses regret over her working days, she seems neither traumatized nor transformed by the experience. The message seems to be: borderline prostitution is OK, but wait until you're 18.

Bernhard gives an atypically subdued performance, balancing her character's toughness with emerging motherly tenderness. Subkoff appears too mature for the lead role of a candy-craving teen. Her characterization lacks vulnerability, a trait that might have raised the stakes of the action. Standouts among the supporting cast are Devine as a brassy masseuse, and Tim Griffin as Jake's first customer, a bashful mechanic who falls in love with her. *(Sexual situations, adult situations, extreme profanity.)*—B.R.

d, Lisa Addario, Joe Syracuse; p, Larry Rattner, Ehud Bleiberg, Yitzhak Ginsberg, Mark Pierce; exec p, Allison Anders; co-p, Ross Hammer, Lansing Parker; w, Lisa Addario, Joe Syracuse; ph, Dean Lent; ed, Poppy Das; m, Mark Kilian; prod d, Elizabeth A. Scott; set d, Heather Gulko; sound, Jason Maltz; casting, Heidi Klein, Robin Klein; cos, Victoria Farrell; makeup, Susan Reiner

Drama/Comedy **(PR: O MPAA: R)**

M

MADELINE ★★★½

(U.S., 1998) 89m Jaffilms; Madeline Films; Columbia TriStar ~ Columbia TriStar c

Frances McDormand *(Miss Clavel)*; Nigel Hawthorne *(Lord Covington)*; Hatty Jones *(Madeline)*; Ben Daniels *(Leopold—the Tutor)*; Stephane Audran *(Lady Covington)*; Arturo Venegas *(Mr. Spanish Ambassador)*; Katia Caballero *(Mrs. Spanish Ambassador)*; Chantal Neuwirth *(Helene—the Cook)*; Kristian De La Osa *(Pepito)*; Clare Thomas *(Aggie)*; Bianca Strohmann *(Victoria)*; Christina Mangani *(Chantal)*; Rachel Dennis *(Lucinda)*; Pilar Garrard *(Beatrice)*; Jessica Mason *(Serena)*; Alix Ponchon *(Lolo)*; Emilie Jessula *(Elizabeth)*; Eloise Eonnet *(Sylvette)*; Alice Lavaud *(Veronica)*; Morgane Farcat *(Marie-Odile)*; Alexis Desseaux *(Louis—the Painter)*; George Harris *(Mr. Liberian Ambassador)*; Marie-Noelle Eusebe *(Mrs. Liberian Ambassador)*; Ash Varrez *(Mr. Indian Ambassador)*; Yayu Naidu *(Mrs. Indian Ambassador)*; Alexandre Arbatt *(Mr. Uzbekhistani Ambassador)*; Katya Tchenko *(Mrs. Uzbekhistani Ambassador)*; Julien Maurel *(Idiot Popopov)*; Raphael Beauville *(Idiot Popopov)*; Choukri Gabteni *(Idiot Popopov)*; Luc Florian *(Chief Gendarme)*; Luca Vellani *(Chauffeur)*; Emile Abossolo M'Bo *(Circus Barker)*; Marianne Groves *(Admitting Nurse)*; Christian Mulot *(Hospital Doctor)*; Christophe Guybet *(Paramedic)*

Director Daisy von Scherler Mayer's episodic adaptation conveys much of the charm contained in Ludwig Bemelmans's *Madeline* series of children's books.

Madeline (Hatty Jones) is a spunky student at a Catholic boarding school. An orphan, she is the favorite of Miss Clavel (Frances McDormand), the nun who runs the school. Madeline serves as a ringleader for her classmates; the group engages in minor mischief on the streets of Paris and within the mansion that serves as their school and home.

When the health of the school's beloved benefactor Lady Covington (Stephane Audran) fails, her husband, Lord Covington (Nigel Hawthorne) plans to withdraw support and sell the mansion. Madeline is subsequently struck by appendicitis, and she bonds with the dying Lady Covington during their concurrent hospitalization. Madeline soon recovers, only to skip headlong into another mishap: she falls into the Seine and is rescued by a stray dog who becomes the girls' secret pet. The very independently minded Miss Clavel tolerates this flagrant violation of Lord Covington's rule against animals on his property.

Meanwhile, the Spanish ambassador to France and his wife move in next door, and their son Pepito (Kristian De La Osa) torments the girls, especially Madeline, with his practical jokes and sultry good looks. Later, while everyone attends a lively carnival, Pepito's greedy tutor kidnaps his charge and Madeline. The young duo must overcome their differences to outsmart their kidnapper and escape his clutches. They soon do, and Madeline is safely reunited with Miss Clavel and her pals. However, Lord Covington's plan to sell the mansion threatens to separate them all for good. Madeline, desperate to remain in Miss Clavel's care, devises a twofold plan. First, she frightens off a diverse parade of prospective buyers—all ambassadors to France from various parts of the world—by enlisting Pepito to take some well-timed spins around the premises on his noisy motorbike, and by assigning the girls the task of hiding the cook's Limburger cheese in strategic locations in the mansion. Next, she confronts Lord Covington directly, and with just one heartfelt speech, convinces him to change his mind in order to honor his wife's memory.

Some viewers, young and not-so-young, may balk at MADELINE's sentimentality, but the film's episodic structure is designed for short attention spans, and thus attempts to also dole out adequate measures of suspense and humor. MADELINE also offers girls a role model of considerable ingenuity, even if she is remarkably similar to the heroine of Mayer's PARTY GIRL (1994)—in that she only plays at being a bad girl, and achieves true happiness only by being a very good girl. (Of course, Madeline's counterpart in PARTY GIRL is an adult—a twentysomething New Yorker who gives up a life devoted to shopping and nightclubbing to become a librarian.)

Amid so much cuteness and cleverness, McDormand's Miss Clavel registers as capable, big-hearted, and more devoted than devout (in addition to having the right amount of prim-and-properness required for an instructor at a Catholic school). Known for her work in much quirkier adult fare (such as her Academy Award-winning performance in the Coen brothers' FARGO), she brings a worldly edge to the role.

Adults may appreciate the film's unexpected visual pleasures, which come courtesy of von Scherler Mayer's talented collaborators. Cinematographer Pierre Aim (who also shot HATE) and production designer Hugo Luczyc-Wyhowski (who worked on MY BEAUTIFUL LAUNDRETTE and PRICK UP YOUR EARS, and the 1998 releases NIL BY MOUTH and COUSIN BETTE) imbue MADELINE with a color palette and composition that's evocative of its dual setting—Paris, on the one hand, and the fanciful world of storybooks and childhood memories on the other. —C.Ch.

d, Daisy von Scherler Mayer; p, Stanley Jaffe, Allyn Stewart, Saul Cooper, Pancho Kohner; exec p, Stanley Jaffe; w, Mark Levin, Jennifer Flackett (from a story by Mark Levin, Jennifer Flackett and Malia Scotch Marmo; based on characters from the children's books by Ludwig Bemelmans); ph, Pierre Aim; ed, Jeffrey Wolf; m, Michel LeGrand; prod d, Hugo Luczyc-Wyhowski; art d, Bertrand Clercq-Roques, Gerard Drolon, Rebecca Holmes; set d, Aline Bonetto; sound, Michael Kharat (mixer); fx, Graham Longhurst, Graham Hills; casting, Karen Lindsay-Stewart; cos, Michael Clancy; makeup, Nathalie Tissier, Beya Gasmi, Dominique Galichet; stunts, Remy Julienne, Daniel Verite, Michel Norman

Children's/Comedy/Adventure (PR: AA MPAA: PG)

MAFIA!

(SEE: JANE AUSTEN'S MAFIA!)

MAGNIFICENT WARRIORS ★★★½

(Hong Kong, 1987) 91m D&B Films Co.,Ltd. ~ Tai Seng c

Michelle Yeoh, billed as Michelle Kheng *(Fok Ming-ming)*; Richard Ng *(Drifter)*; Derek Yee, billed as Yee Tung Shing *(Paulina Wong/Lilly Wang)*; Lowell Lo *(Youda)*; Chindy Lau *(Chin Chin)*; Tetsuya Matsui *(General Toga)*; Hwang Jang Lee *(Japanese Leader)*; Lo Mang *(Japanese Collaborator)*; Ku Feng *(Grandpa)*; Feng Ko An *(Phony Agent #003)*

Michelle Yeoh stars in a rousing and well-mounted historical action picture, playing a female Indiana Jones roaming a early 1940s rendition of a spaghetti western landscape.

In a Japanese-occupied province of China in 1938, mercenary gun-running pilot Fok Ming-ming (Michelle Yeoh) is hired to retrieve Youda (Lowell Lo), leader of the city of Kaal, who has information about a poison gas plant the Japanese are planning to build. After shooting down a pursuing Japanese plane, Fok arrives in time to rescue a person she thinks is her local contact, but is in fact a self-interested drifter (Richard Ng). The pair of them are then caught by Japanese agents and saved by Fok's real contact, Paula Wong (Derek Yee). Together they spirit Youda away, along with his sort-of-girlfriend, Chin-chin (Chindy Lau).

But they need fuel for Fok's plane, and Wong has sworn to kill the Japanese leader, General Toga (Tetsuya Matsui). Heading back into town, they are ambushed and, despite a valiant fight, are captured and sentenced for execution. The townspeople rally to save them and drive Toga from Kaal; he soon returns with troops and besieges the town. With guns, spears, arrows and rocks the townspeople defend themselves, capturing Toga, then mercifully set him free. He returns the favor by warning them of a huge incoming army, and the locals burn their town to keep it from Japanese hands.

Director David Chung (who helmed Yeoh's previous picture, ROYAL WARRIORS), delivers a modern swashbuckler, filling the wide screen with strong compositions and high production values (model planes notwithstanding), matched by an appropriately epic orchestral score. The script not only includes an overload of visceral action but a genuine emotional payoff, building to a crescendo when the townspeople rebel, followed by a bloody climax when they defend their homeland. Rousing moments abound, as when comic relief Richard Ng and Lowell Lo (better known for his many film soundtracks, including one for John Woo s trendsetting THE KILLER) separately graduate from cowards to heroes, and when a jeep full of the leads fight their way past the enemy and promptly turn around to rescue a fallen comrade. Even the aggressive Japanese leader develops a twinge of conscience at the end, an anomalous occurrence for a Chinese film.

Filmed in Taiwan on a three-week shoot that stretched to three grueling and expensive months, it was released in Asia in 1987 and on US video in 1998. Michelle Yeoh (billed as Michelle Kheng, distilled from her given Malaysian name) would star in only one more non-action role before a short-lived marriage and temporary retirement. Co-star Derek Yee had starred in a series of elaborate swordplay fantasies for the Shaw Brothers studio starting in the late 1970s, going on to become a more serious actor and, beginning in 1986 with THE LUNATICS, a highly respected director. Never overly skilled in combat, he was nonetheless terrifically charismatic, and shines as a romantic lead. *(Violence, profanity.)*—A.B.

d, David Chung; p, John Shum, billed as John Sham; exec p, Dickson Poon; assoc p, Yan T. Wong; w, Tsang Kan Cheong; ph, Ma Chun Wah, Law Wan Shing; ed, Chang Kwok Kuen; m, Chan Wing Leung; prod d, Oliver Wong

Action **(PR: C MPAA: NR)**

MAJOR LEAGUE: BACK TO THE MINORS ★★
(U.S., 1998) 90m Morgan Creek; Warner Bros. ~ Warner Bros. c

Scott Bakula *(Gus Cantrell)*; Corbin Bernsen *(Roger Dorn)*; Dennis Haysbert *(Pedro Cerrano)*; Takaaki Ishibashi *(Taka Tanaka)*; Jensen Daggett *(Maggie Reynolds)*; Eric Bruskotter *(Rube Baker)*; Bob Uecker *(Harry Doyle)*; Ted McGinley *(Leonard Huff)*; Walton Goggins *("Downtown" Anderson)*; Kenneth Johnson *(Lance Pere)*; Judson Milles *(Hog Ellis)*; Lobo Sebastian *(Carlos Liston)*; Thom Barry *(Pops Morgan)*; Peter Mackenzie *(Doc Windgate)*; Tim DiFilippo *(Juan #1)*; Tom DiFilippo *(Juan #2)*; Ted DiFilippo *(Juan #3)*; Steve Yeager *(Coach Duke Temple)*; Larry Brandenburg *(Chuck Swartebs)*; Jack Baun *(Chuck Ledbetter)*; Mike Schatz *(Renegades Batter)*; Joe Kelly *(Miracles Catcher)*; J. Don Ferguson *(Umpire)*; Brian Beegle *(Young Player)*; Ted Hanson *(Miracles Manager)*; Ronald "Buzz" Bowman *(Miracles Announcer)*; Alex Van *(Billy Bear)*; Tim Ware *(Hot Dog Vendor)*; Robert M. Egan *(Rockcats Announcer)*; Michael A. Lynch *(Chief Umpire)*; Richard Bruce Doughty *(Boll Weevils Announcer)*; Al Hamacher *(Diner Cook)*; Nathalie Hendrix *(Reporter #1)*; Stephen Hardig *(Reporter #2)*; Letroy Myers *(Reporter #3)*; Gary P. Pozsik *(Reporter #4)*; Andre Tardieu *(Maitre D')*; Brien Straw *(Waiter)*; R.J. Kackley *(1st Base Umpire)*; Bradley Crable *(Twins Runner)*; Ken Medlock *(Twins Assistant Coach)*; Lucinda Whitaker *(Bar Girl #1)*; Kimberly Herndon *(Bar Girl #2)*; Elizabeth Diane Wells *(Diner Waitress)*; Gary Murphy *(Home Umpire)*; Scott Foxhall *(2nd Base Umpire)*; Warren Pepper *(TV Reporter)*; Dee Thompson *(Head Umpire)*; Raymond Sterling *(1st Base Umpire)*; Ron Clinton Smith *(Tote Man #1)*; Richie Dye *(Tote Man #2)*; Dolan Wilson *(Tote Man #3)*; Laura-Shay Griffin *(Stewardess)*; Mark Storm *(Mr. Buzz)*; Bayani Ison *(Ishibashi Photo Double)*

More than a title, MAJOR LEAGUE: BACK TO THE MINORS is a mission statement that encapsulates the lowered sights and diminished expectations of this sequel. That's not necessarily a bad thing; this installment is mostly harmless and as inoffensive as a lazy summer afternoon at the ballpark.

Gus Cantrell (Scott Bakula) is a washed-up minor-league pitcher when Roger Dorn (Corbin Bernsen), owner of the Minnesota Twins, approaches him to manage the minor-league Buzz. Encouraged by his girlfriend Maggie (Jensen Daggett) and egged on by his rivalry with Twins manager Leonard Huff (Ted McGinley), Gus takes the job.

Dorn wants Gus to baby-sit star player "Downtown" Anderson (Walton Goggins), whose bat is dwarfed only by his ego. Though the Buzz are otherwise populated by a collection of misfits, Gus's emphasis on teamwork leads them into a winning season. He recruits Pedro Cerrano (Dennis Haysbert), who is making a comeback, and lures Taka Tanaka (Takaaki Ishibashi) out of retirement.

When Gus claims his team can beat the Twins because they have more team unity, Dorn sets up an exhibition game. Huff exhorts his team to humiliate Gus, who tells his guys to have fun. With the Twins on the verge of losing the game, Huff fakes a "power outage" to avoid further humiliation.

When hotshot Anderson is called up to the Twins, Gus begs him to stay because he's not ready, but the kid thinks Gus is simply jealous. The Buzz go into a tailspin, and Anderson struggles in the majors. The Buzz pull together and get back on a winning streak. Chastened by his experience in the majors, Anderson returns to the Buzz, asking for Gus's help.

The Buzz finish in first place, and Gus again challenges the Twins, this time putting up his annual salary against Huff's job. Using the lessons they have learned, the Buzz win the game. But Gus turns down the Twins job in order to keep teaching young talent. He marries Maggie.

This sequel is most notable for what it lacks compared to earlier MAJOR LEAGUE entries: Charlie Sheen, Tom Berenger, or any bankable big-screen names. Instead we get former top-TV names like Bernsen and Bakula. The film also switches venues to concentrate primarily on the seedier minor leagues.

Writer-director John Warren played some semi-pro ball, so he has a feel for the backwaters of the national pastime. But the film is weak on character development and story conflict. The Buzz aren't a team so much as a collection of walking character flaws whose obstacles (and the film's finale) are telegraphed from the moment they're introduced.

Bakula, so appealing on TV's "Quantum Leap", hits one out of the park here, loping through his role as a likable guy with practiced ease. He's convincing as the world-weary charmer with enough experience and charisma to lead by example. Bernsen ("LA Law") and Haysbert know their roles cold in their third go-round. They're joined once again by Bob Uecker as play-by-play man Doyle, who is overused; the camera jumps to him for a comment in almost every other scene. The strikingly attractive Daggett manages to make an impression in a surprisingly old-fashioned role: the unquestioning, supportive girlfriend.

MAJOR LEAGUE: BACK TO THE MINORS focuses major-league effort on a minor-leauge accomplishment. It may not be a hit for the cycle, but it manages a broken-bat single. *(Profanity.)*—J.Di.

d, John Warren; p, James G. Robinson; exec p, Bill Todman Jr., Michael I. Rachmil, Gary Barber; w, John Warred; ph, Tim Suhrstedt; ed, O. Nicholas Brown, Bryan H. Carroll; m, Robert Folk; prod d, David Crank; set d, Frank Galline; sound, Carl Rudisill (mixer); casting, Pam Dixon Mickelson; cos, Mary E. McLeod; makeup, Vivian Baker; stunts, Cal Johnson

Sports/Comedy **(PR: A MPAA: PG-13)**

MAKER, THE ★★

(U.S., 1997) 98m Millennium Films; Maker Productions; Demitri Samaha Productions; Mad Chance ~ Nu Image c

Matthew Modine *(Walter)*; Jonathan Rhys Meyers *(Josh Minnell)*; Mary-Louise Parker *(Officer Emily Peck)*; Fairuza Balk *(Della Soto)*; Michael Madsen *(Skarny)*; Jesse Borrego *(Felice)*; Kate McGregor-Stewart *(Mother Minnell)*; Lawrence Pressman *(Father Minnell)*; Jeff Kober *(Rubicon)*; Matthew David James *(Ike)*; Marc Worden *(Simon)*; Joel McKinnon Miller *(Customs Officer)*; Robert Gossett *(Partner)*; Kimberly Wallis *(Saleswoman)*; Kate Murtagh *(Large Matron)*; Carrie Boren *(Nurse)*; Ben Scott *(Cowboy)*; Scott Kraft *(Cowboy)*; Jason Kane *(Man)*; Jennifer Griffin *(Woman)*; Teddy Lane Jr. *(Cop)*; Ray Quartermus *(Bartender)*; Francis Du Bois *(Bar Patron)*; Starletta Dupois *(Technician)*; Michael Meinert *(Khaki)*; Shannon Escher *(Cheerleader)*

An impressionable teen flirts with the knowledge that he may have the genes of a thief in THE MAKER. The criminal seduction of innocence has been more chillingly delineated in AT CLOSE RANGE (1986) and more colorfully acted in TRAVELLER (1997). Erring on the side of artiness, THE MAKER overworks its nihilistic philosophizing for an audience that's already seen better versions of this blood-is-thicker-than-water morality play.

Adopted many years ago into a loving home after the death of his parents, teenager Josh Minell (Jonathan Rhys Meyers) wins a college scholarship with little effort and spends his spare time getting high with pals. His bright future is interrupted by the reappearance of his big brother Walter (Matthew Modine), an ex-con. Having bided his time until Josh was old enough to become an accomplice, Walter preys on Josh's rebellious curiosity. Not only does he involve Josh in a moving van scam fronted by his accomplice Felice (Jesse Borrego), but Walter also reveals that their real parents were murdered because their papa was a welshing felon. Having grown up believing they died in a car accident, Josh now wonders whether he has inherited lawbreaking genes.

Walter cuts his fence Skarny (Michael Madsen) out of a deal involving the hijacking of a heart for an illegal organ transplant. During the aftermath of this hospital heist, Felice and another member of Walter's gang are massacred in a parking garage by Skarney's crew; Walter is seriously wounded. Although unable to kill the wounded Skarny, Josh does remove his money belt. Skarny pursues Josh and dying Walter to the Minnell home. Cornered in the garage, Josh pretends to be dead. With a gun positioned in the sleeve of deceased Walter's jacket, Josh guns down Skarny. The cops arrive; Josh allows himself to be viewed as an innocent bystander and turns his back on Walter's bloody legacy.

Visually inventive, THE MAKER is a superficially compelling film that adds nothing new to the environment-vs.-heredity debate. Skimming over Josh's dilemma, the screenplay never allows us to anguish with this callow protagonist over his attraction to a get-rich-quick lifestyle. Instead, it wastes our time with a subplot about Josh's crush on a female cop. What partially redeems the film are two superlatively directed action sequences. The first involves a stolen furniture van stalled on a hill in full view of a curious patrolman. Even more dynamic is the parking garage ambush. Fitfully coming to life, THE MAKER makes its presence felt as a heist caper but doesn't measure up as a meditation on crime as a family business worth deserting. *(Graphic violence, extreme profanity, substance abuse.)*—R.P.

d, Tim Hunter; p, Andrew Lazar, Demitri Samaha; exec p, Elie Samaha, Danny Dimbort, Trevor Short, Avi Lerner; co-p, Rand Ravich, Jody Hedien, Boaz Davidson; w, Rand Ravich; ph, Hubert Taczanowski; ed, Scott Chestnut; m, Paul Buckmaster; prod d, Jane Ann Stewart; art d, Maria C. Connors; set d, Karen Manthey; sound, Lee Howell (mixer); casting, Mary Jo Slater, Bruce Newberg; cos, Rosanna Norton; makeup, Jill Cady; stunts, Gary Baxley

Action/Drama **(PR: C MPAA: R)**

MAN IN THE IRON MASK, THE ★★

(U.S., 1998) 132m United Artists ~ MGM/UA c

Leonardo DiCaprio *(King Louis XIV/Philippe)*; Jeremy Irons *(Aramis)*; John Malkovich *(Athos)*; Gerard Depardieu *(Porthos)*; Gabriel Byrne *(D'Artagnan)*; Anne Parillaud *(Queen Anne)*; Judith Godreche *(Christine)*; Edward Atterton *(Lieutenant Andre)*; Peter Sarsgaard *(Raoul)*; Hugh Laurie; David Lowe *(King's Advisors)*; Brigitte Boucher *(Madame Rotund)*; Matthew Jocelyn *(Assassin)*; Karine Belly *(Wench)*; Emmanuel Guttierez *(King's Friend)*; Christian Erickson *(Ballroom Guard)*; Francois Montagut *(Blond Musketeer)*; Andrew Wallace *(Peasant Boy)*; Cecile Auclert; Sonia Backers *(Serving Women)*; Vincent Nemeth *(Customer)*; Joe Sheridan *(Fortress Keeper)*; Olivier Hemon *(Fortress Head Guard)*; Michael Morris *(Bastille Gate Guard)*; Emmanuel Patron *(Fortress Guard)*; Leonor Varela *(Ballroom Beauty)*; Michael Hofland *(Ruffian)*; Laura Fraser *(Bedroom Beauty)*; Brigitte Auber *(Queen Anne's Attendant)*; Jean-Pol Brissart *(Monk)*

Leonardo DiCaprio plays dual roles in THE MAN IN THE IRON MASK, yet another version of the oft-filmed Dumas classic that's perfectly adequate in most respects, but also thoroughly bland and uninspired as well.

Paris, 1662. Starving peasants are rioting in the streets as the tyrannical young King Louis XIV (Leonardo DiCaprio) wages war throughout Europe and sends all of the fresh food to his troops. Louis purposely gives the peasants rotten food, against the advisement of the former musketeer D'Artagnan (Gabriel Byrne), who's now captain of the king's guards and also the lover of Louis's mother, Queen Anne (Anne Parillaud). Louis orders the court's priest Aramis (Jeremy Irons), who's also a former musketeer, to kill the Jesuit rebel who is leading the revolt against him. Meanwhile, when Louis takes a fancy to a young lady named Christine (Judith Godreche), who's engaged to a soldier named Raoul (Peter Sarsgaard), the son of the former musketeer Athos (John Malkovich), he sends Raoul back into battle, where he's killed. A vengeful Athos tries to kill Louis, but he's stopped by his old comrade D'Artagnan.

Aramis calls a meeting with Athos, D'Artagnan and the fourth ex-musketeer Porthos (Gerard Depardieu) and reveals that he is the Jesuit rebel leader and that he has a plan to replace Louis. All except D'Artagnan agree to help, who remains fiercely loyal to his king. In disguise, Aramis and the others go to the Bastille and manage to bring out a prisoner who's wearing an iron mask, leaving a masked corpse in his place. The prisoner turns out to be Philippe (DiCaprio), Louis's twin brother, who was exiled by King Louis XIII when he was born and then sent to prison when his brother learned of his existence. After training Philippe, the musketeers abduct Louis during a masquerade ball and put Philippe in his place, but a suspicious D'Artagnan rescues Louis and captures Philippe, allowing the musketeers to escape.

When D'Artagnan learns who Philippe really is, he pleads with Louis to let him go, but Louis sends him back to prison. D'Artagnan gets word to the musketeers to meet him at the Bastille, and when they arrive, he arranges for them to free Philippe. He then reveals that he is the real father of the twins, and when Louis and his guards trap them all inside the prison, he joins in their fight and the guards lay down their weapons out of loyalty to their captain. Louis tries to stab Philippe, but D'Artagnan throws himself in front of the dagger and is killed. The musketeers put Louis in the mask and send him to prison, and the new King Philippe appoints them to be his royal council.

Making his directorial debut, writer Randall Wallace (who scripted BRAVEHEART) is obviously much more interested in, and comfortable with, words rather than images, resulting in a visually drab and exceedingly slow and talky costume drama which sorely lacks the panache and swashbuckling thrills that the material demands. The first swordfight doesn't even occur until almost 90 minutes into the film, making one sympathize with the pugnacious Porthos's frustrations about always having to wait for some excitement. In lieu of traditional action, Wallace concentrates on the tale's themes of loyalty, honor, and father-son bonds, which produces some rewards, but like almost everything else in the film, these are stated rather too explicitly, becoming text rather than subtext.

Another problem is that what would appear to be a dream cast of musketeers—Gerard Depardieu, Gabriel Byrne, Jeremy Irons, John Malkovich—turns out to be rather disappointing, with their disparate accents and acting styles clashing in a jarring manner. Irons, and especially Byrne, come off the best, possessing the necessary dash and style the roles require, but a very somber Malkovich seems out of place, and most surprisingly, the genuinely Gallic Depardieu sounds like an American doing a bad French accent, while his buffoonish performance as the earthy Porthos (given to "comic" farting and horniness) is more hammy than the three Ritz Brothers put together in the 1939 version of THE THREE MUSKETEERS. DiCaprio's androgynous pretty-boy looks and high-pitched voice are well suited for the hedonistic Louis, but he does virtually nothing, physically or otherwise, to distinguish his characterization of Philippe, and his superficial performance doesn't erase fond memories of Douglas Fairbanks and Louis Hayward. The Dumas novel provides such an indestructible, fool-proof narrative that it can survive even a mediocre adaptation such as this, but it could have easily been so much better. *(Violence, profanity, sexual situations.)*—M.S.

d, Randall Wallace; p, Randall Wallace, Russell Smith; exec p, Alan Ladd Jr.; co-p, Paul Hitchcock, Rene Dupont; w, Randall Wallace (based on the novel by Alexandre Dumas); ph, Peter Suschitzky; ed, William Hoy; m, Nick Glennie-Smith; prod d, Anthony Pratt; art d, Francois de Lamothe, Albert Rajau; set d, Philippe Turlure; sound, David A. Stephenson (recordist), Tony Lamberti (design), Randy Kelley (design); fx, George Gibbs, Kent Houston, Rob Hodgson; casting, Amanda Mackey, Cathy Sandrich; cos, James Acheson; makeup, Giannetto De Rossi; stunts, Philippe Guegan, Yannick Derrien

Historical/Adventure/Drama (PR: C MPAA: PG-13)

MARIE BAIE DES ANGES ★★½

(France, 1998) 90m Les Films de la Suane;
La Sept Cinema; Lelia Film; Les Films des Tournelles ~
Sony Pictures Classics c

Vahina Giocante *(Marie)*; Frederic Malgras *(Orso)*; Amira Casar *(Young Woman)*; David Kilner *(Larry)*; Jamie Harris *(Jim)*; Frederic Westerman *(Ardito)*; Nicolas Welbers *(Goran)*; Swan Carpio *(Jurec)*; Patrick Gomez *(Claude)*; Aladin Riebel *(Hairdresser)*; Andrew Clover; John Dowling; David Gregg *(GIs)*

From France, the country that has seemingly perfected the coming-of-age movie, comes this under-scripted but still distinctive tale of teenage love. In his feature debut, filmmaker Manuel Pradal exhibits quite a knack for expressive visuals; one wishes his overly familiar story line could have been half as sublime.

Orso (Frederic Malgras) is a 17-year-old resident of the Riviera who steals for a living. He gives his friend Goran (Nicolas Welbers) money to purchase a gun for him, but Goran spends some of the money on liquor, and is unable to bargain with the gun dealer. Despite the setback, Orso continues to pick the pockets of local tourists and visiting American sailors, until he is finally caught and put in a reform school.

Marie (Vahina Giocante) is a 15-year-old flirt who keeps company with the American sailors. The sailors have their fun with Marie and then cruelly reject her; she is subsequently roughed up by a group of local teens, who were angered by her pursuit of the Americans. Orso escapes from the reform school during a session of work in an orange grove. He encounters Marie, and the two (who had previously met when Orso robbed a sailor dating Marie) immediately begin hanging out together. She helps him steal a rowboat, and they journey to a nearby island. Orso asks Marie to get him a handgun from the sailors; she sleeps with one of them, and nabs a Magnum.

Now armed, the two teens rob a married couple who own a local eaterie, obtaining only a cursory amount of money from the job. As they exit the premises, the husband draws a gun and fatally shoots Marie. Orso carries her corpse to a luxurious villa he had robbed once before. He hesitates there to watch a car race on TV, and is startled by the flash of a security camera located inside the villa. He snaps, and shoots up the living room. He leaves the villa, races to find his friend Goran, and upon discovering the boy swimming in a lake, shoots him to death.

Pradal stated in interviews that he fashioned MARIE as a "fairy tale" intended to have a "timeless, mythical quality." As it stands, the film calls to mind every adolesecent odyssey from FORBIDDEN GAMES (1952) to THE FOUR HUNDRED BLOWS (1959) to THE BLUE LAGOON (1949/1980). Pradal posits a kingdom of adolescence, in which the parents of these rogue teens don't make a single appearance. This is clearly intended to "purify" the narrative, but one wishes Pradal hadn't exercised his minimalist instincts to obscure the last few plot twists; he uses a series of briefly seen, oblique images to convey Marie's death and Orso's invasion of the villa (the figure of the villa's owner, an English-speaking woman who is aware of Orso's previous invasion of her property, remains a complete cipher).

The film's chief saving grace is Pradal's immaculate visual sense. His use of kinetic camerawork (which is admirably smooth and not jumpy in the MTV manner) is meant to convey what Pradal has termed the "immediacy" of adolescence. It does indeed capture the swift changes in mood that mark youthful indulgence; thus MARIE's most effective sequences are those nearly peripheral moments (in a narrative sense) that convey the characters' joy (as in a drunken ride on bumper cars), terror (the sudden rape of one of Marie's contemporaries), and exhiliration (the requisite bucolic moments of first love enacted by Orso and Marie).

Vahina Giocante and Frederic Malgras do wonders with the roles of Marie and Orso, given the mostly iconic nature of the characters and the fact that both young people had never acted before. Pradal's casting instincts were uncommonly sound, as Malgras's real-life nomadic background as a Russian gypsy surely reinforced his depiction of the rootless Orso, while Giocante's prior experience as a dancer for the Marseilles Opera adds an innocently sensual dimension to Marie. Giocante's command of the role was so secure that Pradal allowed her to improvise in many of her scenes with the American sailors and local boys (played by other nonprofessionals that Pradal and company enountered while filming on the Riviera).

MARIE BAIE DES ANGES thus serves, curiously enough, as a bold announcement of new acting and filmmaking talent; the film itself, unfortunately, is uneven, uncertain, and hopelessly derivative. *(Sexual situations, adult situations, profanity, violence.)*—E.G.

d, Manuel Pradal; p, Philippe Rousselet; exec p, Pascal Judelewicz; w, Manuel Pradal; ph, Christophe Pollock; ed, Valerie Deseine; m, Carlo Crivelli; prod d, Javier Po; art d, Veronique Mellery; sound, Gita Serveira; casting, Marion Gervais, Frank Sant Cast; cos, Claire Gerard-Hirne

Drama **(PR: C MPAA: R)**

MARIUS AND JEANNETTE ★★★

(France, 1997) 102m Agat Films; Le Sept Cinema ~ New Yorker Films c
(MARIUS ET JEANNETTE)

Ariane Ascaride *(Jeannette)*; Gerard Meylan *(Marius)*; Pascale Roberts *(Caroline)*; Jacques Boudet *(Justin)*; Frederique Bonnal *(Monique)*; Jean-Pierre Darroussin *(Dede)*; Laetitia Pesenti *(Magali)*; Miloud Nacer *(Malek)*; Pierre Banderet *(M. Ebrard)*; Marie Darroussin; Hedi Hamzaoui; Madeleine Guediguian; Matthieu Facella; Farid Ziane; Aiani Madjibounou; Monique Meylan; Michele Camizuli; Blanche Guichou; Jacques Menichetti *(Children)*

"You don't say much, but you talk well," says Jeannette to Marius after they make love for the first time, an observation that can apply equally to the whole of MARIUS AND JEANNETTE, a charming tale of love, fate, and political protest in which romance triumphs over all in an impoverished Marseilles neighborhood.

Jeannette (Ariane Ascaride), a single mother raising a teenage daughter (Laetitia Pesenti) and a young, half-Arab son (Miloud Nacer), is fired from her job as a supermarket clerk after fighting with her boss (Pierre Banderet). Jeannette then meets Marius (Gerard Meylan), who works as a security guard at a disused cement factory, while trying to steal some paint from the factory. Marius chases her away, but later brings her the paint and helps redecorate her apartment. She tells him that she doesn't smoke because her son's father went out for cigarettes and was killed, and also that her daughter's father walked out on her; he tells her that he doesn't drink, but won't reveal the reason why. A romantic relationship gradually develops between them, but Jeannette can't believe that he really loves her and remains wary that he will abandon her.

Following a day at the beach with Jeannette's children, Marius fails to show up for dinner at her apartment, and several days go by without any contact from him. One night, two of Jeannette's Communist neighbors, Justin (Jacques Boudet) and Dede (Jean-Pierre Darroussin), go to the cement factory and find Marius drunk. They all go to a bar for some more drinking and start a barroom brawl with the other patrons. Afterwards, Marius reveals to them that the reason he left Jeannette is because her children were constant reminders of his own two children, who were killed in a car accident along with his wife, who was driving drunk at the time. Marius then passes out, and Justin and Dede carry him back to Jeannette's apartment and put him in her bed. When they both wake up, he tells her that he loves her.

MARIUS AND JEANNETTE is a perfect example of the so-called "plotless" European art film in which nothing happens, but everything happens. Essentially a series of humorous conversations, the film is given dramatic weight and romantic warmth through the depth of its character detail and the socio-political context in which the story is grounded. Set in the rundown district of l'Estaque, Jeannette and her neighbors are a bunch of socialist misfits and outcasts forever grousing about strikes, the Pope, and economic inequities, but taking life on its own terms and never acting bitter or losing their sense of humor. The portraits of all the characters are fully rounded, and the entire cast is superb. Ariane Ascaride's Jeannette is a wonderful mixture of scrappiness and vulnerability, while Gerard Meylan's Marius is a big teddy bear of a man whose giant stature and laconic facade mask a terrible pain. Most scenes take place in the courtyard, where the characters have shared experiences and their lives intertwine as they gossip about love and politics. Nothing earth-shattering happens, but events, as they do in reality, pass by in a manner that seems inconsequential, but add up to what constitutes a life: Jeannette's daughter tells her that she wants to move to Paris to be a journalist; Justin whiles away the day by having philosophical and theological discussions with Jeannette's son and the other neighborhood boys, who are only interested in sports; and in a funny running gag, the women buy lingerie from a traveling salesman, who turns out to be Jeannette's mean old supermarket boss (who also turns up later as a waiter).

Writer-director Robert Guediguian has a fine ear for pithy, naturalistic dialogue and an eye for social realism, while his unpretentious camera style is punctuated with some amusingly New Wave-ish touches, such as irising-in and -out of scenes. The film's carefree rhythm, generosity of spirit, and gentle radicalism are reminiscent of Jean Renoir's films, while its whimsical musicality (a ball floating down a river accompanied by song, Marius and Jeannette singing "O Sole Mio" while painting, an impromptu dance during a picnic; a barroom brawl counterpointed with classical music) recalls the work of Rene Clair. Though the film may be slight in incident, it offers a rich and rewarding slice of life, revealing much about a rarely seen part of France. *(Profanity, sexual situations.)*—M.S.

d, Robert Guediguian; p, Gilles Sandoz, Robert Guediguian; assoc p, Pierre Chevalier; w, Robert Guediguian, Jean-Louis Milesi; ph, Bernard Cavalie; ed, Bernard Sasia; sound, Laurent Lafran (recordist), Jean-Yves Rousseaux (mixer), Jean-Pierre Laforce (mixer); casting, Maya Sevleyan; makeup, Maite Alonso

Romance/Comedy/Drama **(PR: C MPAA: NR)**

MARS ★

(U.S., 1998) 88m Mahagonny Productions; Conquistador Entertainment c

Olivier Gruner *(Caution Templer)*; Shari Belafonte *(Doc Halliday)*; Alex Hyde-White *(Clement)*; Lindsay Lee Ginter *(Ike Ringo)*; Gabriel Dell *(Buckskin Greenburg)*; Scott Valentine *(Pete the Hermit)*; Lee de Broux *(Bascom)*; Amber Smith

(Sheila); Nils Allen Stewart *(Fargo)*; Jeff Wolfe *(Ino Templer)*; Michael Dinelli *(Male Nurse)*; Voyo Goric *(Pinrake)*; Duke Valenti *(Johnny)*; Kathryn Dwyer *(Passport Clerk)*; Paul Dallas *(Hood)*

Apparently not having learned his lesson, martial arts star Olivier Gruner reunites with the team responsible for his previous direct-to-video feature SAVAGE (1997) for this sorry sci-fi/western set on the lawless frontier of the red planet.

Mars, the mid-21st century. Caution Templer (Olivier Gruner) is a member of a quasi-religious order of lawmen-for-hire called "The Keepers." He arrives at Alphacity to avenge the death of his brother Ino (Jeff Wolfe), also a Keeper, which occurred under suspicious circumstances a few days earlier. Alphacity is a domed mining colony where "The Company" extracts Silex, a coal-like superfuel, for spaceshipping back to a needy Earth.

From Clement (Alex Hyde-White), the Company man who runs the mining operation, Templer learns that the outpost town is really run by Ike Ringo (Lindsay Lee Ginter), a crime boss who controls the dome's android prostitution and drug traffic. When he learns that Ringo is responsible for his brother's death, Templer scours several seedy dives and beats up many goons looking for him. He is joined on his search by Doc Halliday (Shari Belafonte), a medico investigating the cause of a deadly plague killing miners.

Templer and Halliday discover that Silex is toxic, and fumes from its burning cause babies to be born mutants. Ino had evidence of the truth about Silex in the form of his own infant, and was trying to smuggle the child to Earth when Clement had Ringo eliminate them both. Templer has a shoot-out with Ringo, and kills him. Clement takes Halliday hostage and tries to escape Mars, but Templer rescues her and kills Clement. The truth about Silex comes out and Alphacity is evacuated.

As if the characters' names weren't obvious enough, endless dialogue likening Alphacity to an Old West gold-rush town hits the viewer over the head with the fact that MARS is a western dressed up in sci-fi garb. The futuristic milieu is so uninspired as to suggest that plastic miners' helmets and jumpsuits were simply cheaper costumes than ten-gallon hats and leather chaps. The filmmakers suggest the Martian locale primarily by flooding occasional scenes with red light.

The direct-to-video answer to Jean-Claude Van Damme, the European-born Gruner specializes in roles that require just a few dozen words of dialogue in each film. (Apparently he can't handle even that much: his voice here is obviously dubbed.) Once its premise is established, MARS consists of Templer getting needed information and fighting various gangs of thugs. It all gets boring fast. The identity of the villain is no surprise, and the 90 minutes it takes this film to get to him seem endless. *(Violence, profanity, nudity.)*—P.R.

d, Jon Hess; p, Avi Nesher; exec p, Pascal Borno; co-p, Kathy Jordan; w, Patrick Highsmith, Steven Hartov (based on a story by Patrick Highsmith); ed, Randy Vandegrift; m, Boris Zelkin; prod d, Deren Abram; art d, Christine O'Malley; set d, Ruth O'Neill; sound, Brad Bryan; fx, Ultimate Effects; cos, Donna Marie; makeup, Melanie Robinett; stunts, Scott Leva

Science Fiction/Action (PR: C MPAA: NR)

MASK OF ZORRO, THE ★★★★

(U.S., 1998) 136m Amblin Entertainment; Columbia TriStar ~ Columbia TriStar c

Antonio Banderas *(Alejandro Murieta/Zorro)*; Anthony Hopkins *(Zorro/Don Diego de la Vega)*; Catherine Zeta-Jones *(Elena)*; Stuart Wilson *(Don Rafael Montero)*; Matt Letscher *(Captain Harrison Love)*; Maury Chaykin *(Prison Warden)*; Tony Amendola *(Don Luiz)*; Pedro Armendariz *(Don Pedro)*; L.Q. Jones *(Three-Fingered Jack)*; William Marquez *(Fray Felipe)*; Jose Perez *(Corporal Armando Garcia)*; Victor Rivers *(Joaquin Murieta)*; Moises Suarez *(Don Hector)*; Humberto Elizondo *(Don Julio)*; Erika Carlson *(Don Pedro's Wife)*; Jose Maria de Tavira *(Young Alejandro Murieta)*; Deigo Sieres *(Young Joaquin Murieta)*; Emiliano Guerra *(Boy Crying)*; Yolanda Orizaga *(Woman Crying)*; Paco Morayta *(Undertaker)*; Pedro Altamirano *(Squad Leader)*; Luisa Huertas *(Nanny)*; Julieta Rosen *(Esperanza de la Vega)*; Raul Martinez *(Heavyset Lieutenant)*; Tony Cabral *(Soldier Holding "Wanted" Poster)*; Tony Genaro *(Watering Station Owner)*; Ivan Rafael *(Small Boy at Watering Station)*; David Villalpando *(Stupid Soldier)*; Paul Ganus *(Prison Guard)*; Sergio Espinosa *(Leper Zorro)*; Conrad Roberts *(Black Zorro)*; Abel Woolrich *(Ancient Zorro)*; Fernando Becerril; Alberto Carrera; Eduardo Lopez; Gonzalo Lora; Rudy Miller; Manolo Pastor *(The Six Dons)*; Diego Sandoval *(Padre at the Beach)*; Enrike Palma *(Bartender)*; Manuel de Jesus Vasquez Morales *(Guitar-Playing Soldier)*; Oscar Zerafin Gonzalez *(Giant Soldier)*; Vanessa Bauche *(Indian Girl)*; Maria Fernandez Cruz; Monica Fernandez Cruz *(Baby Elena de la Vega)*; Kelsie Kimberli Garcia; Kaylissa Keli Garcia *(Baby Joaquin)*

The legendary masked hero rides again in this well-acted and superbly directed action-adventure gem that seems like it may have come to theaters direct from 1955. En garde!

On the eve of Spain's surrender of California to Mexico, Governor Rafael Montero (Stuart Wilson) stages the public executions of three innocents in a last-ditch effort to capture his mortal enemy, the masked hero known as Zorro. Sure enough, Zorro appears to foil the executions and escapes, a feat assisted by two young brothers. His mission accomplished, Zorro returns to his life as nobleman Diego de la Vega (Anthony Hopkins), to his wife, Esperanza (Julieta Rosen), and infant daughter, Elena. He is followed by Rafael, though, who kills Esperanza, jails Diego, and takes Elena back to Spain to raise as his own.

Twenty years later, Rafael returns from Spain; prompted by his enemy's return, Diego breaks out of jail, intent on revenge. . . until he sees Elena (Catherine Zeta-Jones), now grown into a beautiful woman who believes Rafael is her true father. Meanwhile, the two brothers, Joaquin and Alejandro Murrieta (Victor Rivers and Antonio Banderas), are doing a booming business as bandits and horse thieves—that is, until they are captured by Rafael's enforcer, one Captain Harrison Love (Matt Letscher); Alejandro escapes, and Joaquin shoots himself rather than be taken to jail. Alejandro vows to avenge Joaquin's death by one day killing Love.

Diego and Alejandro meet, and Diego offers to train Alejandro in the arts required to take his revenge on Love with skill and honor. In the underground lair below his former home, Diego teaches Alejandro speed, agility, and charm—the attributes he will need to infiltrate Rafael's inner circle and avenge Joaquin. Alejandro disguises himself as a Spanish nobleman, winning entrance to one of Rafael's rich parties; there, he is introduced to Elena, with whom he shares instant, fiery chemistry. Rafael shares with Alejandro the reason for his return: he will purchase California from General Santa Anna using gold extracted from a California mine but stamped to look like Spanish treasure. With Rafael, Alejandro visits the gold mine, worked by hundreds of peasant-slaves.

No longer simply a matter of revenge, Alejandro at last dons the legendary mask and becomes Zorro. He steals the map to the gold mine, evidence that will show Santa Anna that the gold is not Spanish after all. Knowing the jig is up, Love suggests they bomb the mine, destroy both the evidence and the slave witnesses. Both Diego and Alejandro speed to the mine to free the slaves and deal with their enemies. After an exhausting swordfight, and with the help of Elena (who has deduced that Diego is her real father), Rafael and Love are dispatched, and the slaves are freed just before an explosion buries the mine. Unable to take the strain of the duel, Diego dies, passing the name of Zorro on to Alejandro.

Directed by Martin Campbell, a film veteran whose career experienced something of a rebirth after 1995's GOLDENEYE, THE MASK OF ZORRO might be the best film of its kind since RAIDERS OF THE LOST ARK (1981). For years, Hollywood seemed to have lost the recipe for the family-friendly action-adventure movie, churning out near-misses like THE ROCKETEER (1991), THE SHADOW (1994), and THE PHANTOM (1996). THE MASK OF ZORRO effectively marries the thrill of the 1930s-40s serial adventure with the slick action filmmaking techniques of the '90s. The result is a thoroughly enjoyable movie that, while not the deepest film ever made, succeeds on every level to which it aspires. The action set pieces are especially entertaining, while the swordplay is nothing short of stunning. (Antonio Banderas apparently displayed a previously unmined gift for fencing during the making of the film.) The final sequence, in which both Diego and Alejandro battle their rivals, should be required viewing for aspiring action directors.

Much was made of the matching of Banderas and the frankly gorgeous Catherine Zeta-Jones by the hype machine, and to be honest, their dancing-as-foreplay and fencing-as-sex scenes are pretty steamy. But the real genius pairing in MASK OF ZORRO is that of Banderas and Anthony Hopkins. Both exude charm and a wealth of natural acting talent, and the chemistry between them—particularly during the training scenes—is delightful. It's a shame we won't see them again in a sequel. (Though who knows: remember Obi-Wan Kenobi?)

The legend of Zorro has been told over the course of several decades and more than fifty films. In an unexpectedly classy move (by Hollywood standards), the makers of MASK OF ZORRO did not scrap that legend in order to make their film. By passing the mask from one man to the next (and thereby implying that Diego may have inherited it in the same fashion), THE MASK OF ZORRO becomes another chapter in the rich epic. Let's hope it's not the last. *(Violence.)*—B.T.

d, Martin Campbell; p, Doug Claybourne, David Foster; exec p, Steven Spielberg, Walter F. Parkes, Laurie MacDonald; assoc p, Tava R. Maloy; co-p, John Gertz; w, Ted Elliott, Terry Rossio, John Eskow; ph, Phil Meheux; ed, Thom Noble; m, James Horner; prod d, Cecilia Montiel; art d, Michael Atwell; set d, Denise Camargo; sound, Pud Cusack (mixer), Greg P. Russell, Kevin O'Connell, David McMoyler; fx, Rocky Gehr, John Stears, Laurencio Cordero; casting, Pam Dixon; cos, Graciela Mazon; makeup, Ken Diaz, Rosa Elisa Duprat, Gabriel Solana; stunts, Glenn Randall Randall

AAN Best Sound: Kevin O'Connell, Greg P. Russell, Pud Cusack; *AAN Best Sound Effects Editing:* David McMoyler

Action/Adventure/Romance (PR: C MPAA: PG-13)

MAT' I SYN
(SEE: MOTHER AND SON)

MEAN GUNS ★½
(U.S., 1997) 110m Filmwerks ~
Film Office/Imperial Entertainment c

Christopher Lambert *(Lou)*; Ice T *(Vincent Moon)*; Michael Halsey *(Marcus)*; Kimberly Warren *(Dee)*; Deborah Van Valkenburgh *(Cam)*; Hunter Doughty *(Lucy)*; Yuji Okumoto *(Hoss)*; Thom Mathews *(Crow)*; Tina Cote *(Barb)*; Terry Rector *(Bob)*; James Wellington *(Rick)*

On the long list of Quentin Tarantino knockoffs, MEAN GUNS ranks near the nadir. Pretentious, stylistically vacuous, and numbingly brutal, this cartoonish ode to violence eschews logic, flirts with self-parody, and embraces cliches.

On the eve of the opening of a maximum security prison, syndicate spokesperson Vincent Moon (Ice T) commandeers the facility for a one-night-only killing competition in which the survivior (or survivors) will split a $10,000,000 bounty. The contest is secretly sponsored by the Mob, which actually expects no one (including Moon) to survive; all are being punished for disloyalty to their employers.

Pooling their resources, pragmatic Marcus (Michael Halsey), super cool Dee (Kimberly Warren), and loose cannon Lou (Christopher Lambert) decide to better their chances with a fourth partner, Cam (Deborah Van Valkenburgh), who has photographic proof of Moon's many crimes. In yet another rule violation, nutty Lou brings along Lucy (Hunter Doughty), a little girl he kidnapped to replace his own daughter. Among the cutthroats slugging it out with Lou's quartet are Hoss (Yuji Okumoto) and Crow (Thom Mathews), bloodbrothers whose bond is tested by Hoss's attraction to gun moll Barb (Tina Cote).

A series of skirmishes levels the playing field until only the major players remain. By lying about having located the loot inside the prison, Lou's bunch entraps and ambushes their gullible rivals. Foolishly deserting her compatriots, greedy Dee is killed before she can locate the bonanza. When Marcus finds the money, he removes and hides it, booby-trapping one briefcase. Hoss and Crow kill each other in an argument about trust, leaving Barb free to nab the explosive-laden briefcase, which blows her up. Marcus critically wounds Lou and then outdraws Moon. Before he expires, Lou retaliates by killing Marcus. Sole survivor Cam collects the money and leaves with Lucy, for whom she will be a surrogate mother.

Even if viewers can survive MEAN GUNS' deafening barrage of bullets, florid but sterile dialogue, and bug-eyed acting, the overlong film will drive them crazy with its exploitation of L'il Lucy as a symbol of innocence. Relying too heavily on catchy Perez Prado dance music to enliven an enervating presentation, the film comes off like a music video financed by the Gunrunners of America. Endless dialogue about redemption and paying for past transgressions makes no sense, given that all the protagonists are conscienceless killers. Nor does the cast possess the savoir faire needed to combine tongue-in-cheek ripostes with predatory menace. The worst offenders are Ice T, who emerges as a gangsta caricature with denture slippage, and Christopher Lambert, who resembles a demented refugee from the German band Kraftwerk. In the final analysis, MEAN GUNS plays like a Road Runner cartoon laden down with an inappropriately nihilistic sensibility. (Graphic violence, extreme profanity.)—R.P.

d, Albert Pyun; p, Tom Karnowski, Gary Schmoeller; exec p, Paul Rosenblum; assoc p, Darren Turbow, Andrew Witham; w, Andrew Witham, Nat Whitcomb; ph, George Mooradian; ed, Ken Morrisey; m, Tony Riparetti; sound, Lee Howell (mixer); casting, Teri Blythe; cos, Shelly Boies; stunts, Paul Eliopoulos

Crime/Action (PR: C MPAA: R)

MEET JOE BLACK ★★
(U.S., 1998) 174m City Light Films; Universal ~
Universal c

Brad Pitt *(Joe Black/Young Man in Coffee Shop)*; Anthony Hopkins *(William Parrish)*; Claire Forlani *(Susan Parrish)*; Jake Weber *(Drew)*; Marcia Gay Harden *(Allison)*; Jeffrey Tambor

(Quince); David S. Howard *(Eddie Sloane)*; Lois Kelly-Miller *(Jamaican Woman)*; Jahnni St. John *(Jamaican Woman's Daughter)*; Richard Clarke *(Butler)*; Marylouise Burke *(Lillian)*; Diane Kagan *(Jennifer)*; June Squibb *(Helen)*; Gene Canfield *(Construction Foreman)*; Suzanne Hevner *(Florist)*; Steve Coats *(Electrician)*; Madeline N. Balmaceda *(Madeline)*; Julie Lund *(Drew's Secretary)*; Kay Gaffney; Anthony Kane; Joe H. Lamb; Robert C. Lee; Jim McNickle; Hardy Phippen Jr. *(Boardmembers)*; Stephen Adly-Guirgis *(Hospital Receptionist)*; Leo Marks *(Party Waiter)*; Michelle Youell *(Party Guest)*; Gene Leverone *(Party Guest)*

MEET JOE BLACK is a bloated and insanely overlong $90 million remake of the quaint 1934 fantasy DEATH TAKES A HOLIDAY, in which the curious spirit of Death (Brad Pitt) comes to Earth in human form and proceeds to fall in love—as well as put the audience to sleep for three solid hours.

Approaching his 65th birthday, media mogul William Parrish (Anthony Hopkins) begins hearing voices and suffers a heart seizure. Later, his daughter Susan (Claire Forlani), is almost picked up by a young man (Brad Pitt) in a coffee shop, but after they go their separate ways, the man is hit and killed by a car. That night, a man (Brad Pitt) who is identical to the one that Susan met in the coffee shop comes to Parrish's home and tells Parrish that he is Death and has come for him, but wants Parrish to be his guide on Earth for a while before they leave. Parrish accepts and introduces him to his family as a business advisor named Joe Black. Although Susan is already engaged to Drew (Jake Weber), one of her father's business executives, she finds herself falling for Joe, and Drew clashes further with Joe over his influence on Parrish. After Susan breaks up with Drew, and Parrish rejects a lucrative buyout bid which Drew has helped engineer, Drew calls a secret board meeting and convinces the members that Parrish is being manipulated by the mysterious Joe.

The board votes to force Parrish into early retirement, but Parrish's son-in-law Quince (Jeffrey Tambor) discovers that Drew has been working as a mole for the company that's been trying to buy Parrish's and vows to expose him. Meanwhile, Susan has fallen madly in love with Joe, despite her father's warnings against it, and Joe finds himself reciprocating. Joe informs Parrish that they re going to be leaving after Parrish's 65th birthday party, and on the day of the party, says that Susan is coming with them, but changes his made after Parrish implores him not to take her. Quince brings Drew to the party and Parrish sets up a secret conference call to his board, during which he gets Drew to admit to his deviousness. Joe forces Drew to resign by telling him that he is an IRS agent who has been working with Parrish. Parrish has a last dance with Susan, then joins Joe and vanishes. Susan runs after them, but they're gone; however, she discovers that the young man from the coffee shop has inexplicably reappeared.

Director Martin Brest used to make quirky, funny films (GOING IN STYLE, BEVERLY HILLS COP, MIDNIGHT RUN) which stood apart from the typical Hollywood product because of their contemplative and perceptive sensibility. However, in the 157 minute-long SCENT OF A WOMAN (1992), the contemplation became ponderous, despite Al Pacino's bravura, Oscar-winning performance, and in MEET JOE BLACK, it has become petrified. There is no dramatic compression in the script and every scene, camera movement, edit, and line is treated with such gravity and a lack of vitality that the entire film seems to be moving in slow motion. The actors are constantly pausing between words, and characters don't just leave rooms, they start to walk away, stop, look back, walk away, stop, look back, and repeat their actions a few more times before exiting. When Parrish occasionally loses his temper and shatters the moribund ambiance by shouting, the other characters look at him with shock as if he has dared to awaken the dead.

The miscast Brad Pitt has two modes of expression—zombie-like stiffness and boyish befuddlement—as his carefully coiffed golden locks invariably fall in his eyes with a calculated casualness that could only have resulted from hours of preparation, and he's downright embarrassing trying to do a Jamaican accent during a ridiculous subplot involving a sick Jamaican woman who can sense that he's Death. Aside from the film's obvious problems of overlength, narrative torpor, and humorlessness, it's only in retrospect that one realizes what its main flaw is: although it purports to be a story about the overwhelming power of love and the idea of making the most of one's life before the grim reaper arrives, the reality is that the film is more concerned with business than romance or metaphysics, and most of the film consists of interminable dialogue scenes involving dull board meetings and dinners, showing characters sitting down to endless meals in underlit and overdressed sets. Surely, Brest had loftier intentions, but this Death has no sting. *(Sexual situations, profanity.)*—M.S.

d, Martin Brest; p, Martin Brest; exec p, Ronald L. Schwary; assoc p, Celia Costas; co-p, David Wally; w, Bo Goldman, Kevin Wade, Jeff Reno, Ron Osborne (Suggested by the play *Death Takes a Holiday* written by Alberto Casella and adapted by Walter Ferris, and the screenplay by Maxwell Anderson and Gladys Lehman); ph, Emmanuel Lubezki; ed, Joe Hutshing, Michael Tronick; m, Thomas Newman; prod d, Dante Ferretti; art d, Bob Guerra; set d, Leslie Bloom; sound, Danny Michael (mixer); fx, Connie Brink; casting, Ellen Lewis, Juliet Taylor; cos, Aude Bronson-Howard, David C. Robinson; makeup, Richard Dean, Randy Houston Mercer; stunts, Buddy Joe Hooker

Romance/Fantasy/Drama (PR: C MPAA: PG-13)

MEET THE DEEDLES ★

(U.S., 1998) 90m DIC Entertainment; Walt Disney Pictures; Peak Productions ~ Buena Vista c

Paul Walker *(Phil Deedle)*; Steve Van Wormer *(Stew Deedle)*; John Ashton *(Captain Douglas Pine)*; A.J. Langer *(Jesse Pine)*; Robert Englund *(Nemo)*; Megan Cavanaugh *(Mo)*; Eric Braeden *(Elton Deedle)*; M.C. Gainey *(Major Flower)*; Dennis Hopper *(Frank Slater)*; Richard Lineback *(Crabbe)*; Ana Gasteyer *(Mel)*; Michael Ruud *(Ludwig)*; Hattie Winston *(Jo-Claire)*; Bob Eric Hart *(Governor)*

Another entry in the parade of BILL & TED/WAYNE'S WORLD wannabes, MEET THE DEEDLES is as brain-dead as its lead characters.

Stew Deedle (Steve Van Wormer) and his brother Phil (Paul Walker) are California surfer dudes who are devoted to partying. On the verge of being kicked out of school, the duo are sent by their wealthy father Elton (Eric Braeden) to a Wyoming summer camp that will, he hopes, whip them into shape. A series of mishaps instead lead them to be mistaken for ranger trainees by Yellowstone Park Capt. Douglas Pine (John Ashton). Their first assignment: ridding the area of a prairie dog infestation that threatens the forthcoming celebration of the one-billionth birthday of the Old Faithful geyser. The boys don't take well to outdoor living, but Phil finds sufficient distraction in Pine's beautiful daughter Jesse (A.J. Langer), their commanding officer.

The prairie dog problem proves to have been engineered by disgraced ex-ranger Frank Slater (Dennis Hopper). He's using the little mammals to dig tunnels that will allow him to shift Old Faithful to a new location in property he owns, upon which he plans to open a theme park. His henchmen, Nemo (Robert Englund) and Crabbe (Richard Lineback), trick the boys into planting explosives that are supposed to destroy the prairie dogs, but instead shut Old Faithful down. Capt. Pine, already angered by his daughter's relationship with Phil, orders the Deedles out of the park. As they are leaving, they witness a boating mishap that has imperiled Capt. Pine; the boys rescue him from drowning. Back at the park, they discover Slater's plot and venture to his underground lair. There, they alter the villian's machinery and restore Old Faithful to operation, in the process delivering Slater to justice and creating and artificial lake that allows for Wyoming's first surfing.

Only Pauly Shore is missing from this inane project, a too-little, too-late attempt to exploit whatever audience might be left for airheaded "dude" humor. As it stands, Van Wormer and Walker are amiable enough, but possess no particular comic gifts; nor are they given much that's clever or original to work with. Jim Herzfeld's contrived and silly script attempts to imitate the absurdist approach of the underrated comedy FREAKED (1993). Unfortunately, debuting feature director Steve Boyum has shot the film with a hard-edged, "realistic" approach that turns the whole thing into an exercise in foolishness.

Needless to say, the film finds time for a youth comedy staple, gross-out humor—as when a laxative gas intended for the prairie dogs ends up afflicting a group of tourists and a flock of birds instead. This aspect also crops up in Phil and Jesse's big romantic scene, which involves the couple eating worms together. Despite this, Langer is an appealing presence, and Ashton tries hard with his stock character. But it's hard to know what possessed Hopper to take on the ludicrous role of the villain. He doesn't seem to know either: the actor spends most of the film looking embarrassed. *(Profanity.)*—M.G.

d, Steve Boyum; p, Dale Pollock, Aaron Meyerson; exec p, Andy Heyward, Artie Ripp; assoc p, Christopher Cronyn, Rick Johnson; w, Jim Herzfeld; ph, David Hennings; ed, Alan Cody; m, Steve Bartek; prod d, Stephen Storer; art d, Harry Darrow; set d, Robin Peyton; sound, David Kelson (mixer), Kim B. Christenssen (design); fx, Tim Landry, Ray Bivins, Camelot Films; casting, Amy Lippens; cos, Alexandra Welker, Karyn Wagner; makeup, Gina Homan; stunts, Lance Gilbert

Comedy **(PR: C MPAA: PG)**

MEN ★★

(U.S., 1997) 96m Shonderosa Prods.; Hillman/Williams Prods. ~ A-Pix Entertainment c

Sean Young *(Stella James)*; John Heard *(George)*; Dylan Walsh *(Teo)*; Richard Hillman *(Frank)*; Karen Black *(Alex)*; Beau Starr *(Tony)*; Shawnee Smith *(Clara)*; Glen Shadix *(Neil)*; Annie McEnroe *(Annie)*; Shannon Conlon *(Callie)*; Robert Lujan *(Zeke)*

Sean Young stars as a fiercely independent woman on a journey of sexual exploration and self-fulfillment in MEN, a well acted, but desultory and trite indie with a shamelessly contrived tear-jerking conclusion.

Stella James (Sean Young) spends her days wandering aimlessly through Manhattan picking up various men while living with her rich ex-lover Teo (Dylan Walsh), who has become an impotent alcoholic. Unwilling to change, Teo gives Stella a one-way ticket to LA and she winds up in Venice Beach, where she gets a job as a chef at a restaurant. Stella begins a casual affair with its married owner, George (John Heard), but still continues to have numerous one-night stands with other men. After learning that Teo has died, Stella begins dating a radical young photographer named Frank (Richard Hillman) and finds herself falling in love with him, and she quits the restaurant after George pressures her to commit to him. After a party in which Frank gets wildly drunk and Stella freaks out over his bizarre group of lesbian friends, she runs away, but returns the next morning. Stella and Frank declare their love for each other, but soon after, he's killed while taking pictures of a convenience store robbery. Stella gets a job at a new restaurant and discovers that her experiences have turned her into a strong and mature woman.

For all of its nudity, "shocking" talk about female masturbation and orgasms, and frank attempts to shatter sexual double standards, MEN ultimately amounts to little more than an explicit and foul-mouthed version of scores of similar TV-movies in which a woman tries to find herself, while also finding Mr. Perfect. Unfortunately, in the meandering script adapted from Margaret Diehl's best-seller, exactly what Stella is searching for is not made very clear, and she comes off as vapid and pretentious. When not being ravished from behind on the apartment floor of some strange guy she met five minutes ago, Stella spends most of the movie walking moodily through trendy Soho and Venice Beach locations while waxing poetically to herself with such profundities as "The air is moist and warm, dripping with the New York sweetness of half-dressed bodies, garbage, and open back doors of restaurants." Most of her dialogue is laughable ("I think I'm gonna believe in sexual anarchy"; "I'm not a caboose you can hook to some man's choo-choo train"), and the shamelessly sappy ending is poorly handled (one minute, Frank is laughing while awaiting surgery for a bullet wound, and the next minute he's dead, with Stella hysterically screaming and cursing at the doctors). This is followed by a cliched coda where Stella muses "I miss Frank, but I got answers to my questions, and this new woman I have found is alive and real," and the film actually concludes with a title card that says "The Beginning."

Disrobing with abandon, Sean Young is quite convincing as an unconventional free spirit, but she's a bit old for the role of a young woman on a journey of self-discovery, and her attempts to look girlish and innocent (such as by putting her hair in pigtails) are faintly risible. Among the supporting cast, John Heard is very good as the beleaguered and miserably married George, and Karen Black (who also co-wrote the script), shows up in a mind-boggling cameo as a blind lesbian with some kind of strange accent, but Richard Hillman (whose father was one of the film's executive producers) is fairly amateurish as the studly Frank, a sensitive photojournalist with long, blond hair and a social consciousness, whose pictures consist of "exposing America's economic unbalance." (Nudity, sexual situations, profanity.)— M.S.

d, Zoe Clarke-Williams; p, Paul Williams; exec p, Richard Hillman Sr., Dennis Ardi; assoc p, William Grillo; w, Zoe Clark-Williams, Karen Black, James Andronica (based on the novel by Margaret Diehl); ph, Susan Emerson; ed, Annamaria Szanto, Stephen Eckelberry; m, Mark Mothersbaugh, Bob Mothersbaugh; prod d, Clovis Chambaret; sound, Neal Spritz; casting, Pamela Rack; cos, Kameron Hartline; makeup, Diana Davison

Romance/Drama **(PR: O MPAA: R)**

MEN WHO MADE THE MOVIES: ALFRED HITCHCOCK

(SEE: ALFRED HITCHCOCK: MASTER OF SUSPENSE)

MEN WITH GUNS ★★★

(U.S., 1998) 128m Lexington Road Productions; Clear Blue Sky Productions ~ Sony Pictures Classics c (HOMBRES ARMADOS)

Federico Luppi *(Dr. Humberto Fuentes)*; Damian Delgado *(Domingo—the Soldier)*; Dan Rivera Gonzalez *(Conejo—the*

Boy); Damian Alcazar *(Padre Portillo—the Priest)*; Tania Cruz *(Graciela—the Mute Girl)*; Mandy Patinkin *(Andrew)*; Kathryn Grody *(Harriet)*; Iguandili Lopez *(Mother)*; Roberto Sosa *(Bravo)*; Nandi Luna Ramirez *(Daughter)*; Rafael De Quevedo *(General)*; Carmen Madrid *(Angela—Dr. Fuentes' Daughter)*; Esteban Soberanes *(Raul—Angela's Fiance)*; Alejandro Springall *(Carlos—Dr. Fuentes' Son)*; Maricruz Najera; Jacqueline Walters Voltaire *(Rich Ladies)*; Ivan Arango *(Cienfuegos)*; Lizzie Curry Martinez *(Montoya)*; Luis Ramirez *(Hidalgo)*; Humberto Romero *(De Soto)*; Gabriel Cosme *(Echevarria)*; Horacio Trujillo *(Arenas)*; Efrine Elfaro; Pedro Hernandez *(Kokal Drivers)*; Dionisios *(Salt Man)*; Lolo Navarro *(Blind Woman)*; Maggie Renzi; Shari Gray *(Tourists by Pool)*; Paco Mauri *(Captain)*; Gilma Tuyub Castillo *(Mother With Baby)*; Armando Martinez Velasquez *(Vendor)*; Luis Felipe Tovar *(Barber)*; Fernando Medel *(Barber's Client)*; David Villalpando; Raul Sanchez *(Gum People)*; Diego Mendez Guzman *(Moises)*; Mariano Lopez De La Cruz *(Gonzalo)*; Antonio De La Torre Lopez *(Isidro)*; Ermenehildo Saenz Guzman *(Sixto)*; Cristobal Guzman Mesa *(Artemio)*; Domingo Perez Sanchez *(Junipero)*; Oscar Garcia Ortega *(Sergeant)*; Miguel Xocua *(Modelo Boy)*; Guadalupe Xocua *(Modelo Woman)*; Celeste Cornelio Sanchez *(Raped Girl)*; Nazario Montiel; Francisco Valdez; Jose Alberto Acosta *(Guerrillas)*

MEN WITH GUNS could well be the title of an exploitation movie, but John Sayles has higher aspirations in this thoughtful, if plodding, tale of a Latin American doctor's odyssey through bloody, dangerous terrain.

In a town near Cienfuegos, the elderly resident physician, Dr. Humberto Fuentes (Federico Luppi), learns that all of his medical students—stationed throughout the country to carry out his program to treat the poor—are missing and presumed dead. Apparently, guerrilla soldiers ("men with guns") have been brutally attacking villages and killing the doctors in order to secure their drugs and other supplies. Fuentes decides to try to find out if any of the doctors have survived.

On his way to Tierra Quemada, Fuentes meets an orphan, Conejo (Dan Rivera Gonzalez) who tells him about how the guerillas abused the children, tortured the adults of his village, and killed the doctor whom he is seeking. Fuentes and the child are then ambushed by a fugitive soldier, Domingo (Damian Delgado), who forces them to take him to the next village, away from the army. On the way, the three travelers meet up with an ex-priest, "The Ghost" (Damian Alcazar), who tells them how the soldiers attacked his village and, once again, the village's doctor. Though he resents taking the padre on their trip, Domingo privately confesses to him about having killed a boy when he was in the army.

The newly formed quartet of travelers arrive at an army post called The Community of Hope, which is actually a recently burned town. The priest is taken away by suspicious guards, but Domingo escapes imprisonment and death by pretending to be a doctor. He continues his charade by help Fuentes tend to the ill detainees. Finally, Fuentes, Domingo, and the boy are allowed to leave, and they take with them a young woman, Graciela (Tania Cruz) who had been raped by a soldier.

Fuentes plans to search for one more student, the last, deep in the rain forest of Cerca del Cielo. Meanwhile, on the road, the young woman softens Domingo's heart; Domingo subsequently talks her out of suicide. Once they all arrive, Fuentes learns that his student may be nearby, but he dies quietly before finding her. When a young Indian girl requests Domingo treat her mother, Domingo decides to assume the role of doctor. Conejo and Graciela rejoice in his decision.

After two creative steps forward (THE SECRET OF ROAN INISH and LONE STAR), John Sayles takes a step backward with MEN WITH GUNS, a serious, solid, but somewhat prosaic work. Though far more accomplished technically and artistically than Sayles's early works (RETURN OF THE SECAUCUS SEVEN, THE BROTHER FROM ANOTHER PLANET), MEN WITH GUNS lacks the tight narrative construction that has marked the writer-director's other recent efforts. Throughout, Sayles spells out his message (about brutality and the human spirit) all too plainly and obviously. MEN WITH GUNS draws from a number of epic texts, including *The Odyssey*, *Candide*, *The Heart of Darkness*, *The Grapes of Wrath*, even THE WIZARD OF OZ (1939), but the film remains oddly languid and low-key (despite the surrounding bloodshed). Also, the liberal doctor is almost too comforting a main character (like a Mexican Marcus Welby) to lead the journey. The troubled Domingo, to whom the doctor imparts or "transfers" his legacy (in lieu of his dead students), makes a more compelling figure, but none of the characters are very well developed, and some of the minor ones—e.g., an arrogant American couple, all the guerrillas—are strict caricatures. In the resolution, Sayles reverts to an old pattern of hopeful but banal humanism as an answer to complicated sociopolitical problems.

Still, Sayles demonstrates a commitment to his subject matter in many admirable ways: by using Spanish and the native languages of Latin America (subtitled in English) throughout the film, refraining from gratuitous violence, and respecting the intelligence and dignity of his main characters with well-written dialogue. Sayles also comes up with some pleasing artistic touches: the early parts of the doctor's road trip are reminiscent of the lyrical driving montage sequence in LONE STAR, and the black-and-white flashbacks to the students' early days have an eerie, haunting quality. In the final analysis, MEN WITH GUNS needed more scenes like these to be truly powerful, let alone magical. *(Violence, adult situations, extreme profanity.)*—E.M.

d, John Sayles; p, Maggie Renzi, R. Paul Miller; exec p, Jody Patton, Lou Gonda, John Sloss; assoc p, Eric Robison, Peter Gilbert, Jim De Nardo, Doug Sayles; co-p, Bertha Navarro; w, John Sayles (inspired by characters in *The Long Night of White Chickens* by Francisco Goldman); ph, Slawomir Idziak; ed, John Sayles; m, Mason Daring; prod d, Felipe Fernandez Del Paso; art d, Salvador Parra; set d, Miguel Angel Alvarez; sound, Judy Karp (mixer); fx, Alex Vazquez; casting, Lizzie Curry Martinez; cos, Mayes C. Rubeo; makeup, Carlos Sanchez

Political/Drama/Adventure (PR: C MPAA: R)

MENDEL ★★★½

(Norway/Denmark/Germany, 1997) 95m Northern Lights; Zentropa Entertainments; Lichtblick Filmproduktion; Norsk Film; NRK ~ First Run Features c

Thomas Jungling Sorensen *(Mendel Trotzig)*; Teresa Harder *(Bela Trotzig)*; Hans Kremer *(Aron Trotzig)*; Martin Meingast *(David)*; Wolfgang Pintzka *(Mr. Freund)*; Charlotte Trier *(Mrs. Freund)*; John Henning Gobring-Hermstad *(Markus)*; Bjorn Sundquist *(Mitten Man)*; Lene Bragli *(Mrs. Rosen)*; Geo Von Krogh *(Mr. Rosen)*; Bjorn Jenseg *(Ugland)*; Ketil Gudim *(The Farmer)*; Gaute Thu Tesli *(Siggen)*

A family of Jewish immigrants leaves postwar Germany to settle in Norway in MENDEL, a poignant coming-of-age story centered on the youngest son's efforts to understand his heritage. MENDEL premiered at the Berlin Film Festival in 1997. Filmed in German and Norwegian with English subtitles, the film received limited release in the US in 1998 and made its home video bow later that year.

Too young to understand the atrocities perpetrated against his people during WWII, nine-year-old Mendel Trotzig (Thomas Jungling Sorensen) cannot fathom why his family leaves their fatherland to settle in a small town in Norway in 1954. Adding to his confusion are his parents' secretiveness and the introduction of such puzzling concepts as Jesus, Santa Claus, and anti-Semitism. Hidden photographs and whispered comments among his parents, Aron (Hans Kremer) and Bela (Teresa Harder), and older brother, David, (Martin Meingast) pique Mendel's curiosity, causing him to ferret out clues and construct his own version of his family's tortured history.

The more Mendel comes to understand what happened during the war, the more he questions the courage of the seemingly passive Jews who submitted without a fight. His determination to be brave turns him into a bully. His anger escalates in a confrontation with his brother, who reveals that the man in a photo his mother keeps hidden is David's real father, who was killed in an uprising. The brothers realize that the time for secrets has come to an end.

Like his title character, writer-director Alexander Rosler is himself a Jewish refugee from Germany who emigrated to Norway as a child in the 1950s. Though MENDEL is not autobiographical, the story contains elements of Rosler's childhood. His bittersweet script avoids being maudlin or heavy-handed. The grim subject matter is leavened by a lively score and ample humorous moments. Aside from the disturbing imagery of Mendel's dream sequences, and a singularly powerful scene in which firefighters pulling the family from their burning apartment late at night conjure up images of Nazis rounding up Jews for deportation, the tone is light.

With an expressive face and spirited delivery, Sorensen is superb as the inquisitive youth. Kremer scores equally well as Mendel's father, an staunch atheist fond of telling jokes. Harder elicits compassion as the soulful mother who sings her nightmare-plagued sons to sleep. Though the film tells Mendel's story, his parents' dilemma provides the core controversy: to keep their son in the dark or tell him the truth, that he may share their nightmares. *(Violence, adult situations, profanity.)*—B.R.

d, Alexander Rosler; p, Axel Helgeland; co-p, Peter Aalbaek Jensen, Helga Bahr; w, Alexander Rosler; ph, Helge Semb; ed, Einar Egeland; m, Geir Bohren, Bent Aserud; prod d, Jack Van Domburg; sound, Gunnar Meidell (design); casting, Heta Mantscheff, Ellen Lande, Nora Ibsen; cos, Anne Pedersen; makeup, Kai Gronberg

Drama **(PR: C MPAA: NR)**

MERCURY RISING ★½

(U.S., 1998) 130m Joseph M. Singer Productions; Imagine Entertainment; Universal Pictures ~ Universal c

Bruce Willis *(Art Jeffries)*; Alec Baldwin *(Lt. Colonel Nicholas Kudrow)*; Miko Hughes *(Simon)*; Chi McBride *(Tommy B. Jordan)*; Kim Dickens *(Stacey)*; Robert Stanton *(Dean Crandell)*; Bodhi Pine Elfman *(Leo Pedranski)*; Carrie Preston *(Emily Lang)*; John Carroll Lynch *(Martin Lynch)*; Kelley Hazen *(Jenny Lynch)*; John Doman *(Supervisor Hartley)*; Richard Riehle *(Edgar Halstrom)*; Chad Lindberg *(James)*; Hank Harris *(Isaac)*; James MacDonald *(SWAT Team Leader Francis)*; Camryn Manheim *(Dr. London)*; Jack Conley *(Detective Nichols)*; Maricela Ochoa *(Charlayne)*; Peter Fontana *(Pasquale)*; Kirk B.R. Woller *(Lieutenant)*; Betsy Brantley *(Special Ed Teacher #2)*; Ashley Knutson *(Samantha)*; Tom Gallop *(Medic)*; Margaret Travolta *(Autism Expert Nurse)*; Tiffany Fraser *(Night Nurse)*; Koko Taylor *(Koko Taylor)*; Matt Levert *(Tommy Jordan Jr.)*; Lisa Summerour *(Dana Jordan)*; Barbara Alexander *(Librarian)*; Gwen McGee *(Security Woman)*; Ned Schmidtke *(Senator)*; Kristina Eliot Johnson *(Special Ed Teacher #1)*; James Krag *(Rookie Agent Roger)*; Wadell Brown *(Bank Security Guard)*; Tim Grimm *(Ted—Security Guard)*; John Scanlon *(South Dakota Helicopter Pilot)*; Annabel Armour *(Ruth)*; Brent Freeman *(Marine Guard)*; Gary Hand *(Kudrow's Assistant)*; Michael Chieffo *(Hostage)*; Steve Key *(Cop at Lynch House)*; Darryl Alan Reed *(Ambulance Driver)*; Steve Rankin *(WGEX Helicopter Pilot)*; Maureen Gallagher *(Flea Market Lady)*; Mark Collins *(Train Conductor)*; Denise Woods *(Nurse in Elevator)*; Kim Robillard *(Motorman)*

Loose cannon FBI agent Bruce Willis protects an autistic boy who's stumbled upon a top military secret from government killers. Low-key in comparison to the DIE HARD series, MERCURY RISING is still a generic and often ridiculous thriller, undoubtedly produced with one eye on the lower expectations held for action movies in foreign markets and on video.

In South Dakota, an attempted bank robbery by a right-wing militia group ends when the Feds storm the bank and gun down the militia's members, including some teenagers. Undercover FBI agent Art Jeffries (Bruce Willis) had infiltrated the militia and believed he could resolve the stand-off without bloodshed. Disgusted by the killing of children, Jeffries punches out a superior, and is subsequently busted down to routine duty in Chicago.

In Chicago, nine-year-old autistic savant Simon Lynch (Miko Hughes) decodes a message in a puzzle magazine, which instructs him to make a phone call. The call alerts Dean Crandell (Robert Stanton) and Leo Pedranski (Bodhi Pine Elfman), two Defense Department cryptographers who placed the puzzle in the magazine on an unauthorized whim: Simon has cracked "Mercury," the government's new, supposedly uncrackable super-code. In the name of national security, Colonel Kudrow (Alec Baldwin) dispatches a hit man to eliminate the Lynch family, but Simon hides and survives.

Jeffries is called in on the case, and when the assassin comes after Simon at the hospital, he takes it on himself to remove the boy from the hospital. Eventually, Jeffries gets the gist of the shadow conspiracy at work. First Crandell, and then Pedranski, attempt to meet with Jeffries to come clean about Mercury, but both are killed at Kudrow's behest. Jeffries finds an accommodating lady named Stacey (Kim Dickens) to take care of Simon while he flies to Washington to confront Kudrow.

Faced with the threat of Jeffries going public with evidence left by Pedranski, Kudrow agrees to place Simon in the Witness Protection Program. Jeffries correctly suspects a double-cross: at the appointed meeting place atop a skyscraper, Kudrow tries to kill Simon. Instead, after a fight with Jeffries, the Colonel is sent plunging to a splattery death.

A reluctant Every-cop who thumbs his nose at his bosses and their rules, but who proves his mettle when his superior sense of honor obliges him to risk life and pension to protect the innocent—that's the generic Bruce Willis character from the DIE HARD movies, and we meet him again in MERCURY RISING. How generic is MERCURY RISING? Meet Tommy, the "best friend/partner character." Surprise! He's an overweight, African-American family man who resists making waves, but who helps the hero anyway out of loyalty.

The script for MERCURY RISING is a formula that makes sense only as long as Willis is at the center of it. Why is Simon targeted for elimination, even though the kid has no idea of what he did and couldn't tell anybody about it if he did? So Bruce Willis can save him. Why would a woman upend her life, and take in an autistic child and a mysterious stranger with a gun? Because he's Bruce Willis, of course.

Often with action movies that tank domestically, Hollywood executives will point to the foreign grosses as redemption. With only the graces of starring a major movie icon and having its well-produced action beats in the right places, MERCURY RISING appears to have been made with overseas salvation in mind all along. *(Violence, profanity.)*—P.R.

d, Harold Becker; p, Brian Grazer, Karen Kehala; exec p, Joseph M. Singer, Ric Kidney; assoc p, Tom Mack; co-p, Maureen Peyrot, Paul Neesan; w, Lawrence Konner, Mark Rosenthal (based on the novel *Simple Simon* by Ryne Douglas Pearson); ph, Michael Seresin; ed, Peter Honess; m, John Barry; prod d, Patrizia Von Brandenstein; art d, James Truesdale, Steve Saklad; set d, Maria Nay; sound, Kim Ornitz (mixer); fx, Guy Clayton, Burt Dalton, Michael Owens, Industrial Light & Magic; casting, Nancy Klopper; cos, Betsy Heimann; makeup, Leonard Engleman; stunts, Joe Dunne

Thriller/Action **(PR: C MPAA: R)**

MERLIN ★★

(U.S./U.K., 1998) 140m NBC TV ~ Hallmark Entertainment c

Sam Neill *(Merlin)*; Miranda Richardson *(Queen Mab/Lady of the Lake)*; Helena Bonham Carter *(Morgan Le Fey)*; John Gielgud *(King Constant)*; Rutger Hauer *(Lord Vortigan)*; Isabella Rossellini *(Nimue)*; Martin Short *(Frik)*; James Earl Jones *(Voice of the Rock of Ages)*; Paul Curran *(Arthur)*; Lena Headey *(Guinevere)*; Jeremy Sheffield *(Lancelot)*; Mark Jax *(Uther Pendragon)*; John McEnery *(Lord Ardente)*; Thomas Lockyer *(Cornwall)*; Jason Done *(Mordred)*; Billie Whitelaw *(Ambrosia)*; Daniel Brocklebank *(Young Merlin)*; Agnieszka Koson *(Young Nimue)*; Emma Lewis *(Elissa)*; Justin Girdler *(Galahad)*; Roger Ashton-Griffiths *(Sir Boris)*; Nicholas Clay *(Lord Leo)*; Sebastian Roche *(Gawain)*; Rachel Colover *(Lady Igraine)*; John Turner *(Lord Lot)*; Keith Baxter *(Sir Hector)*; Janine Eser *(Lady Elaine)*; Peter Woodthorpe *(Soothsayer)*; Robert Addie *(Sir Gilbert)*; Nickolas Grace *(Sir Egbert)*; Peter Benson *(First Architect)*; John Tordoff *(New Architect)*; Timothy Bateson *(Father Abbott)*; Alice Hamilton *(Young Morgan Le Fey)*; Peter Eyre *(Chief Physician)*; Vernon Dobtcheff *(First Physician)*; Peter Bayliss *(Second Physician)*; Talula Sheppard *(Lady Friend)*

Awash in special effects that overshadow its underwhelming human leads, MERLIN offers a decidedly mundane take on the Arthurian legend. The film was produced as a miniseries for network television, and was released in an edited version on home video in 1998.

As paganism is rejected by the ruling class in favor of Christianity, a wizard named Merlin is created by evil Queen Mab (Miranda Richardson), in order to ensure that the citizenry will still believe in the Old Ways. As an adult, Merlin (Sam Neill) is recruited to help the current ruler, Lord Vortigan (Rutger Hauer), in his war against Uther Pendragon (Mark Jax); in the meantime, Merlin is united with his true love Nimue (Isabella Rossellini). Alas, Nimue is to be sacrificed to a dragon, and despite Merlin's attempts to avert the tragedy, she ends up being terribly scarred.

Merlin is given the sword Excalibur by the Lady of the Lake (Richardson). He uses the sword to kill Vortigan (whose evil he opposes), and then passes it onto Uther, the new king. But when Uther doesn't live up to Merlin's hopes—after he seduces the married Igraine (Rachel Colover) with magic—Merlin imbeds Excalibur into a stone. The offspring of the illicit union between Uther and Igraine is Arthur (Paul Curran), who is tutored by Merlin, and eventually pulls the sword from the stone, thereupon becoming king. Meanwhile, Mab's gnome Frik (Martin Short) befriends Igraine's daughter Morgan Le Fey (Helena Bonham Carter), and she eventually, unknowingly makes love to half-brother Arthur.

While Arthur builds Camelot and marries Guinevere (Lena Headley), Morgan gives birth to the villainous Mordred (Jason Done), who is versed in the Old Ways by Mab. Mordred then exposes Guinevere's adultery with Round Table knight Lancelot (Jeremy Sheffield), and in a final battle, Arthur and Mordred kill each other. Afterward, Merlin returns Excalibur to the lake and destroys Mab by simply ignoring her. As an old man, he's reunited with Nimue.

The character of Merlin has been translated to the screen countless times, but here he finally takes center stage. Strangely, outside of a generic love interest, nothing interesting has been added. Originally telecast as a four-hour miniseries (which did well in the ratings), the edited home-video version delivers merely a few imaginative special effects and a talented troupe of actors attempting to breathe life into their stillborn roles. Dramatically flat, the script also takes major liberties with the legend (e.g., Queen Mab is borrowed from other early literature, and was usually referred to as the nonhostile Queen of the Fairies).

The film's strength is due to Neill, who brings much-needed vulnerability and compassion to the title role. The remaining cast, however, comprises something of a mixed bag. John Gielgud appears for only a few seconds, Richardson hams it up as raspy puppetmistress Mab, and Bonham Carter rates as one of the few cast members who seems comfortable in her role. As Mab's assistant, Short provides unnecessary comic shtick, and plays much of his role as an anachronistic swashbuckler. Filmed in Wales, Scotland, and England, the film is indeed sumptuous on a visual level, even though the CGI effects are only intermittently successful, and the unsubtle performances would be perfectly at home at a modern-day Renaissance Faire. Given all of the resources at his disposal, it's rather unfortunate that director Steve Barron (TEENAGE MUTANT NINJA TURTLES) is unable to make an exciting—and more importantly, original—film out of this potentially rousing yarn. *(Violence.)*—S.P.

d, Steve Barron; p, Dyson Lovell; exec p, Robert Halmi Sr.; w, David Stevens, Peter Barnes (based on the story by Edward Khmara); ph, Sergi Kozlov; ed, Colin Green; m, Trevor Jones; prod d, Roger Hall; art d, Michael Boone; set d, Karen Brookes; sound, Peter Glossop; fx, Tim Webber, Jim Henson's Creature Shop; casting, Lynn Kressel, Noel Davis; cos, Ann Hollowood

Fantasy **(PR: A MPAA: NR)**

MERRY WAR, A ★★★½

(U.K., 1997) 101m Aspidistra Productions, Ltd.; United British Artists; John Wolstenholme Film and TV Entertainment ~ First Look Pictures c

Richard E. Grant *(Gordon Comstock)*; Helena Bonham Carter *(Rosemary)*; Jim Carter *(Erskine)*; Harriet Walter *(Julia Comstock)*; Lill Roughley *(Mrs. Trilling)*; Julian Wadham *(Ravelston)*; Lesley Vickerage *(Hermoine)*; John Clegg *(McKechnie)*; Barbara Leigh Hunt *(Mrs. Wisebeach)*; Grant Parsons *(Beautiful Young Man)*; Dorothea Alexander *(Old Woman)*; Peter Stockbridge *(Old Man)*; Malcolm Sinclair *(Paul Doring)*; Derek Smee *(Lecturer)*; Ben Miles *(Ravenscroft Waiter)*; Richard Dixon *(Head Waiter)*; Roger Morlidge *(Policeman)*; Roland Oliver *(Magistrate Croom)*; Bill Wallis *(Cheeseman)*; Liz Smith *(Mrs. Meakin)*; Roger Frost *(Orton the Undertaker)*; Harri Alexander *(Dora)*; Lucy Speed *(Factory Girl)*; Joan Blackman *(Librarian)*; Roy Evans *(Cabby)*; Maggie McCarthy *(Customer)*; Eve Ferrett *(Barmaid)*; Lone Vidahl *(Girl in Modigliani's)*; Steven Crossley *(Man at CLub)*

A MERRY WAR is a respectful, almost literal transcription of George Orwell's astute, witty, and poignant 1936 novel *Keep the Aspidistra Flying*, the story of a young chap who renounces a lucrative career in advertising to become "a free man."

Gordon Comstock (Richard E. Grant) resigns his position as one of London's top advertising copywriters to pursue a career as a poet. With the help of Ravelston (Julian Wadham), his publisher, Gordon takes a low-paying job as a bookstore clerk and a dreary room in a nearby boarding house. The young man's hand-to-mouth existence and lack of success in getting his new work published increasingly anger and depress him. One Sunday, Gordon and his girlfriend, Rosemary (Helena Bonham Carter), make an excursion into the countryside, where they hope to consummate their relationship, but Gordon's inability to afford contraceptives ruins the couple's big moment.

Back in the city, Gordon receives a hefty acceptance check from an American literary magazine and takes Rosemary and Ravelston out on the town. The evening ends in a shambles when Gordon, flushed with success, gets blind drunk, squanders all his cash, and lands in jail. His fine is paid by Ravelston the next morning but the scandal costs Gordon his day job and his lodgings.

After finding another job and room in the London slums, Gordon slides into a state of near dereliction. Although the long-suffering Rosemary has all but given up on him, she finally agrees to sleep with him. When she subsequently tells him she's pregnant, Gordon becomes a changed man, throws away his work in progress, and returns to his old job at the ad agency. He and Rosemary marry and happily, hopefully move into a middle-class apartment complex to begin their life together.

In the semiautobiographical *Keep the Aspidistra Flying*, Orwell argued that pennilessness is so debilitating, it sours every aspect of life, even such ostensibly unrelated pleasures as sex—and rarely has a novel proclaimed its theme so blatantly or hammered it home so relentlessly. In the words of an American reviewer, "The book projects as do few others the desperate expedients and blind rage of the educated moneyless."

Though hardly inspired, A MERRY WAR (Orwell's term for the battle between the sexes) is a faithful adaptation of a splendid work. The filmmakers wisely chose not to update the book, retaining not only its mid-1930s setting but also the more conservative social and sexual mores of the era. The language has become a bit more profane than that of Orwell—who was probably hampered by the chaste publishing standards of the times—but not anachronistically so. Producer Peter Shaw's express delight with the atypically sunny weather that greeted the London shoot may have been misplaced—the movie's gorgeous, bright exteriors tend at times to clash with its protagonist's spiritually drizzly descent into the lower depths.

In 1986, Richard E. Grant gave a career-defining performance as Withnail in WITHNAIL AND I, a performance that announced he was born to play Orwell's Gordon Comstock, who might well have been Withnail's grandfather. An actor with enormous talent and almost limitless charm, Grant, like Peter O'Toole, is blessed with an attractive streak of feminine vulnerability as well as a gift for delivering scathingly witty lines with sufficient neurotic self-loathing to render him sympathetic rather than merely vicious.

One yearned to see Gordon embark on a long, ranting monologue like the one with which Grant closed WITHNAIL AND I, and at the end of A MERRY WAR's Sunday sequence he seems on the verge of doing so, but the opportunity is not exploited. Given director Robert Bierman's confessed attraction to emotionally "supercharged" characters (as evidenced by Nicolas Cage's overdone turn in his 1989 film VAMPIRE'S KISS), Grant's relative restraint here is somewhat surprising and a bit disappointing. He is nonetheless irreplaceable, particularly when mining Gordon's vast reserves of spite and envy to rail at the idle rich ("I want to know why *I* can't have sex in the afternoon!"). No less sensitive but infinitely more sensible than Gordon, Rosemary has been perfectly cast with Helena Bonham Carter. *(Violence, profanity.)*—D.T.

d, Robert Bierman; p, Peter Shaw; exec p, Robert Bierman, John Wolstenholme; assoc p, Joyce Herlihy; w, Alan Plater (based on the novel *Keep the Aspidistra Flying* by George Orwell); ph, Giles Nuttgens; ed, Bill Wright; prod d, Sarah Greenwood; art d, Philip Robinson; sound, Patrick Quirk (recordist); casting, Michelle Guish; cos, James Keast; makeup, Marilyn MacDonald

Comedy/Drama/Romance (PR: C MPAA: R)

MIDAQ ALLEY ★★★

(Mexico, 1994) 140m Universidad de Guadalajara; Instituto Mexicano de Cinematografia; Fondo de Fomento a la Calidad Cinematografica; Alameda Films ~ Northern Arts Entertainment c
(EL CALLEJON DE LOS MILAGROS)

Ernesto Gomez Cruz *(Don Rutilio)*; Maria Rojo *(Dona Cata)*; Salma Hayek *(Alma)*; Bruno Bichir *(Abel)*; Delia Casanova *(Eusebia)*; Daniel Gimenez-Cacho *(Jose Luis)*; Claudio Obregon *(Don Fidel)*; Luis Felipe Tovar *(Guicho)*; Tiare Scanda *(Maru)*; Margarita Sanz *(Susanita)*; Juan Manuel Bernal *(Chava)*

Before Hollywood discovered Mexican bombshell Salma Hayek (DESPERADO, FROM DUSK TILL DAWN, and 1998's 54), she starred in MIDAQ ALLEY, a richly textured melodrama. Originally released in Mexico back in 1994 (but receiving a US premiere in 1998), this two-and-a-half-hour soap follows the despairing residents of a low-rent neighborhood in Mexico City.

Don Rutilio (Ernesto Gomez Cruz), a gruff cantina owner, treats Eusebia (Delia Casanova), his wife of 30 years, with disdain. The patriarch's amorous longings lie elsewhere; he coddles and seduces a male clothing salesman. Rutilio's suspicious son, Chava (Juan Manuel Bernal), bursts into a public bathhouse and sees his father in a naked embrace with a man. Chava cracks the young retailer's skull against the wall. On the run from his crazed father, Chava goes to his best friend, Abel (Bruno Bichir), a hairdresser, in search of a partner for his planned flight to the US.

Abel was about to consummate his love with his virginal sweetheart, Alma (Salma Hayek). The hairdresser decides to join his desperate friend, but, before leaving, he vows to return with enough money to buy a salon and marry Alma. While Abel is away, Alma falls under the spell of a wealthy charmer, Jose Luis (Daniel Gimenez-Cacho), who introduces her to the high life. She loses her virginity with this depraved Lothario, and it isn't long before she's working as a prostitute at his exclusive brothel.

Susanita (Margarita Sanz), a plain woman with hideous teeth, pines for Chava. She finances his trip to the US, succumbing to his sweet nothings and a deep kiss. This fleeting sexuality melts the spinster, and she soon comes on to the handsome Guicho (Luis Felipe Tovar), who tends bar for Don Rutilio. After Susanita fixes her teeth, the unlikely couple marry. The bride soon learns that her lazy husband loves her for her money.

Abel finally returns to Midaq Alley to marry Alma. He finds his beloved in Jose Luis's brothel, coked up and mingling with the clientele. Distraught, the starry-eyed hairdresser returns with a razor and slashes the pimp's face. Jose Luis has Abel repeatedly shot. Abel, still hopeful that he can save Alma, dies in her arms.

Employing countless plot twists and turns, scripter Vincente Lenero, who based his screenplay on a novel by Egyptian Nobel laureate Naguib Mahfouz, successfully does everything he can to keep the viewing audience away from the concession stand.

Though Lenero and director Jorge Fons pack MIDAQ ALLEY with well-worn elements—the sweet virgin lured into a life of prostitution, the victimized old maid, the lover blinded by his obsession—they avoid predictability with a fast pace and a convoluted, PULP FICTION-like structure.

The film is divided into thirds, with each part highlighting a different character: Don Rutilio, Alma, and Susanita. Time shifts back and forth as the characters move between the foreground and background. The same events, like Chava's exodus, are repeated from different points of view. This device, which was first used explicitly in RASHOMON (1950) as a strident statement about truth and form, has now become a commonplace in the movies, used in comedies (GROUNDHOG'S DAY; HE SAID, SHE SAID) as well as a number of post-Tarantino crime films. Lenero utilizes this strategy quite well here, playfully mingling the plot strands so that the viewer will see intriguing aspects of a supporting story line (say, Abel's courting of Alma), and later on, see the whole thing played in much greater detail.

Though the affair between Abel and Alma affair isn't terribly original and becomes fairly corny at points, it stands as the focal point of the movie. Bruno Bichir wrings every drop of pathos from the role of Abel, going over the top at many points, especially during his character's death scene. And who can blame him? If Salma Hayek's Alma is a sweet temptation when she's the good girl, then she's even more irresistible as the hooking bad girl—and, yes, Hayek acquits herself nicely here, proving to be more than just a sultry, photogenic brunette; she also turns in a credible performance.

The film's intricate plotting may turn some viewers off, but at its core, MIDAQ ALLEY is an absorbing "meller," the cinematic equivalent of a good trashy novel. *(Violence, nudity, profanity.)*—T.Y.

d, Jorge Fons; w, Vincente Lenero (based on the novel by Naguib Mahfouz); ph, Carlos Marcovich; ed, Carlos Savage; m, Lucia Alvarez; sound, David Baksht

Romance/Drama **(PR: C MPAA: NR)**

MIDAS TOUCH, THE ★★

(U.S., 1998) 87m The Kushner-Locke Company ~ Paramount c

Trevor O'Brien *(Billy Bright)*; Ashly Lyn Cafagna *(Hannah)*; Joey Simmrin *(Leon)*; David Jeremiah *(Willy)*; Marla Cotovsky *(Cora)*; Donna Hansen *(Granny Bright)*; Shannon Welles *(Eleanor Latimer)*; Ilinca Goia *(Miss Henderson)*; Joseph Whipp *(Guard)*; Theodor Danetti; Peter Laci; Mihai Radulescu; Michael Larkin; Gabriel Mican; Mark Headley; Madalina Constantinescu

THE MIDAS TOUCH is a tedious straight-to-video kiddie fantasy.

Billy Bright (Trevor O'Brien) is an orphan living with his Granny (Donna Hansen), a frail ex-shopkeeper in need of a pacemaker. At school, Billy is bullied by parasitic "friend" Leon (Joey Simmrin), who, dared by schoolmate Hannah (Ashley Lyn Cafagna) forces Billy to break into a spooky old house for him. Inside, Billy meets witchlike Eleanor Latimer (Shannon Welles), who offers to grant him one wish. Seeking money for Granny's operation, Billy requests the fabled touch of King Midas. Sure enough, after Billy dashes out of the place, his index finger converts ordinary objects to solid gold, including a pet gerbil, a baseball cap, and a soda can. Billy reveals the power to Leon and Hannah. Leon takes charge, bringing various glittering items to a pawnshop run by sleazy siblings Willy (David Jeremiah) and Cora (Marla Cotovsky). Unhappy at the pittance Leon reaps, Billy goes home to Granny, who has just suffered cardiac arrhythmia. Touching her in concern, Billy accidentally changes the old woman into gold. Eleanor Latimer cannot undo the boys' wish—although she does "curse" obnoxious Leon with unnatural politeness. Consulting the complete tale of Midas, the three kids determine that Billy must retouch every single object he transmuted. But Willy and Cora have followed them, and, mistaking the golden grandmother for the motherlode, steal her to melt her down. By the time the kids invade the pawnshop, Granny is liquified; moreover, Billy himself is slowly and painfully becoming solid gold. The trio tote the buckets of gold back to Billy's home and add a few stray golden objects that earlier escaped notice. Billy touches the tubful, and everything, including Granny, returns to normal. But Billy is still metamorphosizing. As per the original Midas legend, Leon and Hannah dunk their friend in a nearby stream, and Billy recovers. Later Billy get a $25,000 check from Eleanor Latimer to make Granny's surgery possible.

Nonsensical lapses in logic are plentiful in THE MIDAS TOUCH: attentive viewers might note how many times Billy touches things that *don't* turn into gold. There are some clever gaglines here and there, small mercies in a feature that pretty much exhausts all its dramatic potential by the midway point, then just reruns tiresome chase sequences with the annoyingly stereotypical white-trash villains Willy and Cora. The child actors gain points for being less overbearing than the adult ones, and the funnier moments involve Leon's excess of civility once he's hexed. Effective computer-generated special effects of people and objects turning into gold demonstrates how advances in imaging technology can put a fresh shine on even the most tarnished story line. Like other family-oriented features from the same production company (JOHNNY MYSTO BOY WIZARD, LITTLE GHOST), THE MIDAS TOUCH was actually shot at a discount in a well-disguised Bucharest, Romania, with principal perfomers imported from the USA.—C.C.

d, Peter Manoogian; p, Vlad Paunescu, Mark Headley; exec p, Peter Locke, Donald Kushner; assoc p, Melanie Weiner; w, Peter Fedorenko, Keith Estrada; ph, Vivi Dragon Vasile; ed, Andy Horvitch; m, John R. Gilmore; prod d, Vali Calinescu; art d, Viorel Ghenea; set d, Ica Varna; sound, Tibi Borcoman; fx, Al Magliochetti; casting, Bob MacDonald, Perry Bullington; cos, Oana Paunescu; makeup, Mihai Stanescu, Dana Busoiu; stunts, Doru Dumitrescu

Children's/Comedy/Fantasy **(PR: A MPAA: PG)**

MIGHTY, THE ★★★

(U.S., 1998) 107m Scholastic Productions; Simon Fields Productions ~ Miramax c

Sharon Stone *(Gwen Dillon)*; Elden Henson *(Maxwell Kane)*; Kieran Culkin *(Kevin Dillon)*; Gena Rowlands *(Gram)*; Harry Dean Stanton *(Grim)*; Gillian Anderson *(Loretta Lee)*; Meat Loaf *(Iggy)*; James Gandolfini *(Kenny Kane)*; Joe Perrino *(Blade)*; Douglas Bisset *(Homeless Man)*; Dov Tiefenbach *(Doghouse Boy #1)*; Michael Colton *(Doghouse Boy #2)*; Eve Crawford *(Mrs. Donelli)*; John Bourgeois *(Mr. Sacker)*; Bruce Tubbe *(Officer)*; Rudy Webb *(Mr. Hampton)*; Ron Nigrini *(Man in Diner)*; Nadia Litz *(Girl in Diner)*; Serena Pruyn *(Girl in Hall)*; Telmo Miranda *(Boy in Hall)*; Jordan Hughes *(Denardo)*; Jenifer Lewis *(Mrs. Addison)*; Bryon Bully *(Fat Boy)*; Charlaine Porter *(Girl with Limp)*; Lisa Marie Chen *(Girl Cafeteria)*; Lisa Mininni *(Cashier)*; Ann Chiu *(Nurse)*; Carl Marotte *(Doctor)*; Nora Sheehan *(Little Girl)*; William Van Allen *(Laundry Worker)*

Based on an acclaimed children's novel, THE MIGHTY is a sentimental melodrama about two outcast kids, one brainy, the other brawny, whose friendship makes them a formidable force.

Well-acted and well-intended, the film features an intense climactic situation that may make the movie inappropriate for some of its target audience.

With his father in prison for killing his mother, Max Kane (Elden Henson) lives with his dour grandparents (Gena Rowlands and Harry Dean Stanton) in a poor section of Cincinnati. Making his third trip through the seventh grade, the hulking Max towers over his classmates, who taunt him endlessly.

Life improves for Max when he gets new neighbors: Kevin Dillon (Kieran Culkin) and his mom, Gwen (Sharon Stone). Kevin has a disease that has stunted the growth of his bones, but not that of his organs, forcing him to rely on crutches. But Kevin is also a genius. He becomes Max's reading tutor, and the two boys become friends.

Dubbing themselves "Freak the Mighty," Kevin rides on Max's shoulders and the two stride the streets of Cincinnati like a modern-day Knight of the Round Table, doing good deeds. One of their quests involves fighting a street gang and returning a stolen purse to its owner, Loretta Lee (Gillian Anderson). When Lee meets Max, she reveals that she and her boyfriend Iggy (Meat Loaf) were members of his father's old gang.

On Christmas Eve, Max is kidnapped by his recently paroled father, Kenny (James Gandolfini), who ties him up and threatens him with a knife. Kevin guesses where Kenny is hiding out, and goes alone to rescue Max. With Loretta's help, Max escapes before his father can harm him, but Kevin is injured and taken to the hospital. When Kevin is released, he and his mother, and Max and his grandparents, all celebrate a belated Christmas together. That night, Kevin dies of his illness. His passing inspires Max to put pen to paper and chronicle their exploits.

THE MIGHTY marks the American directing debut of British filmmaker Peter Chelsom, whose previous efforts, HEAR MY SONG (1991) and FUNNY BONES (1995), were decidedly offbeat comedies. They were also movies with heart, as is THE MIGHTY, a heart that lies in very affecting performances from the film's two young leads. Elden Henson (THE MIGHTY DUCKS movies) and Kieran Culkin (Macauley's brother) go beyond the simplistic stereotypes of precocious cripple and dim-witted hulk, and invest their characters with an appealing three-dimensionality. Lending star power to the production, Sharon Stone and Gillian Anderson are both good in their supporting roles.

Based on Rodman Philbrick's young adult novel *Freak the Mighty*, THE MIGHTY is certainly not exclusively for children, but that's generally the audience this inspirational tale is aimed at, and therein lies a problem. When Max and Kevin first team up, their concerns are dealing with tough bullies, giving Kevin the chance to play basketball on Max's shoulders, and gaining acceptance at school. With the duo's visions of imaginary knights on horseback flanking them as they roam Cincinnati, these are elements that will appeal to pre-teens, but which may strike older kids as simple and corny. But the movie's third act, in which Max is terrorized by his father and threatened with violence, may be too intense for younger viewers. While recommended, THE MIGHTY should be screened under some adult supervision. *(Violence.)*—P.R.

d, Peter Chelsom; p, Simon Fields, Jane Startz; exec p, Bob Weinstein, Harvey Weinstein, Julie Goldstein; co-p, Don Carmody; w, Charles Leavitt, Charles Leavitt (based on the novel *Freak the Mighty* by Rodman Philbrick); ph, John de Borman; ed, Martin Walsh; m, Trevor Jones; prod d, Caroline Hanania; art d, Dennis Davenport; set d, Cal Loucks; sound, Bruce Carwardine (mixer); fx, Michael Kavanagh; casting, Barbara Cohen, Mary Gail Artz; cos, Marie Sylvie Deveau; makeup, Christine Hart; stunts, Rick Forsayath

Children's/Drama **(PR: C MPAA: PG-13)**

MIGHTY JOE YOUNG ★★½

(U.S., 1998) 115m Jacobson Company;
Walt Disney Pictures; RKO Pictures;
Radiant Productions ~ Buena Vista c

Charlize Theron *(Jill Young)*; Bill Paxton *(Gregg O'Hara)*; Rade Sherbedgia *(Strasser)*; Peter Firth *(Garth)*; David Paymer *(Harry Ruben)*; Regina King *(Cecily Banks)*; Robert Wisdom *(Kweli)*; Naveen Andrews *(Pindi)*; Lawrence Pressman *(Dr. Baker)*; Linda Purl *(Dr. Ruth Young)*; Mika Boorem *(Young Jill)*; Geoffrey Blake *(Vern)*; Christian Clemenson *(Jack)*; Cory Buck *(Jason)*; Liz Georges; Richard Riehle *(Commander Gorman)*; Cynthia Allison *(News Reporter)*; Ken Taylor *(News Reporter)*; Ray Harryhausen *(Gentleman at Party)*; Terry Moore *(Elegant Woman at Party)*; Judson Mills *(Impatient Driver)*; Tony Genaro *(Boxer Shorts Man)*; Flo Di Re *(Bambi's Owners)*; Kaylan Romero; Hernan Ruiz; Jenilee Deal; Matt Deal *(Street Kids)*; Bethany Bassler; Vicki Davis; Deborah Kellner; Marguerite Moreau *(Cabriolet Girls)*; Tracey Walter *(Conservancy Girl)*; Larry Brandenburg *(Animal Control Duty Officer)*; Damien Leake *(Cop)*; Neal Kopit *(Cop)*; Janet Eilber *(Concerned Mother)*; Wiley Pickett *(Police Sharpshooter)*; John T. Bower *(Carjack Man)*; Hannah Swanson *(Toddler)*; Laurie Kilpatrick *(Toddler's Mom)*; Richard McGonagle *(Panda Owner)*; Reno Wilson *(Poacher)*; Theodore R. Hartley *(Society Man)*; Dina Merrill; Lily Mariye; John Alexander *(Joe Young)*

Following THE LION KING, THE JUNGLE BOOK (both 1994), GEORGE OF THE JUNGLE (1997), and several other African-set children's adventures, Disney's lucrative transformation of what used to be called "the Dark Continent" into a benign jungle theme park continues with MIGHTY JOE YOUNG, a glossy remake of the 1949 kiddie classic about a giant gorilla, which despite impressive special effects, comes off as even more corny and mechanical than the original.

Dr. Ruth Young (Linda Purl) and her young daughter Jill (Mika Boorem) are studying the behavior of apes in Africa, including a baby gorilla named Joe which Jill has befriended, and whose rare genetic mutation makes him grow faster than his peers. A pack of poachers led by Strasser (Rade Sherbedgia) kills Joe's mother and Ruth is also fatally wounded during the attack. Joe and Jill manage to escape after Joe bites off Strasser's thumb and trigger finger. Twelve years later, the adult Jill (Charlize Theron) and the 15-foot-tall Joe live in peace in their mountain retreat, but when American conservationist Gregg O'Hara (Bill Paxton) arrives and discovers Joe, the poachers also return and Gregg persuades Jill to move the gorilla to a California wildlife preserve, where she will remain Joe's caretaker. The preserve's director Dr. Harry Ruben (David Paymer) tries to push Jill out of the picture, but the preserve chairman Dr. Baker (Lawrence Pressman) realizes that Joe will be a great fund-raising tool and he lets Jill stay.

However, news of Joe's arrival reaches Strasser, who comes to California, and posing as a conservationist, tries to persuade Jill to bring Joe to his own "preserve," which is actually a front for black market trading in endangered animals. During a fancy fund-raising banquet, Strasser secretly provokes Joe into going on a rampage and Baker has the ape sedated and incarcerated. Jill decides to accept Strasser's invitation and she arranges for a truck to take Joe away, but soon realizes who Strasser really is after seeing his mangled hand. During a struggle, the truck crashes and Joe escapes. He runs through downtown LA and winds up at a carnival, where a fire starts. Jill and Gregg arrive, followed by Strasser, who is killed by Joe after he tries to shoot Jill. The police prepare to shoot Joe, but stop when he climbs to the top of a stuck Ferris wheel to rescue a child. Joe saves the boy just as the Ferris wheel collapses and crushes Joe, but he revives after a moment and returns to a wildlife preserve in Africa with Jill and Gregg.

MIGHTY JOE YOUNG seems to be suffering from an identity crisis, not sure if it wants to be a wholesome Disney family film, an Indiana Jones-style jungle adventure, or a high-tech homage to the 1949 film, featuring such references as the welcome return of the old RKO radio-tower logo—now in color—and cameos by the original's star, Terry Moore, and special-effects legend Ray Harryhausen. As a result, the film lacks a cohesive tone and style, and its mood varies wildly from innocuous to frightening. The opening sequence in the jungle featuring Jill and her Dian Fossey-like mother has a nice sense of mystery and wonder, but then the evil poachers show up (in a scene that's way too scary for young kids) sporting the usual assortment of stereotyped German-Russian-South African-Australian accents and the film thereafter becomes mired in one cliche after another. Chortling with venomous glee, his mutilated hand clad in a black leather holster, Strasser is one of the most laughably caricatured villains since the days of Snidely Whiplash, while the depiction of the savage natives as subservient to the beautiful white goddess Jill (who's lent an unfortunate subtext by being played by the South African Charlize Theron) is surprisingly un-PC for Disney. The special effects, melding computer animation, animatronics engineering, and Rick Baker's gorilla suit, are undeniably convincing, giving the impression that Joe is real, but the filmmakers' efforts are defeated by the fact that the gorilla is hunched over to such a degree that he doesn't appear to be that big. The final chase through Hollywood featuring such landmarks as the Chinese Theatre is well done, but the shameless ending is cornball beyond belief: after the apparently dead Joe suddenly opens his eyes, the little boy he saved reaches into his pocket for some change, followed by the cops and everyone else at the carnival, so that Jill can buy a preserve in which Joe can live. *(Violence.)* —M.S.

d, Ron Underwood; p, Tom Jacobson, Ted Hartley; exec p, Gail Katz; assoc p, Jackie Rubin Levine, Jim Chory; w, Lawrence Konner, Mark Rosenthal (based on the original screenplay by Ruth Rose and Merian C. Cooper); ph, Don Peterman, Oliver Wood; ed, Paul Hirsch; m, James Horner; prod d, Michael Corenblith; art d, Charlie Daboub; set d, Meredith Boswell; anim, Chris Bailey; sound, Richard Bryce Goodman (mixer); fx, Allen Hall, Hoyt Yeatman, Jim Mitchell; casting, Pam Dixon Mickelson; cos, Molly Maginnis; makeup, Deborah K. Larsen, Rick Baker (effects); stunts, Terry Leonard

AAN Best Visual Effects: Rick Baker, Hoyt Yeatman, Allen Hall, Jim Mitchell

Fantasy/Adventure/Action (PR: A MPAA: PG)

MIGHTY KONG, THE ★★

(U.S., 1998) 72m The LANA Film Company ~ Warner Home Video c

Voice Cast: Dudley Moore *(C.B. Denham)*; Jodi Benson *(Ann Darrow)*; Randy Hamilton *(Jack Driscoll)*; William Sage III *(Roscoe)*; Jason Gray-Stanford *(Ricky)*; Richard Newman *(Captain)*; Don Brown; Ian James Corlett; Michael Dobson; Paul Dobson

An animated musical comedy-adventure for children, THE MIGHTY KONG is (no surprise) based on the 1933 classic KING KONG. Cheaply produced and boasting a number of forgettable songs, the film was released straight to video in 1998.

Flamboyant, egotistical showman C.B. Denham (voice of Dudley Moore) charters the S.S. Java Queen for an expedition that will serve as the subject of his next film which will star Ann Darrow (voice of Jodi Benson), a struggling movie extra he rescued from the streets of Depression-era New York. On board the ship are first mate Jack Driscoll (voice of Randy Hamilton), cabin boy Ricky (voice of Jason Gray-Stanford), C.B.'s bumbling assistant Roscoe (voice of William Sage III), and an apprehensive crew.

They reach Skull Island in the South Seas, reputed home of a legendary "Monkey God." The initial trip to the island is cut short by hostile natives. At night, following a romantic duet by Ann and Jack, the natives steal aboard the ship and abduct Ann, whom they wish to sacrifice to their god, Kong. The crew races to the island in pursuit and gets there in time to see Kong, a giant ape, pick Ann up in his hand and take her into the jungle. Jack goes on his own through a cavern to the island's interior to head off Kong and try and rescue Ann, while C.B. and Roscoe follow to try to capture Kong on film, an effort consistently undercut by Roscoe's clumsiness. Jack rescues Ann and hurries back to the beach where the crewmen manage to knock out Kong with gas bombs, just as the island's volcano erupts. In New York City, C.B. presents Kong on Broadway, but the commotion of the opening excites Kong who breaks free in a search for Ann. After a series of misadventures on the streets of New York, Kong finds Ann and climbs with her to the top of the Empire State Building only to get knocked off by a pair of dirigibles trying to snare him in a net. As C.B. proclaims that "it was Beauty that killed the Beast," the wounded Kong opens his eyes.

The best that can be said for this witless, misguided cartoon adaptation is that it will doubtless spur disgruntled parents and guardians to expose their children to the original KING KONG (which gets not one word of acknowledgement in this production's credits). Although it follows the original story closely, with one scene lifted from Dino De Laurentiis' modernized 1976 remake, THE MIGHTY KONG leaves out all the excitement and suspense, not to mention the death and destruction, by interjecting a series of light-hearted songs and inappropriate gags, and transforming Carl Denham (played so memorably in the original by Robert Armstrong) from an adventure-seeking, glory-hungry showman into C.B. Denham, a blithely unflappable narcissist with a British accent. It's all tossed together like a Saturday morning cartoon and wastes the talents of Moore, Benson (1989's THE LITTLE MERMAID) and songwriters Richard M. and Robert B. Sherman, who've fallen a long way from the heights of MARY POPPINS (1964). The animation was farmed out to China and Korea, and the voice dubbing to an oft-used Canadian dubbing house.—B.C.

d, Art Scott; p, Lyn Henderson, Denis De Vallance; exec p, Koichi Motohashi, George W. Drysdale; assoc p, Bob Meister; w, William J. Keenan; ed, Tony Hayman; m, Richard M. Sherman, Robert B. Sherman, David Seibels; prod d, Lyn Henderson, Brendan De Vallance; anim, Emily Kong, Iwao Takamoto; casting, Eddie Foy III

Animated/Adventure/Musical (PR: A MPAA: G)

MILO ★★

(U.S., 1998) 90m Treehouse Films; Filmwave Pictures ~ Sterling Home Entertainment c

Jennifer Jostyn *(Claire Mullins)*; Antonio Fargas *(Mr. Kelso)*; Paula Cale *(Marian)*; Maya McLaughlin *(Abigail)*; Vincent Schiavelli *(Dr. Matthew Jeeder)*; Asher Metchik *(Milo)*; Rae'ven

Larrymore Kelly *(Kendra)*; Jordan Blake Warkol *(Evan)*; Walter Olkewicz *(Jack Wyatt)*; Richard Portnow *(Lt. Parker)*; Christel Khalil *(Young Claire)*; Paige Tarnada *(Young May)*; Fiona Landers *(Young Abigail)*; Ashley Nation *(Young Ruth)*; Jennifer Regli *(Young Marian)*; Jill Andre *(Mrs. Dover)*; Darin Heames *(Young Custodian)*; David Robinson *(Officer Tibits)*

To the roster of horror villains with ordinary names like Jason, Michael, and Freddy, one can't quite add Milo, a promising character underserved by this movie.

Five young girls are lured by a boy named Milo Jeeder (Asher Metchik) to the office of his gynecologist father, where he murders one and wounds another. Sixteen years later, the injured girl, Claire (Jennifer Jostyn), is a schoolteacher who returns to her hometown for the wedding of Ruth, one of her old pals, only to discover when she arrives that Ruth has been killed in a car accident. Taking over Ruth's class, Claire starts seeing the rain-slickered Milo lurking around the school. The other survivors of the doctor's office incident, Abigail (Maya McLaughlin) and Marian (Paula Cale), put down her fears, as Milo apparently drowned years before. Soon, however, Abigail is assaulted by Milo and disappears.

Claire and Marian go to see Dr. Jeeder (Vincent Schiavelli), who shows them Milo's grave. That night, the two women spot Milo and follow him, only to have Milo attack Marian and drag her off. Later, while Dr. Jeeder is meeting with Claire after school, Milo stabs custodian Mr. Kelso (Antonio Fargas), and Dr. Jeeder takes Claire and Kelso to his clinic. There, he reveals that Milo was a stillbirth he was able to bring back to life, and the boy attacks Claire. As she is chased through the house, Claire discovers the freshly murdered Dr. Jeeder, and Kelso attempts to protect her, only to be killed himself. Claire finally dispatches Milo in the cellar.

A final scene suggesting that Milo is still alive is as half-hearted as most of what has preceded it. It's a shame that a movie that starts so strongly can end so weakly. The opening scene with Milo and the girls in Dr. Jeeder's clinic is unnerving, and sets up promising possibilities for the main story to come, but the movie doesn't follow through. The idea of an ageless young boy haunting a small town is dramatized in Craig Mitchell's script in too literal a fashion to be believable; Pascal Franchot's direction is equally half-hearted and unimaginative. Nor is Jennifer Jostyn convincing enough in the lead—perhaps a clue as to why she's third-billed in the movie and on the video packaging. Milo himself cuts a fairly creepy figure, pedaling an old bicycle and wearing a yellow raincoat (calling up memories of the young, slickered killer in 1977's cult favorite ALICE, SWEET ALICE). Yet the more the movie insists the viewer accept him at face value, rather than as a manifestation of Claire's fears, the less effective he becomes. *(Graphic violence, adult situations, profanity.)* —M.G.

d, Pascal Franchot; p, Jeff Kirshbaum, Hans Bauer; exec p, Oliver Eberle, Fuminori Hayashida; assoc p, Susi Seydelmann; w, Craig Mitchell; ph, Yuri Neyman; ed, Donn Aron, Ross Guidici; m, Kevin Manthei; prod d, Frank Bollinger; art d, Angela Trujillo, Terri Phillips; set d, Eden Barr; sound, Coleman Metts, Ben Patrick, Leonard Marcel; casting, Betsy Fels; makeup, Tarra Day, Terese Vest; stunts, Ignacio Alvarez

Horror **(PR: O MPAA: R)**

MIRROR, THE ★★★½

(Iran, 1997) 95m Rooz Films ~ Celuloid Dreams c (AYNEH)

Mina Mohammad-Khani *(Little Girl/Mina)*; Kazem Mojdehi; Naser Omuni; M. Shirzad; T. Samadpour

Rendered in an approximation of real time, THE MIRROR abruptly shifts midway from an involving exercise in slice-of-life neorealism to a mock documentary in the cinema-verite style. Both segments of the film concern a little girl trying to make her way home through the busy streets of Tehran.

When her mother fails to pick her up after first-grade class lets out, a small girl (Mina Mohammad-Khani) embarks on a journey to find her way home. Despite lots of hustle and bustle to and fro, she makes very little progress and remains lost. Ultimately, the worried girl finds herself on a bus that she hopes will take her close to her house. Among the passengers are an old woman who complains that her ungrateful children are ashamed of her country ways and won't let her see her grandchild.

"Don't look at the camera, Mina," a voice says. "I'm not acting anymore!" replies the girl, who is not really lost but is playing a part in a movie. After all efforts to change her mind fail, the child walks off the movie to find her own way home. Still miked for sound, she is followed by the cameras of the film crew, who want to see what they can salvage from the situation.

Mina's homeward odyssey proves to be just as frustratingly willy-nilly as that of her fictional counterpart. At one point she encounters the old woman who was on the bus. The lonely woman reveals that she is not a professional actress but was playing herself. Eventually, the lost child finds her way to the shop of the man who recruited her for the film. He urges her to return to work, but to no avail. Safe at home at last, Mina is visited by a member of the film crew, who tells her she must finish the movie they are shooting. Again she refuses.

Jafar Panahi's THE MIRROR begins in the mode of his sleeper hit THE WHITE BALLOON (1996), then radically changes stylistic gears about 40 minutes in, when the central figure steps out of character. Panahi said he had been toying with this idea but did not commit to it until the first little girl he had cast refused to play her role as written and had to be replaced. (She appears only in the finished film's opening shot, a lengthy establishing shot that crosses and recrosses a busy street before finally alighting on the movie's small protagonist.)

THE MIRROR's two distinct segments are shot in radically different styles. Part one, like THE WHITE BALLOON, is a fluid and controlled stretch of film that has been carefully crafted to simulate the spontaneity of everyday life. Part two, though possibly just as precisely planned as the first part, fakes the appearance of off-the-cuff, on-the-fly filmmaking through jumpy hand-held camerawork that seems to be even farther off course than the little girl it is attempting to follow—for long intervals the girl totally eludes the camera's range and for a time the soundtrack goes dead, as if the mike is malfunctioning.

At first one is tempted to feel betrayed by this conceit; one wants to know what happens to the fictional girl. What saves THE MIRROR from being nothing more than an extended and somewhat cruel prank on its audience is the "mirroring" of the two stories. Story two essentially continues the narrative of story one on a different level—the movie is still about a little girl trying to get home. Thus, THE MIRROR has its fun and keeps its promises too.

Although many will wish that the running times of the film's two sections were reversed—much of part two, the longer section, is spent watching cars blur by the clueless cameraman's lens—THE MIRROR is a charming adventure on both its levels. Especially appealing is its involving real-time structure, unsullied by background music, and also welcome are the insights into contemporary Iranian society glimpsed along the way.—D.T.

d, Jafar Panahi; p, Jafar Panahi, V. Nikkhah-Azad; w, Jafar Panahi; ph, Farzad Jodat; ed, Jafar Panahi; sound, Yadollah Najafi, M Delpak

Comedy **(PR: A MPAA: NR)**

MISBEGOTTEN ★½

(U.S., 1998) 97m American World Pictures ~ CFP Distribution c

Kevin Dillon *(Billy Crapshoot)*; Nick Mancuso *(Paul Bourke)*; Lysette Anthony *(Caitlin Bourke)*; Robert Lewis *(Detective Cross)*; Matthew Walker *(Dr. Dotterweigh)*; Stefan Arngrim *(Conan Cornelius)*; Kate Luyben *(Myrna)*; Megan Leitch *(Serena)*; Jo Bates *(Dr. Rory Sorenson)*; Claire Riley *(Detective Gandy)*; J.B. Bivens *(Detective Helfand)*; Felicia Shulman *(Lamaze Instructor)*; Robert Weiss *(Florist)*; Claudio DeVictor *(Dispatcher)*; Amanda O'Leary *(Nurse)*; Adrienne Arsenault *(TV Anchor)*; Owen Walstrom *(Partial Burn Cop)*; Jon Bak *(Chop Shop Owner)*; Rick Perce *(Roof Sniper)*

A disappointment from the pen of cult fave Larry Cohen, MISBEGOTTEN is an unpleasant, topsy-turvy flick about a spermicidal maniac who donates his seed and then insists that an unsuspecting couple reward him with a Daddy's rights.The film premiered on cable before being released on home video.

In the course of a car-jacking, serial killer Billy Crapshoot (Kevin Dillon) murders songwriter Conan Cornelius (Stefan Arngrim) and assumes his identity. After keeping Cornelius's appointment to be an anonymous sperm donor, Billy enjoys the high life at the late musician's home. He murders Cornelius's girlfriend Myrna (Kate Luyben) when she impugns his sexual prowess.

Paul (Nick Mancuso) and Caitlin (Lysette Anthony), an infertile couple, unwittingly become the recipients of Billy's demented gene pool after Caitlin is artificially inseminated with Billy's seed which she believes is Conan Cornelius's. At the clinic run by oleaginous Dr. Dotterweigh (Matthew Walker), Billy tortures a physician into revealing Caitlin's whereabouts.

Tiring of merely sending flowers in Cornelius's name, expectant father Billy stalks Caitlin, threatens her shaky marriage, and confronts a jealous Paul. Billy slays Paul and sends his head in a gift box to Caitlin's baby shower. Later, he kidnaps Caitlin from a maternity hospital. Although Billy emerges victorious from a shootout with cops, Caitlin grabs a fallen officer's gun and blows off his private parts. Using a falsified blood test, Dr. Dotterweigh convinces the emotionally fragile Caitlin that Nick is the father of the child she gives birth to.

MISBEGOTTEN is an aptly titled scare-mongering tale about not putting all your fertile eggs in one demented basket. Ridiculously plotted in Larry Cohen's typically imaginative but slapdash manner, the film doesn't measure up to Cohen's other outre genre pieces like GOD TOLD ME TO (1976). Camp quickly gets the upper hand and quells any chills. Besides the jokey tone, the film is hurt by a minefield of plot-holes. Why does Billy bother to keep Cornelius's donor appointment? Why doesn't Caitlin double check on Dr. Dotterweigh's claims about her infant's bloodline? Memorable for a few sick scenes, MISBEGOTTEN is a souped-up slasher flick that bastardizes its own intriguing bad seed premise. *(Graphic violence, extreme profanity, nudity, sexual situations.)*—R.P.

d, Mark L. Lester; p, Mark L. Lester, Dana Dubovsky; exec p, Jeff Sackman; w, Larry Cohen (based in the book by James Gabriel Berman); ph, Mark Irwin; ed, David Berlatsky; m, Paul Zara; prod d, Paul Joyal; set d, Gail Luining; sound, John Laing; fx, Al Benjamin; casting, Rosemary Welden, Susan Taylor Brouse; cos, Margaret Loveniuk; makeup, Dana Michelle Hamel; stunts, Owen Walstrom

Horror/Thriller **(PR: C MPAA: R)**

MR. JEALOUSY ★★½

(U.S., 1998) 105m Joel Castleberg Productions ~ Lions Gate Films c

Eric Stoltz *(Lester Grimm)*; Annabella Sciorra *(Ramona Ray)*; Chris Eigeman *(Dashiell Frank)*; Carlos Jacott *(Vince)*; Marianne Jean-Baptiste *(Lucretia)*; Brian Kerwin *(Stephen)*; Peter Bogdanovich *(Dr. Poke)*; Bridget Fonda *(Irene)*; John Lehr *(Lint)*; Jay McInerney; Dean Wareham

Though often clever and literate, MR. JEALOUSY lacks much of the charm and focus that made filmmaker Noah Baumbach's debut feature KICKING AND SCREAMING (1995) so successful. Baumbach's reliance on a number of stylistic devices, including flashy editing and and an intrusive third-person narration, winds up alienating the viewer from the story line and characters—never a good thing for a romantic comedy.

At the age of 15, Lester (Eric Stoltz) loses his first girlfriend to an older man. From that point on, he becomes jealous and possessive of everyone he dates, to the extent that he loses one girlfriend because he spends so much time following her ex-boyfriend that he has hardly any time left to spend with her.

By the time he is 30, Lester lives in Brooklyn, where he ekes out a living as a substitute teacher, having decided to pursue a career as a writer instead of his intended goal of attending graduate school. He starts a relationship with Ramona (Annabella Sciorra); though they get along well, he is disturbed by thoughts of her past. He becomes obsessed with one of her ex-boyfriends, a currently fashionable young writer named Dashiell Frank (Chris Eigeman), he begins following Dashiell around town, and even joins Dashiell's therapy group.

In therapy, Lester takes on the persona of his friend Vince (Carlos Jacott), and spends more time criticizing Dashiell than talking about himself. Eventually, Dashiell, who appreciates the fact that "Vince" is unafraid to challenge him, invites "Vince" to coffee and they become friends. Though Ramona isn't a big part of Dashiell's past, she does come up in conversation, and Lester's jealousy grows. Eventually, the lies that Lester comes up with to explain the time he's spending in group therapy arouse Ramona's suspicion, and she comes looking for him, only to meet with Dashiell again. Lester, Ramona, Dashiell, and the real Vince all meet outside of the therapist's office and the truth comes out. Dashiell punches Lester and Ramona leaves him. Lester goes to graduate school to write. He comes back to New York for Vince's wedding and sees Ramona again, after four years apart. The two still have fond feelings for each other, and begin to explore the possibility of dating again.

While KICKING AND SCREAMING worked as a simple parable about dating trends in the 1990s, MR. JEALOUSY doesn't have a complex enough story line to sustain the same "sociological" slant. For instance, though Lester and Ramona are both driven characters, their relationship is never fleshed out: its only defining features are Lester's jealousy and Ramona's ties to her past. We never know what they see in each other, or what they do when they're together.

The film relies on more third-person narration than any other film in recent memory, and often it seems as if Baumbach opted for the narration simply to hurry the story along. In other words, much of the film's plot is *told* rather than shown. Baumbach utilizes jump cuts, freeze frames, and quick transitions between scenes in the same way, ensuring that the film resembles a snapshot album rather than a moving picture.

Baumbach has assembled an outstanding cast, but his dialogue is so unnatural-sounding in this instance, it's impossible for audience members to warm up to the characters. Eigeman, who impressed in another 1998 film, THE LAST DAYS OF DISCO, appears more concerned with his dialogue than his character's emotions. Former Academy Award nominee Marianne Jean-Baptiste (SECRETS AND LIES) is unfortunately given an uneventful role as Vince's fiancee. Bridget Fonda has a scene-stealing role as Dashiell's girlfriend, a young woman overcoming a severe stutter. Fonda is lucky enough not to be victimized by the dialogue, as her character's lines are, by necessity, simpler and sparer than everyone else's.

Though the film is mostly a serious study of an obsessive whose passion and paranoia ruins the things he holds dearest, certain scenes are light enough to elicit a few chuckles, as when the real Vince joins thc therapy group with a silly British accent, or when Ramona's superstitions are explored. This lighter touch might have been the key to success; as it sits, however, the film is well-intentioned and mildly likable, but severely lacking in energy. Much like Lester, Baumbach demonstrates that he needs to have more faith in himself; less reliance on narrative gimmicks, and the film could have been a far more endearing creation. *(Sexual situations, profanity.)*—A.M.

d, Noah Baumbach; p, Joel Castleberg; exec p, Eric Stoltz; w, Noah Baumbach; ph, Steven Bernstein; ed, J. Kathleen Gibson; m, Luna, Robert Een; prod d, Anne Stuhler; art d, Roswell Hamrick; set d, Candis Heiland; sound, Jeff Pullman (mixer); casting, Todd Thaler; cos, Katherine Jane Bryant

Romance/Comedy/Drama (PR: C MPAA: R)

MR. NICE GUY ★★★

(Hong Kong, 1997) 113m Golden Harvest ~ New Line c
(YATGO HO YAN; YIGE HAO REN)

Jackie Chan *(Jackie)*; Richard Norton *(Giancarlo)*; Miki Lee *(Miki)*; Karen McLymont *(Lakeisha)*; Gabrielle Fitzpatrick *(Diana)*; Vince Poletto *(Romeo)*; Barry Otto *(Baggio)*; Sammo Hung *(Cyclist)*; Emil Chau *(Ice Cream Vendor)*; Mina Godenzi *(Cook Show Audience)*; Peter Houghton *(Richard)*; Peter Lindsay *(Gronk)*; David No *(Victor)*; Rachel Blakely *(Sandy)*; Judy Green *(Tina)*; Stephan Friedrich; Jonathan Isgar; Steve Kahlua; Matthew Meersbergen; Stuart Ritchie; Kyne Sedgman; Matt Trihey; Les Uzice *(Demons)*; Karl Ajami; Bradley Allan; Paul Andreovski; David Baldwin; Kerry Blakeman; Mark Campbell; Terry Carter; Dennis Christensen; Tony Doherty; Cameron Douglas; Paul Douglas; Stuart Ellis; Mark Fitzpatrick; Stuart Fraser; Michael Hammad; Habby Heske; Brent Houghton; Richard Huggett; Graham Jahne; Chris Kemp; Robert Lowe; Frederick MacClure; Douglas "Rocky" MacDonald; Ian Mall; Den McCoy; Mike Menzies; Jason Murphy; Michael John Noonan; George Novak; Grant Page; Puven Pather; Harry Pavlidis; George Popovic; John Raaen; Joseph Sayah; Gary Shambrooke; Vess Svorcan; Davin Taylor; Darko Tuskan; Jade Weitering; Chris Wilson; Damon Young *(Giancarlo's Men)*; Aaron Notarfrancesco *(Sonny)*; Jake Notarfrancesco *(Nancy)*; Frederick Miragliotta *(NEA Head Officer)*; Nick Carrafa; Rod Catteral; Ben Mitchell; Mark Neal; Jerome Pride *(NEA Agents)*; Keith Agius *(Specal Action Team Leader)*; Greg Jamieson *(Priest)*; Matthew Dytynski *(Floor Manager)*; Salik Silverstein *(Cook Show Director)*; Lynn Murphy *(Babysitter)*; Nicholas Bufalo *(Passerby)*

Jackie Chan is reunited with longtime associate Sammo Hung (star of TV's "Martial Law") for this amiable action comedy set in Melbourne, Australia. Hung handled directorial chores on this Chan vehicle, which features Jackie as a TV chef who unwittingly gets caught in the middle of a gang war.

When a confrontation between Melbourne drug lord Giancarlo (Richard Norton) and the Demons, a gang that stole his latest cocaine shipment, erupts into a shooting spree, it is videotaped by reporter Diana (Gabrielle Fitzpatrick). As Giancarlo's goons chase her through the streets, she runs into Jackie (Jackie Chan) on his way home from taping his TV show. Jackie helps her get away from the thugs, but her tape gets mixed up with a batch he gives to the grandchildren of his partner Baggio (Barry Otto). Along with his assistant Lakeisha (Karen McLymont) and his girlfriend Miki (Miki Lee), who is visiting from China, Jackie repels attacks from both Giancarlo and the Demons.

Jackie doesn't understand what is going on until he finds Diana ransacking his apartment for the missing tape. They escape Jackie's apartment just before Giancarlo's men arrive and are blown up by the Demons. The Demons kidnap Miki to force Jackie to give them the tape, but police officers at the scene of the exchange scare the kidnappers away, and Jackie decides to do without their help. At a construction site where the Demons have arranged to sell Giancarlo the tape and his drugs, Giancarlo instead kills most of the Demons, retrieves his drugs, and captures Jackie and Lakeisha, whom he takes back to his secluded mansion. After being beaten by Giancarlo, Jackie escapes and uses a giant construction truck to destroy the mansion. The police arrive to find the fleeing Giancarlo covered in spilled cocaine, and arrest him and his men.

For better or worse, MR. NICE GUY is a look at the future of Jackie Chan. Except for a few scenes in which he converses in Chinese with costar Miki Lee, Jackie speaks in English throughout. He's clearly not comfortable with the language, but it's what the market demands. Fortunately, despite his increasing age, he remains comfortable with the kinetic style that made him famous around the world. The difference is that the fight scenes are increasingly comic; he has almost entirely abandoned martial arts except as a general basis for slapstick gags. That's probably also why he decided to work again with Sammo Hung (who has a funny cameo as an irate cyclist); Hung favors broad, knockabout comedy, and doesn't let the film get bogged down in plot. Of course, at times the plot goes right out the window, but if you're watching one of these movies for the story line, you have been misdirected.

Like most Chan vehicles, MR. NICE GUY consists essentially of a series of action set pieces, all smoothly executed. The best is a fight between Chan and Giancarlo's men set on a construction site, which offers plenty of the props Chan likes to work with (a la the warehouse scene in 1994's RUMBLE IN THE BRONX) . The poorest is the finale, which doesn't even truly involve Chan, as a massive truck (the tires alone appear to be about 12 feet high) is used to level the mansion. Apparently gone are the days when Chan movies ended with a battle royale between him and some well-chosen opponent.

The American release of MR. NICE GUY lacks ten minutes of footage from the original release, mostly having to do with the film's three female characters. Little of it is missed, except for a scene showing what has become of Diana and a female Demon leader (after the scene at the construction site, they are seen in the hospital telling the police where to find Jackie.) It is also worth noting that the American version of MR. NICE GUY lacks the hip-hop and rock songs that have been welded onto previous Chan films when they were shown here. *(Violence.)*—M.F.

d, Sammo Hung, billed as Samo Hung; p, Chua Lam; exec p, Leonard Ho; assoc p, Chow Chun Tung; co-p, Tso Kin Nam; w, Edward Tang, billed as Edward Tang King Sang, Fibe Ma; ph, Raymond Lam; ed, Peter Cheung; m, J. Peter Robinson, Peter

Kam; prod d, Horace Ma; art d, Chau Sai Hung; set d, Jill Eden; sound, Gretchen Thornburn (mixer); fx, Peter Stubbs; casting, Maura Fay; cos, Lui Fung Shan; makeup, Poon Men Wah, Jose Perez, Paul Pattison; stunts, Cho Wing, Jackie Chan Stuntmen Team

Action/Comedy **(PR: C MPAA: PG-13)**

MOBILE SUIT GUNDAM I ★★★½

(Japan, 1981) 139m Sunrise ~ Anime Village c

Japanese Voice Cast: Toru Furuya *(Amuro Ray)*; Shuichi Ikeda *(Char Aznable)*; Hirotaka Suzuoki *(Noah Bright)*; Fuyumi Shiraishi *(Mirai Yashima)*

MOBILE SUIT GUNDAM I, the first movie in the GUNDAM series, was released on US home video in 1998, giving American fans of Japanese animation and science fiction the opportunity to enjoy the initial segments of the longest continuous science fiction franchise in Japanese history. A story of war between the earth and outer space colonists and the manned mobile fighting suits which dominate the space battles, the GUNDAM series offers exciting storytelling, expert animation, well-written characters, and spectacular action.

In Universal Century 79 (in the 22nd century), after Earth has built orbiting space colonies called "Sides," a civil war breaks out between the Earth Federation and a group of rebel space colonists calling itself the Zeon Archduchy. After a series of destructive battles which take millions of civilian lives, the opposing sides resort to smaller manned robotic weapons called Mobile Suits. During a battle on Side 7, young Amuro Ray climbs into the Gundam, a prototype for a new Federation mobile suit, and successfully fends off the attacking Zeon mobile suits, led by Char Aznable, a rising young officer in the Zeon military. Because the senior officers are all killed or wounded in the battle, the Federation ship White Base leaves Side 7 piloted by a youthful crew, led by Lieutenant Noah Bright, and housing dozens of refugees.

The White Base heads for Federation Territory on Earth, but is subjected to numerous attacks along the way. During these battles, Amuro gradually learns the skills needed to operate the Gundam to maximum effect and grows more confident in his abilities. But he has moments of great anguish at having to kill at such a tender age. Meanwhile, Zeon consistently underestimates the Federation weapons and their young pilots, and there is growing talk of "New Types," young people with heightened psychic sensibilities and skills.

In one of the battles, the heir to the Zeon throne, Garma Zabi, is killed, throwing the Zeon elite into turmoil. Char Aznable watches from the sidelines and recognizes Amuro as a future—and most worthy—opponent.

This first GUNDAM movie was compiled from the first 13 episodes of the 1979 TV series of the same name and released theatrically in Japan in 1981. It was followed by two other movies compiled, in part, from the TV series, and numerous subsequent TV series, movies, and original animation video (OAV) releases, which continue to this day.

"Gundam" was not the first serious animated space sci-fi series in Japan, but it raised the level of technical sophistication, character development, and animated storytelling to a new high. It also created a plausible, well-thought-out science fiction future, eschewing the fantastic alien elements of other animated Japanese TV series of the era. Credit goes to series creator Yoshiyuki Tomino, who directed the TV series and most of the subsequent theatrical films and guided many of the later Gundam incarnations. He also wrote three well-received science fiction novels based on the TV series. *(Violence.)*—B.C.

d, Ryoji Fujiwara; w, Hiroyuki Hoshiyama, Yoshihisa Araki; art d, Mitsuki Nakamura; anim, Yoshikazu Yasuhiko

Animated/Science Fiction **(PR: A MPAA: NR)**

MOBILE SUIT GUNDAM II: SOLDIERS OF SORROW ★★★

(Japan, 1981) 133m Sunrise ~ Anime Village c

Japanese Voice Cast: Toru Furuya *(Amuro Ray)*; Shuichi Ikeda *(Char Aznable)*; Hirotaka Suzuoki *(Noah Bright)*; Fuyumi Shiraishi *(Mirai Yashima)*

MOBILE SUIT GUNDAM II, compiled from the middle section of the celebrated 1979 Japanese animated TV series, continues the action-packed saga of the space ship White Base and its battles with the Zeon Archduchy.

The adventures of the Federation battleship White Base continue on earth as the young crew gains more experience and learns to work comfortably as a team. At one point, however, Amuro Ray overhears the news that he'll be removed as pilot of the Gundam mobile suit and he reacts by taking the Gundam and flying off into the desert. When the White Base is attacked, he returns, successfully defends the ship, and is reinstated.

In Belfast, where the ship stops to refuel, Ensign Kai Shiden gets involved with Michelle, a Zeon spy. Michelle has a change of heart and opts to join Kai, sacrificing herself in a battle with other Zeon spies. The White Base finally arrives at underground Federation headquarters in the Amazon jungle, where General Revil congratulates the crew for having survived so many battles. He announces their formation as an Independent New Type Squadron. Several of the possible "New Types," individuals who have heightened intuition and insight, begin to experience regular psychic flashes, including messages from dead comrades.

Zeon officer Char Aznable leads a spy mission into the underground base to determine what new weapons the Federation is preparing, then launches a major attack. Amuro and Char have their second major confrontation, the Zeon forces are thwarted.

The second "Mobile Suit Gundam" movie was released in 1981 and compiled from episodes 16 to 30 of the original TV series with about 30% new animation. As the second part of a trilogy, it's not as dramatically compelling as the first film, which introduced all the youthful characters by unceremoniously plunging them into wartime peril, nor as spectacular as Part III (Encounters in Space), which emphasizes the flourishing of the characters' New Type capabilities, but it still boasts numerous twists and turns, tragic deaths, explosive battle action, and occasional quiet moments. It also deftly charts the shifting, deepening relationships of a solid cast of characters. *(Violence.)*—B.C.

d, Yoshiyuki Tomino; w, Hiroyuki Hoshiyama, Yoshihisa Araki, Masaru Yamamoto, Ken'ichi Matsuzaki; art d, Mitsuki Nakamura; anim, Yoshikazu Yasuhiko

Animated/Science Fiction **(PR: A MPAA: NR)**

MOBILE SUIT GUNDAM III: ENCOUNTERS IN SPACE ★★★

(Japan, 1982) 140m Sunrise ~ Anime Village c

Japanese Voice Cast: Toru Furuya *(Amuro Ray)*; Shuichi Ikeda *(Char Aznable)*; Hirotaka Suzuoki *(Capt. Noah Bright)*; Fuyumi Shiraishi *(Lt. Mirai Yashima)*; Keiko Han *(Lalah Sun)*

The third in the series of Gundam movies compiled from the 1979 Japanese animated TV series, MOBILE SUIT GUNDAM III was released in 1982 and included some new animation to tidy up its epic saga of a future civil war in space. After refueling on earth, the Federation battleship White Base heads into space to link up with the larger Federation Army. The ship makes a stop on Side 6, a neutral space colony where Gundam pilot Amuro Ray meets Char Aznable (as well as Char's beautiful protege Lalah Sun) face-to-face for the first time. Behind-the-scenes political machinations within the Zeon Archduchy result in Degin Zabi, the ruler of Zeon, being caught in Zeon's solar ray while petitioning for peace with the Federation. In a subsequent battle, Amuro feels a psychic connection with Lalah Sun, who is piloting the new Zeon craft, and determines they are both "New Types" (young people with heightened psychic sensibilities and skills); Lalah is killed in the battle.

Federation and Zeon forces engage in fierce battle in space over the moon; the destruction is so complete that the combatants wind up fighting hand-to-hand on the surface of the moon, amidst the ruins of an old base. As the moon base is set to explode, Amuro psychically contacts the rest of the White Base crew and directs each of them to appropriate escape routes. The crew members all receive his signals and make it off the moon in a small launch as the moon base and White Base explode.

In this edition, compiled from the last 13 episodes of the original 43-part series with substantial new animation, the characters become more aware of their New Type capabilities and Amuro Ray has his fateful meeting with his beautiful New Type counterpart Lalah Sun. The condensation of the narrative and the inclusion of so many technical details and political maneuvers leads to some confusion and awkward jumps in the narrative. Still, it ranks as a superb representative sample of one of the best animated series to come out of Japan and was followed by subsequent "Gundam" TV programs, OAV (original animation video) series, and two more movies, including CHAR'S COUNTERATTACK (1988) which finishes up the story of Amuro and Char. *(Violence.)*—B.C.

d, Yoshiyuki Tomino; w, Hiroyuki Hoshiyama, Yoshihisa Araki, Masaru Yamamoto, Ken'ichi Matsuzaki; art d, Mitsuki Nakamura; anim, Yoshikazu Yasuhiko

Animated/Science Fiction (PR: A MPAA: NR)

MODULATIONS: CINEMA FOR THE EAR ★★½

(U.S., 1998) 75m Caipirinha Productions ~ Strand Releasing c/bw

Afrika Bambaataa; Alec Empire; Alvin Toffler; Armand Van Helden; Arthur Baker; Autechre; Bill Laswell; Brian Eno; Bundy Brown; Calvin Bush; Carl Cox; Carl Craig; Christian Marclay; Danny Tenaglia; Darren Emerson; David Toop; DB; Derrick Carter; Derrick May; DJ Atrak; DJ Funk; DJ Pierre; DJ Sneak; DJ Spooky; Doc Scott; DXT; Ed Rush; Eddie Fowlkes; Florian Schneider; Frankie Bones; Fumiya Tanaka; Future Sound of London; Genesis P-Orridge; Giorgio Moroder; Hardfloor; Holger Czukay; Irmin Schmidt; Invisibl Skratch Piklz; Jesse Saunders; Joey Beltram; Jonah Sharp; Jonathon More; Juan Atkins; Karlheinz Stockhausen; Ken Ishii; Kevin Saunderson; Kid Koala; Kodwo Eshun; Kraftwerk; Lee Ranaldo; LTJ Bukem; Markus Popp; Marshall Jefferson; Matt Black; Meat Beat Manifesto; Mike Dearborn; Mixmaster Morris; Moby; Money Mark; O Yuki Conjugate; Orbital; Oval; Panacea; Paul Johnson; Photek; Pierre Henry; Prodigy; Prototype 909; Ralf Hutter; Rob Playford; Robert Moog; Robert Pepperell; Roni Size; Sasha; Scanner; Sensorband; Simon Reynolds; Squarepusher; Stacey Pullen; Surgeon; Talvin Singh; Teo Macero; Terre Thaemlitz; Tetsu Inoue; Westbam; X-ecutioners

Using an imagery-barrage technique slightly more refined than was found in her debut feature SYNTHETIC PLEASURES (1996), Korean-Brazilian-American filmmaker Iara Lee here examines the phenomenon, stars, and pioneers of electronic pop music.

House, trance, acid jazz, techno, jungle, electro-funk—all are subspecies of music generated electronically, usually by instruments whose keyboards may vaguely resemble pianos, but whose inner circuit boards are closer to computers. The rhythmic, droning, stimulating sounds address what Mixmaster Morris calls "pre-millenial tension" of modern youth. It is almost always dance-oriented, and Lee's cameras travel the world, from a colorful concert at the misty foot of Japan's Mount Fuji to an illegal "rave" in New York City, busted by cops. Hordes of fans gyrate to music played by inexpressive artists who stand like factory workers at their machines onstage. Sometimes you're lucky to even get that: the Future Sounds of London refuse to perform, or even be interviewed except via Internet uplink. When Lee's inquiries offend them, they snarkily switch off the digital camera connection.

The movie traces electronica back to a 1913 essay "The Art of Noise" by philosopher Luigi Russolo. In the late 1930s, the American John Cage added electrical machine noises to his avant-garde compositions. Karlheinz Stockhausen in East Germany employed synthetically-generated tones and even radio static on a grand scale. West Germany's Kraftwerk and England's Throbbing Gristle were the first pop bands who found success with sound samples, computers, and new instruments like Moog and Roland synthesizers. But more improvisational, less monied club DJs made use of everything from obsolete record turntables to commercially unsuccessful instruments (the Roland TB-303 was a favorite bargain-bin find) to create new sounds. Lee ends with a sequence of toddlers banging on musical instruments; the stated implication being that electronic artists deconstruct musical tradition and have the innocence and creativity of small children as they seek fresh audio stimuli.

Perhaps, but small children are far less pretentious. The trouble with a music documentary like MODULATIONS is that its cutting-edge participants, spouting diverse manifestos and silly generalizations about the "culture of amnesia" and so forth, come across as a comical collection of preening poseurs each trying to out-cool the other. Even though he fronted two cutting-edge bands, Throbbing Gristle and Psychic TV, it's hard to take a guy with a name like Genesis P-Orridge seriously about much of anything. And there is interesting information here, like the assertion that Detroit's techno-funk sound was a followup to the city's race riots of the 1960s—a revolution on the dance floor, fought with drum machines and sequencers. German trendsetters like Ralf Hutter and Florian Schneider of Kraftwerk come across as two of the more personable and articulate of the bunch. Watching Holger Czukay of the group Can, gray and pudgy but still gyrating delightedly at his keyboard, one is struck by how much his evident joy in performing seems to elude younger competitors, most of whom mill around their stacks of gadgets as though they would rather be elsewhere. One wishes the film might comment on this, or anything else that pierces the shallow soundbytes and MTV-montage of visuals. Someone watching MODULATIONS as an introduction to the topic might download a little cultural enlightenment—or go out and buy more Sinatra.—C.C.

d, Iara Lee; p, George Gund; w, Peter Shapiro; ph, Marcus Burnett, Paul Yates; ed, Paula Heredia; sound, Antonio Arroyo (mixer)

Documentary/Musical (PR: C MPAA: NR)

MONTANA ★★

(U.S., 1998) 96m Zeta Entertainment; No Bones Production ~ Initial Entertainment Group c

Kyra Sedgwick *(Claire)*; Stanley Tucci *(Nick)*; Robin Tunney *(Kitty)*; Robbie Coltrane *(The Boss)*; Philip Seymour Hoffman *(Duncan)*; John Ritter *(Wexler)*; Ethan Embry *(Jimmy)*; Keenan Shimizu *(Koo)*; Mark Boone Jr. *(Stykes)*; Paul Calderon *(Boulez)*; Jerry Grayson *(Benny)*; Ajay Naidu *(Ives)*; Karl Geary *(Bosch)*; Alan Manson *(Paul)*; Raynor Scheine *(Fuller)*; Richard Zobel *(Simms)*; Jonathan Hadray *(St. John)*; Peter Francis James *(Lawrence)*; Matt O'Toole *(Montoya)*; Rick Washburn *(Capshaw)*; Erik Jensen *(Earl)*; Deirdre Wallace *(Sharon)*; Walt MacPherson *(Mr. Presser)*; Kathleen Doyle *(Mrs. Presser)*; Tovah Feldshuh *(Greta)*; Elisa Pugliese *(Stephanie)*; Natsuko Ohama *(Mr. Koo)*; Michael E. Knight *(Doctor)*; Liam Aiken *(Kid)*; Peter Gerety *(Mike)*; Phyllis Somerville *(Waitress)*; Rowena Guinness *(Receptionist)*; Wass M. Stevens *(Jackson)*

Yet another attempt to emulate the nihilistic hipness and showy cinematography of PULP FICTION (1995), MONTANA lacks both idiosyncratic dialogue and an individualistic directorial world-view.

Leader of a criminal empire, the Boss (Robbie Coltrane) assigns his most trusted foot-soldiers, Claire (Kyra Sedgwick) and Nick (Stanley Tucci), to locate a bag man, Koo (Keenan Shimizu), who has stolen money under the orders of the Boss's scheming accountant, Duncan (Phillip Seymour Hoffman), and the Boss's partner, Dr. Wexler (John Ritter); the latter duo are planning a takeover.

Koo is captured by Claire and Nick and brought to the boss's headquarters, but the money is not recovered. The Boss's mistress, Kitty (Robin Tunney), has been so alienated by the Boss that she slips Koo a gun in order to have him kill the Boss. Although he has been diagnosed with a terminal illness, quick-thinking Nick has the strength to foil this impromptu hit. After Nick kills Koo, Kitty runs away. Demoting paid killers Nick and Claire to the status of mere kidnappers as punishment for the Koo slip-up, the Boss orders them to give his dim-witted son Jimmy (Ethan Embry) on-the-job training while tracking down Kitty.

Subsequently, Kitty is captured by the trio. When Jimmy tries to sexually assault Kitty when they're left alone at one point, Kitty kills him with his own gun. Seizing the opportunity to allay the Boss's suspicion of him, Duncan suggests Claire deliberately killed Jimmy. The Boss orders Claire's execution, but she gets the drop on Duncan and his henchman. Refusing devious Wexler's offer of support, Claire is reunited with Nick, who had gone off on his own to search for the missing money. The Boss sends his assassin to kill Claire and Nick. After giving Claire the money he has located (thanks to Koo's widow), Nick dies in the ongoing melee. Returning to the Boss's headquarters, Claire fatally shoots the Boss, then sets Kitty free and drives off to Montana.

Stumbling over its own deadpan attitude, MONTANA handles its gangster plot mechanics skillfully without being involving or amusing. Riddled with bullets and borrowed seduction-of-power concepts, this film is a far cry from the droll humor of PRIZZI'S HONOR (1985), a more stylish black comedy about dishonor among thieves. Screeching their uninteresting lines, the cast tries to inflate flat ideas with energy but winds up defeated by cliched notions, like the whore with a heart of gold and the vocational killer capable of last-minute self-sacrifice. MONTANA boasts some attention-getting camerawork, but it never delivers either the suspense or the cynical kicks for which the audience has been primed. *(Graphic violence, extreme profanity, substance abuse, adult situations.)*—R.P.

d, Jennifer Leitzes; p, Mark Yellen, Sean Cooley, Zane Levitt; exec p, Cindy Cowan; assoc p, Jon Hoeber, Kyra Sedgwick, Ronnie Yeskel, Erich Hoeber; w, Jon Hoeber, Erich Hoeber; ph, Ken Kelsch; ed, Norman Buckley; m, Cliff Eidelman; prod d, Daniel Ross; art d, Mark Ricker; set d, Roberta Holinko; sound, Paul Ratajczak; fx, William Traynor; casting, Ronnie Yeskel, Richard Hicks; cos, Michael Clancy; makeup, Judy Chin, Lizz Scalise; stunts, G.A. Aguilar

Crime **(PR: C MPAA: R)**

MONUMENT AVE. ★★★½

(U.S., 1998) 93m Spanky Pictures; Apostle ~ Lions Gate Films c

Denis Leary *(Bobby O'Grady)*; Martin Sheen *(Hanlon)*; Billy Crudup *(Teddy)*; Jeanne Tripplehorn *(Annie)*; Jason Barry *(Seamus)*; Lenny Clarke *(Skunk)*; John Diehl *(Digger)*; Noah Emmerich *(Red)*; Ian Hart *(Mouse)*; Famke Janssen *(Katie)*; Kevin Chapman *(Mickey Pat)*; George MacDonald *(Gallivan)*; Lyndon Byers *(Fitzie)*; Herbie Ade *(Herbie)*; Melissa Fitzgerald *(Sheila)*; Don Gavin *(Brosnihan)*; Colm Meaney *(Jackie O'Hara)*; Greg Dulli *(Shang)*; Brian Goodman *(Gavin)*; Victor Chan *(Lee)*; Marilyn Murphy Meardon *(Mrs. O'Grady)*; Bill McDonald *(Father Donahue)*; Gene Boles *(John Kelsey)*; Sandra Shippley *(Mrs. Timmons)*; Karen White *(Marcy)*; Francois Joseph *(Kid)*; Sue McGinnis *(Mrs. Turbody)*; Jackie Sullivan *(Bar Owner)*

The independent film scene may not need any more clones of Martin Scorsese and Quentin Tarantino, but there's always room for a crime drama as well-written and acted as MONUMENT AVE. Despite the familiarity of the story, director Ted Demme, writer Mike Armstrong, and a strong ensemble cast evoke the desperation of life on the mean streets of Boston.

Bobby O'Grady (Denis Leary) grew up and lives in Charlestown, an Irish ghetto of Boston. While life offers him few choices besides crime or factory labor, he and his friends and family share a strong sense of community, extending to close ties with relatives in Ireland. With his friend Mouse (Ian Hart), Bobby introduces his recently-arrived cousin Seamus (Jason Barry) to the car theft ring they work for, run by local tough guy Jackie (Colm Meany). But Bobby, who still lives with his mother, is beginning to feel deadened by this life of drink, drugs, and hanging around the local bar. His mood isn't helped by an affair with Jackie's substance-abusing girlfriend Katie (Famke Janssen).

When Bobby's cousin Teddy (Billy Crudup) shows up at the bar, unexpectedly paroled from prison, Jackie worries that he may have ratted him out and murders him in front of the others. Everyone denies having seen anything to Detective Hanlon (Martin Sheen), who is frustrated by his inability to bring Jackie down. Jackie is suspicious of everyone except Bobby, who he regards as his second-in-command and heir. Seamus decides to return to Ireland, but before he can, he is picked up by Hanlon for questioning—and then killed by paranoid Jackie. Disgusted at what he has done in the name of "business," Bobby kills Jackie. Hanlon lets him get away, but Bobby realizes he will never escape the neighborhood.

Especially in its first half, MONUMENT AVE. unfolds with a loose, spontaneous feeling, more interested in the ambiance of this community than a story. One scene of Bobby, Mouse, and Seamus sitting around the living room, drinking and talking macho talk, looks to have been the result of improvisation: it goes on a bit too long, but it deftly establishes these characters and their view of the world they're trapped in. When Bobby's mother moans about all the mothers whose sons have been killed, we make a not-inappropriate comparison to Northern Ireland. The characters' community, in essence, is insular to the point of inbreeding. In a particularly shocking scene, Bobby attempts to show up a friend who is making racist remarks by forcing a black pedestrian into their car and threatening to kill him. As his rant progresses, it becomes clear that Bobby (the nominal hero of the film) is not free of the attitudes he despises.

MONUMENT AVE. begins to lag when it gets caught up in its story, though to its credit it avoids making its climax into an action sequence. Leary is excellent in a role that lets him rise above his familiar, sarcastic, comic persona without losing his identity. The script offers meaty roles for most of the cast, including Billy Crudup as a coked-up felon rightly afraid that he's worse off outside prison than in; Famke Janssen as a young woman who despises the role this life offers her; and John Diehl as a dim-witted cabbie. *(Graphic violence, nudity, sexual situations, adult situations, substance abuse, extreme profanity.)*—M.F.

d, Ted Demme; p, Jim Serpico, Nicolas Clermont, Elie Samaha; exec p, Ted Demme, Joel Stillerman; w, Mike Armstrong; ph, Adam Kimmel; ed, Jeffrey Wolf; prod d, Ruth Ammon; casting, Avy Kaufman; cos, Deborah Newhall; stunts, Brian Ricci

Crime/Drama **(PR: C MPAA: NR)**

MOON OVER BROADWAY ★★½

(U.S., 1998) 98m Pennebaker Hegedus Films/McEttinger Films; Bravo Cable; IN Pictures ~ Artistic License Films c

Carol Burnett; Philip Bosco; Ken Ludwig; Tom Moore; Elizabeth Williams; Rocco Landesman; Heidi Ettinger

Filmmakers D.A. Pennebaker and Chris Hegedus (THE WAR ROOM) dissect the making of a Broadway play in MOON OVER BROADWAY, a lightly engaging cinema-verite documentary. Theater and film audiences may respond to certain parts of this effort, but, sadly, the insights are minimal and often incidental.

MOON OVER BROADWAY begins with a March 1995 press conference to announce that Carol Burnett is returning to Broadway after a 30-year hiatus to star in a new play written by Ken Ludwig called *Moon Over Buffalo*. Ludwig's play, set in the early 1950s, concerns the attempts by a bickering, married theater duo (Burnett and Philip Bosco as the couple) to win a movie contract from Frank Capra, who is visiting Buffalo, New York, where they are appearing in a second-rate play.

A sense of doom hangs over the *Moon Over Buffalo* project when the show's director, Tom Moore, fails to attend the initial press conference. A reading of the play takes place in a Manhattan loft space in July, but despite general enthusiasm by the cast, crew, and producers, Moore and Ludwig worry that Burnett's "television" persona will hurt the production.

In Boston, before moving the show to Broadway, the actors work tirelessly through the obligatory "try-out" rehearsals, but the director and writer become further upset with Burnett and Bosco, when they attempt to ad-lib lines. The Boston audiences enjoy *Moon Over Buffalo* on opening night, but the critics—who appreciate Burnett's performance—complain about the play itself, giving it mixed reviews. The producers consider bringing in a joke writer, but Ludwig rewrites his lines himself, adding more humor.

In September, back in New York, the company prepares for the Broadway opening with a considerably altered text. Up until the very last minute, Ludwig hands the actors scene rewrites. The preview audience enjoys Burnett's performance, particularly when she performs an impromptu stand-up routine while technicians fix a main winch jam backstage. The much-anticipated opening attracts many celebrities, and it is followed by a banquet celebration. The next morning, the giddy feelings are quashed when the company reads the mostly negative reviews. The producers extrapolate the best lines—again, mostly bestowed on Burnett—to sell the show to the public, and, on the strength of Burnett's name, *Moon Over Buffalo* runs several months before closing.

Films about the theater world and the process of producing a Broadway play often contain a built-in snappy sophistication, from the mordant ALL ABOUT EVE (1950) to the multi-layered KISS ME KATE (1953) to the quirky ACT ONE (1963). Even MOON OVER BROADWAY, though a cinema-verite documentary, features its share of funny lines and moments: playwright Ludwig wailing after the Boston opening, "It looked like a heart attack!," and, after the New York opening, "It's like the bar mitzvah from hell!"; an overly made-up Burnett glancing into her backstage mirror and exclaiming, "I look like the Joker in BATMAN," and later parodying her friend Julie Andrews in *Victor, Victoria*, a hit show playing down the street.

Such scenes provide genuine entertainment—ironically much more than what *Moon Over Buffalo* seemed to offer critics and audiences (Ms. Burnett notwithstanding). But like the other "showbiz" documentaries of D.A. Pennebaker (JANE, 1962; COMPANY, 1973) and Pennebaker with Chris Hegedus (ROCKABY, 1981), MOON OVER BROADWAY finds the filmmakers effectively playing the fly on the wall, but that's about it. Naturally, some surprises occur, but the revelations are of a superficial nature (the fact the producers consider hiring a joke-writer—a dentist from Long Island, no less); and the filmmakers appear to miss the irony of the "bad"-play-within-the-bad-play situation.

Unlike the documentaries of Frederick Wiseman, MOON OVER BROADWAY takes no critical stance toward its subject matter and in fact appears to exhibit a celebratory attitude towards the elitist side of the theater. Like Pennebaker and Hegedus's most acclaimed film, THE WAR ROOM (1993), which recorded the Clinton presidential campaign in full gear, MOON OVER BROADWAY wants to please and amuse more than anything else; for that, one could just as well watch reruns of "The Carol Burnett Show" (which are, in fact, excerpted here and are among the highlights of this film). Just as the theater folk in the film seemingly foiled their big chance to have Carol Burnett perform on Broadway in a worthy vehicle, the filmmakers have passed up an opportunity to make more profound comments about show business, art, and culture. *(Profanity.)*—E.M.

d, D.A. Pennebaker, Chris Hedegus; p, Frazer Pennebaker, Wendy Ettinger; exec p, Jaimie Ader-Brown, Suzanne Fedak; ph, D.A. Pennebaker, Nick Doob, James Desmond; ed, Chris Hegedus, D.A. Pennebaker; sound, Chris Hegedus, John McCormick

Documentary **(PR: C MPAA: NR)**

MOONDANCE ★★

(Ireland/Germany/U.K., 1995) 92m Majestic Films; Little Bird; MFG; Lodge ~ Miramax c

Ruaidhri Conroy *(Dominic)*; Ian Shaw *(Patrick)*; Julia Brendler *(Anya)*; Marianne Faithfull *(Mother)*; Brendan Grace *(Murphy)*; Jasmine Russell *(Rose)*; Darren Monks *(Chalky)*; David Kelly *(Mr. Dunwoody)*; Tom Hickey *(Mr. Dunbar)*; Kate Flynn *(Aunt Dorothy)*; Alan Devlin *(John Joe)*; Gerard McSorley *(Fr. McGrath)*; P.J. Brady *(Murray)*; Joan O'Hara *(Nun)*; Blink *(The Band)*

The close relationship between two young brothers is ruptured by a beautiful young woman in this handsome but underplotted film, funded by the Eurimage Fund of the Council of Europe.

Brothers Patrick (Ian Shaw) and Dominic (Ruaidhri Conroy) have lived alone in the west country of Ireland since the loss of their father (who died) and mother (who dealt with her grief by running off to Africa to study a lost tribe). Although Patrick had to drop out of school to support his young brother, the two live happily. Their Aunt Dorothy (Kate Flynn) pays a visit, bringing with her Anya (Julia Brendler), a German girl working on her horse ranch for the summer. Dominic develops a crush on Anya, who in turn is smitten with Patrick, and she moves in with the two brothers. Patrick and Dominic's mother (Marianne Faithfull) returns. Anya admits that she loves Patrick but must leave soon for Dublin, where she will be going to university. Patrick asks her to marry him and she agrees, but on the day of the wedding backs out, saying it is too fast. Blaming his mother for turning Anya against him, Patrick decides to go with her to Dublin; Dominic comes as well.

The three are given an apartment over a bar owned by Murphy (Brendan Grace), who is dating a friend of Anya's; he also gets Patrick a sales job. While Patrick spends his days at work, Dominic and Anya grow closer. When Patrick catches on, his drunken accusations cause Anya to try to seduce Dominic, who turns her down rather than hurt his brother. Though underage, Dominic gets a job on a ship bound for Africa, while Anya returns to Germany. Advised by his mother, Dominic makes up with his brother before boarding ship.

For at least its first half, MOONDANCE looks splendid, as one presumes any film set in the Irish countryside inevitably must. It's also a delight to listen to, scored mostly by Irish-tinged adaptations of songs by Van Morrison (one of which gives the film its otherwise meaningless title). But as far as story goes, it can only be assumed that a lot of novel on which this was based was trimmed by the scripters. Everything about it is vague, and the characters are so underdeveloped that its impossible to get any feel for the passion we're supposed to be witnessing. (If the film is supposed to be about youth mistaking infatuation and glandular reaction for true love, it fails to make that clear as well.) A subplot about a pet dog the two brothers hope to turn into a racer adds little to the film, while a "comic" scene featuring nasty stereotypes of both Catholics and homosexuals is particularly ill-advised. MOONDANCE is recommended only to Eirephiles in serious need of a fix. *(Nudity, sexual situations, profanity.)*—M.F.

d, Dagmar Hirtz; p, Jonathan Cavendish; exec p, James Mitchell, Guy East, Rainer Soehnlein; assoc p, Jane Doolan; co-p, Dagmar Hirtz; w, Burt Weinshanker, Matt Watters (based on the novel *The White Hare* by Francis Stuart); ph, Steven Bernstein; ed, Dagmar Hirtz; m, Fiancha Trench, Van Morrison; prod d, Tom Conroy; art d, Denis Bosher; fx, Gerry Johnston; cos, Sheena Napier; makeup, Ken Jennings; stunts, Philippe Zone

Drama **(PR: C MPAA: R)**

MOTHER AND SON ★★★½

(Russia/Germany, 1997) 73m Zero Film; 0-Film; Severnyj Fond ~ International Film Circuit c
(MAT' I SYN)

Gudrun Geyer *(Mother)*; Alexei Ananishnov *(Son)*

A son cares for his dying mother in this poignant, artful Russian film where, sometimes, the pictoral beauty overwhelms the drama.

In an isolated rural setting along the Russian countryside, a young man (Alexei Ananishnov) nurses his sick, feeble mother (Gudrun Geyer) in her small home. While she tries to hide her approaching death from her son, he feeds her, sits her out on a bench in front of the house, and reads postcards aloud to her. They reminisce about his childhood, a time when she was often afraid of letting him out of her sight. She asks to go for a walk, hoping to see other people, but she is unable to rise to her feet. Instead, the son carries her through the empty countryside, and they find no other inhabitants.

Back at the house, the mother finally discusses her impending death with her son, and they debate the idea of an afterlife. While she goes to sleep, he walks out of the house to a field, where he watches a train go by, and to a forest, where he sits down to cry. Back at the house again, the son realizes his mother has finally died, remaining alone in a world that can offer him little comfort or solace.

Alexander Sokurov's oeuvre demands attention and respect, from his documentaries (SIMPLE ELEGY, 1990; SPIRITUAL VOICES, 1995) to his story films (SECOND CIRCLE, 1990; WHISPERING PAGES, 1993). As an example of the latter, which have utilized what has been called a transcendental style, MOTHER AND SON validates Sokurov's ability to create philosophical discourse out of dense imagery. In a series of tableaux (mainly inspired by the German Romantic landscape paintings of Caspar David Friedrich), Sokurov explores the nature of love, life, death, nature, afterlife, and, primarily, the ancient, deeply resonant relationship between parent and child.

Formally, MOTHER AND SON is exquisite: Sokurov and his cinematographer, Alexei Fyodorov, use highly inventive ways to create a stunningly ominous landscape with muted colors, including special lenses and actual hand-painting on glass and mirrors. Sokurov also integrates eerie ambient sound effects—a dust storm, grass rustling, ocean waves—evoking the haunting meteorological undercurrent of Victor Seastrom's 1928 classic, THE WIND. Likewise, the few fragments of music (by Mikhail Glinka, Otmar Nussio, and Giuseppe Verdi) complement the heartfelt pictures.

But like his mentor, Andrei Tarkovsky, and his contemporary, Theodoros Angelopoulos, Sokurov emphasizes visual art above all else. The results may be rich but they are also laborious, heavy-going, and less emotionally moving than had the story been told in a more straightforward way (the film runs only 73 minutes but feels much, much longer). The problem lies not in the spareness of Yuri Arabov's story—which is rooted in Russian poetry and folktales—as much as in Sokurov's oppressively serious treatment, which causes a distancing that may *not* have been intended. Like some museum paintings, even some magnificent museum paintings, MOTHER AND SON possesses a faraway, even musty, remoteness, despite the continuously beautiful expression of universal ideas and issues. *(Adult situations.)*—E.M.

d, Alexander Sokurov; p, Thomas Kufus; exec p, Katrin Schlosser, Martin Hagemann, Alexander Golutva; w, Yuri Arabov; ph, Alexei Fyodorov; ed, Leda Semyonova; m, Mikhail Glinka, Otmar Nussio, Giuseppe Verdi; art d, Vera Zelinskaya, Esther Ritterbusch; sound, Vladimir Persov, Martin Steyer

Drama **(PR: C MPAA: NR)**

MRS. DALLOWAY ★★★★

(U.K./Netherlands, 1997) 97m Mrs. D Productions; Bergen Film ~ First Look Pictures c

Vanessa Redgrave *(Mrs. Clarissa Dalloway)*; Natascha McElhone *(Young Clarissa)*; Rupert Graves *(Septimus Warren Smith)*; Michael Kitchen *(Peter Walsh)*; Alan Cox *(Young Peter)*; Sarah Badel *(Sally Seton—Lady Rosseter)*; Lena Headey *(Young Sally)*; John Standing *(Richard Dalloway)*; Robert Portal *(Young Richard)*; Oliver Ford Davies *(Hugh Whitbread)*; Hal Cruttenden *(Young Hugh)*; Amelia Bullmore *(Rezia Warren Smith)*; Katie Carr *(Elizabeth Dalloway)*; Phyllis Calvert *(Aunt Helena)*; John Franklyn-Robbins *(Lionel—Clarissa's Father)*; Selina Cadell *(Miss Kilman)*; Robert Hardy *(Sir William Bradshaw)*; Margaret

Tyzack *(Lady Bruton)*; Alistair Petrie *(Herbert)*; Rupert Baker *(Joseph Breitkopf)*; Amanda Drew *(Lucy)*; Oscar Pearce *(Bookshop Assistant)*; Janet Henfrey *(Miss Pym)*; Polly Pritchett *(Nursemaid)*; Hilda Braid *(Elderly Woman)*; Derek Smee *(Man on Bench)*; Jane Whittenshaw *(1st Woman by Fountain)*; Susie Fairfax *(2nd Woman by Fountain)*; Fanny Carby *(Old Woman—Singer)*; Jonathan Firth

Vanessa Redgrave shines in this exquisite adaptation of Virginia Woolf's complex 1925 novel about a middle-aged woman who reevaluates her life while preparing to host a party. Screenwriter Eileen Atkins and director Marleen Gorris capture the essence of Woolf's literary technique—particularly her idiosyncratic use of flashbacks and interior monologues—while also satirizing the cattiness and hypocrisy of the stodgy British upper class at the turn of the century.

During one summer day in June, 1923, Clarissa Dalloway (Vanessa Redgrave), a refined upper-class wife, prepares one of her famous parties. Married to prominent Parliament member Richard Dalloway (John Standing), Clarissa's parties are splendid affairs to which only the creme de la creme of London society is invited. But on this particular morning, Clarissa's frantic activity triggers many memories of her youth, when she made many decisions that seemed carefully thought out, but were in fact ploys to delay the inevitability of marriage. She thinks of her younger years, of a time when she (Natascha McElhone) was being ardently pursued by Peter Walsh (Alan Cox), a businessman who was hopelessly in love with her. Clarissa, however, finds greater love with her girlfriend Sally Seton (Lena Headey), a free spirit who shares her desire for independence. One night at a dance, Sally and Clarissa experience a sexual awakening when they kiss passionately in the moonlight. Shocked at the occurrence, they never speak of it again. Soon, Clarissa's interest turns to the dashing young Richard Dalloway (Robert Portal), whose smoldering authority promises stability and comfort. When she agrees to marry Richard, Peter pleads with her to change her mind, but to no avail.

Clarissa's thoughts come back to the present. While buying flowers, she observes Septimus Warren Smith (Rupert Graves), a shell-shocked veteran of WWI, who reacts very violently to a car backfiring. For their part, Septimus and his Italian-born wife Rezia (Amelia Bullmore) have struggled to regain a stable life, but he suffers from horrible flashbacks of the incident in which he watched his friend die in the battlefield. When one psychiatrist can't help him, Rezia persuades him to see Sir William Bradshaw (Robert Hardy), a doctor who specializes in war-related mental afflictions. Bradshaw suggests that Septimus be institutionalized. At home, while waiting for attendants to take him away, Septimus leaps to his death. Meanwhile, as Mrs. Dalloway's party nears, she receives a surprise visitor: Peter Walsh (Michael Kitchen). Clarissa impulsively invites him to the party after he confesses how he's been living an unhappy life in India, where he's in love with a married woman.

Later, as her guests arrive, Mrs. Dalloway assumes the role of a happy hostess, but underneath, she's sure that the party is a "complete failure." After many years apart, Sally Seton (Sarah Badel) shows up with her husband, but Clarissa has no time to speak to her since the Prime Minister has arrived. But Clarissa is disturbed by Bradshaw's callous mention of Septimus's suicide. Horrified by his disregard, Clarissa retreats to the balcony to regain her composure. There, she obsessess over what she has heard and what it was that would have driven Septimus to commit suicide. Regaining her composure, she rejoins her party guests.

Redgrave, always a superlative but emotionally distant actress, sinks her teeth into the role of Mrs. Dalloway. She's absolutely captivating in a part that seems tailor-made to her trademark regal bearing and intensity. Though her performance is sublimely understated, her radiance comes through, thanks to the smooth and structured scripting of Atkins. Redgrave and Atkins previously collaborated on another Woolf project, in which they both costarred in Atkins's off-Broadway play *Vita and Virginia*, based on Woolf's diaries during the period of her romance with writer Vita Sackville-West. It's to their credit that they've reunited to tackle a Woolf novel that seems utterly unfilmable, with its constantly shifting narrative, a profusion of flashbacks, and seemingly unrelated subplots. And given the angry feminist polemics of her past work, Marleen Gorris (ANTONIA'S LINE) seems a surprising choice to direct a period piece that would seem more like an assignment for the Merchant-Ivory team.

Yet Gorris's approach here is restrained and respectful, as if she were an admiring child in awe of a great work of art. In finding the significant symbolism in the everyday—a vase of flowers, a car backfiring, a chance glimpse at a stranger—Gorris vividly explores Clarissa Dalloway's internal struggles, and exposes her outward determination to maintain her stiff-upper-lip facade. Gorris also elicits fine performances from the supporting cast, particularly Graves, who brings intensity to a role that could have been disastrously overplayed by a lesser actor, and McElhone, who bears a striking resemblance to a younger Redgrave.

MRS. DALLOWAY is a rare achievement: a screen adaptation that is equally as compelling as its literary source. *(Adult themes.)*—D.O.

d, Marleen Gorris; p, Lisa Katselas Pare, Stephen Bayly; exec p, Hans de Weers; assoc p, Paul Frift; co-p, Chris J. Ball, William Tyrer, Simon Curtis, Bill Shepherd; w, Eileen Atkins (based on the novel by Virginia Woolf); ph, Sue Gibson; ed, Michiel Reichwein; m, Ilona Sekacz; prod d, David Richens; art d, Alison Wratten, Nik Callan; set d, Carlotta Barrow, Jeanne Vertigan; sound, Peter Glossop (mixer), Brian Simmons (mixer); fx, John Horton; casting, Celestia Fox; cos, Judy Pepperdine; makeup, Joan Hills, Maggie Webb; stunts, Andreas Patrides

Drama **(PR: C MPAA: PG-13)**

MULAN ★★½

(U.S., 1998) 86m Walt Disney ~ Buena Vista c

VOICES OF: Ming-Na Wen *(Mulan)*; Lea Salonga *(Mulan—Singing)*; Eddie Murphy *(Mushu)*; B.D. Wong *(Captain Li Shang)*; Donny Osmond *(Captain Li Shang—Singing)*; Harvey Fierstein *(Yao)*; Jerry Tondo *(Chien-Po)*; Gedde Watanabe *(Ling)*; James Hong *(Chi Fu)*; Miguel Ferrer *(Shan-Yu)*; Soon-Tek Oh *(Fa Zhou)*; Freda Foh Shen *(Fa Li)*; Noriyuki "Pat" Morita, billed as Pat Morita *(Emperor)*; June Foray *(Grandmother Fa)*; George Takei *(First Ancestor)*; James Shigeta *(General Li)*; Miriam Margoyles *(The Matchmaker)*

MULAN, the Disney rendition of a Chinese folk tale about a young woman who disguises herself as a male warrior, is a splendidly animated but unexceptional entertainment.

When the Huns, led by the malevolent Shan-Yu (voice of Miguel Ferrer), invade China, the Chinese Emperor (voice of Pat Morita) declares that one male from every family must join the imperial army. The elderly Fa Zhou (voice of Soon-Tek Oh) prepares to join, but his daughter Mulan (voice of Ming-Na Wen) secretly disguises herself as a male and goes in his place. Upon learning what she has done, her family calls on ancestral spirits to protect her, but the spirits inadvertently send a tiny dragon, Mushu (voice of Eddie Murphy) as her guardian.

With Mushu's assistance, Mulan successfully conceals her sex at the army training camp. Although she and her fellow trainees are initially inept, under the arduous training of Commander Shang (voice of B.D. Wong), they become quality soldiers. In a mountain pass, they encounter the Huns and are nearly routed until Mulan fires a cannon at a snow-covered peak, triggering an avalanche that buries the enemy. When Shang is almost killed in the avalanche as well, Mulan saves him, but is injured in the effort. An attendant doctor discovers her sex, and Shang discharges her from his force. Left at the battle scene, Mulan sees that Shan-Yu and other Huns have survived. She races to the imperial city to warn Shang, who is being honored for his apparent victory. Mulan is not believed until Shan-Yu disrupts the ceremony, taking the emperor hostage and demanding that he be proclaimed ruler of China. Shang, Mulan, and her army friends overpower Shan-Yu's guards, and Shang fights Shan-Yu. Shan-Yu is about to kill Shang when Mulan intervenes and again saves Shang's life. An enraged Shan-Yu chases Mulan to the roof of the imperial palace where, with Mushu's aid, Mulan destroys Shan-Yu with fireworks.

The emperor gratefully invites Mulan to join his council, but she chooses to return home, where her family warmly receives her. Shang, who had been reluctant to acknowledge his debt to Mulan, visits her and accepts an invitation to dinner. Mushu, meanwhile, is chosen by the ancestral spirits to be the Fa family guardian.

The ninth entry in the renaissance of Disney feature animation (which began in 1989 with THE LITTLE MERMAID), MULAN suggests that the creative resurgence at Disney has begun to ebb. As always, anyone looking to Disney for a faithful adaptation will be profoundly disappointed. The story on which MULAN is based emphasizes filial piety, but, as with ANASTASIA (1997), the creators of MULAN have chosen to modify the legend in order to exploit its feminist potential. The heroine of this translation is motivated less by devotion to her family than by a desire to determine her own fate. Calculated perhaps to make the story more palatable (not to mention salable) to contemporary audiences, the thematic shift is nonetheless commendable in that this time around, it is Snow White who rescues Prince Charming. And whereas Disney's two previous attempts to infuse a modern sensibility into an old tale—THE HUNCHBACK OF NOTRE DAME (1996) and HERCULES (1997)—perverted their sources in order to make them fashionable, MULAN at least does not contradict the meaning of the original.

That said, it must be noted that the animation in MULAN is outstanding. Purists may be put off by the high amount of computer-generated animation, but even the computer work in MULAN is beautiful, as in the stunning segment in which the Chinese and Hun armies clash; and the computer animation has been almost seamlessly integrated with the traditional cel technique. The trend in virtually all mainstream studio animation towards hyperkinetic movement continues here, but given the rapid pace of the narrative, it's less disconcerting than usual.

Beyond its feminist twist and strong visual quality, though, MULAN is mostly uninspired. The film draws heavily upon elements that have worked well in previous Disney features, most obviously Eddie Murphy's voice characterization for the jive-talking dragon Mushu, clearly modeled after Robin Williams's similarly anachronistic genie in ALADDIN (1992). The songs by Matthew Wilder and David Zippel are immediately forgettable, and for all its pseudo-Chinese touches—backgrounds that resemble watercolor landscape paintings, and Jerry Goldsmith's attempt at an Oriental score—MULAN remains much closer to The Magic Kingdom than it does to The Monkey King.

MULAN includes a single exceptional sequence, a musical number called "A Girl Worth Fighting For," in which the predominant graphic style of the film momentarily changes to become like a Chinese watercolor painting. This sequence recalls the delirious "Pink Elephants on Parade" number from DUMBO (1941), and it stands apart from the rest of the film in its originality.

That MULAN is a quality piece of filmmaking is undeniable, as is the sense that the folks at the Disney animation studio have begun to avoid taking creative risks and become dependent on tried-and-true formulas.—D.C.

d, Barry Cook, Tony Bancroft; p, Pam Coats; assoc p, Robert S. Garber; w, Rita Hsiao, Jodi Ann Johnson, Alan Ormsby (from a story by Chris Sanders); m, Jerry Goldsmith; prod d, Ric Sluiter, Hans Bacher; anim, Ruben Aquino (supervisor), Dan Haskett, Mark Henn, Press Romanillos, Barry Temple, Alex Kupershmidt, Broose Johnson, Aaron Blaise, Jefrey Varab, Joe Haider

AAN Best Original Musical or Comedy Score: Matthew Wilder, David Zippel, Jerry Goldsmith

Animated/Children's/Musical (PR: AA MPAA: G)

MURDER IN MIND ★

(U.S./U.K., 1998) 89m Live Entertainment; Lakeshore International; Evergreen Entertainment; BBC Films & Alva Motion Pictures; Storyteller Films ~ Hallmark Home Entertainment c

Nigel Hawthorne *(Dr. Ellis)*; Mary-Louise Parker *(Caroline)*; Jimmy Smits *(Peter)*; Jason Scott Lee *(Halloway)*; Gailard Sartain *(Charlie)*; Jon Ceda *(Superior Officer)*; Ibgo Neuhaus *(Officer)*; Art Metrano *(Judge)*; Rob Labelle *(Lecturer)*; Mitch Ward *(Court Clerk)*; Anne De Salvo *(Flustered Attorney)*; Jodi Long *(Secretary Helen)*; Eric Cadora *(Secretary Patrick)*; Nicholas Cascone *(Prosecutor)*; Elizabeth Normant *(Dr. Beck)*; James Handy *(Dr. Harvard)*; Roman Wyden *(Deli Server)*; Aaron Lustig *(Defense Attorney)*; James Maitland *(Medic)*; John Marrott *(Detective)*; Tim Bales *(Detective at Accident)*; Glenn Schechter *(Detective at Accident)*; Richard McCune *(Officer at Accident)*; Ken Christmas *(Officer at Accident)*

MURDER IN MIND is a confusing muddle about a psychiatrist using hypnosis to investigate whether a woman murdered her husband. The film is so bogged down with deliberately confusing flashbacks and false memories that it ultimately collapses under the weight of its own cleverness.

Detective Halloway (Jason Scott Lee) arrests Caroline Walker (Mary-Louise Parker) for the gruesome murders of her wealthy husband Peter (Jimmy Smits) and their handyman Charlie (Gailard Sartain). She claims to remember nothing, despite a recording of her 911 call confessing to the crime.

Psychiatrist Dr. Ellis (Nigel Hawthorne) uses hypnosis to help Caroline remember that night. She brings up memories of arguments with Peter over a pregnancy and miscarriage which, she insists when fully conscious, never existed. With the help of Ellis, she begins to recall certain memories about the night of the murder: returning home unexpectedly after a car crash, she had overheard Peter hiring Charlie to kill her. In the ensuing struggles, she killed both men in self-defense.

These memories, however, are hypnotic implants given to Caroline by Ellis. Eventually she does recall the truth of the situation: the killer was Ellis. He met Caroline, whose real name is Mary Quinn, years earlier in a rehab clinic. He used hypnosis to reinvent her as "Caroline" and implanted memories to create a woman tailored to appeal to his wealthy friend, Peter. He arranged a prenuptial agreement that divided the estate between Caroline and Ellis in the event of Peter's death. Now, Ellis tries to erase "Caroline" and restore "Mary," and to convince her to kill herself. Confused between illusion and reality, Caroline tries to shoot Ellis and chases him outside just as Halloway arrives. Witnessing Ellis threaten Caroline, Halloway shoots Ellis. Before he dies, Ellis completes the hypnotic trigger that restores Mary. Pretending to be Caroline, Mary gives a statement to the police.

The main problem with MURDER IN MIND is the confusion over what is real and what isn't. Since so many sequences turn out to be hypnotic regressions—and implanted memories within regressions—the viewer quickly learns to dismiss everything it sees as potential fantasy, and not care about the characters. Since the central conceit of the movie is to keep the audience off-balance, the result is a cold, distant experience that is thoroughly uninvolving. The red herrings and contradictory information are never explained away.

Director Andrew Morahan seems to be in over his head. The convoluted flashback/flashforward plot line would be difficult for any director to keep straight, and so Morahan settles for keeping individual chunks of the story watchable—even if the vignettes don't mesh into a coherent whole.

Hawthorne turns in a classy performance in material that is clearly beneath him (though as an associate producer, he is presumably watching out for his investment). Parker is believable as the vulnerable Caroline, much less so as the tough Mary. She's just attractive enough, and her scratchy voice just pitiable enough, to evoke sympathy.

MURDER IN MIND simply doesn't manage to get across whatever it is the filmmakers had in mind. *(Graphic violence, profanity.)*—J.Di.

d, Andrew Morahan; p, Vicki Slotnick, Jeremy Paige; exec p, Rena Ronson, Paul Rich, Alan Howden; assoc p, Nigel Hawthorne, Kelly Feldsott Reynolds, Steve Beeks, Sara Lewis, Glenn Ross; w, Michael Cooney (based on the play by Cooney); ph, John Aronson; ed, Andrea MacArthur; m, Paul Buckmaster; prod d, Ben Morahan; art d, Stephen Sinclair; sound, Larry Scharf; casting, Sheila Jaffe, Georgianne Walken; cos, Merrie Lawson; makeup, Jill Cady; stunts, Kurt Bryant

Crime/Drama **(PR: C MPAA: R)**

MUSIC FROM ANOTHER ROOM ★★½

(U.S., 1998) 104m Motion Picture Corporation of America; Orion Pictures ~ Orion/MGM c

Brenda Blethyn *(Grace)*; Jude Law *(Danny)*; Jennifer Tilly *(Nina)*; Martha Plimpton *(Karen)*; Gretchen Mol *(Anna)*; Jon Tenney *(Eric)*; Jeremy Piven *(Billy)*; Vincent Laresca; Jane Adams *(Irene)*; Bruce Jarchow

A lovestruck artist pursuing a young woman encounters her screwy family in this romantic comedy. A talented supporting cast can't overcome a formulaic script that substitutes a fast pace for inspiration.

Five-year-old Danny (Cory Buck) and his father (Kevin Kilner) are having Thanksgiving dinner with the family of his late mother's best, friend Grace (Brenda Blethyn). When she unexpectedly goes into labor, Danny helps his father with the delivery, and afterwards says he'll marry the girl, Anna, when they grow up.

Years later, back in the US after having been raised in England, Danny (Jude Law) is forced by a streak of bad luck to take a temporary job as a delivery boy before starting work restoring a mosaic. A chance meeting with Grace's family convinces him that fate plans for him and Anna (Gretchen Mol) to be together, even if she is engaged to marry Eric (Jon Tenney). Biding his time, he spends time with her siblings: blind Nina (Jennifer Tilly), who has been overly protected by her family; Karen (Martha Plimpton), a militant feminist who thinks Danny is just what uptight Anna needs, and sister-in-law Irene (Jane Adams), who struggles to cope with the stress of marriage to Anna's brother, Billy (Jeremy Piven). Grace, who is seriously ill, worries about all of her children but wishes that Anna would break out of her role as mother hen and find a little passion.

Danny declares his feelings for Anna, who doesn't take him seriously. But when she sees the passion her once-repressed sister Nina is enjoying with the boyfriend she met through Danny's efforts to bring her out, she changes her mind and spends the night with him. Grace's sudden death causes her to go back to Eric, but Nina persuades her that she belongs with Danny, whom she catches as he is about to leave on a train.

MUSIC FROM ANOTHER ROOM, which was produced for theatrical distribution but wound up being dumped onto home video, was written and directed by Charlie Peters, scripter of a long list of lame comedies including KRIPPENDORF'S TRIBE (1998), JUNGLE 2 JUNGLE (1997), MY FATHER THE HERO (1994), and HOT TO TROT (1988), all of which should serve as fair warning to potential viewers. It's not as bad as any of those films, but it does display the same formulaic approach, as if Peters believes that content comes out of form. The film starts well enough, with the scene of young Danny helping his father deliver a baby; but once Peters gets all of his quirky characters together, he doesn't seem to know what to do with them, simply bouncing them off each other for an hour or so until it's time to bring everything to its pre-ordained conclusion. This is a shame because the supporting cast is so much more interesting than the leads. Gretchen Mol makes for an chilly, uninspiring heroine, and her physical similarity to co-star Jude Law detracts from both of them: in this case, more contrast was definitely needed. Unable to generate any real romanticism, the film resorts to what feels like endless replays of Savage Garden's hit song "Truly Madly Deeply," which topped the charts while the film sat in a can waiting for a theatrical release that never came. *(Sexual situations, adult situations, profanity.)*—M.F.

d, Charlie Peters; p, Brad Krevoy, Steven Stabler, John Bertolli, Bradley Thomas; co-p, Marc S. Fischer, J.B. Rogers; w, Charlie Peters; ph, Richard Crudo; ed, Tim O'Meara; prod d, Charles Breen; art d, Chris Gorak; set d, Denise Pizzini; sound, Peter Bentley (mixer); casting, Mary Gail Artz, Barbara Cohen; cos, Mary Claire Hannan

Romance/Comedy **(PR: C MPAA: PG-13)**

MY BROTHER'S WAR ★★

(U.S., 1997) 84m New Concorde ~ New Horizons Home Video c

James Brolin *(John Hall)*; Jennie Garth *(Mary)*; Salvator Xuereb *(Liam Fallon)*; Patrick Foy *(Gerry Fallon)*; Cristi Conaway *(Kelly Hall)*; Josh Brolin *(Pete)*; Gary Cooke *(Brian)*; Tony Boston *(Aidan)*; Seamus Fox *(Bobby)*; Lesley Conroy *(Frances)*; Emma O'Neill *(Sinead)*; Mike Regan *(Michael Fallon)*; Conal O'Fatharta *(12 Year Old Gerry)*; Michael McNally *(8 Year Old Liam)*; Craig Warnock *(Conal Byrne)*; Amber O'Connor *(Lucy)*; Dick Holland *(Feeney)*; William Walker *(Colm)*; Dick Donoghue *(US State Secretary)*; Conor Maguire *(Loyalist Commander)*; Michael Boyle *(Republican Commander)*; James McHale *(Ericson)*; Mouse McHugh *(Armed Guard)*; Oison McGreal *(Daniel)*; Sean Brewster *(Liam Lad)*; Mike Duggan *(Prison Guard 1)*; Kieran Taylor *(Prison Guard 2)*; Anna Broad *(Warden)*; Mike Finn *(Special Security Man)*; John Keyes *(Sir Philip)*; Eamon Rohan *(Paddy)*; Ray Diamond; Roger Brady; Paul Totman; Tom McEvoy *(R&B Band)*; Philip Gettigan *(Ice Cream Vendor)*;

Kasie Prendergast *(Young Pete)*; Sean Salmon *(Older Boy)*; Rico Shea *(Rolly)*; Little John Nee *(Rolly's Mate)*; Turlough Moore *(Club Singer)*; Sean O'Brien *(Police Officer)*; John Slattery *(Devlin)*; Ruth Dillon *(Guitarist)*; Fergus Feeley *(Guitarist)*; Alan Daveron *(Van Driver)*; Carol Hunt *(Newscaster)*

Actor James Brolin's feature film directorial debut pits brother against brother in a political thriller set in Ireland. After festival showings failed to secure a theatrical distributor, MY BROTHER'S WAR was released to home video in 1998. It was named Best Feature Film with a budget over $1 million at the 1997 Hollywood Film Festival.

As children, Gerry and Liam Fallon witnessed their father's murder by a terrorist sniper. Now adults, they are members of an IRA group plotting to kill a British dignitary as his cavalcade drives through Belfast. Gerry (Patrick Foy) calls off the attack when he discovers that the dignitary's wife and children are also in the car. Liam (Salvator Xuereb) turns on his comrades, seriously wounding Gerry and killing the others. He detonates a bomb that kills not only the royal family, but also several bystanders. Gerry survives his wounds and is sentenced to life in prison, while Liam goes free. Liam organizes a new band of followers and commits a rash of terrorist acts designed to stop the peace talks. Retired CIA agent John Hall (James Brolin), whose sister was one of the victims of the bombing, is recruited by British intelligence to stop Liam. Gerry agrees to help Hall capture Liam in exchange for his release from prison. Gerry wants to settle down with his girlfriend, Mary (Jennie Garth), but risks his own happiness to stop his bloodthirsty brother. Liam's gang infiltrates the peace meetings and holds several government officials hostage. As Hall's men subdue the terrorists, Gerry flees with Liam on a boat. Liam thinks his brother has rejoined him in his cause, but Gerry reveals he has taped the explosives intended for the hostages to his own body. Hugging his brother close, Gerry presses the detonator.

MY BROTHER'S WAR is an adequate but undistinguished film perhaps most interesting for its against-type casting of Jennie Garth (from TV's "Beverly Hills, 90210") as an Irish single mother who clings to hope despite the violence that surrounds her. Garth does a commendable job with the material. Xuereb and Foy give a pair of powerful performances as the brothers. In contrast, Brolin appears too laid back for a man pursuing his sister's killer. Hall's hesitance at partnering with Gerry, also involved in the crime, is too quickly overcome. Standing out from the large supporting cast is Josh Brolin (son of James) as a former bully who tormented Liam as a youth and tries to overthrow the group.

Brolin's direction is as lackluster as his performance in this piece. With plodding pacing and little excitement despite a surfeit of action scenes, MY BROTHER'S WAR feels overlong and uninspired. The soundtrack includes Irish standbys "Danny Boy" and "Too-ra-loo-ra-loo-ral" as well as some less obvious choices. Though uninspiring as a thriller, the film at least does boast real Irish locations. *(Violence, sexual situations, adult situations, profanity.)*—B.R.

d, James Brolin; p, Mary Ann Fisher; exec p, Roger Corman, Lance H. Robbins; co-p, Darin Spillman, Cheryl Parnell, Edward G. Reilly; w, Alex Simon; ph, Michael Bucher; ed, Michael Thibault; m, John R. Graham, William Anderson, Gordon Goodwin; prod d, Billy Jett; art d, Tim Zeug; set d, Steve Walton; sound, D.J. Ritchie; casting, Jan Glaser; cos, Freddie Kirk; makeup, Grainne Daly; stunts, Neville Tough

Drama/Political/Thriller **(PR: C MPAA: R)**

MY FIRST NAME IS MACEO ★★★½

(U.S., 1996) 88m Rhythm 'N' Pictures ~ Rhapsody Films c

Maceo Parker; Fred Wesley; Afred "Pee Wee" Ellis; Will Boulware; Bruno Speight; Jerome Preston; Jamal Thomas; Kym Mazelle; George Clinton; Pedro Abrunhosa; Melvin Parker; John "Jabo" Starks; The Rebirth Brass Band

This documentary captures three of modern funk's chief architects (Maceo Parker, Alfred "Pee Wee" Ellis, and Fred Wesley) in superb live performances with assorted guests.

The band is seen onstage playing powerful versions of terrific songs, and in rehearsal stretching out. Guest performers Kym Mazelle, George Clinton, Pedro Abrunhosa, and the Rebirth Brass Band join them live, and are briefly interviewed individually. Also interviewed are the band members and several acquaintances, including Maceo's brother Melvin and John "Jabo" Starks, both formerly of James Brown's band. Intertitles emphasize certain lines from songs or interviews, such as "Funk is what you don't play," and "Chaos with a groove."

James Brown's influence is inescapable—several of his songs anchor the set and Parker often belts out catchphrases and hiccups rather than singing over the driving, syncopated rhythms. Influenced by the soulful arrangements of Ray Charles, alto saxophonist Parker had joined Brown in the "hardest working band in show business" during the mid-1960s, and his wildly expressive playing immediately pushed them to new levels of creativity, not to mention commercial success. Ellis, a tenor sax disciple of Sonny Rollins, joined Brown's band in 1965. Wesley, a self-described "frustrated be-bop trombonist," originally came aboard strictly for the paycheck, going on to discover a true calling and become Brown's musical arranger for many years. All three later played in various permutations of George Clinton's band Parliament, including Bootsy's Rubber Band, thus going on to influence a generation of black music (and provide further generations with an inexhaustible wellspring for sampling).

Interview snippets with Melvin Parker and "Jabo" recall the players' early days, as do visits to the bandmembers' old neighborhoods. Clinton offers an interesting contrast between the early James Brown band in their matching suits and the later Parliament wearing the most outrageous costumes imaginable. The songs run the gamut from smooth jazz to blues, but the bulk of the set is dedicated to pure, organic funk, with a plethora of solos from the three principals and short showcases for their hugely talented sidemen (bassist/singer Jerome Preston being a particular revelation). Sophisticated and intelligently arranged, tight yet fluid, the set climaxes with Fred leading the audience in a rousing "House Party," which would have been an appropriate title for the entire film. Beautifully shot, it wisely digresses from the obvious to include revealing moments such as Wesley lubricating and exercising his lips while Parker takes a solo, and accurately depicts three aging, overweight men with gray hair and glasses as the absolute epitome of cool.—A.B.

d, Markus Gruber; p, Markus Gruber, Stephen Meyner, Maceo Parker; ph, Robert Berghoff; ed, Wolf-Ingo Romer; sound, Pit Lenz, Kai Wickens

Documentary/Musical **(PR: A MPAA: NR)**

MY GIANT ★½

(U.S., 1998) 97m Face Productions; Castle Rock ~ Columbia c

Billy Crystal *(Sammy)*; Kathleen Quinlan *(Serena)*; Gheorghe Muresan *(Max)*; Joanna Pacula *(Lillianna)*; Zane Carney *(Nick)*; Jere Burns *(Weller)*; Harold Gould *(Milt)*; Dan Castellaneta

(Partlow); Raymond O'Connor *(Eddie)*; Rider Strong *(Justin)*; Doris Roberts *(Rose)*; Carl Ballantine *(Rabbi)*; Eric Lloyd *(Young Sammy)*; Jay Black *(Jay)*; Lorna Luft *(Joanne)*; Tony Belton *(Man on Street)*; Lindsay Crystal *(Stephanie)*; Peter Schindler *(Don)*; Martin Falty'n *(Cinema Manager)*; Miroslav Dubsky *(Cameraman)*; Dale Wyatt *(Dialogue Coach)*; David Steinberg *(Himself)*; Ajay Naidu *(Hot Dog Vendor)*; Estelle Harris *(Aunt Pearl)*; Elaine Kagan *(Myrna)*; Philip Sterling *(Uncle Nate)*; Max Goldblatt *(Jerry)*; E.E. Bell *(Ring Announcer)*; Michael Papajohn *(Tough Guy No. 1)*; Lincoln Simonds *(Tough Guy No. 2)*; Steven Seagal *(Himself)*; Heather Thomas *(Showgirl)*; Rick Overton *(Director)*; Richard Portnow *(Producer)*; Nicki Micheaux *(PA Jeannie)*; Lawrence Pressman *(Doctor)*; Yvonne De La Paix *(Cleaning Woman)*; Miroslava Baburkova *(Peasant Woman No. 1)*; Zoja Oubramova *(Peasant Woman No. 2)*; Vaclav Kotva *(Max's Father)*; Lena Birkova *(Max's Mother)*

MY GIANT, the tale of a self-centered Hollywood talent agent and the over-seven-feet-tall "giant" he attempts to make into a movie star, is a comedy top-heavy with forced charm, feeble humor, and telegraphed plot points. Despite its lead character's size, the film just doesn't measure up.

Hollywood talent agent Sammy (Billy Crystal) travels to Romania to hand-hold Justin (Rider Strong), a fresh-faced, rising teen star. Justin is the culmination of Sammy's career, a career spent nurturing the deeply buried talents of has-been rock stars and jingle-crooners. Immediately upon arrival at the set of a paint-by-numbers medieval action picture, Sammy is dumped by Justin, his one promising client. Lost in the byzantine byways of rural Romania, Sammy gets into a car wreck and is pulled from a swelling river by two giant hands. Believing that he's been spared personally by God, Sammy expects to awake in Heaven, but instead finds a monastery that's home to Maximus (Gheorghe Muresan), a Shakespeare-spouting caretaker with a heart of gold. Convinced he's found the next "big thing" in motion-picture villains, Sammy persuades Max to take a small role in the medieval film, and then to accompany him to America, where he's sure to become a star.

Max has no real interest in being a star, however. He's seeking a reunion with his long-lost childhood love, Lillianna (Joanna Pacula), who moved years ago to New Mexico and forgot about Max. Sammy, paying lip service to Max's desire to see the object of his affection, gets Max paying gigs as a professional wrestler and as the bad guy in a Steven Seagal flick shooting in Vegas. But Max can't pass the requisite physical for anyone doing dangerous stunts. It seems the giant is dying of an enlarged heart, a common problem in those of his size. A hasty faux reunion with Sammy's wife (Kathleen Quinlan) standing in for Lillianna is whipped up and then Sammy, suddenly growing a conscience, reunites Max instead with his estranged parents back home in Romania, turning down a big payday from Seagal's producers.

As the by-the-numbers plot of MY GIANT unfolds, dread disbelief grows into the awful certainty that the untalented 7'7" tall NBA star Muresan, who walks through the film like an automaton, is being used by the filmmakers in every bit as craven and manipulative a manner as is the character he portrays. MY GIANT was originally developed as a vehicle for Crystal (here playing a character clearly named after the protagonist of Budd Schulberg's classic *What Makes Sammy Run?*) and his costar in THE PRINCESS BRIDE, the late Andre the Giant, a far more effectively comic and touching on-screen presence than Muresan. This fact can't erase the squirm-inducing sight of a real-life giant with zero acting skills starring in a film about a giant with zero acting skills who's forced to star in films. Evidently, this was thought to be cute by director Michael Lehmann (who will seemingly never do a comedy as original as his 1989 sleeper HEATHERS), scripter David Seltzer (best known for THE OMEN and unintentional laugh riots like SIX WEEKS and SHINING THROUGH), and Crystal (who co-wrote the original story).

The ugliness doesn't stop there, however. The mere presence of the loathsome Steven Seagal as his smarmy self drags the film down even further. And the fact that Max is given a fatal condition similar (if not identical) to that possessed by Muresan in real life—and the same condition that killed Andre the Giant—is the nauseating cherry on top of this lifeless, sawdust-sprinkled sundae of a film.

The self-congratulatory nature of the film's sentimental approach, its predictable scripting, and wholly inaccurate reproduction of the comic formulas of Hollywood's golden era link it to preceding Crystal comedies including CITY SLICKERS II (1994), FORGET PARIS (1995), and FATHERS' DAY (1997). MY GIANT wants desperately to be clever and touching, but the film's insincere schmaltz and its unwillingness to rise above the level of a freak show (despite lip service to the "humanity" of the "giant"), results in an end product creepier and more revolting than the most effective horror films. *(Profanity.)*—K.W.

d, Michael Lehmann; p, Billy Crystal; exec p, Peter Schindler; assoc p, Lynne Boyarsky; w, David Seltzer (from a story by David Seltzer and Billy Crystal); ph, Mike Coulter; ed, Stephen Semel; m, Marc Shaiman; prod d, Jack DeGovia; art d, Tom Reta; set d, Kathe Klopp; sound, Jeff Wexler, Don Coufal, Scott Sherline, Mark C. Grech; fx, Richard Ratliff, Joe Gareri, Pacific Title Digital; casting, Pam Dixon Mickelson; cos, Rita Ryack; makeup, Peter Montagna; stunts, John Branagan

Comedy **(PR: A MPAA: PG)**

MY KNEES WERE JUMPING: REMEMBERING THE KINDERTRANSPORTS ★★½

(U.S., 1998) 75m National Center for Jewish Film c/bw

Joanne Woodward *(Narration)*

One of few American films to address the kindertransports—the pre-WWII trains which moved Jewish children from Nazi-occupied territories to safety in England—MY KNEES WERE JUMPING: REMEMBERING THE KINDERTRANSPORTS recounts this little-documented occurrence through archival footage, family photographs, and the recollections of those who experienced it. Produced by the daughter of one of the kindertransport refugees, this documentary is earnest and dedicated, but diminished in impact by sketchiness and problematic structuring.

In 1990, surviving members of the *kindertransports*—Jews born in Europe who as children were granted refuge in England—gather at a reunion. Among the attendees is Ruth Morley, a Hollywood costume designer and mother of filmmaker Melissa Hacker. At the gathering, Ruth addresses the crowd, recalling the time when she and thousands of other children left their parents and boarded trains bound for England.

In the 1930s, Nazi terror and its attendant anti-Semitism spread through Germany and its neighboring countries. Ruth, a native Austrian, remembers that she fainted (or her "knees jumped," as she puts it) when her father, a Jew, was arrested. While most countries, including the United States, refused entry to Jews, England granted refuge to a few thousand children between the ages of five and 17. Many of the children were too young to understand fully what was happening, and found the journey exciting. Upon arrival in England, the children were set up in camps throughout the country. Some were taken in by families, and a few maintained contact with their families through letters. When WWII ended, most of the children, learning that their parents had perished in the Holocaust, immigrated to America.

At a New York City meeting of the children of *kindertransport* evacuees, the children, now adults, discuss their parents' reluctance to talk about this part of their lives, and comment on how pessimistic and overprotective their parents often were. When Melissa asks her mother about why she had hidden this part of her past, Ruth says that she did so for Melissa's protection. In response, Melissa explains that once she learned the truth, she felt obliged to protect her mother.

In the manner of such contemporary documentary filmmakers as Ross McElwee and Alan Berliner, Melissa Hacker works to present the world from the perspective of a family member, to better to evaluate how the forces of history affect the individual. Using her mother's experiences as a focal point, Hacker recounts an historical event, and she also records the toll that this event has taken as it has rippled through two generations of family. Her film, then, attempts to demonstrate how an increasingly remote past continues to impose itself on the present.

As a filmmaker, however, Hacker, doesn't quite seem up to the complex task she's created for herself, for her film is neither strong enough as a history of the *kindertransports* nor incisive enough an analysis of its aftermath. While the period is effectively evoked through the eerily distinct recollections of its survivors—whose comments are punctuated by inserts of ghostly black-and-white family photos—the broader aspects of the movement are too slightly detailed, comprised more of general historical information than specific facts.

The film is more successful at capturing the incident's reverberative effect, as when the evacuees reveal as elderly adults the guilt they have always carried with them for escaping what their parents could not. Or when their children, as young adults, talk about inherited pessimism, not knowing until they were past childhood why their parents instilled in them such a negative worldview. But even these moments are not as powerful as they should have been, for Hacker never convincingly integrates the personal chronicles into the objective history (a problem reflected in the film's voice-over narration, which alternates awkwardly between Hacker's first-person observations and more tradition third-person descriptions by Joanne Woodward).

Nonetheless, one can sympathize with Hacker for her heartfelt and deeply sensitive attempt to fill gaps in both historical and familial records. And if her film has fallen short of its aims, Hacker still merits credit for calling attention to an underreported episode. *(Adult situations.)*—D.C.

d, Melissa Hacker; p, Melissa Hacker; ph, John Foster, Kevin Keating, Jill Johnson, Eric Schmidt; ed, Melissa Hacker; m, Joel Goodman; sound, Alexandra Balthazuk, Susan Korda, Trisha Gouvanis, Paul Koronkeiwicz

Documentary/Historical **(PR: C MPAA: NR)**

MY VERY BEST FRIEND ★★★

(U.S., 1996) 92m Once and Future Films ~ Viacom c

Jaclyn Smith *(Dana Griffin)*; Jill Eikenberry *(Barbara Wilkins)*; Tom Irwin *(Alex Wilkins)*; Tom Mason *(Ted Marshall)*; Mary Kay Place *(Molly Butler)*; Kimberly Warnat *(Kate Wilkins)*; Beverley Elliott *(Rose)*; Garwin Sanford *(Jay Drucker)*; Robert Lewis *(Trooper Russo)*; Steve Makaj *(Trooper Harris)*; Ryan Taylor *(Bobby)*

This watchable woman's film is a revisionist take on melodramas like OLD ACQUAINTANCE (1943), in which feuding characters endure middle age and each others' company. Unlike such sudsy updates of '40's soap operas as BETWEEN FRIENDS (1983), MY VERY BEST FRIEND takes a different tack: what if one of the squabbling pals really means every bit of her bitchy repartee?

Always supportive of her glamorous friend Dana Griffin (Jaclyn Smith), reserved Barbara Wilkins (Jill Eikenberry) is somewhat relieved when Dana becomes engaged to tycoon Ted Marshall (Tom Mason). Invited to the wedding along with her increasingly distant husband Alex (Tom Irwin) and her teen daughter Kate (Kimberly Warnat), Barbara is stunned when Ted blurts out that Dana is pregnant: she knows that a college abortion left Dana sterile, but keeps quiet.

When Ted discovers that Dana deceived him and threatens to annul the marriage, she deliberately pushes him off his yacht and watches him drown. To allay suspicions of murder, penniless Dana waives her rights to Ted's fortune and is forced to depend on Barbara's kindness. Barbara's housekeeper Rose (Beverley Elliott) isn't keen on Dana joining the Wilkins household.

Worming her way into Kate's confidence, Dana makes subtle plays for Alex's affections and even bugs the Wilkins' home in order to uncover information she can use to break up Barbara's marriage. Resentful of Alex's emotional bonding with Dana, Barbara shreds his skydiving gear; Rose forgets to have it repaired. On Alex's birthday, Dana diverts Barbara with a fake phone call about Kate becoming ill during an out-of-town school outing. When Barbara returns the next morning, she catches Alex and Dana in bed. Alex then rushes out for a skydiving trip with the torn gear; his accidental death casts suspicion on jealous Barbara. Unable to persuade police that Barbara acted intentionally, Dana is finally arrested for Ted's murder. Rose uncovers Dana's recording equipment which taped her confession to Alex that she had killed her own husband and wouldn't hesitate to add Alex to her casualty list; she plays this tape for the police.

This chilling evocation of misplaced trust is an above average soap thriller, expertly directed by Joyce Chopra, who helmed the women's film classic SMOOTH TALK (1985). If this film has a flaw, it's the extremity of Barbara's unwarranted faith in Dana. Still, Dana is a practiced chameleon, and Barbara seems more gullible than unbelievably loyal. The teleplay intelligently pictures the Wilkins marriage as shaky, a battleground vulnerable to Dana's final scourge. Echoing Gene Tierney's vacant-souled heroine in LEAVE HER TO HEAVEN (1945), Jaclyn Smith gives a fine performance by incorporating her delicate beauty into her portrayal of a gamesplayer who manipulates people like chess pieces. She craves the security of Barbara's marriage, but lacks the self-awareness to realize that such relationships are earned, not acquired. Dana kills to fill a void in herself; the tragedy is that she betrays the one person who ever recognized any humanity in her. In examining this cancerous coveting, the film suggests that all our friends should come complete with a psychological profile attached. *(Violence, adult situations.)*—R.P.

d, Joyce Chopra; p, Laurette Hayden, Richard Davis, Sandra Saxon Brice; exec p, Fred Silverman, David Dizenfeld; co-p, Michael Miller, Patti Obrow White; w, Lindsay Harrison, John Robert Bensink; ph, James Glennon; ed, Paul Dixon; m, Patrick Williams; prod d, Perri Gorrara; set d, Ane Christensen; sound, William Butler (mixer); fx, Rae Reedyk; casting, Beth Klein; cos, Vicky Mulholland, Jim Echerd; makeup, Lili Marchenski; stunts, Scott Ateah, Marc Akerstream

Thriller/Drama **(PR: C MPAA: PG)**

NAKED ACTS ★★★

(U.S., 1998) 107m Kindred Spirits Productions; Sirron Communications ~ Kindred Spirits Productions c

Jake-ann Jones (Cicely); Patricia DeArcy (Lydia Love); John McKie (Marcel Brown); Ron Cephas Jones (Joel); Renee Cox (Diana); Sandye Wilson (Winsome); Natalie Robinson (Randi); Marantha Quick (Grandmama); Ajene Washington (Ronnie); Annette Myrie (Little Cece); Rodney Charles (Leading Man); Simone Hunt (Baby Cece); Jairus Hunt (Daddy); Sabrina Lamb (Comic); Laura Washington (Comedy Club Waitress); Jerome Bailey (Homeboy); Beatrice Brazoban (Street Artist); Peekoo A. Lewis (Bathouse Attendant); Tara Greenway (Sauna Woman #1); Leslie Hoffman (Sauna Woman #2); Bridgett Davis (Rae); ATMOSPHERE: Glenn Evans; K. Bradley Davis; Karen L. Glover; Deborah J. Evans; Charles Henderson; Carl Hancock Rux; David Daniel Pleasant; Saul Williams; Tammy Hunte; Ivor Alleyne; Corine Oliver; Eugene Holley; Gracye Nance; Cheryl Rozie; Bethany White; Tracie Morris; Tynia D. Richard; John Morris; Lena Glenn; Andrea Harris; Suzanne C. Cooke; Thelma Paula Fernandez; Sandra M. Stevenson

N

An extremely low-budget, self-distributed production, NAKED ACTS surmounts its financial limitations with talent and ingenuity, and emerges as an affecting portrait of a young black woman who learns to appreciate the beauty of her own body.

After not having seen her for four years, Cicely (Jake-ann Jones) visits her mother, former blaxploitation star Lydia Love (Patricia DeArcy), at the video store she manages. Cicely tells Lydia of her plans to be a film actress, but Lydia warns Cicely that the film industry exploits women. Cicely dismisses Lydia's concerns, claiming that she has landed a part in a serious film.

Cicely is shocked, however, when she learns that she is expected to appear nude in the film. She appeals to the producer, Marcel (John McKie), who is firm about performing the script as written, and to the director, Joel (Ron Cephas Jones)—an ex-boyfriend of Cicely's—who cannot change Marcel's mind. Cicely finally convinces Marcel to change the script, by figuring a way to reduce production costs if she does not disrobe. That night, Cicely and Joel rekindle their relationship and make love, although Cicely does so clothed. Cicely begins to talk with a photographer friend, Diana (Renee Cox), about her discomfort with her body. Diana offers to help Cicely overcome her reluctance and takes her to a public steambath where, with Diana's gentle coaxing, she removes all her clothing. That night, she takes her clothes off in front of Joel before the two engage in sex.

On the first day of shooting, Cicely learns that her lead role has been given away, and that she has been assigned a supporting role. In a rage, she quits. She heads to her mother's store and confronts Lydia with her history of neglect as a mother, revealing to Lydia that she had been sexually abused as a child by one of Lydia's boyfriends. Later, Cicely goes by herself to Diana's studio, where she photographs herself nude. In a gesture of reconciliation, she sends the pictures to Lydia.

Although working with a miniscule budget and a no-name cast, first time writer-director Bridgett M. Davis has managed to put together a thought-provoking, meaningful little film. NAKED ACTS is truly cut-rate filmmaking. In scene after scene, actors stand or sit in front of an unmoving camera, advancing the film's narrative through dialogue. The story's more active moments have been shot silently, with music or voice over narration on the soundtrack. The film's economic liabilities also manifest themselves technically: the sound recording is often so poor that the actors are hardly audible.

But these shortcomings do not undermine the film's worth, thanks to Davis's intelligent script and a fine, spirited cast. Addressing a subject that is resolutely ignored in commercial filmmaking—the self-image of African-American women—Davis shows considerable sensitivity and wit in defining Cicely's problem. For the most part, she avoids tidy resolutions and soapbox moralizing, and while the film criticizes the marginalization of black women in American media (thus acknowledging its own marginalization), Davis does not permit NAKED ACTS to degenerate into a diatribe. This is an essentially positive film, more a story of a woman's personal triumph over self-doubt than a reproach of mainstream culture.

The cast is fine. Jake-ann Jones is splendid as the reticent Cicely, making Cicely's lack of confidence in her body believable and moving. DeArcy and Ron C. Jones lend solid support, and McKie is particularly good as the pretentious, pompous Marcel (who speaks of filming "nudity in the European sense"). Only Cox is problematic, but the trouble may be more with the character than the actress. Diana is the least credible of the characters in NAKED ACTS, and Cox is left with the unfortunate task of mouthing the film's more pedantic dialogue.

On the whole, though, Davis deserves admiration for successfully bringing off a film about an issue that the mainstream film industry pretends doesn't exist. NAKED ACTS is a creditable accomplishment, and a film that deserves to be seen. *(Extensive nudity, sexual situations, adult situations, extreme profanity.)*—D.C.

d, Bridgett M. Davis; p, Bridgett M. Davis; exec p, Henry E. Norris; assoc p, Michele Blackwell, Rita R. Davis, Rob Fields, Jake-ann Jones; w, Bridgett M. Davis; ph, Herman Lew; ed, Brunilda Torres; m, Cecilia Smith; prod d, Donn Thompson; art d, Fred Holland; sound, Pam Demetruis; casting, E/Quality Imaging; cos, Nikki Doss, Tracie L. Garvin; makeup, Anthony Jones

Drama **(PR: O MPAA: NR)**

NAKED LIES ★★

(U.S., 1998) 93m Magic Hour Pictures ~ Filmo Imagen c

Shannon Tweed *(Cara Landry)*; Fernando Allende *(Damian Medina)*; Jay Baker *(Mitch Kendall)*; Salvador Pineda *(Lt. Rivas)*; Steven Bauer *(Kevin)*; Michael Edward Rose *(Garrett Scott)*; Mineko Mori *(Laura)*; Hugo Stieglitz *(Santiago)*; Jaqueline Fernandez *(Carmen)*; Gerardo Samaripa *(Carlos)*; Eliezer Zaldana *(Angel)*; Gerardo Valdivia *(Ernesto)*; Enrique Flores *(Armando)*; Ricarda Edelsbacher *(Goddess)*; Juan Bueno *(Political Leader)*; Mario Valdez *(Cab Driver)*; Ricardo Gandara *(Guard)*; Carlos Aragon *(Guard)*

Male and female hardbodies flex their muscles in this combination of action and softcore erotica. Though she's been in this genre for some time, top-billed Shannon Tweed holds her own against her younger co-stars.

After accidentally killing a child during a DEA drug bust, guilt-ridden agent Cara Landry (Shannon Tweed) plunges into a perilous assignment for her former lover, Treasury Department boss Mitch Kendall (Jay Baker). To ferret out Mexican crime king Damian Medina (Fernando Allende), Cara goes undercover as a croupier at Medina's Mexican casino.

Posing as a croupier, Cara attracts the lustful eye of Medina, along with the mistrust of his partner Garrett Scott (Michael Edward Rose) and the jealousy of his girlfriend Laura (Mineko Mori). To undermine Medina's counterfeiting enterprise, Cara allows herself to get arrested by local policeman Lt. Rivas (Salvador Pineda), who actually works for Mitch. When Rivas opens courier Cara's money case, he finds only gambling chips.

Cara's willingness to take the fall allows her to penetrate Medina's inner circle. She and Medina begin a torrid affair which piques Mitch's jealousy and jeopardizes Cara's mission. Unfortunately, on the day of a mega-million money transfer, Garrett catches snooping Cara red-handed. Forced to kill Garrett, Cara is then taken hostage by Medina as Mitch, Lt. Rivas, and the Policia sweep through Medina's estate. Cara frees herself, Mitch shoots Medina to death, and the Mexican police arrest Medina's accomplices.

NAKED LIES isn't really interested in Cara's redemption as a Treasury Dept. spy. Nor is it concerned with revving up action fans with its spyjinks and shootouts, although it handles these sequences satisfactorily. Instead, NAKED LIES concentrates on peeling off clothing to reveal lovingly lit, titillatingly posed flesh. Shannon Tweed is best in vehicles like SCORNED (1995) where she plays characters driven by a thirst for revenge; here, her only driving force is an overwhelming desire to disrobe. This soft porn outing disguised as a crime thriller sandwiches in just enough plot to fool the gullible. With luscious Tweed leading the undraped pack of playmates, this arousing film meets the requirements of the target audience of lecherous males. *(Graphic violence, extensive nudity, extreme profanity, substance abuse.)*—R.P.

d, Ralph Portillo; p, Ralph Portillo, James Elliot; exec p, Marc Greenburg; assoc p, Shannon Tweed; co-p, Adolfo Martinez Solares; w, Jalee Baily, Michael Edwards, D. Avelo; ph, Keith Hullard; ed, Nicholas Zennaiter; art d, Gabriela Paredes; sound, Richard Mercado (mixer); fx, Arturo Godinez; makeup, Eduardo DeLeon; stunts, Bernabe Palma

Action/Crime **(PR: C MPAA: R)**

NAPOLEON ★★½

(Australia/Japan/U.S., 1997) 81m Film Australia; Furry Feature; Herald Ace; Nippon Herald; Fuji Television; Pony Canyon; Samuel Goldwyn Company; Australian Film Finance Corp. ~ MGM/UA c

VOICES OF: Adam Wylie *(Napoleon)*; Bronson Pinchot *(Birdo Lucci)*; Barry Humphries, billed as Dame Edna Everage *(Kangaroo)*; David Ogden-Stiers *(Koala/Owl)*; Carol Kane *(Spider)*; David Argue *(Frill-Necked Lizard)*; Joan Rivers *(Mother Penguin)*; Steven Vidler *(Turtle/Snake)*; Brandan Little *(Owl/Wombat)*; Stuart Pankin *(Father Penguin)*; Wendy Maaxena *(Napoleon's Mother)*; Debra Mooney *(Black Cat)*; Ashley Malinger *(Sid)*; Olivia Hack *(Nancy)*; Blythe Danner *(Mother Dingo)*; Casey Siemaszko *(Pengi)*

NAPOLEON is a cute, if highly derivative, kids' movie about a pampered little puppy (who, of course, can talk) that heeds the call of the wild and leaves his cushy life in the city to go on an incredible journey in the Australia outback. The Australian-Japanese-US coproduction was made in 1994, and received a very brief US theatrical release in 1997 before finding its natural home on video in 1998 (with a substantially new voice cast from the original version).

Muffin (voice of Adam Wylie) is a gentle golden retriever puppy who wants to be a fearless warrior and calls himself Napoleon. During a child's birthday party, he hears the distant howls of dingoes, jumps into a basket to which several balloons are attached and is whisked away to Sydney Harbor. When he lands, Napoleon is befriended by a parrot named Birdo Lucci (voice of Bronson Pinchot), who teaches the pooch how to fend for himself in the bush country and helps him overcome his fear of water. During his quest to find the dingoes, Napoleon is followed by a nasty black cat (voice of Debra Mooney) who thinks he's an overgrown mouse; he also has some misadventures with a spider, a koala bear, an owl, a wallaby, a frog, a porcupine, a snake, exotic birds, rabbits, and lizards.

After escaping a fire in a sugar-cane field, Napoleon takes refuge in a cave during a storm and discovers a pair of dingo puppies, Sid (voice of Ashley Malinger) and Nancy (voice of Olivia Hack). He saves the pups from drowning and when their mother (voice of Blythe Danner) returns, she introduces him to a friendly kangaroo (voice of Barry Humphries), who puts him in her pouch and takes him to the shore. The black cat makes one last attempt to attack Napoleon, but the cat is dumped into the water by Napoleon, Birdo, and a penguin (voice of Casey Siemaszko). Napoleon then rides on the back of a large turtle across the water to his home, but after reuniting with his mother (voice of Wendy Maaxena), the black cat shows up again.

NAPOLEON hews to the same foolproof anthropomorphic formula which recently proved to be a box-office bonanza for Disney in HOMEWARD BOUND: THE INCREDIBLE JOURNEY (1993): telling a story through the eyes of adorable animals who converse amongst themselves via celebrity voiceovers. Although it's also similar to the more technically accomplished Australian hit BABE (1995), NAPOLEON's old-fashioned, low-tech use of well-trained animals, voice-overs that don't even try to match the animals' lip movements, and clever editing, somehow seems more appealing than the mechanical perfection of animatronics and computer wizardry.

Napoleon's encounters with virtually every animal to be found in Australia—including a frill-necked lizard that sleeps in the middle of the highway as giant trucks drive over it—are sure to delight kids. For adults, the spectacular scenery of the Australian outback is strikingly captured by the expert cinematography, and there are a few amusing film-buff in-jokes thrown in by director Mario Andreacchio (Birdo Lucci and his cousins Vittorio and Federico; the dingoes named Sid and Nancy).

Much of the largely Aussie voice-over cast of the original has been replaced for video with more easily understandable American voices, apart from Barry Humphries who plays the kangaroo using his Dame Edna Everage persona (which means nothing to kids, or even most American adults for that matter). The film's one curious note for a kids' movie is its undue emphasis on death and killing (albeit in a humorous vein): Napoleon constantly talks about wanting to be a savage warrior that kills its own food, and his repeated fights with the relentless cat are truly frightening and invariably end with the cat being violently "killed," only to return with one more of its nine lives like some sort of crazed "Jason" or "Freddy" monster. After Napoleon finally makes it home and kisses his mother for the heartwarming finale, the cat shows up once again and hisses the film's last line: "This dog must die!"— M.S.

d, Mario Andreacchio; p, Mario Andreacchio, Michael Bourchier, Naonari Kawamura, Mark Saltzman; exec p, Masato Hara, Ron Saunders; w, Michael Bourchier, Mario Andreacchio, Mark Saltzman; ph, Roger Dowling; ed, Edward McQueen-Mason; m, Bill Conti; prod d, Vicki Niehus; sound, James S. Currie (design), Craig Carter (design); casting, Christine King

Children's/Adventure **(PR: AA MPAA: G)**

NEGOTIATOR, THE ★★½
(U.S., 1998) 135m New Regency; Mandeville ~ Warner Bros. c

Samuel L. Jackson *(Danny Roman)*; Kevin Spacey *(Chris Sabian)*; David Morse *(Commander Adam Beck)*; Ron Rifkin *(Commander Grant Frost)*; John Spencer *(Chief Al Travis)*; Regina Taylor *(Karen Roman)*; J.T. Walsh *(Inspector Terence Niebaum)*; Siobhan Fallon *(Maggie)*; Paul Giamatti *(Rudy)*; Bruce Beatty *(Markus)*; Michael Cudlitz *(Palermo)*; Carlos Gomez *(Eagle)*; Tim Kelleher *(Argento)*; Dean Norris *(Scott)*; Nestor Serrano *(Hellman)*; Doug Spinuzza *(Tonray)*; Leonard Thomas *(Allen)*; Stephen Lee *(Farley)*; Lily Nicksay *(Omar's Daughter)*; Lauri Johnson *(Chief's Wife)*; Sabi Dorr *(Bartender)*; Gene Wolande *(Morewitz)*; Rhonda Dotson *(Linda Roenick)*; Donald Korte *(Officer at Funeral)*; Anthony T. Petrusonis *(Officer at Funeral)*; John McDonald *(Pipes and Drums Leader)*; Jack Mclaughlin Gray *(Priest)*; John Lordon *(Linda's Attorney)*; Jack Shearer *(D.A. Young)*; Donna Ponterotto *(Secretary)*; Michael Shamus Wiles *(Taylor)*; Mik Scriba *(Bell)*; Joey Perillo *(Tech 1)*; Mary Page Keller *(Lisa Sabian)*; Kelsey Mulrooney *(Stacy Sabian)*; Brad Blaisdell *(FBI Agent Grey)*; Bruce Wright *(FBI Agent Moran)*; Robert David Hall *(Cale Wangro)*; Guy Van Swearingen *(Officer)*; Bernard Hocks *(Sniper)*; Carol-Anne Touchberry; Robert Jordan; Geoff Morrell; Janna Tezlaff; Millie Santiago; Jay Levine; Mark Giangreco; Rick Scarry; Mary Ingersoll; McNally Sagal; Mary Major; Lynn Rondell; Edwina Moore; Lynn Forslund *(Reporters)*; Muriel Clair; Mary Ann Childers; Diann Burns; Carla Sanchez *(News Anchors)*; Charles Valentino *(FBI Agent)*; Robert Baier *(Officer at HBT)*; Ted Montue *(Officer at IAB)*; John Buckley *(Detective)*; Darius Aubry *(Detective)*; Steven Mainz *(TAC Officer)*; Caine *(Raoul)*; Max *(Raoul)*; Paul Guilfoyle *(Nate)*

A fine cast is held hostage by a poor script in THE NEGOTIATOR, in which an honest hostage negotiator takes some hostages of his own to avoid taking the fall for some corrupt cops.

Lt. Danny Roman (Samuel L. Jackson) of the Chicago Police Department is esteemed for his skillful bravado as a hostage negotiator. Having brought a life-or-death situation to a close earlier in the day, Roman modestly shrugs off both media attention and the backslapping of his peers at the police chief's birthday party, while rumors of a mysteriously depleted police disability fund begin to swirl. Roman is himself a member of the disability fund board, but in a festive mood, also shrugs off the rumored shenanigans. His partner, Nate (Paul Guilfoyle), following a lead that could point to the culprits, turns up dead, and circumstantial evidence points to Roman, who lacks an alibi. A little planted evidence threatens to seal the case: Roman finds himself accused of not only murder, but also of stealing the missing money.

Instead of waiting for his day in court to prove his innocence, Roman sets out to beat the corrupt system at its own game. Following a hunch, he pulls off a dramatic hostage-taking scene of his own. With Internal Affairs Inspector Niebaum (J. T. Walsh) and Roman's friend Commander Frost (Ron Rifkin), whom he eventually releases, as well as couple of bystanders as his captives, Roman buys himself some time. He demands that Chris Sabian (Kevin Spacey), whose reputation as a negotiator is as lauded as his own but whose tactics are polar opposite, be called in. Wrenched away from an evening with his family, Sabian is steely and irritable; to make matters worse, his efforts to control the situation are undermined by some trigger-happy cops. Roman makes some progress in his impromptu investigation using Niebaum's computer files, but an apparent attempt to bring Roman down leaves Niebaum dead just after he confesses his complicity in the embezzlement.

As the FBI takes over the negotiation, Sabian helps Roman escape. They make it to the Niebaum's home to search his personal files for hard evidence just ahead of the police. In the nick of time, Sabian, pretending to want a piece of the action himself, tricks Frost into a confession that he manages to record, exonerating Roman.

Jackson brings to his role the brashness audiences have come to expect from him, but style alone can't keep THE NEGOTIATOR from sinking into a predictable game of cat-and-mouse, punctuated by a string of red herrings. Spacey is the perfect picture of tight-lipped calm in the face of chaos, but the wooden dialogue he is given veers too close to parody. Helpful hostages played by Regina Taylor and Paul Giamatti provide some welcome comic relief, but F. Gary Gray's direction actually minimizes both dialogue and action. Instead, he all too often becomes preoccupied with fetishizing the paraphernalia of police work. The camera lingers over police cruisers and helicopters, handguns and handcuffs, the telephones connecting the negotiators, and the listening devices that clutter the police command center, as if Gray's task were to direct an advertisement for these items, rather than use them to drive the narrative forward. His choices suggest that these inanimate devices might be more interesting to look at than the actors. Unfortunately, they come close. *(Graphic violence, extreme profanity.)*— C.Ch.

d, F. Gary Gray; p, Arnon Milchan, David Hoberman; exec p, David Nicksay, Robert Stone, Webster Stone; w, James De Monaco, Kevin Fox; ph, Russell Carpenter; ed, Christian Adam Wagner; m, Graeme Revell; prod d, Holger Gross; art d, Kevin Ishioka; set d, Richard Goddard; sound, Russell Williams (mixer); casting, David Rubin; cos, Francine Jamison-Tanchuk

Action/Thriller/Crime **(PR: C MPAA: R)**

NEIL SIMON'S THE ODD COUPLE II ★★
(U.S., 1998) 99m Cort/Madden Company ~ Paramount c
(AKA: ODD COUPLE II, THE)

Jack Lemmon *(Felix Ungar)*; Walter Matthau *(Oscar Madison)*; Richard Riehle *(Detective)*; Jonathan Silverman *(Brucey Madison)*; Lisa Waltz *(Hannah Ungar)*; Mary Beth Peil *(Felice)*; Christine Baranski *(Thelma)*; Jean Smart *(Holly)*; Rex Linn *(Jay Jay)*; Jay O. Sanders *(Leroy)*; Barnard Hughes *(Beaumont)*; Ellen Geer *(Frances Ungar Melnick)*; Doris Belack *(Blanche Madison Povitch)*; Lou Cutell *(Abe)*; Mary Fogarty *(Flossie)*; Alice Ghostley *(Esther)*; Peggy Miley *(Millie)*; Rebecca Schull *(Wanda)*; Florence Stanley *(Hattie)*; Estelle Harris *(Flirting Woman)*; Joaquin Martinez *(Truck Driver)*; Amy Yasbeck *(Stewardess)*; Francesca P. Roberts *(Woman Passenger)*; Amy Parrish *(Computer Girl)*; Liz Torres *(Maria)*; Myles Jeffrey *(Little Boy)*; Carmen Mormino; Chuck Montgomery *(California Troopers)*; Earl Boen *(Fred)*; Ron Harper *(Jack)*; Edmund Shaff *(Ralph)*; Daisy Velez *(Conchita)*; Beecey Carlson *(Waitress)*; Terry L. Rose *(Bartender)*; Alfred Dennis *(Morton)*; Armando Ortega *(Detective #2)*; Peter Renaday *(Justice of the Peace)*; David Jean-Thomas *(Bus Driver)*; Daniel Zacapa *(Lead Cop)*; Cliff Bemis *(Dance Partner)*; Frank Roman *(Bellman)*; Lonnie McCullough *(Roadblock Officer)*; Matt McKenzie *(Pilot)*; Heath Hyche *(Policeman)*; Irene Olga Lopez *(Cafe Waitress)*; Jerry Rector *(Detective #3)*; Martin Grey *(Immigration Officer)*; Michelle Johnston *(Bridesmaid/Airline Employee)*; Michelle Matthow *(Wedding Guest)*; Mark McGee *(Wedding Bartender)*; Barry Thompson *(Male Passenger)*; Joanna Sanchez; Catherine Paolone *(Passengers)*; Laura Russo *(Stewardess #2)*

Jack Lemmon and Walter Matthau reprise their famous roles of fussy Felix and messy Oscar in NEIL SIMON'S THE ODD

COUPLE II, a belated sequel to the 1968 hit that's pleasant enough to watch despite the fact that it's not very funny, and wastes its stars's talents on a tired and derivative script.

Retired NY sportswriter Oscar Madison (Walter Matthau) is living in Florida when he receives a call from his son Brucey (Jonathan Silverman) in California, who informs him that he's marrying Hannah Ungar (Lisa Waltz), the daughter of Oscar's old friend and ex-roommate Felix, whom he hasn't seen in 17 years. After Oscar meets Felix at the LA airport, they rent a car and start to drive to the desert town of San Molina where the wedding is to take place, but Felix immediately gets on Oscar's nerves with his numerous phobias and restroom stops. When Felix discovers that Oscar has neglected to bring along his suitcase containing a $6,000 wedding gift and $10,000 in cash, he angrily smacks the car and it rolls down a hill and catches fire. Stuck in the middle of the desert, the two are finally picked up by a Mexican truck driver, but he turns out to be smuggling illegal aliens and they're all arrested.

When Felix and Oscar are released, they go to a hotel bar and dance with two flirtatious bikers, Thelma (Christine Baranski) and Holly (Jean Smart), who are on the run from their violent husbands. The next morning, a kindly old gent (Barnard Hughes) who lives in San Molina offers Oscar and Felix a ride, but the man dies while driving and they wind up back in jail again. Back on the road, they get on a bus and run into Thelma and Holly, and are dragged off by the ladies' gun-toting convict husbands, Leroy (Jay O. Sanders) and Jay Jay (Rex Linn). Oscar and Felix are rescued by the police and put on a plane to San Molina. When they arrive, a panicked Brucey is hiding on the roof to escape going through with the wedding; Oscar convinces him to follow his initial instincts and marry Hannah. Afterwards, Felix says goodbye to Oscar and goes off with Oscar's ex-sister-in-law Felice (Mary Beth Peil) whom he's fallen for. A few weeks later, Oscar is back home in Florida when Felix arrives unexpectedly, telling him that things didn't work out with Felice, and asking if he can move in for a little while, since he's sold his apartment in New York.

Even if this sequel to THE ODD COUPLE had an original premise or sparkling dialogue (which it doesn't), its thunder has already been stolen by the two GRUMPY OLD MEN films, which were essentially unofficial sequels, with Lemmon and Matthau plying their standard combative shtick as longtime feuding friends. Similarly, the plot of the second GRUMPY (which was also directed by Howard Deutch) also involved the wedding of Lemmon's character's daughter to Matthau's character's son, and the 1993 TV-movie sequel, THE ODD COUPLE: TOGETHER AGAIN (with Jack Klugman and Tony Randall), dealt with the nuptials of Felix's daughter as well. In any case, Neil Simon's cliched script also borrows freely from his own work (Brucey freaking out and hiding before the wedding comes directly from PLAZA SUITE's story line), and the humor relies heavily on the elderly duo's "shocking" use of four-letter words and jokes about old age, peeing, and farting.

In their 11th film together, (including KOTCH, which Lemmon directed, and cameos in JFK), Lemmon and Matthau are so familiar and at ease with one another that their presence alone unfailingly creates a sense of fun and good spirits. Their efforts are in vain, however, as Simon presents an old-fashioned sitcom view of the world that is so innocuous it can't be called racist or sexist; it, nevertheless, is filled with stereotyped Mexican characters and redneck criminals, middle-aged biker babes who wear tight leather outfits and find Felix and Oscar irresistible, and Oscar, whose struggle to pronounce Spanish names is supposed to be hilarious. The concept of a geriatric road movie is not exactly rife with comic possibilities, and the direction by Deutch is as lethargic and uninventive as the script. The tacked-on ending is an obvious set up for another sequel, but if that happens, one can only hope that someone will pump some fresh ideas into the formula, even if that means Neil Simon will have to forego his customary possessive credit in the title. *(Profanity.)*—M.S.

d, Howard Deutch; p, Robert W. Cort, David Madden, Neil Simon; assoc p, Elena Spiotta; w, Neil Simon (based on characters created by Neil Simon); ph, Jamie Anderson; ed, Seth Flaum; m, Alan Silvestri; prod d, Dan Bishop; art d, Jeff Knipp; set d, Kristen Toscano Messina; sound, Lee Orloff (mixer); fx, Robert L. Knott; casting, Jane Shannon-Smith, Alex Rosenberg; cos, Lisa Jensen; makeup, Steve Artmont; stunts, Charlie Brewer

Comedy (PR: C MPAA: PG-13)

NEMESIS 4: CRY OF ANGELS ★

(U.S., 1998) 80m Karnowski/Schmoeller Productions ~ Imperial Entertainment/Filmwerks c

Sue Price (Alex Sinclair); Norbert Weisser (Tokuda); Nicholas Guest (Earl Typhoon); Simon Poland (Johnny Impact); Andrew Divoff (Bernardo); Michal Gucik (Priest); Blanka Copikova (Woman in Black—Mother); Juro Rasla (Carlos Jr.); Bob Brown (Thug Bob); Jon Epstein (Thug Jon); Hracko Pavol; Andrej Lehota; Miroslav Gabaj (Thugs); Monica Haladova (Thug Double)

NEMESIS 4: CRY OF ANGELS is standard straight-to-video, low-budget action fare with a wafer-thin story line spiced up by shootings, sex sequences, and cheesy special effects.

In 2082, an unsteady peace exists between humans and cyborgs. After executing a target, cyborg assassin Alex (Sue Price) is given one last assignment by her boss Bernardo (Andrew Divoff). She does the deed, but is forced to also kill fellow assassin Earl (Nicholas Guest), who threatens her, explaining that she has mistakenly executed the son of a wealthy crime lord. After each killing, Alex sees a dark apparition that she believes is an angel. Later, Alex shoots down a helicopter full of killers before Bernardo's "cleaner," Tokuda (Norbert Weisser), arrives. He tries to kill Alex and admits that the crime boss has put a $100 million bounty on her head. Alex manages to kill Tokuda and two other hit men, but believing things are hopeless, she asks her friend Johnny Impact (Simon Poland) to shoot her and collect the bounty. While embracing Johnny, Alex sees the angel aiming a gun at them. She draws and kills the angel, who is actually Bernardo's partner, Mother (Blanka Copikova). Realizing that Bernardo was behind a set-up all along, they force him to call off the hit before killing him.

The films of veteran action-schlock director Albert Pyun may not be good, but they always have their odd quirks. His fourth installment in the NEMESIS series is no different—it even has a cyborg-human sex encounter with graphic (and very strange) penetration shots. Lensed in 1995, the film is a choppy, exploitative action stew loaded with Pyun regularities such as dark, claustrophobic settings and languid pacing. For some inexplicable reason, it's shot in widescreen (like most of Pyun's films), making for a brutal series of close-ups when this dreck is seen in its pan-and-scan home-video version. Sue Price reprises her role as Alex Sinclair, a brooding, muscle-bound creature whose role consists solely of exposing her saline-enhanced attributes or blowing away cyborg goons. Ironically, although she plays a human in the film, her chiseled appearance and stony acting make her seem more robotic than the actors playing the cyborgs. Other performers, including Andrew Divoff, Simon Poland and Nicholas Guest (the only veteran of all four NEMESIS films), are equally amusing in their cartoonish roles. The special effects are of the lowest order, but makeup work by Dan Rebert deserves some note for his colorful gore and interesting cyborg facials. On a positive note, this film is still better than Pyun's theatrically released ADRENALIN: FEAR THE RUSH (1996), which is the work of a sadist. *(Graphic violence, profanity, extensive nudity, sexual situations.)*—P.L.

d, Albert Pyun; p, Gary Schmoeller, Tom Karnowski; exec p, Paul Rosenblum; w, Albert Pyun; ph, George Mooradian; ed, Ken Morrisey; art d, Nenad Pecur; sound, Patrick M. Griffith; casting, Teri Blythe; cos, Elizabeth Jett; makeup, Maurine Schlenz, Dan Rebert (effects); stunts, Bob Brown, Jon Epstein

Science Fiction/Action (PR: O MPAA: R)

NEMURI KYOSHIRO: ENGETSUGIRL
(SEE: SLEEPY EYES OF DEATH: FULL CIRCLE KILLING)

NEMURI KYOSHIRO JOYOKEN
(SEE: SLEEPY EYES OF DEATH: SWORD OF SEDUCTION)

NEMURI KYOSHIRO—SHOOBU
(SEE: SLEEPY EYES OF DEATH: SWORD OF ADVENTURE)

NEVADA ★★
(U.S., 1998) 107m Keystone Film Partners; Storm Entertainment ~ Cineville c

Amy Brenneman *(Chrysty Bucks)*; Ben Browder *(Shelby)*; James Wilder *(Rip)*; Keith Anthony Bennett *(Nate)*; Bridgette Wilson *(June)*; Gabrielle Anwar *(Linny)*; Kirstie Alley *(McGill)*; Saffron Burrows *(Quinn)*; Dee Wallace Stone *(Ruby)*; Dawn Ferry *(Cashier)*; Kathy Najimy *(Ruth)*; Barbara Burton *(Katie)*; Emily Miller *(Melanie)*; Jordan Craddock *(Derrick Jr.)*; Rachel Reber *(Paula)*; Cory Riback *(Clown)*; Charlie Crandell *(Kimberly Bucks)*; Garrette Henson *(Weston Bucks)*; Angus MacFadyen *(West Bucks)*; Nathan Garcia *(Cody Bucks)*; David Darmstaedter; Paul Greenstein; Lacy Drew

NEVADA is the sort of overheated psychodrama that gives feminism a bad name, and feminist movies a worse one.

An attractive woman named Chrysty (Amy Brenneman) enters a tiny Nevada settlement called Silver, populated almost entirely by females. The men in town work for weeks at a time on a dam that will make the parched community a vast reservoir, and thus the women spend idle hours in the town, under the thumb of self-styled sheriff McGill (Kirstie Alley). Chrysty assists housewife June (Bridgette Wilson) in giving birth; June has had many children of different races, and her chronic faithlessness is all the more glaring because her husband Rip (James Wilder) is impotent. Despite this helpful deed and the fact that Chrysty gets a steady job delivering milk in the town, McGill continues to cast a suspicious eye on her. McGill does some digging and finds that the sexy stranger is a runaway housewife from Idaho. McGill phones Chrysty's husband West (Angus MacFadyen) who drives to Silver with their three children to force a reconciliation. Instead, West is attacked by Rip, who declares himself in love with Chrysty, and then is surrounded by the women of Silver—including a rifle-toting McGill—who stand in solidarity with Chrysty's bid for freedom. Urged even by his own children to give up, West retreats, leaving Chrysty to mope in scenic splendor.

Gorgeous to look at and vapid at its core, NEVADA opens with Chrysty sashaying into Silver on such a ponderously solemn note that an air of pretension is virtually guaranteed. From Ibsen's *A Doll's House* onwards, dramatists have explored the stifling bonds of marriage and championed heroines who flee it, but somehow American moviemakers seem uniquely ham-handed when they portray distaff domestic desertion as a courageous revolutionary act. Sympathy for NEVADA's heroine completely dries up with the news that Chrysty fled the hearth just because a son cursed her for ruining the meatloaf. While husband "West" (symbolism runs rampant here) is an underwritten, unshaven nonentity, he still seems undeserving of the shabby treatment accorded him by the sisterly lynch mob in the finale. Brenneman, wearing immaculate mascara and various sexy dresses, is too young and glamorous for the kitchen refugee she plays; ditto for nearly everyone else in the cast (exception: a bloated and blowsy Alley). Female viewers may be more receptive to NEVADA, if only because they will get a laugh from the film's apparent contention that multiple births and shack hovels do wonders for one's complexion. The inevitable lesbian subtext is present but marginal, and the near-nudity in certain scenes has all the erotic power of a mid-1960s sexploitation feature. The soundtrack, for reasons best known to the filmmakers, contains several repetitions of the traditional tune "Danny Boy." *(Adult situations, sexual situations, substance abuse, profanity)*—C.C.

d, Gary Tieche; p, Kathryn Arnold; exec p, H. Michael Heuser, Daniel K.S. Suh, Carl Colpaert, Susan Shapiro, Thomas D. Adelman; assoc p, Bernice M. Chu, Vanessa Lasky, Caradoc Ehrenhalt, Jody Levine; w, Gary Tieche; ph, Nancy Schreiber; ed, Rebecca Ross; m, Robert Perry; prod d, Bryce Perrin; art d, Dawn Ferry; sound, Patrick M. Griffith, Jon Ailetcher; fx, Gary Tunnicliffe; casting, Marilyn Black, Steve Brooksbank; cos, Wendy Range Rao; makeup, Debra-Lee Davidson; stunts, Jon Epstein

Drama (PR: O MPAA: R)

NEW ADVENTURES OF KIMBA THE WHITE LION, THE ★★½
(Japan, 1989) 60m TV Tokyo; Nihon Keizaisha; Gakken; Pioneer Entertainment; Ocean Studios ~ Pioneer Entertainment c

ENGLISH VOICE CAST: Ben Baxter; Don Brown; Paul Dobson; Saffron Henderson; Andrea Libman; Scott McNeil; Ricard Neuman; Gerry Plunkett; Alvin Sanders; Kelly Sheridan; Robert O. Smith; Brad Swaile; French Tickner

THE NEW ADVENTURES OF KIMBA THE WHITE LION is a lively reworking of the classic Japanese animated TV series from 1965. The plot line begins with the birth of Kimba and chronicles his later struggle to take his rightful place as king of the jungle.

Panja, the great white lion of the African jungle, is killed by a hunter who captures Panja's pregnant wife, Eliza. Aboard the ship heading across the Atlantic, the captive Eliza gives birth and names her son Kimba. She tells Kimba all about his father and his destiny, which is to return to the jungle to take his father's place. At her insistence, Kimba escapes from the cage and leaps overboard to swim back home.

After a harrowing journey, Kimba makes it back to the jungle only to find strong opposition from Jamar, a scar-faced lion who was Panja's rival, and Shaka, a black panther. Kimba meets a female lion cub, Raya, and befriends an antelope, T.K., and a parrot, Koko. He proves his worth to the other animals of the jungle during a forest fire by diverting the water from a waterfall to extinguish the fire. In his final confrontation with Jamar, Kimba is aided by Old Dice, a rhinoceros who was close to Panja.

This 1998 home video feature was compiled from a 1989 Japanese animated TV series that was a new version of the popular 1965 series, "Kimba the White Lion" (shown in Japan as "Jungle Taitei"). It was produced by Tezuka Productions and created by pioneer Japanese animator/manga artist Osamu Tezuka (who died the year this premiered on Japanese television). Three episodes of the 1989 series are credited on the tape, although the first six were reportedly compressed to make up this 60-minute feature. NEW ADVENTURES was dubbed and re-scripted for US viewers, in an effort to appeal to small children. The result has none of the original series' edge and serves anime fans poorly by cutting out huge chunks of the narrative.

Still, this incarnation of Kimba is a bit more fluidly animated than its fondly-remembered predecessor. The film also generates a good deal of suspense as Kimba faces long odds in his effort to fulfill his destiny. Since no move has been made to officially release the original Kimba TV series on home video in the US (although the show's second Japanese season has appeared in a different form on video under the title "Leo the Lion"), NEW ADVENTURES does something to fill that void. The more Kimba programs that become available in the US, the clearer it becomes how extensively Tezuka's creation influenced Disney's THE LION KING (1994).—B.C.

d, Takashi Ui; p, Ryohei Nakamura, Daisuke Baba, Kuniaki Ohnishi; exec p, Yosuke "James" Kobayashi (English Language Version); w, Mitsuru Majima, Takashi Ui (based on the comic book by Osamu Tezuka), Meredith Bain Woodward (English Language Version); ph, Hisao Shirai; ed, Masaki Sakamoto; m, Tom Keenlyside (English Language Version), John Mitchell (English Language Version); art d, Hageshi Katsumata, Masami Saito; anim, Junji Kobayashi, Osamu Tezuka, Yoshiaki Kawajiri

Animated/Children's/Adventure (PR: AA MPAA: NR)

NEWTON BOYS, THE ★★

(U.S., 1998) 113m Detour Filmproduction ~ 20th Century Fox c

Matthew McConaughey *(Willis Newton)*; Ethan Hawke *(Jess Newton)*; Vincent D'Onofrio *(Dock Newton)*; Skeet Ulrich *(Joe Newton)*; Julianna Margulies *(Louise Brown)*; Dwight Yoakam *(Brentwood Glasscock)*; Chloe Webb *(Avis Glasscock)*; Charles Gunning *(Slim)*; Bo Hopkins *(K.P. Aldrich)*; Gail Cronauer *(Ma Newton)*; Jena Karam; Casey McAuliffe *(Orphan Singers)*; Regina Mae Matthews *(Orphan Fiddler)*; Lew Temple *(Waiter)*; Glynn Williams *(Farmer Williams)*; Charles "Chip" Bray *(Bank Teller)*; Gary Moody *(Crooked Banker)*; Robert Iannaccone *(Tailor)*; Jennifer Miriam *(Catherine)*; Anne Stedman *(Madeline)*; Marjorie Carroll *(Old Woman)*; Katie Gratson *(Young Hotel Clerk)*; Angie Chase *(Kat)*; Lynn Mathis *(Arthur Adams)*; Becket Gremmels *(Lewis)*; Ed Dollison *(Night Guard)*; Boots Southerland *(Wagon Driver)*; Tommy Townsend *(Omaha Detective)*; Mary Love *(Hotel Maid)*; A.G. Zeke Mills *(Old Usher)*; Abra Moore *(Argosy Ballroom Singer)*; Lori Heuring *(Flapper)*; Joe Stevens *(Bank Association President)*; Eddie Matthews; Scott Roland; J.P. Schwan *(Bank Messengers)*; Rooster McConaughey *(Tool Pusher)*; Bo Franks *(Barker)*; Ali Nazary *(Thug)*; Ron De Roxtra *(Murray)*; David Jensen *(William Fahy)*; Brad Arrington *(Hobo)*; Richard A. Jones *(Engineer)*; Randy Stripling *(Fireman)*; Harold Suggs *(Old Brakeman)*; Chamblee Ferguson *(Head Postal Clerk)*; F.W. Post *(Postal Turkey)*; Grant James *(Gangland Doctor)*; Mark Fickert *(Chicago Sergeant)*; Kerry Tartack *(Chicago Detective)*; Luke Askew *(Chief Schoemaker)*; Blue McDonnell *(Nurse)*; Eduardo Cavasos Garza *(Mexican Cab Driver)*; Ken Farmer *(Frank Hamer)*; Daniel T. Kamin *(District Attorney)*; Ross Sears *(Judge)*

Though it boasts a cast of some of Hollywood's most talented young actors, THE NEWTON BOYS is hobbled by a mediocre script, featuring overly familiar characters and a plot that isn't particularly interesting, even in the hands of director Richard Linklater.

Willis Newton (Matthew McConaughey) isn't back home from prison more than a few days before he hooks up with Slim (Charles Gunning) and Brentwood Glasscock (Dwight Yoakam), who have a plan to rob the local bank in broad daylight. The heist goes poorly, but it inspires Willis to plan a series of more ambitious robberies, using nitroglycerine to blow the doors off safes. He enlists the aid of his brothers, Dock (Vincent D'Onofrio), Jess (Ethan Hawke), and Joe (Skeet Ulrich), and along with Brent, the Newton boys successfully rob more than 30 banks from Texas to Illinois.

After a botched job in Toronto in which the Newtons are forced to break their unspoken rule of not hurting anybody during their robberies, Willis decides to quit the robbery business and concentrate on becoming an oil baron. However, the well into which he has sunk all his ill-gotten cash is a duster, and he once again assembles the family for one last job—against the wishes of both youngest brother Joe and Willis's girlfriend, Louise (Julianna Margulies). Rather than a bank, the job is to relieve a train of more than a million dollars en route to Chicago from the Federal Reserve. From the start, the train robbery goes badly, and in the confusion Brent accidentally shoots Dock, wounding him gravely. With the sloppy job, it doesn't take long for the authorities to catch up with the Newtons; at the trial, though, they come across as contrite and congenial, and receive remarkably light sentences. Despite an occasional brush with the law, all four eventually live to a ripe old age.

Fans of director Linklater's films (SLACKER, DAZED AND CONFUSED, BEFORE SUNRISE) have come to expect—even welcome—a lot of talk and very little action. Unfortunately, the brothers Newton don't have a whole lot to say. Instead of featuring an entertaining mixture of intelligent and eccentric characters, THE NEWTON BOYS gives us four charming, largely interchangeable, and ultimately vapid pretty faces. The tremendous acting horsepower available to the film's four leads is all but defused by their characters' oafishness and sheer stupidity; add in the sad underuse of Ethan Hawke and Vincent D'Onofrio, and it's no surprise all four are outshone by Dwight Yoakam—yes, Dwight Yoakam.

The chief failing of THE NEWTON BOYS is the fact that it concentrates on Willis, the least interesting Newton brother portrayed by the least interesting actor, Matthew McConaughey. As essayed by McConaughey, Willis Newton comes off as shallow and not a little crazy; it's hard to see why his brothers feel any familial bond to this reckless and greedy lunatic. Without a sympathetic central character, Linklater cannot achieve the Butch-and-Sundance effect he's obviously going for. By the time the Newton boys are caught, we're rooting for the cops, if only to get it over with already. *(Violence.)*—B.T.

d, Richard Linklater; p, Anne Walker-McBay; exec p, John Sloss; assoc p, Keith Fletcher; co-p, Clark Lee Walker; w, Claude Stanush, Clark Lee Walker, Richard Linklater (from the book *The Newton Boys: Portrait of an Outlaw Gang* by Claude Stanush and David Middleton, based on a story by Willis Newton and Joe Newton); ph, Peter James; ed, Sandra Adair; m, Edward D. Barnes, Bad Livers; prod d, Catherine Hardwicke; art d, Randy Moore; set d, Jeanette Scott; sound, John Pritchett (mixer); fx, John McLeod, Matte World; casting, Don Phillips; cos, Shelley Komarov; makeup, Patty York; stunts, Fred Lerner

Western (PR: C MPAA: PG-13)

NEXT STEP, THE ★★

(U.S., 1997) 87m Closing Notice Productions; Wavelength ~ Phaedra Cinema c

Rick Negron *(Nick Mendez)*; Kristin Moreu *(Amy)*; Denise Faye *(Heidi)*; Taylor Nichols *(Peter)*; Gerry McIntyre *(Sean)*; Aubrey Lynch *(Steven)*; Michelle Pertier *(Michelle)*; Donald Byrd *(Austin)*; Fuschia Walker *(Rolanda)*; Jane Edith Wilson *(Greta)*; Barry McNabb *(Owen)*; Yvonne Racz *(Veronica)*; Jamie Bishton *(Kevin)*; Michael Donaghy *(Luis)*; Howard Wesson *(Louie)*; Fredrick Deane *(Scott)*; Richard Stegman *(Agent)*; Chris Eigeman *(David)*; Peter Reffie *(Frankie)*; John Battista *(Sal)*; Julio Munge *(Ramon)*; Ted Neuhoff *(Husband in Restaurant)*; Yvonne Trinkwater *(Wife in Restaurant)*; Pamela Berkeley *(Woman in Hotel)*; Mio Morales *(Prem)*; David Turley *(Beefcakes Waiter)*; Max Miller *(Dr. Astin)*; Joan Ranquet *(Woman in Bar)*; Thomas Gibson *(Bartender)*; Star Reese *(Videographer)*; Lisa Johnson *(Dance Captain)*

An aging theatrical "gypsy" faces professional and romantic crises when he refuses to hang up his dancing shoes in THE NEXT STEP, an earnest low-budget indie that's saddled with a cliched script but uplifted by choreography by the renowned Donald Byrd, and a credible depiction of the backstage Broadway milieu.

Nick Mendez (Rick Negron), a Broadway dancer in his mid-30s, has a backstage fling with fellow dancer Heidi (Denise Faye), then learns that the show they're in is closing. When he tells his live-in girlfriend Amy (Kristin Moreu), she suggests he should retire, but he's not ready to quit. Nick's agent drops him after getting him an audition for a revival of a musical called "Gangland." Since Nick starred in the original production and is friends with the director/choreographer Austin (Donald Byrd), he's sure he'll get the part. At the audition, Nick finds himself overshadowed by a young challenger named Steven (Aubrey Lynch), but convinces Austin to let him come to the final callback. Meanwhile, at her physical therapy job, Amy meets Peter (Taylor Nichols), a stockbroker having his knee rehabilitated who's immediately attracted to her, and Amy's boss offers her a job working in his new clinic in Connecticut.

While awaiting the callback, Nick returns to his old restaurant job to make some money. Amy begins to pressure him to get married and move to Connecticut with her, but Nick cannot commit, and begins a fling with an attractive French dancer named Michelle (Michelle Pertier) who is waitressing at the restaurant. At the callback, Nick loses out to Steven, and angrily turns down an offer from Austin to help him coach the younger dancers in the show. That night, Nick is fired from the restaurant for showing favoritism to Michelle, and when Amy finds evidence of Nick's affair with Michelle, she throws him out. Nick sublets Heidi's apartment, but is unable to pay the rent and is forced to take a job as a waiter in a male strip club. Broke and desperate, Nick tries hustling after hours, but the attempt turns disastrous. Nick runs back to Amy in the middle of the night, but she tells him she's marrying Peter. Nick shows up the next day at the dance rehearsal studio and accepts Austin's offer to work as a dance coach for "Gangland."

Filmed in 1995, THE NEXT STEP borrows elements from such modern musical-dramas as ALL THAT JAZZ (1979), FAME (1980), and *A Chorus Line,* and comes off like Bob Fosse-lite, replete with fantasy sequences and frequent steamy sex scenes that are staged like dances and intercut with actual dance numbers. Its erotically charged, psychoanalytical portrait of a dancer lacks Fosse's style or substance, however, due to its student film-like execution and a fairly predictable script by co-producer Aaron Reed, who based it on his own experiences as a Broadway dancer. Although it does manage to make some insightful points about aging and performing, the plot frequently grinds to a halt for a number of superfluous scenes (at the restaurant, at the physical therapy clinic, even a Central Park softball game) which drag the story out and make the film seem much longer than its 97 minutes. Additionally, the likable cast struggles valiantly with their stereotyped characters, such as the vixenish chorines who can't keep their hands off the "irresistible" Nick, whose aggressive heterosexuality is relentlessly contrasted with the other male dancers, who are all flamboyantly gay caricatures.

In the critical lead role, Broadway musical veteran Rick Negron proves himself an accomplished dancer, but is less capable as an actor, failing to generate any sympathy for the arrogant, womanizing Nick until the very end, which makes his plight less than compelling since his comeuppance seems well-deserved. Among the supporting cast, Denise Faye stands out as the seductive Heidi, and Donald Byrd, whose choreography gives the shoestring production a professional sheen, gives a relaxed and natural performance as Austin. Taylor Nichols (who was also one of the associate producers) doesn't have much to do in the bland role of the stockbroker for whom Amy leaves Nick. Nichols's fellow Whit Stillman-regular Chis Eigeman pops up in an amusing cameo; while the appearance of Thomas Gibson—who subsequently struck it big in the 1997 hit sitcom "Dharma and Greg"—in a bit part as a bartender is a giveaway as to the film's true age. *(Nudity, sexual situations, profanity.)*—M.S.

d, Christian Faber; p, Aaron Reed, Hank Blumenthal; assoc p, Rafael Moreu, Taylor Nichols; w, Aaron Reed; ph, Zack Winestine; ed, Judd Maslansky, David Codron; m, Roni Skies, Mio Morales, Brian Otto; prod d, Elise Bennett; art d, Catherine Eng; set d, Sarah Baldocchi; ch, Donald Byrd; sound, Andrew Moran (mixer); casting, Elizabeth Marx; cos, Nancy Brous, Ivan Ingerman; makeup, Joanne Ottaviano

Drama/Musical **(PR: O MPAA: NR)**

NEXT STOP, WONDERLAND ★★★½

(U.S., 1998) 104m Robbins Entertainment ~ Miramax c

Hope Davis *(Erin Castleton)*; Alan Gelfant *(Alan Monteiro)*; Victor Argo *(Frank)*; Jon Benjamin *(Eric)*; Cara Buono *(Julie)*; Philip Seymour Hoffman, billed as Phil Hoffman *(Sean)*; Roger Rees *(Ray Thornback)*; Sam Seder *(Kevin Monteiro)*; Robert Stanton *(Robert)*; Holland Taylor *(Piper Castleton)*; Callie Thorne *(Cricket)*; Jose Zuniga *(Andre De Silva)*; Paul Wagner *(Bob)*; Robert Klein *(Arty Lesser)*; Lyn Vaus *(Daryl)*; Larry Gilliard Jr. *(Brett)*; Jason Lewis *(Rory)*; Jimmy Tingle *(Lowrey the Bartender)*; E. Katherine Kerr *(Candice)*; Ernest Thompson *(Nathan)*; Charlie Broderick *(Desmond)*; Aleksander Wierzbicki *(Barry)*; Bronwyn Sims *(Traci)*; Paula Plum *(Denise Shebola)*; Steve Sweeney *(Cab Driver)*; Ken Cheeseman *(Rick)*; Wayne Pretlow *(Oliver)*; Pamela Hart *(Berit)*; Diane Beckett *(Seana)*; Neil Gustafson *(Yuri Spinov)*; Luz Alenandra *(Thalia)*; Kemp Harris *(Ben)*; Dave Gilloran *(Aquarium Volunteer)*; Emme Shaw *(Bailey)*; Greg Watson *(Frank's Crony)*; Robert Larkin *(Arty Lesser's Crony)*; Elizabeth Lindsay *(Lucy Bidwell)*; Jack Sweet *(Sal)*; Jeremy Geidt *(Bookseller)*; Todd Robinson *(Society Photographer)*; Andrea Grano *(Pub Waitress)*; Lori Haims *(Restaurant Waitress)*; Frank T. Wells *(Alan's Father)*; Paula Lyons *(TV News Anchor)*; Arnie Reisman *(Field Reporter)*; Renita Whited *(Arizona Reporter)*; James O'Connell *(Linoleum Man)*; Charles Laquidara; Will Lebow; Eric Roemele; Eric Ruben; Scott Richards; Tom Cotter; Al Ducharme; Ed Regine; Bob Druwing; Ken Mason *(Phone Dates)*

Two lonely hearts who are fated to meet and fall in love keep *almost* doing so, over and over. With a clever script by Lyn Vaus and director Brad Anderson, and a disarming performance by Hope Davis, NEXT STOP, WONDERLAND is a charming treat.

Erin Castleton (Davis), a Boston nurse in her thirties, finds herself single when her politically correct boyfriend Sean (Phil Hoffman), takes off to help an Arizona Indian tribe save their sacred land. At a friend's behest, Erin attends a benefit at Boston's aquarium and almost meets Alan Monteiro (Alan Gelfant), a man who would be perfect for her. Alan is an aquarium volunteer, who at 35 has quit the family plumbing business to attend college and study marine biology.

In Boston for a visit, Erin's globetrotting mother (Holland Taylor) secretly takes out a personal ad on Erin's behalf. Initially outraged, Erin decides to meet the respondents. Three of the interested men are lawyer buddies holding a contest to see who can seduce Erin first; one of the sleazy trio is Alan's brother. A loan shark approaches Alan with an offer to settle his father's gambling debts: all Alan has to do is kill a balloon fish that serves as the mascot for the aquarium, as a favor for a real-estate developer (Robert Klein) who lost a desired plot of land to an aquarium expansion project. Instead, Alan steals Puff and makes it look like the fish was killed.

While Boston mourns Puff, Erin figures out the lawyers' scam and sets a trap for them. She dates Andre (Jose Zuniga), and the two get along very well until he decides to return to his native Brazil. Alan dates Julie (Carla Buono), one of his young classmates, until he realizes that she's just using him for his homework. To Beantown's relief, Alan returns Puff to its tank.

The return of Sean, disillusioned by his Arizona experience, prompts Erin to accept Andre's offer to accompany him to Brazil. On the train to the airport, Erin faints and is helped by Alan. The two have instant chemistry, and Erin decides not to go to Brazil, but to go for a walk with Alan instead.

NEXT STOP, WONDERLAND has basically the same plot as the overly baroque 'TIL THERE WAS YOU (1997). It is also similar in spirit to, but less gimmicky than, SLIDING DOORS (1998). What sets WONDERLAND apart is the full and rich characterization of its leads. The question of how and when the star-crossed couple will finally meet is almost incidental: the characters themselves are sufficiently interesting.

The ruggedly handsome Gelfant makes the sensitive and struggling Alan an appealing suitor, but WONDERLAND is primarily a stage on which Davis (THE DAYTRIPPERS) really shines. Erin is a melancholic romantic searching for a man who's the equal of her late father, and Davis conveys both the neuroticism and poignancy of that situation. An unconventional beauty, Davis makes Erin an engaging mix of dry cynicism and fragile optimism.

WONDERLAND's cute quotient is thankfully low, but Anderson does include some piquant touches. One is the soundtrack of Brazilian bossa nova music; what initially seems inappropriate to the film's chilly Boston locales becomes a surprisingly apt fit. There's also a device Erin uses to predict her fate—randomly picking a word out of a book to serve as a daily signpost. Imagine her surprise when "linoleum" proves to be the guide to her romantic destiny.*(Profanity.)*—P.R.

d, Brad Anderson; p, Mitchell B. Robbins; assoc p, Ari Newman; co-p, Laura Bernieri, Rachel Horovitz; w, Brad Anderson, Lyn Vaus; ph, Uta Briesewitz; ed, Brad Anderson; m, Claudio Ragazzi; prod d, Chad Detweiller; casting, Sheila Jaffe, Georgianne Walken

Comedy/Romance/Drama (PR: C MPAA: R)

NIAGARA NIAGARA ★★½

(U.S., 1998) 96m Shooting Gallery ~ Shooting Gallery c

Robin Tunney *(Marcy)*; Henry Thomas *(Seth)*; Michael Parks *(Walter)*; Stephen Lang *(Claude—Pharmacist)*; John MacKay *(Seth's Father)*; Alan Pottinger *(Sanitation Lot Cop)*; Sol Frieder *(Pawnbroker)*; Candy Clark *(Sally)*; Andrew L. Phillips *(Sally's Policeman)*; Jeffrey Howard *(Liquor Store Clerk)*; Shawn Hatosy *(Lead High School Punk)*; Adam T. Lauricella *(High School Punk #2)*; Jaime Lynn O'Hara *(High School Girl)*; John Ventimiglia *(Doug)*; Clea DuVall *(Convenience Store Clerk)*; Mark Chandler Bailey *(Toy Store Employee)*; Dwight Ewell *(Toy Store Manager)*; Larry Meistrich; Michael D. Rath *(Police Officers)*; Matthew Weiss *(Target Practice Cop)*

Although it bears the trendy stamp of "independent" cinema and knee-jerk critical raves, the tragicomic NIAGARA NIAGARA is in its own way as contrived and formulaic as any mainstream Hollywood production.

Seth (Henry Thomas), a zombielike boy under the thumb of a domineering ex-con father, is shoplifting one day when he bumps, literally, into Marcy (Robin Tunney). She's also stealing, even though she comes from a prosperous, if shady, family in the New York State sanitation rackets. Aggressive and impulsive, Marcy takes the lead in their relationship, introducing sheltered Seth to the joy of sex and revealing she has a variety of neurological ailments, including Tourette's Syndrome, barely suppressed via prescription drugs. Without pills she'll abruptly shout obscenities, lash out violently, and fixate on trivial things—like the fact that none of the "racist" local toy stores carry a black "Bobby Styling Head."

Deciding that more liberal Canada, across the border, will stock the item, Marcy drags Seth into an impromptu cross-country trek in his Plymouth Fury. Marcy deliberately discards her medication, trying to quell her tics with bourbon and lovemaking. When the symptoms start getting too severe en route, they seek the critical drugs at a mall-town pharmacy. Since the owner won't hand pills over to two ragged youths with no doctor's authorization, Marcy and Seth break into the place by night, and escape under a hail of gunfire that wounds Seth and shoots out his tires.

Their overturned car catches the attention of Walter (Michael Parks), an eccentric tow-truck driver and gun fancier, lonely after his wife's death. He nurses Seth and hides the pair from a police dragnet, becoming a sort of father figure, even as Marcy's condition worsens. At last Marcy, after blurting profanities about Walter's wife, beats the man senseless. Seth and Marcy flee in his truck, Marcy enjoying the sensation of Walter's gun in her hand; she says she feels like Farrah Fawcett from "Charlie's Angels."

After a few holdups, the fugitives reach the border at Niagara Falls, where Marcy flushes her remaining medication down the toilet, lest customs agents discover it. The Toronto Galleria only has one of the "Bobby" heads in a store display not for sale. Marcy throws a fit that brings security men, and when she grabs one guard's gun another shoots her in the head. Seth eventually rebounds from the trauma of losing Marcy, and mails Walter all he can spare—$20—in compensation.

NIAGARA NIAGARA goes to extremes to be madly offbeat and outrageous. So why does it feel so stale and artificial? Maybe by the mid-1990s there had just been too many trips to the well of whimsically violent dysfunction, too many campy pop-culture references, too many callow slacker lovers flipping the bird to society's values by going on cross-country crime sprees at the drop of a hat, in the likes of NATURAL BORN KILLERS (1994), LOVE AND A .45 (1994), WILD AT HEART (1990), TRUE ROMANCE (1993), and GUNCRAZY (1992). It says something for the warped mindset of such look-ma-we're-indie features that at least one gas station attendant in NIAGARA NIAGARA actually seems to enjoy being robbed at gunpoint, and flirts openly toward Seth during the raid.

The challenge here is to make ill-fated misfit protagonists (with whom you wouldn't want to spend a minute in real life) appear sympathetic, enlightened, or at least compelling, in spite of themselves. Thomas, as the poor bewildered sap with a distinctly fuzzy sense of right and wrong, is there primarily for audience identification, and he seldom rises above being a blank narrative device, Marcy's driver and foil. Tunney won the Best Actress Award at the 1997 Venice Film Festival for manifesting the more freakish aspects of Tourette's Syndrome. Good as she is, that's more a pathology than a performance. If Marcy's eruptions and manias represent some sort of unchained id, cutting through the crap, then she's an even more appalling and pointless rebel than she appears.

Marcy's murderous attack on Walter, by far the most likeable person onscreen, is, wisely, neither rationalized nor mythologized by first-time director Bob Gosse. Gosse earlier worked extensively with Hal Hartley, whose own material (FLIRT, AMATEUR, SIMPLE MEN, TRUST) serves up determinedly eccentric characters and arch dialogue that sometimes works, sometimes just feels like weird words on a page. NIAGARA NIAGARA, alas, alas, largely falls into the latter category. The feature certainly looks great, and was reportedly lensed for a mere $1.65 million. *(Adult situations, sexual situations, profanity, violence, substance abuse.)*—C.C.

d, Bob Gosse; p, David L. Bushell; exec p, Larry Meistrich; assoc p, Daniel J. Victor; w, Matthew Weiss; ph, Michael Spiller; ed, Rachel Warden; m, Michael Timmins, Jeff Bird; prod d, Clark Hunter; art d, Max Biscoe; set d, Traci Kirshbaum; sound, Jeff Pullman (mixer), Jeff Kushner (design); fx, Peter Kunz; casting, Sheila Jaffe, Georgianne Walken; cos, Laura Jean Shannon; makeup, Kate Morgan Biscoe; stunts, Phil Neilson

Romance/Drama (PR: C MPAA: R)

NIGHT AND THE MOMENT, THE ★★½

(U.K./Italy/France, 1998) 90m CGG Tiger Cinematografica; Societe Francaise de Production; Arthur Pictures ~ Miramax c

Willem Dafoe *(La Chevalier—The Writer)*; Lena Olin *(Le Marquise)*; Miranda Richardson *(Julie)*; Jean-Claude Carriere *(Gouverneur)*; Carole Richert *(Armande)*; Christine Pireyzol *(Justine)*; Guy Verame *(Official)*; Ivan Bacciocchi *(Prison Guard)*

THE NIGHT AND THE MOMENT almost turns into a mini-camp classic, but never quite establishes itself as either a send-up of costume pictures or a genuine attempt at frou-frou gone very wrong. This international coproduction was acquired by Miramax for theatrical distribution, but wound up making its US debut on home-video in 1998.

In mid-1700s France, a Georgian aristocrat, the Marquise (Lena Olin) plays host to a group of weekend houseguests. During the night, a dashing writer (Willem Dafoe) sneaks into the Marquise's bedroom to begin an elaborate, night-long seduction. The Marquise resists the writer's advances. The writer then tries to impress the beautiful woman by telling her several tales of erotic intrigue.

In one story, the writer tells how he ravaged the young, coquettish Armande (Carole Richert). In another story, he tells how he tangled with the older Julie (Miranda Richardson), disproving her theory of physics—that heat drains desire—by making love to her. Finally, the writer tells how he was imprisoned by the Governor (Jean-Claude Carriere) for his licentious writing and, during his time in jail, came to fall in love with a mystery woman in an adjoining cell, with whom he shared love notes but could never see.

Near the end of the evening, after repeatedly rebuffing the writer, the Marquise welcomes his declarations of love. They make passionate love the rest of the night. At dawn, the Marquise informs the writer that she was the mystery woman in prison and had asked the Governor to put her in the cell because she had always loved the writer and wanted to be near him. With their feelings being mutual, the Marquise and the writer decide to go public with their secret affair.

THE NIGHT AND THE MOMENT circumnavigates two subgenres at once: the revisionist costume picture (like Ettore Scola's LA NUIT DE VARENNES) and the steamy soft-porn-styled "women's picture" found most often on late night cable television. The big mystery of the film is not the identity of the writer's cellmate (the solution is obvious), but rather just what such recognizable, established talent had in mind making such a flimsy potboiler. Since most of the elements are so badly handled, it is hard to figure out whether the people involved were way off their stride or merely spoofing the material. Coscreenwriter Jean-Claude Carriere, Bunuel's great, frequent collaborator, surely must be winking at the viewer with the excess of flowery lines such as the Marquise's assertion, "I admire men and I often reflect with fright how impulsive they can be." Carriere's cameo as the crusty Governor provides an additional layer of irony in that his performance far outshines the (deliberately?) miscast main stars, Dafoe and Olin, who are both dreadful in their attempts at a declamatory style. The results are like a high school production of DANGEROUS LIAISONS (1988) with the supposedly roguish Dafoe looking more foppish and foolish than ever.

Even if one accepts THE NIGHT AND THE MOMENT as a minimalist, cartoon version of either THAT OBSCURE OBJECT OF DESIRE (the 1977 Bunuel-Carriere classic), with its frustrating and seemingly endless seduction-rejection plot, or THE DRAUGHTSMAN'S CONTRACT (1982), with its deconstruction of its mystery plot, why then did Carriere and director-cowriter Anna Maria Tato allow the climactic consummation and banal happy ending? What's to make of Tato's absurd, repeating 360-degree pan during the first kiss or Ennio Morricone's pseudo-Baroque score, capped by the florid end-title song? It's all unfathomable, which may be the point. But, then, as the Marquise says, "This is very unfunny clowning." *(Violence, nudity, sexual situations, profanity.)*—E.M.

d, Anna Maria Tato; p, Pierre Noval, Boudjemaa Dahmane; exec p, Ernst F. Goldschmidt; assoc p, Bernard Vilgrain, Marina Gefter; w, Jean-Claude Carriere, Anna Maria Tato (based on the novel by Crebillon Fils); ph, Giusepppe Rotunno; ed, Ruggero Mastroianni; m, Ennio Morricone; prod d, Richard Cunin, Arianna Attaom; sound, David Stephenson, Joel Faure; cos, Gabriella Pecucci

Erotic/Comedy/Drama (PR: O MPAA: R)

NIGHT AT THE ROXBURY, A ★★½

(U.S., 1998) 86m SNL Studios; Lorne Michaels and Amy Heckerling Production; Paramount ~ Paramount c

Will Ferrell *(Steve Butabi)*; Chris Kattan *(Doug Butabi)*; Dan Hedaya *(Kamehl Butabi)*; Molly Shannon *(Emily Sanderson)*; Richard Grieco *(Himself)*; Loni Anderson *(Barbara Butabi)*; Chazz Palminteri *(Zadir—uncredited)*; Dwayne Hickman *(Fred Sanderson)*; Elisa Donovan *(Cambi)*; Gigi Rice *(Vivica)*; Raquel Gardner *(Hot Girl)*; Viveca Paulin *(Porsche Girl)*; Paulette Braxton *(Porsche Girl)*; Michael M. Horton *(Security Guard)*; Richard Francese *(Security Guard)*; Jennifer Coolidge *(Hottie Cop)*; Michael Clarke Duncan *(Roxbury Bouncer)*; Trish Ramish *(Roxbury Club Girl)*; Gina Mari *(Saturday Night Fever Girl)*; Roy

Jenkins (Flower Customer #1); Meredith Scott Lynn (Credit Vixen); Kip King (Flower Customer #2); Lochlyn Munroe (Craig); Mary Ann Kellogg (Aerobics Instructor); Maree Cheatham (Mabel Sanderson); Kristen Dalton (Grieco's Lady); Colin Quinn (Dooey); Deborah Kellner (Topless Woman); Robin Krieger (Mrs. Manicotti); Betty Bridges-Nicasio (Zadir Receptionist); Yoshio Be (Japanese Man #1); Victor Kobayashi (Japanese Man #2); Twink Caplan (Crying Flower Customer); Eva Mendez (Bridesmaid); Mark McKinney (Father Williams); Chad Bannon (New Club Bouncer); Jim Wise; Patrick Ferrell; Dorian Spencer (New Club Waiters); Tina Weisinger (New Club Waitress)

The latest in an uneven succession of feature films based on "Saturday Night Live" skits, A NIGHT AT THE ROXBURY falls squarely in the middle of its limited genre: it's funnier than some "SNL"-derived movies, but not as funny as others.

The Butabi brothers are Doug (Chris Kattan) and Steve (Will Ferrell), inseparable pals who still live at home, work in the artificial flower shop of their father (Dan Hedaya) and spend most of their free time attempting entree to the best nightclubs in Los Angeles, especially the exclusive Roxbury. Though Doug and Steve usually spend their nights on the pavement outside, they dream of opening their own club, all the while keeping constant time to Haddaway's song "What Is Love?" with their incessantly jerking heads.

After their flower shop van is struck from behind one night by their idol, actor Richard Grieco (playing himself), the former "21 Jump Street" thespian helps the brothers get into the Roxbury in exchange for their tacit agreement not to sue for damages. There, the Butabis befriend the club's oddball owner (Chazz Palminteri), relate to him their theme club ideas, and pick up a pair of attractive "hotties" who mistake them for wealthy businessmen. The Butabis lose their virginity but are quickly dumped when the truth is revealed to their new "girlfriends."

At his father's urging, Steve embarks on a sexually charged relationship with Emily Sanderson (Molly Shannon), the wealthy daughter of a fellow storeowner and a woman who's been pursuing the elder Butabi brother for years. She quickly arranges their engagement and drives a wedge between Steve and Doug. At their poolside wedding ceremony, Doug intervenes and stops his brother while best man Richard Grieco looks on. The brothers vow to remain best friends and never let a woman come between them again—and then discover that the owner of the Roxbury has been looking for them for weeks. It seems he's created the very club they dreamed of, it's a financial smash, and the Butabis are co-owners. Their dream has come true, with little effort on their parts.

The first act, which relies solely on reintroducing Doug and Steve to audience members who haven't seen their shtick on "SNL," is horribly weak, based as it is on the slightest of sketches (the original "SNL" bits never actually contained even a line of dialogue). But A NIGHT AT THE ROXBURY builds a head of steam by the finale through lampooning other films—the final 10 minutes offers riffs on JERRY MAGUIRE (1996), THE GRADUATE (1967), and SAY ANYTHING (1989). If its beginning assumes its audience is so woefully out of touch with TV and film culture that the entire sketch needs to be revisited, then the film's final act assumes an equal and opposite knowledge of cinematic pop culture, with co-scripters Ferrell, Kattan, and Steve Koren rivaling the quote-ridden work of the Zucker-Abrahams-Zucker team for quick citations.

The shameless absconding of material from better films, as well as Grieco's zealous lampoon of himself (his emotion-baring backyard chat with Hedaya, which ends with Hedaya tearfully intoning, "Richard Grieco, you see right through me," is a real gem) bend A NIGHT AT THE ROXBURY toward more humorous, if not more original, territory. Shannon, who has already proven herself a pro on "SNL" with characters that are mentally unstable and desperate, steals every scene she's in with an actual performance, as does Hedaya. Loni Anderson, as the Butabis' mother, simply provides window-dressing.

While A NIGHT AT THE ROXBURY is not as funny as it wishes it were, the filmmakers seem well aware of the fact. The worst one can say about the film is that its tale of two dunderheads making good by club hopping would have had a better chance of success in the 1980s, when more of the audience fit the same description. *(Sexual situations, profanity, substance abuse.)*—K.W.

d, John Fortenberry, Peter Markle (uncredited); p, Lorne Michaels, Amy Heckerling; exec p, Robert K. Weiss; assoc p, Erin Fraser; co-p, Marie Cantin, Steve Koren; w, Steve Koren, Will Ferrell, Chris Kattan; ph, Francis Kenny; ed, Jay Kamen; m, David Kitay; prod d, Steve Jordan; art d, Carl Stensel; set d, John Philpotts; ch, Mary Ann Kellogg; sound, Jim Tanenbaum (mixer); fx, Kam Cooney; casting, Jeff Greenberg; cos, Mona May; makeup, Alan "Doc" Friedman; stunts, Pat Romano

Comedy **(PR: C MPAA: PG-13)**

NIGHT VISION ★½

(U.S., 1998) 97m Po'Boy Productions ~ Peachtree Entertainment c

Fred Williamson *(Dakota Smith)*; Cynthia Rothrock *(Kristin O'Connor)*; Robert Forster *(Teak Taylor)*; Frank Pesce *(Mike Mahoney)*; Willie Gault *(FBI Agent Coleman)*; Amanda Welles *(Julie Paulson)*; Rodger Boyce *(Chief Williams)*; Mary Kapper *(Allison Mathison)*; Robin McGee *(Allison's Lover)*; Nina Richardson *(Elizabeth Richards)*; Bushwick Bill *(Newt)*; Cliff Stephans *(Detective Bigelow)*; Willie Minor *(Detective Johnson)*; Robert Prentiss *(Video Stalker)*; Jonathan Hayes *(Muscles)*; Akin Babatunde *(Liquor Store Owner)*; Phyliss Cicero *(Pathologist)*; Tony Arangio *(Anthony Garibaldi)*; Randal Reeder *(Big Boy)*; Ben E. Loggins *(Little Man)*; Gil Glasgow *(TV Director)*; Lynn Mathis *(Priest)*; Ralph Joseph *(TV Station Guard)*; Paul Pender *(Assistant Director)*; Grover Coulson *(A.A. Meeting Leader)*; Roy Morgan *(Police Helicopter Pilot)*; Rupert Reyes *(Cop on Street)*; Veharar Gashaw *(Cop Next to Dak)*; Kaitlin Graves *(Jennifer)*; Daniel Sherman *(Cameraman in Helicopter)*; J.T. Prigmore *(Thug 1)*; Mike Shanks *(Thug 2)*

NIGHT VISION is a cheaply made, straight-to-video throwback to 1970s blaxploitation that contains a threadbare plot, bad performances, and some of the lamest action sequences ever put on film.

Having first videotaped a woman's sexual exploits, a serial killer known as "the Video Stalker" (Robert Prentiss) then abducts her. Dakota "Dak" Smith (Fred Williamson), a cop with a "Dirty Harry"-attitude and a drinking problem, attempts to pull the killer's van over, resulting in a major shoot-out. The killer escapes and dumps the woman's body. An autopsy reveals she was killed by Dak's return gunfire. Angry that he didn't kill the woman, the Stalker sends three thugs to beat up Dak's best friend, but they kill the man instead. Dak and his new partner Kristin O'Connor (Cynthia Rothrock) are called to the scene of the crime, and gun down two of the assailants.

The Stalker calls Dak and reveals the plans for his next victim. They race to find the woman, but the Stalker kills her along with her lover. Dak and O'Connor discover the Stalker is making snuff videos and distributing them through the mob. He also has an alliance with dirty cop Mike Mahoney (Frank Pesce). After killing a news reporter (Amanda Welles) with a videotape containing a bomb, the Stalker abducts O'Connor and prepares to move his operation to Mexico. Dak forces Mahoney to reveal the killer's whereabouts. As they arrive with enforcements, O'Connor escapes and beats up several thugs while Dak kills the Stalker.

A flaccid imitation of the formulaic blaxploitation and crime films of the '70s, NIGHT VISION has too little sleaze to be considered exploitation and too much cheese to give it any kind of edgy quality. The blame for this trash can be evenly distributed between Michael Thomas Montgomery, who wrote the ludicrous screenplay, and Gil Bettman, who directs in a lackluster fashion. Leads Williamson and Rothrock work well together, but both are blessed with better physical abilities than acting skills. Robert Forster (JACKIE BROWN) is solid, but has little to do aside from scolding Dak to keep a low profile and stay away from booze. The supporting cast may as well be invisible, with the exception of Robert Prentiss, who apparently studied the moves of every direct-to-video psycho killer in existence to play his one-note Video Stalker. The film's technical attributes are even worse. The action sequences are slow, overextended, and poorly choreographed. Also, the editing is sloppy, leaving large holes in the plot line. An unintended virtue: the laughably awful soundtrack, which includes original songs ("Hey Dakota, I Know You Can Do It"), which puntuate a '70s style porn-like score by Tony Camillo. *(Extreme profanity, violence, sexual situations.)*—P.L.

d, Gil Bettman; p, Fred Williamson, Linda Williamson; w, Michael Thomas Montgomery; ph, Trey Smith; ed, Robert J. Castaldo; m, Tony Camillo; sound, Pete Verrando; fx, Tom Ford; casting, Shirley Abrams; makeup, Rene L'Ecuyer; stunts, Ben E. Loggins

Crime/Drama (PR: O MPAA: R)

NIGHTWATCH ★★½

(U.S., 1998) 106m Dimension ~ Dimension c

Nick Nolte *(Inspector Cray)*; Patricia Arquette *(Katherine)*; Ewan McGregor *(Martin)*; Josh Brolin *(James)*; Lauren Graham *(Marie)*; Alix Koromzay *(Joyce)*; John C. Reilly *(Deputy Inspector Bill)*; Brad Dourif *(Duty Doctor)*; Erich Anderson *(Newscaster)*; Lonny Chapman *(Old Watchman)*; Scott Burkholder *(College Professor)*; Michael Matthys *(Guy in Pub)*; Alison Gale *(Girlfriend of Guy in Pub)*; Robert LaSardo; Mongo *(Pub Thugs)*; Candy Brown Houston *(Female Paramedic)*; Michelle Csitos *(Leanne Singer)*; Lennie Loftin *(Man in Theater)*; Bradley Gregg *(Theater Actor)*; Nicholas Sadler *(Theater Director)*; Jeff Davis *(Stagehand)*; Nicholas Cascone *(Male Paramedic)*; Ben Skortstad *(Helicopter Pilot)*

Following in the footsteps of Dutch filmmaker George Sluizer, who directed a watered-down big-budget American remake of his thriller THE VANISHING, director Ole Bornedal helmed this US remake of his Danish original. The result is a less compromised effort than Sluizer's, but one that still lacks the punch of its Scandinavian source material.

Law student Martin Bells (Ewan McGregor) takes a job as a night watchman at a hospital morgue. His predecessor (Lonny Chapman) shows him around and reveals that a previous worker was fired for necrophilia. Martin's reckless best friend, James (Josh Brolin), suggests that they indulge in a series of dares. At the same time, a serial killer has been slaying prostitutes, with police Inspector Cray (Nick Nolte) heading up the investigation. One night while Martin is on guard, an alarm rings from inside the morgue, but it proves to have been triggered by James, who sneaked in. James reveals that he has been seeing an underaged prostitute named Joyce (Alix Koromzay); Martin accepts his challenge to join them for dinner. The next night at work, Martin finds the corpse of a murder victim dragged into the hall, but it is back in place by the time Cray arrives. Joyce begins contacting Martin's girlfriend Katherine (Patricia Arquette). When a corpse is abused at the morgue, the evidence points to Martin. Katherine goes to Joyce's apartment, finds that Joyce has been murdered, and escapes just before the killer—Cray—steps out of the bathroom and plants evidence framing Martin.

When Deputy Inspector Bill (John C. Reilly) wants to arrest Martin, Katherine convinces him of Martin's innocence. At the morgue, Martin discovers that Cray was the necrophiliac worker who was fired. Cray soon arrives, as do Katherine, James, and Davis. Cray ties up Martin and Katherine, shoots Davis, and handcuffs James to a pipe. Katherine tries in vain to escape, and Cray is about to kill her and Martin when James, who has cut off his thumb to escape, shoots him.

The new NIGHTWATCH was filmed in 1996, two years after the European success of Bornedal's original NATTEVAGTEN. The remake took two years to reach US screens, following a series of test screenings and reshoots. (As a result, the character of James's girlfriend Marie, played by Lauren Graham, was pared down and a somewhat more satisfying final scene was inserted.) The result is a modestly gripping film with two key flaws that prevent it from being as suspenseful as it might have been.

One is a problem carried over from the original: The identity of the killer is revealed too early and in too off-handed a manner. The other mistake is a miscasting unique to the American version. In the original, James's counterpart was older than Martin, and his obsession with testing the limits seemed related to his fading youth. With the casting of the young, virile Brolin, who fails to suggest any hidden layers of the character, James comes off as obnoxiously cocky and insensitive, and it's hard to believe Martin's tolerance of his borderline sadistic games.

Martin himself remains a sympathetic hero as played by Scottish actor McGregor (with a convincing American accent), while Nolte finds the right insinuating, threatening manner for Cray. Bornedal does have a flair for staging mayhem and creating tension, and the sequences of Martin nervously walking the morgue's empty halls and rooms create the necessary creepy feeling. (Richard Hoover's scary designs for the morgue do much to add to this atmosphere.) But NIGHTWATCH's major disadvantage is that—unlike the original, which had few Danish predecessors—it comes in the wake of too many superior American films dealing with serial killers. *(Graphic violence, nudity, sexual situations, profanity.)*—M.G.

d, Ole Bornedal; p, Michael Obel; exec p, Bob Weinstein, Harvey Weinstein, Cary Granat; w, Ole Bornedal, Steven Soderbergh (based on the film NATTEVAGTEN by Ole Bornedal); ph, Dan Laustsen; ed, Kant Pan, Salle Menke; m, Joachim Holbek; prod d, Richard Hoover; art d, Kathleen McKernin, Adam Scher; set d, Brian Kasch; sound, Stephen Halbert (mixer), Charles Maynes (design), Paul Berolzheimer (design); fx, Dale Newkirk; casting, Rick Pagano; cos, Louise Mingenbach; makeup, Debra Denson, XFX (effects); stunts, Cliff Cudney

Horror/Thriller (PR: C MPAA: R)

NIL BY MOUTH ★★½

(U.K./U.S., 1997) 128m The Smoking Room;
SE8 Group; Seaside Productions; Les Films du Dauphin ~
Sony Pictures Classics c/bw

Ray Winstone *(Raymond)*; Kathy Burke *(Valerie)*; Charlie Creed-Miles *(Billy)*; Laila Morse *(Janet)*; Edna Dore *(Kath)*; Chrissie Cotterill *(Paula)*; Jon Morrison *(Angus)*; Jamie Forman *(Mark)*; Steve Sweeney *(Danny)*; Terry Rowley *(MC in Club)*; Sam Miller *(Club Comic)*; Leah Fitzgerald *(Michelle)*; Gerry

Bromfield *(Drug Dealer)*; Neil Maskell *(Schmuddie)*; Sid Golder *(Old Guy in Window)*; John Blundell *(Man with Knife)*; Kenan Hudaverdi *(Laundrette Owner)*; Everton Nelson *(Street Violinist)*; Ronny Fox *(Peter/Pool Player)*; Frances Ashman *(Club Singer)*; Martin Watson; Dan Carey; Giuseppe Acunzo; Edmund Scott *(Club—Band Musicians)*

Actor Gary Oldman's debut as a writer-director, NIL BY MOUTH is a hyperrealistic look at the sordid and hopeless lives of the members of a London working-class family. Kathy Burke's portrayal of the abused wife won her the Best Actress award at the 1997 Cannes Film Festival.

Ray (Ray Winstone), an alcoholic lout, and his pregnant wife, Valerie (Kathy Burke), live with their six-year-old daughter, Michelle (Leah Fitzgerald), and Valerie's drug-addicted younger brother, Billy (Charlie Creed-Miles). Janet (Laila Morse), Valerie and Billy's mother, wonders why her daughter doesn't leave her brutal husband and reluctantly funds her son's dope habit. After Billy steals and sells a picture belonging to his brother-in-law, Ray beats him up, and Billy finds himself in the streets begging for spare change.

When Ray finds Valerie in a local pub playing a harmless game of billiards with a male acquaintance of hers (Ronny Fox), he goes into a drunken, jealous rage and beats his wife so severely that she has a miscarriage. After getting out of the hospital, Valerie takes Michelle and moves in with Janet. When Ray finds out, he terrorizes them but eventually calms down and asks his wife to take him back. At first, she adamantly refuses, but ultimately she weakens and returns to Ray and the family sits down to discuss what to do about Billy, who has landed in jail.

Slice-of-life filmmakers almost invariably reach for the smallest, most rancid slice, and Oldman—who may be doing self-inflicted penance for overplaying the campy archvillain in the frivolous THE FIFTH ELEMENT (1997)—is no exception. Burdened with the least audience-friendly title since the Joe E. Brown comedy EARTHWORM TRACTORS (1936), NIL BY MOUTH (which could have been called "This Unhappy Breed") is correspondingly uningratiating in its text and tone. Much of the dialogue is, in fact, monologue, and most of it is unintelligible. (English actors must salivate when they read the word "cockney" next to their characters' names in scripts—the way American actors do when they see "Brooklyn," and American actresses, "Southern.") For some reason, NIL BY MOUTH's female cast members are more understandable than their male counterparts and, surprisingly, it is the cast's principal amateur, Laila Morse, who is the most comprehensible of all. By comparison, the cast of the English film SHOPPING (1996) managed to bring crystal-clear line readings to comparable working-class territory with little if any sacrifice of authority or authenticity.

The movie's communication skills are further blunted by long stretches that appear to be improvised. The players do this well, but they do it more for their own benefit than for the audience's. Oldman's indulgence of his fellow actors is understandable, but his film suffers for it. And surely this movie breaks all existing records for the invocation of the word "fucking"—a dubious achievement.

It's difficult to empathize with NIL BY MOUTH's characters, because at no point in the movie's 128 minutes is the viewer allowed to glimpse any vestige of hope or potential for peace and happiness behind their brutalized facades. And, as gritty and unflinchingly honest as it is, the film is not entirely free of cliche: it implies that *both* Ray and Billy are the wretches they are because their fathers didn't love them.

NIL BY MOUTH was generally overpraised by the critics; still, Oldman is to be respected for essaying such a personal and uncompromising work. Best in its final (and most conventional) half-hour and blessed with an all-too-convincing performance by Ray Winstone, NIL BY MOUTH is the kind of down-and-dirty, antiescapist project that producers should continue to support—only not too often. *(Graphic violence, nudity, substance abuse, extreme profanity.)*—D.T.

d, Gary Oldman; p, Luc Besson, Douglas Urbanski, Gary Oldman; assoc p, Marc Frydman; co-p, Hilary Heath; w, Gary Oldman; ph, Ron Fortunato; ed, Brad Fuller; m, Eric Clapton; prod d, Hugo Luczyc-Wyhowski; art d, Luanna Hanson; sound, Jim Greenhorn (recordist); casting, Sue Jones; cos, Barbara Kidd; makeup, Pebbles, Fae Hammond; stunts, Rod Woodruff

Drama **(PR: O MPAA: R)**

NIRVANA ★★½

(Italy/France, 1997) 108m Cecci Gori Group Tiger Cinematografica ~ Miramax c

Diego Abatantuono *(Solo)*; Christopher Lambert *(Jimi Dini)*; Sergio Rubini *(Joystick)*; Stefania Rocca *(Naima)*; Emmanuelle Seigner *(Lisa)*; Amanda Sandrelli *(Maria)*; Claudio Bisio *(Red Rover)*; Gigio Alberti *(Doctor)*; Antonio Catania *(Paranoia Vendor)*; Ugo Conti *(Sicilian Tourist)*; Silvio Orlando *(Indian Desk Clerk)*; Leonardo Gajo *(Gaz Gaz)*; Paolo Rossi *(Joker)*; Fabio Sartor *(Policeman)*; Bebo Storti *(Meditator)*; Gianni Palladino *(Trucker)*

This cleverly scripted, multilayered cyber-thriller concerns an inventor of computer games whose latest creation develops a personality of its own. Clever plot twists (think BLADE RUNNER lite) are nearly sabotaged by Christopher Lambert's lifeless lead performance.

In 2005, computer-game designer Jimi Dini (Christopher Lambert) is ready to deliver his latest creation, "Nirvana," to the all-powerful Okosama Starr conglomerate. Despite being comfortable financially, Jimi is depressed from the loss of his wife, Lisa (Emmanuelle Seigner). He escapes his sadness by playing his game, journeying into the virtual world of Nirvana's lead character, Solo (Diego Abatantuono). Jimi gets quite a surprise when the character begins questioning his commands, the result of a computer virus that has imparted self-awareness into the character. Soon, Solo pleads with Jimi to be deleted from his cyber-world, as the recurring plot complications he's enduring get increasingly violent.

Having promised to delete Solo from Nirvana (and thus put him out of a miserable state) before the game hits the marketplace, Jimi needs to hack into Okosama Starr's databank, since they possess the original copy of the game. He visits the seedier outskirts of the city to get help from underground liaisons Joystick (Sergio Rubini) and Naima (Stefania Rocca). While he's there, Jimi learns that Lisa's consciousness was downloaded onto a cerebral-implant chip before she died. After eluding Okosama's henchmen, Jimi invades their database, and is slowed by various defense system scenarios. Pushing through these barriers, aided by Lisa's downloaded memory, Joystick and Naima are able to siphon off a secret slush fund, while Jimi cancels Solo and learns how much Lisa loved him.

Although the level of acting in NIRVANA is wildly uneven, director Gabriele Salvatores maintains an even pace throughout the proceedings. He and his coscripters (Pino Cacucci and Gloria Corica) effectively sketch an amusing vision of the future, liberally borrowing notions from the "cyber-punk" school of literature (whose most notable member is novelist William Gibson). The labyrinthine story line often appears to be stretching the film's small budget to the snapping point.

Lambert is the film's central problem: even though the script gives him every opportunity to emote, he remains stiff, as if he's mistaken his character's melancholy for catatonia. Thankfully, the supporting actors who enact the roles of cyber-riffraff save the day, providing some genuinely colorful characterizations. Ultimately, it becomes easier to forgive the film's deficits as one becomes drawn in by its intriguing background elements—from organ donors who sell off their body parts while they're still alive, to cerebrally-connected web-surfers who fry their brains online. NIRVANA may not offer many fresh ideas, but it's still fitfully compelling, well-constructed fun. *(Graphic violence, substance abuse, extreme profanity.)*—S.P.

d, Gabriele Salvatores; p, Vittorio Cecchi Gori, Rita Cecchi Gori, Maurizio Totti; exec p, Antonio Tacchia; w, Gabriele Salvatores, Pino Cacucci, Gloria Corica; ph, Italo Petriccione; ed, Massimo Fiocchi; m, Mauro Pagani, Federico De Robertis; prod d, Giancarlo Basili; set d, Mauro Venturini; sound, Jean-Christophe Casalini; fx, Fabrizio Donvito; cos, Patrizia Chericoni, Florence Emir

Science Fiction/Thriller **(PR: O MPAA: R)**

NO LOOKING BACK ★★★

(U.S., 1998) 96m Marlboro Road Gang/Good Machine/South Fork Pictures ~ Gramercy Pictures c

Lauren Holly *(Claudia)*; Edward Burns *(Charlie)*; Jon Bon Jovi *(Michael)*; Connie Britton *(Kelly)*; Blythe Danner *(Claudia's Mom)*; Kathleen Doyle *(Mrs. Ryan)*; Jennifer Esposito *(Teresa)*; Nick Sandow *(Goldie)*; Kaili Vernoff *(Alice)*; Stuart Rudin *(The Foot)*; Matty Delia *(Bugsy)*; Ellen McElduff *(Waitress)*; Welker White *(Missy)*; John Ventimiglia *(Tony)*; Shari Albert *(Shari)*; Marcia DeBonis *(Marcia)*; Leah Gray *(Leah)*; Kevin Heffernan *(Sco)*; Chris McGovern *(Chris)*; Margaret O'Neill *(Maggie)*; Susan Pratt *(Annie)*; Glenn D. Sanford *(Glenn)*; Mark Schulte *(Bno)*

Despite the familiarity of its working-class Long Island milieu, this third film by Edward Burns represents a departure for the actor-writer-director. Where his previous efforts were (almost farcical) romantic comedies with large ensembles, NO LOOKING BACK is a pensive and melancholic drama about a young woman's life and choices.

After having abruptly left town several years ago, Charlie (Edward Burns) returns to his oceanside home on Long Island. He moves back in with his none-too-pleased mother (Kathleen Doyle), and gets a part-time job pumping gas. When he left, he abandoned his longtime girlfriend, Claudia (Lauren Holly), right after she had an abortion. Now, Claudia is living with Charlie's former best friend, Michael (Jon Bon Jovi). Charlie visits Claudia at the diner where she waitresses, apologizes for the past, and asks her to come with him when he leaves again in a few weeks. She declines firmly.

Some days later, when he knows Michael is absent, Charlie surprises Claudia at home and weakens her resolve by seductively telling her how much he missed and still loves her. When the thirtysomething Charlie later shows up at the local bar with a college-age companion, Claudia discovers that she's jealous.

Despite being warned off by Michael, Charlie continues to pursue Claudia. They meet several times, and Claudia takes a harder look at her life: the same friends, the same job since high school, with no change on the horizon. She looks at her mother (Blythe Danner) who, waiting for the return of Claudia's estranged father, hasn't left the house in months. Claudia feels comfortable with Michael, who's solid and dependable, but complacent and unromantic. Having assumed that she would someday marry Michael (as he has repeatedly asked her to do), she now starts to feel trapped in a routine.

Uncertain of where they're going, but planning to go far away, Claudia and Charlie take off, but after only one night, they return. Michael is waiting for Claudia when she gets home, and accepting no explanations, he kicks her out. In the end, Claudia packs a bag, hops in her car, and heads west alone, as Charlie has decided to stay put and take a full-time job at the gas station.

Coming as it does 24 years after the landmark 1974 film ALICE DOESN'T LIVE HERE ANYMORE, a woman's self-actualization drama like NO LOOKING BACK may seem to some as out of place in 1998 as a WIN button (or even as out of place as Lauren Holly looks waitressing in a greasy spoon). But even in this age of post-feminism, many women still feel pressure to settle for settling down.

In strong contrast to his previous, talkier efforts (THE BROTHERS MCMULLEN, 1995; SHE'S THE ONE, 1996), Burns artfully uses sound and image to create the somber atmosphere of imploded dreams that envelope Claudia's life. Burns indirectly indicates what those dreams were, and why Charlie springs hope in Claudia, through his use of Bruce Springsteen songs. (They're all over the soundtrack, and Claudia and Charlie talk about them.) In its own plaintive and lamenting way, NO LOOKING BACK demythologizes Springsteen's paeans to racing cars, passion's throes, and eternal summer nights by catching up with their young men and women when the winter sun comes up on them 10 years later. In those anthems to youth's immortality like "Born to Run" and "Thunder Road," the answer for girls was always simple: Get in *his* car, ride with *him*. Charlie and Michael seem to present Claudia with different choices. But with their rusted-out muscle cars, they're really just two sides of the same macho coin and the only salvation Claudia sees; until she realizes that she owns her own car. . . and doesn't need the rearview mirror. *(Profanity.)*— P.R.

d, Edward Burns; p, Ted Hope, Michael Nozik, Edward Burns; exec p, Robert Redford; w, Edward Burns; ph, Frank Prinzi; ed, Sue Graef; m, Joe Delia; prod d, Therese Deprez; set d, Diane Lederman; sound, Matthew Price (mixer); casting, Laura Rosenthal; cos, Sara Jane Slotnick; makeup, Michal Bigger; stunts, Douglas Crosby

Romance/Drama **(PR: C MPAA: R)**

NO ORDINARY LOVE ★

(U.S., 1998) 104m No Ordinary Limited Partnership; Picture This! Entertainment; Eli Kabillio ~ Phaedra Cinema c

Smith Forte *(Kevin Smith)*; Ericka Klein *(Wendy)*; Robert Pecora *(Andy)*; Mark S. Larson *(Ben)*; Dan Frank *(Tom)*; Koing Kuoch *(Vinny)*; Antonio Rosas *(Ramon)*; Kathleen Gibson *(Rona)*; Marina Palmier *(Gloria)*

An alleged comedy about the mixed-up sex lives of five Los Angeles roommates, Doug Witkins' NO ORDINARY LOVE segues gracelessly from sex romp to murder mystery. Unfortunately, neither Witkins nor the cast have the audacity and panache to pull off the transformation.

After the sudden death of their roommate Tom (Dan Frank), a group of friends—Kevin (Smith Forte), a designer; Wendy (Ericka Klein), a singer; Vinny (Koing Kuoch), a student; and Andy (Robert Pecora), an exotic dancer—look for someone new to share their apartment. Tom left behind plenty of memories: he was carrying on both a sadomasochistic affair with Kevin and was also dallying with Wendy, whom he made pregnant just before his demise. In between interviewing potential replacements, Kevin, the owner of the house, has trouble telling his mother that he's gay and also keeping the other roommates' chaotic lives in check. Wendy can't face being a single mother;

Vinny, who's also gay, struggles with his feelings for his best friend, Ramon (Antonio Rosas), a major closet case who eventually succumbs to Vinny's charms, and then can't face him again; and Andy, who's having an affair with Ramon's married mother Gloria (Marina Palmier). When her husband discovers the affair, his violent rage lands him in jail, and Gloria and Ramon in financial jeopardy.

Into this mix comes Ben (Mark S. Larson), a bank clerk whom Kevin chooses as the new roommate. Bursting with perpetual perkiness, Ben seems the perfect roommate and housemother. But Ben's cheery facade masks a sinister past: Ben was involved in a bank heist—with Andy and Tom—and is hiding all the money in the basement of the house. Andy immediately demands his share of the money, but Ben soon discovers that it's missing. Chaos erupts, and in the struggle that ensues the police arrest Ben, while Andy, having accidentally killed Wendy, goes on the lam. Meanwhile Vinny, who secretly seized the money and kept it in his schoolbag for safekeeping, makes Ramon and Gloria an offer: move in with him and Kevin.

From its cast of unpleasant characters to the inept direction and acting, NO ORDINARY LOVE comes off with all the grace of a hoary old B-movie melodrama, but without the camp humor factor, although Witkins seems to be trying his best to make it funny. He follows Robert Altman's "tapestry" model of filmmaking and attempts to layer the film with subplot after subplot. In the process, he proves that he's no Altman, having written a screenplay that's for the most part incoherent, supremely difficult to follow, and laced with laughable dialogue (that was clearly not intended to be funny).

Viewers shouldn't risk blinking, as characters seem to disappear with alarming regularity. This actually winds up becoming one of the film's few virtues, however, since Witkin has introduced such a plethora of stereotypes that any chance to shed a few of them is welcome. The most offensive and irritating performance comes from Larson, who portrays Ben as a limp-wristed, sexless fairy who makes fun of his own obesity. Klein, who doesn't have much to work with, tries valiantly to make Wendy into a vulnerable young woman hiding behind a riot grrrl facade, while Forte, playing Kevin (the character whom Witkins seems to think is the stable one), is devoid of any charisma. Koing Kuoch manages to rise above the material, and conveys Vinny's conflicts over his sexual feelings with taste and tenderness. If Witkins had only guided his other actors in the same direction as Kuoch, NO ORDINARY LOVE might have been the witty satire on contemporary gay and straight relationships that it wants to be, instead of the contemptible muddle that it is. *(Sexual situations, profanity, nudity.)*—D.O.

d, Doug Witkins; p, Eli Kabillio; exec p, Adam Fast; w, Doug Witkins; ph, Armando Basulto; ed, John Orland; m, Bob Christianson; prod d, Scott Carruth; art d, Anthony Bashford; set d, Bryce Holtshousen; sound, Dan Slider; cos, Sabina Huber

Comedy/Drama **(PR: O MPAA: NR)**

NO WAY HOME ★★★½

(U.S., 1997) 93m Back Alley Productions; Orenda Films ~ LIVE Entertainment c

Tim Roth *(Joey)*; James Russo *(Tommy)*; Deborah Unger, billed as Deborah Kara Unger *(Lorraine)*; Joseph Ragno *(Ralphie Scolaro)*; Catherine Kellner *(Denise)*; Saul Stein *(Brick)*; Bernadette Penotti *(Ronnie)*; Gareth Williams *(Ken Tiemo)*; Jerry Dean *(Jackie)*; Larry Romano *(Carter)*; Mike Grief *(Gastank)*; Brian Burke *(Jason)*; James Starace *(Jeremy)*; James Shue *(Louie)*; Heather Gottlieb *(Candy)*; Geraldine Abbate *(Artie's Wife)*; Bart Darby *(Artie)*; Jerome LePage *(Hamstring)*; Huckleberry Fox *(Danny)*; Jose Soto *(Nume)*; David S. Howard *(Mr. Davis)*; Victor Steinbach *(Mr. Winograd)*; Shawn Wayne Hatosy *(Sean)*; Frank John Hughes *(Bobby)*; Edward S. Dougherty *(Bartender)*; Carmine Giovinazzo *(Frankie Hamm)*; James Saxenmeyer *(Police Officer James)*; Peter Corby *(TV Shop Owner)*; Ron Ryan *(Detective Walters)*; Cheryl Clifford *(Mother on Bus)*; Krista Bonura *(Little Girl on Bus)*; Nikki Krieger *(Barmaid)*

NO WAY HOME is an outstanding, character-driven drama, steeped in a skid-row sense of reality. Boasting a trio of excellent lead performances, director-writer Buddy Giovinazzo's street-wise tale of two brothers in turmoil contains no false notes. The film unfortunately went the straight-to-video route in the US.

Joey (Tim Roth) is released from prison after serving six years for murder. He is invited to live in his family's home in Staten Island by his older brother Tommy (James Russo). Tommy's wife Lorraine (Deborah Unger) is reluctant about the arrangment, since money is tight. Slow-witted but thoughtful, Joey looks for an honest job—as Lorraine worries that her husband's drug dealing will send Joey back to prison if his parole officer shows up. Paying her no heed, Tommy continues to get his brother into trouble, while blowing off his long-overdue debts to a local loan shark, Ralphie Scolaro (Joseph Ragno). Exploring his past, Joey visits a former fiancee, Denise (Catherine Kellner), who deserted him after he went to prison. When Joey asks her why she didn't wait for him, she explains that she couldn't deal with the fact that he took the blame for a crime he didn't commit. After Joey escorts Lorraine to one of her stripping jobs, she asks Joey what caused him to commit the murder that sent him into prison, the killing of a store owner during a botched robbery. Though he doesn't admit the truth to her, it was in fact Tommy who was responsible for the cold-blooded crime.

After being attacked in his home by Scolaro's thugs, Tommy inadvertently kills Joey's parole officer when he pays a surprise visit. Lorraine and Joey come back home and discover the body. When Scolaro's men return, Joey fends them off and Lorraine shoots one of them. The police arrive, and Tommy suddenly orders his wife to blame Joey for the murders. Overhearing this, Joey says that he plans to tell the truth, *this* time around. During a final pang of conscience, Tommy declares his guilt, and is killed by the police. Free for the first time, Joey boards a bus and escapes his deadening past.

Buddy Giovinazzo's feature debut, COMBAT SHOCK (1986), proved he was capable of making a shocking, no-budget drama. His long-overdue sophomore effort accomplishes that same goal, while bringing a more complex human dimension to a similarly dysfunctional landscape. Filmed under the title GASOLINE ALLEY (which was changed due to copyright problems involving the classic comic strip), this ode to brotherly love—and the consequences of abusing that trust—plays like a Mike Leigh rendition of TAXI DRIVER (1976). Although the film is punctuated by sudden moments of violence and bloodshed, Giovinazzo never allows these elements to overwhelm the cooler, more intimate aspects of the drama.

The film's story line has a familiar aspect, but writer-director Giovinazzo transcends that potential liability with a quiet understanding of these battered souls. The lead trio contribute achingly-true performances, with Russo a scene-stealer as Tommy, a man so blissfully self-destructive that he ignores the toll this takes on those around him. Roth is uncommonly reserved, and brings a weary sensitivity and regret to the role of Joey. Unger's long-suffering Lorraine is the most complex of the lot, struggling as she does with uncontrollable forces and family secrets. Giovinazzo's realistic bent is further reflected in the outstanding production design, which sets the action in urban locales as weathered on the exterior as the characters are on the interior.

Steeped in emotional and physical brutality, and offering no easy answers, NO WAY HOME is a raw, unflinching portrait of family life at its most corrosive. (Graphic violence, extensive nudity, sexual situations, substance abuse, extreme profanity.)— S.P.

d, Buddy Giovinazzo; p, Lisa Bruce, Robert Nickson; exec p, John Quested, Guy Collins; co-p, Marcia Shulman; w, Buddy Giovinazzo; ph, Claudia Raschke; ed, Stan Warnow; m, Rick Giovinazzo; prod d, Phyllis Cedar; art d, Stacey Tanner; set d, Ondine Karady; sound, Tom Paul (mixer, design); fx, Drew Jiritano; cos, Ane Crabtree; makeup, Jane DiPersio, Rob Benevides (effects); stunts, Peter Bucossi

Drama/Crime **(PR: C MPAA: NR)**

NORTH SHORE FISH ★★
(U.S., 1997) 93m Showtime ~ Hallmark Home Entertainment c

Mercedes Ruehl *(Florence)*; Peter Riegert *(Porker)*; Tony Danza *(Sal)*; Wendie Malick *(Shimma)*; Carroll Baker *(Arlyne)*; Cordelia Richards *(Ruthie)*; Rusty Schwimmer *(Josie)*; Elizabeth Brown *(Maureen)*; Devon Pierce *(Marlena)*; Louis Del Grande *(Markie)*; Catherine Disher *(Carole)*; Israel Horovitz *(Dr. Berkowitz)*; Tony De Santis *(Eddie Asaro)*

Based on Israel Horovitz's play of the same name, NORTH SHORE FISH boasts character development and witty dialogue, but remains too stagy to make a successful adaptation to film. Like its protagonists, the tale stays trapped between the walls of a fish processing plant over the course of a single day. This made-for-cable film was released on home video in 1998.

North Shore Fish is a small-town Massachusetts institution, a processing and packaging plant where generations of the same families have worked. Hard times have reduced it to a handful of workers repackaging their product under other labels for resale. One morning, the workers learn that plant manager Sal (Tony Danza) expects a new government inspector to show up. Aware that owner Markie (Louis Del Grande) is considering selling the business, Sal is worried.

Sal's got other problems. Married, he is having an affair with one of his employees, Flo (Mercedes Ruehl), who's pregnant. He pushes her toward abortion, but Flo's uncertain. Everyone at North Shore Fish harbors pain. Obese Josie (Rusty Schwimmer) has been living alone since her husband ran off with a younger woman. Lonely handyman Porker (Peter Riegert) has proposed to every woman in the plant. Ruthie (Cordelia Richards), is pregnant and a month overdue. There's also Arlyne (Carroll Baker), Ruthie's conservative mother, and Maureen (Elizabeth Brown), who's training her cousin Marlena (Devon Pierce) to replace her while she's on vacation.

The inspector, Shimma (Wendie Malick), doesn't like what she sees and refuses to pass the plant. Sexist Sal tries to seduce her, to no avail. Tension mounts and Sal battles with his employees, even punching Porker when he steps between the boss and Flo during an argument. The consternation sends Ruthie into labor, and she has a girl. Sal breaks the bad news: given Shimma's negative evaluation, Markie will sell North Shore Fish to a company that wants to turn it into a fitness center. As the employees pack their things for the last time, Flo contemplates the abortion, but Porker, no longer a lackey, hits Sal and proposes to Flo.

While NORTH SHORE FISH is peppered with witty dialogue, the characters sometimes register like condescending impressions of earthy blue-collar workers, quick to anger and to use their fists or sexuality as negotiating tools. Horovitz also apes David Mamet with a profusion of profanity, which doesn't seem appropriate for characters who at other times display traditional small-town virtues. Director Steve Zuckerman can't do much with the little he has to work with. The one-location setting of NORTH SHORE FISH is to be expected from its origins on the stage, but the drab factory surroundings are confining and oppressive. Zuckerman tries to break things up with a few trips outside, but a parking lot and a hot-dog truck stir up zero visual excitement.

The cast is mostly terrific, particularly Danza as a sexist pig with a Yankee accent. Riegert is appealing in a role similar to his pickle man from CROSSING DELANCEY (1988). Schwimmer is a standout, by turns raging and wounded. Only Ruehl, so skilled at portraying characters of intelligence, struggles. She seems artificial and cloying when playing more limited women, and Flo's decision to settle for Porker seems less a triumph than an act of desperation. NORTH SHORE FISH is an okay effort for television that could have benefited from a more comprehensive rewrite. *(Adult situations, profanity.)*—K.W.

d, Steve Zuckerman; p, Allan Kassir, Daniel Paulsen; w, Israel Horovitz; ph, Levie Isaacks; ed, Norman Buckley; prod d, Terry Wareham; art d, Lisa Lev

Drama/Comedy **(PR: C MPAA: R)**

NOT IN THIS TOWN ★★★
(U.S., 1997) 98m Universal ~ Universal c

Kathy Baker *(Tammie Schnitzer)*; Adam Arkin *(Brian Schnitzer)*; Ed Begley Jr. *(Henry Whitcomb)*; Max Gail Jr. *(Wayne Inman)*; Douglas Greer *(Isaac Schnitzer)*; Hannah Driggs *(Rachael Schnitzer)*; Anne Sward *(Carla Inman)*; Char Nelson *(Margie McDonald)*; Bradford Tatum *(Roy Flanders)*; Tayva Patch *(Joan)*; Scott Wilkinson *(Deke)*; Ryne Sanborn *(Stephen)*; Oscar Rowland *(Grandpa Lembke)*; Janice R. Knickrehm *(Grandma Lembke)*; David Valenza *(Jimmy Dades)*; Shannah Foster *(Sally Morningstar)*; William Sargent *(Amnon Shimoni)*; Mary D. Pederson *(Hannah)*; Tom Nibley *(Mark Walton)*; Reverend France A. Davis *(Reverend Manning)*; Frank Gerrish *(Scott Gessel)*; Thom Dillon *(Mayor Forester)*; Stephen Cracroft *(Board Member)*; Anthony Leger *(Rabbi)*; Randy King *(Paul Bernhardt)*; Craig Clyde *(Detective Joe Sumner)*; Sandra Shotwell *(Mrs. Lester)*; Corey Ewan *(Nazi Speaker)*; Mary Bishop *(Second Woman)*; Frank Kanig *(Desk Officer)*; Eric Robertson *(Police Officer #1)*; Ward Wright *(Hospital Guard)*; Elizabeth Hansen *(Businessperson #1)*; Duane Stephens *(Businessman #2)*; Glenn Robards *(Businessman #3)*; Jeff Olson *(Council Member)*; Saul Korewa *(Cantor)*; J. Scott Bronson *(Coach)*; Joan Robinson *(Helen)*; Russell Peacock *(Gang Member #1)*; Brenda Anderson *(Congregational Singer)*; Mary Ethel Gregory *(Synagogue Woman)*

When a spate of hate crimes plagues a Montana town, a housewife rallies her neighbors to take a stand in NOT IN THIS TOWN. Based on a true story, this made for-TV-movie approaches outright preachiness, but manages to strike a number of emotional chords.

Brian Schnitzer (Adam Arkin), a Jewish doctor from the East Coast, settles in Billings, MT, with his wife Tammy (Kathy Baker), and their children Isaac (Douglas Greer) and Rachel (Hanna Driggs). The Schnitzers soon become aware of a growing white supremacist movement in Billings, which has gotten a boost from Henry Whitcomb (Ed Begley Jr.), a traveling, charismatic white-power leader.

A gang of thugs under Whitcomb's tutelage, led by young tough Roy Flanders (Bradford Tatum), distribute anti-Semitic tracts near a synagogue and paint graffiti on the exterior of a

Native American woman's home. Tammy is outraged and demands a meeting with the Police Chief Wayne Inman (Max Gail Jr.). Carrying a load of guilt over a previous incident in which he failed to stop a string of hate crimes before they led to murder, Inman springs into action: he pulls in TV news crews and educates his officers in how to handle hate crimes. Tammy spontaneously founds the Montana Coalition for Human Rights, despite the fact that her husband and grandparents disapprove of her newfound activism.

Whitcomb's thugs escalate their activities, performing various acts of vandalism around town. When a concrete block is thrown through Isaac's bedroom window, Brian can no longer deny the threat to his own children and vows to Tammy that he will no longer ignore or run from prejudice.

While neighbors celebrate their renewed friendships at the Schnitzers' holiday party, Flanders leads his buddies on a tirade of vandalism wherever they find a "Happy Hanukkah" banner, or an antihate poster. Coalition sympathizers simply clean up the mess, and bravely replace each sign. Whitcomb admits defeat and hits the road, leaving Flanders and his gang behind.

The most annoying aspect of NOT IN THIS TOWN is the fact that characters give speeches rather than engage in conversation. As a result, Tammy's righteous anger and Chief Inman's visionary liberalism sound one-dimensional. Begley's character appears only briefly, thus undercutting the possiblity of a grand confrontation between the forces of good and evil; however, with the emphasis taken off of Whitcomb's outside influence, the film is thus free to focus on the banal-seeming, local sources of hatred. With a satisfying degree of realism, the movie's conclusion does not suggest that the do-gooders have actually won the war against the haters in their community, only that they have recognized the enemy and have withstood the battle. Earnest performances all around—especially from Baker (best known for her role on the TV series "Picket Fences") and Gail (who seems comfortably transplanted straight out of his old "Wojo" character on "Barney Miller")—also help prop up a plot otherwise vulnerable to several "message-movie" cliches. *(Profanity, violence, adult situations.)*—C.Ch.

d, Donald Wrye; exec p, Robert Harris, Jim Korris; w, Adam Gilad; ph, Reed Smoot; ed, Bill Butler; m, Don Davis; prod d, Gary Constable; sound, Thomas Brandau, Les Udy; cos, Robin Lewis-West

Drama **(PR: C MPAA: NR)**

NOTES FROM UNDERGROUND ★★★

(U.S., 1995) 87m Renegade Films;
Walkow-Gruber Pictures ~ NFU Film Partners c

Henry Czerny *(The Underground Man)*; Sheryl Lee *(Liza)*; Eammon Roche *(Simon)*; Charlie Stratton *(Jerry)*; Geoffrey Rivas *(Tom)*; Jon Favreau *(Zerkov)*; Seth Green *(Punk Neighbor)*

Henry Czerny's riveting performance as a lonely and misanthropic civil servant propels NOTES FROM UNDERGROUND, an impressive modern-day adaptation of Dostoevsky's novella about the confessions of a self-described "sick and spiteful" man.

In his cramped and dingy basement apartment, the Underground Man (Henry Czerny) sets up a video camera and, in an attempt to free himself of unpleasant memories, records a series of monologues in which he recalls past incidents when he did "ugly things." He is shown working as a low-level clerk at the city's Building Dept., where he takes pleasure in tormenting architects and contractors who need his approval for their plans. He then goes to visit some well-off college acquaintances, and even though they openly despise him, he invites himself to a party they're throwing that night. To humiliate him, they change the time of the party and purposely don't tell him about it, and when they finally arrive, he goes into a drunken tirade and insults them. They all leave him to go to a brothel, and he follows them with the intention of starting a fight, but instead winds up with a prostitute named Liza (Sheryl Lee).

After having sex with Liza, the Underground Man is filled with a mix of pity and disgust and decides to toy with her emotions. He tells her that she is degrading herself working there and makes her cry. He then gives her his address and tells her to quit and come live with him, but later regrets doing so, and dreads the idea that she might actually show up. When she does, he berates her for believing that he really cared about her, and he breaks down and starts crying. They spend the night together and make love, and in the morning he gives her a key to his apartment. When he comes home from work, she has cleaned the apartment and tells him she has found a real job and a place to live near him. Horrified at the idea of having a real relationship with her, he throws her on the floor and brutally rapes her to prove how despicable he is. She leaves him and he runs after her in the rain, but is unable to find her. Back in the present, he says that all of this happened years ago and that he hasn't seen her since, then shuts off the video camera.

NOTES FROM UNDERGROUND triumphs over its obviously low budget through incisive writing and extraordinary acting, particularly by Henry Czerny, who manages to make his character both pathetic and repulsive. He's a mass of contradictions—intelligent yet stuck in a deadening job, self-aware yet unable to change his self-destructive behavior, desirous of human contact yet incapable of love—and Czerny fearlessly captures every nuance of the character, a man who can only express himself through domination and whose only true emotions are negative. Sheryl Lee is also very good as the vulnerable prostitute searching for some warmth and compassion, and writer-director Gary Alan Walkow's use of the video camera is a clever device which allows him to get inside the Underground Man's head, as he flashes back and provides voice-over for a series of stylized, minimalist vignettes.

Some sections of the film are so broad that they border on caricature (such as the party with his four obnoxious yuppie lawyer "friends"), while others are admittedly weak fantasies where the Underground Man gets revenge on people who have wronged him; many others, however, are bitingly satirical. Though Dostoevsky's novella was published in 1846, its themes dealing with the worst traits of human behavior are universal and timeless, and will resonate powerfully with anyone who has ever felt excluded or inferior or socially awkward. The film's strongest and most disturbing accomplishment is how it makes the viewer confront the fact that the petty feelings of hate, spite, and sadism which destroy the Underground Man exist to some degree in everyone. *(Profanity, nudity, sexual situations.)*—M.S.

d, Gary Alan Walkow; p, Frank J. Gruber, Alicia A. Dollard, Chris Beckman; exec p, Gary Alan Walkow; assoc p, Randall Fukunaga, Steven Siegel; w, Gary Alan Walkow (based on the novella by Fyodor Dostoevsky); ph, Dan Gillham; ed, Peter B. Ellis; m, Mark Governor; prod d, Michael Rizzo; art d, Mark Benson, Cindy Vance; sound, Yehuda Maayan; casting, Bonita Pietila; cos, Alina Panova; makeup, Miranda

Drama **(PR: O MPAA: NR)**

NOTHING TO LOSE

(SEE: TEN BENNY)

O

O-LITA 2000
(SEE: LOLIDA 2000)

OBJECT OF MY AFFECTION, THE ★★
(U.S., 1998) 111m Laurence Mark Productions; 20th Century Fox ~ 20th Century Fox c

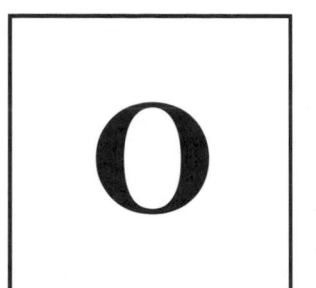

Jennifer Aniston *(Nina)*; Paul Rudd *(George Hanson)*; Tim Daly *(Dr. Robert Joely)*; Alan Alda *(Sidney Miller)*; Nigel Hawthorne *(Rodney Fraser)*; John Pankow *(Vince McBride)*; Kali Rocha *(Melissa Marx)*; Lena Cardwell; Natalie B. Kikkenborg *(Girls at Community Center)*; Lauren Varija Pratt *(Sally Miller)*; Hayden Panettiere *(Mermaid)*; Lauren Chen *(Violin Player)*; Liam Aiken *(Nathan)*; Allison Janney *(Constance Miller)*; Janet Zarish; Ellen Tobie; Virl Andrick; Robert C. Lee *(Dinner Guests)*; Bradley White *(Stephen Saint)*; Marilyn Dobrin *(Mrs. Sarni)*; Midori Nakamura *(Nina's Colleague)*; Joan Copeland *(Madame Reynolds)*; Steve Zahn *(Frank Hanson)*; Kate Jennings Grant *(Kennedy)*; Bruce Altman *(Dr. Goldstein)*; Salem Ludwig *(Mr. Shapiro)*; Antonia Rey *(Mrs. Ochoa)*; Danny Darrow *(Nina's Dance Partner)*; Sean Rademaker; Heather Thompson *(School Children)*; Mary McIlvaine; Lisa-Erin Allen; Fanni Green *(Nurses)*; Samia Shoaib *(Suni)*; Douglas Wert *(Father)*; Michael Phelan *(Son)*; Edward James Hyland *(Doctor)*; Gabriel Macht *(Steve Casillo)*; John Roland *(TV Anchor)*; Rosanna Scotto *(TV Anchor)*; Miguel Maldonado *(Colin Powell)*; Peter Maloney *(Desk Clerk)*; Bette Henritze *(Mrs. Skinner)*; Amo Gulinello *(Paul James)*; Iraida Polanco *(Carmelita)*; Kevin Carroll *(Lewis Crowley)*; Sarah Knowlton *(Caroline Colucci)*; Steven Ochoa *(Waiter)*; Kia Joy Goodwin *(Juliet)*; Daniel Cosgrove *(Trotter Bull)*; Damian Young *(Romeo & Juliet Director)*; Rebecca Eichenberger; Jane Bodle *(Wedding Guests)*; Audra McDonald *(Wedding Singer)*; Sarah Hyland *(Molly)*; Paz De La Huerta *(13-Year-Old Sally)*; Jeffrey Marchett; Susan Bradford *(Parents)*; Sylvia Ader; Howard Atlee; Jerome Bynder; Liz Chrystea; Howard Cutler; Virginia Emerson; Edward Furs; Vernon Gray; Arthur W. Guenther; Miriam Hamilton; Betty Hudson; June Kawai; Dana Lorge; T. Scott Nonnon; Sally Parrish; Larney Rutledge; Catherine Saliba *(Ballroom Dancers)*; Matthew Savage Aibel; Carmen Andino; Vera Butcher; Bienka Jean-Charles; Joseph M. Christensen; Alfredo Cosme; Namibia Donadio; Tyler Flagg; Gilda Flores; Sofia Flores; Brighid Gannon; Kevin Gannon; Kyla Garcia; Olivia Harrington; Ashli Haynes; Gabriel Hernandez; Heather Ichihashi; Max Kelly; Francis Kenny; Lily Norton; Jatze-Rae Ramos; David Sanchez; Skye Lilly Torres; Emily Turonis; Jackie Ventre; Zom Westhof; Kadie Winckelmann *(Brooklyn School Singers)*; Natasha Edwards; Fani Lopez; Roxie Maizler; Sanjae Manbauman; Victoria Marie Thomas *(Community Center Girls)*

Parochial, predictable, and inappropriately R-rated, THE OBJECT OF MY AFFECTION is one of those depressingly hermetic comedies about young New Yorkers of the educated class—a genre created essentially for the comfort and amusement of older New Yorkers of the same class. This time the subject is an unmarried pregnant woman who falls in love with her gay male roommate.

Dropped by his boyfriend (Tim Daly) and in need of a place to stay, George (Paul Rudd), a schoolteacher, moves in with Nina (Jennifer Aniston), a social worker. Nina's sweetheart, Vince (John Pankow), is somewhat irked by this arrangement and becomes more so when he learns that she is carrying his child and intends to raise it in partnership with George.

As Nina and George become fast friends, the young woman grows increasingly attracted to her roomie. When George embarks on a romance with a young actor named Paul (Amo Gulinello), Nina, who is no longer seeing Vince, becomes jealous and ultimately confesses to her roommate that she loves and wants to marry him. He tells her that he loves Paul.

When Nina has her baby, both George and Vince are by her side to provide affection and support. Five years later, Nina's little girl (Sarah Hyland) is a student at George's school. George, now the school's principal, is still involved with Paul. Nina is living with Lewis (Kevin Carroll), a policeman. Everyone is happy, even Vince.

"Heterosexual-homosexual romances don't work out" is the unremarkable, almost tautological conclusion reached by THE OBJECT OF MY AFFECTION. If Nina and George had been written as *much* younger, perhaps mid-teen members of a less sexually sophisticated class, some pathos might have been elicited from the movie's truistic premise.

Deeply mired in upper-middle-class Manhattan provincialism, the film proceeds from a set of such rigid social assumptions that it bypasses preaching to the converted in favor of pandering to the initiated. A small example: the script bends over backwards to include within a wedding reception scene a line of dialogue designed to reassure the film's core audience that the newlyweds will embark on their marriage properly, righteously hyphenated. This isn't satire; it's self-congratulation. There must be a massive pool of moviegoers in the southern half of Manhattan, or pictures like this one would never be made; it's hard to imagine anyone else paying to see them.

The almost uniformly pedestrian cast is enhanced by Jennifer Aniston, an actress with talent, spirit, and one of the screen's cutest figures since Olga San Juan. *(Profanity, adult situations.)*—D.T.

d, Nicholas Hytner; p, Laurence Mark; w, Wendy Wasserstein (based on the novel by Stephen McCauley); ph, Oliver Stapleton; ed, Tariq Anwar; m, George Fenton; prod d, Jane Musky; art d, Patricia Woodbridge; set d, Susan Bode; sound, Michael Barosky (mixer); casting, Daniel Swee; cos, John Dunn; makeup, Naomi Donne; stunts, George Aguilar

Romance/Comedy **(PR: C MPAA: R)**

ODD COUPLE II, THE
(SEE: NEIL SIMON'S THE ODD COUPLE II)

OFF THE MENU: THE LAST DAYS OF CHASEN'S ★★½
(U.S., 1998) 90m A La Carte Films; Lobo Grande Pictures ~ Northern Arts Entertainment c/bw

Steve Allen; Jayne Meadows; Army Archerd; Maureen Arthur; James Bacon; Angela Bassett; Jeff Berg; David Brown; Brett Butler; Gary Coleman; Jackie Collins; Pierre Cossette; Bo Derek; Angie Dickinson; Matt Dillon; Cristina Ferrari; President Gerald Ford; Mrs. Betty Ford; Chuck Fries; Ava Fries; Jodie Foster; Michael J. Fox; David Frost; Neal Gabler; Hugh Grant; Elizabeth Hurley; Merv Griffin; Monty Hall; Charlton Heston; Bob Hope; Holly Hunter; Samuel Jackson; Jessica Lange; Ethel Kennedy; Quincy Jones; Nastassja Kinski; Sally Kellerman; Sally Kirkland; Martin Landau; Jack Lemmon; Jay Leno; Michael Lerner; Art Linkletter; Courtney Love; A.C. Lyles; Carol Lynley; Madonna; Johnny Mathis; Marilyn McCoo; Billy Davis Jr.; Ed McMahon; Margaret O'Brien; Dale Olson; Chazz Palmenteri; Sarah Jessica Parker; Suzanne Pleshette; Colin Powell; Nancy Reagan; Miranda Richardson; Don Rickles; Jennifer

Jones, billed as Mrs. Norton Simon; Tom Snyder; Rod Steiger; Sharon Stone; Donna Summer; Quentin Tarantino; Jennifer Tilly; John Travolta; Kelly Preston; Mrs. Rudy Vallee; Yanni; Robert Wagner; Lew Wasserman; Dianne Wiest; Norm Winter; Fay Wray; Jane Wyman; Ronnie Clint; Tommy Gallagher; Pepe Ruiz; Raymond Bilbool

OFF THE MENU: THE LAST DAYS OF CHASEN'S is a diverting and well-produced but overlong documentary which chronicles the closing of a legendary Beverly Hills eatery.

The announcement that Chasen's, a favorite restaurant of celebrities, will go out of business on April 1, 1995 is met with sadness by its famous patrons. Fay Wray comments that Chasen's is "a haven of tradition, warmth, and dependability." Tom Snyder lauds its durability and laments the failure of the entertainment community to support it. Rod Steiger, meanwhile, speaks highly of Chasen's roast beef and chili, while Ed McMahon enjoys a drink at the bar.

Staff members at Chasen's also regret the closing. They pay tribute to one another and their esprit de corps, and they relate anecdotes about encounters they've had with such famous customers as Jimmy Stewart, Alfred Hitchcock (a generous tipper), Elizabeth Taylor, Queen Elizabeth II, and Richard Nixon. They also discuss the pride and care they take in their jobs and give (sometimes unflattering) opinions of other staff members. Celebrities, in turn, offer comments on their favorite Chasen's employees.

Film historian Neil Gabler briefly recounts the history of the restaurant, which was founded in 1936 by Dave Chasen, a former vaudevillian. Rather downscale at first, its popularity grew and it began to attract movie stars and politicians. When Dave died, ownership passed to his wife, Maude, and then to his grandson, Scott.

News of the closing prompts a surge in business, as people rush to visit the landmark before it closes. The staff is heavy-spirited on the last business day, but go about their work as usual. When the night ends, workers gather up their belongings and leave, and the doors of Chasen's close for the last time. A few months later, Tommy Gallagher, a longtime Chasen's waiter, dies. His co-workers reunite at his funeral service, and he is buried in his waiter's tuxedo, a Chasen's menu tucked under his arm.

Intended as an elegy, OFF THE MENU: THE LAST DAYS OF CHASEN'S offers a glimpse into the dining fashions of the rich and famous. At its most engaging, the film playfully looks at how an institution that caters to the pleasures of the privileged functions, showing Chasen's in everyday operation as reservations are accepted or denied, tables are exactingly arranged, and delicate dishes are prepared. Staff is shown interacting confidently with celebrities, unintimidated by the wealth and power of those they serve. Highlights of OFF THE MENU include a sequence in which the Chasen's bartender prepares his specialty for a gleefully anticipatory Ed McMahon, and an amusing explanation by film producer David Brown of how the garrulous Tommy Gallagher kept him to his diet by threatening to tell Brown's wife (former *Cosmopolitan* editor Helen Gurley Brown) if he cheated. Moments like these demonstrate why Chasen's was beloved and why it will be missed; but they are not enough to sustain a feature-length film.

OFF THE MENU seems padded with digressive matters such as internal disputes among staff, how employees balance the demands of work and family, and even (at the film's most glib) the importance of myth-making in Hollywood. These elements, inserted between sequences of daily activity and the preparations that are made for the imminent closing, are extraneous and only detract from the film's efforts to effect a melancholic tone. Also, while the film includes an entertaining assemblage of historic stills and film clips of Chasen's celebrated clientele, the restaurant's history is dealt with cursorily, and it's nearly impossible to determine why the establishment caught on with the Hollywood crowd.

The film is quite well crafted, with lively camerawork by Ken Kobland and Sandra Chandler. Snippets of old popular songs are also used well on the soundtrack, effectively evoking the past without wallowing in nostalgia. Yet the film's stylistic strengths cannot make up for its structural weakness. OFF THE MENU has the makings of a terrific short. At 90 minutes, it outlasts its appeal. *(Profanity.)*—D.C.

d, Robert Pulcini, Shari Springer Berman; p, Julia Strohm; exec p, Diandra Douglas, Alicia Sams; ph, Ken Kobland, Sandra Chandler; ed, Robert Pulcini; m, Mark Suozzo; sound, John Halaby

Documentary **(PR: A MPAA: NR)**

OGRE, THE ★★½

(France/Germany/U.K./Poland, 1996) 118m Studio Babelsberg; Recorded Picture Co.; Westdeutscher Rundunk; Heritage Films; Renn Productions; France 2 Cinema; Canal + ~ Kino International c/bw
(DER UNHOLD)

John Malkovich *(Abel)*; Armin Mueller-Stahl *(Count of Kaltenborn)*; Gottfried John *(Chief Forester)*; Marianne Sagebrecht *(Frau Netta)*; Caspar Salmon *(Young Abel)*; Volker Spengler *(Reichsmarshall Hermann Goring)*; Heino Ferch *(SS Officer Raufeisen)*; Dieter Laser *(Prof. Blattchen)*; Agnes Soral *(Rachel)*; Sasha Hanau *(Martine)*; Vernon Dobtcheff *(Lawyer)*; Simon McBurney *(Brigadier)*; Ilja Smoljanski *(Ephraim)*; Luc Florian; Laurent Spielvogel; Marc Duvet; Phillipe Stubelle *(Prisoners of War)*

Made in 1996, but unreleased in the US until 1998, Volker Schlondorff's THE OGRE is a well-made, but heavy-handed and rather pointless parable starring a miscast John Malkovich as a simple-minded Frenchman who drifts into a collaboration with the Nazis.

While attending Catholic school in 1925 Paris, young Abel (Caspar Salmon) prays for the school to burn down in order to save him from being punished by the sadistic headmaster, and it does, leading Abel to believe that fate is on his side. Fourteen years later, Abel (John Malkovich) is a garage mechanic who loves to play with all of the children in the neighborhood, but when he's falsely accused of molesting one of them, he's sent to jail. However, due to the outbreak of war, Abel is sent to the front, where his platoon is captured by the Nazis. Abel manages to sneak out of the POW camp to go to a nearby cabin every night, where he befriends a gigantic caribou, but he always returns to the camp. One day, Abel is caught at the cabin by a Nazi (Gottfried John), who, later picks Abel from the camp to be a servant at Hermann Goering's (Volker Spengler) hunting lodge in the Bavarian forest.

Abel ingratiates himself with the Nazis and is assigned to work at a castle owned by the aristocratic Count Kaltenborn (Armin Mueller-Stahl), who's not a Nazi, but whose home has been turned into an army training school. Because of his affinity with children, Abel is assigned to travel the countryside and bring back boys to be trained in the army, whether or not they want to join. Abel rounds up the boys, believing that he's helping them, but as the war continues and the Russians advance on Germany, many of them are killed in battle. After Count Kaltenborn is arrested for his attempts to overthrow Hitler, Abel discovers a young Jewish refugee who has escaped from a concentration camp and he learns about the Nazi gas chambers. Abel hides the boy in the school and tries to convince the other boys to surrender to the rapidly approaching Russians, but they turn on him and nearly beat him to death. When the Russians arrive, they destroy the school and kill everyone inside when the boys refuse to surrender, but Abel manages to escape, carrying the Jewish refugee to safety.

THE OGRE might uncharitably, although not inaccurately, be described as "FORREST GUMP meets TRIUMPH OF THE WILL," what with the half-witted Abel finding himself inadvertently involved with momentous world events and interacting with famous historical personages such as Goering, accompanied by mock-rhapsodic Hitler youth military training montages and satirical depictions of Nazi nobility and pageantry. There is also more than a little touch of Louis Malle's LACOMBE LUCIEN (1974), also about a Frenchman who collaborates with the Nazis, which is acknowledged by Schlondorff, who was once Malle's assistant, with an end credit dedicating the film "To Our Late Friend Louis Malle." The film aims to be a grown-up fairy tale about fate, corruption, and the purity of children and animals, filled with symbolic references to the Brothers Grimm (such as Abel's mystical adventures in the forest with the mysterious caribou, who's also called the Ogre, and a bloody hunting sequence which looks awfully realistic, and is *not* accompanied by a "no animals were harmed. . . " disclaimer at the end).

It's obvious that Schlondorff's intent is to show how easy it is to be seduced by evil without even knowing it, and that the Ogre is really us, but the metaphors are not very subtle and the Nazis are such caricatures that they inspire laughter rather than fear, particularly the grotesquely porcine Goering and an eye-rolling, Dr. Frankenstein-like mad scientist who's obsessed with genetic purity. Additionally, the film is severely compromised by Abel's metaphysical narration which constantly reminds us about his "magical nature" without ever actually dramatizing it, and by being set and filmed in Europe, but made in English, resulting in a disconcertingly dubbed mixture of American, British, and German accents. Malkovich gives a thoughtful, introspective performance that's more restrained than much of his recent work, but he's too old and physically wrong for the role, which, as written, is a gentle giant type of character such as Lenny in *Of Mice and Men,* and which could have been played much more convincingly by someone like Vincent D'Onofrio. The film is interesting, but it's definitely not on the level of THE TIN DRUM, Schlodorff's brilliant 1979 anti-Nazi allegory. *(Violence, profanity, sexual situations.)* —M.S.

d, Volker Schlondorff; p, Ingrid Windisch; exec p, Claude Berri, Jeremy Thomas, Lew Rywin; assoc p, Chris Auty, Pierre Couveinhes; w, Volker Schlondorff, Jean-Claude Carriere (based on the novel *Le Roi Des Aulnes* by Michel Tournier); ph, Bruno de Keyzer; ed, Nicholas Caster; m, Michael Nyman; prod d, Ezio Frigerio; art d, Didier Naert; set d, Bernard Heinrich; sound, Karl-Heinz Laabs (mixer); cos, Anna Sheppard; makeup, Axel Zornow

Drama/War **(PR: O MPAA: NR)**

OLIVER TWIST ★★½

(U.S./U.K./Ireland, 1998) 91m Disney ~ Disney c

Alex Trench *(Oliver Twist)*; Richard Dreyfuss *(Fagin)*; Elijah Wood *(Jack "Dodger" Hawkins)*; David O'Hara *(Bill Sikes)*; Antoine Byrne *(Nancy)*; Anthony Finnegan *(Mr. Brownlow)*; Olivia Caffrey *(Rose Maylie)*; Maria Charles *(Widow Corney)*; Des Braiden; Eileen Colgan; Eilish Moore; Conor Evans; A.J. Kennedy

Shot in Ireland, this revisionist version of the Dickens classic was produced for television by the Disney organization. The film was released on home video in 1998.

In 1825 a nameless vagrant woman dies after giving birth to a baby whom the county orphanage arbitrarily names Oliver Twist. Oliver grows up in the workhouse, fixated on a locket his mother possessed. When adolescent Oliver (Alex Trench) is expelled for daring to ask for more food, he sets out for London and the Grosvenor Square address engraved on the locket.

In the city, Oliver is befriended by Jack "Dodger" Hawkins (Elijah Wood), a young pickpocket who introduces Oliver to Fagin (Richard Dreyfuss), an ingratiating lowlife who gives shelter and fellowship to runaway boys, putting them to work as sneak thieves. Dodger accompanies Oliver on a pocket-picking expedition, but the would-be victim sounds an alarm, and Oliver is captured. The noble Rose Maylie (Olivia Caffrey) testifies that Dodger was the culprit and charitably takes Oliver to the Grosvenor Square mansion of her uncle, Mr. Brownlow (Anthony Finnegan). Oliver realizes he is Brownlow's grandson, by a daughter who fled after becoming pregnant with a married lover's child. Only the locket can prove his heritage, and it's in Fagin's treasure horde. Fagin himself wants Oliver back for fear he'll inform police of his criminal outfit, and Fagin's adult associate Bill Sikes (David O'Hara) has no objection to killing Oliver to ensure silence. Pretending to rejoin the gang, Oliver carefully plays Sikes's greed against Fagin's fear of a murder charge to survive long enough to get the locket. It's Dodger who unwittingly brings down the law when he helps contact Rose Maylie over the danger Oliver is in. Sikes apparently kills Fagin, then accidentally hangs himself trying to escape a lynch mob. Before being reunited with the Brownlow household, Oliver gets a final affectionate farewell from rascally Fagin, who survived after all.

Leaving aside the Disney cartoon bowdlerization OLIVER & COMPANY (1988), one might say the old-style Disney treatment of *Oliver Twist* already arrived in a non-Disney production, Carol Reed's OLIVER! (1968), with its colorful production, spirited songs, and Ron Moody's sugar-coated Fagin (the latter element being a whimsical undermining of Dickens's original depiction of the character, done full justice by Alec Guiness in David Lean's classic 1948 version). What was left for this TV version? Dickens purists will cringe at the rewrites; missing, along with most of the novel's rich dialogue, is Oliver's innate innocence. The literary hero would never dream of dishonesty, but this Oliver is a kid crafty enough to pit his enemies against each other.

The film could have been compelling for viewers who are new to the story, but Tony Bill's rather prosaic direction and the small-scale sets fight against sustaining viewer interest. Newcomer 10-year-old Alex Trench is fine in the lead role, as is Elijah Wood as Dodger. As Fagin, Richard Dreyfuss (who also co-produced) gives in to his hammy tendencies. His character has also been toned down—Dreyfuss's Fagin is even more kid-friendly than was Moody's. This was done, presumably, in an effort to combat charges that the character is an anti-Semitic stereotype; by softening Fagin's behavior, however, an essential component of Oliver's struggle to survive is sacrificed. *(Violence.)*—C.C.

d, Tony Bill; p, Steve North; exec p, Lawrence Mark, John Baldecchi, Stephen Sommers; co-p, Richard Dreyfus, Morgan O'Sullivan; w, Monte Merrick (based on the novel by Charles Dickens); ph, Bing Sokolsky; ed, Axel Hubert; m, Van Dyke Parks; prod d, Keith Wilson; art d, James Hambridge; casting, John Hubbard, Ros Hubbard; makeup, Ken Jennings, Matthew Mungle

Drama/Children's **(PR: A MPAA: NR)**

ON CONNAIT LA CHANSON
(SEE: SAME OLD SONG)

ONE-SEVENTH FARMERS, THE
(SEE: INHERITORS, THE)

ONE TOUGH COP ★★
(U.S., 1998) 90m Bregman Productions; MDP Worldwide; Patriot Pictures ~ Stratosphere Entertainment c

Stephen Baldwin *(Bo Dietl)*; Chris Penn *(Duke Finnerty)*; Gina Gershon *(Joey O'Hara)*; Mike McGlone *(Rickie La Cassa)*; Frank Pellegrino *(Lieutenant Raggio)*; Paul Calderon *(Sergeant Diaz)*; Victor Slezak *(FBI Agent Bruce Payne)*; Amy Irving *(FBI Agent Jean Devlin)*; Christopher Bregman *(Gang Banger #1)*; Mike Santana *(Gang Banger #2)*; Vita Rezza *(Cop #1)*; Marium Carvell *(Cop #2)*; Luis Guzman *(Gunman Popi)*; Dana Dietl *(Little Girl)*; Deirdre Coleman *(EMS Worker)*; Harvey Atkin *(Andy)*; Paul Guilfoyle *(Frankie "Hot" Salvano)*; Lori Alter *(Wife Terry)*; Jason Blicker *(Philly Nase)*; Frank Gio *(Sally Resio)*; Edmonte Salvato Jr. *(Big Jolly)*; Bo Dietl *(Detective Benny Levine)*; David Filippi *(Uniform Cop Scarfacci)*; Michael Rispoli *(Detective Lt. Denny Regan)*; Saundra McClain *(Rowdy Woman)*; Ezra Knight *(Toulouse)*; Ingrid Rogers *(Toulouse's Bride)*; Karen Robinson *(Sherese)*; Larry Gilliard Jr. *(Curtis Wilkins)*; Barbara Barnes-Hopkins *(Ka'reem's Mother)*; Lloyd Adams *(Ka'reem)*; David Sparrow *(Uniform Cop)*; Mary Hammett *(Frankie's Hot Girlfriend)*; Monica Talma *(Girlfriend #2)*; Marlow Vella *(Taxi Driver)*; Philip Akin *(Inspector Cheney)*

ONE TOUGH COP is one dull cop movie, a highly fictionalized yet strangely banal and unexciting account of the "real-life" heroics of renegade NYPD detective Bo Dietl, which aspires to hard-boiled realism, but is actually far less gritty and authentic than a typical episode of a contemporary television police drama.

New York City police detectives Bo Dietl (Stephen Baldwin) and his partner Duke Finnerty (Chris Penn) go to a party at a restaurant owned by Bo's lifelong best friend Rickie LaCassa (Mike McClone), a mobster whose mistress, Joey O'Hara (Gina Gershon), is the restaurant's proprietor. Later, Bo is questioned by two FBI agents (Amy Irving, Victor Slezak) who have pictures of him hugging Rickie and accuse him of corruption and consorting with known criminals. They tell Bo that they'll let him off the hook if he agrees to install a recording device in Rickie's car, but when he refuses, they threaten to destroy his career. Meanwhile, against the orders of their publicity-seeking bosses, Bo and Duke begin to probe the high-profile case of a nun in an East Harlem convent school who was viciously raped and tortured. Based on a tip provided by Rickie's underworld sources, Bo and Duke eventually crack the case and catch the perpetrators, but are suspended after attacking a superior officer during a press conference in which he takes all of the credit.

Bo begins dating Joey after she breaks up with Rickie, and the alcoholic Duke goes on a bender and ends up being murdered by Frankie (Paul Guilfoyle), one of Rickie's crew, to whom Duke owed thousands of dollars. The vengeful Bo asks Rickie to help him find Frankie, but Rickie refuses, and has a fight with Bo after finding out about his affair with Joey. Bo follows Rickie when the latter picks up Frankie, but when Bo tries to apprehend Frankie, he holds Rickie hostage and forces Bo to put down his gun. As Frankie is about to shoot Bo, Rickie hits Frankie's arm and ends up taking a bullet in the gut. Rickie dies in Bo's arms and Bo kills Frankie. At the Internal Affairs hearing, Bo is reinstated to the force and then continues his relationship with Joey.

Though the ads for ONE TOUGH COP proudly trumpeted it as being "from the producer of SERPICO, DOG DAY AFTERNOON, and SCARFACE," they naturally fail to mention that the responsible party—Martin Bregman—only got the initial gigs because he was Al Pacino's agent at the time. And Bregman is the only thing this new run-of-the-mill effort (co-produced with his son Michael) has in common with those films—it certainly lacks Sidney Lumet's social commentary and study of loyalty, as well Brian De Palma's stylistic bravura. Based on Dietl's self-aggrandizing autobiographical novel, the story is oddly set in the present day, despite the fact that Dietl served in the 1980s, and the case involving the nun is based on a real-life 1981 incident. Given this hodgepodge of truth and fantasy, it comes as no shock when an end-credit states, "Except for the character of Bo Dietl, all characters and situations portrayed are fictional"; the only surprise is that since Dietl was the film's coexecutive producer and the screenwriter was not burdened by the restraints of factual accuracy, they couldn't come up with a more original and imaginative scenario with which to portray Dietl as a supercop. Instead, the by-the-numbers script steals from scores of better movies, while the characterizations are all racial and ethnic stereotypes and the self-consciously foul-mouthed dialogue is a virtual primer of cop-movie cliches.

Stephen Baldwin tries hard to act rugged and soulfully intense, but even with a beard and dark hair, he still looks like a stoned surfer and literally seems to be acting with a wad of cotton in his cheeks while affecting a labored De Niro-esque dialect. The other performances are negligible, including a grossly obese Chris Penn in the type of burned-out compulsive-everything role he's played way too often. As in his previous film, FOUR DAYS IN SEPTEMBER (1997), Bruno Baretto's rudimentary point-and-shoot direction lacks a visual or thematic point-of-view. His impassive style not only fails to explore the personal, political, or legal ramifications of the story, it doesn't even deliver the requisite genre thrills and is completely oblivious to the obvious homoeroticism displayed by Bo, Rickie, and Duke, who hug and kiss each other to an excessive degree in virtually every scene. *(Violence, profanity.)*—M.S.

d, Bruno Barreto; p, Michael S. Bregman, Martin Bregman; exec p, Michael Mendelsohn, Mark Damon, Bo Dietl; co-p, Judy Stevens; w, Jeremy Iacone (based on the novel by Bo Dietl); ph, Ron Fortunato; ed, Ray Hubley; set d, Megan Less; sound, Bryan Day (mixer); fx, Brock Jolliffe, Reginald Ashby; makeup, Marlene Aarons; stunts, Branko Racki (coordinator-Toronto), Frank Ferrara (coordinator-NY)

Action/Crime/Drama **(PR: O MPAA: R)**

ONE TRUE THING ★★★½
(U.S., 1998) 127m Ufland Productions; Monarch Pictures; Diamond Heart Productions; Universal ~ Universal c

Meryl Streep *(Kate Gulden)*; Renee Zellweger *(Ellen Gulden)*; William Hurt *(George Gulden)*; Tom Everett Scott *(Brian Gulden)*; Lauren Graham *(Jules)*; Nicky Katt *(Jordan Belzer)*; James Eckhouse *(District Attorney)*; Patrick Breen *(Mr. Tweedy)*; Gerrit Graham *(Oliver Most)*; David Byron *(Senator Sullivan)*; Stephen Peabody *(Harold)*; Lizabeth MacKay *(Dr. Cohen)*; Mary Catherine Wright *(Clarice)*; Sloane Shelton *(Mrs. Best)*; Michele Shay *(June)*; Bobo Lewis *(Muriel)*; Marylouise Burke *(Louisa)*; Marcia Jean Kurtz *(Marcia)*; Diana Canova *(Diana)*; John Deyle *(Santa/Mayor)*; Hallee Hirsch *(8 Year Old Ellen)*; Jeffrey Scaperrotta *(4 Year Old Brian)*; Todd Cerveris *(Casey)*; Anna Alvim *(Nurse Teresa)*; Julie Janney *(Hospital Nurse)*; Susan Stout *(Tweedy's Secretary)*; Greg Hedtke *(Magazine Executive)*; Christian James *(Magazine Executive)*; Lauren Toub *(Halloween Girl)*; Ashley Remy *(Halloween Girl)*; Saul Stacy

Williams *(Graduate Student)*; Julianne Nicholson *(College Student)*; Amber Kain *(College Student)*; Yolande Bavan *(Nari)*; Benjamin Andrews *(Party Kid)*; Kathryn Walsh *(Party Kid)*; James E. Graseck *(Violinist)*; Doug Allen *(Club Band Leader)*; Kirk Driscoll; Paul Pimsler; Scott Spray; Jay Stollman *(Club Band Members)*; CHRISTMAS CHOIR: Cathy Comiskey; Ruth Egner; Phil Gamble; David Hutchings; Linda Hutchings; Wilbur Lewis; Rich Morin; Annette Mulholland; Rosemary Palmer; Gina Piccolo; Rebecca Raines; Barbara Russell; Joanna Hoty Russell; Barbara Savino; Normana Schaaf; Paul Schroeder; Mary G. Sims; Wolodymyr Smishkewych; Chris Sterling; Nancy Tkacs; Peter Zimmerman

Restrained and superbly performed, ONE TRUE THING is an effective tearjerker that never sacrifices credibility to tug at the heartstrings. Thanks to Carl Franklin's skilled direction and fine work from leads Meryl Streep, William Hurt, and Renee Zellweger, the film stands heads above the usual "women's drama."

Ellen Gulden (Renee Zellweger), an investigative journalist based in Manhattan, has largely cut herself off from her family in Langhorne, PA. While she idolizes her father George (William Hurt), a professor of literature, she is annoyed by her mother Kate (Meryl Streep), a prim-and-proper homemaker. After going home for a birthday party for her father, Ellen is asked by George to move home and care for Kate: she has been diagnosed with cancer, and George can't interrupt his busy mid-term schedule. Though annoyed that her father doesn't seem to regard her job as a real career, Ellen agrees.

Over the few next months, Ellen acquires a new perspective on her parents. Kate is the nexus of a group of craft-making, event-planning local women, who rely on Kate for everything from leadership to private emotional support—as does the whole Gulden family. George, on the other hand, is a frustrated novelist who will probably never complete the book he's been editing and rewriting for years. Initially suspecting him of cheating on Kate, Ellen discovers that he spends his evenings at a local bar, drowning his sorrows over his lack of talent.

As Kate's condition worsens, Ellen grows to admire her strength, especially when Kate insists on dying in her own home. Unable to move from her bed, Kate begs Ellen to help her end her life, but Ellen can't bring herself to help her mother commit suicide. After Kate finally dies, Ellen discovers an emptied bottle of pain medication in a kitchen waste basket. Ellen is questioned by the authorities, who have determined that Kate died from an overdose of painkillers. Assuming that George gave Kate the pills, Ellen lies and tells the district attorney that he wasn't home when Kate died. The case is dropped with no charges brought. George and Ellen meet at Kate's grave, where they discover each think the other gave Kate the pills: in reality, knowing both her daughter and husband were too weak to administer the painkillers, Kate must have managed to crawl out of bed and take the overdose on her own.

Though it won't leave many dry eyes, ONE TRUE THING never descends into mawkishness. Franklin and his cast are clearly more interested in discovering emotional truths than they are in delivering platitudes about a mother's love. The script by Franklin and Karen Croner (adapting a novel by *New York Times* columnist Anna Quindlen) powerfully conveys the chill at the core of many WASP families. While every serious performance by Streep seems to be hailed as "Oscar caliber," the phrase is appropriate here (and she was in fact nominated for Best Actress for this role). Her perfectly nuanced turn highlights the proceedings, and once again, she does some of her best work without even a line of dialogue—as when Kate wordlessly registers disappointment over the strained relations between Ellen and George. Zellweger and Hurt embody their characters with a range of realistically conflicted emotions, although Hurt, playing a bookish, distant intellectual, has clearly been down this road before (particularly in 1988's THE ACCIDENTAL TOURIST).

At first glance, ONE TRUE THING might appear to be little more than a feature-length soap opera, but the film's grasp of the emotional issues plaguing its fictional family is deep and remarkably resonant. *(Adult situations, profanity.)*—K.W.

d, Carl Franklin; p, Harry Ufland, Jesse Beaton; exec p, William W. Wilson III, Leslie Morgan; w, Carl Franklin, Karen Croner (based on the novel by Anna Quindlen); ph, Declan Quinn; ed, Carole Kravetz; m, Cliff Eidelman; prod d, Paul Peters; art d, Jefferson Sage; set d, Leslie A. Pope, Elaine O'Donnell; sound, Allan Byer (mixer); casting, Rick Pagano; cos, Donna Zakowska; makeup, Sharon Ilson

AAN Best Actress: Meryl Streep

Drama **(PR: C MPAA: R)**

ONI NO HANZO YAWAHADA KOBAN
(SEE: RAZOR: WHO'S GOT THE GOLD?, THE)

ONLY THRILL, THE ★½

(U.S., 1998) 103m Prestige Productions; Laureate Films; Gallery Motion Pictures; Moonstone Entertainment; Tennessee Valley Productions; G&G Entertainment ~ Legacy Releasing c

Diane Keaton *(Carol Fritzsimmons)*; Sam Shepard *(Reece McHenry)*; Diane Lane *(Katherine Fritzsimmons)*; Robert Patrick *(Tom McHenry)*; Sharon Lawrence *(Joleen Quillet)*; Stacey Travis *(Lola Jennings)*; Tate Donovan *(Eddie)*

Sam Shepard and Diane Keaton head a cast that deserves better than the telemovie-like material of THE ONLY THRILL, a sentimental tale of star-crossed lovers that covers three decades in the lives of a man and woman whose romance is continually thwarted while their children develop a similar relationship.

In 1966 Texas, used-clothing story owner Reece McHenry (Sam Shepard) hires widowed seamstress Carol Fritzsimmons (Diane Keaton), who is newly arrived in town. They begin an affair, which is centered around weekday matinees at the movies, but Reece's heart remains loyal to his wife, who lies in the hospital in a coma from which she'll never recover. Twelve years later, Reece's son Tom (Robert Patrick) begins dating Carol's daughter Katherine (Diane Lane). Carol and Reece are still together, but she is frustrated by his lack of commitment; after learning that her sister in Canada is terminally ill, she decides to move up there. Reece is stunned, as is Tom when Katherine tells him that she is leaving town to pursue an acting career. Carol moves to Canada, and after Reece visits her once, he makes no further attempt to contact her.

In 1990, Carol returns to Texas after her sister's death and meets Reece for a drink. Katherine is also briefly back in town and she picks up her affair with Tom, who's now a successful businessman who owns a chain of video stores. After Carol and Reece have a nasty fight about her leaving years before, during which she gets him to admit that his comatose wife was the love of his life, Carol and Katherine leave town again. Six years later, Reece and Tom are visited by Carol and Katherine, but Carol is now very ill, and Reece tells her that *she* was the love of his life. After Carol's funeral, Tom tells Reece that Katherine is leaving again and Reece screams at him to declare his love for her. Reece throws Tom into his car and chases Katherine down on the highway. They find her at a gas station and Tom asks her to stay. She agrees and they get married.

THE ONLY THRILL is the kind of trite talk-fest that comes into being only because a group of successful Hollywood stars are looking to do a low-budget indie about the "common folk" out there in the heartland. Unfortunately, Larry Ketron's script, based on his play "The Hitching Post," is schematic, poorly structured, and superficial, while Peter Masterson's direction is flat and stagy, with virtually no attention to detail in the depiction of the different eras. It's filled with the kind of artifice that is much more suited to the theatre than to film, such as condensing 30 years into under two hours by having a series of disconnected blackout scenes, and having the characters age via a variety of hokey wigs and makeup effects. Even worse is the theatrical technique of referring to major characters who are never seen and having important events occur offstage. Because Reece's wife is never shown, it's impossible to understand why he is so faithful to her that he would ruin his life, which negates the entire premise of the story. We also never see Carol's sister or learn what disease they both die from, nor the "momentous" first meeting between Tom and Katherine when they exchanged their first kiss as teenagers without knowing that their parents were dating.

Diane Lane is very appealing (and the only cast member who ages convincingly), and Sam Shepard is skillful at suggesting the bottled-up emotions of the inexpressive Reece, but both Robert Patrick and Diane Keaton seem too old and miscast for their roles. In any case, it would be impossible for any actor to triumph over the thin material. The only attempt at any sort of larger statement about the times is the obscure running gag that contrasts "movies" and "videos"—beginning with Reece seeing a VCR in the mid-70s after one his matinees with Carol, and continuing with Tom owning 10 video stores—which is presumably a metaphor for the loss of meaning in the world. After 90 minutes of banality, the film does generate some emotion at the end, when the aged Reece and the married Tom and Katherine are looking at their wedding pictures which are mixed in with pictures of a young Reece and Carol, but the effect is more depressing than poignant. *(Profanity, nudity, sexual situations.)*—M.S.

d, Peter Masterson; p, Yael Stroh, James Holt, Gabriel Grunfeld; exec p, Ernst "Etchie" Stroh, Peter Masterson, Carol Baum, Erin Martin Gorman; w, Larry Ketron (based on his play "The Hitching Post"); ph, Don E. FauntLeRoy; ed, Jeff Freeman; m, Peter Rodgers Melnick; prod d, John Frick; sound, Skip Frazee (mixer); casting, Ellen Kanner, Barbara Brinkley; cos, Jean-Pierre Dorleac

Romance/Drama **(PR: C MPAA: R)**

OPERATION CONDOR 2: THE ARMOUR OF THE GODS
(SEE: ARMOUR OF GOD)

OPERATION DELTA FORCE II: MAYDAY
(SEE: OPERATION DELTA FORCE 2)

OPERATION DELTA FORCE 2 ★★
(U.S., 1998) 98m Nu Image; Nu World Services ~ Nu Image c
(AKA: OPERATION DELTA FORCE II: MAYDAY)

Michael McGrady *(Capt. Skip Lang)*; J. Kenneth Campbell *(Lukash)*; Dale Dye *(Admiral Halsey Lang)*; Greg Melvill-Smith *(Sergei)*; Robert Whitehead *(Mikhail)*; Simon Jones *(Vickers)*; Robert Patteri *(McKinney)*; Todd Jensen *(Lombardi)*; Spencer Rochfort *(Hutch)*; Gavin Hood *(Sparks)*; James Whyle *(Bagley)*; Terence Reis *(Co-Pilot 1)*; Michael Brunner *(Capt. Lazareu)*; Brian O'Shaughnessy *(Admiral Henshaw)*; Danny Keogh *(Tuck)*; Dale Cutts *(Capt. Radchenkov)*; Iain Winter Smith *(Officer Alexiev)*; Douglas Bristo *(Ted Niles)*; Keith van Hoven *(Robert Malcom)*; Dehan Leibenberg *(Chet Hoskins)*; David Sherwood *(Capt. Beleve)*; Vadim Dobrin *(Ships Officer 2)*; Chris Buchanan *(Alexiev Sonar Officer)*; Clare Marshall *(Ruth Lang)*; Emily McArthur *(Annie Lang)*; Robbie Swaizland *(Tuck Lackey 1)*; Campbell Dalziel *(Tuck Lackey 2)*; Waddah Abdul Hassan *(Iraqui Officer)*; Wayne Giles *(Officer 1)*; Stephen Jennings *(Jack)*; Adrian Waldron *(Sonar Officer Bremov)*; Patrick Myhardt *(Vladimir)*; Victor Melleney *(Russian Military Officer)*

Despite a procession of violent set-tos, OPERATION DELTA FORCE 2 emerges as a sluggish action pic with only the "special forces team" concept in common with its predecessor. Bone-crusher flicks like this one need a star figure in firm command, but top-billed Michael McGrady makes no more of an impression than several of his supporting players.

The Kursk, a Russian nuclear submarine in the Bering Sea, is commandeered by master criminal Lukash (J. Kenneth Campbell) in league with Soviet traitors. At the same time, Lukash's partners hijack an ocean liner, planning to use the ship as a shield to prevent another Russian submarine (under authorization of the UN) from bombing the Kursk. They are also after the ship's captain, retired Admiral Halsey Lang (Dale Dye), the world's leading expert on nuclear subs. Lukash demands $25 billion in exchange for not striking at America's West Coast and several Russian cities. The meet his goal, Lukash has Admiral Lang transfered to the Kunsk and forces him to assume command of the sub.

To stop Lukash, The Pentagon assigns risk-taking Army Captain Skip Lang (Michael McGrady), the estranged son of of the kidnapped Admiral. Skip and his team of special forces soldiers are dropped onto the ship by helicopter; Skip leads the men in regaining control from Lukash's mercenaries. In return for Lukash's promise not to blow up the ocean liner, Admiral Lang agrees to pilot him and the Kursk to his destination, a Russian sub base.

Skip next attacks the sub base, and Lukash is wounded in the attack. He returns to the Kursk, where Admiral Lang prevents him from overriding the missiles' fail-safe system. While Skip grapples with Lukash and fatally stabs him, Admiral Lang sends out a Morse Code signal notifying the nearby U.N.-authorized Russian sub that the defused situation no longer necessitates that the Kursk be destroyed. Skip reconciles with his father.

In its desire to lend vigor to a strictly S.O.S. storyline, OPERATION DELTA FORCE 2 multiplies its rescue attempts to diminishing returns. Moreover, the screenplay is loaded with happenstance (such as the fact that Admiral Lang's wife and daughter are sailing on his luxury vessel). Aside from scripting detritus, this action-packed time-waster sprawls over so many international settings that viewers will be unsure of where they are at any given time. Although glint-eyed J. Kenneth Campbell enjoys quoting Poe while promising nuclear catastrophes, his co-stars appear to have matriculated at the I'll-Just-Collect-My-Paycheck branch of the Actors' Studio. They lack the wherewithal to elevate this above the level of a standard adventure tale.*(Graphic violence, extreme profanity.)*—R.P.

d, Yossi Wein ; p, Danny Lerner; exec p, Danny Dimbort, Trevor Short, Avi Lerner; w, David Sparling; ph, Peter Belcher; ed, Felix Meyburgh Jr.; m, Russell Stirling, Wessel van Rensburg; prod d, David Varod; art d, Carlos Da Silva; sound, Henry Prentice; fx, Janine Weinand; casting, Craig Campobasso; cos, Frances Susan Howie; makeup, Debra Fouche; stunts, Wade Eastwood

Action **(PR: C MPAA: R)**

OPPOSITE OF SEX, THE ★★★½
(U.S., 1998) 105m Original Voices ~
Sony Pictures Classics c

Christina Ricci *(Dedee Truitt)*; Martin Donovan *(Bill Truitt)*; Lisa Kudrow *(Lucia Dalury)*; Lyle Lovett *(Sheriff Carl Tippett)*; Johnny Galecki *(Jason Bock)*; Ivan Sergei *(Matt Mateo)*; William Scott Lee *(Randy)*; Megan Blake *(Bobette)*; Colin Ferguson *(Tom Dalury)*; Dan Bucatinsky *(Timothy)*; Chauncey Leopardi *(Joe)*; Rodney Eastman *(Ty)*; Heather Fairfield *(Jennifer)*; Amy Atkins *(TV Reporter)*; Leslie Grossman *(Girl Student)*; Emily Newman *(Marcia)*; Harrison Young *(Medical Examiner)*; Pancho Demmings *(Police Officer)*; Terry L. Rose *(Harley Man)*; Richard Moore *(Harley Man 2)*; Susan Leslie *(Judy Zale, Policewoman)*; Margaux St. Ledger *(Reporter)*; Leslie Bevis *(World News Reporter)*; Nicole Tocantins *(Bobette's Lawyer)*; Becky Wahlstrom *(Cashier)*; Peter Spears *(Doctor Allen)*; Kristine Keever *(Nurse)*; David Phelps-Williams *(School Principal)*; Todd Eckert *(Parole Office)*; Joyce Kurtz; Linda O. Cook; Malcolm Groome; Tim Dornberg; Robert Clotworthy; Tina Hart *(Group Voices)*

An art-house hit, THE OPPOSITE OF SEX is a wickedly funny black comedy about affairs of the loins and heart. It is marked by Christina Ricci in one of several attention-grabbing appearances she made in 1998, as a brazen bad girl with a scorched-earth policy regarding sex.

Immediately after her abusive stepfather's funeral, 16-year-old Dedee Truitt (Christina Ricci) flees Louisiana and lands on the doorstep of her openly gay half-brother Bill (Martin Donovan), an Indiana high-school teacher whose longtime companion, Tom, recently died of AIDS. Bill's current live-in lover is Matt (Ivan Sergei), a none-too-bright but very handsome young stud. Dedee convinces Matt that his homosexuality is just a theory based in prejudice, and seduces him. Soon after, Dedee announces she's pregnant.

Tom's sister Lucia (Lisa Kudrow), still very involved in Bill's life, convinces him to throw Dedee and Matt out. On the way, Dedee steals $10,000 and Tom's ashes. Matt's previous lover, Jason (Johnny Galecki), shows up looking for him. When Bill pleads ignorance, Jason, in a pique, makes false molestation charges against him. Local sheriff Carl Tippett (Lyle Lovett) tries to protect Bill, but soon he is embroiled in scandal.

Bill and Lucia track down Matt and Dedee in Los Angeles. He has married her, even though it is clear to everyone else that her advanced pregnancy predates his involvement with her. Dedee demands a ransom for Tom's ashes, so Bill and Lucia try to steal them back. In so doing, they catch Dedee having sex with Randy (William Scott Lee), her boyfriend from back home; exposed, the two run off. Sheriff Carl, who likes Lucia, has followed his friends to LA, and when they catch up with Dedee, she has shot and killed Randy; once again, she absconds with Matt.

Months pass. Jason reappears in Bill's life with the intention of extorting more money from him on Dedee's behalf. Instead, Bill forces Jason to take him to where Dedee and Matt have been hiding out. Lucia follows them, and Carl follows her. All wind up in Canada, and are on hand when Dedee has her baby. Jason and Matt reunite, Lucia and Carl get married and have a baby, and Dedee leaves her child in the care of Bill and his new lover (her parole officer), while she hits the road on her own.

The directorial debut of writer Don Roos, THE OPPOSITE OF SEX is an absolute hoot, filled with vicious behavior, cynical observation, and caustic wit. It's the kind of harsh and screwy affair the great Preston Sturges might have concocted, had he been freed from the constraints of the Production Code. Roos cements the film's mordant point of view by having Dedee provide a voice-over narration that mixes hilarious, politically incorrect invective with sardonic self-commentary ("I don't have a heart of gold, and I don't grow one later, okay?"). Dedee's contempt extends even to us, the audience. Through her, Roos plays a cat-and-mouse game, taunting us with phony, heart-tugging moments (Dedee tragically dies during labor), then mocking us for falling for it ("I didn't die, I'm the narrator. . . *duh*.").

With her performances here and the concurrent BUFFALO '66, Ricci firmly established herself in 1998 as not just an actress of immense talent, but a tremendous screen presence as well. Fleshy and voluptuous, with a platinum blonde dye-job topping her moon-pie face, Ricci is a wonder to behold, at once childlike and baleful, vulnerable and petulant.

THE OPPOSITE OF SEX also contains a terrific, eye-opening performance by Lisa Kudrow. Exploding her ditsy persona from the TV sitcom "Friends," Kudrow pulls off the difficult feat of making Lucia a complex, funny, and sympathetic character instead of a stock villain, and Roos rewards her with some of the movie's best lines. *(Profanity, sexual situations, violence.)*—P.R.

d, Don Roos; p, David Kirkpatrick, Michael Besman; exec p, Jim Lotfi, Steve Danton; w, Don Roos; ph, Hubert Taczanowski; ed, David Codron; m, Mason Daring; prod d, Michael Clausen; set d, Kristen V. Peterson; sound, Jon Ailetcher; casting, Amanda Mackey Johnson, Cathy Sandrich; cos, Peter Mitchell; makeup, Sergio Lopez-Rivera; stunts, Gary Weston

Comedy/Drama **(PR: C MPAA: R)**

ORGAZMO ★★½
(U.S., 1998) 90m Kuzui Enterprises; Avenging Concience Productions; MDP Worldwide ~ October Films c

Trey Parker *(Joe Young)*; Robyn Lynne Raab *(Lisa)*; Dian Bachar *(Ben Chapleski)*; Michael Dean Jacobs *(Maxxx Orbison)*; Ron Jeremy *(Clark)*; Andrew W. Kemler *(Rodgers)*; David Dunn *(A-Cup)*; Matt Stone *(Dave "The Lightning Guy")*; Toddy Walters *(Georgi)*; Chasey Lain *(Candi)*; Juli Ashton *(Saffi)*; Masao "Maki" San *(G-Fresh)*; Joseph Arsenault *(Jimmy "The Fish")*; Jeff Schubert *(Tommy "The Shark")*; Desi Singh *(Randy "The Guppy")*; Stan Sawicki *(Robert White)*; Ken Merckx *(Original Orgazmo)*; Buff Grey *(Security Guard)*; Cathy Fitzpatrick *(Older Porn Actress)*; Marcus Vaughn *(White Stunt Cock)*; Anna Kazuki *(Nasuko)*; Eve *(Haruko)*; Jeffery Bowman *(Porn Actor)*; T-Rex *(The Fat Lady Stripper)*; Shayla Laveaux *(Greek Porno Actress)*; John Marlo *(Sancho)*; Stanley L. Kaufman *(Doctor)*; Jill Kelly *(Nurse)*; Miyu Natsuki *(G-Fresh's Daughter)*; Mao Yamada *(G-Fresh's Daughter)*

Before cocreating the animated TV series "South Park," Trey Parker scripted, directed, and starred in this low-budget, high-spirited cult comedy. Short on big laughs but chock-full of subversive charms, the film features Parker as a mild-mannered Mormon who becomes an adult-movie superstar, and ultimately, a real-life superhero.

While bringing door-to-door religion to the residents of Los Angeles, Mormon missionary Joe Young (Trey Parker) accidentally interrupts porno-magnate Maxxx Orbison (Michael Dean Jacobs) in the middle of a shoot. When bodyguards go after Joe, he turns into a kickboxing dervish, and Maxxx is so impressed that he offers this Latter-Day Saint the lead in his latest effort, playing a costumed superhero named Orgazmo, who immobilizes villains with his orgasm-producing Orgazmorator. When Joe is hesitant, Maxxx offers him $20,000 (as well as a "stunt-cock", so Joe won't have to have sex). Since this money will allow Joe and fiancee Lisa (Robyn Lynne Raab) to be married in Salt Lake City's expensive Mormon Temple, he accepts.

Using the pseudonym Tom Hung, Joe is initiated into the world of adult moviemaking, befriending costar Ben Chapleski (Dian Bachar), a scientific whiz who plays Orgazmo's dildo-helmeted sidekick, Choda Boy. Later, Ben shows Joe his newest invention, an actual, working Orgazmorator. When the movie "Orgazmo" is released, it quickly becomes the third largest-grossing film of all time, and even spawns a line of action toys. Still, Joe never receives the money promised to him by Maxxx, who begins cajoling him to star in a sequel.

Complicating matters, Lisa surprises Joe with a visit to Los Angeles, unaware of her fiance's occupation. But when Joe tries to quit his job, Maxxx induces him to finish the film by kidnapping Lisa. Having reached his breaking point, Joe invade's Maxxx's estate with Ben. The two are armed with Ben's amazing inventions. Beating Maxxx's henchmen senseless, and repeatedly using the Orgazmorator on Maxxx, Lisa is saved and Maxxx is in need of medical help. Ditching their plans to move back to Salt Lake City, Joe and Lisa decide to stay in LA and fight crime.

Beginning with a hilarious title tune that spoofs machismo, ORGAZMO proudly wears its wiseass sense of humor like a badge of honor. Thus, even if individual jokes fall flat, certain scenes are saved by the good-naturedness of the whole enterprise. More playfully humorous than the acerbic "South Park," this is closer in spirit to Parker's likable feature debut CANNIBAL! THE MUSICAL (1996), with its refreshingly uncynical characters. In addition to unleashing a barrage of nonstop puns (when someone swears "Jesus!", Joe suddenly looks about and asks "Where?"), Parker uses his fish-out-of-water scenario to spoof different movie cliches and the cut-rate aspirations of adult movies.

Parker makes a sincerely amiable leading man, as his character does all he can to retain his religious convictions—even when a 400 pound, nearly naked woman is straddling him. The rest of the cast is appropriately cartoonish, with gravity-challenged porn legend Ron Jeremy playing one of Orgazmo's on- and off-screen nemeses, and real-life porn starlets Chasey Lain, Juli Ashton, and Shayla LaVeaux providing the pulchritude. Meanwhile, Parker's "South Park" partner Matt Stone steals every scene he's in as a slow-witted, perpetually overexcited crew member. ORGAZMO is quite possibly the most benign film to ever receive an NC-17 rating.

Despite its porn-industry backdrop, the film never indulges in blatant sex and nudity, even though they're a constant topic of conversation (there are countless views of bare derrieres, but no breasts or privates on display). More likely, the MPAA rated the film based on its sophomoric view of the porno world and its casual deviance. Parker obviously did his research in the adult-movie profession, as evidenced by several in-jokes, including an explanation of the obscure adult-film term "DVDA" (a definition that's best left out of these pages). Parker is on safest ground, however, when spoofing superhero conventions; where else but in ORGAZMO can you find crimefighters who drive a Buick Century stationwagon? *(Graphic violence, nudity, sexual situations, extreme profanity.)*—S.P.

d, Trey Parker; p, Jason McHugh, Fran Rubel Kuzui, Matt Stone; exec p, Kaz Kazui, Mark Damon, Noriaki Nakagawa; assoc p, Farrell Timlake, Anthony Mindel; w, Trey Parker; ph, Kenny Gioseffi; ed, Trey Parker, Michael Miller; m, Paul Robb; prod d, Tristan Paris Bourne; set d, Mandana Yamin; sound, Jon Ailetcher; casting, Katy Wallin, T. Edwin Klohn; cos, Kristen Anacker

Comedy/Action **(PR: O MPAA: NC-17)**

OSCAR WILDE

(SEE: WILDE)

OTHER SIDE OF SUNDAY, THE ★★★★

(Norway, 1996) 103m NRK Drama ~ First Look Pictures c

(SONDAGS ENGLER)

Marie Theisen *(Maria)*; Bjorn Sundquist *(Father)*; Sylvia Salvesen *(Mother)*; Hildegunn Riise *(Fru Tunheim)*; Martin Dahl Garfalk *(Olav)*; Ina Sofie Brodahl *(Anna)*; Ann Kristin Rasmussen *(Birgit)*; Jorgen Langhelle *(Young Priest)*; Hallvard Holmen *(Seaman)*; Kai Kennet Hanson *(Bard)*; Peter Width Kristiansen *(Pal Hedge)*; Henriette Engesaeth; Kristian Aaby *(Stian)*

Delicately extracted from the famous Norwegian novel *Sunday*, this 1996 Oscar nominee for Best Foreign Language Film is that rarity: a successful female coming-of-age movie. Skillfully directed and written with uncommon sensitivity, THE OTHER SIDE OF SUNDAY bursts at the seams with life.

In 1959, impressionable 16-year-old Maria (Marie Theisen) bristles under the regimented code of behavior imposed by her father, the Vicar (Bjorn Sundquist). When she earns a B grade at school, he rigidly insists on tutoring; when her mother suffers from ulceritis, he forbids Maria's favorite pastime, playing the piano.

Marie begins to rebel by questioning the instruction classes she is required to attend for her upcoming Confirmation. She becomes friends with widowed Mrs. Tunheim (Hildegunn Riise), the church organist, who proves to be a kindred spirit. She is shocked to overhear her self-righteous father breaking off a secret relationship with Mrs. Tunheim. She responds to her father's hypocrisy by challenging him with blasphemous reasoning and cutting her religious classes to hang out with her worldlier school chums. She is encouraged by Mrs. Tunheim, who begs Maria not to follow her life of self-sacrifice. Opting to keep peace for her family's sake, Maria docilely prepares for her Confirmation. But after the despairing Mrs. Tunheim drowns herself, Maria recalls her advice to "do what I never dared" and walks away from her Church and its demand for self-denial.

This alternately humorous and mournful saga studies the incubation of a teen's self-identity. With passion and compassion, it salutes a free spirit who survives peer pressure and parental emotional abuse to accept her own individuality. Where more superficial films about adolescent angst incorporate narration as a colorful addendum, THE OTHER SIDE OF SUNDAY makes Maria's interior monologues an integral, ongoing part of its psychological journey. Surrounded by inferior role models, Maria discovers herself by trial and error. Played with subtle power by the iridescent Marie Theisen, the sensibly heroic Maria is a remarkable protagonist, an unfinished woman who refuses to have her personality "completed" by her father's repressive standards. Nor does THE OTHER SIDE OF SUNDAY caricature its adult characters; the audience appreciates how Maria's mother came by her ulcer and understands that Maria's father is himself a victim of the Church.

What gives this evocative movie its forward thrust is its celebration of Maria's progress from dutiful daughter to a woman with a will of her own. Rejecting the slow death of martyrdom, Maria achieves maturity not through sexual experience but via a decision to worship her God with music, sensuality, and an intuitive affinity for expressing love openly. *(Extreme profanity, nudity, sexual situations, adult situations, substance abuse.)*—R.P.

d, Berit Nesheim; p, Grete Rypdal, Oddvar Bull-Tuhus; w, Berit Nesheim, Lasse Glomm (based on the novel *Sunday* by Reidun Nortvedt); ph, Arne Borsheim; ed, Lillian Fjellvaer; m, Bent

Aserud, Geir Bohren; prod d, Grethe Heier; art d, Grethe Heier; sound, Jan Lindvik; cos, Gro Gillesen

AAN Best Foreign Language Film

Drama/Comedy **(PR: C MPAA: NR)**

OUT OF SIGHT ★★★½

(U.S., 1998) 129m Jersey Films; Universal ~ Universal Pictures c

George Clooney *(Jack Foley)*; Jennifer Lopez *(Karen Sisco)*; Ving Rhames *(Buddy Bragg)*; Don Cheadle *(Maurice (Snoopy) Miller)*; Dennis Farina *(Marshall Sisco)*; Albert Brooks *(Richard Ripley)*; Michael Keaton *(Ray Nicolette—Uncredited)*; Samuel L. Jackson *(Hejira—Uncredited)*; Jim Robinson *(Bank Employee)*; Elgin Marlow *(Bank Customer)*; Donna Frenzel *(Loretta Bank Teller)*; Manny Suarez *(Cop in Bank 1)*; Keith Hudson *(Cop in Bank 2)*; Luis Guzman *(Chino)*; Paul Soileau *(Lulu)*; Scott Allen *(Pup)*; Catherine Keener *(Adele)*; Susan Hatfield *(Parking Lot Woman)*; Steve Zahn *(Glenn Michaels)*; Brad Martin *(White Boxer)*; James Black *(Himey)*; Wendell B. Harris Jr. *(Daniel Burdon, FBI)*; Chuck Castleberry *(Library Guard)*; Chic Daniel *(Fourth FBI Man)*; Connie Sawyer *(Old Elevator Lady)*; Phil Perlman *(Old Elevator Gent)*; Keith Loneker *(Bob, White Boy)*; Isaiah Washington *(Kenneth)*; Paul Calderon *(Raymond Cruz)*; Gregory H. Alpert *(Officer Grant)*; Viola Davis *(Moselle)*; Mark Brown *(Ripley Personnel)*; Sandra Ives *(Receptionist)*; Joe Hess *(Ripley Guard)*; Betsy Monroe *(Celeste, Waitress)*; Wayne Pere *(Executive Guy/Philip)*; Joe Chrest *(Andy, Executive Guy)*; Joe Coyle *(Executive Guy 3)*; Nancy Allen *(Midge)*; Stephen M. Horn *(Federal Marshall)*

Jersey Films, the production team behind 1995's GET SHORTY, mine another Elmore Leonard novel to serve up a second helping of hip crime entertainment with OUT OF SIGHT. While not as lighthearted, OUT OF SIGHT offers the same combination of appealing characters and snappy dialogue that made GET SHORTY a hit, as well as breakout performances by both George Clooney and Jennifer Lopez.

Bank robber and frequent incarceree Jack Foley (George Clooney) sees a clumsy prison break attempt as his ticket out of a Florida penitentiary. Tipping the guards to the breakout, Jack uses the ensuing confusion as cover and with the help of his friend Buddy Bragg (Ving Rhames) manages to get outside the fence. Unfortunately, they are surprised by US Marshal Karen Sisco (Jennifer Lopez), and are forced to throw her in the trunk of the car where Jack is hiding as Buddy drives to safety. While locked in the trunk together, a strange chemistry bubbles between Karen (who has a thing for unsavory types) and Jack (who is actually a pretty nice guy). They meet up with their partner, a bumbling stoner named Glenn (Steve Zahn), but Karen bullies Glenn into driving away, leaving Buddy and Jack standing by the road.

On the run, Jack and Buddy head north to Detroit for one last big score—a rich banker who, while in jail in Florida for inside trading, revealed that he keeps millions of dollars in uncut diamonds in his home. When they get to the Motor City, though, they find that Glenn has arrived ahead of them and has fallen in with another former Florida con, Maurice "Snoopy" Miller (Don Cheadle), and his murderous partner Kenneth (Isaiah Washington); what's more, Karen's interest in Jack—both romantic and professional—has led her to Detroit as well. Jack and Karen finally meet again in a hotel bar, where they decide to spend one night together as a "time out"—no cops, no robbers, just two regular people. The next day, though, it's back to business: Jack and Buddy, along with Snoopy and Kenneth, go to the rich man's house, with Karen close behind. Knowing things are going to get ugly, Jack sends Buddy out of harm's way. When Snoopy tries to doublecross Jack, the ensuing shootout dispatches both Snoopy and Kenneth, leaving Jack to deal with Karen. Determined not to go back to jail, Jack tries to convince Karen to shoot him, which she does. . . in the leg. Though she arrests him, Karen arranges for Jack to share the long ride back to Florida with an accomplished prison break artist (an uncredited Samuel L. Jackson), hoping he can pick up some tips so they might someday be reunited.

In an interview shortly before the release of OUT OF SIGHT, novelist Elmore Leonard explained the secret to adapting his fiction: leave it alone. Evidently, screenwriter Scott Frank already knew this. Just as he did with GET SHORTY, Frank lets Leonard do much of the talking in OUT OF SIGHT, taking large portions of dialogue from the novel word-for-word. Instead of tough talk, Leonard's characters speak from a combination of experience and ignorance; instead of relying on Schwartzeneggerian one-liners for humor, they exhibit a not-unfamiliar quirkiness—Buddy calls his sister after (and sometimes before) each heist to assuage his guilt, while Karen's protective father gives her a new gun for her birthday.

OUT OF SIGHT treats viewers to superb performances by both George Clooney and Jennifer Lopez, two actors who have been looking for breakout roles. Clooney, in particular, needed a character like Jack Foley to put behind him his good work in mediocre films (FROM DUSK TILL DAWN, ONE FINE DAY) and mediocre performances in terrible films (BATMAN & ROBIN). Here, Clooney is finally able to play savvy, funny, and sexy all at once (the kind of combination that got him noticed on television's "ER" in the first place). Lopez, too, can use the tough Karen Sisco as a means to forget about ANACONDA and U TURN (both 1997). The supporting cast—including Ving Rhames, Don Cheadle, and Dennis Farina—is simply stellar, especially Steve Zahn as the drug-addled Glenn.

Though advertised as something of a GET SHORTY sequel, OUT OF SIGHT has a much darker feel, largely due to director Steven Soderbergh's (SEX, LIES, AND VIDEOTAPE) use of handheld cameras, grainy filmstock, and super-saturated colors. His film is also more violent than GET SHORTY, though not excessively so. Still, Soderbergh's flashy style and dry comic touch fits nicely alongside director Barry Sonnenfeld's GET SHORTY, giving us hope for possible future Jersey Films-Elmore Leonard collaborations. *(Violence, profanity.)*—B.T.

d, Steven Soderbergh; p, Danny DeVito, Michael Shambert, Stacey Sher; exec p, Barry Sonnenfeld, John Hardy; w, Scott Frank (based on the novel by Elmore Leonard); ph, Elliot Davis; ed, Anne V. Coates; m, Cliff Martinez; prod d, Gary Frutkoff; art d, Phil Messina; set d, Maggie Martin; sound, Paul Ledford (mixer); fx, Carol Lynn Wenger, Clifford P. Wenger; casting, Francine Maisler; cos, Betsy Heimann; makeup, Katherine James

AAN Best Adapted Screenplay: Scott Frank; *AAN Best Film Editing:* Anne V. Coates

Crime/Romance/Comedy **(PR: C MPAA: R)**

OUT OF THE PAST ★★★

(U.S., 1998) 65m Inverted Pictures ~ Zeitgeist Films/Unapix Films c/bw

Kelli Peterson; George Chauncey; Lillian Faderman; Reverend Peter Gomes; Linda Hunt *(Narrator)*; VOICES OF: Stephen Spinella *(Michael Wigglesworth)*; Gwyneth Paltrow *(Sarah Orne Jewett)*; Cherry Jones *(Annie Adams Fields)*; Edward Norton *(Henry Gerber)*; Leland Gantt *(Bayard Rustin)*

By the late 1990s, documentaries on the gay-lesbian experience in America were old news. The virtue of Jeff Dupre's prosaically entitled OUT OF THE PAST is making a potentially shopworn topic fresh and urgent.

Dupre hangs his selective chronicle of homosexual rights on the framework of a well-publicized court case in Utah in 1995. High school student Kelli Peterson tried to establish a "Gay-Straight Alliance" for teenagers and their families in the school district, to promote dialogue and prevent any potential problems in the community. The school administration, in conservative Salt Lake City, rejected Peterson's application to use their facilities. Peterson took legal action, supported by a variety of gay activists, claiming her club had as much right as anyone to meet on school property.

"I thought about killing myself," goes Peterson's voice-over narration. "If I would have known that history was full of people like me I would have been different," cueing segments about prominent gay Americans, mostly obscure, and the persecution they faced (tacitly compared to Kelli's problems). Michael Wigglesworth (voice of Stephen Spinella), a 17th-century Puritan minister and early Harvard instructor, penned fire-and-brimstone religious tracts—but in his personal diary entries, admitted his own homosexual urges and torment. A few centuries later, popular writer Sarah Orne Jewett (voice of Gwyneth Paltrow) was able to enjoy a "Boston marriage" to her companion Annie Fields. A backlash at the turn of the 20th century made such same-sex unions socially unacceptable, and Jewett was unable to find a publisher for her collected love letters to Annie. In 1924, Chicago's Henry Gerber (voice of Edward Norton) started the "Society for Human Rights," the first known American homosexual advocacy group. Police confiscated his newsletter, and Gerber was fired from his job for "conduct unbecoming of a postal worker." In the 1960s, Bayard Rustin (voice of Leland Gantt) was a black civil rights pioneer and key advisor to Martin Luther King. He was also a homosexual, and has been carefully marginalized in mainstream accounts of Afro-American emancipation. In a return to Kelli Peterson's story, the case goes to the Utah state legislature which, rather than recognize the Gay-Straight Alliance's right to exist, took the dire step of banning *all* student extracurricular clubs.

One might accuse Ms. Peterson of being a trifle disingenuous. This is, after all, Salt Lake City, Utah, not a place normally associated with social liberalism and rainbow-colored diversity. Nonetheless, the authorities' "solution" to punish everyone in order to keep one gay group out of school demonstrates how deep homophobia runs in the white, affluent gentry. Still, one is struck by the busloads of picketers who carpetbag into the Beehive State to protest (on camera) on behalf of Peterson, who does seem a bit overwhelmed by the controversy. Henry Gerber certainly never enjoyed such support.

The short running time is just about right. Filmmaker Dupre formerly worked for documentary historian Ken Burns, whose influence clearly shows in the montages of vintage photographs and documents used to bring the past to life. One is struck by the fact that, especially in Bayard Rustin's case, history is written not just by the winners, but by the winners' censors, and OUT OF THE PAST does its modest part in setting the record straight. *(Adult situations.)*—C.C.

d, Jeff Dupre; p, Jeff Dupre; exec p, Andrew Tobias; assoc p, Kevin Jennings; co-p, Eliza Starr Byard, Michelle Ferrari; w, Michelle Ferrari; ph, Buddy Squires; ed, George O'Donnell, Toby Shimin; m, Matthias Gohl

Documentary **(PR: C MPAA: NR)**

OUTSIDE OZONA ★½

(U.S., 1998) 99m Millenium Films ~ Columbia TriStar c

Robert Forster *(Odell Parks)*; Kevin Pollak *(Wit Roy)*; Sherilyn Fenn *(Marcy Duggan)*; David Paymer *(Alan Defaux)*; Penelope Ann Miller *(Earlene Demers)*; Swoosie Kurtz *(Rosalee)*; Taj Mahal *(Dix Mayal)*; Meat Loaf *(Floyd Bibbs)*; Lucy Webb *(Agent Deene)*; Lois Red Elk *(Effie Twosalt)*; Kateri Walker *(Reba Twosalt)*; F.J. Flynn *(Percy)*; Beth Ann Styne *(Bonnie Mimms)*; Kirk Baily *(Agent Cole)*; Jack Leal *(Agent Caloca)*; Michael Homes *(Truck Stop Owners)*; Bert Emmett *(Agent Krich)*; Benjamin Lum *(Convenience Store Clerk)*; Merideth Mills *(Rhonda)*; Ed Anders *(Strip Club Patron)*; Matt Prescott Morton *(Patrolman)*; Forest Freedom Guider *(Garage Attendant)*; Tony Bernard *(Red)*; Kendall Leigh Wyman *(Lorraine)*; David Carpenter *(Trucker)*; Heidi Jo Markel *(Secretary)*; Ben McCain *(Monty Radio Caller)*; Dylan Tarason *(Strip Club D.J.)*; Butch McCain *(Radio Furniture Salesman)*; Ben McCain *(Radio Furniture Salesman)*; Ray Pichette *(Otto)*; Patti Duce *(Margaret Chanute)*; Fergie *(Girl)*

It's hard to believe that J.S. Cardone, who wrote and directed the 1996 straight-to-video gem BLACK DAY BLUE NIGHT, was responsible for this misfire about a psychopathic serial killer on the loose. When J.T. Walsh died suddenly three days before his scheduled first day on the set of OUTSIDE OZONA, Robert Forster stepped in and assumed his friend's role.

As an unidentified serial killer stalks the badlands of Oklahoma, radio DJ Dix Mayal (Taj Mahal) embarks on a vitriolic broadcast while his insecure station manager (Meat Loaf) frets. Among Dix's legions of listeners are Odell Parks (Robert Forster), a recently widowed truckdriver en route to El Paso. During his trip, Odell meets Reba Twosalt (Kateri Walker), a Navajo woman who is taking her dying grandmother (Lois Red Elk) to see the Gulf of Mexico. Strongly attracted to Reba, the lonely trucker promises to look her up later.

Also on the road are Wit Roy (Kevin Pollak), a circus clown, and his girlfriend Earlene Demers (Penelope Ann Miller). Wit has just been fired for punching out his boss Otto (Ray Pichette) after learning that Earlene has slept with Otto to advance Wit's career. En route to Las Vegas, Earlene takes a job as a stripper, but Wit forces her to quit on her first night of employment. Now very low on cash, Wit holds up a liquor store, but Earlene makes him return the money he has stolen.

Meanwhile, two bickering sisters on their way to their father's funeral (Sherilyn Fenn and Beth Ann Styne) pick up Alan Defaux (David Paymer), a psychiatrist whose car has apparently broken down. Defaux kills and mutilates both women, then calls Dix's listener call-in line, on which he reveals himself to be a religious fanatic. Odell, Wit, Earlene, Reba, her grandmother, and Defaux are involved in a massive four-vehicle accident outside Ozona. All except the mad killer survive.

A road movie in disrepair, OUTSIDE OZONA is tatty, preachy, and unoriginal. Nor is it enhanced by its underlit photography, except in a scene set in a disquietingly dark roadside rest room. A couple of touching moments are contributed by Penelope Ann Miller when Earlene boldly but lovingly stands up to her rather imperious boyfriend, but Cardone makes very little effort to generate suspense or thrills (perhaps a blessing in a film whose villain is a mad slasher). And far too much emphasis is given to Dix's attack on such safe targets as Ku Klux Klanners, Nazis, killers of abortion doctors, and crazed religious fundamentalists. Even the viewer who endorses every one of the stock liberal pieties reiterated in OUTSIDE OZONA may feel badgered by the movie's mindless political filibustering. Other viewers not likely to be fans of OUTSIDE OZONA are those Native

Americans who are getting tired of being represented on the screen as saints.

If one can assume that the film's characters were not meant to be inarticulate, one must conclude that a great deal of OUTSIDE OZONA's dialogue in unintentionally clumsy. For example, when Wit complains to Earlene that one of her strip club patrons "was looking right up your name and address," does the inclusion of the word *right* signal a screenwriting gaffe, or Wit's inability to tell a joke? And what is one to make of the following portion of Dix's film-ending monologue: "The big game was just knocking on my door—I had the whole nine yards by the fucking tail and I let it go. I let it go cause I didn't have the brass balls to move in the fast lane." Here, metaphors have not merely been mixed, they've been stirred, whipped, and beaten. *(Violence, nudity, extreme profanity.)*—D.T.

d, J.S. Cardone; p, Scott Einbeinder, Carol Kottenbrook; exec p, Avi Lerner, Trevor Short, Boaz Davidson, Danny Dimbort, John Thompson; w, J.S. Cardone; ph, Irek Hartowicz; ed, Amanda Kirpaul; m, Taj Mahal, Johnny Lee Schell; prod d, Martina Buckley; art d, Hector Velez; set d, Ivana Letica; sound, George Bruton Goen II; casting, Abra Edelman, Elisa Goodman; cos, Bonnie Stauch; makeup, Carlan Matz; stunts, Ed Anders

Crime/Thriller/Drama **(PR: C MPAA: R)**

OVERNIGHT DELIVERY ★½

(U.S., 1998) 88m New Line Cinema ~ New Line c

Reese Witherspoon *(Ivy Miller)*; Paul Rudd *(Wyatt Trips)*; Larry Drake *(Hal Ipswich)*; Christine Taylor *(Kimberly)*; Tobin Bell *(John Dwayne Beezly)*; Carl Anthony Payne II *(Wheels)*; Gary Wolf *(Snake)*; Kurt Schweikhardt *(Cop #1)*; Buffy Sedlachek *(Teacher)*; Tim McNiff *(TV Anchor)*; Gale Plewacki *(Roving Reporter)*; Tamara Mello *(Marita)*; John Sylvain *(Deejay)*; William Byrd Wilkins *(Bouncer)*; John Beasley *(Baker)*; John Walsh *(Dick)*; Stephen Yoakam *(SWAT Leader)*; Bruce Bohne *(Sniper)*; Maile Flanagan *(Gas Jockey)*; Peter Schmitz *(Ticket Agent)*; Grant Richey *(Waiter)*; Bill Schoppert *(Officer #1)*; Barbara Kingsley *(Waitress)*; Emil Herrera *(Short Order Cook)*; Jay Gjernes *(Drunk Man)*; John Clay Scott *(Florist)*; Matthew Klemp *("The Ricker")*

A mismatched couple hit the road, searching for a wrongfully-mailed package, in this misguided comic-romance. Despite a genial cast, this straight-to-video movie offers little that's new; it instead makes a classic like IT HAPPENED ONE NIGHT (1934) look more innovative than ever.

Minnesota college freshman Wyatt Trips (Paul Rudd) is frustrated that longtime girlfriend Kimberly (Christine Taylor) won't go all the way. Wrongfully thinking that Kimberly, who is 1000 miles away at her Memphis college, is cheating on him, Wyatt gets drunk at a local strip bar and meets student/exotic-dancer Ivy Miller (Reese Witherspoon). With her help, he sends a vicious break-up letter to Kimberly, via overnight delivery, only to learn that the "other man" he suspected she was seeing is actually a dog she's taking care of.

With only one day to stop the package's delivery, and with every imaginable obstacle in their path, panic-stricken Wyatt and hard-boiled Ivy hit the road. They attempt to steal the letter back from a slow-witted, Global Express driver (Larry Drake), without any luck. Later the couple deal with uncooperative airport personnel, the destruction of Ivy's car, and, amidst much squabbling, Ivy's developing affection for the lovelorn Wyatt. After being arrested for ditching their tab at a roadside diner, they accidentally blow up the Global Express truck containing the package—-which still doesn't stop the driver from his mission. Making it to the Memphis campus at the last possible moment, Wyatt swings into action and stops the delivery—-only to realize that he's in love with Ivy, and Kimberly has been unfaithful after all. Allowing his venomous letter to be delivered, Ivy and Wyatt ponder their next destination together.

This "comic" road-movie contains no real laughs, but it does have a carload of generic, sitcom-like plot twists. The premise, of course, couldn't be sustained if any of the lead characters had a lick of common sense—-or if Wyatt would simply make a calm, rational phone call, explaining the situation. The filmmakers clearly banked on the fact that the lead performers are so charming that the viewer wouldn't take the time to notice the cliches trotted out. Rudd and Witherspoon do indeed have natural appeal, but they're given little chance to show it here, as director Jason Bloom piles one outlandish situation onto another. And, in spite of the surface tension between the characters, it's evident from the first that they are going to wind up together. Though filled to overflowing with "screwball" developments (when attempting to take a flight at one point, Wyatt is instead taken hostage by a wanted killer) and physical slapstick (Wyatt is dragged down a highway until the backside of his pants disappear), OVERNIGHT DELIVERY's strained attempts at comic quirkiness only serve to irritate. *(Violence, sexual situations, profanity.)*—S.P.

d, Jason Bloom; p, Brad Krevoy, Steven Stabler, Dan Etheridge; exec p, Roger Birnbaum, Brad Jenkel; assoc p, Amanda Moose; w, Marc Sedaka, Steve Bloom; ph, Edward J. Pei; ed, Luis Colina; m, Andrew Gross; prod d, Marek Dobrowolski; art d, Scott Meehan; set d, Diana L. Stoughton; cos, Kathleen Detoro

Comedy/Romance **(PR: C MPAA: PG-13)**

OYSTER AND THE WIND, THE ★★★½

(Brazil, 1997) 112m Ravina Filmes; Rio Filmes c

(A OSTRA E O VENTO)

Lima Duarte *(Jose)*; Leandra Leal *(Marcela)*; Fernando Torres *(Daniel)*; Floriano Peixoto *(Roberto)*; Castrinho *(Pepe)*; Debora Bloch *(Mother)*; Arduino Colasanti; Marcio Vito; Ricardo Marecos *(Sailors)*

THE OYSTER AND THE WIND is a provocative and often mesmerizing film. Set entirely on a small island, the film examines a father-and-daughter relationship destroyed by emerging sexuality and repressed passion.

A group of men in a supply boat arrives on a small island which serves as a lighthouse station. They find no trace of the island's three inhabitants: the lighthouse keeper, Jose (Lima Duarte); his teenaged daughter, Marcela (Leandra Leal); and Jose's simple-minded assistant, Roberto (Floriano Peixoto). In an effort to learn the whereabouts of the three, the men read through Jose's log and Marcela's diary. The writings reveal that Marcela is an intensely lonely girl on the verge of womanhood, who sees herself as trapped on the island. Jose is insensitive to his daughter's feelings, and makes things worse through a jealousy that manifests itself as overprotection. Roberto's assignment to the island provokes a crisis between the two. Marcela is excited by the young man's arrival, and although Roberto sometimes taunts her childishly, she finds him charming. Jose, though, considers him a danger to his daughter, and warns Roberto to stay away from her.

Marcela, exasperated by her father's possessiveness, plots his demise. On a stormy night, she tells her father that a shipwreck has occurred just off the island. Jose hears nothing but takes his daughter at her word. He and Roberto climb into a lifeboat, unaware that Marcela has cut a hole in it. Marcela at first rejoices as she sees her father go off into the dark, choppy waters, unconcerned that she is endangering Roberto as well. She experiences a change of heart, however, and cries out to Jose that she has lied. Jose cannot hear her and continues into the storm.

Sometime later, the group of men from the supply boat find the bodies of Jose and Roberto rolling in the surf. They take the corpses back to the mainland, but their leader, Daniel (Fernando Torres) stays behind to search for Marcela. He continues to read through her diary for clues, but suffers a fatal heart attack and dies without learning her fate.

THE OYSTER AND THE WIND is set up as a mystery, but Brazilian director Walter Lima Jr. (a veteran of the *cinema novo* movement) seems less interested in solving a puzzle than in exploring and analyzing the feelings and motivations of his characters. The film employs a fragmented narrative that frustrates an easy comprehension of events, abruptly shifting between time periods, points of view, and real and imagined happenings—sometimes within the same shot. The effect is jarring, and at times confusing, but this approach succeeds in moving one's attention away from the question of what happened to why it did. In this, Lima risks incoherence, but he maintains such masterful control over the proceedings that by the film's end, the details that lead to the tragic resolution of a troubled relationship between Jose and Marcela all come together.

Visually and aurally, THE OYSTER AND THE WIND is exquisite. Lima and cinematographer Pedro Farkas manage to make the island both alluring and threatening, the island's natural beauty contrasting with its otherworldliness. The sound of waves and wind are heard constantly on the soundtrack through the film's duration, enhancing the magical and vexing atmosphere in which the island's inhabitants live. Indeed, the island is so fully delineated that it effectively becomes an active character in the story.

The acting is generally solid, and the young Leal is a standout. Her performance is an astonishingly forthright depiction of inchoate sexuality, a delicate mixture of hesitation and passion. Duarte makes Jose's failure to recognize the harm he does his daughter in the name of love understandable, if not somewhat sympathetic. His Jose is overly severe, but never cruel. Piexoto does less well with his role, playing Roberto rather like a stereotypical simpleton.

Overall, though, Lima and company deserve admiration for handling difficult subject matter that challenges the audience and respects its intelligence. THE OYSTER AND THE WIND is a confounding but finally rewarding film. *(Violence, adult situations.)*—D.C.

d, Walter Lima Jr.; p, Flavio R. Tambellini; co-p, Rio Filmes; w, Walter Lima Jr., Flavio R. Tambellini Jr. (based on a novel by Moacir C. Lopes); ph, Pedro Farkas; ed, Sergio Mekler; m, Wagner Tiso, Chico Buarque; prod d, Clovis Bueno; sound, Marcio Camara; cos, Rita Murtinho

Drama/Fantasy **(PR: C MPAA: NR)**

PQ

PALMETTO ★★½

(Germany/U.S., 1998) 113m Neverland Films; Rialto Films; Castle Rock Entertainment ~ Columbia c
(DUMME STERBEN NICHT AUS)

Woody Harrelson *(Harry Barber)*; Elisabeth Shue *(Mrs. Donnelly—aka Rhea Malroux)*; Gina Gershon *(Nina)*; Chloe Sevigny *(Odette Malroux)*; Michael Rapaport *(Donnelly)*; Tom Wright *(DA John Renick)*; Rolf Hoppe *(Felix Malroux)*; Marc Macaulay *(Miles Meadows)*; Joe Hickey *(Lawyer)*; Ralph Wilcox *(Judge)*; Peter Paul DeLeo *(Bartender)*; Mal Jones *(Ed)*; Salvador Levy *(Driver)*; Richard Booker *(Billy Holden)*; Mikki McKeever *(Alda)*; Bill Larson *(Parking Lot Man)*; Tim W. Terry *(Prison Guard)*; Jim Janey *(Policeman)*; Brett Rice *(Crash Site Cop)*; Vince Cecere *(Tow Truck Driver)*; Don Bright *(Crime Scene Cop)*; Ernie Garrett *(TV Anchor)*; Karin J. Ivester *(Forensic Detective)*; Marcus Thomas *(Courtroom Photographer)*; Douglas J. Mann II *(Courtroom Reporter)*; Jim Coleman *(1st Reporter)*; Victoria Tan *(2nd Reporter)*; Stephen McGruder *(Convict)*; Annabelle Weenick *(Ted)*; Wil Kilmer *(Bungalow Cop)*; Ginger King *(The Real Rhea)*; Corey Blevins *(Motel Clerk)*; Duncan Chamberlain *(Gallery Maitre D')*; Peggy Sheffield *(Woman Customer)*; Karen Fraction *(Plainclothes Cop)*; Gary Lowe; Kenneth L. Bright; Jay Ridings; Graig Himes; James Gaunt *(Boathouse Cops)*

PALMETTO is a fairly light and likable entry in the venerable dame-dupes-dope division of crime movies. A routine film that never quite lives up (or down) to its R rating, it earns higher marks for taste than for originality.

Halfway through a four-year term in prison, a reporter named Harry Barber (Woody Harrelson), who was framed after writing a civic expose, is told that his conviction has been overturned. He returns to his small Florida town and moves in with his girlfriend, Nina (Gina Gershon). A woman who calls herself Rhea Malroux (Elisabeth Shue) offers Harry big money and hot sex to participate in a bogus kidnapping. He accepts.

Harry deposits Rhea's 17-year-old stepdaughter, Odette (Chloe Sevigny), who is in on the scheme, in a Miami motel room and collects the ransom money from her wealthy father (Rolf Hoppe) according to plan—then discovers he's been duped when he finds Odette's dead body in a bungalow he has rented, and opens the ransom briefcase to find nothing but scrap paper. Things get even stickier when the corpse of a *second* Odette materializes at Harry's place. When he goes to Malroux's home to tell his story, he is introduced to the *real* Mrs. Malroux (Ginger King)—and he realizes that the women he knew as Rhea and Odette Malroux were imposters.

After falling into the hands of the phony Rhea and her husband-accomplice Donnelly (Michael Rapaport), Harry and Gina are about to be murdered when the police, whom Harry has tipped off, arrive in the nick of time. Donnelly is killed, his wife is arrested, and Harry is sent back to jail. He uses the opportunity to write a screenplay based on his amazing criminal escapade.

Director Volker Schlondorff had long been a specialist in the mounting of such imposingly grim fare as THE TIN DRUM (1979) and THE LOST HONOR OF KATHARINA BLUM (1975). "I decided it was time to take a break from the heavier subject matter," he said, "and have a little fun." The result was PALMETTO, an unpretentious and enjoyable time killer to which Schlondorff applied an unexpectedly light touch. But his lack of experience in formula filmmaking may have caused him to stick too close to the formula. Because this particular genre has been exhaustively mined and remined since it first surfaced in the early 1940s, new entries require somewhat fresh approaches. About the only change Schlondorff rang on its basic notes was an excellent scene in which Harry, after discovering the bogus Odette's body and driving off with it, undergoes a panic attack and hysterically swerves off the road—in refreshing contrast to the genre's traditional protagonist, who may lose nearly everything he has in the world but never his cool.

The rest of PALMETTO is pretty much by-the-numbers. The picture suffers from an absence of memorable lines, a serious shortcoming in this genre, but it does boast one nifty little visual gag: when the fetching (fake) Odette comes on to him, Harry walks smack into a post.

Although it would be difficult to accept the casting of Woody Harrelson as an idealist, the screwed-up, none-too-bright ex-idealist he plays here is comfortably within his range. The ladylike Elisabeth Shue as a femme fatale is a bit harder to buy, but the sight of her, still five delightful pounds too large and in a wardrobe two sizes too small, is more than adequate compensation for any miscasting. *(Violence, sexual situations, profanity.)*—D.T.

d, Volker Schlondorff; p, Matthias Wendlandt; exec p, Al Corley, Bart Rosenblatt, Eugene Musso; w, E. Max Frye (based on the novel *Just Another Sucker* by James Hadley Chase); ph, Thomas Kloss; ed, Peter Przygodda; m, Klaus Doldinger; prod d, Claire Jenora Bowin; set d, Jane B. Johnson; sound, Mark Weingarten (mixer); fx, Richard Lee Jones; casting, Dianne Crittenden; cos, Terry Dresbach; makeup, Kimberly Greene; stunts, Tim Trella

Crime/Thriller **(PR: C MPAA: R)**

PARALLEL SONS ★★½

(U.S., 1996) 93m Black Brook Films; Eureka Pictures ~ Greycat Films c

Gabriel Mann *(Seth Carlson)*; Laurence Mason *(Knowledge Johnson)*; Murphy Guyer *(Sheriff Mott)*; Graham Alex Johnson *(Peter Carlson)*; Heather Gottlieb *(Kristen Mott)*; Josh Hopkins *(Marty)*; Maureen Shannon *(Francine)*; Julia Weldon *(Sally Carlson)*; Johnathan Charles *(Malik)*; Tim Dumas *(Bud)*; Michael J. Allard *(Lars)*; Jack Novak *(Jay)*; Karren Abrams *(Doris Mott)*; Eric P. Granger *(Corrections Officer)*; Kim Snow *(Woman on Street)*; Alice J. Mick *(Seth's Mother)*; Michael Barton Sweeney *(Young Seth)*; Dimitri Kollias *(Bartender)*; Daniel Ferguson; Douglas B. Lansing; John Osborn; Robert Sanson; Ward K. Segrist; Lauren Singer; Theron Snow *(State Troopers)*; William Sedgwick; Charles Terry *(Ambulance Drivers)*

PARALLEL SONS is for most of its length an intriguing dramatic study of an unlikely friendship, before it moves towards a contrived, violent resolution.

Seth Carlson (Gabriel Mick) yearns to leave his sleepy little upstate New York village to study art in New York City, against the wishes of his stern father (Graham Alex Johnson). One morning, as Seth prepares to open a local diner where he works, he is confronted by Knowledge (Laurence Mason), who intends to rob the diner. Bleeding from a wound, Knowledge collapses before he can complete the robbery, and Seth takes him to a shack in a remote wood to recover. Going through Knowledge's clothes, Seth finds a prison identification card. Although he realizes that Knowledge is an escaped convict, Seth decides to keep him hidden. Knowledge initially distrusts and is hostile towards Seth, but as he recuperates, he accepts Seth's friendship.

At work one day, Seth accidentally drops Knowledge's identification card, which he had been carrying, and it is found by a co-worker who contacts the town's sheriff (Murphy Guyer). Seth and Knowledge, meanwhile, become increasingly close, Seth finding that he can relate better to Knowledge than he can to any of his neighbors. One night, Seth allows Knowledge to stay at his house, without his father's awareness. The two drink, talk, and listen to music, but when Knowledge invites Seth to engage in sex, Seth gently rejects him.

The next day, the sheriff arrives at Seth's house to demand that he turn Knowledge over, and Seth shoots and kills him. Seth and Knowledge flee towards Canada, with the law and Seth's father in pursuit. When their car runs out of gas, they proceed on foot. During the night, they take refuge in a lean-to, and make love. In the morning they continue their flight, but as they near the Canadian border, Seth's father catches up with them and shoots Seth in an attempt to gun down Knowledge. Knowledge halts his flight in a futile attempt to aid his dying friend, and waits until lawmen close in around him and take him back to prison.

More widely seen on the festival circuit than in theatrical release, PARALLEL SONS is an admirable independent production with several strong points, chief among them its splendid location shooting and fine cast. PARALLEL SONS makes expert use of its rural location, imbuing the film with a keen sense of place. Writer-director John G. Young effectively turns the small town in which most of the film is set into an omniscient, ever-present character, reassuring in its constancy, yet ominous in its constriction. The location is also used to define the other characters, its agreeable simplicity and disquieting uniformity reflecting the paradoxical qualities of the people who inhabit the town.

The film's performances are equally impressive. Young puts a great deal of trust in his actors, especially the two leads, to carry the dramatic weight of the film. Mick, Mason, and the rest of the cast prove that Young's trust is well founded. Mick is near perfection as Seth. In contrast to the standard depiction of youthful angst—usually played in a rebellious James Dean mode—Mick gives a restrained and subtly intelligent performance while still conveying the depth of Seth's frustration and anger at being trapped in a place where his art and sexuality are denied. He makes Seth a bright, sympathetic, and completely believable young man. While Mason is a bit over the top in his early scenes, his skill comes through as his character becomes more defined, and Mason reveals the intelligence, emotional strength, and tenderness that lie behind Knowledge's tough-talking, streetwise facade. PARALLEL SONS is at its best when focusing on these two actors as the relationship between their characters deepens. The film's most engrossing scene, Knowledge's initial attempt to seduce Seth, is startlingly simple—just two characters talking—yet made deeply affecting because of the graceful interplay between the Mick and Mason.

Unfortunately, PARALLEL SONS works towards an unimaginative finale about the law's effort to capture Knowledge. The forced quality of the story's conclusion is contrary to the delicate tone that Young has established and maintained, and the characters, so genuine through most of the film, suddenly seem inauthentic. Yet the disappointing wrap up does not negate the film's virtues, nor does it cast doubt on the potential of Young and his cast. The talent on display in PARALLEL SONS, in its writing, directing, and acting, shows terrific promise. *(Violence, nudity, sexual situations, extreme profanity.)*—D.C.

d, John G. Young; p, James Spione, Nancy Larsen; w, John G. Young; ph, Matthew M. Howe; ed, John G. Young, James Spione; m, Emile Menasche ; prod d, Cindi Sfinas; art d, Joanne Berman; set d, Chris Schiavo; sound, Harrison Williams (mixer), Jeff Kushner (design); casting, Kathleen Chopin; cos, Leonardo Iturregui; makeup, Evelyn A. Ortmann; stunts, Arthur M. Jolly

Drama **(PR: C MPAA: NR)**

PARALYZING FEAR: THE STORY OF POLIO IN AMERICA, A ★★½

(U.S., 1997) 90m ~ PBS Home Video c

Olympia Dukakis *(Narrator)*; Mrs. Jonas Salk; Marilyn Rogers; Carol Boyer; Hugh Gallagher; John Troan; Dr. Robert Nix

A PARALYZING FEAR: THE STORY OF POLIO IN AMERICA documents the history of the painful and crippling disease with heartfelt care. But with so much information dispensed, this worthy investigation proves exhausting.

The film begins with the first polio epidemic in 1916, and the way in which immigrants, particularly Italian immigrants, were wrongly blamed for spreading the disease through their supposed lack of hygiene. The discrimination was reinforced in the medical community by the way patients were isolated in wards. In 1921, at age 39, Governor (and future President) Franklin D. Roosevelt fell victim to the disease, which undermined the theory that only children were susceptible (polio was then called infantile paralysis).

FDR attempted to combat his affliction by purchasing and running Warm Springs, a spa in Georgia for polio victims, fundraising for scientific research, and disguising his inability to walk in public. The Kolmer experiment, the first significant test to find an antibody immunity, ended in disaster when several children died. Later, during the FDR administration of the 1930s, prevention was emphasized over cure, and the March of Dimes, the research organization, enlisted many Hollywood celebrities to spread helpful information about sanitation and to promote the countrywide drive, the Mothers' March on Polio.

During WWII and throughout the next decade, two rival scientists, Jonas Salk and Albert Sabin, worked on vaccines that they thought could eradicate the disease. In the meantime, Elizabeth Kenny (or "Sister Kenny"), an Australian nurse who came to America, popularized a form of polio therapy that combined heat application with repetitive movement. When postwar America realized that adults were *more* susceptible to the disease in clean environments, where they had no chance of building up an immunity, the pressure mounted for Salk and Sabin to deliver the goods.

In 1953, the government chose to use Salk's "Kill the Virus" vaccine over Sabin's "Live Virus" method in a massive field trial that was mostly successful. Due to some faulty lab work, however, some deaths occurred during the celebrated study and Salk was criticized. Still, the government continued using Salk's formula until more epidemics sprang up, at which point Sabin's vaccine was substituted with much greater success (in 1961). Today, the disease has been eliminated wherever the vaccines are used, although some parts of the world do not have access to the vaccine, and those who have survived the disease in the US still remember a time when there were no effective treatments at all.

Using survivor interviews, newsreel footage, archival photographs, and historical data incorporated into the narration read by Olympia Dukakis, A PARALYZING FEAR: THE STORY OF POLIO IN AMERICA sheds light on the once dreaded and mysterious disease of poliomyelitis. Many parts of Nina Seavey's documentary contain insights into society as well as the history of the disease and its eventual cure. The most interesting portions come early, as Seavey clearly demonstrates that xenophobia was a major part of early 20th century America. Some of the newsreels are also fascinating, including one chiller that makes polio as frightening as the reputed Communist menace, and others, produced by the March of Dimes, that use actors like Greer Garson, Eddie Cantor, Mickey Rooney, and Judy Garland, in awkward but well-meaning public service announcements.

The full story of polio, however, includes too many subplots for this simple, traditional documentary to cover in a mere 90 minutes. A PARALYZING FEAR overambitiously tries to cover all aspects of the disease's effect on society. As a result, sometimes, the facts gets jumbled or glossed over (for example, the US government's late and lackluster involvement is not clearly elucidated), and, by the final section, viewers may have lost interest in the subject.

Technically, A PARALYZING FEAR meets PBS documentary standards, although the use of music for particular historical periods is either blandly generic or simply incorrect. The film was released in 1998, the same year that a searing, intimate portrait of disease was captured in the documentary SICK: THE LIFE AND DEATH OF BOB FLANAGAN (1998). By comparison, A PARALYZING FEAR is more like a competent college thesis paper translated to film. *(Adult situations.)*—E.M.

d, Nina Gilden Seavey; p, Paul Wagner, Nina Gilden Seavey; w, Nina Gilden Seavey, Stephen Chodorov; ph, Allen Moore, Reuben Aaronson; ed, Catherine Shields; m, Paul Christianson

Documentary **(PR: A MPAA: NR)**

PARENT TRAP, THE ★★★

(U.S., 1998) 124m Stansbury Productions; Meyers/Shyer; Walt Disney Pictures ~ Buena Vista c

Lindsay Lohan *(Hallie Parker/Annie James)*; Dennis Quaid *(Nick Parker)*; Natasha Richardson *(Elizabeth James)*; Elaine Hendrix *(Meredith Blake)*; Lisa Ann Walter *(Chessy)*; Simon Kunz *(Martin)*; Polly Holliday *(Marva Kulp Sr.)*; Ronnie Stevens *(Grandfather)*; Maggie Wheeler *(Marva Kulp Jr.)*; Joanna Barnes *(Vicki)*; Hallie Meyers-Shyer *(Lindsay)*; Maggie Emma Thomas *(Zoe)*; Courtney Woods *(Nicole)*; Katerina Graham *(Jackie)*; Michael Lohan *(Lost Boy at Camp)*; Rachel Sullivan; Katie Deshan; Brighton Hertford; Jennifer Lin; Amy Centner; Mia Tramz *(Navajo Bunk Girls)*; Christina Toral *(Cell Phone Girl)*; Dana Ponder *(Cell Phone Girl)*; Brianne Mercier *(Cell Phone Girl)*; Danielle Sherman *(Girl at Poker Game)*; Natasha Melnick *(Girl at Poker Game)*; Amanda Hampton *(Girl at Poker Game)*; Lisa Iverson *(Bugler)*; Lisa Cloud *(Camp Counselor)*; Lisa Foster *(Camp Counselor)*; Heidi Boren *(Camp Counselor)*; Marissa Leigh *(Fencing Girl)*; Heather Wayrock *(Fencing Girl)*; John Atterbury *(Gareth—The James' Chauffeur)*; Hamish McColl *(Photographer)*; Vendela K. Thommessen *(Bridal Gown Model)*; Alexander Cole *(Richard—Meredith's Assistant)*; J. Patrick McCormack *(Les Blake)*; William Akey *(Bellhop with Flowers)*; David Doty *(Hotel Bartender)*; Roshanna Baron *(Lady at Pool)*; Annie Meyers-Shyer *(Towel Girl)*; Brian Fenwick *(Desk Clerk)*; Jonneine Hellerstein *(Ship Photographer)*; Troy Christian *(QE2 Dancer)*; Denise Holland *(QE2 Dancer)*; Terry Kerr *(Living Statue)*; Bruce Block *(Tourist)*

Disney strikes baby boomer gold again with this glossy and sentimental remake of their 1961 hit THE PARENT TRAP (which had already inspired three made-for-TV sequels starring the original's Hayley Mills). The skillful dual-role performance by newcomer Lindsay Lohan and the customarily slick blend of laughs and tears from the husband-and-wife filmmaking team of Charles Shyer and Nancy Myers makes this more charming and enjoyable than it should be.

American Nick Parker (Dennis Quaid) and Englishwoman Elizabeth James (Natasha Richardson) impulsively get married after meeting on a cruise ship, but they're divorced shortly thereafter and split custody of their twin baby daughters, who are never told about the existence of the other. Eleven years and nine months later, Nick sends 11-year-old daughter Hallie (Lindsay Lohan) to a Maine summer camp, and Elizabeth unwittingly sends 11-year-old Annie (Lindsay Lohan) to the same camp. After an initial rivalry, the girls discover that they're twins and decide to switch identities so that each one can get to see the parent they've never met, as well as allow them to try to get their folks back together. Hallie goes to London and Annie goes to California and they successfully pull off their ruse for awhile, but when Nick announces his intention of getting married to the beautiful but bitchy gold digger, Meredith Blake (Elaine Hendrix), Hallie admits the truth to her mother and they fly to California together.

Hallie and Annie arrange a romantic reunion dinner for their parents, but in the morning, the kids refuse to identify which twin they are until they all go on a camping trip together. The parents reluctantly agree, but when Meredith objects, Elizabeth lets her go instead. During the trip, the girls torment Meredith by hiding rocks in her backpack and placing a lizard in her hair. After they put her inflatable sleeping bag in a lake while she's asleep, a furious Meredith demands that Nick choose between her and them, and he chooses them. Nevertheless, Elizabeth decides to return home with Annie, but when they arrive in London, they're shocked to see Nick and Hallie already there. And Nick and Elizabeth are subsequently remarried.

The world according to Disney circa 1998 is very similar to the world of 1961—a great big wonderful place full of fun and hijinks, as long as you're young, rich, and white, that is. Based on a foolproof story from a German book irresistibly titled *Das Doppelte Lottchen,* and previously filmed in Germany in 1950 and in England in 1953, the 1961 version of THE PARENT TRAP was one of Disney's biggest hits of the '60s and made a star of young Hayley Mills. The new version follows it fairly closely (even giving its writer-director David Swift a screenplay credit), updating it with digital wizardry for flawless "twin" effects, and offering an even more fantasized and materialistic depiction of hearth and home. Ruggedly handsome dad now owns a fabulous Napa Valley vineyard, a Range Rover, and of course, a wisecracking servant, while mom is now an elegant English mum, who is chauffeured around London to her fancy wedding-gown design studio in a Rolls Royce, and surprise, also has a wisecracking servant, who naturally falls in love with Nick's. In place of Tommy Sands and Annette Funicello singing the original's title song and Hayley warbling "Let's Get Together" ("yay, yay, yay") we now have an incessant stream of Motown music and other pop songs jackhammered into the action to back up the countless montages that only pad the absurdly long running time.

Yet somehow, the whole sticky, idealized thing works, at least for well-bred young girls and hopeless romantics, with amusing slapstick scenes and very appealing performances by the entire cast. Affecting a British accent for one of the twins, Lindsay Lohan is no less impressive than the British Mills was in doing American accents, while Dennis Quaid, who hasn't seemed so relaxed and likable in ages, and the always classy Natasha Richardson, have such good chemistry that they make you forget these "wonderful" people selfishly split up their family and concealed the fact from their children. Elaine Hendrix is perfect as Meredith, Lisa Ann Walter and Simon Kunz steal every scene they're in as the comical servants, and a nice touch is lent by having Joanna Barnes, who played the gold digger in the original, portray Meredith's mother here. The whole movie is a testament to the seductive power of hokum and to Hollywood's eternal knowledge that most people, despite their protestations, are suckers for fairy tales about perfect families.—M.S.

d, Nancy Meyers; p, Charles Shyer; assoc p, Julie B. Crane; co-p, Bruce A. Block; w, David Swift, Nancy Meyers, Charles Shyer (based on the novel *Das Doppelte Lottchen* by Erich Kastner); ph, Dean A. Cundey; ed, Stephen A. Rotter; m, Alan Silvestri; prod d, Dean Tavoularis; art d, Alex Tavoularis; set d, Gary Fettis;

sound, Sean Rush (mixer); fx, Cliff Wenger, Jim Rygiel; casting, Ilene Starger; cos, Penny Rose; makeup, Karen Blynder, Bradley Wilder; stunts, Freddie Hice

Comedy **(PR: AA MPAA: PG)**

PASS, THE ★
(U.S., 1998) 81m Dream Entertainment ~ Peachtree Entertainment c

William Forsythe *(Charles Duprey)*; James LeGros, billed as James Le Gros *(Hunter)*; Elizabeth Pena *(Zeena)*; Michael McKean *(Willie)*; Nancy Allen *(Shirley)*; John Doe *(Bus Station Clerk)*; Jamie Kennedy *(Deputy Bank)*; Richard Fleming *(Motel Manager)*; Chris Shearer *(Worker #1)*; Robert Keith *(Worker #2)*; Jaason Simmons *(Blackjack Dealer)*; Robin Klein *(Comely Woman)*

Perennial cinematic psycho William Forsythe is boringly miscast as a nice guy who gets embroiled in a thoroughly stupid and illogical murder plot in THE PASS, a plodding straight-to-video "thriller" devoid of thrills or suspense.

Charles Duprey (William Forsythe) is having a mid-life crisis. His job as a comic strip salesman for a syndication agency is going nowhere and his wife Shirley (Nancy Allen) is leaving him after 12 years. Duprey's friend Willie (Michael McKean) convinces him to drive to Reno to help him get over the breakup. Along a treacherous highway, Duprey is forced to swerve to avoid a stalled car. The driver, a man called Hunter (James Le Gros), asks Duprey for a ride and Duprey agrees, but after Hunter tells him that he once killed his girlfriend, Duprey ditches him. However, Duprey is forced to turn around after a storm causes a landslide, and he checks into a roadside motel. Hunter arrives at the motel and kills the manager (Richard Fleming) and a barmaid (Elizabeth Pena), then goes after Duprey and reveals that he has been hired by Shirley and Willie to kill him for his insurance policy. Duprey escapes during a struggle and is pursued by Hunter into the woods, but eventually manages to kill Hunter by throwing gasoline on him and setting him on fire, after which, he puts his ID in Hunter's pocket and goes to Reno. Back home, Shirley and Willie wait for the insurance check to arrive and receive a package which explodes when they open it.

Aside from being talky, uneventful, and glacially paced, THE PASS is so convoluted and implausible that it defies coherent description. Starting with the absurdity of a character who's a comic strip salesman (?!), we are asked to believe that instead of simply hiring someone to bump off Duprey at home, Willie and Shirley plotted to have him drive to Reno (knowing which road he'd travel) and pick up a stranded driver, who, instead of just killing him, first tells him that he's a killer in order to make him suspicious. Then, Duprey goes to a gas station restroom, but instead of using his cell phone to call the cops, he amazingly agrees to take Hunter to the next town before abandoning him. The film takes some laughable stabs at philosophy that only come off as pretentious (Hunter is reading a book called "Existentialism Made Easy" and engages in endless discussions about the meaning of life before killing people), and it's also ponderously mannered, with much use of pointless and irritating jumpcuts and extreme close-ups of inanimate objects meant to convey some sort of deep meaning. Forsythe, who's always a memorable heavy, is all wrong here, wearing wire-rimmed glasses and employing a barely audible monotone voice, while his so-called transformation where he "switches" identities with Hunter after killing him and becomes a swinging gambler with a sexy babe on his arm is ridiculously contrived. *(Graphic violence, profanity, sexual situations, substance abuse.)*—M.S.

d, Kurt Voss; p, Ehud Bleiberg, Yitzhak Gisnberg; co-p, Raimond Reynolds; w, Kurt Voss; ph, Denis Maloney; ed, John Rosenberg; m, Vinny Golia; prod d, Rando Schmook, Mandana Yamin; sound, Lee Howell; fx, Lou Carlucci; casting, Robin Klein, Heidi Klein; cos, Anita Cabada; makeup, Vera Zay

Thriller **(PR: O MPAA: NR)**

PASSION IN THE DESERT ★★
(U.K., 1998) 93m Roland Films ~ Fine Line c

Ben Daniels *(Augustin Robert)*; Michel Piccoli *(Jean-Michel Venture de Paradis)*; Paul Meston *(Grognard)*; Kenneth Collard *(Officer)*; Nadi Odeh *(Bedouin Bride)*; Auda Mohammed Badoul *(Shepherd Boy)*; Mohammed Ali *(Medicine Man)*; Habis Hussein; Tasheen Kwalda; Ismael Al-Hamd *(Bedouins)*; James Peck; Nicolas Sagalle; Abdul Latif Salazar *(Soldiers)*

Based on a story by Honore de Balzac, PASSION IN THE DESERT is an attractive but remote drama about a man's bizarre relationship with a leopard.

During Napoleon's Egyptian campaign, Augustin Robert (Ben Daniels), a military officer, is assigned to accompany Jean-Michel Venture de Paradis (Michel Piccoli), who has been commissioned to sketch monuments in the Egyptian desert. The two meet and encamp with a French regiment, but are separated from it during an attack. Lacking provisions, they continue through the desert. Augustin eventually abandons de Paradis, who kills himself.

Augustin comes to a tent in which he finds water. As he drinks, a woman enters and screams, attracting the attention of nearby Bedouins. They chase Augustin, who finds refuge in an abandoned cave temple. Safe, he sleeps, but is later awakened by a roaring leopard. Although frightened, he is unharmed by the animal.

The next morning, a Bedouin comes to kill Augustin, but the leopard attacks and kills the Bedouin instead. The fearful Augustin tries to flee, but is kept from doing so by the leopard. Later, the leopard kills another animal and brings it to Augustin to eat. When he realizes that the leopard is protecting him, Augustin overcomes his fear, and he and the leopard, which he names Simoom, live peaceably together in the temple.

One day, another leopard appears and Simoom divides her attention between it and Augustin. Jealous, Augustin paints himself with sandstone and charcoal to make himself look like a leopard. Days later, the regiment reaches the temple. When a soldier tries to shoot Simoom, Augustin assaults him to save Simoom's life. The regiment moves on, and Augustin prepares to rejoin it for fear of being branded a deserter. As he leaves the temple, he is attacked by Simoom, and stabs her to death in self-defense. Having killed his beloved leopard, the distraught Augustin picks up its body and wanders into the blazing desert.

The debut feature of writer-director Lavinia Currier, PASSION IN THE DESERT is as technically strong as it is uninspired. Currier takes full advantage of the aesthetic potential that her material offers, and has come up with a film that looks and sounds beautiful. The desert locations (shooting sites included Jordan and Moab, Utah), brilliantly rendered by cinematographer Alexei Rodionov, are appropriately brutal yet mysteriously alluring. The film is equally impressive aurally, the desert sounding simultaneously natural and mystical. Yet for all its beauty, PASSION IN THE DESERT is surprisingly dispassionate, never really developing a sense of the exotic that the subject demands. Given the uncivilized setting, the film's several spiritual allusions, and the almost bestial central relationship, an appreciation of the outlandish seems essential. Currier's treatment, however, is detached and pedestrian throughout, and PASSION IN THE

DESERT comes across less like a story about the seductive and transcendent capabilities of untamed nature than a photo spread for *National Geographic*.

The performance of Daniels is a measure of the opportunity this film misses. Unlike his director, Daniels immerses himself in his environment. He expertly carries the burden of playing what amounts to the only (human) role of substance in the film, and makes Augustin's gradual entrancement believable and involving. Scenes in which Augustin lovingly caresses Simoom, or the sequence in which he makes himself up as a leopard might have been awkward or even embarrassing were it not for the conviction that Daniels brings to the part. Piccoli, in the type of small, unchallenging character role that marked the last years of Laurence Olivier's film career, is entertaining as always.

At the very least, PASSION IN THE DESERT earns distinction for being one of very few films in which leopard trainers are prominently credited. Rick and Judy Glassey deserve top marks for making Simoom the most personable of movie leopards. *(Graphic violence, extensive nudity.)* —D.C.

d, Lavinia Currier; p, Jamil Dehlavi, Lavinia Currier; exec p, Joel McCleary, Stephen Dembitzer; assoc p, Emmanuelle Castro; w, Lavinia Currier, Martin Edmunds (adapted from the novella *A Passion in the Desert* by Honore de Balzac); ph, Alexei Rodionov; ed, Nicolas Gaster; m, Jose Nieto; prod d, Amanda McArthur; set d, Daphne Becket; sound, Godfrey Kirby (recordist), Michael Stearns (design); fx, Randy Pope, Colin Arthur; casting, Daphne Becket; cos, Shuna Harwood; makeup, Anne Spiers; stunts, Stuart St. Paul

Romance/Drama/Historical (PR: C MPAA: PG-13)

PATCH ADAMS ★★½

(U.S., 1998) 120m Farrell/Minoff Productions; Bungalow 78 Productions; Blue Wolf Productions ~ Universal c

Robin Williams *(Hunter "Patch" Adams)*; Daniel London *(Truman)*; Monica Potter *(Carin)*; Philip Seymour Hoffman *(Mitch)*; Bob Gunton *(Dean Walcott)*; Josef Sommer *(Dr. Eaton)*; Irma P. Hall *(Joletta)*; Frances Lee McCain *(Judy)*; Harve Presnell *(Dean Anderson)*; Daniella Kuhn *(Adelane)*; Jake Bowen *(Bryan)*; Peter Coyote *(Bill Davis)*; James Greene *(Bile)*; Michael Jeter *(Rudy)*; Harold Gould *(Arthur Mendelson)*; Bruce Bohne *(Trevor Beene)*; Harry Groener *(Dr. Prack)*; Barry "Shabaka" Henley *(Emmet)*; Stephen Anthony Jones *(Charlie)*; Richard Kiley *(Dr. Titan)*; Douglas Roberts *(Larry)*; Ellen Albertini Dow *(Aggie)*; Alan Tudyk *(Everton)*; Ryan Hurst *(Neil)*; Peter Siiteri *(Chess Man)*; Tim Wiggins *(Scared Customer)*; Helen Tourtillott *(Feeble Woman)*; On West *(Instructor)*; Domenique Lozano *(Passerby)*; Ralph Peduto *(Organizer)*; Ken Hoffman *(Big Texan)*; Jim Antonio *(E.R. Doctor)*; Roy Conrad *(E.R. Doctor)*; Jay Jacobus *(Jack Walton)*; Dot-Marie Jones *(Miss Meat)*; Geoff Fiorito *(3rd Year Student)*; Samuel Sheng *(3rd Year Student)*; Kathleen Stefano *(Margery)*; Piers Mackenzie *(Dr. Hashman)*; Alex Gonzalez *(Hispanic Boy)*; Ismael "East" Carlo *(Hispanic Father)*; Cameron Brooke Stanley; Jamieson G. Downes; Jena Marie Thomas; Wesley G. Haines *(Children's Ward Patients)*; Richard J. Silberg; William Joseph Scharff; James Anthony Cotton; Michael Rae Sommers; Howard Allison Williams; David Fine; James Carraway; J. Stephen Coyle *(Psych Patients)*; Wanda McCadden *(Woman in Lobby)*; Wanda Christine *(Nurse Klegg)*; Lorri Holt *(Pediatric Nurse)*; Stephanie Smith *(Laughing Nurse)*; Mary Delorenzo *(Nurse)*; Vivis *(Hysterical Woman)*; Donna Kimball *(Waitress)*; Norman Alden *(Truck Driver)*; Lydell M. Cheshier *(Younger Man)*; Diane Amos *(Older Waitress)*; Sonya Eddy *(Older Waitress)*; Kelvin Yee *(Orderly)*; Doreen Chou Croft *(Asian Woman)*; Bill Roberson *(Fred Jarvis)*; Randy Oglesby *(Pinstriped Man)*; Vilma Vitanza *(Maria)*; Bonnie Johnson *(Walcott's Secretary)*; Jack Ford *(Lecturer)*; Christine Pineda *(Hispanic Girl)*; Karen Michel *(Mrs. Davis)*; James Allen *(Ed)*; Katherine A. Fitzhugh *(Mrs. O'Bannon)*; Kyle Timothy Smith *(Davis Son)*; Jonathan Holder *(Davis Son)*; Renee Rogers *(Receptionist)*; Shanon Orrock *(Receptionist)*; Don Rizzo *(Minister)*; Andrew Clement *(Puppeteer)*; George Lee Masters; Daniel P. Hannafin; Roger W. Durrett *(Boardroom Doctors)*; Richard C. Adkins; Ralph David Westfall; Bob Feaster; Thom McIntyre; Alfred Salley; Michael Kennedy *(Gynecologists)*

Based on the true story of an unconventional medical student who treats patients with humor and compassion, PATCH ADAMS almost drowns in its own sincerity. While extremely funny, it is also melodramatic and emotionally manipulative.

In 1969, after a suicide attempt, Hunter Adams (Robin Williams) voluntarily enters a mental hospital. While there, he discovers that his sense of humor helps him to bring joy to a variety of troubled people. He checks out of the hospital, and two years later, sporting the nickname "Patch," he enters medical school. His goal is to become a doctor who will help enrich people's lives by developing personal relationships with his patients.

Most of the people he encounters in med school, including roommate Mitch (Philip Seymour Hoffman), classmate Carin (Monica Potter), and humorless Dean Walcott (Bob Gunton), disapprove of his ideas, but he does make one friend, Truman (Daniel London), who is also frustrated by the school's by-the-book structure. When Carin discovers that Patch is a straight-A student, she, too, begins to warm up to him.

Though medical students are not allowed to spend time with actual patients until their third year, Patch sneaks into the hospital to entertain children. His continued flaunting of the rules brings him into conflict with the school's administration, though Dean Anderson (Harve Presnell) stands up for him.

In his third year, Patch opens the "Gesundheit Institute," an off-campus clinic where he and fellow students, including Truman and Carin, provide free care and housing for the sick and troubled. Patch's dream is to expand the clinic when he graduates, but when Carin is murdered by a troubled patient, he questions his ideas and thinks about closing the clinic. However, when, days before graduation, he is threatened with expulsion and legal action for treating patients without a license, he becomes determined to fight to continue his medical career. He gives an emotional courtroom speech about his ideals that wins over the judges, and he is allowed to graduate. After graduation, he expands the Gesundheit Institute.

PATCH ADAMS wants desperately to be a crowd-pleaser, with elaborate jokes such as Patch greeting a group of visiting gynecologists by surrounding a building's entrance with huge legs in stirrups. A scene where Patch and Truman sneak into a meat-packers' convention is particularly hilarious. Unfortunately, the film works just as hard to wrench tears from the audience. The character of Carin was created for the film, and her death artificially creates melodrama in a film that doesn't need it. Patch's battles with the school administration create enough conflict without lessening the impact of his eventual success. Worst is the final half hour, culminating with Patch walking down the graduation aisle naked; it's an embarrassment that makes it hard to take the rest of the film seriously.

Tom Shadyac's direction has no subtlety whatsoever, lingering too long on shots of sick children and focusing in dramatically on Patch, then his admirers, during the courtroom speech, as if Patch were the second coming. Combined with Steve Oedekerk's crisis-a-minute script and Marc Shaiman's grating score, it creates a state of perpetual emotional manipulation that will anger rather than win over intelligent viewers. It's no surprise, really, that the union of Shadyac and Oedekirk, the directors of the ACE VENTURA films, would be so unrealistic and unsubtle—but it leaves one wondering how good the film might have been with a better script and a more refined presentation.

The role of Patch Adams is old hat for Robin Williams, who is consistently cast in roles that call for two parts crazy humor, one part sickly sweet pathos. It's to his credit that he continues to play these roles with such energy and care, and though the film eventually takes its melodrama beyond the point of no return, his performance in the first part of the film is outstanding. Monica Potter is charming as Carin, and Philip Seymour Hoffman shows his versatility, playing a complex role that is completely different from his equally admirable performances in HAPPINESS, NEXT STOP WONDERLAND (both 1998) and BOOGIE NIGHTS (1997). Though PATCH ADAMS was savaged by critics, it was a huge hit at the box office, suggesting either that audiences were hard up for a few good laughs or that they prefer blatant emotional manipulation to good filmmaking. *(Nudity, adult situations, profanity.)*—A.M.

d, Tom Shadyac; p, Mike Farrell, Charles Newirth, Marvin Minoff, Barry Kemp; exec p, Marsha Garces Williams, Tom Shadyac; assoc p, Alan B. Curtiss, Allegra Clegg; co-p, Steve Oedekerk, Devorah Moos-Hankin; w, Steve Oedekerk (based on book *Gesundheit, Good Health Is a Laughing Matter* by Hunter Doherty Adams and Maureen Mylander); ph, Phedon Papamichael; ed, Don Zimmerman; m, Marc Shaiman; prod d, Linda DeScenna; art d, Jim Nedza; set d, Ric McElvin; sound, Nelson Stoll (mixer); fx, David Blitstein; casting, Debbie Zane; cos, Judy Ruskin-Howell; makeup, Hallie D'Amore

AAN Best Original Musical or Comedy Score: Marc Shaiman

Comedy/Drama **(PR: C MPAA: PG-13)**

PAUL MONETTE: THE BRINK OF SUMMER'S END ★★★★

(U.S., 1998) 90m Brink of Summer's End ~ First Run Features c

Paul Monette; Jonathan Fried; Linda Hunt *(Narrator)*; Bob Monette; Judith Light; Robert Desiderio; Larry Kramer; Star Black

PAUL MONETTE: THE BRINK OF SUMMER'S END is a beautifully realized documentary chronicling the life of the award-winning writer who died of AIDS in 1995. Insightful and moving, this portrait speaks to the heart, and is a quiet call to arms against the tyranny of homophobia.

Through interviews with family and friends and extensive home-movie footage, filmmaker Monte Bramer makes Monette live once again. Born on Oct. 16, 1945, in Lawrence, Massachusetts, Monette had a childhood that, though far from ideal, was still relatively happy. He was especially close to his brother Bob who was born with a serious deformity that left him wheelchair bound. A popular and attractive student, Monette excelled in school. He attended Phillips Andover and then went on to Yale, where he had a chance to flourish as a writer. But even with all of his outward successes, Monette couldn't come to terms with, or write about, the core aspect of his identity: his homosexuality.

During the years following the 1969 riot in NYC's Stonewall Inn, Monette gradually came out of the closet, wrote his first novel dealing explicitly with gay sex, *Taking Care of Mrs. Carroll,* and began a long and fruitful relationship with lawyer Roger Horwitz. Their happiness lasted until Horwitz contracted AIDS in 1985. A year later, he was dead. This devastating loss prompted Monette into action. His writings became outspoken and eloquently polemic about the gay experience and the presence of AIDS as an everyday threat. In 1988, he wrote the painful memoir *Borrowed Time* about his ordeal with Horwitz—even as he coped with the mental anguish of his own HIV-positive status. In 1988, Monette met Stephen Kolzak and began a relationship with him, which lasted until 1990 when Kolzak died of AIDS. Widowed a second time, Monette began his autobiography *Becoming a Man,* which went on to win the prestigious National Book Award. At a book-signing, he met Winston Wilde, who remained with Paul and nurtured him as he gradually succumbed to a series of AIDS-related diseases. All the while, he was still writing daily. In 1995, he died with Wilde by his side.

Harrowing, witty, and powerful, PAUL MONETTE is peppered with remarkable home-movie footage that comes from various periods in Monette's life. Monette's joy for living and loving is infectious as we see, for instance, he and Kolzak acting like a couple of giddy schoolboys as they tour Europe. But in the shocking footage depicting Monette in his final years, we see how the once handsome and vital writer became a shell of his former self. In explaining his endless variety of treatments and drugs, Monette speaks in the detached tone of a soldier back from war, worn out and defeated from too many battles. That he shared such private moments on film is a testament to his courage and his belief that people must be shaken out of their complacency in order to face the horror of AIDS. In their raw power, these sequences prove to be a far more effective weapon aginst the disease than the wearing of symbolic red ribbons or glamorous celebrities speaking on behalf of the dying.

As sobering and candid as the film is, it's unfortunate that director Monte Bramer places so much emphasis on the interviews, which are too often arbitrarily placed within the film's framework. With a few exceptions, the interviewees don't add anything particularly enlightening to the tale of Monette's life. Monette's brother Bob offers the most revealing insights into his childhood and his brave character as when he recalls a poignant incident from their childhood in which Paul, who wasn't allowed to visit Bob in the hospital, snuck around to the window of the room he was staying in just to cheer him up. Because they were both outsiders, theirs was a relationship that was solid and enduring.

Actress-activist Judith Light and her husband Robert Desiderio, though warm and sincere, offer only perfunctory recollections of their friendship with Monette. The playwright and feisty AIDS activist Larry Kramer is grandly articulate as always, but doesn't reveal anything earth-shattering. And whatever possessed Bramer to include the recollections of Monette's friend, photographer Star Black? Her embarrasing "I'm-a-moody-artist" pretentions don't suit the respecful tone of the documentary. This structural problem doesn't, however, mar the film's power or diminish Monette's legacy. *(Adult situations.)*—D.O.

d, Monte Bramer; p, Lesli Klainberg; w, Monte Bramer; ed, Chris Riess; m, John Ehrlich

Biography/Documentary **(PR: O MPAA: NR)**

PAULIE ★★½

(U.S., 1998) 105m Mutual Film Company; DreamWorks SKG ~ DreamWorks SKG c

Gena Rowlands *(Ivy)*; Tony Shalhoub *(Misha)*; Cheech Marin *(Ignacio)*; Bruce Davison *(Dr. Reingold)*; Trini Alvarado *(Adult Marie)*; Jay Mohr *(Voice of Paulie/Benny)*; Buddy Hackett *(Artie)*; Hallie Kate Eisenberg *(Marie)*; Matt Craven *(Warren Alweather)*; Tia Texada *(Ruby/Voice of Lupe)*; Laura Harrington *(Lila Alweather)*; Bill Cobbs *(Virgil)*; Charles Parks *(Gerald)*;

Peter Basch *(Grad Student)*; Emily Mura-Smith *(Grad Student #2)*; Hal Robinson *(Grandpa)*; Seth Mumy *(Jeremy)*; Francesca Federico-O'Murchu *(Molly)*; Jerry Winsett *(Mr. Tauper)*; Dig Wayne *(Research Assistant #1)*; Michael Leydon Campbell *(Research Assistant #2)*; Nicole Chamberlain *(Shirley)*; Tamara Zook *(Speech Therapist)*; Kristie Transeau *(Veterinarian #2)*

A parrot who can talk—not merely mimic human speech, but communicate with humans—is the star of this pleasant but unmemorable release from DreamWorks SKG.

Misha (Tony Shalhoub) is a Russian emigre starting a new job as a janitor in a California animal research facility. In the basement he accidentally discovers a caged parrot named Paulie (voice of Jay Mohr) who can speak but refuses to do so. After gaining his trust, he hears the bird's story: in New York, Paulie was the pet of Marie (Hallie Kate Eisenberg), a five-year-old girl whose stammering kept her from making human friends. Paulie learns to talk from Marie's lessons, and helps her overcome her problem. But when her parents fear she is becoming too attached to her pet, they get rid of Paulie. After several owners he is purchased by Ivy (Gena Rowlands), a lonely widow who agrees to return him to Marie. When they find Marie's family has moved to Los Angeles, Ivy and Paulie travel across the country in her mobile home, a trip cut short by Ivy's failing eyesight. Paulie stays as a companion to the now-blind woman, resuming his search for Marie after Ivy's death.

In LA, he joins a troupe of performing parrots working with street artist Ignacio (Cheech Marin). Paulie is kidnapped by Benny (Jay Mohr), a small-time grifter who uses him in larcenous pursuits. Captured in a house he is attempting to burgle, Paulie is sold to Dr. Reingold (Bruce Davison), who sees the talking bird as his passport to a Nobel Prize. But when Paulie learns that Reingold lied about returning him to Marie, he refuses to speak, leading to his banishment to the basement. Eager to help a kindred lonely soul, Misha breaks him out of the facility and returns him to Marie—whom Paulie initially doesn't recognize: his journey has taken 20 years, and Marie (Trini Alvarado) is now a grown woman.

The story of an animal searching for its lost master is one of the oldest in the book, and PAULIE is a fairly standard example of the genre. The film's creators have created a wholly convincing talking bird, using 14 different Blue-crown Conures and animatronic parrots by Stan Winston; Jay Mohr's Arnold Stangish voice was fed into a computer that matched it to the birds' beak movements. But neither cinematic trickery (the way in which the passing of the years is disguised creates quite a few plot gaps, including the cause of Ivy's death) nor a good cast can compensate for a dull script, PAULIE's chief failing. The film does have an effectively touching finale: the now-adult Marie (the film subtly disguises the length of time that has elapsed) proves who she is by singing the song her mother used as a lullaby, Randy Newman's almost painfully lovely "Marie." *(Profanity.)*—M.F.

d, John Roberts; p, Mark Gordon, Gary Levinsohn, Allison Lyon Segan; exec p, Ginny Nugent; co-p, Michele Weisler; w, Laurie Craig; ph, Tony Pierce-Roberts; ed, Bruce Cannon; m, John Debney; prod d, Dennis Washington; art d, Tom Taylor; set d, Denise Pizzini; sound, Joseph Geisinger (mixer); fx, Dave Kelsey, Michael "Tony" Meagher, Charles Linehan, Stan Winston; casting, Risa Bramon Garcia, Randi Hiller, Sarah Finn; cos, Mary Zophres; makeup, Tracey Levy; stunts, Al Jones

Children's/Comedy/Fantasy (PR: A MPAA: PG)

PEACEKEEPER, THE ★★

(Canada/U.S., 1997) 98m Film Line Inc. ~ Nu Image c

Dolph Lundgren *(Major Cross)*; Michael Sarrazin *(Murphy)*; Roy Scheider *(President)*; Montel Williams *(Lt. Colonel Northrop)*; Monika Schnarre *(Jane)*; Christopher Heyerdahl *(Hettinger)*; Allen Altman *(McGarry)*; Tim Post *(Nelson)*; Serge Houde *(Secretary of Defense)*; Chip Chiupka *(Davis)*; Roc LaFortune *(Abbott)*; Phil Chiu *(Kong)*; David Francis *(Maj. General Harding)*; Alan Fawcett *(Samuels)*; Andy Bradshaw *(Johnson)*; Dave Nichols *(Air Force Chief of Staff)*; Vlasta Vrana *(General Douglas)*; Michel Perron *(Space Command)*; Mark Camacho *(Presidential Aide)*; Susan Glover *(Presidential Aide)*

Once again, world peace rests on the shoulders of monolith Dolph Lundgren. This is the kind of jingoistic drek in which filmmakers lovingly depict the blasting of Mt. Rushmore; on the other hand, that monument carved in muscles, Mr. Lundgren, escapes relatively unscathed.

Fearless Major Frank Cross (Lundgren) is pressured into a high-risk assignment: the US President (Roy Scheider) requires Cross's services as keeper of the "Black Bag," a briefcase that houses the launch codes for America's thermonuclear deterrents. Using high-tech espionage, terrorists separate Cross from the nuclear capability case on his first day of work.

In a wild car chase that leads through parking garages and across several rooftops, Cross pursues the extremists to a missile facility. Inside, military personnel are gassed to death by the invaders; only one, Lt. Col. Northrop (Montel Williams) survives by donning a space suit. Cross and Northrop team up to defeat the terrorists, who are led by renegade Lt. Colonel Murphy (Michael Sarrazin). Murphy bears a personal grudge against the President, who, as a general in the Gulf War, left special operative Murphy to die following a cancelled hit on Sadaam Hussein. Instead of the ransom money his partners were planning on, Murphy wants the President to commit suicide on live television; to prove his seriousness, Murphy nukes Mt. Rushmore and then aims another missile at Washington DC. Northrop and Cross battle Murphy's thugs while attempting to dismantle the nuclear arsenal. Decimating the ranks of terrorists, Cross nabs Murphy and reobtains the launch code case, even as Murphy launches the second rocket. As Murphy plummets to his death from a rocket pad, Cross neutralizes the nuclear missile in flight.

In the annals of atomic scaremongering, radicals have played nuclear tag for profit, for power, and for political purposes. Never has any antagonist nuked 300 people and a national treasure to get even with a former commander. That unbelievable plot-hook is only the most preposterous element in this eminently silly bomb-a-thon. Why, for instance, do the venal terrorists continue to pummel Cross after realizing their psychotic boss isn't interested in collecting a ransom for them? Tedious scene after scene of attempted bomb disarmament defuses any suspense.

In a large and unimpressive cast (which includes one-time Oscar nominee Roy Scheider), talk-show host Montel Williams shakes things up with some of the dynamism he exudes on TV. However, THE PEACEKEEPER is awash in top-of-the-line special effects and rib-crunching martial arts; it's also energized by a spectacular chase across rooftops. These distracting destructive moments save THE PEACEKEEPER from its inherent idiocy. *(Graphic violence, extreme profanity.)* —R.P.

d, Frederic Forestier; p, Nicolas Clermont; exec p, Elie Samaha, Avi Lerner; co-p, Stewart Harding; w, James H. Stewart, Robert Geoffrion; ph, John Berrie; ed, Yves Langlois; m, Francois Forestier; prod d, John Meighen; art d, David Blanchard; set d, Josiane Noreau; fx, Andre Pelchay; casting, Vera Miller; cos, Francois Barbeau; makeup, Michele Dion; stunts, Shane Cardwell

Action (PR: C MPAA: R)

PECKER ★★½

(U.S., 1998) 87m Polar Productions; Fine Line ~ Fine Line c

Edward Furlong *(Pecker)*; Christina Ricci *(Shelly)*; Martha Plimpton *(Tina)*; Brendan Sexton III *(Matt)*; Lauren Hulsey *(Little Chrissy)*; Mary Kay Place; Lili Taylor; Jean Schertler *(Memama)*; Bess Armstrong *(Dr. Klompus)*; Mark Joy *(Jimmy)*; Mink Stole *(Precinct Captain)*; Patricia Hearst *(Lynn Wentworth)*; Maureen Fischer *(T-Bone)*; Donald Neal *(Mr. Bozak)*; Carolyn Stayer *(Miss Betty)*; Jack Webster *(Outsider Al)*; Alan J. Wendl *(Mr. Nellbox)*; Judith Knight Young *("Fat & Furious" Lady)*; Anthony Rogers *(Billy Heckman, "Death Row Dave")*; Billy Tolzman *(Seafood Sam)*; Brian Thomas *(Larry the Lughead)*; Tim Caggiano *(Lester Hallbrook)*; Betsy Ames *(Venetia Keydash)*; Scott Morgan *(Jed Coleman)*; Valerie Karasek *(Redd Larchmont)*; Cindy Sherman *(Herself)*; Joyce Flick Wendl *(Street Lady)*; Liam Hughes *(Wild Man of 22nd Street)*; Greg Gorman *(Himself)*; Irving Jacobs *(Guzzels)*; Mary Vivan Pierce *(Homophobic Lady)*; Kennen Sisco *(Art Fan A)*; Jennifer Zakroff *(Art Fan B)*; Angela Calo *(Pregnant Girl)*; Susan Duvall *(Saleswoman)*; Ruth Lawson Walsh *(Sneaky Customer)*; Adin Alai *(Body Builder)*; Emmy Collins *(Hippie)*; Brigid Berlin *(Super Market Rich Lady)*; Kimberlee Suerth *(Beautiful Girl)*; John Badilla *(Irate Manager)*; R. Scott Williams *(Stylist)*; Susan Lowe *(Hairdresser)*; Marisa Zalabak *(Makeup Artist)*; Andreas Kraemer *(Junkie)*; Sharon Nelsp *(Bouncer)*; Delany Williams *(Construction Worker)*; Bobby Brown *(Average Joe)*; Regi Davis *(Cop A)*; Tyler Miller *(Randy, Blind Photographer)*; Channing Wilroy *(Wise Guy Neighbor)*; Rosemary Knower *(Friend of Mary A)*; Kate Kiley *(Friend of Mary B)*; Jack French *(Old Fart Customer)*; Doug Roberts *(Mr. Heckman, Death Row Dave's Father)*; Holly Twyford *(Straight Girl)*; Joshua Shoemaker *(Channel 11 Anchor)*; Sloane Brown *(Sloane Brown, Channel 45 Anchor)*; Thomas Korzeniowski *(Toupe Man)*; Susan Greenhill *(Voice of Miraculous Virgin Mary)*; Lola Pashalinski *(Voice of Pelt Room Announcer)*

Further evidence that former enfant terrible John Waters has turned into an old softie, PECKER is a suprisingly saccharine parable about a small-town boy whose life is nearly ruined by sudden celebrity status and the fawning attention of NYC's irony-obsessed art world.

Blithely innocent Pecker (Edward Furlong) is a fry cook at the "Sub Pit" who obsessively photographs everyone and everything he sees. Subjects include his neighbors in the Baltimore neighborhood of Hampden, his oddball relatives, his sneak-thief friend Matt (Brendan Sexton III), and his girlfriend, Shelley (Christina Ricci), who doggedly manages a local laundromat.

New York art dealer Rorey (Lili Taylor) attends an exhibit of Pecker's photographs at the Sub Pit and invites him to have a show at her Manhattan gallery. Pecker and his family and friends suffer culture shock when they travel to NYC to attend the exhibit, but are pleased that the art world embraces his photography (his emphasis on offbeat subject causes them to label him "a more humane Diane Arbus.") Upon their return to Baltimore, however, they find that his fame has brought unwanted attention from the press. Other problems arise: Matt's thievery has been exposed in the photos; Pecker's gay-friendly sister Tina (Martha Plimpton) loses her job at a local male strip joint also featured in Pecker's work; a neighbor threatens to sue Pecker for using her in his photographs; and Shelley is embarrassed by the attention Pecker's photos have brought her, and annoyed at the attention showered on him by Rorey. Although Rorey has presented him with a new high-tech camera and encourages his work as a photographer, Pecker opts against her offer of a solo show at NY's Whitney Museum of Art. Before he can notify his friends and family of his decision, however, Shelley sees him receiving a kiss from Rorey; he subsequently pursues Shelley to a polling place, and the young couple settle their differences by making love in a voting booth.

Pecker ultimately decides on a way to stay true to his original dream: he opens a nightclub in Baltimore where his photos will be displayed. His first show—for which buses of art aficionados are brought in from NYC—is a collection of revealing and embarrassing photos he took of gallery owners, artists, and critics who attended his first Manhattan show.

PECKER is not the work of the agent provocateur who made PINK FLAMINGOS (1972) and FEMALE TROUBLE (1975); instead, it's the product of the kinder, gentler eccentric who came up with the offbeat, but still very reassuring HAIRSPRAY (1988) and SERIAL MOM (1994). To say that Waters has "lost his edge" is to deny the fact that he didn't make comedies in the conventional sense back in his "underground" heyday: he made tacky, episodic acts of provocation (blessed with some of the most memorably acidic dialogue in American cinema). The mainstream, post-POLYESTER John Waters does, however, make comedies, and therein lies the biggest problem with PECKER: when dealing with conventional story structure, he has to follow certain narrative rules, and by doing so, he produces a film that is uncommonly naive, and is doomed to be only as entertaining as the next wacky character or kooky situation.

The film's simplistic message—that insincere big-city trend-purveyors shouldn't despoil the genuine home-grown tackiness that breeds in smaller cities and towns—is obviously commendable, but it quickly turns the film into a sort of warped Chamber of Commerce ad for Baltimore. It must also be noted that Waters covered similar ground (and in a much more savage, and effective, fashion) in FEMALE TROUBLE, in the sequences where Divine's "ugliness" is exploited by an upscale art-loving couple.

The weakest moments in PECKER are those in which Waters goes entirely "mainstream" and presents choreographed chaos. At three different points, he has characters running around in a closed space wreaking havoc, and the results are strictly sub-Touchstone-level humor. He also takes care to include a running gag—Pecker's younger sister's love of sugary foods—that qualifies as comic relief, a rather conventional notion for a film that's already a comedy.

The film's most amusing bit of business is Pecker's grandmother's fixation with a Virgin Mary statue that she claims speaks to her. Using the statue as a ventriloquist dummy, the old lady parrots stock phrases like "Full of grace!" showing that Waters, a lapsed Catholic, still has some degree of his old bad-boy instincts intact. (A later sequence in which other Maryites unmask the grandmother's delusion is a most unfortunate choice on Waters' part, as outsiders from the "real world" should play no part in his imaginary universe.)

The cast uniformly play their parts with glee, attempting to lend a suitably cartoonish dimension to their roles; Ricci gets highest marks for playing Shelley as fully and completely obsessed wtih her job. As for Furlong, his sticky-sweet (and oddly androgynous) presence fits Pecker to a tee; the fact that the character is the biggest innocent in Waters's work to date (and thus not exactly the most sympathetic young man) should not go unmentioned.

In the final analysis, PECKER is a pleasant enough experience, but Waters the comedy filmmaker runs a very distant second as an artist to Waters the provocateur. *(Extensive nudity, profanity, sexual situations.)*— E.G.

d, John Waters; p, John Fiedler, Mark Tarlov; exec p, Mark Ordesky, Joe Revitte, Jonathan Weisgal, Joe Caraccilo Jr.; w, John Waters; ph, Robert Stevens; ed, Janice Hampton; m, Stewart Copeland; prod d,

Vincent Peranio; art d, Scott Pina; set d, Pat Burgee; sound, Rick Angelella, Carol Everson; casting, Pat Moran, Hopkins-Smith-Barden; cos, Van Smith

Comedy **(PR: C MPAA: R)**

PENTAGON WARS, THE ★★★½

(U.S., 1998) 103m Jersey Films ~ HBO c

Kelsey Grammer *(Major General Partridge)*; Cary Elwes *(Colonel Burton)*; Viola Davis *(Fanning)*; John C. McGinley *(Colonel J.D. Bock)*; Tom Wright *(Major William Sayers)*; Clifton Powell *(Sgt. Benjamin Dalton)*; Dewey Weber *(Spec-4 Ganger)*; Richard Schiff *(General Smith)*; J.C. MacKenzie *(Jones)*; Richard Benjamin *(Casper Weinberger)*; Olympia Dukakis *(Madam Chairwoman)*; Christopher Grove *(Congressman #1)*; Sam Anderson *(Congressman #2)*; Dwayne Macopson *(USMC Guard at Subway)*; Dominic D. DeNiro *(Guard at Military Base)*; Daniel Raymont *(Unknown Officer)*; Randy Oglesby *(Test Range General)*; Billie Worley *(Test Range Lieutenant)*; Dann Florek *(General #1)*; Beau Billingslea *(General #2)*; Richard Riehle *(General #3)*; Roberto Alvarez *(First Soldier in Bradley)*; Chris Ellis *(General Keane)*; Charles Parks *(General Cushing)*; Drew Snyder *(Admiral Marchouse)*; Laura Skill *(Soldier Delivering Message)*; Kevin Scannell *(Collins)*; James DuMont *(Young Officer)*; Freez Luv *(Clean Up Soldier)*; Bruce French *(General De Grasso)*; Ralph P. Martin *(Factory Manager)*; Matt Champagne *(Partridge's Aide)*; Tim DeKay *(Jr. Officer Embassy Party)*; Adam Paul *(Waiter at Fancy Restaurant)*; Brian Carroll *(Range Officer in Tower)*

The military bureaucracy takes it on the chin in this comedy, made for HBO and based on the true story of an Army weapons project that spent a staggering amount of money on a vehicle that didn't work. Crisply directed by Richard Benjamin, THE PENTAGON WARS delivers its best punches subtly.

In 1983, Air Force Lt. Col. James Burton (Cary Elwes) is assigned to oversee the testing of new military hardware at an Army testing post under Major General Partridge (Kelsey Grammer). Alerted by an anonymous phone caller, Burton learns that, despite efforts by Partridge's staff to distract him, tests on the Bradley Fighting Vehicle were done with ammunition that wouldn't dent a paper bag. Examining the voluminous paperwork on the Bradley, he reads that it has been in development since 1968, during which time it has gone from an economical troop transport vehicle to a monster designed to do too many different things. He discovers that his secret phone caller is General Smith (Richard Schiff), who guided the Bradley for years and is afraid to ruin his career by going public with his knowledge that it is a death trap. Burton's attempts to openly test the Bradley are stymied by Partridge, whose own career is on the line. By convincing Smith to leak a story to the newspapers, Burton gets the matter before a Congressional panel, which is horrified to learn that the Bradley project has already cost $14 billion. The panel demands a live-fire test. Partridge orders base personnel to correct problems in the vehicle scheduled to be tested, and stages the test as a public relations event. But unknown to him, the mechanics have returned the test Bradley to its original state, and in what is supposed to be a demonstration of its "invulnerability," it is destroyed.

The story of the Bradley Fighting Vehicle is probably not the worst example of military misspending, and the limitations of a feature film require the script to condense its history rather too much. And the characters are a shade too broad, though Kelsey Grammer invests General Partridge with just the right combination of oily charm and calculated bluster. (As Burton, however, Cary Elwes looks uncomfortably like Oliver North). The best parts of THE PENTAGON WARS demonstrate the greater problem, that the American military is a colossal, overfed bureaucracy where, as in every bureaucracy, the goal of the organization often takes a back seat to the needs of its members. A caption at the end of the film notes that, despite the monumental waste in the Bradley program, most of the officers involved were either promoted or went on to high-paying defense industry jobs, while the Pentagon budgeted another $1 billion for "capability upgrades" on the Bradley. The humor in THE PENTAGON WARS, which, like many HBO productions, is adult in the best sense of the word, mitigates a bitter pill, but that bitterness leaves an aftertaste. *(Profanity.)*—M.F.

d, Richard Benjamin; p, Howard Meltzer; exec p, Martyn Burke, Danny DeVito, Michael Shamberg, Stacy Sher, Gail Lyon; co-p, Gary Daigler; w, Jamie Malanowski, Martyn Burke (based on the book by Col. James G. Burton); ph, Robert Yeoman; ed, Jacqueline Cambas; m, Joseph Vitarelli; prod d, Vincent J. Cresciman; sound, Glenn Micallef; fx, David Simmons; casting, Nancy Foy; cos, Amy Stofsky; makeup, Jo-Anne Smith; stunts, Rick Avery

Comedy **(PR: C MPAA: R)**

PEREIRA DECLARES ★★½

(Italy/France/Portugal, 1995) 104m Jean Vigo International/K.G. Productions; Mikado Film; Fabrica De Imagens ~ Mikado Film c
(AKA: PEREIRA HOLDS; ACCORDING TO PEREIRA; SOSTIENE PEREIRA; AFIRMA PEREIRA)

Marcello Mastroianni *(Pereira)*; Stefano Dionisi *(Monteiro Rossi)*; Nicoletta Braschi *(Marta)*; Daniel Auteuil *(Dottor Cardoso)*; Joaquim De Almeida *(Manuel)*; Marthe Keller *(Signora Delgado)*; Teresa Madruga *(Portiera)*; Nicolau Breyner *(Padre Antonio)*; Filipe Ferrer *(Silva)*; Mario Viegas *(Direttore del Giornale)*; Joao Grosso *(Capo della Polizia Politica)*; Teresa Gouveia *(Moglie di Pereira)*

In one of his final roles before his death in 1996, Marcello Mastroianni gives a powerful performance as an aging journalist who's drawn into political intrigue in 1930s Portugal. Unfortunately, the potentially fascinating, fact-based story is given a prosaic and over-literary treatment that drains most of its interest and suspense.

Pereira (Marcello Mastroianni) is an elderly, widowed culture page editor at a Lisbon newspaper in 1938. He devotes his column to translations of French literature and scrupulously avoids anything political which might antagonize the dictatorial government, which is allied with the fascist regimes of Spain and Italy. Pereira hires a young man named Monteiro (Stefano Dionisi) to prepare advance obituaries for aging writers, but it turns out that Monteiro and his girlfriend Marta (Nicoletta Braschi) are involved with the underground revolutionaries, and they both try to convince Pereira to help their cause. Pereira's conscience is also roused from its apathy by a chance encounter with a persecuted Jewish woman (Marthe Keller) who's fleeing the country and asks him to write about the injustices being committed.

Monteiro convinces Pereira to let his fugitive revolutionary cousin hide out at Pereira's apartment while he goes away to a health clinic for treatments on his weak heart. At the clinic, the conflicted Pereira strikes up a friendship with a doctor (Daniel Auteuil), who encourages him to follow his conscience and speak out against the dictatorship. After Pereira publishes an anti-Nazi short story, his apartment is raided by some police goons and they beat Pereira and kill Monteiro when he won't reveal Marta's whereabouts. Pereira writes a blistering article about the incident, accusing the police and the government of being fascist murderers, and after tricking the printer into putting it on the front page, he flees the country using one of Monteiro's fake passports.

Earnest, but unremarkable, PEREIRA DECLARES is like a TV-movie with subtitles. The filmmakers apparently believe that good intentions and worthy messages automatically result in a good movie and preclude the need for cinematic imagination. Its pace is lumbering and its mise-en-scene is uninspired (including an atypically flat Ennio Morricone score), largely consisting of long, static scenes featuring a plethora of talk. The only time the film really springs to life is during its violent finale when Pereira and Monteiro are beaten and the tense scenes involving Pereira's escape from the country, indicating that director Roberto Faenza (CORRUPT) is capable of excitement but somehow felt is was unnecessary.

Instead of attempting to dramatize Pereira's conflicts and mental transformation, the film employs the tired novelistic device of having an omnipresent narrator provide Pereira's thoughts by constantly breaking in to state "Pereira declares" this and "Pereira declares" that, no doubt reading passages directly from the book on which the film is based. Marcello Mastroianni's intelligent performance sustains interest in the film and even manages to make it compelling through his quietly understated dignity. Whether Pereira is commiserating with the photo of his late, beloved wife, talking philosophy with his priest and doctor, or discussing politics with the young radicals, Mastroianni brings substance and a sense of humor to the character. His is the dominant force in the film, and he single-handedly saves it from being an unsuccessful piece of agitprop and turns it into a fairly interesting character study. It's a worthy late role for the great actor. *(Violence.)*—M.S.

d, Roberto Faenza; p, Elda Ferri; w, Roberto Faenza, Sergio Vecchio, Antonio Tabucchi (based on the novel *Sostiene Pereira* by Antonio); ph, Blasco Giurato; ed, Ruggero Mastroianni; m, Ennio Morricone; prod d, Giantito Burchiellaro; art d, Giantito Burchiellaro; sound, Eric Vaucher (mixer); cos, Elisabetta Beraldo

Political/Drama/Historical (PR: C MPAA: NR)

PERFECT MURDER, A ★★½

(U.S., 1998) 110m Kopelson Entertainment;
Warner Bros. ~ Warner Bros. c

Michael Douglas *(Steven Taylor)*; Gwyneth Paltrow *(Emily Bradford Taylor)*; Viggo Mortensen *(David Shaw)*; David Suchet *(Detective Mohamed Karaman)*; Constance Towers *(Sandra Bradford)*; Sarita Choudhury *(Raquel)*; Michael P. Moran *(Detective Bobby Fain)*; Novella Nelson *(Ambassador Wills)*; Will Lyman *(Jason Gates)*; Maeve McGuire *(Ann Gates)*; Stephen Singer *(Effete Man at Met)*; Laurinda Barrett *(Met Woman #1)*; Aideen O'Kelly *(Met Woman #2)*; Reed Birney *(Merchant Prince #1)*; Robert Vincent Smith *(Merchant Prince #2)*; Bill Ambrozy *(Merchant Prince #3)*; George S. Blumenthal *(Merchant Prince #4)*; Iris Alten; Marion Blumenthal; Andrew Sussman; Robynn N. Sussman; Radney Tucker; Beverly Tucker; Bradford Billet *(Guests at Met)*; Robert Bosco Cokljat *(Croatian Delegate)*; Marat Yusim *(Russian Delegate)*; Lee Wong *(Japanese Diplomat)*; Roberta Orlan *(Italian Diplomat)*; Francis Dumaurier *(French Delegate)*; Deen Badarou *(African Delegate)*; Peter Benson *(Hansen)*; Jeff Williams *(Nolan)*; David Eigenberg *(Stein)*; Jean Debaer *(Secretary)*; Michel Moinot *(Maitre D')*; Gerrit Vooren *(Waiter)*; Monica Parker *(Janice Moran)*; Michael H. Ingram *(Albert)*; Scott Dillin *(Detective Scott)*; Starla Benford *(Police Technician)*; Bob Bowersox *(Police Photographer)*; Joanna P. Adler *(Vyczowski)*; James Georgiades *(Policeman #2)*; Jose Ramon Rosario *(Policeman #1)*; Gerry Becker *(Roger Brill)*; William Bogert *(Harrington)*; Adrian Martinez *(Young Tough)*; Dexter Brown *(Porter)*; John Cenatiempo

A PERFECT MURDER is a much-less-than-perfect remake of Hitchcock's classic DIAL M FOR MURDER (1954). The film has some eye-catching visuals, but the characters act foolishly this time around, draining most of the suspense from the proceedings.

Emily Taylor (Gwyneth Paltrow) is the attractive wife of a seemingly wealthy Wall Street investor, Steven (Michael Douglas). But Emily, who holds an important job as an interpreter at the United Nations, often feels alone in her marriage and seeks the comfort of David (Viggo Mortensen), a struggling young artist who appears to genuinely love her. Steven finds out about the affair, yet keeps quiet about what he knows. Instead, he plans to use jealousy as an impetus to kill Emily in order to inherit her family fortune and pay back the many debts he owes. He meets with David at the artist's Brooklyn loft and offers him $500,000 to kill Emily. At first he refuses, but when Steven threatens to reveal incriminating information about David's background as an embezzler, David agrees to the scheme, not really having loved Emily anyway.

Steven works out an elaborate plan for letting David into their Fifth Avenue apartment on a night when Emily stays home alone. But David secretly hires a friend to play intruder, and during that evening, a startled Emily kills the man who was supposed to kill her. When he arrives home from playing cards with friends, Steven realizes that his plan has fallen apart. He defends and comforts a distraught Emily in front of the police, including the suspicious chief detective, Mohamed Karaman (David Suchet); later, Steven accompanies Emily to her family home, where she confides to her mother (Constance Towers) that she plans to leave Steven.

Back in the city, Steven questions David about the failed murder, and David—after playing him a tape of their previous discussion, counter-blackmails Steven for more money. Steven uses the last of his savings in order to pay off David, who plans to leave town with the loot. Steven surprises David in his overnight train compartment, murders him, and steals the money back. That night, Emily returns to the apartment, where she confronts Steven with her suspicions that he was in some way responsible for the attempted murder. Steven shifts the blame to David, but Emily's suspicions are confirmed when she discovers that the latchkey the intruder used to enter could only have come from Steven. After a violent fight, Emily shoots and kills Steven.

The team behind THE FUGITIVE (including the director, three of the producers, the editor, and the composer) update DIAL M FOR MURDER with more sex, more violence, a few extra plot twists, and lots of cellular phones. But in many ways, A PERFECT MURDER is best when it sticks to the deviously clever original (based on the play by Frederick Knott). The Hitchcock film was a deadly cat-and-mouse game played out like drawing-room comedy, while the new film is a jangly action picture chockful of over-the-top emoting.

Hitchcock buffs will miss the more subtle suspense techniques, the grim ironic humor, his experiments with perspective (for 3-D showings of the film) and the nattier, superior cast—particularly Ray Milland and Grace Kelly as the married couple and John Williams as the inspector. This time, the characters make too many mistakes: Steven throws away his cellular phone (with traceable numbers) into the street during a moment of crisis; later, he meets David in a place where they could easily be spotted by the police; and the police themselves make ineffectual moves to catch their suspect. While it is Emily who finally figures out Steven's plot, up to that moment, she seems thoroughly duped by both men in her life. Her willingness to confront Steven about her suspicions (without police backup or even the assistance of her girlfriend, played by Sarita Choudhury), shows a lack of common sense, as opposed to nervy bravado.

The idea of remaking and updating DIAL M FOR MURDER is not bad, but, ironically, much of A PERFECT MURDER seems disconnected to the modern-day world. To wit, Emily's UN job serves little function in terms of plot or character, and David Suchet's detective anachronistically resembles the actor's PBS appearances as Hercule Poirot. In its favor, the cold, dark film at least looks the way it should (even if the magnificent production design steals scenes from the actors), and the Taylor's luxurious Fifth Avenue apartment makes a perfect setting for a thriller. A PERFECT MURDER also generates the same sort of emotional (if prurient) intensity that made Michael Douglas's FATAL ATTRACTION (1987) such a big hit a decade earlier. Thus, contemporary movie fans who ignore the impressive pedigree might enjoy A PERFECT MURDER. *(Violence, nudity, sexual situations, adult situations, profanity.)*—E.M.

d, Andrew Davis; p, Arnold Kopelson, Anne Kopelson, Christopher Mankiewicz, Peter MacGregor-Scott; exec p, Stephen Brown; assoc p, Lowell Blank, Lisa Reardon, Teresa Tucker-Davies; co-p, Nana Greewald, Mitchell Dauterive; w, Patrick Smith Kelly (based on the play "Dial M For Murder" by Frederick Knott); ph, Dariusz Wolski; ed, Dennis Virkler, Dov Hoenig; m, James Newton Howard; prod d, Philip Rosenberg; art d, Patricia Woodbridge; set d, Debra Schutt; sound, Tom Nelson (mixer), Lance Brown (design); fx, Jeffrey S. Brink; casting, Amanda Mackey Johnson, Cathy Sandrich; cos, Ellen Mirojnick; makeup, Naomi Donne; stunts, Michael Runyard

Thriller/Crime/Drama **(PR: C MPAA: R)**

PERMANENT MIDNIGHT ★★

(U.S., 1998) 85m JD Productions;
Artisan Entertainment ~ Artisan Entertainment c

Ben Stiller *(Jerry Stahl)*; Elizabeth Hurley *(Sandra)*; Janeane Garofalo *(Jana)*; Maria Bello *(Kitty)*; Owen C. Wilson *(Nicky)*; Lourdes Benedicto *(Vola)*; Fred Willard *(Craig Ziffer)*; Liz Torres *(Dita)*; Douglas Spain *(Miguel)*; Charles Fleischer *(Allen from Mr. Chompers)*; Cheryl Ladd *(Pamela Verlaine)*; Peter Greene *(Gus)*; Jerry Stahl *(Dr. Murphy)*; Jay Paulson *(Phoenix Punk)*; Spencer Garrett *(Brad/Tim from Mr. Chompers)*; Chauncey Leopardi *(Jerry at 16)*; Mary Thompson *(Grandma Whittle)*; Connie Nielsen *(Dagmar)*; Sandra Oh *(Friend)*; Scott Williamson *(Gary Warren)*; Nancye Ferguson *(Nurse)*; Sam Anderson *(Dr. Olsen)*; Regina Nichols *(Scrub Nurse)*; John Prosky *(Cop)*; Francois Giroday *(Peter)*

Based on the actual experiences of writer Jerry Stahl, PERMANENT MIDNIGHT is a somber, uninvolving film about a man's hellish journey through drug addiction.

In a motel outside Los Angeles, Jerry (Ben Stiller) tells Kitty (Maria Bello)—a woman who has just picked him up—of his life as a drug addict. Wanting to be a writer, the young Jerry Stahl moves to Los Angeles. Desperate for money, he accepts payment to marry a British woman, Sandra (Elizabeth Hurley), so that she can get a green card. Sandra, who works in the television industry, assists Jerry in landing a job, as a writer for a popular comedy series, "Mr. Chompers." Drawing upon personal experiences for comic inspiration, Jerry is a success.

When he learns that his mother has committed suicide, Jerry goes to a bar to drink. There, he meets a German woman (Connie Nielsen) who introduces him to heroin. He quickly becomes addicted and, as his addiction strengthens, his life falls apart. He loses his job, ruins both an opportunity to write for another show—despite the support of Pamela (Cheryl Ladd), the show's star—and the chance to be represented by a top agent, Jana (Janeane Garofalo). With Sandra, Jerry becomes a father, but when he is arrested for bringing the baby with him while on a drug binge, he realizes that his drug use must stop.

Having told his story, Jerry leaves Kitty to catch a bus for Los Angeles. In LA, he accepts menial jobs as he works his way through rehabilitation. He visits Sandra and his daughter at Sandra's home, but she is cool to him and he leaves. At Jerry's rented room, Kitty surprises him with a visit. The two make love and she leaves town the next morning. Resuming his career as a writer, Jerry details his experiences in a book, *Permanent Midnight.* In promotional appearances on television talk shows, Jerry tells of how he survived, and how he will continue to do so.

PERMANENT MIDNIGHT is never as harrowing as it means to be. Stiller and writer-director David Veloz work arduously at making Stahl's autobiographical nightmare palpable, at manifesting the horror of an all-enveloping addiction. For all their effort, though, the film remains distant and unaffecting. Part of the problem is Stiller. Stiller is an earnest, talented performer, but he's disastrously miscast as Stahl. His amiable lead performances in FLIRTING WITH DISASTER (1996) and THERE'S SOMETHING ABOUT MARY (1998) were aided in no small part by the upbeat nature of the material and terrific, well-used supporting casts. Here, his performance is intense and concentrated, but he seems continually ill at ease with the sullen nature of the character. He simply isn't the right actor for a brooding dramatic role.

Most of the problem with PERMANENT MIDNIGHT, however, rests with Veloz. Veloz has obviously put a great deal of care into giving his film the right look. Jerry's world is one of perpetual darkness. Much of the action takes place at night or in windowless rooms, and Robert D. Yeoman's excellent cinematography manages to keep Stiller shrouded in shadow even in daylight sequences. The pervasive darkness of the film is striking, but Veloz seems to have developed it at the expense of everything else. He fails to define Jerry as anything but a drug addict, and he makes little of the ironic contrast between Jerry's self-destructive lifestyle and the feel-good drivel he writes to make money. Veloz also fails to take full advantage of a great supporting cast, leaving such splendid performers as Janeane Garofalo, Owen Wilson, and Fred Willard to flounder in brief, underdeveloped roles.

Perhaps Veloz's preoccupation with technique is due to his association with Oliver Stone—Veloz co-scripted NATURAL BORN KILLERS (1994). Unlike Stone, though, Veloz lacks the experience (PERMANENT MIDNIGHT is his first feature) to make style substantive enough to carry a film. Time will tell if he will ever have the ability. *(Violence, nudity, sexual situations, adult situations, substance abuse, extreme profanity.)*—D.C.

d, David Veloz; p, Jane Hamsher, Don Murphy; exec p, Yalda Yehranian; co-p, Robert Leveen; w, David Veloz (based on novel by Jerry Stahl); ph, Robert Yeoman; ed, Steven Weisberg, Cara Silverman; m, Daniel Licht; prod d, Jerry Fleming; art d, Ryan Ong; sound, Eric Enroth (mixer); casting, Ronnie Yeskel, Richard Hicks; cos, Louise Mingenbach, Lori Eskowitz; makeup, Christina Bartolucci; stunts, Eddie Perez

Drama/Biography **(PR: O MPAA: R)**

PHANTASM: OBLIVION ★★

(U.S., 1998) 90m Starway International Inc. ~
Orion Home Video c

A. Michael Baldwin *(Mike)*; Reggie Bannister *(Reggie)*; Bill Thornbury *(Jody)*; Heidi Marnhout *(Jennifer)*; Bob Ivy *(Demon

Trooper); Angus Scrimm *(The Tall Man)*; Chloe Kay; Sylvia Flammer; David Gasster; Sasha Kassel; Aidan Kassel

The fourth installment of Don Coscarelli's horror franchise returns the focus to the grave-robbing shenanigans of the eerie Tall Man. With all of the original leads returning 19 years after the series debut, the filmmakers skillfully integrate unused footage from the first PHANTASM in order to beef up the lackluster story line.

A fiend nicknamed the Tall Man (Angus Scrimm) continues to transport human corpses through a dimensional portal to another planet, aided by half-pint drones and flying metallic spheres equipped with retractable spikes. Mike (A. Michael Baldwin), who has been haunted by this villain since he was a boy, is slowly being transformed into one of the Tall Man's minions. Mike's old pal, ice cream vendor Reggie (Reggie Bannister) has his own problems: first, he has a fight with a possessed policeman, and then is visited by Mike's dead brother Jody (Bill Thornbury), who is an incorporeal being, possibly in league with the Tall Man.

Using one of the Tall Man's strange portals, Mike travels back in time to the mid-1800's, where he learns that the Tall Man began as an undertaker, who entered an experimental rift and emerged as an insidious monster. Reggie and Mike drive to a location in Death Valley; undead Jody appears in the same location via a nearby portal. Mike uses one of the portals in the desert to travel back in time, in hopes of putting a stop to the origin of the Tall Man. Unsuccessful, he's forced to kill the possessed Jody, and escapes back to the desert (and Reggie)—followed by the Tall Man. When Mike loses his face-off against the Tall Man, the heavily armed Reggie follows the Tall Man through the gateway, leaving the injured Mike behind and promising him he'll put an end to this nightmare.

Picking up exactly where PHANTASM 3 left off, director-writer Coscarelli weaves together several parallel story threads here, each following its own internal (often hazy) logic. And while fans will be amused to see all of these characters in their old, familiar roles, newcomers will find it just about impossible to understand the plot. On the positive side, Coscarelli makes ingenious use of the clips from the original film, and comes up with the occasional creepy moment. But more often, PHANTASM: OBLIVION is extremely slow-paced and works only on a scene-by-scene basis rather than as a coherent whole. In a misguided move, Coscarelli attempts here to offer concrete explanations for the plot devices that made the original film such a success—when, in fact, the original was successful specifically because so much was left to one's imagination.

Despite obvious budgetary constraints, the film has a convincing production design and the performances are workmanlike—with the cast members deserving special credit for keeping straight faces during the goofiest moments. When compared to the other films in the PHANTASM series, OBLIVION is strictly middling horror fare; when considered on its own, it's indeed difficult to endure. Though it is reportedly the final installment in the series, the open-ended finale leaves the door open for more adventures. *(Graphic violence, nudity, sexual situations, profanity.)*—S.P.

d, Don Coscarelli; p, Don Coscarelli; co-p, A. Michael Baldwin; w, Don Coscarelli; ph, Chris Chomyn; ed, Scott J. Gill; m, Christopher Stone, Steven Morrell; prod d, Naython Vane; art d, Michael Roth; sound, Enzo Treppa; fx, D. Kerry Prior, K.N.B. EFX Group; cos, Shelley Kay; stunts, Bob Ivy

Horror **(PR: O MPAA: R)**

PHANTOMS ★★

(U.S., 1998) 94m NEO Motion Pictures; Raven House ~ Dimension c

Peter O'Toole *(Timothy Flyte)*; Joanna Going *(Dr. Jennifer Pailey)*; Rose McGowan *(Lisa Pailey)*; Ben Affleck *(Sheriff Bryce Hammond)*; Liev Schreiber *(Deputy Stu Wargle)*; Clifton Powell *(General Leland Cooperfield)*; Nicky Katt *(Deputy Steve Shanning)*; Michael DeLorenzo *(Soldier Velazquez)*; Rick Otto *(Scientist Lockland)*; Rachel Shane *(Scientist Yamaguchi)*; Adam Nelson *(Scientist Burke)*; John Hammil *(Scientist Talbot)*; John Scott Clough *(Scientist Shane)*; William Hahn *(Scientist Borman)*; Robert Himber *(Scientist Walker)*; Bo Hopkins *(Agent Hawthorne)*; Rob Knepper *(Agent Wilson)*; Paul Schmidt *(Church Soldier)*; Dean Hallo *(Sergeant Harker)*; Clive Rosengren *(Commanding Officer)*; Edmund Wilson *(Guthrie)*; Luke Eberl *(Tunnel Boy)*; Rich Beall *(Security Guard)*; Judith Drake *(Hilda)*; Yvette Nipar *(Cowgirl)*; Ruger *(Phantom Dog)*

Horror novelist Dean Koontz has railed long and hard against the lackluster film versions of his work, but with this adaptation, which he himself scripted, he has no one to blame but himself.

Jennifer Pailey (Joanna Going) brings her troubled sister Lisa (Rose McGowan) to stay with her in her hometown of Snowfield, CO. Upon arriving, they find the town deserted, save for a few disfigured bodies (or parts of them). Sheriff Bryce Hammond (Ben Affleck) turns up with deputies Wargle (Liev Schreiber) and Shanning (Nicky Katt), and at a hotel they discover more bodies and the name "Timothy Flyte" scrawled on a mirror. Night falls, and Shanning is killed by a mysterious force, followed by Wargle. Hammond is able to radio for help, and when the Army arrives with a scientific team, they also bring Flyte (Peter O'Toole). Now a tabloid reporter, Flyte was a distinguished scientist who was discredited for his beliefs about an Ancient Enemy that has been responsible for mass disappearances throughout history.

Soon, the Ancient Enemy (which spawns "phantoms," imitations of its victims) appears and wipes out the soldiers and scientists. The women, Flyte, and Hammond hide in a mobile science lab, where they determine that the creature is petroleum-based and can be killed with a certain chemical. Theorizing that the Enemy, which absorbs the thoughts of its victims, believes it is the Devil himself, Flyte appeals to its ego and talks it into showing itself, whereupon the chemical is fired into it. The beast succumbs, and Jennifer and Lisa destroy an attacking "phantom" version of Wargle. Flyte's reputation is restored—but Wargle's "phantom" has somehow survived.

In this, his first film since the misbegotten HALLOWEEN: THE CURSE OF MICHAEL MYERS (1995), direct Joe Chappelle does offer some good, chilling moments, mostly in the opening sequences where Jennifer and Lisa explore the ominously empty Snowfield. Unfortunately, the women are relegated to the sidelines once Hammond and the deputies show up, and the characters who take their place are bland. Two exceptions to this are Wargle, who's eccentrically interpreted by Schreiber (more's the pity that the character is transformed into a generic wisecracking monster, who gets to participate in the lame open ending, borrowed from 1981's THE HOWLING), and Flyte, as Peter O'Toole brings the film a welcome touch of class. The character is mostly around for exposition, but the monologue he delivers to lure the monster out is well-written and well-played.

The idea of a monster with delusions of grandeur is a fresh and interesting one, but the movie as a whole suffers from a reliance on cliches. Particularly annoying is the overuse of functional dialogue of the "So what you're saying is. . ." variety. And like so many other 1990s chillers, PHANTOMS pours on the makeup effects (plus a few lackluster CGI shots), while its only truly effective moments are those in which no effects are involved. For example, a bit involving a dog warily eyeing Hammond builds a lot more suspense than a sequence in which the same pooch disgorges a slimy monster that kills off some of the scientists. *(Graphic violence, extreme profanity.)*—M.G.

d, Joe Chappelle; p, Joel Soisson, Michael Leahy, Robert Pringle, Steve Lane; exec p, Dean Koontz, Bob Weinstein, Harvey Weinstein; w, Dean Koontz (based on his novel); ph, Richard Clabaugh; ed, Randolph K. Bricker; m, David Williams; prod d, Deborah Raymond, Dorian Vernacchio; art d, Daniel Bradford, Ken Larson; set d, Barbara Cole Kaye; sound, Larry Scharf (mixer), Dean Beville (design), Harry Cohen (design); fx, Robert Kurtzman, Greg Nicotero, Howard Berger, Steve Johnson XFX; casting, Don Phillips; cos, Dana C. Litwack; makeup, Leah Rial, Amanda Carroll, Tom Rainone (effects), K.N.B. EFX Group (effects); stunts, Dan Bradley

Horror **(PR: O MPAA: R)**

PHOENIX ★★

(U.S., 1998) 113m Lakeshore Entertainment; Graham/Nevinny Production ~ Trimark c

Ray Liotta *(Harry Collins)*; Anthony LaPaglia *(Mike Henshaw)*; Daniel Baldwin *(James Nutter)*; Jeremy Piven *(Fred Shuster)*; Anjelica Huston *(Leila)*; Royce D. Applegate *(Dickerman)*; Xander Berkeley *(Lieutenant Clyde Webber)*; Tamara Clatterbuck *(Waitress)*; Vanessa Munday *(Betsy)*; Al Sapienza *(Cop)*; Yvette Cruise *(Maria)*; John Henry Whitaker *(Husband)*; Glenn Morshower *(Anti-Abortionist)*; Brittany Murphy *(Veronica)*; George Murdock *(Sid)*; Kathryn Joosten *(Esther)*; Giancarlo Esposito *(Louie)*; Ernest M. Garcia *(Chubby)*; David Dunard *(Murray)*; Earl Carroll *(Seymour)*; Sandra Taylor *(Video Game Stripper)*; George Aguilar *(Mr. Fat)*; Frank Clem *(Mr. Skinny)*; Tom Noonan *(Chicago)*; Kari Wuhrer *(Katie Shuster)*; Maria Stanton *(Photographer)*; Murphy Dunn *(Carl)*; Sibel Ergener *(Carl's Wife)*; Giovanni Ribisi *(Joey Schneider)*; Dig Wayne *(Norm)*; Simi Mehta *(New Girl)*; Annie Fitzgerald *(Heist Stripper)*; Gordon Jennison Noice *(Manny)*; Carmen Filpi *(Locksmith)*; Margaret Chavez *(Dolores)*; L. Christian Mixon *(Hustler)*

Ray Liotta coproduced and stars in PHOENIX, a crime thriller that boasts a top-notch cast and a stylish look, but is undone by a predictable and derivative script that like so many other post-modern neo-noirs, worships at the moldy altar of Tarantino. After premiering on HBO (which destroyed its widescreen visuals), the film received token theatrical release only two months before going to video.

Harry Collins (Ray Liotta), Mike Henshaw (Anthony LaPaglia), Fred Schuster (Jeremy Piven), and James Nutter (Daniel Baldwin) are Phoenix police detectives who are also close friends. Harry is a gambling addict who's in debt to a bookie named Chicago (Tom Noonan) for $16,000 and is given seven days to pay. The corrupt Henshaw, who works after hours as an enforcer for strip club owner and loan shark Louie (Giancarlo Esposito), suggests that they bust Chicago, but Harry's principles won't allow him to welsh on a bet. After Harry rescues a young girl named Veronica (Brittany Murphy) from an abortion clinic protest, she tries to come on to him, but he drives her home and begins a tentative relationship with her mother Leila (Anjelica Huston). When Harry loses $16,000 more, Chicago tells him that he'll forget it if Harry bumps off a crook named Joey who's been arrested and is planning to testify against Chicago, but Harry refuses.

Meanwhile, Lt. Clyde Webber (Xander Berkeley) learns that Henshaw has been working for Louie and begins tailing him. He takes pictures of Henshaw sleeping with Schuster's wife Katie (Kari Wuhrer) and uses them to convince Schuster to help him nail Henshaw. A desperate Harry decides to rob Louie's club and enlists the help of Henshaw, Nutter, and Schuster. During the heist, Louie recognizes the masked Henshaw's voice, and Henshaw kills him. Afterwards, when Harry and Schuster return to a trailer to meet the others, Webber is waiting there and Harry realizes that Schuster set them up. However, Webber grabs the loot and kills Schuster, then shoots Harry in the stomach, but he manages to drive away. Soon after, Henshaw and Nutter are killed in a police shootout. Playing a hunch, Harry goes to Webber's house and finds him there having sex with Schuster's wife, who has him handcuffed to the bed. Harry calls the police and turns in Webber, then retrieves the money and burns most of it, but takes some with him and mails an envelope full of cash to Leila. He pays Chicago the $32,000, but kills him after Chicago admits that he had Joey murdered anyway, then stumbles back to his car and dies.

Under the atmospheric direction of Danny Cannon (JUDGE DREDD, I STILL KNOW WHAT YOU DID LAST SUMMER), PHOENIX has a genuinely nasty ambiance and gritty style to burn to go along with an A-line cast that's atypical for this kind of B-movie genre piece. But the script is a depressingly familiar compendium of borrowed ideas which, themselves, have been derived from older, better movies to begin with. The opening credits feature a slow-motion shot of the four cops dressed in black suits as they stride down the street (copying the credits for RESERVOIR DOGS, which was copying OCEANS 11), and in another nod to Tarantino's debut, an early scene has the four cops in a diner using obscenities to dissect the sexual subtext of Loony Tunes cartoons (a la the "Like a Virgin" diner scene). What passes for character development are the usual personality quirks (Harry's superstitions, Chicago's lisp, etc.) and pseudo-hip dialogue that consists of heavy-handed pop-culture references on everything from KING KONG (1933) to Dostoyevsky to bluesman Robert Johnson.

The script's other main flaw is that it portrays all the cops as loathsome lowlifes who are no different than the criminals, which negates one of film noir's tenets—to show gradual moral decay—and therefore, there is no dramatic contrast or climactic sense of tragedy. Also, until the heist, which occurs in the final half-hour, there's really no plot, just an episodic series of scenes following the sleazy daily routines of the cops. Liotta does a good job playing another inherent nice guy who becomes devoured by corruption, and he has nice chemistry with Anjelica Huston, who unfortunately, is only in a few brief scenes, but the rest of the cast just goes through the tough-guy, gun-blasting motions, while the film's depiction of women ranks among the most unremittingly misogynistic in a long time, with all of them, besides Leila, being perfidious whores, adulterers, junkies, and nymphets. *(Extreme profanity, graphic violence, nudity, sexual situations.)*—M.S.

d, Danny Cannon; p, Tracie Graham-Rice, Victoria Nevinny; exec p, Michael Mendelsohn, Tom Rosenberg, Sigurjon Sighvatsson, Ted Tannebaum; co-p, Andre Lamal, Ray Liotta, Candace Veach; w, Eddie Richey; ph, James L. Carter; ed, Zach Staenberg; m, Graeme Revell; prod d, Charles Breen; set d, Jeffrey Kushon; sound, Dane A. Davis; fx, Ultimate Effects; casting, Debi Manwiller, Richard Pagano; cos, Alexandra Welker; makeup, Jill Cady; stunts, Gregg Brazzel

Crime/Drama/Thriller **(PR: O MPAA: R)**

PHOTOGRAPHING FAIRIES ★★½

(U.K., 1997) 104m Starry Night Film Company; Dogstar Films ~ PolyGram Video c
(AKA: APPARITION)

Toby Stephens *(Charles Castle)*; Emily Woof *(Linda)*; Ben Kingsley *(Reverend Templeton)*; Philip Davis *(Roy)*; Frances Barber *(Beatrice Templeton)*; Hannah Bould *(Clara Templeton)*; Miriam Grant *(Miriam Grant)*; Edward Hardwicke *(Sir Arthur Conan Doyle)*; Rachel Shelley *(Anne-Marie)*; Clive Merrison *(Gardener)*

Handsome, moody, and foreboding, this flawed film offers an adult perspective on the story told in the feature FAIRY TALE: A TRUE STORY (1997). The tale introduces fictional characters into the matter of the real-life 1917 "Cottingley fairies" hoax in which two English girls produced photos which they claimed proved the existence of fairies. The photos were actually whimsical cutout drawings, but they were taken by occultists at the time to be "scientific" proof of the supernatural.

The widespread publicity surrounding the Cottingley fairy photos, spearheaded by none other than writer Sir Arthur Conan Doyle (Edward Hardwicke), interest portrait photographer Charles Castle (Toby Stephens), who's suffering from the loss of his wife Anne-Marie (Rachel Shelley), who died in an ice fissure on their Alpine honeymoon. Crashing an assembly at the Theosophical Society of London, rationalist Charles denounces the Cottingley photos. Nonetheless, Bea Templeton (Frances Barber), a woman in the audience, tells Castle that *her* two children cavorted with genuine fairies and captured the otherworldly entities on film. When Charles grudgingly scrutinizes the pictures, doubt yields to fascination; something exists in the humanoid blurs. To the dismay of his assistant Roy (Philip Davis), Charles goes to the Templetons' little village to investigate. Bea's husband, the Reverend Templeton (Ben Kingsley), remains aloof, but Mrs. Templeton tells Charles that she's made a breakthrough and can see fairies herself. Suddenly Bea dies in the forest, apparently having fallen from an old tree where her daughters play. Queries to the girls and their sympathetic nanny, Linda (Emily Woof), help Charles learn that the secret to seeing the fairies is to eat a mind-altering flower apparently growing only in the tree trunk. His heightened senses now perceive the fairies around him—and when they pass through his body, Charles experiences the sensation of loving Anne-Marie again. Roy and Linda help Charles erect an array of cameras, but he faces hostility from Rev. Templeton. During a delirious night of fairy-photographing, Charles must be restrained from climbing the tree and repeating Bea's ecstatic, fatal fall. The next day, however, he catches Templeton destroying his equipment and burning the tree, fairies perishing in an invisible holocaust. Charles grapples with the cleric, accidentally killing him. Arrested, the photographer makes no defense, and embraces the death penalty. Before his hanging, Linda gives Charles one last flower to ingest. At the instant of execution he is suddenly back with Anne-Marie in the mountains, but now he saves her from the ice.

That wishful finale, suggesting that everything you've just seen has been a hysterical delusion, badly subverts the spell cast by the rest of the film. PHOTOGRAPHING FAIRIES begins with Stephens (son of eminent actress Maggie Smith and actor Robert Stephens) effectively portraying a soul-damaged hero who himself, via photographic trickery, creates sham "resurrection" portraits of WWI casualties to comfort grieving relatives. An ominous atmosphere prevails as Castle's loss makes him obsess over the prospect of communion with his mate's spirit, and there's a frisson of Antonioni's BLOW-UP (1966) when Castle's lab overflows with countless fairy enlargements after a manic night in the darkroom. The sprites themselves are strikingly introduced, but resemble computer-generated, nude Barbie dolls more than anything else. In fact, first-time director Nick Willing can't seem to figure out what to do upon finally reaching fairyland, and thus Ben Kingsley's sketchy character arbitrarily mutates into an ill-motivated antagonist. Plus, solemn scenes of Anne-Marie and Charles's fates are played out in painfully phony-looking artificial snow.

Viewing this back to back with the upbeat FAIRY TALE: A TRUE STORY yields a RASHOMON-like feeling of storytellers with different agendas tackling the same material. Here Charles Castle uses basic camera principles to discredit the Cottingley stills; in FAIRY TALE, a similar scene has an expert citing the same details to authenticate the pictures. Similarity between the two features was more than coincidence, reported American author Steve Szilagyi, who claimed that a script adaptation of his 1992 novel *Photographing Fairies*, supposedly rejected by an initial production company, was developed into the PG-rated clone released by Paramount. Meanwhile, Polygram's PHOTOGRAPHING FAIRIES allegedly went through 23 script drafts, discarding much of Szilagyi's original text anyway. In 1998, after both movies had played out, the original Cottingley fairy photographs sold to a book dealer at auction in London for the equivalent of $35,000. *(Nudity, sexual situations, adult situations, violence, substance abuse.)*—C.C.

d, Nick Willing; p, Michele Camarda; exec p, Mike Newell, Alan Greenspan; co-p, Fonda Snyder, Lawrence Weinberg; w, Nick Willing, Chris Harrald (based on the novel Steve Szilagyi); ph, John de Borman; ed, Sean Barton; m, Simon Boswell; prod d, Laurence Dorman; sound, Annie Spiers; casting, Susie Figgis; cos, Hazel Pethig

Historical/Drama/Fantasy (PR: O MPAA: R)

PI ★★½

(U.S., 1998) 85m Protozoa Pictures; Truth and Soul Pictures; Harvest Filmworks; Plantain Films ~ Artisan Entertainment bw

Sean Gullette *(Maximillian Cohen)*; Mark Margolis *(Sol Robeson)*; Ben Shenkman *(Lenny Meyer)*; Pamela Hart *(Marcy Dawson)*; Stephen Pearlman *(Rabbi Cohen)*; Samia Shoaib *(Devi)*; Ajay Naidu *(Farrouhk)*; Kristyn Mae-Anne Lao *(Jenna)*; Espher Lao Nieves *(Jenna's Mom)*; Joanne Gordon *(Mrs Ovadia)*; Lauren Fox *(Jenny Robeson)*; Stanley Herman *(Moustacheless Man)*; Clint Mansell *(Photographer)*; Tom Tumminello *(Ephraim)*; Ari Handel; Oren Sarch; Lloyd Schwarz; Richard "Izzi" Lifschutz; David Strahlberg *(Kabbalists)*; Peter Cheyenne *(Brad)*; David Tawil *(Jake)*; J.C. Islander *(Man Presenting Suitcase)*; Abraham Aronofsky *(Man Delivering Suitcase)*; Ray Seiden *(Transit Cop)*; Scott Franklin *(Voice of Transit Cop)*; Chris Johnson *(Limo Driver)*; Sal Monte *(King Neptune)*

PI ambitiously tells the tale of the way in which a brilliant mathematician nearly destroys his life by uncovering the secrets behind the New York stock market. Initially intriguing, this "Twilight Zone"-style film crashes and burns before it gets to the climax.

Maximillian Cohen (Sean Gullette), a disturbed young genius, pursues his lifelong dream of decoding the numerical patterns of Wall Street by renovating his small Chinatown apartment into a supercomputer named Euclid. But, just as Max gets closer to his auspicious discovery, he receives threats from the outside world. One mysterious brokerage firm tries to entice Max with an important "chip" device as a way to make Max part of their quest for financial domination. A Hasidic sect seeks Max to exploit his knowledge, which they believe will help them unlock the secrets of their holy Kabbalah texts. In order to pacify both groups, Max promises to help them when he finishes his work, but during the constant pursuits, Max becomes ill from chronic migraine headaches, which result in paranoid hallucinations. Desperate and scared, Max looks up his mentor, the mathematical guru Sol Robeson (Mark Margolis), but Sol sees Max heading down a dangerous path and tries to stop him from carrying out his goals. Later, Max is beaten up by the Wall Street "suits" when they find out he has been withholding key information. The Hasidim save Max from the corrupt business people, only to viciously interrogate him themselves. Determined more than ever, Max escapes from his captors and returns home to Euclid to finally crack the coveted code. But just as Euclid spits out the number pattern Max has so long sought, he collapses from another hallucinatory spell. In the end, Max fails to find ultimate meaning in the numbers, but learns to appreciate life beyond his enclosed world.

Much like PI's protagonist, Max, Darren Aronofsky's first-time feature loses its way despite a great degree of promise. Aronofsky's story is immediately involving, and, while none of the characters are especially sympathetic (with the exception of Max's neighbor, played by Kristyn Mae-Anne Lao), they are all interesting and colorful. Best of all, Aronofsky uses a controlled noir style to tell the nightmarish tale: he is aided greatly by Matthew Libatique's black-and-white camerawork (reminiscent of ERASERHEAD's look), Oren Sarch's sharp editing, and Clint Mansell's eerie music score.

But rather than gain momentum or create suspense, PI becomes oddly remote. The sense of menace dissipates from lack of development and pervasive presence (Max's tormentors conveniently disappear by the end). The climactic discovery of the code (the big MacGuffin itself) turns into a confusing jumble of numbers in Max's hallucinatory episode. And the denouement, where Max learns to love nature over numbers, smacks of sappy humanism—a Hollywood happy ending. Technically, Aronofsky also falters a few times: Max's scar changes places, and a subway set doubles for more than one place. For a better, more Borgesian film that connects mathematics and mysticism, viewers should seek out MOEBIUS, the 1996 Argentinean film, which contains similarly creepy scenes set in a subway. Still, PI reveals more than a few flashes of a mature, accomplished filmmaking style. *(Graphic violence, extreme profanity.)*—E.M.

d, Darren Aronofsky; p, Eric Watson; exec p, Randy Simon; assoc p, Scott Franklin; w, Darren Aronofsky (from a story by Darren Aronofsky, Sean Gullette, and Eric Watson); ph, Matthew Libatique; ed, Oren Sarch; m, Clint Mansell; prod d, Matthew Maraffi; sound, Brian Emrich (design), Ken Ishii (recordist), Mark Enette (mixer); fx, Ariyela Wald-Cohain; makeup, Ariyela Wald-Cohain; stunts, Marc Vivian

Science Fiction/Thriller **(PR: C MPAA: R)**

PLACE CALLED CHIAPAS, A ★★★

(Canada, 1998) 90m Canadian Wild Productions; Canadian Broadcasting Corp. c

Marcos; Bishop Samuel Ruiz Garcia; Ramona

A Canadian filmmaker looks at Mexico's Zapatista uprising in A PLACE CALLED CHIAPAS, a vigilant but straightforward documentary.

On January 1, 1994, the day after the NAFTA treaty went into effect, a group of Indian peasants of Chiapas, in southern Mexico, revolts, claiming the ruling Mexican leaders, the Institutional Revolutionary Party (or PRI), are depriving them of basic rights (land, education, healthcare). Calling themselves the Zapatista National Liberation Army (after Emiliano Zapata's 1910 revolt against the Mexican government), these Mayan Indians take over five towns and 500 farms and send their message to the world via the Internet.

The Zapatistas are lead by Subcommander Marcos, a masked guerilla poet who enjoys appearing on fashion magazine covers. Through their high-tech recruitment, the revolutionaries attract many outsiders to join their movement, but, despite calling for an official ceasefire, the government assists paramilitary death squads to quell the uprising. On camera, these "Peace and Justice" fighters blame the country's troubles on the Zapatistas. Off camera, they threaten to kill the film crew. Finally, the government allows one Zapatista representative, Ramona, to travel to Mexico City to protest in the President's Square. Meanwhile, the "Peace and Justice" group attacks Ramona's fellow villagers. Still in a standoff with the government, some of the Chiapas Indians try to carry on with their lives.

There's a sense of urgency, minus any hysteria, behind Nettie Wild's A PLACE CALLED CHIAPAS, one of the few films—fiction or nonfiction—to document the recent sociopolitical troubles in Mexico. Wild, an outsider from Canada, illuminates the point of view of the oppressed Indians, yet occasionally critiques the Zapatistas, whose charismatic leader, Marcos, she admits not fully understanding and even suspects (at one point) of having sold out some of his people in order to reach the ceasefire agreement. Mostly, Wild reserves her harshest judgments for the Zedillo government and the NAFTA treaty, which led to the initial injustices in Chiapas.

A PLACE CALLED CHIAPAS benefits from Wild's access to so many people and places (with the notable exception of Marcos), her clear-eyed story-telling techniques, some vivid moments caught on film (Ramona's lone protest in the President's Square, a wealthy farm family's rant against the Zapatista takeover), and some vivid moments *not* caught on film (the "Peace and Justice" group's attack on the villagers, during which Wild is forced to turn the camera off).

Both Marcel Ophuls and Michael Moore might have wrung more irony out of what was called "the first post-modern revolution" by *The New York Times*, as they might have gone after more corrupt officials for interviews (including Zedillo and representatives of the US government). In A PLACE CALLED CHIAPAS, however, Nettie Wild details the facts in her own articulate and ardent fashion. *(Violence.)*—E.M.

d, Nettie Wild; p, Nettie Wild, Betsy Carson, Kirk Tougas; w, Nettie Wild, Manfred Becker; ph, Kirk Tougas; ed, Manfred Becker; m, Joseph Pepe Danza, Salvador Ferreras, Celso Machado, Laurence Mollerup; sound, Velcrow Ripper

Documentary/Political **(PR: C MPAA: NR)**

PLAN B ★★½

(U.S., 1998) 102m Puny but Loud Productions ~ Monarch Home Video c

Jon Cryer *(Stuart Winer)*; Lisa Darr *(Clare Sadler)*; Lance Guest *(Jack Sadler)*; Mark Mathiesen *(Ricky Stone)*; Sara Mornell *(Gina Ferris)*; Stacy Katzin *(Emily Fishbach)*; Ilia Volokh *(Flash)*; John Kozeluh *(Randy Elliot)*; Claudia Carey *(Marie)*; Annie Grindlay *(Candace)*; Candace DeSarro *(Angela)*; Justin Ross *(Tony/Carrot Man)*; Nicole Chamberlain *(Cheryl)*; Christine Mitges *(Maggie)*; Jose Heredia *(Jose)*; Heather Harris *(Jill)*; Roger LaPage *(Optometrist/Santa Claus)*; Libby *(Receptionist)*; Andi Hughes *(Melonie)*; Lulu Baskins-Leva *(Woman on Plane)*; Stirling Gardner *(Man on Plane)*; Jack Gordon *(Doctor)*; William Norton *(College Sensualist)*; Jason Horst *(High School Boy)*; Zeo Bain *(Little Gina/Kitten)*; Jonathan Perry-Mark *(Timmy/Little Ghost)*; Donna Wieczorkowski *(Liz)*; Kate Capps *(Little Fairy Princess)*; Kit Mattson *(Monster)*; Satosha Ramsey *(Cat)*; Marta Carlson *(Starlet)*; Joanna Liner *(Ghost)*; Patricia Varela *(Ghost)*; Joanie Wallenberg *(Cavegirl)*; Alan Pekrul *(Jacques)*; Gary Leva *(Would-Be Novelist)*; Nancy Joslin *(Elf/Ghost)*; Kenneth Wayne *(Jack's Assistant)*; Kurt Knutzen *(Waiting Man at Plane)*; Erin Braus *(Waiting Woman at Plane)*; Eran Levi *(Store Owner)*; Rafael Correa *(Chef)*

Mildly likable but wholly forgettable, PLAN B contains a few good, character-derived moments. The programmatic scenario involves a group of friends dealing with lives that aren't going the way they had hoped.

At their modest house in suburban LA, Jack (Lance Guest) and Clare Sadler (Lisa Darr) host a Halloween party. Their guests include Jack's longtime friends Stuart Winer (Jon Cryer) and Ricky Stone (Mark Mathiesen), and Clare's sister Gina (Sara Mornell). Stuart is an aspiring writer who has just completed the manuscript of a book calculated to be a best seller. Ricky is an aspiring actor with an eye for women. Gina has a successful sales career but is obsessed with finding a mate. And Jack and Clare having been trying for months to get pregnant.

In the ensuing weeks, Ricky gets a part in a major TV commercial, while Jack (who teaches flying in his small plane) learns that poor eyesight will prevent him from his dream of being a commercial pilot. When the five friends gather for Thanksgiving, they are joined by Gina's latest date, heavy metal musician Flash (Ilia Volokh). As do most of her dates, he leaves before the end of the party. Jack finds financial success turning his plane into a flying honeymoon suite. Stuart, desperate that he can't get a publisher for his novel, takes it to a vanity press. And Ricky fails to get a big part he auditioned for.

At Christmas, Gina shows up with a new date, Marie (Claudia Carey). Clare is distraught when she finds out that she is not pregnant, as she had thought. Ricky collapses and nearly dies of an ulcer he has been hiding from his friends. At the hospital, Stuart and Clare confess a mutual attraction, one they act on at the Sadler's New Year's Eve party, where the hosts announce they have decided to adopt a child. Stuart starts a new novel, written from the heart rather than the pocketbook.

If not for occasional splotches of dialogue in which the characters discuss sex (how they like it, what they fantasize about when they masturbate, what they look for in a partner), PLAN B could be a Disney movie. There's nothing particularly wrong with it; it just doesn't have enough of an edge to remain in the viewer's memory. The performers are all likable but unchallenged, with little to do but react as any decent people would be expected to do in these circumstances. A few gay stereotypes might be enough to tilt some viewers toward active dislike, but it hardly seems worth the trouble. Copyrighted in 1996, PLAN B was released to home video in 1998. *(Sexual situations, adult situations, profanity.)*—M.F.

d, Gary Leva; p, Gary Leva, Nancy Joslin, Lulu Baskins-Leva; exec p, Burr Joslin, Elizabeth Joslin, Shelly Leva, Sally Leva; w, Gary Leva (based on the story by Gary Leva, Nancy Joslin, and Lulu Baskins-Leva); ph, Yoram Astrakhan; ed, Jane Allison Fleck; m, Andrew Rose; prod d, Carol Strober; set d, Natalie Cohen; ch, Justin Ross; sound, Arnold Braun (mixer); cos, Kelly Knutzen; makeup, Erin Braus

Comedy/Drama/Romance **(PR: C MPAA: R)**

PLAYBOY'S STORY OF X

(SEE: STORY OF X, THE)

PLAYERS CLUB, THE ★★★½

(U.S., 1998) 103m Ice Cube/Pat Charbonnet Productions; Ghetto Bird Productions ~ New Line c

LisaRaye *(Diana Armstrong/Diamond)*; Monica Calhoun *(Ebony)*; Bernie Mac *(Dollar Bill)*; Jamie Foxx *(Blue)*; Chrystale Wilson *(Ronnie)*; Adele Givens *(Tricks)*; A.J. Johnson *(Li'l Man)*; Ice Cube *(Reggie)*; Alex Thomas *(Clyde)*; Faizon Love *(Peters)*; Charles O. Murphy *(Brooklyn)*; Tracy C. Jones *(Tina)*; Terrence Howard *(K.C.)*; Larry McCoy *(St. Louis)*; Ronn Riser *(Professor Mills)*; Dick Anthony Williams *(Mr. Armstrong)*; Badja Djola *(The Doctor)*; Tiny Lister *(XL)*; John Amos *(Freeman)*; Judy Ann Elder *(Mrs. Armstrong)*; Jimmy Woodard *(Miron)*; Monte Russell *(Lance)*; Oren Williams *(Jamal at 4 Years)*; Jossie Harris *(Stripper #1)*; Lalanya Masters *(Stripper #2)*; Ursula Y. Houston *(Dancer #2)*; Annie O'Donnell *(Lady)*; Satari *(Girl)*; Bettina Rae *(Vanilla)*; Big Boy *(Joe)*; Gregg McDonald *(Cop)*; Brett Wagner *(Guy/Cop Party)*; Kenya Williams *(Student)*; Nigel Thatch *(Morehouse Guy)*; Michael Clarke Duncan *(Bodyguard)*; Luther Campbell *(Luke)*; Samuel Monroe Jr. *(Junior)*; Master P *(Guy)*; Keith Burke *(Guy at Party)*

The writing/directing debut of controversial rap artist Ice Cube, THE PLAYERS CLUB is one of the most satisfying surprises of 1998, a hard-edged ensemble piece set in a strip club that ventures into territory where other Hollywood productions have come up short.

Diana Armstrong (LisaRaye) is a single parent enrolled in college journalism courses while working at a shoe store. When Ronnie (Chrystale Wilson) and Tricks (Adele Givens), dancers at the Players Club, boast while shopping for shoes about the easy money they're making, Diana decides to give it a try. She is hired by club owner Dollar Bill (Bernie Mac), who gives her the stage name "Diamond." Overcoming her initial fear and disgust, Diana gets hardened to the routine, weathering the disapproval of her family and her live-in boyfriend Lance (Monte Russell), whom she met at the club.

Diana's teen cousin Ebony (Monica Calhoun) pays her a visit, begins hanging out at the club, and gets hired as Ronnie's protege. Diana comes to her cousin's rescue when she follows Ronnie's example by turning tricks in the parking lot, but throws her out when she finds her in bed with Lance (who also gets the boot). Diana grows close to Blue (Jamie Foxx), the club's DJ. Ebony is badly beaten when Ronnie sets her up to work at a bachelor party for her brother. Diana confronts Ronnie in the club dressing room, sending her away in an ambulance. Dollar Bill is taken away, never to be seen again, by the henchmen of mobster St. Louis (Larry McCoy), to whom he owes $60,000. Before he's led off, he destroys the club with a shoulder-launched rocket. Years later, Diana is a successful TV newscaster, still dating Blue, while Ebony, recovered and wiser, works in the shoe store.

THE PLAYERS CLUB carefully avoids the trap of SHOWGIRLS (1995) and STRIPTEASE (1996), films that tried to explore this milieu but eventually embraced the vulgar male fantasies that fuel the commercial sex industry. Ice Cube, who based his script on strip joints he saw during a rap tour in Atlanta, makes clear that stripping is a job, not an erotic adventure: Diana just wants to earn enough to pay for her tuition, apartment, and kids. Cube endows the material with strong female roles down the line, and keeps the onscreen nudity to a necessary minimum. He smartly cast his lead role with a relative unknown, LisaRaye, who still has the credibility that a better-known actress couldn't fake.

If some slime-and-punishment aspects of THE PLAYERS CLUB are way too obvious, the sly wit is a bonus. When the slippery Dollar Bill first interviews Diana, he makes a bogus Afro-centric speech hailing the striptease as a native invention. Later Ronnie does a sadomasochist-laced party for white police officers, spanking one with a paddle (decorated with a map of Africa) as he shouts "I'm black and I'm proud!" Former stand-up comic Foxx is a rather colorless nice guy, but there is considerable humor at the expense of the undersized, much-abused doorman (A.J. Johnson) and a couple of burly beat cops (one of them played by John Amos, whose "Good Times" TV sitcom is the basis of a rather labored gag). *(Adult situations, profanity, nudity, violence, substance abuse.)*—C.C.

d, Ice Cube; p, Patricia Charbonnet, Carl Craig; exec p, Ice Cube; w, Ice Cube; ph, Malik Sayeed; ed, Suzanne Hines; m, Frank Fitzpatrick, Hidden Faces; prod d, Dina Lipton; art d, Keith Neely; set d, Cheryle Grace; sound, Russell Williams (mixer); fx, John Hardigan; casting, Kimberly Hardin; cos, Dahlia Foroutan; makeup, Stacye Branche; stunts, William Washington

Crime/Drama **(PR: O MPAA: R)**

PLAYING BY HEART ★★½

(U.S./U.K., 1998) 121m Hyperion Entertainment; InterMedia Film; Morpheus; Miramax ~ Miramax c
(AKA: DANCING ABOUT ARCHITECTURE)

Gillian Anderson *(Meredith)*; Ellen Burstyn *(Mildred)*; Sean Connery *(Paul)*; Anthony Edwards *(Roger)*; Angelina Jolie *(Joan)*; Jay Mohr *(Mark)*; Ryan Phillippe *(Keenan)*; Dennis Quaid *(Hugh)*; Gena Rowlands *(Hannah)*; Jon Stewart *(Trent)*; Madeleine Stowe *(Gracie)*; Patricia Clarkson *(Allison)*; April Grace *(Valery)*; Alec Mapa *(Lana)*; Jeremy Sisto *(Malcolm)*; Matt Malloy *(Desk Clerk)*; Christian Mills *(Philip)*; Kellie Waymire *(Jane)*; Tim Halligan *(Director—Cook Show)*; Michael Emerson *(Bosco)*; Nastassja Kinski *(Melanie)*; John Patrick White *(Pete)*; David Clennon *(Martin)*; Amanda Peet *(Amber)*; David Ferguson *(Drag Queen)*; Joel McCrary *(Bartender—Drag Bar)*; Worthie Meacham *(2nd Drag Queen Performer)*; Michael Buchman Silver *(Max)*; Hal Landon Jr. *(Actor "Commissioner")*; Marc Allen Lewis *(Actor "Harpagon")*; Ron Boussom *(Actor "Jacques")*; Daniel Chodos *(Actor "Anselme")*; Mark Lewis *(Waiter)*; Jim Abele *(Doctor)*; Chris Conner *(Harry)*; Marcus Printop *(Trumpet Player)*; Larry Antonio *(Bass Player)*; Tom Chuchvara *(Drummer)*; Robert English *(Saxophonist)*; Ryo Okumuto *(Pianist)*

PLAYING BY HEART is a well-acted, but superficial, drama which boasts an impressive ensemble cast. Unfortunately, they can only occasionally transcend a cliched and gimmicky script which presents a sprawling look at that crazy little thing called love as it's experienced in the big, bad dysfunctional '90s among a large group of characters in the City of Angels.

While a mother, Mildred (Ellen Burstyn), keeps vigil over her gay son, Mark (Jay Mohr) who's dying of AIDS, several Los Angeles couples suffer romantic misadventures: TV producer Paul (Sean Connery) and his wife Hannah (Gena Rowlands), the host of a cooking-show, are going through a crisis in their 40-year marriage because of his recently being diagnosed with a brain tumor and her discovery of an affair he had years before; theater director Meredith (Gillian Anderson), whose husband dumped her for a man, begins a halting affair with architect Trent (Jon Stewart), who persistently pursues her despite her constantly rejecting him; the married Gracie (Madeline Stowe) happily engages in a strictly sexual affair with the married and guilt-ridden Roger (Anthony Edwards) in a series of hotel trysts; a man named Hugh (Dennis Quaid) wanders from one bar to another regaling women with incredibly tragic stories in which he pretends to be different people; and Joan (Angelina Jolie), a punky aspiring actress, continually tries to hook up with a young mystery man named Keenan (Ryan Phillippe), whom she keeps running into at dance clubs, but he refuses to date her, or anyone else for that matter.

Eventually, it's revealed that Mark was Meredith's gay ex-husband and that Gracie is married to Hugh, whose bizarre impersonations were actually part of an acting class improv exercise. Keenan and Joan finally become intimate after he breaks down and tells her that the reason he's been afraid to love anyone is because his first and only girlfriend has recently died of AIDS from leading a double-life as a drug addict. After Meredith returns from Mark's funeral in Chicago, she admits that she loves Trent and brings him to a party at the home of her parents, who turn out to be Paul and Hannah. Meredith's other sisters, who are revealed to be Joan and Gracie, arrive with Keenan and Hugh, and they all watch as Paul and Hannah reaffirm their wedding vows during a ceremony which is presided over by Roger, who's a minister. While everyone dances afterwards, Hugh tells Gracie that he wants to work at healing their marriage and she agrees to try.

PLAYING BY HEART was originally titled DANCING WITH ARCHITECTURE, a phrase which is uttered symbolically several times in the film in a paraphrased version of the musicians's maxim that "talking about music is like dancing about architecture," with the word "love" substituted for "music." Unfortunately, writer-director Willard Carroll does nothing *but* talk about love and ironically proves the accuracy of the adage with a screenplay that's filled with incessantly gabby scenes that pointlessly crisscross between the mopey characters who spend all of their time at chic bars, fancy restaurants, and luxurious homes straight out of "Martha Stewart Living" magazine. The film's explicitly stated theme of emotional "honesty"—or the lack thereof—and how it impacts on relationships, smacks of one too many LA therapy sessions, featuring embarrassing laughing-through-your-tears-style sentimentality and glib psych-speak dialogue ("Don't look at me in that tone of voice"; "You're the tenant of my heart. . . sometimes in arrears, but impossible to evict"; "I'm damaged goods and I won't let you love me"; along with several characters describing others as "anger balls").

And though one of the characters decries "calculated artificiality," the film's self-conscious style of setting most scenes at night, punctuated by quick shots of cityscapes dissolving from day back into night, and intercutting between the various characters until revealing the family link among them at the end is a totally calculated and artificial gimmick (as well as not being very surprising and unintentionally hilarious when we see that the adulterous Roger is a man of the cloth) that's obviously designed to sustain interest in what otherwise would rate as typical TV soap opera fodder, Vilmos Zsigmond's luscious widescreen cinematography notwithstanding. The cast does what it can with their cliched roles (the heartbroken woman/man who's afraid of being hurt again, the tough punk hiding a mushy center, et al.), but only Angelina Jolie really makes her character come alive and connect with an audience, giving a wonderfully vibrant and fully dimensional performance that seems guaranteed to make her a star. *(Profanity, sexual situations.)*—M.S.

d, Willard Carroll; p, Willard Carroll, Meg Liberman, Tom Wilhite; exec p, Bob Weinstein, Harvey Weinstein, Guy East, Nigel Sinclair, Paul Feldsher; assoc p, Kacy Andrews; co-p, Kurt Albrecht; w, Willard Carroll; ph, Vilmos Zsigmond; ed, Pietro Scalia; m, John Barry; prod d, Melissa Stewart; art d, Charles Daboub; set d, Cindy Carr; sound, Arthur Rochester; casting, Meg Liberman; cos, April Ferry; makeup, Christina Smith; stunts, Dan Bradley

Romance/Comedy/Drama **(PR: C MPAA: R)**

PLEASANTVILLE ★★★½

(U.S., 1998) 116m Larger Than Life Productions ~ New Line c/bw

Joan Allen *(Betty)*; William H. Macy *(George)*; Tobey Maguire *(David)*; Reese Witherspoon *(Jennifer)*; Jeff Daniels *(Mr.*

Johnson); Don Knotts *(TV Repairman)*; J.T. Walsh *(Big Bob)*; Natalie Ramsey *(Mary Sue)*; Kevin Connors *(Bud)*; Heather McGill *(Girl in School Yard)*; Paul Morgan Stetler *(College Counselor)*; Denise Dowse *(Health Teacher)*; McNally Sagal *(Science Teacher)*; Jane Kaczmarek *(David's Mom)*; Giuseppe Andrews *(Howard)*; Marissa Ribisi *(Kimmy)*; Jenny Lewis *(Christin)*; Justin Nimmo *(Mark)*; Kai Lennox *(Mark's Lackey #1)*; Jason Behr *(Mark's Lackey #2)*; Robin Bissel *(Commercial Announcer)*; Harry Singleton *(Mr. Simpson)*; John Ganun *(Fireman #1)*; Paul Walker *(Skip)*; Dawn Cody *(Betty Jean)*; Maggie Lawson *(Lisa Anne)*; Andrea Taylor *(Peggy Jane)*; Lela Ivey *(Miss Peters)*; Jim Patric *(Tommy)*; Marc Blucas *(Basketball Hero)*; Stanton Rutledge *(Coach)*; Jason Maves *(Paper Boy)*; Gerald Emmerick *(TV Weatherman)*; Charles C. Stevenson Jr. *(Dr. Henderson)*; Nancy Lenehan *(Marge Jenkins)*; Weston Blakesley *(Gus)*; Patrick T. O'Brien *(Roy)*; Jim Antonio *(Ralph)*; Danny Strong *(Juke Box Boy)*; Kristin Rudrud *(Mary)*; Laura Carney *(Bridge Club Lady)*; Dan Gillies *(Fireman #2)*; Marley Shelton *(Margaret)*; Erik MacArthur *(Will)*; Adam Carter *(Boy in Soda Shop)*; David Tom *(Whitey)*; Johnny Moran *(Pete)*; Jeanine Jackson *(Woman)*; J. Patrick Lawlor *(Thug)*; James Keane *(Police Chief Dan)*

Visually stunning and featuring a number of appealing performances, PLEASANTVILLE is an entertaining and thought-provoking challenge to the claim that things were better back in the "good old days." Though writer-director Gary Ross goes a little too far to deliver his message, a preachy conclusion is not enough to mar this fine film.

The world today is a rough place to be a teenager—career prospects are low, AIDS is on the rise, and the environment is a mess. David (Tobey Maguire) takes refuge in "Pleasantville," a squeaky-clean 1950s sitcom that plays in reruns on a campy cable network. On the night of the "Pleasantville" marathon, David and his sister, Jennifer (Reese Witherspoon), are visited by a mysterious television repair man (Don Knotts) who gives them a remote control that transports them into the innocent, black-and-white world of Pleasantville.

They soon find that the citizens of Pleasantville know nothing of what lies beyond their town, and in fact are practically incapable of doing anything outside the narrow definitions of their whitebread sitcom characters. This doesn't stop Jennifer from seducing the captain of the basketball team—an act that upsets the very fabric of Pleasantville. This starts a chain reaction in the community: released from their sitcom bonds, kids begin reading books, listening to jazz and rock music, and having lots of sex. The most stunning side effect is the introduction, little by little, of color to Pleasantville, indelibly marking those who have experienced these new sensations.

The black-and-whites are shocked and horrified by the transformation happening all around them. Conservative teens prowl the streets harassing the "coloreds," and offensive books are tossed on a bonfire. Hoping to bring his town back to normal, the mayor (J. T. Walsh) defines a community code banning music, books, and colors other than black, white, and shades of gray. In an act of rebellion, the local soda shop owner, Mr. Johnson (Jeff Daniels), who has recently discovered a love of painting, paints a colorful mural on the side of the police station. A trial follows, in which David urges the citizens of Pleasantville to give in to their hearts, to let themselves feel real emotion. His speech finally bursts the dam, and color floods into Pleasantville. Finally, David must go back to the real world, though Jennifer elects to stay behind in Pleasantville.

For his directorial debut, writer-director Ross (who wrote BIG and DAVE) crafts a killer premise: what if 1990s teenagers were let loose in the Ozzie-and-Harriet 1950s? For a while it looks as if PLEASANTVILLE will simply riff on the obvious jokes, which it does quite entertainingly. But Ross has more to say here: he reminds us, subtly at first, that the '50s were also a time of racial inequality and cultural intolerance, and it's only through the lens of fond reminiscence—or through a television screen—that this often stifling world is transformed into the idyllic "good old days." By the time we get to Mr. Johnson's trial, PLEASANTVILLE starts to get a bit tiresome, beating viewers over the head with its message, but by then Ross has done something that is almost unprecedented, at least in Hollywood: he suggests that things have actually gotten better in the past four decades. The fact that Ross tries a little too hard to get this message across is much better than his not having tried at all.

In addition to crafting a clever and original story, Ross creates in PLEASANTVILLE a film that is visually remarkable. Spot-coloring is not a new technique by any means, but here it is used not as an artistic gimmick but as an essential element of the story: the appearance of color on flowers, buildings, and faces conveys Pleasantville's emergence from its cocoon of blissful ignorance more elegantly than any dialogue ever could. In addition, it provides Ross with a clever means to draw parallels to the turbulent Civil Rights movement of the 1950s and '60s by splitting the citizens into "colored" and "noncolored." All told, the contrast of black-and-white and vibrant colors is stunning, establishing some unforgettable images.

Further supporting Ross's written and visual material is a splendid cast. Toby Maguire (THE ICE STORM) and Reese Witherspoon (FREEWAY) register as somewhat annoying when their characters dwell in the present day, but they come into their own as socially precocious teens in the '50s. Of the adults, Jeff Daniels stands out, playing the soda jerk who at first cannot contemplate upsetting the daily routine; once he does, though, he cannot contemplate ever going back. PLEASANTVILLE also receives the benefit of several of Hollywood's finest character actors, notably Joan Allen, William H. Macy, and the late J. T. Walsh (appearing here in one of his last screen roles), all of whom turn in the kind of solid performances upon which we've come to rely. With all elements working in its favor, PLEASANTVILLE is a unique and thoroughly enjoyable fantasy. *(Violence, sexual situations, profanity.)*—B.T.

d, Gary Ross; p, Gary Ross, Jon Kilik, Robert J. Degus, Steven Soderbergh; exec p, Michael De Luca, Mary Parent; assoc p, Robin Bissell; co-p, Allen Alsobrook, Allison Thomas, Edward Lynn, Andy Borowitz, Susan Borowitz; w, Gary Ross; ph, John Lindley; ed, William Goldenberg; m, Randy Newman; prod d, Jeannine Oppewall; art d, Diane Wager; set d, Jay Hart; sound, Robert Anderson Jr. (mixer); fx, Chris Watts (visual effects), Michael Southard (color effects); casting, Ellen Lewis, Debra Zane; cos, Judianna Makovsky; makeup, Susan A. Cabral; stunts, Ernie Orsatti

AAN Best Art Direction: Jeannine Oppewall, Jay Hart; *AAN Best Costume Design:* Judianna Makovsky; *AAN Best Original Dramatic Score:* Randy Newman

Comedy/Drama **(PR: C MPAA: PG-13)**

PLUMP FICTION ★★½

(U.S., 1998) 85m Rhino Films ~ Legacy Releasing c

Tommy Davidson *(Julius)*; Julie Brown *(Mimi)*; Paul Dinello *(Jimmy Nova)*; Sandra Bernhard *(Bunny Roberts)*; Dan Castellaneta *(Bumpkin)*; Colleen Camp *(Viv)*; Kevin Meaney *(Les)*; Pamela Segall *(Vallory)*; Matthew Glave *(Nicky)*; Philippe Bergeron *(Jean-Claude)*; Jennifer Rubin *(Kandi Kane)*; Robert Costanzo *(Montello)*; Jennifer Coolidge *(Sister Sister)*; Nada Despotovich *(Sister Batril)*; Karla Tamburrelli *(Sister Ruth)*;

Simbi Khali (Sister Sledge); Lezlie Deane (Jodi); Paul Provenza (Crispin Maraschino); Lea De Laria (Mr. Purple); Tim Kazurinsky (Priscilla); Shawn Michael Howard (Lee); Molly O'Leary (Waitress); Kane Picoy (Christopher Walken Character); Scott LaRose (Karaoke Customer); Riki Rachtman (Clerk #2); Al Septien (Cop #1); Judy Tenuta (Rhonda); Jimmie Walker (Stingy Customer)

Though primarily a parody of PULP FICTION (1996), the fun and clever PLUMP FICTION goofs on most things Tarantino, as well as a whole bunch of other movies.

At a restaurant, Bunny (Sandra Bernhard) gives the Forrest Gump-ish Bumpkin (Dan Castellaneta) a movie screenplay to deliver to director Crispin Maraschino (Paul Provenza). The pages are scattered when Bumpkin runs into Julius (Tommy Davidson) and Jimmy Nova (Paul Dinello), two "hit men" who work for Montello's Pest Extermination.

Jimmy and Julius attempt to spray the apartment of the "Natural Blonde Killers," tag team wrestlers Nicky and Vallory Cox (Matthew Glave and Pamela Segall). On the previous night, Nicky and Vallory double-crossed crime boss Montello (Robert Costanzo) after agreeing to take a dive.

Jimmy is ordered to take Montello's wife Mimi (Julie Brown), a compulsive overeater, out for a good time. They go to an Independent Film theme restaurant where Priscilla the Queen of the Desserts (Tim Kazurinsky) is their waitperson. Jimmy and Mimi stop at a Kwiki-Mart and are held prisoner by its owner, but are rescued by a woman who reveals herself to be the NELL-ish Jodi (Lezlie Deane).

Making their escape, Jimmy and Mimi carjack a group of strippers disguised as nuns. These "Reservoir Nuns" had planned to rob Montello's club, but after Mimi shoots one of them, they retreat to a warehouse. The Sisters turn on each other and draw guns in a noisy standoff, until Maraschino, who's shooting his film next door, comes in and kills them all. After chasing away Jimmy and Julius, Nicky and Vallory realize they left a briefcase full of money they stole from Montello at the Independent Film Cafe. There, they find that Bunny has it. All draw guns in a standoff, until Julius shows up, shoots Bunny, and takes the money. Bumpkin delivers the script with the pages all mixed up to Maraschino, who decides to film the movie that way. Bumpkin meets Jodi, and they fall in love .

Probably no film in recent movie history is riper for parody than PULP FICTION (1994). Quentin Tarantino's crime saga was both excessive and specific, and indelibly memorable. PLUMP FICTION doesn't generate howling laughs, but its unexpected cinematic forays are undeniably fun. Mimi walks into the black-and-white convenience store from CLERKS (1994), into which comes an approximation of the REALITY BITES (1994) crew. The Reservoir Nuns ape the opening montage of "The Monkees" tv show. Especially funny is the Independent Film Cafe, where one of the waiters is a Christopher Walken impersonator (Kane Picoy) obsessed with all the things he's held up his rectum.

Writer-director Bob Koherr makes clever mockery of PULP FICTION's loopy time structure, and does a great job of sending up Tarantino's trademark over-the-top dialogue laced with profanity and pop culture references. Of the cast, Pamela Segall deserves to be singled out for her hilarious, dead-on impression of Juliette Lewis. *(Extreme profanity, graphic violence.)*—P.R.

d, Bob Koherr; p, Gary Binkow; exec p, Stephen Nemeth; assoc p, Patrick J. Clifton; co-p, Mark Roberts, Lorena David; w, Bob Koherr; ph, Rex Nicholson; ed, Neil Kirk; prod d, Jacques Herbert; art d, Robert La Liberte; set d, Nicole Lee; sound, Eric Enroth; fx, John Lambert, Greg Landerer; casting, Gary Oberst; cos, Vincent Lapper; makeup, Ania Harasimiak; stunts, Brad Bovee

Comedy **(PR: C MPAA: R)**

POCAHONTAS II: JOURNEY TO A NEW WORLD ★★

(U.S., 1998) 72m Walt Disney Television Animation ~ Buena Vista Home Video c

VOICES OF: Irene Bedard *(Pocahontas)*; Judy Kuhn *(Pocahontas—singing)*; Billy Zane *(John Rolfe)*; David Ogden Stiers *(Ratcliffe)*; Jean Stapleton *(Mrs. Jenkins)*; Russell Means *(Powhatan)*; Linda Hunt *(Grandmother Willow)*; Donal Gibson *(John Smith)*

Disney continues its recent series of direct-to-video sequels to its big-screen animated hits with POCAHONTAS II: JOURNEY TO A NEW WORLD, which is fairly well made by the studio's Japanese and Canadian TV animation units, but suffers from the usual defects of an uncompelling plot and weak songs that add nothing but extra length to the proceedings.

In colonial Jamestown, the villainous British official Ratcliffe (voice of David Ogden Stiers) tries to arrest Capt. John Smith (voice of Donal Gibson) for treason and Smith falls off a roof and is presumed dead. Later, Smith's lover, the Native American Princess Pocahontas (voice of Irene Bedard) goes to England to dissuade the king from starting a war with her people. Accompanying Pocahontas is John Rolfe (voice of Billy Zane), a royal emissary who is sympathetic to Pocahontas's cause, and the two find themselves falling for each other.

In England, the king invites Pocahontas to a royal ball on the advice of the scheming Ratcliffe, who has convinced the king that all Indians are savages and plans to show him how uncivilized Pocahontas is. Rolfe teaches Pocahontas to act, dance, and dress like an English lady and she charms the king at the ball, but Ratcliffe tricks her into attacking him by mistreating a bear in front of her. The king has her locked up, but she's freed by Rolfe and John Smith, who has recently resurfaced. Pocahontas and Rolfe convince the king that Ratcliffe has been lying to him about the Indians's savagery. The king calls off the British armada and Ratcliffe is arrested. Realizing that she's now in love with Rolfe, Pocahontas bids adieu to Smith, and she returns to Jamestown with Rolfe.

Despite the customary limited motion and sparse backgrounds of the direct-to-video cartoon genre, the animation in POCAHONTAS II: JOURNEY TO A NEW WORLD is a cut above most of its ilk, featuring a nice blend of traditional draftsmanship with judicious use of computer imagery for the action scenes. The film contains annoying fade-outs every 15 minutes or so (obviously intended for future TV showings), but all of the characters from the original and the depictions of Jamestown and London are well rendered. The story is completely formulaic and unmemorable, however, designed primarily to appeal to preteen girls with its romantic triangle plot, while the lame songs sprinkled throughout, boasting generically mystical lyrics about the wind, nature, and spirits, only serve to irritate kids by interrupting the action. And though the film is as reverent as the original in its portrayal of the nobility of Native Americans, it's not quite as stringently PC as its predecessor—using Pocahontas's Indian warrior bodyguard for some cheap comic relief as he clashes with British high society. Most of the original's voice cast members have returned, with the notable exception of Mel Gibson, who's replaced here by his brother Donal (hey, you get what you pay for), but the new cast does include the ubiquitous Billy Zane, who not only does a creditable English accent, but also belts out some songs as if he were auditioning for the opera.—M.S.

d, Bradley Raymond, Tom Ellery; p, Alan Zaslove; co-p, Jeannine Roussel; w, Allen Estrin, Cindy Marcus, Flip Kobler; ed, Colleen Halsey; m, Lennie Niehaus; prod d, Dennis Greco; art d, James Gallego; sound, Ivan Johnson

Animated/Children's **(PR: AA MPAA: NR)**

POLICE ASSASSINS
(SEE: ROYAL WARRIORS)

POLISH WEDDING ★½
(U.S., 1998) 107m Addis-Wechsler;
Lakeshore Entertainment ~ Fox Searchlight c

Lena Olin *(Jadzia Pzoniak)*; Gabriel Byrne *(Bolek Pzoniak)*; Claire Danes *(Hala Pzoniak)*; Adam Trese *(Russell Schuster)*; Mili Avital *(Sofie Pzoniak)*; Daniel LaPaine *(Ziggy Pzoniak)*; Rade Serbedzija *(Roman Kroll)*; Ramsey Krull *(Kris)*; Steven Petrarca *(Witek)*; Jeffrey Nordling *(Father Don)*; Brian Hoyt *(Kaz)*; Christina Romana Lypeckyj *(Kaszia)*; Peter Carey *(Piotrusz)*; Jon Bradford *(Sailor)*; Robert Daniels *(Roman's Business Partner)*; Ryan Spahn *(Kid)*; Randy Godwin *(Nosy Neighbor)*; Mitchell Mandeberg *(Stanley Mislinski)*; Sheldon Alkon *(Man in Church)*; Laurie V. Logan *(Helga)*; Joanna Woodcock *(Woman in Bakery)*; Joseph Haynes *(Mr. Schuster)*; Judy Dery *(Mrs. Schuster)*; Sparks of Fire *(Band at Festival)*; Rick Thompson *(Heckler)*; Seamus McNally *(Heckler #2)*; Cassidy Cirka *(Hala's Baby)*; Rebecca Morrin; Rachel Morrin *(Ziggy and Sofie's Baby)*

In POLISH WEDDING, first time writer-director Theresa Connelly shows us that even families that appear screwed up on the surface can draw upon an inner strength to stay together. Though it features a terrific performance by Claire Danes, POLISH WEDDING spends too much time developing a few characters and not enough time telling an interesting story.

Set in the largely Polish Detroit neighborhood of Hamtramck, POLISH WEDDING centers on the Pzoniak family: father Bolek (Gabriel Byrne), mother Jadzia (Lena Olin), and their five children—four sons and one beautiful, willful daughter, Hala (Claire Danes). Though she values her children above all else, Jadzia is no longer in love with her husband, whom she married because she was pregnant; in order to feel like a woman, she carries on an affair with a businessman, Roman (Rade Serbedzija). Like his father before him, Ziggy Pzoniak (Daniel LaPaine) marries his pregnant girlfriend, and the two live in the Pzoniak home, relying on the family to help care for the child. So when Hala learns she is pregnant with the child of a local cop, Russell (Adam Trese), she must decide whether or not to perpetuate this ignominious family tradition, which has seemingly brought her parents only misery.

Bolek suspects that his wife is having an affair, and ultimately discovers with whom; at the same time, Roman offers to take Jadzia to Paris with him—an offer which startles Jadzia into admitting that she values her family over her affair. Bolek confronts Jadzia, who realizes that she does, in fact, still love her husband. Seeing that the so-called "Polish wedding" can work after all, Hala goes to Russell to beg him to marry her; at first he refuses, which sends her four brothers to his house with hockey sticks to "persuade" him. Russell, not surprisingly, runs away, but returns shortly to marry Hala and raise their child in the Pzoniak home.

Writer-director Theresa Connelly devotes much of POLISH WEDDING (which derives its title from an old joke about a pregnant bride) to young Hala and her mother Jadzia, establishing a level of intimacy between the audience and these characters so that, by the end of the film, we understand the conflict they feel when deciding between family and freedom. Unfortunately, this intimacy is gained at the expense of the rest of the cast: father Bolek is a one-dimensional sap who can't win back his wife, while the rest of the family is neglected altogether. Because it concentrates so much on two characters, rather than the whole of the story, it takes a good hour for POLISH WEDDING to really get moving, by which time many viewers may have tuned out.

Those who stick with POLISH WEDDING will see yet another dynamite performance by Claire Danes, whose portrayal of Hala is by turns angelic and sensual, here escaping the house at night to prowl the streets looking for men to conquer, there choosing to participate in the church's parade of virgins despite her gravid state. With her long blonde tresses and penchant for wispy, gauzy outfits, Danes is almost mystical as the girl entering womanhood. Lena Olin is well cast as Hala's mother, still stunning after five children and possessing that same slightly wicked sensuality. Still, two performances—even good ones—do not a movie make, and POLISH WEDDING offers little else to recommend it. *(Sexual situations, profanity.)*—B.T.

d, Theresa Connelly; p, Tom Rosenberg, Julia Chasman, Geoff Stier; exec p, Nick Wechsler, Sigurjon Sighvatsson, Ted Tannebaum; co-p, Gregory Goodman, Richard S. Wright; w, Theresa Connelly; ph, Guy Dufaux; ed, Curtiss Clayton, Suzanne Fenn; m, Luis Bacalov; prod d, Kara Lindstrom; set d, Ethel Robins Richards; sound, John Sisti (supervisor), Ron Ayers (mixer); casting, Owens Hill; cos, Donna Zakowska

Romance/Comedy/Drama (PR: C MPAA: PG-13)

POLTERGEIST REPORT: YUYU HAKUSHO ★★★
(Japan, 1994) 90m Toho Co. Ltd.; Studio Pierrot;
Movic ~ US Manga Corps c

ENGLISH VOICE CAST: Rik Nagel *(Yusuke)*; Cliff Lazenby *(Kuwahara)*; Elisa Wain *(Hinageshi)*; Hideo Seaver *(Kurama)*; James Stanley *(Hiei)*; Bruce Winant *(Yakumo)*; Caryl Marder *(Genkai)*; Peter Patrikios *(Raiko)*; Jack Taylor *(Majari)*; Eric Stuart *(Kuronue/Lord Koenma)*; Veronica Taylor *(Botan/Yukina)*; George Leaver; Shannon Conley; John P. Poppler; Ed Kissel

Yet another example of the time-honored anime tradition of tales about youths with spiritual powers who are called on to defend Tokyo from demon attacks, POLTERGEIST REPORT: YUYU HAKUSHO offers some spectacular animation to support an exciting, if overstuffed, story line.

In contemporary Tokyo, Yusuke (voice of Rik Nagel), an intermediary between the human and spirit worlds, is alerted by Botan (voice of Veronica Taylor), an emissary from the spirit world's Lord Koenma (voice of Eric Stuart), that the spirit world has been engulfed by the River Styx. As a result, the evil Lord Yakumo (voice of Bruce Winant) seeks to revive the long-dormant Netherworld, which was destroyed eons ago in a battle with the spirit world.

Yusuke and his band of spirit-powered teen warriors race to unseal the five elemental sites in Tokyo in order to block the Netherworld from entering the human world, but Lord Yakumo and his three demon gods beat the teens to each site and successfully seal off a portion of the city and stake it out as Netherworld territory.

Lord Yakumo captures Botan and manages to retrieve the power sphere of the Netherworld from its hiding place within her body. He then transforms a skyscraper into a sprawling Netherworld palace. After a harrowing battle with the demon gods, Yusuke and his mates manage to take back the sphere from Yakumo and use it to transform its power into spiritual energy and vanquish Yakumo in a massive blast of spirit power.

A theatrical film released in Japan in 1994, POLTERGEIST REPORT: YUYU HAKUSHO is based on a popular TV series and comic book (*YuYu Hakusho*) and presupposes a certain amount of foreknowledge on the part of the Japanese viewer, while putting American audiences at a keen disadvantage when trying to determine who Yusuke and his party actually are, where they came from, and how they got their powers. Some opening text or narration would have been helpful to American fans.

That said, the film does indeed offer imaginative design and fluid animation, particularly in its climactic battle atop the devastated skyscraper transformed into the lavish demon palace. It is also relatively milder in tone than most entries in this genre, while still managing to be both entertaining and engrossing. *(Violence.)*—B.C.

d, Masakatsu Iijima; p, Haru Sai, Ken Hagino, Naoharu Honokideni, Stephanie Shalofsky (English Version); exec p, John O'Donnell (English Version); assoc p, Peter Bavaro (English Version); w, Yukiyoshi Ohashi, Sukehiro Tomita, Hiroshi Hashimoto (based on the comics by Yoshihiro Togashi); ph, Toshiyuki Fukushima; m, Yusuke Homma; art d, Yuji Ikeda; anim, Ryo Tanaka, Hiroki Kanno; sound, Kan Mizumoto

Animated/Fantasy (PR: A MPAA: NR)

POST COITUM, ANIMAL TRISTE ★★★★½

(France, 1997) 97m Ognon Pictures/Pinou Film; Canal Plus; Gan Foundation; Club Med ~ New Yorker Films c

Brigitte Rouan *(Diane Clovier)*; Patrick Chesnais *(Philippe Clovier)*; Boris Terral *(Emilio)*; Nils Tavernier *(Francois Narou)*; Jean-Louis Richard *(Weyoman-Lebeau)*; Francoise Arnoul *(Madame LePluche)*; Emmanuelle Bach *(Caroline)*; Carmen Chaplin *(Copine Narou)*; Gaelle Le Furr *(Isabelle)*; Elodie Pong *(Designer)*; Roberto Plate *(Miguel)*; Olivier Lechat *(Victor)*; Felix Dedet-Rouan *(Basile)*; Jean de la Valade *(Dede)*; Jean-Claude Chapuis *(Musical Glasses Player)*; Jean-Francois Rouan *(Sales Manager)*; Bernard Budaga *(Emilio's Grandfather)*; Nicolas Dedet *(Homeless Person)*; Jacques Disses *(Monsieur LePluche)*; Ali Rostand *(Cafe Owner)*; Michel Polac; Gisele Casadesus; Lucien Pascal; Nicole Garcia *(Voice)*

A married Parisian book editor indulges in an affair with a young man in POST COITUM, ANIMAL TRISTE, a lively, engaging, and refreshingly candid piece of work by actress-director Brigitte Rouan.

Forty-year-old Diane Clovier (Brigitte Rouan) seemingly has it all: a great job, an adoring husband, two charming children. On the day Diane visits one of her author-clients, Francois (Nils Tavernier), at his home, she meets his roommate, Emilio (Boris Terral), a dashing, 20-year-old hydraulics engineer who works for a humanitarian organization. The two fall instantly in love.

The May-December affair is doomed from the start, but Diane sincerely believes she has awakened to a new life. Secretly, Diane arranges rendezvous and getaways with Emilio, creating elaborate lies for her husband, Philippe (Patrick Chesnais), a lawyer defending a woman (Francoise Arnoul) who has murdered her husband. Eventually, however, Diane makes mistakes on her job and fails to properly cover up her romance. Her relationship with Emilio also suffers: she becomes demanding, he becomes remote.

Finally, the affair ends as Emilio decides to leave Paris on a humanitarian mission. Diane tries to remain amicable with Emilio, but raw emotions get in the way. She tries to resume a normal home life, but her husband and older child resent what she has done. She also tries to finish working with Francois on his book, but gets fired for accidentally starting a fire in her office.

Depressed and left alone on Mother's Day, Diane takes to drink. Francois visits her and helps stop her downward spiral by taking her out. Once Philippe returns home and starts practicing his closing argument in his defense case, he realizes he still loves Diane, and awaits her return. Much later, Diane takes a trip and jumps off a cliff into the sea—in the same manner as Sappho, the heroine of Francois's book. Her survival after the jump signals a new beginning.

Unlike so many mainstream romantic melodramas about extramarital affairs, POST COITUM takes an intensely personal, amoral tone. Brigitte Rouan's performance makes Diane a thoroughly believable character, and her literally naked honesty in a scene where Diane assesses herself by standing nude in front of a mirror never feels exploitative. The subplots about Philippe's murder case and Francois's book reinforce the theme about the onerous demands placed on women in a patriarchal society. The unfortunate conclusion to the younger man-older woman liaison may seem predictable (if not conventional) but in a film that never condemns the transgression, the story line strengthens the enlightened outlook.

Otherwise, as a film, the delightful POST COITUM plays with generic devices and viewer expectations in clever ways. In only her second film as director, Rouan uses a variety of techniques to explore Diane Clovier's messy but fascinating life, including cinema verite shots during the early stages of illicit sex (for a change, it's the heroine who fumbles about during foreplay). Striking flashforwards of Diane suffering at the end of the affair punctuate the more carefree romantic passages, including a fantasy sequence with Diane floating on a cloud through the city streets and a memorable shot of Emilio and Diane stopping traffic on the Champs-Elysees with a spontaneous kiss. There are also heartfelt references to such classics as ANNA KARENINA (1935), THE EARRINGS OF MADAME DE (1953), and JEANNE DIELMAN 23 QUAI DE COMMERCE 1080 BRUNELLES (1975). POST COITUM deserves to share a spot with these films as a noble and refined achievement in its own right. *(Graphic violence, extensive nudity, sexual situations, adult situations, substance abuse, extreme profanity.)*—E.M.

d, Brigitte Rouan; p, Humbert Balsan; assoc p, Jean-Francois Rouan; w, Brigitte Rouan, Santiago Amigorena, Jean-Louis Richard, Guy Zilberstein, Philippe Le Guay; ph, Pierre Dupouey, Arnaud Leguy, Bruno Mistretta; ed, Laurent Rouan; prod d, Roland Deville; sound, Dominique Vieillard, Philippe Heissler (mixer); casting, Paula Chevalet, Lissa Pilu, Claire Le Saint; cos, Florence Emir, Marika Ingrato

Romance/Comedy/Drama (PR: C MPAA: NR)

PRACTICAL MAGIC ★★★

(U.S., 1998) 105m DiNovi Pictures; Fortis Films; Warner Bros. ~ Warner Bros. c

Sandra Bullock *(Sally Owens)*; Nicole Kidman *(Gillian Owens)*; Stockard Channing *(Aunt Frances)*; Dianne Wiest *(Aunt Jet)*; Aidan Quinn *(Gary Hallet)*; Goran Visnjic *(Jimmy Angelov)*; Evan Rachel Wood *(Kylie)*; Lucinda Jenney *(Sara, as an Adult)*; Alexandra Artrip *(Antoina)*; Mark Feuerstein *(Michael)*; Caprice Benedetti *(Maria Owens)*; Annabella Price *(Lovelorn Lady)*; Camilla Belle *(Sally, Aged 11)*; Lora Anne Criswell *(Gillian, Aged 10)*; Margo Martindale *(Linda Bennett)*; Chloe Webb *(Carla)*; Martha Graham *(Patty)*; Cordelia Richards *(Nan)*; Mary Gross *(Debbie)*; Jack Kirschke *(Old Man Wilkes)*; Herta Ware *(Old Lady Wilkes)*; Ellen Geer *(Pharmacist)*; Courtney Dettrich *(Young Sara)*; John McLeod *(Puritan Minister)*; Trevor Duncan *(Sara's Boy)*; Colby Cochran *(Ice Cream Boy)*; Caitlyn Holley *(Ice Cream Girl)*; Ken Serratt Jr. *(Lovelorn's Lover)*; Rich Sickler *(Dwight)*; Jeanne Robinson *(PTC Moms)*; Deborah Kancher *(PTC Moms)*; Peter Shaw *(Jack)*; Caralyn Kozlowski *(Regina)*

A mixed bag of fantasy, comedy, romance, and a dash of horror, PRACTICAL MAGIC, a tale of two sister witches and the men in their lives, is redeemed from total triviality by the deft touch of director Griffin Dunne and by the charm and smashing good looks of its three leading players.

Sally Owens (Sandra Bullock) and her sister Gillian (Nicole Kidman) are the descendants of a long line of witches. An old curse on men who love Owens women seems to have been unleashed when Sally's husband is killed in a traffic accident. Following the tragedy Sally, takes her two small daughters and moves in with her Aunt Jet (Dianne Wiest) and Aunt Frances (Stockard Channing).

When Gillian, who has moved down to Florida, phones her sister in New England to plead for help, Sally flies south and discovers that Gillian has been beaten by her unstable boyfriend Jimmy (Goran Visnjic). The sisters' attempts to subdue Jimmy, who is now terrorizing both of them, result in his death. After burying the body, Sally and Gillian return to New England.

One day Gary (Aidan Quinn), a police investigator from Tucson, arrives at the Owens home in search of Jimmy, who is wanted for murder. Although the sisters deny any knowledge of Jimmy's whereabouts, Gary gradually deduces the truth about his death. He also begins to fall for Sally, who returns his affections.

The situation comes to a head when Jimmy's ghost suddenly appears and invades the soul and body of Gillian. With the help of the local townswoman, Sally performs an exorcism and Jimmy's evil spirit is banished for good. Although Sally confesses the Florida slaying to Gary, in his official report to Tucson he declares Jimmy's death accidental. The curse of the Owens lifted at last, Sally and Gary wind up in each other's arms.

PRACTICAL MAGIC (a title that could serve as a catch phrase for the film industry's stock in trade) suffers from a weak story line and a shortage of interesting secondary characters—but fortunately Sandra Bullock, Nicole Kidman, and Aidan Quinn have enough charisma among them to carry the movie. Blessed with soft, sensuous features and an air of innate warmth, Bullock commands automatic empathy whenever she plays an average woman—even an average witch-woman like Sally. In contrast, Kidman boasts a kind of exotic Celtic beauty that is—to invoke the title of her best film—"to die for." Her too brief appearance, at picture's end, in full witch regalia (topped with a traditional pointy hat to match her nose and tarted up with a little decolletage) makes a visual impression that is worthy of an archetypal Halloween picture book. An actor who has inherited Montgomery Clift's classic handsomeness as well as, alas, Clift's rather thick voice, Quinn has neutralized his vocal shortcomings here with a slight but attractive Southwestern drawl.

In addition to its trio of stars, what makes PRACTICAL MAGIC ultimately succeed, if only barely, is Dunne's lively yet sensitive directing. Without resorting to shock effects, gratuitous ugliness, or other signposts of directorial desperation, he keeps his film moving from one brief scene to the next with commendable efficiency, allowing himself momentary stops along the way for modest poetic flourishes. Dunne's peak moment, achieved in collaboration with editor Elizabeth Kling and composer Michael Nyman, occurs at the dazzlingly Eisensteinian climax of the film's exorcism sequence.

Entertaining if hardly memorable, PRACTICAL MAGIC proves that reasonably satisfying movies can be made with little more than a few beautiful faces and a modicum of imagination and taste. *(Violence, profanity.)*—D.T.

d, Griffin Dunne; p, Denise DiNovi; exec p, Sandra Bullock, Mary McLaglen, Bruce Berman; co-p, Robin Swicord; w, Robin Swicord, Akiva Goldsman, Adam Brooks (based on the novel by Alice Hoffman); ph, Andrew Dunn; ed, Elizabeth Kling; m, Michael Nyman; prod d, Robin Standefer; art d, Keith P. Cunningham, Stephen Alesch; set d, Claire Jenora Bowin; sound, Richard Goodman; fx, Burt Dalton; casting, Amanda Mackey Johnson, Cathy Sandrich; cos, Judianna Makovsky; makeup, Pamela Westmore; stunts, Jeffrey J. Dashnaw

Fantasy/Romance/Comedy (PR: C MPAA: PG-13)

PRICE ABOVE RUBIES, A ★★★

(U.S., 1998) 120m A Band Apart; GreeneStreet Films; Pandora Cinema; Channel Four Films ~ Miramax c

Renee Zellweger *(Sonia Horowitz)*; Christopher Eccleston *(Sender Horowitz)*; Glenn Fitzgerald *(Mendel Horowitz)*; Julianna Margulies *(Rachel)*; Allen Payne *(Ramon)*; Kathleen Chalfant *(Beggar Woman)*; Edie Falco *(Feiga)*; John Randolph *(Rebbe)*; Kim Hunter *(Rebbitzn)*; Jackie Ryan *(Young Sonia)*; Shelton Dane *(Yossi)*; Peter Jacobson *(Schmuel)*; Tim Jerome *(Dr. Bauer)*; Phyllis Newman *(Mrs. Gelbart)*; Joyce Reehling *(Shaindy)*; Faran Tahir *(Hrundi Kapoor)*; Martin Shakar *(Mr. Berman)*; Teodorina Bello *(Mrs. Garcia)*; Glenn Flesher *(Chief Gabbal)*; Adam Dannheisser *(Young Gabbal #1)*; Stephen Singer *(Gabbal #2)*; Marvin Einhorn *(Gabbal #3)*; Mark Zimmerman *(Doctor)*; Richard "Izzy" Lifschutz *(The Moel)*; David Deblinger *(Baruch)*; Sam Jennings *(Heshle)*; Erin Rakow *(Tsipi)*; Asher Tabak *(Yechlel)*; Allen Swift *(Mr. Fishbein)*; Daryl Edwards *(Nelson)*; Peter Slutsker *(Mr. Sugarman)*; Lauren Klein *(Sonia's Mother)*; Tonye Patano *(Earring Woman)*; Don Wallace *(Ty)*; Asia Minor *(Homegirl)*; Roseanna Plasencia *(Homegirl #2)*; Jerry Matz *(Mr. Engelberg)*; Michael Sthulbarg *(Young Hassid)*; Karen Contreras *(Young Woman)*; Wai Ching Ho *(Lady Vendor)*; Mel Duane Gionson *(Paranoid Vendor)*; Paul J.Q. Lee *(Smooth Vendor)*; Leyla Aalam *(Israeli Woman)*

Understandably mislabeled by many critics as a feminist film, A PRICE ABOVE RUBIES depicts one woman's attempt to retain her independence despite the colossal societal pressure of Jewish tradition.

New bride Sonia Horowitz (Renee Zellweger) tries but cannot seem to adjust to the restrictive expectations of her husband Mendel's (Glenn Fitzgerald) orthodox Jewish family. When they have a baby, Sonia becomes all but a prisoner in her home while Mendel spends days—and often nights—at yeshiva learning to become a rabbi. Her only confidantes are a pair of mystical guides: the spirit of her dead brother Yossi (Shelton Dane), and a strange bag lady (Kathleen Chalfant). After a panic attack, Sonia visits the elder Rebbe, describing her frustration as a "fire inside" her; when the Rebbe dies shortly after her visit, Sonia is convinced she is cursed with a terrible, destructive power.

In order to get out of the house once in a while, Sonia takes a job as a gemologist with Mendel's brother, Sender (Christopher Eccleston), an under-the-table jewelry dealer; in the process, she also becomes Sender's lover. During her work, she encounters Ramon (Allen Payne), a gifted artist who sees Sonia as his muse. Sonia tries to act as Ramon's agent and manager, but Mendel's family suspects she is having an affair with the young man. Sender's wife, Rachel (Julianna Margulies), takes the baby and informs Sonia that her marriage to Mendel is over. After a night spent alone in an abandoned building, Sonia finds the inner strength to go back home and demand her things before setting out on her own. She is later visited by Mendel, who admits that their marriage was not meant to be, but asks her to visit so that their son can know both his parents.

Despite the geographic proximity, the inner circle of New York's orthodox Jewry is about as far as one can get from the crack houses depicted in writer-director Boaz Yakin's debut film, FRESH (1994). Yet the two films are not entirely dissimilar: each presents a character who strives to reject a destiny assigned them by their peers—be it drug dealer or patient, silently suffering housewife. Though initially dubbed a "feminist" film, A PRICE ABOVE RUBIES does not place its sympathies solely with the character of Sonia: her inner fire is infectious, inspiring the elder Rebbe to embrace his wife with passion after years of chaste familiarity, and giving Mendel the strength to defy his family in asking Sonia again into their home. In A PRICE ABOVE RUBIES, Renee Zellweger gives moviegoers a glimpse at a depth of talent only hinted at in her strong but essentially unchallenging role in 1996's JERRY MAGUIRE. Here Zellweger is by turns frightened and furious, wrong and wronged. Her emotional outpouring is balanced by a tremendously icy performance by Julianna Margulies, whose embodiment of the "proper" Jewish wife serves both to fan Sonia's inner fire and justify her anger.

Viewers not familiar with the customs and practices of orthodox Jews may have trouble following A PRICE ABOVE RUBIES, since Yakin makes no attempt to bring such viewers "up to speed," as it were. Unfortunately, neither does Yakin really delve deeply enough into the fascinating and arcane-seeming rituals of orthodox Jewry to really teach us much about the *why* behind these time-honored traditions—a missed opportunity to give audiences more than just a story. *(Profanity, sexual situations.)*—B.T.

d, Boaz Yakin; p, Lawrence Bender, John Penotti; exec p, Bob Weinstein, Harvey Weinstein; co-p, Joann Fregalette Jansen; w, Boaz Yakin; ph, Adam Holender; ed, Arthur Coburn; m, Lesley Barber; prod d, Dan Leigh; set d, Leslie E. Rollins; sound, William Sarokin (mixer); fx, John M. Ottesen; casting, Douglas Aibel; cos, Ellen Lutter; makeup, Lori Hicks

Drama/Religious (PR: C MPAA: R)

PRIMARY COLORS ★★★

(U.S., 1998) 135m Mutual Film Co.; Icarus Productions; Universal ~ Universal c

John Travolta *(Governor Jack Stanton)*; Emma Thompson *(Susan Stanton)*; Billy Bob Thornton *(Richard Jemmons)*; Adrian Lester *(Henry Burton)*; Kathy Bates *(Libby Holden)*; Maura Tierney *(Daisy)*; Larry Hagman *(Governor Fred Picker)*; Paul Guilfoyle *(Howard Ferguson)*; Caroline Aaron *(Lucille Kaufman)*; Rebecca Walker *(March Cunningham)*; Diane Ladd *(Mamma Stanton)*; Tommy Hollis *(Fat Willie)*; Rob Reiner *(Izzy Rosenblatt)*; Ben Jones *(Arlen Sporken)*; J.C. Quinn *(Uncle Charlie)*; Allison Janney *(Miss Walsh)*; Robert Klein *(Norman Asher)*; Mykelti Williamson *(Dewayne Smith)*; Jamie Denton *(Mitch)*; Leontine Guilliard *(Ruby)*; Monique L. Ridge *(Tawana Carter)*; Ned Eisenberg *(Brad Lieberman)*; Brian Markinson *(Randy Culligan)*; Geraldo Rivera; Charlie Rose; Larry King *(Themselves)*; O'Neal Compton *(Sailorman Shoreson)*; Kevin Cooney *(Lawrence Harris)*; Bonnie Bartlett *(Martha Harris)*; Cynthia O'Neal *(Elegant Woman)*; Chelcie Ross *(Charlie Martin)*; John Vargas *(Lorenzo Delgado)*; Tony Shalhoub *(Eddie Reyes)*; Bianca Lawson *(Loretta)*; Robert Cicchini *(Jimmy Ozio)*; Stan Davis *(Jack Mandela Washington)*; Harrison Young *(Sam)*; Rolando Molina *(Anthony Ramirez)*; Ross Benjamin *(Peter Goldsmith)*; Stacy Edwards *(Jennifer Rogers)*; Kristoffer Ryan Winters *(Terry Hicks)*; Susan Kussman *(Ella Louise)*; Vickilyn Reynolds *(Amalee)*; Robert Symonds *(Bart Nilson)*; Gia Carides *(Cashmere McLeod)*; Robert Easton *(Dr. Beauregard)*; Scott Burkholder *(Danny Scanlon)*; Bill Maher *(Himself)*; Lu Elrod *(Chubby Woman)*; R.M. Haley *(Shipyard Announcer)*; Henry Woronicz *(Pundit)*; Darice Richman *(Linda Feldstein)*; Rosalie Peck *(Retiree)*; Susan Forristal *(Bugger Bugger Woman)*; James Earl Jones *(CNN Voiceover)*

After their successful reunion for 1996's THE BIRDCAGE, writer Elaine May and director Mike Nichols team up again on PRIMARY COLORS, a political comedy adapted from the controversial novel by "Anonymous," supposedly inspired by then-governor Bill Clinton's 1992 presidential campaign. Despite fine performances and glowing reviews, the badly-timed release of PRIMARY COLORS coincided with a major real-life presidential scandal.

Jack Stanton (John Travolta), governor of an unnamed Southern state, has all the makings of a successful presidential candidate: charisma, empathy, and a great handshake. Unfortunately, he's also a lying womanizer, a fact his campaign staff go to great lengths to suppress. Newest staff member Henry Burton (Adrian Lester) agrees to join Stanton's team because he believes Stanton could be a good president; however, despite Stanton's climbing numbers, a few of the candidate's ghosts are about to be dragged out of the closet, including his attempt to evade service in Vietnam and an affair with his wife's hairdresser. Stanton hires two new people to help out: a political analyst, Richard Jemmons (Billy Bob Thornton), whose job is to keep the campaign on track; and a "dustbuster," Libby Holden (Kathy Bates), whose job is to clean up any dirt Stanton's opponents dig up.

The campaign soon narrows to two Democratic candidates: Stanton, and the former governor of Florida, Fred Picker (Larry Hagman). Knowing the Picker people will eventually discover Stanton's latest scandal—that he quite possibly impregnated a 14-year-old girl—Henry and Libby do some defensive investigation of Picker. They find out that Picker was once a major cocaine addict who had an affair with his male dealer. Though Stanton has to this point refused to run a smear campaign against his opponents, he gladly accepts the chance to humiliate Picker—destroying Henry and Libby's faith, and ultimately precipitating Libby's suicide. Shocked by Libby's act, Stanton decides not to release the Picker story to the press, and goes on to win the presidency cleanly.

Two unforeseeable factors contributed to PRIMARY COLORS's poor box office showing: the phenomenal success of James Cameron's TITANIC (1997), which destroyed competing films for months after its release; and the media saturation surrounding President Clinton's sex scandal involving White House intern Monica Lewinsky. By the time PRIMARY COLORS opened, most Americans just didn't want to hear any more sordid stories about the President. (Ironically, it had been this same promise of scandal that put the novel by "Anonymous"—actually columnist Joe Klein—at the top of the bestseller list two years earlier.)

Moviegoers who avoided PRIMARY COLORS missed a number of fine performances, beginning with John Travolta as the distinctly Clinton-esque Jack Stanton. With his grayed hair and raspy near-drawl, Travolta is obviously doing his best Clinton impression, and doing a pretty good job even when hobbled by purple, flag-waving prose. As the idealistic but ethically dubious politician, Travolta turns in another in a string of performances whose sheer range is pretty gutsy for a Hollywood A-lister. Kathy Bates, Billy Bob Thornton, and Larry Hagman all turn in crucial supporting performances that are dead-on perfect. The only disappointment is Stanton's wife, a woman willing to overlook her husband's improprieties in order to gain the White House. Written as clueless bordering on stupid, even Emma Thompson's considerable talents can't bring the character to life.

Audiences looking for "the real thing" should pick up THE WAR ROOM (1993), Chris Hegedus and D. A. Pennebaker's riveting documentary featuring Bill Clinton and his staff (many of whom inspired characters in PRIMARY COLORS) on the presidential campaign trail in 1992. *(Profanity, adult situations.)*—B.T.

d, Mike Nichols; p, Mike Nichols; exec p, Neil Machlis, Jonathan D. Krane; assoc p, Michael Haley; co-p, Michelle Imperato; w, Elaine May (based on the novel *Primary Colors: A Novel of Politics* by Anonymous, aka Joe Klein); ph, Michael Ballhaus; ed, Arthur Schmidt; m, Ry Cooder; prod d, Bo Welch; art d, Tom Duffield; set d, Cheryl Carasik; sound, Chris Newman (mixer); fx, Alan Lorimer, Brad Kuehn, Cinesite; casting, Juliet Taylor, Ellen Lewis, Juel Bestrop; cos, Ann Roth; makeup, J. Roy Helland; stunts, Mark Riccardi

AAN Best Adapted Screenplay: Elaine May; *AAN Best Supporting Actress:* Kathy Bates

Political/Comedy/Drama (PR: C MPAA: R)

PRINCE OF EGYPT, THE ★★★
(U.S., 1998) 93m Patchwork Productions;
DreamWorks Feature Animation ~ DreamWorks SKG c

VOICES OF: Val Kilmer *(Moses/God))*; Sandra Bullock *(Miriam)*; Ralph Fiennes *(Rameses)*; Danny Glover *(Jethro)*; Jeff Goldblum *(Aaron)*; Steve Martin *(Hotep)*; Helen Mirren *(Queen)*; Michelle Pfeiffer *(Tzipporah)*; Martin Short *(Huy)*; Patrick Stewart *(Pharaoh Seti)*

DreamWorks studios follows up their first computer-animation film, ANTZ, with their first traditional animated movie, THE PRINCE OF EGYPT. Although it will put most small children to sleep with its solemn retelling of the Biblical tale of the Ten Commandments, it's a must-see for animation buffs and represents the strongest challenge to date of Disney's hegemony of the genre.

In ancient Egypt, the Israelites are enslaved by the Pharaoh Seti (voice of Patrick Stewart), who issues an edict to round up Hebrew children. To save her infant's life, an Israelite mother puts her son Moses in a basket and sets it adrift in the Nile. The baby is found and adopted by the Pharaoh's wife (voice of Helen Mirren); the grown Moses (voice of Val Kilmer) comes to believe that he is the blood-brother of Rameses (voice of Ralph Fiennes), the true heir to the throne. One day, Moses has a chance meeting with his enslaved sister Miriam (voice of Sandra Bullock), who tells him about his true lineage. He refuses to believe her, but the Pharaoh later admits the truth to him and Moses becomes horrified by the treatment of the Hebrews at the hands of his "father." After accidentally killing an overseer while intervening on behalf of a slave who was being whipped, Moses flees to the desert, joins a tribe of nomadic shepherds and marries an Israelite named Tzipporah (voice of Michelle Pfeiffer).

Later, the voice of God (voice of Val Kilmer) tells Moses to go back to Egypt and free the Hebrews. To prove his power, God shows Moses a burning bush and gives him a magical staff. Moses returns to Egypt and asks Rameses, now the Pharaoh, to "let my people go," but Rameses refuses, even after Moses turns the Nile to blood. God then sends more plagues, including frogs and locusts, but Rameses only relents after a plague kills all of the first born of Egypt, including Rameses's own son. Moses leads his people out of Egypt, and God parts the Red Sea so they can cross it, but when the deceitful Rameses pursues them with his army, the sea washes back and wipes out the army. When the Israelites reach Mount Sinai, Moses brings down to them the holy tablets containing the word of God: the Ten Commandments.

Eschewing the giddy gaudiness of Cecil B. DeMille's two versions of THE TEN COMMANDMENTS (1923, 1956), as well as the anthropomorphic cuteness and juvenile humor of typical Disney cartoons, the serious and dignified THE PRINCE OF EGYPT is consistent with the born again-Judaism sensibility of DreamWorks toppers Jeffrey Katzenberg, who personally supervised the production and described it as a "labor of love," and Steven Spielberg, who suggested THE TEN COMMANDMENTS when Katzenberg was looking for a Biblical subject. Curiously, however, the J-word—"Jew"—is never uttered, the Israelites are always referred to as Hebrews, and there are other telling signs of political and commercial correctness (and timidity), such as the depiction of the female characters as strong-willed and independent, having villainous British voices for the two Pharaohs, and even using a black actor (Danny Glover) to provide the voice of a Hebrew high priest.

Though the plot hews closely to the Bible story, as well as the previous film versions, it also contains an obvious subtext which makes an analogy between the treatment of Jews in ancient Egypt and the genocide during WWII, most explicitly in a nightmare sequence where the hieroglyphic wall paintings come to life to tell the bloody story of how the Pharaoh murdered and enslaved the Israelites. New Age theosophy—and the requisite prosaic song numbers—aside, the film represents a high level of artistic achievement in its draftsmanship, flawlessly blending painted animation with 3-D style computer effects. The rendering of fast motion (a chariot race, a sandstorm, the attack at sea) is very realistic, even to the point of adding momentary blurriness, as in real cinematography, and the sense of depth, perspective, and detail throughout is exceptional. There are several excellent set pieces, including the expected "miracle" sequences of the burning bush, the plagues, and the parting of the Red Sea, but the most dazzling of all is the terrifying hieroglyphic nightmare where the paintings on the wall begin to move. Even with Val Kilmer's blandly-voiced Moses, which is easily outshone by Ralph Fiennes's forceful Rameses, the film is a fine addition to the art of animation and raises the visual bar for mainstream American animated features.—M.S.

d, Brenda Chapman, Steve Hickner, Simon Wells; p, Penney Finkelman Cox, Sandra Rabins; exec p, Jeffrey Katzenberg; assoc p, Ron Rocha; w, Philip LaZebnik; ed, Nick Fletcher; m, Hans Zimmer; prod d, Derek Gogol; art d, Kathy Alteri, Richard Chavez; anim, Kelly Asbury, Lorna Cook, Lorenzo E. Martinez; fx, Don Paul, Dan Philips

AA Best Original Song: "When You Believe"; Stephen Schwartz; *AAN Best Original Musical or Comedy Score:* Stephen Schwartz, Hans Zimmer

Religious/Children's/Animated (PR: A MPAA: PG)

PRINCE OF JUTLAND
(SEE: ROYAL DECEIT)

PRINCE VALIANT ★★½
(Germany/Ireland/U.K., 1997) 92m Constantin Film;
Legacy Film Productions; Celtridge Ltd.; Babelsberg
Film ~ 20th Century Fox Home Entertainment c
(PRINZ EISENHERZ)

Stephen Moyer *(Prince Valiant)*; Katherine Heigl *(Princess Ilene)*; Thomas Kretschmann *(Thagnar)*; Edward Fox *(King Arthur)*; Udo Kier *(Sligon)*; Joanna Lumley *(Morgan Le Fey)*; Ron Perlman *(Boltar)*; Warwick Davis *(Pechet)*; Ben Pullen *(Prince Arn)*; Zach Galligan *(Sir Kay)*; Marcus Schenkenberg *(Tiny)*; Anthony Hickox *(Sir Gawain)*; Gavan O'Herlihy; Walter Gotell; Hamish Campbell-Robertson; Chesney Hawkes; Guy Farley; Christian Thornley; Carl Justin; Kristen Hartwig; Eddie Hocking

This clunky international coproduction adapts the popular Arthurian newspaper comic strip. The budget is low, but the film boasts some moments of dizzy, kitschy fun.

While King Arthur (Edward Fox) reigns in Camelot, his hostile sorcerer sister Morgan Le Fey (Joanna Lumley) has allied herself with the Viking tyrant Sligon (Udo Kier) in the realm of Thule. They send raiders, led by Sligon's barbarous brother Thagnar (Thomas Kretschmann), to steal the mystic sword Excalibur, symbol of Arthur's authority. In the meanwhile, Arthur asks Valiant (Stephen Moyer), squire to Sir Gawain (Anthony Hickox), to escort visiting Princess Ilene (Katherine Heigl) back to her native Wales.

After defending the princess against a few potential kidnappers, Valiant divines that Thagnar took Excalibur, and he attempts to inform King Arthur. In the process, he winds up having a duel of honor with Ilene's jealous fiance, Prince Arn (Ben Pullen). A quelled Arn, Valiant, and an armored Ilene (who's been learning about the ways of knighthood from Valiant) converge on a Viking camp where one Knight of the Round Table is being held hostage. But the barbarians overwhelm them, killing Arn, capturing Ilene, and leaving Valiant for dead. Recovering, Valiant is informed of his heritage: the mysterious Boltar (Ron Perlman) tells him that he is really a prince, survivor of a noble Thule dynasty overthrown by Sligon; already their army-in-exile awaits Valiant to lead them in a siege against the villain's castle. Once they begin, however, they learn that Sligon has been slain by Thagnar, who wants the throne—and a harem of captive brides, including newcomer Ilene—for himself. Morgan tries to tempt Valiant into an alliance of their own, but while trying to elimate meddlesome Ilene, Morgan falls into a boiling cauldron. After various traps and escapes, Valiant cuts down Thagnar, but the usurper's swordstroke has already killed Ilene. Valiant's agonized appeal to God resurrects her. Prince Valiant delivers Excalibur to King Arthur just in time to prevent the disconsolate monarch from abdicating.

This is lively folderol, lavishly mounted despite the filmmakers' cost-cutting technique of resorting to cartoon animation (nicely done in the manner of Harold Foster's painstakingly detailed comic art) for transitions and scenic vistas of Camelot. The budget, such as it is, is well applied to a meticulous production design by Crispian Sallis (ALIENS) that offers wondrous medieval armor and fortifications, and Age-of-Chivalry gadgets that a feudal 007 could envy. If the story line were more straightforward and the principal actors were more than merely serviceable (all the colorful parts go to the baddies, although Fox does make a disturbingly doddering Arthur), this would be a swashbuckler worthy of comparison to THE CRIMSON PIRATE (1952). As it is, PRINCE VALIANT parries, thrusts, and occasionally stumbles over its own feet in a manner nearer to ROBIN HOOD: PRINCE OF THIEVES (1991), with liberated princess Heigl as campily anachronistic as was Kevin Costner in Sherwood Forest, and Lumley spooky but underused as Morgan Le Fey. Unlike that well- promoted Hollywood blockbusters, PRINCE VALIANT went quietly to home video in the US in 1998. *(Violence, adult situations, substance abuse.)*—C.C.

d, Anthony Hickox; p, Carsten Lorenz; exec p, Bernd Eichinger, Jim Gorman, Robert Kulzer; w, Anthony Hickox, Michael Frost Beckner, Carsten Lorenz (based on the comic strip "Prince Valiant" by Harold Foster); ph, Roger Lanser; ed, Denis Papillon; m, David Bergeaud; prod d, Crispian Sallis; fx, Bob Keen; casting, Lee Ann Groff; cos, Lindy Hemming; makeup, Robert McCann

Adventure **(PR: C MPAA: PG-13)**

PRINCE, THE ★★½
(Canada, 1995) 89m Prince Productions ~ Curb Entertainment c

Michael Riley *(Roy Timmons)*; Billy Dee Williams *(Jamie Hicks)*; Henry Silva *(Marshall Stern)*; Alex Morrison *(Ruth Di Marco)*; Duane Taniguchi *(Ted)*; Earl Boen *(Mr. Howlle)*; Saul Stein *(Frank)*; Timothy Bottoms *(John)*; Edie McClurg *(Marge)*; William G. Schilling *(Ed)*; B.W. Wiff *(Dick)*; Kurt Paul *(Melvin)*; Lou Rawls *(Jazz Singer)*; Tony Haney *(Detective)*; Bill Everett White *(Charlie)*; Alex Lombardo *(Carlos)*; Liat Goodson *(Angie)*; Lorna Scott *(Mary)*; Doria Rone *(Stripper)*; Tom Billet *(Thug)*; Tim Lounibos *(Thug)*; Jean Hubbard Boone *(Waitress)*; Forbes Riley *(Reporter)*; Clayton Norcoss *(Reporter)*; Jody Barr DiSalvo *(Barfly)*; George Henry Hill *(Custodian)*; Fran Harrison *(Nurse)*; Jess Gargiulo *(Cop)*

Touting itself as an update of Machiavelli's same-named blueprint for success, this upward-mobility drama is a fairly gripping expose of blind ambition. But it coasts too much on the gimmick of adapting Machiavelli's strategies for the 1990s, and would have benefited from sharper direction and a more consistently mordant tone.

Executive Roy Timmons (Michael Riley) is up to his new job of revitalizing the Gally Toy Co. in every way but one: he lacks the proper degree of suspicion of his ambitious co-workers, particularly V.P. Marshall Stern (Henry Silva) and Stern's manipulative account executive, and bedmate, Ruth Di Marco (Alex Morrison).

While keeping several office cut-throats at bay and fending off Ruth's attempts to replace him, Roy acquires a mentor in nearby bar owner Jamie Hicks (Billy Dee Williams). Teaching Roy the intricacies of one-upmanship, Jamie suggests proposing Ruth for a transfer and fudging sales figures. With the financial finagling of his friend and Gally Co. accountant Ted (Duane Taniguchi), Roy fakes a red ink crisis which he then solves to his advantage. But Roy is forced to fire Ted when a suspicious Ruth starts sniffing around for info.

Buoyed by his new aggressiveness, Roy starts neglecting his wife and indulging in recreational drugs. He is beaten by some street thugs, whom he believes are hired by Stern. Under the influence of drugs, a paranoid Roy shoots Stern; wounding him. Regretting his action, he rushes off to dial 911. Ruth, who's been waiting in the shadows, fatally shoots Stern and leaves evidence pointing to Roy. Roy is arrested and Ruth is promoted to CEO, the end result of a master plan put into action by Ruth and her father—Jamie.

THE PRINCE is a modest drama fueled by the bloodsport of corporate politics. It's fun to watch Roy learn to swim with the sharks, even if the film doesn't sufficiently camouflage Jamie Hick's hidden agenda. More suspense would have been engendered if the character of Roy weren't so naive; he's too clearly out of his league in these white-collar Olympics. Despite a few plot zingers, the scenario falls into place too neatly in chronicling Roy's rise and fall. The film deserves a snappier pace; it's weighed down by too many bull sessions between Roy and his conscienceless advisor. As a formal exercise in civilized betrayal, THE PRINCE just misses being royally entertaining. *(Violence, extreme profanity, extensive nudity, substance abuse.)*—R.P.

d, Pinchas Perry; p, Pinchas Perry; assoc p, Hanania Baer, Marc Oren; co-p, Jody Barr DiSalvo; w, Pinchas Perry, Amentha Dymally, Bill Everett White (based on the story by Machiavelli); ph, Hanania Baer; ed, Irit Raz; m, David Michael Frank; prod d, Allen Jones; set d, Martina Buckley; sound, Adam Joseph (mixer); fx, Larry Fioritto; casting, Patricia Rose; cos, Judi Jensen; makeup, Kathy Crouse

Drama **(PR: C MPAA: NR)**

PRINZ EISENHERZ
(SEE: PRINCE VALIANT)

PRODIGAL SON, THE ★★★½
(Hong Kong, 1982) 100m Golden Harvest ~ Tai Seng c
(AKA: PULL NO PUNCHES)

Yuen Biao *(Chang)*; Frankie Chan *(Ngai Fai)*; Lam Ching Ying, billed as Lam Cheng Ying *(Leung Yee-Tai)*; Sammo Hung, billed as Samo Hung *(Wong Wa Po)*; Chung Fat *(Master Sun)*; Dick Wei, billed as Dick Wai *(Master Law)*; Wei Pai *(Kwai)*, billed as Wai Pak; Chan Lung *(Yee Tong-Choi)*; Wu Ma *(Brick Breaker)*; Li Hai-sheng *(Chang's Teacher)*; Chien Yueh-sheng *(Chang's Teacher)*; James Tien *(Broken-Armed Fighter)*; Wong Hap

Also known as PULL NO PUNCHES, this 1982 gem, which was released to US home video in 1998, masterfully juggles comedy, history, and mindblowing martial arts.

Cocky youngster Chang (Yuen Biao), despite a reputation as an undefeated fighter, is soundly thrashed by Leung Yee-Tai (Lam Chen Ying), a performer in a traveling Peking Opera troupe. Informed that all his previous opponents were paid by his wealthy father to take a dive, Chang begs Leung to teach him real kung fu. When attackers compel Leung to reveal his abilities during an Opera performance, audience member Ngai Fai (Frankie Chan) decides Leung is a worthy opponent for a "friendly match." He pressures Leung into a fight, which is cut short by Leung's asthma attack. Later Ngai's bodyguards, instructed by his nobleman father to protect the youth, enlist ninja-like warriors to burn the Opera and kill all the performers, but Chang and Leung escape.

The two take up residence next to Leung's competitive former schoolmate, Wong Wa Po (Sammo Hung), and the two old rivals teach Chang the Wing Chun style of kung fu. Returning home, Leung and Chang are confronted by Ngai, whose bodyguards kill Leung. Shocked, Ngai has them beheaded, then fights a "friendly match" with Chang and is soundly thrashed.

The real Chang was renowned as one of Wing Chun's finest early practitioners. Director Sammo Hung had tackled the character's final years in WARRIORS TWO (1978); here he concerns himself with a young, rebellious Chang, and how he acquired his skills and ethics. In the four whirlwind years between the films, Hung progressed from talented kung fu moviemaker to a genuine world-class action master. The fights here are fast and intricate, and while the basic plot is a kung fu cliche (reluctant *sifu* [master] teaches student, who then avenges *sifu*'s death), the characters are given depth and motivation, the story filled with subplots and details that make it much more than just a western without guns. It is a hugely Chinese film, rich in accurate martial arts styles, Opera lore, and contextual references. The early fights in particular are staged in the manner of Opera routines, even to having tradional Chinese singing and percussion accompaniment; action escalates until the spectacular ninja fight adds flaming daredevil stunts to the stage acrobatics. After the surprisingly brutal scene of mass-murder, the tone shifts drastically back to the light comedy of the opening before returning for a finale that never quite regains the lost momentum. Hung includes sly references to his own films, and adds an interesting parallel between Chang and Ngai, both spoiled youths protected by their parent's money.

It's no surprise the Opera dynamics are so prominent and well-represented. The magnificently limber Yuen and Hung had been classmates in Opera school as youths, while Lam had studied at a "rival" school with several of the bit players. The real Leung Yee-Tai was a noted Opera performer, and Wing Chun is frequently perceived as a feminine style; Hung combined the two elements by having Leung specialize in female Opera roles. Lam, with his slight, wiry frame, had done exactly that in his stage career, going on to double frequently for women in his early days as film stuntman. *(Graphic violence, profanity.)*—A.B.

d, Sammo Hung; exec p, Raymond Chow; w, Sammo Hung, Barry Wong Bing-Yiu; ph, Lau Kwun Wai; ed, Peter Cheung; m, Frankie Chan, Philip Chan; set d, Chien Sum; makeup, Chan Kwok Hung; stunts, Sammo Hung, Yuen Biao, Lam Ching-ying, Billy Chan, Lai Ying Chau

Action/Comedy **(PR: C MPAA: NR)**

PRONTO ★★★
(U.S., 1998) 100m Showtime ~ Showtime c

Peter Falk *(Harry Arno)*; James Le Gros, billed as James LeGros *(Raylan Givens)*; Glenne Headly *(Joyce Patton)*; Sergio Castellito *(Tommy "The Zip" Bucks)*; Bradford Tatum *(Nicky Testa)*; Walter Olkewicz *(Jimmy Cap)*; Glenn Plummer *(Robert Gee)*; Therese Kablan *(Gloria)*; Luis Guzman *(Detective Torres)*

Another witty Elmore Leonard adaptation, PRONTO, features original characters and geography that set it apart from most crime flicks. Made for the Showtime network in 1997, PRONTO was subsequently released on home video in 1998.

Harry Arno (Peter Falk) is a Miami bookie in the indirect employ of mobster Jimmy Cap (Walter Olkewicz). When the FBI looks to nail Jimmy, they set Harry up as a target, spreading the rumor that he's skimming. Jimmy sends a fresh-off-the-boat Sicilian hit man named Tommy Bucks (Sergio Castellito), who everybody refers to simply as "the Zip," to kill Harry. Knowing Harry's in danger, the Feds send Deputy US Marshal Raylan Givens (James Le Gros) to protect him. Seven years earlier, Harry—then a witness in a federal case—gave Raylan the slip, forever marring the deputy's record. When Harry once again disappears, Raylan is determined to get him back.

Harry sneaks off to Rapallo, Italy, a spot he discovered during his service in WWII. After hiring another expatriate named Robert Gee (Glenn Plummer) to run errands for him, Harry sends for his girlfriend, Joyce (Glenne Headly), who travels to Italy, with Raylan following her and the Zip following *him*. Raylan first encounters Joyce in an outdoor cafe, and an instant bond forms between them. He follows her to Harry's villa, but seeing he's being tailed by the Zip's thugs, he pulls off and kills two of them. Knowing the Zip will be back, Raylan sends Harry and Joyce back to Miami; he stays behind to find Robert, who has been kidnapped by the Zip. After asking Raylan at gunpoint for Harry's whereabouts, the Zip shoots Robert and lets the deputy go.

Back in Miami, the Zip and Raylan meet again. The two face off in a restaurant, and when the Zip pulls a gun Raylan kills him. Harry goes back to his bookie business, and Raylan and Joyce leave Florida together.

Though missing the breezy attitude that characterized Barry Sonnenfeld's Leonard adaptation GET SHORTY (1995), PRONTO offers up a number of refreshingly original characters. When first introduced, Raylan appears to be the stereotypical "modern cowboy," with his spotless white cowboy hat and "much obliged, ma'am" demeanor; however, by the end of the film, he has exposed a ruthless streak that doesn't fit into the good ol' boy mold. The same can be said for the Zip, who turns out to be much more interesting than the average crime-movie hit man, particularly when he and his Italian buddies are ridiculing a would-be goodfella from Miami.

The least interesting character is Harry, in no small part due to Peter Falk's less-than-inspired portrayal (which isn't so bad, since by PRONTO's halfway mark, Harry's story has taken a backseat to that of Raylan and the Zip). The most nuanced performance comes from Sergio Castellito as the hitman Tommy "the Zip" Bucks, an authentic Italian mobster who can't believe the clowns pretending to be wise guys in Miami.

Like the Zip, PRONTO itself benefits from its international settings. When the action switches to Rapallo (actually Greece standing in for Italy), director Jim McBride (THE BIG EASY) achieves a whole new feel, depicting the Americans, and Raylan in particular, as starkly out of place without resorting to "ugly American" cliches. By jumping to Italy, PRONTO energizes what could have been a tired premise; by the time the action returns to Miami, the once-flat characters are fully formed, setting up a very satisfying climax. *(Violence, extensive nudity, sexual situations, profanity.)*—B.T.

d, Jim McBride; p, Dick Berg, Allan Marcil; w, Michael Butler (based on the novel by Elmore Leonard); ph, Affonso Beato; ed, Milton Ginsberg; m, John Altman; prod d, John J. Moore; casting, Beth Klein, Alysa Wishingrad

Crime/Comedy/Drama **(PR: C MPAA: R)**

PROPHECY II, THE ★½

(U.S., 1998) 83m Dimension Films; Overseas Film Group; Neo Motion Pictures ~ Dimension Home Video c

Christopher Walken *(Gabriel)*; Jennifer Beals *(Valerie Rosales)*; Russell Wong *(Danyael)*; Eric Roberts *(Michael)*; Brittany Murphy *(Izzy)*; Glenn Danzig *(Samayel)*; Bruce Abbott *(Thomas Daggett)*; William Prael *(Rafayel)*; Steve Hytner *(Joseph)*; Renee Victor *(Nana)*; Elizabeth Dennehy *(Kathy Kimball)*; J.G. Hertzler *(Father William)*; Nicki Micheaux *(Detective Kreibel)*; Danny Strong *(Julian)*; Michael Raimi *(Danyael Jr.)*

A typically off-the-wall performance by Christopher Walken is the only virtue of THE PROPHECY II, a dull and cheap-looking direct-to-video sequel to the 1995 cult film about a group of warring angels who come to Earth to raise hell.

While driving to work, LA nurse Valerie Rosales (Jennifer Beals) accidentally hits a homeless man named Danyael (Russell Wong) and takes him to the hospital. When he recovers, he goes home with Valerie, where they make love. The next day, Valerie learns she's pregnant. Meanwhile, the archangel Gabriel (Christopher Walken) arrives in LA and goes to Valerie's house to kill her, but Danyael rescues her and they take refuge in a church. He tells her that he is an angel, revealing his wings to prove it, and explains that Gabriel is leading an army of evil angels that are trying to destroy mankind because he's jealous of God's affection for humans. He also says that she has been chosen to carry a half human-half angel baby which will unite the angels and end their war.

Danyael takes Valerie to the remnants of Eden, which is inside a burned-out industrial park and seeks the help of Michael (Eric Roberts) the leader of the good angels, but when Gabriel arrives, Michael lets him inside. During a fight with Gabriel, Danyael is killed, but when Gabriel catches Valerie on the top of a high beam, the voice of God tells her to jump, and she leaps into the air, taking Gabriel with her. Gabriel is impaled on a spike and Valerie is unharmed. She tells Michael that she's keeping the baby, even though she's aware that the angels will probably come and take it away someday. Five years later, Valerie kisses her son Danyael Jr. (Michael Raimi) goodbye and puts him on a school bus. As it drives away, Gabriel, who's now a homeless drunk, sits on the streetcorner and watches the bus go by.

THE PROPHECY was far from classic, but at least its premise was offbeat and somewhat original, offering an intriguing mixture of Old Testament mysticism and contemporary horror, as well as Christopher Walken's amusing turn as a tongue-in-cheek maniac. Unfortunately, the sequel recycles the same elements in a thoroughly unimaginative way and jumps from scene to scene with little attempt to present a coherent or interesting story. The whole movie has the look of a low-budget music video, with a plethora of tilted angles, blue smoke, flash-cuts, and slo-mo explosions, and the special effects are pretty shoddy (Danyael's wings are shown only in shadow; there are visible outlines on matte shots; and Gabriel's arrival on Earth from Hell is via a highly unconvincing earthquake in a parking lot, replete with phony looking cracked asphalt and orange lighting). With the rest of the cast behaving as if they're actually making a serious film, Walken's bemused performance is the only reason it's at all watchable, as he seems to be acting in his own private comedy, making snide wisecracks about the idiocy of the situations and the characters like some kind of supernatural Greek chorus. Walken has defended his appearances in bad movies by stating that he likes to work and takes whatever he's offered, but it's a sad sight to see him wasting his prodigious talent on junk like this. *(Graphic violence, profanity, nudity, sexual situations.)*—M.S.

d, Greg Spence; p, Joel Soisson, W.K. Border; exec p, Gregory Widen, Robert Little, Bob Weinstein, Harvey Weinstein; assoc p, Matthew Greenberg; co-p, Denise Leong; w, Matthew Greenberg, Greg Spence (based on characters created by Gregory Widen); ph, Richard Clabaugh; ed, Christopher Cibelli, Ivan Ladizinsky; m, David Williams; prod d, Shay Austin; sound, Larry Scharf, Rick Waddell; fx, David Waine; casting, Mark Tillman; cos, Pennie Fien; makeup, Nacoma Whobrey

Horror **(PR: O MPAA: R)**

PROPOSITION, THE ★★★

(U.S., 1998) 111m Interscope Communications; PolyGram ~ PolyGram c

Kenneth Branagh *(Father Michael McKinnon)*; Madeleine Stowe *(Eleanor Barret)*; William Hurt *(Arthur Barret)*; Neil Patrick Harris *(Roger Martin)*; Robert Loggia *(Hannibal Thurman)*; Blythe Danner *(Syril Danning)*; Josef Sommer *(Father Dryer)*; Bronia Wheeler *(Sister Mary Frances)*; Ken Cheeseman *(Wayne Fenton)*; Jim Chiros *(Timothy)*; Dee Neslon *(Susan Vicar)*; Pamela Hart *(Skip Taylor)*; Wendy Feign *(Maid)*; Dossy Peabody *(Hannibal's Secretary)*; Tom Downey *(Torrey Harrington)*; Tom Kemp *(Arthur's Chauffeur)*; Father Frank Toste *(Father Frank Timothy)*; David Byrd *(Dr. Jenkins)*; Lawrence Bull *(Butler Captain)*; Michael Bradshaw *(Butler)*; Willy O'Donnell *(Andre)*; Frank T. Wells *(Coroner)*

A married couple hire a young man to sire them a child in THE PROPOSITION, a movie that begins as a naughty joke and evolves into a sensitive, intelligent, villainless melodrama with a mild feminist slant.

It is the 1930s. When Arthur Barret (William Hurt), a rich and prominent Bostonian, and his wife Eleanor (Madeleine Stowe), a writer of somewhat scandalous novels, realize that Arthur is sterile, they hire a young man named Roger Martin (Neil Patrick Harris) to impregnate Eleanor. After more than one try, Roger gets the job done, but in the process, falls for his beautiful client and refuses to go away. Eventually, Arthur and Roger exchange threats.

When the pregnant Eleanor, who feels guilty about the situation, learns of Roger's death, she falls and loses her baby and, when it is revealed that the young man was murdered, she suspects her husband of the crime. Father Michael (Kenneth Branagh), the Barrets' new pastor, finds himself being drawn deeper and deeper into the whole messy matter. When a second surrogate (Tom Downey) is hired to service Eleanor, she sends him away and winds up in bed with Father Michael instead. Soon, they have embarked on a serious affair.

Eleanor dies giving birth to twins. Father Michael decides to leave the priesthood and fight for the custody of the twin boys he has propagated because he believes that Arthur was responsible for Roger's death. The priest changes his mind, however, when he overhears Syril (Blythe Danner), the Barrets' longtime secretary and zealously loyal confidante, confess to Arthur that she is Roger's murderer.

The story is narrated by Father Michael nearly 20 years after the fact. Written for the screen, the project, for better or worse, feels like it was adapted from a novel. Although it is equipped with one or two plot intricacies too many (Michael's father turns out to be Arthur's brother, *and,* for good measure, his mother had once been Arthur's fiancee), and the precise role of Syril in the complicated backstory remains somewhat shrouded, THE PROPOSITION is an interesting tale fairly well told.

The film peaks in its first act, in which Eleanor and Roger's initial assignation is very deftly presented as tasteful, ribald comedy. As the story grows increasingly somber, the movie comes uncomfortably close to high-hatting the bulk of its audience when it allows its characters to intellectualize about Shakespeare's sister and Virginia Woolf, but fortunately these misplaced literary allusions are kept in check and not allowed to swamp the film's emotive surge. However, the picture does lose some of its rhythm and thrust in its last stages, which could well have been tightened. THE PROPOSITION's feminist message is explicitly stated at several points in Father Michael's surprisingly worldly narration, but this bald petitioning is so reasonable, pertinent, and straightforwardly presented that it emerges not as intrusive and manipulative but as almost quaintly old-fashioned—in a "pre-postmodern" way.

Amid a generally competent cast, Stowe is especially appealing, but Hurt, an actor who is uncomfortable portraying men of power, comes across as oddly strangulated, particularly when Arthur is shown within the context of the kind of structured social situations such men thrive on. *(Sexual situations, adult situations.)*—D.T.

d, Leslie Linka Glatter; p, Ted Field, Diane Nabatoff, Scott Kroopf; exec p, Lata Ryan; w, Rick Ramage; ph, Peter Sova; ed, Jacqueline Cambas; m, Stephen Endelman; prod d, David Brisbin; art d, Kenneth A. Hardy; set d, Tracey Doyle; sound, T.J. O'Mara (mixer), Weddington Productions (design); fx, Brian Ricci; casting, Johanna Ray, Elaine J. Huzzar; cos, Anna Sheppard; makeup, Jeff Goodwin; stunts, Paul Marini

Romance/Crime/Drama (PR: C MPAA: R)

PRYATYEL PAKOYNIKA

(SEE: FRIEND OF THE DECEASED, A)

PSYCHO ★★

(U.S., 1998) 110m Imagine; Universal ~ Universal c

Vince Vaughn *(Norman Bates)*; Anne Heche *(Marion Crane)*; Julianne Moore *(Lila Crane)*; William H. Macy *(Milton Arbogast)*; Viggo Mortensen *(Sam Loomis)*; Robert Forster *(Dr. Simon)*; Philip Baker Hall *(Sheriff Chambers)*; Anne Haney *(Mrs. Chambers)*; Chad Everett *(Tom Cassidy)*; Rance Howard *(Mr. Lowery)*; Rita Wilson *(Caroline)*; James Remar *(Patrolman)*; James LeGros *(Car Dealer)*; Steven Clark Pachosa *(Police Guard)*; O.B. Babbs *(Mechanic)*; Flea *(Bob Summerfield)*; Marjorie Lovett *(Woman Customer)*; Ryan Cutrona *(Chief of Police)*; Ken Jenkins *(District Attorney)*

"Let me get my Walkman!" is a sample of the updated dialogue in the 1998 edition of PSYCHO. Otherwise, this remake of the Alfred Hitchcock classic stays obsessively close to the original, copying many of Hitch's edits, camera movements, and set details. The only thing that hasn't been reproduced is the original film's jarring sense of originality.

Marion Crane (Anne Heche), an Arizona bank clerk, gets a chance to start a new life with her boyfriend, hardware store owner Sam Loomis (Viggo Mortensen), when a wealthy bank customer, Tom Cassidy (Chad Everett), hands her $400,000 for safekeeping. She flees town with the money, planning to contact Sam later, but during a rainy night on the road, Marion is forced to stop at the remote roadside Bates Motel, run by the shy, well-mannered Norman Bates (Vince Vaughn).

Norman invites Marion to have dinner with him and he tells her about his invalid mother, who lives with Norman in a big house overlooking the motel. During their talk, Norman develops an attraction for Marion, and Marion decides to return to Arizona and repay the money. But Marion never gets the chance to return the money because Norman's mother, presumably in a rage of jealousy, stabs Marion to death while Marion takes a late-night shower. Norman cleans up after the murder and inadvertently throws out the money when he sinks Marion's body and her belongings in her car in a nearby swamp.

Marion's disappearance prompts an investigation by a private detective, Milton Arbogast (William H. Macy). After a broad search of highway motels, Arbogast tracks down Norman and questions him about Marion's motel stay. Believing Norman is hiding something and that Norman's mother knows about Marion's whereabouts, Arbogast sneaks into the Bates's home, but he is killed upon entering by Norman's knife-wielding mother.

Sam and Marion's concerned sister, Lila Crane (Julianne Moore), follow up Arbogast's leads and confront Norman about Marion. To gather information, Sam detains Norman while Lila searches the Bates's home to talk to Norman's mother. Norman knocks out Sam and hunts down Lila. But Lila has already reached the Bates' fruit cellar, where she discovers that Norman's mother is only a well- preserved corpse. Norman, then, dressed as his mother, lunges at Lila with a knife, but Sam subdues him in time.

Later, at a police station, a psychiatrist, Dr. Simon (Robert Forster), explains that Norman had taken on the personality of his late mother when he killed Marion because of the sexual feelings Marion aroused in Norman. Meanwhile, Norman, awaiting his fate, chastises himself in the third person (assuming the thoughts of his mother) as the police locate Marion's car in the swamp.

Remaking Hitchcock often seems like a foolhardy idea, perhaps because Hitchcock's style was so incredibly distinct (DIAL M FOR MURDER—as A PERFECT MURDER—and a TV-movie REAR WINDOW were two other bland 1998 knockoffs). In remaking PSYCHO, auteur wannabe Gus Van Sant genuflects before the famous original, but gets most things wrong anyway. Perhaps if Van Sant had envisioned PSYCHO in a totally new way, he might have justified his jarring changes. But, strangely, Van Sant retains nearly every line of Joseph Stefano's script while he mucks about needlessly with the aesthetics.

On a purely visual level, Van Sant saturates Hitchcock's most expressionistic work (very deliberately designed in black-and-white) with day-glo Pop-Art colors that are sometimes pretty but totally inappropriate. Only two of the night scenes—Marion's ride in the rain and Norman's sinking of the car—capture some of the original chill.

In the most infamous scenes—the two murders—Van Sant uses tricky camera effects and inserts symbolic shots (of clouds, a nude woman, a cow) during the stabbings. Van Sant also gratuitously develops Norman's character by establishing him as a Country-Western fan (Lila finds a Tammy Wynette record instead of Beethoven's "Emperor Concerto" in his room) and by including the sounds of Norman masturbating as he spies on Marion.

A *USA Today* newsstand, the retro '70s clothing (even on Norman!), and that damned Sony Walkman constitute Van Sant's other notions of revisionism, but the new PSYCHO cannot be viewed with the innocence of 1960 eyes: too many sequels, imitations, and more reflexive thrillers (e.g., SCREAM) have been produced, reducing any sense of suspense or surprise, and contemporary social issues stand out glaringly by being ignored. Meanwhile, no one in the cast brings anything fresh to the roles, only accentuating how good the originals were (although Mortensen, who was also in A PERFECT MURDER, matches John Gavin's stiffness). Vaughn is out of his depth imitating Anthony Perkins's class act, and Heche lacks the prerequisite star frisson that had made Janet Leigh's midway demise so shocking (Vaughn and Heche costarred to much better advantage in RETURN TO PARADISE, also in 1998). They and the other actors read the same clever lines as before, but make them sound studied and stilted. Halfway through, you'll be reaching for your Walkman, too. *(Graphic violence, nudity, sexual situations, adult situations.)*—E.M.

d, Gus Van Sant; p, Brian Grazer, Gus Van Sant; exec p, Dany Wolf; assoc p, James Whitaker; w, Joseph Stefano (based on the novel by Robert Bloch); ph, Christopher Doyle; ed, Amy Duddleston; m, Bernard Herrmann; prod d, Tom Foden; art d, Carlos Barbosa; set d, Rosemary Brandenburg; sound, Ron Judkins; fx, Erick Brennan; casting, Howard Feuer; cos, Beatrix Aruna Pasztor; makeup, Elaine Offers, Matthew Mungle (special effects); stunts, Mickey Giacomazzi

Thriller/Horror/Drama (PR: C MPAA: R)

PULL NO PUNCHES
(SEE: PRODIGAL SON, THE)

QIN SONG
(SEE: EMPEROR'S SHADOW, THE)

QUEST FOR CAMELOT ★★
(U.S., 1998) 86m Warner Bros. Feature Animation ~ Warner Bros. c

VOICES OF: Jessalyn Gilsig *(Kayley)*; Andrea Corr *(Kayley—Singing)*; Cary Elwes *(Garrett)*; Bryan White *(Garrett—Singing)*; Gary Oldman *(Baron Ruber)*; Don Rickles *(Cornwall—Two-Headed Dragon)*; Eric Idle *(Devon—Two-Headed Dragon)*; Jane Seymour *(Lady Juliana)*; Pierce Brosnan *(King Arthur)*; John Gielgud *(Merlin)*; Bronson Pinchot *(The Griffin)*; Jaleel White *(Bladebeak)*; Gabriel Byrne *(Sir Lionel)*; Jessica Hathaway *(Lynnit)*; Adam Pascal; Frank Welker

Disney's hegemony in the animation field is in no danger from QUEST FOR CAMELOT, a routine cartoon feature from Warner Bros. about a young girl who aspires to find the legendary sword Excalibur and become a Knight of the Round Table.

Sir Lionel (voice of Gabriel Byrne), a Knight of the Round Table, is killed while protecting King Arthur (voice of Pierce Brosnan) from the evil knight Ruber (voice of Gary Oldman), who's trying to steal the magic sword Excalibur. Ten years later, Lionel's daughter Kayley (voice of Jessalyn Gilsig) wants to be a knight like her father. Ruber finally succeeds in stealing Excalibur, but loses the sword in the Forbidden Forest and takes Kayley's mother Lady Juliana (voice of Jane Seymour) hostage as part of his scheme to retrieve it. Kayley eludes Ruber and sets off for Camelot to find Excalibur. Along the way, she encounters a blind young hermit named Garrett (voice of Cary Elwes) who was trained by Sir Lionel to be a knight years earlier, but had lost his sight in a fire.

Garrett agrees to join Kayley in her quest and they're accompanied by a bickering two-headed dragon named Devon (voice of Eric Idle) and Cornwall (voice of Don Rickles). Kayley manages to rescue Excalibur from the clutches of a giant ogre who's using it as a toothpick, but the dejected Garrett tells her to take it to Arthur alone, convinced that he'll never be able to become a knight. Ruber forces Lady Juliana to help him sneak into Camelot and he also captures Kayley. After using a magical potion to weld Excalibur to his hand, Ruber tries to kill King Arthur, but Garrett, who has changed his mind and come to Camelot, helps Kayley save Arthur, and Ruber is killed after Excalibur is put back into the legendary stone from which only Arthur can pull it out. Kayley and Garrett are married and Arthur makes them both Knights of the Round Table.

QUEST FOR CAMELOT, which was publicized as being Warner Bros.' first animated theatrical feature (not counting compilations and TV-generated items like BATMAN: MASK OF THE PHANTASM), is all the more disappointing in that the studio that was once renowned for the originality of its marvelously irreverent Merrie Melodies/Looney Tunes shorts of the 1930s, '40s, and '50s, has now decided to challenge Disney merely by slavishly copying the worst elements of the Mouse-house's modern formula. In this case, that means limited-motion animation that leans heavily on CGI effects, a sappy romantic story that's demographically designed to appeal to young girls (nothing inherently wrong with that, except that it means that the swordplay action that appeals to boys is given short shrift and reduces the Knights of the Round Table to peripheral characters), and worst of all, the torturous trend of inserting insipid songs into the plot every five minutes, whether or not they're motivated by the story. The fact that these songs are cowritten by Carol Bayer Sager (who just happens to be married to Warner co-CEO Bob Daly) makes them all the more annoying. At least Fox's animated ANASTASIA (1997) had a decent score and took some chances with its opulent widescreen design. For the most part, the animation in QUEST is jerky and stilted, with the usual "cute" anthropomorphism (a hatchet-chicken called Bladebeak, the comical Devon-Cornwall) and blandly heroic, saucer-eyed "humans."

The movie's most impressive scenes are all highly derivative (such as the SWORD IN THE STONE-like finale, and the plethora of bizarre creatures in the Forbidden Forest, which are very reminiscent of those in Disney's ALICE IN WONDERLAND). The roster of stars enlisted to provide the voices of the supporting cast is quite impressive (particularly if you've been dying to hear Gary Oldman sing), but their dialogue is witless and their characters take a back seat to the robotic leads and their sidekicks's de rigueur wisecracks (tiresome Elvis impersonations, lame in-jokes about Warner Bros.' SUPERMAN, and their R-rated DIRTY HARRY, not to mention the TAXI DRIVER "You-talkin'-to-me" routine, which was already done much better in THE LION KING). The action scenes are not badly done, but there's simply not enough of them, and every time the story starts to pick up some momentum, it grinds to a halt so that a celebrity vocalist like Celine Dion can belt out a tune to boost the soundtrack sales. Like too many so-called kid's movies, this is just another merchandising product designed to market toys, games, and other ancillaries.—M.S.

d, Frederik Du Chau; p, Frank Gladstone, Dalisa Cooper Cohen; assoc p, Dowlatabadi; w, William Schifrin, Kirk De Micco (from a story by Jacqueline Feather and David Seidler, based on the novel *The King's Damsel* by Vera Chapman); ed, Stan Allen; m, Patrick Doyle; art d, Carol Police, Michael Spooner, Steve Pilcher; anim, John McKenna (supervisor)

AAN Best Original Song: "The Prayer"; Carole Bayer Sager, David Foster, Tony Renis, Alberto Testa

Animated/Children's (PR: AA MPAA: G)

QUICKSILVER HIGHWAY ★★

(U.S., 1998) 90m National Studios, Inc. ~ 20th Century Fox Home Entertainment c

Christopher Lloyd *(Aaron Quicksilver)*; Matt Frewer *(Dr. Charlie George)*; Raphael Sbarge *(Gary/Bill)*; Missy Crider *(Olivia)*; Silas Weir Mitchell; Bill Nunn *(Lynn)*; Veronica Cartwright; Bill Bolender; Amelia Heinle; Clive Barker *(Anesthesiologist)*; Cynthia Garris *(Ellen)*; Kevin Grevioux *(Police Sergeant)*; Christopher Hart *(Lefty)*; William Knight *(Rhinoplasty Man)*; John Landis *(Surgical Assistant)*; Shawn Nelson *(Driver)*; Sherry O'Keefe *(Harriet DaVinci)*; Dana Waters *(Hand Chaser)*; Constance Zimmer *(Female Patient)*

Compiled as a feature for home video, QUICKSILVER HIGHWAY is two episodes of a failed horror anthology TV series featuring Christopher Lloyd as a spooky storyteller.

In the first segment, young bride Olivia (Missy Crider) is stranded in the desert as her husband Gary (Raphael Sbarge) goes for help. She meets traveling carney Aaron Quicksilver (Christopher Lloyd). He tells her a story about a traveling salesman Bill Hogan (also played by Sbarge) who foolishly tries to drive through a desert sandstorm. At a truck stop, he picks up a birthday present for his son, an oversized pair of chattering teeth with legs. He also picks up a hitchhiker, who tries to rob him. Bill is saved by the teeth, which kill the hitcher and drag his body off into the desert. After the story, Olivia hears the returned Gary being struck and killed by a passing motorist, and steps outside to see his body being dragged away by the teeth.

While running a sideshow in a carnival, Quicksilver meets plastic surgeon Charlie George (Matt Frewer), who is the star of the story he hears: Taking his hands for granted, Charlie notices them when they start acting oddly, trying to turn the wheel of his car into oncoming traffic. As he sleeps, the hands talk to each other, plotting to break free of Charlie's body. The next evening, as he sleeps, they strangle his wife before he can stop them. Charlie's hands pull him to his kitchen, where one grabs a meat cleaver and severs the other. Charlie is taken to a hospital and his liberated hand follows, inciting other hands to "join the revolution." Pretending to speak for his remaining hand, Charlie leads the swarm of hands to the roof and orders them to follow him as he jumps to his death. As he leaves Quicksilver's sideshow, Dr. George is compelled to pinch a policeman.

It's almost a shame QUICKSILVER HIGHWAY didn't get picked up as a series, if more of it would have been as silly as what's here. It's hard to tell if the original stories by Stephen King and Clive Barker (who appears in a cameo) were meant to be taken seriously, or if adapter Mick Garris intended to add a little humor. But the climactic sight of a swarm of detached hands leaping off a rooftop, screaming "Free!" in high-pitched voices, is sublimely ridiculous. (Given to exhorting "Join me and be free! Leave the tyranny of the body! The revolution is at hand!", the hands have some of the best monster dialogue since bloodthirsting plant Audrey Jr. in Roger Corman's 1960 LITTLE SHOP OF HORRORS.) On the other hand, there's no such redeeming moment in the Stephen King story, "Chattering Teeth." Otherwise, these are a pair of tired fright exercises which happily abandon sense or logic any time there's a chance to score another cheap shock. (Violence, adult situations.)—M.F.

d, Mick Garris; p, Mick Garris, Ron Mitchell; exec p, John McTiernan, Donna Dubrow, Sandra Rush, Tarquin Gotch, Bob Lemchen; w, Mick Garris (based on "The Body Politic" by Clive Barker and "Chattery Teeth" by Stephen King); ph, Shelly Johnson; ed, Norman Hollyn; m, Mark Mothersbaugh; prod d, Craig Stearns; set d, Ellen Tottleben; sound, Richard Schexnayder; fx, William Mesa, Joe Fordham; casting, Lynn Kressel; cos, Warden Neil; makeup, Leigh Mitchell, Douglas Noe; stunts, Dan Bradley

Horror/Fantasy (PR: C MPAA: NR)

QUIEN DIABLOS ES JULIETTE?

(SEE: WHO THE HELL IS JULIETTE?)

R

RABID DOGS ★★★

(Italy, 1998) 96m La Spera Cinematrografica ~ Lucertola Media c (AKA: SEMAFORO ROSSO; CANI ARRIBBIATI)

Riccardo Cucciolla *(Riccardo)*; Lea Lander *(Greta)*; Maurice Poli *(Doc)*; Luigi Montefiori *(32)*; Aldo Caponi *(Blade)*; Erika Dario *(Maria)*

Long considered to be a lost film, Mario Bava's RABID DOGS was made in 1974 but got entangled in a legal dispute which kept it in limbo until it was restored for a 1998 video release. The wait was well worth it, as the riveting crime thriller proves to be one of Bava's best films, albeit in a totally different vein than his usual metiers of horror and fantasy.

During an armed robbery, four violent criminals kill two people. When their getaway car runs out of gas, they grab a woman hostage (Lea Lander), then jump into another car, forcing an old man named Riccardo (Riccardo Cucciolla) to drive them out of town. However, Riccardo has an unconscious child in the back of the car and pleads with them to let him take the boy to a hospital for an emergency operation. Doc (Maurice Poli), the gang's leader, refuses, and the two other robbers, nicknamed 32 (Luigi Montefiori) and Blade (Aldo Caponi), sadistically taunt Riccardo by pretending to stab the little boy. Blade and 32 also torment the woman—whom they call Greta Garbo—with lewd remarks and physical advances. When they reach the outskirts of Rome, Greta tries to run away during a bathroom stop. Blade and 32 catch her, then humiliate her by making her urinate in front of them.

Back in the car, 32 exposes himself to Greta and Doc warns him to leave her alone, but after getting drunk, 32 tries to rape her. Doc is forced to shoot him, but he doesn't die right away. When they stop for gas, a woman named Maria (Erika Dario) asks them for a ride, but when she sees the dying and blood-covered 32, Blade kills her. Her body is dumped on the side of the road, along with the still-breathing 32, who has to be shot again. When they reach their safe house, where a car is waiting, Doc prepares to kill the hostages, but Riccardo whips out a pistol and shoots Doc and Blade. Before dying, Blade fires back and kills Greta. Riccardo grabs the money and drives away with the child in the new car. He then stops to phone someone, from whom he demands 3 million lire in ransom for the life of the child that he's got in the car.

The rescue from oblivion of RABID DOGS is a major rediscovery for Bava fans, for it reveals that even at the age of 60, the horror maestro was capable of moving beyond the realm of his customary genre. Although Bava had finished principal photography and assembled a work print, he had no money to cover the final editing following the death of his producer's financial backer. This resulted in the producer filing for bankruptcy and the film elements being impounded in a property dispute. More than 20 years later, a production company run by actress Lea Lander (who plays "Greta") bought the film and reconstructed it based on Bava's original notes. The only scene not originally filmed was a brief prelude, in which an unknown woman is seen sobbing. This was shot in 1997 and has been placed under the new opening titles. Considering that the film had been languishing in a vault somewhere, it's in surprisingly good condition, with the expected grain and faded colors actually adding to its raw power.

The film itself is a taut, nihilistic thriller without a trace of pity or sentimentality, as Bava wrings every ounce of terror out of what was obviously a very low budget, and thankfully keeps his sometimes excessive use of zooms to a minimum. The opening heist sequence is superbly handled, employing tilted angles, aerial shots, and slow-motion, and the entire film moves at a breakneck pace, even though most of it takes place inside the speeding car. Bava's inventive editing and stylish compositions never allows the tension to flag and creates a sweaty, claustrophobic atmosphere that's filled with dread, while the script is structured to allow for pit stops along the way, adding to the suspense. The film's most impressive accomplishment is how it cleverly contrasts the criminals' loathsome appearance, crude language, and barbaric behavior with that of the "normal" looking Riccardo, the seemingly loving father whose rational demeanor is revealed to be a disguise for his cold-blooded ruthlessness. Even without this great final twist, the film would be an expert crime thriller, but the twist adds an ironical extra dimension to the story's exploration of the true nature of evil. *(Graphic violence, extreme profanity, sexual situations.)*—M.S.

d, Mario Bava; p, Roberto Loyola; w, Alessandro Parenzo, Cesare Frugoni (based on the short story "Man and Boy" in *Ellery Queen Mystery Magazine*); ph, Emilio Varriano, Mario Bava; ed, Carlo Reali, Angelo Marzullo; m, Stelvio Cipriani; sound, Mario Bramonti; fx, Franco Ponzo

Crime/Thriller **(PR: O MPAA: NR)**

RACE TO SAVE 100 YEARS, THE ★★★

(U.S., 1998) 57m Warner Bros.; Turner Entertainment ~ Warner Bros. Classics c

Peter Brooks *(Narrator)*; Martin Scorsese; Kevin Brownlow; Robert Rosen; Mary Lea Bandy; James H. Billington

The Turner Entertainment Company promotes film preservation and their own library of goods in THE RACE TO SAVE 100 YEARS, a sort of THAT'S ENTERTAINMENT! with a mission.

This 57-minute documentary runs briskly through the history of film preservation and illustrates its points with film clips. Most classical Hollywood films are considered lost or in need of preservation because the nitrate base of the film stock that was once used caused explosions and because the studios carelessly threw away material, even deliberately burning their libraries in order to recover the silver compounds.

Though most silent films have disintegrated over the years, some early films, including Thomas Edison's turn-of-the-century shorts and D.W. Griffith's first film (THE ADVENTURES OF DOLLIE, 1908), have been salvaged, because filmmakers at the time could only copyright their prints, a material that outlasted the flammable nitrate-based stock. Other films long-thought lost have turned up in archives recently, including a fragment from THE DIVINE WOMAN (1928), starring Greta Garbo, which was discovered in Russia in 1995.

Early sound film preservation has been complicated by those films that used separate sound disks: in some cases, the soundtracks have survived without the film, but in other cases the film has survived without the soundtracks. Finding and restoring early color film prints has been an equally daunting task. Also, some original negative prints of films were not well-protected by the studios, and have been restored only recently by labs (including TOP HAT, 1935, starring Astaire and Rogers). In the 1950s, acetate replaced nitrate as a film base, and the some preservation efforts began by the transfer of classic films to the new "safety stock." Meanwhile, however, many nonclassics perished and some aficionados complained they missed the luminous quality of the nitrate. Technicians also realized that acetate could decompose, too, and that the popular new color processes of the 1950s period faded more rapidly than the three-strip Technicolor technique of yore. By the 1980s, the Library of Congress, Turner Entertainment, and many other organizations expanded their preservation efforts to all kinds of films, hoping to save as many as possible.

THE RACE TO SAVE 100 YEARS is a respectable documentary about the importance of saving the American film heritage. The clips and interviews are well-chosen and well-edited into the mostly chronological story. The highlights include the glimpses of early works saved, including the Edison and Griffith films and the bit from the Garbo picture. Interestingly, fragments of one film cited as completely "lost," Theda Bara's version of CLEOPATRA (1917), was recently discovered but not included here.

It's also fun to see and *hear* early sound films thought lost, including a 1926 short Al Jolson made *before* THE JAZZ SINGER (1927) and a short scene with Laurel and Hardy from THE ROGUE SONG (1930). THE RACE TO SAVE 100 YEARS also shows a little of the process of how films are saved (the bad print of TOP HAT and the color restoration of MEET ME IN ST. LOUIS, 1944, are examples), although more lab and technical information might have been illuminating. Other highlights include the discovery of cut footage and the way alternate prints are used in the reconstruction. The stories behind the restoration of TARZAN, THE APE MAN (1932), THE BIG SLEEP (1946), and A STREETCAR NAMED DESIRE (1951), are actually more entertaining than the restored versions of the films are.

In its desire to stay positive, however, THE RACE TO SAVE 100 YEARS skirts around some of the sins of the past by the studios and gives too much credit to the institutions today, without properly explaining the financial and commercial reasons behind the preservation efforts. Also, it's tiring to hear always from director-collector Martin Scorsese on the issue of saving films—how about an interview with one of the lab people? Historian Kevin Brownlow and Mary Lea Bandy (of the Museum of Modern Art) briefly discuss some of the larger cultural issues, but the thoughts of one more historian or even a film fan might have better rounded out the documentary. As it is, THE RACE TO SAVE 100 YEARS is completely entertaining, partly informative, and just slightly thought-provoking.—E.M.

d, Scott Benson; p, Mary Adair Kaiser; exec p, James Gentilcore, Richard P. May, Roger L. Mayer, Patrick Murphy; w, Mary Adair Kaiser, John DeGroot; ph, Joseph Montgomery, John Simmons

Documentary **(PR: AA MPAA: PG)**

RAGE, THE ★½

(Canada, 1998) 95m ITASCA Productions ~
Norstar Entertainment c

Lorenzo Lamas *(Nick Travis)*; Roy Scheider *(Taggart)*; Gary Busey *(Gacy)*; Kristen Cloke *(Kelly McCord)*; David Carradine *(Lucas)*; Mark G. Allen *(Mechanic)*; Brandon Smith *(Len)*; Tiani Warden *(Gacy's Girlfriend)*; Dell Yount *(Bobby Joe)*; David Jensen *(Agent Green)*; Russ McGinn *(Coroner)*; Dick Kyker *(Militia Leader)*; Ashlee Nicole *(Sgt. Greta)*; Kaye Wade *(Lucille Gacy)*; Terra Allen *(Sheila Cramer)*; Jeff Doucette *(Dr. Arnold)*; Richard Mitchell *(Club President)*; Jim Platt *(Speaker)*; Lynn Peterson *(Driver)*; Gary Gingold *(Deputy Gray)*; Shannon Lavender *(Mother)*

Weighed down by a subplot about internecine FBI rivalry, this gruesome serial-killer flick is guaranteed to make your skin crawl with its obsession with grisly murder details. (That is not intended as a recommendation.)

FBI agent Nick Travis (Lorenzo Lamas) has been butting heads with superior officer Taggart (Roy Scheider) ever since Taggart interfered in a standoff with gunmen, precipitating an unnecessary massacre. When mutilated corpses of tourists start turning up in the Pacific Northwest, Taggart is forced to pair Travis with up-and-coming profiler Kelly McCord (Kristen Cloke).

Travis and McCord discover that the murdered tourists were merely a warm-up for a revenge war planned by discharged soldiers whose V.A. psychiatric rehabilitation program has been cancelled. Led by a depraved ex-CIA agent named Gacy (Gary Busey), the dozen disgruntled veterans plan to massacre military and governmental officials at a nature retreat. McCord is captured by Gacy's militia, and though Travis rescues her, Taggart removes the two agents from the case.

As Taggart's team follows a false lead elsewhere, Gacy's militia invades the retreat. Despite having been taken off the case, Travis and McCord trail Gacy and blunt his attack. Gacy and his girlfriend capture McCord and flee by boat. Travis follows and boards Gacy's boat; in the ensuing fight, McCord is freed while Gacy and his girlfriend are killed. Realizing that Travis's suspicions about Gacy were correct, power-mad Taggart travels to the outskirts of the nature retreat. Not content to share the glory of Gacy's demise, Taggart aims his weapon at Travis; providentially, a local sheriff shoots Taggart to death.

Slammed across energetically, this ill-conceived militia opus will fail to satisfy its one potential audience, antigovernment zealots. Contributing to the movie's moronic approach is the central figure of Gary Busey, a star so over-the-top he can never be taken seriously. Even if the film had better acting, THE RAGE would still suffer from such plot incredulities as survivalists practicing on tourists for a political assassination and a career FBI chief attempting to murder an agent who was willing to give him credit for a major case solution. Logic is not this film's imperative; sadism propelled by Busey's eye-popping menace is the real raison d'etre. *(Graphic violence, extreme profanity, sexual situations, substance abuse.)*—R.P.

d, Sidney J. Furie; p, Robert Snukal, Dan Grodnik; exec p, Peter Simpson; w, Gregg Mellott; ph, Donald Morgan; ed, Nick Rotundo; m, Paul Zara; prod d, Dan Lomino; art d, Timothy Kirkpatrick; sound, Jonathan Earl Stein (mixer); fx, Dan Lester; casting, Libby A. Goldstein; cos, Glenn A. Ralston; makeup, Monet Monsano; stunts, Dick Butler

Action/Crime **(PR: O MPAA: R)**

RAT PACK, THE ★★

(U.S., 1998) 120m HBO Productions ~
HBO Home Video c

Ray Liotta *(Frank Sinatra)*; Joe Mantegna *(Dean Martin)*; Don Cheadle *(Sammy Davis Jr.)*; Angus MacFadyen *(Peter Lawford)*; William Petersen *(John Kennedy)*; Zeljko Ivanek *(Robert Kennedy)*; Bobby Slayton *(Joey Bishop)*; Megan Dodds *(May Britt)*; Deborah Kara Unger *(Ava Gardner)*; Veronica Cartwright *(Rocky Cooper)*; Dan O'Herlihy *(Joe Kennedy)*; Robert Miranda *(Momo Giancana)*; Barbara Niven *(Marilyn Monroe)*; Michelle Grace; Tyress Allen *(George Jacobs)*; John Diehl *(Joe DiMaggio)*; Tom Dreesen *(Himself)*; Michael Townsend Wright *(Walter Winchell)*

Flashy, often ridiculous made-for-cable movie centered around the quintet of performers who ruled Las Vegas in the early 1960s. Gossip-mongering writ large, the film's biggest sin is that it's not so bad it's funny.

Frank Sinatra (Ray Liotta) watches with fascination as charismatic politician John F. Kennedy (William Petersen) makes his bid for the Democratic Presidential nomination. Sinatra's entree into the Kennedy inner circle is an old acquaintance, actor Peter

Lawford (Angus MacFadyen). Sinatra, Lawford, and their show business compadres Dean Martin (Joe Mantegna), Sammy Davis Jr. (Don Cheadle), and Joey Bishop (Bobby Slayton) perform benefits for Kennedy's campaign once he clinches the nomination; the five performers develop into a tightly-knit clique dubbed "The Rat Pack" by the press. The Pack finally work together professionally on a caper movie Sinatra produces called OCEAN'S ELEVEN (1960); simultaneous to the shooting of the movie, they undertake a nightly five-man gig at the Sands hotel, which they call "the Summit."

As the Presidential election looms, Sinatra finds that he has become beholden to the Kennedy family, especially JFK's father, Joe Kennedy (Dan O'Herlihy). Although he is informed that his attendance at the event will hurt Kennedy at the polls, Sinatra refuses to back out of serving as Best Man at Davis's wedding to Swedish actress May Britt (Megan Dodds). Davis, seeing his friend's difficulties, postpones the wedding until after the election.

Soon after Kennedy wins the Presidency, he follows the advice of his brother, Attorney General Robert Kennedy (Zeljko Ivanek), and distances himself from Sinatra because of the singer's mob ties. Sinatra feels the heat from gangster Sam "Momo" Giancana (Robert Miranda), who had helped swing a Presidential primary in Kennedy's favor at Sinatra's request. Giancana decides not to exact retribution against the singer. Kennedy, on the other hand, infuriates Sinatra by announcing that he will stay with him when he visits California, and—after the singer does major construction on his house to accomodate the President—snubs him to stay with Bing Crosby, a noted Republican. The bad news is entrusted to Lawford; Sinatra never speaks to him again. The Pack drift apart as the "Camelot" era comes to a close.

THE RAT PACK has two central problems. First, screenwriter Kario Salem seems uncertain who the main character should be. One assumes that Sinatra will be singled out, given the film's prologue in which the aged Old Blue Eyes waits to go on stage alone, saying to himself "I miss my guys!" Instead, Salem attempts a group-portait encompassing Sammy Davis Jr.'s crises of conscience, JFK's affairs with Marilyn Monroe and Judith Exner, and other related issues equally.

The film's second major problem becomes most apparent in the extended "Summit at the Sands" performance sequences. Each of the five actors operates at a different level of performance: Mantegna offers a cartoon version of Martin's public persona; Cheadle foresakes a Davis impression, instead depicting the "man within" the glitzy star; Liotta affects some of Sinatra's mannerisms, but can't seem to tap into the lighter, "swingin'" side of his personality; MacFadyen does nothing to evoke Lawford, beyond a British accent; and standup comic Slayton offers a letter-perfect Bishop—which does him little good, as Bishop is seen as a minor player in the events depicted here.

The central virtue of celebrity biopics—namely their laughability—is in short supply. Two scenes do qualify for the Hall of Shame: In one, Davis fantasizes that he's performing outside a nightclub for cross-burning Klansmen and rednecks (as a giant neon sign flashes the word "nigger" behind him)—rarely do "message movies" reach this nadir of taste. Another sequence attempts to chronicle the nighttime activities of the Pack and their friends, panning past Sands hotel windows—various couplings are seen (Davis and May Britt, Frank with two women, Lawford admiring himself in a mirror as he makes love), while the laidback Martin drinks milk and watches a western on TV. If the whole movie exhibited the same trashy sensibility, it could've become a cult favorite. As it stands, it's a washout, distinguished by a few good performances (Cheadle, Mantegna's comic work) and the fact that the hedonism depicted may indeed make younger viewers check out the work of the real Pack. *(Violence, sexual situations, nudity, profanity.)*—E.G.

d, Rob Cohen; p, Fred Caruso; exec p, Neal H. Moritz; assoc p, Creighton Bellinger; co-p, Stokely Chaffin ; w, Kario Salem; ph, Shane Hurlbut; ed, Eric Sears; m, Mark Adler; prod d, Hilda Stark Manoos; art d, Kathleen M. McKernin; set d, Linda Spheeris; ch, Savion Glover; sound, Felipe Borrero; casting, Nancy Foy; cos, Jodie Tillen; makeup, Kandace Westmore; stunts, Ian Quinn

Drama **(PR: C MPAA: R)**

RATCHET ★½

(U.S., 1997) 114m Ratchet Productions; Altar Rock Films ~ Phaedra Cinema c

Tom Gilroy *(Elliot Callahan)*; Mitchell Lichtenstein *(Tim Greenleaf)*; Margaret Welsh *(Catherine Ripley)*; Matthew Dixon *(Henry Carver)*; Nurit Koppel *(Julia Webb)*; Neal Jones *(Sam O'Leary)*; Robert Whaley *(Deputy Ed)*; John A. MacKay *(Chief Groves)*; David Dossey *(Man in Airplane)*; Isabelle Fortea *(Kitty Webb)*; Anthony Greanleaf *(Photographer)*; Timothy Britten Parker *(Jeffrey Kahn)*; Shari-Lyn Safir *(Margaret Dickson)*

An initially intriguing neo-noir indie about a filmmaker with writer's block who gets involved in murder, RATCHET gradually unravels under the weight of its plodding pace, pretentious dialogue, and illogical plot developments, and is ultimately as devoid of meaning as its pointless title.

Filmmaker Elliot Callahan (Tom Gilroy) signs a contract with a major studio after making a violent low-budget cult hit that featured a nail-gun torture scene. Afflicted with writer's block, Elliot rents a beach house on Nantucket Island so he can work on his new script. In Nantucket, Elliot befriends a real-estate agent named Catherine (Margaret Welsh), and runs into an old friend named Tim (Mitchell Lichtenstein). Elliot also encounters a strange man named Henry (Matthew Dixon) who asks him to read a screenplay he's written. When Elliot reads Henry's script—which is about a serial killer—he finds it to be surprisingly good and decides to plagiarize it. Henry is not home when Elliot goes to his house to return the script, and when he goes inside he finds a scrapbook containing bondage photos and newspaper clippings about Henry being a murder suspect.

When Henry discovers that Elliot has stolen his script, he attacks him. Elliot shoots Henry with a spear gun and calls 911, then passes out, but when the police arrive, Henry's body has vanished. Later, Elliot sleeps with Tim's flirtatious girlfriend Julia (Nurit Koppel), and when Tim finds out, he drugs Elliot and shoots his hands with a nail-gun. Elliot then finds a videotape of Henry involved in the S&M death of a woman, along with an unidentified third party, whom he comes to believe is Police Chief Groves (John A. MacKay), but in actuality is Catherine. Catherine then kills Julia and stabs herself to make it look like she was also attacked. Tim is then shot by the police when they find him at the crime scene. Catherine recovers, and when Chief Groves discovers she's the real killer, she stabs him to death and reveals to Elliot that the serial killer script was hers and she planned everything just to get Elliot's help. She and Elliot then go to LA and she becomes his agent.

RATCHET is a pretentious mess that strains to be more than just a standard psychological thriller but ends up being substantially less. The plot is so contrived and confusing that even Elliot's self-consciously ironic narration can't explain it, although he does offer such profundities as "There are two kinds of angels—the ones in heaven and the ones who have fallen." Debuting writer-director John Johnson's treatment is visually uninspired and the script is filled with such howlers as "If your life was a movie, what would the title be?" The "mystery" plot is ludicrous beyond belief and the behavior of the characters makes no sense (such as Elliot's ridiculously nonchalant reaction to his murder of Henry and his subsequent disappearance). After Tim shoots Elliot with the nail-gun (in a predictable bit of life-imitating-art symbolism), the last half of the film becomes drearily unwatchable and impossible to follow, with all of the characters skulking in and out of darkened rooms, and unexplained events unfolding with absolutely no logic or plausibility. Johnson's attempts at satire are also sophomoric, such as the risible ending when Catherine kills the police chief and tells Elliot, "I don't know about you, but I'm going to Hollywood," which is then revealed to be the last scene of his new film as it's being screened for a bunch of wildly applauding phonies.

Equally ineffective are Johnson's potshots at Quentin Tarantino. Elliot is obviously modeled on Tarantino, and references are made to Elliot stealing ideas from a Hong Kong actioner (shades of Tarantino's use of elements of the HK film CITY ON FIRE in his RESERVOIR DOGS); Elliot's film also features a character singing while torturing someone with a nail-gun (a la Michael Madsen's turn in Tarantino's film). While amusing to film buffs, this whole analogy is puzzling since it only gives the viewer more reasons to dislike Elliot, who's obnoxious to begin with. It is to Tom Gilroy's credit that the actor is able to engender even a modicum of interest in a plagiarizing writer whose alleged brilliance is never displayed (we know he's an artist because he drinks a lot and never takes off his black leather jacket, even on the beach). Like too many other first films, RATCHET is essentially a solipsistic celebration of the cinematic and sexual fantasies of its author, who ostensibly despises the artificiality of Hollywood, but in actuality, wants nothing more than to be a part of it. *(Graphic violence, profanity, nudity, sexual situations, substance abuse.)*—M.S.

d, John S. Johnson; p, George Belshaw, John S. Johnson; exec p, Hank Blumenthal; w, John S. Johnson; ph, Joaquin Baca-Asay; ed, James Lyons, Keith Reamer; m, Paul Schwartz; prod d, Debbie Devilla; art d, Virginia Tougas; set d, Chris Desmarias; sound, Steve Hamilton; fx, Drew Jiritano; casting, Susan Shopmaker; cos, Jana Rosenblatt; makeup, Aneta Mowel-Hindley

Crime/Drama/Thriller **(PR: O MPAA: NR)**

RAT'S TALE, A ★★

(Germany/U.S., 1998) 89m Monty Film; Warner Bros. ~ Warner Bros. c

Beverly D'Angelo *(Mrs. Dollart)*; Jerry Stiller *(Professor Plumpingham)*; Josef Ostendorf *(Lou Dollart)*; Lauren Hutton *(Evelyn Jellybelly)*; Steffen Wink *(Assistant Nick McRafferty)*; Andreas Herder *(Assistant Tom O'Dooley)*; Yoshinori Yamamoto *(Futon San)*; Jackie Recknitz *(Mr. Adams)*; Natja Brunckhorst *(Mrs. Lucy)*; Klaus Herzog *(Gallery Customer)*; Kati Farkas *(Bank Robber)*; Sam Morales *(Taxi Driver)*; Michael Schreiber *(Toxic Truck Driver)*; Stefan Frings *(Toxic Sprayer No. 1)*; Erik Meyer *(Toxic Sprayer No. 2)*; Heinz Dumbgen *(Security Guard)*; Thermond Pressley *(Hot Dog Vendor)*; VOICES OF: Dee Bradley Baker *(Monty Mad-Rat Jr.)*; Lynsey Bartilson *(Isabella Noble-Rat)*; Ray Guth *(Old Monty Senior)*; Scott MacDonald *(Rudi Rake-Rat)*; Donald Arthur *(Canalligator Jean-Paul/Doc Medicine-Rat/Walter Democrat)*; Danny Wells *(Mr. Dollart)*; Channing Chase *(Aunt Charlotte)*; Daamen Krall *(President Noble Rat)*; Chris Soldevilla *(Laurat Ladida)*; Wally Wingert *(Arnie Pack-Rat)*; Daran Norris *(Dormouse Giuseppe/Eddi Pack-Rat)*; Marianne Muellerleile *(Mother Noble Rat)*; John Moschitta Jr. *(Father Mad-Rat)*; Scott Weil *(Assistant Nick McRafferty)*; Nicholas Benson *(Assistant Tom O'Dooley)*

This German-US co-production, containing a very odd mixture of live-action and an archaic form of animation, was bound to fail. Behold slick modern cinematography and computer graphics, Frankensteined together with the ancient art of string puppetry.

Monty (voice of Dee Bradley Baker), a youthful rodent in New York City's bustling animal underworld, meets Isabella (voice of Lynsey Bartilson), aristo*crat*ic daughter of the rodent president. It's a romance that could never be, because sensitive, artistic Monty comes from a family of sewer-dwellers whose eccentricities have earned them the surname "Mad-Rat" (Isabella is, naturally, a "Noble-Rat"). But rats of every stripe are threatened when human developer Lou Dollart (Josef Ostendorf) orders the vermin poisoned, to clear for wharfside development. Rats know that money is all the greedy homo sapiens understand, so they use their foraging talents to raise a "rat rent" in lost coins and bills, to pay off Dollart. Elderly Uncle Monty Mad-Rat (voice of Ray Guth) is ahead of the game: in partnership with Rudy Rake-Rat (voice of Scott McDonald), an escaped laboratory test specimen, he's been selling trinkets to Mrs. Jellybelly (Lauren Hutton), an eccentric human gallery owner who markets the tiny pieces as art-nouveau jewelry. Eventually joined by Isabella, the rats decide young Monty's seashell paintings will fetch an even greater price, especially when they discover the shells he used are enchanted (blessed by a rat witch-doctor of the tropics). Mrs. Jellybelly gladly pays $150,000 cash for sample shells, but her gallery assistants see the bizarre transaction and try to kill the rats for the money. All the rats scatter, and Uncle Monty is fatally frozen in an air conditioner. By chance, Monty and Isabella happen to be present when Lou Dollart, inspecting the sewers, accidentally gets sprayed with his own toxin. The magic shells, when shattered, release curative powers, and the rats use them to save Dollart. Realizing the "he who accepts nature is accepted by nature," Dollart ceases his extermination campaign. Rudy, before setting off to find his rat-destiny, slips a pair of engagement rings onto the tails of Monty and Isabella.

A RAT'S TALE has genuine novelty value, if little else. Picture a glorious widescreen vista of intricate miniature sets, an entire subterranean kingdom painstakingly conceived and built—and into the picture staggers an expressionless, anthropomorphized rat puppet, no effort made to conceal the black strings holding the marionette upright, waving and jerking up out of the frame. It's difficult for one to accept these ungainly entities, most of whom look nearly identical, as character personalities. One exception is Jean-Paul (voice of Donald Arthur), a friendly New York sewer alligator with a Cajun accent, who has the virtue of a mouth that actually opens when he speaks. Then there's the script, a very clumsy narrative based on a semi-famous, ill-translated European children's novel that presses some very familiar buttons indeed (environmentalism, animal rights, class distinction) and a few new ones (the death of Uncle Monty and Rudy Rake-Rat's subsequent soul-searching are played with utmost sobriety). Very young children might be amused by A RAT'S TALE, but they'd be far better off with the deft and quirky antics of Jim Henson's Muppets, or, for that matter, a live puppet show having the intimacy and playfulness of the real thing. A RAT'S TALE was designed and performed by the Augsburger Puppenkists, an eminent German puppet theater who marked their 50th anniversary in 1998. In the USA, where the Augsburger Puppenkists are barely known, the feature played a few big screens but largely went straight to video. It's neither the first nor the the best-known all-marionette movie; interested viewers should check out Britain's more streamlined and popular sci-fi spinoffs THUNDERBIRDS ARE GO and THUNDERBIRD 6 (both 1968) and their trademark "Supermarionation."—C.C.

d, Michael F. Huse; p, Hans Peter Clahsen; exec p, Christa-Maria Klein; w, Werner Morganrath, Peter Scheerbaum (from the novel by Tor Seidler); ph, Piotr Lenar; ed, Timothy McLeish; m, Frederic Talgorn; prod d, Austen Spriggs; art d, Georg Muhleisen, Giles Masters, Sarah Horton; set d, Chantal Giuliani; sound, Olav Gross (recordist), Josef Porzchen (recordist); fx, Karl-Heinz Bochnig; casting, Thomas Biehl, Outcast; cos, Eun-Young Kim; makeup, Farnaz Moshir Akhbari

Children's/Fantasy **(PR: AA MPAA: G)**

RAZOR: THE SNARE, THE ★★★

(Japan, 1973) 89m Katsu Productions ~
Toho International c
(KAMISORI HANXO JIGOKUZEME)

Shintaro Katsu *(Hanzo "The Razor" Itami)*; Toshio Kurosawa; Akira Nishimura; Kei Satoo; Kazuko Inemo; Hoosei Komatsu; Keiko Aikawa; Masimi Muneta; Daigo Kusano; Mori Kishida; Keizo Kanie

Hanzo "The Razor" Itami returns in the second of three outrageous samurai films about the adventures of the Japanese police constable on a one-man crusade to eradicate crime and corruption by employing a swift sword and a huge penis. The 1973 film received its first official US release on home video in 1998.

While chasing some criminals, Hanzo "The Razor" Itami (Shintaro Katsu) runs into a procession that's carrying Finance Commissioner Okubo and insults him, prompting a duel with his bodyguard. Later, during an investigation into the death of a woman due to an illegal abortion, Itami discovers that a priestess at a Buddhist Temple is auctioning off virgins for S&M orgies. Itami captures the priestess and takes her to his "torture room," where he rapes her until she confesses that Okubo is the mastermind behind the criminal activities. She also tells him that Okubo has been stealing from the treasury by issuing watered down currency.

Meanwhile, a master thief named Shoobei is raiding mints across the country. Itami goes to see Niku, the manager of the mint for the Shogunate, and while lying in wait for Shoobei to arrive, overhears Okubo tell Niku to issue twice as many coins with more lead and less gold. When Shoobei arrives, Itami kills his whole gang, and after Shoobei takes Niku hostage and rapes her, Itami kills him as well. Okubo is arrested after Itami accuses him of corruption and Itami then kills Okubo's vengeful bodyguard in a duel.

THE RAZOR: THE SNARE is the most graphic and perverse of the three films in the series, with a tone that's set during its gory pre-credits sequence where Itami massacres dozens of bandits, followed by a scene where he examines a naked corpse and determines that she died of an abortion by sticking his fingers inside of her and smelling them. The film's original title, which translates as "Hanzo the Razor's Torture from Hell," is an apt description of its tone. The abortion ceremony sequence, featuring a demonic priestess screaming "Purge the unborn" is pretty wild stuff, even for this series, as is the auction of the virgins, in which depraved elderly men bind and viciously whip their willing slaves. And of course, there's Itami's infamous "torture room," where he takes the priestess and alternates "torture of pain"—putting concrete slabs on her knees—with "torture of pleasure"—raping her while she spins in his notorious rope basket.

These elements are made palatable, however, by being woven into the fabric of the plot, which is probably the most intriguing of the series, dealing with such issues as poverty and inflation. There is also less of a tongue-in-cheek attitude than in the two other films, while the myriad swordfights are stylishly staged for maximum bloody impact, as demonstrated in Itami's fortress-like house, which is rigged with knives, spears, and swords that shoot out of the walls and floors at the touch of a button. The widescreen cinematography by the great Kazuo Miyagawa (UGETSU, RASHOMON) is also exceptional, and the effective music score thankfully eschews the 1970s Western-style pop sound of the others in the series. *(Graphic violence, nudity, sexual situations, profanity.)*—M.S.

d, Yasuzo Masamura; p, Shintaro Katsu, Kozen Nishioka; w, Yasuzo Masamura; ph, Kazuo Miyagawa; ed, Toshio Taniguchi; m, Isao Tomita; art d, Seiichi Oota; sound, Iwao Ooya; cos, Natsu Itoo; makeup, Hideo Yumoto

Action/Crime **(PR: O MPAA: NR)**

RAZOR: WHO'S GOT THE GOLD?, THE ★★½

(Japan, 1974) 84m Katsu Productions ~
Toho International c
(ONI NO HANZO YAWAHADA KOBAN)

Shintaro Katsu *(Hanzo "The Razor" Itami)*; Ko Nishimura; Mako Midori; Asao Koike; Erushi Takahashi; Mikio Narita; Keizo Kanie; Daigo Kusano; Akira Yamauchi

The final entry in the campy samurai trilogy about a preternaturally well-endowed, corruption-fighting Japanese police constable, THE RAZOR: WHO'S GOT THE GOLD? is reasonably engaging, but is probably the crudest and least interesting of the series. The film received its first official US release on home video in 1998.

In feudal Japan, police constable Hanzo "The Razor" Itami (Shintaro Katsu) discovers that gold is being smuggled out of the Shogunate treasury and goes after the mastermind behind the scheme. When Elder Hotta, a powerful government official, orders Itami to arrest a physician named Sugino for claiming that Western weapons are superior to those of the Japanese military, Itami instead befriends the man and learns that he only has one month to live. Itami hides Sugino at his home and asks him to build a Western-style cannon. Itami then tells Hotta that Sugino has escaped, but promises to capture him in one month. Itami has his servants tail a suspiciously wealthy blind High Priest named Ishiyama, and learns that he loans money to poor samurai and then charges them exorbitant interest, and that he lives in a luxurious mansion protected by guards. Itami sneaks into Ishiyama's house and overhears him planning another gold robbery from the treasury. He also observes an orgy in which young blind priests have sex with a group of neglected royal wives, one of whom is Lady Yumi, the wife of Elder Hotta.

Meanwhile, Hanzo's samurai friend Heisuke is killed by one of Ishiyama's guards for defaulting on a loan and refusing to turn over a priceless spear in lieu of payment. Itami sneaks into Lady Yumi's bedroom and has sex with her while Ishiyama is there. Hiding under the bedsheets, Itami sees the priest give Heisuke's spear to Elder Hotta as a bribe to get a "loan" from the treasury. When Itami goes to Ishiyama's house and accuses him of stealing gold, Ishiyama's guards attack Itami, but he kills them all. Instead of arresting Ishiyama, he orders him to destroy all of the loan contracts which he's made to the samurai. Itami also takes the copper roof tiles from Ishiyama's mansion and gives them to Sugino, who melts them down to build his cannon. Itami and the dying Sugino take the cannon to Elder Hotta's house and use it to fire at him and his guards. Itami then takes the stolen spear from Hotta and uses it to slay the samurai who killed Heisuke.

The "Razor" series—with its outrageous premise of an incorruptible cop who rapes female suspects (who all love it) with his freakishly large member—is an undeniably entertaining blend of samurai swordplay and softcore kinkiness, but THE RAZOR:

WHO'S GOT THE GOLD? is the weakest of the series due to its prosaic execution. The story touches on some interesting topics, such as samurai becoming corrupted, and the plight of Japanese women who are tossed aside by their husbands once they reach the age of 30, but the mystery plot is overly complicated and not very surprising. Apart from the opening scene where Hanzo rapes the "ghost" who's found near the treasury, the sex scenes are actually discreet in comparison to the earlier entries. Yet because the film is less stylish than its predecessors, and its script more vulgar, the overall effect seems much more lurid, resulting in an exploitative debasement of the samurai genre, which is further exacerbated by the egregiously anachronistic 1970s pop-music score (even copying "Jumpin Jack Flash" at one point!). As Itami, Shintaro Katsu's performance is as enjoyably tongue-in-cheek as ever, but director Yoshio Inoue's staging of the swordfights lacks panache and his handling of the sexual elements is coarse and heavy-handed. *(Graphic violence, nudity, sexual situations, profanity.)*—M.S.

d, Yoshio Inoue; p, Shintaro Katsu, Kozen Nishioka; w, Yasuzo Masamura (based on a story by Kazuo Koike and Takeshi Kanda); ph, Chishi Makiura; ed, Toshio Taniguchi; m, Hideaki Sakurai; art d, Narinori Shimoishizaka; sound, Tsuchitaroo Hayashi; cos, Natsu Itoo; makeup, Hideo Yumoto

Action/Crime **(PR: O MPAA: NR)**

REACH THE ROCK ★★★

(U.S., 1998) 100m Great Oaks Entertainment ~ Gramercy Pictures c

William Sadler *(Phil Quinn)*; Alessandro Nivola *(Robin Fleming)*; Bruce Norris *(Ernie)*; Karen Sillas *(Donna)*; Brooke Langton *(Lise)*; Richard Hamilton *(Ed)*; Norman Reedus *(Danny)*

Set in a generic midwestern town, REACH THE ROCK records a duel of wills between a police officer and a 22-year-old malcontent over the course of a single night. A well-shaped movie of modest ambition and means (seven cast members; no extras), the film is a change of pace for writer John Hughes, previously identified with mainstream comedies like SIXTEEN CANDLES (1984) and HOME ALONE (1990).

Late one summer night, Robin Fleming (Alessandro Nivola) breaks a store window and waits for cops to come get him. He gets his wish when officer Phil Quinn (William Sadler) arrests him and locks him in a cell. Quinn believes that Robin's irresponsible and rebellious attitude was responsible for the drowning death of Quinn's nephew Danny (Norman Reedus) four years earlier. Twice during the night, Robin phones Lise (Brooke Langton), his old high-school sweetheart, to ask her to come spring him, but she refuses. He also manages to sneak out of and back in jail on two occasions. During these absences he breaks two more windows, both of which, like the first, are front businesses owned by Lise's father, the richest and most powerful man in town.

Quinn is convinced that Robin committed the vandalisms but baffled about how he did it. Determined to keep an eye on his slippery prisoner, Quinn engages Robin in a series of rather hostile conversations. At one point the policeman tells a story about a poor boy who fell in love and got involved with a rich girl—only to discover she was merely using him to spite her father. Although Robin doesn't know this, Quinn is telling his own story—and, by extension, Robin's. The boy, in turn, tells Quinn the truth about Danny's accident—far from contributing to his friend's death, Robin had tried to prevent it.

Lise finally shows up at the police station, where she spurns Robin's affections, telling him that although she still finds him attractive, there is no place in her future for an aimless and bitter ne'er-do-well like him. After she leaves, Quinn, perhaps offended by the girl's superior attitude, lets Robin go free. During the course of the night, the older man has acquired a measure of sympathy for the boy, whom he has come to see as a younger version of himself. As for Robin, chances are that he is finally ready to drop his habitual posture of anger and self-pity and attempt to do something constructive with his life.

As dramas go, REACH THE ROCK is refreshingly light, muted, and unoppressive. Structured as a comedy of intrigue, the entire first half of the film is devoted to an ingenious series of antiauthoritarian pranks played by the rebellious Robin—while out-and-out comic relief is supplied by a subplot in which Quinn's frustrations are aggravated by the ineptitude of his deputy (Bruce Norris), whose efforts to consummate his friendship with the town's most bodacious babe (Karen Sillas) are distracting him from his duties.

Hughes's most important contribution to REACH THE ROCK is not what he put into his script, but what he left out. By refusing to plant several standard narrative time bombs—e.g., by making Quinn Danny's uncle rather than his father—he precludes the emotional bloodbaths that mar so many dramas. Most importantly, by eschewing physical violence altogether, he closes the door on the emotive extremism and thematic righteousness that violence invites and even fosters. Oblique without being obscure, REACH THE ROCK's screenplay verges on the overexplicit only in the climactic scene between Robin and Lise.

Director William Ryan has cast his two leading roles very discerningly. One of the film's strengths is that it includes no "powerful" performances—its portrayals are keyed to subtlety rather than capital "s" sensitivity. William Sadler gives a notably delicate performance as Quinn, and Alessandro Nivola's Robin is not far behind. Nivola has an almost wicked knack for conveying mock-ingenuous malice (though he should be told that the only Americans who pronounce "either" with a long "i" are actors).

Set entirely after dark in a sleepy town with little or no neon, REACH THE ROCK probably would have looked better in black-and-white—but it succeeds nevertheless as a good tale, well told, complete with a sound moral—attractive and sexy as it may be, rebellion-without-a-cause has an expiration date. *(Profanity, sexual situations.)*—D.T.

d, William Ryan; p, John Hughes, Ricardo Mestres; exec p, Christopher Cronyn; assoc p, James Giovannetti Jr.; co-p, Chris Cronyn; w, John Hughes; ph, John Campbell; ed, Jerry Greenberg; m, John McEntire; prod d, Jeffrey Townsend; art d, Caty Maxey; set d, Joe Bristol; sound, Richard Lightstone (mixer); fx, Kevin Pike; casting, Billy Hopkins, Suzanne Smith, Kerry Barden; cos, Ellen Ryba; makeup, Jamie Weiss; stunts, Rick LeFevour

Drama/Comedy **(PR: C MPAA: R)**

REAL BLONDE, THE ★★

(U.S., 1998) 105m Lemon Sky Productions; Marcus Viscidi Productions; Lakeshore Entertainment ~ Paramount c

Matthew Modine *(Joe)*; Catherine Keener *(Mary)*; Daryl Hannah *(Kelly)*; Maxwell Caulfield *(Bob)*; Elizabeth Berkley *(Tina)*; Marlo Thomas *(Blair)*; Bridgette Wilson *(Sahara)*; Buck Henry *(Dr. Leuter)*; Christopher Lloyd *(Ernst)*; Kathleen Turner *(Dee Dee Taylor)*; Denis Leary *(Doug)*; Beatrice Winde *(Wilma)*; Schecter Lee *(Chang)*; John Tormey *(Harassing Man)*; Wayne Parent *(Blair's Assistant)*; Peter Rex *(Biker Boy Pete)*; Kendall Knights *(Biker Boy Ken)*; Daniela Olivieri *(Kiki)*; Bronson

Picket *(Rubio)*; Arturo Fresolone *(Javier)*; Ray Trail *(Dirty Old Man)*; Joe D'Angerio *(Porno Clerk)*; Kedar Brown *(Playful Waiter)*; David Thornton *(Alex)*; Alexandra Wentworth *(Raina)*; Sheila Hewlett *(Waitress in Restaurant)*; Timm Zemanek *(Man in Restaurant)*; Joan Heney *(Wife in Restaurant)*; Jonathan Wilson *(Young Man in Restaurant)*; Deborah Swanson *(Young Woman in Restaurant)*; Moynan King; Gloria Slade; Kathryn Haggis; Dawn Roach *(Biker Chicks)*; Debra McGrath *(Cis)*; Tony Hendra *(Soap Director)*; Jim Fyfe *(Roy)*; Sean Orr *(Stagehand)*; Tom Harvey *(Whipped Cream Man)*; Nahanni Johnstone *(Young Woman)*; Alex Appel *(Sheila)*; Djanet Sears *(Chantal)*; Steve Buscemi *(Nick)*; Dave Chappelle *(Zee)*; Landy Cannon *(Beach Boy)*; Katie Griffin *(Empty V Interviewer)*; Brian Frank *(Chet)*; Vincent Laresca *(Trey)*; Missy Yager *(Lisa)*; Karen Woolridge *(Nadia)*; Peter Keleghan *(Successful Actor)*; Daniel Von Bargen *(Devon)*; Colin Mocherie *(Renny)*

Nothing quite clicks in THE REAL BLONDE, a semisatirical look at the attempts of several twenty- and thirtysomethings to find love and success in Manhattan's glamour industries.

A struggling actor of 35 who survives by waitering, Joe (Matthew Modine) is too idealistic to audition for high-paying but unchallenging gigs—unlike his friend Bob (Maxwell Caulfield), who lands a major role on a soap opera. Joe's anxieties about his career and finances are causing a rift in his relationship with Mary (Catherine Keener), his girlfriend and roommate. Mary, a makeup artist, is currently working on an ad campaign featuring Sahara (Bridgette Wilson), a naive young model who has just been beaten and spurned by her current flame—who, as it happens, is Bob.

After being hired as a chorus boy in a Madonna video, Joe is fired for criticizing the assistant director for making a bigoted remark. Meanwhile, Bob launches an affair with his soap costar Kelly (Daryl Hannah), whom he sees as the ideal woman: "The Real Blonde." When Bob experiences a spell of impotence, and Kelly is unsympathetic, he convinces the program's writer to kill off her character, and he returns to Sahara. After they become engaged, she tells him that she's not a real blonde.

Mary's increasing repugnance for the boorish and aggressive attitudes of men toward women is exacerbated when both her psychiatrist (Buck Henry) and her self-defense instructor (Denis Leary) come on to her. Things begin to look up, however, when Joe wins a good role in a movie. The couple celebrate by sharing their first satisfying sexual experience in two months.

In THE REAL BLONDE, writer-director Tom DiCillo largely downplays narrative, characterization, and mood in favor of thematic observations, namely, that people want most what they need least, and that men treat women badly. If DiCillo had put more emphasis on the latter, more provocative theme, the focus of this film would have shifted, to its benefit, from Joe to Mary—and Keener, who had just given one of 1997's most affecting performances in DiCillo's BOX OF MOONLIGHT, would have had more time and space to exhibit her remarkable talents.

The satiric points scored by the movie are not particularly sharp or fresh. Typical targets include the self-defense instructor who encourages his students to increase their "rage release quotient" and the advertising photographer who, after panicking when her top model reports for work with a badly bruised face, saves the day by repitching the campaign to appeal to S&M tastes.

A comedy that doesn't try for big laughs, THE REAL BLONDE's small chuckles are few and fleeting: the preppy boxer trunks worn by Joe, the only one of countless beach boys in a music video not in bikini briefs; Bob goosing a passing actress costumed as a nun. Even Steve Buscemi, an actor who almost can't help being droll, is unfunny in his cameo.

THE REAL BLONDE's poignant moments are equally ephemeral. When a heartbreakingly diffident member of Mary's self-defense class is called forward by the teacher, the movie explodes with feeling for a minute or two. And after the story proper concludes with Joe and Mary's joyous romp in the sack (the 1990s equivalent of deep, peaceful sleep in earlier eras: a signal to the audience that "everything's going to be all right"), the movie ends with a wonderful but incongruous coda in which a missing dog is shown limping home to his lonely and bereaved mistress. This is a touching and inventive metaphor—but for what? *(Profanity, nudity, sexual situations.)*—D.T.

d, Tom DiCillo; p, Marcus Viscidi, Tom Rosenberg; exec p, Sigurjon Sighvatsson, Ted Tannenbaum, Terry McKay; co-p, Meredith Zamsky; w, Tom DiCillo; ph, Frank Prinzi; ed, Camilla Toniolo, Keiko Deguchi; m, Jim Farmer; prod d, Christopher Nowak; art d, Paul Austerberry; set d, Gordon Sim, Marlene Rain; sound, Tom Mather (mixer); casting, Avy Kaufman; cos, Jennifer Von Mayrhauser; makeup, Lori Hicks; stunts, Jamie Jones, George Aguilar

Comedy/Romance **(PR: C MPAA: R)**

REAL HOWARD SPITZ, THE ★★
(Canada/U.K., 1998) 93m Imagex; Metrodome ~
Artisan Entertainment c

Kelsey Grammer *(Howard Spitz)*; Genevieve Tessier *(Samantha)*; Joseph Rutten *(Lou)*; Amanda Donohoe *(Laura)*; Kay Tremblay *(Theodora Winkle)*; Cathy Lee Crosby *(Librarian)*; Gary Levert *(Allen)*; Glen Wadman *(Salesclerk)*; Nancy Marshall *(Customer)*; Joanne Hagen *(Deli Waitress/Chinese Restaurant Waitress)*; Adam Bent *(Stuart)*; George LeBlum *(Gerald)*; John Poultin *(Chauffeur)*; Chris Shore *(Photographer)*; Patrick McKenna *(Roger)*; Lex Gigeroff *(Ronnie Relish)*; Jeff Hirschfeld *(Lawrence, Primrose Rep.)*; Denny Doherty *(Balthazar Mishkin)*; Edward Gregson *(Aaron)*; John Loverin *(Bartender, Cop Bar)*; John Fulton *(Ted the Cop)*; Claude Jean *(Waiter, French Restaurant)*; David Cristofel *(Bill Sellars)*; Jennifer Overton *(Aaron's Mother)*; Alexandra McDonald *(Little Girl, Library)*; Paul Ash *(Parking Ticket Officer)*; Deborah Allen *(Shopper, Supermarket)*; Angus Duncan *(Manager, Supermarket)*; Kim Jenkins *(Sample Lady, Supermarket)*; Diane Marie Regan *(Blonde, Cop Bar)*; Heather Blackburn *(Brunette, Cop Bar)*; Jody Myers *(Mime Artist)*; Josh McDonald *(Mark)*; Tom Scott *(Larry)*; Michael David Hirschbach *(Charlie)*; Justin Friesen *(Lionel, TV Show Kid)*; Sydney Little *(Lilly, TV Show Kid)*; Tom Haney *(Mover 1)*; John Dunsworth *(Clown, Amusement Park)*; Ted Soutar *(Newspaper Man, Book Fair)*; Ian Gillmore *(Page, Book Fair)*; Daniel MacMillan *(Boy, Book Fair)*; Carlos Jacott *(Door Guard, LA)*; Jim Gaffigan *(Storekeeper, LA)*; Dean Cooper *(Newspaper Boy With Bike, LA)*; Dwayne L. Barnes *(Gang Member)*; Jose Urbina *(Gang Member)*; Jurgen Wolff *(Man in Deli)*

THE REAL HOWARD SPITZ is an artificially sweetened dessert, intended for small fries, that mistakes labored comedy for whimsy and homilies for revelations. It is directed so ineptly that you feel sorry for the hard-working cast, overlooking its deficiencies due to its puppydog eagerness to please.

Downtrodden detective novelist Howard Spitz (Kelsey Grammer) is perplexed when his agent Lou (Joseph Rutten) informs him his publisher no longer needs Howard's unpopular potboilers as a tax write-off. Locked into his identity as a writer, Howard explores more lucrative genres such as self-help tomes or children's books. Combing the children's library for inspiration, he meets precocious Samantha (Genevieve Tessier), who dreams of locating her dad, even though he abandoned her and her mom Laura (Amanda Donohoe).

Trading favors, Howard agrees to use his retired PI skills to aid her search if Samantha will evaluate his literary projects for youngsters. By the time Howard's "Crafty Cow Detective" books attain popularity, Howard has reluctantly bonded with Samantha and Laura. Uncomfortable around most kids, curmudgeonly Howard hires a stand-in for personal appearances.

When a Los Angeles public relations tour beckons, Samantha, Laura, and Lou accompany spotlight-shunning Howard. At a mall, Samantha is devastated when she overhears her long-lost father confess to Howard that he is remarried and wants no contact with Samantha. Samantha's faith in grown-ups in crushed. However, at a children's book awards banquet, publicity-shy Howard reveals his true identity and accepts his own prize. Proving himself honest in Samantha's eyes, Howard now becomes her surrogate dad.

Full of sentimental folderol about persisting in daydreams, THE REAL HOWARD SPITZ leavens its domestic heart-tugging with old-fashioned sight gags and pratfalls. Thus, Kelsey Grammer regales himself in a Crafty Cow outfit or spastically runs up and down a kiddie slide. TV's beloved "Frasier Crane" has a field day as this crotchety soulmate of W. C. Fields and saves the movie for his fans. Unfortunately, this flick's performances are severely compromised by a director whose framing is often at the level of a home movie. Unfortunately, the feel-good script doesn't overflow with creativity, either. Still, the entire family can safely retire to this benign madcap adventure without fear of being offended. *(Mild profanity.)*—R.P.

d, Vadim Jean; p, Paul Brooks, Chris Zimmer; exec p, Alan Martin; assoc p, Sara Giles, William Ritchie; w, Jurgen Wolff; ph, Glen MacPherson; ed, Pia Di Ciaula; m, John Murphy, David Hughes; prod d, Chris Townsend; art d, Angela Murphy, Charles Infante; set d, Caroline Smith; sound, Aidan Hobbs, Stephen Halbert; fx, Anna Laurie; casting, Jon Comerford; cos, Martha Curry; makeup, Cathy O'Connell; stunts, Julius LeFlore

Comedy/Children's (PR: AA MPAA: PG)

REAL THING, THE ★★

(U.S., 1996) 89m LAC; LP Productions; WT Entertainment; Cutting Edge ~ Windy City International c (AKA: LIVERS AIN'T CHEAP)

James Russo *(Rupert)*; Jeremy Piven *(John)*; Fabrizio Bentivoglio *(Alfredo)*; Robert LaSardo *(Eric)*; Ashley Laurence *(Carla)*; Dave Buzzotta *(James)*; Rod Steiger *(Victor)*; Esai Morales *(Collin)*; Pat Gallagher *(Dexter)*; Gary Busey *(Foreman)*; Emily Lloyd *(Lisa)*; Barbara Nickell *(Bartender)*; Scott Lowy *(Bouncer No. 1)*; Jimmy Steger *(Bouncer No. 2)*; Jane Danford *(Cop No. 1)*; Brendan Burns *(Cop No. 2)*; Lou Rawls *(Emcee)*; Robert Knott *(Dr. Lawson)*; John Zurlo *(Big Tony)*; Anthony Ferar *(Rocky)*; Bob Pennetta *(Franko)*; Hugh McAfee *(Bruno)*; Paul De Angelo *(Buddy)*; Max Perlich *(Tom)*

Despite its title, THE REAL THING is yet another Quentin Tarantino clone, an exercise in fatalistic cinema stripped of surprise and power, but loaded with shoot-'em-ups, numbingly slangy repartee, and freeze-dried acting.

While stuck in a holding cell, smartass punk James (Dave Buzzotta) overhears a heist plan concocted by vicious career criminal Dexter (Pat Gallagher) and his outside man Collin (Esai Morales). Resisting efforts by his ex-con brother Rupert (James Russo) to reform him, released James brags all over town about usurping Dexter's plan to rob a trendy disco on New Year's Eve. On that busy night, club owner Victor (Rod Steiger) will carry two suitcases of cash to a limo.

The still-jailed Dexter orders Collin to wipe out blowhard James, but Collin only manages to shoot James badly enough to destroy his liver. To acquire funds for a liver transplant, Rupert decides to do the robbery himself. He puts together a gang of small timers, including his buddy John (Jeremy Piven); John's girlfriend, Carla (Ashley Laurence); Alfredo (Fabrizio Bentivoglio); Eric (Robert LaSardo); and Rupert's former girlfriend Lisa (Emily Lloyd). Rupert intends for Carla, Alfredo, and Eric to create a diversion in the club while he, John, and Lisa bust through a wall connecting an abandoned bagel shop to the disco. Rupert doesn't know that Dexter has broken out of prison and is also planning to hit the dance club with his more professional crew.

Rupert's scheme unfolds smoothly, until they encounter Dexter's thugs in Victor's office, just after they have massacred Victor's guards and most of the club's patrons.) In the ensuing bloodbath, Eric, John, and Collin are shot; the police arrest Alfredo; Carla gets away; and Lisa is killed during a police chase. The wounded Dexter pursues Rupert as he flees with the money. In an alley, Rupert knocks down Dexter with the case and shoots him. He is then run over by a passing truck.

THE REAL THING is proficient on a grinding level of familiar crime-film bloodletting and may satisfy the cravings of hungry gangster-holics. What it fails to do is to create a single character either sympathetic or memorably nasty enough to engage the viewer. The principals are all stamped "generic lawbreakers." Rupert's bunch exhibit one personality trait apiece, while Dexter's thugs are cut from a cookie-cutter pattern of nihilism. Rendered complacent, the audience neither cheers nor boos.

As a result, the film never establishes a dialectic between its two contrasting criminal philosophies: Rupert breaks the law out of economic necessity, while Dexter exemplifies the bandit as vocational desperado. The movie might still have gotten by on directorial verve, but there's none to be found. What THE REAL THING does have is a surfeit of histrionics by three of Hollywood's biggest hams (Russo, Steiger, and Gary Busey, ridiculously shoehorned in as Russo's ex-employer). *(Graphic violence, extreme profanity, adult situations, substance abuse.)*— R.P.

d, James Merendino; p, Kurt MacCarley; assoc p, James Langford III, Martin Carlton; co-p, David Glasser; w, James Merendino; ph, Gregg Littlewood; ed, Esther Russell; m, Peter Leinheiser; prod d, Charlotte Malmlof; art d, Sandy Grass; set d, Segolen Koschu; sound, Tom Moor (mixer), Melisa Hoffman (mixer), Don Summer (mixer); fx, Larry Fioritto; casting, Geno Havens, Roe Baker; cos, Megan Heath; makeup, Sheri Short; stunts, Gary Jensen

Crime/Action/Thriller (PR: C MPAA: R)

REBOUND: THE LEGEND OF EARL "THE GOAT" MANIGAULT ★★★

(U.S., 1997) 111m HBO Pictures; Way Out Pictures; The Badham Co. ~ HBO Home Video c

Don Cheadle *(Earl Manigault)*; James Earl Jones *(Dr. McDuffie)*; Michael Beach *(Legrand)*; Ronny Cox *(Coach Scarpelli)*; Loretta Devine *(Miss Mary)*; Glynn Turman *(Coach Powell)*; Monica Calhoun *(Evonne)*; Colin Cheadle *(Young Earl)*; Michael Ralph *(Dion)*; Daryl Mitchell *(Memminger)*; Nicole Parker *(Wanda)*; Tamara Tunie *(Miss Marcus)*; Kareem Abdul-Jabbar; Chick Hearn *(Themselves)*; Cress Williams *(Kimbrough)*; Clarence Williams III *(Coach Pratt)*; Eriq La Salle *(Diego)*;

Forest Whitaker *(Mr. Rucker)*; Kevin Steward *(Cedrick)*; James Allodi *(ER Doctor)*; Karen Arruda *(Harlem Girl #1)*; Sherri Arruda *(Harlem Girl #2)*; Harvey Atkin *(Marly Glickman)*; Wren T. Brown *(Pluckis)*; Kevin Garnett *(Wilt "The Stilt" Chamberlain)*; Mitchell Butler *(Earl "The Pearl" Monroe)*

Though plagued by uneven scripting, REBOUND: THE LEGEND OF EARL "THE GOAT" MANIGAULT remains a compelling treatise on wasted talent. The film was made for cable and subsequently released on home video.

In 1959 Harlem, young Earl Manigault (Colin Cheadle) is a shy student at Benjamin Franklin High School who stuns the local basketball players with his athletic prowess. With local organizer Mr. Rucker (Forest Whitaker) eyeing his progress on the court, the slightly older Earl (Don Cheadle) is swept into the wild off-court lifestyle of fellow ballplayers Legrand (Michael Beach), Diego (Eriq La Salle), and Dion (Michael Ralph). In trouble and expelled from school, Earl takes Rucker's advice and attends a prep school in South Carolina. He makes progress there, both in his studies and with fellow student Evonne (Monica Calhoun), whom he impregnates.

Earl is granted a college scholarship, but has troubles obeying his new coach. After he learns of Rucker's death, he becomes distraught and heads back to Harlem, where he winds up doing heroin with Dion, who is murdered. He begins buying drugs from Legrand and shooting up with Diego, who lost his hands in Vietnam. Within six months, Earl turns to begging and theft. Suffering from withdrawal, Diego overdoses and dies. Earl is then arrested, and two years pass. He goes cold turkey and comes out clean. He later makes peace with Evonne. Finally, he meets with Legrand, who has been controlling the steady drug traffic in the neighborhood park. Legrand agrees to remove his dealers from the park, giving Manigault the chance to start a children's basketball league as the first step in his new life.

Based on a true story and featuring the real Earl Manigault in a short appearance as a cleaning man, REBOUND is a winning effort from first-time actor-turned-director Eriq La Salle ("E.R."). The film falters slightly, due to annoying plot holes and familiar sports-movie cliches. Overall, though, its excellent pacing, stark visuals, and relevant subject matter elevate it head and shoulders above the regular crop of made-for-cable movies. Early sequences in the film parallel the careers of Manigault and Kareem Abdul-Jabbar, who in a pre-credits sequence reveals that "The Goat" was the best he ever played against. Oddly, this comparison isn't sustained, and Abdul-Jabbar's name is never mentioned in the latter half of the film. Another structural incongruity involves the film's first scene: a specific incident, involving Manigault being saved from a drug-addled spree by some children, is depicted at the outset, and then never mentioned again. Given the dramatic nature of the scene, and the fact that the incident would have occurred at about the midpoint of the film's chronology, it's a jarring omission.

Leading man Don Cheadle (BOOGIE NIGHTS) does an excellent job capturing the self-destructive side of Manigault, but surprisingly, the film falters during the sparse hoop-action scenes, with flaccid camerawork and editing. This misstep can be overlooked, though, thanks to the superb acting. La Salle, as a heroin-addicted Vietnam vet who lost his hands in the war, and Michael Beach as a stereotypical street pusher, both do fine jobs portraying the two ends of the drug spectrum—the user and the dealer. The soundtrack, highlighted by Stevie Wonder's "A Place in the Sun," is full of classic Motown tunes that provide the film with a fittingly nostalgic backdrop. *(Adult situations, profanity, sexual situations, violence.)*—P.L.

d, Eriq La Salle; p, David Coatsworth; exec p, D.J. Caruso, Mark Bakshi, Rick Singer, John Badham; co-p, St. Clair Bourne, Alan Swyer; w, Alan Swyer, Larry Golin; ph, Alar Kivilo; ed, Gary Karr; m, Kevin Eubanks; prod d, Charles M. Lagola; art d, Rocco Matteo; sound, Rolf Pardula; casting, Jaki Brown-Karman, Robyn M. Mitchell; cos, Denise Cronenberg; makeup, Suzanne Benoit; stunts, Branko Racki

Drama **(PR: O MPAA: R)**

RED BLOODED AMERICAN GIRL II
(SEE: HOT BLOODED)

RED CHERRY ★★★
(China, 1995) 121m Beijing Youth Film Studio; Beijing Economic Development Investment Co.; Beijing Time Cultural Consulting Firm ~ Fox Lorber Home Video c

Guo Ke-Yu *(Chuchu)*; Xu Xiaoli *(Luo Xiaoman)*; Vladimir Nizmiroff *(Dr. Von Dietricht)*

A box-office record-breaker in China, RED CHERRY is a fractured war parable purportedly based on actual events. The film's truly affecting sequences and intriguing metaphorical scenarios are undermined by persistent transitions between two episodic stories.

1940. To escape the turmoil in China, Luo Xiaoman (Xu Xiaoli) and Chuchu (Guo Ke-Yu) are sent to the Ivanov International School in Russia. There they make friends and engage in pranks before Chuchu leaves for summer camp while Luo stays at the school. Immediately the Germans invade, with Chuchu and her classmates captured; Luo, too young to enlist as a soldier, lives hand-to-mouth in the streets.

Ultimately Luo is given a job delivering notices to families that a relative has been killed. He adopts a young orphan girl and begins replacing the notices with phony letters from the dead. Later he practices shooting German prisoners-of-war with his slingshot and eventually leads them into a deathtrap, committing fiery suicide.

Meanwhile, Chuchu has become a maid to a Nazi general, Dr. Von Dietricht (Vladimir Nizmiroff). Against her will, he tattoos an elaborate swastika motif across her back, finishing just as the war ends. Killing himself, he sets her free, and a shamed Chuchu unsuccessfully tries to burn the tattoo off, later undergoing extensive skin-grafting. She is later hailed as a heroine.

Shot entirely in Russia, RED CHERRY won multiple awards at home, including best actress at the Shanghai International Film Festival. Guo Ke-Yu underplays nicely, beginning as a shy peasant forced by her teacher to reveal an anguished past to the class, including seeing her father literally sawn in half by the Kuomintang. The camera holds on Guo's stoically tearful face as she relives the moment, succinctly defining her character. For the bulk of the film she quietly perseveres through increasing hardships, until finally she cracks and shrieks in terror at Von Dietricht's handiwork. Upon her rescue, she fights frantically to keep away from the showers but is stripped by well-meaning social workers; it's a chilling moment when they freeze in shock and she scurries across the room to cower and beg for her clothes back.

Unfortunately the children's stories tend to interrupt rather than complement one another. Luo's sequences are intriguing but disjunctive, culminating in an unconvincing end sequence which shows him building a symbolic slingshot out of a rifle and playing a deadly Pied Piper. The last third of the script is particularly rife with powerful ideas and allegory, some obvious, some oblique: the Nazi, a crippled doctor, is entranced by Chuchu's smooth Chinese skin and uses it as a canvas for his cruel work of art, so that she will "carry his soul." The title, said to be from a Chinese expression for youth and innocence, is reflected when

Chuchu, wearing the initial marks of her shame, begs to be killed and has her face mashed in a plate of cherries. Bright red streaming down her cheeks, she is forced to watch as her fellow students are shot, until she submits to her tormenter and agrees to bear the Nazi banner. Later, as the Third Reich goes kaput, she is led narcoleptically past bloody bodies in the snow while wearing a thin white nightgown—a layered allusion, with white representative of death in Chinese lore. *(Graphic violence, extensive nudity, adult situations, profanity.)*— A.B.

d, Ye Ying; p, Jin Ji-Wu; exec p, Ye Ying, Jiang Qitao; w, Jiang Qitao; ph, Zhang Li

Drama/Historical/War **(PR: O MPAA: NR)**

RED HAWK: WEAPON OF DEATH ★★★
(South Korea, 1995) 86m Dai-Wan Animation; ZRO Limit Productions; Animaze ~ Manga Entertainment c

ENGLISH VOICE CAST: Jimmy Theodore; David Swift; Charles Douglas; Tom Charles; Darian Sewell; Doug Stone; David Lucas; Richard Hayworth; Mark Turner Canadian; Gil Starberry; Mona Marshall; Peter Spellos; George C. Cole; Jackson Daniels; Simon Isaacson; Wendee Lee; Richard Barnes; Sparky Thornton; Jonathan Charles; Tessa Ariel; Melissa Williamson; Joe Romersa; Dorothy Melendez; Bambi Darro; Julie Pickering; Phil Brewster; Dougary Grant

RED HAWK is only the second Korean animated feature to be officially released in the US, but its colorful, action-packed tale of young super-powered heroes fighting demonic villains in ancient Korea matches its Japanese models in almost every department.

In the land of Chung Won, a corrupt noble, Lord Sibong seeks to destabilize the country and cause Emperor Won Woo to be driven from the throne. Aided by his enuch Liu, Sibong stages a campaign of terror against the countryside led by his henchmen, the Five Dragons. After three years, a mysterious, costumed young man calling himself Red Hawk comes forward to defend powerless villages from Sibong's assassins.

A female martial artist, Yun Yung, investigates a series of murders of craftsmen. She is soon joined by Hon Yong, a maiden whose father is among the victims, and Hon Yong's male friends, Jun Chon and Mon Yon. The group travels to Siman, where they soon come under attack by outlaws working for Sibong, but are rescued by the timely arrival of Red Hawk. It is revealed to the group that Red Hawk was originally a boy named Dan Yung who was one of the Five Dragons, along with his older brother Muk Yung. Dan Yung objected to the senseless killing and broke with the others, with the help of Muk Yung, who was then taken by the assassins and transformed by potion into an insane killer.

Hon Yong is abducted and taken to the castle of Lord Sibong. An attempt to free her leads to a series of final confrontations with Red Hawk and Yun Yung fighting the remaining Five Dragons, the eunuch Liu, Lord Sibong himself, and Muk Yung. At the start of the battle, Red Hawk is revealed to be Jun Chon (Dan Yung's disguise). Dying from a mortal wound inflicted by a reluctant Red Hawk, Muk Young insists that Red Hawk and he keep fighting until Red Hawk finishes him off. After all the foes are vanquished, Red Hawk bids his friends goodbye so he can seek out new enemies.

Produced in 1995, RED HAWK came out on US home video in 1998 following ARMAGEDDON, another Korean animated feature, which was actually produced later, in 1996. RED HAWK (given the subtitle WEAPON OF DEATH for its US release) is the better of the two, with a more cohesive plot and a set of compelling heroes and villains. The historical settings and costumes are nicely executed. The design scheme is clean, bright, and simple, although the story line is overpacked with detail, in the Japanese tradition. Korea, which boasts a number of animation production companies doing work for American cartoon series, appears to be developing its own animated body of work that could eventually compete with Japan. Unfortunately, the scripter for the English-language dubbing decided to fill the mouths of the bad guys with gratuitous modern-day obscenities, thus limiting the audience for a relatively clean adventure that was otherwise quite suitable for younger viewers. *(Violence, profanity.)*—B.C.

d, Quint Lancaster (English version); p, Kyoung Tae Hwang, Yutaka Maseba (English version), Haruyo Kanesaku (English version); exec p, Wook Jung, Hyung Dong Ahn, Laurence Guiness (English version); w, Ju Wan So, Sang Wol Ji; ph, Sung Woo Lee; ed, Byungtae Chun, Jangsoo Kim; m, Chul Shin, Changkwan Kim; art d, Sung Pil Park; anim, Sang Il Sim

Animated/Action **(PR: A MPAA: NR)**

REDLINE ★★½
(U.S., 1997) 96m Mondofin ~ Nu Image c

Rutger Hauer (John Anderson Wade); Mark Dacascos (Merrick); Yvonne Scio (Marina K.); Randall William Cook (Vanya, Special Prosecutor); Patrick Dreihauss (Mishke); Michael Mehlman (Serge); John Thompson (Udo); Ildiko Szucs (Antonia); Istvan Kanizsai (Assistant Prosecutor); Gabor Peter Vincze (Lieutenant Lo); Agnes Banfalvi (President); Scott Ateah (Brett); Attila Arpa (Yamoto); Jak Osmond (Assassin); Roger LaPage (Beggar); Gabor Nagy (Priest); Magda Scheer (Concierge); Zoltan Koppany (Vigo); Gabor Kosco (Pilot); Pal Makray (Head Scavenger); Gabor Salinger (Scavenger 2); Gabor Varadi (Surgeon); Mercedes Szinkora (Nurse 1); Eva Gyetvai (Nurse 2); Agi Margitai (Old Woman); Mark Suveg (Buttonhead); Eszter Tanka (Dirt Girl); Szilvia Bizek (Female Soldier); Gyula Szekely (Male Soldier); Krisztina Desi (Newscaster); Levente Lezsak (Attendant)

Despite a tendency to repeat itself, REDLINE is a fairly imaginative action pic. This post-Glasnost corruption adventure delivers plot twists that keep viewers off guard, set decoration that envelops the audience with a sense of rotting tradition, and a cynical tone that suggests rampant capitalism is more of a moral plague than communism ever was.

Moscow, the near future. Petty criminal John Anderson Wade (Rutger Hauer) is shot to death by his partner, Merrick (Mark Dacascos) during his last smuggling run prior to retirement. Wade is selected for official resurrection by shadowy bureaucrat Vanya (Randall William Cook). Head of a corruption task force, Vanya misleads Russia's president about the true purpose of his scientific program that brings criminals back from the dead. Claiming that vengeful Wade will lead authorities to the Mafia Troika protected by Merrick, crooked Vanya actually intends to have Wade eliminate the leaders of the Troika and then usurp its power for himself. Allowed to escape from Vanya's clinic, Wade touches base with former colleague Mishke (Patrick Dreihauss), who then tells Merrick about Wade's rebirth. Wade's only ally is Marina K. (Yvonne Scio), a self-serving hooker who nonetheless rescues Wade on several occasions. Meanwhile, Merrick is pressured by leaders of the Troika—tycoon Serge (Michael Mehlman) and Army Commandant Udo (John Thompson)—to kill Wade.

Zeroing in on his enemies at an Extreme Fighting match, Wade pays back Mishke by shooting him in the leg. Wade is then arrested and tortured by Udo's men, but gets released through Vanya's intervention. Using Marina K. as sexual bait, Wade infiltrates a society party where he finally executes Merrick. Later, gunning down Udo in front of fellow Troika member

Serge, Wade insists Serge pay him money owed by Merrick. At a pay-off rendezvous, Vanya turns on Serge and his bodyguards, only to be killed by Marina K., who turns out to be a CIA agent. Grabbing his back pay, Wade retires with Marina K.

With enough plot for three Russian Mob exposes, REDLINE is a Yankee gangster pic transplanted to the financially shaky terrain of the former Soviet Union. Sly suggestive visual touches portray a culture being eaten away from within: the opening and closing scenes transpire against a backdrop of toppled statues of Communist heroes, lying on their sides like fallen Olympian gods; a crime re-enactment on "Moscow's Most Wanted" copies the Odessa Steps sequence from THE BATTLESHIP POTEMKIN (1925). REDLINE is filled with clever approximations of a desperate economic future. Ambitiously indicting capitalism in the format of an action flick, REDLINE does hit a few snags. Gratuitous martial arts interruptions and sex scenes pad out the running time. And while Yvonne Scio makes for an indelibly ballsy heroine, the script features too many reversals about her character, including a coda that hints she is the reborn version of Wade's murdered girlfriend from the film's opening. Despite these plotting hiccups, REDLINE offers action buffs both brain and brawn. *(Graphic violence, extreme profanity, extensive nudity.)*—R.P.

d, Tibor Takacs; p, Brian Irving; exec p, Danny Dimbort, Sam Perlmutter; co-p, Gabor Nagy; w, Tibor Takas, Brian Irving; ph, Zoltan David; ed, Neil Grieve; m, Guy Zerafa; prod d, Istavan Ocztos; art d, Janos Szabolcs, Zsusza Borvendeg; sound, Giovanni DiSimone (mixer); fx, Jak Osmond; casting, Michelle Guillermin; cos, Natalie Chanin; makeup, Kati Jakots; stunts, Scott Ateah

Action/Science Fiction **(PR: C MPAA: R)**

REGENERATION ★★½

(U.K./Canada, 1997) 113m Rafford Films; Norstar Entertainment; BBC Films; Scottish Arts Council Lottery Fund ~ Alliance Releasing c

Jonathan Pryce *(Dr. Wiliam Rivers)*; James Wilby *(Siegfried Sassoon)*; Jonny Lee Miller *(Billy Prior)*; Stuart Bunce *(Wilfred Owen)*; Tanya Allen *(Sarah)*; David Hayman *(Dr. Bryce)*; Dougray Scott *(Robert Graves)*; John Neville *(Dr. Yealland)*; Paul Young *(Dr. Brock)*; Alastair Galbraith *(Campbell)*; Eileen Nichols *(Miss Crowe)*; Julian Fellowes *(Timmons)*; David Robb *(Dr. McIntyre)*; Kevin McKidd *(Callan)*; Rupert Proctor *(Burns)*; Angela Bradley *(Nurse Alison)*; Finlay McLean *(Huntley)*; Jeremy Child *(Balfour Graham)*; Jenny Ryan *(Madge)*; Andrew Woodall *(Willard)*; Russell Barr *(Sassoon's Soldier)*; Kate Donnelly *(Lizzie)*; Lee Brown *(Logan)*; Joel Strachan *(Martin)*; Bob Docherty *(Man in Pub)*; James McAvoy *(Anthony Balfour)*

REGENERATION is a well-acted and well-made adaptation of Pat Barker's Booker Prize-winning novel about a group of WWI soldiers recovering at a mental hospital. Unfortunately, it's too stagy and talky to make much of an emotional impact, resulting in a film that's intelligent, but dramatically indifferent.

In 1917, famed poet and decorated British war hero Siegfried Sassoon (James Wilby) is declared mentally unstable and sent to Craiglockhart Hospital in the Scottish countryside after publishing a denouncement of the war's transformation from one of defense to aggression. He's treated by Dr. William Rivers (Jonathan Pryce), who confirms Sassoon's sanity, but is pressured to persuade him to recant his protest. Also being treated by Rivers are aspiring poet Wilford Owen (Stuart Bunce), whom Sasson befriends and encourages to write, and Billy Prior (Jonny Lee Miller), a bitter working-class officer whose brutal battlefield experiences have left him mute and an amnesiac. Through his sessions with Rivers, Prior eventually regains his speech and has a brief affair with a sympathetic munitions-factory worker (Tanya Allen) he meets in town. Meanwhile, Sassoon's continued adversarial relationship with Rivers and the stress of the job starts to wear on the doctor and he goes to London to visit a colleague, Dr. Yealland (John Neville), but he's further horrified by observing Yealland's sadistic electro-shock therapy methods. Back at the hospital, Prior fully regains his memory during a breakthrough therapy session and decides that he wants to return to active duty, but the medical board only clears him for home service. When the defiant Sassoon goes before the medical board, he tells them that he feels it's his duty to return to combat, but he refuses to recant his war protest. He's sent back to the front, where he captures a German platoon; later, he sends a letter to Rivers telling him of Owen's death in battle.

Despite its psychological approach and modern sensibility, REGENERATION is essentially old hat British stiff-upper-lip "war-is-hell" stuff familiar from such classic WWI movies as JOURNEY'S END (1930) and THE DAWN PATROL (1930). It's admirable and dignified, but rarely moving, due to a wandering and slow-moving narrative that's virtually plotless and never settles on telling the story from a single character's point of view. Though fleshed out with some potent battlefield flashbacks as the characters recall their harrowing experiences, the film is basically a series of verbose and uncinematic therapy sessions set in Dr. Rivers's dimly lit office, along with moral arguments about war (most of which are drowned out by the insistent musical score) and graphic observation of the pitiful patients' various breakdowns (a soldier who goes into the woods naked and rips apart bloody animals, an officer vomiting up his food, et al.)

Additionally, the bland characters have reportedly been toned down from the novel, which is said to be more frank about Sassoon and Owen's homosexuality, as well as Prior's bisexuality and his ultimate death, both of which are completely absent from the film. Given these limitations and the relentlessly somber tone, the film's only real dramatic sparks are produced by its skillful cast. Like the emotionally repressed characters, the script is rather too restrained, while director Gillies MacKinnon (TROJAN EDDIE) adopts a remote and stagnant style that makes the film seem like it's an adaptation of a play. The exceptions are the battlefield flashbacks, which are powerfully staged and beautifully shot by cinematographer Glen MacPherson, whose crystalline images are superb throughout. Using desaturated color, and Steadicam and aerial shots to explore the nightmarishly muddy and bloody trenches as corpses pile up, these scenes capture the true horror of war more eloquently than all of the words in the prolix script. *(Violence, profanity, nudity, sexual situations, adult situations.)*—M.S.

d, Gillies MacKinnon; p, Allan Scott, Peter R. Simpson; exec p, Saskia Sutton, Mark Shivas; w, Allan Scott (based on the novel by Pat Barker); ph, Glen MacPherson; ed, Pia Di Ciaula; m, Mychael Danna; prod d, Andy Harris; art d, John Frankish; sound, Louis Kramer (recordist); fx, Joss Williams (advisor), Kevin Draycott (supervisor), Garry Cohen, Jody Taylor; casting, Sarah Trevis; cos, Kate Carin; makeup, Irene Napier, Dianne Jamieson, Stephanie Wedge; stunts, Gareth Milne

War/Drama **(PR: O MPAA: NR)**

REPLACEMENT KILLERS, THE ★★

(U.S., 1998) 88m Brillstein-Grey Entertainment; WCG Entertainment; Columbia TriStar ~ Columbia TriStar c

Chow Yun-Fat (John Lee); Mira Sorvino (Meg Coburn); Michael Rooker (Stan "Zeedo" Zedkov); Jurgen Prochnow (Michael Kogan); Til Schweiger (Ryker); Carlos Gomez (Sammy Hunt);

Danny Trejo (Collins); Kenneth Tsang (Mr. Terence Wei); Clifton Gonzalez Gonzalez (Loco); Frank Medrano (Rawlins); Patrick Kilpatrick (Pryce); Randall Duk Kim (Alan Chan); Yau-Gene Chan (Peter Wei); Leo Lee (Lam); Andrew J. Marton (Stevie); Sydney Coberly (Sara); Carlos Leon (Romero); Nicki Micheaux (Technician); Max Daniels (Smuggler); James Wing Woo (Priest); Albert Wong (Old Man); Chris Doyle; Joey Bucaro III; Bob Apisa; Norm F. Compton (Thugs); Cle Shaheed Sloan; Paul Higgins (Bangers); James Lew (Bodyguard); Thomas Rosales Jr.; Eddie Perez; Mario Roberts; Jimmy Ortega; Richard Duran (Gangsters); David Gene Gibbs; Rodger LaRue (Helicopter Pilots)

Like an extended trailer for a potentially entertaining movie, the sketchily plotted THE REPLACEMENT KILLERS consists solely of cardboard characters engaging in a succession of flashy shootouts with increasingly destructive firepower.

In the course of a drug bust, policeman Stan Zedkov (Michael Rooker) winds up killing the son of underworld kingpin Terence Wei (Kenneth Tsang). Wei in turn hires Chinese immigrant John Lee (Chow Yun-Fat) to exact revenge by killing Zedkov's son, but Lee feels pangs of conscience and spares the boy. He approaches forger Meg Coburn (Mira Sorvino) for a phony passport so he can get out of town, but Wei sends assassins after the wayward hitman, forcing Lee and Coburn to shoot their way out of her apartment. Following several more gun battles in unlikely surroundings, Wei hires a set of replacement killers to carry out the original hit on Zedkov's son, while Wei and Coburn score a cache of heavy arms to protect the child. Another gunfight ensues in a theater during which the couple save the boy. Afterwards, the dynamic duo set their sights on Wei, killing him and all his cronies.

THE REPLACEMENT KILLERS is, to put it bluntly, a stupid title for a stupid film filled with stupid people doing stupid things: for example, Lee's buddy Eddie is the only one who knows that Lee went to see Coburn; after a small army of killers suddenly show up and blow her apartment apart, Lee's first reaction is to go back to Eddie for more help. Naturally, he's captured. Naturally, he escapes. Thereafter the "plot" is simply a matter of somehow getting the characters from the gunfight in the carwash to the gunfight in the video arcade to the gunfight in the movie theater. Lee and Coburn face off against an armed gang of punks in order to increase their armory; then they race through the streets, get caught in traffic, run through crowds with their guns drawn, burst into the theater and engage in a shootout. All this rather than picking up the phone and telling Zedkov, "Don't go to the movie." At one point, when one of Lee's buddies is found severely beaten as in countless badly written scripts since the very dawn of film, the man offers an important line of exposition and promptly dies in his friend's arms. The lone surprise in the film's leaden and formulaic story line was given away in every ad and promo for the film: initially we're supposed to believe that Lee is hired to kill Zedkov; instead it is revealed, after nearly an hour, that the child was the target. It's the key to Lee's mono-dimensional character—although it gets diluted with some leaky nonsense about Lee's family back in Shanghai and his having to choose between saving them and saving the boy (he chooses the boy; it's more melodramatic).

But director Antoine Fuqua clearly isn't concerned with the film's plot. He's concerned with kinetic action and slick visual style, tailored to the undeniable screen allure of Chow Yun-Fat. A superstar in Asia and a cult favorite in the West for his hypercool gangster elegies (including several made with John Woo), Chow came to Hollywood with the express intention of breaking away from that mold. Instead, after fielding second-rate script offers for several years, he wound up making his American debut in this John Woo-produced film that plays like a glossy compilation of Hong Kong's greatest hits.

Here, all the trademarks of that once-vibrant cinema are reduced to badly executed cliches: Chow spinning in slow motion with guns in both fists, blasting villains while sliding away on his back; a cop and a killer connecting on a mystical (yet still macho) level; and groups of people in a Mexican standoff, pointing guns at one another's heads. Playing Lee's major nemesis is Hong Kong character actor Kenneth Tsang, who worked with Chow in the mid-1980s TV serial "The Radio Tycoon" and in numerous subsequent crime films. Chow, an actor whose cinematic wardrobe has inspired entire fashion trends in Asia, certainly looks terrific and exudes charisma in a role reminiscent of 1970s-vintage Clint Eastwood, requiring him simply to look intense and speak mainly with his eyes (a wise script decision). Music-video alumnus Fuqua directs with all the requisite elan, but ultimately the film is all surface and no substance. *(Violence.)*—A.B.

d, Antoine Fuqua; p, Brad Grey, Bernie Brillstein; exec p, John Woo, Terence Chang, Christopher Godsick, Matthew Baer; co-p, Michael McDonnell; w, Ken Sanzel; ph, Peter Lyons Collister; ed, Jay Cassidy; m, Harry Gregson-Williams; prod d, Naomi Shohan; art d, David Lazan; set d, Evette Knight; sound, Douglas B. Arnold (mixer); fx, Joe Ramsey, Kelley Ray, Sony Pictures Imageworks; casting, Wendy Kurtzman; cos, Arianne Phillips; makeup, Zoltan Elek; stunts, Allan Graf

Action/Crime **(PR: C MPAA: R)**

RESCUERS: STORIES OF COURAGE—TWO COUPLES ★★½

(U.S., 1998) 109m Barwood Films ~ Showtime/Viacom c

"Aart and Joht Je Vos": Dana Delany (Joht Je Vos); Martin Donovan (Aart Vos); Jan Rubes (Hendrick de Vries); Hugo Haenen (S.S. Lieutenant); Tom Jansen (Ginkel); Marilyn Lightstone (Joht Je's Mother); Nigel Bennett (Kurt); Harry Spiegel (Herkos); Cayda Rubin (Barbara); Michael Seater (Peter); Hayley Lochner (Hetty); Nicole Zarry (Alice); Carly Wijs (Rebecca); Richard Clarkin (Simon); James Kidnie (Arnold); David Eisner (Brecht); Chelsea Moore (Moana); Richard McMillan (Dutchman); Oliver Becker (Forger); Michael Vieira (Nap); "Marie Taquet": Linda Hamilton (Marie Taquet); Alfred Molina (Emile Taquet); Nicholas Kilbertus (German Major); Paulo Costanzo (Yaakov/Gaston); Scott Speedman (Patric); Jonathan Kroeker (Etienne); Jake Goldsbie (Abraham/Albert); Ashton Moore (David/Daniel); Asa Perlman (Allie/Julien); Marc Donato (Paul); Duncan Ollerenshaw (Comblain); Susan Coyne (Marie-Madeleine); Diana Belshaw (CDJ Woman); Chandler Nicol (Fredrich); Len Doncheff (Truck Driver); Larry Mannel (Mr. Inowlocki); Carol Lempert (Mrs. Inowlocki); Stefan Rollpiller (Lieutenant); Valerie Boyle (Mrs.Leon); Graham McPherson (Father Herdy)

This particular salute to Holocaust heroes is a marked improvement over earlier entries in the Showtime-produced RESCUERS series. Both parts of TWO COUPLES exhibit a smoother narrative flow and a fuller depiction of European settings.

In "Aart and Joht Je Vos," Dutch couple Aart Vos (Martin Donovan) and Joht Je Vos (Dana Delany) save Jewish musicians at their wedding. Subsequently, with the aid of a sympathetic cop who signals them about Nazi visits, the couple makes a wartime career of hiding Jews in their home. While Aart obtains forged identification papers from the Resistance fighters, Joht Je endures house searches by an S.S. Lieutenant. Suspicious but unable to blow her cover, the Lieutenant turns Joht Je's neighbors against her by revealing her German ancestry and making a display of giving her preferential ration treatment. The Vos's mission faces exposure when a family friend is caught; but rather than denounce them, he submits to a firing squad to protect their network of salvation, which thrives until the liberation of Holland.

In "Marie Taquet," Belgian school administrator Marie Taquet (Linda Hamilton) is stunned to learn that her husband Emile (Alfred Molina) has turned their school for the sons of gentile POWs into a refuge for Jewish children. Despite the lack of comprehension on the part of younger wards, Marie indoctrinates the Jewish boys into new Catholic identities. While placating Nazi officers, Marie molds one anti-Semitic student into the youngsters' greatest protector and cautions a Jewish teen that his decision to flaunt his religion endangers the lives of everyone. At the war's end, the childless Taquets sadly hand over their pupils to grateful parents and refugee organizations. A coda notes that the rescued children held a reunion in Marie Taquet's honor in 1988, the year before she died.

Although this series of films made for cable TV has much to learn about creating a histrionically convincing rendition of European history, these period pieces overcome some of the awkwardness of American actors caught in this bind. Sidestepping the flat-footed direction and coyness that marred the RESCUERS entry TWO WOMEN, these yarns combine suspenseful scenes of Nazi inspections with touching human interest. Of the two morality plays, "Marie Taquet" is the more trenchant, a sort of wartime GOOD MORNING MISS DOVE (1958) saga climaxing in the heartbreaking finale of Marie bidding adieu to her charges. In chronicling quiet courage, both segments shine a spotlight on the sort of unostentatious bravery that doesn't get highlighted in history texts. *(Violence, profanity, adult situations.)*—R.P.

d, Tim Hunter ("Aart and Joht Je Vos"), Lynne Litman ("Marie Taquet"); p, Jeff Freilich; exec p, Cis Corman, Barbra Streisand; w, Paul Monash ("Aart and Joht Je Vos"), Francine Carroll, Cy Chermack ("Aart and Joht Je Vos" and "Marie Taquet"; based on the book *Rescuers: Portraits of Moral Courage in the Holocaust* by Malka Drucker and Gay Block); ph, Miroslaw Baszak; ed, Peter Basinski; m, Pino Donaggio, Hummie Mann; prod d, Franco de Cotiis; art d, Mary Lavelle; set d, Zeljka Alosinac; sound, Dan Munroe; fx, Jim McGillivary; casting, Todd Thaler, Gary Zuckerbrod; cos, Eydi Caines-Floyd; makeup, Jacqueline Hinks; stunts, Steve Lucescu

Historical/War/Drama **(PR: A MPAA: PG)**

RESCUERS: STORIES OF COURAGE—TWO WOMEN ★★

(U.S., 1997) 107m Barwood Films ~ Viacom c

"Mamusha": Elizabeth Perkins *(Mamusha)*; Nicky Gudagni *(Lydia Stolowitzky)*; Michael Cameron *(Young Mickey)*; Fraser McGregor *(Older Mickey)*; Al Waxman *(Dr. Jacob Weinstock)*; Mark Humphery *(Tomas Kolchak)*; Pixie Bigelow *(Mrs. Kolchak)*; Gerard Parks *(Father Daniel)*; Stuart Stone *(Aaron Weinstock)*; Nancy Beatty *(Ella Weinstock)*; "Woman on a Bicycle": Sela Ward *(Marie-Rose Geneste)*; Anne Jackson *(Maman)*; Fritz Weaver *(Bishop Theas)*; Michael Landes *(Rene Klein)*; Theresa Tova *(Abbess)*; Brian Paul *(Inspector Fernera)*; L.B. Straten *(Annette)*; Ed Sahely *(Maurice Hirschorn)*; Antonia Bogdonovich *(Nicole Bloch)*; Barna Moricz *(Jules Debret)*; Marvin Karon *(Armand Alkimov)*

This first entry in a series of omnibus films made for Showtime (and produced by Barbra Streisand), showcasing true stories of men and women who offered resistance to Nazi oppression, runs the gamut from the stilted nobility of the first episode to the inappropriate coyness of the second. The valor of these people deserved more expressive direction and less mundane writing.

In "Mamusha," gentile nanny Mamusha (Elizabeth Perkins) risks her life by unofficially adopting her Jewish charge Mickey Stolowitzky (played at different ages by Michael Cameron and Fraser McGregor). Initially, Mamusha's employer Lydia Stolowitzky (Nicky Gudagni) waits for her missing husband in the Russian-held town of Vilna. After Vilna falls to the anti-Semites, Mrs. Stolowitzky suffers a stroke but extracts a promise from Mamusha to pass off Mickey as her own child.

Drilling the boy with a new code of behavior (without having him deny his heritage in private), Mamusha maintains Mickey's bogus identity while making a living as a translator for her Jew-hating neighbors. Risking detection by slipping supplies to the Jewish underground, Mamusha also bravely slips a Jewish doctor through the sewers to avoid the risk of bringing the boy to a gentile doctor. At the war's end, she keeps her promise to Lydia by moving with Mickey to Israel.

In "Woman on a Bicycle," pious Catholic rectory secretary Marie-Rose Geneste (Sela Ward) is compelled by her religious convictions to do resistance work, even though she's never so much as met a Jewish person. Prompted by local church leader, Bishop Theas (Fritz Weaver), Marie-Rose prints and delivers anti-Nazi propaganda. She helps hide Jews in a convent and delivers Bishop Theas's latest polemic, a sermon that results in his death by firing squad. Filling the void left by the Bishop's death, Marie-Rose even sequesters Jewish refugees in her house after they jump off a concentration camp-bound train. She continues defying the Germans until the Allies are victorious.

Resolutely on the side of the angels, RESCUERS: STORIES OF COURAGE: TWO WOMEN functions as a sort of blazing flashback through a darkened corner of world history. It's invaluable as a teaching aid, but as drama, it's regrettably uninspired. Director Peter Bogdanovich does little to mold his material, failing to move the audience in the emotionally draining way these stories demand. "Mamusha" offers ample opportunities for suspense as Mamusha improvises motherhood, but Bogdanovich doesn't build on them. "Woman on a Bicycle" is even more lackluster because it treats its heroine's defiant deeds with a wink. Instead of dramatizing this simple woman's dawning of conscience, we get a blandly narrated run-down of her courage under fire. As Marie-Rose, Sela Ward is unbearably precious. Neither she nor any cast member is convincing as a European. Ultimately, the oppressed Jews and their partisan Gentile underground deserve a revisitation of history that heals old wounds, not the superficial application of a bandage that is supplied by RESCUERS. *(Violence, profanity, adult situations.)*—R.P.

d, Peter Bogdanovich; p, Jeff Freilich; exec p, Barbra Streisand, Cis Corman; w, Susan Nanus ("Mamusha"), Ernest Kinoy ("Woman on a Bicycle"; based on the book *Rescuers: Portraits of Moral Courage in the Holocaust* by Gay Block and Malka Drucker); ph, Miroslaw Baszak; ed, Dianne Ryder-Rennolds; m, Hummie Mann; prod d, Franco de Cotiis; art d, Benno Tutter; set d, Zeljka Alosinac; sound, Doug Johnson; fx, Jim McGillivary; casting, Todd Thaler; cos, Eydi Caines-Floyd; makeup, Jacqueline Hinks; stunts, Steven Lucescu

Historical/War/Drama **(PR: A MPAA: PG-13)**

RETROACTIVE ★★★½

(U.S., 1998) 91m Cohiba Pictures ~ Orion c

James Belushi *(Frank)*; Kylie Travis *(Karen)*; Shannon Whirry *(Rayanne)*; Frank Whaley *(Brian)*; Jesse Borrego *(Jesse)*; M. Emmet Walsh *(Sam)*; Guy Boyd *(Bud)*; Sherman Howard

(Trooper); Kristina Coggins *(Martha)*; Robbie Thibault Jr. *(Paul)*; Roger Clinton *(Truck Driver)*

A police psychiatrist gets the chance to go back in time to prevent a murder in RETROACTIVE, a fast-paced thriller that runs out of steam before it ends.

Working alone in an isolated lab in rural Texas, government scientist Brian (Frank Whaley) has discovered how to reverse time for brief periods. Nearby, Karen (Kylie Travis) is on the road after quitting her job as a police psychiatrist when a hostage situation she was negotiating turned into a massacre. When her car breaks down, she is picked up by Frank (James Belushi), a small-time crook, and his tense wife Rayanne (Shannon Whirry). When he learns from truckstop owner Sam (M. Emmet Walsh) that Rayanne has been seeing another man, Frank shoots her to death. Before he can shoot her too, Karen escapes into Brian's lab, and is caught up in a test run that sends her 20 minutes into the past.

Attempting to defuse the situation as it replays, Karen instead escalates it, and several other people are killed along with Rayanne. She returns to Brian's lab and convinces him to accompany her on another trip back. The results are even more dire. Trying to save Karen from Frank, who is perplexed at her knowledge of certain things, Brian blurts out the potential of his machine. In another run, they are all sent back, though the weakening machine is only able to move them 10 minutes, not enough time for Karen and Frank to save any of the victims of Frank's increasingly murderous spree. Karen persuades Brian to send them back 60 minutes, even though to do so will destroy the machine. This time, Karen refuses to accept Frank's offer of help, setting off a different chain of events in which Frank is killed by Rayanne.

Most films about time travel make the mistake of letting too much creep into their exposition, a fatal mistake given that you can't possibly make plausible such an inherently illogical activity. RETROACTIVE has the sense to keep moving at a quick enough clip that the viewer doesn't have time to ponder the logical flaws of what he's seeing. It's also to the film's benefit that the script isn't ambitious enough to play too much with the metaphysical aspects of attempting to change the past: it wants nothing more than to be a bracing thriller with an unusual premise. (It might, however, have done a bit more with the comical aspect of a situation that gets worse rather than better the harder professional hostage negotiator Karen tries to mend it.) RETROACTIVE's biggest problem is its weak, anticlimactic ending. Even if the filmmakers couldn't concoct a juicier plot twist, it would have helped immeasurably had they shown us the turn of events in which long-suffering Rayanne (a good performance by former sexploitation star Shannon Whirry), who gets killed several times during the film, gets to triumph. *(Violence, profanity.)* —M.F.

d, Louis Morneau; p, Brad Kewvoy, Steve Stabler, David Bixler, Michael Nadeau; exec p, Jeffrey D. Ivers; co-p, Kelley Feldcott-Reynolds, Jesse Donnelly; w, Michael Hamilton-Wright, Robert Strauss, Philip Badger; ph, George Mooradian; ed, Glenn Garland; m, Tim Truman; prod d, Philip Duffin; set d, Kelly Potter; sound, Pat Toma; fx, John Hartigan; casting, Michelle Lang; cos, Alexandra Welker; makeup, Jacqueline Dobbie; stunts, Gregg Brazzel

Science Fiction/Thriller/Action (PR: C MPAA: R)

RETURN OF THE KING, THE ★★

(U.S., 1993) 70m Colossal Mountain Pictures ~ Independent Cinema Inc. c/bw

Steve Strangio *(Brad Willard)*; Barney Weil *(Elvis)*; Michael Calomino *(Dr. Baxter/Mobster)*; Joseph Sikorski *(Dr. Morton Figg)*; Dan Walsh *(Clem Mildermo)*; Jennifer McGinn *(Kay Willagher)*; Paul Mookie *(Stumpy/Caveman/Scientist)*; Al Isaacs *(Interviewer)*; Glenn Otton *(Store Manager)*; Anthony DeBlasio *(Mobster)*; Bob McGuire *(Zak)*; Barry Weil *(Bubba)*; John O'Hanlon *(Jethro)*; Mike Kirschenheiter *(Billy Jo Bob)*; John Dorcic *(Elvis in White)*; Bob DiRienzo *(Elvis in Black)*; Pam Eaton *(Mrs. Pollock)*; William Walsh *(Henry Pollock)*; Dawn Graziano *(Cavegirl/Scientist)*; Chris Calomino *(Bigfoot)*; Pete Kata *(Victor Minscoff)*; Ian Penk *(Man with Dog)*; Murph *(Himself)*; Barry Weil *(Voice-Over)*; Susan Howard *(Voice-Over)*

THE RETURN OF THE KING would have made a clever film school short. Drawn out to 70 minutes, the finished product reveals the pitfalls of parodying subjects that have been lampooned ad nauseum.

In the form of a true-life TV expose program, THE RETURN OF THE KING examines the Elvis Presley sightings that have proliferated since his death on August 16, 1977. Hosted by smarmy Brad Willard (Steve Strangio), this mockumentary dredges up conspiracy theories by questionable sources like supermarket clerk Clem Mildermo (Dan Walsh), who received a crank phone call from "The King." In addition to resurrecting the rumor that Elvis is in a witness protection program because of blabbing against mobsters, this mockumentary contends that large footprints in the backwoods belong to Elvis, and not, as previously assumed, to Bigfoot.

Professor Baxter (Michael Calomino) unequivocally states that evidence of an Elvis-like figure dates back to prehistoric cave drawings. Was the original Elvis part of a vanguard of alien visitors? Are extraterrestrials now cloning Elvis in record numbers? As the film's suppositions pile up, THE RETURN OF THE KING grasps at one last straw; Elvis is indeed deceased, but can be photographed by ghost-shutterbug Kay Willagher (Jennifer McGinn). Unfortunately, Kay's snapshots of Elvis's spirit on the toilet don't develop at Fotomat. Dead or alive, which is it? All that remains is the collective hope of the faithful that Elvis still swivels among us.

Sporadically amusing, THE RETURN OF THE KING suffers from its creators' amateurishness. Although their glee in trashing Elvis devotees is infectious, any goof-ball tabloid gets just as much of a response with only a sensational headline. On the plus side, the filmmakers fashion a dead-on parody of cheesy, talking head documentaries. They also hit hilarious heights in the Sasquatch section, particularly when a Bigfoot travel pattern turns out to be a foot impression of Elvis's Vegas choreography. Scattershot in its approach, this likable misfire milks lousy dramatizations and shoestring reenactments for cheap laughs, but chooses to broadly lampoon rather than intelligently satirize the ghoulish Elvis death cult.—R.P.

d, Joseph Sikorski; w, Elmo Birch, Hubie Giblets; ed, Joseph Sikorski; m, Chris Calamino; sound, Alex Kuc (mixer), Felicia Standel (mixer)

Comedy (PR: A MPAA: NR)

RETURN TO PARADISE ★★½

(U.S., 1998) 110m Propoganda Films; Tetragram; Lava Films ~ PolyGram c

Vince Vaughn *(Sheriff)*; Anne Heche *(Beth Eastern)*; Joaquin Phoenix *(Lewis)*; David Conrad *(Tony)*; Jada Pinkett, billed as Jada Pinkett Smith *(M.J. Major)*; Vera Farmiga *(Kerrie)*; Nick Sandow *(Ravitch)*; Ming Lee *(Mr. Chandran)*; Joel De La Fuente *(Mr. Doramin)*: Richard Chang *(Prosecutor)*; James Michael MaCauley *(Famous Divorce Lawyer)*; Brettanya Friese *(Young Woman in Limo)*; Deanna Yusoff *(Woman in Bar)*; David Zayas

(Construction Foreman); Amy Wong *(Ticket Agent)*; Is Issariya *(Malaysian Woman in Hammock)*; Ed Hodson *(Features Editor)*

RETURN TO PARADISE is an initially thoughtful and intriguing exploration of friendship, moral fiber, and personal responsibility that suffers from a slackly handled narrative and eventually falls apart during some absurd third act plot developments.

Buddies Tony (David Conrad) and Sheriff (Vince Vaughn) befriend another American named Lewis (Joaquin Phoenix) while vacationing in Malaysia and the trio share a house there for a few weeks of partying. Before returning to the United States with Tony, Sheriff throws some hashish into a trash can and Lewis stays on at the house. Two years later in New York, Sheriff is working as a limo driver and Tony is a successful architect with a wealthy fiancee. They're both visited by a woman named Beth (Anne Heche) who claims to be Lewis's lawyer and informs them that Lewis was arrested after they both left Malaysia when police found the hashish which Sheriff had discarded. She also tells them that because the hash weighed more than 100 grams, Lewis was tried as a drug dealer and sentenced to hang, which is due to be carried out in eight days. However, if the two of them return and serve three years apiece in jail, or six years if only one of them returns, then Lewis will only have to serve jail time. Tony agrees to go back if Sheriff goes, but Sheriff refuses. Sheriff gradually changes his mind, however, after he starts to fall for Beth and comes to realize the emptiness of his life. The three of them fly to Malaysia, but after Sheriff visits Lewis, whose mental condition has badly deteriorated, Beth admits that she's actually Lewis's sister. Feeling betrayed and misled, Tony convinces Sheriff to leave with him, but when they get to the airport, Sheriff cannot get on the plane and Tony flies home alone. Sheriff goes to Lewis's court hearing and pleads guilty, and the judge agrees to reduce Lewis's sentence, but after a recess, he's angered by an American newspaper story about the case which criticizes Malaysian justice, and he reverses his decision. Sheriff is locked up and watches helplessly as Lewis is hanged. Afterwards, Sheriff is visited by Beth, who tells him that the US ambassador has assured her that he'll be released from prison in six months after the publicity dies down, and she promises to wait for him.

RETURN TO PARADISE admirably resists the temptation to be a visceral MIDNIGHT EXPRESS-style thriller in favor of probing character studies which examine ethics, soul searching, and the concept of conscience. While its contemplative, idea-driven approach is no doubt due to the fact that it's a remake of a 1989 French film called FORCE MAJEURE, it's still surprisingly thought-provoking, at least while it's posing questions about principles and ideals, and ironically contrasting the Third World "hellhole" with the "civilized" decadence of Manhattan. Unfortunately, the film starts to bog down and become monotonous during the long, repetitive middle section where Beth tries to convince Sheriff and Tony into going back, resulting in a series of static scenes (usually set at restaurants) in which the characters argue back and forth ad nauseam. And despite a compelling performance by Vince Vaughn and intelligent direction by Joseph Ruben, there's only so much visual and dramatic excitement that can be gleaned from endless over-the-shoulder shots.

Also, the filmmakers regrettably found it necessary to cook up a conventional romance between Beth and Sheriff (the lawyer was a male in the French film), which allows Anne Heche to be seen in various stages of undress, but weakens the film's ostensible argument about moral imperatives and the notion that Sheriff's selfish character is transformed because he realizes how vacuous his life is and longs to find something more meaningful. The revelation that Beth is really Lewis's sister is a melodramatic contrivance, as is the introduction of a nosy reporter character who pesters Beth for exclusive rights to the story and is responsible for causing the Malaysian judge to punish Lewis, thus turning the story into a cliched media-bashing tale. Still, it's a generally interesting film that actually challenges a viewer to think about different cultures and examine one's own lifestyle and choices, something that's pretty rare in contemporary American films. *(Violence, profanity, substance abuse, nudity, sexual situations.)*—M.S.

d, Joseph Ruben; p, Steve Golin, Alain Bernheim; exec p, Ezra Swerdlow, David Arnold; w, Wesley Strick, Bruce Robinson; ph, Reynaldo Villalobos; ed, Andrew Mondshein, Craig McKay; m, Mark Mancina; prod d, Bill Groom; art d, Dennis Bradford; set d, Betty Klompus; sound, William Sorkin (mixer); casting, Kathleen Chopin; cos, Juliet Polcsa

Drama **(PR: O MPAA: R)**

RETURN TO SAVAGE BEACH ★

(U.S., 1998) 98m Skyhawk Films; Malibu Bay Films ~ Monarch Home Video c

Julie Strain *(Willow Black)*; Shae Marks *(Tiger)*; Christian Letelier *(J. Tyler Ward)*; Carrie Westcott *(Sofia)*; Julie K. Smith *(Cobra)*; Paul Logan *(Doc Austin)*; Gerald Okamura *(Fu)*; Rodrigo Obregon *(Rodrigo Martinez)*; Marcus Bagwell *(Warrior)*; Kevin Eastman *(Harry the Cat)*; Ava Cadell *(Ava)*; Carolyn Liu *(Silk)*; Chuck Tam *(Kabuki #2)*; Lelagi Togisala *(Kabuki #3)*; David Hopper *(Ninja #2)*; Jeff McMahen *(Ninja #3)*; Beau Parker *(Terrorist #1)*; Art Isles *(Terrorist #2)*; Joe Jester *(Pilot)*; Abe Rich *(Pilot)*; David Hadder *(Co-Pilot)*; Ken Meeks *(Cycle Bandit #2)*; Jefferson Hendricks *(Guard)*; Alan Blakeney *(Yacht Guard)*; Elizabeth O'Donnell *(Receptionist)*; Beebe Smilow *(Office Manager)*; Christian Drew Sidaris *(Cycle Bandit #1)*; Marcus Young *(Lead Kabuki/Lead Ninja)*

Exploitation auteur Andy Sidaris continues his series of silicone-enhanced espionage pastiches with RETURN TO SAVAGE BEACH, starring his usual roster of singularly inexpressive ex-Playboy and Penthouse magazine models, along with an assortment of even more spectacularly untalented, though well-sculpted, musclemen, wrestlers, and martial artists.

Willow Black (Julie Strain) leads the L.E.T.H.A.L. Force (Legion to Ensure Total Harmony and Law), a covert government agency comprised of the world's most beautiful undercover agents, including Tiger (Shae Marks), Tyler (Christian Letelier), Cobra (Julie K. Smith), and Doc (Paul Logan). When one of two computer disks containing the secret to the location of a hidden treasure is stolen, the L.E.T.H.A.L. agents travel from Louisiana to Beverly Hills to Hawaii to retrieve it. The disk, which was stolen by Sofia (Carrie Westcott), is delivered to Martinez (Rodrigo Obregon), who tries to find the second disk, but it's found first by Tiger and Tyler.

Tyler is then abducted by Sofia and some ninjas, and they take him by submarine to the location of the hidden treasure, but the rest of the L.E.T.H.A.L. team is already there and they rescue Tyler. Sofia reveals that she is actually an Interpol agent, and she and the L.E.T.H.A.L. agents retrieve the treasure, which includes a priceless golden Buddha. Willow and the L.E.T.H.A.L. agents go to arrest Martinez, who tries to persuade them that he's a Philippine government official who is trying to rightfully reclaim the treasure for his country, which was stolen by the Japanese during WWII. However, Tiger discovers that he's actually Martinez's outlaw nephew in disguise, and they arrest him.

For the uninitiated, Andy Sidaris is a former television sports director who turned to softcore features in the mid-1970s and whose family affair oeuvre (with wife Arlene and son Christian) consists of about a dozen babes, beefcake 'n' bullets sagas which are sort of like what James Bond movies might look like if they were directed by Russ Meyer—albeit if Russ had no sense of humor and only rudimentary filmmaking skills. The films are beyond traditional criticism, since their sole raison d'etre is to allow the Sidaris's to vacation in Hawaii and display the twin talents of their preternaturally (if surgically created) pneumatic females, with virtually every scene beginning or ending with them getting dressed or undressed and entering or exiting showers.

RETURN TO SAVAGE BEACH carries on this noble tradition with clockwork efficiency, along with the requisite chases, shootouts, kung fu fights, and explosions, alternating with slow-mo fireplace and waterfall sex scenes. Unfortunately, however, Sidaris seems to be under the impression that his viewers are actually interested in a story, and thus, there is far too much plot (although none of it makes much sense), even including flashbacks to the original SAVAGE BEACH (1990), and constant pauses for characters to deliver convoluted exposition and backstory in hilariously ham-fisted fashion. Though the film is merely meant to be tongue-in-cheek, campy fun, the "actors" are too inept to pull it off, as the wooden, bikini-clad male and female bimbos struggle to spit out ludicrous techno-babble and exchange in such witty repartee as "I love women in leather. . . you smell like a new car"—"Yeah, well too bad you'll never get a test drive." But what can you expect from a movie that actually gives a screen credit to a supplier of "Lingerie and adult marital aids." *(Violence, profanity, nudity, sexual situations.)*—M.S.

d, Andy Sidaris; p, Arlene Sidaris; exec p, Christian Sidaris; w, Andy Sidaris; ph, Howard Wexler; ed, Anthony Dalesandro; m, Ron DiIulio; art d, William Pryor; sound, Greg Clark; fx, Randy Stevens; cos, Warden Neil; makeup, Angela Mayelian

Action **(PR: O MPAA: R)**

RICHIE RICH'S CHRISTMAS WISH ★★

(U.S., 1998) 84m Saban Entertainment; Harvey Entertainment Co. ~ Warner Bros. c

David Gallagher *(Richie Rich)*; Martin Mull *(Mr. Rich)*; Keene Curtis *(Cadbury)*; Lesley Ann Warren *(Mrs. Rich)*; Eugene Levy *(Professor Keenbean)*; Jake Richardson *(Reggie Van Dough)*; Marla Maples *(Mrs. Van Dough)*; Richard Fancy *(Mr. Van Dough)*; Kathleen Freeman *(Mrs. Peabody)*; Don McLeod *(Irona)*; Richard Riehle *(Sgt. Mooney)*; Michelle Trachtenberg *(Gloria)*; Blake Jeremy Collins *(Freckles)*; Austin Stout *(Pee Wee)*

The venerable "I wish I were never born" plot of IT'S A WONDERFUL LIFE (1946) gets another holiday movie workout in RICHIE RICH'S CHRISTMAS WISH, a silly, but serviceable, made-for-video sequel to 1994's bigscreen RICHIE RICH, which featured aging moppet Macaulay Culkin.

On Christmas Eve, 12-year-old Richie Rich (David Gallagher), the richest boy in the world, prepares to deliver some presents to the Richville orphanage, which, along with everything else in town, is owned by his tycoon father (Martin Mull). While Richie drives a motorized sleigh invented by Professor Keenbean (Eugene Levy), the spoiled brat Reggie Van Dough (Jake Richardson) steals the remote control and causes the sleigh to crash, destroying the toys and injuring Richie's butler Cadbury (Keene Curtis). After Reggie and everyone else in town blame Richie for the accident, Richie hides in Keenbean's laboratory and wishes that he had never been born, unaware that Keenbean's newly invented wishing machine is nearby. Richie is sucked into the machine and when he emerges, discovers that his father and mother (Lesley Ann Warren) now work for Reggie, who owns the whole town and has turned it into a police-state and a slum. Reggie tries to have Richie arrested, but he escapes, and with the help of Cadbury and some friends, he tracks down Keenbean and they steal a giant dinosaur wishbone from a museum to make his wishing machine work. Richie wishes that he was born and is successfully transported to the real Richville, where his family and friends warmly welcome him back.

RICHIE RICH'S CHRISTMAS WISH is pretty much par for the course for what passes for family entertainment these days: an innocuous merchandising and marketing product by a comic-book company (Harvey) that owns the rights to a character, in partnership with a leading supplier of kids television programs, Saban Entertainment ("The Power Rangers," "Beetleborgs," et al.) The result is like an extended Saturday-morning TV show, with calculated fantasy elements involving dinosaurs, ninja costumes, skateboards, various electronic gadgets, and a luxurious mansion that's like a gigantic toystore, as well as rudimentary cartoon-like sets and not-so-special effects that look like they could have come straight from "The Power Rangers" (especially a robotic, fire-breathing maid). Though the film is overlong and slows down too much to deal with the dull adult characters, kids should be moderately entertained by Richie's misadventures, while older viewers can only sigh at the sad fact that two erstwhile great satirists (Martin Mull and Eugene Levy), are now playing second fiddle to a blond-haired, blue-eyed moppet in a kids video which also costars that noted thespian Marla Maples, Donald Trump's ex-wife. The story pays lip service to morals about "responsibility" and the concept of "noblesse oblige," but the real message is revealed at the end, as the happy citizens of Richville gather around a Christmas tree and sing a carol, and the camera pans up to show a golden angel sitting atop the tree, holding a dollar sign in its hand.—M.S.

d, John Murlowski; p, Mike Elliott; exec p, Haim Saban, Lance H. Robbins, Jeffrey A. Montgomery; assoc p, Nathan Rotmensz; co-p, Rob Kerchner, Amy Goldberg ; w, Mark Furey (based on a story by Rob Kerchner and Jason Feffer); ph, Christian Lebaldt; ed, John Gilbert; m, Deddy Tzur; prod d, Nava; sound, Marcus Ricaud, Al Samuels; fx, Dennis Dion; casting, Julie Ashton Barson; cos, Ryck Schmidt; makeup, Yolanda Halston

Children's/Fantasy **(PR: AA MPAA: G)**

RIDE ★★½

(U.S., 1998) 90m Hudlin Bros. Productions ~ Dimension c

Malik Yoba *(Poppa)*; Melissa DeSousa *(Leta Evans)*; Fredro Star *(Geronimo)*; John Witherspoon *(Roscoe)*; Cedric the Entertainer *(Bo)*; Guy Torry *(Indigo)*; Sticky Fingaz *(Brotha X)*; Kellie Williams *(Tuesday)*; Idalis De Leon *(Charity)*; The Lady of Rage *(Peaches)*; Dartanyan Edmonds *(Byrd)*; Luther "Luke" Campbell *(Freddy B)*; Snoop Doggy Dog *(Mente)*; Julia Garrison *(Blacke)*; Reuben Asher *(Casper)*; Downtown Julie Brown *(Bleau)*; Doctor Dre *(Eight)*; Ed Lover *(Six)*; Kirsten Camille Hill *(Sexy Woman)*; Thalia Baudin *(#65)*; Gary Anthony Williams *(Tiny)*; Gene Chen *(Store Owner)*; Glenn Morel *(Groom)*; Fred Williamson *(Casper's Dream Dad)*; Michael Pilver *(Restroom Attendant)*; Tom Chapman *(Farmer)*; Jon Bergholz *(Sheriff)*; George Collier *(Mechanic)*; Michael Balin *(James)*; Amber Pyfrom *(Little Girl)*; Dave Hollister; Redman; Keith Murray; Erik Sermon *(Themselves)*; Terri Lester *(Yes Girl #50)*; Tonya Oliver *(Montage Girl)*

Freshman director Millicent Shelton gets a passing grade with RIDE, a thin but likable comedy that follows a hapless bus journey from New York to Florida.

Just out of film school, Leta Evans (Melissa DeSousa) lands a job with a company that produces music videos. Her first assignment is to chaperone a busload of rowdy rap music hopefuls from New York City to Florida, where they will serve as extras for a production shoot. She gathers the group for departure from Harlem with the assistance of Poppa (Malik Yoba), their street-wise leader.

As they travel, the group experiences various mishaps. The dilapidated bus rented for the trip breaks down repeatedly, and the clownish bus operators, Roscoe (John Witherspoon) and Bo (Cedric the Entertainer), resort to increasingly outlandish means to hold the bus together. Tuesday (Kellie Williams) learns that she's pregnant by Brotha (Sticky Fingaz), who refuses to accept responsibility for the pregnancy. Poppa's younger brother Geronimo (Fredro Starr), who is prone to trouble, is pursued by Peaches (The Lady of Rage) and Byrd (Dartanyan Edmonds), a pair of inept hoodlums from whom Geronimo has stolen money.

Upon arrival in Florida, members of the group resolve their difficulties. Tuesday heeds the advice of her traveling companions and ends her relationship with the faithless Brotha. Peaches and Byrd are arrested and Geronimo uses the money he had taken from them to pay a repair bill for the bus. Poppa interests record producer Freddy B (Luther "Luke" Campbell) in financing a self-discipline program for urban youth. Leta and Poppa—who had quarreled throughout the trip on how to handle the group—become romantically involved. On their first full day in Miami Beach, the group gathers for the video shoot. When Leta's boss Bleau (Downtown Julie Brown) congratulates her for having successfully transported the "riff raff," Leta takes offense and insists that her charges be given quality transportation for their trip home. Bleau balks and threatens to fire Leta for insubordination, but the youths rally behind her, refusing to work unless Leta directs them. Bleau relents, and Leta begins her career as a music video director.

Literally and figuratively all over the map, RIDE is hardly more disciplined than any of its many rambunctious characters. Writer-director Shelton betrays her background as a director of music videos both in her ability to introduce characters and situations quickly and economically, and in her inability (or disinclination) to create and sustain a consistent narrative thread through the duration of a feature. While her approach permits RIDE to proceed at jaunty pace, it undercuts any meaningful plot or character development. Lacking any truly substantial story line or characterizations, RIDE depends mainly on a steady stream of one-shot gags and momentary, easily resolved conflicts to fill its running time.

Yet, while RIDE is not an especially noteworthy piece of filmmaking, its amiability and fresh, talented cast keep it watchable. Despite the blizzard of rough language and overreliance on crude bathroom jokes, RIDE is too easygoing to offend. The gags, such as they are, are amusing and tossed off with aplomb by a very game cast. Indeed, the real worth of RIDE lies with its cast, an energetic assemblage whose appeal comes through even when their material fails them. Standouts are DeSousa, who is utterly charming as the slightly dazed Leta, and Yoba, who brings quiet dignity to the underdeveloped role of Poppa. Starr, Witherspoon, Edmonds, The Lady of Rage, and Cedric the Entertainer all lend confident, capable comic support to the film, and Dr. Dre, Ed Lover, and Fred Williamson each turn in a delightful cameo.

A high point of RIDE is a hilarious parody of a rap music video (as dreamt by one of the characters), all brashness, easy cash, and beautiful women. This inspired moment and a few mild gibes at the treachery of the music industry suggest what this film could have been if it had some integrity, or perhaps if Shelton had more faith in her audience. As it is, RIDE is easy to enjoy, and just as easy to forget. *(Sexual situations, extreme profanity.)*—D.C.

d, Millicent Shelton; p, Reginald Hudlin, Warrington Hudlin; exec p, Bob Weinstein, Harvey Weinstein, Cary Granat; co-p, S. Bryan Hickox; w, Millicent Shelton; ph, Frank Byers; ed, Earl Watson; m, Dunn Pearson Jr.; prod d, Bryan Jones; art d, Vera Mills; set d, Rick Ambroise, Cynthia Wigginton; sound, Al McGuire (mixer); fx, Bob Vasquez; casting, Eileen Mack Knight; cos, Richard Owings; makeup, Angela Johnson; stunts, Cal Johnson

Comedy **(PR: C MPAA: R)**

RIEN NE VA PLUS
(SEE: SWINDLE, THE)

RIGET II
(SEE: KINGDOM, PART 2, THE)

RIGHT CONNECTIONS, THE ★½

(U.S., 1997) 95m Heartbreak Films; Once & Future Films; Shaken Not Stirred Inc. ~ Viacom c

MC Hammer *(Kendrick Brags)*; Belinda Metz *(Gail Tompkins)*; Elizabeth Hart *(Jamie Tompkins)*; Brian Hart *(Chase Tompkins)*; Emily Hart *(Marnie Tompkins)*; Alexandra Hart-Gilliams *(Kayla Tompkins)*; Meshach Taylor *(Lionel Clark)*; Scott Vicaryous *(Eric)*; Melissa Joan Hart *(Melanie Cambridge)*; Jano Frandsen *(Anthony Springer)*; Bill Switzer *(Gary Fleming)*; Chris Lovick *(Peter)*; J.R. Bourne *(Douglas Freeman)*; Biski Gugushe *(Blake Ingram)*; Ron Robinson *(Bouncer)*; Doron Bell *(A.J. Jackson)*; Peter Kelamis *(Sales Guy)*; Benz Antione *(Bartender)*; Carolyn Tweedle *(Mrs. Kolbe)*; Lucia Walters *(Sassy Lady)*; Tony Bailey *(Buffalo Wings Guy)*; Chad Dormer *(Josh)*

THE RIGHT CONNECTIONS is a sticky kiddie film about racial harmony along the innocuous lines of TV's "Different Strokes." Subjecting the viewer to sitcom pieties and soulless Caucasian renditions of hip-hop music, its wholesomeness could backfire and drive music-loving tykes right to the Marilyn Manson bin at the nearest CD store.

Struggling single mom Gail Tompkins (Belinda Metz) lovingly raises her latchkey brood: Jamie (Elizabeth Hart), Chase (Brian Hart), Marnie (Emily Hart), and Kayla (Alexandra Hart-Gilliams). When she gets laid off, Gail gambles her meager savings on returning to school to ensure her family's future. To prevent their mom from sacrificing her education, her children withhold an IRS notice about $5000 in back taxes.

Meanwhile, former recording superstar Kendrick Brags (MC Hammer) endures a career slump as he ignores the advice of his agent Lionel Clark (Meshach Taylor) to abandon performing and become a talent manager. A chance meeting with Kendrick at the mall convinces the Tompkins kids to enlist his help in winning a local amateur contest that offers a $5000 prize. Against his better judgment, Kendrick bonds with the kids and trains them to be cool.

Teenaged Jamie, who has the lion's share of singing talent, is pressured by her boyfriend to blow off the try-out. But she prioritizes her family responsibility, and leads her family to a smashing debut at the competition. They don't win first place, but Kendrick offers to loan Gail tuition and generously moves the Tompkins clan in with him, as he begins his new career as an impresario.

How quickly the glitzy celebs of yesteryear must refashion themselves as spokesmen for family values! Ex-rapper MC Hammer does his darndest to adapt to the sap content of domestic comedy as big brother to a brat pack of honky kids. The film's real raison d'etre becomes clear, however, when actress Melissa Joan Hart, star of TV's "Sabrina, the Teenage Witch" first appears in a supporting role as a friendly (surprisingly young looking) cabbie who helps the kids out by shepherding them around town (and accepting her cab fare in homemade meals). Hart is the real-life sibling of the film's stars, and the film appears to have been mom Paula Hart's attempt to jumpstart the careers of her other children by luring in "Sabrina" fans interested in catching Melissa's appearance (her character functions as an older sister to the confused kids in the final nightclub scene, somewhat like her real-life role as the actors' big sis).

The film sticks to the tried-and-true formula of alternating one-liners and tear jerking so scrupulously that one can almost see the scripters sitting around a conference table debating the topic "How to map out family fun." Nothing about THE RIGHT CONNECTIONS registers as spontaneous. It has that oppressively preachy air of sanctimonious TV shows like "Touched by an Angel." Warning: when these youngsters sunnily perform their suburban hip-hop specialty, they make the Brady Bunch and Partridge Family singers of yesteryear seem positively cutting-edge. *(Sexual situations.)*— R.P.

d, Chuck Vinson; p, Richard Davis, Mary Burch; exec p, Paula Hart, Paul Bernbaum; assoc p, Ted Rich; co-p, Spencer Proffer; w, Chuck Vinson, Paul Birnbaum; ph, Richard Leiterman; ed, Christopher Ellis; m, Michel Colombier, Spencer Proffer; prod d, Andrew Wilson; art d, Maya Ishiura; set d, Grant Pearse; ch, Eddie Garcia; sound, William Butler (mixer); fx, A.B.I. Industries; casting, Beth Klein; cos, Cynthia Summers; makeup, Lili Marchenski; stunts, Garvin Cross

Comedy/Children's (PR: A MPAA: PG)

RINGMASTER ★½

(U.S., 1998) 95m Motion Picture Corporation of America ~ Artisan Entertainment c

Jerry Springer *(Jerry Farrelly)*; Jamie Pressly *(Angel Zorzak)*; William McNamara *(Troy)*; Molly Hagan *(Connie Zorzak)*; John Capodice *(Mel Riley)*; Wendy Raquel Robinson *(Starletta)*; Ashley Holbrook *(Willie)*; Tangie Ambrose *(Vonda)*; Nicki Micheaux *(Leshawnette)*; Krista Tesreau *(Catherine)*; Dawn Maxey *(Natalie)*; Maximilliana *(Charlie/Claire)*; Michael Jai White *(Demond)*; Michael Dudikoff *(Rusty)*; Jerry Giles *(Floyd Merkel)*; Jason Lewis *(Tim)*; Reamy Hall *(Stage Manager)*; Thea Vidale *(Juanita)*; Korrine St. Onge *(Desiree)*; M.C. Gainey *(Trucker)*; Robert H. Harvey *(Businessman)*; Roxanne Enright *(Pregnant Fan)*; Conrad Goode *(Sexy Male Neighbor)*; Rebecca Broussard *(Suzanne)*; Kimberly Pullis *(Fiona)*; Ron Orbach *(Man in Diner)*; Lucia Sullivan *(College Girl #1)*; Nicole Richard *(College Girl #2)*; Joel Farar *(Boy in Booth)*; Frank Woods *(Emcee)*; VOICES: Vanessa De La Rocha; Randall Kirby; Peter Renaday; Steve Staley; Christina Challey; Diane Michelle; Angie Harper; Seth Isler; Karl Iglesias; Sharon Houston; Marietta Sirleaf

Quickly produced to cash in on the tremendous popularity of "The Jerry Springer Show," RINGMASTER is a sleazy little number that pretends to explore the tangled personal lives of the show's guests. One decent lead performance (by actress Molly Hagan) can't compensate for the fact that the movie isn't exploitative enough to appeal to the show's regular viewers, who comprise its only potential audience.

Both Broward County trailer-park resident Connie (Molly Hagan) and her nubile daughter Angel (Jamie Pressly) are sleeping with Connie's shiftless husband Rusty (Michael Dudikoff). Connie becomes so frustrated by this unstated but understood arrangement that she has sex with Angel's fiance Willie (Ashley Holbrook). When that rash act does nothing to change Angel and Rusty's behavior, she decides to air their situation in public by bringing her clan on an outlandish daytime talk show run by a sensitive host (Jerry Springer).

In Detroit, the feisty Starletta (Wendy Raquel Robinson) is outraged when she discovers that her boyfriend Demond (Michael Jai White) is sleeping with her friend Vonda (Tangie Ambrose). Starletta also applies to be on the "Jerry Show" to discuss her situation. Connie, Angel, Rusty, and Willie fly out to LA to be on the show, as do Starletta, Demond, Vonda, and their friend Leshawnette (Nicki Micheaux). The two groups meet during an orientation session for the show's guests. Angel is attracted to Demond, who winds up coming to her hotel room that evening to have sex. Jealous of her daughter's good fortune, Connie makes a play for Demond after he emerges from Angel's room, but Demond and she wind up merely dancing together; Vonda and Leshawnette catch a glimpse of this interaction.

The next day on the show, Connie and Angel's segment sags, due to the fact that Rusty has refused to participate, and has flown back home to Florida. Willie spices things up, however, when he announces that he and Angel have never consummated their relationship, and their forthcoming marriage is a sham, meant to cover up the fact that Angel is pregnant by Rusty. Seated in the audience, Vonda and Leshawnette then confront Connie about her supposed tryst with Demond. A scuffle breaks out on the set.

Starletta and friends decide that their friendship is more important than doing their segment on the show, and thus leave LA for Detroit. Connie and Angel make amends, and vow to become more responsible. Back in Florida, having realized that Rusty has left them both, the women revert to their old ways and flirt with their hunky new neighbor in the trailer court.

RINGMASTER procceds on the mistaken assumption that the viewers of Springer's show are interested in the behind-the-scenes melodrama leading up to the explosive moments of confrontation that are the show's stock in trade. Though marketed as a comedy, the movie is rife with serious sequences in which doleful music plays while the trailer-trash protagonists rue their sorry romantic choices and dead-end existences. This sort of ennobling approach might have worked if the film had been made as a documentary, detailing the real-life dilemmas of actual daytime talk-show guests (an approach already taken in stories by more than one network newsmagazine). Instead, scripter John Bernstein presents us with a group of incredibly stupid characters who are presumably redeemed by occasional bouts of conscience, and the populist concerns of Springer's character. Along these lines is a sequence that qualifies as the worst bit in the film—an evangelical in the show's audience condemns the guests, whereupon Springer launches into an impassioned speech about the way in which the media delights in exposing the sleazy affairs of the rich and famous, while his show balances that out by detailing the sleazy affairs of the poor and unknown ("they hurt just as much," opines Jerry).

Springer served as executive producer, so many of the film's worst indulgences can be traced back to him. The most dispensible sequences all involve his character—singing country music at a local nightclub, pontificating to a reporter who comments on the show's "bleak" view of humanity, and having sex while watching his show (a purportedly comic moment which should have been left on the cutting room floor). While Pressly has the demeanor and vocal pattern of Springer's real guests, Hagan alone emerges unscathed from the film's sorry attempts at moralizing. Her sympathetic depiction of Connie is the only element in the film that even begins to justify Bernstein's humanist concerns.

Most likely, many viewers attended RINGMASTER thinking they were going to be seeing the "uncensored" side of Springer's show, which had already been spotlighted in the bestselling 1997 home video "Too Hot for TV," a garish and unapologetic sampling of the sleazier moments from the program. Not contained on the tape, unfortunately, is "Hands off my lover!" the episode that (despite a blatant denial in the movie's end credits) clearly inspired RINGMASTER's plot. *(Profanity, nudity, sexual situations.)*—E.G.

d, Neil Abramson; p, Jerry Springer, Gina Rugolo-Judd, Brad Jenkel, Steven Stabler, Gary W. Goldstein; exec p, Brent Baum, Don Corsini, Richard Dominick, Erwin More, Brian Medavoy, Donald Kushner, Peter Locke; assoc p, Mark Morgan; co-p, Jade Ramsey, David Bales; w, John Bernstein; ph, Russell Lyster; ed, Suzanne Hines; m, Kennard Ramsey; prod d, Dorian Vernacchio, Deborah Raymond; sound, Shawn Holden; casting, Carmen Tetzlaff; cos, Gail McMullen; makeup, Jojo Meyers Proud, Vanessa Dionne Browning; stunts, Chris Howell

Comedy/Drama **(PR: O MPAA: R)**

R.I.P. REST IN PIECES: A PORTRAIT OF JOE COLEMAN ★★½

(Austria, 1998) 90m Prisma Filmproduktion ~ Media Luna c

Joe Coleman; Bill Coleman; Katherine Gates; Dian Hanson; Jim Jarmusch; Manuel De Landa; Nancy Pivar; Hasil Adkins; Harold Schechter; Martin Wilner; G.G. Allin

Notorious for his disturbing paintings of serial killers, freaks, and various human grotesqueries, cult-artist Joe Coleman is celebrated in this expertly constructed love letter, aimed squarely at the already converted.

Opening with one of his apocalyptic rants, the short, bearded Coleman, now in his 40s, explains that his artwork's fixations are deeper than simple cheap thrills. He describes the process of how one of his paintings evolves, and openly discusses the events in his life which shaped his obsessions—-including a Catholic upbringing and his childhood identification with actual freaks. Filmed around Manhattan and the Coney Island boardwalk, we visit Coleman's home, decorated with human skulls, grotesque bric-a-brac, and a pickled deformed fetus ("Junior, my adopted kid"). He also dresses up as a cripple and a sideshow barker, performs an autopsy, visits a strip club, and recalls his infamous stage performances (accompanied by old film clips) in which he'd bite the heads off live mice and ignite explosives hidden in his shirt. At one such gig in Boston, he ended up being arrested.

Sprinkled throughout are interviews with friends. There's friendly ex-wife Nancy Pivar, who discusses their performance art and breakup due to Coleman's heroin addiction; filmmaker Jim Jarmusch and Coleman sit in a church, recalling their religious roots (Joe admits that he once falsely confessed a murder to his priest); and defiantly demented West Virginian rockabilly musician Hasil Adkins whose home is visited by Coleman (and who's heavily featured in the soundtrack). Only at the very end do we meet a family member, Coleman's brother, and uncover his small-town Connecticut roots, which includes driving a taxi cab before his painting career took off.

Director Robert Pejo delivers an expertly constructed profile of an artist, but unlike a breakthrough documentary such as CRUMB, R.I.P. captures only the surface level of its subject. Still, even a lightweight look at a career like Coleman's is fascinating enough to keep one amused. Containing far-too-lengthy looks at Coleman's artwork and his rambling view of the world, we're also told he's less interested in external gruesomeness than in the internal pain which causes it. Oddly, this comes from a guy who considers a serial killer's actions a form of "communication," and compares humankind to a cancer upon the Earth. Unfortunately, most of the interviews offer only laudatory comments or lightweight observations, while the film's only tension comes in the sequences which feature Coleman's ex-girlfriend, porn publisher Dian Hanson, who obviously still has issues with the guy. In a bad move, Pejo assumes the viewer is knowledgeable about Coleman's career at the outset, and then tackles the surface details, accepting everything the loquacious Coleman (and his friends) say without question. It would have been more interesting to hear a few dissenting views of his work and world view, instead of unanimous praise for his genius—-making the film seem like an extended vanity piece.

Only 88 minutes long, R.I.P. is padded out with unfocused discussions, belabored insights, and long explanations of his technique, best appreciated by hardcore fans. Coleman is a terrific subject for a film, but R.I.P. only occasionally hits the target. *(Violence, adult situations, profanity.)*—S.P.

d, Robert Pejo; p, Michael Seeber, Heinz Stussak; w, Walt Michelson; ph, Wolfgang G. Lehner; ed, Robert Pejo; m, Hasil Adkins, Charlie Feathers, Link Wray, Wanda Jackson; sound, Nils Petersen

Documentary **(PR: O MPAA: NR)**

RIPUI B'HAREG

(SEE: HEALING BY KILLING)

RIVER RED ★★½

(U.S., 1998) 103m Frontier Films; Drilling Films; Miller Entertainment Group ~ Castle Hill c

Tom Everett Scott *(Dave Holden)*; David Moscow *(Tom Holden)*; Cara Buono *(Rachel)*; David Lowery *(Billy)*; Denis O'Hare *(Father)*; Michael Kelly *(Frankie)*; Leo Burmester *(Judge Perkins)*; Tibor Feldman *(Dr. Harry Fields)*; James Murtaugh *(Chief Bascomb)*; Michael Angarano *(Young Tom)*; Peter Tambakis *(Young Dave)*; Ted Travelstead *(Gas Attendant)*; Marcia DeBonis *(Sara)*; Christopher Cantwell *(Mr. Taylor)*; Andrew VanDusen *(Convenience Store Clerk)*; Jefferson Taffett *(Young Store Clerk)*; Mella Fazzoli *(Timmy the Mechanic)*; Charle Landry *(Mike Sanel)*; Christopher Petrosino *(Store Clerk's Son)*; Jenni Gallagher *(Denise)*; Chris McGinn *(Woman in Store)*; Andrew Sikking *(Liquor Store Clerk)*; Louis Ludwig *(Elderly Clerk)*; John Lally *(Mr. Orton)*; Trudy Lally *(Mrs. Orton)*; Gary Kauffman *(Prosecutor)*; Pete "Conan" Winebrake *(Defense Attorney)*; John McLaughlin *(Guy in Store)*; Daniel Prucell *(Boy at Sara's)*; Ceili *(Mocha)*

RIVER RED is an engrossing but flawed drama about the psychic toll taken on a young man who allows his brother to accept responsibility for a crime he committed.

At his home in rural New Hampshire, Dave Holden (Tom Everett Scott) watches in horror as his younger brother Tom (David Moscow) is regularly brutalized by their alcoholic father (Denis O'Hare). One night, Dave sneaks into his father's bedroom and stabs him to death. The grateful Tom claims responsibility for the killing, and is sentenced to a juvenile detention center until age 21.

After Tom's trial, Dave learns that his father was heavily in debt. To earn money he accepts a job from Billy (David Lowery), a local tavern owner, but when Billy refuses to co-sign a loan for him, he quits. Desperately in need of cash, Dave begins robbing gas stations and small stores at gunpoint. At the same time, he ceases all contact with Tom.

On the day of Tom's release, Dave picks Tom up and brings him home. Tom is angry with Dave for failing to call or visit him, and the relationship between the brothers is strained. Dave starts to drink heavily, and when asked by Tom about why he neither called nor visited, Dave advises Tom to forget the past.

When Tom learns how his brother gets money, however, he offers to assist Dave with the robberies. During their first stick-up together, Dave shoots and kills the proprietor. The two return home, and Tom, without Dave's knowledge, summons the police. As the police arrive, Tom says quietly to Dave, "I didn't do anything. You did it."

Writer-director Eric Drilling's debut feature is an unconventional and ambitious effort that doesn't quite come together. Drilling has chosen to emphasize mood over action, and the sparse plot he has concocted serves primarily to provoke an emotional crisis in the lead character. Much of the film is devoted to chronicling the cancerous effect that Dave's guilt has on him, how it leads him from righteous anger to self-destruction. Sustaining a disquietingly subdued tone as the story progresses, Drilling credibly establishes the unnerving confusion and helplessness that overtake Dave as his inner turmoil envelops him, and he ably employs the acting and cinematography towards this same end. The two lead actors give superior performances, Scott convincingly alternating between brooding silences and explosive outbursts; and Moscow making his character a sympathetic yet unwitting accomplice to his brother's psychological undoing. Stephen Schlueter's masterful cinematography also contributes to a growing sense of despair, shifting from autumnal to wintry as Dave becomes increasingly antisocial.

Despite its many good qualities, though, RIVER RED is never fully engaging. It's as though Drilling was so intent on getting the mood right that he neglected to develop other aspects of the film. The narrative structure is awkward and the story line has several strong improbabilities, such as the ease with which Dave gets away with a string of armed robberies. It's often difficult to tell how much time has passed between sequences, and Drilling frequently resorts to the cheap ploy of bridging incongruous segments with soundtrack songs. Character development is also a problem; besides Dave and Tom, none of the characters is fully realized, so that, for example, a romantic subplot about a woman who falls for Dave goes nowhere.

But Drilling deserves praise for taking on a considerable creative challenge, making a film in which emotional consequences are conveyed more through tone than through plot. That RIVER RED is not entirely successful does not make it any less admirable an attempt, especially for a first-time filmmaker. *(Violence, sexual situations, adult situations, extreme profanity.)*—D.C.

d, Eric Drilling; p, Eric Drilling, Stephen Schlueter, Avram Ludwig; exec p, David Miller, Gary Kauffman; w, Eric Drilling (based on play by Drilling); ph, Stephen Schlueter; ed, Paul Streicher, Paige Lauman, Steve LaMorte; m, Johnny Hickman; prod d, Roshelle Berliner; art d, Josh Outerbridge; sound, Robert Ghiraldini (recorder); fx, Greg Jiritano; casting, Gabriela Leff; cos, Cindy Evans; makeup, Cassandra Mucha; stunts, John McLaughlin, Elliot Santiago

Crime/Drama (PR: C MPAA: R)

RONIN ★★½

(U.S., 1998) 121m FGM Entertainment; United Artists ~ MGM/UA c

Robert De Niro *(Sam)*; Jean Reno *(Vincent)*; Natascha McElhone *(Deirdre)*; Stellan Skarsgard *(Gregor)*; Jonathan Pryce *(Seamus O'Rourke)*; Sean Bean *(Spence)*; Skipp Sudduth *(Larry)*; Michael Lonsdale *(Jean-Pierre)*; Jan Triska *(Dapper Gent)*; Bernard Bloch *(Sergi)*; Feodor Atkine *(Mikhi)*; Katerina Witt *(Natacha Kirilova)*; Ron Perkins *(The Man with the Newspaper)*; Dominic Gugliametti *(Clown Iceskater)*; Alan Beckworth *(Clown Iceskater)*; Daniel Breton *(Sergi's Accomplice)*; Amidou Ben Messaoud *(Man at Exchange)*; Tolsty *(The "Boss")*; Gerard Moulevrier *(Tour Guide)*; Lionel Vitrant *(The "Target")*; Vincent Schmitt *(Arles Messenger)*; Leopoldine Serre *(Arles Little Girl)*; Lou Maraval *(Arles Little Girl)*; Frederic Schmalzbauer *(German Tour Guide)*; Julia Maraval *(Girl Hostage)*; Laurent Spielvogel *(Tourist in Nice)*; Ron Hiatt *(Fishmonger)*; Steve Suissa *(Waiter in Nice)*; Katia Tchenko *(Woman Hostage)*; Dyna Gauzy *(Little Screaming Girl)*; Lilly-Fleur Pointeaux *(Little Girl)*; Amanda Spencer *(Little Girl)*; Dimitri Rafalsky *(Russian Interpreter)*; Vladimir Tchernine *(Russian Mechanic)*; Gerard Touratier *(Ice Rink Security Guard)*; Cyril Prenout *(Mikhi's Bodyguard)*; Henry Moati *(Bartender)*; Christophe Maratier *(Armed Police Officer)*; Pierre Forest *(C.R.S. Captain)*

Classic spy fare from a director with a track record of espionage and suspense classics, RONIN is the story of a group of secret agents-turned-mercenaries in a race to capture a mysterious briefcase. Though he nearly reawakens the comatose car-chase genre, director John Frankenheimer squanders a cast of A-list character actors in the process.

In order to steal a heavily-guarded briefcase, Irish Republican Army agent Dierdre (Natascha McElhone) hires a cadre of freelance former intelligence agents—Sam (Robert De Niro), Vincent (Jean Reno), Gregor (Stellan Skarsgard), Larry (Skipp Sudduth), and Spence (Sean Bean). Though an early screwup gets Spence kicked out, the rest go on to track the briefcase to a village in France. After a firefight and car chase, Gregor captures the case, then ditches the others to sell it to the highest bidder. Sam taps an old CIA buddy to locate Gregor, just before he sells the case to the Russians. They nearly recover the briefcase, but are interrupted by Dierdre's boss, Seamus O'Rourke (Jonathan Pryce), a high-ranking member of the IRA who kills Larry and takes the case. After another white-knuckle car chase, Gregor manages to flee with the briefcase.

Determining that Gregor still has ties to the KGB (his former employers), Sam and Vincent wait for him at the opening performance of a prominent Russian skater (Katarina Witt) whose coach, Mikhi (Feodor Atkine), is also a KGB operative. Gregor is doublecrossed and shot by Mikhi, who is in turn killed by Seamus, who takes the briefcase. Sam admits to Vincent that he is not freelance at all but still an active CIA agent, and that Seamus has been his target all along. Sam hunts Seamus and kills him, collecting the briefcase for the CIA.

RONIN (the name means "masterless Samurai") is an old-fashioned Cold War type thriller in the vein of John Le Carre, and director Frankenheimer captures that same feel—secret hideouts, rainy European villages, and of course the ubiquitous Russians. Add the truly heart-pounding but oddly anachronistic car chases (and RONIN boasts no less than three) and the whole affair seems like the lost Sean Connery Bond film. Which is not to say that RONIN is a bad movie: in addition to the hair-raising chases, RONIN has in its corner a nicely complex plot and a handful of characters that are more than capable of keeping your interest for two hours. But alongside the high-tech, special effects-laden brand of thrillers of the 1990s, RONIN looks dated.

To his credit, Frankenheimer has collected in RONIN some of the international film scene's coolest character actors, including Robert De Niro, Jean Reno (THE PROFESSIONAL, GODZILLA), Stellan Skarsgard (GOOD WILL HUNTING), Sean Bean (PATRIOT GAMES), and Jonathan Pryce (TOMORROW NEVER DIES). For the first half-hour or so, the interaction of these highly charged personalities creates an additional dynamic, a swirling current that threatens to send the action spinning in different directions. It's unfortunate that Bean is dispatched so soon, and that much of the remainder of the film relies on the overlong car chases. The film's ending may seem a bit forced, but the scenes that feature De Niro and Reno are themselves worth the price of admission. *(Violence, profanity.)*—B.T.

d, John Frankenheimer; p, Frank Mancuso Jr.; exec p, Paul Kelmenson; assoc p, Ethel Winant; w, J.D. Zeik, David Mamet, billed as Richard Wiesz (based on the stort by J.D. Zeik); ph, Robert Fraisse; ed, Tony Gibbs; m, Elia Cmiral; prod d, Michael Z. Hanan; art d, Gerard Viard; set d, Robert LeCorre; sound, Bernard Bats (recorder); fx, Georges Demetrau; casting, Amanda Mackey Johnson, Cathy Sandrich, Margot Capelier, Sue Jones; cos, May Routh; makeup, Paul Le Marinel; stunts, Joe Dunne

Action/Spy/Thriller **(PR: C MPAA: R)**

ROUNDERS ★★½

(U.S., 1998) 120m Spanky Pictures;
Miramax ~ Miramax c

Matt Damon (Mike McDermott); Edward Norton (Worm); Gretchen Mol (Jo); John Malkovich (Teddy KGB); John Turturro (Joey Knish); Martin Landau (Abe Peterovsky); Famke Janssen (Petra); Michael Rispoli (Grama); Vernon E. Jordan Jr. (Judge McKinnon); Paul Cicero (Russian Thug); Ray Iannicelli (Kenny); Merwin Goldsmith (Sy); Sonny Zito (Tony); Josh Mostel (Zagosh); Mal Z. Lawrence (Irving); Lenny Clarke (Savino); Peter Yoshida (Henry Lin); Jay Boryea (Russian Thug #2); Lenny Venito (Moogie); Richard Mawe (Professor Eisen); Michael Lombard (D.A. Shields); Tom Aldredge (Judge Marinacci); Beeson Carroll (Judge Kaplan); Matthew Yavne (Professor Green); Erik LaRay Harvey (Roy); Dominic Marcus (Dowling); Brian Anthony Wilson (Derald); George Kmeck (Prison Guard); Joe Parisi (Property Guard); Melina Kanakaredes (Barbara); Kohl Sudduth (Wagner); Charlie Matthes (Birch); Hank Jacobs (Steiny); Chris Messina (Higgins); Michael Ryan Segal (Griggs); Kerry O'Malley (Kelly); Slava Schoot (Roman); Goran Visnjic (Maurice); Michele Zanes (Taj Dealer); Allan Havey (Guberman); Joe Vega (Freddy Face); Neal Hemphill (Claude); John C. Chan (Johnny Chan); Lisa Gorlitsky (Sherry); John DiBenedetto (LaRossa); Nicole Brier (Sunshine); Bill Camp (Eisenberg); Tony Hoty (Taki); Mario Mendoza (Zizzo); Joe Zaloom (Cronos); Sal Richards (Johnny Gold); Josh Pais (Weitz); John Gallagher (Bartender); Adam LeFevre (Sean Frye); P.J. Brown (Vitter); David Zayas (Osborne); Michael Arkin (Bear); Murphy Guyer (Detweiler); Alan Davidson (Cabbie)

Although well done and good looking, ROUNDERS is undermined by narration and dialogue that too often wallow shamelessly in the mystique and lingo of the subculture being depicted: the world of big-time poker. What's more, the movie lacks the charismatic central character and delicious plot twists that helped make two of director John Dahl's previous pictures, RED ROCK WEST (1993) and the THE LAST SEDUCTION (1994), so memorably entertaining.

A master of high stakes poker, Mike McDermott (Matt Damon) lives with Jo (Gretchen Mol), his girlfriend and law school classmate. After losing all his tuition money to a Russian hood known as Teddy KGB (John Malkovich), Matt swears off cards and takes a job driving a truck.

Worm (Edward Norton), Mike's old high school buddy, is released from prison. Confronted with heavy gambling debts, Worm lures Mike back into the poker scene. Eventually, Jo, unhappy with Mike's relapse, leaves him. His debts increasing by the day, the reckless and irresponsible Worm is roughed up by Grama (Michael Rispoli), a thug who as bought up all of Worm's IOUs. Later, involved in a card game with state policeman, the two pals are beaten up when the cops catch Worm cheating. Worm suggests that they skip out on his debts and leave town, but Mike, who has vouched for his friend to Grama, remains behind to try to pay off the money Worm owes.

When Mike calls on Grama to negotiate for time, he discovers that Grama is a front for Teddy KGB, Worm's actual creditor. Mike borrows $10,000 from his favorite law professor (Martin Landau) and challenges KGB to a no-limit game. After winning enough to pay off his and Worm's debts, Mike is tempted to call it a night but KGB goads him into continuing. Knowing that if he loses, he loses everything—maybe even his life—Mike plays on and cleans KGB out. Realizing at last that he was born to play poker, Mike quits law school and jubilantly heads for Las Vegas, where the big action is.

The structure of the film resembles that of one of its prototypes, THE HUSTLER (1961). At the beginning and end of each movie a young hotshot player faces off with a wily veteran; the youth loses the first showdown but wins the rematch. But like THE HUSTLER's 1986 sequel, THE COLOR OF MONEY, ROUNDERS eschews, if not reverses, the original film's moral message in order to comply with the less idealistic values of the times. THE HUSTLER was about living by the Golden Rule; ROUNDERS is about looking for the Golden Fleece. Poker, an all but unphotographable game, lacks the physical contact and kinetic beauty of athletics, and even the minor visual graces of pool and golf. This built-in handicap has impelled the depictors of screen poker to up the machismo ante with overdoses of argot and supercool mystique. Movies about cardplaying are corny, and ROUNDERS is no exception; it piles on the jargon, tough talk, and gutter aphorisms to an overweening degree. Didn't the writers realize the "Let's play some *fucking cards*" lacks the true grit of "Fill your hands, you son of a bitch!"?

Edward Norton's loose-limbed, very assured portrayal of Worm, a New Jersey Irish version of Robert De Niro's Johnny Boy in MEAN STREETS (1973), makes his foolhardy character almost likable. John Malcovich's over-the-top performance as Teddy KGB—complete with an exaggerated Russian accent that would have made Akim Tamiroff blush—might have been annoying in a first-rate movie but is quite amusing here. As Mike, Matt Damon wisely plays against the script's braggadocio but is not endowed with sufficient presence to triumph over it. At no point does he match the subtle but overwhelming charisma of the screen's most prominent poker player, Steve McQueen as THE CINCINNATI KID (1965)—or the matter of fact manner in which McQueen, with the absolute sincerity born of total self-confidence, made this ordinary line unforgettable: "I don't have to cheat to beat *you*, pal." *(Violence, nudity, extreme profanity.)*—D.T.

d, John Dahl; p, Ted Demme, Joel Stillman; exec p, Bob Weinstein, Harvey Weinstein, Bobby Cohen, Kerry Orent; assoc p, Tracy Falco, Christopher Goode; w, David Levien, Brian Koppleman; ph, Jean-Yves Escoffier; ed, Scott Chestnut; m, Christopher Young; prod d, Rob Pearson; art d, Rick Butler; set d, Beth Kushnik; sound, Mark Weingarten; casting, Avy Kaufman; cos, Terry Dresbach; makeup, Carla White; stunts, Jery Hewitt

Drama/Crime **(PR: C MPAA: R)**

ROYAL DECEIT ★★★½

(Denmark/U.K./Germany/France, 1998) 85m Les Films Ariane; Woodline Films; Kenneth Madsen Filmproduktion; Films Roses ~ Miramax c
(AKA: PRINCE OF JUTLAND)

Gabriel Byrne *(Fenge)*; Helen Mirren *(Queen Geruth)*; Christian Bale *(Prince Amled)*; Brian Cox *(Aethelwine, Duke of Lindsey)*; Steven Waddington *(Ribold)*; Kate Beckinsale *(Ethel)*; Tom Wilkinson *(King Hardvendel)*; Tony Haygarth *(Radnar)*; Saskia

Wickham *(Gunvor)*; Brian Glover *(Caedman)*; Mark Williams *(Aslak)*; Andy Serkis *(Torsten)*; Philip Rham *(Aelfred)*; Freddie Jones *(Bjorn)*

A reworking of Shakespeare's *Hamlet*, ROYAL DECEIT may lack the Bard's lyrical dialogue, but it does boast some sensational action sequences and a truly top-notch cast.

In 6th century Denmark, young Prince Amled (Christian Bale), son of King Hardvendel (Tom Wilkinson), discovers that his uncle Fenge (Gabriel Byrne) murdered his father in order to gain the throne and the hand of his mother, Queen Geruth (Helen Mirren). Seething with rage, Amled pretends to be mad in order to gain sympathy while he secretly plots revenge.

Believing that Amled is faking his madness, Fenge and his henchmen set him up with a woman—to whom they hope he'll confess his masquerade—but he acts in the same manner while in her company. In a moment alone with his mother, Amled discovers one of the henchmen under the bed trying to eavesdrop, but Amled promptly kills him. He tells Geruth that he is quite sane and that Fenge is her husband's murderer. Disbelieving at first, Geruth promises Amled that she will act as if nothing is wrong in Fenge's presence, until the time that Amled can take his revenge.

When Fenge discovers the body of his henchman, he arranges to have Amled exiled on the pretence that his health needs to be seen to. Fenge actually sends the young man to his good friend the Duke of Lindsey with two escorts, Aslak and Torsten, and a stone tablet etched with orders to kill Amled. Amled manages to change the writing on the tablet so that it orders the Duke to kill the escorts. Amled wins the duke's admiration by leading a bloody but victorious battle against a rival duke and then marrying his daughter Ethel (Kate Beckinsale); then heads back to Jutland to exact his vengeance. Fenge is shocked to see the prince return, but holds a public celebration in a town meeting place to welcome him home. At the celebration, Amled seizes the opportunity to attack Fenge's henchmen and set the meeting place on fire. In the flames, Fenge and Amled struggle until Amled finally kills his uncle. The next day, Geruth crowns her son and his wife the king and queen of Jutland.

Originally titled PRINCE OF JUTLAND, ROYAL DECEIT is epic in structure, but has an intimacy worthy of a small character study. As directed by Danish director Gabriel Axel (1987's BABETTE'S FEAST), the film proves that it is possible to tell a straightforward story about bravery, treachery, and revenge in a period setting without a large budget. Axel makes remarkable use of a small cast, a few extras, limited location shooting, and surprisingly violent but bloodless battle scenes. Without great fanfare, Axel's variation on "Hamlet" takes the familiar story back to its roots, in this case an ancient Danish legend. The cast perfectly incarnate their morally black-and-white roles: Byrne's dark Irish looks provide the perfect mask for Fenge's faked warmth and underlying ruthlessness, while Bale turns in a surprisingly complex performance as Amled, avoiding flashy heroic moves (and, of course, Hamlet's sullen compulsion to muse on his fate). Unfortunately, the normally compelling Mirren gives a by-the-numbers, woman-standing-by-her-man performance that is unworthy of her immense talents. *(Violence, nudity.)*—D.O.

d, Gabriel Axel; p, Kees Kasander; exec p, Terry Glinwood, Sylvaine Sainderichin, Denis Wigman; co-p, Kenneth Madsen; w, Gabriel Axel, Erik Kjersgaard; ph, Henning Kristiansen; ed, Jean Francois Naudon; m, Per Norgaard; prod d, Sven Wichmann; set d, Torben Bekmark; sound, Volker Zeigermann; fx, Herbert Blank, Peter Wiemketz; casting, Kate Dowd; cos, Gisele Tanalias; makeup, Werner Puthe, Petra Lober

Drama/Adventure **(PR: C MPAA: R)**

ROYAL WARRIORS ★★★½

(Hong Kong, 1986) 95m D&B Films ~ Century Pacific Entertainment c
(AKA: IN THE LINE OF DUTY; POLICE ASSASSINS; YES MADAM II)

Michelle Yeoh, billed as Michelle Khan *(Michelle)*; Henry Sanada *(Peter Yamamoto)*; Michael Wong *(Michael Wong)*; David Lam, billed as Lam Wai *(Blackie)*; Chan Wai Man *(Harvey)*; Paul Chun *(Police Escort on Plane)*; Kenneth Tsang *(Police Chief Lau Chi Shing)*; Dennis Chan *(Photographer on Plane)*; Eddie Maher *(Gun Dealer)*; Reiko Niwa; Pak Ying; Kam Hing Ying

Made in 1986 but unreleased in America until 1998, Michelle Yeoh's second starring action vehicle (following YES, MADAM in 1985) is a nonstop action classic chock full of terrific battles and exciting stunts.

When a gun-toting passenger on an airplane kills several people and attempts to free a prisoner being extradited to Hong Kong, three strangers—former Japanese policeman Peter Yamamoto (Henry Sanada), airline security agent Michael (Michael Wong), and Hong Kong cop Michelle (Michelle Yeoh)—band together to kill the prisoner and his intended savior. Later, another criminal (David Lam), an associate of the two on the plane, decides to avenge their deaths by blowing up the wife and child of Yamamoto; the criminal then escapes in a frantic car chase. Yamamoto uses Michael and Michelle to lure the assassin to a bar, where the murderer is killed in a protracted, violent battle.

Another criminal associate remains. It is revealed that the four men were soldiers who swore an oath of fealty to one another on the battlefield. The remaining criminal snatches Michael and dangles him from a rooftop as bait to catch Michelle; rather than be used, Michael intentionally plunges to his death. After the funeral, the criminal digs up Michael's corpse and dangles it as bait yet again, bringing Michelle and Yamamoto to an abandoned quarry where they fight with guns, cars, tanks, fists, feet, and chainsaws. Killing the criminal, Michelle and Yamamoto escape as the quarry, wired by the criminal, explodes.

Nominally an ensemble piece for the three heroes, the film is actually a showcase for the dynamic Ms. Yeoh, tailored specifically for her by D&B Films, owned by her then-fiance, multimillionaire Dickson Poon. She kicks it off (literally) by thrashing some Japanese thugs in an unrelated prologue, and ends by rescuing her pals (one of whom is dead!) and killing the villain. Henry Sanada, a martial arts star in Japan, fares second best, both in his well-choreographed fights and his dramatic scenes as a hardboiled cop-cum-family man. Amerasian Michael Wong is a good-looking but wooden actor, utilized convincingly as a good-looking but wooden playboy. Playing a character imaginatively named Michael Wong, he tries at one point to bluff the criminal and is told "your acting is rather bad"—the picture's biggest laugh. Often cast as a romantic lead, he's a nonstarter as a martial artist, and consequently gets wounded early in the film to excuse him from the action. In a peculiarly Asian concept, Yamamoto and Michelle don't really like him when he's alive, but once he's dead, they'll risk their lives for his mortal remains.

David Chung, a cinematographer-director who worked on numerous classics including Tsui Hark's DANGEROUS ENCOUNTER OF THE FIRST KIND (1979), offers a nice understated style, building not only excitement but genuine suspense, a rarity in Hong Kong filmmaking. Yeoh suffered the first of numerous on-set injuries during a fight scene in this film. Along with YES, MADAM, ROYAL WARRIORS has also been released overseas as part of the POLICE ASSASSINS and ULTRA FORCE series, and as IN THE LINE OF DUTY (its title on the current domestic print of the film), the first in a long-running and confusingly numbered series of female action flicks from D&B. *(Graphic violence.)*— A.B.

d, David Chung; p, John Sham; exec p, Dickson Poon; assoc p, Chan Kiu Ying; w, Sammy Tsang; ph, Wan Man Kit, Ma Chun Wah; ed, Cheong Kwok Kuen; m, Romeo Diaz; prod d, Oliver Wong, Dominique Lo, Yang Wong; stunts, Mang Hoi, Or Sau Leung

Action/Crime **(PR: C MPAA: NR)**

RUDOLPH THE RED-NOSED REINDEER: THE MOVIE ★★

(U.S., 1998) 90m Tundra Productions; GoodTimes Entertainment ~ Legacy Releasing c

VOICES OF: John Goodman *(Santa Claus)*; Whoopi Goldberg *(Stormella, The Evil Ice Queen)*; Debbie Reynolds *(Mrs. Claus)*; Bob Newhart *(Leonard the Polar Bear)*; Richard Simmons *(Boone)*; Eric Idle *(Slyly the Fox)*; Eric Popisil *(Young Rudolph)*; Kathleen Barr *(Grown-Up Rudolph)*; Alec Willows *(Doggle)*; Lee Tockar *(Ridley)*; Garry Chalk *(Blitzen)*; Christopher Gray *(Arrow)*; Vanessa Morley *(Young Zoey)*; Myriam Sircos *(Older Zoey)*

Probably setting a new record by being released to video less than one month after receiving a token theatrical release, RUDOLPH THE RED-NOSED REINDEER: THE MOVIE is an unsophisticated and old-fashioned cartoon aimed squarely at pre-schoolers, but is perfectly pleasant and good-natured entertainment for its target group.

A reindeer named Rudolph (voice of Kathleen Barr) is born in Santa's village in the North Pole, but is teased by all of his schoolmates, except for a young doe named Zoey (voice of Myriam Sircos), for having a red glowing nose. When some of Santa's elves accidentally smash up the ice garden of wicked Queen Stormella (voice of Whoopi Goldberg), she demands that the elves be turned over to her, but Santa (voice of John Goodman) refuses, so Stormella forbids anyone from using her ice bridge and promises to ruin Christmas with a storm if anyone tries to cross it. During some Christmas Eve reindeer games to qualify to become one of Santa's sleigh-pullers, Rudolph is cheated out of a win by Zoey's boyfriend Arrow (voice of Christopher Gray), who's jealous of Zoey's friendship with Rudolph.

After being unfairly disqualified because of his nose, Rudolph runs away and befriends a fox named Slyly (voice of Eric Idle) and a polar bear named Leonard (voice of Bob Newhart). Zoey breaks up with Arrow and tries to find Rudolph, but when she crosses the ice bridge, she's captured by Stormella and locked up in her dungeon. Some sprites inform Rudolph about Zoey's capture, and with the aid of Slyly and Leonard, they save her, but Stormella retaliates by conjuring up a blizzard, causing Santa to cancel his delivery of Christmas presents. Rudolph uses his nose as a searchlight to return with the others to Santa's village, and when Santa sees the glow from his nose, he asks Rudolph to guide his sleigh that night, ensuring that all of the presents are delivered on time.

RUDOLPH THE RED-NOSED REINDEER: THE MOVIE is a throwback to the age of kind, gentle, and innocuous holiday cartoons that used to be a TV staple before the era of high-tech, digital razzle-dazzle took over, bombarding kids with a nonstop sensory overload of violent sight gags and nasty wisecracks. Produced by the video company Goodtimes, the cassettes of RUDOLPH were probably all boxed up and ready to ship even before it played in theaters for about a week (a good two months before Christmas), and while it will never win any awards for its artistry, especially for a big-screen production, the animation is certainly no worse than most of its made-for-video ilk and a lot better than some (e.g., the execrable SWAN PRINCESS III). Although the running time is padded by the usual addition of irrelevant songs (including one that tries to update the story by having Santa sing about how "everyone has a spot in my extended family tree"), at least they're short, and include several renditions of the irresistible, classic title song, as well as "Wonderful Christmastime" performed by Paul McCartney. The herky-jerky movement and simplistic visual design is compensated for by the film's overall sweetness and the way it soft-pedals homilies to kids about tolerance, forgiveness, and being just plain nice. The voice cast is not asked to do very much, and plays it all very straight, but Eric Idle is amusing as the fox who sounds exactly like Jimmy Durante, and Whoopi Goldberg spices up Stormella with her usual quota of "honey," "baby," and "girl" ad-libs.—M.S.

d, William R. Kowalchuk; p, William R. Kowalchuk, Michael Lloyd; exec p, Eric Ellenbogen, Seth Willenson, Andy Greenburg; assoc p, Jean Rogers; co-p, Jonathn Flom; w, Michael Aschner (based on the story by Robert L. May and the song by Johnny Marks); ed, Tom Hok; m, Michael Lloyd, Al Kasha; anim, William R. Kowalchuk; sound, Doug Pearce; casting, Mary Jo Slater

Animated/Children's/Fantasy **(PR: AA MPAA: G)**

RUGRATS MOVIE, THE ★★★

(U.S., 1998) 85m Nickelodeon Movies; Klasky/Csupo Inc. ~ Paramount c

VOICES OF: David Spade *(Ranger Frank)*; Whoopi Goldberg *(Ranger Margaret)*; E.G. Daily *(Tommy Pickles)*; Christine Cavanaugh *(Chuckie Finster)*; Kath Soucie *(Phillip Deville, Lillian Deville, Betty Deville)*; Tara Charendoff *(Dylan Pickles)*; Cheryl Chase *(Angelica Pickles)*; Melanie Chartoff *(Minka, Didi Pickles)*; Jack Riley *(Stu Pickles)*; Joe Alaskey *(Grandpa Lou Pickles)*; Michael Bell *(Chas Finster, Drew Pickles, Grandpa Boris)*; Tim Curry *(Rex Pester)*; Busta Rhymes *(Reptar Wagon)*; Roger Clinton *(Air Crewman)*; Margaret Cho *(Lt. Klavin)*; Laurie Anderson; Beck; B Real; Jakob Dylan; Phife; Gordon Gano; Iggy Pop; Lenny Kravitz; Lisa Loeb; Lou Rawls; Patti Smith; Dawn Robinson; Fred Schneider; Kate Pierson; Cindy Wilson *(Newborn Babies)*; Phil Proctor *(Howard Delville, Igor)*; Cree Summer *(Susie Carmichael)*; Andrea Martin *(Aunt Miriam)*; Tress Macneille *(Charlotte Pickles)*; Tony Jay *(Dr. Lipshitz)*; Edie McClurg *(Nurse)*; Hattie Winston *(Dr. Lucy Carmichael)*; Gregg Berger *(Circus TV Announcer)*; Abe Benrubi *(Serge)*; Charlie Adler *(United Express Driver)*; Mary Gross *(Woman Guest)*; Kevin McBride *(Male Guest)*; Steve Zirnkilton *(Reporter)*; Robin Groth *(Reporter)*; Angel Harper *(Reporter)*

Those phenomenally popular talking toddlers from the Nickelodeon cartoon series finally get their own movie, titled, appropriately enough, THE RUGRATS MOVIE, and as a pleasant change from the usual cheap cash-ins on successful TV shows, the film's animation is actually superior to what's been seen on the tube.

In a suburban neighborhood, young Tommy Pickles (voice of E.G. Daily) is the leader of a group of precocious babies: his cowardly best friend Chuckie (voice of Christine Cavanaugh) and bickering twins Phil and Lil (both voiced by Kath Soucie). Their various misadventures are invariably sabotaged by

Tommy's bratty cousin Angelica (voice of Cheryl Chase), and now, the arrival of Tommy's new baby brother Dil (voice of Tara Charendoff), who steals all of Tommy's toys and does nothing but cry. When Tommy's inventor father Stu (voice of Jack Riley) creates a toddler transportation vehicle called the Reptar Wagon to enter in a contest, Dil, Tommy, and his friends take it for a ride and wind up getting lost in a spooky forest. Angelica goes after them, along with Spike the dog, because Dil had stolen her beloved doll.

In the forest, the kids face numerous perils, including encounters with rapids and a waterfall, some mischievous escaped circus monkeys who temporarily abduct Dil, and a scary wolf that's on the prowl for food. Meanwhile, the kids' parents take off in hot pursuit, led by Stu in a flying pterodactyl-like contraption he's invented, and they're followed by throngs of tabloid news reporters. Eventually, Angelica finds the babies just as the wolf has them trapped on a bridge, and Spike comes to the rescue by attacking the wolf. Drew spots the babies from the sky and rescues them, and after all of the kids are safely returned to their homes, the ordeal has resulted in forging a loving bond between Dil and Tommy and instilling Chuckie with bravery.

Since its debut in 1991, "The Rugrats" has proven to be Nickelodeon's most durable and successful cartoon, utilizing a simple, but surprisingly effective premise of showing the world through the eyes of babies who can converse intelligently amongst themselves (that must be the reason for their abnormally large heads), and depicting their fantasy world in vividly realistic terms; as in the movie's Indiana Jones parody prologue in which a whip-wielding Tommy leads the babies into a cave to search for a golden treasure, which turns into a banana split in his kitchen. For parents and older viewers, the adult characters are amusingly portrayed: the overprotective liberal mother, the yuppie couple, the doting-but-dozing grandpa, the crazy neighbors, et al, which results in a messy, but loving, portrait of family life that everyone can relate to. THE RUGRATS MOVIE throws in a new baby to the mix, but otherwise follows the established formula and uses the larger screen to expand on the fluid visual effects of the series, with several striking set pieces, including extensive "tracking shots" through Tommy's house, and impressive rapid motion showing the Reptar Wagon roaring down the highway and floating on a river, and Drew flying through the air in his invention.

The humor is generally on the same level as the series, featuring lots of juvenile puns and malapropisms (such as Detective Angelica calling Spike the dog her "butthound"), and references to "poopy" and other bodily functions which never fail to crack kids up, but there is also some broad satire designed to appeal to adults, such as the numerous pop-culture music/movie/television references. Additionally, the tone of the series, which treads a fine line between hipness and innocence without ever resorting to smugness or condescension, translates quite well to the big screen, particularly in the spoofy musical numbers (under the direction of the series composer Mark Mothersbaugh), which include a nursery scene where infants create a rainbow by urinating into the air, Angelica's variation on "One Way or Another," and the monkeys' manic rendition of "Witch Doctor" (performed by Devo). While it may not go down in history as a classic of animation, the film is short and sweet, and unlike so many contemporary cartoon features, doesn't take itself at all seriously and has no sociological axe to grind.—M.S.

d, Igor Kovalyov, Norton Virgien; p, Arlene Klasky, Gabor Csupo; exec p, Albie Hecht, Debby Beece; co-p, Hal Waite, Eryk Casemiro, Julia Pistor; w, J. David Stem, David N. Weiss (based on the characters created by Arlene Klasky, Gabor Csupo, and Paul Germain); ed, Peter Tomaszewicz; m, Mark Mothersbaugh; art d, Dima Malanitchev; anim, Arlene Klasky, Gabor Csupo, Peter Chung, Andrei Svislotski, Mark Marren, Panagiotis Rappas; sound, Kurt Vanzo; casting, Barbara Wright

Children's/Animated **(PR: AA MPAA: G)**

RUN FOR COVER ★

(U.S., 1998) 80m New Wave Films Inc. ~ New Wave Films Distribution Inc. c

Thomas Dunne *(Jay Fleming)*; Adam West *(Senator Prescott)*; Viveca Lindfors *(Senator Anderson)*; Edward I. Koch *(Mayor of New York)*; Curtis Sliwa *(Himself)*; Lynn Samuels *(Activist)*; Rev. Al Sharpton *(Himself)*; Rudolf Martin *(Spengel)*; David Paterson *(Helmut)*; Anthony Michaels *(Heinrich)*; Naira Soibatian *(Susan)*; Dina Ipavic *(Anne Sommers/Sarah Lerner)*; Natasha Espiedra *(Lissette)*; Don Demico *(Agent West)*; John Knox *(FBI Director/Corey)*; Mark McIlraith *(Kyle)*; Koby Benvenisti *(Yuri)*

Terrorists threaten New York in 3D. As a straight action thriller, RUN FOR COVER is so tepid that its advertising attempted to pass it off as "camp," emphasizing the marginal cameo contributions of three colorful NYC figures: ex-Mayor Ed Koch, the Rev. Al Sharpton, and Guardian Angel leader Curtis Sliwa, along with the appearance of former Batman Adam West in a supporting role.

TV-news cameraman Jay Fleming (Thomas Dunne) sees a woman he recognizes as Anne Sommers (Dina Ipavic), a key witness in a federal antiterrorism investigation, gunned down in the streets. After being arrested and questioned by the FBI, Fleming is abducted by a small but deadly band of terrorists led by a man named Helmut (David Paterson). Innocent of Sommers's murder, the terrorists unsuccessfully grill Fleming about the actual killer's identity. Eventually they release him but have him tailed. After shaking his pursuer, Fleming arrives at the TV station where he and his ex-girlfriend Susan (Naria Soibatian) work. Susan provides him with a haven in her apartment, where they resume their affair.

Fleming's terrorist pursuer finds him in Susan's flat and chases him into a paint-gun arcade. There the terrorist is killed by a resurrected Anne Sommers, whose murder had been faked by the FBI, and who is in reality an intelligence agent attempting to avenge the assassination of her father, an Israeli diplomat.

The terrorists announce that if they do not receive $10,000,000 from the city, they will kill 1,500 people. When the Mayor (Edward I. Koch) refuses to comply, they detonate a bomb in the Queens Midtown Tunnel. No commuters are hurt, all the terrorists are captured or killed, and an official announcement is made that Fleming has died in the blast. In reality he is unhurt and embarks on a romantic vacation with Susan.

Richard R. Haines, the authority on motion picture processes who masterminded RUN FOR COVER, maintained that his film boasted the most advanced and realistic sub-70mm three-dimensional technology to date. In truth, the movie's 3D photography is quite weak, the major problem being the completely disorienting tendency of objects in the background to look "closer" to the viewer than objects in the foreground. Accompanying the film at its NYC screenings was an untitled one-reeler devoted to skateboarding, snowboarding, and surfing. Presumably shot in the same process as the feature, this short showcased 3D much more successfully than RUN FOR COVER did.

Technology aside, the movie has very little to offer. Saddled with a tired formula-bound plot and performances that generally are not merely bad but *loud*, RUN FOR COVER fails to live up to its end-credit dedication "to Mike Todd, William Castle, and the spirit of motion picture showmanship." One has to wonder why Haines, burdened with a very low budget, would opt to make his 3D debut in a genre that ideally requires a Bruce Willis-sized overhead, rather than essaying a simple little horror movie or psychological thriller. *(Violence.)*—D.T.

d, Richard W. Haines; p, Miljan Peter Ilich, Peter Lewnes, Grace Pettijohn; co-p, Richard W. Haines; w, Richard W. Haines; ph, Brendan C. Flynt; ed, Richard W. Haines; m, Gary Schreiner

Action/Thriller **(PR: C MPAA: NR)**

RUNNING WOMAN, THE ★★½
(U.S., 1998) 87m Concorde; New Horizons ~ New Horizons Home Video c

Theresa Russell *(Emily Russo)*; Andrew J. Robinson *(Capt. Don Gibbs)*; Gary Graham *(John Delaney)*; Eddie Velez *(Reuben Alvarez)*; Anthony Crivello *(Det. Harris)*; Castulo Guerra *(Father Talou)*; Robert La Sardo *(Manuel)*; Melinda Songer *(Det. Steward)*; David McCurley *(Sam)*; Gregory Norman Cruz *(Enrico)*; Christopher Pennock *(William Dayton)*; Richard Joseph Paul *(Det. Caprio)*; Seidy Lopez *(Carmela)*; Julio Dolce Vita *(Jesus)*

Theresa Russell stars in RUNNING WOMAN, an above-average made-for-video thriller produced by Roger Corman. The film was disguised in its promotional materials as a murder mystery, but is actually a disturbing drama dealing with racism, civic corruption, and the dark side of contemporary LA.

After working on a painting at a Hispanic church in East LA, art restorer Emily Russo (Theresa Russell) drives home with her young son Sam (David McCurley). Emily is pulled over by a police car, but the drivers turn out to be carjackers in disguise. Emily fights with them and gets away, but falls off a highway overpass and Sam is shot and killed during the struggle. Emily wakes up in the hospital and is questioned by Capt. Gibbs (Andrew J. Robinson), who comes to regard her as a suspect after a gun is found outside her condo which matches the bullet holes in her car. After being released from the hospital, Emily goes undercover in disguise and tells her story to her ex-husband John (Gary Graham), a newspaper reporter.

Emily then goes to East LA and uncovers evidence of foul play involving a defense contractor and philanthropist named Dayton (Christopher Pennock). She learns that Dayton is saving money by burying deadly nerve gas in various Hispanic churches and housing projects, instead of incinerating it, and that he ordered the fake carjacking which killed her son because he was afraid she would discover traces of the nerve gas on the church painting she was restoring. Emily sneaks into the church and is caught by Gibbs, who tells her he's working for Dayton and that he's doing it in order to kill off Hispanics who will grow up to be criminals. Emily manages to escape and tells John about Dayton, but after fleeing to San Diego, she learns that John's expose of Dayton has been killed and she sees a TV report announcing that 15 more Dayton housing projects will be built.

Boasting a complicated narrative dealing with such social issues as gang violence, missing kids, carjackings, the exploitation of minorities by big business, police brutality, and the environment, RUNNING WOMAN is highly atypical made-for-video fodder. It's not always successful, as the plot is often murky and contrived, but it's thoughtful and its heart is in the right place. Perhaps the most startling aspect of the story is how it unflinchingly faces up to LA's Hispanic "problem," making the clean-cut Gibbs a Mark Fuhrman-like fanatic who practices ethnic cleansing and is backed by a revered philanthropist billionaire who's friends with politicians and celebrities. That the bad guys get away with it and plan to continue more genocide at the film's end is also fairly shocking. Theresa Russell, a long way from THE LAST TYCOON (1976) and BAD TIMING (1980), is not a particularly convincing action heroine, but she's quite good at conveying maternal anguish, and still looks great in a variety of wigs and disguises. And it's always fun to see Andrew Robinson, whose racist cop is almost as chilling as his legendary psycho killer in DIRTY HARRY (1971). *(Violence, profanity.)*—M.S.

d, Rachel Samuels; p, Roger Corman; assoc p, Matthew Dresden; co-p, Darin Spillman, Marta M. Mobley; w, Rachel Samuels; ph, Chris Manley; ed, Sonya Polonsky; m, Christopher Lennertz; prod d, Dave Blass; sound, John R.F. Halaby, Aletha Rodgers, James H. Coburn IV; fx, Albert Lannutti; casting, Jan Glaser; cos, Jayme Bohn; makeup, Tonie Keyton, Marie Sherwood

Thriller/Drama **(PR: O MPAA: R)**

RUSH HOUR ★★½
(U.S., 1998) 94m New Line; Caravan ~ New Line c

Jackie Chan *(Lee)*; Chris Tucker *(Carter)*; Tom Wilkinson *(Griffin/Juntao)*; Elizabeth Pena *(Johnson)*; Tzi Ma *(Consul Han)*; Julia Hsu *(Soo Yung)*; Ken Leung *(Sang)*; Robert Littman *(First Caucasian)*; Michael Chow *(Dinner Guest)*; Chris Penn *(Clive)*; Kai Lennox *(Cop at Diner)*; Larry Sullivan Jr. *(Cop at Diner)*; Yan Lin *(Consul Secretary)*; Roger Fan *(Soo Yung's Bodyguard)*; George Kee Cheung *(Soo Yung's Driver)*; Lucy Lin *(Exposition Official)*; Rex Lin *(Agent Whitney)*; Mark Rolston *(Agent Russ)*; Philip Baker Hall *(Captain Diel)*; Jason Davis *(Kid at Theatre)*; John Hawkes *(Stucky)*; Jean Lebell *(Taxi Driver)*; Wayne A. King *(Cigaweed Man)*; Manny Perry *(Bartender)*; Kevin Jackson *(Pool Player)*; Ronald D. Brown *(Pool Hall Doorman)*; Clifton Powell *(Luke)*; Matt Barry *(Market Clerk)*; Stanley DeSantis *(FBI Gate Guard #1)*; Dan Martin *(FBI Gate Guard #2)*; Kevin Lowe *(Another Agent)*; Billy Devlin *(FBI Agent at Building)*; Tommy Bush *(Bomb Practice Sergeant)*; Barry "Shabaka" Henley *(Bobby)*; Albert Wong *(Chin)*; Al Wan *(Foo Chow Hostess)*; Lydia Look *(Foo Chow Waitress)*; Sumiko (Osumi) Chan *(Japanese Tourist)*; Man Ching Chan *(Japanese Tourist)*; Kenneth Houi Kan Low; Stuart Yee; Nicky Chung Chi Li; Andy Kai Chung Cheng; Man Ching Chan *(Juntao's Men)*; Christine Mg Wing Mei *(Flight Attendant #1)*; Frances Fong *(Socialite)*; Robert Kotecki *(Convention Center Agent)*; Mike Ashley *(Male Flight Attendant)*; Ada Tai *(Flight Attendant #2)*; Arlene Tai *(Flight Attendant #3)*

RUSH HOUR was hailed as "the best Jackie Chan movie yet," apparently by critics who had only seen the watered-down Chan films released theatrically in the US. This second attempt by Chan to conquer the American market on its own terms (following the 1985 washout THE PROTECTOR) was a box-office success, pairing him with comedian Chris Tucker in a paint-by-numbers buddy-cop plot designed to stitch together a series of generally uninspired action and comedy sequences.

In Hong Kong, Detective Inspector Lee (Jackie Chan) breaks up the operation of unseen criminal mastermind Juntao and retrieves the priceless Chinese artifacts he has been stealing. Several months later, he is summoned to Los Angeles by his friend Consul Han (Tzi Ma), when his young daughter Soo Yung (Julia Hsu) is kidnapped. Unwilling to have a foreigner underfoot, the FBI agents in charge ask the LAPD for someone to keep Lee out of their way. The job goes to Detective James Carter (Chris Tucker), largely as punishment for his ongoing refusal to follow departmental procedures. Insulted by this babysitting assignment but determined to impress the FBI, Carter launches his own investigation while trying to keep Lee distracted. But Lee easily outsmarts both him and the FBI and makes his way to Han.

At the site of an explosion staged by the kidnappers as a warning, Lee recognizes Sang (Ken Leung), one of Juntao's henchmen. Carter's sources confirm that Juntao, who has set up shop in LA as a dealer in illegal explosives, is behind the kidnapping. Lee and Carter raid a restaurant which they have learned is Juntao's headquarters, not realizing that they are interfering with the FBI's ransom drop. Juntao raises his ransom demands, and Lee shamefully prepares to return to Hong Kong. But the conscience-stricken Carter talks him into taking another shot at Juntao.

At a dedication ceremony for an exhibit of the Chinese artifacts retrieved by Lee, Carter recognizes Han's friend, British businessman Griffin (Tom Wilkinson) as having been at the restaurant. Adding up the clues, Lee realizes that Griffin is indeed the mysterious Juntao. Carter locates Soo Yung and, with the help of LAPD Officer Johnson (Elizabeth Pena) defuses the explosive vest the kidnapped girl is wearing. Lee fights and defeats Griffin and his bodyguards. Carter is offered a job with the FBI, but turns it down to visit Hong Kong with his new friend Lee.

A popular hit starring two non-Caucasian performers would be more of a cause for celebration if RUSH HOUR weren't so loaded with racial cliches. Chris Tucker is a charismatic screen presence, but his persona relies rather uncomfortably on black cliches that wouldn't be out of place in a Rudy Ray Moore movie. And while it made sense to partner Chan, whose command of the English language is weak, with a fast-talking costar, the expected culture clash between the two is voiced in a string of Asian stereotypes (Carter takes Lee to Mann's Chinese Theater, refers to him as "ricki" man, offers him a cup of noodles) that are insulting rather than funny. And while it's unfair to expect Chan, who has been abusing his body onscreen for more than 25 years, to maintain that furious pace forever (who'd have thought he could have carried on this long?), RUSH HOUR screams out for the comic invention he brings to his own work. There's just enough of it here, as Chan casually runs over a 10-foot wall or fights off two opponents in a museum while trying not to damage any of the valuable pottery around him, to whet the appetite. Hopefully stateside success will bring Chan a larger degree of creative control in future projects, in which case RUSH HOUR will happily be forgotten as the trivial effort it is. *(Violence, adult situations, profanity.)*—M.F.

d, Brett Ratner; p, Roger Brinbaum, Arthur Sarkissian, Jonathan Glickman; exec p, Jay Stern; assoc p, James M. Freitag, Wayne Morris; co-p, Art Schaefer; w, Ross LaManna, Jim Kouf (based on the story by Ross LaManna); ph, Adam Greenberg; ed, Mark Helfrich; m, Lalo Schifrin; prod d, Robb Wilson King; art d, Thomas Fichter; set d, Lance Lombardo; sound, Kim Ornitz (mixer); fx, Dennis King; casting, Matthew Barry, Nancy Green-Keyes; cos, Sharen Davis; makeup, Melanie Hughes; stunts, Terry Leonard, Jackie Chan

Action/Crime/Comedy (PR: C MPAA: PG-13)

RUSHMORE ★★★½

(U.S., 1998) 95m American Empirical; Touchstone Pictures ~ Buena Vista c

Bill Murray *(Mr. Blume)*; Olivia Williams *(Miss Cross)*; Jason Schwartzman *(Max Fischer)*; Brian Cox *(Dr. Guggenheim)*; Seymour Cassel *(Bert Fischer)*; Mason Gamble *(Dirk Calloway)*; Sara Tanaka *(Margaret Yang)*; Stephen McCole *(Magnus Buchan)*; Luke Wilson *(Dr. Peter Flynn)*; Deepak Pallana *(Mr. Adams)*; Andrew Wilson *(Coach Beck)*; Marietta Marich *(Mrs. Guggenheim)*; Ronnie McCawley *(Ronny Blume)*; Keith McCawley *(Donny Blume)*; Hae Joon Lee *(Alex)*; Adebayo Asabi *(Mr. Obiamiwe)*; Connie Nielsen *(Mrs. Calloway)*; Al Fielder *(Ernie)*; Colin Platt *(Boy Portraying Frank Serpico)*; George Farish *(O'Reilly)*; Francis Fernandez *(Burnum)*; McCauley Penderdast *(Fields)*; Eric Weems *(Willie)*; Dalton Tomlin *(Wrestler)*; Wally Wolodarsky *(Referee)*; Kim Terry *(Mrs. Blume)*; Ella Pryor *(Woman Back Stage)*; Paul Schiff *(Waiter)*; Antoni Scarana *(Small Boy Artist)*; Brian Tenenbaum *(Contractor)*; Thayer McClanahan *(School Reporter)*; Patricia Winkler *(Mrs. Whitney)*; Manning Mott *(Mr. Holstead)*; J.J. Stonebraker *(Woody)*; Donny Caicedo *(40 Ounce)*; Ali Ktiri *(Benjamin)*; Michael Maggart *(Concierge)*; Robbie Lee *(Issac)*; Morgan Redmond *(Bellman)*; Ed Geldart *(Security Guard)*; David Moritz *(Dynamite Salesman)*; J.J. Killalea *(Tommy Stalling)*; William Lau *(Mr. Yang)*; Lucille Sadikin *(Mrs. Yang)*; Steve Eckelman *(Tennis Pro)*; Eric Anderson *(Architect)*; Danny Fine *(Coach Fritz)*; Kyle Ryan Urquhart *(Regis)*; Kumar Pallana *(Mr. LittleJeans)*; Stephen Dignan *(Reuben)*

Though not as fine as his modest but memorable debut feature, BOTTLE ROCKET (1996), writer-director Wes Anderson's second film—the story of an obsessive preppy's unrequited love for both his school and a beautiful widow—displays the same benevolent qualities of bemused affection for its characters and magnanimous indulgence of their foibles.

Fifteen-year-old Max Fischer (Jason Schwartzman), a barber's son, is a scholarship student at Rushmore Academy, a prestigious prep school. Though a compulsive organizer of extracurricular activities, he is poor student.

Max befriends Mr. Blume (Bill Murray), a rich Rushmore benefactor, and falls in love with Miss Cross (Olivia Williams), a first-grade teacher who is still mourning the death of her husband. Although he is gently but firmly rebuffed by the object of his affection, the boy proceeds with plans to erect an aquarium in her honor (and with Mr. Blume's money) on school grounds. For this, along with low grades, he is expelled from Rushmore and compelled to enroll in the local public high school.

Meanwhile, Miss Cross and Mr. Blume, who is unhappily married, are falling in love. After the jealous Max informs on Mr. Blume to Mrs. Blume (Kim Terry), who immediately sues for divorce, a small war erupts between the two former friends.

When Mr. Blume and Miss Cross drift apart, Max has a change of heart and tries to reunite them. He shows further signs of maturation by apologizing to a friend (Mason Gamble) he has hurt, and dropping the pretense that his father (Seymour Cassel) is a neurosurgeon.

Max writes, directs, and stars in an ambitious school play about the Vietnam War. At the party following the spectacular premiere he contentedly dances with Margaret (Sara Tanaka), a schoolmate whose interest in him he has previously spurned. Also dancing together are Mr. Blume and Miss Cross, who seem to be ready to resume their romance.

Were he not such an original talent in his own right, Anderson could be called the Whit Stillman of Middle America. Like Stillman (METROPOLITAN, THE LAST DAYS OF DISCO), he genuinely loves the "white-bread" youth he affectionately satirizes—the kind of people other filmmakers savage or ignore. This tradition, represented at its best by Booth Tarkington and at its worst by Andy Hardy, is long overdue for revival. (A movie version of Tarkington's immortal *Seventeen*, as adapted by Anderson or Stillman, would be a godsend.)

To maintain that RUSHMORE is not as consistently funny, poignant, and surprising as Anderson's first film is not an indictment—BOTTLE ROCKET was a hard act to follow. RUSHMORE's central flaw is the miscasting of the main character. Jason Schwartzman, who resembles Dustin Hoffman in THE GRADUATE (1967) but lacks Hoffman's air of vulnerability, comes across as a brainy kid who doesn't go in for school activities, when the role of Max as written requires the exact opposite.

What was needed was a mid-teen version of the Wilson brothers (costars of BOTTLE ROCKET): Luke, who appears in RUSHMORE as a friend of Miss Cross, and Owen, who wrote the movie in collaboration with the director. Although Anderson looked at 1,800 boys before choosing his Max, Schwartzman fails to convey the hunger and desperation that would explain Max's obsessive behavior. On the other hand, to his great credit, Schwartzman *never* begs us for our pity and does manage to score in the scenes in which Max bluntly insults Miss Cross's dinner escort—the most hilarious sequence in the film.

Bill Murray, one of the drollest actors in America, gets a lot of mileage out of a passive role that offers him few opportunities to display his great comic talents, both verbal and behavioral. He nonetheless makes a strong impression, perhaps because, as Olivia Williams observes, "he has a kind of tragedy in his eyes." *(Adult situations, profanity.)*—D.T.

d, Wes Anderson; p, Barry Mendel, Paul Schiff; exec p, Wes Anderson, Owen Wilson; co-p, John Cameron; w, Wes Anderson, Owen Wilson; ph, Robert Yeoman; ed, David Moritz; m, Mark Mothersbaugh; prod d, David Wasco; art d, Andrew Laws; set d, Alexandra Reynolds-Wasco; anim, David Ridlen; sound, Pawel Wdowczak (mixer); fx, Ron Trost; casting, Mary Gail Artz, Barbara Cohen; cos, Karen Patch; makeup, Robert W. Harper, Sally J. Harper; stunts, David Sanders

Comedy/Drama **(PR: C MPAA: R)**

RUSTY: A DOG'S TALE
(SEE: RUSTY: THE GREAT RESCUE)

RUSTY: THE GREAT RESCUE ★
(U.S., 1998) 92m Saban Entertainment ~ 20th Century Fox Home Entertainment c
(AKA: RUSTY: A DOG'S TALE)

Laraine Newman *(Bertha Bimini)*; Charles Fleischer *(Bart Bimini)*; Hal Holbrook *(Boyd Callahan)*; Rue McClanahan *(Edna Callahan/Voices of Zelda the Duck/Latte the Cow)*; Lucille Oliver *(Wanda)*; Blake Foster *(Jory)*; Danielle Wiener *(Tess)*; Michael Jamon Pagan *(Dylan)*; Beau Billingslea *(Sherriff Wilson)*; Vincent Schiavelli *(Carny Boss)*; Ken Kercheval *(Carl Winthorpe)*; Damara Reilly; Gwendolyn Sanford; Rob Flynn; Lisa Varga; James Mathers; Voices of: Matthew Lawrence *(Rusty the Dog)*; Doug E. Doug *(Turbo the Turtle)*; Bobcat Goldthwaite *(Jet the Turtle)*; Melissa Disney *(Boo the Cat)*; Jennifer Darling *(Mrs. Cluck)*; Jane Singer *(Ellie the Elephant/Koo the Pigeon)*; Suzanne Somers *(Malley)*; Patrick Duffy *(Cap)*; Rodney Dangerfield *(Bandit the Rabbit)*; Charlie Adler *(Agent the Snake)*; Mary Kay Bergman *(Myrtle the Duck)*; Frank Welker *(Boss Duck)*; Tony Oliver *(Gabby the Goat/Rebel)*; Nick Jameson *(Ratchet the Racoon)*; Wendee Lee; Michael Sorich; Julie Maddalena; James Cummings; Steve Kramer; Chad Einbinder; Brianne Siddall

Saban Entertainment, the company behind TV's "Mighty Morphin Power Rangers" and other downmarket kiddie diversions, crafted this cloying talking-critter comedy.

A combination animal-shelter/farm run by kindly Boyd and Edna Callahan (Hal Holbrook, Rue McClanahan) is visited by their younger clodhopper "cousins" Bart and Bertha Bimini (Charles Fleischer, Laraine Newman). The duo demand custody of the Callahan's grandchildren, Tess and Jory (Danielle Wiener, Blake Foster), and with them control of the rich trust fund set up for the children by their parents who died. Vowing to get the kids, the pair slink off, and later spy wealthy Karl Winthorpe (Ken Kercheval) shopping for a puppy for his own ailing little girl. Winthrope's promise of $300 will help finance the Bimini's evil schemes, so they sneak back to the Callahan farm and abduct a whole litter of puppies to offer the millionaire. The loss is noticed first by the farm animals—who speak to each other out loud in English. Rusty the dog (voice of Matthew Lawrence), mixed-breed elder brother of the pups, leads the rescue, even enlisting the aid of wild beasts he meets along the way. He traces the scent to the Bimini's hovel, and Tess and Jory remove the pups, while Rusty rallies all the farm animals in an attack. The strength of Ellie the Elephant and some well-aimed guano by Koo the Pigeon (both voiced by Jane Singer) send the Bimini's shabby van crashing into a pond, and Bart and Bertha are arrested.

Saban (which also acquired the rights to the character of Casper, the Friendly Ghost for a series of direct-to-video features) has seldom been noted for subtlety or thoughtfulness, but even by their frenetic standards RUSTY: THE GREAT RESCUE is awful. A bunch of goggle-eyed performances, syrupy sentiment, and dumb scripting demonstrate clearly why underaged viewers often prefer the R-rated company of Freddy Kreuger or the Terminator to such wholesome fare as this. Seemingly inspired by profitable talking-animal features like BABE (1996) and Disney's HOMEWARD BOUND series (canine lead Lawrence sounds like the latter's mutt hero vocalized by Michael J. Fox), the feature uses high-tech puppetry and computer graphics to make the various species' mouths flawlessly mimic human lips—a refinement of trick-film techniques using live barnyard animals that were masterminded by cartoonists like Tex Avery decades ago. In addition, the presence of exotic tropical fauna (elephants, alligators) in an American setting passes without comment.

There's a touch of imagination in the offscreen cast, like reuniting Suzanne Somers and Patrick Duffy of the TV sitcom "Step by Step" as husband-and-wife dogs; at least they're less obnoxious by far than Newman and Fleischer (the voice of "Roger Rabbit"), who are way overboard as yahoo villains. Director Shuki Levy has composed music for many productions, perhaps explaining why the whole film is set to a nonstop score that telegraphs every emotion with blaring bombast or bothersome ballads. The suitable capper is a closing montage that is accompanied by the notoriously painful novelty tune, "Disco Duck" (written and performed by Rick Dees).—C.C.

d, Shuki Levy; p, Craig Golin; exec p, Haim Saban, Shuki Levy, Tony Oliver; assoc p, J.B. Levine, Lisa Krantz; w, Shuki Levy, Shell Danielson; ph, Frank Byers; ed, Priscilla Nedd-Friendly; m, Inon Zur; prod d, Yuda Ako; art d, Steve Miller; sound, Robert R. Rutledge, William M. Fiege, Yehuda Maayan; fx, Tom Burton, Loni Peristere; casting, Katy Wallin, Thom Klohn; cos, Marcelle McKay; makeup, Lily Gart; stunts, Brad Bovee

Children's/Comedy **(PR: A MPAA: G)**

S

SAFE MEN ★★
(U.S., 1998) 99m Andell Entertainment; Blue Guitar Films ~ October Films c

Sam Rockwell *(Sam)*; Steve Zahn *(Eddie)*; Mark Ruffalo *(Frank)*; Josh Pais *(Mitchell)*; Harvey Fierstein *(Good Stuff Leo)*; Michael Lerner *(Big Fat Bernie Gayle)*; Paul Giamatti *(Veal Chop)*; Christina Kirk *(Hannah)*; Michael Schmidt *(Bernie Jr.)*; Mark Shanahan *(Party Coordinator)*; Raymond Serra *(Barber)*; Ray Iannicelli *(Swoop)*; Jacob Reynolds *(Cousin Ira)*; Peter Dinklage *(Leflore)*; Michael Showalter *(Larry)*; Adam Morenoff *(Victor)*; John Tormey *(Older Guy)*; Don Picard *(Gunter)*; Carl Don *(Hyman)*; Allen Swift *(Sol)*; John Hamburg *(Philip)*; Ali Marsh *(Sherry)*; Emily Doubilet *("Sweet" Denise Schneider)*; Sidney Zubrow *(Pappy)*; Mr. Blue *(M.C. Victor)*; Ellen M. Hauptman *(Joyce Kaufman)*; Dee Dee Friedman *(Barbara)*; Seth Herzog *(Gold Trophy)*; Richard Bolster *(Gold Trophy)*; Brian Mullen *(Himself)*; Ian Helfer *(Janusz)*; Eric Bogosian *(Voice of Edward Templeton Sr.)*

SAFE MEN is a mildly amusing and well-acted but undistinguished little comedy about a pair of bungling safe crackers.

Sam (Sam Rockwell) and Eddie (Steve Zahn) are tricked into appearing before crime boss "Big Fat" Bernie (Michael Lerner) and his assistant Veal Chop (Paul Giamatti), who have mistaken the two for professional safe crackers. Though Sam and Eddie are aware of Bernie's error, for fear of him they agree to go along with his plan for a series of burglaries.

On their first assignment, Sam and Eddie break into an upscale home, but are caught by Hannah (Christina Kirk), a young woman who lives there. Although Hannah knows what they are up to, she lets them go when they agree not to steal anything. Bernie excuses the failure but warns that the subsequent robberies must be successful. On their second effort, Sam and Eddie unwittingly compete with another pair of thieves, who empty the safe ahead of them. When Bernie learns what has happened, he threatens to kill the two if they fail again. Sam, meanwhile, begins to court Hannah, and meets her gangster father, "Goodstuff" Leo (Harvey Fierstein), a rival of Bernie's.

On their third try, the duo successfully break into a safe in a synagogue, simultaneously with the bar mitzvah of Bernie's son in the same building. Bernie is pleased with the theft and orders another, of The Stanley Cup from Leo. Sam tells Hannah of the planned robbery and in anger, she breaks off their relationship. Although the theft goes according to plan, Sam has the Cup returned to its "rightful" owner, Leo, in order to placate Hannah. Having become an accomplished safe cracker, Eddie joins a professional gang. Hannah, meanwhile, demonstrates her forgiveness of Sam by dancing with him at a party for Bernie's son.

SAFE MEN could be described as a professional student film. The feature debut of writer-director John Hamburg has the spirited but unpracticed quality of a work produced by an ambitious bunch of film students who have outdone themselves in an effort to impress their professor. Many of Hamburg's crew are newcomers, including producers Ellen Bronfman and Andrew Hauptman, cinematographer Michael Barrett, and production designer Anthony Gasparro. Their collective lack of professional experience manifests itself in the film's tame, prescriptive approach to filmmaking, and so while SAFE MEN is competently made, it's not particularly impressive.

SAFE MEN also evinces the most unfortunate of recent independent film trends in its aping of Quentin Tarantino's films. Hamburg stocks the film with rock songs, references to cultural trivia, and characters who are supposed to be amusingly amoral, in obvious deference to RESERVOIR DOGS (1992), TRUE ROMANCE (1993), and of course, PULP FICTION (1994). Hamburg probably intends to show that he is as hip and attuned to the eminence of pop culture as his forebear (of half a decade), but more often than not, the inclusion of such material makes his film seem sophomoric and derivative.

Yet Hamburg does seem to have a way with actors, and SAFE MEN's cast is its chief asset. Low-budget film perennials Sam Rockwell (BOX OF MOONLIGHT) and Steve Zahn (SUBURBIA) are funny and likable as the lovable losers of the title. Michael Lerner, Harvey Fierstein, and Paul Giamatti are ingratiating, as always, each giving a thoroughly enjoyable performance. Hamburg deserves credit for maintaining a high level of inspiration among his actors, a level that is consistent from such seasoned veterans as Lerner to such relative novices as Christina Kirk.

On the whole, though, SAFE MEN is too conventional and imitative to make it notable. It's a film that strives to be offbeat and quirky, but it ultimately plays things a bit too safely. *(Violence, extreme profanity.)*—D.C.

d, John Hamburg; p, Andrew Hauptman, Ellen Bronfman, Jeffrey Clifford, Jonathan Cohen; assoc p, Rain Kramer; w, John Hamburg; ph, Michael Barrett; ed, Suzanne Pillsbury; m, Theodore Shapiro; prod d, Anthony Gasparro; art d, Ondine Karady; sound, Coll Anderson (mixer); casting, Avy Kaufman; cos, Cat Thomas; makeup, Kyra Panchenko

Crime/Comedy **(PR: C MPAA: NR)**

SALTMEN OF TIBET, THE ★★½
(Switzerland/Germany, 1997) 110m Captics Coproductions; Duran Film ~ Zeitgeist Films c
(DIE SALZMANNER VON TIBET)

THE SALTMEN OF TIBET provides a rare, inside look at the vanishing world of Tibetan nomads. This meditative documentary misses opportunities to develop a wider story or a particular point of view, but makes a painstaking attempt to cover a culture's rough method of survival.

Director Ulrike Koch begins THE SALTMEN OF TIBET by interviewing the villagers of northern Tibet before their annual spring pilgrimage to the Himalayan lakes, where they gather their most precious trading commodity, raw salt. Koch discovers that the women are forbidden to travel with the men, because of superstitious legends.

During the three-month trip along flat terrain, the tribesmen fight against snow and hail and the ailing health of one of their yaks, which eventually dies. Finally, the men reach Lake Tsentso, where they begin the process of raking up the wet salt, letting the heaps dry, then packing and sewing up the salt into bags, which the yaks carry back to the village. Before leaving the lake, however, the tribesmen pray to a Tibetan Goddess, Matsenten, for success with their bounty. Finally, the tribesmen solemnly return to the village.

THE SALTMEN OF TIBET appears to be a labor of love of director Koch, an ethnographer who shot this film secretly with a digital video camera so as not to alert disapproving Chinese authorities. Koch clearly is fascinated with the ancient but still active "saltman" culture, and her documentary reverently reflects a desire to preserve and record their lives for posterity. The sad, mournful undertone of a civilization lost is best captured in the beautiful, haunting vistas that provide a backdrop to the tribesmen's journey (the lengthy final shot of the travelers, accompanied by discordant yak sounds, is the most memorable).

It's too bad that Koch, who is thorough but not conceptual, chose not to document the political and economic realities that have directly influenced the lives of the Tibetan tribe. It would have been much more topical (and dramatic) to have included something about the Chinese oppression of Tibet, which also apparently affected the course of Koch's filming approach. Likewise, the German-born Koch should have included more of herself in the film, rather than pretend, a la Robert Flaherty, that she wasn't present on the journey (plus her problems getting the film made might have made fascinating on-screen material).

Still, Koch's humanist ideals (and feminism in the scenes with the women villagers) give dignity to documentary subjects that might have been less well treated by a different filmmaker.—E.M.

d, Ulrike Koch; exec p, Alfi Sinniger; co-p, Christophe Bicker, Knut Winkler; w, Ulrike Koch; ph, Pio Corradi; ed, Magdolna Rokob; m, Stefan Wulff, Frank Wulff; sound, Andreas Koppen, Uve Haussig

Documentary **(PR: A MPAA: NR)**

SAME OLD SONG ★★★½

(France, 1997) 120m Arena Films; Camera One; France 2 Cinema; Vega Films; Greenpoint; Canal+; Cofimage 9; Sofineurope; Alia Film; Television Suisse Romande; European Coproduction Fund c
(ON CONNAIT LA CHANSON)

Pierre Artidi *(Claude)*; Sabine Azema *(Odile Lalande)*; Jean-Pierre Bacri *(Nicolas)*; Andre Dussollier *(Simon)*; Agnes Jaoui *(Camille Lalande)*; Lambert Wilson *(Marc Duveyrier)*; Jane Birkin *(Jane)*; Jean-Paul Roussillon *(Father)*

A musical comedy from one of the *Nouvelle Vague*'s most rigorous aesthetes? Densely plotted and endearingly neurotic, SAME OLD SONG is Alain Resnais's tribute to the work of brilliant British tele-playwright Dennis Potter (THE SINGING DETECTIVE). As befits Resnais's past work, the film is an intricately structured piece, but its good-natured charm and likeable cast of characters ensure that it will strike a chord in the hearts of lovestruck city-dwellers everywhere.

In present-day Paris, tour guide Camille (Agnes Jaoui) encounters Nicolas (Jean-Pierre Bacri), who's newly arrived in town, and is interested in meeting with his ex-girlfriend, Camille's sister Odile (Sabine Azema). Nicolas has dinner with Odile and her husband Claude (Pierre Artidi), and discusses how he's looking for an apartment for himself, his wife, and their two children. He also talks about the fact that he's been unable to find a doctor who can diagnose the unspecified malady from which he's suffering.

In the meantime, Camille has been busily preparing her doctoral thesis on an obscure historical topic; while doing research, she meets Simon (Andre Dussollier), who has been frequenting Camille's tour groups. He is infatuated with her, but treads lightly. Camille soon meets and falls for Odile's realtor Marc (Lambert Wilson), who has found a dream apartment, with a marvelous view of the Parisian skyline, for Odile and Claude.

Simon becomes a close friend and confidante of Camille, but he continues to tell her about a sideline of his (writing radio plays), rather than admit to his more staid job—he, in fact, works for the very bossy Marc at the realty office. Camille's moment of truth arrives: she makes the presentation of her doctoral thesis, and has a panic attack afterwards. Though she has no life-threatening malady, her unnameable "nervous disorder" comes to dominate her life. Simon attempts to lift her depressed spirits, but is hurt by the discovery that Marc is her boyfriend. Claude and Odile, meanwhile, are preparing to move into their new apartment. What the always-in-control Odile doesn't know is that Claude is planning to leave her for another woman. Nicolas also has marital troubles: his wife Jane (Jane Birkin) arrives in town to check on his progress in finding an apartment; he reveals that he still hasn't settled on anything. The two argue, and Jane returns home.

The night of Odile and Claude's housewarming party arrives, and various truths emerge. Firstly, Nicolas and Camille speak about their respective maladies, and find strength in the fact that they both suffer from the same mixture of depression and anxiety. Then, Simon reveals to Nicolas the "secret" about Odile's dream apartment: its idyllic view will soon be blocked by a housing project. Nicolas informs Odile, and in a complete turnabout, Claude comforts her and tells off Marc, instead of saying farewell to Odile. Having learned of Marc's duplicity, Camille breaks with him, leaving Simon a chance to become more central in her life. Nicolas speaks on the phone to Jane, attempting to iron out their difficulties.

While honoring the spirit of Dennis Potter's musical fantasies (PENNIES FROM HEAVEN, "Lipstick on Your Collar"), Resnais adds a new wrinkle to Potter's powerful technique of having characters suddenly lip-synch to popular music: the characters here only mouth *parts* of the songs chosen by Resnais and scripters Agnes Jaoui and Jean-Pierre Bacri. The lyrics serve as supplementary dialogue to illuminate their feelings about a situation; often, only a few short lines of a song are used, and the characters immediately return to the "reality" of the situation. Resnais's approach thus integrates the music more fully into the proceedings, but also proves mildly frustrating, as songs are introduced and then quickly discarded. One can only surmise from this that Resnais's connection to the music being played is not as strong or emotional as Potter's was. Resnais's love of "standard" popular music shone through in "Gershwin," his 1991 television documentary about the life of the composer, but SAME OLD SONG goes for long stretches without any musical "punctuation," thus almost negating the evocative strength of Potter's technique. In addition, American viewers will be further intrigued and frustrated by the sudden disposal of the music, as the songs contained in the film are a range of French pop hits from the 1930s to the '80s, none being familiar to American ears.

This single stylistic quirk aside, the film is a delightful study of modern love that benefits from a top-notch ensemble cast and witty scripting. Jaoui and Bacri (who also scripted UN AIR DE FAMILLE, released in the US in 1998) offer some perceptive insights about various types (the control freak, the constant worrier, the user) in a surprisingly light and airy package. They also turn in fine performances as the most angst-ridden of the bunch.

The film's careful structure obviously originated with the screenplay, but Resnais's consistent approach to the material, and his emphasis on the hope that love offers each of the characters, makes this one of the most accessible, and strictly entertaining, projects he's ever worked on. Thus it was no surprise the film was his most popular in Europe since his last comedy, MON ONCLE D'AMERIQUE (1980). And with its profusion of characters, plots, and snippets of songs, SAME OLD SONG qualifies as yet another Resnais film that becomes richer with repeated viewings. *(Adult situations.)*—E.G.

d, Alain Resnais; exec p, Bruno Pesery; assoc p, Michael Seydoux, Ruth Waldburger; w, Agnes Jaoui, Jean-Pierre Bacri; ph, Renato Berta; ed, Herve de Luze; m, Bruno Fontaine; prod d, Jacques Saulnier; sound, Pierre Lenoir; cos, Jackie Budin

Musical/Comedy/Drama **(PR: C MPAA: NR)**

SAND TRAP ★★★½

(U.S., 1998) 100m Marjan Street Entertainment; Looking Glass Films ~ PM Entertainment c

David John James *(Nelson Yeagher)*; Brad Koepenick *(Jack)*; Elizabeth Morehead *(Margo Yeagher)*; Bob Thompson *(Sheriff)*; Kirk Woller *(Carl)*; Sharon Stelling *(Tilly)*; David Gibbs *(Helicopter Pilot)*; Terry Palmer *(Gas Attendant)*; Steve Brownyard *(Zeke)*

A wounded man is hunted in the desert by his murderous wife and her lover in this satisfying, darkly-humored suspense thriller.

The day after nebbishy Nelson Yeagher (David John James) is nearly killed in his house by a masked intruder, his best friend and lawyer Jack (Brad Koepenick) drives him and his sexy wife Margo (Elizabeth Morehead) to the desert to look at an investment property. Jack takes Nelson up a cliff for the view and then pushes him over the side; it was he who tried to shoot Nelson the night before. Jack and Margo are longtime lovers who have planned to kill him for his money and insurance. But when they bring the sheriff (Bob Thompson), to the scene of the "accident" the next morning, there's no body; Nelson survived the fall and walked away, only to become lost in the desert. A cat-and-mouse game ensues in which Jack and Margo attempt to find and kill Nelson without causing the sheriff to become suspicious as he also searches. As Nelson grows more resourceful from his ordeal, Jack and Margo begin to bicker. The sheriff figures out Jack and Margo's plan, and is killed by a bullet meant for Nelson. Jack dies when he falls into a mine shaft where Nelson is hiding. In a final confrontation, Nelson tries to offer forgiveness to his wife, but she is killed by backfire when she tries to shoot him with a gun whose barrel is clogged with dirt.

SAND TRAP isn't quite up to the level of films like Joel and Ethan Coen's BLOOD SIMPLE (1984), Sam Raimi's THE EVIL DEAD (1983), or John Dahl's RED ROCK WEST (1993), but it's in that class: a smart thriller from an obviously intelligent filmmaker with an ability to work well with a small budget and unknown cast. Debuting director and cowriter Harris Done, a former cinematographer (whose credits range from straight-to-video titles like SINFUL INTRIGUE to the prestigious, Spielberg-produced 1999 documentary THE LAST DAYS), avoids letting his material become either too nasty or too comic, though he could probably have mined more humor from this pair of oversexed murderers who aren't nearly as smart as they think they are. The one scene in the film that rings false is one that occurs before we know that Jack and Margo are lovers: he enters her room, pretending to rape her in what turns out to be a sex game they play. (It wasn't any better in 1969 when it was done in BUTCH CASSIDY AND THE SUNDANCE KID.) All of the leads are good, particularly Elizabeth Morehead in a juicily villainous role. SAND TRAP was voted the audience favorite at the 1997 Newport Beach International Film Festival. *(Violence, nudity, sexual situations, adult situations, substance abuse, profanity.)*—M.F.

d, Harris Done; p, Erik Done, Harris Done, Jerry Rapp; exec p, Kevin S. Bogart, Garrett P. Kreditor; assoc p, Cain DeVore, Elizabeth Hooper; co-p, Linda Miller; w, Harris Done, Jerry Rapp; ph, Roy Unger, Mark W. Gray; ed, Michael Mayhew; m, Bennet Salvay; prod d, Naython Vane; art d, Daniel Harrison Bornstein; sound, Patrick Rideaux; fx, Wayne Beauchamp; cos, Sevilla Granger; makeup, Gail Bailey Brownyard; stunts, Chuck Borden

Drama/Thriller **(PR: C MPAA: R)**

SAVING PRIVATE RYAN ★★★★

(U.S., 1998) 170m DreamWorks SKG; Mutual Film; Paramount ~ DreamWorks SKG c

Tom Hanks (Captain Miller); Tom Sizemore (Sergeant Horvath); Edward Burns (Private Reiben); Barry Pepper (Private Jackson); Adam Goldberg (Private Mellish); Vin Diesel (Private Caparzo); Giovanni Ribisi (T/4 Medic Wade); Jeremy Davies (Corporal Upham); Matt Damon (Private Ryan); Ted Danson (Captain Hamill); Paul Giamatti (Sergeant Hill); Dennis Farina (Lieutenant Colonel Anderson); Joerg Stadler (Steamboat Willie); Maximilian Martini (Corporal Henderson); Dylan Bruno (Toynbe); Daniel Cerqueira (Weller); Demetri Goritsas (Parker); Ian Porter (Trask); Gary Sefton (Rice); Julian Spencer (Garrity); Steve Griffin (Wilson); William Marsh (Lyle); Marc Cass (Fallon); Markus Napier (Major Hoess); Neil Finnighan (Ramelle Paratrooper); Peter Miles (Ramelle Paratrooper); Paul Garcia (Field HQ Major); Seamus McQuade (Field HQ Aide); Ronald Longridge (Coxswain); Adam Shaw (Delancey); Rolf Saxon (Lieutenant Briggs); Corey Johnson (Radioman); Loclann Aiken; John Barnett; MacLean Burke; Victor Burke; Aiden Condron; Paschal Friel; Shane Hagan; Paul Hickey; Shane Johnson; Laird MacIntosh; Brian Maynard; Martin McDougall; Mark Phillips; Lee Rosen; Andrew Scott; Matthew Sharp; Vincent Walsh; Grahame Wood (Soldiers on the Beach); John Sharian (Corporal); Glenn Wrage (Boyle); Crofton Hardester (Senior Medical Officer); Martin Hub (Czech Wermacht Soldier); Raph Taylor (Goldman); Nigel Whitmey (Private Boyd); Sam Ellis (Private Hastings); Erich Redman (German No 1); Tilo Keiner (German No 2); Stephan Grothgar (German No 3—Voice on Bullhorn); Stephan Cornicard (Jean); Michelle Evans (Jean's Wife); Martin Beaton (Jean's Son); Anna Maguire (Jean's Daughter); Nathan Fillion (Minessota Ryan); Leland Orser (Lieutanant DeWindt); Michael Mantas (Paratrooper Lieutenant); David Vegh (Paratrooper Oliver); Ryan Hurst (Paratrooper Michaelson); Nick Brooks (Paratrooper Joe); Sam Scudder (Paratrooper No 1); John Walters (Old French Man); Dorothy Grumbar (Old French Woman); James Innes-Smith (MP Lieutenant); Harve Presnell (General Marshall); Dale Dye (War Department Colonel); Bryan Cranston (War Department Colonel); David Wohl (War Department Captain); Eric Loren (War Department Lieutenant); Valerie Colgan (War Department Clerk); Amanda Boxer (Mrs. Margaret Ryan); Harrison Young (Ryan as Old Man); Kathleen Byron (Old Mrs. Ryan); Rob Freeman (Ryan's Son); Thomas Gizbert (Ryan's Grandson)

Shunning the usual war movie hokum, Steven Spielberg suffuses his WWII epic with an air of grim necessity. SAVING PRIVATE RYAN, a bravura display of filmmaking, gives patriotism and glory a back seat to stomach-turning reality, particularly during the opening 25-minute re-creation of the D-Day landing on Omaha beach. The film won five Oscars, including Best Director.

June 6, 1944. American soldiers nervously prepare for the invasion of Normandy. Landing by water, they scramble up the beach, the majority downed by German snipers. A few finally gain cover. Captain Miller (Tom Hanks), with help from his right-hand man Sergeant Horvath (Tom Sizemore) and sharpshooter Private Jackson (Barry Pepper), leads a battalion that finally crushes German resistance and takes the beach.

Back in the US, the army informs a middle-aged mother that three of her four sons have been killed in combat during the same week. General Marshall (Harve Presnell) orders that the fourth son, James Patrick Ryan (Matt Damon), who parachuted into Normandy behind enemy lines, be rescued and sent home. Captain Miller is assigned the duty. Not knowing where to find one soldier among so many, he marches across the French countryside with Horvath, Jackson and six other men, including Private Mellish (Adam Goldberg), cynical Brooklynite Private Reiben

(Edward Burns), and the clumsy, bookish translator Corporal Upham (Jeremy Davies).

Along the way, Miller loses several of his men; first in an incident involving a French family whose pleas for help cause one of the soldiers to fatally let down his guard, and later when they attack a German machine gun post. Miller's men argue over what to do with the one German survivor, and when Upham talks them out of executing him, Reiben mutinies, fed up with the sacrifices they are making for the sake of one unknown man. Miller defuses the situation by revealing his background, which has been the subject of curiosity (and a betting pool); he is not a veteran military man, but rather a schoolteacher from Pennsylvania.

When they finally find Ryan, the private refuses to leave his post, where he and a few comrades are protecting an important bridge. Miller decides to deploy his men alongside these survivors, on what appears to be a hopeless but important mission. Undermanned and poorly armed, they try to defend the bridge against a swarm of well-equipped Germans. One of them, the soldier freed through Upham's intercession, cruelly murders Mellish while Upham watches, paralyzed with fear. All seems lost until an air strike saves the day. Upham captures and executes the German soldier he now regrets setting free. The planes, and a safe Private Ryan, are the last images seen by a dying Captain Miller. Fifty years later, Ryan, now an old man (Harrison Young), visits Miller's grave with his children and grandchildren and weeps, wondering if he has earned what was done for him.

Reversing the tide of too many films, Spielberg sets about to make violence repellent again. SAVING PRIVATE RYAN resensitizes the audience, not only through authentically grisly recreations of battle, but also by creating an atmosphere of fear and randomness. A lucky GI examines his helmet after a bullet glanced off of it; a second later another bullet pierces his brain. Audience expectations formed from years of Hollywood cliches are repeatedly subverted as Spielberg tries to depict the reality rather than the myth of war.

Oscar winners Spielberg and cinematographer Janusz Kaminski shoot the battles as if the cameraman is in as much danger as the combatant. The subjective camera bounces near the surface water (a la Spielberg's JAWS, 1975) and then moves for cover on the beach, blood and water splattering onto the lens. Forget about flying bicycles and computer-generated velociraptors; Hollywood's favorite son has abandoned escapism. He's intent on transporting us back to the blood-soaked beaches and bombed-out cities of 1944.

One Spielbergism continues to hold: he's never met a tear duct he didn't like. In SCHINDLER'S LIST (1993), Spielberg maintained an air of tense reality until the overwrought "I could've done more" sequence when Schindler gets a gold ring from his charges on the tear-drenched train tracks. SAVING PRIVATE RYAN suffers from the amateurish framing device of the elder Ryan crying at Miller's grave. Tom Hanks's performance as Miller brings consistent truth to every moment: to cut from his world to a stiff old man delivering corny lines that question the goodness of his life, elicits the wrong kind of pain. However, it's easy to overlook such sentimental wrongheadedness from a film that attains such memorable heights. *(Extreme violence, profanity.)*—T.Y.

d, Steven Spielberg; p, Steven Spielberg, Ian Bryce, Mark Gordon, Gary Levinsohn; assoc p, Mark Huffam, Kevin De La Noy; co-p, Bonnie Curtis, Allison Lyon Segan; w, Robert Rodat; ph, Janusz Kaminski; ed, Michael Kahn; m, John Williams; prod d, Tom Sanders; art d, Daniel T. Dorrance, Ricky Eyres, Tom Brown, Chris Seagers, Alan Tomkins; set d, Lisa Dean Kavanaugh; sound, Gary Rydstrom (design), Ronald Judkins (mixer), Gary Summers, Andy Nelson, Richard Hymns; fx, Neil Corbould, Carol McAulay; casting, Denise Chamian; cos, Joanna Johnston; makeup, Lois Burwell, Conor O'Sullivan, Daniel C. Striepeke; stunts, Simon Crane; tech, Effects

AA Best Director: Steven Spielberg; *AA Best Cinematography:* Janusz Kaminski; *AA Best Film Editing:* Michael Kahn; *AA Best Sound:* Gary Rydstrom, Gary Summers, Andy Nelson, Ronald Judkins; *AA Best Sound Effects Editing:* Gary Rydstrom, Richard Hymns; *AAN Best Picture; AAN Best Actor:* Tom Hanks; *AAN Best Original Screenplay:* Robert Rodat; *AAN Best Art Direction:* Tom Sanders, Lisa Dean Kavanaugh; *AAN Best Makeup:* Lois Burwell, Conor O'Sullivan, Daniel C. Striepeke; *AAN Best Original Dramatic Score:* John Williams

War/Drama **(PR: O MPAA: R)**

SAVIOR ★★

(U.S., 1998) 103m Ixtlan Productions; Initial Entertainment Group ~ Lions Gate Films c

Dennis Quaid *(Joshua Rose/Guy)*; Nastassja Kinski *(Maria Rose)*; Stellan Skarsgard *(Dominic)*; Natasa Ninkovic *(Vera)*; Sergej Trifunovic *(Goran)*; Nebojsa Glogovac *(Vera's Brother)*; Vesna Trivalic *(Woman on Bus)*; Pascal Rollin *(Paris Priest)*; Catlin Foster *(Christian Rose)*; John McLaren *(Colonel)*; Irfan Mensur *(Drill Sergeant)*; Kosta Andrejevic *(Boy on Bridge)*; Ljiljana Krstic *(Old Lady)*; Sanja Zogovic *(Girl on Bridge)*; Veljko Otasevic *(Orthodox Priest)*; Marina Bukvicki *(Muslim Girl)*; Dusan Perkovic *(Uncle Ratko)*; Dajana Radevic; Sanja Borodenko; Aleksandra Bordenko; Toskovic Darka *(Babies)*; Ljiljana Blagojevic *(Vera's Mother)*; Modrag Krstovic *(Vera's Father)*; Dusan Janicijevic *(Old Man)*; Renata Ulmanski *(Old Woman)*; Svetozar Cvetkovic *(Croat Officer)*; Josif Tatic *(Chief Executioner)*; Cedo Dragovic *(Driver)*

Ambitiously conceived but unimaginatively written and directed, SAVIOR views the Serbo-Croatian conflict through the eyes of a disillusioned soldier of fortune as he reluctantly escorts an outcast Serbian woman through her ravaged country.

In 1987, after his wife and son are slain in a Muslim Fundamentalist bomb attack in Paris, US military officer Josh Rose (Dennis Quaid) vengefully opens fire on innocent Muslim worshippers at a mosque. Whisked away from the crime scene by his comrade Dominic (Stellan Skarsgard), Josh joins the Foreign Legion with Dominic (who's later killed by a Muslim girl).

In 1993, hired gun Josh and his vicious Serbian trainee Goran (Sergej Trifunovic) participate in a Muslim-Serb prisoner exchange in Bosnia. Xenophobic Goran takes personal custody of Vera (Natasa Ninkovic), a girl from his village who had been raped and impregnated by a Muslim soldier. On the way home, Muslim-hating Goran repeatedly kicks Vera in the stomach to dispose of both her and her unborn child. When the beating hastens the onset of childbirth, Josh shoots Goran to prevent him from slaying Vera and her baby girl.

Josh drives them home, but Vera's father (Modrag Krstovic) shuns her for disgracing the family. While Josh is accompanying Vera and the baby to a refugee camp, Goran's corpse is discovered and Vera's father and brother (Nebojsa Glogovac) are ordered to hunt her down. Although he wounds the interfering Josh, Vera's father cannot bring himself to kill his daughter and granddaughter.

Vera and Josh cannot prevent enemy soldiers from rounding up her family and neighbors for a firing squad. Driving until they run out of gas, Josh and Vera encounter a Serb peasant and his Croat wife, who nurse Josh and give him their boat.

Arriving at a port with bus service, Vera seeks transportation, while Josh hides with the baby in an abandoned boat. Vera and other civilians are rounded up by soldiers who brutally execute them while outnumbered Josh watches helplessly. Escaping detection by the soldiers, Josh walks to the bus and pays his fare with a crucifix that belonged to his dead wife. Instead of abandoning Vera's child at a Red Cross center, unexpected father Josh allows a kindly stranger to drive him and the infant to a hospital.

Alternately brutal and sentimental, this true-life saga relates a redemptive fable in the form of a picaresque war adventure, but sententiousness overrides suspense and action. Every encounter between embittered Josh and battered Vera schematically documents their emotional progress. It's far too obvious when they will hit certain emotional guideposts on their journey back to full humanity. Instead of gleaning insight from the saga of a mercenary seizing a second chance at decency, the writer squeezes this fable (with its Nativity angle) through a wringer of Hollywood formulas. Vera rejects her child; Josh renounces compassion; both end up embracing the pain of others and rediscovering their own dormant virtue.

Although SAVIOR has its assets (e.g., stunning cinematography, believable support from the foreign supporting cast, authentic local color), the script is simplistic and the direction pedestrian, framing every dramatic climax in obvious setups. There are so many close-ups of Quaid fingering his late wife's crucifix, that his inevitable sacrifice of this heirloom becomes meaningless.

Clearly, the filmmakers' hearts were in the right place when they chose this real-life parable to edify the audience. However, although we comprehend the poignancy of a soul-dead soldier learning to love a motherless babe, his instant fatherhood is not particularly challenging for an audience primed for more compelling insights from a distillation of the Serb-Croat-Muslim hostilities. Instead of enlightening us about this ongoing tragedy, the screenwriter tells us what we already know. *(Graphic violence, extreme profanity, adult situations.)*—R.P.

d, Peter Antonijevic; p, Oliver Stone, Janet Yang; exec p, Cindy Cowan; assoc p, Molly M. Mayeux, Scott Moore; co-p, Naomi Despres, Joseph Bruggeman; w, Robert Orr; ph, Ian Wilson; ed, Ian Crafford, Gabriella Cristiani; m, David Robbins; prod d, Vladislav Lasic; set d, Jovan Radomirovic, Ljubomir Mrsovic; sound, Bill Fiege (mixer); fx, Louis Craig; casting, Mary Vernieu; cos, Boris Caksiran, Ginette Magny; makeup, Giancarlo Del Brocco, Martina Subic; stunts, David McKeown

War/Drama **(PR: O MPAA: R)**

SCARRED CITY ★½

(U.S., 1998) 95m Millenium Films ~ Nu Image c

Stephen Baldwin *(John Trace)*; Chazz Palminteri *(Lt. Laine Devon)*; Tia Carrere *(Candy)*; Michael Rispoli *(Sammy Bandusky)*; Larry Manetti *(Paul)*; Bray Poor *(Zero)*; Dana Eskelson *(Janice)*; Gary Dourdan *(Sgt. Creedy)*; Steven Flynn *(Bobby)*; D.B. Woodside *(Forrest)*; Herschel Sparber *(Tito)*; James Villemaire *(Speedy)*; Matt Saha *(Bad Boy)*; Dexter Locke *(Long Coat)*; Andy Duppin *(Short Coat)*; Al Thompson *(Ski Jacket)*; Jalil Lynch *(Denim)*; Jerry Walsh *(Bar Heckler)*; Heidi Jo Markel *(Faith)*; Sarah Carone *(Georgy)*; Lou Cantres *(Rafael Soto)*; Mick O'Rourke *(Mike)*; Mike Massa *(Flaco)*; Dylan Price *(Ted Crewe)*; Chuck Zito *(Guard)*; Sharon Scruggs *(Bartender)*; Frank Ferrara *(Terry)*; Renee Estevez *(Cop)*; David Zayas *(Cop)*; Jeffrey Buehl *(Dealer)*; Chad Courtney *(Druggy)*; Manny Silverio *(Druggy)*; Andrew Davoli *(Paramedic)*; Collette Wilson *(Paramedic)*; Bobby Unser Jr. *(Ted)*

This slapped-together, excessive-force flick uses an anti-vigilante springboard to celebrate police brutality. The violent sequences aren't imaginatively stylized; the good-cop vs. bad-cop situations aren't freshly realized; the filmmakers are half in love with what they're condemning.

Although gung-ho police detective John Trace (Stephen Baldwin) has killed four suspects in the line of duty, he's spared an Internal Affairs investigation when Lt. Laine Devon (Chazz Palminteri) selects him for his unconventional task force, SCAR (Select Unit Armed Response). Resented by his less principled comrades like Zero (Bray Poor) who kill blindly without asking questions, Trace can't sanction Lt. Devon's orders to take no prisoners.

In a strike on a druglord's mansion, the SCAR commandos exterminate not only the dealers, but also two hookers who witnessed the carnage. Trace is able to let one prostitute, Candy (Tia Carrere) escape; but her pimp Paul (Larry Manetti) and his mob boss Sammy Bandusky (Michael Rispoli) agree to turn her over to Lt. Devon in the hopes he'll steer clear of their illegal franchises.

Sammy blabs about Trace's good samaritanism to Devon, who orders that Trace be ambushed during a routine assault. But Trace gets away and rescues Candy from Paul's strip joint. When SCAR officers attack Candy's house, Trace guns them down. After forcing Paul to set up a rendezvous for Sammy and Devon, Trace wounds Sammy's henchmen and shoots Devon to death. With the SCAR ringleader dead, Trace and Candy drive off to a fresh start.

Practically drooling over its own mayhem, SCARRED CITY barely disguises its caveman ideology, with the filmmakers getting their jollies by dwelling on how much the cretinous cops enjoy their killing duties. There is little or no effort to link the gangsters and police in a chain of amorality. The anti-vigilante stance is an excuse to whet the audience's appetite for blood, a tactic that wouldn't be so repellent if the screenplay didn't insert bits of gallows humor, with Trace and Candy cracking wise as the bullets fly and the bodies splatter. SCARRED CITY wants to have its cake of tainted justice and eat it, too. *(Graphic violence, nudity, extreme profanity, substance abuse.)* —R.P.

d, Ken Sanzel; p, Avi Lerner, Elie Samaha; exec p, Trevor Short, Danny Dimbort; assoc p, Adam Silverman; co-p, John Ashley; w, Ken Sanzel; ph, Michael Slovis; ed, Troy Takaki; m, Anthony Marinelli; prod d, Anne Stuhler; art d, Roswell Hamrick; set d, Jennifer Alex; sound, Felix Andrew; fx, Ken Speed; casting, Hughs Moss, Jessica Gilburne; cos, Katherine Jane Bryant; makeup, Hariette Landau; stunts, Cort Hessler Hessler

Crime/Action **(PR: C MPAA: R)**

SCOOBY-DOO ON ZOMBIE ISLAND ★★½

(U.S., 1998) 77m Hanna-Barbera Cartoons Inc.; Warner Bros. ~ Warner Home Video c

VOICES OF: Scott Innes *(Scooby-Doo)*; Billy West *(Shaggy)*; Mary Kay Bergman *(Daphne)*; Frank Welker *(Fred)*; B.J. Ward *(Velma)*; Adrienne Barbeau *(Simone)*; Tara Charendoff *(Lena)*; Cam Clarke *(Beau)*; Jim Cummings *(Jacques)*; Mark Hamill *(Snakebite Scruggs)*; Jennifer Leigh Warren *(Chris)*; Ed Gilbert *(Mr. Beeman)*

The timorous and articulating (sort of) cartoon dog is back in SCOOBY-DOO ON ZOMBIE ISLAND, a watchable made-for-video feature that immediately sets out to establish that this is not your parents' Scooby-Doo by having Third Eye Blind perform a rocking new rendition of the immortal theme song "Scooby-Doo, Where Are You?" under the opening credits.

Daphne (voice of Mary Kay Bergman), the host of a TV show about supernatural phenomena, and her cameraman-boyfriend Fred (voice of Frank Welker) round up their old gang: Shaggy (voice of Billy West), his dog Scooby-Doo (voice of Scott Innes), and Velma (voice of B.J. Ward), to accompany them to look for a haunted house. In New Orleans, they meet a woman named Lena (voice of Tara Charendoff), who takes them to the supposedly haunted home of Simone (voice of Adrienne Barbeau), whose mansion is filled with hundreds of cats and a mysterious gardener named Beau (voice of Cam Clarke). Strange incidents begin to occur, including levitations and the appearance of pirate ghosts, but Velma suspects that Beau is just trying to scare them away, until they're menaced by some real zombies that rise out of a bayou.

When Fred, Daphne, and Velma go back to Simone's mansion, they discover an underground passage and see Simone and Lena practicing voodoo rituals. Simone ties them up and reveals that she's a cat creature who's more than 200 years old and plans to preserve her immortality by draining their blood during the Harvest Moon. Shaggy and Scooby-Doo stumble onto the cave and free their friends during a fight with Simone and Lena, who decompose when the Harvest Moon passes, and the zombies, who were actually Simone and Lena's past victims, thank the gang for avenging their spirits. Beau reveals that he's an undercover detective and agrees to go on Daphne's TV show. In the meantime, Fred has dropped his camera—the camera that videotaped evidence of the ghosts and zombies.

The animation in ZOMBIE ISLAND is somewhat more sophisticated than it was in the old Saturday-morning TV series, effecting a slightly anime look with soft, rounded contours and lots of noirish shadows and dark borders. The rudimentary slapstick is obviously geared for kids, but they're likely to get fidgety over the fairly complicated plot, taking more than 20 minutes to set up the story and utilizing a lengthy monochrome flashback to show how Simone became an immortal cat creature. Taking over from Casey Kasem for the high-pitched, squealing Shaggy, cartoon voice veteran Billy West ("Ren & Stimpy") sounds more like Casey than Casey ever did, and there is also some tongue-in-cheek comedy for older viewers which pokes fun at the series' absurdities, such as an amusing running gag centering on the talking Scooby's incredulity at being called a dog by strangers. Still, there's no getting around the fact that the show is primarily based on the rather limited comic possibilities of overeating (Scooby-Doo and Shaggy are constantly stuffing themselves with their beloved Scooby Snax), and of being scared, with Velma endlessly exclaiming "Jinkys," Scooby chewing his nails, and Shaggy screaming "Zoinks" at every opportunity.— M.S.

d, Jim Stenstrum; p, Cos Anzilotti; exec p, Jean MacCurdy; assoc p, Victoria McCullum; w, Glenn Leopold (based on the story by Glenn Leopold and Davis Doi); ed, Paul Douglas; m, Steven Bramson; sound, Jeff O. Collins

Animated/Children's **(PR: AA MPAA: NR)**

SECRET KINGDOM, THE ★½

(U.S./Romania, 1997) 82m Full Moon; The Kushner-Locke Company ~ Full Moon c

Billy O'Sullivan, billed as Billy O' *(Mark)*; Tricia Dickson *(Callie)*; Gerald S. O'Laughlin *(Chartwell)*; Jamieson K. Price *(Regent)*; Andrew Ducote *(Zak)*; Andreea Macelaru *(Catherine)*; Florin Chiriac *(Captain)*; Constantin Barbulescu *(Chief Constable)*; Gueydan T. Verret *(Lightning Rod Salesman)*; Bogdan Voda; Eugen Christea; Marius Galea; Mihai Niculescu; Mona Telega; Lelia Ciubotaru; Alina Sirbu; Adrian Pavel; Daniel Pisleaga; Dora Ortelecan; Ion Haiduc; Silviu Geamanu; Ronald Dulan; Joe "Cool" Davis; Rasheed Ali Akbar; Troy Michael Andrews

THE SECRET KINGDOM is a strange, off-kilter children's feature that dwindles into a state of ennui.

New Orleans teen Mark (Billy O') is followed home one day by a mysterious old lightning-rod salesman (Gueyden T. Verret). His sister Callie (Tricia Dickson) is minding their little brother Zak (Andrew Ducote) during their parents' absence. Zak's toy walkie-talkie picks up a distress-call originating from beneath their home's kitchen sink. There sits a tiny, thriving city, surrounded by other tiny lands and bodies of water. Zak shows Mark the marvel, and the older boy is suddenly teleported into the place—called Relkin—by technician Chartwell (Gerald S. O'Laughlin). He explains that Relkin has been cut off from the outside world for a long time, and that with Mark's help Chartwell and his rebels hope to overthrow their tyrant Regent (Jamieson K. Price). Mark doesn't trust Chartwell, but when he escapes he finds Relkin filled with eyeless or otherwise mutilated serfs, all products of the Regent's "Ministry of Perfection," intended to keep everyone in their place. Captured by the Regent, Mark is threatened with the surgery, but he's rescued from the operating table by Chartwell. The Regent locates Chartwell's apparatus and uses it to bring in another human: Callie, who falls for the Regent's promises of instant beauty in the Ministry of Perfection. To save his sister, Mark contacts Zak in the kitchen and has the boy fling a food tin into Relkin during a battle with the rebels. The colossal can falling into their sea scares the Regent's men into surrendering. A grateful Chartwell returns Mark and Callie back to their world, where they notice for the first time a long-forgotten lightning-rod terminus also under the sink. Using it, the siblings release a flash of energy that takes Relkin back to its original realm. Outside the house the lightning-rod man departs, satisfied.

THE SECRET KINGDOM is a product of busy producer Charles Band's Full Moon company, which itself has been transported from Los Angeles to Italy to Bucharest—not because of freak energy bolts, but rather bad debts and the low cost of movie production in Romania. As with many a feature ground out under the prolific low-budget mogul, it's often difficult to tell whether the film's scattered virtues arise via design or sheer accident. Opening footage (shot on location in Louisiana) is full of lyrical juxtapositions and curt dialogue that recalls the surreal fantasy fiction of Ray Bradbury and Rod Serling's "The Twilight Zone." Even though the realm under the kitchen sink is a painfully obvious model, the Relkin scenes take advantage of impressive Eastern European palaces and grandiose socialist public-building interiors to evoke a mild Terry Gilliam (BRAZIL) vibe. But the low-energy plot never gets in gear, and even the principle actors sleepwalk through mannered performances as though indifferent to their characters' plights.

At 82 minutes THE SECRET KINGDOM is padded by pointless sequences of young Zak surrounding the kitchen cabinet with toy soldiers for some kind of invasion that never happens, surely a letdown for the younger viewers at whom this material was aimed. The movie arrived directly on home video at much the same time as the same producers' THE SHRUNKEN CITY, *another* juvenile fantasy concerning a miniaturized civilization, although in terms of content the films themselves bear little resemblance to one another except for the fact that both are not very good. *(Violence.)*—C.C.

d, David Schmoeller; p, Vlad Paunescu, Christopher Landry; exec p, Peter Locke, Donald Kushner; co-p, Dana Scanlan; w, Benjamin Carr; ph, Gabriel Kosuth; ed, Barry Taylor; m, Carl Dante; prod d, Radu Corciova; art d, Viorel Ghenea; set d, Ica Varna; sound, Tiberiu Borcoman; casting, Bob MacDonald, Perry Bullington; cos, Iona Corciova; makeup, Gabe Bartalos; stunts, Doru Dimitrescu

Children's/Fantasy **(PR: A MPAA: PG)**

SECRET OF NIMH 2: TIMMY TO THE RESCUE, THE ★★

(U.S., 1998) 68m MGM Family Entertainment ~ MGM/UA Home Video c

VOICES OF: Dom DeLuise *(Jeremy)*; Andrew Ducote *(Timmy at 10)*; Eric Idle *(Martin)*; Harvey Korman *(Floyd)*; Ralph Macchio *(Timmy at 19)*; Peter MacMicol *(Narrator)*; William H. Macy *(Justin)*; Arthur Malet *(Mr. Ages)*; Andrea Martin *(Muriel)*; Meshach Taylor *(Cecil)*; Debi Mae West; Hynden Walsh *(Jenny)*; Steve Marshall *(Dr. Valentine)*

THE SECRET OF NIMH 2: TIMMY TO THE RESCUE is a belated, direct-to-video sequel to Don Bluth's 1982 animated feature, THE SECRET OF NIMH, which was marked by its superior animation and a surprisingly grim story about animal experimentation. The sequel features animation that's fairly simplistic, but not bad by made-for-video standards; the original film's disturbing theme, however, has been predictably neutered to make it much more kid-friendly.

A young mouse named Timmy (voice of Andrew Ducote) is chosen to follow in his late father's footsteps to help save animals from being tortured at NIMH, the National Institute for Mental Health. Timmy ventures out of the forest and goes to Thorn Valley, where he is taught how to be a brave warrior by Mr. Ages (voice of Arthur Malet) and Justin (voice of William H. Macy). As time goes by, the now grown Timmy (voice of Ralph Macchio) meets and falls in love with Jenny (voice of Hynden Walsh), whose parents are among those who have been captured and experimented on at NIMH by the evil Dr. Valentine (voice of Steve Marshall). Timmy learns that his brother Martin is also being held captive at NIMH, and with the aid of Cecil the caterpillar (voice of Meshach Taylor) and Timmy's old crow friend Jeremy (voice of Dom DeLuise), he and Jenny go to NIMH. When he gets there, however, he's shocked to discover that Martin (voice of Eric Idle) has taken over NIMH and become a crazed tyrant because of too much shock therapy. After knocking Martin unconscious, Timmy and Jenny free her parents and flee, but when a fire breaks out, Timmy goes back and rescues Martin, who's later restored to his old friendly self.

THE SECRET OF NIMH 2: TIMMY TO THE RESCUE is pretty innocuous stuff designed for very young children, but at least it's a marginal improvement over director Paul Sabella's previous 1998 cartoon for MGM/UA Home Video, the wretched AN ALL DOGS CHRISTMAS CAROL. The lively animation has some color and bounce to it, and even though the shots involving complicated motion are awkwardly achieved through computers, at least there's some action, such as in the fiery finale where NIMH explodes. Even the songs are tolerable, particularly an "Under the Sea"-like calypso number by Cecil the caterpillar and all of the other forest creatures, although the song attempted by the ex-"Karate Kid" Ralph Macchio is lamentable. The truly scary elements from the original and its message about genetic experimentation and animal testing have been toned down considerably, starting with the appearance of the mice and rats, who now look more like cuddly brown chipmunks than ugly gray rodents, and including the testing scenes at NIMH, which have been made farcical rather than frightening. The voice cast is better than average, with Dom DeLuise and Arthur Malet reprising their roles from the original, Harvey Korman and Andrea Martin hamming it up as comically villainous alley cats, and Eric Idle continuing his recent cartoon career renaissance.—M.S.

d, Dick Sebast; p, Paul Sabella, Jonathan Dern; exec p, William Stuart; co-p, Robert Winthrop; w, Sam Graham, Chris Hubbell (based on characters created by Robert C. O'Brien); ed, Jeffrey Patch; m, Lee Holdridge, Richard Sparks

Animated/Children's **(PR: A MPAA: G)**

SEMAFORO ROSSO

(SEE: RABID DOGS)

SENSELESS ★½

(U.S., 1998) 90m Mandeville Films; Gold/Miller; Senseless Productions ~ Dimension c

Marlon Wayans *(Darryl Witherspoon)*; Matthew Lillard *(Tim LaFlour)*; David Spade *(Scott Thorpe)*; Rip Torn *(Randall Tyson)*; Brad Dourif *(Professor Wheedon)*; Tamara Taylor *(Janice Baker)*; Richard McGonagle *(Robert Bellweather)*; Esther Scott *(Denise Witherspoon)*; Ken Lerner *(Dean Barlow)*; Kenya Moore *(Lorraine)*; Ernie Lively *(Coach Brandau)*; Debra Jo Rupp *(Fertility Clinic Attendant)*; Vicellous Shannon *(Carter)*; Michael Weatherred *(Kern)*; Mark Christopher Lawrence *(Wig Shop Owner)*; John Ingle *(Economics Professor)*; Jenette Goldstein *(Nurse Alvarez)*; Constance Zimmer *(Zestfully Clean Woman)*; Patrick O'Neill *(Waiter #1)*; Ross Rayburn *(Waiter #2)*; Jeanne Diehl *(Banquet Guest)*; Jennie Vaughn *(Pastry Chef)*; Cee-Cee Harshaw *(Tonya)*; Michael Dean Ester *(Chet)*; Greg Grunberg *(Steve)*; Mike Butters *(Hockey Referee)*; Orlando Brown *(Brandon Witherspoon)*; Angelique Parry *(April Witherspoon)*; Tino Williams *(Darius Witherspoon)*; Brenden Richard Jefferson *(Lyndell Witherspoon)*; Greg Wilson *(Monte Card Shark)*; Jeff Garlin *(Arlo Vickers)*; Patrick Ewing *(Himself)*; Michelle Brookhurst; Alexander Enberg; Manu Intiraymi *(Drug Intervention Students)*; Kevin Cooney *(Mr. Thorpe)*; Ivar Brogger *(Economics Coach)*; Cyia Batten *(Punk Waitress)*; Jack Shearer *(Vice-Chair—Federal Reserve)*; Joe Basile *(Security Guard)*; Darrel M. Heath *(Shady Guy)*; Thom Gossom Jr. *(Clothing Salesman)*; Sierra Pasteur *(Smythe/Bates Receptionist)*; Len Costenza *(Board Member)*; Jeremy Paul Meldrum; Kevin Downes; Branden Morgan *(Smythe/Bates Finalists)*; Sherman Hemsley *(Smythe/Bates Doorman)*

SENSELESS is an aptly titled juvenile slapstick comedy of ill manners and gross behavior. Though the farcical plot hinges on the effectiveness of molecular science, it is the film's stars who ironically lack chemistry.

Stratford University business student Darryl Witherspoon (Marlon Wayans) works several jobs to support himself, his mother, and his siblings. He hopes to win a competition for a fellowship, sponsored by the Smythe-Bates investment firm, as a junior analyst. His main rival is rich brat Scott Thorpe (David Spade). Desperate for money, Darryl becomes a guinea pig for Dr. Wheedon (Brad Dourif), who has developed a potion to increase human senses tenfold.

The first injection of the potion works so well that Darryl's heightened senses make him unable to concentrate on an important exam. Failing it causes him to be passed over as a finalist for the Smythe-Bates position. Posing as a waiter, he sneaks into an SB banquet and uses his powers to charm boss Tyson (Rip Torn). Tyson is impressed enough by Darryl's apparent knowledge to make him an extra finalist in the competition. Darryl's new powers also get him a spot on the school hockey team and a date with Janice (Tamara Taylor).

But when Darryl makes the mistake of taking a double dose, his overwhelmed brain reacts by shutting down his senses one at a time. He alienates Janice and blows a big hockey game, while his roommate Tim (Matthew Lillard) starts to suspect he's a junkie. He recovers by the morning of the final SB exam, and wins. But Darryl admits that he used an experimental drug to better his chances at scoring the fellowship. Tyson withdraws the junior analyst job, but gives Darryl a job in the mailroom; within a year, he has worked his way up to the position of junior analyst.

Wayans, while a talented physical comedian, needs work on his acting. His slapstick performance works best when he's stumbling into walls and drooling uncontrollably rather than emoting. Spade plays his usual snarky persona, and while he's definitely too long in the tooth to be playing college students, his icy attitude makes him easy to hate.

While harmless, SENSELESS wallows in juvenile jokes about bodily fluids, rectal itches, pierced genitalia, and premature ejaculation. Thus preoccupied, the writing and direction never rise above sitcom blandness. With some cleaned-up language and plot elements, this project might have worked better in the less-demanding environment of the small screen. It's basically a one-joke story: See Darryl lose his sense of touch at the worst possible moment. Whoops! Now he can't see! Wow, that's a bad time to go deaf! Blame director Penelope Spheeris for setting her sights so low on a film that could have benefited from a lighter touch. *(Profanity, sexual situations.)*—J.Di.

d, Penelope Spheeris; p, David Hoberman; exec p, Eric L. Gold, Don Carmody, Bob Weinstein, Harvey Weinstein, Cary Granat; assoc p, Scott Wilder, Terry Austin, Mike Karz; w, Greg Erb, Craig Mazin; ph, Daryn Okada; ed, Ross Albert; m, Yello; prod d, Peter Jamison; art d, Ann Harris; set d, Linda Spheeris; sound, Susumu Tokunow (mixer), John Pospisil (design); fx, F. Lee Stone, Brian Jennings; casting, Junie Lowry Johnson; cos, Betsy Cox; makeup, Jeanne Van Phue, Jo-Anne Smith; stunts, Shane Dixon

Comedy **(PR: O MPAA: R)**

SEPARATION, THE
(SEE: LA SEPARATION)

SEVEN DOORS OF DEATH
(SEE: BEYOND, THE)

SEVENTH HEAVEN ★★★
(France, 1997) 91m Dacia Films; Cinea; La Sept ~ Zeitgeist Films c
(LE SEPTIEME CIEL)

Sandrine Kiberlain *(Mathilde)*; Vincent Lindon *(Nico)*; Francois Berleand *(Doctor)*; Francine Berge *(Mathilde's Mother)*; Pierre Cassignard; Leo Le Bevillon; Sylvie Loeillet; Florence Loiret; Philippe Magnan

Director Benoit Jacquot (A SINGLE GIRL) serves up another stylish domestic drama in SEVENTH HEAVEN, a peculiar triangle "romance" between a wife, her husband, and her therapist.

In Paris, Mathilde (Sandrine Kiberlain), a 29-year-old wife and mother, inexplicably begins stealing objects from stores and fainting in public. She seeks comfort from her 39-year-old husband, Nico (Vincent Lindon), an orthopedic surgeon, but his only response is to prescribe antidepressive drugs. Mathilde also tries to find answers from her mother, who runs the law firm where she works, but her mother (Francine Berge), like her husband, lacks compassion. Finally, Mathilde gets help from a mysterious doctor (Francois Berleand) she meets at a party. At a quiet lunch, the doctor questions Mathilde thoroughly and discovers that her recent kleptomania and fainting spells relate to her father's death years earlier, which her mother had called an accident but Mathilde suspects was a suicide.

Mathilde continues seeing the doctor, who performs sexually-charged hypnosis on his patient and suggests she employ the Eastern art of *feng shui* (rearranging her furniture in harmony with nature) as a way to improve her sex life with Nico, who has been cheating on Mathilde. Unfortunately, Nico reacts angrily to the changes in Mathilde as she becomes more confident, both socially and sexually. Mathilde's mother, too, worries about her daughter's growing strength, and tells Nico about the hypnosis-therapy sessions in order to get him more involved in the situation. Nico responds by seeing a hypnotist himself, but his session ends unsatisfactorily. Later, he confronts Mathilde and insists she take him to see her therapist. But Nico misses the doctor at his apartment, and he leaves Mathilde to sort out his feelings after she admits her sessions were sexual in nature. Finally, Nico returns home, where he humbly reconciles with Mathilde and their son.

Benoit Jacquot's examination of psychoanalyis—specifically, hypnotherapy—and marital fidelity alternates between the serious and the funny, the studied and the jaunty. As in some of his previous films, Jacquot takes a deliberate but elliptical approach to a slender narrative that explores contemporary social angst. Though the screenplay (cowritten by Jerome Beaujour) is not as compelling as it could have been, the film contains a rich subtext about gender relations, effectively embodied by the leading players, Kiberlain and Lindon. The film begins with Mathilde's point of view and then surreptitiously shifts to Nico's, a subtle departure that allows Jacquot to inquire as much about the male psyche as the female.

However, some of Jacquot's previous films (including THE DISENCHANTED and especially A SINGLE GIRL), made similar points while drawing viewers more closely into the drama. This time, the items that are ellipsed and the clean, precise mise-en-scene keep viewers from truly caring about Mathilde (the only really sympathetic character). On the other hand, the dispassionate storytelling appropriately underlines the ambivalent attitude Jacquot accords the subject of analysis. Though never spoofed or parodied, the two therapists depicted represent strange, slightly silly characters; yet, their hypnosis works when their patients are willing. Sadly for Jacquot, SEVENTH HEAVEN follows the plot line of the *very* silly 1997 American feature, BLISS, starring Terence Stamp as the meddling sex therapist. Viewers are advised to avoid the latter film in order to better enjoy the former, an assured, sophisticated, albeit minor work. *(Nudity, sexual situations, adult situations, extreme profanity.)*—E.M.

d, Benoit Jacquot; p, Georges Benayoun, Philippe Carcassonne; exec p, Francoise Guglielmi; assoc p, Chantal Poupaud; w, Benoit Jacquot, Jerome Beaujour; ph, Romain Winding; ed, Pascale Chavance; prod d, Patrice Arrat; sound, Michel Vionnet; casting, Frederique Moidon; cos, Caroline De Vivaise

Drama/Comedy **(PR: C MPAA: NR)**

SHADOWBUILDER
(SEE: BRAM STOKER'S SHADOWBUILDER)

SHADRACH ★★½
(U.S., 1998) 90m Millenium; Phoenician ~ Columbia c

Harvey Keitel *(Vernon Dabney)*; Andie MacDowell *(Trixie Dabney)*; John Franklin Sawyer *(Shadrach)*; Scott Terra *(Paul)*; Daniel Treat *(Little Moe)*; Monica Bugajski *(Edmonia)*; Deborah Hedwall *(Mrs. Whitehurst)*; Darrell Larson *(Mr. Whitehurst)*; Erin Underwood *(Lucinda)*; Edward Bunker *(Joe Thorton)*; Alice Rogers *(Cloris)*; Michael Ruff *(Smut)*; Jonathan Parks Jordan *(Middle Mole)*; Ginnie Randall *(Virginia)*; Muse Watson

(Captain); Doug Chancey *(Dock Worker)*; Rick Warner *(Presbyterian Minister)*; Clarinda Hollmond *(Chapel Singer)*; Melvin Cauthen *(Earvin Williams)*; Richard Olsen *(Seddon Washington)*; Olivia Bost *(Sweet Betty)*; Bill Nelson *(Fautleroy)*; Walter Hand *(Preacher)*; Martin Sheen *(Narrator)*

SHADRACH is the story of events that transpire when a 99-year-old ex-slave returns to his hometown to die. Based on a semi-autobiographical tale by William Styron, SHADRACH was filmed with taste and faithfulness by the writer's daughter, Susanna Styron.

Tidewater, Virginia; the summer of 1935. While his parents (Darrell Larson and Deborah Hedwall) are away in Baltimore, 10-year-old Paul (Scott Terra), an only child, stays with the Dabneys, a poor neighboring family of nine headed by Vernon Dabney (Harvey Keitel) and his wife, Trixie (Andie MacDowell).

One day, while Paul and the youngest Dabney boy (Daniel Treat) are shooting marbles in the yard, their game is interrupted by the sudden appearance of a frail and ancient man named Shadrach (John Franklin Sawyer), who has walked 600 miles from Alabama to die and be buried on the site where he had been born into slavery 99 years earlier. Vernon Dabney's aristocratic ancestors had been his slave masters.

The next day the Dabneys, Paul, and Shadrach, who is failing fast, drive to the Dabneys' scrabbly summer "farm," a property that incorporates the family burial grounds and Vernon's illegal still. There, the local sheriff informs Vernon that it is against the law to bury a body on private property, and that when the old man dies he must be interred in a black churchyard by a black undertaker. That afternoon, Shadrach asks to be taken down to the old millpond where, Paul speculates, he may have enjoyed the only fully happy moments of his life almost a century ago,

Shadrach dies that night. Vernon angrily shells out the $35 burial fee, which he can ill afford, and the old man's coffin is interred according to law. Back at the farm, everyone is overjoyed to learn that Vernon has pulled a fast one: The coffin was empty. That night, Shadrach is laid to rest, as he so dearly wished, on Dabney property.

William Styron's 40-page story—the perfect length for a feature film adaptation—ends with Shadrach's demise and Vernon's heated declaration that "Death ain't much. . . .It's life that's fearsome!" Realizing that moviegoers would require a brighter and more conclusive ending, Susanna Styron shrewdly extended the narrative in order to honor Shadrach's last request. Otherwise, the movie is virtually an illustrated edition of the original story.

Its most resonant moments, however, are provided by two added interludes—both very brief, narratively peripheral, and shot in slow motion: the outdoor baptism by immersion of 12-year-old Edmonia Dabney (Monica Bugajski), whose manifest joy in both the dunking and the occasion is exhilarating; and Vernon's drive into the Negro district, where he uneasily glimpses dark, alien figures on all sides of him.

SHADRACH's virtues are many, though minor. The portrayal of the "white trash" Dabneys as decent and worthy human beings is unusual and refreshing. The title character is an interesting symbol of "the White Man's Burden" and guilt. The film's narration is beautifully read by a Dixie-accented Martin Sheen. The color photography is splendidly mellow and soothing.

Despite all this, SHADRACH doesn't approach the richness of RAMBLING ROSE (1991), an earlier film based on another Southern writer's memories of his boyhood in 1935—largely because William Styron lacks the vision, vivacity, and genius of RAMBLING ROSE's author Calder Willingham.

Prior to playing Shadrach, John Franklin Sawyer, an 83-year-old retired postal worker, had acted only in church theatricals.*(Nudity, profanity.)*—D.T.

d, Susanna Styron; p, Bridget Terry, Boaz Davidson, John Thompson; exec p, Johnathan Demme, Steven Shareshian, Avi Lerner, Trevor Short, Danny Dimbort, Elie Samaha; w, Susanna Styron, Bridget Terry (based on the short story by William Styron); ph, Hiro Narita; ed, Colleen Sharp; m, Van Dyke Parks; prod d, Burton Rencher; set d, Valerie Fann; sound, Larry Long (mixer), Carl Rudisill; casting, Tracy Kilpatrick; cos, Dona Granata; makeup, Rudolph Eavey III; stunts, John Copeman

Drama (PR: A MPAA: PG-13)

SHAKESPEARE IN LOVE ★★★★

(U.S., 1998) 120m United International Pictures ~ Miramax c

Gwyneth Paltrow (Viola De Lesseps); Joseph Fiennes (Will Shakespeare); Colin Firth (Lord Wessex); Geoffrey Rush (Philip Henslowe); Judi Dench (Queen Elizabeth); Tom Wilkinson (Hugh Fennyman); Ben Affleck (Ned Alleyn); Simon Callow (Tilney, Master of the Revels); Jim Carter (Ralph Bashford); Martin Clunes (Richard Burbage); Imelda Staunton (Nurse); Steven O'Donnell (Lambert); Tim McMullen (Frees); Steven Beard (Makepeace, The Peacemaker); Antony Sher (Dr. Moth); Patrick Barlow (Will Kempe); Sandra Reinton (Rosaline); Rupert Everett (Christopher Marlowe); Bridget McConnel (Lady in Waiting); Georgie Glen (Lady in Waiting); Nicholas Boulton (Henry Condell); Desmond McNamara (Crier); Barbany Kay (Nol); Paul Bigley (Peter, The Stage Manager); Jason Round (Actor in Tavern); Rupert Farley (Barman); Adam Barker (First Auditionee); Joe Roberts (John Webster); Harry Gostelow (Second Auditionee); Alan Cody (Third Auditionee); Mark Williams (Wabash); David Curtiz (John Hemmings); Gregor Truter (James Hemmings); Simon Day (First Boatman); Jill Baker (Lady De Lesseps); Amber Glossop (Scullery Maid); Robin Davies (Master Plum); Hywel Simons (Servant); Nicholas Le Prevost (Sir Robert De Lesseps); Timothy Knightley (Edward Pope); Mark Saban (Augustine Philips); Bob Barrett (George Bryan); Roger Morlidge (James Armitage); Daniel Brocklebank (Sam Gosse); Roger Frost (Second Boatman); Rebecca Charles (Chambermaid); Richard Gold (Lord in Waiting); Rachel Clarke (First Whore); Lucy Speed (Second Whore); Patricia Potter (Third Whore); John Ramm (Makepeace's Neighbor); Martin Neeley (Paris/Lady Montague); The Choir of St. George's School, Windsor (Choir)

Literate, witty, and beautifully produced, SHAKESPEARE IN LOVE is a fictional account of the inspiration behind the Bard's penning of *Romeo and Juliet*. The film fetched seven Oscars, including Best Picture, Best Actress (Gwyneth Paltrow), and Best Supporting Actress (Judi Dench).

London, 1593. Young playwright Will Shakespeare (Joseph Fiennes), suffering from writer's block and badly in need of a hit, auditions actors for an unfinished play. Among those auditioning is Viola De Lesseps (Gwyneth Paltrow), disguised as a man since women are prohibited from acting. Will is fooled by the disguise and selects Viola for the male lead. Later, at a ball, Will again meets Viola, not recognizing her as the auditioner. He is immediately drawn to her, and soon learns that she and the young actor are the same person. The two become lovers, Will's block breaks, and he begins to write furiously. Viola, her gender known only to Will, continues to rehearse the play as a man.

Viola, however, has been promised by her father to Lord Wessex (Colin Firth), whom she does not love. When Wessex presents Viola publicly to Queen Elizabeth (Judi Dench), Will disguises himself and sneaks into the presentation, at which he accepts a wager from Wessex over whether a play can "show the truth and nature of love." Will completes the play, titled *Romeo and Juliet*, but before it opens, Viola's sex becomes known and the theater is ordered closed. Another theater offers to stage the play, but without Viola.

The play finally opens, the same day as Viola's wedding, and she heads directly from the ceremony to see the production. The actor playing Juliet is unable to play the role and Viola agrees to play the part. The play is a smashing success but just after it ends, authorities come to close the theater, as Viola's appearance has been reported. Elizabeth, who has been in the audience, steps forward and dismisses the charges. She tells Wessex that he has lost the wager and orders him to pay Will, but she also tells Viola that her place is with her husband. Having lost the woman he loves, Will sets to writing his next work—*Twelfth Night*.

SHAKESPEARE IN LOVE is a rare treat, a fun, robust movie that plays up, not down, to its audience. This film has been made by people who assume that contemporary moviegoers can appreciate Shakespeare without having to arm his characters with guns (*a la* the Leonardo DiCaprio starrer WILLIAM SHAKESPEARE'S ROMEO & JULIET). In concocting a mock biography of the Elizabethan playwright, Oscar-winning co-scenarists Marc Norman and Tom Stoppard have cleverly strung together plot strands from several of Shakespeare's works, and have the characters speaking in the playwright's own dialogue. They have fun with these elements, sometimes through gentle parody (the working title of Will's play is "Romeo and Ethel, the Pirate's Daughter"), occasionally by contemporizing the period, Mel Brooks style (Will tries therapy to help him with his writer's block), but mostly by deferring to the Bard. SHAKESPEARE IN LOVE is as funny, as action-packed, and often as witty as Shakespeare itself. The film is filled with lusty romance, sword fights, stumbling buffoons, wisecracking servants, reptilian villains, midnight rendezvous, and so on. Without compromising or perverting their source of inspiration, Norman and Stoppard knowingly exploit Shakespeare, not as rarefied high-brow culture, but as entertainment.

Director John Madden, for his part, expertly exploits what Norman and Stoppard have given him. He sorts out and makes perfect sense of the rather complicated plot, and keeps it all moving at a quick, steady pace. He accentuates but never overemphasizes the humor, the action, or the romance, gracefully tempering exuberance with restraint. Most importantly, he maintains a consistently high spirited tone through the duration of the movie.

The cast is uniformly excellent. Oscar-winner Paltrow shines as Will's strong-willed muse; Geoffrey Rush, Ben Affleck, and Tom Wilkinson all lend fine comic support, and Best Supporting Actress Dench anchors the film with a regal presence. The surprise of SHAKESPEARE IN LOVE is Joseph Fiennes (Ralph's younger brother), who in his first major starring role, ably and with total confidence bears the twin burdens of carrying the lead and playing the English language's greatest author.

Technically, SHAKESPEARE IN LOVE is perfectly polished, with the production design by Martin Childs and the costuming by Sandy Powell (both of whom won Oscars for their work on the film) steeping the film in the world of Elizabethan England. The entire enterprise gives the impression that everyone involved was caught up in the fanciful conceit that Shakespeare's own life was as dramatic and romantic as his work. The result of their labors is a delightful triumph. *(Violence, nudity, sexual situations, profanity.)*— D.C.

d, John Madden; p, David Parfitt, Donna Gigliotti, Harvey Weinstein, Edward Zwick, Marc Norman; exec p, Bob Weinstein, Julie Goldstein; w, Marc Norman, Tom Stoppard; ph, Richard Greatrex; ed, David Gamble; m, Stephen Warbeck; prod d, Martin Childs; art d, Steve Lawrence; set d, Jill Quertier; ch, Quinny Sacks; sound, Peter Glossop (mixer), Robin O'Donoghue, Dominic Lester; fx, Stuart Brisdon; casting, Michelle Guish; cos, Sandy Powell; makeup, Lisa Westcott

AA Best Picture; AA Best Actress: Gwyneth Paltrow; *AA Best Supporting Actress:* Judi Dench; *AA Best Costume Design:* Sandy Powell; *AA Best Art Direction:* Martin Childs, Jill Quertier; *AA Best Original Musical or Comedy Score:* Stephen Warbeck; *AA Best Original Screenplay:* Marc Norman, Tom Stoppard; *AAN Best Supporting Actor:* Geoffrey Rush; *AAN Best Director:* John Madden; *AAN Best Cinematography:* Richard Greatrex; *AAN Best Film Editing:* David Gamble; *AAN Best Makeup:* Lisa Westcott, Veronica Brebner; *AAN Best Sound:* Robin O'Donoghue, Dominic Lester, Peter Glossop

Comedy/Romance/Historical (PR: C MPAA: R)

SHAMPOO HORNS ★★½

(Spain/U.S., 1998) 90m Alta Films ~ Elias Querejeta/Esicma c

Jason Reeves *(Dennis)*; Cheyenne Besch *(Cheyenne)*; Jonathan Lawrence *(Junky Jonathan)*; Jason Anthony *(Mark)*; Andrew Galuppi *(Tony)*; Brie Koyanagi *(Brie)*; Michael Alig *(Michael Alig)*; James St. James *(James St. James)*; Lahoma Van Zandt *(Lahoma Van Zandt)*; Tobell Von Cartier *(Tobell)*; Tiffany Shepis *(Amy)*; Kenny Kenny *(Kenny Kenny)*; Atsushi Sakai *(Sushi)*; Sue Banshee *(Sue)*; Rob Ransom *(Freez)*; Ivette Mercedes *(Maid)*; Robert Sorce *(Robert Twin)*; Tim Duperron *(Tim Twin)*; Sophia Lamar *(Sophia Lamar)*; Jacquee Rivera *(Jacquee Rivera)*; Codie Leone *(Codie)*; Richie Rich *(Richie Rich)*; Gabriella Voigt *(Gaby)*; Lawrence Thom *(Larry Tee)*; Desiree *(Desiree)*

Writer-director Manuel Toledano's authentic, low-budget portrait of the Manhattan club kid scene is technically uneven and generally tedious, but there are affecting moments.

Preparing for a night at Disco 2000 are club impresario Michael Alig (himself), Junky Jonathan (Jonathan Lawrence), and drag queens such as Lahoma Van Zandt (herself), Brie (Brie Koyanagi), and Tobell (Tobell Von Cartier). Older drag queen Dennis (Jason Reeves) tells Cheyenne (herself) he doesn't feel well and will leave the city. In their NYU dorm, Amy (Tiffany Shepis) over-indulges in a heroin-laced beverage before taking roommate Tony (Andrew Gallupi) on his first night clubbing.

At the club, Lahoma mc's the stage show but is stuck when Dennis, who has checked-in to an Atlantic City hotel, doesn't show. Other club regulars are introduced, including Mark (Jason Anthony), a handsome, straight Brooklynite who's only interested in mooching cocaine. On stage, Lahoma is heckled. Meanwhile, Dennis befriends the hotel maids, writes letters, and ponders his life. While bathing, he likens the urge to don drag with children making horns with their shampoo-covered hair. Tony takes a wasted Amy back to the dorm and puts her to bed; she gets up and wanders the streets. Lahoma and other club regulars are interviewed in mock-documentary segments. Tony returns to the club looking for Amy and does drugs. In Atlantic City, Dennis takes a fatal dose of pills.

At an afterhours club, Michael talks about his plans to make a movie. Amy dies in an accident. Patricia Fried, Jennytalia, Keoki, Michael Musto, and Jennifer Gatien comment (as themselves) on the club scene. Attracted to Mark, Jonathan has a drug-induced fantasy that includes the major characters in a Last Supper tableau at Michael's birthday party. Jonathan dreams that Mark saves his life and they have a whirlwind courtship, marriage, and honeymoon. The dream ends when Cheyenne learns via letter of Dennis' death. It is morning now. Tony is afraid to confront Amy's parents. Brie, who has been mothering Tony, takes him home with her. Jonathan dies from an overdose in the after-hours spot. Mark, scrounging for cocaine, robs him. But the bouncer insists Mark get rid of Jonathan's body. So he puts him into a cardboard box, drags him through the streets to a self-storage locker, and leaves him there.

Perhaps in homage to the 1990 documentary hit PARIS IS BURNING, director Manuel Toledano often uses interviews and voiceover narration to reveal his characters's emotions and the all-too-apparent themes of SHAMPOO HORNS. These segments don't really work, but they underscore Toledano's censorious sympathy for his troubled, drug-addled subjects. Unfortunately, some incredibly poor acting (especially by Jason Reeves in the one key role) makes the film appear unfinished. One could argue that the film's lack of energy mirrors the listlessness and boredom of the club kids, who randomly indulge in drugs. There's little electricity or wit, and only fleeting signs of a genuine camp sensibility. Michael Alig's real-life conviction for the 1996 murder of his former roommate underscores the moral and intellectual vacuity of the milieu. (Alig, who shot his scenes before the murder, was sentenced to 10 to 20 years.)

The film's best element is Jonathan's story, which nobly attempts to illustrate the theme of rejection. Club kids, it's implied, are compelled by the rest of society to remain outsiders, cloaked in eccentric personas. The viewer can sympathize with Jonathan's yearning for a "normal" relationship with Mark, and the indifference with which he is treated. Also, while Mark's descent into a cold, emotionless state is somehow inevitable, the sequence in which he gently kisses Jonathan's corpse hints that the often destructive illusions of club kids are not so far-fetched or hopeless.

In the final analysis, it's possible that if Toledano had resisted using verite devices to present his wayward children, SHAMPOO HORNS might be more compelling. *(Violence, nudity, profanity.)*— J.M.

d, Manuel Toledano; p, Elias Querejeta; exec p, Thomas Bidegain; co-p, Jennifer Gatien, Andrew Chiaras, Brilliant Mistake; w, Manuel Toledano; ph, Alfredo Mayo; ed, Nacho Ruiz Capillas; m, Angel Illarramendi; sound, David Powers; cos, Martha Gretsch; makeup, Gabriella Voigt

Drama/Comedy **(PR: O MPAA: NR)**

SHAOLIN TEMPLE, THE ★★★½

(China/Hong Kong, 1981) 94m Chung Yuen Motion Picture Company ~ SYS Entertainment c

Jet Li, billed as Jet Lee *(Jue Yuan)*; Ding Lan *(Bai Wu Xia)*; Yu Hai *(Shi Fu)*; Hu Jian Qiang *(Wu Kong)*; Sun Jian Kui *(Se Kong)*; Liu Huai Liang *(Liao Kong)*; Wang Jue *(Ban Kong)*; Du Chuan Yang *(Wei Kong)*; Chi Zhi Qiang *(Xuan Kong)*; Xun Feng *(Dao Kong)*; Pan Han Guang *(Zhi Cao)*; Fang Ping *(Hui Neng)*; Jiang Hong Bo *(Hui Yin)*; Shan Qi Bo Tong *(Hui Yang)*; Zhang Jian Wen *(Fang Zhang)*; Yang Di Hua *(Seng Zhi)*; Wang Guang Kuan *(Li Shi Min)*; Yu Cheng Hui *(Wang Ren Ze)*; Ji Chun Hua *(Tu Ying)*; Pan Qingfu; Su Fei; Chen Guo An; Bian Li Chang; Wang Guo Yi; Kong Fan Yan; Sun Sheng Jun *(General)*

Judged by its plot, this 1981 China-Hong Kong coproduction is tired and hackneyed. But judged by its exquisitely choreographed fighting, it's a thrilling and truly monumental achievement, with a terrific Jet Li in his film debut.

In early seventh-century China, the population suffers under a despotic Sui ruler. After being badly injured in a fight with the evil Wang Ren Ze (Yu Cheng Hui) and seeing his father killed, Jue Yuan (Jet Li) flees, collapsing at the gates of the Shaolin Temple. There, the mischievous youngster is taken in by the kindly monk Shi Fu (Yu Hai) and trained in the rudimentary martial arts. When Shi Fu's daughter Bai Wu Xia (Ding Lan) is captured by Wang, Jue Yuan rescues her. Later, with Bai's help, he helps prisoner Li Shi Min (Wang Guang Kuan) escape his Sui captors.

Knowing that Wang will be furious when he hears that Shaolin has aided Li, Shi Fu expels his daughter and Jue Yuan for their own safety. Wang does attack the temple and a heated battle ensues, with Shi Fu killed. But Jue Yuan and Bai return to help, as do rebel troops led by Li, wiping out the enemy soldiers and chasing Wang to the river where, after a terrific brawl, Jue Yuan kills him.

Chairman Mao's death in 1976 was followed by a gradual liberalization in the arts, with this the first martial arts film shot in China since he nationalized the cinema. The Shaw Brothers had enjoyed great success with a popular film series about the legendary temple and its heroes, filmed on backlots; the producers of THE SHAOLIN TEMPLE spent a reported three years and ten million US dollars to capture the epic vistas and spectacular architecture of real China. Interiors and some of the fights were actually filmed in Hong Kong, on stages rented from Shaw studios, with advice and encouragement from Shaw directors. Cinematically, the film is less advanced than many of those made concurrently in Hong Kong, which contained unimaginative camera setups and a preponderance of cheap zooms. Nonetheless, it was a huge hit in Asia.

Impish Jue Yuan is quickly forgiven by Bai for (accidentally) killing her dog and (maybe) eating it. The bad guys, on the other hand, are so mean they *intentionally* kill Bai's defenseless little lambs. Bai, portrayed by skilled Peking Opera performer Ding Lan, instantly becomes a whirlwind of eye-popping action, taking on the enemy troops singlehandedly and only succumbing to superior numbers. Also starring are an array of outstanding martial artists from Beijing's acclaimed *wu shu* (martial arts) team. Hu Jian Qiang, China's 1981 national champion, is a particular standout, as is Li's main nemesis Yu Cheng Hui; "Iron Fist" Pan Qingfu, who portrayed himself in Mark Salzman's spiritual paean IRON & SILK (1991) has a villainous role and helped design the action. The boyish and charming Li, still a teen when this was released, went on to make two official sequels, receiving only a paltry state subsidy for his work. *(Violence, adult situations.)*—A.B.

d, Chang Hsin Yen; p, Liu Yet Yuen; exec p, Lau Fong, Fu Chi; assoc p, Chan Man; w, Shih Hou, Lu Shau Chang; ph, Chau Pak Ling, Lau Fung Lam; ed, Chang Hsin Yen, Wong Ting, Li Yuk Wai, Ku Chi Wai; m, Wang Li Ping; art d, Wong Hok Sun; sound, Wong Kwan Sai; cos, Wong Kwai Ping, Tong Yuet Fung; stunts, Ma Xian Da, Yu Hai, Pan Qing Fu, Wang Chang Kai

Martial Arts/Adventure **(PR: C MPAA: NR)**

SHATTERED IMAGE ★★★

(U.S., 1998) 103m Seven Arts Pictures; Schroeder Hoffman; Fireworks Entertainment; MDP Worldwide; CineVisions; Silverman Productions; Legacy Filmworks ~ Lions Gate Films c

William Baldwin *(Brian)*; Anne Parillaud *(Jessie)*; Lisanne Falk *(Paula/Laura)*; Graham Greene *(Conrad/Mike)*; Billy Wilmott *(Lamond)*; O'Neil Peart *(Simon)*; Leonie Forbes *(Isabel)*; Bulle Ogier *(Mrs. Ford)*

Is Jessie Markham a frightened heiress who dreams of being a professional assassin? Or is she a heartless assassin dreaming of being a heiress? That uncertainty drives SHATTERED IMAGE, which seems to be an attempt by veteran experimental filmmaker Raul Ruiz to work within the cinema mainstream while continuing to play games with dissecting conventional narrative. The film follows two parallel stories involving the two Jessies, with Ruiz perpetually complicating our attempts to decide which is the real story and which the dream. Those familiar with his past work will appreciate the level of cinematic subversion here, though viewers who haven't been clued in are likely to be left scratching their heads in befuddlement.

In a Seattle restaurant, Jessie Markham (Anne Parillaud) coolly dispatches the man she has been paid to kill. She is jolted awake to find herself on a plane, headed to St. Croix on her honeymoon with new husband Brian (William Baldwin). As they make love in their room, Brian caresses the scars on her wrists from a suicide attempt after she was raped, and promises to protect her. Jessie awakens in Seattle and begins her next assignment; since being raped, she kills only men.

While stalking her assignment in Seattle, Jessie meets and begins an affair with Brian (William Baldwin). In Jamaica, Jessie fears she is being stalked by the man who raped her, though her husband assures her this is impossible. Elements appear in both stories, as do some people: Laura (Lisanne Falk), Jessie's client in Seattle, is also Paula, a fellow vacationer who monitors her actions in Jamaica. Conrad (Graham Greene), the man she has been hired to kill, is also Mike, stalking her in Jamaica and (she fears) her never-caught attacker. In reality, he is a detective hired to protect her. After Jessie kills Conrad in Seattle, she learns she had the wrong man—her real target is Brian. In Jamaica, Jessie comes to suspect that it was Brian who raped her as part of a plan to murder her for her money. Jessie wakes up in a psychiatric hospital six months after an overdose of pills fed to her by Brian and coconspirator Paula. In a scene similar to the film's opening, she shoots Brian in a restaurant bathroom, and then shoots her own image in the mirror.

Prior to the early 1990s, Raul Ruiz seemed only slightly less likely than underground icon Stan Brakhage to try the waters of commercial filmmaking. With a prodigious output in film, video, and television in a career stretching back to 1968, this Chilean-born expatriate, who has lived and worked in France since Allende's overthrow, has staked out his own territory with largely experimental films questioning the nature of storytelling, perspective, and criticism. But despite the theoretical basis of his work, his films can be quite entertaining.

SHATTERED IMAGE, Ruiz' second American film (after 1990's little-seen THE GOLDEN BOAT), seems to be equal parts parody, homage, and game playing. But while Parillaud and Baldwin play characters similar to those they played in LA FEMME NIKITA (1990) and SLIVER (1993), respectively, they don't seem to have been let in on the joke, playing Duane Poole's flat (and often laughable) dialogue as if they don't know what to make of it. In fact, dubbing this film into French for Ruiz' home audience will probably help, adding another level of ironic detachment to offset what most American reviewers took as botched realism. While not nearly as bad as its notices would indicate, SHATTERED IMAGE can't be called a success, as the essentially gimmicky script eventually gets the better of Ruiz. Still, there are more than enough moments along the way as Ruiz and Poole tease us as to which story is reflecting which to make it worthwhile viewing for those who enjoy a good game. *(Violence, nudity, sexual situations, adult situations, profanity.)*—M.F.

d, Raul Ruiz; p, Peter Hoffman, Barbet Schroeder, Susan Hoffman, Lloyd A. Silverman; exec p, Jack Baran, Jay Fireston, James Michael Vernon, Bastiaan Gleben; co-p, Lisanne Falk; w, Duane Poole; ph, Robby Muller; ed, Michael Duthie; m, Jorge Arriagada; prod d, Robert De Vico; casting, Sue Brouse; cos, Francine Lecoultre

Thriller/Mystery/Drama (PR: C MPAA: NR)

SHOOTING FISH ★★½

(U.K., 1997) 93m Gruber Brothers; Winchester Films; Tomboy Films; Arts Council of England ~ Fox Searchlight c

Dan Futterman (Dylan); Stuart Townsend (Jez); Kate Beckinsale (Georgie); Nickolas Grace (Mr. Stratton-Luce); Claire Cox (Floss); Ralph Ineson (Mr. Ray); Dominic Mafham (Roger); Peter Capaldi (Mr. Gilzean); Annette Crosbie (Mrs. Cummins); Jane Lapotaire (Dylan's Headmistress); Phyllis Logan (Mrs. Ross); Rowena Cooper (Jez's Teacher); Scott Charles (Samuel—age 8); Antonia Corrigan (Antonia—age 8); Myles Anderson (Jez—age 8); Harry Ditson (IRS Man); Jacob Macoby (Dylan—age 8); Tom Chadbon (Mr. Greenaway); Vicki Bensted (Bank Clerk); Peter McNamara (Geoff); Nicola Duffett (Mrs. Ray); Larry Randall; Neil Peplow (Golfers); Arabella Weir (Mrs. Stratton-Luce); Alan Cooke (Car Park Attendant); Andree Evans (Mrs. Furnival-Jones); Ralph Watson; Harry Gostelow (Vigilantes); Wolf Christian (Mr. Thor); Louis Schwartz (Bandaged Baby); Alan Sollinger (Gasometer Foreman); Cosmo Scurr (Boy with Tennis Ball); Paul Kynman (Chauffeur); Philip York (Detective); Nicholas Woodeson (Mr. Collyns); Louis Mahoney (Magistrate); John Clegg (Church Vicar); Darren Renouf (Robin); Emily Braham (Bridesmaid); Phil Evans; Otto Jarman (Prison Guards); Adam Fogerty (Bruiser); David Glover (Prison Governor); Frankie; Sally; Angie (Blow-up Dolls); Catherine Russell (Crematorium Cleaning Lady); Ronald Markham (Crematorium Vicar); Dickie Graydon (Racehorse Trainer); Tim Stern (Panfield); Paul Williamson (Weighing-in Official); Peter O'Sullevan (Race Commentator); Geoffrey Whitehead (1st Owner); Linda Spurrier (The Hon. Mrs. Wescot); Ahmed Khalil (Prince Ahmed); Barry Woolgar (Friend of Lady Georgina)

Two swinging con men and their perky Girl Friday team up to fleece some rich and stuffy Britishers in SHOOTING FISH, a would-be retro comedy that tries too hard to recapture the spirit of 1960s Swinging London caper movies, and only partially succeeds, although costar Kate Beckinsale is an utter delight.

Dylan (Dan Futterman), a smooth-talking Amcrican orphan with a head for numbers, goes to England and hooks up with shy electronics expert Jez (Stuart Townsend), also an orphan. Living together in a converted oil tank, they both dream of owning a stately mansion, and earn money by pulling cons and entering contests. They hire a temp named Georgie (Kate Beckinsale)—whom they both fall for—to help them with an elaborate computer scam, but assure her that their profits will go toward an orphanage they're building. After their computer is stolen, they track down the thieves and steal their van , which belongs to an insulation company, then pose as employees of the company and pull a loft insulation scam. However, when they go to pick up a check for a bogus invention, they're both arrested when the accountant turns out to be one of the victims of their insulation scam.

Jez and Dylan are sentenced to serve three months in jail, and Georgie, who's actually a member of the gentry, is coerced into becoming engaged to the boobish Roger (Dominic Mafham) when he threatens to close down the treatment center at her financially troubled home which cares for her Down syndrome-afflicted brother. While in prison, Dylan and Jez learn that the money they've accumulated will become worthless before they're released, due to the government withdrawing the 50-pound note because it has an unflattering picture of the queen. Desperate, they ask Georgie to exchange the banknotes for them, and during her wedding ceremony, Georgie learns from her sister Floss (Claire Cox) that Roger still intends to close down the Down syndrome treatment center.

She leaves him at the altar and runs to the prison to see Dylan and Jez, but after discovering that they aren't giving the money to charity, she pulls a complicated scam of her own. She uses the money to buy one of Roger's racehorses out of spite after he pays off the lien on her home and tries to close it down, but the horse turns out to be a rundown nag. However, when Dylan and Jez are released, they use helium to inflate the jockey's clothes and the horse wins a big race. They sell the horse back to Roger at an inflated price and reclaim Georgie's stately home. In a double wedding, Jez marries Georgie, while Dylan marries her sister Floss.

SHOOTING FISH is only mildly amusing at best and gratingly arch at worst, as it strenuously flails about in a rather desperate attempt to achieve a kind of effervescent irreverence. Virtually every element of the film seems to have been compiled from a checklist marked "cool," from the lead characters' names, the '60s-style pop-art animated credits, and the relentlessly trendy soundtrack, consisting of everything from rock to Burt Bacharach ("Do You Know the Way to San Jose" is heard and sung repeatedly—and annoyingly), to the unbearably "cute" gargantuan oil tank house(!), decorated with toys and gadgets (blow-up dolls, electronically-locked briefcases full of money, etc.). Added to this is an absurdly overplotted script in which all of the scams are meticulously detailed, but still manage to be confusing and not especially clever, and a smugly cartoonish directorial style that's heavy on distorted lenses and tilted angles (not to mention a telephoto shot of Dylan and Jez being chased down the street that's straight out of A HARD DAY'S NIGHT).

The story is never plausible to begin with, but it becomes ludicrous by the time Georgie manages to sneak Jez and Dylan out of prison and use blow-up dolls in their place at a fake funeral (don't ask), and the film descends into terminal bathos by shamelessly dragging in the Down syndrome subplot, succumbing to the "charity" impulse which it mocks at the beginning. Although Dylan is an obnoxious and overbearing stereotype of a Yuppie Yank (replete with rollerblades and a backwards Yankees cap), all of the performances are quite jaunty, and the film's saving grace is Beckinsale, whose natural charm, talent, and beauty go a long way toward keeping the whole thing afloat and making it seem more enjoyable than it has earned the right to be. (Profanity.)—M.S.

d, Stefan Schwartz; p, Richard Holmes, Glynis Murray; exec p, Gary Smith; assoc p, Lesley McNeil; co-p, Neil Peplow; w, Stefan Schwartz, Richard Holmes; ph, Henry Braham; ed, Alan Strachan; m, Stanislas Syrewicz; prod d, Max Gottlieb; art d, Sue Ferguson; sound, Simon Clark (recordist); casting, Sarah Beardsall, Dianne Crittenden; cos, Stewart Meachem; makeup, Susie Adams, Luisa Abel; stunts, Clive Curtis, Wayne Michaels

Comedy/Romance/Crime **(PR: C MPAA: PG)**

SHOPPING FOR FANGS ★★½

(Canada/U.S., 1998) 90m De/Center Communications ~ Margin Films c

Radmar Jao *(Phil)*; Jeanne Chin *(Katherine Nguyen/Trinh)*; Clint Jung *(Jim Lee)*; Lela Lee *(Naomi)*; John Cho *(Clarence)*; Peggy Ahn *(Grace)*; Scott Eberlein *(Matt)*; Daniel Twyman *(Dr. Suleri)*; Jennifer Hengstenberg *(Sammi)*; Dana Pan *(May)*; Roxanne Coyne *(Dr. Hali)*

SHOPPING FOR FANGS is an intermittently amusing dark comedy from first-time Asian-American filmmakers Quentin Lee and Justin Lin.

The intensely shy Katherine (Jeanne Chin) tells her therapist (Daniel Twyman) of her troubled marriage to Jim (Clint Jung) and of amnesiac spells she's had lately, during one of which she has lost her wallet. The wallet is found and mailed back by Trinh (also Jeanne Chin), a flamboyant coffeeshop waitress. In an accompanying letter, Trinh expresses a desire to meet Katherine.

Meanwhile, Phil (Radmar Jao), a lonely bachelor, begins to experience strange physical changes, including accelerated hair growth and a craving for meat. Although a doctor gives him a rational explanation for the changes, Phil is worried. One night, he meets a woman in a bar and brings her back to his apartment for sex. When he awakens the next morning, the woman is gone and Phil hears a pair of police investigators outside questioning his neighbors about a missing woman. Believing that he may be responsible, Phil seeks counsel from his sister's boyfriend, Matt (Scott Eberlein), an expert in lycanthropy. While Matt tells Phil that werewolves exist, he assures him that he is not one.

Katherine responds to Trinh's invitation and leaves Jim. The outraged Jim blames Katherine's therapist and kills him in his office. Phil, who has been recommended to the same therapist, arrives soon after and finds the corpse. Fearing that he has killed the man as a werewolf, Phil returns home and chains himself up for the night. Trinh is confronted at her job by Jim, who accuses her of stealing his wife. They fight and Trinh knocks Jim unconscious. Walking away, Trinh removes the wig and sunglasses she always wears to reveal that she is Katherine. She calls her home and leaves a message for Jim asking for a divorce.

The next morning, Phil is relieved to find that he hasn't changed into a werewolf. He shaves off his excess hair, leaves his apartment, and starts to hitchhike. Katherine, who is driving by, picks him up, and the two drive off together.

A very modest independent production, SHOPPING FOR FANGS functions in a quirky, low-key vein, rather like a Hal Hartley film. Like Hartley, writer-directors Lee and Lin are inventive enough so that their lack of budget is not a hindrance and actually contributes to the film's offbeat sensibility. The understated manner of SHOPPING FOR FANGS is continually contrasted to the film's outlandish plot turns, in which unassuming characters find their lives turned upside-down. This oppositional clash effects an agreeably oddball tone that makes the film, at its best, wryly amusing.

As novice feature filmmakers, Lee and Lin demonstrate an astute sense of structure. They cultivate both the characters and several narrative threads so that no one character or story line dominates another. When the various characters and plot threads are finally pulled together, it's plausible because of the care that has gone into their development, and the film has a satisfactory sense of closure. And Lee and Lin reveal a keen understanding of genre, cleverly exploring the film's main themes—assimilation anxiety (among Asian-Americans) and sexual repression—by evoking both the horror and action-adventure genres, while never actually entering either.

However, they also exhibit an overeagerness to flaunt their knowledge of trendy cinema. Parts of SHOPPING FOR FANGS seem to have been culled from (among other films) SAFE (1995), THE ADDICTION (1995), CHUNGKING EXPRESS (1994) (the character of Trinh—bedecked at all times in a curly blond wig and dark sunglasses—is a dead ringer for the Brigitte Lin character in Wong Kar-wai's film), and several of John Woo's movies. Although intended, perhaps, as tribute to the world's more audacious filmmakers, this grab bag of appropriation comes across pretentiously, and even as homage, it's handled clumsily.

The principal shortcoming of SHOPPING FOR FANGS, though, is its prevailing lack of energy. The temperate quality that characterizes the film and colors its comic sensibility also has an enervating affect. Lee and Lin don't appear to have the skill to sustain such a tone over the course of a feature while keeping things consistently interesting. They seem to confuse moderation with enervation, and too often their film flags to a point near inertia. SHOPPING FOR FANGS shows that its cocreators have ideas on how to make a virtue of modesty, but that they haven't yet developed the ability to make it sufficiently entertaining. *(Violence, nudity, sexual situations, adult situations, extreme profanity.)*—D.C.

d, Quentin Lee, Justin Lin; p, Quentin Lee; w, Dan Alvarado, Quentin Lee, Justin Lin; ph, Lisa Wiegand; ed, Quentin Lee, Justin Lin, Sean Yeo; m, Steven Pranoto; art d, Deeya Loram; sound, Jeffrey Liu (mixer); casting, Josh Diamond; makeup, Ray W. Lau

Comedy/Drama/Thriller (PR: C MPAA: R)

SHRUNKEN CITY, THE ★½

(U.S./Romania, 1997) 90m Full Moon; The Kushner-Locke Company ~ Full Moon c

Michael Malota *(George)*; Agnes Bruckner *(Lori)*; Jules Mandel *(Prime)*; Steve Valentine *(Leader)*; Ray Laska *(Mordan)*; Dorina Lazar *(Ramona)*; Lula Malota *(George's Mom)*; Andreea Macelaru *(Lori's Mom)*; Christopher Landry; Ion Haiduc; Mihai Baranga; Silviu Biris; Florin Chevorchian; Lucien Pavel

The law of diminishing returns definitely applies to THE SHRUNKEN CITY, a tiresome sci-fi yarn for kids.

"Shandar" is the name of an advanced, peace-loving metropolis under threat from reptilian space invaders called the Ood. To protect themselves, the Shandarians use the "Powerlink," an inexhaustible energy source sought by the Ood, to shrink their city down to a portable, domed orb. Thus camouflaged, Shandar voyages throughout time and space to hide in suspended animation on Earth.

Twenty-six thousand years later, in Cochrane Hills, Pennsylvania, a construction crew unearths the city, which is discovered by inquistive teen George (Michael Malota) and his friend Lori (Agnes Bruckner). But the boy disconnects the Powerlink, and a projected image of Shandar's awakened guardian Prime (Jules Mandel) complains that in a dozen hours or so the shrunken city will run out of energy and grow with apocalyptic force. Worse, the persistent Ood have detected Shandar and are on the way, hypnotizing everyone into seeing them as benign authority figures (surveyors, truant officers, etc.) as George and Lori flee with the city.

Returning to the construction site, the kids find and reattach the Powerlink—but it's damaged, risking a cosmic explosion. George and Lori are both teleported by Prime into Shandar itself, where they frantically connect this thingamabob to that whatzit until the power stabilizes. The Ood, who follow the children inside, are zapped to some faraway exile, and Shandar can return to its rightful place in the universe.

The SHRUNKEN CITY's plot boils down to a basic game of keep-away between two plucky but colorless teens and the swaggering, unhurried baddies (it may or may not matter that "Ood" was the name of a mad doctor in THE HEAD, a 1961 German cult horror flick).

A feeble sense of wonder arises from the fact that the object of contention is a miniaturized alien city. The prop looks like a roundish, rococo lava lamp, and when the viewer finally enters its interior the cramped, depopulated sets are underwhelming. Way too much screen time goes to tedious squabbling between the juvenile heroes and the imperious, impatient Prime, who can't understand why two 14-year-olds can't muster their world's full military might against the Ood. Prime's endless kvetching seems a far more tangible menace than the mighty explosions and expansions threatened in the dialogue.

The special effects are rickety computer graphics, but Bucharest, Romania, where the production was filmed, does a credible impersonation of a bland Pennsylvania suburb. THE SHRUNKEN CITY came out of the prolific, straight-to-video fantasy-cheapie production company originated by (uncredited) producer Charles Band, who relocated to Eastern Europe in the early 1990s to take advantage of cut-rate production costs. *(Violence.)*—C.C.

d, Ted Nicolaou; p, Vlad Paunescu; exec p, Peter Locke, Donald Kushner; co-p, Dana Scanlan; w, Benjamin Carr; ph, Vivi Dragan Visile; ed, Gregory Sanders; m, Carl Dante; prod d, Iona Corciova; art d, Viorel Ghenea; sound, Tiberiu Borcoman; cos, Oana Paunescu; makeup, Mark Rappaport; stunts, Doru Dimitrescu

Children's/Science Fiction (PR: A MPAA: PG)

SIEGE, THE ★★★

(U.S., 1998) 124m 20th Century Fox; Lynda Obst; Edward Zwick ~ 20th Century Fox c

Denzel Washington *(Anthony "Hub" Hubbard)*; Annette Bening *(Elise Kraft/Sharon Bridger)*; Bruce Willis *(General William Devereaux)*; Tony Shalhoub *(Frank Haddad)*; Sami Bouajila *(Samir Nazhde)*; Ahmed Ben Larby *(Sheik Ahmed Bin Talal)*; Mosleh Mohamed *(Muezzin)*; Liana Pai *(Tina Osu)*; Mark Valley *(Mike Johanssen)*; Jack Gwaltney *(Fred Darius)*; David Proval *(Danny Sussman)*; Lance Reddick *(Floyd Rose)*; Jeremy Knaster *(INS Official)*; William Hill *(INS Uniform)*; Aasif Mandvi *(Khalil Saleh)*; Frank DiElsi *(Officer Williams)*; Wood Harris *(Officer Henderson)*; Ellen Bethea *(Anita)*; David Costabile *(Fingerprint Expert)*; Glenn Kessler *(Fiber Expert)*; Jeffrey Allen Waid *(Video Agent)*; Tom McDermott *(Phone Bank Agent)*; Sherry Ham-Bernard *(Hub's Secretary)*; Joseph Hodge *(Landlord)*; Joey Naber *(Rashad)*; Said Faraj *(Yousuf)*; Alex Dodd *(Ali)*; Jacqueline Antaramian *(Najiba Haddad)*; Helmi Kassim *(Frank Haddad, Jr.)*; Ghoulam R. Rasoully *(Frank Jr.'s Teacher)*; Joseph Badalucco Jr. *(EMT)*; Diana Naftal *(Injured Woman)*; Insben Shenkman *(Kaplan)*; A.A. Barton Tinapp *(Mayoral)*; Neal Jones *(NYPD Representative)*; Donna Hanover *(District Attorney)*; Peter Schindler *(Johnson, FAA)*; Hany Kamal *(Arab Spokesman)*; Chip Zien *(Chief of Staff)*; Dakin Matthews *(Senator Wright)*; John Rothman *(Congressman Marshall)*; John Henry Cox *(Speaker of the House)*; E. Katherine Kerr *(Attorney General)*; Jimmie Ray Weeks *(Army General)*; Will Lyman *(FBI Director)*; Ray Godshall *(CIA Director)*; Victor Slezak *(Colonel Hardwick)*; Chris Messina *(Corporal)*; Gilbert Rosales *(Mechanic)*; Amro Salama *(Tariq Husseini)*; Jim Shankman *(ACLU Lawyer)*; Matt Servitto *(Journalist #1)*; Jourdan Fremin *(Journalist #2)*; Anjua Warfield *(March Organizer)*; Susie Essman *(Protest Speaker)*; Rory J. Aylward *(Lieutenant)*; Jeff Beatty *(FBI Agent Undercover)*; Graham J. Larson *(FBI Agent)*; Arianna Huffington *(Capital Week Pundit)*; Robert Scheer *(Capital Week Pundit)*; Matt Miller *(Capital Week Pundit)*; NEWSCASTERS: John F. Beard; Stan Brooks; Alex Chadwick; Epi Colon; Judy de Angelis; Luis Jimenez; Sean Hannity; Ronald Kuby; Daniel Schorr; Curtis Sliwa; Susan Stamberg; Mary Alice Williams

Purposefully schizophrenic, THE SIEGE is both an action-charged thriller about domestic terrorism, and a cautionary tale about the fear-inspired over-reaction to it. Fortunately, director Edward Zwick has put Denzel Washington in charge of protecting our freedom on all fronts. So while it's neither fish nor fowl, THE SIEGE is consistently entertaining.

Somewhere in the Middle East, Sheik Ahmed Bin Talal (Ahmed Ben Larby), the head of an Islamic terrorist organization, is captured in a covert US military operation under the direction of General William Devereaux (Bruce Willis). In New York City, Arab terrorists respond by blowing up a bus filled with hostages. Anthony Hubbard (Denzel Washington), the head of the Joint FBI/NYPD Terrorism Task Force, leads the hunt for the bombers, along with his partner, Frank Haddad (Tony Shalhoub). Their chase crosses paths with that of Elise Kraft (Annette Bening), a CIA agent who knows more than she's letting on. Her secret lover, Samir (Sami Bouajila), is a double-agent who has infiltrated the terrorist underground.

Although those who carried out the bus bombing are caught, a crowded Broadway theater is bombed, and the attempted bombing of a school is narrowly thwarted by Hubbard. As fear grips the city, Hubbard's team makes little headway; they can track down various functionaries, but not the terrorists' leader. After the FBI headquarters itself is bombed (killing more than 600 people), martial law is declared in New York. Devereaux is put in charge of the military occupation. Brooklyn is sealed off, and Arabs and Arab-Americans, including Haddad's son, are rounded up and placed in an internment camp. Here, under Devereaux's interpretation of martial law, prisoners are tortured and even executed. Opposed to Devereaux's suspension of civil rights, Hubbard presses Kraft for the "classified" information she's been concealing. She is really a NSA agent named Sharon Bridger; the terrorists are Iraqis she helped train. Samir, a triple-agent who has been masterminding the attacks all along, has duped her. When Samir is found out, he kills Bridger, and Hubbard kills him. Hubbard moves to arrest Devereaux for murder and civil rights violations and end the martial law. After a tense standoff in which Hubbard's and Devereaux's men hold each other at gunpoint, Hubbard talks the general into backing down, and all his prisoners are released.

When our republic comes under attack, we cannot protect it by dismantling our democracy. That's the point Zwick is making with THE SIEGE; and anyone who doubts that should read up on the internment of Japanese-Americans during WWII. The movie also makes the point that though some Islamic Arabs have declared a jihad against the US, the overwhelming majority of Arabs in the US are good and decent people. Nonetheless, THE SIEGE came under attack from antidefamation groups for its depiction of Arabs as killers.

The action-thriller is, ideologically, a right-wing form of expression (think DIRTY HARRY, 1971). It's Zwick's intention to give us his best impression of a high-octane popcorn movie, then pull the rug out from under our feet and slap us in the face with a left-of-center message about the sanctity of the Constitution. That Zwick would proffer such thematically complicated work isn't too much of a surprise—COURAGE UNDER FIRE (1996) tried to be both pro-Gulf War and anti-war in general. And Zwick has Washington, who excels at portraying ethical righteousness, to guide us by the nose through the proceedings. Unfortunately, the movie sets us up for a confrontation between Washington and Willis that never comes. Willis sneers through his scenes, and once his villainy is firmly established, the audience's collective reactionary bone is looking for our hero to take him down hard. Zwick fails us by ending THE SIEGE, which has so many bangs, with a whimper. *(Violence, profanity, sexual situations.)*— P.R.

d, Edward Zwick; p, Edward Zwick, Lynda Obst; exec p, Peter Schindler; assoc p, Robin Budd; w, Lawrence Wright, Menno Meyjes, Edward Zwick (based on a story by Lawrence Wright); ph, Roger Deakins; ed, Steven Roseblum; m, Graeme Revell; prod d, Lily Kilvert; art d, Chris Shriver; set d, Gretchen Rau; sound, Allan Byer (mixer); fx, Paul Lombardi; casting, Mary Goldberg, Mary Colquhoun; cos, Ann Roth; makeup, Kathryn Bihr; stunts, Joel J. Kramer

Drama/Political/Thriller (PR: C MPAA: R)

SILVER SCREEN: COLOR ME LAVENDER, THE ★★★

(U.S., 1998) 101m Couch Potato Productions ~ Planet Pictures c/bw

Dan Butler *(Narrator)*

Filmmaker Mark Rappaport's video essay (which received a theatrical release in 1998) about the gay subtext that ran through many films in Hollywood's Golden Age is witty, incisive, and amusing. At points it also seems like too much of a good thing, with certain points being elaborated at length; however, the questions Rappaport raises, and his immaculate ability to reedit Hollywood classics to his own advantage, make SILVER SCREEN a very watchable and entertaining act of deconstruction.

SILVER SCREEN consists of film clips that span a period from the 1930s to the early 1960s, edited together to reinforce certain points about Hollywood's covert depiction of seemingly gay characters and attitudes. Rappaport focuses first on the prissy character actors who populated the sophisticated comedies of the 1930s: Edward Everett Horton, Eric Blore, Franklin Pangborn, et al. In this way, Hollywood is seen to have stereotyped effeminate behavior as an upperclass affectation. When America became involved in WWII, attitudes changed and these characters disappeared. They were replaced by a pervasive strain of innuendo in the vehicle comedies of the 1940s and '50s: Bob Hope's cowardly-but-vain screen persona produced a large number of jokes dealing with gender preference and "nontraditional" male behavior (especially in his ROAD movies with Bing Crosby); Danny Kaye, Red Skelton, and Martin and Lewis also toyed with this concept of the childish/foppish adult male. It's suggested that perhaps American audiences could tolerate this behavior from comedians as they are known to go to any lengths for a laugh, whereas the stars of westerns and crime films were identified more explicitly with their macho roles.

After a discussion of "epicene" actor Clifton Webb, Rappaport turns to a lengthy analysis of the sidekick character in action films, most notably as incarnated by Walter Brennan. These figures are seen to be domestic partners of a sort—they devote themselves entirely to the welfare of the western/criminal hero, to the extent of cooking and keeping house for them.

Jumping away from Hollywood, Rappaport next includes a discussion of the European cinema of roughly the same period, spotlighting how the work of Cocteau, Visconti, and others fetishized the male image as Hollywood had done with the female. Returning to America, the career of Randolph Scott is analyzed in light of certain facts about his private life—including his having lived with Cary Grant for some time as "carefree bachelors" when both actors were big-name stars. The final topic is the military; a series of comic sequences from war/army films illustrate Rappaport's concept of the "Hollywood telegraph system," in which gay signals and codes could be conveyed but never acknowledged consciously on screen.

Though narrator Dan Butler (of TV's "Frasier") does note at the outset of SILVER SCREEN that what will be offered up is an "incomplete" survey of Hollywood films, the piece's length (and the short duration of the majority of the clips) makes it seem as if this essay is longer than it actually is. When it's at its best, though, Rappaport scores some tremendous points against Hollywood's twisted history. As he did in his earlier video essay ROCK HUDSON'S HOME MOVIES (1993), he essentially uses the evidence found in the films themselves to illustrate his conclusions. The section that covers gay innuendo in the work of Hope, Kaye, et al, is truly eye-opening: one laughs not at the particular jokes being excerpted, but at Rappaport's skillful juxtaposition of the clips, showing that gay gags were indeed pervasive and were in fact pretty bold for the period under consideration (especially in light of the way that the heterosexual innuendo of such performers as Mae West had been blunted by the Hays Office).

Other sections of SILVER SCREEN prove equally absorbing, but some problems do arise as a result of Rappaport's method. His inclusion of European filmmakers (among them Cocteau and Visconti, who were open about their own homosexuality) takes the video in a very different direction. The point about the vast difference between the depiction of the male image in American and European cinema has much validity, but there seems little reason to return to the trite double entendres of Hollywood's creations after viewing the fully realized works of master filmmakers. Rappaport also unfortunately hammers home one of his themes for far too long: the "grizzled sidekick" section of the video comprises literally a quarter of the film's entire running time, proving brilliantly funny at first and then wearing down the viewer with what appears to be every single instance in which a Walter Brennan character acted in an oddly over-protective way (and there appear to be *plenty* of such instances).

These structural problems aside, SILVER SCREEN has much to commend it. In fact, the final section in which a series of film clips depicts male couples dancing, reminds one of Rappaport's skill and talent as an eccentrically lyrical filmmaker. And then there are the clips themselves—their inclusion in this often wonderfully amusing assemblage ensures that they can never be viewed in the same way again.—E.G.

d, Mark Rappaport; w, Mark Rappaport; ph, Nancy Schreiber; ed, Mark Rappaport

Documentary **(PR: C MPAA: NR)**

SIMON BIRCH ★★★

(U.S., 1998) 110m Hollywood Pictures; Caravan Pictures; Roger Birnbaum; Laurence Mark ~ Buena Vista c

Ian Michael Smith *(Simon Birch)*; Joseph Mazzello *(Joe Wenteworth)*; Ashley Judd *(Rebecca Wenteworth)*; Oliver Platt *(Ben Goodrich)*; David Strathairn *(Reverend Russell)*; Dana Ivey *(Grandmother Wenteworth)*; Beatrice Winde *(Hildie Grove)*; Jan Hooks *(Miss Leavey)*; Ceciley Carroll *(Marjorie)*; Sumela-Rose Keramidopulos *(Ann)*; Sam Morton *(Stuart)*; Jim Carrey *(Adult Joe Wenteworth)*; John Mazzello *(Simon Wenteworth)*; Holly Dennison *(Mrs. Birch)*; Peter MacNeil *(Mr. Birch)*; Addison Bell *(Doctor Wells)*; Roger McKeen *(Coach Higgins)*; Sean McCann *(Chief Al Cork)*; John Robinson *(Mr. Baker)*; Guy Sanvido *(Janitor)*; Gil Filar *(Eddie)*; Marcello Meleca *(Howard Ellis)*; Tim Hall *(Pitcher)*; Tom Redman *(First Baseman)*; Mark Skrela *(Third Baseman)*; Kevin White *(Shortstop)*; Terry V. Hart *(Umpire)*; Alan Markfield *(Umpire)*; Chrisopher Marren *(Rival Baseball Coach)*; Tommy Dorrian *(Teammate #1)*; Justin Marangoni *(Teammate #2)*; Tyler Cairns *(Sheep)*; Gino Giacomini *(Wise Man)*; Barbara Stewart *(Delivery Room Nurse)*; David Rigby *(Bus Driver)*; Sam Aaron *(Old Man #1)*; David Chapman *(Old Man #2)*; Wendy Fleming *(Mrs. Russell)*; Junior Lambs: Paul De Fibo; Cameron Croughwell; Scotty Leavenworth; Joshua Titen; Joshua Croughwell; Dalton Rondell; Logan Holladay; Devon Alan; Tony Orr; Jeffrey Schoeny; Derek Montgomery; Devon Borisoff; Brian McLaughlin; Sean Flynn Amir; Blake Hubbell; Ramiro Gonzalez III; Trevor Habberstad; Sean Sullivan; Taylor Emerson; Nicholas Andrew; Patrick McTavish; Cody Gill; Mitchell Orr

A story of a small boy with a big heart, SIMON BIRCH isn't as inspiring as it would like to be, but still manages to be sentimental without turning mawkish.

Joe Wenteworth (Jim Carrey) reminisces about his childhood best friend Simon while visiting his grave: The diminutive Simon (Ian Michael Smith) always believed that, despite his tiny stature, God would make him a hero, though he shies away from religious activities run by the Rev. Russell (David Strathairn).

Joe (Joseph Mazzello) and Simon attend junior high, where Simon is infatuated with classmate Marjorie (Ceciley Carroll). He also has a crush on Joe's unmarried mother, Rebecca (Ashley Judd), who has never revealed the identity of Joe's father. She starts dating the amiable Ben (Oliver Platt), who gives Joe a stuffed armadillo.

During a Little League game, Simon hits a foul ball that kills Rebecca. Devastated, Simon gives the distraught Joe his precious baseball card collection; Joe gives Simon his armadillo. With only his Grandma (Dana Ivey) for family, Joe becomes obsessed with learning who his father is. After Simon's antics disrupt the church Christmas pageant, he is expelled by Rev. Russell, who confiscates his baseball cards and orders him and Joe to chaperone third-graders at the church retreat. But Simon gets sick and cannot go. After the others leave, he breaks into Rev. Russell's office to retrieve his baseball cards. There, he finds evidence that the Reverend is Joe's father. Simon and Ben race to the retreat, where the Rev. Russell has already revealed his guilty secret to his son.

Simon joins the others on the bus ride home, where Joe suggests that his destiny was to help him find his father. An accident sends the bus into a raging river. Rev. Russell is knocked unconscious and the driver flees as the bus begins to sink. Simon calms the panicked kids and organizes an orderly evacuation as Joe and Ben ferry children to shore. Simon just manages to save the last child before he sinks with the bus. Joe drags his unconscious body out of the river. In the hospital, after the two best friends say goodbye, Simon dies. After Joe's grandmother dies the following June, he is adopted by Ben; Simon did help him find a real father.

Back in the present, Joe is joined by his own son, and leaves the beloved armadillo at Simon's grave.

SIMON BIRCH offers hope that amid the horrifying capriciousness of life, some of us may have been put here for a reason—even if it's not the reason we think it is. While the destination of the film is fairly predictable, it's still unexpected in execution. We're sure Simon is bound for glory, but we're caught off-guard by the means, and the high stakes of his struggle to fulfill his destiny.

Adapted by director Mark Steven Johnson from a segment of John Irving's novel *A Prayer for Owen Meany*, Johnson maintains an earnest tone that avoids bathos; things never get weepy until the very end. But the pacing does lag in places, and there is some confusion about the passage of time—is it months, weeks or days between some events? The photography cloaks the action in deep, thick shadows, but bathes characters in brilliant light. Scenes are also framed amidst wonderfully atmospheric winter tableaux.

Johnson evokes sympathetic but not pitiable performances from his talented cast. Smith is a surprisingly talented non-actor who has a disability that has affected his growth; as Simon, he maintains a sense of bemused attachment and quiet authority, playing the character not as a victim, but rather as a hero-in-waiting. Mazzello is engaging in a difficult part—the point-of-view buddy who's important but incidental to events. Judd is simply luminous as the life force of the picture. Platt offers a wonderful, quiet strength and dignity; it's pleasant to see a big man in a romantic role.

SIMON BIRCH tries to remind us that no matter how certain we may be of our place in the universe, we can never really be sure. God works in mysterious ways, and the only thing we can count on is that we'll never see it coming. *(Profanity.)*—J.Di.

d, Mark Steven Johnson; p, Laurence Mark, Roger Birnbaum; exec p, John Baldecchi; assoc p, Howard Ellis; co-p, Billy Higgins; w, Mark Steven Johnson (suggested by the novel *A Prayer for Owen Meany* by John Irving); ph, Aaron E. Schneider; ed, David Finfer; m, Marc Shaiman; prod d, David Chapman; art d, Dennis Davenport; set d, Carolyn A. Loucks; sound, Glen Gauthier (mixer); fx, Joe Bauer, Modern Videofilm; casting, Mary Gail Artz, Barbara Cohen; cos, Betsy Heimann, Abram Waterhouse; makeup, Marilyn Terry; stunts, Alison Reid

Comedy/Religious/Drama (PR: C MPAA: PG)

SIMPLE PLAN, A ★★★½
(U.S., 1998) 120m Scott Rudin Productions; Mutual Film Co; Paramount Pictures ~ Paramount c

Bill Paxton *(Hank Mitchell)*; Billy Bob Thornton *(Jacob Mitchell)*; Bridget Fonda *(Sarah Mitchell)*; Brent Briscoe *(Lou Chambers)*; Becky Ann Baker *(Nancy)*; Chelcie Ross *(Carl)*; Gary Cole *(Baxter)*; Jack Walsh *(Mr. Pederson)*; Bob Davis *(FBI Agent Renkins)*; Peter Syvertson *(FBI Agent Freemont)*; Tom Carey *(Dwight Stephanson)*; John Paxton *(Mr. Schmitt)*; Marie Mathay *(News Reporter)*; Paul Magers *(Anchorman)*; Joan Steffand *(Anchorwoman)*; Jill Sayre *(Hospital Nurse)*; Wayne A. Evenson *(Bartender)*; Timothy Storms *(Drinker)*; Terry Hempleman *(Dead Pilot)*; Jay Gjernes *(Bearded Man)*; Grant Curtis; Solomon Abrams; Nina Kaczorowiski *(Bar Patrons)*; Thomas Boedy *(Priest)*; Mary Woolever *(Linda)*; Rhiannon R. Savers *(Girl on Sled)*; Christopher Gallus *(Boy on Sled)*; Eric Cegon *(Tommy)*; Robert Martin Halverson *(Detective)*; Roger Watton *(Barber)*

Adapted by Scott B. Smith from his 1994 bestseller of the same name, A SIMPLE PLAN is the story of a group of decent people who are destroyed by their own greed. Impeccably photographed in Snow Belt country, the movie succeeds by reintroducing narrative clarity and a moral spine to a genre that increasingly had been eschewing both.

Hank Mitchell (Bill Paxton) is a young accountant who lives and works in a country town. One snowy day Hank, his slightly simpleminded brother Jacob (Billy Bob Thornton), and Lou (Brent Briscoe), a friend, find a small plane that has crashed in the woods. Inside the plane is more than $4,000,000 in cash. The men decide to hide the money until spring, then split it or, if anyone's looking for it, burn it.

Hank's wife Sarah (Bridget Fonda) advises him to return half a million dollars to the plane, to avert future suspicion. As he is doing so, an old farmer (Tom Carey) approaches, Jacob panics and clubs him, Hank finishes him off, and together the brothers dispose of the body. Later, a newspaper story reveals that the cash in the plane was ransom money.

Shortly thereafter, Sarah gives birth to a baby girl. Lou, who is heavily in debt, becomes impatient to divvy up the dough. In order to keep him quiet, Hank and Jacob, at Sarah's suggestion, trick him into making a recorded confession to the slaying of the old farmer. When Lou pulls out a shotgun and demands the tape, a shootout ensues and the brothers kill Lou and his wife (Becky Ann Baker). Carl (Chelcie Ross), the local sheriff, accepts Hank and Jacob's alibi of self-defense.

Hank, Jacob, Carl, and Baxter (Gary Cole), a thief posing as an FBI agent, go out into the woods to inspect the plane. There, after killing Carl, Baxter is killed by Hank. Deeply depressed by the situation, Jacob urges his brother to shoot him in the head and Hank reluctantly complies.

Hank discovers that the serial numbers of one-tenth of the bills he is hoarding were copied before being turned over to pay the ransom. Realizing he can never safely pass the money, he burns it. Guilt ridden, he and Sarah return to their workaday world, but their lives will never again be as happy and contented as they were before last winter.

A SIMPLE PLAN was to have been directed by John Boorman, who contributed substantial input to the project before a scheduling conflict forced him off the picture. After the gifted John Dahl came and went, Sam Raimi took over, and it's hard to imagine Dahl or even Boorman doing a better job. Known for directing such flamboyant cult films as THE EVIL DEAD (1983) and such underrated action pictures as DARKMAN (1990) and THE QUICK AND THE DEAD (1995), Raimi reportedly welcomed the opportunity to make a movie that would not be dependent on dazzling cinematics, a movie that was actor-driven rather than action-driven. His success with A SIMPLE PLAN establishes him as one of the most talented and versatile directors of his time.

The film's most conspicuous virtue is the clarity of its plot line; at no point does sloppy construction obscure what is happening to whom, when, where, and why. Though never convoluted, the story is nonetheless complex enough to sustain interest and provide an involving plot twist every reel or two. What's more, A SIMPLE PLAN is a thriller with a conscience and a heart worn not on its sleeve, like so many Hollywood potboilers, but in the right place.

Much of this compassionate quality can be credited to Billy Bob Thornton's portrayal of the unsophisticated, unemployed, and unloved Jacob. At once modest and inventive in his approach to the role, Thornton not only plays Jacob more effectively than most actors would have, he plays him quite differently.

Among A SIMPLE PLAN's other rewards are a scary scene involving crows in a cockpit, a robust supporting performance by Becky Ann Baker, interesting intimations of the class differences that subtly distance Hank from his hometown friends and neighbors, and the deliciously ambiguous remark Sarah makes to her worried husband in an attempt to cheer him up: "Nobody would ever believe that you'd be capable of doing what you've done." *(Graphic violence, extreme profanity.)* —D.T.

d, Sam Raimi; p, Adam Schroeder, James Jacks; exec p, Mark Gordon, Gary Levinsohn; co-p, Michael Polaire; w, Scott B. Smith, Susana Preston (based on the novel by Scott B. Smith); ph, Alar Kivilo; ed, Arthur Coburn, Eric Beason; m, Danny Elfman; prod d, Patrizia Von Brandenstein; art d, James F. Truesdale; set d, Hilton Rosemarin; sound, Ed Novick (mixer); fx, John D. Milinac; casting, Ilene Starger; cos, Julie Weiss; makeup, Lynne Eagan; stunts, Chris Doyle

AAN Best Supporting Actor: Billy Bob Thornton; *AAN Best Adapted Screenplay:* Scott B. Smith

Thriller/Crime/Drama (PR: O MPAA: R)

SIN AND REDEMPTION ★½
(U.S., 1994) 94m Stonehenge Productions; Viacom Productions ~ Paramount Home Video c

Cynthia Gibb *(Billie Simms)*; Richard Grieco *(Jim McDaniel)*; Ralph Waite *(Cal Simms)*; Concetta Tomei *(Mrs. McDaniel)*; Cheryl Pollak *(Mary Ann Simms)*; Chapelle Jaffe *(Emma Simms)*; Brittany Tiplady *(Katie-Aged One Year)*; Colleen Rennison *(Katie-Aged Five Years)*; Ashley Rogers *(Sally Simms)*; Kelly Sheridan *(Sarah Simms)*; Alex Bruhanski *(Mr. Farley)*; Walter Marsh *(Jack McDaniels)*; Jay Ono *(Sammy)*; Jason

Gaffney *(Boy One)*; Jed Rees *(Boy Two)*; Lossen Chambers *(Connie)*; Todd Dulmage *(Frank)*; Sheelah Megill *(Nurse One)*; Andrew Wheeler *(J.P.)*; Gillian Carfa *(Linda)*; William MacDonald *(Fred)*; Steve Hilton *(Dr. Graham)*; Taylor McLellyn *(Jimmy)*; Vicki Dahl *(Nurse Two)*; Sandra Grant *(Doctor)*; Lorena Gale *(Nurse Three)*

The premise of this unsavory made-for-TV sudser is so sexist and preposterous that the mind reels: A virginal young woman is raped and unwittingly marries her repentant attacker! Maybe Pedro Almodovar could get away with this psycho-sexual melodrama, but, as morosely executed here, the movie's central dramatic peg is merely and clearly offensive.

Taking a short-cut home from work, high-schooler Billie Simms (Cynthia Gibb) is raped. Not only does the incident cause an unwanted pregnancy that damages her college expectations, but it also outrages her smugly religious father Cal Simms (Ralph Waite), who unsuccessfully pressures her to give up the baby. Sir Galahad arrives in the person of upper-middle-class Jim McDaniel (Richard Grieco), who falls for and marries blue-collar Billie, much to the chagrin of his snooty mother (Concetta Tomei).

Strains on the marriage quickly surface: ne'er-do-well Jim can't hold a job, and Billie becomes pregnant a second time. Oldest daughter Katie is diagnosed with progressive kidney deterioration. By the time Billie bears a third sickly child, critically ill Katie needs an organ donor. Jim refuses to take a compatibility test, even though he is not supposed to be a blood relative to the girl. When he relents, and proves a perfect tissue match, Billie realizes the truth: it was Jim who raped her, later marrying her out of guilt. Billie is grateful to Jim for donating his kidney to save Katie's life. Independent at last, Billie realizes her dream of a writing career. Although she doesn't deny Jim his parental rights, she divorces him and returns to pursue her education.

Every opportunity for legitimate emotional development is undercut by the luridness of SIN AND REDEMPTION's low-down high concept. Within its tasteless perimeters, this sex opera pays lip service to important considerations like the smothering effects of early marriage and religious hypocrisy about unwed mothers. The leading players tackle their roles superficially, barely hinting at the lack of self-esteem that ruins Billie and Jim's lives. The sleazy treatment of such a serious subject makes the film even more of a distasteful viewing experience. Although this film is dressed up as a made-for-TV issues movie, it has more in common with old exploitation flicks like CHILD BRIDE (1937) and MARRIED TOO YOUNG (1961), which blanket their prurient interest with twaddle about social significance for the audience. *(Violence, sexual situations, substance abuse.)*—R.P.

d, Neema Barnette; p, Loucas George; exec p, Allan Marcil, Dick Berg; co-p, Ellie Ashburn; w, Ellen Weston; ph, Tobias A. Schliessler; ed, Victor Dubois; m, David Bell; prod d, William Heslup; art d, Ken Rabehl; set d, Michael O'Connor; sound, Daryl Powell (mixer); fx, Rory Cutler; casting, Beth Klein; cos, Jane Still; makeup, Connie Parker; stunts, Jacob Rupp

Drama **(PR: C MPAA: PG-13)**

SIX DAYS, SEVEN NIGHTS ★★½

(U.S., 1998) 101m Caravan Pictures; La Luna Films ~ Buena Vista c

Harrison Ford *(Quinn Harris)*; Anne Heche *(Robin Monroe)*; David Schwimmer *(Frank Martin)*; Jacqueline Obradors *(Angelica)*; Temuera Morrison *(Jager)*; Allison Janney *(Marjorie)*; Douglas Weston *(Philippe)*; Cliff Curtis *(Kip)*; Danny Trejo *(Pierce)*; Ben Bode *(Helicopter Pilot)*; Derek Basco *(Ricky)*; Amy Sedaris *(Robin's Secretary)*; Long Nguyen; John Koyama; Jake Feagai; Jen Sung Outerbridge *(Pirates)*; Michael Chapman *(Handsome Mechanic)*; E. Kalani Flores *(Tahitian Priest)*; Ping Wu *(Infirmary Orderly)*; Greg Gorman *(Photographer)*; Hoyt Richards; Odile Broulard *(Models)*; Cynthia Langbridge *(Resort Greeter)*; Jody Kono *(Hotel Clerk)*; Michael Lushing *(Front Desk Clerk)*; Pua Kaholokula *(Waitress)*; Ron Dinson Jr. *(Bellboy)*; Don Nahaku *(Bellboy No. 2)*; Priscilla Lee Taylor *(Bathing Suit Girl)*; Reri Tava Jobe; Natalie Goss *(Flight Attendants)*; Christian Martson *(French Airport Security No. 1)*; James Edward Sclafani *(French Airport Security No. 2)*; Jason S. Nichols *(Runway Traffic)*; Taj Mahal *(Himself)*; Fred Lunt; Kester Smith; Wayne Jacintho; Rudy Costa; Carlos Andrade; Pat Cockett; Michael Barretto; Pancho Graham *(Band Members)*; Mervyn Lilo; Afa Thompson; Gordon Lilo; Javan Kaiama; Nicole Maldonado *(Dancers)*; Iele; Eric Laufiso; Vise Vitale; Aldo Paro; Wayne Aqino; Lloyd Chandler *(Musicians)*; Elliot M. Kaplan *(Man at Bar)*; Stephen James Conteh *(Newspaper Salesman)*

This pleasant, albeit predictable, summer comedy—about mismatched, bickering castaways who fall in love—created more fireworks offscreen than on, thanks to all the press attention lavished on costar Anne Heche's high-profile lesbian relationship. The merits of the film itself ultimately played second fiddle to all the second-guessing about whether a gay star could convincingly portray hetero passion.

In wintery Manhattan, Robin Monroe (Anne Heche), the busy associate editor of a fashion magazine, looks forward to a week's vacation with her boyfriend, Frank (David Schwimmer), in Kauai, an Hawaiian island. Upon their arrival, Frank proposes marriage and Robin accepts, but their celebration is cut short when Robin's boss, Marjorie (Allison Janey), asks her to oversee an emergency photo-shoot in Tahiti. Reluctantly, Robin leaves Frank, and takes off in a rickety aircraft with Quinn Harris (Harrison Ford), a laid-back aviator. An unexpected storm forces Quinn to land the plane on a deserted island, wrecking his landing gear in the process. Stranded, Quinn and Robin become quickly irritated with each other but try to make the best of the situation. While waiting for a rescue party, they gather food and share resources. Meanwhile, back in Kauai, Frank worries about Robin and joins Quinn's dancer-girlfriend, Angelica (Jacqueline Obradors), in a series of futile helicopter rescue missions.

As Robin displays an unexpected survival skill, Quinn begins taking a liking to the young woman. After a scary ordeal with a group of modern-day pirates (Temuera Morrison, Cliff Curtis, Danny Trejo, Long Nguyen) from whom they barely escape, Quinn and Robin grow closer, but stop short of starting a romance. Yet, back at the resort, Frank and Angelica think their mates have died, so they consummate a sexual relationship. When Quinn finds an old aircraft on the island, he and Robin renovate it and fly back to Kauai. During an island "funeral" service, Robin and Quinn relieve the mourners as they land on the beach, alive and safe. Before leaving Kauai with Frank, Robin tries to ascertain where she stands with Quinn, but the hard-bitten island regular gives her no promise of developing their friendship. On her way home, Robin learns of Frank's infidelity and breaks off the engagement. Just before their plane departs, she gets off the craft—with Quinn waiting for her on the runway, and ready to face the future together.

SIX DAYS, SEVEN NIGHTS presents an inventory of every sort of comic and dramatic bit of business from a whole range of stranded castaway movies, including WE'RE NOT DRESSING (1934), ON AN ISLAND WITH YOU (1948), ATOLL K (1950), HEAVEN KNOWS, MR. ALLISON (1957), and, most prominently, ROMANCING THE STONE (1984), which itself borrowed heavily from RAIDERS OF THE LOST ARK (1981). At times, SIX DAYS, SEVEN NIGHTS even borrows from such disparate sources as SWEPT AWAY... BY AN UNUSUAL DESTINY IN THE BLUE SEA OF AUGUST (1974) and the more mundane (but ubiquitous) castaway saga, "Gilligan's Island."

With its characters' class lines erased, SIX DAYS represents a traditional battle-of-the-sexes; here, the woman comes out the loser in that she gives up her home, job, income, and whatever authority she possesses to stay with her father-figure lover on the island. (Robin even starts uttering foolish lines like, "I need you to be my confident captain.") Scripter Michael Browning and director Ivan Reitman treat the island natives and pirate characters in a similarly retrograde way, making the film feel very dated at times. (Morrison as the lead pirate takes a step backward from his better performance and role in ONCE WERE WARRIORS.)

Still, Ford and Heche measure up to the challenge of the grade-B material. Though neither performer is noted as a comedian, both show a natural affinity in their timing and expressions (it's the flat dialogue and sexually gauche situations that let *them* down). Ford and Heche are also nicely supported by Schwimmer (of "Friends" fame), Obradors, and Janey, all of whom make something out of their cardboard characters.

The film, unfortunately, may best be remembered in relation to Heche's real-life revelation of her relationship with sitcom star Ellen DeGeneres. A tidal wave of publicity followed this proclamation (made initially in relation to DeGeneres's own public coming out). Heche neatly confounded the silly "advance word" that predicted she would not be able to pull off love scenes with Ford because of her real-life proclivities. This revelation colors certain moments in the film (at one point, for example, when Robin asks Quinn if he wonders why she doesn't find him attractive), but certainly is not the reason SIX DAYS, SEVEN NIGHTS ultimately wound up as a critical and commercial flop—in fact, Heche is easily the best part of the film. *(Violence, sexual situations, profanity.)*—E.M.

d, Ivan Reitman; p, Ivan Reitman, Wallis Nicita, Roger Birnbaum; exec p, Joe Medjuck, Daniel Goldberg, Julie Bergman Sender; assoc p, Terry Norton, Michael Palmieri; co-p, Gordon Webb, Sheldon Kahn; w, Michael Browning; ph, Michael Chapman; ed, Sheldon Kahn, Wendy Greene Bricmont; m, Randy Edelman; prod d, J. Michael Riva; art d, David F. Klassen, Richard F. Mays; set d, Lauri Gaffin; sound, Gene Cantamessa (mixer), John Pospisil (design); fx, Larry Cavanaugh, Bruce Steinheimer, Richard M. Zarro, Jean S. Tom, David McCullough; casting, Michael Chinich, Bonnie Timmerman; cos, Gloria Gresham; makeup, Ken Chase; stunts, Doug Coleman

Romance/Adventure/Comedy (PR: C MPAA: PG-13)

SIX O'CLOCK NEWS ★★★½

(U.S., 1997) 103m Homemade Movies; Channel 4 ~ First Run Features c

Ross McElwee; Marilyn Levine; Adrian McElwee; Mariah McElwee; Charleen; Steve Im; John Noeding; Caroline Noeding; Salvador Pena

South Carolina-born, Boston-based filmmaker Ross McElwee continues his series of diary films, the best known of which is SHERMAN'S MARCH (1986), with this record of his quest to learn more about people whose shattered lives he sees on television news broadcasts. The conclusion—that people pick up and carry on with their lives as best they can—isn't too surprising. Unfortunately, neither is much else in this film. McElwee meanders, ready as always to pursue any interesting digressions, but few come his way.

1993. Since his last film, TIME INDEFINITE (1991), McElwee and his new wife Marilyn have had a son, Adrian. Confined to the house, he becomes obsessed with watching the news on TV, which offers a seemingly endless parade of people in the worst moments of their lives. When he sees that Hurricane Hugo has devastated the Carolina island where his old friend Charleen lives, he goes there with Charleen's son to be with her. Having suffered the death of her husband and the loss of her previous house to fire, Charleen wonders if she can start again, and says that if she knew about the unpredictability of life when she was younger she would never have had children.

After diversions with a neighbor who obsessively tapes old television shows, and a tabloid TV show that interviews him for a segment, McElwee decides to hit the road and get a closer look at some of the people he has seen on the news. He meets Steve Im, a Korean immigrant whose wife was brutally murdered; John and Caroline Noeding, residents of an Arizona trailer park that was destroyed by a tornado; and Salvador Pena, who survived the collapse of a parking garage in a Los Angeles earthquake. In between, he entertains an offer to direct a fictional film for Miramax, and (while in Los Angeles) observes the filming of an episode of "Baywatch." Three years later, as he edits the film we are watching, violence strikes his neighborhood in the form of a shooting at an abortion clinic; soon after, he films Charleen meeting her grandchild for the first time.

Like Woody Allen and Henry Jaglom at their best, Ross McElwee has the rare gift of being able to share his self-absorption in a way that makes it universal. So what SIX O'CLOCK NEWS lacks is something that would be a drawback in most films—there is too little of the filmmaker. Aside from the usual worries of a first-time parent about the state of the world that the child is entering, McElwee seems to be at a happy point in his life, and it's a sad cliche that happiness is dull, at least in art. McElwee's concern about what he sees on television come across as too much a matter of form, that the few seconds of people suffering from this or that tragedy in no way paint an adequate picture of their lives; his feelings don't provide a base or inform the film the way his loneliness did in SHERMAN'S MARCH, or his fear of nuclear war did in TIME INDEFINITE.

Still, even if SIX O'CLOCK NEWS is a lesser McElwee film, there is enough dry wit to please his fans, particularly during his encounters with Hollywood and when he is interviewed for a TV show and finds himself jockeying with the show's cameraman for position. (As always, McElwee films everything.) It's nice to renew our acquaintance with both him and his friend Charleen (though it saddens us to hear of the troubles she has been through). Like the seven Brits whose lives have been charted in the series of 7 UP films, McElwee has become a friend we enjoy catching up with every few years, even if (because he operates his own camera), we seldom actually *see* him. *(Adult situations.)*—M.F.

d, Ross McElwee; ph, Ross McElwee; ed, Ross McElwee; sound, Richard Bock

Documentary (PR: C MPAA: NR)

SIX-STRING SAMURAI ★★

(U.S., 1998) 81m HSX Films; Palm Pictures ~ Palm Pictures c

Jeffrey Falcon *(Buddy)*; Justin McGuire *(The Kid)*; Stephane Gauger *(Death)*; John Sakisian *(Russian General)*; Gabrille Pimenter *(Little Man)*; Zuma Jay *(Clint)*; Monti Ellison *(Head Pin Pal)*; Kim de Angelo *(Mother)*; Clifford Hugo *(Psycho)*

While technically polished, this low-budget sci-fi saga rates as ambitious but overly derivative.

In 1957, after the Russians bombed the US, "Lost Vegas" became the last refuge of freedom and Elvis Presley was named King of the Free World. Forty years later Elvis has died, and among the many would-be new Kings trekking toward Vegas is the guitar-playing, sword-wielding Buddy (Jeffrey Falcon). As he fights his way across the post-apocalyptic wasteland, he picks up a young orphaned boy (Justin McGuire), whom he reluctantly allows to join him. During the journey, they encounter and fight off a gang of bowlers-cum-bounty hunters, the whacked-out, cannibalistic Cleaver clan, and other threatening types; all the while, Buddy is stalked by Death (Stephane Gauger) and his minions.

As Buddy and the kid near Vegas, they run into a Russian general (John Sakisian) and his military outpost. Buddy takes on the general and his soldiers, and manages to slaughter them all. He is then confronted by Death, who engages Buddy in a pitched sword fight. Buddy is defeated, but before he dies, he passes on his guitar and his legacy to the kid, who heads through the gates of Vegas in Buddy's place.

SIX STRING SAMURAI does have a sharp, stylish look, but as much as one wants to applaud writer-director Lance Mungia and writer-star Falcon for pulling this movie together by hook or by crook, it's disappointing to realize that their efforts were all in the service of a second-hand vision. They seem to have drawn their inspiration from a marathon viewing of samurai films, spaghetti Westerns, and Hong Kong actioners, with a couple of Elvis movies thrown in for good measure; the central story line (loner plus feral kid in a post-apocalyptic landscape) is borrowed directly from THE ROAD WARRIOR (1982). Instead of being presented in a spirit of either conscious homage or satire, these influences are simply appropriated outright, with an unfortunate lack of fresh ideas.

Better action sequences and a stronger hero at the film's center might have helped. Despite Falcon's background as a stunt man and "assistant action director" on Hong Kong action movies, he is a surprisingly uncharismatic lead as Buddy. Admittedly, there's not much to the character beyond his strong, silent, antagonistic attitude and his talents with a guitar and a sword. Some of the fight scenes are flashy, but they qualify more as demonstrations of technique than as involving set pieces. The film's finale does have some resonance, but only because it's one of the few times the film treats its characters as people, rather than props in a genre exercise. *(Graphic violence, adult situations, substance abuse, profanity.)* —M.G.

d, Lance Mungia; p, Michael Burns, Leanna Creel; w, Lance Mungia, Jeffrey Falcon; ph, Kristian Bernier; ed, James Frisa; m, Brian Tyler; prod d, Jeffrey Falcon; art d, Casey Lurie, Scooter Schamus; sound, Robert Backus; casting, Ross Lacy; cos, Jeffrey Falcon

Fantasy/Action **(PR: C MPAA: PG-13)**

SKIN
(SEE: UNDER THE SKIN)

SKIN & BONE **No Stars**
(U.S., 1998) 114m Film Research Unit ~ Jour de Fete Films c/bw

b. Wyatt *(Harry)*; Alan Boyce *(Dean)*; Susannah Melvoin *(Lovely Girl)*; Garret Scullin *(Billy)*; Clark Bolly *(Frankie)*; Chad Kula *(Bruno)*; Nicole Dillenberg *(Ghislaine)*; Gregory Sporleder *(Hadadasher)*; Richard Mitrani *(Herb)*; Chris Wetzel *(Assistant)*; Michael Nehring *(Harry's Manager, Michael)*; Michael Haynes *(Billy's Killer)*; Greg Jackson *(Mr. Donut Audition/Producer #1)*; Chris Reahm *(Satanic Youth Star)*; Andrea Beane *(Junkie with Pierced Nipples)*; Mark Sawicki *(Powerful Casting Agent)*; Joseph Dalough *(TV Cop)*; Fernando Arguelles *(TV Psycho)*; Rebecca Little *(Producer #2)*; James Michael White *(Zack at the Morgue)*; David Arquette *(Buzzhead)*; Wynston A. Jones *(General Wayne)*; Kimberly Cardinali *(Executrix)*; Alexx Carroll *(Insecure Female John)*; John Cork *(Angry John)*; Mollena Williams *(Scientist #1, Masters)*; Damien Kaner *(Scientist #2, Johnson)*; Jon Leichter *(George)*; VOICES: Andrew McGarrigan *(The Veteran)*; Mickey Cotrell *(Self Esteem)*; Everett Lewis *(Voyeur)*; Matt McChristy *(Man in the Street)*

Sorely lacking in cartilage, muscle, or any kind of consistent tone, SKIN & BONE is a tedious and derivative study of the rise and fall of three young male hustlers.

In Los Angeles, madam Ghislaine (Nicole Dillenberg) runs a male prostitution ring catering to men who are into sadomasochistic role-playing. Harry (b. Wyatt), a very macho actor who makes ends meet working for Ghislaine, has a loyal following, particularly an older man known as the General (Wynston A. Jones) who has a penchant for military and cop fantasies. Fellow hustler Billy (Garret Scullin), a sweet, lanky surfer type, is so inexperienced that he mistakenly picks up non-johns when he is supposed to meet clients. Into this mix comes Dean (Alan Boyce), an actor whose pretty-boy good looks quickly make him popular with Ghislaine's male and female clients. Harry is chosen to train him in the fine art of bondage, whipping, and role-playing. Dean learns quickly.

Though Harry has steady customers, Ghislaine complains that he's losing his touch. Harry, for his part, feels disillusioned with his acting career, as he meets rejection after rejection. Most of the parts for which he auditions require nudity, which he steadfastly refuses to do. After he is violently raped by the General during one of their regular appointments, Harry angrily confronts Ghislaine, saying he's fed up with working for her. He calls his agent to demand a job. The agent quickly hooks him up with a casting agent who promises him a role if Harry will sleep with him. He lands the role and tries to go straight, but discovers that Ghislaine doesn't take no for an answer.

Billy, meanwhile is having problems identifying his clients. During one job, he's supposed to meet a man in a dark car that has the top down. Instead, he picks up the bisexual Bruno (Chad Kula) who falls for Billy and wants him to go away with him. Billy agrees, but still needs to attend to one final client. On his way to the appointment, he picks up a gay-basher in a men's room who stabs him and leaves him for dead.

Dean has better luck. His first client is a young woman whose low self-esteem is quickly elevated by his lovemaking skills. Another client wants to simply watch him mop the floor while naked. Even two women who are studying human sexuality ask for Dean's services. But Dean's bravado vanishes when he makes a call home, and lies to his family about being in a play. He and Harry, who've become close friends, decide that they want out. But Ghislaine, still enraged over Harry's angry tirade, agrees if they will do one more job. Dean, playing an interrogator, is supposed to torture and "shoot" Harry with blanks for the sexual delectation of a kinky customer. What the two don't know is that Ghislaine, watching with the client behind a one-way mirror, has exchanged the fake gun for a real one. Dean is horrified when he sees that he's shot Harry dead. Months later, Ghislaine spots a homeless Dean in the street and persuades him to come back to "the life."

If director Everett Lewis aimed to deliver a statement about how prostitution is an ugly, dehumanizing business, he would have done well to have studied a masterpiece like MIDNIGHT COWBOY (1969) to learn about subtlety and nuanced characterization. Instead, Lewis seems to have modeled his film after CRUISING (1980), which, like SKIN & BONE, has a dark undercurrent of sleaze presented in the guise of an artistic statement. Shot on 16mm film that's so grainy it becomes hard to tell one character from another, SKIN & BONE hammers home its single, solitary message—that prostitution leads to destruction—over and over again. The graphic sex scenes, which are seemingly meant to evoke sympathy and horror, instead make one squirm and feel sorry for the actors. Most bothersome is the indirect undercurrent of homophobia running throughout the film. The supposedly heterosexual Harry fantasizes about an ideal woman he visualizes while he's with his male clients, implying that a woman would somehow set his life on the straight (so to speak) and narrow. Harry's not gay or anything; he's just turning tricks while waiting for the right woman.

Even with an attractive cast doing copious nude scenes, it's hard not to be disturbed by the irony that Lewis has good-looking actors exploiting themselves to play good-looking actors exploiting themselves. Gay or straight audiences expecting to see a serious treatise on the dangers of prostitution should steer clear of trash like SKIN & BONE; those in need of a bout of self-loathing can always re-rent CRUISING. *(Violence, extensive nudity, sexual situations, extreme profanity.)*—D.O.

d, Everett Lewis; p, Gardner Monks, Claudia Lewis; w, Everett Lewis; ph, Fernando Arguelles; ed, Everett Lewis; m, Pansy Division, Geoff Hhaba, Mark Jan Wlodarkowicz; sound, Garrett Scullin, Tom Scurry, Mark Jan Wlodarkowicz

Drama **(PR: O MPAA: NR)**

SLAM ★★★

(U.S., 1998) 100m Offline Entertainment Group ~ Trimark c

Saul Williams *(Ray Joshua)*; Sonja Sohn *(Lauren Bell)*; Bonz Malone *(Hopha)*; Beau Sia *(Jimmy Huang)*; Lawrence Wilson *(Big Nike)*

The Grand Jury Prize winner at the 1998 Sundance Film Festival, SLAM is an energetic and involving drama about a young, inner-city black poet who gets entangled in the criminal justice system.

A resident of Washington, DC, Ray (Saul Williams) spends his days writing rap poems. For cash, he sells small amounts of marijuana. One night, Ray is arrested and charged with drug possession. Unable to post bail, he is incarcerated. After he gets into a fight with several inmates, he is moved from his original cell into another. His new cellmate, Hopha (Bonz Malone), advises Ray that the prisoners are divided into two opposing factions. He offers to let Ray join his group, but Ray declines. Later, in the prison yard, Ray is pressured by prisoners from both groups to choose a side, but instead he performs a rap about the oppression of blacks in America. When finished, he is left alone.

Ray befriends Lauren (Sonja Sohn), who teaches a writing class in the prison, and impresses her with his poetry. He also impresses Hopha, who arranges Ray's bail. Upon release, Ray visits a friend, Big Mike (Lawrence Wilson). Big Mike demands Ray's assistance in avenging an injury that has left him blind, but Ray refuses. He then locates Lauren and attends a party at her house, where he entertains her guests with his rap poetry. After the party, Ray and Lauren make love. The following day, however, they engage in a bitter argument over what Ray should do next, Ray not wanting to face trial and a likely prison sentence. That night, at Lauren's behest, Ray attends a "slam," a poetry contest. Although he has never performed before an audience, Ray wins over the crowd, which gives him a standing ovation and demands an encore. Instead of returning to the stage, Ray exits the club and heads into the streets, running through them until he reaches and embraces the base of the Washington Monument.

Director Marc Levin's fiction feature debut is a gratifying change of pace. Despite its milieu, SLAM is neither a "gangsta" film nor a naively uplifting piece about a ghetto kid who beats the odds. It's a character study, and a thoughtful consideration of the nature of creativity. SLAM is not particularly strong on plot, but the plot isn't what's important here. What matters is establishing and maintaining the atmosphere through which Ray moves. To do so, Levin dwells on seemingly minor details, and lets rambling dialogue exchanges go on for minutes at a time. Considered separately, these elements seem digressive, but collectively they coalesce into the charged yet credible environment that provokes Ray's poetic expressions.

In creating a film in which words are privileged, Levin has cast performers who appreciate their power. Several of the leads contributed to their own dialogue, including Williams, Sohn, and Malone; and Williams, a real-life poet (and a star of the slam circuit), wrote the poetry that his character delivers. SLAM has a few rough touches, including jumpy editing and the tepid acting of its many nonprofessional cast members; even these factors work to the film's advantage, though, giving SLAM an unpolished, edgy quality that aptly characterizes the world Ray inhabits.

The film has one major defect, however: the tired and implausible romantic subplot involving Lauren and Ray, in which, once again, an angry young man finds redemption through a morally upright woman. In a film where everything else is fresh, this cliche is all the more irritating. This flaw isn't significant enough, though, to undermine the film's better attributes. Most of the talents involved in SLAM are relative newcomers to feature filmmaking. This film marks a very promising start. *(Violence, nudity, sexual situations, extreme profanity.)*—D.C.

d, Marc Levin; p, Henri M. Kessler, Marc Levin, Richard Stratton; exec p, Henri M. Kessler, David Peipers; assoc p, Daphne Pinkerson; w, Marc Levin, Bonz Malone, Sonja Sohn, Richard Stratton, Saul Williams; ph, Mark Benjamin; ed, Emir Lewis; m, Paul Miller

Drama **(PR: C MPAA: R)**

SLAMNATION ★★★

(U.S., 1998) 91m ~ Cinema Guild c

Saul Williams; Jessica Care Moore; Beau Sia; muMs the Schemer; Taylor Mali; Daniel Ferri; Marc Smith; Patricia Smith; Alexandra Oliver

The competitive spoken word movement is the focus of SLAMNATION, a surprisingly lively and enjoyable documentary.

Twenty-seven US city spoken-word teams compete with each other in Portland, OR, the mecca of the annual National Poetry Slam, an event that was started in the mid-1980s by entrepreneur Marc Smith. The film focuses on the preparations and performances by key poet-speakers within each group over a four-day period. On day one, Taylor Mali, an upstart who mimics other poets, discusses the chances of his team from Providence, RI. Meanwhile, the Boston team, lead by fiery Patricia Smith, loses a preliminary round to team Austin.

On day two, New York's member, Sean Williams, discusses his recent celebrity as a poet, while the Vancouver team loses in a preliminary round due to a time violation. By day three, the Austin team leads the other groups going into the semifinals, and a rivalry heats up between the Boston and New York groups. Finally, on day four, during a meeting just before the final performances, Marc Smith chastises Taylor Mali for writing a collaborative effort without his fellow members (and, thus, exploiting the rules of the group poetry segment). Still, Mali's Providence group prevails in the final judging and wins the contest.

SLAMNATION looks affectionately at the cultish stand-up poetry movement and quickly draws even indifferent viewers into this scene. The performances, of course, constitute the best parts of the film, and many of the poets are irresistible, both onstage and off. Sean Williams proves his deserved star-power with eloquent, spiritually inspired reading (he was profiled in *The New York Times* and has since starred in a dramatic role in the film, SLAM). Fellow New York City member (and SLAM costar) Beau Sia rants amusingly about dreams of success. Taylor Mali, of Providence, steals the show with his riffs on the other poets, his contentious final poem about modern-day vernacular, and his abrasive, off-the-cuff comments on the slam movement.

Though SLAMNATION fails to profile the women as evenly as the men, several stand out, including Vancouver's Alexandra Oliver, a deadpan artist who addresses a love-gone-wrong, and Patricia Smith, the angry rhetorician of racial matters. (Interestingly, the film was made well before—but released soon after—Smith, a *Boston Globe* columnist, was fired from her newspaper for fabricating human interest stories.)

SLAMNATION also develops suspense by building up to the final contest, crosscutting from rehearsals to the shows to reflections after the final results, but never revealing (until the end) the winning performance. Director Paul Devlin wisely embroiders the drama with some Greek Chorus commentary about the purpose and procedures of the event, including the interesting controversy over the group poetry rules and some criticism from an African-American poet that the outcome is "lily white."

Still, Devlin could have delved more into the odd, contradictory concept of a competition in poetry reading and what effect this has on the poems and poets. On a purely expository level, the film also gets somewhat chaotic explicating the order of the preliminary rounds and how the judging works. Otherwise, SLAMNATION takes a static, potentially deadly idea for a documentary and turns it into a spirited, entertaining profile. *(Nudity, extreme profanity.)*—E.M.

d, Paul Devlin; p, Paul Devlin; assoc p, Michael Shaw; co-p, Tom Poole; ph, John Anderson; ed, Paul Devlin; m, Chris Parker; md, Chris Parker; sound, John Kayne

Documentary **(PR: C MPAA: NR)**

SLAPPY AND THE STINKERS ★½

(U.S., 1998) 78m The Bubble Factory; Sheinberg Productions; TriStar ~ TriStar c

B.D. Wong *(Morgan Brinway)*; Bronson Pinchot *(Roy)*; Jennifer Coolidge *(Harriet)*; Joseph Ashton *(Sonny)*; Gary LeRoi Gray *(Domino)*; Carl Michael Linder *(Witz)*; Scarlett Pomers *(Lucy)*; Travis Tedford *(Loaf)*; David Dukes *(Spencer Dane Sr.)*; Spencer Klein *(Spencer Dane Jr.)*; Sam McMurray *(Broccoli)*; Terry Cain *(Nancy)*; Bodhi Pine Elfman *(Tag)*; Terri Garber *(Witz's Mom)*; Rick Lawless *(Tommy)*; Richard Taylor Olson *(Max Straus)*; Fred Asparagus *(Dockhand)*; Jamie Donnelly *(Aquarium Information Woman)*; Arturo Gil *(Goateed Man)*; Barbara Howard *(Sonny's Mom)*; Tim Hutchinson *(Domino's Dad)*; Thomas H. Middleton *(Aquarium Security Guard)*; Jill Remez *(Newsweek Reporter)*; Jonathan Slavin *(Fish 'n' Chips Delivery Boy)*; Marina Vain *(Tattooed Woman)*; Craig Rudnick *(Special Animal Voices)*

An apparent attempt to create an "Our Gang"-like series for the 1990s, SLAPPY AND THE STINKERS replaces the innocence of Spanky, Alfalfa, and friends with crass calculation.

Sonny (Joseph Ashton), Domino (Gary LeRoi Gray), Witz (Carl Michael Lindner), Lucy (Scarlett Pomers), and Loaf (Travis Tedford) are preteen students at Dartmoor Academy, where their prank-happy ways have earned them the nickname "The Stinkers." After one stunt, headmaster Brinway (B.D. Wong) puts them on double probation—one more slipup, and they're all expelled. On a subsequent field trip to a nearby aquarium, they decide to free the park's sea lion, Slappy. Interrupting an attempt by animal broker Broccoli (Sam McMurray) to steal Slappy, the Stinkers are able to spirit him away, hiding him first in Brinway's hot tub and then Witz's bedroom.

The next day, the kids attempt to return him to the sea, but Slappy refuses to go due to the local killer whale population. Realizing that they must return Slappy to the aquarium, the Stinkers first honor a commitment to attend Dartmoor's Parent's Day, where Slappy gets loose. Thanks to the attempts of addled groundskeeper Roy (Bronson Pinchot) to apprehend Slappy (who he thinks is a giant gopher), havoc ensues, and Brinway expels the Stinkers. Broccoli appears and spirits Slappy away, and the kids set out to save the seal from Broccoli's mountain cabin. After being bashed around by the Stinkers, Broccoli chases after them—a pursuit that Brinway becomes caught up in—before he is finally laid low. Slappy is returned to the aquarium, and the Stinkers are honored as heroes.

With a plot that might have sufficed for an "Our Gang" short but here is tediously stretched out to 78 minutes, SLAPPY AND THE STINKERS attempts to combine elements of 1993's FREE WILLY (which is referenced more than once in the dialogue) and 1990's HOME ALONE. Unfortunately for the target audience, it lacks the genuine heart of the former, the identifiability of the latter, and the polish of both. The thin plot is cluttered (or, more accurately, padded) with pointless subplots, including Roy's campaign against gophers, which is lifted wholesale from CADDYSHACK (1980).

Director Barnet Kellman incorporates an occasional amusing flourish, but he and the scriptwriters mostly deliver haphazard plotting and unimaginative slapstick set pieces, with a generous supply of fart, belch, poop, vomit, and crotch jokes. The Stinkers are given no distinguishing characteristics (except for the fact that Witz complains all the time), and mouth dialogue that has little or nothing to do with the way real kids talk. The adults are equally one-dimensional, flailing and mugging to compensate for a lack of anything genuinely funny to say or do. "This is getting boring," one kid says about 50 minutes in, and it's hard not to imagine even young viewers agreeing with him by that point. *(Violence, mild profanity.)*—M.G.

d, Barnet Kellman; p, Sid Sheinberg, Jon Sheinberg; exec p, Martha Chang; co-p, Michele Weisler; w, Bob Wolterstorff, Mike Scott; ph, Paul Maibaum; ed, Jeff Wishengrad; m, Craig Safan; prod d, Ivo Cristante; art d, Ken Larson; set d, Michael Claypool; sound, Mark Hopkins McNabb (mixer); fx, David Waine, Ultimate Effects, Alterian Studios, Inc.; casting, Shari Rhodes, Joseph Middleton, Ronnie Yeskel, Mary Vernieu; cos, Jami Burrows; makeup, Tracey Levy, Debra Denson; stunts, Jeff Cadiente

Children's/Comedy **(PR: A MPAA: PG)**

SLAYERS: THE MOTION PICTURE ★★½

(Japan, 1995) 67m Slayers Sponsorship Committee; Kadokawa Shoten; Bandai Visual; Marubeni; King Records; A.D. Vision ~ A.D.V. Films c

ENGLISH VOICE CAST: Cynthia Martinez *(Lina Inverse)*; Kelly Manison *(Nahga)*; Tristan MacAvery *(Joyrock)*; Phil Ross *(Rowdy)*; David Bell *(Young Rowdy)*; Jessica Calvello *(Meliroon)*; Guil Lunde *(Julianne Jubibieno)*; Bryan Bounds *(Lagos)*;

Grag Stanley *(Sorcerer A)*; Rob Mungle *(Thief 1/Hooligan 1)*; Brett Weaver *(Thief 2)*; Michael Zaragarov *(Thief 3)*; Kurt Stoll *(Pickpocket)*; Randy Fox *(Hooligan 2/Zombie Villager)*; Bryan Bounds *(Hooligan 3)*; Brian Granveldt *(Hooligan 4)*; Phil Ross *(Elderly Lady)*; Kira *(Shampoo)*; Meridth Dahl *(Rinse)*; Tiffany Grant *(Loofa)*; Paul Sidello *(King)*; Angela Lorio *(Queen)*; John Swasey *(Growth Spring Villager)*

A feature spun off from a popular animated Japanese TV series, SLAYERS is a comic fantasy adventure of two unpredictable young sorceresses who join forces to rid a mystical island of demons.

The rival sorceresses Lina Inverse (voice of Cynthia Martinez) and Nahga (voice of Kelly Manison) vacation together on the legend-shrouded island of Mipross which was once occupied by a race of elves. Lina has persistent dreams of a human boy romancing an elf girl, with the voice of Lina's grandfather, Rowdy (voice of Phil Ross), urging Lina to take specific actions.

Lina is called on by the island's king (voice of Paul Sidello) and queen (voice of Angela Lorio) to visit the northern ruins and rout the demons who have stopped the flow of hot spring water, the island's chief tourist attraction. Grandpa Rowdy shows up to assist the girls as they confront Joyrock (voice of Tristan MacAvery), a reptilian demon king who manages to resist the girls' best efforts. Grandpa is able to open the Gates of Time, enabling Lina to journey back in time to slay Joyrock at the beginning of his rampage by using her most powerful spell. Lina learns that the boy in the dream is indeed her grandfather. When she returns to her time, the demon threat has vanished and the king and queen no longer recognize Lina and refuse to pay her.

Based on a popular 1995 TV series, SLAYERS employs a more comical mode of anime character design to tell a fanciful tale of two impossibly cute magical girls who smite their opponents without working up a sweat. Although one of the two is scantily clad in a black bikini, boots, and cape, there is never any overt sexual innuendo. The violent encounters with demons and bandits are all bloodless. Young anime fans will enjoy the antics of the goofy female leads who are as apt to fight each other as any bad guys, but will gladly put down their swords in the presence of food. *(Violence.)*—B.C.

d, Hiroshi Watanabe, Matt Greenfield (English Language Version); p, Tohru Suzuki, Matt Greenfield (English Language Version); exec p, Tsuguhiko Kadokawa, John Ledford (English Language Version); w, Kazuo Yamazaki (based on the novel by Hazime Kanzaka), Matt Greenfield (English Language Version); ph, Takashi Yazuhata; m, Takayuki Hattori; prod d, Hitoshi Kato; anim, Takahiro Yoshimatsu; sound, Katsuhiko Kobayashi

Animated/Fantasy/Comedy (PR: A MPAA: NR)

SLEEPY EYES OF DEATH: FULL CIRCLE KILLING ★★★

(Japan, 1964) 85m Daiei ~ Daiei c
(AKA: KYOSHIRO NEMURI: FULL MOON-CUT; NEMURI KYOSHIRO: ENGETSUGIRL)

Raizo Ichikawa *(Kyoshiro Nemuri)*; Yuuko Hamada; Kyooko Azuma; Taroo Marui; Jun'ichiroo Narita; Kenjiroo Nemura; Saburo Date; Koochi Mizuhara; Tahamaru Sasaki; Shintaroo Nanjoo

SLEEPY EYES OF DEATH: FULL CIRCLE KILLING is the strong second entry in the unusual Japanese series about the adventures of Kyoshiro Nemuri, a wandering outcast samurai who's haunted by his past and employs a deadly swordfighting technique known as the "Full Moon Cut."

Kyoshiro Nemuri (Raizo Ichikawa) witnesses Takayuki, an illegitimate son of the Shogun, testing his new sword by beheading a peasant farmer. Meanwhile, Takayuki's ruthlessly ambitious mother is bumping off the Shogun's other prospective heirs in order to assure that Takayuki will be the next Shogun. Tajuu, the son of the dead farmer, kidnaps the sister of Takayuki's lover Konami, in an attempt to force a duel with Takayuki, but Nemuri convinces him to return the child. When Nemuri takes her home, Komani insults him and he humiliates her by slashing off her clothes and sleeping with her.

Konami hires a samurai to kill Nemuri, and after failing to talk him out of a duel, Nemuri kills him. When Tajuu kidnaps Konami, Takayuki captures him and is about to kill him, but stops when Nemuri agrees to trade his sword in exchange for Tajuu's life. After Takayuki's mother arranges a meeting between Takayuki and the Shogun, she begs him not to duel Nemuri, but he defies her, egged on by Konami's admission that she allowed Nemuri to have her. Takayuki is killed during the duel, and his mother is then arrested for the murder of the Shogun's other heirs.

In keeping with this entry's colorful title, which refers to Nemuri's trademark swordfighting technique, FULL CIRCLE KILLING is more violent than other films in the SLEEPY EYES series, focusing on the oppressed peasants at the hands of the decadent rich. Takayuki's imperiousness brings out the best and the worst in Nemuri and his innate sense of justice, inspiring him to new heights (or depths) of retribution, which is reflected in his unusual brutishness (forcing himself on Konami) and the spectacularly bloody duels. After the shocking opening sequence where Takayuki callously beheads the farmer, Nemuri is challenged by one of Takayuki's samurai using the Iai swordfighting technique (a duel from the seated position) and calmly chops off the man's arm.

The later attempts on Nemuri's life are all ingeniously staged, including an attack on a house from a moving boat; a knife through the floor; and Nemuri running up an enormous flight of steps and chopping down dozens of assassins. Nemuri's duel with the samurai who's hired by Konami takes place in a forest at dawn which is filled with blue-colored mist and is beautifully shot and choreographed, as is the furious finale, set on a burning bridge, where Nemuri vanquishes dozens of samurai, deflects arrows with his sword, and then kills Takayuki as they're engulfed by a torrent of flames. Despite the emphasis on gore, there are also the customary reflective, philosophical moments, such as when Nemuri and the samurai hired to kill him discuss principles and codes of honor, while the dialogue is rife with poetic and existential observations that are typical of the series, such as "The wind is a voice from the void," and "My karma is a bottomless pit of darkness." *(Graphic violence, nudity, sexual situations.)*—M.S.

d, Kimiyoshi Yasuda; w, Kiyoshi Hoshikawa; ph, Chishi Makiura; ed, Kanji Suganuma; m, Ichiro Saito; art d, Shigeru Katoo; sound, Iwao Ooya

Action (PR: O MPAA: NR)

SLEEPY EYES OF DEATH: SWORD OF ADVENTURE ★★★½

(Japan, 1964) 83m Daiei ~ Daiei c
(NEMURI KYOSHIRO—SHOOBU)

Raizo Ichikawa *(Kyoshiro Nemuri)*; Shiho Fujimura; Miwa Takada; Naoko Kubo; Yoshi Katoo; Junichiroo Narita; Matasaburo Tamba; Yutaroo Gomi; Fujio Suga

SLEEPY EYES OF DEATH: SWORD OF ADVENTURE is an outstanding entry in the 1960s samurai series known as "Son of the Black Mass," in reference to the heritage of the protagonist, a red-haired ronin named Kyoshiro Nemuri who is damned to be an eternal outcast because he was the progeny of a satanic ritual in which his Japanese mother was raped by a European monk.

Wandering swordsman Kyoshiro Nemuri (Raizo Ichikawa) befriends an old man named Asahina who turns out to be the Finance Commissioner for the Shogunate. Asahina's economic reforms bring him into conflict with the Shogun's spoiled daughter Princess Takahime. When he eliminates the Princess's extravagant allowance, she plots to have him killed, along with Nemuri, who has decided to protect Asahina. Nemuri is lured into a trap by Uneme, a fortune teller who has agreed to help the Princess in exchange for the release of her incarcerated foreign missionary husband. Uneme drugs Nemuri's tea and ties him up, but he manages to escape, and Uneme later finds herself falling in love with Nemuri.

The Princess and her stewards then plot to eliminate Nemuri and Asahina by inviting Nemuri to participate in an official duel, where he will be given a sword that has been tampered with so that its blade will detach and fly into Asahina. Despite Asahina's suspicions, Nemuri agrees to the duel, and during it, the blade does indeed detach, but it flies into one of the Princess' stewards and kills him. When the Shogun hears of the Princess' murderous conspiracies, he has her exiled. Nemuri then goes to see Uneme, who has been captured by dozens of samurai, and after freeing her, Nemuri kills them all in duels. Asahina and Uneme asks Nemuri to stay, but he refuses, and disappears into the woods.

The SLEEPY EYES OF DEATH series is unique in the samurai genre in that while it includes plenty of action, it concentrates mostly on character development and solid plotting. Nemuri may be an invincible swordsman, but he's vehemently antiheroic. The story of SWORD OF ADVENTURE is fascinating in its depiction of ancient Japanese politics, and even somewhat radical in that the Finance Commissioner is attempting to take some wealth away from the corrupt ruling warrior-class in order to help the peasants. It also deals with the Japanese concept of racial purity, which is central to Nemuri's character, most memorably in the powerful flashback where Uneme's Western-missionary husband is arrested for preaching Christianity, and as he's being dragged to jail, he picks Nemuri out of a crowd and speaks to him because he recognizes pain and misfortune in Nemuri's face.

In keeping with Nemuri's tortured and rebellious nature, the films also place a strong emphasis on philosophy, as he and other characters often engage in conversations about religion, race, bravery, cowardice, and what it means to be a man or a woman. These discussions are always an intrinsic part of the narrative, and only add to the film's rich texture of exotic physical beauty. As with other films in the series, the cinematic style is also somewhat different from the norm, employing many static shots and long takes instead of quick cutting, even during the duels themselves, and using objects such as trees, walls, and even snow, to split the widescreen frame into sections, creating marvelously expressive compositions. *(Violence.)*—M.S.

d, Kenji Misumi; w, Seiji Hoshikawa (based on the novel by Renzaburo Shibata); ph, Chishi Makiura; ed, Kanji Suganuma; m, Ichiro Saito; art d, Akira Naito; sound, Masahiro Okumura

Action **(PR: O MPAA: NR)**

SLEEPY EYES OF DEATH: SWORD OF SEDUCTION ★★★

(Japan, 1964) 81m Daiei ~ Daiei c
(NEMURI KYOSHIRO JOYOKEN)

Raizo Ichikawa *(Kyoshiro Nemuri)*; Kenzaburo Joo *(Chen Sun)*; Shiho Fujimura; Naoko Kubo; Katssuhiko Kobayashi; Masumi Harukawa; Akemi Negishi; Ikuko Moori; Michiko Ai; Ichiruo Nakaya

Chapter four of the stylish 1960s samurai series about the outcast ronin Kyoshiri Nemuri finds our antihero mixed up in a labyrinthine plot involving persecuted Christians, opium smuggling, a murderous princess, and a search for a "saint" who supposedly knows the dark secret of his mysterious birth.

Princess Kiku is killing off her ladies-in-waiting by giving them overdoses of opium, which is being smuggled into Japan by the Inner Court's physician and a rice-dealer named Bizenya. Meanwhile, Torizo, a member of an underground Christian group, pleads with wandering samurai Kyoshiro Nemuri (Raizo Ichikawa) to find and save a priestess called "Virgin Shima," who, Torizo claims, knows about the circumstances of Nemuri's birth. After Nemuri finds out about Bezinya's smuggling and confronts him, he foils several attempts on his life, including one by Princess Kiku. During a Noh-dance performance, Nemuri rips off Kiku's mask to reveal her horribly disfigured face, which is the reason she was murdering her beautiful ladies-in-waiting. Kiku demands Nemuri's head and one of her guards follows him, but is killed by Nemuri.

Nemuri eventually finds Shima on Bezinya's smuggling ship, and after he vanquishes Bezinya's guards and a Chinese boxing master named Chen Sun (Kenzaburo Joo), Shima admits that she's a fake employed by the authorities to catch Christians. As Nemuri is about to kill her, she tells him that her mother was his wet nurse when he was a baby and that he was conceived as part of a Satanic ritual performed by a Christian missionary who raped his mother. Nemuri then kills Shima and walks away, followed by a stray dog.

SWORD OF SEDUCTION is an even more somber contemplation on alienation and loneliness than the previous three series entries, and the first to actually depict the Black Mass rape of Nemuri's mother during which he was conceived, which is the basis for his status as an outcast character. The flashback is brilliantly handled, masterfully utilizing the entire widescreen frame—as does virtually every shot in the series—by shifting the images of Nemuri, his mother, and Shima to different parts of the frame, showing the mother lying in a coffin surrounded by flickering candles as the demonic missionary violates her. It's a chilling sequence that more than compensates for the sometimes disjointed and confusing narrative that precedes it. It is complemented by several other stunning images: Kiku's shadow laughing as her dying ladies-in-waiting wail in pain; Nemuri decapitating an old man (who turns out to be his father) after he rapes a woman; Kiku's hideously mutilated face; bloody water dissolving into a red sky; and the finale where Nemuri slashes Shima as she runs toward him and her white dressing gown slowly turns crimson with her own blood. The numerous swordfights and duels are equally stylish, placing the characters on the extreme edges and employing angles from overhead and underneath, while in slow motion, Nemuri's blade is shown moving in psychedelic trails as he flashes his sword in preparation for his infamous Full Moon Cut. *(Violence, sexual situations.)*—M.S.

d, Kazuo Ikehiro; p, Sadoa Zaizen; w, Kiyoshi Hoskikawa (based on the novel by Renzaburo Shibata); ph, Yasukazu Takemura; ed, Toshio Taniguchi; m, Ichiro Saitoo; art d, Yoshinobu Nishioko; sound, Masao Oosum

Action **(PR: O MPAA: NR)**

SLIDING DOORS ★★

(U.K./U.S., 1998) 105m Mirage Enterprises; InterMedia Film Equities; Big Deal Pictures ~ Miramax c

Gwyneth Paltrow *(Helen)*; John Hannah *(James)*; John Lynch *(Gerry)*; Jeanne Tripplehorn *(Lydia)*; Zara Turner *(Anna)*; Douglas McFerran *(Russell)*; Paul Brightwell *(Clive)*; Nina Young *(Claudia)*; Virginia McKenna *(James' Mother)*; Phylidda Law; Kevin McNally

The Fickle Finger of Fate activates SLIDING DOORS, a glum romantic drama about a woman whose life takes two turns at once.

In contemporary London, Helen (Gwyneth Paltrow), an English PR executive, discovers one morning she has been dismissed by her firm over a misunderstanding. On her way home, Helen races to catch the closing doors of the local subway train. In one moment, Helen catches the train, and continues on her way. In another moment, Helen just misses the train, and is stuck on the platform. This opens the way for Helen to pursue two different courses, in what appear to be two different realities. The Helen who does make it onto the train sits next to a charming stranger, James (John Hannah), who flirts with her to no avail. When Helen finally arrives at her flat, she discovers her live-in boyfriend, Gerry (John Lynch), a struggling novelist, in bed with his American mistress, Lydia (Jeanne Tripplehorn). The Helen who missed the train, however, walks home from the station, and gets mugged on the way. She is taken by the police to a hospital for treatment of her injuries before arriving home, where Gerry has already hidden all traces of Lydia's presence.

The first Helen walks out on Gerry and stays with her best friend, Anna (Zara Turner). She applies for a small business loan to start a catering company, and she celebrates her new life by cutting her long locks and going blonde. Eventually, she runs into James again, and begins to date the persistent young man. Meanwhile, the second Helen continues her dissatisfying relationship with Gerry, while she hunts for and finds a lowly waitressing job.

Gerry tries to win back the first Helen by approaching her at a major event she is catering. Briefly, she considers returning to Gerry, who seems genuinely repentant, but their reunion is disrupted again by Lydia. The first Helen returns to dating James, but is mortified to discover that he is married. In the meantime, the second Helen finally realizes that Gerry has been cheating on her with Lydia.

James explains to the first Helen that he is separated from his wife, while Gerry tries to mollify the furious second Helen, but at the same moment both Helens are seriously hurt in accidents, which land them in the hospital. The first Helen dies that night, with James mourning her at the operating table; but the second Helen survives her injuries, and eventually leaves the facility. On the day of her discharge, she runs into James, and they flirt with each other: the possibility of a romance resonates in their exchange.

In his feature debut, writer-director Peter Howitt attempts a different kind of storytelling, although SLIDING DOORS owes something to the metaphysical musings of A MATTER OF LIFE AND DEATH (1946), the looking-glass gimmick of A CRACK IN THE MIRROR (1960), and the separate but interrelated *roman-fleuve* style of Krzysztof Kieslowski's "Three Colors Trilogy" (1993-94).

Still, what keeps SLIDING DOORS from making its own mark is that the parallel stories never play off each other in an interesting way, and there's rarely any suspense over whether or not they will ever connect. In fact, if it weren't for the first Helen s midway-through makeover (shades of THE MIRROR HAS TWO FACES), it would be hard to tell which story is which! (The movie cries out for the use of split-screen.) It is also annoying that the intriguing premise is undercut by Helen's passivity: the two scenarios evolve from events enacted upon her, while little is instigated by her pro-active decision-making.

No one in the cast emerges unscathed by this "accident" of a movie: Paltrow adds a bit of Cockney to her "Emma Woodhouse" (see 1996's EMMA), but her Brit act seems more like a vain star turn this time; the normally gifted John Lynch (see CAL, 1984) overplays the nervously philandering boyfriend gambit; John Hannah (of FOUR WEDDINGS AND A FUNERAL, 1994) makes little impression as the wisecracking Scottish lothario; and Jeanne Tripplehorn (WATERWORLD, BASIC INSTINCT) gets too little to do as a shrewish vamp.

The slick-looking Tony Blair-ized London makes the right setting for the fairy-tale scenarios, although devotees of the work of Mike Leigh and Ken Loach won't recognize this new "swinging" city (even the significant cultural differences among the leading characters are never addressed!). But the production values are more than adequate, and the catchy pop tunes assure the music videos will live on in perpetuity. *(Violence, nudity, sexual situations, substance abuse, profanity.)*—E.M.

d, Peter Howitt; p, William Horberg, Philippa Braithwaite, Sydney Pollack; exec p, Guy East, Nigel Sinclair; assoc p, Sandy Poustie; w, Peter Howitt; ph, Remi Adefarasin; ed, John Smith; m, David Hirschfelder; prod d, Maria Djurkovic; art d, John Martyn; sound, John Midgley (mixer); casting, Michelle Guiche; cos, Jill Taylor; makeup, Tina Earnshaw; stunts, Helen Caldwell

Romance/Drama/Fantasy (PR: C MPAA: R)

SLUMS OF BEVERLY HILLS ★★★

(U.S., 1998) 91m South Fork Pictures; Fox Searchlight ~ Fox Searchlight c

Natasha Lyonne *(Vivian Abramowitz)*; Alan Arkin *(Murray Abramowitz)*; Marisa Tomei *(Rita)*; Kevin Corrigan *(Eliot)*; Jessica Walter *(Doris)*; Rita Moreno *(Belle)*; David Krumholtz *(Ben)*; Eli Marienthal *(Rickey)*; Carl Reiner *(Mickey)*; Bryna Weiss *(Saleslady)*; Charlotte Stewart *(Landlady)*; Brendan Burns *(Cop in Station)*; Harris Laskawy *(Charlie the Cook)*; Mena Suvari *(Rachel)*; Marley McClean *(Brooke)*; Mary Portser *(Mrs. Hoffman)*; Jock MacDonald *(Man at Brymans)*; Rich Willis *(EMS Guy #1)*; Rock Reiser *(EMS Guy #2)*; Jack Tracy *(Cop #1)*; Jay Patterson *(Dr. Grossman)*; Natalie Karp *(Nurse Curtrell)*; Sally Schaub *(Waitress)*

A smart and funny filmmaking debut by writer-director Tamara Jenkins, SLUMS OF BEVERLY HILLS is a semiautobiographical, coming-of-age story about blossoming teen Vivian and her eccentric family, who live on the outskirts of the famously fashionable zip code.

July 1976. Fifteen-year-old Vivian Abramowitz (Natasha Lyonne) has two big problems. Her breasts have "sprouted overnight" to what she considers grotesque proportions. And her divorced father, Murray (Alan Arkin), a hapless, 65-year-old car salesman, moves the family every few months in order to evade the rent of yet another seedy apartment. The Abramowitzes always remain within the Beverly Hills city limits, so that Vivian and her two brothers can attend the district's good schools.

At one dingy apartment complex, Vivian meets Eliot (Kevin Corrigan), a pot- selling dropout obsessed with Charles Manson. Eliot becomes Vivian's de facto boyfriend after she lets him go to second base in the laundry room. Vivian's older cousin Rita (Marisa Tomei), who has just run away from a rehab facility, joins the family, securing them financial support from her wealthy father so long as Murray can keep Rita off drugs and in school.

The Abramowitzs move into much better digs. The girls bond as Rita instructs Vivian in the use of a vibrator and depilatory cream. She also confesses that she's secretly carrying a baby fathered by an actor she met in rehab. Rita enrolls in nursing school and Murray orders Vivian to look after her, but while Vivian is occupied with losing her virginity to Eliot, Rita relapses and overdoses.

The next day, Rita's father Mickey (Carl Reiner) pays a visit. At a contentious dinner, he berates his brother Murray so foully that Vivian stabs him in the thigh with a fork, and Rita announces her pregnancy. Mickey takes Rita back home with him, leaving Vivian and her nomadic family broke and on their own again.

SLUMS OF BEVERLY HILLS is the flipside of CLUELESS, and like that 1995 hit, SLUMS could inspire a sitcom. The movie's narrative is episodic, and the characters are broadly drawn and appropriately kooky in a sitcom-ready way. The humor is quirky, running the gamut from sharp and observed to broad and zany.

What the film does especially well is capture the vagaries of Vivian's relationship to her body and her family. Straddling tomboyishness and womanhood, Vivian's mortification at her sexual development is only exasperated by the embarrassing attention she receives from her overbearing father and brothers. Jenkins does an admirable job of keeping SLUMS unsentimental, while still signaling how much the family loves each other, and how Vivian will look back in 22 years on the freakiness of 1976 with fondness. The film's stars elevate the material with rich performances. Lyonne shines at the center of the film, displaying a wonderful gift for comedy and a winning personality. Arkin is solid in the role that could have come off as *really* pathetic—still boasting about the time when he owned a restaurant and caught the cook stealing steaks. Arkin conveys that Murray's bravado is a necessary mask for his kids' sake and how much he needs them in his life. This keeps the character sympathetic, the movie buoyant, and any potential pathos at bay. *(Sexual situations, profanity, nudity.)*—P.R.

d, Tamara Jenkins; p, Michael Nozik, Stan Wlodkowski; exec p, Robert Redford; w, Tamara Jenkins; ph, Tom Richmond; ed, Pamela Martin; m, Rolfe Kent; prod d, Dena Roth; art d, Scott Plauche; set d, Robert Greenfield; sound, Ken Segal (mixer); casting, Sheila Jaffe, Georgianne Walken; cos, Kirsten Everberg

Comedy/Drama **(PR: C MPAA: R)**

SMALL SOLDIERS ★★★

(U.S., 1998) 105m Universal; DreamWorks SKG ~ DreamWorks SKG c

Denis Leary *(Gil Mars)*; Kirsten Dunst *(Christy Fimple)*; Gregory Smith *(Alan Abernathy)*; Ann Magnuson *(Irene Abernathy)*; Phil Hartman *(Phil Fimple)*; David Cross *(Irwin Wayfair)*; Jay Mohr *(Larry Benson)*; Alexandra Wilson *(Ms. Kegel)*; Gregory Itzin *(Mr. Florens)*; Dick Miller *(Joe)*; Jacob Smith *(Timmy Fimple)*; Jonathan David Bouck *(Brad)*; Kevin Dunn *(Stuart Abernathy)*; Wendy Schaal *(Marion Fimple)*; Archie Hahn III *(Satellite Dish Installer)*; Robert Picardo *(Clean Room Technician)*; Julius Tennon *(Toy World Supervisor)*; Belinda Balaski *(Neighbor)*; Rance Howard *(Husband)*; Jackie Joseph *(Wife)*; Marcia Mitzman Gaven *(Globotech Announcer)*; VOICES OF: Tommy Lee Jones *(Chip Hazard)*; Frank Langella *(Archer)*; Ernest Borgnine *(Kip Killagin)*; Jim Brown *(Butch Meathook)*; Bruce Dern *(Link Static)*; George Kennedy *(Brick Bazooka)*; Clint Walker *(Nick Nitro)*; Christopher Guest *(Slamfist/Scratch-It)*; Michael McKean *(Insaniac/Freakenstein)*; Harry Shearer *(Punch-It)*; Jim Cummings *(Ocula)*; Sarah Michelle Gellar *(Gwendy Doll)*; Christina Ricci *(Gwendy Doll)*

Ironic twist on the action genre for youngsters or message film gone awry? Either way, SMALL SOLDIERS provides a handful of harrowing clashes between an assortment of human and doll characters—and some wry commentary on our dual obsessions with technology and violence.

Irwin (David Cross) and Larry (Jay Mohr) are toy designers whose firm has been acquired by Globotech Industries, a munitions manufacturer diversifying its holdings in the post-Cold War defense slump. Globotech's CEO Gil Mars (Denis Leary) isn't impressed by their designs for pacifistic, educational action figures called Gorgonites, and sends them back to the drawing board to create a corresponding set of adversaries. Accordingly, Larry scams some computer chips meant for advanced weaponry from another division of the conglomerate to fuel the enemy Commandos with realistic motion—and mercenary sensibilities.

Teen Alan Abernathy (Gregory Smith) is left temporarily in charge of his family's failing nonviolent, educational toyshop, the Inner Child. Alan, whose parents (Kevin Dunn, Ann Magnuson) enjoy the simpler pleasures of life, has a crush on his neighbor Christy Fimple (Kirsten Dunst), whose father (Phil Hartman) revels in the latest electronic gear. Christy's little brother wants to be the first kid on the block with his own Commandos and Gorgonites, so Alan persuades a deliveryman (Dick Miller) to give him a set before their release date—and without his parents' knowledge. In the shop overnight, the toys reek havoc, for the Commandos, led by Chip Hazard (voice of Tommy Lee Jones), are programmed to seek and destroy Gorgonites. Hiding in Alan's room, Archer (voice of Frank Langella), the gentle dog-faced leader of the Gorgonites, reveals to Alan that his kooky menagerie of friends are not robotic toys but intelligent beings programmed to lose the battle against the brutal Commandos.

With a phone call, Alan convinces Globotech to withhold the figures from the market, but it is not so easy to stop the Commandos already on the loose, who are busily transforming household appliances and lawn mower parts into flamethrowers and nail-spitting bazookas—and "enlisting" Christy's Barbie-like Gwendy dolls into their ranks. Once the devastation of the suburban neighborhood is in full swing, Alan manages to rally both of their once-skeptical families to fight off the Commandos' increasingly violent attacks. While most of the Gorgonites are unable to overcome their programming in order to defend themselves, and spend the final firefight hiding under a toppled satellite dish, Alan persuades Archer that it is his duty to protect his comrades so that they can continue to search for their homeland. Together, they undertake a risky but ultimately triumphant plan to disable the Commandos' chips with a magnetic jolt (from which the Gorgonites are spared by cover of the satellite dish). While Mars drops by the neighborhood to pacify the adults with big checks, Alan faces the hard task of saying goodbye to the Gorgonites. He sends them on their way to search for the land of Gorgon on a makeshift boat down a peaceful river that poses no threat—at least not from the Commandos.

Promoted primarily as an action movie for kids, SMALL SOLDIERS rankled some parents who were taken aback by the considerable brutality of the Commandos, which was only exacerbated by a load of licensed merchandise that mistook Chip Hazard for the hero. The film also took some flack for criticizing the cynical use of violence to sell children's toys while doing the same thing itself. It would be hard to argue otherwise, as the film's critique of violence in children's entertainment is drowned out by all the explosions. At the same time, Alan, a sensitive kid trying to live down his reputation as a troublemaker, makes a decent enough role model.

Message (or lack thereof) aside, animatronic wizardry and special effects bring the Gorgonites and Commandos fully to life, giving them great expressiveness. Not to be outdone, human performers Magnuson and Hartman (in his last role) ham up their roles with pleasing results. Director Joe Dante, who first turned cuddly creatures into menaces in GREMLINS (1984), sprinkles his film with jokey homages to other films that may add a layer of pleasure for film trivia buffs. (One example: The voices of the Commandos and the Gorgonites are provided by members of the casts of THE DIRTY DOZEN (1967) and THIS IS SPINAL TAP (1984) respectively. Sometimes clunky in terms of plot and pacing, often cartoonish, SMALL SOLDIERS may be too frightening for some small children, but its wit may appeal to those older kids and adults who don't mind a film that may be making a little fun of its own audience. *(Violence.)*—C.Ch.

d, Joe Dante; p, Michael Finnell, Colin Wilson; exec p, Walter F. Parkes; co-p, Paul Deason; w, Gavin Scott, Adam Rifkin, Ted Elliott, Terry Rossio; ph, Jamie Anderson; ed, Marshall Harvey; m, Jerry Goldsmith; prod d, William Sandell; art d, Mark W. Mansbridge, Bradford Ricker; set d, Rosemary Brandenburg; anim, David Andrews, Stefen Fangmeier; sound, Ken King (mixer); fx, Stan Winston, Leslie Barnett, Kenneth D. Pepiot, Erik Mattson, Alexandra Altrocchi, Amanda Montgomery, Michele Spina, Industrial Light & Magic; casting, Denise Chamian; cos, Carole Brown-James; makeup, Christina Smith; stunts, Jim Arnett

Action/Fantasy **(PR: A MPAA: PG-13)**

SMOKE SIGNALS ★★★½

(U.S., 1998) 89m ShadowCatcher Entertainment ~ Miramax c

Adam Beach *(Victor Joseph)*; Evan Adams *(Thomas Builds-the-Fire)*; Gary Farmer *(Arnold Joseph)*; Tantoo Cardinal *(Arlene Joseph)*; Irene Bedard *(Suzy Song)*; Cody Lightning *(Young Victor Joseph)*; Simon Baker *(Young Thomas Builds-the-Fire)*; Monica Mojica *(Grandma Builds-the-Fire)*; John Trudell *(Randy Peone)*; Leonard George *(Lester Fallsapart)*; Michael Greyeyes *(Junior Polatkin)*; Darwin Haine *(Boo)*; Michelle St. John *(Velma)*; Elaine Miles *(Lucy)*; Cynthia Geary *(Cathy the Gymnast)*; Gary Taylor *(Cowboy)*; Perrey Reeves *(Holly)*; Nicolette Vajtay *(Julie)*; Molly Cheek *(Penny)*; Robert Miano *(Burt)*; Tom Skerritt *(Police Chief)*; Todd Jamieson *(Jesuit #1)*

Adapted by Sherman Alexie from his short-story collection, "The Lone Ranger and Tonto Fistfight in Heaven," director Chris Eyre's Native American-themed SMOKE SIGNALS won both an Audience Award and a Filmmaker's Trophy at the 1998 Sundance Film Festival. Though its pace and energy flag occasionally due to a plot that's stretched too thin, the film is an overdue modern examination of a people usually relegated in movies to wearing period dress and spouting revisionist New Age wisdom.

Victor Joseph (Adam Beach) is a Coeur d'Alene youth who has lived on an Idaho reservation with his single mother Arlene (Tantoo Cardinal) since his likable but hard-drinking father Arnold (Gary Farmer) abandoned the family when Victor was a boy. Thomas Builds-the-Fire (Evan Adams) is his nerdy former classmate, also raised by a single woman (his grandmother) since losing his parents in a tragic Fourth of July fire. Thomas styles himself a traditional storyteller, one whose parable-like stories have healing properties. Thomas also idolizes the absent Arnold (to Victor's annoyance) for saving him from that same fire.

News of Arnold's death in Phoenix arrives. Victor initially rejects Thomas's suggestion that the two of them travel to Arizona to get his ashes. But a desire to put painful memories of his father to rest and pity for the socially awkward Thomas (who is paying for the trip) persuade Victor to change his mind. The duo travel by bus to Phoenix, where they meet Arnold's neighbor, Suzy Song (Irene Bedard). They also learn the truth about the fire: A drunken Arnold accidentally started it with the irresponsible use of fireworks. Guilt drove Arnold to drink and to the abandonment of his family.

Driving home in Arnold's pickup truck, Victor proves himself at least the man his father was by rescuing traffic accident victims, and facing the racism of a local sheriff (Tom Skeritt) who detains the Native American duo. The sheriff is at first convinced that they must have been responsible for the accident; lacking any evidence, he eventually lets them go. Rising above the intolerance, Victor and Thomas reconcile with Arnold's memory and each other as they scatter the dead man's ashes on the reservation.

What makes SMOKE SIGNALS special is not its mundane plot about confronting the demons of the past, but rather the insight it provides into modern Native American attitudes. Encouraging Thomas to change his geek image, Victor advises him to "get stoic," demonstrating with a cliched Native American pose of silent strength and poker face. At a rest stop, Victor even persuades Thomas to literally let his hair down, and when Eyre depicts the now-handsome Thomas emerging from the bathroom in slow motion, it's just the right stylistic choice. These are funny, insightful moments, and SMOKE SIGNALS has enough of them to sufficiently entertain.

But there are slow points in the film where little is said or accomplished. SMOKE SIGNALS has a feeling of being padded for length, reflecting its roots as a short story. Alexie and Eyre also make too liberal use of quirky, eccentric characters in the first half: the obvious influence of TV's "Northern Exposure" is made clear by the presence of two of that show's stars, Elaine Miles and Cynthia Geary, in small roles. SMOKE SIGNALS works best when it concentrates instead on the relationship between Victor and Thomas, and their very different ideas about what it means to be Native American. Victor, who's considered "cool," affects a cliched, Hollywood-influenced demeanor, while Thomas, a reservation reject, is more "authentic" in his faith that stories heal; the film itself, a story about healing, comes down on Thomas's side.

Had Alexie and Eyre focused on the cultural tension between Victor and Thomas this might have been an indie classic, but SMOKE SIGNALS drifts from its strengths too many times. Solid and entertaining, the film makes valid and interesting points about the state of Native America in the 1990s, but too much is left unsaid in the film's been-there, done-that quest for broader emotional truths. *(Violence, adult situations.)*—K.W.

d, Chris Eyre; p, Larry Estes, Scott Rosenfelt; exec p, David Skinner, Carl Bressler; assoc p, Roger Baerwolf, Randy Suhr; co-p, Sherman Alexie, Chris Eyre; w, Sherman Alexie (based on stories from his book *The Lone Ranger and Tonto Fistfight in Heaven*); ph, Brian Capener; ed, Brian Berdan; m, B.C. Smith; prod d, Charles Armstrong; art d, Jonathon Saturen; set d, Dawn Ferry; sound, Douglas Tourtelot (mixer), Patrick O'Sullivan (design); fx, Ray Brown; casting, Coreen Mayrs; cos, Ron Leamon; makeup, Cynthia Bornia; stunts, Ron Otis

Drama/Comedy **(PR: C MPAA: PG-13)**

SNAKE EYES ★★½

(U.S., 1998) 91m Paramount; DeBart ~ Paramount c

Nicolas Cage *(Rick Santoro)*; Gary Sinise *(Kevin Dunne)*; Carla Gugino *(Julia Costello)*; Kevin Dunn *(Lou Logan)*; Joel Fabiani *(Charles Kirkland)*; Luis Guzman *(Cyrus)*; John Heard *(Gilbert Powell)*; David Anthony Higgins *(Ned Campbell)*; Michael Rispoli *(Jimmy George)*; Stan Shaw *(Lincoln Tyler)*; Chip Zien *(Mickey Alter)*; Mike Starr *(Walt Mcgahn)*; Christain Napoli *(Michael Santoro)*; Adam C. Flores *(Jose Pacifico Ruiz)*; Tamara Tunie *(Anthea)*; Mark Camacho *(C.J.)*; Peter McRobbie *(Pritzker)*; Jayne Heitmeyer *(Serena)*; Chip Chuipka *(Zietz/Drunk)*; Eric Hoziel *(Rabat)*; Michaella Bassey *(Tyler's Party Girl #2)*; Paul Joseph Bernardo *(Casino Security #1)*; Jernard Burks *(Tyler's Bodyguard)*; Desmond Campbell *(Arena Security #1)*; Jean-Paul Chartrand *(Ring Announcer)*; Deano Clavet *(Arena Security)*; Tara Ann Culp *(Lady at Elevator)*; Kelly Deadmon *(Blonde Reporter)*; Frederick DeGrandpre *(College Boy #1)*; Sebastien Delorme *(College Boy #4)*; George Fourniotis *(Blue Shirt #3)*; Christina Fulton *(Roundgirl)*; Kenneth Glegg *(Referee)*; Alain Goulem *(PPV Director)*; Dean Hagopian *(Latecomer)*; Byron Johnson *(College Boy #2)*; Guy Kelada *(Blue Shirt)*; Sylvain Landry *(Remote Producer)*; Cary Lawrence *(Powell's Aide)*; Robert Norman Lemieux *(FBI Agent)*; Richard Lemire *(Agent #2)*; Christopher MacCabe *(Couple #2)*; Sylvain Masse *(Cop)*; Patrick F. McDade *(Lawyer)*; William J. McKeon III *(Anthea's Cameraman)*; Lance E. Nichols *(Cop #3)*; Jason Nuzzo *(Coin Cup Grabber)*; Patrick Parent *(Detective)*; Peter Patrikios *(Coin Cup Decoy)*; Jacynthe Rene *(Couple #1)*; Stephen Spreekmeester *(College Boy #3)*; Eva Tep *(Tyler's Party Girl #1)*; John Thaddeus *(Cop #2)*; James Whelan *(Mayor)*; Brian A. Wilson *(Casino Security #2)*; Richard Zeman *(Agent #1)*; Gerard Max Desilus *(Tyler's Party Crash Guy)*

Brian De Palma's SNAKE EYES is a flashy, but disappointing, high-concept thriller that seems to have been designed primarily to provide De Palma with several opportunities to show off his indisputable command of cinematic grammar; he unfortunately fails to back up his visual flashes of brilliance with a credible script and sympathetic characters.

Corrupt Atlantic City cop Rick Santoro (Nicolas Cage) is asked by his boyhood friend Navy Comdr. Kevin Dunne (Gary Sinise) to assist him with security for a prize fight taking place at a casino during a tropical storm, which Secretary of Defense Kirkland (Joel Fabiani) is attending. During the fight, Dunne leaves to follow a suspicious-looking redhead (Tamara Tunie), and a woman in a blonde wig (Carla Gugino) sits next to Santoro and gives Kirkland an envelope. Suddenly, the champ, Lincoln Tyler (Stan Shaw), is knocked out and two gunshots ring out, the first killing Kirkland and the second grazing the arm of the "blonde," whose wig falls off, and who grabs back the envelope and scrambles away during the ensuing pandemonium. In the upper deck, Dunne shoots and kills the assassin, who's an alleged Palestinian terrorist. Santoro checks a tape of the fight and sees that Tyler was "knocked out" by a phantom punch. Tyler admits he took a dive after the redhead offered to pay off his huge gambling debts. After Santoro tells Dunne that he suspects a conspiracy, Dunne goes to the casino's basement, where he calmly shoots the redhead and another associate.

Santoro finds the "blonde" (whose name is Julia), and she tells him that she works for a defense contractor owned by industrialist Gilbert Powell (John Heard)—who also owns the casino—and that she had alerted Kirkland that Powell's new missile tests were doctored. She shows Santoro photos of the tests, and also tells him that she saw Dunne talking with the alleged assassin before the shooting. Santoro is shocked when a surveillance tape confirms her story, and he hides her away. Dunne confronts Santoro and erases the tape, then offers him $1 million to tell him where he's stashed Julia. When Santoro refuses, Tyler beats him up and Dunne plants a tracking device on the unconscious Santoro, who unwittingly leads Dunne to Julia. As Dunne is about to shoot Julia, a police van driving on the boardwalk is blown by the violent storm and crashes through the casino's wall. The cops order Dunne to put down his gun and he shoots himself. Later, Santoro is commended for heroism, but he's subsequently indicted for corruption and sentenced to a short prison term. Before going to jail, he runs into Julia, who tells him she's just testified against Powell, then thanks Santoro and gives him a kiss.

After the impersonal commercial chore of MISSION: IMPOSSIBLE (1996), SNAKE EYES, though a dazzling stylistic exercise, represents another step back for De Palma; this is unfortunate, given that he exhibited a newfound maturity in his previous film, the underrated CARLITO'S WAY (1993), in which he applied his technical expertise to a story that had real emotional resonance. Cowritten by David Koepp (who also scripted CARLITO), SNAKE EYES fails to leave much of an impression due to its superficially drawn characters, its implausibility (the finale and epilogue are particularly contrived), and the artificiality of its set up (in which an enclosed space and compressed time frame are expanded with fragmented flashbacks and other narrative tricks). Nicolas Cage's strident performance as the hyperactive hustler makes his moral conversion hard to swallow, while Gary Sinise (in a role initially offered to Will Smith and then Al Pacino), is too obviously sinister from the start.

The set pieces, however, are superbly done, such as Santoro and Dunne's intercut pursuit of Julia through the casino via surveillance monitors, and the bravura 12-minute opening Steadicam shot that follows Santoro as he talks on a cell phone, meets various people, goes down an escalator, shakes down a punk for some cash, goes into the boxing arena, and culminates with the assassination. The various RASHOMON-like flashbacks, including the fight (which is not shown the first time) are seen from multiple POV's and offer some nimble cinematic footwork by De Palma, who even employs two of his old trademarks: elaborate split-screen effects, and overhead tracking shots, with the camera soaring above a row of ceilingless hotel rooms, creating a vertiginous reminder of REAR WINDOW (1954) and De Palma's own HI, MOM! (1970). The film is always visually entertaining, but it catches the eye without engaging the mind and is ultimately as ponderous as it is clever. *(Violence, profanity, sexual situations.)*—M.S.

d, Brian De Palma; p, Brian De Palma; exec p, Louis A. Stroller; assoc p, Jeff Levine; w, David Koepp, Brian De Palma; ph, Stephen H. Burum; ed, Bill Pankow; m, Ryuichi Sakamoto; prod d, Anne Pritchard; art d, James Fox, Isabelle Guay, Real Proulx; set d, Daniel Carpenter; sound, Patrick Rousseau (mixer); fx, Garry Elmendorf, Industrial Light & Magic; casting, Mary Colquhoun; cos, Odette Gadoury; makeup, Lucille Demers; stunts, Peter Bucossi, Michael Nomad, Mike Scherer, Eddie Yansick

Thriller/Mystery **(PR: C MPAA: R)**

SNOWBOUND ★★★

(U.S./Canada, 1998) 92m Pacific Motion Pictures; Spectator Films; Jaffe/Braunstein Films, Ltd. ~ Bonneville Worldwide Entertainment c

(AKA: SNOWBOUND: THE JIM AND JENNIFER STOLPA STORY)

Neil Patrick Harris *(Jim Stolpa)*; Kelli Williams *(Jennifer Stolpa)*; Susan Clark *(Muriel)*; Michael Gross *(Kevin)*; Richard Cox; Duncan Fraser; Andrew Arlie *(Dr. Bonaldi)*; Alexander Anhert *(Clay Stolpa)*; Zachary Anhert *(Clay Stolpa)*; Shannon Beaty *(Megan Mulligan)*; Heather Beaty *(Megan Mulligan)*; Joy Coghill *(Dr. Jorgenson)*; Kevin McNulty *(Joe Tirado)*; Roger Barnes *(Steve)*; J.B. Bivens *(Roadblock CHP)*; John B. Destry

(Redinger); Beverley Elliott *(Terri)*; Tina Gilbertson *(Reporter)*; Mitchell Kosterman *(Deputy)*; Catherine Lough *(Paramedic)*; Randi Lynne *(CHP Sergeant)*; Walter Marsh *(Sherriff Watkins)*; Hrothgar Mathews *(Rick Frazier)*; Arlin McFarlane *(Roberta Patterson)*; Douglas Newell *(Tommy)*; Rick Poltaruk *(Mechanic)*; Phil Reimer *(Weatherman)*; Robert Toohey *(Doug Farley)*; Arnie Walters *(Uncle Clay)*; Shawn Webster *(Weatherwoman)*; Dale Wilson *(Lt. Jack Reynolds)*; Donna Yamamoto *(Nurse)*

The true story of a young couple and their five-month-old son who survived a week stranded in the snow was the basis for this interesting, if seldom compelling, 1994 made-for-television film. The film was released to home video in 1998.

Young marrieds Jim (Neil Patrick Harris) and Jennifer Stolpa (Kelli Williams) spend Christmas with his mother Muriel (Susan Clark) and her husband Kevin (Michael Gross). The visit is interrupted when Muriel gets a call that her mother has had a heart episode; by the time she gets there, her mother has died. Wanting to comfort her, Jim gets five days leave from his army base and borrows a truck from Jennifer's brother so that they and their son Clay can drive the 1000 miles to the funeral in Idaho. When the main route is blocked by a snowstorm, they take an alternate route, choosing not to tell Jim's parents so as not to worry them. After taking the noisy chains off the trucks tires so that the baby can sleep, a wrong turn leaves them stuck in snow on an untraveled mountain road. After a few days, they decide to walk 18 miles to the next town. Meanwhile, after finding the police unwilling to launch a search effort, Kevin uses his experience as a sports publicist to rally a public effort to find the Stolpas.

An exhausting walk brings the Stolpas to the realization that they are lost. After resting for the night in a cave, Jennifer is still unable to walk. Jim decides to retrace his steps to the truck and walk the 40 miles back to the previous town while Jennifer waits with Clay. The walk takes several days. Rescuers guided by Jim's directions retrieve mother and child just before another major blizzard. Clay survives, and while Jim and Jennifer lose portions of their feet to frostbite, both fulfill a promise to walk on the beach with Clay on his first birthday.

While the ordeal endured by the real-life Stolpas (who are seen in the film's closing shot) was undoubtedly terrifying, it's not all that dramatic, at least not as presented in SNOWBOUND. Given that this was made for television, it's entirely possible that some things were toned down a bit for a family audience—the film isn't as exploitative as it might have been. (There are two exceptions, both involving baby Clay, when the viewer is led to suspect that the infant may be dead or injured, and both are unforgivably manipulative.) Because not a whole lot happens to the characters for long stretches, scripter Jonathan Rintels wisely chose to focus on the emotional aspect of a couple, already facing doubts that they may be too young to have started a family, confronting what appears to be a failure in their responsibilities. Effectively photographed in and around Vancouver, SNOWBOUND features good performances and is well paced, though it may be a bit grim for younger viewers. *(Adult situations.)*—M.F.

d, Christian Duguay; p, Lisa Richardson, Matthew O'Connor; exec p, Howard Braunstein, Christine A. Sacani; w, Jonathan Rintels; ph, Peter Woeste; ed, George Appleby; m, Lou Natale; prod d, Michael Joy; art d, David Hay; set d, Mary Lou Storey; sound, Rick Patton; fx, Randy Shymkiw; casting, Shana Landsburg, Sid Kozak; cos, Susan de Laval; makeup, Dianne Pelletier; stunts, Melissa Stubbs

Docudrama **(PR: C MPAA: NR)**

SOLDIER ★★

(U.S./U.K., 1998) 96m Jerry Weintraub Productions; Impact Pictures; Warner Bros. ~ Warner Bros. c

Kurt Russell *(Sgt. Todd)*; Jason Scott Lee *(Caine 607)*; Connie Nielsen *(Sandra)*; Gary Busey *(Captain Church)*; Michael Chiklis *(Jimmy Pig)*; James Black; Jason Isaacs *(Col. Mekum)*; Sean Pertwee *(Mace)*; Tom O'Brien; Brenda Wehle *(Hawkins)*; Wyatt Russell *(Young Todd)*; Jared Thorne *(Nathan)*; Taylor Thorne *(Nathan)*; Mark Bringelson *(Rubrick)*; KK Dodd *(Sloan)*

It's SHANE (1953) in space, with Kurt Russell as a combination of Rambo and the Terminator. Stylishly piecing together cliches from some of the best action movies of the 1980s, SOLDIER entertains, but lacks the spark of originality.

In 1996, the United States initiates the Adam Project, indoctrinating select male infants into lifelong military service. Weaned on fear and discipline, young Todd (Wyatt Russell) is trained to be a merciless killing machine with total loyalty to his superiors. A mature Todd (Kurt Russell) proves himself an exceptional soldier in numerous battles both on Earth and in outer space.

In 2036, Colonel Mekum (Jason Isaacs) introduces a new breed of soldier, genetically engineered to be bigger, faster, and stronger. Sgt. Todd, the best of the old guard, is pitted in a brutal contest against one of the new, Caine 607 (Jason Scott Lee). Todd is defeated and his now-obsolete carcass is dumped along with the rest of the Earth's refuse on waste disposal planet Arcadia 234. There, colonist families, whose ship had crashed on the desert planet, rescue the fallen warrior. Todd is taken in by Mace (Sean Pertwee), his beautiful wife Sandra (Connie Nielsen), and their mute son Nathan (Jared and Taylor Thorne). As Todd regains his health, his training reasserts itself, making any assimilation into the ragtag community impossible.

Todd is exiled just as Mekum and his soldiers land on Arcadia 234 for a routine security sweep. Mekum decides to exterminate the colonists rather than deal with the paperwork entailed by rescuing them. After Mace is killed, Todd returns and launches a one-man guerrilla defense of the colonists. Using his guile and battle-honed skills, Todd kills all of Mekum's genetically-engineered soldiers except Caine 607, whom Todd faces and defeats in a rain-soaked *mano a mano* battle. Todd leaves Mekum and his lieutenants to die on Arcadia 234, and flies Sandra, Nathan, and the rest of the colonists off to a new future.

SOLDIER's screenplay is by David Webb Peoples, who scripted the sci-fi noir BLADE RUNNER (1982) and the western UNFORGIVEN (1992). Its genre-mixing is no surprise, but its failure to add anything new to the stew is. It's a mix that uses an all-time American classic (SHANE) as its base, adding elements of the Stallone and Schwarzenegger oeuvres, THE ROAD WARRIOR (1981), echoes of the Ewoks battle on Endor from RETURN OF THE JEDI (1983) and even a little WITNESS (1985).

Having previously directed MORTAL KOMBAT (1995) and EVENT HORIZON (1997), Paul Anderson here cements his reputation as a filmmaker who delivers violent sci-fi eye candy, rapidly paced so as to keep audiences from thinking too much about it. SOLDIER is a terrific looking movie, thanks in large measure to the production design of David L. Snyder, an Oscar-winner for BLADE RUNNER.

Kurt Russell is basically on hand to lend the marquee value of his name to the film. Russell grunts out precious few words of dialogue in the movie, and his part could easily have been played by any actor willing to buff up for the role and able to stare intently through many scenes. (Graphic violence, profanity.)—P.R.

d, Paul Anderson; p, Jerry Weintraub; exec p, R.J. Louis, Susan Ekins; assoc p, Fred Fontana; co-p, Jeremy Bolt; w, David Webb Peoples; ph, David Tattersall; ed, Martin Hunter; prod d, David L. Snyder; art d, Tom Valentine; set d, Kate Sullivan; sound, Andy Wiskes; fx, Clay Pinny; casting, Mindy Marin; cos, Erica Phillips

Science Fiction/Action/Drama (PR: C MPAA: R)

SOLDIER'S DAUGHTER NEVER CRIES, A ★★★½

(U.S., 1998) 120m Merchant-Ivory; RHI Entertainment; Nayeem Hafizika ~ October Films c

Kris Kristofferson *(Bill Willis)*; Barbara Hershey *(Marcella Willis)*; Leelee Sobieski *(Channe Willis)*; Jesse Bradford *(Billy Willis)*; Jane Birkin *(Mrs. Fortescue)*; Dominique Blanc *(Candida)*; Virginie Ledoyen *(Billy's Mother)*; Anthony Roth Costanzo *(Francis Fortescue)*; Harley Cross *(Keith Carter)*; Isaac de Bankole *(Mamadou)*; Macha Meril *(Madame Beauvier)*; Nathalie Richard *(Mademoiselle Fournier)*; Bob Swaim *(Bob Smith)*; Luisa Conlon *(Young Channe)*; Samuel Gruen *(Benoit/Young Billy)*; Frederic Da *(Stephane)*; Antoine Chain *(Billy's Father)*; Michelle Fairley *(Miss O'Shaunessy)*; Sarah Haxaire *(Mademoiselle Devereux)*; Marie Henriau *(Social Worker)*; Pierre-Michel Sivadier *(Mr. Flowers)*; Scott Thomas *(1st Jock)*; Dominic Gould; Susan Gutfreund; Stephanie Levin; Louis Niedleman; Anna Niedleman; Louis St. Calbre *(Poker Players, Paris)*; Freddy Stracham *(Dancer)*; Veronique Bellegarde *(Test Monitor)*; Miranda Raimondi *(Melissa)*; Anne-Cecile Crapie *(Mademoiselle Picot)*; Eric Naccache *(Lawyer)*; Elizabeth Villeminot *(Cassandra Smith)*; Catherine Villeminot *(Mary-Ellen Smith)*; Florence Villeminot *(Gillis Smith)*; Emma Scaife *(Bethany)*; Anthony Decadi *(Schoolyard Tease)*; Valerie Toledano *(Mademoiselle Fauchon)*; Daniel Tepfer *(Kevin)*; Alycia Fashae *(Salome)*; Marcos Pujol *(Herod)*; Catherine Alcover *(Herodias)*; Tammy Arnold *(Real Estate Agent)*; Loretta Anawalt; Bruce Anawalt; Tammy Helm; Don Baker *(Poker Players, Wilmington)*; Mitch Eakins *(2nd Jock)*; Christopher Berry *(Steve Bates)*

A SOLDIER'S DAUGHTER NEVER CRIES is a sensitive, carefully paced coming-of-age story about the daughter of a famous writer as she grows from childhood to teenhood.

In 1960s Paris, an American couple—a renowned war novelist, Bill Willis (Kris Kristofferson) and his wife Marcella (Barbara Hershey)—adopt a six-year-old French boy named Benoit (Samuel Gruen). The boy's mother (Virginie Ledoyen) leaves with the Willises a diary she wrote when she was pregnant at 15. Benoit is renamed Billy (his own choice) and immediately gets into conflict with the Willises' only other child, the headstrong preteen Channe (Luisa Conlon). Billy's stubbornness also gets him into trouble at school. Gradually Channe and Billy develop a warm relationship and both get into trouble together.

Five years later, as adolescents, Channe (LeeLee Sobieski) and Billy (Jesse Bradford) go to separate schools. At her American school, Channe meets and befriends Francis (Anthony Roth Costanzo), an aspiring opera singer and free spirit who is derided by the other boys for his effeminate manner and eccentric ways. He and Channe bring out each other's wildest impulses as they travel the city, and sing and dance, and act out in their homes. Willis has heart trouble and decides to move back with his family to the United States to complete a novel. They settle in a small, picturesque town where both Channe and Billy have difficulty adjusting. Hurt at school by taunts based on his nationality, Billy gradually withdraws into himself. Channe embarks on a number of brief affairs with local boys. Willis is hospitalized, but continues his work by having Channe type as he dictates his novel. He soon comes home, but must take it easy. When Channe settles down with a nice boy, Keith Carter (Harley Cross), her father gives his approval of their sleeping together.

As Channe prepares to go to a party on New Year's Eve, 1973, Marcella tells her that this will be Willis's last New Year—he will not last the year. Reluctantly, Channe goes to the party, but she calls from a pay phone at midnight. Willis dies soon after. Marcella digs out the diary of Billy's mother and gives it to him, but he refuses to read it, still angry at the mother who abandoned him. However, a chance opening to the line, "I hope he will be loved, as is his right," makes him realize how lucky he was to have the family he's had.

Based on a novel by Kaylie Jones, daughter of James Jones (author of *From Here to Eternity* and *The Thin Red Line*), A SOLDIER'S DAUGHTER NEVER CRIES is a rare foray into a (relatively) contemporary setting for the Merchant-Ivory-Jhabvala team. Equally rare, this is a story told from the viewpoint of children. The customary sensitivity the team has shown to characters trying to find their identity in the midst of difficult relationships is even richer and more delicate here as they show a precocious girl slowly maturing from childhood to adolescence and the tricky negotiations with boys she undertakes during that crucial time. The actors are more than equal to the task of fleshing out these richly drawn characters. Channe is played by two remarkable young actresses—Luisa Conlon, who has a timeless face that transcends her young age, and LeeLee Sobieski, who should strike a chord with girls of all ages as they cope with the joyous, often perilous landscape of childhood and adolescence.

Kristofferson, at the age of 62, gives what is arguably his best performance, as a man who leads a comfortable existence and is free to be himself, share his philosophy, and speak openly in front of the kids. (Some viewers may be alarmed at the father's easy acceptance of his teen daughter's sex life.) Barbara Hershey is very good at making an unsympathetic character human and accessible. The deck is stacked against her (she's given a grotesque hairdo and makeup job), but she invests the character with humanity and complexity. As the flighty Francis, Anthony Roth Costanzo deliberately recalls Sal Mineo's outcast Plato from REBEL WITHOUT A CAUSE (1955), though without the tragic dimensions of that character. Jesse Bradford, as the teenaged Billy, has the most underwritten role, but presents a realistic portrayal of a teen who has the hardest time coping with the dislocation of the move to America despite the fact that he's completely rid himself of his accent. *(Profanity.)*—B.C.

d, James Ivory; p, Ismail Merchant; exec p, Richard Hawley, Nayeem Hafizka; co-p, Paul Bradley; w, James Ivory, Ruth Prawer Jhabvala (based on the novel by Kaylie Jones); ph, Jean-Marc Fabre; ed, Noelle Boisson; m, Richard Robbins; prod d, Jacques Bufnoir (France), Pat Garner (USA); sound, Ludovic Henault; casting, Annette Trumel (France), Tricia Tomey (USA), Celestia Fox (UK); cos, Carol Ramsey

Drama (PR: C MPAA: R)

SOMEWHERE IN THE CITY ★★

(U.S., 1998) 93m Sideshow Inc. ~ Artistic License Films c

Sandra Bernhard *(Betty)*; Ornella Muti *(Marta)*; Robert John Burke *(Frankie)*; Peter Stormare *(Graham)*; Bai Ling *(Lu Lu)*; Paul Anthony Stewart *(Che)*; Bulle Ogier *(Brigitte)*; Linda Dano *(Television Producer)*; William Sage *(Bill Sage)*; Steve Schub *(Steven Schub)*; Kim Walker *(Molly—Texas Acting Student)*; John Fugelsang *(Henry)*; Robert Shapiro *(Larry)*; Dupre Kelly *(2-Kool)*; Jimmy Noonan *(Brian)*; Victoria Bastel *(Johanna)*; David Pittu *(Graham's Agent)*; Paolina Weber *(Nine)*; Mike Danner *(George)*; Ed Koch *(Himself)*

Billing itself as a "noir screwball comedy" inspired by Maxim Gorky's "Lower Depths," SOMEWHERE IN THE CITY is as jumbled and tiresome as that description would suggest—a plotless indie talkathon about the intersecting, albeit uninteresting, lives of a group of "wacky" New Yorkers which is made barely watchable because of its surprisingly good cast.

Among the denizens of a Lower East Side, New York tenement are Betty (Sandra Bernhard), a neurotic sex therapist who acts more like a patient; Marta (Ornella Muti), a beautiful Italian who's married to the building's slovenly super, but who's cheating with her neighbor Frankie (Robert John Burke), who's a scam artist and car thief; Graham (Peter Stormare), an unemployed Russian gay actor who supports himself by giving acting lessons to young men; Chinese immigrant Lu Lu (Bai Ling), who is seeking a paper marriage in order to get her green card; and Che (Paul Anthony Stewart), a rich kid who fancies himself a Marxist revolutionary, but who's constantly being interrupted by calls from his mother on his cell phone.

Betty takes the shy Lu Lu under her wing and tries to find her a mate, but Lu Lu goes too far in trying to Americanize herself and transforms into a club-hopping punk; Marta becomes a soap opera star after Frankie goes on the lam following a botched jewel heist; Graham thinks that he's got a job in a big Hollywood movie, but is shattered to learn that the project has been canceled. Che eventually falls in love with Lu Lu and marries her after giving up being a revolutionary when one of his partners goes berserk and kidnaps Ed Koch (Himself), whom he believes is still the mayor of New York.

The feature film debut by Iranian-born director and co-writer Ramin Niami (a former documentary filmmaker), SOMEWHERE IN THE CITY is a cliched collection of quirks in search of real characters and an engaging story. The result is strained whimsy, with all the familiar New York indie stereotypes assembled by rote, including the eccentric, whip-wielding sex-therapist; the trust fund Communist; the gay actor; coke-snorting neighbors staring into the mirror and reciting Travis Bickle dialogue; apartment doors with dozens of bolts and chain locks; and padding scenes of visits to rock clubs featuring appearances by real-life bands (in this case, The Voluptuous Horror of Karen Black). There's even the requisite lame attempt at satirizing LA and the emptiness of big-budget Hollywood movies, in a scene where Graham goes to see his trendy agent (who constantly says "Ciao ciao," of course) to discuss his role in a big-screen remake of "I Dream of Jeannie," starring Madonna and Keanu Reeves, and directed by Ron Howard and written by Joe Eszterhas.

The film's only redeeming feature is the presence of its notable cast, and with such a shallow script, it's hard to believe that Niami was able to attract such international names as Ornella Muti, Bai Ling, and even Bulle Ogier in a small role, and persuade them to degrade themselves. The performances are generally understated and good-natured, in contrast to the self-consciously "zany" and unpleasant proceedings, although Ed Koch shamelessly hams it up in his cameo where he's bound to a chair and held captive, which, along with the casting of a manic-motormouthed Sandra Bernhard, conjures up (intentionally, no doubt) memories of another darkly humorous tale of New Yorkers on the fringe of society, the infinitely superior THE KING OF COMEDY (1983). *(Profanity, sexual situations, nudity, violence, substance abuse.)* —M.S.

d, Ramin Niami; p, Ramin Niami, Karen Robson; exec p, Paula Brancato; assoc p, Patrick Dillon, Ken Greenblatt, Robert Sturm, Iona de Macedo; co-p, Karen Jaronecki; w, Patrick Dillon, Ramin Niami; ph, Igor Sunara; ed, Elizabeth Gazzara, Ramin Niami; m, John Cale; prod d, Lisa Albin; sound, Antonio L. Arroyo; casting, Caroline Sinclair; cos, S. Betim Balaman

Comedy/Romance **(PR: O MPAA: NR)**

SONATINE ★★★★

(Japan, 1994) 94m Bandai Visual; Shochiku Dai-Ichi Kogyo; Office Kitano; Right Vision ~ Rolling Thunder c

Takeshi Kitano, billed as "Beat" Takeshi *(Murakama)*; Aya Kokumai *(Miyuki—the Village Girl)*; Tetsu Watanabe *(Uechi—the Okinawan Gangster)*; Masanobu Katsumura *(Ryoji)*; Susumu Terashima *(Ken)*; Ren Ohsugi *(Katagiri)*; Tonbo Zushi *(Kitajima)*; Kenichi Yajima *(Takahashi)*; Eiji Minakata *(The Hit Man)*

The second movie directed by and starring Japanese super-celebrity Takeshi Kitano to receive an official US release in 1998 (after FIREWORKS), SONATINE solidifies Mr. Kitano's standing as a master of the crime-story-cum-character-study. The film's winning mixture of wry humor and sudden, brutal violence makes it one of the most uniquely original gangster movies in recent memory.

Low-ranking *yakuza* boss Murakawa (Takeshi Kitano) is thinking of retiring. His higher-up, Kitajima (Tonbo Zushi), asks him to undertake a special mission: bring a group of his men to Okinawa, where a gang war has erupted between the Aran clan and that of Nakamatsu, Kitajima's close friend. Murakawa and his band are to "restore peace" by negotiating a settlement between the two sides; Kitajima emphasizes that the situation is desperate. The hesitant Murakawa complies, but his suspicions are aroused when he arrives in Okinawa with his men, only to be informed by Nakamatsu that the feud is "nothing serious." The Murakawa clan soon become the victims of violent attacks: a bomb is thrown through the window of the shabby office that serves as their provisional headquarters, killing some of the men. A short time later, more lives are lost in a bloody shootout in a local bar. Murakawa and the other survivors drive to a seaside house owned by the brother of a sympathetic local mobster, Uechi (Tetsu Watanabe). There, they will lay low and consider their options.

To keep their spirits up, the *yakuza* begin playing games, incorporating everything from frisbees to fireworks. They are joined in these pastimes by Miyuki (Aki Kokumai), a local woman whom Murakawa rescued from a date rapist.

It soon becomes apparent that the Murakawa clan has been abandoned by their bosses in Tokyo. The group is finally contacted by Nakamatsu, who passes on the news that Katajima has forged a truce with the Aran clan, and has decided that the Murakawa clan must be banished. Soon after, a hitman disguised as a fisherman kills two of Murakawa's men on the beach, in front of Murakawa and Miyuki.

Murakawa sets out for revenge. He finds the hitman in a local hotel and kills him, then abducts Kitajima's right-hand man, Takahashi (Kenichi Yajima). Before he is killed by one of Murakawa's men, Takahashi reveals what Murakawa suspected: that the Okinawa assignment was a setup. Takahashi also informs Murakawa that Kitajima is coming to Okinawa to have a meeting with the Anan clan.

Murakawa says farewell to Miyuki and his remaining comrade, and goes to the site of the conference. He enters the building and proceeds to wipe out all of the assembled mobsters. Bloody, he leaves the scene and drives to a secluded spot near the beach. There, he shoots himself in the head.

Released through Quentin Tarantino's cult-movie division of Miramax, Rolling Thunder Pictures, SONATINE provided American cinephiles with one of their first glimpses at a major filmmaking talent. Known in Japan for his extensive work on television (as a variety show host, quizmaster, and even political pundit), Takeshi Kitano had directed three films before this one, in which he forged a bold style which combined an aesthete's visual concerns with the sardonic humor that had been a trademark of his work as a performer.

Given Kitano's beginnings as a standup comedian, it's no surprise that he exhibits a master's touch with the humorous portions of SONATINE. Rarely has a film presented such a vivid portrait of the childlike side of gangsters—while hiding out in their seaside refuge, Murakawa's gang behaves like a band of aggressive little boys who are bored out of their minds, and have to rely on their skewed imaginations to fight the tedium. The result is an uncommonly endearing portrait of cold-blooded killers, which shows the juvenile impulses that belie their professional tough-guy posture.

This strong vein of humor makes the film's violent interludes all the more startling. Kitano and cinematographer Katsumi Yanagishima frame their subjects in static shots which emphasize both their placid surroundings and their business-like attitude towards their work. This spartan visual style is complemented by the silence that punctuates every major action—counterpointed by Joe Hasaishi's vibrant synthesizer musical score, which buoys up the film's cheerier moments.

The cast fill their roles admirably, but their central function, naturally enough, is to lend support to Kitano. Having been seen by American audiences only in two supporting roles—in MERRY CHRISTMAS, MR. LAWRENCE (1983) and JOHNNY MNEMONIC (1995)—there was little preparation for the one-two punch offered by the 1998 release of both his FIREWORKS and SONATINE (GONIN, a gangster drama in which he acted only, also appeared in the USA in '98). Here, he elicits viewer sympathy for his character by making him a sacrificial lamb whose sense of humor (coupled with a metaphysical desire for death) enables him to make the best out of the doomed situation in which he's been placed. Kitano's deadpan visage, his aggressive demeanor, and his assured physicality provoke one set of viewer expectations—that Murakawa is a ruthless and emotionless gunman—while the character's nasty sense of humor (embodied in the many pranks he pulls on his cohorts) and his bittersweet take on his profession ("I shoot first because I get scared first," he tells Miyuki) make him an endearing antihero.

For a resolutely tough-looking individual, "Beat" Takeshi (a nickname from his days as a comedian, used for his onscreen billing as an actor) has a wonderfully luminous smile. He uses this trait in both the film's silliest moments and its most jarring—as he blows his brains out in a suicidal nightmare that prefigures the film's stark conclusion.

SONATINE truly qualifies as a thinking man's action film, which reworks crime-movie cliches while presenting a pungent commentary on the cult of machismo. *(Violence, nudity, profanity.)*—E.G.

d, Takeshi Kitano; p, Masayuki Mori, Hisao Nabeshima, Takio Yoshida, Ritta Saito; exec p, Kazuyoshi Okuyama; w, Takeshi Kitano; ph, Katsumi Yanagishima; ed, Takeshi Kitano; m, Joe Hisaishi; art d, Osamu Saseki; set d, Hirohide Shibata; sound, Senji Horiuchi (recordist); makeup, Kyoko Toyokawa, Tomoo Haraguchi (effects), Hisashi Oda (effects)

Crime/Drama/Comedy (PR: C MPAA: R)

SONDAGS ENGLER
(SEE: OTHER SIDE OF SUNDAY, THE)

SOSTIENE PEREIRA
(SEE: PEREIRA DECLARES)

SOULER OPPOSITE, THE ★½
(U.S., 1998) 105m Buffalo Jump Productions ~ Curb Entertainment c

Christopher Meloni *(Barry Singer)*; Timothy Busfield *(Robert Levin)*; Janel Moloney *(Thea Douglas)*; Joshua Keaton *(Young Barry)*; Jed Rhein *(Young Robert)*; Bruce Nozick *(Barry's Dad)*; J.J. Rodgers *(Charisse)*; Catrin Zack *(Call Girl)*; Rachel Winfree *(Biker Chick)*; Joe Rose *(Biker Boyfriend)*; Tom McTigue *(Joey Kagan)*; Robert Fields *(Jay Smiley)*; Devon Meade *(Sandra)*; Mariangela Pino *(Rita)*; Cynthia Lynch *(Yoga Instructor)*; Michael Kagan *(Max Luckstein)*; Steven Kravitz *(Arnold)*; Steve Landesberg *(Himself)*; Buddy Winston *("A" Table Comic)*; Mark Clifton *(Man in Clinic)*; Lenora May *(Doctor in Clinic)*; Jeffrey Anderson-Gunter *(Evan)*; Allison Mackie *(Diane)*; Rutanya Alda *(Thea's Mom)*; Richard Rifkin *(Argus)*; John Putch *(Lester)*; Jon Stafford *(Bar Patron)*; Sarah Scott Davis *(Campaign Worker #1)*; Sheila Creal *(Campaign Worker #2)*; Roger Nolan *(Political Analyst)*; Cindy Kalmenson *(Folk Singer)*; Danny Hartigan *(Van Driver)*; Julian Neil *(Reporter)*; Kathleen Garret *(Julianne)*; Suzanne Krull *(Vanessa)*; Daran Norris *(Young Man "Actor")*; Gene Borkan *(Father "Actor")*; Casey Kalmenson *(Young Girl in Hearse)*; Bill Kalmenson *(Dad in Hearse)*

Based largely on writer-director Bill Kalmenson's own experiences, THE SOULER OPPOSITE chronicles the romantic ups and downs of a struggling stand-up comic. A self-distributed film, Kalmenson's debut feature is monotonous and self-indulgent, and at its length, nearly unendurable.

Though in his mid-30s, Barry Singer (Christopher Meloni) still hopes to make it big as a comedian on the Los Angeles club circuit. One night, in the parking lot of a club where he performs, he meets Thea (Janel Moloney), a young student who comes to his aid after he's been assaulted by an audience member he'd offended. Barry is immediately attracted to Thea, but she tells him she's not interested in a relationship. Undeterred, Barry pursues her, and even bribes an astrologist to concoct a chart showing that they are perfect for each other because they are "solar opposites." Eventually, Barry wins Thea over.

The two begin to spend all their time together, Barry accompanying Thea when she visits her parents for Christmas. When Thea suggests, however, that Barry and she move in together, Barry expresses strong reservations. Angry and hurt, Thea ends the relationship.

Meanwhile, Barry's career as a comedian founders. Max (Michael Kagan), the manager of a popular club, steadfastly refuses to book him. In time, he gets an opportunity to perform at Max's and he impresses the crowd, but afterward, he is accused of stealing material from a rival and ejected from the club.

Thea finds work as a political campaign consultant and leaves Los Angeles to travel for her job. When Barry learns of this, he tracks her down and asks her to marry him, but she turns him down. Thea moves to Washington, DC, while Barry returns home and takes a job giving tours of sites where celebrities have died. Returning home from work one night, Thea finds and opens an envelope from Barry containing the "solar opposites" astrological chart. She immediately returns to Southern California and proposes to Barry that they resume their relationship, a proposal Barry gladly accepts.

THE SOULER OPPOSITE has all the quality of a failed television pilot. The central character is intended to be lovably hip and irreverent, as full of snappy wisecracks off stage as he is on. He meets his match in the form of an attractive, levelheaded woman, and they verbally banter their way to romantic bliss. And as is the case with many a failed pilot, the filmmaker has neglected to imbue his creation with anything witty, original, or interesting.

Nothing much out of the ordinary happens during the course of THE SOULER OPPOSITE, nor is there anything special about its main character. Of course, some filmmakers—Eric Rohmer, Hou Hsiao-hsien—have made an art of the ordinary, but in Kalmenson's inexperienced hands, the ordinary seems even less so. Perhaps because Barry's story is based on his own experiences, Kalmenson was reluctant to embellish his narrative, or perhaps he felt its dramatic value was self-evident. Either way, he has failed to convey what makes Barry or his experiences worthy of a feature film. It is never clear why Thea (or a moviegoer) should care about or be attracted to Barry, a second-rate comic and emotional adolescent. Even the film's romantic aspect is dull—the relationship between Barry and Thea, once established, goes nowhere, as the pair mouth boring, repetitive dialogue and keep on redefining their relationship.

Kalmenson actually had the elements to make a good film. The cast is fine, and Moloney is outstanding. Technically, the film is assured, and it has a lovely blues score that ideally complements Los Angeles nighttime scenery. Unfortunately, Kalmenson seems more interested in prolonged self-portraiture than he is in entertaining an audience. *(Violence, nudity, sexual situations, extreme profanity.)*—D.C.

d, Bill Kalmenson; p, Tani Cohen; w, Bill Kalmenson; ph, Amin Bhattacharya; ed, Timothy Snell; m, Peter Himmelman; prod d, Jane Ann Stewart; set d, Renee Davenport; sound, Ed White (mixer); casting, Laura Adler, Shana Landsburg; cos, Lynn Bernay

Romance/Comedy/Drama (PR: C MPAA: R)

SOUR GRAPES ★★★

(U.S., 1998) 92m Castle Rock ~ Columbia c

Steven Weber *(Evan Maxwell)*; Craig Bierko *(Richie)*; Matt Keeslar *(Danny Pepper)*; Karen Sillas *(Joan)*; Robyn Peterman *(Roberta)*; Viola Harris *(Selma)*; Orlando Jones *(Digby)*; Jack Burns *(Eulogist)*; Scott Erik *(Teenage Richie)*; Michael Resnick *(Teenage Evan)*; Jennifer Leigh Warren *(Millie)*; Anthony Parziale *(Blackjack Dealer)*; Abraham Kessler *(Crap Dealer)*; Fred Goehner *(Floor Manager)*; Amy Hohn *(Waitress)*; Denise Bessette *(Cocktail Waitress)*; Angelo Tiffe *(Chauffeur)*; Bari K. Willerford; Alan Wilder *(Irwin)*; Hiram Kasten *(Male Co-Worker)*; Kari Coleman *(Female Co-Worker)*; Rosanna Huffman *(Mr. Bell's Assistant)*; Philip Baker Hall *(Mr. Bell)*; Harry Murphy *(Anesthesiologist #1)*; Deirdre Lovejoy *(Nurse Wells)*; Iqbal Theba *(Dr. Alagappan)*; Tamara Clatterbuck *(Nurse Donato)*; Helen Anzalone *(Nurse Jamison)*; Richard Gant *(Det. Crouch)*; James MacDonald *(Det. Frehill)*; Ann Guilbert *(Mrs. Drier)*; Harper Roisman *(Mr. Drier)*; Edith Varon *(Fran)*; Jack Kehler *(Jack)*; John Toles-Bey *(Lee)*; Michael Krawic *(Larry)*; Sonya Eddy *(Nurse Loder)*; Jill Talley *(Lois)*; Bryan Gordon *(Doug)*; Rachel Crane *(Allie)*; Julie Claire *(Matisse)*; Patrick Fabian *(Palmer)*; Kevin Shinick *(Conner)*; Meredith Salenger *(Degan)*; Kristin Davis *(Riggs)*; Larry David; Jon Hayman; Linda Wallem *(TV Producers)*; Ron West *(Dr. Isner)*; Bruce Jarchow *(Dr. Dean)*; Marvin Braverman *(Bartender)*; Arthur Chobanian *(Man in Bar)*; Jack O'Connell *(Homeless Man)*; Tucker Smallwood *(Anesthesiologist #2)*; Mark Chaet *(Dr. Michaels)*; Rande Leaman *(Hospital Worker)*; Larry Brandenburg *(Landlord)*; James Gallery *(Mr. Lesser)*; Tom Dahlgren *(Mr. Havelock)*

Though soundly dismissed by both the critics and the ticket-buying public, SOUR GRAPES is an underrated comedy that recaptures the cruelty at the black heart of the best episodes of TV's "Seinfeld." That's no surprise, since the film marks the feature directorial debut of "Seinfeld" cocreator Larry David, the man responsible for penning that program's funniest episodes.

Evan Maxwell (Steven Weber), a brain surgeon, and his cousin Richie (Craig Bierko), a sneaker designer, have been best friends since childhood. Evan considers Richie and his doting mother Selma (Viola Harris) a pair of certified eccentrics, but tolerates their behavior because they're family. When the cousins go to Atlantic City for a weekend with their girlfriends, Richie runs out of money playing slots and Evan lends him two quarters. When the pull of the handle results in a $436,000 jackpot, Richie doesn't share the money with Evan.

Enraged, Evan tries to coax his cousin to part with some of the money. When that results in Richie merely presenting him with a jogging suit, Evan plays a vengeful prank on his hypochondriac cousin by telling Richie that he's dying of a terminal brain disease. Evan leaves Richie a message setting the record straight, but it's too late. In the meantime, Richie has decided that his mother would be so traumatized by hearing the news about his medical condition that he has hired a homeless man to break into Selma's house, in hope of giving his ailing mother a terminal heart attack and ending her life quickly rather than having her feel grief over his fate. Richie is convinced that the shock of losing her beloved son will kill Selma anyway, and he can't bear to break the bad news. Although she barely survives, Selma indeed suffers a heart attack. The homeless man and some of his friends occupy Selma's empty house and destroy it, while two detectives look into the break-in, and quickly cast a suspicious eye on Richie.

A guilt-ridden Evan's work is affected. Though the brain is his surgical specialty, he's been convinced to perform the delicate removal of a cancerous testicle from major television star Danny Pepper (Matthew Keeslar). But Evan accidentally removes the wrong one and is forced to castrate Danny, ruining the actor's career. Meanwhile, the cousins are both left by their girlfriends and Richie, convinced he no longer needs to work, gets fired. He breaks down and gives Evan half the money to operate on his mother, and the cousins reconcile. But Evan is attacked by Danny Pepper and his money is flung from a window, landing practically in the homeless man's lap. Selma returns home, sees her wrecked house, and promptly expires; Richie's remaining half of the jackpot is spent restoring his mother's house. At Selma's funeral, Richie lends Evan some change for a parking meter, leaving both to ponder what they've lost over 50 cents.

Using his sitcom success as a template, David has created two characters in Evan and Richie who closely resemble Jerry and George from "Seinfeld," and many of the events in the film could easily have been transformed into plots for the classic TV show. Misunderstandings, neurotic behavior, cruel observations, odd sexual proclivities (Richie is able to orally gratify himself), and authority figures who are amazed at the lack of morality in the main characters were all hallmarks of "Seinfeld," and all can be found here. Most obviously, Evan and Richie's greed, the shallow, unapologetic self-interest that prevents them from simply doing the right thing by each other, stands as the plot element directly borrowed from David's work on "Seinfeld."

Perhaps the box-office failure of SOUR GRAPES stemmed from the very fact that the film so closely resembles David's hit TV series. It must be pointed out, however, that the series' uniquely dark outlook on the selfish aspects of humanity and its shrewd observations about the desperation with which we cling to our private peccadilloes came from David in the first place, so it's somewhat unreasonable to believe that he would change his comic approach upon making his first movie.

The most important similarity between SOUR GRAPES and "Seinfeld," however, is that, in the final analysis, both are sophisticated and funny. David pulls no punches in offering up characters who are cravenly, unabashedly out for their own interests. The film also skewers popular sacred cows, like the TV show "Friends," which aired after "Seinfeld" for a time, and which David mercilessly satirizes in a few clips of Danny Pepper's show. SOUR GRAPES demonstrates that David is a unique talent, unafraid of taking comedic risks. *(Adult situations, sexual situations, profanity.)*—K.W.

d, Larry David; p, Laurie Lennard; exec p, Barry Berg; assoc p, Yoli Poropat; w, Larry David; ph, Victor Hammer; ed, Priscilla Nedd-Friendly; prod d, Charles Rosen; art d, Chas. Butcher; set d, Anne D. McCulley; sound, Robert Janiger (mixer); fx, Mike Thompson; casting, Liberman/Hirschfeld Casting; cos, Debra McGuire; makeup, Brad Wilder; stunts, Roydon Clark

Comedy **(PR: O MPAA: R)**

SPACEJACKED ★

(U.S./Ireland, 1998) 89m Pacific Trust; New Concorde ~ New Horizons Home Video c

Corbin Bernsen *(Alex Barnes)*; Steve Bond *(Ryan Taylor)*; Amanda Pays *(Dawn Taggart)*; Matt Holland *(Mac)*; Des Kenny *(Gibson)*; Bill Murphy *(Jack)*; Fiedhlim Hillery *(Vincent Miles)*; Ciara O'Callaghan *(Monica Miles)*; Anita McFarlane *(Anna Koros)*; Vincent Dunlea *(Warren Wayne)*; Frank Melia *(Carlo)*; Richard Farrell *(Mr. Putnam)*; Donncha Crowley *(Katz)*; Shawn Brewster *(Brayson)*; Conor Maguire *(Phillips)*; Rico Shea *(Freighter Pilot)*; Brian Monaghan *(VR Caveman)*; Jonathan Jeffes *(VR Cop)*; Noelle Swan *(Mrs. Marshall)*; Mick Nolan *(Mr. Bohm)*

Veteran independent producer Roger Corman has a reputation for making do with very little, but the raw materials that went into SPACEJACKED were apparently too little even for his thrifty genius. The actors wouldn't make the cut-offs for "Star Search," the sets resemble a fourth-grade science fair project; the direction gives life to a new cinematic term: mess-en-scene.

In the near future, filthy rich pleasure-seekers get their kicks flying to the Moon. Fawned over by androids like Mac (Matt Holland) and Gibson (Des Kenny), the jaded travelers are in for a rude awakening in Outer Space. Having reprogrammed Gibson, greedy second mate Alex Barnes (Corbin Bernsen) damages the Moon-bound ship. As the passengers float helplessly in space, Barnes extorts money from them in exchange for safe passage.

However, only one escape pod (with room for seven passengers) remains; secretly Barnes intends to take the passengers' money, kill them, and escape to a neutral space station. As he delivers ultimatums to the passengers, first mate Ryan Taylor (Steve Bond) and enterprising passenger Dawn Taggart (Amanda Pays) scramble to get to the escape pod. Thwarted by Barnes, Dawn nearly drifts out of the ship into outer space and Ryan nearly implodes from depressurizing. While Dawn outwits and detonates Gibson, Ryan temporarily regains control of the ship. After leading the survivors to the getaway pod, Dawn heads for the captain's bridge. Ryan kills Barnes by cutting off his oxygen, as the escape vehicle takes off without him and Dawn. They are rescued by a freighter which picked up Mac after he was blasted into space and used his memory bank to locate the ship.

Filmed in Ireland and conceived in desperation, this derivative Yankee-Irish coproduction doesn't possess a single original thought. Worse, it has no idea what to do with the ones it has borrowed. (It extracts minimal excitement from the plot contrivance about too many passengers for one lifeboat, for example.) Slapdash art direction and skeletal screenwriting contribute to a Poverty Row enterprise, whose artistic resources are even more limited than its budget. *(Graphic violence, profanity, extensive nudity, substance abuse.)*—R.P.

d, Jeremiah Cullinane; p, Mary Ann Fisher; exec p, Roger Corman; co-p, Goly Jamshidi, Darin Spillman; w, Brendan Broderick, Daniella Purcell; ph, Laurence Manly; ed, Folmer Wiesinger; m, Siobhan Cleary; prod d, Billy Jett; art d, Tim Zeug; set d, Steve Walton; ch, Grainne Daily; sound, Peter Slater (mixer); casting, Jan Glaser; cos, Aisling Byrne; stunts, Neville Tough

Science Fiction **(PR: C MPAA: R)**

SPANISH PRISONER, THE ★★★½

(U.S., 1998) 112m Jean Doumanian Productions; Jasmine Productions ~ Sony Pictures Classics c

Campbell Scott *(Joe Ross)*; Rebecca Pidgeon *(Susan Ricci)*; Steve Martin *(Jimmy Dell)*; Ben Gazzara *(Mr. Klein)*; Ricky Jay *(George Lang)*; Felicity Huffman *(Pat McCune)*; Richard L. Freidman; Jerry Graff; G. Roy Levin *(Businessmen)*; Hilary Hinckle *(Resort Concierge)*; David Pittu *(Resort Manager)*; Christopher Kaldor *(Dell's Bodyguard)*; Gary McDonald *(Ticket Agent)*; Michael Robinson *(Security Person)*; Olivia Tecosky *(Flight Attendant)*; Charlotte Potok *(Bookstore Woman)*; Paul Butler *(Bookbinder)*; J.J. Johnston *(Doorman)*; Emily Weisberg *(Secretary)*; Stephanie Ross *(Receptionist)*; Elliot Cuker *(Antique Car Dealer)*; Scott Zigler *(Car Dealer's Assistant)*; Steven Hawley *(Restaurant Manager)*; Jordan Lage *(Maitre D')*; Steven Goldstein; Jonathan Katz *(Lawyers)*; Paul Dunn III *(Jailer)*; Tony Mamet *(FBI Agent Levy)*; Jack Wallace *(Sanitation Man)*; Ed O'Neill *(FBI Team Leader)*; Clark Gregg *(FBI Sniper)*; Lionel Mark Smith *(Detective Jones)*; Jim Frangione *(Detective Luzzio)*; Allen Soule *(Fingerprint Technician)*; Mary McCann *(Policewoman)*; Gus Johnson *(Property Clerk)*; Isiah Whitlock Jr. *(Trooper)*; Harriet Voyt *(Airline Employee)*; Kristin Reddick *(Airport Mother)*; Andrew Murphy *(Airport Child)*; Jeremy Geidt *(Timid Man)*; Carolyn "Coco" Kallis *(Timid Woman)*; Neil Pepe *(Airport Security)*; Charles Stransky *(Deckhand)*; Takeo Matsushita; Seiko Yoshida *(United States Marshals)*; Mimi Jo Katano *(Japanese Tour Guide)*

Writer-director David Mamet shifts gears from his usual, character-driven dramas for this ingeniously plotted thriller. A cool, stylized mystery in a Hitchcock vein, it revolves around an innocent man pulled into a maelstrom of industrial espionage, seduction, and misdirection that often leaves the viewer as perplexed as its lead character.

Inventor Joe Ross (Campbell Scott) arrives on the Caribbean island of St. Estephe for a business meeting concerning his immensely lucrative, "hush-hush" formula known as The Process; though fully supporting Joe (financially as well as morally), company executive Klein (Ben Gazzara) worries about potential industrial espionage. After flirting with secretary Susan Ricci (Rebecca Pidgeon), Joe bonds with mysterious businessman Jimmy Dell (Steve Martin). Later, as Joe is leaving for New York, Jimmy asks him to deliver a package to his sister. On the airplane home, Joe becomes suspicious of this package, secretly opens it, and sees it's only a book—-which he feels compelled to replace once he accidentally damages it. As Susan's affections for Joe escalate, his attention is elsewhere; he quizzes Klein about specific compensation for his Formula. After getting nothing but vague promises, Jimmy offers to help Joe obtain an appropriate share of the huge profits.

Learning Jimmy actually has no sister, Joe becomes additionally suspicious when asked to bring the only copy of the formula to a meeting. He contacts an FBI agent, who also happened to have been in St. Estephe at the time that his business meeting took place. The FBI agrees to help Joe. He is equipped with a wire before the meeting, but in the end, discovers his notebook has been switched and he has been taken—the FBI agent was part of Jimmy's confidence game.

When the police are called in to investigate the theft, their suspicions lie with Joe. After his lawyer-friend George (Ricky Jay) is murdered with Joe's knife, he runs from the police and goes to Susan for help. She convinces him to head back to St. Estephe, in order to uncover evidence of the illusive Jimmy. She drives him to the airport. What Joe doesn't realize is that Susan has secretly planted a gun on him. Before he's apprehended by airport security, however, Joe observes several odd actions made by Susan (including her speaking to the FBI agent who'd been helping him), and his suspicions are aroused—he believes she may be in league with Jimmy. As Joe confronts Susan, Jimmy turns up and prepares to kill him. A pair of US Marshals save the day; it seems they'd been following Joe the entire time.

With THE SPANISH PRISONER, Pulitzer Prize-winning playwright Mamet has concocted one of his more purely entertaining films. Offering up a world filled with characters who are never what they seem to be, Mamet returns to the cinematic slight-of-hand he first displayed in HOUSE OF GAMES (1987), mixing in elements from his play-turned-cable-movie THE WATER ENGINE (which also focused on a naive inventor at odds with outside forces). It should be noted that the film lacks a single prisoner and there's nary a Spaniard in sight—the oblique title instead refers to a classic confidence game, further proof of Mamet's playful efforts to misdirect the viewer in the way that Joe is misdirected by Jimmy's clan of con artists. The plot line centers around a classic Hitchcockian McGuffin ("The Process") that's continually referred to, yet never once explained. Beginning slowly and gradually picking up speed, the film multiplies its deceptions and duplicity, pointing up the manner in which anyone can be corrupted with the right words at the right time.

The dialogue is delivered in the trademark Mamet fashion: a flatly unsentimental, staccato delivery which transforms the proceedings, making the character's actions both patently artificial and (thanks to the fact that the characters' matter-of-fact demeanor belies their status as actor-con men) completely comprehensible. Scott starts out as a rather bland dupe, yet slowly earns the viewer's sympathy, as his character's naive faith in humanity quickly unravels, turning into a severe case of (justified) paranoia. In support, Martin effectively submerges his familiar comedic personality, giving the unpredictable, ever-charming Dell a slightly menacing edge. The film's only weak spot is a somewhat forced performance by Rebecca Pidgeon (Mamet's real-life wife).

Suspension of disbelief is necessary for viewing THE SPANISH PRISONER. A few plot twists are less than plausible, but the film contains enough genuine surprises to make it worth the effort. Mamet's triumph here is one of deft writing over the "committee" mentality evident in contemporary mainstream Hollywood thrillers. The film benefits from repeated viewings—during which the performances emerge as richer than initially suspected, and the underlying manipulations become crystal clear. *(Violence.)*—S.P.

d, David Mamet; p, Jean Doumanian; exec p, J.E. Beaucaire; co-p, Sarah Green; w, David Mamet; ph, Gabriel Beristain; ed, Barbara Tulliver; m, Carter Burwell; prod d, Tim Galvin; art d, Kathleen Rosen; set d, Jessica Lanier; sound, John Patrick Pritchett; casting, Billy Hopkins, Suzanne Smith, Kerry Barden; cos, Susan Lyall; makeup, Carla White; stunts, Bill Anagnos

Thriller/Drama/Mystery **(PR: C MPAA: PG)**

SPECIES II ★½

(U.S., 1998) 94m FMG Productions; MGM Pictures ~ MGM/UA c

Michael Madsen *(Press Lennox)*; Marg Helgenberger *(Dr. Laura Baker)*; Natasha Henstridge *(Eve)*; Mykelti Williamson *(Astronaut Dennis Gamble)*; Justin Lazard *(Astronaut Patrick Ross)*; James Cromwell *(Senator Ross)*; George Dzundza *(Colonel Carter Burgess Jr.)*; Myriam Cyr *(Anne Sampas)*; Sarah Wynter *(Melissa)*; Baxter Harris *(Dr. Orinsky)*; Scott Morgan *(Harry Sampas)*; Nancy La Scala *(Debutante)*; Raquel Gardner *(Debutante's Sister)*; Henderson Forsythe; Robert Hogan; Ted Sutton *(Pentagon Personnel)*; Gwen Briley-Strand; Valerie Karasek; Jane Beard *(Biologists)*; Nancy Young *(Tether Console Guard)*; Beau James *(Administrator)*; Tracy Metro *(Prostitute)*; Irv Ziff *(Seedy Motel Clerk)*; Melanie Pearson *(Hooker)*; Felicia Deel *(Stripper)*; Norman Aronovic *(Medical Examiner)*; Kim Adams *(Darlene)*; Dustin Turner *(Kid at Supermarket)*; Susan Duvall *(Woman Shopper)*; Andreas Kraemer *(Male Teenager)*; Lauren Ziemski *(Female Teenager)*; Donna Sacco *(Woman in Crowd)*; Sondra Williamson *(Woman with Gamble)*; Kevin Grantz *(Federal Agent)*; Zite Bidanie *(Press Assistant)*; Nat Benchley *(Squad Leader)*; Mike Gartland *(Cobra Pilot)*; John C. Pratt; John T. Scanlon; Herbert R. Schutt Jr. *(Pilots)*; Evelyn Ebo *(Gorgeous Nurse)*; Bill Boggs *(Himself)*; Richard Belzer *(US President)*; Alesia Newman-Breen *(News Announcer)*; Vincent Hammond *(Patrick Creature Performer)*; Monica Staggs *(Eve Creature Performer)*; Peter Boyle *(uncredited)*

Though it contains some promising ideas, this sequel to the 1995 sex-and-violence hit quickly devolves into tacky schlock.

Patrick Ross (Justin Lazard), head astronaut of the first manned mission to Mars, returns home infected by alien DNA—which had earlier been used in the creation of a half-human, half-alien creature that ultimately ran amok. He becomes sexually aggressive, but any woman he has intercourse with becomes pregnant with a monstrous embryo that rapidly matures and rips out of its mother's womb. Meanwhile, molecular biologist Dr. Laura Baker (Marg Helgenberger) has grown a clone of the original human-alien hybrid which she calls Eve (Natasha Henstridge), and is studying her in a government lab. It becomes evident that Eve has a telepathic connection with Ross, and Dr. Baker realizes that if the two were to meet and mate, their offspring would be unstoppable. She is reteamed with security expert Press Lennox (Michael Madsen), with whom she pursued and destroyed the first hybrid creature.

While Dr. Baker monitors Eve, Lennox and Ross's fellow astronaut Dennis Gamble (Mykelti Williamson) attempt to track down Ross, who has been keeping his alien children in a barn on his family's estate. Ross eludes them and kills his senator father (James Cromwell), and Eve escapes from the lab. Dr. Baker, Lennox, and Gamble follow her to the barn, where they destroy the offspring as Ross and Eve mutate into monstrous form and begin to mate. Eve's human side begins to rebel, and the Ross creature kills her before being vanquished itself. Dr. Baker, Lennox, and Gamble leave the scene, unaware that one of the alien children has survived.

Given that the worst aspect of the first SPECIES was its overly simplistic script, one is initially encouraged that SPECIES II seems to have taken the premise in a whole new direction. The film proceeds, however, as if it had been edited down to its barest essentials (namely action sequences), leaving any nuances of plot or characterization on the cutting room floor. What's left becomes increasingly unpleasant and misogynist; the first movie was hardly a feminist tract, but its depiction of a female sexual predator was certainly preferable to the sequel's focus on Ross's sexual victims, who die in bloody agony as his extraterrestrial progeny explode from their bodies.

Director Peter Medak brought a subtle sense of horror to THE CHANGELING (1980) and a bracing vitality to the crime films THE KRAYS (1990) and ROMEO IS BLEEDING (1994), so it's especially dispiriting that his work here is on the basest straight-to-video level. Henstridge and Lazard seem game to explore deeper levels of their characters, but are barely given a chance; ditto Williamson's supposedly experienced astronaut, who comes to be defined by his desire for "booty." Madsen simply looks bored, while Helgenberger tries too hard to invest her dialogue with drama or meaning. In one telling moment, Dr. Baker comes upon a grotesque death scene, and can only intone, "This is awful. This is awful." Any film that would include an audience-baiting line like that is exactly the type of film that shouldn't. *(Graphic violence, extensive nudity, sexual situations, adult situations, extreme profanity.)*—M.G.

d, Peter Medak; p, Frank Mancuso Jr.; exec p, Dennis Feldman; w, Chris Brancato (based on characters created by Dennis Feldman); ph, Matthew F. Leonetti; ed, Richard Nord; m, Edward Shearmur; prod d, Miljen Kreka Kljakovic; art d, Mark Zuelzke; set d, Suzette Sheets; sound, Steve Nelson (recordist); fx, Jeff Jarvis, Steve Johnson, Joseph Grossberg, Ralph Maiers, Steve Johnson's XFX, The Digital Magic Company; casting, Cathy Sandrich, Amanda Mackey, Pat Moran; cos, Richard Bruno; makeup, Perri Sorel, Steve Johnson (effects); stunts, David M. Barrett

Science Fiction/Horror/Thriller (PR: O MPAA: R)

SPHERE ★½

(U.S., 1998) 130m Baltimore Pictures; Constant C; Punch Productions; Warner Bros. ~ Warner Bros. c

Dustin Hoffman *(Dr. Norman Goodman)*; Sharon Stone *(Dr. Beth Halperin)*; Samuel L. Jackson *(Dr. Harry Adams)*; Peter Coyote *(Harold C. Barnes)*; Liev Schreiber *(Dr. Ted Fielding)*; Queen Latifah *(Fletcher)*; Marga Gomez *(Jane Edmunds)*; Huey Lewis *(Helicopter Pilot)*; Barnard Hocke *(Seaman)*; James Pickens Jr. *(OSSA Instructor)*; Michael Keyes Hall *(OSSA Official)*; Ralph Tabakin *(OSSA Official)*

A bloated and pretentious sci-fi thriller, directed by Barry Levinson and starring an A-list cast including Dustin Hoffman, Samuel L. Jackson, and Sharon Stone, SPHERE is not just bad; it's an embarrassing squandering of talent and effort.

Psychologist Norman Goodman (Dustin Hoffman), biochemist Beth Halperin (Sharon Stone), mathematician Harry Adams (Samuel L. Jackson), and astrophysicist Ted Fielding (Liev Schrieber) comprise a team of "experts" summoned to investigate when the 288-year-old sunken wreckage of a spacecraft is found on the Pacific Ocean floor. Along with a military commander, Barnes (Peter Coyote), and a technician, Fletcher (Queen Latifah), the scientists descend 1000 feet to a habitat that has been constructed beside the spaceship.

Upon entering the spaceship, they discover it is not extraterrestrial in origin, but American. They conclude that it was launched in the future, took a wrong turn at a black hole, and time-traveled to the past. They also discover a huge golden sphere. The sphere has no openings, but Adams is somehow taken inside the object and later returned unconscious. A sudden storm severs the habitat's contact with the surface. Fletcher is killed in a jellyfish attack.

When Adams revives, he discovers a mathematical encryption in the computer system, which he decodes as a message from an alien intelligence identifying itself as "Jerry." Later, while Adams naps, monstrous squid attack the habitat resulting in flooding, fires, and the deaths of Barnes and Fielding. Goodman realizes that Jerry and the attacks are manifestations of Adams's unconscious thoughts and fears. He and Halperin drug Adams for their own protection. More events of this nature convince Goodman that Halperin has also entered the sphere; she believes the same is true of him.

The trio finally conclude that they all entered the sphere, and are all seeing their darkest thoughts manifested. Before mutual suspicion kills them all, they decide to escape together in a minisub. Upon reaching the surface, they agree to end the nightmare by forgetting about the sphere; as this thought is manifested, the sphere zooms back out into space.

SPHERE begins interestingly enough. As we meet the scientists, revelations emerge that Fielding and Adams are bitter professional rivals, and that Goodman had an extramarital affair with Halperin when she was his patient. It's also revealed that "The Goodman Report" recommending these so-called experts was just a joke Goodman submitted to the government for some fast grant money, based on his research of watching science-fiction movies.

The opening scenes of SPHERE promise suspense and wonder like a combination of CONTACT (1997) and THE ABYSS (1989). That promise quickly disappears as the film succumbs to a series of cliches and frights that harken back to the same old sci-fi flicks Goodman probably studied, like THE THING (1951) and FORBIDDEN PLANET (1956). Based on a novel by *Jurassic Park* author Michael Crichton, SPHERE offers the same cautionary moral as that dinosaur tale and THE DAY THE EARTH STOOD STILL (1951): Disaster will follow if humans allow technological advancement to outpace the evolution of the species.

The game cast makes a go of it. Hoffman and Jackson deliver the dialogue, which is often little more that a mixture of psychobabble and technobabble, with aplomb. On the other hand, Stone gives her performance much more emotional investment than is called for. And Levinson, whose previous collaboration with Hoffman, the incisive black comedy WAG THE DOG, was released mere months before this, is completely out of his element with this genre. *(Violence, profanity.)*—P.R.

d, Barry Levinson; p, Barry Levinson, Michael Crichton, Andrew Wald; exec p, Peter Giuliano; assoc p, Pat Churchill; w, Stephen Hauser, Paul Attanasio (based on the novel by Michael Crichton as adapted by Kurt Wimmer); ph, Adam Greenberg; ed, Stu Linder; m, Elliot Goldenthal; prod d, Norman Reynolds; art d, Mark Mansbridge, Jonathan McKinstry; set d, Anne Kuljian; sound, Steve Cantamessa (mixer); fx, Kenneth Pepiot; casting, Ellen Chenoweth; cos, Gloria Gresham; makeup, Allan Apone; stunts, Ronnie Rondell

Science Fiction/Thriller (PR: C MPAA: PG-13)

SPICE WORLD ★★★

(U.K., 1998) 93m Spice Girls/Fragile Films; PolyGram Filmed Entertainment ~ Sony Pictures Entertainment c

Melanie Brown, billed as Mel B *(Scary Spice)*; Victoria Adams *(Posh Spice)*; Melanie Chisholm, billed as Mel C *(Sporty Spice)*; Emma Bunton *(Baby Spice)*; Geri Halliwell *(Ginger Spice)*; Richard E. Grant *(Clifford)*; Elvis Costello *(Himself)*; Jennifer Saunders *(Fashionable Woman)*; Naoko Mori *(Nicola)*; George Wendt *(Martin Barnfield—Film Producer)*; Mark McKinney *(Graydon)*; Richard O'Brien *(Damien)*; Claire Rushbrook *(Deborah)*; Alan Cumming *(Piers Cutherton-Smyth)*; Roger Moore *(The Chief)*; Meat Loaf *(Dennis)*; Barry Humphries *(Kevin McMaxford)*; Steven O'Donnell *(Jess)*; Kevin Allen *(TV Director)*; Devon Anderson *(Jack)*; Michael Barrymore *(Mr. Step)*;

Richard Briers *(Bishop)*; Simon Chandler *(Hospital Parent)*; The Dream Boys *(Themselves)*; David Fahm *(Enzo)*; Jason Flemyng *(Brad)*; Neil Fox *(Voice of Radio DJ)*; Stephen Fry *(Judge)*; Bob Geldof *(Himself)*; Llewella Gideon *(Nurse)*; Guy Gowan *(Waiter)*; Jools Holland *(Musical Director)*; Bob Hoskins *(Himself)*; Elton John *(Himself)*; Craig Kelly *(Nervous Guy)*; Hugh Laurie *(Poirot)*; Marian McLoughlin *(Hospital Parent)*; Kevin McNally *(Policeman)*; Neil Mullarkey *(Barnaby)*; Bill Paterson *(Brian)*; Jonathan Ross *(Himself)*; Simon Shepherd *(Doctor)*; Cathy Shipton *(Midwife)*; Peter Sissons *(Newsreader)*; Denise Stephenson *(Jack/Evie's Mother)*; Perdita Weeks *(Evie)*; Dominic West *(Photographer)*; Simon Ellis; Andy Gangadeen; Paul Gendler; Fergus Gerrand; Steve Lewinson; Michael Martin *(The Spice Band)*

The Spice Girls, those lovable, loudmouthed, and overexposed British pop tarts who dominated international music charts in 1997, fill the big screen with good cheer, sassy charm, and self-deprecating humor in a film debut that may leave viewers craving for—believe it or not—*more.*

With their first-ever concert just days away, smash hit pop band the Spice Girls—"Posh Spice" Victoria (Victoria Adams), "Scary Spice" Mel B. (Melanie Brown), "Baby Spice" Emma (Emma Bunton), "Sporty Spice" Mel C. (Melanie Chisholm), and "Ginger Spice" Geri (Geri Halliwell)—struggle through rehearsals. Chaos ensues as unauthorized documentarian Piers (Alan Cumming) gets underfoot; ruthless media mogul McMaxford (Barry Humphries) hires notorious paparazzo Damien (Richard O'Brien) to catch the women in compromising positions; and Hollywood producer Barnfield (George Wendt) and his idea man, Graydon (Mark McKinney), ply the band's high-strung manager, Clifford (Richard E. Grant), with silly cinematic concepts. Meanwhile, the Girls' collective hyperactivity—as well as their attentiveness to their pal Nicola's (Naoko Mori) pregnancy—cause neurotic Clifford to constantly call his mentor, the Chief (Roger Moore).

The Spice Girls live in the Spicebus, which stops only for photo shoots, television appearances, and parties, which the Girls greet with exhaustion and enthusiasm. When the worn-out Girls worry that their concert will be a bust, Damien overhears, and McMaxford gets the scoop. Later the band takes two young contest winners for a boat ride on the Thames, and the girls accidentally go overboard. Damien gets it on film, creating more anti-Spice propaganda for McMaxford.

The day before the concert, Clifford lambastes the Girls over the bad publicity—and one by one, they walk out. Soon the band members—and Nicola—instinctively gather at the old diner where they used to rehearse. Agreeing to give the show a go, they head out for a wild night on the town. Nicola realizes she's about to have her baby; the Girls rush Nicola to the hospital, staying overnight to attend the birth. Suddenly they realize the concert is about to start. While Clifford has a near-nervous breakdown at the packed Royal Albert Hall, Barnfield and Graydon babble about more possible movie projects. The Girls make a daring race against time through the streets of London in the Spicebus, and every wild step of it is described, in exact detail, by Graydon—complete with the discovery of a bomb in the bus and a jump over the London Bridge. The band makes it intact, the show is a smash, and they get a movie deal with Barnfield.

Packed with enough rock-film in-jokes (including the presences of Humphries, O'Brien, and Meat Loaf, all alumni of THE ROCKY HORROR PICTURE SHOW and SHOCK TREATMENT) and Brit-star cameos (including Elton John, Elvis Costello, Hugh Laurie, Stephen Fry, Bob Hoskins, and Jennifer Saunders) to make the heads of music-movie devotees and Anglophiles alike spin like mad, SPICE WORLD is junk-food viewing with a nutritious and welcome dose of smarts, thanks to director Bob Spiers (THAT DARN CAT), whose impressive television credits include "Fawlty Towers" and "Absolutely Fabulous," as well as screenwriter Kim Fuller (brother of the band's then-manager) of "Red Dwarf" and "The Tracey Ullman Show." The pacing is fast, the tone is relentlessly upbeat, the adorably dopey jokes fly by too quickly for most to notice how dopey they are, and logic is *verboten.* There's a wee bit of social satire found here, largely in cookie-cutter-evil McMaxford (a parody of every tabloid king from Robert Maxwell to Rupert Murdoch) and his power-mad, paparazzi-dependent world; ironically, a reference to Princess Diana had to be cut from the film upon her death. Even so, the focus is all on the Spice Girls, how many songs they get to sing, and how many outfits they get to wear. (Answer: a lot.)

As would be expected here, the set design is beyond reproach in its futuristic gaudiness (the Girls' shared "dorm" in the Spicebus is impossibly large), and the montage sequences are cheeky and plentiful (dressing up as "Charlie's Angels," Bond girls, and each other). As for the Spice Girls. . . well, they do just fine playing exaggerated versions of themselves.

Even if the departure of "Ginger Spice" Geri in mid-1998 spells the end of the band's cinematic ouevre, at least they've managed to star in a film which rests comfortably between the Village People vehicle CAN'T STOP THE MUSIC (1980) and the Monkees' HEAD (1968) on the camp-art scale for movies featuring pre-fab music groups. Not a bad place to be, really. *(Nudity.)*—K.S.

d, Robert Spiers, billed as Bob Spiers; p, Uri Fruchtmann, Barnaby Thompson; exec p, Simon Fuller; assoc p, Kim Fuller; co-p, Peter McAleese; w, Kim Fuller (based on an idea by the Spice Girls and Kim Fuller); ph, Clive Tickner; ed, Andrea MacArthur; m, Paul Hardcastle; prod d, Grenville Horner; art d, David Walley, Colin Blaymires; set d, Linda Wilson; sound, Colin Nicolson (mixer); fx, Stuart Brisdon; casting, Vanessa Pereira, Simone Ireland; cos, Kate Carin; makeup, Graham Johnston; stunts, Peter Brayham

Musical/Comedy (PR: C MPAA: PG)

SPOOKY ENCOUNTERS
(SEE: ENCOUNTER OF THE SPOOKY KIND)

SPREE, THE ★★½
(U.S., 1998) 98m MGM Worldwide Television; Pacific Motion Pictures ~ Orion Home Video c

Jennifer Beals *(Xinia Kelly)*; Powers Boothe *(Bram Hatcher)*; Garry Chalk *(Colin)*; John Cassini *(Ray)*; Nathaniel Deveaux *(Salvador)*; Eric Keenleyside *(Madden)*; Rita Moreno *(Irma)*; Jano Frandsen *(Homeowner)*; Linda Ko *(Suzi)*; Don Thompson *(Cop)*; Akiko Morison *(Cocktail Waitress)*; Warren Takeuchi *(Salesman)*; Terence Kelly *(Captain Richie)*; Alex Green *(Detective)*; Johnny Mah *(Madden's Bodyguard)*

A cop and a burglar generate sexual heat before deciding to go into business together in this crime thriller that is saved in its third act with a twist on its fairly standard plot. The film was first shown on cable television in 1998, and was subsequently released to home video.

"Gardening consultant" Xinia Kelly (Jennifer Beals) is really a burglar with a specialty in getting past high-tech alarms. At a bar, she meets and flirts with snake rancher Bram Hatcher (Powers Boothe). Intrigued, she tracks him to his ranch, and the two make love. Checking out his place while he's asleep, Xinia discovers that Bram is really a cop who has been tailing her. After she vengefully tries to incriminate him in another robbery, Bram tells Xinia he's more interested in bedding her than arresting her, and gives her his incriminating file on her. Bram becomes intrigued by Xinia's profession, and asks her to teach him. They become partners, scoring well until they are interrupted and nearly caught on a job by Bram's former partner Colin (Garry Chalk). Wanting to leave town but lacking the funds to start over, Gram suggests that they hit Madden (Eric Keenleyside), a sleazy lawyer with a safe full of undeclared cash from his drug-dealing clients. When Madden catches them in the act, Bram shoots him dead. Splitting up to tie up their loose ends, Xinia accidentally learns that her fence Ray (John Cassini), has been working for Bram: Bram has long planned to rob Madden, and enlisted Xinia for her particular skills. Bram kills both Ray and Colin, and tracks Xinia down. He is about to kill her when she beats him to it with a bomb planted in what he thinks is the bundle of loot. Xinia drives off to a new life with Bram's favorite snake.

Eroticism should be left to the pros, as the weakest aspects of THE SPREE are the endless make-out scenes between Powers Boothe and Jennifer Beals (or more precisely, Boothe and Beals's body double, in the tradition of Beals's 1983 big-screen breakthrough, FLASHDANCE.) They're made particularly laughable by trite seduction dialogue and the use of a snake that couldn't be more obvious if it had the words "phallic symbol" painted on its body (and which gives the ending a presumably unintentional echo of Lorena Bobbit). Nor does a subplot involving Xinia's dying father do anything except provide a role for Rita Moreno as her grieving mother. Fortunately, THE SPREE improves when it becomes a variant on the standard noir plot of a straight arrow tricked into a criminal venture by a femme fatale, with Boothe as the "bad girl." This half of the film moves at a crisp pace, and is least interesting even if obvious once Gram's true nature becomes apparent. *(Violence, nudity, sexual situations, adult situations, profanity.)* —M.F.

d, Tommy Lee Wallace; exec p, Marcy Gross, Ann Weston, Albert Berger, Ron Yerxa; w, Livia Linden, Percy Angress; ph, Richard Leiterman; ed, Judy Andreson; m, Peter Manning Robinson; prod d, David Fischer; art d, Ken Rabehl; set d, David Chiasson; sound, Bill Skinner (mixer); fx, Rory Cutler; casting, Mary Jo Slater; cos, Tish Monaghan; makeup, Norma Hill-Patton; stunts, Dawn Stofer

Crime/Drama/Romance (PR: O MPAA: R)

STAR KID ★★

(U.S., 1998) 101m Jenny Lew Tugend/Trimark Pictures ~ Trimark c

Joseph Mazzello *(Spencer Griffith)*; Richard Gilliland *(Roland Griffith)*; Corinne Bohrer *(Janet Holloway)*; Joey Simmrin *(Turbo Bruntley)*; Ashlee Levitch *(Stacey Griffith)*; Lauren Eckstrom *(Michelle)*; Alex Daniels *(Cyborsuit)*; Jack McGee *(Hank Bruntley)*; Arthur Burghardt *(Cyborsuit Voice)*; Danny Masterson *(Kevin)*; Brian Simpson *(Broodwarrior)*; Christine Weatherup *(Nadia)*; Yumi Adachi *(Mika)*; Alissa Ann Smego *(Burgerworld Girl)*; Fred Kronenberg *(Officer 1)*; Joshua Fardon *(Rookie Cop)*; Bobby Porter *(Trelkin/Nath)*; Larry Nicholas *(Trelkin/Tenris)*; Rusty Hanson *(Trelkin)*; Terry Castillo-Faass *(Trelkin)*

Japanese science-fiction conventions meet American kid-flick cliches in this serviceable fantasy, filmed in 1996 as "The Warrior of Waverly Street."

In a distant galaxy, the peaceful Trelkans are engaged in a war with the savage Broodwarriors. A new Trelkan device, the Cyborsuit, is blasted into space before the Broodwarriors can get their hands on it. The Cyborsuit lands on Earth and is discovered by Spencer Griffith (Joseph Mazzello), a lonely seventh grader trying to deal with his distant, recently widowed father, Roland (Richard Gilliland), his obnoxious older sister, Stacey (Ashlee Levitch), and a bully named Turbo (Joey Simmrin). Spencer climbs into the Cyborsuit, whereupon it seals up around him and begins to speak to him (voice of Arthur Burghardt). It explains that it is designed to operate symbiotically with its wearer, and Spencer, delighted by the Cyborsuit's powers, uses it to get even with Turbo. Not entirely in control of the suit, he also causes havoc at an amusement park and his own house.

When "Cy," as Spencer calls it, reveals that the suit cannot be removed until it is tested in battle, he runs to the house of teacher Janet Holloway (Corinne Bohrer) for help. A Broodwarrior sent to Earth to retrieve the Cyborsuit appears and engages Cy/Spencer in battle. Spencer escapes and sheds the suit, but when no one will believe his story, he sets out to find it again. Upon discovering the suit has disappeared, he convinces Turbo to help him and tracks the Broodwarrior and Cy to the junkyard. There, Spencer dons the suit again; when it is badly damaged in the ensuing fight, he exits the Cyborsuit, and he and Turbo destroy the Broodwarrior in a car-crusher. Reunited with his father and sister, Spencer is also greeted by a detachment of Trelkans, who retrieve the suit and present him with an extraterrestrial trinket.

All the usual problems of a modern kid in the world of family films are present and accounted for in STAR KID: Spencer's mother has just died, he drowns his loneliness in comic books, his father is more concerned with work than his feelings, his sister calls him "Fungus," he's got a crush on a pretty classmate, and he's antagonized by a bigger boy whose playground handle (Turbo) masks a wimpy real name (Manfred, an odd choice for writer-director Manny Coto). While STAR KID is just as formulaic as Coto's previous DR. GIGGLES (1992), at least this formula is a less objectionable one, although that still doesn't compensate for the fact that Coto has absolutely no surprises in store for the viewing audience. The film does have its moments, though, however brief; when the Cyborsuit scans a computer, its observation is "Intelligence limited," and one touching moment has Cy tapping into Spencer's memories and giving him a chance to "see" his mother again.

Mostly, though, STAR KID plays like a watered-down version of *The Guyver*, the Japanese *anime* (which inspired two American movies in the '90s) about a young man and his living battle armor. The Americanization of the concept is embodied in the film's unfortunate obviousness, its overreliance on lowbrow humor (much is made of Spencer's inability to urinate while inside the Cyborsuit), and cheap characterizations (most egregiously, a young Chinese girl is defined by her pidgin English and ever-present camera). The special effects supervised by Thomas C. Rainone get the job done on a relatively low budget; too bad the film got stuck with a title that sounds like it belongs on a cheap Italian import from the '60s. *(Violence, adult situations, profanity.)*—M.G.

d, Manny Coto; p, Jennie Lew Tugend; exec p, Mark Amin; co-p, Jonathon Komack Martin, Cami Winikoff; w, Manny Coto; ph, Ronn Schmidt; ed, Bob Ducsay; m, Nicholas Pike; prod d, C.J. Strawn; art d, Michael D. Welch; set d, Irina Rivera; fx, Lou Carlucci, Thomas C. Rainone, Film Technical Services, Inc.; cos, Ileane Meltzer; makeup, Tina K. Roesler, Thomas R. Burman (effects), Bari Dreiband-Burman (effects)

Children's/Science Fiction (PR: A MPAA: PG)

STAR TREK: INSURRECTION ★★½

(U.S., 1998) 103m Rick Berman Production ~ Paramount c

Patrick Stewart *(Picard)*; Jonathan Frakes *(Riker)*; Brent Spiner *(Data)*; LeVar Burton *(Geordi)*; Michael Dorn *(Worf)*; Gates McFadden *(Beverly)*; Marina Sirtis *(Troi)*; F. Murray Abraham *(Ru'afo)*; Donna Murphy *(Anij)*; Anthony Zerbe *(Dougherty)*; Gregg Henry *(Gallatin)*; Daniel Hugh Kelly *(Sojef)*; Michael Welch *(Artim)*; Mark Deakins *(Tournel)*; Stephanie Niznik *(Perim)*; Michael Horton *(Lt. Daniels)*; Bruce French *(Son'a Officer #1)*; Breon Gorman *(Lt. Curtis)*; John Hostetter *(Bolian Officer)*; Rick Worthy *(Elloran Officer #1)*; Larry Anderson *(Tarlac Officer)*; D. Elliot Woods *(Starfleet Officer)*; Jennifer Tung *(Female Ensign)*; Raye Birk *(Son'a Doctor)*; Peggy Miley *(Regent Cuzar)*; Lee Arnone-Briggs *(Librarian)*; Claudette Nevins *(Son'a Officer #2)*; Max Grodenchik *(Alien Ensign)*; Greg Poland *(Elloran Officer #2)*; Kenneth Lane Edwards *(Ensign)*; Joseph Ruskin *(Son'a Officer #3)*; Zachary Williams *(Ba'ku Child)*; McKenzie Westmore *(Ba'ku Woman)*; Phillip Glasser *(Young Ru'afo)*

The ninth STAR TREK film and the third featuring "The Next Generation" cast is a retread of themes familiar to regular viewers. This installment's action and hammy humor make it mildly diverting at best.

Captain Picard (Patrick Stewart), Commander Riker (Jonathan Frakes), and the rest of the *Enterprise* crew are ordered to intervene when their android crewmate Data (Brent Spiner) malfunctions during a surveillance mission. Arriving at the lush home of the peaceful Ba'ku people, Picard devises a way to deactivate Data without destroying him. He then learns that Data was not malfunctioning at all, but attempting to protect the Ba'ku from a forced relocation scheme devised by Federation bureaucrats and the Sona, a militant race that covets the Ba'ku's world.

The Sona are a long-lived species that ages very badly: they fall apart so rapidly they need daily face-lifts and tissue stretchings. With the amorous help of his lovely Ba'ku guide Anij (Donna Murphy), Picard finds that their planet is bathed in a therapeutic radiation that confers perpetual youth. The Federation hopes to revolutionize medical science with the discovery; the Sona, under the fanatical leadership of Ru'afo (F. Murray Abraham) seek a cure for their chronic decrepitude.

Ordered to leave the area immediately, Picard chooses to risk court-martial and help the Ba'ku to defend themselves. His crew enthusiastically joins in the "insurrection." Picard, Worf (Michael Dorn), Data, et al. direct the ground-based resistance; Riker and the *Enterprise* head off to find support among sympathetic Federation authorities.

His patience exhausted, Ru'afo dispatches two warships to destroy the *Enterprise* and attempts to remove the Ba'ku by force. Riker's innovative battle tactics thwart the Sona attack, while Picard leads the refugees to the comparative safety of the mountains. Dr. Crusher (Gates McFadden) then makes a startling discovery: the Ba'ku and the Sona are of the same race. Captured at last, Picard confronts Ru'afo and learns how deeply the Sona yearn for revenge for being exiled from "paradise."

Ru'afo's resentment against his youthful relatives grows so vicious that he alienates his lieutenant, Dougherty (Anthony Zerbe); Dougherty then helps Picard to escape. The *Enterprise* returns, and Ru'afo's gang is captured via a transporter trick. Ru'afo escapes in turn, but Picard destroys his vessel before he can damage the Ba'ku planet.

Despite a wealth of plot, INSURRECTION contains little that's new. The themes of searching for perpetual youth, of rural "paradise" vs. techno-militarism, were explored repeatedly in the original "Star Trek" TV-series. Having an *Enterprise* crew mutiny against official orders is also a familiar plot line, enacted at length in the third film, THE SEARCH FOR SPOCK (1984). What *is* surprising is the film's implicit sympathy for sun-tanned Luddites like the Ba'ku: as recently as 1994's STAR TREK: GENERATIONS, the series has always shown a mistrust for heavenly utopias.

One problem has emerged as "The Next Generation" cast have taken over the theatrical franchise: whereas the movies featuring the original "Trek" cast had a core troika of Kirk, Spock, and McCoy, this ensemble could best be described as Capt.-Picard-plus-a-sidekick. Patrick Stewart is a better actor than any of the actors in the original TV series, but it becomes evident in INSURRECTION that the squeaky-clean Picard shouldn't be shouldering the dramatic weight of the feature-length installments of the "Trek" saga.

The "Next Generation" crew does resemble the original cast in two respects: the friendly chemistry between the performers and their increasing paunch. INSURRECTION does have its virtues, however: several comedic scenes, such as Picard's bid to distract the rebellious Data by joining him in a rousing chorus from Gilbert and Sullivan's *H.M.S. Pinafore,* are corny and jarring in just the right way. There's nothing in INSURRECTION that makes one feel there's a need for another STAR TREK film, but its comic touch at least assures most of us won't be dreading it. *(Violence, profanity.)*—N.N.

d, Jonathan Frakes; p, Rick Berman; exec p, Martin Hornstein; assoc p, Patrick Stewart; co-p, Peter Lauritson, Michael Piller; w, Michael Piller (based on "Star Trek" created by Gene Roddenberry); ph, Matthew F. Leonetti; ed, Peter E. Berger; m, Jerry Goldsmith; prod d, Herman Zimmerman; art d, Ron Wilkinson; set d, John Dwyer; sound, Thomas Causey (mixer); fx, Terry Frazee; casting, Junie Lowry-Johnson, Ron Surma; cos, Sanja Milkovic Hays; makeup, Michael Westmore; stunts, Rick Avery

Science Fiction **(PR: C MPAA: PG)**

STEAM: THE TURKISH BATH ★★★

(Italy/Turkey/Spain, 1996) 101m Sorpasso Films; Promete Film; Asbrell Productions ~ Strand Releasing c
(AKA: TURKISH BATH, THE; HAMAM: IL BAGNO TURCO)

Alessandro Gassman *(Francesco)*; Francesca D'Aloja *(Marta)*; Carlo Cecchi *(Oscar)*; Halil Ergun *(Osman)*; Serif Sezer *(Perran)*; Mehmet Gunsur *(Mehmet)*; Basak Koklukaya *(Fusun)*; Alberto Molinari *(Paolo)*; Zozo Toledo *(Zozo)*; Lodovoca Modungno *(Voice of Aunt Anita)*

STEAM: THE TURKISH BATH is a predictable but well-crafted film about a young married couple whose lives are transformed by a visit to Istanbul.

When Francesco (Alessandro Gassman), an Italian workaholic, learns that an aunt in Istanbul has died, he heads to Turkey to sell property she owned there. Although he hopes to handle matters quickly, complications ensue and Francesco finds that he must remain in Istanbul for at least a few days.

A Turkish family residing in a house his aunt owned invites Francesco to stay with them for the duration of his visit, and Francesco accepts. He is pleasantly surprised to discover that the residence includes a *hamam*—a Turkish sauna, and is so taken with the house that he decides not to sell it, although a local attorney, Zozo (Zozo Toledo), warns him that criminals want the property. Ignoring the warning, Francesco starts to renovate the steam bath. He also begins to learn Turkish and otherwise immerses himself in Turkish culture, usually in the company of the family's teenaged son, Mehmet (Mehmet Gunsur).

One day, Francesco's wife Marta (Francesca d'Aloja) arrives unexpectedly from Rome. The Turkish family receives her warmly, but Francesco practically ignores her. On her second night in Istanbul, Marta comes upon Francesco and Mehmet in the *hamam*, locked in an intimate embrace. The next evening, Marta confronts Francesco with her knowledge of his homosexuality, and demands a divorce. Telling her that he is happy with his new life, Francesco agrees.

The next day, however, Francesco is fatally stabbed in retaliation for his refusal to sell the building. Marta, who had been preparing to return to Rome, changes her mind and stays. In honor of Francesco, she acquires the house and preserves the steam bath. In time, she becomes as enamored of Istanbul as her husband was.

Stories about chic people who renounce their lives in favor of tradition have themselves become traditional. A sly film like LOCAL HERO (1983) may gently play with the notion, but most such works unquestioningly respect the formula's well-defined parameters and buy into its nostalgic myth. STEAM is such a film, and in spite of contemporary touches like male nudity and gay romance, it is ultimately conventional.

Given that limitation, though, STEAM is quite enjoyable. As depicted here, the concept of tradition is so remote to present-day Europeans that it can only be manifested in a foreign culture, Turkish in this case. Director Ferzan Ozpetek does a fine job in setting up Istanbul as the antithesis to everything that Francesco and Marta understand, a place that could credibly provoke great personal change. Aided by Pasquale Mari's rich cinematography and an evocative score by Aldo and Pivio De Scalzi, Ozpetek makes Istanbul inviting and intimate, but also lived in and realistic. The exoticism is omnipresent but it isn't overdone, and the city is alluring yet entirely believable.

Along with co-scenarist Stefano Tummolini, Ozpetek has prepared a solid script with a well-rounded, satisfying plot, serviceable dialogue, and a nice balance of sentiment and sharp humor. They have also come up with a wittily concise exemplification of the whole tradition versus modernity theme: a sequence in which Francesco and Marta are frustrated in their effort to contact each other by cel phone (even though they are only blocks apart) while neighborhood women are shown communicating effectively by shouting to one another out of windows.

Otherwise, nothing much unexpected happens as the story runs its course. Ozpetek, however, is clever enough a director to make up in atmosphere what his film lacks in originality. STEAM might not have anything new to say, but it's entertaining all the same. *(Violence, nudity, sexual situations, profanity.)*—D.C.

d, Ferzan Ozpetek; p, Marco Risi, Marco Tedesco; exec p, Paolo Buzzi, Ozan Ergun; co-p, Cengiz Ergun, Aldo Sanbrell; w, Stefano Tummolini, Ferzan Ozpetak (based on the story by Ozpetak); ph, Pasquale Mari; ed, Mauro Bonanni; m, Pivio De Scalzi, Aldo De Scalzi; art d, Virginia Vianello, Mustafa Ziya Ulgenciler; sound, Marco Grillo; cos, Metella Raboni, Selda Cicek; makeup, Gaja Banchelli

Romance/Drama **(PR: C MPAA: NR)**

STEEL SHARKS ★½

(U.S., 1998) 94m Cabin Fever Productions ~ Royal Oaks Entertainment c

Gary Busey *(Cmdr. McKay)*; Billy Dee Williams *(Adm. Perry)*; Billy Warlock *(Bob Rogers)*; Shaun Toub *(Reza Lashgar)*; Robert Miranda *(Gregorov)*; David Roberson *(Lt. Zamborski)*; Barry Livingston *(Dr. Van Tasset)*; Tim Abell *(Cord)*; Matthew St. Patrick *(Mattox)*; Eric Lawson *(Adm. Evans)*; Tim Lounibos *(Mack)*; Matthew R. Anderson *(Kaplan)*; Larry Poindexter *(Dobbins)*; Anthony Griffith *(Bernie)*; Miranda Wolfe *(Lt. Hickey)*; Ahmed Ahmed *(Noussavi)*; Curnal Aulisio; Jeff Burnett *(Montiero)*; Thomas R. Martin *(Radio Man)*; Bill Langlois Monroe *(News Reporter)*

STEEL SHARKS is a modestly entertaining, if predictable, direct-to-video potboiler. With a linear plot, TV-caliber acting, and static camera, it doesn't aim very high and so manages to hit its target.

After a military coup in Iran, revolutionary elements kidnap Dr. Van Tasset (Barry Livingston), an American expert in chemical weapons. The "Steel Sharks," an elite squad of Navy SEALs led by Lt. Zamborski (David Roberson), is assigned to rescue him. Joining the team at the last minute is neophyte Bob Rogers (Billy Warlock), who wonders if he will be able to live up to the SEALs high standards. The team is taken to Iran on the submarine *USS Oakland,* commanded by Capt. McKay (Gary Busey).

The Sharks infiltrate the base where Van Tasset is being held, and find him being tortured by guards. They free him and attempt to flee, but are captured and held prisoner on an Iranian submarine commanded by Capt. Reza Lashgar (Shaun Toub). The *Oakland* is ordered to shadow the Iranian submarine.

Lashgar interrogates Zamborski, executing him when he refuses to cooperate. The other Sharks overpower their guards and take their weapons. The *Oakland's* sonar picks up the sound of gunfire, and radios for help, thus alerting the Iranians as to their position. Lashgar fires on the *Oakland,* confident that the Americans won't return fire while hostages are on board. The *Oakland* avoids the torpedoes and runs, intending to lure the enemy sub into the teeth of the Fifth Fleet.

Dr. Van Tasset helps the Sharks concoct tear gas and napalm from supplies in the sub's galley. Rogers seizes the radio and sends a Morse code signal to the *Oakland* that they're escaping. The *Oakland* leads the Iranian submarine through the narrow Strait of Hormuz. Lashgar fires more torpedoes that miss the *Oakland* and strike the undersea canyon wall, collapsing it on the Iranian sub. The Sharks reach the sub's hatch, and Rogers covers their escape. When the Sharks are clear, the *Oakland* radios for rescue helicopters who pluck them out of the sea. The *Oakland* leads the Iranian sub away before destroying it with torpedoes.

STEEL SHARKS is a by-the-numbers military thriller with few surprises. Some feeble attempts are made at characterization, such as making Zamborski and McKay old friends, and having Rogers express doubts about his fitness, but these moments feel forced and out of place. Warlock, while appearing earnest, suffers because he is a full head shorter than everyone else on the team, giving the impression of a child chasing after his big brothers. There is impressive stock footage of American military might at work, but the sets used are generic warehouses and unlighted submarine companionways. And where is the crew of the Iranian sub? The escaping SEALs creep through pitch-dark passages without encountering anyone except a cook and a radio man. *(Violence.)*—J.Di.

d, Rodney McDonald; p, Ashok Amritraj, Andrew Stevens; exec p, Alan B. Bursteen; w, William C. Martell, Rodney McDonald; ph, Bryan Greenberg; ed, W. Peter Miller; m, David Lawrence; prod d, Steve Ralph; art d, William Paine; set d, Nicki Roberts; sound, Arnold Braun (mixer), Joe Perez (mixer); fx, Dale Newkirk; casting, Mr. Nickel; cos, Emily Harris; makeup, Megan M. Johnson

Action/Adventure **(PR: C MPAA: R)**

STEPHEN KING'S THE NIGHT FLIER ★½

(U.S., 1997) 99m New Amsterdam Entertainment; Stardust International; Medusa Film ~ New Line c

Miguel Ferrer *(Richard Dees)*; Julie Entwisle *(Katherine Blair)*; Dan Monahan *(Merton Morrison)*; Michael H. Moss *(Dwight*

Renfield); John Bennes *(Ezra Hannon)*; Beverly Skinner *(Selida McCamon)*; Rob Wilds *(Buck Kendall)*; Richard Olsen *(Claire Bowie)*; Elizabeth McCormick *(Ellen Sarch)*; J.R. Rodriguez *(Terminal Cop #1)*; Bob Casey *(Terminal Cop #2)*; Ashton Stewart *(Nate Wilson)*; William Neely *(Ray Sarch)*; Windy Wenderlich *(Henry Gates)*; General Fermon Judd Jr. *(Policeman)*; Deann Korbutt *(Linda Ross)*; Rachel Lewis *(Libby Grant)*; Kristen Leigh *(Dottie Walsh)*; Simon Elsworth *(Duffery Bartender)*; Jim Grimshaw *(Gas Station Attendant)*; Matthew Johnson *(Caretaker)*; Terry Neil Edlefsen *(Drunk)*; Joy Knox; Randal Brown; Laurie Wolf; Keith Shepard; Ruth Reid *(Dream Vampires)*; Matt Webb; David Zum Brunnen; April Turner; Manya K. Rubinstein *(Reporters)*; Kelley Sims *(Intern)*

An above-average Stephen King adaptation, THE NIGHT FLIER (which premiered on HBO in 1997 prior to its '98 theatrical and video releases) also showcases a terrific lead performance by Miguel Ferrer.

Cynical, misanthropic Richard Dees (Miguel Ferrer) is the top writer/photographer at the *Inside View* tabloid. Dees turns down an assignment from editor Merton Morrison (Dan Monahan) to cover a pair of gruesome murders which took place at small airfields. The story is given to new reporter Katherine Blair (Julie Entwisle), but when another slaying occurs, Dees decides to pursue it as well. As he flies his private plane to the scenes of the crimes and interviews witnesses, Dees receives warnings from the killer—a vampire who calls himself Dwight Renfield (Michael H. Moss). He has been piloting his own black Cessna into remote airports and slaughtering anyone he finds there.

When Dees discovers Katherine still on the trail, he proposes that they team up to cover the story together, but later locks her in a closet at their motel and sets out alone. He catches up to Renfield at the site of his latest slaughter. The vampire first threatens Dees, then subjects him to a hallucination in which the previous victims attack him. Grabbing a fire axe to defend himself, Dees is mistaken for the killer by arriving police and shot dead. As Renfield departs, Katherine appears on the scene and, apparently on the way to becoming as cynical as Dees, files the whole story to *Inside View*.

More effectively fleshed out than most films derived from King's short stories, THE NIGHT FLIER (a novella collected in King's own *Nightmares and Dreamscapes* from an earlier appearance in a horror anthology) is a back-to-basics horror film that avoids humor and instead works towards creating a successfully creepy atmosphere. The real secret to its success, however, is the riveting work done by Ferrer, who has been memorable in supporting roles (most significantly 1987's ROBOCOP) and here proves himself a major talent. Dees is burned-out and driven only by his obsession to get a good story; usually, such a character in a horror movie exists only to get his comeuppance near the end. Making Dees the protagonist of the piece is a bracing change of pace, one that risks alienating the audience but delivers fully, thanks to Ferrer's nuanced characterization. He finds just enough humanity in the character to keep responding to him no matter what he's doing, without making him strictly likable.

Since the story is told from Dees's perspective, the horrific material in the first hour is told via a series of flashbacks, which prevents it from being as fully suspenseful as it might have been. There are compensations, however, in the subplot about Dees's rivalry with Katherine (the capable Entwisle), and the amusing turn by PORKY'S star Monahan as their stupid editor. But the majority of the movie's running time serves as a simple preamble for the finale: the last 20 minutes or so are genuinely chilling, drenched in both eerie atmospherics and gut-wrenching gore. The film's two most memorable scenes occur at this point—a nightmarish hallucination (which appears to have been inspired by Italian frightmeister Lucio Fulci) and a great horror sight gag (the vampire, invisible in a mirror, urinating blood in a bathroom). The revelation of Renfield's monstrous face is a bit disappointing—the KNB EFX team's makeup work isn't bad, it's simply that this straight-on moment of horror isn't nearly as effective as when the villain is only seen hovering around the edges of the screen. But the dark-humored irony of the final scene (Katherine's assumption of Dees's jaded demeanor) wraps up the story perfectly. *(Graphic violence, extreme profanity.)*—M.G.

d, Mark Pavia; p, Richard P. Rubinstein, Mitchell Galin; exec p, David Kappes; assoc p, Neal Stevens; co-p, Alfredo Cuomo, Jack O'Donnell; w, Mark Pavia, Jack O'Donnell (based on a story by Stephen King); ph, David Connell; ed, Elizabeth Schwartz; m, Brian Keane; prod d, Burton Rencher; set d, Timothy Smithwick Stepeck; sound, Jay Meagher (mixer); fx, Oliver Rockwell; casting, Leonard Finger, Lyn Richmond; cos, Pauline White; makeup, Jeff Goodwin, Robert Kurtzman (effects), Greg Nicotero (effects), Howard Berger (effects), K.N.B. EFX Group (effects); stunts, John Copeman

Horror **(PR: C MPAA: R)**

STEPMOM ★★

(U.S., 1998) 124m Wendy Finerman Production; 1492 Production; Chris Columbus Production ~ Columbia c

Susan Sarandon *(Jackie Harrison)*; Julia Roberts *(Isabel Kelly)*; Ed Harris *(Luke Harrison)*; Jena Malone *(Anna Harrison)*; Liam Aiken *(Ben Harrison)*; Lynn Whitfield *(Dr. Sweikert)*; Darrell Larson *(Duncan Samuels)*; Mary Louise Wilson *(School Counselor)*; Andre Blake *(Cooper)*; Russel Harper *(Photo Assistant)*; Jack Eagle *(Craft Service Man)*; Lu Celania Sierra; Lauma Zemzare; Holly Schenck; Michelle Stone; Annett Esser; Monique Rodrique *(Photo Shoot Models)*; Sal Mistretta; Rex Hays; Alice Liu; Chuck Montgomery *(Ad Executives)*; Mak Gilchrist *(Rapunzel)*; Dylan Michaels *(Prince)*; David Zayas *(Policeman)*; Jose Ramon Rosaio *(Policeman)*; Lee Shepard *(Desk Sergeant)*; George Masters *(Maitre'd)*; Anthony Grasso *(Waiter)*; Robert F. Alvarado *(Soccer Coach)*; Sebastian Rand *(Tucker)*; Michelle Hurst *(Nurse)*; Jason Maves *(Brad Kovitsky)*; Julie Lancaster *(Flight Attendant)*; Charlie Christman *(Stone Fox)*; Amina Asep; Naama Katz; Jennifer Best; Robin Fusco; Jessica M. Oasis; Electra Telesford; Michelle L. Brady *(Anna's Friends)*; Zachary M. Hasak; Jordan Gochros; Rob London; James Ostrofsky; Chad Lavinio *(Brad's Friends)*; John Sadowski *(Ben's Friend)*; Matthew Doudounis *(Ben's Friend)*; Andrea Dolloff *(Cocktail Waitress)*

Supermom Susan Sarandon clashes with her ex-husband's new girlfriend, Julia Roberts, over the care of her children, until tragedy brings them together as a family. STEPMOM begins as a light comedy but ends as a tearjerker whose sappiness is only partially redeemed by the efforts of the film's first-rate cast.

Photographer Isabel Kelly (Julia Roberts) shares a Manhattan loft with divorced, workaholic lawyer Luke Harrison (Ed Harris), and is often stuck babysitting Luke's two children, 12-year-old Anna (Jena Malone) and 7-year-old Ben (Liam Aiken). Isabel tries her best, but that can't compare to the care given by Luke's imperious ex-wife, Jackie (Susan Sarandon), whose mothering is practically perfect in every way. Making matters worse is Anna, who is still stewing over her parents' divorce and lashes out at Isabel at every turn—a resentment Jackie is only too pleased to foster.

Jackie learns that she has cancer, and though she keeps her condition a secret, the restrictions of chemotherapy require that Isabel, who is now Luke's fiancee, be trusted more and more with the children. Anna starts to appreciate Isabel as a sort of big sister, and Jackie sees how much Isabel cares about the children's welfare after Ben injures himself at a playground.

Isabel discovers Jackie's secret, and helps her keep it. But before too long, Jackie finds out that she is terminal and breaks the news to Anna, Ben, and Luke. Isabel's increasing devotion to Anna and Ben costs her her job, and Jackie is troubled when Anna chooses Isabel's advice on handling boys over hers. As Jackie's health declines, she is forced to accept her passing, and Isabel's emerging, role in the children's lives. On Christmas morning, Jackie says her good byes to her children, and presents each of them with a unique scrapbook of family photos taken by Isabel.

STEPMOM starts out as an enjoyable comic catfight with Sarandon and Roberts trading verbal digs. But before too long, the movie takes an abrupt turn, with the revelation of Jackie's illness the first of a series of phony moments designed to wrench the guts of viewers. This culminates in a scene in which Mother Earth-incarnate Jackie passes the maternal baton to Isabel in a speechy, life-affirming scene, with Sarandon gazing into the camera, fighting back tears and daring the audience to stop theirs.

Director Chris Columbus is best known for family-friendly, crowd-pleasing entertainment like HOME ALONE (1990) and MRS. DOUBTFIRE (1993). His skill at effective (and affective) button pushing is well displayed here. But it requires the considerable talents and conviction of Sarandon, Roberts and young Jena Malone (who acts her little heart out) to put the material over.

STEPMOM is the work of five credited screenwriters, and it probably took a committee of at least that many to cook up a script consisting of behavior so foreign to that of known human beings. Divorced parents and custody fights are real issues in the real world, but you wouldn't know it from STEPMOM. Harris barely figures into the proceedings (this is, after all, a female-bonding picture), but usually absentee dads with live-in lovers aren't so demanding of visits from the kids. And few kids have to suffer the exquisite anguish of shuttling between a glitzy Manhattan pad and a country home in the Hudson River Valley. *(Adult situations.)*—P.R.

d, Chris Columbus; p, Wendy Finerman, Chris Columbus, Mark Radcliffe, Michael Barnathan; exec p, Patrick McCormick, Ron Bass, Margaret French Isaac, Julia Robert, Susan Sarandon, Pliny Porter; assoc p, Gigi Levangie, Jessie Nelson, Steven Rogers, Karen Leigh Hopkins, Ron Bass, Paula Dupre Pesmen; w, Gigi Levangie, Jessie Nelson, Steven Rogers, Karen Leigh Hopkins, Ron Bass; ph, Donald M. McAlpine; ed, Neil Travis; m, John Williams; prod d, Stuart Wurtzel; art d, Raymond Kluga; set d, George DeTitta Jr.; sound, Tod Maitland; fx, Todd R. Wolfeil, Robert J. Scupp; casting, Ellen Lewis; cos, Joseph G. Aulisi; makeup, Michal Bigger; stunts, Phil Neilson

Drama **(PR: C MPAA: PG-13)**

STILL BREATHING ★★★

(U.S., 1998) 109m Fresh Produce Company; Zap Pictures; Seattle Pacific Investments ~ October Films c

Brendan Fraser *(Fletcher McBracken)*; Joanna Going *(Roz Willoughby)*; Celeste Holm *(Ida McBracken)*; Ann Magnuson *(Elaine)*; Toby Huss *(Cameron)*; Angus MacFadyen *(Philip)*; Lou Rawls *(Tree Man)*; Paolo Seganti *(Tomas De Leon)*; Michael McKean *(Roz's New Mark)*; Junior Brown *(Wrong Texan)*; Chao-Li Chi *(Formosa Bartender)*; Wendy Benson *(Brigitte)*; Jeff Schweickert *(Slammin' Sammy)*; Bill Gundry *(Man with Painting)*; Joyce Schweickert *(Mary)*; Kathleen Couser *(Frances)*; Melinda Martinez *(Birthday Girl)*; Jennifer Lauray *(Birthday Girl's Mother)*; Tom Balmos *(Beer Delivery Man)*; Margaret Bush *(Dress Shop Sales Woman)*; Liz Mamana *(Coffee House Girl)*; Katie Hagan *(Little Girl in Dream)*; A.J. Mallett *(Little Boy in Dream)*; Steve Lambert *(Man in Alley)*; Mara *(Barking Dog)*; Jim Cullum *(Jazz Band Leader)*; Evan Christopher; Howard Elkins; Don Mopsick; Mike Pittsley; John Sheridan; Ed Torres *(Jazz Band)*; Scott Land *(Puppeteer)*

STILL BREATHING is a simple, single-minded tale about "love and mystery trying to take root in an age of cynicism and ambition," in the words of its publicists. Pure but not mindless romance, it will be welcomed with open arms by aficionados of the genre. Others are advised to pass it by.

Fletcher (Brendan Fraser) is a street performer from San Antonio. One night, his ideal mate comes to him in a vision, along with the word "formosa." The woman whom Fletcher has fantasized is Roz (Joanna Going), a cynical con artist living in Los Angeles. Roz's MO is to entice a wealthy man like Tomas (Paolo Seganti) into buying her an expensive painting, collecting the commission on the sale, and then scaring off her mark by pretending to be HIV-positive. In her off hours, she hangs out with friends at the Formosa Cafe.

Fletcher embarks for China in search of his dreams. During a layover in LA, he happens upon the Formosa Cafe and, in it, Roz. Realizing that his quest is over, he goes home with her. Having mistaken Fletcher for a rich Texan she was supposed to meet, Roz tries to seduce him. In addition, she's slowly becoming attracted to him. Not wishing to rush the progress of the most important relationship of his life, Fletcher resists her advances, confusing and galling her.

Fletcher takes Roz to San Antonio and introduces her to his family and friends and to a tranquil, altruistic world she has never known. Eventually, she tells him her only interest in him was the bucks she erroneously thought he had and angrily returns to LA. After briefly reverting to her old lifestyle, she has a change of heart and flies back to Texas to share her future with Fletcher.

The story ends with a hokey shot of the two lovers, hand in hand, idyllically floating down a river in a pair of inner tubes. In an attempt to preempt the scorn of schmaltz detectors, writer-director James F. Robinson inserted after the end credits a snippet in which a friend of Fletcher's criticizes the artificiality of that final image. Fletcher, speaking for Robinson, replies, "What do movies have to do with real life?" a response that is at once quite insightful and a bit of a cop-out. For its breed, however, the film is relatively low in hokum—though when Roz asks a jazz musician (Lou Rawls) where he plays and he answers, "Inside myself," one wants to jump into the frame and say, "No, no, she means where *literally.* Some will find the film antifeminist, but the values STILL BREATHING attacks—urbanism, egoism, ambition—although often associated with feminism, are not intrinsic to it. The movie is, however, almost uniquely conservative for a film of its era.

Joanna Going makes a sharper impression than costar Fraser, perhaps because it's easier to play a bad girl than a good guy. Whereas Fraser's Fletcher comes across as a kind of drag, Going's Roz at times amusingly suggests a mean little stewardess on her fifth cup of coffee. Had Going given even more of an edge to Roz's hard-bitten side, her performance might have been memorable. Celeste Holm, who portrays the hero's grandmother (and who in real-life was, as reported in the film's press notes, "recently honored as national Grandparent of the Year"), was, in her prime, one of the few actresses who could register intelligence and radiance simultaneously. Pushing 80 at the time of STILL BREATHING, she has lost amazingly little of that gift.

Those who can't take their romance straight will wish that Robinson had taken a tip from Preston Sturges's script for the similarly plotted REMEMBER THE NIGHT (1940) and laced the love interest with hefty doses of comedy. Still, Robinson's debut feature fulfills the requisites of its genre, and what more can one ask of a movie than that? *(Violence, sexual situations.)*—D.T.

d, James F. Robinson; p, James F. Robinson, Marshall Persinger; exec p, Joyce Schweickert; assoc p, Julie Lynn, Amy Lippens, Michael Moody, Cuba Craig; w, James F. Robinson; ph, John Thomas; ed, Sean Albertson; m, Paul Mills; prod d, Denise Pizzini; art d, Bob West; set d, Lisa Lopez; sound, J. Byron Smith (mixer); fx, Bob Engelsiepen, Kim Bajorek, View Studios; casting, Amy Lippens; cos, Susanna Puisto; makeup, Ann Masterson, Jo-Anne Smith; stunts, Russell Towery

Romance/Comedy/Drama (PR: C MPAA: PG-13)

STIR ★

(U.S., 1997) 92m RGN Production ~ York Home Video c

Traci Lords *(Kelly Bekins)*; Andrew Heckler *(Michael Novic)*; Daniel Roebuck *(Joseph Bekins)*; Seth Adkins *(Matt Bekins)*; Tony Todd *(Bubba)*; Karen Black *(Dr. Gabrielle Kessler)*; Michael J. Pollard *(Hotel Manager)*; Reno Wilson; Robert Wisdom *(Williams)*; Slavitza Jovan *(Gypsy Woman)*; Channon Roe *(Cab Driver)*; Angel Aviles *(Hotel Maid)*; Darryl Jones *(Street Vendor)*; Rodion Nakhapetov *(Russian Mobster)*

Despite its title and prominent featuring of star Traci Lords in its advertising, STIR is not a women-in-prison movie, but rather a poorly scripted straight-to-video release about a psychic child and a missing computer disk.

Biochemist Joseph Bekins (Daniel Roebuck) returns to the hotel room where he and his wife Kelly (Traci Lords) spent their honeymoon. He completes his work on a medical breakthrough, and is thereafter murdered. Some days later, Kelly and her six-year-old son Matt (Seth Adkins) check into the same hotel room "looking for closure." Joseph's best friend and colleague, Michael Novic (Andrew Heckler) follows soon after. All are under surveillance by Bubba (Tony Todd), a member of the hotel staff.

Matt has nightmares in which he is visited by his father and sees the murder. Novic arranges for the boy to visit Dr. Kessler (Karen Black), who will probe the visions. When Matt realizes that the killer he witnessed is Novic, he runs away and ends up with Bubba, who is really an FBI agent. Novic takes Kelly prisoner in an abandoned building and demands the computer disk on which Joseph saved his research. Though she knew nothing about it, Joseph had discovered a cure for AIDS, which Novic plans to sell to the Russian mafia for $20 million.

Bubba helps save Kelly, leading to a chase in which Novic is killed in an abandoned building as it is demolished. Matt receives a psychic message from his father, guiding him to discover the disk hidden in his pillow.

If there's an audience for movies in which Traci Lords keeps her clothes on and emotes, then STIR is for them. All others will want to give it a wide berth. This is the kind of movie where it takes you an hour to figure out what's going on, by which time you don't care anymore. And once the explanations come, none of them make any sense. How could the FBI be guarding the country's best scientist and let him be murdered right under it's nose? Why would Dr. Bekins be doing research in a hotel room? How could Kelly have *no* idea what her husband was working on? What's with all the psychic mumbo-jumbo? And what the heck does the title mean? *(Violence, profanity.)*—P.R.

d, Rodion Nakhapetov; p, Natasha Shliapnikoff; exec p, John Whelpley, Rodion Nakhapetov; w, Eric Lee Bowers, Rodion Nakhapetov; ph, Darko Suvak; ed, James Frisa; m, Keith Bilderbeck; prod d, Paul Bickel; sound, Itamar Ben Jacob; cos, Melissa Guerrero; stunts, Victor Ivanov

Thriller (PR: C MPAA: R)

STOLEN MOMENTS ★★★

(Canada, 1997) 92m National Film Board of Canada ~ First Run Features c

Audre Lorde; Leslie Feinberg; Kitty Tsui; Joan Nestle; Judy Grahn; Nicole Brossard; Sheila Gilhooly; Kate Nelligan *(narrator)*

STOLEN MOMENTS offer what few documentaries about lesbian culture have offered before: an in-depth study of an often invisible but always vibrant community.

Filmmaker Margaret Westcott hammers home two points in STOLEN MOMENTS: first, that lesbians have been around since the beginning of time, and second, that they've had a more difficult time nurturing an identity than any other minority group. Sexism has had alot to do with it—even gay history tends to skim over lesbian contributions. To rectify these omissions, Wescott packs a great amount of information and anecdotes into the film, to the extent that the viewer is, at points, almost overwhelmed by the breadth of the material. Elegantly narrated by actress Kate Nelligan, STOLEN MOMENTS begins on a positive note, with extensive footage of a convergance of women on motorcyles at a recent Gay Pride Parade in New York City. But as the film makes clear, this kind of public visibility has come at a very high price. Even though psychiatric and social forces were at work in past periods of history condemning lesbianism as a sickness, many lesbian communities managed to spring up and thrive. At the turn of the century, several European cities had bustling lesbian communities. In Paris, long-time companions Gertrude Stein and Alice B. Toklas, and poet-salon hostess Natalie Barney (referred to as the "notorious lesbian") were at the vanguard of a lifestyle that was literary, elegant, and proudly celebratory of their homosexuality. In Berlin, Germany's gay capital, homosexuality was an accepted lifestyle. Though still on the books as a criminal offense, the gay lifestyle was encouraged by the bustling cabarets, bars, and prevalent practice of crossdressing among women.

The film also focuses on the ways in which many societies have viewed homosexuality as a criminal activity, with lesbians becoming easy targets for hostile behavior. Transgendered author Leslie Feinberg recalls in appalling detail how in the 1950s lesbian bars were repeatedly raided and the women arrested. At the police station, they were often sexually harassed and subject to groping and rape. Even in the more lenient European cities such as Amsterdam, being a lesbian was literally life-threatening: in the 1700s, any woman caught crossdressing was punished in the town square by strangulation, drowning, and being burned alive. Those spared this fate were sent to prison or simply banished. In post-WWI Germany, the Nazi party began targeting homosexuals, sending many of them to concentration camps. Even after the camps were liberated, gay prisoners were forced to serve out the sentences that they were given under the country's anti-homosexual law.

While STOLEN MOMENTS is an important contribution to lesbian "herstory," the film disappoints in many respects. Director Wescott clearly has a passion for the subject, but this passion often overwhelms her good judgment as a filmmaker. She includes so much information that certain subjects get short shrift—for instance, the life of a lesbian archetype, the Greek poet Sappho, is given a brief glance, and then it's onto the next topic. Other frustrating inclusions are the all-too-brief interviews with pioneering lesbian author-activists Joan Nestle and the late Audre Lorde; excluded entirely are the "Boston marriage" and "romantic friendship" arrangements of the 18th- and 19th-century, in which American society accepted women living together as couples.

In the final analysis, STOLEN MOMENTS presents much valuable information and serves as a good primer for the unitiated. Westcott's fascination with the material may have caused a certain uneveness in the presentation of historical detail, but what she has offered up certainly qualifies as food for thought. *(Adult situations.)*— D.O.

d, Margaret Wescott; ph, Zoe Dirse

Documentary **(PR: C MPAA: NR)**

STOREFRONT HITCHCOCK ★★★★

(U.S., 1998) 81m Clinica Estetico; Orion Pictures ~ Orion/MGM c

Robyn Hitchcock *(Himself/Guitar,Harmonica, Vocals)*; Tim Keegan *(Himself/Guitar,Backing Vocals)*; Deni Bonet *(Herself/Violin)*

British singer-songwriter Robyn Hitchcock, a cult icon revered for his darkly humored and intensely surreal work, is the focus of this warm, intimate valentine of a concert film by longtime fan Jonathan Demme, director of the formidable STOP MAKING SENSE (1984).

Filmed over two days and nights in a run-down, vacant furniture store on 14th Street in New York City, STOREFRONT HITCHCOCK features the singer-songwriter performing fifteen songs culled from four different sets executed on a makeshift stage before small (and unseen) audiences. With his back to the shop window, Hitchcock works mostly solo, switches from acoustic guitar to electric, and brings out recent collaborators Deni Bonet (violin) and Tim Keegan (guitar) to perform with him for a few numbers.

Behind Hitchcock, traffic and passersby stream in and out of frame; every once in a while a crowd gathers, but for the most part, the public in the space "outside" goes about its business, unaware. Over the course of the film, day seems to turn to night, then back to day, thanks to backdrops—a filmy black curtain, an opaque black background—which are drawn over the window, then pulled away to reveal a change in ambient light; in the case of "The Yip! Song," the backdrop is pulled away mid-song to reveal stained-glass-like panels of color which have been surreptitiously added to the window. Littering the stage are traffic cones, which Hitchcock absentmindedly moves around between songs; candles are brought out for his more raw, deeply emotional material ("I'm Only You," "Glass Hotel"); a disco ball whirls throughout the fragile "Element of Light;" bare lightbulbs ("You and Oblivion") and a sculpture of a tomato ("Alright, Yeah") are suspended from the ceiling—in-jokes for Hitchcock fans, as he's addressed both items in past songs.

It's not surprising that Demme would be a Hitchcock fan. The British singer has been buzzing under the radar for over two decades, first with the Soft Boys in the '70s through his '80s work with the Egyptians, with countless solo projects scattered throughout. Not only is he an acclaimed songwriter and guitarist (and perpetual underdog, despite his almost-hits "Balloon Man" and "So You Think You're in Love"), he's also an author of short stories and an accomplished painter and illustrator. Hitchcock's concerts are known for his stream-of-consciousness monologues; thus, Demme gives these as much weight as the music. While Hitchcock, now in his mid-40s, doesn't deliver them with the manic speed he formerly exhibited (if he *did*, he'd scare off uninitiated viewers), they're still quite remarkable. He describes rock-and-roll as a willful teenager with serious biological-scatalogical issues, while the simple act of extinguishing a candle inspires a meditation on minotaurs, duct tape, and traffic congestion on London's A4. Hitchcock introduces "The Yip! Song" (dedicated to his late father) as "the most upbeat song I've ever written—it's about death from cancer," directly addresses computerized lifeforms of the future ("We created you. . . .We are God, and we're sorry."), and compares organized religion to pornography. But Hitchcock exudes enough warmth, intelligence, and humor to avoid coming off as lunatic fringe. While his psycho-folk music has led him to be oft-compared to Pink Floyd acid casualty Syd Barrett, his spoken improvisations share much in common with the scabrously witty monologues of British comedian Peter Cook (whom Hitchcock also resembles physically), especially when he makes such straightfaced observances as, "I don't know what kind of church you like to imagine, but I like to imagine a church full of carcasses."

Demme presents Hitchcock with a minimum of visual flash; no quick-cut editing, no sharply-executed stage production, and absolutely no big white suits. Even so, Demme's presentation befits his subject, as was the case with his groundbreaking (and superstar-making) Talking Heads concert film, STOP MAKING SENSE. That said, STOREFRONT HITCHCOCK relies primarily on the considerable charms of its subject to generate electricity, and its off-the-cuff, small-scale, low-budget intimacy proves it's a grassroots labor of love on Demme's part. If viewers don't "get" Hitchcock—or, more accurately, are unwilling to try—the film itself won't do much to convince them otherwise. And considering the troubles of Orion Pictures, there's little chance that audiences will get the opportunity to see for themselves. Along with BELOVED, this leaves Demme batting .000 this year in terms of financial success; with STOREFRONT HITCHCOCK, the blame can easily be placed upon its distributor—though that's hardly a consolation. *(Profanity.)*—K.S.

d, Jonathan Demme; p, Peter Saraf; exec p, Edward Saxon, Gary Goetzman; assoc p, Steven Shareshian; ph, Anthony Jannelli; ed, Andy Keir; m, Robyn Hitchcock; sound, Jonathan Porath (mixer); makeup, Carl Fullerton

Documentary/Musical **(PR: C MPAA: PG-13)**

STORY OF X, THE ★★★

(U.S., 1997) 82m Calliope Films ~ Playboy Entertainment c/bw
(AKA: PLAYBOY'S STORY OF X)

Buck Henry *(Host/Narrator)*; Russ Meyer; Bernardo Bertolucci; Jack Valenti; Al Goldstein; Camille Paglia; Hugh Hefner; Dave Friedman

As a catchy inventory of dirty movies, THE STORY OF X squeezes in a lot of material. Although it might be better titled: "The Story of R, Leading to Some X," this well-researched Playboy production hits the highlights of an industry that has always operated under a Puritannical cloud of suspicion, while providing guilty pleasure for admitted devotees and hypocrites alike.

Genially hosted by Buck Henry, THE STORY OF X lets us sample forbidden fruit that is as old as the movies themselves. In fact, it's even older—Eadweard James Muybridge (1830-1904), the photographic innovator whose experiments led to the discovery of motion pictures, shot test footage of nude subjects. Interrupting its overview with commentary from fans, the X story heats up with silent stag films with titles like FREE RIDE (1915). In the talkie era, adult cinema became the strange bedfellow of educational shorts and exploitative flicks protected by a social message.

By the late 1950, Supreme Court rulings on the issue of obscenity began to liberalize what could be shown in American moviehouses. Enterprising hucksters like Herschel Gordon Lewis expanded the marketplace by taking their "roadshow" productions to America's heartland. When more daring foreign films drew away the faithful, American smut peddlers responded with "roughies," in which violence blurred the lines of sexual pleasure. When Hollywood took advantage of censorship inroads (in films like 1969's MIDNIGHT COWBOY and 1973's LAST TANGO IN PARIS), the X-industry crafted erotic classics like THE DEVIL IN MISS JONES (1972) and BEHIND THE GREEN DOOR (1972) which brought hardcore pornography into the popular vernacular. And in the 1980s, the home-video boom allowed couples to watch anything-goes erotica in the privacy of their boudoirs.

Informative and amusing, THE STORY OF X occasionally pays lip service to antiporn crusaders, but it's clearly a ringing endorsement of a skin trade that now encompasses Vegas trade shows, amateur home videos, and an X-rated Hall of Fame. Filmmaker Chuck Workman, best known for his rapid-fire compressions of film history (shown on Academy Award broadcasts) saves his quick-cut magic for this film's "climax," while utilizing a less exhausting approach in detailing the early rise of erotic cinema. Interviews with veteran filmmakers like Dave Friedman and Russ Meyer offer fascinating anecdotes, though the opinions proffered by viewers at an LA midnight screening of antique erotica are a waste of time.

On the downside, THE STORY OF X does tend to pile up its history, blurring its time line as it explains how various factions jumped on the X-rated bandwagon. Still, Workman does a yeoman's job of covering everything from Russ Meyer's mammary fixation to the impact of AIDS. Oddly enough, the one thing this entertaining documentary never does is to arouse. Slyly affectionate and subversively educational, this would-be masturbatory marathon lets us giggle under the bedcovers. *(Violence, extreme profanity, extensive nudity, sexual situations, substance abuse.)*—R.P.

d, Chuck Workman, Nancy Schreiber (host sequences); p, Chuck Workman; assoc p, John Leonetti, Jennifer McGonigal; ph, John Sharaf, Michael Messenheimer; ed, Chuck Workman, Jeremy Workman; art d, Marc Greville-Masson; sound, Tom Orsi

Documentary/Erotic **(PR: O MPAA: NR)**

STRAY BULLET ★

(U.S., 1998) 86m Concorde; New Horizons ~ New Horizons Home Video c

Robert Carradine *(John Burnside)*; Rebecca Staab *(Stella Crosby)*; Fred Dryer *(Forest Mason)*; Ian Beattie *(Pryke)*; Lorraine McCourt *(Francesca)*; Tim Murphy *(Morris)*; Kieran Hurley *(Doyle)*; Berts Folan *(Kimble)*; Ben Gaule *(Brown)*; Shawn Brewster *(Teller)*; Mick Nolan *(Lilus)*; Stuart Dunne *(Chester)*; Glen Mulhern *(Troy)*; Sabina Brennan *(Receptionist)*; Robert Boyd *(Forestry Worker #1)*; Paddy Sweeney *(Forestry Worker #2)*; Carol Hunt *(Sales Woman)*; Brian Begley *(Wayne)*; Eileen Dunne *(B&B Lady)*

STRAY BULLET is a terrible mistaken-identity thriller, churned out in Ireland by Roger Corman's made-for-video factory, that makes absolutely no sense and is populated by some of the dumbest characters in movie history.

Attorney John Burnside (Robert Carradine) gets off a plane in Maine and gets his suitcase mixed up with a woman named Stella Crosby (Rebecca Staab), who gives him a ride and invites him to a party at her house that night. At the party, Stella tells Burnside that her husband Tom couldn't make it and she introduces him to a friend named Mason (Fred Dryer). When Burnside goes outside, he's kidnapped by some gunmen who take him to a warehouse where he's questioned by a man named Pryke (Ian Beattie), who thinks that he's Tom Crosby and tells him that he has 48 hours to pay the $2 million that he and Stella owe him. Burnside goes to the cops, but they don't believe him, especially when Stella arrives and claims he's her husband. She explains that she and Tom are in trouble over a money-laundering scheme and begs him to help her by pretending to be Tom for a while. Burnside agrees and sleeps with Stella, who says that she's leaving Tom after the deal. Stella and Burnside go to pick up the money from a man she says is Tom, but Stella shoots him. After splitting up, Burnside goes back to Stella's house and finds Mason and his two bodyguards shot to death. He's captured by Pryke, but manages to escape and tracks Stella down to a hotel, where he finds her in bed with a woman. Pryke and his gang arrive and a shootout ensues, but he's killed by the police and Stella gets away with the money. Burnside is arrested, but then released after the police receive an anonymous call from a woman who clears him.

One might think that it would be impossible to rip off NORTH BY NORTHWEST (1959) and produce a movie that's incredibly dull and totally devoid of entertainment, but STRAY BULLET proves that otherwise. STRAY lifts NORTH's premise of a character who's mistaken for someone who's nonexistent, steals some lines of dialogue verbatim, and makes Burnside devoted to his mother, as was Cary Grant's character, but forgot to borrow such necessary little items as logic, humor, and excitement. The so-called crosses, double-crosses, and triple-crosses are literally impossible to follow, since the filmmakers make no attempt to connect the narrative dots or provide any reasonable explanation for the characters' mystifying actions. Burnside is a mind-numbingly idiotic character, agreeing to pose as Stella's husband even after his life has been threatened, and his credulity is not helped by Robert Carradine's somnambulistic acting style and his curious mannerism of turning away and looking down as he speaks to people, though it is somewhat comforting to know that he's carrying on his family's sleaze-movie tradition. *(Violence, profanity, sexual situations.)*—M.S.

d, Rob Spera; p, Mary Ann Fisher; exec p, Roger Corman; co-p, Darin Spillman, Frances Doel; w, Christopher Wood; ph, Jules Labarthe; ed, Ian Ladizinsky; m, Arthur Kempel; prod d, Dave Blass; sound, D.J. Ritchie; casting, Jan Glaser; cos, Ashling Byrne; makeup, Grainne Daly

Mystery/Thriller **(PR: O MPAA: R)**

SUB DOWN ★★★

(U.S., 1998) 91m Muraglia; Sladek Filmworks ~ Carousel Picture Co. c

Stephen Baldwin *(Rick Postley)*; Tom Conti *(Harry Rheinhardt)*; Gabrielle Anwar *(Laura Dyson)*; Chris Mulkey *(Commander John Kirsch)*; Tony Plana *(Lt. Commander Meiges)*; Joe Dain *(Sonar Chief)*; Chris Taafe *(Lt. Hayes)*; Kevin Connally *(Petty Officer Holliday)*; Doug McKeon *(Chief of Boat)*; Eugene Wiliams *(Lt. Weston)*; Matt Kennedy *(Navigator)*; Paul Abbott *(Ballast)*; Joel Traywick *(Dive)*; Michael Caradonna *(Miller)*; Twirlie Delite Dollison *(Francis)*; Nikki Cox *(Holliday's Girlfriend)*; Joyce Brooks *(Ellie Weston)*; Courtney Gore *(Weston's Daughter)*; Daniel Sladek *(Gate Guard)*; Thambo Kasinathan *(Sonar Asst.)*; Steve Darne; Cort Hessler; Anthony Besselle *(Sailor)*

Research scientists race to save a sinking nuclear submarine in SUB DOWN, an entertaining if routine thriller.

The *USS Portland* sets sail from Washington with three civilian scientists aboard: Harry Rheinhardt (Tom Conti) and his assistant Rick Postley (Stephen Baldwin), who will be testing an ice profiler mounted in "Marvyn," a minisub they have developed; and Laura Dyson (Gabrielle Anwar), who will be tracking whale migrations. They are welcomed cordially by Commander John Kirsch (Chris Mulkey), a career military man struggling to maintain his standards against political notions of the role of a peacetime army.

When the *Portland* is under the polar ice cap, Harry and Rick take Marvyn out for a test, accompanied by a curious Laura. The minisub's sonar confuses a Russian submarine, causing a collision with the *Portland*. Damaged, the *Portland* settles on the ocean floor at 2500 feet, well below the depth at which it is safe from being crushed by water pressure. The three scientists return to the sub and make it to the control room. Harry takes Marvyn to look for a break in the ice, but he is killed when Marvyn develops a leak. Rick and Laura receive a Morse code message from the surviving crew, trapped in another part of the sub. Rick restores electrical power to the ship and Kirsch sacrifices his life to repair the damaged reactor so that the ship will have enough power to escape. With air almost gone, Laura hears whales on sonar and has Rick follow them to a break in the ice.

In between the plot points mentioned above, the characters in SUB DOWN spend most of their time listening to the ships' hull creak, struggling against the confined spaces in which they are trapped, and looking worried and sweaty about the lack of oxygen. In other words, SUB DOWN is pretty much everything you could ask for in a submarine movie. As such, it's hard to know why director Greg Champion had his name taken off the film and replaced with the fictitious Alan Smithee. Barring any of the innumerable disputes that can trouble a film, one can only assume that he had something better in mind that what is seen here. The only real weakness is the script, which doesn't seem to know what to do with the characters on their way to getting trapped under the polar ice cap: the sexual flirtation between Laura and Rick is obviously here only to kill time, while a scene in which Rick, Kirsch, and some of the others argue over the role of the military in the post-Cold War era plays like nothing better than an attempt by the scriptwriters to show off how many books they've read. *(Adult situations.)*—M.F.

d, Alan Smithee; p, Daniel Sladek, Silvio Muragila, Jeffery White; exec p, Tom Reeve, Romain Schroeder; assoc p, Tom Piskura, Howard Chesley, Sterling Belefant, Cam Jones; w, Howard Chelsey; ph, Hiro Narita; ed, Cary Shott; m, Stefano Mainetti; art d, Peter Powis; set d, Beck Taylor; fx, Harry Wiessenhaan; cos, Lisa Johnson; makeup, Vincenzo Mastrantonio

Disaster/Thriller **(PR: C MPAA: PG-13)**

SUBSPECIES IV: BLOODSTORM ★★

(U.S., 1998) 85m Full Moon Pictures ~ Full Moon c
(AKA: BLOODSTORM: SUBSPECIES IV)

Anders Hove *(Radu)*; Denice Duff *(Michelle)*; Jonathon Morris *(Ash)*; Ioana Abur *(Dr. Ana Lazar)*; Mihai Dinvale *(Dr. Nicolescu)*; Floriella Grappini *(Cassandra)*; Dan Astileanu, billed as Dan Astilean *(Dr. Lupu)*; Ion Haiduc *(Lt. Marin)*; Camelia Zorlescu *(Gypsy Woman)*; Eugenia Bosanceanu *(Caretaker)*; Cristi Zorlescu *(Gypsy Woman)*; Oana Voicu *(Rebecca)*; Dorina Lazar *(Old Woman)*; Gelu Nitu *(Detective Voda)*; Luminita Erga *(Nurse)*; Dan Istrate *(Boy)*; Eugenia Pavel *(Girl)*; Radu Badica *(Guard)*; Silviu Geamanu

Better than most other fourth entries in straight-to-video series, this vampire adventure does eventually wind up descending into the formulaic.

Having escaped a fiery fate, Radu Vladislas (Anders Hove) travels from Transylvania to Bucharest in search of Michelle (Denice Duff), who was rescued from him by her sister and a friend. Doctor Ana Lazar (Ioana Abur) finds Michelle at a car crash that killed her saviors. Ana's colleague Dr. Nicolescu (Mihai Dinvale) recognizes Michelle as a vampire's victim and says he can help her. Arriving at the lair of vampire Ash (Jonathon Morris), Radu takes over, seducing Ash's protege Cassandra (Floriella Grappini). Dr. Nicolescu begins Michelle's treatment—but he is a vampire himself, and hopes to use her blood to synthesize the Bloodstone's serum, which can grant him eternal life.

Spurned by Radu, Cassandra encourages Ash to destroy him and claim the Bloodstone. She follows Radu to the clinic, where Dr. Nicolescu springs a trap and stakes him. Overwhelmed by Radu's influence, Michelle frees him, and the two vampires vanish. Cassandra offers to help Ana kill Radu and rescue Michelle, giving her a key to the Vladislas crypt. Ana discovers Nicolescu's vampiric nature, but he quells her fears and joins her in entering Radu's lair; once inside, however, he offers Ana to Radu in exchange for a taste of the Bloodstone. Radu kills him and offers Ana to Michelle, but she fights off Radu's influence, and the women decapitate Radu. They are confronted by Ash and Cassandra, but manage to escape into daylight.

The SUBSPECIES films have always been the best-looking films to come from the Full Moon studio, and such is the case with this sequel, as writer-director Ted Nicolaou wrings effective atmosphere out of the Romanian locations. And unlike the previous films in the series, this entry features a busy plot that, for the first half, helps to disguise how tired the basic material has become. Dr. Nicolescu is a fun addition to the overcrowded plot, and Dinvale plays him in the great tradition of crazed scientists.

The longer the film goes on, though, the more it emphasizes the struggle between the possessive Radu and the no-longer-innocent Michelle—a war of wills that quickly wears out its welcome. The movie actually could have been longer, and could have done more with the character of Ash (from the 1987 Full Moon production THE VAMPIRE JOURNALS); as it is, his inclusion here seems a mere gimmick, and his potential is wasted. Still, his survival at the film's (abrupt) conclusion presumably points to yet another entry in the series. (Graphic violence, extensive nudity, sexual situations, profanity.)—M.G.

d, Ted Nicolaou; p, Vlad Paunescu, Kirk Edward Hansen; exec p, Charles Band; assoc p, Gabi Antal; w, Ted Nicolaou; ph, Adolfo Bartoli; ed, Gregory Sanders; m, Richard Kosinski, John Zeretzke; prod d, Radu Corciova; art d, Viorel Ghenea; sound, Tibi Borcoman; fx, David A. Wagner, John R. Ellis; casting, Robert MacDonald, Perry Bullington, Catalin Dordea; cos, Oana Paunescu; makeup, Mark A. Rappaport (effects), Dana Busoiu

Horror **(PR: O MPAA: R)**

SUBSTITUTE 2: SCHOOL'S OUT, THE ★

(U.S., 1998) 90m Live Film and Mediaworks;
Dinamo Entertainment; Gun for Hire Films ~
Artisan Entertainment c

Treat Williams *(Thomasson)*; B.D. Wong *(Drummond)*; Angel David *(Joey 6)*; Michael Michele *(Kara)*; Larry Gilliard Jr. *(Duncan X)*; Edoardo Ballerini *(Danny)*; The Guru *(Little B.)*; Daryl Edwards *(Bartee)*; Antonio David Lyons *(Sodaboy)*; Eugene Byrd *(Mose)*; Owen Stadele *(Joel)*; Christopher Cousins *(Randall)*; Chuck Jeffreys *(Willy)*; Susan May Pratt *(Anya)*; Camille Gaston *(Keysham)*; Paul Lazar *(Weathers)*; Cisco Davis *(A.K.)*; Schooly-D *(Tail #1)*; Shawn McLean *(Badass)*; Julie R. Pearl *(Faculty Lounge Teacher)*; Michael Knowles *(Man Moving Ta-*

ble); Samantha Brown *(Auto Shop Student)*; Reuben Seid *(Cop)*; Harold Baines *(Lavatory Hood #1)*; Howard "Stick" Baines *(Lavatory Hood #2)*; David Lomax *(Warehouse Hood)*; Jalil Jay Lynch *(Driver)*

This name-only sequel has nothing in common with its 1996 predecessor other than the idea of a mercenary working undercover as a teacher in a tough high school. And the story worked much better the first time around.

Mercenary Carl Thomasson (Treat Williams) returns to Brooklyn when he gets word that his brother Randall was shot to death while trying to prevent a carjacking. Enlisting the help of past associate Joey (Angel David), Carl learns that the thieves were members of the Brotherhood, a gang based at the high school where Randall taught Special Ed. With the help of his niece Anya (Susan May Pratt) and her teacher Kara (Michael Michele), Carl gets a job (under an alias) as a substitute teacher with the same ghetto hard cases his brother taught.

In between trying to get the attention of his students, romantic encounters with Kara, and dodging attacks by the Brotherhood, Carl learns that the gang has been running a chop shop for stolen cars out of the school's auto shop. He suspects that shop teacher Warren Drummond (B.D. Wong) is behind the operation. Kara pulls his background file, but Drummond kills her while Carl is on his way over to read it. The file reveals that Drummond was a Marine staff sergeant drummed out of the Corps for black marketeering. While fending off seduction by her boyfriend Danny (Edouardo Ballerini), Anya discovers that it was he who murdered her father in the carjacking. Carl and Joey head to school for a showdown with Drummond. After a shootout with the Brotherhood, Carl confronts Drummond in front of his class, and in a one-on-one fight using shop tools, Drummond is killed.

Unlike the first SUBSTITUTE, which arguably had a sense of its own ridiculousness, SUBSTITUTE 2 simply *is* ridiculous. The script is awful, plodding listlessly from plot element to plot element, with dialogue that reads like the scripters' notes for the purpose it is supposed to fill in advancing the plot. (Needing to set up that Anya knows karate in order that she can use it later to subdue her murderous boyfriend, the script shoehorns a mention of it into a tearful tirade to uncle Carl about how he abandoned his family.) It's never clear whether or not Drummond ordered Randall killed, or why, or for that matter what white Danny was doing jacking cars with a black gang. And why does Drummond kill Kara for what she knows about him, then leave his file behind for Carl to see? SUBSTITUTE 2 is most of all a waste of the talents of Treat Williams, who manages to retain a screen presence even in crap like this, and B.D. Wong, whose role as macho Drummond is as far as he could ever want to get from his transvestite in the Broadway version of *M. Butterfly*. *(Violence, sexual situations, adult situations, profanity.)*—M.F.

d, Steven Pearl; p, Morrie Eisenman, Robert Salerno; exec p, Steven Bakalar, Devorah Cutler-Rubenstein; w, Roy Frumkes, Rocco Simonelli; ph, Larry Banks; ed, Mayin Lo; m, Joe Delia; prod d, Wing Lee; art d, Mark White; set d, Stacey Tanner; sound, Pete Conlin, David Novack (mixer); fx, Drew Jiritano; casting, Lina Todd; cos, Kim Marie Druce; makeup, Sabine Roller, Kelly Gleason; stunts, Phil Neilson

Crime/Drama **(PR: C MPAA: R)**

SUE ★★★½

(Israel/U.S., 1998) 90m Amko Productions ~ Amko Productions c

Anna Thomson *(Sue)*; Matthew Powers *(Ben)*; Tahnee Welch *(Lola)*; Tracee Ellis Ross *(Linda)*; John Ventimiglia *(Larry)*; Edoardo Ballerini *(Eddi)*; Matthew Faber *(Sven)*; Robert Kya Hill *(Willie)*; Austin Pendelton *(Bob)*; Alice Liu *(Lisa)*; Dechen Thurman *(Interviewer)*; Joshua Kaplan *(Sydney)*; Lazaro Perez *(Pedro/Phil)*; Dechen Thurman *(Interviewer/Office Manager)*; James Mulholland *(Man in Cinema)*; Smadar Levy *(1st Interviewer)*; Joan Price Rahav *(2nd Interviewer)*; Sarah Zhang *(Chinese Takeout Lady #1)*; Sylvia Wong *(Chinese Takout Lady #2)*; Phil La Rocco *(Hotel Receptionist)*; Lon Waterford *(Homeless Man)*; Mike Delassario *(Diner Owner)*; Frances Ensemplari *(Diner Patron)*; Joe McLaughlin *(Rude Walker)*; Dale Lawyer *(Sue's Mother)*; Dana Jared *(Piano Man)*; Rizwan Manji *(Newsstand Owner)*; Kevin Keane Murphy *(Barman)*; Dimitri Todarek *(Delivery Boy)*; Robert S. Brown *(Doctor)*; Mohinder Singh *(Cab Driver)*; Harvey Kaufman *(Person in Crowd)*; Amelia Fouler *(Person in Crowd)*; Adam Vignola *(Young Man on Phone)*; Barbara Rand *(Coffee Shop Customer)*

A critical and commercial hit in Germany and France, SUE barely received an American release. It's a shame, for this Manhattan-set portrait of one woman's crushing loneliness is remarkable, and features a great performance by Anna Thomson.

Unemployed and lonely, Sue (Anna Thomson) spends her days going to museums or sitting in parks, where she starts up conversations with strangers. In a coffee shop, she meets and chats with Ben (Matthew Powers), a travel writer, and gives him her phone number. Later, Sue meets a young woman, Lola (Tahnee Welch), and offers to buy her a drink. When they get to the bar, however, Lola tells Sue that she is an armed robber, and robs the bar. Eventually, Sue and Ben begin to date. The couple is happy for a while, but Ben breaks up with Sue when she inadvertently offends him. In Ben's absence, Sue begins drinking heavily and picking up men for casual sexual encounters. Ben finally reconciles with Sue, but soon after leaves again when he gets a job in India.

One night, Eddie (Edoardo Ballerini), a boyfriend of Lola's, comes by Sue's apartment and demands to know Lola's whereabouts. Sue tells him that she doesn't know, then invites him in and sleeps with him. She finally gets a job, as a coffee shop waitress, but does not make enough money to pay her back rent. In short time, she is evicted and begins spending nights in a cheap hotel. One afternoon, she runs into Lola, who is working as a prostitute, but Lola does not remember her. Moments later, Lola is dead, having been struck by a car.

Ben returns from India and is eager to resume his relationship with Sue, but Sue is evasive with him. She also neglects to tell him about her financial problems. The next day, Sue goes to a park to eat lunch. She sits down on a bench, and passes out.

Shot on a shoestring and self-distributed, SUE is a truly independent work, not only by virtue of its noncommercial status, but also in its spirit. Unimaginable as a mainstream studio release, the film often plays like a cheap exploitation flick. It's crudely made, poorly shot, and could even be described as ugly looking. The performances (except for the lead) are broad and unreal, and the dialogue is absurd. SUE also has the grittiness and audacity of some of the better exploitation films—like the early work of Abel Ferrara—and a blunt, almost affronting approach to distasteful subject matter.

As graphic as some of the material is, however, SUE does not have the sensational character of exploitation. Israeli director Amos Kollek's intent is clearly not salaciousness, but a harsh study of urban isolation. Kollek's direction is as inelegant as the film's title, and he goes at his material head-on, putting no buffer between the audience and the character as her behavior becomes bizarre and self-destructive. Eschewing a standard cause-and-effect narrative, Kollek relates Sue's story in bits and pieces, as if his script were prepared by culling together random pages from someone's dairy. The overall effect is often startling in its directness, and if unmoving, the film provokes a voyeuristic fascination with Sue's deterioration.

Essential to making SUE work is a strong central performance, and Thomson is more than up to the task. Although best-known through such small roles as the face-slashing victim in UNFORGIVEN (1992), she shows herself here to be a world-class actress. Unreserved yet totally in control, Thomson immerses herself in her unglamorous, strung-out wreck of a character, and yet she constantly emanates dignity and intelligence, and even traces of humor. It's a brave, intuitive, and hugely rewarding performance.

Without any real plot, SUE is a bit long for what it is, and moves into tedium towards the end. And its lack of a conventional resolution may frustrate some viewers. But Kollek and Thomson's creative collaboration is a bold, unusual, and unsettling work, a film that deserves a better chance at finding an audience. *(Extensive nudity, sexual situations, adult situations, substance abuse, extreme profanity.)*—D.C.

d, Amos Kollek; p, Amos Kollek; assoc p, Osnat Shalev; co-p, Rene Bastian, Linda Moran; w, Amos Kollek; ph, Ed Talavera; ed, Liz Gazzara; m, Chico Freeman; prod d, Charlotte Burke; art d, Kirsten Kearse; sound, Theresa Radka (mixer); cos, Seth Hanson; makeup, Evelyn Ortman

Drama **(PR: O MPAA: NR)**

SUICIDE KINGS ★★½

(U.S., 1998) 106m LIVE Entertainment ~ LIVE Entertainment c

Christopher Walken *(Charles Barrett/Carlo Bartolucci)*; Denis Leary *(Lono Vecchio)*; Sean Patrick Flanery *(Max Minot)*; Johnny Galecki *(Ira Reder)*; Jay Mohr *(Brett Campbell)*; Jeremy Sisto *(T.K.)*; Henry Thomas *(Avery Chasten)*; Laura San Giacomo *(Lydia)*; Mark Watson *(Doorman)*; Nina Seimaszko *(Jennifer)*; Jay Fiondella *(Bartender)*; Nathan Dana *(Marcus)*; Frank Medrano *(Heckle)*; Brad Garrett *(Jeckyll)*; James Peter "JP" O'Fallon Jr. *(Kid #1)*; Nicholas Huttloff *(Kid #2)*; Trent Bross *(Maitre D')*; Cliff DeYoung *(Marty)*; Lisanne Falk *(Marty's Wife)*; Louis Lombardi *(Mickey)*; Barry Sherman *(Window Washer)*; Lenny Citrano *(Barrio Bennie)*; Laura Harris *(Elise "Lisa" Chasten)*; Spike Silver *(Masked Man #1)*; Corey Eubanks *(Masked Man #2)*; Kevin Crowley *(Security Guard)*; Joseph Cali *(Nick the Nose)*; Joseph Whipp *(Harry)*; Sean Whalen *(Windowmaker)*; Karen Rosin *(Emergency Room Nurse)*; Bryan Swerling *(Doctor)*; Will Klipstine *(Protesting Orderly)*; Virginia Madsen

One of the more credible RESERVOIR DOGS-inspired independent films, SUICIDE KINGS is an ensemble piece about a group of young men who kidnap a retired crime boss in order to force his help in settling another kidnapping. The premise of a wily Mafioso exploiting his captors' weaknesses is promising, but the unfocused script contains too many empty interludes that were seemingly concocted simply to pass the time until the film's "surprise" ending is unveiled.

Manhattan businessman Charlie Barrett (Christopher Walken), aka Mafia capo Carlo Bartolucci, is kidnapped and held hostage in a Long Island mansion by a group of young men, all from rich families. They want him to aid in freeing another kidnap victim, Elise (Laura Harris), whose parents are unable to pay her ransom of $2 million. The group includes Elise's brother Avery (Henry Thomas); her boyfriend Max (Sean Patrick Flanery); Brett (Jay Mohr), a hot-headed control freak; T.K. (Jeremy Sisto), the drug-addicted son of a doctor; and nebbishy Ira (Johnny Galecki), who didn't realize what his friends had in mind when they asked to use his parent's summer home. To duplicate what Elise's kidnappers have done, T.K. severs Charlie's ring finger.

Charlie phones his lawyer Marty (Cliff DeYoung) and bodyguard Lono (Denis Leary), who begin to search for both Elise and Charlie. Marty discovers that Elise's kidnapping involved an "inside player"—one of the five young men. Though tied to a chair, Charlie uses this knowledge to drive a wedge through the group, all the while playing on their fear and uncertainty at the situation they have gotten themselves into. Shortly after Marty sends word that he has made arrangements for the ransom to be paid and the girl released at a hospital emergency room, Charlie succeeds in making Avery admit that he is behind the kidnapping, planned by thugs to whom Avery owes a substantial gambling debt. Lono arrives, having tracked the group down; after a brief standoff, they agree to let Charlie go, trusting his promise that he will finish the plan to free Elise. Guilt-ridden at what he has put his sister through, Avery races to the hospital where she is supposed to be returned, but she isn't there. Charlie and Lono find the two thugs who collected the ransom and kill them after they swear they never took the girl. The plot was actually concocted by Elise and Max, who hired the thugs that approached Avery, as a way to get enough cash to get away from their feuding families. Charlie and Lono track them to their boat and, after admonishing them for lying to their friends, kill them.

Director Peter O'Fallon fails to get the most out of the many intriguing elements that are introduced in SUICIDE KINGS. The underlying ironic premise is that Charlie and Lono share a strong sense of morality that their young captors, all children of privilege, lack. In scenes that work harder than necessary to establish the point, Lono and Charlie are shown dispensing rough justice to those who deserve it. But the script doesn't do quite so much to show the equivalent moral weakness of the five young men; they merely seem spoiled and weak.

Walken is as watchable as always in a role that forces him to act only with his face. His young costars do what they can with their roles, none of which is terribly challenging. (Did no one involved remember that Jay Mohr used to do a pretty credible Walken impression on "Saturday Night Live"?) The film's considerable amount of slack is taken up by Denis Leary, who often seems to be doing one of his stand-up routines. SUICIDE KINGS is a mildly entertaining film with too many random bits that don't contribute to the whole.

An alternate ending for the film, in which Elise and Max get away with their plan, appeared as a "bonus" on the later DVD release of the film. *(Violence, nudity, adult situations, substance abuse, profanity.)*—M.F.

d, Peter O'Fallon; p, Morrie Eisenman, Wayne Rice; exec p, Stephen Drimmer; assoc p, Charles A. Chiara, Adam Mills; co-p, Patrick Peach; w, Wayne Rice, Josh McKinney, Gina Goldman (based on the short story "The Hostage" by Don Stanford); ph, Christopher Baffa; ed, Chris Peppe; m, Graeme Revell; prod d, Clark Hunter; art d, Max Biscoe; set d, Traci Kirshbaum; sound, Eric Enroth (mixer), Clive Taylor (design); fx, John Hartigan, Ultimate Effects; casting, Wendy Kurtzman, Roger Mussenden; cos, Genevieve Tyrrell; makeup, Pamela Roth; stunts, Hubie Kerns Kerns

Crime/Thriller/Comedy **(PR: C MPAA: R)**

SUMMER FLING ★★

(Ireland/U.K./Denmark, 1997) 104m Parallel Film Productions; Northolme Entertainment; Nordisk Film ~ Miramax c

(AKA: LAST OF THE HIGH KINGS)

Jared Leto *(Frankie Griffin)*; Christina Ricci *(Erin)*; Catherine O'Hara *(Ma Griffin)*; Gabriel Byrne *(Da Griffin)*; Stephen Rea *(Taxi Driver)*; Lorraine Pilkington *(Jayne Wayne)*; Jason Barry *(Nelson Fitzgerald)*; Emily Mortimer *(Romy Thomas)*; Karl Hayden *(Hopper Delaney)*; Ciaran Fitzgerald *(Noelie Griffin)*; Colm Meaney *(Jim Davern)*; Des Braden *(Teacher)*; Darren Monks *(Davy Dudley)*; Peter Keating *(Ray Griffin)*; Renee Weldon *(Maggie Griffin)*; Alexandra Haughey *(Dawn Griffin)*; Vincent Walsh *(Bobby Gallo)*; Ken Russell; Lisa Russell *(Figgis Twins)*; Mal White *(Mr. Figgis)*; Kay Creighton *(Mrs. Figgis)*; Gabriel Brady *(Television Reporter)*; Clodagh Reid *(Mo)*; Emma Stewart *(Jo)*; Don Wycherley *(Peter Colcannon)*; Amanda Shun *(Rainbow)*; Joe Savino *(Bus Conductor)*; Jack Lynch *(Returning Officer)*; Mark O'Regan *(Father Michael)*; Oliver Maguire *(Billy)*; Graham Wilkinson *(Henchman)*; Luke Hayden *(Fireman)*; Murphy *(Parnell the Dog)*

Originally titled THE LAST OF THE HIGH KINGS, SUMMER FLING is yet another coming-of-age story about teen boys fumbling toward maturity with one hand on their zippers. Set in the 1970s, it benefits from a plethora of rock 'n' roll tunes that blessedly drown out the script's warmed-over political debate. The film was acquired by Miramax for theatrical distribution but was dumped onto home video in 1998.

In 1977 Dublin, young Frankie Griffin (Jared Leto) isn't quite ready to forgo high-school joyriding and girl-watching with his callow pals to leave home and attend University. When his dad (Gabriel Byrne) departs for an acting stint in a Broadway play, Frankie's firebrand Ma (Catherine O'Hara) must care for her large brood while canvassing for her favorite candidate in a local race, Jim Davern (Colm Meaney).

Frankie is annoyed that he has to postpone his much-anticipated beach party when the Griffins play host to the visiting children of Da's Yank producer. While serving as tour guide for American teenager Erin (Christina Ricci), Catholic Frankie catches the eye of two Protestant schoolmates, Jayne Wayne (Lorraine Pilkington) and Romy Thomas (Emily Mortimer).

A fund-raiser at the Griffin home for Davern turns ugly when Frankie refuses to vote as his Ma demands, particularly after Davern makes a pass at her. Frankie then takes a step toward manhood when he loses his virginity to Jayne. Discovering that her son had sex with a Protestant girl, Ma temporarily tosses him out of the house, but they patch up their differences before Da returns to see Frankie off to college. Fiercely proud of their son, they accept Frankie's independent spirit, and at the long-awaited beach bash, Frankie initiates a lasting romantic encounter with Romy.

Coadapted by Gabriel Byrne, from a popular novel, SUMMER FLING plays out like an ersatz Ireland valentine. It's unbearable to watch brilliant sketch comedienne Catherine O'Hara sink in a Brenda Fricker role by resorting to histrionic cliches that were probably already old when "Abie's Irish Rose" made its Broadway debut in 1919. The rest of the cast offers equally stereotypical performances.

Prettily photographed and flamboyantly acted, SUMMER FLING means to be an upbeat yet bittersweet recollection, but audiences have seen adolescence fade this way too many times before—only not this clamorously. *(Violence, extreme profanity, nudity, sexual situations, substance abuse.)* —R.P.

d, David Keating; p, Tim Palmer; exec p, John Wolstenholme, Keith Northrop, Paul Feldsher, Gabriel Byrne; co-p, Martha O'Neill, Alan Moloney, Lars Kolvig; w, David Keating, Gabriel Byrne (based on the novel *Last of the High Kings* by Ferdia MacAnna); ph, Bernd Heinl; ed, Ray Lovejoy; m, Michael Convertino; prod d, Frank Conway; art d, John Paul Kelly; sound, Simon Willis (recordist), Henrik Garnov (design); fx, Kevin Hannigan (supervisor); casting, Nuala Moiselle, Karen Lindsay Stewart; cos, Mary Zophres; makeup, Maire O'Sullivan; stunts, Philippe Zone

Drama/Comedy **(PR: C MPAA: R)**

SWAN PRINCESS III: AND THE MYSTERY OF THE ENCHANTED TREASURE, THE ★½

(U.S., 1998) 72m Rich Animation Studios;
Swan III Inc. ~ Nest Entertainment Inc. c

VOICES OF: Michelle Nicastro *(Princess Odette)*; Brian Nissen *(Prince Derek)*; Katja Koch *(Zelda)*; Christy Landers *(Queen Uberta)*; Donald Sage McKay *(Jean-Bob)*; Doug Stone *(Speed)*; Steve Vinovich *(Puffin)*; Joseph Medrano *(Lord Rogers)*; Paul Masonson *(Whizzer)*; Owen Miller *(Bromley)*; Sean Wright *(Rothbart)*

The second straight-to-video sequel to the theatrical feature THE SWAN PRINCESS (1994) was made right after the first follow-up THE SWAN PRINCESS: ESCAPE FROM CASTLE MOUNTAIN (1997). Evidently, little time was taken between the two productions to actually come up with a different script.

Prince Derek (voice of Brian Nissen) and Princess Odette (voice of Michelle Nicastro) plan to celebrate the kingdom's victory over the previous films' warlocks Rothbart and Clavius, and the now- annihilated crystal ball known as the Forbidden Arts. But their joy is premature. The sorceress Zelda (voice of Katja Koch) invented the Forbidden Arts in partnership with Rothbart. Now she covets his notes, supposedly still hidden in Derek's castle. Derek found the papers, but, hoping some good could come of the spells someday, concealed his discovery from Odette, who twice before was turned into a swan by Rothbart's evil. Zelda visits the kingdom masquerading as a ditzy refugee from some faraway tyrant, and she charms Derek's poltroon counselor Lord Rogers (voice of Joseph Medrano) into disclosing the location of the notes. With the papers Zelda becomes very nearly all-powerful; Derek kept a scrap of the most important spell just in case. Zelda thus kidnaps Odette, transforming the princess once *again* into a swan. Derek rides to the rescue, and by impersonating Odette, the villainess is able to obtain that final piece of parchment. Nonetheless, Derek challenges her to a showdown in which Zelda wields deadly, guided-missile-like fireballs. Derek succeeds in breaking Zelda's wand and destroying her, but not before one of the fireballs consumes the Swan Princess. Dejected Derek finally burns Rothbart's notes, and miraculously Odette reappears, phoenix-like and restored, from the flames. The kingdom goes ahead with the celebration.

Only late in the movie, when Zelda's pyrotechnics are introduced, does the film's animation achieve anything spectacular. Otherwise this Swan Princess is a recidivist Ugly Duckling, heavy with unsympathetic talking animals and tiresome humans. Questions arise as the series continues: among others, was Rothbart an evil wizard or head of a law firm? With every sequel (ground out by former Disney animator Richard Rich) another "partner" of the deceased warlock comes out of the woodwork, and the filmmakers show true lack of ambition by padding this feature out with flashbacks to earlier SWAN PRINCESS installments. What juice the first film had came from Jack Palance's lusty portrayal of Rothbart; here Sean Wright voices the character in flashbacks and in a "surprise" moment at the film's conclusion. Brian Nissen, manly voice of Prince Derek in this outing, is credited for the scenerio, which reworks ESCAPE FROM CASTLE MOUNTAIN, which was pretty insubstantial itself. However, by drawing the bedraggled fairy-tale franchise out further the filmmakers were able to insert a few more forgettable musical numbers by Lex de Azevedo.—C.C.

d, Richard Rich; p, Richard Rich, Jared F. Brown; exec p, Sheldon O. Young, Jared F. Brown, K. Douglas Martin; co-p, Thomas J. Tobin, Terry L. Noss; w, Brian Nissen (based on the story by Richard Rich); ed, James D. Koford, Paul Murphy; m, Lex deAzevedo; casting, Bernard Van de Yacht

Animated/Children's/Musical (PR: AA MPAA: G)

SWEPT FROM THE SEA ★★
(U.K./U.S., 1997) 115m Phoenix Pictures; Tapson Steel Films ~ TriStar c

Vincent Perez *(Yanko Gooral)*; Rachel Weisz *(Amy Foster)*; Ian McKellen *(Dr. James Kennedy)*; Joss Ackland *(Mr. Swaffer)*; Kathy Bates *(Miss Swaffer)*; Tom Bell *(Isaac Foster)*; Zoe Wanamaker *(Mary Foster)*; Tony Haygarth *(Mr. Smith)*; Fiona Victory *(Mrs. Smith)*; William Scott Masson *(Mr. Wilcox)*; Eve Matheson *(Mrs. Wilcox)*; Dave Hill *(Jack Vincent)*; Roger Ashton-Griffiths *(Canon Van Stone)*; Matthew Scurfield *(Thackery)*; Margery Withers *(Widow Cree)*; Janine Duvitski *(Mrs. Finn)*; Willie Ross *(Preble)*; Janet Henfrey *(Mrs. Rigby)*; Paul Whitby *(Stefan)*; Bob Smith *(Nikolas)*; Angela Morant *(Iryna)*; Gerardo Silano *(Brother Bodan)*; Neil Rutherford *(Brother Peter)*; Sandra Huggett *(Brother Bodan's Wife)*; Frederique Feder *(Peter's Wife)*; Ellis Fernandez *(Amy's Son—Stefan)*

Joseph Conrad's short story "Amy Foster," about the love of two outsiders in a harsh British town in the late 19th century, is here adapted as an exercise in masochism by scripter Tim Willocks and director Beeban Kidron.

On route to America from his home in the Carpathian mountains, Yanko Gooral (Vincent Perez) is the only survivor of a shipwreck off the coast of Cornwall. He makes his way to the house of farmer Smith (Tony Haygarth), who, as intolerant of the unknown as are all of his neighbors, beats the Russian-speaking Yanko senseless and locks him in his woodshed. His wounds are tended by Amy Foster (Rachel Weisz), the Smiths' servant girl. Smith gives Yanko to his neighbor Swaffer (Joss Ackland), who keeps him in virtual slavery as an unpaid laborer. It isn't until Dr. Kennedy (Ian McKellen) discovers Yanko's ability to play chess that anyone realizes his unrecognizable sounds are a language. Kennedy teaches him English, and helps improve his situation with Swaffer.

Yanko draws closer to Amy, who was conceived out of wedlock and consigned to the Smiths by her shamed parents. Despite the hatred of the local villagers, Amy and Yanko marry. They are given a small house and a little land by Swaffer and his crippled daughter (Kathy Bates), and Amy soon has a child. Yanko and the baby both contract pneumonia, and her husband's delirium leads Amy to fear he will injure the baby if she leaves it with him while she goes for medicine. When her parents refuse her request for help, she is forced to walk miles in a storm to take the baby to the Swaffers' house before setting out for the doctor. She and Dr. Kennedy return just in time to hear Yanko's dying words.

Apparently conceived with an eye on the box-office successes of THE ENGLISH PATIENT and BREAKING THE WAVES (both 1996), SWEPT FROM THE SEA captures all of the melodramatic excesses of those films but none of the mitigating humanity. The characters are abused less by the elements and their neighbors as they are by the filmmakers, who torture them for the purpose of provoking a reaction from audiences. The insane hatred with which the villagers react to Amy and Yanko is unexplained and inexplicable, more so given that Kidron chose to cast them with a pair of actors who look more like fashion models than country workers. Apparently afraid that the story and actors might be insufficient to reduce viewers to tears, Kidron keeps turning up the volume with hurricane-like storms, gorgeous photography of the English countryside (Dick Pope's cinematography is by far the best thing about the film), and a deafening score by John Barry, a composer who has never been able to leave well enough alone. Even viewers who enjoy a good cry at a movie (and who doesn't?) will simply feel abused by this. *(Sexual situations, adult situations.)*—M.F.

d, Beeban Kidron; p, Polly Tapson, Charles Steel, Beeban Kidron; exec p, Garth Thomas, Tim Willocks; assoc p, Devon Dickson; w, Tim Willocks (based on the short story "Amy Foster" by Joseph Conrad); ph, Dick Pope; ed, Alex Mackie, Andrew Mondshein; m, John Barry; prod d, Simon Holland; art d, Clinton Cavers; set d, Neesh Ruben; sound, George Richards (recordist); fx, Stuart Brisdon; casting, Gail Stevens, Andy Prior; cos, Caroline Harris; makeup, Amanda Knight; stunts, Tom Lucy, Terry Forrestal

Historical/Romance/Drama (PR: C MPAA: PG-13)

SWINDLE, THE ★★★
(France/Switzerland, 1997) 105m MK2 Productions; TF1 Films Production; CAB Productions; Television Suisse Romande; Teleclub; Rhone-Alps Cinema ~ New Yorker Films c
(RIEN NE VA PLUS)

Isabelle Huppert *(Betty)*; Michel Serrault *(Victor)*; Francois Cluzet *(Maurice)*; Jean-Francois Balmer *(Monsieur K)*; Jackie Berroyer *(Chatillon)*; Jean Benguigui *(Guadeloupe Gangster)*; Mony Dalmes *(Signora Trotti)*; Thomas Chabrol *(Swiss Desk Clerk)*; Greg Germain *(Chatty Man)*; Nathalie Kousnetzoff *(Blond Woman)*; Pierre Martot; Eric Bonicatto; Pierre-Francois Dumeniaud; Philippe Dana *(Conventioneers)*; Yves Verhoeven *(Pickpocket)*; Henri Attal *(Greek Vendor)*; Gunther Germain *(Chatty Man's Friend)*; Maurice Debranche *(Guadaloupe Taxi Driver)*; Stefan Witschi *(Swiss Maitre d')*; Rodolphe Ittig *(Belgian Dentist)*; Dodo Deer *(Hungarian Dentist)*; Barbara-Magdalena Ahren *(Wife of Hungarian Dentist)*; Alexander Seibt *(Chair-Lift Worker)*; James Hauduroy *(Barman at Hotel Waldhaus)*; Elie Axas *(Flight Attendant)*; Emmanuel Guttierez *(Barman at the Park Hotel)*; Gilbert Laumord *(Tall Black Man)*; Yvon Crenn *(Mafioso)*; Marie Dubois *(Dedette)*; Brygida Ochaim *(Dancer)*

In his 50th feature film, New Wave veteran Claude Chabrol brings a touch of pre-New Wave classiness to a sleek comedy of intrigue about a pair of con artists who stumble onto the biggest score of their careers. Characterized by Chabrol as "light entertainment," THE SWINDLE won Michel Serrault the 1997 Lumieres de Paris award for Best Actor.

Victor (Michel Serrault) is an aging confidence man who plies his trade in collaboration with his much younger disciple, Betty (Isabelle Huppert), who may or may not be his lover. Together they make a comfortable living and avoid their comeuppance by keeping their goals modest and their greed in check.

In the Swiss mountain resort of Sils-Maria, Victor discovers that Betty has become involved with Maurice (Francois Cluzet), a young executive who is transporting $5,000,000 in Swiss francs. Betty tells Victor that she believes Maurice is planning to steal the money from his firm. Betty and Maurice fly to Geneva with an attache case containing the cash. Also on the plane, unknown to Maurice, is Victor, with an identical case filled with blank paper. Betty pulls a switch and sticks Maurice with the fake cash.

Now in Guadaloupe with their haul, Victor and Betty are visited by two thugs who take them to Maurice's boss, a gangster known as Monsieur K (Jean-Francois Balmer). After K shows them Maurice's corpse and breaks Victor's finger, Betty divulges the combination of the attache case. Although the case is missing over a third of the $5,000,000, K lets Victor and Betty go free.

When Victor disappears that night, Betty feels betrayed. A good deal of time passes before he summons her to his chateau in the mountains, where he admits that he has the cash that was missing from the attache case. The angry Betty drives off but immediately has a change of heart and returns to Victor. The two partners in crime embrace.

Chabrol maintained that "of all the characters in all my films, Victor is the one that most closely resembles me." He also confessed to deliberately obscuring Victor and Betty's exact relationship so that individual viewers could determine it for themselves. Quite aware that THE SWINDLE was his 50th feature, the director admitted to inserting "plenty of little details and vague references to past films for the loyal few who want to have a good laugh finding them."

Although a leading figure of the French New Wave, Chabrol said, in a famous statement, that in the cinema there are no waves, there is only ocean. So it should not be too surprising that THE SWINDLE resembles and evokes many glossy Hollywood movies of the 1950s, as well as the slick Universal films produced by Ross Hunter (PILLOW TALK, MIDNIGHT LACE, etc.). Dry, droll, discreet, THE SWINDLE is as attentive to fashionable clothes, scenic vistas, and fine dining as it is to the lightweight tale it is telling so adroitly. Indeed it is impossible to imagine a 1990s film in which a convention of dentists would hire, instead of a stripper, a Martha Graham-type dancer draped from head to toe in yards of billowing white fabric.

THE SWINDLE's most compelling sequence is the amusingly sinister M. K's third degree of Victor and Betty in Guadaloupe. If the film as a whole, good as it is, lacks the degree of sparkle it ought to have, it's because Isabelle Huppert's forte is not vivaciousness. *(Violence, profanity.)*—D.T.

d, Claude Chabrol; p, Marin Karmitz; assoc p, Jean-Louis Porchet, Gerard Ruey; w, Claude Chabrol; ph, Eduardo Serra; ed, Monique Fardoulis; m, Mathieu Charbol; prod d, Francoise Benoit-Fresco; sound, Jean-Bernard Thomasson, Claude Villand; cos, Corinne Jorry

Crime/Comedy **(PR: C MPAA: NR)**

T

TALES FROM A PARALLEL UNIVERSE: EATING PATTERN ★½

(Canada/Germany, 1997) 93m Salter Street Films; Telefilm Canada; TiMe Film und TV Produktions ~ Showtime c

Brian Downey *(Stanley Tweedle)*; Eva Habermann *(Zev)*; Michael McManus *(Kai)*; Rutger Hauer *(Bog)*; Jerry Hirschfield *(790/Freeman)*; Doreen Jacobi *(Wist)*; Gerry Wolff *(Snik)*; Holger Kunkel *(Boork)*; Hans Dieter Bruckner *(Grullek)*; Jerry Hirschfield *(Freeman)*; Clancy King *(Coozunk)*

Unlike its impenetrable predecessors in the four-part TALES FROM A PARALLEL UNIVERSE series (renamed from the original title LEXX for airings on US cable TV), EATING PATTERN has a relatively comprehensible plot. But clarity isn't everything. The creative team's imagination went entirely into computer-generated production design and special effects, leaving a detritus of sketchy characters and wobbly plot construction in its wake. The PARALLEL UNIVERSE series initially aired on European TV under the title "Lexx" and retitled for US cable airings; this entry in the series was released on home video in 1998.

Space boob Stanley Tweedle (Brian Downey) and space babe Zev (Eva Habermann) pilot their super ship, the *Lexx*, through the cosmos' Dark Zone. When their vessel runs out of the fuel that it needs to manufacture food, they land on a deserted garbage dump of a planet. Here, they bury the apparently lifeless corpse of their comrade Kai (Michael McManus).

Unfortunately, the famished travelers have landed on a cannibal planet. While scrounging for food, Zev is kidnapped, and Stanley falls victim to local seductress Wist (Doreen Jacobi), who inserts a mind-controlling parasitic worm into Stanley's mouth by kissing him. As worms feast on the interred Kai, their bodily secretions reanimate him. Zev discovers that the planet's residents are addicted to "Pattern," a pleasurable drug synthesized from human beings that have been tossed into a meat grinder. Cannibal king Bog (Rutger Hauer) schedules Zev for the Pattern machine. The resurrected Kai searches the planet for his spacemates and resists the charms of Wist, who is the manifestation of a larger Worm Queen. After the local cannibals feast on the last batch of Pattern, they rest near a large hole from which the parasitic worms extract the Pattern and feed it to the Worm Queen (a transaction which results in the death of the Pattern addicts). Kai saves Zev from the Pattern mill, but cannot free worm-hosting Stanley unless he destroys the mega-Worm Queen. As Kai, Zev, and Stanley take off, the shape-shifting Worm Queen attaches itself to the *Lexx* and begins incorporating it into her own bodily structure. Fortunately, a storm of asteroids shakes loose the Worm Queen and obliterates it. With the Worm Queen dead, Stanley's worm is destroyed.

Is EATING PATTERN the best film you'll ever see about a gigantic alien, cannibal annelid? Probably, but that's worm-like praise, indeed. As a visual exercise in grotesquerie, EATING PATTERN deserves kudos for its ability to rise to ever more disgusting displays of grossness. Although the film functions on the level of the Garbage Pail Kids trading cards, it's much too sadistic and sexual for youngsters. At the same time, adult sci-fi fans will be put off by the filmmakers' witlessness, the cast's total lack of charm, and the screenplay's epidemic of happenstance. Recommended for inveterate space junkies, EATING PATTERN resembles something Beavis and Butthead might concoct after being forced to read Arthur C. Clarke for a book report. Still, the film's outre climax does provoke a bit of awe: The sight of the Big Mama Worm merging with the enormous spacecraft is a weird spectacle bordering on the surreal. *(Graphic violence, sexual situations, profanity, substance abuse.)* —R.P.

d, Rainer Matsutani; exec p, Paul Donovan, Wolfram Tichy; co-p, Bill Fleming; w, Lex Gigeroff, Jerry Hirschfield, Paul Donovan; ph, Les Krizsan; ed, Kimberlee McTaggart; m, Marty Simon; prod d, Ingolf Hetscher, Mark Liang, Nigel Scott, Emanuel Junnasch, Frank Weimann; art d, Gerry Kunz, Tim Bider; set d, Udo Reinschi; sound, John Megill (mixer); fx, Die Hefzers; casting, Jon Comerford; cos, Jill Aslin; makeup, Holdo Hass, Ulriko Bruns; stunts, Hold Stuer

Science Fiction/Action **(PR: O MPAA: R)**

TALES FROM A PARALLEL UNIVERSE: GIGA SHADOW ★½

(Canada/Germany, 1997) 93m CHUM Television; Salter Street Productions; TiMe Film und TV Produktions ~ Showtime c

Brian Downey *(Stanley Tweedle)*; Eva Habermann *(Zev)*; Michael McManus *(Kai)*; Walter Borden *(Divine Shadow)*; Malcolm McDowell *(Yottskry)*; Jerry Hirschfield *(790)*; Andy Jones *(Emoor)*; Michael Habeck *(Feppo)*; Anna Cameron *(Time Prophet)*; David Renton *(Soshua)*; Robert Sigl *(Petrif)*; Jamie Bradley *(Jood)*; Jim Pettrie *(Garrett)*; Cherie Devanney *(Kyytra)*; Joel Sapp *(Bleeding Cleric)*; John Dunsworthy *(Running Man)*; Jennifer Overton *(Customs Officer)*; Shaun Clarke *(Reteep)*; David Woods *(Yoyal)*; David McClelland *(Benediction Clerk)*; Lionel Doucette *(Judge)*; Sanjay Talwar *(Honar)*

Although only a series devotee could plumb the depths of this conclusion to the wretched TALES FROM A PARALLEL UNIVERSE series (renamed from the original title LEXX for US cable airings), the uninitiated will recognize this galactic misfire as a true clinker. Whereas the previous entry in the series, EATING PATTERN, at least offered the novelty value of a weird cannibal plot line, this unimaginative conclusion merely replays events from the first three films out of sequence and rehashes old story elements.

Aboard the super spaceship *Lexx*, cosmic coward Stanley Tweedle (Brian Downey) refuses the request of Zev (Eva Habermann) to return to their homebase in the Fractile Core in order to obtain proto-blood to save the life of their failing comrade Kai (Michael McManus). As Kai languishes, a rebirth of the dastardly divinity known as Divine Shadow (Walter Borden) unfolds. Attended to by clerics, the dormant brain of this despotic god is ready to resume human form and begin a new reign as an agent for the mysterious Giga Shadow. Heretics led by Yottskry (Malcolm McDowell) squelch the resurrection of the Divine Shadow, the resident deity in the Fractile Core. The heretics fail to totally destroy his brain, however. Meanwhile, space mercenaries Emoor (Andy Jones) and Feppo (Michael Habeck) plot to wrest control of the *Lexx* from their old nemesis Stanley.

Finally persuading Stanley to pilot them to their former homeland, Zev and Kai land there with new-found pet Squish, a brain-digesting, baby cluster lizard. Meanwhile, Feppo and Emoor lure Stanley aboard their ship from the *Lexx* where Stanley had remained. As Zev and Kai search for the proto-blood source, the Divine Shadow infiltrates the body of rebel Yottskry and travels toward the Giga Shadow (which turns out to be a mega-insect bent on universal domination). Kai orders Squish to locate and feed on the Divine Shadow's brain before it can completely merge with the Giga Shadow. Summoning his super vessel, Stanley orders the *Lexx* to swallow up and deposit them on a desolate planet, while Stanley is safely sucked back aboard the *Lexx*. After Squish fatally munches the Divine Shadow's brain, Zev nurses Kai back to health after discovering a supply of proto-blood.

It is not the far-fetched plot that destroys the credibility of GIGA SHADOW, but the screenwriters' lazy execution of their own space jam. For no discernible reason, the story's time layout is juggled until you cannot tell a flashback from a flash-forward. Scenes from previous PARALLEL UNIVERSE films entries pad out the running time of an exceedingly misshapen screenplay. Despite all the expository juxtapositions, the film is your basic yarn about a well-preserved brain plugging into a colossal insect planning to overrun the universe with a race of brainy bug-beings. The film's high point features a singing choir of pickled brains chanting the limmericked praises of Stanley Tweedle in bawdy fashion. Aside from that low humor and Eva Habermann's spectacular physical allure, GIGA SHADOW is a brainless cosmic shuffle. *(Graphic violence, profanity.)*—R.P.

d, Robert Sigl; p, Wolfram Tichy, Paul Donovan; co-p, Bill Fleming; w, Paul Donovan, Lex Gigeroff, Jerry Hirschfield; ph, Les Krizsan; ed, Bruce Lange; m, Marty Simon; prod d, Ingolf Hetscher, Mark Laing, Nigel Scott, Emmanuel Junnasch, Frank Weimann; art d, Tim Bider; set d, Patricia Larman; sound, John Megill (mixer); fx, Cordell Wynne (visual), A. Scott Hamilton (makeup); casting, Jon Comerford; cos, Jill Aslin; makeup, Babette Broseke

Science Fiction **(PR: C MPAA: R)**

TALES FROM A PARALLEL UNIVERSE: SUPER NOVA ★½

(Canada/Germany/U.S., 1998) 93m Salter Street Films; TiME Film und TV Producktions ~ Showtime c

Brian Downey *(Stanley Tweedle)*; Eva Habermann *(Zev)*; Michael McManus *(Kai)*; Tim Curry *(Poet Man)*; Ellen Dubin *(Giggerota)*; Jerry Hirschfield *(790)*; Kate Rose *(Hold Woman)*; Rachel Grover *(Zev's Mother)*; Shaun Clark *(Zev's Father)*; Jennifer Overton *(Matron)*; Rainer Matsutani *(Brunnen-G General)*; Anna Cameron *(Time Prophet)*

This second segment of the four-part German-Canadian sci-fi series LEXX (retitled TALES FROM A PARALLEL UNIVERSE for US airings on The Movie Channel) is a cinematic black hole about a dying planet in which plot issues are raised and then left unresolved. Despite an introduction summing up the events of the first installment, I WORSHIP HIS SHADOW (1997), this is all but incomprehensible.

The intergalactic adventures of the crew of the *Lexx* continue as Captain Stanley Tweedle (Brian Downey) pilots his cohorts away from danger. Because Kai (Michael McManus), the last of the "Brunnen G." warriors, is wasting away due to a proto-blood deficiency, galactic gladiator Zev (Eva Habermann) inveigles Tweedle to head for Kai's homeland. As griping Tweedle pilots the *Lexx* toward the planet Brunnis, he's unaware that itinerant cannibal gal Giggerota (Ellen Dubin) has stowed away for the purpose of hijacking his super-space vessel.

On deserted Brunnis, Kai and Zev discover a memory-storage facility presided over by Poet Man (Tim Curry), a vengeful hologram. Back aboard the *Lexx*, the stored brains of the high priests of the Shadow religion promise Giggerota unlimited human goodies if she thwarts the recovery of their enemy, Kai. When Tweedle doesn't cooperate with Giggerota, she rips off his hand, which is imprinted with a code for navigating the *Lexx*.

Meanwhile, Zev and Kai are tricked into captivity by Poet Man, who plans to slice them up and store their souls on discs. An enemy of human life, Poet Man initiates a countdown for a super nova explosion and attempts to download himself elsewhere. Subsequently, wounded Tweedle flies his auxiliary vessel to Brunnis; after landing on the planet, Tweedle rescues Zev, and Kai is restored to life by the healing power of a blue star. The Shadow priests' brains dupe Giggerota into traveling to Brunnis, which explodes (along with Poet Man) right after Tweedle, Zev, and Kai return to the *Lexx*. Aboard the *Lexx*, Tweedle's hand is restored by the *Lexx's* talking android head, 790 (Jerry Hirschfield).

This chowder-head adventure is precipitated by a quest to preserve Kai's life; yet, at the film's conclusion, slowly dying Kai pops back into his cryogenic tube with no new medical hope. Aside from developing a romance between Kai and Zev, this dismally acted flick accomplishes nothing; if viewers haven't seen other series entries, SUPER NOVA registers as fairly confusing. As bad as they are, the three stars can't match the hamminess of guest villain Tim Curry, whose scenes as a holographic menace appear to have been filmed in a single day on a soundstage nowhere near the rest of the production. At least one scene, in which lovestruck Kai and Zev break into an Andrew Lloyd Webber-style ballad, reaches a level of inspired camp silliness; perhaps the only way to save the TALES FROM A PARALLEL UNIVERSE series would have been to rework it as a full-scale space operetta. *(Graphic violence, profanity, adult situations.)*—R.P.

d, Ron Oliver; p, Paul Donovan, Wolfram Tichy; exec p, Paul Donovan, Wolfram Tichy; co-p, Bill Fleming; w, Paul Donovan, Lex Gigeroff, Jerry Hirschfield; ph, Les Krizsan; ed, David Ostry; m, Marty Simon; prod d, Tim Bider, Ingolf Hetscher, Alexander Knop, Nigel Scott, Frank Wiemann; set d, Patricia Lamman; sound, John McGill (mixer); fx, Bob Munroe; casting, Jon Comerford; cos, Jill Aslin; makeup, Heidi Hass, A. Scott Hamilton

Science Fiction **(PR: C MPAA: R)**

TALISMAN ★

(U.S., 1998) 73m Full Moon Pictures ~ Full Moon c

Billy Parish *(Elias Storm)*; Walter Jones *(Jacob)*; Jason Adelman *(Burke)*; Ilinca Goia *(Elizabeth)*; Costi Barbulescu *(Black Angel)*; Oana Stefanescu *(Mrs. Greynitz)*; Claudiu Trandafir *(Dr. Jarod)*; Mircea Caraman *(John)*; Iuliana Ciuguilea *(Sharon)*; George Duta *(Young Elias)*; Livia Constantin *(Young Elizabeth)*; Dana Saviuca *(Woman)*; Sandu Teodor *(Grimes)*; Adrian Leu *(Colby)*; Vlad Dulea *(Willis)*; Flavia Fitoi *(Girl)*; Paul Grigoriu *(Sanders)*

Though several of the characters in TALISMAN are the victims of ritualized sacrifice, the only thing that's truly sacrificed in this by-the-numbers horror outing is the element of surprise. It's all been done before elsewhere—and to a finer turn.

Teenaged Elias (Billy Parish) arrives at the Gornek International School for Boys, where overbearing administrator Mrs. Greynitz (Oana Stefanescu) warns against fraternizing with her daughter Elizabeth (Ilinca Goia). Elias has been plagued by nightmares about his parents, who died after conjuring up a black angel (Costi Barbulescu)—who is now stalking the school, pulling out the boys' hearts. Dr. Jarod (Claudiu Trandafir) tells Elias that a talisman he has seen in his dreams is the key to a ritual involving seven sacrificial victims that will plunge the world into eternal darkness. Elias later finds out that Elizabeth is only Mrs. Greynitz's adopted daughter.

The black angel kills two more boys, and Elias sees Mrs. Greynitz and Elizabeth in the room from whence their screams came. He reveals to Dr. Jarod that he was led to the school by a letter from his sister, whom he previously thought dead. Mrs.

Greynitz kills Dr. Jarod, and Elias finds himself on an altar with Elizabeth standing over him. She is in fact his sister, possessed by evil forces. The black angel kills Mrs. Greynitz; Elizabeth tries to convince Elias to join her in completing the ritual, but he kills her instead.

Utilizing a plot similar to another production from the Full Moon company, SHRIEKER (1998)—and quite similar to the previously produced DEAD WATERS (also 1998)—TALISMAN whisks us off to a school so exclusive that it only has seven students, yet more than half of them vanish before anyone notices that something's amiss. The film then attempts to involve us in a mystery whose answers are transparently obvious from the get-go (who could Elias's grown-up sister be? Could she be the only teenaged girl in the entire place?) and to scare us with a demonic fiend who resembles THE ADDAMS FAMILY's Uncle Fester after a three-day drunk. As are many Full Moon productions, the film was shot on location in Romania, but even the picturesque locations can't add life to the proceedings.

Director Victoria Sloan (a.k.a. David DeCoteau) seems more concerned with showing off his young actors in their underwear than bringing any variety to his staging of their deaths: Each time, the black angel plunges his hand into the victim's chest, and the boy screams as blood sprays all over him from various directions (yet there's none on either the victim or the killer in the reverse shots). The lack of a music credit indicates that the score was patched together out of bits and pieces from other Full Moon movies—an approach entirely in keeping with the rest of TALISMAN. *(Graphic violence, profanity.)*—M.G.

d, David DeCoteau, billed as Victoria Sloan; p, Vlad Paunescu; exec p, Charles Band; co-p, Kirk Edward Hansen; w, Benjamin Carr; ph, Viorel Sergovici Jr.; ed, Poppy Das; prod d, Cristian Niculescu; art d, Viorel Ghenea, Serban Porupea; sound, Tibi Borcoman; fx, David A. Wagner, Lucian Iordache; casting, Robert MacDonald, Perry Bullington; cos, Mihaela David; makeup, Mark Williams, Dana Busoiu, Letita Stoenciu

Horror **(PR: O MPAA: R)**

TALK OF ANGELS ★★

(U.S., 1998) 97m Miramax ~ Miramax c
(FALANDO DE ANJOS)

Polly Walker *(Mary Lavelle)*; Vincent Perez *(Francisco Areavaga)*; Franco Nero *(Dr. Vicente Areavaga)*; Frances McDormand *(Conlon)*; Ruth McCabe *(O'Toole)*; Francisco Rabal *(Don Jorge)*; Marisa Paredes *(Dona Consuelo)*; Penelope Cruz *(Pilar)*; Ariadna Gil *(Beatriz)*; Rossy de Palma *(Elena)*; Britta Smith *(Duggan)*; Anita Reeves *(Harty)*; Veronica Duffy *(Keogh)*; Leire Berrocal *(Milagros)*; Jorge de Juan *(Jaime)*; Ellea Ratier *(Leonor)*

TALK OF ANGELS is an earth-bound bore, a vapid romance set against a Spanish Civil War backdrop.

In mid-1930s Spain, as conflict reigns between the Loyalists and Franco's Rightists, a pretty young Irish woman, Mary (Polly Walker), arrives in the north of the country to work as a governess in the wealthy Areavaga household. Mary bonds instantly with her two teenage wards and the patriarch, Dr. Vicente (Franco Nero), a Loyalist supporter. She is treated coldly, however, by the lady of the house, Dona Consuelo (Marisa Paredes), a champion of the Right. Mary sees the same split in political philosophy between the Areavaga's visiting son, Francisco (Vincent Perez), a Loyalist like his father, and Beatriz (Ariadna Gil), Francisco's conservative bride.

Drawn to Francisco, Mary helps the handsome young man hide an injured Loyalist in the Areavaga stable. Rumors begin about Francisco and Mary after they dance together in the town square, an act that scandalizes both Mary's Irish compatriots and many of the townspeople. Only the governesses, Conlon (Frances McDormand) and O'Toole (Ruth McCabe), overlook the incident with humor. Sometime later, Conlon admits she has a "crush" on Mary, which remains an unrequited love.

When the newspapers expose him for consorting with Anarchists, Francisco prepares for a trip with Beatriz back to their home in Madrid. Blind to the budding romance, the family encourages Mary and the children to also go to Madrid. During her stay in the city, Mary and Francisco enjoy some private time together, finally kissing on a mountaintop.

The family returns together to Northern Spain, where the priest, Don Jorge (Francisco Rabal) puts pressure on Vicente and Francisco by threatening to expose their political sympathies. Not wanting to destroy Francisco's marriage or add to his troubles, Mary plans to leave Spain, and writes a goodbye postcard to her love. But the postcard gets lost, imperiling them both. Just before leaving, Francisco and Mary meet one last time, and consummate their romance with an afternoon of love-making. Soon after, the Rightists kill Vicente, and Mary joins the funeral procession before saying her last goodbye to her friends and the Areavagas. While boarding a train to the boat back to Ireland, Mary is greeted by the family's gardener, who returns the incriminating postcard to her.

Few films have taken on the topic of the Spanish Civil War, so it's all the more disappointing that TALK OF ANGELS is so uninformed about its subject matter. As with most old Hollywood war movies, TALK OF ANGELS uses war as an excuse to bring together its romantic leads for passionate excitement, then separate them for heartbreaking drama. Based on Kate O'Brien's novel, *Mary Lavelle*, TALK OF ANGELS at least get the politics correct (bad Rightists, good Loyalists), but even the glossy classic FOR WHOM THE BELL TOLLS (1943) integrated the particulars of this bloody conflict better into the romance between the US mercenary (Gary Cooper) and the Loyalist peasant (Ingrid Bergman). By contemporary standards, Ken Loach's LAND AND FREEDOM (1995) has it all over TALK OF ANGELS by eschewing the romantic element.

The real surprise is that even as a bodice-ripper, TALK OF ANGELS is all talk and no action. The leads are pretty, but they fail to generate much heat, only kissing chastely three-quarters of the way into the story. And their climactic love-making scene exists mostly off-screen. Much more interest surrounds the supporting characters (e.g., the Queen Bee Dona Consuelo and the closet lesbian Conlon), but they are given so little screen time, they almost emerge as "Saturday Night Live"-style caricatures. The actors try their best, though some awkward dubbing and the dull look of the film makes their jobs even harder. Ruth McCabe steals the show, however, with the liveliest, most convincing portrait, playing a governess past her prime.

Finally, TALK OF ANGELS owes the most to old romance fiction like Marcia Davenport's *The Valley of Decision* and the recent spate of films about governesses falling for their employers (e.g., another 1998 release THE GOVERNESS). But, politics aside, the film misses the boat even in the area of eroticism. *(Violence, nudity, sexual situations, adult situations, profanity.)*—E.M.

d, Nick Hamm; p, Patrick Cassavetti; exec p, Harvey Weinstein, Bob Weinstein, Donna Gigliotti; w, Ann Guedes, Frank McGuinness (based on the novel *Mary Lavelle* by Kate O'Brien); ph, Alexei Rodionov; ed, Gerry Hambling; m, Trevor Jones; prod d, Michael Howells; art d, Eduardo Hidalgo; set d, Totty Whately; sound, Peter Glossop (recordist); casting, Mary Selway,

Camilla-Valentine Isola; cos, Liz Waller, Lala Huete; makeup, Peter King

Romance/Drama **(PR: C MPAA: PG-13)**

TALK TO ME ★½
(U.S., 1998) 87m Pug Films ~ Northern Arts Entertainment c

Cheryl Clifford *(Betty)*; Peter Welch *(Arnold)*; Elizabeth Landis *(Ronnie Goldstein)*; Gary Navicoff *(Michael Dowling)*; Rick Poli *(Jerry)*; Judith Boxley *(Dolores)*; Ralph Romeo *(Frederick)*; George Esguerra *(The Editor)*; Heather Quick *(Zina's Voice)*; Jeff Montaigne *(Moderator's Voice)*; Thomas Blake *(Stuart Sherwood)*; Christy Tully *(Stuart's Fiancee)*; Burt Wright *(Arnold's Pa)*; Ruth Ray *(Arnold's Ma)*; Deborah Lanino *(Receptionist)*; George Esguerra Sr. *(Maitre d')*; Michael Roderick *(Guy with Dog)*

An independent film by first-time director George Esguerra, TALK TO ME is a flat comedy about a pair of lonely New Yorkers whose romance begins on an adult chat line.

Frustrated at being unable to find a boyfriend, the thirtyish Betty (Cheryl Clifford) dials an adult party line and hits it off with Arnold (Peter Welch). As they talk, the usually reserved Arnold reveals a little about himself, but Betty, wary of identifying herself, gives a false name. Their conversation becomes intimate and leads to phone sex, but Betty hangs up before the two can make arrangements to talk again.

In the days that follow, each tries to contact the other. Using the information he had given her, Betty locates Arnold and mails him her phone number. He calls, and among other things, they discuss previous failed romances. Arnold tells of a particularly devastating experience, a relationship ruined because of the woman's dishonesty. Betty and Arnold begin to call each other constantly, but as they become closer, Betty's anxiety grows, since she continues to misidentify herself.

They arrange a date which doesn't go well, but Betty remains determined to win Arnold over. She quits smoking (a habit that Arnold finds offensive), and makes a surprise visit to Arnold's apartment, where she helps him realize a sexual fantasy. The next day, however, Arnold accidentally learns Betty's real name, and feeling deceived, breaks off their relationship. Betty pursues and tries to reconcile with him, but he resists. One night, Betty is called by the monitor of the party line, who tells her that a distraught friend of hers is trying to reach her. The friend, Ronnie (Elizabeth Landis), rages over the line about her loneliness. Fearing that Ronnie is suicidal, Betty races to her apartment, but finds that Ronnie has only destroyed her phone. Betty returns home to find Arnold, who had been listening on the party line, waiting in front of her building. They reconcile, and walk hand in hand into Betty's building.

TALK TO ME struggles mightily to be a hip romantic farce. George Esguerra's debut feature is loaded with all the requisite details: single professionals, cel phones, 1-900 telephone services, red wine, and nicely decorated New York apartments. And the script (cowritten by Esquerra and Robert Foulkes) is filled with attempts at snappy dialogue and cynical one-liners. TALK TO ME, however, never rises above the level of a situation comedy, despite its fashionable content. It plays at being candid and provocative—especially in its inclusion of graphic sex scenes—but at heart it's really conventional and contrived. The two principal characters are well-defined and generally believable, and the actors who play them are earnest and likable. Clifford is especially good, making Betty's desperate effort to bring romance into her life funny but never ridiculous. All the other characters in the film, however, are completely one-dimensional, serving either as sounding boards for the leads or as targets for sophomoric jokes about loneliness and sexual need. Esquerra's lack of attention to the secondary characters is indicative of the film's overall creative shortcomings.

While TALK TO ME is not badly made, it's undistinguished as filmmaking. Esquerra's formulaic structure never wavers from a routine cause-and-effect narrative which, though serviceable, renders the film dull and predictable. As the film wears on, even the cat-and-mouse game between Betty and Arnold becomes a bore. Esquerra and Foulkes have hit upon a timely and interesting topic, namely, the difficulty of commitment in modern times. It's a shame that the simplistic approach they take to their material prevents them from giving it anything more than superficial consideration. *(Extensive nudity, sexual situations, extreme profanity.)*—D.C.

d, George Esguerra; p, George Esguerra; assoc p, Deborah Lanino, Robert Foulkes; w, George Esguerra, Robert Foulkes; ph, Randy Drummond; ed, Tom McArdle; m, David McLary; prod d, Jori Adam; art d, Dixie Thomas, Deborah Lanino; set d, Susan Loughlin; sound, Peter Schneiden (recordist), Boaz Atzmon (mixer); makeup, Debra Edelman

Romance/Comedy **(PR: O MPAA: NR)**

TA'M E GUILASS
(SEE: TASTE OF CHERRY)

TARANTELLA ★★
(U.S., 1998) 84m Tarantella Productions ~ BWE c

Mira Sorvino *(Diana Di Sorella)*; Rose Gregorio *(Pina De Nora)*; Matthew Lillard *(Matt)*; Frank Pellegrino *(Lou)*; Stephen Spinella *(Frank)*; Antonia Rey *(Grandmother)*; James Georgiades *(Bartender)*; Melissa Maxwell *(Young Diana)*; Maryann Urbano *(Mother)*; Magda Lang; Sean Baldwin *(Home Buying Couple)*; Derek Contreras *(Home Buying Young Man)*; A.J. Lopez *(Home Buying Young Man)*; Gaetano Lisco *(Father)*; Carol Dante *(Tarantella Dancer)*

Filmed in the fall of 1994, TARANTELLA—named for an Italian folk dance believed to drive away poison—quietly disappeared after scattered festival showings in 1995. But within weeks of the announcement of star Mira Sorvino's Academy Award nomination for MIGHTY APHRODITE in 1996 (she subsequently won the award), the film was dusted off for a limited run in movie theaters. It's a testament to Sorvino's continuing appeal and the rising star status of Matthew Lillard (1996's SCREAM) that this unremarkable story of self-discovery and ethnic identity managed to find a home video distributor in 1998.

Diana Di Sorella (Mira Sorvino) is a professional photographer who has distanced herself from her family and her Italian-American heritage. She returns to her old neighborhood after her widowed mother dies suddenly. Confronted with the sights and sounds and smells of her childhood, Diana finds that the task of selling her mother's house and disposing of its contents isn't as cut and dried as she had presumed.

Armed with gnocchi, her mother's best friend Pina (Rose Gregorio) imposes herself on Diana's life. Though the two women clash at first, they develop a close friendship over the succeeding weeks, as Pina tries to help Diana understand and appreciate her heritage. Pina translates for Diana her mother's *libro di casa*—a scrapbook of family mementos and history. The book reveals a long-buried secret: Diana's grandmother poisoned her abusive husband back in Italy before emigrating to the US. Diana believes the secret explains the silent reserve her mother and grandmother maintained throughout their lives. As

Diana comes to embrace her "Italian-ness," the transformation goes deeper than just learning how to cook tomato sauce. Diana's boyfriend Matt (Matthew Lillard) comes for a visit and tries to persuade her to go back home with him. But Diana's journey isn't over: She stays to finish learning her mother's story, and to help Pina, who is terminally ill, end her own life with an overdose of pills.

Other than as a curio of Sorvino and Lillard's pre-stardom careers, TARANTELLA offers little to recommend it. In their first feature film, director Helen De Michiel and screenwriter Richard Hoblock clearly lucked out in the casting department. TARANTELLA isn't an embarrassment—it just isn't very good. Sorvino is likable in an undemanding role. (If this is the worst of her early acting efforts to be unearthed and exploited, she can be counted among the lucky ones.) Lillard displays a goofy charm in a more-restrained precursor of roles to come (SCREAM, SENSELESS, SHE'S ALL THAT). Gregorio—familiar from the films of her husband, director Ulu Grosbard—is believable as the meddling mentor.

The film's only unique convention is the use of puppetry to illustrate the grandmother's story: these vignettes are well-executed and visually striking, but they stand in jarring contrast to the naturalistic style of the narrative and the surrealism of Diana's childhood memories. This hodge-podge of visual styles, coupled with a slow moving script, subvert what emotional resonance the story contains. *(Sexual situations.)*—B.R.

d, Helen De Michiel; p, George La Voo; assoc p, Laura Gabbert; co-p, James Calabrese; w, Helen De Michiel, Richard Hoblock; ph, Teodoro Maniaci; ed, Richard Gordon; m, Norman Noll; prod d, Diane Lederman; art d, Tina Khayat; set d, Ondine Karady, Orna Yaary; sound, Daniel Baldwin; casting, Adrienne Punter Stern, Ellen Parks; cos, Suzanne Schwarzer

Drama **(PR: C MPAA: NR)**

TARZAN AND THE LOST CITY ★

(Australia/U.S., 1998) 83m Village Roadshow Pictures ~ Warner Bros. c

Casper Van Dien *(Tarzan/John Clayton)*; Jane March *(Jane Porter)*; Steven Waddington *(Nigel Ravens)*; Winston Ntshona *(Mugambi)*; Rapulana Seiphemo *(Kaya)*; Ian Roberts *(Captain Dooley)*; Sean Taylor *(Wilkes)*; Gys De Villiers *(Schiller)*; Russel Savadier *(Archer)*; Paul Buckby *(Jerjynski)*; Zane Meas *(Knowles)*; Barry Berk *(Burke)*; Michael Gritten *(Devlin)*; Dimitri Cassar *(Klemmer)*; Tony Caprari *(Ritter)*; Kurt Wurstman *(Sykes)*; Chris Olley *(Ackerman)*; Joshua Lindberg *(Edwards)*; Henry van der Berg *(Lucas)*; Pete Janschk *(Laconte)*; Danie van Reinsberg *(Devoors)*; Aubrey Lovett *(Brooks)*; Paolo Tocha *(Fitt)*; Nickie Grigg *(Stonehouse)*; Neville Strydom *(Dodd)*; Dieter Hoffman *(Lutz)*; Pierre van Rensburg *(Dorr)*; Bismulah Mdaka *(Jeremiah)*; Sello Sebotiane *(Dube)*; Sello Dlamini *(Scout)*; Chester Fukazi *(Waiter)*; Grant Swanby *(Douglas)*; Adam Crousdale *(Lewis)*; Nick Rujewick *(Andrew)*; Brendan Stapelton; Amy Pearson; Jeneane Wyatt-Mair; Cheryl Lang; Flash Trobajane *(Apes)*

If every generation gets the Tarzan it deserves, then this glassy-eyed Lord Greystoke suits the gloss-over-substance '90s. A loose sequel to GREYSTOKE : THE LEGEND OF TARZAN, LORD OF THE APES (1984), it is occasionally nice to look at but lacks energy and imagination.

Raised by apes in the jungles of Africa, John Clayton returned to England to claim his title as Lord Greystoke. In 1913, John (Casper Van Dien) is set to marry Jane Porter (Jane March) when he receives a telepathic distress call from his old friends the Mbiko. The tribesmen are being menaced by white adventurers led by Nigel Ravens (Steven Waddington), who seeks the "cradle of civilization," the hidden city of Opar.

John postpones his marriage to return to central Africa, reclaim his Tarzan identity and consult with Mbiko shaman Mugambi (Winston Ntshona) and warrior Kaya (Rapulana Seiphemo). Jane follows her fiance to Africa, and together they track Ravens toward Opar. Tarzan is bitten while saving Jane from a cobra. She is captured by Ravens while diverting him away from Tarzan, who is later magically healed by Mugambi.

Pursued by Kaya and his warriors, Ravens finds the gateway to Opar and blasts it open with dynamite. He ties Jane and a stick of dynamite to a rock to flush out the pursuing Tarzan. Kaya distracts Ravens so that Tarzan can free Jane. Mugambi conjures magical skeleton warriors to help Tarzan, Jane, and Kaya battle the mercenaries. Tarzan chases Ravens into the throne room of Opar's magical pyramid. After knocking out Tarzan, Ravens sits on the throne and is enveloped in light, which disintegrates him. Tarzan and Jane get married at a Mbiko wedding.

Neither as good as GREYSTOKE nor as bad as the Bo Derek vehicle, TARZAN THE APE MAN (1981), this imagination-starved adventure is at least periodically pretty when the camera focuses on the South African locales or the chiseled Van Dien and angelic March.

The script is a cliched mishmash of Edgar Rice Burroughs stories stitched together with no room for logic. (Why do the Mbiko need Tarzan when they have Mugambi and his seemingly limitless magical powers?) The finale, which shamelessly steals from RAIDERS OF THE LOST ARK (1982), is made unforgivable by a puzzling execution.

Van Dien (STARSHIP TROOPERS, 1997), who appears to have been carved out of marble, looks the part, but his acting is as stony as his rippling pecs. His body is exposed more than that of his costar, the ethereally beautiful March, whose part doesn't stretch her limited range. The film feels like an overblown TV movie; instead of a "lost city," there's one empty pyramid. From its sub-TV- quality special effects— including men in ape suits—to its desolate destination, it's rife with missed opportunities, and should have been called "Tarzan and the Lost Box Office." *(Violence.)*—J.Di.

d, Carl Schenkel; p, Stanley Canter, Dieter Geissler, Michael Lake; exec p, Greg Coote, Peter Ziegler, Kurt Silberschneider, Lawrence Mortorff; assoc p, Marina Glass; w, Bayard Johnson, J. Anderson Black (from characters created by Edgar Rice Burroughs); ph, Paul Gilpin; ed, Harry Hitner; m, Christopher Franke; prod d, Herbert Pinter; art d, Emilia Roux, Anna Lenox; sound, Nigel Olland; fx, Julian Parry; casting, Nicole Arbusto, Celestia Fox, Moonyeen Lee; cos, Jo Katsaras-Barklem; makeup, Annie Bartels; stunts, Roly Jansen

Action/Adventure **(PR: A MPAA: PG-13)**

TASTE OF CHERRY ★★½

(Iran, 1997) 98m Abbas Kiarostami Productions ~ Zeitgeist Films c
(TA'M E GUILASS)

Homayoun Ershadi *(Mr. Badii)*; Abdolhossein Bagheri *(Taxidermist)*; Afshin Khorshidbakhtair *(Worker)*; Safar Ali Moradi *(Soldier)*; Mir Hossein Noori *(Seminarian)*; Ahman Ansari *(Factory Guard)*; Hamid Massomi *(Man in Phone Booth)*; Elham Imani *(Woman in Front of Museum)*

Another small-scale fable from Iranian director Abbas Kiarostami, TASTE OF CHERRY tells the tale of a suicidal man's last days. The film is refreshingly without sentiment, but it's almost too subdued artistically (despite the grave subject matter) to stay with viewers.

A man driving a van, Mr. Badii (Homayoun Ershadi), searches a desert area outside Tehran looking for a laborer to help him with a mysterious job. None of the workers he meets are willing to get into his van until he picks up a hitchhiking soldier (Safar Ali Moradi), who is heading toward his barracks. Badii takes the soldier a long way up a hill before he finally tells him that he will pay the young man a large amount of money to come back to the area the following morning and throw earth on him in a ditch after making sure he has successfully killed himself with sleeping pills. The soldier recoils at the idea of helping Badii commit suicide and runs away. Badii drives on and picks up an Afghan seminarian (Mir Hossein Noori), who works as a laborer to make extra money. Despite his need for money, however, the seminarian objects on religious grounds to helping Badii kill himself. After some philosophical debating, Badii drops off the seminarian at a friend's house and drives off. Finally, he picks up a museum taxidermist (Abdolhossein Bagheri), who questions Badii about his reasons for killing himself and tries to convince him that the joys of nature alone (the taste of cherries) are reasons enough to continue living.

But the taxidermist neither changes Badii's mind nor finds out why he wants to commit suicide. Instead, he agrees to help him. That night, before a brewing storm, Badii prepares for his demise. At his home, he takes the sleeping pills then drives himself to the ditch on the hill, where he lies down and watches the clouds pass over the moon. The next morning, we see the actor playing Badii walking past the film crew on the hill as a group of soldiers settle around the set location.

TASTE OF CHERRY seems to tell a rather simple story with a plain moral message of carpe diem (espoused in the title and by the taxidermist character). But like his other films, including THROUGH THE OLIVE TREES (1995), writer-director-producer-editor Kiarostami adds a reflexive element and some wistful nuance. The open-ended resolution, which refuses to determine Badii's fate or even explain his actions, becomes all the more cerebral—if quizzical—by the on-location epilogue.

But as with the film-within-the-film framework of THROUGH THE OLIVE TREES, Kiarostami uses the self-reflexivity in an innocuous way that indeed creates a distancing effect to the story and characters but adds little more than another layer of playful whimsy. This breaking down of the "fourth wall" can no longer be considered an innovation in narrative film when even made-for-television dramas have incorporated the once-"radical" technique.

Likewise, TASTE OF CHERRY makes a tentative socio-political statement about modern Iran, touching on the differences of secular and religious beliefs, the influx of different cultures, the demands of the military on the youth of the nation, and the uncertainty of the country's future. But as happens with the film's finale, these issues are not addressed in a clear way. Though adeptly made, TASTE OF CHERRY is just *too* open-ended. *(Adult situations.)*—E.M.

d, Abbas Kiarostami; p, Abbas Kiarostami; w, Abbas Kiarostami; ph, Homayon Payvar; ed, Abbas Kiarostami; sound, J. Mrshekari

Drama **(PR: C MPAA: NR)**

TEKKEN: THE MOTION PICTURE ★★

(Japan, 1997) 57m Foursome Co. Ltd; Studio DEEN ~ A.D.V. Films c

ENGLISH LANGUAGE VOICE CAST: Edi Patterson *(Jun Kazuma)*; Adam Dudley *(Kazuya Mishima)*; Gray G. Haddock *(Lei Wulong)*; David Stokey *(Lee Chaolan)*; John Paul Shepard *(Heihachi Mishima)*; Ellie McBride *(Nina Williams/Operator 3)*; Claire Hamilton *(Anna Williams/Operator 2)*; Lucy Faris *(Young Jun)*; Jacob Franchek *(Young Kazuya/Jin)*; Jessica Robertson *(Michelle Chang)*; Mark O'Brien *(Jack 2)*; Jessica Schwartz *(Jack 2's Little Girl)*; David Jones *(Narrator)*; Douglas Taylor *(WWWC Chief)*; Ken Webster *(Dr. Boskonovich)*; Peter Harrell Jr. *(Bruce Iervin)*; Charles Campbell *(Thug 1)*; L.B. Bartholomee *(Thug 2/Competition Fighter)*; Gary Dehan *(Thug 3)*; Amy L. Gamber *(Operator 1)*; Rolee Rios *(Operator 4)*

Another in the long line of animated versions of Japanese video games, TEKKEN's tale of a lethal fighting contest staged by an evil tycoon boasts attractive animation and design, but fewer of the ferocious game-style fight scenes that are normally the heart of such films.

Jun Kazama (voice of Edi Patterson), an agent for the international police agency WWWC, and Hong Kong policeman Lei Wulong (voice of Gray G. Haddock) are invited to participate in the Tekken Iron Fist Tournament on an offshore island owned by defense contractor Heihachi Mishima (voice of John Paul Shepard). Their undercover assignment is to identify secret experiments in biological weaponry being performed at an underground base on the island. Also attending the tournament is Kazuya Mishima (voice of Adam Dudley), the son of Heihachi, who has vowed to kill his father for abandoning him as a child.

The island tournament begins with the participants facing off against each other in the jungle and fighting to get to a central tower where the winner is to confront Heihachi himself. Lei Wulong teams with Jack 2 (voice of Mark O'Brien), a giant robot warrior seeking his creator, Dr. Boskonovich (voice of Ken Webster), and enters the massive underground plant. Jun partners with Kazuya to try to dissuade him from his mission of vengeance. Heihachi's adopted son Lee Chaolan (voice of David Stokey) sends genetically created dinosaurs into the jungle to stop the fighters. Kazuya makes it to the central tower for the final battle with Heihachi. He manages to defeat his father, but is prevented from killing him by Jun's intervention. Lee Chaolan initiates Program 13, which results in the destruction of the island. Most of the principals escape the island safely.

TEKKEN: THE MOTION PICTURE suffers in comparison to other anime versions of video games (most notably the "Street Fighter II" Japanese movie and TV series), thanks in part to its truncated story line and weakly sketched main characters. Although the animation is distinguished by some dramatic imagery (employing obvious computer effects at certain points) and straightforward character design, there is not enough of the intense action such productions need to draw in their adolescent target audience. The few bouts we see are all too short and rather conventionally staged, with insipid philosophical banter often traded back and forth. Given the evil industrialist Mishima's avowed goal of destroying the world, Jun's insistence that his life be spared is somewhat misguided. The intrusive rock soundtrack added for the US video release makes a bid for further teen appeal by spotlighting songs by a number of contemporary bands (The Offspring, Stabbing Westward, Corrosion of Conformity). *(Violence, profanity.)*—B.C.

d, Kunihisa Sugishima; p, Tomiyo Hiruta, Ken Kindaichi, Yumiko Masujima, Yoshimasa Mori, Akira Saigoku, Gary Dehan (English Language Version); exec p, John Ledford (English Language Version); w, Ryota Yanagisawa (based on the Namco fighting game series "Tekken"); m, Kazuhiko Toyama; anim, Masaaki Kannan

Animated/Martial Arts **(PR: C MPAA: NR)**

TEN BENNY ★½

(U.S., 1998) 98m Palisades Pictures; Cubb Productions; Visland Entertainment; Trans Atlantic ~ Artistic License Films c
(AKA: NOTHING TO LOSE)

Adrien Brody *(Ray)*; Michael Gallagher *(Mike)*; Sybil Temchen; Tony Gillan *(Butchie)*; James E. Moriarty *(Donny)*; Frank Vincent *(Ray Sr.)*; Lisa Roberts *(Linda)*; Gayle Scott *(Donna)*; Jill Bross *(Sue)*; Jay Galione *(Young Ray)*; Jason Peterson *(Young Mike)*; Greg Zittel *(Al)*; David Deblinger *(Cosmo)*; Jerry Moore *(Tony)*

The feature debut of director Eric Bross, TEN BENNY is a hackneyed, flagrantly derivative drama about a New Jersey lowlife.

Ray (Adrien Brody), an inveterate gambler, barely makes enough salary at the shoe store where he works to meet his creditors' demands. When he gets a hot tip on a horse race, he goes to Donny (James E. Moriarty), a loan shark, who gives Ray $10,000 and a deadline for repaying the loan. The horse loses and Ray panics. He borrows money from his friend Butchie (Tony Gillan) and drives to Atlantic City to take part in a backroom card game. Ray is on a winning streak when he's called away from the card table to meet the gambling house's owner—Donny. Donny confiscates Ray's winnings and gives him a few days to repay the remainder of the loan. Meanwhile, Ray's girlfriend, Joanne (Sybil Temchen), feeling neglected, begins an affair with another of Ray's friends, Mike (Michael Gallagher). At her birthday party, Ray, having just returned from Atlantic City, fails to give Joanne a gift, while Mike presents her with an expensive bracelet. Later that night, Mike calls Joanne at home and professes his love for her, unaware that Ray is with Joanne when she receives the call. The next day, Ray finds Mike and the two begin to fight. Their brawl is interrupted, however, by the arrival of Donny's henchmen, who bring the pair to Donny's hideout. There, Donny threatens to kill them as the deadline for repaying the loan nears, but Ray's father (Frank Vincent) arrives just in time and successfully bargains for their release.

Soon after, Ray leaves his home for Florida, while Joanne and Mike enroll in a nearby college. In class, Joanne listens as Mike reads a composition he has written about Ray which concludes, "I hope he finds happiness. I hope he finds forgiveness."

TEN BENNY is yet another entry in the seemingly endless Scorsese sweepstakes. Virtually devoid of originality (except for the title, which is hipster's lingo for a shoe size), the film is populated with "realistic" thick-accented small timers who hate working, wear gold chains, and use truckloads of profanity. Characters communicate principally by screaming at or hitting each other. An inordinate amount of time is taken showing how these folk hang out—smoking, drinking, putting each other down, and talking about sex, usually while a mobile camera zips around them. The object of all this, of course, is to lend the film veracity and atmosphere, but the only reality that TEN BENNY evokes is the reality of other movies. Even real-life do-nothings are more interesting than the bunch featured here.

Bross has certainly done his homework. Moments of TEN BENNY specifically recall MEAN STREETS (1973) and GOODFELLAS (1990), and Bross has gotten the shady milieu, the fluid camera movements, and the half-admiring/half-aghast voice-over narration down pat. But although he proves himself a first-rate imitator, Bross also shows that his appreciation doesn't go below the surface. His film apes Scorsese's style to good effect, but has absolutely none of the texture.

The actors don't fare much better, and have apparently been encouraged to ham it up. Brody, often a fine actor, mugs ridiculously through the film, Moriarty plays Donny as little more than a tough-guy cartoon, and most of the other performers barely register. Vincent (a Scorsese veteran, who appeared in RAGING BULL and GOODFELLAS) is the lone exception. Coolly professional while the actors around him overheat, he's a fresh, authentic talent in an otherwise stale movie.

It's tough not to root for a feature that cost only $200,000, for such films are usually the result of intense drive and devotion. But a low budget isn't always telling of a fervent, independent spirit. . . the way MEAN STREETS was. TEN BENNY is little more than a calling card film, and a mediocre one at that. *(Violence, extensive nudity, sexual situations, extreme profanity.)*—D.C.

d, Eric Bross; p, H.M. Coakley, Eric Bross; exec p, Paul D. Wheaton, Lisa Roberts, Michael Brysh; assoc p, Tom Cudworth, Carla Zackson, Larry Tuorto, Peter Giblin, Wendy McKernon, Malia Damon; co-p, Mark D. Severini, Robert Mitchell; w, Tom Cudworth, Eric Bross; ph, Horacio Marquinez; ed, Keith Reamer; m, Chris Hajian; prod d, J.C. Svec; art d, Amy Scholte; sound, John Bross (mixer); casting, Lauren Nadler; cos, Jana Lee Fong; makeup, Virna Mejia, Sherry Rosse; stunts, Marc Brackett

Crime/Drama **(PR: C MPAA: R)**

TERMINAL JUSTICE ★★

(U.S., 1996) 95m Partners Film Co; Skyvision Entertainmnet ~ Promark Entertainment c
(AKA: TERMINAL JUSTICE: CYBERTECH P.D.)

Lorenzo Lamas *(Chase)*; Chris Sarandon *(Reggie Matthews)*; Peter Coyote *(Dr. Vivyan)*; Kari Wuhrer, billed as Kari Salin *(Pamela Travis)*; Barry Flatman *(Phillips)*; Tod Thawley *(Hiroshi)*; Barry Yourgrau *(Brady)*; Calvin Green *(Efram)*; Catherine Blythe *(Marie)*; Lynne Cormack *(Polansky)*; Christopher Kennedy *(Goatee)*; Roy Lewis *(Tillbrook)*; Kelly Grando *(Monica)*; Dana Brooks *(Chasier)*; Earl Mann *(Attorney)*; Ronnie King *(Sonny)*; Robert Bidaman *(Uniform 1)*; Chris Marren *(Desk Sergeant)*; Lori Heath *(Alice)*; Ron Small *(Leon)*; Bryan Renfro *(Deputy)*; Henry Chan *(Executive)*

Criminal scientists use cloning to develop disposable sex slaves in TERMINAL JUSTICE, an action exercise whose direction and writing aren't nearly as imaginative as its weird central concept.

Eager to outdo the sexual thrills available in the virtual reality market, depraved adult toymaker Reggie Matthews (Chris Sarandon) and mad scientist Dr. Vivyan (Peter Coyote) have concocted the next big thing. Dipping into his own gene pool for a modified version of cloning, Dr. Vivyan creates female equivalents of himself. Matthews molests and murders two of them.

Eager to move up a step, Matthews sends two goons to steal DNA from soft-core porn star Pamela Travis (Kari Wuhrer). When a police investigation uncovers Matthews's plan, Travis hires a moonlighting police detective, Sgt. Chase (Lorenzo Lamas), as a bodyguard; he protects her when Matthews's men invade her home. Subsequently, Chase's partner Phillips (Barry Flatman) is slain by one of Matthews's henchmen. Pressured by his Metro division superior, Chase teams up with cyber-genius Hiroshi (Tod Thawley) to foil Matthews's genetic theft of Travis's DNA. After Chase locates the corpse of one of Matthews's genetically-created victims, Matthews retaliates by unsuccessfully ambushing Chase and Travis at a restaurant. Tracing him through Matthews's low-level thugs, Chase arrests Dr. Vivyan and saves the newest clone from being sold overseas.

After Matthews abducts Travis, Chase is forced to pursue him through a deadly virtual reality game called Hellraiser. Despite being badly wounded during the virtual competition, Chase eliminates the assassins, rescues Travis, and arrests Matthews.

Dr. Vivyan is released when a court accepts his legal argument that one cannot be tried for killing oneself (i.e., a cloned version of oneself). His sole surviving clone takes advantage of that argument by grabbing a cop's gun and shooting her creator to death.

This outre but undisciplined action pic is full of neat gimmicks, like a remote control pheromone-seeker that attacks Chase in the restaurant. If only it weren't so stuffed with macho movie cliches like avenging the cop buddy's death and putting the haughty female lead in her (submissive) place. The direction of this deja-vu-ish material is thoroughly routine; quality actors Peter Coyote and Chris Sarandon grope for that ham overkill level set by Jack Nicholson in BATMAN (1989). Although it has a few delirious moments, TERMINAL JUSTICE does little to revitalize stale cliches. Instead, it trashes scientific wizardry to jazz up overly familiar cops-and-gene-robbers schlock. *(Graphic violence, extreme profanity, extensive nudity, sexual situations, substance abuse.)*—R.P.

d, Rick King; p, David Lancaster; exec p, David Newlon, Jon Kramer; assoc p, Amy Krell; w, Wynne McLaughlin, Frederick Bailey; ph, Chris Holmes Jr.; ed, Jeff Bessner; m, Michael Hoenig; prod d, Tim Bider; art d, Benno Tutter; set d, Terry Roberts; sound, Doug Johnston; fx, Laird McMurray; casting, Pat Di Stefano; cos, Trish Venema; makeup, Monet Monsano; stunts, Jim Dunn

Science Fiction/Action/Crime (PR: C MPAA: R)

TERMINAL JUSTICE: CYBERTECH P.D.
(SEE: TERMINAL JUSTICE)

THEORY OF FLIGHT ★★½
(U.K./U.S., 1998) 100m BBC Films; Distant Horizon ~ Fine Line c

Kenneth Branagh *(Richard)*; Helena Bonham Carter *(Jane Hatchard)*; Gemma Jones *(Anne)*; Holly Aird *(Julie)*; Ray Stevenson *(Gigolo)*

Far too whimsical for its own good, THE THEORY OF FLIGHT tells the story of a terminally ill, physically deteriorating woman and an imbalanced, quixotic man, whose love for each other brings them renewed hope. Kenneth Branagh and Helena Bonham Carter are unable to breathe life into the film's unlikely protagonists.

Richard (Kenneth Branagh), an eccentric artist captivated with flight, leaps off of a building with his homemade hang glider. Not only does his contraption fail, but he's sentenced to 120 hours community service for being a public nuisance. He must, twice a week, take care of Jane (Helena Bonham Carter), a wheelchair bound young woman suffering from ALS, a terminal motor-neuron disease. Jane, fed up with condescending do-gooders, gives Richard a hard time until she realizes that he's as much of a misfit as she is.

Jane surfs the Net in search of a sexual partner; the severely handicapped woman wants to lose her virginity before she dies. Meanwhile, Richard designs and welds together an airplane reminiscent of the Wright brothers' creation. He invites Jane to a candlelight dinner to unveil his master work. Jane asks Richard to help her find a partner. Richard says he can't do it, and they stop seeing each other. He tries to fly his plane and fails. She treats a volunteer rudely and argues with her mother, Anne (Gemma Jones). Eventually Richard agrees to help Jane.

They find a gigolo (Ray Stevenson) who will sleep with Jane for two thousand pounds, a sum Richard plans to raise by robbing a bank. As the gigolo tries to relax a terrified Jane in a hotel room, Richard pulls a stocking over his face and enters the bank. Before he can pull out his gun, he runs into his ex-girlfriend Julie (Holly Aird). She screams. He runs out of the bank and up to the hotel room, where Jane writhes with repulsion. Richard, still armed, scares away the hapless gigolo before consummation.

Unable to fulfill her dream, the couple board his biplane, a potential suicide machine, and attempt to defy gravity. When the plane gets off the ground, Richard and Jane blissfully float over the rolling hills before crashing, without injury, back to earth. They make love.

Some time later, he builds a monument out of the smashed plane atop her grave.

One of the central problems with THEORY OF FLIGHT is that Richard's obsession with flight is way too obvious a metaphor for his head-in-the-clouds existence, his inability to deal with things as they are down here on Earth. Scripter Richard Hawkins drives the metaphor home with stilted dialogue like "taking flight has more than the one meaning." There is also the rather predictable moment in the narrative where Richard suddenly realizes that he is more of a cripple (in an emotional sense) than Jane. And then (to completely exhaust the metaphor) we see that Richard is finally able to fly successfully when he's learned to love.

As for Branagh's performance, he appears to be playing a different character than the one Hawkins intended. Whereas the actions of leaping off of a building or attempting a bank robbery demand manic intensity, Branagh registers only a breezy detachment. Take the Bard's words out of his mouth (HENRY V, MUCH ADO ABOUT NOTHING, HAMLET) and Branagh is left to do a poor Woody Allen impression (CELEBRITY) or the bloodless Richard in this film.

His costar, and real-life love interest, Bonham Carter fares a bit better. She trades in the period costumes from her Merchant-Ivory days (ROOM WITH A VIEW, MAURICE) for a wheelchair, playing the disabled Jane with a continually cocked head and slurred speech. Her vibrant turn gives the film a much-needed dose of adrenaline. One of the more affecting moments involving her character occurs when Jane's mother complains that she too has lost her life in a sense to Jane's disease. The mixture of defiance and regret that Bonham Carter registers makes it possible for the viewer to truly understand Jane's tormented behavior and not merely feel a base sympathy for her character (the emotion most generally elicited in movies about disabled persons).

It's interesting to consider that no one involved in the production recognized how horribly miscalculated the film's comedy sequences are—particularly Richard's blighted bank robbery. The film only truly takes off when the two leads are soaring in the air, but by that point the story line has been left far behind on the tarmac. *(Sexual situations, profanity.)*—T.Y.

d, Paul Greengrass; p, Anant Singh, Helena Spring, Ruth Caleb, David M. Thompson; w, Richard Hawkins; ph, Ivan Strasburg; ed, Mark Day; m, Rolfe Kent; prod d, Melanie Allen; sound, John Taylor, Robert Farr; casting, John Hubbard, Ros Hubbard; cos, Dinah Collin

Drama/Comedy/Romance (PR: C MPAA: R)

THERE'S SOMETHING ABOUT MARY ★★★½
(U.S., 1998) 120m 20th Century Fox ~ 20th Century Fox C

Ben Stiller *(Ted Stroehmann)*; Cameron Diaz *(Mary Jenson)*; Matt Dillon *(Pat Healy)*; Chris Elliott *(Dom)*; Lin Shaye *(Magda)*; Lee Evans *(Tucker/Norm)*; Jeffrey Tambor *(Sully)*; W. Earl Brown *(Warren)*; Markie Post *(Mary's Mom)*; Keith David

(Mary's Stepfather); Sarah Silverman *(Brenda)*; Khandi Alexander *(Joanie)*; Marnie Alexenburg *(Lisa)*; Dan Murphy *(Boss' Brother)*; Richard M. Tyson *(Detective Krevoy)*; Rob Moran *(Detective Stabler)*; Jackie Flynn *(South Carolina Police)*; Hillary Matthews *(Dom's Wife)*; Willie Garson *(Doctor Zit Face/High School Pal)*; David Shackelford *(Coconut Guy)*; David Goryl *(Petey)*; Lori Glick *(Friend 3)*; Jeffrey P. Lerner *(Car Hood Kid)*; Cory Pendergast *(Car Hood Kid)*; Brett Farve *(Himself)*; Warren Tashjian *(Freddie)*; Kelly Roarke *(Girl)*; Herbie Flynn *(Homeless Man)*; Caryl West *(Medical Assistant 1)*; Ken Rogerson *(Pants at Ankles Guy)*; Brad Blank *(Paramedic)*; Steve Sweeney *(Police Officer)*; Cindy Oliver *(Renise)*; Steve Tyler *(TV News Reporter)*; Maureen Griffin *(Wine Waitress)*; Bob Farrelly *(Hot Dog Stud)*; Mariann Farrelly *(Driving Range Sweetie)*; Jonathan Richman *(Jonathan)*; Tommy Larkins *(Drummer)*; Lenny Clarke *(Fireman)*; Daniel Greene *(Pizza House Man)*; Lagena Greene *(Pizza House Woman)*; Michael Budge *(Joe Bishop Look-Alike)*; James Gifford *(Jimmy)*; Sean P. Gildea *(Prison Warden)*; Zen Gesner *(Bartender)*; Tracy Anne George *(Dancer)*; Jesse Farrelly *(Dom's Kid)*; Anna Farrelly *(Dom's Kid)*; Zack Lee *(Mary's Little Friend)*; Valerie Bruce *(Nimord's Cafe Patron)*; Kelly O'Brien *(Office Assistant)*; Mike Charpentier; Peter Grundy; Michael Gannon; Peter Conway; Ann Conway; Susan O'Day; Heather Rosebeck *(Hot Club Patrons)*; Jack Shields; Fallon Shields; Bob Grundy *(Hot Club Barkeeps)*; Nancy Farrelly *(Boardroom Babe)*; Billy Beauchene; Kathy Beauchene; Manny Barrows *(Insurance Spitballers)*; Michael Murphy *(Office Worker)*; Sheila Moore *(Officer Worker)*; Barbara O'Connor *(Ashtray Babe)*; Tim Sheehan *(Camera Hog)*; Richie Balsbaugh *(Cigar Smoker)*; Jim "Sunshine" Blake; Tim Robbie; Providence Wissel; Ruth Michelle Meyer; Billy Meyer; Brian McGlaughlin; Brian Moore; John Stroehman; Pete Anicelli *(Architect Partiers)*; Duana Knight; Kelley Schneider; Meda Thomas *(Architect Babes)*; Jeanie Flynn; Kevin Civali; Tom Leasca; Mercy Lopez *(Cuban Dancer)*; Michael Cheney *(Cell Block Bitch)*; Scott Rosenberg; George Bedard; Terry Mullany; Rick Coleman; Michael Burke; Kris Meyer; Emilio Diaz; Billy Smith; Ed Nelson; Brian Stube; Don Daley *(Jail Bird)*; Clem Frank; Julia Hissom; Sport Ahern; Robin Gau *(Strip Club Perverts)*; Paul Pelletier *(Cordosa Gawker)*; Monique Pelletier *(Cordosa Gawker)*; Johnny Mone *(Comic Book Kid)*; Nick Greenbury *(Fish Hook Kid)*; Andrew Greenbury *(Fish Hook Kid)*; Phil Rosenberg *(Cell Block Masseuse)*; John-Eliot Jordan; John Adamonis; Kyle Adamonis; Neil Pomfret; Ruth Pomfret; Josh Miller *(Buttercup Singers)*

Peter and Bobby Farrelly (KINGPIN, DUMB AND DUMBER) serve up their best work to date with THERE'S SOMETHING ABOUT MARY, an aggressively tasteless but immensely enjoyable comedy about *l'amour fou*.

Although he hasn't seen her in 13 years, Ted (Ben Stiller) still longs for Mary (Cameron Diaz), the girl he loved in high school. On the advice of his friend Dom (Chris Elliot), Ted hires a shady insurance claims investigator, Healy (Matt Dillon), to determine Mary's current whereabouts. Healy finds Mary living in Miami, but is so smitten with her himself that he lies to Ted to dissuade him from contacting her. Healy relocates to Miami and begins to pursue Mary, using information he had gathered about her to win her over. They start to date, although Mary is warned about Healy by her uppercrust British friend, Tucker (Lee Evans).

When Ted learns that he's been lied to, he impulsively leaves his home in Providence and drives towards Miami. Along the way, he is mistaken for a serial killer and jailed. Bailed out by Dom, Ted reaches Miami and finds Mary. The two arrange a date and spend a pleasant evening together, Ted never revealing how he has located her. Healy, meanwhile, aware that Tucker is suspicious of him, tails Tucker and discovers that he's really a pizza delivery man named Norm, and is similarly infatuated with Mary.

The next day, Mary receives an anonymous letter informing her that Ted had hired Healy to spy on her. Furious, Mary orders Ted to get out of her life. Ted confronts Healy and Norm about the letter, but both deny writing it. The three go to Mary's apartment and find her there with Dom—the author of the letter—who is also madly in love with Mary. Healy demands that Mary choose from among them when her old boyfriend, Brett Farve (Himself) arrives. Ted explains that he has summoned Farve because he believes Mary loves him best, and that her happiness is what matters most. Ted then leaves but is followed by Mary, who tells him that it's he whom she truly loves.

In their brief filmmaking careers, Peter and Bobby Farrelly have made abundantly clear that their films are for neither the acutely sensitive nor the easily embarrassed. Like their earlier efforts, DUMB & DUMBER (1994) and the underrated KINGPIN (1996), THERE'S SOMETHING ABOUT MARY is rife with the crassest humor permissible in a mainstream studio release. This latest outing spews audaciously unfashionable jokes about the mentally and physically impaired, gays, the elderly, police brutality, masturbation, and even a cute border terrier. Not since the heyday of Blake Edwards has Hollywood seen comedy as gleefully vulgar as that of the Farrellys.

But they have demonstrated just as clearly that their films are more than mere assaults on good taste. The Farrellys create whole movies, with complete stories and fully developed, functional characters. THERE'S SOMETHING ABOUT MARY succeeds not only through its beautifully executed gags, but also because the gags have been worked into a well-rounded and coherent (if highly improbable) plot, with characters who serve a purpose beyond being comic props. As a result, the film is involving and finally engaging as its principals stumble their way through comically hazardous romantic pursuits.

The Farrellys also show that they are capable directors of actors, making the most of a very game cast. Stiller is an endearing if schleppish hero, Diaz makes Mary a prize worthy of Ted's Odyssean effort, and Elliot is an amusingly creepy foil to Stiller's noble-minded nice guy. Best of all are Dillon and Evans. Dillon proves as he did in IN & OUT (1997) that he is a first-rate comic performer, and Evans is as cleverly droll here as he was in FUNNY BONES (1995).

The film's only real flaw is its length. At two hours, THERE'S SOMETHING ABOUT MARY outlasts its energy, and its last section plods as the film works towards a drawn-out finale that is at odds with the well-paced farce that precedes it.

Musician Jonathan Richman pops up periodically as a wandering troubadour who summarizes in insipid lyric what has just transpired on screen. Richman's intentional discordance and mock sincerity characterize the movie perfectly. *(Violence, nudity, extreme profanity.)*—D.C.

d, Peter Farrelly, Bobby Farrelly; p, Charles Wessler, Bradley Thomas, Frank Beddor, Michael Steinberg; exec p, Peter Farrelly, Bobby Farrelly; assoc p, Patrick Healy, Mark Charpentier; co-p, Marc S. Fischer, James B. Rogers; w, Peter Farrelly, Bobby Farrelly, Ed Decter, John J. Strauss (from a story by Ed Decter and John J. Strauss); ph, Mark Irwin; ed, Christopher Greenbury; m, Jonathan Richman; art d, Arlen Jay Vetter; set d, Scott Jacobson; sound, Jonathan Earl Stein (mixer); fx, Kevin Harris; casting, Rick Montgomery; cos, Mary Zophres; makeup, Cindy Jane Williams; stunts, Rick Barker

Romance/Comedy **(PR: O MPAA: R)**

THIEF, THE ★★★½
(Russia, 1997) 90m NTV-Profit; Productions Le Pont; Roissy Films ~ Stratosphere Entertainment c
(VOR)

Vladimir Mashkov *(Tolyan)*; Ekaterina Rednikova *(Katya)*; Misha Philipchuk *(Sanya)*; Amalia Mordvinova *(Doctor's Wife)*; Dima Shigarev *(Sanya, 12 years-old)*; Yuri Belyaev *(Sanya, 48 years-old)*; Lidiya Savchenko *(Baby Sanya)*; Ania Shtukaturova *(Gammy Girl)*; Olga Peshkova *(Actress)*; Anatoliy Koscheev *(Bootmaker)*; Lyudmila Selyanskaya *(Alcoholic)*; Viktor Bunakov *(Engineer)*; Natalia Pozdniakova *(Accountant's Wife)*; Yevgeni Popov *(Vagrant)*; Yulia Artamonova *(Engineer's Wife)*; Galina Petrova *(Varvara)*; Yervant Arzumanian *(Accountant)*

A con man captures the hearts of a desperate mother and her child in this memorable Russian import. THE THIEF, an Oscar nominee for Best Foreign Film, succeeds as both an involving character study and as a metaphorical critique of Stalin and his bitter legacy.

Pregnant, impoverished, and alone, Katya (Ekaterina Rednikova) stumbles across the Russian tundra until she collapses and gives birth. Six years later, in 1952, Katya and her son Sanya (Misha Philipchuk) ride a crowded train, their prospects bleak. An army captain, Tolyan (Vladimir Mashkov) swaggers over to them and instructs the boy to watch his gun as he seduces Katya. Tolyan makes love to the young mother between two cars on the train.

The three pose as a family to get a room in a boarding house. While Tolyan rules his "family" with an iron hand, Sanya does everything he can to get between the soldier and his mother. After Sanya is bullied by some local boys, Tolyan beats one boy's father, then grabs one of the bullies and forces Sanya to repeatedly hit the bigger boy. To solidify the six-year old's burgeoning respect, Tolyan claims to be Stalin's son.

The lies continue. Katya soon realizes her lover isn't really a soldier but a thief. Tolyan steals from the boarding house, and drags his so-called family to another village, where he once again poses as a respectable citizen to gain the trust of the neighbors before robbing them. During one heist, he even pushes Sanya to aid him. Katya, though she loves Tolyan, decides to leave the brute when he refuses to go straight. While waiting for a train, though, Katya can't work up the resolve to depart. Just then Tolyan is nabbed by the police. Katya unsuccessfully attempts to bribe the authorities and free her man. Darkness ensues: Tolyan is sent to a gulag for seven years; Katya dies of complications during an abortion; and Sanya is raised in an orphanage.

Years later, a teenage Sanya runs into a seedier but still dishonest Tolyan. Pleased to see his old surrogate father, Sanya is deflated when the thief barely recognizes him and lumps his mother in with a long series of other women. In the end, Sanya sneaks up behind Tolyan and shoots him in the back.

When the Soviet era ended in Russia, the fate of the country's cinema remained in question. Despite several years of a weak, corrupt economy and ineffective political rule, fine films have continued to emerge from the beleaguered country—to wit, BURNT BY THE SUN (1994), PRISONER OF THE MOUNTAINS (1997), and THE THIEF.

Though he was a ruthless despot who killed millions, "Uncle Joe," it should be remembered, was also revered by millions. In THE THIEF, Tolyan echoes Joseph Stalin's prime credo when he instructs Sanya that "if you scare people, they will respect you." Tolyan's extreme form of tough love wins over Katya and her son in the same way that Stalin won over the country. To hammer home this point, writer-director Pavel Chukhari has Tolyan sport a Stalin tattoo on his chest—admittedly an unsubtle detail, but one that can be easily forgiven in an otherwise understated movie. The charismatic Vladmir Mashkov plays the thief with well-calculated charm and frightening authority. On the surface, with his neatly pressed captain's uniform and suave demeanor, Tolyan represents the shining representation of Russian manhood. Underneath, he's nothing more than a two-bit con man.

The method in which this lowlife captures Sanya's psyche is the core of this sharply written allegory. Though he needs a father, Sanya (depicted in an unerringly naturalistic fashion by eight-year-old Misha Philipchuk) is wary of the thief. While his mother does her best to accept Tolyan's evil actions, the boy resists, trying to remain true to the memory of his natural father, who died before Sanya was born. When Sanya finally proclaims his loyalty to Tolyan, it's evident to the viewer that he's made the wrong decision in a moral sense—it also seems to be the only natural choice to make. Chukhrai implicates the audience; THE THIEF shows what it's like, on a base level, to be seduced by a dictator.

After the thief's inevitable betrayal, there's no attendant note of triumph when Sanya shoots him in the back and announces that he's nothing like him. Now, Chukhrai points out with perverse satisfaction, Sanya is more like him than ever. *(Adult situations.)*—T.Y.

d, Pavel Chukhrai; p, Igor Tolstunov; exec p, Sergei Kozlov; w, Pavel Chukhrai; ph, Vladimir Klimov; ed, Marina Dobryanskaya, Natalia Kucherenko; m, Vladimir Dashkevich; prod d, Victor Petrov; sound, Yulia Egorova (engineer); cos, Natalya Alexandrova, Natalya Moneva; makeup, Nina Kolodkina

AAN Best Foreign Language Film

Drama **(PR: C MPAA: R)**

THIN RED LINE, THE ★★★★
(U.S., 1998) 166m Fox 2000 Pictures; Phoenix Pictures ~ 20th Century Fox c

Sean Penn *(First Sergeant Welsh)*; Adrien Brody *(Corporal Fife)*; Jim Caviezel *(Pvt. Witt)*; Ben Chaplin *(Bell)*; George Clooney *(Bosche)*; John Cusack *(Gaff)*; Woody Harrelson *(Keck)*; Elias Koteas *(Captain "Bugger" Staros)*; Jared Leto *(Whyte)*; Dash Mihok *(Doll)*; Tim Blake Nelson *(Tills)*; Nick Nolte *(Colonel Tall)*; John C. Reilly *(Storm)*; Larry Romano *(Mazzi)*; John Savage *(McCron)*; John Travolta *(Qintard)*; Arie Verveen *(Dale)*; Nick Stahl *(Bead)*; David Harrod *(Queen)*; Paul Gleason *(Band)*; Shawn Hatosy *(Tella)*; Travis Fine *(Weld)*; Matt Doran *(Coombs)*; Jarrod Dean *(Throne)*; Donal Logue *(Marl)*; Dan Wylie *(First Medic)*; Simon Westaway *(Stack)*; Sam Rockwell *(Peale)*; Don Harvey *(Becker)*; Gordon MacDonald *(Gordon/Earl)*; Danny Hoch *(Carni)*; John Dee Smith *(Train)*; Stephen Spacek *(Jenks)*; Will Wallace *(Hoke)*; Felix Williamson *(Private Drake)*; Ben Hines *(Assistant Pilot)*; Todd Wallace *(Pilot)*; Kirk Acevedo *(Kirk/Guide)*; Robert Roy Hofmo *(Sico)*; Jace Phillips *(S-1)*; Randall Duk Kim *(Nisei Interpreter)*; David Paschall *(General)*; Norman Patrick Brown *(Pvt. Henry)*; Thomas Jane *(Pvt. Ash)*; Penny Allen *(Witt's Mother)*; Benjamin *(Melanesian Villager)*; Simon Billig *(Lt. Col. Billig)*; Mark Boone Jr. *(Pvt. Peale)*; Kengo Hasuo *(Japanese Prisoner)*; Jack *(Melanesian Man Walking)*; Jimmy *(Melanesian Villager)*; Polyn Leona *(Melanesian Woman with Child)*; Simon Lyndon *(Medic #2)*; Kazuki Maehara *(Japanese Pvt. #1)*; Marina Malota *(Marina)*; Michael McGrady *(Pvt. Floyd)*; Ken Mitsuishi *(Japanese Officer #1)*; Ryushi Mizukami *(Japanese Pvt. #4)*; Larry Neuhaus *(Crewman)*; Taiju Okayasu *(Japanese Pvt. #6)*; Takamitsu Okubo *(Japanese Soldier)*; Miranda Otto *(Marty Bell)*; Kazuyoshi Sakai *(Japanese Prisoner #2)*; Masayuki Shida *(Japanese Officer #2)*; Hiroya Sugisaki *(Japanese Pvt. #7)*; Kouji Suzuki *(Japanese Pvt. #3)*; Tomohiro Tanji *(Japanese Pvt.*

#2); Minoru Toyoshima *(Japanese Sgt.)*; Terutake Tsuji *(Japanese Pvt. #5)*; Steven Vidler *(2nd Lt. Gore)*; Vincent *(Melanesian Guide)*; Joe Watanabe *(Japanese Officer #3)*; Yasoumi Yoshino *(Young Japanese)*; Melanesian Extras: John Augwata; Joshua Augwata; John Bakotee; Immanuel Dato; Michael Iha; Emmunual Konai; Stephen Konai; Peter Morosiro; Amos Niuga; Jennifer Siugali; Carlos Tome; Selina Tome

The long-awaited third film of director Terrence Malick (his second, DAYS OF HEAVEN, was released in 1978), THE THIN RED LINE is the story of a US Army infantry company mounting an offensive on the island of Guadalcanal during WWII. Based on the novel by James Jones, the movie is an unusually ambitious and accomplished exploration of the anatomy, strategy, morality, ecology, and terrible gravity of warfare.

It is 1942. US Army Pvt. Witt (Jim Caviezel) is absent without official leave on an island in the Solomons. This idyllic interlude is interrupted when his company arrives to launch a major offensive in the area. Witt is upbraided by First Sergeant Welsh (Sean Penn) and is allowed to rejoin his divisioin. Their objective is to take a key airfield being built by the Japanese on Guadalcanal. Among the personnel of Charlie Company are Lt. Col. Tall (Nick Nolte), who has been put in charge of the operation, Capt. Staros (Elias Koteas), Welsh, and Pvt. Bell (Ben Chaplin), a former officer who resigned his commission in order to spend more time with his wife (Miranda Otto).

Charlie Company charges the Guadalcanal beachhead and moves inland with no resistance from the enemy. The only indication of Japanese is the mutilated bodies of two Marines. The battle is launched when the American infantrymen attempt to seize a hill protected by enemy machine-gun fire emanating from a deeply entrenched bunker. Many GIs are killed or wounded in the assault. At one point Capt. Staros refuses to accept Col. Tall's order to send his men on a direct frontal attack on the Japanese bunker, an attack the junior officer thinks would be suicidal.

The next day the Americans take the hill and secure the surrounding area. Much Japanese blood is shed. Believing Staros to be too soft-hearted, Tall relieves him of his command but also promises him a Silver Star. Later, Bell receives a "Dear John" letter from his wife, and Witt is killed during a reconnaissance mission. Having successfully completed their part of the Guadalcanal campaign, the surviving members of Charlie Company ship out.

Both Jones and Malick created their masterworks on the first attempt—Jones with his 1951 novel *From Here to Eternity* and Malick with his debut film BADLANDS (1973). Unlike Booth Tarkington and Orson Welles (THE MAGNIFICANT AMBERSONS) and Cornell Woolrich and Alfred Hitchcock (REAR WINDOW), Jones, the WWII veteran who was wounded on Guadalcanal, and Malick, the former philosophy professor, would seem to be an imperfect matchup. And indeed Jones would have been startled by Malick's representation of Pvt. Witt, the hardhead hillbilly, "going native" among Solomon Islanders and musing about humanity, nature, and evil. ("How did we lose the good that was given us?" Witt wonders in voice-over. "What's keeping us from reaching out, touching the glory?")

Jones had a gift for psychological conflict, both inter- and intra-personal—something that is outside Malick's areas of expertise and interest. But Malick, though he has not done full justice to Jones, has his own muses to heed and they are rarer and far more precious than those followed by most of his filmmaking contemporaries; a viewing of BADLANDS will establish that only he (and maybe John Boorman) could have summoned the spirituality to make a transcendent masterpiece out of the tabloid story of a redneck serial killer and his semi-moronic girlfriend.

For all his contemplativity, Malick, with THE THIN RED LINE, proves himself to be an action director in a class with Sam Peckinpah. Fans of combat movies will not be disappointed in the film, which incorporates more than an hour of straight action, superbly photographed by roving cameras that always seem to know where the significant activity is occurring. As a re-creation of the fight for Guadalcanal, THE THIN RED LINE is vastly superior to GUADALCANAL DIARY (1943), a film that runs aground in a sea of Brooklyn jokes.

The true protagonist of this ensemble piece is not any individual soldier, but Charlie Company collectively. Amidst a large and impressive male cast, Nick Nolte, equipped with a mid-American twang, contributes another in a long line of authoritative portrayals. Also giving a strong performance, Sean Penn qualifies as the only "name" performer who appears on screen for the lion's share of the film's running time; his character, however, has little influence over events and remains relegated to the periphery (his most significant role is that of conscience-antagonist for Witt). George Clooney is adequate in a cameo, but John Travolta, in an apparent attempt at an offbeat characterization, doesn't merely walk through his bit, he sleepwalks through it. Several little-known actors, particularly Jim Caviezel who has what amounts to the film's pivotal role, manage to hold their own amongst the more familiar faces. Witt and Welsh are close counterparts of Prewitt and Warden, characters of *From Here to Eternity*. An earlier version of THE THIN RED LINE (1964) featured Keir Dullea and Jack Warden. *(Graphic violence, nudity, profanity.)* —D.T.

d, Terrence Malick; p, Robert Michael Geisler, John Roberdeau, Grant Hill; exec p, George Stevens Jr.; assoc p, Michael Stevens; w, Terrence Malick (based on the novel by James Jones); ph, John Toll; ed, Bill Weber, Leslie Jones, Saar Klein; m, Hans Zimmer; prod d, Jack Fisk; art d, Ian Gracy; set d, Suza Maybury; sound, Paul "Salty" Brincat (mixer), Andy Nelson, Anna Behlmer; fx, Brian Cox; casting, Dianne Crittenden; cos, Margot Wilson; makeup, Viv Mepham

AAN Best Picture; AAN Best Director: Terrence Malick; AAN Best Adapted Screenplay: Terrence Malick; AAN Best Cinematography: John Toll; AAN Best Film Editing: Billy Weber, Leslie Jones, Saar Klein; AAN Best Original Dramatic Score: Hans Zimmer; AAN Best Sound: Andy Nelson, Anna Behlmer, Paul Brincat

War/Action **(PR: C MPAA: R)**

3 NINJAS: HIGH NOON AT MEGA MOUNTAIN ★½

(U.S., 1998) 88m Sheen Productions; Leeds/Ben-Ami Productions ~ TriStar c

Hulk Hogan (Dave Dragon); Loni Anderson (Medusa); Jim Varney (Lothar Zogg); Mathew Botuchis (Rocky Douglas); Michael J. O'Laskey II (Colt Douglas); James Paul Roeske II (Tum Tum Douglas); Victor Wong (Grandpa Mori); Chelsey Earlywine (Amanda Morgan-Green); Lindsay Felton (Jennifer); Alan McRae (Sam Douglas); Margarita Franco (Jessica); Kirk Baily (Carl); Travis McKenna (Buelow); Brendan O'Brien (Zed); Pat Mahoney (Harry Jacobson); Emily Roeske (Little Karate Girl); Syntrell Ryder (Jennifer's Friend); Anthony Fiorino (Lars); Walter Newton (Moving Man)

While this fourth series installment pumps up the star power, 3 NINJAS: HIGH NOON AT MEGA MOUNTAIN delivers primarily the kind of high jinx—karate kids, adults hollering and falling down—that will amuse only young kids.

Brothers Rocky (Mathew Botuchis), Colt (Michael J. O'Laskey II), and TumTum (J.P. Roeske II) stay with their Grandpa Mori (Victor Wong) for a summer vacation, during which they undergo his rendition of ninja training. The boys return home to discover a new neighbor: feisty Amanda (Chelsey Earlywine), who is as expert with her new toy helicopter as she is with computers.

The kids, plus Rocky's girlfriend Jennifer (Lindsay Felton), go to Mega Mountain Amusement Park to see martial-arts hero Dave Dragon (Hulk Hogan), whose TV show has just been canceled. Meanwhile, terrorist Medusa (Loni Anderson) and her minions, led by Lothar (Jim Varney), infiltrate the seaside park, seize control, and hold the unsuspecting patrons hostage for a $10 million ransom.

After rescuing Dragon from Lothar's goons, who have shot him with a tranquilizer gun, the kids and Dragon deduce that the park is being held by terrorists. Amanda finds a villain's walkie-talkie and the kids summon the police. As Dragon investigates, Amanda uses her computer skills to prevent Medusa from turning rides into death traps. The villains kidnap Jennifer and tie her to the roller coaster tracks to flush Rocky out. He bests Lothar in a fight that takes them to the top of the roller coaster tracks.

The park owner drops the ransom payment from a helicopter, as instructed. But Amanda uses her toy chopper to intercept a falling bag of cash, slash it open, and scatter money into the crowd, in order to cause confusion and prevent the terrorists from escaping. Medusa takes Amanda hostage, handcuffing the child to a railing next to a bomb. The brothers face off against the remaining terrorists. Before fleeing back out to sea, Medusa shoots out the lights, but the brothers remember Grandpa's training, and dispatch the goons in the dark. Unable to defuse the bomb, the boys turn it into a homemade torpedo and use it to sink Medusa's escape boat. The boys give the credit to Dragon, whose show gets renewed.

The wafer-thin plot of HIGH NOON AT MEGA MOUNTAIN requires its villains to be such idiots that viewers over the age of 7 will find it hard to suspend their disbelief. In addition, every story element is shamelessly foreshadowed—can there be any doubt that the darkness training or toy helicopter will figure in the climax? On the other hand, the story is easy for tots to follow; the good guys and bad guys clearly delineated.

The slapstick action is fast and furious, aided by aggressive sound effects, and while it seems violent, there is no blood, and every blow is clearly cartoon overkill. Lots of bullets fly, but nobody is hurt.

It is pointless to discuss the acting in a film like this; suffice to say the adults ham it up shamelessly—squealing and rolling their eyes—and the aging Hogan's earnest sincerity as a fading, balding hero wins out over Varney's mugging and Anderson's posturing. The boys, all making their feature debuts, were obviously cast for their martial-arts aptitude, not their penchant to recite lines as woodenly as any school play.

This film will appeal to those youngsters trapped indoors on a rainy Saturday afternoon following their own karate classes, but nonmartial artists would do better to look elsewhere to get their kicks. *(Violence.)*—J.Di.

d, Sean McNamara; p, James Kang, Yoram Ben-Ami; exec p, Simon Sheen, Arthur Leeds; w, Sean McNamara, Jeff Phillips; ph, Blake T. Evans; ed, Annamaria Szanto; m, John Coda; prod d, Chuck Connor; art d, Chase Harlan; fx, Tim Drnec; casting, Joey Paul; cos, Miye Matsumoto; makeup, Nancy Bassett; stunts, Brett Jones, Charlie Kao (fights), Jason Liu (fights)

Children's/Action/Comedy (PR: A MPAA: PG)

THURSDAY ★½

(U.S., 1998) 82m Propaganda Films ~ Gramercy Pictures c

Thomas Jane *(Casey)*; Aaron Eckhart *(Nick)*; Paulina Porizkova *(Dallas)*; James LeGros, billed as Jamie Le Gros *(Billy Hill)*; Mickey Rourke *(Kasarov)*; Glenn Plummer *(Rasta Man)*; Michael Jeter *(Dr. Jarvis)*; Paula Marshall *(Christine)*; Luck Hari *(Cashier)*; Bari Willerford *(Cop)*; Richard Wong *(Mr. Wong)*; Shawn Michael Howard *(Jimmy)*; Gary Dourdan *(Ballpean)*; Brian Hooks *(Jary)*; Jeff Sanders *(Ballpean's Bodyguard)*; Eugene Collier *(Domino Player)*; Michael Darnell *(Domino Player)*; Marjean Holden *(Pregnant Woman)*; Tony Colon *(Allen)*; Sam Miona *(Businessman)*

Like too many other independent films made in the wake of Quentin Tarantino, this grindingly violent pastiche apes all the Tarantino mannerisms without connecting to them in any meaningful fashion.

Shaking off his partners Dallas (Paulina Porizkova) and Billy Hill (James Le Gros), LA felon Nick (Aaron Eckhart) drops by the Houston home of his reformed, happily married brother Casey (Thomas Jane). Nick hides a cache of stolen heroin there, leaves his car at his brother's, borrows his brother's car, and drives off to kill the dope-peddlers he's ripping off.

Casey, who is awaiting the arrival of adoption agency counselor Dr. Jarvis (Michael Jeter), discovers the heroin and angrily dumps it down the sink. When Rasta Man (Glenn Plummer), a drug dealer/user who's been trailing Nick, invades Casey's house, Casey pretends to get high with him and hangs the doped-up dealer upside down in the garage. Doing his damndest to impress Jarvis, Casey's dream of fatherhood evaporates when Dallas drops by and regales Jarvis with Casey's criminal past. Jarvis storms out.

Billy Hill arrives, shoots Dallas, and prepares to torture Casey, who overcomes him and suspends him upside down in the garage next to Rasta Man. Fatally wounded by the drug dealers he ripped off, Nick calls and drops hints about the whereabouts of $2 million of drug money. Casey is next visited by Kasarov (Mickey Rourke), a crooked cop who kills Rasta Man and Billy Hill and demands that Casey give him the stolen money. When the dealers Nick has robbed also converge on the house, Casey plays them against Kasarov's contingent; the two groups annihilate each other. Having deduced that Nick hid the money in the hubcaps of Nick's car, Casey retrieves the dough. When his wife returns home from a business trip, Casey persuades her to run away with him to France.

It takes more than gruesome violence and caustic snippets of humor to build a proper weltanschauung. Smug and unfocused, THURSDAY is yet another style-obsessed exercise in smarty-pants noir. While it provides a showcase for talented players who know how to pounce on brittle dialogue, it puts them to work in a vacuum. Where Tarantino at his best develops quirky protagonists and then tests them in violent arenas, THURSDAY hypnotizes viewers with trendy brutality and then expects that the desensitized audience won't care about the characters. The film's haphazardly inserted flashbacks and critique of suburban values add up to naught. *(Graphic violence, extreme profanity, sexual situations, extensive nudity, substance abuse.)*—R.P.

d, Skip Hill; p, Alan Poul; co-p, Skip Woods, Christine Sheaks; w, Skip Woods; ph, Denis Lenoir; ed, Paul Trejo, Peter Schink; m, Luna; prod d, Chris Anthony Miller; art d, Benjamin Ball; set d, Greta Grigorian; sound, Cameron Hanza, Christopher Taylor; fx, John Gray; casting, Christine Sheaks; cos, Mark Bridges; makeup, Heidi Grotsky, Pamela Phillips; stunts, B.L. Richmond

Crime/Drama (PR: O MPAA: R)

TIAN MIMI

(SEE: COMRADES, ALMOST A LOVE STORY)

TIETA OF AGRESTE ★★½
(Brazil, 1996) 116m Skylight Cinema; Serene Productions; Sony; Columbia Pictures ~ Fox Lorber Home Video c

Sonia Braga *(Tieta)*; Marilia Pera *(Perpetua)*; Chico Anisio *(Tieta's Father)*; Claudia Abreu *(Leonora)*; Zeze Motta *(Carmosina)*; Jece Valadao *(Dario)*; Heitor Martinez Mello *(Ricardo)*; Patricia Franca *(Imaculada/Young Tieta)*; Leon Goes *(Ascanio)*; Jorge Amado *(Narrator)*; Andre Valle; Noelia Montanhas; Debora Adorno; Caco Monteiro; Joao Phellippe; Andre Vale; Frank Menezes

Three of Brazil's top talents—Sonia Braga, director Carlos Diegues (BYE BYE BRAZIL, 1981) and Jorge Amado, on whose novel DONA FLOR AND HER TWO HUSBANDS (1978) was based—collaborated on this tepid comedy-drama about a woman's return to her family's country village 26 years after she was kicked out.

After years of letters telling about her life as the wife of a rich Sao Paolo industrialist, Tieta (Sonia Braga) writes to say her husband has died and she and her stepdaughter Leonora (Claudia Abreu) will be coming to visit. Tieta's older sister Perpetua (Marila Pera), who was responsible for snitching on the sexual activities that got Tieta sent packing, nevertheless schemes to get her hands on some of the money by getting Tieta to adopt one or both of her sons.

Tieta arrives, and immediately wins the good will of the villagers by calling in a favor from a senator she knows and having the village wired for electricity. She tries to hook up the sad Leonora with serious young Ascanio (Leon Goes), secretary to the village mayor. Tieta seduces Perpetua's virtuous son Ricardo (Heitor Martinez Mello), who is studying to be a priest. Ascanio regrets a deal he brokered to bring a factory to town when Tieta reveals that it will spoil the beautiful area with highly toxic pollutants. Tieta is upset when Ricardo stands her up for a young girl; soon after, he quits the seminary and catches the bus to Salvador. When Ascanio proposes to Leonora, she tells him the truth: Tieta is actually the madame of a successful brothel, and brought Leonora here to hide from the police after her lover was arrested for drugs. She and Tieta leave town, but at the last minute Ascanio runs after the bus and begs Leonora to stay, which she does.

One can only assume either that Amado's novel was better fleshed out or that there's something about the story that doesn't transfer culturally, because this film does a lot of huffing and puffing without ever going anywhere. The plot is certainly busy enough, in fact too busy—there are so many things going on that the script can't do justice to any of them. The big revelation of Tieta's true occupation is so plainly foreshadowed that it has no impact (in fact, until then it seems obvious that the viewer was intended to see through Tieta's story). And if this character is supposed to have a tragic dimension, no one told Sonia Braga, who plays her with little sense of either tragedy or vengefulness, but simply as a woman with money in her pocket and some harmless mischief on her mind. The film is colorful and lively, which is what we have come to expect of Brazilian imports, but never enough to sustain interest in the story. Author Amado appears as himself at the beginning of the film, introducing it from a park bench as a story he reads from a book. *(Nudity, sexual situations, adult situations, profanity.)*—M.F.

d, Carlos Diegues; p, Bruno Stroppiana, Donald K. Ranvaud; exec p, Miguel Faria Jr., Telmo Maia; assoc p, Renata Almeida Magalhaes; co-p, Sonia Braga, Carlos Diegues; w, Joao Ubaldo, Antonio Calmon , Carlos Diegues (based on the novel *Tieta do Agreste* by Jorge Amado); ph, Edgar Moura; ed, Karen Harley, Mair Tavares; m, Caetano Veloso; prod d, Lia Renha; sound, Rolf Pardula; cos, Luciana Buarque, Ocimar Versolato

Comedy/Drama **(PR: O MPAA: NR)**

TIMOTHY LEARY'S DEAD ★★★
(U.S., 1997) 80m Davids and Mills Productions ~ Strand Releasing c/bw

Timothy Leary; Richard Alpert; Ralph Metzner; Zach Leary; Vicki Marhall; Michael Bowen

This informative overview of the life and high-times of legendary LSD advocate Timothy Leary bounces from the psychedelic '60s to his death in the '90s, and offers a one-of-a-kind trip into his turbulent and often illegal lifestyle.

Opening with news broadcasts of Leary's death from inoperable prostate cancer at the age of 75, accompanied by The Moody Blues' classic tune "Timothy Leary's Dead," this portrait strives to follow a chronological pattern, as it intermingles film clips, photos, and interviews. Beginning as a square Harvard professor in the early 1960s, Leary describes his first, enlightening encounter with magic mushrooms, and the profound changes this brought about—the least of which was getting booted out of Harvard. Warning that an individual should only take LSD if they are psychologically prepared "to go out of their mind," Leary entertains visitors from the fields of religion, psychedelia, and entertainment at his Millbrook, New York, home; the same location was the site of a mid-1960s late-night raid by two dozen sheriffs and future Nixon aide G. Gordon Liddy.

Proclaiming his mantra "turn on, tune in, and drop out," Leary becomes a modern-day guru, and after announcing his plan to run for Governor against Ronald Reagan, he's suddenly arrested for having two roaches (which he alleges were planted) in his ashtray. Escaping from prison in 1970, Leary shaves his head, poses as a Republican, and winds up in Algiers with Eldridge Cleaver—until he's finally hauled back to America and placed in a cell next to Charles Manson. After touring on the college lecture circuit in the 1980s, Leary is ravaged with illness in the 1990s. Despite his problems, he continues to declare that death is the greatest event in any individual's life. After his death, Leary's wish to have his brain cryogenically frozen is honored: his head is surgically removed from his body, put on ice, and carted off.

Although the film doesn't offer much new information for anyone versed in Leary's legacy, TIMOTHY LEARY'S DEAD is a loving look back at this "high priest of the drug revolution" and his unique allure. Respectful, but never so reverential that he ignores Leary's more ludicrous side, director Paul Davids does a fine job of charting Leary's exuberant existence, with excellent use of archival news footage, intimate images of turned-on gatherings, Congressional hearings about LSD use, and filmed comments from his admirers and enemies (of course, when then-President Nixon labels Leary "the most dangerous man alive," it's difficult *not* to consider that a compliment). Skillfully editing these random elements into a cohesive portrait, Davids also includes footage of Leary articulately speaking at length about his beliefs and his work with mind-altering chemicals. While the film certainly won't win over any of Leary's detractors, the assembled evidence makes it difficult to deny that the man was an extremely charismatic figure.

Unfortunately, there are a few small missteps: the comments from Leary's long time followers seem a bit half-baked (as do the followers), while Davids also avoids such difficult subjects as Leary's daughter's suicide, or his son Jack's public denouncement of him, for being a prison informer. When Davids does see fit to include a negative comment about Leary, it comes from a blowhard LAPD cop, who's an easy target for derision. The times at which the movie truly falters, however, are when Davids strays from the topic of Leary's life and philosophy, offering up sidebars about modern-day misfits, or the legal problems the filmmakers faced when filming Leary's death. Still, when Leary is shown laughing about his upcoming passing, the film truly captures the essence of the man. The outrageous finale, in fact, feels like nothing less than Leary's own cosmic raspberry from the grave. *(Nudity, adult situations, substance abuse.)*—S.P.

d, Paul Davids; p, Todd Easton Mills, Paul Davids; assoc p, Claire Burch, Hollace Davids; w, Paul Davids, Todd Easton Mills; ph, Paul Helling; ed, David J. Wilson, Mark Deimel; m, The Moody Blues, Jimmie Rodgers, Ray Thomas, John Selby, Leon Rubenhold, Errol G. Spencer, Steve Weissner, Dennis Martinez, Claire Burch, Randi McMathew, Mark Kapner, Lauri-anne Fiorentino, Joe Weissman; sound, Ted Gordon

Documentary **(PR: C MPAA: NR)**

TOKYO FIST ★★★

(Japan, 1997) 90m Kaijyu Theater Company ~ Manga Entertainment c

Shinya Tsukamoto *(Tsuda Yoshiharu)*; Kahori Fujii *(Hizuru)*; Kohji Tsukamoto *(Kojima Takuji)*; Naomasa Musaka *(Hase—Trainer)*; Naoto Takenaka *(Ohizumi—Trainer)*; Koichi Wajima *(Shirota—Gym Owner)*; Tomoroh Taguchi *(Tattoo Master)*; Nobu Kanaoka *(Nurse)*

From the maker of TETSUO: IRON MAN (1990) and TETSUO II: BODY HAMMER (1991) comes this surreal, frequently hellish account of an obsessive love triangle that involves boxing and self-mutilation. Although it eschews the science-fiction trappings of the earlier films, the film is no less exotic, like a combination of David Lynch and Takeshi Kitano.

In Tokyo, the lives of a plodding insurance salesman, Tsuda (Shinya Tsukamoto), and his attractive fiancee, Hizuru (Kahori Fujii), are thrown into disarray after a chance encounter with Tsuda's high school friend Kojima (Kohji Tsukamoto), a pro boxer. Kojima begins visiting Hizuru while Tsuda is out, provoking a confrontation which results in Kojima beating and bloodying Tsuda. Tsuda confronts Hizuru over Kojima's affections and forces a breakup. She moves in with Kojima.

Deeply angered and humiliated, Tsuda begins boxing lessons at the same gym where Kojima trains and throws himself into the sport with a maniacal fervor. Hizuru begins to pierce her body in different places and has tattoos applied. Kojima is set to fight a boxer named Kumakagi, but has second thoughts after watching Kumakagi disable an opponent. Kojima reveals to Hizuru that in high school he witnessed a girl's murder by a gang of boys and he responded by vowing, along with Tsuda, to avenge the girl by learning boxing so they could give the girl's killers a beating when they got out of jail. But Tsuda never followed through—until now.

Tsuda confronts Hizuru and bangs his own head against a wall; she, in turn, beats him with her fist. Tsuda spars with Kojima at the gym and beats him badly until Kojima rallies and knocks Tsuda out, sending him to the hospital. The three troubled souls, Tsuda, Kojima, and Hizuru, simultaneously engage in different acts of bloodletting: at the hospital, Tsuda bleeds in an out-of-control fashion, as the doctors work furiously to stop it; in the ring, Kojima fights ferociously and beats Kumakagi but, at the moment of triumph, blood flows from his eyes; out in a field in the moonlight, Hizuru cuts herself open in a ritualistic fashion.

No plot synopsis can do justice to the dizzying array of bizarre images director Shinya Tsukamoto employs to tell his story. Fans of TETSUO I and II will appreciate the themes of self-mutilation and sudden bursts of violence underlying the strict social order. Although it contains no elements of science fiction, TOKYO FIST maintains a futuristic aura with its blue-lit exteriors, blood-red interiors, high-speed skyline shots, and frequent long shots of Tsuda, alone and catatonic in the midst of modern cityscapes and bustling crowds. The frenzied boxing and self-mutilation on display can be interpreted as a metaphor for the suppressed rage of Japan's yuppie/professional class.

This Japanese arthouse film of the '90s stands out for its perverse charm, black humor, and unmistakable visual flair. It may not be for all tastes, but it ranks with the work of such other New Wave Japanese filmmakers as Takeshi Kitano (FIREWORKS), Sogo Ishii (ANGEL DUST) and Takashi Ishii (GONIN). *(Graphic violence, profanity.)*—B.C.

d, Shinya Tsukamoto; p, Shinya Tsukamoto; assoc p, Kiyo Joo; w, Shinya Tsukamoto (based on a story by Hisashi Saito and Shinya Tsukamoto); ph, Shinya Tsukamoto; ed, Shinya Tsukamoto; m, Chu Ishikawa; prod d, Shinya Tsukamoto; art d, Shinya Tsukamoto; sound, Yukio Sekiya (mixer), Ichiro Kawashima (recordist); fx, Takashi Oda, Hiroshi Sagae; cos, Hiroko Iwasaki; makeup, Kaori Sasaki, Akira Fukaya (effects), Tadahiro Inoue (effects)

Drama/Romance/Horror **(PR: O MPAA: NR)**

TOP OF THE WORLD ★½

(U.S., 1998) 98m Millennium Films ~ Nu Image c

Peter Weller *(Ray Mercer)*; Tia Carrere *(Rebecca)*; Dennis Hopper *(Steve Atlas)*; Joe Pantoliano *(Vince)*; Martin Kove *(Carl)*; Peter Coyote *(The Butcher)*; David Allan Grier *(Detective Augustus)*; Cary-Hiroyuki Tagawa *(Capt. Heller)*; Julie McCollough *(Ginger)*; Kevin Bernhardt *(Dean)*; Eddie Mekka *(Joe Burns)*; Ed Lauter *(Ridgenfield)*; Derek Annunciation *(Fredo)*; Dell Yount *(Mac)*; Alexander Mervin *(Benny)*; Michael Delano *(Lt. De Rosa)*; Gavan O'Herlihy *(Lt. Detective Logan)*; Brenda Cavalie *(Maid)*; Roger Rhu *(Count Room Guard)*; Andrew Jarrell *(Casino Guard)*; Larry Mannetti *(Morgan)*; Sly Smith *(Fipps)*; Frank Patton *(Franco)*; Don Mirault *(Surveillance Technicians)*; Michael Weller *(Surveillance Technicians)*; Rusty Meyers *(Swat Cop)*; Dick Butler *(Elevator Corridor Guard)*

The term "kitchen sink" used to refer to a style of cinematic naturalism. In the case of TOP OF THE WORLD, it signifies a commercial enterprise that throws in every filmmaking style but the kitchen sink; this film shifts tone, crossbreeds genres, and pumps up its violence quotient to distract an audience it has long since lost. The film premiered on HBO and was subsequently released on home video.

Newly released ex-con Ray Mercer (Peter Weller) spends his first day of freedom accompanying his estranged wife Rebecca (Tia Carrere) to Las Vegas for a divorce. Killing time at a casino managed by Rebecca's new boyfriend Steve Atlas (Dennis Hopper), Mercer gets a big payoff on a slot machine. Before he can collect, Ray gets caught in the middle of a carefully timed robbery of the casino. Heading a dimwitted crew disguised as security guards, trigger-happy Carl (Martin Kove) makes off with $12 million from the counting room.

The heist is being masterminded by Atlas and his partner Vince (Joe Pantoliano) to conceal millions they've already siphoned away from their Mafia bosses. When quick police intervention traps the thieves inside the casino hotel, Atlas decides to play parolee Mercer for his patsy because Mercer has a prison record. The owner of the casino, nicknamed the Butcher (Peter Coyote), comes gunning for the burglars personally. As a SWAT team peppers the building with bullets, Mercer shoots the

Butcher in self-defense before clutching the bottom of a getaway copter carrying Rebecca, Carl, Atlas, and Vince. When he discovers a shortage in the cash taken from the counting room, a suspicious Atlas murders Vince. Upon landing, Carl flees, while Mercer, Rebecca, and Atlas chase each other to Hoover Dam. Atlas plunges to his death in a scuffle, and Rebecca reveals she masterminded a pre-robbery skimming of Atlas's payload; she stashed the millions in her car at the casino parking garage.

This smirking film is infuriating, because its cynicism isn't earned; a smarty-pants attitude is slathered on top of this double-crosser's Dagwood sandwich like mayonnaise covering stale lunch meat. Everything about this caper is past its expiration date, from the dishonor-among-thieves subtext to the barely breathing performances to the plot reversals any idiot could figure out. TOP OF THE WORLD doesn't merely fashion a tongue-in-cheek overview, it changes stylistic gears and turns the crime aftermath into a robbery vaudeville. When a movie fires salvos from the opening credits, the audience soon learns to duck for cover. *(Graphic violence, extreme profanity, nudity, substance abuse.)* —R.P.

d, Sidney J. Furie; p, Elie Samaha, Avi Lerner; exec p, Danny Dimbort, Trevor Short, Bob Misiorowski; co-p, Kevin Bernhardt, Warren Zide; w, Bart Madison; ph, Alan Caso; ed, Alain Jakubowicz; m, Robert O. Ragland; prod d, Aaron Osborne; sound, Douglas Schulman; fx, Dan Lester; casting, Geno Havens; cos, Dalia Saydah-Dokter; makeup, Dalia Saydah-Dokter; stunts, Dick Butler

Crime/Action **(PR: C MPAA: R)**

TOUCH OF EVIL: THE DIRECTOR'S CUT ★★★★★

(U.S., 1998) 111m Universal ~ October Films bw

Charlton Heston *(Ramon Miguel "Mike" Vargas)*; Janet Leigh *(Susan Vargas)*; Orson Welles *(Hank Quinlan)*; Joseph Calleia *(Pete Menzies)*; Akim Tamiroff *("Uncle Joe" Grandi)*; Val DeVargas *(Pancho)*; Ray Collins *(District Attorney Adair)*; Dennis Weaver *(Motel Clerk)*; Joanna Moore *(Marcia Linnekar)*; Mort Mills *(Schwartz)*; Marlene Dietrich *(Tanya)*; Victor Millan *(Manolo Sanchez)*; Lalo Rios *(Risto)*; Michael Sargent *(Pretty Boy)*; Mercedes McCambridge *(Gang Leader)*; Joseph Cotten *(Detective)*; Zsa Zsa Gabor *(Owner of Strip Joint)*; Phil Harvey *(Blaine)*; Joi Lansing *(Blonde)*; Harry Shannon *(Gould)*; Rusty Wescoatt *(Casey)*; Wayne Taylor; Kenny Miller; Raymond Rodriguez *(Gang Members)*; Arlene McQuade *(Ginnie)*; Dominick Delgarde *(Lackey)*; Joe Basulto *(Young Delinquent)*; Jennie Dias *(Jackie)*; Yolanda Bojorquez *(Bobbie)*; Eleanor Dorado *(Lia)*; Keenan Wynn *(Man)*

Forty years after being truncated by Universal Studios and dumped into theaters on the bottom half of a double bill, and some 10 years after being released on video in the '80s in a longer "restored" version, Orson Welles's classic film noir TOUCH OF EVIL finally got the treatment it deserved in 1998, reissued in a beautifully reconstructed "director's cut" that incorporates about 50 editing and soundtrack alterations which were based on a rediscovered 58-page memo written by Welles to heedless studio executives in 1957.

Mexican lawman Vargas (Charlton Heston) and his new American bride Susie (Janet Leigh) are in a small town along the US-Mexico border when a car bomb kills an important local businessman. While Vargas helps police detective Hank Quinlan (Orson Welles) investigate, Susie is lured away by a gang of Mexicans who take her to see Grandi (Akim Tamiroff), a drug dealer who tries to scare Susie into keeping Vargas from testifying against his jailed brother. Immersed in the investigation, Vargas has to postpone his honeymoon and he drives Susie to a motel in the desert. Quinlan interrogates a suspect named Sanchez (Victor Millan), and discovers a shoebox filled with dynamite in Sanchez's bathroom. However, Vargas claims that the box was empty when he had knocked it over earlier, and he accuses Quinlan of planting evidence.

At the motel, Susie is terrorized and drugged by a gang of junkies working for Grandi, who has made a deal with Quinlan to get Vargas off his back. When Vargas finds out that Quinlan recently bought some dynamite, and also uncovers evidence of other possible frame-ups, he tries to talk Quinlan's loyal partner Menzies (Joseph Calleia) into helping him, but Menzies refuses. Quinlan then strangles Grandi and frames Susie for his murder. Menzies finally agrees to help Vargas after finding Quinlan's cane in the hotel room where Grandi's body was found. Wearing a hidden microphone, Menzies gets Quinlan to admit his guilt, but hearing an echo coming from Vargas's recording device, Quinlan realizes that he is being set up and he shoots Menzies. Quinlan then aims at Vargas, but Menzies, still barely alive, fires a fatal shot at Quinlan. As Vargas is reunited with Susie, he receives word that Sanchez has confessed and that Quinlan was right all along about his guilt.

The new version of TOUCH OF EVIL is not so much a restoration as it is a revivification, presenting the film according to Welles's original intentions for the first time, and changing the film in subtle, but very real, ways without including any new footage. The most significant change is the removal of the superimposed credits from the legendary opening crane shot, a spectacular three-minute continuous take in which a bomb is placed in a car trunk and the camera follows Vargas and Susie along the streets of the border town until the car explodes. With the credits now gone, the technical virtuosity of the shot is no longer obscured, but more importantly, the love between Vargas and Susie, which is so important to the rest of the film, is immediately established by being able to see them nuzzling and hear them talk. Also removed from the opening is Henry Mancini's jazzy Latin bongo theme (though it can still be heard in the background throughout the film), and while the original music was great, its absence now allows for Welles's dense soundtrack, consisting of a montage of music blasting from loudspeakers, footsteps, laughter, Vargas's and Susie's voices, sirens, and even a pack of goats, to be clearly heard. Similarly, the soundtrack for the entire picture has been remixed, permitting Welles's mastery of overlapping dialogue and multiple conversations to come through with crystal clarity, and also contributing immeasurably to the film's dizzying and disorienting atmosphere.

The other major alteration is the intercutting of the stories of the separated honeymooners, Vargas and Susie, which had originally been more linear, but now cuts back and forth between the two of them to create a greater sense of tension. Taken separately, all of the changes don't seem that radical, but together, their impact on the final film makes the story easier to follow and results in a movie that now seems less like a pulpy crime thriller and more of a tragic character study. It's as if a layer of haze had been peeled away to reveal all of the buried social comment and subtext involving prejudice, poverty, and abuse of power.

Visually, the film has never looked so pristine, allowing Russell Metty's protean cinematography to shine in its feverish depiction of an inferno-like milieu of neon stripjoints and bars, and during the bravura set pieces (the hallucinatory strangling of Grandi, the distorted wide-angle shots of the gang terrorizing Susie, the stunningly choreographed climax where Vargas follows Menzies and Quinlan through a maze of sewers and canals). The performances also seem fresher than ever, from Welles's towering portrayal of the dissolute, gargantuan Quinlan, to Heston's self-righteous Vargas (of whom everyone keeps amusingly observing "He doesn't sound Mexican"), and the hilarious support provided by Dennis Weaver as a neurotic hotel nightman, and Akim Tamiroff's Grandi, whose "rug" keeps falling off. The film was always ahead of its time in technique, subject matter, treatment, and characterization, but it now seems more modern than ever and is arguably Welles's most brilliant film after CITIZEN KANE (1941). *(Violence, substance abuse.)*—M.S.

d, Orson Welles, Harry Keller (uncredited); p, Albert Zugsmith, Rick Schmidlin (director's cut); w, Orson Welles (based on the novel *Badge of Evil* by Whit Masterson); ph, Russell Metty; ed, Virgil Vogel, Aaron Stell, Walter Murch (director's cut); m, Henry Mancini; md, Joseph Gershenson; art d, Alexander Golitzen, Robert Clatworthy; set d, Russel A. Gausman, John Austin; sound, Bill Varney (director's cut), Peter Reale (director's cut), Walter Murch (director's cut); cos, Bill Thomas

Crime/Thriller (PR: C MPAA: NR)

TRACKED ★★

(U.S./Canada, 1998) 92m Goodstuff Entertainment ~ Showtime/Viacom c
(AKA: DOGBOYS, THE)

Bryan Brown *(Capt Brown)*; Dean Cain *(Julian Talyor)*; Tia Carrere *(Jennifer Dern)*; Ken James *(Wakefield)*; Richard Chevolleau *(Willy B)*; Sean McCann *(Pappy)*; Hardee Lineham *(Wilkins)*; Von Flores *(Miguel)*; Robbie Rox *(Bull)*; Jody Racicot *(Rego)*; Matthew Bennett *(Carl Ewing)*; Jim Bearden *(J.B. Diggs)*; Robert Collins *(Cates)*; Bruce Tubbe *(Bus Guard)*; Scott Wickware *(Prison Guard One)*; Billy Otis *(Smitty)*; Rick Demas *(Monster)*; Bernard Browne *(Tower Guard)*; Wayne Best *(Prison Guard Two)*; Roger McKeen *(Guard One)*; Raymond Hunt *(Guard Two)*; Jerry Knight *(Newscaster One)*; Joe Matheson *(Newscaster Two)*

Filmed under the more descriptive title "The Dogboys," this hell-hole movie is an amalgam of THE MOST DANGEROUS GAME (1932) and horror schlock like THE PACK (1977). Action pic cliches clog this escapism's suspense arteries.

After taking part in a barroom brawl, cocky ex-marine Julian Taylor (Dean Cain) gets shoved in a Southern slammer where the convicts, as part of their work duties, help train bloodhounds to discourage prison breakouts. Although the Dogboy program at Retrieve Prison is the brainchild of Capt. Brown (Bryan Brown), Taylor is trained by Pappy (Sean McCann) and Willy B. (Richard Chevolleau).

Willy B. is actually an assistant to local D.A. Jennifer Dern (Tia Carrere), posing as a prisoner in order to investigate Brown, whose bank account is too large for his meager salary. Unable to elicit Taylor's cooperation, Willy B. is bitten to death by Brown's killer-dog, Clyde, after someone undoes the latch on Clyde's pen. After Willy B.'s demise, Dern confides her suspicions about Brown's financial improprieties to Warden Wakefield (Ken James), not realizing that the Warden and Brown are in cahoots.

Upset about mysteriously disappearing cellmates, Taylor snoops in an off-limits cabin on the prison grounds and learns that Brown has been allowing paying customers to hunt down prisoners for sport. When Dern pays an unannounced visit to the prison, Wakefield reveals to her his true colors. Brown prepares to eliminate both her and Taylor. Warden Wakefield plans to frame Brown for all the crimes, including the murders of Dern and Taylor. Before Brown can strike back, Wakefield shoots Clyde; Brown retaliates by shooting Wakefield. As he flees Brown, Taylor gives the dog-pack some clothing coated with Brown's scent; the animals track him down, and Dern arrests him.

Delete all the colorful background matter about dog-training, and TRACKED is just another rip-off of the action world's most recycled screenplay: THE MOST DANGEROUS GAME (1932). (It's time for some enterprising huckster to do an all-female version or to reset the story in outer space.) On its own rough-house terms, TRACKED packs a nasty punch in a repetitiously gory way and revs up for some exciting hound pursuits. On the minus side, a snarling Bryan Brown bares his teeth as often as the dogs, and the script fails to camouflage Warden Wakefield's complicity. Recommended for macho-holics with a high tolerance for brutality and barking. *(Graphic violence, extreme profanity, adult situations.)*—R.P.

d, Ken Russell; exec p, Hugh Martin, Rob Stork, Bob Rubin; w, Rob Stork, David Taylor; ph, Jamie Thompson; ed, Xavier Russell; m, John Altman; prod d, Ed Hanna; art d, Bob Sher; set d, Doug McCullough; sound, Stuart French (mixer); fx, Tim Good; casting, Beth Klein; cos, Csilla Marki; makeup, Lynda McCormack; stunts, John Stoneham Stoneham

Action/Prison (PR: C MPAA: NR)

TRANCEFORMER: A PORTRAIT OF LARS VON TRIER ★★★

(Sweden, 1997) 52m AB Memfis Film; Svergis Television Dokumentar; Swedish Film Institute; Bengt Forslund; Film Vast; Danish Film Institute; Jorgen Ljungdalh; Danmarks Radio; TV-Fakta ~ Cowboy Booking International c/bw

Lars von Trier *(Himself)*; Stig Bjorkman *(Interviewer)*; Fredrik von Krusenstjerna *(Interviewer)*

Elusive cult director Lars von Trier gets his due in TRANCEFORMER: A PORTRAIT OF LARS VON TRIER. This spirited documentary features a rare interview with von Trier and clips from several of his films.

Through interviews with the director (shot over a two-year period), we learn about how von Trier was born to Jewish parents in Denmark (the "radical middle class," as he puts it), how he became a child star of Danish television in the late 1960s, and how he experimented making super-8 films as a boy. We also hear from ex-classmates about his struggles with authority in Danish film school.

Von Trier reviews his work as a mature filmmaker, as we see clips from THE ELEMENT OF CRIME (1984), EPIDEMIC (1987), ZENTROPA (1992), BREAKING THE WAVES (1996), and THE KINGDOM, PART 1 (1994). On a personal note, von Trier discusses his self-hatred, his legendary phobias, and his enigmatic persona. Positive and negative anecdotes from colleagues round out the portrait.

Lars von Trier has emerged as a major filmmaker over the last few years, but, as a person, he has remained resolutely remote (even in 1998, he showed up at the Cannes Film Festival to promote IDIOTS, his latest film, but ended up skipping the attendant press conference). For this reason, TRANCEFORMER: A PORTRAIT OF LARS VON TRIER offers a rare glimpse of the director, who, as it turns out, reveals a surprisingly loquacious side. Yet, throughout this efficient documentary, von Trier never seems completely straightforward, either about his beliefs or his autobiography. Thus, some may find this smirking enfant terrible frustrating, while others will find him amusing (his story about seeing a UFO as a child is highly suspect). The rare footage of von Trier as a child actor and the scenes from his earliest films (including a school project, THE ORCHID GARDEN, and his first two features, ELEMENT OF CRIME and EPIDEMIC) highlight the profile. Otherwise, there is an imbalanced emphasis on BREAKING THE WAVES (including many behind-the-scenes glimpses) because TRANCEFORMER was shot during the filming of WAVES. The comments from the actors and colleagues from this production abet some understanding of von Trier, but the emphasis diminishes the importance of von Trier's other (sometimes better) work, including EPIDEMIC. And where is MEDEA, his provocative 1988 video staging of the classic myth? Even THE KINGDOM, his magnum opus (a miniseries which premiered on Danish television) is treated as an afterthought. Happily, most of von Trier's work has become available on home video, so viewers can fill in the gaps of this playful if uneven biographical sketch. *(Violence, profanity.)*—E.M.

d, Stig Bjorkman, Fredrik von Krusenstjerna; p, Lars Jonsson; ph, Jan Roed, Anthony Dod Mantle, Bjorn Blixt; ed, Leon Flamholc; sound, Ragnar Samuelson, Steen K. Anderson, Thomas Langballe

Documentary **(PR: C MPAA: NR)**

TREKKIES ★★★

(U.S., 1997) 87m Neo Motion Pictures ~ Paramount c

INTERVIEWEES: Denise Crosby; Leonard Nimoy; James Doohan; Brent Spiner; Barbara Adams; William Shatner; LeVar Burton; Kate Mulgrew; John De Lancie; George Takai; Majel Barrett; Denis G. Bourguignon; Gabriel Koerner; Michael Dorn; Chase Masterson; Nichelle Nichols; DeForest Kelley; Douglas Marcks; Fred Travalina; Jeri Taylor; Walter Koenig; Wil Wheaton; Edwin A. "Buzz" Aldrin; Jonathan Frakes; Anne Murphy; Ethan Phillips; Grace Lee Whitney; Robert O'Reilly; Terry Farrell; Brannon Braga; Richard Arnold

This 16mm documentary on the insatiable fan-followers of TV's "Star Trek" can be taken two ways: as a celebration of the Trek phenomenon, or as a cautionary display for those who believe, as actor William Shatner once notoriously asserted, that all these people should simply "get a life."

Host and executive producer Denise Crosby claims (disingenuously) that she had no idea what she was in for when she won a short-lived part on the successful 1987 revival series "Star Trek: The Next Generation." Now Crosby, plus Shatner and other prominent performers in Trek programs and movies, are venerated at fan conventions on virtually any given weekend. In interview snippets the original "Star Trek" cast recount the first "con" in New York in 1972, just a few years after NBC's cancellation of the low-rated sci-fi show. Shatner, Leonard Nimoy, DeForest Kelley, and others came to the hotel expecting 300 well-wishers. Instead 3,000 zealous "Trekkies" materialized, applauding their every syllable. It was only the beginning. Nichelle "Lt. Uhura" Nichols and George "Mr. Sulu" Takei visited NASA and found themselves idolized by real-life space scientists and astronauts that their media images had inspired. James Doohan (Chief Engineer Scott) emotionally recalls that while on the Trek-con circuit he talked a despondent young woman out of suicide; he has become emotionally attached to his fan-base ever since.

But the focus is on the fans themselves, like teenaged Gabriel Koerner suiting up for the latest Los Angeles con and creating a Trek feature screenplay and movie on his home computer—just for his own Trekkie club. Or Barbara Adams of Arkansas, a bindery worker assigned to jury duty during the 1990s Whitewater scandal that reached the White House. A serious Trekker (sometimes a preferred designation over "Trekkie"), Adams made national news by wearing her "Next Generation" uniform to the trial, insisting it symbolized her devotion to civic duty. Adams's case only seems to be the tip of the iceberg: some of these folks seem pretty warped, like the subculture of "Klingons," fans dressed as the fictional warrior race who even teach themselves its nonexistent language (one paid $1,400 for a Westmore-created Klingon forehead worn on "Star Trek: Deep Space Nine"). Another collector allegedly hoarded blood samples from cast members. One crazed fan drank from a glass used by ill "Next Generation" actor John De Lancie, in hopes of contracting his virus. Despite the upbeat tone, there are times when Crosby herself seems ready to panic, especially in the Florida offices of "Starbase Dental," a company run by Dr. Denis G. Bourguignon D.M.D. who conducts business in an elaborate *USS Enterprise* sickbay motif. Crosby also finds Trek thespians depicted in sex-fantasy art and prose circulated among fans who prefer not to be identified on camera.

The sex angle is about as dark as TREKKIES ever get, but for the initiated, it's probably enough. Interestingly, the movie makes no mention of the infamous "Heaven's Gate" cult (which included Nichelle Nichols's brother) who committed mass-suicide in 1997; reportedly "Star Trek's" played a large part in their cosmology.

Interviewees declare "Star Trek's" enduring appeal rests on an optimistic future, promulgated by original producer Gene Roddenberry as a triumph of interplanetary humanism—every ethnic, religious, and even species difference is tolerated and respected. Other recent Hollywood portrayals of tomorrow foresee post-apocalyptic hells or technological nightmares, as in ALIEN (1979), MAD MAX (1979), BLADE RUNNER (1982), and THE TERMINATOR (1984). Only "Star Trek," like a religion, offers a life better and more enlightened than this one (argue the participants in the Trek cult). Even with that sort of appealing message, TREKKIES stands as a rather one-note affair for the nonconverted, a happy photo album of eccentrics in which each individual tops the last. Fortunately, these folks are a lot more amusing than many evangelical types. In terms of pop-cultural anthropology, the feature is worth comparing to TIE-DIED, Andrew Behar's 1995 documentary on fans of the band The Grateful Dead. *(Sexual situations.)*—C.C.

d, Roger Nygard; p, W.K. Border; exec p, Michael Leahy, Joel Soisson, Denise Crosby; assoc p, Scott Nimerfro; ph, Harris Done; ed, Roger Nygard; m, Walter Werzowa, Jimmy Wood, J.J. Holiday, Billy Sullivan; sound, Larry Scharf

Documentary **(PR: C MPAA: NR)**

TRICKS ★★★

(U.S., 1997) 96m Gunning/Taylor Productions ~ Viacom c

Mimi Rogers *(Jackie Simpson)*; Tyne Daly *(Sarah)*; Ray Walston *(Big Sam)*; Callum Keith Rennie *(Adam)*; David Kaye *(Joseph)*; Ron Halder *(Tommy)*; Kevin McNulty *(Henry Rinaldi)*; Tom McBeath *(Mike)*; Don S. Davis *(Man)*; Elizabeth Carol Savenkoff *(Daria)*; Mark Brandon *(Frank)*; Marilyn Norry *(Freda)*; Hiro Kanagawa *(Matsuba)*; Frank C. Turner *(Dr. Olsen)*; Constance Barnes *(Shirley)*; Carol Alexander *(Bobbie)*; Iris Quinn *(April)*; Yoko Sakai *(Japanese Woman)*; Carrie Cain Sparks *(Unemployment Woman)*; Suzanne Zelmer *(Young Showgirl)*; Deanne Henry *(Melanie)*; Jaayda Ellingham *(Brianne)*; Robin Palmer *(Rickie)*

TRICKS is a feminist midlife crisis foray imbued with harsh truths about sexism and ageism. Having much more impact than exploitative adventures in hookerdom like WHORE (1991), this evocative woman's film is equal parts soap opera, revenge pic, and show biz tragedy.

Now too old to strut her stuff onstage, former Vegas showgirl Jackie Simpson (Mimi Rogers) barely makes ends meet as a salesclerk in a Reno boutique. In order to provide for her sickly child, Jackie turns tricks at a casino hotel in an arrangement with hotel bell captain Tommy (Ron Halder). One night, Tommy sets her up with a sadist, who unbeknownst to her, is a Reno power broker named Henry Rinaldi (Kevin McNulty). After humiliating her, Rinaldi gets his kicks by viciously beating Jackie. Befriended by a cabbie, Adam (Callum Keith Rennie), who drives her to a doctor, Jackie bounces back only to learn she cannot find employment anywhere in town. Her roommate Sarah (Tyne Daly) introduces her to retired leg-breaker Big Sam (Ray Walston), but Jackie doesn't know the identity of her assailant. Using information from Big Sam about Tommy's illegal gambling activities, she blackmails him into revealing Rinaldi's identity. But because Rinaldi is one of Reno's major concessionaires, Big Sam is afraid to help her. Tipped off by Tommy, Rinaldi threatens to harm Jackie's young son. Armed with a pistol, Jackie stalks and terrorizes Rinaldi at his mansion, but cannot sink to murdering him. Bidding adieu to Adam and to Sarah (who moves in with Big Sam), Jackie renounces the past and moves on to a quieter life as a computer programmer in Texas.

This update of old Constance Bennett/Kay Francis weepies that once flooded the 1930s is refreshingly uncompromising. Without turning its back entirely on those whore-with-the-heart-of-gold cliches, TRICKS remains clear-eyed about the realities of the skin trade. Admittedly, the film veers into misplaced adorableness with the Golden Ager romance of Big Sam and Sarah, and stacks the deck by saddling Jackie's child with poor health. But TRICKS never ducks the ugly nature of Jackie's part-time job. In an incredibly nasty scene, Tommy and a hotel official argue about what to do with the battered woman, as if she were roadkill to be disposed of. Despite the melodramatic denouement, TRICKS succeeds in exposing the indignities women like Jackie must endure. As the dethroned Vegas showgirl, Rogers brilliantly conveys a character whose self-esteem is wholly linked to a fading allure, a woman who can't see her options clearly after staring too many years into a spotlight. It's a subtle turn in a sober-minded movie about life after 30 in a culture that worships the young. *(Violence, nudity, extreme profanity, sexual situations.)*—R.P.

d, Kenneth Fink; p, Grazka Taylor, Barbara Gunning; exec p, Mimi Rogers, Stephen Gelber, Julie Silverman Yorn; co-p, Colleen Nystedt; w, Deborah Amelon; ph, John S. Bartley ; ed, Jay Friedkin; m, Patrick Seymour; prod d, Michael Nemirsky; set d, Andrea French; sound, Gord Anderson; fx, James G. Fisher; casting, Abra Edelman, Elisa Goodman, Stuart Aikins; cos, Gregory Mah; makeup, Victoria Down; stunts, Melissa Stubbs

Drama **(PR: C MPAA: R)**

TRUCE, THE ★★½

(Italy/France/Germany/Switzerland/U.K., 1997) 145m
Capitol Films; 3 Emme Cinematografica; Stephan Films/UGC Images/France 2 Cinema; DaZu Film; T&C Film ~ Miramax c
(LA TREGUA)

John Turturro *(Primo Levi)*; Rade Serbedzija *(The Greek)*; Massimo Ghini *(Cesare)*; Stefano Dionisi *(Daniele)*; Teco Celio *(Col. Rovi)*; Roberto Citran *(Unverdorben)*; Claudio Bisio *(Ferrari)*; Andy Luotto *(D'Agata)*; Agnieszka Wagner *(Galina)*; Lorenza Indovina *(Flora)*; Marina Gerasymenko *(Maria Fiodorovna)*; Igor Bezgin *(Egorov)*; Alexandr Ilijn *(The Mongol)*; Viachesslav Olhovsky *(Lt. Sergei)*; Anatoliy Vassiliev *(Dr. Gotlieb)*; Tatiana Meshcherkina *(Irina)*; Franco Trevisi *(Marshall)*; Federico Pacifici *(Lieutenant)*; Ernesto Lama *(Carmine)*; Gerda Maria Jurgens *(Brigitte)*; Kaspar Weiss *(Kapo)*; Vitalij Rozstalnyj *(Gen. Timoshenko)*; Joachim Wormsdorf *(German General)*; Konstiantyn Artemenko; Igor Chernezkyj; Valentyna Derbasova; Olexandr Grynko; Tetiatana Jelciuk

A labored adaptation of Primo Levi's post-Holocaust memoir, THE TRUCE follows the author's alternately exhilarating and arduous journey home to Italy after his release from Auschwitz. Studied visuals, an episodic structure, and slight but seminal alterations of the book weigh down this international coproduction.

It's January 1945, and, as the Russians approach Auschwitz, the Nazis burn evidence and shoot down or evacuate the "healthy" prisoners, leaving behind only the sick. Among the infirm is Primo Levi (John Turturro), one of the relatively few Jews to survive imprisonment in the infamous death camp. Freed from hell, Levi begins a long, circuitous journey through war-torn Europe, trying to get back to his family in Turin.

Joining the mass of refugees streaming through Poland, Levi teams with The Greek (Rade Serbedzija), a mercenary Greek. As Levi limps along in his ragged shoes, The Greek flashes his own sturdy footwear and proclaims that, in a world perpetually at war, good shoes are the linchpin of survival. Before the two go their separate ways, in a rare burst of altruism, The Greek gives Levi a better pair.

Next, the Italian Jew gets waylaid in a Russian transit camp where, using his chemistry background, he does some pharmaceutical work. He falls for Galina (Agnieszka Wagner), his gorgeous Russian assistant. To the chemist's dismay, she finds affection elsewhere. WWII ends and Levi leaves the camp amid a wave of festivities, never having expressed his love.

For the remainder of the journey, Levi unites with several of his compatriots, including a colorful rogue, Cesare (Massimo Ghini), and an introspective young man, Daniele (Stefano Dionisi), whose entire family was slaughtered by the Nazis. Stalled for months by destroyed rail lines and endless red tape, the group makes countless detours in the Soviet Union before finally making a beeline for Italy. The crew bonds as they scrounge for food and drink in the heavily wooded countryside.

Nine months after leaving Auschwitz, Levi finally arrives in Turin. Away for a seeming lifetime, the survivor adjusts to the resounding normalcy of his home. With memories tattooed on both his forearm and brain, Levi feels compelled to sit down, pen in hand, and share his harrowing experience with the world.

At or near the pinnacle of Holocaust writers, Primo Levi did a brilliant job capturing what went on around him during the prolonged nightmare. Like many fine writers, he was a consummate observer. Unfortunately, by making an observer a protagonist, THE TRUCE acquires an unavoidable air of detachment. Turturro is given little to do except watch and listen. As Levi, he creates an intelligent, reticent character, always respectable, though rarely compelling.

The film's lifeblood, therefore is comprised of the colorful characters Levi meets. Numerous scenes consist solely of Levi listening to another person relate his situation or philosophy. This works when Rade Serbedzija bursts on the screen as the brash Greek, announcing that "war is always," or later, when he exhibits his gaggle of oversized prostitutes. More often, the tactic backfires, and it becomes difficult to differentiate the characters. Why should the viewer even try when a character is likely to disappear after a scene or two?

In an effort to stir up the drama, the movie diverges from its source material, Levy's book *The Reawakening,* in depicting a few fictional interactions. Soon after leaving the concentration camp, Levi is seen offering some of his meager food to a begging waif. Though a man of integrity, Levi is foremost a survivor, who never mentions such falsely self-sacrificing gestures in his book. Director and cowriter Francesco Rosi is under the misguided impression that an Auschwitz survivor needs to be made more sympathetic, even at the price of reality.

Rosi commits a far more serious transgression near the end of the film, when the train makes a stop in the defeated Germany. The downtrodden refugees stare out the windows at several

German laborers. Levi opens his shirt revealing his striped prison uniform, complete with its dehumanizing number. Full of shame, one German kneels before the victims. Compare this false sentimentality with Levi's description of the actual incident: ". . . no one looked us in the eyes, no one accepted the challenge; they were deaf, blind and dumb. . . still strong, still capable of hatred and contempt, still prisoners of their old tangle of pride and guilt." Sometimes, filmmakers would do better to honor the sanctity of history. *(Adult situations.)*—T.Y.

d, Francesco Rosi; p, Leo Pescarolo; exec p, Guido De Laurentiis; assoc p, Dominique Green; co-p, Vera Belmont, Daniel Zuta, Marcel Hoehn; w, Francesco Rosi, Stefano Rulli, Sandro Petraglia (from Francesco Rosi and Tonino Guerra's adaptation of the book by Primo Levi); ph, Pasqualino De Santis, Marco Pontecorvo; ed, Ruggero Mastroianni, Bruno Sarandrea; m, Luis Bacalov; prod d, Andrea Crisanti; sound, Alain Curvelier, Steven Ghouti (design); cos, Alberto Verso; makeup, Francesco Freda

Historical/Drama **(PR: C MPAA: R)**

TRUCKS ★★½

(U.S./Canada, 1998) 99m Trucks Productions; Leider-Reisberg; Credo Entertainment; USA Pictures ~ Trimark Home Video c

Timothy Busfield *(Ray)*; Brenda Bakke *(Hope)*; Aidan Devine *(Trucker Bob)*; Roman Podhora *(Thad)*; Jay Brazeau *(Jack)*; Brendan Fletcher *(Logan)*; Amy Stewart *(Abby)*; Victor Cowie *(George)*; Sharon Bajer *(June)*; Jonathan Barrett *(Brad)*; Rick Skene *(Trucker Pete)*; Don Cranberry *(Sheriff)*; Barbara Lee Edwards *(TV Reporter)*; Gene Pyrz *(Refrigerator Truck Driver)*; Kirk Harper *(Lino)*; Harry Nelken *(Phil)*

People at a desert truckstop are terrorized by driverless trucks in this adaptation of a story previously filmed by its author, Stephen King, as MAXIMUM OVERDRIVE (1986). The film is all premise and no plot, a problem made worse by the clumsy addition of extraneous gory sequences. After premiering on the Sci-Fi Channel, the film was released on home video in 1998.

Ray (Timothy Busfield) and his son Logan (Brendan Fletcher) operate a desert truckstop just outside of Area 51. Hope (Brenda Bakke), who runs a hiking service nearby, is heading home after picking up some clients, including ex-Air Force officer Thad (Roman Podhora) and his rebellious teen daughter Abby (Amy Stewart), when they are attacked by a large truck with no driver. On his way to help, Ray is harassed by another truck whose driver he can't see.

When Ray and the others return to the truckstop, they find a group of driverless trucks terrorizing people trapped there. Attempts to escape or otherwise deal with the trucks result in death. Ray is puzzled when the trucks attempt to kill his son and Abby, yet fall back when he goes to help them. He realizes that they need him to "feed" them with gas, and will let him live so long as he does so. At night, Thad and Abby head for the government base at Area 51 to get a helicopter, while the others hide in the woods. The next morning, Ray, Hope, and Logan are picked up and flown away by a helicopter containing a shocked Abby—and no pilot.

Alfred Hitchcock's classic THE BIRDS (1963) explored the terror that is produced when a normally benign presence turns lethal; George Romero also toyed with this concept in various sequences to the original NIGHT OF THE LIVING DEAD (1968). In his original story "Trucks," Stephen King dealt simply with the question of whether trucks that had become imbued with intelligence (never mind how) could indeed conquer humanity. But fantasy elements that can enthrall in a short story aren't always translatable to the screen—particularly if the filmmaker in question has less of a grasp on his material than did Hitchcock and Romero. Here, Brian Taggert's script tries to fuel viewers' paranoia by having the characters discuss possible explanations for the phenomenon of the possessed trucks; this strategy only serves to frustrate and confuse, since the horror genre depends largely on well-crafted thrills, and not necessarily well-founded explanations of the supernatural curiosities depicted. Taggert does leave some loose ends dangling—the most irritating of which is the introduction of a deadly toxic cloud formed by an army chemical research project which seems to vanish halfway through the film.

What really demolishes TRUCKS, though, are a number of scenes which were tacked onto the film (per the end credits, which single out contributors to the "extra scenes"). The sequences depict characters who have nothing to do with the story being attacked and gruesomely murdered by other animated objects. Presumably the film's producers felt that more gore was needed (and didn't care how shoddy it looked), but these clumsy insertions only serve to extend uncomfortably the film's running time and drain away the tension from the movie's otherwise claustrophobic setting. *(Graphic violence, profanity.)* —M.F.

d, Chris Thomson; p, Jerry Leider, Richard S. Reisberg, William Wesley, David Bradstreet; exec p, Mark Amin, Derek Mazur; assoc p, Moses Theimer; co-p, Michael Scott, Bruce David Eisen, Jonathon Komack Martin, Phillip B. Goldfine; w, Brian Taggert (based on the short story "Trucks" by Stephen King); ph, Rob Draper, Keith Holland; ed, Lara Mazur, Dexter Adriano; m, Michael Richard Plowman; prod d, David Ferguson, Nathan Ogilvie, Regina Acuna; set d, Kim Forrest; sound, Gael MacLean; fx, Rory P.M. Cutler, Norman Cabrera, Enrich Martin Hicks, Gary Bentley; casting, Ellen Meyer, Bette Chadwick, Gary Oberst, Moses Theimer; cos, Darena Snowe, Warden Neil, Julieann Getman; makeup, Pamela Athayde, Tyson Fontaine; stunts, Shane Cardwell, Terence S. Kelley, Michael Kruzel

Science Fiction/Thriller **(PR: O MPAA: R)**

TRUMAN SHOW, THE ★★★★

(U.S., 1998) 102m Scott Rudin Productions ~ Paramount c

Jim Carrey *(Truman Burbank)*; Laura Linney *(Meryl)*; Noah Emmerich *(Marlon)*; Natascha McElhone *(Lauren/Sylvia)*; Holland Taylor *(Truman's Mother)*; Ed Harris *(Christof)*; Brian Delate *(Kirk—Truman's Father)*; Paul Giamatti *(Simeon—Control Room Director)*; Harry Shearer *(Mike Michaelson—Interviewer)*; Blair Slater *(Young Truman)*; Peter Krause *(Lawrence)*; Heidi Schanz *(Vivien)*; Ron Taylor *(Ron)*; Don Taylor *(Don)*; Ted Raymond *(Spencer)*; Judy Clayton *(Travel Agent)*; Fritz Dominique; Angel Schmiedt; Nastassja Schmiedt *(Truman's Neighbors)*; Muriel Moore *(Teacher)*; Mal Jones *(News Vendor)*; Judson Vaughn *(Insurance Co-Worker)*; Earl Hilliard Jr. *(Ferry Worker)*; David Andrew Nash *(Bus Driver/Ferry Captain)*; Jim Towers *(Bus Supervisor)*; Savannah Swafford *(Little Girl in Bus)*; Antoni Corone; Mario Ernesto Sanchez *(Security Guards)*; John Roselius *(Man at Beach)*; Kade Coates *(Truman—4 years)*; Marcia DeBonis *(Nurse)*; Sam Kitchin *(Surgeon)*; Sebastian Youngblood *(Orderly)*; Dave Corey *(Hospital Security Guard)*; Mark Alan Gillott *(Policeman at Power Plant)*; Jay Saiter; Tony Todd *(Policemen at Truman's House)*; Marco Rubeo *(Man in Christmas Box)*; Daryl Davis; Robert Davis *(Couple at Picnic Table)*; R.J. Murdock *(Production Assistant)*; Matthew McDonough; Larry McDowell *(Men at Newstand)*; Joseph Lucus *(Ticket Taker)*; Logan Kirksey *(TV Host)*; Adam Tomei *(Control Room Director)*; Una Damon *(Chloe)*; Philip Baker Hall; John Pleshette *(Network Executives)*; Philip Glass; John Pramik

(Keyboard Artists); O-Lan Jones; Krista Lynn Landolfi *(Bar Waitresses)*; Joe Minjares *(Bartender)*; Al Foster; Zoaunne LeRoy; Millie Slavin *(Bar Patrons)*; Terry Camilleri *(Man in Bathtub)*; Dona Hardy; Jeanette Miller *(Senior Citizens)*; Joel McKinnon Miller; Tom Simmons *(Garage Attendants)*; Susan Angelo *(Mother)*; Carly Smiga *(Daughter)*; Yuji Okumoto; Kiyoko Yamaguchi; Saemi Nakamura *(Japanese Family)*

A man discovers that his entire life has been a TV show in THE TRUMAN SHOW. Deftly mixing light entertainment with heavier themes, director Peter Weir's film is a terrific seriocomic fantasy as well as a showcase for star Jim Carrey, who puts himself at the service of the film instead of vice versa.

Truman Burbank (Jim Carrey) works as an insurance salesman and lives with his wife Meryl (Laura Linney) on picturesque Seahaven Island. . . or so he believes. Seahaven is actually a gigantic, domed television studio, an artificial world created to be Truman's reality. The brainchild of Christof (Ed Harris), "The Truman Show" has been broadcasting live to a global audience every moment of Truman's life for 30 years. Everyone else in Seahaven, including Meryl and Truman's lifelong best friend Marlon (Noah Emmerich), is an actor.

One day, Truman spots on the street the actor who played his father (Brian Delate), whom Christof killed off in a boating accident when Truman was a child. This and such strange occurrences as a klieg light falling out of the sky start Truman questioning if things in Seahaven are what they seem.

In college, Truman fell in love with an extra named Sylvia (Natascha McElhone) When she threatened to disrupt the show by telling Truman the truth, Christof had her abruptly removed. Truman wants to find Sylvia (he was told she moved to Fiji), but every time he tries to leave Seahaven, Christof puts obstacles in his way. Truman's increasingly manic behavior is too much for Meryl to take and she leaves the show. To appease Truman, his father is returned to the show with the excuse that he had amnesia, and Truman seems to return to normal.

But one night, Truman tunnels out of his basement, escapes Christof's cameras for the first time in his life, and sets sail for the horizon. Christof creates a terrible storm to force him to turn back, to no avail. Reaching the edge of his world, Truman crashes into the wall of the dome. Christof reveals himself and the truth about the show to Truman, imploring him to stay anyway. As Truman takes a bow and exits his artificial world through a doorway, Sylvia rejoices, watching the event on television—and puts on her coat to go meet him. Hundreds of millions of other viewers cheer the finale, then flip the channel to see what else is on.

Along with being compelling entertainment, THE TRUMAN SHOW operates on many metaphoric levels. It's an allegory about one man testing his free will against a godlike determinism. It's a parable primer on epistemology and the divide between subjective and objective realities. It's a commentary on the wages of fame in the age of celebrity-stalking paparazzi, and a cautionary tale about the threat to privacy in a culture of voyeurism.

Ingeniously sly, THE TRUMAN SHOW is also the most subversive critique of commercial television since NETWORK (1976). Merging the carrot and the cart, Christof's "The Truman Show" thrives on product placement. The blandly unthreatening Seahaven is a commercial utopia for the promotion of consumerism and the ideal of comfortable sameness. As the most boringly sanitized place on Earth, it's a perfect forum for Meryl (a Stepford spokesmodel with a plasticine smile, terrifically played by Linney) to hawk the saving graces of an improved cocoa or the latest kitchen gadget. And all those ridiculous people tuning in to watch Truman take naps and mow the lawn. . . they are us.

Andrew Niccol, who wrote and directed GATTACA (1997), in which a natural man struggled to *conform* to an unnatural society, wrote THE TRUMAN SHOW; and here, unraveling the film's premise is the plot. The machinations of "The Truman Show" (most of which concern Christof's efforts to convince Truman that there's no place like home) won't stand up to much logical scrutiny, so a great part of Weir's achievement is constantly deflecting our attention from the story's seams. It's a task akin to revealing the man behind the curtain and then convincing the audience to ignore him for the sake of the drama, and it's a task Weir pulls off with panache.

Jim Carrey would seem like an odd choice for an Everyman role, but the "off-casting" is really a masterstroke. What he brings to the part, even more than considerable ability, is his considerable persona. When Carrey isn't mugging, we know he's dying to, and so his suppressed id becomes the very emblem of Truman's painful repression, and the root of our desire to root for his escape. *(Profanity.)*—P.R.

d, Peter Weir; p, Scott Rudin, Andrew Niccol, Edward S. Feldman, Adam Schroeder; exec p, Lynn Pleshette; co-p, Richard Luke Rothschild; w, Andrew Niccol; ph, Peter Biziou; ed, William Anderson, Lee Smith; m, Burkhard Dallwitz, Philip Glass; prod d, Dennis Gassner; art d, Richard L. Johnson; set d, Nancy Haigh; sound, Arthur Rochester (mixer), Lee Smith (design); fx, Michael J. McAlister, Larz Anderson, Craig Barron, Cinesite; casting, Howard Feuer; cos, Marilyn Matthews; makeup, Ron Berkeley, Brad Wilder; stunts, Pat Banta

AAN Best Supporting Actor: Ed Harris; *AAN Best Director:* Peter Weir; *AAN Best Original Screenplay:* Andrew Niccol

Drama/Fantasy/Comedy **(PR: A MPAA: PG)**

TURKISH BATH, THE

(SEE: STEAM: THE TURKISH BATH)

12 ANGRY MEN ★★★★

(U.S., 1997) 117m MGM Worldwide Television ~ Orion Home Video c

Courtney B. Vance *(Number One)*; Ossie Davis *(Number Two)*; George C. Scott *(Number Three)*; Armin Mueller-Stahl *(Number Four)*; Dorian Harewood *(Number Five)*; James Gandolfini *(Number Six)*; Tony Danza *(Number Seven)*; Jack Lemmon *(Number Eight)*; Hume Cronyn *(Number Nine)*; Mykelti Williamson *(Number Ten)*; Edward James Olmos *(Number Eleven)*; William Petersen *(Number Twelve)*; Mary McDonnell *(Judge)*; Tyress Allen *(Guard)*; Douglas Spain *(Accused)*

An excellent cast and intelligent direction by William Friedkin are more than sufficient reasons for this made-for-cable remake of a classic American drama, first produced for television and later adapted for the movies by Sidney Lumet in 1957.

After receiving instructions from the judge (Mary McDonnell), twelve men enter a jury room to pass judgment on a Hispanic youth accused of murdering his father. Everyone is immediately ready to vote guilty, except for Juror Eight (Jack Lemmon), who argues that a case which potentially involves the death penalty at least deserves some discussion. He reminds the others of the judge's instructions, that in order to hand down a verdict of guilty they must be persuaded beyond a reasonable doubt of the boy's guilt. The foreman (Courtney B. Vance) agrees, despite grumblings from the others, particularly Jurors Three (George C. Scott), Seven (Tony Danza), and Ten (Mykelti Williamson). Examining the evidence and the testimony of the two witnesses, Juror Eight provokes discussion in a way that the boy's attorney, a public defender who seemed to assume that his client was guilty, failed to do. He begins to receive support, first from Juror Nine (Hume Cronyn), who thinks the boy is guilty but feels Eight should have his say, and then from others who come to doubt the state's case. As the more reasonable jurors come around, others become more stubborn, revealing the prejudices that blind them. Losing his temper, Juror Ten reveals himself to be a racist, while Juror Three is seen to be taking out his frustrations with his own son on the defendant. No longer convinced by any of the evidence offered against the defendant, the jury returns a verdict of not guilty.

The deliberations of a jury trying a criminal case is such an excellent source of drama that it's surprising it isn't used more often. But then, why bother when it was done so well here? Although writer Reginald Rose made minor adjustments for this adaptation, the issues addressed in 12 ANGRY MEN are as important as they were four decades earlier. (They may even be more so, in an era when publicity generated by the mass media so often affects trials.) Although Jack Lemmon initially seems an odd choice for the role taken by Henry Fonda in 1957, it turns out to have been wise casting: his age and his characteristic reasonableness are an appropriate tonic to the era, and Lemmon gives one of his best performances in years. Rose gets good use out of all 12 characters, continually finding new ways to juxtapose them. It's a mark of the teleplay's quality that excellent actors like Ossie Davis were willing to appear in smaller roles. As did Sidney Lumet in the 1957 film, director William Friedkin works with the claustrophobic environment rather than against it, making the oppressive setting a 13th character in the drama. *(Profanity.)*— M.F.

d, William Friedkin; p, Terence A. Donnelly; w, Reginald Rose; ph, Fred Schuler; ed, Augie Hess; m, Kenyon Hopkins, Charlie Haden; prod d, Bill Malley; set d, Donald Elmblad; sound, Russell Williams II; fx, Paul Staples; casting, Mary Jo Slater; cos, Dan Moore; makeup, Rick Sharp

Drama **(PR: C MPAA: PG-13)**

TWENTYFOURSEVEN ★★★

(U.K., 1997) 96m Scala Productions; BBC Films ~ October Films bw

Bob Hoskins *(Alan Darcy)*; Jimmy Hynd *(Meggy)*; Mat Hand *(Fagash)*; Danny Nussbaum *(Tim)*; Karl Collins *(Stuart)*; James Hooton *(Knighty)*; Darren Campbell *(Daz)*; Justin Brady *(Gadget)*; James Corden *(Tonka)*; Bruce Jones *(Tim's Dad—Geoff)*; Annette Badland *(Tim's Mum—Pat)*; Krishan Beresford *(Young Darcy)*; Anthony Clarke *(Youngy)*; Johann Myers *(Benny)*; Lord Dominic Dillon of Eldon *(Court Security Man)*; Ian Smith *(Prosecutor)*; Tanya Myers *(Sally the Judge)*; Frank Harper *(Ronnie)*; Tony Nyland *(Gadget's Dad)*; Colin Higgins *(Knighty's Dad)*; Jo Bell *(Jo)*; Pamela Cundell *(Auntie Iris)*; Gina Aris *(Sharon)*; Sammy Pasha *(Jimmy)*; Paul Fraser *(Photographer)*; Ladene Hall *(Daz's Girlfriend)*; Dena Smiles *(Meggy's Girlfriend)*; John Baxter *(Man Outside Shop)*; Maureen O'Grady *(Knighty's Mum)*; Lord Shane Meadows of Eldon *(Man With Saucepan on Head)*; Ben Rothwell *(Man Selling Flowers)*; Ron Bissell; Mick Bleakley; Derek Osborne *(Boxing Match Judges)*; Derek Groomsbridge *(Staffordshire Coach)*; Liam Walsh; Kevin Wallace *(Staffordshire Boxers)*; Dave Miller *(Phil "The Animal" Yeats)*; Ginger Keane *(Stephen S. Stephenson)*

Set in a dreary, dead-end town in the English Midlands, TWENTYFOURSEVEN, the debut full-length feature from 26-year-old Shane Meadows, traces the efforts of a middle-aged resident to motivate the aimless young men around him. Bob Hoskins's portrayal of the central character earned him the citation of European Actor of the Year at the 1997 European Film Awards.

Tim (Danny Nussbaum) comes upon an ailing derelict he recognizes as old acquaintance Darcy (Bob Hoskins), takes him home, puts him to bed, and begins to read from a diary in Darcy's possession. The entries begin several years earlier: Darcy springs Fagash (Mat Hand) from a drug charge by promising the court he will include the young man in a boxing club he is organizing to provide an outlet for the suppressed energy and thwarted ambitions shared by the lads of the area. Soon, Darcy has recruited Fagash, Tim, and many others into the club. During breaks in their rigorous training schedule, Darcy takes the boys on an excursion to Wales, escorts his Auntie Iris (Pamela Cundell) to dances, and tries to get up the nerve to ask out Jo (Jo Bell), a local salesclerk. Major setbacks occur when Fagash reverts to drug-taking, and the club's sponsor (Frank Harper), irate at not getting his name in the paper, knocks Darcy unconscious—but eventually the big night of the club's maiden match arrives.

The first two bouts are lost by Fagash and Knighty (James Hooton), who is disqualified for kicking. After admonishing Knighty for losing his cool, Darcy himself goes berserk when Geoff (Bruce Jones), Tim's cynical and abusive father, forbids his son to enter the ring for the third fight. Darcy gives Geoff a savage beating, and the evening ends in shambles. The club dissolves, the kids go back to soccer, and the bitterly disillusioned Darcy descends into alcoholism.

Here, the diary ends. Tim goes to Darcy's bedside to check on his former mentor just as Darcy is dying. Tim calls the other lads to tell them the sad news, and on the day of Darcy's funeral, the town's small chapel is nearly filled with mourners.

"Twenty-four seven" is shorthand for the deadly routineness of life as it is lived by Darcy's boys, who have become resigned to seeing and doing the same old thing 24 hours a day, seven days a week. This note of blighted hopes and dreams is loudly sounded in the opening pages of the derelict's diary, which (like the film itself) begins as a sort of sociological essay, then quickly changes into a tragicomic fable. At times quite funny and ultimately rather touching, TWENTYFOURSEVEN, which Meadows described as "utterly positive," is in many ways a throwback to the old Hollywood formula in which a Pat O'Brien type would goad a gang of dead-end kids into finding the light at the end of the tunnel. All that's missing is the light itself.

The movie recalls also Tony Richardson's THE LONELINESS OF THE LONG DISTANCE RUNNER (1962), another English film about young proles in a funk. Paradoxically, TWENTYFOURSEVEN is the more old-fashioned in its root values, positing sports as beneficial—as one of the few exit ramps on the working-class highway to nowhere—rather than as an instrument wielded by the haves to distract the have-nots, as the earlier movie argued. Unfortunately, TWENTYFOURSEVEN has a softer narrative spine than Richardson's hard-nosed classic, and owes less to it, perhaps, than to Richard Lester's charming, plotless A HARD DAY'S NIGHT (1964), a good movie but a bad influence.

In addition to taking a few Lesteroid side trips, Meadows allowed improvisation, sometimes a good idea in rehearsal, to extend beyond preproduction into the shoot, almost always a mistake. The result: too many people talking too often at the same time, usually to no avail.

It's a pleasure to see Hoskins, after years of impersonating Yanks in American movies, back on home ground. Regrettably, none of the young men in the cast match his charisma—not a Tom Courtenay in the bunch. Nevertheless, any picture that can induce audiences to cry at its protagonist's funeral must have done something right. *(Violence, profanity, substance abuse.)*—D.T.

d, Shane Meadows; p, Imogen West; exec p, George Faber, David Thompson, Stephen Woolley, Nik Powell; w, Shane Meadows, Paul Fraser; ph, Ashley Rowe; ed, William Diver; m, Boo Hewerdine, Neill MacColl; prod d, John-Paul Kelly; casting, Abi Cohen; cos, Phillip Crichton

Sports/Drama **(PR: C MPAA: R)**

TWILIGHT ★★★

(U.S., 1998) 96m Cinehaus; Scott Rudin Productions ~ Paramount c

Paul Newman *(Harry Ross)*; Susan Sarandon *(Catherine Ames)*; Gene Hackman *(Jack Ames)*; Stockard Channing *(Verna)*; Reese Witherspoon *(Mel Ames)*; James Garner *(Raymond Hope)*; Giancarlo Esposito *(Reuben)*; Liev Schreiber *(Jeff Willis)*; M. Emmet Walsh *(Lester Ivar)*; Margo Martindale *(Gloria Lamar)*; John Spencer *(Captain Phil Egan)*; Peter Gregory *(Verna's Partner)*; Rene Mujica *(Mexican Bartender)*; Jason Clarke *(Young Cop #1)*; Patrick Y. Malone *(Younger Cop)*; Lewis Arquette *(Water Pistol Man)*; Michael Brockman *(Garvey's Bartender)*; April Grace *(Police Stenographer)*; Clint Howard *(EMS Worker)*; John Cappon *(Paramedic)*; Neil Mather *(Young Cop #2)*; Ronald C. Sanchez *(Crime Scene Detective)*; Jack Wallace *(Interrogation Officer)*; Jeff Joy *(Carl)*

A veteran cast of aging stars, including Paul Newman, Gene Hackman, and James Garner, lend their considerable iconic weight to Robert Benton's TWILIGHT, a small-scale, but richly textured, LA detective story that's flawlessly acted and deliberately old-fashioned.

At the request of his wealthy friend Jack Ames (Gene Hackman), cop-turned-private eye Harry Ross (Paul Newman) retrieves Jack's 17-year-old daughter Mel (Reese Witherspoon), who has run away with her sleazy boyfriend Jeff (Liev Schreiber). Harry is accidentally shot in the groin by Mel during a struggle. Two years later, the formerly alcoholic Harry is broke and living in Jack's LA estate. Jack, a popular 1970s movie star, is dying of cancer, and his wife Catherine (Susan Sarandon), also a former movie star, is attracted to Harry, but even though they slept together once, she remains loyal to her husband. Jack asks Harry to deliver a package to a woman named Gloria (Margo Martindale) who's blackmailing him, but he won't say what about. At Gloria's house, Harry encounters a bullet-ridden man (M. Emmet Walsh) who shoots at him, then dies; the man turns out to be an ex-cop named Ivar.

After being interrogated by the police, including a lieutenant who is a former lover of Harry's named Verna (Stockard Channing), Harry learns from friend and fellow PI Raymond Hope (James Garner) that Ivar was the original investigating officer on a case involving the apparent suicide and mysterious disappearance of Catherine's first husband Bruce in the 1970s. When Harry finally meets with Gloria, he's beaten up by her companion, who's Mel's ex-boyfriend Jeff. Later, Harry tracks Gloria and Jeff down and they admit they're blackmailing Jack about Bruce's disappearance and have been digging up Jack's country house in an attempt to find the body. Suddenly, somebody bursts inside and kills Jeff and Gloria, then gets away without Harry seeing who it was.

Harry goes to the country house and finds a buried skull with a bullet hole in it. Jack tells Harry that Bruce had fallen into an empty swimming pool and cracked his skull during a fight, and that Catherine had called Raymond, who was a movie studio security chief at the time, to take care of it. Harry goes to see Raymond, who admits that he shot Bruce, who was still alive after falling, and that he's been covering up the crime with subsequent murders. In return, he's been receiving payoffs from the Ames's ever since. When Harry says he has to turn him in, Raymond shoots at Harry but misses, and Harry fires back, killing Raymond. Harry tells the whole story to the cops, but they're unable to arrest the Ames's since they never actually committed a crime. Harry and Verna decide to take a vacation together.

TWILIGHT is a pensive meditation on mortality that's both rueful and dark humored, and brings to mind Jean Cocteau's famous observation about cinema being the only art form that shows death at work. It's about Los Angeles and movies and money and houses, but mostly it's about growing old and the disintegration of the human mind, body, and spirit. The cast itself is a poignant manifestation of this, as the mere presence of a 73-year-old Paul Newman with white hair and a raspy voice, a balding Gene Hackman, a heavy-set James Garner wearing thick glasses, and a middle-aged Susan Sarandon is a constant reminder of the theme. The Ames's mansion is filled with pictures of them as glamorous young stars, which are actual publicity photos of Hackman and Sarandon. In one scene, the ailing Jack is watching a video of one of his old movies, which is really DOWNHILL RACER (1969). The effect created by this use of doubling is an integral part of the film and gives it a further layer of depth.

Appropriately enough for a film about stars from the past, both fictionally and in real-life, Robert Benton employs a restrained and leisurely cinematic style that reinforces the idea of old age and recalls the low-key, character-driven mysteries of the 1970s. Technically, the film is beautifully crafted, with the noirish cinematography providing moody and poetic shots of LA at its duskiest, while the superb art direction makes excellent use of the various houses which define the characters and their standings in society. Admittedly, the film is totally—but intentionally—out of touch with the style and sensibility of today's movies, meaning its dialogue is pithy and meaningful, its characters are three-dimensional people with moral ambiguities, and it tells a complicated story in a concise, coherent, and entertaining manner while also possessing emotional and thematic resonance. In an era of narratively impaired movies with bloated running times and more flash than substance, that is no mean feat. *(Violence, profanity, nudity, sexual situations.)*—M.S.

d, Robert Benton; p, Scott Rudin, Arlene Donovan; exec p, Michael Hausman; assoc p, Scott Ferguson, David McGiffert; w, Robert Benton, Richard Russo; ph, Piotr Sobocinski; ed, Carol Littleton; m, Elmer Bernstein; prod d, David Gropman; art d, David Bomba; set d, Beth Rubino; sound, David R.B. McMillan; fx, Larry Fioritto; casting, Ilene Starger; cos, Joseph G. Aulisi; makeup, Bron Roylance; stunts, Stan Barrett

Crime/Thriller/Mystery **(PR: C MPAA: R)**

TWISTED ★★★

(Australia, 1996) 86m Newton Films ~ Southern Star Sales c

"Bonus Mileage": Geoffrey Rush *(Harry Chisholm)*; Shane Briant *(Jay Condon)*; Peter Carmody; Kate Fischer; Tottie Goldsmith; Jacek Koman; Alan Zitner; Natalie McCurry; Anthony Martin; "Third Party": Marshall Napier *(Tom)*; Rachel Ward *(Sara)*; Mitchell Butel; Anthony Hayes; "The Confident Man": Bryan Brown *(Jack)*; Josephine Byrne *(Jack's Girlfriend)*; Mark Lee *(Clerk)*; Steve Bastoni; Aaron Blabey; Andrew Chapman; Minh Tamtran; Jill McKay; "Directly From My Heart to You": Kimberley Davies *(Betty)*; Gary Day; Simon Westaway; Salvatore Coco; Kate Fitzpatrick; Caroline Gan; Mercia Dean-Jones; Grant Piro

This whacked-out omnibus may have been deemed a poor bet for wide release, because it defies commercial pigeonholing. Providing each of its four stories with a distinct identity and visual style, TWISTED twists its way from the supernatural to the blackly comic to the ironic to the creepily futuristic.

"Bonus Mileage": Foul-tempered, frequent flyer Harry Chisholm (Geoffrey Rush) converses with suspiciously friendly first-class passenger Jay Condon, collector of souls (Shane Briant), who is wanted by the police for embezzlement. Condon is looking for souls he can subsume just by giving his intended target his calling card. Having traded places with crooked CEO Condon, Harry, who now inherits Condon's fate, flees from the cops and avoids a prison stretch only by flipping the magical card to his cabbie.

"Third Party": Secretive Tom (Marshall Napier) and provocative Sara (Rachel Ward) exchange dating videos and meet for an assignation, even though a serial killer is striking through the personal ads. Could kinky Tom or insatiable Sara be the lovelorn maniac? The morning after, we learn that this happily married couple were only spicing up their lovemaking routine.

"The Confident Man" is Jack (Bryan Brown), who can smooth talk his way in or out of anything. His plans to upgrade his liquor store are derailed when the store is robbed by a coked-up thief. Holding what he believes is only a drill, con man Jack uses his salesmanship to convince the rattled robber he must surrender or die. When Jack pulls the trigger, his weapon turns out to be a real gun, after all.

"Directly From My Heart to You": A lethal blonde named Betty (Kimberley Davies) cold-bloodedly guns down three renowned scientists, before emptying her revolver into a pizza delivery boy. Her creator, who ordered Betty only to eliminate his patent partners in robot manufacturing, now plans to replace this haywire prototype with a newer model. Although malfunctioning murderess Betty executes him first, she learns that her Maker, himself, was also an android.

Uncanny and unsettling, TWISTED is a sort of Aussie "Twilight Zone." This spooky kaleidoscope offers viewers a journey through time, space, and our own preconceived notions of where the narrative is wending itself. Starting on a skin-crawling note with that airborne identity-snatching yarn, this visually elegant film deftly combines the macabre with the droll. The film noir shadows of "Third Party" prove a bold contrast to the cheery circusy colors that complement "The Confident Man" or the grainy photography that suits the atmosphere of panic in "Bonus Mileage." The most accomplished of the four tales, "Directly From My Heart to You," boasts the deepest saturated color, the blood hues of a fairy tale gone awry. Satirizing contemporary culture's empty obsession with "plastic" beauty, it uses off-kilter camera angles and expressionistic art direction to suggest an innately malevolent environment. In each episode, human beings are at the mercy of other-worldly influences or their own uncontrollable impulses. Only Betty the killer robot can cope with a universe this TWISTED. *(Graphic violence, profanity, sexual situations, substance abuse.)*—R.P.

d, Christopher Robin-Collins ("Bonus Mileage"), Samantha Lang ("Third Party"), Gregor Jordan ("The Confident Man"), Catherine Millar ("Directly From My Heart To You"); p, Helen Watts; exec p, Bryan Brown, Kris Noble; w, Simon D. Hoenger ("Bonus Mileage"), Neil Burman ("Third Party"), Tim Rolfe ("The Confidant Man"), Louis Nowra ("Directly From My Heart To You"); ph, James Bartle; ed, Richard Hindley, Mark Perry; m, Nerida Tyson-Chew; prod d, Jim Ferrier; art d, Charles Reval; set d, Glen Johnson, Kerrie Brown; sound, Phil Judd (mixer); casting, Maura Fay & Associates; cos, Annie Marshall; makeup, Paul Pattison; stunts, Andy Clarke

Thriller/Science Fiction (PR: C MPAA: PG-13)

TWO FOR TEXAS ★★½

(U.S., 1998) 96m Bleeker Street Films ~ Warner Home Video c

Kris Kristofferson (Hugh Allison); Scott Barstow (Son Holland); Tom Skerritt (Sam Houston); Irene Bedard (Sana); Peter Coyote (Jim Bowie); Victor Rivers (Emile Landry); Thomas Schuster (Alcide Landry); Rodney A. Grant (Iron Jacket); Marco Rodriguez (General Santa Ana); Karey Green (Susanah Dickinson); Richard Jones (Deaf Smith); Richard Nance (Pike the Outlaw); Lonnie Rodriguez (Sergeant Major); Julio Cesar Cedillo (Lieutenant Herrera); Woody Watson (Lieutenant Burnett); Carlos Compean (Captain Trejo); Alex Morris (Rex the Slave); Terry McIlvain (Trusty Lake); Mark Dalton (Snake Bite Convict); Larry Brothers (Clay the Outlaw); Rick Dennis (Mac the Outlaw); Roy Burger (Matt); Billy L. "Butch" Frank (Hank); Rodger Boyce (Ned the Cook); Daniel O'Callaghan (Jones the Picket); Robert Lott (Messenger Kelly); Stephen Madrid (Mexican Pheasant); Yvette Ancira (Emily Morgan); Gatlin Boone Smith (Baby Dickson)

This story of two ex-cons who join Texas's struggle for independence from Mexico is strong on historical detail but weak in dramatic development. The 1997 made-for cable feature was released on home video in 1998.

Hugh Allison (Kris Kristofferson) and Son Holland (Scott Barstow) escape from a brutal Louisiana prison and head into the Mexican territory of Texas. They plan to join the rebel army of Sam Houston, as much for protective covering as for the land and cash he has promised to every man who helps him fight the Mexican government. They trade some stolen Army horses to a Choctaw tribe in exchange for food and shelter. The Choctaws also throw in Sana (Irene Bedard), a slave woman from another tribe.

The Indians trade the stolen horses to Mexican soldiers; when the Mexicans cheat them, the tribe gives Hugh and Son six horses in exchange for their help in getting revenge.

Although Tennessean Holland hates Indians (his parents were murdered by drunken Shawnee), his consciousness is raised by Sana, who tells him how she was captured and raped by Americans, her initial captors. The two make love, but Hugh insists that she join a nearby friendly tribe before he and Son find the Army.

That happens quickly, as they rendezvous with Houston (Tom Skerritt), where Hugh is delighted to meet up with his old friend Jim Bowie (Peter Coyote) among Houston's troops. Inflamed by the cause, Bowie leaves to join the forces at the Alamo, where Santa Ana's troops slaughter every man. This massacre causes many more Texans to join Houston's army, and Houston's newly bolstered forces are able to surprise a Mexican force at San Jacinto. As ex-miner Hugh uses his knowledge of explosives to demolish the bridge that offers the only chance of escape, Houston's army overcomes the Mexicans and captures Santa Ana. Son retrieves Sana to live with him on the land he is given for his service.

At the battle of San Jacinto, depicted in the climax of TWO FOR TEXAS, 630 Mexican solders were killed by Texans, who suffered only 9 casualties in a fight that lasted a mere 18 minutes. Yet what ought to have been a stirring climax to a slice of American history is reduced to a few minutes at the end of a film that spends more time with the ho-hum exploits of a pair of blandly drawn adventurers. Presumably the novel by James Lee Burke on which this was based offered richer historical detail that couldn't be supplied on a cable-movie budget. But Hugh and Son's escapes from the prison master who chases them until the end of the movie (when he is dispatched in surprisingly anticlimactic fashion), their stay with a Choctaw tribe, and Son's growing admiration for Sana do nothing but waste time prior to a historical re-creation that is hardly worth the effort. *(Graphic violence, sexual situations, profanity.)*—M.F.

d, Rod Hardy; p, Dennis Bishop; exec p, Lois Bonfiglio; assoc p, Ari Sloane; w, Larry Brothers (based on the novel by James Lee Burke); ph, David Connell; ed, Michael Ornstein; m, Lee Holdridge; prod d, Cary White; art d, Edward Vega; set d, Barbara Haberecht; sound, John Patrick Pritchett; fx, Matt Vogel; casting, Julie Selzer; cos, Dan Moore; makeup, Phyllis Temple; stunts, Norman Howell

Historical/Adventure/Western **(PR: C MPAA: NR)**

TWO GIRLS AND A GUY ★★

(U.S., 1998) 92m Edward R. Pressman; Muse Productions; Bigel/Mailer Films ~ Fox Searchlight c

Robert Downey Jr. *(Blake Allen)*; Heather Graham *(Carla)*; Natasha Gregson Wagner *(Lou)*; Angel David *(Tommy)*; Frederique Van Der Wal *(Carol)*

Robert Downey Jr. stars as a compulsive liar and womanizer whose two "exclusive" girlfriends (well-played by Heather Graham and Natasha Gregson Wagner) team up to take revenge on him in James Toback's TWO GIRLS AND A GUY, another of the writer-director's intriguing, but ultimately unsatisfying paeans to his own unbridled libido and renowned ego.

While waiting in front of a loft building in SoHo for their boyfriends, two strangers, Carla (Heather Graham) and Lou (Natasha Gregson Wagner), discover that they're actually dating the same man: struggling actor Blake Allen (Robert Downey Jr.). They sneak into Blake's loft and wait for him to return from LA, and when he comes home, they confront him about his deception. Blake tries to defend himself by claiming that he really loves them both, but after being berated by the two women, he goes into the bathroom and pretends to shoot himself, complete with stage blood.

While Blake calls his mother, to whom he's uncommonly devoted, Lou and Carla get drunk and decide to stay and find out why Blake is such a pathological liar. Later, Carla has sex with Blake, and Lou suggests that if he had been truthful all along, she might have willingly been part of a menage a trois. During a frank discussion of their relationships, Blake is shocked to learn that Lou is bisexual and that Carla has slept with other men while they were dating. After several more calls to his mother, Blake begins to worry about her deteriorating health and he goes to see her. Lou gives Carla her number and leaves her there alone. When Blake returns, he starts crying about his mother's death and tries to call a funeral home to make arrangements, but is so distraught that Carla makes the call and then comforts him as he plays the piano.

Filmed in sequence in just 11 days during a break in Downey's 1997 drug rehabilitation, TWO GIRLS AND A GUY feels less like a movie than an actual part of that rehab program. The story shares some superficial elements with Toback's excellent FINGERS (1979) (mother-fixation, piano-playing) and Downey is essentially incarnating an adult version of the compulsive womanizer that he played in Toback's THE PICK-UP ARTIST (1987). But 10 years later, the once happy-go-lucky kid has become bloated and debauched, and the character is now inextricably entwined with Downey's own spiral of self-destruction. Watching someone onscreen going through a personal meltdown is hard enough, but when one knows that the actor and character are virtually the same, it becomes an uncomfortably voyeuristic experience, particularly during the numerous embarrassing improvisations where Downey stares in the mirror, making grotesque faces and screaming to himself about "getting it together."

Unfolding in "real time" on a single set, the film has the cramped, low-budget look and feel of an Off-Broadway play, and one could excuse the crude technical work (blatant overdubs, out-of-focus shots) and prolix script if the sexually explicit dialogue were more insightful. The notorious sex scene where Blake and Carla engage in reciprocal oral sex has been trimmed to garner the film an R rating after the MPAA gave it an NC-17 on 14 separate occasions, but it seems implausible in the context of the story and feels like a contrived attempt to shock. At times, the whole film plays like a combination group therapy session and acting class exercise, as the three protagonists sit around and yell obscene pseudo-psychological jargon at one another, each actor looking for his or her own "big moment." The talented Downey truly appears to be at the end of his tether, but both Graham and Wagner are very good, with the coolly elegant Graham capturing Carla's combination of intellect and sexuality, and the vivacious Wagner looking and sounding eerily like her mother Natalie Wood at certain moments.

Toback's script throws in some token explanations for Blake's behavior ("Actors lie," he claims; "You Don't Know Me" is his favorite song, there's a JULES AND JIM poster on his wall), while theorizing that fidelity and monogamy are controlled by chemicals and hormones (thus rationalizing his own well-documented womanizing). But the film is really just another of Toback's sexual fantasies disguised as a brutally honest confessional, wherein a man has two beautiful girlfriends (one of whom turns out to be bisexual), who stay with him in his luxurious loft (conveniently explained as being an inheritance) and give him sex even after finding out that he's a lying, cheating pig. *(Extreme profanity, sexual situations.)*—M.S.

d, James Toback; p, Edward R. Pressman, Chris Hanley; exec p, Michael Mailer, Daniel Bigel; w, James Toback; ph, Barry Markowitz; ed, Alan Oxman; prod d, Kevin Thompson; set d, Alisa Grifo; sound, Brian Miksis, Itamar Ben Jacob; casting, Sheila Jaffe, Georgianne Walken

Drama/Comedy **(PR: O MPAA: R)**

UGLY, THE ★★★

(New Zealand, 1998) 93m Essential Films; New Zealand Film Commission ~ Trimark Home Video c

Paolo Rotundo *(Simon Cartwright—the Killer)*; Rebecca Hobbs *(Dr. Karen Schumaker—the Interviewer)*; Jennifer Ward-Lealand *(Evelyn Cartwright—Simon's Mother)*; Roy Ward *(Dr. Marlowe—the Warden)*; Cath McWhirter *(Helen Ann Miller)*; Carolyn Beaver *(Helen's Friend)*; Caelem Pope *(Simon—Age 4)*; Vanessa Byrnes *(Julie—age 25)*; Paul Glover *(Philip—Orderly No. 1)*; Chris Graham *(Robert—Orderly No. 2)*; Jon Brazier *(Frank—the Vet)*; Darien Takle *(Marge—Elderly Patient)*; Finn Johnson; Phillip Brown; Tau Luke *(Future Cops)*; Tim Barlow *(Police Photographer)*; Sam Wallace *(Simon—Age 13)*; Aaron Buskin *(Roland—Ringleader Bully)*; John Steemson *(Bully #2)*; Oliver Hodges *(Bully #3)*; Beth Allen *(Julie—Age 13)*; Chris Bailey *(Ed Daley)*; Gary Mackay *(Man in Park)*; Steve Hall *(Worker Thug #1)*; Shane Bessant *(Worker Thug #2)*; Katrina Browne *(Woman in the Floral Dress)*; Yvonne Dudman *(Melinda Jackson)*; Frances Chan; Scott Wills; Jenny Ashton; Matt Cornelius *(Simon's Victims)*; Hugh D'Calveley *(Victim in Alleyway)*; Sara Pivac *(Deaf Girl)*; Michael Dwyer *(Alex)*; David Baxter *(Clive)*

UV

Stylish first-time filmmaker Scott Reynolds adopts a distinctive new approach to the serial-killer genre in this 1996 New Zealand import.

Psychiatrist Dr. Karen Schumaker (Rebecca Hobbs) visits a mental hospital to interview incarcerated serial killer Simon Cartwright (Paolo Rotundo) in preparation for a sanity hearing. Simon, who sees himself as a deformed figure he calls "The Ugly," recounts his story: While growing up, he was dyslexic, lived with his domineering single mother Evelyn (Jennifer Ward-Lealand), and was routinely bullied by schoolmates. His only friend was Julie (Beth Allen), a young girl whose relationship with Simon was frowned upon by Evelyn. After Julie revealed to Simon that a letter from his absent father did not claim hatred for him but was rather seeking custody of him, Evelyn forbade Simon to see her again, and Simon killed his mother.

After spending time in an institution, Simon began a series of murders, claiming he was spurred on by the ghosts of his past victims. By chance, he met Julie (Vanessa Byrnes) again, and their friendship was rekindled. But when her brother came for a visit, Simon mistook him for a boyfriend and killed him; some time later, Simon murdered Julie as well. Eventually captured, Simon now insists he still has visions of the dead, and during their last session, Karen sees them too. She returns home, and dreams of Simon escaping the asylum and killing her. When she wakes up, she finds that Simon is in fact in her bedroom, and has just slit her throat.

The idea of depicting a killer's background and rampage in a series of flashbacks isn't a new one, but it has rarely been presented in as gripping a fashion as it is here. Young writer-director Reynolds, a longtime horror film fan, adopts a stream-of-consciousness approach to Simon's story, and often inserts the "older" Simon into his own flashbacks, giving them an immediacy that heightens the tension. Reynolds also plays with perceptions of reality, juxtaposing Karen's interview of Simon with the flashbacks and also violent fantasies taking place within both Karen and Simon's minds.

By the end of the film, all these conscious nightmares get to be a bit much; the climactic dream-that-becomes-reality, however much of a piece it is with the rest of the movie, still comes off as too much of a genre cliche. Nonetheless, Reynolds's aggressive filmmaking commands attention throughout, and the murder setpieces are genuinely suspenseful and shocking. In an unusual gambit, all the blood in these scenes is an inky black instead of red, perhaps to reflect Simon's off-kilter point of view and also to avoid censorship problems. (Nonetheless, the MPAA bestowed an NC-17 rating on the movie, which was released unrated in its US theatrical release before being trimmed to an R for home video.) Gratifyingly, all of Reynolds's visual and narrative experimentation is ably supported by the strong performances of the two leads. Hobbs is solid as the doctor who finds that her subject's state of mind is not as cut and dried as she thought, while Rotundo makes his killer a three-dimensional character. Reynolds ably abets him in this regard: from the lengthy flashbacks of Simon's childhood to scenes in which he is tormented by a pair of sadistic asylum attendants, Reynolds aims and succeeds at creating an understanding of (if not quite sympathy for) his frankly murderous protagonist. *(Graphic violence, nudity, adult situations, profanity.)*—M.G.

d, Scott Reynolds; p, Jonathan Dowling; w, Scott Reynolds; ph, Simon Raby; ed, Wayne Cook; m, Victoria Kelly; prod d, Grant Major; art d, Gary Mackey; sound, Dick Reade (recordist), Dave Whitehead (design); fx, Weta Ltd.; casting, Gaye Donnellan, Maura Fay, Maura Fay & Associates; cos, Emily Carter; makeup, Dominie Till, Richard Taylor (effects); stunts, Sam Williams

Horror **(PR: O MPAA: NC-17)**

UN AIR DE FAMILLE ★★★

(France, 1996) 107m Telema; Canal Plus; France 2 Cinema; Cofimage 7 ~ Leisure Time Features c

Agnes Jaoui *(Betty Menard)*; Jean-Pierre Bacri *(Henri Menard)*; Jean-Pierre Darroussin *(Denis)*; Catherine Frot *(Yolande—Philippe's Wife)*; Claire Maurier *(Mother)*; Wladimir Yordanoff *(Philippe Menard)*; Alain Guillo *(TV Presenter)*; Sophie Simon *(Mother—1967)*; Cedric Klapisch *(Father—1967)*; Antoine Chappey *(Neighbor)*; Chantal Gouard; Viviane Ordas *(Mother's Friends)*; Aurelie Renacle *(Betty—1967)*; Nicolas Taieb *(Henri—1967)*; Ludovic Taieb *(Philippe—1967)*; Romain Legrand *(Kevin—Philippe's Son)*; Hugo Charpiot *(Mikael—Philippe's Son)*; Zinedine Soualem; Walter Debeigh; Denis Falgoux; Albert Parisio *(Cafe Customers)*; Elimoez Jalouli; Olivier Rageoonauth; Louis Espert; Alexandre Garcia; Lyamin Jamel; Diatta Ibrahima; Yann Brunelles; Christophe Bademis; Stephane Pouillade; Patricia Eridan *(Youths at Housing Project)*

UN AIR DE FAMILLE is an incisive adaptation of a hit French play about a disastrous family gathering, that's imaginatively directed by Cedric Klapisch (WHEN THE CAT'S AWAY) and sharply acted by an excellent cast, including the play's authors, Agnes Jaoui and Jean-Pierre Bacri.

Betty Menard (Agnes Jaoui) goes to a cafe that's owned by her brother Henri (Jean-Pierre Bacri), to await the arrival of her mother (Claire Maurier), her other brother Philippe (Wladimir Yordanoff), and his wife Yolande (Catherine Frot), whose 35th birthday they are celebrating that night. Betty tells the bartender Denis (Jean-Pierre Darroussin) that she wants to break off their clandestine affair, and Henri is upset because his wife has not yet arrived for the party. When the others arrive, Philippe, who's an executive at a computer company, is only concerned about a TV appearance he's made that morning, which is criticized by his fatuous wife and overbearing mother. The mother also berates Betty for her crude language and the fact that she's 30-years-old and still not married, as well as Henri, whom she considers to be the family idiot, for not having more ambition.

Things only get worse when Henri receives a call from his wife Arlette, who informs him that she's leaving him because of the inconsiderate way he treats her. Henri tries to keep the news from the others and tells them to go to a restaurant without him, but they stay after finding out. Later, Yolande hurts the mother's feelings by insulting her birthday gift, which is a coupon for a dog. At the urging of Betty and Denis, Henri decides to go to Arlette to apologize, but she refuses to talk to him. Philippe, still worried about his TV appearance, calls his boss for his opinion, and learns that Betty, for whom he had gotten a job at the computer company, had fought with the boss earlier that day. Philippe and Betty have a big argument and Denis ends up hitting Philippe. Denis and Betty then leave together and passionately kiss in front of the others, and after the rest of the family leaves, Arlette calls Henri and he promises to change.

UN AIR DE FAMILLE transcends its obvious stage origins and idiomatic French milieu through clever direction and trenchant writing and performances that make its familial themes universal in nature. Rather than trying to "open up" the play by traditional means (adding exteriors, cutting between different locations, rapid-fire editing), Klapisch employs expressive widescreen photography (including refracted shots using glass and mirrors) to explore the mostly one-set location, and uses dramatic shifts in lighting and astutely timed close-ups to create tension and psychological, rather than visual, claustrophobia. There are a sufficient number of exteriors and other locations so that it never feels like a piece of filmed theater (the mother's apartment building where she yells out the window to tell her neighbors to watch Philippe on TV; Henri standing outside a house and screaming to Arlette while being hassled by a gang of kids), as well as fleeting, slow-motion flashbacks of Philippe, Henri, and Betty as children jumping on their parents' bed, which seem idyllic at first, but are gradually revealed not to be, as the father starts spanking them and they cower beneath the sheets.

Inside the cafe, the biting dialogue is broken up by awkward silences and pregnant pauses which are filled with cutaways to insects being fried by a bug-zapper and wryly amusing reaction shots of Henri's arthritic dog watching the whole mess. For all of the simmering angst and bitter recriminations, there is also a good deal of humor, as when Henri denies that he's mean to his wife, claiming that he works so hard that "I don't have time to treat her badly," or when the sweet, but dim, Yolande (who's called YoYo by the others for good reason) finds out about Arlette leaving Henri and laments, "It's terrible for the children. Fortunately they don't have any," and when she asks if her gift of a dog comes with instructions. Along with its other virtues, where the film really excels is its three-dimensional portrayals of the various characters, who could have come off as stereotypes (castrating mother, rebel daughter, weak son, et al.), but come alive through the perceptive writing and vibrant acting, all adding up to a convincing argument that dysfunctional families are the only kind there are. *(Profanity.)*—M.S.

d, Cedric Klapisch; p, Charles Gassot; assoc p, Jacques Hinstin; w, Agnes Jaoui, Jean-Pierre Bacri, Cedric Klapisch (based on the play by Agnes Jaoui and Jean-Pierre Bacri); ph, Benoit Delhomme; ed, Francine Sandberg; m, Philippe Eidel; art d, Francois Emmanuelli; set d, Perine Batre; sound, Francois Waledisch, Jean-Pierre Laforce (mixer); cos, Corinne Jorry; makeup, Irene Ottavis

Comedy/Drama **(PR: C MPAA: NR)**

UNAGI

(SEE: EEL, THE)

UNCLE SAM ★★½

(U.S., 1998) 89m Gable Productions ~ A-Pix Entertainment c

Leslie Neale *(Sally Baker)*; Christopher Ogden *(Jody Baker)*; Isaac Hayes *(Jed Crowley)*; David Shark Fralick *(Sam Harper)*; Bo Hopkins *(Sgt. Twining)*; Anne Tremko *(Louise Harper)*; Timothy Bottoms *(Donald Crandall)*; Matthew Flint *(Phil)*; Tim Grimm *(Ralph)*; Zachary McLemore *(Barry Cronin)*; P.J. Soles *(Madge Cronin)*; Thom McFadden *(Mac Cronin)*; Morgan Paul *(Mayor)*; Robert Forster *(Congressman Cummings)*; Richard Cummings Jr. *(Dan)*; William Smith *(Major)*; Frank Pesce *(Barker)*; Jason Adelman *(Jesse)*; Abby Ball *(Rick)*; Stanton Barrett *(Clete)*; Mark Chadwick *(Willie on Stilts)*; Desirae Klein *(Barbeque Girl)*; Laura Alcalde *(Park Mother)*; Raquel Allessi *(Girl Student)*; Taylor Jones *(Boy Student)*; Chris Durand *(Sergeant)*; Jason Lustig *(Undertaker)*; Joseph Vitale *(Kuwaiti Captain)*

The writer and director behind the MANIAC COP movies reteamed for a film that could be retitled "Maniac Patriot."

The body of Sam Harper (David Shark Fralick), a soldier killed by friendly fire, is found on a Desert Storm battlefield and shipped back to his small hometown. There, both his wife Louise (Anne Tremko) and her sister, divorcee Sally Baker (Leslie Neale), are still living with memories of Sam's violent nature. Sally's young son Jody (Christopher Ogden) idolizes his uncle and hopes to follow him into the Army; local veteran Jed (Isaac Hayes) tries to dissuade him. A trio of young punks burn an American flag over the grave where Sam is to be buried, and the corpse comes to life, killing two of them. Sam then steals an Uncle Sam costume and slays its owner.

The next day, the disguised Sam invades a Fourth of July celebration, where he kills a number of people who have betrayed their country, including draft-dodging teacher Donald Crandall (Timothy Bottoms); Phil (Matthew Flint), a tax cheat who's been courting Sally; the last of the flag-burning punks; and a crooked visiting congressman (Robert Forster). Barry (Zachary McLemore), a friend of Jody's who was blinded in a fireworks accident, senses Sam's presence, and the ghoul soon confronts Louise at her house. While Jody distracts Sam, Jed brings over an antique cannon that he uses to blow Sam away. But Sam's spirit may live on in Jody. . .

The idea of a dead soldier who comes to life to kill in the name of patriotism was a natural for director William Lustig and writer Larry Cohen, after their explorations of undead justice in the MANIAC COP trilogy. The result is an entertaining film, though a fairly schematic and predictable one; Cohen's script spends the first half establishing how its supporting characters have done wrong to the spirit of America, and the second bumping them off (through such appropriate implements as flagpoles and fireworks). Ironically, there's more than a bit of an antimilitary slant in the film itself: Sam's battlefield heroics are linked directly to a lust for violence that Sally, Louise, and Jed try to wean out of Jody.

Lustig keeps the action moving, with convincing special effects and stuntwork and a fun supporting cast of character actors, including Forster, Bottoms, Bo Hopkins, P.J. Soles, and William Smith. As the kindly, regretful veteran, Hayes is solid and sympathetic, though it's hard not to think of Hayes's "Chef" role on the "South Park" TV series during his bonding scenes with Jody. While he keeps a sense of fun about the proceedings, Lustig never descends into an outright spoof; a closing homage and dedication to Italian goremeister Lucio Fulci seem a bit out of place, though, as UNCLE SAM isn't nearly as singlemindedly gruesome as Fulci's work. *(Graphic violence, adult situations, nudity, substance abuse, profanity.)*—M.G.

d, William Lustig; p, George G. Braunstein; assoc p, Gina Fortunato; w, Larry Cohen; ph, James Lebovitz; ed, Bob Murawski; m, Mark Governor; prod d, Charlotte Malmlof; art d, Sue Savage; set d, Piper Renee Ferguson; sound, Jon Ailetcher; fx, Ultimate Effects, John Hartigan; casting, Karen Rea; cos, Amy Wetherbee; makeup, Debi Davidson, SOTA Effects (effects), Roy Knyrim (effects), Jerry Macaluso (effects); stunts, Sprio Razatos

Horror **(PR: O MPAA: R)**

UNDER HEAVEN ★★½
(U.S., 1998) 112m Banner Entertainment ~
Banner Entertainment c
(AKA: WINGS OF AN ANGEL)

Aden Young *(Buck Henson)*; Joely Richardson *(Eleanor Dunston)*; Molly Parker *(Cynthia Loomis)*; Kevin Phillip *(John)*; Krisha Fairchild *(Cynthia's Mother)*; Marjorie Nelson *(Mrs. Fletcher)*; Alisa Mackay; Elsie Vance; Kevin Rosinebun

A solid and promising debut from writer-director Meg Richman, UNDER HEAVEN is based on the Henry James novel *The Wings of the Dove*, adding about a hundred years and 5,000 miles to the setting. Unfortunately, Richman's work must stand in the shadow of last year's lavish, Oscar-nominated, period adaptation of the same story.

Occasionally employed and less occasionally sober, Cynthia Loomis (Molly Parker) and Buck Henson (Aden Young) subsist in Seattle. The young lovers travel by bus to visit Cynthia's mother (Krisha Fairchild) on her birthday, and arrive stoned on cough syrup. Thrice divorced from alcoholics, Mrs. Newhouse warns her daughter against involvement with a man like Buck. Soon after their return to Seattle, Cynthia leaves Buck, and sets out to go straight.

Cynthia finds employment as a live-in caregiver for wealthy, terminally ill Eleanor Dunston (Joely Richardson). The extroverted Cynthia and timid Eleanor become close friends. One day, Cynthia runs into Buck, who has stopped drinking and kicked drugs. Introducing Buck as her half-brother, Cynthia convinces Eleanor to hire him on as a gardener, and Buck moves into a cottage on the estate.

Cynthia comes up with a plan for Buck to seduce and marry Eleanor, who has no other family, and thus inherit her fortune when she dies. Eleanor, who's had a double mastectomy, never thought a man could be interested in her again, so when Buck flirts with her, she falls for him quickly.

When her housekeeper, Mrs. Fletcher (Marjorie Nelson), catches Buck and Cynthia in bed together, she reports what she has seen to Eleanor. Eleanor tells Buck that she knows what he and Cynthia are doing, but that she doesn't care. Buck confesses that he has really fallen in love with her. This prompts a jealous Cynthia to attempt suicide with a drug overdose. Eleanor tells Cynthia not to worry because she knows she is just borrowing Buck. Eleanor offers to marry Buck but he refuses.

When Eleanor dies, she leaves everything to Buck, who doesn't want it. He gives it all to Cynthia, and goes off to start a landscaping business. Cynthia invites her mother and stepsisters to come live with her in the Dunston mansion.

Even with the change of time and place, the story is a good one and Richman tells it well, but UNDER HEAVEN can't help but suffer in comparison to 1997's THE WINGS OF THE DOVE. The problem is that changing the setting to contemporary times robs the work of its edge. There's something in the earlier film about Victorian mores and the sight of Helena Bonham Carter in a big hat that gives the goings-on between the trio of lovers shock value. The same amoral behavior taking place in post-grunge Seattle seems not just acceptable, but expectable.

UNDER HEAVEN benefits from good performances by its leads. Richardson may be a bit too beatific, but it's easy to understand why a young woman facing death would care more about the happiness of her final days than the disposition of her estate after she's gone. Australian actor Young is charming in a role that requires him to be just that, while Parker gives a strong performance that centers the movie, playing her character with the right mix of deviousness and desperation. *(Sexual situations, nudity, profanity.)* —P.R.

d, Meg Richman; p, Robin Schorr, Brian Swardstrom, Mickey Liddell; co-p, Paddy Cullen; w, Meg Richman (based on the novel *The Wings of the Dove* by Henry James); ph, Claudio Rocha; ed, Debbie Zeitman; m, Marc Olsen; prod d, Sharon Lomofsky; art d, Natalie Beauchene; set d, Chris Karges; sound, Doug Tourtelot (mixer); casting, Laurel Smith; cos, Ron Leamon

Drama/Romance **(PR: C MPAA: R)**

UNDER THE SKIN ★★★½
(U.K., 1997) 83m Strange Dog Productions; Rouge Films; British Film Institute/Channel Four Television ~
Arrow Releasing c
(AKA: IRIS AND ROSE; SKIN)

Samantha Morton *(Iris Kelley)*; Claire Rushbrook *(Rose)*; Rita Tushingham *(Mum)*; Stuart Townsend *(Tom)*; Christine Tremarco *("Vron"—Veronica)*; Matthew Delamere *(Gary)*; Mark Womack *(Frank)*; Clare Francis *(Elena)*; Daniel O'Meara *(Max)*; Crissy Rock *(Compere)*; Joe Tucker *(Sam)*; Lisa Millet *(Sylvia)*; John Whitehall *(Man at Station)*; Marie Jelliman *(Manageress)*; Michelle Byatt *(Mrs. Smith—Woman in Lost Property)*; Stella Scragg *(Customer)*; David Brice *(Man in Bed)*; Jack Marsden *(Builder)*; Sean Cauldwell *(Man in Club)*; Sandie Lavell *(Woman at Phone Box)*; Jill Broadber *(Conductor)*; Castle Singers *(Choir)*

British director Carine Adler makes an impressive debut with UNDER THE SKIN, a compelling and dark examination of a young woman's tormented search for self-identity.

Nineteen-year-old Iris (Samantha Morton), a daughter in a working-class family, is envious of her older sister Rose's (Claire Rushbrook) relationship with their terminally ill mother (Rita Tushingham), believing that mother favors Rose because, married and pregnant, Rose leads a conventional life. When mother dies, Iris impulsively quits her job, breaks up with her boyfriend, and gets her own apartment. She also begins having casual sexual encounters with men.

Over a series of days, Iris sees and receives a phone call from her mother, who expresses regret that she can no longer be with Iris. One morning, Rose arrives at Iris's to find her in bed with Tom (Stuart Townsend), a man she had picked up in a movie theater. Rose reminds Iris that they were scheduled to dispose of their mother's ashes, which Iris had been keeping. Iris cavalierly claims to have lost them, and when an irate Rose scolds her, Iris orders both her and Tom to leave.

One night, Iris is robbed of her purse. She catches Rose at a train station before Rose leaves for a trip and explains her predicament. Rose is about to give her money when Iris notices their mother's ring on Rose's finger. Iris demands to know how Rose got it, and when Rose says that it was their mother's wish that she have it, Iris accuses her of lying, and Rose leaves without giving her any cash. Iris then heads to Rose's home, where Rose's husband, Frank (Mark Womack) agrees to let her spend the night. When a drunken Iris later makes sexual advances, Frank stops her, and she leaves.

Days later, Rose arrives at Iris's and admits that she took the ring without mother's consent. Iris, in turn, reveals that she had been keeping mother's ashes for herself. In the following days, Iris assists Rose with the delivery of her baby, and the sisters dispose of the ashes, Rose by burying some, Iris by scattering the remainder to the wind.

UNDER THE SKIN has the feel of a Mike Leigh or Ken Loach film, not only because of its gritty view of British working-class life, but also because of its empathy and the respect it shows for its characters. Writer-director Adler has created a sensitive and often harrowing portrait of a person who earns compassion despite obnoxious and even cruel behavior. Maintaining an nonjudgmental view of Iris as she works her way to self-awareness through a maze of bitterness, confusion, and anger, Adler permits an acute understanding of Iris's actions, which, given Adler's objectivity, come across as anguished rather than debased.

The intensity of UNDER THE SKIN as a character drama is heightened through its structure. The character of Iris appears in virtually every scene, the camera remaining fixed on her as her (primarily sexual) behavior becomes increasingly self-destructive. The fine camerawork of Barry Ackroyd (Loach's regular cinematographer) reinforces the constancy of Iris's presence by moving as she moves, even when she stumbles drunkenly or wanders aimlessly. At times, the portrait of Iris is so sharply intimate that it would provoke claustrophobic discomfort were it not for Adler's command over Iris's characterization.

Greatly abetting Adler in her forceful depiction of Iris is Samantha Morton (a veteran of several British television miniseries), who gives a daring and vivid performance. Morton in no way works to make Iris likable, remaining wholly true to her character's wretchedness, but as an actress she is so persuasive that one is entranced rather than offended by Iris's descent. The supporting cast is equally fine. Rushbrook (the white daughter in SECRETS AND LIES) is outstanding as the alternately cool and loving Rose, and Tushingham's serene performance as mother interestingly counterbalances Morton's storminess.

The meandering story line of UNDER THE SKIN, while appropriate to the principal character, is at times difficult to follow, and the film is occasionally confusing. This is a minor fault, however, in a film that offers an honest, unblinking but ultimately optimistic view of someone who discovers her worth at the end of a long, painful road. *(Extensive nudity, sexual situations, adult situations, substance abuse, extreme profanity.)*—D.C.

d, Carine Adler; p, Kate Ogborn; exec p, Ben Gibson; w, Carine Adler; ph, Barry Ackroyd; ed, Ewa J. Lind; m, Ilona Sekacz; prod d, John-Paul Kelly; art d, Niall Moroney; sound, Gary Desmond (recordist); casting, Vanessa Pereira, Simone Ireland; cos, Frances Tempest; makeup, Jenny Sharpe

Drama **(PR: O MPAA: NR)**

UNDERTAKER'S WEDDING, THE ★★★

(U.S./Canada, 1998) 85m Anna Pics; S. Entertainment ~ Cabin Fever Entertainment c

Adrien Brody *(Mario Bellini)*; Jeff Wincott *(Rocco)*; Kari Wuhrer *(Maria)*; Burt Young *(Alberto)*; Holly Gagnier *(Louise)*; Nicholas Pasco *(Michael Caprelli)*; Darren Andrea *(Taxi Driver)*; Paul Arno *(Doctor)*; Steve Bloom *(Grave Digger 1)*; Lisa Drew *(Waitress Agnes)*; Edmund *(Enzio Caprielli)*; Ralph George *(Giuseppe)*; Anna Giannotti *(Mrs. Bellini)*; Louie Jannetta *(Frederico Caprelli)*; Bill Kyros *(Ship's Captain)*; Frank Mansillo *(Alberto's Bodyguard)*; Peter Marino *(Gravedigger 2)*; Phil Morrison *(Lt. Green)*; Cam Natalie *(Assassin)*; Ron Pecca *(Driver)*; Nilo Picchi *(Priest)*

A lonely undertaker is saddled with a mobster for a house guest in THE UNDERTAKER'S WEDDING, a rough-edged comedy made enjoyable by an ingratiating cast.

As if Mario Bellini (Adrian Brody) didn't having enough trouble trying to find a woman willing to be the wife of a funeral director, he gets an offer he can't refuse from local mobster Alberto (Burt Young): In order to defuse an ongoing mob war, Alberto needs to fake the death of his hotheaded brother Rocco (Jeff Wincott). He wants Mario to provide a fake funeral, and to give Rocco a hiding place for a few days.

Rocco isn't happy about being cooped up, and Mario has trouble restraining him. So Alberto sends over Rocco's sexpot wife Maria (Kari Wuhrer) to calm him down (though in doing so she inflames lonely Mario). Warming to his host, Rocco tries to help him win back his most recent girlfriend, Louise (Holly Gagnier). But his advice only brings Louise into his own arms. Distraught, Mario spills his heart to Maria, who accidentally kills Rocco in a jealous rage. Tired of being a mob pawn and unwilling to see Maria go to jail for murder, Mario arranges for Rocco's mob enemies to think they have killed him. The ruse works, leaving Mario and Maria happily sailing away on a ship for Sicily.

What THE UNDERTAKER'S WEDDING lacks in big laughs, it compensates for with sheer likability. Despite a tendency of the plot to lurch from scene to scene, it's pleasant enough so that it's a bit jarring when broken-hearted Mario watches Rocco in bed with the woman he tried so desperately to win, and when Rocco (who isn't such a bad guy, as cold-blooded killers go) is killed. Brody (despite a haircut that makes him resemble David Schwimmer) and Wincott (taking a break from action roles) make a good team as the shy, sad-sack undertaker and the extroverted, dim-bulb mobster, while Wuhrer has no trouble looking sexy, which is about all the script requires of her. *(Violence, sexual situations, adult situations, profanity.)*—M.F.

d, John Bradshaw; p, Nicolas Stiliadis; co-p, Paco Alvarez; w, John Bradshaw; ph, Edgar Egger; ed, Ron Wisman; m, Varouje; prod d, Michael Close; set d, Mayuko Udea; fx, Brock Jolliffe; casting, Michael Jannetta; cos, Alex Kavanagh; makeup, Christina Del Grande, Charlene Cordoba; stunts, Tony Cordiero

Comedy **(PR: C MPAA: R)**

UNMADE BEDS ★★★★

(U.S., 1997) 93m Baltic Media; BBC-Modern Times; HBO-Cinemax; La Sept/Arte; Post Perfect ~ Chelsea Pictures c

Brenda Monte; Michael De Stefano; Aimee Copp; Michael Russo

Four lonely New Yorkers look for their soulmates by using the personal ads in UNMADE BEDS, a witty yet haunting blend of fiction and nonfiction. British director Nicholas Barker views modern-day urban angst with a smart and skewed, but passionate, sensibility.

The four "participants" in Barker's study of the contemporary singles scene include two women and two men who reveal intimate facts about their lives to the director throughout a nine-month period in 1996. Brenda, a divorced receptionist and former lap dancer, seeks a man to support her and her teenage daughter, but is more interested in the money than the relationship.

Michael, a bitter 40-year-old bachelor, yearns to meet and marry a woman who will accept his 5'4" height. Aimee Copp, a 28-year-old conference organizer, tries to understand her poor success finding a man while she gives herself until age 30 to find a husband. Mikey Russo, a 54-year-old security director and aspiring screenwriter, uses the personals to get dates with attractive women, but usually ends up rejecting or being rejected by his escorts.

By the end of the nine months, Mikey regrets having lost the beautiful women of his youth, and sadly turns to the singles bar scene to find companionship. Aimee, who takes the advice of Laurie, her slimmer, more attractive best friend, considers using a dating service, her last resort to finding a husband. Michael also gives up using the personals, and gets help from a dating coach, who suggests he take a "Cooking for Singles" class. Finally, Brenda finds a man, an immigrant, who provides her with marriage and $10,000, but no personal commitment.

Barker, a former anthropologist, created this fascinating survey of today's dating game by interviewing over 1000 single New Yorkers in 1996, then selecting the four finalists here and developing their life stories into mock-cinema verite script form. The blurring of the lines between documentary and story film is not new—in fact all documentaries depend upon some degree of manufacture—but rarely has a film been quite so successful in making the lines so completely disappear. Despite Barker's use of nonprofessional actors (playing themselves—a difficult task), there is not one false moment in UNMADE BEDS.

Still, the film, like true cinema verite, raises questions about the exploitation of people and the invasion of their privacy: whether scripted or not, all four subjects reveal their deepest feelings, and Brenda even reveals her nude body. One might also argue that Barker makes fun of his characters by laughing at their hopes and fears. Yet, in a larger way, Barker laughs at and rightly criticizes a myriad of social foibles—through Michael, the desire for status and acceptance by being seen with beautiful women; through Aimee, the obsession with marriage as a utopian solution to her problems; through Mikey, his fear and hatred of homosexuality; and through Brenda, her forthright xenophobia, and her association of relationships with money. Cleverly, the film traces the negative and destructive attitudes with the individual's failure to connect interpersonally.

Along the way, the four subjects make some very funny comments about their plights, but Barker also intercuts shots of other lonely New Yorkers through their bedroom windows and accompanies their mini-narratives with plaintive jazz music (evoking Hitchcock's REAR WINDOW); the result constantly reminds the viewer of the pain behind the pathos. Edward Hopper's painting, *Early Sunday*, becomes another recurring motif, symbolizing the anomie and despair of modern city living. By challenging the film form and taking chances, UNMADE BEDS goes farther than most in depicting an ailing and alienating society. *(Extensive nudity, extreme profanity.)*—E.M.

d, Nicholas Barker; p, Steve Wax; assoc p, Sam Bickley; w, Nicholas Barker; ph, William Rexer II; ed, Paul Binns; sound, Brad Bergbom (recordist)

Docudrama **(PR: O MPAA: NR)**

UNVEILING, THE ★

(U.S., 1998) 81m Miasma Films c/bw

Dixie Evans; Michele Watley; Eldad Sahar; Erin Watley; Michelle Levy

THE UNVEILING is an inept and wearying documentary on exotic dancing, as experienced by three people who work or have worked as strippers.

Former dancer Dixie Evans, now in her 70s, relates the history of the striptease, its roots in burlesque stage shows, and subsequent development on the nightclub circuit. She also recounts her own career, as well as the careers of such striptease legends as Tempest Storm and Sally Rand.

Michele Watley, an African-American single mother, demonstrates the careful preparation that goes into each show and explains her various routines. She comments on how she tailors her performance to suit specific audiences, how performing for a male audience differs from performing for a female audience, and the quality of her own dancing.

Eldad Sahar, a gay dancer, discusses the atmosphere at the club where he works, where both the clientele and other dancers are primarily gay and Latino. He explains his dancing technique and the care he puts into his performances, and comments on sexual harassment he has experienced on the job. Both Michele and Eldad discuss their dynamic interactions with audience members and the common misconceptions about the work they do. They also talk about what their futures may hold, Michele expressing reservations about her young daughter following in her footsteps, and Eldad expressing his desire to become a legitimate actor.

At the close of the annual Miss Exotic World contest, emcee Dixie asserts the importance of exotic dancing as an American tradition, and proclaims its legitimacy.

THE UNVEILING, the first feature film by Rodney Evans, is a well-intentioned attempt to de-exoticize what is generally referred to as "exotic dancing." Evans's choice of interviews is good, the three principals proving to be highly engaging and earnest about their profession. In fact, the choice of one of the interview subjects provided some free publicity for the film, when it was revealed that Michele Watley was the sister of pop star Jody Watley.

Evans's support for what Michele and her confederates do is obvious, and he succeeds in presenting their provocative line of work forthrightly without ever being exploitive.

THE UNVEILING, however, completely lacks structure, amounting more or less to a hodgepodge of random discussions which are intercut with poorly shot performance footage. The interviewees raise a broad range of topics, among them the significance of race and sexuality for both dancers and audience members, but no one issue is ever given enough consideration for a meaningful conclusion to be drawn. The film never develops momentum, and tapers into tedium once the novelty of the subject matter has worn off.

Technically, THE UNVEILING is dreadful. Besides amateurish cinematography, the soundtrack is often barely audible, and the editing is choppy, with many scenes beginning and ending very abruptly. The archival footage included to illustrate the history of stripping is fascinating, and a stag short starring a young Dixie Evans (titled "Trying to Break into the Movies") is priceless, but even here, Evans (the filmmaker) undermines the material by intercutting it with wholly unnecessary contemporary footage of Dixie describing her performance in it.

Evans clearly intended to illuminate an often reviled profession, but the light shed by THE UNVEILING is hopelessly dim. *(Extensive nudity, sexual situations, adult situations, profanity.)*— D.C.

d, Rodney Evans; p, Rodney Evans; ph, Rodney Evans, Lauri King, Chris Robertson, Aaron Kirsch, Eric Wussie; ed, Rodney Evans; sound, Elyzabeth Dunnebacke (recordist), Colin Gagon (recordist)

Documentary **(PR: O MPAA: NR)**

URBAN LEGEND ★★

(U.S., 1998) 97m Phoenix Films; Original Films ~ Columbia TriStar c

Jared Leto *(Paul)*; Alicia Witt *(Natalie)*; Michael Rosenbaum *(Parker)*; Joshua Jackson *(Damon)*; Tara Reid *(Shasha)*; Rebecca Gayheart *(Brenda)*; Loretta Devine *(Reese)*; John Neville *(Dean Adams)*; Julian Richings *(Janitor)*; Robert Englund *(Professor Wexler)*; Danielle Harris *(Tosh)*; Natasha Gregson Wagner *(Michelle Mancini)*; Gord Martineau *(Newsman)*; Kay Hawtrey *(Library Attendant)*; Angela Vint *(Bitchy Girl)*; J.C. Kenny *(Weather Woman)*; Vince Corrazza *(David Evans)*; Balazs Koos *(Nerdy Guy)*; Stephanie Mills *(Felicia)*; Danny Comden *(Blake)*; Nancy McAlear *(Jenny)*; Shawn Mathieson *(Hippie Guy)*; Cle Bennett *(Dorky Guy)*; Danielle Brett *(Trendy Girl)*; Roberta Angelica *(Swimming Woman)*; Matt Birman *(Killer)*

Columbia Pictures and producer Neil Moritz followed up their 1997 thriller hit I KNOW WHAT YOU DID LAST SUMMER in 1998 not only with a sequel but also this lackluster lookalike which borrowed the same ad campaign, scare setups, and juvenile target audience for its rehashed plot of young adults stalked by a mystery maniac.

Michelle Mancini (Natasha Gregson Wagner), a girl attending Pendleton College in New England, is slain by an ax murderer hiding in her car's backseat. Although a gas station clerk (Brad Dourif) is arrested for the crime, there seems more to it than that. At Pendleton, Prof. Wexler (Robert Englund), a folklore expert, teaches a course on "urban legends," horrific tales of dubious validity which are nevertheless widely accepted as fact. Thirty years ago, Pendleton's Stanley Hall gave birth to such a legend when a psychology instructor supposedly went on a murderous rampage. Students plan a big keg blast for the anniversary.

Student Natalie (Alicia Witt) is worried: she and Michelle were high school friends who once pulled a traffic prank that caused the death of a teenaged boy. Now Natalie seems surrounded by gruesome mayhem. On a date with class clown Damon (Joshua Jackson), he is attacked and killed by an unseen figure. With no corpse to be found, the authorities put it down to a prank. Next her much-disliked roommate (Danielle Harris) is found with her wrists cut, and Natalie doubts the verdict of suicide. When ambitious student reporter Paul (Jared Leto) learns that Wexler was the sole survivor of the Pendleton massacre, Natalie realizes that a serial killer, possibly Wexler, is patterning new murders after established urban legends.

On the night of the party the killer claims several other victims. Natalie is knocked out and strapped down inside Stanley Hall, where she learns that the killer is her best friend Brenda (Rebecca Gayheart), secretly the bereaved lover of the youth who died in the traffic prank. All this time Brenda has been plotting her revenge, setting up Wexler to take the rap. Natalie is saved from vivisection by Paul, and the two flee the determined Brenda, who pursues despite being shot, stabbed, and bludgeoned. A car chase catapults her into a storm-swept river, but no corpse is found. A new generation of students discuss the urban legend that has grown up around the story; among the listeners is Brenda.

Pendleton College (actually the University of Toronto, where URBAN LEGEND was filmed) is one of those learning institutions seen only in movies, where classes and studying never seem to get in the way of nonstop sex, drinking, parties and practical jokes. And that's still more credible than the silly murder plot, with the culprit's identity becoming painfully obvious midway through—even if Brenda's fatal schemes are patently ridiculous once the viewer applies real-world logic to her recurring appearance as a phantom figure in a fur-collared parka. Hauling in a wagonload of these thrice-told tales as a post-modern serial killer's signature proves a better idea in concept than execution. The killer may as well have based her murders on French Impressionist paintings, famous TV commercials, or whatever; the depressing agenda remains the same, as an ensemble of good-looking young actors are slaughtered for your entertainment dollar. Anyone over 30 in this cast is disposable, though Robert "Freddy Krueger" Englund at least tries to put some spirit into the exposition. Debuting director Jamie Blanks overemphasizes such cheap shock tactics as hands tapping on shoulders and faces unexpectedly popping into the frame, accompanied by a "boo!" from the equally-tiresome, nonstop orchestral-music score. *(Violence, profanity, adult situations, sexual situations, substance abuse.)*—C.C.

d, Jamie Blanks; p, Neal H. Moritz, Gina Matthews, Michael McDonnell; exec p, Brad Luff; w, Silvio Horta; ph, James Chressanthis; ed, Jay Cassidy; m, Christopher Young; prod d, Charles Breen; art d, Benno Tutter; set d, Cal Loucks; sound, Tom Mather (mixer); fx, Dean Stewart; casting, John Papsidera; cos, Mary Claire Hannan; makeup, Leslie Sebert; stunts, Matt Birman

Horror/Thriller **(PR: O MPAA: R)**

URBAN SAFARI ★½

(Canada/Switzerland, 1995) 92m Full Circle Films ~ G.L.A.S.S. Films c

David Naughton *(Joe)*; Linda Kash *(Candy)*; Andrea Nemeth *(Heather)*; Donnelly Rhodes *(Harry)*; Art Brazeau *(Carl Johnson)*; Charles Siegel *(George Winkler)*; Rebecca Toolan *(Louise Winkler)*; David Palffy *(Art)*; Teryl Rothery *(Faye)*; Barry Pepper *(Rico)*; Adriana Tripa *(Eva)*; Akiko Morison *(Gloria, the Reporter)*; Nick Misura *(Taxi Driver)*; Tom Pickett *(Albert)*; Darren Moore *(Video Editor)*; Richard Side *(Alex)*; Joely Collins *(Girl Friend)*; Kim Kondrashoff *(Pavel)*; Paul Bittante *(Lt. Snyder)*; Jed Rees *(Delivery Boy)*; Art Irizawa *(Mr. Kwong)*; Lillian Carlson *(Mrs. Pelegrini)*

Tasteless and frenetic, URBAN SAFARI spins its vulgarian wheels in a story line that makes increasingly less sense as it reaches its climax. The cast scampers about in a farce-manque that lacks lunatic logic and comic precision.

Angling for a promotion for her husband Joe (David Naughton), social-climbing Candy (Linda Kash) prevaricates about Joe's invention of a low-flow toilet. She impresses Joe's boss George Winkler (Charles Siegel), but ruffles the feathers of Joe's rival Art (David Palffy) and his competitive wife Faye (Teryl Rothery). Boasting about taking an African safari vacation to travel-loving Mr. Winkler, Candy and Joe actually head for the Catskills, where Joe plans to perfect his still-unrealized toilet design.

Having forgotten their resort reservations, they sneak home, where they are unexpectedly joined by their teenaged daughter Heather (Andrea Nemeth) who's cutting school, and by Joe's dad, Harry (Donnelly Rhodes). Because Mr. Winkler lives in the same building, Joe and Candy are forced to stay in their apartment, lest their lie be exposed. They lose even the full use of the apartment when building handyman Carl Johnson (Jay Brazeau) takes over their supposedly vacant residence to transact the smuggling of rhino horns with Russian Mafiosi. The couple hide in the closet and unoccupied rooms.

Carl isn't the only one with plans for the "empty" apartment: Joe and Candy also are forced to hide from Art, who is carrying on an affair with Mr. Winkler's wife Louise (Rebecca Toolan). Other unwelcome guests include Heather's beau Rico (Barry Pepper) and Mr. Winkler, who sexually harasses Carl's cousin Eva (Adriana Tripa) until Candy conks him from behind. Assuming he was attacked by a burglar, Mr. Winkler installs a security gate outside the apartment. When Rico climbs down the building to get help from the police, he's arrested. Tipped off by Rico at the police station, a snoopy reporter breaks the story about the

Rhino Horn racket. The police arrive, and rescue the trapped family from the apartment. Tired of clawing his way up the corporate ladder, Joe quits Winkler's firm for a City Hall post; Candy pens a runaway best-seller about family survival techniques.

Although the premise of a couple caught in a deceitful web of their own devising promises merriment, URBAN SAFARI soon gets caught in a taffy-pull of extraneous mishaps and salacious pandering. Despite a few bright zingers, the film is sidetracked by Carl's criminal slapstick shtick and by dated blue humor about adultery. Nor are its protagonists particularly sympathetic: chronic opportunists Joe and Candy are just as whorish as Faye and Art, when it comes to career advancement. As a wallow in tastelessness, URBAN SAFARI doesn't score many laughs, but it does strike a death blow against office politics. *(Violence, extreme profanity, substance abuse, sexual situations.)* —R.P.

d, Reto Salimbeni; p, Michael Collier; exec p, Reto Salimbeni; assoc p, John Cumming; co-p, Martin Schmassmann, Alfred Nathan; w, P.J. Reece, James J. Desmarais, Alison Rosenfeld Desmarais; ph, Vic Sarin; ed, Jana Frisch; m, Brahm Wenger; art d, Peter Hinton, Kathy Henderson; set d, Al Schedler; sound, Daryl Powell (mixer); casting, Akiko Morison; cos, David Lisle; makeup, Jacky Wilkinson, Anne Ross; stunts, Bill Stewart

Comedy **(PR: C MPAA: R)**

U.S. MARSHALS ★★

(U.S., 1998) 133m Arnold Kopelson/Keith Barish; Warner Bros. ~ Warner Bros. c

Tommy Lee Jones *(Chief Deputy Marshal Samuel Gerard)*; Wesley Snipes *(Mark Sheridan)*; Robert Downey Jr. *(John Royce)*; Joe Pantoliano *(Deputy Marshal Cosmo Renfro)*; Kate Nelligan *(US Marshal Walsh)*; Irene Jacob *(Marie)*; Daniel Roebuck *(Deputy Marshal Biggs)*; Tom Wood *(Deputy Marshal Newman)*; Latanya Richardson *(Deputy Marshal Cooper)*; Patrick Malahide *(Lamb)*; Rick Snyder *(Barrows)*; Michael Paul Chan *(Chen)*; Johnny Lee Davenport *(Deputy Henry)*; Donald Li *(Detective Kim)*; Marc Vann *(Deputy Jackson)*; Michael Guido *(Distracted Driver)*; Robert Mohler *(Young Cop)*; Richard Lexsee *(Fireman)*; Dado *(Female Cop)*; Karen Vaccaro *(Hospital Cashier)*; David Kersnar *(Desk Sergeant)*; Tony Fitzpatrick *(Greg Conroy)*; Don Gibb *(Mike Conroy)*; Cynthia S. Baker *(Mama Conroy)*; Susan Hart *(Greg's Girlfriend)*; Vaitiare Bandera *(Stacia Vela)*; Don Herlon *(Detective Caldwell)*; Len Bajenski *(Deputy Hollander)*; Matt Decaro *(Deputy Stern)*; Thomas Rosales Jr. *(727 Prisoner)*; James Sie *(Ling)*; Christian Payton *(1st 727 Deputy)*; Steve King *(727 Pilot)*; Tracy Letts *(Sheriff Poe)*; Mark Morettini *(1st Cop)*; Kent Reed *(Trooper with Dogs)*; Ray Toler *(Earl)*; Brenda Pickelman *(Martha)*; Max Maxwell *(Roadblock Trooper)*; Peter Burns *(State Trooper Captain)*; Roy Hytower *(Tracker)*; Ian Barford *(Royce's Guide)*; Robert Kurcz *(Kidnapped Man)*; Rose M. Abdoo *(Donna)*; Lorenzo Clemons *(Stark)*; Stephen A. Cinabro *(Undercover Deputy)*; Clifford T. Frazier *(Minister)*; Mindy Bell *(Deputy Holt)*; Richard Thomsen *(Doorman)*; Yasen Peyanikow *(Janitor)*; Meg Thalken *(Saks Saleswoman)*; Lennox Brown *(Man in Green Cap)*; Varen Black *(Network Reporter)*; Ammar Daraiseh *(Drugstore Clerk)*; Romanos Isaac *(Ship's First Officer)*; Richard Pickren *(Prosecutor)*; Lynn Wilde *(Caldwell's Wife)*; Amy E. Jacobsen *(New York Reporter)*; Cliff Teinert *(Swamp Tracker)*; Ellen Hearn *(4th Reporter)*; Janet Contursi *(Chicago Nurse)*; George J. Hynek Jr. *(New York Paramedic)*; Wendell Thomas *(New York Paramedic)*; E. Glenn Ward Jr. *(Elderly Resident)*; Marie Ware *(Elderly Resident)*; Rick Lefevour *(10th Deputy)*; Jim Fierro *(6th Deputy)*; Michael Braun *(727 Co-pilot)*; Perry D. Sullivan *(727 Navigator)*; Terry G. Rochford *(NTSB Agent)*; Tony Paris *(Newman's Guide)*; Ed Fernandez *(Detective)*; Richard Wilkie *(Detective)*; Chick Bernhardt *(Royce's Guide)*; Tressana Alouane *(Mike's Girlfriend)*; Ralph J. Lucci *(Bartender)*; Louis Young *(3rd Reporter)*; David A. Bales *(Man in Taxi)*; Vince DeMentri *(Reporter)*; Chris Bean *(Bar Patron)*

Tommy Lee Jones reprises his Oscar-winning role from THE FUGITIVE (1993) in U.S. MARSHALS, a routine and overlong spin-off that slavishly tries to copy elements of the original blockbuster, but sorely lacks its solid plotting and plausibility, not to mention the sympathetic star-power of Harrison Ford.

Chicago tow-truck driver Mark Sheridan (Wesley Snipes) is arrested when a gun is found in his truck with fingerprints that are said to match those from a weapon that was used to murder two diplomatic Secret Service agents in the United Nations parking lot some months earlier. Sheridan is put on a plane which will take him to a Federal penitentiary; also on board is US Marshal Sam Gerard (Tommy Lee Jones), who's escorting one of his own prisoners. During the flight, a prisoner goes into the bathroom and returns with a zip-gun that was hidden there. He shoots at Sheridan but misses and blows a hole in the fuselage. The plane crashes in a lake, and Sheridan escapes during the confusion.

Gerard and his crew begin their manhunt, and he's forced by his superiors to take along special agent Royce (Robert Downey Jr.). Sheridan makes his way to New York and rents an apartment across from the UN and sets up surveillance cameras. He also calls his girlfriend (Irene Jacob) in Chicago and reveals that he used to work for the government, but that he was set up and had to kill the two UN agents in self-defense. Gerard starts to question Sheridan's guilt when he learns about the planted zip-gun and checks the tapes of the murder from the parking lot security cameras and sees that the shooter was wearing gloves, meaning fingerprints should not have been found on the gun. In New York, Sheridan tails a Chinese operative named Chen (Michael Paul Chan) and sees him switch suitcases with someone, then follows the second man to a cemetery in Queens. Gerard and his team are also following them, having come to New York and found Sheridan's apartment and the surveillance tapes of Chen.

At the cemetery, Sheridan catches an ex-colleague, Agent Barrows (Rick Snyder) picking up the suitcase, which is filled with money. Barrows admits that he has been selling information to the Chinese and that he and his "mystery" partner set up Sheridan. Just then, Chen arrives and kills Barrows, but Sheridan escapes and is chased by Gerard and his crew. When Agent Newman (Tom Wood) is about to capture Sheridan, Royce kills him, then tells Gerard that Sheridan did it. Sheridan escapes again, but Gerard later tracks him down at a shipyard. During a fight, Sheridan is shot by Royce and rushed to the hospital. At the hospital, Gerard becomes suspicious of Royce when he sees the gun that Sheridan supposedly used to kill Newman. Gerard pretends to leave, and when he returns, he sees Royce trying to murder Sheridan. Gerard shoots Royce and Sheridan is subsequently exonerated.

Tommy Lee Jones is a fine actor and always fun to watch, but his dour, dyspeptic charm is much more suited to the role of a supporting player than a leading man, as the plodding U.S. MARSHALS proves. The film manages to be predictable and slow moving, even while offering nonstop crash-and-burn action for the yahoo crowd. After a maladroit first half-hour that has virtually nothing to do with the story, the film turns into a pure chase movie. Still, time is found for political correctness: Gerard has a new black female agent and a female boss, a "good" Chinese agent counterbalances the Fu Manchu-ish Chen character, and Sheridan has a white girlfriend (the hilariously miscast and misused Irene Jacob, who looks quite ludicrous running through a Queens cemetery wearing a tight designer dress.)

The film is essentially a series of action set pieces designed to recall THE FUGITIVE (a plane crash instead of the original's train wreck; an aerial shot of Sheridan jumping from a roof onto a moving train in lieu of Harrison Ford's jump into the waterfall) which are technically well staged, but lack suspense because they're so mechanically done. The convoluted script depends on numerous coincidences and contrivances, and fails to make clear the reason why Sheridan was set up in the first place, why he had to kill the agents in self-defense, or exactly how Gerard deduces that the gun used to kill Newman was Royce's. There's also little doubt as to the identity of Barrows's "mystery" partner: as soon as the smarmy Royce shows up with his fancy suit, sunglasses, laptop, and cell phone, we know he's not to be trusted. *(Violence, profanity.)*—M.S.

d, Stuart Baird; p, Arnold Kopelson, Anne Kopelson; exec p, Keith Barish, Roy Huggins; assoc p, Glenn Richard Cote, Linda Warren; co-p, Stephen Brown; w, John Pogue (based on characters created by Roy Huggins); ph, Andrzej Bartkowiak; ed, Terry Rawlings; m, Jerry Goldsmith; prod d, Maher Ahmad; art d, Bruce Alan Miller; set d, Gene Serdena; sound, Scott D. Smith (mixer); fx, Mike Meinardus, Peter Donen; casting, Amanda Mackey, Cathy Sandrich, Jane Alderman; cos, Louise Frogley; makeup, June Westmore; stunts, Gary Davis, Dick Ziker

Action/Thriller/Crime (PR: C MPAA: R)

VAMPIRES

(SEE: JOHN CARPENTER'S VAMPIRES)

VELVET GOLDMINE ★★

(U.K./U.S., 1998) 120m Killer Films; Zenith Productions; Single Cell Picture ~ Miramax c

Ewan McGregor *(Curt Wild)*; Christian Bale *(Arthur Stuart)*; Jonathan Rhys Meyers *(Brian Slade)*; Toni Collette *(Mandy Slade)*; Eddie Izzard *(Jerry Divine)*; Emily Woof *(Shannon)*; Michael Feast *(Cecil)*; Mariad McKinley *(Wilde Housemaid)*; Janet McTeer *(Female Narrator)*; Luke Morgan Oliver *(Oscar Wilde-8)*; Osheen Jones *(Jack Fairy-7)*; Micko Westmoreland *(Jack Fairy)*; Damian Suchet *(BBC Reporter)*; Danny Nutt *(Kissing Sailor)*; Wash Westmoreland *(Young Man)*; Don Fellows *(Lou)*; Ganiat Kasumu *(Mary)*; Ray Shell *(Murray)*; Alastair Cumming *(Tommy Stone)*; Zoe Boyce *(Girl on the Subway)*; Jim Whelan *(Mr. Stuart)*; Sylvia Grant *(Mrs. Stuart)*; Tim Hans *(Manchester Teacher)*; Ryan Pope *(Arthur's Teacher)*; Stuart Callaghan *(Boy in Record Shop 1)*; James Francis *(Boy in Record Shop 2)*; Callum Hamilton *(Brian Slade-7)*; Lindsay Kemp *(Pantomime Dame)*; Carlos Miranda *(Pianist)*; Emma Handy *(Mod Girlfriend)*; Matthew Glamour *(Mimosa)*; Daniel Adams *(Curt Wild-13)*; Brian Torfeh *(Bartender)*; Joe Beattie *(Cooper)*; Sarah Cawood *(Angel)*; David Hoyle *(Freddi)*; Winston Austin *(Micky)*; Ivan Cartwright *(Cecil's Friend 1)*; Peter King *(Cecil's Friend 2)*; Justin Salinger *(Rodney)*; Roger Alborough *(Middle Age Man)*; Peter Bradley Jr. *(30's Style Singer)*; Jonathan Cullen *(Reporter 1)*; William Key *(Reporter 2)*; Vincent Marzello *(US Reporter 1)*; Corey Skaggs *(US Reporter 2)*; Nathan Osgood *(US Reporter 3)*; Nadia Williams *(Teenage Girl)*; FLAMING CREATURES: Brian Molko *(Malcolm)*; Anthony Langdon *(Ray)*; Xaf *(Pearl)*; Steve Hewitt *(Billy)*; THE VENUS IN FURS: Guy Leverton *(Trevor)*; Vinney Reck *(Reg)*; Keith-Lee Castle *(Harley)*; THE WYLDE RATTTZ: Alan Fordham *(Bass Guitar)*; Jono McGrath *(Lead Guitar)*; Perry Clayton *(Drummer)*; POLLY SMALL'S BAND: Donna Matthews *(Polly Small)*; Ritz *(Lead Guitar)*; Stefan Olsday *(Bass Guitar)*; Trevor Sharpe *(Drummer)*

Director Todd Haynes (POISON, SAFE) prizes style over substance in this atmospheric but comatose fictional history of the relationship between glam-rock icon David Bowie and punk godfather Iggy Pop. Skip the film and buy the soundtrack.

London, 1974: Glittery pop idol Brian Slade (Jonathan Rhys Meyers), in the guise of his alter-ego, Maxwell Demon, is shot and killed onstage. Among the shocked onlookers is Arthur Stuart (Christian Bale), whose love for his androgynous glam-rock heroes has distanced him from his parents (Jim Whelan, Sylvia Grant), who shun him after he's discovered masturbating to one of Slade's album covers.

New York, 1984: A right-wing pop star, Tommy Stone (Alastair Cumming), is all the rage, and Stuart, now a newspaper reporter, is assigned the task of finding out what happened to Brian Slade, whose onstage murder turned out to be a hoax.

Stuart seeks out Cecil (Michael Feast), Slade's first manager. Cecil describes how he took Slade, then a hippie type, under his wing and got him a gig with incendiary American rocker Curt Wild (Ewan McGregor), whose onstage antics—including dropping his pants and setting the stage on fire—inspired Slade to reinvent himself as a glitzy gender-bender. Once Slade attracted the attention of Bijou Records' Jerry Divine (Eddie Izzard) and landed on "Top of the Pops," Cecil became *persona non grata*. He urges Stuart to find Slade's crass American ex-wife, Mandy (Toni Collette), for the rest of the story.

Mandy, divorced from Slade for seven years, fills in the blanks: how she introduced Slade to androgynous style maven Jack Fairy (Micko Westmoreland); how Slade took Fairy's fabled brooch, which was proported to have once belonged to Oscar Wilde; and how Slade, at the peak of superstardom, was allowed to produce an album by Wild. While the creative—and sexual—relationship between Slade and Wild flourished, the project was a disaster, causing Wild to walk out on Slade forever. Depressed, Slade allowed himself to be "executed;" the revelation of the hoax tarnished his image; and Slade, washed up and coked out, was served divorce papers. The last time Mandy had seen Slade was at a "Death of Glitter" concert—a concert which Stuart himself attended, and which ended with Stuart engaging in rooftop sex with Wild.

Stuart attempts to get in touch with Wild, but he's turned down. He investigates further, and discovers that Slade changed his name to "Thomas" in 1979. Even though the story's been dropped, Stuart perseveres. He gets backstage at a Tommy Stone concert and asks Stone about Slade. Stone is shocked by the question, and Stuart is kicked out. Stuart goes to a bar, where he runs into Wild. "I guess, in the end, he got what he wanted," Wild says in regards to Slade. He then reveals the fabled brooch, which he says was given to him by "a friend of mine that kind of disappeared some years back." Stuart and Wild then wordlessly share memories of their rooftop encounter. Wild gives Stuart the brooch, saying he's had it too long, but Stuart declines. After Wild leaves with a smile, Stuart finds the brooch in his beer bottle.

It's hard to resist VELVET GOLDMINE's supercharged opening credit sequence, which features Stuart and a plethora of period-costumed extras gearing up for Slade/Demon's ill-fated 1974 concert to the tune of Brian Eno's "Needle in the Camel's Eye," but it's all downhill from there. Haynes, who also gets sole writer credit, must believe that a sense of "mystical" ambiguity (most evident in the film's preamble, in which the brooch is bequeathed to Oscar Wilde and then to a youthful Jack Fairy) and a CITIZEN KANE-like frame device can add weight to a flimsy story; all his flashy music-video-sequence padding, while lovely to look at, isn't much more than a fleeting distraction to behold. The price of fame—not to mention the nature of celebrity and charisma—may be the film's central theme, if, indeed, we are to believe that Slade and Stone are one and the same; but what does it matter when the road to our conclusion has all the sonambulant flash of a heroin nod?

The Bowie/Pop comparisons are thinly veiled: Wild performs "T.V. Eye," a Pop classic; Demon is an obvious reference to Bowie's alter-ego, Ziggy Stardust; and the pains taken by Haynes to (unsuccessfully) get permission to use Bowie's music have been well-documented. But in Haynes's hands, these archetypes become nothing more than Ken dolls, whose sole function is to dress up and look pretty. (And in a cheeky scene referencing his notorious Karen Carpenter biopic, SUPERSTAR, Haynes does just that.)

VELVET GOLDMINE's saving grace is its rousing soundtrack, which features originals by Eno, Roxy Music, T-Rex, and Lou Reed, in addition to some fine period-appropriate originals by the likes of Shudder to Think and Grant Lee Buffalo. Rhys Meyers and McGregor supply their own vocals; their respective rock-star impersonations are thoroughly impressive (though workmanlike), as is Collette, whose Angie Bowie/Marianne Faithfull manque could easily define "obnoxious." Even so, Collette manages to render herself completely sympathetic during Mandy's wrenching final confrontation with Slade. It could be because she's finally discovered what the audience has known all along—that Slade's vainglorious appeal is virtually nonexistent. *(Violence, nudity, sexual situations, adult situations, substance abuse, profanity.)*—K.S.

d, Todd Haynes; p, Christine Vachon; exec p, Michael Stipe, Scott Meek, Sandy Stern; co-p, Olivia Stewart; w, Todd Haynes; ph, Maryse Alberti; ed, James Lyons; m, Carter Burwell; prod d, Christopher Hobbs; art d, Andrew Munro; ch, Lea Anderson; sound, Peter Lindsay (recordist); fx, Evolution FX; casting, Susie Figgis (UK), Laura Rosenthal (US); cos, Sandy Powell; makeup, Peter King

AAN Best Costume Design: Sandy Powell

Musical/Fantasy/Drama (PR: C MPAA: R)

VERY BAD THINGS ★½

(U.S., 1998) 101m Initial Entertainment Group; Interscope Communications; Ballpark Productions ~ Polygram Films c

Jon Favreau *(Kyle Fisher)*; Leland Orser *(Charles Moore)*; Cameron Diaz *(Laura Garrety)*; Christian Slater *(Robert Boyd)*; Rob Brownstein *(Man)*; Jeremy Piven *(Michael Berkow)*; Daniel Stern *(Adam Berkow)*; Jeanne Tripplehorn *(Lois Berkow)*; Joey Zimmerman *(Adam Berkow Jr.)*; Tyler Malinger *(Timmy Berkow)*; Carla Scott *(Tina)*; Russell B. McKenzie *(Security Guard)*; Pancho Demings *(Cop)*; Blake Gibbons *(Suit)*; Angelo Di Mascio Jr. *(Clerk)*; Lawrence Pressman *(Mr. Fisher)*; Steve Fitchpatrick *(Cop at Hospital)*; Brian Grandison *(Doctor #1)*; John Cappon *(Doctor #2)*; Linda Klein *(Doctor #3)*; Byrne Piven *(Rabbi)*; Bob Bancroft *(Barry Morris)*; Trey Davis *(Receptionist)*; Marilyn McIntyre *(Judge Tower)*

Actor Peter Berg (THE LAST SEDUCTION) makes a potentially career-killing writing-directing debut with VERY BAD THINGS, an appalling black comedy that's very bad indeed, and is so intent on being shocking that it forgets to be funny.

Before his wedding to Laura (Cameron Diaz), LA stockbroker Kyle (Jon Favreau) sets off for a wild bachelor party in Las Vegas with his four buddies: brothers Adam (Daniel Stern) and Michael (Jeremy Piven), real-estate agent Robert Boyd (Christian Slater), and mechanic Charles (Leland Orser). After some drugs and booze, Robert brings a hooker (Carla Scott) up to their hotel room, but during some rough sex with Michael, she's killed when he accidentally smashes her skull into a coat hook. Adam wants to call 911, but Boyd convinces them to bury her in the desert, along with a suspicious security guard (Russell B. McKenzie) who comes to the room and is killed by Boyd. The men chop up the bodies and bury them in the desert, but after returning to LA, Adam is wracked with guilt, and he's eventually run down and killed by Michael during an argument.

Adam's wife Lois (Jeanne Tripplehorn) finds a letter in which Adam confesses to what happened in Las Vegas, and when she confronts the other men, Boyd strangles her and then shoots Michael to make it look like a murder-suicide. Kyle is appointed as the guardian of Adam and Lois's two kids, one of whom is crippled, and awarded some money from Adam's insurance policy. Cracking under the pressure, Kyle tells Laura about the hooker and says he wants to postpone the wedding, but she refuses to allow anything to interfere with her plans. The day of the wedding, Boyd demands his cut of the insurance money from Kyle, and a fight ensues between them, ending when Laura kills Boyd with a coat tree. After the ceremony, Laura tells Kyle to bury Boyd's body, and to bump off Charles while he's at it, but Kyle can't go through with it. Driving back from the desert, Kyle has a head-on collision with another car, and the miserable Laura is left tending to the wheelchair-bound Kyle and Charles, along with Adam's kids.

VERY BAD THINGS inexplicably ignited a bidding war from distributors, who no doubt were hoping that memories of Cameron Diaz and her role in the summer's surprise smash hit, THERE'S SOMETHING ABOUT MARY, would result in lightning striking twice. Unfortunately, while MARY was a genuinely funny black comedy because of its fearless tastelessness, there was also something curiously sweet about it, while BAD is simply rancid and amoral. It's not unfunny because it's amoral, but rather, it's amoral because it's not funny. VERY BAD THINGS is also not very original: the plot line of the murdered hooker at a bachelor party was done as recently as 1997 in an HBO movie called STAG (which treated the subject seriously), while the juvenile Tom Hanks movie BACHELOR PARTY (1984) offered a lot more laughs and served up the out-of-control hotel room antics with much more gusto. There is nothing inherently funny about ridiculing the handicapped, but Berg seems to think that the mere sight of a child falling off his crutches or a three-legged dog hopping around is hilarious and cutting edge.

As the hooker is Asian and the security guard an African-American, perhaps Berg thought he could camouflage the nastiness by positioning the story as a social allegory about the oppression of minorities at the hands of white middle-class males (using Boyd's self-empowerment real-estate philosophy to rationalize his heinous behavior), but the execution is such that the audience is ultimately supposed to sympathize with the men. Berg's idea of biting satire is to show pictures of Don Rickles and Julio Iglesias in the hotel room while the men are chopping up the corpses, and to take easy potshots at suburban squares, soccer moms, and mini vans. The performances are all pitched at an obnoxiously hysterical one-note level, with lots of aimless, self-indulgent improv scenes. Berg's cinematic style is equally tiresome, with a plethora of mannered slow-motion shots and "ironic" use of lightweight pop songs to counterpoint the grisly mayhem. In MARY and A LIFE LESS ORDINARY (1997), Cameron Diaz has already proven that she's a good sport and isn't afraid of risky roles, but her thankless part here as a marriage-obsessed harridan is beyond the call of duty and she should really think twice about putting her career in the hands of a neophyte trying to prove how outrageous he can be. *(Graphic violence, extreme profanity, nudity, sexual situations, substance abuse.)*—M.S.

d, Peter Berg; p, Michael Schiffer, Diane Nabatoff, Cindy Cowan; exec p, Ted Field, Scott Kroopf, Michael Helfant, Christian Slater ; w, Peter Berg; ph, David Hennings; ed, Dan Lebental; m, Stewart Copeland; prod d, Dina Lipton; art d, Michael Atwell; set d, Kathy Lucas; sound, Matthew Iadarola, Gary Gegan; fx, Larry Fioritto; cos, Terry Dresbach; makeup, Nancy Baca; stunts, Chris Howell

Comedy/Drama (PR: O MPAA: R)

VIAGEM AO PRINCIPIO DO MUNDO
(SEE: VOYAGE TO THE BEGINNING OF THE WORLD)

VILLAGE OF DREAMS ★★★
(Japan, 1995) 112m Siglo; Japan Arts Fund ~ Milestone Film c
(E NO NAKA NO BOKU NO MURA)

Mieko Harada *(Mizue Tashima)*; Keigo Matsuyama *(Seizo Tashima)*; Shogo Matsuyama *(Yukihiko Tashima)*; Kyozo Nagatsuka *(Kenzo Tashima)*; Hosei Komatsu *(Jimma)*; Kaneko Iwasaki *(Toshie)*; Tokuko Sugiyama *(Ushibamba)*; Koichi Ueda *(The Principal)*; Mizuki Mamada *(Ikuko)*; Takehiro Nakajima *(The Mayor)*; Yukihiko Tashima; Hideko Tashima; Seizo Tashima *(Themselves)*

Set in a bucolic country village, this unfocused yet evocative adaptation of the memoirs of Japanese artist Seizo Tashima is a whimsical "autobiography" that includes talking fish and a Greek chorus which rides the wind bestowing tonsillitis and bad eyesight. Largely eschewing linear plot, the film comes off like a series of lyrical diary entries, most of which could be removed or shuffled around without appreciably affecting the whole.

In 1948, young identical twin brothers Seizo and Yukihiko (Keigo and Shogo Matsuyama) reside in a Kochi prefecture while their father lives and works most of the year away from home. Their mother, a teacher, spoils the kids terribly, and they create all manner of mischief, chopping up their neighbors' harvests, breaking things, and getting into fights with one another. Most of the time, however, they are so preternaturally close that they simultaneously dream about the same fish and wet their beds in unison. They also share visions of *shibaten* (demons), hear voices, and are constantly watched by three mysterious old women who offer commentary from a tree. When a prank on the school principal results in an innocent student being blamed, they remain silent as he is beaten and sent home, never to return. Similarly, when a female classmate who had treated them kindly is ridiculed by bullies, the twins join in to insult and shun her. In return, the three mysterious women punish them with illness and a need for eyeglasses, but years later reluctantly admit that the kids grew up alright after all.

Winner of the Silver Bear Award at the Berlin Film Festival, VILLAGE OF DREAMS was made in 1995—not coincidentally the fiftieth anniversary of the end of the war—and concerns itself with the immediate post-war years as perceived by a child. As such, it comes complete with casual supernatural occurrences and the matter-of-fact cruelty of both young and old. Adult males come off particularly poorly, from the intolerant principal to the largely absent father who laughs at his son's pain.

The twins, fiercely protective of each other and of their family even as the rest of the world looks down upon them as precocious misfits, suffer all the growing pains and sharp emotions of youth, experiencing joy and anger and discovering new feelings like jealousy and guilt. They also develop a sexual curiosity, amusingly depicted when one of the twins "accidentally" brushes against their older sister's breast—the same sister who earlier sparked their imaginations by warning them that the Thunder God would steal their penises if they didn't put on some clothes. Water and fish (and fish out of water) figure prominently in the palate of images, painting an impressionistic portrait of innocent yet mischievous youth, and of provincial Japan on the brink of drastic change. *(Violence, extensive nudity.)*—A.B.

d, Yoichi Higashi; p, Tetsujiro Yamagami, Koshiro Sho; w, Yoichi Higashi, Takehiro Nakajima (based on the autobiography *The Village of My Paintings* by Seizo Tashima); ph, Yoshio Shimizu; ed, Yoichi Higashi; m, Catherina Early Music Consort; art d, Akira Naito; set d, Shoichi Yasuda; sound, Hiroshi Tsurumaki

Drama (PR: C MPAA: NR)

VIOLET'S VISIT ★★
(U.S., 1995) 72m Spandau Films c

Rebecca Smart *(Violet)*; Graham Harvey *(Alec)*; David Franklin *(Peter)*; Caleb Packham *(Wayne)*; May Lloyd *(Sharon, Scooter's Mom)*; Tom Pender *(Man in McDonalds)*

The life of a gay couple is turned turned upside-down when the daughter one of them sired 15 years earlier turns up on their doorstep in this minor Australian comedy, filmed in 1995 and released on US home video in 1998.

Fifteen-year-old Violet (Rebecca Smart), who prefers to be called Scooter, has left her small-town home and come to Sydney to find the father she's never met. That man is Alec (Graham Harvey), who has been aware of Violet's existence, but has stayed out of communication with her. Alec now lives with a male lover, Peter (David Franklin). He wants Violet to return home immediately, but she refuses and at Peter's insistence, they allow Violet to move in with them on a trial basis. They get on well and Violet develops a crush on Wayne (Caleb Packham), one of her father's gay friends; she has her suspicions about his proclivities, but still her hopes run high.

Although Alec takes to parenting, Peter is dismayed to find that having a teenaged girl in the house puts a crimp in his and Alec's partying and sex life. After spying Wayne on a date with a man, a broken-hearted Violet decides to return home. Alec now wants her to stay, but Peter wants her to go. When her mother (May Lloyd) shows up with yet another potential husband in tow, Violet balks and demands to stay put. This prompts Peter to move out. Believing she has ruined her father's life, Violet runs away. The crisis reunites Alec and Peter; soon after, Wayne finds Violet living in the park and brings her home.

VIOLET'S VISIT is not an unenjoyable piece of entertainment, but it is a rather inconsequential one. It plays like the pilot for a new, very open-minded version of the sitcom "My Two Dads." Young Rebecca Smart (THE COCA-COLA KID) is neither particularly cute nor charismatic in the central role, and provides little depth for a character who obviously has a lot of "issues." A major problem with the film is that its timeframe is so uncertain. Violet seems to be in Sydney quite a while before her mother expresses any concern about her having left home; but at the same time, Alec and Peter's attitudes about having Violet live with them seem to turn around pretty quickly. *(Sexual situations.)*—P.R.

d, Richard Turner; p, Andrew Steuart; exec p, Oscar Scherl; w, Barry Lowe, Andrew Creagh (based on the story by Richard Turner); ph, Edmund Milts; ed, Kathryn Fenton; m, Paul Anthony Smith; art d, Colleen Forde

Comedy (PR: C MPAA: NR)

VOR
(SEE: THIEF, THE)

VOYAGE AU DEBUT DU MONDE
(SEE: VOYAGE TO THE BEGINNING OF THE WORLD)

VOYAGE TO THE BEGINNING OF THE WORLD ★★★
(Portugal/France, 1997) 95m Madragoa Filmes;
Gemini Films ~ Strand Releasing c
(GB: JOURNEY TO THE BEGINNING OF THE WORLD; VIAGEM AO PRINCIPIO DO MUNDO; VOYAGE AU DEBUT DU MONDE)

Marcello Mastroianni *(Manoel)*; Jean-Yves Gautier *(Afonso)*; Leonor Silveira *(Judite)*; Diego Doria *(Duarte)*; Isabel de Castro *(Maria Afonso)*; Isabel Ruth *(Olga)*; Cecile Sanz de Alba *(Cristina)*; Jose Pinto *(Jose Afonso)*

Marcello Mastroianni's final dramatic feature, made before his death in 1997, is an uneven yet graceful meditation on exile and nostalgia by aged and revered Portuguese filmmaker Manoel de Oliviera.

An aged and revered Portuguese filmmaker, Manoel (Marcello Mastroianni), is about to work on a television production. He tours the region where he grew up, accompanied by a carload of prized actors and friends. The sight of his old Jesuit school, a ruined hotel where Manoel and his brother romped after girls, a folk-art sculpture of a burdened, kneeling man whose significance has been long forgotten—all these fill Manoel with romantic melancholy called *soudade*, defined by him as "nostalgia. . . when you have lost your sense of irony."

One traveling companion is a French actor of Portuguese descent, Afonso (Jean-Yves Gautier). His father—also called Manoel—came from an obscure mountain village not far away. In contrast to the old filmmaker's privileged background, this Manoel was born to peasant stock during years of political turmoil. He fled to France, fought the Nazis, married, and died young in a car crash. The trip becomes a journey into Afonso's origins, as the small group sets out to contact Portuguese relatives who have never heard of him. At an ancient homestead, visitors find an insular clan headed by Afonso's aunt, Maria Afonso (Isabel de Castro), the family matriarch, uncomprehending and suspicious of these unannounced strangers, especially the one claiming to be her nephew (why, she repeatedly asks, can't he speak Portuguese?). Only when Afonso makes her hold his arm does the old woman tearfully accept him. She remembers his father in wildly contradictory terms, as irresponsible, as heroic, and begs Afonso to visit again and bring more of his side of the family. But first the show must go on; Manoel and his actors prepare for the soundstage.

A coda states that this story is based on the true experiences of French thespian Yves Afonso, when he visited Portugal in 1987 to act in a Manoel de Oliveira film.

A race-car driver and gymnast in his youth, Manoel Candido Pinto de Oliveira, son of a prosperous factory owner, had a remarkably durable cinematic career, dating his onscreen roles as actor and director as far back as the 1920s. Not until the 1960s was he noticed outside of Portugal; he was approaching his 80s when he finally gained wide recognition not only for his talent but as one of the oldest active filmmakers. Indeed, VOYAGE TO THE BEGINNING OF THE WORLD is a work of unhurried maturity—hence slow-moving, verbose, and contemplative. And just as Federico Fellini used Marcello Mastroianni as his on-screen alter ego, Oliveira employs the ever-urbane Italian star to serve as a stand-in for Oliveira himself. Though an old man may be granted his indulgences, Manoel's self-referential musings (including an incongruous lament over civil strife in Bosnia) are the lesser moments in the movie, even as foreknowledge of Mastroianni's demise give the rather static scenes a decidedly bittersweet tone. It all pales, however, before the second half of the narrative, when Afonso takes the spotlight. His fragile introduction to the lost branch of his family tree is a truly spellbinding piece of drama, a meeting of two worlds; the cosmopolitan acting troupe and the timeless, isolated peasants, most of whom are dressed in black, mourning for a deceased relation. The climax is a moment of elemental screen magic, as the pinched face of Maria Afonso hovers in darkness, illuminated only by firelight as she recalls a painful legacy of impoverished local men uprooted from home by war, economics, or wanderlust, many never to return.

It's an unforgettable sequence, even if it reduces the great Mastroianni to a bystander in what would turn out to be his farewell film. Oliveira manages to tie the distinct halves of VOYAGE TO THE BEGINNING OF THE WORLD together with the theme of exile, connectedness and *soudade*, although not as neatly as one might hope. Still, its transcendent moments reside in memory, and vindicate Manoel de Oliveira's less-than-overnight critical acclaim.—C.C.

d, Manoel de Oliveira; p, Paulo Branco; w, Manoel de Oliveira; ph, Renato Berta; ed, Valerie Loiseleux; prod d, Ze Branco; sound, Jean-Paul Mugel, Jean-Francois Auger (mixer)

Drama **(PR: A MPAA: NR)**

WAKING NED DEVINE ★★½

(U.K./France, 1998) 91m Tomboy Films ~ Fox Searchlight c

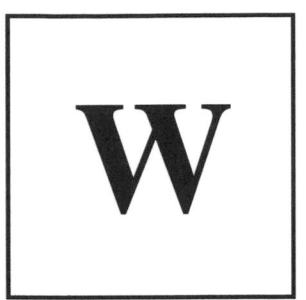

Ian Bannen *(Jackie O'Shea)*; David Kelly *(Michael O'Sullivan)*; Fionnula Flanagan *(Annie O'Shea)*; Susan Lynch *(Maggie)*; James Nesbitt *(Pig Finn)*; Maura O'Malley *(Mrs. Kennedy)*; Robert Hickey *(Maurice)*; Paddy Ward *(Brendy)*; James Ryland *(Dennis Fitzgerald)*; Fintan McKeown *(Pat Mulligan)*; Matthew Devitt *(Tom Tooney)*; Eileen Dromey *(Lizzy Quinn)*; Kitty Fitzgerald *(Kitty)*; Dermot Kerrigan *(Father Patrick)*; Jimmy Keogh *(Ned Devine)*; Brendan F. Dempsey *(Jim Kelly/Lotto Man)*; Larry Randall *(Father Mulligan)*; Eamonn Doyle *(Dicey, The Fiddleman)*; Raymond MacCormac *(Baudron Player)*; Rennie Campbell *(Rennie)*

Even the late Barry Fitzgerald couldn't have helped WAKING NED DEVINE, an alternately cloying and perfunctory comedy about a pair of superannuated Irish geezers and their efforts to scam a piece of a winning lottery ticket.

Life is fairly dull in the tiny rural village of Tully More, whose population of 52 has a median age well past 50. So when retired farmer Jackie O'Shea (Ian Bannen) reads in the national paper that a winning ticket for this week's lottery was sold in town, he and old friend Michael O'Sullivan (David Kelly) plan to find the lucky winner (who has not yet claimed his or her prize) and buddy up in hopes of some reciprocal generosity. Their initial picks—pig farmer Finn (James Nesbitt), his inamorata Maggie (Susan Lynch), who loves him but can't stand the smell of pigs, and horny postmistress Mrs. Kennedy (Maura O'Malley)—all prove to be dead ends.

Their search finally brings them to the isolated cottage of Ned Devine, who holds the winning ticket in his dead hand—apparently having suffered a fatal heart attack while watching the drawing on television. A vague dream in which Ned appears is enough to convince Jackie that Ned would have wanted him and Michael to cash in the ticket. Planning to pass Michael off as Ned just long enough to cash the ticket, they place a call to the lottery office, which sends representative Jim Kelly (Brendan F. Dempsey) to Tully More. Jackie and Michael are shocked to find out that Ned's is the sole winning ticket on a prize of 7 million pounds. Because of the size of the prize, Kelly will return in a few days to do some background checking to ensure that "Ned" is really who he says he is.

Jackie and Michael are forced to enlist the rest of the town in their deception, agreeing to split the prize 52 ways. The only holdout is cranky old Lizzy Quinn (Eileen Dromey), who threatens to turn them all in unless she is given 10 percent of the winnings. Assuming that she is bluffing, they refuse. Lizzy tries to call the lottery office to report the fraud, but the phone box she is calling from is struck by a van and sent flying over a cliff. The town holds a funeral for the well-liked Ned. When Kelly returns just as Jackie is making a eulogy speech, he turns it into one for his friend Michael. Persuaded that all is in order, Kelly signs over the check and the villagers celebrate.

The idea of the inhabitants of a remote village in the British islands collaborating on a scam has served as a good comic springboard in the past, in films like WHISKEY GALORE/TIGHT LITTLE ISLAND (1949), THE ENGLISHMAN WHO WENT UP A HILL BUT CAME DOWN A MOUNTAIN (1995), and especially LOCAL HERO (1983). But WAKING NED DEVINE lacks the eccentric characters and solid plotting that made those film so charming. It's praiseworthy that stars Ian Bannen and David Kelly eschew making their characters into Irish stereotypes. But the script (by English director Kirk Jones, whose feature debut this is after a career in commercials), doesn't give them much else to do; the film's comic highlight is a pointless skinny-dipping scene. The imaginary town of Tully More, shot in the fairy-tale environs of the Isle of Man, seems to have even fewer than the 52 residents who are supposed to live there; the bland supporting characters scarcely figure into the plot, and seem to be here only to give the stars an occasional break. (The exception is Fionnula Flanagan, whose few scenes as Jackie's wife makes one wish she had more to do in the film.)

Films set in Ireland hold a special place in the hearts of many filmgoers, and this one is not without its charms. But even the most ardent Eirephile is likely to doze through WAKING NED DEVINE. *(Nudity, sexual situations, adult situations, profanity.)*—M.F.

d, Kirk Jones; p, Glynis Murray, Richard Holmes; exec p, Alexandre Heylen; assoc p, Miara Martell; co-p, Neil Peplow; w, Kirk Jones; ph, Henry Braham; ed, Alan Strachan; m, Shaun Davey; prod d, John Ebden; art d, Mark Tanner; sound, John Downer (Editor); casting, Ros Hubbard, John Hubbard; cos, Rosie Hackett; makeup, Anne Oldham

Comedy **(PR: C MPAA: PG)**

WALKING THUNDER ★★

(U.S., 1997) 95m Sunset Hill Productions ~ Majestic Entertainment c

David Tom *(Jacob McKay)*; James Read *(Abner Murdock)*; John Denver *(John McKay)*; Klara Irene Miracle *(Mrs. McKay)*; Christopher Neame *(Ansel Richter)*; Chief Ted Thin Elk *(Dark Wind)*; Kevin Conners *(Toby McKay)*; Billy Oscar *(Weasel)*; Don Shanks *(Blood Coat)*; Bart the Bear *(Walking Thunder)*; Danny McKay *(Kasey Clyde)*; Carolyn Hurlbrut *(Anne McKay)*; Brian Keith *(Narrator)*; Robert Doqui; Duane Stephens; Roy J. Cohoe; Wayne Brennan; John Aspiras; Ivan Long; David Kirk Chambers; Joseph Kelly Lookinland; Utah Mountain Men Association

A scenic tale of pioneer days, the family feature WALKING THUNDER blazes few fresh trails.

In the present, a boy sulks because his parents, the McKays, leave him with his grandmother during a trip away. But the wise old lady has the kid read the journal of his ancestor, Jacob McKay (David Tom), 14 years old in 1850 and unwillingly uprooted from his New Hampshire home and dragged west with the rest of the family by father John (John Denver), a former shipbuilder who imagines prosperity in the California goldfields. Oncoming winter and the pregnancy of Mrs. McKay (Klara Irene Miracle) strands the family in the mountains en route—perhaps for good when a legendary grizzly bear, named Walking Thunder by the Indians, attacks and disables their wagon. Help comes to the McKays via Abner Murdock (James Read) a friendly mountain man, and Dark Wind (Chief Ted Thin Elk), an old Sioux medicine man tragically linked to Walking Thunder; his son mistakenly killed the bear's mate, so W.T. killed the brave in retaliation, and now the old man and the bear commune regularly amidst the trees. Among the various dangers in the territory is Ansel Richter (Christopher Neame) and his renegade partners, determined to rob the McKays and slaughter Walking Thunder for his valuable pelt. Again and again, Abner and the McKays beat off the marauders, John proving, surprisingly, that he can fight. Finally, with Dark Wind shot and Jacob unable to use a gun on Richter, things look hopeless—until the avenging Walking Thunder comes to the rescue and crashes down upon the villain. The journal concludes with a legend that

Dark Wind and Walking Thunder recovered from their wounds and wandered the mountains doing good deeds for decades afterwards.

There are times when WALKING THUNDER resembles nothing so much as a movie version of the popular educational computer game "The Oregon Trail," as Jacob McKay, surrogate for the (presumably juvenile) viewer, learns through experience how to best feed, provision, and defend a family in the untamed wilderness. But the three dumb bad guys are more like something out of a cheap cartoon, raiding the McKays with the tiresome regularity of Wile E. Coyote after the Roadrunner, clearly a convenience for instances in which the writers couldn't think up an interesting crisis to send the characters' way. Animal actor Bart the Bear is more compelling as the truly fearsome beast who, for Dark Wind, embodies the unsentimental spirit of nature (though, as with most movie treatments of the topic, WALKING THUNDER's greeting-card version of native American mysticism verges on the cloying and condescending). Singer-actor John Denver is also quite well cast as the tenderfoot dad out of his element. WALKING THUNDER was shot in co-writer/director Craig Clyde's home base of Utah and completed in 1993, but not until several years later did it emerge on home video, as a melancholy footnote for two of its performers. John Denver had perished in a 1997 crash of a plane he was piloting over Monterey. Veteran actor Brian Keith, who narrates as the voice of the mature Jacob McKay, also died that same year, a suicide. *(Violence.)*—C.C.

d, Craig Clyde; p, Bryce Fillmore, Ray Tremblay; exec p, Joe Brady; assoc p, Troy Rohovit; w, Craig Clyde, James Hennessy; ph, Gary Eckert; ed, Stephen L. Johnson; m, John Scott; art d, Jim Sherman; sound, Douglas Cameron; casting, Billy Da Mota; cos, Barbara Nelson; makeup, Ryan Marie McCormick; stunts, Don Shanks

Children's/Western (PR: A MPAA: PG)

WAR ZONE ★★★

(U.S./Germany, 1998) 76m Film Fatale; Hank Levine Film GmbH c/bw

Maggie Hadleigh-West

City sidewalks are a WAR ZONE in this guerrilla-style documentary which features filmmaker Maggie Hadleigh-West turning the tables on catcalling males. A confrontational piece, the film raises important and disturbing issues but also blunders slightly as a cinematic sociology experiment.

Walking down the streets of New York, San Francisco, Chicago, and New Orleans, Hadleigh-West interviews the many men who make sexually-suggestive remarks while walking by her on the street. Hadleigh-West hopes to reveal both the rude and complimentary comments as insulting, aggressive, and even threatening. One man says "Your film is not gonna make any difference" in terms of enlightening people, while another simply calls her a "Nazi" for asking pointed questions.

While visiting these cities, Hadleigh-West also interviews several women who talk about their experiences of verbal abuse on the street: Lori in Chicago and Gina in New Orleans both talk about how their ethnicity also motivate racist slurs amid the sexual taunting; Natasha and Sheila, a mother and daughter in New York, differ over whether the men's comments are cruel or benign.

After one man punches her camera, Hadleigh-West recalls her own near-rape experience and recounts how she has had to find mutual respect in her current relationship with her boyfriend. Finally, she tracks down and interrogates a man named Joe, whom she finds harassing women on the street. An emergency call to 911 of a woman, Karen, being raped, makes a final statement about the end result of male-to-female hostility.

The WAR ZONE braves new, rough territory by trying to capture the real-life gender war waged daily in cities across the country. Maggie Hadleigh-West's cinema-verite technique is not new (she is trailed by a camerawoman while she walks up to the offending males), but the subject matter has rarely been looked at with so much depth and anger.

WAR ZONE makes the provocative argument that catcalling and even complimenting strangers disturbs a zone of privacy and may result in (or encourage an atmosphere of) male-to-female violence. In some instances, Hadleigh-West proves her point (e.g., the man who punches her camera head on); in other ways, she takes some poetic leaps of faith (e.g., the 911 call played over a shot of rain drops).

Generally, WAR ZONE works as an experiment to see how men react when confronted with their own insensitive behavior (many feel threatened and try to escape), but there are some aspects that set the director up for unneeded criticism: the revealing way she dresses to attract attention; her equation of a look with verbal and physical taunting; and her questioning of an elderly man who seems to be telling the truth when he says he is staring at her arm band (not her breasts). For a 76-minute film, there are also some repetitive moments and a few so inaudible, they would have been better off excised.

The strongest portions of WAR ZONE actually consist of the interviews with the various women around the country, including the argument between the mother and daughter, which reveals an interesting cultural and generational gap. Still, Hadleigh-West's bold attempt at "fighting back" against a sexist tradition, while still trying to explore its social dynamics and implications, makes compelling viewing. *(Violence, nudity, sexual situations, adult situations, extreme profanity.)*—E.M.

d, Maggie Hadleigh-West; p, Hank Levine; exec p, Maggie Hadleigh-West, Hank Levine, Missouri Davenport Lobrano; ph, Todd Liebler, Eileen Schreiber; ed, Kelly Korzan, Fernando Villena, Tula Goenka, Emily Gumpel, Sara Thorson; m, Cindy Wall, Jack Wall, David Plakke, Paul Steinman; sound, Dawn Colello, Peter Levin

Documentary (PR: O MPAA: NR)

WATCHERS REBORN ★½

(U.S., 1998) 88m Concorde ~ New Horizons Home Video c

Mark Hamill *(Murphy)*; Lisa Wilcox *(Dr. Grace Hudson)*; Stephen Macht *(Lem Johnson)*; Gary Collins *(Gus Brody)*; Lou Rawls *("Doc" Grimes)*; Robert Clendenin *(Barnes)*; Melissa Cross *(Kristin)*; Shawn David Thompson *(Researcher #1)*; Lucy Lin *(Researcher #2)*; Milton Kahn *(Agent)*; Tony Guma *(Agent #1)*; Gary Wayton *(Agent #2)*; Kane Hodder *(Clerk)*; Floyd Levine *(Captain Dekker)*; Larry Cedar *(Driver #2)*; Deirdre Coleman *(Reporter)*; Lloyd Garroway *(Officer)*; Robert Peters *(Driver #1)*; Gerald Brodin *(Cop)*

Clearly, Roger Corman's production team intends to keep adapting Dean Koontz's novel *Watchers* until they get it right; if this fourth attempt is any indication, they're still a long way from that goal.

During a fire at a genetics lab, a humanoid creature called the Outsider and a golden retriever escape. The monster kills a zoo security guard, a slaying investigated by homicide cops Murphy (Mark Hamill) and Gus Brody (Gary Collins). Murphy meets Dr. Grace Hudson (Lisa Wilcox) at the scene, not knowing at first that she was the scientist in charge of the Outsider project. She later briefs Lem Johnson (Stephen Macht) and his National

Security Agency team: The dog has been engineered for superior intelligence, and the creature (with which it is telepathically linked) intended to follow it into enemy encampments during wartime. Murphy, meanwhile, has found the dog, and Brody takes it home, only to be killed by the Outsider.

Murphy again encounters the dog, and becomes convinced of its intelligence. He calls Grace over, and after she is attacked by the Outsider, the two flee with the dog to a mountain cabin. There they are set upon by both the Outsider and Johnson and his men, who have been ordered to kill Murphy and Grace. Instead, all the NSA men except Johnson are killed and Grace is abducted by the Outsider. With the dog's help, Murphy tracks her down to a warehouse where the creature is beginning to speak to her. Johnson arrives, shoots the Outsider and prepares to burn the building down with Murphy and Grace inside. Instead, the Outsider revives and attacks Johnson; Murphy, Grace and the dog flee just before the warehouse explodes.

With dialogue taking precedence over action (so much so that the movie could have easily been titled TALKERS), this is a tedious exercise in thrill-making. As would be expected, makeup effects artist-turned-director John Buechler's approach emphasizes graphic gore. But the occasional gushes of blood fail to pump any life into his pedestrian storytelling. Monotonous music and some abrupt transitions (evidently the result of scene deletions) don't help. Nor does Sean Dash's script, which renders Koontz's original concept implausible and shoehorns in an unbelievable romance between the two leads.

For their part, Hamill looks like he has just come off a three-day bender, while Wilcox, a spunky, appealing presence in the fourth and fifth NIGHTMARE ON ELM STREET films, is ill-served by the material. By the end, when Hamill is studying an orange and intoning, "This means something," and the Outsider is imploring Wilcox to "Pet me," it's hard to imagine *anyone* who'd want to keep watching. *(Graphic violence, profanity.)*—M.G.

d, John Carl Buechler; p, Darin Spillman; exec p, Roger Corman; co-p, Mark Hamill; w, Sean Dash (based on the novel *Watchers* by Dean Koontz); ph, Michael Mickniewicz; ed, Daniel Holland; m, Terry Plumeri; prod d, Mark Harper; set d, Jennifer Fraser; sound, John R.F. Halaby, Jonathan Catala; fx, Magical Media Industries, John Carl Buechler, Albert Lannutti; casting, Jan Glaser; cos, Jayme Bohn; makeup, Erin M. Braus; stunts, Gary Wayton

Horror **(PR: O MPAA: R)**

WATERBOY, THE ★★

(U.S., 1998) 86m The Robert Simonds Company; Touchstone ~ Buena Vista c

Adam Sandler *(Bobby Boucher)*; Henry Winkler *(Coach Klein)*; Kathy Bates *(Mama Boucher)*; Fairuza Balk *(Vicki Vallencourt)*; Jerry Reed *(Red Beaulieu)*; Larry Gilliard Jr. *(Derek Wallace)*; Blake Clark *(Farmer Fran)*; Peter Dante *(Gee Grenouille)*; Jonathan Loughran *(Lyle Robideaux)*; Al Whiting *(Casey Bugge)*; Clint Howard *(Paco)*; Allen Covert *(Walter)*; Rob Schneider *(Townie)*; Todd Holland *(Greg Meaney)*; Robert Kokol *(Professor)*; Frank Coraci *(Roberto)*; Jennifer Bini Taylor *(Rita)*; James Bates *(West Mississippi Lineman)*; Kelly Hare *(Drunk Cheerleader)*; Dawn Birch *(Red's Watergirl)*; Steve Raulerson *(Sheriff Loughran)*; Chris Mugglebee *(Sheriff Jack)*; Brett Rice *(Laski)*; John Farley *(Tony Dodd)*; Kevin Farley *(Jim Simonds)*; Paul "The Giant" Wright *(Captain Insano)*; Jamie Williams *(Young Bobby)*; Marc Kittay *(Youngest Bobby)*; Matt Baylis *(Student)*; Jack Carroll *(Bible College Coach)*; Tom Nowicki *(Community College Coach)*; Ric Swezey *(Male Cheerleader)*; Matthew Lussier *(Redneck)*; Haven Gaston *(Tina)*; Michael Hold *(Central Kentucky Quarterback)*; Kevin Reid *(West Mississippi Quarterback)*; Mattie Wolf *(Cajun Lady)*; Phyllis Alia *(Assistant)*; Dave Wagner *(Announcer)*; Tina Barr *(Cheerleader)*; Michael Giarraputo *(Bourbon Bowl Statistician)*; Marty Eli Schwartz *(Moderator)*; AS THEMSELVES: Lee Corso; Bill Cowher; Dan Fouts; Chris Fowler; Jimmy Johnson; Brent Musburger; Dan Patrick; Lynn Swann; Lawrence Taylor

With the broad appeal of his earlier 1998 release THE WEDDING SINGER as a springboard, Adam Sandler entered the movie-star stratosphere (and stunned the entertainment industry) when this simple-minded comedy about a moron who becomes a football star grossed nearly $40 million on its opening weekend.

Cajun simpleton Bobby Boucher (Adam Sandler) is a 31-year-old waterboy for perennial college football champs the University of Louisiana Cougars. He takes his job as "water distribution engineer" *very* seriously, good-naturedly accepting the abuse heaped upon him by the Cougar players. Considering the oddball Boucher a distraction to the team, UL's mean-spirited head coach Red Beaulieu (Jerry Reed) fires him.

Bobby approaches Coach Klein (Henry Winkler), the troubled leader of perennial losers the South Central Louisiana State University Mud Dogs, to become SCLSU's new waterboy. When the SCLSU players start making fun of his stuttering, Bobby is encouraged by Klein to fight back. As he unleashes years of pent-up rage, the waterboy reveals an incredibly fierce tackling ability. Klein puts Bobby on the team, the Mud Dogs start winning, and the waterboy becomes a college football sensation.

All the while, Bobby has to keep his gridiron exploits a secret from his over-protective Mama (Kathy Bates). He also has to keep secret his romance with fortune-telling felon Vicki Vallencourt (Fairuza Balk), because Mama says, "girls are the devil."

When the Mud Dogs are set to face the Cougars in the Bourbon Bowl, Coach Beaulieu digs up evidence that Bobby never graduated high school, and the waterboy must take the GED to regain his eligibility. Bobby passes the test, but when Mama finds out he's been playing football (of which she disapproves), she fakes an illness to keep her son from the game.

A rally in his honor convinces Mama that she was wrong to shelter Bobby from the world, and she delivers him to the Bourbon Bowl in time for him to make the big plays that win the Mud Dogs the game. The victory spoils the Cougars national championship bid, and provides a personal vindication for Coach Klein over his longtime rival Beaulieu. With Mama's blessing, Bobby marries Vicki.

With a touch of heartfelt romance, and a hint of maturity added to his character, THE WEDDING SINGER expanded Sandler's audience beyond the teen and young adult male demographic loyal to his rude and crude previous efforts, BILLY MADISON (1995) and HAPPY GILMORE (1996). That broadened audience turned out in droves for THE WATERBOY, which is really a return to form for Sandler.

THE WATERBOY is primitive filmmaking, made to appeal to the juvenile sensibilities of a 13-year-old boy, at which it succeeds modestly. The sports movie cliche of redemption for the underdog versus the bully is executed strictly by the numbers. The comedy is not just low brow (not necessarily a bad thing), but *uninspired* and low brow (a combo that shoots for mediocrity at best). Most of the laughs come from some Cajun caricatures (Clint Howard, Rob Schneider, Blake Clark) that might offend Louisiana's bayou citizenry.

It's only Sandler's good-natured performance as this goony man-child that keeps THE WATERBOY from being utterly grating. Kathy Bates appears to have a good time overacting as

Mama, and her presence at least ensures THE WATERBOY's future as the answer to the trivia question: In what movie does a Best Actress Oscar winner play badminton with a mule? *(Profanity, violence.)*—P.R.

d, Frank Coraci; p, Robert Simonds, Jack Giarraputo; assoc p, Phyllis Alia, Rita Smith, Michelle Holdsworth; co-p, Ira Shuman; w, Adam Sandler, Tim Herlihy; ph, Steven Bernstein; ed, Tom Lewis; m, Alan Pasqua; prod d, Perry Andelin Blake; art d, Alan Au; set d, Barbara Peterson; sound, Jay Meagher (mixer); casting, Roger Mussenden; cos, Tom Bronson; makeup, Erin B. Koplow, Lee A. Grimes; stunts, Allan Graf

Comedy/Sports (PR: C MPAA: PG-13)

WEDDING SINGER, THE ★★½

(U.S., 1998) 95m The Robert Simonds Company; Brillstein-Grey Entertainment; New Line ~ New Line c

Adam Sandler *(Robbie Hart)*; Drew Barrymore *(Julia)*; Christine Taylor *(Holly)*; Allen Covert *(Sammy)*; Angela Featherstone *(Linda)*; Matthew Glave *(Glenn)*; Alexis Arquette *(George)*; Frank Sivero *(Andy)*; Christina Pickles *(Angie)*; Ellen Albertini Dow *(Rosie)*; Jodi Thelen *(Kate)*; Steve Buscemi *(Drunken Best Man—Uncredited)*; Patrick McTavish *(Tyler)*; Gemini Barnett *(Petey)*; Teddy Castellucci; Randy Razz; John Vana *(Robbie Hart Band)*; Billy Idol *(Himself)*; Kevin Nealon *(Mr. Simms)*; Marnie Schneider *(Joyce—Flight Attendant)*; Carmen Filpi *(Old Man in Bar)*; Robert Smigel *(Andre)*; Todd Hurst *(Drunken Teenager)*; Peter Dante *(David's Friend)*; Phyllis Alia *(Mrs. Harold Veltri)*; Paul Thiele *(Mr. Harold Veltri)*; Jack Nisbet *(Father of Groom)*; Sally Pierce *(Grandma Molly)*; Earl Carroll *(Justice of the Peace)*; Jenna Byrne *(Cindy Castellucci)*; Jason Cottle *(Scott Castellucci)*; Mark Lonow *(Father of the Bride)*; Bill Elmer *(Fat Man)*; Jackie R. Challet *(Sideburns Lady)*; Jimmy Karz *(Studliest Kid at Bar Mitzvah)*; Al Hopson *(Grandpa at Bar Mitzvah)*; Michael Shuman *(Bar Mitzvah Boy)*; Steven Brill *(Glenn's Buddy)*; Angela Payton *(Faye)*; Jon Lovitz *(Jimmy Moore (uncredited))*; Mike Thompson; Michael Jay; John Sawaski; Chris Alan; Kimberly Schwartz; Sanetta Y. Gipson *(Jimmy Moore's Band)*; Timothy P. Herlihy *(Rudy the Bartender)*; Matthew Kimble *(Drunk at Bar)*; Sid Newman *(Frank)*; Mark Beltzman *(Vegas Air Ticket Agent)*; Andrew Shaifer *(Flight Attendant #2)*; Shanna Moakler *(Flight Attendant #3)*; Maree Cheatham *(Nice Lady on Plane)*; Al Burke *(Large Billy Idol Fan)*; Bob Hackl; Gabe Veltri; Josh Oppenheimer *(David's Band)*

THE WEDDING SINGER is a romantic comedy in which Adam Sandler and Drew Barrymore meet sweet, and then spend the next 90 minutes working up the courage to admit they're in love. That's the romantic part. The comedy part comes from endless references to pop culture of the 1980s, when this is set.

1985. Robbie Hart (Adam Sandler) is the genial frontman of a combo popular on the suburban New Jersey wedding circuit. Robbie is friends with catering waitress Julia (Barrymore). Both are engaged; Robbie to longtime girlfriend Linda (Angela Featherstone), Julia to Glenn (Matthew Glave), a junk bond trader.

On their wedding day, Linda strands Robbie at the altar, later explaining that she doesn't love him anymore because he's a failure, "just a wedding singer." Robbie's depression spills over into his next gig, where he harangues the newlyweds with a version of "Love Stinks" and provokes the bride's father into a fight. Subsequently, Robbie's band works bar mitzvahs only.

Julia and Glenn set a date, and she asks Robbie, to help her plan the wedding. As they spend time together, Julia and Robbie grow closer and fall for each other, but deny their feelings. When Glenn admits to Robbie that he cheats on Julia and plans to continue doing so, Robbie decides to confess his love to her, but feels inadequate and chickens out. Julia realizes her true feelings and goes to confess her love to Robbie, but finds Linda with him. Julia assumes the two are a couple once more—an assumption Linda encourages.

While performing at a 50th wedding anniversary party, Robbie has an epiphany: he truly loves Julia and wants to marry her. He chases after her, but she has eloped with Glenn to Las Vegas. When he realizes they are on the same plane as he, Robbie enlists the aid of another passenger, snarling rocker Billy Idol (Himself) who convinces Robbie that he should serenade Julia in order to win her. Robbie sings a love song to Julia over the plane's intercom, and while Idol's roadies "take care" of Glenn, Julia and Robbie make plans to grow old together.

In Adam Sandler's previous starring vehicles, BILLY MADISON (1995) and HAPPY GILMORE (1996), he reveled in the juvenile antics of an attention-hungry class clown. Having entered his 30s, Sandler is outgrowing his arrested adolescent persona, and in THE WEDDING SINGER he builds on his alternate comic trademark (from his year's on TV's "Saturday Night Live") as a goofy singer.

The plot of THE WEDDING SINGER is a contrivance of cliches that were already getting stale when Barrymore's grandfather was in his heyday, and the movie requires nothing more of Drew than that she look adorable. Nonetheless, the love story sneaks up on and engages a viewer with an unironic and totally disarming sweetness.

All the comedy in THE WEDDING SINGER stems from the movie's '80s setting, and your reaction to it will depend entirely on how much camp value you find in the fashions and music of that decade. Julia's friend Holly (Christine Taylor) is a Madonna wannabe; Robbie's friend Sammy (Allen Covert) dresses in "Thriller"-era Michael Jackson clothes. There's a gay Boy George look-alike (Alexis Arquette), and Glenn sports the "Miami Vice" look. The soundtrack is a collection of New Wave's greatest hits. References to '80s cultural touchstones abound ("Who Shot J.R.," New Coke, breakdancing), though very few are specific to 1985. There's no punchline to any of it, unless one considers "Look! The guys are wearing skinny ties, and the girls are wearing pastel eyeshadow!" a punchline. *(Profanity.)*—P.R.

d, Frank Coraci; p, Robert Simonds, Jack Giarraputo; exec p, Brad Grey, Sandy Wernick; assoc p, Rita Smith, Michelle Holdsworth; co-p, Ira Shuman; w, Tim Herlihy; ph, Tim Suhrstedt; ed, Tom Lewis; m, Teddy Castellucci; prod d, Perry Andelin Blake; art d, Alan Au; set d, Lisa Deutsch; sound, Kim H. Ornitz (mixer), L. Mo Weber (design); casting, Roger Mussenden; cos, Mona May; makeup, Ann Pala, Kimberly Greene; stunts, Michael Runyard

Comedy/Romance (PR: C MPAA: PG-13)

WELCOME TO WOOP WOOP ★★½

(U.K./Australia, 1997) 103m Scala Productions; Unthank Films ~ Goldwyn Films/MGM c

Johnathon Schaech *(Teddy)*; Rod Taylor *(Daddy O)*; Susie Porter *(Angie)*; Dee Smart *(Krystal)*; Barry Humphries *(Bling Wally)*; Richard Moir *(Reggie)*; Mark Wilson *(Duffy)*; Paul Mercutio *(Midget)*; Rachel Griffiths *(Sylvia)*; Maggie Kirkpatrick *(Ginger)*; Tina Louise *(Bella)*

Stephan Ellliott, the director of the outrageous THE ADVENTURES OF PRISCILLA, QUEEN OF THE DESERT (1994), unleashes another bizarre fantasy about life Down Under in WELCOME TO WOOP WOOP, a demented black comedy-cum-musical about a New Yorker who's shanghaied to a remote Australian hellhole where the alcoholic denizens make dog food out of kangaroos and sing Rodgers & Hammerstein tunes 24-hours a day.

New York con man Teddy (Johnathon Schaech) flees to Australia hoping to escape his troubles and meets a sexy hitchhiker named Angie (Susie Porter). After having sex with her, she knocks him out, drugs him, and takes him home to Woop Woop, a former asbestos mining town which has been all but wiped off the map, and now only has 50 residents. When Teddy awakens, Angie tells him that they're married, and he meets her father, Daddy-O (Rod Taylor), who runs the whole town and warns Teddy that nobody is allowed to ever leave it, which he immediately proves by shooting another son-in-law who tries to escape.

Teddy becomes Angie's sex-slave and a virtual prisoner, but after Angie announces that she's pregnant with twins, he finds himself falling for her sister Krystal (Dee Smart), who also wants to leave the town. Teddy learns that Angie lied about being pregnant, and following the death of her mother, Krystal and Teddy run away and flee in a construction vehicle. Daddy-O and Angie pursue them across the Outback, but Daddy-O smashes his van into a giant, mythical kangaroo called Big Red, and Teddy and Krystal escape. Fifteen years later, two teens named Sonny and Cher show up at a pet store in Manhattan owned by Teddy and Krystal, and introduce themselves to Teddy as being his kids.

WELCOME TO WOOP WOOP is one of most gleefully tasteless and vulgar films in quite a while, obsessed with messy bodily functions and reveling in politically incorrect scenes of comical animal abuse (pistol-packing New Yorkers shooting at rare Australian cockatoos; little kids in Woop Woop trying to kill dogs; kangaroos being chain-sawed and bulldozed into a meat grinder to make dog food) that are guaranteed to leave most viewers in a daze. Its viciously satirical depiction of the residents of Woop Woop as foul-mouthed (their favorite incredulous exclamation is an innocent "Fuck me dead"), beer-swilling, gun-toting, incestuous rednecks is like something out of a Russ Myer movie, but it's also obviously meant to serve as a microcosm of Australian society in general, culminating in the hilariously cheesy special effects scene where Daddy-O finally encounters the legendary 20-foot-tall kangaroo, Big Red.

As with Elliott's kitschy use of ABBA pop songs in PRISCILLA, the use of Rodgers & Hammerstein here is pure camp, and would undoubtedly have their creators spinning in their graves if they saw their songs accompanying the most scabrous behavior (e.g., "Happy Talk" while kangaroos are being slaughtered, "You'll Never Walk Alone" during a funeral procession where the corpse is carried on a beer-can cross). Yet it's also oddly affectionate, as the only time the residents can relieve the misery and ugliness of their lives is when they happily spend their nights at a makeshift drive-in and sing along with Julie Andrews in THE SOUND OF MUSIC (1965) and Mitzi Gaynor in SOUTH PACIFIC (1958). Elliott's flamboyant widescreen visual style is well suited to the caricatured milieu and the over-the-top performances are all amusing, with 1960s matinee idol Rod Taylor (THE BIRDS, THE TIME MACHINE) easily stealing the movie and having a hell of a time hamming it up as the tattooed and grizzled Daddy-O. Although the film is ultimately more original than it is good, it deserves some kind of credit for fearlessly trying to offend everyone, and it certainly is unforgettable. *(Extreme profanity, nudity, sexual situations, violence .)*— M.S.

d, Stephan Elliott; p, Finola Dwyer; exec p, Stephen Woolley, Nik Powell; co-p, Antonia Barnard; w, Michael Thomas (based on the book *The Dead Heart* by Douglas Kennedy); ph, Mike Molloy; ed, Martin Walsh; m, Stewart Copeland; prod d, Owen Paterson; art d, Colin Gibson; sound, Tony Johnson (recordist); casting, Prototype Casting; cos, Lizzy Gardiner

Comedy/Musical **(PR: O MPAA: R)**

WEST NEW YORK ★½

(U.S., 1998) 86m White Whale Films C

Frank Vincent *(Tom Coletti)*; Brian McCormack *(Frank Ryan)*; Gloria Darpino *(Diane Ryan)*; Victor Collichio *(Berto)*; Vincent Pastore *(Carmine)*; Brian Burke *(Zeller)*; Daniel Grimaldi *(Police Captain)*; Gian DiDonna *(Jimmy Vero)*; Benny Nieves *(Joaquin)*; Mike Squicciarini *(Paulie)*

WEST NEW YORK is an amateurish and ultra-low budget, sub-Scorsesian, Italianate crime saga—boasting a star turn by character actor and Scorsese regular Frank Vincent—that takes a jaw-dropping detour into mysticism for an outlandish finale that has to be seen, but still might not be believed.

Ex-New York City cop Tom Coletti (Frank Vincent) was dismissed from the force under a cloud and became an alcoholic. Now working as a security officer for a New Jersey bank, Tom decides to help his daughter Diane (Gloria Darpino), who's married to violent local cop Frank (Brian McCormack), by stealing some corporate bonds he's supposed to destroy and have a fence find a buyer for them. Local mob boss Carmine (Vincent Pastore), angry because he's not cut in on the deal, has the fence brutally murdered and orders the hitman Zeller (Brian Burke) to find the buyer. Tom is contacted by the buyer's middlemen, Berto (Victor Colicchio) and Joaquin (Benny Nieves), who tell him that they want more bonds.

Meanwhile, Tom's ex-partner Jimmy (Gian DiDonna), who once loved Diane and now owns a music store, resumes his affair with Diane and helps Tom pull off the deal. But Tom is killed by the middlemen during a botched exchange and Jimmy and Diane go through with the deal. Frank is revealed to be the buyer and he shoots Zeller, the middlemen, and Jimmy, but Diane then shoots Frank. Jimmy recovers and he and Diane get away with the money.

Although WEST NEW YORK's minuscule budget ($130,000) may excuse its cheap look and shoddy production values (even though far more stylish and accomplished work has been achieved with much less), it doesn't explain its cliched script, featuring stereotyped ethnic characters and dialogue that makes daytime soaps sound like paradigms of originality—Diane to a priest, who happens to be Frank's brother: "I don't dream anymore. It's like I die every night and in the morning I only remember the blackness." Priest: "Darling, we all feel like that sometimes." And even on its own level, there isn't much filmmaking talent on display, with clumsily staged action, murky lighting, and shaky handheld camerawork being the norm.

Apart from veteran character actor Vincent, the cast is pretty stiff, but the student-film level acting, writing, and direction, all pale in comparison to its stupefying climax, in which Jimmy—who's been profoundly affected by an encounter with a guitarist customer (with long hair and a beard who says stuff like "It's one connected universe, man" and "Be cool. Go deep inside") who tells him about a spiritual experience he's had with an African shaman—is shot by Frank and is about to die. Via some crude special effects, Jimmy's body is surrounded by a blue aura and he travels down a long tunnel to a white light, then comes upon the dead Tom standing in a park (and quite nattily attired in a turtle neck and sports jacket), who tells Jimmy to "Go back." Jimmy promptly does so and literally rises from the dead to fight Frank and save the day. It's a bizarre and unforgettable touch that at least earns the film a place in the bad movie hall of fame. *(Graphic violence, extreme profanity, nudity, sexual situations.)* —M.S.

d, Phil Gallo; p, Donna Miller; exec p, Tami Lione, Trade Martin, Eugene Vazquez; assoc p, Greg Lamberson, Clem Vicari Jr.; co-p, Steve Bretschneider, Marc Makowski; w, Steve Bretschneider, Phil Gallo; ph, Jonathan Rho; ed, Phil Gallo; prod d, Steve Bretschneider; sound, Betsy Nagler, Dave Powers; casting, Nancy Hancock

Crime/Drama **(PR: C MPAA: NR)**

WESTERN ★★★

(France, 1996) 110m Salome Productions; Diaphana Productions ~ New Yorker Films c

Sergi Lopez *(Paco Cazale)*; Sacha Bourdo *(Nino)*; Elizabeth Vitali *(Marinette)*; Marie Matheron *(Nathalie)*; Daphne D'Gaudefroy *(Hitch-Hiker)*; Karine Lelievre *(Voice of Mr. Letour's Secretary)*; Jean-Louis Dupont *(Policeman)*; Olivier Herveet *(Hospital Doctor)*; Alain Luc Guhur *(Hospital Attendant)*; Bernar d'Mazzinghi *(Roland—Marinette's Brother)*; Alain Denniel *(Bearded Man in Hospital Ward)*; Serge Raiboukine *(Van Driver)*; Michel Vivier *(Car Driver)*; Melanie Leray *(Guenaelle)*; Catherine Riaux *(Guenaelle's Friend)*; Carole Ledreau *(Friend at Wedding)*; Basile Siekoua *(Baptiste)*; Helene Foubert *(Baptiste's Girlfriend)*; Marilyne Canto *(Marilyne)*; Helene Berrou *(Helene)*; Monette Cardinaux *(Monette)*; Ghislaine Jegou *(Ghislaine)*; Sophie Kervadel *(Sophie)*; Angelina Pochie *(Angelina)*; Diane Valsonne *(Diane)*; Helene Moreau *(Helene)*; Vanina Delannoy *(Fougere—Hysterical Woman)*; Marie Lounici *(Cafe Patron)*; Veronique Bellegarde *(Cafe Patron)*; Fabien Kachev *(New Salesman)*; Guy Abgrall *(Farmer)*; Jean-Jacques Vanier *(Dr. Yvon Le Marrec)*; Brigitte Legal *(Pharmacist)*; Michel LeCossec *(Bar Patron/Nathalies' Child)*; Johan LeSaux *(Johan)*; Tudy Bernard *(Tudy)*; Lena Bernard *(Lena)*; Rudi Desseaux *(Rudi)*; Maxime Guggenbuhl *(Maxime)*; Olivier Guehenneux *(Antoine)*; Maeva Privat *(Antoine's Sister)*; Arthur Privat *(Antoine's Brother)*; Theo Vigouroux *(Antoine's Brother)*; Gerard Privat *(Antoine's Father)*; Karine Hascoet *(Post Office Clerk)*; Jean-Bernard Batina *(Child at Meal)*; Olivia Berthelot *(Child at Meal)*; Yacine Elboo-Abdellatti *(Child at Meal)*; Perina Janvier *(Child at Meal)*; Clara Quiros-Debroise *(Child at Meal)*; Marion Signor *(Child at Meal)*; Laura Wang *(Child at Meal)*; Gilles Marchais *(Vocals/guitar/banjo for La Cambuse—Band at Wedding)*; Joel Tymen *(Accordion in La Cambuse—Band at Wedding)*; Christopher Runarvot *(Bass in La Cambuse—Band at Wedding)*; Emmanuel LeRoy *(Guitar in La Cambuse—Band at Wedding)*

Two mismatched friends—one a womanizing Spaniard, the other a love-starved Russian immigrant—take a picaresque journey through France in search of romance in Manuel Poirier's WESTERN, a rambling, but amusing, seriocomic road movie.

Paco (Sergi Lopez), a Spanish traveling shoe salesman, picks up a Russian immigrant hitchhiker, Nino (Sacha Bourdo), while driving through Brittany. Nino thanks Paco by stealing his car, along with his merchandise. Paco is saved by a woman named Marinette (Elisabeth Vitali), who picks him up and takes him back to her home. The next day, Paco spots Nino on the street and attacks him, but a friendship develops between them when Paco goes to visit Nino at the hospital to apologize. Nino explains that he stole the car because he has no luck with women and felt that a vehicle would help him find love. Fired from his job, Paco stays with Marinette for a few more days and they gradually fall in love, but she suggests that they test their commitment to each other by separating for three weeks. Paco reluctantly agrees and hits the road with Nino.

They stop at a hotel, where Nino tries to pick up a waitress named Guenaelle (Melanie Leray), but she prefers Paco, as does her girlfriend (Catherine Riaux), both of whom sleep with Paco during a drunken party. Attending a wedding reception for one of Guenaelle's friends, Nino is rejected by some more women and bitterly lashes out at them. To placate Nino, Paco cooks up a plan to find him the perfect mate by going to a town and canvassing women for a fake opinion poll on their ideal man, but the scheme backfires and Nino is once again rejected. At another town, Paco meets Nathalie (Marie Matheron), a single mother with five children, and he begins to fall for her despite his still pining for Marinette. Nathalie tentatively returns Paco's advances, but when she meets Nino, she falls instantly in love and asks him to spend the night with her, which causes a temporary rift between Paco and Nino. Paco returns to Marinette, but is crushed to learn that she has gotten involved with someone else. He goes back to Nathalie's house and joins Nino and Nathalie for a family meal.

Aside from its no doubt symbolic, but mystifying and unexplained title, WESTERN is an affectionate and enjoyable exploration of the vicissitudes of love. It's too long and basically plotless, consisting of a series of episodic encounters on the road, and its ultra-French sensibility and reliance on local slang makes it somewhat difficult for non-Europeans to get into at first (with virtually every scene centering on drinking, smoking, and eating), but the understated observational humor is universal in nature and the peripatetic story picks up steam as one gets to know the characters.

The relationship between the odd couple-like Paco and Nino is an interesting study in the dynamics of male bonding and romantic rivalry, and one comes to care about the fate of these two men who seem so outwardly different from each other. The movie's ultimate joke is that the handsome Paco, who's always so sure of himself (well played with a combination of charm and goofiness by Sergi Lopez), ends up losing the two women he cares for most, one of them to the scrawny loser Nino (played with wiry intelligence by Sacha Bourdo), but learns humility and becomes a better man for it.

In addition to the fine performances by Lopez and Bourdo, the widescreen cinematography and the flamenco guitar score impressively capture the sights and sounds of Brittany's picturesque coastal towns. There are also some very funny scenes, particularly when Paco and Nino do the fake opinion poll and Nino ends up with a neurotic women who decides that she can't sleep with him because he's *too* good for her. The film's female characters are refreshingly portrayed as smart and independent, if fearful of being betrayed by their lovers, typified by Nathalie's confession to Nino that all of her kids have been fathered by different men who were just passing through. The final scene, where the humbled Paco sits at the dinner table with Nathalie as the beaming Nino happily plays with her kids, is a fitting and touching image that encapsulates the film's concept of extended families and the search for friendship and identity. *(Profanity, violence, sexual situations.)*—M.S.

d, Manuel Poirier; p, Maurice Bernart, Michel Saint-Jean; w, Jean-Francois Goyet, Manuel Poirier (based on an idea by Manuel Poirier); ph, Nara Keo Kosal; ed, Yann Dedet; m, Barnardo Sandoval; art d, Roland Mabille; sound, Patrick Sigwalt (engineer), Jean-Paul Bernard, Christian Fontaine (mixer); cos, Sophie Dwernicki; makeup, Francoise Bosc

Comedy/Drama **(PR: O MPAA: NR)**

WHAT DREAMS MAY COME ★★

(U.S., 1998) 106m Metafilmics Inc; Interscope Communications ~ Polygram c

Robin Williams *(Chris Nielsen)*; Cuba Gooding Jr. *(Albert)*; Annabella Sciorra *(Annie Nielsen)*; Max Von Sydow *(The Tracker)*; Rosalind Chao *(Leona)*; Jessica Brooks Grant *(Marie Nielsen)*; Josh Paddock *(Ian Nielsen)*; Lucinda Jenney *(Mrs. Jacobs)*; Wilma Bonet *(Angie)*; Maggie McCarthy *(Stacey Jacobs)*; Matt Salinger *(Reverend Hanley)*; Carin Sprague *(Best Friend Cindy)*; June Lomena *(Woman in Car Accident)*; Paul P. Card IV *(Paramedic)*; Werner Herzog *(Face)*; Clara Thomas *(Emily)*; Benjamin Brock *(Billy)*

Robin Williams abandons Heaven and makes like Orpheus, traveling to the underworld to rescue his wife from Hell, in WHAT DREAMS MAY COME, an exploration of the afterlife and the spiritual power of love that is as dramatically shallow as it is visually stunning.

Chris Nielsen (Robin Williams) meets his soul mate Annie (Annabella Sciorra) on a lake in the Swiss Alps. Many years later, Chris, a doctor, and Annie, a painter, are happily married and have two children, Ian (Josh Paddock) and Marie (Jessica Brooks Grant). The children are killed in an auto accident and Annie suffers a nervous breakdown. Chris works to help Annie recover for four years, until he is also killed in a traffic accident.

After watching his own funeral, Chris enters the afterlife and is met by an angelic guide named Albert (Cuba Gooding Jr.)., who has taken the form of Chris's medical school mentor. Together they explore the personal heaven of Chris's own imagination, recreated from the idyllic pastoral scenes of Annie's color-saturated canvases. Chris meets Leona (Rosalind Chao), who escorts him to a shining city with Greco-Roman columns. This is the heaven of his daughter Marie, and Leona is the woman that Marie never got to grow up to be.

Albert informs Chris that Annie has committed suicide and gone to Hell. Chris insists on rescuing her, so they enlist the aid of a Tracker (Max Von Sydow). Albert reveals that he is really his son Ian, in the guise of a man Chris would respect. On the journey to Hell, they sail on stormy seas and cross plains choked with the damned. The Tracker warns Chris that he runs the risk of getting trapped in Annie's reality, instead of bringing her back to his.

Chris enters Annie's hell, a grim and rubble-strewn church turned upside-down, but she doesn't recognize him. When he can't convince her to leave with him, he decides to stay with her. The power of love demonstrated by that choice transports both of them back to his heaven, where Ian and Marie join them. Chris and Annie decide to be reincarnated, so they can meet and fall in love all over again.

As a display of state-of-the-art computer-generated effects, WHAT DREAMS MAY COME is dazzling, even amazing to look at. Unfortunately, it is also boring to watch. It is based on the 1977 novel by Richard Matheson, whose *Somewhere in Time*, adapted as a 1980 film of the same name, was also about the power of love transcending death. But although it encompasses grief and loss, familial and romantic love, utter despair and exuberant joy, the movie is as emotionally barren as its landscapes (and dreamscapes) are rich and spectacular.

With the help of too many artists and technicians to list here, visionary director Vincent Ward (THE NAVIGATOR, MAP OF THE HUMAN HEART) has realized the afterlife as an amalgam of images from art history. Chris's paradise mixes the Romanticism of Caspar David Friedrich with the bold and vibrant coloring of the French Fauvists. Marie's city is like an Italian Renaissance fresco come to life. There's a field of screaming heads (one of them played by director Werner Herzog) reminiscent of H.R. Giger's horrific babies' heads landscapes. And Hell is a surreal nightmare by way of Hieronymus Bosch.

It's a shame that all this effort and imagination was put in service of so little. Williams doesn't do much more than gape throughout the movie, while Sciorra wears different wigs to indicate her mood, and there's no visceral connection between them. The movie's New Age metaphysics is rather murky. The notion of a subjective afterlife is intriguing, but the movie's gumbo of mysticism with only an oblique reference to God may offend some people. *(Adult situations.)*—P.R.

d, Vincent Ward; p, Stephen Deutsch, billed as Stephen Simon, Barnet Bain; exec p, Ronald Bass, Ted Field, Scott Kroopf, Erica Huggins; co-p, Alan C. Blomquist; w, Ronald Bass (based on the novel by Richard Matheson); ph, Eduardo Serra; ed, David Brenner, Maysie Hoy; m, Michael Kamen; prod d, Eugenio Zanetti; art d, Thomas Voth, Christian Wintter; set d, Cindy Carr; sound, Nelson Stoll (mixer); fx, Roy Arbogast, Joel Hynek, Nicholas Brooks, Stuart Robertson, Kevin Mack; casting, Heidi Levitt; cos, Yvonne Blake; makeup, Cheri Minns; stunts, Charles Croughwell

AA Best Visual Effects: Joel Hynek, Nicholas Brooks, Stuart Robertson, Kevin Mack; *AAN Best Art Direction:* Eugenio Zanetti, Cindy Carr

Drama/Fantasy **(PR: C MPAA: PG-13)**

WHATEVER ★★★

(U.S., 1998) 112m Circle/DuArt Films;
Anyway Productions ~ Sony Pictures Classics c

Liza Weil *(Anna Stockard)*; Chad Morgan *(Brenda Talbot)*; Frederic Forrest *(Mr. Chaminsky)*; Gary Wolf *(Eddie)*; Dan Montano *(Zak)*; Marc Riffon *(Martin)*; John G. Connolly *(John Woods)*; Kathryn Rossetter *(Carol Stockard)*; Tony Torn *(Mr. Stanley)*; Trey Compton *(Sam)*; Joe Mantranga *(Chris)*; Matt Rumbaugh *(Tony)*; Jim Neville *(Rob)*; Garret Spencer *(Joe)*; Destiny Matranga *(Lynn)*; Mary Jo Roth *(Amy Peck)*; Evie Mazzone *(Mrs. Wilson)*; Michelle Yahn *(Principal)*; Lenora Nemetz *(Principal)*; Peter Gannon *(Henry Talbot)*; Jean Cardello *(Karen Talbot)*; Harold Herthum *(Howard)*; Sean O'Brien *(Mr. Tibbets)*; Frank Licato *(Real Estate Agent)*; Charlie Schroeder *(Tom)*; Zach Chapman *(Gus)*; Susan Skoog *(Roxanne)*; Ed Mattson *(Danny Boy)*

Since most movies about teenagers dote on stereotypes and play difficult life situations for laughs, it's refreshing to see a film that treats its teenage characters as human and flawed. WHATEVER is so sincere and straightforward that it's often painful to watch, making older viewers remember the awkwardness and isolation of being a teen.

The year is 1981. Anna (Liza Weil) and Brenda (Chad Morgan) are New Jersey high school seniors. Both young women have troubled home lives, and neither one is very interested in school. They spend their days drinking, doing drugs, and getting in trouble; Brenda courts trouble by sleeping around. The only adult they respect is Mr. Chaminsky (Frederic Forrest), a teacher who encourages Anna to pursue her interest in art by applying to Cooper Union.

At a party, Anna runs into Martin (Marc Riffon), an older boy who had been away for a few years, "finding himself." She likes him, and soon, with Brenda's encouragement, has her first sexual experience with him. He doesn't call Anna again after that encounter, and when she drops in on him unannounced, she discovers that he's dating a woman his own age.

Anna and Brenda skip school one day and take the train to New York City. The girls fantasize about living in Manhattan, and decide to flirt with two older men. When they return home,

Anna finds out she was not accepted to Cooper Union. She tells Mr. Chaminsky that she has no future in art, and quits his class.

Later, things reach a head when Brenda's abusive stepfather molests and batters her. Unable to live with his abuse any longer, Brenda convinces Anna to run away to Florida with John (John G. Connolly) and Zak (Dan Montano), two ex-cons they had met at a party. As the girls steal money from Brenda's home, Brenda's stepfather catches her and begins assaulting her. Brenda hits him repeatedly with a poker, seriously wounding but not killing him.

In a hotel that same evening, as Brenda makes out with John, Zak mistakenly gives Anna some angel dust. She begins hallucinating, and awakens the next day on the beach, naked. Zak finds her and assures her he didn't take advantage of her. He gives her money to take the bus home, and she decides to leave Brenda with the two men. Anna returns home, attempts to make up with her mom, and begins to straighten out her life. She stops selling drugs, turns in an English paper she had planned not to finish, and begins painting again.

Susan Skoog's first film, WHATEVER starts out as a depressing account of the lives of unlikeable teenagers, but as it progresses the honesty and accuracy of the characterizations make us warm to the young leads. While Anna and Brenda appear to be living their lives in an amoral and decadent fashion, they are simply going through the motions, souls adrift who obtain no lasting thrills as they stay too long at parties that never seem to end.

WHATEVER's main flaw is in its treatment of adults. The foolishness and abusiveness of the older characters does provide an explanation for Brenda's self-hatred and Anna's general frustration, but it also unfortunately represents the one way in which Skoog took an easy out. By setting up an us-against-them situation, WHATEVER is reminiscent of films like THE BREAKFAST CLUB (1985) and PUMP UP THE VOLUME (1990), which age poorly as their original target audience grows older.

This problem aside, there is much to commend in the film. Skoog wisely uses a gritty, low-gloss visual style that sharply conveys the bleak world inhabited by the characters. Liza Weil's sensitive performance rates as one of the film's strongest assets, although the rest of the young cast exhibit an equally solid sense of authenticity. The adult performers unfortunately don't fare as well, especially Frederic Forrest, who is unable to lend any shadings to his turn as aging hippie Mr. Chaminsky. WHATEVER does an outstanding job of portraying the way many teenagers get caught up in the wrong lifestyle simply because of peer pressure or lack of support from friends and family. It also encourages adolescent viewers to think about the ramifications of their decisions, and avoid writing it all off with the trendy titular utterance. *(Sexual situations, substance abuse, extreme profanity, nudity, violence, adult situations.)*—A.M.

d, Susan Skoog; p, Susan Skoog, Ellin Baumel, Michelle Yahn, Kevin Segalla; exec p, Jim Pedas, Ted Pedas, Irwin Young, Bill Durkin, George P. Pelecanos; w, Susan Skoog; ph, Michael Mayers, Michael Barrow; ed, Sandy Guthrie; m, Walter Salas-Humara; prod d, Dina Goldman; set d, Lisa Schilling; sound, Curtis Mattikow; casting, Adrienne Stern; cos, Jill Kilber; makeup, Nuria Sitja

Drama **(PR: C MPAA: R)**

WHEN DANGER FOLLOWS YOU HOME ★★

(U.S., 1997) 92m Two Oceans Entertainment; Spinnaker Films ~ Universal Television c

JoBeth Williams *(Anne Werden)*; Michael Manasseri *(Gogol)*; William Russ *(Detective Barnes)*; Nicolas Surovey *(Harold Rhodes)*; Julie Patzwald *(Elaine)*; Bill Switzer *(Andrew Werden)*; Vanessa King *(Julie Werden)*; Susan Hogan *(Alicia)*; Duncan Fraser *(Dr. Lensky)*; Rob Freeman *(George)*; Teryl Rothery *(Detective Seigel)*; Roman Podhora *(Detective Roman)*; Linda Darlow *(Isabel Benchley)*; John MacLaren *(Oscar Somner)*; Fred Henderson *(Rhodes' Lawyer)*; April Telek *(Pam)*; Selina Rachel Williams *(Becka)*; Judith Maxie *(Judge)*; Mitchell Kosterman *(Jack)*; Patrick Pon *(Chinese Man)*; Brad Loree *(TBX Guard)*; Darren Flint *(Hospital Guard)*

This improbable made-for-cable mystery yarn starring JoBeth Williams as a psychology student who gets involved in a murder case stretches credulity way past the breaking point. Viewers won't buy the finale in which our middle-aged heroine (a onetime high school gymnast) uses her rusty balance beam skills to drop down on a predator from a second-floor railing!

Back in college after a bitter divorce, Anne Werden (JoBeth Williams) juggles raising her children with studies and working as an intern for psychologist Dr. Lensky (Duncan Fraser) at a minimum security prison. Anne's penchant for personal involvement flares up as she cares for brilliant young schizophrenic Gogol (Michael Manasseri), a computer nerd arrested for breaking into TBX, the corporation run by his stepfather Harold Rhodes (Nicolas Surovy), who had murdered Gogol's father in order to usurp his empire.

After crossing swords with rigid Dr. Lensky over Gogol's medication, Anne is surprised when the newly released Gogol seeks refuge at her home. Through Detective Barnes (William Russ), the sympathetic cop handling the investigation of the TBX break-in, Anne learns about a confidential file on Gogol. From his teenaged sister Elaine (Julie Patzwald), Anne discovers Gogol's job history as a computer hacker following the suicide of his father after an embezzlement scandal.

Gogol dies from a drug interaction. Sued for interfering in his treatment, Anne is powerless to prevent a distraught Elaine from over-medicating herself, at Rhodes's suggestion. Anne's attempts to clear her name jeopardize her family when Gogol's enemies kidnap her son Andrew (Bill Switzer). At a remote rendezvous to rescue Andrew, Anne encounters Gogol's stepfather Rhodes, who eliminated Gogol for compiling incriminating evidence about Rhodes's murder of his father. Breaking free, Andrew dashes for help with Rhodes and his bodyguard in pursuit. While he's distracted, Anne knocks the bodyguard off a balcony. Jumping down on Rhodes from a second-story ledge, Anne calls the police.

Although this low-key mystery is occasionally gripping, its credibility problems extend beyond the souped-up climax in which JoBeth Williams acts like an aging Mary Lou Retton. Why would a seasoned killer-CEO tip his hand by kidnapping a child? Why bump off Gogol when his tall tales were always considered the by-product of his mental illness? Although the mature romance between Williams and William Russ is affecting, the film squanders too much footage on the heroine's strained relations with her children. A slack lady-in-peril thriller, WHEN DANGER FOLLOWS YOU HOME is watchable primarily for the appealing Williams. *(Violence, profanity, adult situations.)*—R.P.

d, David Peckinpah; p, John L. Roman; exec p, Meryl Marshall, Mae Woods; w, Sharon Elizabeth Doyle (based on a story by Sara Paretsky); ph, Robert A. Hudececk; ed, Hibah Sherif Frisina; m, Charles Bernstein; prod d, David Fischer; set d, Louise Roper; ch, Joe Laughlin; sound, William Skinner (mixer); fx, Andrew Cotton Chamberlayne; casting, Abra Edelman, Elisa Goodman; cos, Stephanie Nolin; makeup, Lisa Roberts; stunts, Danny Virtue

Thriller/Mystery **(PR: C MPAA: PG-13)**

WHEN I CLOSE MY EYES ★★★★½
(Japan, 1995) 116m Fuji Television Network ~ Fine Line c
(AKA: LOVE LETTER)

Miho Nakayama *(Hiroko Watanabe/Itsuki Fujii)*; Etsushi Toyokawa *(Shigeru Akiba)*; Akiba Bunjaku Han *(Female Itsuki's Mother)*; Katsuyuki Shinohara *(Female Itsuki's Grandfather)*; Takashi Kashiwabara *(Itsuki Fujii—As a Young Boy)*; Mariko Kaga *(Male Itsuki's Mother)*; Miki Sakai *(Itsuki Fujii—As a Young Girl)*; Ken Mitsuishi *(Abekasu)*; Kumi Nakamura *(Hamaguchi the Teacher)*; Ranran Suzuki *(Sanae Oikawa)*; Emiko Osada *(Librarian)*; Kaori Oguri *(Girl in Akiba's Workshop)*; Teppei Wataru *(Yoshida)*; Keiichi Suzuki *(Male Itsuki's Father)*; Sansei Shiomi *(Kajioyaji)*; Tomoro Taguchi *(Female Itsuki's Father)*

WHEN I CLOSE MY EYES (originally entitled LOVE LETTER) is a hauntingly poetic and beautifully made Japanese love story with supernatural undertones, which was virtually ignored in the US due to the incompetence of its American distributor, Fine Line Features. After acquiring the film, which was acclaimed at various film festivals in 1995, they let it sit on the shelf collecting dust for three years while trying to set up an American remake (to purportedly star Meg Ryan), then changed its title and unceremoniously dumped it into a few theaters with no publicity.

A young Japanese woman named Hiroko (Miho Nakayama) attends a memorial service in Kobe for her late fiance Itsuki Fujii, who was killed two years earlier in a mountain climbing accident. After the ceremony, Hiroko goes home with Itsuki's mother, and while looking through his high school graduation yearbook, impulsively writes down the address of his boyhood home in Otaru. Still mourning his death, Hiroko then writes a love letter to Itsuki "in heaven" and sends it to his old address in an attempt at closure. To her astonishment, she receives a reply from another Itsuki Fujii (Miho Nakayama), who unbeknownst to her, is actually a woman who grew up with the male Itsuki and went to school with him. The two women begin to correspond with each other and Hiroko eventually goes to Otaru to track "him" down, but when she learns that Itsuki is a woman and that she looks a lot like her, she realizes that her late fiance only loved her because of her resemblance to Itsuki.

Hiroko then writes Itsuki and asks her about her school days with the male Itsuki, and flashbacks depict them as children, showing how they shunned each other and were both teased by classmates because of their names, but developed a tentative relationship nevertheless. Back in the present, Itsuki visits her old school and meets some students who have seen her and the male Itsuki's name written on numerous library cards. Later, Hiroko and a friend make a pilgrimage to the mountain where Itsuki was killed to say goodbye to him. Meanwhile, the female Itsuki succumbs to the fever she's had from a persistent cold and her grandfather puts her on his back and carries her to the hospital during a blizzard. After recovering, Itsuki writes her last letter to Hiroko, and when some schoolgirls bring Itsuki a book from the school library which contains a picture of her as a girl that was drawn by the male Itsuki, she realizes that he really did love her.

Ravishingly filmed in snow-covered northern Japan and stunningly acted by Miho Nakayama in a dual role, the deeply emotional WHEN I CLOSE MY EYES is a superb feature-film debut by writer-director-editor Shunji Iwai, who's clearly a talent to watch. Alternating hand-held camerawork and jump-cuts with stately compositions and seamlessly integrated flashbacks, Iwai imbues a fragile tale of memory, loss, and grief with a powerful sense of fate and mysticism. Somewhat reminiscent of the films of Alain Resnais and Krzysztof Kieslowski (though more naturalistic), and featuring specific references to Proust's *Remembrance of Things Past,* the richly metaphorical story is a lyrical and tender exploration of destiny, identity, and the past. The complexly structured script gracefully moves back and forth between scenes in the present of Hiroko and Itsuki communicating via computer and letter (imaginatively shot so that their correspondence is never depicted in a static fashion) and flashbacks depicting the childhood of the two Itsukis, as well as a subplot involving the grown female Itsuki's chronic cold and memories of her late father, who died of pneumonia.

Visually, the film boasts magnificent widescreen images: Hiroko lying in the snow during the memorial service, Itsuki's dreams of her father in the hospital, Hiroko and Itsuki unwittingly passing each other in the street amidst a giant crowd and slowly turning as they sense who the other is and realize that they're practically twins, and Hiroko's profoundly moving pilgrimage to the mountain where she screams "How are you?" to Itsuki's ghost, which is brilliantly intercut with the female Itsuki in the hospital answering "Very well."

The film's commercial plight is sadly indicative of the ignominious way that foreign films are now treated in the US, which are usually only imported in the first place if they're deemed to be remake fodder. Yet despite the lack of support by its distributor, WHEN I CLOSE MY EYES was easily one of the best films released in the US in 1998. *(Adult situations)*—M.S.

d, Shunji Iwai; p, Suji Abe, Koichi Murakami, Hajime Shigemura, Juichi Horiguchi, Jiro Komaki, Tomoki Ikeda, Masahiko Nagasawa; assoc p, Shinya Kawai; co-p, Takaaki Kabuto; w, Shunji Iwai; ph, Noboru Shinoda; ed, Shunji Iwai; m, Remedios; prod d, Terumi Hosoishi; sound, Masato Yano; cos, Chikae Takahashi

Romance/Drama (PR: C MPAA: PG-13)

WHEN PIGS FLY ★½
(U.K./Germany/Japan, 1993) 94m Panorama Entertainment; Allarts; Sultan; Driver Films ~ Nippon Films c

Alfred Molina *(Marty)*; Marianne Faithfull *(Lilly)*; Seymour Cassel *(Frank)*; Maggie O'Neill *(Sheila)*; Rachel Bella *(Ruthie)*; Freddie Gibbs *(Stretch)*; Matyelok Gibbs *(Mrs. Cleary)*; Carl Dennie *(Tony)*; Ruth Sheen *(Marge)*; George Lannan *(Police Chief)*; Gil Peleg; Matt Dahms *(Two Teens)*; Barry Stevenson *(Drunk)*; Pim Tjujermans *(Postman)*; Christopher Porter *(Steve)*; Bob Brady *(Drinker)*

Heavy-handed and lugubrious, WHEN PIGS FLY is a ghost story that lacks any of the traditional virtues of the genre. It was made in 1993, but reached its first major audience with a home video release in 1998.

In a tight-knit village, foul-tempered bar owner Frank (Seymour Cassel) orders his barmaid/exotic dancer Sheila (Maggie O'Neill) to perform menial chores like locking up his shed. There, Sheila spots a discarded antique chair, which she takes as a present to cheer up her depressed landlord, Marty (Alfred Molina). Sheila doesn't know that the chair comes with its own resident poltergeists. Transported to Marty's musty basement, Lilly (Marianne Faithfull), the ghost of Frank's wife, and Ruthie (Rachel Bella), her child-spirit guardian, raise an ectoplasmic ruckus until a bewildered Marty moves the chair to his cosy living room.

Ruthie and Lilly reveal themselves to Marty and Sheila and tell them that Lilly was seated in the chair when abusive Frank beat her to death. After Lilly and Ruthie unnerve Frank with mischievous pranks at his bar, Marty and Sheila agree to exact revenge against Frank. Lilly shows them where Frank has hidden his hoarded fortune. When Frank catches Marty and Sheila stealing it, he causes a disturbance that attracts the police. On the verge of a breakdown, Frank confesses to Lilly's slaying in front of the cops. Keeping some of Frank's loot for themselves, Marty and Sheila deliver the bulk of it to Lilly's married daughter, then take Ruthie and Lilly to their new resting place—the deck of Lilly's son-in-law's houseboat.

WHEN PIGS FLY was directed by former Jim Jarmusch associate Sara Driver, whose debut feature SLEEPWALK (1987) was similarly slow moving. Famed cinematographer Robby Muller was the wrong choice to photograph this: although his colors are breathtaking, the compositions are static and the photography has a somber look, lending this wispy ghost pageant an unsuitable gravity. Insufferable screenwriting and club-footed direction make this woebegone movie a clumsily coy salute to ghostly enterprise and human accountability. Although we're supposed to cheer as the spirits revitalize depressed Marty's life-force, our goodwill is siphoned off by extraneous special effects and the cluttered plot. One promising sequence, in which the spirits and Marty review ghostly scenes of his childhood, winds down without capitalizing on Marty's reaction to the sight of his beloved father dancing in a bar. Haunted by vague concepts concerning the supernatural and its connection to memory, WHEN PIGS FLY loses much of its emotional power when it unnecessarily drags out its story. *(Violence, extreme profanity, adult situations.)*—R.P.

d, Sara Driver; p, Kees Kasander; exec p, Denis Wigman, Jim Jarmusch; assoc p, Hisami Kurowa; co-p, Susan Sultan, Demetra MacBride; w, Ray Dobbins; ph, Robby Muller; ed, Jay Rabinowitz; m, Joe Strummer; prod d, Jocelyn Beaudoin; art d, Florian Langmaack; set d, Bernard Homann; sound, Drew Kunin (mixer); fx, Udo Engel; casting, Ellen Lewis; cos, Kathleen Mobley; makeup, Rolf Bauman

Comedy/Fantasy **(PR: A MPAA: NR)**

WHEN TIME EXPIRES ★½

(U.S., 1998) 93m Regent Entertainment ~ Evergreen c

Richard Grieco *(Travis Beck)*; Cynthia Geary *(June Kelly)*; Mark Hamill *(Bill Thermot)*; Tim Thomerson *(Rifkin Koss)*; Ron Masak *(TV Evangelist)*; Pat Corley *(TV Car Salesman)*; Chad Everett *(Walter Kelly)*; Gary Lee Davis *(Assassin #1)*; Rick Cramer *(Assassin #2)*; Matthew Mahaney *(Tom Holten)*; Joyclyn O'Brian *(TV Housewife)*; Eric Lawson *(Sheriff Holten)*; Bill Rosier *(Bartender)*; David Rowden *(Redneck #1)*; Mark Ginther *(Redneck #2)*; David Wiley *(TV Repairman)*; Marvin Braverman *(Hotel Guest)*; Richard Gross *(Trucker)*; Phil Redrow *(Ticket Officer)*; Glen Vernon *(Old Man)*; Christopher Boyer *(Gun Dealer)*

Watchable but unmemorable, WHEN TIME EXPIRES is base-level science fiction centered around a very tenuous premise. The film premiered on The Movie Channel prior to a release on home video.

Space alien Travis Beck (Richard Grieco) arrives in a small town on Earth with a simple mission: insert a quarter in a parking meter at a specified time. He meets and falls for local girl June Kelly (Cynthia Geary)—something strictly forbidden by his bosses at an alien faction called "The Ministry," since any interaction with an Earthling could affect the planet's future. Meeting up with his former partner Bill (Mark Hamill), Travis discovers that not only is the Ministry planning to infiltrate Earth, but that three assassins from another alien faction, called "The League," are after him. Travis tells June who he really is, but she doesn't believe him until her father, Walter (Chad Everett), reveals his own alien past—he is, in fact, an ex-member of the Ministry who chose to resign after landing on Earth. Meanwhile, Travis finds out something the Ministry didn't want him to know: his seemingly innocuous mission will, if executed, prevent a chain of events that would lead to a nuclear disaster.

Realizing that Bill is involved with the assassins, Travis kills him in self-defense and confronts the killers. Their leader, Rifkin Koss (Tim Thomerson), explains that the League wants to use Travis to expose the Ministry's error. Koss allows Travis several hours to collect proof of the cover-up, but instead, Travis returns to June and they make love. Travis kills Koss and his henchmen in a shoot-out, but he is beaten unconscious by Tom (Matthew Mahaney), an ex-boyfriend of June's (who had threatened him previously), just as he is nearing the meter. June fulfills Travis's mission and deposits the quarter in the meter herself, thereby preventing disaster. Seeing Travis on the ground, she passes out. When she awakens, the future has changed so that June is living out her dream of owning a horse ranch with her father. Travis, now a stranger, appears asking for riding lessons and they begin a new relationship.

WHEN TIME EXPIRES is a harmless time-passer that can only sustain the viewer's interest for a short period of time; it's the sort of thing that fills up pay-cable schedules in the late-evening hours. Obviously dealing with a low budget, the moviemakers wisely avoid sci-fi trappings for the most part; instead, the film plays like a western-comedy-romance hybrid with one of the silliest premises in recent memory (the fact that a quarter placed in a parking meter could avert a nuclear war—because it would prevent a certain individual from getting a parking ticket, no less—is pretty shaky terrain for a sci-fi thriller to start from).

Richard Grieco, the star of many such bargain-bin obscurities, and Cynthia Geary both perform well enough, but writer-director David Bourla's script is such a minimalist affair that the two barely have any character traits to latch onto. Even the subplots provided to strengthen the two characters are hopelessly derivative: it is revealed that Travis was the Ministry's star employee before being wrongfully blamed for a tragic accident that was actually partner Bill's fault; June, meanwhile, is shocked to discover she's really half alien. A few of the supporting performers, particularly Tim Thomerson and Pat Corley (playing Travis's alien computer interface) distinguish themselves, but they can't do anything to improve this muddled fantasy. *(Violence, sexual situations.)*— P.L.

d, David Bourla; p, Larry Estes; exec p, Paul Colichman, Mark R. Harris, Stephen P. Jarchow; co-p, Sam Irvin; w, David Bourla; ph, Dean Lent; ed, Bruce Wescott; m, Todd Hayen; prod d, Stuart Blatt; set d, Melissa Levander; sound, Pat Toma; fx, Ultimate Effects; casting, Donald Paul Pemrick, Dean E. Fronk; cos, Charmian Schreiner; makeup, Jennifer Montgomery; stunts, Tom Dewier

Science Fiction/Drama **(PR: C MPAA: PG-13)**

WHEN TRUMPETS FADE ★★

(U.S., 1998) 92m Citadel Entertainment;
HBO NYC ~ HBO Home Video c

Ron Eldard *(David Manning)*; Zack Orth *(Warren Sanderson)*; Frank Whaley *(Medic Chamberlain)*; Martin Donovan *(Captain Pritchett)*; Dwight Yoakam *(Lt. Colonel)*; Dylan Bruno *(Sergeant Talbot)*; Timothy Olyphant *(Lieutenant Colonel)*; Jeffrey Donovan *(Bobby)*; Dan Futterman *(Despin)*; Devon Gummersall *(Lonnie)*; Steven Petrarca *(Baxter)*; Bobby Cannavale *(Captain Zenek)*; Frank Kobe *(German Sergeant)*; Andras Stohl *(Wounded Soldier)*; Matthew Ruston Cooney *(Driver)*; Peter Thomas *(News Footage Narrator)*; Anthony Rapp

This made-for-HBO feature aims to document a forgotten chapter in the history of WWII, the protracted fight for a forest straddling the border between Belgium and Germany. Unfortunately, there's not much here to distinguish WHEN TRUMPETS FADE from most other WWII flicks—particularly in a year that saw the release of SAVING PRIVATE RYAN and THE THIN RED LINE.

November 1944. By virtue of his having survived a full week of hellish battle in the Hurtgen forest—during which the rest of his company were killed—Private David Manning (Ron Eldard) is promoted to sergeant, despite rumors of cowardice and his own request for a dismissal. Manning is ordered to lead a group of very green replacement soldiers to the front line, where they scout enemy positions. At one point, the soldiers' inexperience leads to one man, Sanderson (Zack Orth), becoming separated from the company and barely escaping detection by a German patrol. The men are included in the attempt to take a bridge guarded by German heavy artillery, a loss that results in heavy American casualties.

Desperate for a break, Manning's commanding officer, Captain Pritchett (Martin Donovan), agrees to grant Manning his dismissal if he'll lead his men in a longshot attempt to burn out the German artillery with flamethrowers. Manning takes his men behind lines and knocks out the big guns, losing three men in the process. However, Pritchett is wounded in the battle and is relieved before Manning can return, negating the deal for a dismissal; furthermore, Manning is again promoted, this time to lieutenant. When a pair of German tanks roll in to replace the artillery, Manning elects to lead a small group of soldiers in a night attack to take them out. His men manage to take out the tanks, but only one man returns—Sanderson, the once-green soldier who got lost on patrol. Before the Battle of Hurtgen Forest ends, 24,000 soldiers will die.

It can be said that WHEN TRUMPETS FADE's intentions are good: telling the story of the battle for Hurtgen forest, a long and bloody fight that came between the liberation of France and the Battle of the Bulge. The implication, of course, is that this battle was one worth remembering. However, neither writer W.W. Vought nor director John Irvin (HAMBURGER HILL, CITY OF INDUSTRY) attempt to explain why this particular battle was strategically pivotal—or even the least bit important—to the course of the war in Europe. To the viewer, it just looks like another prolonged combat, complete with scared recruits, dirt-flinging land mines, and the bloody stumps of soldiers' blown-off limbs (a visual that has become a staple of the 1990s war movie).

Star Ron Eldard doesn't help matters much: as a frightened soldier whose knack for self-preservation is mistaken for battle smarts, he is offered a role with some emotional range to it; it's too bad he doesn't choose to explore that range. Perhaps hoping to convey shell shock, Eldard wears a stone-faced expression throughout—except for the moments in which he's shouting at the replacement soldiers. Overall, Eldard's overly stoic performance is as forgettable as the battle itself—after all, if the main character doesn't seem to care about the events, why should we? *(Extreme violence, profanity.)*—B.T.

d, John Irvin; p, John Kemeny; exec p, David R. Ginsberg, Gavin Polone, Judy Hofflund; w, W.W. Vought; ph, Thomas Burstyn; ed, Ian Crafford; m, Geoffrey Burgon; prod d, Laszlo Rajk; sound, Brian Simmons; fx, Joe Lombardi; casting, Mindy Marin; cos, Gyorgy Homonnay; makeup, Stephen Dupuis; stunts, Bela Unger

Drama/War **(PR: O MPAA: R)**

WHITE RAVEN, THE ★★

(U.S./Poland, 1998) 92m Royal Oaks Entertainment; Cabin Fever Entertainment; Hermes Filmstudio ~ Artisan Entertainment c/bw

Ron Silver *(Tully Windsor)*; Joanna Pacula *(Julia Konneman)*; Elizabeth Sheppard *(Hannah Rothschild)*; Roy Scheider *(Tom Heath)*; Hannes Jaenicke *(Dockmonish)*; Jack Recknitz *(Inspector Zielinski)*; Doug Lennox *(General Dodd)*; Jan Rubes *(Markus Straud)*; Larry Poindexter *(Kreisler)*; Agnieszka Wagner *(Zofia)*; Monikz Switaj *(Wanda)*; Jerzy Zydkiewicz *(Uncle Boy/Erwin Koch)*; Joanna Kasperska *(Mildred)*; Wladyslaw Byrdy *(Lou)*; Jerry Flynn *(Alain Levon)*; D. Paul Thomas *(Ambassador Kennedy)*; Peter Snider *(Sgt. Paul)*; Jacek Samojlowicz; Anais Granofsky; Wenanty Nosul; Joanna Samojlowicz

A good cast goes through the motions in this cloak-and-dagger tale.

Incarcerated in Poland, Nazi war criminal Markus Straud (Jan Rubes) breaks decades of silence to announce that he will do an interview; he demands to speak to Tully Windsor (Ron Silver), Chicago reporter for *The Christian Science Monitor.* During WWII, Straud hid a diamond called the White Raven, and as Windsor arrives in Warsaw, various cabals have their agents poised. Police Inspector Zielinski (Jack Recknitz) wants the rock to help finance his resurgent fascist movement. American General Dodd (Doug Lennox) wants it to fund his retirement. And wealthy Zionist Hannah Rothschild (Elizabeth Sheppard) wants it because it's hers—she gave up the White Raven in the Treblinka death camp to avoid rape by a vicious underling of Straud's. After the war, the assailant wound up in Windsor's family as childlike, brain-damaged "Uncle Boy" (Jerzy Zydkiewicz); it was Windsor's sentimental article about him that got Straud's attention.

In their big meeting, Straud recites a cryptic series of numbers; the assorted factions after the diamond pursue Windsor for the precious information. The least disagreeable is Rothschild—and her grown daughter Julia (Joanna Pacula), who has been watching Windsor all along. She gets the reporter safely back to Chicago, but Dodd and Zielinski soon follow. Even pathetic Uncle Boy turns up, interrogated to death by the Polish cop. Breaking Straud's code—and doing some crude surgery—Windsor locates the diamond, long crammed under the plate in his uncle's skull. Dodd subsequently nabs Windsor, but is himself killed by Zielinski. Windsor manages to shoot Zielinski in a struggle, then brings the White Raven back to Hannah and Julia, while the *Monitor* prints a cover story which states that the gem was never found.

The politically potent idea of neo-Nazis on the rise in Poland gets a slight treatment in THE WHITE RAVEN. Canadian actor Jan Rubes steals the show as the sinister Straud, while Roy Scheider has a feisty but abbreviated role as Tully Windsor's bulldog boss at *The Christian Science Monitor*. Media-savvy viewers may be amused at the portrayal of that eminent paper as sort of scrappy tabloid like Chicago's famously competing *Tribune* and *Sun Times*.

The film is colored by hyperbole and contrivance, from a silly erzatz action sequence which shows Tully pursued by mobs of zealous newshounds to Uncle Boy conveniently dumped in the hero's lap, just in time for Windsor to deduce the jewel's whereabouts. When, in the course of his role, Ron Silver has to use a kitchen blade to slice an old man's skull, one can readily make allowances for his somewhat dispirited performance.

The film's callow spy-jinks and far-flung locales seem like a throwback to the Cold War espionage B-movies of the 1960s. In terms of subject matter, however, the international coproduction is a step up for actor/director Andrew Stevens (NIGHT EYES,

THE SEDUCTION) and Royal Oaks Entertainnment, the low-budget production company he cofounded with former tennis champ Ashok Amritraj. Stevens keeps the proceedings lively and watchable, if not always logical, but characteristically finds a leather-heavy Warsaw music club to visit for some gratuitous kink. No MALTESE FALCON (1941), THE WHITE RAVEN bypassed theaters for video and cable-TV markets. *(Adult situations, violence, nudity, profanity.)*—C.C.

d, Andrew Stevens; p, Ashok Amritraj, Andrew Stevens; exec p, Jorg Hermes, Alan B. Bursteen; assoc p, Kajtek Kowalski, Jacek Samojlowicz, Larry Poindexter; w, Michael Blodgett (based on the novel by Blodgett); ph, Michael Slovis; ed, Brett Hedlund; m, David Wurst, Michael Wurst; art d, Michael Borthwick, Katarzyna Boczek; fx, Brett Hollund; casting, Marjorie Lecker, Wendell Speer, Andrzej Bednarski; cos, Marya DuPlaga, Magda Rutkiewicz-Luterek; stunts, John Stoneham Stoneham

Thriller **(PR: O MPAA: R)**

WHO IS HENRY JAGLOM? ★★★

(U.S., 1995) 52m Calliope Films ~ First Run Features c

Henry Jaglom; Gary Lasdun; Andrea Marcovicci; Candice Bergen; Peter Bogdanovich; John Landis; Ross McElwee; Milos Forman; Louis Malle; Alan Rudolph; Seymour Cassel; Zack Norman; Karen Black; Michael Emil Jaglom; Dennis Hopper; Bob Rafelson; Lee Grant; Molly Haskell; Andrew Sarris; Bruce Williamson; Sally Kellerman; Martha Plimpton

Fimmakers H. Alex Rubin and Jeremy Workman don't entirely answer the question they pose in the title of this short documentary, made in 1995 and released to home video in 1998. While they interview the director and many of his friends and associates, they don't arrive at much that isn't obvious from watching Jaglom's films.

But that may be the point. As many of the interview subjects note, Jaglom's films are his way of viewing the world; anything he can't capture on film is less valid to him. He regularly records and films the people he knows, not always with their permission. (Orson Welles, for whom Jaglom tried for years to raise financing to make another film, was reportedly highly upset to learn a few days before his death that Jaglom had regularly tape-recorded their conversations.)

Jaglom is seen openly welcoming the makers of this documentary, which he hopes will be like his own work—an avenue to explore feelings and emotional truths. Clips are included from Jaglom's dozen films made since 1970, most of them semi-improvisational works in which he encourages the actors to react to given situations, saying, "I'll fit the script later into what they give me." Although he distinguishes between himself and the character he plays in many of his films, he says, "If there's one thing I'm trying to prove, it's that there's no such thing as too personal." One of his best films, ALWAYS (1985), is essentially a reenactment of the breakup of his marriage, starring himself, his ex-wife, and members of their families.

Jaglom is particularly interested in women's issues, and refers to himself as a "male lesbian." While neither homosexual nor effeminate, he and his films value the open emotionality associated with the feminine nature. His relentless probing for openness and honesty, at all times and with all people, strikes some as liberating and others as an inappropriate form of aggression. Speaking in favor of his methods, Candice Bergen comments that "If I'd had Henry as a father or a husband, I could probably have taken Poland."

While WHO IS HENRY JAGLOM? merely confirms what any viewer of Jaglom's oeuvre will have surmised, its brevity makes it a good primer for those who haven't been introduced to the work of this truly independent filmmaker, which can be equally fascinating and maddening. Oddly, it fails to address the financial side of Jaglom's independence—his films are entirely self-financed and distributed, an increasingly difficult feat in an era when major chains dominate theatrical exhibition. *(Adult situations, profanity.)*—M.F.

d, H. Alex Rubin, Jeremy Workman; exec p, Richard Lundun; assoc p, Mary Apostolon; w, H. Alex Rubin, Jeremy Workman; ph, H. Alex Rubin, Jeremy Workman; sound, H. Alex Rubin, Jeremy Workman

Documentary **(PR: C MPAA: NR)**

WHO THE HELL IS JULIETTE? ★★

(Mexico, 1997) 91m December Error; Alameda Films ~ Kino International c (QUIEN DIABLOS ES JULIETTE?)

Yuliet Ortega; Fabiola Quiroz; Oneida Ramirez; Obdulia Fuentes; Yolanda Barajas; Victor Ortega; Marco O Mark; Jose "Don Pepe" Breuil; Jorge Quiroz; Michele Ortega; Guillermo; Billy Joe Landa; Kirenia Rosa; Glenda Rayna; Salma Hayek; Benny; Francesco Clemente; Manolin

Mexican music video director Carlos Marcovich makes his feature debut with this highly stylized, ultimately empty documentary about two gorgeous young women: a teenaged Cuban prostitute and a Mexican model. Marcovich seems particularly taken with his subjects; this apparently lustful approach to character-study can drive a three-minute video, but WHO THE HELL IS JULIETTE? seems to prove that such feelings aren't enough to propel a full-length project.

When Marcovich went to Cuba to shoot a music video which features an acting turn by model Fabiola Quiroz, 23, he needs a lookalike to play her younger sister. Enter the documentary's life-blood: 16-year-old Juliette (Yuliet) Ortega. Marcovich follows his two subjects after the shoot, from October 1995 to January 1997, but we only see them together in clips from the music video. The film moves between Fabiola, as she continues her modeling career in New York City, and Juliette, as she survives in Havana. The sullen Fabiola has little to say, and the only way she seems able to hold the viewer's attention is to flash her breasts at the camera. Marcovich devotes more screen-time to the bouncy, irreverent Juliette.

Against the backdrop of a sordid, decaying city, Juliette basks in the spotlight, intent on making every minute of her momentary fame count. She sparkles for the camera, sharing the details of her harsh life with the glee of a toddler describing a visit to the circus. Typically mischievous, Juliette flirts with the technical crew as she speaks about what it's like to prostitute herself to Italian tourists.

It's the teenager's family life, however, that provides the meandering film with its only shred of drama. Soon after Juliette was born, her father headed to America via the Mariel boat lift. A year later, her mother committed suicide. Raised by an iron-fisted grandmother, Juliette blames her father for her mother's death and claims to have no interest in meeting him. Now settled in New Jersey with a new wife and baby, Victor Ortega recounts how Juliette's mother stonewalled him when he tried to get his Cuban family to come to America. Ortega's keen interest in Juliette is emphasized by a sequence in which he begins to cry as he watches her scenes in the music video. The filmmaker sets up a phone call between the errant father and his daughter, and later orchestrates a reunion so his film can have a climax. Though the reunion may have elicited deep feelings for the family members, none of these emotions appear in the footage. Instead, the moment comes off as stagy and uninvolving.

Proving himself edit-crazy throughout the film, Marcovich enhances a self-conscious feel of the material with repeated shots of his crew in action. Move from Juliette to the camera, cut to New York and Fabiola, jump to a music video, and then on to another jokey, insipid interview clip. High on form, low on content, Marcovich's style seems better suited to providing promos for Mexican ballads than for creating an interesting documentary. *(Nudity, profanity.)*—T.Y.

d, Carlos Marcovich; p, Carlos Marcovich; assoc p, Gerardo Garza, Eduardo Barajas, Simon Bross, Judith Padlog, Alameda Films, Cuatro Y Medio; w, Carlos Marcovich; ph, Carlos Marcovich; ed, Carlos Marcovich; m, Alejandro Marcovich; sound, Juan Carlos Prieto, Antonio Diego

Documentary **(PR: C MPAA: NR)**

WHY DO FOOLS FALL IN LOVE? ★★½
(U.S., 1998) 111m Rhino Films; Warner Bros. ~ Warner Bros. c

Larenz Tate *(Frankie Lymon)*; Halle Berry *(Zola Taylor)*; Lela Rochon *(Emira Eagle)*; Vivica A. Fox *(Elizabeth Waters)*; Little Richard *(Himself)*; Miguel A. Nunez Jr. *(Young Little Richard)*; Paul Mazursky *(Morris Levy)*; Alexis Cruz *(Herman Santiago)*; David Barry Gray *(Peter Markowitz)*; Pamela Reed *(Judge Lambrey)*; Clifton Powell *(Lawrence Roberts)*; Lane Smith *(Ezra Grahme)*; Ben Vereen *(Richard Barrett)*; Paula Jai Parker *(Paula King)*; Marcello Tedford *(Coop)*; Norris Young *(Jimmy)*; J. August Richards *(Sherman)*; Jon Huertas *(Joe)*; Aries Spears *(Redd Foxx)*; Craig Kirkwood *(Eddie Williams)*; Lucille M. Oliver *(Linda)*; Alex Thomas Jr. *(Jimmy Mac)*; Mary Pat Green; Carlase Burke; Erik Dahlberg *(Guard)*; Ray Laska *(Bailiff)*; Renee Raudman *(Waitress)*; Frankie Jai Allison *(Undercover Cop)*; Raymond O'Keefe *(Desk Sergeant)*; Cerita Monet Bicklemann *(Laura)*; Loretta Fox *(Pam)*; Darrell Eisman; Sam Mountain; Ric Borelli; Douglas Seagraves *(Control Room Workers)*; Mark Paulk; Martin Paulk; Ron Jaxson; Gary L. Neal *(The Platters)*; Yorgo Constantine *(Announcer)*; Shirley Caesar *(Herself)*; James Gleason *(Stage Manager)*; Brandon D. Morgan *(Young Singer in Church Choir)*; Charles Walker *(Driver)*; Kevin Fry *(MP)*; Ray Proscia *(Security Man)*; Keith Amos *(Man in Hot Tub)*; J.W. Smith *(Postman)*; Shashawnee Hall *(Preacher)*; Shari Albert *(Mossis Secretary)*; John West *(Singer)*

WHY DO FOOLS FALL IN LOVE? tells the story of the three very different women who married 1950s doo-wop singer Frankie Lymon. Unfortunately, this would-be tragedy fails to answer its own title question.

The rapid rise and fall of composer-performer Frankie Lymon (Larenz Tate) is told through the eyes of three women who each claim to be his widow during a mid-1980s trial held to determine Lymon's royalty credit.

The initial demand for estate ownership comes from Elizabeth Waters (Vivica A. Fox) who, after finishing out a prison term for theft, hires a lawyer who takes her to see Morris Levy (Paul Mazursky), Lymon's former manager, in order to collect Lymon's royalties. Yet during the meeting, two other women who purport to be Lymon's widows also arrive: former Platters singer Zola Taylor (Halle Berry) and Southern school teacher Emira Eagle (Lela Rochon). Levy and the women proceed to court in order to determine the rightful heir.

Before the widows get on the stand, however, several witnesses, including Levy, Richard Barrett (Ben Vereen), and Little Richard (as himself), tell the story of how Lymon and his group, The Teenagers, were discovered in the streets of New York and found instant fame performing on the Alan Freed Show in 1956. Taylor then relates how she met the young Lymon backstage during the show and soon fell in love with him. Lymon went ont to experience fleeting fame with his song, "Why Do Fools Fall in Love?" but by the late 1950s, doo-wop music became passe. Taylor says that they married during a reunion in Los Angeles after she became a solo star and he had fallen on hard times.

Next on the stand, Waters confirms that Lymon had hit the skids by the time they met—he was already using heroin while she was a shoplifter during their courtship. Nevertheless, Lymon and Waters set up house and established a common-law marriage arrangement before he fled to Los Angeles to marry Taylor. During Taylor's next tour, however, a desperate Lymon trashes Taylor's hillside home and depletes her bank account, thus ending their relationship.

Lymon next finds himself drafted into the Army, stationed in Georgia, and romancing an officer friend's sister, Eagle, a prim school teacher. Right after Lymon marries Eagle, he is carted off by MPs for being AWOL. Later, Lymon leaves Eagle to jumpstart his career in New York, but his plan fails, and he dies from a heroin overdose. On the stand, Eagle seems the most believable of the widows, because the other women lack evidence of their marriages. But, in the end, the judge awards Waters the royalties, because her common-law marriage status supersedes the other marital assertions. Eagle wins an appeal of the case, but she gets little of the money.

WHY DO FOOLS FALL IN LOVE? starts with an interesting, non-linear framing device. But screenwriter Tina Andrews's RASHOMON ploy wears thin over time because the three women's perspectives barely differ, and we still never get to really know or understand the late singer (the "ghost" singing voice supplied for Tate creates even more distance from Lymon) or the women who claim to be his wives. Larenz Tate imbues the fictional Lymon with charisma and good looks, but otherwise our "hero" seems to be little more than a drug-addicted loser whose talent is too limited to compensate for his character flaws. Moreover, the real Lymon (seen performing under the closing credits in archival footage) appears physically like the "flat-footed little weirdo" one of his wives had called him earlier.

Fortunately, the film does entertain at points, in spite of itself. Gregory Nava directs FOOLS with more liveliness than his last cliched biopic (SELENA). The script contains anachronisms, but Cary White's production design and Ed Lachman's eye-catching photography add historical nuance. And the three female leads (particularly Berry and Fox in a riotous cafeteria encounter) have fun with their showy parts, even though all the cussing, hair-pulling, and golddigging hardly enhances big-screen representation of African-American women. In the end, WHY DO FOOLS FALL IN LOVE? may start another round of lawsuits from the real-life individuals so glamorously maligned in this hollow, albeit sprightly, docudrama. *(Violence, nudity, sexual situations, substance abuse, extreme profanity.)*—E.M.

d, Gregory Nava; p, Paul Hall, Stephen Nemeth, Harold Bronson; exec p, Gregory Nava, Mark Allan; assoc p, Bruce Franklin; w, Tina Andrews; ph, Edward Lachman; ed, Nancy Richardson; m, Stephen James Taylor; prod d, Mayne Berke; art d, John Chichester; set d, Jackie Carr; ch, Russell Clark; sound, Veda Campbell; casting, Reuben Cannon; cos, Elizabeth Beraldo; makeup, Mark Sanchez; stunts, William Washington

Biography/Musical/Drama **(PR: C MPAA: R)**

WIDE AWAKE ★★
(U.S., 1998) 86m Woods Entertainment; Miramax ~ Miramax c

Denis Leary *(Mr. Beal)*; Dana Delany *(Mrs. Beal)*; Rosie O'Donnell *(Sister Terry)*; Robert Loggia *(Grandfather)*; Joseph Cross

(Joshua Beal); Timothy Reifsnyder *(Dave O'Hara)*; Camryn Manheim *(Sister Sophia)*; Vicki Giunta *(Sister Beatrice)*; Julia Stiles *(Neena Beal)*; Heather Casler *(Hope)*; Dan Lauria *(Father Peters)*; Stefan Niemczyk *(Frank Benton)*; Michael Pacienza *(Freddie Waltman)*; Michael Shulman *(Robert Brickman)*; Jaret Ross Barron *(Dan)*; Jarrett Abello *(John)*; Joseph Melito Jr. *(Billy)*; Peter A. Urban Jr. *(Newman)*; Jahmal Curtis *(Student)*; Michael Craig Bigwood *(Little Boy)*; Gil Robbins *(Cardinal Geary)*; Marc H. Glick *(Father Sebastian)*; Robert K. O'Neill *(Young Priest)*; Deborah Stern *(Mrs. Waltman)*; Joey Perillo *(Mr. Waltman)*; Jerry Walsh *(Football Coach)*; Liam Mitchell *(Gym Teacher)*; Charles Techman *(Janitor)*; Antoine McLean *(Wilson)*; Arleen Goman *(Mrs. Pitman)*; Mets Suber *(Race Starter)*

Rather bland and ultimately too pat, WIDE AWAKE is the story of a 10-year-old, bereaved by his grandfather's death, who goes out in search of God.

Following the death of his beloved grandfather (Robert Loggia), Joshua Beal (Joseph Cross) recalls many loving moments the two of them shared and launches a mission to find God and ask Him if his grandfather is safe in Heaven. Josh solicits help from several of the nuns and priests who comprise the faculty of his school, but as sympathetic as they are to the boy's cause, they are unable to offer him any concrete advice.

Josh's quest motivates him to experiment with Islam, Judaism, and fasting—he even seeks out God on his computer. In addition to his theological efforts, he finds time to hang out with Dave (Timothy Reifsnyder), his best friend, develop his first crush on a girl (Heather Casler), and befriend the school bully (Michael Pacienza) and misfit (Stefan Niemczyk).

On the last day of fifth grade, Josh, all but resigned to the failure of his mission, reads aloud a paper in which he reports on how much he has learned in the past year about life and growing up. Later, in the corridor, a mysterious schoolmate assures him that his grandfather is all right. Josh realizes to his joy that the boy is an angel.

WIDE AWAKE may be of some comfort to children who have recently lost grandparents, but will probably induce naps in most of the rest. The film's sweetest and most amusing scene occurs when an unscheduled meeting of the entire Beal family transpires in Mom and Dad's bed. Comedian and TV personality Rosie O'Donnell contributes a solid, unexpectedly measured portrayal as Sister Terry, Josh's favorite teacher.

Many adult viewers of WIDE AWAKE will find the movie's ending too blatantly miraculous, and the Protestant ones, in particular, might prefer Josh to find God through the series of good works he performs late in the school year (accepting the friendship of the unattractive classmate he had been avoiding, bidding the chastened school bully a let-bygones-be-bygones goodbye, etc.) than through divine intervention. But this *is,* after all, essentially a kids' movie, and children require more tangible proof of God's existence than grownups are willing to settle for.

Twenty-six-year-old writer-director M. Night Shyamalan based WIDE AWAKE, his second feature, on memories of his Philadelphia boyhood. Some of the scenes were shot at the same parochial school he attended as a child. *(Profanity.)*—D.T.

d, M. Night Shyamalan; p, Cary Woods, Cathy Konrad; exec p, Randy Ostrow, Bob Weinstein, Harvey Weinstein, Meryl Poster; assoc p, Timothy Lonsdale; co-p, James Bigwood; w, N. Night Shyamalan; ph, Adam Holender; ed, Andrew Mondshein; m, Edmund Choi; prod d, Michael Johnston; set d, Andrea Fenton; sound, Brian Miksis (mixer); fx, Edward A. Drohan III, Norm Dodge; casting, Avy Kaufman; cos, Bridget Kelly; makeup, Joseph Hurt; stunts, Bill Anagnos

Children's/Drama/Religious **(PR: A MPAA: PG)**

WILD MAN BLUES ★★★

(U.S., 1998) 105m Cabin Creek Films ~ Fine Line c

Woody Allen; Dan Barrett; Simon Wettenhall; John Gill; Cynthia Sayer; Greg Cohen; Eddy Davis; John Doumanian; Richard Jones; Letty Aronson; Soon-Yi Previn; Jean Doumanian

Oscar-winning documentarian Barbara Kopple (HARLAN COUNTY U.S.A., AMERICAN DREAM) trains her probing cameras on Woody Allen for a European tour with his jazz band in WILD MAN BLUES, an irresistibly entertaining goldmine of gossip, comedy, and music for both Woody-lovers and Woody-haters.

The film consists of concert footage of Woody and his New Orlean-style jazz band performing in Madrid, Geneva, Vienna, Venice, Milan, Bologna, Turin, Rome, Paris, and London. This is intercut with private glimpses of Woody and his inner-circle entourage (including then girlfriend Soon-Yi Previn [whom he subsequently married], friend and producer Jean Doumanian, and his sister Letty Aronson) at various hotels and parties as they travel through each city. Upon returning to New York, Woody and Soon-Yi visit his elderly parents for what he calls a "lunch from hell."

The most fascinating aspect of WILD MAN BLUES, aside from the obvious voyeuristic opportunities it affords, is why the notoriously private Woody Allen would allow himself to be followed around with a camera in the first place. The most likely explanation is that he thought it would be a further step in his public-relations rehabilitation in the wake of the sordid Mia Farrow-Soon-Yi scandal. Ever since that incident, Allen has been much more accessible and open to the media than ever before, giving interviews and appearing on television programs to defend himself. Perhaps he felt that a documentary would be a chance to show that, yes, he may be neurotic, eccentric, and weird (he hates animals, travel, and sun; he takes numerous medications and carries a bathmat with him when he travels because his feet can't touch marble floors), but he's no pedophiliac pervert. The film certainly accomplishes this, but by no means is the portrait entirely flattering, as he comes off as funny and intelligent, but also sometimes quite caustic and mean-sprited.

His relationship with Soon-Yi (whom he introduces at a party as "the notorious Soon-Yi") naturally becomes the focal point of the film, and it's interesting how they both seem to relate to each other as a parent would to a child. She gives him motherly advice on how to behave with other people and deal with the public, while he sometimes acts like her father (discussing ANNIE HALL, which she hasn't seen, he tells her to "go see it with one of your teenage twitty friends," and comments that "the kid used to be eating out of garbage cans in Korea" while she's in a luxurious Italian hotel room). How much of his persona is an act and how much is the truth is debatable, since the mere presence of a camera invariably creates a "performance," but his self-described "Anhedonia" (the inability to enjoy oneself) and string of witty one-liners seem genuine and certainly make for an amusing experience.

Kopple's intimate, yet unobtrusive, directorial style is so self-effacing that its subject's personality becomes the dominant force and it ultimately feels like another Woody Allen movie. Though the film offers plentiful concert footage, it's actually more effective and interesting as a study of fame and what it means to be a celebrity, albeit one who's more popular in Europe than he is in his own country. The irony of this is not lost on Allen, who, while riding in a gondola and being gawked at by camera-wielding tourists, wryly says: "They won't pay 10 cents to see one of my movies, but in a gondola, they love me."

As for his musicianship, Woody plays a pretty mean clarinet and speaks passionately about his love of playing, which he says he enjoys because there is no cerebral element to it. The concert scenes are quite enjoyable, though they tend to become repetitious and cause the film to be slightly overlong. However, the finale back in New York when he visits his aged father and mother is priceless. We see his Oscars and other awards on their mantle, hear him complain that they made him go to Hebrew school as a boy ("a complete waste of time"), and best of all, watch in amazement as his mother casually dismisses his accomplishments by saying that when he was young "he was interested in a lot of things, but never pursued any of them," and how she wishes that "he would have married a nice Jewish girl" while Soon-Yi (whom she thinks is Chinese) is sitting right there in the room. For hardcore Woody-philes and amateur psychologists, this scene alone is worth the price of admission. *(Profanity.)*—M.S.

d, Barbara Kopple; p, Jean Doumanian; exec p, J.E. Beaucaire; assoc p, Kathleen Bambrick Meier; ph, Tom Hurwitz; ed, Lawrence Silk; sound, Peter Miller (recordist)

Documentary/Musical **(PR: C MPAA: PG)**

WILD THINGS ★★★

(U.S., 1998) 113m McNaughton/Jones Motion Pictures; Mandalay Entertainment ~ Columbia c

Kevin Bacon *(Ray Duquette)*; Matt Dillon *(Sam Lombardo)*; Neve Campbell *(Suzie Toller)*; Denise Richards *(Kelly Van Ryan)*; Daphne Rubin-Vega *(Gloria Perez)*; Bill Murray *(Ken Bowden)*; Theresa Russell *(Sandra Van Ryan)*; Robert Wagner *(Tom Baxter)*; Carrie Snodgress *(Ruby)*; Jeff Perry *(Bryce Hunter)*; Cory Pendergast *(Jimmy Leach)*; Marc Macaulay *(Walter)*; Toi Svane *(Nicole)*; Dennis Neal *(Art Maddox)*; Diane Adams *(School Secretary)*; Paulo Benedeti *(Kirk)*; Eduardo Yanez *(Frankie Condo)*; Jennifer Bini *(Barbara Baxter)*; Victoria Bass *(Judge)*; Ted Bartsch *(Bailiff)*; Leonor Anthony *(Ken's Secretary)*; Antoni Cornacchione *(Police Chief)*; Robert Deacon *(Prisoner)*; Tony Giaimo *(Dave)*; Manny Suarez *(Georgie)*; Janet Bushor *(Barmaid)*; Gina LaMarca *(Hooker)*; Nancy Duerr *(Reporter #1)*; Margo Peace *(Reporter #2)*; Keith Wilson *(Reporter #3)*; Nelson Oramos *(Policeman #1)*; Michael Dean Walker *(Policeman #2)*; Jesse Muson *(Policeman #3)*; Kimberly Lamaze *(Policewoman #1)*; Rebecca White *(Policewoman #2)*

Trashy, gimmicky, and unapologetically exploitative, WILD THINGS is film noir for the SCREAM generation. The movie combines a double helix, keeps-you-guessing plot with R-rated, soft-core flesh peddling into an adrenaline rush of entertainment that revels in the very act of making you feel guilty for enjoying it.

Lady-killer Sam Lombardo (Matt Dillon) is a respected high school teacher in Blue Bay, FL, until one of his students, sexpot Kelly Van Ryan (Denise Richards), accuses him of rape. Kelly's mother is boozy heiress Sandra Van Ryan (Theresa Russell), one of Lombardo's former paramours. She uses her considerable influence to see that Lombardo loses his job, his home, and his socialite girlfriend. Another student, grungy loner Suzie Toller (Neve Campbell), also comes forward to claim that Lombardo raped her the previous year.

At his trial, Sam is defended by Ken Bowden (Bill Murray), a sleazy lawyer who specializes in phony whiplash cases. Under cross-examination, Bowden gets Suzie to recant her rape charge and admit that Kelly is lying as well. Lombardo quickly collects a multimillion dollar settlement from Sandra. Later, Kelly and Suzie join Lombardo in his motel room to celebrate what was in fact a scam concocted to get money from Kelly's mother.

Police detective Ray Duquette (Kevin Bacon) is suspicious. He browbeats Suzie to determine what information she knows, and spies on the girls making love. Fearing Suzie will talk, Lombardo bludgeons her with a bottle and disposes of her body in a swamp. Duquette goes to Kelly's home to persuade her to confess. She shoots him, and he kills her in self-defense.

Lombardo moves to the Caribbean. There, he's met by Duquette, who it turns out was his partner in crime (and perhaps more) all along. Out sailing, Lombardo attempts to throw Duquette overboard, but fails, until Suzie (surprisingly alive) pops up and does the job. She and Lombardo embrace, and for a moment the lovers bask in their greedy success; then, Suzie kills Lombardo as well. Suzie, it turns out, is an iron-willed genius who pretending to be a troubled loser, master-minded and guided the entire plot.

WILD THINGS is full of double- and triple-crosses, twists and turns, but it's the curves—of its female stars—that are this movie's drawing card. To say that WILD THINGS plays head games with its male audience is definitely a double entendre. While Neve Campbell, aspiring to a legitimate career, remains reasonably demurely clad, former swimsuit model Denise Richards seizes her chance to get noticed, a la Uma Thurman in DANGEROUS LIAISONS (1989).

There are other, less prurient, noteworthy aspects to WILD THINGS. All the performances are good. Bill Murray is great fun as Bowden, and you can't help but be pleased when he shows up at the end as Suzie's only surviving accomplice. Visually, WILD THINGS lacks the sweat-and-shadows atmospherics of PALMETTO, another 1998 Florida-based noir that takes the more classic approach to sensuality. But give director John McNaughton credit for squeezing in all that plot in less than two hours. *(Extensive nudity, sexual situations, profanity, violence.)*—P.R.

d, John McNaughton; p, Rodney Liber, Steven A. Jones; exec p, Kevin Bacon; w, Stephen Peters; ph, Jeffrey L. Kimball; ed, Elena Maganini; m, George S. Clinton; prod d, Edward T. McAvoy; art d, Bill Hiney; set d, Bill Cimino; sound, Peter J. Devlin (mixer); fx, Kevin Harris; casting, Linda Lowry, Brace John; cos, Kimberly A. Tillman; makeup, Jeni Lee Dinkel; stunts, Chick Bernhardt

Thriller **(PR: O MPAA: R)**

WILDE ★★½

(U.K., 1997) 116m Samuelson Productions; Dove International; NDF International; Pony Canyon; Pandora Film; Capitol Films; BBC Films ~ Sony Pictures Classics c
(OSCAR WILDE)

Stephen Fry *(Oscar Wilde)*; Jude Law *(Lord Alfred Douglas)*; Jennifer Ehle *(Constance Wilde)*; Vanessa Redgrave *(Lady Speranza Wilde)*; Gemma Jones *(Lady Queensberry)*; Judy Parfitt *(Lady Mount-Temple)*; Michael Sheen *(Robert Ross)*; Zoe Wanamaker *(Ada Leverson)*; Tom Wilkinson *(Marquess of Queensberry)*; Ioan Gruffudd *(John Gray)*; Matthew Mills *(Lionel Johnson)*; Jason Morell *(Ernest Dowson)*; Peter Barkworth *(Charles Gill)*; Robert Lang *(C.O. Humphreys)*; Philip Locke *(Judge)*; David Westhead *(Edward Carson)*; Jack Knight *(Cyril Wilde)*; Jackson Leach *(Cyril Wilde—Aged 4)*; Laurence Owen *(Vyvyan Wilde)*; Benedict Sandiford *(Alfred Wood)*; Mark Letheren *(Charles Parker)*; Michael Fitzgerald *(Alfred Taylor)*; Orlando Bloom *(Rentboy)*; Bob Sessions *(Mine Owner)*; Adam Garcia *(Jones)*; Joseph May *(First Miner)*; Jamie Leene *(Second Friend)*; James D'Arcy *(First Friend)*; Orlando Wells *(Undergraduate)*; Robin Kermode *(George Alexander)*; Avril Elgar *(Lady Bracknell)*; Jean Ainslie *(Miss Prism)*; Andrew Havill

(Algernon); Biddy Hodson *(Gwendolen)*; Judi Maynard *(Mrs. Allonby)*; Hugh Munro *(Chasuble)*; Michael Simkins *(Lord Illingworth)*

Stephen Fry gives a remarkable performance as Oscar Wilde (to whom he bears an uncanny likeness) in WILDE, the third film biography of the legendary Irish wit, and the first to deal candidly with his homosexuality. The film's honesty is commendable, but otherwise it's as glossy and superficial as the previous biopics.

During an 1882 lecture tour of the US, writer Oscar Wilde (Stephen Fry) visits a Colorado silver mine and finds himself attracted to the young miners. Oscar returns home to England and marries Constance Lloyd (Jennifer Ehle) and has a son with her, but allows himself to be seduced by their Canadian houseguest Robbie Ross (Michael Sheen). As the years pass, Constance gives birth to another son, and Oscar leads a double life as a loving husband while having a series of homosexual affairs. Following the success of *The Picture of Dorian Gray*, Oscar writes *Lady Windermere's Fan* and meets the young and handsome Lord Alfred Douglas—known as "Bosie"—(Jude Law) at a first-night party. Oscar immediately falls in love with the wild and childish young man, who introduces Oscar to a male brothel he frequents. Their tempestuous affair is marked by numerous fights, however, as Bosie takes advantage of Oscar's financial generosity and continues to sleep with other men.

Bosie's tyrannical father, the Marquess of Queensberry (Tom Wilkinson) orders Bosie to stay away from Oscar and after failing to disrupt the premiere of *The Importance of Being Earnest*, he publicly accuses Oscar of behaving as a "Sodomite." Against the advice of Robbie, Bosie convinces Oscar to sue Queensberry for libel, but after the trial is over, Oscar is arrested and sentenced to two years' hard labor when some prostitutes from the male brothel testify against him. In jail, Oscar's health rapidly deteriorates and he is visited by Constance, who promises to stand by him on condition that he never see Bosie again. Oscar agrees and writes Bosie a letter severing their relationship, but when he's released, he finds that Constance has died and he's barred from seeing his children. He goes to France with Robbie, who still loves Oscar, but can't forget Bosie and travels to Italy to find him. A postscript states that Oscar left Bosie for good three months later and died in 1900, while Bosie died in 1945. Robbie died in 1918 and his ashes were reinterred alongside Oscar's in 1950.

After an unlikely and somewhat campy prologue, in which Oscar rides through the American West and ogles a group of virile, bare-chested miners, WILDE settles down to being a generally absorbing and honest biography that unfortunately never exhibits the wit and fearlessness that was characteristic of Wilde. The film is physically handsome and well acted, but it winds up being only a more sexually explicit, though similarly tasteful, type of Merchant-Ivory/"Masterpiece Theatre" production that's ultimately as conventional as previous Wilde biopics.

While Wilde's (initially repressed) homosexuality is undoubtedly the key to his personality and the trial that led to his downfall is certainly a pivotal event, by concentrating almost entirely on his sexual proclivities to the exclusion of his art, the filmmakers don't do justice to his genius. It may be impossible to demonstrate the brilliance of his writing with a film, but all we get here are a few brief glimpses of stage productions, Oscar's bon mot-filled dialogue, and repeated voice-overs in which he symbolically reads a fairytale to his children about "trespassers being eaten by a giant," set to montages that skim over his complex relationship with his wife and his life in prison.

The entire cast is exceptionally good, particularly Tom Wilkinson as the viciously homophobic Queensberry, Michael Sheen as the loyal and loving friend Robbie, and Vanessa Redgrave in a cameo as Wilde's sympathetic mother. But despite the fact that Stephen Fry is a dead ringer for Wilde and gives a witty and touching performance, Jude Law's Bosie (who unwisely becomes the story's focal point) is so obnoxious and dislikable that it's hard to understand Wilde's stated love for him, which ironically undermines the film's lofty intentions and leaves the audience with the same smirking suspicion that Queensberry had: Wilde merely likes sleeping with young boys. *(Nudity, profanity, sexual situations.)*—M.S.

d, Brian Gilbert; p, Marc Samuelson, Peter Samuelson; exec p, Michiyo Yoshizaki, Michael Viner, Deborah Raffin, Alan Howden, Alex Graham; assoc p, Rachel Cuperman; w, Julian Mitchell (from the biography *Oscar Wilde* by Richard Ellmann); ph, Martin Fuhrer; ed, Michael Bradsell; m, Debbie Wiseman; prod d, Maria Djurkovic; art d, Martyn John; sound, Jim Greenhorn (mixer); fx, Bob Hollow; casting, Sarah Bird; cos, Nic Ede; makeup, Pat Hay

Biography/Drama **(PR: C MPAA: R)**

WINGS OF AN ANGEL
(SEE: UNDER HEAVEN)

WITHOUT LIMITS ★★½
(U.S., 1998) 117m CW Productions; Warner Bros. ~ Warner Bros. c

Billy Crudup *(Steve Prefontaine)*; Donald Sutherland *(William Bowerman)*; Monica Potter *(Mary Marckx)*; Jeremy Sisto *(Frank Shorter)*; Gabe Olds *(Don Kardong)*; Judith Ivey *(Barbara Bowerman)*; Dean Norris *(Bill Dellinger)*; Billy Burke *(Kenny Moore)*; Adam Setliff *(Mac Wilkins)*; Nicholas Oleson *(Russ Francis)*; William Mapother *(Bob Peters)*; Matthew Lillard *(Roscoe Devine)*

Arriving one year after Disney's failed pseudo-docudrama PREFONTAINE (1997), WITHOUT LIMITS, Robert Towne's much-delayed biography of runner Steve Prefontaine (originally titled PRE) is much better made and boasts a bigger budget, but it's only marginally more interesting due to the intrinsic problem of trying to fascinate the general public in the story of a virtually forgotten nonprofessional athlete who actually lost the big race.

In 1969, Steve Prefontaine (Billy Crudup), a track star from Coos Bay, OR, accepts an athletic scholarship to attend the University of Oregon in order to work under the legendary coach Bill Bowerman (Donald Sutherland), who designs his own running shoes with spiked-rubber soles made with a waffle-iron. The cocky and good-looking Prefontaine instantly becomes a school hero and sets numerous college records despite ignoring Bowerman's advice to pace himself and not always be a frontrunner. Prefontaine romantically pursues a pretty student named Mary (Monica Potter), but she rejects him because of her religious beliefs and his constant womanizing. In 1971, Prefontaine goes to Finland and clashes with the unethical and dictatorial Amateur Athletic Union, against which he begins a crusade.

In 1972, Prefontaine and Bowerman go to Munich with the American Olympic team; while there, they are all shaken by the massacre of Israeli athletes at the hands of Palestinian terrorists. During the 5,000 meter race, Prefontaine pulls into the lead, but wears out at the end and only finishes in fourth place. Back home, the impoverished and despondent Prefontaine quits the track team and takes a job at a bar, but Mary renews her relationship with him and Bowerman talks him into coming back. In 1975, after Prefontaine rejects a $200,000 offer to play for a professional track team, and starts training for the 1976 Montreal Olympics, he's killed in a car crash. During a memorial service at the college, a huge crowd applauds as a hearse carrying his body drives laps around the track.

Similar in theme to PERSONAL BEST (1982), the first film directed by the illustrious screenwriter Robert Towne, which also dealt with the Olympics and the psychology of sports, WITHOUT LIMITS is a definite improvement over his only other directorial outing, TEQUILA SUNRISE (1988), and is meters ahead of the amateurish PREFONTAINE, yet is still not totally satisfying. While PREFONTAINE presented a more detailed historical account of Prefontaine's running career, based on exclusive ABC Olympic footage owned by Disney, WITHOUT LIMITS spends more time dealing with his personal life and his complex relationships with Mary and Bowerman. It also heavily promotes the philosophy of supreme confidence, bordering on arrogance (as when Mary asks Prefontaine if he believes in God and he shoots back: "I believe in myself"), which also could be read as being the theosophy of the film's co-producer Tom Cruise. The textured script includes allusions to Plato and is guided by Bowerman's belief that athletic competition is a metaphor for finding meaning in life and to test the limits of the human heart and spirit. More interesting than the differences between the two films, however, are the similarities, as both of them pretty much boil down to comparable montages of races, newspaper headlines, and the intercutting of archival track footage of the real Prefontaine with actors made up to look like him.

Most critically, like PREFONTAINE, Towne has not been able to successfully solve the seemingly insuperable dilemma of how to convince nontrack aficionados that Prefontaine really was the mythic and important figure that the fanatical publicity asserts he was (variously described as the "James Dean of track" and an "athletic Beatle"). All the slow-motion shots of the handsome golden boy huffing and puffing around the track to the adoration of swooning teeny-boppers, accompanied by a pulsating rock soundtrack, cannot erase the persistent feeling that Prefontaine was merely a local Northwest college legend, and a cult hero only in the world of racing. Still, the film is technically quite accomplished, with superbly staged re-creations of races (integrating Olympic footage from the BBC and outtakes from the 1973 documentary VISIONS OF EIGHT) featuring excellent editing and sound work that delivers the exhilaration and adrenaline rush of the sport. While Jared Leto in PREFONTAINE looked more like the real man, Billy Crudup is more convincing at creating a three-dimensional character, and Donald Sutherland gives one of his best performances in a long time as the cagey and eccentric Bowerman, who eventually used his waffle-iron-made sneaks to help found a little company called "Nike." *(Profanity, sexual situations.)*—M.S.

d, Robert Towne; p, Paula Wagner, Tom Cruise; exec p, Kenny Moore, Jonathan Sanger; w, Robert Towne, Kenny Moore; ph, Conrad L. Hall; ed, Claire Simpson, Robert K. Lambert; m, Randy Miller; prod d, William Creber; art d, William Durrell Jr.; set d, Roberta Holinko; sound, Bruce Bisenz (mixer); fx, Bobby Riggs; casting, Rick Pagano, Keri Peyton; cos, Grania Preston

Biography/Sports/Drama (PR: C MPAA: PG-13)

WOO ★½

(U.S., 1998) 80m New Deal/Gotham Entertainment ~ New Line c

Jada Pinkett, billed as Jada Pinkett Smith *(Darlene "Woo" Bates/Off the Wall Babe)*; Tommy Davidson *(Tim)*; Dave Chappelle *(Lenny)*; Paula Jai Parker *(Claudette)*; LL Cool J *(Darryl)*; Darrel M. Heath *(Hop)*; Michael Ralph *(Romaine)*; Duane Martin *(Frankie)*; Foxy Brown *(Fiancee)*; Aida Turturro *(Tookie)*; Dartanyan Edmonds *(Shakim)*; Lance Slaughter *(Lamar)*; Sam Moses *(Cabbie)*; Tiffany Hall *(Denise)*; Girlina *(Celestrial)*; Denosh Bennett *(Sister at Concert)*; Joanna Bacalso *(Stunning Woman)*; Mia Pitts *(Voluptuous Woman)*; Catherine Burdon *(Alluring Woman)*; Lenny Solomon *(Violin Player)*; Silvio Oliviero *(Waiter #1)*; Nick Corri *(Maitre D')*; Victor Chan *(Delivery Biker)*; Lisa Scarola *(Latina Woman)*; Philip Akin *(Roger Smith)*; Stu "Large" Riley *(Beast)*; David "Rumble" Morgan *(Patron #2)*; Fawn Boardley *(Shanay)*; Natalie Venetia Belcon *(Hootchie)*; Buddy Lewis *(Bartender)*; Nicci Gilbert *(Crayola)*; Christian Maelen *(Officer #1)*; Desmond Campbell *(Officer #2)*; Kelley Grando *(Barry—Bouncer)*; Orlando Jones *(Sticky Fingas)*; Esther Jones *(Shorty)*; Tyree Michael Simpson *(Big Brother #1)*; Roland Rothchild *(Big Brother #2)*; Martin Roach *(West Indian Brother)*; Wilfredo A. Crispin; Jessica Nahar; James De Jesus; Eustace Dunbar IV *(Salsa Band)*; Sergio Trujillo *(Ricardo/Salsa Dancer)*; Shyla Marlin *(Niece)*; Robinne Fanfair *(Fine Sister at Restaurant)*; John Stoneham Jr. *(Fine Sister's Date)*; Russell Hornsby *(Guy)*; Marc Desourdy *(Waiter with Pasta)*; Billy Linders *(Waiter with Flambee)*; Frank Ferrara *(Construction Guy)*; Silvana Gatica *(Rosa)*; David Roberts *(Disco Girl #1)*; Kirk Pickersgill *(Disco Girl #2)*; Drake Thorens *(Delivery Biker #2)*; Kevin Louis *(Door Person)*; A.J. Johnson *(Doorman)*; Pat Dias *(Salsa Party Photographer)*; Pam Grier; Isaac Hayes

How can a surefire comedy premise, a disastrous date between two opposite types, turn into a disastrous movie? WOO provides the answer.

Darlene "Woo" Bates (Jada Pinkett Smith) turns heads everytime she walks down the New York City streets, but the take-charge young beauty can't seem to attract the man of her dreams. Following the advice of her psychic friend, Celestrial (Girlina), Woo looks out for the next Virgo she can find. That same day, her cousin, Claudette (Paula Jai Parker), sets her up on a blind date with a friend who happens to be a Virgo—a meek law clerk named Tim (Tommy Davidson). Woo drops everything and swings by Tim's place for a night of fun and romance. But Woo and Tim's starkly different personalities get in the way of the plans. At first, Woo is impressed when Tim lies about being a lawyer, but later she's insulted when Tim's rambunctious buddies (Duane Martin, Michael Ralph, Darrel M. Heath) stop by and assume Woo is a prostitute. Eventually, Woo and Tim go out on the town, but their romantic dinner plans fail when Woo interrupts the tete-a-tete to complain about her seat, then accidentally sets the establishment on fire.

The evening becomes even more frantic after Woo and Tim head to a nightclub where Woo's ex-boyfriend starts a fight and ends up socking Tim. On the way out of the club, Tim realizes his expensive sports car has been stolen. He and Woo report the theft at the local police station, where they get into an argument when Tim admits he is only a law clerk. Woo takes a cab home, but can't help thinking about her date and how much nicer Tim was than most of the men she has met. Tim, meanwhile, tries to get home on his own, but is nearly mugged on the way.

Finally, Woo realizes some of ways she has been selfish in the past. She visits her brother to tell him and his fiancee that she blesses their impending marriage. She also tries to set things right with Tim, whom she thanks for "opening her eyes." As a measure of her gratitude, and a way to restore his manhood, she helps him retain a car he co-signed to a former girlfriend. However, once they successfully secure the vehicle, they step out into the street for a slow dance, and a fast-moving truck turns the car into a wreck. Still, their future together seems assured.

WOO might sound like a hip-hop update of Jane Austen, but in every way this supposed comedy of manners fumbles over itself. First, there's the script (by David C. Johnson), a flat, unfunny series of poorly developed scenes depicting the night on the town between free-spirited Woo and introverted Tim. Second, there's Daisy von Scherler Mayer's listless direction, which tries to camouflage itself with lots of loud, frenetic party bits (remember Mayer's overrated debut, PARTY GIRL?).

But WOO is much worse than a rehash of Martin Scorsese's AFTER HOURS (1985), Blake Edwards's BLIND DATE (1987), or even Jeff Pollack's BOOTY CALL (1997, also with Davidson). There is nothing remotely funny about all the gender and racial stereotypes that are meant to suggest an urban hip attitude on the filmmakers' part. Echoing long-thought dead cultural racism, the film portrays mostly libidinous black males drooling after sluttish, mercenary black women. In a small part, for example, a poorly used Dave Chappelle plays a man who likes fried chicken so much, he dresses as a pimp called "Big Daddy" and demands his "ho" wife dress in a chicken outfit during sex. There are also lots of homophobic laughs at the expense of transvestites which include dated jokes about THE CRYING GAME (1992).

But apart from the deeply troubling subtext (the pandering to African-Americans with jokes at their expense), WOO is just a foolish waste of time. Maybe the Wayans Brothers could have turned the stereotypes on their heads, but without them, WOO is a bad-date movie your significant other won't soon let you forget! *(Violence, sexual situations, extreme profanity.)*—E.M.

d, Daisy von Scherler Mayer, billed as Daisy V.S. Mayer; p, Beth Hubbard, Michael Hubbard; exec p, John Singleton, Howard Hobson, Bradford W. Smith; assoc p, Stephanie Koules; co-p, David C. Johnson, Bill Carraro; w, David C. Johnson; ph, Jean Lepine; ed, Nicholas Eliopoulos, Janice Hampton; m, Michel Colombier; prod d, Ina Mayhew; art d, Vlasta Svoboda; set d, Mike Harris; sound, Owen "Sound" Langevin; fx, Jordan Craig; casting, Robi Reed-Humes; cos, Michael Clancy; makeup, Judy Murdock; stunts, Alison Reid

Romance/Comedy **(PR: C MPAA: R)**

WOUNDED ★½

(U.S./Canada, 1996) 91m Wounded Pictures ~ Keystone Pictures/Republic Pictures c

Madchen Amick *(Julie Clayton)*; Adrian Pasdar *(Hanaghan)*; Graham Greene *(Rollins)*; Richard Joseph Paul *(Don Powell)*; Daniel Kash *(David Boyd)*; Jim Beaver *(Eric Ashton)*; Francois Chau *(Mr. Lee)*; Michael Rawlins *(Agent Clark)*; J.B. Bivens Jr. *(Richard Pearson)*; Greg Rogers *(Dr. Jay Voight)*; Jerry Wasserman *(Dr. Sam Cohen)*; Frank Crudele *(Bill Gillespie)*; Michael Dobson *(Lee's Attorney)*; Akiko Morison *(Nurse)*; Constance Barnes *(Nurse)*; Patrick Gorman *(Paramedic)*; Adam Harrington *(Paramedic)*; Kelly Benson *(Cohen's Secretary)*; Eric Breker *(Security Guard)*; Marc Akerstream *(Agent Waring)*; Lauro Chartrand *(Agent Eagan)*; Randy Lee *(Hiking Man)*; Peter Mac Innes *(Doctor)*; David Neale *(Cop)*; Claude Kananack *(Hotel Clerk)*; Rod McDonald *(Homeless Man)*

After roles in WOUNDED and HUNTED (1998), Madchen Amick seems to have cornered the market in vulnerable heroines being stalked in the wilderness. Why would this stylish actress appear in one rip-off of THE MOST DANGEROUS GAME (1932), let alone two? High heels suit her better than hiking boots. The film premiered on HBO, and was subsequently released on home video.

Can animal conservationist Julie Clayton (Madchen Amick) and her partner/boyfriend Don Powell (Richard Joseph Paul) head off the critter-poaching problem in their once-idyllic forest? Flanked by federal agents, Julie and Don, nonetheless, find themselves outsmarted by outlaw poacher Hanaghan (Adrian Pasdar), who provides grizzly bear organs for organ-trafficker Mr. Lee (Francois Chau).

One by one, the agents fall victim to diabolical Hanaghan's deadly booby traps. Promising Julie he will spare Don if she drops her gun, duplicitous Hanaghan guts Don and shoots her twice, but rescuers later save her. When he discovers she has survived, Hanaghan travels to the city to eliminate Julie and to threaten Mr. Lee, who is seeking immunity by cooperating with the Feds. Hanaghan eludes the agents long enough to torture and kill Lee.

Trailing Julie to the home of FBI agent Rollins (Graham Greene) who is guarding her, Hanaghan eviscerates Rollins. As a result of the arrival of other agents, Hanaghan is unable to kill Julie. Refusing to be intimidated by Hanaghan any longer, Julie returns to her work in the forest. Deciding to play by Hanaghan's kill-or-be-killed rules, Julie conceals her gun and allows him to track her. Toppling with him into the river, Julie pretends to drown and then shoots Hanaghan when he climbs back onto the river bank.

There's something inherently silly about Madchen Amick tip-toeing through the fearsome woods in camouflage makeup like a model for the J. Peterman Catalogue of Wilderness Fashions. Is WOUNDED scary? No, because its victims are sitting ducks. Is the atmosphere even mildly creepy as madman Hanaghan stalks his human prey? No, because the cinematography and direction don't even attempt to use screen space to create tension. What does that leave? Just another run-of-the-forest action pic with a few low-impact thrills. Wallowing in mindless brutality, WOUNDED reminds us of how escapist entertainment has been devalued since 1932's version of THE MOST DANGEROUS GAME. *(Graphic violence, profanity, adult situations.)*—R.P.

d, Richard Martin; p, Robert Vince, William Vince; exec p, Michael Strange; assoc p, Don Woodman; w, Harry S. Longstreet, Lindsay Bourne; ph, Greg Middleton; ed, Kerry Uchida; m, Ross Vannelli; prod d, Al Benjamin; art d, Pamela Neelands; set d, Francesca Courtois; sound, Marc Benoit (mixer); fx, Roy Schultz; casting, Abra Edelman, Elisa Goodman; cos, Druh Ireland; makeup, Nicole Demers, Toby Lindala (special makeup effects); stunts, Marc Akerstream

Action **(PR: C MPAA: R)**

WRATH OF THE NINJA: THE YOTODEN MOVIE ★★★½

(Japan, 1989) 87m JVC ~ US Manga Corps c

ENGLISH VOICE CAST: Rose Markisello *(Ayame)*; Hideo Seaver *(Sakon)*; Peter Patrikios *(Ryoma)*; Vinnie Penna *(Ranmaru)*; Flavio Romeo *(Nobunaga)*; Jack Taylor *(Ryoan)*; Bruce Winant *(Jinnai)*; Greg Wolfe *(Genyusai)*; Nick Sullivan *(Kiheji)*; Sharon Becker *(Kikyo)*; Frank Frankson *(Jinpei)*; Shannon Conley *(Kayo)*; Bill Blechingberg; George Leaver; Socko Jones

An epic historical fantasy of noble young ninjas fighting an evil conqueror in feudal Japan, WRATH OF THE NINJA is a better-than-average Japanese animated adventure, boasting a strong story, compelling characters, imaginative supernatural touches, and plenty of action. This 1989 feature received its first official US release on home video in 1998.

In 1580 Japan, Lord Nobunaga Oda (voice of Flavio Romeo) seeks to "attain the power of a true demon god" by conquering all resisting provinces. He sends his army of riflemen on a campaign of destruction, until only Iga remains as the last stronghold of resistance. Arrayed against Nobunaga are the three Shadow Warriors, survivors of the three Shadow Ninja schools: the female ninja Ayame of the Kasumi school (voice of Rose

Markisello), Sakon the Whirlwind of the Hyuga school (voice of Hideo Seaver), and Ryoma of the Hagakure school (voice of Peter Patrikios). Gradually, Iga is isolated as its allies submit to Nobunaga or are destroyed by his army of monsters, including a three-headed dragon and the demonic Seven Oboro Ninja. When Iga's last ally, Koga, surrenders to Nobunaga, Iga seems doomed. To make matters worse, Sakon deserts the group, convinced of their impending loss and his unwillingness to die for a lost cause.

The monk Ryoan (voice of Jack Taylor), who had originally brought the three ninjas together, pleads with Sakon and reminds him of an ancient prophecy, the Legend of the Sword, which dictates that the three ninjas must combine their weapons—a long sword, a short sword, and a halberd—in order to defeat the demons. Only when the three finally reunite for an attack on Nobunaga's castle are they able to summon up the power to destroy Nobunaga, his evil sidekick Ranmaru (voice of Vinnie Penna), and the remaining demons once and for all in a spectacular final battle that leaves all but Ayame dead.

A Japanese theatrical release made up of three made-for-video episodes flawlessly edited together, WRATH OF THE NINJA creates an epic tale of ninjas, armies, civil war, and raging demon monsters. Parts of it are based on history; Nobunaga was a real historical figure, but the rest is purely imaginary.

There's a hint of romance between Ayame and Sakon in a brief, tender kissing scene, very rare in anime, done in beautifully rendered closeups. There is little time for romance, however, as Sakon has a crisis of faith midway through and, uncharacteristically for Japanese heroes, questions the validity of dying to fulfill a preordained destiny. It's all very well animated and produced with expert design in all departments.

There are bursts of graphic, bloody violence and some imaginatively grotesque monsters that may put off casual viewers of anime and Japanese history buffs drawn to the subject matter. Devoted fans, however, will rank this alongside such later, similarly themed anime as RAVEN TENGU KABUTO (1992) and NINJA SCROLL (1993). *(Extreme violence, nudity.)*—B.C.

d, Osamu Yamazaki; p, Yoshiaki Aihara, Tomoyuki Miyato, Stephanie Shalofsky (English version); exec p, Makoto Hasegawa, John O'Donnell (English version); w, Sho Aikawa (based on the story by Osamu Yamazaki); m, Seiji Hano; art d, Geki Katsumata; sound, Yasunori Honda

Animated/Fantasy **(PR: C MPAA: NR)**

WRONGFULLY ACCUSED ★½

(U.S./Germany, 1998) 85m Morgan Creek; Constantin Films; Westbay Entertainment ~ Warner Bros. c

Leslie Nielsen *(Ryan Harrison)*; Kelly LeBrock *(Lauren Goodhue)*; Michael York *(Hibbing Goodhue)*; Richard Crenna *(US Marshal Fergus Falls)*; Sandra Bernhard *(Dr. Fridley)*; Gerald Plunkett *(UN Secretary General)*; Aaron Pearl *(One-Armed, One-Legged, One-Eyed Killer)*; Melinda McGraw *(Cass Lake)*; Leslie Jones *(Sgt. Tina Bagley)*; Benjamin Ratner *(Sgt. Orono)*; Duncan Fraser *(Sgt.McMacDonald)*; John Walsh *(John Walsh)*; Maury Hannigan *(Commissioner Hannigan)*; Chick Hearn *(Basketball Announcer)*; Brian Arnold *(News Reporter)*; Guy Bews *(Security Guard #1)*; Mary Black *(Woman with IV)*; Michael Bolton *(TV Stage Manager)*; Jacques Bourassa *(Teenager With Backpack)*; Ken Boyd *(Usher)*; Alexander Boynton *(Security Guard #2)*; Johnathon Bruce *(Hospital Janitor)*; Rick Burgess *(Prisoner)*; Charn *(Bus Convict)*; Brian Cochrane *(Cop #1)*; Arthur Corber *(Percussionist)*; Rick Cross *(Ben Hur Oarsman)*; Cory Dagg *(Reporter #3)*; Alex Daikun *(Daikun)*; Rob Daprocida *(Security Guard #1)*; Thea Nielsen Disney *(Party Guest #2)*; Adrien Dorval *(Proctor)*; Mark Fox *(Butcher)*; Mark Francis *(Abe Lincoln)*; Christopher L. Gibson *(Paramedic)*; Calvin Guo *(Japanese Gardener)*; Michelle Hart *(Reporter #2)*; Ellie Harvie *(Ruth the News Anchor)*; Noah Heney *(Parking Attendant)*; Ingrid Henningsen *(Party Guest Out of Focus)*; Derek Hurst *(Patient with Liquid Ears)*; Maura Nielsen Kaplan *(Party Guest #1)*; Ellen Kennedy *(Bow in the Eye Musician)*; P.J. Lespance *(Yo-yo Double)*; Wallace Leung *(Conductor)*; Bev Martin *(Mary Lincoln)*; Mina E. Mina *(Arab Diplomat)*; Kanlayaporn Neelaphamorn *(Party Guest #3)*; Barbaree Earl Neilsen *(Fainting Pedestrian)*; Robin Nielsen; Jason Payn *(Wanted Poster Boy)*; Charles Paymer *(Paramedic #1)*; David Priestly *(Paramedic)*; Pat Proft *(Window Technician)*; Marco Roy *(Paramedic #2)*; Patty Sachs *(Waitress at Crash Site)*; Yoko Sakai *(Reporter #1)*; Veena Sood *(Nurse)*; Bill Tarling *(Bus Convict)*; Ingrid Tesch *(Reporter #4)*; Stephen Tibbetts *(Patient)*; French Tickner *(Doctor in ICU)*; Kenneth "Brother" Vils *(Detective Van Adir)*; Henry O. Watson *(Mayor)*

Wrongfully accused of murder, Leslie Nielsen goes on the run, stumbling and bumbling his way through this lame parodic pastiche of the Harrison Ford movies THE FUGITIVE (1993) and PATRIOT GAMES (1992).

Concertmaster Ryan Harrison (Leslie Nielsen), the "Lord of the Violin," begins an affair with his passionate patron Lauren Goodhue (Kelly LeBrock). Her husband, Hibbing Goodhue (Michael York), has a mysterious relationship with artist Cass Lake (Melinda McGraw). One night, Lauren summons Harrison to her home, where he finds Hibbing dead at the hand of a one-armed, one-legged, one-eyed man (Aaron Pearl). The killer escapes, and Harrison is convicted of the murder.

After his prison bus is hit by a train, Harrison goes on the lam, with US Marshall Fergus Falls (Richard Crenna) hot on his trail. Harrison seeks out Lake, who he believes hired the handicapped hit man. She denies his accusations, and they fall in love. Harrison infiltrates an artificial limb hospital seeking information to lead him to the one-armed, one-legged, one-eyed man. He learns that the killer is in league with Lauren: they are Irish terrorists out to assassinate the UN Secretary General (Gerald Plunkett). With Lake's help, Harrison foils the assassination attempt, and turns Lauren and the rest of the terrorists over to Falls.

Pat Proft cowrote the three NAKED GUN movies, in which the comedy derived from slapstick and wordplay, and he cowrote and produced the HOT SHOTS movies, which were more gag-oriented and parody-driven. WRONGFULLY ACCUSED is Proft's first directorial effort, and it appears his strategy was to split the difference between those two comedy styles. Unfortunately, the result is the least, rather than the best, of both worlds.

WRONGFULLY ACCUSED includes parodies of famous scenes from MISSION: IMPOSSIBLE (1996), NORTH BY NORTHWEST (1959), and A CLEAR AND PRESENT DANGER (1994)—to name but a few. The problem is that none of them are particularly clever. There are a *lot* of sight gags referencing various movies ranging from THE EMPIRE STRIKES BACK (1980) to FIELD OF DREAMS (1989) to ANACONDA (1997) (again, to name only a few), which elicit what amusement value they possess from their very absurdity. A sequence with TV criminal hunter John Walsh ("America's Most Wanted") in a bit lifted from THE USUAL SUSPECTS (1995) is the best one in the film.

The rest of WRONGFULLY ACCUSED's attempts to glean comedy from its PATRIOT GAMES/FUGITIVE story line are woeful. Tersely delivering hard-boiled double-talk that mangles just about everything Bogart ever said, Nielsen raises a smile as we remember how much funnier he was doing the same shtick in the NAKED GUN films. Most of the time he simply flails about, mugging and pratfalling. Crenna fares even worse with an awful aping of Tommy Lee Jones that is so unfunny it's amazing.

Along with JANE AUSTEN'S MAFIA! and BASEKETBALL, WRONGFULLY ACCUSED was one of a triumvirate of 1998 summer comedies that can trace their pedigree back to AIRPLANE! (1980). All three suffered at the box office, suggesting that too many people are going to the well too often to maintain this genre of movie comedy. *(Violence.)*— P.R.

d, Pat Proft; p, Pat Proft, James G. Robinsom, Bernd Eichinger; exec p, Robert L. Rosen, Martin Moskowicz, Robert Kulzer; assoc p, Martin Moszkowicz, Warren Carr, Elizabeth Wang-Lee, Sara Risher; co-p, Bobby Herbeck; w, Pat Proft; ph, Glen MacPherson; ed, James R. Symons; m, Bill Conti; prod d, Michael Bolton; art d, Sandy Cochrane; set d, Lin MacDonald; ch, Mairead O'Brien-Kent; sound, Rob Young; fx, Bill Schirmer, Tony Lazarowich, Lee Wilson; casting, Karen Rea; cos, Jori Woodman; makeup, L. Taylor Roberts; stunts, Guy Bews

Comedy **(PR: C MPAA: PG-13)**

XYZ

X-FILES, THE ★★★
(U.S., 1998) 121m Ten Thirteen Productions; 20th Century Fox ~ 20th Century Fox c

David Duchovny *(FBI Special Agent Fox Mulder)*; Gillian Anderson *(FBI Special Agent Dana Scully)*; Martin Landau *(Dr. Alvin Kurtzweil)*; Armin Mueller-Stahl *(Strughold)*; Mitch Pileggi *(FBI Assistant Director Walter Skinner)*; Terry O'Quinn *(Michaud)*; Blythe Danner *(Cassidy)*; William B. Davis *(The Cigarette-Smoking Man)*; John Neville *(The Well-Manicured Man)*; Jeffrey DeMunn *(Dr. Ben Brohnshweig)*; Glenne Headly *(Barmaid)*; Lucas Black *(Stevie)*; Dean Haglund *(Lone Gunman Ringo Langley)*; Tom Braidwood *(Lone Gunman Melvin Frohike)*; Bruce Harwood *(Lone Gunman John Byers)*; Chris Fennell *(Boy)*; Cody Newton *(Boy)*; Blake Stokes *(Boy)*; Don S. Williams *(Group Elder)*; George Murdock *(2nd Elder)*; Michael Shamus Wiles *(Black-Haired Man)*; Craig Davis *(Primitive)*; Carrick O'Quinn *(Primitive)*; Tom Woodruff Jr. *(Creature 2)*; Gregory B. Ballora *(Creature 2)*; T.W. King *(FBI Agent on Roof)*; Luis Beckford *(FBI Agent)*; Steve Rankin *(Field Agent)*; Gary Grubbs *(Fire Captain Cooles)*; Steven M. Gagnon *(Last Agent Out)*; Lawrence Joshua *(DC Cops)*; Glendon Rich *(DC Cops)*; Gunther Jensen *(Security Guard)*; Scott Smith *(Technician)*; Ian Ruskin *(The Well-Manicured Man's Valet)*; Paul Welterien *(Control Room Operator)*; Jack Traywick *(Young Naval Guard)*; Milton Johns *(British Valet)*; Paul Turpei *(Paramedic)*; Michael Krawic *(Paramedic)*; Larry Rippenkroeger *(Towncar Driver)*; Josh McLaglen *(Buzz Milhoe)*; Randy Hall *(Windbreakered Agent)*; T.C. Badalato *(Fireman)*; Amine Zary *(Tunisian)*

It took Gene Roddenberry 10 years to bring "Star Trek" to the big screen; Chris Carter, creator of the wildly successful Fox series "The X-Files," struck while the iron was hot, releasing THE X-FILES while the series was still in production, thus drawing fans at the peak of his series' popularity.

In rural Texas, a group of young boys accidentally discovers a strange black oil in an ancient cave; a government emergency team quickly arrives on the scene to quarantine the area. Days later, in Dallas, FBI agents Fox Mulder (David Duchovny) and Dana Scully (Gillian Anderson) are on the scene of the bombing of a federal building in which agents are killed. Formerly of the "X files," a branch of the Bureau that investigated unexplainable cases (often dealing with extraterrestrials or the paranormal), they have been reassigned to counter-terrorism following the shutdown of the X files. Hoping to avoid a Waco/Ruby Ridge media blitz, the FBI elects to offer up Mulder and Scully to a special investigatory hearing as scapegoats for the mishandled Dallas bombing. As their careers hang in the balance, Mulder is approached by a man, Dr. Alvin Kurtzweil (Martin Landau), who suggests that the bomb was planted by the government to destroy a lab that contained evidence of a biological weapon, "the black oil." Mulder and Scully head back to Texas to investigate, discovering a mysterious complex in the middle of the desert containing millions of bees. Putting two and two together, they surmise that the bees are being engineered as a delivery system for the government's biological weapon.

In Washington, the hearing is not going well. Threatened with yet another reassignment, Scully elects to resign; as Mulder begs her to reconsider, she is stung by one of the engineered bees, and collapses. Mulder's call to 911 is answered by conspiracy agents who abduct Scully and shoot Mulder, wounding but not killing him. After leaving the hospital, Mulder is visited by the Well-Manicured Man (John Neville); a member of the inner circle of international puppetmasters, he explains to Mulder that the black oil is extraterrestrial, a byproduct of the alien race that populated the Earth before man. However, the oil has mutated, and now uses those humans infected with it as hosts to gestate a new race of vicious aliens. The Well-Manicured Man gives Mulder the location where Scully is held—in Antarctica—and provides him with an experimental vaccine that they had been developing as a contingency. Mulder races to the location, discovering a vast underground annex housing thousands of frozen black oil victims, all harboring growing aliens. Mulder locates Scully and injects her with the vaccine, ridding her of the black oil; however, the aggressive vaccine travels through Scully's i.v. into the complex's systems, bringing it crashing down around them. Mulder and Scully escape just as the complex—actually a grounded spacecraft—lifts out of the ice and sails away. The agents return to Washington to tell their story to the hearing committee; faced with more questions than answers, the committee has no choice but to reopen the X files.

Though it has become common for television shows to make the leap to films, it's odd that "The X-Files" would do so while the series was still in production. One of the most common questions about THE X-FILES film was whether a moviegoer not familiar with the series could follow the intricate story line. The answer: yes . . . mostly. The basic premise—an international conspiracy to hide evidence of aliens—has become commonplace in movies and television. What's more, series creator Chris Carter deftly avoids the more complicated facets of Mulder and Scully's history (including Scully's own abduction). While a few characters' motivations (particularly the nameless Well-Manicured Man and Cigarette Smoking Man) probably seem confusing to the uninitiated, the screenplay for the film is really no more inexplicable than an average episode of the series.

If THE X-FILES occasionally reads like the TV show, it looks like . . . well, like a movie. Director Rob Bowman (a frequent contributor to the series) does everything in his power to make the feature film more than just a really big "X Files" episode. Cinematographer Ward Russell (DAYS OF THUNDER) frames scenes expertly, here closing in on Duchovny and Anderson so they tower, there placing them in the corner of the screen, dwarfed by the landscape. The special effects, though used sparingly, also demonstrate a vision—and budget—that would not have fit on a TV screen. (The sequence in which the bomb destroys the Dallas building is nothing short of stunning.) The addition of silver screen veterans like Martin Landau and Armin Mueller-Stahl also helps compensate for the somewhat dubious acting chops of the series regulars. The result is that most viewers did not feel they had just spent eight bucks on a television show—a good omen for Carter, who immediately expressed a desire to make more "X-Files" movies. Surprise, surprise. *(Violence, profanity.)*—B.T.

d, Rob Bowman; p, Chris Carter, Daniel Sackheim; exec p, Lata Ryan; assoc p, Mary Astadourian; co-p, Frank Spotnitz; w, Chris Carter (from a story by Chris Carter and Daniel Sackheim); ph, Ward T. Russell; ed, Stephen Mark; m, Mark Snow; prod d, Christopher Nowak; art d, Gregory Bolton, Hugo Santiago; set d, Jackie Carr; sound, Geoffrey Patterson (mixer); fx, Paul Lombardi; casting, Liberman/Hirschfeld; cos, Marlene Stewart; makeup, Greg Nelson; stunts, Tim Davison

Science Fiction/Action **(PR: C MPAA: PG-13)**

YES MADAM II
(SEE: ROYAL WARRIORS)

YIGE HAO REN
(SEE: MR. NICE GUY)

YINGXIONG WULEI
(SEE: HEROES SHED NO TEARS)

YOU DON'T KNOW WHAT LOVE IS
(SEE: HEAVEN'S BURNING)

YOUNG HERCULES ★★★
(U.S., 1998) 93m Renaissance Pictures ~ Universal Home Video c

Ian Bohen *(Young Hercules)*; Dean O'Gorman *(Young Iolaus)*; Chris Conrad *(Young Jason)*; Johna Stewart *(Yvenna)*; Kevin Smith *(Ares)*; Meighan Desmond *(Discord)*; Nathaniel Less *(Cheiron)*; Rachel Blakely *(Alcmene)*; King Aeson *(Mike McGee)*

A spin-off from the popular TV show "Hercules: The Legendary Journeys," which is also coexecutive produced by Sam Raimi, YOUNG HERCULES is an enjoyable video prequel to the series that features the same type of imaginative special effects, robust action sequences, and tongue-in-cheek humor.

Trying to impress his father Zeus, 18-year-old half human-half god Hercules (Ian Bohen) is always getting into trouble and is sent by his human mother (Rachel Blakely) to a fighting academy. At the academy, Hercules is reluctantly partnered with a petty thief named Iolaus (Dean O'Gorman), and he also befriends Jason (Chris Conrad), who's the son of King Aeson of Corinth, and a girl cadet named Yvenna (Johna Stewart). Hercules's evil half-brother Ares (Kevin Smith) poses as King Aeson's long-lost brother and plots to become king by making Aeson seriously ill. When Jason learns that his father is dying, he goes home, joined by Iolaus and Hercules. During their journey, they repel an attack on their lives, and when they reach the palace, they're told by Ares that the only thing that can save Aeson is the Golden Fleece.

Jason, Hercules, and Iolaus set out to find the Fleece, accompanied by Yvenna and some other cadets. During the trip, they encounter a deadly Siren—who's actually Hercules's evil half-sister Discord (Meighan Desmond)—and defeat her attempt to have them kill each other. They eventually find the Fleece and slay a giant who's protecting it, but Yvenna is killed during the battle. Back at the palace, Jason cures his father with the Fleece, but Ares then kills Aeson and stabs Jason. Hercules and Ares fight each other and Hercules temporarily vanquishes Ares. The wounded Jason is saved by the Golden Fleece and becomes the new king, and Hercules and Iolaus set off for new adventures.

YOUNG HERCULES is simply a juvenile version of the weekly syndicated TV series starring Kevin Sorbo as the grown Hercules, offering the same exact New Zealand locations and mixture of amusing special effects (a huge, slithering snake; a giant with dagger-like teeth; a half man-half horse; hallucinations brought on by the siren), energetic stunts (a cyclone scene with Herc and Iolaus twisting in the air; a terrific battle on the beach against marauders riding chariots with spiked wheels; the final Kung Fu-like fight between Herc and Ares while standing on top of burning poles), and campy, anachronistic dialogue ("let's get ready to rumble, little brother") spoken by a cast of Valley Dudes and Dudettes. Director T.J. Scott's music-video style technique becomes annoying and excessive (replete with slow-mo, strobe lighting, jittery camerawork, and step-printing), but the pace never slows down and the action scenes are exciting and well-staged. Sam Raimi's visual influence is evident in the frenetic comic-book compositions and the Ray Harryhausen-like effects, featuring lots of skeletons and rotting skulls. The whole thing is pure Saturday matinee fantasy fodder, and a teenage boy's wet dream, filled with plentiful sword fights and buxom young damsels. Taken on that level, it's quite entertaining. *(Violence.)*—M.S.

d, T.J. Scott; p, Liz Friedman, Eric Gruendemann; exec p, Sam Raimi, Robert Tapert; co-p, Bernadette Joyce; w, Andrew Dettmann, Daniel Truly (based on a story by Robert Tapert, Andrew Dettmann, and Daniel Truly); ph, John Mahaffie; ed, Steve Polivka; m, Joseph LoDuca; prod d, Robert Gillies; fx, Kevin O'Neill; casting, Beth Hymson-Ayer, Marie Adams; cos, Ngila Dickson; makeup, Annie Single

Action/Fantasy **(PR: C MPAA: PG-13)**

YOUR FRIENDS & NEIGHBORS ★★★½
(U.S., 1998) 100m Polygram; Propaganda Films; Fleece ~ Gramercy Pictures c

Amy Brenneman *(Mary)*; Aaron Eckhart *(Barry)*; Catherine Keener *(Terri)*; Nastassja Kinski *(Cheri)*; Jason Patric *(Cary)*; Ben Stiller *(Jerry)*; Lola Glaudini; Joshua Dotson

A dark comedy of manners, YOUR FRIENDS & NEIGHBORS portrays contemporary gender relations with razor-sharp insight. Director Neil LaBute's follow-up to IN THE COMPANY OF MEN (1997) turns bourgeois social ills into tragic farce.

Trouble starts for two urban, middle-class couples after a dinner party when Jerry (Ben Stiller), a flirtatious theater instructor, secretly makes a pass at Mary (Amy Brenneman), a writer and the wife of his best friend, Barry (Aaron Eckhart), an executive. Feeling unfulfilled in her marriage, Mary accepts the date to meet Jerry later at a hotel. Meanwhile, Terri (Catherine Keener), Jerry's equally unfulfilled wife, who is also a writer, meets Cheri (Nastassja Kinski), an art gallery worker, and begins an affair with her.

Jerry and Mary's rendezvous becomes a disaster when Jerry fails to get aroused during foreplay. Mary abruptly ends the "affair" and feels even more miserable when Barry unwittingly takes her to the same hotel room to rekindle *their* romance. Barry fails to understand Mary's attitude until Cary (Jason Patric), a mutual friend and a caddish doctor, forces Jerry to tell Barry about his would-be tryst during a verbal mind game in a gym steamroom. Later, Barry confronts Mary over dinner just as Terri accidentally finds out about Jerry's indiscretion and eventually confronts him, too.

Both couples subsequently split up: Terri moves in with Cheri, although she finds her annoyingly needy; Jerry continues philandering with his young students; and Mary moves in with Cary, leaving Barry miserable with himself. Sometime later, Mary expects to have a baby but she feels just as unhappy in her new relationship as her old one.

With a spare narrative and a small handful of characters, LaBute creates a modern-day combination of RULES OF THE GAME (1939) and *Les Liaisons Dangereuses.* LaBute also refers directly to the plays of William Wycherley, including *The Country Wife* and *The Plain Dealer*, and draws on Arthur Schnitzler's play, *Reigen*, Ingmar Bergman's TV-film, SCENES FROM A MARRIAGE (1973), Mike Nichols's CARNAL KNOWLEDGE (1971), the plays of David Mamet, and some of the novels of John Updike and John Cheever. By using smart verbal badinage within a series of studied tableaux (foreshadowed in Alex Katz's title portrait art), LaBute expertly captures the clumsy, contentious communication between the sexes and illustrates how minute behavior packs powerful meaning.

The actors brilliantly flesh out the somewhat sketchy parts, leaving lasting impressions: Jason Patric (who also coproduced) stands out playing a predatory pediatrician who delivers a chilling soliloquy about his best sexual experience—raping a high school classmate. Ben Stiller adds a new dimension to his screen persona by playing a charming but essentially loathsome scoundrel. Aaron Eckhart (the villain of IN THE COMPANY OF MEN) changes his image (adding a paunch to his waistline) to portray the sad-sack Barry. Amy Brenneman draws some sympathy out of the pathetic Mary. And Catherine Keener sizzles as the weary, sarcastic Terri.

Still, at points, LaBute appears to be struggling to find his form. A few plot lines go nowhere (e.g., Mary's stint writing an article on couples), and some sequences are less realistic than others (the characters too often shout about—or even act out—their secret affairs in public places). The two structural allusions to *Reigen* (filmed by Max Ophuls in 1950 as LA RONDE) also fail because one, involving a bracelet being passed around, is underutilized, and the other, a series of attempted pick-ups of the Nastassja Kinski character, is overdone.

Finally, it also must be asked why Kinski, the only weak link among the actors here, keeps getting good parts in interesting films. Minor frustrations aside, YOUR FRIENDS & NEIGHBORS represents fine work that will prompt heated debate—hopefully with happier results for the off-screen audience than the onscreen characters. *(Nudity, sexual situations, adult situations, extreme profanity.)*—E.M.

d, Neil LaBute; p, Steve Golin, Jason Patric; exec p, Alix Madigan-Yorkin, Stephen Pevner; co-p, Philip Steuer; w, Neil LaBute (based on the play *Lepers*); ph, Nancy Schreiber; ed, Joel Plotch; prod d, Charles Breen; set d, Jeffrey Kushon; sound, Felipe Borrero (mixer); casting, Mali Finn; cos, April Napier; makeup, Desne Holland

Drama/Comedy (PR: O MPAA: R)

YOU'VE GOT MAIL ★★½

(U.S., 1998) 118m Shuler Donner/Donner Productions; Warner Bros.; Lauren Shuler Donner Production ~ Warner Bros. c

Tom Hanks *(Joe Fox)*; Meg Ryan *(Kathleen Kelly)*; Greg Kinnear *(Frank Navasky)*; Parker Posey *(Patricia Eden)*; Jean Stapleton *(Birdie)*; Steve Zahn *(George Pappas)*; David Chappelle *(Kevin Scanlon)*; Dabney Coleman *(Nelson Fox)*; John Randolph *(Schuyler Fox)*; Heather Burns *(Christina)*; Deborah Rush *(Veronica Grant)*; Hallee Hirsh *(Annabel Fox)*; Jeffrey Scaperrotta *(Matt Fox)*; Cara Seymour *(Gillian, Nelson's fiancee)*; Katie Finneran *(Maureen, the Nanny)*; Michael Badalucco *(Charlie, Lift Attendant)*; Veanne Cox *(Miranda Magulies, Children's Author)*; Sara Ramirez *(Rose, Zabar's Cashier)*; Howard Spiegel *(Henry, Irate Zabars Shopper)*; Diane Sokolow *(Zabars Shopper)*; Julie Kaas *(Zabars Shopper)*; Reiko Aylesworth *(Thanksgiving Guest)*; Katie Sagona *(Young Kathleen Kelly)*; Kathryn Maisle *(Cecilia Kelly)*; Nina Zoie Lam *(Sidne Anne, TV Reporter)*; Maggie Murphy *(Theatre Patron)*; Michelle Blakely; Meredith White; Dianne Dreyer; Julie Galdieri; Leila Nichols *(Shoppers)*; Mary Kelly *(Fox Books Shopper)*; Chris Messina *(Fox Salesperson)*; Ronobir Lahiri *(Man at Cafe Lalo)*; Andre Sogliuzzo *(Waiter at Cafe Lalo)*; Peter A. Mian *(Capeman at Starbucks)*; Richard Cohen *(Starbucks Customer)*; Enzo Angileri *(Starbucks Customer)*; Nick Brown *(Juggler)*; Ann Fleuchaus *(Sarah Mancini)*; Neil Bonin *(Party Guest)*; Bill McHugh *(Party Guest)*; Santiago Quinones *(Decorator)*; Lynn Grossman *(Yvette Fox)*; Dolores Sirianni *(Mother of Twins)*; Nicole Bernadette *(Florist)*; Bonnie *(Brinkley the Dog)*; Clovis *(Brinkley the Dog)*; Lucy *(Dog in Elevator)*

The superficially charming YOU'VE GOT MAIL neatly updates THE SHOP AROUND THE CORNER (1940) for the Internet age, reducing the Ernst Lubitsch classic to sitcom dimensions.

In current-day Manhattan, Kathleen Kelly (Meg Ryan) runs "The Shop Around the Corner," an Upper West Side children's book shop founded by her late mother. Kathleen's independence and livelihood are threatened by a mega-book store chain, Fox Books, whose owners plan to build one of their discount superstores on the same block. Little does Kathleen know that she has been carrying on an e-mail flirtation with the heir of the chain, Joe Fox (Tom Hanks), a man she despises in person, but only knows as "NY152" on the Internet.

For his part, Joe remains equally unaware that Kathleen, the rival he is trying to put out of business, is the same "Shopgirl" he met in a chatroom on his computer. The pen-pals refrain from meeting each other, because both are involved with other people: Kathleen with Frank Navasky (Greg Kinnear), a journalist, and Joe with Patricia (Parker Posey), a book editor. Through the encouragement of her Internet friend, Kathleen decides to protest the Fox Books chain, using Frank to write critical articles.

"NY152" and "Shopgirl" finally decide to meet at a restaurant, but when Joe sees that his dream woman is none other than Kathleen, he greets her as himself and doesn't reveal his online identity. They wind up getting into an argument and Joe leaves, but he soon acknowledges to himself that he loves Kathleen and spends his days trying to befriend her, while subtlely undermining her affection for her phantom Internet mate. At the same time, both Joe and Kathleen also break up with their respective partners, Patricia and Frank. Kathleen slowly warms to Joe, despite the fact that he indeed puts her out of business. Joe finally sets up a meeting between Kathleen and "NY152," where she confesses to Joe that she was hoping all along that he was the man of her cyberdreams.

Regrouping the team that had made SLEEPLESS IN SEATTLE (1993) a hit, YOU'VE GOT MAIL cheerfully glosses THE SHOP AROUND THE CORNER retaining the basic premise of two people who dislike each other in person, but anonymously carry on a pen-pal romance (this time via e-mail). Some of the changes actually improve upon the original (and subsequent musical remakes, IN THE GOOD OLD SUMMERTIME [1949] and *She Loves Me* [1963]); taking a leaf from the Doris Day-Rock Hudson sex comedies of the 1960s, director Nora Ephron (cowriting with her sister, producer Delia Ephron) cleverly turn the protagonists from feuding coworkers to professional rivals with competing businesses. And New York City makes the perfect new setting for this bouncy battle-of-the-sexes.

But the bright, slickly packaged film misses the crucial qualities that had made THE SHOP AROUND THE CORNER a haunting tragicomedy about a bygone era and people (of old Budapest). More like an episode of "Friends," YOU'VE GOT MAIL emphasizes the lighter side of the lonelyheart protagonists' lives, eliminating entirely the touching details of their coworkers lives (played here by Jean Stapleton, Steve Zahn, Heather Burns, and David Chappelle in underwritten roles). Leads Tom Hanks and Meg Ryan make an overly cute pair (he's gruff to her plucky), but at no time do they show the range of either Jimmy Stewart or Margaret Sullavan, the originals.

The other defects are symptomatic of 1990s Big Studio releases. Although the production quality is quite competent, there is nothing particularly artful about the staging, design, or cinematography of Ephron's film. The decision to quash the independent Kelly (while she falls for her enemy) too happily validates the triumph of both patriarchy and vertical integration (this is the most sexist version of the tale, despite the presence of the female writer-director-producer combo). And the commercial plugs—from IBM laptops to American Online to Starbucks

Coffee to Visa credit cards to Warner Bros. rerelease of THE WIZARD OF OZ (1939) ("Over the Rainbow" closes this WB film)—reinforce the greedy capitalist themes, undercutting any hope that the filmmakers might have maintained some independence for themselves. *(Profanity.)*—E.M.

d, Nora Ephron; p, Lauren Shuler-Donner, Nora Ephron; exec p, Julie Durk, Delia Ephron, G. Mac Brown; w, Nora Ephron, Delia Ephron (based on the play *Parfumerie* by Miklos Laszlo); ph, John Lindley; ed, Richard Marks; m, George Fenton; prod d, Dan Davis; art d, Ray Kluga; set d, Ellen Christiansen; sound, Christopher Newman; casting, Francine Maisler; cos, Albert Wolsky

Romance/Comedy/Drama **(PR: A MPAA: PG)**

ZAKIR AND HIS FRIENDS ★★½

(Switzerland/Germany, 1997) 90m Interartes Mediengestaltung Filmproduktion; Horizonte Film; Swiss Films c

Zakir Hussain; Les Freres Coulibali; George Brooks; Renegades; Koko; Suar Agung; Boys and Girls of Cahauo

ZAKIR AND HIS FRIENDS takes viewers on a world music tour with Indian-born percussionist, Zakir Hussain. While the music is great, the movie is surprisingly prosaic.

Zakir Hussain talks about his youth and musical influences before embarking on travels through many lands, where we see him perform with native musicians and learn about the origin of music of different places. The film follows Zakir from San Francisco to India to Japan to Venezuela to Trinidad to Burkina Faso to Bali. In Bali, Zakir's last stop, the musicians pay special tribute to their visiting colleague.

Swiss director Lutz Leonhardt honors "global music" by eschewing narrative and loosely tieing together the various segments with Zakir Hussain's touring program. Fortunately, Zakir merits his "starring role"; he is a pleasant personality and a talented musician (who perfected his tabla-playing with the help of Ali Akbar Khan, Ravi Shankar, the Grateful Dead's Mickey Hart, jazz guitarist John McLaughlin, and his own father, legendary percussionist Alla Rakha).

But Hussain is also dangerously close to becoming a trendy celebrity (like "new age" musician Yanni) and some of his music is blandly benign. Thus, the best musical portions of the film exclude Hussain, instead featuring everyday people (e.g., Venezuelan children slapping their palms against their puffed cheeks). Other highlights show how rhythm emerges from daily work and play (e.g., the thrashing of clothes against stone, or food being crushed by a wooden mortar).

The sad fact is that Leonhardt lacks the skills to articulate his "rhythm experience" (the film's subtitle). The sequences showing the daily creation of rhythm recalls the great opening of Rouben Mamoulian's LOVE ME TONIGHT (1932), but in no scene in the film does Leonhardt edit to these rhythms in an effective way. ZAKIR AND HIS FRIENDS also patterns itself after BARROCCO (1989), another travelogue-music anthology sans narrative, but one that emphasized greater cultural awareness and visual flair. If anything, Leonhardt's ethnographic framing is too reminiscent of John Fitzpatrick's "Traveltalks" of the 1930s and Irving Penn's arty but racially insensitive photographs of the 1960s. ZAKIR AND HIS FRIENDS contains pleasant moments, but it also inadvertently reveals a troubling subtext.—E.M.

d, Lutz Leonhardt; p, Lutz Leonhardt, Klaus Armbruster; exec p, Lutz Leonhardt; co-p, Klaus Armbruster; w, Lutz Leonhardt; ph, Felix von Muralt; ed, Claudia Gleisner; m, Zakir Hussain, Ali Akbar Khan, Ravi Shankar, Mickey Hart, John McLaughlin; sound, Hans Castrop, Thomas Guthoff

Documentary **(PR: A MPAA: NR)**

ZAPOMENUTE SVETLO

(SEE: FORGOTTEN LIGHT)

ZERO EFFECT ★★½

(U.S., 1998) 115m Manifest Film Co.; Castle Rock Entertainment ~ Columbia c

Bill Pullman *(Daryl Zero)*; Ben Stiller *(Steve Arlo)*; Ryan O'Neal *(Gregory Stark)*; Kim Dickens *(Gloria Sullivan)*; Angela Featherstone *(Jess)*; Hugh Ross *(Bill)*; Sara Devincentis *(Daisy)*; Matt O'Toole *(Kragen Vincent)*; Michele Mariana *(Maid)*; Robert Katims *(Gerald Auerbach)*; Tyrone Henry *(Staffer #1)*; Aleta Barthell *(Staffer #2)*; Tapp Watkins *(Firefighter)*; Wendy Westerwelle *(Motel Clerk)*; Lauren Hasson *(Little Kid)*; Daniel Pershing *(Rahim)*; David Doty *(Officer Hagans)*; J.W. Crawford *(Convention Employee)*; Fred Parnes *(Chuck)*; Luisa Sermol *(Waitress)*; Marvin L. Sanders *(Astronomer #1)*; Doug Baldwin *(Astronomer #2)*; Robert Blanche *(Paramedic #1)*; Margot Demeter *(Clarissa Devereau)*

ZERO EFFECT, the filmmaking debut of writer-director Jake (son of Lawrence) Kasdan, is a comedy-mystery about a Sherlock Holmes/Nero Wolfe-style detective in which the twist is that the super sleuth is also a total wacko. It's a moderately entertaining effort that never lives up to the comic potential of its premise.

Daryl Zero (Bill Pullman) is the world's greatest and most eccentric private investigator. A nutty recluse, he regularly solves cases without ever having to leave his penthouse vault. His begrudging sidekick is Steve Arlo (Ben Stiller), who does the legwork and serves as go-between with the clients.

Gregory Stark (Ryan O'Neal), an Oregon timber baron who lost his key to a safe deposit box and is now being blackmailed over its contents, hires Zero to discover the extortionist's identity. Zero quickly surmises from available information about Stark that the situation has to do with a dark secret from Stark's past and a mysterious "K.V." Zero makes one of his rare journeys outside to go to Portland and, incognito, meets Stark in a gym and quickly sizes him up as a liar and cretin. There, he also makes the acquaintance of paramedic Gloria Sullivan (Kim Dickens). Zero follows Stark on a money drop and identifies Sullivan as the blackmailer. He decides to dig deeper before reporting to Stark.

Posing as an accountant, Zero does Sullivan's taxes, and takes the opportunity to search her apartment. He has Arlo keep Stark busy while he searches the businessman's office, and finds the missing key under the sofa cushions—the blackmailer never had it after all. Stark offers Arlo $5 million to betray Zero's law-abiding philosophy and kill the blackmailer, but Arlo steadfastly refuses.

Zero's investigation reveals that Sullivan is Stark's illegitimate daughter. Her mother was a woman he had raped in college whom Stark later had killed when she threatened to expose and ruin him. Sullivan is blackmailing him with evidence by Kragen Vincent—"K.V."—the killer Stark hired to murder her mother. At the final drop, Stark has a heart attack and Sullivan saves his life. Zero sees it all. He returns the key to the safe deposit box and its incriminating contents to Stark. Then he nobly helps Sullivan escape the country with the blackmail money. The case now closed, Arlo quits to get married.

Before we ever meet Daryl Zero, we're offered two portraits of him, courtesy of Arlo. To Stark, he describes his boss with deep admiration as an amazing, though unusual, genius. Venting in a bar, Arlo paints Zero detestably as a tyrannical psychopath.

When we meet Zero, he's an unkempt and paranoid hermit, a la Howard Hughes. Thus, the movie takes a decisive turn away from the Holmes/Wolfe bachelor-detective archetype (the connection to Rex Stout's sleuth is underscored not only by the nature of the two protagonists, but by their names, which mirror those of Nero Wolfe and his partner, Archie Goodwin).

The major problem is that Zero goes from being crazy to merely quirky far too fast. Pullman gives a nice comic performance, but this social misfit is able to fit in and flirt at the gym too easily; his burgeoning romance should be much more comically problematic. The mystery is interesting, and while its broad outline (Sullivan is Stark's child), won't surprise anyone, the details get filled in with entertaining invention.

The best parts of the movie are those pairing Zero and Arlo, played by Stiller in a perpetual state of slow-burning indignation. But there aren't enough of them. Kasdan holds back on exploring their twisted symbiosis, as if this was intended as the first installment in a series. Given that ZERO EFFECT had almost zero effect at the box office, that possibility seems very unlikely. *(Profanity, sexual situations.)*—P.R.

d, Jake Kasdan; p, Lisa Henson, Janet Yang, Jake Kasdan; exec p, Jim Behnke; co-p, Naomi Despres; w, Jake Kasdan; ph, Bill Pope; ed, Tara Timpone; m, The Greyboy Allstars; prod d, Gary Frutkoff; art d, Philip J. Messina; set d, Maggie Martin; sound, Glenn Berkovitz (mixer); fx, Bob Riggs; casting, Mary Vernieu; cos, Kym Barrett; makeup, John Caglione Jr.; stunts, Diamond Farnsworth

Mystery/Comedy **(PR: C MPAA: R)**

ZERO WOMAN ★★

(Japan, 1995) 84m Toru Shinohara; Gaga Communications; Vision Sugimoto ~ Tokoyo Shock c

Natsuki Ozawa *(Zero Woman)*; Saori Iwama *(Kyosuke Kishima)*; Kane Kosugi *(Ken)*; Hiroyuki Watari; Tomomi Miyauch; Hiromitsu Kiho; Minoru Toyoshima; Yoshitaka Yanagida; Mitsuhiro Matsumoto; Seitaro Fujii; Shigeki Kato; Yukio Yamato; Jiro Dan; Takanori Kikuchi; Tokuma Nishioka

An exploitative made-for-video Japanese crime thriller about an undercover female cop searching for stolen stock certificates, ZERO WOMAN is in actuality little more than a showcase for an attractive Japanese centerfold model-cum-starlet.

Zero Woman, a female undercover cop in Tokyo, is assigned to recover an attache case containing stock certificates which was stolen by a trio of young hoodlums from a member of the Diet (Japanese parliament). Her partner is Kyosuke Kishima (Saori Iwama), with whom she has a brief affair. They track the thieves to a female psychic, Ann, who is the sister of Ken (Kane Kosugi), one of the thieves. Unbeknownst to Zero, Kishima is actually behind the theft of the stocks and plans to sell them to industrialist/crime boss Kosei and use the proceeds to flee the country with Ann, his girlfriend.

Kishima gets the stocks from Ken's partner Ryu and kills Ryu. Kosei has Ann kidnapped to force Kishima to turn over the stocks. Zero and Ken locate the warehouse where Ann is being held and the two of them battle Kosei's men in order to free Ann. As the battle ends and Kosei and his men are killed, Kishima appears and shoots both Ann and Ken. He reveals to Zero that he's suffering from lung cancer and will soon be dead. A coughing fit enables the policewoman to retrieve a gun and shoot and kill Kishima.

With its emphasis on a slender young woman with a penchant for gunplay, ZERO WOMAN comes across as a deliberate knock-off of LA FEMME NIKITA (1990) and its Hong Kong variation, BLACK CAT (1991), as well as numerous other Hong Kong girls-with-guns thrillers of the early 1990s. While the star of ZERO WOMAN, Natsuki Ozawa, is arguably more beautiful than some of her predecessors, the film lacks the high-octane action sequences of its HK counterparts (replaced here by greater doses of sex) and suffers from a poorly conceived plot, haphazard editing, and unremarkable visuals (the film is shot in a video process that boasts a film-like texture). Ozawa, however, poses well, looks great in (and out of) mini-dresses, and has attitude to spare, particularly when she utters her trademark line, "Do you believe in Heaven?" before shooting her victims in the head. *(Violence, nudity, sexual situations.)*—B.C.

d, Daisuke Gotoh; p, Shinsuke Yamazaki, Yoshinori Chiba; exec p, Hiroshi Yamaji, Hideo Sugimoto, John Sirabella (English Version); w, Chiaki Hashiba, Daisuke Gotoh (based on the novel by Toru Shinohara), Tokyo Rose (English Version); ph, Yoichi Shiga; ed, Natao Komatsu; m, Ryuji Murayama; art d, Seiki Kobayashi

Crime/Thriller **(PR: O MPAA: R)**

Academy Awards

ACADEMY AWARDS

71st AWARDS OF THE ACADEMY OF MOTION PICTURE ARTS AND SCIENCES
(Listings in italics indicate winners)

Best Picture
David Parfitt, Donna Gigliotti, Harvey Weinstein, Edward Zwick, Marc Norman, SHAKESPEARE IN LOVE
Alison Owen, Eric Fellner, Tim Bevan, ELIZABETH
Elda Ferri, Gianluigi Braschi, LIFE IS BEAUTIFUL
Steven Spielberg, Ian Bryce, Mark Gordon, Gary Levinsohn, SAVING PRIVATE RYAN
Robert Michael Geisler, John Roberdeau, Grant Hill, THE THIN RED LINE

Best Performance by an Actor in a Leading Role
Roberto Benigni, LIFE IS BEAUTIFUL
Tom Hanks, SAVING PRIVATE RYAN
Ian McKellen, GODS AND MONSTERS
Nick Nolte, AFFLICTION
Edward Norton, AMERICAN HISTORY X

Best Performance by an Actress in a Leading Role
Gwyneth Paltrow, SHAKESPEARE IN LOVE
Cate Blanchett, ELIZABETH
Fernanda Montenegro, CENTRAL STATION
Meryl Streep, ONE TRUE THING
Emily Watson, HILARY AND JACKIE

Best Performance by an Actor in a Supporting Role
James Coburn, AFFLICTION
Robert Duvall, A CIVIL ACTION
Ed Harris, THE TRUMAN SHOW
Geoffrey Rush, SHAKESPEARE IN LOVE
Billy Bob Thornton, A SIMPLE PLAN

Best Performance by an Actress in a Supporting Role
Judi Dench, SHAKESPEARE IN LOVE
Kathy Bates, PRIMARY COLORS
Brenda Blethyn, LITTLE VOICE
Rachel Griffiths, HILARY AND JACKIE
Lynn Redgrave, GODS AND MONSTERS

Best Achievement in Directing
Steven Spielberg, SAVING PRIVATE RYAN
Roberto Benigni, LIFE IS BEAUTIFUL
John Madden, SHAKESPEARE IN LOVE
Terrence Malick, THE THIN RED LINE
Peter Weir, THE TRUMAN SHOW

Best Screenplay Written Directly for the Screen
Marc Norman, Tom Stoppard, SHAKESPEARE IN LOVE
Warren Beatty, Jeremy Pikser, BULWORTH
Vincenzo Cerami, Roberto Benigni, LIFE IS BEAUTIFUL
Robert Rodat, SAVING PRIVATE RYAN
Andrew Niccol, THE TRUMAN SHOW

Best Screenplay Based on Material Previously Produced or Published
Bill Condon, GODS AND MONSTERS
Scott Frank, OUT OF SIGHT
Elaine May, PRIMARY COLORS
Scott B. Smith, A SIMPLE PLAN
Terrence Malick, THE THIN RED LINE

Best Foreign Language Film
LIFE IS BEAUTIFUL (Italy)
CENTRAL STATION (Brazil)
CHILDREN OF HEAVEN (Iran)
THE GRANDFATHER (Spain)
TANGO (Argentina)

Best Achievement in Art Direction
Martin Childs, Jill Quertier, SHAKESPEARE IN LOVE
John Myhre, Peter Howitt, ELIZABETH
Jeannine Oppewall, Jay Hart, PLEASANTVILLE
Tom Sanders, Lisa Dean Kavanaugh, SAVING PRIVATE RYAN
Eugenio Zanetti, Cindy Carr, WHAT DREAMS MAY COME

Best Achievement in Cinematography
Janusz Kaminski, SAVING PRIVATE RYAN
Conrad L. Hall, A CIVIL ACTION
Remi Adefarasin, ELIZABETH
Richard Greatrex, SHAKESPEARE IN LOVE
John Toll, THE THIN RED LINE

Best Achievement in Costume Design
Sandy Powell, SHAKESPEARE IN LOVE
Colleen Atwood, BELOVED
Alexandra Byrne, ELIZABETH
Judianna Makovsky, PLEASANTVILLE
Sandy Powell, VELVET GOLDMINE

Best Achievement in Documentary Features
James Moll, Ken Lipper, THE LAST DAYS
Matthew Diamond, Jerry Kupfer, DANCEMAKER
Jonathan Stack, Liz Garbus, THE FARM: ANGOLA, U.S.A.
Robert B. Weide, LENNY BRUCE: SWEAR TO TELL THE TRUTH
Barbara Sonneborn, Janet Cole, REGRET TO INFORM

Best Achievement in Documentary Short Subjects
Keiko Ibi, THE PERSONALS: IMPROVISATIONS ON ROMANCE IN THE GOLDEN YEARS
Charles Guggenheim, A PLACE IN THE LAND
Shui-Bo Wang, Donald McWilliams, SUNRISE OVER TIANANMEN SQUARE

Best Achievement in Film Editing
Michael Kahn, SAVING PRIVATE RYAN
Simona Paggi, LIFE IS BEAUTIFUL
Anne V. Coates, OUT OF SIGHT
David Gamble, SHAKESPEARE IN LOVE,
Billy Weber, Leslie Jones, Saar Klein, THE THIN RED LINE

Best Achievement in Makeup
Jenny Shircore, ELIZABETH
Lois Burwell, Conor O'Sullivan, Daniel C. Striepeke, SAVING PRIVATE RYAN
Lisa Westcott, Veronica Brebner, SHAKESPEARE IN LOVE

Best Achievement in Music (Original Dramatic Score)
Nicola Piovani, LIFE IS BEAUTIFUL
David Hirschfelder, ELIZABETH
Randy Newman, PLEASANTVILLE
John Williams, SAVING PRIVATE RYAN
Hans Zimmer, THE THIN RED LINE

Best Achievement in Music (Original Musical or Comedy Score)
Stephen Warbeck, SHAKESPEARE IN LOVE
Randy Newman, A BUG'S LIFE
Matthew Wilder, David Zippel, Jerry Goldsmith, MULAN
Marc Shaiman, PATCH ADAMS
Stephen Schwartz, Hans Zimmer, THE PRINCE OF EGYPT

Best Achievement in Music (Original Song)
Stephen Schwartz, "When You Believe" THE PRINCE OF EGYPT
Diane Warren, "I Don't Want to Miss a Thing" ARMAGEDDON
Carole Bayer Sager, David Foster, Tony Renis, Alberto Testa, "The Prayer"
QUEST FOR CAMELOT
Allison Moorer, Gwil Owen, "A Soft Place to Fall" THE HORSE WHISPERER
Randy Newman, "That'll Do" BABE: PIG IN THE CITY

Best Achievement in Animated Short Films
Chris Wedge, BUNNY
Christopher Grace, Jonathan Myerson, THE CANTERBURY TALES
Mark Baker, JOLLY ROGER
Mark Osborne, Steve Kalafer, MORE
Karsten Kiilerich, Stefan Fjeldmark, WHEN LIFE DEPARTS

Best Achievement in Live Action Short Films
Kim Magnusson, Anders Thomas Jensen, ELECTION NIGHT (Valgaften)
Will Speck, Josh Gordon, CULTURE
Alexander Jovy, J.J. Keith, HOLIDAY ROMANCE
Vivian Goffette, LA CARTE POSTALE (The Postcard)
Simon Sandquist, Joel Bergvall, VICTOR

Best Achievement in Sound
Gary Rydstrom, Gary Summers, Andy Nelson, Ronald Judkins, SAVING PRIVATE RYAN
Kevin O'Connell, Greg P. Russell, Keith A. Wester, ARMAGEDDON
Kevin O'Connell, Greg P. Russell, Pud Cusack, THE MASK OF ZORRO
Robin O'Donoghue, Dominic Lester, Peter Glossop, SHAKESPEARE IN LOVE
Andy Nelson, Anna Behlmer, Paul Brincat, THE THIN RED LINE

Best Achievement in Sound Effects Editing
Gary Rydstrom, Richard Hymns, SAVING PRIVATE RYAN
George Watters II, ARMAGEDDON
David McMoyler, THE MASK OF ZORRO

Best Achievement in Visual Effects
Joel Hynek, Nicholas Brooks, Stuart Robertson, Kevin Mack, WHAT DREAMS MAY COME
Richard R. Hoover, Pat McClung, John Frazier, ARMAGEDDON
Rick Baker, Hoyt Yeatman, Allen Hall, Jim Mitchell, MIGHTY JOE YOUNG

Honorary Award
Elia Kazan

Irving G. Thalberg Memorial Award
Norman Jewison

Obituaries

OBITUARIES

(January 1 to December 31, 1998)

By Joe Frazzetta and Stephen Pell

Abbott, Philip

born: Philip Abbott Alexander, c. 1924, Lincoln, NE
died: Feb. 23, 1998, Los Angeles, CA, age 73
educ: Pasadena Junior College

Actor, known for playing solid, trustworthy characters.

After serving in WWII as a decorated bomber pilot, Philip Abbott established himself as an actor in New York, appearing on the stage and in prestigious television dramas. His Broadway debut was in the short-lived Harvest of Years (1948), but he later had success as a replacement in the hits The Detective Story (1949) and Two for the Seesaw (1958). He appeared in early teleplays on anthology series such as "The Philco Television Playhouse," "Studio One," and "The Armstrong Circle Theatre."

His movie career started with two 1957 releases. He was the groom-to-be in Paddy Chayefsky's THE BACHELOR PARTY and the scientist-father of the boy who becomes the victim of a computer robot gone berserk in THE INVISIBLE BOY. Other movies include SWEET BIRD OF YOUTH (1962), THE SPIRAL ROAD (1962), MIRACLE OF THE WHITE STALLIONS (1963), THOSE CALLOWAYS (1965), and HANGAR 18 (1980). In STARRY NIGHT, a film he completed before he died, Abbott appeared with his son, actor David Abbott Alexander.

Abbott was best known, however, for his television work. On the series, "The FBI," which ran from 1965 to 1974 on ABC, he was FBI assistant director Arthur Ward. He was also on two long-running soap operas: "General Hospital," as Dr. Alex Baker, and "Search for Tomorrow," as Dr. Dan Walton.

In addition to making several TV movies, Abbott was a frequent guest on a number of episodic dramas.

Active in California theater, Abbott was a co-founder of Theatre West and appeared in several of their productions.

Abbott died of cancer.

Addison, John

born: c. 1920, England
died: December 7, 1998, Bennington, VT, age 78

Composer of numerous film and television scores.

Beginning his career during WWII, John Addison earned popularity as a concert hall composer. At the end of the war, he began composing for film, eventually scoring more than 70 films, including REACH FOR THE SKY (1956), LOOK BACK IN ANGER (1959), THE ENTERTAINER (1960), TORN CURTAIN (1966), THE SEVEN PERCENT SOLUTION (1976), and A BRIDGE TOO FAR (1977). He received an Oscar nomination for SLEUTH (1972), and he won the Academy Award for TOM JONES (1963).

In addition to his film work during this period, he composed for many theatrical productions on London's West End. In 1976, Addison moved to the United States, where he wrote music for such television series as "Murder, She Wrote" and "Nero Wolfe," and for the made-for television production of PHANTOM OF THE OPERA (1990).

In addition to his scoring of films and television shows, Addison enjoyed a lengthy career as an orchestral conductor both in the United States and in England.

Addison died of a stroke at the Southern Vermont Medical Center in Bennington.

Aiken, Elaine

born: Elena Arizmendi, July 12, 1927, Cordoba, Spain
died: July 12, 1998, New York, NY, age 71

Actress and teacher.

After Elaine Aiken emigrated with her parents to New York from Spain at the time of the Spanish Civil War, she embarked on a stage career, becoming a pupil of famed acting teacher Lee Strasberg. Aiken joined the Actors Studio in 1954; in later years she would become a producer of Studio stage productions. She taught acting at the Lee Strasberg Theater Institute and was one of the founders of the Actors Conservatory, where she also taught.

The well-respected teacher found time to act on a few occasions. She appeared in New York and regional theater plays, and her films include the 1957 western THE LONELY MAN with Anthony Perkins and Jack Palance. She had a considerably less important part in the 1980 comedy CADDYSHACK.

Aiken died of cancer.

Algar, James

born: June 11, 1912, Modesto, CA
died: Feb. 26, 1998, Carmel, CA, age 85
educ: Stanford University, BA, MA (journalism)

Director, writer, producer, and animator who worked for 43 years at Walt Disney productions.

James Algar developed an interest in animation in college, working on the school's humor magazine. He joined the Walt Disney organization in 1934 and spent virtually his entire career there. He started as an animator on SNOW WHITE AND THE SEVEN DWARFS (1937) and then directed a segment ("The Sorcerer's Apprentice") of FANTASIA (1940), and sequences for BAMBI (1942). He was also involved in the training and morale films Disney made for the government during WWII, the most significant being the highly regarded VICTORY THROUGH AIR POWER (1942), for which Algar directed a sequence.

The enormous success of the Disney feature-length True-Life nature series was due, in large part, to Algar. He directed and contributed to the screenplays for THE LIVING DESERT (1953) and THE VANISHING PRAIRIE (1954), each of which won an Academy Award as Best Documentary Feature. Other successes in the series include THE AFRICAN LION (1955), SECRETS OF LIFE (1956), WHITE WILDERNESS (1958), and JUNGLE CAT (1960).

The versatile Algar occasionally produced or coproduced live-action Disney narrative movies, including THE INCREDIBLE JOURNEY (1963), THE GNOME-MOBILE (1967), and RASCAL (1969). Algar worked extensively on the TV series "The Wonderful World of Disney" and wrote and produced shows at Disneyland and Walt Disney World.

Algar died after a brief illness; no cause of death was reported.

Allen, Robert

aka: Robert "Tex" Allen, Bob Allen
born: Irvine E. Theodore Baehr, Mar. 28, 1906, Mt. Vernon, NY
died: Oct. 9, 1998, Oyster Bay, NY, age 92
educ: Dartmouth College

Actor, best known for a series of low-budget westerns in which he played "Texas Ranger Bob."

After graduating from college in 1929, Robert Allen went into banking, but the onset of the Depression forced him to seek work elsewhere. Allen tried other careers, including acting. He initially worked on the stage, and then moved into film.

Allen appeared in supporting roles in many films; he scored more prominent parts in low-budget westerns and programmers. Among his early films were LOVE ME FOREVER, CRIME AND PUNISHMENT (both 1935), and CRAIG'S WIFE (1936). His biggest success came when Columbia Pictures cast him in the Texas Ranger series. He played Bob Allen, Ranger in THE UNKNOWN RANGER (1936), RIO GRANDE RANGER, THE RANGER STEPS IN, RANGER COURAGE, LAW OF THE RANGER, and RECKLESS RANGER (all 1937). While he worked on these programmers in the mid-1930s, he also made several other films, including LET'S GET MARRIED, THE AWFUL TRUTH (both 1937), and UP THE RIVER (1938). He continued in films over the next several decades, mostly in small roles.

Returning to the stage, Allen was on Broadway in I Killed the Count (1942), Kiss Them for Me (1945), Show Boat (1946 revival), and Auntie

Mame (1956), among others. He also appeared in several television shows and commercials.

Allen died of cancer and a collapsed lung.

Alvarez, Santiago

born: Mar. 18, 1919, Havana, Cuba
died: May 20, 1998, Havana, Cuba, age 79

Prolific documentarian.

A supporter of the 1959 Cuban revolution, Santiago Alvarez chronicled many important events in the country's political life, including Fidel Castro's rise to power and his foreign tours. Alvarez also documented everyday life in Cuba in films like CICLON (1963), which showed the devastating results of Hurricane Flora.

In a career that spanned more than four decades, Alvarez made over 80 documentaries, including NOW (1965), a study of race problems in the United States, which was awarded the Golden Dove at the Leipzig DOK Festival. He was also honored by that same festival in 1997, at which he was given an honorary award in recognition of his service to the development of the documentary genre.

Alvarez, who was suffering from Parkinson's disease, died from a lung infection.

Ambler, Eric

born: June 28, 1909, London, England
died: Oct. 22, 1998, London, age 89
educ: London University

Spy novelist and screenwriter whose books were often adapted for movies and television.

After studying to be an engineer, Eric Ambler worked in advertising as a copywriter for six years. He then turned to fiction-writing, producing six acclaimed novels between 1936 and 1940. His books were critically praised for bringing realism and a gritty sense of atmosphere to the spy thriller.

His introduction to filmmaking was as a script consultant for producer Alexander Korda in 1938. Although Ambler later worked as a screenwriter, his early novels were adapted by others. The films produced from his books included the Orson Welles' production JOURNEY INTO FEAR (1942; remade in 1976), BACKGROUND TO DANGER (1943), THE MASK OF DIMITRIOS (1944), and HOTEL RESERVE (1946).

During WWII, Ambler served in the British War Office, working on training, morale, and propaganda films for the Army. After the war, he worked for the Rank Organization. His first produced screenplay was a collaboration with actor Peter Ustinov, THE IMMORTAL BATTALION (1944). Ambler also adapted his own THE OCTOBER MAN (1948), serving as producer for the film. His other screenwriting credits included HIGHLY DANGEROUS, THE CLOUDED YELLOW (both 1950), THE MAGIC BOX (1952), THE CRUEL SEA (1953; for which he received an Academy Award nomination), THE PURPLE PLAIN, LEASE OF LIFE (both 1954), BATTLE HELL (1957), A NIGHT TO REMEMBER (1958), and THE WRECK OF THE MARY DEARE (1959). His novel *The Light of Day* was filmed by Jules Dassin as the stylish TOPKAPI (1964).

In 1981, Ambler was made an Officer of the Order of the British Empire by Queen Elizabeth. He remained a prolific novelist and wrote about his life in *Here Lies: An Autobiography* (1985). The writer's second wife was Joan Harrison, a producer and screenwriter who often worked with Alfred Hitchcock. She died in 1994.

Ambler died after a long illness. No cause of death was reported.

Amory, Cleveland

born: Sept. 2, 1917, Nahant, MA
died: Oct. 14, 1998, New York, NY, age 81
educ: Harvard University

Writer and longtime animal-rights activist.

From a privileged background, Cleveland Amory began his public life as a newspaper reporter. He later became the youngest man to serve as editor of the *Saturday Evening Post.*

Amory was in the Army Intelligence during WWII. After the war was over, he began writing books that took a humorous look at society's foibles. One of the most popular was the massive *Who Killed Society?* Amory also wrote novels and books about animals, including a trio of best-sellers about cats.

The self-described curmudgeon was chief critic for *TV Guide* for thirteen years, until 1963. He wrote a column for *The Saturday Review*, was a contributing editor for *Parade Magazine*, and a radio essayist on "Curmudgeon at Large."

For television, Amory co-created a short-lived sitcom, "O. K. Crackerby!", starring Burl Ives, and for eleven years was a social commentator on the "Today" show. He acted in the film MR. NORTH (1988), playing the character of Mr. Danforth.

As the unpaid president of The Fund for Animals, which he founded, Amory was a significant figure in the animal-rights movement.

No cause of death was reported.

Anderson, Bill

aka: William H. Anderson
born: c. 1911, Smithfield, UT
died: Dec. 28, 1997, San Francisco, CA, age 86

Prolific producer of Disney features.

Bill Anderson worked for the Disney organization for more than four decades, starting in 1943. He served in several capacities at the studio, including production manager and vice president in charge of studio operations. In the early 1960s, Anderson became involved in several Disney television shows, including the "Zorro" series and "The Wonderful World of Disney."

After his initial stint as an associate producer on OLD YELLER (1957), Anderson produced or coproduced an impressive number of Disney films, including SWISS FAMILY ROBINSON, THE SIGN OF ZORRO (both 1960), MOON PILOT (1962), A TIGER WALKS, THE MOON-SPINNERS (both 1964), THE ADVENTURES OF BULLWHIP GRIFFIN, THE HAPPIEST MILLIONAIRE (both 1967), THE ONE AND ONLY, GENUINE ORIGINAL FAMILY BAND, SMITH! (both 1968), THE COMPUTER WORE TENNIS SHOES (1969), THE BAREFOOT EXECUTIVE, $1,000,000 DUCK (both 1971), SUPERDAD (1974), THE STRONGEST MAN IN THE WORLD, THE APPLE DUMPLING GANG (both 1975), and THE SHAGGY D.A. (1976).

Anderson retired in 1975, but remained on the board of directors for Walt Disney Productions until 1984.

Anderson died of a brain hemorrhage which resulted from a fall.

Apstein, Theodore

born: c. 1917, Kiev, Russia
died: July 26, 1998, Los Angeles, CA, age 80

Playwright, screenwriter, and playwriting instructor.

While writing for television, Theodore Apstein began his career as a playwright for the New York stage. His plays *The Innkeepers* (1956) and *Come Share My House* (1960) weren't hits; however, he was successful with a series of one-acts that were produced internationally. While continuing his work for television, Apstein wrote for films and later took up teaching.

Apstein was one of four screenwriters who collaborated on WITHOUT EACH OTHER (1962), a modest drama that was filmed in Florida and never released theatrically, although it was shown out of competition at the Cannes film festival. He scripted the successful thriller WHAT EVER HAPPENED TO AUNT ALICE? (1969) and wrote BLOOD LINK (1982).

His work in television included the TV movie BAFFLED! (1972) and scripts for numerous dramas, including "Studio One," "Dr. Kildare," "Marcus Welby, MD," and "The Waltons." As a longtime, well-respected teacher of playwriting and play analysis, Apstein taught at Columbia University, the American Theater Wing, and the University of California at Berkeley.

Apstein died of a stroke.

Asparagus, Fred

aka: Freddy Asparagus
born: Fred Reveles, c. 1946
died: June 29, 1998, Panorama City, CA, age 51

Character actor and comedian.

Fred Asparagus started acting in television dramas and sitcoms during the early 1980s, often cast as an Hispanic character. Among his credits are roles on "CHiPs," "Falcon Crest," "Wiseguy," "Hunter," "Cheers," and "Roseanne."

Films he appeared in include THIS IS SPINAL TAP (1984), THREE AMIGOS! (1986), FATAL BEAUTY (1987), COLORS (1988), HAVANA (1990), THE FIVE HEARTBEATS (1991), STEAL BIG, STEAL LITTLE (1995), SLAPPY AND THE STINKERS, and SELENA (both 1998).

Asparagus died of a heart attack.

Auerbach, Arnold

born: May 23, 1912, New York, NY
died: October 19, 1998, New York, NY, age 86

Comedy writer for radio, television, film, and theater.

Educated at Columbia University, Arnold Auerbach began his long career in comedy writing working for Fred Allen on his very popular radio show. He also served as gag-writer for such show business legends as Al Jolson, Frank Sinatra, and Milton Berle. Following this, Auerbach moved to Hollywood, where he was employed by Paramount, Warner Brothers, and MGM studios, providing gags and extra dialogue for numerous light comedies and musicals, such as LADY BE GOOD (1941). During WWII, Auerbach served in the army, where he wrote skits for Special Services shows. He later contributed sketches for Broadway revues, including *Call Me Mister, Inside U.S.A.,* and *Bless You All.*

Auerback also wrote for a number of television shows and, in 1955, won an Emmy Award for best comedy writing for the Phil Silvers show, "You'll Never Get Rich." He recounted his career in his autobiography, *Funny Men Don't Laugh.*

Auerbach was reported to have died from natural causes.

Autry, Gene

born: September 29, 1907, Tioga, TX
died: October 2, 1998, Studio City, CA, age 91

Legendary singing cowboy who wore numerous hats: during a lengthy career he was an actor, producer, songwriter, recording artist, and highly successful businessman.

Although Gene Autry's original ambition was professional baseball, he turned to show business not long after graduating high school. His earliest taste of success was on radio as "Oklahoma's Yodeling Cowboy." It was around this time that he began writing and recording his own songs, eventually totaling over 200. Among the most famous were "That Silver-Haired Daddy of Mine," "Tumbling Tumbleweeds," " Back in the Saddle Again," "Mexicali Rose," "Peter Cottontail," and "Here Comes Santa Claus." His recordings of "South of the Border" (not one of his own compositions) and "Rudolph the Red-Nosed Reindeer" became two of the top-selling records of all time.

Autry's film career began in 1931 with Ascott (later Republic) Studios, where he became a major cowboy star in rural and western America. Among the 56 films he made for Republic were IN OLD SANTA FE (1934), TUMBLING TUMBLEWEEDS (1935), THE SINGING COWBOY (1936) and SPRINGTIME IN THE ROCKIES (1937). After a contractual dispute with Republic, Autry went to make films at other studios. Among these were SHOOTING HIGH (1940) and SIOUX CITY SUE (1946).

During this period, he maintained an equally successful career as a radio and recording star. He also toured extensively. After service in the armed forces during WWII, he made numerous personal appearances for the USO. He accumulated a fortune from the combined incomes of his films, records, radio shows, tours, and product endorsements, augmented by the ownership of recording studios, music publishing houses, and a chain of movie houses.

With the growing popularity of television, Autry abandoned films and embarked on a new career as producer and star of his own TV series, "The Gene Autry Show." The series lasted from 1950 to 1956 and spawned several spinoffs, including "Annie Oakley." Autry's television empire also produced a children's series, "Buffalo Bill, Jr." and the hit "Death Valley Days."

Autry's business interests eventually came to include a baseball team (the California Angels), television and radio stations, a chain of hotels, and vast land holdings, making him one of Hollywood's wealthiest citizens. In 1988 he opened the Gene Autry Western Heritage Museum in Los Angeles' Griffith Park, which remains a popular tourist destination.

The exact cause of Autry's death was not reported; he had, however, been suffering from a long illness.

Babb, Dorothy

born: c. 1927, Amarillo, TX
died: May 13, 1998, Thousand Oaks, CA, age 71

Actress and dancer.

As a pre-teen, Dorothy Babb made an impressive debut in YOU CAN'T TAKE IT WITH YOU (1938), doing a lively swing dance with James Stewart. She went on to appear in small roles in such films as SCANDAL STREET (1938), THE STAR MAKER (1939), PLAYMATES (1941), and THE TALK OF THE TOWN (1942).

During the 1940s, Babb joined the Jivin' Jacks and Jills dance troupe, with whom she performed in low-budget, modest Universal musicals. Three of them were in support of the Andrews Sisters: WHAT'S COOKIN'?, GIVE OUT SISTERS (both 1942) and ALWAYS A BRIDESMAID (1943). Her other films include HOW ABOUT IT? (1943), EARL CARROLL SKETCHBOOK (1946) and WHEN MY BABY SMILES AT ME (1948).

Babb appeared onstage in the Los Angeles, New York, and Chicago companies of the revue *Lend an Ear* in the early 1950s. She retired from show business in 1959.

Babb died of complications resulting from heart surgery.

Barer, Marshall

born: Feb. 19, 1923, Astoria, NY
died: Aug. 25, 1998, Santa Fe, NM, age 75

Songwriter of considerable wit, well-known for his work on Broadway.

Marshall Barer started out as a successful graphic artist-illustrator for magazines. He entered show business by writing special material for night club performers and lyrics for popular songs.

Barer began writing for the theater in the 1950s. He collaborated on a series of revues, including *Walk Tall* (1954), *New Faces of 1956* (1956), and *Ziegfeld Follies* (1957). Barer was the lyricist for the 1959 Broadway hit *Once Upon a Mattress,* a musical version of *The Princess and The Pea* (Mary Rodgers supplied the music); the show made a star of Carol Burnett. Barer was less successful with some other musicals he worked on, including a collaboration with Duke Ellington on a stage version of the classic 1930 movie THE BLUE ANGEL, called *Pousse-Cafe* (1966).

For television, Barer's facile wit was shown to great advantage on several television shows, including the satirical "That Was the Week That Was." His *Once Upon a Mattress* was adapted for TV in 1964 and 1972, both times with Carol Burnett. With Ellington providing the music, Barer wrote the words to "I Want to Love You," used in the television version of "The Asphalt Jungle" (1961). His best-known composition for TV was the Mighty Mouse theme: "Here I Come to Save the Day" (which Barer claimed to have dashed off while riding in the back of a taxi cab).

Barer wrote song lyrics for the campy movie SCARECROW IN A GARDEN OF CUCUMBERS (1972), several of which were sung by Bette Midler. He also composed the song "Milly's On the Methadone," heard in NORMAN ... IS THAT YOU? (1976). In Henry Jaglom's VENICE/VENICE (1992), Barer played the part of Mark, a singer; the scene in which he auditions his song was filmed in Barer's Venice, California home.

A man of varied talents and interests, Barer operated an art gallery in Los Angeles and often performed his songs in a cabaret act.

Barer retired to New Mexico, where he died of cancer.

Barnes, Binnie

born: Gitelle Gertrude Maude Barnes, Mar. 25, 1903 or 1905, London, England
died: July 27, 1998, Beverly Hills, CA, age 93 or 95

Character actress with a unique style of delivering snappy dialogue.

In her native England, Binnie Barnes worked her way up through the ranks as a chorus girl, dance hostess, and vaudevillian before making her stage debut with Charles Laughton in *Silver Tassie* (1929). Shortly afterwards, she entered films, appearing in a series of comedy shorts with famed comedian Stanley Lupino.

Barnes appeared in more than a dozen features before playing Catherine Howard in Alexander Korda's THE PRIVATE LIFE OF HENRY VIII (1933). The popularity of that film led to more important roles in films like 1934's THE PRIVATE LIFE OF DON JUAN (Douglas Fairbanks's last movie) and a Hollywood career. Throughout her almost four decades of Hollywood moviemaking, Barnes was seldom cast as a leading lady. She was, however, in the top echelon of supporting players, bringing style, authority, and often wit to her characterizations. Some of her memorable roles include singer Lillian Russell in DIAMOND JIM (1935), the flighty Miriam in THREE BLIND MICE (1938), the exotic Nazama in THE ADVENTURES OF MARCO POLO (1938), the wicked Milady De Winter in THE THREE MUSKETEERS (1939), and pirate Anne Bonney in THE SPANISH MAIN (1945).

After more than 75 films, Barnes retired temporarily in the mid-1950s. She returned to the screen in Ida Lupino's THE TROUBLE WITH ANGELS (1966), playing Sister Celestine, a role she reprised for WHERE ANGELS GO, TROUBLE FOLLOWS (1968). In her final film, 40 CARATS (1973), she played Liv Ullmann's mother. That movie was produced by Barnes's husband, M. J. (Mike) Frankovich. Barnes had married Frankovich, a former UCLA football star, radio producer, and commentator, in 1940. He produced or coproduced several films in which she appeared, including DECAMERON NIGHTS (1953), and FIRE OVER AFRICA (1954). Frankovich, who was an executive at Columbia Pictures, died in 1992.

Barnes died of natural causes. There is some disagreement about the year of her birth; some sources list it as 1903, others as 1905.

Barnes, Walter

born: Jan. 26, 1918, Parkersburg, W VA
died: Jan. 6, 1998, Woodland Hills, CA, age 79
educ: Louisiana State University

Character actor who had the nickname "Piggy."

While in college, Walter Barnes studied drama and was a member of the football team. He eventually realized careers in both fields: he played professional football with the Philadelphia Eagles from 1948 to 1951, and became a movie actor in 1958 when he appeared in REVOLT IN THE BIG HOUSE and OREGON PASSAGE.

He appeared in several westerns and adventure movies, including WESTBOUND (1959), CAPTAIN SINBAD, (1963), FRONTIER HELLCAT, THE BIG GUNDOWN (both 1966), THE TRAVELING EXECUTIONER (1970), and the Clint Eastwood films HIGH PLAINS DRIFTER (1973), EVERY WHICH WAY BUT LOOSE (1978), and BRONCO BILLY (1980).

Among the many television shows in which Barnes appeared were "Mission Impossible," "The Dukes of Hazzard," "Bonanza," "Gunsmoke," "Zane Grey Theater," and "Walking Tall."

Barnes was hospitalized for several months before he died of complications from diabetes.

Barry, Jr, Philip

born: Aug. 8, 1923, New York, NY
died: May 16, 1998, New York, NY age 74
educ: Yale University

Producer and son of noted playwright Philip Barry.

Philip Barry Jr. started his show business career in 1946 as a production associate for the London mounting of his father's play *The Animal Kingdom*. Continuing in the theater, Barry worked in theater companies in New York, Connecticut, and Rochester.

In the early 1950s, Barry worked as a story editor in television. He soon became an associate producer and later a producer on such shows as "Center Stage," "The Alcoa Hour," and "The Goodyear Playhouse."

He produced two Hollywood films, the comedies THE MATING GAME (1959) and SAIL A CROOKED SHIP (1961), then returned exclusively to television.

Barry was involved in the production of a number of prestigious TV movies, including THE GLASS HOUSE (1972), THE AUTOBIOGRAPHY OF MISS JANE PITTMAN (1974), QUEEN OF THE STARDUST BALLROOM (1975), FIRST YOU CRY (1978), and FRIENDLY FIRE (1979), which won a Peabody Award and an Emmy Award.

Barry was a vice president of Tomorrow Entertainment, a board member of the American Film Institute, a board member of the Eugene O'Neill Theater Center, and a dramaturge at the National Playwrights Conference.

Barry died of cancer.

Bartok, Eva

born: Eva Ivanova Szoeke, June 18, 1926, Kecskemet, Hungary
died: Aug. 1, 1998, London, England, age 72

Hungarian actress who had a brief fling at international stardom.

As a teenager, Eva Bartok was coerced into marriage with a Nazi, a union that was later annulled. She was also interred in a concentration camp during WWII. Bartok entered films in her native Hungary in the late 1940s and quickly moved over to the British cinema, appearing briefly in MADELINE (1950) and most significantly in A TALE OF FIVE WOMEN (1951). Bartok's first American film, made in Europe, was the adventure-comedy THE CRIMSON PIRATE (1952), opposite Burt Lancaster. She continued as a leading lady in several British films, including SPACEWAYS, NORMAN CONQUEST, THE ASSASSIN (all 1953), THE BREAK IN THE CIRCLE (1955), and THE GAMMA PEOPLE (1956).

After a few more German and British films, Bartok appeared with Dean Martin in TEN THOUSAND BEDROOMS (1957). It was while Bartok was making this comedy in Hollywood that she met Frank Sinatra, with whom she claimed to have had a romantic liaison that produced a child. At the time, Bartok was wed to actor Curt Jurgens; they later divorced. The child, a daughter, was never acknowledged by Sinatra to be his.

Bartok's film career during the next ten years was in European movies. She left the industry in the late 1960s, opting to study religion and philosophy with the Pak Subuh sect in Indonesia.

No cause of death was reported, but Ms. Bartok had a history of heart trouble.

Beechman, Laurie

born: Apr. 4, 1954, Philadelphia, PA
died: Mar. 8, 1998, White Plains, NY, age 43
educ: New York University

Powerhouse singer best known for her work on the Broadway stage, the cabaret circuit, and recordings.

In 1977, Laurie Beechman was a supporting player in her first Broadway musical, *Annie*. Her breakthrough was as the Narrator in 1982's *Joseph and the Technicolor Dreamcoat.* She joined the cast of *Cats* in 1983, as Grizabella, and in 1989, toured as Fantine in *Les Miserables*. She sang "You'll Never Walk Alone" at President Clinton's 1997 inaugural gala.

Her only movie was HAIR (1979), in which she and a group of young women sing "Black Boys."

Beechman died of complications from ovarian cancer.

Behn, Noel

born: Jan. 6, 1928, Chicago, IL
died: July 27, 1998, New York, NY, age 70
educ: Stanford Univ. (BA, 1950)

Raconteur and popular New York show business figure.

Noel Behn was a pioneer in the early days of off-Broadway, producing important works by Samuel Beckett and Sean O'Casey. Behn was also a novelist, wrote for television, and appeared in several films.

Behn's first novel, the best-selling thriller *The Kremlin Letter*, was the basis for the 1970 movie of the same name, directed by John Huston. THE BRINK'S JOB (1978) was adapted from Behn's *The Big Stick-Up at Brinks.* Woody Allen cast his friend Behn in small parts in the films STARDUST MEMORIES (1980) and ANOTHER WOMAN (1988).

For television, Behn wrote for the short-lived series "Tattinger's," which he also produced. At the time of his death, he was a creative consultant for the hit drama series "Homicide: Life on the Street," and also wrote several episodes.

Behn, who had cancer, died of a heart attack.

Bell, Ralph

born: 1916, New York, NY
died: August 2, 1998, New York, NY, age 82

Actor, television writer, and voice-over artist.

Ralph Bell began his radio career in the 1940s, when he was heard on countless radio shows, specials, series, and soap operas. Notable among these were "This Is Nora Drake" (1947), "Yours Truly, Johnny Dollar" (1949), "Dimension X (1950), "Barrie Craig, Confidential Investigator" (1951-1955), and "The Marriage," with Hume Cronyn and Jessica Tandy (1953-1954). He also starred in the television production of "Dr. Jekyll and Mr. Hyde" (1950).

After a career slump during the McCarthy era, Bell returned to television, writing scripts for "The Loretta Young Show," and "The

George Sanders Show." He also did numerous voice-overs for major commercial advertisers throughout the country. Among his film credits are EDGE OF THE CITY (1957), WOLFEN (1981), and ZELIG (1983).

In 1965, Bell became a National Board member of the Screen Actors Guild, a position he held until 1994. He also served as a trustee of the Motion Picture Players Welfare Fund.

Bell died of a heart attack.

Benair, Jonathan

born: July 4, 1950, Los Angeles, CA
died: July 1, 1998, Van Nuys, CA, age 47

Self-taught film historian and screenwriter.

Although he sold a few screenplays that were not produced during his lifetime, and provided the voice of the black-and-white TV set for the animated feature THE BRAVE LITTLE TOASTER (1987), Jonathan Benair made his mark during his lifetime as an expert on film history.

For many years Benair was responsible for the film programs at the Los Angeles County Museum of Art. His scholarly knowledge of film and his status as a first-rate cinema historian also made him popular on the lecture circuit.

Benair died of a heart attack and a cerebral hemorrhage.

Berger, Richard H.

born: c. 1904
died: October 8, 1998, Los Angeles, CA, age 94

Film, theatrical, and television producer.

Richard H. Berger began his career on Broadway in the 1920s as assistant to producer Lawrence Schwab, but went on to produce a number of musicals on his own. Leaving Broadway in the 1930s, he moved to St. Louis, where he ran the Municipal Opera House, an outdoor theater.

Berger relocated to Hollywood in 1941, where he produced several films for Metro-Goldwyn-Mayer. He later moved to RKO, where he produced his best-known films, including A LIKELY STORY (1947), RACHEL AND THE STRANGER (1948), ROUGHSHOD (1949), and ADVENTURE IN BALTIMORE (1949).

After his stint in Hollywood, Berger returned to New York City, where he produced "The Perry Como Show" for television. Following this, he moved to Kansas City, where he established an outdoor summer stock venue, The Starlight Theater, which he ran until his retirement in 1971.

Berger's son Richard has served as president of both MGM and Disney Studios.

Berger died of natural causes.

Bickman, Stan

born: c. 1931
died: May 30, 1998, New York, NY, age 66
educ: University of Southern California Film School

Producer and production manager.

Stan Bickman's early experience in the film industry was working for Roger Corman on several films including MACHINE GUN KELLY (1958) and THE INTRUDER (1962).

Bickman also served as the associate producer for the 1958 low-budget sci-fi thriller THE BRAIN EATERS, and SAVAGE LUST (1993), a slasher horror movie.

He and his wife were the models for the cover art of a Frank Sinatra album, "Songs for Swingin' Lovers."

Bickman died of complications from emphysema.

Bixby, Jerome

aka: Jay Lewis Bixby
born: c. 1922, Lincoln, NE
died: Apr. 28, 1998, San Bernardino, CA, age 75

Writer who specialized in both science-fiction and action-adventure stories.

During his long career, Jerome Bixby wrote more than 1,300 stories, starting as a short-story writer for sci-fi magazines. Moving to television, Bixby wrote for the series "The Twilight Zone" and the original "Star Trek."

Films for which he wrote or co-wrote the screenplays include THE LOST MISSILE, IT! THE TERROR FROM BEYOND SPACE, CURSE OF THE FACELESS MAN (all 1958), and the "It's a Good Life" segment of TWILIGHT ZONE: THE MOVIE (1983). FANTASTIC VOYAGE (1966) was based on a novel Bixby co-authored.

Bixby died of complications from quadruple bypass surgery.

Blair, Nicky

born: Nicholas Macario, c. 1928, Brooklyn, NY
died: Nov. 22, 1998, Los Angeles, CA, age 70

Bit player whom Frank Sinatra referred to as his all-time favorite.

Nicky Blair was a genuine Hollywood celebrity. Although he was a supporting actor for over 40 years, appearing in probably more than 150 movies and television shows, his real fame came as a charismatic restaurateur. Because of his expert culinary skills and dynamic personality, he was encouraged by his show business friends to open an Italian restaurant, which he first did in 1971. One of his eateries was the popular Sunset Boulevard, whose loyal clientele numbered some of the biggest stars in the business. Another was Las Vegas Nicky Blair's.

His many film credits include ROGUE COP (1954), HOLD BACK THE NIGHT (1956), UNTIL THEY SAIL (1957), OPERATION PETTICOAT (1959), OCEAN'S ELEVEN (1960), THE MANCHURIAN CANDIDATE (1962), VIVA LAS VEGAS (1964), DIAMONDS ARE FOREVER (1971), NEW YORK, NEW YORK (1976), THAT'S LIFE (1986), BEACHES (1988), ROCKY V (1990), THE GODFATHER, PART III (1990), and A BRONX TALE (1993).

Blair appeared on several episodic television dramas, such as "Wagon Train," "The Wild, Wild West," and "Hunter," as well as in some television movies, including THE LINDBERGH KIDNAPPING CASE (1976), CONTRACT ON CHERRY STREET (1977), and PORTRAIT OF A SHOWGIRL (1982).

Blair died of liver cancer.

Blake, Walter

born: c. 1903, New York, NY
died: Jan. 1, 1998, Woodland Hills, CA, age 94

Art director and associate producer.

Walter Blake started as a commercial artist and later joined the film industry as an art director for advertising and publicity, working for almost all the major studios. He turned to television in the late 1940s While at CBS in 1950, he became friendly with fledgling director Robert Aldrich, leading to a professional association and Blake's involvement with the Aldrich Company.

Blake served as an associate producer on the Aldrich-directed movies ATTACK! (1956), HUSH ... HUSH, SWEET CHARLOTTE (1964), THE FLIGHT OF THE PHOENIX (1965), THE KILLING OF SISTER GEORGE (1968), TOO LATE THE HERO (1970), THE GRISSOM GANG (1971), and ...ALL THE MARBLES (1981). He was the title designer for Aldrich's THE DIRTY DOZEN (1967) and producer of the 1972 documentary about encounter groups, HERE COMES EVERY BODY.

Blake's many television credits include "You Are There," "The Doctor," and "Richard Diamond, Private Detective."

Blake died of natural causes.

Bono, Sonny

born: Salvatore Bono, Feb. 16, 1935, Detroit, MI
died: Jan. 5, 1998, South Lake Tahoe, CA, age 62

Versatile performer whose various professions included songwriter, recording artist, television personality, film actor, mayor of Palm Springs, and, at the time of his death, congressman.

Sonny Bono began his show business career in the late fifties as singer and songwriter with Specialty Records, working with such artists as Sam Cooke and Little Richard. In collaboration with record producer Phil Spector, he wrote several popular songs including "You Bug Me, Baby," and "Needles and Pins."

His teaming with Cherilyn Sarkisian, then 16 years old, resulted in several modestly successful recordings until 1965 when, under the names Sonny and Cher, the pair hit the big time with their recording of "I Got You, Babe."

Married at the time to Donna Rankin, with whom he had a daughter, Christy, Bono obtained a divorce; he and Cher did not marry for several years, though, until after the birth of their daughter, Chastity. In the meantime, they recorded several more hit songs, including "The Beat Goes On."

Trading on their success as recording stars, the pair starred in several films, including GOOD TIMES (1967) and CHASTITY (1969). Appearances on a number of television shows, especially "This Is Tom Jones," not only widened their recognition with the general public, but gave them a chance to display a flair for comedy. Their own television show, "The Sonny and Cher Comedy Hour," began as a summer replacement and went on to run for four seasons, ending when the couple divorced in 1974. Bono's attempt to carry on a solo career as comedy star with his own series, "The Sonny Comedy Hour," failed, as did a brief re-teaming with Cher.

While Cher went on to a distinguished film career, Bono suffered a major slump, appearing in unsuccessful films like ESCAPE TO ATHENA (1979) and the low-budget horror movie TROLL (1986). He also appeared in the moderately successful AIRPLANE II: THE SEQUEL (1982). During this time, he was briefly married to actress Susie Coelho.

Bono settled in Palm Springs during the 1980s and was running his own restaurant when a disagreement with local authorities concerning the sign for his restaurant gave him the idea of running for the office of Mayor. In 1988, he was elected to that office. One of his accomplishments as mayor was to establish the Nortel Palm Springs International Film Festival.

A Republican in a highly conservative Republican district, Bono made an unsuccessful bid for a Senate seat, but was successful when he ran for Congress in 1994; he was re-elected in 1996. He married his fourth wife, Mary Whitaker in 1985, and they had two children, Chesare and Chianna. After his death, Mary was popularly elected to succeed him in Congress.

Bono was killed in a skiing accident while on vacation in Lake Tahoe, suffering massive head injuries after colliding with a tree.

Boutross, Tom

aka: Thomas Cassarino
born: c. 1929
died: June 24, 1998, Kansas City, MO, age 69
educ: University of Southern California, School of Cinema (Master's degree, communications)

Director, editor, and producer.

Tom Boutross was the editor and one of three directors on THE HIDEOUS SUN DEMON (1959), a cult science-fiction film. Later, Boutross worked mostly as a film editor and occasionally coproduced low-budget movies. These include RAT FINK (1965), A MAN CALLED DAGGER (1967), THE SAVAGE WILD (1970), THE LEGEND OF BOGGY CREEK (1973), BOOTLEGGERS (1974), THE TOWN THAT DREADED SUNDOWN (1977), WISHBONE CUTTER (1978), APPOINTMENT WITH FEAR (1985), FREE RIDE (1986), and DARK BEFORE DAWN (1989).

For television, Boutross was an editor for the series "Gunsmoke" and an editor-writer on "Disney's Wonderful World of Color."

While Boutross was in South America working as an associate producer on a film, he contracted a fever that is believed to have contributed to the heart condition that caused his death.

Bradley, Owen

born: Oct. 21, 1915, Westmoreland, TX
died: Jan. 8, 1998, Nashville, TN, age 82

Veteran country music producer.

Owen Bradley was largely responsible for bringing country music into the mainstream. When the Nashville Sound emerged during the 1950s and '60s, Bradley, an accomplished musician and savvy businessman, was in the creative forefront of the movement. He and his brother, Harold, established Nashville as an important recording center when they opened a recording studio there in 1954. Bradley became vice president of Decca Records' Nashville Division, and guided the careers of many great artists. He later became an independent producer, and in 1974 was elected to the Country Music Hall of Fame.

Two of those whose careers he helped were singers Loretta Lynn and Patsy Cline. Appropriately, he was the musical director on COAL MINER'S DAUGHTER (1980) and SWEET DREAMS (1985), the films based on their lives.

Bradley had been experiencing a respiratory problem and was in the hospital for tests to determine its cause when he died.

Bradley, Tom

born: Dec. 29, 1917, Calvert, TX
died: Sept. 29, 1998, West Los Angeles, CA, age 80
educ: Univ. of California at Los Angeles, Southwestern Univ.

The first African-American mayor of Los Angeles.

A soft-spoken, handsome, and dignified man, Tom Bradley was the grandson of slaves and was born on a cotton plantation. Bradley initially worked as a member of the Los Angeles Police Department. After 21 years there, he started his mayoral tenure in 1973 and served for five terms, until 1993. After his retirement from politics, Bradley became associated with a San Francisco law firm. Bradley had a small part playing himself in NICK OF TIME, John Badham's 1995 thriller set in Los Angeles.

Bradley, who had been in ill health for more than two years prior to his death, died of a heart attack.

Bragaglia, Carlo Ludovico

born: July 8, 1894
died: January 4, 1998, Rome, Italy, age 103

Film and theater director, scriptwriter, and poet.

A prolific filmmaker, Carlo Ludovico Bragaglia remained active to the end of his life. Decorated for bravery in WWI, his film career began in 1930 at Cines Studio, which was then run by his father, who was active in the early days of the Italian film industry.

After learning the varied aspects of filmmaking, Bragaglia made documentaries before making his first feature, O LA BORSA O LA VITA (1933). Combining craftsmanship with speed, he went on to direct 64 films and write the screenplays for 21 more. Among his films are CASANOVA FAREBBE COSI (1942), NON TI PAGO (1943), LA VITA E BELLA starring Anna Magnani (1943), and I QUATTRO MONACI (1947). Although his films spanned many genres, he was best known for a series of hits he made with the popular Neapolitan comic, Toto, among which were TOTO LE MOKO (1949), FIGARO QUA...FIGARO LA (1950), and TOTO CERCA MOGLIE (1950).

Later in his life, Bragaglia turned to writing poetry, publishing several volumes. He also wrote an autobiography, *Bragaglia raconta Bragaglia.* He continued making films, including GLI AMORE DI ERCOLE (1960), THE LOVES OF HERCULES starring Jayne Mansfield (1960) and I QUATTRO MOSCHETTIERI with Aldo Fabrizi (1963). A number of his films were screened in 1994 at the Locarno Film Festival to mark his 100th birthday.

Bragaglia died of complications following hip surgery.

Braginsky, Emil

born: 1921, Moscow, Russia
died: May 26, 1998, Moscow, Russia, age 77

Soviet screenwriter, playwright.

Although he studied law, Emil Braginsky's career was as a successful writer of film scripts and stage plays in the Soviet Union. For more than 35 years, most of his almost two dozen movies were collaborative writing efforts with director Eldar Ryazanov.

Their films were unusual, as they dealt with the country's political ideology in a satiric and humane fashion. One of the team's early successes was 1966's BEWARE AUTOMOBILES, a provocative comment on sharing. In it, the protagonist is a Robin Hood-type who steals cars from dishonest wealthy officials and sells them to help subsidize children's homes. Other films include AN UNCOMMON THIEF (1967), GARAGE (1979), A TRAIN STATION FOR TWO (1982), and GAME OF IMAGINATION (1995).

Braginsky died after suffering a heart attack at Moscow's Sheremetyevo Airport.

Brandt (Sr.), Jerrold T.

born: June 10, 1913, New York, NY
died: May 3, 1998, age 85
educ: University of Pennsylvania (Wharton School graduate)

Enterprising producer.

Jerrold Brandt started out as a film cutter at Columbia Pictures, a studio that was co-founded by his father Joe Brandt (along with Jack and Harry Cohen). He then worked as an assistant director and a producer at RKO. Brandt produced that studio's "Scattergood" movies (based on the popular radio series): SCATTERGOOD BAINES, SCATTERGOOD PULLS

THE STRINGS, SCATTERGOOD MEETS BROADWAY (all 1941), CINDERELLA SWINGS IT, SCATTERGOOD RIDES HIGH, and SCATTERGOOD SURVIVES A MURDER (all 1942). Brandt also produced AT SWORDS POINT (1952) and coproduced THE BELL JAR (1979).

Forming Jerry Brandt Productions in 1945, he moved his operations to Europe in the 1950s, producing and packaging movies for European distribution companies.

As a young man, Brandt had served as an officer in the US Navy, and in his later years, he was active in Veterans of Foreign Wars causes.

Brandt died of heart failure.

Brasno, Olive

aka: Olive Brasno Wayne
born: c. 1917, Old Bridge, NJ
died: January 25, 1998, Lakeland, FL, age 80

Diminutive actress, vaudevillian, and night club performer.

Olive Brasno was a popular stage performer at an early age, appearing with her brothers Richard and George on the vaudeville circuit. As little people, they had limited opportunities in the movies.

Brasno started in films with a bit part in SITTING PRETTY (1933), and appeared in an "Our Gang" short, "Shrimps for a Day" (1934). Brother George had the part of General Tom Thumb in THE MIGHTY BARNUM (1934) and Olive was his wife, Lavinia. In CARNIVAL (1935), she and George played themselves. Again with George, they were the "dancing midgets" in CHARLIE CHAN AT THE CIRCUS (1936). In LITTLE MISS BROADWAY (1938), she and George were themselves. Olive and her brothers were asked to appear in THE WIZARD OF OZ (1939), but declined the offer, preferring to earn twice as much playing vaudeville.

During the 1950s and '60s, Brasno was a favorite of Las Vegas audiences, performing frequently at the Sahara Hotel with Donald O'Connor.

Brasno died of heart failure two days after the death of her husband of 37 years and fellow little person, actor Gus Wayne.

Brickhouse, Jack

born: c. 1916, Peoria, IL
died: Aug. 6, 1998, Chicago, IL, age 82

Baseball Hall of Fame sportscaster.

Chicago-based Jack Brickhouse was primarily known as a radio and television broadcast play-by-play announcer for the Chicago White Sox and the Chicago Cubs baseball teams.

The very popular Brickhouse appeared briefly as a ring announcer in the modestly produced 1950 boxing movie THE GOLDEN GLOVES STORY (1950), which achieved some degree of authenticity by incorporating real footage of a Golden Gloves event.

Brickhouse died of cardiac arrest.

Bridges, Lloyd

born: January 15, 1915, San Leandro, CA
died: March 10, 1998, Los Angeles, CA, age 85

Busy star of films and television.

In a career that spanned six decades, Lloyd Bridges attained real stardom as Mike Nelson on the hugely popular television series, "Sea Hunt," which ran for 156 episodes from 1957 to 1961 and reran for years in syndication.

Although his majors at UCLA were political science and pre-law, Bridges' interest in acting drew him to the University Dramatic Society, of which he became president. After graduation, he spent years touring in plays and working with regional stock companies. He supplemented his income by recording plays, poetry, and portions of the Bible for the American Foundation for the Blind.

His first break in movies came when Columbia Studios signed him to a contract. He played small roles in HERE COMES MR. JORDAN (1941), TALK OF THE TOWN (1942), THE MASTER RACE (1944), and A WALK IN THE SUN (1945). Breaking his contract with Columbia to freelance, Bridges at first played lead roles in "B" pictures such as THE SOUND OF FURY and WHISTLE AT EATON FALLS (both 1951), but also got substantial roles in such quality films as HOME OF THE BRAVE (1949), HIGH NOON, and PLYMOUTH ADVENTURE (both 1952).

While continuing to work in theater as a member of the Actor's Lab, as well as doing stints on several television series, Bridges found himself blacklisted by the House Un-American Activities Committee for alleged Communist leanings. He managed, however, to clear his name and his career suffered only a temporary setback. Ahead of him were several of his finest films, including THE RAINMAKER (1956) and THE GODDESS (1958).

Although proficient in many sports, Bridges had never tried skin-diving until "Sea Hunt," but became a major enthusiast. In fact, the series did much to promote the sport. Following "Sea Hunt," Bridges went on to star in several other television series including "The Lloyd Bridges Show," "The Loner," and "Harts of the West," but none of these enjoyed a major success. He returned to the stage, this time on Broadway, and appeared in a fairly large number of TV movies and miniseries, most notably "Roots" in 1977. His big screen credits were at this time largely forgettable, including such films as AROUND THE WORLD UNDER THE SEA (1966) and THE HAPPY ENDING (1969).

Late in his career, Bridges displayed a surprising flair for broad comedy in the film AIRPLANE! (1980). It brought him new recognition, and he followed with AIRPLANE II: THE SEQUEL (1982), HOT SHOTS! (1991), HOT SHOTS! PART DEUX (1995), and one of his final screen roles, the mob patriarch in JANE AUSTEN'S MAFIA! (1998).

Bridges' greatest success may have been in his private life. His marriage to Dorothy Simpson lasted for 59 years and produced three sons, two of whom, Jeff and Beau, are film stars in their own rights.

Bridges died of natural causes, stemming from a long-time heart condition.

Burge, Gregg

born: Nov. 14, 1957, New York, NY
died: July 4, 1998, Atlanta, GA, age 40
educ: Julliard School

Dancer who was also an accomplished singer, actor, and choreographer.

Before he entered his teen-age years, Gregg Burge was a skillful dancer and a three-time winner on TV's "The Ted Mack Amateur Hour." Shortly thereafter he turned professional, appearing in television commercials and as a regular in the PBS children's series "The Electric Company."

Among his many stage shows, Burge was on Broadway in 1975's *The Wiz* (as a replacement), *Sophisticated Ladies* (1981), and the shows for which he was honored with Fred Astaire Awards: *Song and Dance* (1985) and *Oh, Kay!* (1991 revival).

Burge often created dances; besides his one-man show, he was involved in music videos, the most celebrated being Michael Jackson's "Bad," for which Burge was one of the choreographers.

Landing the role of Richie in the movie version of A CHORUS LINE (1985) did little to further the dancer's film career. He was one of several performers in Spike Lee's comedy with music, SCHOOL DAZE (1988); and in the HBO telefilm BASEBALL IN BLACK AND WHITE (1996), Burge played song-and-dance man Bill Robinson.

Burge died of complications from a brain tumor.

Bykov, Rolan

born: 1930
died: October 6, 1998, Moscow, Russia, age 68

Actor and director.

An actor of great versatility, Rolan Bykov appeared in more than 80 films, playing an enormous range of character roles. Making his debut in 1955, his film credits as an actor include THE OVERCOAT (1959), and COMMISSAR (1968). His best-known screen credit was the highly regarded ANDREI RUBLEV (1966), withheld by Soviet authorities until 1971. Among his directorial efforts was the Russian film SCARECROW (1985), which was hailed by critics as "the Soviet 'Lord of the Flies.'"

No cause of death was reported.

Cable, Bill

born: c. 1945
died: Mar. 7, 1998, Los Angeles, CA, age 52

Actor and stuntman.

Among Bill Cable's film credits are appearances in THE LAST TANGO IN ACAPULCO (1975), PEE-WEE'S BIG ADVENTURE (1985), ELVIRA, MISTRESS OF THE DARK (1988), and BASIC INSTINCT (1992).

Cable's death was the result of complications from injuries sustained in a motorcycle accident a year and a half earlier.

Caccialanza, Gisella

born: c. 1915, San Diego, CA
died: July 16, 1998, Daly City, CA, age 83
American ballet dancer who appeared briefly in movies.

Classically trained in the Italian school of ballet with the legendary teacher Enrico Cecchetti, Gisella Caccialanza later joined famed choreographer George Balanchine's American Ballet in 1934. With that company, she created many celebrated parts. Though Balanchine was committed to classical dance, he would often cross over and choreograph a Broadway musical or movie. Caccialanza was part of his ensemble for two of these: THE GOLDWYN FOLLIES (1938) and ON YOUR TOES (1939).

In addition to being an original member of the American Ballet, Caccialanza performed with Ballet Caravan, the San Francisco Ballet, and Ballet Society, which became the New York City Ballet. She retired from dancing in 1953 and became a teacher.

Caccialanza died of a stroke.

Calamai, Clara

born: c. 1909, Prato, Italy
died: Sept. 21, 1998, Rimini, Italy, age 89
Popular Italian actress.

Although Clara Calamai appeared in more than 30 films in a career that spanned almost 50 years, she will probably be best remembered for two films made during Italy's Fascist regime. In Alessandro Blasetti's LA CENA DELLE BEFFE (1941), Calamai became the first actress to expose her breasts in an Italian movie. And in the 1942 film OSSESSIONE (US release in 1959, in a truncated version), she was the lusty, adulterous innkeeper; adapted from the sensational James Cain novel *The Postman Always Rings Twice*, the film was the debut of director Luchino Visconti.

Though she first appeared in films in 1938 and worked with some of Italy's top directors and stars, Calamai was most prominent during the Italian cinema's neorealist period, which came shortly after WWII. Some of her films include L'AVVENTURIERA DEL PIANO DI SOPRA (1941) costarring Vittorio De Sica, LA GUARDIA DEL CORPO (1942), IL MONDO VUOLE COSI (1946), Visconti's LE NOTTI BIANCHE (1957); and the De Sica-directed segment of the anthology film LE STREGHE (1966). After the 1940s, her most productive decade, Calamai appeared in only a few films, in supporting roles.

Calamai died of a stroke.

Cameron, Hope

born: 1920
died: November 20, 1998, New York, NY, age 78
Stage, film, and television actress.

A longtime member of the Actor's Studio, Hope Cameron spent most of her career on the stage, appearing in productions of *The Philadelphia Story* with Katharine Hepburn and *Captain Carvallo* with Katharine Cornell. She created the role of Letty in *Death of a Salesman* and was also in the original Broadway production of *All My Sons,* both directed by Elia Kazan.

She appeared on the screen as Ruth in THE CHAPMAN REPORT (1962), in TALES OF ORDINARY MADNESS (1982), and in IN THE SPIRIT (1990), as a new age lecturer.

In the 1960s, she made a number of television appearances in such shows as "Hazel," "The Patty Duke Show," and "The Defenders."

Cameron's death was caused by cancer.

Campanis, Al

born: Allesandro Sebastian Campani, Nov. 2, 1916, Kos, Dodecanese Islands, Greece
died: June 21, 1998, Fullerton, CA, age 81
educ: New York University (graduated 1940)
Baseball player, scout, and manager.

Al Campanis played briefly for the Brooklyn Dodgers baseball team in the early 1940s and was the general manager of the Los Angeles Dodgers from 1968-87. He guided the team to four National League pennants (1974, 1977, 1978) and a 1981 World Series win. He was forced to resign as general manager two days after he appeared on a 1987 TV talk show where he made comments about blacks in baseball that were perceived to be racist.

Campanis was in the first feature film directed by Robert Aldrich, the MGM programmer, BIG LEAGUER (1953). The film is primarily set in the (then) New York Giants Florida baseball training camp, and Campanis, in what amounts to little more than a bit part, played himself.

Campanis died of coronary artery disease.

Cannon, Vince

born: Vincent Aloysius Carrelli Jr., c. 1937, Philadelphia, PA
died: Aug. 15, 1998, Los Angeles, CA, age 61
educ: Villanova University
Actor, producer, and personal manager.

Before acting in features, Vince Cannon could be seen on television in the series "Love Is a Many Splendored Thing" and the telefilms EARTH II (1971) and THE BAIT (1973). His theatrical films include BLADE (1973), TRACKDOWN (1976), YOUNGBLOOD (1978), and FAST FORWARD (1985).

Cannon was actress Dyan Cannon's personal manager for many years. (Though they shared the same professional surname, they were not related.) He was the associate producer on her film COAST TO COAST, and coproduced two films she directed, THE END OF INNOCENCE (1991) and the Oscar-nominated short "Number One" (1976).

In addition to managing the career of his wife, the artist Artis Lane, and producing her gallery exhibitions, Cannon did guest stints on several television series, including "McMillan and Wife," "The Love Boat," and "The Golden Girls."

Cannon was active in many social causes, including SHARE and Artists for a Free South Africa.

No cause of death was reported.

Carlile, Clancy

born: Clarence Lawson Carlile, 1930, Choctaw Indian Reservation, OK
died: June 4, 1998, Austin, TX, age 68
educ: San Francisco State University (MA degree)
Novelist, screenwriter.

While in the Army, Clancy Carlile, the son of a sharecropper, developed his appreciation for literature. Soon after he completed his education, he published his first novel, *As I Was Young and Easy* (1958). His second book was *Spore 7* (1979).

Clint Eastwood's HONKYTONK MAN (1982), the story of a fatally ill country singer, was adapted by Carlile from his 1980 book. Carlile's novel, *Children of the Dust*, became a 1995 TV miniseries of the same name, aka "A Good Day to Die," starrring Sidney Poiter.

Carlile died of cancer.

Cates, Joseph

born: Joseph Katz, Aug. 10, 1924, New York, NY
died: Oct. 10, 1998, New York, NY, age 74
educ: New York University
Broadway, movie, television producer and director.

After completing his WWII service flying rescue missions in the Pacific, Joseph Cates entered television in the mid-1940s, with a Dumont show called "Look Upon a Star."

Cates worked with all the top television performers, and is credited with teaming Art Carney with Jackie Gleason for "The Honeymooners," as well as designing the show's original set. Cates was also one of the creators of the game show "The $64,000 Question," which won a 1955 Emmy Award. Cates himself won two Emmys, as the executive producer of "Annie, the Women in the Life of a Man" (1970), starring Anne Bancroft; and again for "Jack Lemmon in 'S Wonderful, 'S Marvelous, 'S Gershwin" (1972).

Although he attained great success in television, Cates was only moderately successful producing for the stage. Among his Broadway shows were *Spoon River Anthology* (1963), *What Makes Sammy Run?* (1964), *A Day in the Death of Joe Egg* (1968), and *Gantry* (1970).

During the 1960s, Cates directed a few low-budget movies: GIRLS OF THE NIGHT (1960), WHO KILLED TEDDY BEAR? (1965), and THE FAT SPY (1965). With his brother Gilbert Cates, who also directed, he executive-produced THE LAST MARRIED COUPLE IN AMERICA (1980). He produced the telefilm THE CRADLE WILL FALL (1983), based on a Mary Higgins Clark novel, and was the executive producer for the TV movie adaptation of Louis L'Amour's western story THE QUICK AND THE DEAD (1987).

A well-liked show business figure, Cates was the father of actress Phoebe Cates.

Cates died of complications from leukemia.

Clark, Dane

born: Bernard Zanville, Feb. 18, 1913, Brooklyn, NY
died: Sept. 11, 1998, Santa Monica, CA, age 85
educ: Cornell University; St. John's University Law School

Actor who worked as a Warner Bros. contract player during the 1940s and '50s, often cast in tough guy roles.

After graduating with a law degree during the Great Depression, Dane Clark chose to pursue a career in the performing arts. Following a bit of radio work and modeling, Clark turned to acting, and he managed to get small parts in a few Broadway dramas.

Entering films in the early 1940s, Clark had small parts in a few movies using his real name, Bernard Zanville. These included MONEY AND THE WOMAN (1940), WAKE ISLAND, PRIDE OF THE YANKEES, and THE GLASS KEY (all 1942). Reportedly, he was given his new name by Humphrey Bogart, whom Clark supported in ACTION IN THE NORTH ATLANTIC (1943). Bogart suggested the young actor use the name Zane Clark before it was finally decided he would be Dane Clark.

Warners gave Clark a publicity build-up and cast him in important roles in DESTINATION TOKYO (1944), PRIDE OF THE MARINES, and GOD IS MY CO-PILOT (both 1945). He was the second male lead, opposite Bette Davis, in A STOLEN LIFE (1946), and occasionally co-starred with other young contract players in modest programmers like HER KIND OF MAN (1946) and THAT WAY WITH WOMEN (1947). Clark was acclaimed for his portrayal of an escaped convict in DEEP VALLEY (1947), with Ida Lupino, and as a guilt-ridden young man in MOONRISE (1948). He finished his Warner contract with two 1950 releases: BACKFIRE and BARRICADE. His movies over the next several years were ordinary fare, except for GO, MAN, GO! (1954), in which he played Abe Saperstein, the man who brought the Harlem Globetrotters into prominence.

As Clark's movie career waned, he returned to the stage and worked regularly in television. Among his plays, the most successful was the off-Broadway *Brecht on Brecht* (1962). Clark made guest appearances on many popular television shows, such as "Wagon Train," "The Twilight Zone," "The Untouchables," "I Spy," "Night Gallery," and "Mission: Impossible." He was a regular on "Wire Service," "Bold Adventure," and "The New Perry Mason." His TV movies include THE FAMILY RICO (1972), SAY GOODBYE, MAGGIE COLE (1972), JAMES DEAN (1976), and CONDOMINIUM (1980).

No cause of death was reported.

Clark, Lon

born: c. 1912
died: Oct. 2, 1998, New York, age 86

Actor.

Lon Clark achieved popularity as a radio actor, portraying the title character in the popular series "Nick Carter, Master Detective." He was also on the air in such shows as "The Thin Man" and "Norman Corwin Presents."

As a theater actor, Clark was on Broadway in such plays as *Church Street* (1948), *Roman Candle* (1960), and as Jason Robards Jr.'s replacement in the 1956 production of *Long Day's Journey Into Night*.

His movie career consisted of a supporting role in THE GENTLE PEOPLE (1966), a romantic drama set in Rio.

No cause of death was reported.

Clifford, Ruth

see: Cornelius, Ruth

Cohen, Ronald M.

aka: Ron Cohen
born: c. 1939
died: Apr. 21, 1998, Los Angeles, CA, age 58

Screenwriter, who, early in his career, wrote scripts for Steve McQueen's TV western series "Wanted: Dead or Alive."

Ronald M. Cohen collaborated on the screenplays for the films BLUE (1968), THE GOOD GUYS AND THE BAD GUYS (1969; also coproduced), and TWILIGHT'S LAST GLEAMING (1977).

For cowriting the well-received telefilm AMERICAN DREAM (1981), Cohen received an Emmy nomination. He collaborated on the teleplays for CALL TO GLORY (1984) and FORTUNE DANE (1986). Cohen also adapted LAST STAND AT SABER RIVER (1997) for TV, which was based on the Elmore Leonard novel.

Cohen died of lung cancer.

Collis, Jack T.

born: c. 1922
died: Feb. 1, 1998, Encino, CA, age 75

Production designer and art designer for numerous movies.

For most of his films, Jack T. Collis was the production designer; occasionally he was the art designer or part of a design team. Some of his early credits include HELL BOUND, THE GIRL IN BLACK STOCKINGS (both 1957), VIOLENT ROAD, MACABRE (both 1958), UP PERISCOPE, BORN RECKLESS (both 1959), THE DELTA FACTOR, DARKER THAN AMBER (both 1970), SAVE THE TIGER and MAGNUM FORCE (both 1973). For 1976's THE LAST TYCOON, Collis shared an Academy Award nomination in the art direction-set direction category. Other films include THE LAST WORD, THE JERK (both 1979), PATERNITY, THE FOUR SEASONS (both 1981), and TEX (1982).

When Collis served as the production designer on IMPULSE (1984), he was cast in the small role of Mr. Anson.

Apparently the designer was a favorite of director Ron Howard; Collis was a designer on the Howard-directed films NIGHT SHIFT (1982), SPLASH (1984), COCOON (1985), and FAR AND AWAY (1992).

Collis reportedly died of natural causes.

Connolly, Norma

born: c. 1927
died: Nov. 18, 1998, Los Angeles, CA, age 71

Actress known primarily for her regular role on the daytime TV drama "General Hospital."

Norma Connolly appeared in several plays on the New York and Los Angeles stages; however, she was most active in television. Besides her role of Aunt Ruby Anderson in "General Hospital," Connolly was in the series "The Young Marrieds" and made guest appearances in several dramas, such as "Naked City," "The Twilight Zone," "The Bionic Woman," and "Charlie's Angels."

Connolly had small parts in the films THE WRONG MAN (1956), THIRD OF A MAN (1962), THE OTHER, THEY ONLY KILL THEIR MASTERS (both 1972), and the telefilm F. SCOTT FITZGERALD IN HOLLYWOOD (1976).

Connolly was married for 31 years to screenwriter Howard Rodman, until his death in 1985.

Connolly died of complications from a stroke.

Cooley, Lee

born: Leland Frederick Cooley, c. 1909
died: Oct. 27, 1998, Napa Valley, CA, age 89

An early trailblazer in television.

After a stint in the US Merchant Marines, Lee Cooley was a radio newscaster and later a foreign correspondent in southern Europe during times of upheaval; he provided radio reports from Italy during the Italian-Ethiopian War and was in Spain at the time of the Spanish Civil War.

In addition to authoring several books, often about his own true-life adventures, Cooley worked primarily in radio and television. One of his long-term jobs was as a writer, producer, and director on "The Perry Como Show."

In the 1937 comedy SWING HIGH, SWING LOW, Cooley had the small part of a radio announcer.

Cooley died of prostate cancer.

Cookson, Catherine

born: c. 1906, Tyne Dock, England
died: June 11, 1998, London, England, age 91

Popular British novelist who was honored with the title of "Dame" in 1993.

Catherine Cookson started her prolific writing career at the age of 40, some time after she and her husband experienced the sadness of four stillborn children. Many of her novels (she wrote more than 90) are about spirited British 19th-century working class poor.

The first of her novels to reach the screen was JACQUELINE (1956), for which she provided additional dialogue to a screenplay adapted by others. Other page-to-screen works include the feature ROONEY (1958), and television movies A HOUSE FULL OF MEN (1977), THE FIFTEEN STREETS (1989), THE BLACK CANDLE (1991), THE BLACK VELVET GOWN (1993) and THE WINGLESS BIRD (1997). The TV miniseries "The Man Who Cried" (1993), "The Cinder Path" (1994), "The Glass Virgin" (1995), "Tide of Life" (1996), and "The Round Tower" (1998) were also based on Cookson novels.

Tom Cookson, Dame Catherine's husband of 58 years, died on June 28, 1998, just seventeen days after his wife. He was 86 years old.

Dame Catherine's death was attributed to a blood disorder and a heart ailment.

Cornelius, Ruth

aka: Ruth Clifford
born: 1900, Pawtucket, RI
died: November 30, 1998, Woodland Hills, CA, age 98

Leading silent film actress whose career spanned nearly fifty years.

Under the name Ruth Clifford, Cornelius appeared in more than fifty films. She began her career in 1914 at the Thomas Edison Studio, and moved to Universal Studios in 1916. Her early successes include A KENTUCKY CINDERELLA (1917), THE KAISER—BEAST OF BERLIN (1918), and ABE LINCOLN (1924), in which she played Ann Rutledge. She starred in THE FACE ON THE BARROOM FLOOR (1924) directed by John Ford, with whom she would make nine more films.

Her marriage to James D. Cornelius brought her career to a halt. She returned to film after her marriage ended in a contentious divorce suit, although she never again played more than minor roles. Among her many films are STAND UP AND CHEER (19340, DANTE'S INFERNO (1935), and KEYS OF THE KINGDOM (1944). For John Ford, she appeared in DRUMS ALONG THE MOHAWK (1939), THREE GODFATHERS (1948), WAGONMASTER (1950), THE SEARCHERS (1956), THE LAST HURRAH (1958), and TWO RODE TOGETHER (1961), among others. In addition to her film work, she was a regular on the television series "Highway Patrol" and "I Led Two Lives."

Cornelius died following a long illness.

Cotes, Peter

born: Sydney Boulting, Mar. 19, 1912, Maidenhead, England
died: Nov. 10, 1998, Chipping Norton, England, age 86

British actor, director, writer and older brother of twins John and Roy Boulting, prominent figures in the British film industry.

Peter Cotes's film work was less celebrated than his accomplishments for the British stage. He acted in several plays, including a stint as Joe Bonaparte in *Golden Boy* (1942); among his directorial successes were the controversial play *Pick-Up Girl* (1946) and Agatha Christie's phenomenally successful *The Mousetrap* (1952). He also had his own theater company, the Peter Cotes Players, which included his late wife, actress Joan Miller. On Broadway, Cotes directed *A Pin to See the Peepshow* (1953) and *Hidden Stranger* (1963).

His films include small acting roles in a handful of British movies, such as PASTOR HALL (which was produced by brother John and directed by brother Roy), FINGERS (both 1940), THE GENTLE SEX (1943), DON'T TAKE IT TO HEART (1944), JOHNNY IN THE CLOUDS (1945), BEWARE OF PITY (1946), and THE UPTURNED GLASS (1947). Cotes directed the film THE YOUNG AND THE GUILTY (1958), as well as some television dramas.

Among his writings is the book *Little Fellow*, written with Thelma Niklaus, about the life and works of Charlie Chaplin.

No cause of death was reported.

Cottafavi, Vittorio

born: January 30, 1914, Modena, Italy
died: December 14, 1998, Anzio, Italy, age 84.

Italian film and television director-writer.

A pioneer film director in Italy, Vittorio Cottafavi directed more than twenty films, and wrote a good many of them. His first film was I NOSTRI SOGNI (1943). The bulk of his career was involved in the making of many highly successful "historical" movies, featuring mythical heroes, gladiators, and the like.

Some of the films which he directed were LA GRANDE STRADA (1948), IL CAVALIERE DI MAISON ROUGE (1953), UNA DONNA LIBERA (1956), REVOLT OF THE GLADIATORS (1958), GOLIATH AND THE DRAGON and MESSALINA (both 1960). As writer-director, he made IL BOIO DI LILLA (1952), AVANZI DI GALERA (1954), LE LEGIONI DI CLEOPATRA (1959), and HERCULES IN ATLANTIS (1961). After the failure of his HUNDRED KNIGHTS (1964), Cottafavi turned his attentions to television, where he directed the miniseries, "Cristoforo Colombo" in 1967. He also directed classical works based on plays by Dostoevsky, Hugo, and Lorca.

No cause of death was reported.

Cresse, Bob

born: 1937
died: April 6, 1998, Miami, FL, age 61

Independent exploitation-film producer, writer, actor, and distributor.

Educated at the University of Miami, Bob Cresse began his film career as a messenger at MGM Studios. Several years later, he and director R. Lee Frost formed Olympic International Films, which produced softcore movies for adult theaters around the country. Among the films in which Cresse (under the name Robert W. Cresse) had a hand as writer-producer were NIGHT ON BARE MOUNTAIN (1962), THE SECRET SOCIETY (1965), MONDO FREUDO, HOT SPUR (both 1968), and THE SCAVENGERS (1971). Cresse also developed a wide distribution of his company's films and owned theaters in many cities.

As an actor, Cresse appeared in SURFTIDE 77 (1962), THE EROTIC ADVENTURES OF ZORRO (1972), and the made-for-television SILENT WITNESS (1985).

Cresse's death was caused by a heart attack.

Cross, Beverley

born: Alan Beverley Cross, Apr. 13, 1931
died: Mar. 20, 1998, London, England, age 66
educ: Balliol College, Oxford University, England

Screenwriter, opera librettist, novelist, stage actor, and stage director.

Although known mainly for his work as a playwright and screenwriter, Beverley Cross started out as a London stage actor in the mid-1950s. As a playwright, he gained some fame with *One More River*, which, after a London engagement, debuted on Broadway in 1960. Several other plays followed over the years, most notably the book for the musical *Half a Sixpence*, which was a West End success in 1963 and a Broadway hit in 1965.

Cross contributed to the writing of the action sequences in David Lean's 1962 film LAWRENCE OF ARABIA. Other movies for which he either wrote or collaborated on the screenplay include JASON AND THE ARGONAUTS (1963), THE LONG SHIPS (1964), GENGHIS KAHN (1965), HALF A SIXPENCE (1967), THE DONKEY RUSTLERS (1969), SINBAD AND THE EYE OF THE TIGER (1977), and CLASH OF THE TITANS (1981).

Cross wrote several opera librettos, a couple of novels, and a few television dramas for the BBC. His "Catherine Howard" episode for the miniseries "The Six Wives of Henry VIII" was seen on PBS stations in 1971.

At the time of his demise, Cross was married to actress Maggie Smith, whom he wed in 1975.

Cross had been treated for a series of aneurysms shortly before his death.

Dalrymple, Jean

born: Sept. 2, 1902, Morristown, NJ
died: Nov. 15, 1998, New York, NY, age 96

Theatrical veteran who worked as an actress, playwright, director, producer, publicist, and manager.

Jean Dalrymple started her writing career early: at the age of nine she sold a short story for $1 to a Newark, NJ newspaper. Although she eventually sold many other stories, her main interest was in the legitimate theater. During her long theatrical career, Dalrymple was most successful as a publicist and a producer of musical revivals.

With her then-husband Ward Morehouse, a newspaper drama critic, she wrote the story "Baghdad on the Hudson," which was adapted for the screen as IT HAPPENED IN NEW YORK (1935).

Dalrymple wrote about her life in a 1963 autobiography, *September Child*; she recounted her years producing successful musicals and plays at New York's famed City Center in a 1975 memoir, *From the Last Row.*

No cause of death was reported.

Dauman, Anatole

born: c. 1924, Warsaw, Poland
died: April 8, 1998, Paris, France, age 73

Producer of many of the most important and influential European films of the last 45 years.

As an independent film producer, Anatole Dauman was responsible for bringing to the world a remarkable number of great films made by some of the most brilliant (and often difficult) directors to come out of Europe since WWII. Establishing his own production company, Argos Films, in 1949, he had an uncanny knack for making commercial successes out of seemingly uncommercial projects. In the early 1950s, he produced several dozen short films by such filmmakers as Agnes Varda, Georges Franju, Jean Aurel, and Alain Resnais.

Resnais' incisive Holocaust documentary NIGHT AND FOG (1955) was Dauman's first big success as a producer. He worked again with Resnais on three equally influential features, HIROSHIMA, MON AMOUR (1959), LAST YEAR AT MARIENBAD (1961), and MURIEL (1963).

Dauman produced filmmaker Chris Marker's critically lauded LA JETEE (1962) and SANS SOLEIL (1982); Dauman's final film as a producer was Marker's LEVEL FIVE (1996). Dauman also produced Jean-Luc Godard's influential films TWO OR THREE THINGS I KNOW ABOUT HER and MASCULINE-FEMININE (both 1966), and two of Robert Bresson's finest works, AU HASARD BALTHAZAR (1966) and MOUCHETTE (1967).

In the 1970s and 1980s, he worked with Polish filmmaker Walerian Borowczyk on IMMORAL TALES (1974) and LA BETE (1975), and with Nagisa Oshima on the critically acclaimed (and quite controversial) IN THE REALM OF THE SENSES (1976), followed by EMPIRE OF PASSION (1978).

Dauman's collaboration with Volker Schlondorff resulted in COUP DE GRACE (1976) and THE TIN DRUM (1979), which won the Academy Award for Best Foreign Language Film. They followed this up with the well-regarded CIRCLE OF DECEIT (1981). He also produced two of the biggest international successes by filmmaker Wim Wenders: PARIS, TEXAS (1984) and WINGS OF DESIRE (1987). Thus, Dauman was a key figure in modern European cinema, supporting the work of the French *Nouvelle Vague,* the New German Cinema, and mavericks who fit into no cinematic movement (Bresson, Oshima, Borowczyk).

Dauman died at his Paris home of an apparent heart attack.

Davis, Donald

born: Feb. 26, 1928, Newmarket, Ontario, Canada
died: Jan. 23, 1998, Toronto, Canada, age 69
educ: St. Andrews College (1946), Univ. of Toronto (BA, 1950)

Stage actor, renowned for his interpretations of the classics.

In 1954, Donald Davis helped establish a repertory company in Canada, The Crest Theater. His Broadway debut was as Agydas in *Tamburlaine the Great* (1956). He recreated his performance as Tiresias in *Oedipus Rex* from the Stratford Shakespearean Festival in Ontario for the US television program "Omnibus." Another triumph for the actor was his Obie Award-winning performance in Samuel Beckett's *Krapp's Last Tape,* which he performed in New York in the acclaimed 1960 off-Broadway production.

Throughout his career, Davis was active primarily in theater, appearing in numerous plays in America and Canada. But he also appeared in a handful of movies, including Stratford-Ontario's filmization of their stage success OEDIPUS REX (1957), JOY IN THE MORNING (1965), and the Canadian films THE MAN INSIDE (1976), AGENCY(1981), and SAMUEL LOUNT (1986). In 1990 he was in two TV movies, MEMORIES OF MURDER and HITLER'S DAUGHTER.

During the 1960s, Davis acted in several episodic television dramas, including "The Nurses," "The Defenders," "Mission: Impossible," "The F.B.I.," and "The Wild, Wild West."

Davis died from emphysema.

Davis, Marvin Aubrey

born: c. 1910
died: Mar. 8, 1998, Santa Monica, CA, age 87

Art director noted for his work on Disney features.

Marvin Aubrey Davis served as an art director for several Disney movies, including DAVY CROCKETT, KING OF THE WILD FRONTIER (1955), WESTWARD HO THE WAGONS! (1956) and THE SIGN OF ZORRO (1960). He shared the art director credit with Carroll Clark for BABES IN TOYLAND (1961), MOON PILOT, BON VOYAGE, BIG RED (all 1962), SAVAGE SAM (1963), A TIGER WALKS (1964), THE UGLY DACHSHUND, and FOLLOW ME, BOYS! (both 1966).

For his art work, Davis won an Emmy Award (honor shared with Clark) for TV's "Walt Disney's Wonderful World of Color."

Davis also worked for the Walt Disney Imagineering team; the team planned and created Disney theme parks.

No cause of death was reported.

Day, Doris

born: c. 1920
died: September 16, 1998, age 78

Actress, aerial stuntwoman, and model.

Not to be confused with the later singing and film star, Doris Day was an actress who starred in minor films and played bit parts in several major ones. She began her career on Broadway in *Dodsworth,* and made her film debut as Roy Rogers' leading lady in SAGA OF DEATH VALLEY (1939). Her other screen appearances include VILLAGE BARN DANCE (also 1939), THOU SHALT NOT KILL (1940), LADY BE GOOD, A WOMAN'S FACE (both 1941), THIS TIME FOR KEEPS (1942), and THEY GOT ME COVERED (1943).

She left films shortly thereafter and became one of the first female aerial daredevils, teaming with speed pilot John Livingston. Day also worked as a model.

Her death resulted from a series of strokes.

Del Prete, Duilio

born: June 25, 1938, Cuneo, Italy
died: February 2, 1998, Rome, Italy, age 61

Popular Italian singer and television entertainer, who also worked as an actor in films and on TV.

Beginning his career on the Italian stage in productions of *Richard III* and *Orlando Furioso,* Duilio Del Prete went on to become a recording artist and television celebrity. Early film credits in his native Italy included I SETTE FRATELLI CERVI (1968), ALFREDO, ALFREDO (1972), VOGLIAMO I COLONNELLI and SESSOMATO (both 1973). Del Prete first attracted great attention as an actor in Mario Monicelli's hit comedy AMICI MIEI (1975). His first appearance outside Italy was in Joseph Losey's THE ASSASSINATION OF TROTSKY (1972). His American film career was subverted when he appeared in Peter Bogdanovich's critical failures DAISY MILLER (1974) and AT LONG LAST LOVE (1975).

Returning to Italy, he made several more films, including DIVINA CREATURA (1976), UNA SPIRALE DI NEBBIA (1977) and LE CADEAU (1981). Although he was primarily a supporting player, he did star in Piero Vivarelli's NELLA MISURA IN CUI...(1979). Despite a less-than-stellar film career, he remained a popular television performer. In a recent return to the stage, he appeared in a successful production of *Born Yesterday,* with Valeria Marini.

Del Prete died following a long illness, the nature of which was unreported.

Del Rio, Evelyn

born: Evelyn Bernadette Janer, c. 1930, Catano, Puerto Rico
died: November 26, 1998, Los Angeles, CA, age 67

Former child actress.

Evelyn Del Rio began her stint in show business at the age of three, with a radio program called "The Baby Evelyn Show." Known as "the Latin Shirley Temple," she toured with Carmen Miranda, and sang and danced in such venues as the Cotton Club and the Apollo Theater until she was thirteen.

She appeared in 17 films, the first one of note being the Spanish-language MIS DOS AMORES (1938). Universal hired her to play an obnoxious child in YOU CAN'T CHEAT AN HONEST MAN (1939), starring W.C. Fields, and the following year she was cast as his obnoxious daughter, Elsie Mae Adele Brunch Souse, in THE BANK DICK (1940). Fans of this film will remember Fields raising his hand as if to strike her, muttering, "She can't tell me I don't love her!"

Del Rio's last film was ALOMA OF THE SOUTH SEAS (1940). During WWII she entertained servicemen, and then retired from show business to be a wife and a mother to four sons.

Her death was caused by complications due to diabetes.

Dempsey, Jerome

born: Mar. 1, 1929, St. Paul, MN
died: Aug. 26, 1998, New York, NY, age 69
educ: Toledo University

Versatile character actor who worked on stage, in movies, and on television.

Jerome Dempsey, a graduate of the American Theater Wing and a member of the Actors Studio, was a well-known and respected actor on the New York theater scene. He appeared on and off Broadway in many plays, including *The Love Nest* (1963) and *An Ordinary Man* (1968). With The Repertory Company of Lincoln Center, Dempsey was in *A Cry of Players* (1968) and *The Crucible* (1972).

Dempsey appeared occasionally on television, most notably in the telefilm GORE VIDAL'S LINCOLN (1988) and the 1990 miniseries "The Kennedys of Massachusetts."

Although his film roles were usually in supporting parts, Dempsey worked fairly regularly over a 20-year period. His credits include MALATESTA'S CARNIVAL (1973), NETWORK (1976), BREWSTER'S MILLIONS (1985), THE IMAGEMAKER (1986), THE WIZARD OF LONELINESS (1988), RACE FOR GLORY (1989), TUNE IN TOMORROW (1990), MISTRESS (1992), and THE HUDSUCKER PROXY (1994).

Dempsey died of heart failure.

Denison, Michael

born: Nov. 1, 1915, Doncaster, Yorkshire, England
died: July 22, 1998, Amersham, England, age 82
educ: Oxford University

Veteran actor who specialized in playing elegant, urbane English gentlemen.

Michael Denison made his London stage debut in 1938. His career was interrupted by WWII, and he served in the British Army from 1940-46. When Denison resumed acting, he appeared in dozens of West End plays, many with his wife, Dulcie Gray, whom he married in 1938. The couple made their Broadway debut in 1996 in *An Ideal Gentleman.* Their last appearance together was on the London stage in *Curtain Up* (1998).

Denison's first movie was 1940s TILLY OF BLOOMSBURY. Some of his other films are HUNGRY HILL (1947), THE BLIND GODDESS (1948), MY BROTHER JONATHAN (1949), THE MAGIC BOX, THE FRIGHTENED BRIDE, ANGELS ONE FIVE (all 1952), THE TRUTH ABOUT WOMEN (1958), FACES IN THE DARK (1960), and his last, SHADOWLANDS (1993).

Denison is best known to American audiences for his work in two popular British films. As the lead in the elaborately produced THE GLASS MOUNTAIN (1950), he played a composer whose wartime experience compels him to write an opera based on a peasant legend. (Denison's wife Gray costarred). And in the 1952 adaptation of Oscar Wilde's THE IMPORTANCE OF BEING EARNEST, Denison was the carefree Algernon.

Denison appeared in dozens of television shows in a wide variety of roles, most notably as the title character in the half-hour drama series "Boyd, QC," which ran from 1956-63.

Denison died of cancer.

Denning, Richard

born: Louis Denninger, Mar. 27, 1914, Poughkeepsie, NY
died: Oct. 11, 1998, Escondido, CA, age 84
educ: Woodbury College

Leading man noted for his blond good looks.

After graduating from college with an accounting degree, Richard Denning took over his father's garment business. However, his interest in performing was sparked by his winning a radio contest, "Do You Want to Be an Actor?", sponsored by Warner Bros. The contest did not result in an expected contract with that studio; instead he was signed by Paramount. Denning's first movie was HOLD 'EM NAVY! (1937), a low-budget comedy-romance.

In 1938, Denning appeared in nine releases, including YOU AND ME, HER JUNGLE LOVE, COLLEGE SWING, and THE BUCCANEER. He was even busier in 1939, showing up in fifteen films, including UNION PACIFIC, TELEVISION SPY, MILLION DOLLAR LEGS, KING OF CHINATOWN, and GERONIMO. His career was interrupted in 1942 by WWII; he was in the US Submarine Service, serving in the South Pacific for three years.

For most of his 30 years in the motion picture industry, Denning played supporting roles, often cast as the non-threatening "other man." Among his 80 movies, Denning was seen to good advantage in such films as NORTHWEST MOUNTED POLICE (1940), BLACK BEAUTY (1946), NO MAN OF HER OWN (1950), THE GLASS WEB (1953), AN AFFAIR TO REMEMBER (1957), and TWICE-TOLD TALES (1963).

Denning was also active in radio. He's best remembered as the male lead, starring opposite Lucille Ball, in "My Favorite Husband." He later successfully made the transition to television, as one of the leads in "Mr. and Mrs. North" and appearing on many dramatic anthology series, including "Ford Theater," "Schlitz Playhouse," and "Lux Video Theater." He continued in episodic TV with "The Flying Doctor," "Michael Shayne," "Going My Way," and "Karen." It was in 1968 that Denning had his most notable success, portraying the Governor of Hawaii for twelve seasons on "Hawaii Five-O."

Actress Evelyn Ankers was Denning's wife from 1942 until the time of her death in 1985.

Denning, who was suffering from emphysema, died of cardiac arrest.

Derek, John

born: Derek Harris, August 12, 1926, Hollywood, CA
died: May 22, 1998, Santa Maria, CA, age 71

Actor, director, producer, writer, cinematographer, and photographer who made a comeback guiding the career of his fourth wife, Bo Derek.

John Derek was the son of one-time actress Dolores Johnson and writer-director Lawson Harris. After a stint in the service during WWII, Derek appeared in small roles in two 1944 David O. Selznick films, SINCE YOU WENT AWAY and I'LL BE SEEING YOU. Under contract to Columbia Pictures, Derek became the prototype of the handsome leading man and had substantial parts in two 1949 releases. He played delinquent Nick Romano in KNOCK ON ANY DOOR and the adopted son of a shady politician in ALL THE KING'S MEN, which won a Best Picture Oscar. After appearances in these "A" features, Derek was cast in a series of inconsequential adventure, costume, and western movies, such as ROGUES OF SHERWOOD FOREST (1950), MASK OF THE AVENGER (1951), THE LAST POSSE (1953), THE OUTCAST and THE ADVENTURES OF HAJJI BABA (both 1954).

A few good supporting parts followed, as John Wilkes Booth in PRINCE OF PLAYERS (1955), Joshua in THE TEN COMMANDMENTS (1956) and Taha in EXODUS (1960), but by the 1960s, Derek's career was in decline. After NIGHTMARE IN THE SUN (1964), which he also produced, Derek turned to still photography, cinematography, and directing. He directed his second wife Ursula Andress in ONCE BEFORE I DIE (1967); his third wife Linda Evans in CHILDISH THINGS (1969, re-released in 1972 as CONFESSIONS OF TOM HARRIS); and his fourth wife, the former Kathleen Collins, in AND ONCE UPON A LOVE (1973); the film was released in 1981 as FANTASIES after Collins achieved notoriety for her work in Blake Edwards's 1979 film 10, under the name Bo Derek.

Thereafter, Derek devoted to his attention to managing the career of Bo. He directed and photographed her in TARZAN, THE APE MAN (1981); did triple duty as director-cinematographer-scripter for BOLERO (1984); and wore the same three hats for GHOSTS CAN'T DO IT (1990), which he edited as well. All three films, which placed Bo in various erotically-charged situations, fared poorly with the critics and the public.

Derek died of heart failure two days after he was admitted to the hospital following a heart attack.

Dior, Rick

aka: Richard Dior
born: c. 1947
died: Oct. 26, 1998, Freehold Township, NJ, age 51

Academy Award-winning sound engineer.

While working as a sound engineer for Todd-AO Sound, Sync Sound, and his own studio, Rick Dior worked on numerous films and television shows. He was variously credited as a sound designer, sound mixer, re-recording mixer, sound re-recordist, or dubbing mixer.

Some of the films Dior worked on include YOU LIGHT UP MY LIFE (1977), BROADWAY DANNY ROSE (1984), DIRTY DANCING (1987), THE ACCUSED (1988), PARENTHOOD (1989), Q & A (1990), MISSISSIPPI MASALA (1991), BOB ROBERTS (1992), THE PELICAN BRIEF (1993), and APOLLO 13 (1995), for which he was part of the sound team that won a Best Sound Oscar. In addition, there was the TV miniseries "With God On Our Side: The Rise of the Religious Right in America" and the feature documentaries MESSAGE TO LOVE (1996) and GREEN CHIMNEY'S (1997).

Dior died of a heart attack.

Dominguez, Wade

born: c. 1966, California
died: Aug. 26, 1998, Los Angeles, CA, age 32

Actor.

Wade Dominquez was a model, a soap opera actor, and appeared in the REM video "Losing My Religion," before being cast as the troubled inner-city student in the hit DANGEROUS MINDS (1995). Dominguez went on to appear in EROTIQUE (1995), John Irvin's film noir CITY OF INDUSTRY (1997), Avi Nesher's action-comedy THE TAX MAN, and Randall Kleiser's SHADOW OF DOUBT (both 1998).

Dominguez died of respiratory failure.

Donegan, Dorothy

born: April 6, 1924, Chicago, IL
died: May 19, 1998, Los Angeles, CA, age 74
educ: Chicago Conservatory, Chicago Musical College

Jazz, blues, boogie-woogie, swing, and ragtime pianist.

As a concert performer, classically trained pianist Dorothy Donegan was an iconoclast on stage. Her flamboyant and outrageous style of acting out songs, poking fun at her contemporaries, and telling profane jokes, was thought by many to be offensive. But her mastery of the piano and the eclecticism of her repertory won her a devoted following.

Early in her career, before her idiosyncratic concert personality came fully to the fore, she was approached by MGM and offered a long-term contract. She refused, but accepted a one-picture deal with United Artists to appear in SENSATIONS OF 1945 (1944), as a specialty performer with Cab Calloway's band. The film, a "B" musical starring Eleanor Powell, is notable as W. C. Fields's last movie. Donegan's only other film appearance was in the musical documentary TEXAS TENOR: THE ILLINOIS JACQUET STORY (1992), a tribute to the jazz saxophonist.

Donegan died from colon cancer.

Downs, Frederic

born: c. 1916
died: May 1, 1998, Los Angeles, CA, age 81

Longtime stage and movie actor.

A well-respected stage actor, Frederic Downs performed in many plays and musicals in New York. He started in the 1940s; some of his appearances were in *Oedipus Rex* (1945), *The Grass Harp* (1953), *The Trip to Bountiful* (1953), *The Threepenny Opera* (1955), and *Fiorello!* (1959).

His film credits include TERROR FROM THE YEAR 5000 (1958), EXPERIMENT IN TERROR (1962), THE HELLCATS (1968), I LOVE MY . . .WIFE (1970), 1776 (1972), BUG (1975), and THE COTTON CLUB (1984).

Downs was a regular on the daytime drama "Days of Our Lives" for many years. He was a guest actor on such series as "Perry Mason," "Bewitched," and "Night Gallery," and was in the TV movies SHADOW ON THE LAND (1968), THE CALIFORNIA KID (1974) and HUCKLEBERRY FINN (1975).

No cause of death was reported.

Drew, Norma

born: c. 1904
died: Aug. 23, 1998, West Hills, CA, age 94

Actress who had small roles in a few films during the 1930s.

In 1930, Norma Drew had a supporting part in a modest romance, WHAT A MAN. She was a model in a bigger-budgeted programmer, OUR BLUSHING BRIDES (1930), sharing screen time with Joan Crawford, who played a fellow mannequin. In the Laurel and Hardy comedy short "Chickens Come Home" (1931), Drew was cast as the wife of Stan Laurel. She lent support in the romantic melodrama FORBIDDEN COMPANY (1932); was a maid in DR. MONICA (1934); and portrayed a nurse in the first MAGNIFICENT OBSESSION (1935).

No cause of death was reported.

Drury, Allen

born: Sept. 2, 1918, Houston, TX
died: Sept. 2, 1998, San Francisco, CA, age 80
educ: Stanford University (BA, 1939)

Pulitzer Prize winner for the 1959 novel *Advise and Consent,* which was made into a 1962 film.

Allen Drury started his professional writing career as an editorial writer, a Washington reporter, and a political correspondent. Of his 20 novels, *Advise and Consent* was the most popular (it spawned six sequels). The bestseller was dramatized for the Broadway stage by Loring Mandel, and opened to good reviews in 1960. The film rights to the novel were obtained by independent producer Otto Preminger.

For the movie, Drury did not adapt his work—the screenplay was by Wendell Mayes—but he did act as technical advisor. Preminger cast Henry Fonda in the lead, and Charles Laughton (in his last role) as an old-time Southern senator. The film was a popular and critical success.

Drury died of cardiac arrest on his 80th birthday.

Duncan, Todd

born: Robert Todd Duncan, February 12, 1903, Danville, KY
died: Feb. 28, 1998, Washington, DC, age 95
educ: Butler University (BA, 1925), Columbia University Teachers College (MA, 1930)

Broadway, concert, opera baritone; teacher and actor.

Blessed with commanding good looks and a strong, refined singing voice, Todd Duncan originated three landmark roles on Broadway: Porgy in George Gershwin's *Porgy and Bess* (1935), the Lord's General in Vernon Duke's *Cabin in the Sky* (1940), and Stephen Kumalo in Kurt Weill's *Lost in the Stars* (1949). Duncan, a classically trained singer, was the first African-American to appear with the New York City Opera, singing Tonio in their 1945 production of *Pagliacci.*

While performing professionally, Todd Duncan was also part of the voice faculty of Howard University, Washington, DC, where he remained until 1945.

The singer's first movie, SYNCOPATION (1942) was a William Dieterle-directed musical about a jazz band on the road. Duncan had a more substantial role in Hall Bartlett's prison melodrama, UNCHAINED (1955), playing an inmate.

Duncan died of a heart condition.

Dunn, Linwood G.

born: Linwood Gale Dunn, c. 1904, Brooklyn, NY
died: May 20, 1998, Burbank, CA, age 93

Innovative and award-winning visual effects cinematographer and photographic equipment designer.

Linwood G. Dunn started in the entertainment business as a projectionist in New York City. Within a few years, he was working in the fledgling movie industry as an assistant cameraman and a director of photography. In 1929 he became a visual effects cinematographer for RKO, and for nearly three decades he created effects for numerous films, including KING KONG, THE MONKEY'S PAW (both 1933), BRINGING UP BABY (1938), CITIZEN KANE (1941), CAT PEOPLE (1942), MIGHTY JOE YOUNG (1949), THE THING (1951), and THE CONQUEROR (1956).

Along with his associate, Cecil Love, Dunn designed the Acme-Dunn Special Effects Optical Printer in 1942. For their achievement, Dunn and Love were honored by the Academy of Motion Picture Arts and Sciences with a 1944 award.

Dunn often worked on films as a consultant, and sometimes provided special photographic effects and title photography. In these capacities he worked on WEST SIDE STORY (1961), IT'S A MAD MAD MAD MAD WORLD (1963), CIRCUS WORLD (1964), HAWAII (1966), DARLING LILI (1970), THE DEVIL'S RAIN (1975) and others. Dunn also worked on the TV series "Star Trek."

In addition to receiving many technical achievement awards, Dunn was honored three more times by the Academy of Motion Picture Arts and Sciences: in 1978, he was recognized for his outstanding service and dedication; in 1980, he was given (along with Love and Acme Tool) an Academy Award of Merit; and in 1984, he received the Academy's Gordon E. Sawyer Award.

Dunn died of natural causes.

Dunphy, Don

born: July 5, 1908, New York, NY
died: July 22, 1998, Roslyn, NY, age 90
educ: Manhattan College

Boxing announcer, sportscaster.

For more than 40 years, Don Dunphy was the voice of boxing, first on radio and then television. He called some of the greatest events in the history of the sport, including the 1941 Joe Louis-Billy Conn bout and the Muhammad Ali-Joe Frazier fight in 1971. Dunphy was also a broadcast announcer for other events, such as baseball, basketball, and football.

His unique style of delivery was captured in a handful of movies in which he played himself or a fictitious sportscaster. These films include BANANAS (1971), MATILDA (1978), THE GREATEST (1977), and RAGING BULL (1980).

Dunphy died of heart failure.

Durand, David

aka: Dave Durand, David Grey Parker
born: David Parker Grey, c. 1921
died: July 25, 1998, Bridgewater, IL, age 77

Actor who worked from the 1920 through the '40s.

David Durand became a movie actor at the age of five when he appeared in the "Our Gang" shorts "The Sun Down Limited" (1924) and "Uncle Tom's Uncle" (1926). In 1929 he appeared in two musicals, THE SONG OF LOVE and INNOCENTS OF PARIS, in which the young Durand sang a song with Chevalier.

All told, Durand made about three dozen films over a period of 15 years. They include THE JAZZ CINDERELLA (1930), RICH MAN'S FOLLY (1931), SILVER DOLLAR (1932), THE LIFE OF JIMMY DOLAN (1933), VIVA VILLA! (1934), LITTLE MEN (1935), ANGELS WITH DIRTY FACES (1938), THE GHOST BREAKERS (1940), GLOVE BIRDS (1942), KID DYNAMITE (1943), and MILLION DOLLAR KID (1944).

Discouraged by his inability to get movie roles, Durand left the business in the mid-1940s.

No cause of death was reported.

Edmonds, Walter D.

born: Walter Dumaux Edmonds, July 15, 1903, Boonville, NY
died: Jan. 24, 1998, Utica, NY, age 94

Popular writer whose books were adapted for the stage, screen, and television.

In 1934, Henry Fonda played the lead in the Broadway production of *The Farmer Takes a Wife,* a play adapted from the Walter D. Edmonds novel about life on the Erie Canal, *Rome Haul.* When Twentieth Century-Fox bought the film rights to the hit show, Fonda was signed to recreate his part, making his movie debut in the 1935 release. THE FARMER TAKES A WIFE was later remade by Fox as a 1953 Betty Grable musical.

Sticking to literature, Edmonds never adapted his novels for other media. Fox turned his most successful book, *Drums Along the Mohawk,* into the popular 1939 John Ford film of the same title. The circus story CHAD HANNA (1940) was adapted from Edmonds' *Red Wheels Rolling.* The Australian TV movie BORN TO RUN (1979) was based on the Edmonds novel *The Boys of Black River.*

Edmonds continued writing for many years; his last book, *Tales My Father Never Told,* was published in 1995.

No cause of death was reported.

Edwards, Penny

born: Millicent Maxine Edwards, Aug. 24, 1928, Jackson Heights, NY
died: Aug. 26, 1998, Friendswood, TX, age 70

Pert actress who projected a strong, confident image.

While still a teenager, Penny Edwards appeared on Broadway in the *Ziegfeld Follies of 1943.* Several other stage appearances followed, including a part in the Olsen and Johnson farce *Laffing Room Only* (1944), before she was signed by Warner Bros. to a starlet contract.

THAT HAGEN GIRL, MY WILD IRISH ROSE (both 1947), and TWO GUYS FROM TEXAS (1948) were the only films Edwards made for Warner Bros. She gained popularity when she moved over to Republic and became Roy Rogers's leading lady in a string of westerns: TRAIL OF ROBIN HOOD, SUNSET IN THE WEST, NORTH OF THE GREAT DIVIDE (all 1950), SPOILERS OF THE PLAINS, IN OLD AMARILLO, and HEART OF THE ROCKIES (all 1951). Republic also paired her with Rex Allen in UTAH WAGON TRAIL (1951) and starred her in the quickie crime melodramas STREET BANDITS, MISSING WOMEN, MILLION DOLLAR PURSUIT (all 1951) and WOMAN IN THE DARK (1952). After THE WILD BLUE YONDER (1952), in which she was relegated to a supporting role, Edwards left the studio.

Other films in which Edwards appeared include PONY SOLDIER (1952), POWDER RIVER (1953), and her last, THE DALTON GIRLS (1957). Among the many popular television series in which she guest starred were "Wagon Train," "Perry Mason," "Wells Fargo," "Cheyenne," and "Playhouse 90." Her association with western films made her a favorite guest at several western film conventions.

Edwards died of lung cancer.

Eliscu, Edward

born: Apr. 2, 1902, New York, NY
died: June 18, 1998, Newtown, CT, age 96
educ: City College of New York (BS, social science)

Screenwriter and Songwriters Hall of Fame lyricist.

Edward Eliscu was hardly out of college when he started acting on Broadway in the early 1920s. He also directed and wrote plays, with little success. When he turned to writing songs and sketches for Broadway musicals, he scored with *Great Day!* (1929), collaborating with Billy Rose on lyrics set to tunes by Vincent Youmans, including the standards "More Than You Know" and "Without a Song." Another writing success was the 1940 revue *Meet the People,* with music by Jay Gorney.

In Hollywood, Eliscu collaborated with Nacio Herb Brown on a song for WHOOPEE (1930). The result wasn't memorable, but when Eliscu and Gus Kahn teamed up with composer Youmans for FLYING DOWN TO RIO (1933), they produced a first-rate score, with such classics as "The Carioca" (which received an Oscar nomination) and "Orchids in the Moonlight." Eliscu also contributed to songs for the non-musicals ROCKABYE (1933) and THE MORE THE MERRIER (1943), as well as the Ann Miller musical HEY, ROOKIE (1944).

For most of his movie career, Eliscu was a screenwriter on low-budget films. Some of his cowriting credits are PADDY, MUSIC IS MAGIC (both 1935), LITTLE TOUGH GUYS IN SOCIETY (1938), CHARLIE MCCARTHY, DETECTIVE (1939), SOMETHING TO SHOUT ABOUT (1943), THE GAY SENORITA (1945), and THREE HUSBANDS (1950).

Because of his political views, Eliscu was blacklisted in Hollywood in the 1950s. Thereafter, he wrote primarily for the theater and television.

Eliscu died of natural causes.

Evans, Gene

born: July 11, 1922, Holbrook, AZ
died: Apr. 1, 1998, age 75

Character actor with a tough yet vulnerable image; a favorite of filmmaker Samuel Fuller.

Gene Evans started his acting career on the stage, first as part of an acting troupe of soldiers during WWII and then in summer stock at the Penthouse Theater in Altadena, CA.

Evans appeared in small roles and bit parts in 10 movies, beginning with UNDER COLORADO SKIES (1947), before Samuel Fuller cast him in the lead role of an infantry sergeant driven to the brink of madness in the Korean War melodrama STEEL HELMET (1951). Four more Fuller films followed, including the writer-director's second Korean War movie FIXED BAYONETS (1951). Evans played a hard-hitting turn-of-the-century newspaper man in Fuller's own personal favorite of his films, PARK ROW (1952), a mercenary in HELL AND HIGH WATER (1954), and a mental-hospital patient in SHOCK CORRIDOR (1963).

In a career of four decades, Evans made more than 50 movies. The versatile actor was well cast in a variety of parts, such as in the westerns CATTLE QUEEN OF MONTANA (1954) and THE WAR WAGON (1967); the contemporary melodramas THE BIG CARNIVAL (1951) and THE HELEN MORGAN STORY (1957); the sci-fi thrillers DONOVAN'S BRAIN (1953) and THE GIANT BEHEMOTH (1959); and the comedies THE SAD SACK (1957) and OPERATION PETTICOAT (1959).

Evans worked extensively in television from the 1950s through the '80s. He played the father in "My Friend Flicka" from 1956-58, and guest starred on many major dramas, including "The Alfred Hitchcock Hour," "Wagon Train," "Gunsmoke," "Bonanza," and "Murder, She Wrote." Before he retired from acting in the late 1980s, Evans worked almost exclusively in television.

Evans spent his retirement years on his farm in Tennessee.

No cause of death was reported.

Falco

born: Johann Holzel, February 19, 1957, Vienna, Austria
died: February 7, 1998, Puerta Plata, Dominican Republic, age 40

Rock star who appeared in several films.

A musical prodigy as a child, Falco turned to pop music in the 1980s. His brand of synthesizer-based rock music proved popular with the 1986 international hit "Rock Me, Amadeus." He also scored major hits with "Der Kommisar" and "Vienna Calling."

He appeared in several music-oriented films such as DER FORMEL EINS FILM aka FEEL THE MOTION (1985), also featuring Meatloaf and Pia Zadora, and GELD ODER LEBER! (1986).

Falco's death was the result of severe head injuries suffered in a car accident.

Faye, Alice

born: Alice Jeanne Leppert, May 5, 1915 (some sources say 1912), New York, NY
died: May 9, 1998, Rancho Mirage, California, age 83

Major star of 1930s and '40s film musicals.

The velvet-voiced singing star of numerous movies, Alice Faye was, for nearly a decade, 20th Century-Fox's hottest property and the "girl back home" to tens of thousands of homesick GI's during the war. The daughter of a New York City policeman, Faye was raised in the Hell's Kitchen neighborhood of Manhattan. Drawn to show business from an early age, she was hired for the chorus of *George White's Scandals* at the age of 16. The star of the show, Rudy Vallee, admired her voice and hired her to sing on his weekly radio show. When Vallee went to Hollywood to do the film version of his Broadway hit, he asked Fox to let her do a song in the film. When the film's female star quit, Faye replaced her and thus made her film debut in the leading role of GEORGE WHITE'S SCANDALS OF 1934 (1934). The following year, she starred in GEORGE WHITE'S SCANDALS OF 1935 (1935). Her relationship with Vallee, which was reputed to be more than professional, led Vallee's wife to name Faye in a stormy divorce case.

Under long-term contract to Fox, Faye appeared in a string of musicals, among them EVERY NIGHT AT EIGHT, MUSIC IS MAGIC (both 1935), KING OF BURLESQUE, and POOR LITTLE RICH GIRL (both 1936) with Shirley Temple. She graduated to higher-budget musicals and scored solid successes with ON THE AVENUE, WAKE UP AND LIVE, and SALLY, IRENE, AND MARY (all 1937). She became a major star in IN OLD CHICAGO (1938) and with ALEXANDER'S RAGTIME BAND (1938) and ROSE OF WASHINGTON SQUARE (1939), she was named Hollywood's biggest box-office star by America's theater owners.

She continued to make musical films, distinguishable only by the leading men cast opposite her (usually Don Ameche, John Payne, or Tyrone Power). These include TIN PAN ALLEY (1940), THAT NIGHT IN RIO, WEEKEND IN HAVANA (both 1941), and HELLO FRISCO, HELLO (1943). In the meantime, she became just as well-known for some of the popular songs she introduced as for her movies. Among her biggest hits were "Goodnight, My Love," "I've Got My Love To Keep Me Warm," and the song most widely associated with her, "You'll Never Know," which won an Oscar in 1943. By the time of her last big Fox musical, Busby Berkeley's bizarre Technicolor confection THE GANG'S ALL HERE (1943), Faye was becoming disenchanted with her image as the sweet and somewhat insipid girl-next-door. She persuaded studio chief, Darryl Zanuck to cast her in the film noir FALLEN ANGEL (1945), and when her part was severely cut, she walked out on her contract. No other studio would hire her and she left the film industry for the next 17 years.

Married and divorced from singer Tony Martin, she married bandleader Phil Harris in 1941, a marriage that surprised many cynics by lasting until his death in 1995. After leaving the movies, she turned to radio, and "The Phil Harris-Alice Faye Show" lasted from 1946 to 1954. Faye also made appearances on television, including numerous Bob Hope specials. She returned to movies with an unsuccessful remake of STATE FAIR (1962) and was featured in THE MAGIC OF LASSIE (1978). In 1973 she starred in a Broadway revival of *Good News,* opposite Gene Nelson. She toured with the show for two years, reunited with former co-stars Don Ameche and John Payne.

The cause of death was cancer.

Fell, Norman

born: March 24, 1924, Philadelphia, PA
died: December 14, 1998, Woodland Hills, CA, age 74

Character actor in film and television.

After graduating from Temple University with a bachelor's degree in drama, Norman Fell moved to New York, where he studied with Stella Adler and later joined the Actor's Studio. His first professional appearances consisted of small parts in theater and television.

Fell's film career began with PORK CHOP HILL (1959), and included such notable films as OCEAN'S ELEVEN (1961), IT'S A MAD MAD MAD MAD WORLD (1964), THE GRADUATE (1967), BULLITT (1968), CATCH-22 (1970), THE STONE KILLER (1973), THE END (1978) and PATERNITY (1981).

Fell, who had been a regular on such television series as "87th Precinct" (1961-64), and "Dan August" (1970-75), achieved fame as landlord Stanley Roper on the hit comedy series "Three's Company." He and co-star Audra Lindley played Mr. and Mrs. Roper from 1977 to 1979, when they were rewarded with their own spinoff series, "The Ropers," which lasted one season. He continued to appear in films, however, including FOR THE BOYS (1991) and THE DESTINY OF MARTY FINE (1995).

The cause of death was cancer.

Feuillere, Edwige

born: Edwige Caroline Cunati, October 29, 1907, Vesoul, France
died: November 13, 1998, Paris, France, age 91

Beloved star of French cinema and theater.

Combining beauty, elegance, charisma, and a distinguished voice, Edwige Feuillere began her film career with LE CORDON BLEU (1930), but first received critical attention as the female lead in Marcel Pagnol's TOPAZE (1932). She gained stardom in Abel Gance's LUCRECE BORGIA (1935), appearing in a brief nude scene. She made several more films in the 1930s, including I WAS AN ADVENTURESS (1938), before turning to the theater.

In 1939 she played Marguerite Gautier in a stage production of Dumas' *La Dame aux Camelias* to enormous success; she was to return to this role frequently over the following decades. Feuillere also scored great recognition for her performances in *L'Aigle a Deux Tetes* and *Partage de Midi.* During this time, she continued to appear in movies, notably DUCHESSE DE LANGEAIS (1941), L'IDIOT (1946), and Jean Cocteau's film version of L'AIGLE A DEUX TETES (1947).

Although she spent most of the rest of her career onstage, she did appear in a number of notable films, including OLIVIA (1950), LE BLE EN HERBE (1953), and EN CAS DE MANCHEUR (1957). Retiring from movies in 1960 to devote herself to the theater, she returned briefly to film in LA CHAIR DE L'ORCHIDE (1974). She continued working up to the age of 84.

No cause of death was reported.

Field, Sylvia

aka: Sylvia Field Truex
born: Harriet Louisa Johnson, Feb. 14, 1901, Allston, MA
died: July 31, 1998, Fallbrook CA, age 97

Versatile character actress who worked on stage, screen, radio, and television; best known as the sweet, unflappable Mrs. Wilson on TV's "Dennis the Menace."

Sylvia Field was a busy Broadway actress, appearing in more than three dozen plays between 1923 and 1951. She appeared in three films in 1929—VOICE OF THE CITY and THE EXALTED FLAPPER, and the short "Stewed, Fried and Boiled." But it was not until the early 1940s that she and her husband, Ernest Truex, relocated to Hollywood. Truex, who died in 1973, became one of filmdom's most popular character actors, appearing in more than 60 movies and numerous television shows. Field's output was much smaller. Her screen appearances included TILLIE THE TOILER (1941), BLONDIE FOR VICTORY (1942), SALOME, WHERE SHE DANCED, JUNIOR MISS (both 1945), ALL MINE TO GIVE (1957), and ANNETTE (1958).

Field was seen regularly on television in an array of popular dramas and sitcoms besides "Dennis the Menace" (on which she worked from 1959 to 1962), including "The Philco Television Playhouse," "The Goodyear Playhouse," "Perry Mason," "Father Knows Best," "Hazel," and "Harry O."

No cause of death was reported.

Forest, Jean-Claude

born: c. 1930
died: December 30, 1998, Paris, France

Creator of stylish science fiction comic strips who worked on the film adaptation of BARBARELLA.

Jean-Claude Forest began his cartooning career at the age of 19 with "The Haunted Ship." He went on to contribute illustrations to magazines, but remains best known for his comics. In 1962, he created what was to become his most infamous character, the 41st-Century space adventuress Barbarella, whose sex-filled exploits tested the limits of censors in France (the strip was, for the most part, unchallenged in other countries). The character became popular around the world.

The comic's potential as a motion picture was evident, and in 1968, courtesy of producer Dino De Laurentiis, BARBARELLA (1968) was born. The film was directed by Roger Vadim and starred his then-wife Jane Fonda; Forest served as the film's "artistic consultant," working on set design and other visual elements. The film was an international success, and Fonda's futuristic costumes caused much interest among fashion designers.

Forest continued with the character for some time after the movie, publishing stories of her intergalactic exploits until 1981.

Forest died of a respiratory illness.

Fowler Jr., Gene

born: May 27, 1917, Denver, CO
died: May 11, 1998, Hollywood Hills, CA, age 80

Award-winning film editor and occasional director, who had a long career in movies and television.

Although born in Denver, Gene Fowler Jr. was raised in New York City and Southern California. His father was a well-known newspaper reporter, screenwriter, and author.

Fowler studied film editing at 20th Century-Fox and worked on films including HANGMEN ALSO DIE, THE OX-BOW INCIDENT (both 1943), PHILO VANCE RETURNS (1947), MAIN STREET TO BROADWAY (1953), WHILE THE CITY SLEEPS (1956), RUN OF THE ARROW, FORTY GUNS (both 1957), A CHILD IS WAITING (1963), HANG 'EM HIGH (1968), CAVEMAN (1981) and SMORGASBORD (1983).

His short-subject documentary "Seeds of Destiny" (1946), which he made while serving in the US Army Special Services during WWII, was awarded an Oscar. Fowler also worked as part of the editing team that was Oscar nominated for IT'S A MAD MAD MAD MAD WORLD (1963). In later years, Fowler edited the documentary WALLS OF FIRE (1971), which won a Golden Globe Award; he also was part of the editing teams that won Emmys for the TV series "The Waltons" and "The Blue Knight."

Fowler edited several TV movies, including THE HOMECOMING: A CHRISTMAS STORY (1971, with his wife, Marjorie Fowler), MOLLY AND LAWLESS JOHN, THE CROOKED HEARTS, PURSUIT (all 1972), and THE GIRLS OF HUNTINGTON HOUSE (1973).

The first movie Fowler directed was the cult-classic I WAS A TEENAGE WEREWOLF (1957), followed by I MARRIED A MONSTER FROM OUTER SPACE (which Fowler also produced), GANG WAR, SHOWDOWN ON BOOT HILL (all 1958), THE OREGON TRAIL (which Fowler also co-wrote and acted in), and THE REBEL SET (both 1959).

Fowler died of natural causes.

Fowley, Douglas

born: Daniel Vincent Fowley, May 30, 1911, New York, NY
died: May 21, 1998, Woodland Hills, CA, age 86

Veteran character actor.

In a career spanning six decades, in which Douglas Fowley made two hundred movies and countless television appearances, he played every kind of role from cowboy to gangster to movie director. He is probably best remembered as the harried director trying to cope with primitive recording equipment and a temperamental female star in SINGIN' IN THE RAIN (1952).

Making his debut in THE MAD GAME (1933), he played roles in such entertaining films as TWO FOR TONIGHT (1935), ON THE AVENUE (1937), ALEXANDER'S RAGTIME BAND (1938), and DODGE CITY (1939). After serving in the navy during WWII, he continued his career with JITTERBUGS (1943), SEE HERE, PRIVATE HARGROVE (1944), THE HUCKSTERS (1947), BATTLEGROUND, MIGHTY JOE YOUNG (both 1949), and THE HIGH AND THE MIGHTY (1954).

Turning to television, Fowley played Doc Holiday in the series "The Life and Legend of Wyatt Earp," which ran from 1955 to 1961. In addition, he was a regular on "Gunsmoke" from 1968 to 1974. He made guest appearances on such shows as "The Streets of San Francisco," "Perry Mason," and "The Rockford Files." Later big screen credits include THE SEVEN FACES OF DR. LAO (1964), WALKING TALL (1973), FROM NOON TILL THREE (1976), and THE NORTH AVENUE IRREGULARS (1978). He also produced and directed MACUMBA LOVE (1960).

Fowley died of natural causes.

Franchina, Sandro

born: c. 1939
died: February 22, 1998, Paris, age 58
educ: Centro Sperimentale di Cinematografia, Rome

Actor, screenwriter, documentary filmmaker.

At the age of 12, Sandro Franchina was cast by Roberto Rossellini in EUROPA '51, aka THE GREATEST LOVE (1954). Franchina had the small but pivotal role of Michele, the boy who commits suicide because he thinks he has lost the love of his mother, played by Ingrid Bergman.

After attending film school, Franchina was quite prolific as a documentarian, producing several portraits of contemporary artists.

The only feature Franchina wrote and directed, MORIRE GRATIS (1968; US release, 1969), about a disillusioned young sculptor on a path of self destruction, won the Max Ophuls Prize. While continuing to make documentaries, Franchina took an occasional acting role, as in 1989's ENIGMA.

Franchina died after a year-long battle with cancer.

Franciosa, Massimo

born: July 23, 1924, Rome, Italy
died: Mar. 30, 1998, Rome, Italy, age 73

One of Italy's most successful screenwriters; also achieved some renown as a director.

Massimo Franciosa cowrote screenplays for some of Italy's most popular films. With his long-time collaborator, director-writer Pasquale Festa Campanile (who died in 1986), Franciosa won the best screenplay award at the 1958 Cannes Film Festival for GIOVANNI MARITI (1957). Franciosa and Feste Campanile were part of a team of screenwriters for the critically acclaimed Luchino Visconti films ROCCO AND HIS BROTHERS (1960) and THE LEOPARD (1963). Franciosa received an Oscar nomination for Best Original Screenplay for his work on THE FOUR DAYS OF NAPLES (1963). Other films he coscripted include

THE CONJUGAL BED (1963), EL GRECO (1966), THE VOYAGE (1974), and FRANKENSTEIN: ITALIAN STYLE (1977).

Franciosa's first few directing efforts were collaborative; with Festa Campanile, Franciosa co-helmed UN TENTATIVE SENTIMENTALE (1963) and WHITE VOICES (1964). He went on to a solo directorial career with such films as IL MORBIDONE (1965), and LA STAGIONE DEI SENSI (1968).

Franciosa also wrote novels and television scripts.

The cause of death was a heart attack.

Franco, Ricardo

born: May 24, 1949, Madrid, Spain
died: May 20, 1998, Madrid, Spain, age 48

Spanish filmmaker.

A successful film artist when barely out of his teens, Ricardo Franco was one of several independent directors who formed the controversial Madrid Independent Cinema in 1968. Extremely versatile, Franco served as writer, director, actor, editor, and composer for his first film, GOSPEL (1969).

It was his second feature, PASCUAL DUARTE (1975), that brought him notoriety. A gruesome film about an illiterate peasant's murderous acts, it caused walkouts at the 1976 Cannes Film Festival, but nevertheless earned its star, Jose Luis Gomez, the Festival's top acting award.

Franco's career took off as he explored different genres, from musicals to romances to adventures. Among his most noteworthy films are REMAINS FROM THE SHIPWRECK (1978), THE DREAM OF TANGIERS (1986), and BERLIN BLUES (1988). One constant in his films was a sympathy for, and understanding of, life's losers. One of his final films, LUCKY STAR (1997), is a moving drama about friendship and dignity using characters that might be regarded as the dregs of society.

Franco died of a heart attack.

Frank, Gerold

born: 1907, Cleveland, OH
died: Sept. 17, 1998, Philadelphia, PA, age 91
educ: Ohio State Univ.

Author and sometimes ghostwriter of books about celebrities.

Gerold Frank started his writing career working for newspapers and magazines. He was a trailblazer in the world of celebrity biography, as the author of several noted biographies and "as-told-to" autobiographies. *I'll Cry Tomorrow,* which Frank wrote with Mike Connolly, was about the singer Lillian Roth; the book was adapted to film in 1955 with Susan Hayward. Diana Barrymore's story was told in *Too Much, Too Soon,* a collaboration between the actress and Frank, filmed in 1958. Gossip columnist Sheila Graham recounted, with Frank's help, her love affair with writer F. Scott Fitzgerald in *Beloved Infidel,* filmed in 1959.

Frank also collaborated with Zsa Zsa Gabor on her autobiography, *My Story.* He twice won the Edgar Award from the Mystery Writers of America, for 1963's *The Deed* and 1966's *The Boston Strangler.* The latter was made into the very successful 1968 movie THE BOSTON STRANGLER, starring Tony Curtis.

Frank was a war correspondent during WWII, working in the Middle East. Some of his later writings dealt with Eastern European Jews in the period before WWII, and the founding of Israel.

No cause of death was reported.

Frann, Mary

born: Mary Frances Luecke, February 27, 1943, St. Louis, MS
died: September 23, 1998, Beverly Hills, CA, age 55

Veteran television actress, best known as the wife of Bob Newhart on the series "Newhart."

Mary Frann began her career in show business as a child model. She went on to appear in many television shows and the series "Return to Peyton Place" before landing a regular role in the soap opera, "Days of our Lives," on which she played Amanda Howard Peters from 1974 to 1979. She continued to guest on countless series including "Hawaii Five-O," "The Mary Tyler Moore Show," "The Rockford Files," and "Cannon," before becoming a familiar face to millions of TV viewers as Joanne Loudon, Bob Newhart's understanding wife on the "Newhart" series, which ran from 1982 to 1990.

Frann also made a large number of made-for-television films, including NIGHTMARE IN CHICAGO (1964), PORTRAIT OF AN ESCORT (1980), GIDGET'S SUMMER REUNION (1985), EIGHT IS ENOUGH: A FAMILY REUNION (1987), SINGLE WOMEN, MARRIED MEN (1989), and Jackie Collins' miniseries "Lucky Chances" (1990). She also appeared in several feature films, including NASHVILLE REBEL (1966) (as the wife of Waylon Jennings) and WOMAN IN THE RAIN (1978).

The cause of death was reported as heart failure.

Gable, Christopher

born: 1940, London, England
died: Oct. 23, 1998, Yorkshire, England, age 58

Internationally famous ballet star who went on to success in theater, film, and television.

Born in a poor section of North London, Christopher Gable's early interest in dance led to his acceptance, at age 11, to the Sadler's Wells Opera (now the Royal) Ballet School. After beginning with the Covent Garden Opera Ballet, he soon joined the Royal Ballet Company, where he eventually became a star. After several successes, many in tandem with dance partner Lynn Seymour, Gable left the ballet due to persistent difficulties with arthritic feet.

Possessing good looks, intelligence and charm, Gable easily made the transition to theater, acting with the Royal Exchange Theater in Manchester for several years and with the Royal Shakespeare Company as Lysander in Peter Brook's production of *A Midsummer Night's Dream.* Turning to television, he began an association with director Ken Russell that spanned over twenty years, during which time Gable appeared (and occasionally starred) in numerous films for Russell, among them WOMEN IN LOVE (1969), THE MUSIC LOVERS (1970), THE BOY FRIEND (1971), THE LAIR OF THE WHITE WORM (1988), and THE RAINBOW (1988); Gable also was featured in THE SLIPPER AND THE ROSE (1976).

Gable returned to ballet in 1982 when he co-founded the Central School of Ballet, with which he worked up to the time of his death. He was also artistic director for the Northern Ballet Company in Leeds, near his home.

The cause of death was cancer.

Gene, Peggy

born: Peggy Eaton, 1894
died: Sept. 15, 1998, Newport Beach, CA, age 104

Named by the *Guinness Book of World Records* as the world's oldest tap dancer.

Peggy Eaton was a professional dancer by the time she was 10 years old. As Peggy Gene, the young dancer was soon performing on the vaudeville circuit with such top acts as W. C. Fields and Will Rogers.

Gene had small parts in THE PHANTOM OF THE OPERA (1925) and THE JAZZ SINGER (1927). Gene later found greater success as a dance teacher; her Peggy Gene Studios of the Dance was notable for training many future stars, including Judy Garland.

Long retired from the dance business, Gene was 85 and a widow when she established herself in the Guinness Book of World Records.

Gene, who was also known as by her married name, Peggy Gene Evans, died of natural causes.

Girard, Bernard

born: Feb. 22, 1918, Vallejo, CA
died: Dec. 30, 1997, Woodland Hills, CA, age 79

Writer and director known for modest youth-oriented films.

Prior to joining the movie industry, Bernard Girard completed a tour of duty with the Army Air Corps during WWII.

During the early part of his film career, Girard worked on the scripts of such B movies as WATERFRONT AT MIDNIGHT, THE BIG PUNCH (both 1948), and BREAKTHROUGH (1950). He then provided the story for the bigger-budgeted Joan Crawford vehicle, THIS WOMAN IS DANGEROUS (1952), and started directing with two low-budget 1957 films, RIDE OUT FOR REVENGE and THE GREEN-EYED BLONDE. Girard continued to work as both a screenwriter and director; his later films included THE PARTY CRASHERS, AS YOUNG AS WE ARE (both 1958), THE REBEL SET (1959), DEAD HEAT ON A MERRY-GO-ROUND (1966), THE MAD ROOM (1969), A NAME FOR EVIL (1970), and THE HAPPINESS CAGE (1972).

Girard's many television credits included "Alfred Hitchcock Presents," "Playhouse 90," "The Twilight Zone," "You Are There," and "Wagon Train."

No cause of death was reported.

Godden, Rumer

born: Dec. 10, 1907, Eastbourne, East Essex, England
died: Nov. 8, 1998, Dumfriesshire, Scotland, age 90

British novelist whose best-known works were adapted for the screen.

Rumer Godden was only 9 months old when her father relocated his family from England to India. Godden spent her childhood and young adult years in colonial India, and used the country as the setting of many of her later fictional works. During her lifetime, the prolific Godden wrote numerous books of fiction, non-fiction, poetry, and children's stories.

Michael Powell's classic BLACK NARCISSUS (1947) was based on Godden's third novel, about a community of Anglican nuns in the Himalayas. Samuel Goldwyn gave a glossy treatment to ENCHANTMENT (1949), a multi-generational romance based on Godden's *Take Three Tenses.* THE RIVER (1951), Jean Renoir's masterful exploration of life along the Ganges River, was also adapted from Godden's novel. Other movies based on her writings include LOSS OF INNOCENCE (1961), THE BATTLE OF THE VILLA FIORITA (1965), and two TV movies: IN THIS HOUSE OF BREDE (1975) and THE PEACOCK SPRING (1995).

Godden co-wrote the screenplay for INNOCENT SINNERS (1958), taken from her novel *An Episode of Sparrows.*

No cause of death was reported.

Goldman, James

born: June 30, 1927, Chicago, IL
died: Oct. 28, 1998, New York, NY, age 71
educ: University of Chicago, Columbia University

Screenwriter, playwright, and novelist.

After serving in the Army from 1952-54, James Goldman became a writer. His first noteworthy item was the play *Blood, Sweat, and Stanley Poole,* which Goldman co-wrote with his younger brother William (who later became a noted screenwriter); the play opened on Broadway in 1961. Goldman's next play, *They Might Be Giants* (1961), was first produced in London. He achieved success on Broadway in 1966 with his play *The Lion in Winter;* one of his later hits was the 1971 musical *Follies,* for which he wrote the book.

Goldman moved into screenwriting in the late 1960s. His screenplay for THE LION IN WINTER (1968) won him an Oscar. His other screenwriting credits include THEY MIGHT BE GIANTS, NICHOLAS AND ALEXANDRA (both 1971), ROBIN AND MARIAN (1976), and WHITE NIGHTS (1986), which he cowrote with Eric Hughes and Nancy Dowd.

For television, Goldman adapted John Collier's story for the musical EVENING PRIMROSE (1966). He also collaborated on the 1987 miniseries "Queenie" (using the name Winston Beard), co-wrote ANNA KARENINA (1985), and scripted OLIVER TWIST (1982) and ANASTASIA: THE MYSTERY OF ANNA (1986). Goldman also wrote several novels and books of nonfiction.

A heart attack was the cause of Goldman's death.

Goldstone, Duke

born: Louis Goldstone, 1914, Omaha, NE
died: Apr. 16, 1998, Los Angeles, CA, age 84

Editor who worked in both film and television.

Upon coming to Hollywood in his late teens, Duke Goldstone was hired to work in the property department at Universal Studios. He soon progressed to film editing; among the many films on which he worked are WOLVES OF THE SEA, ON THE GREAT WHITE TRAIL (both 1938), several "Hedda Hopper's Hollywood" shorts (1941-42), and the George Pal-directed movies THE GREAT RUPERT and DESTINATION MOON (both 1950).

He tried feature-film directing with the low-budget quasi-musical HOLLYWOOD BURLESQUE (1949), and was the executive producer for THE HARRAD SUMMER (1974).

In the 1950s, Goldstone moved over to television, becoming involved as a producer and director in several musical variety shows, including "The Connie Haines Show," "Horace Heidt's Bandwagon," "The Frankie Laine Show," and "The Lawrence Welk Show." He later produced and directed military, corporate, industrial, and educational films.

Goldstone died at his home of heart failure.

Gora, Claudio

born: Emilio Giordana, July 27, 1913, Genoa, Italy
died: Mar. 13, 1998, Italy, age 84

Italian actor, writer, and director.

Claudio Gora began acting on stage and screen during the late 1930s. He was in the forefront of his country's emergence, shortly after WWII, as a vital European film center. In a career that spanned several decades, Gora acted in numerous movies, directed and wrote a small number of films, appeared on television, and performed frequently onstage.

He started acting in European films in 1939, and often made several films in one year. In 1942 he met actress Marina Berti while working with her on the movie SIGNORINETTE; the two later married. Gora's films include LUXURY GIRLS (1953), THE GODDESS OF LOVE (1958), THE FACTS OF MURDER (1959), THE SWORDSMAN OF SIENA (1962), GIDGET GOES TO ROME, THE EASY LIFE, (both 1963), WHITE VOICES (1965), MADE IN ITALY (1967), CONFESSIONS OF A POLICE CAPTAIN (1971), and LION OF THE DESERT (1981).

Included among Gora's non-acting credits are the acclaimed FEBBRE DI VIVERE (1953) and L'ODIO E IL MIO DIO (1967), both of which he cowrote and directed.

Gora died of heart failure in his home near Rome.

Goring, Marius

born: May 23, 1912, Newport, Isle of Wight
died: Sept. 30, 1998, West Sussex, England, age 86

Actor prominent in British theater, film, and television for over 60 years.

Although best known as star of the long running BBC series "The Expert," and as Julian Craster, the earnest young composer in that most beloved of ballet films, THE RED SHOES (1948), Marius Goring enjoyed a long career that encompassed nearly every aspect of show business.

Trained at the Old Vic Dramatic School, Goring began playing roles in Shakespearean plays as a teenager, and continued doing so for many years with the Old Vic (now the National Theater) and with many other distinguished companies, including the Royal Shakespeare company. His many appearances on the West End include *The Madwoman of Chaillot* as the ragpicker, and *Sleuth,* which he played for three seasons.

In his early films Goring was typecast as either German officers or decadent aristocrats. He was also featured in a number of interesting, quirky, and occasionally excellent films such as REMBRANDT (1936), STAIRWAY TO HEAVEN (1946), ODETTE (1951), THE MAGIC BOX (1952), THE BAREFOOT CONTESSA (1954), THE MOONRAKER (1958), and EXODUS (1960).

During the war he made British broadcasts to Germany and was the voice of Adolph Hitler in the radio serial "The Shadow of the Swastika." In addition to his success with "The Experts," Goring played the title role in the 1956 syndicated series "The Adventures of the Scarlet Pimpernel." Other television work includes the miniseries "Edward and Mrs. Simpson" (as King George V), and the TV movie "Holocaust."

A founding member of British Actors' Equity, Goring served as its president from 1963-65 and from 1975-82.

The cause of death was cancer.

Grade, Lew

born: Lewis Winogradsky, 1906, Tokmak, the Ukraine
died: Dec. 13, 1998, London, England, age 91

Flamboyant British film and television mogul.

A larger-than-life showman and one of Britain's most successful entrepreneurs, Lew Grade made his name in many areas of the entertainment industry. The son of a Ukrainian tailor, Grade fled czarist Russia with his family when he was six. In London he joined his father in the rag business, later pursuing a career as a music hall dancer. In 1926, on the stage of the Albert Hall, he won a contest and became the Charleston Champion of the World. He toured Europe with his dancing, until an injury cut short this phase of his career.

In 1934, he joined his brother Leslie in founding the Grade Organization, a theatrical agency which became Britain's biggest, representing such stars as Laurence Olivier, John Gielgud and Ralph Richardson; he was also responsible for booking American celebrities like Judy Garland, Danny Kaye, and Jack Benny into the London Palladium. He later founded Associated Television, the first commercially-financed company in Britain, and BBC's major competitor. This company produced some of England's most successful series, including "Robin Hood," "The Saint," "Thunderbirds," "The Muppet Show," and "Coronation Street," the most popular soap opera in British TV history.

As chairman and chief executive of Embassy Communications, Grade branched out into other areas of show business, coproducing Andrew Lloyd Weber's *Starlight Express* in London's West End and on Broadway. He was 70 years old when he first turned his attention to the movies.

Producing over a dozen films in less than eight years, Grade was as known for his extravagant failures as for his successes. As he himself said, "My shows are all great. Some of them are bad, but they are all great." Among his hits were VOYAGE OF THE DAMNED (1976), THE CASSANDRA CROSSING (1977), THE BOYS FROM BRAZIL (1978), MOVIE, MOVIE (1978), ON GOLDEN POND (1981), and SOPHIE'S CHOICE (1982). When his movies failed, they did so on a grand scale. About his most resounding flop, the $30 million RAISE THE TITANIC (1980), the always quotable Grade quipped, "It would have been easier to raise the Atlantic."

Grade was knighted in 1963 and given a life peerage in 1976.

The cause of death was reported as heart failure.

Gunsberg, Sheldon

born: c. 1919, Jersey City, NJ
died: June 18, 1998, New York, NY, age 78

Theater chain president, producer, distributor, and publicist.

After completing service during WWII in the Merchant Marines, Sheldon Gunsberg entered the film business as a publicist for United Artists and Universal. He eventually became the chief operating officer and then president of the Walter Reade Organization, a nationwide theater chain.

Gunsberg served as the head of Walter Reade's Continental Distributing, the organization's distribution and producing division. Continental was responsible for bringing many foreign-produced films to the United States, such as Jacques Tati's MY UNCLE (1958, which won the Oscar for Best Foreign-Language Film), Karel Reisz's SATURDAY NIGHT AND SUNDAY MORNING (1961), Tony Richardson's A TASTE OF HONEY, Sidney Lumet's A VIEW FROM THE BRIDGE (both 1962), Pietro Germi's SEDUCED AND ABANDONED (1964), Sergei Bondarchuk's WAR AND PEACE (1968), and Pier Paolo Pasolini's TEOREMA (1969).

Gunsberg was also chairman of the Walter Reade Foundation and a vice chairman of the Film Society of Lincoln Center.

Gunsberg died of a heart attack.

Gunther, Lee

born: c. 1935
died: Aug. 25, 1998, Woodland Hills, CA, age 63

Award-winning producer of animated films and television shows.

Starting out as a film editor at Warner Bros., Lee Gunther later joined the DePatie-Freleng studio, producers of the popular "Pink Panther" series. He was a film editor on the Academy Award-winning cartoon short, "The Pink Phink" (1964). Stints at Marvel Productions and Gunther-Wahl Productions followed, with Gunther working on shows that aired on the Fox Children's Network and Nickelodeon.

Gunther was on the production team for "Jim Henson's Muppet Babies," which won four consecutive Emmy Awards, starting with the 1984-85 season.

He worked as a film editor on over a hundred animated shorts and was on the production end of such popular children's TV series as "The Transformers," "G. I. Joe," "G. I. Joe Extreme," and "Angry Beavers." Gunther was the co-executive producer of the animated feature film MY LITTLE PONY (1986).

Gunther died of a stroke.

Hahn, Jess

born: 1922, Terre Haute, IN
died: June 30, 1998, France, age 76

American actor who made a career playing tough guys in European films.

Jess Hahn's film persona was that of a thug, an authoritarian figure, or other aggressive, threatening presences. He played this stereotype in a large and rather remarkable assortment of movies, from exploitation to prestige films.

He made his first film, THE MOST WANTED MAN IN THE WORLD (1953), in France, and remained there for most of his career. At first playing minor roles in such films as LES HUSSARDS (1955) and THE HAPPY ROAD (1957), Hahn went on to become a familiar figure in more important supporting roles. Among his notable films were Julien Duvivier's LA FEMME ET LE PANTIN (1958), Phillipe de Broca's CARTOUCHE (1962), Orson Welles' THE TRIAL (1963), Jules Dassin's TOPKAPI (1964), and WHAT'S NEW, PUSSYCAT? (1965).

Within the next 20 years, Hahn appeared in over thirty films, mostly crime, action and horror films. Among the more notable ones were NIGHT OF THE FOLLOWING DAY (1968), THE MYSTERIOUS ISLAND OF CAPTAIN NEMO (1972), MEAN FRANK AND CRAZY TONY (1973), THREE TOUGH GUYS (1974), and MAMMA DRACULA (1980).

No cause of death was reported.

Haller, Michael D.

aka: Michael Haller
born: c. 1938
died: July 11, 1998, Los Angeles, CA, age 60
educ: Chionard Art College, Los Angeles, CA

Production designer who started out as a director of television commercials.

Michael D. Haller began his career in film production design when he was hired for George Lucas's first feature, THX 1138 (1971). Haller then worked on several of director Hal Ashby's films: HAROLD AND MAUDE (1971), THE LAST DETAIL (1973), COMING HOME (1978), BEING THERE (1979), and 8 MILLION WAYS TO DIE (1986). Other Haller credits include PERFECT (1985), COOKIE (1989), and two films directed by actor Sean Penn, THE INDIAN RUNNER (1991) and THE CROSSING GUARD (1995). Haller also worked on STEAL BIG, STEAL LITTLE (1995), and HURLYBURLY (1998).

Haller died of cancer.

Hampton, Henry

born: Jan. 8, 1940, St. Louis, MO
died: Nov. 22, 1998, Boston, MA, age 58
educ: Washington University, Boston University

Award-winning documentary producer-director.

Henry Hampton is best remembered as creator, executive producer, and director of the six-hour PBS series, "Eyes on the Prize." The series won Emmy Awards for writing, and one segment, BRIDGE TO FREEDOM 1965 (1987), earned an Academy Award nomination as Best Feature Documentary. Hampton also wrote the companion volume to the series, *Voices of Freedom: An Oral History of America's Civil Rights Movement.*

Hampton also served as executive producer of "The Great Depression," a seven-hour PBS series which won numerous awards, including a DuPont-Columbia Silver Baton, a Columbus International Film and Video Festival Award, and an Emmy Award. Other highly lauded documentaries produced by Hampton include "America's War on Poverty" and "Malcolm X: Make it Plain."

As founder and president of the production company Blackside, Inc., Hampton produced or otherwise had major input on over sixty film and media projects. In 1990 he was one of five Americans honored by the National Endowment for the Arts for their work in making history, literature, philosophy, and other humanities more accessible to the public.

Hampton's death was the result of lung cancer.

Hartman, Phil

born: Philip Edward Hartmann, Sept. 24, 1948, Branford, Ontario, Canada
died: May 28, 1998, Encino, CA, age 49

Comic actor, prolific voice-over artist, expert impressionist, and television personality.

Raised in Connecticut and Los Angeles, Phil Hartman was studying graphic design and creating album covers when he turned his talents toward improvisational comedy with the group The Groundlings in 1975.

Working with comic Paul Reubens led to Hartman's sole credit as screenwriter with PEE-WEE'S BIG ADVENTURE (1985). He would later appear as Kap'n Karl on Reubens' children's series, "Pee-wee's Playhouse."

Through the early 1980s, Hartman did commercials, voice-overs, and small roles in such films as PANDEMONIUM (1982) and WEEKEND PASS (1984). He achieved celebrity, however, with NBC's "Saturday Night Live," on which he was a regular from 1986-94. SNL offered him the opportunity to display his talent for mimicry, playing such personalities as Frank Sinatra, the Rev. Jimmy Swaggart, Ted Kennedy, and Bill Clinton. During this period he also appeared in numerous films, including THREE AMIGOS, JUMPIN' JACK FLASH (both 1986), BLIND DATE (1987), FLETCH LIVES (1989), SO I MARRIED AN AXE MURDERER, and THE CONEHEADS (both 1993).

After SNL Hartman guested on television shows like "The Larry Sanders Show" and "The Dennis Miller Show" and created numerous voice-over characters on the cartoon series "The Simpsons." On the big screen, he went on to play major roles in JINGLE ALL THE WAY and SGT. BILKO (both 1996), as well as the made-for-television movie THE SECOND CIVIL WAR (1997). His last film appearance was as Phil Fimple in Joe Dante's SMALL SOLDIERS (1998). From 1994-98, Hartman was a regular on the sitcom "NewsRadio," playing anchorman Bill McNeal.

Hartman, who was regarded as a gentle, funny and generous man, met a tragic death when he was murdered in his sleep by his wife, Brynn, who then committed suicide with a self-inflicted gunshot wound.

Hatfield, Hurd

born: Willian Rukard Hurd Hatfield, Dec. 7, 1918, New York, NY
died: Dec. 25, 1998, Monktown, Ireland, age 80
educ: Columbia University, NY

Actor in film, stage, and television.

Though born in the United States, Hurd Hatfield made his professional show business debut on the London stage. Returning to America, he made his first screen appearance in DRAGON SEED (1944). The following year, he played the title role in the movie for which he is best known, THE PICTURE OF DORIAN GRAY (1945). The film costarred the young Angela Lansbury, with whom Hatfield would reunite many years later for several guest appearances on the television series "Murder, She Wrote."

Hatfield went on to act in a number of films, including DIARY OF A CHAMBERMAID (1946), THE BEGINNING OR THE END (1947), JOAN OF ARC (1948), THE LEFT-HANDED GUN (1958), KING OF KINGS (1961), MICKEY ONE (1965), THE BOSTON STRANGLER (1968), CRIMES OF THE HEART (1986), and HER ALIBI (1989).

In the 1950s, Hatfield did a good deal of theater work, appearing with Rex Harrison and Lilli Palmer in *Venus Observed,* directed by Laurence Olivier, and playing the title role in *Julius Caesar* at the American Shakespeare Festival in Stratford, Connecticut. On Broadway he played Don Juan in John Gielgud's production of *Much Ado About Nothing.* He also portrayed Don Quixote and Lord Byron in Tennessee Williams' *Camino Real.*

On television, Hatfield played the title roles in "The Count of Monte Cristo" and "Don Juan in Hell," as well as in the made-for-television movies THIEF (1970), THE NORLISS TAPES (1973), THE WORD (1978), and YOU CAN'T GO HOME AGAIN (1979). In recent years, Hatfield toured Europe in a one-man show about James McNeill Whistler called *The Son of Whistler's Mother.*

No cause of death was reported.

Hayes, Patricia

born: Dec. 22, 1909, Camberwell, London
died: Sept. 19, 1998, age 88
educ: Royal Academy of Dramatic Art, England

British character actress with a high-pitched voice, renowned for her portrayal of cockney women.

Encouraged by her parents to seek a career in show business, Patricia Hayes made her acting debut at the age of 12, in radio, usually playing little boys. After finishing her dramatic training at the Royal Academy of Dramatic Art (with honors) she spent 10 years in repertory theatre. Shortly afterwards, Hayes won acclaim when she was chosen by famed playwright J. B. Priestly to act in his play *When We Are Married.*

During the WWII years, Hayes turned to radio and established herself as a comedienne of the first rank. Her popularity continued when she moved over to television, appearing in several shows including "The Benny Hill Show," the sitcoms "Till Death Us Do Part" and "In Sickness and in Health," and the title character in "Edna, the Inebriate Woman." For her portrayal of Edna, Hayes won the 1972 Actress of the Year Award.

While Hayes appeared frequently on stage, including two seasons with the Royal Shakespeare Company, she also made over two dozen films. These include WHEN WE ARE MARRIED (1943), NICHOLAS NICKLEBY (1947), THE BATTLE OF THE SEXES (1960), THE SICILIANS (1964), GOODBYE MR. CHIPS(1969), THE NEVERENDING STORY (1984), WILLOW, LITTLE DORRIT, and A FISH CALLED WANDA (all 1988). Among her TV movies were THE CORN IS GREEN (1979), CYMBELINE (1983), THE HOUSE OF BERNARDA ALBA (1991), and LORD OF MISRULE (1996).

In 1987, Hayes was made an Officer of the Order of the British Empire, an honor bestowed by Queen Elizabeth.

No cause of death was reported.

Hayes, Peter Lind

born: Joseph Conrad Lind, June 25, 1915, San Francisco, CA
died: Apr. 21, 1998, Las Vegas, NV, age 82

Versatile entertainer who started in vaudeville and successfully segued to the legitimate stage, radio, movies, and television.

Trained by his mother, vaudevillian Grace Hayes, Peter Lind Hayes joined her act when he was nine years old. He was a child actor on the stage, and as a young adult appeared in small roles in several light film comedies, including MILLION DOLLAR LEGS (1939), SEVENTEEN (1940), PLAYMATES (1941), COLLEGE SWEETHEARTS(1942), WINGED VICTORY (1944), and THE SENATOR WAS INDISCREET (1947).

Hayes and his wife, Mary Healy (whom he married in 1940), had a very successful act on the night-club circuit. The couple also hosted a popular daily radio program, "The Peter Lind Hayes-Mary Healy Show." Hayes and Healy became frequent performers on television, starting in 1949 and continuing for over two decades. They debuted with the variety show "Inside the USA with Chevrolet," and went on to "The Peter Lind Hayes Show," "Star of the Family" and "Peter Loves Mary." Hayes also appeared on several variety-talk shows, including "The Stork Club," "The Perry Como Show," "The Ed Sullivan Show," and "The Dinah Shore Show."

While continuing to work on TV Hayes would make an occasional movie, such as the cult favorite THE 5,000 FINGERS OF DR. T. (1953), or star on Broadway, as in the 1958 comedy *Who Was That Lady I Saw You With?.*

No cause of death was reported.

Hayward, Chuck

born: 1920, Nebraska
died: Feb. 23, 1998, North Hollywood, CA, age 77

Stuntman and stunt coordinator.

From the age of 16, Chuck Hayward worked as a horse trainer and bronco rider. He was a rodeo worker until 1947 when he settled in California to become a stuntman in the movies. He struck up a friendship with John Wayne while doing stunt work in the star's THE FIGHTING KENTUCKIAN (1949), and appeared with Wayne in several other films.

Besides doubling for many stars, Hayward had small character parts in over two dozen movies. He worked often with John Ford, appearing in the director's WAGON MASTER (1950), THE HORSE SOLDIERS (1959), SERGEANT RUTLEDGE (1960), TWO RODE TOGETHER (1961), THE MAN WHO SHOT LIBERTY VALANCE (1962), and CHEYENNE AUTUMN (1964).

Hayward also worked on several television westerns. Beginning in 1958 he appeared in such series as "Zane Grey Theater," "Gunsmoke," "Wichita Town," "Wanted: Dead or Alive," and "Bonanza."

Recognized as one of the industry's leading stuntmen, Hayward was inducted into the Stuntmen's Hall of Fame, and was a member of the Stuntmen's Association of Motion Pictures.

Hayward succumbed to Hodgkin's disease.

Hecht Lucari, Gianni

born: 1922, Vienna, Austria
died: Aug. 27, 1998, Rome, Italy, age 76

Producer of many European films that had wide distribution.

After serving with the British Army as an Italian Intelligence liaison officer during WWII, Gianni Hecht Lucari entered the film industry in 1950. His company, Documento Films, produced numerous features, documentaries, and television programs, several of which were Italian-French coproductions.

In 1954, Hecht Lucari released TOO BAD SHE'S BAD, a crime farce which was based on a story by Antonio Moravia and featured the first screen teaming of Sophia Loren, Marcello Mastroianni, and Vittorio De Sica. Other films he produced include THE WARRIOR EMPRESS (1961), RUN WITH THE DEVIL (1963) and three anthology films featuring some of Europe's biggest sex symbols: HIGH INFIDELITY (1965), featuring Monica Vitti and Claire Bloom; BAMBOLE!, aka THE DOLLS (1965), featuring Vitti, Lisi, and Gina Lollobrigida; and THE QUEENS (1968), featuring Vitti, Claudia Cardinale, and Raquel Welch. Vitti was also in Hecht Lucari's production THE GIRL WITH A PISTOL (1968), and Lisi co-starred with Ursula Andress in his ANYONE CAN PLAY (1968).

Hecht Lucari's most prestigious production was the Oscar-winning Best Foreign Language Film THE GARDEN OF THE FINZI-CONTINIS (1971), which Hecht Lucari coproduced with Arthur Cohen.

No cause of death was reported.

Herthum, Harold G.

born: 1929
died: July 4, 1998, Baton Rouge, LA, age 69

Character actor who entered the movies in his later years.

Baton Rouge inhabitant Harold G. Herthum was a businessman in insurance (and the former owner of a radio station) when he landed a job as an extra in the Richard Pryor-Jackie Gleason movie THE TOY (1982). Herthum had acted locally before that experience, and was later able to land small roles in other films, including BLAZE (1989), JFK (1991), COBB, FOREST GUMP (both 1994), and TIN CUP (1996).

Herthum died of a heart attack.

Hervey, Irene

born: Irene Herwick, July 11, 1910, Los Angeles, CA
died: Dec. 20, 1998, Calabasas, CA, age 89

Film, television and stage actress.

Known for her dimpled beauty and lady-like demeanor, Irene Hervey was featured in over a dozen films in the late 1930s and early 1940s. She is perhaps best remembered as the girlfriend (and eventually wife) of James Stewart in the western comedy, DESTRY RIDES AGAIN (1939). Under contract to Universal Studios, she played small roles in STRANGER RETURNS (1933), THE COUNT OF MONTE CRISO (1934), and THE THREE GODFATHERS (1936) before playing her first lead in THE GIRL SAID NO (1937).

After a secondary role in THE BOYS FROM SYRACUSE (1940), Hervey was relegated by Universal to leads in B pictures such as UNSEEN ENEMY, NIGHT MONSTER, and DESTINATION UNKNOWN (all 1942). She left Hollywood to appear on Broadway, and on tour, with the play *State of the Union.* Over the next 30 years she made sporadic appearances on the screen, playing in such films as MR. PEABODY AND THE MERMAID (1948), TEENAGE REBEL (1956), CACTUS FLOWER (1969), and PLAY MISTY FOR ME (1971).

In television, Hervey made guest appearances on "Charlie's Angels," "My Three Sons" (for which she received an Emmy nomination), "Perry Mason" and "The Twilight Zone." She also played Anne Francis' Aunt Meg in the series "Honey West."

Her second marriage, to screen tenor Allan Jones, lasted for 21 years (they divorced in 1957) and produced a son, singer Jack Jones.

The cause of death was reported as heart failure.

Hickson, Joan

born: Aug. 5, 1906, Kingsthorpe, Northamptonshire, England
died: Oct. 17, 1998, Colchester, Essex, age 92
educ: Royal Academy of Dramatic Arts

British character actress who gained international fame as TV's Miss Marple.

Joan Hickson studied drama for three years and made her acting debut at the age of 20. She appeared in many West End shows, including a 1945 production of Agatha Christie's *Appointment With Death.* Although Hickson was most active in her native England she did appear on Broadway, winning a Tony Award for her performance in *Bedroom Farce* (1979).

Hickson had dozens of supporting roles in film, including WIDOW'S MIGHT (1934), THE MAN WHO COULD WORK MIRACLES (1937), THE OUTSIDER (1949), SEVEN DAYS TO NOON (1950), THE MAGIC BOX (1951), and THE PROMOTER (1952). She appeared in two of the popular "DOCTOR" films starring Dirk Bogarde: DOCTOR IN THE HOUSE (1954) and DOCTOR AT SEA (1955); she also had roles in several of the "CARRY ON" series, including CARRY ON NURSE (1959) and CARRY ON REGARDLESS (1961).

Hickson had a small part in one of the first Miss Marple movies, MURDER SHE SAID (1961), starring Margaret Rutherford as the famous amateur sleuth. She later played the role of Jane Marple in the BBC television series from 1984-92. Hickson played Marple in a quieter fashion than Rutherford, making the sleuth more of an observer. Hickson soon became an international star, as the show was aired in more than 30 countries. Her artistry was recognized in 1987 when she was awarded the Order of the British Empire by Queen Elizabeth.

No cause of death was reported.

Ho, Leonard

born: Leonard Ho Koon Cheung, c. 1924
died: February 16, 1998, Hong Kong, age 74

Major producer and movie mogul in the Hong Kong film industry.

Influential in Hong Kong's film industry for over forty years, Leonard Ho began his career writing for newspapers. In 1958, his friend and future partner, Rayond Chow, helped him secure a position at Shaw Brothers Studio as head of promotion and production. He remained with Shaw Brothers for eleven successful years, at which time he and Chow broke off to form the Golden Harvest film organization, which was to become Asia's largest production, distribution, and theater management group. Ho would go on to produce more than four hundred films.

Golden Harvest's first film was ANGRY RIVER (1971), but it achieved major success with THE BIG BOSS (1972), the film that launched the career of Bruce Lee. In the mid-1970s, Ho discovered a young kung fu maestro, Jackie Chan, and a long and successful collaboration began. Among the films that the two made together were THE YOUNG MASTER (1980), DRAGON STRIKE (1983), POLICE STORY 2 (1986), MIRACLE (1989), and OPERATION CONDOR (1991). It was RUMBLE IN THE BRONX (1995) that made Chan a major star in the United States, and was Hong Kong's highest grossing film of the year.

With as many films as Golden Harvest turned out, there were as many failures as successes, but a number of Ho's films were singled out for prestigious awards and film festival honors. Among these were ROUGE (1988), A FISHY STORY (1990), ACTRESS (1993), and CHRIST OF NANJING (1996). His last film was Jackie Chan's WHO AM I? (1998).

The cause of death was a heart attack.

Hobson, Valerie

born: 1917, Larne, Northern Ireland
died: Nov. 13, 1998, London, England, age 81

British film star.

Valerie Hobson studied acting at the Royal Academy of Dramatic Art, and began her career on the London stage. After appearing in a handful of small British films, she was signed by Universal Studios in 1934 and moved to Hollywood. Her first Universal feature was THE MAN WHO RECLAIMED HIS HEAD (1934); she went on to star in a series of horror films, including THE BRIDE OF FRANKENSTEIN, THE MYSTERY OF EDWIN DROOD, and THE WEREWOLF OF LONDON (all 1935).

Disappointed with the way her career in Hollywood was going, Hobson returned to England in 1937. With her patrician bearing and speech, she graced a number of quality films over the next fifteen years, among them DRUMS (1938), THE SPY IN BLACK (1939), THE ADVENTURES OF TARTU (1943), THE ROCKING HORSE WINNER (1949), and THE PROMOTER (1952). Her most memorable appearances were in David Lean's classic GREAT EXPECTATIONS (1946) and the delightful black comedy KIND HEARTS AND CORONETS (1949).

In 1939, Hobson married a baronet, Sir Anthony Havelock-Allen, who produced several of her films. The marriage ended in 1952, and the following year Hobson scored a great personal triumph playing Anna Leonowens in the London stage production of *The King and I.* On this high note, she chose to end her career.

In 1954, Hobson married politician John Profumo. In 1963, while serving as Secretary of State for War, Profumo became involved in a highly publicized scandal involving his affair with call girl Christine Keeler, who was also involved with a Soviet military attache; Profumo wound up resigning in disgrace. Hobson stood by her husband, and the two of them involved themselves in a great deal of charity work. Profumo eventually redeemed himself to the extent that he and his wife were invited to Buckingham Palace, where he was honored for his good works by being made a Commander, Order of the British Empire.

The cause of Hobson's death was a heart attack.

Hopkins, John R.

aka: John Hopkins
born: Jan. 27, 1931, London, England
died: July 23, 1998, Woodland Hills, CA, age 67
educ: St. Catherine's College, Cambridge University

Screenwriter, playwright, and writer for television.

Shortly after graduating college, John R. Hopkins joined the BBC as a studio manager. He eventually became a writer, and over the next several years saw one hundred of his scripts produced on TV, including several dozen for the popular police drama "Z Cars," which he also created. Hopkins also wrote the popular 1966 miniseries "Talking to a Stranger," which he later adapted for American television. The American version starred Shirley Knight, whom he married in 1972.

Hopkins also wrote for the stage. His first play was *This Story of Yours*, produced on the West End in 1969; he later adapted it for the screen as THE OFFENCE (1973), which starred Sean Connery and was directed by Sidney Lumet. Michael Moriarty won a best actor Tony Award for Hopkins's first Broadway play, *Find Your Way Home* (1974). Of the many plays that Hopkins wrote, several featured his wife Knight.

Several of Hopkins's screenplays were collaborative efforts, including the sex comedy TWO LEFT FEET, the James Bond adventure THUNDERBALL (both 1965), the comedy-drama THE VIRGIN SOLDIERS (1970), and the spy thriller THE HOLCROFT COVENANT (1985), based on Robert Ludlum's thriller. He also scripted the Sherlock Holmes mystery MURDER BY DECREE (1979)and served as codirector, coproducer, and coscreenwriter for the slasher thriller TORMENT (1986).

Some of the writer's notable TV scripts include the miniseries "The Gambler" (1971), "Divorce; his/Divorce; hers," (1973) and "Smiley's People" (1982), and the telefilms CODENAME: KYRIL (1988), and (as cowriter) HIROSHIMA (1995).

Hopkins died of a head injury that was the result of a fall.

Horvitch, Eric

born: c. 1922
died: Aug. 10, 1998, Johannesburg, South Africa, age 76

South African cinematographer.

A longtime member of the American Society of Cinematographers, Eric Horvitch was the only member of the society to live and work exclusively on the African continent. He was also a member of British Cinematographic Society, the Society of Motion Picture and Television Engineers, and the South African Society of Cinematographers.

In addition to his early work as a cinematographer, Horvitch formed the largest and most successful motion picture and photographic supply houses in his country. Always supportive of, and influential in, local film industry development, he was instrumental in bringing in the latest equipment and technological innovations to filmmakers in the region.

Horvitch died of complications following heart surgery.

Hutchinson, Josephine

born: Oct. 12, 1903, Seattle, WA
died: June 4, 1998, New York, NY, age 94

Actress who went from playing ingenues to mature character parts.

As a child, Josephine Hutchinson was encouraged in her show business pursuits by her actress mother. Through her mother's connections, young Hutchinson obtained a role in the Mary Pickford vehicle THE LITTLE PRINCESS (1917).

Hutchinson turned to the stage after this experience, joining Eva Le Gallienne's prestigious Civic Repertory Theatre. It was while Hutchinson was on the road with this troupe that she won a short-term contract with Warner Bros.

Though her first role at the studio was in the Mervyn Le Roy musical HAPPINESS AHEAD (1934) opposite Dick Powell, Hutchinson was primarily cast in inconsequential programmers like the melodrama I MARRIED A DOCTOR (1936). Her performance as Marie Pasteur in THE STORY OF LOUIS PASTEUR (1936) garnered her good reviews, but the studio continued to neglect her, and she subsequently worked with other companies in films like SON OF FRANKENSTEIN (1939), TOM BROWN'S SCHOOL DAYS (1940), and HER FIRST BEAU (1941).

Hutchinson was off the screen until 1946, when she returned in a supporting role in the film noir SOMEWHERE IN THE NIGHT. Her later roles were supporting ones in films like ADVENTURE IN BALTIMORE (1949), LOVE IS BETTER THAN EVER, RUBY GENTRY (both 1952), and GUN FOR A COWARD (1957).

Hutchinson was more active in television in the 1960s and '70s. She acted in the telefilms STORM OVER ELVERON (1968) and THE HOMECOMING: A CHRISTMAS STORY (1971), as well as many drama series, including "Gunsmoke," "Perry Mason," "Wagon Train," "The Twilight Zone," "Bonanza," "The Name of the Game," and "Little House on the Prairie."

No cause of death was reported for Hutchinson, who died in a nursing home.

Innes, Hammond

born: Ralph Hammond Innes, 1913
died: June 10, 1998, Kersey, England, age 84

Author of adventure thrillers which were adapted for the screen.

Before he became famous as a novelist, Hammond Innes was a journalist for London's *Financial News* (later known as the *Financial Times*). His first book, *Attack Alarm,* came out in 1940 while he was serving in Britain's Royal Artillery. Innes was a seasoned traveler and an accomplished sailor with a keen sense of adventure—characteristics that inspired the story lines of his almost three dozen thrillers.

Some of Innes's novels were turned into feature films. *The Lonely Skier* was filmed as SNOWBOUND (1949), followed by HELL BELOW ZERO (1954), CAMPBELL'S KINGDOM (1957), and Gary Cooper's second-to-last film, THE WRECK OF THE MARY DEARE (1959), a high-seas adventure about insurance fraud.

No cause of death was reported.

Jenkins, Megs

born: Muguette Mary Jenkins, April 21, 1917, Birkenhead, Chesire, England
died: Oct. 5, 1998, England, age 81
educ: School of Dancing and Dramatic Art, Liverpool

Veteran character actress.

Megs Jenkins initially dreamed of being a ballerina, but as she possessed what she termed an "unsylphlike" figure, she settled for acting. She was quickly typecast as the lovable matron, a part she played quite effectively for more than half a century.

In some of her London stage performances she had the opportunity to portray more complex characters, in plays like *Summer and Smoke* (1951) and *School Mistress* (1954). She made her film debut in the 1939 spy melodrama THE SILENT BATTLE (aka CONTINENTAL EXPRESS) and then appeared in close to three dozen films over the next several decades, including POISON PEN (1941), GREEN FOR DANGER (1946), THE MONKEY'S PAW (1948), THE HISTORY OF MR. POLLY, SARABAND (both 1949), SECRET PEOPLE, IVANHOE (both 1952), THE CRUEL SEA (1953), THE STORY OF ESTHER COSTELLO (1957), and INDISCREET (1958). The most notable films she appeared in were MURDER MOST FOUL (1964), BUNNY LAKE IS MISSING (1965), OLIVER! (1968), and ASYLUM (1972).

Some of her memorable television work includes the kindly Mrs. Peggotty in DAVID COPPERFIELD (1970); appearances in "All Creatures Great and Small"; the sitcom "Young at Heart," opposite John Mills; and the miniseries "A Woman of Substance."

No cause of death was reported.

Jewell, Austin

born: c. 1915
died: Sept. 24, 1998, Vista, CA, age 83
educ: University of California, Los Angeles

Child actor who eventually moved into production.

As a youngster, Austin Jewell appeared in GREED (1925), BLOOD WILL TELL, KING OF KINGS (both 1927), CITY LIGHTS (1931), and some Tom Mix westerns. Following a stint in the US Navy during WWII, Jewell returned to the movie industry, working at Columbia Pictures and the Disney organization. He later became a production manager.

Jewell died of cancer.

John, Rosamund

aka: Rosamund Jones
born: Nora Rosamund Jones, Oct. 19, 1913, London, England
died: Oct. 27, 1998, England, age 85

Popular redheaded British actress.

Although she was not very well known in America, Rosamund John enjoyed a career in British films. She also worked on stage, with her most notable performance being in a 1940 revival of George Bernard Shaw's *The Devil's Disciple*.

Her film debut was in THE SECRET OF THE LOCH (1934), an early fantasy about Scotland's Loch Ness monster. John co-stared in SPITFIRE (1943) with Leslie Howard, who also directed and coproduced; Howard produced another film with John, THE LAMP STILL BURNS (1943), before his untimely death. Many of John's films were propagandistic WWII dramas, including THE GENTLE SEX (1943), SOLDIER, SAILOR (1944), JOHNNY IN THE CLOUDS (1945), and GREEN FOR DANGER (1946).

After the war years, John was featured in tearjerkers like WHEN THE BOUGH BREAKS (1947); crime melodramas like THE UPTURNED GLASS (also 1947); and dramas, including NO PLACE FOR JENNIFER (1950), NEVER LOOK BACK (1952), and BOTH SIDES OF THE LAW (1953). After OPERATION MURDER (1957), John retired from films.

No cause of death was reported.

Kane, Bob

born: Bob Kahn, Oct. 24, 1915, New York, NY
died: Nov. 3, 1998, Los Angeles, CA, age 83

Comic book artist and writer most famous as the creator of Batman.

Bob Kane's Batman character has been one of the most popular comic creations of the 20th century, on a par with Superman, Mickey Mouse, and Bugs Bunny. Kane created the character over a single weekend for a debut in *Detective Comics* in 1939; his intention was to create a hero without super-human powers, but who relied on his own mental and physical skills (and a very unique style) in dealing with a bizarre assortment of villains, many of whom became almost as famous as Batman himself. Though the original idea of Batman was drawn from several sources, the "bat" angle was, according to Kane, inspired by a Da Vinci painting of a flying machine with bat wings. Robin, Batman's sidekick, made his first appearance a year after Batman's debut.

The success of the character led to a daily comic strip, as well as two fifteen-episode film serials released by Columbia Pictures. In the 1960s, Batman reappeared on the television screen in a hugely successful—and very campy—series starring Adam West, which, ironically, spawned a big screen feature, BATMAN (1966), using the cast from the TV series.

Director Tim Burton's BATMAN (1989) was the next big-screen incarnation of the Caped Crusader. BATMAN RETURNS (1992) followed the success of the first, and the character returned the next year in an animated feature, BATMAN: MASK OF THE PHANTASM (1993), based on a daily TV cartoon series. The last two of the live-action series of films to appear in Kane's lifetime were BATMAN FOREVER (1995) and BATMAN AND ROBIN (1997). For all of the proceeding motion pictures, Kane served as project consultant, in addition to being credited as the creator of the characters.

Other comic character created by Kane include Courageous Cat and Minute Mouse, and Cool McCool. At the time of his death, Kane had finished a screenplay, "The Silver Fox," about a new superhero.

Kane died of natural causes.

Kaye, Stubby

born: Dec. 11, 1918, Bronx, NY
died: Dec. 14, 1998, Rancho Mirage, CA, age 79

Musical comedy, film, and television actor.

After graduating from DeWitt Clinton High School, Stubby Kaye won on "the Major Bowes Amateur Hour" radio show, launching his career as a traveling vaudevillian. During the war he toured with Bob Hope and the USO, and after worked mostly as a comedian and emcee.

Kaye's big break came in 1950, when he created the role of Nicely-Nicely Johnson in the Broadway megahit *Guys and Dolls,* wherein he stopped the show with his rendition of the song, "Sit Down, You're Rocking the Boat." As "Marryin' Sam" in the Broadway hit *Li'l Abner* he once again had a show-stopper with the number "Jubilation T. Cornpone." During this period, he guested on many television variety shows, including those hosted by Dinah Shore, Perry Como, and Marge and Gower Champion, as well as on such series as "Love and Marriage" and "My Sister Eileen."

He made his film debut in TAXI (1953), going on to repeat his Broadway roles in GUYS AND DOLLS (1955) and LI'L ABNER (1959). Among his other screen credits were FORTY POUNDS OF TROUBLE (1963), SEX AND THE SINGLE GIRL (1965), THE WAY WEST (1967), SWEET CHARITY (1969), SIX PACK ANNIE (1975), and WHO FRAMED ROGER RABBIT? (1988). He had a memorable turn in CAT BALLOU (1965), in which he and Nat "King" Cole sang onscreen the film's musical narration.

No cause of death was reported.

Keaton, Eleanor Norris

born: c. 1918
died: Oct. 19, 1998, California, age 80

Dancer and widow of comedian Buster Keaton

When Buster Keaton died in 1966, he and his wife Eleanor Norris Keaton had been married for 26 years. They met at MGM, where she was working as a dancer and he was working as a gagman for various studio comedies. Later, the couple worked together for many years on television and the stage.

On her own after her husband's death, Keaton became a beautician and then bred St. Bernard dogs, some of them appearing in the "Beethoven" films.

Keaton died of emphysema and lung cancer.

Khambatta, Persis

born: Oct. 2, 1950, Bombay, Maharashtra, India
died: Aug. 18, 1998, Bombay, age 47

Miss India of 1965; model, actress, humanitarian.

A natural beauty, Persis Khambatta appeared in films in her native India before working in British and American productions. She was featured in two 1975 British movies, THE WILBY CONSPIRACY and CONDUCT UNBECOMING, then appeared in STAR TREK—THE MOTION PICTURE (1979), in which she made an impression on moviegoers as the bald-headed Lieutenant Ilia.

Usually cast as an exotic or an Indian national, Khambatta's other films include NIGHTHAWKS (1981), MEGAFORCE (1982), WARRIOR OF THE LOST WORLD (1984), FIRST STRIKE (1985), MY BEAUTIFUL LAUNDRETTE (1986), PHOENIX THE WARRIOR (1987), and DEADLY INTENT (1988).

Khambatta was occasionally seen as a guest star on American TV series, including "Hunter," "MacGyver," and "Lois & Clark: The New Adventures of Superman."

The former Air India and Revlon spokeswoman was once described by India's prime minister Indira Gandhi as the "pride of India." The appellation was used by Khambatta as the title of her 1997 book, which chronicles the stories of several beauties who held the title of Miss India.

Khambatta died of a heart attack.

Kinoshita, Keisuke

born: Dec. 5, 1912, Hamamatsu, Japan
died: Dec. 30, 1998, Tokyo, Japan, age 86

Japanese film director and screenwriter.

Equally adept at tragedy, comedy, domestic drama, and social satire, Keisuke Kinoshita was a highly regarded film artist whose work, regrettably, remained largely unknown in the United States.

Kinoshita joined what is now the Shochiku Company, one of Japan's major movie studios, in 1933. His first directorial effort was THE BLOSSOMING PORT (1943), the first of over forty films he would direct and often write. Kinoshita's versatility is evident from a filmography that includes such satires as CARMEN COMES HOME (1951), a musical comedy about a bubbly stripper, and CANDLE IN THE WIND (1957), a humorous film about the dissolution of a Japanese family, alongside such dramas as A JAPANESE TRAGEDY (1953), THE BALLAD OF NARAYAMA (1958), and LOVELY FLUTE AND DRUM (1967). Kinoshita's biggest international success was TWENTY-FOUR EYES (1954), a chronicle of 20 years in the life of a schoolteacher and a dozen of her pupils; the film examines the topics of youth, innocence (and the loss thereof) and, inevitably, sorrow.

The cause of death was a stroke.

Kinskey, Leonid

born: April 18, 1903, St. Petersburg, Russia
died: Sept. 9, 1998, Fountain Hills, AZ, age 95

Veteran Hollywood character actor.

Best remembered for his portrayal of Sascha, the bartender at Rick's Cafe in CASABLANCA (1942), Leonid Kinskey was recommended for the role by Humphrey Bogart. By the time he acted in that film, playing eccentric Russian characters had already become Kinskey's stock-in-trade. He is well-remembered as a comic gigolo in DOWN ARGENTINE WAY (1940) and as one of the seven professors in Howard Hawks' takeoff on "Snow White," BALL OF FIRE (1942). Other credits include TROUBLE IN PARADISE (1932), DUCK SOUP (1933), LES MISERABLES (1935), THE GENERAL DIED AT DAWN (1936), ALGIERS (1938), SO ENDS OUR NIGHT (1941), and MONSIEUR BEAUCAIRE (1946).

Kinskey retired from acting in the late 1940's, but returned in the fifties, appearing in films like THE MAN WITH THE GOLDEN ARM (1955) and GLORY (1956).

He ran a restaurant called Bublitchki on the Sunset Strip, which catered to the Hollywood crowd. During this time, he made guest appearances on such television shows as "The Man From U.N.C.L.E.," "Hogans Heroes," and "Perry Mason." He later made a living as producer, director, and writer of industrial films.

Kiskey was married three times. His second wife, Viennese beauty Iphigenie Castiglioni, played many distinguished cameo roles.

Kinskey's death was caused by complications from a stroke.

Korvin, Charles

born: Geza Korvin Karpathi, Nov. 21, 1907, Piestany, Hungary
died: June 18, 1998, New York, NY, age 90

Actor who worked in stage, screen, and television.

Educated at the Sorbonne, the Hungarian-born Charles Korvin remained in Paris for ten years as a photographer and documentary filmmaker. Moving to America in 1940, he began a career on the stage, making his Broadway debut in *Dark Eyes* in 1943. Spotted in this production by producer Charles K. Feldman, Korvin was signed as a contract player for Universal Studios. He returned occasionally to the stage, most notably for a particularly long run in the play *Barefoot in the Park,* but did most of his later work in film.

He made his film debut in the title role of ENTER ARSENE LUPIN (1945). Korvin made a specialty of playing cads, gentleman thieves, and philandering husbands; early in his screen career he was paired in three films with Merle Oberon: THIS LOVE OF OURS (1945), TEMPTATION (1946) and BERLIN EXPRESS (1948). Other notable titles include THE KILLER THAT STALKED NEW YORK (1950), LYDIA BAILEY (1952), and SANGAREE (1953).

In the early 1950s, Korvin ran afoul of the House Committee on Un-American Activities for refusing to cooperate and did not make another film until Stanley Kramer signed him for a prominent role in the star-studded SHIP OF FOOLS (1965). He continued to make films, among them THE MAN WHO HAD POWER OVER WOMEN (1970) and INSIDE OUT (1975), but worked primarily in television. He guest-starred on shows like "Zorro," "U.S. Steel Hour," "I Spy," and "Holocaust;" fans of classic sitcoms will remember him as Carlos the mambo teacher on an episode of "The Honeymooners." From 1959-60 Korvin starred in the series "Interpol Calling."

No cause of death was reported.

Kosberg, Marvin I.

born: c. 1930
died: Mar. 18, 1998, Henderson, NV, age 67

Versatile sound expert.

As a sound or dialogue editor, Marvin I. Kosberg worked on many films, including LITTLE BIG MAN, THE LANDLORD (both 1970), BEYOND THE POSEIDON ADVENTURE (1979), ENDLESS LOVE (1981), and MR. NORTH (1988).

Kosberg was also a specialist in dialogue looping, the post-production re-recording of dialogue also known as automatic dialogue replacement (ADR). His ADR editing credits include THE JERK (1979), TAPS, DOCTOR DETROIT (both 1981), and SWEET LIBERTY (1986).

His television work encompassed sitcoms, dramas and TV movies, such as "The Partridge Family," "Bewitched," "Magnum P.I.," "Simon and Simon," and BRIAN'S SONG (1971). Kosberg was one of several on the sound editing team that won Emmy Awards for a 1975 "Medical Story" episode and the 1975 miniseries "QB VII;" he was also on the team that received two Emmy Award nominations, for an episode of "Police Woman," and the 1976 telefilm THE LINDBERGH KIDNAPPING CASE.

Kosberg died of heart failure.

Kren, Kurt

born: c. 1928
died: June 23, 1998, Vienna, Austria, age 69

Avant-garde filmmaker who was in the forefront of Europe's structuralist movement.

While his short movies were not generally known to mainstream filmgoers, Kurt Kren was active as a film director, producer, cinematographer, and editor in Austria and Germany for three decades. The prolific filmmaker turned out more than 50 shorts that have a modernist structure. Some representative works are "2/60: 48 Heads from the Szondi-Test" (1960), "6/64: Mom and Dad (An Otto Muhl Happening)" (1964), "31/75: Asyl" (1975), "32/76: To W + B" (1976), and his last film, "50/96: Snapshots (for Bruce)" (1996). In addition, he was the animator for his "26/71 Cartoon: Balzac and the Eye of God" (1971).

Several of Kren's films were well received at film festivals and societies; "Thousand-Years-Cinema" (1995), which he also edited, received critical acclaim.

Kren occasionally worked as an actor, appearing in the telefilm THE LOVE OF A HOODLUM (1966) and the feature EXIT . . . NUR KEINE PANIK (1980).

Kren died of pneumonia.

Kurosawa, Akira

born: March 23, 1910, Tokyo, Japan
died: Sept. 6, 1998, Tokyo, age 88

Japanese director, considered one of the greatest filmmakers in the annals of world cinema.

The son of a soldier and proudly possessing a Samurai heritage, Akira Kurosawa is credited with bringing Japanese cinema to world audiences. Often out of favor with purists in his own country for being "too Western," it was precisely this universality which enabled Kurosawa to make Japanese history and culture accessible to filmgoers everywhere. He is indeed regarded as the most Western of Asian directors, and his influence has been felt by generations of filmmakers, especially in America. Kurosawa himself was influenced by John Ford, to whom he often paid homage; he also professed an admiration for the work of Frank Capra.

Initially intent on becoming an artist, Kurosawa studied painting at the Tokyo School of Fine Arts. When this pursuit failed him, he happened upon movies rather by accident, answering an ad from a studio (the future Toho Film Company) seeking an assistant director. His experience as a painter was not wasted, though, as some of the hallmarks of his work as a filmmaker included an exquisite sense of composition, a flair for dramatic lighting, and moody cinematography.

He remained an assistant director for 8 years, learning the basics of filmmaking and scriptwriting. His first film as director was SANSHIRO SUGATA (1943), which ran into censorship problems, being considered unpatriotic by the Japanese military. Working on his next film, THE MOST BEAUTIFUL (1944), he met actress Yoko Yaguchi, whom he eventually married; the two remained together for the next four decades, until her death in 1985.

He was again censored by the military for his next film, THEY WHO STEP ON THE TIGER'S TAIL (1945), but finally won acceptance with his tender romance ONE WONDERFUL SUNDAY (1947). He began his twenty-year association with actor Toshiro Mifune in his next film, DRUNKEN ANGEL (1948); Mifune appeared in many of Kurosawa's masterpieces until their falling out in 1965.

Kurosawa came to international prominence with the film RASHOMON (1950), which won the 1951 Academy Award for Best Foreign Film. He followed this with an adaptation of Dostoevsky's THE IDIOT (1951) and soon after made what may be his most famous movie, THE SEVEN SAMURAI (1954), which was later remade by director John Sturges as the hugely successful western THE MAGNIFICENT SEVEN (1960). Kurosawa continued to make critically lauded, and internationally popular, films, such as THE HIDDEN FORTRESS (1958) and YOJIMBO (1961), but in the late 1960s and early '70s he suffered setbacks with a number of failed or aborted projects. However, he made a considerable comeback with the Soviet-financed DERSU UZALA (1975), which won him his second Academy Award.

Falling from favor with backers in his own country for his "profligate" ways, Kurosawa often had to turn to foreign money for support. When he failed to obtain financing for his film KAGEMUSHA (1980), it was Francis Ford Coppola and George Lucas who persuaded Twentieth Century-Fox to put up completion funds. For what Kurosawa (and many critics) considered his greatest work, RAN (1985), French producer Serge Silberman worked with him on what would turn out to be the most expensive film in Japanese history...and one of the most successful. It was also the only film that earned him an Oscar nomination as Best Director. In 1990, Kurosawa was honored with an honorary Academy Award for Lifetime Achievement.

Known as "The Emperor" because of his toughness and perfectionism on the set, many coworkers felt that Kurosawa was fully in his element only when making movies. "When I die," he once said, "I prefer to just drop dead on the set...I will be the happiest man if I die at the precise moment when I am saying, 'Yoi...staato' (Ready . . . start)."

Immediately after Kurosawa's death was reported (prompting much grieving around the world), the Japanese government announced plans to give him a People's Honor Award for his contribution to Japanese life. He would be the first director and only the 14th person to receive that honor.

Kurosawa's death was caused by a stroke.

Labby, Sherman

born: 1929, Hollywood, CA
died: May 31, 1998, Los Angeles, CA, age 68

Production artist.

After a stint in the US Navy, Sherman Labby worked in advertising and television, becoming part of the motion picture industry in 1963.

For the 60 films he worked on over the next three decades, Labby was usually credited as a storyboard artist, sketch artist, or production illustrator. He worked on such films as INVASION OF THE BODY SNATCHERS (1978), PROPHECY (1979), BLADE RUNNER (1982), THE RIVER (1984), OUT OF BOUNDS (1986), THE WITCHES OF EASTWICK (1987), SEA OF LOVE (1989), DOWNTOWN (1990), BODY OF EVIDENCE (1993), NORTH (1994), THELMA & LOUISE (1991), and THE HORSE WHISPERER (1998).

Labby died of natural causes.

Lang, Charles

aka: Charles Lang Jr., Charles B. Lang, Charles B. Lang Jr
born: March 27, 1902, Bluff, UT
died: April 3, 1998, Santa Monica, CA, age 96
educ: University of Southern California

Innovative cinematographer who worked on more than 150 movies.

Charles Lang began his career in Paramount's film laboratory, worked his way up to the position of assistant cameraman, and eventually became a director of photography. After more than two decades photographing numerous Paramount films, Lang launched his freelance career in 1952, continuing for many years as one of the industry's most highly regarded cinematographers.

Because of his mastery of actress-flattering lighting techniques and camera angles, Lang was categorized as a "woman's photographer." Among the beauties he photographed were Marlene Dietrich in DESIRE (1936), ANGEL (1937) and A FOREIGN AFFAIR (1948); Claudette Colbert in several films, including TOVARICH (1937), MIDNIGHT, ZAZA (both 1939), SKYLARK (1941) and NO TIME FOR LOVE (1943); and Paulette Goddard in THE CAT AND THE CANARY (1939), THE GHOST BREAKERS (1940), NOTHING BUT THE TRUTH (1941), and THE FOREST RANGERS (1942).

Lang's first nomination for a Best Cinematography Oscar was for THE RIGHT TO LOVE (1931). He won the award for 1932's A FAREWELL TO ARMS, and was subsequently nominated in the black-and-white category for ARISE MY LOVE (1940), SUNDOWN (1941), SO PROUDLY WE HAIL! (1943), THE UNINVITED (1944), A FOREIGN AFFAIR (1948), SUDDEN FEAR (1952), SABRINA (1954), QEEEN BEE (1955), SEPARATE TABLES (1958), SOME LIKE IT HOT (1959) and THE FACTS OF LIFE (1960); and in the color category for ONE-EYED JACKS (1961) and HOW THE WEST WAS WON (1963), for which he shared the nomination. By the late 1960s (when the award was no longer color-specific), Lang was still receiving nominations for his work on such films as BOB & CAROL & TED & ALICE (1969) and BUTTERFLIES ARE FREE (1972). Lang appeared onscreen in a small role in ONE CROWDED NIGHT (1940), and the American Film Institute documentary VISIONS OF LIGHT: THE ART OF CINEMATOGRAPHY (1993) as one of several interviewees.

In 1991, Lang was honored with a Lifetime Achievement Award by the American Society of Cinematographers.

The cause of Lang's death was pneumonia.

Leeds, Phil

aka: Philip Leeds
born: c. 1916, New York, NY
died: Aug. 16, 1998, Los Angeles, CA, age 82
educ: City College of New York

Offbeat character actor and comedian who was employed in both film and television.

Before turning to acting, Phil Leeds was a stand-up comedian. He made his Broadway debut in the 1942 revue *Of V We Sing*. After serving in the Army's Special Services Unit during WWII he resumed his show business career, appearing in night clubs and over two dozen stage shows in New York and across the country. His versatility was demonstrated in such Broadway entries as the musicals *Make a Wish* (1951) and *Can Can* (1953); the comedies *The Matchmaker* and *Romanoff and Juliet* (1957); and the drama *Inquest* (1970). In 1973 he was in the Los Angeles production of *Two Gentlemen of Verona* and decided to stay on and work in films and television.

With his rather comic appearance and strong, authoritative speaking voice, Leeds worked steadily in numerous movies and TV shows, especially in his mature years. His first film was the horror classic ROSEMARY'S BABY (1968), in which he played a mute warlock. Among his other credits: DON'T DRINK THE WATER (1969), MASTERMIND (1976), BEACHES (1988), ENEMIES, A LOVE STORY (1989), GHOST (1990), SOAPDISH (1991), CLEAN SLATE (1994), and KRIPPENDORF'S TRIBE (1998).

Leeds guested on many of the top television comedy-variety shows, working with Milton Berle, Jimmy Durante, Jackie Gleason, and Jack Parr. He could also be seen regularly on many hit TV sitcoms, including "I Love Lucy," "Car 54, Where Are You?", "The Monkees," "The Odd Couple," "Happy Days," "Alice," "Three's Company," "Coach," "Roseanne," "Murphy Brown," and "Mad About You"; he also made appearances on dramas like "thirtysomething." In his last years, Leeds had recurring roles on different series, including "The Larry Sanders Show," "Everybody Loves Raymond," and "Ally McBeal."

Leeds died of pneumonia.

Leopold, Ethelreda

born: 1917, Chicago, IL
died: January 26, 1998, North Hollywood, CA, age 80

Chorus girl, bit player, and frequent foil to the Three Stooges.

Ethelreda Leopold was spotted by a Warner Bros. talent scout while modeling teen fashions at the age of 17, signing a contract and appearing immediately in the chorus of DAMES (1934). A standout among 110 other chorus girls, Leopold was voted best in five categories, including most popular. This vote earned her a cross-country tour, the key to 15 cities, numerous proposals of marriage, and expensive gifts from admirers.

It also earned her chorus work in more Warner Bros. musicals choreographed by Busby Berkeley, including GOLDDIGGERS OF 1935

(1935), READY WILLING AND ABLE, HOLLYWOOD HOTEL (both 1937), and GOLDDIGGERS OF PARIS (1938). From then on she played walk-on roles in such distinguished films as TRADEWINDS (1938), YOU CAN'T CHEAT AN HONEST MAN (1939), CITY FOR CONQUEST, ANGELS OVER BROADWAY, THE GREAT DICTATOR (all 1940), and BALL OF FIRE (1941). She occasionally took roles in B pictures like VOODOO MAN (1944), GEORGE WHITE'S SCANDALS, and LITTLE GIANT (both 1946), and was frequently featured with the Three Stooges in their comedy shorts. Leopold's last major film was Preston Sturges' MAD WEDNESDAY (also 1947).

During the 1950s, '60s and '70s, Leopold mostly worked in commercials and on television shows, including "The Mary Tyler Moore Show."

Leopold died of natural causes.

Levy, Edmond

born: Sept. 26, 1929, Toronto, Ontario, Canada
died: Oct. 10, 1998, New York, NY, age 69
educ: Harvard University, Yale University

Award-winning documentary filmmaker and TV movie director.

Raised in Buffalo, New York, Edmond Levy aspired to be an actor and director early on, going on to study at the Yale School of Drama and the Actors Studio.

Levy made over 100 documentaries and directed several television movies. His 1966 documentary "A Year Toward Tomorrow," narrated by Paul Newman and produced in conjunction with the Office of Economic Opportunity, won an Academy Award in the Short Subjects category. Two other of his short documentaries were Oscar-nominated: "Beyond Silence" (1960) and "While I Run This Race" (1967).

One of his most notable TV movies was MOM, THE WOLFMAN AND ME (1980), starring Patty Duke.

Levy died of cancer.

Lewis, Bobo

born: 1926, Miami, FL
died: November 6, 1998, New York, NY, age 72

Stage, film, and television actress.

An accomplished performer with a range that extended from light comedy to Shakespearean drama, Bobo Lewis spent twenty-five years as a member of New York's prestigious Circle Repertory company, for which she appeared in such plays as e.e. cummings' *him,* Milan Stitt's *Runner Stumbles* (opposite William Hurt) and Jim Leonard's *Diviners.* On Broadway she appeared in *42d Street, Twigs, The Women, Lorelei,* and *On the Twentieth Century.* In 1978 Lewis won a Drama Desk Award for her performance in Studs Terkel's *Working.*

Unlike her theater work, Lewis' appearances on screen consisted mostly of bit parts. Among her screen credits are IT'S A MAD, MAD, MAD, MAD WORLD (1964), THE WILD PARTY (1975), LE SAUVAGE (1975), RUNNING ON EMPTY (1988), and THE PAPER (1994). One of her last roles was in the Andy Garcia-Andie MacDowell romantic comedy JUST THE TICKET (1999).

Lewis also appeared on television in shows like "That Girl" and "Bewitched," in which she played the sister to Agnes Moorehead's Endora. She was also a regular on the PBS children's series "Shining Time Station" in the role of Midge Smoot.

The cause of death was cancer.

Lord, Jack

born: John Joseph Patrick Ryan, Dec. 30, 1920, New York, NY
died: Jan. 21, 1998, Honolulu, HI, age 77

Actor in theater and film and star of the hugely successful television series "Hawaii Five-0."

Jack Lord decided to become an actor immediately after studying at New York University on a football scholarship. He worked as a car salesman by day, while studying acting at the Neighborhood Playhouse by night.

Lord's early film credits include PROJECT X (1949) and CRY MURDER (1950). He was also active in television, appearing on such series as "Philco Television Playhouse," "Studio One," and "Suspense." He was featured in several Broadway plays, including *The Traveling Lady* and *Cat on a Hot Tin Roof,* in which he took over the principle role of Brick.

Lord left Broadway for Hollywood, where he divided his time between film and television appearances. Among the films in which he played supporting roles were THE COURT-MARTIAL OF BILLY MITCHELL (1955), GOD'S LITTLE ACRE (1958), WALK LIKE A DRAGON (1960), DR. NO (1962), RIDE TO HANGMAN'S TREE (1967), and THE COUNTERFEIT KILLER (1968). During this period, Lord also made guest appearances on many popular series like "Gunsmoke," "The Untouchables," "Bonanza," "Rawhide," "Twelve O'Clock High," "Wagon Train," and "The Fugitive."

Having starred in the 1962-63 series, "Stony Burke," Lord was ready for another TV vehicle, and he found it in "Hawaii Five-0," playing the role of detective Steve McGarrett. The combination of crime stories and an exotically beautiful locale was a winning one, and the series ran for an outstanding twelve years (1968-80). In addition to playing the main character, Lord occasionally directed episodes; he also directed the made-for-television M STATION: HAWAII (1980).

After the success of "Hawaii Five-O" Lord found it difficult to get any further projects going. Disillusioned with Hollywood, Lord retired to his beloved Hawaii, where he lived a reclusive life with his wife of 45 years, Marie. In the last years of his life, Lord suffered from Alzheimer's disease and his health deteriorated severely.

The cause of death was reported as congestive heart failure.

Luckman, Sid

born: Nov. 21, 1916, Brooklyn, NY
died: July 5, 1998, North Miami Beach, FL, age 81
educ: Columbia University

Professional football player who made one movie.

In 1948, near the end of Sid Luckman's career as a star quarterback for the Chicago Bears, he and other pro football players appeared in a minor movie about the sport, TRIPLE THREAT. His small part served to lend some authenticity to a story that followed the career of a somewhat arrogant player (portrayed by Richard Crane).

Hall of Famer Luckman was with the Bears for 12 seasons, leading the team to four NFL championships.

Luckman was hospitalized at the time of his demise; no cause of death was reported.

Lyden, Pierce

born: Jan. 8, 1908, Nebraska
died: Oct. 10, 1998, Orange, CA, age 90

Character actor who often played heavies in westerns.

Even though most moviegoers didn't know his name, Pierce Lyden was so typecast in badman roles that in 1944 he was named in a poll of movie fans as the "Villain of the Year." Born on a ranch, Lyden went to Hollywood while still in his 20s. An accomplished horseman, he started in the film industry by playing bit parts before moving up to substantial character roles in low-budget westerns and serials; along the way he played the bad guy against such western heroes as Wild Bill Elliott, Tex Ritter, Don "Red" Barry, William Boyd (Hopalong Cassidy), Gene Autry, Sunset Carson, and Roy Rogers. Some of his films during this time include KING OF DODGE CITY (1941), UNDERCOVER MAN (1942), RIDERS OF THE DEADLINE (1943), SAN FERNANDO VALLEY (1944), THE CHEROKEE FLASH (1945), ROLL ON TEXAS MOON (1946), THE BIG SOMBRERO (1949), and WAGON TEAM (1952).

Lyden appeared in almost 100 films; besides westerns, he worked in comedies like BABY FACE MORGAN (1942) and THE FIRST TRAVELING SALESLADY (1956). His last film was THE WILD WESTERNERS (1962).

Lyden was also a familiar figure on television, appearing in many popular adventure and western series, including "The Roy Rogers Show," "Adventures of Wild Bill Hickock," "The Gene Autry Show," and "Sergeant Preston of the Yukon."

Before retiring in 1973, Lyden worked as a crew person for popular local stage presentations. He was a welcomed guest at western film festivals and conventions, and during the 1980s wrote of his early Hollywood days in the books *Camera! Roll 'em! Action, From the B's to T.V.'s* and *The Movie Badmen I Rode With.*

Lyden died of cancer.

MacLeod, David

born: David Leigh MacLeod, c. 1944, Ontario, Canada
died: December 6, 1998, Montreal, Canada, age 54

Film producer.

David MacLeod, who served as associate producer on several films made by his cousin, Warren Beatty, was better known to police authorities and tabloid journalists for his private activities than to the public for his professional accomplishments. He was listed as associate producer for the films REDS (1981) and ISHTAR (1987), and as producer for the THE PICK-UP ARTIST (1987), from which Beatty had his name removed.

MacLeod's sad personal life came to the attention of the media in 1989, when he was arrested in the Bronx for the transportation of young runaway boys over state lines for acts of prostitution. It was discovered at this time that he was already on probation for having committed similar acts in Manhattan three years earlier. MacLeod managed to escape from the courthouse and became a fugitive from the law.

MacLeod's body was found on the streets of Montreal, where he had allegedly committed suicide by drinking lighter fluid.

Maher, Joseph

born: Dec. 29, 1933, Westport, County Galway, Ireland
died: July 17, 1998, Los Angeles, CA, age 64

Veteran character actor.

Joseph Maher's first job upon emigrating from his native Ireland to Canada was working for an oil company. He developed an interest in theater and was soon touring Canada doing Shakespearean plays. Upon moving to New York, Maher appeared on and off-Broadway in such plays as *The Hostage, The Local Stigmatic,* and *The Prime of Miss Jean Brodie.* But it was his association with the plays of Joe Orton and director John Tillinger that he made his mark. His performances in *Loot, What the Butler Saw,* and *Entertaining Mr. Sloane* gave Maher a respectable reputation on Broadway. He acted in several other critically acclaimed roles in plays like *The Royal Family, Night and Day,* and *American Buffalo.* For his efforts, Maher established the record for the most Tony nominations for supporting actor in Broadway history.

Maher made his film debut in IT AIN'T EASY (1972); other credits include JUST TELL ME WHAT YOU WANT (1980), I'M DANCING AS FAST AS I CAN (1981), MY STEPMOTHER IS AN ALIEN (1988), BULLETPROOF HEART (1994), and IN AND OUT (1997). His best-remembered screen performances were as Warren Beatty's butler in HEAVEN CAN WAIT (1978) and as Bishop O'Hara in SISTER ACT (1992).

He also worked on television, guesting on several series and playing a regular role on the sitcom "Anything But Love" from 1989-90.

Maher's death was caused by a brain tumor.

Mankowitz, Wolf

born: Cyril Wolf Mankowitz, Nov. 7, 1924, London, England
died: May 20, 1998, County Cork, Ireland, age 73
educ: Cambridge University, London

Screenwriter, novelist, poet, and impresario.

As the son of a Russian-Jewish emigre to England, Wolf Mankowitz's upbringing was enriched with tales of Jewish folklore and the vagaries of the antiques business—both of which would figure into his later writings. After college, young Mankowitz became an antiques and porcelain dealer; he used this experience as the basis for a successful comic novel, *Make Me An Offer.* Mankowitz's novel was adapted as a film in 1954 (for which Mankowitz wrote the screenplay), as London musical in 1959, and as a TV movie in 1965. The Carol Reed-directed A KID FOR TWO FARTHINGS (1956), a fable about a young boy searching for a unicorn, had a screenplay by Mankowitz, again based on his own novel. "The Bespoke Overcoat," a 1956 short film about a Jewish tailor, was adapted by Mankowitz from his novel, and won an Academy Award as that year's best two-reel short subject. EXPRESSO BONGO (1959) was a London musical before it became a film; Mankowitz scripted both versions.

Mankowitz also produced plays for the London stage and wrote for television, most notably the 1976 miniseries "Dickens of London." His many screenplays, either written alone or in collaboration with others, include THE LONG AND THE SHORT AND THE TALL (1961), THE DAY THE EARTH CAUGHT FIRE (1961; for which he won the British Academy Award), WALTZ OF THE TOREADORS (1962), WHERE THE SPYS ARE (1965), CASINO ROYALE (1967), BLACK BEAUTY (1971), THE HERO (1972; which he also coproduced), THE HIRELING (1973), and ALMONDS AND RAISINS (1984).

After having had tax problems with the British government, Mankowitz settled in Ireland. Between 1982-88 he taught at the University of New Mexico, while living in Santa Fe.

Mankowitz had continued as a novelist, writing his last book, *A Night with Casanova,* in 1991; in it he revealed that he had terminal cancer.

Manners, David

born: Rauff de Ryther Duan Acklom, April 30, 1901, Halifax, Nova Scotia
died: Dec. 23, 1998, Santa Barbara, CA, age 97

Actor best known for appearances in several classic horror films.

Promoted by the Universal Studios publicity department as a direct descendant of William the Conqueror, David Manners was usually cast in handsome leading man parts. He is most widely remembered as Jonathan Harker in DRACULA (1931), starring Bela Lugosi. Manners also continued his connection the Universal horror cycle by playing the juvenile foil for Boris Karloff in THE MUMMY (1932), appearing with Karloff and Lugosi in THE BLACK CAT (1934), and essaying the title role in THE MYSTERY OF EDWIN DROOD (1935). Manners did play in other sorts of films, however: he was the caliph in KISMET (1930) and was the leading man in a variety of dramas and comedies, including THE RIGHT TO LOVE (1930), Frank Capra's THE MIRACLE WOMAN (1931), THE GREEKS HAD A WORD FOR THEM (1932), and ROMAN SCANDALS (1933). He appeared as Katharine Hepburn's fiance in A BILL OF DIVORCEMENT (1932) and worked with her again in A WOMAN REBELS (1936), after which he retired from the screen.

In the years following, Manners made occasional stage appearances and wrote several novels.

Manners died of natural causes.

Manners, Dorothy

born: July 30, 1903, Fort Worth, TX
died: Aug. 25, 1998, Palm Springs, CA, age 95

Hollywood gossip columnist.

As a teenager, Dorothy Manners moved with her divorced mother to California and found work as a bit player in several films featuring stars like Douglas Fairbanks and Gloria Swanson. Manners soon realized she was not star material and eventually settled into a career as a writer.

After having worked at a couple of newspapers she was hired by *Motion Picture* magazine and in 1935 became the assistant to the powerful columnist Louella Parsons. Manners worked with Parsons for 30 years and succeeded her in the Hearst Corporation after the syndicated columnist died. By the time Manners was on her own the heyday and influence of the Hollywood columnist was on the wane, which fit in nicely with Manners own benign style of reporting.

No cause of death was reported.

Marais, Jean

born: Jean Villain-Marais, Dec. 11, 1913, Cherbourg, France
died: Nov. 8, 1998, Cannes, France, age 84

Strikingly handsome French actor, noted for his professional and personal connection with artist Jean Cocteau.

Jean Marais, the son of a physician, abandoned his formal studies when he was 16 years old to study acting, but was rejected by two of France's most prestigious drama schools. While never giving up the hope of becoming an actor, he earned his living at odd jobs, including a stint as an apprentice photographer, until he met Jean Cocteau in 1937. At the time, Cocteau was one of France's most well-known and respected modernists: a surrealist poet, novelist, playwright, artist, and draftsman. Soon Marais became not only Cocteau's lover but his inspiration. Under Cocteau's guidance Marais became a beloved and popular actor. (Cocteau, who died in 1963, was 23 years older than Marais.)

Although he appeared to great advantage in CARMEN (1942), Marais's career as a romantic leading man was established when he acted one of the leads in Cocteau's modern version of the Tristan and Isolde legend, filmed as THE ETERNAL RETURN (1943). Among the many films in which Marais starred, the ones for which he is best known were those written and directed by Cocteau: BEAUTY AND THE BEAST (1946), LES PARENTS TERRIBLES (1948), ORPHEUS (1950), and THE TESTAMENT OF ORPHEUS (1955).

Marais also had a notable film career outside of his work with Cocteau. In his more than 60 films, he worked with several of Europe's top directors: he was in Jean Renoir's EAGLE WITH TWO HEADS (1948) and ELENA AND HER MEN (1956); Sacha Guitry's NAPOLEON (1955), IF PARIS WERE TOLD TO US (1956) and ROYAL AFFAIRS IN VERSAILLES (1957); Abel Gance's AUSTERLITZ (1959); Luchino Visconti's WHITE NIGHTS (1961); Claude Lelouch's LES MISERABLES (1995); and Bernardo Bertolucci's STEALING BEAUTY (1996).

Marais attained matinee-idol status in swashbuckler roles like THE COUNT OF MONTE CRISTO (1954) and LE CAPITAINE FRACASSE (1960), and the FANTOMAS crime-adventure series (consisting of three features made in the mid-1960s).

The actor appeared often on the stage, and in his later years, when there were fewer and smaller movie roles, he starred in the famed cabaret show *Les Folies Bergeres* and in successful theatre productions such as *The Tempest, Bacchus*, and *Monstres Sacres*.

Marais died of pulmonary disease.

Marasco, Robert

born: c. 1936, Bronx, NY
died: Dec. 6, 1998, Manhasset, NY, age 62
educ: Fordham University

Playwright and novelist whose aim in writing *Child's Play* was to "scare the hell out of everybody."

While writing, Robert Marasco made a living teaching classical languages and English at a Catholic high school (Regis) in Manhattan. When he received much acclaim for his first Broadway play *Child's Play* (1970), which concerned evil doings in a Catholic boys' school, he concealed the identity of the school he worked at from the press, noting that the play's story line wasn't influenced by his own experiences but rather by Ingmar Bergman's script for TORMENT (1944).

Marasco adapted the play for the screen in 1972; the film starred Robert Preston and James Mason. Marasco's successful 1973 novel *Burnt Offerings,*,about a house inhabited by nasty ghouls that prey on a family, was the basis for the 1976 film of the same name, starring Bette Davis and Oliver Reed.

Marasco died of lung cancer.

Marshall, E.G.

born: Everett G. Marshall, June 18, 1914, Owatonna, MN
died: Aug. 24, 1998, Mount Kisco, NY, age 84

Highly respected actor who worked in stage, film and television.

Usually cast as knowledgeable professionals, elder statesmen and other authority figures, E. G. Marshall had a long and distinguished career. Extremely secretive about his background and private life, he nonetheless became a familiar face to millions of Americans.

His stage credits included the Broadway productions of such classics as *The Skin of Our Teeth, The Iceman Cometh, The Crucible, The Little Foxes* and *Waiting for Godot.* This last, which premiered in 1956, remained the achievement of which Marshall was most proud.

His film career including such top-notch fare as HOUSE ON 92ND STREET (1945), CALL NORTHSIDE 777 (1948), THE CAINE MUTINY (1954), THE LEFT HAND OF GOD (1955), TWELVE ANGRY MEN, BACHELOR PARTY (both 1957), THE BUCCANEER (1958), COMPULSION (1959), THE BRIDGE AT REMAGEN (1969), INTERIORS (1978), CONSENTING ADULTS (1992), and NIXON (1995).

Marshall achieved his greatest fame, however, working in television. He won two Emmy awards for his starring role as a lawyer in the series "The Defenders," which ran from 1961-65. He followed this by playing a chief of hospital research in "The New Doctors" series of "The Bold Ones" (1969-73). He also appeared in many made for television movies, specials and docudramas playing historical figures like Harry S. Truman, Dwight D. Eisenhower, John Mitchell, and Joseph P. Kennedy.

Marshall died following a short illness, the nature of which was not specified.

Massey, Daniel

born: Oct. 10, 1933, London, England
died: Mar. 25, 1998, London, age 64
educ: King's College, Cambridge University, London

Urbane British actor who worked on the stage and in film.

The son of Canadian actor Raymond Massey and British actress Adrianne Allen, Daniel Massey made his movie debut at the age of eight playing the son of Noel Coward's character in the 1942 British drama IN WHICH WE SERVE (which Coward also scripted and directed).

After finishing his education, the dapper Massey made his debut on the London stage. Among the notable plays he acted in over the next four decades were the Broadway production of the musical *She Loves Me* (1963), the (London) National Theatre's four-hour version of *Man and Superman* (1981; for which he won the Olivier Award as Actor of the Year), and the London and Broadway productions of *Taking Sides* (1996).

GIRLS AT SEA (1958) marked Massey's first film as an adult; his other screen appearances include THE ENTERTAINER (1960), UPSTAIRS AND DOWNSTAIRS (1961), THE QUEEN'S GUARDS (1963; the only film in which he appeared with his father Raymond), THE AMOROUS ADVENTURES OF MOLL FLANDERS (1965) and THE JOKERS (1967). Massey drew much critical attention in Robert Wise's STAR! (1968), in which he played his godfather, Noel Coward; Massey was nominated for an Oscar as Best Supporting Actor for the performance, and won a Golden Globe. He was in the "Midnight Mess" segment of THE VAULT OF HORROR, aka TALES FROM THE CRYPT II (1973), a film that costarred his sister, actress Anna Massey. His movie appearances over the next few years were sporadic; they include THE DEVIL'S ADVOCATE (1977), VICTORY (1981), SCANDAL (1989), and IN THE NAME OF THE FATHER (1993).

Massey appeared often on television on shows like "CBS Playhouse," "Bonanza," "Mystery: Inspector Morse," and "Mystery: The Casebook of Sherlock Holmes." He was also in the TV movies LOVE WITH A PERFECT STRANGER (1986), INTIMATE CONTACT (1987; for which he won an ACE Award as Best Actor in a Dramatic Special) and STALIN (1992).

Massey died of Hodgkin's disease, which he had been battling for several years.

Masters, George

born: c. 1935
died: Mar. 6, 1998, Los Angeles, CA, age 62

Makeup artist, hair stylist, and beauty expert.

Before he dropped out of high school, George Masters received some valuable advice from his guidance counselor, who suggested that Masters try hairdressing as a career. He did, and thus found his niche in the beauty industry. For more than 40 years Masters was at the top of his profession as a hair stylist and makeup artist, enhancing the beauty of some of the world's most celebrated women.

Masters worked on several movies, but often without screen credit because he reportedly wouldn't join the union. Among his films, Masters is credited with creating the hair styles for TENDER IS THE NIGHT (1961) and accomplishing the daunting task of transforming Dustin Hoffman into Dorothy Michaels for TOOTSIE (1982).

Masters was a particular favorite of Ann-Margret, and he worked on her films THE TRAIN ROBBERS (1973), A TIGER'S TALE (1988), and the TV movie OUR SONS (1991).

In a 1978 book, *The Masters Way to Beauty,* Masters shared his beauty tips and wrote about his life in the glamour business.

No cause of death was revealed by his family.

Mathews, Pamela

See: Morris, Lana

Mattingly, Hedley

born: c. 1914, London, England
died: Mar. 3, 1998, Encino, CA, age 83

British character actor who appeared regularly in American films.

Hedley Mattingly's long career as an actor started with his early work on the British stage and, after WWII, work in Canadian television dramas.

Settling in the US in the early 1960s, Mattingly could be seen frequently as a character actor in movies and on television. His film credits include THE THRILL OF IT ALL (1963), MARRIAGE ON THE ROCKS, STRANGE BEDFELLOWS, KING RAT, THE COLLECTOR (all 1965), TORN CURTAIN (1966), LOST HORIZON (1973), and ALL OF ME (1984). He appeared in the TV series "The Travels of Jaimie McPheeters" and "Daktari," as well as in such episodic dramas as "Perry Mason," "The Rogues" and "Night Gallery."

Mattingly died of cancer.

Mayne, Ferdy

aka: Ferdinand Mayne
born: Ferdinand Philip Mayer-Horckel, Mar. 11, 1916, Mayence, Germany
died: Jan. 30, 1998, London, England, age 81

Character actor who worked internationally.

In well over a hundred movies, telefilms, and stage plays, Ferdinand Mayne proved his versatility portraying a variety of ethnic types in dramas, comedies and musicals. The wide variety of nationalities Mayne played is reflected in the names of his characters: Slant-Eyes in MEET SEXTON BLAKE (1944), Yusef in HOTEL SAHARA (1951), a sheikh in THE CAPTAIN'S PARADISE (1953), Mario Satargo in WHITE FIRE (1953), Dr. Harraz in STORM OVER THE NILE (1955), Dimitri Aperghis in THE BIG CHANCE (1957), Sanchez in OUR MAN IN HAVANA (1960), Vittorio Fettucini in PROMISE HER ANYTHING (1966), Count von Krolock in THE FEARLESS VAMPIRE KILLERS (1967), Marcus Kaplan in INNOCENT BYSTANDERS (1973), Abu Ben Ishak in THE BLACK STALLION RETURNS (1983), and General Karl von Weber in THE KILLERS WITHIN (1995).

Mayne appeared in numerous television movies and series for German, British, and American TV, including HAROLD ROBBINS' THE PIRATE (1978), DEATH OF A CENTERFOLD: THE DOROTHY STRATTEN STORY (1981), SADAT (1983), and the miniseries "The Winds of War."

Mayne died of Parkinson's disease.

McCartney, Linda

born: born Linda Eastman, Sept. 24, 1941, New York, NY
died: Apr. 17, 1998, Tucson, AZ, age 56
educ: University of Arizona (fine arts major)

Best-known as the wife and onstage partner of rocker Paul McCartney; also noted in her own right as an award-winning photographer, animal-rights activist, and environmental advocate.

Self-taught photographer Linda Eastman received attention during the 1960s with her photographs of musicians, which appeared in various publications, including *Town and Country* and *Rolling Stone.* Her work was much in demand and eventually appeared worldwide as part of photographic exhibitions.

Eastman married former Beatle Paul McCartney in 1969, and throughout most of the 1970s performed with him as part of the band Wings, providing vocals and playing keyboard. They appeared together, playing themselves, in the films LET IT BE (1970), ROCK SHOW (1979), GIVE MY REGARDS TO BROAD STREET (1984), and GET BACK (1991). She and Paul received an Oscar nomination for their song "Live and Let Die," written for the 1973 James Bond adventure of the same name.

Recognized as an authority on vegetarianism, McCartney wrote a book 1989, *Linda McCartney's Home Cooking,* which became a bestseller. As a humorous aside to her commitment to the cause, in 1995 she lent her voice to the "Lisa the Vegetarian" episode of TV's "The Simpsons."

One of her last projects was a posthumously-released film short based on a song she wrote, "Wide Prairie." McCartney and artist Oscar Grillo created the animated film, which had its 1998 world premiere at the Edinburgh Film Festival.

The official statement concerning McCartney's death was that she died of natural causes related to metastatic breast cancer.

McDowall, Roddy

born: Roderick Andrew Anthony Jude McDowall, Sept. 17, 1928, London, England
died: Oct. 3, 1998, Studio City, CA, age 70

Child star who enjoyed a six-decade-long career on stage, screen, and in television.

By the time he acted in John Ford's HOW GREEN WAS MY VALLEY (1941) at the age of thirteen, Roddy McDowall was already a seasoned pro, having appeared in over a dozen films in his native England before his family emigrated to America during the Battle of Britain. His first featured role was in SCRUFFY (1938), and his first Hollywood film was MAN HUNT (1941), but VALLEY truly made young McDowall a star. He subsequently appeared in SON OF FURY, THE PIED PIPER (both 1942), KEYS OF THE KINGDOM, and THE WHITE CLIFFS OF DOVER (both 1944), but he is better remembered for a series of films in which he played opposite animal actors, including MY FRIEND FLICKA (1943), THUNDERHEAD—SON OF FLICKA (1945), and LASSIE COME HOME (1943). The last-mentioned costarred a young Elizabeth Taylor, with whom McDowall would maintain a close lifelong friendship.

He played his first adult role in Orson Welles' MACBETH (1948); this led to starring roles in low-budget items like TUNA CLIPPER (1949), and KILLER SHARK (1950). In the 1950s, McDowall abandoned the screen to begin a stage career, making his Broadway debut opposite Ethel Barrymore in Shaw's *Misalliance.* After a few years of working off-Broadway and in summer stock he returned to Broadway in hits like *Compulsion, No Time for Sergeants* and *Camelot,* in which he played the evil Mordred. During this period McDowall made frequent appearances on television shows like "Playhouse 90" and "The Hallmark Hall of Fame," and in 1961 won an Emmy award for his performance in "Not Without Honor."

He returned to film with MIDNIGHT LACE (1960), and then worked on wildly diverse fare, including THE LONGEST DAY (1962), CLEOPATRA (1963), THE LOVED ONE (1965) and LORD LOVE A DUCK (1966), THE POSEIDON ADVENTURE (1972), LASERBLAST (1978), EVIL UNDER THE SUN (1982), FRIGHT NIGHT (1985), GOING UNDER (1991), and THE GRASS HARP (1996). Perhaps his most famous film was the incredibly successful science-fiction film PLANET OF THE APES (1968); the film's success led to his re-appearance in three sequels and the television spinoff. McDowall's final contribution to film was as "Mr. Soil" in the Disney cartoon, A BUG'S LIFE (1998).

McDowall also maintained a side career as a photographer, publishing four volumes of his work (spotlighting celebrity portraits). A movie fan as much as a movie star, he was also well-known for possessing an astonishing collection of screen memorabilia; he was also active with the National Film Preservation Board and was on the boards of the Screen Actors Guild and The Academy of Motion Picture Arts and Sciences.

McDowall's death was caused by cancer.

McEnroe, Robert E.

born: c. 1915
died: Feb. 6, 1998, West Hartford, CT, age 82

Playwright.

Robert E. McEnroe wrote plays while working full time at United Aircraft in Hartford, Connecticut. Although he wrote dozens of plays, only two were produced on Broadway—the very successful *The Silver Whistle* (1948) with Jose Ferrer, and the 1961 musical *Donnybrook!* which was inspired by John Ford's THE QUIET MAN (1952).

The Silver Whistle was adapted for the screen in 1951 as MR. BELVEDERE RINGS THE BELL, the third and last of the Mr. Belvedere series starring Clifton Webb. The main character in McEnroe's play was not the fastidious Mr. Belvedere, but a likeable tramp named Oliver Erwenter; the character was re-tailored by screenwriter Ranald MacDougall to fit the persona of the prissy, brilliant Mr. Belvedere, as popularized by Webb in SITTING PRETTY (1948).

The Silver Whistle was later seen on television, largely in its original form, when McEnroe adapted it for a 1959 "Playhouse 90" presentation starring Eddie Albert.

No cause of death was reported for McEnroe, who died in a convalescent home.

Merrill, Bob

born: May 17, 1920, Atlantic City, NJ
died: Feb. 17, 1998, Beverly Hills, CA, age 77
educ: Temple Univ.

Composer and lyricist.

During Bob Merrill's long and distinguished career, he produced an impressive array of hit songs. After a military stint during WWII he worked at various jobs in the entertainment industry, performing in a night club and writing and composing for radio. His career took off when he provided the lyrics for a blockbuster novelty song, "If I Knew You Were Coming I'd've Baked a Cake." Merrill subsequently wrote numerous pop tunes on his own.

When MGM was planning a movie musical of playwright Eugene O'Neill's *Anna Christie,* Merrill was assigned to write the songs. The film was never made, but O'Neill's story and Merrill's songs made it to Broadway as *New Girl in Town* (1957). Merrill then specialized in writing musical scores for shows based on films or other plays: *Take Me Along* (1959) was a musical adaptation of O'Neill's *Ah, Wilderness; Carnival*

(1961) was based on MGM's LILI (1953); *Henry, Sweet Henry* was based on THE WORLD OF HENRY ORIENT (1964); and *Sugar* (1972), for which Merrill wrote tunes with Jule Styne, was an adaptation of SOME LIKE IT HOT (1959). Merrill's biggest success, however, was an original based on the life of Fanny Brice, *Funny Girl* (1964), for which he wrote the lyrics and Styne wrote the melodies. The show made a star out of Barbra Streisand and produced the hit song "People."

Before establishing himself as a songwriter, Merrill had a small role in the minor musical SENORITA FROM THE WEST (1945). He wrote the songs for the biopic THE WONDERFUL WORLD OF THE BROTHERS GRIMM (1962); and for television, he and Styne provided songs for the musical THE DANGEROUS CHRISTMAS OF RED RIDING HOOD (1965). The film of FUNNY GIRL (1968) brought Merrill an Academy Award nomination for the title song, expressly written for the movie. As a screenwriter, Merrill wrote W. C. FIELDS AND ME (1976) and the TV movie PORTRAIT OF A SHOWGIRL (1982). His last work was an animated version of TOM SAWYER for television, for which he wrote the book, music, and lyrics.

Merrill had been experiencing physical ailments, including gastrointestinal problems, when he reportedly ended his life with a self-inflicted pistol shot.

Merritt, Theresa

born: Sept. 24, 1922, Emporia or Newport News (sources vary), VA
died: June 12, 1998, Bronx, NY, age 75
educ: Temple University, New York University

Character actress and singer.

As a teen, Theresa Merritt was a singer in a church choir and appeared on a local radio show. She studied to be an opera singer, but the closest she came to performing in that mode was when she appeared in a 1946 stage revival of *Carmen Jones,* Oscar Hamerstein II's adaptation of the Bizet opera, *Carmen.* She later appeared in the Gospel musical *Trumpets of the Lord* (1969). Over the years, Merritt worked extensively in the theater, portraying Mammy in the Los Angeles production of Harold Rome's musical *Gone With the Wind* (1973), before obtaining the lead in the TV sitcom "That's My Mama" (1974-75). After that show was cancelled, Merritt went back to Broadway to portray the wicked witch Evillene in *The Wiz* (1976). Merritt's most acclaimed performance was in August Wilson's first Broadway play, *Ma Rainey's Black Bottom* (1984).

Merritt made her movie debut in THEY MIGHT BE GIANTS (1971). Her other films include THE GOODBYE GIRL (1977), THE WIZ (1978), THE GREAT SANTINI, ALL THAT JAZZ (both 1979), THE BEST LITTLE WHOREHOUSE IN TEXAS (1982), and BILLY MADISON (1995).

She appeared in several television shows, including "Police Story," "The Love Boat," "NYPD Blue," "Cosby" and "Law and Order."

Merritt died of skin cancer.

Milhaupt, Charles

born: c. 1949
died: Mar. 13, 1998, New York, NY, age 48

Production worker and associate producer.

Charles Milhaupt worked as a production assistant on F.I.S.T.(1978) and was associate producer of three films, A SOLDIER'S STORY, ICEMAN (both 1984) and AGNES OF GOD (1985). He was also a coproducer of the TV movie PARENT TRAP HONEYMOON (1989).

In his last years, Milhaupt worked as an executive in the paper industry.

Milhaupt died of complications from AIDS.

Miller, Sigmund

born: 1910, Austria, Vienna
died: Aug. 5, 1998, New York, NY, age 87

Playwright, novelist, and blacklisted screenwriter.

Austrian-born Sigmund Miller grew up in Brooklyn. He served in the Army Signal Corps during WWII, after which he pursued a writing career, starting in radio and becoming the chief scripter for the popular horror show "The Inner Sanctum."

In the early 1950s Miller became a playwright, but his career was hindered when he was blacklisted for supposed Communist beliefs. Although his plays *One Bright Day* (1952) and *Masquerade* (1959) were still produced on Broadway, Miller relocated to England, where he had great success on the London stage.

After losing movie jobs because of the blacklist, Miller often worked as a script doctor under a pseudonym. He was credited, however, as one of scripters of the lurid melodrama PORTRAIT IN SMOKE, aka WICKED AS THEY COME (1957), and as the screenwriter for the British air-disaster film JET STORM (1959).

Miller authored several books, including *The Snow Leopard* and *The Conquest of Aging.*

The cause of Miller's death was complications from pneumonia.

Minetti, Bernhard

born: Jan. 26, 1905
died: Oct. 12, 1998, Frankfurt, Germany, age 93

Stage and film actor.

A popular actor in the German theater, Bernhard Minetti began his career in the early 1930s with the Prussian State Theatre. He gave several acclaimed performances in plays like Samuel Beckett's Krapp's Last Tape, Goethe's Faust, and Bertolt Brecht's The Resistible Rise of Arturo Ui.

Minetti's films include KARAMAZOV (1931), BERLIN ALEXANDERPLATZ (1933), DER FREISCHUTZ (1970), THE LEFT-HANDED WOMAN (1980), and FRANCESCA (1987).

No cause of death was reported.

Misraki, Paul

born: Paul Misrachi, 1908, Constantinople, Turkey
died: Oct. 29 or 30, 1998, Paris, France, age 90

Composer of film scores and popular songs.

Schooled in Paris, Paul Misraki did the majority of his work in France; he did, however, have a period of exile during WWII in which he resided in South America and then Hollywood.

In addition to numerous popular songs, Misraki wrote over one hundred film and television scores. He began writing film scores before WWII, and was a member of Les Collegiens, a popular band. Misraki's early specialty was swing music, and he often performed with well-known swing artist Ray Ventura.

Misraki played a role in one of the films for which he supplied a musical score, WHIRLWIND OF PARIS (1946). The other films he scored include HEARTBEAT (1946), NOUS IRONS A PARIS (1949), MANON (1950), CRAZY FOR LOVE (1952), MONTE CARLO BABY (1953), OBSESSION, THE FRENCH TOUCH (both 1954), and Orson Welles's MR. ARKADIN (1955).

Misraki had great success working with directors who were part of (or who influenced) France's "new wave" school of filmmaking. He scored Luis Bunuel's DEATH IN THE GARDEN (1956); Roger Vadim's AND GOD CREATED WOMAN (1956); Claude Chabrol's THE COUSINS (1959), and WEB OF PASSION (1961); and Jean-Luc Godard's ALPHAVILLE (1965).

Misraki died after a long, undisclosed illness.

Monica, Corbett

born: c. 1930, New York, NY
died: July 22, 1998, North Miami, FL, age 68

Stand-up comic who found fame as the opening act for some of show business's leading entertainers on the nightclub circuit.

Corbett Monica spent his adolescence and early adult years in St. Louis, where he honed his comedic talents at local night spots. He eventually worked his way to prestigious engagements at famous New York clubs like the Latin Quarter and the Copacabana and other top spots in Las Vegas, Atlantic City, and Miami.

He frequently appeared on television variety shows, including "The Ed Sullivan Show" and "The Tonight Show." As an actor, Monica was a regular on the sitcom "The Joey Bishop Show" and was in the short-lived "Call Her Mom."

Monica had substantial supporting parts in the movies THE GRASSHOPPER (1970) and Woody Allen's BROADWAY DANNY ROSE (1984).

Onstage, Monica often performed in *Catskills on Broadway*, a long-running comedy revue.

The cause of Monica's death was cancer.

Montana, Montie

aka: Monte Montana, Monty Montana
born: Owen Harlan Mickel, June 21, 1910, Wolf Point, MT
died: May 20, 1998, Los Angeles, CA, age 87

Rodeo star and occasional actor who was a regular at the Pasadena Tournament of Roses Parade.

After a small part in STAND UP AND CHEER (1934), Montie Montana was the hero of the low-budget CIRCLE OF DEATH (1935) and the producer of the equally modest GUN SMOKE (1936). He had small roles in other action films, including RIDERS OF THE DEADLINE (1943), MAN FROM FRISCO (1944), DOWN DAKOTA WAY (1949), THE MAN WHO SHOT LIBERTY VALANCE (1962), HUD (1963), and ARIZONA BUSHWHACKERS (1968). As the technical director for THE STORY OF WILL ROGERS (1952), Montana instructed the performers in lasso and roping techniques.

Montana caused a bit of a stir at President Dwight D. Eisenhower's 1953 inaugural parade. Montana had received the president's permission to lasso him, as a joke; the president's Secret Service agents, however, were not amused.

Montana toured the rodeo circuit for many years. He wrote about his life—from a sod house in Montana to a career in the entertainment industry—in a 1993 autobiography, *Montie Montana: Not Without My Horse!*

Montana died from complications after a series of strokes.

Moore, Archie

born: Archibald Lee Wright, Dec. 13, 1913, Benoit, MS
died: Dec. 9, 1998, San Diego, CA, age 84

Boxing great who acted in several films.

Winning his first professional fight in 1936, Archie Moore had a remarkably long career in the ring, lasting an astounding 27 years and holding the light-heavyweight title for eleven. He fought in 228 bouts, with 194 wins, 26 losses and 8 draws, and is credited with setting the record for knockout punches (numbering 141). Moore was also the only boxer to fight both Rocky Marciano and Muhammad Ali.

Moore did sporadic acting work while he was still active in the ring, appearing on several television shows, including "Wagon Train" and "Perry Mason;" he also played Jim in THE ADVENTURES OF HUCKLEBERRY FINN (1960), co-starring with Eddie Hodges and Tony Randall. After his retirement from prizefighting in 1963, Moore concentrated his energies on acting, making guest appearances on such TV shows as "Batman," "A Family Affair," and "The Fall Guy." His film credits include THE CARPETBAGGERS (1964), THE FORTUNE COOKIE (1966), THE OUTFIT (1974), and BREAKHEART PASS (1976), and the telefilms THE HANGED MAN (1964) and MY SWEET CHARLIE (1970).

Moore died of heart failure, following several years of heart problems.

Morris, Edmund

born: Sept. 22, 1912
died: Jan. 6, 1998, Seattle, WA, age 85

Theatre personality who had a few roles in film.

Edmund Morris worked in many capacities in the theater world: he wrote plays, acted, directed, and taught playriting. His most ambitious play, *The Wooden Dish,* was not well received on Broadway when it opened in 1955, but Morris did receive acclaim for the drama when it was produced in several European countries and adapted for television for the "Play of the Week" series in 1961.

In film, Morris shared screenplay credit on the drama A WALK ON THE WILD SIDE (1962) and wrote the scripts for the western THE SAVAGE GUNS (1962), and the sci-fi thriller PROJECT X (1968).

No cause of death was reported.

Morris, Lana

aka: Mathews, Pamela
born: 1930, England
died: May 28, 1998, Windsor, Berkshire, England, age 68

British film and television actress.

Sometimes credited as Pamela Mathews, Lana Morris appeared as the perky romantic interest in several dozen films between 1948 and 1969. American fans of "Masterpiece Theater" will remember her in the superb PBS miniseries "The Forsyte Saga." In it she played the ill-fated Helene, a sympathetic German governess who marries a Forsyte and, for her sin, suffers ostracism, mental deterioration, and, ultimately, death.

Morris's film work consisted primarily of minor thrillers and light romantic comedies (often starring Norman Wisdom) in which she frequently played featured roles. Among her more notable credits were SPRING IN PARK LANE (1948), THE GAY LADY (1949), TRIO (1950), A TALE OF FIVE WOMEN (1951), TROUBLE IN STORE (1953), HOME AND AWAY (1956), and I START COUNTING (1969).

No cause of death was reported.

Moss, Jeffrey

born: 1942, New York, NY
died: Sept. 24, 1998, New York, NY, age 56
educ: Princeton Univ.

Writer and composer for children's television.

Jeffrey Moss started out in show business as a production assistant for TV's "Captain Kangaroo" and later wrote for the show. In 1969 he helped develop "Sesame Street," creating, among other things, the character of the Cookie Monster. Several of the other Muppets were given distinctive characteristics by the songs Moss wrote for them, which included "I Love Trash," "Rubber Duckie," and "Captain Vegetable."

Moss received many awards during his lifetime: his work on "Sesame Street" as head writer and composer-lyricist brought him fourteen Emmy Awards; he wrote songs for four albums that won Grammy Awards; and he was nominated for an Academy Award for his musical score for THE MUPPETS TAKE MANHATTAN (1984).

He wrote numerous best-selling children's books, including *Hieronymus White,* and also authored poetry collections like the popular *The Butterfly Jar.*

Moss died of colon cancer.

Nardino, Gary

born: Aug. 26, 1935, Garfield, NJ
died: Jan. 31, 1998, Los Angeles, CA, age 62
educ: Seton Hall University

Film producer and television production executive.

Before becoming a executive in the television industry, Gary Nardino started as an agent, representing such high profile companies as Lorimar Productions, Talent Associates and Granada Television. When he became president of Paramount TV Production in 1977, Nardino's division was responsible for such hit sitcoms as "Happy Days," "Laverne and Shirley," "Mork and Mindy," "Taxi," and "Cheers." The miniseries "Shogun" (1980) and "The Winds of War" (1983) and the telefilm A WOMAN CALLED GOLDA (1982) were also made during his tenure at Paramount.

In 1983 he formed Gary Nardino Productions, which was involved in developing television shows and films. He served as executive producer for STAR TREK III: THE SEARCH FOR SPOCK (1984) and produced the romance FIRE WITH FIRE (1986).

Nardino later held high-level executive positions at Orion, Lorimar and Warner Bros., during which time he supervised several shows and was part of the team producing the series "Marblehead Manor," "Time Trax," and "Pacific Blue."

Nardino died several days after suffering a stroke.

Newey, Murray

born: c. 1952
died: Apr. 8, 1998, Auckland, New Zealand, age 45

Filmmaker.

Murray Newey worked as an assistant director on the films BEYOND REASONABLE DOUBT (1980), RACE FOR THE YANKEE ZEPHYR, DEAD KIDS (both 1981), THE PIRATE MOVIE (1982), and THE MAN FROM SNOWY RIVER (1983).

Newey later served as producer, coproducer, or executive producer for several films, including DEATH WARMED UP (1985), MY GRANDPA IS A VAMPIRE (1992), JACK BE NIMBLE (1994), BONJOUR TIMOTHY (1995) and THE WHOLE OF THE MOON (1996), which was honored as the best picture by the New Zealand Film Awards in 1995.

Newey then forged an association with Lucasfilms, serving as the New Zealand production manager for WILLOW (1988). At the time of his death, Newey was employed as a production executive for George Lucas' "Star Wars" prequels.

Newey's death was reported as a suicide.

Nolan, Jeanette

born: Dec. 30, 1911, Los Angeles, CA
died: June 5, 1998, Los Angeles, CA, age 86
educ: Los Angeles Community College

Beloved character actress known for work in films, television, and radio.

In the 1930s, Jeanette Nolan was a sought-after radio actress, valued for her mastery of ethnic dialects and her ability to incarnate a variety of characters. She often performed with her husband, actor John McIntire, whom she married in 1935; the versatile couple performed in such popular dramatic shows as "Crime Doctor," "Cavalcade of America," and "Perfect Crime."

Nolan's film debut was in Orson Welles' MACBETH (1948), playing Lady Macbeth. She subsequently appeared, over a period of 50 years, in hundreds of movies and television shows. Her film appearances include THE SECRET OF CONVICT LAKE (1951), THE BIG HEAT (1953), TRIBUTE TO A BAD MAN (1956), TWO RODE TOGETHER (1961), THE MAN WHO SHOT LIBERTY VALENCE (1962), THE RELUCTANT ASTRONAUT (1967), THE RESCUERS (1977), TRUE CONFESSIONS (1981), and THE HORSE WHISPERER (1998).

The four-time Emmy Award-nominated Nolan appeared in many TV episodes and telefilms, often with husband McIntire (as on "The Virginian" and "Wagon Train"). Nolan was a regular on "The Richard Boone Show" and had her own western series, "Dirty Sally" (a spin-off of "Gunsmoke"), in which she played the character of Sally Fergus.

Nolan died after having suffered a stroke.

Norden, Joseph

born: c. 1914, New York, NY
died: March 30, 1998, Woodland Hills, CA, age 84

Actor.

Joseph Norden became a contract player at Universal Studios in 1938 and continued acting in small roles and walk-ons for over fifty years. Among the numerous films in which he appeared was DILLINGER (1945).

During the 1950s, Norden worked as personal secretary to the on-screen/off-screen team of Howard Duff and Ida Lupino and, remarkably, served as a stand-in for both of them in films and on the set of their television show, "Mr. Adams and Eve." He played various roles on that series and Duff's subsequent vehicle "Felony Squad" (1966-69).

Norden died following an extended illness.

Norman, Maidie

born: c. 1912, Georgia
died: May 2, 1998, San Jose, CA, age 85

Actress whose housekeeper character in WHAT EVER HAPPENED TO BABY JANE? provided the film with a dose of sanity.

Even though her opportunities in film and television were limited (she was often cast as a domestic), Maidie Norman sought to bring truth and dignity to the parts she played. Her first important film was the social drama THE WELL (1951); other credits include TORCH SONG, FOREVER FEMALE, BRIGHT ROAD (all 1953), ABOUT MRS. LESLIE, SUSAN SLEPT HERE (both 1954), TARZAN'S HIDDEN JUNGLE (1955), and WRITTEN ON THE WIND (1956).

Norman is probably best remembered as Elvira the caring housekeeper who tries to rescue Blanche (Joan Crawford) from the cruelty of her sister Jane (Bette Davis) in WHAT EVER HAPPENED TO BABY JANE? (1962). Reportedly, Norman rewrote Elvira's dialogue to eliminate what the actress called "old slavery-time talk."

Norman's other films included AIRPORT (1977), MOVIE MOVIE (1978), HALLOWEEN III: SEASON OF THE WITCH (1982), and IN THE HANDS OF THE ENEMY (1994).

She appeared on television on several dramatic series, including "Alfred Hitchcock Presents," "Perry Mason" and "Ben Casey," and in the telefilms A DREAM FOR CHRISTMAS (1973), BARE ESSENCE (1982), and HIS MISTRESS (1984).

Norman taught acting at the University of California, and in 1977 was inducted into the Black Filmmakers Hall of Fame.

Norman died of lung cancer.

Noris, Assia

born: Anastasia Noris von Gerzeld, Feb. 26, 1912, St. Petersburg, Russia
died: Jan. 27, 1998, San Remo, Italy, age 85

Italian film star of the 1930s and '40s.

One of the most popular film stars in Italy before WWII, Assia Noris' work is virtually unknown outside her adopted country due to the Fascist Party's practice of keeping Italian films from being exported. However, Noris' shy, wholesome image made her a favorite among Italian moviegoers of that era.

Often playing up her somewhat mysterious, aristocratic origins, Noris' family did indeed flee Russia during the Revolution, settling first in Paris, then in Italy. Noris made her film debut with TRE UOMINI IN FRAC (1932), but it was with her third movie, GIALLO (1933), that she began an association with director Mario Camerini, to whom she was briefly married. They made seven films together, mostly light romantic comedies. Three of them—DARO UN MILIONE (1936), IL SIGNOR MAX (1937), and I GRANDI MAGAZZINI (1939)—co-starred Vittorio De Sica, and made him a film star before he began his illustrious career as a director. Other films Noris made with Camerini include BATTICUORE (1939), UNA ROMANTICA AVVENTURA (1940), and UNA STORIA D'AMORE (1942). Two of her most popular films were made with other directors: DORIA NELSON (1939) and UN COLPA DI PISTOLA (1941).

Noris' wholesome image did not survive the transition to the grittier feel of post-war Italian neo-realism, and after WWII her career began to fade. She did some theater work in the 1940s and appeared in several films such as LA PECCATRICE BIANCA (1949), but never regained her popularity. Her last film was LA CELESTINA (1964), which she also cowrote.

Noris died after a brief illness, the exact nature of which was unreported.

O'Connor, Kendall

born: 1908, Perth, Western Australia
died: May 27, 1998, Burbank, CA, age 90

One of the top creative talents in the field of animation for more than fifty years.

In the course of working for Disney Studios from 1935 to 1974, Kendall O'Connor made creative contributions to 13 animated features and nearly 100 shorts, among them some of the studio's most beloved classics.

Working as a layout artist, designer, and art director, he was responsible for the evil witch's demise sequence in SNOW WHITE AND THE SEVEN DWARFS (1937), the "Dance of the Hours" sequence in FANTASIA (1940), the coach in CINDERELLA (1950), the marching cards in ALICE IN WONDERLAND (1951), and Skull Rock in PETER PAN (1953).

During WWII, O'Connor worked on training films, making some with the Disney Studio and others with director Frank Capra. He also made a number of educational cartoons, including "Toot, Whistle, Plunk, and Boom," which went on to win an Oscar in 1953. With the Disney organization, he served as art director for a trio of landmark space "factuals" for television; these were "Man in Space," "Man and the Moon," and "Mars and Beyond." Although O'Connor retired from Disney in 1974, he continued to work on projects for Disney's theme parks, including the World of Motion and the Universe of Energy for Epcot Center, and "Back to Neverland" for Disney-MGM.

Among the many honors O'Connor received for his distinguished work were an Annie Award, a Golden Award from the Motion Picture Screen Cartoonists in 1985, and a Disney Legends Award in 1992.

O'Connor died of natural causes.

O'Day, Molly

born: Suzanne Noonan, c. 1910, Bayonne, NJ
died: Oct. 15, 1998, Arroyo Grande, CA, age 88

Actress who started her movie career in the "Our Gang" shorts.

After the death of her father, Molly O'Day's mother relocated Molly and her ten siblings to Hollywood, where she and her sister (later to be known professionally as Sally O'Neil) became actresses. O'Day was still in high school when Hal Roach placed her under contract, featuring her in "Our Gang" shorts and movies with such comedians as Laurel and Hardy.

O'Day was still a teenager when she made her first feature, 1927's THE PATENT LEATHER KID. She also appeared in three other films released that year: HARD-BOILED HAGGERTY, THE LOVELORN, and THE SHEPHERD OF THE HILLS. Other films that followed, made mostly at "poverty-row" studios, include SISTERS (1930), SEA DEVILS (1931), GIGOLETTES OF PARIS (1933), BARS OF HATE (1936), and SKULL AND CROWN (1938).

She was still a young, attractive woman in the late 1930s when her movie career ended. She reportedly left the movie business due to health problems that resulted from radical surgery she had undergone in an effort to reduce her weight. O'Day later became a very successful California real estate agent.

No cause of death was reported.

O'Driscoll, Martha

born: Mar. 4, 1922, Tulsa, OK
died: Nov. 3, 1998, Indian Creek Village, FL, age 76

Studio starlet of the 1940s.

Martha O'Driscoll was a child performer and model before entering movies in the late 1930s. The first of her nearly three dozen film appearances was a bit in the 1936 college musical COLLEGIATE. She played small roles in SHE'S DANGEROUS (1937), MAD ABOUT MUSIC (1938), THE SECRET OF DR. KILDARE, and JUDGE HARDY AND SON (both 1939). She was Daisy Mae in the first LI'L ABNER (1940), a modest programmer, and played supporting roles in a few bigger-budgeted films, including THE LADY EVE (1941), THE REMARKABLE ANDREW, REAP THE WILD WIND (both 1942), and THE FALLEN SPARROW (1943).

In 1943, Universal cast O'Driscoll and Noah Berry Jr. in supporting roles in the WWII drama WE'VE NEVER BEEN LICKED. Universal then costarred them in four low-budget films: ALLERGIC TO LOVE (1943), WEEKEND PASS, HI, BEAUTIFUL! (both 1944), and UNDER WESTERN SKIES (1945). O'Driscoll also did studio duty in popular genre films: HOUSE OF DRACULA, the Abbott and Costello vehicle HERE COME THE CO-EDS, and the western THE DALTONS RIDE AGAIN (all 1945). Her last film was the 1947 feature CARNEGIE HALL, after which she left the industry.

In later years, O'Driscoll raised a family and was involved in community activities. She was also one of the founders of the Appleton Museum of Art.

No cause of death was reported.

Olvis, William Edward

born: c. 1928, Hollywood, CA
died: November 27, 1998, Redlands, CA, age 70
education: University of Southern California and Occidental College

Operatic tenor who also starred on the concert stage and Broadway, and appeared in one feature film.

Abandoning his original ambition to become a lawyer, William Edward Olvis studied music and voice in Los Angeles and Rome. He was drafted into the Navy in 1949. An admiral's wife who heard him sing predicted that "in 10 years, you'll be singing at the Metropolitan Opera." Her prophecy turned out to be correct.

Olvis first came to national attention when he was hired to replace temperamental tenor Mario Lanza for a guest appearance in MGM's film biography of Sigmund Romberg, DEEP IN MY HEART (1954). This led to his stint in the leading role of Edward Grieg in the Broadway production of *Song of Norway,* a role he also played in the national tour.

In 1959, he sang the lead role of Don Jose in the Metropolitan Opera's production of *Carmen.* He would also sing the leads in the operas *Aida, Madame Butterfly, La Boheme,* and *The Flying Dutchman.* For several seasons, he sang leading roles with the highly respected Dusseldorf Opera Company. His later professional career consisted mostly of concert work.

Throat cancer was reported as the cause of death.

O'Neill, Dick

born: 1928, New York, NY
died: November 17, 1998, Santa Monica, CA, age 70

Character actor who worked in theater, film, and television.

Dick O'Neill's career began on the stage. He appeared in Broadway productions of *Promises, Promises, The Unsinkable Molly Brown,* and *The Front Page.* Among his screen credits are THE TAKING OF PELHAM ONE TWO THREE (1974), THE FRONT PAGE (1974) (repeating his stage role), THE JERK, THE BUDDY HOLLY STORY (both 1978), WOLFEN (1981), and PRIZZI'S HONOR (1985).

It was in television, however, that O'Neill achieved his greatest recognition. On the police drama "Cagney and Lacey," he had his best-remembered role—that of Chris Cagney's father, Charlie. He also acted in such shows as "M.A.S.H.," "Falcon Crest," "Magnum, P.I.," and "St. Elsewhere." In the 1990s, he appeared on shows including "Home Improvement," "Mad About You," "Cybill," "Fresh Prince of Bel Air," and "Dharma and Greg."

For the last seven years of his life, O'Neill served on the Screening Committee for the Academy of Motion Picture Arts and Sciences.

The cause of death was heart failure.

O'Neill, Thomas F.

born: c. 1916
died: March 14, 1998, Greenwich, CT, age 82

Longtime film and television executive; pioneer in broadcast of movies on television.

After serving in the navy during WWII, Thomas F. O'Neill combined the Yankee Network, a radio chain owned by his father's General Tire and Rubber Company, with WNAC-TV, an early New York television station, to form General Teleradio. He continued to buy up television and radio stations until the mid-'50s.

Around this time, he came up with the idea of airing movies on television once daily and four times on weekends, just as theaters did. The result was "Million Dollar Movie," a resounding success on New York's WOR-TV. He bought the rights to many films and later syndicated them to other stations, another first.

In 1954, he purchased the entire RKO film library from Howard Hughes for $25 million. He renamed the company RKO General, and remained active with it until 1985. O'Neill is also credited as a pioneer in the testing of pay television.

The cause of death was heart failure.

O'Sullivan, Maureen

born: May 17, 1911, Boyle, County Roscommon, Ireland
died: June 23, 1998, Scottsdale, AZ, age 87

Actress best-known as "Jane" opposite Johnny Weissmuller's "Tarzan" in six movies made between 1932 and 1942.

Maureen O'Sullivan was only 18 when she played tenor John McCormack's daughter in SONG O' MY HEART (1930), a 20th Century- Fox movie shot in Dublin. This performance resulted in a short-term contract with Fox; among the six films she made at that studio was A CONNECTICUT YANKEE (1931) starring Will Rogers. She then signed with MGM, and scored her best-remembered role, that of Jane Parker, a refined British beauty who captures the heart of a jungle hero in TARZAN, THE APE MAN (1932). The pair were reunited in five sequels: TARZAN AND HIS MATE (1934), TARZAN ESCAPES (1936), TARZAN FINDS A SON (1939), TARZAN'S SECRET TREASURE (1941), and TARZAN'S NEW YORK ADVENTURE (1942).

Aside from her stint as Jane, O'Sullivan primarily played secondary parts, supporting such MGM stars as Marie Dressler in TUGBOAT ANNIE (1933), William Powell and Myrna Loy in THE THIN MAN, Norma Shearer and Charles Laughton in THE BARRETTS OF WIMPOLE STREET (both 1934), W. C. Fields in DAVID COPPERFIELD, Greta Garbo in ANNA KARENINA (both 1935), The Marx Brothers in A DAY AT THE RACES (1937), and Robert Taylor in A YANK AT OXFORD (1938).

When the Tarzan series moved over to RKO, O'Sullivan was asked to continue. By this time, however, she had retired (temporarily) from the movies. She married director John Farrow, with whom she had seven children. Her return to the screen in 1948 was in a film directed by Farrow: THE BIG CLOCK (1948), starring Ray Milland. Sullivan worked with her husband again two years later in the melodrama WHERE DANGER LIVES (1950).

During the 1950s, O'Sullivan appeared on television in the syndicated series "Irish Heritage." She then turned to the stage, with a successful summer stock engagement in *A Roomful of Roses.* She made her Broadway debut in 1962 with the hit comedy *Never Too Late.*

After her husband's death in 1962, she devoted herself to work on the stage, making only occasional appearances in film and television. In 1963, she served as a host of the "Today" show, and in 1965 starred in the film adaptation of NEVER TOO LATE (1965). After a layoff of two decades, she returned to the screen for sporadic roles in the late '80s, most notably Francis Ford Coppola's PEGGY SUE GOT MARRIED and Woody Allen's HANNAH AND HER SISTERS (both 1986); in the latter, Sullivan played the mother of her real-life daughter Mia Farrow.

O'Sullivan died of natural causes.

Pakula, Alan J.

born: April 7, 1928, Bronx, NY
died: November 19, 1998, Plainview, NY, age 70

Highly respected and successful producer, writer, and screenwriter.

Raised in Manhattan and on Long Island, Alan J. Pakula attended Yale University. After graduating, he went to Hollywood, where he worked as an assistant in the cartoon department at Warner Brothers. At MGM he worked as a script reader. When MGM producer Don Hartman became head of production at Paramount, he took Pakula with him. In 1956, Pakula began his own production company.

Pakula made his producing debut with the sports biopic FEAR STRIKES OUT (1957), directed by Robert Mulligan. The two continued to work together, with Pakula producing Mulligan's popular and critically lauded TO KILL A MOCKINGBIRD (1962), LOVE WITH THE PROPER STRANGER (1963), INSIDE DAISY CLOVER (1965), BABY, THE RAIN MUST FALL (1965), and UP THE DOWN STAIRCASE (1967).

In 1969, Pakula began his own career as a director with THE STERILE CUCKOO (1969). He eventually made 15 other films, many of which he produced and scripted as well. Among his biggest successes were KLUTE (1971), THE PARALLAX VIEW (1974), ALL THE PRESIDENT'S MEN (1976), COMES A HORSEMAN (1978), STARTING OVER (1979), SOPHIE'S CHOICE (1982), PRESUMED INNOCENT (1990), and THE PELICAN BRIEF (1993). His last film was THE DEVIL'S OWN (1997). At the time of his death, Pakula was working on a screenplay based on Doris Kearns Goodwin's Pulitzer Prize-winning biography, *No Ordinary Time,* about Eleanor and Franklin Roosevelt. He had intended to direct the film as well.

Known as an actor's director, Pakula's films typically showcased several performers. Many actors won Oscars in films directed by Pakula, including Jane Fonda, Meryl Streep, Jason Robards, Jr., and Gregory Peck. Well-regarded by his casts, Pakula made, and in some cases resuscitated, the careers of his actors—Liza Minnelli (whose first starring dramatic role was in Pakula's THE STERILE CUCKOO) and Candice Bergen (whose turn in STARTING OVER demonstrated her flair for light comedy) are prime examples. Often nominated for the Academy Award, Pakula never won the prize, although he received critical accolades for his films' challenging subjects and psychological underpinnings.

Pakula was married to actress Hope Lange in 1963. They divorced in 1969, and, in 1973, he wed Hannah Cohn Boornstein, a writer of historical biographies, who survived him.

Pakula's untimely death was the result of a bizarre accident on the Long Island Expressway, in which a metal pipe flew through the windshield of his car, hitting and killing him.

Palca, Alfred

born: c. 1919, New York, NY
died: June 18, 1998, New York, NY, age 78
educ: New York University

Screenwriter who was blacklisted in the 1950s.

Although Alfred Palca proclaimed that he was not a Communist, his screenwriting career came to a screeching halt during the HUAC witch-hunts of the 1950s. He admitted under questioning merely to having been "attracted by the Soviet Union's socialist ideals," but he was still considered unemployable by the heads of the major studios.

Palca had just finished scripting and coproducing GO, MAN, GO! (1954), the classic film about the Harlem Globetrotters, when he was accused of being a Communist. Because of the controversy, the film was unable to find a distributor until Palca removed his name, giving screenwriting credit to his pediatrician and producing credit to his brother-in-law. In that way, the film was eventually distributed by United Artists.

In 1997, Palca's screenwriting credit for GO, MAN, GO! was restored at a Los Angeles 50th-anniversary ceremony that honored blacklisted Hollywood screenwriters and directors.

Prior to GO, MAN, GO!, Palca had scripted THE HARLEM GLOBETROTTERS (1951), a modest programmer that was similar in style and tone to the later picture.

Palca continued as a writer, but never returned to the film world.

He died of cancer.

Pandit, Korla

born: c. 1922, New Delhi, India
died: Oct. 1, 1998, San Mateo County, CA, age 76

Distinctive, exotic musician.

Pandit Korla's virtuosity on the piano and organ made him a favorite guest on several early TV shows, including those hosted by Kay Kyser and Rudy Vallee. He had his own television show at one point on a Los Angeles station, titled "Adventures in Music." He was a prolific recording artist and appeared in a few movies. He played a Hindu man in both SOMETHING TO LIVE FOR (1952) and WHICH WAY IS UP? (1977). In a musical appearance in ED WOOD (1994), he essentially played himself.

Pandit died from complications following a stroke.

Paz, Octavio

born: Mar. 31, 1914, Mexico City, Mexico
died: Apr. 19, 1998, Mexico City, Mexico, age 84

Poet, essayist, social critic, diplomat, and biographer.

One of Mexico's leading intellectuals and perhaps its foremost writer, Octavio Paz's published works ran mostly to poetry and essays, two forms not particularly suited to cinematic adaptation. His book *Sor Juana Ines De La Cruz* was the basis for the 1990 Argentinean movie YO, LA PEOR DE TODAS aka I, THE WORST OF ALL.

Paz received some of literature's most prestigious awards, including the Miguel Cervantes Prize in 1982, the T. S. Eliot Award in 1987, and the Nobel Prize for literature in 1990.

No cause of death was reported.

Pearlman, Stephen

born: c. 1935, Brooklyn, NY
died: Sept. 30, 1998, New York, NY, age 63
educ: Dartmouth College

Stage, film, and television actor.

After his graduation from college, where he majored in philosophy, Stephen Pearlman studied acting with Stella Adler; he soon joined the famed Second City comedy troupe in Chicago, where he worked with future luminaries such as Alan Arkin and Barbara Harris. He made his New York stage debut in the long-running off-Broadway production of *The Threepenny Opera.* His Broadway credits included *Barefoot in the Park, Children of a Lesser God,* and *Six Degrees of Separation.* Pearlman also had a leading role in the short-lived musical version of Fellini's *La Strada,* which starred Bernadette Peters.

On television, Pearlman starred in the series "Husbands, Wives, and Lovers" and guested on shows like "Seinfeld" and "LA Law." His film credits include THE ICEMAN COMETH (1973), ROLLERCOASTER (1977), GREEN CARD (1990), THE CEMETERY CLUB (1993), QUIZ SHOW (1994), DIE HARD WITH A VENGEANCE (1995), THE FIRST WIVES CLUB (1996), PRIVATE PARTS (1997), and THE HORSE WHISPERER (1998).

Pearlman's death was caused by cancer.

Penn, Leo

born: Aug. 27, 1921, Lawrence, MA
died: Sept. 5, 1998, Santa Monica, CA, age 77
educ: Univ. of California, Los Angeles

Actor, director, and father of actors Sean and Christopher and singer-songwriter Michael.

After serving in the Army Air Corps as a bombardier during WWII, Leo Penn was signed to a Paramount contract in the mid-1940s. His acting career stalled when he was dropped by the studio because of his support of leftist causes. During this period, Penn acted in only two films, the noir THE UNDERCOVER MAN and Ida Lupino's independently produced NOT WANTED (both 1949).

Penn turned to the stage and television, where the blacklist was less influential. In New York he appeared in several plays, including *Dinosaur Wharf* (1951) and *A View From the Bridge* (1955). He also acted in live TV shows, such as "The Philco Television Playhouse" in 1948, and series dramas like "The Untouchables" and "Ben Casey."

Penn started to gain recognition as a stage director with *Midnight Caller* and *John Turner Davis* (both 1958). His greatest success came as a director of episodic television, starting with "Gunsmoke" and "Bonanza" in the late 1950s. Throughout the next three decades, Penn directed episodes of such hit as "Ben Casey," "The Fugitive," "I Spy," "Star Trek," "Magnum, P.I.," "Fame," "Remington Steele," and "Diagnosis Murder." He won an Emmy Award for his direction of the "Columbo" telefilm ANY OLD PORT IN A STORM in 1973; among his other telefilms were DARK SECRET OF HARVEST HOME (1978) and HELLINGER'S LAW (1981).

Penn returned to acting in films with THE STORY ON PAGE ONE (1959); he also made an uncredited appearance in BIRDMAN OF ALCATRAZ (1962). In the ensuing years he worked sporadically in films. He directed A MAN CALLED ADAM (1966) and directed and coscripted JUDGMENT IN BERLIN (1988), which starred his son Sean. Penn acted in SIXTH AND MAIN (1977), and played the father of his son Christopher in THE WILD LIFE (1984).

Penn acted on television in a few episodes of the Andy Griffith series "Matlock" and the telefilms NORTH BEACH AND RAWHIDE (1985) and THE RETURN OF MICKEY SPILLANE'S MIKE HAMMER (1986). Penn's last acting appearance was with his wife Eileen Ryan in THE CROSSING GUARD (1995), written and directed by their son Sean.

Penn died of lung cancer.

Perkins, Carl

born: Apr. 9, 1932, Tiptonville, TN
died: Jan. 19, 1998, Jackson, TN, age 65

Influential rockabilly guitarist, singer, and songwriter.

A self-taught musician, Carl Perkins was a trailblazer of the rock'n'roll/country hybrid that came to be known as "rockabilly." He wrote numerous songs, most notably "Blue Suede Shoes," which became an enormous hit for Elvis Presley. Perkins's style and musicianship influenced generations of singers, including Paul McCartney, Bob Dylan, and Paul Simon.

When Perkins wasn't recording or appearing in concert, he managed to make a few movies. He played himself in JAMBOREE (1957) and the documentary JOHNNY CASH! THE MAN, HIS WORLD, HIS MUSIC (1969). He appeared as a thug in John Landis's farce INTO THE NIGHT (1985). He also contributed to the musical score of the biker flick LITTLE FAUSS AND BIG HALSY (1970). Perkins also appeared in several television and video documentaries about the history of rock 'n' roll and country music.

Perkins died of complications related to a series of strokes.

Perrin, Nat

born: c. 1905, New York, NY
died: May 12, 1998, Los Angeles, CA, age 93

Film and television comedy writer, noted for his collaborations with the Marx Brothers.

Trained as a lawyer, Nat Perrin abandoned the legal profession to write comedy for the theater. Finding it difficult to gain a foothold, he wrote a sketch which he submitted directly to Groucho Marx, who liked his material; before long, Perrin had a contract with Paramount Studios as gag writer. This led to a long association with the Marx Brothers, in particular Groucho, with whom he maintained a lifelong friendship. His first film for the brothers was MONKEY BUSINESS (1931). Although not always given screen credit, Perrin had substantial input on other Marx Brothers films including HORSE FEATHERS (1932), DUCK SOUP (1933), and GO WEST (1940). He was also head writer for Groucho and Chico's 1933-34 radio program "Flywheel, Shyster, and Flywheel." Other film credits include ROMAN SCANDALS (1933), KID MILLIONS (1934), DIMPLES (1936), the film version of HELLZAPOPPIN' (1941) which he had collaborated on during its Broadway run, WHISTLING IN DIXIE (1942), SONG OF THE TIN MAN (1947), MISS GRANT TAKES RICHMOND, TELL IT TO THE JUDGE (both 1949), I'LL TAKE SWEDEN (1965), and FRANKIE AND JOHNNY (1966).

During the 1950s, Perrin worked almost exclusively in television, producing such shows as "The Red Skelton Show" and "Death Valley Days." He was also producer and head writer for "The Addams Family."

Indebted always to Groucho Marx, Perrin became temporary conservator for Marx during his years of declining health. In 1991, he appeared on a television special about his friend, "The One, The Only....Groucho."

No cause of death was reported.

Perrin, Sam

born: Aug. 15, 1901
died: Jan. 8, 1998, Woodland Hills, CA, age 96

Radio and television comedy writer.

Sam Perrin's greatest success was as a writer for Jack Benny. He was with the comedian for more than 40 years, winning Emmy Awards for "The Jack Benny Show" in 1959 and 1960.

Early in his career, Perrin supplied gags for a few films, including Samuel Goldwyn's big-budget musical THE GOLDWYN FOLLIES (1938) and the modest Warner Brothers tunefest NAVY BLUES (1941). The carnival musical ARE YOU WITH IT? (1948), was based on a 1945 Broadway show with a book cowritten by Perrin.

Perrin died after an extended illness.

Petersen, Don

born: c. 1927, Davenport, IA
died: Apr. 25, 1998, Pittsfield, MA, age 70
educ: University of New Mexico

Stage and screen writer.

Don Petersen started his career in show business playing violin in a local orchestra when he was 15. He subsequently served in the Navy during WWII, and then the Army during the Korean conflict. After attending college in the 1960s, Petersen took a job teaching English at drug rehabilitation centers in New York City, an experience that influenced his first Broadway play, *Does a Tiger Wear a Necktie?* (1969). A critical and popular success, the production made a star of actor Al Pacino, who won a Tony for his role.

While Petersen wrote many screenplays, including one for *Does a Tiger Wear a Necktie?*, only three of his efforts were produced during his lifetime. He wrote the cop thriller DEADLY HERO (1976), and collaborated on the scenarios for the romantic comedy AN ALMOST PERFECT AFFAIR (1979) and the thriller TARGET (1985).

Petersen died of lung and liver disease.

Peterson, Louis S.

born: c. 1921, Hartford, CT
died: Apr. 27, 1998, New York, NY, age 76
educ: Morehouse College, Yale School of Drama, New York University

Playwright, screenwriter, actor, and teacher.

While a graduate student at New York University, Louis Peterson became a stage actor. He appeared in a few New York plays, but was frustrated by the lack of opportunity afforded black actors. He turned to playwriting, studying with famed playwright Clifford Odets.

Peterson's first Broadway play was the semi-autobiographical *Take A Giant Step,* about a young black man coming of age in middle-class white America. The play opened to very favorable reviews in 1953, but had a short run; it fared considerably better three years later in an off-Broadway production. The play was made into a film in 1959; Peterson coscripted with Julius J. Epstein. Peterson's other produced screenwriting credit was as a collaborator on the film TEMPEST (1958).

Peterson was nominated for an Emmy Award for his teleplay "Joey," presented in 1956 on the "Goodyear Playhouse."

For more than 25 years, Peterson taught in the theater arts department of the State University of New York, while continuing to write plays.

Peterson died of lung cancer.

Phillips, Webster

born: c. 1915
died: May 13, 1998, Los Angeles, CA, age 83

Makeup artist for film and television.

Webster Phillips was the last of a noted family of film makeup artists. His father, Festus, started during the silent era, while he and his brothers carried on the family tradition for the next six decades.

Under contract to MGM Studios for many years, he made up many of its biggest stars, including John Barrymore, Clark Gable, and Greta Garbo, who called him "the miracle man." Some of the films on which he worked were MUTINY ON THE BOUNTY, A NIGHT AT THE OPERA (both 1935), and ROMEO AND JULIET (1936). Later credits include DESTINATION MOON (1950), RUN FOR THE HILLS (1953), THE COLOR PURPLE (1985), and PLANET OF THE APES (1968), for which he helped develop the remarkably genuine-looking simian visages.

Phillips was also active in television, serving as the head makeup artist on "Lou Grant" as well as such series as "L.A. Law," " Hill Street Blues," and "Bay City Blues." A respected judge in the makeup division of the Academy Awards, Phillips was, in 1996, recognized as "Show Biz Man of the Year" by the Southern California Motion Picture Council.

Phillips' death was caused by cancer.

Preston, William

born: August 26, 1921, Columbia, PA
died: July 10, 1998, New York, NY, age 77
educ: Pennsylvania State University, Pennsylvania

Stage and film actor, best known as the character Carl "Oldy" Olsen on "Late Night with Conan O'Brien."

After receiving a masters degree, William Preston worked for years as a bookkeeper for a trucking firm, dabbling in theater. It was not until he reached the age of 50 that he became a full-time actor, after scoring a role in the Circle in the Square production of Joseph Heller's *We Bombed in New Haven.* He went on to appear in several Broadway productions, including *Arsenic and Old Lace, Our Town,* and *Ivanov.* Off-Broadway, he appeared in *The Fantastiks, Volpone, The Rivals,* and *The Golem,* with the New York Shakespeare Festival.

Preston's film credits include small roles in GOODBYE, NEW YORK (1985), FAMILY BUSINESS (1989), THE EXORCIST III (1990), THE FISHER KING (1991), FAR AND AWAY (1992), WATERWORLD (1995), THE CRUCIBLE, and I'M NOT RAPPAPORT (both 1996).

He gained notoriety in his last years as a regular on "The Conan O'Brien Show," where he appeared in more than 100 comic segments from 1993 until the month before his death. His television work also included a number of daytime dramas, commercials, and the made-for-television film LADY IN THE CORNER (1989).

Preston died following a brief illness.

Price, Loren E.

born: c. 1921
died: Dec. 28, 1998, Tampa, FL, age 77

Theatrical producer.

Loren Price began producing off-Broadway shows in 1959. His first Broadway production was *The Natural Look* (1967), a musical about cosmetics tycoon Helena Rubinstein starring Gene Hackman, Brenda Vaccaro and Jerry Orbach. Price scored his first big success with *George M,* based on the life of George M. Cohan, starring Joel Grey and Bernadette Peters. Other Broadway shows included *Show Me the Good Times,* based on Moliere's *The Imaginary Invalid,* and *Seesaw,* which won Tony Awards for its choreographer, Michael Bennett, and its star, Tommy Tune.

Price produced a rock documentary, FREE (1972), which chronicled a concert on New York's Randall's Island and featured such luminaries as Janis Joplin, Jimi Hendrix and the Who. Since no record exists of a theatrical showing of the film, it may be assumed that it remains unreleased.

Price died of Parkinson's disease.

Questel, Mae

born: 1908, Bronx, NY
died: January 4, 1998, New York, NY, age 89

Actress, singer, comedienne, and voice-over artist.

Familiar to cartoon fans as the voice of Betty Boop, Mae Questel began her career as an impressionist, imitating Fanny Brice, Maurice Chevalier, Rudy Vallee, and Marlene Dietrich. When animator Max Fleischer heard her imitation of "boop-boop-a-doop" singer Helen Kane, he hired her as the voice of his Betty Boop character. She did the character from 1932 to 1939, and repeated the voice for Woody Allen's ZELIG (1983) and WHO FRAMED ROGER RABBIT? (1988). Questel created the voice of Popeye's girlfriend, Olive Oyl, which she continued on and off from 1933 to 1967. She was also the voice of Swee'pea in the 1930s Popeye radio program.

On Broadway, Questel appeared in *Dr. Social, A Majority of One,* and *Enter Laughing.* On the big screen, she had a memorable role as Woody Allen's ghostly mother in NEW YORK STORIES (1989). Other films include A MAJORITY OF ONE, IT'S ONLY MONEY (both 1962), FUNNY GIRL (1968), MOVE (1970), and NATIONAL LAMPOON'S CHRISTMAS VACATION (1989).

Questel died of a lingering illness; she also had suffered from Alzheimer's disease.

Rabinowitz, Mort

aka: Morton Rabinowitz
born: c. 1920
died: Jan. 9, 1998, Ventura, CA, age 77

Art director and production designer.

In a career that spanned more than three decades, Mort Rabinowitz worked on theatrical films and TV movies as an illustrator, art director, and production designer. His many credits include CRIME AND PUNISHMENT, USA (1959), CASTLE KEEP (1969), THE BABY MAKER, FLAP (both 1970), MOLLY AND LAWLESS JOHN (1972), SANTEE (1973), THE FUNHOUSE (1981), and LET'S GET HARRY (1987). He also worked in television, on the technical crews of the TV miniseries "Salem's Lot" (1979) and "The Mystic Warrior" (1984).

Rabinowitz died of respiratory failure.

Raymond, Gene

born: Raymond Guion, Aug. 13, 1908, New York, NY
died: May 2, 1998, Los Angeles, CA age 89

Handsome supporting player and husband of Jeanette MacDonald.

Gene Raymond started out as a child performer on the stage. He made his Broadway debut as a young adult in 1920. After appearing in several plays, he headed for Hollywood, making his movie debut in PERSONAL MAID (1931).

Raymond's blond good looks and upper-class bearing made him a perfect foil for stronger female and male leads. He had featured roles in RED DUST (1932) with Clark Gable and Jean Harlow; EX-LADY (1933) with Bette Davis; FLYING DOWN TO RIO with Dolores Del Rio; ZOO IN BUDAPEST (1933) with Loretta Young; SADIE MCKEE (1934) with Joan Crawford; and THE WOMAN IN RED (1935) with Barbara Stanwyck.

In 1941, Raymond made his only screen appearance alongside his spouse Jeanette MacDonald as the romantic lead in the lavish musical SMILIN' THROUGH. After a prominent supporting role in Alfred Hitchcock's MR. AND MRS. SMITH (1941), Raymond was off the screen for the next five years. He and MacDonald pursued other interests, including traveling. He returned to the movies with a small role in THE LOCKET (1946). In 1948, he tried his hand at directing, with the "B" comedy MILLION DOLLAR WEEKEND, in which he also appeared.

Starting in 1949, Raymond made several appearances on television. He was the host and star of the series "Fireside Theater," and went on to host "TV Reader's Digest" and "Hollywood Summer Theater."

Raymond occasionally returned to the stage. He was on Broadway in *Shadow of My Enemy* (1957) and had a leading role in the tour of *The Best Man* (1960). One of Raymond's last screen appearances was a small part in THE BEST MAN (1964).

Raymond was married to MacDonald for 38 years until her death in 1965.

Pneumonia was the cause of Raymond's death.

Reder, Gigi

born: Luigi Schroeder, 1928, Naples, Italy
died: October 8, 1998, Rome, Italy, age 70

Italian character actor.

Gigi Reder's career spanned five decades and some 70 films, many with some of Italy's leading directors. After making his stage debut with one of Italy's most prestigious repertory companies in 1950, Reder appeared in several minor films before achieving notice in Vittorio De Sica's INDISCRETION OF AN AMERICAN WIFE (1953). He went on to appear in such films as BREAD, LOVE, AND DREAMS (also 1953), De Sica's GOLD OF NAPLES (1954), Alessandro Blasetti's TOO BAD

SHE'S BAD (1955), FAST AND SEXY (1958), Fellini's TV movie THE CLOWNS (1971), CAFE EXPRESS (1980), and THE GREAT PUMPKIN (1993).

It was alongside popular Italian comedian Paolo Villaggio in the "Fantozzi" series of films that Reder became a star. In these, Reder played Filini, a bossy colleague to Villagio's hapless office clerk, Fantozzi. The first installment was FANTOZZI (1975), and a total of nine sequels followed, from FANTOZZI IN PARADISE (1993) to FANTOZZI—THE RETURN (1996). Reder teamed with Villagio on 34 films in all, including the "Frachia" series. In addition to his film and stage roles, Reder worked extensively in television and radio, and as a dubbing actor.

Reder died after a long illness, the exact nature of which was unspecified.

Reed, Bruce

born: c. 1943
died: Feb. 20, 1998, Los Angeles, CA, age 54

Character actor.

In 1974, Bruce Reed appeared in THE LORDS OF FLATBUSH as a gang member. His other film credits included FADE TO BLACK (1980), CLUB LIFE (1987), TAXI DANCERS (1993), and CONFESSIONS OF A HIT MAN (1994).

Reed acted in the television soap opera "Search for Tomorrow," was a guest performer in episodic dramas, including "Cagney and Lacey," and was in the telefilm CRIME OF INNOCENCE (1985).

Reed, who had been the recipient of a heart transplant in 1994, died of heart failure.

Regen, Stuart

born: c. 1959, New York, NY
died: Aug. 18, 1998, Los Angeles, CA, age 39
educ: Skidmore College

Art dealer turned film producer.

When Stuart Regen opened an art gallery in Hollywood in 1989, he became interested in the world of motion pictures. His first film credit was as associate producer of the road movie BRIGHT ANGEL (1991).

A few years later, Regen was drawn to John O'Brien's novel *Leaving Las Vegas* because of the stylish art on the book's dust jacket. He subsequently read the novel and secured the film rights. Despite many obstacles, Regen helped bring LEAVING LAS VEGAS(1995) in on a modest budget of $3.6 million. The film was nominated for four Academy Awards and star Nicolas Cage scored a Best Actor Oscar. Regen had a bit part in the movie, playing a man at the bar. He had another small role in FOXFIRE (1996).

Regen died of non-Hodgkin's lymphoma.

Reilly, Hugh

born: c. 1916, Newark, NJ
died: July 17, 1998, Burbank, CA, age 82
educ: Northwestern Univ.

Actor who played the patriarch of Lassie's TV family for six seasons (1958-64).

Following WWII service in the US Army Air Corps., Hugh Reilly began his acting career on the Broadway stage. The dapper actor was cast in several leading roles, including *Dear Charles* (1954) and *Fair Game* (1957).

Reilly did little film work. He had supporting roles in JOHNNY STOOL PIGEON (1949), THE SLEEPING CITY (1950), and BRIGHT VICTORY (1951). In 1960, he starred in THE DISAPPEARANCE, a "Lassie" TV movie. LASSIE'S GREAT ADVENTURE (1963) was a compilation of four episodes of the series. Reilly was also in the western feature CHUKA (1967).

Reilly's other television work included roles in anthology series, such as "Goodyear Television Playhouse" and "Playhouse 90." He hosted the 1955 series "TV Reader's Digest."

Reilly died of emphysema.

Rio, Larry

born: c. 1915, Brooklyn, NY
died: July 26, 1998, Thousand Oaks, CA, age 83

A former vaudevillian who formed, with his two brothers, the Rio Brothers Comedy Dance Troupe.

After successfully touring in vaudeville, Larry Rio became a dancer and actor in the movies. Many of his films were made for Warner Brothers, where he was a contract player and choreographer. Rio appeared in more than two dozen movies, including THE SKY'S THE LIMIT (1943), THE DOUGHGIRLS, COVER GIRL, LADY IN THE DARK (all 1944), MILDRED PIERCE (1945), A KISS IN THE DARK, JOHN LOVES MARY (both 1949), YOUNG MAN WITH A HORN (1950), CASA MANANA (1951), and THE BUSTER KEATON STORY (1957).

Rio died of lung cancer.

Robbins, Jerome

born: Jerome Rabinowitz, Oct. 11, 1918, New York, NY
died: July 29, 1998, New York, NY, age 79
educ: New York University

Noted choreographer who received an Academy Award for codirecting his first and only feature.

Although his background was in classical ballet, Jerome Robbins made a tremendous impact on Broadway as a director and choreographer of popular musicals; he also contributed his talents to a few very noteworthy films.

Robbins studied dance as a young man. In 1940, he became a member of Ballet Theater. Robbins worked with several major ballet companies for the next six decades. His first fame as a choreographer came from his work on the 1944 ballet *Fancy Free.*

He made his Broadway debut as the choreographer of *On the Town* (1944); other shows followed, including the very successful *The King and I* (1951). Robbins assumed greater creative control as the director as well as choreographer of such Tony-winning Broadway productions as *Peter Pan* (1954), *West Side Story* (1957), *Gypsy* (1959), and *Fiddler on the Roof* (1964).

Robbins recreated his original choreography for the film adaptation of Rodgers and Hammerstein's THE KING AND I (1956). Director Robert Wise brought in Robbins to codirect the movie adaptation of WEST SIDE STORY in 1961. An enormous success, the film won 10 Academy Awards, including Best Picture; Wise and Robbins shared Best Director honors. Robbins was also given an Oscar "for his brilliant achievements in the art of choreographing on film."

After WEST SIDE STORY, Robbins never returned to films, instead remaining active in the world of ballet and musical theater.

His television work included the 1955 NBC telecast of his production of *Peter Pan* starring Mary Martin; the show won an Emmy Award as the year's best single program. The 1993 television adaptation of GYPSY (1993), starring Bette Midler, featured recreations of Robbins's choreography by Bonnie Walker.

Robbins died shortly after suffering a stroke.

Robertson, Peggy

born: c. 1916
died: Feb. 6, 1998, Woodland Hills, CA, age 81

Script supervisor and chief assistant to Alfred Hitchcock.

Peggy Robertson served as script supervisor on Alfred Hitchcock's UNDER CAPRICORN (1949), which was shot in England, and worked as his assistant on his next British project, STAGE FRIGHT (1950). Thus began a 30-year relationship, with Robertson functioning as both a professional associate of Hitchcock's and a close family friend.

Robertson came to America in 1958 to work as a script supervisor for VERTIGO (1958), and continued with Hitchcock as his assistant for the remainder of his career, which included such classic thrillers as PSYCHO (1960) and THE BIRDS (1963). In her work for the director, she had creative input into all facets of his movies' production.

Robertson later had a professional association with director Peter Bogdanovich, serving as an associate producer on MASK (1985) and an executive producer on ILLEGALLY YOURS (1988).

No cause of death was reported.

Rogers, Adam

born: c. 1963
died: January 25, 1998, New York, NY, age 36

Independent film distributor.

Starting his career at the age of 22 in theatrical sales at Castle Hill Productions, Adam Rogers learned the ins and outs of film distribution. Two years later, he became marketing vice-president for Miramax Films.

With a keen eye for quality in the independent market, Rogers joined Cinepix Film Properties in 1991. Through his enthusiasm and experience, he made the small, Toronto-based firm (later known as CFP distribution) into an important player in the United States indie film market. In only a few years, he was responsible for the acquisition and marketing of a number of films by both well-regarded and fledgling independent directors, including Doris Dorrie's NOBODY LOVES ME (1994), Roberto Begnini's THE MONSTER (both 1994), James Mangold's HEAVY, Peter Greenaway's THE PILLOW BOOK (both 1996), Greg Mottola's THE DAYTRIPPERS, Jonathan Nossiter's SUNDAY, Kirby Dick's SICK: THE LIFE AND DEATH OF BOB FLANAGAN, SUPERMASOCHIST (all 1997), and Richard Kwietniowski's LOVE AND DEATH ON LONG ISLAND (1998).

In 1997, Rogers was made vice-president of distribution at Cinepix. Shortly before his death, he was hired as senior vice-president and general manager of Alliance Releasing, the domestic distribution operation for Canadian entertainment giant Alliance Communications.

No cause of death was reported.

Rogers, Roswell

born: c. 1911, South Dakota
died: Aug. 6, 1998, Monterey County, CA, age 87
educ: University of Missouri, Sioux Falls College

Writer for radio, television, and films.

Roswell Rogers started his professional writing career in the mid-1930s, providing scripts for many popular radio programs. He cowrote the screenplays for two 1943 RKO programmers based on radio characters Lum 'n' Abner, TWO WEEKS TO LIVE and SO THIS IS WASHINGTON. He also coscripted the romantic comedy JUST ACROSS THE STREET (1952). He enjoyed his greatest success (and four Emmy nominations) writing for the radio and television series "Father Knows Best."

After retiring from television, Roswell returned to screenwriting. He scripted two very popular Disney live-action comedies, $1,000,000 DUCK (1971) and CHARLEY AND THE ANGEL (1973).

Rogers died of complications from Parkinson's disease.

Rogers, Roy

born: Leonard Franklin Slye, November 5, 1912, Cincinnati, OH
died: July 6, 1998, Apple Valley, CA, age 86

Legendary singing cowboy star who worked in film, television, and recordings.

Hollywood's number one "King of the Cowboys" for more than ten years, Roy Rogers came from humble beginnings. His family moved from Ohio to California in 1930, where they worked as migrant fruit-pickers. Rogers began entertaining at parties and square dances, eventually joining several musical groups, including The Rocky Mountaineers and the O-Bar Cowboys. A stint with a Roswell, New Mexico radio station led to the formation of the country-western group Sons of the Pioneers, who had a hit recording with "The Last Roundup" in 1935.

Rogers began to play bit parts in "B" westerns such as TUMBLING TUMBLEWEEDS (1935) and THE OLD CORRAL (1937) under the names Len Slye and Dick Weston. He got his big break at Republic Studios, replacing Gene Autry in UNDER WESTERN SKIES (1937). Rogers went on to star in dozens of low-budget westerns with his sidekick "Gabby" Hayes and Trigger, "The Smartest Horse in the Movies." Films like BILLY THE KID RETURNS (1938), THE ARIZONA KID (1939), RED RIVER VALLEY (1941), ROMANCE ON THE RANGE (1942), and KING OF THE COWBOYS (1943) made Rogers America's top cowboy star.

Rogers first worked with singer Dale Evans in THE COWBOY AND THE SENORITA (1944); they subsequently made 26 films together, including DON'T FENCE ME IN (1945), APACHE ROSE (1947), THE EYES OF TEXAS (1948), and HEART OF THE ROCKIES (1951). In 1947, the year following the death of Rogers' first wife, the former Arlene Wilkins, he and Evans married.

Rogers virtually retired from the movies after an amusing self-parody in the Bob Hope film SON OF PALEFACE (1951). He and Evans began their popular television series, "The Roy Rogers Show" in 1951; the show costarred the ever-present Hayes and Trigger. With its familiar theme song, "Happy Trails to You," the series ran until 1957. A variety show, "The Roy Rogers and Dale Evans Show," lasted only one season in 1962.

When Trigger died in 1965 at the age of 33, Rogers had him mounted (not stuffed); the horse remains on display at the Roy Rogers-Dale Evans Museum in Victorville, California. Rogers and Evans continued to make recordings; their output exceeded 400 songs. Rogers is a member of the Country Music Hall of Fame.

In addition to the money he earned off his work in film, TV, and recordings, Rogers also profited from the merchandising of products bearing his likeness, including clothing, souvenirs, and comic books. He also maintained extensive real estate holdings, a television production company, a music publishing company, and a chain of fast-food restaurants. At the time of his death, his fortune was estimated at more than $100 million.

Humble and simple to the end, Rogers was quoted as saying, "When my time comes, just skin me, and put me right there on top of Trigger, just as though nothing has changed."

Rogers died of congestive heart failure.

Roland, Rita

born: Oct. 5, 1914
died: Aug. 17, 1998, Los Angeles, CA, age 84

Film editor.

Rita Roland worked in various European countries as an editor. After she assembled the German film BOEFJE (1939), her career stalled with the outbreak of WWII.

She relocated to Hollywood after the war and continued to hone her craft. Her career flourished during the 1960s, when she was worked as an editor on several MGM films, including HONEYMOON HOTEL (1964), A PATCH OF BLUE, GIRL HAPPY (both 1965), THE SINGING NUN, SPINOUT, PENELOPE (all 1966), WHERE WERE YOU WHEN THE LIGHTS WENT OUT?, and THE SPLIT (both 1968).

Roland's later work included the films MOVE (1970), THE BETSY (1978), RESURRECTION (1980), FORT APACHE, THE BRONX (1981), and THE NEW KIDS (1985).

She also edited television movies, including THE LINDBERGH KIDNAPPING CASE (1976), ELEANOR AND FRANKLIN: THE WHITE HOUSE YEARS (1977), A PIANO FOR MRS. CIMINO (1982), and THE DOLLMAKER (1984).

Roland died of a stroke.

Rolle, Esther

born: November, 1920, Pompano Beach, FL
died: November 17, 1998, Culver City, CA, age 78

Actress and crusader against black stereotypes.

The daughter of a vegetable farmer, Esther Rolle developed her interest in acting early on. As a teen, she moved to New York, where she became a member of the Negro Ensemble Company. She appeared in a number of plays over the years, including *The Amen Corner, A Raisin in the Sun,* and *Dame Lorraine.*

It was in the Broadway production of *Don't Play Me Cheap* that she was spotted by producer Norman Lear, who offered her the role of maid Florida Evans in the sitcom "Maude." She appeared for two seasons (1972-74) and received so much attention that, in 1974, Lear offered her a spinoff series, "Good Times," which focused on Florida's struggles to raise a family in a Chicago ghetto. Although the series ran until 1979, Rolle left after three seasons in protest of the negative image projected by the character of her TV son, J.J., played by actor Jimmie Walker. She was persuaded to return to the series for its final season.

It is ironic that a woman who deplored stereotypes should have gained fame and respect playing servants, but Rolle took care to inject a note of strength and dignity into such portrayals. She received the Emmy Award for Oustanding Supporting Actress as a maid in the TV movie THE SUMMER OF MY GERMAN SOLDIER (1978). She played the sagacious housekeeper in a New York theater production of *The Member of the Wedding* (1988), and was the long-suffering housekeeper in the film DRIVING MISS DAISY (1989). Her final film roles were in ROSEWOOD (1997) and in DOWN IN THE DELTA (1998), directed by Maya Angelou.

In 1990, Rolle was the first woman to receive the N.A.A.C.P. Chairman's Civil Rights Leadership Award for helping to raise the image of blacks.

Although no specific cause of death was reported, she was known to have been suffering from diabetes, and was undergoing dialysis at the time of her death.

Ross, Sam
born: c. 1911, Russia
died: Mar. 30, 1998, Laguna Beach, CA, age 86
educ: Northwestern Univ.
Novelist and scriptwriter.

A Russian emigre, Sam Ross started his professional career as a sportswriter. He turned to writing fiction in the late 1940s, and published his first novel, *He Ran All the Way,* in 1947. The book was adapted for the screen in 1951, with John Garfield (in his last film role) and Shelley Winters.

While continuing to write novels, Ross also worked as a scripter for various television shows, including "The Naked City," "Rawhide," "The Fugitive," "Mannix," and "Hawaiian Eye."

Ross died of heart failure.

Rothschild, Jon
born: c. 1943
died: Jan. 30, 1998, age 54
Production designer, set builder, and producer.

Early in his career, Jon Rothschild worked as an actor with the Los Angeles Art Theater. He then turned to designing and building houses; he later used his design skills on film and television projects. He was the production designer for THE NIGHT VISITOR (1990), DEAD ON: RELENTLESS 2 (1991), and MORTUARY ACADEMY (1992).

Making a final career switch, Rothschild coproduced a film STAND INS, and was seeking a distributor for it at the time of his death.

Rothschild died of heart failure.

Roux, Michel
born: 1924, Angouleme, France
died: February 4, 1998, Paris, France, age 73
Operatic baritone who worked as an actor on stage and in film.

Michel Roux enjoyed great success in both opera and film. He made his opera debut in 1948 at the Opera-Comique, and went on to sing with the Paris Opera, the Glyndebourne Opera Company, La Scala, the Vienna Staatsoper, and the Deutsche Oper. He sang the leads in many operas, primarily those written by Mozart and Rossini.

He made his film debut with a small role in LA CAVALCADE DES HEURES (1943). After BLANC COMME NEIGE (1947), his second film, he began to play more important roles. In the 1950s he appeared in several films by Julien Duvivier, including LA FETE A HENRIETTE (1952) and LA FEMME ET LE PANTIN (1958), a remake of Josef von Sternberg's THE DEVIL IS A WOMAN (1936).

Among Roux's other films are MATERNITE CLANDESTINE (1953), CROQUEMITOUFLE (1958), and PAS TRES CATHOLIQUE (1994). In 1977, he starred in the French television series "Recherche dans l'interet des Familles," as Inspector Matthieu.

No cause of death was reported.

Rowe, Arthur
born: c. 1924, Los Angeles, CA
died: Aug. 8, 1998, Beverly Hills, CA, age 74
Writer for radio, television, and the movies.

After serving as a Marine during WWII, Arthur Rowe settled into a career as a gag writer for radio shows, providing jokes for such popular comedians as Jack Benny and Eddie Cantor.

He later wrote for television. His many credits include "Gunsmoke," "Fantasy Island," "Starsky & Hutch," and "Mission: Impossible."

In the world of film, Rowe collaborated on the screenplay for the WWI adventure ZEPPELIN (1971), and wrote the screenplays for THE MAGNIFICENT SEVEN RIDE! (1972) and the horror film LAND OF THE MINOTAUR (1976).

Rowe died after a lengthy illness; no cause of death was reported.

Ryan, Chico
born: David-Allen Ryan, c. 1948
died: July 26, 1998, Beverly, MA, age 50
educ: Boston Univ., Emerson College
Singer and bass player with the 1950s revival band Sha-Na-Na for 25 years.

Before joining Sha-Na-Na in 1972, Chico Ryan performed with a number of groups, including the Minutemen, the Rockin' Ramrods, Rainface, and The Happenings, who had a major hit with "See You in September."

As part of Sha-Na-Na, the theatrical group that helped spearhead the 1950s rock'n'roll revival, Ryan appeared in GREASE (1978).

No cause of death was reported for Ryan, who died in a nursing home.

Sabbatini, Enrico
born: January 7, 1932, Spoleto, Italy
died: November 25, 1998, Ouarzazate, Morocco, age 66
Oscar-nominated costume designer who also worked as a production designer and art director in film, theater, and television.

A specialist in historical productions, Enrico Sabbatini was noted for his ability to re-interpret period styles in modern modes. He began his career in the 1960s, designing for operatic productions at Milan's La Scala. He went on to work for many of Italy's best known filmmakers. His earliest film work was as a costumer for Elio Petri's THE TENTH VICTIM (1965) and Mario Monicelli's CASANOVA 70 (1966). He designed Sophia Loren's costumes for Francesco Rosi's MORE THAN A MIRACLE (1967).

Sabbatini designed the costumes for Vittorio De Sica's A PLACE FOR LOVERS (1968) and SUNFLOWER (1970); SACCO AND VANZETTI (1971), Ettore Scola's A SPECIAL DAY (1977), and CHRIST STOPPED AT EBOLI (1978). In Hollywood, he designed costumes for SIDNEY SHELDON'S BLOODLINE (1979). Roland Joffe's THE MISSION (1986), for which he earned an Oscar nomination, CUTTHROAT ISLAND (1995), and SEVEN YEARS IN TIBET (1997).

Sabbatini worked as a production designer for Dario Argento's thriller FOUR FLIES ON GREY VELVET (1971), and also served as art director on (as well as designing the exotic costumes for) Radley Metzger's CAMILLE 2000 (1969) and THE LICKERISH QUARTET (1970).

For television, Sabbatini was a costume designer on JESUS OF NAZARETH and the production designer for a series of bible films produced by the TNT cable network, including JOSEPH (1994), JACOB (1995), and MOSES (1996). In 1982, he won an Emmy Award for his costume design for the miniseries "Marco Polo" (1982). At the time of his death, he was working on the Hallmark/ABC miniseries Cleopatra."

Sabbatini died in an automobile accident while on location in Morocco.

Salem, Murray
born: c. 1950, Cleveland, OH
died: Jan. 6, 1998, Los Angeles, CA, age 47
educ: Miami University
Actor and screenwriter.

After graduating college, Murray Salem studied acting at London's Drama Studio and acted in several plays with repertory companies.

He went on to act in movies and on television. Salem's credits include the films LET'S GET LAID!, THE SPY WHO LOVED ME (both 1977), and HUSSY (1980); the TV miniseries "Jesus of Nazareth" (1977) and "Holocaust" (1978); the TV movies INSTITUTE FOR REVENGE (1979) and BRAVE NEW WORLD (1980); and the television series "Magnum PI."

Salem coscripted the Arnold Schwarzenegger comedy KINDERGARTEN COP (1990).

Salem died of complications from AIDS.

Sampson, Caleb
born: c. 1953, Lewiston, ME
died: June 8, 1998, Cambridge, MA, age 45
educ: Wesleyan University (1976)
Musician and composer.

After graduating from college, Caleb Sampson worked as a jazz pianist and became one of the founders of the Alloy Orchestra, a popular Boston ensemble. In 1991, they were asked to create a contemporary score for a presentation of the Fritz Lang classic METROPOLIS (1926) in Brookline, Massachusetts. That success led to appearances at several international film festivals, including the Telluride Film Festival and Italy's Pordenone Silent Film Festival, where they performed distinctive modern scores for classic silent films.

Sampson also scoresd a number of documentaries, including LEONA'S SISTER GERRI (1995), MY FATHER'S GARDEN (1996), THE MYSTERIES OF THE LAST TSAR (1997), and FAST, CHEAP &

OUT OF CONTROL (1997). He also wrote music for several television shows, including "Sesame Street."

Sampson's death was reported as an apparent suicide.

Samuelson, Michael

born: c. 1931
died: Aug. 26, 1998, London, England, age 67
Producer of documentaries.

After working with a theatrical repertory company, Michael Samuelson turned to a career in the film industry. He began as a cameraman, and later served as a director of the Samuelson Film Service, which was started by his brother.

Samuelson was involved in the production of two acclaimed sports documentaries: GOAL: THE OFFICIAL FILM OF THE 1966 WORLD CUP (1966), which concerned the competition held in England; and WHITE ROCK (1977), about the 1976 Innsbruck Austria Winter Olympics. He was a photographic consultant at the 1984 Los Angeles Olympics.

Samuelson died of a blood clot in the lung.

Sanders, Lawrence

born: c. 1920, New York, NY
died: Feb. 14, 1998, Pompano Beach, FL, age 78
educ: Wabash College (Indiana)
Prolific, popular novelist.

After serving in the Marines during WWII, Lawrence Sanders contributed to several magazines as a journalist. He later turned to writing fiction, and published his first novel, *The Anderson Tapes,* in 1970. The book was enormously successful and received the Edgar Award for Best First Novel from the Mystery Writers of America. It was adapted into a hit film of the same name by Sidney Lumet in 1971.

Sanders' book *The First Deadly Sin* was adapted into a 1980 film, starring Frank Sinatra and Faye Dunaway, which was a success with neither critics nor the public.

No cause of death was reported.

Sanders, Steve

born: Sept. 17, 1952, Richland, GA
died: June 10, 1998, Cape Coral, FL, age 45
Lead singer and rhythm guitarist of the country vocal group the Oak Ridge Boys.

Steve Sanders sang gospel music as a child. When he was 13 years old, he appeared on Broadway playing the lead in *The Yearling* (1965), a musical version of the popular Marjorie Kinnen Rawlings novel.

In 1967, he played Faye Dunaway and John Philip Law's son in Otto Preminger's turgid melodrama HURRY SUNDOWN (1967).

Sanders occasionally appeared on television, most notably in the series "Gunsmoke" and "Matt Helm" and the ABC Stage 67 production of "Noon Wine."

Sanders joined the Oak Ridge Boys in 1981, the year the band had its biggest hit, "Elvira." He left the group in 1995.

Sanders died from a gun-shot wound, apparently self-inflicted.

Saperstein, Henry G.

born: June 2, 1918, Chicago, IL
died: June 24, 1998, Beverly Hills, CA, age 80
educ: University of Chicago
Film and television producer and distributor.

From 1943-45, Henry G. Saperstein was a theater owner in Chicago. He became involved in television production in the 1950s. He served as president of Television Personalities, president of Glen Films, and president and owner of UPA (United Productions of America). Saperstein was responsible for the distribution or production of such television shows as "All-Star Golf," "Championship Bowling," "Ding Dong School," and the cartoon series "Mr. Magoo," "Gerald McBoing Boing," and "Dick Tracy."

In 1962, Saperstein moved into the film world, producing the animated musical GAY PURR-EE (1962). He was the executive producer of the unusual WHAT'S UP, TIGER LILY? (1966), Woody Allen's English-dubbed comic reworking of the Japanese spy film KEY OF KEYS (1964). Saperstein also served as executive producer on John Boorman's taut war drama HELL IN THE PACIFIC (1968).

Saperstein was best known among cult-film fans for his distribution of a number of Japanese science fiction-fantasy films during the 1960s and '70s; these included FRANKENSTEIN CONQUERS THE WORLD (1964), MONSTER ZERO, WAR OF THE GARGANTUAS (both 1970), and TERROR OF MECHAGODZILLA (1975). He was responsible for the American television and video licensing of Toho's very popular Godzilla character.

Saperstein was also associated with the nearsighted cartoon character Mr. Magoo. He produced the primetime series, "The Famous Adventures of Mr. Magoo" and several popular specials featuring the character, including the beloved "Mr. Magoo's Christmas." Many years later, Saperstein was the executive producer of the live-action feature MR. MAGOO (1997).

Saperstein died of cancer.

Schamoni, Ulrich

born: November 9, 1939, Berlin, Germany
died: March 9, 1998, Berlin, Germany, age 59
Award-winning filmmaker of the "New German Cinema" movement.

An influential German filmmaker in the 1960s and '70s, Ulrich Schamoni began his career with the short film "Hollywood in Deblatchka Pescara" (1965) and the feature ES (1966). His next film, ALLE JAHRE WIEDER (1967), garnered critical acclaim and won the Silver Bear award at the 1967 Berlin Film Festival.

His other films include QUARTETT IM BETT (1968), EINS (1971), and CHAPEAU CLAQUE (1974), which attracted the attention of Germany's intellectuals; he scripted as well as directed the latter two titles. His last film was DAS TRAUMHAUS (1980).

Schamoni died of cancer.

Schnittke, Alfred

born: November 24, 1934, Engels, Volga Republic (former Soviet Union)
died: August 3, 1998, Hamburg, Germany, age 63
education: Moscow Conservatory
Major Soviet composer of contemporary classical music; prolific film composer.

Alfred Schnittke, who studied in his early years in both Vienna and the Soviet Union, was one of the outstanding musical figures of his time. Known for his hallmark "polystylistic" idiom, he displayed a genius for juxtaposing older musical styles with distinctly contemporary sounds. Sometime in disfavor with the official Soviet musical hierarchy for his stylistic experimentation, he nonetheless achieved fame and popularity throughout the world, where his music was celebrated in festivals and in concerts by leading orchestras.

His classical output included 9 symphonies, 6 concerti grossi, 4 violin concertos, ballet scores, operas, chamber music, and choral works. He also composed extensively for the Soviet cinema, scoring more than 60 films. Among his most significant film scores were KOMISSAR (1967), UNCLE VANYA (1970), AUTUMN (1974), THE CREW (1979), and AGONY (1981). He also composed extensively for Soviet television.

Schnittke won numerous awards for his work, among them the Austrian State Prize in 1991, and Japan's Imperial Prize in 1992. Shortly before his death, he won the prestigious Slava-Gloria-Prize, organized by his longtime friend, Msistlav Rostropovich. Following his death, the parade of tributes was led by Russian president Boris Yeltsin, who credited the composer for "a genuine revolution in music."

After more than a decade of ill health, Schnittke died after a series of strokes.

Sessa, Alejandro

born: c. 1937
died: July 10, 1998, Buenos Aires, Argentina, age 60
Argentinian producer/director.

An important figure in the Argentine film industry, Alejandro Sessa was educated in American film schools. Before becoming a filmmaker, Sessa ran Laboratorios Alex, a top film lab, with his brother Aldo. He later joined with several other producers to form Aries Cinematografia, a major production company in Argentina from the mid-1960s to the mid-'80s.

Sessa produced two major films for Aries: NO HABRA MAS PENAS NI OLVIDO (1983) and PASAJEROS DE UNA PESADILLA (1984). In the United States, Sessa produced and directed AMAZONS (1986) and coproduced HIGHLANDER II: THE QUICKENING (1991).

The cause of death was heart failure.

Shdanoff, George

born: c. 1906, Russia
died: Aug. 14, 1998, Los Angeles, CA, age 92

Acting coach who acted and wrote plays.

Before moving to the United States, George Shdanoff was an established figure in the European theater. Upon his arrival in America, he coestablished the Chekhov Theater, which performed to critical acclaim around the country. Although he primarily worked in theater as an actor and a playwright, Shdanoff also played small roles in the films A ROYAL SCANDAL (1945) and SPECTER OF THE ROSE (1946).

In his later years, Shdanoff was known primarily for his work as an acting coach and master teacher.

Shdanoff died of natural causes.

Shipstad, Eddie

born: c. 1907, MN
died: August 20, 1998, Los Angeles, CA, age 91

Cofounder of the Ice Follies.

Along with his younger brother Roy and his comic ice-skating partner Oscar Johnson, Eddie Shipstad created the first traveling ice show, the Ice Follies, an idea that grew into a major show-business success story.

The Shipstads and Johnson had attracted local fame since childhood with their skating performances; they later worked up elaborate routines and, during the Depression, tried them out in larger venues. They eventually gathered national attention with a five-year stint at Madison Square Garden. This taste of notoriety prompted the trio to form the Shipstad and Johnson Ice Follies in 1936; the touring show proved to be enormously popular with Depression-era audiences.

Their success led to an MGM film, ICE FOLLIES OF 1939 (1939). The film was a flop, but the Ice Follies continued to score with audiences nation-wide. So popular were they that, when they refused to form a second touring company, arena managers joined forces in 1940 to form a copycat company called Ice-Capades. The partners sold the Ice Follies in 1954 for $3.5 million. It was eventually absorbed by the "Disney on Ice" subsidiary of Walt Disney Productions.

Shipstad died of natural causes.

Sinatra, Frank

born: Francis Albert Sinatra, December 12, 1915, Hoboken, NJ
died: May 14, 1998, Los Angeles, CA, age 82

Versatile performer, widely considered to be the most influential male pop singer of the 20th century.

Singer, actor, recording artist, producer, philanthropist—Frank Sinatra covered a lot of ground in his sixty years in show business. His show business career was jump-started when he won first prize on "Major Bowes' Amateur Radio Hour" in 1937. Within two years, he was a big-band singer, first with Harry James and then with Tommy James. In 1941, Sinatra went solo, and quickly bacame a nationwide sensation.

While attendance at his concerts and his record sales continued to soar, Sinatra turned to film. Although his early film appearances were negligible, fans of his music attended in droves. In 1945, he signed with MGM Studios, where he appeared in movies ranging from good—ANCHORS AWEIGH (1945)—to atrocious—THE SINGING BANDIT (1948)—to classic—ON THE TOWN (1949).

By 1950, Sinatra's career was flagging. His contract with MGM was broken, and he lost fans to the younger, hotter singing sensations of the day. He further alienated his fans by maintaining a very public affair with MGM star Ava Gardner while still married to his first wife, Nancy Barbato.

Sinatra achieved a miraculous comeback in 1953 with a one-two punch. First, he joined with legendary arranger Nelson Riddle to record a series of enormously popular "swingin'" singles. At the same time, he scored a straight dramatic role in the film version of James Jones's FROM HERE TO ETERNITY (1953), and received an Academy Award as Best Supporting Actor for his performance.

A bankable movie star once more, Sinatra followed ETERNITY with two of his best dramatic performances, playing an assassin waiting to kill the President in SUDDENLY (1954) and a drug-addicted musician in Otto Preminger's controversial THE MAN WITH THE GOLDEN ARM (1955). At this point, Sinatra settled into a pattern, alternating big-budget musicals like GUYS AND DOLLS (1955), HIGH SOCIETY (1956), PAL JOEY (1957), and CAN CAN (1960) with lesser adaptations of bestselling novels, including NOT AS A STRANGER (1955), THE PRIDE AND THE PASSION (1957), and KINGS GO FORTH (1958). Two exceptions were his sincere turn as comedian Joe E. Lewis in THE JOKER IS WILD (1957) and his strong work in Vincente Minnelli's SOME CAME RUNNING (1958).

In the 1960s, films like OCEANS 11 (1960), SERGEANTS 3 (1962), FOUR FOR TEXAS (1963) , and ROBIN AND THE SEVEN HOODS (1964) were mostly vehicles for the notorious "Rat Pack," a loose-knit aggregation consisting primarily of Sinatra and his Vegas pals Dean Martin, Sammy Davis Jr., Peter Lawford, and Joey Bishop. At the same time, Sinatra appeared in what many critics consider his best role, as a Korean War-era soldier who tries to help a brainwashed ex-comrade, in John Frankheimer's Cold War thriller THE MANCHURIAN CANDIDATE (1962). The film was just as much of a critical and popular success when it was re-released theatrically in 1987.

In 1965, Sinatra made his only triple-threat movie, NONE BUT THE BRAVE (1965), a war film which he produced, directed, and starred in. A series of hard-boiled detective films—TONY ROME (1967), THE DETECTIVE, and LADY IN CEMENT (both 1968)—made little impact at the box office, and after the comic western DIRTY DINGUS MCGEE (1970), he essentially retired from movies. Aside from two more appearances as police detectives, in the telefilm CONTRACT ON CHERRY STREET (1977) and THE FIRST DEADLY SIN (1980), Sinatra was seen only as himself in the documentaries THAT'S ENTERTAINMENT (1974) and LISTEN UP: THE LIVES OF QUINCY JONES (1991), and in a cameo as "The Chairman" in THE CANNONBALL RUN II (1983).

As a recording artist, Sinatra enjoyed the distinction of placing records at the top of the charts in each of the six decades in which he worked. His records were phenomenally successful in the 1950s, even as rock'n'roll dominated the charts. After a series of hits in the mid-1960s, including "Strangers in the Night" and "It Was a Very Good Year," his recordings dipped in popularity until 1980, when his recording of "New York, New York" hit the Top Ten and led to a resurgence of interest. All the while, however, his concert appearances continued to sell out, particularly in the showrooms of Las Vegas. Despite a short-lived "retirement" from 1971 to 1973, he continued to perform in concerts through the early '90s, when age and ill health caught up with him.

Sinatra's personal life had its peaks and valleys as well. His first marriage produced three children: Nancy, Frank Jr., and Christine (Tina). His marriage to Ava Gardner lasted two years. In the 1950s and early 1960s, he was seriously involved with several noted actresses and public figures including Lauren Bacall and Juliet Prowse. In 1966, at the age of 50, he married 21-year-old Mia Farrow; the couple were officially separated in less than a year-and-a-half. Sinatra devoted his later years to his final love, fourth wife Barbara Marx (the former wife of Zeppo Marx), whom he married in 1976. The couple remained together until the singer's death.

In 1971, the Academy of Motion Picture Arts and Sciences gave Sinatra the Jean Hersholt Humanitarian Award, for his many charitable enterprises. In 1994, the Grammy Awards honored him with a special lifetime achievement award.

Sinatra died of an acute heart attack, following years of severe health problems.

Sitka, Emil

born: c. 1914, Johnstown, PA
died: Jan. 16, 1998, Camarillo, CA, age 83

Slapstick comedian who often served as a comic foil for the Three Stooges.

Emil Sitka had the distinction of having acted with all six of the men who were members of the Three Stooges. His first screen encounter with the immortal comedy team came when he had already been in Hollywood a decade, and was working in odd jobs in and out of the theater and film. He was cast in the Stooges's 98th Columbia short, "Half-Wits Holiday" (1947), which was also Curly Howard's last appearance before his death.

Sitka was a supporting player in almost three dozen of the Stooges' two-reelers; he also appeared with the trio in THE THREE STOOGES MEET HERCULES, THE THREE STOOGES IN ORBIT (both 1962), THE THREE STOOGES GO AROUND THE WORLD (1963), and THE

OUTLAWS IS COMING (1965). Often on the receiving end of punches, sprays of seltzer, or hurled cream pies, Sitka claimed to have played about 70 different characters in the shorts. His favorite was Old Man Flint in "All Gummed Up" (1947), but he is better known for his turn as the frazzled justice of the peace in "Brideless Groom" (1947), the use of a clip from which in PULP FICTION (1994) prompted Quentin Tarantino to credit Sitka in the film's cast list.

Although Sitka was never an official Stooge, he came close. He signed a contract in 1974 to replace Larry Fine in a Stooges feature, but before the film could be made, Moe Howard died and the project was abandoned.

Besides the Stooges movies, Sitka appeared in several other films, including a few comedies with the Bowery Boys.

Sitka supplemented his small income from bit parts in the movies with work as a structural and civil engineer. He had an agreement with his employer that enabled him to take time off whenever he had a role in a movie.

Sitka had suffered a stroke several months prior to his death.

Snyder, William L.

born: c. 1917
died: June 3, 1998, Livingston, NY, age 80

Producer and distributor of foreign films.

William L. Snyder was influential in revitalizing the film industry in postwar Eastern Europe, particularly in Czechoslovakia. In 1949 he organized Rembrandt Films, which was initially an importer of European movies. One of the company's early successes was Hans Christian Andersen's THE EMPEROR AND THE NIGHTINGALE (1949), an animated puppet feature by the Czechoslovakian director Jiri Trnka; the English-language narration was supplied by Boris Karloff. Other notable items distributed by Rembrandt included the short French films "White Mane" (1952) and "The Red Balloon" (1956), which won an Oscar for Best Original Screenplay.

With animator Gene Deitch, Snyder started producing cartoons in Prague in 1959. He received an Academy Award (for Best Animated Short Subject) for Jules Feiffer's "Munro" (1960), an eight-minute film about a four-year-old boy who is drafted into the Army by mistake. Three other shorts he produced were honored with Oscar nominations: "Self Defense—for Cowards" (1962), "Nudnik #2," and "How to Avoid Friendship" (both 1964).

Rembrandt Films also distributed animated versions of children's classics and the popular "Tom and Jerry" and "Popeye" cartoons.

Snyder died as a result of complications from Alzheimer's disease.

Spies, Adrian

born: c. 1920, Newark, NJ
died: Oct. 2, 1998, Los Angeles, CA, age 78
educ: University of North Carolina, Columbia University

Acclaimed television writer.

Trained as a journalist, Adrian Spies was a writer for newspapers and magazines before turning to script writing for radio and television. He contributed scripts to many popular shows, including "Climax," "Playhouse 90," "Dr. Kildare," "The Defenders," "Ironsides," "Hawaii Five-O," and "Star Trek"; his "Miri" script for the last-named is considered one of the best-written episodes in the series.

For one of his dramatic scripts, written for the live "Studio One" series, Spies was given the Mystery Writers of America's Edgar Award.

He collaborated on the scripts of several TV movies, including THE SCORPIO LETTERS (1967), HAUSER'S MEMORY (1970), and THE FAILING OF RAYMOND (1971). Spies also cowrote the screenplay for the 1968 film DARK OF THE SUN, aka THE MERCENARIES.

It was reported that Spies died while undergoing heart surgery.

Squires, Dorothy

born: Edna May Squires, March 25, 1915, Llwynypia, Rhondda, Wales
died: April 14, 1998, Llwynypia, Rhondda, Wales, age 83

British musical star.

The daughter of a Welsh steelworker, Dorothy Squires moved to London in 1938, where she worked with bandleader Billy Reid. Their 13-year relationship, which was personal as well as professional, resulted in a number of hit recordings, beginning with "The Gypsy" in 1945. Squires went on to become a favorite on the music hall and concert stages, and her records sold millions, both in Britain and the United States. During this period, she starred on the television show "Wit and Wisdom," alongside fellow music hall stars Norman Wisdom and Beryl Reid.

One of her biggest hits was "I'm Walking Behind You" in 1953, and it was in that year that she married actor Roger Moore, of future "Saint" and James Bond fame. While his career took off, hers only seemed to decline. She made one of her only film appearances at this point, in the British musical STARS IN YOUR EYES (1956). Despite a wide age difference between Squires and Moore (he was 13 years her junior), the marriage endured until 1968. From that time on, Squires was plagued by hard luck—bankruptcies, evictions, loss of property. It was through the help of a fan that she found a home in her later years, back in her native Wales.

Squires died of cancer.

Sterling, Philip

born: c. 1922, Philadelphia, PA
died: November 30, 1998, Woodland Hills, CA, age 76
educ: University of Pennsylvania and The Wharton School of Business

Character actor in film, theater, and television.

A familiar face to millions of TV viewers, Philip Sterling enjoyed a long and distinguished career. Before turning to acting, he was a jazz pianist and a radio personality.

He made his Broadway debut in Cole Porter's *Silk Stockings,* and went on to appear in *Summertree* and Gore Vidal's *An Evening With Richard Nixon.* His most prominent role was as the adulterous father in Neil Simon's *Broadway Bound.*

On the big screen, he was featured in movies including ME, NATALIE (1969), THE GANG THAT COULDN'T SHOOT STRAIGHT (1971), HESTER STREET (1975), AUDREY ROSE (1977), METEOR (1979), THE COMPETITION (1980), MOVERS AND SHAKERS (1985), and MY GIANT (1998). He appeared in many made-for-television movies, including RAINBOW (1977), BEST KEPT SECRETS (1984), VITAL SIGNS (1986), and FATAL JUDGMENT (1988),

Sterling's work in television included live TV dramas, including "Studio One" and "Kraft Television Theater." He played George Hayes on the soap opera "Guiding Light" from 1963 to 1968. He had recurring roles on such series as "L.A. Law," "NYPD Blue," and "Barney Miller." He was attorney Michael Brimm on the series "City of Angels," and Judge Truman Ventnor on "Sisters" from 1991 to 1995.

Sterling was a member of the national board of the Screen Actors Guild, the first president of the Screen Actors Guild Foundation, and a trustee of the Guild's health and pension plan.

Sterling died from complications of myelofibrosis, a bone marrow disease.

Stevens, Leslie

born: February 3, 1924, Washington, D.C.
died: April 24, 1998, Los Angeles, CA, age 74
educ: Royal College of Westminster, London

Playwright, producer, director, and writer who worked in film and television.

Leslie Stevens's career as playwright began at the age of 15, when he sold his first play, *The Mechanical Bat* to Orson Welles' Mercury Theater. After serving in WWII, Stevens worked for *Time* magazine before turning his full attention to writing. His Broadway plays included *The Marriage-Go-Round* and *The Pink Jungle.*

Stevens's first produced screenplay was for Arthur Penn's THE LEFT-HANDED GUN (1958). He wrote and produced the films PRIVATE PROPERTY (1959), THE MARRIAGE-GO-ROUND (1960, adapted from his play), HERO'S ISLAND (1962), BUCK ROGERS IN THE 21ST CENTURY (1979), and SHEENA (1984). He wrote and directed THREE KINDS OF HEAT (1987) and scripted RETURN TO THE BLUE LAGOON (1991).

Stevens's greatest successes were in the field of television. He created, produced, and served as writer-director of the popular series "The Outer Limits," and created and produced the hit shows "It Takes a Thief," and "McCloud," Other shows in which he had creative input included "Stony Burke," "Battlestar Galactica," and "The Name of the Game."

Stevens died of a heart attack.

Stickney, Dorothy

born: June 21, 1897, Dickinson, ND
died: June 9, 1998, New York, NY, age 101

Celebrated stage actress, who also worked in film and television.

Best-known for creating the role of Vinny (Mother) in *Life with Father,* Dorothy Stickney enjoyed a long career on the Broadway stage. She made her debut in *The Squall* in 1926. The following year she married writer Howard Lindsay, who was to become one of Broadway's most successful playwrights. She created the role of prostitute Molly Molloy in Ben Hecht's and Charles MacArthur's 1929 classic, *The Front Page.*

In 1939, Lindsay (along with partner Russell Crouse) wrote *Life with Father,* and, with Stickney, costarred in the play for four years and a total of 1600 performances, making them one of the most celebrated acting couples in America.

Stickney made only rare appearances in films. Among her screen credits are WAYWARD (1932), MURDER AT THE VANITIES, THE LITTLE MINISTER (both 1934), THE UNINVITED (1944), THE CATERED AFFAIR (1956), and I NEVER SANG FOR MY FATHER (1970). She made occasional forays into television, appearing as the Queen in Rodgers and Hammerstein's 1957 "Cinderella," starring Julie Andrews. She also played the role of a bootlegger on the series "The Waltons."

Her theatrical work remained her focus. In 1960, she wrote and appeared in a one-woman show, *A Lovely Light,* about poet Edna St. Vincent Millay.

No cause of death was reported.

Tasker, William

born: c. 1943
died: May 13, 1998, Santa Monica, CA, age 54

Composer of film soundtracks.

William Tasker had many careers in his lifetime: in addition to working in film music, he also wrote scores for TV shows and commercials, taught, and worked as a photographer for magazines. He also wrote about trains, a subject for which he had great fondness.

Among his film credits are the music for 1977's JOHN HUS and Russ Meyer's erotic BENEATH THE VALLEY OF THE ULTRA-VIXENS (1979). Tasker also wrote a new score for the D. W. Griffith silent western "The Battle of Elderbush Gulch" (1914).

Tasker died of a heart condition.

Taylor, Don

born: Dec. 13, 1920, Pittsburgh, PA
died: Dec. 29, 1998, Los Angeles, CA, age 78

Actor, writer, and director who worked in film and television.

Don Taylor made his acting debut in Moss Hart's stage production of *Winged Victory.* During the run of the show, he was offered a contract at MGM Studios, where he played supporting roles in a number of features. He repeated his stage role in the film WINGED VICTORY (1944), and later appeared in SONG OF THE THIN MAN (1947), THE NAKED CITY (1948), BATTLEGROUND (1949), FLYING LEATHERNECKS (1951), I'LL CRY TOMORROW (1955), and THE BOLD AND THE BRAVE (1956), among others. He is most familiar to audiences as Elizabeth Taylor's bridegroom in FATHER OF THE BRIDE (1950) and its sequel, FATHER'S LITTLE DIVIDEND (1951), and as the persecuted war hero in STALAG 17 (1953).

He turned from acting to directing with the comedy EVERYTHING'S DUCKY (1961), starring Mickey Rooney, Buddy Hackett, and Jackie Cooper. He went on to direct a number of genre films, including RIDE THE WILD SURF (1964), JACK OF DIAMONDS (1967), ESCAPE FROM THE PLANET OF THE APES (1971), THE ISLAND OF DR. MOREAU (1977), DAMIEN: OMEN II (1973), and THE FINAL COUNTDOWN (1979). During this period Taylor worked in television as well, directing more than 400 television dramas, as well as the series "Night Gallery" and "Mobil One." Utilizing his talent as a writer (he had previously written several one-act plays, radio dramas, and short stories), he both wrote and directed the TV movie biography of Errol Flynn, MY WICKED, WICKED WAYS (1985); other TV movies directed by Taylor include GOING FOR THE GOLD: THE BILL JOHNSON STORY (1985) and THE DIAMOND TRAP (1988). His script for the "Night Gallery" episode "They're Tearing Down Tim Riley's Bar" was nominated for an Emmy Award.

Twice married, both times to actresses, Taylor divorced his first wife Phyllis Avery in 1955 and later married Hazel Court, whom he had directed in a play he had written for Alcoa Theater, "The Tweed Hat."

The cause of death was reported as heart failure.

Taylor, Robert Lewis

born: c. 1910, Carbondale, IL
died: Sept. 30, 1998, Southbury, CT, age 88
educ: Univ. of Illinois

Prolific writer.

Robert Lewis Taylor was an author noted for his wit, style, adventurous spirit, and eccentric behavior. He started his writing career as a newspaper journalist and then worked for many years writing stories for *The New Yorker,* in which he also published a series of brilliant character profiles.

His 1959 Pulitzer Prize-winning novel, *The Travels of Jaimie McPheeters,* was made into a television series that ran during the 1963-64 season. Set in 1849, the book told the story of a 14-year-old boy's adventures in the Wild West; Kurt Russell starred as Jaimie in the TV series.

Taylor's novel *A Journey to Matecumbe,* an adventure yarn about two boys looking for buried treasure, was made into the 1976 Disney movie TREASURE OF MATECUMBE.

Among Taylor's many critically lauded books was the much-praised anecdotal autobiography *W. C. Fields: His Follies and Fortunes.*

No cause of death was reported.

Terry, W. Benson

born: c. 1922
died: Mar. 24, 1998, age 76

Character actor.

W. Benson Terry made his entry into the world of film late in life; prior to his work as an actor, he was a prizefighter and a union organizer. He had small parts in WHERE'S POPPA (1970), HARRY AND TONTO (1974), the telefilm CINDY (1978), HER ALIBI (1989), and FOREST GUMP (1994).

Terry often worked on the stage and was part of the acclaimed Arena Stage (Washington's regional theater) production of *The Cherry Orchard.*

Terry died of cancer.

Thomas, Crawford John

born: c. 1928
died: June 3, 1998, Pasadena, CA, age 69

Producer best known for his work with no-budget filmmaker Edward D. Wood Jr.

Crawford John Thomas, the son of a 1930s character actor, first encountered Ed Wood while working with him on the 1947 play "The Blackguard Returns," in which both were actors. Subsequently the two formed a company, Wood-Thomas Pictures. They initially worked on television commercials before making a short movie, "Crossroads of Laredo," aka "Streets of Laredo" (1948). Thomas coproduced and acted in the movie, along with Wood, who also wrote and directed. It was with this movie that Wood established his *modus operandi:* the first take of every scene was the one used in the finished film. Thomas was also coproducer of the 1995 documentary THE HAUNTED WORLD OF EDWARD D. WOOD, JR.

Thomas died of liver cancer.

Thomas, Michele

born: Sept. 23, 1969, Boston, MA
died: Dec. 22, 1998, New York, NY, age 29

Television and film actress.

Raised in New York, Michele Thomas was the daughter of Phynjuar Thomas, an actress, and Dennis Thomas, a member of the music group Kool and the Gang. She attended the Montclair School of the Arts and the Broadway Dance Center, and came to prominence playing Callie on the soap opera, "The Young and the Restless." For her work on the series, she was nominated by the N.A.A.C.P. as outstanding actress in a daytime drama series.

On primetime television, Thomas played Malcolm Jamal Warner's girlfriend Justine on "Cosby," and Urkel's girlfriend, Myra, on "Family Matters" from 1994-98. She also appeared in a number of films, including

HANGING WITH THE HOMEBOYS (1991), CAGED HEARTS (1995) and UNBOWED (1998), as well as the TV movie DREAM DATE (1989).
Thomas' death was caused by cancer.

Thompson, Kay

born: Nov. 9, 1905 (sources inexact), St. Louis, MO
died: July 2, 1998, New York, NY, age believed to be between 92 and 95

Actress, vocalist, vocal arranger, composer, and author.

Kay Thompson is best known as the author of four books about the adventures of Eloise, an unsupervised, bratty six-year-old living in the Plaza Hotel in Manhattan. The character first appeared in the early 1950s, and the popularity of the Eloise books provided Thompson with material for a night-club act, recordings, and teleplays. In 1956 TV's "Playhouse 90" presented a dramatization of the character, appropriately entitled "Eloise."

Thompson began her show business career as a pianist with the St. Louis Symphony and later became a band singer, making regular appearances on radio. With her group, The Kay Thompson Ensemble, she had a guest stint in a low-budget 1937 Republic musical, MANHATTAN MERRY-GO-ROUND (which also featured her first husband, bandleader-trombonist Jack Jenny). Thompson wrote songs, made recordings, and continued to make live appearances while becoming one of the movie industry's top vocal and choral arrangers. In 1946, Thompson created the vocal arrangements for the Danny Kaye musical THE KID FROM BROOKLYN, in which she also appeared in a small role; that same year Thompson worked on ZIEGFELD FOLLIES as a writer, composer and the vocal arranger. She was also the vocal arranger for THE HARVEY GIRLS (1946), TILL THE CLOUDS ROLL BY (1947), GOOD NEWS (1947), and (with Roger Edens and Robert Tucker) THE PIRATE (1948).

After her MGM experience, Thompson returned to performing, enjoying great success in nightclubs with the Williams Brothers (Andy, Dick, Don, and Bob). She returned to the screen in FUNNY FACE (1957) as the fashion editor who urged American women to "think pink," and had a supporting role in TELL ME THAT YOU LOVE ME, JUNIE MOON (1970).

Thompson was living in a New York City apartment with her goddaughter, Liza Minnelli, when she died. The cause of death was not revealed, nor was her age. Apparently Thompson refused to discuss how old she was; however, it was generally speculated that she was between 92 and 95 years old.

Tillman, Harrel

born: Harrel Gordon Tillman, c. 1925
died: June 19, 1998, Houston, TX, age 73
education: Livingstone College, Salisbury, NC

Film and stage actor.

After graduating college, Harrel Tillman moved to New York, where he had a brief career on the stage. In 1947 he moved to Hollywood, where he appeared in several low-budget films, including LOVE IN SYNCOPATION (1947), THAT MAN OF MINE (1947), and THE FIGHT NEVER ENDS (1949) starring champion boxer Joe Louis.

Tillman left the film industry in the early 1950s and moved to Houston, where he was ordained a Methodist minister and helped organize a church. He later studied law and practiced in Houston for over thirty years before being appointed a municipal court judge—the first black man in Texas to be accorded that honor.

Tillman's death was caused by cancer.

Tors, Peter

born: c. 1957, Beverly Hills, CA
died: July 29, 1998, Miami, FL, age 41

Actor, director, and stuntman.

Peter Tors had early exposure to the world of filmmaking as the son of producer, writer, and director Ivan Tors. Although Tors acted in the feature ESCAPE FROM ANGOLA (1976), he worked primarily as a stuntman, appearing in such films as SPRING BREAK (1983), AMERICAN TIGER (1989), SOUTH BEACH (1993), and BAD BOYS (1995). He later served as writer, production chief and codirector of LOOKING FOR TROUBLE (1996), a kiddie comedy about a baby elephant named Trouble.

Tors died of a heart attack.

Tromberg, Sheldon

born: c. 1930
died: July 5, 1998, Richmond, CA, age 68

Radio personality, film producer, and entertainment reporter.

A major figure in Washington, DC show business circles, Sheldon Tromberg began his career as a sales trainee for Republic Pictures; he soon turned to film distribution for Continental Films and Embassy Pictures, then founded his own firm, Box Office Attractions. Tromberg also worked as an entertainment reporter for ABC's Washington affiliate. Tromberg also produced several low-budget films, including THE REDEEMER (1978), and appeared in Tony Brown's message movie about cocaine abuse, THE WHITE GIRL (1990).

Tromberg's entry into radio history occurred while he was hosting a late night radio call-in show for station WRC in Washington in the early 1970s. One remarkable night, shortly after Iranian terrorists seized the American embassy in Tehran, Tromberg placed a call to the embassy and conversed with an English-speaking revolutionary on the air. It was soon clear that Tromberg's call had actually preceded any from the U.S. State Department.

Tromberg died of a heart attack.

Trow, Bob

born: Feb. 6, 1926
died: Nov. 2, 1998, New Alexandria, PA, age 72

Actor best known for his thirty-year stint on the PBS children's show "Mr. Rogers' Neighborhood."

Bob Trow got his start in show business on Pittsburgh radio stations WWSW and WDKA, delighting morning commuters with an assortment of comic characters on Rege Cordic's morning talk show.

Trow's work in film was minimal: he appeared in two early films directed by Pittsburgh filmmaker George Romero, SEASON OF THE WITCH and THERE'S ALWAYS VANILLA (both 1972). By the time he worked for Romero, however, he had already joined the hit television series, "Mr. Rogers' Neighborhood," which began in 1968. For the next three decades Trow played the characters Robert Troll and Bob Dog, as well as himself. Trow also wrote and produced television and radio commercials.

Trow's death was caused by a heart attack.

Turney, Catherine

born: c. 1906
died: Sept. 9, 1998, Los Angeles, CA, age 92

Screenwriter who specialized in stories about strong, willful women.

Catherine Turney scripted several classic examples of what were called "women's pictures" in Hollywood' Golden Age. She didn't receive screen credit for her work on MILDRED PIERCE (1945)—Ronald MacDougall did—but film historians believe she had a great deal to do with bringing the James Cain novel to the screen. After that film, Turney continued writing screenplays for some of the era's top female stars like Bette Davis, Ann Sheridan, Ida Lupino, and Barbara Stanwyck; the films she scripted (sometimes in collaboration with others) included ONE MORE TOMORROW, OF HUMAN BONDAGE, MY REPUTATION, THE MAN I LOVE, A STOLEN LIFE (all 1946), CRY WOLF (1947), WINTER MEETING (1948), and NO MAN OF HER OWN (1950). Turney later wrote the scripts for two lower-budgeted movies: JAPANESE WAR BRIDE (1952) and BACK FROM THE DEAD (1957), which was based on her novel, *The Other One.*

For TV, Turney provided the script for LITTLE DOG LOST (1963). In her later years she wrote romance novels and biographies.

No cause of death was reported.

Tuttle, Dorothy

born: c. 1918
died: Aug. 12, 1998, Encino, CA, age 80

Longtime Hollywood bit player.

Dorothy Tuttle's career, which spanned some fifteen years, consisted mostly of uncredited bit parts in a number of big-budget musicals and costume dramas. Under contract to Metro-Goldwyn-Mayer, she appeared in ROSALIE (1937), MARIE ANTOINETTE (1938), ZIEGFELD GIRL (1941), MEET ME IN ST. LOUIS (1944), THE HARVEY GIRLS

(1946), SUMMER STOCK (1950), and AN AMERICAN IN PARIS (1951). One of her few credited appearances was as a court lady in JOAN OF ARC (1948), starring Ingrid Bergman.

Tuttle died of natural causes.

Ulanova, Galina

born: Jan. 10, 1910, St. Petersburg, Russia
died: Mar. 21, 1998, Moscow, age 88

Prima ballerina whose performances were preserved in various films.

Considered one of the greatest ballerinas of the 20th century, Galina Ulanova was, for most of her 32-year career, a leading soloist, first with Leningrad's Maryinsky Ballet and then with Moscow's Bolshoi Ballet.

Ulanova documented her artistry on film on a few occasions. In RUSSIAN BALLERINA (1947) she did a portion of her acclaimed performance from *Swan Lake.* Ulanova was also one of several Soviet dancers in THE GRAND CONCERT (1952). In a segment of STARS OF THE RUSSIAN BALLET (1954) she danced Maris in "Fountain of Bakhchisarai," a dramatic dancing role she had done originally in 1934 and which had established her as a front-ranking ballerina. ROMEO AND JULIET (1954), made when Ulanova was in her 40s, saw the dancer recreating the role she had first played in 1940. When she appeared with the Bolshoi in London in 1956, a film was made, THE BOLSHOI BALLET (1957), which documented the company's engagement.

After retiring from ballet in 1960, Ulanova became a teacher.

She died after a lengthy, unidentified illness.

Vanselow, Robert A.

born: c. 1920, Milwaukee, WI
died: March 30, 1998, Los Angeles, CA, age 79

Actor and singer in films and television shows.

Perhaps best remembered for his role as Starky in the Broadway production of *Peter Pan,* Robert A. Vaneslow had a long career on the stage. Other theatrical productions in which he appeared were *Annie Get Your Gun, Jollyanna,* and *Red, White and Blue.*

Vanselow's film appearances include THE MALE ANIMAL (1942), PETE KELLY'S BLUES (1955), and THE TEN COMMANDMENTS (1956). On television, Vanselow was featured on such series as "The Virginian," "Death Valley Days," "Thriller," and "Perry Mason." In addition to his film, theater, and television work, Vanselow appeared in nightclubs and hotels across the United States.

Vanselow's death followed a lengthy, heart-related illness.

Veitch, John

born: c. 1920
died: Dec. 8, 1998, Los Angeles, CA, age 78

Actor, producer, assistant director, head of production, and CEO at several companies.

Injured in combat in WWII, John Veitch came to Hollywood to be treated for war-related leg wounds. While hospitalized he met actor Alan Ladd, who suggested he try his hand at acting in movies. Veitch decided to follow Ladd's advice, and subsequently appeared in several films, including STALAG 17, FROM HERE TO ETERNITY (both 1953), CRIME WAVE, and RIVER OF NO RETURN (both 1954).

Finding himself more at home behind the scenes, Veitch worked as location manager on such films as THE HORSE SOLDIERS (1959); he quickly graduated to assistant director, a position he filled on the movie SHIP OF FOOLS (1965). As production manager he worked with some of the best directors in the business, including Stanley Kramer, George Stevens, Billy Wilder, and John Ford.

In 1968, Veitch was elevated to senior vice-president, and later president in charge of worldwide production, at Columbia Pictures. In this capacity he oversaw the production of over 300 films, including such blockbusters as TAXI DRIVER (1976), CLOSE ENCOUNTERS OF THE THIRD KIND (1977), KRAMER VS. KRAMER (1979), and TOOTSIE (1982). In 1987, Veitch set up his own production unit at Columbia; the unit produced, among others titles, SUSPECT (1987), the made-for-television RAINBOW DRIVE (1990), BRAM STOKER'S DRACULA (1992), MARY SHELLEY'S FRANKENSTEIN (1994), and FLY AWAY HOME (1996).

Shortly before his death, Veitch was named co-chairman of LG Pictures, a division of the Toronto-based Lions Gate Entertainment. He was also a member of the Academy of Motion Picture Arts and Science's executive branch for thirty years.

Veitch died of pancreatic cancer.

Villiers, James

born: James Michael Lyle Villiers, Sept. 29, 1933, London, England
died: Jan. 18, 1998, Arundel, Sussex, England, age 64

British film, stage, and television actor.

After graduating from London's Royal Academy of Dramatic Art, James Villiers began a successful career on the London stage, starting at the Old Vic (now the National Theater Company). For the next seven years he appeared in a wide assortment of plays on the West End, ranging from Shakespeare to *Peter Pan,* in which he played Captain Hook. He made his Broadway debut in *Richard III* in 1956.

Villiers made his film debut in CARRY ON SERGEANT (1959) and went on to appear in over 40 films, usually typecast as an upper-class, snooty Brit; he particularly excelled in villainous roles. Among his more notable credits are THE DAMNED (1963), NOTHING BUT THE BEST (1964), REPULSION (1965), THE RULING CLASS (1972), JOSEPH ANDREWS (1977), UNDER THE VOLCANO (1984), and MOUNTAINS OF THE MOON (1990). His last film was THE TICHBORNE CLAIMANT (1998).

Villiers' television work was extensive. He appeared in several adaptations of such classic plays as "The Millionairess," "Lady Windemere's Fan," and "Pygmalion," and was particularly memorable as Charles II in the British miniseries "The First Churchills."

Villiers died of cancer.

Walsh, J. T.

born: James Patrick Walsh, Sept. 28, 1943, San Francisco, CA
died: Feb. 27, 1998, La Mesa, CA, age 54
educ: University of Rhode Island (BA in sociology)

Accomplished supporting actor who specialized in portraying average individuals, many with a dark side.

J. T. Walsh worked at various jobs, including social worker, school teacher and reporter, before he turned to professional acting. He was just entering his 30s when he started his career on the New York stage, making his debut with the Manhattan Theatre Club as Kit Carson in *Yucca Flats* (1973). Over the next decade, Walsh acted in over two dozen plays on Broadway and in regional theaters around the country before making a solid impression in David Mamet's *Glengarry Glen Ross* (1984) on Broadway.

Walsh's first film role was a bit in EDDIE MACON'S RUN (1983). Thereafter he worked almost exclusively in film, sometimes in as many as six films in one year. He was in Woody Allen's HANNAH AND HER SISTERS (1986); scored significantly as the hard-nose sergeant in GOOD MORNING, VIETNAM (1987); and reunited with Mamet for HOUSE OF GAMES (1987) and THINGS CHANGE (1988). Other early Walsh credits include TEQUILA SUNRISE (1988), THE BIG PICTURE, WIRED (both 1989), CRAZY PEOPLE, NARROW MARGIN, THE GRIFTERS, MISERY (all 1990), TRUE IDENTITY, and BACKDRAFT (both 1991).

Walsh' most impressive role during this period was the weak, suicidal Lt. Col. Markinson in A FEW GOOD MEN (1992). Walsh also appeared in two John Dahl movies that were planned for theatrical release but debuted on cable TV: THE LAST SEDUCTION and RED ROCK WEST (both 1994). Other films he appeared in include MIRACLE ON 34th STREET (1994), THE BABYSITTER, NIXON (both 1995), SLING BLADE (1996), BREAKDOWN (1997), THE NEGOTIATOR, and PLEASANTVILLE (both 1998).

Among Walsh's numerous television appearances are the miniseries "Little Gloria . . . Happy at Last" (1982), "Sidney Sheldon's Windmills of the Gods" (1988), the telefilms ARTHUR MILLER'S THE AMERICAN CLOCK (1993), GANG IN BLUE, and CRIME OF THE CENTURY (both 1996). He also was a guest star on many episodic dramas.

Walsh died of a heart attack while at a San Diego-area resort.

Wayne, Gus

born: Oct. 16, 1920, Bronx, NY
died: Jan. 23, 1998, Lakeland, FL, age 77

Midget character actor.

Although he wasn't prominently seen in THE WIZARD OF OZ (1939), Gus Wayne played a Munchkin soldier, making him one of the 124 little people employed for the classic film. It was his only film appearance.

Wayne's greatest success came as a corporate spokesperson: he was a diminutive chef for a biscuit company, and "Mr. Lucky" for a Las Vegas casino.

Wayne left the entertainment industry in 1973 to work for Piper Aircraft, where he was employed until he retired in 1980.

Wayne, who was in poor health after having suffered a stroke three years prior to his death, succumbed to heart failure. His wife of 37 years, actress Olive Brasno, died two days later.

Weidman, Jerome

born: Apr. 14, 1913, New York, NY
died: Oct. 6, 1998, New York, NY, age 85
educ: City College of New York, New York University

Novelist, playwright, and screenwriter.

Before he started college, Jerome Weidman worked as an office boy in New York's garment district—an experience he drew upon for his first novel, *I Can Get It for You Wholesale,* published in 1937. The popular book established Weidman as an important novelist, and later served as the basis for a movie and a Broadway musical.

Weidman's initial experience with the movie industry came when his novel *I'll Never Go There Any More* was made into the 1949 film HOUSE OF STRANGERS (later remade as the 1954 western BROKEN LANCE). His first novel was transformed into a vehicle for Susan Hayward, I CAN GET IT FOR YOU WHOLESALE (1951), by screenwriters Abraham Polonsky and Vera Caspary. Weidman coscripted the Joan Crawford vehicle THE DAMNED DON'T CRY (1950) and THE EDDIE CANTOR STORY (1953); provided the story for INVITATION (1952); and wrote the screenplay for SLANDER (1956).

Weidman collaborated with George Abbott on the book for the hit Broadway musical *Fiorello!* (1959), for which the team received the Pulitzer Prize for Drama. Less successful were the musicals *Tenderloin* (1960), *I Can Get It for You Wholesale* (1962; which featured Barbra Streisand in an impressive Broadway debut), and *Pousse-Cafe* (1966).

Weidman also wrote 22 novels and numerous short stories. His memoir, *Praying for Rain,* was published in 1986.

No cause of death was reported.

Wells, Robert

born: Oct. 15, 1922
died: Sept. 23, 1998, Santa Monica, CA, age 76

Prolific song lyricist and Emmy-winning television producer and writer.

Though he provided lyrics for more than 400 songs during his five-decade career, Robert Wells is probably best known for providing the lyrics to "The Christmas Song," which was originally recorded by his longtime song-writing partner and friend, Mel Torme; "The Christmas Song" went on to become the second highest-grossing holiday song of all time, next to "White Christmas." Wells and Torme wrote many other songs together as well, including "County Fair" for the Disney film SO DEAR TO MY HEART (1949). He also cowrote (with author James Jones) the song "Reenlistment Blues" for the movie FROM HERE TO ETERNITY (1953). Wells received an Oscar nomination for the lyrics to "It's Easy to Say" for Blake Edwards' 10 (1979). Other films for which he wrote songs include THE FRENCH LINE (1954) and WATERHOLE #3 (1967). Wells also made brief appearances in several films, such as THE FIGHTER (1952).

Wells also made a name for himself in later years as a television producer and writer. He won Emmy awards as producer and head writer for "The Dinah Shore Chevy Show" for four years. He also won two Emmy awards for his work on the television special, "Shirley MacLaine: If They Could See Me Now." He contributed lyrics and special material for television specials starring Gene Kelly, Julie Andrews, and Ann-Margret. In addition, Wells created nightclub material for such diverse performers as Nat "King" Cole, Peggy Lee, and Harry Belafonte.

The cause of death was cancer.

Wendelken, George

born: c. 1917
died: Jan. 3, 1998, Toms River, NJ, age 81

Former child actor.

A child star who went on to become a war hero, George Wendelken was "Freckles" in the original "Our Gang," whose silent one-reel comedies were popular program-fillers during the 1920s. After appearing in a number of shorts, Wendelken retired from the screen before the age of ten.

He became a prominent figure again, however, for his distinguished service record in WWII, during which he was wounded on Guadalcanal. Upon his return home, Wendelken was appointed as the first Enlisted Men's Representative in Washington for the Navy, Marine Corps and the Coast Guard. He is also credited with having raised over $200 million in war bonds. After the war, Wendelken created the Publicity Searchlight Company, which provided Army surplus searchlights for film premieres and other events.

No cause of death was reported.

Westcott, Helen

born: Myrthas Helen Hickman, 1928, Hollywood, CA
died: Mar. 17, 1998, Edmunds, WA, age 70
educ: Los Angeles Junior College

Actress noted for several supporting roles, including the steadfast wife in THE GUNFIGHTER (1950).

At the age of 7, Helen Westcott was acting onstage in *The Drunkard* and in radio plays, and later was in the long-running *God's Little Acre*. Her first film appearance was in the low-budget western THUNDER OVER TEXAS (1934); she then had a role in the elaborate Max Reinhardt production of A MIDSUMMER NIGHT'S DREAM (1935).

Westcott appeared in a number of films made at major studios, usually in supporting roles. As an adult actress she started appearing regularly in films in the late 1940s, and in 1949 alone appeared in eight films, including Otto Preminger's WHIRLPOOL and MR. BELVEDERE GOES TO COLLEGE. Westcott's most notable role was Peggy, the long-suffering schoolteacher wife of outlaw Jimmy Ringo, in THE GUNFIGHTER (1950). Perhaps the essentially unglamorous nature of the character worked against Westcott, as she continued to play supporting roles in films like THREE CAME HOME (1950), THE SECRET OF CONVICT LAKE (1951), PHONE CALL FROM A STRANGER, RETURN OF THE TEXAN, LOAN SHARK, and WITH A SONG IN MY HEART (all 1952). She had nominal leads in various B westerns, including BATTLES OF CHIEF PONTIAC (1952), COW COUNTRY, GUN BELT, and THE CHARGE AT FEATHER RIVER (all 1953).

Westcott continued to make movies for many years and retired after her work in two 1970 releases, PIECES OF DREAMS and I LOVE MY WIFE. After leaving films, she taught and was active with her local theatre group.

Westcott died of complications from cancer.

Whitehead, O. Z.

born: Mar. 1, 1911, New York
died: Jul. 29, 1998, Dublin, Ireland, age 87

Versatile character actor.

In his early 20s, O. Z. Whitehead began a successful career on the stage, acting in several Broadway plays. He also began to act in films, most notably THE SCOUNDREL (1935). He continued onscreen as a supporting player for more than three decades, appearing in approximately 30 movies.

Whitehead worked in several genres, appearing in such titles as MY BROTHER TALKS TO HORSES (1946), THE ROMANCE OF ROSY RIDGE (1947), A SONG IS BORN (1948), MAN AND PA KETTLE (1949), BEWARE MY LOVELY (1952), and JULIUS CAESAR (1953). He was in several films directed by John Ford, including THE GRAPES OF WRATH (1940), THE LAST HURRAH (1958), THE HORSE SOLDIERS (1959), TWO RODE TOGETHER (1961), and THE MAN WHO SHOT LIBERTY VALANCE (1962). Whitehead's last movie was THE LION IN WINTER (1968).

He also appeared occasionally on television, acting in episodes of "Gunsmoke" and "Perry Mason," as well as the 1981 miniseries "The Manions of America."

Whitehead died of cancer.

Williams, Mark

born: c. 1960
died: May 27, 1998, Panorama City, CA, age 38

Special effects and makeup effects artist.

Mark Williams began his career in special effects working in the field of video games, entering filmmaking as a technician on ALIENS (1986). He helped devise creature effects for THE FLY (1986) and BLUE MONKEY (1987). In 1987, Williams opened a "creature shop" in which he created effects for RETURN TO SALEM'S LOT (1987), THE ABYSS (1989), and TERMINATOR II: JUDGMENT DAY (1991). He eventually created effects for some sixty films, working with such directors as James Cameron, Larry Cohen, and Samuel Fuller.

Williams also made significant contributions to the genre films PSYCHO COP 2 (1992), RELENTLESS 3 (1993), BLUE FLAME (1994), WEREWOLF (1997), and KRAAA! THE SEA MONSTER (1998). He was later named head of special effects for Full Moon Pictures, for which he created effects for the film SHRIEKER (1998).

Williams' death resulted from respiratory failure.

Williams, Wendy O.

born: Wendy Orleans Williams, May 28, 1949, Rochester, NY
died: Apr. 6, 1998, Storrs, CT, age 48

Best known as lead singer for the punk band The Plasmatics.

Wendy O. Williams, one of the most notoriously outrageous performers in rock, made her show business debut at age 6 tap-dancing on "The Howdy Doody Show." Brought up in Webster, New York, a small town outside Rochester, Williams took to the road in search of new experiences while still in her mid-teens. She eventually landed in New York City and went to work for Captain Kink's Sex Fantasy Theater, run by Rod Swenson, who later became her manager and remained her lifelong friend and companion.

Williams participated in the live sex shows at Captain Kink's and is credited with at least one adult film, CANDY GOES TO HOLLYWOOD (1979). It was at this time that Williams and Swenson organized The Plasmatics, which debuted at the New York punk mecca CBGBs. With Williams' trademark Mohawk hairstyle and striking dress (on one occasion, she performed wearing only shaving cream), the band quickly made a name for themselves by blowing up cars, firing gunshots into amplifiers and sledge-hammering TV sets—in fact, the band seemed to make headlines less for its music than for its behavior and run-ins with the law. Nevertheless, Williams was nominated for a Grammy Award in 1985 as best female vocalist.

Williams went on to make several movies, appearing as Charlie, a leather-clad Lesbian, in REFORM SCHOOL GIRLS (1986), and as Butch in PUCKER UP AND BARK LIKE A DOG (1990). As The Plasmatics drifted apart, Williams released several solo albums, which failed to receive any recognition. In 1991, she and Swenson moved to a small town in Connecticut, where she worked in a natural foods co-op.

Despondent for some time, Williams died of a self-inflicted gunshot wound.

Williamson, Bruce

born: c. 1927, Cadillac, MI
died: Oct. 6, 1998, New York, NY, age 71

Film critic.

After graduating from college, Bruce Williamson moved to New York where he pursued a career as an actor, appearing in several off-Broadway shows. He soon turned to writing and, during the 1950s, wrote topical humor for Julius Monk's long-running comedy cabaret revue, *Upstairs at the Downstairs.*

Williamson began writing film criticism for *Time* magazine during the 1960s, then worked briefly for *Life* magazine; in 1968 he joined *Playboy,* where he remained a film critic, columnist and interviewer for the next thirty years. Williamson retired from the position in June of 1998, but continued to supply a movie column for *New Woman* magazine.

The cause of death was bladder cancer.

Wilson, Carl

born: Dec. 21, 1946, Hawthorne, CA
died: Feb. 7, 1998, Los Angeles, CA, age 51

Singer and lead guitarist for the Beach Boys.

The Beach Boys got their start in 1961, when brothers Brian, Dennis, and Carl Wilson, along with their cousin Mike Love and friend Alan Jardine, recorded "Surfin'," a song whose popularity attracted the attention of Capitol Records. The group's distinct sound and optimistic lyrics made them one of the most popular musical acts of the 1960s. They had numerous top-10 hits, including "Good Vibrations," "Surfin' U.S.A.," "Wouldn't It Be Nice," and "Surfer Girl," many of which featured Carl on lead vocal.

The band worked primarily on stage and in the recording studio, but at the height of their popularity they made a guest appearance in a college comedy, GIRLS ON THE BEACH (1965). Wilson later appeared in several documentary and home-video productions, among them THE BEACH BOYS—AN AMERICAN BAND (1987), 1960s: MUSIC, MEMORIES AND MILESTONES (1989), BRIAN WILSON: I JUST WASN'T MADE FOR THESE TIMES, and HISTORY OF ROCK 'N' ROLL (both 1995). He also performed in episodes of the TV series "Baywatch" and "Home Improvement."

For a time in the 1980s, Carl left The Beach Boys and tried a solo career. He eventually rejoined the group and was with them when they were inducted into the Rock and Roll Hall of Fame in 1988.

Wilson, who was the group's youngest member, died of complications from lung cancer.

Wilson, Flip

born: Clerow Wilson, Dec. 8, 1933, Jersey City, NJ
died: Nov. 25, 1998, Malibu, CA, age 64

Standup comedian who hosted an immensely popular TV variety series in the early 1970s.

Wilson, whose comic characters contributed several catch phrases into the American pop lexicon, was the first black to host a weekly variety show. His most beloved creation was the character of Geraldine Jones, a sassy, wisecracking woman whose trademark quips, "What you see is what you get!", "The devil made me do it," and "When you're hot, you're hot—when you're not, you're not!" passed into common usage.

Born into abject poverty, Wilson was the 10th of at least 18 children (some sources claim the number of siblings to be as many as 24). He joined the Air Force as a teenager, and was soon chided by his fellow servicemen for "flipping out," telling outrageous stories and acting them out in dialects. Thus, the origin of his famous nickname.

After leaving the service, Wilson worked as a bellboy at a San Francisco hotel. He persuaded the management to let him try out some comedy routines in the hotel nightclub, and his success there led to appearances in black nightclubs around the country, including a successful stint as master of ceremonies at the Apollo Theater in Harlem.

In the late 1960s, Wilson appeared to great acclaim on various TV series, including "The Tonight Show," "Laugh-In," "The Ed Sullivan Show," and "The Merv Griffin Show." He became a regular at the most important nightclubs on both coasts, and also made several comedy albums. In 1970, NBC offered Wilson his own television series. "The Flip Wilson Show" earned him two Emmy Awards, and his picture on the cover of *Time* magazine.

During his time as a successful TV host (his show ran from 1970-74), Wilson made appearances in several films, including CANCEL MY RESERVATIONS (1972) and UPTOWN SATURDAY NIGHT (1974). Wilson ended his show's run while it was still in the top 10, ostensibly to raise his family. Having had a half interest in the show, he was financially comfortable, and thus began to appear onscreen less frequently. He did, however, take leading roles in two later films, SKATETOWN, U.S.A. and THE FISH THAT SAVED PITTSBURGH (both 1979).

Wilson's later TV work included a short-lived sitcom "Charlie & Co." (1985-86), presumably intended to capitalize on the success of "The Cosby Show," and various guest shots on shows like "227," Living Single," and "The Drew Carey Show." His low profile was occasionally disrupted by the publicity surrounding several "palimony" suits, and a widely reported drug bust in 1981.

Wilson's death was caused by liver cancer.

Wilson, Orlandus

born: c. 1917, Chesapeake, VA
died: Dec. 30, 1998, Paris, France, age 81

Bass vocalist, and later manager and arranger, for the Golden Gate Quartet, an influential gospel-pop singing group.

Orlandus Wilson began singing with the Golden Gate Jubilee Singers in 1934, when the four members were still high school students. Within a few years, the group was a regular attraction on local radio and had signed a recording contract with RCA's Bluebird label.

In 1941, the group shortened its name to the Golden Gate Quartet, and signed with Columbia Records, where they produced pop as well as gospel music. Their fame spread to national radio, where they had their own show, and to Hollywood, where they did guest shots in a number of movies. In STAR-SPANGLED RHYTHM (1942), the Quartet performed "Hit the Road to Dreamland" with Dick Powell and Mary Martin, and in HOLLYWOOD CANTEEN (1944), they sang "The General Jumped at Dawn." Other films in which the group made notable appearances were HIT PARADE OF 1943 (1943), BRING ON THE GIRLS (1945), and Howard Hawks' A SONG IS BORN (1948), which starred Danny Kaye.

The Quartet continued to perform for decades, although Wilson retired from performing in 1997. In their long career, the group was accorded numerous honors; they sang at the inauguration of Franklin Delano Roosevelt, and performed for the Roosevelts and their guests at the White House. In 1994, they were inducted into the hall of fame of United in Group Harmony, an organization devoted to preserving the history of vocal harmony.

No cause of death was reported.

Worth, Marvin

born: c. 1925, Brooklyn, NY
died: Apr. 27, 1998, Los Angeles, CA, age 72

Producer and writer who worked in film and television.

Marvin Worth started in the entertainment field while still a teenager, and over the next three decades dabbled in a number of behind-the-scenes capacities: he managed and promoted jazz legends such as Charlie Parker and Billie Holiday; wrote comedy material for stand-up comedians like Joey Bishop and Buddy Hackett; was Lenny Bruce's first manager; wrote for TV series like "The Steve Allen Show" (for which Worth won a 1958 Peabody Award), "The Milton Berle Show" and "Get Smart"; coproduced the acclaimed Broadway play *Lenny* (1971); and entered the movie industry as a writer (with Arne Sultan), providing the stories for BOYS NIGHT OUT (1962), THREE ON A COUCH and PROMISE HER ANYTHING (both 1966).

He coproduced the black comedy WHERE'S POPPA? (1970) and the documentary MALCOLM X (1972), which was nominated for an Academy Award. Worth produced Bob Fosse's LENNY (1974), which was nominated for a Best Picture Oscar, and Alan Arkin's black comedy FIRE SALE (1977). Over the next several years Worth produced a number of films, including THE ROSE (1979), UNFAITHFULLY YOURS, RHINESTONE (both 1984), PATTY HEARST (1988), FLASHBACK (1990), Spike Lee's MALCOLM X (1992), DIABOLIQUE (1996), and CRIMINAL LAW (1998).

Worth returned to television as the executive producer of the cable movies NORMA JEAN AND MARILYN (1996) and GIA (1998).

The cause of death was lung cancer.

Wynette, Tammy

born: Virginia Wynette Pugh, May 5, 1942, Itawamba County, MS
died: Apr. 6, 1998, Nashville, TN, age 55

One of country music's all-time top female vocalists.

Tammy Wynette had a career that catapulted her from small-town beautician to being the "first lady of country music." Born on a cotton farm in Mississippi, she visited Nashville in the mid-1960s; there her singing impressed country star Porter Wagoner, who asked her to join him on his road tours. Shortly afterward she met record producer Billy Sherrill, with whom she cowrote the song that would be her first big hit (and her signature song), "Stand By Your Man." The incredible success of the song brought Wynette from obscurity to stardom. She subsequently recorded more than fifty albums worth of material and scored more than 30 million in record sales. Among her biggest hits were "D-I-V-O-R-C-E," "I Don't Want to Play House," "Womanhood," "Till I Can Make It on My Own," and "Your Good Girl's Gonna Go Bad." During her biggest period of success she was named female vocalist of the year three times running (1968-70) by the Country Music Association.

Although mostly a concert and recording artist, Wynette did make a few big-screen appearances, playing herself in FROM NASHVILLE WITH LOVE (1969) and in BEACH BOYS: THE NASHVILLE SOUNDS (1996), and singing the theme song for the biker film RUN, ANGEL, RUN (1969). She was also the voice of Tilly Hill on several episodes of the animated television series "King of the Hill."

Throughout her career, Wynette was plagued by bouts of ill health, and was hospitalized in the late 1970s for addiction to pain-killing drugs. She was also renowned for her stormy marriages—five in all—but, despite her problems, refused to let negativity get the best of her. "I've had a wonderful life," she said in a 1981 Associated Press interview.

Wynette died of a blood clot to the lungs.

Young, Freddie

aka: Frederick Young, Fred Young, F. A. Young
born: Oct. 9, 1902, London, England
died: Dec. 1, 1998, London, age 96

Award-winning cinematographer.

Leaving school at 14, Freddie Young went to work in a munitions factory before becoming an apprentice in the film industry. Beginning as a stuntman, Young developed an interest in the camera itself; by the 1930s he had photographed 25 mostly undistinguished films. His first successes were with BLUE DANUBE (1932) and BITTER SWEET (1933), but his breakthrough came with the high-budget VICTORIA THE GREAT (1937). This was followed by such hits as GOODBYE, MR. CHIPS (1939), Michael Powell's FORTY-NINTH PARALLEL (1941), YOUNG MR. PITT (1942), THE WINSLOW BOY (1948), and EDWARD, MY SON (1949).

In great demand, Young worked with some of the screen's finest directors, including John Ford on MOGAMBO (1953), Vincente Minnelli on LUST FOR LIFE (1956), George Cukor on BHOWANI JUNCTION (1956), and King Vidor on SOLOMON AND SHEBA (1959). He is best-remembered, however, for his collaborations with David Lean on LAWRENCE OF ARABIA (1962), DR. ZHIVAGO (1965), and RYAN'S DAUGHTER (1970). Young won Oscars for his work on all three films.

Other notable films shot by Young include INVITATION TO THE DANCE (1956), INN OF THE SIXTH HAPPINESS (1958), LORD JIM (1965), YOU ONLY LIVE TWICE (1967) NICHOLAS AND ALEXANDRA (1971), LUTHER (1974), STEVIE (1978), and INVITATION TO THE WEDDING (1984). His television work includes a production of *Macbeth,* for which he won an Emmy Award. Young made his directorial debut at the age of 82 with the made-for-television movie ARTHUR'S HALLOWED GROUND (1985).

In 1972, Young was named a Fellow of the British Academy for Film and Television Arts, the only person to receive that honor since Alfred Hitchcock.

Young died of natural causes.

Young, Robert

born: Feb. 22, 1907, Chicago, IL
died: July 21, 1998, Westlake Village, CA, age 91

Longtime Hollywood leading man, later one of television's most successful and beloved stars.

Known by many as "father to the country" on the long-running television series "Father Knows Best" (1954-60), Robert Young displayed an easygoing charm and amiability that, for twenty years, made him one of the screen's most reliable leading men.

Young began acting after he graduated high school, appearing in over thirty productions at the Pasadena Playhouse. Discovered by an agent from MGM Sudios, Young was signed to a contract and, for the next two decades, appeared in over sixty films, mostly for MGM. While many of his films were forgettable, he did play opposite many of Hollywood's biggest female stars, including Norma Shearer, Claudette Colbert, Janet Gaynor, Loretta Young, Katharine Hepburn, and Joan Crawford. Some of the more prominent titles he appeared in during this period were THE SIN OF MADELON CLAUDET (1931), STRANGE INTERLUDE (1932), HOUSE OF ROTHSCHILD (1934), and THE BRIDE WORE RED (1937). Three of his best roles were in films in which he costarred with Margaret Sullavan: THREE COMRADES, THE SHINING HOUR (both 1938), and THE MORTAL STORM (1940). Young distinguished himself in his first starring role, H. M. PULHAM, ESQ. (1941), as well as in the charming comedy CLAUDIA (1943).

In 1947, Young and his partner, Eugene Rodney, created a radio show about a "typical" American family, which they called "Father Knows Best?" (The question mark was dropped at the behest of a sponsor.) The show first aired in 1949 and ran until 1954, when it made the transition to television. For years, Young, as Jim Anderson, projected the image of the wise, sympathetic and always good-humored father. What the audience didn't see was Young's real-life 30-year battle with alcoholism, a problem he managed to bring under control and later spoke about quite frankly. His professional life continued quite well, however; "Father Knows Best" (which he also coproduced) made him a big star and a wealthy man.

After a shot-lived series, "Window on Main Street," Young scored another remarkable success as a warm, sagacious and reassuring suburban doctor in "Marcus Welby, M.D." (1969-76). Unlike Jim Anderson, whom Young admitted was a fantasy figure, Dr. Welby was, to him, very real and very much his own role model.

Young died of respiratory failure.

Youngman, Henny

born: Henry Youngman, Jan. 12, 1906, Liverpool, England
died: Feb. 24, 1998, New York, NY, age 92

Stand-up comedian famous for his rapid-fire one-liners.

After a stopover in England, Henny Youngman's Russian immigrant parents settled in Brooklyn. Youngman was encorged to be a musician by his father; though he didn't continue with the study of classical music, Youngman utilized his violin skills in his own band, the Syncopaters.

Youngman soon found that he enjoyed telling jokes onstage more than playing music. He spent two years on the Kate Smith radio show in the mid-1930s, and for many years toured his vaudeville act, appearing in hundreds of venues across the country. Youngman made an early bid for movie stardom in a B musical at Monogram, executive produced by Lou Costello, A WAVE, A WAC AND A MARINE (1944), in which Youngman had the role of an agent. Other movies Youngman appeared in include YOU CAN'T RUN AWAY FROM IT (1956), NASHVILLE REBEL (1966), THE GORE-GORE GIRLS (1972), SILENT MOVIE (1976), HISTORY OF THE WORLD, PART 1 (1981), THE COMEBACK TRAIL (1982), AMAZON WOMEN ON THE MOON (1987), and GOODFELLAS (1990).

Television played a more important part in keeping Youngman's never-changing comedic style before the public. Over the years he appeared on all the popular variety shows, including "The Ed Sullivan Show," "Texaco Star Theater," "The Jackie Gleason Show," "Rowan & Martin's Laugh-In," "Hee-Haw," and "The Flip Wilson Show." He even acted character parts on such shows as "The U. S. Steel Hour" and "Batman."

Youngman wrote several books of jokes, recorded a few comedy albums and penned an autobiography, *Take My Wife . . . Please! My Life and Laughs* (1973).

Youngman died of pneumonia.

Zanville, Bernard

See: Clark, Dane

Zaslow, Michael

born: Nov. 1, 1944, Inglewood, CA
died: Dec. 6, 1998, New York, NY, age 54

Actor who worked on the stage, in film, and in television.

Early on in his career, Michael Zaslow appeared in the Broadway productions of *Cat on a Hot Tin Roof, Boccaccio,* and *Fiddler on the Roof.* During this period he also made a number of guest appearances on the television series "Star Trek." His first role in a soap opera was as Dick Hart in "Search for Tomorrow" (1970-71). In 1971, Zaslow was cast in the role of suave villain Roger Thorpe on "The Guiding Light," a role he played until 1980, and then again from 1989 to 1997; he scored a big following in the part, and became a much-beloved figure amongst soap fans. Between his two stints as Thorpe he appeared as pianist David Renaldi on "One Life to Live" (1983-86).

Zaslow's film work included a starring role in YOU LIGHT UP MY LIFE (1977) and smaller parts in METEOR (1979), SEVEN MINUTES IN HEAVEN (1985), and STAR TREK: FIRST CONTACT (1996). He also played the recurring role of Ben Hollings in the primetime series "Law and Order."

Diagnosed with amyotrophic lateral sclerosis (also know as Lou Gehrig's Disease) in 1996, Zaslow was dismissed from "Guiding Light" when symptoms of his illness caused his speech to slur. He then returned to "One Life to Live" in his original role, incorporating his disorder into the life of his character in order to raise awareness of the disease. He also co-founded Zazangels, an organization that works under the umbrella of the Greater New York Chapter of the Amyotrophic Lateral Sclerosis Association and aids its efforts to find a cure.

Despite his bout with Lou Gehrig's disease, the cause of Zaslow's death was reported as a heart attack.

Indices

MASTER INDEX FOR MPG ANNUALS

Listed below are the titles of all films reviewed in the Motion Picture Guide since 1984. The date following each title is the year of the *Motion Picture Guide* annual in which the review appears, not the year of the film's release. All films released in 1984 can be found in the second half of volume IX of the original *Motion Picture Guide.*

If a film has been reviewed, but is absent from the list below, the title in question was released prior to 1984 and can be found in the original ten-volume set, which is arranged alphabetically by title.

A

B

C

D

E

F

G

H

I

L

M

N

O

P

Q

R

S

T

U

V

X

Y

Z

FILMS BY COUNTRY OF ORIGIN

A bullet before the title indicates a film co-produced by more than one country

Argentina

• LOVE WALKED IN

Australia

• ABERRATION
BABE: PIG IN THE CITY
• FERNGULLY 2: THE MAGICAL RESCUE
• HEAVEN'S BURNING
JOEY
• NAPOLEON
• TARZAN AND THE LOST CITY
TWISTED
• WELCOME TO WOOP WOOP

Austria

FUNNY GAMES
INHERITORS, THE
JAMES ELLROY: DEMON DOG OF AMERICAN CRIME FICTION
R.I.P. REST IN PIECES: A PORTRAIT OF JOE COLEMAN

Brazil

CENTRAL STATION
OYSTER AND THE WIND, THE
TIETA OF AGRESTE

Canada

• ACT OF WAR
• AIR BUD: GOLDEN RECEIVER
BLACK LIGHT
BLACKJACK
• BLEEDERS
BREAKOUT
• BUFFALO '66
• CAPTIVE
• CHILE, OBSTINATE MEMORY
CUBE
DEAD END
• EBENEZER
ESCAPE, THE
• FALLING FIRE
• FUTURE FEAR
HANGING GARDEN, THE
HARD CORE LOGO
• HOSTILE INTENT
• HUNTED, THE
• IN HIS FATHER'S SHOES
• JACK HIGGINS' MIDNIGHT MAN
• JACK HIGGINS' THE WINDSOR PROTOCOL
• JACK LONDON'S THE CALL OF THE WILD: DOG OF THE YUKON
• LOUISA MAY ALCOTT'S LITTLE MEN
• LOVE AND DEATH ON LONG ISLAND
• PEACEKEEPER, THE
PLACE CALLED CHIAPAS, A
PRINCE, THE
RAGE, THE
• REAL HOWARD SPITZ, THE
• REGENERATION
• SHOPPING FOR FANGS
• SNOWBOUND
STOLEN MOMENTS
• TALES FROM A PARALLEL UNIVERSE: EATING PATTERN
• TALES FROM A PARALLEL UNIVERSE: GIGA SHADOW
• TALES FROM A PARALLEL UNIVERSE: SUPER NOVA
• TRACKED
• TRUCKS
• UNDERTAKER'S WEDDING, THE
• URBAN SAFARI
• WOUNDED

China

• EAST PALACE, WEST PALACE
• EMPEROR'S SHADOW, THE
• FROZEN
RED CHERRY
• SHAOLIN TEMPLE, THE

Czech Republic

• ACT OF WAR
FORGOTTEN LIGHT

Denmark

CELEBRATION, THE
• JERUSALEM
• JUNK MAIL
KINGDOM, PART 2, THE
KRZYSZTOF KIESLOWSKI: I'M SO-SO
• MENDEL
• ROYAL DECEIT
• SUMMER FLING

Egypt

• DESTINY

Finland

• JERUSALEM

France

• ARTEMISIA
• CHAMBERMAID ON THE TITANIC, THE
• CHILE, OBSTINATE MEMORY
• CHINESE BOX, THE
• CLASSIFIED X
• COUSIN BETTE
• DESTINY
DISENCHANTED, THE
• EAST PALACE, WEST PALACE
• EL CHE: INVESTIGATING A LEGEND
• FRIEND OF THE DECEASED, A
FULL SPEED
GADJO DILO
GENEALOGIES OF A CRIME
• HOSTILE WATERS
• INSIDE/OUT
LA SEPARATION
• LAND GIRLS, THE
LIFE OF JESUS, THE
• LIVE FLESH
• LOLITA
MARIE BAIE DES ANGES
MARIUS AND JEANNETTE
• NIGHT AND THE MOMENT, THE
• NIRVANA
• OGRE, THE
• PEREIRA DECLARES
POST COITUM, ANIMAL TRISTE
• ROYAL DECEIT
SAME OLD SONG
SEVENTH HEAVEN
• SWINDLE, THE
• TRUCE, THE
UN AIR DE FAMILLE
• VOYAGE TO THE BEGINNING OF THE WORLD
• WAKING NED DEVINE
WESTERN

Germany

• ARTEMISIA
BEYOND SILENCE
• BREAK, THE
• CARLA'S SONG
DIDN'T DO IT FOR LOVE
• GENERAL CHAOS: UNCENSORED ANIMATION
• HOSTILE WATERS
• KILLER CONDOM, THE
• KRISTIN LAVRANSDATTER
• LITTLE DIETER NEEDS TO FLY
• MENDEL
• MOONDANCE
• MOTHER AND SON
• OGRE, THE
• PALMETTO
• PRINCE VALIANT
• RAT'S TALE, A
• ROYAL DECEIT
• SALTMEN OF TIBET, THE
• TALES FROM A PARALLEL UNIVERSE: EATING PATTERN
• TALES FROM A PARALLEL UNIVERSE: GIGA SHADOW
• TALES FROM A PARALLEL UNIVERSE: SUPER NOVA
• TRUCE, THE
• WAR ZONE
• WHEN PIGS FLY
• WRONGFULLY ACCUSED
• ZAKIR AND HIS FRIENDS

Hong Kong

ARMOUR OF GOD
BEAUTY INVESTIGATOR
BODYGUARD FROM BEIJING
COMRADES, ALMOST A LOVE STORY
DRAGONS FOREVER
• EMPEROR'S SHADOW, THE
ENCOUNTER OF THE SPOOKY KIND
FALLEN ANGELS
• FROZEN
HEROES SHED NO TEARS
HONG KONG 1941
KICK BOXER'S TEARS
KILLER ANGELS
MAGNIFICENT WARRIORS
MR. NICE GUY
PRODIGAL SON, THE
ROYAL WARRIORS
• SHAOLIN TEMPLE, THE

Iceland

• JERUSALEM

Iran

MIRROR, THE
TASTE OF CHERRY

Ireland

• BREAK, THE

- BUTCHER BOY, THE
- • DANCING AT LUGHNASA
- • GENERAL, THE
- • MOONDANCE
- • OLIVER TWIST
- • PRINCE VALIANT
- • SPACEJACKED
- • SUMMER FLING

Israel

- HEALING BY KILLING
- • SUE

Italy

- • ARTEMISIA
- BEST MAN, THE
- BEYOND, THE
- • CHAMBERMAID ON THE TITANIC, THE
- • DAY OF THE BEAST, THE
- • FROM A FAR COUNTRY
- LIFE IS BEAUTIFUL
- • NIGHT AND THE MOMENT, THE
- • NIRVANA
- • PEREIRA DECLARES
- RABID DOGS
- • STEAM
- • TRUCE, THE

Japan

- • BREAK, THE
- • CHINESE BOX, THE
- • DOUBLE EDGE
- DRAGON BALL Z THE MOVIE: DEAD ZONE
- DRAGON BALL Z THE MOVIE: THE TREE OF MIGHT
- DRAGON BALL Z THE MOVIE: THE WORLD'S STRONGEST
- EEL, THE
- FIREWORKS
- GODZILLA AND MOTHRA: THE BATTLE FOR EARTH
- GODZILLA VS. KING GHIDORAH
- GOLGO 13: QUEEN BEE
- GONIN
- • HEAVEN'S BURNING
- JUNK FOOD
- KIKI'S DELIVERY SERVICE
- MOBILE SUIT GUNDAM I
- MOBILE SUIT GUNDAM II: SOLDIERS OF SORROW
- MOBILE SUIT GUNDAM III: ENCOUNTERS IN SPACE
- • NAPOLEON
- NEW ADVENTURES OF KIMBA THE WHITE LION, THE
- POLTERGEIST REPORT: YUYU HAKUSHO
- RAZOR: THE SNARE, THE
- RAZOR: WHO'S GOT THE GOLD?, THE
- SLAYERS: THE MOTION PICTURE
- SLEEPY EYES OF DEATH: FULL CIRCLE KILLING
- SLEEPY EYES OF DEATH: SWORD OF ADVENTURE
- SLEEPY EYES OF DEATH: SWORD OF SEDUCTION
- SONATINE
- TEKKEN: THE MOTION PICTURE
- TOKYO FIST
- VILLAGE OF DREAMS
- WHEN I CLOSE MY EYES
- • WHEN PIGS FLY
- WRATH OF THE NINJA: THE YOTODEN MOVIE
- ZERO WOMAN

Mexico

- MIDAQ ALLEY
- WHO THE HELL IS JULIETTE?

Netherlands

- CHARACTER
- DRESS, THE
- • EAST PALACE, WEST PALACE
- • FROZEN
- • MRS. DALLOWAY

New Zealand

- UGLY, THE

Norway

- INSOMNIA
- • JERUSALEM
- • JUNK MAIL
- • KRISTIN LAVRANSDATTER
- • MENDEL
- OTHER SIDE OF SUNDAY, THE

Poland

- • FROM A FAR COUNTRY
- • OGRE, THE
- • WHITE RAVEN, THE

Portugal

- • PEREIRA DECLARES
- • VOYAGE TO THE BEGINNING OF THE WORLD

Romania

- • SECRET KINGDOM, THE
- • SHRUNKEN CITY, THE

Russia

- • ADVENTURES OF MOWGLI
- BROTHER
- • DEAD WATERS
- • MOTHER AND SON
- THIEF, THE

South Korea

- RED HAWK: WEAPON OF DEATH

Spain

- • CARLA'S SONG
- • CHAMBERMAID ON THE TITANIC, THE
- • DAY OF THE BEAST, THE
- • EL CHE: INVESTIGATING A LEGEND
- • LIVE FLESH
- • SHAMPOO HORNS
- • STEAM

Sweden

- • JERUSALEM
- • KRISTIN LAVRANSDATTER
- TRANCEFORMER: A PORTRAIT OF LARS VON TRIER

Switzerland

- • KILLER CONDOM, THE
- • SALTMEN OF TIBET, THE
- • SWINDLE, THE
- • TRUCE, THE
- • URBAN SAFARI
- • ZAKIR AND HIS FRIENDS

Turkey

- • STEAM

U.K.

- • ABERRATION
- BIG ONE, THE
- BORROWERS, THE
- • BREAK, THE
- BRYLCREEM BOYS, THE
- • CARLA'S SONG
- • CLAY PIGEONS
- CLOCKWATCHERS
- • COUSIN BETTE
- DAD SAVAGE
- • DANCING AT LUGHNASA
- • DEAD WATERS
- • DEJA VU
- • DISAPPEARANCE OF KEVIN JOHNSON, THE
- DIVORCE IRANIAN STYLE
- ELIZABETH
- • FIRELIGHT
- • FROM A FAR COUNTRY
- • GENERAL CHAOS: UNCENSORED ANIMATION
- • GENERAL, THE
- GO NOW
- GOVERNESS, THE
- HILARY AND JACKIE
- • HOSTILE WATERS
- I WENT DOWN
- INNOCENT SLEEP, THE
- • JACK HIGGINS' ON DANGEROUS GROUND
- • JACK HIGGINS' THE WINDSOR PROTOCOL
- KILLING TIME
- KURT AND COURTNEY
- • LAND GIRLS, THE
- LAWN DOGS
- LEADING MAN, THE
- LIKE IT IS
- • LITTLE DIETER NEEDS TO FLY
- LITTLE VOICE
- • LOVE AND DEATH ON LONG ISLAND
- LOVE IS THE DEVIL: STUDY FOR A PORTRAIT OF FRANCIS BACON
- • MERLIN
- MERRY WAR, A
- • MOONDANCE
- • MRS. DALLOWAY
- • MURDER IN MIND
- • NIGHT AND THE MOMENT, THE
- • NIL BY MOUTH
- • OGRE, THE
- • OLIVER TWIST
- PASSION IN THE DESERT
- PHOTOGRAPHING FAIRIES
- • PLAYING BY HEART
- • PRINCE VALIANT
- • REAL HOWARD SPITZ, THE
- • REGENERATION
- • ROYAL DECEIT
- SHOOTING FISH
- • SLIDING DOORS
- • SOLDIER
- SPICE WORLD
- • SUMMER FLING
- • SWEPT FROM THE SEA
- • THEORY OF FLIGHT
- • TRUCE, THE
- TWENTYFOURSEVEN
- UNDER THE SKIN
- • VELVET GOLDMINE
- • WAKING NED DEVINE
- • WELCOME TO WOOP WOOP
- • WHEN PIGS FLY
- WILDE

U.S.

- • ADVENTURES OF MOWGLI
- AFFLICTION
- • AIR BUD: GOLDEN RECEIVER
- ALARMIST, THE
- ALFRED HITCHCOCK: MASTER OF SUSPENSE
- ALL DOGS CHRISTMAS CAROL, AN
- ALL THE RAGE
- ALMOST HEROES

ALMOST PARTNERS
ALONE IN THE WOODS
ALWAYS OUTNUMBERED
AMERICAN HISTORY X
ANOTHER DAY IN PARADISE
ANTZ
APT PUPIL
ARGUING THE WORLD
ARMAGEDDON
ASYLUM
ATOMIC DOG
AVENGERS, THE
AYN RAND: A SENSE OF LIFE
BAD MANNERS
BARNEY'S GREAT ADVENTURE—THE MOVIE
BARRIERS
BASEKETBALL
BATMAN & MR. FREEZE: SUBZERO
BATMAN/SUPERMAN MOVIE, THE
BELLY
BELOVED
BEST OF THE BEST: WITHOUT WARNING
BIG HIT, THE
BIG LEBOWSKI, THE
BILLBOARD DAD
BILLY'S HOLLYWOOD SCREEN KISS
BLACK DOG
BLACK THUNDER
BLADE
• BLEEDERS
BLUES BROTHERS 2000
BODY COUNT
BODY COUNT
BONE DADDY
BOOGIE BOY
BOYS IN LOVE 2
BOYS WILL BE BOYS
BRAM STOKER'S SHADOWBUILDER
BRAM STOKER'S THE MUMMY
BRANDON TEENA STORY, THE
BRAVE LITTLE TOASTER GOES TO MARS, THE
BREAST MEN
BRIDE OF CHUCKY
BRIGHT SHINING LIE, A
BROADWAY DAMAGE
• BUFFALO '66
BUG'S LIFE, A
BULLET ON A WIRE
BULWORTH
BURN HOLLYWOOD BURN
BUSTER & CHAUNCEY'S SILENT NIGHT
CALL TO REMEMBER, A
CAN'T HARDLY WAIT
CAN'T YOU HEAR THE WIND HOWL?: THE LIFE AND MUSIC OF ROBERT JOHNSON
• CAPTIVE
CASPER MEETS WENDY
CATHERINE'S GROVE
CAUGHT UP
CELEBRITY
CHAIRMAN OF THE BOARD
CHARLIE HOBOKEN
CHICAGO CAB
CHILDREN OF THE CORN V: FIELD OF TERROR
• CHINESE BOX, THE
CHOSEN ONE: LEGEND OF THE RAVEN, THE
CITY OF ANGELS
CIVIL ACTION, A
• CLASSIFIED X
• CLAY PIGEONS
CLOCKMAKER
CLUB VAMPIRE
COLONY, THE
COMEDY'S DIRTIEST DOZEN
CON, THE
COURTING COURTNEY
• COUSIN BETTE
CRACKING UP
CROSSING FIELDS
CRUISE, THE
CURSE OF THE PUPPET MASTER
DANCE WITH ME
DANCER, TEXAS POP. 81
DANGEROUS BEAUTY
DARK CITY
DAVID SEARCHING
DAY AT THE BEACH
DEAD MAN ON CAMPUS
DEAR JESSE
DECAMPITATED
DECEIVER
DECLINE OF WESTERN CIVILIZATION PART III, THE
DEE SNIDER'S STRANGELAND
DEEP IMPACT
DEEP RISING
DEFENDERS: PAYBACK, THE
• DEJA VU
DENNIS THE MENACE STRIKES AGAIN
DESPERATE MEASURES
DESTINY OF MARTY FINE, THE
DETONATOR
DETOUR
DIARY OF A SERIAL KILLER
DIGGING TO CHINA
DIRTY LAUNDRY
DIRTY WORK
• DISAPPEARANCE OF KEVIN JOHNSON, THE
DISTURBING BEHAVIOR
DR. DOLITTLE
DOGWATCH
DON KING: ONLY IN AMERICA
• DOUBLE EDGE
DOWN IN THE DELTA
DREAM FOR AN INSOMNIAC
• EBENEZER
EDEN
EIGHTEENTH ANGEL, THE
ELIA KAZAN: A DIRECTOR'S JOURNEY
ELMORE LEONARD'S GOLD COAST
ELVIS MEETS NIXON
ENEMY
ENEMY OF THE STATE
ERNEST IN THE ARMY
EVER AFTER
FACE DOWN
FACE THE EVIL
FACULTY, THE
FALLEN
• FALLING FIRE
FARM: ANGOLA, U.S.A., THE
FATAL PURSUIT
FEAR AND LOATHING IN LAS VEGAS
• FERNGULLY 2: THE MAGICAL RESCUE
54
• FIRELIGHT
FIRESTORM
FIRST LOVE, LAST RITES
FIXER, THE
FLINTSTONES: I YABBA-DABBA DOO!, THE
FORMER CHILD STAR
FREE TIBET
FRENCH EXIT
FULL TILT BOOGIE
• FUTURE FEAR
• GENERAL CHAOS: UNCENSORED ANIMATION
GEORGE WALLACE
GIA
GINGERBREAD MAN, THE
GIRLS IN PRISON
GODS AND MONSTERS
GODSON, THE
GODZILLA
GREAT EXPECTATIONS
GUN, A CAR, AND A BLONDE, A
HALF BAKED
HALLELUJAH!
HALLOWEEN H20: TWENTY YEARS LATER
HANDS ON A HARDBODY
HAPPINESS
HARD RAIN
HAV PLENTY
HE GOT GAME
HENRY FOOL
HENRY: PORTRAIT OF A SERIAL KILLER PART 2
HERCULES AND XENA THE ANIMATED MOVIE: THE BATTLE FOR MOUNT OLYMPUS
HIGH ART
HIJACKING HOLLYWOOD
HI-LIFE
HI-LO COUNTRY, THE
HIT ME
HOLLYWOOD CONFIDENTIAL
HOLY MAN
HOME BEFORE DARK
HOME FRIES
HOMEGROWN
HOPE FLOATS
HORSE WHISPERER, THE
HORTON FOOTE'S ALONE
• HOSTILE INTENT
• HOSTILE WATERS
HOT BLOODED
HOW STELLA GOT HER GROOVE BACK
HUMAN BOMB
• HUNTED, THE
HURLYBURLY
HURRICANE STREETS
HUSH
I GOT THE HOOK UP
I LOVE YOU, DON'T TOUCH ME!
I MARRIED A STRANGE PERSON!
I STILL KNOW WHAT YOU DID LAST SUMMER
I THINK I DO
I'LL BE HOME FOR CHRISTMAS
ILLTOWN
IMPOSTORS, THE
IN GOD'S HANDS
• IN HIS FATHER'S SHOES
INCOGNITO
INDISCREET
INFORMANT, THE
• INSIDE/OUT
INTERLOCKED: THRILLED TO DEATH
INVADER, THE
INVISIBLE DAD
INVISIBLE MOM
JACK FROST
• JACK HIGGINS' ON DANGEROUS GROUND
JACK HIGGINS' THUNDER POINT
• JACK HIGGINS' MIDNIGHT MAN

- • JACK LONDON'S THE CALL OF THE WILD: DOG OF THE YUKON
- JANE AUSTEN'S MAFIA!
- JOHN CARPENTER'S VAMPIRES
- JOHNNY MYSTO BOY WIZARD
- JOHNNY SKIDMARKS
- JUNGLE BOOK: MOWGLI'S STORY, THE
- KID IN ALADDIN'S PALACE, A
- KINGDOM OF SHADOWS
- KISSING A FOOL
- KNOCK OFF
- KRAA! THE SEA MONSTER
- KRIPPENDORF'S TRIBE
- LAND OF THE FREE
- LANDLADY, THE
- LAST ASSASSINS
- LAST BIG THING, THE
- LAST BREATH
- LAST DAYS OF DISCO, THE
- LAST LIVES
- LAST SEDUCTION II, THE
- LAVENDER LIMELIGHT: LESBIANS IN FILM
- LENA'S DREAMS
- LENNY BRUCE: SWEAR TO TELL THE TRUTH
- LES MISERABLES
- LETHAL WEAPON 4
- LET'S KILL ALL THE LAWYERS
- LET'S TALK ABOUT SEX
- LETTER FROM DEATH ROW, A
- LEWIS & CLARK & GEORGE
- LION KING II: SIMBA'S PRIDE, THE
- LITTLE BIGFOOT 2: THE JOURNEY HOME
- LITTLE BOY BLUE
- LITTLE GHOST
- LIVING IN PERIL
- LIVING OUT LOUD
- LOLIDA 2000
- • LOLITA
- LOS LOCOS
- LOST IN SPACE
- LOST WORLD, THE
- LOU REED: ROCK AND ROLL HEART
- • LOUISA MAY ALCOTT'S LITTLE MEN
- LOVE TO KILL
- • LOVE WALKED IN
- LOVELIFE
- LOVER GIRL
- MADELINE
- MAJOR LEAGUE: BACK TO THE MINORS
- MAKER, THE
- MAN IN THE IRON MASK, THE
- MARS
- MASK OF ZORRO, THE
- MEAN GUNS
- MEET JOE BLACK
- MEET THE DEEDLES
- MEN
- MEN WITH GUNS
- MERCURY RISING
- • MERLIN
- MIDAS TOUCH, THE
- MIGHTY, THE
- MIGHTY JOE YOUNG
- MIGHTY KONG, THE
- MILO
- MISBEGOTTEN
- MR. JEALOUSY
- MODULATIONS: CINEMA FOR THE EAR
- MONTANA
- MONUMENT AVE.
- MOON OVER BROADWAY
- MULAN
- • MURDER IN MIND
- MUSIC FROM ANOTHER ROOM
- MY BROTHER'S WAR
- MY FIRST NAME IS MACEO
- MY GIANT
- MY KNEES WERE JUMPING: REMEMBERING THE KINDERTRANSPORTS
- MY VERY BEST FRIEND
- NAKED ACTS
- NAKED LIES
- • NAPOLEON
- NEGOTIATOR, THE
- NEIL SIMON'S THE ODD COUPLE II
- NEMESIS 4: CRY OF ANGELS
- NEVADA
- NEWTON BOYS, THE
- NEXT STEP, THE
- NEXT STOP, WONDERLAND
- NIAGARA NIAGARA
- NIGHT AT THE ROXBURY, A
- NIGHT VISION
- NIGHTWATCH
- • NIL BY MOUTH
- NO LOOKING BACK
- NO ORDINARY LOVE
- NO WAY HOME
- NORTH SHORE FISH
- NOT IN THIS TOWN
- NOTES FROM UNDERGROUND
- OBJECT OF MY AFFECTION, THE
- OFF THE MENU: THE LAST DAYS OF CHASEN'S
- • OLIVER TWIST
- ONE TOUGH COP
- ONE TRUE THING
- ONLY THRILL, THE
- OPERATION DELTA FORCE 2
- OPPOSITE OF SEX, THE
- ORGAZMO
- OUT OF SIGHT
- OUT OF THE PAST
- OUTSIDE OZONA
- OVERNIGHT DELIVERY
- • PALMETTO
- PARALLEL SONS
- PARALYZING FEAR: THE STORY OF POLIO IN AMERICA, A
- PARENT TRAP, THE
- PASS, THE
- PATCH ADAMS
- PAUL MONETTE: THE BRINK OF SUMMER'S END
- PAULIE
- • PEACEKEEPER, THE
- PECKER
- PENTAGON WARS, THE
- PERFECT MURDER, A
- PERMANENT MIDNIGHT
- PHANTASM: OBLIVION
- PHANTOMS
- PHOENIX
- PI
- PLAN B
- PLAYERS CLUB, THE
- • PLAYING BY HEART
- PLEASANTVILLE
- PLUMP FICTION
- POCAHONTAS II: JOURNEY TO A NEW WORLD
- POLISH WEDDING
- PRACTICAL MAGIC
- PRICE ABOVE RUBIES, A
- PRIMARY COLORS
- PRINCE OF EGYPT, THE
- PRONTO
- PROPHECY II, THE
- PROPOSITION, THE
- PSYCHO
- QUEST FOR CAMELOT
- QUICKSILVER HIGHWAY
- RACE TO SAVE 100 YEARS, THE
- RAT PACK, THE
- RATCHET
- • RAT'S TALE, A
- REACH THE ROCK
- REAL BLONDE, THE
- REAL THING, THE
- REBOUND: THE LEGEND OF EARL "THE GOAT" MANIGAULT
- REDLINE
- REPLACEMENT KILLERS, THE
- RESCUERS: STORIES OF COURAGE—TWO COUPLES
- RESCUERS: STORIES OF COURAGE—TWO WOMEN
- RETROACTIVE
- RETURN OF THE KING, THE
- RETURN TO PARADISE
- RETURN TO SAVAGE BEACH
- RICHIE RICH'S CHRISTMAS WISH
- RIDE
- RIGHT CONNECTIONS, THE
- RINGMASTER
- RIVER RED
- RONIN
- ROUNDERS
- RUDOLPH THE RED-NOSED REINDEER: THE MOVIE
- RUGRATS MOVIE, THE
- RUN FOR COVER
- RUNNING WOMAN, THE
- RUSH HOUR
- RUSHMORE
- RUSTY: THE GREAT RESCUE
- SAFE MEN
- SAND TRAP
- SAVING PRIVATE RYAN
- SAVIOR
- SCARRED CITY
- SCOOBY-DOO ON ZOMBIE ISLAND
- • SECRET KINGDOM, THE
- SECRET OF NIMH 2: TIMMY TO THE RESCUE, THE
- SENSELESS
- SHADRACH
- SHAKESPEARE IN LOVE
- • SHAMPOO HORNS
- SHATTERED IMAGE
- • SHOPPING FOR FANGS
- • SHRUNKEN CITY, THE
- SIEGE, THE
- SILVER SCREEN: COLOR ME LAVENDER, THE
- SIMON BIRCH
- SIMPLE PLAN, A
- SIN AND REDEMPTION
- SIX DAYS, SEVEN NIGHTS
- SIX O'CLOCK NEWS
- SIX-STRING SAMURAI
- SKIN & BONE
- SLAM
- SLAMNATION
- SLAPPY AND THE STINKERS
- • SLIDING DOORS
- SLUMS OF BEVERLY HILLS
- SMALL SOLDIERS
- SMOKE SIGNALS
- SNAKE EYES
- • SNOWBOUND

- • SOLDIER
- SOLDIER'S DAUGHTER NEVER CRIES, A
- SOMEWHERE IN THE CITY
- SOULER OPPOSITE, THE
- SOUR GRAPES
- • SPACEJACKED
- SPANISH PRISONER, THE
- SPECIES II
- SPHERE
- SPREE, THE
- STAR KID
- STAR TREK: INSURRECTION
- STEEL SHARKS
- STEPHEN KING'S THE NIGHT FLIER
- STEPMOM
- STILL BREATHING
- STIR
- STOREFRONT HITCHCOCK
- STORY OF X, THE
- STRAY BULLET
- SUB DOWN
- SUBSPECIES IV: BLOODSTORM
- SUBSTITUTE 2: SCHOOL'S OUT, THE
- • SUE
- SUICIDE KINGS
- SWAN PRINCESS III: AND THE MYSTERY OF THE ENCHANTED TREASURE, THE
- • SWEPT FROM THE SEA
- • TALES FROM A PARALLEL UNIVERSE: SUPER NOVA
- TALISMAN
- TALK OF ANGELS
- TALK TO ME
- TARANTELLA
- • TARZAN AND THE LOST CITY
- TEN BENNY
- TERMINAL JUSTICE
- • THEORY OF FLIGHT
- THERE'S SOMETHING ABOUT MARY
- THIN RED LINE, THE
- 3 NINJAS: HIGH NOON AT MEGA MOUNTAIN
- THURSDAY
- TIMOTHY LEARY'S DEAD
- TOP OF THE WORLD
- TOUCH OF EVIL: THE DIRECTOR'S CUT
- • TRACKED
- TREKKIES
- TRICKS
- • TRUCKS
- TRUMAN SHOW, THE
- 12 ANGRY MEN
- TWILIGHT
- TWO FOR TEXAS
- TWO GIRLS AND A GUY
- UNCLE SAM
- UNDER HEAVEN
- • UNDERTAKER'S WEDDING, THE
- UNMADE BEDS
- UNVEILING, THE
- URBAN LEGEND
- U.S. MARSHALS
- • VELVET GOLDMINE
- VERY BAD THINGS
- VIOLET'S VISIT
- WALKING THUNDER
- • WAR ZONE
- WATCHERS REBORN
- WATERBOY, THE
- WEDDING SINGER, THE
- WEST NEW YORK
- WHAT DREAMS MAY COME
- WHATEVER
- WHEN DANGER FOLLOWS YOU HOME
- WHEN TIME EXPIRES
- WHEN TRUMPETS FADE
- • WHITE RAVEN, THE
- WHO IS HENRY JAGLOM?
- WHY DO FOOLS FALL IN LOVE?
- WIDE AWAKE
- WILD MAN BLUES
- WILD THINGS
- WITHOUT LIMITS
- WOO
- • WOUNDED
- • WRONGFULLY ACCUSED
- X-FILES, THE
- YOUNG HERCULES
- YOUR FRIENDS & NEIGHBORS
- YOU'VE GOT MAIL
- ZERO EFFECT

Ukraine

- • FRIEND OF THE DECEASED, A

Venezuela

- BATTLE OF CHILE: THE STRUGGLE OF AN UNARMED PEOPLE—PART 2: THE COUP D'ETAT, THE

FILMS BY DISTRIBUTOR

A-PIX ENTERTAINMENT
BLEEDERS
DIARY OF A SERIAL KILLER
FACE THE EVIL
LAST ASSASSINS
LAST BREATH
LOVE TO KILL
MEN
UNCLE SAM

A.D.V. FILMS
SLAYERS: THE MOTION PICTURE
TEKKEN: THE MOTION PICTURE

ALLIANCE RELEASING
REGENERATION

AMAZING FANTASY ENTERTAINMENT
CLOCKMAKER
KRAA! THE SEA MONSTER
LOLIDA 2000

AMERICAN HOME ENTERTAINMENT
FATAL PURSUIT

AMKO PRODUCTIONS
SUE

ANIME VILLAGE
MOBILE SUIT GUNDAM I
MOBILE SUIT GUNDAM II: SOLDIERS OF SORROW
MOBILE SUIT GUNDAM III: ENCOUNTERS IN SPACE

ARROW RELEASING
DAY AT THE BEACH
UNDER THE SKIN

ARTISAN ENTERTAINMENT
ABERRATION
BELLY
BONE DADDY
CRUISE, THE
PERMANENT MIDNIGHT
PI
REAL HOWARD SPITZ, THE
RINGMASTER
SUBSTITUTE 2: SCHOOL'S OUT, THE
WHITE RAVEN, THE

ARTISTIC LICENSE FILMS
HALLELUJAH!
MOON OVER BROADWAY
SOMEWHERE IN THE CITY
TEN BENNY

ATTITUDE FILMS
DRESS, THE
FUNNY GAMES

AVALANCHE HOME ENTERTAINMENT
ELVIS MEETS NIXON

AVALANCHE RELEASING
DREAM FOR AN INSOMNIAC
KILLING TIME

BANNER ENTERTAINMENT
UNDER HEAVEN

BARRISTER FILMS
LET'S KILL ALL THE LAWYERS

BEDFORD ENTERTAINMENT
DISAPPEARANCE OF KEVIN JOHNSON, THE
LOVER GIRL

BLACKWATCH RELEASING
CAPTIVE

BMG
LEADING MAN, THE
LEWIS & CLARK & GEORGE

BMG INDEPENDENTS
CLOCKWATCHERS

BONNEVILLE WORLDWIDE ENTERTAINMENT
SNOWBOUND

BROKEN TWIG PRODUCTIONS
COURTING COURTNEY
HIJACKING HOLLYWOOD

BUENA VISTA
Walt Disney Productions
Hollywood Pictures
Touchstone Pictures

ARMAGEDDON
BELOVED
BUG'S LIFE, A
BURN HOLLYWOOD BURN
CIVIL ACTION, A
DEEP RISING
ENEMY OF THE STATE
HE GOT GAME
HOLY MAN
HORSE WHISPERER, THE
I'LL BE HOME FOR CHRISTMAS
JANE AUSTEN'S MAFIA!
KRIPPENDORF'S TRIBE
MEET THE DEEDLES
MIGHTY JOE YOUNG
MULAN
PARENT TRAP, THE
RUSHMORE
SIMON BIRCH
SIX DAYS, SEVEN NIGHTS
WATERBOY, THE

BUENA VISTA HOME ENTERTAINMENT
BEST OF THE BEST: WITHOUT WARNING
LION KING II: SIMBA'S PRIDE, THE

BUENA VISTA HOME VIDEO
GIRLS IN PRISON
KIKI'S DELIVERY SERVICE
POCAHONTAS II: JOURNEY TO A NEW WORLD

BWE
ALMOST PARTNERS
FROM A FAR COUNTRY
TARANTELLA

CABIN FEVER ENTERTAINMENT
HOSTILE INTENT
UNDERTAKER'S WEDDING, THE

CAROUSEL PICTURE CO.
SUB DOWN

CASTLE HILL
BREAK, THE
CHICAGO CAB
ELIA KAZAN: A DIRECTOR'S JOURNEY
HIT ME
LITTLE BOY BLUE
RIVER RED

CBS FOX VIDEO
FERNGULLY 2: THE MAGICAL RESCUE

CELULOID DREAMS
MIRROR, THE

CENTURY PACIFIC ENTERTAINMENT
ROYAL WARRIORS

CFP DISTRIBUTION
LOVE AND DEATH ON LONG ISLAND
MISBEGOTTEN

CHELSEA PICTURES
UNMADE BEDS

CIBY SALES
BRYLCREEM BOYS, THE

CINEMA GUILD
SLAMNATION

CINEMA PARALLEL
INSIDE/OUT

CINETEL FILMS
BODY COUNT

CINEVILLE
FRENCH EXIT
NEVADA

COLUMBIA
DANCE WITH ME
I STILL KNOW WHAT YOU DID LAST SUMMER
KNOCK OFF
LES MISERABLES
MY GIANT
PALMETTO
SHADRACH
SOUR GRAPES
STEPMOM

WILD THINGS
ZERO EFFECT

COLUMBIA TRISTAR
BUSTER & CHAUNCEY'S SILENT NIGHT
CAN'T HARDLY WAIT
DANCER, TEXAS POP. 81
GODZILLA AND MOTHRA: THE BATTLE FOR EARTH
GODZILLA VS. KING GHIDORAH
HOMEGROWN
JOHN CARPENTER'S VAMPIRES
MADELINE
MASK OF ZORRO, THE
OUTSIDE OZONA
REPLACEMENT KILLERS, THE
URBAN LEGEND

COWBOY BOOKING INTERNATIONAL
DEAR JESSE
TRANCEFORMER: A PORTRAIT OF LARS VON TRIER

CULTURE Q CONNECTION
VIOLET'S VISIT

CURB ENTERTAINMENT
PRINCE, THE
SOULER OPPOSITE, THE

CZECH TELEXPORT
FORGOTTEN LIGHT

DAIEI
SLEEPY EYES OF DEATH: FULL CIRCLE KILLING
SLEEPY EYES OF DEATH: SWORD OF ADVENTURE
SLEEPY EYES OF DEATH: SWORD OF SEDUCTION

DIMENSION
AIR BUD: GOLDEN RECEIVER
BLACKJACK
FACULTY, THE
FULL TILT BOOGIE
HALLOWEEN H20: TWENTY YEARS LATER
I GOT THE HOOK UP
NIGHTWATCH
PHANTOMS
RIDE
SENSELESS

DIMENSION HOME VIDEO
CHILDREN OF THE CORN V: FIELD OF TERROR
PROPHECY II, THE

DISNEY
OLIVER TWIST

DREAMWORKS SKG
ANTZ
PAULIE
PRINCE OF EGYPT, THE
SAVING PRIVATE RYAN
SMALL SOLDIERS

ELIAS QUEREJETA/ESICMA
SHAMPOO HORNS

ENGLEWOOD ENTERTAINMENT
DETOUR

EVERGREEN
WHEN TIME EXPIRES

F.C.P. MEDIA VENTURES
HOT BLOODED

FILM OFFICE/IMPERIAL ENTERTAINMENT
MEAN GUNS

FILMO IMAGEN
NAKED LIES

FINE LINE
HURLYBURLY
LET'S TALK ABOUT SEX
PASSION IN THE DESERT
PECKER
THEORY OF FLIGHT
WHEN I CLOSE MY EYES
WILD MAN BLUES

FIRST LOOK PICTURES
JERUSALEM
MERRY WAR, A
MRS. DALLOWAY
OTHER SIDE OF SUNDAY, THE

FIRST RUN FEATURES
ARGUING THE WORLD
BOYS IN LOVE 2
DIDN'T DO IT FOR LOVE
DISENCHANTED, THE
INSOMNIA
JAMES ELLROY: DEMON DOG OF AMERICAN CRIME FICTION
KRZYSZTOF KIESLOWSKI: I'M SO-SO
LAVENDER LIMELIGHT: LESBIANS IN FILM
LIKE IT IS
MENDEL
PAUL MONETTE: THE BRINK OF SUMMER'S END
SIX O'CLOCK NEWS
STOLEN MOMENTS
WHO IS HENRY JAGLOM?

FIRST RUN FEATURES/ICARUS FILMS
BATTLE OF CHILE: THE STRUGGLE OF AN UNARMED PEOPLE—PART 2: THE COUP D'ETAT, THE
CHILE, OBSTINATE MEMORY

FOX LORBER
EMPEROR'S SHADOW, THE
LIFE OF JESUS, THE
LOU REED: ROCK AND ROLL HEART

FOX LORBER HOME VIDEO
ALFRED HITCHCOCK: MASTER OF SUSPENSE
CLASSIFIED X
RED CHERRY
TIETA OF AGRESTE

FOX SEARCHLIGHT
COUSIN BETTE
IMPOSTORS, THE
POLISH WEDDING
SHOOTING FISH
SLUMS OF BEVERLY HILLS
TWO GIRLS AND A GUY
WAKING NED DEVINE

FULL MOON
CURSE OF THE PUPPET MASTER
SECRET KINGDOM, THE
SHRUNKEN CITY, THE
SUBSPECIES IV: BLOODSTORM
TALISMAN

G.L.A.S.S. FILMS
URBAN SAFARI

GOLDEN HARVEST
COMRADES, ALMOST A LOVE STORY
HEROES SHED NO TEARS

GOLDWYN FILMS/MGM
WELCOME TO WOOP WOOP

GOOD MACHINE
HAPPINESS

GRAMERCY PICTURES
BIG LEBOWSKI, THE
CLAY PIGEONS
ELIZABETH
GO NOW
HI-LO COUNTRY, THE
LAND GIRLS, THE
LAST DAYS OF DISCO, THE
NO LOOKING BACK
REACH THE ROCK
THURSDAY
YOUR FRIENDS & NEIGHBORS

GREYCAT FILMS
PARALLEL SONS

HALLMARK ENTERTAINMENT
HORTON FOOTE'S ALONE
JACK LONDON'S THE CALL OF THE WILD: DOG OF THE YUKON
MERLIN
MURDER IN MIND
NORTH SHORE FISH

HBO
ALWAYS OUTNUMBERED
BREAST MEN
PENTAGON WARS, THE

HBO HOME VIDEO
BRIGHT SHINING LIE, A
DON KING: ONLY IN AMERICA
GIA
HOSTILE WATERS
RAT PACK, THE
REBOUND: THE LEGEND OF EARL "THE GOAT" MANIGAULT
WHEN TRUMPETS FADE

HOLLYWOOD PRODUCTIONS
DIRTY LAUNDRY

HOME VISION CINEMA
KRISTIN LAVRANSDATTER

HOUSE OF SCOOTER PRODUCTIONS
FORMER CHILD STAR

IMPERIAL ENTERTAINMENT/FILMWERKS
NEMESIS 4: CRY OF ANGELS

INDEPENDENT CINEMA INC.
RETURN OF THE KING, THE

INITIAL ENTERTAINMENT GROUP
MONTANA

INTERNATIONAL FILM CIRCUIT
FROZEN
MOTHER AND SON

INVESTEC BANK LTD
ERNEST IN THE ARMY

ISLAND VISUAL ARTS
COMEDY'S DIRTIEST DOZEN

JOUR DE FETE FILMS
ALL THE RAGE
BROADWAY DAMAGE
SKIN & BONE

KEYSTONE PICTURES/REPUBLIC PICTURES
WOUNDED

KINDRED SPIRITS PRODUCTIONS
NAKED ACTS

KINO INTERNATIONAL
BROTHER
FALLEN ANGELS
OGRE, THE
WHO THE HELL IS JULIETTE?

KINO ON VIDEO
KINGDOM OF SHADOWS

L4LTD PRODUCTIONS/JOUR DE FETE
DAVID SEARCHING

LEGACY RELEASING
DIGGING TO CHINA
EDEN
HANDS ON A HARDBODY
LOUISA MAY ALCOTT'S LITTLE MEN
ONLY THRILL, THE
PLUMP FICTION
RUDOLPH THE RED-NOSED REINDEER: THE MOVIE

LEISURE TIME FEATURES
DESTINY
UN AIR DE FAMILLE

LIBRA PICTURES
DEAD END

LIONS GATE FILMS
AFFLICTION
ALARMIST, THE
BUFFALO '66
GADJO DILO
GODS AND MONSTERS
HI-LIFE
I MARRIED A STRANGE PERSON!
JOHNNY SKIDMARKS
JUNK MAIL
MR. JEALOUSY
MONUMENT AVE.
SAVIOR
SHATTERED IMAGE

LIVE ENTERTAINMENT
CAUGHT UP
INVADER, THE
NO WAY HOME
SUICIDE KINGS

LUCERTOLA MEDIA
RABID DOGS

MAJESTIC ENTERTAINMENT
WALKING THUNDER

MANGA ENTERTAINMENT
GENERAL CHAOS: UNCENSORED ANIMATION
RED HAWK: WEAPON OF DEATH
TOKYO FIST

MARGIN FILMS
HENRY: PORTRAIT OF A SERIAL KILLER PART 2
SHOPPING FOR FANGS

MAVERICK ENTERTAINMENT
ENEMY

MEDIA ASIA DISTRIBUTION LTD.
ENCOUNTER OF THE SPOOKY KIND

MEDIA LUNA
R.I.P. REST IN PIECES: A PORTRAIT OF JOE COLEMAN

MGM HOME ENTERTAINMENT
ALL DOGS CHRISTMAS CAROL, AN

MGM/GOLDWYN
LIVE FLESH

MGM/UA
DECEIVER
DIRTY WORK
DISTURBING BEHAVIOR
HANGING GARDEN, THE
HURRICANE STREETS
I LOVE YOU, DON'T TOUCH ME!
MAN IN THE IRON MASK, THE
NAPOLEON
RONIN
SPECIES II

MGM/UA HOME VIDEO
ESCAPE, THE
JOEY
SECRET OF NIMH 2: TIMMY TO THE RESCUE, THE

MICHAELS ENTERTAINMENT GROUP
LETTER FROM DEATH ROW, A

MIKADO FILM
PEREIRA DECLARES

MILESTONE FILM
FIREWORKS
VILLAGE OF DREAMS

MIRAMAX
BEYOND SILENCE
BIG ONE, THE
CELEBRITY
DOWN IN THE DELTA
54
FIRELIGHT
HAV PLENTY
LIFE IS BEAUTIFUL
LITTLE VOICE
MIGHTY, THE
MOONDANCE
NEXT STOP, WONDERLAND
NIGHT AND THE MOMENT, THE
NIRVANA
PLAYING BY HEART
PRICE ABOVE RUBIES, A
ROUNDERS
ROYAL DECEIT
SHAKESPEARE IN LOVE
SLIDING DOORS
SMOKE SIGNALS
SUMMER FLING
TALK OF ANGELS
TRUCE, THE
VELVET GOLDMINE
WIDE AWAKE

MIRAMAX ZOE
ARTEMISIA

MONARCH HOME VIDEO
PLAN B
RETURN TO SAVAGE BEACH

MRG ENTERTAINMENT
INDISCREET

NEST ENTERTAINMENT INC.
SWAN PRINCESS III: AND THE MYSTERY OF THE ENCHANTED TREASURE, THE

NEW HORIZONS HOME VIDEO
ALONE IN THE WOODS
BLACK THUNDER
CLUB VAMPIRE
DETONATOR
FALLING FIRE
FUTURE FEAR
INVISIBLE MOM
MY BROTHER'S WAR
RUNNING WOMAN, THE
SPACEJACKED
STRAY BULLET
WATCHERS REBORN

NEW LINE
AMERICAN HISTORY X
BLADE
DARK CITY
LIVING OUT LOUD
LOST IN SPACE
MR. NICE GUY
OVERNIGHT DELIVERY
PLAYERS CLUB, THE
PLEASANTVILLE
RUSH HOUR
STEPHEN KING'S THE NIGHT FLIER
WEDDING SINGER, THE
WOO

NEW LINE HOME VIDEO
LIVING IN PERIL

NEW WAVE FILMS DISTRIBUTION INC.
RUN FOR COVER

NEW YORKER FILMS
EEL, THE
HEALING BY KILLING
MARIUS AND JEANNETTE
POST COITUM, ANIMAL TRISTE

SWINDLE, THE
WESTERN

NFU FILM PARTNERS
NOTES FROM UNDERGROUND

NIPPON FILMS
WHEN PIGS FLY

NORSTAR ENTERTAINMENT
ASYLUM
RAGE, THE

NORTHERN ARTS ENTERTAINMENT
CHARLIE HOBOKEN
MIDAQ ALLEY
OFF THE MENU: THE LAST DAYS OF CHASEN'S
TALK TO ME

NU IMAGE
MAKER, THE
OPERATION DELTA FORCE 2
PEACEKEEPER, THE
REDLINE
SCARRED CITY
TOP OF THE WORLD

OCTOBER FILMS
BEST MAN, THE
CELEBRATION, THE
HIGH ART
HILARY AND JACKIE
KINGDOM, PART 2, THE
ORGAZMO
SAFE MEN
SOLDIER'S DAUGHTER NEVER CRIES, A
STILL BREATHING
TOUCH OF EVIL: THE DIRECTOR'S CUT
TWENTYFOURSEVEN

OLYMPIA PICTURES
LENA'S DREAMS

ORION
RETROACTIVE

ORION HOME VIDEO
DOUBLE EDGE
PHANTASM: OBLIVION
SPREE, THE
12 ANGRY MEN

ORION/MGM
MUSIC FROM ANOTHER ROOM
STOREFRONT HITCHCOCK

PALM PICTURES
SIX-STRING SAMURAI

PARAMOUNT
DEAD MAN ON CAMPUS
DEEP IMPACT
HARD RAIN
HOLLYWOOD CONFIDENTIAL
JOHNNY MYSTO BOY WIZARD
LITTLE GHOST
MIDAS TOUCH, THE
NEIL SIMON'S THE ODD COUPLE II
NIGHT AT THE ROXBURY, A
REAL BLONDE, THE
RUGRATS MOVIE, THE
SIMPLE PLAN, A
SNAKE EYES
STAR TREK: INSURRECTION
TREKKIES
TRUMAN SHOW, THE
TWILIGHT

PARAMOUNT HOME VIDEO
CON, THE
JACK HIGGINS' ON DANGEROUS GROUND
SIN AND REDEMPTION

PBS HOME VIDEO
PARALYZING FEAR: THE STORY OF POLIO IN AMERICA, A

PEACHTREE ENTERTAINMENT
BLACK LIGHT
NIGHT VISION
PASS, THE

PHAEDRA CINEMA
BAD MANNERS
CRACKING UP
GONIN
LA SEPARATION
NEXT STEP, THE
NO ORDINARY LOVE
RATCHET

PIONEER ENTERTAINMENT
DRAGON BALL Z THE MOVIE: DEAD ZONE
DRAGON BALL Z THE MOVIE: THE TREE OF MIGHT
DRAGON BALL Z THE MOVIE: THE WORLD'S STRONGEST
NEW ADVENTURES OF KIMBA THE WHITE LION, THE

PLANET PICTURES
SILVER SCREEN: COLOR ME LAVENDER, THE

PLAYBOY ENTERTAINMENT
STORY OF X, THE

PLAZA ENTERTAINMENT
DESTINY OF MARTY FINE, THE
EBENEZER

PM ENTERTAINMENT
CATHERINE'S GROVE
LAND OF THE FREE
LITTLE BIGFOOT 2: THE JOURNEY HOME
SAND TRAP

POLYGRAM
BARNEY'S GREAT ADVENTURE—THE MOVIE
BORROWERS, THE
GINGERBREAD MAN, THE
PROPOSITION, THE
RETURN TO PARADISE
VERY BAD THINGS
WHAT DREAMS MAY COME

POLYGRAM VIDEO
BODY COUNT
DAD SAVAGE
LOS LOCOS
PHOTOGRAPHING FAIRIES

PROMARK ENTERTAINMENT
LAST LIVES
TERMINAL JUSTICE

RAINBOW RELEASING
DEJA VU

RAUCUS RELEASING
DEE SNIDER'S STRANGELAND

REAL ENTERTAINMENT
DOGWATCH

RHAPSODY FILMS
MY FIRST NAME IS MACEO

ROLLING THUNDER
BEYOND, THE
HARD CORE LOGO
SONATINE

ROXIE RELEASING
KURT AND COURTNEY

ROYAL OAKS ENTERTAINMENT
STEEL SHARKS

RYSHER ENTERTAINMENT
EIGHTEENTH ANGEL, THE

S. ENTERTAINMENT
BREAKOUT

SACIS ENTERTAINMENT/UNAPIX
INVISIBLE DAD

SAMUEL GOLDWYN COMPANY
CHAMBERMAID ON THE TITANIC, THE
LOLITA

SEVENTH ART RELEASING
FARM: ANGOLA, U.S.A., THE

SHADOW DISTRIBUTION
CARLA'S SONG

SHOOTING GALLERY
FREE TIBET
ILLTOWN
NIAGARA NIAGARA

SHOWCASE ENTERTAINMENT
GUN, A CAR, AND A BLONDE, A

SHOWTIME
FACE DOWN
FIXER, THE
JACK HIGGINS' THUNDER POINT
JACK HIGGINS' THE WINDSOR PROTOCOL
PRONTO
TALES FROM A PARALLEL UNIVERSE: EATING PATTERN
TALES FROM A PARALLEL UNIVERSE: GIGA SHADOW
TALES FROM A PARALLEL UNIVERSE: SUPER NOVA

SHOWTIME/HALLMARK
IN HIS FATHER'S SHOES

SHOWTIME/VIACOM
ATOMIC DOG
DEFENDERS: PAYBACK, THE
HUMAN BOMB
HUNTED, THE
INFORMANT, THE
JACK HIGGINS' MIDNIGHT MAN

RESCUERS: STORIES OF COURAGE—TWO COUPLES
TRACKED

SONY PICTURES CLASSICS
CENTRAL STATION
CHARACTER
DANCING AT LUGHNASA
FRIEND OF THE DECEASED, A
GENERAL, THE
GOVERNESS, THE
HENRY FOOL
MARIE BAIE DES ANGES
MEN WITH GUNS
NIL BY MOUTH
OPPOSITE OF SEX, THE
SPANISH PRISONER, THE
WHATEVER
WILDE

SONY PICTURES ENTERTAINMENT
SPICE WORLD

SOUTHERN STAR SALES
TWISTED

SPECIFIC FILMS
LAST SEDUCTION II, THE

STERLING HOME ENTERTAINMENT
BOOGIE BOY
BRAM STOKER'S SHADOWBUILDER
GODSON, THE
MILO

STRAND RELEASING
AYN RAND: A SENSE OF LIFE
EAST PALACE, WEST PALACE
FIRST LOVE, LAST RITES
FULL SPEED
GENEALOGIES OF A CRIME
I THINK I DO
LAWN DOGS
LOVE IS THE DEVIL: STUDY FOR A PORTRAIT OF FRANCIS BACON
MODULATIONS: CINEMA FOR THE EAR
STEAM
TIMOTHY LEARY'S DEAD
VOYAGE TO THE BEGINNING OF THE WORLD

STRATOSPHERE ENTERTAINMENT
INHERITORS, THE
LAST BIG THING, THE
ONE TOUGH COP
THIEF, THE

SYS ENTERTAINMENT
SHAOLIN TEMPLE, THE

TAI SENG
ARMOUR OF GOD
BEAUTY INVESTIGATOR
DRAGONS FOREVER
HONG KONG 1941
KICK BOXER'S TEARS
KILLER ANGELS
MAGNIFICENT WARRIORS
PRODIGAL SON, THE

TAPESTRY FILMS
BILLBOARD DAD
KID IN ALADDIN'S PALACE, A

TOHO INTERNATIONAL
RAZOR: THE SNARE, THE
RAZOR: WHO'S GOT THE GOLD?, THE

TOKOYO SHOCK
ZERO WOMAN

TRIDENT RELEASING
INNOCENT SLEEP, THE

TRIMARK
ANOTHER DAY IN PARADISE
BILLY'S HOLLYWOOD SCREEN KISS
CHAIRMAN OF THE BOARD
CHINESE BOX, THE
CUBE
DAY OF THE BEAST, THE
PHOENIX
SLAM
STAR KID

TRIMARK HOME VIDEO
COLONY, THE
HEAVEN'S BURNING
LANDLADY, THE
LOST WORLD, THE
LOVELIFE
TRUCKS
UGLY, THE

TRISTAR
APT PUPIL
BIG HIT, THE
DESPERATE MEASURES
GODZILLA
HUSH
IN GOD'S HANDS
SLAPPY AND THE STINKERS
SWEPT FROM THE SEA
3 NINJAS: HIGH NOON AT MEGA MOUNTAIN

TRIUMPH RELEASING
LOVE WALKED IN

TROMA
CHOSEN ONE: LEGEND OF THE RAVEN, THE
DECAMPITATED
KILLER CONDOM, THE

TSC RELEASING
ADVENTURES OF MOWGLI

TSG PICTURES
I WENT DOWN20TH CENTURY FOX
BULWORTH
CASPER MEETS WENDY
DR. DOLITTLE
EVER AFTER
FIRESTORM
GREAT EXPECTATIONS
HOPE FLOATS
HOW STELLA GOT HER GROOVE BACK
NEWTON BOYS, THE
OBJECT OF MY AFFECTION, THE
SIEGE, THE
THERE'S SOMETHING ABOUT MARY
THIN RED LINE, THE
X-FILES, THE

20TH CENTURY FOX HOME ENTERTAINMENT
PRINCE VALIANT

QUICKSILVER HIGHWAY
RUSTY: THE GREAT RESCUE

UNAPIX
BOYS WILL BE BOYS
BRAM STOKER'S THE MUMMY
INTERLOCKED: THRILLED TO DEATH

UNIVERSAL
BABE: PIG IN THE CITY
BASEKETBALL
BLACK DOG
BLUES BROTHERS 2000
BRIDE OF CHUCKY
FEAR AND LOATHING IN LAS VEGAS
HALF BAKED
KISSING A FOOL
MEET JOE BLACK
MERCURY RISING
NOT IN THIS TOWN
ONE TRUE THING
OUT OF SIGHT
PATCH ADAMS
PRIMARY COLORS
PSYCHO

UNIVERSAL HOME VIDEO
HERCULES AND XENA THE ANIMATED MOVIE: THE BATTLE FOR MOUNT OLYMPUS
YOUNG HERCULES

UNIVERSAL TELEVISION
WHEN DANGER FOLLOWS YOU HOME

URBAN VISION ENTERTAINMENT
GOLGO 13: QUEEN BEE

US MANGA CORPS
POLTERGEIST REPORT: YUYU HAKUSHO
WRATH OF THE NINJA: THE YOTODEN MOVIE

UTE INC.
CALL TO REMEMBER, A

VIACOM
ELMORE LEONARD'S GOLD COAST
MY VERY BEST FRIEND
RESCUERS: STORIES OF COURAGE—TWO WOMEN
RIGHT CONNECTIONS, THE
TRICKS

WALT DISNEY HOME VIDEO
BRAVE LITTLE TOASTER GOES TO MARS, THE
JUNGLE BOOK: MOWGLI'S STORY, THE

WARNER BROS.
ALMOST HEROES
AVENGERS, THE
BUTCHER BOY, THE
CITY OF ANGELS
DANGEROUS BEAUTY
FALLEN
GEORGE WALLACE
HOME FRIES
INCOGNITO
JACK FROST
LETHAL WEAPON 4
MAJOR LEAGUE: BACK TO THE MINORS
NEGOTIATOR, THE
PERFECT MURDER, A
PRACTICAL MAGIC

QUEST FOR CAMELOT
RAT'S TALE, A
RICHIE RICH'S CHRISTMAS WISH
SOLDIER
SPHERE
TARZAN AND THE LOST CITY
U.S. MARSHALS
WHY DO FOOLS FALL IN LOVE?
WITHOUT LIMITS
WRONGFULLY ACCUSED
YOU'VE GOT MAIL

WARNER BROS. CLASSICS

RACE TO SAVE 100 YEARS, THE

WARNER HOME VIDEO

BATMAN & MR. FREEZE: SUBZERO
BATMAN/SUPERMAN MOVIE, THE
DENNIS THE MENACE STRIKES AGAIN
FLINTSTONES: I YABBA-DABBA DOO!, THE
MIGHTY KONG, THE
SCOOBY-DOO ON ZOMBIE ISLAND
TWO FOR TEXAS

WHITE STAR

EL CHE: INVESTIGATING A LEGEND

WINDY CITY INTERNATIONAL

REAL THING, THE

WINSTAR HOME ENTERTAINMENT

CAN'T YOU HEAR THE WIND HOWL?: THE LIFE AND MUSIC OF ROBERT JOHNSON

WOMEN MAKE MOVIES

DIVORCE IRANIAN STYLE

WORLD VIDEO

BODYGUARD FROM BEIJING

YORK HOME VIDEO

ACT OF WAR
DEAD WATERS
STIR

ZEITGEIST FILMS

BRANDON TEENA STORY, THE
SALTMEN OF TIBET, THE
SEVENTH HEAVEN
TASTE OF CHERRY

ZEITGEIST FILMS/UNAPIX FILMS

OUT OF THE PAST

FILMS BY GENRE

Films belonging to more than one genre are listed under each appropriate category

Action

ACT OF WAR
ANOTHER DAY IN PARADISE
ARMAGEDDON
ATOMIC DOG
BATMAN & MR. FREEZE: SUBZERO
BATMAN/SUPERMAN MOVIE, THE
BIG HIT, THE
BLACK DOG
BLACK THUNDER
BLACKJACK
BLADE
BODYGUARD FROM BEIJING
BOOGIE BOY
BREAK, THE
BREAKOUT
CHOSEN ONE: LEGEND OF THE RAVEN, THE
DESPERATE MEASURES
DETONATOR
DOGWATCH
DOUBLE EDGE
DRAGONS FOREVER
ELMORE LEONARD'S GOLD COAST
ENEMY
ENEMY OF THE STATE
ERNEST IN THE ARMY
FACE THE EVIL
FIRESTORM
FUTURE FEAR
HARD RAIN
HEAVEN'S BURNING
HEROES SHED NO TEARS
HOSTILE INTENT
HUNTED, THE
JACK HIGGINS' ON DANGEROUS GROUND
JACK HIGGINS' THUNDER POINT
JACK HIGGINS' MIDNIGHT MAN
JACK HIGGINS' THE WINDSOR PROTOCOL
JOHN CARPENTER'S VAMPIRES
KNOCK OFF
LAND OF THE FREE
LAST ASSASSINS
LETHAL WEAPON 4
LOST IN SPACE
MAGNIFICENT WARRIORS
MAKER, THE
MARS
MASK OF ZORRO, THE
MEAN GUNS
MERCURY RISING
MIGHTY JOE YOUNG
MR. NICE GUY
NAKED LIES
NEGOTIATOR, THE
NEMESIS 4: CRY OF ANGELS
ONE TOUGH COP
OPERATION DELTA FORCE 2
ORGAZMO
PEACEKEEPER, THE
PRODIGAL SON, THE
RAGE, THE
RAZOR: THE SNARE, THE
RAZOR: WHO'S GOT THE GOLD?, THE
REAL THING, THE
RED HAWK: WEAPON OF DEATH
REDLINE
REPLACEMENT KILLERS, THE
RETROACTIVE
RETURN TO SAVAGE BEACH
RONIN
ROYAL WARRIORS
RUN FOR COVER
RUSH HOUR
SCARRED CITY
SIX-STRING SAMURAI
SLEEPY EYES OF DEATH: FULL CIRCLE KILLING
SLEEPY EYES OF DEATH: SWORD OF ADVENTURE
SLEEPY EYES OF DEATH: SWORD OF SEDUCTION
SMALL SOLDIERS
SOLDIER
STEEL SHARKS
TALES FROM A PARALLEL UNIVERSE: EATING PATTERN
TARZAN AND THE LOST CITY
TERMINAL JUSTICE
THIN RED LINE, THE
3 NINJAS: HIGH NOON AT MEGA MOUNTAIN
TOP OF THE WORLD
TRACKED
U.S. MARSHALS
WOUNDED
X-FILES, THE
YOUNG HERCULES

Adventure

ACT OF WAR
ALMOST HEROES
ARMAGEDDON
ARMOUR OF GOD
AVENGERS, THE
BARNEY'S GREAT ADVENTURE—THE MOVIE
BLACK THUNDER
BORROWERS, THE
DEEP IMPACT
GODZILLA
HERCULES AND XENA THE ANIMATED MOVIE: THE BATTLE FOR MOUNT OLYMPUS
HOSTILE INTENT
IN GOD'S HANDS
JACK LONDON'S THE CALL OF THE WILD: DOG OF THE YUKON
JOHNNY MYSTO BOY WIZARD
JUNGLE BOOK: MOWGLI'S STORY, THE
KID IN ALADDIN'S PALACE, A
LITTLE BIGFOOT 2: THE JOURNEY HOME
LOST IN SPACE
LOST WORLD, THE
MADELINE
MAN IN THE IRON MASK, THE
MASK OF ZORRO, THE
MEN WITH GUNS
MIGHTY JOE YOUNG
MIGHTY KONG, THE
NAPOLEON
NEW ADVENTURES OF KIMBA THE WHITE LION, THE
PRINCE VALIANT
ROYAL DECEIT
SHAOLIN TEMPLE, THE
SIX DAYS, SEVEN NIGHTS
STEEL SHARKS
TARZAN AND THE LOST CITY
TWO FOR TEXAS

Animated

ADVENTURES OF MOWGLI
ALL DOGS CHRISTMAS CAROL, AN
ANTZ
BATMAN & MR. FREEZE: SUBZERO
BATMAN/SUPERMAN MOVIE, THE
BRAVE LITTLE TOASTER GOES TO MARS, THE
BUG'S LIFE, A
BUSTER & CHAUNCEY'S SILENT NIGHT
DRAGON BALL Z THE MOVIE: DEAD ZONE
DRAGON BALL Z THE MOVIE: THE TREE OF MIGHT
DRAGON BALL Z THE MOVIE: THE WORLD'S STRONGEST
FERNGULLY 2: THE MAGICAL RESCUE
FLINTSTONES: I YABBA-DABBA DOO!, THE
GENERAL CHAOS: UNCENSORED ANIMATION
GOLGO 13: QUEEN BEE
HERCULES AND XENA THE ANIMATED MOVIE: THE BATTLE FOR MOUNT OLYMPUS
I MARRIED A STRANGE PERSON!
KIKI'S DELIVERY SERVICE
LION KING II: SIMBA'S PRIDE, THE
MIGHTY KONG, THE
MOBILE SUIT GUNDAM I
MOBILE SUIT GUNDAM II: SOLDIERS OF SORROW
MOBILE SUIT GUNDAM III: ENCOUNTERS IN SPACE
MULAN
NEW ADVENTURES OF KIMBA THE WHITE LION, THE
POCAHONTAS II: JOURNEY TO A NEW WORLD
POLTERGEIST REPORT: YUYU HAKUSHO
PRINCE OF EGYPT, THE
QUEST FOR CAMELOT
RED HAWK: WEAPON OF DEATH
RUDOLPH THE RED-NOSED REINDEER: THE MOVIE
RUGRATS MOVIE, THE
SCOOBY-DOO ON ZOMBIE ISLAND
SECRET OF NIMH 2: TIMMY TO THE RESCUE, THE
SLAYERS: THE MOTION PICTURE
SWAN PRINCESS III: AND THE MYSTERY OF THE ENCHANTED TREASURE, THE
TEKKEN: THE MOTION PICTURE
WRATH OF THE NINJA: THE YOTODEN MOVIE

Biography

ARTEMISIA
AYN RAND: A SENSE OF LIFE

DON KING: ONLY IN AMERICA
ELIZABETH
GENERAL, THE
GEORGE WALLACE
JAMES ELLROY: DEMON DOG OF AMERICAN CRIME FICTION
LOVE IS THE DEVIL: STUDY FOR A PORTRAIT OF FRANCIS BACON
PAUL MONETTE: THE BRINK OF SUMMER'S END
PERMANENT MIDNIGHT
WHY DO FOOLS FALL IN LOVE?
WILDE
WITHOUT LIMITS

Children's

ADVENTURES OF MOWGLI
AIR BUD: GOLDEN RECEIVER
ALL DOGS CHRISTMAS CAROL, AN
ALMOST PARTNERS
ALONE IN THE WOODS
ANTZ
BARNEY'S GREAT ADVENTURE—THE MOVIE
BATMAN/SUPERMAN MOVIE, THE
BILLBOARD DAD
BORROWERS, THE
BOYS WILL BE BOYS
BRAVE LITTLE TOASTER GOES TO MARS, THE
BREAKOUT
BUG'S LIFE, A
BUSTER & CHAUNCEY'S SILENT NIGHT
CASPER MEETS WENDY
CLOCKMAKER
DENNIS THE MENACE STRIKES AGAIN
DR. DOLITTLE
FERNGULLY 2: THE MAGICAL RESCUE
FLINTSTONES: I YABBA-DABBA DOO!, THE
HERCULES AND XENA THE ANIMATED MOVIE: THE BATTLE FOR MOUNT OLYMPUS
IN HIS FATHER'S SHOES
INVISIBLE DAD
INVISIBLE MOM
JACK FROST
JOEY
JOHNNY MYSTO BOY WIZARD
JUNGLE BOOK: MOWGLI'S STORY, THE
KIKI'S DELIVERY SERVICE
LION KING II: SIMBA'S PRIDE, THE
LITTLE BIGFOOT 2: THE JOURNEY HOME
LITTLE GHOST
LOUISA MAY ALCOTT'S LITTLE MEN
MADELINE
MIDAS TOUCH, THE
MIGHTY, THE
MULAN
NAPOLEON
NEW ADVENTURES OF KIMBA THE WHITE LION, THE
OLIVER TWIST
PAULIE
POCAHONTAS II: JOURNEY TO A NEW WORLD
PRINCE OF EGYPT, THE
QUEST FOR CAMELOT
RAT'S TALE, A
REAL HOWARD SPITZ, THE
RICHIE RICH'S CHRISTMAS WISH
RIGHT CONNECTIONS, THE
RUDOLPH THE RED-NOSED REINDEER: THE MOVIE
RUGRATS MOVIE, THE
RUSTY: THE GREAT RESCUE
SCOOBY-DOO ON ZOMBIE ISLAND
SECRET KINGDOM, THE
SECRET OF NIMH 2: TIMMY TO THE RESCUE, THE
SHRUNKEN CITY, THE
SLAPPY AND THE STINKERS
STAR KID
SWAN PRINCESS III: AND THE MYSTERY OF THE ENCHANTED TREASURE, THE
3 NINJAS: HIGH NOON AT MEGA MOUNTAIN
WALKING THUNDER
WIDE AWAKE

Comedy

AIR BUD: GOLDEN RECEIVER
ALARMIST, THE
ALL THE RAGE
ALMOST HEROES
ALONE IN THE WOODS
ARMOUR OF GOD
BASEKETBALL
BEST MAN, THE
BIG HIT, THE
BIG LEBOWSKI, THE
BIG ONE, THE
BILLBOARD DAD
BILLY'S HOLLYWOOD SCREEN KISS
BLUES BROTHERS 2000
BOYS IN LOVE 2
BOYS WILL BE BOYS
BREAST MEN
BRIDE OF CHUCKY
BROADWAY DAMAGE
BUFFALO '66
BULWORTH
BURN HOLLYWOOD BURN
CAN'T HARDLY WAIT
CASPER MEETS WENDY
CELEBRATION, THE
CELEBRITY
CHAIRMAN OF THE BOARD
CHARLIE HOBOKEN
CHICAGO CAB
CLAY PIGEONS
CLOCKWATCHERS
COMEDY'S DIRTIEST DOZEN
CON, THE
COURTING COURTNEY
COUSIN BETTE
CRACKING UP
DANCER, TEXAS POP. 81
DANCING AT LUGHNASA
DAVID SEARCHING
DAY AT THE BEACH
DAY OF THE BEAST, THE
DEAD MAN ON CAMPUS
DENNIS THE MENACE STRIKES AGAIN
DIGGING TO CHINA
DIRTY LAUNDRY
DIRTY WORK
DISAPPEARANCE OF KEVIN JOHNSON, THE
DR. DOLITTLE
DREAM FOR AN INSOMNIAC
DRESS, THE
ELVIS MEETS NIXON
ENCOUNTER OF THE SPOOKY KIND
ERNEST IN THE ARMY
FALLEN ANGELS
FEAR AND LOATHING IN LAS VEGAS
FORMER CHILD STAR
FRENCH EXIT
GADJO DILO
GODSON, THE
HALF BAKED
HANGING GARDEN, THE
HAPPINESS
HARD CORE LOGO
HAV PLENTY
HENRY FOOL
HIJACKING HOLLYWOOD
HI-LIFE
HOLY MAN
HOME FRIES
HOMEGROWN
HOW STELLA GOT HER GROOVE BACK
HURLYBURLY
I GOT THE HOOK UP
I LOVE YOU, DON'T TOUCH ME!
I MARRIED A STRANGE PERSON!
I THINK I DO
I WENT DOWN
I'LL BE HOME FOR CHRISTMAS
IMPOSTORS, THE
INVISIBLE DAD
INVISIBLE MOM
JANE AUSTEN'S MAFIA!
JUNK MAIL
KILLER CONDOM, THE
KINGDOM, PART 2, THE
KISSING A FOOL
KRIPPENDORF'S TRIBE
LAST BIG THING, THE
LAST DAYS OF DISCO, THE
LEADING MAN, THE
LETHAL WEAPON 4
LET'S KILL ALL THE LAWYERS
LEWIS & CLARK & GEORGE
LIFE IS BEAUTIFUL
LITTLE GHOST
LITTLE VOICE
LIVING OUT LOUD
LOVE AND DEATH ON LONG ISLAND
LOVE TO KILL
LOVELIFE
LOVER GIRL
MADELINE
MAJOR LEAGUE: BACK TO THE MINORS
MARIUS AND JEANNETTE
MEET THE DEEDLES
MERRY WAR, A
MIDAS TOUCH, THE
MIRROR, THE
MR. JEALOUSY
MR. NICE GUY
MUSIC FROM ANOTHER ROOM
MY GIANT
NEIL SIMON'S THE ODD COUPLE II
NEXT STOP, WONDERLAND
NIGHT AND THE MOMENT, THE
NIGHT AT THE ROXBURY, A
NO ORDINARY LOVE
NORTH SHORE FISH
OBJECT OF MY AFFECTION, THE
OPPOSITE OF SEX, THE
ORGAZMO
OTHER SIDE OF SUNDAY, THE
OUT OF SIGHT
OVERNIGHT DELIVERY
PARENT TRAP, THE
PATCH ADAMS
PAULIE
PECKER
PENTAGON WARS, THE
PLAN B
PLAYING BY HEART
PLEASANTVILLE

PLUMP FICTION
POLISH WEDDING
POST COITUM, ANIMAL TRISTE
PRACTICAL MAGIC
PRIMARY COLORS
PRODIGAL SON, THE
PRONTO
REACH THE ROCK
REAL BLONDE, THE
REAL HOWARD SPITZ, THE
RETURN OF THE KING, THE
RIDE
RIGHT CONNECTIONS, THE
RINGMASTER
RUSH HOUR
RUSHMORE
RUSTY: THE GREAT RESCUE
SAFE MEN
SAME OLD SONG
SENSELESS
SEVENTH HEAVEN
SHAKESPEARE IN LOVE
SHAMPOO HORNS
SHOOTING FISH
SHOPPING FOR FANGS
SIMON BIRCH
SIX DAYS, SEVEN NIGHTS
SLAPPY AND THE STINKERS
SLAYERS: THE MOTION PICTURE
SLUMS OF BEVERLY HILLS
SMOKE SIGNALS
SOMEWHERE IN THE CITY
SONATINE
SOULER OPPOSITE, THE
SOUR GRAPES
SPICE WORLD
STILL BREATHING
SUICIDE KINGS
SUMMER FLING
SWINDLE, THE
TALK TO ME
THEORY OF FLIGHT
THERE'S SOMETHING ABOUT MARY
3 NINJAS: HIGH NOON AT MEGA MOUNTAIN
TIETA OF AGRESTE
TRUMAN SHOW, THE
TWO GIRLS AND A GUY
UN AIR DE FAMILLE
UNDERTAKER'S WEDDING, THE
URBAN SAFARI
VERY BAD THINGS
VIOLET'S VISIT
WAKING NED DEVINE
WATERBOY, THE
WEDDING SINGER, THE
WELCOME TO WOOP WOOP
WESTERN
WHEN PIGS FLY
WOO
WRONGFULLY ACCUSED
YOUR FRIENDS & NEIGHBORS
YOU'VE GOT MAIL
ZERO EFFECT

Crime

ALARMIST, THE
ANOTHER DAY IN PARADISE
BEAUTY INVESTIGATOR
BELLY
BEST OF THE BEST: WITHOUT WARNING
BIG HIT, THE
BLACKJACK
BODY COUNT
BODYGUARD FROM BEIJING
BONE DADDY
BOOGIE BOY
BROTHER
BULLET ON A WIRE
CAPTIVE
CAUGHT UP
CHARACTER
CHARLIE HOBOKEN
CLAY PIGEONS
DAD SAVAGE
DAY AT THE BEACH
DECEIVER
DEE SNIDER'S STRANGELAND
DESPERATE MEASURES
DESTINY OF MARTY FINE, THE
DETOUR
DOGWATCH
DOUBLE EDGE
ELMORE LEONARD'S GOLD COAST
FACE DOWN
FALLEN
FALLEN ANGELS
FIRESTORM
FIREWORKS
FIXER, THE
FRIEND OF THE DECEASED, A
GENERAL, THE
GINGERBREAD MAN, THE
GODSON, THE
GONIN
GUN, A CAR, AND A BLONDE, A
HARD RAIN
HIT ME
HOLLYWOOD CONFIDENTIAL
HOMEGROWN
HOT BLOODED
I WENT DOWN
ILLTOWN
INDISCREET
INSOMNIA
JANE AUSTEN'S MAFIA!
JOHNNY SKIDMARKS
JUNK MAIL
KICK BOXER'S TEARS
KILLER ANGELS
KILLING TIME
KNOCK OFF
LAST SEDUCTION II, THE
LETHAL WEAPON 4
LETTER FROM DEATH ROW, A
LEWIS & CLARK & GEORGE
LITTLE BOY BLUE
LOVE WALKED IN
MEAN GUNS
MONTANA
MONUMENT AVE.
MURDER IN MIND
NAKED LIES
NEGOTIATOR, THE
NIGHT VISION
NO WAY HOME
ONE TOUGH COP
OUT OF SIGHT
OUTSIDE OZONA
PALMETTO
PERFECT MURDER, A
PHOENIX
PLAYERS CLUB, THE
PRONTO
PROPOSITION, THE
RABID DOGS
RAGE, THE
RATCHET
RAZOR: THE SNARE, THE
RAZOR: WHO'S GOT THE GOLD?, THE
REAL THING, THE
REPLACEMENT KILLERS, THE
RIVER RED
ROUNDERS
ROYAL WARRIORS
RUSH HOUR
SAFE MEN
SCARRED CITY
SHOOTING FISH
SIMPLE PLAN, A
SONATINE
SPREE, THE
SUBSTITUTE 2: SCHOOL'S OUT, THE
SUICIDE KINGS
SWINDLE, THE
TEN BENNY
TERMINAL JUSTICE
THURSDAY
TOP OF THE WORLD
TOUCH OF EVIL: THE DIRECTOR'S CUT
TWILIGHT
U.S. MARSHALS
WEST NEW YORK
ZERO WOMAN

Dance

DANCE WITH ME

Disaster

DEEP IMPACT
HARD RAIN
SUB DOWN

Docudrama

FROM A FAR COUNTRY
SNOWBOUND
UNMADE BEDS

Documentary

ALFRED HITCHCOCK: MASTER OF SUSPENSE
ARGUING THE WORLD
AYN RAND: A SENSE OF LIFE
BATTLE OF CHILE: THE STRUGGLE OF AN UNARMED PEOPLE—PART 2: THE COUP D'ETAT, THE
BIG ONE, THE
BRANDON TEENA STORY, THE
CAN'T YOU HEAR THE WIND HOWL?: THE LIFE AND MUSIC OF ROBERT JOHNSON
CHILE, OBSTINATE MEMORY
CLASSIFIED X
COMEDY'S DIRTIEST DOZEN
CRUISE, THE
DEAR JESSE
DECLINE OF WESTERN CIVILIZATION PART III, THE
DIDN'T DO IT FOR LOVE
DIVORCE IRANIAN STYLE
EL CHE: INVESTIGATING A LEGEND
ELIA KAZAN: A DIRECTOR'S JOURNEY
FARM: ANGOLA, U.S.A., THE
FREE TIBET
FULL TILT BOOGIE
HALLELUJAH!
HANDS ON A HARDBODY
HEALING BY KILLING
JAMES ELLROY: DEMON DOG OF AMERICAN CRIME FICTION

KINGDOM OF SHADOWS
KRZYSZTOF KIESLOWSKI: I'M SO-SO
KURT AND COURTNEY
LAVENDER LIMELIGHT: LESBIANS IN FILM
LENNY BRUCE: SWEAR TO TELL THE TRUTH
LET'S TALK ABOUT SEX
LITTLE DIETER NEEDS TO FLY
LOU REED: ROCK AND ROLL HEART
MODULATIONS: CINEMA FOR THE EAR
MOON OVER BROADWAY
MY FIRST NAME IS MACEO
MY KNEES WERE JUMPING: REMEMBERING THE KINDERTRANSPORTS
OFF THE MENU: THE LAST DAYS OF CHASEN'S
OUT OF THE PAST
PARALYZING FEAR: THE STORY OF POLIO IN AMERICA, A
PAUL MONETTE: THE BRINK OF SUMMER'S END
PLACE CALLED CHIAPAS, A
RACE TO SAVE 100 YEARS, THE
RETURN OF THE KING, THE
R.I.P. REST IN PIECES: A PORTRAIT OF JOE COLEMAN
SALTMEN OF TIBET, THE
SILVER SCREEN: COLOR ME LAVENDER, THE
SIX O'CLOCK NEWS
SLAMNATION
STOLEN MOMENTS
STOREFRONT HITCHCOCK
STORY OF X, THE
TIMOTHY LEARY'S DEAD
TRANCEFORMER: A PORTRAIT OF LARS VON TRIER
TREKKIES
UNVEILING, THE
WAR ZONE
WHO IS HENRY JAGLOM?
WHO THE HELL IS JULIETTE?
WILD MAN BLUES
ZAKIR AND HIS FRIENDS

Drama

AFFLICTION
ALARMIST, THE
ALL THE RAGE
ALWAYS OUTNUMBERED
AMERICAN HISTORY X
ANOTHER DAY IN PARADISE
APT PUPIL
ARTEMISIA
BAD MANNERS
BARRIERS
BELLY
BELOVED
BEST MAN, THE
BEYOND SILENCE
BLACK DOG
BODY COUNT
BOOGIE BOY
BOYS IN LOVE 2
BREAK, THE
BREAST MEN
BRIGHT SHINING LIE, A
BROADWAY DAMAGE
BROTHER
BRYLCREEM BOYS, THE
BUFFALO '66
BULLET ON A WIRE
BUTCHER BOY, THE
CALL TO REMEMBER, A
CARLA'S SONG
CAUGHT UP
CELEBRATION, THE
CELEBRITY
CENTRAL STATION
CHAMBERMAID ON THE TITANIC, THE
CHARACTER
CHICAGO CAB
CHINESE BOX, THE
CITY OF ANGELS
CIVIL ACTION, A
CLOCKWATCHERS
COMRADES, ALMOST A LOVE STORY
COUSIN BETTE
CRACKING UP
CROSSING FIELDS
DANCER, TEXAS POP. 81
DANCING AT LUGHNASA
DANGEROUS BEAUTY
DAVID SEARCHING
DAY AT THE BEACH
DEAD END
DEEP IMPACT
DEFENDERS: PAYBACK, THE
DEJA VU
DESTINY
DESTINY OF MARTY FINE, THE
DETOUR
DIGGING TO CHINA
DISENCHANTED, THE
DON KING: ONLY IN AMERICA
DOWN IN THE DELTA
DRESS, THE
EAST PALACE, WEST PALACE
EBENEZER
EDEN
EEL, THE
EMPEROR'S SHADOW, THE
FALLEN ANGELS
FEAR AND LOATHING IN LAS VEGAS
54
FIRELIGHT
FIREWORKS
FIRST LOVE, LAST RITES
FIXER, THE
FORGOTTEN LIGHT
FRIEND OF THE DECEASED, A
FROM A FAR COUNTRY
FROZEN
FULL SPEED
GADJO DILO
GEORGE WALLACE
GIA
GO NOW
GODS AND MONSTERS
GOVERNESS, THE
GREAT EXPECTATIONS
GUN, A CAR, AND A BLONDE, A
HANGING GARDEN, THE
HAPPINESS
HARD CORE LOGO
HE GOT GAME
HENRY FOOL
HIGH ART
HILARY AND JACKIE
HI-LIFE
HI-LO COUNTRY, THE
HIT ME
HOLLYWOOD CONFIDENTIAL
HOLY MAN
HOME BEFORE DARK
HOMEGROWN
HONG KONG 1941
HOPE FLOATS
HORSE WHISPERER, THE
HORTON FOOTE'S ALONE
HOSTILE WATERS
HOT BLOODED
HOW STELLA GOT HER GROOVE BACK
HURLYBURLY
HURRICANE STREETS
HUSH
I WENT DOWN
ILLTOWN
IN GOD'S HANDS
IN HIS FATHER'S SHOES
INFORMANT, THE
INHERITORS, THE
INSIDE/OUT
JERUSALEM
JOEY
JUNK FOOD
KINGDOM, PART 2, THE
KRISTIN LAVRANSDATTER
LA SEPARATION
LAND GIRLS, THE
LAST ASSASSINS
LAST BIG THING, THE
LAST BREATH
LAST DAYS OF DISCO, THE
LAST SEDUCTION II, THE
LAWN DOGS
LEADING MAN, THE
LENA'S DREAMS
LES MISERABLES
LET'S TALK ABOUT SEX
LETTER FROM DEATH ROW, A
LIFE IS BEAUTIFUL
LIFE OF JESUS, THE
LIKE IT IS
LITTLE BOY BLUE
LITTLE VOICE
LIVE FLESH
LIVING OUT LOUD
LOLITA
LOUISA MAY ALCOTT'S LITTLE MEN
LOVE AND DEATH ON LONG ISLAND
LOVE IS THE DEVIL: STUDY FOR A PORTRAIT OF FRANCIS BACON
LOVER GIRL
MAKER, THE
MAN IN THE IRON MASK, THE
MARIE BAIE DES ANGES
MARIUS AND JEANNETTE
MEET JOE BLACK
MEN
MEN WITH GUNS
MENDEL
MERRY WAR, A
MIDAQ ALLEY
MIGHTY, THE
MR. JEALOUSY
MONUMENT AVE.
MOONDANCE
MOTHER AND SON
MRS. DALLOWAY
MURDER IN MIND
MY BROTHER'S WAR
MY VERY BEST FRIEND
NAKED ACTS
NEVADA
NEXT STEP, THE
NEXT STOP, WONDERLAND
NIAGARA NIAGARA
NIGHT AND THE MOMENT, THE
NIGHT VISION

NIL BY MOUTH
NO LOOKING BACK
NO ORDINARY LOVE
NO WAY HOME
NORTH SHORE FISH
NOT IN THIS TOWN
NOTES FROM UNDERGROUND
OGRE, THE
OLIVER TWIST
ONE TOUGH COP
ONE TRUE THING
ONLY THRILL, THE
OPPOSITE OF SEX, THE
OTHER SIDE OF SUNDAY, THE
OUTSIDE OZONA
OYSTER AND THE WIND, THE
PARALLEL SONS
PASSION IN THE DESERT
PATCH ADAMS
PEREIRA DECLARES
PERFECT MURDER, A
PERMANENT MIDNIGHT
PHOENIX
PHOTOGRAPHING FAIRIES
PLAN B
PLAYERS CLUB, THE
PLAYING BY HEART
PLEASANTVILLE
POLISH WEDDING
POST COITUM, ANIMAL TRISTE
PRICE ABOVE RUBIES, A
PRIMARY COLORS
PRINCE, THE
PRONTO
PROPOSITION, THE
PSYCHO
RAT PACK, THE
RATCHET
REACH THE ROCK
REBOUND: THE LEGEND OF EARL "THE GOAT" MANIGAULT
RED CHERRY
REGENERATION
RESCUERS: STORIES OF COURAGE—TWO COUPLES
RESCUERS: STORIES OF COURAGE—TWO WOMEN
RETURN TO PARADISE
RINGMASTER
RIVER RED
ROUNDERS
ROYAL DECEIT
RUNNING WOMAN, THE
RUSHMORE
SAME OLD SONG
SAND TRAP
SAVING PRIVATE RYAN
SAVIOR
SEVENTH HEAVEN
SHADRACH
SHAMPOO HORNS
SHATTERED IMAGE
SHOPPING FOR FANGS
SIEGE, THE
SIMON BIRCH
SIMPLE PLAN, A
SIN AND REDEMPTION
SKIN & BONE
SLAM
SLIDING DOORS
SLUMS OF BEVERLY HILLS
SMOKE SIGNALS
SOLDIER
SOLDIER'S DAUGHTER NEVER CRIES, A
SONATINE
SOULER OPPOSITE, THE
SPANISH PRISONER, THE
SPREE, THE
STEAM
STEPMOM
STILL BREATHING
SUBSTITUTE 2: SCHOOL'S OUT, THE
SUE
SUMMER FLING
SWEPT FROM THE SEA
TALK OF ANGELS
TARANTELLA
TASTE OF CHERRY
TEN BENNY
THEORY OF FLIGHT
THIEF, THE
THURSDAY
TIETA OF AGRESTE
TOKYO FIST
TRICKS
TRUCE, THE
TRUMAN SHOW, THE
12 ANGRY MEN
TWENTYFOURSEVEN
TWO GIRLS AND A GUY
UN AIR DE FAMILLE
UNDER HEAVEN
UNDER THE SKIN
VELVET GOLDMINE
VERY BAD THINGS
VILLAGE OF DREAMS
VOYAGE TO THE BEGINNING OF THE WORLD
WEST NEW YORK
WESTERN
WHAT DREAMS MAY COME
WHATEVER
WHEN I CLOSE MY EYES
WHEN TIME EXPIRES
WHEN TRUMPETS FADE
WHY DO FOOLS FALL IN LOVE?
WIDE AWAKE
WILDE
WITHOUT LIMITS
YOUR FRIENDS & NEIGHBORS
YOU'VE GOT MAIL

Erotic

FATAL PURSUIT
INTERLOCKED: THRILLED TO DEATH
LAST SEDUCTION II, THE
LOLIDA 2000
NIGHT AND THE MOMENT, THE
STORY OF X, THE

Fantasy

ANTZ
AVENGERS, THE
BABE: PIG IN THE CITY
BARNEY'S GREAT ADVENTURE—THE MOVIE
BORROWERS, THE
CASPER MEETS WENDY
CHOSEN ONE: LEGEND OF THE RAVEN, THE
CITY OF ANGELS
DARK CITY
DR. DOLITTLE
DRAGON BALL Z THE MOVIE: DEAD ZONE
DRAGON BALL Z THE MOVIE: THE TREE OF MIGHT
DRAGON BALL Z THE MOVIE: THE WORLD'S STRONGEST
ENCOUNTER OF THE SPOOKY KIND
GODS AND MONSTERS
GUN, A CAR, AND A BLONDE, A
IN HIS FATHER'S SHOES
JACK FROST
JOHNNY MYSTO BOY WIZARD
KID IN ALADDIN'S PALACE, A
KIKI'S DELIVERY SERVICE
LETTER FROM DEATH ROW, A
LITTLE BIGFOOT 2: THE JOURNEY HOME
LITTLE GHOST
MEET JOE BLACK
MERLIN
MIDAS TOUCH, THE
MIGHTY JOE YOUNG
OYSTER AND THE WIND, THE
PAULIE
PHOTOGRAPHING FAIRIES
POLTERGEIST REPORT: YUYU HAKUSHO
PRACTICAL MAGIC
QUICKSILVER HIGHWAY
RAT'S TALE, A
RICHIE RICH'S CHRISTMAS WISH
RUDOLPH THE RED-NOSED REINDEER: THE MOVIE
SECRET KINGDOM, THE
SIX-STRING SAMURAI
SLAYERS: THE MOTION PICTURE
SLIDING DOORS
SMALL SOLDIERS
TRUMAN SHOW, THE
VELVET GOLDMINE
WHAT DREAMS MAY COME
WHEN PIGS FLY
WRATH OF THE NINJA: THE YOTODEN MOVIE
YOUNG HERCULES

Historical

ALMOST HEROES
BELOVED
BRIGHT SHINING LIE, A
CHAMBERMAID ON THE TITANIC, THE
COUSIN BETTE
DANGEROUS BEAUTY
DESTINY
ELIZABETH
EMPEROR'S SHADOW, THE
EVER AFTER
FIRELIGHT
FROM A FAR COUNTRY
HONG KONG 1941
LES MISERABLES
MAN IN THE IRON MASK, THE
MY KNEES WERE JUMPING: REMEMBERING THE KINDERTRANSPORTS
PASSION IN THE DESERT
PEREIRA DECLARES
PHOTOGRAPHING FAIRIES
RED CHERRY
RESCUERS: STORIES OF COURAGE—TWO COUPLES
RESCUERS: STORIES OF COURAGE—TWO WOMEN
SHAKESPEARE IN LOVE
SWEPT FROM THE SEA
TRUCE, THE
TWO FOR TEXAS

Horror

ABERRATION
ASYLUM

BEYOND, THE
BLADE
BLEEDERS
BRAM STOKER'S SHADOWBUILDER
BRAM STOKER'S THE MUMMY
BRIDE OF CHUCKY
CHILDREN OF THE CORN V: FIELD OF TERROR
CLUB VAMPIRE
CUBE
CURSE OF THE PUPPET MASTER
DAY OF THE BEAST, THE
DEAD WATERS
DECAMPITATED
DEE SNIDER'S STRANGELAND
DEEP RISING
DISTURBING BEHAVIOR
EIGHTEENTH ANGEL, THE
ENCOUNTER OF THE SPOOKY KIND
FACULTY, THE
FALLEN
FUNNY GAMES
HALLOWEEN H20: TWENTY YEARS LATER
HENRY: PORTRAIT OF A SERIAL KILLER PART 2
I STILL KNOW WHAT YOU DID LAST SUMMER
JOHN CARPENTER'S VAMPIRES
KILLER CONDOM, THE
KINGDOM OF SHADOWS
KINGDOM, PART 2, THE
LANDLADY, THE
MILO
MISBEGOTTEN
NIGHTWATCH
PHANTASM: OBLIVION
PHANTOMS
PROPHECY II, THE
PSYCHO
QUICKSILVER HIGHWAY
SPECIES II
STEPHEN KING'S THE NIGHT FLIER
SUBSPECIES IV: BLOODSTORM
TALISMAN
TOKYO FIST
UGLY, THE
UNCLE SAM
URBAN LEGEND
WATCHERS REBORN

Martial Arts

BEST OF THE BEST: WITHOUT WARNING
BODYGUARD FROM BEIJING
DRAGON BALL Z THE MOVIE: DEAD ZONE
DRAGONS FOREVER
KICK BOXER'S TEARS
SHAOLIN TEMPLE, THE
TEKKEN: THE MOTION PICTURE

Musical

BLUES BROTHERS 2000
BUSTER & CHAUNCEY'S SILENT NIGHT
CAN'T YOU HEAR THE WIND HOWL?: THE LIFE AND MUSIC OF ROBERT JOHNSON
DESTINY
HARD CORE LOGO
LION KING II: SIMBA'S PRIDE, THE
MIGHTY KONG, THE
MODULATIONS: CINEMA FOR THE EAR
MULAN
MY FIRST NAME IS MACEO
NEXT STEP, THE
SAME OLD SONG
SPICE WORLD
STOREFRONT HITCHCOCK
SWAN PRINCESS III: AND THE MYSTERY OF THE ENCHANTED TREASURE, THE
VELVET GOLDMINE
WELCOME TO WOOP WOOP
WHY DO FOOLS FALL IN LOVE?
WILD MAN BLUES

Mystery

ALMOST PARTNERS
ASYLUM
BIG LEBOWSKI, THE
CAPTIVE
FACE DOWN
INDISCREET
INNOCENT SLEEP, THE
LITTLE BOY BLUE
SHATTERED IMAGE
SNAKE EYES
SPANISH PRISONER, THE
STRAY BULLET
TWILIGHT
WHEN DANGER FOLLOWS YOU HOME
ZERO EFFECT

Political

BRIGHT SHINING LIE, A
BULWORTH
DEAR JESSE
ENEMY
GEORGE WALLACE
HOSTILE WATERS
HUMAN BOMB
INFORMANT, THE
JACK HIGGINS' THE WINDSOR PROTOCOL
LAND OF THE FREE
MEN WITH GUNS
MY BROTHER'S WAR
PEREIRA DECLARES
PLACE CALLED CHIAPAS, A
PRIMARY COLORS
SIEGE, THE

Prison

BRYLCREEM BOYS, THE
ESCAPE, THE
GIRLS IN PRISON
TRACKED

Religious

FORGOTTEN LIGHT
PRICE ABOVE RUBIES, A
PRINCE OF EGYPT, THE
SIMON BIRCH
WIDE AWAKE

Romance

BEST MAN, THE
BILLY'S HOLLYWOOD SCREEN KISS
BOYS IN LOVE 2
BROADWAY DAMAGE
CAN'T HARDLY WAIT
CARLA'S SONG
CHAMBERMAID ON THE TITANIC, THE
CHINESE BOX, THE
CITY OF ANGELS
COMRADES, ALMOST A LOVE STORY
CON, THE
COURTING COURTNEY
DANCE WITH ME
DANGEROUS BEAUTY
DAVID SEARCHING
DEJA VU
DREAM FOR AN INSOMNIAC
ESCAPE, THE
EVER AFTER
FIRELIGHT
FRENCH EXIT
GO NOW
GREAT EXPECTATIONS
HAV PLENTY
HOME FRIES
HONG KONG 1941
HOPE FLOATS
HORSE WHISPERER, THE
HOW STELLA GOT HER GROOVE BACK
I LOVE YOU, DON'T TOUCH ME!
I THINK I DO
KISSING A FOOL
LAND GIRLS, THE
LEADING MAN, THE
LIKE IT IS
LIVING OUT LOUD
LOLITA
LOVELIFE
MARIUS AND JEANNETTE
MASK OF ZORRO, THE
MEET JOE BLACK
MEN
MERRY WAR, A
MIDAQ ALLEY
MR. JEALOUSY
MUSIC FROM ANOTHER ROOM
NEXT STOP, WONDERLAND
NIAGARA NIAGARA
NO LOOKING BACK
OBJECT OF MY AFFECTION, THE
ONLY THRILL, THE
OUT OF SIGHT
OVERNIGHT DELIVERY
PASSION IN THE DESERT
PLAN B
PLAYING BY HEART
POLISH WEDDING
POST COITUM, ANIMAL TRISTE
PRACTICAL MAGIC
PROPOSITION, THE
REAL BLONDE, THE
SHAKESPEARE IN LOVE
SHOOTING FISH
SIX DAYS, SEVEN NIGHTS
SLIDING DOORS
SOMEWHERE IN THE CITY
SOULER OPPOSITE, THE
SPREE, THE
STEAM
STILL BREATHING
SWEPT FROM THE SEA
TALK OF ANGELS
TALK TO ME
THEORY OF FLIGHT
THERE'S SOMETHING ABOUT MARY
TOKYO FIST
UNDER HEAVEN
WEDDING SINGER, THE
WHEN I CLOSE MY EYES
WOO
YOU'VE GOT MAIL

Science Fiction

ABERRATION
ARMAGEDDON
ATOMIC DOG

CLOCKMAKER
COLONY, THE
CUBE
DARK CITY
DISTURBING BEHAVIOR
FACULTY, THE
FALLING FIRE
FUTURE FEAR
GODZILLA
GODZILLA AND MOTHRA: THE BATTLE FOR EARTH
GODZILLA VS. KING GHIDORAH
HOSTILE INTENT
INVADER, THE
INVISIBLE DAD
INVISIBLE MOM
KRAA! THE SEA MONSTER
LAST LIVES
LOST IN SPACE
LOST WORLD, THE
MARS
MOBILE SUIT GUNDAM I
MOBILE SUIT GUNDAM II: SOLDIERS OF SORROW
MOBILE SUIT GUNDAM III: ENCOUNTERS IN SPACE
NEMESIS 4: CRY OF ANGELS
NIRVANA
PI
REDLINE
RETROACTIVE
SHRUNKEN CITY, THE
SOLDIER
SPACEJACKED
SPECIES II
SPHERE
STAR KID
STAR TREK: INSURRECTION
TALES FROM A PARALLEL UNIVERSE: EATING PATTERN
TALES FROM A PARALLEL UNIVERSE: GIGA SHADOW
TALES FROM A PARALLEL UNIVERSE: SUPER NOVA
TERMINAL JUSTICE
TRUCKS
TWISTED
WHEN TIME EXPIRES
X-FILES, THE

Sports

AIR BUD: GOLDEN RECEIVER
BASEKETBALL
HE GOT GAME
IN GOD'S HANDS
MAJOR LEAGUE: BACK TO THE MINORS
TWENTYFOURSEVEN
WATERBOY, THE
WITHOUT LIMITS

Spy

AVENGERS, THE
JACK HIGGINS' ON DANGEROUS GROUND
JACK HIGGINS' THUNDER POINT
JACK HIGGINS' MIDNIGHT MAN
JACK HIGGINS' THE WINDSOR PROTOCOL
RONIN

Thriller

APT PUPIL
BEAUTY INVESTIGATOR
BLACK LIGHT
BODY COUNT
BONE DADDY
BREAK, THE
CATHERINE'S GROVE
CAUGHT UP
CLAY PIGEONS
CUBE
DAD SAVAGE
DARK CITY
DEAD END
DECEIVER
DEEP RISING
DESPERATE MEASURES
DETOUR
DIARY OF A SERIAL KILLER
DISTURBING BEHAVIOR
DOUBLE EDGE
ENEMY
ENEMY OF THE STATE
ESCAPE, THE
FACE THE EVIL
FACULTY, THE
FALLEN
FATAL PURSUIT
FIREWORKS
FUNNY GAMES
FUTURE FEAR
GENEALOGIES OF A CRIME
GINGERBREAD MAN, THE
GODZILLA
GOLGO 13: QUEEN BEE
HENRY: PORTRAIT OF A SERIAL KILLER PART 2
HOME FRIES
HOSTILE WATERS
HOT BLOODED
HUMAN BOMB
HUNTED, THE
HUSH
INCOGNITO
INNOCENT SLEEP, THE
INSOMNIA
INTERLOCKED: THRILLED TO DEATH
JOHN CARPENTER'S VAMPIRES
JOHNNY SKIDMARKS
KILLER ANGELS
KILLING TIME
LAND OF THE FREE
LAST BREATH
LEWIS & CLARK & GEORGE
LIVING IN PERIL
LOVE WALKED IN
MERCURY RISING
MISBEGOTTEN
MY BROTHER'S WAR
MY VERY BEST FRIEND
NEGOTIATOR, THE
NIGHTWATCH
NIRVANA
OUTSIDE OZONA
PALMETTO
PASS, THE
PERFECT MURDER, A
PHOENIX
PI
PSYCHO
RABID DOGS
RATCHET
REAL THING, THE
RETROACTIVE
RONIN
RUN FOR COVER
RUNNING WOMAN, THE
SAND TRAP
SHATTERED IMAGE
SHOPPING FOR FANGS
SIEGE, THE
SIMPLE PLAN, A
SNAKE EYES
SPANISH PRISONER, THE
SPECIES II
SPHERE
STIR
STRAY BULLET
SUB DOWN
SUICIDE KINGS
TOUCH OF EVIL: THE DIRECTOR'S CUT
TRUCKS
TWILIGHT
TWISTED
URBAN LEGEND
U.S. MARSHALS
WHEN DANGER FOLLOWS YOU HOME
WHITE RAVEN, THE
WILD THINGS
ZERO WOMAN

War

BRIGHT SHINING LIE, A
BRYLCREEM BOYS, THE
CARLA'S SONG
LAND GIRLS, THE
LITTLE DIETER NEEDS TO FLY
OGRE, THE
RED CHERRY
REGENERATION
RESCUERS: STORIES OF COURAGE—TWO COUPLES
RESCUERS: STORIES OF COURAGE—TWO WOMEN
SAVING PRIVATE RYAN
SAVIOR
THIN RED LINE, THE
WHEN TRUMPETS FADE

Western

EBENEZER
HI-LO COUNTRY, THE
LOS LOCOS
NEWTON BOYS, THE
TWO FOR TEXAS
WALKING THUNDER

FILMS BY MPAA RATING

The Motion Picture Association of America (MPAA) currently grades films according to the following codes:

G GENERAL AUDIENCES (All ages admitted)
PG PARENTAL GUIDANCE SUGGESTED (Some material may not be suitable for children)
PG-13 PARENTS STRONGLY CAUTIONED (Some material may be inappropriate for children under 13)
R RESTRICTED (Under 17 requires accompanying parent or adult guardian)
NC-17 NO CHILDREN UNDER 17 ADMITTED
NR NOT RATED

G

ALL DOGS CHRISTMAS CAROL, AN
BABE: PIG IN THE CITY
BARNEY'S GREAT ADVENTURE—THE MOVIE
BRAVE LITTLE TOASTER GOES TO MARS, THE
BUG'S LIFE, A
BUSTER & CHAUNCEY'S SILENT NIGHT
DENNIS THE MENACE STRIKES AGAIN
FERNGULLY 2: THE MAGICAL RESCUE
JUNGLE BOOK: MOWGLI'S STORY, THE
KID IN ALADDIN'S PALACE, A
KIKI'S DELIVERY SERVICE
LITTLE GHOST
MIGHTY KONG, THE
MULAN
NAPOLEON
QUEST FOR CAMELOT
RAT'S TALE, A
RICHIE RICH'S CHRISTMAS WISH
RUDOLPH THE RED-NOSED REINDEER: THE MOVIE
RUGRATS MOVIE, THE
RUSTY: THE GREAT RESCUE
SECRET OF NIMH 2: TIMMY TO THE RESCUE, THE
SWAN PRINCESS III: AND THE MYSTERY OF THE ENCHANTED TREASURE, THE

PG

AIR BUD: GOLDEN RECEIVER
ALONE IN THE WOODS
ANTZ
BEST MAN, THE
BILLBOARD DAD
BORROWERS, THE
BOYS WILL BE BOYS
CASPER MEETS WENDY
CLOCKMAKER
DANCE WITH ME
DANCER, TEXAS POP. 81
DANCING AT LUGHNASA
DIGGING TO CHINA
EBENEZER
ERNEST IN THE ARMY
HANDS ON A HARDBODY
HERCULES AND XENA THE ANIMATED MOVIE: THE BATTLE FOR MOUNT OLYMPUS
HOLY MAN
HOSTILE WATERS
I'LL BE HOME FOR CHRISTMAS
IN HIS FATHER'S SHOES
INVISIBLE MOM
JACK FROST
JACK LONDON'S THE CALL OF THE WILD: DOG OF THE YUKON
JOEY
JOHNNY MYSTO BOY WIZARD
KRAA! THE SEA MONSTER
LITTLE BIGFOOT 2: THE JOURNEY HOME
LOUISA MAY ALCOTT'S LITTLE MEN
MADELINE
MEET THE DEEDLES
MIDAS TOUCH, THE
MIGHTY JOE YOUNG
MY GIANT
MY VERY BEST FRIEND
PARENT TRAP, THE
PAULIE
PRINCE OF EGYPT, THE
RACE TO SAVE 100 YEARS, THE
REAL HOWARD SPITZ, THE
RESCUERS: STORIES OF COURAGE—TWO COUPLES
RIGHT CONNECTIONS, THE
SECRET KINGDOM, THE
SHOOTING FISH
SHRUNKEN CITY, THE
SIMON BIRCH
SLAPPY AND THE STINKERS
SPANISH PRISONER, THE
SPICE WORLD
STAR KID
STAR TREK: INSURRECTION
3 NINJAS: HIGH NOON AT MEGA MOUNTAIN
TRUMAN SHOW, THE
WAKING NED DEVINE
WALKING THUNDER
WIDE AWAKE
WILD MAN BLUES
YOU'VE GOT MAIL

PG-13

ALMOST HEROES
ARMAGEDDON
ATOMIC DOG
AVENGERS, THE
BIG ONE, THE
BLACK DOG
BLUES BROTHERS 2000
BRYLCREEM BOYS, THE
CAN'T HARDLY WAIT
CHAIRMAN OF THE BOARD
CITY OF ANGELS
CIVIL ACTION, A
CLOCKWATCHERS
CON, THE
DEEP IMPACT
DIRTY WORK
DR. DOLITTLE
DOWN IN THE DELTA
ELVIS MEETS NIXON
EVER AFTER
GODSON, THE
GODZILLA
HOME FRIES
HOPE FLOATS
HORSE WHISPERER, THE
HUMAN BOMB
HUSH
IN GOD'S HANDS
JANE AUSTEN'S MAFIA!
JERUSALEM
KRIPPENDORF'S TRIBE
LES MISERABLES
LIFE IS BEAUTIFUL
LOST IN SPACE
MAJOR LEAGUE: BACK TO THE MINORS
MAN IN THE IRON MASK, THE
MASK OF ZORRO, THE
MEET JOE BLACK
MIGHTY, THE
MR. NICE GUY
MRS. DALLOWAY
MUSIC FROM ANOTHER ROOM
NEIL SIMON'S THE ODD COUPLE II
NEWTON BOYS, THE
NIGHT AT THE ROXBURY, A
OVERNIGHT DELIVERY
PASSION IN THE DESERT
PATCH ADAMS
PLEASANTVILLE
POLISH WEDDING
PRACTICAL MAGIC
PRINCE VALIANT
RESCUERS: STORIES OF COURAGE—TWO WOMEN
RUSH HOUR
SHADRACH
SIN AND REDEMPTION
SIX DAYS, SEVEN NIGHTS
SIX-STRING SAMURAI
SMALL SOLDIERS
SMOKE SIGNALS
SPHERE
STEPMOM
STILL BREATHING
STOREFRONT HITCHCOCK
SUB DOWN
SWEPT FROM THE SEA
TALK OF ANGELS
TARZAN AND THE LOST CITY
12 ANGRY MEN
TWISTED
WATERBOY, THE
WEDDING SINGER, THE

WHAT DREAMS MAY COME
WHEN DANGER FOLLOWS YOU HOME
WHEN I CLOSE MY EYES
WHEN TIME EXPIRES
WITHOUT LIMITS
WRONGFULLY ACCUSED
X-FILES, THE
YOUNG HERCULES

R

ABERRATION
AFFLICTION
ALARMIST, THE
ALWAYS OUTNUMBERED
AMERICAN HISTORY X
ANOTHER DAY IN PARADISE
APT PUPIL
ARMOUR OF GOD
ARTEMISIA
ASYLUM
BAD MANNERS
BARRIERS
BASEKETBALL
BELLY
BELOVED
BEST OF THE BEST: WITHOUT WARNING
BEYOND SILENCE
BIG HIT, THE
BIG LEBOWSKI, THE
BLACK THUNDER
BLACKJACK
BLADE
BLEEDERS
BODY COUNT
BODY COUNT
BONE DADDY
BOOGIE BOY
BRAM STOKER'S SHADOWBUILDER
BRAM STOKER'S THE MUMMY
BREAK, THE
BREAST MEN
BRIDE OF CHUCKY
BRIGHT SHINING LIE, A
BUFFALO '66
BULWORTH
BURN HOLLYWOOD BURN
BUTCHER BOY, THE
CALL TO REMEMBER, A
CATHERINE'S GROVE
CAUGHT UP
CELEBRATION, THE
CELEBRITY
CENTRAL STATION
CHARACTER
CHICAGO CAB
CHILDREN OF THE CORN V: FIELD OF TERROR
CHINESE BOX, THE
CLAY PIGEONS
CLUB VAMPIRE
COLONY, THE
COUSIN BETTE
CUBE
CURSE OF THE PUPPET MASTER
DAD SAVAGE
DANGEROUS BEAUTY
DARK CITY
DAY OF THE BEAST, THE
DEAD END
DEAD MAN ON CAMPUS
DECEIVER
DECLINE OF WESTERN CIVILIZATION PART III, THE
DEE SNIDER'S STRANGELAND
DEEP RISING
DEFENDERS: PAYBACK, THE
DESPERATE MEASURES
DETONATOR
DIARY OF A SERIAL KILLER
DIRTY LAUNDRY
DISAPPEARANCE OF KEVIN JOHNSON, THE
DISTURBING BEHAVIOR
DOGWATCH
DON KING: ONLY IN AMERICA
DOUBLE EDGE
DREAM FOR AN INSOMNIAC
EDEN
EIGHTEENTH ANGEL, THE
ELIZABETH
ELMORE LEONARD'S GOLD COAST
ENEMY
ENEMY OF THE STATE
FACE DOWN
FACE THE EVIL
FACULTY, THE
FALLEN
FALLEN ANGELS
FALLING FIRE
FATAL PURSUIT
FEAR AND LOATHING IN LAS VEGAS
54
FIRELIGHT
FIRESTORM
FRENCH EXIT
FRIEND OF THE DECEASED, A
FULL TILT BOOGIE
FUTURE FEAR
GENERAL, THE
GIA
GINGERBREAD MAN, THE
GIRLS IN PRISON
GODS AND MONSTERS
GOVERNESS, THE
GREAT EXPECTATIONS
GUN, A CAR, AND A BLONDE, A
HALF BAKED
HALLOWEEN H20: TWENTY YEARS LATER
HANGING GARDEN, THE
HAPPINESS
HARD CORE LOGO
HARD RAIN
HAV PLENTY
HE GOT GAME
HEAVEN'S BURNING
HENRY FOOL
HENRY: PORTRAIT OF A SERIAL KILLER PART 2
HIGH ART
HIJACKING HOLLYWOOD
HILARY AND JACKIE
HI-LIFE
HI-LO COUNTRY, THE
HIT ME
HOLLYWOOD CONFIDENTIAL
HOMEGROWN
HOSTILE INTENT
HOT BLOODED
HOW STELLA GOT HER GROOVE BACK
HUNTED, THE
HURLYBURLY
HURRICANE STREETS
I GOT THE HOOK UP
I LOVE YOU, DON'T TOUCH ME!
I STILL KNOW WHAT YOU DID LAST SUMMER
I THINK I DO
I WENT DOWN
ILLTOWN
IMPOSTORS, THE
INCOGNITO
INDISCREET
INFORMANT, THE
INHERITORS, THE
INNOCENT SLEEP, THE
INTERLOCKED: THRILLED TO DEATH
JACK HIGGINS' ON DANGEROUS GROUND
JACK HIGGINS' THUNDER POINT
JACK HIGGINS' MIDNIGHT MAN
JACK HIGGINS' THE WINDSOR PROTOCOL
JOHN CARPENTER'S VAMPIRES
JOHNNY SKIDMARKS
KISSING A FOOL
KNOCK OFF
LAND GIRLS, THE
LAND OF THE FREE
LANDLADY, THE
LAST ASSASSINS
LAST BIG THING, THE
LAST BREATH
LAST DAYS OF DISCO, THE
LAST LIVES
LAST SEDUCTION II, THE
LEADING MAN, THE
LETHAL WEAPON 4
LET'S KILL ALL THE LAWYERS
LET'S TALK ABOUT SEX
LEWIS & CLARK & GEORGE
LITTLE BOY BLUE
LITTLE VOICE
LIVE FLESH
LIVING IN PERIL
LIVING OUT LOUD
LOLITA
LOS LOCOS
LOST WORLD, THE
LOVE AND DEATH ON LONG ISLAND
LOVE IS THE DEVIL: STUDY FOR A PORTRAIT OF FRANCIS BACON
LOVE TO KILL
LOVE WALKED IN
LOVELIFE
LOVER GIRL
MAKER, THE
MARIE BAIE DES ANGES
MEAN GUNS
MEN
MEN WITH GUNS
MERCURY RISING
MERRY WAR, A
MILO
MISBEGOTTEN
MR. JEALOUSY
MONTANA
MOONDANCE
MURDER IN MIND
MY BROTHER'S WAR
NAKED LIES
NEGOTIATOR, THE
NEMESIS 4: CRY OF ANGELS
NEVADA
NEXT STOP, WONDERLAND
NIAGARA NIAGARA
NIGHT AND THE MOMENT, THE
NIGHT VISION
NIGHTWATCH
NIL BY MOUTH
NIRVANA
NO LOOKING BACK
NORTH SHORE FISH
OBJECT OF MY AFFECTION, THE
ONE TOUGH COP

ONE TRUE THING
ONLY THRILL, THE
OPERATION DELTA FORCE 2
OPPOSITE OF SEX, THE
OUT OF SIGHT
OUTSIDE OZONA
PALMETTO
PEACEKEEPER, THE
PECKER
PENTAGON WARS, THE
PERFECT MURDER, A
PERMANENT MIDNIGHT
PHANTASM: OBLIVION
PHANTOMS
PHOENIX
PHOTOGRAPHING FAIRIES
PI
PLAN B
PLAYERS CLUB, THE
PLAYING BY HEART
PLUMP FICTION
PRICE ABOVE RUBIES, A
PRIMARY COLORS
PRONTO
PROPHECY II, THE
PROPOSITION, THE
PSYCHO
RAGE, THE
RAT PACK, THE
REACH THE ROCK
REAL BLONDE, THE
REAL THING, THE
REBOUND: THE LEGEND OF EARL "THE GOAT" MANIGAULT
REDLINE
REPLACEMENT KILLERS, THE
RETROACTIVE
RETURN TO PARADISE
RETURN TO SAVAGE BEACH
RIDE
RINGMASTER
RIVER RED
RONIN
ROUNDERS
ROYAL DECEIT
RUNNING WOMAN, THE
RUSHMORE
SAND TRAP
SAVING PRIVATE RYAN
SAVIOR
SCARRED CITY
SENSELESS
SHAKESPEARE IN LOVE
SHOPPING FOR FANGS
SIEGE, THE
SIMPLE PLAN, A
SLAM
SLIDING DOORS
SLUMS OF BEVERLY HILLS
SNAKE EYES
SOLDIER
SOLDIER'S DAUGHTER NEVER CRIES, A
SONATINE
SOULER OPPOSITE, THE
SOUR GRAPES
SPACEJACKED
SPECIES II
SPREE, THE
STEEL SHARKS
STEPHEN KING'S THE NIGHT FLIER
STIR
STRAY BULLET
SUBSPECIES IV: BLOODSTORM
SUBSTITUTE 2: SCHOOL'S OUT, THE
SUICIDE KINGS
SUMMER FLING
TALES FROM A PARALLEL UNIVERSE: EATING PATTERN
TALES FROM A PARALLEL UNIVERSE: GIGA SHADOW
TALES FROM A PARALLEL UNIVERSE: SUPER NOVA
TALISMAN
TEN BENNY
TERMINAL JUSTICE
THEORY OF FLIGHT
THERE'S SOMETHING ABOUT MARY
THIEF, THE
THIN RED LINE, THE
THURSDAY
TOP OF THE WORLD
TRICKS
TRUCE, THE
TRUCKS
TWENTYFOURSEVEN
TWILIGHT
TWO GIRLS AND A GUY
UNCLE SAM
UNDER HEAVEN
UNDERTAKER'S WEDDING, THE
URBAN LEGEND
URBAN SAFARI
U.S. MARSHALS
VELVET GOLDMINE
VERY BAD THINGS
WATCHERS REBORN
WELCOME TO WOOP WOOP
WHATEVER
WHEN TRUMPETS FADE
WHITE RAVEN, THE
WHY DO FOOLS FALL IN LOVE?
WILD THINGS
WILDE
WOO
WOUNDED
YOUR FRIENDS & NEIGHBORS
ZERO EFFECT
ZERO WOMAN

NC-17

ORGAZMO
UGLY, THE

NR

ACT OF WAR
ADVENTURES OF MOWGLI
ALFRED HITCHCOCK: MASTER OF SUSPENSE
ALL THE RAGE
ALMOST PARTNERS
ARGUING THE WORLD
AYN RAND: A SENSE OF LIFE
BATMAN & MR. FREEZE: SUBZERO
BATMAN/SUPERMAN MOVIE, THE
BATTLE OF CHILE: THE STRUGGLE OF AN UNARMED PEOPLE—PART 2: THE COUP D'ETAT, THE
BEAUTY INVESTIGATOR
BEYOND, THE
BILLY'S HOLLYWOOD SCREEN KISS
BLACK LIGHT
BODYGUARD FROM BEIJING
BOYS IN LOVE 2
BRANDON TEENA STORY, THE
BREAKOUT
BROADWAY DAMAGE
BROTHER
BULLET ON A WIRE
CAN'T YOU HEAR THE WIND HOWL?: THE LIFE AND MUSIC OF ROBERT JOHNSON
CAPTIVE
CARLA'S SONG
CHAMBERMAID ON THE TITANIC, THE
CHARLIE HOBOKEN
CHILE, OBSTINATE MEMORY
CHOSEN ONE: LEGEND OF THE RAVEN, THE
CLASSIFIED X
COMEDY'S DIRTIEST DOZEN
COMRADES, ALMOST A LOVE STORY
COURTING COURTNEY
CRACKING UP
CROSSING FIELDS
CRUISE, THE
DAVID SEARCHING
DAY AT THE BEACH
DEAD WATERS
DEAR JESSE
DECAMPITATED
DEJA VU
DESTINY
DESTINY OF MARTY FINE, THE
DETOUR
DIDN'T DO IT FOR LOVE
DISENCHANTED, THE
DIVORCE IRANIAN STYLE
DRAGON BALL Z THE MOVIE: DEAD ZONE
DRAGON BALL Z THE MOVIE: THE TREE OF MIGHT
DRAGON BALL Z THE MOVIE: THE WORLD'S STRONGEST
DRAGONS FOREVER
DRESS, THE
EAST PALACE, WEST PALACE
EEL, THE
EL CHE: INVESTIGATING A LEGEND
ELIA KAZAN: A DIRECTOR'S JOURNEY
EMPEROR'S SHADOW, THE
ENCOUNTER OF THE SPOOKY KIND
ESCAPE, THE
FARM: ANGOLA, U.S.A., THE
FIREWORKS
FIRST LOVE, LAST RITES
FIXER, THE
FLINTSTONES: I YABBA-DABBA DOO!, THE
FORGOTTEN LIGHT
FORMER CHILD STAR
FREE TIBET
FROM A FAR COUNTRY
FROZEN
FULL SPEED
FUNNY GAMES
GADJO DILO
GENEALOGIES OF A CRIME
GENERAL CHAOS: UNCENSORED ANIMATION
GEORGE WALLACE
GO NOW
GODZILLA AND MOTHRA: THE BATTLE FOR EARTH
GODZILLA VS. KING GHIDORAH
GOLGO 13: QUEEN BEE
GONIN
HALLELUJAH!
HEALING BY KILLING
HEROES SHED NO TEARS
HOME BEFORE DARK
HONG KONG 1941
HORTON FOOTE'S ALONE
I MARRIED A STRANGE PERSON!
INSIDE/OUT
INSOMNIA
INVADER, THE
INVISIBLE DAD

JAMES ELLROY: DEMON DOG OF AMERICAN CRIME FICTION
JUNK FOOD
JUNK MAIL
KICK BOXER'S TEARS
KILLER ANGELS
KILLER CONDOM, THE
KILLING TIME
KINGDOM OF SHADOWS
KINGDOM, PART 2, THE
KRISTIN LAVRANSDATTER
KRZYSZTOF KIESLOWSKI: I'M SO-SO
KURT AND COURTNEY
LA SEPARATION
LAVENDER LIMELIGHT: LESBIANS IN FILM
LAWN DOGS
LENA'S DREAMS
LENNY BRUCE: SWEAR TO TELL THE TRUTH
LETTER FROM DEATH ROW, A
LIFE OF JESUS, THE
LIKE IT IS
LION KING II: SIMBA'S PRIDE, THE
LITTLE DIETER NEEDS TO FLY
LOLIDA 2000
LOU REED: ROCK AND ROLL HEART
MAGNIFICENT WARRIORS
MARIUS AND JEANNETTE
MARS
MENDEL
MERLIN
MIDAQ ALLEY
MIRROR, THE
MOBILE SUIT GUNDAM I
MOBILE SUIT GUNDAM II: SOLDIERS OF SORROW
MOBILE SUIT GUNDAM III: ENCOUNTERS IN SPACE
MODULATIONS: CINEMA FOR THE EAR
MONUMENT AVE.
MOON OVER BROADWAY
MOTHER AND SON
MY FIRST NAME IS MACEO
MY KNEES WERE JUMPING: REMEMBERING THE KINDERTRANSPORTS
NAKED ACTS
NEW ADVENTURES OF KIMBA THE WHITE LION, THE
NEXT STEP, THE
NO ORDINARY LOVE
NO WAY HOME
NOT IN THIS TOWN
NOTES FROM UNDERGROUND
OFF THE MENU: THE LAST DAYS OF CHASEN'S
OGRE, THE
OLIVER TWIST
OTHER SIDE OF SUNDAY, THE
OUT OF THE PAST
OYSTER AND THE WIND, THE
PARALLEL SONS
PARALYZING FEAR: THE STORY OF POLIO IN AMERICA, A
PASS, THE
PAUL MONETTE: THE BRINK OF SUMMER'S END
PEREIRA DECLARES
PLACE CALLED CHIAPAS, A
POCAHONTAS II: JOURNEY TO A NEW WORLD
POLTERGEIST REPORT: YUYU HAKUSHO
POST COITUM, ANIMAL TRISTE
PRINCE, THE
PRODIGAL SON, THE
QUICKSILVER HIGHWAY
RABID DOGS
RATCHET
RAZOR: THE SNARE, THE
RAZOR: WHO'S GOT THE GOLD?, THE
RED CHERRY
RED HAWK: WEAPON OF DEATH
REGENERATION
RETURN OF THE KING, THE
R.I.P. REST IN PIECES: A PORTRAIT OF JOE COLEMAN
ROYAL WARRIORS
RUN FOR COVER
SAFE MEN
SALTMEN OF TIBET, THE
SAME OLD SONG
SCOOBY-DOO ON ZOMBIE ISLAND
SEVENTH HEAVEN
SHAMPOO HORNS
SHAOLIN TEMPLE, THE
SHATTERED IMAGE
SILVER SCREEN: COLOR ME LAVENDER, THE
SIX O'CLOCK NEWS
SKIN & BONE
SLAMNATION
SLAYERS: THE MOTION PICTURE
SLEEPY EYES OF DEATH: FULL CIRCLE KILLING
SLEEPY EYES OF DEATH: SWORD OF ADVENTURE
SLEEPY EYES OF DEATH: SWORD OF SEDUCTION
SNOWBOUND
SOMEWHERE IN THE CITY
STEAM
STOLEN MOMENTS
STORY OF X, THE
SUE
SWINDLE, THE
TALK TO ME
TARANTELLA
TASTE OF CHERRY
TEKKEN: THE MOTION PICTURE
TIETA OF AGRESTE
TIMOTHY LEARY'S DEAD
TOKYO FIST
TOUCH OF EVIL: THE DIRECTOR'S CUT
TRACKED
TRANCEFORMER: A PORTRAIT OF LARS VON TRIER
TREKKIES
TWO FOR TEXAS
UN AIR DE FAMILLE
UNDER THE SKIN
UNMADE BEDS
UNVEILING, THE
VILLAGE OF DREAMS
VIOLET'S VISIT
VOYAGE TO THE BEGINNING OF THE WORLD
WAR ZONE
WEST NEW YORK
WESTERN
WHEN PIGS FLY
WHO IS HENRY JAGLOM?
WHO THE HELL IS JULIETTE?
WRATH OF THE NINJA: THE YOTODEN MOVIE
ZAKIR AND HIS FRIENDS

FILMS BY PARENTAL RECOMMENDATION (PR)

AA – good for children; A – acceptable for children;
C – cautionary, some scenes may be objectionable for children; O – objectionable for children

AA

ADVENTURES OF MOWGLI
ALL DOGS CHRISTMAS CAROL, AN
ALMOST PARTNERS
BARNEY'S GREAT ADVENTURE—THE MOVIE
BATMAN & MR. FREEZE: SUBZERO
BILLBOARD DAD
BORROWERS, THE
BRAVE LITTLE TOASTER GOES TO MARS, THE
BUSTER & CHAUNCEY'S SILENT NIGHT
CLOCKMAKER
DENNIS THE MENACE STRIKES AGAIN
ERNEST IN THE ARMY
FERNGULLY 2: THE MAGICAL RESCUE
FLINTSTONES: I YABBA-DABBA DOO!, THE
KIKI'S DELIVERY SERVICE
LION KING II: SIMBA'S PRIDE, THE
MADELINE
MULAN
NAPOLEON
NEW ADVENTURES OF KIMBA THE WHITE LION, THE
PARENT TRAP, THE
POCAHONTAS II: JOURNEY TO A NEW WORLD
QUEST FOR CAMELOT
RACE TO SAVE 100 YEARS, THE
RAT'S TALE, A
REAL HOWARD SPITZ, THE
RICHIE RICH'S CHRISTMAS WISH
RUDOLPH THE RED-NOSED REINDEER: THE MOVIE
RUGRATS MOVIE, THE
SCOOBY-DOO ON ZOMBIE ISLAND
SWAN PRINCESS III: AND THE MYSTERY OF THE ENCHANTED TREASURE, THE

A

AIR BUD: GOLDEN RECEIVER
ALONE IN THE WOODS
ANTZ
ARGUING THE WORLD
BATMAN/SUPERMAN MOVIE, THE
BLUES BROTHERS 2000
BOYS WILL BE BOYS
BREAKOUT
BUG'S LIFE, A
CASPER MEETS WENDY
CHILE, OBSTINATE MEMORY
CLASSIFIED X
DANCER, TEXAS POP. 81
DESTINY
DR. DOLITTLE
DOWN IN THE DELTA
DRAGON BALL Z THE MOVIE: DEAD ZONE
DRAGON BALL Z THE MOVIE: THE TREE OF MIGHT
DRAGON BALL Z THE MOVIE: THE WORLD'S STRONGEST
EBENEZER
EVER AFTER
GODZILLA AND MOTHRA: THE BATTLE FOR EARTH
GODZILLA VS. KING GHIDORAH
HANDS ON A HARDBODY
HERCULES AND XENA THE ANIMATED MOVIE: THE BATTLE FOR MOUNT OLYMPUS
HOPE FLOATS
HORTON FOOTE'S ALONE
HUMAN BOMB
I'LL BE HOME FOR CHRISTMAS
IN HIS FATHER'S SHOES
INVISIBLE DAD
INVISIBLE MOM
JACK FROST
JACK LONDON'S THE CALL OF THE WILD: DOG OF THE YUKON
JOEY
JOHNNY MYSTO BOY WIZARD
JUNGLE BOOK: MOWGLI'S STORY, THE
KID IN ALADDIN'S PALACE, A
KRAA! THE SEA MONSTER
LITTLE BIGFOOT 2: THE JOURNEY HOME
LITTLE GHOST
LOST IN SPACE
LOUISA MAY ALCOTT'S LITTLE MEN
MAJOR LEAGUE: BACK TO THE MINORS
MERLIN
MIDAS TOUCH, THE
MIGHTY JOE YOUNG
MIGHTY KONG, THE
MIRROR, THE
MOBILE SUIT GUNDAM I
MOBILE SUIT GUNDAM II: SOLDIERS OF SORROW
MOBILE SUIT GUNDAM III: ENCOUNTERS IN SPACE
MY FIRST NAME IS MACEO
MY GIANT
OFF THE MENU: THE LAST DAYS OF CHASEN'S
OLIVER TWIST
PARALYZING FEAR: THE STORY OF POLIO IN AMERICA, A
PAULIE
POLTERGEIST REPORT: YUYU HAKUSHO
PRINCE OF EGYPT, THE
RED HAWK: WEAPON OF DEATH
RESCUERS: STORIES OF COURAGE—TWO COUPLES
RESCUERS: STORIES OF COURAGE—TWO WOMEN
RETURN OF THE KING, THE
RIGHT CONNECTIONS, THE
RUSTY: THE GREAT RESCUE
SALTMEN OF TIBET, THE
SECRET KINGDOM, THE
SECRET OF NIMH 2: TIMMY TO THE RESCUE, THE
SHADRACH
SHRUNKEN CITY, THE
SLAPPY AND THE STINKERS
SLAYERS: THE MOTION PICTURE
SMALL SOLDIERS
STAR KID
TARZAN AND THE LOST CITY
3 NINJAS: HIGH NOON AT MEGA MOUNTAIN
TRUMAN SHOW, THE
VOYAGE TO THE BEGINNING OF THE WORLD
WALKING THUNDER
WHEN PIGS FLY
WIDE AWAKE
YOU'VE GOT MAIL
ZAKIR AND HIS FRIENDS

C

ACT OF WAR
AFFLICTION
ALARMIST, THE
ALFRED HITCHCOCK: MASTER OF SUSPENSE
ALMOST HEROES
ALWAYS OUTNUMBERED
APT PUPIL
ARMAGEDDON
ARMOUR OF GOD
ARTEMISIA
ATOMIC DOG
AVENGERS, THE
AYN RAND: A SENSE OF LIFE
BABE: PIG IN THE CITY
BAD MANNERS
BARRIERS
BASEKETBALL
BATTLE OF CHILE: THE STRUGGLE OF AN UNARMED PEOPLE—PART 2: THE COUP D'ETAT, THE
BEAUTY INVESTIGATOR
BELOVED
BEST MAN, THE
BEST OF THE BEST: WITHOUT WARNING
BEYOND SILENCE
BIG HIT, THE
BIG LEBOWSKI, THE
BIG ONE, THE
BLACK DOG
BLACK LIGHT
BLACKJACK
BLADE
BODYGUARD FROM BEIJING
BRANDON TEENA STORY, THE
BREAK, THE
BROADWAY DAMAGE
BROTHER
BRYLCREEM BOYS, THE
BUFFALO '66
BULLET ON A WIRE
BULWORTH
CALL TO REMEMBER, A
CAN'T HARDLY WAIT
CAN'T YOU HEAR THE WIND HOWL?: THE LIFE AND MUSIC OF ROBERT JOHNSON
CAPTIVE

CARLA'S SONG
CATHERINE'S GROVE
CENTRAL STATION
CHAIRMAN OF THE BOARD
CHAMBERMAID ON THE TITANIC, THE
CHARACTER
CHARLIE HOBOKEN
CHICAGO CAB
CHINESE BOX, THE
CITY OF ANGELS
CIVIL ACTION, A
CLAY PIGEONS
CLOCKWATCHERS
COLONY, THE
COMEDY'S DIRTIEST DOZEN
COMRADES, ALMOST A LOVE STORY
CON, THE
COURTING COURTNEY
CRACKING UP
CROSSING FIELDS
CRUISE, THE
DANCE WITH ME
DANCING AT LUGHNASA
DARK CITY
DAY AT THE BEACH
DEAR JESSE
DECLINE OF WESTERN CIVILIZATION PART III, THE
DEEP IMPACT
DEFENDERS: PAYBACK, THE
DEJA VU
DESPERATE MEASURES
DESTINY OF MARTY FINE, THE
DETONATOR
DETOUR
DIGGING TO CHINA
DIRTY LAUNDRY
DIRTY WORK
DISAPPEARANCE OF KEVIN JOHNSON, THE
DISENCHANTED, THE
DISTURBING BEHAVIOR
DIVORCE IRANIAN STYLE
DON KING: ONLY IN AMERICA
DRAGONS FOREVER
DREAM FOR AN INSOMNIAC
DRESS, THE
EAST PALACE, WEST PALACE
EDEN
EEL, THE
EL CHE: INVESTIGATING A LEGEND
ELIA KAZAN: A DIRECTOR'S JOURNEY
ELIZABETH
ELMORE LEONARD'S GOLD COAST
ELVIS MEETS NIXON
EMPEROR'S SHADOW, THE
ENCOUNTER OF THE SPOOKY KIND
ENEMY
ENEMY OF THE STATE
FACE DOWN
FALLEN ANGELS
FARM: ANGOLA, U.S.A., THE
FIRELIGHT
FIRESTORM
FIREWORKS
FIXER, THE
FORGOTTEN LIGHT
FORMER CHILD STAR
FREE TIBET
FRENCH EXIT
FRIEND OF THE DECEASED, A
FROM A FAR COUNTRY
FROZEN
FULL SPEED
FULL TILT BOOGIE

GADJO DILO
GENEALOGIES OF A CRIME
GEORGE WALLACE
GINGERBREAD MAN, THE
GIRLS IN PRISON
GODS AND MONSTERS
GODSON, THE
GODZILLA
GONIN
GOVERNESS, THE
GREAT EXPECTATIONS
HALF BAKED
HALLOWEEN H20: TWENTY YEARS LATER
HANGING GARDEN, THE
HARD CORE LOGO
HARD RAIN
HAV PLENTY
HE GOT GAME
HEALING BY KILLING
HEAVEN'S BURNING
HENRY FOOL
HEROES SHED NO TEARS
HIGH ART
HIJACKING HOLLYWOOD
HILARY AND JACKIE
HI-LIFE
HI-LO COUNTRY, THE
HIT ME
HOLLYWOOD CONFIDENTIAL
HOLY MAN
HOME BEFORE DARK
HOME FRIES
HOMEGROWN
HONG KONG 1941
HORSE WHISPERER, THE
HOSTILE INTENT
HOSTILE WATERS
HOT BLOODED
HOW STELLA GOT HER GROOVE BACK
HUNTED, THE
HUSH
I LOVE YOU, DON'T TOUCH ME!
I STILL KNOW WHAT YOU DID LAST SUMMER
I THINK I DO
I WENT DOWN
IMPOSTORS, THE
IN GOD'S HANDS
INDISCREET
INFORMANT, THE
INSIDE/OUT
INSOMNIA
JACK HIGGINS' ON DANGEROUS GROUND
JACK HIGGINS' THUNDER POINT
JACK HIGGINS' MIDNIGHT MAN
JACK HIGGINS' THE WINDSOR PROTOCOL
JAMES ELLROY: DEMON DOG OF AMERICAN CRIME FICTION
JANE AUSTEN'S MAFIA!
JERUSALEM
JOHNNY SKIDMARKS
JUNK MAIL
KICK BOXER'S TEARS
KILLER ANGELS
KILLING TIME
KINGDOM OF SHADOWS
KINGDOM, PART 2, THE
KISSING A FOOL
KNOCK OFF
KRIPPENDORF'S TRIBE
KRISTIN LAVRANSDATTER
KRZYSZTOF KIESLOWSKI: I'M SO-SO
KURT AND COURTNEY
LA SEPARATION

LAND GIRLS, THE
LANDLADY, THE
LAST ASSASSINS
LAST BIG THING, THE
LAST DAYS OF DISCO, THE
LAST LIVES
LAVENDER LIMELIGHT: LESBIANS IN FILM
LENA'S DREAMS
LES MISERABLES
LETHAL WEAPON 4
LET'S KILL ALL THE LAWYERS
LEWIS & CLARK & GEORGE
LIFE IS BEAUTIFUL
LITTLE DIETER NEEDS TO FLY
LITTLE VOICE
LIVE FLESH
LIVING OUT LOUD
LOST WORLD, THE
LOU REED: ROCK AND ROLL HEART
LOVE AND DEATH ON LONG ISLAND
LOVE WALKED IN
LOVELIFE
MAGNIFICENT WARRIORS
MAKER, THE
MAN IN THE IRON MASK, THE
MARIE BAIE DES ANGES
MARIUS AND JEANNETTE
MARS
MASK OF ZORRO, THE
MEAN GUNS
MEET JOE BLACK
MEET THE DEEDLES
MEN WITH GUNS
MENDEL
MERCURY RISING
MERRY WAR, A
MIDAQ ALLEY
MIGHTY, THE
MISBEGOTTEN
MR. JEALOUSY
MR. NICE GUY
MODULATIONS: CINEMA FOR THE EAR
MONTANA
MONUMENT AVE.
MOON OVER BROADWAY
MOONDANCE
MOTHER AND SON
MRS. DALLOWAY
MURDER IN MIND
MUSIC FROM ANOTHER ROOM
MY BROTHER'S WAR
MY KNEES WERE JUMPING: REMEMBERING THE KINDERTRANSPORTS
MY VERY BEST FRIEND
NAKED LIES
NEGOTIATOR, THE
NEIL SIMON'S THE ODD COUPLE II
NEWTON BOYS, THE
NEXT STOP, WONDERLAND
NIAGARA NIAGARA
NIGHT AT THE ROXBURY, A
NIGHTWATCH
NO LOOKING BACK
NO WAY HOME
NORTH SHORE FISH
NOT IN THIS TOWN
OBJECT OF MY AFFECTION, THE
ONE TRUE THING
ONLY THRILL, THE
OPERATION DELTA FORCE 2
OPPOSITE OF SEX, THE
OTHER SIDE OF SUNDAY, THE
OUT OF SIGHT

OUT OF THE PAST
OUTSIDE OZONA
OVERNIGHT DELIVERY
OYSTER AND THE WIND, THE
PALMETTO
PARALLEL SONS
PASSION IN THE DESERT
PATCH ADAMS
PEACEKEEPER, THE
PECKER
PENTAGON WARS, THE
PEREIRA DECLARES
PERFECT MURDER, A
PI
PLACE CALLED CHIAPAS, A
PLAN B
PLAYING BY HEART
PLEASANTVILLE
PLUMP FICTION
POLISH WEDDING
POST COITUM, ANIMAL TRISTE
PRACTICAL MAGIC
PRICE ABOVE RUBIES, A
PRIMARY COLORS
PRINCE VALIANT
PRINCE, THE
PRODIGAL SON, THE
PRONTO
PROPOSITION, THE
PSYCHO
QUICKSILVER HIGHWAY
RAT PACK, THE
REACH THE ROCK
REAL BLONDE, THE
REAL THING, THE
REDLINE
REPLACEMENT KILLERS, THE
RETROACTIVE
RIDE
RIVER RED
RONIN
ROUNDERS
ROYAL DECEIT
ROYAL WARRIORS
RUN FOR COVER
RUSH HOUR
RUSHMORE
SAFE MEN
SAME OLD SONG
SAND TRAP
SCARRED CITY
SEVENTH HEAVEN
SHAKESPEARE IN LOVE
SHAOLIN TEMPLE, THE
SHATTERED IMAGE
SHOOTING FISH
SHOPPING FOR FANGS
SIEGE, THE
SILVER SCREEN: COLOR ME LAVENDER, THE
SIMON BIRCH
SIN AND REDEMPTION
SIX DAYS, SEVEN NIGHTS
SIX O'CLOCK NEWS
SIX-STRING SAMURAI
SLAM
SLAMNATION
SLIDING DOORS
SLUMS OF BEVERLY HILLS
SMOKE SIGNALS
SNAKE EYES
SNOWBOUND
SOLDIER
SOLDIER'S DAUGHTER NEVER CRIES, A
SONATINE
SOULER OPPOSITE, THE
SPACEJACKED
SPANISH PRISONER, THE
SPHERE
SPICE WORLD
STAR TREK: INSURRECTION
STEAM
STEEL SHARKS
STEPHEN KING'S THE NIGHT FLIER
STEPMOM
STILL BREATHING
STIR
STOLEN MOMENTS
STOREFRONT HITCHCOCK
SUB DOWN
SUBSTITUTE 2: SCHOOL'S OUT, THE
SUICIDE KINGS
SUMMER FLING
SWEPT FROM THE SEA
SWINDLE, THE
TALES FROM A PARALLEL UNIVERSE: GIGA SHADOW
TALES FROM A PARALLEL UNIVERSE: SUPER NOVA
TALK OF ANGELS
TARANTELLA
TASTE OF CHERRY
TEKKEN: THE MOTION PICTURE
TEN BENNY
TERMINAL JUSTICE
THEORY OF FLIGHT
THIEF, THE
THIN RED LINE, THE
TIMOTHY LEARY'S DEAD
TOP OF THE WORLD
TOUCH OF EVIL: THE DIRECTOR'S CUT
TRACKED
TRANCEFORMER: A PORTRAIT OF LARS VON TRIER
TREKKIES
TRICKS
TRUCE, THE
12 ANGRY MEN
TWENTYFOURSEVEN
TWILIGHT
TWISTED
TWO FOR TEXAS
UN AIR DE FAMILLE
UNDER HEAVEN
UNDERTAKER'S WEDDING, THE
URBAN SAFARI
U.S. MARSHALS
VELVET GOLDMINE
VILLAGE OF DREAMS
VIOLET'S VISIT
WAKING NED DEVINE
WATERBOY, THE
WEDDING SINGER, THE
WEST NEW YORK
WHAT DREAMS MAY COME
WHATEVER
WHEN DANGER FOLLOWS YOU HOME
WHEN I CLOSE MY EYES
WHEN TIME EXPIRES
WHO IS HENRY JAGLOM?
WHO THE HELL IS JULIETTE?
WHY DO FOOLS FALL IN LOVE?
WILD MAN BLUES
WILDE
WITHOUT LIMITS
WOO
WOUNDED
WRATH OF THE NINJA: THE YOTODEN MOVIE
WRONGFULLY ACCUSED
X-FILES, THE
YOUNG HERCULES
ZERO EFFECT

O

ABERRATION
ALL THE RAGE
AMERICAN HISTORY X
ANOTHER DAY IN PARADISE
ASYLUM
BELLY
BEYOND, THE
BILLY'S HOLLYWOOD SCREEN KISS
BLACK THUNDER
BLEEDERS
BODY COUNT
BODY COUNT
BONE DADDY
BOOGIE BOY
BOYS IN LOVE 2
BRAM STOKER'S SHADOWBUILDER
BRAM STOKER'S THE MUMMY
BREAST MEN
BRIDE OF CHUCKY
BRIGHT SHINING LIE, A
BURN HOLLYWOOD BURN
BUTCHER BOY, THE
CAUGHT UP
CELEBRATION, THE
CELEBRITY
CHILDREN OF THE CORN V: FIELD OF TERROR
CHOSEN ONE: LEGEND OF THE RAVEN, THE
CLUB VAMPIRE
COUSIN BETTE
CUBE
CURSE OF THE PUPPET MASTER
DAD SAVAGE
DANGEROUS BEAUTY
DAVID SEARCHING
DAY OF THE BEAST, THE
DEAD END
DEAD MAN ON CAMPUS
DEAD WATERS
DECAMPITATED
DECEIVER
DEE SNIDER'S STRANGELAND
DEEP RISING
DIARY OF A SERIAL KILLER
DIDN'T DO IT FOR LOVE
DOGWATCH
DOUBLE EDGE
EIGHTEENTH ANGEL, THE
ESCAPE, THE
FACE THE EVIL
FACULTY, THE
FALLEN
FALLING FIRE
FATAL PURSUIT
FEAR AND LOATHING IN LAS VEGAS
54
FIRST LOVE, LAST RITES
FUNNY GAMES
FUTURE FEAR
GENERAL CHAOS: UNCENSORED ANIMATION
GENERAL, THE
GIA
GO NOW
GOLGO 13: QUEEN BEE

GUN, A CAR, AND A BLONDE, A
HALLELUJAH!
HAPPINESS
HENRY: PORTRAIT OF A SERIAL KILLER PART 2
HURLYBURLY
HURRICANE STREETS
I GOT THE HOOK UP
I MARRIED A STRANGE PERSON!
ILLTOWN
INCOGNITO
INHERITORS, THE
INNOCENT SLEEP, THE
INTERLOCKED: THRILLED TO DEATH
INVADER, THE
JOHN CARPENTER'S VAMPIRES
JUNK FOOD
KILLER CONDOM, THE
LAND OF THE FREE
LAST BREATH
LAST SEDUCTION II, THE
LAWN DOGS
LEADING MAN, THE
LENNY BRUCE: SWEAR TO TELL THE TRUTH
LET'S TALK ABOUT SEX
LETTER FROM DEATH ROW, A
LIFE OF JESUS, THE
LIKE IT IS
LITTLE BOY BLUE
LIVING IN PERIL
LOLIDA 2000
LOLITA
LOS LOCOS
LOVE IS THE DEVIL: STUDY FOR A PORTRAIT OF FRANCIS BACON
LOVE TO KILL
LOVER GIRL
MEN
MILO
NAKED ACTS
NEMESIS 4: CRY OF ANGELS
NEVADA
NEXT STEP, THE
NIGHT AND THE MOMENT, THE
NIGHT VISION
NIL BY MOUTH
NIRVANA
NO ORDINARY LOVE
NOTES FROM UNDERGROUND
OGRE, THE
ONE TOUGH COP
ORGAZMO
PASS, THE
PAUL MONETTE: THE BRINK OF SUMMER'S END
PERMANENT MIDNIGHT
PHANTASM: OBLIVION
PHANTOMS
PHOENIX
PHOTOGRAPHING FAIRIES
PLAYERS CLUB, THE
PROPHECY II, THE
RABID DOGS
RAGE, THE
RATCHET
RAZOR: THE SNARE, THE
RAZOR: WHO'S GOT THE GOLD?, THE
REBOUND: THE LEGEND OF EARL "THE GOAT" MANIGAULT
RED CHERRY
REGENERATION
RETURN TO PARADISE
RETURN TO SAVAGE BEACH
RINGMASTER
R.I.P. REST IN PIECES: A PORTRAIT OF JOE COLEMAN
RUNNING WOMAN, THE
SAVING PRIVATE RYAN
SAVIOR
SENSELESS
SHAMPOO HORNS
SIMPLE PLAN, A
SKIN & BONE
SLEEPY EYES OF DEATH: FULL CIRCLE KILLING
SLEEPY EYES OF DEATH: SWORD OF ADVENTURE
SLEEPY EYES OF DEATH: SWORD OF SEDUCTION
SOMEWHERE IN THE CITY
SOUR GRAPES
SPECIES II
SPREE, THE
STORY OF X, THE
STRAY BULLET
SUBSPECIES IV: BLOODSTORM
SUE
TALES FROM A PARALLEL UNIVERSE: EATING PATTERN
TALISMAN
TALK TO ME
THERE'S SOMETHING ABOUT MARY
THURSDAY
TIETA OF AGRESTE
TOKYO FIST
TRUCKS
TWO GIRLS AND A GUY
UGLY, THE
UNCLE SAM
UNDER THE SKIN
UNMADE BEDS
UNVEILING, THE
URBAN LEGEND
VERY BAD THINGS
WAR ZONE
WATCHERS REBORN
WELCOME TO WOOP WOOP
WESTERN
WHEN TRUMPETS FADE
WHITE RAVEN, THE
WILD THINGS
YOUR FRIENDS & NEIGHBORS
ZERO WOMAN

NAME INDEX

Individuals included in the cast or credit sections of the film reviews in this volume are listed below. Names are arranged alphabetically by function as follows:

- Actors
- Animators
- Art Directors
- Associate Producers
- Casting
- Choreographers
- Cinematographers
- Co-producers
- Costumes
- Directors
- Editors
- Executive Producers
- Makeup/ FX makeup
- Music Composers
- Producers
- Production Designers
- Screenwriters
- Set Decorators
- Sound
- Source Authors
- Special Effects
- Stunts

ACTORS

Aeson, King
YOUNG HERCULES
Affif, Ron
CELEBRITY
Affleck, Ben
ARMAGEDDON
PHANTOMS
SHAKESPEARE IN LOVE
Afrika Bambaataa
MODULATIONS: CINEMA FOR THE EAR
Agie, Awaovieyi
I'LL BE HOME FOR CHRISTMAS
Agis, Gaby
LOVE IS THE DEVIL: STUDY FOR A PORTRAIT OF FRANCIS BACON
Agius, Keith
MR. NICE GUY
Aguilar, George
ALMOST HEROES
PHOENIX
Agung, Suar
ZAKIR AND HIS FRIENDS
Ahern, Sport
THERE'S SOMETHING ABOUT MARY
Ahmed, Ahmed
STEEL SHARKS
Ahmed, Ali
JUNK FOOD
Ahn, Peggy
SHOPPING FOR FANGS
Ahray, Sonsee
LAST DAYS OF DISCO, THE
Ahren, Barbara-Magdalena
SWINDLE, THE
Ai, Michiko
SLEEPY EYES OF DEATH: SWORD OF SEDUCTION
Aibel, Matthew Savage
OBJECT OF MY AFFECTION, THE
Aiello, Ricky
HOLLYWOOD CONFIDENTIAL
Aikawa, Keiko
RAZOR: THE SNARE, THE
Aikawa, Sho
EEL, THE
Aiken, Liam
HENRY FOOL
MONTANA
OBJECT OF MY AFFECTION, THE
STEPMOM
Aiken, Loclann
SAVING PRIVATE RYAN
Ainslie, Jean
LOVE AND DEATH ON LONG ISLAND
WILDE
Aird, Holly
THEORY OF FLIGHT
Ajami, Karl
MR. NICE GUY
Akbar, Rasheed Ali
SECRET KINGDOM, THE
Akerman, Jeremy
LOVE AND DEATH ON LONG ISLAND
Akerstream, Marc
WOUNDED
Akey, William
PARENT TRAP, THE
Akhurst, Lucy
LAND GIRLS, THE
Akin, Philip
DOWN IN THE DELTA
ONE TOUGH COP
WOO
Akwri, Noella
HIJACKING HOLLYWOOD
Al-Hamd, Ismael
PASSION IN THE DESERT
Alai, Adin
PECKER
Alan, Chris
WEDDING SINGER, THE
Alan, Devon
SIMON BIRCH
Alan, Sayda
CIVIL ACTION, A
Alaskey, Joe
RUGRATS MOVIE, THE
Alazraqui, Carlos
GODSON, THE
Alban, Allisa
HOPE FLOATS
Alban, Carlo
HI-LIFE
HURRICANE STREETS
Albe, Paul
HENRY FOOL
Albert, Shari
NO LOOKING BACK
WHY DO FOOLS FALL IN LOVE?
Alberti, Gigio
NIRVANA
Alborough, Roger
VELVET GOLDMINE
Albright, Ariauna
CURSE OF THE PUPPET MASTER
Albright, Gerald
LIVING OUT LOUD
Alcalde, Laura
UNCLE SAM
Alcazar, Damian
MEN WITH GUNS
Alcott, Todd
CRACKING UP
Alcover, Catherine
SOLDIER'S DAUGHTER NEVER CRIES, A
Alda, Alan
OBJECT OF MY AFFECTION, THE
Alda, Rutanya
SOULER OPPOSITE, THE
Alden, Norman
PATCH ADAMS
Alderson, Jude
LIKE IT IS
Aldredge, Tom
LAWN DOGS
ROUNDERS
Aldrin, Edwin A. "Buzz"
TREKKIES
Alec Empire
MODULATIONS: CINEMA FOR THE EAR
Alenandra, Luz
NEXT STOP, WONDERLAND
Aleong, Aki
LEWIS & CLARK & GEORGE
Alessi, Joseph
JACK HIGGINS' ON DANGEROUS GROUND
Alexander, Barbara
MERCURY RISING
Alexander, Carol
TRICKS
Alexander, Caroline
LOLIDA 2000
Alexander, Dorothea
MERRY WAR, A
Alexander, Erika
54
Alexander, Harri
MERRY WAR, A
Alexander, John
MIGHTY JOE YOUNG
Alexander, Kathryn
FEAR AND LOATHING IN LAS VEGAS
Alexander, Khandi
THERE'S SOMETHING ABOUT MARY
Alexander, Lee
DAVID SEARCHING
Alexander, Terry
HURRICANE STREETS
Alexenburg, Marnie
THERE'S SOMETHING ABOUT MARY
Alexis, Kim
HOLY MAN
Alfonsi, Claudio
LIFE IS BEAUTIFUL
Alfonsi, Lydia
LIFE IS BEAUTIFUL
Alfredson, Hans
JERUSALEM
Ali, Mohammed
PASSION IN THE DESERT
Alia, Phyllis
WATERBOY, THE
WEDDING SINGER, THE
Alianak, Hrant
DIRTY WORK
Alice, Mary
DOWN IN THE DELTA
Alig, Michael
SHAMPOO HORNS
Aling, Marilka
KNOCK OFF
Alkon, Sheldon
POLISH WEDDING
Allan, Bradley
MR. NICE GUY
Allan, Danielle
INCOGNITO
Allar, Daniel
HENRY: PORTRAIT OF A SERIAL KILLER PART 2
Allard, Michael J.
PARALLEL SONS
Allaux, Berangere
INSIDE/OUT
Allen, Alfie
ELIZABETH
Allen, Beth
UGLY, THE
Allen, Deborah
REAL HOWARD SPITZ, THE
Allen, Doug
ONE TRUE THING
Allen, Elizabeth
BABE: PIG IN THE CITY
Allen, James
PATCH ADAMS
Allen, Joan
PLEASANTVILLE
Allen, Joe
ARMAGEDDON
Allen, Kevin
SPICE WORLD
Allen, Lily
ELIZABETH
Allen, Lisa-Erin
OBJECT OF MY AFFECTION, THE
Allen, Mark G.
RAGE, THE
Allen, Nancy
LAST ASSASSINS
OUT OF SIGHT
PASS, THE
Allen, Naomi Lee
IN HIS FATHER'S SHOES
Allen, Penny
THIN RED LINE, THE
Allen, Ray
HE GOT GAME
Allen, Robert
FEAR AND LOATHING IN LAS VEGAS
Allen, Sage
ARMAGEDDON

Allen, Scott
OUT OF SIGHT
Allen, Steve
LENNY BRUCE: SWEAR TO TELL THE TRUTH
OFF THE MENU: THE LAST DAYS OF CHASEN'S
Allen, Tanya
REGENERATION
Allen, Terra
RAGE, THE
Allen, Tim
COMEDY'S DIRTIEST DOZEN
Allen, Tyress
RAT PACK, THE
12 ANGRY MEN
Allen, Woody
ANTZ
IMPOSTORS, THE
WILD MAN BLUES
Allende, Fernando
NAKED LIES
Allendorfer, John
ENEMY OF THE STATE
Allessi, Raquel
UNCLE SAM
Alley, Kirstie
NEVADA
Alleyne, Ivor
NAKED ACTS
Allison, Cynthia
MIGHTY JOE YOUNG
Allison, Frankie Jai
WHY DO FOOLS FALL IN LOVE?
Allison, Stayce
BRAM STOKER'S THE MUMMY
Allodi, James
REBOUND: THE LEGEND OF EARL "THE GOAT" MANIGAULT
Allsberry, David
BABE: PIG IN THE CITY
Almario, Justo
LIVING OUT LOUD
Almeida, Al
DESTINY OF MARTY FINE, THE
Alonso, Daniel
HOMEGROWN
Alonso, Maria Conchita
CATHERINE'S GROVE
Alouane, Tressana
U.S. MARSHALS
Alpert, Arnie
ENEMY OF THE STATE
Alpert, Gregory H.
GINGERBREAD MAN, THE
OUT OF SIGHT
Alpert, Richard
TIMOTHY LEARY'S DEAD
Altamirano, Pedro
MASK OF ZORRO, THE
Altaras, Adrian
KILLER CONDOM, THE
Alten, Iris
PERFECT MURDER, A
Alter, Lori
ONE TOUGH COP
Altman, Allen
PEACEKEEPER, THE
Altman, Bruce
OBJECT OF MY AFFECTION, THE
Alvarado, Angela
HOLLYWOOD CONFIDENTIAL
Alvarado, Robert F.
STEPMOM
Alvarado, Trini
PAULIE
Alvarez, George
INTERLOCKED: THRILLED TO DEATH
Alvarez, Roberto
PENTAGON WARS, THE
Alvim, Anna
ONE TRUE THING
Alvin, Martin
GREAT EXPECTATIONS
Amado, Jorge
TIETA OF AGRESTE
Amalric, Mathieu
GENEALOGIES OF A CRIME
Amandes, Tom
BILLBOARD DAD
Amber
54
Ambercrombie, Ian
JOHNNY MYSTO BOY WIZARD
Ambrose, Lauren
CAN'T HARDLY WAIT
Ambrose, Tangie
I GOT THE HOOK UP
RINGMASTER
Ambrozy, Bill
PERFECT MURDER, A
Amendola, Tony
MASK OF ZORRO, THE
Ames, Betsy
PECKER
Ames, Kenner
IN HIS FATHER'S SHOES
Ami, Shoshana
HENRY FOOL
Amick, Madchen
FRENCH EXIT
HUNTED, THE
WOUNDED
Amico, Robert
COLONY, THE
Amir, Sean Flynn
SIMON BIRCH
Amis, Suzy
FIRESTORM
Amodei, Joe
ALMOST PARTNERS
Amos, Diane
PATCH ADAMS
Amos, Emma
FIRELIGHT
Amos, John
PLAYERS CLUB, THE
Amos, Keith
WHY DO FOOLS FALL IN LOVE?
Amsing, Sean
DISTURBING BEHAVIOR
Amsterdam, Lisa
BILLBOARD DAD
Ana, Doru
JOHNNY MYSTO BOY WIZARD
Ananishnov, Alexei
MOTHER AND SON
Anawalt, Bruce
SOLDIER'S DAUGHTER NEVER CRIES, A
Anawalt, Loretta
SOLDIER'S DAUGHTER NEVER CRIES, A
Ancira, Yvette
TWO FOR TEXAS
Anders, Ed
OUTSIDE OZONA
Anderson, Bob
LAST ASSASSINS
Anderson, Brenda
NOT IN THIS TOWN
Anderson, Carol
DOWN IN THE DELTA
Anderson, Clark
LIVING OUT LOUD
Anderson, Daryl
I GOT THE HOOK UP
Anderson, Devon
SPICE WORLD
Anderson, Eric
RUSHMORE
Anderson, Erich
NIGHTWATCH
Anderson, Georgine
FROM A FAR COUNTRY
Anderson, Gillian
CHICAGO CAB
MIGHTY, THE
PLAYING BY HEART
X-FILES, THE
Anderson III, Haskell Vaughn
CIVIL ACTION, A
Anderson, Isabelle
GREAT EXPECTATIONS
Anderson, Jason
AIR BUD: GOLDEN RECEIVER
Anderson, Julie
HENRY FOOL
Anderson, Keith
INCOGNITO
Anderson, Kevin
FIRELIGHT
Anderson, Larry
STAR TREK: INSURRECTION
Anderson, Laurie
LOU REED: ROCK AND ROLL HEART
RUGRATS MOVIE, THE
Anderson, Loni
NIGHT AT THE ROXBURY, A
3 NINJAS: HIGH NOON AT MEGA MOUNTAIN
Anderson, Matthew R.
STEEL SHARKS
Anderson, Michael J.
CLUB VAMPIRE
Anderson, Myles
SHOOTING FISH
Anderson, Nathan
GODZILLA
Anderson, Richard
BREAKOUT
Anderson, Sam
PENTAGON WARS, THE
PERMANENT MIDNIGHT
Anderson, Scott
ALMOST HEROES
Anderson, Sherry
CRACKING UP
Anderson, Stanley
ARMAGEDDON
Anderson, Steve
CLAY PIGEONS
Anderson, Todd
JOHN CARPENTER'S VAMPIRES
Anderson-Gunter, Jeffrey
SOULER OPPOSITE, THE
Andino, Carmen
OBJECT OF MY AFFECTION, THE
Andolini, Mike
ENEMY OF THE STATE
Andon, Kurt
DON KING: ONLY IN AMERICA
Andrade, Carlos
SIX DAYS, SEVEN NIGHTS
Andrade, Roberto
CENTRAL STATION
Andre, Jill
MILO
Andre, Robert
INVADER, THE
Andrea, Darren
UNDERTAKER'S WEDDING, THE
Andreeff, Starr
CLUB VAMPIRE

Andrei, Damir
HOSTILE INTENT
Andrejevic, Kosta
SAVIOR
Andreovski, Paul
MR. NICE GUY
Andrew, Nicholas
SIMON BIRCH
Andrews, Benjamin
ONE TRUE THING
Andrews, Giuseppe
AMERICAN HISTORY X
PLEASANTVILLE
Andrews, Jason
54
Andrews, Joey
INVISIBLE MOM
Andrews, Matt
ELIZABETH
Andrews, Naveen
MIGHTY JOE YOUNG
Andrews, Troy Michael
SECRET KINGDOM, THE
Andrick, Virl
OBJECT OF MY AFFECTION, THE
Angarano, Michael
RIVER RED
Angel, Vanessa
KISSING A FOOL
Angela, June
KIKI'S DELIVERY SERVICE
Angelica, Roberta
URBAN LEGEND
Angelo, Susan
TRUMAN SHOW, THE
Angie
SHOOTING FISH
Angileri, Enzo
YOU'VE GOT MAIL
Angulo, Alex
DAY OF THE BEAST, THE
LIVE FLESH
Anhert, Alexander
SNOWBOUND
Anhert, Zachary
SNOWBOUND
Anicelli, Pete
THERE'S SOMETHING ABOUT MARY
Anisio, Chico
TIETA OF AGRESTE
Aniston, Jennifer
DREAM FOR AN INSOMNIAC
OBJECT OF MY AFFECTION, THE
Anker, Jack
DEEP RISING
Anne-Simone
DEEP RISING
Annunciation, Derek
TOP OF THE WORLD
Ansara, Michael
BATMAN & MR. FREEZE: SUBZERO
JOHNNY MYSTO BOY WIZARD
Ansari, Ahman
TASTE OF CHERRY
Anscombe, Mike
DIRTY WORK
Ant, Adam
FACE DOWN
Antaramian, Jacqueline
SIEGE, THE
Anthony, Jason
SHAMPOO HORNS
Anthony, Leonor
WILD THINGS
Anthony, Lysette
MISBEGOTTEN
Antione, Benz
RIGHT CONNECTIONS, THE
Antonio, Jim
PATCH ADAMS
PLEASANTVILLE
Antonio, Larry
PLAYING BY HEART
Antrobus, Yvonne
JACK HIGGINS' ON DANGEROUS GROUND
Anwar, Gabrielle
NEVADA
SUB DOWN
Anzalone, Helen
SOUR GRAPES
Anzilotti, Perry
AIR BUD: GOLDEN RECEIVER
Apisa, Bob
REPLACEMENT KILLERS, THE
Appel, Alex
REAL BLONDE, THE
Applebaum, Bill
DANCE WITH ME
Applegate, Christina
BIG HIT, THE
JANE AUSTEN'S MAFIA!
Applegate, Royce D.
DR. DOLITTLE
PHOENIX
Appleton, Dudi
JACK HIGGINS' ON DANGEROUS GROUND
April
LOVE IS THE DEVIL: STUDY FOR A PORTRAIT OF FRANCIS BACON
Apsion, Annabelle
LOLITA
Aqino, Wayne
SIX DAYS, SEVEN NIGHTS
Aragon, Carlos
NAKED LIES
Arangio, Tony
NIGHT VISION
Arango, Ivan
MEN WITH GUNS
Arbatt, Alexandre
MADELINE
Arce, Robert
LOVELIFE
Archerd, Army
OFF THE MENU: THE LAST DAYS OF CHASEN'S
Archie, John
HOLY MAN
Arcoraci, Vene
ENEMY OF THE STATE
Ardant, Fanny
ELIZABETH
Ardeatini, Valentina
DANGEROUS BEAUTY
Arenberg, Lee
JOHNNY SKIDMARKS
Argiro, Vinny
BULWORTH
Argo, Victor
NEXT STOP, WONDERLAND
Argue, David
NAPOLEON
Arguelles, Fernando
SKIN & BONE
Arguello, Jimmy Jose
CARLA'S SONG
Argueta, Luis
BREAK, THE
Ariel, Tessa
RED HAWK: WEAPON OF DEATH
Ariola, Julie
I LOVE YOU, DON'T TOUCH ME!
Aris, Gina
TWENTYFOURSEVEN
Arkin, Adam
HALLOWEEN H20: TWENTY YEARS LATER
NOT IN THIS TOWN
Arkin, Alan
SLUMS OF BEVERLY HILLS
Arkin, Michael
ROUNDERS
Arlie, Andrew
SNOWBOUND
Arluck, Neal
CELEBRITY
Arlyn, Nikki
CLAY PIGEONS
Armand, Gisken
INSOMNIA
Armendariz, Pedro
MASK OF ZORRO, THE
Armour, Annabel
MERCURY RISING
Armstrong, Bess
PECKER
Armstrong, Chris
HUMAN BOMB
INNOCENT SLEEP, THE
Armstrong, Curtis
ELVIS MEETS NIXON
Armstrong, Neil
KILLING TIME
Arnette, Jeanetta
FIRST LOVE, LAST RITES
Arngrim, Stefan
MISBEGOTTEN
Arno, Paul
BREAKOUT
UNDERTAKER'S WEDDING, THE
Arnold, Brian
WRONGFULLY ACCUSED
Arnold, Melanie
LOVE IS THE DEVIL: STUDY FOR A PORTRAIT OF FRANCIS BACON
Arnold, Richard
TREKKIES
Arnold, Tammy
SOLDIER'S DAUGHTER NEVER CRIES, A
Arnold, Terry
LAST SEDUCTION II, THE
Arnold, Tom
BUSTER & CHAUNCEY'S SILENT NIGHT
Arnone-Briggs, Lee
STAR TREK: INSURRECTION
Arnoul, Francoise
POST COITUM, ANIMAL TRISTE
Aron, Michael
FALLEN
Aronofsky, Abraham
PI
Aronovic, Norman
SPECIES II
Aronson, Letty
WILD MAN BLUES
Aronzon, Frederick
LOLIDA 2000
Arpa, Attila
REDLINE
Arquette, Alexis
BRIDE OF CHUCKY
CHILDREN OF THE CORN V: FIELD OF TERROR
I THINK I DO
WEDDING SINGER, THE
Arquette, David
ALARMIST, THE
SKIN & BONE
Arquette, Lewis
ALARMIST, THE

Avis, Mark
DISTURBING BEHAVIOR
Avital, Mili
KISSING A FOOL
POLISH WEDDING
Awanzino, Erick
EVER AFTER
Axas, Elie
SWINDLE, THE
Axelrod, Robert
FATAL PURSUIT
Ayer, Debbon
LAST DAYS OF DISCO, THE
Aykroyd, Dan
ANTZ
BLUES BROTHERS 2000
Aylesworth, Reiko
YOU'VE GOT MAIL
Aylward, John
ARMAGEDDON
EDEN
ESCAPE, THE
Aylward, Rory J.
SIEGE, THE
Ayoung, Lin Que
HE GOT GAME
Ayres, Rosalind
GODS AND MONSTERS
Aza, Sebastian
JANE AUSTEN'S MAFIA!
Azaria, Hank
CELEBRITY
GODZILLA
GREAT EXPECTATIONS
HOMEGROWN
Azeff, Michael
LOUISA MAY ALCOTT'S LITTLE MEN
Azema, Sabine
SAME OLD SONG
Azimov, Richard
LOUISA MAY ALCOTT'S LITTLE MEN
Azizi, Rahi
DEEP IMPACT
Azman, Yank
BONE DADDY
Azuma, Kyooko
SLEEPY EYES OF DEATH: FULL CIRCLE KILLING
Azur, Sybil
LIVING OUT LOUD
Azzab, Rayek
DESTINY
Azzara, Candice
LAND OF THE FREE
Azzopardi, Kyra
BONE DADDY
B Real
RUGRATS MOVIE, THE
Babalis, Mia
FEAR AND LOATHING IN LAS VEGAS
Babatunde, Akin
NIGHT VISION
Babatunde, Obba
FATAL PURSUIT
Babbs, O.B.
PSYCHO
Babcock, John C.
LOLIDA 2000
Babcock, Todd
GODS AND MONSTERS
Babich, Michaline
LET'S TALK ABOUT SEX
Baburkova, Miroslava
MY GIANT
Bacalso, Joanna
WOO
Bacciocchi, Ivan
NIGHT AND THE MOMENT, THE
Bach, Emmanuelle
POST COITUM, ANIMAL TRISTE
Bachar, Carmit
LIVING OUT LOUD
Bachar, Dian
BASEKETBALL
ORGAZMO
Bachmann, Conrad
CHOSEN ONE: LEGEND OF THE RAVEN, THE
Backers, Sonia
MAN IN THE IRON MASK, THE
Bacon, James
OFF THE MENU: THE LAST DAYS OF CHASEN'S
Bacon, Kevin
DIGGING TO CHINA
WILD THINGS
Bacon, Stephanie
LEWIS & CLARK & GEORGE
Bacri, Jean-Pierre
SAME OLD SONG
UN AIR DE FAMILLE
Badalato, T.C.
X-FILES, THE
Badalucco Jr., Joseph
GODZILLA
SIEGE, THE
Badalucco, Michael
LOVE WALKED IN
YOU'VE GOT MAIL
Badarou, Deen
PERFECT MURDER, A
Badel, Sarah
MRS. DALLOWAY
Bademis, Christophe
UN AIR DE FAMILLE
Bader, Sheila
FALLEN
Bader, Terry
DARK CITY
Badger, Jennifer
CHILDREN OF THE CORN V: FIELD OF TERROR
Badica, Radu
SUBSPECIES IV: BLOODSTORM
Badilla, John
PECKER
Badin, Jean
GENEALOGIES OF A CRIME
Badland, Annette
LITTLE VOICE
TWENTYFOURSEVEN
Badoul, Auda Mohammed
PASSION IN THE DESERT
Badu, Erykah
BLUES BROTHERS 2000
Baer, G. Gordon
INVISIBLE DAD
Baez, Rafael
ELMORE LEONARD'S GOLD COAST
Bagheri, Abdolhossein
TASTE OF CHERRY
Bagley, Lorri
CELEBRITY
54
Bagley, Tim
CHOSEN ONE: LEGEND OF THE RAVEN, THE
Bagwell, Marcus
RETURN TO SAVAGE BEACH
Bai Yefu
FROZEN
Bai Yu
FROZEN
Baier, Robert
DESPERATE MEASURES
NEGOTIATOR, THE
Bailey, Chris
UGLY, THE
Bailey, D'Army
HOW STELLA GOT HER GROOVE BACK
Bailey, Janet
BLACKJACK
Bailey, Jerome
NAKED ACTS
Bailey, Mark Chandler
NIAGARA NIAGARA
Bailey, Tony
RIGHT CONNECTIONS, THE
Bailleul, Sebastien
LIFE OF JESUS, THE
Baily, Kirk
INDISCREET
OUTSIDE OZONA
3 NINJAS: HIGH NOON AT MEGA MOUNTAIN
Baily, Lisa
BABE: PIG IN THE CITY
Bain, Trevor
DIRTY WORK
Bain, Zeo
PLAN B
Baines, Harold
SUBSTITUTE 2: SCHOOL'S OUT, THE
Baines, Howard "Stick"
SUBSTITUTE 2: SCHOOL'S OUT, THE
Baio, Scott
DETONATOR
Baird, Benjamin V.
GODZILLA
Baisho, Mitsuko
EEL, THE
Baiss, Bridget
DISAPPEARANCE OF KEVIN JOHNSON, THE
Bajenski, Len
U.S. MARSHALS
Bajer, Sharon
TRUCKS
Bak, Jon
MISBEGOTTEN
Baka, Jeremy
BURN HOLLYWOOD BURN
Baker, Arthur
MODULATIONS: CINEMA FOR THE EAR
Baker, Becky Ann
CELEBRITY
SIMPLE PLAN, A
Baker, Brandon
JUNGLE BOOK: MOWGLI'S STORY, THE
Baker, Brett
DISAPPEARANCE OF KEVIN JOHNSON, THE
Baker, Carly
I WENT DOWN
Baker, Carroll
NORTH SHORE FISH
Baker, Cynthia S.
U.S. MARSHALS
Baker, Damani
BELOVED
Baker, Dee Bradley
RAT'S TALE, A
Baker, Don
SOLDIER'S DAUGHTER NEVER CRIES, A
Baker, Dylan
CELEBRITY
HAPPINESS
Baker, Frank
HOSTILE WATERS
Baker, Gale
FEAR AND LOATHING IN LAS VEGAS
Baker, George Anthony
CAUGHT UP

Barlow, Tim
COUSIN BETTE
LES MISERABLES
UGLY, THE
Barnes, Adilah
BULWORTH
Barnes, Avis-Marie
CATHERINE'S GROVE
Barnes, Constance
TRICKS
WOUNDED
Barnes, Dwayne L.
REAL HOWARD SPITZ, THE
Barnes, Joanna
PARENT TRAP, THE
Barnes, Lynne
LOLIDA 2000
Barnes, Priscilla
CATHERINE'S GROVE
Barnes, Richard
RED HAWK: WEAPON OF DEATH
Barnes, Roger
SNOWBOUND
Barnes, Sean
HORTON FOOTE'S ALONE
Barnes, Susan
DOGWATCH
LOVER GIRL
Barnes-Hopkins, Barbara
ONE TOUGH COP
Barnett, Craig
GODSON, THE
Barnett, Gemini
WEDDING SINGER, THE
Barnett, John
SAVING PRIVATE RYAN
Barnwell, Ysaye M.
BELOVED
Baron, Chuck
HAV PLENTY
Baron, Roshanna
PARENT TRAP, THE
Baron, Sandy
HI-LO COUNTRY, THE
Barondes, Elizabeth
LOVE TO KILL
Barone, Diane
HAV PLENTY
Baroni, Gil
LIFE IS BEAUTIFUL
Barquin, Pedro
GREAT EXPECTATIONS
Barr, Kathleen
RUDOLPH THE RED-NOSED REINDEER: THE MOVIE
Barr, Russell
LAND GIRLS, THE
REGENERATION
Barr, Tina
WATERBOY, THE
Barrera, David
ALMOST HEROES
Barrett, Bob
SHAKESPEARE IN LOVE
Barrett, Dan
WILD MAN BLUES
Barrett, David
CIVIL ACTION, A
Barrett, Jonathan
TRUCKS
Barrett, Laurinda
PERFECT MURDER, A
Barrett, Majel
TREKKIES
Barrett, Ray
HEAVEN'S BURNING
Barrett, Stanton
UNCLE SAM
Barretto, Michael
SIX DAYS, SEVEN NIGHTS
Barron, Barbara Hubbard
HOLY MAN
Barron, Jaret Ross
WIDE AWAKE
Barrow, Andrew
LOVE AND DEATH ON LONG ISLAND
Barrows, Keith
BOYS WILL BE BOYS
Barrows, Manny
THERE'S SOMETHING ABOUT MARY
Barry, Alan
BRYLCREEM BOYS, THE
Barry, Jason
MONUMENT AVE.
SUMMER FLING
Barry, Matt
RUSH HOUR
Barry, Thom
MAJOR LEAGUE: BACK TO THE MINORS
Barrymore, Drew
EVER AFTER
HOME FRIES
WEDDING SINGER, THE
Barrymore, Jaid
LAST DAYS OF DISCO, THE
Barrymore, Michael
SPICE WORLD
Barsaraba, Gary
LAST BREATH
Barstow, Scott
TWO FOR TEXAS
Bart, Peter
BURN HOLLYWOOD BURN
Bart the Bear
WALKING THUNDER
Bartel, Paul
BILLY'S HOLLYWOOD SCREEN KISS
LEWIS & CLARK & GEORGE
Barth, Eddie
BABE: PIG IN THE CITY
Barthell, Aleta
ZERO EFFECT
Bartholomee, L.B.
TEKKEN: THE MOTION PICTURE
Bartilson, Lynsey
RAT'S TALE, A
Bartlett, Bonnie
PRIMARY COLORS
Bartlett, Robin
CITY OF ANGELS
Bartlett, Victoria
LOVE IS THE DEVIL: STUDY FOR A PORTRAIT OF FRANCIS BACON
Bartok, Jayce
ALMOST PARTNERS
Barton, Mischa
LAWN DOGS
Bartsch, Ted
WILD THINGS
Barty, Billy
BURN HOLLYWOOD BURN
Basch, Peter
PAULIE
Basco, Derek
SIX DAYS, SEVEN NIGHTS
Basile, Joe
GIA
SENSELESS
Baskins-Leva, Lulu
PLAN B
Basoli, Anna
HURRICANE STREETS
Bass, Ben
BRIDE OF CHUCKY
Bass, George
BREAK, THE
Bass, Victoria
WILD THINGS
Bassel, Valeriy
DEAD WATERS
Bassett, Angela
HOW STELLA GOT HER GROOVE BACK
OFF THE MENU: THE LAST DAYS OF CHASEN'S
Bassey, Michaella
SNAKE EYES
Bassler, Bethany
MIGHTY JOE YOUNG
Bastel, Victoria
SOMEWHERE IN THE CITY
Bastoni, Steve
TWISTED
Bastos, Othon
CENTRAL STATION
Basulto, David
AMERICAN HISTORY X
Basulto, Joe
TOUCH OF EVIL: THE DIRECTOR'S CUT
Batalla, Rick
GIA
Bates, James
WATERBOY, THE
Bates, Jo
MISBEGOTTEN
Bates, Kathy
PRIMARY COLORS
SWEPT FROM THE SEA
WATERBOY, THE
Bates, Nancy Ann
BASEKETBALL
Bateson, Timothy
LES MISERABLES
MERLIN
Batina, Jean-Bernard
WESTERN
Batista, Lloyd
BOYS WILL BE BOYS
Batten, Cyia
SENSELESS
Battista, John
NEXT STEP, THE
Battista, Rich
GODZILLA
Batyr, Christopher
HAV PLENTY
Bauche, Vanessa
MASK OF ZORRO, THE
Baudin, Thalia
RIDE
Bauer, Robert
BOOGIE BOY
Bauer, Steven
NAKED LIES
Baun, Jack
MAJOR LEAGUE: BACK TO THE MINORS
Baur, Mark
INVADER, THE
Bavan, Yolande
ONE TRUE THING
Baxter, Ben
NEW ADVENTURES OF KIMBA THE WHITE LION, THE
Baxter, David
UGLY, THE
Baxter, Jeff
BLUES BROTHERS 2000
Baxter, John
TWENTYFOURSEVEN
Baxter, Keith
MERLIN
Baxter, Tommie
CELEBRITY
Bay, Frances
KRIPPENDORF'S TRIBE

Bayley, Arnold
HAV PLENTY
Baylis, Matt
WATERBOY, THE
Bayliss, Peter
MERLIN
Bayne, Lawrence
BRAM STOKER'S SHADOWBUILDER
Be, Yoshio
NIGHT AT THE ROXBURY, A
Beach, Adam
SMOKE SIGNALS
Beach, Michael
JOHNNY SKIDMARKS
REBOUND: THE LEGEND OF EARL "THE GOAT" MANIGAULT
Beachwood, Kermit
FERNGULLY 2: THE MAGICAL RESCUE
Beall, Rich
PHANTOMS
Beals, Jennifer
LAST DAYS OF DISCO, THE
PROPHECY II, THE
SPREE, THE
Bean, Chris
U.S. MARSHALS
Bean, Sean
RONIN
Beane, Andrea
SKIN & BONE
Beane, Jibby
LOVE IS THE DEVIL: STUDY FOR A PORTRAIT OF FRANCIS BACON
Bear, R.H.
DEE SNIDER'S STRANGELAND
Beard, Jane
SPECIES II
Beard, John F.
SIEGE, THE
Beard, Steven
SHAKESPEARE IN LOVE
Bearden, Jim
TRACKED
Beasley, Alyson E.
GINGERBREAD MAN, THE
Beasley, Angela
GINGERBREAD MAN, THE
Beasley, John
OVERNIGHT DELIVERY
Beastie Boys
FREE TIBET
Beaton, Martin
SAVING PRIVATE RYAN
Beattie, Ian
STRAY BULLET
Beattie, Joe
VELVET GOLDMINE
Beattie, Ron
KISSING A FOOL
Beatty, Bruce
NEGOTIATOR, THE
Beatty, Jeff
SIEGE, THE
Beatty, Nancy
RESCUERS: STORIES OF COURAGE—TWO WOMEN
Beatty, Ned
HE GOT GAME
Beatty, Warren
BULWORTH
Beaty, Heather
SNOWBOUND
Beaty, Shannon
SNOWBOUND
Beauchene, Billy
THERE'S SOMETHING ABOUT MARY
Beauchene, Kathy
THERE'S SOMETHING ABOUT MARY
Beaudene, Raquel
GREAT EXPECTATIONS
Beaudoin, David
INSIDE/OUT
Beaumont, Jacqueline
LET'S KILL ALL THE LAWYERS
Beauville, Raphael
MADELINE
Beaver, Carolyn
UGLY, THE
Beaver, Jim
WOUNDED
Becerril, Fernando
MASK OF ZORRO, THE
Bechir, Pierre
ARTEMISIA
Beck
FREE TIBET
RUGRATS MOVIE, THE
Beck, Joel
DECAMPITATED
Beckel, Graham
BLACK DOG
BULWORTH
Becker, Gerry
CELEBRITY
HAPPINESS
PERFECT MURDER, A
Becker, Meret
KILLER CONDOM, THE
Becker, Oliver
RESCUERS: STORIES OF COURAGE—TWO COUPLES
Becker, Sharon
WRATH OF THE NINJA: THE YOTODEN MOVIE
Beckett, Diane
NEXT STOP, WONDERLAND
Beckford, Luis
X-FILES, THE
Beckhurst, Garry
KNOCK OFF
Beckinsale, Kate
LAST DAYS OF DISCO, THE
ROYAL DECEIT
SHOOTING FISH
Beckworth, Alan
RONIN
Bedard, George
THERE'S SOMETHING ABOUT MARY
Bedard, Irene
POCAHONTAS II: JOURNEY TO A NEW WORLD
SMOKE SIGNALS
TWO FOR TEXAS
Bedelia, Bonnie
BAD MANNERS
Bednarz, Mark
GINGERBREAD MAN, THE
Bee, Kenny
ARMOUR OF GOD
Beegle, Brian
MAJOR LEAGUE: BACK TO THE MINORS
Beehner, Scott
LAST DAYS OF DISCO, THE
Beekman, Bunny
LAST DAYS OF DISCO, THE
Beener, Yada
BELOVED
Begley, Brian
STRAY BULLET
Begley Jr., Ed
HORTON FOOTE'S ALONE
JOEY
NOT IN THIS TOWN
Behr, Dani
LIKE IT IS
Behr, Jason
PLEASANTVILLE
Behr, Melissa
LANDLADY, THE
Beigi, Maryam
I GOT THE HOOK UP
Beint, Michael
ELIZABETH
Beiser, Brendan
I'LL BE HOME FOR CHRISTMAS
Beith, Jeff
GENERAL CHAOS: UNCENSORED ANIMATION
Belack, Doris
ALMOST PARTNERS
KRIPPENDORF'S TRIBE
NEIL SIMON'S THE ODD COUPLE II
Belafonte, Shari
MARS
Belance, Alerte
BELOVED
Belcon, Natalie Venetia
WOO
Belcourt, Dominique
FIRELIGHT
Beley, Lisa Ann
DRAGON BALL Z THE MOVIE: DEAD ZONE
DRAGON BALL Z THE MOVIE: THE WORLD'S STRONGEST
Bell, Addison
SIMON BIRCH
Bell, Ann
LAND GIRLS, THE
Bell, Daniel
ARGUING THE WORLD
Bell, David
SLAYERS: THE MOTION PICTURE
Bell, Doron
RIGHT CONNECTIONS, THE
Bell, E.E.
LEWIS & CLARK & GEORGE
MY GIANT
Bell, Jo
TWENTYFOURSEVEN
Bell, Michael
FLINTSTONES: I YABBA-DABBA DOO!, THE
RUGRATS MOVIE, THE
Bell, Mindy
U.S. MARSHALS
Bell, Nicholas
DARK CITY
Bell, Steve
LIKE IT IS
Bell, Tobin
BEST OF THE BEST: WITHOUT WARNING
OVERNIGHT DELIVERY
Bell, Tom
SWEPT FROM THE SEA
Bella, Rachel
WHEN PIGS FLY
Belle, Camilla
PRACTICAL MAGIC
Bellegarde, Veronique
SOLDIER'S DAUGHTER NEVER CRIES, A
WESTERN
Bellisario, Troian
BILLBOARD DAD
Bellissimo, Tommy L.
AMERICAN HISTORY X
Bello, Maria
PERMANENT MIDNIGHT
Bello, Teodorina
PRICE ABOVE RUBIES, A
Belly, Karine
MAN IN THE IRON MASK, THE

Bernardo, Paul Joseph
SNAKE EYES
Bernbaum, Sharon
BLACKJACK
Bernhard, Sandra
BURN HOLLYWOOD BURN
LOVER GIRL
PLUMP FICTION
SOMEWHERE IN THE CITY
WRONGFULLY ACCUSED
Bernhardt, Chick
U.S. MARSHALS
Bernhardt, Kevin
TOP OF THE WORLD
Bernhardt, Lisa
LET'S KILL ALL THE LAWYERS
Bernheim, Shirl
BROADWAY DAMAGE
Berns, Judy Jean
I GOT THE HOOK UP
Bernsen, Corbin
MAJOR LEAGUE: BACK TO THE MINORS
SPACEJACKED
Bernstein, Jack
JANE AUSTEN'S MAFIA!
Berrocal, Leire
TALK OF ANGELS
Berrou, Helene
WESTERN
Berroyer, Jackie
SWINDLE, THE
Berry, Christopher
SOLDIER'S DAUGHTER NEVER CRIES, A
Berry, Dave
LOVE IS THE DEVIL: STUDY FOR A PORTRAIT OF FRANCIS BACON
Berry, Halle
BULWORTH
WHY DO FOOLS FALL IN LOVE?
Berry, Sydney
HOPE FLOATS
Bershevitz, Vladimir
DEJA VU
Bertelot, Suzanne
LIFE OF JESUS, THE
Berthelot, Olivia
WESTERN
Bertolucci, Bernardo
STORY OF X, THE
Berwick, Arthur
CELEBRITY
Besch, Cheyenne
SHAMPOO HORNS
Beshlian, Harout
CIVIL ACTION, A
Bessant, Shane
UGLY, THE
Besselle, Anthony
SUB DOWN
Bessette, Denise
SOUR GRAPES
Bessho, Tetsuya
GODZILLA AND MOTHRA: THE BATTLE FOR EARTH
Best, Jennifer
STEPMOM
Best, Travis
HE GOT GAME
Best, Wayne
BONE DADDY
TRACKED
Bethea, Ellen
SIEGE, THE
Bettany, Paul
LAND GIRLS, THE
Betts, Jack
GODS AND MONSTERS

Bevan, Daisy
ELIZABETH
Bevan, Tim
ELIZABETH
Beverly, Trazana M.
BELOVED
Bevis, Leslie
OPPOSITE OF SEX, THE
Bews, Guy
WRONGFULLY ACCUSED
Bey, John Toles
KID IN ALADDIN'S PALACE, A
Beyer, Troy
GINGERBREAD MAN, THE
LET'S TALK ABOUT SEX
Beymer, Richard
DISAPPEARANCE OF KEVIN JOHNSON, THE
ELVIS MEETS NIXON
Bezace, Didier
CHAMBERMAID ON THE TITANIC, THE
Bezgin, Igor
TRUCE, THE
Bian Li Chang
SHAOLIN TEMPLE, THE
Biase, Mike
CIVIL ACTION, A
Bibb, Sarah
ALONE IN THE WOODS
Bibic, Vladimir
CELEBRITY
Bichir, Bruno
MIDAQ ALLEY
Bick, Stewart
CAPTIVE
Bick, Suzie
LOVE IS THE DEVIL: STUDY FOR A PORTRAIT OF FRANCIS BACON
Bickerton, Melissa
CATHERINE'S GROVE
Bicklemann, Cerita Monet
WHY DO FOOLS FALL IN LOVE?
Bidaman, Robert
TERMINAL JUSTICE
Bidanie, Zite
SPECIES II
Biehn, Michael
DOUBLE EDGE
Biel, Jessica
I'LL BE HOME FOR CHRISTMAS
Bierko, Craig
FEAR AND LOATHING IN LAS VEGAS
SOUR GRAPES
Big Boy
PLAYERS CLUB, THE
Bigelow, Pixie
RESCUERS: STORIES OF COURAGE—TWO WOMEN
Bigley, Paul
SHAKESPEARE IN LOVE
Bigwood, Michael Craig
WIDE AWAKE
Bilancio, Vincent J.
ALARMIST, THE
Bilbool, Raymond
OFF THE MENU: THE LAST DAYS OF CHASEN'S
Bilderback, Nicole
CAN'T HARDLY WAIT
Bill, Bushwick
NIGHT VISION
Billet, Bradford
PERFECT MURDER, A
Billet, Tom
ASYLUM
PRINCE, THE
Billig, Simon
THIN RED LINE, THE

Billing, Lisa
DANCER, TEXAS POP. 81
Billings, Earl
LIVING IN PERIL
Billingslea, Beau
HALLOWEEN H20: TWENTY YEARS LATER
PENTAGON WARS, THE
RUSTY: THE GREAT RESCUE
Billingsley, John
EDEN
Billington, James H.
RACE TO SAVE 100 YEARS, THE
Biltcliffe, Martin
INNOCENT SLEEP, THE
Bini, Gentuca
LOVE IS THE DEVIL: STUDY FOR A PORTRAIT OF FRANCIS BACON
Bini, Jennifer
WILD THINGS
Binkley, James
DIRTY WORK
54
Binney, Chris
ACT OF WAR
Binnie, Alex
HALLELUJAH!
Binns, T. David
I GOT THE HOOK UP
Binswanger, Dr. Harry
AYN RAND: A SENSE OF LIFE
Birardi, Barbara
EIGHTEENTH ANGEL, THE
Birch, Dawn
WATERBOY, THE
Birch, James
LOVE IS THE DEVIL: STUDY FOR A PORTRAIT OF FRANCIS BACON
Birchard, Paul
HOSTILE WATERS
Bird, Emma
GOVERNESS, THE
Biris, Silviu
SHRUNKEN CITY, THE
Birk, Raye
STAR TREK: INSURRECTION
Birkett, Jeremiah
LENA'S DREAMS
Birkin, David
LES MISERABLES
Birkin, Jane
SAME OLD SONG
SOLDIER'S DAUGHTER NEVER CRIES, A
Birkova, Lena
MY GIANT
Birman, Matt
URBAN LEGEND
Birney, Frank
JANE AUSTEN'S MAFIA!
Birney, Reed
PERFECT MURDER, A
Birt, Cecelia Ann
BELOVED
Bishop, Jennifer
HARD CORE LOGO
Bishop, Kirsten
BONE DADDY
Bishop, Mary
NOT IN THIS TOWN
Bishop, Nancy
ACT OF WAR
Bishop, Rummy
DIRTY WORK
Bishton, Jamie
NEXT STEP, THE
Bisio, Claudio
NIRVANA
TRUCE, THE

Bissel, Robin
PLEASANTVILLE
Bissell, Ron
TWENTYFOURSEVEN
Bisset, Douglas
MIGHTY, THE
Bisset, Jacqueline
DANGEROUS BEAUTY
Bisson, Jean Marc
CAPTIVE
Bittante, Paul
URBAN SAFARI
Bitten, Roosevelt
ANOTHER DAY IN PARADISE
Bittiker, Brad
DETOUR
Bivens, J.B.
ESCAPE, THE
MISBEGOTTEN
SNOWBOUND
Bivens Jr., J.B.
WOUNDED
Bivens, Mary Lucy
BODY COUNT
Bizek, Szilvia
REDLINE
Bjork
FREE TIBET
Bjorkman, Stig
TRANCEFORMER: A PORTRAIT OF LARS VON TRIER
Bjorn-Andersen, Michelle
KINGDOM, PART 2, THE
Bjornson, Maira
LOVE IS THE DEVIL: STUDY FOR A PORTRAIT OF FRANCIS BACON
Blabey, Aaron
TWISTED
Black, Jack
ENEMY OF THE STATE
JOHNNY SKIDMARKS
Black, James
DON KING: ONLY IN AMERICA
GODZILLA
OUT OF SIGHT
SOLDIER
Black, Jay
BELLY
MY GIANT
Black, Jordan
CLUB VAMPIRE
Black, Karen
INVISIBLE DAD
MEN
STIR
WHO IS HENRY JAGLOM?
Black, Louis
FACULTY, THE
Black, Lucas
X-FILES, THE
Black, Mary
WRONGFULLY ACCUSED
Black, Matt
MODULATIONS: CINEMA FOR THE EAR
Black, Royana
ALMOST PARTNERS
Black, Shane
BURN HOLLYWOOD BURN
Black, Star
PAUL MONETTE: THE BRINK OF SUMMER'S END
Black, Varen
U.S. MARSHALS
Blackburn, Heather
REAL HOWARD SPITZ, THE
Blackburn, Richard
DOWN IN THE DELTA
Blacker, David
DEFENDERS: PAYBACK, THE
54
Blackman, Joan
MERRY WAR, A
Blackmon, Shantele
I GOT THE HOOK UP
Blades, Ruben
CHINESE BOX, THE
Blaevoet, Helene
LIFE OF JESUS, THE
Blagojevic, Ljiljana
SAVIOR
Blair, John Patrick
DOGWATCH
Blair, Selma
CAN'T HARDLY WAIT
Blaisdell, Brad
NEGOTIATOR, THE
Blake, Andre
STEPMOM
Blake, Craig
HOW STELLA GOT HER GROOVE BACK
Blake, Geoffrey
MIGHTY JOE YOUNG
Blake, Grace
BELOVED
Blake, Jim "Sunshine"
THERE'S SOMETHING ABOUT MARY
Blake, Jonathan
FROM A FAR COUNTRY
Blake, Megan
OPPOSITE OF SEX, THE
Blake, Thomas
TALK TO ME
Blakely, Brien
DIARY OF A SERIAL KILLER
Blakely, Michelle
YOU'VE GOT MAIL
Blakely, Rachel
MR. NICE GUY
YOUNG HERCULES
Blakeman, Kerry
MR. NICE GUY
Blakeney, Alan
RETURN TO SAVAGE BEACH
Blakesley, Weston
PLEASANTVILLE
Blakey, Don
GEORGE WALLACE
Blalock, Steve
JOHN CARPENTER'S VAMPIRES
Blame, Judy
LOVE IS THE DEVIL: STUDY FOR A PORTRAIT OF FRANCIS BACON
Blanc, Dominique
SOLDIER'S DAUGHTER NEVER CRIES, A
Blancard, Jarred
DISTURBING BEHAVIOR
Blanch, Jaime
DAY OF THE BEAST, THE
Blanchard, Claude
JACK HIGGINS' ON DANGEROUS GROUND
Blanchard, David
HALLOWEEN H20: TWENTY YEARS LATER
Blanchard, Tara
AMERICAN HISTORY X
Blanche, Robert
ZERO EFFECT
Blanchett, Cate
ELIZABETH
Bland, Steven
DANCER, TEXAS POP. 81
Blank, Brad
THERE'S SOMETHING ABOUT MARY
Blankenship, Connie
DISAPPEARANCE OF KEVIN JOHNSON, THE
Blanks, Michael
DON KING: ONLY IN AMERICA
Blassfield, Tony
LAND OF THE FREE
Blatchley, Joseph
INCOGNITO
Blaylock, Jeannie
ELMORE LEONARD'S GOLD COAST
Blazer, Judy
BUSTER & CHAUNCEY'S SILENT NIGHT
Bleakley, Mick
TWENTYFOURSEVEN
Blechingberg, Bill
WRATH OF THE NINJA: THE YOTODEN MOVIE
Bleeth, Yasmine
BASEKETBALL
Blethyn, Brenda
LITTLE VOICE
MUSIC FROM ANOTHER ROOM
Blevins, Corey
PALMETTO
Blicker, Jason
ONE TOUGH COP
Blink
MOONDANCE
Bloch, Bernard
RONIN
Bloch, Debora
OYSTER AND THE WIND, THE
Block, Bruce
PARENT TRAP, THE
Bloom, Orlando
WILDE
Bloom, Steve
UNDERTAKER'S WEDDING, THE
Bloomfield, Sedley
BARRIERS
Blount, Will
FEAR AND LOATHING IN LAS VEGAS
Bloz, Alexandra
BEYOND SILENCE
Blucas, Marc
PLEASANTVILLE
Blue, Mr.
SAFE MEN
Bluestein, David
HALF BAKED
Bluhm, Brady
ALONE IN THE WOODS
Blum, Mark
DEFENDERS: PAYBACK, THE
Blum, Steven Jay
BRAM STOKER'S SHADOWBUILDER
Blumberg, Ted
IMPOSTORS, THE
Blumenthal, George S.
PERFECT MURDER, A
Blumenthal, Marion
PERFECT MURDER, A
Blundell, John
NIL BY MOUTH
Bluthal, John
DARK CITY
Bluto, Tony
INNOCENT SLEEP, THE
Blythe, Catherine
TERMINAL JUSTICE
Boakye, Adusah
GREAT EXPECTATIONS
Boardley, Fawn
WOO
Boas, Erna
CELEBRATION, THE

Boas, John
CELEBRATION, THE
Bobby, Anne
HAPPINESS
Bobesiu, Doru
CLOCKMAKER
Bocaletti, Andrea
54
Boccaccio, Gil
FEAR AND LOATHING IN LAS VEGAS
Bochner, Lloyd
BRAM STOKER'S THE MUMMY
Bode, Ben
SIX DAYS, SEVEN NIGHTS
Bode, Georg-Martin
KILLER CONDOM, THE
Bodle, Jane
OBJECT OF MY AFFECTION, THE
Bodner, Michael
BLACKJACK
Bodrov Jr., Sergei
BROTHER
Body, Leslie
HURRICANE STREETS
Boe, Drew
LETTER FROM DEATH ROW, A
Boedy, Thomas
SIMPLE PLAN, A
Boeheim, Coach Jim
HE GOT GAME
Boen, Earl
LIVING IN PERIL
NEIL SIMON'S THE ODD COUPLE II
PRINCE, THE
Boensch, Jim
BASEKETBALL
Boey, Brandon
HENRY FOOL
Bogdanovich, Peter
54
MR. JEALOUSY
WHO IS HENRY JAGLOM?
Bogdonovich, Antonia
RESCUERS: STORIES OF COURAGE—TWO WOMEN
Bogert, William
PERFECT MURDER, A
Boggs, Bill
SPECIES II
Bogosian, Eric
BRIGHT SHINING LIE, A
SAFE MEN
Bohen, Ian
YOUNG HERCULES
Bohne, Bruce
OVERNIGHT DELIVERY
PATCH ADAMS
Bohrer, Corinne
STAR KID
Bohringer, Romane
CHAMBERMAID ON THE TITANIC, THE
Boidin, Samuel
LIFE OF JESUS, THE
Boisen, Ole
KINGDOM, PART 2, THE
Bojorquez, Yolanda
TOUCH OF EVIL: THE DIRECTOR'S CUT
Bokor, Sylvia
AYN RAND: A SENSE OF LIFE
Bolender, Bill
QUICKSILVER HIGHWAY
Boles, Gene
MONUMENT AVE.
Bollard, Natalie
DARK CITY
Bollen, Paul
LETHAL WEAPON 4
Bolly, Clark
SKIN & BONE
Bologna, Joseph
BATMAN/SUPERMAN MOVIE, THE
Bologna, Marlene
FEAR AND LOATHING IN LAS VEGAS
Bolster, Richard
SAFE MEN
Bolton, Michael
WRONGFULLY ACCUSED
Bon Jovi, Jon
HOMEGROWN
LEADING MAN, THE
NO LOOKING BACK
Bon, Ross
KISSING A FOOL
Bonanni, Maud
DANGEROUS BEAUTY
Bond, Steve
SPACEJACKED
Bondam, Klaus
CELEBRATION, THE
Bondar, Michael
BLUES BROTHERS 2000
Bonds, Gary U.S.
BLUES BROTHERS 2000
Bondy, Ken
FULL TILT BOOGIE
Bone, Kevin
CHARLIE HOBOKEN
Bones, Frankie
MODULATIONS: CINEMA FOR THE EAR
Bonet, Deni
STOREFRONT HITCHCOCK
Bonet, Lisa
ENEMY OF THE STATE
Bonet, Wilma
WHAT DREAMS MAY COME
Bonham Carter, Helena
MERLIN
MERRY WAR, A
THEORY OF FLIGHT
Boni, Gabrielle
LOUISA MAY ALCOTT'S LITTLE MEN
Bonicatto, Eric
SWINDLE, THE
Bonifant, J. Evan
BLUES BROTHERS 2000
BREAKOUT
Bonilla, Michelle
HOMEGROWN
Bonin, Neil
YOU'VE GOT MAIL
Bonnal, Frederique
MARIUS AND JEANNETTE
Bonnevie, Maria
INSOMNIA
JERUSALEM
Bonnie
YOU'VE GOT MAIL
Bonura, Krista
NO WAY HOME
Boobleswang, Helena
LAST SEDUCTION II, THE
Boocock, Paul
HENRY FOOL
Booker, Jessica
DIRTY WORK
Booker, Richard
PALMETTO
Bookwalter, J.R.
CURSE OF THE PUPPET MASTER
Boone, Jean Hubbard
PRINCE, THE
Boone Jr., Mark
ARMAGEDDON
I STILL KNOW WHAT YOU DID LAST SUMMER
JOHN CARPENTER'S VAMPIRES
MONTANA
THIN RED LINE, THE
Boone, Lesley
I'LL BE HOME FOR CHRISTMAS
Boorem, Mika
JACK FROST
MIGHTY JOE YOUNG
Booth, Bronwen
JACK LONDON'S THE CALL OF THE WILD: DOG OF THE YUKON
Boothe, Powers
SPREE, THE
Borden, Chuck
CLOCKWATCHERS
LITTLE BIGFOOT 2: THE JOURNEY HOME
Borden, Rainbow
CITY OF ANGELS
Borden, Walter
TALES FROM A PARALLEL UNIVERSE: GIGA SHADOW
Bordenko, Aleksandra
SAVIOR
Borders, Theodore
CITY OF ANGELS
Bordon, Victor
EL CHE: INVESTIGATING A LEGEND
Borelli, Ric
WHY DO FOOLS FALL IN LOVE?
Boren, Carrie
MAKER, THE
Boren, Heidi
PARENT TRAP, THE
Borg, Annika
JERUSALEM
Borge, Ana Victoria
CARLA'S SONG
Borgnine, Ernest
ALL DOGS CHRISTMAS CAROL, AN
BASEKETBALL
SMALL SOLDIERS
Borisoff, Devon
SIMON BIRCH
Borkan, Gene
SOULER OPPOSITE, THE
Borodenko, Sanja
SAVIOR
Borowiec, Kazimierz
FROM A FAR COUNTRY
Borrego, Jesse
MAKER, THE
RETROACTIVE
Borriello, Bobby
ENEMY OF THE STATE
Boryea, Jay
ROUNDERS
Bosa, John
HOLY MAN
Bosanceanu, Eugenia
SUBSPECIES IV: BLOODSTORM
Bosco, Mario
54
Bosco, Philip
MOON OVER BROADWAY
Bose-Smith, Jason
AMERICAN HISTORY X
Bosley, Tom
LITTLE BIGFOOT 2: THE JOURNEY HOME
Bosschaert, Alisa
HUMAN BOMB
Bossell, Simon
ABERRATION
Bost, Olivia
SHADRACH
Boston, Michael
LITTLE BOY BLUE
Boston, Tony
MY BROTHER'S WAR

Boswell, Anthony
I GOT THE HOOK UP
Boswell Sr., Donnie
LOLITA
Bosworth, Catherine
HORSE WHISPERER, THE
Bosworth, Martin
ENEMY OF THE STATE
Bottoms, Timothy
PRINCE, THE
UNCLE SAM
Botuchis, Mathew
3 NINJAS: HIGH NOON AT MEGA MOUNTAIN
Bouajila, Sami
ARTEMISIA
SIEGE, THE
Bouchard, Ray
LAST LIVES
Boucher, Brigitte
MAN IN THE IRON MASK, THE
Bouchez, Elodie
FULL SPEED
Bouchner, Vitezslav
ACT OF WAR
Bouck, Jonathan David
SMALL SOLDIERS
Boudet, Jacques
MARIUS AND JEANNETTE
Bougere, Teagle F.
IMPOSTORS, THE
Bould, Hannah
PHOTOGRAPHING FAIRIES
Boulton, Nicholas
SHAKESPEARE IN LOVE
Boulware, Will
MY FIRST NAME IS MACEO
Bounds, Bryan
SLAYERS: THE MOTION PICTURE
SLAYERS: THE MOTION PICTURE
Bourassa, Jacques
WRONGFULLY ACCUSED
Bourdo, Sacha
WESTERN
Bourgeois, John
MIGHTY, THE
Bourguignon, Denis G.
TREKKIES
Bourne, J.R.
RIGHT CONNECTIONS, THE
Boussom, Ron
PLAYING BY HEART
Boutoussov, Viatcheslav
BROTHER
Bovingloh, Don
JANE AUSTEN'S MAFIA!
Bowdler Roger
LOVE IS THE DEVIL: STUDY FOR A PORTRAIT OF FRANCIS BACON
Bowen, Jake
PATCH ADAMS
Bowen, Michael
DON KING: ONLY IN AMERICA
TIMOTHY LEARY'S DEAD
Bowens, Harry
DANCE WITH ME
Bower, Hugo
INCOGNITO
Bower, John T.
MIGHTY JOE YOUNG
Bowersox, Bob
PERFECT MURDER, A
Bowie, David
LOU REED: ROCK AND ROLL HEART
Bowles, Hamish
LOVE IS THE DEVIL: STUDY FOR A PORTRAIT OF FRANCIS BACON

Bowlin, Brandon N.
BULWORTH
Bowman, Alan
KURT AND COURTNEY
Bowman, Jeffery
ORGAZMO
Bowman, Ronald "Buzz"
MAJOR LEAGUE: BACK TO THE MINORS
Bowman, Vincent
BILLBOARD DAD
Boxer, Amanda
SAVING PRIVATE RYAN
Boxer, Michael
BABE: PIG IN THE CITY
Boxley, Judith
TALK TO ME
Boy, Gouchy
CAPTIVE
ESCAPE, THE
Boyar, Lombardo
GIA
Boyce, Alan
SKIN & BONE
Boyce, Rodger
NIGHT VISION
TWO FOR TEXAS
Boyce, Todd
HOSTILE WATERS
Boyce, Zoe
VELVET GOLDMINE
Boyd, Guy
RETROACTIVE
Boyd, Jerry
CAUGHT UP
Boyd, Ken
WRONGFULLY ACCUSED
Boyd, Lynda
DISTURBING BEHAVIOR
INVADER, THE
Boyd, Robert
STRAY BULLET
Boyden, Peter
CELEBRITY
Boyer, Carol
PARALYZING FEAR: THE STORY OF POLIO IN AMERICA, A
Boyer, Christopher
WHEN TIME EXPIRES
Boyer, Scott
CURSE OF THE PUPPET MASTER
Boyett, William
GIRLS IN PRISON
Boyle, Alan
BUTCHER BOY, THE
Boyle, Ken
ARMOUR OF GOD
Boyle, Lara Flynn
HAPPINESS
Boyle, Marie
LET'S KILL ALL THE LAWYERS
Boyle, Michael
MY BROTHER'S WAR
Boyle, Peter
DR. DOLITTLE
SPECIES II
Boyle, Valerie
RESCUERS: STORIES OF COURAGE—TWO COUPLES
Boynton, Alexander
WRONGFULLY ACCUSED
Boys and Girls of Cahauo
ZAKIR AND HIS FRIENDS
Bozonnet, Marcel
DISENCHANTED, THE
Bracco, Elizabeth
IMPOSTORS, THE
Bradbury, Stephen
ALONE IN THE WOODS

Bradecki, Tadeusz
FROM A FAR COUNTRY
Braden, Des
SUMMER FLING
Braden, Don
LENA'S DREAMS
Bradfield, Dawn
DANCING AT LUGHNASA
Bradford, Conor
INFORMANT, THE
Bradford, Doug
BOYS IN LOVE 2
Bradford, James
JACK HIGGINS' THE WINDSOR PROTOCOL
LOUISA MAY ALCOTT'S LITTLE MEN
Bradford, Jesse
SOLDIER'S DAUGHTER NEVER CRIES, A
Bradford, Jon
POLISH WEDDING
Bradford, Liberty
BILLBOARD DAD
Bradford, Richard
ELMORE LEONARD'S GOLD COAST
Bradford, Susan
OBJECT OF MY AFFECTION, THE
Bradford, Toby
BREAK, THE
Bradley, Angela
REGENERATION
Bradley, Christopher
BILLY'S HOLLYWOOD SCREEN KISS
Bradley, George
LITTLE VOICE
Bradley, Jamie
TALES FROM A PARALLEL UNIVERSE: GIGA SHADOW
Bradley Jr., Peter
VELVET GOLDMINE
Bradley, Justin
LOUISA MAY ALCOTT'S LITTLE MEN
Bradshaw, Andy
DEAD END
PEACEKEEPER, THE
Bradshaw, Michael
PROPOSITION, THE
Bradway, Kim
BUFFALO '66
Brady, Angela
DEAR JESSE
Brady, Bob
WHEN PIGS FLY
Brady, Don
LOLITA
Brady, Gabriel
SUMMER FLING
Brady, Justin
TWENTYFOURSEVEN
Brady, Michelle L.
STEPMOM
Brady, P.J.
MOONDANCE
Brady, Rachel
I WENT DOWN
Brady, Roger
MY BROTHER'S WAR
Braeden, Eric
MEET THE DEEDLES
Braga, Brannon
TREKKIES
Braga, Sonia
TIETA OF AGRESTE
Bragg, Bobby
LAND OF THE FREE
Bragli, Lene
MENDEL
Braham, Emily
SHOOTING FISH

Braid, Hilda
MRS. DALLOWAY
Braiden, Des
INFORMANT, THE
OLIVER TWIST
Braidwood, Kate
DISTURBING BEHAVIOR
Braidwood, Tom
X-FILES, THE
Branagh, Kenneth
CELEBRITY
GINGERBREAD MAN, THE
PROPOSITION, THE
THEORY OF FLIGHT
Branaman, Rustam
LOVE TO KILL
Brancato, Lillo
ENEMY OF THE STATE
Brand, Marlon
HOSTILE INTENT
Brandenburg, Larry
FEAR AND LOATHING IN LAS VEGAS
MAJOR LEAGUE: BACK TO THE MINORS
MIGHTY JOE YOUNG
SOUR GRAPES
Brandenburg, Otto
KINGDOM, PART 2, THE
Brandon, Mark
AIR BUD: GOLDEN RECEIVER
TRICKS
Brandon, Michael
DEJA VU
DISAPPEARANCE OF KEVIN JOHNSON, THE
Brandt, Max
I MARRIED A STRANGE PERSON!
Brandt, Victor
BABE: PIG IN THE CITY
Brandt, Walker
INDISCREET
Brandy
I STILL KNOW WHAT YOU DID LAST SUMMER
Branklyn, Charles A.
DR. DOLITTLE
Brannen, George Lyndel
GINGERBREAD MAN, THE
Brantley, Betsy
DEEP IMPACT
MERCURY RISING
Brantley, Whitt
BLACK DOG
Branzea, Nicu
BLACKJACK
Braschi, Nicoletta
LIFE IS BEAUTIFUL
PEREIRA DECLARES
Brask, Cecilie
KINGDOM, PART 2, THE
Brass, Lorne
JACK HIGGINS' THE WINDSOR PROTOCOL
Braugher, Andre
CITY OF ANGELS
Braun, Craig
GREAT EXPECTATIONS
Braun, Michael
U.S. MARSHALS
Braunstein, Terry
BUFFALO '66
Braus, Erin
PLAN B
Braverman, Marvin
SOUR GRAPES
WHEN TIME EXPIRES
Braxton, Paulette
NIGHT AT THE ROXBURY, A
Bray, Charles "Chip"
NEWTON BOYS, THE
Bray, Wilfrid
DIRTY WORK
Brayton, Morgan
HARD CORE LOGO
Brazeau, Art
URBAN SAFARI
Brazeau, Jay
AIR BUD: GOLDEN RECEIVER
DISTURBING BEHAVIOR
TRUCKS
Brazier, Jon
UGLY, THE
Brazleton, Conni Marie
DOGWATCH
Brazoban, Beatrice
NAKED ACTS
Breathnach, Paraic
BUTCHER BOY, THE
Breed, Helen Lloyd
HOME BEFORE DARK
Breen, Conor
BRYLCREEM BOYS, THE
Breen, Danny
LAND OF THE FREE
Breen, Patrick
ONE TRUE THING
Bregman, Christopher
ONE TOUGH COP
Breker, Eric
WOUNDED
Breland, Mark
HE GOT GAME
Brendemuhl, Alex
LAST SEDUCTION II, THE
Brendler, Julia
MOONDANCE
Brener, Shirley
HIJACKING HOLLYWOOD
Brenna, Dwayne
BLACK LIGHT
Brennan, Brid
DANCING AT LUGHNASA
Brennan, Kevin
HALF BAKED
Brennan, Sabina
STRAY BULLET
Brennan, Stephen
GENERAL, THE
Brennan, Wayne
CLAY PIGEONS
WALKING THUNDER
Brenneman, Amy
NEVADA
YOUR FRIENDS & NEIGHBORS
Brennen, Paul
INCOGNITO
Breton, Daniel
RONIN
Brett, Danielle
URBAN LEGEND
Brettingham, Steve
KNOCK OFF
Breuer, Jim
HALF BAKED
Breuil, Jose "Don Pepe"
WHO THE HELL IS JULIETTE?
Brewster, Jordana
FACULTY, THE
Brewster, Paget
LET'S TALK ABOUT SEX
Brewster, Phil
RED HAWK: WEAPON OF DEATH
Brewster, Sean
MY BROTHER'S WAR
Brewster, Shawn
SPACEJACKED
STRAY BULLET
Breyner, Nicolau
PEREIRA DECLARES
Brezner, China
KRIPPENDORF'S TRIBE
Briant, Shane
TWISTED
Brice, David
UNDER THE SKIN
Bridges, Beau
DEFENDERS: PAYBACK, THE
Bridges, Jeff
BIG LEBOWSKI, THE
Bridges, Lloyd
JANE AUSTEN'S MAFIA!
Bridges, Todd
LOVE TO KILL
Bridges-Nicasio, Betty
NIGHT AT THE ROXBURY, A
Bridgewater, Stephen
FEAR AND LOATHING IN LAS VEGAS
Brien, Mark Stephen
LITTLE BIGFOOT 2: THE JOURNEY HOME
Brier, Nicole
ROUNDERS
Briers, Richard
SPICE WORLD
Briganti, William
LOLIDA 2000
Briggs, Tony
JOEY
Bright, Don
PALMETTO
Bright, Kenneth L.
PALMETTO
Brightwell, Paul
INNOCENT SLEEP, THE
SLIDING DOORS
Briley-Strand, Gwen
SPECIES II
Brill, Charlie
FLINTSTONES: I YABBA-DABBA DOO!, THE
Brill, Jason
CRACKING UP
Brill, Steven
FRENCH EXIT
WEDDING SINGER, THE
Bringelson, Mark
SOLDIER
Brisbin, David
ALARMIST, THE
FEAR AND LOATHING IN LAS VEGAS
Briscoe, Brent
ANOTHER DAY IN PARADISE
SIMPLE PLAN, A
Brissart, Jean-Pol
MAN IN THE IRON MASK, THE
Bristo, Douglas
OPERATION DELTA FORCE 2
Britton, Connie
NO LOOKING BACK
Broad, Anna
MY BROTHER'S WAR
Broadbent, Jim
AVENGERS, THE
BORROWERS, THE
LITTLE VOICE
Broadber, Jill
UNDER THE SKIN
Brobbey, John
GO NOW
Brock, Benjamin
JACK FROST
WHAT DREAMS MAY COME

Brocklebank, Daniel
MERLIN
SHAKESPEARE IN LOVE
Brockman, Michael
TWILIGHT
Brocksmith, Roy
ALMOST PARTNERS
Brodahl, Ina Sofie
OTHER SIDE OF SUNDAY, THE
Broderick, Beth
FRENCH EXIT
Broderick, Charlie
NEXT STOP, WONDERLAND
Broderick, Erin
BLACK DOG
Broderick, Matthew
GODZILLA
LION KING II: SIMBA'S PRIDE, THE
Brodie, Colin
ENEMY OF THE STATE
Brodin, Gerald
WATCHERS REBORN
Brody, Adrien
TEN BENNY
THIN RED LINE, THE
UNDERTAKER'S WEDDING, THE
Brody, Raymond
GOVERNESS, THE
Brogger, Ivar
SENSELESS
Brolin, James
LEWIS & CLARK & GEORGE
MY BROTHER'S WAR
Brolin, Josh
MY BROTHER'S WAR
NIGHTWATCH
Brolly, Clark
ARMAGEDDON
Bromfield, Gerry
NIL BY MOUTH
Bromley, Joe
GOVERNESS, THE
Bronson, J. Scott
NOT IN THIS TOWN
Brookhurst, Michelle
CAN'T HARDLY WAIT
SENSELESS
Brooklyn, Ranger
ACT OF WAR
Brooks, Albert
DR. DOLITTLE
OUT OF SIGHT
Brooks, Annabel
LOVE IS THE DEVIL: STUDY FOR A PORTRAIT OF FRANCIS BACON
Brooks, Avery
AMERICAN HISTORY X
BIG HIT, THE
Brooks, Bill
DANCER, TEXAS POP. 81
Brooks, Dana
TERMINAL JUSTICE
Brooks, Diana
GOVERNESS, THE
Brooks, George
ZAKIR AND HIS FRIENDS
Brooks, Joyce
SUB DOWN
Brooks, Lonnie
BLUES BROTHERS 2000
Brooks, Melissa
HAV PLENTY
Brooks, Nick
SAVING PRIVATE RYAN
Brooks, Peter
RACE TO SAVE 100 YEARS, THE
Brooks, Stan
SIEGE, THE
Brookshire, Evante
LETTER FROM DEATH ROW, A
Brophy, Anthony
INFORMANT, THE
Brophy, Brian
ARMAGEDDON
LOVE TO KILL
Brosnan, James
BROADWAY DAMAGE
Brosnan, Pierce
QUEST FOR CAMELOT
Brosnon, Charlotte
DISAPPEARANCE OF KEVIN JOHNSON, THE
Bross, Jill
TEN BENNY
Bross, Trent
SUICIDE KINGS
Brossard, Nicole
STOLEN MOMENTS
Brothers, Larry
TWO FOR TEXAS
Broughton, Paul
LIKE IT IS
Broulard, Odile
ARMAGEDDON
SIX DAYS, SEVEN NIGHTS
Broussard, Rebecca
FRENCH EXIT
RINGMASTER
Browder, Ben
BOOGIE BOY
NEVADA
Brown, Arnold
LAND GIRLS, THE
Brown, Ben
DOGWATCH
I STILL KNOW WHAT YOU DID LAST SUMMER
Brown, Big Skinny
CON, THE
Brown, Bill Lee
JOHNNY SKIDMARKS
Brown, Bob
NEMESIS 4: CRY OF ANGELS
Brown, Bobbie
GODSON, THE
Brown, Bobby
PECKER
Brown, Bryan
TRACKED
TWISTED
Brown, Bundy
MODULATIONS: CINEMA FOR THE EAR
Brown, Chloe
DEFENDERS: PAYBACK, THE
Brown, Clancy
BATMAN/SUPERMAN MOVIE, THE
JUNGLE BOOK: MOWGLI'S STORY, THE
Brown, David
OFF THE MENU: THE LAST DAYS OF CHASEN'S
Brown, Dexter
PERFECT MURDER, A
Brown, Don
ADVENTURES OF MOWGLI
DRAGON BALL Z THE MOVIE: DEAD ZONE
DRAGON BALL Z THE MOVIE: THE TREE OF MIGHT
DRAGON BALL Z THE MOVIE: THE WORLD'S STRONGEST
MIGHTY KONG, THE
NEW ADVENTURES OF KIMBA THE WHITE LION, THE
Brown, Donna Marie
APT PUPIL
Brown, Downtown Julie
RIDE
Brown, Dwier
DENNIS THE MENACE STRIKES AGAIN
Brown, Elizabeth
ALMOST PARTNERS
NORTH SHORE FISH
Brown, Foxy
WOO
Brown III, L.P.
FATAL PURSUIT
Brown, James
BLUES BROTHERS 2000
HOLY MAN
Brown, Jim
HE GOT GAME
SMALL SOLDIERS
Brown, John
FARM: ANGOLA, U.S.A., THE
Brown, Julie
PLUMP FICTION
Brown, Junior
STILL BREATHING
Brown, Karen
DEAR JESSE
Brown, Kedar
REAL BLONDE, THE
Brown, Kevin
CRACKING UP
Brown, Lee
REGENERATION
Brown, Lennox
BLADE
ENEMY OF THE STATE
U.S. MARSHALS
Brown, Mark
ELMORE LEONARD'S GOLD COAST
HOLY MAN
OUT OF SIGHT
Brown, Melanie
SPICE WORLD
Brown, Nick
YOU'VE GOT MAIL
Brown, Norman Patrick
THIN RED LINE, THE
Brown, Orlando
SENSELESS
Brown, P.J.
ROUNDERS
Brown, Pat Crawford
JACK FROST
JOHNNY SKIDMARKS
Brown, Peter
ASYLUM
Brown, Philip Martin
HOSTILE WATERS
Brown, Phillip
UGLY, THE
Brown, Randal
STEPHEN KING'S THE NIGHT FLIER
Brown, Robert S.
SUE
Brown, Ronald D.
RUSH HOUR
Brown, Samantha
SUBSTITUTE 2: SCHOOL'S OUT, THE
Brown, Shony Alex
DESTINY OF MARTY FINE, THE
Brown, Sloane
PECKER
Brown, Tracey
ENEMY
Brown, Victor
54
Brown, W. Earl
THERE'S SOMETHING ABOUT MARY
Brown, Wadell
MERCURY RISING

Brown, Wren T.
REBOUND: THE LEGEND OF EARL "THE GOAT" MANIGAULT
Browne, Bernard
DOWN IN THE DELTA
TRACKED
Browne, Katrina
UGLY, THE
Browne, Roscoe Lee
BABE: PIG IN THE CITY
Brownlee, Mongo
BULWORTH
Brownlow, Kevin
RACE TO SAVE 100 YEARS, THE
Brownstein, Rob
VERY BAD THINGS
Brownyard, Steve
SAND TRAP
Brubaker, Christine
IN HIS FATHER'S SHOES
Bruce, Honey
LENNY BRUCE: SWEAR TO TELL THE TRUTH
Bruce, Johnathon
WRONGFULLY ACCUSED
Bruce, Kitty
LENNY BRUCE: SWEAR TO TELL THE TRUTH
Bruce, Reginald
HAV PLENTY
Bruce, Shane
DAVID SEARCHING
Bruce, Shannon
DETONATOR
Bruce, Steve
BAD MANNERS
Bruce, Susan
DAVID SEARCHING
Bruce, Valerie
THERE'S SOMETHING ABOUT MARY
Bruckner, Agnes
SHRUNKEN CITY, THE
Bruckner, Hans Dieter
TALES FROM A PARALLEL UNIVERSE: EATING PATTERN
Bruglio, Julia
I LOVE YOU, DON'T TOUCH ME!
Bruhanski, Alex
SIN AND REDEMPTION
Bruhier, Catherine
BRAM STOKER'S SHADOWBUILDER
Brull, Pamela
LIVING IN PERIL
Brummond, Sheri
FATAL PURSUIT
Brunanski, Craig
INVADER, THE
Brunckhorst, Natja
RAT'S TALE, A
Bruneau, Laura
LITTLE GHOST
Brunelle, Thomas
YOUR FRIENDS & NEIGHBORS
Brunelles, Yann
UN AIR DE FAMILLE
Brunet, Michelle
BLEEDERS
Brunnen, David Zum
STEPHEN KING'S THE NIGHT FLIER
Brunner, Michael
OPERATION DELTA FORCE 2
Bruno, Dylan
SAVING PRIVATE RYAN
WHEN TRUMPETS FADE
Bruno, Gary
FEAR AND LOATHING IN LAS VEGAS
Bruno, Tony
BOOGIE BOY
Bruns, Phillip
JOHNNY SKIDMARKS
Bruskotter, Eric
MAJOR LEAGUE: BACK TO THE MINORS
Bruton, Ian
KNOCK OFF
Bruynbroek, Frank
GODZILLA
Bry, Ellen
DEEP IMPACT
Bryant, John "B.J."
BELLY
Bryant, Kurt
LOVER GIRL
Bryant, Lee
HOLY MAN
Bryant, Peter
HUNTED, THE
Bryce, Mackenzie
HARD RAIN
Brygmann, Lars
CELEBRATION, THE
Brynolfsson, Reine
JERUSALEM
LES MISERABLES
Bryon, Ron
LAST ASSASSINS
Bubriski, Peter
ALL THE RAGE
Bucaro III, Joey
REPLACEMENT KILLERS, THE
Bucatinsky, Dan
OPPOSITE OF SEX, THE
Buccille, Ashley
LAST ASSASSINS
Buchanan, Chris
OPERATION DELTA FORCE 2
Buchholz, Horst
LIFE IS BEAUTIFUL
Buck, Cory
MIGHTY JOE YOUNG
Buckby, Paul
TARZAN AND THE LOST CITY
Buckford, Kenneth
HOW STELLA GOT HER GROOVE BACK
Buckley, A.J.
DISTURBING BEHAVIOR
Buckley, David
JACK HIGGINS' MIDNIGHT MAN
Buckley, Ellen
LIVING OUT LOUD
Buckley, John
NEGOTIATOR, THE
Budaga, Bernard
POST COITUM, ANIMAL TRISTE
Budayova, Irena
KNOCK OFF
Budge, Michael
THERE'S SOMETHING ABOUT MARY
Buehl, Jeffrey
SCARRED CITY
Bueno, Juan
NAKED LIES
Bufalo, Nicholas
MR. NICE GUY
Buff, Sarah
CELEBRITY
Bugajski, Monica
SHADRACH
Buggy, Niall
BUTCHER BOY, THE
Bugin, Mary
BIG LEBOWSKI, THE
Buhr, Gavin
FIRESTORM
Bukvicki, Marina
SAVIOR
Bull, Lawrence
PROPOSITION, THE
Bull, Tommy
FATAL PURSUIT
Bullmore, Amelia
MRS. DALLOWAY
Bullock, Gary
CHILDREN OF THE CORN V: FIELD OF TERROR
Bullock, Sandra
HOPE FLOATS
PRACTICAL MAGIC
PRINCE OF EGYPT, THE
Bully, Bryon
MIGHTY, THE
Bulos, Burt
GODZILLA
Bunakov, Viktor
THIEF, THE
Bunce, Stuart
REGENERATION
Bunch, Jarrod
DON KING: ONLY IN AMERICA
Bunker, Edward
SHADRACH
Bunton, Emma
SPICE WORLD
Buono, Cara
NEXT STOP, WONDERLAND
RIVER RED
Burdette, Nicole
DIGGING TO CHINA
Burdon, Catherine
WOO
Burger, Roy
TWO FOR TEXAS
Burgess, Fison
LAST SEDUCTION II, THE
Burgess, Rick
WRONGFULLY ACCUSED
Burghardt, Arthur
STAR KID
Burgio, Danielle
JOHN CARPENTER'S VAMPIRES
Burke, Adam
LITTLE BOY BLUE
Burke, Al
WEDDING SINGER, THE
Burke, Billy
JANE AUSTEN'S MAFIA!
WITHOUT LIMITS
Burke, Brian
NO WAY HOME
WEST NEW YORK
Burke, Carlase
WHY DO FOOLS FALL IN LOVE?
Burke, Kathy
DANCING AT LUGHNASA
ELIZABETH
NIL BY MOUTH
Burke, Keith
PLAYERS CLUB, THE
Burke, MacLean
SAVING PRIVATE RYAN
Burke, Marylouise
CELEBRITY
MEET JOE BLACK
ONE TRUE THING
Burke, Michael
THERE'S SOMETHING ABOUT MARY
Burke, Robert John
BRIGHT SHINING LIE, A
FIRST LOVE, LAST RITES
SOMEWHERE IN THE CITY
Burke, Stephen
LIKE IT IS

Burke, Tim
LOVE IS THE DEVIL: STUDY FOR A PORTRAIT OF FRANCIS BACON
Burke, Tom
HOMEGROWN
Burke, Victor
SAVING PRIVATE RYAN
Burkholder, Scott
NIGHTWATCH
PRIMARY COLORS
Burks, Jernard
SNAKE EYES
Burmester, Leo
RIVER RED
Burn, Tam Dean
LEADING MAN, THE
Burnett, Carol
MOON OVER BROADWAY
Burnett, Jeff
STEEL SHARKS
Burnette, Billy
CASPER MEETS WENDY
Burnette, Elizabeth
CIVIL ACTION, A
Burnette, Olivia
CHILDREN OF THE CORN V: FIELD OF TERROR
Burney, Staurt
DIRTY LAUNDRY
Burns, Brendan
REAL THING, THE
SLUMS OF BEVERLY HILLS
Burns, Diann
NEGOTIATOR, THE
Burns, Edward
NO LOOKING BACK
SAVING PRIVATE RYAN
Burns, Heather
YOU'VE GOT MAIL
Burns, Jack
SOUR GRAPES
Burns, Jackson Earl
CON, THE
Burns, Jere
MY GIANT
Burns, Peter
U.S. MARSHALS
Burroughs, Hayley
ELIZABETH
Burroughs, Jackie
BLEEDERS
ELVIS MEETS NIXON
Burrows, Darren
HI-LO COUNTRY, THE
Burrows, Saffron
LOVELIFE
NEVADA
Burrus, Swan
LETTER FROM DEATH ROW, A
Burson, Greg
FLINTSTONES: I YABBA-DABBA DOO!, THE
Burstyn, Ellen
DECEIVER
PLAYING BY HEART
Burstyn, Mike
DOGWATCH
Burton, Barbara
NEVADA
Burton, Corey
KIKI'S DELIVERY SERVICE
Burton, Kate
CELEBRITY
Burton, LeVar
STAR TREK: INSURRECTION
TREKKIES
Burton, Noel
CAPTIVE
Burton, Terrance
BIG LEBOWSKI, THE
Bury, Karl
ASYLUM
Busby, Linda
LOVE AND DEATH ON LONG ISLAND
Buscemi, Steve
ARMAGEDDON
BIG LEBOWSKI, THE
IMPOSTORS, THE
REAL BLONDE, THE
WEDDING SINGER, THE
Busch, Ian
KRIPPENDORF'S TRIBE
Busch, Inga
KILLER CONDOM, THE
Busey, Gary
DIARY OF A SERIAL KILLER
FEAR AND LOATHING IN LAS VEGAS
RAGE, THE
REAL THING, THE
SOLDIER
STEEL SHARKS
Busey, Jake
ENEMY OF THE STATE
HOME FRIES
Busfield, Timothy
SOULER OPPOSITE, THE
TRUCKS
Bush, Calvin
MODULATIONS: CINEMA FOR THE EAR
Bush, Margaret
STILL BREATHING
Bush, Robert L.
JOHN CARPENTER'S VAMPIRES
Bush, Tommy
RUSH HOUR
Bushor, Janet
WILD THINGS
Buskin, Aaron
UGLY, THE
Bussieres, Pascale
JACK HIGGINS' THUNDER POINT
Bustric, Sergio
LIFE IS BEAUTIFUL
Butcher, Randy
HOSTILE INTENT
Butcher, Vera
OBJECT OF MY AFFECTION, THE
Butel, Mitchell
DARK CITY
TWISTED
Butkus, Dick
LET'S KILL ALL THE LAWYERS
Butler, Brett
OFF THE MENU: THE LAST DAYS OF CHASEN'S
Butler, Chelsea
DECEIVER
Butler, Dan
ENEMY OF THE STATE
SILVER SCREEN: COLOR ME LAVENDER, THE
Butler, Dick
TOP OF THE WORLD
Butler, Dollie
I GOT THE HOOK UP
Butler, Genevieve
DECEIVER
Butler, Jean
BRYLCREEM BOYS, THE
Butler, Kevin
KNOCK OFF
Butler, Maria
KNOCK OFF
Butler, Mitchell
REBOUND: THE LEGEND OF EARL "THE GOAT" MANIGAULT
Butler, Paul
SPANISH PRISONER, THE
Butler, Peter
ERNEST IN THE ARMY
Buttafuoco, Joey
CELEBRITY
GODSON, THE
Buttafuoco, Mary Jo
CELEBRITY
Butterbean
CHAIRMAN OF THE BOARD
Butterfield, Alexander
ELVIS MEETS NIXON
Butterfield, Neil
LAST DAYS OF DISCO, THE
Butterfield, Richard
LEWIS & CLARK & GEORGE
Butters, Mike
SENSELESS
Buttimore, Simon
BRYLCREEM BOYS, THE
Buzick, William
FATAL PURSUIT
Buzzi, Ruth
BOYS WILL BE BOYS
FLINTSTONES: I YABBA-DABBA DOO THE
Buzzotta, Dave
CHILDREN OF THE CORN V: FIELD OI TERROR
REAL THING, THE
Byatt, Michelle
UNDER THE SKIN
Bye, John Ivar
JUNK MAIL
Byers, Lyndon
MONUMENT AVE.
Bynder, Jerome
OBJECT OF MY AFFECTION, THE
Byrd, David
PROPOSITION, THE
Byrd, Donald
NEXT STEP, THE
Byrd, Eugene
SUBSTITUTE 2: SCHOOL'S OUT, THE
Byrd, Thomas Jefferson
BULWORTH
HE GOT GAME
Byrd, William "Buddy"
HORSE WHISPERER, THE
Byrdy, Wladyslaw
WHITE RAVEN, THE
Byrne, Antoine
I WENT DOWN
OLIVER TWIST
Byrne, Chris
LAND OF THE FREE
Byrne, David
LOU REED: ROCK AND ROLL HEART
Byrne, Gabriel
BRYLCREEM BOYS, THE
ENEMY OF THE STATE
MAN IN THE IRON MASK, THE
POLISH WEDDING
QUEST FOR CAMELOT
ROYAL DECEIT
SUMMER FLING
Byrne, Jason
GENERAL, THE
I WENT DOWN
Byrne, Jenna
WEDDING SINGER, THE
Byrne, John
LOVE IS THE DEVIL: STUDY FOR A PORTRAIT OF FRANCIS BACON
Byrne, Josephine
TWISTED

Byrne, Michael
APT PUPIL
Byrne, Michael P.
CIVIL ACTION, A
I STILL KNOW WHAT YOU DID LAST SUMMER
Byrne, Patsy
LES MISERABLES
Byrne, Stephen
BRYLCREEM BOYS, THE
Byrnes, C.J.
HORSE WHISPERER, THE
Byrnes, Jon
ADVENTURES OF MOWGLI
Byrnes, Vanessa
UGLY, THE
Byron, David
ONE TRUE THING
Byron, Kathleen
FROM A FAR COUNTRY
LES MISERABLES
SAVING PRIVATE RYAN
Caan, Scott
ENEMY OF THE STATE
Caballero, Katia
MADELINE
Caban, Angel
CELEBRITY
Cabezas, Oyanka
CARLA'S SONG
Cabral, Tony
MASK OF ZORRO, THE
Cabrinha, Peter
IN GOD'S HANDS
Cadell, Ava
RETURN TO SAVAGE BEACH
Cadell, Selina
MRS. DALLOWAY
Cadora, Eric
MURDER IN MIND
Cael, Jordan
BELOVED
Caesar, Shirley
WHY DO FOOLS FALL IN LOVE?
Cafagna, Ashly Lyn
MIDAS TOUCH, THE
Cafferty, Frankie
INFORMANT, THE
Caffrey, Olivia
OLIVER TWIST
Caffrey, Peter
I WENT DOWN
Cage, Nicolas
CITY OF ANGELS
SNAKE EYES
Caggiano, Tim
PECKER
Cahill, Lynn
GENERAL, THE
Caicedo, Donny
RUSHMORE
Cail, John Harold
BLEEDERS
Cain, Burl
FARM: ANGOLA, U.S.A., THE
Cain, Dean
TRACKED
Cain, Robbie
BILLY'S HOLLYWOOD SCREEN KISS
Cain, Terry
SLAPPY AND THE STINKERS
Caine
NEGOTIATOR, THE
Caine, Charlie
LIKE IT IS
Caine, Michael
LITTLE VOICE
Cairns, Adrian
JACK HIGGINS' ON DANGEROUS GROUND
Cairns, Tyler
SIMON BIRCH
Caise, Yule
DR. DOLITTLE
Cajzl, Pavel
ACT OF WAR
Calderisi, David
BRAM STOKER'S SHADOWBUILDER
Calderon de Calero, Josefa
CARLA'S SONG
Calderon, Paul
MONTANA
ONE TOUGH COP
OUT OF SIGHT
Caldwell, Sandra
DOWN IN THE DELTA
Cale, John
LOU REED: ROCK AND ROLL HEART
Cale, Paula
MILO
Calfa, Don
DR. DOLITTLE
Calhoun, Monica
PLAYERS CLUB, THE
REBOUND: THE LEGEND OF EARL "THE GOAT" MANIGAULT
Cali, Joseph
SUICIDE KINGS
Calicchio, Larry
HENRY: PORTRAIT OF A SERIAL KILLER PART 2
Call, Allyson
JANE AUSTEN'S MAFIA!
Callaghan, Stuart
VELVET GOLDMINE
Callahan, E.J.
CITY OF ANGELS
Callahan, Greg
GODZILLA
Callan, Carmel
I WENT DOWN
Callan, Margaret
I WENT DOWN
Callan, Peter
BABE: PIG IN THE CITY
DARK CITY
Calleia, Joseph
TOUCH OF EVIL: THE DIRECTOR'S CUT
Callen, Christopher
FEAR AND LOATHING IN LAS VEGAS
Callender, L. Peter
DR. DOLITTLE
Callow, Simon
SHAKESPEARE IN LOVE
Calnan, Richard
CIVIL ACTION, A
Calo, Angela
PECKER
Calomino, Chris
RETURN OF THE KING, THE
Calomino, Michael
RETURN OF THE KING, THE
Caloz, Michael
LOUISA MAY ALCOTT'S LITTLE MEN
Calvello, Jessica
SLAYERS: THE MOTION PICTURE
Calvert, Phyllis
MRS. DALLOWAY
Calvert, William
YOUR FRIENDS & NEIGHBORS
Calypso, Anthony S.
BELOVED
Camacho, Art
LITTLE BIGFOOT 2: THE JOURNEY HOME
Camacho, Mark
LOUISA MAY ALCOTT'S LITTLE MEN
PEACEKEEPER, THE
SNAKE EYES
Camargo, Christano
CENTRAL STATION
Camarina, Kelli
BASEKETBALL
Cameron, Anna
TALES FROM A PARALLEL UNIVERSE: GIGA SHADOW
TALES FROM A PARALLEL UNIVERSE: SUPER NOVA
Cameron, Dean
HI-LIFE
Cameron, Earl
DEJA VU
Cameron, Michael
RESCUERS: STORIES OF COURAGE—TWO WOMEN
Camilleri, Terry
TRUMAN SHOW, THE
Camizuli, Michele
MARIUS AND JEANNETTE
Camp, Andrew
I LOVE YOU, DON'T TOUCH ME!
Camp, Bill
ROUNDERS
Camp, Colleen
PLUMP FICTION
Camp, Hamilton
ALMOST HEROES
DR. DOLITTLE
LET'S KILL ALL THE LAWYERS
Campbell, Andrew
DEAD END
Campbell, Bill
BRYLCREEM BOYS, THE
Campbell, Charles
TEKKEN: THE MOTION PICTURE
Campbell, Colin
ALARMIST, THE
Campbell, Darren
TWENTYFOURSEVEN
Campbell, David
COLONY, THE
Campbell, Desmond
SNAKE EYES
WOO
Campbell, Emma
LOUISA MAY ALCOTT'S LITTLE MEN
Campbell, J. Kenneth
BULWORTH
OPERATION DELTA FORCE 2
Campbell, Julia
DIARY OF A SERIAL KILLER
Campbell, Ken
ARMAGEDDON
Campbell, Larkin
LETHAL WEAPON 4
Campbell, Luther
PLAYERS CLUB, THE
RIDE
Campbell, Mark
MR. NICE GUY
Campbell, Michael Leydon
PAULIE
Campbell, Naomi
BURN HOLLYWOOD BURN
Campbell, Nell
GREAT EXPECTATIONS
Campbell, Neve
54
LION KING II: SIMBA'S PRIDE, THE
WILD THINGS
Campbell, Rennie
WAKING NED DEVINE

Campbell, Rob
HOSTILE WATERS
Campbell, Saskia
BABE: PIG IN THE CITY
Campbell, Scott Michael
BULWORTH
Campbell, Sean
FIRESTORM
HUNTED, THE
Campbell-Robertson, Hamish
PRINCE VALIANT
Campisi, Tony
DOGWATCH
Camuso, Angela
DANGEROUS BEAUTY
Canadian, Mark Turner
RED HAWK: WEAPON OF DEATH
Candela, Michael
I LOVE YOU, DON'T TOUCH ME!
Candelario, Wanda
HAV PLENTY
Canfield, Gene
LOVE WALKED IN
MEET JOE BLACK
Cannata, T.J.
JANE AUSTEN'S MAFIA!
Cannavale, Bobby
WHEN TRUMPETS FADE
Canning, Lisa
BURN HOLLYWOOD BURN
Cannon, Landy
REAL BLONDE, THE
Cano, Daniel
ENEMY OF THE STATE
Canonica, Sybille
BEYOND SILENCE
Canova, Diana
ONE TRUE THING
Cant, Peter
HUMAN BOMB
Cantanese, Kerry
BULWORTH
Cantarelli, Dario
BEST MAN, THE
Cantarini, Giorgio
LIFE IS BEAUTIFUL
Canto, Marilyne
WESTERN
Canton, Abigail
LOST IN SPACE
Cantona, Eric
ELIZABETH
Cantres, Lou
SCARRED CITY
Cantwell, Christopher
RIVER RED
Cantwell, John
BOYS IN LOVE 2
Capaldi, Peter
SHOOTING FISH
Capatch, Blaine
LAST BIG THING, THE
Capizzi, Bill
BABE: PIG IN THE CITY
Caplan, Twink
BILLBOARD DAD
NIGHT AT THE ROXBURY, A
Capodice, John
ENEMY OF THE STATE
RINGMASTER
Capone, Nadia
DOUBLE EDGE
Caponi, Aldo
RABID DOGS
Cappon, John
TWILIGHT
VERY BAD THINGS

Capps, Kate
PLAN B
Caprari, Tony
TARZAN AND THE LOST CITY
Caprita, David
CATHERINE'S GROVE
Capshaw, Kate
ALARMIST, THE
Caradonna, Michael
SUB DOWN
Caraman, Mircea
TALISMAN
Caravetta, Julio
AIR BUD: GOLDEN RECEIVER
Carbo, Henry
GODSON, THE
Carby, Fanny
MRS. DALLOWAY
Card IV, Paul P.
WHAT DREAMS MAY COME
Cardellini, Linda
DEAD MAN ON CAMPUS
DEE SNIDER'S STRANGELAND
Cardello, Jean
WHATEVER
Carden, Paul
GINGERBREAD MAN, THE
Cardinal, Tantoo
SMOKE SIGNALS
Cardinali, Kimberly
SKIN & BONE
Cardinaux, Monette
WESTERN
Cardona, Helene
BILLBOARD DAD
Cardona Jr., Rene
DIDN'T DO IT FOR LOVE
Cardwell, Lena
OBJECT OF MY AFFECTION, THE
Carey, Claudia
PLAN B
Carey, Dan
NIL BY MOUTH
Carey, David
GENERAL, THE
Carey, Geoffrey
COUSIN BETTE
Carey, Matthew
BILLBOARD DAD
Carey, Peter
POLISH WEDDING
Carey, Tom
SIMPLE PLAN, A
Carfa, Gillian
SIN AND REDEMPTION
Carides, Gia
LAST BREATH
PRIMARY COLORS
Carl, Jann
BULWORTH
Carlo, Ismael "East"
PATCH ADAMS
Carlo, Johann
HAPPINESS
Carlson, Beecey
NEIL SIMON'S THE ODD COUPLE II
Carlson, Dylan
KURT AND COURTNEY
Carlson, Erika
MASK OF ZORRO, THE
Carlson, K.C.
LETTER FROM DEATH ROW, A
Carlson, Lillian
URBAN SAFARI
Carlson, Marta
PLAN B

Carlton, Darryl
HALLELUJAH!
Carlton, Jerry
DOGWATCH
Carlton, Lloyd
LAST SEDUCTION II, THE
Carlyle, Robert
CARLA'S SONG
GO NOW
Carmichael, Jason
CAUGHT UP
Carmody, Peter
TWISTED
Carnes, Tara
FALLEN
Carney, Laura
PLEASANTVILLE
Carney, Zane
MY GIANT
Caron, Jean-Luc
INCOGNITO
Carone, Antoni
CATHERINE'S GROVE
Carone, Sarah
SCARRED CITY
Carpenter, David
OUTSIDE OZONA
Carpentieri, Renato
ARTEMISIA
Carpezza, Mark
DEAD MAN ON CAMPUS
Carpio, Maria Alejandra
HOLY MAN
Carpio, Swan
MARIE BAIE DES ANGES
Carr, Howie
CIVIL ACTION, A
Carr, Katie
INNOCENT SLEEP, THE
MRS. DALLOWAY
Carr, Melanie
DEEP RISING
Carradine, David
CHILDREN OF THE CORN V: FIELD OF TERROR
RAGE, THE
Carradine, Robert
BREAKOUT
STRAY BULLET
Carrafa, Nick
MR. NICE GUY
Carraway, James
PATCH ADAMS
Carreno, Ignacio
DAY OF THE BEAST, THE
Carrera, Alberto
MASK OF ZORRO, THE
Carreras, Nora
CHARLIE HOBOKEN
Carrere, Tia
SCARRED CITY
TOP OF THE WORLD
TRACKED
Carrey, Jim
SIMON BIRCH
TRUMAN SHOW, THE
Carrier, Don
54
Carriere, Jean-Claude
NIGHT AND THE MOMENT, THE
Carrigan, Caroline
CIVIL ACTION, A
Carroll, Alexx
SKIN & BONE
Carroll, Beeson
ROUNDERS
Carroll, Brian
PENTAGON WARS, THE

Carroll, Ceciley
SIMON BIRCH
Carroll, Earl
PHOENIX
WEDDING SINGER, THE
Carroll, Jack
WATERBOY, THE
Carroll, James
DIRTY WORK
Carroll, Jim
LOU REED: ROCK AND ROLL HEART
Carroll, Jolene
HUSH
Carroll, Kevin
ALWAYS OUTNUMBERED
OBJECT OF MY AFFECTION, THE
Carroll, Marjorie
NEWTON BOYS, THE
Carrot Top
CHAIRMAN OF THE BOARD
DENNIS THE MENACE STRIKES AGAIN
Carruthers, Christopher
GODZILLA
Carson, L.M. Kit
HURRICANE STREETS
Carson, Steve
GIA
Carter, Adam
PLEASANTVILLE
Carter, Clarence
ANOTHER DAY IN PARADISE
Carter, Craig
DANCER, TEXAS POP. 81
HI-LO COUNTRY, THE
Carter, Derrick
MODULATIONS: CINEMA FOR THE EAR
Carter, Jamaal
ALWAYS OUTNUMBERED
Carter, Jim
MERRY WAR, A
SHAKESPEARE IN LOVE
Carter, Joelle
HORSE WHISPERER, THE
Carter, John
CELEBRITY
Carter, Lynn
DANCER, TEXAS POP. 81
Carter, Mandy
DEAR JESSE
Carter, Myra
BREAK, THE
Carter, Richard
BABE: PIG IN THE CITY
Carter, Terry
MR. NICE GUY
Carter, Vercy
I GOT THE HOOK UP
Cartlidge, Katrin
HI-LIFE
Cartmell, Charles
ELIZABETH
Cartwright, Angela
LOST IN SPACE
Cartwright, Ivan
VELVET GOLDMINE
Cartwright, Jon
INCOGNITO
Cartwright, Nancy
GODZILLA
JUNGLE BOOK: MOWGLI'S STORY, THE
Cartwright, Peter
INNOCENT SLEEP, THE
Cartwright, Veronica
QUICKSILVER HIGHWAY
RAT PACK, THE
Caruana, Michael
BONE DADDY
Carubia, Saverio
JANE AUSTEN'S MAFIA!
Carucci, Pat
CHARLIE HOBOKEN
Caruso, David
BODY COUNT
ELMORE LEONARD'S GOLD COAST
Carvell, Marium
DOWN IN THE DELTA
ONE TOUGH COP
Casadesus, Gisele
POST COITUM, ANIMAL TRISTE
Casanova, Delia
MIDAQ ALLEY
Casar, Amira
MARIE BAIE DES ANGES
Cascio, Will
HI-LO COUNTRY, THE
Cascone, Nicholas
MURDER IN MIND
NIGHTWATCH
Case, Johnie
DIRTY WORK
Casel, Nitanju Bolade
BELOVED
Caserta, Clem
GREAT EXPECTATIONS
Caserta Jr., Clem
GREAT EXPECTATIONS
Casey, Bob
STEPHEN KING'S THE NIGHT FLIER
Casey, Donna
FACULTY, THE
Casey, John P.
GREAT EXPECTATIONS
Casey, Julian
LOST WORLD, THE
Casey, Nollaig
BRYLCREEM BOYS, THE
Casino, John
JOHN CARPENTER'S VAMPIRES
Casler, Heather
WIDE AWAKE
Casnoff, Philip
HOW STELLA GOT HER GROOVE BACK
Cass, Crystal
DISTURBING BEHAVIOR
DOUBLE EDGE
Cass, Marc
SAVING PRIVATE RYAN
Cassadie, Alberto
CHAMBERMAID ON THE TITANIC, THE
Cassar, Dimitri
TARZAN AND THE LOST CITY
Cassar, Raymond
HENRY FOOL
Cassel, Seymour
DREAM FOR AN INSOMNIAC
RUSHMORE
WHEN PIGS FLY
WHO IS HENRY JAGLOM?
Cassel, Vincent
ELIZABETH
Casseus, Gabriel
BLACK DOG
DON KING: ONLY IN AMERICA
FALLEN
Cassidy, Joanna
DANGEROUS BEAUTY
Cassignard, Pierre
SEVENTH HEAVEN
Cassini, John
HALLOWEEN H20: TWENTY YEARS LATER
SPREE, THE
Cassola, Carla
DANGEROUS BEAUTY
Castaldo, Craig A.
GODZILLA
Castellaneta, Dan
MY GIANT
PLUMP FICTION
Castellarin, Stephanie
HOME BEFORE DARK
Castellito, Sergio
PRONTO
Castellucci, Teddy
WEDDING SINGER, THE
Castelotti, Pete
CELEBRITY
Castian, Hazvan
JOHNNY MYSTO BOY WIZARD
Castillo, Enrique
HI-LO COUNTRY, THE
Castillo, Gilma Tuyub
MEN WITH GUNS
Castillo-Faass, Terry
STAR KID
Castle, Keith-Lee
VELVET GOLDMINE
Castle, Ramona
BELOVED
Castle, Robert
BELOVED
Castle Singers
UNDER THE SKIN
Castleberry, Chuck
OUT OF SIGHT
Castoldi, Karen E.
FEAR AND LOATHING IN LAS VEGAS
Castrinho
OYSTER AND THE WIND, THE
Castro, Fidel
EL CHE: INVESTIGATING A LEGEND
Catalano, Laura
54
Catania, Antonio
NIRVANA
Catano, Adriana
HOLY MAN
Cates, Demo
BLUES BROTHERS 2000
Cates, Georgina
CLAY PIGEONS
Cates Jr., Gil
LOVELIFE
Catillon, Brigitte
ARTEMISIA
Catlett, Mary Jo
BRAM STOKER'S THE MUMMY
Catone, Magda
JOHNNY MYSTO BOY WIZARD
Cattell, Todd
KRIPPENDORF'S TRIBE
Catteral, Rod
MR. NICE GUY
Caudell, Toran
BILLBOARD DAD
JOHNNY MYSTO BOY WIZARD
Cauldwell, Sean
UNDER THE SKIN
Caulfield, Maxwell
REAL BLONDE, THE
Caunter, Nicholas
LAST SEDUCTION II, THE
Cauthen, Melvin
SHADRACH
Cavalie, Brenda
TOP OF THE WORLD
Cavanah, Robert
INFORMANT, THE
Cavanaugh, Christine
RUGRATS MOVIE, THE

Cavanaugh, Megan
MEET THE DEEDLES
Cavanaugh, Michael
BLACK THUNDER
BREAST MEN
Cavasos Garza, Eduardo
NEWTON BOYS, THE
Cavett, Dick
ELVIS MEETS NIXON
Caviezel, James
THIN RED LINE, THE
Cawood, Sarah
VELVET GOLDMINE
Cawthorne, Russell
CHINESE BOX, THE
Cayouette, Laura
ENEMY OF THE STATE
KRIPPENDORF'S TRIBE
LOVELIFE
Cazenove, Christopher
FROM A FAR COUNTRY
Cecchi, Carlo
STEAM
Cecere, Fulvio
DISTURBING BEHAVIOR
DOUBLE EDGE
HUNTED, THE
Cecere, Vince
PALMETTO
Ceda, Jon
MURDER IN MIND
Cedar, Larry
FEAR AND LOATHING IN LAS VEGAS
LAND OF THE FREE
WATCHERS REBORN
Cedillo, Julio Cesar
TWO FOR TEXAS
Cedric the Entertainer
RIDE
Cegon, Eric
SIMPLE PLAN, A
Ceili
RIVER RED
Celea, Serban
CLOCKMAKER
Celio, Teco
TRUCE, THE
Cenatiempo, John
ENEMY OF THE STATE
PERFECT MURDER, A
Ceniceroz, Jonathan
BOYS IN LOVE 2
Centner, Amy
PARENT TRAP, THE
Cephers, Troy Anthony
ENEMY OF THE STATE
Cerabolini, Linda
EIGHTEENTH ANGEL, THE
Cerqueira, Daniel
SAVING PRIVATE RYAN
Cerruti, Nino
HOLY MAN
Cerveris, Todd
ONE TRUE THING
Cervi, Valentina
ARTEMISIA
Cervo, Pascal
FULL SPEED
Cesario, Jeff
JACK FROST
Chaatouf, Kader
LIFE OF JESUS, THE
Chaatouf, M
LIFE OF JESUS, THE
Chaatouf, Mme
LIFE OF JESUS, THE
Chabert, Lacey
LOST IN SPACE
Chabrol, Thomas
SWINDLE, THE
Chadbon, Tom
SHOOTING FISH
Chadwick, Alex
SIEGE, THE
Chadwick, Mark
UNCLE SAM
Chae, Sunny
HORSE WHISPERER, THE
Chaet, Mark
SOUR GRAPES
Chai Chun
KILLER ANGELS
Chaifetz, Dana
DIRTY LAUNDRY
Chain, Antoine
SOLDIER'S DAUGHTER NEVER CRIES, A
Chaio, Roy
DRAGONS FOREVER
Chaksam-Pa
FREE TIBET
Chalfant, Kathleen
DAVID SEARCHING
LAST DAYS OF DISCO, THE
PRICE ABOVE RUBIES, A
Chalfoun, Carine
LITTLE BOY BLUE
Chalk, Garry
DISTURBING BEHAVIOR
RUDOLPH THE RED-NOSED REINDEER: THE MOVIE
SPREE, THE
Challet, Jackie R.
WEDDING SINGER, THE
Challey, Christina
RINGMASTER
Challier, Claudine
LA SEPARATION
Chalupa, Vaclav
LES MISERABLES
Chamber, Tom
HANGING GARDEN, THE
Chamberlain, Duncan
PALMETTO
Chamberlain, Nicole
PAULIE
PLAN B
Chambers, Cullen
LOVER GIRL
Chambers, David Kirk
WALKING THUNDER
Chambers, Jacob
ENEMY OF THE STATE
Chambers, Lossen
SIN AND REDEMPTION
Chambers, Monique
LIVING OUT LOUD
Chambers, Stephen
DECLINE OF WESTERN CIVILIZATION PART III, THE
Champagne, Connie
FERNGULLY 2: THE MAGICAL RESCUE
Champagne, Matt
PENTAGON WARS, THE
Chan, Anthony
ARMOUR OF GOD
Chan, Dennis
KNOCK OFF
ROYAL WARRIORS
Chan Fai-hung
FALLEN ANGELS
Chan, Frances
UGLY, THE
Chan, Frankie
PRODIGAL SON, THE
Chan, Henry
DIRTY WORK
TERMINAL JUSTICE
Chan, Jackie
ARMOUR OF GOD
BURN HOLLYWOOD BURN
DRAGONS FOREVER
MR. NICE GUY
RUSH HOUR
Chan, John C.
ROUNDERS
Chan, Kim
LETHAL WEAPON 4
Chan Lau
KILLER ANGELS
Chan Lung
ENCOUNTER OF THE SPOOKY KIND
PRODIGAL SON, THE
Chan Man Cheong
KNOCK OFF
Chan, Michael Paul
U.S. MARSHALS
Chan, Moses
KNOCK OFF
Chan, Victor
MONUMENT AVE.
WOO
Chan Wai Man
ROYAL WARRIORS
Chan, William
KNOCK OFF
Chan, Yau-Gene
REPLACEMENT KILLERS, THE
Chancey, Doug
SHADRACH
Chandler, Dave
LETTER FROM DEATH ROW, A
Chandler, Lloyd
SIX DAYS, SEVEN NIGHTS
Chandler, Simon
INCOGNITO
SPICE WORLD
Chaney, Coach John
HE GOT GAME
Chaney, Eoin
BUTCHER BOY, THE
Chang, Chaplin
CHINESE BOX, THE
Chang, Dr. Julian
CHINESE BOX, THE
Chang, Jen Wei
LETHAL WEAPON 4
Chang, Ray
LETHAL WEAPON 4
Chang, Richard
RETURN TO PARADISE
Chang, Thomas
FACE THE EVIL
Channing, Carol
BRAVE LITTLE TOASTER GOES TO MARS, THE
Channing, Stockard
PRACTICAL MAGIC
TWILIGHT
Chao, Brendan
HOLLYWOOD CONFIDENTIAL
Chao, Harvey
GIRLS IN PRISON
Chao, Rosalind
WHAT DREAMS MAY COME
Chapdelaine, Morris
EBENEZER
Chaplain, Hanna Josesina
KNOCK OFF
Chaplin, Ben
THIN RED LINE, THE
Chaplin, Carmen
POST COITUM, ANIMAL TRISTE

Chaplin, Geraldine
COUSIN BETTE
Chapman, Andrew
TWISTED
Chapman, David
SIMON BIRCH
Chapman, Kevin
MONUMENT AVE.
Chapman, Lonny
NIGHTWATCH
Chapman, Michael
SIX DAYS, SEVEN NIGHTS
Chapman, Sam
LOVE IS THE DEVIL: STUDY FOR A PORTRAIT OF FRANCIS BACON
Chapman, Tom
RIDE
Chapman, Victoria
CLUB VAMPIRE
Chapman, Zach
WHATEVER
Chappelle, Dave
HALF BAKED
REAL BLONDE, THE
WOO
YOU'VE GOT MAIL
Chappey, Antoine
UN AIR DE FAMILLE
Chapuis, Jean-Claude
POST COITUM, ANIMAL TRISTE
Charendoff, Tara
RUGRATS MOVIE, THE
SCOOBY-DOO ON ZOMBIE ISLAND
Charleen
SIX O'CLOCK NEWS
Charles, Emile
LIKE IT IS
Charles, Johnathan
PARALLEL SONS
Charles, Jonathan
RED HAWK: WEAPON OF DEATH
Charles, Maria
OLIVER TWIST
Charles, Rebecca
SHAKESPEARE IN LOVE
Charles, Rodney
NAKED ACTS
Charles, Scott
SHOOTING FISH
Charles, Tom
RED HAWK: WEAPON OF DEATH
Charn
WRONGFULLY ACCUSED
Charof, Alan
ASYLUM
Charpentier, Mike
THERE'S SOMETHING ABOUT MARY
Charpiot, Hugo
UN AIR DE FAMILLE
Chartoff, Melanie
RUGRATS MOVIE, THE
Chartrand, Jean-Paul
SNAKE EYES
Chartrand, Lauro
WOUNDED
Chase, Angie
NEWTON BOYS, THE
Chase, Channing
RAT'S TALE, A
Chase, Cheryl
RUGRATS MOVIE, THE
Chase, Chevy
DIRTY WORK
Chase, Johnie
BONE DADDY
DOWN IN THE DELTA
Chase, Maraya
HENRY FOOL
Chatman, Glenndon
BOYS WILL BE BOYS
Chau, Emil
MR. NICE GUY
Chau, Francois
LETHAL WEAPON 4
WOUNDED
Chauncey, George
OUT OF THE PAST
Chavez, Margaret
PHOENIX
Chavis, Benjamin
BELLY
Chayanne
DANCE WITH ME
Chaykin, Maury
LOVE AND DEATH ON LONG ISLAND
MASK OF ZORRO, THE
Cheadle, Colin
REBOUND: THE LEGEND OF EARL "THE GOAT" MANIGAULT
Cheadle, Don
BULWORTH
OUT OF SIGHT
RAT PACK, THE
REBOUND: THE LEGEND OF EARL "THE GOAT" MANIGAULT
Cheatham, Maree
NIGHT AT THE ROXBURY, A
WEDDING SINGER, THE
Cheek, Molly
SMOKE SIGNALS
Cheeseman, Ken
NEXT STOP, WONDERLAND
PROPOSITION, THE
Chen, Dick T.
LEWIS & CLARK & GEORGE
Chen, Gene
RIDE
Chen Guo An
SHAOLIN TEMPLE, THE
Chen, Kimball
LAST DAYS OF DISCO, THE
Chen, Lauren
OBJECT OF MY AFFECTION, THE
Chen, Lisa Marie
MIGHTY, THE
Chen Man Lei
FALLEN ANGELS
Chen So Aie
BEAUTY INVESTIGATOR
Chen Yue Sang
HEROES SHED NO TEARS
Cheney, Michael
THERE'S SOMETHING ABOUT MARY
Cheng, Becky
FACE DOWN
Cheng, Kent
BODYGUARD FROM BEIJING
Cheng, Mark
KICK BOXER'S TEARS
Chepovetsky, Dimitry
I'LL BE HOME FOR CHRISTMAS
Chernezkyj, Igor
TRUCE, THE
Chernov, Jacqueline
HOLY MAN
Cherot, Christopher Scott
HAV PLENTY
Cherry, Josh
ERNEST IN THE ARMY
Cheshier, Lydell M.
PATCH ADAMS
Cheshire, Denise
JACK FROST
Chesnais, Patrick
POST COITUM, ANIMAL TRISTE
Chester, Craig
DAVID SEARCHING
Cheung, Daphne
JACK HIGGINS' ON DANGEROUS GROUND
JACK HIGGINS' MIDNIGHT MAN
Cheung, Emotion
CHINESE BOX, THE
Cheung, George Kee
LETHAL WEAPON 4
RUSH HOUR
Cheung, Joseph
COMRADES, ALMOST A LOVE STORY
Cheung, Leslie
KNOCK OFF
Cheung, Maggie
CHINESE BOX, THE
COMRADES, ALMOST A LOVE STORY
Cheung Ti-Hong
ENCOUNTER OF THE SPOOKY KIND
Chevolleau, Richard
TRACKED
Chevorchian, Florin
SHRUNKEN CITY, THE
Chevrier, Arno
CHAMBERMAID ON THE TITANIC, THE
Chew, Joshua
I GOT THE HOOK UP
Cheyenne, Peter
PI
Chi, Chao-Li
STILL BREATHING
Chi Zhi Qiang
SHAOLIN TEMPLE, THE
Chibas, Marissa
HENRY FOOL
Chieffo, Michael
BREAST MEN
MERCURY RISING
Chien Yueh-sheng
PRODIGAL SON, THE
Chiklis, Michael
SOLDIER
Chilcott, Barbara
FACE THE EVIL
Chilcutt, Pete
AIR BUD: GOLDEN RECEIVER
Child, Jeremy
REGENERATION
Child, Les
LOVE IS THE DEVIL: STUDY FOR A PORTRAIT OF FRANCIS BACON
Childers, Bill
CATHERINE'S GROVE
Childers, Mary Ann
NEGOTIATOR, THE
Chilli
HAV PLENTY
Chilvers, Patrick
HOSTILE INTENT
Chin, Glen
KNOCK OFF
LOVE TO KILL
Chin, Jeanne
LETHAL WEAPON 4
SHOPPING FOR FANGS
Chinchilla, Chris
BREAKOUT
Chinn, Alva
GREAT EXPECTATIONS
Chiriac, Florin
CLOCKMAKER
LITTLE GHOST
SECRET KINGDOM, THE
Chiros, Jim
PROPOSITION, THE
Chisholm, Anthony
BELOVED

Chisholm, Marcia
ARMOUR OF GOD
Chisholm, Melanie
SPICE WORLD
Chiu, Ann
MIGHTY, THE
Chiu, Phil
PEACEKEEPER, THE
Chiu Wah Lee
CHINESE BOX, THE
Chiupka, Chip
PEACEKEEPER, THE
Chivers, Robin
BURN HOLLYWOOD BURN
Cho, John
SHOPPING FOR FANGS
Cho, Margaret
RUGRATS MOVIE, THE
Chobanian, Arthur
SOUR GRAPES
Chocol, Tara
CHICAGO CAB
Chodos, Daniel
PLAYING BY HEART
Choe, Dean
DOUBLE EDGE
Choir of St. George's School, Windsor, The
SHAKESPEARE IN LOVE
Chong, Phil
LETHAL WEAPON 4
Chong, Tommy
HALF BAKED
Chorale, Faith
BLUES BROTHERS 2000
Choudhury, Sarita
PERFECT MURDER, A
Chow, Billy
DRAGONS FOREVER
KICK BOXER'S TEARS
Chow, China
BIG HIT, THE
Chow Kam Kong
HEROES SHED NO TEARS
Chow, Michael
LETHAL WEAPON 4
RUSH HOUR
Chow, Peter
BEAUTY INVESTIGATOR
Chow, William
KNOCK OFF
Chow Yun-Fat
HONG KONG 1941
REPLACEMENT KILLERS, THE
Choy, Cordelia
KNOCK OFF
Chrest, Joe
CLOCKWATCHERS
OUT OF SIGHT
Chriss, Sandra
DON KING: ONLY IN AMERICA
Christea, Eugen
SECRET KINGDOM, THE
Christensen, David
LET'S KILL ALL THE LAWYERS
Christensen, Dennis
MR. NICE GUY
Christensen, Joseph M.
OBJECT OF MY AFFECTION, THE
Christensen, Laura
KINGDOM, PART 2, THE
Christensen, Sean
EDEN
Christian, Troy
PARENT TRAP, THE
Christian, Wolf
SHOOTING FISH

Christiansen, Margaret
BABE: PIG IN THE CITY
Christianson, Anne
EDEN
Christine, Wanda
CITY OF ANGELS
PATCH ADAMS
Christman, Charlie
STEPMOM
Christmas, Ken
MURDER IN MIND
Christofferson, Debra
BILLBOARD DAD
GODSON, THE
Christopher, Dyllan
ARMAGEDDON
Christopher, Evan
STILL BREATHING
Christopher, June
DR. DOLITTLE
Christopher, Mike
HOLY MAN
Chrystea, Liz
OBJECT OF MY AFFECTION, THE
Chu Din Mo
KILLER ANGELS
Chu, William
BODYGUARD FROM BEIJING
Chuchvara, Tom
PLAYING BY HEART
Chuck D
BURN HOLLYWOOD BURN
Chuipka, Chip
SNAKE EYES
Chun, Paul
HONG KONG 1941
ROYAL WARRIORS
Chung Chi Li, Nicky
RUSH HOUR
Chung, Christy
BODYGUARD FROM BEIJING
Chung Fat
BEAUTY INVESTIGATOR
DRAGONS FOREVER
ENCOUNTER OF THE SPOOKY KIND
PRODIGAL SON, THE
Chung, Leta
KNOCK OFF
Chunn, Tommy
I GOT THE HOOK UP
Chuvalo, George
DIRTY WORK
Ciampi, Daniele
DANGEROUS BEAUTY
Ciarrocchi, Pat
FALLEN
Cibo Matto
FREE TIBET
Cibrian, Eddie
LIVING OUT LOUD
Cicchetti, Mike
FALLEN
Cicchini, Robert
CIVIL ACTION, A
DOGWATCH
PRIMARY COLORS
Ciccolella, Jude
BELOVED
Cicero, Paul
ROUNDERS
Cicero, Phyliss
NIGHT VISION
Cicetti, Rick
GIRLS IN PRISON
Cienfuegos, Juan Carlois
DANCE WITH ME
Cilberg, Frank
GODZILLA

Cinabro, Stephen A.
U.S. MARSHALS
Cinis, Alan
DARK CITY
Cirdler, Justin
HUMAN BOMB
Cirillo, Joe
ALMOST PARTNERS
Cirka, Cassidy
POLISH WEDDING
Citran, Roberto
TRUCE, THE
Citrano, Lenny
SUICIDE KINGS
Ciubotaru, Lelia
SECRET KINGDOM, THE
Ciucur, Manuela
JOHNNY MYSTO BOY WIZARD
Ciuguilea, Iuliana
TALISMAN
Civali, Kevin
THERE'S SOMETHING ABOUT MARY
Cividanes, Robert
CELEBRITY
Clair, Muriel
NEGOTIATOR, THE
Claire, Julie
SOUR GRAPES
Clapczynski, Stefan
FUNNY GAMES
Clapton, Eric
BLUES BROTHERS 2000
CAN'T YOU HEAR THE WIND HOWL?: THE LIFE AND MUSIC OF ROBERT JOHNSON
Clark, Bill
FALLEN
Clark, Blake
ALONE IN THE WOODS
WATERBOY, THE
Clark, Candy
NIAGARA NIAGARA
Clark, Dave Allen
BULWORTH
Clark, Eugene
FACE DOWN
JACK HIGGINS' THE WINDSOR PROTOCOL
Clark, Israel "Wink"
CAN'T YOU HEAR THE WIND HOWL?: THE LIFE AND MUSIC OF ROBERT JOHNSON
Clark, Jonathan
LITTLE VOICE
Clark, Joseph
FUTURE FEAR
Clark, Krystee
ALONE IN THE WOODS
Clark, Madison
HOLLYWOOD CONFIDENTIAL
Clark, Matt
HOMEGROWN
Clark, Mystro
CHAIRMAN OF THE BOARD
Clark, Shaun
TALES FROM A PARALLEL UNIVERSE: SUPER NOVA
Clark, Susan
SNOWBOUND
Clark, William G.
GIRLS IN PRISON
Clarke, Anthony
TWENTYFOURSEVEN
Clarke, Basil
BABE: PIG IN THE CITY
Clarke, Cam
SCOOBY-DOO ON ZOMBIE ISLAND

Clarke, Christopher
ACT OF WAR
Clarke, Eugene
DOWN IN THE DELTA
Clarke, George
LOVE IS THE DEVIL: STUDY FOR A PORTRAIT OF FRANCIS BACON
Clarke, Ian
KNOCK OFF
Clarke, Jason
TWILIGHT
Clarke, Lenny
MONUMENT AVE.
ROUNDERS
THERE'S SOMETHING ABOUT MARY
Clarke, Liz
LOVE IS THE DEVIL: STUDY FOR A PORTRAIT OF FRANCIS BACON
Clarke, Madison
DISAPPEARANCE OF KEVIN JOHNSON, THE
Clarke, Matt
ATOMIC DOG
Clarke, Melody
LITTLE BIGFOOT 2: THE JOURNEY HOME
Clarke, Patsy
DEAR JESSE
Clarke, Rachel
SHAKESPEARE IN LOVE
Clarke, Richard
MEET JOE BLACK
Clarke, Shaun
TALES FROM A PARALLEL UNIVERSE: GIGA SHADOW
Clarke, Warren
FROM A FAR COUNTRY
Clarkin, Richard
RESCUERS: STORIES OF COURAGE—TWO COUPLES
Clarkson, Patricia
HIGH ART
PLAYING BY HEART
Clatterbuck, Tamara
GIRLS IN PRISON
LEWIS & CLARK & GEORGE
PHOENIX
SOUR GRAPES
Clavet, Deano
JACK HIGGINS' THUNDER POINT
SNAKE EYES
Claxton, Jack
BUFFALO '66
Clay, Nicholas
MERLIN
Clay, Ray
HE GOT GAME
Clayton, Judy
TRUMAN SHOW, THE
Clayton, Perry
VELVET GOLDMINE
Clegg, John
MERRY WAR, A
SHOOTING FISH
Cleghorne, Ellen
ARMAGEDDON
Clem, Frank
PHOENIX
Clemenson, Christian
ALMOST HEROES
ARMAGEDDON
BIG LEBOWSKI, THE
MIGHTY JOE YOUNG
Clement, Andrew
PATCH ADAMS
Clemente, Francesco
WHO THE HELL IS JULIETTE?
Clementon-Smith, Christine
LENA'S DREAMS

Clemons, Clarence
BLUES BROTHERS 2000
Clemons, Lorenzo
U.S. MARSHALS
Clendenin, Robert
WATCHERS REBORN
Clennon, David
PLAYING BY HEART
Clifford, Cheryl
NO WAY HOME
TALK TO ME
Clifton, Mark
SOULER OPPOSITE, THE
Clint, Ronnie
OFF THE MENU: THE LAST DAYS OF CHASEN'S
Clinton, George
MY FIRST NAME IS MACEO
Clinton, Roger
RETROACTIVE
RUGRATS MOVIE, THE
Cloke, Kristen
RAGE, THE
Clooney, George
FULL TILT BOOGIE
OUT OF SIGHT
THIN RED LINE, THE
Clotworthy, Robert
OPPOSITE OF SEX, THE
Cloud, Lisa
PARENT TRAP, THE
Clough, John Scott
PHANTOMS
Clover, Andrew
MARIE BAIE DES ANGES
Clovis
YOU'VE GOT MAIL
Clunes, Martin
SHAKESPEARE IN LOVE
Cluzet, Francois
SWINDLE, THE
Clyde, Craig
NOT IN THIS TOWN
Clydesdale, Gareth
BABE: PIG IN THE CITY
Coassin, Cinzia
DARK CITY
Coates, Dorothy Love
BELOVED
Coates, Kade
TRUMAN SHOW, THE
Coats, Steve
MEET JOE BLACK
Cobain, Kurt
KURT AND COURTNEY
Cobbs, Bill
ALWAYS OUTNUMBERED
HOPE FLOATS
I STILL KNOW WHAT YOU DID LAST SUMMER
PAULIE
Coberly, Sydney
REPLACEMENT KILLERS, THE
Coburn, James
AFFLICTION
Cochran, Colby
PRACTICAL MAGIC
Cochrane, Brian
WRONGFULLY ACCUSED
Cochrane, Michael
INCOGNITO
Cockburn, Arlene
GOVERNESS, THE
Cockett, Pat
SIX DAYS, SEVEN NIGHTS
Cockrum, Dennis
ALARMIST, THE
DESPERATE MEASURES

Coco, Salvatore
TWISTED
Cody, Alan
SHAKESPEARE IN LOVE
Cody, Dawn
PLEASANTVILLE
Coen, Alexis Rose
AMERICAN HISTORY X
Coffey, Scott
DISAPPEARANCE OF KEVIN JOHNSON, THE
Cogger, Matt
LOVE IS THE DEVIL: STUDY FOR A PORTRAIT OF FRANCIS BACON
Coggins, Kristina
RETROACTIVE
Coghill, Joy
SNOWBOUND
Cohen, Adam
BOYS IN LOVE 2
Cohen, Amy
FULL TILT BOOGIE
Cohen, Ellen
JACK HIGGINS' MIDNIGHT MAN
Cohen, Greg
WILD MAN BLUES
Cohen, Lynn
HURRICANE STREETS
Cohen, Ray
CELEBRITY
Cohen, Richard
YOU'VE GOT MAIL
Cohen, Scott
GIA
Cohoe, Roy J.
WALKING THUNDER
Cokljat, Robert Bosco
PERFECT MURDER, A
Colasanti, Arduino
OYSTER AND THE WIND, THE
Cold, Ulrik
KINGDOM, PART 2, THE
Cole, Alexander
PARENT TRAP, THE
Cole, Eric Michael
GIA
Cole, Gary
I'LL BE HOME FOR CHRISTMAS
SIMPLE PLAN, A
Cole, George C.
RED HAWK: WEAPON OF DEATH
Cole, Israel
DON KING: ONLY IN AMERICA
Cole, Kevin Anthony
ASYLUM
Cole, Natalie
ALWAYS OUTNUMBERED
Cole, Ted
DRAGON BALL Z THE MOVIE: THE TREE OF MIGHT
Cole, Virginia
INFORMANT, THE
Coleman, Bill
R.I.P. REST IN PIECES: A PORTRAIT OF JOE COLEMAN
Coleman, Brady
CON, THE
HOME FRIES
Coleman, Clarke
JOHN CARPENTER'S VAMPIRES
Coleman, Dabney
YOU'VE GOT MAIL
Coleman, Deirdre
ONE TOUGH COP
WATCHERS REBORN

Coleman, Gary
DIRTY WORK
OFF THE MENU: THE LAST DAYS OF CHASEN'S
Coleman, Jack
LANDLADY, THE
Coleman, Jim
ELMORE LEONARD'S GOLD COAST
PALMETTO
Coleman, Joe
R.I.P. REST IN PIECES: A PORTRAIT OF JOE COLEMAN
Coleman, Kalena
BOYS IN LOVE 2
Coleman, Kari
SOUR GRAPES
Coleman, Rick
THERE'S SOMETHING ABOUT MARY
Coleman, Signy
LAND OF THE FREE
Coleman, Townsend
BUSTER & CHAUNCEY'S SILENT NIGHT
Colgan, Eileen
OLIVER TWIST
Colgan, Valerie
SAVING PRIVATE RYAN
Colicchio, Victor
CELEBRITY
Colicos, John
JACK HIGGINS' THUNDER POINT
JACK HIGGINS' THE WINDSOR PROTOCOL
Colina, Luis
BIG LEBOWSKI, THE
Colitti, Rik
ALMOST PARTNERS
Collard, Kenneth
PASSION IN THE DESERT
Collette, Toni
CLOCKWATCHERS
VELVET GOLDMINE
Collichio, Victor
WEST NEW YORK
Collier, Denorvell "Dee"
DON KING: ONLY IN AMERICA
Collier, Eugene
DON KING: ONLY IN AMERICA
THURSDAY
Collier, George
RIDE
Collier, Marian
LETHAL WEAPON 4
Collins, Blake Jeremy
RICHIE RICH'S CHRISTMAS WISH
Collins, Emmy
PECKER
Collins, Gary
WATCHERS REBORN
Collins, Greg
ARMAGEDDON
ENEMY OF THE STATE
GODZILLA
Collins, Jackie
OFF THE MENU: THE LAST DAYS OF CHASEN'S
Collins, Jessica
BEST OF THE BEST: WITHOUT WARNING
Collins, Joely
URBAN SAFARI
Collins, Karl
TWENTYFOURSEVEN
Collins, Kyle
EBENEZER
Collins, Mark
MERCURY RISING
Collins, Ray
TOUCH OF EVIL: THE DIRECTOR'S CUT
Collins, Robert
TRACKED
Colomby, Scott
DESPERATE MEASURES
JACK FROST
Colon, Epi
SIEGE, THE
Colon, Tony
THURSDAY
Colover, Rachel
MERLIN
Colton, Michael
BEST OF THE BEST: WITHOUT WARNING
MIGHTY, THE
Coltorti, Ennio
EIGHTEENTH ANGEL, THE
Coltrane, Andrew
LOVE IS THE DEVIL: STUDY FOR A PORTRAIT OF FRANCIS BACON
Coltrane, Robbie
MONTANA
Colvey, Catherine
CAPTIVE
Colwell, Joshua
DEEP IMPACT
Comar, Richard
EBENEZER
Combs, Jeffrey
CAUGHT UP
I STILL KNOW WHAT YOU DID LAST SUMMER
Comden, Danny
URBAN LEGEND
Comiskey, Cathy
ONE TRUE THING
Como, Frankie
JANE AUSTEN'S MAFIA!
Compean, Carlos
TWO FOR TEXAS
Compton, Norm F.
REPLACEMENT KILLERS, THE
Compton, O'Neal
DEEP IMPACT
PRIMARY COLORS
Compton, Trey
WHATEVER
Conard, Steven Brian
HORSE WHISPERER, THE
Conaway, Cristi
COLONY, THE
MY BROTHER'S WAR
Condon, Dominic
BABE: PIG IN THE CITY
Condron, Aiden
SAVING PRIVATE RYAN
Conley, Corinne
DEFENDERS: PAYBACK, THE
Conley, Jack
MERCURY RISING
Conley, Mark
INTERLOCKED: THRILLED TO DEATH
Conley, Shannon
POLTERGEIST REPORT: YUYU HAKUSHO
WRATH OF THE NINJA: THE YOTODEN MOVIE
Conlon, Luisa
SOLDIER'S DAUGHTER NEVER CRIES, A
Conlon, Shannon
MEN
Connally, Kevin
SUB DOWN
Connell, Steven Gererd
ANOTHER DAY IN PARADISE
Connelly, Jennifer
DARK CITY
Conner, Chris
PLAYING BY HEART
Conner, Holly
FERNGULLY 2: THE MAGICAL RESCUE
Conners, Kevin
WALKING THUNDER
Connery, Sean
AVENGERS, THE
PLAYING BY HEART
Connick Jr., Harry
HOPE FLOATS
Connolly, Billy
IMPOSTORS, THE
Connolly, John G.
WHATEVER
Connolly, Maria
JACK HIGGINS' ON DANGEROUS GROUND
Connolly, Nora
INCOGNITO
Connolly, Pat
DON KING: ONLY IN AMERICA
Connor, Toy
HENRY FOOL
Connors, Kevin
PLEASANTVILLE
Conrad, Chris
YOUNG HERCULES
Conrad, David
RETURN TO PARADISE
Conrad, Roy
PATCH ADAMS
Conrath, Malcolm
DISENCHANTED, THE
Conrish, Neil
KID IN ALADDIN'S PALACE, A
Conroy, Brendan
BUTCHER BOY, THE
Conroy, Kevin
BATMAN & MR. FREEZE: SUBZERO
BATMAN/SUPERMAN MOVIE, THE
Conroy, Lesley
MY BROTHER'S WAR
Conroy, Neile
GENERAL, THE
Conroy, Ruaidhri
MOONDANCE
Considine, John
GIA
Constantin, Livia
TALISMAN
Constantine, Yorgo
WHY DO FOOLS FALL IN LOVE?
Constantinescu, Madalina
JOHNNY MYSTO BOY WIZARD
MIDAS TOUCH, THE
Conteh, Stephen James
SIX DAYS, SEVEN NIGHTS
Conti, Pier Luigi
BEYOND, THE
Conti, Tom
SUB DOWN
Conti, Ugo
BEST MAN, THE
NIRVANA
Contreras, Derek
TARANTELLA
Contreras, Karen
PRICE ABOVE RUBIES, A
Contursi, Janet
U.S. MARSHALS
Conway, Ann
THERE'S SOMETHING ABOUT MARY
Conway, Denis
I WENT DOWN
Conway, Lyle
BLADE
Conway, Peter
THERE'S SOMETHING ABOUT MARY

Conway, Tim
AIR BUD: GOLDEN RECEIVER
Coogan, Keith
GODSON, THE
Cook, A.J.
IN HIS FATHER'S SHOES
Cook, Ben
LOUISA MAY ALCOTT'S LITTLE MEN
Cook, Christopher
DAVID SEARCHING
Cook, Leslie
HI-LO COUNTRY, THE
Cook, Linda O.
OPPOSITE OF SEX, THE
Cook, Rachael Leigh
DEFENDERS: PAYBACK, THE
EIGHTEENTH ANGEL, THE
LIVING OUT LOUD
Cook, Randall William
REDLINE
Cooke, Alan
SHOOTING FISH
Cooke, Chris
I MARRIED A STRANGE PERSON!
Cooke, Gary
MY BROTHER'S WAR
Cooke, Michael
DISAPPEARANCE OF KEVIN JOHNSON, THE
Cooke, Suzanne C.
NAKED ACTS
Cooley, David
APT PUPIL
Cooley, Terry
BULWORTH
Coolidge, Jennifer
NIGHT AT THE ROXBURY, A
PLUMP FICTION
SLAPPY AND THE STINKERS
Coolio
BURN HOLLYWOOD BURN
Cooney, Kevin
BULWORTH
CLOCKWATCHERS
PRIMARY COLORS
SENSELESS
Cooney, Matthew Ruston
WHEN TRUMPETS FADE
Cooney, Tim
LETHAL WEAPON 4
Cooper, Chris
BREAST MEN
GREAT EXPECTATIONS
HORSE WHISPERER, THE
HORTON FOOTE'S ALONE
Cooper, Dean
REAL HOWARD SPITZ, THE
Cooper, Garry
HOSTILE WATERS
Cooper, Jeremy
GINGERBREAD MAN, THE
Cooper, Justin
DENNIS THE MENACE STRIKES AGAIN
Cooper, Rowena
SHOOTING FISH
Copeland, Joan
OBJECT OF MY AFFECTION, THE
Copikova, Blanka
NEMESIS 4: CRY OF ANGELS
Copp, Aimee
UNMADE BEDS
Coraci, Frank
WATERBOY, THE
Corazza, Vincent
BRIDE OF CHUCKY
LOVE AND DEATH ON LONG ISLAND
Corber, Arthur
WRONGFULLY ACCUSED
Corbiletto, Robert
DANGEROUS BEAUTY
Corby, Peter
NO WAY HOME
Corcoran, Jay
ALL THE RAGE
Corcoran, John
BURN HOLLYWOOD BURN
Cordasco, Nicholas
CHARLIE HOBOKEN
Corday, Bill
LOUISA MAY ALCOTT'S LITTLE MEN
Corden, James
TWENTYFOURSEVEN
Cordero, Maria
CHINESE BOX, THE
Cordoba, Carmen
EL CHE: INVESTIGATING A LEGEND
Cordova, Amanda
HI-LO COUNTRY, THE
Cordova, Laura
JOHN CARPENTER'S VAMPIRES
Corduner, Allan
IMPOSTORS, THE
Corey, Dave
HOLY MAN
TRUMAN SHOW, THE
Corirossi, Nick
CATHERINE'S GROVE
Cork, John
SKIN & BONE
Corlett, Ian James
ADVENTURES OF MOWGLI
MIGHTY KONG, THE
Corley, Pat
WHEN TIME EXPIRES
Cormack, Lynne
TERMINAL JUSTICE
Corman, Maddie
I THINK I DO
Cornacchione, Antoni
HOLY MAN
WILD THINGS
Cornelius, Matt
UGLY, THE
Cornell, Caroline
INTERLOCKED: THRILLED TO DEATH
Cornicard, Stephan
SAVING PRIVATE RYAN
Corone, Antoni
TRUMAN SHOW, THE
Corr, Andrea
QUEST FOR CAMELOT
Corrazza, Vince
URBAN LEGEND
Correa, Rafael
PLAN B
Correa, Roberto
INVISIBLE DAD
Corrente, Damian
HURRICANE STREETS
Corri, Nick
WOO
Corrigan, Antonia
SHOOTING FISH
Corrigan, Kevin
BUFFALO '66
HENRY FOOL
ILLTOWN
SLUMS OF BEVERLY HILLS
Corrigan, Michael
BODY COUNT
Corso, Lee
WATERBOY, THE
Cortese, Joe
AMERICAN HISTORY X
Cortez, Juila
EL CHE: INVESTIGATING A LEGEND
Cosentino, Giancarlo
LIFE IS BEAUTIFUL
Cosgrove, Daniel
OBJECT OF MY AFFECTION, THE
Cosme, Alfredo
OBJECT OF MY AFFECTION, THE
Cosme, Gabriel
MEN WITH GUNS
Cosmo, James
BABE: PIG IN THE CITY
Cossette, Pierre
OFF THE MENU: THE LAST DAYS OF CHASEN'S
Costa, James
JANE AUSTEN'S MAFIA!
Costa, Rudy
DON KING: ONLY IN AMERICA
SIX DAYS, SEVEN NIGHTS
Costabile, David
SIEGE, THE
Costanzo, Anthony Roth
SOLDIER'S DAUGHTER NEVER CRIES, A
Costanzo, Paulo
RESCUERS: STORIES OF COURAGE—TWO COUPLES
Costanzo, Robert
AIR BUD: GOLDEN RECEIVER
BATMAN & MR. FREEZE: SUBZERO
BATMAN/SUPERMAN MOVIE, THE
PLUMP FICTION
Costas, Bob
BASEKETBALL
Costello, Elvis
SPICE WORLD
Costelloe, Joe
CELEBRITY
Costenza, Len
SENSELESS
Costescu, Petre
GADJO DILO
Costigan, Ken
IMPOSTORS, THE
Costrini, Angela
GINGERBREAD MAN, THE
Cote, Robert-Pierre
JACK LONDON'S THE CALL OF THE WILD: DOG OF THE YUKON
Cote, Tina
MEAN GUNS
Cotovsky, Marla
MIDAS TOUCH, THE
Cotrell, Mickey
SKIN & BONE
Cotten, Joseph
TOUCH OF EVIL: THE DIRECTOR'S CUT
Cotter, Jemima
LOVE IS THE DEVIL: STUDY FOR A PORTRAIT OF FRANCIS BACON
Cotter, Tom
NEXT STOP, WONDERLAND
Cotterill, Chrissie
NIL BY MOUTH
Cottle, Jason
WEDDING SINGER, THE
Cotton, Anthony
LOVE IS THE DEVIL: STUDY FOR A PORTRAIT OF FRANCIS BACON
Cotton, James Anthony
PATCH ADAMS
Cotton, Jerry
LITTLE BOY BLUE
Cotton, Oliver
INNOCENT SLEEP, THE
Cottreel, Genevieve
LIFE OF JESUS, THE
Cottreel, Marjorie
LIFE OF JESUS, THE

Cottrell, Mickey
APT PUPIL
Coulson, Bernie
HARD CORE LOGO
Coulson, Grover
NIGHT VISION
Coulter, Bridgid
ALWAYS OUTNUMBERED
Council, Richard
BREAK, THE
Countryman, Eric
JOHNNY MYSTO BOY WIZARD
Couprie, Denis
KNOCK OFF
Courier, David
DAVID SEARCHING
Court, Alyson
ELVIS MEETS NIXON
Courtney, Chad
SCARRED CITY
Couser, Clifford
DON KING: ONLY IN AMERICA
Couser, Kathleen
STILL BREATHING
Cousins, Brian
LIVING IN PERIL
Cousins, Christopher
SUBSTITUTE 2: SCHOOL'S OUT, THE
Cover, Franklin
ALMOST HEROES
Covert, Allen
WATERBOY, THE
WEDDING SINGER, THE
Cowen, Shulie
CHICAGO CAB
Cowher, Bill
WATERBOY, THE
Cowie, Victor
TRUCKS
Cowling, Paul
ATOMIC DOG
Cox, Alan
MRS. DALLOWAY
Cox, Brian
DESPERATE MEASURES
ROYAL DECEIT
RUSHMORE
Cox, Carl
MODULATIONS: CINEMA FOR THE EAR
Cox, Claire
LEADING MAN, THE
SHOOTING FISH
Cox, Greg
HANDS ON A HARDBODY
Cox, Jennifer Elise
FEAR AND LOATHING IN LAS VEGAS
Cox, Johanna
INSIDE/OUT
Cox, John Henry
SIEGE, THE
Cox, Nikki
SUB DOWN
Cox, Renee
NAKED ACTS
Cox, Richard
SNOWBOUND
Cox, Ronny
REBOUND: THE LEGEND OF EARL "THE GOAT" MANIGAULT
Cox, Veanne
CHARLIE HOBOKEN
HENRY FOOL
YOU'VE GOT MAIL
Coyle, Brendan
GENERAL, THE
Coyle, Eliza
COURTING COURTNEY
Coyle, J. Stephen
PATCH ADAMS
Coyle, James
FROM A FAR COUNTRY
Coyle, Joe
OUT OF SIGHT
Coyne, Roxanne
SHOPPING FOR FANGS
Coyne, Susan
EBENEZER
RESCUERS: STORIES OF COURAGE—TWO COUPLES
Coyote, Peter
INDISCREET
PATCH ADAMS
SPHERE
TERMINAL JUSTICE
TOP OF THE WORLD
TWO FOR TEXAS
Crabb, Bill
GINGERBREAD MAN, THE
Crable, Bradley
MAJOR LEAGUE: BACK TO THE MINORS
Crabtree, Michael
DANCER, TEXAS POP. 81
Cracknell, Ruth
JOEY
Cracroft, Stephen
NOT IN THIS TOWN
Craddock, Billie
DANCER, TEXAS POP. 81
Craddock, Jordan
NEVADA
Craig, Carl
MODULATIONS: CINEMA FOR THE EAR
Craig, Daniel
ELIZABETH
LOVE IS THE DEVIL: STUDY FOR A PORTRAIT OF FRANCIS BACON
Cramer, Kendal
GOVERNESS, THE
Cramer, Rick
WHEN TIME EXPIRES
Crampton, Barbara
GODSON, THE
Cranberry, Don
TRUCKS
Crandell, Charlie
NEVADA
Crane, Carol
LAST ASSASSINS
Crane, Chilton
FIRESTORM
Crane, Rachel
SOUR GRAPES
Crane, Vanessa
EIGHTEENTH ANGEL, THE
Cranham, Kenneth
JACK HIGGINS' ON DANGEROUS GROUND
JACK HIGGINS' MIDNIGHT MAN
Cranitch, Lorcan
DANCING AT LUGHNASA
Cranston, Bryan
SAVING PRIVATE RYAN
Crapie, Anne-Cecile
SOLDIER'S DAUGHTER NEVER CRIES, A
Craven, Matt
PAULIE
Craven, Mimi
DOGWATCH
Crawford Brown, Patrick
JOHNNY MYSTO BOY WIZARD
Crawford, Cindy
54
Crawford, Eve
MIGHTY, THE
Crawford, George
FARM: ANGOLA, U.S.A., THE
Crawford, J.W.
ZERO EFFECT
Crawford, Rachael
IN HIS FATHER'S SHOES
Crawford, Shontonette
HAV PLENTY
Crawford, Sophia
BEAUTY INVESTIGATOR
Cray, Robert
CAN'T YOU HEAR THE WIND HOWL?: THE LIFE AND MUSIC OF ROBERT JOHNSON
Creal, Sheila
SOULER OPPOSITE, THE
Crecco, Michael
CELEBRITY
Creech, Don
HENRY FOOL
Creed, Ben
COMEDY'S DIRTIEST DOZEN
Creed-Miles, Charlie
NIL BY MOUTH
Cregg, Ian
LES MISERABLES
Creighton, Kay
SUMMER FLING
Cremins, Coach Robert "Bobby"
HE GOT GAME
Crenn, Yvon
SWINDLE, THE
Crenna, Richard
WRONGFULLY ACCUSED
Crenshaw, Patrick
ALMOST HEROES
Crenshaw, Randy
FLINTSTONES: I YABBA-DABBA DOO!, THE
Crescenzo, James
DOUBLE EDGE
Crewson, Wendy
EIGHTEENTH ANGEL, THE
Crider, Missy
GIRLS IN PRISON
QUICKSILVER HIGHWAY
Crisp, Quentin
BARRIERS
Crispin, Wilfredo A.
WOO
Cristea, Eugen
CLOCKMAKER
Cristensen, Alisa
LAND OF THE FREE
Cristin, Tomi
CLOCKMAKER
Cristofel, David
REAL HOWARD SPITZ, THE
Criswell, Lora Anne
PRACTICAL MAGIC
Crivello, Anthony
JANE AUSTEN'S MAFIA!
RUNNING WOMAN, THE
Croft, Doreen Chou
PATCH ADAMS
Croft, Jamie
JOEY
Crompton, Ben
LES MISERABLES
Cromwell, James
BABE: PIG IN THE CITY
DEEP IMPACT
SPECIES II
Cronauer, Gail
LITTLE BOY BLUE
NEWTON BOYS, THE
Cronin, Jeanette
DARK CITY

Cronin, Pat
BREAST MEN
Cronyn, Hume
HORTON FOOTE'S ALONE
12 ANGRY MEN
Crooks, Tara
BRAM STOKER'S SHADOWBUILDER
Cropper, Steve
BLUES BROTHERS 2000
Crosbie, Annette
SHOOTING FISH
Crosby, Cathy Lee
REAL HOWARD SPITZ, THE
Crosby, Denise
DEEP IMPACT
TREKKIES
Cross
HALLELUJAH!
Cross, Ben
INVADER, THE
Cross, David
SMALL SOLDIERS
Cross, Garvin
HUNTED, THE
Cross, Harley
SOLDIER'S DAUGHTER NEVER CRIES, A
Cross, Joseph
DESPERATE MEASURES
JACK FROST
WIDE AWAKE
Cross, Melissa
WATCHERS REBORN
Cross, Rick
WRONGFULLY ACCUSED
Cross, Roger R.
DOUBLE EDGE
Crossley, Steven
MERRY WAR, A
Croughwell, Cameron
SIMON BIRCH
Croughwell, Joshua
SIMON BIRCH
Crousdale, Adam
TARZAN AND THE LOST CITY
Crow, Sheryl
54
Crowden, Graham
INNOCENT SLEEP, THE
Crowder, Daniel
AVENGERS, THE
Crowder, Rico
I GOT THE HOOK UP
Crowe, Russell
HEAVEN'S BURNING
Crowley, Amelia
I WENT DOWN
Crowley, Donncha
SPACEJACKED
Crowley, Kevin
SUICIDE KINGS
Crowley, Lawrence
ASYLUM
Crowson, Hilary
INNOCENT SLEEP, THE
Crowther, Hal
DEAR JESSE
Crowther, John
EIGHTEENTH ANGEL, THE
Crudele, Frank
BLACKJACK
WOUNDED
Crudup, Billy
HI-LO COUNTRY, THE
MONUMENT AVE.
WITHOUT LIMITS
Cruise, Yvette
PHOENIX
Crum, Coach Denny
HE GOT GAME
Crumb, Chrisopher
FACE DOWN
Cruttenden, Hal
MRS. DALLOWAY
Cruz, Alexis
WHY DO FOOLS FALL IN LOVE?
Cruz, Anthony "Az"
BELLY
Cruz, Anthony Jesse
JANE AUSTEN'S MAFIA!
Cruz, Diana
ELMORE LEONARD'S GOLD COAST
Cruz, Gary
GODZILLA
Cruz, Gregory Norman
ALMOST HEROES
RUNNING WOMAN, THE
Cruz, Marcelino
CARLA'S SONG
Cruz, Penelope
HI-LO COUNTRY, THE
LIVE FLESH
TALK OF ANGELS
Cruz, Ricardo
EVER AFTER
Cruz, Tania
MEN WITH GUNS
Cruzat, Liza
KISSING A FOOL
Cryer, Jon
HOLY MAN
PLAN B
Crystal, Billy
MY GIANT
Crystal, Jennifer
DON KING: ONLY IN AMERICA
Crystal, Lindsay
MY GIANT
Csitos, Michelle
NIGHTWATCH
Csokas, Marton
BOYS IN LOVE 2
Cuccioli, Robert
CELEBRITY
Cucciolla, Riccardo
RABID DOGS
Cucinotta, Maria Grazia
DAY OF THE BEAST, THE
Cudlitz, Michael
NEGOTIATOR, THE
Cuervo, Alma
CELEBRITY
Cuevas, Elizabeth Strong
LAST DAYS OF DISCO, THE
Cuevas, Jose-Luis
DIDN'T DO IT FOR LOVE
Cuker, Elliot
SPANISH PRISONER, THE
Culbertson, Rod
ELIZABETH
Culkin, Kieran
MIGHTY, THE
Culkin, Michael
DANGEROUS BEAUTY
LOLITA
Cullen, Glen
FUTURE FEAR
Cullen, Jonathan
VELVET GOLDMINE
Cullen, Juana
HAV PLENTY
Cullum, Jim
STILL BREATHING
Culotta, Phil
BOOGIE BOY
Culp, Joe
LOS LOCOS
Culp, Tara Ann
SNAKE EYES
Cumming, Alan
SPICE WORLD
Cumming, Alastair
VELVET GOLDMINE
Cummings, Brenda
DAVID SEARCHING
Cummings, James
RUSTY: THE GREAT RESCUE
Cummings, Jim
ANTZ
BABE: PIG IN THE CITY
BUSTER & CHAUNCEY'S SILENT NIGHT
SCOOBY-DOO ON ZOMBIE ISLAND
SMALL SOLDIERS
Cummings Jr., Richard
UNCLE SAM
Cumyn, Steve
FACE DOWN
Cundell, Pamela
TWENTYFOURSEVEN
Cunningham, Bill
GINGERBREAD MAN, THE
Cunningham, Jocelyn
HANGING GARDEN, THE
LOVE AND DEATH ON LONG ISLAND
Cunningham, Matt
DECAMPITATED
Curran, Paul
MERLIN
Curran, Tony
GO NOW
Currie, Brian Hayes
ARMAGEDDON
Curry, Christopher
BULWORTH
Curry, Mark
ARMAGEDDON
Curry, Tim
RUGRATS MOVIE, THE
TALES FROM A PARALLEL UNIVERSE: SUPER NOVA
Curtin, Jane
ANTZ
Curtis, Andy
ATOMIC DOG
Curtis, Charlie
ENEMY OF THE STATE
Curtis, Cliff
DEEP RISING
SIX DAYS, SEVEN NIGHTS
Curtis, Clint
BLADE
DEEP RISING
Curtis, Grant
SIMPLE PLAN, A
Curtis Hall, Vondie
DON KING: ONLY IN AMERICA
Curtis, Jahmal
WIDE AWAKE
Curtis, Jamie Lee
HALLOWEEN H20: TWENTY YEARS LATER
HOMEGROWN
Curtis, Janis
HANDS ON A HARDBODY
Curtis, Keene
RICHIE RICH'S CHRISTMAS WISH
Curtis, Liz
DANCE WITH ME
Curtis, Tony
ELVIS MEETS NIXON
Curtiz, David
SHAKESPEARE IN LOVE

Dante, Carol
TARANTELLA
Dante, Peter
WATERBOY, THE
WEDDING SINGER, THE
Danticat, Edwidge
BELOVED
Danton, Steve
HOW STELLA GOT HER GROOVE BACK
Danyliu, Andre
DISTURBING BEHAVIOR
Danza, Tony
ILLTOWN
LOVE TO KILL
NORTH SHORE FISH
12 ANGRY MEN
Danzig, Glenn
PROPHECY II, THE
Dapkunaite, Ingeborg
JACK HIGGINS' ON DANGEROUS GROUND
Daprocida, Rob
WRONGFULLY ACCUSED
Daprocida, Ron
DOUBLE EDGE
Darabont, Frank
JOHN CARPENTER'S VAMPIRES
DaRae, Eric
DISAPPEARANCE OF KEVIN JOHNSON, THE
Daraiseh, Ammar
U.S. MARSHALS
Darby, Bart
NO WAY HOME
Darga, Christopher
DEEP IMPACT
Dario, Erika
RABID DOGS
Darius
DECLINE OF WESTERN CIVILIZATION PART III, THE
Dark, Peter
CELEBRITY
Darka, Toskovic
SAVIOR
Darling, Jennifer
RUSTY: THE GREAT RESCUE
Darlow, Linda
WHEN DANGER FOLLOWS YOU HOME
Darmstaedter, David
DESTINY OF MARTY FINE, THE
NEVADA
Darne, Steve
SUB DOWN
Darnell, Chad
GINGERBREAD MAN, THE
Darnell, Michael
THURSDAY
Darpino, Gloria
WEST NEW YORK
Darr, Lisa
GODS AND MONSTERS
LAND OF THE FREE
PLAN B
Darro, Bambi
RED HAWK: WEAPON OF DEATH
Darroussin, Jean-Pierre
MARIUS AND JEANNETTE
UN AIR DE FAMILLE
Darroussin, Marie
MARIUS AND JEANNETTE
Darrow, Danny
OBJECT OF MY AFFECTION, THE
Darrow, Oliver
LAST ASSASSINS
Darrow, Tony
CELEBRITY
Darst, Danny
GINGERBREAD MAN, THE
Dasilva, Danielle
FUTURE FEAR
Date, Saburo
SLEEPY EYES OF DEATH: FULL CIRCLE KILLING
Dato, Immanuel
THIN RED LINE, THE
Davenport, Johnny Lee
U.S. MARSHALS
Daveron, Alan
MY BROTHER'S WAR
David, Angel
SUBSTITUTE 2: SCHOOL'S OUT, THE
TWO GIRLS AND A GUY
David, Ingolf
KINGDOM, PART 2, THE
David, Keith
ARMAGEDDON
DON KING: ONLY IN AMERICA
THERE'S SOMETHING ABOUT MARY
David, Larry
SOUR GRAPES
David, Zdenek
LES MISERABLES
Davidovich, Lolita
GODS AND MONSTERS
Davids, Christo
ERNEST IN THE ARMY
Davidson, Alan
ROUNDERS
Davidson, Josephine
HERCULES AND XENA THE ANIMATED MOVIE: THE BATTLE FOR MOUNT OLYMPUS
Davidson, Richard
BROADWAY DAMAGE
Davidson, Tommy
PLUMP FICTION
WOO
Davidtz, Embeth
FALLEN
GINGERBREAD MAN, THE
Davies, Eleanor
DIRTY WORK
Davies, Jeremy
SAVING PRIVATE RYAN
Davies, John S.
CON, THE
Davies, Kimberley
TWISTED
Davies, Robin
SHAKESPEARE IN LOVE
Davis, Bob
SIMPLE PLAN, A
Davis, Bridget D.
HAV PLENTY
Davis, Bridgett
NAKED ACTS
Davis, Cisco
SUBSTITUTE 2: SCHOOL'S OUT, THE
Davis, Coach Tom
HE GOT GAME
Davis, Craig
X-FILES, THE
Davis, Daryl
TRUMAN SHOW, THE
Davis, Don S.
TRICKS
Davis, Duane
BURN HOLLYWOOD BURN
KNOCK OFF
Davis, Eddy
WILD MAN BLUES
Davis, Edgar
INSIDE/OUT
Davis, Everton
DON KING: ONLY IN AMERICA
Davis, Felix
LAND GIRLS, THE
Davis, Frank
FALLEN
Davis, Gary Lee
WHEN TIME EXPIRES
Davis, Glynis
DISTURBING BEHAVIOR
Davis, Hope
IMPOSTORS, THE
NEXT STOP, WONDERLAND
Davis, Jason
JANE AUSTEN'S MAFIA!
RUSH HOUR
Davis, Jeff
NIGHTWATCH
Davis, Joe "Cool"
SECRET KINGDOM, THE
Davis, John T.
BLUES BROTHERS 2000
Davis Jr., Billy
OFF THE MENU: THE LAST DAYS OF CHASEN'S
Davis, Judy
CELEBRITY
Davis, Julie
I LOVE YOU, DON'T TOUCH ME!
Davis, K. Bradley
NAKED ACTS
Davis, Karen
FORMER CHILD STAR
Davis, Kristin
SOUR GRAPES
Davis, Ossie
DR. DOLITTLE
12 ANGRY MEN
Davis, Paula
LOLITA
Davis, Philip
PHOTOGRAPHING FAIRIES
Davis, Regi
PECKER
Davis, Reverend France A.
NOT IN THIS TOWN
Davis, Robert
TRUMAN SHOW, THE
Davis, Sarah Scott
DON KING: ONLY IN AMERICA
SOULER OPPOSITE, THE
Davis, Stan
CITY OF ANGELS
PRIMARY COLORS
Davis, Susan
LETTER FROM DEATH ROW, A
Davis, Tom
BLUES BROTHERS 2000
Davis, Trey
VERY BAD THINGS
Davis, Vicki
MIGHTY JOE YOUNG
Davis, Viola
OUT OF SIGHT
PENTAGON WARS, THE
Davis, Warwick
PRINCE VALIANT
Davis, William B.
X-FILES, THE
Davis-Williams, Shanesia
CHICAGO CAB
Davisan, Michelle
COLONY, THE
Davison, Bruce
APT PUPIL
LOVELIFE
PAULIE

Davoli, Andrew
SCARRED CITY
Davy, Susan
BLUES BROTHERS 2000
Dawkins, Harold
HOW STELLA GOT HER GROOVE BACK
Dawson, Deacon
BODY COUNT
Dawson, Rosario
HE GOT GAME
Day, Gary
TWISTED
Day, Larry
CAPTIVE
DEAD END
Day, Nicholas
HUMAN BOMB
Day, Simon
SHAKESPEARE IN LOVE
Daydoge, Billy
ALMOST HEROES
DB
MODULATIONS: CINEMA FOR THE EAR
De Almeida, Joaquim
PEREIRA DECLARES
de Angelis, Judy
SIEGE, THE
de Angelo, Kim
SIX-STRING SAMURAI
De Angelo, Paul
REAL THING, THE
de Bankole, Isaac
SOLDIER'S DAUGHTER NEVER CRIES, A
de Boer, Nicole
CUBE
de Broux, Lee
MARS
de Caro, Vincenzo
CHAMBERMAID ON THE TITANIC, THE
de Castro, Isabel
VOYAGE TO THE BEGINNING OF THE WORLD
De Crispino, Sam
ENEMY OF THE STATE
De Falco, Steve
LOLIDA 2000
De Fibo, Paul
SIMON BIRCH
de Gooyer, Rijk
DRESS, THE
de Guzman, Nino
EL CHE: INVESTIGATING A LEGEND
de Habsburgo, Inmaculada
LAST DAYS OF DISCO, THE
De Jesus, James
WOO
de Jesus Vasquez Morales, Manuel
MASK OF ZORRO, THE
De Jesus, Wanda
ELMORE LEONARD'S GOLD COAST
de Johnette, Jacques
BLUES BROTHERS 2000
de Juan, Jorge
TALK OF ANGELS
De La Cruz, Mariano Lopez
MEN WITH GUNS
De La Cruz, Mark
I'LL BE HOME FOR CHRISTMAS
De La Fuente, Joel
RETURN TO PARADISE
De La Huerta, Paz
OBJECT OF MY AFFECTION, THE
De La Osa, Kristian
MADELINE
De La Paix, Yvonne
MY GIANT
De La Rocha, Vanessa
RINGMASTER
De La Soul
FREE TIBET
De La Torre Lopez, Antonio
MEN WITH GUNS
de la Valade, Jean
POST COITUM, ANIMAL TRISTE
De Lancie, John
TREKKIES
De Landa, Manuel
R.I.P. REST IN PIECES: A PORTRAIT OF JOE COLEMAN
De Laria, Lea
PLUMP FICTION
De Leon, Idalis
RIDE
de Leon, Phillip
BOYS IN LOVE 2
de Lint, Derek
DEEP IMPACT
De Lizia, Cara
DON KING: ONLY IN AMERICA
De Luca, Aaron
ARTEMISIA
De Marchi, Laura
BEYOND, THE
De Mornay, Rebecca
CON, THE
de Nava, Giovanni
BEYOND, THE
De Niro, Drena
GREAT EXPECTATIONS
De Niro, Robert
GREAT EXPECTATIONS
LENNY BRUCE: SWEAR TO TELL THE TRUTH
RONIN
de Oliveira, Vinicius
CENTRAL STATION
De Ortega y Gasca, Felipe
DANCER, TEXAS POP. 81
de Palma, Rossy
TALK OF ANGELS
De Quevedo, Rafael
MEN WITH GUNS
De Ravenel, Ariel
LOVE IS THE DEVIL: STUDY FOR A PORTRAIT OF FRANCIS BACON
de Razza, Armando
DAY OF THE BEAST, THE
De Roxtra, Ron
NEWTON BOYS, THE
De Salvo, Anne
MURDER IN MIND
De Santis, Silvia
ARTEMISIA
De Santis, Tony
BLACKJACK
NORTH SHORE FISH
De Sapio, Francesca
EIGHTEENTH ANGEL, THE
De Silva, Pietro
LIFE IS BEAUTIFUL
De Stefano, Michael
UNMADE BEDS
de Tavira, Jose Maria
MASK OF ZORRO, THE
De Villiers, Gys
TARZAN AND THE LOST CITY
De Vincentis, D.V.
BLADE
De Vincenzis, Ilaria
DANGEROUS BEAUTY
De Wees, Rusty
BLACK DOG
De Winter, Jo
INDISCREET
De Young, Cliff
GEORGE WALLACE
Deacon, Robert
WILD THINGS
Deadmon, Kelly
SNAKE EYES
Deakins, Mark
STAR TREK: INSURRECTION
Deal, Jenilee
MIGHTY JOE YOUNG
Deal, Matt
MIGHTY JOE YOUNG
Dealey, Fiona
LOVE IS THE DEVIL: STUDY FOR A PORTRAIT OF FRANCIS BACON
Dean, Erin J.
LOLITA
Dean, James F.
DR. DOLITTLE
Dean, Jarrod
THIN RED LINE, THE
Dean, Jason
CURSE OF THE PUPPET MASTER
Dean, Jerry
NO WAY HOME
Dean, Loren
ENEMY OF THE STATE
Dean, Rick
CASPER MEETS WENDY
DETONATOR
Dean, Ron
CHICAGO CAB
Dean-Jones, Mercia
TWISTED
Deane, Freddy
LOVE TO KILL
Deane, Fredrick
NEXT STEP, THE
Deane, Lezlie
PLUMP FICTION
Dearborn, Mike
MODULATIONS: CINEMA FOR THE EAR
DeArcy, Patricia
NAKED ACTS
Deavers, Dorothy
LOLITA
Deayton, Angus
ELIZABETH
Debaer, Jean
PERFECT MURDER, A
Debatin, Jackie
I LOVE YOU, DON'T TOUCH ME!
Debeigh, Walter
UN AIR DE FAMILLE
DeBlasio, Anthony
RETURN OF THE KING, THE
Deblinger, David
PRICE ABOVE RUBIES, A
TEN BENNY
DeBonis, Marcia
NO LOOKING BACK
RIVER RED
TRUMAN SHOW, THE
Debranche, Maurice
SWINDLE, THE
Debray, Regis
EL CHE: INVESTIGATING A LEGEND
Decadi, Anthony
SOLDIER'S DAUGHTER NEVER CRIES, A
Decaro, Matt
U.S. MARSHALS
Dechent, Antonio
DAY OF THE BEAST, THE
Deckert, Blue
CON, THE
HOME FRIES
Decleir, Jan
CHARACTER

Desure, Francis
LIFE OF JESUS, THE
Dettrich, Courtney
PRACTICAL MAGIC
Devanney, Cherie
TALES FROM A PARALLEL UNIVERSE: GIGA SHADOW
DeVargas, Val
TOUCH OF EVIL: THE DIRECTOR'S CUT
Deveau, David
BLEEDERS
LOUISA MAY ALCOTT'S LITTLE MEN
Deveaux, Nathaniel
ESCAPE, THE
SPREE, THE
DeVenere, Carmen
INNOCENT SLEEP, THE
DeVictor, Claudio
MISBEGOTTEN
Devincentis, Sara
ZERO EFFECT
Devine, Aidan
TRUCKS
Devine, Alicia
CARLA'S SONG
Devine, Loretta
DON KING: ONLY IN AMERICA
DOWN IN THE DELTA
LOVER GIRL
REBOUND: THE LEGEND OF EARL "THE GOAT" MANIGAULT
URBAN LEGEND
Devine, Margaret
LAST BREATH
DeVito, Danny
LIVING OUT LOUD
Devitt, Matthew
WAKING NED DEVINE
Devlin, Alan
MOONDANCE
Devlin, Billy
ARMAGEDDON
RUSH HOUR
Devos, Emmannuelle
ARTEMISIA
DeVuono, Michelle
LET'S KILL ALL THE LAWYERS
Dewitt, Fay
KIKI'S DELIVERY SERVICE
Dexter, Annabelle Raine
HANGING GARDEN, THE
Dexter, Melissa
DANCE WITH ME
Dexter, Sally
FIRELIGHT
Deyle, John
ONE TRUE THING
DeYoung, Cliff
SUICIDE KINGS
deZarn, Tim
I LOVE YOU, DON'T TOUCH ME!
Di Dio, Barbara
DANGEROUS BEAUTY
Di Guoqiang
EMPEROR'S SHADOW, THE
Di Mascio Jr., Angelo
VERY BAD THINGS
Di Re, Flo
MIGHTY JOE YOUNG
Diamandi, Aristita
CLOCKMAKER
Diamond, Keith
DESPERATE MEASURES
Diamond, Ray
MY BROTHER'S WAR
Dias, Jennie
TOUCH OF EVIL: THE DIRECTOR'S CUT
Dias, Pat
WOO
Diaz, Cameron
FEAR AND LOATHING IN LAS VEGAS
THERE'S SOMETHING ABOUT MARY
VERY BAD THINGS
Diaz, Emilio
THERE'S SOMETHING ABOUT MARY
Diaz, Guillermo
ELMORE LEONARD'S GOLD COAST
HALF BAKED
I THINK I DO
Diaz, Sully
CLOCKWATCHERS
Dib, Mohammed
FULL SPEED
Dibben, Damian
LOVE IS THE DEVIL: STUDY FOR A PORTRAIT OF FRANCIS BACON
DiBenedetto, John
ROUNDERS
DiCaprio, Leonardo
CELEBRITY
MAN IN THE IRON MASK, THE
Dick, Andy
LION KING II: SIMBA'S PRIDE, THE
Dickens, Kim
GREAT EXPECTATIONS
MERCURY RISING
ZERO EFFECT
Dickerson, Pamela
LAST BIG THING, THE
Dickinson, Angie
OFF THE MENU: THE LAST DAYS OF CHASEN'S
Dickson, Tricia
SECRET KINGDOM, THE
DiConcetto, Karen
HENRY FOOL
Diddley, Bo
BLUES BROTHERS 2000
Didier, Celia
HAV PLENTY
DiDonna, Gian
WEST NEW YORK
Diehl, Jeanne
SENSELESS
Diehl, John
DESTINY OF MARTY FINE, THE
HI-LO COUNTRY, THE
MONUMENT AVE.
RAT PACK, THE
DiElsi, Frank
SIEGE, THE
Dienst, Jonathan
GODZILLA
Dierkop, Charles
INVISIBLE DAD
Diesel, Vin
SAVING PRIVATE RYAN
Dietl, Bo
ONE TOUGH COP
Dietl, Dana
ONE TOUGH COP
Dietrich, Marlene
TOUCH OF EVIL: THE DIRECTOR'S CUT
DiFilippo, Ted
MAJOR LEAGUE: BACK TO THE MINORS
DiFilippo, Tim
MAJOR LEAGUE: BACK TO THE MINORS
DiFilippo, Tom
MAJOR LEAGUE: BACK TO THE MINORS
DiGennaro, Julius
BUFFALO '66
Diggs, Taye
HOW STELLA GOT HER GROOVE BACK
Dignam, Arthur
GODS AND MONSTERS
Dignan, Stephen
RUSHMORE
Dill, Guy
BILLBOARD DAD
Dillane, Stephen
DEJA VU
FIRELIGHT
Dillen, Lori
JOHN CARPENTER'S VAMPIRES
Dillenberg, Nicole
SKIN & BONE
Diller, Phyllis
BUG'S LIFE, A
Dilley, Leslie
DEEP IMPACT
Dillin, Scott
PERFECT MURDER, A
Dillon, Hugh
HARD CORE LOGO
Dillon, Kevin
MISBEGOTTEN
Dillon, Matt
OFF THE MENU: THE LAST DAYS OF CHASEN'S
THERE'S SOMETHING ABOUT MARY
WILD THINGS
Dillon of Eldon, Lord Dominic
TWENTYFOURSEVEN
Dillon, Paul
CHICAGO CAB
Dillon, Ruth
MY BROTHER'S WAR
Dillon, Thom
NOT IN THIS TOWN
DiMaggio, John
GOLGO 13: QUEEN BEE
Dimitri, Michael
INCOGNITO
Dimoupolous, Stephen
INVADER, THE
Dinelli, Michael
MARS
Dinello, Paul
PLUMP FICTION
Ding Lan
SHAOLIN TEMPLE, THE
Dinklage, Peter
SAFE MEN
Dinson Jr., Ron
SIX DAYS, SEVEN NIGHTS
Dinvale, Mihai
SUBSPECIES IV: BLOODSTORM
Diomande, Laurent
FULL SPEED
Dionisi, Stefano
PEREIRA DECLARES
TRUCE, THE
Dionisios
MEN WITH GUNS
Dionisotti, Paola
LES MISERABLES
Director, Kim
HE GOT GAME
DiRienzo, Bob
RETURN OF THE KING, THE
DiSalvo, Jody Barr
PRINCE, THE
Disher, Catherine
NORTH SHORE FISH
Disney, Melissa
RUSTY: THE GREAT RESCUE
Disney, Thea Nielsen
WRONGFULLY ACCUSED
Disses, Jacques
POST COITUM, ANIMAL TRISTE
DiTocco, Robyn
CATHERINE'S GROVE

Ditson, Harry
SHOOTING FISH
Divoff, Andrew
NEMESIS 4: CRY OF ANGELS
Dixon, Jerry
I GOT THE HOOK UP
Dixon, Matthew
RATCHET
Dixon, Phil
KILLING TIME
Dixon, Richard
MERRY WAR, A
Dixon, Steve
LET'S KILL ALL THE LAWYERS
Dixon, Terrell
BABE: PIG IN THE CITY
DJ Atrak
MODULATIONS: CINEMA FOR THE EAR
DJ Funk
MODULATIONS: CINEMA FOR THE EAR
DJ Pierre
MODULATIONS: CINEMA FOR THE EAR
DJ Sneak
MODULATIONS: CINEMA FOR THE EAR
DJ Spooky
MODULATIONS: CINEMA FOR THE EAR
Djola, Badja
PLAYERS CLUB, THE
Dlamini, Sello
TARZAN AND THE LOST CITY
Doba, Wayne
DOGWATCH
Dobrin, Marilyn
OBJECT OF MY AFFECTION, THE
Dobrin, Vadim
OPERATION DELTA FORCE 2
Dobrovolskaya, Tanya
DEAD WATERS
Dobrowolski, Tony
LET'S KILL ALL THE LAWYERS
Dobson, Michael
MIGHTY KONG, THE
WOUNDED
Dobson, Paul
DRAGON BALL Z THE MOVIE: DEAD ZONE
DRAGON BALL Z THE MOVIE: THE TREE OF MIGHT
DRAGON BALL Z THE MOVIE: THE WORLD'S STRONGEST
MIGHTY KONG, THE
NEW ADVENTURES OF KIMBA THE WHITE LION, THE
Dobtcheff, Vernon
DEJA VU
HILARY AND JACKIE
MERLIN
OGRE, THE
Docherty, Bob
REGENERATION
Doctor Dre
RIDE
Dodd, Alex
GODZILLA
SIEGE, THE
Dodd, KK
SOLDIER
Dodds, Jake
LOVE IS THE DEVIL: STUDY FOR A PORTRAIT OF FRANCIS BACON
Dodds, Megan
EVER AFTER
RAT PACK, THE
Doe, John
PASS, THE
Doerner, Darrick
IN GOD'S HANDS
Dogg, Snoop Doggy
CAUGHT UP
HALF BAKED
Doherty, Colom
BRYLCREEM BOYS, THE
Doherty, Denny
ELVIS MEETS NIXON
REAL HOWARD SPITZ, THE
Doherty, Tony
MR. NICE GUY
Dohring, Jason
DEEP IMPACT
Dolan, John
LENNY BRUCE: SWEAR TO TELL THE TRUTH
Dolan, Julie
BASEKETBALL
Dolan, Michael
LOLITA
Dollaghan, Patrick
HOLLYWOOD CONFIDENTIAL
Dolleris, Helle
CELEBRATION, THE
Dollison, Ed
NEWTON BOYS, THE
Dollison, Twirlie Delite
SUB DOWN
Dolloff, Andrea
STEPMOM
Dolven, Rolf
JUNK MAIL
Doman, John
LITTLE BOY BLUE
MERCURY RISING
Dominigue, Norris
DEAD END
Dominique
KNOCK OFF
Dominique, Fritz
TRUMAN SHOW, THE
Don, Carl
SAFE MEN
Donadio, Namibia
OBJECT OF MY AFFECTION, THE
Donaghy, Michael
NEXT STEP, THE
Donahue, Phil
AYN RAND: A SENSE OF LIFE
Donahue, Ryan
ANOTHER DAY IN PARADISE
Donald, Juli
CIVIL ACTION, A
Donato, Marc
BONE DADDY
RESCUERS: STORIES OF COURAGE—TWO COUPLES
Donatto, Jean
HOME FRIES
Donavan, Robert
CURSE OF THE PUPPET MASTER
Doncheff, Len
RESCUERS: STORIES OF COURAGE—TWO COUPLES
Done, Jason
MERLIN
Donegan, Mike
LETTER FROM DEATH ROW, A
Donella, Chad E.
DISTURBING BEHAVIOR
Donnelly, Jamie
CAN'T HARDLY WAIT
SLAPPY AND THE STINKERS
Donnelly, Kate
REGENERATION
Donnelly, Tony Michael
FALLEN
Donner, Jack
JOHNNY MYSTO BOY WIZARD
Donoghue, Dick
MY BROTHER'S WAR
Donohoe, Amanda
REAL HOWARD SPITZ, THE
Donohue, John F.
LIVING OUT LOUD
Donovan, Brian
GIA
Donovan, Elisa
NIGHT AT THE ROXBURY, A
Donovan, Jamie
LETHAL WEAPON 4
Donovan, Jeffrey
CATHERINE'S GROVE
WHEN TRUMPETS FADE
Donovan, Martin
LIVING OUT LOUD
OPPOSITE OF SEX, THE
RESCUERS: STORIES OF COURAGE—TWO COUPLES
WHEN TRUMPETS FADE
Donovan, Robert
INVISIBLE DAD
Donovan, Tate
ONLY THRILL, THE
Doohan, James
TREKKIES
Dooley, Paul
CLOCKWATCHERS
Dooley, Sean
LIVING OUT LOUD
Doqui, Robert
WALKING THUNDER
Dorado, Eleanor
TOUCH OF EVIL: THE DIRECTOR'S CUT
Doran, Matt
THIN RED LINE, THE
Dorcic, John
RETURN OF THE KING, THE
Dore, Edna
LES MISERABLES
NIL BY MOUTH
Dorff, Stephen
BLADE
Dorfmeister, Tom
LOS LOCOS
Doria, Diego
VOYAGE TO THE BEGINNING OF THE WORLD
Dorian, Patrick Shane
IN GOD'S HANDS
Dorkin, Cody
LAND OF THE FREE
Dormer, Chad
RIGHT CONNECTIONS, THE
Dormer, Richard
BREAK, THE
Dorn, Cynthia
CON, THE
Dorn, Michael
STAR TREK: INSURRECTION
TREKKIES
Dornberg, Tim
OPPOSITE OF SEX, THE
Dorr, Sabi
NEGOTIATOR, THE
Dorrian, Tommy
SIMON BIRCH
Dorsey, Ayoka
BELOVED
Dorval, Adrian
FIRESTORM
Dorval, Adrien
WRONGFULLY ACCUSED
Dossey, David
RATCHET
Dotson, Joshua
YOUR FRIENDS & NEIGHBORS

Dotson, Rhonda
CITY OF ANGELS
NEGOTIATOR, THE
Doty, David
JOHNNY SKIDMARKS
PARENT TRAP, THE
ZERO EFFECT
Doubilet, Emily
SAFE MEN
Doubleday, Portia
BRAM STOKER'S THE MUMMY
Doucette, Jeff
DR. DOLITTLE
RAGE, THE
Doucette, Lionel
TALES FROM A PARALLEL UNIVERSE: GIGA SHADOW
Douche, David
LIFE OF JESUS, THE
Doudounis, Matthew
STEPMOM
Doug, Doug E.
RUSTY: THE GREAT RESCUE
Doughan, Jim
ALONE IN THE WOODS
Dougherty, Edward S.
NO WAY HOME
Doughty, Hunter
MEAN GUNS
Doughty, Kenny
ELIZABETH
Doughty, Richard Bruce
MAJOR LEAGUE: BACK TO THE MINORS
Douglas, Cameron
MR. NICE GUY
Douglas, Charles
RED HAWK: WEAPON OF DEATH
Douglas, James B.
BRAM STOKER'S SHADOWBUILDER
Douglas, Jerry
GODSON, THE
Douglas, Michael
PERFECT MURDER, A
Douglas, Paul
MR. NICE GUY
Douglas, Sarah
ASYLUM
Douglas, Shirley
BARNEY'S GREAT ADVENTURE—THE MOVIE
Douglas, Suzzanne
HOW STELLA GOT HER GROOVE BACK
Douglas, Tyrone
ASYLUM
Douglass, Jim A.
DON KING: ONLY IN AMERICA
Doumanian, Jean
WILD MAN BLUES
Doumanian, John
CELEBRITY
WILD MAN BLUES
Doupe, Tony
EDEN
Dourdan, Gary
SCARRED CITY
THURSDAY
Dourif, Brad
BRIDE OF CHUCKY
NIGHTWATCH
SENSELESS
Douthitt, Buff
HI-LO COUNTRY, THE
Dow, Ellen Albertini
54
PATCH ADAMS
WEDDING SINGER, THE
Dowd, Ann
APT PUPIL
Dowling, John
MARIE BAIE DES ANGES
Down, Gerald
LAND GIRLS, THE
Downes, Jamieson G.
PATCH ADAMS
Downes, Kevin
SENSELESS
Downey, Brian
TALES FROM A PARALLEL UNIVERSE: EATING PATTERN
TALES FROM A PARALLEL UNIVERSE: GIGA SHADOW
TALES FROM A PARALLEL UNIVERSE: SUPER NOVA
Downey, Jim
DIRTY WORK
Downey Jr., Robert
GINGERBREAD MAN, THE
TWO GIRLS AND A GUY
U.S. MARSHALS
Downey, Tom
PROPOSITION, THE
Downing, J.
HOLLYWOOD CONFIDENTIAL
Dowse, Denise
CIVIL ACTION, A
PLEASANTVILLE
Doyle, Ann
GENERAL, THE
Doyle, Chris
LOVE TO KILL
REPLACEMENT KILLERS, THE
Doyle, Christopher
ANOTHER DAY IN PARADISE
COMRADES, ALMOST A LOVE STORY
Doyle, Eamonn
WAKING NED DEVINE
Doyle, Kathleen
CELEBRITY
MONTANA
NO LOOKING BACK
Doyle Kennedy, Maria
BREAK, THE
Doyle, Tony
EVER AFTER
I WENT DOWN
Doyle-Murray, Brian
BRAVE LITTLE TOASTER GOES TO MARS, THE
DENNIS THE MENACE STRIKES AGAIN
DR. DOLITTLE
JUNGLE BOOK: MOWGLI'S STORY, THE
Dr. John
BLUES BROTHERS 2000
Drago, Joe
DESPERATE MEASURES
Dragovic, Cedo
SAVIOR
Drai, Victor
BURN HOLLYWOOD BURN
Drake, David
DAVID SEARCHING
Drake, Dolores
I'LL BE HOME FOR CHRISTMAS
Drake, Judith
ARMAGEDDON
PHANTOMS
Drake, Larry
OVERNIGHT DELIVERY
Draudt, Kristin
FEAR AND LOATHING IN LAS VEGAS
Drayton, Stanley
BELLY
Dream Boys, The
SPICE WORLD
Dreesen, Tom
RAT PACK, THE
Dreihauss, Patrick
REDLINE
Drew, Amanda
MRS. DALLOWAY
Drew, J.D.
HANDS ON A HARDBODY
Drew, Lacy
NEVADA
Drew, Lisa
UNDERTAKER'S WEDDING, THE
Drewry, Amanda
HUMAN BOMB
Drewry, Mark
HOSTILE WATERS
Drewy, Chris
HOPE FLOATS
Dreyer, Dianne
YOU'VE GOT MAIL
Dreyfuss, Richard
JACK LONDON'S THE CALL OF THE WILD: DOG OF THE YUKON
KRIPPENDORF'S TRIBE
OLIVER TWIST
Driggs, Hannah
NOT IN THIS TOWN
Driscoll, Kirk
ONE TRUE THING
Driscoll, Robyn
FIRESTORM
Driver, John
DIRTY LAUNDRY
Driver, Minnie
GOVERNESS, THE
HARD RAIN
Dromey, Eileen
WAKING NED DEVINE
Droog, Bernhard
CHARACTER
Drozd, Georgiy
DEAD WATERS
Drozda, Peter
ACT OF WAR
Drummond, Chad
DECAMPITATED
Druwing, Bob
NEXT STOP, WONDERLAND
Dryer, Fred
STRAY BULLET
Du Bois, Francis
MAKER, THE
Du Chuan Yang
SHAOLIN TEMPLE, THE
Duarte, Herbie
HENRY FOOL
Duarte, Lima
OYSTER AND THE WIND, THE
Dubin, Ellen
TALES FROM A PARALLEL UNIVERSE: SUPER NOVA
Dubois, Marie
SWINDLE, THE
Dubone, Aisha
LIVING OUT LOUD
Dubsky, Miroslav
MY GIANT
Duce, Patti
OUTSIDE OZONA
Ducey, John
DEEP IMPACT
Ducharme, Al
NEXT STOP, WONDERLAND
Duchovny, David
X-FILES, THE
Duck, Cindy Lee
BOYS WILL BE BOYS

Ducote, Andrew
SECRET KINGDOM, THE
SECRET OF NIMH 2: TIMMY TO THE RESCUE, THE
Dudikoff, Michael
BLACK THUNDER
RINGMASTER
Dudley, Adam
TEKKEN: THE MOTION PICTURE
Dudman, Yvonne
UGLY, THE
Duering, Carl
DEJA VU
Duerr, Nancy
HOLY MAN
WILD THINGS
Duff, Denice
SUBSPECIES IV: BLOODSTORM
Duff, Hilary
CASPER MEETS WENDY
Duffett, Nicola
SHOOTING FISH
Duffy, Donna M.
DESPERATE MEASURES
Duffy, Helen
HIJACKING HOLLYWOOD
Duffy, Jack
DEFENDERS: PAYBACK, THE
Duffy, Karen
CELEBRITY
Duffy, Patrick
RUSTY: THE GREAT RESCUE
Duffy, Phillip
KNOCK OFF
Duffy, Veronica
TALK OF ANGELS
Duffy, Victoria
FRENCH EXIT
Dugan, James
EBENEZER
Duggan, James
JACK HIGGINS' MIDNIGHT MAN
Duggan, Judy
LOLITA
Duggan, Mike
MY BROTHER'S WAR
Duggan, Patrick
INNOCENT SLEEP, THE
Dugger, Robin
BURN HOLLYWOOD BURN
Duhaney, Kevin
DOWN IN THE DELTA
IN HIS FATHER'S SHOES
Dukakis, Olympia
JANE AUSTEN'S MAFIA!
JERUSALEM
PARALYZING FEAR: THE STORY OF POLIO IN AMERICA, A
PENTAGON WARS, THE
Duke, Bill
ALWAYS OUTNUMBERED
Dukes, David
GODS AND MONSTERS
SLAPPY AND THE STINKERS
Dulan, Ronald
SECRET KINGDOM, THE
Dulea, Vlad
TALISMAN
Duling, Dan
LAST LIVES
Dulli, Greg
MONUMENT AVE.
Dulmage, Todd
SIN AND REDEMPTION
Dumas, Charles
DEEP IMPACT
Dumas, Tim
PARALLEL SONS
Dumaurier, Francis
GREAT EXPECTATIONS
PERFECT MURDER, A
Dumaurier, Isabella
LOLIDA 2000
Dumbgen, Heinz
RAT'S TALE, A
Dumeniaud, Pierre-Francois
SWINDLE, THE
DuMont, James
PENTAGON WARS, THE
Dun, Dennis
DOGWATCH
Dunard, David
PHOENIX
Dunaway, Faye
GIA
Dunbar, Adrian
GENERAL, THE
Dunbar IV, Eustace
WOO
Dunbar, John
LOVE IS THE DEVIL: STUDY FOR A PORTRAIT OF FRANCIS BACON
Dunbar, William
LOVE IS THE DEVIL: STUDY FOR A PORTRAIT OF FRANCIS BACON
Duncan, Angus
REAL HOWARD SPITZ, THE
Duncan, Michael Clarke
ARMAGEDDON
BULWORTH
CAUGHT UP
NIGHT AT THE ROXBURY, A
PLAYERS CLUB, THE
Duncan, Trevor
PRACTICAL MAGIC
Dunford, Andrew
BORROWERS, THE
Dungey, Merrin
DEEP IMPACT
Dunlea, Vincent
SPACEJACKED
Dunlop, Darcy
EBENEZER
Dunn, David
ORGAZMO
Dunn, Donald
BLUES BROTHERS 2000
Dunn III, Paul
SPANISH PRISONER, THE
Dunn, Kevin
ALMOST HEROES
GODZILLA
SMALL SOLDIERS
SNAKE EYES
Dunn, Morrissey
LOVE AND DEATH ON LONG ISLAND
Dunn, Murphy
PHOENIX
Dunn, Nicholas
INVISIBLE DAD
Dunn, Nora
AIR BUD: GOLDEN RECEIVER
BULWORTH
Dunn-Hill, John
BLEEDERS
Dunne, Dominick
BURN HOLLYWOOD BURN
Dunne, Eileen
STRAY BULLET
Dunne, Murphy
BLUES BROTHERS 2000
Dunne, Robin
BIG HIT, THE
Dunne, Stuart
STRAY BULLET
Dunne, Thomas
RUN FOR COVER
Dunphy, Jerry
BULWORTH
Dunst, Kirsten
KIKI'S DELIVERY SERVICE
SMALL SOLDIERS
Dunsworth, Christine
HANGING GARDEN, THE
Dunsworth, John
REAL HOWARD SPITZ, THE
Dunsworthy, John
TALES FROM A PARALLEL UNIVERSE: GIGA SHADOW
Dunye, Cheryl
LAVENDER LIMELIGHT: LESBIANS IN FILM
Duong, Anh
HIGH ART
Duperron, Tim
SHAMPOO HORNS
Dupois, Starletta
HORTON FOOTE'S ALONE
MAKER, THE
Dupont, Jean-Louis
WESTERN
Duppin, Andy
SCARRED CITY
Dupree, Whitney
HOLY MAN
Dupuis, Roy
BLEEDERS
Duque, Chris
KRIPPENDORF'S TRIBE
Duran, James
BREAK, THE
Duran, Richard
REPLACEMENT KILLERS, THE
Durand, Chris
HALLOWEEN H20: TWENTY YEARS LATER
UNCLE SAM
Durano, Giustino
LIFE IS BEAUTIFUL
Durante, Morris
FALLING FIRE
Duris, Romain
GADJO DILO
Durning, Charles
HI-LIFE
Durrett, Roger W.
PATCH ADAMS
Dusay, Marj
LOVE WALKED IN
Dussollier, Andre
SAME OLD SONG
Duta, George
TALISMAN
Dutton, Anthony
FIRELIGHT
Dutton, Charles
BLACK DOG
Dutton, Simon
DANGEROUS BEAUTY
FROM A FAR COUNTRY
Duva, Chris
DAVID SEARCHING
DuVall, Clea
ALARMIST, THE
CAN'T HARDLY WAIT
DEFENDERS: PAYBACK, THE
FACULTY, THE
NIAGARA NIAGARA
Duvall, Robert
CIVIL ACTION, A
DEEP IMPACT
GINGERBREAD MAN, THE

Duvall, Shelley
CASPER MEETS WENDY
HOME FRIES
HORTON FOOTE'S ALONE
Duvall, Susan
PECKER
SPECIES II
Duvall, Wayne
HARD RAIN
Duvet, Marc
OGRE, THE
Duvitski, Janine
SWEPT FROM THE SEA
Dwarves, The
KURT AND COURTNEY
Dwyer, Kathryn
MARS
Dwyer, Michael
UGLY, THE
DXT
MODULATIONS: CINEMA FOR THE EAR
Dye, Dale
OPERATION DELTA FORCE 2
SAVING PRIVATE RYAN
Dye, Richie
GINGERBREAD MAN, THE
MAJOR LEAGUE: BACK TO THE MINORS
Dyktynksi, Matthew
HEAVEN'S BURNING
Dylan, Jakob
RUGRATS MOVIE, THE
Dyrholm, Trine
CELEBRATION, THE
Dysart, Richard
HARD RAIN
Dyson, Anne
FROM A FAR COUNTRY
Dytynski, Matthew
MR. NICE GUY
Dzundza, George
BATMAN & MR. FREEZE: SUBZERO
BATMAN/SUPERMAN MOVIE, THE
SPECIES II
Eagle, Jack
STEPMOM
Eakins, Mitch
SOLDIER'S DAUGHTER NEVER CRIES, A
Earl, Elizabeth
EVER AFTER
Earlywine, Chelsey
3 NINJAS: HIGH NOON AT MEGA MOUNTAIN
Earnhart, Dale
BASEKETBALL
Eastin, Steve
LITTLE BIGFOOT 2: THE JOURNEY HOME
Eastman, Kevin
RETURN TO SAVAGE BEACH
Eastman, Rodney
OPPOSITE OF SEX, THE
Easton, Robert
PRIMARY COLORS
Easton, Sheena
ALL DOGS CHRISTMAS CAROL, AN
Eastwood, Adam
COURTING COURTNEY
Eaton, Leigh
DANCER, TEXAS POP. 81
Eaton, Pam
RETURN OF THE KING, THE
Eaton, Robert Vernon
BIG HIT, THE
Eaves, Dashiell
BELOVED
Ebbe, Annevig Shelde
KINGDOM, PART 2, THE
Eberhard, Ben
CALL TO REMEMBER, A
Eberl, Luke
PHANTOMS
Eberlein, Scott
SHOPPING FOR FANGS
Ebo, Evelyn
SPECIES II
Eccleston, Christopher
ELIZABETH
PRICE ABOVE RUBIES, A
Echevarria, Nicholas
DIDN'T DO IT FOR LOVE
Eckard, Beth
GINGERBREAD MAN, THE
Eckelman, Steve
RUSHMORE
Eckert, Todd
OPPOSITE OF SEX, THE
Eckhart, Aaron
THURSDAY
YOUR FRIENDS & NEIGHBORS
Eckhouse, James
ONE TRUE THING
Eckstrom, Lauren
STAR KID
Eddy, Sonya
GODSON, THE
PATCH ADAMS
SOUR GRAPES
Edelman, Gregg
BUSTER & CHAUNCEY'S SILENT NIGHT
Edelsbacher, Ricarda
NAKED LIES
Edelson, Kenneth
CELEBRITY
Edelstein, Lisa
BATMAN/SUPERMAN MOVIE, THE
INDISCREET
Edlefsen, Terry Neil
STEPHEN KING'S THE NIGHT FLIER
Edmonds, Dartanyan
RIDE
WOO
Edmonds, Kenneth "Babyface"
HAV PLENTY
Edmonds, Tracey E.
HAV PLENTY
Edmund
UNDERTAKER'S WEDDING, THE
Edward-Stevens, Michael
BABE: PIG IN THE CITY
Edwards, Anthony
PLAYING BY HEART
Edwards, Barbara Lee
TRUCKS
Edwards, Blue
AIR BUD: GOLDEN RECEIVER
Edwards, Daryl
PRICE ABOVE RUBIES, A
SUBSTITUTE 2: SCHOOL'S OUT, THE
Edwards, David
BELLY
Edwards, Don
HORSE WHISPERER, THE
Edwards, Edward
CHILDREN OF THE CORN V: FIELD OF TERROR
Edwards, Eric
BLADE
Edwards, Honeyboy
CAN'T YOU HEAR THE WIND HOWL?: THE LIFE AND MUSIC OF ROBERT JOHNSON
Edwards, Kenneth Lane
STAR TREK: INSURRECTION
Edwards, Natasha
OBJECT OF MY AFFECTION, THE
Edwards, Neville
DOWN IN THE DELTA
Edwards, Stacy
PRIMARY COLORS
Egan, Aeryk
DEAD MAN ON CAMPUS
Egan, Robert M.
MAJOR LEAGUE: BACK TO THE MINORS
Egner, Ruth
ONE TRUE THING
Ehle, Jennifer
WILDE
Ehrlich, Joy
ENEMY OF THE STATE
Eichenberger, Rebecca
OBJECT OF MY AFFECTION, THE
Eigeman, Chris
LAST DAYS OF DISCO, THE
MR. JEALOUSY
NEXT STEP, THE
Eigenberg, David
CHARLIE HOBOKEN
PERFECT MURDER, A
Eikenberry, Jill
MY VERY BEST FRIEND
Eilber, Janet
MIGHTY JOE YOUNG
Einbinder, Chad
DR. DOLITTLE
RUSTY: THE GREAT RESCUE
Einhorn, Marvin
PRICE ABOVE RUBIES, A
Einhorn, Trevor
BASEKETBALL
Eisenberg, Hallie Kate
PAULIE
Eisenberg, Ned
CELEBRITY
CIVIL ACTION, A
PRIMARY COLORS
Eisman, Darrell
WHY DO FOOLS FALL IN LOVE?
Eisner, David
RESCUERS: STORIES OF COURAGE—TWO COUPLES
Eizenia, Laura
ENEMY OF THE STATE
Ejogo, Carmen
AVENGERS, THE
Eke, Robert Baynton
KNOCK OFF
Ekstrand, Laura
HIGH ART
El Adl, Hassan
DESTINY
El Cherif, Nour
DESTINY
El Duce
KURT AND COURTNEY
El Emary, Safia
DESTINY
El Nabaoui, Khaled
DESTINY
Elam, Kiant
AMERICAN HISTORY X
Elbaum, Don
DON KING: ONLY IN AMERICA
Elbaz, Aaron
HOLY MAN
Elboo-Abdellatti, Yacine
WESTERN
Eldard, Ron
DEEP IMPACT
WHEN TRUMPETS FADE
Elder, Judy Ann
PLAYERS CLUB, THE
Eldridge, Lehla
INNOCENT SLEEP, THE

Electra, Carmen
CHOSEN ONE: LEGEND OF THE RAVEN, THE
Eleniak, Erika
CAPTIVE
Elfaro, Efrine
MEN WITH GUNS
Elfman, Bodhi Pine
ARMAGEDDON
ENEMY OF THE STATE
GODZILLA
MERCURY RISING
SLAPPY AND THE STINKERS
Elfman, Jenna
CAN'T HARDLY WAIT
DR. DOLITTLE
KRIPPENDORF'S TRIBE
Elgar, Avril
WILDE
Elias, Hector
DISAPPEARANCE OF KEVIN JOHNSON, THE
Elias, Jeannie
BABE: PIG IN THE CITY
Elisa, Gillian
LAST SEDUCTION II, THE
Elise, Kimberly
BELOVED
Elizondo, Humberto
MASK OF ZORRO, THE
Elk, Lois Red
OUTSIDE OZONA
Elkins, Howard
STILL BREATHING
Ellertsen, Dan
CELEBRATION, THE
Ellin, Doug
KISSING A FOOL
Ellingham, Jaayda
TRICKS
Elliot, Antonio
INCOGNITO
Elliot, Simon
LEADING MAN, THE
Elliott, Beverley
MY VERY BEST FRIEND
SNOWBOUND
Elliott, Chris
THERE'S SOMETHING ABOUT MARY
Elliott, David James
CLOCKWATCHERS
Elliott, Sam
ADVENTURES OF MOWGLI
BIG LEBOWSKI, THE
DOGWATCH
HI-LO COUNTRY, THE
Elliott, Shawn
HURRICANE STREETS
Ellis, Afred "Pee Wee"
MY FIRST NAME IS MACEO
Ellis, Chris
ARMAGEDDON
GODZILLA
HOME FRIES
PENTAGON WARS, THE
Ellis, Leland
I GOT THE HOOK UP
Ellis, Sam
SAVING PRIVATE RYAN
Ellis, Simon
SPICE WORLD
Ellis, Stuart
MR. NICE GUY
Ellison, Monti
SIX-STRING SAMURAI
Ellroy, James
JAMES ELLROY: DEMON DOG OF AMERICAN CRIME FICTION
Elman, Lawrence
HOSTILE WATERS
JACK HIGGINS' ON DANGEROUS GROUND
Elmecky, Khaldoun
DRESS, THE
Elmer, Bill
WEDDING SINGER, THE
Eloui, Laila
DESTINY
Elrod, Lu
BIG LEBOWSKI, THE
PRIMARY COLORS
Elspas, Jacob
HUSH
Elspas, Rebecca
HUSH
Elspas, Sarah
HUSH
Elsworth, Simon
LETTER FROM DEATH ROW, A
STEPHEN KING'S THE NIGHT FLIER
Elvin, Justin
HAPPINESS
Elwes, Cary
INFORMANT, THE
PENTAGON WARS, THE
QUEST FOR CAMELOT
Embry, Ethan
CAN'T HARDLY WAIT
DANCER, TEXAS POP. 81
DISTURBING BEHAVIOR
MONTANA
Emelle, Michelyn
DOWN IN THE DELTA
Emerick, Gerald
JANE AUSTEN'S MAFIA!
Emerson, Darren
MODULATIONS: CINEMA FOR THE EAR
Emerson, Michael
IMPOSTORS, THE
PLAYING BY HEART
Emerson, Taylor
ALL DOGS CHRISTMAS CAROL, AN
SIMON BIRCH
Emerson, Virginia
OBJECT OF MY AFFECTION, THE
Emin, Tracey
LOVE IS THE DEVIL: STUDY FOR A PORTRAIT OF FRANCIS BACON
Emmerich, Noah
MONUMENT AVE.
TRUMAN SHOW, THE
Emmerick, Gerald
PLEASANTVILLE
Emmerson, Geoffrey
LITTLE VOICE
Emmett, Bert
OUTSIDE OZONA
Emoto, Akira
EEL, THE
Enberg, Alexander
GIA
SENSELESS
Endre, Lena
JERUSALEM
KRISTIN LAVRANSDATTER
Eng, Melinda
CELEBRITY
Engesaeth, Henriette
OTHER SIDE OF SUNDAY, THE
Engle, Marie
HORSE WHISPERER, THE
English, Robert
PLAYING BY HEART
Englund, Robert
DEE SNIDER'S STRANGELAND
MEET THE DEEDLES
URBAN LEGEND
Ennals, Roger
KID IN ALADDIN'S PALACE, A
Ennis, John
JACK FROST
Eno, Brian
MODULATIONS: CINEMA FOR THE EAR
Enos III, John
BLADE
Enright, Roxanne
RINGMASTER
Enriquez, Jocelyn
54
Ensemplari, Frances
SUE
Ensign, Michael
FATAL PURSUIT
Entwisle, Julie
STEPHEN KING'S THE NIGHT FLIER
Enuke, Amy
BILLBOARD DAD
Eonnet, Eloise
MADELINE
Epp, Gary
KID IN ALADDIN'S PALACE, A
Epperson, Van
BABE: PIG IN THE CITY
Epstein, Jon
NEMESIS 4: CRY OF ANGELS
Erga, Luminita
SUBSPECIES IV: BLOODSTORM
Ergener, Sibel
LAST BIG THING, THE
PHOENIX
Ergun, Halil
STEAM
Erickson, Christian
MAN IN THE IRON MASK, THE
Eridan, Patricia
UN AIR DE FAMILLE
Erik, Scott
SOUR GRAPES
Erl
BLADE
Erlich, Laura
FERNGULLY 2: THE MAGICAL RESCUE
Ernsberger, Duke
ERNEST IN THE ARMY
Ernsberger, Virginia
BODY COUNT
Erpichini, Mario
BEST MAN, THE
Ersgard, Patrick
LIVING IN PERIL
Ershadi, Homayoun
TASTE OF CHERRY
Erskine, Howard
CELEBRITY
Ervolino, Tony
CLUB VAMPIRE
Esary, Doreen
AIR BUD: GOLDEN RECEIVER
Escher, Shannon
MAKER, THE
Escobar, Junior
CARLA'S SONG
Escovedo, Peter Michael
LIVING OUT LOUD
Eser, Janine
MERLIN
Esguerra, George
TALK TO ME
Esguerra Sr., George
TALK TO ME
Eshun, Kodwo
MODULATIONS: CINEMA FOR THE EAR

Eskelson, Dana
SCARRED CITY
Espenoza, James
LOS LOCOS
Esperanza, Katia
HALLELUJAH!
Espert, Louis
UN AIR DE FAMILLE
Esphagen, Claes
JERUSALEM
Espiedra, Natasha
RUN FOR COVER
Espinosa, Salvador
CARLA'S SONG
Espinosa, Sergio
MASK OF ZORRO, THE
Espinoza, Gil
CLUB VAMPIRE
Espinoza, Micah
CATHERINE'S GROVE
Esposito, Destiny
LEWIS & CLARK & GEORGE
Esposito, Giancarlo
PHOENIX
TWILIGHT
Esposito, Jennifer
CHARLIE HOBOKEN
HE GOT GAME
I STILL KNOW WHAT YOU DID LAST SUMMER
NO LOOKING BACK
Esposito, Phyllis J.
CHARLIE HOBOKEN
Esser, Annett
STEPMOM
Essman, Susie
SIEGE, THE
Ester, Michael Dean
SENSELESS
Estevez, Joe
FATAL PURSUIT
I GOT THE HOOK UP
Estevez, Renee
SCARRED CITY
Estrem, David
EDEN
Eszterhas, Joe
BURN HOLLYWOOD BURN
Eszterhas, Naomi
BURN HOLLYWOOD BURN
Etienne, Yanick
BELOVED
Ettinger, Cynthia
DEEP IMPACT
Ettinger, Heidi
MOON OVER BROADWAY
Eubanks, Corey
SUICIDE KINGS
Eusebe, Marie-Noelle
MADELINE
Evangelista, Daniella
DISTURBING BEHAVIOR
Evans, Andree
SHOOTING FISH
Evans, Auriol
HILARY AND JACKIE
Evans, Conor
OLIVER TWIST
Evans, Deborah J.
NAKED ACTS
Evans, Dixie
UNVEILING, THE
Evans, Ella Mae
I GOT THE HOOK UP
Evans, Glenn
NAKED ACTS
Evans, Lee
THERE'S SOMETHING ABOUT MARY
Evans, Michelle
SAVING PRIVATE RYAN
Evans, Phil
SHOOTING FISH
Evans, Robert
BURN HOLLYWOOD BURN
Evans, Roy
MERRY WAR, A
Evans, Spencer
BLEEDERS
Evans, Stephanie
ARMOUR OF GOD
Evans, Troy
FEAR AND LOATHING IN LAS VEGAS
Evans, Wanda-Lee
CITY OF ANGELS
Eve
ORGAZMO
Evenson, Wayne A.
SIMPLE PLAN, A
Everett, Chad
PSYCHO
WHEN TIME EXPIRES
Everett III, Morris
ENEMY
Everett, Lee
BOYS IN LOVE 2
Everett, Rupert
SHAKESPEARE IN LOVE
Everett Scott, Tom
DEAD MAN ON CAMPUS
RIVER RED
Evetts, H.P.
HI-LO COUNTRY, THE
Ewan, Corey
NOT IN THIS TOWN
Ewell, Dwight
NIAGARA NIAGARA
Ewing, Patrick
SENSELESS
Eyraud, Matthew R.
I LOVE YOU, DON'T TOUCH ME!
Eyre, Peter
DANGEROUS BEAUTY
MERLIN
Ezrin, Bob
LOU REED: ROCK AND ROLL HEART
Faber, Matthew
SUE
Fabian, Patrick
SOUR GRAPES
Fabiani, Joel
SNAKE EYES
Fabrizio, David
GODS AND MONSTERS
Facella, Matthieu
MARIUS AND JEANNETTE
Facinelli, Peter
CAN'T HARDLY WAIT
DANCER, TEXAS POP. 81
Faddis, Jon
BLUES BROTHERS 2000
Faderman, Lillian
OUT OF THE PAST
Fagerbakke, Bill
ALMOST PARTNERS
Fagerholm, Vylette Jezel
GIA
Fahey, Dennis S.
ENEMY OF THE STATE
Fahey, Jeff
CATHERINE'S GROVE
Fahm, David
SPICE WORLD
Fair, Andrea
FRENCH EXIT
Fair, William
DEEP IMPACT
Fairbrass, Craig
KILLING TIME
Fairchild, Krisha
UNDER HEAVEN
Fairchild, Morgan
HOLY MAN
Fairfax, Susie
MRS. DALLOWAY
Fairfield, Heather
OPPOSITE OF SEX, THE
Fairhurst, Angus
LOVE IS THE DEVIL: STUDY FOR A PORTRAIT OF FRANCIS BACON
Fairley, Michelle
SOLDIER'S DAUGHTER NEVER CRIES, A
Fairlie, Kristine
DEFENDERS: PAYBACK, THE
Faison, Donald
CAN'T HARDLY WAIT
Faithfull, Marianne
MOONDANCE
WHEN PIGS FLY
Falco, Edie
HURRICANE STREETS
PRICE ABOVE RUBIES, A
Falcon, Jeffrey
SIX-STRING SAMURAI
Falgoux, Denis
UN AIR DE FAMILLE
Falk, Andrew
LAST BIG THING, THE
Falk, Lisanne
SHATTERED IMAGE
SUICIDE KINGS
Falk, Peter
PRONTO
Fallick, Mary
DOWN IN THE DELTA
Fallon, Siobhan
KRIPPENDORF'S TRIBE
NEGOTIATOR, THE
Faltisco, Robert
GODZILLA
Falty'n, Martin
MY GIANT
Fan, Roger
RUSH HOUR
Fancy, Richard
RICHIE RICH'S CHRISTMAS WISH
Fanfair, Robinne
WOO
Fang Ping
SHAOLIN TEMPLE, THE
Fanti, Francesca
EIGHTEENTH ANGEL, THE
Farabaugh, Brian
GODZILLA
Faraday, Jim
HANGING GARDEN, THE
Faragallah, Ramsey
CELEBRITY
Faraj, Said
SIEGE, THE
Farar, Joel
RINGMASTER
Farcat, Morgane
MADELINE
Fardon, Joshua
STAR KID
Fargas, Antonio
MILO
Fargier, Frederic
FULL SPEED
Farina, Carolyn
LAST DAYS OF DISCO, THE

Farina, Dennis
OUT OF SIGHT
SAVING PRIVATE RYAN
Faris, Anna
EDEN
Faris, Lucy
TEKKEN: THE MOTION PICTURE
Farish, George
RUSHMORE
Farkas, Kati
RAT'S TALE, A
Farley, Chris
ALMOST HEROES
Farley, Guy
PRINCE VALIANT
Farley, John
ALMOST HEROES
WATERBOY, THE
Farley, Kevin
DIRTY WORK
WATERBOY, THE
Farley, Rupert
SHAKESPEARE IN LOVE
Farmer, Bill
CASPER MEETS WENDY
Farmer, Gary
SMOKE SIGNALS
Farmer, Ken
FARMIGA, VERA
NEWTON BOYS, THE
RETURN TO PARADISE
Farmiga, Vera
RETURN TO PARADISE
Farrell, Richard
SPACEJACKED
Farrell, Terry
TREKKIES
Farrelly, Anna
THERE'S SOMETHING ABOUT MARY
Farrelly, Bob
THERE'S SOMETHING ABOUT MARY
Farrelly, Jesse
THERE'S SOMETHING ABOUT MARY
Farrelly, Mariann
THERE'S SOMETHING ABOUT MARY
Farrelly, Nancy
THERE'S SOMETHING ABOUT MARY
Farson, Danlel
LOVE IS THE DEVIL: STUDY FOR A PORTRAIT OF FRANCIS BACON
Farve, Brett
THERE'S SOMETHING ABOUT MARY
Fashae, Alycia
SOLDIER'S DAUGHTER NEVER CRIES, A
Fate, Jayson
KISSING A FOOL
Faulkner, James
KID IN ALADDIN'S PALACE, A
Faurschou, Jannie
KINGDOM, PART 2, THE
Faust, Joe
LOS LOCOS
Favreau, Jon
DEEP IMPACT
NOTES FROM UNDERGROUND
VERY BAD THINGS
Fawcett, Alan
BARNEY'S GREAT ADVENTURE—THE MOVIE
JACK HIGGINS' THE WINDSOR PROTOCOL
PEACEKEEPER, THE
Fawcett, Farrah
BRAVE LITTLE TOASTER GOES TO MARS, THE
Fawkes, Sandy
LOVE IS THE DEVIL: STUDY FOR A PORTRAIT OF FRANCIS BACON
Faye, Denise
NEXT STEP, THE
Fazzio, Dan
HARD CORE LOGO
Fazzoli, Mella
RIVER RED
Feagai, Jake
SIX DAYS, SEVEN NIGHTS
Feast, Fred
LITTLE VOICE
Feast, Michael
VELVET GOLDMINE
Feaster, Bob
PATCH ADAMS
Featherstone, Angela
HALF BAKED
ILLTOWN
WEDDING SINGER, THE
ZERO EFFECT
Fedele, Jon
KRAA! THE SEA MONSTER
Feder, Frederique
SWEPT FROM THE SEA
Federici, Federica
DANGEROUS BEAUTY
Federico-O'Murchu, Francesca
PAULIE
Federman, Wayne
JACK FROST
Fee, Kathleen
LOUISA MAY ALCOTT'S LITTLE MEN
Feeley, Fergus
MY BROTHER'S WAR
Feeney, Caroleen
BAD MANNERS
Fegarotti, Flaminia
DANGEROUS BEAUTY
Fehr, Brendan
DISTURBING BEHAVIOR
Feichtner, Michael
LOLIDA 2000
Feign, Wendy
PROPOSITION, THE
Fein, Amanda
DEEP IMPACT
Fein, Caitlin
DEEP IMPACT
Feinberg, Leslie
STOLEN MOMENTS
Feldman, Tibor
RIVER RED
Feldshuh, Tovah
CHARLIE HOBOKEN
MONTANA
Felice, Lina
54
Felkins, Rick
FORMER CHILD STAR
Fell, Norman
DESTINY OF MARTY FINE, THE
Fellowes, Julian
REGENERATION
Fellows, Don
VELVET GOLDMINE
Feltham, Piers
LOVE IS THE DEVIL: STUDY FOR A PORTRAIT OF FRANCIS BACON
Felton, Lindsay
3 NINJAS: HIGH NOON AT MEGA MOUNTAIN
Felton, Tom
BORROWERS, THE
Feng Ko An
DRAGONS FOREVER
MAGNIFICENT WARRIORS
Fenn, Sherilyn
LOVELIFE
OUTSIDE OZONA
Fennell, Chris
X-FILES, THE
Fenton, Kim
HUMAN BOMB
Fenwick, Brian
PARENT TRAP, THE
Feore, Colm
CITY OF ANGELS
ESCAPE, THE
HOSTILE WATERS
Ferar, Anthony
REAL THING, THE
Ferch, Heino
OGRE, THE
Fergerson, Pearline
CIVIL ACTION, A
Fergie
OUTSIDE OZONA
Fergo, Bob
BOYS WILL BE BOYS
Ferguson, Chamblee
NEWTON BOYS, THE
Ferguson, Colin
OPPOSITE OF SEX, THE
Ferguson, Daniel
PARALLEL SONS
Ferguson, David
PLAYING BY HEART
Ferguson, J. Don
MAJOR LEAGUE: BACK TO THE MINORS
Ferguson, Myles
AIR BUD: GOLDEN RECEIVER
Ferguson, Nancye
PERMANENT MIDNIGHT
Ferguson, Sandra
INTERLOCKED: THRILLED TO DEATH
Ferlan, Carmen
BLEEDERS
Fernandes, Maria
CENTRAL STATION
Fernandez, Agustin
ELMORE LEONARD'S GOLD COAST
Fernandez Cruz, Maria
MASK OF ZORRO, THE
Fernandez Cruz, Monica
MASK OF ZORRO, THE
Fernandez, Ed
U.S. MARSHALS
Fernandez, Ellis
SWEPT FROM THE SEA
Fernandez, Esteban
BREAK, THE
Fernandez, Evelina
HOLLYWOOD CONFIDENTIAL
Fernandez, Francis
RUSHMORE
Fernandez, Jaqueline
NAKED LIES
Fernandez, Thelma Paula
NAKED ACTS
Fernandez, Victoria
LOVE IS THE DEVIL: STUDY FOR A PORTRAIT OF FRANCIS BACON
Fernando
EL CHE: INVESTIGATING A LEGEND
Ferrabee, Gillian
BLEEDERS
CAPTIVE
JACK HIGGINS' THUNDER POINT
Ferrara, Frank
SCARRED CITY
WOO
Ferrara, Juan
DIDN'T DO IT FOR LOVE
Ferrari, Cristina
OFF THE MENU: THE LAST DAYS OF CHASEN'S

Ferre, Cameron
JACK FROST
Ferrell, Brenda
DOGWATCH
Ferrell, Patrick
NIGHT AT THE ROXBURY, A
Ferrell, Will
NIGHT AT THE ROXBURY, A
Ferrelli, Robert J.
KRAA! THE SEA MONSTER
Ferrer, Filipe
PEREIRA DECLARES
Ferrer, Miguel
MULAN
STEPHEN KING'S THE NIGHT FLIER
Ferrero, Martin
GODS AND MONSTERS
Ferrett, Eve
MERRY WAR, A
Ferri, Claudia
HARD CORE LOGO
Ferri, Daniel
SLAMNATION
Ferrigno, Lou
GODSON, THE
Ferro, Carlos
GOLGO 13: QUEEN BEE
Ferry, Dawn
NEVADA
Ferry, Lucy
LOVE IS THE DEVIL: STUDY FOR A PORTRAIT OF FRANCIS BACON
Feuer, Cindra
HIGH ART
Feuerstein, Mark
PRACTICAL MAGIC
Fichtner, William
ARMAGEDDON
Fickert, Mark
NEWTON BOYS, THE
Fiddes, David
KNOCK OFF
Field, Arabella
GODZILLA
Field, Susan
EVER AFTER
Fielder, Al
RUSHMORE
Fields, Duggie
LOVE IS THE DEVIL: STUDY FOR A PORTRAIT OF FRANCIS BACON
Fields, Robert
SOULER OPPOSITE, THE
Fiend
I GOT THE HOOK UP
Fiennes, Joseph
ELIZABETH
SHAKESPEARE IN LOVE
Fiennes, Ralph
AVENGERS, THE
PRINCE OF EGYPT, THE
Fierro, Jim
U.S. MARSHALS
Fierstein, Harvey
MULAN
SAFE MEN
Figenschow, Kristian
INSOMNIA
Figueroa, Azucena
CARLA'S SONG
Figueroa, Efrain
DESPERATE MEASURES
Fiig, Henrik
KINGDOM, PART 2, THE
Filar, Gil
SIMON BIRCH
Filderman, Alan
BROADWAY DAMAGE
Filipone, Jim
INVADER, THE
Filippi, David
ONE TOUGH COP
Fillebeen, Bernard
LIFE OF JESUS, THE
Fillion, Nathan
SAVING PRIVATE RYAN
Fillmore, Bruce
LOVE AND DEATH ON LONG ISLAND
Filpi, Carmen
PHOENIX
WEDDING SINGER, THE
Fils-Aime, Jacqueline Celestin
BELOVED
Filth
DECLINE OF WESTERN CIVILIZATION PART III, THE
Final Conflict
DECLINE OF WESTERN CIVILIZATION PART III, THE
Finch, Charles
FRENCH EXIT
Finch, Larry
LITTLE BIGFOOT 2: THE JOURNEY HOME
Finch, Nick
LITTLE BIGFOOT 2: THE JOURNEY HOME
Fine, Danny
RUSHMORE
Fine, David
PATCH ADAMS
Fine, Travis
THIN RED LINE, THE
Fink, Eric
IN HIS FATHER'S SHOES
Finkel, Fyvush
BRAVE LITTLE TOASTER GOES TO MARS, THE
Finley, Cameron
HOPE FLOATS
Finley, Felicia
HE GOT GAME
Finley, Frank
FROM A FAR COUNTRY
Finn, Mike
MY BROTHER'S WAR
Finnegan, Amy "Blue"
INTERLOCKED: THRILLED TO DEATH
Finnegan, Anthony
OLIVER TWIST
Finnegan, John
BUTCHER BOY, THE
Finneran, Katie
YOU'VE GOT MAIL
Finnighan, Neil
SAVING PRIVATE RYAN
Fiondella, Jay
LETHAL WEAPON 4
SUICIDE KINGS
Fionte, John
CATHERINE'S GROVE
Fiore, Antimo
KISSING A FOOL
Fiorentino, Linda
BODY COUNT
Fiorino, Anthony
3 NINJAS: HIGH NOON AT MEGA MOUNTAIN
Fiorito, Geoff
PATCH ADAMS
Fiorucci, Elio
54
Firmin, Tyne
BOYS IN LOVE 2
Firth, Colin
SHAKESPEARE IN LOVE
Firth, Jonathan
MRS. DALLOWAY
Firth, Peter
MIGHTY JOE YOUNG
Fiscella, Andy
CATHERINE'S GROVE
Fischer, Kate
TWISTED
Fischer, Maureen
PECKER
Fischnaller, Eddie
INHERITORS, THE
Fishburne, Laurence
ALWAYS OUTNUMBERED
Fisher, Robert
CHARLIE HOBOKEN
Fisher, Simon
LAST SEDUCTION II, THE
Fisher, Thomas
FIRELIGHT
Fishman, Michael
LITTLE BIGFOOT 2: THE JOURNEY HOME
Fitchpatrick, Steve
VERY BAD THINGS
Fite, Mark
GODZILLA
Fitoi, Flavia
TALISMAN
Fitzgerald, Annie
PHOENIX
Fitzgerald, Ciaran
GENERAL, THE
INFORMANT, THE
SUMMER FLING
Fitzgerald, Dan
HOLY MAN
Fitzgerald, Donegal
CELEBRITY
Fitzgerald, Glenn
PRICE ABOVE RUBIES, A
Fitzgerald, Gregg
BUTCHER BOY, THE
Fitzgerald, Helen
CLOCKWATCHERS
Fitzgerald, Kitty
WAKING NED DEVINE
Fitzgerald, Leah
NIL BY MOUTH
Fitzgerald, Melissa
MONUMENT AVE.
Fitzgerald, Michael
WILDE
Fitzgerald, Patrick
DAY AT THE BEACH
Fitzgerald, Rob Roy
CAN'T HARDLY WAIT
Fitzgerald, Wilbur T.
GINGERBREAD MAN, THE
Fitzgibbon, Ian
INFORMANT, THE
Fitzhugh, Katherine A.
PATCH ADAMS
Fitzpatrick, Cathy
ORGAZMO
Fitzpatrick, Gabrielle
MR. NICE GUY
Fitzpatrick, James
LITTLE GHOST
Fitzpatrick, Kate
HEAVEN'S BURNING
TWISTED
Fitzpatrick, Leo
ANOTHER DAY IN PARADISE
Fitzpatrick, Mark
MR. NICE GUY
Fitzpatrick, Tony
U.S. MARSHALS
Flagg, Tyler
OBJECT OF MY AFFECTION, THE

Flaherty, Lanny
HOME FRIES
Flammer, Sylvia
PHANTASM: OBLIVION
Flanagan, Fionnula
WAKING NED DEVINE
Flanagan, Jesse
BIG LEBOWSKI, THE
Flanagan, John
FIRELIGHT
Flanagan, Maile
OVERNIGHT DELIVERY
Flanders, Keeley
HILARY AND JACKIE
Flanery, Sean Patrick
EDEN
SUICIDE KINGS
Flatman, Barry
TERMINAL JUSTICE
Flea
BIG LEBOWSKI, THE
DECLINE OF WESTERN CIVILIZATION PART III, THE
FEAR AND LOATHING IN LAS VEGAS
PSYCHO
Flees, Anthony
BEYOND, THE
Fleischer, Charles
PERMANENT MIDNIGHT
RUSTY: THE GREAT RESCUE
Fleming, Cliff
DESPERATE MEASURES
HORSE WHISPERER, THE
Fleming, Emily
DEFENDERS: PAYBACK, THE
Fleming, Richard
PASS, THE
Fleming, Shara P.
HAV PLENTY
Fleming, Wendy
SIMON BIRCH
Flemyng, Jason
DEEP RISING
SPICE WORLD
Flender, Rodman
CASPER MEETS WENDY
Flesher, Glenn
PRICE ABOVE RUBIES, A
Fletcher, Brendan
TRUCKS
Fletcher, Louise
BREAST MEN
LOVE TO KILL
Fleuchaus, Ann
YOU'VE GOT MAIL
Flick, David
DESPERATE MEASURES
Flint, Darren
WHEN DANGER FOLLOWS YOU HOME
Flint, Matthew
UNCLE SAM
Flippo, Michael
DECEIVER
Floberg, Bjorn
INSOMNIA
Flood, Kevin
GENERAL, THE
Florek, Dann
HARD RAIN
PENTAGON WARS, THE
Flores, Adam C.
SNAKE EYES
Flores, Alberto
CARLA'S SONG
Flores, E. Kalani
SIX DAYS, SEVEN NIGHTS
Flores, Enrique
NAKED LIES
Flores, Gilda
OBJECT OF MY AFFECTION, THE
Flores, Jose
DIDN'T DO IT FOR LOVE
Flores, Leila
DANCE WITH ME
Flores, Roberto
CARLA'S SONG
Flores, Sofia
OBJECT OF MY AFFECTION, THE
Flores, Von
TRACKED
Florian, Luc
MADELINE
OGRE, THE
Flowers, Kim
ANOTHER DAY IN PARADISE
FEAR AND LOATHING IN LAS VEGAS
Floyd, Billy
CLOCKMAKER
Floyd, Eddie
BLUES BROTHERS 2000
Floyd, Kari Leigh
KRIPPENDORF'S TRIBE
Floyd, Robert
GODZILLA
Flygare, Claus
KINGDOM, PART 2, THE
Flynn, F.J.
OUTSIDE OZONA
Flynn, Herbie
THERE'S SOMETHING ABOUT MARY
Flynn, Jackie
THERE'S SOMETHING ABOUT MARY
Flynn, Jeanie
THERE'S SOMETHING ABOUT MARY
Flynn, Jerry
WHITE RAVEN, THE
Flynn, Kate
MOONDANCE
Flynn, Kimberly
CRACKING UP
Flynn, Rob
RUSTY: THE GREAT RESCUE
Flynn, Steven
SCARRED CITY
Flythe, Mark
APT PUPIL
Foch, Nina
HUSH
Fodor, Julia
LOVE IS THE DEVIL: STUDY FOR A PORTRAIT OF FRANCIS BACON
Foehrweisser, Guido
GIA
Fogarty, Mary
NEIL SIMON'S THE ODD COUPLE II
Fogel, Peter
INTERLOCKED: THRILLED TO DEATH
Fogerty, Adam
INCOGNITO
SHOOTING FISH
Fok, Clarence
ARMOUR OF GOD
Folan, Berts
STRAY BULLET
Foley, Dave
BUG'S LIFE, A
Foley, Jeremy
CASPER MEETS WENDY
Foley, Liam
ELIZABETH
Folk, Alexander
CITY OF ANGELS
DISAPPEARANCE OF KEVIN JOHNSON, THE
Fonda, Bridget
MR. JEALOUSY
SIMPLE PLAN, A
Fong, Frances
RUSH HOUR
Fong, Tig
BIG HIT, THE
Fontaine, Frank
LOUISA MAY ALCOTT'S LITTLE MEN
Fontana, Peter
MERCURY RISING
Fontani, Amerigo
LIFE IS BEAUTIFUL
Foo Fighters
FREE TIBET
Foote, Hallie
HORTON FOOTE'S ALONE
Foray, June
FLINTSTONES: I YABBA-DABBA DOO!, THE
MULAN
Forbes, Andrew
INCOGNITO
Forbes, Belinda
CARLA'S SONG
Forbes, Leonie
SHATTERED IMAGE
Ford, Bette
LANDLADY, THE
Ford, Clebert
CELEBRITY
Ford Davies, Oliver
MRS. DALLOWAY
Ford, Harrison
SIX DAYS, SEVEN NIGHTS
Ford, Jack
PATCH ADAMS
Ford, Maria
CASPER MEETS WENDY
FUTURE FEAR
Ford, Mrs. Betty
OFF THE MENU: THE LAST DAYS OF CHASEN'S
Ford, President Gerald
OFF THE MENU: THE LAST DAYS OF CHASEN'S
Ford, Steven
ARMAGEDDON
Fordham, Alan
VELVET GOLDMINE
Foreman, Amanda
BREAST MEN
Foreman, Jamie
ELIZABETH
Forest, Pierre
RONIN
Forge, Scarlet
ARMAGEDDON
Forgerty, Adam
LITTLE VOICE
Forget, Mark
CARLA'S SONG
Forlani, Claire
MEET JOE BLACK
Forman, Jamie
NIL BY MOUTH
Forman, Milos
WHO IS HENRY JAGLOM?
Formicola, Fil
LIVING OUT LOUD
Forner, Lola
ARMOUR OF GOD
Forrest, Frederic
BLACK THUNDER
BOOGIE BOY
HORTON FOOTE'S ALONE
WHATEVER
Forristal, Susan
PRIMARY COLORS

Forsey, Norman
ABERRATION
Forshind, Constance
CLOCKWATCHERS
Forslund, Lynn
NEGOTIATOR, THE
Forster, Keith
DOGWATCH
Forster, Robert
NIGHT VISION
OUTSIDE OZONA
PSYCHO
UNCLE SAM
Forsythe, Henderson
SPECIES II
Forsythe, William
FIRESTORM
PASS, THE
Forte, Marlene
LENA'S DREAMS
Forte, Smith
NO ORDINARY LOVE
Fortea, Isabelle
RATCHET
Fortuna, Nadio
JACK HIGGINS' ON DANGEROUS GROUND
Foskett, Tawnya
FATAL PURSUIT
Foster, Al
TRUMAN SHOW, THE
Foster, Benim
BROADWAY DAMAGE
Foster, Blake
CASPER MEETS WENDY
RUSTY: THE GREAT RESCUE
Foster, Catlin
SAVIOR
Foster, Jodie
OFF THE MENU: THE LAST DAYS OF CHASEN'S
Foster, Lisa
LETTER FROM DEATH ROW, A
PARENT TRAP, THE
Foster, Robert
ERNEST IN THE ARMY
Foster, Shannah
NOT IN THIS TOWN
Foster, Susanna
DETOUR
Foubert, Helene
WESTERN
Fouler, Amelia
SUE
Fountidakis, Plato
FUTURE FEAR
Fourniotis, George
SNAKE EYES
Fouts, Dan
WATERBOY, THE
Fowells, Julie
HALLELUJAH!
Fowler, Chris
WATERBOY, THE
Fowler, Hal
BRYLCREEM BOYS, THE
Fowler Jr., Jonathan
AMERICAN HISTORY X
Fowler, Monique
CELEBRITY
LAST BREATH
Fowlkes, Eddie
MODULATIONS: CINEMA FOR THE EAR
Fox, Alejandro Acosta
HOLY MAN
Fox, Billy
CHOSEN ONE: LEGEND OF THE RAVEN, THE
Fox, Colin
JACK HIGGINS' THE WINDSOR PROTOCOL
Fox, Edward
LOST IN SPACE
PRINCE VALIANT
Fox, Huckleberry
NO WAY HOME
Fox, John
COMEDY'S DIRTIEST DOZEN
Fox, Kerry
HANGING GARDEN, THE
Fox, Lauren
PI
Fox, Loretta
WHY DO FOOLS FALL IN LOVE?
Fox, Mark
WRONGFULLY ACCUSED
Fox, Michael J.
OFF THE MENU: THE LAST DAYS OF CHASEN'S
Fox, Neil
SPICE WORLD
Fox, Paul
ELIZABETH
Fox, Randy
SLAYERS: THE MOTION PICTURE
Fox, Rick
HE GOT GAME
Fox, Ronny
NIL BY MOUTH
Fox, Seamus
MY BROTHER'S WAR
Fox, Vivica A.
WHY DO FOOLS FALL IN LOVE?
Foxhall, Scott
MAJOR LEAGUE: BACK TO THE MINORS
Foxx, Jamie
PLAYERS CLUB, THE
Foy, Patrick
MY BROTHER'S WAR
Foye, Janet
BABE: PIG IN THE CITY
Foyt, Victoria
DEJA VU
Fraade, Robert
DON KING: ONLY IN AMERICA
Fraction, Karen
PALMETTO
Fraim, Tracy
GEORGE WALLACE
Frain, Ben
ELIZABETH
Frain, James
ELIZABETH
HILARY AND JACKIE
Frakes, Jonathan
STAR TREK: INSURRECTION
TREKKIES
Fralick, David Shark
BEST OF THE BEST: WITHOUT WARNING
UNCLE SAM
Franca, Patricia
TIETA OF AGRESTE
Francese, Richard
NIGHT AT THE ROXBURY, A
Franchek, Jacob
TEKKEN: THE MOTION PICTURE
Francis, Clare
UNDER THE SKIN
Francis, David
PEACEKEEPER, THE
Francis, Jacklyn
FALLING FIRE
Francis, James
VELVET GOLDMINE
Francis, Lynne
KNOCK OFF
Francis, Mark
WRONGFULLY ACCUSED
Franco, Chris
DOUBLE EDGE
Franco, Margarita
3 NINJAS: HIGH NOON AT MEGA MOUNTAIN
Frandsen, Jano
RIGHT CONNECTIONS, THE
SPREE, THE
Frangione, Jim
SPANISH PRISONER, THE
Frank, Billy L. "Butch"
TWO FOR TEXAS
Frank, Brian
REAL BLONDE, THE
Frank, Clem
THERE'S SOMETHING ABOUT MARY
Frank, Dan
NO ORDINARY LOVE
Frank, David Roland
HURRICANE STREETS
INSIDE/OUT
Frank, Diana
CLUB VAMPIRE
Frank, Elan
LOVE TO KILL
Frank, Tony
CON, THE
Frankfurter, William
DIARY OF A SERIAL KILLER
Frankie
ARMAGEDDON
SHOOTING FISH
Franklin, Aretha
BLUES BROTHERS 2000
Franklin, Candide
BLUES BROTHERS 2000
Franklin, Cherie
DR. DOLITTLE
Franklin, David
VIOLET'S VISIT
Franklin, Gary
BURN HOLLYWOOD BURN
Franklin, Jonathan
ENEMY
Franklin, Paula Bellamy
I GOT THE HOOK UP
Franklin, Scott
PI
Franklyn-Robbins, John
FROM A FAR COUNTRY
MRS. DALLOWAY
Franks, Bo
NEWTON BOYS, THE
Frankson, Frank
WRATH OF THE NINJA: THE YOTODEN MOVIE
Franz, Alan
INVADER, THE
Franz, Dennis
CITY OF ANGELS
Frasca, Jason
DEEP IMPACT
Frasco, Joan
LETHAL WEAPON 4
Fraser, Brendan
GODS AND MONSTERS
STILL BREATHING
Fraser, Duncan
SNOWBOUND
WHEN DANGER FOLLOWS YOU HOME
WRONGFULLY ACCUSED
Fraser, Laura
COUSIN BETTE
MAN IN THE IRON MASK, THE
Fraser, Paul
TWENTYFOURSEVEN

Fraser, Stuart
MR. NICE GUY
Fraser, Tiffany
MERCURY RISING
Fratkin, Stuart
GODZILLA
Frazer, Jonathan
LIVING IN PERIL
Frazer, Rupert
FROM A FAR COUNTRY
Frazier, Clifford T.
U.S. MARSHALS
Frazier, John
ARMAGEDDON
Frederick, Rick
LET'S KILL ALL THE LAWYERS
Fredericks, David
FIRESTORM
Fredo, Sgt. Gary
DECLINE OF WESTERN CIVILIZATION PART III, THE
Freeman, Brent
MERCURY RISING
Freeman, David
BORROWERS, THE
Freeman, Dee
LANDLADY, THE
Freeman Jr., Al
DOWN IN THE DELTA
Freeman, Kathleen
BLUES BROTHERS 2000
I'LL BE HOME FOR CHRISTMAS
RICHIE RICH'S CHRISTMAS WISH
Freeman, Morgan
BIG HIT, THE
DEEP IMPACT
54
HARD RAIN
Freeman, Rob
SAVING PRIVATE RYAN
WHEN DANGER FOLLOWS YOU HOME
Freeman-Atwood, Roz
LEADING MAN, THE
Freidman, Richard L.
SPANISH PRISONER, THE
Freitas, Stela
CENTRAL STATION
Frejkova, Hana
FORGOTTEN LIGHT
Fremin, Jourdan
SIEGE, THE
French, Bruce
PENTAGON WARS, THE
STAR TREK: INSURRECTION
French, Jack
PECKER
French, Leigh
HOMEGROWN
YOUR FRIENDS & NEIGHBORS
French, Michael Bryan
I STILL KNOW WHAT YOU DID LAST SUMMER
Frenzel, Donna
OUT OF SIGHT
Freshwater, Geoffrey
LEADING MAN, THE
Fresolone, Arturo
REAL BLONDE, THE
Frewer, Matt
BREAST MEN
QUICKSILVER HIGHWAY
Friberg, Ulf
JERUSALEM
Fribo, Louise
KINGDOM, PART 2, THE
Fricke, David
LOU REED: ROCK AND ROLL HEART

Fried, Jonathan
PAUL MONETTE: THE BRINK OF SUMMER'S END
Fried, Manny
BUFFALO '66
Frieder, Sol
NIAGARA NIAGARA
Friedman, Bruce Jay
CELEBRITY
54
Friedman, Dave
STORY OF X, THE
Friedman, Dee Dee
SAFE MEN
Friedman, Glenn
LETHAL WEAPON 4
Friedman, Joel
CHARLIE HOBOKEN
Friedman, Nan
FEAR AND LOATHING IN LAS VEGAS
Friedrich, Stephan
MR. NICE GUY
Friedrich, Su
LAVENDER LIMELIGHT: LESBIANS IN FILM
Friel, Anna
LAND GIRLS, THE
Friel, Greg
CARLA'S SONG
Friel, Paschal
SAVING PRIVATE RYAN
Friels, Colin
DARK CITY
Frier-Dryden, Rosie
CALL TO REMEMBER, A
Frierson, Eddie
DR. DOLITTLE
KIKI'S DELIVERY SERVICE
YOUR FRIENDS & NEIGHBORS
Fries, Ava
OFF THE MENU: THE LAST DAYS OF CHASEN'S
Fries, Chuck
OFF THE MENU: THE LAST DAYS OF CHASEN'S
Friese, Brettanya
RETURN TO PARADISE
Friesen, Justin
REAL HOWARD SPITZ, THE
Frings, Stefan
RAT'S TALE, A
Frisch, Arno
FUNNY GAMES
Frith, Gary
HE GOT GAME
Frogner, Lars
JUNK MAIL
Frost, David
OFF THE MENU: THE LAST DAYS OF CHASEN'S
Frost, Roger
MERRY WAR, A
SHAKESPEARE IN LOVE
Frot, Catherine
UN AIR DE FAMILLE
Fruitman, Jason
54
Fry, Cory
AIR BUD: GOLDEN RECEIVER
Fry, Ed
LIVING OUT LOUD
Fry, Kevin
BILLBOARD DAD
CIVIL ACTION, A
WHY DO FOOLS FALL IN LOVE?
Fry, Stephen
CIVIL ACTION, A
SPICE WORLD
WILDE

Frye, Steve
HORSE WHISPERER, THE
Fuchs, Jason
JANE AUSTEN'S MAFIA!
Fuentes, Obdulia
WHO THE HELL IS JULIETTE?
Fugees
FREE TIBET
Fugelsang, John
SOMEWHERE IN THE CITY
Fugle, Susie
GO NOW
Fuhrman, Lisa
HARD RAIN
Fujii, Kahori
TOKYO FIST
Fujii, Seitaro
ZERO WOMAN
Fujimura, Shiho
SLEEPY EYES OF DEATH: SWORD OF ADVENTURE
SLEEPY EYES OF DEATH: SWORD OF SEDUCTION
Fukazi, Chester
TARZAN AND THE LOST CITY
Fukuzaki, Rob
GODZILLA
Fulci, Lucio
BEYOND, THE
Fuller, Amanda
DON KING: ONLY IN AMERICA
Fuller, Kurt
FRENCH EXIT
Fullerton, Andrew
BUTCHER BOY, THE
Fullerton, Richard
BODY COUNT
LAST LIVES
Fulton, Christina
SNAKE EYES
Fulton, John
REAL HOWARD SPITZ, THE
Fultz, Mona Lee
HOME FRIES
HOPE FLOATS
Funck, Susanne
CELEBRATION, THE
Fung Shui-fan
DRAGONS FOREVER
Fuqua, Joseph
DAVID SEARCHING
Furey, John
LAND OF THE FREE
Furlong, Anthony
KRAA! THE SEA MONSTER
Furlong, Edward
AMERICAN HISTORY X
PECKER
Furlong, John
JOHN CARPENTER'S VAMPIRES
Furman, Allison
HAPPINESS
Furs, Edward
OBJECT OF MY AFFECTION, THE
Furst, Stephen
LITTLE BIGFOOT 2: THE JOURNEY HOME
Furuta, Arata
JUNK FOOD
Furuya, Toru
MOBILE SUIT GUNDAM I
MOBILE SUIT GUNDAM II: SOLDIERS OF SORROW
MOBILE SUIT GUNDAM III: ENCOUNTERS IN SPACE
Fusco, Cosimo
EIGHTEENTH ANGEL, THE
Fusco, Robin
STEPMOM

Garcia, Saturnino
DAY OF THE BEAST, THE
Garcia, Tomasa
CARLA'S SONG
Garcia, Virginia
EVER AFTER
Garcin, Henri
DRESS, THE
Garcy, Geoff
BARRIERS
Gardner, Jerry
LEWIS & CLARK & GEORGE
Gardner, Micah
ATOMIC DOG
Gardner, Raquel
NIGHT AT THE ROXBURY, A
SPECIES II
Gardner, Stacia
I GOT THE HOOK UP
Gardner, Stirling
PLAN B
Gareis, Jennifer
LAST BREATH
Garello, Stefania Orsola
CHAMBERMAID ON THE TITANIC, THE
Garfalk, Martin Dahl
OTHER SIDE OF SUNDAY, THE
Garfunkel, Art
54
Gargiulo, Jess
PRINCE, THE
Gargula, Milan
ACT OF WAR
Garito, Ken
CHARLIE HOBOKEN
Garland, Julia
LOUISA MAY ALCOTT'S LITTLE MEN
Garlin, Jeff
SENSELESS
Garner, James
TWILIGHT
Garner, Rees
DECAMPITATED
Garnett, Kevin
REBOUND: THE LEGEND OF EARL "THE GOAT" MANIGAULT
Garofalo, Janeane
CLAY PIGEONS
HALF BAKED
KIKI'S DELIVERY SERVICE
PERMANENT MIDNIGHT
Garr, Teri
CASPER MEETS WENDY
Garrard, Pilar
MADELINE
Garrel, Maurice
ARTEMISIA
Garret, Kathleen
SOULER OPPOSITE, THE
Garrett, Brad
BUG'S LIFE, A
DON KING: ONLY IN AMERICA
SUICIDE KINGS
Garrett, Ernie
PALMETTO
Garrett, Spencer
PERMANENT MIDNIGHT
Garris, Cynthia
QUICKSILVER HIGHWAY
Garrison, Julia
RIDE
Garroway, Lloyd
WATCHERS REBORN
Garson, Willie
ALONE IN THE WOODS
DESTINY OF MARTY FINE, THE
LIVING OUT LOUD
THERE'S SOMETHING ABOUT MARY
Garth, Jennie
MY BROTHER'S WAR
Gartland, Mike
SPECIES II
Garvey, Steve
BASEKETBALL
Gashaw, Veharar
NIGHT VISION
Gassant, Denise
BELOVED
Gassman, Alessandro
STEAM
Gasster, David
PHANTASM: OBLIVION
Gasteyer, Ana
COURTING COURTNEY
MEET THE DEEDLES
Gaston, Camille
SUBSTITUTE 2: SCHOOL'S OUT, THE
Gaston, Haven
WATERBOY, THE
Gates, Katherine
R.I.P. REST IN PIECES: A PORTRAIT OF JOE COLEMAN
Gates, Ransom
FEAR AND LOATHING IN LAS VEGAS
Gatica, Silvana
WOO
Gatien, Jennifer "Nen"
BELLY
Gatins, John
ANOTHER DAY IN PARADISE
GODS AND MONSTERS
Gatiss, Dean
LOVE AND DEATH ON LONG ISLAND
Gau, Robin
THERE'S SOMETHING ABOUT MARY
Gaudet, Alphonse
BLACK LIGHT
Gauger, Stephane
SIX-STRING SAMURAI
Gaule, Ben
JACK HIGGINS' MIDNIGHT MAN
STRAY BULLET
Gault, Willie
HOLY MAN
NIGHT VISION
Gaunt, Fred
LITTLE VOICE
Gaunt, James
PALMETTO
Gaup, Mikkel
INSIDE/OUT
Gautier, Jean-Yves
GENEALOGIES OF A CRIME
VOYAGE TO THE BEGINNING OF THE WORLD
Gauzy, Dyna
RONIN
Gavin, Don
MONUMENT AVE.
Gavin, James W.
LETHAL WEAPON 4
Gay, Benjamin T.
GINGERBREAD MAN, THE
Gayheart, Rebecca
URBAN LEGEND
Gayle, Jackie
LENNY BRUCE: SWEAR TO TELL THE TRUTH
Gaynor, Joey
COMEDY'S DIRTIEST DOZEN
Gaze, Christopher
ADVENTURES OF MOWGLI
Gazzara, Ben
BIG LEBOWSKI, THE
BUFFALO '66
HAPPINESS
SPANISH PRISONER, THE
Ge Qingxiang
EMPEROR'S SHADOW, THE
Ge You
EMPEROR'S SHADOW, THE
Geamanu, Silviu
SECRET KINGDOM, THE
SUBSPECIES IV: BLOODSTORM
Geary, Caron
LOVE IS THE DEVIL: STUDY FOR A PORTRAIT OF FRANCIS BACON
Geary, Cynthia
SMOKE SIGNALS
WHEN TIME EXPIRES
Geary, Karl
MONTANA
Gebuhr, Vera
KINGDOM, PART 2, THE
Geer, Ellen
NEIL SIMON'S THE ODD COUPLE II
PRACTICAL MAGIC
Geffner, Deborah
LIVING OUT LOUD
Geidt, Jeremy
NEXT STOP, WONDERLAND
SPANISH PRISONER, THE
Geiger, Kirk
GODZILLA
Gelard, Frederic
LA SEPARATION
Geldart, Ed
RUSHMORE
Gelder, Ian
INFORMANT, THE
Geldof, Bob
SPICE WORLD
Gelfant, Alan
DESTINY OF MARTY FINE, THE
NEXT STOP, WONDERLAND
Gellar, Sarah Michelle
SMALL SOLDIERS
Gelose, Norma
BUFFALO '66
Genaro, Tony
MASK OF ZORRO, THE
MIGHTY JOE YOUNG
Gendler, Paul
SPICE WORLD
Genereux, Jean Marc
DANCE WITH ME
Genesis P-Orridge
MODULATIONS: CINEMA FOR THE EAR
Genest, Edmond
GIA
Genkinger, Scott
GIA
George, Andrew
DEAR JESSE
George, Jason Winston
FALLEN
George, Kent
GODS AND MONSTERS
George, Leonard
SMOKE SIGNALS
George, Lovette
BROADWAY DAMAGE
George, Matt
IN GOD'S HANDS
George, Melissa
DARK CITY
George, Ralph
BREAKOUT
UNDERTAKER'S WEDDING, THE
George, Tracy Anne
THERE'S SOMETHING ABOUT MARY
Georges, Liz
MIGHTY JOE YOUNG

Gillmore, Ian
REAL HOWARD SPITZ, THE
Gilloran, Dave
NEXT STOP, WONDERLAND
Gillott, Mark Alan
TRUMAN SHOW, THE
Gilmore, Jimmie Dale
BIG LEBOWSKI, THE
Gilmore, Peter
JACK HIGGINS' ON DANGEROUS GROUND
Gilmore, Susan
INNOCENT SLEEP, THE
Gilmour, Alexa
BIG HIT, THE
Gilpin, Jack
LAST BREATH
Gilroy, Tom
INSIDE/OUT
RATCHET
Gilsfort, Peter
KINGDOM, PART 2, THE
Gilshenan, Darren
DARK CITY
Gilsig, Jessalyn
HORSE WHISPERER, THE
QUEST FOR CAMELOT
Gimenez-Cacho, Daniel
MIDAQ ALLEY
Gingerich, Peter
BOYS IN LOVE 2
Gingold, Gary
RAGE, THE
Ginter, Lindsay Lee
MARS
Ginther, Mark
WHEN TIME EXPIRES
Gio, Frank
ONE TOUGH COP
Giocante, Vahina
MARIE BAIE DES ANGES
Gioiello, Bruno
CELEBRITY
Gionson, Mel Duane
PRICE ABOVE RUBIES, A
Giovinazzo, Carmine
BILLY'S HOLLYWOOD SCREEN KISS
NO WAY HOME
Gipson, Sanetta Y.
WEDDING SINGER, THE
Girdler, Justin
MERLIN
Girlina
WOO
Giroday, Francois
GODZILLA
PERMANENT MIDNIGHT
Giunta, Vicki
WIDE AWAKE
Giuntoli, Neil
HENRY: PORTRAIT OF A SERIAL KILLER PART 2
Givens, Adele
PLAYERS CLUB, THE
Giverin, Daniel
JACK HIGGINS' THUNDER POINT
Gizbert, Thomas
SAVING PRIVATE RYAN
Gjernes, Jay
OVERNIGHT DELIVERY
SIMPLE PLAN, A
Glabczyncka, Liliana
FROM A FAR COUNTRY
Glahn, Therese
CELEBRATION, THE
Glamour, Matthew
VELVET GOLDMINE

Glantzman-Leib, Lila
HAPPINESS
Glasgow, Gil
NIGHT VISION
Glass, Philip
LOU REED: ROCK AND ROLL HEART
TRUMAN SHOW, THE
Glasser, Phillip
STAR TREK: INSURRECTION
Glassman, Andrew
ARMAGEDDON
Glaudini, Lola
YOUR FRIENDS & NEIGHBORS
Glave, Matthew
PLUMP FICTION
WEDDING SINGER, THE
Glazer, Nathan
ARGUING THE WORLD
Gleason, James
WHY DO FOOLS FALL IN LOVE?
Gleason, Paul
BEST OF THE BEST: WITHOUT WARNING
DAY AT THE BEACH
THIN RED LINE, THE
Gleeson, Brendan
BREAK, THE
BUTCHER BOY, THE
GENERAL, THE
I WENT DOWN
Glegg, Kenneth
SNAKE EYES
Glen, Georgie
SHAKESPEARE IN LOVE
Glenn, Charles
BELOVED
Glenn, DeFoy
DOWN IN THE DELTA
Glenn, Lena
NAKED ACTS
Glenn, Scott
CARLA'S SONG
FIRESTORM
Gless, Sharon
AYN RAND: A SENSE OF LIFE
Glick, Lori
THERE'S SOMETHING ABOUT MARY
Glick, Marc H.
WIDE AWAKE
Glogovac, Nebojsa
SAVIOR
Glossop, Amber
SHAKESPEARE IN LOVE
Glover, Brian
ROYAL DECEIT
Glover, Danny
ANTZ
BELOVED
CAN'T YOU HEAR THE WIND HOWL?: THE LIFE AND MUSIC OF ROBERT JOHNSON
LETHAL WEAPON 4
PRINCE OF EGYPT, THE
Glover, David
SHOOTING FISH
Glover, Joan
LOLITA
Glover, Karen L.
NAKED ACTS
Glover, Paul
UGLY, THE
Glover, Susan
PEACEKEEPER, THE
Gluck, Wolfgang
FUNNY GAMES
Glymph, Avery
HE GOT GAME
Gobbi, Giorgio
CHAMBERMAID ON THE TITANIC, THE

Gobring-Hermstad, John Henning
MENDEL
Gochros, Jordan
STEPMOM
Goddard, Beth
LAST SEDUCTION II, THE
Goddard, Mark
LOST IN SPACE
Goddard, Trevor
DEEP RISING
Godenzi, Mina
MR. NICE GUY
Godfrey, Julie
BABE: PIG IN THE CITY
Godfrey, Patrick
EVER AFTER
Godley, Michael
AVENGERS, THE
Godreche, Judith
DISENCHANTED, THE
MAN IN THE IRON MASK, THE
Godshall, Ray
SIEGE, THE
Godsiff, Anna
GO NOW
Godwin, Christopher
AVENGERS, THE
Godwin, Randy
POLISH WEDDING
Goede, Jay
54
Goehner, Fred
SOUR GRAPES
Goes, Leon
TIETA OF AGRESTE
Goessens, Fred
CHARACTER
Goetsch, Brett R.
BOOGIE BOY
Goggins, Walton
MAJOR LEAGUE: BACK TO THE MINORS
Gogin, Michael Lee
FEAR AND LOATHING IN LAS VEGAS
Goia, Ilinca
MIDAS TOUCH, THE
TALISMAN
Going, Joanna
EDEN
PHANTOMS
STILL BREATHING
Gold, Claudia
LOVELIFE
Gold, Jeremy
LAST BREATH
Gold, L. Harvey
CALL TO REMEMBER, A
Gold, Richard
SHAKESPEARE IN LOVE
Goldberg, Adam
BABE: PIG IN THE CITY
SAVING PRIVATE RYAN
Goldberg, Simon
LOVE IS THE DEVIL: STUDY FOR A PORTRAIT OF FRANCIS BACON
Goldberg, Whoopi
BURN HOLLYWOOD BURN
HOW STELLA GOT HER GROOVE BACK
RUDOLPH THE RED-NOSED REINDEER: THE MOVIE
RUGRATS MOVIE, THE
Goldblatt, Max
MY GIANT
Goldblum, Jeff
HOLY MAN
PRINCE OF EGYPT, THE
Golden, Annie
BARRIERS

Golder, Sid
NIL BY MOUTH
Goldin, Nan
LOU REED: ROCK AND ROLL HEART
Goldman, Lorry
GODZILLA
Goldman, Michael
LOVE TO KILL
Goldring, Danny
CHILDREN OF THE CORN V: FIELD OF TERROR
Goldsbie, Jake
RESCUERS: STORIES OF COURAGE—TWO COUPLES
Goldschmidt, Kate
CELEBRATION, THE
Goldsmith, Merwin
ROUNDERS
Goldsmith, Tottie
TWISTED
Goldstein, Al
STORY OF X, THE
Goldstein, Jenette
FEAR AND LOATHING IN LAS VEGAS
LIVING OUT LOUD
SENSELESS
Goldstein, Mark
JANE AUSTEN'S MAFIA!
Goldstein, Steven
SPANISH PRISONER, THE
Goldthwaite, Bobcat
RUSTY: THE GREAT RESCUE
Goman, Arleen
WIDE AWAKE
Gomersalt, Barry
LITTLE VOICE
Gomes, Manoel
CENTRAL STATION
Gomes, Reverend Peter
OUT OF THE PAST
Gomez, Alicia
DANCE WITH ME
Gomez, Carlos
ENEMY OF THE STATE
NEGOTIATOR, THE
REPLACEMENT KILLERS, THE
Gomez Cruz, Ernesto
MIDAQ ALLEY
Gomez, Ian
COURTING COURTNEY
Gomez, Jaime
CLOCKWATCHERS
Gomez, Marga
SPHERE
Gomez, Michael
BIG LEBOWSKI, THE
Gomez, Mike
DANCE WITH ME
Gomez, Patrick
MARIE BAIE DES ANGES
Gomez, Raul
DANCE WITH ME
Gomi, Yutaroo
SLEEPY EYES OF DEATH: SWORD OF ADVENTURE
Gong Li
CHINESE BOX, THE
Gonsalves, Kiran
LAST ASSASSINS
Gonzales, Alcides
CARLA'S SONG
Gonzalez, Alex
PATCH ADAMS
Gonzalez Gonzalez, Clifton
REPLACEMENT KILLERS, THE
Gonzalez III, Ramiro
SIMON BIRCH
Gonzalez, Monica
DANCE WITH ME
Gonzalez, Narciso
CARLA'S SONG
Gonzalez, Rudy
DANCE WITH ME
Goodall, Louise
CARLA'S SONG
Goode, Conrad
RINGMASTER
Gooding Jr., Cuba
WHAT DREAMS MAY COME
Goodman, Brian
MONUMENT AVE.
Goodman, John
BIG LEBOWSKI, THE
BLUES BROTHERS 2000
BORROWERS, THE
FALLEN
RUDOLPH THE RED-NOSED REINDEER: THE MOVIE
Goodson, Liat
PRINCE, THE
Goodwin, Kia Joy
OBJECT OF MY AFFECTION, THE
Goodwin, Michael
LOLITA
Goody, Bob
BORROWERS, THE
Goorjian, Michael
HARD RAIN
Gorby, Maebh
GENERAL, THE
Gorden, Henry
FLINTSTONES: I YABBA-DABBA DOO!, THE
Gordon, Amy
DECAMPITATED
Gordon, Barbara
FIXER, THE
Gordon, Bryan
SOUR GRAPES
Gordon, Danso
AMERICAN HISTORY X
Gordon, Eve
I'LL BE HOME FOR CHRISTMAS
Gordon, J.J.
HOSTILE WATERS
Gordon, Jack
PLAN B
Gordon, Joanne
PI
Gordon, Joel
DOWN IN THE DELTA
Gordon, Liz
BLUES BROTHERS 2000
Gordon, Pamela
ANOTHER DAY IN PARADISE
Gore, Courtney
SUB DOWN
Goric, Voyo
MARS
Goritsas, Demetri
SAVING PRIVATE RYAN
Gorlitsky, Lisa
ROUNDERS
Gorman, Bradley J.
ALARMIST, THE
Gorman, Breon
STAR TREK: INSURRECTION
Gorman, Greg
PECKER
SIX DAYS, SEVEN NIGHTS
Gorman, Patrick
WOUNDED
Goryl, David
THERE'S SOMETHING ABOUT MARY
Goshmir, Simon
DEJA VU
Goss, Natalie
SIX DAYS, SEVEN NIGHTS
Gosselaar, Mark Paul
DEAD MAN ON CAMPUS
Gossett Jr., Louis
BRAM STOKER'S THE MUMMY
IN HIS FATHER'S SHOES
Gossett, Robert
MAKER, THE
Gossom Jr., Thom
SENSELESS
Gostelow, Harry
SHAKESPEARE IN LOVE
SHOOTING FISH
Gotell, Walter
PRINCE VALIANT
Goto, Al
LOVE TO KILL
Gottfried, Gilbert
DR. DOLITTLE
Gottlieb, Heather
NO WAY HOME
PARALLEL SONS
Gouard, Chantal
UN AIR DE FAMILLE
Gould, Dana
COURTING COURTNEY
Gould, Dominic
SOLDIER'S DAUGHTER NEVER CRIES, A
Gould, Elliott
AMERICAN HISTORY X
BIG HIT, THE
Gould, Graydon
DEJA VU
Gould, Harold
MY GIANT
PATCH ADAMS
Goulem, Alain
CAPTIVE
SNAKE EYES
Gouveia, Teresa
PEREIRA DECLARES
Gowan, Guy
SPICE WORLD
Gowen, Peter
BUTCHER BOY, THE
DANCING AT LUGHNASA
Goz, Harry
BUSTER & CHAUNCEY'S SILENT NIGHT
Grace, April
CHICAGO CAB
PLAYING BY HEART
TWILIGHT
Grace, Brendan
MOONDANCE
Grace, Howard
LITTLE VOICE
Grace, Michelle
RAT PACK, THE
Grace, Nickolas
MERLIN
SHOOTING FISH
Grady, Ed
LOLITA
Graff, Jerry
SPANISH PRISONER, THE
Graham, Chris
UGLY, THE
Graham, Currie
BLACK LIGHT
Graham, Gary
RUNNING WOMAN, THE
Graham, Gerrit
ONE TRUE THING

Graham, Heather
LOST IN SPACE
TWO GIRLS AND A GUY
Graham, Katerina
PARENT TRAP, THE
Graham, Lauren
NIGHTWATCH
ONE TRUE THING
Graham, Martha
PRACTICAL MAGIC
Graham, Pancho
SIX DAYS, SEVEN NIGHTS
Graham, Prince "Blunt"
BELLY
Graham, Richard
HOSTILE WATERS
Graham, Robert
HOME FRIES
Graham, Stuart
BUTCHER BOY, THE
INFORMANT, THE
Grahn, Judy
STOLEN MOMENTS
Grainger, Gawn
LOVE AND DEATH ON LONG ISLAND
Grammer, Kelsey
PENTAGON WARS, THE
REAL HOWARD SPITZ, THE
Granath, Bjorn
JERUSALEM
Grandison, Brian
VERY BAD THINGS
Grandison, Pippa
BABE: PIG IN THE CITY
Grando, Kelley
WOO
Grando, Kelly
TERMINAL JUSTICE
Granger, Eric P.
PARALLEL SONS
Granli, Elisabeth
HOW STELLA GOT HER GROOVE BACK
Grano, Andrea
NEXT STOP, WONDERLAND
Granofsky, Anais
WHITE RAVEN, THE
Grant, Beth
DANCE WITH ME
DR. DOLITTLE
LAWN DOGS
Grant, Breanne
BREAKOUT
Grant, Dougary
RED HAWK: WEAPON OF DEATH
Grant, Gaye
HI-LO COUNTRY, THE
Grant, Hugh
OFF THE MENU: THE LAST DAYS OF CHASEN'S
Grant II, Edward
DARK CITY
Grant, Jessica Brooks
WHAT DREAMS MAY COME
Grant, Kate Jennings
OBJECT OF MY AFFECTION, THE
Grant, Lee
WHO IS HENRY JAGLOM?
Grant, Leon W.
KRAA! THE SEA MONSTER
Grant, Lisa Ann
DEEP IMPACT
Grant, Matt
KNOCK OFF
Grant, Miriam
PHOTOGRAPHING FAIRIES
Grant, Oli
BELLY
Grant, Richard E.
MERRY WAR, A
SPICE WORLD
Grant, Rodney A.
TWO FOR TEXAS
Grant, Sandra
SIN AND REDEMPTION
Grant, Sylvia
VELVET GOLDMINE
Grant, Tiffany
SLAYERS: THE MOTION PICTURE
Grant, Tom
KURT AND COURTNEY
Grant, Vince
FRENCH EXIT
Grantz, Kevin
SPECIES II
Granveldt, Brian
SLAYERS: THE MOTION PICTURE
Grappini, Floriella
SUBSPECIES IV: BLOODSTORM
Graseck, James E.
ONE TRUE THING
Grassi, Alessandra
LIFE IS BEAUTIFUL
Grasso, Anthony
STEPMOM
Gratson, Katie
NEWTON BOYS, THE
Graver, Gary
INVISIBLE DAD
Graves, Kaitlin
NIGHT VISION
Graves, Rupert
INNOCENT SLEEP, THE
MRS. DALLOWAY
Gray, Christopher
RUDOLPH THE RED-NOSED REINDEER: THE MOVIE
Gray, David Barry
LAWN DOGS
WHY DO FOOLS FALL IN LOVE?
Gray, Frances
BELOVED
Gray, Gary LeRoi
SLAPPY AND THE STINKERS
Gray, Jack Mclaughlin
NEGOTIATOR, THE
Gray, Leah
NO LOOKING BACK
Gray, Mackenzie
FALLING FIRE
Gray, Rick
HUSH
Gray, Sam
CELEBRITY
Gray, Shari
MEN WITH GUNS
Gray, Vernon
OBJECT OF MY AFFECTION, THE
Gray-Stanford, Jason
ESCAPE, THE
MIGHTY KONG, THE
Graydon, Dickie
SHOOTING FISH
Grayson, Jerry
BREAK, THE
MONTANA
Graziano, Dawn
RETURN OF THE KING, THE
Greanleaf, Anthony
RATCHET
Greatches, Phil John
KNOCK OFF
Greaves, Kristoffer
BABE: PIG IN THE CITY
Greco, Paul
HENRY FOOL
Green, Alex
SPREE, THE
Green, Calvin
TERMINAL JUSTICE
Green, Clinton
DOWN IN THE DELTA
Green, Fanni
OBJECT OF MY AFFECTION, THE
Green, Johnny
GIA
Green, Josh
CURSE OF THE PUPPET MASTER
Green, Judy
MR. NICE GUY
Green, Karey
TWO FOR TEXAS
Green, Mary Pat
WHY DO FOOLS FALL IN LOVE?
Green, Robyn M.
HAV PLENTY
Green, Seth
CAN'T HARDLY WAIT
ENEMY OF THE STATE
NOTES FROM UNDERGROUND
Green, Vince
CHICAGO CAB
Greenberg, Paul
GODSON, THE
Greenburg, Mitch
LIVING OUT LOUD
Greenbury, Andrew
THERE'S SOMETHING ABOUT MARY
Greenbury, Nick
THERE'S SOMETHING ABOUT MARY
Greene, Daniel
THERE'S SOMETHING ABOUT MARY
Greene, Daniel E.
AYN RAND: A SENSE OF LIFE
Greene, Graham
SHATTERED IMAGE
WOUNDED
Greene, H. Richard
ARMAGEDDON
Greene, Jaki Shelton
DEAR JESSE
Greene, James
PATCH ADAMS
Greene, Lagena
THERE'S SOMETHING ABOUT MARY
Greene, Peter
PERMANENT MIDNIGHT
Greenhill, Susan
PECKER
Greenstein, Paul
NEVADA
Greenway, Tara
NAKED ACTS
Greenwood, Bruce
DISTURBING BEHAVIOR
Greer, Douglas
NOT IN THIS TOWN
Greer, Judy
KISSING A FOOL
Greer, Stuart
BLACK DOG
GINGERBREAD MAN, THE
Greet, Christopher
JACK HIGGINS' ON DANGEROUS GROUND
Gregg, Bradley
NIGHTWATCH
Gregg, Clark
SPANISH PRISONER, THE
Gregg, David
MARIE BAIE DES ANGES
Gregor, Simon
LAST SEDUCTION II, THE

Guggenbuhl, Maxime
WESTERN
Gugino, Carla
LOVELIFE
SNAKE EYES
Gugliametti, Dominic
RONIN
Gugushe, Biski
RIGHT CONNECTIONS, THE
Guhur, Alain Luc
WESTERN
Guichou, Blanche
MARIUS AND JEANNETTE
Guidall, George
IMPOSTORS, THE
Guider, Forest Freedom
OUTSIDE OZONA
Guidera, Anthony
ARMAGEDDON
Guido, Michael
U.S. MARSHALS
Guilbert, Ann
SOUR GRAPES
Guilfoyle, Paul
NEGOTIATOR, THE
ONE TOUGH COP
PRIMARY COLORS
Guillaume, Robert
LION KING II: SIMBA'S PRIDE, THE
Guillermo
WHO THE HELL IS JULIETTE?
Guilliard, Leontine
PRIMARY COLORS
Guillo, Alain
UN AIR DE FAMILLE
Guinee, Tim
BLADE
JOHN CARPENTER'S VAMPIRES
Guinness, Peter
HOSTILE WATERS
Guinness, Rowena
MONTANA
Gulager, Tom
CLOCKMAKER
Gulinello, Amo
OBJECT OF MY AFFECTION, THE
Gulka, Jeff
AIR BUD: GOLDEN RECEIVER
Gullette, Sean
PI
Guma, Tony
WATCHERS REBORN
Gumbert, Noah
DARK CITY
Gumbert, Satya
DARK CITY
Gummersall, Devon
WHEN TRUMPETS FADE
Gundry, Bill
STILL BREATHING
Gunn, Anna
ENEMY OF THE STATE
Gunn, Michael
LEADING MAN, THE
Gunn, Peter
EVER AFTER
Gunning, Charles
NEWTON BOYS, THE
Gunsur, Mehmet
STEAM
Gunther, Dan
LEWIS & CLARK & GEORGE
Gunton, Bob
ELVIS MEETS NIXON
PATCH ADAMS
Guo, Calvin
WRONGFULLY ACCUSED
Guo Ke-Yu
RED CHERRY
Gurganus, Allan
DEAR JESSE
Gurrola, Juan-Jose
DIDN'T DO IT FOR LOVE
Guru, The
SUBSTITUTE 2: SCHOOL'S OUT, THE
Gusenbauer, Christoph
INHERITORS, THE
Gusta, Lee
LET'S KILL ALL THE LAWYERS
Gustafson, Neil
NEXT STOP, WONDERLAND
Gutfreund, Susan
SOLDIER'S DAUGHTER NEVER CRIES, A
Guth, Ray
RAT'S TALE, A
Guthorsen, Lena
DANGEROUS BEAUTY
Guttierez, Emmanuel
MAN IN THE IRON MASK, THE
SWINDLE, THE
Guttman, Ronald
LENA'S DREAMS
Guy, Buddy
FREE TIBET
Guybet, Christophe
MADELINE
Guyer, Murphy
PARALLEL SONS
ROUNDERS
Guzman, Diego Mendez
MEN WITH GUNS
Guzman, Ermenehildo Saenz
MEN WITH GUNS
Guzman, Luis
ONE TOUGH COP
OUT OF SIGHT
PRONTO
SNAKE EYES
Guzman, Patricio
CHILE, OBSTINATE MEMORY
Guzzo, Francesco
LIFE IS BEAUTIFUL
Gwaltney, Jack
SIEGE, THE
Gwaltney, Robert
CATHERINE'S GROVE
Gyetvai, Eva
REDLINE
Gyllenhaal, Jake
HOMEGROWN
Gyllenhaal, Maggie
HOMEGROWN
Gyorgy, Chobi
FEAR AND LOATHING IN LAS VEGAS
Ha, Benita
HARD CORE LOGO
LOVE AND DEATH ON LONG ISLAND
Haas, Richard
ACT OF WAR
Habberstad, Trevor
SIMON BIRCH
Habeck, Michael
TALES FROM A PARALLEL UNIVERSE: GIGA SHADOW
Habel, Jeannette
EL CHE: INVESTIGATING A LEGEND
Habermann, Eva
TALES FROM A PARALLEL UNIVERSE: EATING PATTERN
TALES FROM A PARALLEL UNIVERSE: GIGA SHADOW
TALES FROM A PARALLEL UNIVERSE: SUPER NOVA
Habich, Matthias
BEYOND SILENCE
Hack, Olivia
NAPOLEON
Hackett, Buddy
PAULIE
Hackl, Bob
WEDDING SINGER, THE
Hackman, Ben
BREAKOUT
Hackman, Gene
ANTZ
ENEMY OF THE STATE
TWILIGHT
Hadder, David
RETURN TO SAVAGE BEACH
Haddock, Gray G.
TEKKEN: THE MOTION PICTURE
Haddon, Dayle
CELEBRITY
Haden-Guest, Anthony
LAST DAYS OF DISCO, THE
Hadland, Sean
LITTLE VOICE
Hadleigh-West, Maggie
WAR ZONE
Hadray, Jonathan
MONTANA
Hadyn-Tovey, Clifford
BRYLCREEM BOYS, THE
Hae Joon Lee
RUSHMORE
Haenen, Hugo
RESCUERS: STORIES OF COURAGE—TWO COUPLES
Hagan, Katie
DEEP IMPACT
STILL BREATHING
Hagan, Marianne
I THINK I DO
Hagan, Molly
FRENCH EXIT
RINGMASTER
Hagan, Shane
SAVING PRIVATE RYAN
Hagar, David
LAST LIVES
Hagen, Joanne
REAL HOWARD SPITZ, THE
Hagen, Ross
INVISIBLE DAD
Hagerty, Julie
BOYS WILL BE BOYS
Haggerty, Joe
INVISIBLE DAD
Haggie, James
LEADING MAN, THE
Haggis, Kathryn
REAL BLONDE, THE
Hagler, Nik
CON, THE
Hagler, Shawna
BULWORTH
Haglund, Dean
X-FILES, THE
Hagman, Larry
PRIMARY COLORS
Hagopian, Dean
SNAKE EYES
Hahn, Archie
DR. DOLITTLE
Hahn III, Archie
SMALL SOLDIERS
Hahn, William
PHANTOMS
Hahn-Petersen, John
KINGDOM, PART 2, THE
Hai Truhong
DISENCHANTED, THE

Haiduc, Ion
SECRET KINGDOM, THE
SHRUNKEN CITY, THE
SUBSPECIES IV: BLOODSTORM
Hails, Chris
BLACK LIGHT
Haims, Lori
NEXT STOP, WONDERLAND
Haine, Darwin
SMOKE SIGNALS
Haines, Wesley G.
PATCH ADAMS
Hakuryu
FIREWORKS
Haladova, Monica
NEMESIS 4: CRY OF ANGELS
Hald, Mette
KINGDOM, PART 2, THE
Halder, Ron
TRICKS
Hale, Embry
LEWIS & CLARK & GEORGE
Haleva, Jerry
BIG LEBOWSKI, THE
JANE AUSTEN'S MAFIA!
Haley, R.M.
PRIMARY COLORS
Hall, Albert
BELOVED
Hall, Brian
CAN'T HARDLY WAIT
Hall, Carol
CHICAGO CAB
Hall, Esther
LAND GIRLS, THE
Hall, Gabriella
INDISCREET
LOLIDA 2000
Hall, Glenn
ELVIS MEETS NIXON
Hall, Irma P.
BELOVED
PATCH ADAMS
Hall, J.D.
BABE: PIG IN THE CITY
Hall, Keana
DON KING: ONLY IN AMERICA
Hall, Ladene
TWENTYFOURSEVEN
Hall, Michael Keyes
SPHERE
Hall, Monty
OFF THE MENU: THE LAST DAYS OF CHASEN'S
Hall, Philip Baker
ENEMY OF THE STATE
HIT ME
PSYCHO
RUSH HOUR
SOUR GRAPES
TRUMAN SHOW, THE
Hall, Randy
X-FILES, THE
Hall, Reamy
RINGMASTER
Hall, Robert David
NEGOTIATOR, THE
Hall, Ron
DON KING: ONLY IN AMERICA
Hall, Shashawnee
KRIPPENDORF'S TRIBE
LAST ASSASSINS
WHY DO FOOLS FALL IN LOVE?
Hall, Steve
UGLY, THE
Hall, Suzanne
LIKE IT IS
Hall, Tiffany
WOO
Hall, Tim
SIMON BIRCH
Hall, Walter C.
HI-LO COUNTRY, THE
Hall, Willie
BLUES BROTHERS 2000
Hallberg, Gry Worre
CELEBRATION, THE
Halliday, Richard
EBENEZER
Hallier, Lori
BLACK LIGHT
Halligan, Tim
KRIPPENDORF'S TRIBE
PLAYING BY HEART
Halliwell, Geri
SPICE WORLD
Hallo, Dean
PHANTOMS
Halsey, Michael
MEAN GUNS
Halsey, Steven
BROADWAY DAMAGE
Halston, Julie
CELEBRITY
DAVID SEARCHING
Halverson, Robert Martin
SIMPLE PLAN, A
Ham-Bernard, Sherry
SIEGE, THE
Hamacher, Al
MAJOR LEAGUE: BACK TO THE MINORS
Hamada, Yuuko
SLEEPY EYES OF DEATH: FULL CIRCLE KILLING
Hamburg, John
SAFE MEN
Hamburger
DECLINE OF WESTERN CIVILIZATION PART III, THE
Hamer, Lille Shaw
ENEMY OF THE STATE
Hamill, Mark
BATMAN/SUPERMAN MOVIE, THE
SCOOBY-DOO ON ZOMBIE ISLAND
WATCHERS REBORN
WHEN TIME EXPIRES
Hamilton, Alice
MERLIN
Hamilton, Callum
VELVET GOLDMINE
Hamilton, Claire
TEKKEN: THE MOTION PICTURE
Hamilton, Derek
DISTURBING BEHAVIOR
FIRESTORM
Hamilton, George
BULWORTH
CASPER MEETS WENDY
Hamilton, Linda
RESCUERS: STORIES OF COURAGE—TWO COUPLES
Hamilton, Lisa Gay
BELOVED
HALLOWEEN H20: TWENTY YEARS LATER
LAST BREATH
Hamilton, Miriam
OBJECT OF MY AFFECTION, THE
Hamilton, Quancetia
DOWN IN THE DELTA
Hamilton, Randy
MIGHTY KONG, THE
Hamilton, Reggie
LIVING OUT LOUD
Hamilton, Richard
REACH THE ROCK
Hamilton, Trip
LOLITA
Hamlin, Harry
HUNTED, THE
Hammad, Michael
MR. NICE GUY
Hammer, MC
RIGHT CONNECTIONS, THE
Hammett, George "Butch"
LOVELIFE
Hammett, Mary
ONE TOUGH COP
Hammil, John
PHANTOMS
Hammond, Blake
JANE AUSTEN'S MAFIA!
Hammond, Darrell
BLUES BROTHERS 2000
Hammond, Drew
FRENCH EXIT
Hammond, Earl
BUSTER & CHAUNCEY'S SILENT NIGHT
Hammond, John
CAN'T YOU HEAR THE WIND HOWL?: THE LIFE AND MUSIC OF ROBERT JOHNSON
Hammond, Louis
LES MISERABLES
Hammond, Mark
BABE: PIG IN THE CITY
Hammond, Vincent
SPECIES II
Hammonds, Margaret
LOLITA
Hampton, Amanda
PARENT TRAP, THE
Hamzaoui, Hedi
MARIUS AND JEANNETTE
Han, Akiba Bunjaku
WHEN I CLOSE MY EYES
Han, David
ENEMY OF THE STATE
Han, Keiko
MOBILE SUIT GUNDAM III: ENCOUNTERS IN SPACE
Hanau, Sasha
OGRE, THE
Hancock, Dick
ANOTHER DAY IN PARADISE
Hancock, Jason Todd
KNOCK OFF
Hancock, Sheila
LOVE AND DEATH ON LONG ISLAND
Hand, Gary
LETHAL WEAPON 4
MERCURY RISING
Hand, Mat
TWENTYFOURSEVEN
Hand, Walter
SHADRACH
Handel, Ari
PI
Handfield, Don
DEEP IMPACT
Handley, Taylor
JACK FROST
Handy, Emma
VELVET GOLDMINE
Handy, Jacob
KRIPPENDORF'S TRIBE
Handy, James
MURDER IN MIND
Handy, Preston B.
HURRICANE STREETS
Handy, Zachary
KRIPPENDORF'S TRIBE

Haney, Anne
PSYCHO
Haney, Tom
REAL HOWARD SPITZ, THE
Haney, Tony
PRINCE, THE
Hankin, Harry
LET'S KILL ALL THE LAWYERS
Hanks, Tom
SAVING PRIVATE RYAN
YOU'VE GOT MAIL
Hann-Byrd, Adam
HALLOWEEN H20: TWENTY YEARS LATER
Hanna, Gillian
LES MISERABLES
Hanna, Lisa
HOW STELLA GOT HER GROOVE BACK
Hanna, William
FLINTSTONES: I YABBA-DABBA DOO!, THE
Hannafin, Daniel P.
PATCH ADAMS
Hannah, Bobby
BIG HIT, THE
Hannah, Daryl
GINGERBREAD MAN, THE
HI-LIFE
REAL BLONDE, THE
Hannah, John
INNOCENT SLEEP, THE
SLIDING DOORS
Hanneman, Lewis
ASYLUM
Hannigan, Alyson
DEAD MAN ON CAMPUS
Hannigan, Maury
WRONGFULLY ACCUSED
Hannity, Sean
SIEGE, THE
Hanover, Donna
CELEBRITY
SIEGE, THE
Hans, Tim
VELVET GOLDMINE
Hansen, Donna
MIDAS TOUCH, THE
Hansen, Elizabeth
NOT IN THIS TOWN
Hansen, Erik
HOSTILE WATERS
Hansen, Holger Juul
KINGDOM, PART 2, THE
Hansen, Kevin
I'LL BE HOME FOR CHRISTMAS
Hansen, Monika
KILLER CONDOM, THE
Hansen, Nyree
KNOCK OFF
Hansen, Stig Poul
CELEBRATION, THE
Hanson, Dian
R.I.P. REST IN PIECES: A PORTRAIT OF JOE COLEMAN
Hanson, Kai Kennet
OTHER SIDE OF SUNDAY, THE
Hanson, Rusty
STAR KID
Hanson, Ted
MAJOR LEAGUE: BACK TO THE MINORS
Harada, Ann
HAPPINESS
Harada, Kiwako
GODZILLA VS. KING GHIDORAH
Harada, Mieko
VILLAGE OF DREAMS
Harden, Marcia Gay
DESPERATE MEASURES
MEET JOE BLACK
Harder, Teresa
MENDEL
Hardester, Crofton
SAVING PRIVATE RYAN
Hardfloor
MODULATIONS: CINEMA FOR THE EAR
Hardig, Stephen
MAJOR LEAGUE: BACK TO THE MINORS
Harding, Ellerine
I STILL KNOW WHAT YOU DID LAST SUMMER
Harding, Jan Leslie
HENRY FOOL
Harding, Peter
KILLING TIME
Hardt, Katreen
HENRY FOOL
Hardwick, Chris
COURTING COURTNEY
GENERAL CHAOS: UNCENSORED ANIMATION
Hardwicke, Edward
ELIZABETH
PHOTOGRAPHING FAIRIES
Hardy, Caroline
LOVE IS THE DEVIL: STUDY FOR A PORTRAIT OF FRANCIS BACON
Hardy, Dona
TRUMAN SHOW, THE
Hardy, Nita
GINGERBREAD MAN, THE
Hardy, Robert
MRS. DALLOWAY
Hardy, Trishalee
LITTLE GHOST
Hare, Kelly
WATERBOY, THE
Harewood, Dorian
12 ANGRY MEN
Hargett, Hester
BLACK DOG
Hargreaves, Christopher
LIKE IT IS
Hargreaves, Janie
COUSIN BETTE
Hari, Luck
THURSDAY
Hariken, "Hurricane Ryu"
GODZILLA AND MOTHRA: THE BATTLE FOR EARTH
Harimoto, Dale
GODZILLA
Harker, Amanda
LAST DAYS OF DISCO, THE
Harkless, Loni-Kaye
DON KING: ONLY IN AMERICA
Harland, Franz
DIDN'T DO IT FOR LOVE
Harlowe, Peter
JACK HIGGINS' ON DANGEROUS GROUND
Harmon, Angie
LAWN DOGS
Harmon, Cynde
DISTURBING BEHAVIOR
Harmon, Mark
FEAR AND LOATHING IN LAS VEGAS
Harms, John
LETHAL WEAPON 4
Harnell, Jess
CASPER MEETS WENDY
Harnoff, Igor
JOHNNY MYSTO BOY WIZARD
Harnos, Christine
HOLLYWOOD CONFIDENTIAL
LOVE TO KILL
Harper, Angel
RUGRATS MOVIE, THE
Harper, Angie
RINGMASTER
Harper, Frank
TWENTYFOURSEVEN
Harper, Hill
BELOVED
HAV PLENTY
HE GOT GAME
Harper, James
ARMAGEDDON
Harper, Kate
HUMAN BOMB
Harper, Kirk
TRUCKS
Harper, Kyra
DEFENDERS: PAYBACK, THE
Harper, Ron
BODY COUNT
NEIL SIMON'S THE ODD COUPLE II
Harper, Russel
STEPMOM
Harper, Tess
DIRTY LAUNDRY
Harrell, James N.
HOPE FLOATS
Harrell Jr., Peter
TEKKEN: THE MOTION PICTURE
Harrelson, Brett
DEE SNIDER'S STRANGELAND
Harrelson, Woody
HI-LO COUNTRY, THE
PALMETTO
THIN RED LINE, THE
Harrington, Adam
WOUNDED
Harrington, John
I STILL KNOW WHAT YOU DID LAST SUMMER
Harrington, Laura
PAULIE
Harrington, Olivia
OBJECT OF MY AFFECTION, THE
Harrington, Pat
FLINTSTONES: I YABBA-DABBA DOO!, THE
Harris, Andrea
NAKED ACTS
Harris, Barbara
BABE: PIG IN THE CITY
Harris, Barbara Eve
IN HIS FATHER'S SHOES
Harris, Baxter
SPECIES II
Harris, Carle
HUMAN BOMB
Harris, Danielle
URBAN LEGEND
Harris, Doc
DRAGON BALL Z THE MOVIE: DEAD ZONE
DRAGON BALL Z THE MOVIE: THE WORLD'S STRONGEST
Harris, Ed
STEPMOM
TRUMAN SHOW, THE
Harris, Estelle
CHAIRMAN OF THE BOARD
MY GIANT
NEIL SIMON'S THE ODD COUPLE II
Harris, George
MADELINE
Harris, Hank
MERCURY RISING

Harris, Heather
PLAN B
Harris, Henry
JANE AUSTEN'S MAFIA!
Harris, J. Todd
LEWIS & CLARK & GEORGE
Harris, Jamie
MARIE BAIE DES ANGES
Harris, Jared
CHINESE BOX, THE
HAPPINESS
HURRICANE STREETS
LOST IN SPACE
Harris, Jill
APT PUPIL
Harris, Jonathan
BUG'S LIFE, A
Harris, Jossie
PLAYERS CLUB, THE
Harris Jr., Wendell B.
OUT OF SIGHT
Harris, Julie
BAD MANNERS
Harris, Keith
DIGGING TO CHINA
LAST LIVES
Harris, Kemp
NEXT STOP, WONDERLAND
Harris, Kim
HAV PLENTY
Harris, Laura
FACULTY, THE
SUICIDE KINGS
Harris, Michael
I LOVE YOU, DON'T TOUCH ME!
Harris, Michael D.
I GOT THE HOOK UP
Harris, Moira
CHICAGO CAB
Harris, Neil Patrick
PROPOSITION, THE
SNOWBOUND
Harris, Pascale
KNOCK OFF
Harris, Phil
LAST SEDUCTION II, THE
Harris, Quinn
HE GOT GAME
Harris, Rachhael
DISAPPEARANCE OF KEVIN JOHNSON, THE
Harris, Reggie
HENRY FOOL
Harris, Ricky
HARD RAIN
Harris, Steve
GEORGE WALLACE
Harris, Viola
SOUR GRAPES
Harris, Wood
CELEBRITY
SIEGE, THE
Harris, Zelda
HE GOT GAME
Harrison, Angela
LITTLE VOICE
Harrison, Cathryn
DEJA VU
Harrison, David
LOVE IS THE DEVIL: STUDY FOR A PORTRAIT OF FRANCIS BACON
Harrison, Emily
CURSE OF THE PUPPET MASTER
Harrison, Fran
PRINCE, THE
Harrison, Gregory
AIR BUD: GOLDEN RECEIVER
Harrison, Hank
KURT AND COURTNEY
Harrison, Jasmine
DEEP IMPACT
Harrison, Noel
DEJA VU
Harrison, Schae
INTERLOCKED: THRILLED TO DEATH
Harrison, Stanley Earl
DIRTY LAUNDRY
Harrod, David
THIN RED LINE, THE
Harrold, Jamie
I THINK I DO
Harrow, Lisa
FROM A FAR COUNTRY
Harryhausen, Ray
MIGHTY JOE YOUNG
Harryson, Annelie
DANGEROUS BEAUTY
Harshaw, Cee-Cee
GIA
SENSELESS
Hart, Anita
JOHN CARPENTER'S VAMPIRES
Hart, Bob Eric
MEET THE DEEDLES
Hart, Brian
RIGHT CONNECTIONS, THE
Hart, Christopher
QUICKSILVER HIGHWAY
Hart, Elizabeth
RIGHT CONNECTIONS, THE
Hart, Emily
RIGHT CONNECTIONS, THE
Hart, Ian
BUTCHER BOY, THE
ENEMY OF THE STATE
MONUMENT AVE.
Hart, Jillian
BLUES BROTHERS 2000
Hart, Melissa Joan
CAN'T HARDLY WAIT
RIGHT CONNECTIONS, THE
Hart, Michelle
WRONGFULLY ACCUSED
Hart, Mike
DECAMPITATED
Hart, Pamela
NEXT STOP, WONDERLAND
PI
PROPOSITION, THE
Hart, Roxanne
HORTON FOOTE'S ALONE
Hart, Susan
U.S. MARSHALS
Hart, Terry V.
SIMON BIRCH
Hart, Tina
OPPOSITE OF SEX, THE
Hart-Gilliams, Alexandra
RIGHT CONNECTIONS, THE
Hartigan, Danny
SOULER OPPOSITE, THE
Hartley, Steven
JOHN CARPENTER'S VAMPIRES
Hartley, Theodore R.
MIGHTY JOE YOUNG
Hartman, Phil
BUSTER & CHAUNCEY'S SILENT NIGHT
KIKI'S DELIVERY SERVICE
SMALL SOLDIERS
Hartman, Steven
BOYS WILL BE BOYS
Hartmann, Peter
KINGDOM, PART 2, THE
Hartner, Rona
GADJO DILO
Hartnett, Josh
FACULTY, THE
HALLOWEEN H20: TWENTY YEARS LATER
Hartney, Brick
ALMOST PARTNERS
Hartridge, Walter
GINGERBREAD MAN, THE
Hartsock, Charlie
DEEP IMPACT
Hartwig, Kristen
PRINCE VALIANT
Hartz, Maria Von
LAST BIG THING, THE
Harukawa, Masumi
SLEEPY EYES OF DEATH: SWORD OF SEDUCTION
Harvey, David
LOVE IS THE DEVIL: STUDY FOR A PORTRAIT OF FRANCIS BACON
Harvey, Don
CON, THE
THIN RED LINE, THE
Harvey, Erik LaRay
ROUNDERS
Harvey, Graham
VIOLET'S VISIT
Harvey, Pat
JANE AUSTEN'S MAFIA!
Harvey, Phil
TOUCH OF EVIL: THE DIRECTOR'S CUT
Harvey, Robert H.
RINGMASTER
Harvey, Tom
REAL BLONDE, THE
Harvie, Ellie
WRONGFULLY ACCUSED
Harwood, Bruce
X-FILES, THE
Hasak, Zachary M.
STEPMOM
Hascoet, Karine
WESTERN
Haskell, Molly
WHO IS HENRY JAGLOM?
Haskins, Coach Clem
HE GOT GAME
Hassan, Waddah Abdul
OPERATION DELTA FORCE 2
Hassen, Kulani
DOWN IN THE DELTA
Hasson, Lauren
ZERO EFFECT
Hastings, Bob
BATMAN & MR. FREEZE: SUBZERO
BATMAN/SUPERMAN MOVIE, THE
Hastings, Jay
FATAL PURSUIT
Hasuo, Kengo
THIN RED LINE, THE
Hatch, Deborah
KRAA! THE SEA MONSTER
Hatfield, Mert
LOLITA
Hatfield, Susan
OUT OF SIGHT
Hathaway, Jessica
QUEST FOR CAMELOT
Hatosy, Shawn
FACULTY, THE
NIAGARA NIAGARA
NO WAY HOME
Hatosy, Shawn Wayne
THIN RED LINE, THE
Hauduroy, James
SWINDLE, THE
Hauer, Rutger
BLEEDERS

BONE DADDY
HOSTILE WATERS
JACK LONDON'S THE CALL OF THE WILD: DOG OF THE YUKON
MERLIN
REDLINE
TALES FROM A PARALLEL UNIVERSE: EATING PATTERN

Haughey, Alexandra
SUMMER FLING

Haughton, Mark
KNOCK OFF

Haugk, Charlie
HOLY MAN

Hauptman, Ellen M.
SAFE MEN

Hauptman, Tara
CHARLIE HOBOKEN

Hauser, Cole
HI-LO COUNTRY, THE

Havens, John C.
LAST DAYS OF DISCO, THE

Havens, Richie
FREE TIBET

Havey, Allan
ROUNDERS

Havill, Andrew
WILDE

Hawes, Keeley
AVENGERS, THE

Hawes, Tony
ERNEST IN THE ARMY

Hawk, Jeremy
ELIZABETH

Hawke, Ethan
GREAT EXPECTATIONS
NEWTON BOYS, THE

Hawken, Pamela
BABE: PIG IN THE CITY

Hawkes, Chesney
PRINCE VALIANT

Hawkes, John
BOOGIE BOY
HOME FRIES
I STILL KNOW WHAT YOU DID LAST SUMMER
RUSH HOUR

Hawkins, Anika
FALLEN

Hawkins, Brittany
BELOVED

Hawkins, Dana
HOLY MAN

Hawkins, Sam
LOVE IS THE DEVIL: STUDY FOR A PORTRAIT OF FRANCIS BACON

Hawles, Terri
BONE DADDY

Hawley, Steven
SPANISH PRISONER, THE

Hawthorne, Nigel
MADELINE
MURDER IN MIND
OBJECT OF MY AFFECTION, THE

Hawtrey, Kay
DIRTY WORK
URBAN LEGEND

Haxaire, Sarah
SOLDIER'S DAUGHTER NEVER CRIES, A

Hay, Colin
HEAVEN'S BURNING

Hay, Jaida
AIR BUD: GOLDEN RECEIVER

Haybeard, Roy
BREAK, THE

Hayden, Cynthia
FALLEN

Hayden, Karl
SUMMER FLING

Hayden, Luke
INFORMANT, THE
SUMMER FLING

Haydn, Lili
JACK FROST

Hayek, Salma
FACULTY, THE
54
MIDAQ ALLEY
WHO THE HELL IS JULIETTE?

Hayes, Anthony
TWISTED

Hayes, Deryl
ATOMIC DOG
FIRESTORM

Hayes, Donald
ANOTHER DAY IN PARADISE

Hayes, Isaac
BLUES BROTHERS 2000
ILLTOWN
UNCLE SAM
WOO

Hayes, Jonathan
NIGHT VISION

Hayes, Laura
I GOT THE HOOK UP

Hayes, Reggie
CHICAGO CAB

Hayes, Sean P.
BILLY'S HOLLYWOOD SCREEN KISS

Haygarth, Tony
ROYAL DECEIT
SWEPT FROM THE SEA

Hayman, David
REGENERATION

Hayman, Jon
SOUR GRAPES

Haynes, Ashli
OBJECT OF MY AFFECTION, THE

Haynes, Joseph
POLISH WEDDING

Haynes, Melanie
CON, THE

Haynes, Michael
SKIN & BONE

Haynes, Tim
BRYLCREEM BOYS, THE

Hays, Rex
STEPMOM

Haysbert, Dennis
MAJOR LEAGUE: BACK TO THE MINORS

Hayward, Charlie
LOVE IS THE DEVIL: STUDY FOR A PORTRAIT OF FRANCIS BACON

Hayward, J.C.
ARMAGEDDON

Hayworth, Richard
RED HAWK: WEAPON OF DEATH

Hazeltine, Sarah
JOHNNY MYSTO BOY WIZARD

Hazen, Kelley
MERCURY RISING

Headey, Lena
MERLIN
MRS. DALLOWAY

Headley, Mark
MIDAS TOUCH, THE

Headly, Glenne
BABE: PIG IN THE CITY
PRONTO
X-FILES, THE

Heald, Anthony
DEEP RISING

Healy, Dermot
BUTCHER BOY, THE

Healy, Dorian
HUMAN BOMB

Heames, Darin
MILO

Heard, John
MEN
SNAKE EYES

Heard, Shawnette
LIVING OUT LOUD

Hearn, Chick
REBOUND: THE LEGEND OF EARL "THE GOAT" MANIGAULT
WRONGFULLY ACCUSED

Hearn, Ellen
U.S. MARSHALS

Hearn, George
BARNEY'S GREAT ADVENTURE—THE MOVIE

Hearst, Patricia
PECKER

Heath, Darrel M.
SENSELESS
WOO

Heath, Lori
TERMINAL JUSTICE

Heche, Anne
GIRLS IN PRISON
PSYCHO
RETURN TO PARADISE
SIX DAYS, SEVEN NIGHTS

Hecker, Gary
LOST IN SPACE

Heckler, Andrew
ARMAGEDDON
STIR

Hector, Jamie
HE GOT GAME

Hedaya, Dan
CIVIL ACTION, A
NIGHT AT THE ROXBURY, A

Hedges, Mark
DARK CITY

Hedtke, Greg
ONE TRUE THING

Hedwall, Deborah
SHADRACH

Heffernan, Kevin
NO LOOKING BACK

Heffernan, Maggie
EDEN

Hefner, Hugh
STORY OF X, THE

Heigl, Katherine
BRIDE OF CHUCKY
PRINCE VALIANT

Heimbinder, Susan
LAST BIG THING, THE

Heinle, Amelia
QUICKSILVER HIGHWAY

Heinrich, Denise
HOLY MAN

Heitmeyer, Jayne
DEAD END
FACE THE EVIL
LOST WORLD, THE
SNAKE EYES

Helfer, Ian
SAFE MEN

Helgenberger, Marg
ELMORE LEONARD'S GOLD COAST
SPECIES II

Hellerstein, Jonneine
PARENT TRAP, THE

Hellmann, Hannes
LIFE IS BEAUTIFUL

Helm, Tammy
SOLDIER'S DAUGHTER NEVER CRIES, A

Helmond, Katherine
FEAR AND LOATHING IN LAS VEGAS

Helms, Grayson "Jim"
CON, THE
Helms, Jesse
DEAR JESSE
Helsel, Dee Ann
I STILL KNOW WHAT YOU DID LAST SUMMER
Hely, Kevin
I WENT DOWN
Hemblen, David
JACK HIGGINS' THUNDER POINT
Hembrow, Mark
HEAVEN'S BURNING
Hemeida, Mahmoud
DESTINY
Hemingson, Brian
INSIDE/OUT
Hemingway, Mariel
LOUISA MAY ALCOTT'S LITTLE MEN
Hemon, Olivier
MAN IN THE IRON MASK, THE
Hemphill, Claire
CARLA'S SONG
Hemphill, Neal
ROUNDERS
Hempleman, Terry
SIMPLE PLAN, A
Hemsley, Sherman
SENSELESS
Henderson, Andrew
EVER AFTER
Henderson, Bill
LETHAL WEAPON 4
Henderson, Charles
NAKED ACTS
Henderson, Florence
HOLY MAN
Henderson, Fred
WHEN DANGER FOLLOWS YOU HOME
Henderson, Michael
54
Henderson, Saffron
DRAGON BALL Z THE MOVIE: DEAD ZONE
DRAGON BALL Z THE MOVIE: THE TREE OF MIGHT
DRAGON BALL Z THE MOVIE: THE WORLD'S STRONGEST
NEW ADVENTURES OF KIMBA THE WHITE LION, THE
Hendley, Elleanor Jean
FALLEN
Hendra, Tony
REAL BLONDE, THE
Hendricks, Jefferson
RETURN TO SAVAGE BEACH
Hendrie, Chris
FEAR AND LOATHING IN LAS VEGAS
Hendrix, Elaine
PARENT TRAP, THE
Hendrix, Natalie
GINGERBREAD MAN, THE
Hendrix, Nathalie
MAJOR LEAGUE: BACK TO THE MINORS
Heney, Joan
REAL BLONDE, THE
Heney, Noah
WRONGFULLY ACCUSED
Henfrey, Janet
EVER AFTER
LES MISERABLES
MRS. DALLOWAY
SWEPT FROM THE SEA
Hengstenberg, Jennifer
SHOPPING FOR FANGS
Henley, Barry "Shabaka"
FALLEN
HOW STELLA GOT HER GROOVE BACK
PATCH ADAMS
RUSH HOUR
Henner, Marilu
BATMAN & MR. FREEZE: SUBZERO
Hennigan, Dee
HOPE FLOATS
Henning, Golden
JACK FROST
Henningsen, Bent
CELEBRATION, THE
Henningsen, Ingrid
WRONGFULLY ACCUSED
Henriau, Marie
SOLDIER'S DAUGHTER NEVER CRIES, A
Henriksen, Bjarne
CELEBRATION, THE
Henriksen, Lance
FACE THE EVIL
LAST ASSASSINS
Henritze, Bette
OBJECT OF MY AFFECTION, THE
Henry, Buck
REAL BLONDE, THE
STORY OF X, THE
Henry, Deanne
TRICKS
Henry, Gregg
STAR TREK: INSURRECTION
Henry, Julie
BARRIERS
Henry, Pierre
MODULATIONS: CINEMA FOR THE EAR
Henry, Tim
INVADER, THE
Henry, Tyrone
ZERO EFFECT
Henson, Elden
MIGHTY, THE
Henson, Garrette
NEVADA
Henstridge, Natasha
SPECIES II
Hentoff, Nat
LENNY BRUCE: SWEAR TO TELL THE TRUTH
Henzel, Richard
HENRY: PORTRAIT OF A SERIAL KILLER PART 2
Herbert, Ric
BABE: PIG IN THE CITY
Herder, Andreas
RAT'S TALE, A
Heredia, Jose
PLAN B
Herek, Lori Viveros
HOLY MAN
Herlihy, Timothy P.
WEDDING SINGER, THE
Herlon, Don
U.S. MARSHALS
Herman, Stanley
PI
Hernandez, Ana
DANCE WITH ME
Hernandez, Coati Mundi
54
Hernandez, Felipe
CARLA'S SONG
Hernandez, Gabriel
OBJECT OF MY AFFECTION, THE
Hernandez, Joel
DANCE WITH ME
Hernandez, Pedro
MEN WITH GUNS
Hernandez, Sam
LOS LOCOS
Herndon, Kimberly
MAJOR LEAGUE: BACK TO THE MINORS
Herod, Geoffrey
LOVE AND DEATH ON LONG ISLAND
Herrera, Emil
OVERNIGHT DELIVERY
Hershey, Barbara
SOLDIER'S DAUGHTER NEVER CRIES, A
Hertford, Brighton
PARENT TRAP, THE
Herth, Lisa
GREAT EXPECTATIONS
Herthum, Harold
WHATEVER
Hertzler, J.G.
PROPHECY II, THE
Herveet, Olivier
WESTERN
Hervey, Shane
LES MISERABLES
Herzog, Klaus
RAT'S TALE, A
Herzog, Seth
SAFE MEN
Herzog, Werner
LITTLE DIETER NEEDS TO FLY
WHAT DREAMS MAY COME
Heske, Habby
MR. NICE GUY
Heskin, Kam
BLACKJACK
HENRY: PORTRAIT OF A SERIAL KILLER PART 2
Heslov, Grant
ENEMY OF THE STATE
Hess, Jayne
HUSH
Hess, Joe
OUT OF SIGHT
Hess, Zdenek
LES MISERABLES
Hesse, Zoe Rose
EBENEZER
Hessler, Cort
SUB DOWN
Heston, Charlton
ADVENTURES OF MOWGLI
ARMAGEDDON
OFF THE MENU: THE LAST DAYS OF CHASEN'S
TOUCH OF EVIL: THE DIRECTOR'S CUT
Hetherington, Jason
JACK HIGGINS' ON DANGEROUS GROUND
Heung Hoi
KNOCK OFF
Heuring, Lori
NEWTON BOYS, THE
Hevner, Suzanne
MEET JOE BLACK
Hewitt, Jennifer Love
CAN'T HARDLY WAIT
I STILL KNOW WHAT YOU DID LAST SUMMER
Hewitt, Michael
BORROWERS, THE
Hewitt, Paul
CIVIL ACTION, A
HIJACKING HOLLYWOOD
Hewitt, Simon
BORROWERS, THE
Hewitt, Steve
VELVET GOLDMINE
Hewlett, David
CUBE
Hewlett, Sheila
REAL BLONDE, THE
Heyerdahl, Christopher
BLEEDERS
PEACEKEEPER, THE

Hogan, Gabriel
ELVIS MEETS NIXON
LOVE AND DEATH ON LONG ISLAND
Hogan, Hulk
3 NINJAS: HIGH NOON AT MEGA MOUNTAIN
Hogan, Rasheed H.
I GOT THE HOOK UP
Hogan, Robert
SPECIES II
Hogan, Susan
DISTURBING BEHAVIOR
WHEN DANGER FOLLOWS YOU HOME
Hogarty, John
HORSE WHISPERER, THE
Hoge, Alicia
GODSON, THE
Hoge, Bob
GODSON, THE
Hogg, B.J.
BREAK, THE
BRYLCREEM BOYS, THE
INFORMANT, THE
Hogg, Kyle
INVADER, THE
Hogg, Pam
LOVE IS THE DEVIL: STUDY FOR A PORTRAIT OF FRANCIS BACON
Hogue, Bill
LAST BREATH
Hohn, Amy
IMPOSTORS, THE
SOUR GRAPES
Hoijtink, Elisabeth
DRESS, THE
Hojfeldt, Solbjorg
KINGDOM, PART 2, THE
Holbrook, Ashley
RINGMASTER
Holbrook, Hal
HUSH
RUSTY: THE GREAT RESCUE
Hold, Michael
WATERBOY, THE
Holden, Alexandra
DANCER, TEXAS POP. 81
Holden, Jill
FALLEN
Holden, Marjean
JOHN CARPENTER'S VAMPIRES
THURSDAY
Holder, Ginny
LEADING MAN, THE
Holder, Jonathan
PATCH ADAMS
Hole, Henrik
JUNK MAIL
Holladay, Logan
SIMON BIRCH
Holland, Buck
FEAR AND LOATHING IN LAS VEGAS
Holland, Denise
PARENT TRAP, THE
Holland, Dick
MY BROTHER'S WAR
Holland, Jools
SPICE WORLD
Holland, Matt
SPACEJACKED
Holland, Todd
WATERBOY, THE
Holley, Caitlyn
PRACTICAL MAGIC
Holley, Eugene
NAKED ACTS
Holliday, Polly
PARENT TRAP, THE
Hollingsworth, John
LET'S KILL ALL THE LAWYERS
Hollis, Tommy
PRIMARY COLORS
Hollister, Dave
RIDE
Hollmond, Clarinda
SHADRACH
Holly, Lauren
NO LOOKING BACK
Holm, Bentine
JUNK MAIL
Holm, Celeste
STILL BREATHING
Holm, Karin
KNOCK OFF
Holman, Bruce
CIVIL ACTION, A
Holmen, Hallvard
OTHER SIDE OF SUNDAY, THE
Holmes, Katie
DISTURBING BEHAVIOR
Holmes, Stephen
DISTURBING BEHAVIOR
Holmes, Tom
HUSH
Holston, Rodger
CASPER MEETS WENDY
Holt, Chris
ENEMY OF THE STATE
Holt, Lorri
PATCH ADAMS
Holt, Nick
54
Holton, Mark
HIJACKING HOLLYWOOD
Homes, Michael
OUTSIDE OZONA
Hong, James
BREAKOUT
CATHERINE'S GROVE
MULAN
Hood, Gavin
OPERATION DELTA FORCE 2
Hooker, John Lee
FREE TIBET
Hooks, Brian
BELOVED
THURSDAY
Hooks, Jan
SIMON BIRCH
Hoosier, James G.
BIG LEBOWSKI, THE
Hooton, James
TWENTYFOURSEVEN
Hoover, Howard
BLUES BROTHERS 2000
Hope, Bob
OFF THE MENU: THE LAST DAYS OF CHASEN'S
Hope, Leslie
BRAM STOKER'S SHADOWBUILDER
Hope, Nicholas
HENRY FOOL
Hopewell, Nancy
LETHAL WEAPON 4
Hopkins, Anthony
MASK OF ZORRO, THE
MEET JOE BLACK
Hopkins, Barbara Barnes
DOWN IN THE DELTA
Hopkins, Bo
NEWTON BOYS, THE
PHANTOMS
UNCLE SAM
Hopkins, Harold
JOEY
Hopkins, Josh
PARALLEL SONS
Hopkins, Kaitlin
LITTLE BOY BLUE
Hopkins, Karen Leigh
JANE AUSTEN'S MAFIA!
Hopkins, Paul
AMERICAN HISTORY X
Hopkins, T. Dan
ALMOST HEROES
Hoppe, Rolf
PALMETTO
Hopper, David
RETURN TO SAVAGE BEACH
Hopper, Dennis
MEET THE DEEDLES
TOP OF THE WORLD
WHO IS HENRY JAGLOM?
Hopson, Al
WEDDING SINGER, THE
Hopson, Charles T.
ENEMY
Hopson, Chole
ENEMY
Hopton, Georgie
LOVE IS THE DEVIL: STUDY FOR A PORTRAIT OF FRANCIS BACON
Horan, Gerard
LES MISERABLES
Horitatsu, Kansai
JUNK FOOD
Horler, Sacha
BABE: PIG IN THE CITY
Horn, Stephen M.
OUT OF SIGHT
Horne, Viviane
ELIZABETH
Hornsby, Russell
WOO
Horovitz, Avrohom
HOLY MAN
Horovitz, Israel
NORTH SHORE FISH
Horrocks, Jane
LITTLE VOICE
Horst, Jason
PLAN B
Horton, Michael
STAR TREK: INSURRECTION
Horton, Michael M.
NIGHT AT THE ROXBURY, A
Hosking, Craig
DESPERATE MEASURES
LETHAL WEAPON 4
Hoskins, Bob
COUSIN BETTE
SPICE WORLD
TWENTYFOURSEVEN
Hostetler, Jay
BROADWAY DAMAGE
Hostetter, John
GOLGO 13: QUEEN BEE
STAR TREK: INSURRECTION
Hotton, Jean
LITTLE VOICE
Hoty, Tony
ROUNDERS
Houde, Serge
DEAD END
JACK HIGGINS' THE WINDSOR PROTOCOL
LOUISA MAY ALCOTT'S LITTLE MEN
PEACEKEEPER, THE
Houghton, Brent
MR. NICE GUY
Houghton, Peter
MR. NICE GUY

Houi Kan Low, Kenneth
RUSH HOUR
Houlihan, Mike
HENRY: PORTRAIT OF A SERIAL KILLER PART 2
Hounsou, Djimon
DEEP RISING
House, Son
CAN'T YOU HEAR THE WIND HOWL?: THE LIFE AND MUSIC OF ROBERT JOHNSON
Houser, Jerry
FLINTSTONES: I YABBA-DABBA DOO!, THE
Houstin, Ursula
I GOT THE HOOK UP
Houston, Candy Brown
NIGHTWATCH
Houston, Sharon
RINGMASTER
Houston, Thelma
BELOVED
54
Houston, Ursula Y.
PLAYERS CLUB, THE
Hove, Anders
KINGDOM, PART 2, THE
SUBSPECIES IV: BLOODSTORM
Hovik, Trond
JUNK MAIL
Howard, Barbara
SLAPPY AND THE STINKERS
Howard, Clint
TWILIGHT
WATERBOY, THE
Howard, David S.
MEET JOE BLACK
NO WAY HOME
Howard, Jean Speegle
LOS LOCOS
Howard, Jeffrey
NIAGARA NIAGARA
Howard, Matthew
HORTON FOOTE'S ALONE
Howard, Rance
LAND OF THE FREE
PSYCHO
SMALL SOLDIERS
Howard, Shawn Michael
PLUMP FICTION
THURSDAY
Howard, Sherman
JUNGLE BOOK: MOWGLI'S STORY, THE
RETROACTIVE
Howard, Susan
RETURN OF THE KING, THE
Howard, Terrence
PLAYERS CLUB, THE
Howard, Tom
LIVING OUT LOUD
Howard, Traylor
DIRTY WORK
Howe, Irving
ARGUING THE WORLD
Howell, C. Thomas
LAST LIVES
Howell, Hoke
ALARMIST, THE
INVISIBLE DAD
Howell, Mark Eric
BOYS IN LOVE 2
Howell, Norm
DESPERATE MEASURES
Howell, Peter
INNOCENT SLEEP, THE
Howey, David
JACK HIGGINS' ON DANGEROUS GROUND

Howze, Duke
DETOUR
Hoyland, William
LOVE IS THE DEVIL: STUDY FOR A PORTRAIT OF FRANCIS BACON
Hoyle, David
VELVET GOLDMINE
Hoyle, Lisa S.
FEAR AND LOATHING IN LAS VEGAS
Hoyos, Terri
CLOCKWATCHERS
Hoyt, Brian
POLISH WEDDING
Hoziel, Eric
SNAKE EYES
Hsu, Julia
RUSH HOUR
Hu Jian Qiang
SHAOLIN TEMPLE, THE
Hu Jun
EAST PALACE, WEST PALACE
Huang, Jessica
BEST OF THE BEST: WITHOUT WARNING
Hub, Martin
ACT OF WAR
SAVING PRIVATE RYAN
Hubbard, Tim
LETTER FROM DEATH ROW, A
Hubbard, Valorie
HENRY FOOL
Hubbell, Blake
SIMON BIRCH
Huber, Dr. Elise
HEALING BY KILLING
Hubley, Season
CHILDREN OF THE CORN V: FIELD OF TERROR
Hudak, Thomas
KNOCK OFF
Hudaverdi, Kenan
NIL BY MOUTH
Huddleston, David
BIG LEBOWSKI, THE
Huddleston, Michael
JOHN CARPENTER'S VAMPIRES
Hudson, Betty
OBJECT OF MY AFFECTION, THE
Hudson, Ernie
BEST OF THE BEST: WITHOUT WARNING
Hudson, Gary
BLACK THUNDER
Hudson, Keith
HAV PLENTY
OUT OF SIGHT
Huertas, Jon
WHY DO FOOLS FALL IN LOVE?
Huertas, Luisa
MASK OF ZORRO, THE
Hues, Matthias
ALONE IN THE WOODS
Huff, Brent
HOLLYWOOD CONFIDENTIAL
Huff, Neal
LOVE WALKED IN
Huffines, Brad
GINGERBREAD MAN, THE
Huffington, Arianna
SIEGE, THE
Huffman, Felicity
SPANISH PRISONER, THE
Huffman, John
ASYLUM
Huffman, Rosanna
SOUR GRAPES
Huggett, Richard
BABE: PIG IN THE CITY
MR. NICE GUY

Huggett, Sandra
SWEPT FROM THE SEA
Hugghins, David
LAST LIVES
Hughes, Andi
PLAN B
Hughes, Barnard
NEIL SIMON'S THE ODD COUPLE II
Hughes, Frank John
NO WAY HOME
Hughes, Jordan
MIGHTY, THE
Hughes, Liam
PECKER
Hughes, Miko
MERCURY RISING
Hughes, Sean
BUTCHER BOY, THE
Hughes, Tresa
DIRTY LAUNDRY
Hugo, Clifford
SIX-STRING SAMURAI
Hui Fan
CHINESE BOX, THE
Hui Li
CHINESE BOX, THE
Hui, Michael
CHINESE BOX, THE
Huie, Kimberly
DEEP IMPACT
Hulsey, Lauren
PECKER
Hume, Gary
LOVE IS THE DEVIL: STUDY FOR A PORTRAIT OF FRANCIS BACON
Hummel, Matt
FUTURE FEAR
Humphery, Mark
RESCUERS: STORIES OF COURAGE—TWO WOMEN
Humphrey, Meleney
GIA
Humphrey, Renee
LOVER GIRL
Humphreys, Alfred E.
ESCAPE, THE
Humphries, Barry
LEADING MAN, THE
NAPOLEON
SPICE WORLD
WELCOME TO WOOP WOOP
Humphries, Harry
ARMAGEDDON
Humpoletz, Paul
HUMAN BOMB
Hundley, Dylan
LAST DAYS OF DISCO, THE
Hung, Sammo
DRAGONS FOREVER
ENCOUNTER OF THE SPOOKY KIND
MR. NICE GUY
PRODIGAL SON, THE
Hung, Shirley
CHINESE BOX, THE
Hungerford, Bob
DECEIVER
Hunt, Barbara Leigh
MERRY WAR, A
Hunt, Bonnie
BUG'S LIFE, A
KISSING A FOOL
Hunt, Carol
MY BROTHER'S WAR
STRAY BULLET
Hunt, Denise
HOW STELLA GOT HER GROOVE BACK
Hunt, Eamonn
I WENT DOWN

Inoue, Tetsu
MODULATIONS: CINEMA FOR THE EAR
Inscoe, Joe
HUSH
Intiraymi, Manu
SENSELESS
Invisibl Skratch Piklz
MODULATIONS: CINEMA FOR THE EAR
Ionescu, Razvan
JOHNNY MYSTO BOY WIZARD
Ipale, Aharon
KID IN ALADDIN'S PALACE, A
Ipavic, Dina
RUN FOR COVER
Ippoliti, Gianni
DAY OF THE BEAST, THE
Irizarry, Alaina
HAV PLENTY
Irizawa, Art
URBAN SAFARI
Irons, Jeremy
CHINESE BOX, THE
LOLITA
MAN IN THE IRON MASK, THE
Irons, Nicholas
KID IN ALADDIN'S PALACE, A
Ironside, Adrienne
CAPTIVE
Ironside, Michael
BLACK LIGHT
CAPTIVE
CHICAGO CAB
DESTINY OF MARTY FINE, THE
Irrera, Dom
BIG LEBOWSKI, THE
GODSON, THE
Irving, Amy
ONE TOUGH COP
Irving, Martha
HANGING GARDEN, THE
Irwin, Jennifer
BLUES BROTHERS 2000
Irwin, Tom
MY VERY BEST FRIEND
Isaac, Romanos
U.S. MARSHALS
Isaacs, Al
RETURN OF THE KING, THE
Isaacs, Jason
ARMAGEDDON
SOLDIER
Isaacson, Simon
RED HAWK: WEAPON OF DEATH
Isabelle, Katharine
DISTURBING BEHAVIOR
Isgar, Jonathan
MR. NICE GUY
Isherwood, Simon
AIR BUD: GOLDEN RECEIVER
Ishibashi, Takaaki
MAJOR LEAGUE: BACK TO THE MINORS
Ishida, Jim
ARMAGEDDON
Ishii, Ken
MODULATIONS: CINEMA FOR THE EAR
Islander, J.C.
PI
Isler, Seth
RINGMASTER
Isles, Art
RETURN TO SAVAGE BEACH
Isomura, Kenji
HEAVEN'S BURNING
Ison, Bayani
MAJOR LEAGUE: BACK TO THE MINORS
Israel, Ishma
ANOTHER DAY IN PARADISE

Issariya, Is
RETURN TO PARADISE
Istrate, Dan
SUBSPECIES IV: BLOODSTORM
Italiano-Zaza, J.N.
LOLIDA 2000
Itsumi, Taro
FIREWORKS
Ittig, Rodolphe
SWINDLE, THE
Itzin, Gregory
FEAR AND LOATHING IN LAS VEGAS
SMALL SOLDIERS
Ivancevic, Danica
INTERLOCKED: THRILLED TO DEATH
Ivanek, Zeljko
CIVIL ACTION, A
RAT PACK, THE
Iverson, Lisa
PARENT TRAP, THE
Ives, Sandra
OUT OF SIGHT
Ivester, Karin J.
PALMETTO
Ivey, Dana
IMPOSTORS, THE
SIMON BIRCH
Ivey, Judith
WITHOUT LIMITS
Ivey, Lela
PLEASANTVILLE
Ivy, Bob
PHANTASM: OBLIVION
Ivy Supersonic & The Groovy Girls
LAST DAYS OF DISCO, THE
Iwama, Saori
ZERO WOMAN
Iwasaki, Kaneko
VILLAGE OF DREAMS
Izzard, Eddie
AVENGERS, THE
VELVET GOLDMINE
Jacintho, Wayne
SIX DAYS, SEVEN NIGHTS
Jack
THIN RED LINE, THE
Jackman, Jim
CASPER MEETS WENDY
Jackson, Aaron
CHILDREN OF THE CORN V: FIELD OF TERROR
Jackson, Andrew
BLACKJACK
BRAM STOKER'S SHADOWBUILDER
Jackson, Anne
RESCUERS: STORIES OF COURAGE—TWO WOMEN
Jackson, Dee Jay
DISTURBING BEHAVIOR
Jackson, Ernie
I'LL BE HOME FOR CHRISTMAS
Jackson, Greg
SKIN & BONE
Jackson, Jeanine
PLEASANTVILLE
Jackson, Joshua
APT PUPIL
URBAN LEGEND
Jackson, Ken
LETTER FROM DEATH ROW, A
Jackson, Kenneth
LETHAL WEAPON 4
Jackson, Kevin
RUSH HOUR
Jackson, Marco
LOVE IS THE DEVIL: STUDY FOR A PORTRAIT OF FRANCIS BACON

Jackson, Mel
GEORGE WALLACE
Jackson, Philip
COUSIN BETTE
LITTLE VOICE
Jackson, Reuben
CELEBRITY
Jackson, Sally
LEWIS & CLARK & GEORGE
Jackson, Samuel
OFF THE MENU: THE LAST DAYS OF CHASEN'S
Jackson, Samuel L.
NEGOTIATOR, THE
OUT OF SIGHT
SPHERE
Jackson, Stoney
DISAPPEARANCE OF KEVIN JOHNSON, THE
Jacob, Irene
INCOGNITO
U.S. MARSHALS
Jacob, Jake Sear
KNOCK OFF
Jacobi, Derek
LOVE IS THE DEVIL: STUDY FOR A PORTRAIT OF FRANCIS BACON
Jacobi, Doreen
TALES FROM A PARALLEL UNIVERSE: EATING PATTERN
Jacobs, Hank
ROUNDERS
Jacobs, Irving
PECKER
Jacobs, Martin
JOEY
Jacobs, Michael Dean
ORGAZMO
Jacobsen, Amy E.
U.S. MARSHALS
Jacobsen, Lasse
CELEBRATION, THE
Jacobsen, Mikkel
CELEBRATION, THE
Jacobson, Alicia
CHARLIE HOBOKEN
Jacobson, Lucy
DANCER, TEXAS POP. 81
Jacobson, Peter
CIVIL ACTION, A
GREAT EXPECTATIONS
PRICE ABOVE RUBIES, A
Jacobus, Jay
PATCH ADAMS
Jacoby, Bobby
CAN'T HARDLY WAIT
Jacott, Carlos
LAST DAYS OF DISCO, THE
MR. JEALOUSY
REAL HOWARD SPITZ, THE
Jaenicke, Hannes
HUNTED, THE
JACK HIGGINS' MIDNIGHT MAN
WHITE RAVEN, THE
Jaffe, Chapelle
SIN AND REDEMPTION
Jaglom, Henry
WHO IS HENRY JAGLOM?
Jaglom, Michael Emil
WHO IS HENRY JAGLOM?
Jaglom, Sabrina
DEJA VU
Jaglom, Simon Orson
DEJA VU
Jahne, Graham
MR. NICE GUY
Jain, Aditi
GREAT EXPECTATIONS

Jennings, Stephen
OPERATION DELTA FORCE 2
Jenseg, Bjorn
MENDEL
Jensen, Birger
KINGDOM, PART 2, THE
Jensen, David
NEWTON BOYS, THE
RAGE, THE
Jensen, Erik
MONTANA
Jensen, Ethan
BOOGIE BOY
Jensen, Gunther
X-FILES, THE
Jensen, Henning
KINGDOM, PART 2, THE
Jensen, Soren Elung
KINGDOM, PART 2, THE
Jensen, Todd
OPERATION DELTA FORCE 2
Jensen, Vita
KINGDOM, PART 2, THE
Jeremiah, David
MIDAS TOUCH, THE
Jeremy, Ron
54
ORGAZMO
Jerome, Howard
DIRTY WORK
Jerome, Tim
PRICE ABOVE RUBIES, A
Jerome, Timothy
CELEBRITY
Jessula, Emilie
MADELINE
Jester, Joe
RETURN TO SAVAGE BEACH
Jeter, Michael
FEAR AND LOATHING IN LAS VEGAS
PATCH ADAMS
THURSDAY
Jett, Joan
BOOGIE BOY
Jewell, Gary
BLEEDERS
Jewison, Norman
BURN HOLLYWOOD BURN
Ji Chun Hua
SHAOLIN TEMPLE, THE
Jia Hongshen
FROZEN
Jian Rui Chao
CHINESE BOX, THE
Jiang Hong Bo
SHAOLIN TEMPLE, THE
Jiang Wen
EMPEROR'S SHADOW, THE
Jianu, Laura
CLOCKMAKER
Jilkes, Sam
LOVE IS THE DEVIL: STUDY FOR A PORTRAIT OF FRANCIS BACON
Jillebo, J. Anders
BRYLCREEM BOYS, THE
Jillette, Penn
FEAR AND LOATHING IN LAS VEGAS
LOU REED: ROCK AND ROLL HEART
Jimenez, Luis
SIEGE, THE
Jimmy
THIN RED LINE, THE
Jo-Ann, Ebony
CHARLIE HOBOKEN
Joaquim, Suzy
DISTURBING BEHAVIOR
Jobe, Reri Tava
SIX DAYS, SEVEN NIGHTS
Jocelyn, Matthew
MAN IN THE IRON MASK, THE
Johannessen, Runar
JUNK MAIL
Johanson, Carl
LETTER FROM DEATH ROW, A
Johansson, Scarlett
HORSE WHISPERER, THE
John, Elton
SPICE WORLD
John, Gordon
LOVE IS THE DEVIL: STUDY FOR A PORTRAIT OF FRANCIS BACON
John, Gottfried
OGRE, THE
John, Pat
LOVE IS THE DEVIL: STUDY FOR A PORTRAIT OF FRANCIS BACON
John, Prakash
BLUES BROTHERS 2000
John, Robert
LOLIDA 2000
Johns, Milton
X-FILES, THE
Johnsen, Geir
JUNK MAIL
Johnsen, John
CELEBRATION, THE
Johnson, A.J.
I GOT THE HOOK UP
PLAYERS CLUB, THE
WOO
Johnson, Alexander
ARMAGEDDON
Johnson, Andray
BLADE
Johnson, Anne Marie
DOWN IN THE DELTA
Johnson, Ariyan
BULWORTH
Johnson, Ashley
DANCER, TEXAS POP. 81
Johnson, Beverly
54
Johnson, Birch "Crimson Slide"
BLUES BROTHERS 2000
Johnson, Bonnie
PATCH ADAMS
Johnson, Byron
SNAKE EYES
Johnson, Calen
BELOVED
Johnson, Chris
PI
Johnson, Corey
SAVING PRIVATE RYAN
Johnson, Crystal N.
BELLY
Johnson, Danny
DON KING: ONLY IN AMERICA
Johnson, Finn
UGLY, THE
Johnson, Graham Alex
PARALLEL SONS
Johnson, Guri
INSOMNIA
Johnson, Gus
HE GOT GAME
SPANISH PRISONER, THE
Johnson, Hassan
BELLY
Johnson, Jack
LOST IN SPACE
Johnson, Jimmy
WATERBOY, THE
Johnson, John
54
Johnson, John H.
ARMAGEDDON
Johnson Jr., Theodore Toure
LETHAL WEAPON 4
Johnson, Karl
LOVE IS THE DEVIL: STUDY FOR A PORTRAIT OF FRANCIS BACON
Johnson, Katie
CLOCKMAKER
Johnson, Ken
BABE: PIG IN THE CITY
Johnson, Kenneth
BLADE
MAJOR LEAGUE: BACK TO THE MINORS
Johnson, Kristina Eliot
MERCURY RISING
Johnson, Lauri
CITY OF ANGELS
NEGOTIATOR, THE
Johnson, Lawrence
I GOT THE HOOK UP
Johnson, Lisa
NEXT STEP, THE
Johnson, Louise
BELOVED
Johnson, Marcus
CAUGHT UP
DARK CITY
Johnson, Marjorie
LAST BREATH
Johnson, Matthew
STEPHEN KING'S THE NIGHT FLIER
Johnson, Michael
BRIDE OF CHUCKY
Johnson, Miles
LOVE IS THE DEVIL: STUDY FOR A PORTRAIT OF FRANCIS BACON
Johnson, Paul
MODULATIONS: CINEMA FOR THE EAR
Johnson, Plas
LIVING OUT LOUD
Johnson, Sean
DOGWATCH
Johnson, Shane
SAVING PRIVATE RYAN
Johnson, Shannon
BLUES BROTHERS 2000
Johnson, Vann
GUN, A CAR, AND A BLONDE, A
Johnston, Darrell
DANCING AT LUGHNASA
Johnston, J.J.
FIXER, THE
SPANISH PRISONER, THE
Johnston, Jay
JACK FROST
Johnston, Jim
FACULTY, THE
Johnston, Michelle
NEIL SIMON'S THE ODD COUPLE II
Johnstone, Nahanni
REAL BLONDE, THE
Jokubeit, Joe
LIVING IN PERIL
Jolani, Wael
DEJA VU
Jolie, Angelina
GEORGE WALLACE
GIA
PLAYING BY HEART
Jonas, Michelle
GIA
Jones, Andy
TALES FROM A PARALLEL UNIVERSE: GIGA SHADOW
Jones, Angela
CHILDREN OF THE CORN V: FIELD OF TERROR

Jones, Ben
PRIMARY COLORS
Jones, Bruce
TWENTYFOURSEVEN
Jones, Cherry
HORSE WHISPERER, THE
OUT OF THE PAST
Jones, Darryl
STIR
Jones, David
TEKKEN: THE MOTION PICTURE
Jones, Dean
BATMAN & MR. FREEZE: SUBZERO
Jones, Dot-Marie
PATCH ADAMS
Jones, Eddie
DANCER, TEXAS POP. 81
Jones, Esther
WOO
Jones, Frank
GEORGE WALLACE
Jones, Freddie
ROYAL DECEIT
Jones, Gemma
THEORY OF FLIGHT
WILDE
Jones, Harry
LEADING MAN, THE
Jones, Hatty
MADELINE
Jones, Illiam
BRYLCREEM BOYS, THE
Jones, Jake-ann
NAKED ACTS
Jones, James Earl
HORTON FOOTE'S ALONE
LION KING II: SIMBA'S PRIDE, THE
MERLIN
PRIMARY COLORS
REBOUND: THE LEGEND OF EARL "THE GOAT" MANIGAULT
Jones, Jason Edwards
GODZILLA
Jones, Jeff
DOWN IN THE DELTA
Jones, Jennifer
OFF THE MENU: THE LAST DAYS OF CHASEN'S
Jones, Judge John
LETTER FROM DEATH ROW, A
Jones, L.Q.
MASK OF ZORRO, THE
Jones, Leslie
WRONGFULLY ACCUSED
Jones, Lewis
ELIZABETH
Jones, Mal
HOLY MAN
PALMETTO
TRUMAN SHOW, THE
Jones, Michael Steve
KRIPPENDORF'S TRIBE
Jones, Nasir
BELLY
Jones, Neal
DAY AT THE BEACH
RATCHET
SIEGE, THE
Jones, Nicola
BIG HIT, THE
Jones, O-Lan
CLOCKWATCHERS
TRUMAN SHOW, THE
Jones, Ora
CHICAGO CAB
Jones, Orlando
SOUR GRAPES
WOO
Jones, Osheen
VELVET GOLDMINE
Jones, Patrick
LEWIS & CLARK & GEORGE
Jones, Quincy
OFF THE MENU: THE LAST DAYS OF CHASEN'S
Jones, Richard
TWO FOR TEXAS
WILD MAN BLUES
Jones, Richard A.
NEWTON BOYS, THE
Jones, Richard T.
HOLLYWOOD CONFIDENTIAL
Jones, Ron Cephas
HE GOT GAME
NAKED ACTS
Jones, Simon
OPERATION DELTA FORCE 2
Jones, Socko
WRATH OF THE NINJA: THE YOTODEN MOVIE
Jones, Stephanie
FUTURE FEAR
Jones, Stephen Anthony
PATCH ADAMS
Jones, Tamala
CAN'T HARDLY WAIT
Jones, Tammi Katherine
HAV PLENTY
Jones, Taylor
UNCLE SAM
Jones, Tiffany
HE GOT GAME
Jones, Timothy
DARK CITY
Jones, Toby
COUSIN BETTE
EVER AFTER
LES MISERABLES
Jones, Tommy Lee
SMALL SOLDIERS
U.S. MARSHALS
Jones, Tony
CATHERINE'S GROVE
Jones, Tracy C.
PLAYERS CLUB, THE
Jones, Ursula
EVER AFTER
Jones, Veryl
ENEMY
Jones, Walker
IMPOSTORS, THE
Jones, Walter
TALISMAN
Jones, William James
CROSSING FIELDS
Jones, William Todd
LOST IN SPACE
Jones, Wynston A.
SKIN & BONE
Jong, Erica
CELEBRITY
Joo, Kenzaburo
SLEEPY EYES OF DEATH: SWORD OF SEDUCTION
Joosten, Kathryn
PHOENIX
Jordan, Alan
HOLY MAN
Jordan, David
GINGERBREAD MAN, THE
Jordan, Don
CAPTIVE
DEAD END
Jordan, J. Matthew
LETHAL WEAPON 4
Jordan, John-Eliot
THERE'S SOMETHING ABOUT MARY
Jordan, Jonathan Parks
SHADRACH
Jordan Jr., Vernon E.
GINGERBREAD MAN, THE
ROUNDERS
Jordan, Kerrie
KNOCK OFF
Jordan, Michael
HE GOT GAME
Jordan, Randy
CELEBRITY
Jordan, Robert
NEGOTIATOR, THE
Jorgensen, Christine Louise
CELEBRATION, THE
Jorgensen, Rosmarie
CELEBRATION, THE
Joseph, Francois
MONUMENT AVE.
Joseph, Harry
FERNGULLY 2: THE MAGICAL RESCUE
Joseph, Jackie
SMALL SOLDIERS
Joseph, Ralph
NIGHT VISION
Josephson, Erland
KRISTIN LAVRANSDATTER
Joshua, Lawrence
X-FILES, THE
Joslin, Nancy
PLAN B
Joss, Jonathan
ALMOST HEROES
Jostyn, Jennifer
DEEP IMPACT
MILO
Jourden, Tom
LOVELIFE
Jovan, Slavitza
STIR
Jover, Arly
BLADE
Jovovich, Milla
HE GOT GAME
Joy, Jeff
TWILIGHT
Joy, Mark
PECKER
Joy, Robert
FALLEN
Joyce, Anne
HORSE WHISPERER, THE
Juan, Jean-Marie
CHAMBERMAID ON THE TITANIC, THE
Jubinville, Kevin
FACE THE EVIL
Judd, Ashley
SIMON BIRCH
Judd Jr., General Fermon
STEPHEN KING'S THE NIGHT FLIER
Jules, Jenny
GO NOW
Julien, Don
CHICAGO CAB
Jumel, Gerard
LA SEPARATION
Jung, Calvin
LETHAL WEAPON 4
Jung, Clint
SHOPPING FOR FANGS
Jungmann, Eric
FACULTY, THE
Junker, Ruth
KINGDOM, PART 2, THE

Junqueira, Caio
CENTRAL STATION
Jupiter, Mark
CHARLIE HOBOKEN
LAST BREATH
Jurado, Katy
HI-LO COUNTRY, THE
Jurgens, Gerda Maria
TRUCE, THE
Jury, Chris
INNOCENT SLEEP, THE
Justin, Carl
PRINCE VALIANT
Kaas, Julie
YOU'VE GOT MAIL
Kabatova, Zita
FORGOTTEN LIGHT
Kablan, Therese
PRONTO
Kabler, Roger
BRAVE LITTLE TOASTER GOES TO MARS, THE
Kachev, Fabien
WESTERN
Kackley, R.J.
MAJOR LEAGUE: BACK TO THE MINORS
Kaczmarek, Jane
PLEASANTVILLE
Kaczorowiski, Nina
SIMPLE PLAN, A
Kada, Hiro
CHILDREN OF THE CORN V: FIELD OF TERROR
Kadlec, Mark
INVISIBLE DAD
Kaga, Mariko
WHEN I CLOSE MY EYES
Kagan, Diane
LAST BREATH
MEET JOE BLACK
Kagan, Elaine
MY GIANT
Kagan, Michael
SOULER OPPOSITE, THE
Kahan, Steve
LETHAL WEAPON 4
Kahler, Wolf
FIRELIGHT
Kahlil, Aisha
BELOVED
Kahlua, Steve
MR. NICE GUY
Kahn, Madeline
BUG'S LIFE, A
Kahn, Milton
WATCHERS REBORN
Kaholokula, Pua
SIX DAYS, SEVEN NIGHTS
Kai Chung Cheng, Andy
RUSH HOUR
Kaiama, Javan
SIX DAYS, SEVEN NIGHTS
Kain, Amber
ONE TRUE THING
Kaiser, Bent
CELEBRATION, THE
Kaiser, Vibeke
CELEBRATION, THE
Kajanus, Georg
DIDN'T DO IT FOR LOVE
Kajanus, Johanne
DIDN'T DO IT FOR LOVE
Kajbaek, Poul
CELEBRATION, THE
Kalani, Jayson
DISAPPEARANCE OF KEVIN JOHNSON, THE

Kaldor, Christopher
SPANISH PRISONER, THE
Kalember, Patricia
HOME BEFORE DARK
Kalensky, Harry
ADVENTURES OF MOWGLI
Kaler, Berwick
GO NOW
Kalin, Nathaniel
LAST BREATH
Kallis, Carolyn "Coco"
SPANISH PRISONER, THE
Kalmenson, Bill
SOULER OPPOSITE, THE
Kalmenson, Casey
SOULER OPPOSITE, THE
Kalmenson, Cindy
SOULER OPPOSITE, THE
Kalonne, Kenna
HIJACKING HOLLYWOOD
Kam Bun
KILLER ANGELS
Kam Hing Ying
ROYAL WARRIORS
Kam To
KILLER ANGELS
Kamaar, Al
HOLY MAN
Kamal, Hany
SIEGE, THE
Kamenoff, Eandy
BABE: PIG IN THE CITY
Kamin, Daniel T.
NEWTON BOYS, THE
Kanagawa, Hiro
DOUBLE EDGE
TRICKS
Kanakaredes, Melina
DANGEROUS BEAUTY
ROUNDERS
Kananack, Claude
WOUNDED
Kanaoka, Nobu
TOKYO FIST
Kancher, Deborah
PRACTICAL MAGIC
Kandel, Paul
BUSTER & CHAUNCEY'S SILENT NIGHT
Kane, Anthony
MEET JOE BLACK
Kane, Billy
DESPERATE MEASURES
HOLLYWOOD CONFIDENTIAL
Kane, Carol
NAPOLEON
Kane, Dyan
GREAT EXPECTATIONS
Kane, Jason
MAKER, THE
Kane, Tom
HALLOWEEN H20: TWENTY YEARS LATER
Kaner, Damien
SKIN & BONE
Kaneshiro, Takeshi
FALLEN ANGELS
Kang Lung Shing
KILLER ANGELS
Kanie, Keizo
RAZOR: THE SNARE, THE
RAZOR: WHO'S GOT THE GOLD?, THE
Kanig, Frank
NOT IN THIS TOWN
Kanizsai, Istvan
REDLINE
Kanter, Marlene
CITY OF ANGELS

Kantor, Calman
GADJO DILO
Kanzawa, Mark
LET'S KILL ALL THE LAWYERS
Kapelos, John
JOHNNY SKIDMARKS
Kaplan, Elliot M.
SIX DAYS, SEVEN NIGHTS
Kaplan, Jonathan
KID IN ALADDIN'S PALACE, A
Kaplan, Joshua
SUE
Kaplan, Marcy
DIARY OF A SERIAL KILLER
Kaplan, Maura Nielsen
WRONGFULLY ACCUSED
Kaplan, Michael
ARMAGEDDON
Kapnist, Maria
DEAD WATERS
Kapper, Mary
NIGHT VISION
Karam, Jena
NEWTON BOYS, THE
Karasek, Valerie
PECKER
SPECIES II
Karen, James
APT PUPIL
Karfo, Robin
KRIPPENDORF'S TRIBE
Karkowsky, Adam
ENEMY OF THE STATE
Karl, Coach George
HE GOT GAME
Karlin, Miriam
INCOGNITO
Karn, Richard
BRAM STOKER'S THE MUMMY
Karon, Marvin
RESCUERS: STORIES OF COURAGE—TWO WOMEN
Karp, Izetta
I GOT THE HOOK UP
Karp, Natalie
SLUMS OF BEVERLY HILLS
Karras, Alex
BUFFALO '66
Kartheiser, Vincent
ANOTHER DAY IN PARADISE
Karz, Jimmy
WEDDING SINGER, THE
Karzis, Alex
FACE DOWN
Kash, Daniel
BONE DADDY
DEFENDERS: PAYBACK, THE
WOUNDED
Kash, Linda
URBAN SAFARI
Kashiwabara, Takashi
WHEN I CLOSE MY EYES
Kasinathan, Thambo
SUB DOWN
Kasperska, Joanna
WHITE RAVEN, THE
Kassel, Aidan
PHANTASM: OBLIVION
Kassel, Sasha
PHANTASM: OBLIVION
Kassim, Helmi
SIEGE, THE
Kasten, Hiram
SOUR GRAPES
Kastner, Gil
FRENCH EXIT
Kasumu, Ganiat
VELVET GOLDMINE

Kelly, David
MOONDANCE
WAKING NED DEVINE
Kelly, Dupre
SOMEWHERE IN THE CITY
Kelly, Eamon A.
I WENT DOWN
Kelly, Jill
HE GOT GAME
ORGAZMO
Kelly, Joe
MAJOR LEAGUE: BACK TO THE MINORS
Kelly, Joseph Patrick
ARMAGEDDON
ENEMY OF THE STATE
Kelly, Lesley
BONE DADDY
Kelly, Lisa Robin
HORTON FOOTE'S ALONE
Kelly, Mary
YOU'VE GOT MAIL
Kelly, Max
OBJECT OF MY AFFECTION, THE
Kelly, Michael
RIVER RED
Kelly, Moira
DANGEROUS BEAUTY
HI-LIFE
LION KING II: SIMBA'S PRIDE, THE
LOVE WALKED IN
Kelly, Rae'ven Larrymore
MILO
Kelly, Simon
JACK HIGGINS' MIDNIGHT MAN
Kelly, Terence
HUNTED, THE
SPREE, THE
Kelly, Terry
FIRESTORM
Kelly-Miller, Lois
MEET JOE BLACK
Kelsey, Herb
GINGERBREAD MAN, THE
Kelsey, Tamsin
DISTURBING BEHAVIOR
Kelty, Gavin
BUTCHER BOY, THE
GENERAL, THE
Kemble, Josh
DESPERATE MEASURES
Kemler, Andrew W.
ORGAZMO
Kemp, Chris
MR. NICE GUY
Kemp, David
LITTLE VOICE
Kemp, Lindsay
VELVET GOLDMINE
Kemp, Sacha
I GOT THE HOOK UP
Kemp, Tom
PROPOSITION, THE
Kempson, Rachel
DEJA VU
Kendrick, Tommy G.
DANCER, TEXAS POP. 81
Keneally, Laura
DARK CITY
Kenia, Sheyla
CENTRAL STATION
Kennedy, A.J.
OLIVER TWIST
Kennedy, Chistopher
ELVIS MEETS NIXON
Kennedy, Christopher
HOSTILE INTENT
TERMINAL JUSTICE

Kennedy, David
LOVE IS THE DEVIL: STUDY FOR A PORTRAIT OF FRANCIS BACON
Kennedy, Ellen
WRONGFULLY ACCUSED
Kennedy, Ethel
OFF THE MENU: THE LAST DAYS OF CHASEN'S
Kennedy, George
DENNIS THE MENACE STRIKES AGAIN
SMALL SOLDIERS
Kennedy, Jamie
CLOCKWATCHERS
ENEMY OF THE STATE
PASS, THE
Kennedy, Maria Doyle
GENERAL, THE
Kennedy, Matt
SUB DOWN
Kennedy, Michael
PATCH ADAMS
Kenney, Eileen
GODSON, THE
Kenny, Des
SPACEJACKED
Kenny, Francis
OBJECT OF MY AFFECTION, THE
Kenny, J.C.
URBAN LEGEND
Kenny, Jack
I'LL BE HOME FOR CHRISTMAS
Kenny, Jon
LES MISERABLES
Kenny Kenny
SHAMPOO HORNS
Kensit, Patsy
HUMAN BOMB
Kent, Anne
I WENT DOWN
Kent, Diana
KID IN ALADDIN'S PALACE, A
Kent, Jennifer
BABE: PIG IN THE CITY
KENTA.S
JUNK FOOD
Keogh, Danny
OPERATION DELTA FORCE 2
Keogh, Jimmy
WAKING NED DEVINE
Keramidopulos, Sumela-Rose
SIMON BIRCH
Kerbes, Hal
ATOMIC DOG
EBENEZER
Kercheval, Ken
RUSTY: THE GREAT RESCUE
Kerman, Janice
JACK HIGGINS' ON DANGEROUS GROUND
Kermode, Robin
WILDE
Kern, Richard
BULLET ON A WIRE
Kerns, Hubie
LOVE TO KILL
Kerr, E. Katherine
IMPOSTORS, THE
NEXT STOP, WONDERLAND
SIEGE, THE
Kerr, Eddie
LOVE IS THE DEVIL: STUDY FOR A PORTRAIT OF FRANCIS BACON
Kerr, James E.
HOSTILE WATERS
Kerr, Terry
PARENT TRAP, THE

Kerrigan, Dermot
INNOCENT SLEEP, THE
WAKING NED DEVINE
Kersnar, David
U.S. MARSHALS
Kervadel, Sophie
WESTERN
Kerwin, Brian
MR. JEALOUSY
Kess, Georgina
54
Kessler, Abraham
SOUR GRAPES
Kessler, Glenn
SIEGE, THE
Kesten, Frederika
DISAPPEARANCE OF KEVIN JOHNSON, THE
Kesting, Hans
CHARACTER
Ketscher, Annette
KINGDOM, PART 2, THE
Keung, Eric
ENEMY OF THE STATE
Key, Malcom
LOVE IS THE DEVIL: STUDY FOR A PORTRAIT OF FRANCIS BACON
Key, Steve
MERCURY RISING
Key, William
VELVET GOLDMINE
Keyes, Irwin
ASYLUM
GODSON, THE
Keyes, John
MY BROTHER'S WAR
Keyes, Steven
ALMOST PARTNERS
Keyes, Tony
LETHAL WEAPON 4
Khaderni, Shahari
AIR BUD: GOLDEN RECEIVER
Khaled, Alaa
CAN'T HARDLY WAIT
Khali, Simbi
PLUMP FICTION
Khalil, Ahmed
SHOOTING FISH
Khalil, Christel
MILO
Khan, Rana
CHICAGO CAB
Khorshidbakhtair, Afshin
TASTE OF CHERRY
Khosla, Surinder
CELEBRITY
Kibbe, David
BOYS IN LOVE 2
Kiberlain, Sandrine
SEVENTH HEAVEN
Kickinger, Roland
LETHAL WEAPON 4
Kid Koala
MODULATIONS: CINEMA FOR THE EAR
Kidd, Kevin
DAD SAVAGE
Kidder, Janet
BRIDE OF CHUCKY
Kidman, Nicole
LEADING MAN, THE
PRACTICAL MAGIC
Kidnie, James
HOSTILE INTENT
RESCUERS: STORIES OF COURAGE—TWO COUPLES
Kiely, Mark
GODS AND MONSTERS

Kier, Udo
ARMAGEDDON
BLADE
KINGDOM, PART 2, THE
PRINCE VALIANT
Kierann, Anthony
DARK CITY
Kiernan, Ford
CARLA'S SONG
Kiernan, Paul
ELMORE LEONARD'S GOLD COAST
Kierney, Tyde
FEAR AND LOATHING IN LAS VEGAS
Kieslowski, Krzysztof
KRZYSZTOF KIESLOWSKI: I'M SO-SO
Kieu-Chinh
CITY OF ANGELS
Kihlstedt, Rya
DEEP IMPACT
Kiho, Hiromitsu
ZERO WOMAN
Kikkenborg, Natalie B.
OBJECT OF MY AFFECTION, THE
Kikuchi, Takanori
ZERO WOMAN
Kilbertus, Nicholas
DEFENDERS: PAYBACK, THE
RESCUERS: STORIES OF COURAGE—TWO COUPLES
Kiley, Kate
PECKER
Kiley, Richard
PATCH ADAMS
Killalea, J.J.
RUSHMORE
Killen, Paula
BULLET ON A WIRE
Killian, Robyn
ENEMY OF THE STATE
Kilmer, Val
PRINCE OF EGYPT, THE
Kilmer, Wil
PALMETTO
Kilner, David
MARIE BAIE DES ANGES
Kilner, Kevin
MUSIC FROM ANOTHER ROOM
Kilpatrick, Laurie
MIGHTY JOE YOUNG
Kilpatrick, Patrick
REPLACEMENT KILLERS, THE
Kilvington, Denzil
HOSTILE WATERS
Kim, James
FACE THE EVIL
Kim, Jin S.
HURRICANE STREETS
Kim, Jonathan Staci
CHARLIE HOBOKEN
Kim, Randall Duk
REPLACEMENT KILLERS, THE
THIN RED LINE, THE
Kim, Simon
FACE THE EVIL
Kimball, Donna
PATCH ADAMS
Kimble, Matthew
WEDDING SINGER, THE
Kimura, Hideo
BURN HOLLYWOOD BURN
Kimura, Kazuya
GONIN
Kinchla, Chan
BLUES BROTHERS 2000
Kind, Richard
BUG'S LIFE, A
Kinery, Micheline
DIDN'T DO IT FOR LOVE
Kinevane, Pat
GENERAL, THE
INFORMANT, THE
King, Alan
BRAVE LITTLE TOASTER GOES TO MARS, THE
King, B.B.
BLUES BROTHERS 2000
King, Benjamin
LETHAL WEAPON 4
King, Clancy
TALES FROM A PARALLEL UNIVERSE: EATING PATTERN
King, Darren
LOVE IS THE DEVIL: STUDY FOR A PORTRAIT OF FRANCIS BACON
King, David
HOSTILE WATERS
King, Erik
BURN HOLLYWOOD BURN
DESPERATE MEASURES
King, George
BLACKJACK
King, Ginger
PALMETTO
King, Jamie
BUFFALO '66
King, Janel
BUFFALO '66
King, Kelly
BONE DADDY
King, Kip
FLINTSTONES: I YABBA-DABBA DOO!, THE
NIGHT AT THE ROXBURY, A
King, Larry
BULWORTH
BURN HOLLYWOOD BURN
ENEMY OF THE STATE
PRIMARY COLORS
King, Moynan
REAL BLONDE, THE
King, Peter
VELVET GOLDMINE
King, Randy
NOT IN THIS TOWN
King, Regina
ENEMY OF THE STATE
HOW STELLA GOT HER GROOVE BACK
MIGHTY JOE YOUNG
King, Ronnie
TERMINAL JUSTICE
King, Stan
FALLEN
King, Steve
U.S. MARSHALS
King, Suzy
LIKE IT IS
King, T.W.
X-FILES, THE
King, Vanessa
WHEN DANGER FOLLOWS YOU HOME
King, Wayne A.
RUSH HOUR
Kingi, Henry
JOHN CARPENTER'S VAMPIRES
Kingi, Tony
BOYS IN LOVE 2
Kingsley, Barbara
OVERNIGHT DELIVERY
Kingsley, Ben
PHOTOGRAPHING FAIRIES
Kingston, Graeme
I'LL BE HOME FOR CHRISTMAS
Kinnear, Greg
YOU'VE GOT MAIL
Kinney, Terry
GEORGE WALLACE
Kino, Lloyd
GODZILLA
Kinsey, Lance
KRIPPENDORF'S TRIBE
Kinski, Nastassja
LITTLE BOY BLUE
OFF THE MENU: THE LAST DAYS OF CHASEN'S
PLAYING BY HEART
SAVIOR
YOUR FRIENDS & NEIGHBORS
Kinsky, Antonin
FORGOTTEN LIGHT
Kira
SLAYERS: THE MOTION PICTURE
Kirby, Bobby
GEORGE WALLACE
Kirby, Bruce
INTERLOCKED: THRILLED TO DEATH
Kirby, Randall
RINGMASTER
Kirchmer, Tom
CELEBRITY
Kirk, Christina
SAFE MEN
Kirkiles, Candice
JOHN CARPENTER'S VAMPIRES
Kirkland, Ajgie
BIG LEBOWSKI, THE
Kirkland, Sally
LITTLE GHOST
OFF THE MENU: THE LAST DAYS OF CHASEN'S
Kirkman, Jerry
DEAR JESSE
Kirkman, Tim
DEAR JESSE
Kirkpatrick, Maggie
WELCOME TO WOOP WOOP
Kirksey, Logan
TRUMAN SHOW, THE
Kirkwood, Craig
WHY DO FOOLS FALL IN LOVE?
Kirkwood, David
ASYLUM
DON KING: ONLY IN AMERICA
Kirsch, David
KID IN ALADDIN'S PALACE, A
Kirschenheiter, Mike
RETURN OF THE KING, THE
Kirschke, Jack
PRACTICAL MAGIC
Kirton, Mike
HOLY MAN
Kishida, Mori
RAZOR: THE SNARE, THE
Kishimoto, Kayoko
FIREWORKS
Kissel, Ed
POLTERGEIST REPORT: YUYU HAKUSHO
Kissner, Jeremy James
GREAT EXPECTATIONS
Kitano, Takeshi
FIREWORKS
GONIN
SONATINE
Kitchen, Michael
MRS. DALLOWAY
Kitchin, Sam
HOLY MAN
TRUMAN SHOW, THE
Kitt, Eartha
JUNGLE BOOK: MOWGLI'S STORY, THE
Kittay, Marc
WATERBOY, THE
Klammer, Clara
MUSIC FROM ANOTHER ROOM

Korikova, Elena
FRIEND OF THE DECEASED, A
Korman, Harvey
SECRET OF NIMH 2: TIMMY TO THE RESCUE, THE
Kornova, Katerina
ACT OF WAR
Koromzay, Alix
NIGHTWATCH
Korsmo, Charlie
CAN'T HARDLY WAIT
Korte, Donald
NEGOTIATOR, THE
Korwin, Anna
INCOGNITO
Korzeniowski, Thomas
PECKER
Kosata, Petr
ACT OF WAR
Koscheev, Anatoliy
THIEF, THE
Kosco, Gabor
REDLINE
Koslo, Corrine
HARD CORE LOGO
Koson, Agnieszka
MERLIN
Kosterman, Mitchell
SNOWBOUND
WHEN DANGER FOLLOWS YOU HOME
Kostychin, Constantin
FRIEND OF THE DECEASED, A
Kosugi, Kane
ZERO WOMAN
Koteas, Elias
APT PUPIL
FALLEN
HIT ME
LIVING OUT LOUD
THIN RED LINE, THE
Kotecki, Robert
RUSH HOUR
Kotilsky, Marge
CON, THE
Kotto, Yaphet
DEFENDERS: PAYBACK, THE
Kotva, Vaclav
MY GIANT
Koulinskyi, The Countess
GOVERNESS, THE
Kousnetzoff, Nathalie
SWINDLE, THE
Kovac, Mario
HALLELUJAH!
Kovacs, Danny
DIARY OF A SERIAL KILLER
Kove, Martin
TOP OF THE WORLD
Koyama, John
BOOGIE BOY
SIX DAYS, SEVEN NIGHTS
Koyanagi, Brie
SHAMPOO HORNS
Kozeluh, John
PLAN B
Kozlowski, Caralyn
PRACTICAL MAGIC
Krabbe, Jeroen
DANGEROUS BEAUTY
EVER AFTER
Kraemer, Andreas
PECKER
SPECIES II
Kraemer, Mattias
ENEMY OF THE STATE
Kraft, Scott
MAKER, THE
Kraftwerk
MODULATIONS: CINEMA FOR THE EAR
Krag, James
MERCURY RISING
Krag, Peter
CELEBRATION, THE
Krah, Kim
BUFFALO '66
Krakowski, Jane
DANCE WITH ME
Krall, Daamen
RAT'S TALE, A
Kramer, Eric Allan
COLONY, THE
Kramer, Larry
PAUL MONETTE: THE BRINK OF SUMMER'S END
Kramer, Peter
KNOCK OFF
Kramer, Steve
RUSTY: THE GREAT RESCUE
Krape, Evelyn
BABE: PIG IN THE CITY
Krassner, Paul
LENNY BRUCE: SWEAR TO TELL THE TRUTH
Krause, Peter
LOVELIFE
TRUMAN SHOW, THE
Kravitz, Lenny
RUGRATS MOVIE, THE
Kravitz, Steven
SOULER OPPOSITE, THE
Krawic, Michael
SOUR GRAPES
X-FILES, THE
Krek, Michael
FUTURE FEAR
Kremer, Hans
MENDEL
Kress, Nathan
BABE: PIG IN THE CITY
Kretschmann, Thomas
PRINCE VALIANT
Krich, Gretchen
HENRY FOOL
Krieger, Nikki
NO WAY HOME
Krieger, Robin
NIGHT AT THE ROXBURY, A
Kriesa, Christopher
LANDLADY, THE
Kriss, Mandy
ENEMY OF THE STATE
ENEMY OF THE STATE
Kristen, Marta
BODY COUNT
LOST IN SPACE
Kristiansen, Peter Width
OTHER SIDE OF SUNDAY, THE
Kristofferson, Kris
BLADE
DANCE WITH ME
SOLDIER'S DAUGHTER NEVER CRIES, A
TWO FOR TEXAS
Kristol, Irving
ARGUING THE WORLD
Krivitska, Tatiana
FRIEND OF THE DECEASED, A
Kroeker, Jonathan
RESCUERS: STORIES OF COURAGE—TWO COUPLES
Krog, Evald
KINGDOM, PART 2, THE
Kronenberg, Fred
STAR KID
Kronenfeld, Ivan
LIVING OUT LOUD
Krstic, Ljiljana
SAVIOR
Krstovic, Modrag
SAVIOR
Krsztoff
DEE SNIDER'S STRANGELAND
Kruk, Richard
BLUES BROTHERS 2000
Krull, Ramsey
POLISH WEDDING
Krull, Suzanne
SOULER OPPOSITE, THE
Krumholtz, David
SLUMS OF BEVERLY HILLS
Kruse, Doug
CAUGHT UP
Krutchey, Phillipe
LOVE IS THE DEVIL: STUDY FOR A PORTRAIT OF FRANCIS BACON
Krystyan, Vieslav
54
Ktiri, Ali
RUSHMORE
Ku Feng
HONG KONG 1941
MAGNIFICENT WARRIORS
Kubecka, Ivo
FORGOTTEN LIGHT
Kubo, Naoko
SLEEPY EYES OF DEATH: SWORD OF ADVENTURE
SLEEPY EYES OF DEATH: SWORD OF SEDUCTION
Kuby, Ronald
SIEGE, THE
Kuchok, Ady
JOHNNY MYSTO BOY WIZARD
Kudoh, Youki
HEAVEN'S BURNING
Kudrow, Lisa
CLOCKWATCHERS
OPPOSITE OF SEX, THE
Kuh, Richard
LENNY BRUCE: SWEAR TO TELL THE TRUTH
Kuhn, Daniella
PATCH ADAMS
Kuhn, Judy
POCAHONTAS II: JOURNEY TO A NEW WORLD
Kula, Chad
SKIN & BONE
Kulich, Vladimir
FIRESTORM
Kulish, Kyle
CELEBRITY
Kum Ho Kon
HEROES SHED NO TEARS
Kumagai, Mika
JUNK FOOD
Kunis, Mila
GIA
KRIPPENDORF'S TRIBE
Kunitz, James
DANCE WITH ME
Kunitz, Janna
DANCE WITH ME
Kunkel, Holger
TALES FROM A PARALLEL UNIVERSE: EATING PATTERN
Kunnecke, Evelyn
KILLER CONDOM, THE
Kunstmann, Doris
FUNNY GAMES
Kunz, Simon
PARENT TRAP, THE
Kuoch, Koing
NO ORDINARY LOVE

Kurcz, Robert
U.S. MARSHALS
Kurosawa, Toshio
RAZOR: THE SNARE, THE
Kurth, Wally
I LOVE YOU, DON'T TOUCH ME!
Kurtz, Joyce
OPPOSITE OF SEX, THE
Kurtz, Marcia Jean
ONE TRUE THING
Kurtz, Swoosie
OUTSIDE OZONA
Kurup, Shishir
CITY OF ANGELS
Kusano, Daigo
RAZOR: THE SNARE, THE
RAZOR: WHO'S GOT THE GOLD?, THE
Kusatsu, Clyde
GODZILLA
Kushell, Lisa
BILLBOARD DAD
Kushner, Celia
I'LL BE HOME FOR CHRISTMAS
Kussman, Susan
PRIMARY COLORS
Kuwabara, Nobutaka
JUNK FOOD
Kuzelka, Jan
LES MISERABLES
Kuznetsov, Yuri
BROTHER
Kuzyk, Mimi
BONE DADDY
DEFENDERS: PAYBACK, THE
Kwalda, Tasheen
PASSION IN THE DESERT
Kwan, Brian
DR. DOLITTLE
Kwan Lee-na
FALLEN ANGELS
Kwan, Rosamund
ARMOUR OF GOD
Kwok, Crystal
DRAGONS FOREVER
Kydd, Johnnie Shand
LOVE IS THE DEVIL: STUDY FOR A PORTRAIT OF FRANCIS BACON
Kyker, Dick
RAGE, THE
Kynman, Paul
SHOOTING FISH
Kyros, Bill
UNDERTAKER'S WEDDING, THE
Kyte, Tyler
DEFENDERS: PAYBACK, THE
L'Harmonie de Bailleul
LIFE OF JESUS, THE
L'Heureux, Gerard
BIG LEBOWSKI, THE
La Croix, Robert
BROADWAY DAMAGE
La Fayette, John
CIVIL ACTION, A
La Fleur, Art
BEST OF THE BEST: WITHOUT WARNING
HIJACKING HOLLYWOOD
LEWIS & CLARK & GEORGE
La Londe, Mike
HORSE WHISPERER, THE
La Lumia, Drinda
GIA
La Rocco, Phil
SUE
La Rosa, Kevin
DEEP IMPACT
La Salle, Eriq
REBOUND: THE LEGEND OF EARL "THE GOAT" MANIGAULT
La Sardo, Robert
RUNNING WOMAN, THE
La Scala, Nancy
SPECIES II
La Valette, Desiree Von
LAST DAYS OF DISCO, THE
La Vecchia, Antoinette
DIRTY LAUNDRY
Labao, Cece Neber
LETHAL WEAPON 4
Labelle, Rob
MURDER IN MIND
Laborit, Emmanuelle
BEYOND SILENCE
Labus, Jiri
FORGOTTEN LIGHT
LaCaprara, Antonella
BLACKJACK
LaChanze
DAVID SEARCHING
Laci, Peter
MIDAS TOUCH, THE
Lacopo, Jay
ALMOST HEROES
GODSON, THE
LaCourt, Fort
DEE SNIDER'S STRANGELAND
Lacroix, Peter
DISTURBING BEHAVIOR
HUNTED, THE
Ladalski, John
ARMOUR OF GOD
Ladd, Cheryl
PERMANENT MIDNIGHT
Ladd, Diane
PRIMARY COLORS
Ladden, Steve
DECAMPITATED
Lady of Rage, The
RIDE
Lafayette, John
BRIGHT SHINING LIE, A
DR. DOLITTLE
INDISCREET
Laffan, Pat
GENERAL, THE
LaFont, Bernadette
GENEALOGIES OF A CRIME
LaFortune, Roc
PEACEKEEPER, THE
Lage, Jordan
SPANISH PRISONER, THE
Lahiri, Ronobir
YOU'VE GOT MAIL
Lai, Benny
DRAGONS FOREVER
Lai, Leon
COMRADES, ALMOST A LOVE STORY
FALLEN ANGELS
Laimene, Missoum
FULL SPEED
Lain, Chasey
ORGAZMO
Lake, Don
ALMOST HEROES
Lake, Michael
DARK CITY
Lala, Joe
GOLGO 13: QUEEN BEE
Lally, John
RIVER RED
Lally, Trudy
RIVER RED
Lam Ching Ying
ENCOUNTER OF THE SPOOKY KIND
HEROES SHED NO TEARS
PRODIGAL SON, THE
Lam, David
DRAGONS FOREVER
ROYAL WARRIORS
Lam Man Cheung
CHINESE BOX, THE
Lam, Nina Zoie
YOU'VE GOT MAIL
Lam, Steven
LETHAL WEAPON 4
Lam, Wilson
KICK BOXER'S TEARS
Lama, Ernesto
TRUCE, THE
Lamar, Sophia
SHAMPOO HORNS
LaMarca, Gina
WILD THINGS
Lamas, Lorenzo
RAGE, THE
TERMINAL JUSTICE
Lamaze, Kimberly
WILD THINGS
Lamb, Carl
INVISIBLE DAD
LAST BIG THING, THE
Lamb, Jennifer
BIG LEBOWSKI, THE
Lamb, Joe H.
MEET JOE BLACK
Lamb, Sabrina
NAKED ACTS
Lambert, Christopher
MEAN GUNS
NIRVANA
Lambert, Michael
KNOCK OFF
Lambert, Steve
STILL BREATHING
Lambton, Anne
AMERICAN HISTORY X
LOVE IS THE DEVIL: STUDY FOR A PORTRAIT OF FRANCIS BACON
Lamert, Jerry
GODSON, THE
Lamkin, Kathy
CON, THE
LaMotta, John
GODSON, THE
Lanasa, Katherine
DESTINY OF MARTY FINE, THE
DISAPPEARANCE OF KEVIN JOHNSON, THE
Lancaster, Julie
STEPMOM
Lancelot, Patrick
ARTEMISIA
Land, Scott
STILL BREATHING
Landa, Billy Joe
WHO THE HELL IS JULIETTE?
Landau, Martin
OFF THE MENU: THE LAST DAYS OF CHASEN'S
ROUNDERS
X-FILES, THE
Lander, John-Michael
ALL THE RAGE
Lander, Lea
RABID DOGS
Lander, Steven
JACK HIGGINS' MIDNIGHT MAN
Landers, Christy
SWAN PRINCESS III: AND THE MYSTERY OF THE ENCHANTED TREASURE, THE
Landers, Fiona
MILO
Landes, Michael
DREAM FOR AN INSOMNIAC

RESCUERS: STORIES OF COURAGE—TWO WOMEN
Landesberg, Steve
SOULER OPPOSITE, THE
Landesman, Rocco
MOON OVER BROADWAY
Landey, Clayton
CIVIL ACTION, A
Landin, Erika
DANCE WITH ME
Landis, Elizabeth
TALK TO ME
Landis, John
QUICKSILVER HIGHWAY
WHO IS HENRY JAGLOM?
Landis, Max
BLUES BROTHERS 2000
Landolfi, Krista Lynn
TRUMAN SHOW, THE
Landon, Dawn
DIARY OF A SERIAL KILLER
Landon Jr., Hal
PLAYING BY HEART
Landre, Lou
CHARACTER
Landry, Charle
RIVER RED
Landry, Christopher
CLOCKMAKER
SHRUNKEN CITY, THE
Landry, J.M.
INVADER, THE
Landry, Sylvain
SNAKE EYES
Lane, Cam
ADVENTURES OF MOWGLI
Lane, Diane
ONLY THRILL, THE
Lane Jr., Teddy
MAKER, THE
Lane, Nathan
LION KING II: SIMBA'S PRIDE, THE
Lang, Cheryl
TARZAN AND THE LOST CITY
Lang, Jonny
BLUES BROTHERS 2000
Lang, Magda
TARANTELLA
Lang, Robert
WILDE
Lang, Stephen
NIAGARA NIAGARA
Langbridge, Cynthia
SIX DAYS, SEVEN NIGHTS
Langdijk, Jack
JACK LONDON'S THE CALL OF THE WILD: DOG OF THE YUKON
Langdon, Anthony
VELVET GOLDMINE
Lange, Artie
DIRTY WORK
Lange, Jessica
COUSIN BETTE
HUSH
OFF THE MENU: THE LAST DAYS OF CHASEN'S
Langedijk, Jack
CAPTIVE
DEAD END
Langella, Frank
LOLITA
SMALL SOLDIERS
Langer, A.J.
MEET THE DEEDLES
Langford, Lisa Louise
HAPPINESS
LAST BREATH
Langhelle, Jorgen
KRISTIN LAVRANSDATTER
OTHER SIDE OF SUNDAY, THE
Langton, Brooke
REACH THE ROCK
Lanino, Deborah
TALK TO ME
Lannan, George
WHEN PIGS FLY
Lano, Jenya
BLADE
Lanoff, Lawrence
CHOSEN ONE: LEGEND OF THE RAVEN, THE
Lanoil, Bruce
JACK FROST
Lansbury, Kate
EVER AFTER
Lansing, Douglas B.
PARALLEL SONS
Lansing, Joi
TOUCH OF EVIL: THE DIRECTOR'S CUT
Lansink, Leonard
KILLER CONDOM, THE
LaPage, Roger
PLAN B
REDLINE
LaPaglia, Anthony
PHOENIX
LaPaine, Daniel
DANGEROUS BEAUTY
54
POLISH WEDDING
LaPalme, Denis
BLEEDERS
Lapatin, Melanie
DANCE WITH ME
Lapicki, Andrej
FROM A FAR COUNTRY
Laplaca, Charlie
CHARLIE HOBOKEN
Lapotaire, Jane
SHOOTING FISH
Laquidara, Charles
NEXT STOP, WONDERLAND
Larby, Ahmed Ben
SIEGE, THE
Laresca, Vincent
MUSIC FROM ANOTHER ROOM
REAL BLONDE, THE
Larkin, Michael
MIDAS TOUCH, THE
Larkin, Robert
NEXT STOP, WONDERLAND
Larkins, Tommy
THERE'S SOMETHING ABOUT MARY
LaRosa, Kevin
LITTLE BIGFOOT 2: THE JOURNEY HOME
LaRose, Scott
PLUMP FICTION
Larrivaz, Estelle
LA SEPARATION
Larrivey, Wayne A.
ENEMY OF THE STATE
Larroquette, John
DEFENDERS: PAYBACK, THE
Larsen, Thomas Bo
CELEBRATION, THE
KINGDOM, PART 2, THE
Larsen, Wayne
DECAMPITATED
Larson, Bill
PALMETTO
Larson, Darrell
SHADRACH
STEPMOM
Larson, Graham J.
SIEGE, THE
Larson, Mark S.
NO ORDINARY LOVE
Larson, Nils
CAN'T HARDLY WAIT
Larson, Tom
I MARRIED A STRANGE PERSON!
Larson, Ulla
LOVE IS THE DEVIL: STUDY FOR A PORTRAIT OF FRANCIS BACON
LaRue, Rodger
REPLACEMENT KILLERS, THE
LaSardo, Robert
NIGHTWATCH
REAL THING, THE
Lascher, David
CALL TO REMEMBER, A
Lasdun, Gary
WHO IS HENRY JAGLOM?
Laser, Dieter
OGRE, THE
Laska, Ray
SHRUNKEN CITY, THE
WHY DO FOOLS FALL IN LOVE?
Laskawy, Harris
SLUMS OF BEVERLY HILLS
Laskin, Michael
DISAPPEARANCE OF KEVIN JOHNSON, THE
Lasky, Richard
ENEMY
Lasser, Louise
HAPPINESS
Lassez, Sarah
HOLLYWOOD CONFIDENTIAL
Laswell, Bill
MODULATIONS: CINEMA FOR THE EAR
Latham, David
HENRY FOOL
Lathan, Philip
FROM A FAR COUNTRY
Lathan, Sanaa
BLADE
Lathom, Michael
CHOSEN ONE: LEGEND OF THE RAVEN, THE
Latifah, Queen
LIVING OUT LOUD
Latshaw, Steve
INVISIBLE DAD
Lau, Carina
ARMOUR OF GOD
Lau Chau Sang
HEROES SHED NO TEARS
Lau, Chindy
MAGNIFICENT WARRIORS
Lau Jia Hui
KILLER ANGELS
Lau Shiu Kwan
KILLER ANGELS
Lau, William
RUSHMORE
Lauer, Andrew
I'LL BE HOME FOR CHRISTMAS
Laufiso, Eric
SIX DAYS, SEVEN NIGHTS
Laumord, Gilbert
SWINDLE, THE
Lauray, Jennifer
STILL BREATHING
Laurence, Ashley
REAL THING, THE
Lauria, Dan
DOGWATCH
WIDE AWAKE
Lauricella, Adam T.
NIAGARA NIAGARA
Laurie, Hugh
BORROWERS, THE

COUSIN BETTE
MAN IN THE IRON MASK, THE
SPICE WORLD
Laurie, Piper
FACULTY, THE
HORTON FOOTE'S ALONE
Laursen, Linda
CELEBRATION, THE
Lauter, Ed
BRIGHT SHINING LIE, A
TOP OF THE WORLD
Lavaud, Alice
MADELINE
Laveaux, Shayla
ORGAZMO
Lavell, Sandie
UNDER THE SKIN
Lavender, Shannon
RAGE, THE
Lavergne, Nestor
EL CHE: INVESTIGATING A LEGEND
Lavia, Lorenzo
ARTEMISIA
Lavinio, Chad
STEPMOM
Lavish, Lea
DETOUR
Lavoo, Bethany
DECAMPITATED
LaVorgna, Adam
I'LL BE HOME FOR CHRISTMAS
Law Jr., Don
CAN'T YOU HEAR THE WIND HOWL?: THE LIFE AND MUSIC OF ROBERT JOHNSON
Law, Jude
MUSIC FROM ANOTHER ROOM
WILDE
Law, Phylidda
SLIDING DOORS
Lawless, Lucy
HERCULES AND XENA THE ANIMATED MOVIE: THE BATTLE FOR MOUNT OLYMPUS
Lawless, Rick
SLAPPY AND THE STINKERS
Lawlor, J. Patrick
PLEASANTVILLE
Lawrence, Aiden
LITTLE VOICE
Lawrence, Andy
JACK FROST
Lawrence, Burke
JACK LONDON'S THE CALL OF THE WILD: DOG OF THE YUKON
Lawrence, Cary
SNAKE EYES
Lawrence, Christopher B.
ENEMY OF THE STATE
Lawrence, Jeremy D.
BOYS IN LOVE 2
Lawrence, Jonathan
SHAMPOO HORNS
Lawrence, Mal Z.
ROUNDERS
Lawrence, Mark Christopher
SENSELESS
Lawrence, Matthew
KIKI'S DELIVERY SERVICE
RUSTY: THE GREAT RESCUE
Lawrence, Sharon
DEFENDERS: PAYBACK, THE
ONLY THRILL, THE
Lawrence, Steve
BLUES BROTHERS 2000
Lawson, Bianca
PRIMARY COLORS
Lawson, Eric
STEEL SHARKS
WHEN TIME EXPIRES
Lawson, Maggie
PLEASANTVILLE
Lawson, Richard
HOW STELLA GOT HER GROOVE BACK
Lawson, Shannon
FACE DOWN
Lawyer, Dale
SUE
Layfield, Crispin
LAND GIRLS, THE
Lazar, Dorina
SHRUNKEN CITY, THE
SUBSPECIES IV: BLOODSTORM
Lazar, Paul
BELOVED
HENRY FOOL
LOS LOCOS
SUBSTITUTE 2: SCHOOL'S OUT, THE
Lazar, Veronica
BEYOND, THE
Lazard, Justin
SPECIES II
Lazarev, Alexandre
FRIEND OF THE DECEASED, A
Lazenby, Cliff
POLTERGEIST REPORT: YUYU HAKUSHO
Lazerine, Loren
ASYLUM
CHICAGO CAB
HIJACKING HOLLYWOOD
Le Bailly, Cecile
HEROES SHED NO TEARS
Le Bevillon, Leo
SEVENTH HEAVEN
Le Furr, Gaelle
POST COITUM, ANIMAL TRISTE
Le Grand, Nathan
LANDLADY, THE
Le Guerrier, Renee Madeleine
BARNEY'S GREAT ADVENTURE—THE MOVIE
Le Prevost, Nicholas
LAND GIRLS, THE
SHAKESPEARE IN LOVE
Lea, Ursula
LIKE IT IS
Leach, Jackson
WILDE
Leach, John Paul
CARLA'S SONG
Leach, Nigel
KILLING TIME
Leadbitter, Bill
LOVE AND DEATH ON LONG ISLAND
Leahan, Catherine
CIVIL ACTION, A
Leake, Damien
MIGHTY JOE YOUNG
Leal, Jack
OUTSIDE OZONA
Leal, Leandra
OYSTER AND THE WIND, THE
Leaman, Rande
SOUR GRAPES
Learned, Michael
ALARMIST, THE
Leary, Denis
BUG'S LIFE, A
LOVE WALKED IN
MONUMENT AVE.
REAL BLONDE, THE
SMALL SOLDIERS
SUICIDE KINGS
WIDE AWAKE
Leary, Timothy
FRENCH EXIT
TIMOTHY LEARY'S DEAD
Leary, Zach
TIMOTHY LEARY'S DEAD
Leasca, Tom
THERE'S SOMETHING ABOUT MARY
Leavenworth, Scotty
BABE: PIG IN THE CITY
SIMON BIRCH
Leaver, George
POLTERGEIST REPORT: YUYU HAKUSHO
WRATH OF THE NINJA: THE YOTODEN MOVIE
Leavins, Chris
HANGING GARDEN, THE
Leavy, Pat
BUTCHER BOY, THE
GENERAL, THE
Lebaron, Brian
FEAR AND LOATHING IN LAS VEGAS
Lebboroni, Raffaella
LIFE IS BEAUTIFUL
Lebell, Jean
RUSH HOUR
LeBlanc, Matt
LOST IN SPACE
LeBlum, George
REAL HOWARD SPITZ, THE
Lebow, Will
NEXT STOP, WONDERLAND
LeBrock, Kelly
WRONGFULLY ACCUSED
Lecesne, James
BROADWAY DAMAGE
GODS AND MONSTERS
Lechat, Olivier
POST COITUM, ANIMAL TRISTE
LeCossec, Michel
WESTERN
Leder, Bryan
LAST DAYS OF DISCO, THE
Ledoyen, Virginie
SOLDIER'S DAUGHTER NEVER CRIES, A
Ledreau, Carole
WESTERN
Lee, Carmen
KNOCK OFF
Lee, Cherish
AMERICAN HISTORY X
Lee, Conan Hutch
LETHAL WEAPON 4
Lee, Dana
INTERLOCKED: THRILLED TO DEATH
LETHAL WEAPON 4
Lee, Fay Ann
HENRY FOOL
Lee, Grace
KRIPPENDORF'S TRIBE
Lee Hoi Suk
HEROES SHED NO TEARS
Lee, Jason
ENEMY OF THE STATE
KISSING A FOOL
Lee, Jason Scott
MURDER IN MIND
SOLDIER
Lee, Jimmy
KICK BOXER'S TEARS
Lee Ka Ding
DRAGONS FOREVER
Lee, Kaiulani
CIVIL ACTION, A
HUSH
Lee, Lela
SHOPPING FOR FANGS
Lee, Leo
REPLACEMENT KILLERS, THE

Lee, Mark
TWISTED
Lee, Miki
MR. NICE GUY
Lee, Ming
RETURN TO PARADISE
Lee, Moon
BEAUTY INVESTIGATOR
KICK BOXER'S TEARS
KILLER ANGELS
Lee, Paul J.Q.
PRICE ABOVE RUBIES, A
Lee, Randy
WOUNDED
Lee, Robbie
RUSHMORE
Lee, Robert
BLACKJACK
Lee, Robert C.
MEET JOE BLACK
OBJECT OF MY AFFECTION, THE
Lee, Robinne
HAV PLENTY
Lee, Roderick
CHINESE BOX, THE
Lee, Schecter
REAL BLONDE, THE
Lee, Shannon
BLADE
Lee, Sheryl
JOHN CARPENTER'S VAMPIRES
NOTES FROM UNDERGROUND
Lee, Simone
KNOCK OFF
Lee Siu Kai
CHINESE BOX, THE
Lee, Stephen
NEGOTIATOR, THE
Lee, Stephen Xavier
GODZILLA
Lee, Tom
CARLA'S SONG
Lee, Wendee
RED HAWK: WEAPON OF DEATH
RUSTY: THE GREAT RESCUE
Lee, William Scott
OPPOSITE OF SEX, THE
Lee, Zack
THERE'S SOMETHING ABOUT MARY
Leeds, Phil
KRIPPENDORF'S TRIBE
Leene, Jamie
WILDE
Leestemaker, Luc
LITTLE GHOST
Lefebvre, Jean-Claude
LIFE OF JESUS, THE
Lefevour, Rick
U.S. MARSHALS
LeFevre, Adam
ROUNDERS
Leffers, Morten Rotne
KINGDOM, PART 2, THE
Legal, Brigitte
WESTERN
Leger, Anthony
NOT IN THIS TOWN
Leggett, Jay
ANOTHER DAY IN PARADISE
HIT ME
Legner, Vaclav
FORGOTTEN LIGHT
Legrand, Romain
UN AIR DE FAMILLE
LeGros, James
DESTINY OF MARTY FINE, THE
ENEMY OF THE STATE
PASS, THE
PRONTO
PSYCHO
THURSDAY
Leguizamo, John
BODY COUNT
DR. DOLITTLE
Lehl, Philip
LAST ASSASSINS
Lehman, Kristin
BLEEDERS
Lehota, Andrej
NEMESIS 4: CRY OF ANGELS
Lehr, John
MR. JEALOUSY
Leibenberg, Dehan
OPERATION DELTA FORCE 2
Leibman, Ron
DON KING: ONLY IN AMERICA
Leichter, Jon
SKIN & BONE
Leigh, Janet
HALLOWEEN H20: TWENTY YEARS LATER
TOUCH OF EVIL: THE DIRECTOR'S CUT
Leigh, Katie
BABE: PIG IN THE CITY
Leigh, Kristen
STEPHEN KING'S THE NIGHT FLIER
Leigh, Marissa
PARENT TRAP, THE
Leigh, Taylor
LIVING OUT LOUD
Leitch, Megan
HARD CORE LOGO
MISBEGOTTEN
Leland, Grace
LAND GIRLS, THE
Leland, Jacob
LAND GIRLS, THE
Lelievre, Karine
WESTERN
LeMat, Paul
AMERICAN HISTORY X
Lemieux, Robert Norman
SNAKE EYES
Lemire, Richard
SNAKE EYES
Lemmon, Chris
BEST OF THE BEST: WITHOUT WARNING
LAND OF THE FREE
Lemmon, Jack
NEIL SIMON'S THE ODD COUPLE II
OFF THE MENU: THE LAST DAYS OF CHASEN'S
12 ANGRY MEN
Lempert, Carol
RESCUERS: STORIES OF COURAGE—TWO COUPLES
Lenancker, Alain
LIFE OF JESUS, THE
Lenandowski, Terese
BUFFALO '66
Lenehan, Nancy
PLEASANTVILLE
Lenihan, J. Zachary
EDEN
Lennix, Harry J.
CHICAGO CAB
Lennon, Maria
INFORMANT, THE
Lennon, Sean
FREE TIBET
Lennox, Alyra
DANCE WITH ME
Lennox, Doug
WHITE RAVEN, THE
Lennox, Kai
PLEASANTVILLE
RUSH HOUR
Lennstrom, Stephen
EDEN
Leno, Jay
OFF THE MENU: THE LAST DAYS OF CHASEN'S
Lenthall, David
LAST LIVES
Lentz, Jerry
KRAA! THE SEA MONSTER
Lenz, Kay
GUN, A CAR, AND A BLONDE, A
Leomiti, K.C.
ARMAGEDDON
Leon, Carlos
BIG LEBOWSKI, THE
REPLACEMENT KILLERS, THE
Leon, Joseph
ALMOST PARTNERS
Leona, Polyn
THIN RED LINE, THE
Leonard, Robert Sean
LAST DAYS OF DISCO, THE
Leone, Codie
SHAMPOO HORNS
Leonet, Patrizia
DANGEROUS BEAUTY
Leonetti, Elisa
DIARY OF A SERIAL KILLER
Leong Po-Chin
HONG KONG 1941
Leoni, Tea
DEEP IMPACT
Leopardi, Chauncey
OPPOSITE OF SEX, THE
PERMANENT MIDNIGHT
LePage, Jerome
NO WAY HOME
Leray, Melanie
WESTERN
Lerel, Laurence
LA SEPARATION
Lerici, Barbara
CHAMBERMAID ON THE TITANIC, THE
Lerner, Jeffrey P.
THERE'S SOMETHING ABOUT MARY
Lerner, Ken
DON KING: ONLY IN AMERICA
SENSELESS
Lerner, Michael
CELEBRITY
GODZILLA
OFF THE MENU: THE LAST DAYS OF CHASEN'S
SAFE MEN
Lerner, Michael Alan
FRENCH EXIT
LeRoy, Emmanuel
WESTERN
LeRoy, Zoaunne
TRUMAN SHOW, THE
Les Freres Coulibali
ZAKIR AND HIS FRIENDS
Les Majorettes de Bailleul
LIFE OF JESUS, THE
LeSaux, Johan
WESTERN
Leschin, Luisa
YOUR FRIENDS & NEIGHBORS
Lescin, Luisa
LANDLADY, THE
Leslie, Susan
OPPOSITE OF SEX, THE
Lespance, P.J.
WRONGFULLY ACCUSED

Less, Nathaniel
YOUNG HERCULES
Lesser, Robert
GODZILLA
Lester, Adrian
PRIMARY COLORS
Lester, Loren
BATMAN & MR. FREEZE: SUBZERO
Lester, Terri
RIDE
Letelier, Christian
RETURN TO SAVAGE BEACH
Letheren, Mark
WILDE
Leto, Jared
SUMMER FLING
THIN RED LINE, THE
URBAN LEGEND
Letscher, Matthew
LOVELIFE
MASK OF ZORRO, THE
Letts, Dennis
LITTLE BOY BLUE
Letts, Tracy
CHICAGO CAB
U.S. MARSHALS
Leu, Adrian
TALISMAN
Leung Chi On
CHINESE BOX, THE
Leung Kar Yan
KILLER ANGELS
Leung, Ken
RUSH HOUR
Leung Mui Chung
KILLER ANGELS
Leung Suet Mai
ENCOUNTER OF THE SPOOKY KIND
Leung, Wallace
WRONGFULLY ACCUSED
Leung Wing-chung
BODYGUARD FROM BEIJING
Leung Yiu Hay
KNOCK OFF
Leva, Gary
PLAN B
Levani
BLADE
Leverington, Shelby
GIA
Leverman, Zerha
FALLING FIRE
Leverone, Gene
MEET JOE BLACK
Levert, Gary
REAL HOWARD SPITZ, THE
Levert, Matt
MERCURY RISING
Leverton, Guy
VELVET GOLDMINE
Levi, Eran
PLAN B
Levin, Charles
CIVIL ACTION, A
Levin, G. Roy
SPANISH PRISONER, THE
Levin, Stephanie
SOLDIER'S DAUGHTER NEVER CRIES, A
Levine, Floyd
WATCHERS REBORN
Levine, Jay
NEGOTIATOR, THE
Levine, Marilyn
SIX O'CLOCK NEWS
Levine, Walter
BLUES BROTHERS 2000
Levinson, Carri
HENRY: PORTRAIT OF A SERIAL KILLER PART 2
Levisette, Emile
DETONATOR
Levitch, Ashlee
STAR KID
Levitch, Timothy "Speed"
CRUISE, THE
Levitt, Joseph Gordon
HALLOWEEN H20: TWENTY YEARS LATER
Levy, Adam
GOVERNESS, THE
Levy, Eugene
ALMOST HEROES
RICHIE RICH'S CHRISTMAS WISH
Levy, Katharine
FIRELIGHT
Levy, Michelle
UNVEILING, THE
Levy, Salvador
PALMETTO
Levy, Smadar
SUE
Lew, James
BOOGIE BOY
LETHAL WEAPON 4
LOVE TO KILL
REPLACEMENT KILLERS, THE
Lewicki, Jennifer
ELIZABETH
Lewinson, Steve
SPICE WORLD
Lewis, Andrea
DOWN IN THE DELTA
Lewis, Antonio
LETTER FROM DEATH ROW, A
Lewis, Bobo
ONE TRUE THING
Lewis, Brian "Skinny B"
LOS LOCOS
Lewis, Buddy
WOO
Lewis, Carol Jean
BELOVED
Lewis, Cornelius
DEEP IMPACT
Lewis, David
AIR BUD: GOLDEN RECEIVER
Lewis, Emma
MERLIN
Lewis, Everett
SKIN & BONE
Lewis, Gary
CARLA'S SONG
Lewis, Huey
SPHERE
Lewis, Jason
NEXT STOP, WONDERLAND
RINGMASTER
Lewis, Jenifer
MIGHTY, THE
Lewis, Jenny
LITTLE BOY BLUE
PLEASANTVILLE
Lewis, Juliette
FULL TILT BOOGIE
Lewis, Marc Allen
PLAYING BY HEART
Lewis, Mark
EVER AFTER
PLAYING BY HEART
Lewis, Peekoo A.
NAKED ACTS
Lewis, Rachel
STEPHEN KING'S THE NIGHT FLIER
Lewis, Robert
DISTURBING BEHAVIOR
MISBEGOTTEN
MY VERY BEST FRIEND
Lewis, Roy
TERMINAL JUSTICE
Lewis, Tyrone
BELLY
Lewis, Vicki
GODZILLA
Lewis, Wilbur
ONE TRUE THING
Lexsee, Richard
U.S. MARSHALS
Leyner, Mark
LOU REED: ROCK AND ROLL HEART
Lezsak, Levente
REDLINE
Li Chi Leih
KICK BOXER'S TEARS
Li, Donald
U.S. MARSHALS
Li Geng
FROZEN
Li Hai-sheng
PRODIGAL SON, THE
Li, Jet
BODYGUARD FROM BEIJING
LETHAL WEAPON 4
SHAOLIN TEMPLE, THE
Li, Katherine
COMRADES, ALMOST A LOVE STORY
Li Meng
EMPEROR'S SHADOW, THE
Libby
PLAN B
Libertini, Richard
BRIGHT SHINING LIE, A
Libman, Andrea
NEW ADVENTURES OF KIMBA THE WHITE LION, THE
Libman, Daniel
EBENEZER
Librizzi, Rosa
KNOCK OFF
Licato, Frank
WHATEVER
Lichtenstein, Mitchell
RATCHET
Lieff, Judith
FEAR AND LOATHING IN LAS VEGAS
Lien, Jennifer
AMERICAN HISTORY X
Lierop, Toy Van
HOLY MAN
Liesa, Cesar
KNOCK OFF
Lifschutz, Richard
PI
PRICE ABOVE RUBIES, A
Lifton, Robert Jay
HEALING BY KILLING
Light, Judith
PAUL MONETTE: THE BRINK OF SUMMER'S END
Lightning, Cody
SMOKE SIGNALS
Lightstone, Marilyn
RESCUERS: STORIES OF COURAGE—TWO COUPLES
Lillard, Matthew
SENSELESS
TARANTELLA
WITHOUT LIMITS
Lillesoe, Britta
KINGDOM, PART 2, THE
Lilly, Kabriel
54

Lilo, Gordon
SIX DAYS, SEVEN NIGHTS
Lilo, Mervyn
SIX DAYS, SEVEN NIGHTS
Lima, Danny
BIG HIT, THE
Limas, Jim Adhi
CHAMBERMAID ON THE TITANIC, THE
Lin, Jennifer
PARENT TRAP, THE
Lin, Lucy
RUSH HOUR
WATCHERS REBORN
Lin, Rex
RUSH HOUR
Lin, Yan
RUSH HOUR
Linard, Steven
LOVE IS THE DEVIL: STUDY FOR A PORTRAIT OF FRANCIS BACON
Lincoln, Scott
LAST ASSASSINS
Lindberg, Chad
CITY OF ANGELS
MERCURY RISING
Lindberg, Joshua
TARZAN AND THE LOST CITY
Lindbjerg, Lalainia
ADVENTURES OF MOWGLI
DISTURBING BEHAVIOR
DRAGON BALL Z THE MOVIE: DEAD ZONE
DRAGON BALL Z THE MOVIE: THE TREE OF MIGHT
DRAGON BALL Z THE MOVIE: THE WORLD'S STRONGEST
Linde, Betty
I'LL BE HOME FOR CHRISTMAS
Linden, Andy
LOVE IS THE DEVIL: STUDY FOR A PORTRAIT OF FRANCIS BACON
Linder, Carl Michael
SLAPPY AND THE STINKERS
Linders, Billy
WOO
Lindfors, Viveca
RUN FOR COVER
Lindgren, Axel
ALMOST HEROES
Lindner, Carl Michael
KRIPPENDORF'S TRIBE
Lindon, Vincent
SEVENTH HEAVEN
Lindsay, Elizabeth
NEXT STOP, WONDERLAND
Lindsay, Peter
MR. NICE GUY
Lindsay-Chapman, Mark
BRAM STOKER'S THE MUMMY
Lindsey, Joseph
CAUGHT UP
Lindstrom, Trish
FACE DOWN
Lineback, Richard
HUSH
MEET THE DEEDLES
Lineham, Hardee
BIG HIT, THE
BRAM STOKER'S SHADOWBUILDER
TRACKED
Lineham, Niamh
GENERAL, THE
Linehan, Rosaleen
BUTCHER BOY, THE
HI-LO COUNTRY, THE
Liner, Joanna
PLAN B
Ling
54
Ling, Bai
SOMEWHERE IN THE CITY
Link, Robin
LETHAL WEAPON 4
Linkletter, Art
OFF THE MENU: THE LAST DAYS OF CHASEN'S
Linn, Rex
HORTON FOOTE'S ALONE
NEIL SIMON'S THE ODD COUPLE II
Linnestad, Eli Anne
JUNK MAIL
Linney, Laura
TRUMAN SHOW, THE
Linville, Larry
FATAL PURSUIT
Liotard, Therese
DISENCHANTED, THE
Liotta, Ray
PHOENIX
RAT PACK, THE
Lipman, David
IMPOSTORS, THE
Lipnicki, Jonathan
DR. DOLITTLE
Lippin, Renee
CELEBRITY
Lipson, Brian
INNOCENT SLEEP, THE
Lipton, Sam
BOYS IN LOVE 2
Lira, Soia
CENTRAL STATION
LisaRaye
PLAYERS CLUB, THE
Lisco, Gaetano
TARANTELLA
Lisi, Joe
HAPPINESS
Liska, Stephen
LETHAL WEAPON 4
Lister, Tiny
BODY COUNT
I GOT THE HOOK UP
PLAYERS CLUB, THE
Lite, MC
BURN HOLLYWOOD BURN
Lithgow, John
CIVIL ACTION, A
HOMEGROWN
JOHNNY SKIDMARKS
Litmus Green
DECLINE OF WESTERN CIVILIZATION PART III, THE
Little, Brandan
NAPOLEON
Little, Rebecca
SKIN & BONE
Little Richard
CHAIRMAN OF THE BOARD
WHY DO FOOLS FALL IN LOVE?
Little, Sydney
REAL HOWARD SPITZ, THE
Little Tommy the Queer
DECLINE OF WESTERN CIVILIZATION PART III, THE
Littman, Robert
BURN HOLLYWOOD BURN
RUSH HOUR
Littrigio, Frank
CHARLIE HOBOKEN
Litz, Nadia
MIGHTY, THE
Liu, Alice
STEPMOM
SUE
Liu, Carolyn
RETURN TO SAVAGE BEACH
Liu, Gordon
KILLER ANGELS
Liu Huai Liang
SHAOLIN TEMPLE, THE
Liu Jie
FROZEN
Liu, Mathew Stephen "Matty"
IN GOD'S HANDS
Liufau, Sidney
BLADE
Lively, Andrea
HOLY MAN
Lively, Ernie
SENSELESS
Livingston, Barry
INVISIBLE MOM
STEEL SHARKS
Livingston, Bill
JANE AUSTEN'S MAFIA!
Livingston, Jennie
LAVENDER LIMELIGHT: LESBIANS IN FILM
Livingston, Paul
BABE: PIG IN THE CITY
DARK CITY
LL Cool J
CAUGHT UP
HALLOWEEN H20: TWENTY YEARS LATER
WOO
Lloyd, Christopher
QUICKSILVER HIGHWAY
REAL BLONDE, THE
Lloyd, Emily
BOOGIE BOY
REAL THING, THE
Lloyd, Eric
BRAVE LITTLE TOASTER GOES TO MARS, THE
MY GIANT
Lloyd, Frank
CHILDREN OF THE CORN V: FIELD OF TERROR
Lloyd, May
VIOLET'S VISIT
Lo Hung
CHINESE BOX, THE
Lo, Ken
KICK BOXER'S TEARS
Lo Lieh
DRAGONS FOREVER
Lo, Lowell
MAGNIFICENT WARRIORS
Lo Mang
MAGNIFICENT WARRIORS
Lo, Ming
DR. DOLITTLE
Loane, Tim
INFORMANT, THE
LoBianco, Tony
JANE AUSTEN'S MAFIA!
Locane, Amy
BRAM STOKER'S THE MUMMY
EBENEZER
LOVE TO KILL
Lochner, Hayley
RESCUERS: STORIES OF COURAGE—TWO COUPLES
Lock, Kate
LAND GIRLS, THE
Locke, Dexter
SCARRED CITY
Locke, Kourtney
I GOT THE HOOK UP
Locke, Philip
WILDE
Lockhart, June
LOST IN SPACE

Lockwood, Robert Jr.
CAN'T YOU HEAR THE WIND HOWL?: THE LIFE AND MUSIC OF ROBERT JOHNSON
Lockwood, Vera
JANE AUSTEN'S MAFIA!
Lockyer, Thomas
INCOGNITO
MERLIN
Loder, Anne Marie
BLACK LIGHT
Loder, Kurt
BELLY
Lodwick, Phil
LOVE TO KILL
Loeb, Lisa
RUGRATS MOVIE, THE
Loeillet, Sylvie
SEVENTH HEAVEN
Loevy, Karen
DEJA VU
Loewen, Jocelyn
EBENEZER
Loewi, Fiona
LOVE AND DEATH ON LONG ISLAND
Loffredo, Phillip
HEROES SHED NO TEARS
Lofgren, Angelica
CHINESE BOX, THE
Loftin, Lennie
NIGHTWATCH
Logan, Laurie V.
POLISH WEDDING
Logan, Patrick
JACK HIGGINS' ON DANGEROUS GROUND
Logan, Paul
RETURN TO SAVAGE BEACH
Logan, Phyllis
SHOOTING FISH
Loggia, Kristina
DESTINY OF MARTY FINE, THE
Loggia, Robert
HOLY MAN
PROPOSITION, THE
WIDE AWAKE
Loggins, Ben E.
NIGHT VISION
Logue, Donal
BLADE
BRIGHT SHINING LIE, A
FIRST LOVE, LAST RITES
THIN RED LINE, THE
Logue, Karina
DECEIVER
Lohan, Lindsay
PARENT TRAP, THE
Lohan, Michael
PARENT TRAP, THE
Lohman, Alison
KRAA! THE SEA MONSTER
Lohman, Lenore
DANGEROUS BEAUTY
Lohmeyer, Peter
KILLER CONDOM, THE
Loiret, Florence
SEVENTH HEAVEN
Lojodice, Giuliana
LIFE IS BEAUTIFUL
Lomax, David
SUBSTITUTE 2: SCHOOL'S OUT, THE
Lombard, Michael
ROUNDERS
Lombardi, Louis
SUICIDE KINGS
Lombardo, Alex
PRINCE, THE
Lombardozzi, Domenick
54
Lomena, June
WHAT DREAMS MAY COME
London, Daniel
PATCH ADAMS
London, Lisa
GODSON, THE
London, Rob
STEPMOM
Loneker, Keith
OUT OF SIGHT
Long, Blake
HANDS ON A HARDBODY
Long, Howie
FIRESTORM
Long, Hudson Lee
LOLITA
Long, Ivan
WALKING THUNDER
Long, Jesse H.
GODS AND MONSTERS
Long, Joanne
LET'S KILL ALL THE LAWYERS
Long, Jodi
CELEBRITY
MURDER IN MIND
Long, Martha
HOPE FLOATS
Long, Mary
IN HIS FATHER'S SHOES
Long, Matthew
FROM A FAR COUNTRY
Long, Nia
HAV PLENTY
Long, Valerie
ALARMIST, THE
Longley, Janine
54
Longo, Tony
LIVING IN PERIL
Longridge, Ronald
SAVING PRIVATE RYAN
Longserre, Linda
CON, THE
Lonow, Mark
WEDDING SINGER, THE
Lonsdale, Michael
RONIN
Look, Lydia
RUSH HOUR
Lookinland, Joseph Kelly
WALKING THUNDER
Looping Group, The
BABE: PIG IN THE CITY
Lopez, A.J.
TARANTELLA
Lopez, Eduardo
MASK OF ZORRO, THE
Lopez, Fani
OBJECT OF MY AFFECTION, THE
Lopez, Iguandili
MEN WITH GUNS
Lopez, Irene Olga
BIG LEBOWSKI, THE
CLOCKWATCHERS
NEIL SIMON'S THE ODD COUPLE II
Lopez, Jennifer
ANTZ
OUT OF SIGHT
Lopez, Mercy
THERE'S SOMETHING ABOUT MARY
Lopez, Rosa Amelia
CARLA'S SONG
Lopez, Seidy
RUNNING WOMAN, THE
Lopez, Sergi
WESTERN
Lora, Gonzalo
MASK OF ZORRO, THE
Lord, Justin
DOWN IN THE DELTA
Lorde, Audre
STOLEN MOMENTS
Lordon, John
NEGOTIATOR, THE
Lords, Traci
BLADE
BOOGIE BOY
STIR
Lorea, Tony
INVISIBLE DAD
Loree, Brad
DOUBLE EDGE
WHEN DANGER FOLLOWS YOU HOME
Loren, Eric
SAVING PRIVATE RYAN
Lorenzetti, Fulvia
DANGEROUS BEAUTY
Lorge, Dana
OBJECT OF MY AFFECTION, THE
Lorinz, James
LAST BIG THING, THE
Lorio, Angela
SLAYERS: THE MOTION PICTURE
Lothar, Susanne
FUNNY GAMES
Lott, Eddie
ANOTHER DAY IN PARADISE
Lott, Robert
TWO FOR TEXAS
Lotti, Sahara
LOVER GIRL
Lough, Catherine
SNOWBOUND
Loughlin, Terry
BODY COUNT
Loughran, Jonathan
WATERBOY, THE
Louis, Kevin
WOO
Louis-Dreyfus, Julia
BUG'S LIFE, A
Louise, Tina
WELCOME TO WOOP WOOP
Lounibos, Tim
PRINCE, THE
STEEL SHARKS
Lounici, Marie
WESTERN
Loup, Jean
BROADWAY DAMAGE
Loustau, Kate
ELIZABETH
Love, Courtney
KURT AND COURTNEY
OFF THE MENU: THE LAST DAYS OF CHASEN'S
Love, Darlene
LETHAL WEAPON 4
Love, Faizon
PLAYERS CLUB, THE
Love, Mary
NEWTON BOYS, THE
Love, Victor
GUN, A CAR, AND A BLONDE, A
Lovejoy, Deirdre
SOUR GRAPES
Lovell, Jacqueline
LOLIDA 2000
Lover, Ed
RIDE
Loverin, John
REAL HOWARD SPITZ, THE

Lovett, Aubrey
TARZAN AND THE LOST CITY
Lovett, Lyle
BREAST MEN
FEAR AND LOATHING IN LAS VEGAS
OPPOSITE OF SEX, THE
Lovett, Marjorie
APT PUPIL
PSYCHO
Lovick, Chris
RIGHT CONNECTIONS, THE
Lovitz, Jon
HAPPINESS
WEDDING SINGER, THE
Low, Victor
CHARACTER
Lowe, David
MAN IN THE IRON MASK, THE
Lowe, Gary
PALMETTO
Lowe, Kevin
RUSH HOUR
Lowe, Louhan
INTERLOCKED: THRILLED TO DEATH
Lowe, Rob
HOSTILE INTENT
JACK HIGGINS' ON DANGEROUS GROUND
JACK HIGGINS' MIDNIGHT MAN
LIVING IN PERIL
Lowe, Robert
MR. NICE GUY
Lowe, Susan
PECKER
Lower, Geoffrey
JOHNNY SKIDMARKS
Lowery, David
RIVER RED
Lowery, Ryan
DECAMPITATED
Lowy, Scott
REAL THING, THE
Loyola
EL CHE: INVESTIGATING A LEGEND
Loza, Richard
CARLA'S SONG
Lozano, Domenique
PATCH ADAMS
Lozano, Ramon
CARLA'S SONG
LTJ Bukem
MODULATIONS: CINEMA FOR THE EAR
Lubaszenko, Edward
FROM A FAR COUNTRY
Lucai, Victoria
FULL TILT BOOGIE
Lucas, David
RED HAWK: WEAPON OF DEATH
Lucas, Ivan
ERNEST IN THE ARMY
Lucas, Michael Shawn
BROADWAY DAMAGE
Lucas, Sarah
LOVE IS THE DEVIL: STUDY FOR A PORTRAIT OF FRANCIS BACON
Lucci, Ralph J.
U.S. MARSHALS
Lucenti, Pat
LENA'S DREAMS
Lucero, Neva
JOHN CARPENTER'S VAMPIRES
Lucia, Emma
CHINESE BOX, THE
Lucidi, Francesca
DANGEROUS BEAUTY
Lucieer, Rudolf
DRESS, THE
Lucre, Andrew
LEADING MAN, THE
Lucus, Joseph
TRUMAN SHOW, THE
Lucy
HANGING GARDEN, THE
YOU'VE GOT MAIL
Ludwig, Bon
LOU REED: ROCK AND ROLL HEART
Ludwig, Ken
MOON OVER BROADWAY
Ludwig, Louis
RIVER RED
Ludwig, Salem
OBJECT OF MY AFFECTION, THE
Luedecke, Mary Ann
DANCER, TEXAS POP. 81
Luetgert, Bailey
BILLBOARD DAD
Luft, Lorna
54
MY GIANT
Lujan, Robert
MEN
Luk, Irene
KNOCK OFF
Lukata, Fofo
DON KING: ONLY IN AMERICA
Luke, Tau
UGLY, THE
Lum, Benjamin
OUTSIDE OZONA
Lumbly, Carl
HOW STELLA GOT HER GROOVE BACK
Lumley, Joanna
PRINCE VALIANT
Lumsden, Richard
AVENGERS, THE
Lund, Joel
BOYS IN LOVE 2
Lund, Julie
MEET JOE BLACK
Lund, Rolf Arly
JUNK MAIL
Lunde, Guil
SLAYERS: THE MOTION PICTURE
Lunderskov, Lasse
CELEBRATION, THE
Lundgren, Dolph
BLACKJACK
PEACEKEEPER, THE
Lunghi, Cheri
BURN HOLLYWOOD BURN
Lunny, Donal
BRYLCREEM BOYS, THE
Lunoe, Lars
KINGDOM, PART 2, THE
Lunt, Fred
SIX DAYS, SEVEN NIGHTS
Luotto, Andy
TRUCE, THE
Luppi, Federico
MEN WITH GUNS
Lusby, Scott
GODZILLA
Lushing, Michael
SIX DAYS, SEVEN NIGHTS
Lussier, Matthew
WATERBOY, THE
Lustig, Aaron
MURDER IN MIND
Lustig, Jason
UNCLE SAM
Lutes, Eric
BRAM STOKER'S THE MUMMY
Lutz, Mark
FACE DOWN
Lutz, Mike
FACULTY, THE
Luv, Freez
PENTAGON WARS, THE
Luyben, Kate
MISBEGOTTEN
Lydon, Gary
INFORMANT, THE
Lyles, A.C.
OFF THE MENU: THE LAST DAYS OF CHASEN'S
Lyles, Leslie
LAST DAYS OF DISCO, THE
Lyman, Will
PERFECT MURDER, A
SIEGE, THE
Lynch, Aubrey
NEXT STEP, THE
Lynch, Cynthia
SOULER OPPOSITE, THE
Lynch, George
AIR BUD: GOLDEN RECEIVER
Lynch, Jack
SUMMER FLING
Lynch, Jalil
SCARRED CITY
SUBSTITUTE 2: SCHOOL'S OUT, THE
Lynch, John
SLIDING DOORS
Lynch, John Carroll
MERCURY RISING
Lynch, Kelly
HOMEGROWN
Lynch, Michael A.
MAJOR LEAGUE: BACK TO THE MINORS
Lynch, Susan
WAKING NED DEVINE
Lyndon, Simon
THIN RED LINE, THE
Lynley, Carol
OFF THE MENU: THE LAST DAYS OF CHASEN'S
Lynn, Amanda
HOLY MAN
Lynn, Debra K.
CRACKING UP
Lynn, Meredith Scott
BILLY'S HOLLYWOOD SCREEN KISS
I LOVE YOU, DON'T TOUCH ME!
NIGHT AT THE ROXBURY, A
Lynn, Sherry
KIKI'S DELIVERY SERVICE
Lynne, Randi
SNOWBOUND
Lynskey, Melanie
EVER AFTER
Lynskey, Michael
LITTLE VOICE
Lyonne, Natasha
KRIPPENDORF'S TRIBE
SLUMS OF BEVERLY HILLS
Lyons, Antonio David
AMERICAN HISTORY X
SUBSTITUTE 2: SCHOOL'S OUT, THE
Lyons, Jennifer
CAN'T HARDLY WAIT
Lyons, John
BLUES BROTHERS 2000
Lyons, Paula
NEXT STOP, WONDERLAND
Lypeckyj, Christina Romana
POLISH WEDDING
Lysenko, Stefan
JANE AUSTEN'S MAFIA!
Ma, Raymond
LETHAL WEAPON 4
Ma Xiaoqing
FROZEN

Ma Ying Chun
HEROES SHED NO TEARS
Maaxena, Wendy
NAPOLEON
Mabe, Ricky
LOUISA MAY ALCOTT'S LITTLE MEN
Mabius, Eric
LAWN DOGS
Mac, Bernie
DON KING: ONLY IN AMERICA
PLAYERS CLUB, THE
MacArthur, Erik
PLEASANTVILLE
Macaulay, Marc
CATHERINE'S GROVE
GREAT EXPECTATIONS
HOLY MAN
PALMETTO
WILD THINGS
MacAvery, Tristan
SLAYERS: THE MOTION PICTURE
MacCabe, Christopher
SNAKE EYES
MacCallum, Heather Lee
EBENEZER
Macchio, Ralph
SECRET OF NIMH 2: TIMMY TO THE RESCUE, THE
Maccione, Aldo
CHAMBERMAID ON THE TITANIC, THE
MacClure, Frederick
MR. NICE GUY
MacColl, Catriona
BEYOND, THE
MacCormac, Raymond
WAKING NED DEVINE
MacDonald, Art
HOT BLOODED
MacDonald, Barry
AIR BUD: GOLDEN RECEIVER
MacDonald, Douglas "Rocky"
MR. NICE GUY
MacDonald, George
MONUMENT AVE.
MacDonald, Gordon
THIN RED LINE, THE
MacDonald, Heather Lyn
LAVENDER LIMELIGHT: LESBIANS IN FILM
MacDonald, James
MERCURY RISING
SOUR GRAPES
MacDonald, Jock
SLUMS OF BEVERLY HILLS
Macdonald, Kelly
COUSIN BETTE
ELIZABETH
MacDonald, Michael James
CASPER MEETS WENDY
Macdonald, Norm
DIRTY WORK
DR. DOLITTLE
MacDonald, Scott
RAT'S TALE, A
MacDonald, William
SIN AND REDEMPTION
MacDowell, Andie
SHADRACH
Macelaru, Andreea
SECRET KINGDOM, THE
SHRUNKEN CITY, THE
Macero, Teo
MODULATIONS: CINEMA FOR THE EAR
MacFadyen, Angus
BRYLCREEM BOYS, THE
NEVADA
RAT PACK, THE
STILL BREATHING
Machado, Mario
BURN HOLLYWOOD BURN
Macht, Gabriel
OBJECT OF MY AFFECTION, THE
Macht, Stephen
WATCHERS REBORN
Maciejewski, Michael
BUFFALO '66
MacIntosh, Laird
SAVING PRIVATE RYAN
MacIntyre, Gandhi
BABE: PIG IN THE CITY
MacIsaac, Ashley
HANGING GARDEN, THE
Mack, Sam
AIR BUD: GOLDEN RECEIVER
Mackay, Alisa
UNDER HEAVEN
Mackay, Gary
UGLY, THE
MacKay, John
NIAGARA NIAGARA
RATCHET
MacKay, Lizabeth
ONE TRUE THING
Mackay, Mathew
LOUISA MAY ALCOTT'S LITTLE MEN
MacKay, Michael Reid
APT PUPIL
MacKechnie, Keith
DOGWATCH
MacKenzie, Donald
LITTLE GHOST
MacKenzie, J.C.
HE GOT GAME
PENTAGON WARS, THE
Mackenzie, Nina
KNOCK OFF
Mackenzie, Peter
MAJOR LEAGUE: BACK TO THE MINORS
MacKenzie, Phillip
BLACKJACK
Mackenzie, Piers
PATCH ADAMS
Mackenzie, Sean
GO NOW
Mackichan, Doon
BORROWERS, THE
Mackie, Allison
GIA
SOULER OPPOSITE, THE
Mackie, David
HERCULES AND XENA THE ANIMATED MOVIE: THE BATTLE FOR MOUNT OLYMPUS
MacKinnon, Scott
BREAKOUT
Mackintosh, Martha
LAND GIRLS, THE
Mackintosh, Steven
LAND GIRLS, THE
Mackriel, Peter
LES MISERABLES
MacLachlan, Kyle
JACK HIGGINS' THUNDER POINT
JACK HIGGINS' THE WINDSOR PROTOCOL
MacLaren, Alyson
AIR BUD: GOLDEN RECEIVER
MacLaren, John
WHEN DANGER FOLLOWS YOU HOME
MacLean, Ali
CAN'T HARDLY WAIT
MacMicol, Peter
SECRET OF NIMH 2: TIMMY TO THE RESCUE, THE
MacMillan, Daniel
REAL HOWARD SPITZ, THE
MacNamara, Oengus
JACK HIGGINS' MIDNIGHT MAN
Macnee, Patrick
AVENGERS, THE
MacNeill, Peter
HANGING GARDEN, THE
SIMON BIRCH
Macneille, Tress
RUGRATS MOVIE, THE
Macoby, Jacob
SHOOTING FISH
Macopson, Dwayne
PENTAGON WARS, THE
MacPherson, Walt
MONTANA
MacVittie, Bruce
54
HI-LIFE
Macy, William H.
CIVIL ACTION, A
CON, THE
HIT ME
PLEASANTVILLE
PSYCHO
SECRET OF NIMH 2: TIMMY TO THE RESCUE, THE
Maddalena, Julie
RUSTY: THE GREAT RESCUE
Maddox, Rose
HI-LO COUNTRY, THE
Madigan, Amy
BRIGHT SHINING LIE, A
Madigan, Anthony
BRYLCREEM BOYS, THE
Madjibounou, Aiani
MARIUS AND JEANNETTE
Madonna
OFF THE MENU: THE LAST DAYS OF CHASEN'S
Madrid, Carmen
MEN WITH GUNS
Madrid, Rob
BLACK THUNDER
Madrid, Salvador
CHAMBERMAID ON THE TITANIC, THE
Madrid, Stephen
TWO FOR TEXAS
Madruga, Teresa
PEREIRA DECLARES
Madsen, Michael
CATHERINE'S GROVE
DIARY OF A SERIAL KILLER
LOVE TO KILL
MAKER, THE
SPECIES II
Madsen, Virginia
SUICIDE KINGS
Mae-Anne Lao, Kristyn
PI
Maehara, Kazuki
THIN RED LINE, THE
Maelen, Christian
I THINK I DO
WOO
Maffi, Joe
INVADER, THE
Maffia, Robert
BULLET ON A WIRE
Maffia, Roma
DEFENDERS: PAYBACK, THE
Mafham, Dominic
SHOOTING FISH
Magdalena, Deborah
HOLY MAN
Mage, Francis
DISENCHANTED, THE
Magers, Paul
SIMPLE PLAN, A

Maggart, Michael
RUSHMORE
Maggenti, Maria
LAVENDER LIMELIGHT: LESBIANS IN FILM
Magnan, Philippe
SEVENTH HEAVEN
Magnuson, Ann
SMALL SOLDIERS
STILL BREATHING
Magnusson, Magnus
LOVE AND DEATH ON LONG ISLAND
Maguire, Anna
EVER AFTER
SAVING PRIVATE RYAN
Maguire, Conor
MY BROTHER'S WAR
SPACEJACKED
Maguire, Michael
LOVELIFE
Maguire, Oliver
SUMMER FLING
Maguire, Tobey
FEAR AND LOATHING IN LAS VEGAS
PLEASANTVILLE
Mah, Johnny
SPREE, THE
Mahal, Taj
OUTSIDE OZONA
Mahan, Kerrigan
DR. DOLITTLE
Mahaney, Matthew
WHEN TIME EXPIRES
Maher, Bill
PRIMARY COLORS
Maher, Cherifa
DESTINY
Maher, Eddie
ROYAL WARRIORS
Mahmoud, Abdallah
DESTINY
Mahmud-Bey, Sheik
BREAK, THE
Mahon, John
ARMAGEDDON
Mahoney, John
ANTZ
Mahoney, Louis
SHOOTING FISH
Mahoney, Pat
3 NINJAS: HIGH NOON AT MEGA MOUNTAIN
Mahoney, Summer
LAST BREATH
Maibock, Gertraud
INHERITORS, THE
Maillard, Carol Lynn
BELOVED
Mainprize, Jesse
FACE DOWN
Mainz, Steven
NEGOTIATOR, THE
Maisle, Kathryn
YOU'VE GOT MAIL
Maisonett, Robert
DAY AT THE BEACH
Maitland, James
MURDER IN MIND
Maizler, Roxie
OBJECT OF MY AFFECTION, THE
Major, Mary
NEGOTIATOR, THE
Makaj, Steve
MY VERY BEST FRIEND
Makin, Nigel
LOVE AND DEATH ON LONG ISLAND
Makinde, Adetoro
DON KING: ONLY IN AMERICA
Makray, Pal
REDLINE
Malahide, Patrick
U.S. MARSHALS
Malanga, Gerard
LOU REED: ROCK AND ROLL HEART
Malau, Lillemor
KILLER CONDOM, THE
Malcolm, Graeme
BREAK, THE
Maldin, Forrest
LEWIS & CLARK & GEORGE
Maldonado, Miguel
OBJECT OF MY AFFECTION, THE
Maldonado, Nicole
SIX DAYS, SEVEN NIGHTS
Maldonado, Norma
GUN, A CAR, AND A BLONDE, A
Maleki, Chris
GODZILLA
Malesh, Darko
LOLIDA 2000
Malet, Arthur
SECRET OF NIMH 2: TIMMY TO THE RESCUE, THE
Malgras, Frederic
MARIE BAIE DES ANGES
Malherbe, Annet
DRESS, THE
Mali, Taylor
SLAMNATION
Malick, Wendie
NORTH SHORE FISH
Malicki-Sanchez, Keram
AMERICAN HISTORY X
Malina, Joshua
BULWORTH
CLOCKWATCHERS
Malinger, Ashley
NAPOLEON
Malinger, Ross
CLUB VAMPIRE
Malinger, Tyler
VERY BAD THINGS
Malipiero, Anna Maria
DANGEROUS BEAUTY
Malkovich, John
MAN IN THE IRON MASK, THE
OGRE, THE
ROUNDERS
Mall, Ian
MR. NICE GUY
Malle, Louis
WHO IS HENRY JAGLOM?
Mallett, A.J.
STILL BREATHING
Mallon, Brian
INFORMANT, THE
Malloy, Matt
ALARMIST, THE
ARMAGEDDON
HAPPINESS
IMPOSTORS, THE
PLAYING BY HEART
Malm, Mona
JERUSALEM
Malone, Bonz
SLAM
Malone, Jena
STEPMOM
Malone, Katherine
APT PUPIL
Malone, Patrick Y.
TWILIGHT
Malone, Tom
BLUES BROTHERS 2000
Maloney, Janel
DESPERATE MEASURES
Maloney, Peter
OBJECT OF MY AFFECTION, THE
Malota, Kristina
CITY OF ANGELS
Malota, Lula
SHRUNKEN CITY, THE
Malota, Marina
THIN RED LINE, THE
Malota, Michael
SHRUNKEN CITY, THE
Maltby, Lauren
I'LL BE HOME FOR CHRISTMAS
Mamada, Mizuki
VILLAGE OF DREAMS
Mamana, Liz
STILL BREATHING
Mamet, Tony
SPANISH PRISONER, THE
Mammone, Robert
HEAVEN'S BURNING
Man, Alex
HONG KONG 1941
Man Ching Chan
RUSH HOUR
RUSH HOUR
Manahan, Kent
FALLEN
Manasseri, Michael
WHEN DANGER FOLLOWS YOU HOME
Manbauman, Sanjae
OBJECT OF MY AFFECTION, THE
Mancini, Al
BABE: PIG IN THE CITY
Mancini, Ray
LOVE TO KILL
Mancuso, Nick
INVADER, THE
MISBEGOTTEN
Mancuso, Sam
JACK HIGGINS' ON DANGEROUS GROUND
Mandeberg, Mitchell
POLISH WEDDING
Mandel, Jules
SHRUNKEN CITY, THE
Mandt, Michael
HIJACKING HOLLYWOOD
Mandt, Neil
HIJACKING HOLLYWOOD
Mandvi, Aasif
SIEGE, THE
Mandylor, Louis
JANE AUSTEN'S MAFIA!
Manesh, Marshall
BIG LEBOWSKI, THE
Manetti, Larry
FATAL PURSUIT
SCARRED CITY
Mangani, Christina
MADELINE
Mangione, Carlotta
LIFE IS BEAUTIFUL
Mangrum, Kelli
HANDS ON A HARDBODY
Manhattan, Mike
GINGERBREAD MAN, THE
Manheim, Camryn
CRACKING UP
DAVID SEARCHING
HAPPINESS
MERCURY RISING
WIDE AWAKE
Maniaci, Jim
ARMAGEDDON
Manison, Kelly
SLAYERS: THE MOTION PICTURE
Manji, Rizwan
SUE

Mankuma, Blu
BONE DADDY
CALL TO REMEMBER, A
Mann, Aimee
BIG LEBOWSKI, THE
Mann, Alex Craig
FEAR AND LOATHING IN LAS VEGAS
Mann, Byron
DOUBLE EDGE
Mann, Danny
BABE: PIG IN THE CITY
Mann, Earl
TERMINAL JUSTICE
Mann, Gabriel
HIGH ART
PARALLEL SONS
Mann II, Douglas J.
PALMETTO
Mannel, Larry
RESCUERS: STORIES OF COURAGE—TWO COUPLES
Mannetti, Larry
TOP OF THE WORLD
Manni, Vic
ARMAGEDDON
ENEMY OF THE STATE
Manning, Michael
BELLY
Manning, Sam
ASYLUM
Manojlovic, Miki
ARTEMISIA
Manolin
WHO THE HELL IS JULIETTE?
Manon, Christian
BABE: PIG IN THE CITY
Manoogian, Brian C.
LET'S KILL ALL THE LAWYERS
Mansell, Clint
PI
Mansfield, Trudy Jane
KNOCK OFF
Mansillo, Frank
UNDERTAKER'S WEDDING, THE
Manson, Alan
MONTANA
Mantas, Michael
LAND GIRLS, THE
SAVING PRIVATE RYAN
Mantegna, Joe
CALL TO REMEMBER, A
CELEBRITY
FACE DOWN
RAT PACK, THE
Mantranga, Joe
WHATEVER
Manza, Ralph
GODZILLA
Mapa, Alec
PLAYING BY HEART
Maples, Marla
HAPPINESS
RICHIE RICH'S CHRISTMAS WISH
Mapother, William
WITHOUT LIMITS
Mapp, Desmond
I GOT THE HOOK UP
Mapp, Greg
I GOT THE HOOK UP
Mapp, Jim
DANCE WITH ME
Mara
STILL BREATHING
Mara, Mary
CIVIL ACTION, A
Marangoni, Justin
SIMON BIRCH
Maratier, Christophe
RONIN
Maraval, Julia
RONIN
Maraval, Lou
RONIN
Marc, Christian
EVER AFTER
Marceau, Sophie
FIRELIGHT
Marcel, Victor
DANCE WITH ME
March, Jane
TARZAN AND THE LOST CITY
Marchais, Gilles
WESTERN
Marchett, Jeffrey
OBJECT OF MY AFFECTION, THE
Marchi, Carl
BUFFALO '66
Marcks, Douglas
TREKKIES
Marclay, Christian
MODULATIONS: CINEMA FOR THE EAR
Marcos
PLACE CALLED CHIAPAS, A
Marcovicci, Andrea
WHO IS HENRY JAGLOM?
Marcus, Dominic
ROUNDERS
Marcus, Dr. Eric
HAPPINESS
Marcus, Michael
DIRTY LAUNDRY
Marder, Caryl
POLTERGEIST REPORT: YUYU HAKUSHO
Marder, Jordan
AMERICAN HISTORY X
Mardon, Alexa
HARD CORE LOGO
INVADER, THE
Marecos, Ricardo
OYSTER AND THE WIND, THE
Margitai, Agi
REDLINE
Margolis, Cindy
CHAIRMAN OF THE BOARD
Margolis, Mark
ALMOST PARTNERS
PI
Margolyes, Miriam
BABE: PIG IN THE CITY
Margoyles, Miriam
MULAN
Margulies, David
CELEBRITY
LAST BREATH
Margulies, Julianna
NEWTON BOYS, THE
PRICE ABOVE RUBIES, A
Marhall, Vicki
TIMOTHY LEARY'S DEAD
Mari, Gina
NIGHT AT THE ROXBURY, A
Mari, Suzanne
LEWIS & CLARK & GEORGE
Maria, Nick Santa
HOLY MAN
Mariana, Michele
ZERO EFFECT
Mariarna
JUNK FOOD
Marich, Marietta
RUSHMORE
Marie, Leilani
DON KING: ONLY IN AMERICA
Marie, Lisa
BREAST MEN
Marienthal, Eli
FIRST LOVE, LAST RITES
JACK FROST
SLUMS OF BEVERLY HILLS
Marigliani, Elide
DANGEROUS BEAUTY
Marin, Cheech
PAULIE
Marine, Laura
JACK HIGGINS' MIDNIGHT MAN
Marini, Lou
BLUES BROTHERS 2000
Marino, Dan
HOLY MAN
Marino, Peter
UNDERTAKER'S WEDDING, THE
Mariye, Lily
MIGHTY JOE YOUNG
Mark, Emmanuel
54
Mark, Marco O.
WHO THE HELL IS JULIETTE?
Markel, Heidi Jo
OUTSIDE OZONA
SCARRED CITY
Markfield, Alan
SIMON BIRCH
Markham, Ronald
SHOOTING FISH
Markham, Stuart Lee
KNOCK OFF
Markie, Biz
FREE TIBET
Markinson, Brian
CITY OF ANGELS
PRIMARY COLORS
Markisello, Rose
WRATH OF THE NINJA: THE YOTODEN MOVIE
Markle, Erin
BUFFALO '66
Marko, Monica
AIR BUD: GOLDEN RECEIVER
Markova, Nadine
DIDN'T DO IT FOR LOVE
Marks, Aviva
DEJA VU
Marks, Leo
MEET JOE BLACK
Marks, Shae
RETURN TO SAVAGE BEACH
Markwood, Bob
BOYS WILL BE BOYS
Marlene, Lydia
GINGERBREAD MAN, THE
Marlene, Maria
CENTRAL STATION
Marlin, Shyla
WOO
Marlo, John
ORGAZMO
Marlo, Oliver
HOSTILE WATERS
Marlow, Elgin
OUT OF SIGHT
Marlow, Janet
CELEBRITY
Marlow, Zuzana
DISTURBING BEHAVIOR
Marlowe, Nora
BELOVED
Marnhout, Heidi
PHANTASM: OBLIVION
Marni, Heather
CELEBRITY

Maroney, Kelli
FACE DOWN
Marotte, Carl
MIGHTY, THE
Marquez, Nelson
DANCE WITH ME
Marquez, William
DANCE WITH ME
MASK OF ZORRO, THE
Marr, Sally
LENNY BRUCE: SWEAR TO TELL THE TRUTH
Marren, Chris
TERMINAL JUSTICE
Marren, Chrisopher
SIMON BIRCH
Marrick, David
INCOGNITO
Marrott, John
MURDER IN MIND
Marrow, Mari
DEAD MAN ON CAMPUS
Marsac, Laure
HIT ME
Marsala, Maria Pia
BEYOND, THE
Marsden, Jack
UNDER THE SKIN
Marsden, James
DISTURBING BEHAVIOR
Marsden, Jason
LION KING II: SIMBA'S PRIDE, THE
Marsh, Ali
SAFE MEN
Marsh, Jon
BRIGHT SHINING LIE, A
Marsh, Walter
SIN AND REDEMPTION
SNOWBOUND
Marsh, William
SAVING PRIVATE RYAN
Marshall, Chris
BLUES BROTHERS 2000
Marshall, Clare
OPERATION DELTA FORCE 2
Marshall, E.G.
DEFENDERS: PAYBACK, THE
Marshall, Ian
EL CHE: INVESTIGATING A LEGEND
Marshall, Mona
RED HAWK: WEAPON OF DEATH
Marshall, Nancy
LOVE AND DEATH ON LONG ISLAND
REAL HOWARD SPITZ, THE
Marshall, Paula
GUN, A CAR, AND A BLONDE, A
THURSDAY
Marshall, Peter
LITTLE VOICE
Marshall, Steve
SECRET OF NIMH 2: TIMMY TO THE RESCUE, THE
Martell, Gillian
COUSIN BETTE
Martell, William C.
INVISIBLE MOM
Marten, Isaac B.
HAV PLENTY
Marti, Billy
HOLLYWOOD CONFIDENTIAL
Martin, Alexander
CAN'T HARDLY WAIT
Martin, Andrea
RUGRATS MOVIE, THE
SECRET OF NIMH 2: TIMMY TO THE RESCUE, THE
Martin, Anthony
TWISTED
Martin, Ben
LOVE IS THE DEVIL: STUDY FOR A PORTRAIT OF FRANCIS BACON
Martin, Bev
WRONGFULLY ACCUSED
Martin, Brad
OUT OF SIGHT
Martin, Christian
LOVE IS THE DEVIL: STUDY FOR A PORTRAIT OF FRANCIS BACON
Martin, Dan
RUSH HOUR
Martin, Dick
AIR BUD: GOLDEN RECEIVER
Martin, Duane
FACULTY, THE
WOO
Martin, Elaine
HOT BLOODED
Martin, Gary
FERNGULLY 2: THE MAGICAL RESCUE
Martin, Gilbert
JACK HIGGINS' ON DANGEROUS GROUND
Martin, Helen
I GOT THE HOOK UP
Martin, Lily
DEJA VU
Martin, Michael
SPICE WORLD
Martin, Ralph P.
PENTAGON WARS, THE
Martin, Richard
AIR BUD: GOLDEN RECEIVER
Martin, Rudolf
HIGH ART
RUN FOR COVER
Martin, Sandy
KRIPPENDORF'S TRIBE
Martin, Steve
BABE: PIG IN THE CITY
PRINCE OF EGYPT, THE
SPANISH PRISONER, THE
Martin, Thomas R.
STEEL SHARKS
Martin, Wondosas "Kilo"
BELLY
Martindale, Margo
PRACTICAL MAGIC
TWILIGHT
Martineau, Gord
DIRTY WORK
URBAN LEGEND
Martinez, Adrian
PERFECT MURDER, A
Martinez, Cynthia
SLAYERS: THE MOTION PICTURE
Martinez, Jaime D.
DAVID SEARCHING
Martinez, Joaquin
NEIL SIMON'S THE ODD COUPLE II
Martinez, Lizzie Curry
MEN WITH GUNS
Martinez, Melinda
STILL BREATHING
Martinez, Olivier
CHAMBERMAID ON THE TITANIC, THE
Martinez, Raul
MASK OF ZORRO, THE
Martini, Maximilian
SAVING PRIVATE RYAN
Martling, Jackie "the Jokeman"
COMEDY'S DIRTIEST DOZEN
Marton, Andrew J.
REPLACEMENT KILLERS, THE
Martot, Pierre
SWINDLE, THE
Martson, Christian
SIX DAYS, SEVEN NIGHTS
Martwick, Thomas
DECAMPITATED
Marufova, Ludmila
DEAD WATERS
Marui, Taroo
SLEEPY EYES OF DEATH: FULL CIRCLE KILLING
Marz, Pablo
I GOT THE HOOK UP
Marzello, Vincent
VELVET GOLDMINE
Masak, Ron
WHEN TIME EXPIRES
Mascarino, Perrino
CLOCKMAKER
Mascoli, Cinia
BEST MAN, THE
Mase, Marino
EIGHTEENTH ANGEL, THE
Mashkov, Vladimir
THIEF, THE
Masi, Andrew
CHARLIE HOBOKEN
Masi, Debbie
CHARLIE HOBOKEN
Masi, Rita
CHARLIE HOBOKEN
Masi, Vera
CHARLIE HOBOKEN
Maskell, Neil
NIL BY MOUTH
Mason, Anthony
CELEBRITY
Mason, David
FACE DOWN
Mason, Jessica
MADELINE
Mason, Ken
NEXT STOP, WONDERLAND
Mason, Laurence
PARALLEL SONS
Mason, Luba
DIRTY LAUNDRY
Mason, Margery
LES MISERABLES
Mason, Raymond Matthew
DR. DOLITTLE
Mason, Tom
MY VERY BEST FRIEND
Mason, Willie
CAN'T YOU HEAR THE WIND HOWL?: THE LIFE AND MUSIC OF ROBERT JOHNSON
Masonson, Paul
SWAN PRINCESS III: AND THE MYSTERY OF THE ENCHANTED TREASURE, THE
Massa, Mike
SCARRED CITY
Massar, Mark
HOLY MAN
Masse, Sylvain
SNAKE EYES
Massey, Anna
DEJA VU
Massomi, Hamid
TASTE OF CHERRY
Masson, William Scott
SWEPT FROM THE SEA
Master P
I GOT THE HOOK UP
PLAYERS CLUB, THE
Masters, George
STEPMOM
Masters, George Lee
PATCH ADAMS

McAlear, Nancy
URBAN LEGEND
McArthur, Emily
OPERATION DELTA FORCE 2
McAuliffe, Casey
NEWTON BOYS, THE
McAvoy, James
REGENERATION
McBeath, Tom
FIRESTORM
TRICKS
McBride, Chi
MERCURY RISING
McBride, Ellie
TEKKEN: THE MOTION PICTURE
McBride, Kevin
RUGRATS MOVIE, THE
McBurney, Simon
COUSIN BETTE
OGRE, THE
McCabe, Pat
BUTCHER BOY, THE
McCabe, Ruth
TALK OF ANGELS
McCabe, Vinnie
BUTCHER BOY, THE
McCadden, Wanda
PATCH ADAMS
McCafferty, Frankie
BREAK, THE
McCain, Ben
OUTSIDE OZONA
McCain, Butch
OUTSIDE OZONA
McCain, Frances Lee
PATCH ADAMS
McCambridge, Mercedes
TOUCH OF EVIL: THE DIRECTOR'S CUT
McCann, Mary
CON, THE
SPANISH PRISONER, THE
McCann, Sean
AFFLICTION
DEFENDERS: PAYBACK, THE
SIMON BIRCH
TRACKED
McCarlie, Colin
DEEP RISING
McCarthy, Francis X.
DEEP IMPACT
McCarthy, Jenny
BASEKETBALL
McCarthy, Maggie
FIRELIGHT
MERRY WAR, A
WHAT DREAMS MAY COME
McCarthy, Patrick
CELEBRITY
McCarthy, Thomas J.
FALLEN
McCarthy, Tyson
DARK CITY
McCartney, Stella
LOVE IS THE DEVIL: STUDY FOR A PORTRAIT OF FRANCIS BACON
McCarty, Walter
HE GOT GAME
McCauley, James Michael
RETURN TO PARADISE
McCawley, Keith
RUSHMORE
McCawley, Ronnie
RUSHMORE
McChristy, Matt
SKIN & BONE
McClain, Saundra
ONE TOUGH COP
McClanahan, Rue
RUSTY: THE GREAT RESCUE
McClanahan, Thayer
RUSHMORE
McClarnon, Zahn
LAST ASSASSINS
McClean, Marley
SLUMS OF BEVERLY HILLS
McClelland, David
TALES FROM A PARALLEL UNIVERSE: GIGA SHADOW
McClure, Robert
DEFENDERS: PAYBACK, THE
McClure, Tane
FEAR AND LOATHING IN LAS VEGAS
McClurg, Edie
BUG'S LIFE, A
HOLY MAN
KIKI'S DELIVERY SERVICE
PRINCE, THE
RUGRATS MOVIE, THE
McCluskey, Michelle
BUFFALO '66
McCole, Stephen
RUSHMORE
McColl, Hamish
PARENT TRAP, THE
McCollough, Julie
TOP OF THE WORLD
McComb, Heather
APT PUPIL
McConaughey, Matthew
NEWTON BOYS, THE
McConaughey, Rooster
NEWTON BOYS, THE
McConnachie, Brian
CELEBRITY
McConnel, Bridget
SHAKESPEARE IN LOVE
McConnell, Shawn
DIARY OF A SERIAL KILLER
McCoo, Marilyn
OFF THE MENU: THE LAST DAYS OF CHASEN'S
McCord, Sarah
IMPOSTORS, THE
McCormack, Brian
CELEBRITY
WEST NEW YORK
McCormack, Catherine
DANCING AT LUGHNASA
DANGEROUS BEAUTY
LAND GIRLS, THE
McCormack, Eric
HOLY MAN
McCormack, J. Patrick
ARMAGEDDON
GIRLS IN PRISON
PARENT TRAP, THE
McCormack, Kevin
BRYLCREEM BOYS, THE
McCormack, Mary
ALARMIST, THE
DEEP IMPACT
McCormick, Elizabeth
STEPHEN KING'S THE NIGHT FLIER
McCormick, Shannon
ACT OF WAR
LES MISERABLES
McCouch, Grayson
ARMAGEDDON
McCourt, Lorraine
STRAY BULLET
McCowan, Ronald
HANDS ON A HARDBODY
McCoy, Den
MR. NICE GUY
McCoy, Larry
PLAYERS CLUB, THE
McCrackin, Joe
HOMEGROWN
McCrary, Darius
DON KING: ONLY IN AMERICA
McCrary, Joel
PLAYING BY HEART
McCrory, Helen
DAD SAVAGE
McCullough, Julie
BREAST MEN
McCullough, Lonnie
NEIL SIMON'S THE ODD COUPLE II
McCullough, Suli
BURN HOLLYWOOD BURN
McCune, Richard
MURDER IN MIND
McCurley, David
RUNNING WOMAN, THE
McCurry, Natalie
TWISTED
McDade, Patrick F.
SNAKE EYES
McDaniel, Drucie
FALLEN
McDermott, Carolyn
CRACKING UP
McDermott, Dean
BONE DADDY
McDermott, Tom
SIEGE, THE
McDonald, Alan
LOVE IS THE DEVIL: STUDY FOR A PORTRAIT OF FRANCIS BACON
McDonald, Alexandra
REAL HOWARD SPITZ, THE
McDonald, Audra
OBJECT OF MY AFFECTION, THE
McDonald, Bill
MONUMENT AVE.
McDonald, Bruce
HARD CORE LOGO
McDonald, Chris
FACULTY, THE
McDonald, Christopher
DIRTY WORK
EIGHTEENTH ANGEL, THE
LAWN DOGS
McDonald, Gary
SPANISH PRISONER, THE
McDonald, Gregg
PLAYERS CLUB, THE
McDonald, John
NEGOTIATOR, THE
McDonald, Josh
REAL HOWARD SPITZ, THE
McDonald, Kevin
GODSON, THE
McDonald, Peter
I WENT DOWN
McDonald, Robert
LEADING MAN, THE
McDonald, Robin
LIVING OUT LOUD
McDonald, Rod
WOUNDED
McDonnell, Blue
NEWTON BOYS, THE
McDonnell, Mary
12 ANGRY MEN
McDonnell, Tommy
BLUES BROTHERS 2000
McDonough, Brenna
ENEMY OF THE STATE
McDonough, Matthew
TRUMAN SHOW, THE

McDormand, Frances
JOHNNY SKIDMARKS
MADELINE
TALK OF ANGELS
McDougall, Martin
SAVING PRIVATE RYAN
McDowall, Roddy
BUG'S LIFE, A
McDowell, Larry
TRUMAN SHOW, THE
McDowell, Malcolm
ASYLUM
FATAL PURSUIT
TALES FROM A PARALLEL UNIVERSE: GIGA SHADOW
McElduff, Ellen
LIVING OUT LOUD
NO LOOKING BACK
McElhatton, Michael
I WENT DOWN
McElhenney, Rob
CIVIL ACTION, A
McElhone, Natascha
MRS. DALLOWAY
RONIN
TRUMAN SHOW, THE
McElvaney, Siobhan
BUTCHER BOY, THE
McElwee, Adrian
SIX O'CLOCK NEWS
McElwee, Mariah
SIX O'CLOCK NEWS
McElwee, Ross
SIX O'CLOCK NEWS
WHO IS HENRY JAGLOM?
McEneaney, Aine
BUTCHER BOY, THE
McEnery, John
MERLIN
McEnroe, Annie
MEN
McEvoy, Tom
MY BROTHER'S WAR
McEwan, Hamish
FACE THE EVIL
McEwan, Russell
HALLELUJAH!
McFadden, Gates
STAR TREK: INSURRECTION
McFadden, Madeline
GODZILLA
McFadden, Thom
UNCLE SAM
McFarlane, Anita
SPACEJACKED
McFarlane, Arlin
SNOWBOUND
McFerran, Douglas
SLIDING DOORS
McFerrin, Julia
JOHN CARPENTER'S VAMPIRES
McGann, Joe
BRYLCREEM BOYS, THE
McGarrigan, Andrew
SKIN & BONE
McGee, Diane
GIRLS IN PRISON
McGee, Dr. Jerry
DEAR JESSE
McGee, Gwen
DON KING: ONLY IN AMERICA
MERCURY RISING
McGee, Jack
I LOVE YOU, DON'T TOUCH ME!
STAR KID
McGee, Mark
NEIL SIMON'S THE ODD COUPLE II
McGee, Robin
NIGHT VISION
McGill, Bruce
LAWN DOGS
McGill, Heather
PLEASANTVILLE
McGinley, John C.
PENTAGON WARS, THE
McGinley, Sean
BREAK, THE
BUTCHER BOY, THE
GENERAL, THE
INFORMANT, THE
McGinley, Ted
MAJOR LEAGUE: BACK TO THE MINORS
McGinn, Chris
RIVER RED
McGinn, Jennifer
RETURN OF THE KING, THE
McGinn, Russ
RAGE, THE
McGinnis, Sue
MONUMENT AVE.
McGlaughlin, Brian
THERE'S SOMETHING ABOUT MARY
McGlone, Mike
ONE TOUGH COP
McGlynn, John
LES MISERABLES
McGlynn, Mary Elizabeth
INVISIBLE DAD
McGonagle, Richard
MIGHTY JOE YOUNG
SENSELESS
McGough, Philip
LES MISERABLES
McGovern, Barry
GENERAL, THE
INFORMANT, THE
McGovern, Chris
NO LOOKING BACK
McGowan, Rose
LEWIS & CLARK & GEORGE
PHANTOMS
McGrady, Michael
OPERATION DELTA FORCE 2
THIN RED LINE, THE
McGrane, Erin
DETOUR
McGrath, Debra
REAL BLONDE, THE
McGrath, Doug
CELEBRITY
HAPPINESS
McGrath, Jono
VELVET GOLDMINE
McGrath, Matt
IMPOSTORS, THE
LAST BREATH
McGrath, Pat
BUTCHER BOY, THE
McGraw, Melinda
WRONGFULLY ACCUSED
McGraw, Sarge
HI-LO COUNTRY, THE
McGreal, Oison
MY BROTHER'S WAR
McGregor, Cal
GO NOW
McGregor, Ewan
LITTLE VOICE
NIGHTWATCH
VELVET GOLDMINE
McGregor, Fraser
RESCUERS: STORIES OF COURAGE—TWO WOMEN
McGregor-Stewart, Kate
LIVING OUT LOUD
MAKER, THE
McGruder, Stephen
PALMETTO
McGuire, Bob
RETURN OF THE KING, THE
McGuire, Elly
HOW STELLA GOT HER GROOVE BACK
McGuire, Justin
SIX-STRING SAMURAI
McGuire, Maeve
PERFECT MURDER, A
McHale, James
MY BROTHER'S WAR
McHugh, Bill
YOU'VE GOT MAIL
McHugh, Mouse
MY BROTHER'S WAR
McIlraith, Mark
RUN FOR COVER
McIlvain, Terry
TWO FOR TEXAS
McIlvaine, Mary
OBJECT OF MY AFFECTION, THE
McInerney, Jay
MR. JEALOUSY
McInnes, Donald
LOVE IS THE DEVIL: STUDY FOR A PORTRAIT OF FRANCIS BACON
McIntosh, Neve
LEADING MAN, THE
McIntosh, Yanna
DOWN IN THE DELTA
McIntyre, Bill
LAST BREATH
McIntyre, Dianne
BELOVED
McIntyre, Gerry
BROADWAY DAMAGE
NEXT STEP, THE
McIntyre, Marilyn
VERY BAD THINGS
McIntyre, Roger
GODZILLA
McIntyre, Thom
PATCH ADAMS
McIvor, LaShawn
DANCER, TEXAS POP. 81
McKane, Matthew
LIVING OUT LOUD
McKay, Danny
WALKING THUNDER
McKay, David
LES MISERABLES
McKay, Donald Sage
SWAN PRINCESS III: AND THE MYSTERY OF THE ENCHANTED TREASURE, THE
McKay, Donette
CAPTIVE
McKay, Jill
TWISTED
McKay, Micky
CARLA'S SONG
McKean, Michael
PASS, THE
SMALL SOLDIERS
STILL BREATHING
McKee, Lonette
HE GOT GAME
McKeen, Roger
BRIDE OF CHUCKY
SIMON BIRCH
TRACKED
McKeever, Mikki
PALMETTO
McKellen, Ian
APT PUPIL

GODS AND MONSTERS
SWEPT FROM THE SEA
McKenna, Alex
JOEY
McKenna, Patrick
REAL HOWARD SPITZ, THE
McKenna, Seana
HANGING GARDEN, THE
McKenna, Travis
CASPER MEETS WENDY
3 NINJAS: HIGH NOON AT MEGA MOUNTAIN
McKenna, Virginia
SLIDING DOORS
McKenzie, Matt
GODS AND MONSTERS
NEIL SIMON'S THE ODD COUPLE II
McKenzie, Russell B.
VERY BAD THINGS
McKeon, Doug
COURTING COURTNEY
SUB DOWN
McKeon III, William J.
SNAKE EYES
McKeown, Fintan
WAKING NED DEVINE
McKern, Roger
GO NOW
McKernan, Peter
JOHNNY SKIDMARKS
McKewley, Robert
LOVE AND DEATH ON LONG ISLAND
McKidd, Kevin
LEADING MAN, THE
REGENERATION
McKie, John
NAKED ACTS
McKinley, Mariad
VELVET GOLDMINE
McKinney, Angie Ray
GIRLS IN PRISON
McKinney, Mark
LAST DAYS OF DISCO, THE
NIGHT AT THE ROXBURY, A
SPICE WORLD
McKnight Jr., Esau
BLADE
McKown, Anna K.
CLUB VAMPIRE
McLaglen, Josh
X-FILES, THE
McLaren, John
SAVIOR
McLaughlin, Brian
SIMON BIRCH
McLaughlin, Cliff
DR. DOLITTLE
McLaughlin, Ian
KILLING TIME
McLaughlin, Joe
SUE
McLaughlin, John
BULWORTH
RIVER RED
McLaughlin, Maya
MILO
McLean, Antoine
HURRICANE STREETS
WIDE AWAKE
McLean, Courtney
CAUGHT UP
McLean, Finlay
REGENERATION
McLean, Shawn
SUBSTITUTE 2: SCHOOL'S OUT, THE
McLellan, B.J.
LOUISA MAY ALCOTT'S LITTLE MEN
McLellyn, Taylor
SIN AND REDEMPTION
McLemore, Zachary
CLOCKMAKER
UNCLE SAM
McLeod, Alister
BRYLCREEM BOYS, THE
McLeod, Don
RICHIE RICH'S CHRISTMAS WISH
McLeod, John
PRACTICAL MAGIC
McLeod, Magnus
BRYLCREEM BOYS, THE
McLeod, Shannon
I LOVE YOU, DON'T TOUCH ME!
McLiam, Eanna
GENERAL, THE
McLoughlin, Marian
SPICE WORLD
McLymont, Karen
MR. NICE GUY
McMadden, Joe
DAD SAVAGE
McMahen, Jeff
RETURN TO SAVAGE BEACH
McMahon, Ed
OFF THE MENU: THE LAST DAYS OF CHASEN'S
McMahon, Erin
GO NOW
McManus, Michael
TALES FROM A PARALLEL UNIVERSE: EATING PATTERN
TALES FROM A PARALLEL UNIVERSE: GIGA SHADOW
TALES FROM A PARALLEL UNIVERSE: SUPER NOVA
McMillan, Babs
BABE: PIG IN THE CITY
McMillan, Gary
FACE DOWN
McMillan, Kelli-Lin
HE GOT GAME
McMillan, Richard
BRAM STOKER'S SHADOWBUILDER
RESCUERS: STORIES OF COURAGE—TWO COUPLES
McMullan, Jim
EIGHTEENTH ANGEL, THE
McMullan, Tim
DANGEROUS BEAUTY
McMullen, Tim
SHAKESPEARE IN LOVE
McMurray, R.L.
KRAA! THE SEA MONSTER
McMurray, Sam
SLAPPY AND THE STINKERS
McNabb, Barry
NEXT STEP, THE
McNally Jr., Seamus
HOMEGROWN
McNally, Kevin
SLIDING DOORS
SPICE WORLD
McNally, Michael
MY BROTHER'S WAR
McNally, Seamus
POLISH WEDDING
McNamara, Desmond
SHAKESPEARE IN LOVE
McNamara, Maureen
CELEBRITY
McNamara, Peter
SHOOTING FISH
McNamara, William
BRYLCREEM BOYS, THE
RINGMASTER
McNeil, Eric Keith
BELLY
McNeil, Marguerite
LOVE AND DEATH ON LONG ISLAND
McNeil, Scott
ADVENTURES OF MOWGLI
DRAGON BALL Z THE MOVIE: DEAD ZONE
DRAGON BALL Z THE MOVIE: THE TREE OF MIGHT
DRAGON BALL Z THE MOVIE: THE WORLD'S STRONGEST
NEW ADVENTURES OF KIMBA THE WHITE LION, THE
McNeil, Timothy
DESTINY OF MARTY FINE, THE
McNeille, Tress
KIKI'S DELIVERY SERVICE
McNickle, Jim Taylor
GREAT EXPECTATIONS
MEET JOE BLACK
McNiff, Tim
OVERNIGHT DELIVERY
McNulty, Kevin
CALL TO REMEMBER, A
SNOWBOUND
TRICKS
McParland, Paul
INFORMANT, THE
McPherson, Conor
I WENT DOWN
McPherson, Graham
RESCUERS: STORIES OF COURAGE—TWO COUPLES
McPherson, Selma
HOW STELLA GOT HER GROOVE BACK
McQuade, Arlene
TOUCH OF EVIL: THE DIRECTOR'S CUT
McQuade, Seamus
HOSTILE WATERS
SAVING PRIVATE RYAN
McQueen, B.J.
DIRTY WORK
McRae, Alan
3 NINJAS: HIGH NOON AT MEGA MOUNTAIN
McRobbie, Peter
CELEBRITY
SNAKE EYES
McShane, Michael
BUG'S LIFE, A
McSorley, Gerard
BUTCHER BOY, THE
DANCING AT LUGHNASA
MOONDANCE
McSwain, Monica
CAN'T HARDLY WAIT
McTaggart, Thomas
CARLA'S SONG
McTavish, Patrick
SIMON BIRCH
WEDDING SINGER, THE
McTeer, Janet
VELVET GOLDMINE
McTigue, Tom
SOULER OPPOSITE, THE
McVicar, Dan
ALONE IN THE WOODS
McWhirter, Cath
UGLY, THE
Mdaka, Bismulah
TARZAN AND THE LOST CITY
Meacham, Worthie
PLAYING BY HEART
Meade, Devon
SOULER OPPOSITE, THE
Meadows, Jayne
OFF THE MENU: THE LAST DAYS OF CHASEN'S

Meadows of Eldon, Lord Shane
TWENTYFOURSEVEN
Meadows, Tim
FREE TIBET
Meaney, Colm
MONUMENT AVE.
SUMMER FLING
Meaney, Kevin
PLUMP FICTION
Means, Russell
POCAHONTAS II: JOURNEY TO A NEW WORLD
Meardon, Marilyn Murphy
MONUMENT AVE.
Meas, Zane
TARZAN AND THE LOST CITY
Meat Beat Manifesto
MODULATIONS: CINEMA FOR THE EAR
Meat Loaf
BLACK DOG
MIGHTY, THE
OUTSIDE OZONA
SPICE WORLD
Mechoso, Julio Oscar
INDISCREET
KRIPPENDORF'S TRIBE
Medel, Fernando
MEN WITH GUNS
Medina, Alma Blanco
CARLA'S SONG
Medlock, Ken
MAJOR LEAGUE: BACK TO THE MINORS
Medrano, Frank
DESTINY OF MARTY FINE, THE
ENEMY OF THE STATE
FALLEN
KISSING A FOOL
REPLACEMENT KILLERS, THE
SUICIDE KINGS
Medrano, Joseph
SWAN PRINCESS III: AND THE MYSTERY OF THE ENCHANTED TREASURE, THE
Medwetz, Anthony
CLOCKMAKER
Meehan, Howard
DESPERATE MEASURES
Meehan, Miles
LAWN DOGS
Meeks, Ken
RETURN TO SAVAGE BEACH
Meenen, Leslie C.
CHOSEN ONE: LEGEND OF THE RAVEN, THE
Meer, Alicia
CELEBRITY
Meersbergen, Matthew
MR. NICE GUY
Megahy, Francis
DISAPPEARANCE OF KEVIN JOHNSON, THE
Megill, Sheelah
SIN AND REDEMPTION
Mehler, Tobias
DISTURBING BEHAVIOR
Mehlman, Michael
REDLINE
Mehoudar, Diana
FEAR AND LOATHING IN LAS VEGAS
Mehrens, Timm
KINGDOM, PART 2, THE
Mehta, Ajay
LAST DAYS OF DISCO, THE
Mehta, Simi
PHOENIX
Meier, John
DESPERATE MEASURES
Meindl, Anthony
DAVID SEARCHING
Meinert, Michael
MAKER, THE
Meingast, Martin
MENDEL
Meister, Martin
LOVE IS THE DEVIL: STUDY FOR A PORTRAIT OF FRANCIS BACON
Meistrich, Larry
NIAGARA NIAGARA
Mejia, Kristine
INTERLOCKED: THRILLED TO DEATH
Mekas, Jonas
LOU REED: ROCK AND ROLL HEART
Mekka, Eddie
TOP OF THE WORLD
Meldrum, Jeremy Paul
SENSELESS
Meleca, Marcello
SIMON BIRCH
Melendez, Dorothy
RED HAWK: WEAPON OF DEATH
Melia, Frank
GENERAL, THE
SPACEJACKED
Melinand, Monique
GENEALOGIES OF A CRIME
Melito Jr., Joseph
WIDE AWAKE
Melleney, Victor
OPERATION DELTA FORCE 2
Mello, Heitor Martinez
TIETA OF AGRESTE
Mello, Tamara
OVERNIGHT DELIVERY
Mellor, Christie
YOUR FRIENDS & NEIGHBORS
Mellor, Steve
CELEBRITY
Melnick, Natasha
PARENT TRAP, THE
Meloni, Chirtopher
FEAR AND LOATHING IN LAS VEGAS
Meloni, Christopher
SOULER OPPOSITE, THE
Meltzer, Adrienne
BILLBOARD DAD
Melvill-Smith, Greg
OPERATION DELTA FORCE 2
Melvoin, Susannah
SKIN & BONE
Men of Fire Island
BOYS IN LOVE 2
Menage, Amanda
LOVE IS THE DEVIL: STUDY FOR A PORTRAIT OF FRANCIS BACON
Menage, Chiara
LOVE IS THE DEVIL: STUDY FOR A PORTRAIT OF FRANCIS BACON
Mendes, Helen
HIGH ART
Mendez, Eva
CHILDREN OF THE CORN V: FIELD OF TERROR
NIGHT AT THE ROXBURY, A
Mendicino, Gerry
BIG HIT, THE
DIRTY WORK
Mendillo, Tag
KISSING A FOOL
Mendoza, Mario
BREAK, THE
ROUNDERS
Meneghel, Susanne
FUNNY GAMES
Meneses, Alex
LIVING IN PERIL
Meneses, Jose
CARLA'S SONG
Menezes, Frank
TIETA OF AGRESTE
Menichetti, Jacques
MARIUS AND JEANNETTE
Mennicucci, Joe
CHARLIE HOBOKEN
Mensur, Irfan
SAVIOR
Menville, Scott
KIKI'S DELIVERY SERVICE
Menza, Jim
LAST ASSASSINS
Menzel, Paul
CON, THE
Menzies, Mike
MR. NICE GUY
Mercedes, Ivette
SHAMPOO HORNS
Merchande, Teal
KRAA! THE SEA MONSTER
Mercier, Brianne
PARENT TRAP, THE
Merckx, Ken
ORGAZMO
Mercutio, Paul
WELCOME TO WOOP WOOP
Meredith, Tony
DANCE WITH ME
Mergenthaler, Carl
ENEMY OF THE STATE
Meril, Macha
SOLDIER'S DAUGHTER NEVER CRIES, A
Merkin, Michelle
KID IN ALADDIN'S PALACE, A
Merlin, Joanna
CITY OF ANGELS
Merrick, Steve
LAST ASSASSINS
Merrill, Dina
MIGHTY JOE YOUNG
Merrill, Norman
GIA
Merrison, Clive
PHOTOGRAPHING FAIRIES
Merritt, Therese
HOME FRIES
Mervin, Alexander
TOP OF THE WORLD
Meryl, Angela
HE GOT GAME
Mesa, Cristobal Guzman
MEN WITH GUNS
Mescolini, Franco
LIFE IS BEAUTIFUL
Meshcherkina, Tatiana
TRUCE, THE
Meskin, Amnon
DEJA VU
Messaoud, Amidou Ben
RONIN
Messick, Don
FLINTSTONES: I YABBA-DABBA DOO!, THE
Messina, Chris
ROUNDERS
SIEGE, THE
YOU'VE GOT MAIL
Messinese, Francesca
LIFE IS BEAUTIFUL
Messing, Debra
CELEBRITY
Meston, Paul
PASSION IN THE DESERT
Metcalf, Laurie
ALWAYS OUTNUMBERED
BULWORTH
CHICAGO CAB

Metcalf, Mark
HIJACKING HOLLYWOOD
Metchik, Asher
MILO
Metrano, Art
HOW STELLA GOT HER GROOVE BACK
MURDER IN MIND
Metro, Tracy
SPECIES II
Mettia, Rudy
ARMAGEDDON
Metz, Belinda
RIGHT CONNECTIONS, THE
Metzler, Jim
GUN, A CAR, AND A BLONDE, A
Metznarowski, Richard
FORGOTTEN LIGHT
Metzner, Ralph
TIMOTHY LEARY'S DEAD
Meyer, Billy
THERE'S SOMETHING ABOUT MARY
Meyer, Breckin
CAN'T HARDLY WAIT
DANCER, TEXAS POP. 81
54
Meyer, Daniel
LOVE TO KILL
Meyer, Daryl
HOLY MAN
Meyer, Erik
RAT'S TALE, A
Meyer, Jeffery
KRAA! THE SEA MONSTER
Meyer, Kris
THERE'S SOMETHING ABOUT MARY
Meyer, Russ
STORY OF X, THE
Meyer, Ruth Michelle
THERE'S SOMETHING ABOUT MARY
Meyering Jr., Ralph
GIRLS IN PRISON
Meyers, Rusty
TOP OF THE WORLD
Meyers, William
INVISIBLE DAD
Meyers-Shyer, Annie
PARENT TRAP, THE
Meyers-Shyer, Hallie
PARENT TRAP, THE
Meylan, Gerard
MARIUS AND JEANNETTE
Meylan, Monique
MARIUS AND JEANNETTE
Meyler, Tony
DIRTY WORK
Mg Wing Mei, Christine
RUSH HOUR
Mhuiri, Aine Ni
BRYLCREEM BOYS, THE
MIA
JUNK FOOD
Mian, Peter A.
YOU'VE GOT MAIL
Miano, Robert
SMOKE SIGNALS
Mican, Gabriel
JOHNNY MYSTO BOY WIZARD
MIDAS TOUCH, THE
Miceli, Justine
DANGEROUS BEAUTY
Michael, Devon
LITTLE BOY BLUE
Michael, Larry
DON KING: ONLY IN AMERICA
Michael, Rebecca
LOVE AND DEATH ON LONG ISLAND
Michaels, Al
BASEKETBALL
Michaels, Anthony
RUN FOR COVER
Michaels, Bret
IN GOD'S HANDS
LETTER FROM DEATH ROW, A
Michaels, Corinne
LEWIS & CLARK & GEORGE
Michaels, David
DIARY OF A SERIAL KILLER
Michaels, Delana
LEWIS & CLARK & GEORGE
Michaels, Dylan
STEPMOM
Michaels, Jimmy
JACK FROST
Michaels, Monica
BELLY
Michaels, Shawn
LETHAL WEAPON 4
Michaels, Ted
COURTING COURTNEY
Michaels, Ted Johan
KNOCK OFF
Michaely, Joel
CAN'T HARDLY WAIT
Micheaux, Nicki
MY GIANT
PROPHECY II, THE
REPLACEMENT KILLERS, THE
RINGMASTER
Michel, Fritz
GREAT EXPECTATIONS
Michel, Karen
PATCH ADAMS
Michele, Lea
BUSTER & CHAUNCEY'S SILENT NIGHT
Michele, Michael
SUBSTITUTE 2: SCHOOL'S OUT, THE
Michelle, Diane
RINGMASTER
Michelson, Charis
HIGH ART
I MARRIED A STRANGE PERSON!
Mick, Alice J.
PARALLEL SONS
Mick, Gabriel
GREAT EXPECTATIONS
Middleton, James
DECEIVER
Middleton, Thomas H.
SLAPPY AND THE STINKERS
Middleton, William
LOVE IS THE DEVIL: STUDY FOR A PORTRAIT OF FRANCIS BACON
Midgley, Jonathan
CHINESE BOX, THE
Midler, Randy
BRAVE LITTLE TOASTER GOES TO MARS, THE
Midori, Mako
RAZOR: WHO'S GOT THE GOLD?, THE
Midwood, Ramsay
HOMEGROWN
Miehe-Renard, Tine
KINGDOM, PART 2, THE
MIF
DIRTY WORK
Mignacio, Darlene
FACE DOWN
Miguel, Bruno
54
Miguel, Nigel
AMERICAN HISTORY X
Miguel Young, Ricardo
HUSH
Mihok, Dash
THIN RED LINE, THE
Mikala, Monica
JANE AUSTEN'S MAFIA!
Milano, Alyssa
BODY COUNT
Milavich, Ivana
ENEMY OF THE STATE
Milder, Andy
ARMAGEDDON
Miles, Ben
MERRY WAR, A
Miles, Elaine
SMOKE SIGNALS
Miles, Joanna
HORTON FOOTE'S ALONE
Miles, Marc
LOS LOCOS
Miles, Peter
SAVING PRIVATE RYAN
Miles, Robin
LAST DAYS OF DISCO, THE
Miley, Peggy
NEIL SIMON'S THE ODD COUPLE II
STAR TREK: INSURRECTION
Milford, Penelope
HENRY: PORTRAIT OF A SERIAL KILLER PART 2
Milicevic, Ivana
HOLLYWOOD CONFIDENTIAL
Millan, Victor
TOUCH OF EVIL: THE DIRECTOR'S CUT
Millbern, David
GODS AND MONSTERS
Miller, Andrew
CUBE
Miller, Carolyn C.
DECAMPITATED
Miller, Corey
I GOT THE HOOK UP
Miller, Dave
TWENTYFOURSEVEN
Miller, Dick
SMALL SOLDIERS
Miller, Emily
NEVADA
Miller, Gary
BILLBOARD DAD
Miller, Jeanette
TRUMAN SHOW, THE
Miller, Jeff
ALL THE RAGE
Miller, Joel McKinnon
MAKER, THE
TRUMAN SHOW, THE
Miller, Jonny Lee
REGENERATION
Miller, Josh
THERE'S SOMETHING ABOUT MARY
Miller, Kenny
TOUCH OF EVIL: THE DIRECTOR'S CUT
Miller, Kristin
DOGWATCH
Miller, Larisa
HALLOWEEN H20: TWENTY YEARS LATER
Miller, Larry
CHAIRMAN OF THE BOARD
Miller, Matt
KIKI'S DELIVERY SERVICE
SIEGE, THE
Miller, Max
NEXT STEP, THE
Miller, Michael
KNOCK OFF
Miller, Michael Clair
LIVING OUT LOUD

Miller, Michele M.
DESTINY OF MARTY FINE, THE
Miller, Owen
SWAN PRINCESS III: AND THE MYSTERY OF THE ENCHANTED TREASURE, THE
Miller, Penelope Ann
OUTSIDE OZONA
Miller, Reggie
HE GOT GAME
Miller, Roxanne
LOLIDA 2000
Miller, Rudy
MASK OF ZORRO, THE
Miller, Ruth
ALARMIST, THE
Miller, Sam
NIL BY MOUTH
Miller, Stephen E.
DISTURBING BEHAVIOR
Miller, Tenny
HOW STELLA GOT HER GROOVE BACK
Miller, Tracy
CIVIL ACTION, A
Miller, Tyler
PECKER
Miller, Valerie Rae
DISAPPEARANCE OF KEVIN JOHNSON, THE
HOLLYWOOD CONFIDENTIAL
Miller, Will
ANOTHER DAY IN PARADISE
Milles, Judson
MAJOR LEAGUE: BACK TO THE MINORS
Millet, Lisa
UNDER THE SKIN
Millgate, Gabby
BABE: PIG IN THE CITY
Millman, Gabriel
CELEBRITY
Mills, A.G. Zeke
NEWTON BOYS, THE
Mills, Christian
PLAYING BY HEART
Mills, Eddie
DANCER, TEXAS POP. 81
Mills, Jessica
KISSING A FOOL
Mills, Judson
GODS AND MONSTERS
MIGHTY JOE YOUNG
Mills, Matthew
WILDE
Mills, Merideth
OUTSIDE OZONA
Mills, Mort
TOUCH OF EVIL: THE DIRECTOR'S CUT
Mills, Pete
HARD CORE LOGO
Mills, Stephanie
URBAN LEGEND
Mills, Walter
BLACK LIGHT
Mills, Zeke
HOME FRIES
Milman, Martin
FROM A FAR COUNTRY
Milos, Sofia
JANE AUSTEN'S MAFIA!
Milova, Jaromira
FORGOTTEN LIGHT
Mimica, Marin
DARK CITY
Mina, Mina E.
WRONGFULLY ACCUSED
Minakata, Eiji
SONATINE
Minati, Anna Maria
DANGEROUS BEAUTY
Miner, Rachel
HENRY FOOL
Mingalone, Dick
CELEBRITY
Minifie, Valerie
FIRELIGHT
Minikus, Amanda
DIGGING TO CHINA
Mininni, Lisa
MIGHTY, THE
Mininni, Sara
BREAKOUT
Minjares, Joe
TRUMAN SHOW, THE
Minns, Daniele
LOVE IS THE DEVIL: STUDY FOR A PORTRAIT OF FRANCIS BACON
Minns, Martyn A.
KNOCK OFF
Minns, Peter
LITTLE VOICE
Minor, Bob
DON KING: ONLY IN AMERICA
GINGERBREAD MAN, THE
Minor, Willie
NIGHT VISION
Miona, Sam
THURSDAY
Mirabella, Michele
BEYOND, THE
Miracle, Klara Irene
WALKING THUNDER
Miragliotta, Frederick
DARK CITY
MR. NICE GUY
Miranda, Carlos
VELVET GOLDMINE
Miranda, Robert
BLACK THUNDER
RAT PACK, THE
STEEL SHARKS
Miranda, Tatiana
CARLA'S SONG
Miranda, Telmo
MIGHTY, THE
Mirault, Don
TOP OF THE WORLD
Miriam, Jennifer
NEWTON BOYS, THE
Mirren, Helen
PRINCE OF EGYPT, THE
ROYAL DECEIT
Mirsky, Eytan
HAPPINESS
Miscisco, Irene
CALL TO REMEMBER, A
Mistretta, Sal
STEPMOM
Misura, Nick
I'LL BE HOME FOR CHRISTMAS
URBAN SAFARI
Mita, Elena
DANGEROUS BEAUTY
Mita, Federico
DANGEROUS BEAUTY
Mitchell, Alexandria
FIRESTORM
I'LL BE HOME FOR CHRISTMAS
Mitchell, Ben
MR. NICE GUY
Mitchell, Brian
FLINTSTONES: I YABBA-DABBA DOO!, THE
Mitchell, C.E.
LEWIS & CLARK & GEORGE
Mitchell, Daryl
HOME FRIES
REBOUND: THE LEGEND OF EARL "THE GOAT" MANIGAULT
Mitchell, Elizabeth
GIA
Mitchell, James
LOVE IS THE DEVIL: STUDY FOR A PORTRAIT OF FRANCIS BACON
Mitchell, John Cameron
DAVID SEARCHING
Mitchell, Liam
WIDE AWAKE
Mitchell, Linda
LEWIS & CLARK & GEORGE
Mitchell, Radha
HIGH ART
Mitchell, Richard
RAGE, THE
Mitchell, Silas Weir
QUICKSILVER HIGHWAY
Mitges, Christine
PLAN B
Mitler, Matt
CRACKING UP
Mitra, Rhona
KID IN ALADDIN'S PALACE, A
Mitrani, Richard
SKIN & BONE
Mitsuishi, Ken
THIN RED LINE, THE
WHEN I CLOSE MY EYES
Mitzman Gaven, Marcia
SMALL SOLDIERS
Mixmaster Morris
MODULATIONS: CINEMA FOR THE EAR
Mixon, L. Christian
PHOENIX
Miyauch, Tomomi
ZERO WOMAN
Mizrahi, Issac
CELEBRITY
Mizuhara, Koochi
SLEEPY EYES OF DEATH: FULL CIRCLE KILLING
Mizukami, Ryushi
THIN RED LINE, THE
Mo', Keb'
CAN'T YOU HEAR THE WIND HOWL?: THE LIFE AND MUSIC OF ROBERT JOHNSON
Moakler, Shanna
WEDDING SINGER, THE
Moan, Bjorn
INSOMNIA
Moan, Henny
KRISTIN LAVRANSDATTER
Moati, Henry
RONIN
Moby
MODULATIONS: CINEMA FOR THE EAR
Mocherie, Colin
REAL BLONDE, THE
Modiano, Patrick
GENEALOGIES OF A CRIME
Modine, Matthew
MAKER, THE
REAL BLONDE, THE
Modugno, Enrica Maria
EIGHTEENTH ANGEL, THE
Modungno, Lodovoca
STEAM
Moench, Monica
CLAY PIGEONS
Moffett, Joel
BOYS IN LOVE 2
Moffett, Michelle
BLACKJACK

Moglia, Ronald
DIDN'T DO IT FOR LOVE
Mohamed, Mosleh
SIEGE, THE
Mohammad-Khani, Mina
MIRROR, THE
Mohler, Robert
U.S. MARSHALS
Mohr, Jay
JANE AUSTEN'S MAFIA!
PAULIE
PLAYING BY HEART
SMALL SOLDIERS
SUICIDE KINGS
Moinot, Michel
PERFECT MURDER, A
Moir, Richard
WELCOME TO WOOP WOOP
Mojdehi, Kazem
MIRROR, THE
Mojica, Monica
SMOKE SIGNALS
Mok, Karen
FALLEN ANGELS
Mokae, Zakes
KRIPPENDORF'S TRIBE
Mokone, Tsepo
HAPPINESS
Mol, Gretchen
CELEBRITY
MUSIC FROM ANOTHER ROOM
ROUNDERS
Moldovan, Florin
GADJO DILO
Molina, Alfred
BREAK, THE
IMPOSTORS, THE
RESCUERS: STORIES OF COURAGE—TWO COUPLES
WHEN PIGS FLY
Molina, Angela
LIVE FLESH
Molina, Rolando
PRIMARY COLORS
Molinari, Alberto
STEAM
Molino III, Louis
JACK FROST
Molko, Brian
VELVET GOLDMINE
Moll, Richard
CASPER MEETS WENDY
LET'S KILL ALL THE LAWYERS
LIVING IN PERIL
Mollo, Nick
LAND GIRLS, THE
Moloney, Janel
SOULER OPPOSITE, THE
Moloney, Robert
DISTURBING BEHAVIOR
HUNTED, THE
Moltena, Luis
DANGEROUS BEAUTY
Molvaer, Skjalg
ENEMY
Monaghan, Brian
SPACEJACKED
Monaghan, Dominic
HOSTILE WATERS
Monahan, Dan
STEPHEN KING'S THE NIGHT FLIER
Monast, Fernard
JACK HIGGINS' MIDNIGHT MAN
Monat, Donald
BRAM STOKER'S THE MUMMY
Mone, Johnny
THERE'S SOMETHING ABOUT MARY
Monette, Bob
PAUL MONETTE: THE BRINK OF SUMMER'S END
Monette, Paul
PAUL MONETTE: THE BRINK OF SUMMER'S END
Money Mark
MODULATIONS: CINEMA FOR THE EAR
Monge, Juio
DAVID SEARCHING
Mongo
NIGHTWATCH
Monjo, Justin
DARK CITY
Monk, Damian
BABE: PIG IN THE CITY
Monk, Gregg Joseph
CIVIL ACTION, A
Monks, Darren
MOONDANCE
SUMMER FLING
Monks, Michael
HARD RAIN
LAST LIVES
Monkton, Patrick
BORROWERS, THE
Monreale, Cinzia
BEYOND, THE
Monroe, Betsy
OUT OF SIGHT
Monroe, Bill Langlois
STEEL SHARKS
Monroe, Carlos
DON KING: ONLY IN AMERICA
Monroe Jr., Samuel
PLAYERS CLUB, THE
Monroe, Steve
CAN'T HARDLY WAIT
Montagut, Francois
MAN IN THE IRON MASK, THE
Montaigne, Jeff
TALK TO ME
Montanhas, Noelia
TIETA OF AGRESTE
Montano, Dan
WHATEVER
Monte, Brenda
UNMADE BEDS
Monte, Sal
PI
Montefiori, Luigi
RABID DOGS
Monteiro, Caco
TIETA OF AGRESTE
Montenegro, Fernanda
CENTRAL STATION
Monterrey, Ramon
CARLA'S SONG
Montez, Ricardo
INCOGNITO
Montgomery, Chuck
CRACKING UP
HENRY FOOL
NEIL SIMON'S THE ODD COUPLE II
STEPMOM
Montgomery, Derek
SIMON BIRCH
Montgomery, Lisa
BILLBOARD DAD
Montgomery, Poppy
DEAD MAN ON CAMPUS
Montgomery, Smokey
CAN'T YOU HEAR THE WIND HOWL?: THE LIFE AND MUSIC OF ROBERT JOHNSON
Montiel, Celia
FULL TILT BOOGIE
Montiel, Nazario
MEN WITH GUNS
Montue, Ted
NEGOTIATOR, THE
Moody, Gary
NEWTON BOYS, THE
Moody, Jim
CELEBRITY
Moog, Robert
MODULATIONS: CINEMA FOR THE EAR
Mookie, Paul
RETURN OF THE KING, THE
Moon, Michael
CELEBRITY
Moon, Philip
BIG LEBOWSKI, THE
Moon, Warren
AIR BUD: GOLDEN RECEIVER
Mooney, Debra
NAPOLEON
Moore, Abra
NEWTON BOYS, THE
Moore, Anthony
APT PUPIL
Moore, Ashton
RESCUERS: STORIES OF COURAGE—TWO COUPLES
Moore, Billy
I GOT THE HOOK UP
Moore, Brian
THERE'S SOMETHING ABOUT MARY
Moore, Chelsea
RESCUERS: STORIES OF COURAGE—TWO COUPLES
Moore, Christina
LOVE IS THE DEVIL: STUDY FOR A PORTRAIT OF FRANCIS BACON
Moore, Darren
URBAN SAFARI
Moore, Deborah
JACK HIGGINS' ON DANGEROUS GROUND
JACK HIGGINS' MIDNIGHT MAN
Moore, Dudley
MIGHTY KONG, THE
Moore, Edwina
NEGOTIATOR, THE
Moore, Eilish
OLIVER TWIST
Moore, Elizabeth Jaye
BLACK DOG
Moore, Jack
GODZILLA
Moore, Jerry
TEN BENNY
Moore, Jessica Care
SLAMNATION
Moore, Joanna
TOUCH OF EVIL: THE DIRECTOR'S CUT
Moore, John Rixy
BRAM STOKER'S THE MUMMY
Moore, Julianne
BIG LEBOWSKI, THE
CHICAGO CAB
PSYCHO
Moore, Kenya
SENSELESS
Moore, Lisa Bronwyn
BLEEDERS
JACK HIGGINS' THE WINDSOR PROTOCOL
Moore, Michael
BIG ONE, THE
Moore, Muriel
TRUMAN SHOW, THE
Moore, Perry
DOGWATCH

Moore, Richard
HUMAN BOMB
OPPOSITE OF SEX, THE
Moore, Roger
SPICE WORLD
Moore, Sam
BLUES BROTHERS 2000
Moore, Sheila
THERE'S SOMETHING ABOUT MARY
Moore, Shemar
HAV PLENTY
Moore, Terry
MIGHTY JOE YOUNG
Moore, Thurston
LOU REED: ROCK AND ROLL HEART
Moore, Tom
MOON OVER BROADWAY
Moore, Turlough
MY BROTHER'S WAR
Moore, William
ENEMY
Moore, Zachary
HOME FRIES
Moorer, Allison
HORSE WHISPERER, THE
Moori, Ikuko
SLEEPY EYES OF DEATH: SWORD OF SEDUCTION
Mopsick, Don
STILL BREATHING
Mora, Camila
GENEALOGIES OF A CRIME
Moradi, Safar Ali
TASTE OF CHERRY
Morales, Brooke
BASEKETBALL
Morales, Esai
DOGWATCH
REAL THING, THE
Morales, Mio
NEXT STEP, THE
Morales, Sam
RAT'S TALE, A
Moran, Dan
CELEBRITY
HAPPINESS
Moran, Janet
BUTCHER BOY, THE
Moran, Johnny
PLEASANTVILLE
Moran, Michael P.
PERFECT MURDER, A
Moran, Rob
THERE'S SOMETHING ABOUT MARY
Morand, Timothy
FROM A FAR COUNTRY
Morant, Angela
SWEPT FROM THE SEA
Moraru, Dan
JOHNNY MYSTO BOY WIZARD
Moraru, Petre
CLOCKMAKER
JOHNNY MYSTO BOY WIZARD
Morato, Nina
LA SEPARATION
Morawski, Cezary
FROM A FAR COUNTRY
Morayta, Paco
MASK OF ZORRO, THE
Mordvinova, Amalia
THIEF, THE
More, Jonathon
MODULATIONS: CINEMA FOR THE EAR
Moreau, Helene
WESTERN
Moreau, Jeanne
EVER AFTER
Moreau, Jennie
DAVID SEARCHING
Moreau, Marguerite
MIGHTY JOE YOUNG
Morehead, Elizabeth
SAND TRAP
Morel, Glenn
RIDE
Morel, Paul
FULL SPEED
Moreland, David
CITY OF ANGELS
Morell, Jason
WILDE
Morely, Jill
HENRY FOOL
Moreno, Helen
JOHN CARPENTER'S VAMPIRES
Moreno, Rita
SLUMS OF BEVERLY HILLS
SPREE, THE
Moreno, Rojelio
DANCE WITH ME
Moreno, Ruben
LEWIS & CLARK & GEORGE
Morenoff, Adam
SAFE MEN
Morettini, Mark
U.S. MARSHALS
Moreu, Kristin
NEXT STEP, THE
Morfogen, George
CHARLIE HOBOKEN
Morgan, Branden R.
SENSELESS
Morgan, Brandon D.
WHY DO FOOLS FALL IN LOVE?
Morgan, Brendan
JACK HIGGINS' MIDNIGHT MAN
Morgan, Chad
WHATEVER
Morgan, David "Rumble"
WOO
Morgan, Denise
HENRY FOOL
Morgan, Diana
BILLBOARD DAD
Morgan, John Paul
INCOGNITO
Morgan, Michele
BULWORTH
Morgan, Roy
NIGHT VISION
Morgan, Scott
PECKER
SPECIES II
Morgan, Trevor
BARNEY'S GREAT ADVENTURE—THE MOVIE
Morgan, Wesley
LOVE IS THE DEVIL: STUDY FOR A PORTRAIT OF FRANCIS BACON
Morhlrein, John
CHICAGO CAB
Mori, Mineko
NAKED LIES
Mori, Naoko
SPICE WORLD
Moriarity, Aoife
GENERAL, THE
Moriarty, Cathy
CASPER MEETS WENDY
DIGGING TO CHINA
Moriarty, Edmund
LAND GIRLS, THE
Moriarty, James E.
TEN BENNY
Moricz, Barna
RESCUERS: STORIES OF COURAGE—TWO WOMEN
Morin, Rich
ONE TRUE THING
Morison, Akiko
SPREE, THE
URBAN SAFARI
WOUNDED
Morissette, Luc
JACK LONDON'S THE CALL OF THE WILD: DOG OF THE YUKON
Morita, Noriyuki "Pat"
MULAN
Moritz, David
RUSHMORE
Moritzen, Henning
CELEBRATION, THE
Morley, Sheridan
LEADING MAN, THE
Morley, Vanessa
RUDOLPH THE RED-NOSED REINDEER: THE MOVIE
Morlidge, Roger
MERRY WAR, A
SHAKESPEARE IN LOVE
Mormino, Carmen
NEIL SIMON'S THE ODD COUPLE II
Mornell, Sara
PLAN B
Moroder, Giorgio
MODULATIONS: CINEMA FOR THE EAR
Morosiro, Peter
THIN RED LINE, THE
Morrell, Geoff
NEGOTIATOR, THE
Morrin, Rachel
POLISH WEDDING
Morrin, Rebecca
POLISH WEDDING
Morris, A. Lee
CELEBRITY
Morris, Alex
TWO FOR TEXAS
Morris, Alex Allen
CON, THE
Morris, Aubrey
BRAM STOKER'S THE MUMMY
Morris, Chris
HIJACKING HOLLYWOOD
Morris, Howie
FLINTSTONES: I YABBA-DABBA DOO!, THE
Morris, Jane
COURTING COURTNEY
Morris, Jeff
BLUES BROTHERS 2000
Morris, John
NAKED ACTS
Morris, Jonathon
SUBSPECIES IV: BLOODSTORM
Morris, Keith
DECLINE OF WESTERN CIVILIZATION PART III, THE
Morris, Mack
I GOT THE HOOK UP
Morris, Michael
MAN IN THE IRON MASK, THE
Morris, Phil
CLAY PIGEONS
Morris, Sarah Ann
GODS AND MONSTERS
Morris, Tracie
NAKED ACTS
Morrison, Alex
PRINCE, THE
Morrison, Campbell
INNOCENT SLEEP, THE

Morrison, Jon
NIL BY MOUTH
Morrison, Phil
UNDERTAKER'S WEDDING, THE
Morrison, Shaun
BELLY
Morrison, Temuera
SIX DAYS, SEVEN NIGHTS
Morrissen, Lori
I GOT THE HOOK UP
Morrissey, David
HILARY AND JACKIE
Morrissey, Erin
HOLY MAN
Morrow, Donald
FEAR AND LOATHING IN LAS VEGAS
Morse, David
NEGOTIATOR, THE
Morse, Laila
NIL BY MOUTH
Morshower, Glenn
GODZILLA
PHOENIX
Morstad, Geir
JUNK MAIL
Mortensen, Viggo
PERFECT MURDER, A
PSYCHO
Mortimer, Emily
ELIZABETH
SUMMER FLING
Mortimore, Jean
LOVE IS THE DEVIL: STUDY FOR A PORTRAIT OF FRANCIS BACON
Mortimore, Nick
LOVE IS THE DEVIL: STUDY FOR A PORTRAIT OF FRANCIS BACON
Mortimore, Tu Tu
LOVE IS THE DEVIL: STUDY FOR A PORTRAIT OF FRANCIS BACON
Morton, Billy
BLACK LIGHT
EBENEZER
Morton, Joe
APT PUPIL
BLUES BROTHERS 2000
Morton, Matt Prescott
OUTSIDE OZONA
Morton, Sam
SIMON BIRCH
Morton, Samantha
UNDER THE SKIN
Moscardini, Paolo Mario
KNOCK OFF
Moschitta Jr., John
RAT'S TALE, A
Moscow, David
HURRICANE STREETS
RIVER RED
Moseley, Bill
JAMES ELLROY: DEMON DOG OF AMERICAN CRIME FICTION
Mosenson, Scott
CLOCKWATCHERS
Moses, Mark
DEEP IMPACT
Moses, Sam
WOO
Moskowitz, Marvin
JOHNNY SKIDMARKS
Mosley, Tony
DARK CITY
Moss, Larry
BABE: PIG IN THE CITY
Moss, Michael H.
STEPHEN KING'S THE NIGHT FLIER
Moss, Paige
CAN'T HARDLY WAIT
Mostel, Josh
GREAT EXPECTATIONS
ROUNDERS
Motiu, Christian
CLOCKMAKER
Motoki, Masahiro
GONIN
Mott, Manning
RUSHMORE
Motta, Bess
DIRTY WORK
Motta, Zeze
TIETA OF AGRESTE
Mottola, Greg
CELEBRITY
Moukhtar, Ahmed
DESTINY
Moulder, Helen
ABERRATION
Moulevrier, Gerard
RONIN
Mounir, Mohamed
DESTINY
Mountain, Sam
WHY DO FOOLS FALL IN LOVE?
Mouritsen, Ryan
CLAY PIGEONS
Mousseau, France
DANCE WITH ME
Moustafa, Samy Sheraf
CHARLIE HOBOKEN
Mowat, Rick
CELEBRITY
Mowling, Panou
BONE DADDY
Moxey, Paul
BABE: PIG IN THE CITY
Moxley, Gina
BUTCHER BOY, THE
Moyer, Mike G.
LIVING OUT LOUD
Moyer, Stephen
PRINCE VALIANT
Moynihan, Daniel
ELIZABETH
Mozes, Alan
DEFENDERS: PAYBACK, THE
Mozes, Patrice
BILLBOARD DAD
Mr. Chips
JACK FROST
Mr. Oh
JANE AUSTEN'S MAFIA!
Mruvka, Alan
DIGGING TO CHINA
Mueller-Stahl, Armin
OGRE, THE
12 ANGRY MEN
X-FILES, THE
Muellerleile, Marianne
BURN HOLLYWOOD BURN
RAT'S TALE, A
Mugglebee, Chris
WATERBOY, THE
Muhe, Ulrich
FUNNY GAMES
Muir, Gregor
LOVE IS THE DEVIL: STUDY FOR A PORTRAIT OF FRANCIS BACON
Mujica, Rene
TWILIGHT
Muldoon, Margaret
HOLY MAN
Mulgrew, Kate
TREKKIES
Mulheren, Michael
DIRTY LAUNDRY
Mulhern, Glen
STRAY BULLET
Mulholland, Annette
ONE TRUE THING
Mulholland, James
SUE
Mulkey, Chris
BULWORTH
SUB DOWN
Mull, Martin
RICHIE RICH'S CHRISTMAS WISH
Mullally, Megan
FLINTSTONES: I YABBA-DABBA DOO!, THE
Mullany, Terry
THERE'S SOMETHING ABOUT MARY
Mullarkey, Neil
SPICE WORLD
Mullen, Brian
SAFE MEN
Mullen, Marie
BUTCHER BOY, THE
DANCING AT LUGHNASA
Muller, David
ERNEST IN THE ARMY
Mulligan, Brian
ARMAGEDDON
Mulligan, Terry David
DISTURBING BEHAVIOR
HARD CORE LOGO
Mulot, Christian
MADELINE
Mulrooney, Kelsey
NEGOTIATOR, THE
muMs the Schemer
SLAMNATION
Mumy, Seth
PAULIE
Munafo, Mark
GODZILLA
Munch, Dr. Hans
HEALING BY KILLING
Munday, Vanessa
PHOENIX
Mundi, Coati
BREAK, THE
HE GOT GAME
Muneta, Masimi
RAZOR: THE SNARE, THE
Munge, Julio
NEXT STEP, THE
Mungle, Rob
SLAYERS: THE MOTION PICTURE
Mungo, Howard
I GOT THE HOOK UP
INTERLOCKED: THRILLED TO DEATH
Munro, Hugh
WILDE
Munro, Lochlyn
DEAD MAN ON CAMPUS
Munro, Ronn
FALLEN
Munroe, Debbie
I LOVE YOU, DON'T TOUCH ME!
Munroe, Lochlyn
NIGHT AT THE ROXBURY, A
Munroe, Richard
DAVID SEARCHING
Mura-Smith, Emily
PAULIE
Murata, Takehiro
GODZILLA AND MOTHRA: THE BATTLE FOR EARTH
Murdock, George
PHOENIX
X-FILES, THE
Murdock, R.J.
TRUMAN SHOW, THE

Muresan, Gheorghe
MY GIANT
Murfi, Mikel
BUTCHER BOY, THE
Murgo, John
INVISIBLE DAD
Murnik, Peter
ARMAGEDDON
HARD RAIN
Murph
RETURN OF THE KING, THE
Murphy
SUMMER FLING
Murphy, Alec
DAY AT THE BEACH
Murphy, Andrew
SPANISH PRISONER, THE
Murphy, Anne
TREKKIES
Murphy, Betty
HORTON FOOTE'S ALONE
Murphy, Bill
SPACEJACKED
Murphy, Brian
HALLELUJAH!
Murphy, Brittany
PHOENIX
PROPHECY II, THE
Murphy, Charles O.
PLAYERS CLUB, THE
Murphy, Dan
THERE'S SOMETHING ABOUT MARY
Murphy, Donna
STAR TREK: INSURRECTION
Murphy, Eddie
DR. DOLITTLE
HOLY MAN
MULAN
Murphy, Elizabeth
LOVE AND DEATH ON LONG ISLAND
Murphy, Eric
BRAM STOKER'S SHADOWBUILDER
Murphy, Gary
MAJOR LEAGUE: BACK TO THE MINORS
Murphy, Harry
SOUR GRAPES
Murphy, Jason
MR. NICE GUY
Murphy, Joe
LITTLE BIGFOOT 2: THE JOURNEY HOME
Murphy, Johnny
I WENT DOWN
Murphy, Kevin Keane
SUE
Murphy, Kim
CITY OF ANGELS
Murphy, Lorcan
BRYLCREEM BOYS, THE
Murphy, Lynn
MR. NICE GUY
Murphy, Maggie
YOU'VE GOT MAIL
Murphy, Matt
BLUES BROTHERS 2000
Murphy, Michael
THERE'S SOMETHING ABOUT MARY
Murphy, Padraigin
BLACKJACK
Murphy, Tim
STRAY BULLET
Murphy, Tom
GENERAL, THE
Murphy, Vinnie
GENERAL, THE
Murray, Bill
RUSHMORE
WILD THINGS
Murray, Keith
RIDE
Murray, Kirk
CATHERINE'S GROVE
Murtagh, Kate
MAKER, THE
Murtaugh, James
LAST DAYS OF DISCO, THE
RIVER RED
Musaka, Naomasa
TOKYO FIST
Musburger, Brent
WATERBOY, THE
Muso, Nonie
COLONY, THE
Muson, Jesse
WILD THINGS
Musselwhite, Charlie
BLUES BROTHERS 2000
Musser, Larry
DISTURBING BEHAVIOR
Mustata, Catalina
JOHNNY MYSTO BOY WIZARD
Mustillo, Louis
LAST BIG THING, THE
Musy, Gianny
DANGEROUS BEAUTY
Muti, Ornella
SOMEWHERE IN THE CITY
Mwine, Ntare
DON KING: ONLY IN AMERICA
Mybrand, Jan
JERUSALEM
Mydcarz, Anthony
BUFFALO '66
Myers, Bruce
GOVERNESS, THE
Myers, Chris
EIGHTEENTH ANGEL, THE
Myers, Jody
REAL HOWARD SPITZ, THE
Myers, Johann
TWENTYFOURSEVEN
Myers, Letroy
MAJOR LEAGUE: BACK TO THE MINORS
Myers, Lou
BULWORTH
HOW STELLA GOT HER GROOVE BACK
Myers, Mike
54
Myers, Tanya
TWENTYFOURSEVEN
Mygind, Peter
KINGDOM, PART 2, THE
Myhardt, Patrick
OPERATION DELTA FORCE 2
Myrgard, Maria
CELEBRATION, THE
Myrie, Annette
NAKED ACTS
Myrin, Arden
IMPOSTORS, THE
Myslik, Pavel
ACT OF WAR
Naber, Joey
SIEGE, THE
Naccache, Eric
SOLDIER'S DAUGHTER NEVER CRIES, A
Nacer, Miloud
MARIUS AND JEANNETTE
Nachtergaele, Matheus
CENTRAL STATION
Naftal, Diana
SIEGE, THE
Nagashima, Toshiyuki
GONIN
Nagatsuka, Kyozo
VILLAGE OF DREAMS
Nagel, Nicole
BURN HOLLYWOOD BURN
FRENCH EXIT
Nagel, Rik
POLTERGEIST REPORT: YUYU HAKUSHO
Nagy, Gabor
REDLINE
Nahaku, Don
SIX DAYS, SEVEN NIGHTS
Nahar, Jessica
WOO
Naidu, Ajay
MONTANA
MY GIANT
PI
Naidu, Yayu
MADELINE
Najera, Maricruz
MEN WITH GUNS
Najimy, Kathy
BRIDE OF CHUCKY
HOPE FLOATS
JUNGLE BOOK: MOWGLI'S STORY, THE
NEVADA
Nakagawa, Anna
GODZILLA VS. KING GHIDORAH
Nakahara-Wallett, Kellye
DR. DOLITTLE
Nakajima, Takehiro
VILLAGE OF DREAMS
Nakamura, Kumi
WHEN I CLOSE MY EYES
Nakamura, Midori
OBJECT OF MY AFFECTION, THE
Nakamura, Saemi
TRUMAN SHOW, THE
Nakamura, Suzy
DEEP IMPACT
Nakaya, Ichiruo
SLEEPY EYES OF DEATH: SWORD OF SEDUCTION
Nakayama, Miho
WHEN I CLOSE MY EYES
Naked Aggression
DECLINE OF WESTERN CIVILIZATION PART III, THE
Nakhapetov, Rodion
STIR
Name, Billy
LOU REED: ROCK AND ROLL HEART
Namer, Nicole
DIGGING TO CHINA
Nance, Gracye
NAKED ACTS
Nance, Richard
HOPE FLOATS
TWO FOR TEXAS
Nanjoo, Shintaroo
SLEEPY EYES OF DEATH: FULL CIRCLE KILLING
Nannerello, George
DECEIVER
Napier, Charles
FATAL PURSUIT
Napier, Markus
SAVING PRIVATE RYAN
Napier, Marshall
TWISTED
Naples, Rachel
BRAM STOKER'S THE MUMMY
Napoli, Christain
SNAKE EYES
Nappo, Tony
DEFENDERS: PAYBACK, THE
Narakbunchai, Pichariva
BRIGHT SHINING LIE, A

Nardi, Andrea
LIFE IS BEAUTIFUL
Narita, Junichiroo
SLEEPY EYES OF DEATH: FULL CIRCLE KILLING
SLEEPY EYES OF DEATH: SWORD OF ADVENTURE
Narita, Mikio
RAZOR: WHO'S GOT THE GOLD?, THE
Naruse, Keigo
JUNK FOOD
Nascarella, Arthur
ENEMY OF THE STATE
54
HAPPINESS
HE GOT GAME
Nash, David Andrew
ELMORE LEONARD'S GOLD COAST
TRUMAN SHOW, THE
Nash, Graham
ELVIS MEETS NIXON
Nassa, Avi
JACK HIGGINS' ON DANGEROUS GROUND
Natale, Alan
ALL THE RAGE
Natalie, Cam
UNDERTAKER'S WEDDING, THE
Nate, Ultra
54
Nation, Ashley
MILO
Nation, Steve
KNOCK OFF
Natsuki, Miyu
ORGAZMO
Naughton, David
URBAN SAFARI
Navarro, Lolo
MEN WITH GUNS
Nave, Steve
LITTLE BIGFOOT 2: THE JOURNEY HOME
Navicoff, Gary
TALK TO ME
Naylor, Anthony
HUMAN BOMB
Nazary, Ali
NEWTON BOYS, THE
Neal, Dennis
WILD THINGS
Neal, Donald
PECKER
Neal, Gary L.
WHY DO FOOLS FALL IN LOVE?
Neal, Jonathan Roger
BULWORTH
Neal Jr., Tom
DETOUR
Neal, Mark
MR. NICE GUY
Neale, David
WOUNDED
Neale, Leslie
UNCLE SAM
Nealon, Kevin
WEDDING SINGER, THE
Neame, Christopher
WALKING THUNDER
Neant, Quque
LAST SEDUCTION II, THE
Nee, Little John
MY BROTHER'S WAR
Needham, Catilin Sarah
MUSIC FROM ANOTHER ROOM
Needham, Peter
FIRELIGHT
Needles, David Paul
GIRLS IN PRISON
Neelaphamorn, Kanlayaporn
WRONGFULLY ACCUSED
Neeley, Martin
SHAKESPEARE IN LOVE
Neely, William
STEPHEN KING'S THE NIGHT FLIER
Neeson, Liam
LES MISERABLES
Neff, Kathy
ARMAGEDDON
Negin, Louis
54
Negishi, Akemi
SLEEPY EYES OF DEATH: SWORD OF SEDUCTION
Negron, Rick
NEXT STEP, THE
Negron, Taylor
CHAIRMAN OF THE BOARD
COURTING COURTNEY
KID IN ALADDIN'S PALACE, A
Nehls, Roger
LIVING OUT LOUD
Nehring, Michael
SKIN & BONE
Neil, Julian
SOULER OPPOSITE, THE
Neil, Richard
DISAPPEARANCE OF KEVIN JOHNSON, THE
Neill, Sam
FROM A FAR COUNTRY
HORSE WHISPERER, THE
MERLIN
Neilsen, Barbaree Earl
WRONGFULLY ACCUSED
Neira, Santiago
CARLA'S SONG
Nelken, Harry
TRUCKS
Nelligan, Kate
STOLEN MOMENTS
U.S. MARSHALS
Nelson, Adam
PHANTOMS
Nelson, Bill
SHADRACH
Nelson, Brodie
CLOCKWATCHERS
Nelson, Char
NOT IN THIS TOWN
Nelson, Ed
THERE'S SOMETHING ABOUT MARY
Nelson, Everton
NIL BY MOUTH
Nelson, Ketema
GEORGE WALLACE
Nelson, Marc
CHICAGO CAB
Nelson, Marjorie
EDEN
UNDER HEAVEN
Nelson, Mike
DEAR JESSE
Nelson, Novella
PERFECT MURDER, A
Nelson, Peter
KNOCK OFF
Nelson, Rebecca
HENRY FOOL
Nelson, Shawn
QUICKSILVER HIGHWAY
Nelson, Tim Blake
THIN RED LINE, THE
Nelson, Willie
HALF BAKED
Nelsp, Sharon
PECKER
Nemejovsky, Jan
ACT OF WAR
Nemeth, Andrea
URBAN SAFARI
Nemeth, Vincent
MAN IN THE IRON MASK, THE
Nemetz, Lenora
WHATEVER
Nemirovsky, Vladimir
INDISCREET
Nemura, Kenjiroo
SLEEPY EYES OF DEATH: FULL CIRCLE KILLING
Nendels, Frank
INCOGNITO
Nepomniaschy, Alex
ALARMIST, THE
Neri, Francesca
LIVE FLESH
Nerman, David
LOST WORLD, THE
Nero, Franco
INNOCENT SLEEP, THE
TALK OF ANGELS
Nesbitt, James
GO NOW
WAKING NED DEVINE
Neslon, Dee
PROPOSITION, THE
Nestle, Joan
STOLEN MOMENTS
Neuhaus, Ibgo
MURDER IN MIND
Neuhaus, Larry
THIN RED LINE, THE
Neuhoff, Ted
NEXT STEP, THE
Neuman, Ricard
NEW ADVENTURES OF KIMBA THE WHITE LION, THE
Neumann, Birthe
CELEBRATION, THE
KINGDOM, PART 2, THE
Neustadt, Ted
CELEBRITY
Neuwirth, Bebe
ALL DOGS CHRISTMAS CAROL, AN
CELEBRITY
FACULTY, THE
Neuwirth, Chantal
MADELINE
Neville, Gaynielle
BELOVED
Neville, Jim
WHATEVER
Neville, John
REGENERATION
URBAN LEGEND
X-FILES, THE
Neville, Roger
LITTLE VOICE
Nevins, Claudette
STAR TREK: INSURRECTION
Nevolina, Angelika
FRIEND OF THE DECEASED, A
Newberger, Marc
CURSE OF THE PUPPET MASTER
Newberry, Shirley
LAND GIRLS, THE
Newbigin, Flora
BORROWERS, THE
Newbill, Ivano
AIR BUD: GOLDEN RECEIVER
Newbold, Richard
LOVE IS THE DEVIL: STUDY FOR A PORTRAIT OF FRANCIS BACON
Newcott, Rosemary
GINGERBREAD MAN, THE

Newell, Douglas
SNOWBOUND
Newfield, Jack
DON KING: ONLY IN AMERICA
Newhart, Bob
RUDOLPH THE RED-NOSED REINDEER: THE MOVIE
Newman, Edwin
ELVIS MEETS NIXON
Newman, Emily
OPPOSITE OF SEX, THE
Newman, Joanne
LET'S KILL ALL THE LAWYERS
Newman, Laraine
ALONE IN THE WOODS
FEAR AND LOATHING IN LAS VEGAS
RUSTY: THE GREAT RESCUE
Newman, Mimi
LES MISERABLES
Newman, Paul
TWILIGHT
Newman, Phyllis
PRICE ABOVE RUBIES, A
Newman, Richard
MIGHTY KONG, THE
Newman, Sid
WEDDING SINGER, THE
Newman-Breen, Alesia
SPECIES II
Newsome, Paula
CHARLIE HOBOKEN
Newson, Marlon "Furry"
HENRY: PORTRAIT OF A SERIAL KILLER PART 2
Newstone, Pauline
ADVENTURES OF MOWGLI
Newth, Jonathan
INCOGNITO
Newton, Cody
X-FILES, THE
Newton, Thandie
BELOVED
LEADING MAN, THE
Newton, Walter
3 NINJAS: HIGH NOON AT MEGA MOUNTAIN
Newton, Wayne
ELVIS MEETS NIXON
Nezu, Jinpachi
GONIN
Ng, Alex
CHINESE BOX, THE
Ng Man Tat
KILLER ANGELS
Ng, Richard
MAGNIFICENT WARRIORS
Ng Wai-kwok
BODYGUARD FROM BEIJING
Ngai Sing
BODYGUARD FROM BEIJING
Ngo, Rosy
BOYS IN LOVE 2
Ngor, Haing S.
HIT ME
Nguyen, Long
SIX DAYS, SEVEN NIGHTS
Nguyen, Tina
LET'S TALK ABOUT SEX
Nibley, Tom
NOT IN THIS TOWN
Nicastro, Michelle
SWAN PRINCESS III: AND THE MYSTERY OF THE ENCHANTED TREASURE, THE
Nicholas, Larry
STAR KID
Nicholas, P.J.
LIKE IT IS
Nicholas, Skylar
LOLIDA 2000
Nicholas, Thomas Ian
KID IN ALADDIN'S PALACE, A
Nichole, Deva
INTERLOCKED: THRILLED TO DEATH
Nicholls, Jeffrey Max
FACE THE EVIL
Nichols, Dave
PEACEKEEPER, THE
Nichols, Eileen
REGENERATION
Nichols, Jason S.
SIX DAYS, SEVEN NIGHTS
Nichols, Lance E.
SNAKE EYES
Nichols, Leila
YOU'VE GOT MAIL
Nichols, Marisol
CAN'T HARDLY WAIT
JANE AUSTEN'S MAFIA!
Nichols, Nichelle
TREKKIES
Nichols, Raymond Leslie
KNOCK OFF
Nichols, Regina
PERMANENT MIDNIGHT
Nichols, Taylor
LAST DAYS OF DISCO, THE
NEXT STEP, THE
Nicholson, Julianne
ONE TRUE THING
Nicholson, Mil
GIRLS IN PRISON
Nickalls, Grant
DIRTY WORK
Nickell, Barbara
REAL THING, THE
Nicksay, Lily
NEGOTIATOR, THE
Nicol, Chandler
RESCUERS: STORIES OF COURAGE—TWO COUPLES
Nicole, Ashlee
RAGE, THE
Nicolea, Petre
GADJO DILO
Niculescu, Mihai
CLOCKMAKER
SECRET KINGDOM, THE
Niedleman, Anna
SOLDIER'S DAUGHTER NEVER CRIES, A
Niedleman, Louis
SOLDIER'S DAUGHTER NEVER CRIES, A
Nielsen, Bjarne G.
KINGDOM, PART 2, THE
Nielsen, Connie
PERMANENT MIDNIGHT
RUSHMORE
SOLDIER
Nielsen, Leslie
WRONGFULLY ACCUSED
Nielsen, Robin
WRONGFULLY ACCUSED
Nielson, Rick
BIG ONE, THE
Niemczyk, Stefan
WIDE AWAKE
Nieves, Benny
WEST NEW YORK
Nieves, Espher Lao
PI
Nieves, Laura
CHARLIE HOBOKEN
Nigrini, Ron
MIGHTY, THE
Nigsch, Dietmar
INHERITORS, THE
Nikaido, Miho
HENRY FOOL
Nikolaev, Valery
ABERRATION
Nimmer, Geoffrey B.
FEAR AND LOATHING IN LAS VEGAS
Nimmo, Justin
PLEASANTVILLE
Nimoy, Leonard
TREKKIES
Ninach, Youcef
FULL SPEED
Ninkovic, Natasa
SAVIOR
Nipar, Yvette
PHANTOMS
Nisbet, Jack
WEDDING SINGER, THE
Nishimura, Akira
RAZOR: THE SNARE, THE
Nishimura, Deborah
ARMAGEDDON
Nishimura, Ko
RAZOR: WHO'S GOT THE GOLD?, THE
Nishioka, Tokuma
GODZILLA VS. KING GHIDORAH
ZERO WOMAN
Nissen, Brian
SWAN PRINCESS III: AND THE MYSTERY OF THE ENCHANTED TREASURE, THE
Nissen, Claus
KINGDOM, PART 2, THE
Nissman, Michael
BOYS IN LOVE 2
Nitu, Gelu
SUBSPECIES IV: BLOODSTORM
Niuga, Amos
THIN RED LINE, THE
Niven, Barbara
RAT PACK, THE
Nivola, Alessandro
REACH THE ROCK
Niwa, Reiko
ROYAL WARRIORS
Nix, Dr. Robert
PARALYZING FEAR: THE STORY OF POLIO IN AMERICA, A
Nixon, Marni
I THINK I DO
Nizmiroff, Vladimir
RED CHERRY
Niznik, Stephanie
STAR TREK: INSURRECTION
No, David
MR. NICE GUY
Nobili, Simona
DANGEROUS BEAUTY
Nobre, Socorro
CENTRAL STATION
Noeding, Caroline
SIX O'CLOCK NEWS
Noeding, John
SIX O'CLOCK NEWS
Noelle, Anne
DANCE WITH ME
Noice, Gordon Jennison
PHOENIX
Nolan, Jeanette
HORSE WHISPERER, THE
Nolan, Mick
SPACEJACKED
STRAY BULLET
Nolan, Roger
SOULER OPPOSITE, THE
Noland, Charles
DESPERATE MEASURES
Nolasco, Vincent
HAV PLENTY

Nolot, Jacques
ARTEMISIA
Nolte, Nick
AFFLICTION
NIGHTWATCH
THIN RED LINE, THE
Nonnon, T. Scott
OBJECT OF MY AFFECTION, THE
Noonan, Jimmy
SOMEWHERE IN THE CITY
Noonan, Michael John
MR. NICE GUY
Noonan, Sarah
COURTING COURTNEY
Noonan, Tom
PHOENIX
Noori, Mir Hossein
TASTE OF CHERRY
Norby, Ghita
KINGDOM, PART 2, THE
Norcoss, Clayton
PRINCE, THE
Nordling, Jeffrey
POLISH WEDDING
Norman, Zack
WHO IS HENRY JAGLOM?
Normant, Elizabeth
MURDER IN MIND
Norring, Jens
CELEBRATION, THE
Norris, Bruce
CIVIL ACTION, A
REACH THE ROCK
Norris, Daran
INVISIBLE DAD
RAT'S TALE, A
SOULER OPPOSITE, THE
Norris, Dean
NEGOTIATOR, THE
WITHOUT LIMITS
Norry, Marilyn
TRICKS
Northcott, Ryan
ATOMIC DOG
Northern, Tim
LETTER FROM DEATH ROW, A
Northup, Harry
BELOVED
Norton, Alex
LES MISERABLES
LITTLE VOICE
Norton, Edward
AMERICAN HISTORY X
OUT OF THE PAST
ROUNDERS
Norton, Jim
AMERICAN HISTORY X
Norton, Ken
DIRTY WORK
Norton, Lily
OBJECT OF MY AFFECTION, THE
Norton, Richard
BLACK THUNDER
MR. NICE GUY
Norton, William
PLAN B
Norvind, Eva
DIDN'T DO IT FOR LOVE
Nossek, Ralph
LES MISERABLES
Nosul, Wenanty
WHITE RAVEN, THE
Notarfrancesco, Aaron
MR. NICE GUY
Notarfrancesco, Jake
MR. NICE GUY
Nottle, Dean
BABE: PIG IN THE CITY
Novak, Danny
HARD CORE LOGO
Novak, George
MR. NICE GUY
Novak, Jack
PARALLEL SONS
Novak, John
JACK LONDON'S THE CALL OF THE WILD: DOG OF THE YUKON
Nowak, Jerzy
FROM A FAR COUNTRY
Nowicki, Tom
WATERBOY, THE
Noyce, Richard
AMERICAN HISTORY X
Noyes, Joanna
BLEEDERS
Nozick, Bruce
SOULER OPPOSITE, THE
Ntshona, Winston
TARZAN AND THE LOST CITY
Nucci, Danny
LOVE WALKED IN
Nudziak, Tareusz
FROM A FAR COUNTRY
Nunez Jr., Miguel A.
WHY DO FOOLS FALL IN LOVE?
Nunn, Bill
ALWAYS OUTNUMBERED
HE GOT GAME
QUICKSILVER HIGHWAY
Nussbaum, Danny
TWENTYFOURSEVEN
Nussbaum, Mike
CON, THE
Nutt, Danny
VELVET GOLDMINE
Nuzzo, Jason
SNAKE EYES
Nykl, David
ACT OF WAR
Nyland, Tony
TWENTYFOURSEVEN
Nymshack, Deborah
LET'S KILL ALL THE LAWYERS
Nystrom, Anders
JERUSALEM
Nystul, Daisy
CLOCKMAKER
O Yuki Conjugate
MODULATIONS: CINEMA FOR THE EAR
O'Blenis Jr., Edward
EDEN
O'Brian, Joyclyn
WHEN TIME EXPIRES
O'Brien, Brendan
3 NINJAS: HIGH NOON AT MEGA MOUNTAIN
O'Brien, Kelly
THERE'S SOMETHING ABOUT MARY
O'Brien, Margaret
OFF THE MENU: THE LAST DAYS OF CHASEN'S
O'Brien, Mark
TEKKEN: THE MOTION PICTURE
O'Brien, Maureen
LAND GIRLS, THE
O'Brien, Patrick T.
PLEASANTVILLE
O'Brien, Richard
DARK CITY
EVER AFTER
SPICE WORLD
O'Brien, Robert
ARMOUR OF GOD
O'Brien, Sean
MY BROTHER'S WAR
WHATEVER
O'Brien, Tom
SOLDIER
O'Brien, Trevor
MIDAS TOUCH, THE
O'Bryan, Sean
I'LL BE HOME FOR CHRISTMAS
O'Callaghan, Ciara
SPACEJACKED
O'Callaghan, Daniel
TWO FOR TEXAS
O'Callaghan, Richard
DANGEROUS BEAUTY
O'Carroll, Robert Harrison
FUTURE FEAR
O'Connell, Chris
HI-LO COUNTRY, THE
O'Connell, Deirdre
CITY OF ANGELS
O'Connell, Jack
IMPOSTORS, THE
SOUR GRAPES
O'Connell, James
NEXT STOP, WONDERLAND
O'Connell, Jerry
CAN'T HARDLY WAIT
O'Connor, Amber
MY BROTHER'S WAR
O'Connor, Barbara
THERE'S SOMETHING ABOUT MARY
O'Connor, Derrick
DEEP RISING
O'Connor, Gavin
INFORMANT, THE
O'Connor, Gerald
CHARLIE HOBOKEN
O'Connor, Jeanette
BODY COUNT
O'Connor, Joseph
ELIZABETH
O'Connor, Kevin J.
CHICAGO CAB
DEEP RISING
GODS AND MONSTERS
HIT ME
O'Connor, Maria Torres
DANCE WITH ME
O'Connor, Raymond
GIRLS IN PRISON
MY GIANT
O'Connor, Renee
HERCULES AND XENA THE ANIMATED MOVIE: THE BATTLE FOR MOUNT OLYMPUS
O'Connor, Shane
BUTCHER BOY, THE
O'Connor, Sinead
BUTCHER BOY, THE
O'Day, Susan
THERE'S SOMETHING ABOUT MARY
O'Donnell, Annie
PLAYERS CLUB, THE
O'Donnell, Elizabeth
RETURN TO SAVAGE BEACH
O'Donnell, Rosie
WIDE AWAKE
O'Donnell, Steven
SHAKESPEARE IN LOVE
SPICE WORLD
O'Donnell, Willy
PROPOSITION, THE
O'Dwyer, Jack
BRYLCREEM BOYS, THE
O'Fallon Jr., James Peter "JP"
SUICIDE KINGS
O'Fatharta, Conal
MY BROTHER'S WAR
O'Fatharta, Macdara
BUTCHER BOY, THE

O'Gorman, Dean
YOUNG HERCULES
O'Grady, Maureen
TWENTYFOURSEVEN
O'Hagan, Michael
GODS AND MONSTERS
O'Hai, Cirian
JACK HIGGINS' MIDNIGHT MAN
O'Hampton, Jack
LAND GIRLS, THE
O'Hanlon, Ardal
BUTCHER BOY, THE
O'Hanlon, John
RETURN OF THE KING, THE
O'Hara, Catherine
HOME FRIES
SUMMER FLING
O'Hara, David
OLIVER TWIST
O'Hara, Jaime Lynn
NIAGARA NIAGARA
O'Hara, Joan
MOONDANCE
O'Hare, Denis
RIVER RED
O'Hea, Brendan
ELIZABETH
O'Herlihy, Cornelia Hayes
GODS AND MONSTERS
O'Herlihy, Dan
RAT PACK, THE
O'Herlihy, Gavan
PRINCE VALIANT
TOP OF THE WORLD
O'Kane, Dierdre
BREAK, THE
O'Kane, Kevin
LET'S KILL ALL THE LAWYERS
O'Keefe, Jodi Lyn
HALLOWEEN H20: TWENTY YEARS LATER
O'Keefe, Raymond
WHY DO FOOLS FALL IN LOVE?
O'Keefe, Sherry
QUICKSILVER HIGHWAY
O'Kelly, Aideen
PERFECT MURDER, A
O'Kelly, Donal
I WENT DOWN
O'Laskey II, Michael J.
3 NINJAS: HIGH NOON AT MEGA MOUNTAIN
O'Laughlin, Gerald S.
SECRET KINGDOM, THE
O'Leary, Amanda
MISBEGOTTEN
O'Leary, Jer
BUTCHER BOY, THE
O'Leary, Molly
PLUMP FICTION
O'Linde, Paul
FATAL PURSUIT
O'Malley, Des
GENERAL, THE
O'Malley, Kerry
ROUNDERS
O'Malley, Maura
WAKING NED DEVINE
O'Malley, Mike
DEEP IMPACT
O'Meara, Daniel
UNDER THE SKIN
O'Morris, Kevin
EDEN
O'Neal, Cynthia
PRIMARY COLORS
O'Neal, Gerard
DIDN'T DO IT FOR LOVE
O'Neal, Jim
CAN'T YOU HEAR THE WIND HOWL?: THE LIFE AND MUSIC OF ROBERT JOHNSON
O'Neal, Redmond
BRAVE LITTLE TOASTER GOES TO MARS, THE
O'Neal, Ryan
BURN HOLLYWOOD BURN
ZERO EFFECT
O'Neal, Shaquille
HE GOT GAME
O'Neil, Michael
DANCER, TEXAS POP. 81
O'Neil, Tricia
GIA
O'Neile, Tara
INFORMANT, THE
O'Neill, Annie
BUTCHER BOY, THE
O'Neill, Colleen
BOYS IN LOVE 2
GENERAL, THE
O'Neill, Con
LAST SEDUCTION II, THE
O'Neill, Ed
SPANISH PRISONER, THE
O'Neill, Emma
MY BROTHER'S WAR
O'Neill, Errol
JOEY
O'Neill, Lorcan
LOVE IS THE DEVIL: STUDY FOR A PORTRAIT OF FRANCIS BACON
O'Neill, Maggie
WHEN PIGS FLY
O'Neill, Margaret
NO LOOKING BACK
O'Neill, Owen
GENERAL, THE
O'Neill, Patrick
SENSELESS
O'Neill, Robert K.
WIDE AWAKE
O'Neill, Tom
BROADWAY DAMAGE
O'Neill, Tommy
GENERAL, THE
O'Quinn, Carrick
X-FILES, THE
O'Quinn, Terry
BREAST MEN
X-FILES, THE
O'Regan, Mark
SUMMER FLING
O'Reilly, Ciaran
BREAK, THE
O'Reilly, Cyril
BLACK DOG
O'Reilly, Robert
TREKKIES
O'Rourke, Mick
SCARRED CITY
O'Rourke, Robert
ENEMY OF THE STATE
O'Shaughnessy, Brian
OPERATION DELTA FORCE 2
O'Shaughnessy, Maureen
DARK CITY
O'Shea, Milo
BUTCHER BOY, THE
O'Sullevan, Peter
SHOOTING FISH
O'Sullivan, Aisling
BUTCHER BOY, THE
O'Sullivan, Billy
SECRET KINGDOM, THE
O'Sullivan, Frank
I WENT DOWN
LES MISERABLES
O'Sullivan, James
FEAR AND LOATHING IN LAS VEGAS
O'Sullivan, Paul
DIRTY WORK
O'Toole, John
GENERAL, THE
O'Toole, Kate
DANCING AT LUGHNASA
O'Toole, Matt
MONTANA
ZERO EFFECT
O'Toole, Peter
PHANTOMS
Oaks, Digory
FERNGULLY 2: THE MAGICAL RESCUE
Oasis, Jessica M.
STEPMOM
Obando, Karla
CARLA'S SONG
Obradors, Jacqueline
SIX DAYS, SEVEN NIGHTS
Obregon, Claudio
MIDAQ ALLEY
Obregon, Rodrigo
RETURN TO SAVAGE BEACH
Ocampo, Yvette
BLADE
Occhino, Murphy
CELEBRITY
Ochaim, Brygida
SWINDLE, THE
Ochoa, Maricela
MERCURY RISING
Ochoa, Steven
OBJECT OF MY AFFECTION, THE
Odaka, Megumi
GODZILLA AND MOTHRA: THE BATTLE FOR EARTH
GODZILLA VS. KING GHIDORAH
Oddy, Christine
DIRTY WORK
Odeh, Nadi
PASSION IN THE DESERT
Odett, Keith
AMERICAN HISTORY X
Offerman, Nick
CITY OF ANGELS
Ogden, Christopher
UNCLE SAM
Ogier, Bulle
SHATTERED IMAGE
SOMEWHERE IN THE CITY
Ogilvy, Ian
DISAPPEARANCE OF KEVIN JOHNSON, THE
Oglesby, Randy
PATCH ADAMS
PENTAGON WARS, THE
Oguri, Kaori
WHEN I CLOSE MY EYES
Oh, Sandra
PERMANENT MIDNIGHT
Oh, Soon-Tek
MULAN
Ohama, Natsuko
MONTANA
Ohlsson, Camilla
LEADING MAN, THE
Ohlsson, Fredrik
JERUSALEM
Ohsugi, Ren
SONATINE
Ohtsji, Kevan
DOUBLE EDGE

Ok, Anne
GREAT EXPECTATIONS
Okamura, Gerald
RETURN TO SAVAGE BEACH
Okamura, Yoichi
JUNK FOOD
Okayasu, Taiju
THIN RED LINE, THE
Okking, Jens
KINGDOM, PART 2, THE
Okonedo, Sophie
GO NOW
Oksen, Lene Laub
CELEBRATION, THE
Okubo, Takamitsu
THIN RED LINE, THE
Okuma, Enuka
HUNTED, THE
Okumoto, Yuji
MEAN GUNS
TRUMAN SHOW, THE
Okumuto, Ryo
PLAYING BY HEART
Olasin, Irena
FATAL PURSUIT
Olbrychski, Daniel
FROM A FAR COUNTRY
Oldman, Gary
LOST IN SPACE
QUEST FOR CAMELOT
Olds, Gabe
WITHOUT LIMITS
Oleson, Nicholas
AMERICAN HISTORY X
WITHOUT LIMITS
Olga
GOVERNESS, THE
Olhovsky, Viachesslav
TRUCE, THE
Olin, Lena
NIGHT AND THE MOMENT, THE
POLISH WEDDING
Oliney, Alan
HOLY MAN
Olivas, Santos
CARLA'S SONG
Oliveira, Jorseba-Sebastiao
CENTRAL STATION
Oliver, Alexandra
SLAMNATION
Oliver, Cindy
THERE'S SOMETHING ABOUT MARY
Oliver, Corine
NAKED ACTS
Oliver, Dave
CHOSEN ONE: LEGEND OF THE RAVEN, THE
Oliver, Deanna
BRAVE LITTLE TOASTER GOES TO MARS, THE
Oliver, James
LETHAL WEAPON 4
Oliver, Lucille
RUSTY: THE GREAT RESCUE
WHY DO FOOLS FALL IN LOVE?
Oliver, Luke Morgan
VELVET GOLDMINE
Oliver, Nicole
I'LL BE HOME FOR CHRISTMAS
Oliver, Roland
MERRY WAR, A
Oliver, Tony
RUSTY: THE GREAT RESCUE
Oliver, Tonya
HOLY MAN
RIDE
Olivier, George
LITTLE VOICE
Olivieri, Daniela
REAL BLONDE, THE
Oliviero, Silvio
DIRTY WORK
WOO
Olkewicz, Walter
MILO
PRONTO
Ollerenshaw, Duncan
RESCUERS: STORIES OF COURAGE—TWO COUPLES
Olley, Chris
TARZAN AND THE LOST CITY
Olley, Ray
LOVE IS THE DEVIL: STUDY FOR A PORTRAIT OF FRANCIS BACON
Ollivier, Alain
ARTEMISIA
Olmos, Edward James
HOLLYWOOD CONFIDENTIAL
12 ANGRY MEN
Olmos, William James
HOLLYWOOD CONFIDENTIAL
Olmstead, Dan
BELOVED
Olney, Warren
ENEMY OF THE STATE
Olofsen, Dorte
CELEBRATION, THE
Olofsen, Kasper
CELEBRATION, THE
Olohan, John
BUTCHER BOY, THE
Olsday, Stefan
VELVET GOLDMINE
Olsen, Ashley
BILLBOARD DAD
Olsen, Mary Kate
BILLBOARD DAD
Olsen, Richard
SHADRACH
STEPHEN KING'S THE NIGHT FLIER
Olson, Coach Lute
HE GOT GAME
Olson, Dale
OFF THE MENU: THE LAST DAYS OF CHASEN'S
Olson, Eric
ENEMY OF THE STATE
Olson, Jeff
CLAY PIGEONS
NOT IN THIS TOWN
Olson, Richard Taylor
SLAPPY AND THE STINKERS
Olynek, Scott
ATOMIC DOG
Olyphant, Timothy
WHEN TRUMPETS FADE
Omar, Farouk Valley
ERNEST IN THE ARMY
Oms, Alba
BREAK, THE
Omundson, Tom
DISAPPEARANCE OF KEVIN JOHNSON, THE
Omuni, Naser
MIRROR, THE
On Kam See
KILLER ANGELS
On On
KILLER ANGELS
Onimaru
JUNK FOOD
Ono, Jay
SIN AND REDEMPTION
Ono, Yoko
FREE TIBET
Ontrup, Martin
HUMAN BOMB
Oparei, Deobie
DARK CITY
Opie, Cathy
HALLELUJAH!
Oppenheimer, Alan
FLINTSTONES: I YABBA-DABBA DOO!, THE
Oppenheimer, Josh
WEDDING SINGER, THE
Oppenheimer, Julie
BABE: PIG IN THE CITY
Oramos, Nelson
WILD THINGS
Orbach, Ron
RINGMASTER
Orbital
MODULATIONS: CINEMA FOR THE EAR
Orchid, Bruce
LETHAL WEAPON 4
Orchid, Christina
LETHAL WEAPON 4
Ordas, Viviane
UN AIR DE FAMILLE
Orefice, Carmen Dell
CELEBRITY
Orenstein, Joan
HANGING GARDEN, THE
Orizaga, Yolanda
MASK OF ZORRO, THE
Orlan, Roberta
PERFECT MURDER, A
Orlando Araque, Jose
LAWN DOGS
Orlando, Silvio
NIRVANA
Orr, Mitchell
ANOTHER DAY IN PARADISE
SIMON BIRCH
Orr, Piper
DANCE WITH ME
Orr, Richard
JACK HIGGINS' ON DANGEROUS GROUND
Orr, Sean
REAL BLONDE, THE
Orr, Tony
SIMON BIRCH
Orrock, Shanon
PATCH ADAMS
Orser, Leland
SAVING PRIVATE RYAN
VERY BAD THINGS
Ortega, Armando
NEIL SIMON'S THE ODD COUPLE II
Ortega, Jimmy
JOHN CARPENTER'S VAMPIRES
REPLACEMENT KILLERS, THE
Ortega, Michele
WHO THE HELL IS JULIETTE?
Ortega, Oscar Garcia
MEN WITH GUNS
Ortega, Victor
WHO THE HELL IS JULIETTE?
Ortega, Yuliet
WHO THE HELL IS JULIETTE?
Ortelecan, Dora
SECRET KINGDOM, THE
Orth, Elisabeth
INHERITORS, THE
Orth, Zack
WHEN TRUMPETS FADE
Oruche, Phina
HOW STELLA GOT HER GROOVE BACK
Osada, Emiko
WHEN I CLOSE MY EYES

Osawa, Sayaka
GODZILLA AND MOTHRA: THE BATTLE FOR EARTH
Osborn, John
PARALLEL SONS
Osborne, Derek
TWENTYFOURSEVEN
Osborne, Holmes
AFFLICTION
Osborne, Kent
KNOCK OFF
Oscar, Billy
WALKING THUNDER
Osgood, Nathan
VELVET GOLDMINE
Oshima, Yukari
BEAUTY INVESTIGATOR
KICK BOXER'S TEARS
Osmond, Donny
MULAN
Osmond, Jak
REDLINE
Osmond, Marie
BUSTER & CHAUNCEY'S SILENT NIGHT
Ossman, David
BUG'S LIFE, A
Ostendorf, Josef
RAT'S TALE, A
Ostrenko, Kim
CATHERINE'S GROVE
Ostrofsky, James
STEPMOM
Ostrow, Ron
BULWORTH
Osugi, Ren
FIREWORKS
Oswill, Chaz
DANCE WITH ME
Otake, Makoto
GODZILLA AND MOTHRA: THE BATTLE FOR EARTH
Otasevic, Veljko
SAVIOR
Otis, Billy
TRACKED
Otis, James
ANOTHER DAY IN PARADISE
HENRY: PORTRAIT OF A SERIAL KILLER PART 2
Otis, Laura
BRAM STOKER'S THE MUMMY
Otori, Rumi
JUNK FOOD
Ottesen, Maja
INCOGNITO
Otto, Barry
MR. NICE GUY
Otto, Miranda
THIN RED LINE, THE
Otto, Rick
PHANTOMS
Ottoman, Mary
APT PUPIL
Otton, Glenn
RETURN OF THE KING, THE
Oubramova, Zoja
LES MISERABLES
MY GIANT
Ousdal, Sverre Anker
INSOMNIA
KRISTIN LAVRANSDATTER
Outerbridge, Jen Sung
SIX DAYS, SEVEN NIGHTS
Outlaw, Paul
ALL THE RAGE
Ouzo
LOVE AND DEATH ON LONG ISLAND
Oval
MODULATIONS: CINEMA FOR THE EAR
Overby, Rhonda
ENEMY OF THE STATE
Overton, Jennifer
REAL HOWARD SPITZ, THE
TALES FROM A PARALLEL UNIVERSE: GIGA SHADOW
TALES FROM A PARALLEL UNIVERSE: SUPER NOVA
Overton, Rick
MY GIANT
Owe, Baard
KINGDOM, PART 2, THE
Owen, Chris
CAN'T HARDLY WAIT
Owen, Laurence
WILDE
Owen, Sarah
ELIZABETH
Owens, Chris
DISTURBING BEHAVIOR
Owens, Ciaran
BUTCHER BOY, THE
Owens, Eamonn
BUTCHER BOY, THE
GENERAL, THE
Oxenberg, Catherine
BOYS WILL BE BOYS
Oz, Frank
BLUES BROTHERS 2000
Ozawa, Natsuki
ZERO WOMAN
Ozawa, Shoichi
EEL, THE
Ozbek, Rifat
LOVE IS THE DEVIL: STUDY FOR A PORTRAIT OF FRANCIS BACON
Ozioi, Hari
BOYS WILL BE BOYS
P., Sweet
HALLELUJAH!
Paalgaard, Suzanne
JUNK MAIL
Pacheco, Ruth
CARLA'S SONG
Pachin, Eugen
FRIEND OF THE DECEASED, A
Pachosa, Steven Clark
PSYCHO
Pacienza, Michael
WIDE AWAKE
Pacifici, Federico
EIGHTEENTH ANGEL, THE
TRUCE, THE
Packer, David
ALMOST HEROES
Packer, Deborah
BABE: PIG IN THE CITY
Packham, Caleb
VIOLET'S VISIT
Pacula, Joanna
MY GIANT
WHITE RAVEN, THE
Paddock, Josh
WHAT DREAMS MAY COME
Paetkau, David
DISTURBING BEHAVIOR
Paetty, Scott
DANCE WITH ME
Paetz, Laurel
CAPTIVE
Pagan, Angelo
DANCE WITH ME
Pagan, Michael J.
FALLEN
HOW STELLA GOT HER GROOVE BACK
Pagan, Michael Jamon
RUSTY: THE GREAT RESCUE
Page, Corey
DEAD MAN ON CAMPUS
Page, Erika
LITTLE BIGFOOT 2: THE JOURNEY HOME
Page, Grant
MR. NICE GUY
Page, Melanie
KNOCK OFF
Pagh, Klaus
KINGDOM, PART 2, THE
Paglia, Camille
HENRY FOOL
STORY OF X, THE
Pai, Liana
SIEGE, THE
Paige, Jordan
54
Paige, Tony
HE GOT GAME
Pais, John
CIVIL ACTION, A
Pais, Josh
ROUNDERS
SAFE MEN
Pak Ying
ROYAL WARRIORS
Paladino, Dennis
GREAT EXPECTATIONS
Palagonia, Al
HE GOT GAME
Palance, Jack
EBENEZER
Palffy, David
URBAN SAFARI
Pall, Subash Sing
CARLA'S SONG
Palladino, Aleska
CELEBRITY
Palladino, Erik
CAN'T HARDLY WAIT
Palladino, Gianni
NIRVANA
Pallana, Deepak
RUSHMORE
Pallana, Kumar
RUSHMORE
Pallenberg, Anita
LOVE IS THE DEVIL: STUDY FOR A PORTRAIT OF FRANCIS BACON
Pallone, Gregory F.
GINGERBREAD MAN, THE
Palma, Enrike
MASK OF ZORRO, THE
Palma, Nicholas
CHARLIE HOBOKEN
Palmer, Andrew
HOW STELLA GOT HER GROOVE BACK
Palmer, Ben
INFORMANT, THE
Palmer, Gretchen
I GOT THE HOOK UP
Palmer, Robin
TRICKS
Palmer, Rosemary
ONE TRUE THING
Palmer, Terry
SAND TRAP
Palmier, Marina
NO ORDINARY LOVE
Palminteri, Chazz
HURLYBURLY
NIGHT AT THE ROXBURY, A
OFF THE MENU: THE LAST DAYS OF CHASEN'S
SCARRED CITY

Palomino, Cris Thomas
JOHN CARPENTER'S VAMPIRES
Palone, Gavin
BURN HOLLYWOOD BURN
Paltrow, Gwyneth
GREAT EXPECTATIONS
HUSH
OUT OF THE PAST
PERFECT MURDER, A
SHAKESPEARE IN LOVE
SLIDING DOORS
Pamintuan, Angelica
ENEMY OF THE STATE
Pan, Dana
SHOPPING FOR FANGS
Pan Han Guang
SHAOLIN TEMPLE, THE
Pan Qingfu
SHAOLIN TEMPLE, THE
Pan Yun Cheung
HEROES SHED NO TEARS
Panacea
MODULATIONS: CINEMA FOR THE EAR
Panaro, Hugh
BROADWAY DAMAGE
Pancake, Sam
GIA
Pandey, Ramesh
I LOVE YOU, DON'T TOUCH ME!
Pandolfo, Tony
FATAL PURSUIT
Panettiere, Hayden
BUG'S LIFE, A
OBJECT OF MY AFFECTION, THE
Pang, Bennett
ARMOUR OF GOD
Pankey, Bill
LETTER FROM DEATH ROW, A
Pankin, Stuart
NAPOLEON
Pankow, Joanne
DIGGING TO CHINA
Pankow, John
OBJECT OF MY AFFECTION, THE
Pantaeva, Irina
CELEBRITY
Pantoliano, Joe
TOP OF THE WORLD
U.S. MARSHALS
Pao Fung
CHINESE BOX, THE
Paolini, Joseph
BOYS IN LOVE 2
Paolone, Catherine
KRIPPENDORF'S TRIBE
NEIL SIMON'S THE ODD COUPLE II
Papa, Carmen
CLOCKMAKER
Papajohn, Michael
MY GIANT
Paquin, Anna
HURLYBURLY
Paras, Dean
HARD CORE LOGO
Pardo, Don
GODSON, THE
Parducci, Paul
GUN, A CAR, AND A BLONDE, A
Pare, Michael
FALLING FIRE
HOPE FLOATS
Paredes, Marisa
LIFE IS BEAUTIFUL
TALK OF ANGELS
Parent, Matthieu
BLEEDERS
Parent, Patrick
SNAKE EYES
Parent, Wayne
REAL BLONDE, THE
Parfitt, Judy
EVER AFTER
WILDE
Parhm, A.J. Alexander O.
HOLY MAN
Parillaud, Anne
MAN IN THE IRON MASK, THE
SHATTERED IMAGE
Paris, Tony
U.S. MARSHALS
Parish, Billy
TALISMAN
Parisi, Joe
ROUNDERS
Parisio, Albert
UN AIR DE FAMILLE
Park, Joong-Hoon
DOUBLE EDGE
Park, Steve
DESPERATE MEASURES
Park, Uni
DIRTY WORK
Parker, Beau
RETURN TO SAVAGE BEACH
Parker, David
LANDLADY, THE
Parker, Doug
DRAGON BALL Z THE MOVIE: THE TREE OF MIGHT
Parker, Gerard
JACK HIGGINS' THUNDER POINT
Parker, Kerri
HANDS ON A HARDBODY
Parker, Leni
BLEEDERS
Parker, Maceo
MY FIRST NAME IS MACEO
Parker, Mary-Louise
MAKER, THE
MURDER IN MIND
Parker, Melvin
MY FIRST NAME IS MACEO
Parker, Molly
UNDER HEAVEN
Parker, Monica
PERFECT MURDER, A
Parker, Nicole
HARD CORE LOGO
REBOUND: THE LEGEND OF EARL "THE GOAT" MANIGAULT
Parker, Norman
BULWORTH
Parker, Paula Jai
WHY DO FOOLS FALL IN LOVE?
WOO
Parker, Sarah Jessica
OFF THE MENU: THE LAST DAYS OF CHASEN'S
Parker, Timothy Britten
ELMORE LEONARD'S GOLD COAST
RATCHET
Parker, Trey
BASEKETBALL
ORGAZMO
Parker, Zane
CLAY PIGEONS
Parker-Jones, Jill
HOME FRIES
Parkinson, Matthew
BABE: PIG IN THE CITY
Parks, Charles
PAULIE
PENTAGON WARS, THE
Parks, Gerard
RESCUERS: STORIES OF COURAGE—TWO WOMEN
Parks, Michael
DECEIVER
FULL TILT BOOGIE
NIAGARA NIAGARA
Parks, Ted
LOS LOCOS
Parnes, Fred
ZERO EFFECT
Paro, Aldo
SIX DAYS, SEVEN NIGHTS
Parris, James
BELLY
Parris, Marriam
CLUB VAMPIRE
Parrish, Amy
NEIL SIMON'S THE ODD COUPLE II
Parrish, Sally
OBJECT OF MY AFFECTION, THE
Parron, Michel
DEAD END
Parry, Angelique
BILLBOARD DAD
SENSELESS
Parsons, Grant
MERRY WAR, A
Parsons, Ian
HANGING GARDEN, THE
Partlow, Richard
LIVING IN PERIL
Parziale, Anthony
SOUR GRAPES
Pascal, Adam
QUEST FOR CAMELOT
Pascal, Lucien
POST COITUM, ANIMAL TRISTE
Paschall, David
THIN RED LINE, THE
Pasco, Nicholas
HOT BLOODED
UNDERTAKER'S WEDDING, THE
Pasdar, Adrian
WOUNDED
Paseka, Lawton
GODZILLA
Pasha, Sammy
TWENTYFOURSEVEN
Pashalinski, Lola
GODZILLA
PECKER
Paskel, Eric
GODZILLA
Pasteur, Sierra
SENSELESS
Pastor, Manolo
MASK OF ZORRO, THE
Pastor, Rosana
BREAK, THE
Pastore, Vincent
JANE AUSTEN'S MAFIA!
WEST NEW YORK
Pastorello, Natascia
DANGEROUS BEAUTY
Patal, Rajan
JUNGLE BOOK: MOWGLI'S STORY, THE
Patano, Tonye
PRICE ABOVE RUBIES, A
Patch, Tayva
NOT IN THIS TOWN
Pate, Curt
HORSE WHISPERER, THE
Pate, Tammy
HORSE WHISPERER, THE
Paterson, Bill
HILARY AND JACKIE
SPICE WORLD
Paterson, Christine
DECAMPITATED

Paterson, David
RUN FOR COVER
Pather, Puven
MR. NICE GUY
Patinkin, Mandy
MEN WITH GUNS
Patocka, Jiri
LES MISERABLES
Paton, Angela
CON, THE
LOLITA
Paton, Eliot
DARK CITY
Patric, Jason
INCOGNITO
YOUR FRIENDS & NEIGHBORS
Patric, Jim
PLEASANTVILLE
Patrick, Dan
WATERBOY, THE
Patrick, Robert
ASYLUM
FACULTY, THE
ONLY THRILL, THE
Patrikios, Peter
POLTERGEIST REPORT: YUYU HAKUSHO
SNAKE EYES
WRATH OF THE NINJA: THE YOTODEN MOVIE
Patron, Emmanuel
MAN IN THE IRON MASK, THE
Patteri, Robert
OPERATION DELTA FORCE 2
Patterson, Edi
TEKKEN: THE MOTION PICTURE
Patterson, Jay
CITY OF ANGELS
CIVIL ACTION, A
HARD RAIN
SLUMS OF BEVERLY HILLS
Patterson, Lance
LOVE IS THE DEVIL: STUDY FOR A PORTRAIT OF FRANCIS BACON
Patterson, Patrick
BLUES BROTHERS 2000
Patti, Thomas
HOLLYWOOD CONFIDENTIAL
Patton, Frank
TOP OF THE WORLD
Patton, Lucille
BROADWAY DAMAGE
Patton, Stephanie
DEEP IMPACT
Patton, Will
ARMAGEDDON
Patzwald, Julie
DISTURBING BEHAVIOR
WHEN DANGER FOLLOWS YOU HOME
Paul, Adam
PENTAGON WARS, THE
Paul, Bonnie
BOYS WILL BE BOYS
Paul, Brian
RESCUERS: STORIES OF COURAGE—TWO WOMEN
Paul, Kurt
PRINCE, THE
Paul, Morgan
UNCLE SAM
Paul, Richard Joseph
RUNNING WOMAN, THE
WOUNDED
Paulin, Viveca
NIGHT AT THE ROXBURY, A
Paulk, Mark
WHY DO FOOLS FALL IN LOVE?
Paulk, Martin
WHY DO FOOLS FALL IN LOVE?

Paulos, Nick
CAN'T HARDLY WAIT
Paulsen, Tiffany
HOMEGROWN
Paulson, Jay
CAN'T HARDLY WAIT
PERMANENT MIDNIGHT
Paun, Jean
GADJO DILO
Paun, Lunitia
GADJO DILO
Pavel, Adrian
SECRET KINGDOM, THE
Pavel, Eugenia
SUBSPECIES IV: BLOODSTORM
Pavel, Lucien
SHRUNKEN CITY, THE
Pavel, Philip
COURTING COURTNEY
Pavement
FREE TIBET
Pavez, Terele
DAY OF THE BEAST, THE
Pavlidis, Harry
MR. NICE GUY
Pavol, Hracko
NEMESIS 4: CRY OF ANGELS
Paxton, Bill
BRIGHT SHINING LIE, A
MIGHTY JOE YOUNG
SIMPLE PLAN, A
Paxton, John
SIMPLE PLAN, A
Payan, Diana
FIRELIGHT
Payeur, Gregoriane Minot
LOST WORLD, THE
Paymer, Charles
WRONGFULLY ACCUSED
Paymer, David
MIGHTY JOE YOUNG
OUTSIDE OZONA
Payn, Jason
WRONGFULLY ACCUSED
Payne, Allen
PRICE ABOVE RUBIES, A
Payne, Bruce
FACE THE EVIL
Payne II, Carl Anthony
OVERNIGHT DELIVERY
Payne, Kendra
DANCER, TEXAS POP. 81
Pays, Amanda
HOLLYWOOD CONFIDENTIAL
SPACEJACKED
Payton, Angela
WEDDING SINGER, THE
Payton, Christian
U.S. MARSHALS
Paz, Jennifer
CAN'T HARDLY WAIT
Peabody, Dossy
PROPOSITION, THE
Peabody, Stephen
ONE TRUE THING
Peace, Joshua
BIG HIT, THE
Peace, Margo
GREAT EXPECTATIONS
WILD THINGS
Peace, Westin
FERNGULLY 2: THE MAGICAL RESCUE
Peacock, Russell
NOT IN THIS TOWN
Pearce, Daniel
GODZILLA
Pearce, Darren
DESPERATE MEASURES

Pearce, Oscar
MRS. DALLOWAY
Pearl, Aaron
EBENEZER
WRONGFULLY ACCUSED
Pearl, Julie R.
SUBSTITUTE 2: SCHOOL'S OUT, THE
Pearl, Steven
COMEDY'S DIRTIEST DOZEN
Pearlman, Stephen
HORSE WHISPERER, THE
PI
Pearlstein, Randy
DEAD MAN ON CAMPUS
Pearson, Amy
TARZAN AND THE LOST CITY
Pearson, Jay S.
GINGERBREAD MAN, THE
Pearson, Melanie
SPECIES II
Peart, O'Neil
SHATTERED IMAGE
Pecararo, Joe
LOVE TO KILL
Pecca, Ron
UNDERTAKER'S WEDDING, THE
Pecha, Jiri
FORGOTTEN LIGHT
Peck, Cecilia
FRENCH EXIT
Peck, George
CURSE OF THE PUPPET MASTER
Peck, James
INNOCENT SLEEP, THE
PASSION IN THE DESERT
Peck, Rosalie
PRIMARY COLORS
Pecora, Robert
NO ORDINARY LOVE
Pederson, Eric
FORMER CHILD STAR
Pederson, Mary D.
NOT IN THIS TOWN
Pedtrchenko, Victor
BLUES BROTHERS 2000
Peduto, Ralph
PATCH ADAMS
Peel, Darren
LETHAL WEAPON 4
Peels, Derek
BIG HIT, THE
Peeples, Nia
BLUES BROTHERS 2000
Peet, Amanda
CHARLIE HOBOKEN
PLAYING BY HEART
Peikoff, Cynthia
AYN RAND: A SENSE OF LIFE
Peikoff, Dr. Leonard
AYN RAND: A SENSE OF LIFE
Peil, Mary Beth
NEIL SIMON'S THE ODD COUPLE II
Peirez, Susan
LENA'S DREAMS
Peixoto, Floriano
OYSTER AND THE WIND, THE
Pekova, Simona
FORGOTTEN LIGHT
Pekrul, Alan
PLAN B
Peldon, Ashley
JUNGLE BOOK: MOWGLI'S STORY, THE
Peleg, Gil
WHEN PIGS FLY
Pellegrino, Frank
CELEBRITY
ONE TOUGH COP
TARANTELLA

Peterson, Melanie
BLACK LIGHT
Peterson, Otto
COMEDY'S DIRTIEST DOZEN
Peterson, Poul
CELEBRATION, THE
Peterson, Seth
CAN'T HARDLY WAIT
GODZILLA
Petrarca, Steven
POLISH WEDDING
WHEN TRUMPETS FADE
Petrie, Alistair
MRS. DALLOWAY
Petrocelli, Richard
HURRICANE STREETS
Petrof, Alita
LITTLE VOICE
Petronijevic, Dan
IN HIS FATHER'S SHOES
Petrosino, Christopher
RIVER RED
Petrova, Galina
THIEF, THE
Petrusonis, Anthony T.
NEGOTIATOR, THE
Pettrie, Jim
TALES FROM A PARALLEL UNIVERSE: GIGA SHADOW
Petty, Dini
DIRTY WORK
Pevsner, David
DAVID SEARCHING
Peyanikow, Yasen
U.S. MARSHALS
Pfeiffer, Michelle
PRINCE OF EGYPT, THE
Phelan, Anthony
BABE: PIG IN THE CITY
HEAVEN'S BURNING
Phelan, Michael
OBJECT OF MY AFFECTION, THE
Phellippe, Joao
TIETA OF AGRESTE
Phelps-Williams, David
OPPOSITE OF SEX, THE
Phife
RUGRATS MOVIE, THE
Phifer, Mekhi
HAV PLENTY
I STILL KNOW WHAT YOU DID LAST SUMMER
Philipchuk, Misha
THIEF, THE
Philippe, Harry
HE GOT GAME
Philips, Gina
LIVING OUT LOUD
Phillip, Kevin
UNDER HEAVEN
Phillippe, Ryan
54
HOMEGROWN
LITTLE BOY BLUE
PLAYING BY HEART
Phillips, Andrew L.
NIAGARA NIAGARA
Phillips, Dionne D.
HE GOT GAME
Phillips, Ethan
TREKKIES
Phillips, Jace
THIN RED LINE, THE
Phillips, Joseph C.
LET'S TALK ABOUT SEX
Phillips, Julian M.
GODZILLA
Phillips, Lara
BULLET ON A WIRE
Phillips, Lou Diamond
BIG HIT, THE
Phillips, Mark
SAVING PRIVATE RYAN
Phillips, Pamela
INVISIBLE MOM
Phinnessee, Darryl
FLINTSTONES: I YABBA-DABBA DOO!, THE
Phippen Jr., Hardy
MEET JOE BLACK
Phipps, Anna Rose
DEAD WATERS
Phoenix, Joaquin
CLAY PIGEONS
RETURN TO PARADISE
Phoenix, Summer
CAN'T HARDLY WAIT
FACULTY, THE
Photek
MODULATIONS: CINEMA FOR THE EAR
Picard, Don
SAFE MEN
Picardo, Robert
SMALL SOLDIERS
Picchi, Nilo
UNDERTAKER'S WEDDING, THE
Piccirillo, Mario
LIVING OUT LOUD
Piccoli, Michel
GENEALOGIES OF A CRIME
PASSION IN THE DESERT
Piccolo, Gina
ONE TRUE THING
Pichette, Ray
OUTSIDE OZONA
Pickard, Raymond
BORROWERS, THE
Pickelman, Brenda
U.S. MARSHALS
Pickelsimer II, David Alan
DECEIVER
Pickens, Jimmy Ray
CON, THE
Pickens Jr., James
BULWORTH
HOW STELLA GOT HER GROOVE BACK
SPHERE
Pickering, Julie
RED HAWK: WEAPON OF DEATH
Pickersgill, Kirk
WOO
Picket, Bronson
REAL BLONDE, THE
Pickett, Cindy
ATOMIC DOG
Pickett, Tom
URBAN SAFARI
Pickett, Wiley
MIGHTY JOE YOUNG
Pickett, Wilson
BLUES BROTHERS 2000
Pickles, Christina
WEDDING SINGER, THE
Pickren, Richard
U.S. MARSHALS
Pickup, Ronald
LOLITA
Picoy, Kane
PLUMP FICTION
Piddock, Jim
BURN HOLLYWOOD BURN
Pidgeon, Rebecca
SPANISH PRISONER, THE
Pierce, Bradley
BORROWERS, THE
Pierce, David Hyde
BUG'S LIFE, A
Pierce, Devon
NORTH SHORE FISH
Pierce, John Patrick
FORMER CHILD STAR
Pierce, Linda
LAST DAYS OF DISCO, THE
Pierce, Mary Vivan
PECKER
Pierce, Sally
WEDDING SINGER, THE
Pierce, Wendell
BULWORTH
Pierre, Olivier
INCOGNITO
Pierrot, Frederic
ARTEMISIA
Pierson, Kate
RUGRATS MOVIE, THE
Pierson, Ronda
HOLY MAN
Pietrangolare, Frank
GREAT EXPECTATIONS
Pilato, Josef
LAST SEDUCTION II, THE
Pileggi, Mitch
X-FILES, THE
Pilkington, Joe
BUTCHER BOY, THE
Pilkington, Lorraine
SUMMER FLING
Pillars, Jeffrey
ERNEST IN THE ARMY
Pilmark, Soren
KINGDOM, PART 2, THE
Pilver, Michael
RIDE
Pimenter, Gabrille
SIX-STRING SAMURAI
Pimsler, Paul
ONE TRUE THING
Pinchot, Bronson
NAPOLEON
QUEST FOR CAMELOT
SLAPPY AND THE STINKERS
Pine, Larry
CELEBRITY
Pine, Robert
BODY COUNT
Pineda, Christine
PATCH ADAMS
Pineda, Salvador
NAKED LIES
Ping, Sinna
KNOCK OFF
Ping Wu
SIX DAYS, SEVEN NIGHTS
Pinilla, David
DAY OF THE BEAST, THE
Pinkett, Jada
RETURN TO PARADISE
WOO
Pinnock, Emil
BELOVED
Pino, Mariangela
LIVING OUT LOUD
SOULER OPPOSITE, THE
Pinque, Joe
DEFENDERS: PAYBACK, THE
Pinto, Barbara Winters
BROADWAY DAMAGE
Pinto, Jose
VOYAGE TO THE BEGINNING OF THE WORLD
Pintzka, Wolfgang
MENDEL

Pinwheel
DECLINE OF WESTERN CIVILIZATION PART III, THE
Pippen, Scottie
HE GOT GAME
Pireyzol, Christine
NIGHT AND THE MOMENT, THE
Pirman Jr., Bill
HENRY: PORTRAIT OF A SERIAL KILLER PART 2
Piro, Grant
TWISTED
Pirozzi, Brett
DEE SNIDER'S STRANGELAND
Piscitelli, Carol
CHARLIE HOBOKEN
Pisleaga, Daniel
SECRET KINGDOM, THE
Pismichenko, Svetlana
BROTHER
Pitillo, Maria
GODZILLA
Pitino, Coach Rick
HE GOT GAME
Pitt, Brad
MEET JOE BLACK
Pittarello, Massimo
ARTEMISIA
Pitts, Mia
WOO
Pitts, Michael
COURTING COURTNEY
Pitts, Wendy
CLOCKWATCHERS
Pittsley, Mike
STILL BREATHING
Pittu, David
SOMEWHERE IN THE CITY
SPANISH PRISONER, THE
Pivac, Sara
UGLY, THE
Pivac, Wayne
BOYS IN LOVE 2
Pivar, Nancy
R.I.P. REST IN PIECES: A PORTRAIT OF JOE COLEMAN
Piven, Byrne
VERY BAD THINGS
Piven, Jeremy
DON KING: ONLY IN AMERICA
MUSIC FROM ANOTHER ROOM
PHOENIX
REAL THING, THE
VERY BAD THINGS
Pizano, Beatriz
FACE DOWN
Place, Mary Kay
MY VERY BEST FRIEND
PECKER
Plana, Tony
SUB DOWN
Planer, Nigel
LAND GIRLS, THE
Plasencia, Roseanna
PRICE ABOVE RUBIES, A
Plasil, Milo
HOMEGROWN
Plate, Roberto
POST COITUM, ANIMAL TRISTE
Platt, Colin
RUSHMORE
Platt, Jim
RAGE, THE
Platt, Oliver
BULWORTH
DANGEROUS BEAUTY
DR. DOLITTLE
IMPOSTORS, THE
SIMON BIRCH
Playford, Rob
MODULATIONS: CINEMA FOR THE EAR
Pleasant, David Daniel
NAKED ACTS
Pleshette, John
TRUMAN SHOW, THE
Pleshette, Suzanne
LION KING II: SIMBA'S PRIDE, THE
OFF THE MENU: THE LAST DAYS OF CHASEN'S
Plewacki, Gale
OVERNIGHT DELIVERY
Plimpton, George
LAST DAYS OF DISCO, THE
Plimpton, Martha
DEFENDERS: PAYBACK, THE
MUSIC FROM ANOTHER ROOM
PECKER
WHO IS HENRY JAGLOM?
Plotnick, Jack
CHAIRMAN OF THE BOARD
GODS AND MONSTERS
Plowright, Joan
DANCE WITH ME
Plum, Mette Munk
KINGDOM, PART 2, THE
Plum, Paula
NEXT STOP, WONDERLAND
Plumb, Eve
BREAST MEN
Plummer, Glenn
DESTINY OF MARTY FINE, THE
PRONTO
THURSDAY
Plunkett, Gerald
NEW ADVENTURES OF KIMBA THE WHITE LION, THE
WRONGFULLY ACCUSED
Pniewski, Mike
GINGERBREAD MAN, THE
Pochie, Angelina
WESTERN
Podhora, Roman
TRUCKS
WHEN DANGER FOLLOWS YOU HOME
Poe, Juliet
BODY COUNT
Pogue, Ken
JACK HIGGINS' THE WINDSOR PROTOCOL
Poindexter, Jeris
CAUGHT UP
Poindexter, Larry
STEEL SHARKS
WHITE RAVEN, THE
Pointeaux, Lilly-Fleur
RONIN
Pointer, Priscilla
HORTON FOOTE'S ALONE
Poirier, Denise
GOLGO 13: QUEEN BEE
Polac, Michel
POST COITUM, ANIMAL TRISTE
Polakova, Belinka
KNOCK OFF
Polan, Claire
INVISIBLE DAD
Polanco, Iraida
OBJECT OF MY AFFECTION, THE
Poland, Greg
STAR TREK: INSURRECTION
Poland, Simon
NEMESIS 4: CRY OF ANGELS
Pole, Edward Tudor
LES MISERABLES
Poletto, Vince
MR. NICE GUY
Poli, Maurice
RABID DOGS
Poli, Rick
TALK TO ME
Polic II, Henry
FLINTSTONES: I YABBA-DABBA DOO!, THE
Polito, Jon
BIG LEBOWSKI, THE
GIRLS IN PRISON
Polivka, Boleslav
FORGOTTEN LIGHT
Polk Jr., Cletus
CHARLIE HOBOKEN
Polk, Patrik Ian
HAV PLENTY
Pollack, Sydney
CIVIL ACTION, A
Pollak, Cheryl
SIN AND REDEMPTION
Pollak, Kevin
BUFFALO '66
OUTSIDE OZONA
Pollard, Michael J.
STIR
Polley, Sarah
HANGING GARDEN, THE
Poltaruk, Rick
SNOWBOUND
Pomales, Ana Sofia
DANCE WITH ME
Pomerance, Hope
HAPPINESS
Pomeroy, Christopher
IMPOSTORS, THE
Pomers, Scarlett
SLAPPY AND THE STINKERS
Pomfret, Neil
THERE'S SOMETHING ABOUT MARY
Pomfret, Ruth
THERE'S SOMETHING ABOUT MARY
Pon, Patrick
WHEN DANGER FOLLOWS YOU HOME
Poncelet, Thomas
DEJA VU
Ponchon, Alix
MADELINE
Ponder, Dana
PARENT TRAP, THE
Ponella, Mike
CELEBRITY
Pong, Elodie
POST COITUM, ANIMAL TRISTE
Ponterotto, Donna
NEGOTIATOR, THE
Pool, Austin John
DIRTY WORK
Pooley, Alex
EVER AFTER
Pooley, Robin
BAD MANNERS
Poon, Alice
HALF BAKED
Poon Sam
KILLER ANGELS
Poor, Bray
SCARRED CITY
Pop, Iggy
RUGRATS MOVIE, THE
Popa, Isabella
BASEKETBALL
Popa, Razvan
LITTLE GHOST
Pope, Caelem
UGLY, THE

Pope, Carly
DISTURBING BEHAVIOR
Pope, Don
HI-LO COUNTRY, THE
Pope, Ralph
CELEBRITY
Pope, Ryan
VELVET GOLDMINE
Popisil, Eric
RUDOLPH THE RED-NOSED REINDEER: THE MOVIE
Popov, Yevgeni
THIEF, THE
Popovic, George
MR. NICE GUY
Popp, Markus
MODULATIONS: CINEMA FOR THE EAR
Popper, John
BLUES BROTHERS 2000
Poppler, John P.
POLTERGEIST REPORT: YUYU HAKUSHO
Popson, Hedy
HIJACKING HOLLYWOOD
Porizkova, Paulina
THURSDAY
Portal, Robert
MRS. DALLOWAY
Porter, Adina
GIA
Porter, Bobby
STAR KID
Porter, Charlaine
MIGHTY, THE
Porter, Christopher
WHEN PIGS FLY
Porter, Ian
SAVING PRIVATE RYAN
Porter, Maria
HENRY FOOL
Porter, Nyree Dawn
HILARY AND JACKIE
Porter, Steven
ALMOST HEROES
Porter, Susie
WELCOME TO WOOP WOOP
Portnow, Richard
ALMOST PARTNERS
FEAR AND LOATHING IN LAS VEGAS
MILO
MY GIANT
Portser, Mary
SLUMS OF BEVERLY HILLS
Posey, Parker
CLOCKWATCHERS
HENRY FOOL
YOU'VE GOT MAIL
Posner, Joel
LAST BREATH
Pospisil, Eric
I'LL BE HOME FOR CHRISTMAS
Post, F.W.
NEWTON BOYS, THE
Post, Markie
THERE'S SOMETHING ABOUT MARY
Post, Tim
PEACEKEEPER, THE
Poster, Tom
ASYLUM
Posterboys, The
CRACKING UP
Poston, Tom
KRIPPENDORF'S TRIBE
Potok, Charlotte
SPANISH PRISONER, THE
Potter, Monica
PATCH ADAMS
WITHOUT LIMITS
Potter, Patricia
SHAKESPEARE IN LOVE
Potteuw, Jean-Paul
LIFE OF JESUS, THE
Pottinger, Alan
NIAGARA NIAGARA
Potts, Faith
HUSH
Potts, Jonathan
HOSTILE INTENT
Potts, Steve
BLUES BROTHERS 2000
Pouillade, Stephane
UN AIR DE FAMILLE
Poultin, John
REAL HOWARD SPITZ, THE
Pouncie, Ocie
DECEIVER
Pounsett, Geoffrey
FALLING FIRE
Poupaud, Melvil
GENEALOGIES OF A CRIME
Powell, Charles
JACK LONDON'S THE CALL OF THE WILD: DOG OF THE YUKON
Powell, Clifton
CAUGHT UP
DEEP RISING
PENTAGON WARS, THE
PHANTOMS
RUSH HOUR
WHY DO FOOLS FALL IN LOVE?
Powell, Colin
OFF THE MENU: THE LAST DAYS OF CHASEN'S
Powell, Sunni Ali
CHICAGO CAB
Powell, Suzette G.
LENA'S DREAMS
Powell, Tim
HOLY MAN
Powell, Willie Mae
CAN'T YOU HEAR THE WIND HOWL?: THE LIFE AND MUSIC OF ROBERT JOHNSON
Powers, Matthew
SUE
Poyer, Jude
KNOCK OFF
Pozdniakova, Natalia
THIEF, THE
Pozsik, Gary P.
MAJOR LEAGUE: BACK TO THE MINORS
Prado
EL CHE: INVESTIGATING A LEGEND
Pradon, Jerome
BRYLCREEM BOYS, THE
Prael, William
PROPHECY II, THE
Praetorius, Helen
KNOCK OFF
Pramik, John
TRUMAN SHOW, THE
Pratt, John C.
SPECIES II
Pratt, Kyla
BARNEY'S GREAT ADVENTURE—THE MOVIE
DR. DOLITTLE
Pratt, Lauren Varija
OBJECT OF MY AFFECTION, THE
Pratt, Susan
NO LOOKING BACK
Pratt, Susan May
SUBSTITUTE 2: SCHOOL'S OUT, THE
Prebble, Simon
CRACKING UP
Prendergast, Kasie
MY BROTHER'S WAR
Prendergast, Paul
HOMEGROWN
Prenout, Cyril
RONIN
Prentiss, Robert
NIGHT VISION
Presnell, Harve
BRIGHT SHINING LIE, A
PATCH ADAMS
SAVING PRIVATE RYAN
Press, Jacob
HUSH
Pressley, Thermond
RAT'S TALE, A
Pressly, Jamie
CAN'T HARDLY WAIT
RINGMASTER
Pressman, David
GODZILLA
Pressman, Lawrence
MAKER, THE
MIGHTY JOE YOUNG
MY GIANT
VERY BAD THINGS
Prester, Nino
LIFE IS BEAUTIFUL
Preston, Billy
BLUES BROTHERS 2000
Preston, Carrie
MERCURY RISING
Preston, Jerome
MY FIRST NAME IS MACEO
Preston, Kelly
HOLY MAN
JACK FROST
OFF THE MENU: THE LAST DAYS OF CHASEN'S
Preston, Madeline
BELOVED
Preston, Stewart
CARLA'S SONG
Pretlow, Wayne
NEXT STOP, WONDERLAND
Previn, Soon-Yi
WILD MAN BLUES
Price, Annabella
PRACTICAL MAGIC
Price, Annie Michele
EDEN
Price, Dylan
SCARRED CITY
Price, Gene
DEAR JESSE
Price, Jamieson K.
SECRET KINGDOM, THE
Price, Sue
NEMESIS 4: CRY OF ANGELS
Price, Tara
HOPE FLOATS
Price, Thommy
BOOGIE BOY
Pride, Jerome
MR. NICE GUY
Priest, Dan
I STILL KNOW WHAT YOU DID LAST SUMMER
Priestley, Jason
LOVE AND DEATH ON LONG ISLAND
Priestly, David
WRONGFULLY ACCUSED
Prigmore, J.T.
NIGHT VISION
Primus, Barry
ELMORE LEONARD'S GOLD COAST
Prince, Daisy
CELEBRITY

Prince, James Hansen
CON, THE
Pringle, Joan
GIA
Prinsloo, P.J.
DISTURBING BEHAVIOR
I'LL BE HOME FOR CHRISTMAS
Printop, Marcus
PLAYING BY HEART
Prinz, Werner
INHERITORS, THE
Prinze Jr., Freddie
I STILL KNOW WHAT YOU DID LAST SUMMER
Prior, Susan
HEAVEN'S BURNING
Prisco, Thomas
LAST BIG THING, THE
Pritchett, Polly
MRS. DALLOWAY
Privat, Arthur
WESTERN
Privat, Gerard
WESTERN
Privat, Maeva
WESTERN
Prochnow, Jurgen
HUMAN BOMB
JACK HIGGINS' ON DANGEROUS GROUND
REPLACEMENT KILLERS, THE
Procter, Emily
BREAST MEN
LOVE TO KILL
Proctor, Phil
DR. DOLITTLE
RUGRATS MOVIE, THE
Proctor, Rupert
REGENERATION
Proctor, Toby
BRAM STOKER'S SHADOWBUILDER
Prodigy
MODULATIONS: CINEMA FOR THE EAR
Proft, Pat
WRONGFULLY ACCUSED
Prokop, Patrick
GINGERBREAD MAN, THE
Proscia, Ray
WHY DO FOOLS FALL IN LOVE?
Prosky, John
COLONY, THE
PERMANENT MIDNIGHT
Prototype 909
MODULATIONS: CINEMA FOR THE EAR
Proval, David
SIEGE, THE
Provencher, Dylan
IN HIS FATHER'S SHOES
Provenza, Paul
PLUMP FICTION
Prucell, Daniel
RIVER RED
Pruckner, Tilo
INHERITORS, THE
Pruner, Karl
FIXER, THE
Pruyn, Serena
MIGHTY, THE
Pryce, Jonathan
REGENERATION
RONIN
Pryor, Ella
RUSHMORE
Pryor, J.F.
HIJACKING HOLLYWOOD
Pudwell, Laura
DIRTY WORK
Pugliese, Elisa
MONTANA
Pujol, Marcos
SOLDIER'S DAUGHTER NEVER CRIES, A
Pullen, Ben
PRINCE VALIANT
Pullen, Stacey
MODULATIONS: CINEMA FOR THE EAR
Pullis, Kimberly
RINGMASTER
Pullman, Bill
ZERO EFFECT
Pultar, Maylin
IN GOD'S HANDS
Purdy, Richard
HI-LO COUNTRY, THE
Purl, Linda
MIGHTY JOE YOUNG
Pursell, Laura
LANDLADY, THE
Purver, Edward
ELIZABETH
Putch, John
CITY OF ANGELS
SOULER OPPOSITE, THE
Putch, Pamela
ALONE IN THE WOODS
Putnam, Mary Allison
LOVE AND DEATH ON LONG ISLAND
Putney, Robert
DIGGING TO CHINA
Pyfrom, Amber
RIDE
Pyl, Jean Vander
FLINTSTONES: I YABBA-DABBA DOO!, THE
Pyper-Ferguson, John
HARD CORE LOGO
Pyrz, Gene
TRUCKS
Qian, Zu-Wu
LETHAL WEAPON 4
Qu Lixin
FROZEN
Quaid, Dennis
PARENT TRAP, THE
PLAYING BY HEART
SAVIOR
Quaid, Randy
HARD RAIN
Quarles, Norma
LAST DAYS OF DISCO, THE
Quartermus, Ray
MAKER, THE
Queen Latifah
SPHERE
Quentin, John
COUSIN BETTE
Quick, Christine
LITTLE VOICE
Quick, Diana
LEADING MAN, THE
Quick, Heather
TALK TO ME
Quick, Marantha
NAKED ACTS
Quidjada, Francisco
CELEBRITY
Quigley, Gerry
HOSTILE INTENT
Quigley, Linnea
BOOGIE BOY
Quinlan, Kathleen
CIVIL ACTION, A
LAWN DOGS
MY GIANT
Quinn, Aidan
PRACTICAL MAGIC
Quinn, Colin
NIGHT AT THE ROXBURY, A
Quinn, Elizabeth
LOVE AND DEATH ON LONG ISLAND
Quinn, Ian
ARMAGEDDON
Quinn, Iris
TRICKS
Quinn, J.C.
DECEIVER
DIGGING TO CHINA
HIT ME
LAST LIVES
PRIMARY COLORS
Quinn, Kasey Lynn
ENEMY OF THE STATE
Quinn, Patrice Pitman
CLOCKWATCHERS
Quinn, Thomas M.
ENEMY OF THE STATE
Quinones, Santiago
YOU'VE GOT MAIL
Quiros-Debroise, Clara
WESTERN
Quiroz, Fabiola
WHO THE HELL IS JULIETTE?
Quiroz, Jorge
WHO THE HELL IS JULIETTE?
Raab, Robyn Lynne
ORGAZMO
Raaberg, Birgitte
KINGDOM, PART 2, THE
Raaen, John
MR. NICE GUY
Rabaeus, Johan
JERUSALEM
Rabal, Francisco
TALK OF ANGELS
Rabal, Liberto
LIVE FLESH
Rabelo, Jose
HAPPINESS
Rabin, Trevor
JACK FROST
Rachlin, Kit
BROADWAY DAMAGE
Rachtman, Riki
PLUMP FICTION
Racicot, Jody
HOSTILE INTENT
TRACKED
Rack, Tom
JACK HIGGINS' THE WINDSOR PROTOCOL
Racz, Yvonne
NEXT STEP, THE
Radecki, Barbara
54
Rademaker, Sean
OBJECT OF MY AFFECTION, THE
Radevic, Dajana
SAVIOR
Radley, Ken
BABE: PIG IN THE CITY
Radley, Xantha
HARD CORE LOGO
Radoncic, Emir
HAV PLENTY
Radu Family, The
GADJO DILO
Radulescu, Mihai
MIDAS TOUCH, THE
Rae, Bettina
PLAYERS CLUB, THE
Rafael, Ivan
MASK OF ZORRO, THE
Rafalsky, Dimitri
RONIN

Rafelson, Bob
WHO IS HENRY JAGLOM?
Rafferty, Barbara
GO NOW
Ragan, Talmadge
LAST LIVES
Rage Against the Machine
FREE TIBET
Rageoonauth, Olivier
UN AIR DE FAMILLE
Ragno, Joseph
DAY AT THE BEACH
NO WAY HOME
Rahav, Joan Price
SUE
Rahm, Kevin
CLAY PIGEONS
Rahman, Seif Abdel
DESTINY
Raiboukine, Serge
WESTERN
Raider-Wexler, Victor
I LOVE YOU, DON'T TOUCH ME!
Railsback, Steve
DISTURBING BEHAVIOR
Raimi, Michael
PROPHECY II, THE
Raimi, Ted
HERCULES AND XENA THE ANIMATED MOVIE: THE BATTLE FOR MOUNT OLYMPUS
Raimondi, Miranda
SOLDIER'S DAUGHTER NEVER CRIES, A
Raines, Rebecca
ONE TRUE THING
Rainey, David "Puck"
DREAM FOR AN INSOMNIAC
Rakow, Erin
PRICE ABOVE RUBIES, A
Ralph, Michael
REBOUND: THE LEGEND OF EARL "THE GOAT" MANIGAULT
WOO
Rambis, Jesse
BURN HOLLYWOOD BURN
Ramcu, Mandra
GADJO DILO
Ramirez, Belkis
CARLA'S SONG
Ramirez, Jose
ELMORE LEONARD'S GOLD COAST
Ramirez, Luis
MEN WITH GUNS
Ramirez, Nandi Luna
MEN WITH GUNS
Ramirez, Oneida
WHO THE HELL IS JULIETTE?
Ramirez, Sara
YOU'VE GOT MAIL
Ramish, Trish
NIGHT AT THE ROXBURY, A
Ramm, John
SHAKESPEARE IN LOVE
Ramone, Joey
HARD CORE LOGO
Ramos, Armando
HOLY MAN
Ramos, Jatze-Rae
OBJECT OF MY AFFECTION, THE
Ramos, Raymond
GODZILLA
Ramrus, Al
AYN RAND: A SENSE OF LIFE
Ramsay, Bruce
HIT ME
Ramsey, Natalie
PLEASANTVILLE
Ramsey, Satosha
PLAN B
Ranaldo, Lee
LOU REED: ROCK AND ROLL HEART
MODULATIONS: CINEMA FOR THE EAR
Rand, Barbara
SUE
Rand, Sebastian
STEPMOM
Randall, Ginnie
SHADRACH
Randall, Larry
SHOOTING FISH
WAKING NED DEVINE
Randazzo, Steven
CELEBRITY
Randle, Charlotte
DANGEROUS BEAUTY
Randle, Kenneth
BULWORTH
Randle, Tony Tomas
BULWORTH
Randolph, John
PRICE ABOVE RUBIES, A
YOU'VE GOT MAIL
Rands, Noel
CHINESE BOX, THE
KNOCK OFF
Ranft, Joe
BUG'S LIFE, A
Rangely, Len
LITTLE VOICE
Rankin, Heather
HANGING GARDEN, THE
Rankin, Louie
BELLY
Rankin, Steve
MERCURY RISING
X-FILES, THE
Ranquet, Joan
NEXT STEP, THE
Ransom, Rob
SHAMPOO HORNS
Rapaport, Michael
ILLTOWN
PALMETTO
Raphael, Marylin
CELEBRITY
Rapp, Anthony
DAVID SEARCHING
WHEN TRUMPETS FADE
Rasla, Juro
NEMESIS 4: CRY OF ANGELS
Rasmussen, Ann Kristin
OTHER SIDE OF SUNDAY, THE
Rasmussen, Frode
INSOMNIA
Rasmussen, Kaj
CELEBRATION, THE
Rasner, David
FERNGULLY 2: THE MAGICAL RESCUE
Rasoully, Ghoulam R.
SIEGE, THE
Ratcliffe, Ken
INNOCENT SLEEP, THE
Rath, Michael D.
NIAGARA NIAGARA
Rathke, Mike
LOU REED: ROCK AND ROLL HEART
Ratier, Ellea
TALK OF ANGELS
Ratner, Benjamin
DOUBLE EDGE
FIRESTORM
WRONGFULLY ACCUSED
Ratner, Ellen
BILLBOARD DAD
Ratzenberger, John
BUG'S LIFE, A
Raudman, Renee
WHY DO FOOLS FALL IN LOVE?
Raulerson, Steve
WATERBOY, THE
Rausch, Leon
HI-LO COUNTRY, THE
Raven, Melissa
ELMORE LEONARD'S GOLD COAST
Raven-Symone
DR. DOLITTLE
Ravenscroft, Thurl
BRAVE LITTLE TOASTER GOES TO MARS, THE
Rawlins, Michael
WOUNDED
Rawls, Lou
BLUES BROTHERS 2000
DON KING: ONLY IN AMERICA
PRINCE, THE
REAL THING, THE
RUGRATS MOVIE, THE
STILL BREATHING
WATCHERS REBORN
Ray, Connie
HOPE FLOATS
Ray, Danny
BLUES BROTHERS 2000
Ray, Fred Olen
INVISIBLE MOM
Ray, George E.
BELOVED
Ray, Jerry
GODSON, THE
Ray, Ruth
I MARRIED A STRANGE PERSON!
TALK TO ME
Ray, Tanika
LIVING OUT LOUD
Rayburn, Ross
SENSELESS
Raymon, Marcia Charity
LOS LOCOS
Raymond, Jennie
LOVE AND DEATH ON LONG ISLAND
Raymond, Ted
TRUMAN SHOW, THE
Raymond, Usher
FACULTY, THE
Raymont, Daniel
PENTAGON WARS, THE
Rayna, Glenda
WHO THE HELL IS JULIETTE?
Rayne, Sarah
HORTON FOOTE'S ALONE
Raynor, Lavita
BELLY
Razack, Noorie
KNOCK OFF
Razz, Randy
WEDDING SINGER, THE
Rea, Joe
INFORMANT, THE
Rea, Stephen
BREAK, THE
BUTCHER BOY, THE
SUMMER FLING
Read, James
INDISCREET
WALKING THUNDER
Read, Kim
INVISIBLE DAD
Read, Rufus
HAPPINESS
Reagan, Nancy
OFF THE MENU: THE LAST DAYS OF CHASEN'S

Reahm, Chris
SKIN & BONE
Reber, Rachel
NEVADA
Rebhorn, James
BRIGHT SHINING LIE, A
Rebirth Brass Band, The
MY FIRST NAME IS MACEO
Reck, Vinney
VELVET GOLDMINE
Recknitz, Jack
RAT'S TALE, A
WHITE RAVEN, THE
Rector, Jeff
KRAA! THE SEA MONSTER
Rector, Jerry
NEIL SIMON'S THE ODD COUPLE II
Rector, Terry
MEAN GUNS
Red Hot Chili Peppers
FREE TIBET
Red, Shortee
HE GOT GAME
Reddick, Kristin
SPANISH PRISONER, THE
Reddick, Lance
GREAT EXPECTATIONS
SIEGE, THE
Reddin, Keith
LOLITA
Redford, Robert
HORSE WHISPERER, THE
Redgrave, Lynn
GODS AND MONSTERS
Redgrave, Vanessa
DEEP IMPACT
DEJA VU
MRS. DALLOWAY
WILDE
Redher, Shane
DECAMPITATED
Redican, Dan
ELVIS MEETS NIXON
Redlyon, Jane
BLACK LIGHT
Redman
RIDE
Redman, Christopher
DEFENDERS: PAYBACK, THE
Redman, Crispin
INNOCENT SLEEP, THE
Redman, Enrich
JACK HIGGINS' MIDNIGHT MAN
Redman, Erich
SAVING PRIVATE RYAN
Redman, Joshua
BLUES BROTHERS 2000
Redman, Tom
SIMON BIRCH
Redmond, Morgan
RUSHMORE
Redmond, Sarah-Jane
DISTURBING BEHAVIOR
Rednikova, Ekaterina
THIEF, THE
Redrow, Phil
WHEN TIME EXPIRES
Reece, Georgia
LEADING MAN, THE
Reece, Keith
DENNIS THE MENACE STRIKES AGAIN
Reed, Bunny
JACK HIGGINS' MIDNIGHT MAN
Reed, Dan
FLINTSTONES: I YABBA-DABBA DOO!, THE
Reed, Darryl Alan
MERCURY RISING
Reed, Jerry
WATERBOY, THE
Reed, Kent
U.S. MARSHALS
Reed, Lou
LOU REED: ROCK AND ROLL HEART
Reed, Pamela
WHY DO FOOLS FALL IN LOVE?
Reed, Tripp
INVISIBLE MOM
Reeder, Randal
NIGHT VISION
Reedus, Norman
REACH THE ROCK
Reehling, Joyce
PRICE ABOVE RUBIES, A
Rees, Jed
SIN AND REDEMPTION
URBAN SAFARI
Rees, Richard
JACK HIGGINS' ON DANGEROUS GROUND
Rees, Roger
NEXT STOP, WONDERLAND
Reese, P.G.
HAV PLENTY
Reese, Star
NEXT STEP, THE
Reeves, Anita
BUTCHER BOY, THE
TALK OF ANGELS
Reeves, Jason
SHAMPOO HORNS
Reeves, Jin-Jin
DON KING: ONLY IN AMERICA
Reeves, Perrey
SMOKE SIGNALS
Reffie, Peter
NEXT STEP, THE
Regan, Diane Marie
REAL HOWARD SPITZ, THE
Regan, Judith
LIVING OUT LOUD
Regan, Liam
I WENT DOWN
Regan, Mike
MY BROTHER'S WAR
Reggie III, Arthur
BULWORTH
Regine, Ed
NEXT STOP, WONDERLAND
Regli, Jennifer
MILO
Reid, Ann
LOVE AND DEATH ON LONG ISLAND
Reid, Bradley
DIRTY WORK
Reid, Clodagh
SUMMER FLING
Reid, Ferguson
GINGERBREAD MAN, THE
Reid, Fiona
IN HIS FATHER'S SHOES
Reid, Kevin
WATERBOY, THE
Reid, R.D.
HALF BAKED
IN HIS FATHER'S SHOES
Reid, Roger
HOLY MAN
Reid, Ruth
STEPHEN KING'S THE NIGHT FLIER
Reid, Tara
BIG LEBOWSKI, THE
URBAN LEGEND
Reid, Valerie
KRIPPENDORF'S TRIBE
Reifsnyder, Timothy
WIDE AWAKE
Reilly, Charles Nelson
ALL DOGS CHRISTMAS CAROL, AN
BOYS WILL BE BOYS
Reilly, Corrinn
CAN'T HARDLY WAIT
Reilly, Damara
RUSTY: THE GREAT RESCUE
Reilly, John C.
CHICAGO CAB
NIGHTWATCH
THIN RED LINE, THE
Reimer, Phil
SNOWBOUND
Reinders, Christopher
BOYS WILL BE BOYS
Reiner, Carl
SLUMS OF BEVERLY HILLS
Reiner, Rob
PRIMARY COLORS
Reinhard, Tim
CHICAGO CAB
Reinhold, Judge
HOMEGROWN
LAST LIVES
Reinton, Sandra
SHAKESPEARE IN LOVE
Reis, Diana
FACE DOWN
Reis, Michelle
FALLEN ANGELS
Reis, Terence
OPERATION DELTA FORCE 2
Reiser, Rock
SLUMS OF BEVERLY HILLS
Reisman, Arnie
NEXT STOP, WONDERLAND
Reitman, Joseph D.
CLAY PIGEONS
Relph, Emma
FROM A FAR COUNTRY
Remar, James
PSYCHO
Remez, Jill
SLAPPY AND THE STINKERS
Remy, Ashley
ONE TRUE THING
Renacle, Aurelie
UN AIR DE FAMILLE
Renaday, Peter
NEIL SIMON'S THE ODD COUPLE II
RINGMASTER
Renaud, Ritch
AIR BUD: GOLDEN RECEIVER
Rene
CELEBRATION, THE
Rene, Jacynthe
SNAKE EYES
Renegades
ZAKIR AND HIS FRIENDS
Renfro, Brad
APT PUPIL
Renfro, Bryan
TERMINAL JUSTICE
Renna, Patrick
JOHNNY MYSTO BOY WIZARD
Rennie, Callum Keith
HARD CORE LOGO
TRICKS
Rennison, Colleen
SIN AND REDEMPTION
Reno, Jean
GODZILLA
RONIN
Reno, Susan
LIVING OUT LOUD

Reno, Warren
HOLLYWOOD CONFIDENTIAL
Renouf, Darren
SHOOTING FISH
Renton, David
TALES FROM A PARALLEL UNIVERSE: GIGA SHADOW
Renzi, Maggie
MEN WITH GUNS
Resistance, The
DECLINE OF WESTERN CIVILIZATION PART III, THE
Resnick, Michael
SOUR GRAPES
Reuben, Gloria
INDISCREET
Reubens, Paul
DR. DOLITTLE
Rex, Peter
REAL BLONDE, THE
Rey, Antonia
OBJECT OF MY AFFECTION, THE
TARANTELLA
Reyes, Judy
LENA'S DREAMS
Reyes, Rupert
NIGHT VISION
Reymond, Dominique
ARTEMISIA
Reynolds, Clarence
HOLY MAN
Reynolds, Debbie
FEAR AND LOATHING IN LAS VEGAS
KIKI'S DELIVERY SERVICE
RUDOLPH THE RED-NOSED REINDEER: THE MOVIE
Reynolds, Jacob
SAFE MEN
Reynolds, Kevin
INFORMANT, THE
Reynolds, Ryan
ALARMIST, THE
Reynolds, Simon
HOSTILE INTENT
MODULATIONS: CINEMA FOR THE EAR
Reynolds, Vickilyn
PRIMARY COLORS
Rezza, Vita
ONE TOUGH COP
Rham, Philip
ROYAL DECEIT
Rhames, Ving
BODY COUNT
DON KING: ONLY IN AMERICA
OUT OF SIGHT
Rhee, Phillip
BEST OF THE BEST: WITHOUT WARNING
Rhee, Simon
LETHAL WEAPON 4
Rhein, Jed
SOULER OPPOSITE, THE
Rhind-Tutt, Julian
LES MISERABLES
Rhindress, Charlie
LOVE AND DEATH ON LONG ISLAND
Rhoads, Terry
LIVING OUT LOUD
Rhodes, Donnelly
URBAN SAFARI
Rhoe, Amal
DEE SNIDER'S STRANGELAND
Rhu, Roger
TOP OF THE WORLD
Rhymes, Busta
RUGRATS MOVIE, THE
Rhys Meyers, Jonathan
GOVERNESS, THE
MAKER, THE
VELVET GOLDMINE
Ri'chard, Robert
IN HIS FATHER'S SHOES
Riach, Ralph
DANGEROUS BEAUTY
GOVERNESS, THE
Riaux, Catherine
WESTERN
Riback, Cory
NEVADA
Ribisi, Giovanni
FIRST LOVE, LAST RITES
PHOENIX
SAVING PRIVATE RYAN
Ribisi, Marissa
PLEASANTVILLE
Ricard, Adrian
BULWORTH
Ricci, Christina
BUFFALO '66
FEAR AND LOATHING IN LAS VEGAS
OPPOSITE OF SEX, THE
PECKER
SMALL SOLDIERS
SUMMER FLING
Riccio, Philip
HOT BLOODED
Rice, Brett
HOLY MAN
PALMETTO
WATERBOY, THE
Rice, Diana
BARNEY'S GREAT ADVENTURE—THE MOVIE
Rice, Gigi
NIGHT AT THE ROXBURY, A
Rice, Nicholas
BLUES BROTHERS 2000
Rice, Robyn
BOYS IN LOVE 2
Rich, Abe
RETURN TO SAVAGE BEACH
Rich, Duffy
I GOT THE HOOK UP
Rich, Glendon
X-FILES, THE
Richard, Jean-Louis
POST COITUM, ANIMAL TRISTE
Richard, Nathalie
SOLDIER'S DAUGHTER NEVER CRIES, A
Richard, Nicole
RINGMASTER
Richard, Tynia D.
NAKED ACTS
Richards, Beah
BELOVED
Richards, Billie Mae
BRAM STOKER'S SHADOWBUILDER
Richards, Cordelia
NORTH SHORE FISH
PRACTICAL MAGIC
Richards, Darryl
ANOTHER DAY IN PARADISE
Richards, Denise
WILD THINGS
Richards, Glenford O.
DARK CITY
Richards, Hoyt
SIX DAYS, SEVEN NIGHTS
Richards, J. August
WHY DO FOOLS FALL IN LOVE?
Richards, Keith
CAN'T YOU HEAR THE WIND HOWL?: THE LIFE AND MUSIC OF ROBERT JOHNSON
Richards, Lou
LIVING OUT LOUD
Richards, Sal
ROUNDERS
Richards, Scott
NEXT STOP, WONDERLAND
Richards, T.R.
ENEMY OF THE STATE
Richardson, Aaron
KNOCK OFF
Richardson, Alex
INNOCENT SLEEP, THE
Richardson, Coach Nolan
HE GOT GAME
Richardson, Ian
DARK CITY
INCOGNITO
Richardson, Jake
RICHIE RICH'S CHRISTMAS WISH
Richardson, Joely
UNDER HEAVEN
Richardson, Latanya
U.S. MARSHALS
Richardson, Miranda
MERLIN
NIGHT AND THE MOMENT, THE
OFF THE MENU: THE LAST DAYS OF CHASEN'S
Richardson, Natasha
PARENT TRAP, THE
Richardson, Nina
NIGHT VISION
Richardson, Shaun D.
LOVE AND DEATH ON LONG ISLAND
Richert, Carole
NIGHT AND THE MOMENT, THE
Richey, Grant
OVERNIGHT DELIVERY
Richie Rich
SHAMPOO HORNS
Richings, Julian
CUBE
HARD CORE LOGO
URBAN LEGEND
Richman, Darice
PRIMARY COLORS
Richman, Jonathan
THERE'S SOMETHING ABOUT MARY
Richman, Stuart
LOVE IS THE DEVIL: STUDY FOR A PORTRAIT OF FRANCIS BACON
Richmond, Elizabeth
HUMAN BOMB
Richmond, Janice
JOHN CARPENTER'S VAMPIRES
Richter, Marc
KILLER CONDOM, THE
Richwood, Patrick
ARMAGEDDON
CASPER MEETS WENDY
Rick
LOLIDA 2000
Ricketts, Conrad
DOGWATCH
Rickles, Don
DENNIS THE MENACE STRIKES AGAIN
DIRTY WORK
OFF THE MENU: THE LAST DAYS OF CHASEN'S
QUEST FOR CAMELOT
Rideau, Stephane
FULL SPEED
Rideau, Wilbert
FARM: ANGOLA, U.S.A., THE
Ridge, Monique L.
PRIMARY COLORS
Ridgeway, Esther
BLUES BROTHERS 2000
Ridgeway, Gloria
BLUES BROTHERS 2000

Ridgeway, Gracie
BLUES BROTHERS 2000
Riding, Anthony
LOVE IS THE DEVIL: STUDY FOR A PORTRAIT OF FRANCIS BACON
Ridings, Jay
PALMETTO
Ridings, Richard
JACK HIGGINS' ON DANGEROUS GROUND
Ridpath, Dr. John
AYN RAND: A SENSE OF LIFE
Riebel, Aladin
MARIE BAIE DES ANGES
Riefenstein, Thure
BEST OF THE BEST: WITHOUT WARNING
Riegert, Peter
FACE DOWN
HI-LIFE
NORTH SHORE FISH
Riehle, Richard
DESPERATE MEASURES
FEAR AND LOATHING IN LAS VEGAS
LETHAL WEAPON 4
MERCURY RISING
MIGHTY JOE YOUNG
NEIL SIMON'S THE ODD COUPLE II
PENTAGON WARS, THE
RICHIE RICH'S CHRISTMAS WISH
Riehs, Milan
FORGOTTEN LIGHT
LES MISERABLES
Riemens, Peter
JACK HIGGINS' MIDNIGHT MAN
Riestra, Dora
I GOT THE HOOK UP
Riffel, Rena
BREAST MEN
Riffon, Marc
WHATEVER
Rifkin, Myers
HALLELUJAH!
Rifkin, Richard
SOULER OPPOSITE, THE
Rifkin, Ron
NEGOTIATOR, THE
Rigby, David
SIMON BIRCH
Rigby, Terence
ELIZABETH
Riise, Hildegunn
OTHER SIDE OF SUNDAY, THE
Riley, Claire
MISBEGOTTEN
Riley, Forbes
PRINCE, THE
Riley, Jack
RUGRATS MOVIE, THE
Riley, Kaitlin
CATHERINE'S GROVE
Riley, Michael
PRINCE, THE
Riley, Sharon
BLUES BROTHERS 2000
Riley, Stu "Large"
WOO
Rimgale, Don
HENRY: PORTRAIT OF A SERIAL KILLER PART 2
Rimmer, Maureen
DEJA VU
Rinaldi, Cristina
DANGEROUS BEAUTY
Rios, Jacqueline
DANCE WITH ME
Rios, Lalo
TOUCH OF EVIL: THE DIRECTOR'S CUT
Rios, Rolee
TEKKEN: THE MOTION PICTURE
Riovega, Elodia
HOLY MAN
Ripley, David
LOVE TO KILL
Rippenkroeger, Larry
X-FILES, THE
Rippy, Rodney Allen
FORMER CHILD STAR
Riser, Ronn
PLAYERS CLUB, THE
Rispoli, Michael
ONE TOUGH COP
ROUNDERS
SCARRED CITY
SNAKE EYES
Ristic, Suzanna
AIR BUD: GOLDEN RECEIVER
Ritchie, Claire
HENRY FOOL
Ritchie, Gina Angela
GODSON, THE
Ritchie, Jill
BEST OF THE BEST: WITHOUT WARNING
Ritchie, Stuart
MR. NICE GUY
Ritter, John
BRIDE OF CHUCKY
GUN, A CAR, AND A BLONDE, A
MONTANA
Ritz
VELVET GOLDMINE
Rivalta, Pablo
EL CHE: INVESTIGATING A LEGEND
Rivas, Geoffrey
NOTES FROM UNDERGROUND
Rivera, Ava
BULWORTH
Rivera, Geraldo
PRIMARY COLORS
Rivera Gonzalez, Dan
MEN WITH GUNS
Rivera, Jacquee
SHAMPOO HORNS
Rivera, Norma
CARLA'S SONG
Rivers, Joan
NAPOLEON
Rivers, Victor
MASK OF ZORRO, THE
TWO FOR TEXAS
Rivett, Julian
INNOCENT SLEEP, THE
Rizo, Alison Paula
CARLA'S SONG
Rizzo, Don
PATCH ADAMS
Rizzo, Ray
DARK CITY
Roach, Dawn
REAL BLONDE, THE
Roach, Martin
WOO
Roarke, Kelly
THERE'S SOMETHING ABOUT MARY
Robards, Glenn
NOT IN THIS TOWN
Robards Jr., Jason
BELOVED
ENEMY OF THE STATE
Robb, David
REGENERATION
Robberts, Derrick
BARRIERS
Robbie, Tim
THERE'S SOMETHING ABOUT MARY
Robbins, Gil
WIDE AWAKE
Robbins, Logan
CASPER MEETS WENDY
Robbins, Stephen
GOVERNESS, THE
Robbins, Wills
GREAT EXPECTATIONS
Roberson, Bill
PATCH ADAMS
Roberson, David
STEEL SHARKS
Robert, Mario
DIARY OF A SERIAL KILLER
Roberts, Conrad
MASK OF ZORRO, THE
Roberts, David
WOO
Roberts, Doris
MY GIANT
Roberts, Doug
ENEMY OF THE STATE
PECKER
Roberts, Douglas
PATCH ADAMS
Roberts, Eliza
DEAD END
Roberts, Eric
DEAD END
PROPHECY II, THE
Roberts, Francesca P.
NEIL SIMON'S THE ODD COUPLE II
Roberts, Ian
TARZAN AND THE LOST CITY
Roberts, J.C.
ATOMIC DOG
EBENEZER
Roberts, Joe
SHAKESPEARE IN LOVE
Roberts, Julia
STEPMOM
Roberts, Kim
DEFENDERS: PAYBACK, THE
DOWN IN THE DELTA
Roberts, Kitty
LITTLE VOICE
Roberts, Layla
ARMAGEDDON
Roberts, Leonard
HE GOT GAME
Roberts, Lisa
TEN BENNY
Roberts, Mario
REPLACEMENT KILLERS, THE
Roberts, Ndehru
BREAK, THE
Roberts, Pascale
MARIUS AND JEANNETTE
Roberts, Robin
HE GOT GAME
Robertson, Bill
JOHNNY SKIDMARKS
Robertson, Cliff
ALFRED HITCHCOCK: MASTER OF SUSPENSE
Robertson, Eric
NOT IN THIS TOWN
Robertson, Jessica
TEKKEN: THE MOTION PICTURE
Robertson Jr., Woody
HUSH
Robillard, Kim
HOME FRIES
MERCURY RISING
Robinson, Aemilia
54
Robinson, Aliya
BELOVED

Robinson, Andrew J.
RUNNING WOMAN, THE
Robinson, Bill
BODY COUNT
Robinson, Carrie
LIVING IN PERIL
Robinson, Charlie
LAND OF THE FREE
Robinson, David
MILO
Robinson, Dawn
RUGRATS MOVIE, THE
Robinson, Eric Thomas
DANCE WITH ME
Robinson, Hal
PAULIE
Robinson, Jeanne
PRACTICAL MAGIC
Robinson, Jim
OUT OF SIGHT
Robinson, Joan
NOT IN THIS TOWN
Robinson, John
SIMON BIRCH
Robinson, Karen
DEFENDERS: PAYBACK, THE
ONE TOUGH COP
Robinson, Lisa
LOU REED: ROCK AND ROLL HEART
Robinson, Michael
SPANISH PRISONER, THE
Robinson, Miles
BOYS WILL BE BOYS
Robinson, Natalie
NAKED ACTS
Robinson, Phil
FERNGULLY 2: THE MAGICAL RESCUE
Robinson, Robby
DON KING: ONLY IN AMERICA
Robinson, Ron
RIGHT CONNECTIONS, THE
Robinson, Todd
NEXT STOP, WONDERLAND
Robinson, Troy
DESPERATE MEASURES
JOHN CARPENTER'S VAMPIRES
Robinson, Wendy Raquel
RINGMASTER
Robison, Ian
I'LL BE HOME FOR CHRISTMAS
Robison, Mark Steven
BLACK DOG
Robson, Wayne
AFFLICTION
CUBE
Rocca, Stefania
INSIDE/OUT
NIRVANA
Rocco, Alex
BUG'S LIFE, A
Rocco, Rinaldo
ARTEMISIA
Rocha, Kali
OBJECT OF MY AFFECTION, THE
Roche, Eammon
NOTES FROM UNDERGROUND
Roche, Jim
BELOVED
Roche, Sebastian
MERLIN
Roche, Tudi
CITY OF ANGELS
Rochester, Matt
BELOVED
Rochford, Terry G.
U.S. MARSHALS
Rochfort, Spencer
OPERATION DELTA FORCE 2
Rochon, Lela
BIG HIT, THE
KNOCK OFF
WHY DO FOOLS FALL IN LOVE?
Rochstar, J.F.
FERNGULLY 2: THE MAGICAL RESCUE
Rock, Chris
COMEDY'S DIRTIEST DOZEN
DR. DOLITTLE
LETHAL WEAPON 4
Rock, Crissy
UNDER THE SKIN
Rocks, Sean
GO NOW
Rockwell, John
LOU REED: ROCK AND ROLL HEART
Rockwell, Sam
CELEBRITY
LAWN DOGS
SAFE MEN
THIN RED LINE, THE
Rodd, Everett J.
LOLIDA 2000
Roderick, Michael
TALK TO ME
Rodger, Straun
INNOCENT SLEEP, THE
Rodgers, J.J.
SOULER OPPOSITE, THE
Rodgers, Michael E.
GIA
Rodriguez, Al D.
LENA'S DREAMS
Rodriguez, Christina
FACULTY, THE
Rodriguez, Elizabeth
I THINK I DO
Rodriguez, Freddy
CAN'T HARDLY WAIT
Rodriguez, J.R.
STEPHEN KING'S THE NIGHT FLIER
Rodriguez, Jose
BROADWAY DAMAGE
Rodriguez, Lonnie
TWO FOR TEXAS
Rodriguez, Marco
TWO FOR TEXAS
Rodriguez, Raymond
TOUCH OF EVIL: THE DIRECTOR'S CUT
Rodriguez, Robert
FULL TILT BOOGIE
Rodriguez, Steve
CLOCKWATCHERS
Rodrique, Monique
STEPMOM
Roe, Channon
CAN'T HARDLY WAIT
STIR
Roebuck, Daniel
STIR
U.S. MARSHALS
Roemele, Eric
NEXT STOP, WONDERLAND
Roemmele, David
IN HIS FATHER'S SHOES
Roeske, Emily
3 NINJAS: HIGH NOON AT MEGA MOUNTAIN
Roeske II, James Paul
3 NINJAS: HIGH NOON AT MEGA MOUNTAIN
Rogell, Gregg
HALF BAKED
Rogen, Laura
INDISCREET
Rogers, Alice
SHADRACH
Rogers, Anthony
PECKER
Rogers, Ashley
DECEIVER
SIN AND REDEMPTION
Rogers, Danny
DESPERATE MEASURES
Rogers, Greg
WOUNDED
Rogers, Ingrid
CELEBRITY
ONE TOUGH COP
Rogers, John
COURTING COURTNEY
Rogers, Marilyn
PARALYZING FEAR: THE STORY OF POLIO IN AMERICA, A
Rogers, Michael
ACT OF WAR
Rogers, Mimi
LOST IN SPACE
TRICKS
Rogers, Renee
PATCH ADAMS
Rogers, Scott
LOVE TO KILL
Rogerson, Ken
THERE'S SOMETHING ABOUT MARY
Rogerson, Ryan
LOVE AND DEATH ON LONG ISLAND
Rohan, Eamon
MY BROTHER'S WAR
Rohr, Tony
BUTCHER BOY, THE
Rois, Sophie
INHERITORS, THE
Roisman, Harper
CITY OF ANGELS
SOUR GRAPES
Rojas III, Rafael
BILLBOARD DAD
Rojas, Luz Maria
DIDN'T DO IT FOR LOVE
Rojo, Maria
MIDAQ ALLEY
Rokicki, Joe
JACK FROST
Roks Chik
KNOCK OFF
Roland, John
OBJECT OF MY AFFECTION, THE
Roland, Scott
NEWTON BOYS, THE
Rold, Dominic
EVER AFTER
Roledar, Gary
ASYLUM
Rolf, Frederick
CELEBRITY
Rolfe, Liz Francis
DOGWATCH
Rolffes, Kirsten
KINGDOM, PART 2, THE
Rolle, Esther
DOWN IN THE DELTA
Rollin, Pascal
SAVIOR
Rollins, Henry
JACK FROST
Rollpiller, Stefan
RESCUERS: STORIES OF COURAGE—TWO COUPLES
Rolls, David
KNOCK OFF
Rolston, Mark
GEORGE WALLACE

HARD RAIN
RUSH HOUR
Rom, Lori
HE GOT GAME
Romaker, Brad
DAVID SEARCHING
Roman, Emilio
DIRTY WORK
Roman, Frank
NEIL SIMON'S THE ODD COUPLE II
Romano, Christy
HENRY FOOL
Romano, Frank
FEAR AND LOATHING IN LAS VEGAS
Romano, Juanita
JOHN CARPENTER'S VAMPIRES
Romano, Larry
NO WAY HOME
THIN RED LINE, THE
Romano, Rino
HOSTILE INTENT
Romanus, Robert
LOVER GIRL
Romanyuk, Sergiy
FRIEND OF THE DECEASED, A
Romeo, Flavio
WRATH OF THE NINJA: THE YOTODEN MOVIE
Romeo, Ralph
TALK TO ME
Romero, Ann
JOHN CARPENTER'S VAMPIRES
Romero, Humberto
MEN WITH GUNS
Romero, Kaylan
HOLLYWOOD CONFIDENTIAL
MIGHTY JOE YOUNG
Romersa, Joe
RED HAWK: WEAPON OF DEATH
Romijn, Rebecca
DIRTY WORK
Romila, Claudiu
JOHNNY MYSTO BOY WIZARD
Ronan, Martin
HUMAN BOMB
Ronan, Paul
BREAK, THE
Roncalli, Guido
ARTEMISIA
Rondell, Dalton
SIMON BIRCH
Rondell, Lynn
NEGOTIATOR, THE
Rone, Doria
PRINCE, THE
Rooker, Michael
BRAM STOKER'S SHADOWBUILDER
DECEIVER
REPLACEMENT KILLERS, THE
Rooney, Mickey
BABE: PIG IN THE CITY
BOYS WILL BE BOYS
Root, Bonnie
EDEN
Root, Stephen
KRIPPENDORF'S TRIBE
Roots, Jamaul
BARRIERS
Ropiejko, Kristie
FUTURE FEAR
Rosa, Kirenia
WHO THE HELL IS JULIETTE?
Rosaio, Jose Ramon
STEPMOM
Rosales, Gilbert
JOHN CARPENTER'S VAMPIRES
SIEGE, THE
Rosales Jr., Thomas
REPLACEMENT KILLERS, THE
U.S. MARSHALS
Rosales, Tommy
JOHN CARPENTER'S VAMPIRES
Rosario, Jose Ramon
PERFECT MURDER, A
Rosas, Antonio
NO ORDINARY LOVE
Rose, Anna
LEADING MAN, THE
Rose, Charlie
PRIMARY COLORS
Rose, Ian
CHARLIE HOBOKEN
LIKE IT IS
Rose, Joe
SOULER OPPOSITE, THE
Rose, Kate
TALES FROM A PARALLEL UNIVERSE: SUPER NOVA
Rose, Lenny
FATAL PURSUIT
Rose, Margot
CIVIL ACTION, A
Rose, Michael Edward
NAKED LIES
Rose, Mitchell
I LOVE YOU, DON'T TOUCH ME!
Rose, Roger
BABE: PIG IN THE CITY
FLINTSTONES: I YABBA-DABBA DOO!, THE
Rose, Skip
CELEBRITY
Rose, Terry L.
NEIL SIMON'S THE ODD COUPLE II
OPPOSITE OF SEX, THE
Rosebeck, Heather
THERE'S SOMETHING ABOUT MARY
Rosefeld, Rudi
CLOCKMAKER
Roselius, John
TRUMAN SHOW, THE
Rosen, Edward J.
LETHAL WEAPON 4
Rosen, Julieta
MASK OF ZORRO, THE
Rosen, Lee
SAVING PRIVATE RYAN
Rosen, Robert
RACE TO SAVE 100 YEARS, THE
Rosenbaum, Michael
URBAN LEGEND
Rosenberg, Alan
ARGUING THE WORLD
Rosenberg, Phil
THERE'S SOMETHING ABOUT MARY
Rosenberg, Richard
INDISCREET
Rosenberg, Scott
THERE'S SOMETHING ABOUT MARY
Rosenburg, Ira
BOYS IN LOVE 2
Rosenfeld, Rudy
LITTLE GHOST
Rosenfield, Nancy
LETHAL WEAPON 4
Rosengren, Clive
PHANTOMS
Rosenthal, Norman
LOVE IS THE DEVIL: STUDY FOR A PORTRAIT OF FRANCIS BACON
Rosier, Bill
KRIPPENDORF'S TRIBE
WHEN TIME EXPIRES
Rosin, Karen
SUICIDE KINGS
Rosinebun, Kevin
UNDER HEAVEN
Ross, Chelcie
PRIMARY COLORS
SIMPLE PLAN, A
Ross, Chris
LIKE IT IS
Ross, Hugh
ZERO EFFECT
Ross, Jonathan
SPICE WORLD
Ross, Justin
PLAN B
Ross, Katharine
HOME BEFORE DARK
Ross, Matt
HOMEGROWN
LAST DAYS OF DISCO, THE
Ross, Phil
SLAYERS: THE MOTION PICTURE
Ross, Sandi
BLUES BROTHERS 2000
BONE DADDY
DOWN IN THE DELTA
Ross, Stanley Ralph
BABE: PIG IN THE CITY
BURN HOLLYWOOD BURN
Ross, Stephanie
SPANISH PRISONER, THE
Ross, Tracee Ellis
SUE
Ross, Willie
SWEPT FROM THE SEA
Rossatti, Alberto
DANGEROUS BEAUTY
Rossellini, Isabella
IMPOSTORS, THE
MERLIN
Rossetter, Kathryn
WHATEVER
Rossi, Paolo
NIRVANA
Rossi, Toni
I MARRIED A STRANGE PERSON!
Rossouw, Zeno
ERNEST IN THE ARMY
Rostand, Ali
POST COITUM, ANIMAL TRISTE
Roth, Mary Jo
WHATEVER
Roth, Matt
CHICAGO CAB
Roth, Tim
DECEIVER
NO WAY HOME
Rothberg, Elise
LIVING IN PERIL
Rothchild, Roland
HOT BLOODED
WOO
Rothenberg, Andrew
CHICAGO CAB
Rothery, Teryl
URBAN SAFARI
WHEN DANGER FOLLOWS YOU HOME
Rothhaar, Will
JACK FROST
Rothlein, William
GREAT EXPECTATIONS
Rothman, John
BREAK, THE
HOSTILE WATERS
SIEGE, THE
Rothrock, Cynthia
NIGHT VISION
Rothstein, Rebecca
ASYLUM

Rothwell, Ben
TWENTYFOURSEVEN
Rottger, John
DESPERATE MEASURES
Rotundo, Paolo
UGLY, THE
Rouan, Brigitte
POST COITUM, ANIMAL TRISTE
Rouan, Jean-Francois
POST COITUM, ANIMAL TRISTE
Roughley, Lill
MERRY WAR, A
Round, Jason
SHAKESPEARE IN LOVE
Rourke, Mickey
BUFFALO '66
THURSDAY
Rousseau, Sophie
54
Roussillon, Jean-Paul
SAME OLD SONG
Rovere, Gina
LIFE IS BEAUTIFUL
Rovere, Liliane
ARTEMISIA
Rowden, David
JOHN CARPENTER'S VAMPIRES
WHEN TIME EXPIRES
Rowe, Brad
BILLY'S HOLLYWOOD SCREEN KISS
Rowe, James
ELIZABETH
Rowland, Oscar
NOT IN THIS TOWN
Rowlands, Gena
HOPE FLOATS
MIGHTY, THE
PAULIE
PLAYING BY HEART
Rowley, Peter
HERCULES AND XENA THE ANIMATED MOVIE: THE BATTLE FOR MOUNT OLYMPUS
Rowley, Terry
NIL BY MOUTH
Rox, Robbie
DIRTY WORK
TRACKED
Roy, Cheryl
LET'S KILL ALL THE LAWYERS
Roy, Marco
WRONGFULLY ACCUSED
Rozelaar-Green, Frank
FIRELIGHT
Rozie, Cheryl
NAKED ACTS
Rozstalnyj, Vitalij
TRUCE, THE
Ruben, Eric
NEXT STOP, WONDERLAND
Rubens, Sergey
DEAD WATERS
Rubeo, Marco
TRUMAN SHOW, THE
Rubes, Jan
MUSIC FROM ANOTHER ROOM
RESCUERS: STORIES OF COURAGE—TWO COUPLES
WHITE RAVEN, THE
Rubicondi, Rossano
EIGHTEENTH ANGEL, THE
Rubin, Alan
BLUES BROTHERS 2000
Rubin, Cayda
RESCUERS: STORIES OF COURAGE—TWO COUPLES
Rubin, David
DEJA VU
Rubin, Jennifer
LAST LIVES
PLUMP FICTION
Rubin-Vega, Daphne
WILD THINGS
Rubinek, Saul
BAD MANNERS
BLACKJACK
HOSTILE INTENT
Rubini, Sergio
NIRVANA
Rubinow, John
INTERLOCKED: THRILLED TO DEATH
Rubinstein, Manya K.
STEPHEN KING'S THE NIGHT FLIER
Ruby, Dave
DEAD MAN ON CAMPUS
Ruckebusch, Sophie
LIFE OF JESUS, THE
Ruckstuhl, Robert
ENEMY
Rudd, Paul
OBJECT OF MY AFFECTION, THE
OVERNIGHT DELIVERY
Rudin, Stuart
NO LOOKING BACK
Rudnick, Craig
SLAPPY AND THE STINKERS
Rudolph, Alan
WHO IS HENRY JAGLOM?
Rudolph, Lars
INHERITORS, THE
Rudrud, Kristin
PLEASANTVILLE
Rue, Sara
CAN'T HARDLY WAIT
Ruehl, Mercedes
GIA
NORTH SHORE FISH
Ruff, Michael
SHADRACH
Ruffalo, Mark
DESTINY OF MARTY FINE, THE
54
LAST BIG THING, THE
SAFE MEN
Ruffini, Gene
HENRY FOOL
Ruffo, A. Frank
DIRTY WORK
Rufo, Joseph Jumbo
JANE AUSTEN'S MAFIA!
Ruger
PHANTOMS
Ruggier, Carole
LIVING OUT LOUD
Ruggiero, Allelon
FALLEN
Ruivivar, Anthony
HIGH ART
Ruiz, Edoardo
ARTEMISIA
Ruiz, Hernan
MIGHTY JOE YOUNG
Ruiz, Nestor
COURTING COURTNEY
Ruiz, Pepe
OFF THE MENU: THE LAST DAYS OF CHASEN'S
Rujewick, Nick
TARZAN AND THE LOST CITY
Rumbaugh, Matt
WHATEVER
Rummel, John
BUFFALO '66
Rumnock, Bob
FALLEN
Runarvot, Christopher
WESTERN
Runte, Kurte Max
I'LL BE HOME FOR CHRISTMAS
Runyan, Tygh
DISTURBING BEHAVIOR
Rupert, Michael
DAVID SEARCHING
Rupp, Debra Jo
CLOCKWATCHERS
SENSELESS
Ruppe, Diana
HENRY FOOL
Rush, Deborah
YOU'VE GOT MAIL
Rush, Ed
MODULATIONS: CINEMA FOR THE EAR
Rush, Geoffrey
ELIZABETH
LES MISERABLES
SHAKESPEARE IN LOVE
TWISTED
Rushbrook, Claire
SPICE WORLD
UNDER THE SKIN
Rushton, Kevin
HOSTILE INTENT
Ruskin, Ian
X-FILES, THE
Ruskin, Joseph
STAR TREK: INSURRECTION
Rusoff, Ted
EIGHTEENTH ANGEL, THE
Russ, William
AMERICAN HISTORY X
WHEN DANGER FOLLOWS YOU HOME
Russell, Anthony
LIVING OUT LOUD
Russell, Barbara
ONE TRUE THING
Russell, Catherine
SHOOTING FISH
Russell, Geoffrey
FROM A FAR COUNTRY
Russell, Grant
DANGEROUS BEAUTY
Russell, Jasmine
MOONDANCE
Russell, Joanna Hoty
ONE TRUE THING
Russell, John Raphael
FALLEN
Russell, Ken
SUMMER FLING
Russell, Kurt
SOLDIER
Russell, Lisa
SUMMER FLING
Russell, Monte
GODZILLA
PLAYERS CLUB, THE
Russell, Theresa
RUNNING WOMAN, THE
WILD THINGS
Russell, Wyatt
SOLDIER
Russo, James
LOVE TO KILL
NO WAY HOME
REAL THING, THE
Russo, John
I MARRIED A STRANGE PERSON!
Russo, Laura
NEIL SIMON'S THE ODD COUPLE II
Russo, Michael
UNMADE BEDS
Russo, Rene
LETHAL WEAPON 4

Russom, Leon
BIG LEBOWSKI, THE
Ruth, Isabel
VOYAGE TO THE BEGINNING OF THE WORLD
Rutherford, Bill
DARK CITY
Rutherford, Neil
SWEPT FROM THE SEA
Rutledge, Larney
OBJECT OF MY AFFECTION, THE
Rutledge, Stanton
PLEASANTVILLE
Ruttan, Susan
KRIPPENDORF'S TRIBE
Rutten, Joseph
REAL HOWARD SPITZ, THE
Ruud, Michael
MEET THE DEEDLES
Rux, Carl Hancock
NAKED ACTS
Ryan, Amanda
ELIZABETH
Ryan, Christopher
BRYLCREEM BOYS, THE
Ryan, Jackie
PRICE ABOVE RUBIES, A
Ryan, James
BRYLCREEM BOYS, THE
Ryan, Jenny
REGENERATION
Ryan, Joal
FORMER CHILD STAR
Ryan, Meg
CITY OF ANGELS
HURLYBURLY
YOU'VE GOT MAIL
Ryan, Ron
NO WAY HOME
Ryan, Shayna
I GOT THE HOOK UP
INVISIBLE DAD
Ryan, Thomas Jay
HENRY FOOL
Ryder, Shaun
AVENGERS, THE
Ryder, Syntrell
3 NINJAS: HIGH NOON AT MEGA MOUNTAIN
Ryder, Winona
CELEBRITY
Ryfle, Steve
FORMER CHILD STAR
Ryland, James
WAKING NED DEVINE
Saban, Mark
SHAKESPEARE IN LOVE
Sabato Jr., Antonio
BIG HIT, THE
Sabbagh, Kahlil
BRAM STOKER'S THE MUMMY
Sabella, Ernie
LION KING II: SIMBA'S PRIDE, THE
Saccarola, Giampaolo
BEYOND, THE
Sacco, Donna
SPECIES II
Sachs, Patty
WRONGFULLY ACCUSED
Sachtlenben, Horst
BEYOND SILENCE
Sack Jr., George
HORSE WHISPERER, THE
Sadiello, Erin
BILLBOARD DAD
Sadikin, Lucille
RUSHMORE
Sadiq, Laara
DRAGON BALL Z THE MOVIE: THE TREE OF MIGHT
Sadler, Nicholas
NIGHTWATCH
Sadler, William
DISTURBING BEHAVIOR
REACH THE ROCK
Sadowski, John
STEPMOM
Saether, Andrine
JUNK MAIL
Safir, Shari-Lyn
RATCHET
Sagal, McNally
NEGOTIATOR, THE
PLEASANTVILLE
Sagalle, Nicolas
PASSION IN THE DESERT
Sage
DECLINE OF WESTERN CIVILIZATION PART III, THE
Sage, Bill
HIGH ART
Sage III, William
MIGHTY KONG, THE
Sage, William
SOMEWHERE IN THE CITY
Sagebrecht, Marianne
OGRE, THE
Sager, Donald
CLUB VAMPIRE
Sagona, Katie
YOU'VE GOT MAIL
Sagouspe, Chantal
DANCE WITH ME
Saha, Matt
SCARRED CITY
Sahar, Eldad
UNVEILING, THE
Sahara, Kenji
GODZILLA VS. KING GHIDORAH
Sahely, Ed
RESCUERS: STORIES OF COURAGE—TWO WOMEN
Saiet, Eric
BODY COUNT
GODZILLA
Saint John, Antoine
BEYOND, THE
Saint Macary, Hubert
GENEALOGIES OF A CRIME
Saiter, Jay
TRUMAN SHOW, THE
Saito, James
HENRY FOOL
Saito, Toru
FALLEN ANGELS
Sakai, Atsushi
SHAMPOO HORNS
Sakai, Kazuyoshi
THIN RED LINE, THE
Sakai, Miki
WHEN I CLOSE MY EYES
Sakai, Yoko
TRICKS
WRONGFULLY ACCUSED
Sakaoduen, Naetdao
HEROES SHED NO TEARS
Saki, Eileen
BOYS WILL BE BOYS
Sakisian, John
SIX-STRING SAMURAI
Salama, Amro
SIEGE, THE
Salama, Hani
DESTINY
Salazar, Abdul Latif
PASSION IN THE DESERT
Saleem, Damon
CAUGHT UP
Salem, Pamela
GODS AND MONSTERS
Salenger, Meredith
SOUR GRAPES
Salerno, Daniel
HARD CORE LOGO
Salerno, Nini
BEST MAN, THE
Salerno, Tiffany
GEORGE WALLACE
Sales, Soupy
HOLY MAN
Saletta, Sam
HENRY: PORTRAIT OF A SERIAL KILLER PART 2
Salgado, Marcus
BLADE
Sali, Richard
DIRTY WORK
FACE DOWN
Saliba, Catherine
OBJECT OF MY AFFECTION, THE
Salimbeni, Enrico
ARTEMISIA
Salinger, Gabor
REDLINE
Salinger, Justin
VELVET GOLDMINE
Salinger, Matt
WHAT DREAMS MAY COME
Salk, Mrs. Jonas
PARALYZING FEAR: THE STORY OF POLIO IN AMERICA, A
Sall, Garmy
DANGEROUS BEAUTY
Salley, Alfred
PATCH ADAMS
Sally
SHOOTING FISH
Salmon, Caspar
OGRE, THE
Salmon, Sean
MY BROTHER'S WAR
Salonga, Lea
MULAN
Salsedo, Frank
ALMOST HEROES
CHOSEN ONE: LEGEND OF THE RAVEN, THE
Salsman, Thomas
DISENCHANTED, THE
Salstrom, Clare
COLONY, THE
Salter, Louise
DEAD WATERS
Salvato Jr., Edmonte
ONE TOUGH COP
Salvato, Laura
LIVING OUT LOUD
Salvesen, Sylvia
OTHER SIDE OF SUNDAY, THE
Salvianti, Massimo
LIFE IS BEAUTIFUL
Samadpour, T.
MIRROR, THE
Samaha, John
BABE: PIG IN THE CITY
Samaripa, Gerardo
NAKED LIES
Samek, Jiri
FORGOTTEN LIGHT
Samel, Udo
KILLER CONDOM, THE

Sammel, Richard
LIFE IS BEAUTIFUL
Samojlowicz, Jacek
WHITE RAVEN, THE
Samojlowicz, Joanna
WHITE RAVEN, THE
Sampson, Holly
GIA
Sampson, Tiffany
HENRY FOOL
Samuels, Lynn
RUN FOR COVER
San Giacomo, Laura
SUICIDE KINGS
San Jose Blackman, Sean
DREAM FOR AN INSOMNIAC
San, Masao "Maki"
ORGAZMO
Sanada, Henry
ROYAL WARRIORS
Sanborn, Ryne
NOT IN THIS TOWN
Sanchez, Carla
NEGOTIATOR, THE
Sanchez, Celeste Cornelio
MEN WITH GUNS
Sanchez, David
OBJECT OF MY AFFECTION, THE
Sanchez, Domingo Perez
MEN WITH GUNS
Sanchez, Joanna
NEIL SIMON'S THE ODD COUPLE II
Sanchez, Mario
CATHERINE'S GROVE
Sanchez, Mario Ernesto
TRUMAN SHOW, THE
Sanchez, Raul
MEN WITH GUNS
Sanchez, Ronald C.
TWILIGHT
Sanchez-Gijon, Aitana
CHAMBERMAID ON THE TITANIC, THE
LOVE WALKED IN
Sancho, Jose
LIVE FLESH
Sand, Shauna
CHOSEN ONE: LEGEND OF THE RAVEN, THE
Sandberg, Laura Kellogg
CHICAGO CAB
Sandberg, Paul Michael
GODS AND MONSTERS
Sander, Otto
KILLER CONDOM, THE
Sanders, Ajai
JACK FROST
Sanders, Alvin
DRAGON BALL Z THE MOVIE: THE TREE OF MIGHT
NEW ADVENTURES OF KIMBA THE WHITE LION, THE
Sanders, Jay O.
NEIL SIMON'S THE ODD COUPLE II
Sanders, Jeff
THURSDAY
Sanders, Marvin L.
ZERO EFFECT
Sanderson, William
GEORGE WALLACE
Sandiford, Benedict
WILDE
Sandler, Adam
WATERBOY, THE
WEDDING SINGER, THE
Sandler, Henry
ENEMY OF THE STATE
Sandman, Paul
GIA
Sando, Daniella
LITTLE BIGFOOT 2: THE JOURNEY HOME
Sandoval, Antony
GIA
Sandoval, Diego
MASK OF ZORRO, THE
Sandoval, Miguel
FIXER, THE
GIRLS IN PRISON
Sandow, Nick
LIVING OUT LOUD
NO LOOKING BACK
RETURN TO PARADISE
Sandrelli, Amanda
NIRVANA
Sands, Kleoka Renee
HOMEGROWN
Sands, Peter
AYN RAND: A SENSE OF LIFE
Sandy, Gary
CROSSING FIELDS
Sanford, Garwin
FIRESTORM
MY VERY BEST FRIEND
Sanford, Glenn D.
NO LOOKING BACK
Sanford, Gwendolyn
RUSTY: THE GREAT RESCUE
Sanson, Robert
PARALLEL SONS
Sansone, John
BUFFALO '66
Santagata, Toni
BEST MAN, THE
Santana, Mike
ONE TOUGH COP
Santarelli, Joe
DAVID SEARCHING
Santiago, Millie
NEGOTIATOR, THE
Santiago, Saundra
HI-LIFE
Santiago, Socorro
HAPPINESS
HURRICANE STREETS
Santoni, Reni
CAN'T HARDLY WAIT
DR. DOLITTLE
Santore, Charles
CHOSEN ONE: LEGEND OF THE RAVEN, THE
Santucci, Marco
HENRY: PORTRAIT OF A SERIAL KILLER PART 2
Sanvido, Guy
SIMON BIRCH
Sanz de Alba, Cecile
VOYAGE TO THE BEGINNING OF THE WORLD
Sanz, Jorge
BREAK, THE
Sanz, Margarita
MIDAQ ALLEY
Saperstein, Richard
LOST IN SPACE
Sapienza, Al
GODZILLA
LETHAL WEAPON 4
PHOENIX
Saponangelo, Teresa
EEL, THE
Sapp, Joel
TALES FROM A PARALLEL UNIVERSE: GIGA SHADOW
Sarafian, Richard
BULWORTH
Sarandon, Chris
LOUISA MAY ALCOTT'S LITTLE MEN
TERMINAL JUSTICE
Sarandon, Susan
STEPMOM
TWILIGHT
Sarch, Oren
PI
Sardella, Andrew
BRAM STOKER'S SHADOWBUILDER
Sardie Jr., Bobby J.
I GOT THE HOOK UP
Sargent, Michael
TOUCH OF EVIL: THE DIRECTOR'S CUT
Sargent, William
NOT IN THIS TOWN
Sarosiak, Ronn
HOSTILE INTENT
Sarrazin, Michael
JACK HIGGINS' THUNDER POINT
JACK HIGGINS' MIDNIGHT MAN
PEACEKEEPER, THE
Sarris, Andrew
WHO IS HENRY JAGLOM?
Sarruf, Valerie
FIRELIGHT
Sarsgaard, Peter
ANOTHER DAY IN PARADISE
MAN IN THE IRON MASK, THE
Sartain, Gailard
MURDER IN MIND
Sartor, Fabio
NIRVANA
Sasaki, Katsuhiko
GODZILLA VS. KING GHIDORAH
Sasaki, Tahamaru
SLEEPY EYES OF DEATH: FULL CIRCLE KILLING
Sasha
MODULATIONS: CINEMA FOR THE EAR
Saso, Theresa
HALLELUJAH!
Sastre, Ines
BEST MAN, THE
Satari
PLAYERS CLUB, THE
Sato, Koichi
GONIN
Sato, Makoto
EEL, THE
Satoo, Kei
RAZOR: THE SNARE, THE
Satsuma, Kenpachiro
GODZILLA AND MOTHRA: THE BATTLE FOR EARTH
GODZILLA VS. KING GHIDORAH
Saunders, Cliff
DIRTY WORK
Saunders, David
KNOCK OFF
Saunders, Fernando
LOU REED: ROCK AND ROLL HEART
Saunders, George P.
I LOVE YOU, DON'T TOUCH ME!
Saunders, Jennifer
SPICE WORLD
Saunders, Jesse
MODULATIONS: CINEMA FOR THE EAR
Saunders, Kendall
DISTURBING BEHAVIOR
Saunderson, Kevin
MODULATIONS: CINEMA FOR THE EAR
Savadier, Russel
TARZAN AND THE LOST CITY
Savage, Fred
JUNGLE BOOK: MOWGLI'S STORY, THE
Savage, John
CLUB VAMPIRE

HOSTILE INTENT
LITTLE BOY BLUE
THIN RED LINE, THE
Savant, Doug
GODZILLA
Savchenko, Lidiya
THIEF, THE
Savenkoff, Elizabeth Carol
TRICKS
Savers, Rhiannon R.
SIMPLE PLAN, A
Savino, Barbara
ONE TRUE THING
Savino, Joe
SUMMER FLING
Saviuca, Dana
TALISMAN
Sawalha, Nadim
AVENGERS, THE
Sawaski, John
WEDDING SINGER, THE
Sawicki, Mark
SKIN & BONE
Sawicki, Stan
ORGAZMO
Sawyer, Connie
OUT OF SIGHT
Sawyer, John Franklin
SHADRACH
Saxenmeyer, James
NO WAY HOME
Saxon, Barry
ENEMY
Saxon, James
LES MISERABLES
Saxon, Rolf
SAVING PRIVATE RYAN
Saxton, Richard
GIRLS IN PRISON
Sayah, Joseph
MR. NICE GUY
Sayer, Cynthia
WILD MAN BLUES
Sayre, Jill
SIMPLE PLAN, A
Sbarge, Raphael
BREAST MEN
QUICKSILVER HIGHWAY
Scaife, Emma
SOLDIER'S DAUGHTER NEVER CRIES, A
Scales, Alonzo
HE GOT GAME
Scales, Melodie
LITTLE VOICE
Scalia, Jack
ACT OF WAR
Scanda, Tiare
MIDAQ ALLEY
Scanlon, Anne
HOT BLOODED
Scanlon, John
MERCURY RISING
Scanlon, John T.
SPECIES II
Scannell, Kevin
PENTAGON WARS, THE
Scanner
MODULATIONS: CINEMA FOR THE EAR
Scaperrotta, Jeffrey
ONE TRUE THING
YOU'VE GOT MAIL
Scarana, Antoni
RUSHMORE
Scarborough, Adrian
LOVE IS THE DEVIL: STUDY FOR A PORTRAIT OF FRANCIS BACON
Scarfe, Jonathan
BOOGIE BOY
Scarola, Lisa
WOO
Scarry, Rick
NEGOTIATOR, THE
Scavano, Larry
COMEDY'S DIRTIEST DOZEN
Schaaf, Normana
ONE TRUE THING
Schaal, Wendy
SMALL SOLDIERS
Schade, Doris
BEYOND SILENCE
Schaech, Johnathon
HUSH
WELCOME TO WOOP WOOP
Schaffel, Marla
I LOVE YOU, DON'T TOUCH ME!
Schanz, Heidi
TRUMAN SHOW, THE
Scharff, William Joseph
PATCH ADAMS
Schatz, Mike
MAJOR LEAGUE: BACK TO THE MINORS
Schaub, Sally
SLUMS OF BEVERLY HILLS
Schechter, Glenn
MURDER IN MIND
Schechter, Harold
R.I.P. REST IN PIECES: A PORTRAIT OF JOE COLEMAN
Scheer, Magda
REDLINE
Scheer, Robert
BULWORTH
SIEGE, THE
Scheider, Roy
PEACEKEEPER, THE
RAGE, THE
WHITE RAVEN, THE
Scheine, Raynor
MONTANA
Schell, Maximilian
DEEP IMPACT
EIGHTEENTH ANGEL, THE
JOHN CARPENTER'S VAMPIRES
Schell, Ronnie
FLINTSTONES: I YABBA-DABBA DOO!, THE
Schenck, Holly
STEPMOM
Schenkenberg, Marcus
PRINCE VALIANT
Scherer, Mike
JACK HIGGINS' THUNDER POINT
Schertler, Jean
PECKER
Schiavelli, Vincent
CASPER MEETS WENDY
MILO
RUSTY: THE GREAT RESCUE
Schiff, Paul
RUSHMORE
Schiff, Richard
DEEP IMPACT
DR. DOLITTLE
LIVING OUT LOUD
PENTAGON WARS, THE
Schiffler, Carrie
ATOMIC DOG
Schilling, William G.
PRINCE, THE
Schindler, Peter
MY GIANT
SIEGE, THE
Schirripa, Steve
FEAR AND LOATHING IN LAS VEGAS
Schlaikjer, Amena Lee
KNOCK OFF
Schliessler, Jochen A.
HARD CORE LOGO
Schluter, Ariane
DRESS, THE
Schluter, Henning
KILLER CONDOM, THE
Schmalzbauer, Frederic
RONIN
Schmidberger, Mary
CELEBRITY
Schmidt, Dwight
GODZILLA
Schmidt, Irmin
MODULATIONS: CINEMA FOR THE EAR
Schmidt, Michael
SAFE MEN
Schmidt, Neils Bruno
BRYLCREEM BOYS, THE
Schmidt, Paul
PHANTOMS
Schmidtberger, Mary
LIVING OUT LOUD
Schmidtke, Ned
MERCURY RISING
Schmiedt, Angel
HOLY MAN
TRUMAN SHOW, THE
Schmiedt, Nastassja
TRUMAN SHOW, THE
Schmitt, Vincent
RONIN
Schmitz, Peter
OVERNIGHT DELIVERY
Schnarre, Monika
PEACEKEEPER, THE
Schneider, Dave
GO NOW
Schneider, Florian
MODULATIONS: CINEMA FOR THE EAR
Schneider, Fred
RUGRATS MOVIE, THE
Schneider, Kelley
THERE'S SOMETHING ABOUT MARY
Schneider, Marnie
WEDDING SINGER, THE
Schneider, Rob
KNOCK OFF
WATERBOY, THE
Schoeny, Jeffrey
SIMON BIRCH
Schombing, Jason
ASYLUM
Schooly-D
SUBSTITUTE 2: SCHOOL'S OUT, THE
Schoot, Slava
ROUNDERS
Schoppert, Bill
OVERNIGHT DELIVERY
Schorpion, Frank
DEAD END
Schorr, Daniel
SIEGE, THE
Schram, Bitty
KISSING A FOOL
Schreiber, Liev
PHANTOMS
SPHERE
TWILIGHT
Schreiber, Michael
RAT'S TALE, A
Schroder, Lise
KINGDOM, PART 2, THE
Schroder, Rick
EBENEZER
Schroeder, Carly
BABE: PIG IN THE CITY

Schroeder, Charlie
WHATEVER
Schroeder, Paul
ONE TRUE THING
Schub, Steve
SOMEWHERE IN THE CITY
Schub, Steven
DESPERATE MEASURES
Schubert, Jeff
ORGAZMO
Schull, Rebecca
NEIL SIMON'S THE ODD COUPLE II
Schulte, Mark
NO LOOKING BACK
Schulz, Mark
LIVING OUT LOUD
Schulze, Matt
BLADE
Schulze, Paul
ILLTOWN
Schumacher, Wendy
DIARY OF A SERIAL KILLER
Schuster, Thomas
TWO FOR TEXAS
Schutt Jr., Herbert R.
SPECIES II
Schuurman, Betty
CHARACTER
Schwab, Kirstin
INHERITORS, THE
Schwan, J.P.
NEWTON BOYS, THE
Schwartz, Jessica
TEKKEN: THE MOTION PICTURE
Schwartz, Kimberly
WEDDING SINGER, THE
Schwartz, Louis
SHOOTING FISH
Schwartz, Marty Eli
WATERBOY, THE
Schwartz, Tyagi
BROADWAY DAMAGE
Schwartzberg, Antoinette
CELEBRITY
Schwartzman, Jason
RUSHMORE
Schwartzman, Maurice
DANCE WITH ME
Schwarz, Austin
HORSE WHISPERER, THE
Schwarz, Dustin
HORSE WHISPERER, THE
Schwarz, Lloyd
PI
Schwarz, Simon
INHERITORS, THE
Schweickert, Jeff
STILL BREATHING
Schweickert, Joyce
STILL BREATHING
Schweiger, Til
REPLACEMENT KILLERS, THE
Schweikhardt, Kurt
OVERNIGHT DELIVERY
Schwimmer, David
APT PUPIL
BREAST MEN
KISSING A FOOL
SIX DAYS, SEVEN NIGHTS
Schwimmer, Rusty
LOS LOCOS
NORTH SHORE FISH
Schwoebel, Kurt
LOLIDA 2000
Scialla, Fred
LIVING OUT LOUD
Scio, Yvonne
REDLINE
Scionti, Steve
INVISIBLE DAD
Sciorra, Annabella
INNOCENT SLEEP, THE
MR. JEALOUSY
WHAT DREAMS MAY COME
Sclafani, James Edward
SIX DAYS, SEVEN NIGHTS
Scofield, Dean
LAST ASSASSINS
Scorsese, Martin
RACE TO SAVE 100 YEARS, THE
Scorsese, Nicolette
GIRLS IN PRISON
Scott, Andrew
SAVING PRIVATE RYAN
Scott, Angela
DECAMPITATED
Scott, Ben
MAKER, THE
Scott, Bob
LITTLE VOICE
Scott, Byron
FALLEN
Scott, Campbell
HI-LIFE
IMPOSTORS, THE
SPANISH PRISONER, THE
Scott, Carla
VERY BAD THINGS
Scott, Colton
KRAA! THE SEA MONSTER
Scott, Darin
CAUGHT UP
Scott, Doc
MODULATIONS: CINEMA FOR THE EAR
Scott, Donna
ENEMY OF THE STATE
Scott, Dougray
DEEP IMPACT
EVER AFTER
REGENERATION
Scott, Edmund
NIL BY MOUTH
Scott, Eric Brice
CAN'T HARDLY WAIT
Scott, Esther
SENSELESS
Scott, Fiona
DISTURBING BEHAVIOR
Scott, Gayle
TEN BENNY
Scott, George C.
12 ANGRY MEN
Scott, Jason-Shane
CURSE OF THE PUPPET MASTER
Scott, John-Clay
GIA
OVERNIGHT DELIVERY
Scott, Jonathan
DECAMPITATED
Scott, Judson
BLADE
Scott, Lorna
PRINCE, THE
Scott, Stuart
HE GOT GAME
Scott Thomas, Kristin
HORSE WHISPERER, THE
Scott, Tom
REAL HOWARD SPITZ, THE
Scott, Tom Everett
ONE TRUE THING
Scott, Willard
HOLY MAN
Scottfield, Robert
GODZILLA VS. KING GHIDORAH
Scotto, Rosanna
OBJECT OF MY AFFECTION, THE
Scragg, Stella
UNDER THE SKIN
Scriba, Mik
CITY OF ANGELS
NEGOTIATOR, THE
Scrimm, Angus
PHANTASM: OBLIVION
Scroope, Doug
DARK CITY
Scruggs, Sharon
LAST DAYS OF DISCO, THE
SCARRED CITY
Scudder, Sam
SAVING PRIVATE RYAN
Scullin, Garret
SKIN & BONE
Scurfield, Matthew
SWEPT FROM THE SEA
Scurr, Cosmo
SHOOTING FISH
Seabrook, Christine
GINGERBREAD MAN, THE
Seacat, Sandra
DESTINY OF MARTY FINE, THE
Seagal, Steven
MY GIANT
Seago, Howie
BEYOND SILENCE
Seagraves, Douglas
WHY DO FOOLS FALL IN LOVE?
Seagren, Steve
KISSING A FOOL
Sealy-Smith, Alison
DOWN IN THE DELTA
Sears, Djanet
IN HIS FATHER'S SHOES
REAL BLONDE, THE
Sears, Ross
NEWTON BOYS, THE
Seater, Michael
FUTURE FEAR
RESCUERS: STORIES OF COURAGE—TWO COUPLES
Seaver, Hideo
POLTERGEIST REPORT: YUYU HAKUSHO
WRATH OF THE NINJA: THE YOTODEN MOVIE
Sebastian, James
COLONY, THE
Sebastian, Lobo
MAJOR LEAGUE: BACK TO THE MINORS
Sebotiane, Sello
TARZAN AND THE LOST CITY
Sedaris, Amy
SIX DAYS, SEVEN NIGHTS
Seder, Sam
NEXT STOP, WONDERLAND
Sedgman, Kyne
MR. NICE GUY
Sedgwick, Kyra
MONTANA
Sedgwick, William
PARALLEL SONS
Sedlachek, Buffy
OVERNIGHT DELIVERY
Seeman, Marina
LET'S KILL ALL THE LAWYERS
Sefton, Gary
SAVING PRIVATE RYAN
Segal, Michael Ryan
ROUNDERS
Segall, Pamela
KIKI'S DELIVERY SERVICE
PLUMP FICTION

Sharif, Bina
HAPPINESS
Sharp, Jonah
MODULATIONS: CINEMA FOR THE EAR
Sharp, Matthew
SAVING PRIVATE RYAN
Sharpe, Trevor
VELVET GOLDMINE
Sharpton, Rev. Al
RUN FOR COVER
Shatner, William
LAND OF THE FREE
TREKKIES
Shaud, Grant
ANTZ
Shaw, Adam
SAVING PRIVATE RYAN
Shaw, Emme
NEXT STOP, WONDERLAND
Shaw, Fiona
AVENGERS, THE
BUTCHER BOY, THE
Shaw, Ian
MOONDANCE
Shaw, Morgana
HOME FRIES
Shaw, Peter
PRACTICAL MAGIC
Shaw, Stan
SNAKE EYES
Shaw, Tara
LAST SEDUCTION II, THE
Shawn, Wallace
JUNGLE BOOK: MOWGLI'S STORY, THE
Shawn-Williams, Nigel
DOWN IN THE DELTA
Shawzin, Gregg
CIVIL ACTION, A
Shay, Michele
HE GOT GAME
ONE TRUE THING
Shaye, Lin
LIVING OUT LOUD
THERE'S SOMETHING ABOUT MARY
Shea, Rico
MY BROTHER'S WAR
SPACEJACKED
Shear, Claudia
LIVING OUT LOUD
Shearer, Chris
PASS, THE
Shearer, Harry
ALMOST HEROES
GODZILLA
SMALL SOLDIERS
TRUMAN SHOW, THE
Shearer, Jack
NEGOTIATOR, THE
SENSELESS
Shearer, Steve
CON, THE
Shebby, Brianna
BOYS IN LOVE 2
Shebby, Danielle
BOYS IN LOVE 2
Sheedy, Ally
HIGH ART
Sheehan, Bobby
BLUES BROTHERS 2000
Sheehan, Nora
MIGHTY, THE
Sheehan, Tim
THERE'S SOMETHING ABOUT MARY
Sheen, Charlie
LETTER FROM DEATH ROW, A
Sheen, Martin
HOSTILE WATERS
LETTER FROM DEATH ROW, A
MONUMENT AVE.
SHADRACH
Sheen, Michael
WILDE
Sheen, Ruth
WHEN PIGS FLY
Sheena
LOVE IS THE DEVIL: STUDY FOR A PORTRAIT OF FRANCIS BACON
Sheffield, Jeremy
MERLIN
Sheffield, Peggy
PALMETTO
Shell, Ray
VELVET GOLDMINE
Shelley, Rachel
PHOTOGRAPHING FAIRIES
Shellist, Lorelei
LETTER FROM DEATH ROW, A
Shelton, Marley
PLEASANTVILLE
Shelton, Sloane
ONE TRUE THING
Shen, Freda Foh
MULAN
Shendi
HANGING GARDEN, THE
Sheng, Samuel
PATCH ADAMS
Shenkel, Leslie
CELEBRITY
Shenkman, Ben
PI
Shenkman, Insben
SIEGE, THE
Shepard, John Paul
TEKKEN: THE MOTION PICTURE
Shepard, Keith
STEPHEN KING'S THE NIGHT FLIER
Shepard, Lee
STEPMOM
Shepard, Sam
ONLY THRILL, THE
Sheperd, Karen Lee
ANOTHER DAY IN PARADISE
BOOGIE BOY
Shepherd, Simon
SPICE WORLD
Shepherd, Suzanne
LIVING OUT LOUD
LOLITA
Shepis, Tiffany
SHAMPOO HORNS
Sheppard, Elizabeth
WHITE RAVEN, THE
Sheppard, Ellen
FALLEN
Sheppard, Talula
MERLIN
Sheppard, W. Morgan
ESCAPE, THE
Sher, Antony
SHAKESPEARE IN LOVE
Sher, Sy
LIVING OUT LOUD
Sheraton III, John
FORMER CHILD STAR
Sherbedgia, Rade
MIGHTY JOE YOUNG
Sheridan, Jim
GENERAL, THE
Sheridan, Joe
MAN IN THE IRON MASK, THE
Sheridan, John
STILL BREATHING
Sheridan, Kelly
NEW ADVENTURES OF KIMBA THE WHITE LION, THE
SIN AND REDEMPTION
Sherman, Barry
SUICIDE KINGS
Sherman, Barry Del
ALMOST HEROES
Sherman, Bob
HUMAN BOMB
Sherman, Cindy
PECKER
Sherman, Daniel
NIGHT VISION
Sherman, Danielle
PARENT TRAP, THE
Sherry, James
I'LL BE HOME FOR CHRISTMAS
Sherwood, David
OPERATION DELTA FORCE 2
Shestack, Marcia Rose
DISTURBING BEHAVIOR
Shida, Masayuki
THIN RED LINE, THE
Shields, Ciara A.
HE GOT GAME
Shields, Fallon
THERE'S SOMETHING ABOUT MARY
Shields, Jack
THERE'S SOMETHING ABOUT MARY
Shigarev, Dima
THIEF, THE
Shigeta, James
MULAN
Shih Kien
HONG KONG 1941
Shiina, Kippei
GONIN
Shimizu, Keenan
MONTANA
Shimizu, Miho
EEL, THE
Shimizu, Misa
EEL, THE
Shimono, Sab
BIG HIT, THE
Shinas, Sofia
HOSTILE INTENT
Shines, Johnny
CAN'T YOU HEAR THE WIND HOWL?: THE LIFE AND MUSIC OF ROBERT JOHNSON
Shing Fui-on
DRAGONS FOREVER
KILLER ANGELS
Shinick, Kevin
SOUR GRAPES
Shinohara, Katsuyuki
WHEN I CLOSE MY EYES
Shinsui, Sansho
EEL, THE
Shiomi, Sansei
WHEN I CLOSE MY EYES
Shipman, Robert
DIRTY WORK
Shippley, Sandra
MONUMENT AVE.
Shipton, Cathy
SPICE WORLD
Shiraishi, Fuyumi
MOBILE SUIT GUNDAM I
MOBILE SUIT GUNDAM II: SOLDIERS OF SORROW
MOBILE SUIT GUNDAM III: ENCOUNTERS IN SPACE
Shire, Talia
LANDLADY, THE

Shirley, Aaron
JACK HIGGINS' MIDNIGHT MAN
Shiroma, Earl Kim
BURN HOLLYWOOD BURN
Shirzad, M.
MIRROR, THE
Shively, Ed
GENERAL CHAOS: UNCENSORED ANIMATION
Shoaib, Samia
OBJECT OF MY AFFECTION, THE
PI
Shodeinde, Fash
KINGDOM, PART 2, THE
Shoemaker, Joshua
PECKER
Shonte, Alicia
ARMOUR OF GOD
Shore, Chris
REAL HOWARD SPITZ, THE
Shore, Pauly
CASPER MEETS WENDY
Short, Martin
MERLIN
PRINCE OF EGYPT, THE
Short, Paul
AMERICAN HISTORY X
Short, Sylvia
I STILL KNOW WHAT YOU DID LAST SUMMER
Shotwell, Sandra
NOT IN THIS TOWN
Showalter, Michael
SAFE MEN
Shroyer, Sonny
GINGERBREAD MAN, THE
Shtempel, Alexander
DEJA VU
Shtukaturova, Ania
THIEF, THE
Shu Chu
KILLER ANGELS
Shu Yaoxuan
EMPEROR'S SHADOW, THE
Shue, Elisabeth
COUSIN BETTE
PALMETTO
Shue, James
NO WAY HOME
Shuerman, Al
COURTING COURTNEY
Shulman, Felicia
BLEEDERS
MISBEGOTTEN
Shulman, Michael
WIDE AWAKE
Shultz, Albert
BLACKJACK
EBENEZER
Shultz, Dwight
GOLGO 13: QUEEN BEE
Shumaker, Scott J.
LET'S KILL ALL THE LAWYERS
Shuman, Michael
WEDDING SINGER, THE
Shun, Amanda
SUMMER FLING
Shuster, Skylar
BOYS WILL BE BOYS
Shuttleworth, Brenda
EBENEZER
Shuttleworth, Darryl
EBENEZER
Si Han
EAST PALACE, WEST PALACE
Sia, Beau
SLAM
SLAMNATION
Sibley, David
FROM A FAR COUNTRY
INCOGNITO
Sicari, Joseph
BABE: PIG IN THE CITY
Sicari, Joseph R.
JANE AUSTEN'S MAFIA!
Sicilia, Joseph
DIRTY WORK
Sicily
CHILDREN OF THE CORN V: FIELD OF TERROR
HOW STELLA GOT HER GROOVE BACK
Sickler, Rich
PRACTICAL MAGIC
Sidaris, Christian Drew
RETURN TO SAVAGE BEACH
Siddall, Brianne
RUSTY: THE GREAT RESCUE
Side, Richard
URBAN SAFARI
Sidello, Paul
SLAYERS: THE MOTION PICTURE
Sie, Allison
ENEMY OF THE STATE
Sie, James
U.S. MARSHALS
Siegel, Charles
CALL TO REMEMBER, A
URBAN SAFARI
Siegel, Eric
LOVER GIRL
Siegler, Ben
FALLEN
Sieh, Jeanette
HOPE FLOATS
Sieker, Richard M.
LETHAL WEAPON 4
Siekoua, Basile
WESTERN
Siemaszko, Casey
NAPOLEON
Sienna, Bridget
CLOCKWATCHERS
Sieres, Deigo
MASK OF ZORRO, THE
Sierra, Gregory
JANE AUSTEN'S MAFIA!
JOHN CARPENTER'S VAMPIRES
Sierra, Lu Celania
STEPMOM
Sietz, Adam
CELEBRITY
Sigl, Robert
TALES FROM A PARALLEL UNIVERSE: GIGA SHADOW
Signor, Marion
WESTERN
Siiteri, Peter
PATCH ADAMS
Sikes, Lori Beth
GINGERBREAD MAN, THE
Sikking, Andrew
RIVER RED
Sikorski, Joseph
RETURN OF THE KING, THE
Silano, Gerardo
SWEPT FROM THE SEA
Silberg, Joshua
EBENEZER
Silberg, Richard J.
PATCH ADAMS
Silberg, Tusse
LOVE AND DEATH ON LONG ISLAND
Sillas, Karen
REACH THE ROCK
SOUR GRAPES
Silva, Henry
PRINCE, THE
Silva, Maria Jose
CARLA'S SONG
Silva, Rebecca
ENEMY OF THE STATE
Silvano, Jerome
BREAKOUT
Silveira, Leonor
VOYAGE TO THE BEGINNING OF THE WORLD
Silveira, Ruth
YOUR FRIENDS & NEIGHBORS
Silver, Michael Buchman
PLAYING BY HEART
Silver, Ron
WHITE RAVEN, THE
Silver, Spike
SUICIDE KINGS
Silverberg, Evan
HAPPINESS
Silverio, Manny
SCARRED CITY
Silverio, Susanne
INHERITORS, THE
Silverman, Jonathan
FRENCH EXIT
NEIL SIMON'S THE ODD COUPLE II
Silverman, Laura
HALF BAKED
Silverman, Sarah
BULWORTH
THERE'S SOMETHING ABOUT MARY
Silverstein, Salik
MR. NICE GUY
Silverstone, Ben
LOLITA
Silvertsen, Mark
JOHN CARPENTER'S VAMPIRES
Simanton, Jon
KRAA! THE SEA MONSTER
Simionescu, Adrian
GADJO DILO
Simkins, Michael
WILDE
Simmons, Earl
BELLY
Simmons, J.K.
CELEBRITY
CROSSING FIELDS
FACE DOWN
LOVE WALKED IN
Simmons, Jaason
PASS, THE
Simmons, Richard
RUDOLPH THE RED-NOSED REINDEER: THE MOVIE
Simmons, Shadia
IN HIS FATHER'S SHOES
Simmons, Sophie
FACE THE EVIL
Simmons, Tom
TRUMAN SHOW, THE
Simmons, Venera
DEAD WATERS
Simmons, Vincent
FARM: ANGOLA, U.S.A., THE
Simmons, Xavier
BELLY
Simmrin, Joey
MIDAS TOUCH, THE
STAR KID
Simms, Tasha
I'LL BE HOME FOR CHRISTMAS
Simola, Liisa
DIDN'T DO IT FOR LOVE
Simon, Cheung
KNOCK OFF

Simon, Georgia
JANE AUSTEN'S MAFIA!
Simon, Jay
JACK HIGGINS' MIDNIGHT MAN
Simon, Phillip
GIA
Simon, Sophie
UN AIR DE FAMILLE
Simonds, Dave
HENRY FOOL
Simonds, Lincoln
MY GIANT
Simonett, Ted
BLACKJACK
Simons, Hywel
SHAKESPEARE IN LOVE
Simpson, Brian
STAR KID
Simpson, Dr. H. Mitch
DEAR JESSE
Simpson, Melanie
LITTLE VOICE
Simpson, Michael Philip
KINGDOM, PART 2, THE
Simpson, Sean
LIKE IT IS
Simpson, Tyree Michael
WOO
Sims, Adam
LOST IN SPACE
Sims, Bronwyn
NEXT STOP, WONDERLAND
Sims, Keely
DISAPPEARANCE OF KEVIN JOHNSON, THE
Sims, Kelley
STEPHEN KING'S THE NIGHT FLIER
Sims, Mary G.
ONE TRUE THING
Sin-D
DEE SNIDER'S STRANGELAND
Sinclair, John Gordon
BRYLCREEM BOYS, THE
Sinclair, Malcolm
MERRY WAR, A
Sinden, Grace
APT PUPIL
Sinden, Marc
BRYLCREEM BOYS, THE
Sinelnikoff, Michael
LOST WORLD, THE
Siner, Guy
DISAPPEARANCE OF KEVIN JOHNSON, THE
Singer, Jane
RUSTY: THE GREAT RESCUE
Singer, Lauren
PARALLEL SONS
Singer, Linda
JACK HIGGINS' THUNDER POINT
Singer, Mildred
APT PUPIL
Singer, Norbert D.
APT PUPIL
Singer, Ritchie
DARK CITY
Singer, Stephen
PERFECT MURDER, A
PRICE ABOVE RUBIES, A
Singer, Susie
LANDLADY, THE
Singh, Desi
ORGAZMO
Singh, Mohinder
SUE
Singh, Talvin
MODULATIONS: CINEMA FOR THE EAR
Singleton, Harry
PLEASANTVILLE
Sinise, Gary
GEORGE WALLACE
SNAKE EYES
Siragusa, Peter
BIG LEBOWSKI, THE
Sirbu, Alina
SECRET KINGDOM, THE
Sircos, Myriam
RUDOLPH THE RED-NOSED REINDEER: THE MOVIE
Sirianni, Dolores
YOU'VE GOT MAIL
Sirico, Tony
CELEBRITY
Sirleaf, Marietta
RINGMASTER
Sirtis, Marina
STAR TREK: INSURRECTION
Sisco, Kennen
PECKER
Siscoe, David
DEAD END
JACK HIGGINS' THE WINDSOR PROTOCOL
Sissons, Peter
SPICE WORLD
Sisto, Jeremy
PLAYING BY HEART
SUICIDE KINGS
WITHOUT LIMITS
Sisto, Meadow
CAN'T HARDLY WAIT
CROSSING FIELDS
Sisto, Rocco
LOVE WALKED IN
Sisto, Rocko
CHARLIE HOBOKEN
Sitter, Karen
BUFFALO '66
Siugali, Jennifer
THIN RED LINE, THE
Sivadier, Pierre-Michel
SOLDIER'S DAUGHTER NEVER CRIES, A
Sivero, Frank
WEDDING SINGER, THE
Siviero, Marco
KISSING A FOOL
Size, Roni
MODULATIONS: CINEMA FOR THE EAR
Sizemore, Tom
ENEMY OF THE STATE
SAVING PRIVATE RYAN
Skagestad, Bjorn
KRISTIN LAVRANSDATTER
Skaggs, Corey
VELVET GOLDMINE
Skalnik, Michelle
DISTURBING BEHAVIOR
Skarga, Alvina
DEAD WATERS
Skarsgard, Stellan
INSOMNIA
KINGDOM, PART 2, THE
RONIN
SAVIOR
Skene, Rick
TRUCKS
Skeriotis, Patricia
DIARY OF A SERIAL KILLER
Skerritt, Tom
SMOKE SIGNALS
TWO FOR TEXAS
Skill, Laura
PENTAGON WARS, THE
Skinner, Beverly
STEPHEN KING'S THE NIGHT FLIER
Skinner, Vicki
INVISIBLE DAD
Skjaerstad, Robert
JUNK MAIL
Skoog, Susan
WHATEVER
Skortstad, Ben
NIGHTWATCH
Skrela, Mark
SIMON BIRCH
Skulski, Brooke
BULWORTH
Skye, Azura
HORTON FOOTE'S ALONE
Skye, Ione
DREAM FOR AN INSOMNIAC
GIRLS IN PRISON
Slade, Gloria
BLUES BROTHERS 2000
REAL BLONDE, THE
Sladek, Daniel
SUB DOWN
Slater, Blair
I'LL BE HOME FOR CHRISTMAS
TRUMAN SHOW, THE
Slater, Callison
ENEMY OF THE STATE
Slater, Christian
HARD RAIN
VERY BAD THINGS
Slater, Thomas A.
DANCE WITH ME
Slattery, John
MY BROTHER'S WAR
Slaughter, Lance
WOO
Slavin, Jonathan
SLAPPY AND THE STINKERS
Slavin, Millie
TRUMAN SHOW, THE
Slayton, Bobby
RAT PACK, THE
Sleep, Wayne
ELIZABETH
Slezak, Victor
ONE TOUGH COP
SIEGE, THE
Sliwa, Curtis
RUN FOR COVER
SIEGE, THE
Sloan, Cle Shaheed
REPLACEMENT KILLERS, THE
Sloan, Tina
CELEBRITY
Sloate, Maynard
LENNY BRUCE: SWEAR TO TELL THE TRUTH
Slutsker, Peter
PRICE ABOVE RUBIES, A
Smagghe, Steve
LIFE OF JESUS, THE
Small, Robert
HOLY MAN
Small, Ron
TERMINAL JUSTICE
Smallman, Nick
ELIZABETH
Smallwood, Tucker
DEEP IMPACT
SOUR GRAPES
Smart, Alexis
GIA
Smart, Amy
DEE SNIDER'S STRANGELAND
Smart, Dee
WELCOME TO WOOP WOOP
Smart, Jean
NEIL SIMON'S THE ODD COUPLE II

Smart, Rebecca
VIOLET'S VISIT

Smashing Pumpkins, The
FREE TIBET

Smee, Derek
MERRY WAR, A
MRS. DALLOWAY

Smego, Alissa Ann
STAR KID

Smidman, David
LEADING MAN, THE

Smiga, Carly
TRUMAN SHOW, THE

Smigel, Robert
WEDDING SINGER, THE

Smiles, Dena
TWENTYFOURSEVEN

Smiley, Leigh
BELOVED

Smiljanic, Bozidar
ARMOUR OF GOD

Smilow, Beebe
RETURN TO SAVAGE BEACH

Smishkewych, Wolodymyr
ONE TRUE THING

Smit, Cate
LAST DAYS OF DISCO, THE

Smith, Adam C.
ARMAGEDDON

Smith, Alan
BURN HOLLYWOOD BURN

Smith, Amber
MARS

Smith, Andrew
LOVE AND DEATH ON LONG ISLAND

Smith, Be-Be
BULWORTH

Smith, Billy
THERE'S SOMETHING ABOUT MARY

Smith, Bob
SWEPT FROM THE SEA

Smith, Brandon
RAGE, THE

Smith, Britta
TALK OF ANGELS

Smith, Buddy
GENERAL CHAOS: UNCENSORED ANIMATION

Smith, Caroline
EDEN

Smith, Cedric
JACK HIGGINS' THUNDER POINT

Smith, Charles Martin
DEEP IMPACT

Smith, Clifford
BELLY

Smith, Coach Dean
HE GOT GAME

Smith, Danny
BIG HIT, THE

Smith, Dari Gerard
DR. DOLITTLE

Smith, Ebonie
LETHAL WEAPON 4

Smith, Edward
I GOT THE HOOK UP

Smith, Errol
HOLY MAN

Smith, Fran
HENRY: PORTRAIT OF A SERIAL KILLER PART 2

Smith, Gatlin Boone
TWO FOR TEXAS

Smith, Gerald L.A.
LET'S KILL ALL THE LAWYERS

Smith, Gregory
KRIPPENDORF'S TRIBE
SMALL SOLDIERS

Smith, Hillary B.
LAST BREATH

Smith, Iain Winter
OPERATION DELTA FORCE 2

Smith, Ian
TWENTYFOURSEVEN

Smith, Ian Michael
SIMON BIRCH

Smith, Isaac
ANOTHER DAY IN PARADISE

Smith, J.W.
WHY DO FOOLS FALL IN LOVE?

Smith, Jaclyn
MY VERY BEST FRIEND

Smith, Jacob
SMALL SOLDIERS

Smith, John Dee
THIN RED LINE, THE

Smith, Julie K.
RETURN TO SAVAGE BEACH

Smith, Kester
SIX DAYS, SEVEN NIGHTS

Smith, Kevin
HERCULES AND XENA THE ANIMATED MOVIE: THE BATTLE FOR MOUNT OLYMPUS
YOUNG HERCULES

Smith, Kieran
INNOCENT SLEEP, THE

Smith, Kurtwood
BRIGHT SHINING LIE, A
DEEP IMPACT

Smith, Kyle Timothy
PATCH ADAMS

Smith, L.H.
GINGERBREAD MAN, THE

Smith, Lane
HI-LO COUNTRY, THE
WHY DO FOOLS FALL IN LOVE?

Smith, Lee
DEAR JESSE

Smith, Leslie L.
DAVID SEARCHING

Smith, Lillian
BELOVED

Smith, Lionel Mark
CON, THE
SPANISH PRISONER, THE

Smith, Lisa Rhianna
LETHAL WEAPON 4

Smith, Liz
MERRY WAR, A

Smith, Marc
SLAMNATION

Smith, Marty
LET'S KILL ALL THE LAWYERS

Smith, Matt
DRAGON BALL Z THE MOVIE: THE TREE OF MIGHT

Smith, Patricia
SLAMNATION

Smith, Patti
LOU REED: ROCK AND ROLL HEART
RUGRATS MOVIE, THE

Smith, Paul
DECEIVER

Smith, Philip R.
KISSING A FOOL

Smith, Robert O.
NEW ADVENTURES OF KIMBA THE WHITE LION, THE

Smith, Robert Vincent
PERFECT MURDER, A

Smith, Roger Guenveur
HE GOT GAME

Smith, Ron Clinton
MAJOR LEAGUE: BACK TO THE MINORS

Smith, Scott
X-FILES, THE

Smith, Sean
DISTURBING BEHAVIOR

Smith, Shawnee
ARMAGEDDON
MEN

Smith, Sly
TOP OF THE WORLD

Smith, Stephanie
PATCH ADAMS

Smith, Taran Noah
LITTLE BIGFOOT 2: THE JOURNEY HOME

Smith, Thomasina
LOVE IS THE DEVIL: STUDY FOR A PORTRAIT OF FRANCIS BACON

Smith, Tommy
LETTER FROM DEATH ROW, A

Smith, Tony
LOU REED: ROCK AND ROLL HEART

Smith, Tucker
HI-LIFE

Smith, Will
ENEMY OF THE STATE

Smith, William
UNCLE SAM

Smits, Jimmy
MURDER IN MIND

Smoljanski, Ilja
OGRE, THE

Smurfitt, Victoria
LEADING MAN, THE

Smythe, Pete
JACK HIGGINS' MIDNIGHT MAN

Snegur, Lubov
DEAD WATERS

Snider, Barry
BREAK, THE

Snider, Dee
DEE SNIDER'S STRANGELAND

Snider, Peter
WHITE RAVEN, THE

Snipes, Wesley
BLADE
DOWN IN THE DELTA
U.S. MARSHALS

Snodgress, Carrie
WILD THINGS

Snoop Doggy Dog
I GOT THE HOOK UP
RIDE

Snow, Cherene
CITY OF ANGELS

Snow, Kim
PARALLEL SONS

Snow, Rachel Lena
HOPE FLOATS

Snow, Theron
PARALLEL SONS

Snowball, Yolanda
LIVING OUT LOUD

Snyder, Drew
PENTAGON WARS, THE

Snyder, Kim
GREAT EXPECTATIONS

Snyder, Rick
U.S. MARSHALS

Snyder, Tom
OFF THE MENU: THE LAST DAYS OF CHASEN'S

Soare, Claudia
LITTLE GHOST

Soares, Malcon
CENTRAL STATION

Sobeck, Tara
HORSE WHISPERER, THE

Soberanes, Esteban
MEN WITH GUNS

Sobieski, Leelee
DEEP IMPACT
SOLDIER'S DAUGHTER NEVER CRIES, A
Sogliuzzo, Andre
YOU'VE GOT MAIL
Sogne, Herve
JACK HIGGINS' MIDNIGHT MAN
Sogreni, Soren
CELEBRATION, THE
Sohn, Sonja
SLAM
Soibatian, Naira
RUN FOR COVER
Soileau, Paul
OUT OF SIGHT
Sokolov, Pavel
DEAD WATERS
Sokolow, Diane
YOU'VE GOT MAIL
Sol, Alex
AMERICAN HISTORY X
Solari, John
DISAPPEARANCE OF KEVIN JOHNSON, THE
LOVE TO KILL
Solari, Matthew
BOYS IN LOVE 2
Solarino, Ken
BREAK, THE
Solberg, Shayn
AIR BUD: GOLDEN RECEIVER
Solda, Maurizio
CHAMBERMAID ON THE TITANIC, THE
Soldevilla, Chris
RAT'S TALE, A
Soles, P.J.
UNCLE SAM
Soles, Paul
BRAM STOKER'S SHADOWBUILDER
Sollenberger, Michael
CURSE OF THE PUPPET MASTER
Sollinger, Alan
SHOOTING FISH
Solomon, Howard
LENNY BRUCE: SWEAR TO TELL THE TRUTH
Solomon, Lenny
WOO
Somera Jr., Leon C.
KNOCK OFF
Somers, Suzanne
RUSTY: THE GREAT RESCUE
Somerville, Phyllis
IMPOSTORS, THE
MONTANA
Sommer, Josef
PATCH ADAMS
PROPOSITION, THE
Sommerfeld, Peter
DARK CITY
Sommers, Jana
DEEP RISING
Sommers, Michael Rae
PATCH ADAMS
Songer, Melinda
RUNNING WOMAN, THE
Songhui, Kwasi
DEAD END
Songhurst, Gregan
BOYS IN LOVE 2
Sonic Youth
FREE TIBET
Sonnabend, Yolanda
LOVE IS THE DEVIL: STUDY FOR A PORTRAIT OF FRANCIS BACON
Sonnenberg, Maurice
CELEBRITY

Sood, Veena
WRONGFULLY ACCUSED
Soral, Agnes
OGRE, THE
Soratorio, Marissa
DANCE WITH ME
Sorbo, Kevin
HERCULES AND XENA THE ANIMATED MOVIE: THE BATTLE FOR MOUNT OLYMPUS
Sorce, Robert
SHAMPOO HORNS
Sorel, Nancy
I LOVE YOU, DON'T TOUCH ME!
Sorensen, Cindy L.
I GOT THE HOOK UP
Sorensen, Thomas Jungling
MENDEL
Sorenson, Kevin
HENRY: PORTRAIT OF A SERIAL KILLER PART 2
Sorge, Paula
LEWIS & CLARK & GEORGE
Sorich, Michael
GOLGO 13: QUEEN BEE
RUSTY: THE GREAT RESCUE
Sorkin, Arleen
BATMAN/SUPERMAN MOVIE, THE
Sornson, Tanisher
DON KING: ONLY IN AMERICA
Soronen, Tim "Stuffy"
FULL TILT BOOGIE
Sorvino, Mira
REPLACEMENT KILLERS, THE
TARANTELLA
Sorvino, Paul
ALMOST PARTNERS
BULWORTH
DOGWATCH
KNOCK OFF
Sosa, Roberto
MEN WITH GUNS
Sosa, Sammy
KISSING A FOOL
Soto, Frank
LOS LOCOS
Soto, Jose
NO WAY HOME
Soto, Roberto
BULWORTH
Sottili, Fabio
DAVID SEARCHING
Soualem, Zinedine
UN AIR DE FAMILLE
Soucie, Kath
BRAVE LITTLE TOASTER GOES TO MARS, THE
KIKI'S DELIVERY SERVICE
RUGRATS MOVIE, THE
Soucy, Jin Hi
GINGERBREAD MAN, THE
Soughan, Josephine
LOVE IS THE DEVIL: STUDY FOR A PORTRAIT OF FRANCIS BACON
Soukhoroukov, Victor
BROTHER
Soule, Allen
SPANISH PRISONER, THE
Soutar, Ted
REAL HOWARD SPITZ, THE
Southerland, Boots
NEWTON BOYS, THE
Sowers, Scott
BOOGIE BOY
Sozzani, Anna
DANGEROUS BEAUTY
Spacek, Sissy
AFFLICTION

Spacek, Stephen
THIN RED LINE, THE
Spacey, Kevin
BUG'S LIFE, A
HURLYBURLY
NEGOTIATOR, THE
Spade, David
RUGRATS MOVIE, THE
SENSELESS
Spahn, Ryan
POLISH WEDDING
Spain, Douglas
PERMANENT MIDNIGHT
12 ANGRY MEN
Spann, Aaron
BABE: PIG IN THE CITY
Spano, Joe
CALL TO REMEMBER, A
Spano, Nick
GIA
Sparber, Herschel
SCARRED CITY
Sparks, Carrie Cain
TRICKS
Sparks, Millicent
BELOVED
Sparks of Fire
POLISH WEDDING
Sparrow, David
ONE TOUGH COP
Sparrow, Walter
EVER AFTER
Speakman, Jeff
LAND OF THE FREE
Spears, Aries
WHY DO FOOLS FALL IN LOVE?
Spears, Peter
OPPOSITE OF SEX, THE
Speed, Lucy
MERRY WAR, A
SHAKESPEARE IN LOVE
Speedman, Scott
RESCUERS: STORIES OF COURAGE—TWO COUPLES
Speight, Bruno
MY FIRST NAME IS MACEO
Spellos, Peter
CITY OF ANGELS
LIVING IN PERIL
RED HAWK: WEAPON OF DEATH
Spence, Bruce
DARK CITY
Spence, Sebastian
FIRESTORM
Spencer, Amanda
RONIN
Spencer, Brant
BELLY
Spencer, C.B.
BASEKETBALL
Spencer, Dorian
NIGHT AT THE ROXBURY, A
Spencer, Garret
WHATEVER
Spencer, John
NEGOTIATOR, THE
TWILIGHT
Spencer, Julian
SAVING PRIVATE RYAN
Spender, Elizabeth
LEADING MAN, THE
Spengler, Sanja
HOSTILE WATERS
Spengler, Volker
OGRE, THE
Sperdakos, George
BLUES BROTHERS 2000
DIRTY WORK

Spiegel, Harry
RESCUERS: STORIES OF COURAGE—TWO COUPLES
Spiegel, Howard
YOU'VE GOT MAIL
Spiegel, James
CHARLIE HOBOKEN
Spielvogel, Laurent
OGRE, THE
RONIN
Spinella, Stephen
DAVID SEARCHING
GREAT EXPECTATIONS
OUT OF THE PAST
TARANTELLA
Spiner, Brent
STAR TREK: INSURRECTION
TREKKIES
Spinner
DECLINE OF WESTERN CIVILIZATION PART III, THE
Spinuzza, Doug
NEGOTIATOR, THE
Spirtas, Kevin
APT PUPIL
Spiteri, John
LOVE IS THE DEVIL: STUDY FOR A PORTRAIT OF FRANCIS BACON
Spitz, Robert
HUMAN BOMB
Spivak, Kristina
DEAD WATERS
Spoke, Suanne
KRIPPENDORF'S TRIBE
Spoon
DECLINE OF WESTERN CIVILIZATION PART III, THE
Spore, Richard
I MARRIED A STRANGE PERSON!
Sporleder, Gregory
CLAY PIGEONS
SKIN & BONE
Sposit, Laurie
LIVING OUT LOUD
Spottag, Jens Jorn
KINGDOM, PART 2, THE
Spradling, Charlie
JOHNNY SKIDMARKS
Sprague, Carin
WHAT DREAMS MAY COME
Spray, Scott
ONE TRUE THING
Spreekmeester, Stephen
SNAKE EYES
Springall, Alejandro
MEN WITH GUNS
Springer, Jerry
KISSING A FOOL
RINGMASTER
Spruill, James
BODY COUNT
Spurrier, Linda
SHOOTING FISH
Spybey, Dina
BURN HOLLYWOOD BURN
Squarepusher
MODULATIONS: CINEMA FOR THE EAR
Squibb, June
MEET JOE BLACK
Squicciarini, Mike
WEST NEW YORK
Squid
DECLINE OF WESTERN CIVILIZATION PART III, THE
Squire, Mike
KISSING A FOOL
Squires, David
LOLIDA 2000
Sripitakulvikai, Samrit
HEROES SHED NO TEARS
Sroka, Jerry
ANTZ
St. Calbre, Louis
SOLDIER'S DAUGHTER NEVER CRIES, A
St. Clair, Taylore
LOLIDA 2000
St. James, James
SHAMPOO HORNS
St. James, Mark
I LOVE YOU, DON'T TOUCH ME!
St. John, Jahnni
MEET JOE BLACK
St. John, Michelle
SMOKE SIGNALS
St. John-Hacker, Trevor
FIRELIGHT
St. Johnston, Kate
LOVE IS THE DEVIL: STUDY FOR A PORTRAIT OF FRANCIS BACON
St. Juste, Margie
HAV PLENTY
St. Ledger, Margaux
OPPOSITE OF SEX, THE
St. Lynne, Maria
CHINESE BOX, THE
St. Onge, Korrine
RINGMASTER
St. Patrick, Matthew
STEEL SHARKS
Staab, Rebecca
STRAY BULLET
Stabile, Nick
BRIDE OF CHUCKY
Stack, Robert
BASEKETBALL
Stack, Tim
BRAVE LITTLE TOASTER GOES TO MARS, THE
Stadele, Owen
SUBSTITUTE 2: SCHOOL'S OUT, THE
Stadlen, Lewis J.
IMPOSTORS, THE
Stadler, Joerg
EVER AFTER
SAVING PRIVATE RYAN
Stadvec, Michael
CHOSEN ONE: LEGEND OF THE RAVEN, THE
Stafford, Jerry
LOVE IS THE DEVIL: STUDY FOR A PORTRAIT OF FRANCIS BACON
Stafford, Jon
SOULER OPPOSITE, THE
Staggs, Monica
SPECIES II
Stahelski, Chad
JOHN CARPENTER'S VAMPIRES
Stahl, Jerry
PERMANENT MIDNIGHT
Stahl, Nick
DISTURBING BEHAVIOR
THIN RED LINE, THE
Stahlbrand, Sandi
BRIDE OF CHUCKY
Staines, Kent
FACE DOWN
Staley, Steve
RINGMASTER
Stallone, Sylvester
ANTZ
BURN HOLLYWOOD BURN
Stamberg, Susan
SIEGE, THE
Stamp, Terence
LOVE WALKED IN
Standing, John
MRS. DALLOWAY
Stanley, Cameron Brooke
PATCH ADAMS
Stanley, Florence
BULWORTH
NEIL SIMON'S THE ODD COUPLE II
Stanley, Grag
SLAYERS: THE MOTION PICTURE
Stanley, James
POLTERGEIST REPORT: YUYU HAKUSHO
Stanton, Harry Dean
FEAR AND LOATHING IN LAS VEGAS
MIGHTY, THE
Stanton, Maria
PHOENIX
Stanton, Robert
MERCURY RISING
NEXT STOP, WONDERLAND
Stapelton, Brendan
TARZAN AND THE LOST CITY
Stapleton, Jean
POCAHONTAS II: JOURNEY TO A NEW WORLD
YOU'VE GOT MAIL
Star, Fredro
RIDE
Starace, James
NO WAY HOME
Starberry, Gil
RED HAWK: WEAPON OF DEATH
Stark, Don
DOUBLE EDGE
Starks, John "Jabo"
MY FIRST NAME IS MACEO
Starr, Beau
MEN
Starr, Mike
SNAKE EYES
Staub, Jack
LAST DAYS OF DISCO, THE
Stauber, Liz
CAN'T HARDLY WAIT
Staunton, Imelda
SHAKESPEARE IN LOVE
Staunton, Kim
HOLY MAN
Stavola, Charlie
CIVIL ACTION, A
Stayer, Carolyn
PECKER
Stearns, Elizabeth
DAY AT THE BEACH
Steccaglia, Giacomo
DANCE WITH ME
Stedman, Anne
NEWTON BOYS, THE
Steemson, John
UGLY, THE
Steen, Jessica
ARMAGEDDON
DOGWATCH
Steen, Paprika
CELEBRATION, THE
Steenstrup, Henriette
JUNK MAIL
Steer, Stanley
DARK CITY
Steers, Burr
LAST DAYS OF DISCO, THE
Stefanescu, Oana
TALISMAN
Stefano, Kathleen
PATCH ADAMS
Stefanson, Leslie
BURN HOLLYWOOD BURN
Steffand, Joan
SIMPLE PLAN, A

Steger, Jimmy
REAL THING, THE
Stegman, Richard
NEXT STEP, THE
Steiger, Jacqueline
DENNIS THE MENACE STRIKES AGAIN
Steiger, Rod
INCOGNITO
KINGDOM OF SHADOWS
OFF THE MENU: THE LAST DAYS OF CHASEN'S
REAL THING, THE
Stein, Ben
CASPER MEETS WENDY
Stein, Mary
BABE: PIG IN THE CITY
Stein, Saul
HE GOT GAME
ILLTOWN
NO WAY HOME
PRINCE, THE
Steinbach, Victor
NO WAY HOME
Steinberg, David
MY GIANT
Steinberg, Eric
DOGWATCH
Steinberg, Matthew
DIRTY WORK
Steiner, Tommy Shane
HOME FRIES
Steinline, Lenny
HUSH
Stelling, Sharon
SAND TRAP
Stender, Thomas
KINGDOM, PART 2, THE
Stender-Petersen, Dorrit
KINGDOM, PART 2, THE
Stepanova, Olga
HAPPINESS
Stephans, Cliff
NIGHT VISION
Stephens, Duane
CLAY PIGEONS
NOT IN THIS TOWN
WALKING THUNDER
Stephens, Nancy
HALLOWEEN H20: TWENTY YEARS LATER
Stephens, Perry
GODSON, THE
Stephens, Toby
COUSIN BETTE
PHOTOGRAPHING FAIRIES
Stephenson, Denise
SPICE WORLD
Stephenson, John
FLINTSTONES: I YABBA-DABBA DOO!, THE
Stepic, Irena
BLADE
Sterk, Michael
DREAM FOR AN INSOMNIAC
Sterling, Chris
ONE TRUE THING
Sterling, Philip
MY GIANT
Sterling, Raymond
MAJOR LEAGUE: BACK TO THE MINORS
Stern, Daniel
VERY BAD THINGS
Stern, Deborah
WIDE AWAKE
Stern, Tim
SHOOTING FISH
Sternard, Mitchell
BOYS IN LOVE 2
Sternhagen, Frances
CON, THE
Stetler, Paul Morgan
PLEASANTVILLE
Stevens, Brinke
INVISIBLE MOM
Stevens, Heather
DISAPPEARANCE OF KEVIN JOHNSON, THE
Stevens, Joe
DANCER, TEXAS POP. 81
NEWTON BOYS, THE
Stevens, Leslie
DREAM FOR AN INSOMNIAC
Stevens, Micaal
BELLY
Stevens, Ronnie
PARENT TRAP, THE
Stevens, Stella
INVISIBLE MOM
Stevens, Wass M.
MONTANA
Stevenson, Barry
WHEN PIGS FLY
Stevenson, Christopher
CIVIL ACTION, A
Stevenson, Cynthia
AIR BUD: GOLDEN RECEIVER
HAPPINESS
Stevenson, Elvira
EVER AFTER
Stevenson Jr., Charles C.
PLEASANTVILLE
Stevenson, Patrick
INVADER, THE
Stevenson, Ray
THEORY OF FLIGHT
Stevenson, Sandra M.
NAKED ACTS
Steward, Kevin
REBOUND: THE LEGEND OF EARL "THE GOAT" MANIGAULT
Stewart, Alice
GINGERBREAD MAN, THE
Stewart, Amy
TRUCKS
Stewart, Ashton
STEPHEN KING'S THE NIGHT FLIER
Stewart, Barbara
SIMON BIRCH
Stewart, Charles
ARMAGEDDON
Stewart, Charlotte
SLUMS OF BEVERLY HILLS
Stewart, Chris
GENERAL CHAOS: UNCENSORED ANIMATION
Stewart, David
LOU REED: ROCK AND ROLL HEART
Stewart, Doug
LITTLE VOICE
Stewart, Emma
SUMMER FLING
Stewart, Johna
YOUNG HERCULES
Stewart, Jon
FACULTY, THE
HALF BAKED
PLAYING BY HEART
Stewart, Mike
IN GOD'S HANDS
Stewart, Nils Allen
MARS
Stewart, Pamela Holden
LAST BREATH
Stewart, Patrick
DAD SAVAGE
PRINCE OF EGYPT, THE
STAR TREK: INSURRECTION
Stewart, Paul Anthony
SOMEWHERE IN THE CITY
Sthulbarg, Michael
PRICE ABOVE RUBIES, A
Stickney, Phyllis Yvonne
HOW STELLA GOT HER GROOVE BACK
Sticky Fingaz
RIDE
Stieglitz, Hugo
NAKED LIES
Stiers, David Ogden
KRIPPENDORF'S TRIBE
NAPOLEON
POCAHONTAS II: JOURNEY TO A NEW WORLD
Stiles, Julia
WIDE AWAKE
Stiles, Ryan
COURTING COURTNEY
Still, Jeff
CHICAGO CAB
Stiller, Ben
PERMANENT MIDNIGHT
THERE'S SOMETHING ABOUT MARY
YOUR FRIENDS & NEIGHBORS
ZERO EFFECT
Stiller, Jerry
RAT'S TALE, A
Stinson, Christopher
CHILDREN OF THE CORN V: FIELD OF TERROR
Stockbridge, Peter
ELIZABETH
MERRY WAR, A
Stockbridge, Sara
GO NOW
Stockhausen, Karlheinz
MODULATIONS: CINEMA FOR THE EAR
Stockwell, Dean
LIVING IN PERIL
Stockwell, John
BREAST MEN
Stockwin, Harvey
CHINESE BOX, THE
Stoffman, Nicole
BRAM STOKER'S SHADOWBUILDER
Stohl, Andras
WHEN TRUMPETS FADE
Stojanovich, Christina
HOPE FLOATS
Stoker, John
BIG HIT, THE
Stokes, Blake
X-FILES, THE
Stokey, David
TEKKEN: THE MOTION PICTURE
Stole, Mink
PECKER
Stoll, Kurt
SLAYERS: THE MOTION PICTURE
Stollman, Jay
ONE TRUE THING
Stoltz, Eric
HI-LIFE
MR. JEALOUSY
Stone, Christopher
INVISIBLE MOM
Stone, Doug
RED HAWK: WEAPON OF DEATH
SWAN PRINCESS III: AND THE MYSTERY OF THE ENCHANTED TREASURE, THE
Stone, James
HALLELUJAH!
Stone, Julian
BRAM STOKER'S THE MUMMY

Stone, Laura
- DIRTY WORK

Stone, Matt
- BASEKETBALL
- ORGAZMO

Stone, Michelle
- STEPMOM

Stone, Sharon
- ANTZ
- MIGHTY, THE
- OFF THE MENU: THE LAST DAYS OF CHASEN'S
- SPHERE

Stone, Stuart
- RESCUERS: STORIES OF COURAGE—TWO WOMEN

Stone, Terrance
- BEST OF THE BEST: WITHOUT WARNING

Stonebraker, J.J.
- RUSHMORE

Stoneham Jr., John
- WOO

Stoneham Sr., John
- BIG HIT, THE

Stoner, Jeremy
- DEJA VU

Storey, Howard
- INVADER, THE

Storm, Mark
- MAJOR LEAGUE: BACK TO THE MINORS

Stormare, Peter
- ARMAGEDDON
- BIG LEBOWSKI, THE
- SOMEWHERE IN THE CITY

Storms, Timothy
- SIMPLE PLAN, A

Storti, Bebo
- NIRVANA

Story, Kim
- BABE: PIG IN THE CITY

Story, Tom
- HUSH

Stout, Austin
- RICHIE RICH'S CHRISTMAS WISH

Stout, Mary
- HOLY MAN

Stout, Susan
- ONE TRUE THING

Stowe, Madeleine
- PLAYING BY HEART
- PROPOSITION, THE

Stowe, Sherry
- ELMORE LEONARD'S GOLD COAST

Stracham, Freddy
- SOLDIER'S DAUGHTER NEVER CRIES, A

Strachan, Joel
- REGENERATION

Strahlberg, David
- PI

Strain, Julie
- RETURN TO SAVAGE BEACH

Stralka, Benjamin
- DEEP IMPACT

Strandgard, Robert
- CELEBRATION, THE

Strang, Deborah
- CHILDREN OF THE CORN V: FIELD OF TERROR

Strangio, Steve
- RETURN OF THE KING, THE

Stransky, Charles
- SPANISH PRISONER, THE

Stransky, Leos
- ACT OF WAR

Straten, L.B.
- RESCUERS: STORIES OF COURAGE—TWO WOMEN

Strathairn, David
- BAD MANNERS
- SIMON BIRCH

Stratt, Jonathan
- LOVE AND DEATH ON LONG ISLAND

Stratton, Charlie
- NOTES FROM UNDERGROUND

Strauss, Kim
- BOYS IN LOVE 2

Straw, Brien
- MAJOR LEAGUE: BACK TO THE MINORS

Streep, Meryl
- DANCING AT LUGHNASA
- ONE TRUE THING

Street, Simon
- HOW STELLA GOT HER GROOVE BACK

Stribling, Rick
- FULL TILT BOOGIE

Strickland, Amzie
- I'LL BE HOME FOR CHRISTMAS
- KRIPPENDORF'S TRIBE

Stringer, Lee
- CON, THE

Stringfield, Sherry
- 54

Stripling, Randy
- NEWTON BOYS, THE

Stritch, Elaine
- KRIPPENDORF'S TRIBE

Strnad, Petr
- LES MISERABLES

Stroehman, John
- THERE'S SOMETHING ABOUT MARY

Strohmann, Bianca
- MADELINE

Strong, Brenda
- BLACK DOG

Strong, Danny
- PLEASANTVILLE
- PROPHECY II, THE

Strong, Jeff
- BULLET ON A WIRE

Strong, Jeff N.
- DIARY OF A SERIAL KILLER

Strong, Rider
- MY GIANT

Stroth, Miles
- HENRY: PORTRAIT OF A SERIAL KILLER PART 2

Strother, Frederick
- BELOVED

Stroud, Don
- DETONATOR

Strydom, Neville
- TARZAN AND THE LOST CITY

Stuart, Eric
- POLTERGEIST REPORT: YUYU HAKUSHO

Stuart, Katie
- ATOMIC DOG

Stuart, Marty
- HI-LO COUNTRY, THE

Stuart Masterson, Mary
- DIGGING TO CHINA

Stube, Brian
- THERE'S SOMETHING ABOUT MARY

Stubelle, Phillipe
- OGRE, THE

Studi, Wes
- DEEP RISING

Sturiano, Terry
- HURRICANE STREETS

Styles, Luke
- DARK CITY

Styne, Beth Ann
- OUTSIDE OZONA

Styron, Alexandra
- FRENCH EXIT

Su Fei
- SHAOLIN TEMPLE, THE

Suarez, Manny
- OUT OF SIGHT
- WILD THINGS

Suarez, Moises
- MASK OF ZORRO, THE

Suber, Mets
- WIDE AWAKE

Subkoff, Tara
- LAST DAYS OF DISCO, THE
- LOVER GIRL

Sucharetza, Marla
- GREAT EXPECTATIONS

Suchet, Damian
- VELVET GOLDMINE

Suchet, David
- PERFECT MURDER, A

Sudduth, Kohl
- 54
- ROUNDERS

Sudduth, Skipp
- 54
- GEORGE WALLACE
- RONIN

Suerth, Kimberlee
- PECKER

Suga, Fujio
- SLEEPY EYES OF DEATH: SWORD OF ADVENTURE

Suggs, Harold
- NEWTON BOYS, THE

Sugisaki, Hiroya
- THIN RED LINE, THE

Sugiyama, Tokuko
- VILLAGE OF DREAMS

Suhr, Jerzy
- FROM A FAR COUNTRY

Sui, Anna
- FREE TIBET

Sui Tak Fu
- KICK BOXER'S TEARS

Suissa, Steve
- RONIN

Sullivan, Charlotte
- BRAM STOKER'S SHADOWBUILDER

Sullivan, Jackie
- MONUMENT AVE.

Sullivan Jr., Larry
- RUSH HOUR

Sullivan, Lucia
- RINGMASTER

Sullivan, Nick
- WRATH OF THE NINJA: THE YOTODEN MOVIE

Sullivan, Perry D.
- U.S. MARSHALS

Sullivan, Quinn
- BULWORTH

Sullivan, Rachel
- PARENT TRAP, THE

Sullivan, Sarah
- LETHAL WEAPON 4

Sullivan, Sean
- 54
- HOSTILE INTENT
- SIMON BIRCH

Sumiko (Osumi) Chan
- RUSH HOUR

Summer, Cree
- RUGRATS MOVIE, THE

Summer, Donna
- OFF THE MENU: THE LAST DAYS OF CHASEN'S

Summerour, Lisa
- BELOVED
- MERCURY RISING

Summers, Cher
BRAM STOKER'S THE MUMMY
Summers, Terey
LOS LOCOS
Sumpton, Christopher R.
DISTURBING BEHAVIOR
Sun Jian Kui
SHAOLIN TEMPLE, THE
Sun Sheng Jun
SHAOLIN TEMPLE, THE
Sundby, Karl
JUNK MAIL
Sundown, Monica
HI-LO COUNTRY, THE
Sundquist, Bjorn
JUNK MAIL
MENDEL
OTHER SIDE OF SUNDAY, THE
Sundstrom, Carl
DISAPPEARANCE OF KEVIN JOHNSON, THE
Sung, Elizabeth
LETHAL WEAPON 4
Suplee, Ethan
AMERICAN HISTORY X
Surgeon
MODULATIONS: CINEMA FOR THE EAR
Suriano, Phil
JANE AUSTEN'S MAFIA!
Surman, John
LES MISERABLES
Surmont, Elisa
FORMER CHILD STAR
Surovey, Nicolas
WHEN DANGER FOLLOWS YOU HOME
Susi, Carol Ann
JANE AUSTEN'S MAFIA!
Sussman, Andrew
PERFECT MURDER, A
Sussman, Robynn N.
PERFECT MURDER, A
Sutherland, Donald
FALLEN
WITHOUT LIMITS
Sutherland, Kiefer
DARK CITY
Sutherland, Victor
54
Suton, Pete
ENEMY OF THE STATE
Sutton, Dudley
INCOGNITO
Sutton, Lisa
LOLIDA 2000
Sutton, Ted
SPECIES II
Suvari, Mena
SLUMS OF BEVERLY HILLS
Suveg, Mark
REDLINE
Suzuki, Keiichi
WHEN I CLOSE MY EYES
Suzuki, Kimmy
GREAT EXPECTATIONS
Suzuki, Kouji
THIN RED LINE, THE
Suzuki, Ranran
WHEN I CLOSE MY EYES
Suzuoki, Hirotaka
MOBILE SUIT GUNDAM I
MOBILE SUIT GUNDAM II: SOLDIERS OF SORROW
MOBILE SUIT GUNDAM III: ENCOUNTERS IN SPACE
Svane, Toi
WILD THINGS
Svarre, Steen
KINGDOM, PART 2, THE
Sveen, Helge
JUNK MAIL
Svorcan, Vess
MR. NICE GUY
Swafford, Savannah
TRUMAN SHOW, THE
Swaile, Brad
NEW ADVENTURES OF KIMBA THE WHITE LION, THE
Swaim, Bob
SOLDIER'S DAUGHTER NEVER CRIES, A
Swain, Dominique
LOLITA
Swaizland, Robbie
OPERATION DELTA FORCE 2
Swan, Noelle
SPACEJACKED
Swan, Paul
LITTLE VOICE
Swanby, Grant
TARZAN AND THE LOST CITY
Swann, Lynn
WATERBOY, THE
Swanson, Deborah
REAL BLONDE, THE
Swanson, Hannah
MIGHTY JOE YOUNG
Swanson, Kristy
LOVER GIRL
Sward, Anne
NOT IN THIS TOWN
Swasey, John
SLAYERS: THE MOTION PICTURE
Swatek, Barret
LETHAL WEAPON 4
Swayze, Patrick
BLACK DOG
Swayzee
LOVE AND DEATH ON LONG ISLAND
Swedberg, Heidi
DENNIS THE MENACE STRIKES AGAIN
Sweeney, Birdy
BUTCHER BOY, THE
Sweeney, Julia
COURTING COURTNEY
Sweeney, Kelley
HORSE WHISPERER, THE
Sweeney, Matthew
CELEBRITY
Sweeney, Michael Barton
PARALLEL SONS
Sweeney, Paddy
STRAY BULLET
Sweeney, Steve
NEXT STOP, WONDERLAND
NIL BY MOUTH
THERE'S SOMETHING ABOUT MARY
Sweet, Jack
NEXT STOP, WONDERLAND
Swerling, Bryan
SUICIDE KINGS
Swezey, Ric
WATERBOY, THE
Swift, Allen
PRICE ABOVE RUBIES, A
SAFE MEN
Swift, David
RED HAWK: WEAPON OF DEATH
Swift, Francie
LAST BREATH
Swingler, Dwayne
GODZILLA
Swinton, Tilda
LOVE IS THE DEVIL: STUDY FOR A PORTRAIT OF FRANCIS BACON
Switaj, Monikz
WHITE RAVEN, THE
Switzer, Bill
CALL TO REMEMBER, A
RIGHT CONNECTIONS, THE
WHEN DANGER FOLLOWS YOU HOME
Sylvain, John
OVERNIGHT DELIVERY
Symonds, Bob
HORTON FOOTE'S ALONE
Symonds, Robert
PRIMARY COLORS
Symons, Annie
LOVE IS THE DEVIL: STUDY FOR A PORTRAIT OF FRANCIS BACON
Symons, David
LOVE IS THE DEVIL: STUDY FOR A PORTRAIT OF FRANCIS BACON
Syson, Steve
KNOCK OFF
Syversen, Marit
JUNK MAIL
Syvertson, Peter
SIMPLE PLAN, A
Syverud, Henning
JUNK MAIL
Syyouk, Igor
BLUES BROTHERS 2000
Szarabajka, Keith
DANCER, TEXAS POP. 81
Szekely, Gyula
REDLINE
Szinkora, Mercedes
REDLINE
Szubanski, Magda
BABE: PIG IN THE CITY
Szucs, Ildiko
REDLINE
T, Jeff
DEAD MAN ON CAMPUS
T-Rex
ORGAZMO
Taafe, Chris
SUB DOWN
Tabak, Asher
PRICE ABOVE RUBIES, A
Tabakin, Ralph
SPHERE
Taborksy, Miroslav
LES MISERABLES
Taczanowski, Hubert
CHICAGO CAB
Taffett, Jefferson
RIVER RED
Tagawa, Cary-Hiroyuki
DOUBLE EDGE
JOHN CARPENTER'S VAMPIRES
TOP OF THE WORLD
Tager, Arron
JACK HIGGINS' THE WINDSOR PROTOCOL
Taguchi, Tomoro
EEL, THE
TOKYO FIST
WHEN I CLOSE MY EYES
Tahash, Brian
JANE AUSTEN'S MAFIA!
Tahir, Faran
PRICE ABOVE RUBIES, A
Tai, Ada
RUSH HOUR
Tai, Arlene
RUSH HOUR
Tai Boa
BEAUTY INVESTIGATOR
Tai Chi Wai
KILLER ANGELS
Tai Po
DRAGONS FOREVER

Taieb, Ludovic
UN AIR DE FAMILLE
Taieb, Nicolas
UN AIR DE FAMILLE
Tait, Matthew
CHILDREN OF THE CORN V: FIELD OF TERROR
Taj Mahal
SIX DAYS, SEVEN NIGHTS
Takada, Miwa
SLEEPY EYES OF DEATH: SWORD OF ADVENTURE
Takahashi, Erushi
RAZOR: WHO'S GOT THE GOLD?, THE
Takai, George
TREKKIES
Takarada, Akira
GODZILLA AND MOTHRA: THE BATTLE FOR EARTH
Takei, George
MULAN
Takenaka, Naoto
GONIN
TOKYO FIST
Takeuchi, Warren
DEEP RISING
DOUBLE EDGE
SPREE, THE
Takle, Darien
UGLY, THE
Talavera, Elba Aurora
CARLA'S SONG
Talavera, Luis
CARLA'S SONG
Taliferro, Michael "Bear"
ARMAGEDDON
Talley, Jill
SOUR GRAPES
Tallman, Bob
HI-LO COUNTRY, THE
Tallulah
LOVE IS THE DEVIL: STUDY FOR A PORTRAIT OF FRANCIS BACON
Talma, Monica
ONE TOUGH COP
Talwar, Sanjay
DIRTY WORK
TALES FROM A PARALLEL UNIVERSE: GIGA SHADOW
Tam, Alan
ARMOUR OF GOD
Tam, Chuck
RETURN TO SAVAGE BEACH
Tam, Lauren
BATMAN/SUPERMAN MOVIE, THE
Tamba, Matasaburo
SLEEPY EYES OF DEATH: SWORD OF ADVENTURE
Tambakis, Peter
RIVER RED
Tamblyn, Amber
JOHNNY MYSTO BOY WIZARD
Tamblyn, Russ
INVISIBLE MOM
JOHNNY MYSTO BOY WIZARD
Tambor, Jeffrey
DR. DOLITTLE
MEET JOE BLACK
THERE'S SOMETHING ABOUT MARY
Tamburrelli, Karla
PLUMP FICTION
Tamez, Art Michael
HOPE FLOATS
Tamiroff, Akim
TOUCH OF EVIL: THE DIRECTOR'S CUT
Tamtran, Minh
TWISTED
Tan, Philip
LETHAL WEAPON 4
Tan, Victoria
PALMETTO
Tanaka, Fumiya
MODULATIONS: CINEMA FOR THE EAR
Tanaka, Sara
RUSHMORE
Tanchon, Daniel
LIFE OF JESUS, THE
Tang, Ian
KNOCK OFF
Tang, Mathew
KNOCK OFF
Taniguchi, Duane
PRINCE, THE
Tanji, Tomohiro
THIN RED LINE, THE
Tanka, Eszter
REDLINE
Tannehill, Eugene "Bishop"
FARM: ANGOLA, U.S.A., THE
Tanner, Jeff
FALLEN
Tannous, Glenn
LETHAL WEAPON 4
Taplin, Terry
LES MISERABLES
Tarantino, Quentin
FULL TILT BOOGIE
OFF THE MENU: THE LAST DAYS OF CHASEN'S
Tarason, Dylan
OUTSIDE OZONA
Tardieu, Andre
MAJOR LEAGUE: BACK TO THE MINORS
Tarling, Bill
WRONGFULLY ACCUSED
Tarnada, Paige
MILO
Tarr, Ronnie
LOLIDA 2000
Tartack, Kerry
NEWTON BOYS, THE
Tarver, Milt
FEAR AND LOATHING IN LAS VEGAS
Tashima, Hideko
VILLAGE OF DREAMS
Tashima, Seizo
VILLAGE OF DREAMS
Tashima, Yukihiko
VILLAGE OF DREAMS
Tashjian, Warren
THERE'S SOMETHING ABOUT MARY
Tate, Lahmard
DON KING: ONLY IN AMERICA
Tate, Larenz
WHY DO FOOLS FALL IN LOVE?
Tate, Margaret
JOHNNY MYSTO BOY WIZARD
Tatic, Josif
SAVIOR
Tattasciore, Fred
GENERAL CHAOS: UNCENSORED ANIMATION
Tatum, Bradford
NOT IN THIS TOWN
PRONTO
Taube, Sven-Bertil
JERUSALEM
Tavernier, Nils
POST COITUM, ANIMAL TRISTE
Tawil, David
PI
Taylor, Andrea
PLEASANTVILLE
Taylor, Brian
LEWIS & CLARK & GEORGE
Taylor, Cherilee
BLACKJACK
Taylor, Christine
OVERNIGHT DELIVERY
WEDDING SINGER, THE
Taylor, Davin
MR. NICE GUY
Taylor, Don
TRUMAN SHOW, THE
Taylor, Douglas
TEKKEN: THE MOTION PICTURE
Taylor, Gary
SMOKE SIGNALS
Taylor, Holland
NEXT STOP, WONDERLAND
TRUMAN SHOW, THE
Taylor, Jack
POLTERGEIST REPORT: YUYU HAKUSHO
WRATH OF THE NINJA: THE YOTODEN MOVIE
Taylor, Jennifer Bini
HOLY MAN
WATERBOY, THE
Taylor, Jeri
TREKKIES
Taylor, Jordan
JOHNNY SKIDMARKS
Taylor, Joseph Lyle
HE GOT GAME
Taylor, Joshua
GODZILLA
Taylor, Ken
MIGHTY JOE YOUNG
Taylor, Kieran
MY BROTHER'S WAR
Taylor, Koko
BLUES BROTHERS 2000
MERCURY RISING
Taylor, Lawrence
WATERBOY, THE
Taylor, Lili
ILLTOWN
IMPOSTORS, THE
PECKER
Taylor, Meshach
RIGHT CONNECTIONS, THE
SECRET OF NIMH 2: TIMMY TO THE RESCUE, THE
Taylor, Michael L.
I GOT THE HOOK UP
Taylor, Patick
54
Taylor, Priscilla Lee
SIX DAYS, SEVEN NIGHTS
Taylor, Raph
SAVING PRIVATE RYAN
Taylor, Regina
HOSTILE WATERS
NEGOTIATOR, THE
Taylor, Robert
BREAK, THE
Taylor, Rocky
LAST SEDUCTION II, THE
Taylor, Rod
WELCOME TO WOOP WOOP
Taylor, Ron
TRUMAN SHOW, THE
Taylor, Russ
BRAVE LITTLE TOASTER GOES TO MARS, THE
Taylor, Russi
BABE: PIG IN THE CITY
FLINTSTONES: I YABBA-DABBA DOO!, THE
Taylor, Ryan
DISTURBING BEHAVIOR
JUNGLE BOOK: MOWGLI'S STORY, THE
MY VERY BEST FRIEND
Taylor, Sam
LOS LOCOS

Taylor, Sandra
PHOENIX
Taylor, Sarah
COURTING COURTNEY
Taylor, Sean
TARZAN AND THE LOST CITY
Taylor, Tamara
SENSELESS
Taylor Thomas, Jonathan
I'LL BE HOME FOR CHRISTMAS
Taylor, Veronica
POLTERGEIST REPORT: YUYU HAKUSHO
Taylor, Wayne
TOUCH OF EVIL: THE DIRECTOR'S CUT
Taylor, Zachary
LAST DAYS OF DISCO, THE
Tayyeb, Shiraz
BLUES BROTHERS 2000
Tchenko, Katia
MADELINE
RONIN
Tchernine, Vladimir
RONIN
Teague, Marshall
ARMAGEDDON
Techman, Charles
WIDE AWAKE
Tecosky, Olivia
SPANISH PRISONER, THE
Tedesco, Laura
DANGEROUS BEAUTY
Tedesco, Tony
CELEBRITY
Tedford, Marcello
WHY DO FOOLS FALL IN LOVE?
Tedford, Travis
SLAPPY AND THE STINKERS
Tedlie, Dan
HAPPINESS
Teegardin, Carol
LET'S KILL ALL THE LAWYERS
Tefelski, Norbert
HOSTILE WATERS
Teinert, Cliff
U.S. MARSHALS
Telega, Mona
SECRET KINGDOM, THE
Telek, April
WHEN DANGER FOLLOWS YOU HOME
Telesco, Dominic
BUFFALO '66
Telesford, Electra
STEPMOM
Tell, Greg
DARK CITY
Tellefsen, Rut
KRISTIN LAVRANSDATTER
Telljohn, Sumiko
BULWORTH
Temchen, Sybil
TEN BENNY
Temple, Lew
NEWTON BOYS, THE
Templeman, Simon
DON KING: ONLY IN AMERICA
Tenaglia, Danny
MODULATIONS: CINEMA FOR THE EAR
Tenenbaum, Brian
RUSHMORE
Tennant, Victoria
BRAM STOKER'S THE MUMMY
Tennessee
DANCER, TEXAS POP. 81
Tenney, Jon
HOMEGROWN
LOVELIFE
MUSIC FROM ANOTHER ROOM
Tennon, Julius
SMALL SOLDIERS
Tensun, Justin
54
Tenuta, Judy
PLUMP FICTION
Teodor, Sandu
TALISMAN
Teodosiu, Valentin
GADJO DILO
Tep, Eva
SNAKE EYES
Tepfer, Daniel
SOLDIER'S DAUGHTER NEVER CRIES, A
Terajima, Susumu
FIREWORKS
SONATINE
Terkel, Studs
BIG ONE, THE
Termo, Larry
LOVER GIRL
Termo, Leonard
GODZILLA
Terra, Scott
SHADRACH
Terral, Boris
POST COITUM, ANIMAL TRISTE
Terry, Charles
PARALLEL SONS
Terry, Herbie
FALLING FIRE
Terry, Kim
RUSHMORE
Terry, Tim W.
PALMETTO
Terzo, Venus
ADVENTURES OF MOWGLI
Tesanovic, Branislav
EIGHTEENTH ANGEL, THE
Tesch, Ingrid
WRONGFULLY ACCUSED
Tesli, Gaute Thu
MENDEL
Tesreau, Krista
RINGMASTER
Tessier, Christian
CALL TO REMEMBER, A
Tessier, Genevieve
REAL HOWARD SPITZ, THE
Testud, Sylvie
BEYOND SILENCE
Texada, Tia
BOYS IN LOVE 2
PAULIE
Tezlaff, Janna
NEGOTIATOR, THE
Thachalom, Choke
HEROES SHED NO TEARS
Thaddeus, John
SNAKE EYES
Thaemlitz, Terre
MODULATIONS: CINEMA FOR THE EAR
Thalken, Meg
U.S. MARSHALS
Thatch, Nigel
PLAYERS CLUB, THE
Thawley, Tod
TERMINAL JUSTICE
Theba, Iqbal
SOUR GRAPES
Thebus, Mary Ann
CHICAGO CAB
Thedford, Marcello
BURN HOLLYWOOD BURN
Theirse, Darryl
CHICAGO CAB
I LOVE YOU, DON'T TOUCH ME!
Theisen, Marie
OTHER SIDE OF SUNDAY, THE
Thelen, Jodi
WEDDING SINGER, THE
Theodore, Jimmy
RED HAWK: WEAPON OF DEATH
Theriault, Janine
BLEEDERS
JACK HIGGINS' THE WINDSOR PROTOCOL
Theriot, Logan "Bones"
FARM: ANGOLA, U.S.A., THE
Theron, Charlize
CELEBRITY
HOLLYWOOD CONFIDENTIAL
MIGHTY JOE YOUNG
Theroux, Justin
BODY COUNT
Thewlis, David
BIG LEBOWSKI, THE
Thibault Jr., Robbie
RETROACTIVE
Thibeaux, Jack
LET'S KILL ALL THE LAWYERS
Thicke, Alan
CASPER MEETS WENDY
JACK HIGGINS' THE WINDSOR PROTOCOL
Thiele, Paul
WEDDING SINGER, THE
Thin Elk, Chief Ted
WALKING THUNDER
Thirkeld, Stephen D.
KILLING TIME
Thom, Lawrence
SHAMPOO HORNS
Thomas, Alex
PLAYERS CLUB, THE
Thomas Baxter, Charles
HUSH
Thomas, Brian
PECKER
Thomas, Carmen
BLADE
Thomas, Clara
WHAT DREAMS MAY COME
Thomas, Clare
MADELINE
Thomas, D. Paul
WHITE RAVEN, THE
Thomas, Drew Lexi
BABE: PIG IN THE CITY
Thomas, G.B.
GREAT EXPECTATIONS
Thomas, Glyn
BLACKJACK
Thomas, Heather
MY GIANT
Thomas, Henry
HIJACKING HOLLYWOOD
NIAGARA NIAGARA
SUICIDE KINGS
Thomas, Jamal
MY FIRST NAME IS MACEO
Thomas, Jay
DIRTY LAUNDRY
Thomas, Jena Marie
PATCH ADAMS
Thomas, JoAnn D.
BULWORTH
Thomas Jr., Alex
WHY DO FOOLS FALL IN LOVE?
Thomas, Leonard
NEGOTIATOR, THE
Thomas, Maggie Emma
PARENT TRAP, THE
Thomas, Marcus
PALMETTO

Thomas, Marlo
REAL BLONDE, THE
Thomas, Meda
THERE'S SOMETHING ABOUT MARY
Thomas, Pat
CURSE OF THE PUPPET MASTER
Thomas, Patrice
FULL SPEED
Thomas, Peter
WHEN TRUMPETS FADE
Thomas, Robin
BULWORTH
Thomas, Scott
HIJACKING HOLLYWOOD
SOLDIER'S DAUGHTER NEVER CRIES, A
Thomas, Sean Patrick
CAN'T HARDLY WAIT
Thomas, Stephanie Knight
BLACK LIGHT
Thomas, Victoria Marie
OBJECT OF MY AFFECTION, THE
Thomas, Wendell
U.S. MARSHALS
Thomerson, Tim
FEAR AND LOATHING IN LAS VEGAS
WHEN TIME EXPIRES
Thommessen, Vendela K.
PARENT TRAP, THE
Thompson, Afa
SIX DAYS, SEVEN NIGHTS
Thompson, Al
SCARRED CITY
Thompson, Andrea
GUN, A CAR, AND A BLONDE, A
Thompson, Andy
HUNTED, THE
Thompson, Barry
NEIL SIMON'S THE ODD COUPLE II
Thompson, Bob
SAND TRAP
Thompson, Coach John
HE GOT GAME
Thompson, Dana
BUFFALO '66
Thompson, Dee
MAJOR LEAGUE: BACK TO THE MINORS
Thompson, Don
SPREE, THE
Thompson, Elspeth
LOVE IS THE DEVIL: STUDY FOR A PORTRAIT OF FRANCIS BACON
Thompson, Emma
PRIMARY COLORS
Thompson, Emmalee
HALLOWEEN H20: TWENTY YEARS LATER
Thompson, Ernest
NEXT STOP, WONDERLAND
Thompson, Heather
OBJECT OF MY AFFECTION, THE
Thompson, John
REDLINE
Thompson, Mark
DON KING: ONLY IN AMERICA
Thompson, Mary
PERMANENT MIDNIGHT
Thompson, Mike
WEDDING SINGER, THE
Thompson, Peter
LITTLE VOICE
Thompson, Randy
DESPERATE MEASURES
Thompson, Rick
POLISH WEDDING
Thompson, Shaun
IN GOD'S HANDS
Thompson, Shawn
FUTURE FEAR
Thompson, Shawn Alex
BRAM STOKER'S SHADOWBUILDER
Thompson, Shawn David
WATCHERS REBORN
Thompson, Sophie
DANCING AT LUGHNASA
Thompson, Tara
BUFFALO '66
Thompson, Tyler
AIR BUD: GOLDEN RECEIVER
Thomsen, Janne
CELEBRATION, THE
Thomsen, Richard
U.S. MARSHALS
Thomsen, Ulrich
CELEBRATION, THE
Thomson, Anna
SUE
Thomson, Cecilia
54
Thomson, R.H.
BONE DADDY
Thomson, Scott
JACK FROST
Thor, Cameron
FACE DOWN
Thorens, Drake
54
WOO
Thornbury, Bill
PHANTASM: OBLIVION
Thorne, Callie
NEXT STOP, WONDERLAND
Thorne, Geoffrey A.
CITY OF ANGELS
Thorne, Jared
SOLDIER
Thorne, Taylor
SOLDIER
Thorne-Smith, Courtney
CHAIRMAN OF THE BOARD
Thornley, Christian
PRINCE VALIANT
Thornton, Billy Bob
ARMAGEDDON
BURN HOLLYWOOD BURN
GUN, A CAR, AND A BLONDE, A
HOMEGROWN
PRIMARY COLORS
SIMPLE PLAN, A
Thornton, David
CIVIL ACTION, A
HIGH ART
HUSH
LAST DAYS OF DISCO, THE
REAL BLONDE, THE
Thornton, Sparky
RED HAWK: WEAPON OF DEATH
Thorp IV, William L.
GINGERBREAD MAN, THE
Thorson, Sven Ole
BEST OF THE BEST: WITHOUT WARNING
Thrush, Michelle
EBENEZER
Thuet, Robbi Jay
ELVIS MEETS NIXON
Thumaraksa, Anchana
HEROES SHED NO TEARS
Thurman, Dechen
I THINK I DO
SUE
SUE
Thurman, Professor Robert
FREE TIBET
Thurman, Uma
AVENGERS, THE
LES MISERABLES
Tibbetts, Blake Anthony
APT PUPIL
Tibbetts, Stephen
WRONGFULLY ACCUSED
Tibetan Nuns Project
FREE TIBET
Tickner, French
CALL TO REMEMBER, A
NEW ADVENTURES OF KIMBA THE WHITE LION, THE
WRONGFULLY ACCUSED
Tiefenbach, Dov
MIGHTY, THE
Tien, James
DRAGONS FOREVER
PRODIGAL SON, THE
Tierney, Brigid
AFFLICTION
Tierney, Jacob
DEAD END
Tierney, Lawrence
ARMAGEDDON
Tierney, Maura
PRIMARY COLORS
Tiffe, Angelo
SOUR GRAPES
Tighe, Darren
GO NOW
Tignini, Eric
DESPERATE MEASURES
Tilden, Peter
KRIPPENDORF'S TRIBE
Tilley, Sue
LOVE IS THE DEVIL: STUDY FOR A PORTRAIT OF FRANCIS BACON
Tilly, Jennifer
BRIDE OF CHUCKY
MUSIC FROM ANOTHER ROOM
OFF THE MENU: THE LAST DAYS OF CHASEN'S
Tilton, Charlene
DETONATOR
Timoney, Ann-Marie
CARLA'S SONG
Tinapp, A.A. Barton
SIEGE, THE
Ting Chow-hin
COMRADES, ALMOST A LOVE STORY
Ting Yu
COMRADES, ALMOST A LOVE STORY
Tingle, Jimmy
NEXT STOP, WONDERLAND
Tinin, Brandie
COURTING COURTNEY
Tinkler, Robert
FUTURE FEAR
Tinter, Phil
JAMES ELLROY: DEMON DOG OF AMERICAN CRIME FICTION
Tiplady, Brittany
SIN AND REDEMPTION
Tippit, Wayne
DANCER, TEXAS POP. 81
Titen, Joshua
SIMON BIRCH
Tittor, Robert
ALMOST HEROES
Tjujermans, Pim
WHEN PIGS FLY
Tkacs, Nancy
ONE TRUE THING
To Siu Ming
ENCOUNTER OF THE SPOOKY KIND
Tobias, Oliver
BRYLCREEM BOYS, THE
Tobie, Ellen
OBJECT OF MY AFFECTION, THE

Tobin, Kim
ALARMIST, THE
Tobolowsky, Stephen
BLACK DOG
BRAVE LITTLE TOASTER GOES TO MARS, THE
BURN HOLLYWOOD BURN
JUNGLE BOOK: MOWGLI'S STORY, THE
Tocantins, Nicole
OPPOSITE OF SEX, THE
Tocha, Paolo
TARZAN AND THE LOST CITY
Tockar, Lee
RUDOLPH THE RED-NOSED REINDEER: THE MOVIE
Toda, Toshi
GODZILLA
Todarek, Dimitri
SUE
Todd, Tony
BRAM STOKER'S SHADOWBUILDER
CAUGHT UP
STIR
TRUMAN SHOW, THE
Todo, Yuta
JUNK FOOD
Toffler, Alvin
MODULATIONS: CINEMA FOR THE EAR
Toft, Mickey
LOUISA MAY ALCOTT'S LITTLE MEN
Togisala, Lelagi
RETURN TO SAVAGE BEACH
Toledano, Valerie
SOLDIER'S DAUGHTER NEVER CRIES, A
Toledo, Zozo
STEAM
Tolentino, Candida
KRAA! THE SEA MONSTER
Toler, Ray
U.S. MARSHALS
Toles-Bey, John
SOUR GRAPES
Tolson, Christine
CON, THE
Tolson, Dickon
LIKE IT IS
Tolsty
RONIN
Tolzman, Billy
PECKER
Tom, David
PLEASANTVILLE
WALKING THUNDER
Tomanovic, Ljubo
ACT OF WAR
Tome, Carlos
THIN RED LINE, THE
Tome, Selina
THIN RED LINE, THE
Tomei, Adam
TRUMAN SHOW, THE
Tomei, Concetta
DEEP IMPACT
SIN AND REDEMPTION
Tomei, Marisa
SLUMS OF BEVERLY HILLS
Tomita, Tamlyn
LIVING OUT LOUD
Tomlin, Dalton
RUSHMORE
Tomlin, Lily
KRIPPENDORF'S TRIBE
Tompkins, Paul F.
JACK FROST
Tondo, Jerry
MULAN
Tonne, Detective Bob
DON KING: ONLY IN AMERICA
Toohey, Robert
SNOWBOUND
Tookes, Lamar
HE GOT GAME
Toolan, Rebecca
URBAN SAFARI
Toop, David
MODULATIONS: CINEMA FOR THE EAR
Tootle, Chip
GINGERBREAD MAN, THE
Tootle, Grace
GINGERBREAD MAN, THE
Toral, Christina
PARENT TRAP, THE
Tordoff, John
INCOGNITO
MERLIN
Torfeh, Brian
VELVET GOLDMINE
Torgan, Kendra
KILLING TIME
Tormey, John
REAL BLONDE, THE
SAFE MEN
Torn, Rip
SENSELESS
Torn, Tony
WHATEVER
Torrance, Ingrid
ACT OF WAR
Torrens, Pip
INCOGNITO
Torres, Albert
DANCE WITH ME
Torres, Angelina Calderon
JOHN CARPENTER'S VAMPIRES
Torres, Ed
STILL BREATHING
Torres, Fernando
OYSTER AND THE WIND, THE
Torres, Liz
NEIL SIMON'S THE ODD COUPLE II
PERMANENT MIDNIGHT
Torres, Robert
CELEBRITY
Torres, Skye Lilly
OBJECT OF MY AFFECTION, THE
Torry, Guy
AMERICAN HISTORY X
RIDE
Torti, Robert
LAND OF THE FREE
Toste, Father Frank
PROPOSITION, THE
Toth, Richard
LES MISERABLES
Totman, Paul
MY BROTHER'S WAR
Toub, Lauren
ONE TRUE THING
Toub, Shaun
STEEL SHARKS
Touchberry, Carol-Anne
NEGOTIATOR, THE
Tougas, Erin
DISTURBING BEHAVIOR
Touratier, Gerard
RONIN
Tourtillott, Helen
PATCH ADAMS
Toussaint, Lorraine
BLACK DOG
Toutebon, Joe
BELOVED
Tova, Theresa
RESCUERS: STORIES OF COURAGE—TWO WOMEN
Tovar, Luis Felipe
MEN WITH GUNS
MIDAQ ALLEY
Tove, Birthe
KINGDOM, PART 2, THE
Towers, Constance
PERFECT MURDER, A
Towers, Jim
TRUMAN SHOW, THE
Towles, Tom
DR. DOLITTLE
GIRLS IN PRISON
Townsend, Henry
CAN'T YOU HEAR THE WIND HOWL?: THE LIFE AND MUSIC OF ROBERT JOHNSON
Townsend, Isabelle
LAST DAYS OF DISCO, THE
Townsend, Stuart
SHOOTING FISH
UNDER THE SKIN
Townsend, Tommy
NEWTON BOYS, THE
Townsley, Andy
CARLA'S SONG
Toyohara, Isao
GODZILLA VS. KING GHIDORAH
Toyokawa, Etsushi
WHEN I CLOSE MY EYES
Toyoshima, Minoru
THIN RED LINE, THE
ZERO WOMAN
Trachta, Jeff
INTERLOCKED: THRILLED TO DEATH
Trachtenberg, Michelle
RICHIE RICH'S CHRISTMAS WISH
Tracy, Jack
SLUMS OF BEVERLY HILLS
Tracy, Virgil
LITTLE VOICE
Trail, Ray
REAL BLONDE, THE
Trainor, Mary Ellen
LETHAL WEAPON 4
Tramz, Mia
PARENT TRAP, THE
Trandafir, Claudiu
TALISMAN
Transeau, Kristie
PAULIE
Travalina, Fred
TREKKIES
Travelstead, Ted
RIVER RED
Travis, Kylie
GIA
RETROACTIVE
Travis, Nigel
LOVE IS THE DEVIL: STUDY FOR A PORTRAIT OF FRANCIS BACON
Travis, Randy
BLACK DOG
BOYS WILL BE BOYS
Travis, Sheila
CASPER MEETS WENDY
Travis, Stacey
ONLY THRILL, THE
Travolta, John
CIVIL ACTION, A
OFF THE MENU: THE LAST DAYS OF CHASEN'S
PRIMARY COLORS
THIN RED LINE, THE
Travolta, Margaret
MERCURY RISING
Travolta, Sam
CIVIL ACTION, A

Traylor, Mike
LOS LOCOS
Traynor, Rosemary
DARK CITY
Traywick, Jack
X-FILES, THE
Traywick, Joel
SUB DOWN
Treat, Daniel
SHADRACH
Tredway, Laura
CARLA'S SONG
Tregenza, Eareckson Mary
INSIDE/OUT
Tregouet, Yahn
ARTEMISIA
Trehearne, James
GO NOW
Trejo, Danny
LOS LOCOS
REPLACEMENT KILLERS, THE
SIX DAYS, SEVEN NIGHTS
Tremarco, Christine
UNDER THE SKIN
Tremblay, Kay
REAL HOWARD SPITZ, THE
Tremblett, Ken
INVADER, THE
Tremko, Anne
UNCLE SAM
Trench, Alex
OLIVER TWIST
Trengrove, David
ERNEST IN THE ARMY
Trese, Adam
ILLTOWN
POLISH WEDDING
Treut, Monika
LAVENDER LIMELIGHT: LESBIANS IN FILM
Treviglio, Leonardo
EIGHTEENTH ANGEL, THE
Trevino, Olivia
CHICAGO CAB
Trevisi, Franco
TRUCE, THE
Trewinnard, Phillip
FROM A FAR COUNTRY
Tribe Called Quest, A
FREE TIBET
Tricky
GO NOW
Trieb, Tatjana
BEYOND SILENCE
Trier, Charlotte
MENDEL
Trifunovic, Sergej
SAVIOR
Trihey, Matt
MR. NICE GUY
Trimasova, Nadezhda
DEAD WATERS
Trimble, Tony
KNOCK OFF
Trindy, Jimmy
LOVE IS THE DEVIL: STUDY FOR A PORTRAIT OF FRANCIS BACON
Trinity Dance Troupe
JANE AUSTEN'S MAFIA!
Trinkwater, Yvonne
NEXT STEP, THE
Tripa, Adriana
URBAN SAFARI
Tripplehorn, Jeanne
MONUMENT AVE.
SLIDING DOORS
VERY BAD THINGS
Triska, Jan
APT PUPIL
RONIN
Tritt, Travis
BLUES BROTHERS 2000
Trivalic, Vesna
SAVIOR
Troan, John
PARALYZING FEAR: THE STORY OF POLIO IN AMERICA, A
Trobajane, Flash
TARZAN AND THE LOST CITY
Troche, Rose
LAVENDER LIMELIGHT: LESBIANS IN FILM
Troll
DECLINE OF WESTERN CIVILIZATION PART III, THE
Trombetta Jr., Vincent
LIVING OUT LOUD
Troughton, Scott
GINGERBREAD MAN, THE
Troutman, Dennis
EDEN
Trowbridge, Caroline
LAST SEDUCTION II, THE
Troy, Bill
BOYS WILL BE BOYS
Troy, Erik
BOYS WILL BE BOYS
Troy, Thomas
ENEMY OF THE STATE
Troya, Verne J.
FEAR AND LOATHING IN LAS VEGAS
Trudell, John
SMOKE SIGNALS
True, Jim
AFFLICTION
True, Rachel
HALF BAKED
Trujillo, Horacio
MEN WITH GUNS
Trujillo, Sergio
WOO
Trump, Donald
CELEBRITY
54
Truter, Gregor
SHAKESPEARE IN LOVE
Tsang, Eric
COMRADES, ALMOST A LOVE STORY
KILLER ANGELS
Tsang, Kenneth
REPLACEMENT KILLERS, THE
ROYAL WARRIORS
Tse, Elaine
HIGH ART
Tse Wai Yin
KNOCK OFF
Tse Yuen Fat
CHINESE BOX, THE
Tsu, Irene
COMRADES, ALMOST A LOVE STORY
Tsuchiya, Yoshio
GODZILLA VS. KING GHIDORAH
Tsui, Kitty
STOLEN MOMENTS
Tsui Zen Aie
BEAUTY INVESTIGATOR
Tsuji, Terutake
THIN RED LINE, THE
Tsukamoto, Kohji
TOKYO FIST
Tsukamoto, Shinya
TOKYO FIST
Tsuneta, Fujio
EEL, THE
Tsurumi, Shingo
GONIN
Tubbe, Bruce
MIGHTY, THE
TRACKED
Tucci, Stanley
ALARMIST, THE
EIGHTEENTH ANGEL, THE
IMPOSTORS, THE
MONTANA
Tucek, Sarabeth
DESTINY OF MARTY FINE, THE
Tuck, Jessica
BILLBOARD DAD
BRAVE LITTLE TOASTER GOES TO MARS, THE
Tucker, Beverly
PERFECT MURDER, A
Tucker, Burnell
JACK HIGGINS' ON DANGEROUS GROUND
Tucker, Chris
RUSH HOUR
Tucker, Joe
UNDER THE SKIN
Tucker, Jon
DECAMPITATED
Tucker, Marcus
AIR BUD: GOLDEN RECEIVER
Tucker, Maureen
LOU REED: ROCK AND ROLL HEART
Tucker, Radney
PERFECT MURDER, A
Tucker, Tony
HARD CORE LOGO
Tuda, Kanji
JUNK FOOD
Tudisco, Joseph
CELEBRITY
Tudyk, Alan
PATCH ADAMS
Tuerpe, Paul
LETHAL WEAPON 4
Tufeld, Dick
LOST IN SPACE
Tufeld, Lynn
CLOCKWATCHERS
Tugend, Jennie Lew
LETHAL WEAPON 4
Tullio, Paolo
BUTCHER BOY, THE
Tully, Christy
TALK TO ME
Tumminello, Tom
PI
Tung, Jennifer
STAR TREK: INSURRECTION
Tunie, Tamara
REBOUND: THE LEGEND OF EARL "THE GOAT" MANIGAULT
SNAKE EYES
Tunney, Robin
MONTANA
NIAGARA NIAGARA
Turk, Brian
CIVIL ACTION, A
Turley, David
NEXT STEP, THE
Turman, Glynn
HOW STELLA GOT HER GROOVE BACK
REBOUND: THE LEGEND OF EARL "THE GOAT" MANIGAULT
Turner, April
STEPHEN KING'S THE NIGHT FLIER
Turner, Arnold F.
DR. DOLITTLE
Turner, Cedric
FALLING FIRE

Turner, Danny
DENNIS THE MENACE STRIKES AGAIN
Turner, Dustin
SPECIES II
Turner, Frank C.
AIR BUD: GOLDEN RECEIVER TRICKS
Turner, Frantz
I GOT THE HOOK UP
Turner, Graham
LITTLE VOICE
Turner, Jewel
GREAT EXPECTATIONS
Turner, John
MERLIN
Turner, Karol
CHARLIE HOBOKEN
Turner, Kathleen
REAL BLONDE, THE
Turner, Michele
HAV PLENTY
Turner, Ophelia M.
BELOVED
Turner, Pamela
CARLA'S SONG
Turner, Rich
BOOGIE BOY
Turner, Tyrin
BELLY
LITTLE BOY BLUE
Turner, Zara
SLIDING DOORS
Turonis, Emily
OBJECT OF MY AFFECTION, THE
Turpei, Paul
X-FILES, THE
Turpin, Bahni
GIRLS IN PRISON
Turturro, Aida
CELEBRITY
WOO
Turturro, John
BIG LEBOWSKI, THE
HE GOT GAME
ROUNDERS
TRUCE, THE
Tushingham, Rita
UNDER THE SKIN
Tuskan, Darko
MR. NICE GUY
Tuturro, Aida
FALLEN
Tweed, Shannon
FACE THE EVIL
NAKED LIES
Tweedle, Carolyn
RIGHT CONNECTIONS, THE
Twyford, Holly
PECKER
Twyman, Daniel
SHOPPING FOR FANGS
Tydings, Alexandra
HERCULES AND XENA THE ANIMATED MOVIE: THE BATTLE FOR MOUNT OLYMPUS
Tyler, Liv
ARMAGEDDON
Tyler, Steve
THERE'S SOMETHING ABOUT MARY
Tyler, Thom
ENEMY
Tylor, Diane
HAPPINESS
Tymen, Joel
WESTERN
Tyson, Cicely
ALWAYS OUTNUMBERED
Tyson, Hayley
ERNEST IN THE ARMY
Tyson, Richard M.
THERE'S SOMETHING ABOUT MARY
Tyzack, Margaret
MRS. DALLOWAY
Tzi Ma
RUSH HOUR
Ubach, Alanna
CLOCKWATCHERS
Udenio, Fabiana
GODSON, THE
Uecker, Bob
MAJOR LEAGUE: BACK TO THE MINORS
Ueda, Koichi
GODZILLA VS. KING GHIDORAH
VILLAGE OF DREAMS
Ufland, Chris
HORTON FOOTE'S ALONE
Uhrig, Steve
ENEMY OF THE STATE
Ulbach, Athena
CLOCKWATCHERS
Ulmanski, Renata
SAVIOR
Ulmschneider, Craig
CELEBRITY
Ulrich, Beth
INVISIBLE MOM
Ulrich, Skeet
NEWTON BOYS, THE
Ulrichsen, Marianne O.
INSOMNIA
Umbers, Mark
LOVE IS THE DEVIL: STUDY FOR A PORTRAIT OF FRANCIS BACON
Underwood, Blair
DEEP IMPACT
Underwood, Erin
DIRTY LAUNDRY
SHADRACH
Underwood, Sheryl
BULWORTH
I GOT THE HOOK UP
Unger, Deborah
NO WAY HOME
RAT PACK, THE
Unger, Jan
LES MISERABLES
Unser Jr., Bobby
SCARRED CITY
Upjohn, William
DARK CITY
Upton, John
BABE: PIG IN THE CITY
Urban Jr., Peter A.
WIDE AWAKE
Urbaniak, James
HENRY FOOL
Urbano, Maryann
TARANTELLA
Urbina, Jose
REAL HOWARD SPITZ, THE
Urla, Joseph
DEEP IMPACT
Urquhart, Kyle Ryan
RUSHMORE
Urquidez, Benny
DRAGONS FOREVER
Ursan, Aurica
GADJO DILO
Usher, David
BIG HIT, THE
Utah Mountain Men Association
WALKING THUNDER
Utay, William
LOVER GIRL
Utt, Angie
BELOVED
Uzice, Les
MR. NICE GUY
Vaccaro, Karen
U.S. MARSHALS
Vacco, Angela
CAN'T HARDLY WAIT
Vaden, Jack
DANCER, TEXAS POP. 81
Vaginal Creme Davis
HALLELUJAH!
Vahle, Dirk
DESPERATE MEASURES
HORSE WHISPERER, THE
Vain, Marina
SLAPPY AND THE STINKERS
Vajakas, Lena
54
Vajtay, Nicolette
SMOKE SIGNALS
Valadao, Jece
TIETA OF AGRESTE
Valdes-Kennedy, Armando
BILLY'S HOLLYWOOD SCREEN KISS
Valdez, Elisa
JOHN CARPENTER'S VAMPIRES
Valdez, Francisco
MEN WITH GUNS
Valdez, Mario
NAKED LIES
Valdivia, Gerardo
NAKED LIES
Valdovinos, Oscar
EL CHE: INVESTIGATING A LEGEND
Vale, Andre
TIETA OF AGRESTE
Valen, Nancy
BLACK THUNDER
Valenti, Duke
ARMAGEDDON
MARS
Valenti, Jack
STORY OF X, THE
Valentine, Dominic
INSIDE/OUT
Valentine, Owen
HUSH
Valentine, Phil
LETTER FROM DEATH ROW, A
Valentine, Scott
MARS
Valentine, Steve
SHRUNKEN CITY, THE
Valentino, Charles
NEGOTIATOR, THE
Valentova, Sona
FORGOTTEN LIGHT
Valenza, David
NOT IN THIS TOWN
Valenzuela, Janette
DANCE WITH ME
Valenzuela, Rick
DANCE WITH ME
Valeska, Etta
I MARRIED A STRANGE PERSON!
Valeta, Thalia
LOVE IS THE DEVIL: STUDY FOR A PORTRAIT OF FRANCIS BACON
Valle, Andre
TIETA OF AGRESTE
Vallee, Mrs. Rudy
OFF THE MENU: THE LAST DAYS OF CHASEN'S
Vallette, Franklin
INTERLOCKED: THRILLED TO DEATH

Valley, Mark
GEORGE WALLACE
SIEGE, THE
Valsonne, Diane
WESTERN
Valverde, Norma
HANDS ON A HARDBODY
Van, Alex
MAJOR LEAGUE: BACK TO THE MINORS
Van Allen, William
MIGHTY, THE
Van Damme, Jean-Claude
KNOCK OFF
van Delden, Lex
INCOGNITO
van den Dop, Tamar
CHARACTER
van der Berg, Henry
TARZAN AND THE LOST CITY
Van Der Veen, Ben
FEAR AND LOATHING IN LAS VEGAS
van der Velden, Naomi
DARK CITY
Van Der Wal, Frederique
CELEBRITY
54
TWO GIRLS AND A GUY
Van Der Wal, Michel
54
Van Dien, Casper
CASPER MEETS WENDY
TARZAN AND THE LOST CITY
van Donk, Eric
DRESS, THE
Van Dyke, Phillip
INVISIBLE MOM
van Dyke, Walter
INCOGNITO
Van Helden, Armand
MODULATIONS: CINEMA FOR THE EAR
Van Horn, Sara
I LOVE YOU, DON'T TOUCH ME!
van Hoven, Keith
OPERATION DELTA FORCE 2
van Huet, Fedja
CHARACTER
Van Keeken, Frank
ARMAGEDDON
Van Lear, Phillip
CHICAGO CAB
van Overbeke, Marie-Josee
LIFE OF JESUS, THE
Van Peebles, Mario
LOS LOCOS
Van Peebles, Melvin
CLASSIFIED X
van Reinsberg, Danie
TARZAN AND THE LOST CITY
van Rensburg, Pierre
TARZAN AND THE LOST CITY
Van Rooyen, Gordon
ERNEST IN THE ARMY
Van Silva, Tony
LIKE IT IS
Van Swearingen, Guy
NEGOTIATOR, THE
Van Valkenburgh, Deborah
MEAN GUNS
van Warmerdam, Alex
DRESS, THE
Van Winkle, Dick
LITTLE VOICE
Van Wormer, Steve
HIJACKING HOLLYWOOD
MEET THE DEEDLES
Van Zandt, Lahoma
SHAMPOO HORNS

Vana, John
WEDDING SINGER, THE
Vance, Courtney B.
12 ANGRY MEN
Vance, Elsie
UNDER HEAVEN
Vanderloo, Mark
CELEBRITY
VanDusen, Andrew
RIVER RED
Vanier, Jean-Jacques
LA SEPARATION
WESTERN
Vann, Marc
U.S. MARSHALS
Varadi, Gabor
REDLINE
Varela, Leonor
MAN IN THE IRON MASK, THE
Varela, Patricia
PLAN B
Varga, Lisa
RUSTY: THE GREAT RESCUE
Vargas, Jacob
HI-LO COUNTRY, THE
Vargas, John
PRIMARY COLORS
Varnedoe, Kirk
LOU REED: ROCK AND ROLL HEART
Varney, Jim
ERNEST IN THE ARMY
3 NINJAS: HIGH NOON AT MEGA MOUNTAIN
Varon, Edith
SOUR GRAPES
Varrez, Ash
MADELINE
Vasile, Marian
CLOCKMAKER
Vasquez, Humberto
EL CHE: INVESTIGATING A LEGEND
Vasquez, Yul
LAST BIG THING, THE
Vassiliev, Anatoliy
TRUCE, THE
Vastine, Lisa
GODS AND MONSTERS
Vasut, Marek
BRYLCREEM BOYS, THE
Vaughan, Greg
CHILDREN OF THE CORN V: FIELD OF TERROR
Vaughan, Jimmie
BLUES BROTHERS 2000
Vaughan, Peter
LES MISERABLES
Vaughn, Betty
HAV PLENTY
Vaughn, Eloise
DEAR JESSE
Vaughn, Jennie
SENSELESS
Vaughn, Judson
TRUMAN SHOW, THE
Vaughn, Marcus
ORGAZMO
Vaughn, Robert
BASEKETBALL
Vaughn, Vince
CLAY PIGEONS
PSYCHO
RETURN TO PARADISE
Vaus, Lyn
NEXT STOP, WONDERLAND
Vazquez, Francisco
DANCE WITH ME
Vazquez, Joby
DANCE WITH ME

Vazquez, Luis
DANCE WITH ME
Vega, Alexa
DENNIS THE MENACE STRIKES AGAIN
Vega, Isidra
HURRICANE STREETS
Vega, Joe
ROUNDERS
Vega, Suzanne
LOU REED: ROCK AND ROLL HEART
Vega, Vladimir
ELIZABETH
Vegh, David
SAVING PRIVATE RYAN
Veinotte, Troy
HANGING GARDEN, THE
Velasquez, Armando Martinez
MEN WITH GUNS
Velasquez, Hector
CITY OF ANGELS
Velez, Daisy
NEIL SIMON'S THE ODD COUPLE II
Velez, Eddie
RUNNING WOMAN, THE
Velez, Lauren
I THINK I DO
Vella, Marlow
ONE TOUGH COP
Vellani, Luca
MADELINE
Velniciuc, Stefan
JOHNNY MYSTO BOY WIZARD
Velter, Francois
EVER AFTER
Veltri, Gabe
WEDDING SINGER, THE
Venable, Janine
I LOVE YOU, DON'T TOUCH ME!
Venantini, Venantino
EIGHTEENTH ANGEL, THE
Vencl, Zdenek
LES MISERABLES
Venegas, Arturo
MADELINE
Venerable Palden Gyatso, The
FREE TIBET
Venito, Lenny
ROUNDERS
Vennera, Chick
ALONE IN THE WOODS
Ventimiglia, John
NIAGARA NIAGARA
NO LOOKING BACK
SUE
Ventola, Carmen
CHARLIE HOBOKEN
Ventre, Jackie
OBJECT OF MY AFFECTION, THE
Venturi, Charles
DANCE WITH ME
Vera, Veronica
DIDN'T DO IT FOR LOVE
Verame, Guy
NIGHT AND THE MOMENT, THE
Verdier, Marco
BEST OF THE BEST: WITHOUT WARNING
DON KING: ONLY IN AMERICA
Verdugo, Vanessa
JOHNNY SKIDMARKS
Vereen, Ben
WHY DO FOOLS FALL IN LOVE?
Verhoeven, Yves
CHAMBERMAID ON THE TITANIC, THE
SWINDLE, THE
Vernoff, Kaili
NO LOOKING BACK

Vernon, Glen
WHEN TIME EXPIRES
Vernon, Kate
BLACKJACK
Vernstad, Alice
DIDN'T DO IT FOR LOVE
Vernstad, Paul
DIDN'T DO IT FOR LOVE
Veronis, Nick
DAY AT THE BEACH
Verret, Gueydan T.
SECRET KINGDOM, THE
Verveen, Arie
THIN RED LINE, THE
Vesey, Melanie
HENRY FOOL
Vessey, Tricia
ALARMIST, THE
Vezina, James
LET'S KILL ALL THE LAWYERS
Vezzoli, Francesco
LOVE IS THE DEVIL: STUDY FOR A PORTRAIT OF FRANCIS BACON
Viali, Stefano
EIGHTEENTH ANGEL, THE
Viard, Karin
LA SEPARATION
Vicaryous, Scott
RIGHT CONNECTIONS, THE
Vickerage, Lesley
MERRY WAR, A
Vicks, Karen Lorraine
BELOVED
Victor, Dan
JOHNNY MYSTO BOY WIZARD
Victor, Renee
PROPHECY II, THE
Victory, Fiona
SWEPT FROM THE SEA
Vidahl, Lone
MERRY WAR, A
Vidal, Eric
I GOT THE HOOK UP
Vidale, Thea
COMEDY'S DIRTIEST DOZEN
RINGMASTER
Vidler, Steven
NAPOLEON
THIN RED LINE, THE
Vidosa, Christian
FALLING FIRE
Viegas, Mario
PEREIRA DECLARES
Vieira, Michael
RESCUERS: STORIES OF COURAGE—TWO COUPLES
Vieluf, Vince
CLAY PIGEONS
Vignola, Adam
BELLY
SUE
Vigouroux, Theo
WESTERN
Villa, Giovanna
LIFE IS BEAUTIFUL
Villacorta, Roberto
DANCE WITH ME
Villalpando, David
MASK OF ZORRO, THE
MEN WITH GUNS
Villari, Libby
FACULTY, THE
Villemaire, James
SCARRED CITY
Villeminot, Catherine
SOLDIER'S DAUGHTER NEVER CRIES, A
Villeminot, Elizabeth
SOLDIER'S DAUGHTER NEVER CRIES, A
Villeminot, Florence
SOLDIER'S DAUGHTER NEVER CRIES, A
Villeneuve, Bernard
FULL SPEED
Vils, Kenneth "Brother"
WRONGFULLY ACCUSED
Vince, Pruitt Taylor
BREAK, THE
Vincent
THIN RED LINE, THE
Vincent, Bob
INVISIBLE DAD
Vincent, Brian
BLACK DOG
BREAK, THE
Vincent, Craig
FRENCH EXIT
Vincent, David
ALL THE RAGE
Vincent, Frank
BELLY
TEN BENNY
WEST NEW YORK
Vincent, Jan-Michael
BUFFALO '66
Vincent, Louis
LA SEPARATION
Vincze, Gabor Peter
REDLINE
Vinovich, Steve
SWAN PRINCESS III: AND THE MYSTERY OF THE ENCHANTED TREASURE, THE
Vinson, Victor
ARMAGEDDON
Vint, Angela
URBAN LEGEND
Vinterberg, Thomas
CELEBRATION, THE
Virgile, Peter
BLACKJACK
Virkner, Helle
KINGDOM, PART 2, THE
Visnjic, Goran
PRACTICAL MAGIC
ROUNDERS
Vita, Julio Dolce
GIA
RUNNING WOMAN, THE
Vitale, Dick
HE GOT GAME
Vitale, Fabrizio
EIGHTEENTH ANGEL, THE
Vitale, Joseph
UNCLE SAM
Vitale, Vise
SIX DAYS, SEVEN NIGHTS
Vitali, Elizabeth
WESTERN
Vitanza, Vilma
PATCH ADAMS
Vitello, Lisa
LOS LOCOS
Viterelli, Joe
JANE AUSTEN'S MAFIA!
Viteychuk, Chris
FACULTY, THE
Vito, Marcio
OYSTER AND THE WIND, THE
Vitrant, Lionel
RONIN
Vivier, Michel
WESTERN
Vivis
PATCH ADAMS
Vlahos, Sam
AMERICAN HISTORY X
Voda, Bogdan
LITTLE GHOST
SECRET KINGDOM, THE
Vogel, Tony
LES MISERABLES
Voges, Torsten
BIG LEBOWSKI, THE
Vogt, K.T.
FERNGULLY 2: THE MAGICAL RESCUE
Voicu, Oana
SUBSPECIES IV: BLOODSTORM
Voight, Jon
BOYS WILL BE BOYS
ENEMY OF THE STATE
FIXER, THE
GENERAL, THE
Voigt, Gabriella
SHAMPOO HORNS
Vokoun, Pavel
LES MISERABLES
Vollans, Michael
DIRTY WORK
Volokh, Ilia
PLAN B
Voltaire, Jacqueline Walters
MEN WITH GUNS
Von Bargen, Daniel
CIVIL ACTION, A
FACULTY, THE
REAL BLONDE, THE
Von Cartier, Tobell
SHAMPOO HORNS
von Franckenstein, Clement
LANDLADY, THE
Von Krogh, Geo
MENDEL
von Krusenstjerna, Fredrik
TRANCEFORMER: A PORTRAIT OF LARS VON TRIER
Von Palleske, Heidi
FALLING FIRE
von Sinnen, Hella
KILLER CONDOM, THE
von Sydow, Max
HOSTILE WATERS
JERUSALEM
WHAT DREAMS MAY COME
von Trier, Lars
TRANCEFORMER: A PORTRAIT OF LARS VON TRIER
von Zallinger II, Monika
FUNNY GAMES
Vooren, Gerrit
PERFECT MURDER, A
Vorsloo, Arnold
DIARY OF A SERIAL KILLER
Vorstman, Frans
CHARACTER
Voyt, Harriet
SPANISH PRISONER, THE
Vrana, Vlasta
JACK HIGGINS' THE WINDSOR PROTOCOL
PEACEKEEPER, THE
Vyvyan, Hugh
BRYLCREEM BOYS, THE
Wachholz, E. Alexander
HOSTILE WATERS
Wachsman, Melanie
I LOVE YOU, DON'T TOUCH ME!
Wada, Jey
LETHAL WEAPON 4
Waddington, Steven
ROYAL DECEIT
TARZAN AND THE LOST CITY
Wade, Kaye
RAGE, THE

Wade, Melinda
DAVID SEARCHING
Wadham, Julian
MERRY WAR, A
Wadman, Glen
REAL HOWARD SPITZ, THE
Wagner, Agnieszka
TRUCE, THE
WHITE RAVEN, THE
Wagner, Brett
PLAYERS CLUB, THE
Wagner, Brian
BOYS WILL BE BOYS
Wagner, Dave
WATERBOY, THE
Wagner, Henrik
COUSIN BETTE
Wagner, Natasha Gregson
FIRST LOVE, LAST RITES
URBAN LEGEND
Wagner, Paul
NEXT STOP, WONDERLAND
Wagner, Rick
LAST LIVES
Wagner, Robert
OFF THE MENU: THE LAST DAYS OF CHASEN'S
WILD THINGS
Wahl, Bob
BUFFALO '66
Wahlberg, Donnie
BODY COUNT
Wahlberg, Mark
BIG HIT, THE
Wahlstrom, Becky
OPPOSITE OF SEX, THE
Wai Ching Ho
HAPPINESS
PRICE ABOVE RUBIES, A
Wai Sing
CHINESE BOX, THE
Waid, Jeffrey Allen
SIEGE, THE
Wain, Elisa
POLTERGEIST REPORT: YUYU HAKUSHO
Waite, Michael
FORMER CHILD STAR
Waite, Ralph
SIN AND REDEMPTION
Wajima, Koichi
TOKYO FIST
Waldo, Janet
FLINTSTONES: I YABBA-DABBA DOO!, THE
Waldron, Adrian
OPERATION DELTA FORCE 2
Walken, Christopher
ANTZ
PROPHECY II, THE
SUICIDE KINGS
Walker, Amanda
EVER AFTER
Walker, Bruce
CHINESE BOX, THE
Walker, Charles
WHY DO FOOLS FALL IN LOVE?
Walker, Charlotte
CATHERINE'S GROVE
Walker, Clint
SMALL SOLDIERS
Walker, Clinton
HOT BLOODED
Walker, Doug
BURN HOLLYWOOD BURN
Walker, Fuschia
NEXT STEP, THE
Walker, Jake
JOHN CARPENTER'S VAMPIRES
Walker, Jeannie
CAPTIVE
Walker, Jiggs
BELOVED
Walker, Jimmie
PLUMP FICTION
Walker, John Haynes
ENEMY OF THE STATE
Walker, Jonathan
BROADWAY DAMAGE
Walker, Kateri
OUTSIDE OZONA
Walker, Kelvin
BOYS IN LOVE 2
Walker, Kim
SOMEWHERE IN THE CITY
Walker, Marjorie
LOVE IS THE DEVIL: STUDY FOR A PORTRAIT OF FRANCIS BACON
Walker, Matthew
MISBEGOTTEN
Walker, Michael Dean
WILD THINGS
Walker, Michael J.
ENEMY OF THE STATE
Walker, Nicholas
BODY COUNT
Walker, Paul
MEET THE DEEDLES
PLEASANTVILLE
Walker, Polly
TALK OF ANGELS
Walker, Rebecca
PRIMARY COLORS
Walker, Robert
HOLY MAN
Walker, William
MY BROTHER'S WAR
Wall, Alison
HERCULES AND XENA THE ANIMATED MOVIE: THE BATTLE FOR MOUNT OLYMPUS
Wall, Christopher
FALLING FIRE
Wall, David
KRAA! THE SEA MONSTER
Wallace, Andrew
MAN IN THE IRON MASK, THE
Wallace, Basil
CAUGHT UP
Wallace, Deirdre
MONTANA
Wallace, Don
PRICE ABOVE RUBIES, A
Wallace, Jack
FIXER, THE
SPANISH PRISONER, THE
TWILIGHT
Wallace, John
HE GOT GAME
Wallace, Kevin
TWENTYFOURSEVEN
Wallace, Laurie
HOLY MAN
Wallace, Mike
AYN RAND: A SENSE OF LIFE
Wallace, Sam
UGLY, THE
Wallace Stone, Dee
INVISIBLE MOM
NEVADA
Wallace, Todd
THIN RED LINE, THE
Wallace, Will
THIN RED LINE, THE
Wallach, Eli
ELIA KAZAN: A DIRECTOR'S JOURNEY
Wallem, Linda
SOUR GRAPES
Wallenberg, Joanie
PLAN B
Walling, Jessica
IMPOSTORS, THE
Wallis, Bill
MERRY WAR, A
Wallis, Kimberly
MAKER, THE
Walls, Kevin Patrick
BLADE
Wallyn, Gerard
LIFE OF JESUS, THE
Walser, Donald R.
HI-LO COUNTRY, THE
Walsh, Andy
LOVE IS THE DEVIL: STUDY FOR A PORTRAIT OF FRANCIS BACON
Walsh, Baillie
LOVE IS THE DEVIL: STUDY FOR A PORTRAIT OF FRANCIS BACON
Walsh, Dan
RETURN OF THE KING, THE
Walsh, Dylan
EDEN
MEN
Walsh, Gerry
INFORMANT, THE
Walsh, Gwynyth
CROSSING FIELDS
Walsh, Hynden
SECRET OF NIMH 2: TIMMY TO THE RESCUE, THE
Walsh, J.T.
NEGOTIATOR, THE
PLEASANTVILLE
Walsh, Jack
SIMPLE PLAN, A
Walsh, Jerry
FALLEN
SCARRED CITY
WIDE AWAKE
Walsh, John
OVERNIGHT DELIVERY
WRONGFULLY ACCUSED
Walsh, Kate
HENRY: PORTRAIT OF A SERIAL KILLER PART 2
Walsh, Kathryn
ONE TRUE THING
Walsh, Laurence
BLACKJACK
Walsh, Liam
TWENTYFOURSEVEN
Walsh, M. Emmet
CHAIRMAN OF THE BOARD
RETROACTIVE
TWILIGHT
Walsh, Ruth Lawson
PECKER
Walsh, Vincent
SAVING PRIVATE RYAN
SUMMER FLING
Walsh, William
RETURN OF THE KING, THE
Walston, Ray
TRICKS
Walstrom, Owen
MISBEGOTTEN
Walter, Harriet
GOVERNESS, THE
MERRY WAR, A
Walter, Jessica
SLUMS OF BEVERLY HILLS
Walter, Lisa Ann
PARENT TRAP, THE

Walter, Tracey
BELOVED
DESPERATE MEASURES
MIGHTY JOE YOUNG
Walters, Arnie
SNOWBOUND
Walters, Brian
DECAMPITATED
Walters, Harriet
LEADING MAN, THE
Walters, Hugh
FIRELIGHT
INNOCENT SLEEP, THE
Walters, John
EVER AFTER
SAVING PRIVATE RYAN
Walters, Keith
HI-LO COUNTRY, THE
Walters, Lucia
RIGHT CONNECTIONS, THE
Walters, Mark
HOME FRIES
Walters, Melora
LOS LOCOS
Walters, Toddy
ORGAZMO
Walton, Bill
HE GOT GAME
Walton, Gary H.
BULWORTH
Walton, John
BABE: PIG IN THE CITY
Waltz, Lisa
NEIL SIMON'S THE ODD COUPLE II
Wameling, Gerd
KILLER CONDOM, THE
Wan, Al
RUSH HOUR
Wanamaker, Zoe
SWEPT FROM THE SEA
WILDE
Wang Guang Kuan
SHAOLIN TEMPLE, THE
Wang Guo Yi
SHAOLIN TEMPLE, THE
Wang Jue
SHAOLIN TEMPLE, THE
Wang, Laura
WESTERN
Wang Ning
EMPEROR'S SHADOW, THE
Wanlass, Lynn
FALLEN
Wantuch, Holly
CHICAGO CAB
Warbeck, David
BEYOND, THE
Ward, B.J.
FLINTSTONES: I YABBA-DABBA DOO!, THE
SCOOBY-DOO ON ZOMBIE ISLAND
Ward, Dave
DRAGON BALL Z THE MOVIE: DEAD ZONE
DRAGON BALL Z THE MOVIE: THE WORLD'S STRONGEST
Ward, Dick
BORROWERS, THE
Ward, Fern
HOW STELLA GOT HER GROOVE BACK
Ward, Fred
DANGEROUS BEAUTY
Ward, Jacklilynn
ENEMY OF THE STATE
Ward, James
CASPER MEETS WENDY
Ward, Joshua
ENEMY OF THE STATE
Ward Jr., E. Glenn
U.S. MARSHALS
Ward Jr., William B.
JOHNNY SKIDMARKS
Ward, Maitland
INTERLOCKED: THRILLED TO DEATH
Ward, Mitch
MURDER IN MIND
Ward, Paddy
WAKING NED DEVINE
Ward, Rachel
TWISTED
Ward, Roy
UGLY, THE
Ward, Sela
54
RESCUERS: STORIES OF COURAGE—TWO WOMEN
Ward, Tim
FALLING FIRE
Ward, Willa
BELOVED
Ward-Lealand, Jennifer
UGLY, THE
Warden, Jack
BULWORTH
CHAIRMAN OF THE BOARD
DIRTY WORK
Warden, Rick
KILLING TIME
Warden, Tiani
RAGE, THE
Ware, Herta
PRACTICAL MAGIC
Ware, Marie
U.S. MARSHALS
Ware, Paul
GODZILLA
Ware, Tim
MAJOR LEAGUE: BACK TO THE MINORS
Wareham, Dean
MR. JEALOUSY
Warfield, Anjua
SIEGE, THE
Warfield, Branch
INSIDE/OUT
Warkol, Jordan Blake
MILO
Warlock, Billy
STEEL SHARKS
Warmouth, Greg
ARMAGEDDON
Warnaby, John
JACK HIGGINS' ON DANGEROUS GROUND
JACK HIGGINS' MIDNIGHT MAN
Warnat, Kimberly
MY VERY BEST FRIEND
Warne, Andrew
BULWORTH
Warner, David
LEADING MAN, THE
Warner, Gary
GODZILLA
Warner, Martin Charles
GIRLS IN PRISON
JANE AUSTEN'S MAFIA!
Warner, Rick
FALLEN
SHADRACH
Warnock, Craig
MY BROTHER'S WAR
Warren, Brad
KNOCK OFF
Warren, Garnett
BEST OF THE BEST: WITHOUT WARNING
Warren, Jennifer Leigh
SCOOBY-DOO ON ZOMBIE ISLAND
SOUR GRAPES
Warren, Kimberly
MEAN GUNS
Warren, Lesley Ann
RICHIE RICH'S CHRISTMAS WISH
Warren, Marc
DAD SAVAGE
Warren, Mervyn
LIVING OUT LOUD
Warry-Smith, Dan
IN HIS FATHER'S SHOES
Warshofsky, David
BRIGHT SHINING LIE, A
Warwick, Michael
FEAR AND LOATHING IN LAS VEGAS
Washburn, Rick
MONTANA
Washington, Ajene
NAKED ACTS
Washington, Anthony
ENEMY
Washington, Denzel
FALLEN
HE GOT GAME
SIEGE, THE
Washington, Isaiah
ALWAYS OUTNUMBERED
BULWORTH
OUT OF SIGHT
Washington, Jascha
ENEMY OF THE STATE
Washington Jr., Grover
BLUES BROTHERS 2000
Washington, Laura
NAKED ACTS
Washington, Pauletta
BELOVED
Wasserman, Jerry
WOUNDED
Wasserman, Lew
OFF THE MENU: THE LAST DAYS OF CHASEN'S
Watanabe, Gedde
MULAN
Watanabe, Joe
THIN RED LINE, THE
Watanabe, Tetsu
FIREWORKS
SONATINE
Watari, Hiroyuki
ZERO WOMAN
Wataru, Teppei
WHEN I CLOSE MY EYES
Waterford, Lon
SUE
Waters, Dana
QUICKSILVER HIGHWAY
Waters, Hilary
INNOCENT SLEEP, THE
Watkins, Steven
INSIDE/OUT
Watkins, Tapp
ZERO EFFECT
Watkins, Tionne
BELLY
Watkins, Tuc
I THINK I DO
Watley, Erin
UNVEILING, THE
Watley, Michele
UNVEILING, THE
Watson, Ashleigh
BELOVED
Watson, Emily
HILARY AND JACKIE

Watson, Greg
NEXT STOP, WONDERLAND
Watson, Henry O.
WRONGFULLY ACCUSED
Watson, Joe
HIJACKING HOLLYWOOD
Watson, Joy
HERCULES AND XENA THE ANIMATED MOVIE: THE BATTLE FOR MOUNT OLYMPUS
Watson, Mark
SUICIDE KINGS
Watson, Martin
NIL BY MOUTH
Watson, Mike
DOGWATCH
Watson, Muse
I STILL KNOW WHAT YOU DID LAST SUMMER
SHADRACH
Watson, Ralph
SHOOTING FISH
Watson, Tom
GO NOW
Watson, Woody
TWO FOR TEXAS
Watt, Raichle
ENEMY OF THE STATE
Wattley, Danny
FIRESTORM
Watton, Roger
SIMPLE PLAN, A
Watts, Naomi
BABE: PIG IN THE CITY
DANGEROUS BEAUTY
Waugh, Scott
DESPERATE MEASURES
Wax, Ruby
BORROWERS, THE
Waxman, Al
RESCUERS: STORIES OF COURAGE—TWO WOMEN
Wayans, Marlon
SENSELESS
Wayborn, Kristina
LITTLE GHOST
Waymire, Kellie
PLAYING BY HEART
Wayne, Big Daddy
DON KING: ONLY IN AMERICA
Wayne, Dig
PAULIE
PHOENIX
Wayne, Kenneth
PLAN B
Wayrock, Heather
PARENT TRAP, THE
Wayton, Gary
WATCHERS REBORN
Wearing, Gillian
LOVE IS THE DEVIL: STUDY FOR A PORTRAIT OF FRANCIS BACON
Weathered, Michael
JOHNNY SKIDMARKS
Weatherly, Michael
COLONY, THE
LAST DAYS OF DISCO, THE
Weatherly, Shawn
DANCER, TEXAS POP. 81
Weatherred, Michael
SENSELESS
Weathers, Doug
GINGERBREAD MAN, THE
Weatherup, Christine
STAR KID
Weaver, Brett
SLAYERS: THE MOTION PICTURE
Weaver, Dennis
TOUCH OF EVIL: THE DIRECTOR'S CUT
Weaver, Doug
LETHAL WEAPON 4
Weaver, Fritz
RESCUERS: STORIES OF COURAGE—TWO WOMEN
Weaver, Lee
BULWORTH
GODZILLA
HOW STELLA GOT HER GROOVE BACK
Weaving, Hugo
BABE: PIG IN THE CITY
Webb, Chloe
NEWTON BOYS, THE
PRACTICAL MAGIC
Webb, Danny
LOVE AND DEATH ON LONG ISLAND
Webb, Gregory Allen
GODSON, THE
Webb, Lucy
OUTSIDE OZONA
Webb, Matt
STEPHEN KING'S THE NIGHT FLIER
Webb, Rudy
MIGHTY, THE
Webb, Veronica
54
HOLY MAN
Webber, David
AVENGERS, THE
Webber, Stephen
INCOGNITO
Weber, Dewey
PENTAGON WARS, THE
Weber, Jake
DANGEROUS BEAUTY
MEET JOE BLACK
Weber, Paolina
SOMEWHERE IN THE CITY
Weber, Steven
ALL DOGS CHRISTMAS CAROL, AN
SOUR GRAPES
Webster, Derek
GODZILLA
Webster, Jack
PECKER
Webster, Ken
TEKKEN: THE MOTION PICTURE
Webster, Shane
DEAR JESSE
Webster, Sharon
DOGWATCH
Webster, Shawn
SNOWBOUND
Wedersoe, Erik
KINGDOM, PART 2, THE
Weedon, Emily
BRIDE OF CHUCKY
Weeks, Jimmie Ray
SIEGE, THE
Weeks, Perdita
SPICE WORLD
Weeks, Willie
BLUES BROTHERS 2000
Weems, Eric
RUSHMORE
Weenick, Annabelle
PALMETTO
Wegener, Klaus
KINGDOM, PART 2, THE
Wehle, Brenda
SOLDIER
Wei, Dick
DRAGONS FOREVER
PRODIGAL SON, THE
Wei Pai
PRODIGAL SON, THE
Wei Ye
FROZEN
Weil, Barney
RETURN OF THE KING, THE
Weil, Barry
RETURN OF THE KING, THE
RETURN OF THE KING, THE
Weil, Liza
WHATEVER
Weil, Scott
RAT'S TALE, A
Weiner, David
I GOT THE HOOK UP
Weinstein, Harvey
BURN HOLLYWOOD BURN
Weinstock, Lotus
LENNY BRUCE: SWEAR TO TELL THE TRUTH
Weintraub, Scott
CIVIL ACTION, A
Weir, Arabella
SHOOTING FISH
Weir, Michael
HANGING GARDEN, THE
Weireter, Peter
DESPERATE MEASURES
Weisberg, Emily
SPANISH PRISONER, THE
Weisinger, Tina
NIGHT AT THE ROXBURY, A
Weiss, Bryna
SLUMS OF BEVERLY HILLS
Weiss, Kaspar
TRUCE, THE
Weiss, Matthew
NIAGARA NIAGARA
Weiss, Robert
MISBEGOTTEN
Weisser, Norbert
NEMESIS 4: CRY OF ANGELS
Weisz, Rachel
LAND GIRLS, THE
SWEPT FROM THE SEA
Weitering, Jade
MR. NICE GUY
Weitz, Bruce
DEEP IMPACT
LANDLADY, THE
Welbers, Nicolas
MARIE BAIE DES ANGES
Welch, Jason
ENEMY OF THE STATE
Welch, Michael
STAR TREK: INSURRECTION
Welch, Peter
TALK TO ME
Welch, Raquel
CHAIRMAN OF THE BOARD
Welch, Susan
LETTER FROM DEATH ROW, A
Welch, Tahnee
BLACK LIGHT
SUE
Weldon, Julia
PARALLEL SONS
Weldon, Renee
SUMMER FLING
Welh, James
LITTLE VOICE
Welker, Frank
FLINTSTONES: I YABBA-DABBA DOO!, THE
JUNGLE BOOK: MOWGLI'S STORY, THE
QUEST FOR CAMELOT
RUSTY: THE GREAT RESCUE
SCOOBY-DOO ON ZOMBIE ISLAND

Weller, Frederick
ARMAGEDDON
ELMORE LEONARD'S GOLD COAST
Weller, Michael
TOP OF THE WORLD
Weller, Peter
TOP OF THE WORLD
Welles, Amanda
NIGHT VISION
Welles, Orson
TOUCH OF EVIL: THE DIRECTOR'S CUT
Welles, Shannon
MIDAS TOUCH, THE
Wellington, James
MEAN GUNS
Wells, Danny
RAT'S TALE, A
Wells, David
BREAST MEN
CRACKING UP
Wells, Elizabeth Diane
MAJOR LEAGUE: BACK TO THE MINORS
Wells, Frank T.
NEXT STOP, WONDERLAND
PROPOSITION, THE
Wells, Hubert
BABE: PIG IN THE CITY
Wells, Junior
BLUES BROTHERS 2000
Wells, Orlando
WILDE
Wells, Tico
BRAM STOKER'S THE MUMMY
Wells, Timothy
KRIPPENDORF'S TRIBE
Welsh, John
FROM A FAR COUNTRY
Welsh, Kenneth
JACK HIGGINS' THUNDER POINT
Welsh, Margaret
RATCHET
Welsh, Russell
HANDS ON A HARDBODY
Welterien, Paul
X-FILES, THE
Wen, Ming-Na
MULAN
Wenderlich, Windy
STEPHEN KING'S THE NIGHT FLIER
Wendl, Alan J.
PECKER
Wendl, Joyce Flick
ENEMY OF THE STATE
PECKER
Wendt, George
DENNIS THE MENACE STRIKES AGAIN
SPICE WORLD
Wenham, David
DARK CITY
Wenn, Joslyn
DIRTY WORK
Wensueen, Barry
KNOCK OFF
Wentworth, Alexandra
REAL BLONDE, THE
Wenz, Tyler Daniel
JANE AUSTEN'S MAFIA!
Werking, Noel
ENEMY OF THE STATE
Werntz, Gary
DEEP IMPACT
Werntz, Hannah
DEEP IMPACT
Wert, Douglas
OBJECT OF MY AFFECTION, THE
Werthmann, Colleen
BREAST MEN

Wescoatt, Rusty
TOUCH OF EVIL: THE DIRECTOR'S CUT
Weseluck, Cathy
ADVENTURES OF MOWGLI
DRAGON BALL Z THE MOVIE: THE TREE OF MIGHT
I'LL BE HOME FOR CHRISTMAS
Wesley, Fred
MY FIRST NAME IS MACEO
Wesley, John
I GOT THE HOOK UP
Wessler, Charles
FRENCH EXIT
Wesson, Howard
NEXT STEP, THE
West, Adam
RUN FOR COVER
West, Billy
SCOOBY-DOO ON ZOMBIE ISLAND
West, Bob
BARNEY'S GREAT ADVENTURE—THE MOVIE
West, Caryl
THERE'S SOMETHING ABOUT MARY
West, Debi Mae
SECRET OF NIMH 2: TIMMY TO THE RESCUE, THE
West, Dominic
SPICE WORLD
West, John
WHY DO FOOLS FALL IN LOVE?
West, On
PATCH ADAMS
West, Pamela
HOLY MAN
West, Randy
HIJACKING HOLLYWOOD
West, Red
I STILL KNOW WHAT YOU DID LAST SUMMER
West, Ron
SOUR GRAPES
West, Tegan
HI-LIFE
West, Timothy
EVER AFTER
West, Troy
CHICAGO CAB
Westaway, Simon
BABE: PIG IN THE CITY
THIN RED LINE, THE
TWISTED
Westbam
MODULATIONS: CINEMA FOR THE EAR
Westcott, Carrie
RETURN TO SAVAGE BEACH
Westerman, Floyd Red Crow
LAST ASSASSINS
Westerman, Frederic
MARIE BAIE DES ANGES
Westerwelle, Wendy
ZERO EFFECT
Westfall, Ralph David
PATCH ADAMS
Westhead, David
WILDE
Westhof, Zom
OBJECT OF MY AFFECTION, THE
Westmore, McKenzie
STAR TREK: INSURRECTION
Westmoreland, Micko
VELVET GOLDMINE
Westmoreland, Stoney
GODZILLA
Westmoreland, Wash
VELVET GOLDMINE
Weston, Celia
CELEBRITY

Weston, Douglas
SIX DAYS, SEVEN NIGHTS
Wetherell, Virginia
LOVE IS THE DEVIL: STUDY FOR A PORTRAIT OF FRANCIS BACON
Wetjen, Bethany
KNOCK OFF
Wettenhall, Simon
WILD MAN BLUES
Wettig, Patricia
DANCER, TEXAS POP. 81
Wetzel, Chris
SKIN & BONE
Wetzel, Jeffrey
HOLY MAN
Whalen, Sean
SUICIDE KINGS
Whaley, Frank
RETROACTIVE
WHEN TRUMPETS FADE
Whaley, Robert
RATCHET
Wheaton, Wil
TREKKIES
Wheeler, Andrew
SIN AND REDEMPTION
Wheeler, Bronia
PROPOSITION, THE
Wheeler, Ed
GODZILLA
Wheeler, Jane
BARNEY'S GREAT ADVENTURE—THE MOVIE
CAPTIVE
Wheeler, Maggie
PARENT TRAP, THE
Wheeler-Nicholson, Dana
LIVING IN PERIL
Whelan, Jim
SNAKE EYES
VELVET GOLDMINE
Whetham, Bradie
DEFENDERS: PAYBACK, THE
Whipp, Joseph
MIDAS TOUCH, THE
SUICIDE KINGS
Whirry, Shannon
FATAL PURSUIT
RETROACTIVE
Whitaker, Forest
BODY COUNT
REBOUND: THE LEGEND OF EARL "THE GOAT" MANIGAULT
Whitaker, John Henry
PHOENIX
Whitaker, Kenn
BULWORTH
Whitaker, Lucinda
MAJOR LEAGUE: BACK TO THE MINORS
Whitby, Paul
SWEPT FROM THE SEA
White, Bernard
CITY OF ANGELS
White, Bethany
NAKED ACTS
White, Betty
DENNIS THE MENACE STRIKES AGAIN
HARD RAIN
HOLY MAN
White, Bill Everett
PRINCE, THE
White, Bradley
OBJECT OF MY AFFECTION, THE
White, Bryan
QUEST FOR CAMELOT
White, Giovahann
BIG HIT, THE

Williams, Gareth
DIGGING TO CHINA
NO WAY HOME
Williams, Gary Anthony
RIDE
Williams, Gigi
CELEBRITY
Williams, Glynn
NEWTON BOYS, THE
Williams, Harland
HALF BAKED
Williams, Heathcote
COUSIN BETTE
Williams, Howard Allison
PATCH ADAMS
Williams III, Clarence
GEORGE WALLACE
HALF BAKED
REBOUND: THE LEGEND OF EARL "THE GOAT" MANIGAULT
Williams, James
BOYS WILL BE BOYS
Williams, Jamie
WATERBOY, THE
Williams, Jeff
PERFECT MURDER, A
Williams, Jermaine
BULWORTH
Williams, Jim Cody
LOS LOCOS
Williams, JoBeth
WHEN DANGER FOLLOWS YOU HOME
Williams, Johnathan
LOVE IS THE DEVIL: STUDY FOR A PORTRAIT OF FRANCIS BACON
Williams, Keith Leon
BLADE
Williams, Kelli
SNOWBOUND
Williams, Kellie
RIDE
Williams, Kenya
PLAYERS CLUB, THE
Williams, Kevin
FRENCH EXIT
Williams, Lawrence
I GOT THE HOOK UP
Williams, Lia
FIRELIGHT
Williams, Mark
BORROWERS, THE
ROYAL DECEIT
SHAKESPEARE IN LOVE
Williams, Mary Alice
SIEGE, THE
Williams, Michelle
HALLOWEEN H20: TWENTY YEARS LATER
Williams, Mollena
SKIN & BONE
Williams, Montel
PEACEKEEPER, THE
Williams, Myron
DEAR JESSE
Williams, Nadia
VELVET GOLDMINE
Williams, Olivia
RUSHMORE
Williams, Oren
PLAYERS CLUB, THE
Williams, R. Scott
PECKER
Williams, Rhys
AIR BUD: GOLDEN RECEIVER
Williams, Robin
PATCH ADAMS
WHAT DREAMS MAY COME
Williams, Ron
KILLER CONDOM, THE
Williams, Rose Vaughn
DEAR JESSE
Williams, Roshumba
CELEBRITY
Williams, Roxanna
GENERAL, THE
Williams, Saul
NAKED ACTS
ONE TRUE THING
SLAM
SLAMNATION
Williams, Selina Rachel
WHEN DANGER FOLLOWS YOU HOME
Williams, Simon
ANOTHER DAY IN PARADISE
Williams, Tino
SENSELESS
Williams, Treat
DEEP RISING
SUBSTITUTE 2: SCHOOL'S OUT, THE
Williams, Vanessa
DANCE WITH ME
Williams, William
ARMOUR OF GOD
Williams, Zachary
STAR TREK: INSURRECTION
Williamson, Bruce
WHO IS HENRY JAGLOM?
Williamson, Dean
LAST SEDUCTION II, THE
Williamson, Felix
BABE: PIG IN THE CITY
THIN RED LINE, THE
Williamson, Fred
BLACKJACK
CHILDREN OF THE CORN V: FIELD OF TERROR
NIGHT VISION
RIDE
Williamson, Kate
HI-LO COUNTRY, THE
Williamson, Kendall
GREAT EXPECTATIONS
Williamson, Melissa
RED HAWK: WEAPON OF DEATH
Williamson, Mykelti
PRIMARY COLORS
SPECIES II
12 ANGRY MEN
Williamson, Paul
SHOOTING FISH
Williamson, Scott
ALMOST HEROES
PERMANENT MIDNIGHT
Williamson, Sondra
SPECIES II
Willis, Bruce
ARMAGEDDON
MERCURY RISING
SIEGE, THE
Willis, Katherine
FACULTY, THE
Willis, Rich
SLUMS OF BEVERLY HILLS
Willis, Susan
FACULTY, THE
Willmann, Heike
INCOGNITO
Willows, Alec
ADVENTURES OF MOWGLI
DRAGON BALL Z THE MOVIE: DEAD ZONE
DRAGON BALL Z THE MOVIE: THE WORLD'S STRONGEST
RUDOLPH THE RED-NOSED REINDEER: THE MOVIE
Wills, Marti
CON, THE
Wills, Scott
UGLY, THE
Wilmot, David
GENERAL, THE
I WENT DOWN
Wilmot, Ronan
BUTCHER BOY, THE
GENERAL, THE
Wilmott, Billy
SHATTERED IMAGE
Wilner, Martin
R.I.P. REST IN PIECES: A PORTRAIT OF JOE COLEMAN
Wilroy, Channing
PECKER
Wilson, Alexandra
SMALL SOLDIERS
Wilson, Amanda
ERNEST IN THE ARMY
Wilson, Andrew
RUSHMORE
Wilson, Brian Anthony
ROUNDERS
SNAKE EYES
Wilson, Bridgette
NEVADA
REAL BLONDE, THE
Wilson, Chris
MR. NICE GUY
Wilson, Chrystale
PLAYERS CLUB, THE
Wilson, Chuck
GODZILLA VS. KING GHIDORAH
Wilson, Cindy
RUGRATS MOVIE, THE
Wilson, Collette
SCARRED CITY
Wilson, Dale
SNOWBOUND
Wilson, Debra
ASYLUM
CRACKING UP
Wilson, Dolan
MAJOR LEAGUE: BACK TO THE MINORS
Wilson, Edmund
PHANTOMS
Wilson, Greg
SENSELESS
Wilson, Jane Edith
NEXT STEP, THE
Wilson, Jeanette H.
HOMEGROWN
Wilson, Jody
HOLY MAN
Wilson, Jonathan
REAL BLONDE, THE
Wilson, Keith
WILD THINGS
Wilson, Kristen
DR. DOLITTLE
Wilson, Lambert
LEADING MAN, THE
SAME OLD SONG
Wilson, Lawrence
SLAM
Wilson, Luke
HOME FRIES
RUSHMORE
Wilson, Mark
WELCOME TO WOOP WOOP
Wilson, Mary Louise
STEPMOM
Wilson, Owen
ARMAGEDDON
PERMANENT MIDNIGHT

Wilson, Reno
DIARY OF A SERIAL KILLER
FALLEN
LOS LOCOS
MIGHTY JOE YOUNG
STIR
Wilson, Rita
PSYCHO
Wilson, Sandye
NAKED ACTS
Wilson, Scott
CLAY PIGEONS
Wilson, Stuart
ENEMY OF THE STATE
MASK OF ZORRO, THE
Wilson, Warren
APT PUPIL
Winant, Bruce
POLTERGEIST REPORT: YUYU HAKUSHO
WRATH OF THE NINJA: THE YOTODEN MOVIE
Winchell, April
ANTZ
Winckelmann, Kadie
OBJECT OF MY AFFECTION, THE
Wincott, Jeff
FUTURE FEAR
UNDERTAKER'S WEDDING, THE
Winde, Beatrice
HORTON FOOTE'S ALONE
REAL BLONDE, THE
SIMON BIRCH
Windle, David
LOVE IS THE DEVIL: STUDY FOR A PORTRAIT OF FRANCIS BACON
Windum, R.L.
CAN'T YOU HEAR THE WIND HOWL?: THE LIFE AND MUSIC OF ROBERT JOHNSON
Winebrake, Pete "Conan"
RIVER RED
Winford
LOVE IS THE DEVIL: STUDY FOR A PORTRAIT OF FRANCIS BACON
Winfree, Rachel
KRIPPENDORF'S TRIBE
SOULER OPPOSITE, THE
Winfrey, Oprah
BELOVED
Wingert, Wally
RAT'S TALE, A
Winget, Drew
BOYS WILL BE BOYS
Wink, Steffen
RAT'S TALE, A
Winkler, Henry
WATERBOY, THE
Winkler, Patricia
RUSHMORE
Winningham, Mare
GEORGE WALLACE
Winsett, Jerry
PAULIE
Winston, Buddy
SOULER OPPOSITE, THE
Winston, Don
DECEIVER
Winston, Hattie
LIVING OUT LOUD
MEET THE DEEDLES
RUGRATS MOVIE, THE
Winston, Matt
HALLOWEEN H20: TWENTY YEARS LATER
Winstone, Ray
NIL BY MOUTH
Wint, Maurice Dean
CUBE
Winter, Alex
BORROWERS, THE
Winter, Gordon
KID IN ALADDIN'S PALACE, A
Winter, Matthew
HOMEGROWN
Winter, Norm
OFF THE MENU: THE LAST DAYS OF CHASEN'S
Winter, Terence
GODZILLA
Winters, April
JOHN CARPENTER'S VAMPIRES
Winters, Dean
LAST BREATH
Winters, Kristoffer Ryan
HOT BLOODED
PRIMARY COLORS
Winters, Michael
DEEP IMPACT
Winters, Time
GUN, A CAR, AND A BLONDE, A
Winwood, Steve
BLUES BROTHERS 2000
Winzenried, Eric
LOS LOCOS
Wirth, Billy
LAST LIVES
Wirtz, Billy
LETTER FROM DEATH ROW, A
Wisdom, Robert
MIGHTY JOE YOUNG
STIR
Wise, Alfie
CATHERINE'S GROVE
Wise, Jim
CLOCKWATCHERS
NIGHT AT THE ROXBURY, A
Wissel, Providence
THERE'S SOMETHING ABOUT MARY
Withers, Margery
SWEPT FROM THE SEA
Witherspoon, Ashanti
FARM: ANGOLA, U.S.A., THE
Witherspoon, John
BULWORTH
I GOT THE HOOK UP
RIDE
Witherspoon, Reese
OVERNIGHT DELIVERY
PLEASANTVILLE
TWILIGHT
Witschi, Stefan
SWINDLE, THE
Witt, Alicia
URBAN LEGEND
Witt, Katerina
RONIN
Wittaker, Carl
LITTLE VOICE
Wohl, David
SAVING PRIVATE RYAN
Wojas, Michael
LOVE IS THE DEVIL: STUDY FOR A PORTRAIT OF FRANCIS BACON
Wolande, Gene
CIVIL ACTION, A
NEGOTIATOR, THE
Wolf, Fred
DIRTY WORK
Wolf, Gary
OVERNIGHT DELIVERY
WHATEVER
Wolf, Laurie
STEPHEN KING'S THE NIGHT FLIER
Wolf, Mattie
WATERBOY, THE
Wolfe, Greg
WRATH OF THE NINJA: THE YOTODEN MOVIE
Wolfe, Jeff
KNOCK OFF
MARS
Wolfe, Miranda
STEEL SHARKS
Wolfe, Traci
LETHAL WEAPON 4
Wolfert, Nicholas
GREAT EXPECTATIONS
Wolff, Gerry
TALES FROM A PARALLEL UNIVERSE: EATING PATTERN
Wolff, Jurgen
REAL HOWARD SPITZ, THE
Wolfgang, Penny
BUFFALO '66
Wolford, Steve
AMERICAN HISTORY X
Woller, Kirk B.R.
MERCURY RISING
SAND TRAP
Wollter, Sven
JERUSALEM
Wolodarsky, Wally
RUSHMORE
Wolter, Ralf
KILLER CONDOM, THE
Womack, Mark
UNDER THE SKIN
Wong, Albert
ARMAGEDDON
ENEMY OF THE STATE
REPLACEMENT KILLERS, THE
RUSH HOUR
Wong, Amy
RETURN TO PARADISE
Wong, B.D.
MULAN
SLAPPY AND THE STINKERS
SUBSTITUTE 2: SCHOOL'S OUT, THE
Wong Chung Yu
KILLER ANGELS
Wong, Donna
BLADE
Wong Hap
PRODIGAL SON, THE
Wong Har
ENCOUNTER OF THE SPOOKY KIND
Wong, Lee
PERFECT MURDER, A
Wong, Melvin
BEAUTY INVESTIGATOR
Wong, Michael
KNOCK OFF
ROYAL WARRIORS
Wong, Richard
THURSDAY
Wong, Russell
PROPHECY II, THE
Wong, Sylvia
SUE
Wong, Victor
3 NINJAS: HIGH NOON AT MEGA MOUNTAIN
Wong, Wyman
KNOCK OFF
Wong Yat-San, Gabriel
KICK BOXER'S TEARS
Wong Yu Wan
DRAGONS FOREVER
Wong Yui Sang
KNOCK OFF
Woo, James Wing
LETHAL WEAPON 4
REPLACEMENT KILLERS, THE

Wood, Elijah
DEEP IMPACT
FACULTY, THE
OLIVER TWIST
Wood, Evan Rachel
DIGGING TO CHINA
PRACTICAL MAGIC
Wood, Grahame
SAVING PRIVATE RYAN
Wood, Jake
DAD SAVAGE
Wood, Jody
HALLOWEEN H20: TWENTY YEARS LATER
Wood, John
AVENGERS, THE
Wood, Julie Tolentino
HALLELUJAH!
Wood, Tom
U.S. MARSHALS
Woodall, Andrew
REGENERATION
Woodard, Alfre
DOWN IN THE DELTA
Woodard, Jimmy
PLAYERS CLUB, THE
Woodbine, Bokeem
ALMOST HEROES
BIG HIT, THE
CAUGHT UP
Woodbury, Judith
LETHAL WEAPON 4
Woodcock, Joanna
POLISH WEDDING
Woodeson, Nicholas
AVENGERS, THE
SHOOTING FISH
Woodhouse, Michael
BELLY
Woodlawn, Holly
BILLY'S HOLLYWOOD SCREEN KISS
LOU REED: ROCK AND ROLL HEART
Woodruff Jr., Tom
X-FILES, THE
Woods, Courtney
PARENT TRAP, THE
Woods, D. Elliot
STAR TREK: INSURRECTION
Woods, Dana
I GOT THE HOOK UP
Woods, David
TALES FROM A PARALLEL UNIVERSE: GIGA SHADOW
Woods, Denise
MERCURY RISING
Woods, Frank
RINGMASTER
Woods, James
ANOTHER DAY IN PARADISE
JOHN CARPENTER'S VAMPIRES
Woods, Michael Jeffrey
ANOTHER DAY IN PARADISE
Woodside, D.B.
SCARRED CITY
Woodthorpe, Peter
MERLIN
Woodward, Joanne
MY KNEES WERE JUMPING: REMEMBERING THE KINDERTRANSPORTS
Woodward, Peter
BRYLCREEM BOYS, THE
Woof, Emily
PHOTOGRAPHING FAIRIES
VELVET GOLDMINE
Woolever, Mary
SIMPLE PLAN, A
Woolf, Alan
DON KING: ONLY IN AMERICA
Woolgar, Barry
SHOOTING FISH
Woolrich, Abel
MASK OF ZORRO, THE
Woolridge, Karen
REAL BLONDE, THE
Woolvert, Gordon M.
BRAM STOKER'S SHADOWBUILDER
Woolvert, Jaimz
BOOGIE BOY
Woolvett, Gordon Michael
BRIDE OF CHUCKY
Worapinrat, Sureeporn
HEROES SHED NO TEARS
Worden, Marc
MAKER, THE
Workman, Fred
HOLY MAN
Worley, Billie
PENTAGON WARS, THE
Wormsdorf, Joachim
TRUCE, THE
Woronicz, Henry
LIVING OUT LOUD
PRIMARY COLORS
Woronov, Mary
LOU REED: ROCK AND ROLL HEART
Worrall, Chaylee
HENRY FOOL
Worret, Christopher
ARMAGEDDON
Worters, Daniel
LEADING MAN, THE
Worthing, Deborah
ASYLUM
Worthington, Wendy
KRIPPENDORF'S TRIBE
Worthy, Rick
STAR TREK: INSURRECTION
Wrage, Glenn
SAVING PRIVATE RYAN
Wray, Fay
OFF THE MENU: THE LAST DAYS OF CHASEN'S
Wren, Joshua
LES MISERABLES
Wright, Arlaine
DIRTY WORK
Wright, Bruce
NEGOTIATOR, THE
Wright, Burt
TALK TO ME
Wright, Cecil
LOVE AND DEATH ON LONG ISLAND
Wright, Jeffrey
CELEBRITY
Wright, Karl T.
DR. DOLITTLE
Wright, Mary Catherine
CELEBRITY
ONE TRUE THING
Wright, Michael Townsend
RAT PACK, THE
Wright, N'Bushe
BLADE
Wright, Paul "The Giant"
WATERBOY, THE
Wright Penn, Robin
HURLYBURLY
Wright, Sean
SWAN PRINCESS III: AND THE MYSTERY OF THE ENCHANTED TREASURE, THE
Wright, Stan
LITTLE VOICE
Wright, Steven
BABE: PIG IN THE CITY
HALF BAKED
Wright, Tom
PALMETTO
PENTAGON WARS, THE
Wright, Ward
NOT IN THIS TOWN
Wu, Gloria
CHINESE BOX, THE
Wu Ma
ENCOUNTER OF THE SPOOKY KIND
HONG KONG 1941
PRODIGAL SON, THE
Wu, Vivan
BRIGHT SHINING LIE, A
Wu Yue Zhu
BEAUTY INVESTIGATOR
Wu-yuk Ho
FALLEN ANGELS
Wuhrer, Kari
DISAPPEARANCE OF KEVIN JOHNSON, THE
HOT BLOODED
KISSING A FOOL
PHOENIX
TERMINAL JUSTICE
UNDERTAKER'S WEDDING, THE
Wurstman, Kurt
TARZAN AND THE LOST CITY
Wyatt, b.
SKIN & BONE
Wyatt, Dale
MY GIANT
Wyatt-Mair, Jeneane
TARZAN AND THE LOST CITY
Wycherley, Don
I WENT DOWN
SUMMER FLING
Wyden, Roman
MURDER IN MIND
Wylie, Adam
CHILDREN OF THE CORN V: FIELD OF TERROR
NAPOLEON
Wylie, Dan
THIN RED LINE, THE
Wyman, Jane
OFF THE MENU: THE LAST DAYS OF CHASEN'S
Wyman, Kendall Leigh
OUTSIDE OZONA
Wynands, Dan
LETHAL WEAPON 4
Wynkoop, Christopher
HE GOT GAME
Wynn, Keenan
TOUCH OF EVIL: THE DIRECTOR'S CUT
Wynter, Sarah
SPECIES II
X, Mia
I GOT THE HOOK UP
X-ecutioners
MODULATIONS: CINEMA FOR THE EAR
Xaf
VELVET GOLDMINE
Xavier, Debra
CHOSEN ONE: LEGEND OF THE RAVEN, THE
Xifo, Ray
ALMOST PARTNERS
DIRTY LAUNDRY
FALLEN
Xocua, Guadalupe
MEN WITH GUNS
Xocua, Miguel
MEN WITH GUNS
Xu Qing
EMPEROR'S SHADOW, THE

Xu, Tony
JACK HIGGINS' ON DANGEROUS GROUND
Xu Xiaoli
RED CHERRY
Xuereb, Salvator
MY BROTHER'S WAR
Xun Feng
SHAOLIN TEMPLE, THE
Yager, Missy
REAL BLONDE, THE
Yagher, Priscilla
CHOSEN ONE: LEGEND OF THE RAVEN, THE
Yahn, Michelle
WHATEVER
Yajima, Kenichi
FIREWORKS
SONATINE
Yakushiji, Yasuei
FIREWORKS
Yakusho, Koji
EEL, THE
Yale, Stan
LIVING IN PERIL
Yamada, Mao
ORGAZMO
Yamaguchi, Akifumi
JUNK FOOD
Yamaguchi, Kiyoko
TRUMAN SHOW, THE
Yamamoto, Donna
SNOWBOUND
Yamamoto, Kay
DR. DOLITTLE
Yamamoto, Shizuko
JUNK FOOD
Yamamoto, Yoshinori
RAT'S TALE, A
Yamamura, So
GODZILLA VS. KING GHIDORAH
Yamato, Yukio
ZERO WOMAN
Yamauchi, Akira
RAZOR: WHO'S GOT THE GOLD?, THE
Yanagida, Yoshitaka
ZERO WOMAN
Yanez, Eduardo
WILD THINGS
Yang Chun
BEAUTY INVESTIGATOR
Yang Di Hua
SHAOLIN TEMPLE, THE
Yang, Jamison
GODZILLA
Yanni
OFF THE MENU: THE LAST DAYS OF CHASEN'S
Yannuzzi Jr., Carmen
BELLY
Yardley, Stephen
INNOCENT SLEEP, THE
Yarmoush, Michael
LOUISA MAY ALCOTT'S LITTLE MEN
Yasbeck, Amy
NEIL SIMON'S THE ODD COUPLE II
Yasotake, Patti
CLOCKWATCHERS
Yates, Cecilia
BABE: PIG IN THE CITY
Yates, Delanie
LAST BREATH
Yavne, Matthew
ROUNDERS
Yeager, Ben
FEAR AND LOATHING IN LAS VEGAS
Yeager, Steve
MAJOR LEAGUE: BACK TO THE MINORS
Yearwood, Richard
DOWN IN THE DELTA
Yee, Derek
MAGNIFICENT WARRIORS
Yee, Kelvin
PATCH ADAMS
Yee, Nancy
ENEMY OF THE STATE
Yee, Stuart
RUSH HOUR
Yenque, Teresa
BREAK, THE
Yeoh, Michelle
MAGNIFICENT WARRIORS
ROYAL WARRIORS
Yerkovich, Anthony
HOLLYWOOD CONFIDENTIAL
Yeung, Kristy
COMRADES, ALMOST A LOVE STORY
Yeung, Michelle
CHINESE BOX, THE
Yeung, Pauline
DRAGONS FOREVER
Yeung Tsui Kuen
HEROES SHED NO TEARS
Yevo
LAST BIG THING, THE
Yiasoumi, George
BORROWERS, THE
ELIZABETH
Yip, Cecilia
HONG KONG 1941
Yip, Danny
ARMOUR OF GOD
Yip, Deannie
DRAGONS FOREVER
Yiu Shiu Chung
KNOCK OFF
Yoakam, Dwight
NEWTON BOYS, THE
WHEN TRUMPETS FADE
Yoakam, Stephen
OVERNIGHT DELIVERY
Yoba, Malik
RIDE
Yohn, Erica
DIARY OF A SERIAL KILLER
Yokoyama, Megumi
GONIN
Yordanoff, Wladimir
UN AIR DE FAMILLE
York, Michael
54
WRONGFULLY ACCUSED
York, Philip
SHOOTING FISH
Yorker, Jade
HE GOT GAME
Yoshida, Peter
ROUNDERS
Yoshida, Seiko
SPANISH PRISONER, THE
Yoshino, Yasoumi
THIN RED LINE, THE
Yoshiyuki
JUNK FOOD
Youell, Michelle
MEET JOE BLACK
Young, Aden
COUSIN BETTE
UNDER HEAVEN
Young, Adrian
LIVING OUT LOUD
Young, Bobby
LOLIDA 2000
Young, Burt
HOT BLOODED
UNDERTAKER'S WEDDING, THE
Young, Charlie
FALLEN ANGELS
Young, Chris
BRAVE LITTLE TOASTER GOES TO MARS, THE
Young, Damian
OBJECT OF MY AFFECTION, THE
Young, Damon
MR. NICE GUY
Young, Gillian
LOVE IS THE DEVIL: STUDY FOR A PORTRAIT OF FRANCIS BACON
Young, Harrison
OPPOSITE OF SEX, THE
PRIMARY COLORS
SAVING PRIVATE RYAN
Young, Jonathon
FIRESTORM
Young, Judith Knight
PECKER
Young, Louis
U.S. MARSHALS
Young, Marcus
RETURN TO SAVAGE BEACH
Young, Nancy
SPECIES II
Young, Nina
SLIDING DOORS
Young, Norris
WHY DO FOOLS FALL IN LOVE?
Young, Paul
REGENERATION
Young, Rozwill
FALLEN
Young, Sean
INVADER, THE
MEN
Young, Vanessa
GINGERBREAD MAN, THE
Youngblood, Sebastian
TRUMAN SHOW, THE
Yount, Dell
RAGE, THE
TOP OF THE WORLD
Yourgrau, Barry
TERMINAL JUSTICE
Yow, David
BULLET ON A WIRE
Yu Cheng Hui
SHAOLIN TEMPLE, THE
Yu Hai
SHAOLIN TEMPLE, THE
Yuan, Roger
LETHAL WEAPON 4
Yuan Yuan
EMPEROR'S SHADOW, THE
Yuen, Anika
KNOCK OFF
Yuen Biao
DRAGONS FOREVER
PRODIGAL SON, THE
Yuen, Corey
BODYGUARD FROM BEIJING
Yuen Hung
KILLER ANGELS
Yuen Lai King
KILLER ANGELS
Yuen, Russell
LOST WORLD, THE
Yuen Wah
DRAGONS FOREVER
Yueng Lam
KILLER ANGELS
Yulin, Harris
HOSTILE WATERS
Yurnet, Julio
HAV PLENTY

Yusim, Marat
PERFECT MURDER, A
Yusoff, Deanna
RETURN TO PARADISE
Z'Dar, Robert
FATAL PURSUIT
Zaborowski, Jan
JUNK MAIL
Zabriskie, Grace
ARMAGEDDON
Zacapa, Daniel
NEIL SIMON'S THE ODD COUPLE II
Zack, Catrin
SOULER OPPOSITE, THE
Zago, Catherine
ARTEMISIA
Zagon, Mandy
HAV PLENTY
Zahn, Steve
OBJECT OF MY AFFECTION, THE
OUT OF SIGHT
SAFE MEN
YOU'VE GOT MAIL
Zakroff, Jennifer
PECKER
Zalabak, Marisa
PECKER
Zaldana, Eliezer
NAKED LIES
Zaloom, Joe
ROUNDERS
Zanden, Philip
KINGDOM, PART 2, THE
Zander, Johnny
CAN'T HARDLY WAIT
Zane, Billy
POCAHONTAS II: JOURNEY TO A NEW WORLD
Zanes, Michele
ROUNDERS
Zang, Leslie
HENRY: PORTRAIT OF A SERIAL KILLER PART 2
Zapasiewicz, Zbigniew
FROM A FAR COUNTRY
Zappa, Ahmet
CHILDREN OF THE CORN V: FIELD OF TERROR
JACK FROST
Zappa, Diva
CHILDREN OF THE CORN V: FIELD OF TERROR
Zappa, Dweezil
JACK FROST
Zappa, Moon
LOVE TO KILL
Zaragarov, Michael
SLAYERS: THE MOTION PICTURE
Zarish, Janet
OBJECT OF MY AFFECTION, THE
Zarnecki, Andrzej
FROM A FAR COUNTRY
Zarry, Nicole
RESCUERS: STORIES OF COURAGE—TWO COUPLES
Zary, Amine
X-FILES, THE
Zavaglia, Richard
DOGWATCH
Zayas, David
LENA'S DREAMS
ROUNDERS
RETURN TO PARADISE
SCARRED CITY
STEPMOM
Zecheru, Traian
JOHNNY MYSTO BOY WIZARD
Zegers, Kevin
AIR BUD: GOLDEN RECEIVER
BRAM STOKER'S SHADOWBUILDER
CALL TO REMEMBER, A
Zeller, Torben
KINGDOM, PART 2, THE
Zellweger, Renee
DECEIVER
ONE TRUE THING
PRICE ABOVE RUBIES, A
Zelmer, Suzanne
TRICKS
Zeman, Richard
SNAKE EYES
Zemanek, Timm
IN HIS FATHER'S SHOES
REAL BLONDE, THE
Zemzare, Lauma
STEPMOM
Zerafin Gonzalez, Oscar
MASK OF ZORRO, THE
Zerbe, Anthony
STAR TREK: INSURRECTION
Zeta-Jones, Catherine
MASK OF ZORRO, THE
Zhang Jian Wen
SHAOLIN TEMPLE, THE
Zhang, Sarah
SUE
Zhang Yongning
FROZEN
Zhukova, Maria
BROTHER
Ziane, Farid
MARIUS AND JEANNETTE
Zickel, Mather
CAUGHT UP
Zidek, Libor
LES MISERABLES
Zidel, Bob
DEFENDERS: PAYBACK, THE
Ziemski, Lauren
SPECIES II
Zien, Chip
SIEGE, THE
SNAKE EYES
Ziff, Irv
SPECIES II
Zigler, Scott
SPANISH PRISONER, THE
Zihenni, Albert
GREAT EXPECTATIONS
Zilkova, Veronika
FORGOTTEN LIGHT
Zimbalist Jr., Efrem
BATMAN & MR. FREEZE: SUBZERO
BATMAN/SUPERMAN MOVIE, THE
Zimmer, Constance
QUICKSILVER HIGHWAY
SENSELESS
Zimmerman, Joey
VERY BAD THINGS
Zimmerman, Mark
PRICE ABOVE RUBIES, A
Zimmerman, Peter
ONE TRUE THING
Zingaretti, Luca
ARTEMISIA
Zirnkilton, Steve
RUGRATS MOVIE, THE
Zitin, Brandon
FALLEN
Zitner, Alan
TWISTED
Zito, Chuck
SCARRED CITY
Zito, Sonny
ROUNDERS
Zittel, Greg
TEN BENNY
Zivanovic, Steven
LOVE IS THE DEVIL: STUDY FOR A PORTRAIT OF FRANCIS BACON
Zivot, Eric
ALARMIST, THE
Zobeida
EL CHE: INVESTIGATING A LEGEND
Zobel, Richard
MONTANA
Zogovic, Sanja
SAVIOR
Zohar, Rita
CALL TO REMEMBER, A
Zook, Tamara
PAULIE
Zoppi, Gaia
DANGEROUS BEAUTY
Zorlescu, Camelia
SUBSPECIES IV: BLOODSTORM
Zorlescu, Cristi
SUBSPECIES IV: BLOODSTORM
Zubrow, Sidney
SAFE MEN
Zuereb, Salvator
LEWIS & CLARK & GEORGE
Zuiderhoek, Olga
DRESS, THE
Zukovic, Dan
DISTURBING BEHAVIOR
LAST BIG THING, THE
Zuniga, Jose
HURRICANE STREETS
NEXT STOP, WONDERLAND
Zurlo, John
REAL THING, THE
Zushi, Tonbo
SONATINE
Zwang, Ron
LAST BIG THING, THE
Zydkiewicz, Jerzy
WHITE RAVEN, THE

ANIMATORS

Andrews, David
SMALL SOLDIERS
Aquino, Ruben
MULAN
Arcadias, Laurence
GENERAL CHAOS: UNCENSORED ANIMATION
Asbury, Kelly
PRINCE OF EGYPT, THE
Bailey, Chris
MIGHTY JOE YOUNG
Bean, Charlie
HERCULES AND XENA THE ANIMATED MOVIE: THE BATTLE FOR MOUNT OLYMPUS
Bevitt, Jayne
GENERAL CHAOS: UNCENSORED ANIMATION
Blaise, Aaron
MULAN
Blyth, Graham
I MARRIED A STRANGE PERSON!
Booth, Mike
GENERAL CHAOS: UNCENSORED ANIMATION
Brinkerhoff, Joel
GENERAL CHAOS: UNCENSORED ANIMATION
Butterworth, Kent
CASPER MEETS WENDY
Chung, Peter
RUGRATS MOVIE, THE
Claerhout, Paul
GENERAL CHAOS: UNCENSORED ANIMATION

Collins, Vince
GENERAL CHAOS: UNCENSORED ANIMATION
Cook, Lorna
PRINCE OF EGYPT, THE
Csupo, Gabor
RUGRATS MOVIE, THE
Destefano, Stephan
HERCULES AND XENA THE ANIMATED MOVIE: THE BATTLE FOR MOUNT OLYMPUS
Donar, David
GENERAL CHAOS: UNCENSORED ANIMATION
Eling, Stefan
GENERAL CHAOS: UNCENSORED ANIMATION
Enright, Amanda
GENERAL CHAOS: UNCENSORED ANIMATION
Fangmeier, Stefen
SMALL SOLDIERS
Fogel, Eric
GENERAL CHAOS: UNCENSORED ANIMATION
Grignon, Rex
ANTZ
Haider, Joe
MULAN
Haskett, Dan
MULAN
Henn, Mark
MULAN
Hui, Raman
ANTZ
Johnson, Broose
MULAN
Johnson, Ewan
BUG'S LIFE, A
Kannan, Masaaki
TEKKEN: THE MOTION PICTURE
Kanno, Hiroki
POLTERGEIST REPORT: YUYU HAKUSHO
Kawajiri, Yoshiaki
NEW ADVENTURES OF KIMBA THE WHITE LION, THE
Kim, Mike
HERCULES AND XENA THE ANIMATED MOVIE: THE BATTLE FOR MOUNT OLYMPUS
Klasky, Arlene
RUGRATS MOVIE, THE
Klein, Burt
GENERAL CHAOS: UNCENSORED ANIMATION
Kobayashi, Junji
NEW ADVENTURES OF KIMBA THE WHITE LION, THE
Kondo, Katsuya
KIKI'S DELIVERY SERVICE
Kondo, Yoshifumi
KIKI'S DELIVERY SERVICE
Kong, Emily
MIGHTY KONG, THE
Kowalchuk, William R.
RUDOLPH THE RED-NOSED REINDEER: THE MOVIE
Kupershmidt, Alex
MULAN
Maeda, Minoru
DRAGON BALL Z THE MOVIE: DEAD ZONE
DRAGON BALL Z THE MOVIE: THE TREE OF MIGHT
DRAGON BALL Z THE MOVIE: THE WORLD'S STRONGEST
Marren, Mark
RUGRATS MOVIE, THE
Martinez, Lorenzo E.
PRINCE OF EGYPT, THE
McKenna, John
QUEST FOR CAMELOT
McKinney, Brandon
GENERAL CHAOS: UNCENSORED ANIMATION
McQueen, Glenn
BUG'S LIFE, A
Montgomery, Tyron
GENERAL CHAOS: UNCENSORED ANIMATION
Morse, Scott
HERCULES AND XENA THE ANIMATED MOVIE: THE BATTLE FOR MOUNT OLYMPUS
Nittoli, Tony
GENERAL CHAOS: UNCENSORED ANIMATION
Otsuke, Shinji
KIKI'S DELIVERY SERVICE
Pair, Greg
I MARRIED A STRANGE PERSON!
Plympton, Bill
GENERAL CHAOS: UNCENSORED ANIMATION
I MARRIED A STRANGE PERSON!
Quade, Rich
BUG'S LIFE, A
Rappas, Panagiotis
RUGRATS MOVIE, THE
Reccardi, Chris
HERCULES AND XENA THE ANIMATED MOVIE: THE BATTLE FOR MOUNT OLYMPUS
Ridlen, David
RUSHMORE
Romanillos, Press
MULAN
Sang Il Sim
RED HAWK: WEAPON OF DEATH
Santucci, Walter
GENERAL CHAOS: UNCENSORED ANIMATION
Scanlon, Neal
BABE: PIG IN THE CITY
Schiff, Brad
GENERAL CHAOS: UNCENSORED ANIMATION
Skinner, Emily
GENERAL CHAOS: UNCENSORED ANIMATION
Staven, Karl
GENERAL CHAOS: UNCENSORED ANIMATION
Stillman, Thomas
GENERAL CHAOS: UNCENSORED ANIMATION
Sturgis, Jeff
GENERAL CHAOS: UNCENSORED ANIMATION
Sugino, Akio
GOLGO 13: QUEEN BEE
Svislotski, Andrei
RUGRATS MOVIE, THE
Takamoto, Iwao
MIGHTY KONG, THE
Tanaka, Ryo
POLTERGEIST REPORT: YUYU HAKUSHO
Temple, Barry
MULAN
Tezuka, Osamu
NEW ADVENTURES OF KIMBA THE WHITE LION, THE
Travers, Kathryn
GENERAL CHAOS: UNCENSORED ANIMATION
Uchida, Hiroshi
GOLGO 13: QUEEN BEE
Varab, Jefrey
MULAN
Wilton, Lee
GENERAL CHAOS: UNCENSORED ANIMATION
Yasuhiko, Yoshikazu
MOBILE SUIT GUNDAM I
MOBILE SUIT GUNDAM II: SOLDIERS OF SORROW
MOBILE SUIT GUNDAM III: ENCOUNTERS IN SPACE
Yoshimatsu, Takahiro
SLAYERS: THE MOTION PICTURE
Yost, Carey
HERCULES AND XENA THE ANIMATED MOVIE: THE BATTLE FOR MOUNT OLYMPUS

ART DIRECTORS

Barbosa, Carlos
PSYCHO
Ackland-Snow, Andrew
AVENGERS, THE
Adams, Jeff
DANCER, TEXAS POP. 81
Alberti, Alessandro
EIGHTEENTH ANGEL, THE
Alesch, Stephen
PRACTICAL MAGIC
Alteri, Kathy
PRINCE OF EGYPT, THE
An Bing
EAST PALACE, WEST PALACE
Arrizabalaga, Jose Luis
DAY OF THE BEAST, THE
Atwell, Michael
MASK OF ZORRO, THE
VERY BAD THINGS
Au, Alan
WATERBOY, THE
WEDDING SINGER, THE
Austerberry, Paul
HALF BAKED
REAL BLONDE, THE
Baker, Melanie J.
BURN HOLLYWOOD BURN
Ball, Benjamin
THURSDAY
Ballance, Jack
GINGERBREAD MAN, THE
Baryski, Tracey
EBENEZER
Bashford, Anthony
NO ORDINARY LOVE
Beauchene, Natalie
UNDER HEAVEN
Bedford, Louise
LIKE IT IS
Benson, Mark
NOTES FROM UNDERGROUND
Berman, Joanne
PARALLEL SONS
Biaffra
DAY OF THE BEAST, THE
Bider, Tim
TALES FROM A PARALLEL UNIVERSE: EATING PATTERN
TALES FROM A PARALLEL UNIVERSE: GIGA SHADOW
Biscoe, Max
CLAY PIGEONS
NIAGARA NIAGARA
SUICIDE KINGS
Black, James Kyler
AMERICAN HISTORY X
Blanchard, David
PEACEKEEPER, THE
Blaymires, Colin
SPICE WORLD

Mansbridge, Mark
SMALL SOLDIERS
SPHERE
Marcus, Caryn
HIGH ART
Martyn, John
SLIDING DOORS
Masson, Jacqueline R.
IN GOD'S HANDS
Masters, Giles
RAT'S TALE, A
Matteo, Rocco
REBOUND: THE LEGEND OF EARL "THE GOAT" MANIGAULT
Maxey, Caty
REACH THE ROCK
Mays, Richard
HARD RAIN
LETHAL WEAPON 4
SIX DAYS, SEVEN NIGHTS
McAteer, James
BRIDE OF CHUCKY
McCullagh, Tom
I WENT DOWN
McGahey, Michelle
DARK CITY
McGillivray, Brent
BRAM STOKER'S SHADOWBUILDER
McKernin, Kathleen M.
APT PUPIL
NIGHTWATCH
RAT PACK, THE
McKinstry, Jonathan
SPHERE
Meehan, Scott
OVERNIGHT DELIVERY
Mellery, Veronique
MARIE BAIE DES ANGES
Messina, Phil
OUT OF SIGHT
Messina, Philip
ZERO EFFECT
Meyer, Philip J.
EDEN
Michaeli, Dani
CURSE OF THE PUPPET MASTER
Mikula, Molly
LAST DAYS OF DISCO, THE
Milenkovic, Carmen
BLACK LIGHT
Miller, Bruce Alan
U.S. MARSHALS
Miller, Steve
RUSTY: THE GREAT RESCUE
Mills, Vera
RIDE
Miquel, Llorenc
CARLA'S SONG
Moore, Christina
LOVE IS THE DEVIL: STUDY FOR A PORTRAIT OF FRANCIS BACON
Moore, Randy
NEWTON BOYS, THE
Morahan, Jim
BORROWERS, THE
Moroney, Niall
UNDER THE SKIN
Morse, Scott
HERCULES AND XENA THE ANIMATED MOVIE: THE BATTLE FOR MOUNT OLYMPUS
Muhleisen, Georg
RAT'S TALE, A
Munro, Andrew
LEADING MAN, THE
VELVET GOLDMINE
Munro, Christa
HOPE FLOATS
Murakami, Glen
BATMAN/SUPERMAN MOVIE, THE
Murakami, James J.
ENEMY OF THE STATE
Murphy, Angela
REAL HOWARD SPITZ, THE
Naert, Didier
COUSIN BETTE
OGRE, THE
Naito, Akira
SLEEPY EYES OF DEATH: SWORD OF ADVENTURE
VILLAGE OF DREAMS
Nakamura, Mitsuki
MOBILE SUIT GUNDAM I
MOBILE SUIT GUNDAM II: SOLDIERS OF SORROW
MOBILE SUIT GUNDAM III: ENCOUNTERS IN SPACE
Nassau, Robert
LENA'S DREAMS
Naylor, Lynne
HERCULES AND XENA THE ANIMATED MOVIE: THE BATTLE FOR MOUNT OLYMPUS
Nedza, Jim
PATCH ADAMS
Neelands, Pamela
WOUNDED
Neely, Keith
PLAYERS CLUB, THE
Neskoromny, Andrew
DEEP IMPACT
Niemi, Colin
BARNEY'S GREAT ADVENTURE—THE MOVIE
Nishioko, Yoshinobu
SLEEPY EYES OF DEATH: SWORD OF SEDUCTION
Norlin, Eric
AIR BUD: GOLDEN RECEIVER
Nursey, Tom
BRIGHT SHINING LIE, A
O'Brien, William F.
BULWORTH
O'Malley, Christine
MARS
Ockley, Walter
INVADER, THE
Olexiewicz, Dan
AMERICAN HISTORY X
Ong, Ryan
PERMANENT MIDNIGHT
Ono, Hiroshi
KIKI'S DELIVERY SERVICE
Oota, Seiichi
RAZOR: THE SNARE, THE
Outerbridge, Josh
RIVER RED
Outrow, Chuck
LAST ASSASSINS
Pain, Keith
DANGEROUS BEAUTY
LOST IN SPACE
Paine, William
STEEL SHARKS
Papalia, Greg
DR. DOLITTLE
JANE AUSTEN'S MAFIA!
Paredes, Gabriela
NAKED LIES
Parise, Tina
DAVID SEARCHING
Parra, Salvador
MEN WITH GUNS
Pauley, Bob
BUG'S LIFE, A
Pearce, Frazer
GO NOW
LAST SEDUCTION II, THE
Pecur, Nenad
NEMESIS 4: CRY OF ANGELS
Perry, Amy
BRAM STOKER'S THE MUMMY
Phillips, Terri
MILO
Pilcher, Steve
QUEST FOR CAMELOT
Pina, Scott
PECKER
Plauche, Scott
SLUMS OF BEVERLY HILLS
Police, Carol
QUEST FOR CAMELOT
Popa, Doina
LITTLE GHOST
Porupea, Serban
TALISMAN
Powis, Peter
SUB DOWN
Proulx, Real
SNAKE EYES
Pryor, William
RETURN TO SAVAGE BEACH
Rabehl, Ken
SIN AND REDEMPTION
SPREE, THE
Rackard, Anna
BREAK, THE
BUTCHER BOY, THE
Raggett, Mark
INCOGNITO
Rajau, Albert
MAN IN THE IRON MASK, THE
Rea, Bill
KRIPPENDORF'S TRIBE
Repkin, P.
ADVENTURES OF MOWGLI
Reta, Tom
MY GIANT
Reval, Charles
TWISTED
Rhodes, Robin
BREAKOUT
Richards, Randall
BLACK DOG
Richardson, Lucy
ELIZABETH
Ricker, Bradford
SMALL SOLDIERS
Ricker, Mark
MONTANA
Riley, Travis
LAST LIVES
Ritenour, Scott
I STILL KNOW WHAT YOU DID LAST SUMMER
Ritterbusch, Esther
MOTHER AND SON
Robinson, Philip
GOVERNESS, THE
MERRY WAR, A
Rosen, Kathleen
SPANISH PRISONER, THE
Roth, Michael
PHANTASM: OBLIVION
Roux, Emilia
TARZAN AND THE LOST CITY
Sage, Jefferson
ONE TRUE THING
Saito, Masami
NEW ADVENTURES OF KIMBA THE WHITE LION, THE
Sakas, Iliana
HURRICANE STREETS

Saklad, Steve
MERCURY RISING
Santiago, Hugo
X-FILES, THE
Saradjian, Valerie
CLASSIFIED X
Saseki, Osamu
SONATINE
Saturen, Jonathon
SMOKE SIGNALS
Savage, Sue
UNCLE SAM
Schalk, Steven
COLONY, THE
Schamus, Scooter
SIX-STRING SAMURAI
Scharnowski, Udo
HOSTILE WATERS
Scher, Adam
NIGHTWATCH
Schmitt, Patrick
CLASSIFIED X
Scholte, Amy
TEN BENNY
Scott, Helen
DEJA VU
Scrignuoli, Armando
FACE THE EVIL
Seagers, Chris
SAVING PRIVATE RYAN
Sheets, Linda Louise
HIJACKING HOLLYWOOD
Sher, Bob
DOWN IN THE DELTA
TRACKED
Sherman, Jim
WALKING THUNDER
Shields, Darlene
HANGING GARDEN, THE
Shimoishizaka, Narinori
RAZOR: WHO'S GOT THE GOLD?, THE
Shriver, Chris
IMPOSTORS, THE
SIEGE, THE
Sinclair, Stephen
MURDER IN MIND
Skinner, William Ladd
GODZILLA
Smith, Russell J.
HI-LO COUNTRY, THE
Snyder, Dawn
HALLOWEEN H20: TWENTY YEARS LATER
Sosnowski, Janusz
FROM A FAR COUNTRY
Spooner, Michael
QUEST FOR CAMELOT
Stearn, Andrew
BIG HIT, THE
Stein, David
HE GOT GAME
Stensel, Carl
NIGHT AT THE ROXBURY, A
Strathum, Ron
KRAA! THE SEA MONSTER
Suchartanun, Kuladee
BRIGHT SHINING LIE, A
Suchet, Frederique
LIFE OF JESUS, THE
Sullivan, Shawn
CRACKING UP
Sung Pil Park
RED HAWK: WEAPON OF DEATH
Svoboda, Vlasta
WOO
Szabolcs, Janos
REDLINE
Tagliaferro, Patrick
ALMOST HEROES
Tanner, Mark
WAKING NED DEVINE
Tanner, Stacey
NO WAY HOME
Tavoularis, Alex
PARENT TRAP, THE
Taylor, Tom
PAULIE
Taylor, Yvette
INVISIBLE DAD
Terry, Allen
ELMORE LEONARD'S GOLD COAST
Thomas, Dixie
TALK TO ME
Tocci, James
HOLY MAN
Tomkins, Alan
SAVING PRIVATE RYAN
Tougas, Virginia
RATCHET
Truesdale, James
HUSH
MERCURY RISING
SIMPLE PLAN, A
Trujillo, Angela
MILO
Tsukamoto, Shinya
TOKYO FIST
Tutter, Benno
RESCUERS: STORIES OF COURAGE—TWO WOMEN
TERMINAL JUSTICE
URBAN LEGEND
Ulgenciler, Mustafa Ziya
STEAM
Valentine, Tom
DEEP IMPACT
SOLDIER
Vallerin, Christian
LA SEPARATION
Vance, Cindy
NOTES FROM UNDERGROUND
Vega, Edward
FACULTY, THE
TWO FOR TEXAS
Velez, Hector
OUTSIDE OZONA
Vetter, Arlen Jay
THERE'S SOMETHING ABOUT MARY
Vianello, Virginia
STEAM
Viard, Gerard
RONIN
Vinokurov, A.
ADVENTURES OF MOWGLI
Voth, Thomas
WHAT DREAMS MAY COME
Wager, Diane
PLEASANTVILLE
Walley, David
SPICE WORLD
Walsh, Frank
LAND GIRLS, THE
Warnke, John
CITY OF ANGELS
Warren, Tom
CELEBRITY
Warter, Fred
LION KING II: SIMBA'S PRIDE, THE
Watkins, Ken
DEFENDERS: PAYBACK, THE
Welch, Michael D.
STAR KID
Wenham, Peter
FIRELIGHT
West, Bob
STILL BREATHING
Westacott, Paul
LITTLE VOICE
Whitaker, Su
INCOGNITO
White, Mark
SUBSTITUTE 2: SCHOOL'S OUT, THE
Wilkinson, Ron
STAR TREK: INSURRECTION
Wilson, Andrew
DOUBLE EDGE
Wimmer, Isi
INHERITORS, THE
Winkler, Sharon
GUN, A CAR, AND A BLONDE, A
Wintter, Christian
WHAT DREAMS MAY COME
Wong Hok Sun
SHAOLIN TEMPLE, THE
Woodbridge, Patricia
OBJECT OF MY AFFECTION, THE
PERFECT MURDER, A
Woodruff, Donald B.
ENEMY OF THE STATE
Wratten, Alison
MRS. DALLOWAY
Yamazaki, Teru
GONIN
Yarhi, Dan
BLUES BROTHERS 2000
Yee Chung-man
COMRADES, ALMOST A LOVE STORY
Zelinskaya, Vera
MOTHER AND SON
Zeug, Tim
MY BROTHER'S WAR
SPACEJACKED
Zhang Daqian
EMPEROR'S SHADOW, THE
Zuelzke, Mark
SPECIES II

ASSOCIATE PRODUCERS

Acuna, Fernando
CHILE, OBSTINATE MEMORY
Akkad, Malek
HALLOWEEN H20: TWENTY YEARS LATER
Alameda Films
WHO THE HELL IS JULIETTE?
Albert, Jeff
LAND OF THE FREE
Alexander, Haven
BATMAN & MR. FREEZE: SUBZERO
BATMAN/SUPERMAN MOVIE, THE
Aley, Judy
CLASSIFIED X
Alia, Phyllis
WATERBOY, THE
Allen, Jacque
BOOGIE BOY
Andrews, Kacy
PLAYING BY HEART
Antal, Gabi
SUBSPECIES IV: BLOODSTORM
Aoki, Yaem
GOLGO 13: QUEEN BEE
Apostolon, Mary
WHO IS HENRY JAGLOM?
Astadourian, Mary
X-FILES, THE
Austin, Terry
SENSELESS
Auty, Chris
OGRE, THE

Baer, Hanania
PRINCE, THE
Baerwolf, Roger
SMOKE SIGNALS
Ballou, Frank "Cat"
ELMORE LEONARD'S GOLD COAST
Barajas, Eduardo
WHO THE HELL IS JULIETTE?
Barber, Catherine
BABE: PIG IN THE CITY
Bark, Andrew M.
DEAD WATERS
Bass, Ron
STEPMOM
Bates, Kenny
ARMAGEDDON
Bavaro, Peter
POLTERGEIST REPORT: YUYU HAKUSHO
Beal, David
CRACKING UP
Beattie, Stuart
JOEY
Beeks, Steve
MURDER IN MIND
Belefant, Sterling
SUB DOWN
Bellinger, Creighton
RAT PACK, THE
Benz, Hilarie Roope
CLAY PIGEONS
Bernacchi, Roberto
LITTLE GHOST
Bernstein, Jack
JANE AUSTEN'S MAFIA!
Bernstein, Karen
LOU REED: ROCK AND ROLL HEART
Bernstein, Michael
DOUBLE EDGE
Berritt, Shannon Rain
LET'S KILL ALL THE LAWYERS
Bickley, Sam
UNMADE BEDS
Bigwood, James B.
BRIGHT SHINING LIE, A
Bissell, Robin
PLEASANTVILLE
Blackwell, Michele
NAKED ACTS
Blank, Lowell
PERFECT MURDER, A
Blinderman, Jonathan
I LOVE YOU, DON'T TOUCH ME!
Borg, Laurie
BREAK, THE
Boyarsky, Lynne
MY GIANT
Brito, Paulo
CENTRAL STATION
Britting, Jeff
AYN RAND: A SENSE OF LIFE
Bross, Simon
WHO THE HELL IS JULIETTE?
Brownstein, Jerome
HENRY FOOL
Buckley, Lauren
BUFFALO '66
Budd, Robin
SIEGE, THE
Burch, Claire
TIMOTHY LEARY'S DEAD
Cagianut, Thierry
HENRY FOOL
Caldwell, Howell
HOMEGROWN
Cantero, Mate
CHAMBERMAID ON THE TITANIC, THE
Carlton, Martin
REAL THING, THE
Carney, Susan
DOGWATCH
Carr, Warren
WRONGFULLY ACCUSED
Carreras, Chris
LOST IN SPACE
Castro, Emmanuelle
PASSION IN THE DESERT
Chag, Lindsay
INDISCREET
Chan Kiu Ying
ROYAL WARRIORS
Chan Man
SHAOLIN TEMPLE, THE
Chan Wai-yee
COMRADES, ALMOST A LOVE STORY
Chapple, John Paul
HUMAN BOMB
Charpentier, Mark
THERE'S SOMETHING ABOUT MARY
Chesley, Howard
SUB DOWN
Chevalier, Pierre
MARIUS AND JEANNETTE
Chiara, Charles A.
SUICIDE KINGS
Chory, Jim
MIGHTY JOE YOUNG
Chow Chun Tung
MR. NICE GUY
Chu, Bernice M.
NEVADA
Churchill, Pat
SPHERE
Clegg, Allegra
PATCH ADAMS
Clifton, Patrick J.
PLUMP FICTION
Cobb, Melissa
EVER AFTER
Costas, Celia
MEET JOE BLACK
Cote, Glenn Richard
U.S. MARSHALS
Couveinhes, Pierre
OGRE, THE
Craig, Cuba
STILL BREATHING
Crane, Julie B.
PARENT TRAP, THE
Crier, Cammie
INCOGNITO
Cronyn, Christopher
MEET THE DEEDLES
Crosby, Cat
HALLELUJAH!
Cruse, Meredith
I LOVE YOU, DON'T TOUCH ME!
Cuatro Y Medio
WHO THE HELL IS JULIETTE?
Cudworth, Tom
TEN BENNY
Cumming, John
URBAN SAFARI
Cuperman, Rachel
WILDE
Curio, Joe
LAST BIG THING, THE
Curtiss, Alan B.
PATCH ADAMS
Dali, Nigel
DEAD WATERS
Damon, Malia
TEN BENNY
Danziger, Amy Grauman
GIRLS IN PRISON
Davids, Hollace
TIMOTHY LEARY'S DEAD
Davidson, J.C.
INSIDE/OUT
Davis, Rita R.
NAKED ACTS
De Garcillan, Fernando
DAY OF THE BEAST, THE
De La Noy, Kevin
SAVING PRIVATE RYAN
de Macedo, Iona
SOMEWHERE IN THE CITY
De Nardo, Jim
MEN WITH GUNS
De Quetteville, Daryl
LIVING IN PERIL
DeVore, Cain
SAND TRAP
Dickson, Devon
SWEPT FROM THE SEA
Dillon, Patrick
SOMEWHERE IN THE CITY
Dofrin, John
COMEDY'S DIRTIEST DOZEN
Donovan, Brian
LOVE AND DEATH ON LONG ISLAND
Doolan, Jane
MOONDANCE
Douglas, Leroy
I GOT THE HOOK UP
Dowlatabadi
QUEST FOR CAMELOT
Dray, Julia
DIRTY WORK
HALF BAKED
Dresden, Matthew
RUNNING WOMAN, THE
Easton, D. Scott
DEEP IMPACT
Ehrenhalt, Caradoc
NEVADA
Ellis, Howard
DEEP RISING
SIMON BIRCH
Engle, Alex
FERNGULLY 2: THE MAGICAL RESCUE
Epstein, Alex
CHILDREN OF THE CORN V: FIELD OF TERROR
Epstein, Robert J.
LAST BREATH
Eyraud, Matthew R.
I LOVE YOU, DON'T TOUCH ME!
Falco, Tracy
ROUNDERS
Feitag, James T.
DON KING: ONLY IN AMERICA
Ferguson, Scott
TWILIGHT
Ferns, Pat
BRYLCREEM BOYS, THE
Fields, Rob
NAKED ACTS
Filon, Richard
DIARY OF A SERIAL KILLER
Flaherty, Vince
GUN, A CAR, AND A BLONDE, A
Fletcher, Keith
NEWTON BOYS, THE
Fodie, Ian
AIR BUD: GOLDEN RECEIVER
Fontana, Fred
SOLDIER
Fortenberry, Tina L.
GIA

Fortunato, Gina
UNCLE SAM
Foulkes, Robert
TALK TO ME
Franklin, Bruce
WHY DO FOOLS FALL IN LOVE?
Franklin, Scott
PI
Franklin, Spencer
LETHAL WEAPON 4
Fraser, Erin
NIGHT AT THE ROXBURY, A
Fraser Milne, Sheila
GO NOW
Freeman, Doug
ELIA KAZAN: A DIRECTOR'S JOURNEY
Freitag, James M.
RUSH HOUR
French, Fuller
LOVELIFE
Frey, James
KISSING A FOOL
Friedman, Mark
FULL TILT BOOGIE
Frift, Paul
MRS. DALLOWAY
Frydman, Marc
NIL BY MOUTH
Fukunaga, Randall
NOTES FROM UNDERGROUND
Fuller, Kim
SPICE WORLD
Gabbert, Laura
TARANTELLA
Gaines, David
DON KING: ONLY IN AMERICA
Gallo, Janet
BUFFALO '66
Ganz, Martin
HUNTED, THE
Garber, Robert S.
MULAN
Garza, Gerardo
WHO THE HELL IS JULIETTE?
Gassot, Charles
FULL SPEED
Gefter, Marina
NIGHT AND THE MOMENT, THE
Gibgot, Jennifer
JANE AUSTEN'S MAFIA!
Giblin, Peter
TEN BENNY
Gibson, Colin
BABE: PIG IN THE CITY
Giducos, Amila
LAST ASSASSINS
Gilbert, Jo
BRYLCREEM BOYS, THE
Gilbert, Peter
MEN WITH GUNS
Giles, Sara
BRYLCREEM BOYS, THE
REAL HOWARD SPITZ, THE
Gilroy, Grace
BLUES BROTHERS 2000
Giovannetti Jr., James
REACH THE ROCK
Glass, Marina
TARZAN AND THE LOST CITY
Golas, Henry J.
CIVIL ACTION, A
Goode, Christopher
ROUNDERS
Grace, Francey
CHINESE BOX, THE
Graf, Patricia
FALLEN
Grant, Maxwell
JOEY
Graves, Richard
CAN'T HARDLY WAIT
Green, Dominique
TRUCE, THE
Greenberg, Matthew
PROPHECY II, THE
Greenblatt, Ken
SOMEWHERE IN THE CITY
Grillo, William
MEN
Gronow, Fritz
LET'S KILL ALL THE LAWYERS
Gustafson, Gordon
CURSE OF THE PUPPET MASTER
Gwartz, Jennifer
LETHAL WEAPON 4
Haley, Michael
PRIMARY COLORS
Hall, Ian
BRAM STOKER'S SHADOWBUILDER
Hammond, Mark
HANGING GARDEN, THE
Harold, Holly
FERNGULLY 2: THE MAGICAL RESCUE
Hastings, Jay
FATAL PURSUIT
Hawthorne, Nigel
MURDER IN MIND
Healy, Patrick
THERE'S SOMETHING ABOUT MARY
Henry, Jeff
CON, THE
Herlihy, Joyce
MERRY WAR, A
Hinstin, Jacques
UN AIR DE FAMILLE
Hirshenson, Michael
I LOVE YOU, DON'T TOUCH ME!
Hoeber, Erich
MONTANA
Hoeber, Jon
MONTANA
Hoerr, Mark S.
KISSING A FOOL
Holdsworth, Michelle
WATERBOY, THE
WEDDING SINGER, THE
Holloway, Ken
ERNEST IN THE ARMY
Holmes, Guy
LIKE IT IS
Hooper, Elizabeth
HOPE FLOATS
SAND TRAP
Hopkins, Karen Leigh
STEPMOM
Houston, David
HIJACKING HOLLYWOOD
Howie, Betsy
CRACKING UP
Hu, Marcus
BILLY'S HOLLYWOOD SCREEN KISS
Huffam, Mark
SAVING PRIVATE RYAN
Hui, Jojo
COMRADES, ALMOST A LOVE STORY
Jannetta, Michael
BREAKOUT
Jennings, Kevin
OUT OF THE PAST
Jensen, Peter Aalbaek
KINGDOM, PART 2, THE
Jessey, Michael
LIKE IT IS
Johnson, Rick
MEET THE DEEDLES
Jones, Cam
SUB DOWN
Jones, Jake-ann
NAKED ACTS
Jones, Susann
HOME FRIES
Joo, Kiyo
TOKYO FIST
Karol, Deverin
ASYLUM
Karz, Mike
SENSELESS
Kaslow, Harmon
FATAL PURSUIT
Kawai, Shinya
WHEN I CLOSE MY EYES
Khan, Nathaniel
LAST BREATH
Kiefer, Corey
CHOSEN ONE: LEGEND OF THE RAVEN, THE
King, Jonathan
54
Kirch, Doris
HUNTED, THE
Kirkwood, Charles
DREAM FOR AN INSOMNIAC
Kluge, Joseph
DOUBLE EDGE
Kohler, Warren
KISSING A FOOL
Koules, Stephanie
WOO
Kowalski, Kajtek
WHITE RAVEN, THE
Krachman Brothers, The
DEE SNIDER'S STRANGELAND
Kramer, Rain
SAFE MEN
Krantz, Lisa
RUSTY: THE GREAT RESCUE
Krell, Amy
TERMINAL JUSTICE
Kurowa, Hisami
WHEN PIGS FLY
Ladden, Philip A.
DECAMPITATED
Ladden, Steve
DECAMPITATED
Lady, Steph
DR. DOLITTLE
Lamberson, Greg
WEST NEW YORK
Lang, Bruce
BROADWAY DAMAGE
Langford III, James
REAL THING, THE
Lanino, Deborah
TALK TO ME
Larrain, Ricardo
CHILE, OBSTINATE MEMORY
Lasky, Vanessa
NEVADA
Law, Norman
FALLEN ANGELS
Leonetti, John
STORY OF X, THE
Levangie, Gigi
STEPMOM
Levine, J.B.
RUSTY: THE GREAT RESCUE
Levine, Jackie Rubin
MIGHTY JOE YOUNG
Levine, Jeff
SNAKE EYES

Levine, Jody
NEVADA
Levy, David
GINGERBREAD MAN, THE
Lew, James
BOOGIE BOY
Lewis, Eric
DECAMPITATED
Lewis, Keith
BROADWAY DAMAGE
Lewis, Sara
MURDER IN MIND
Licata, Richard
GIA
Lintinger, Melissa
DAY AT THE BEACH
Lippens, Amy
STILL BREATHING
Lonsdale, Timothy
WIDE AWAKE
Lynn, Julie
STILL BREATHING
Mack, Tom
MERCURY RISING
Madragoa Filmes
GENEALOGIES OF A CRIME
Magalhaes, Renata Almeida
TIETA OF AGRESTE
Maloy, Tava R.
MASK OF ZORRO, THE
Mandt, Maura
HIJACKING HOLLYWOOD
Mandt, Michael
HIJACKING HOLLYWOOD
Margolis, Stephen
BRYLCREEM BOYS, THE
Martell, Miara
WAKING NED DEVINE
Martin, Alan
KILLING TIME
Mayeux, Molly M.
SAVIOR
McBride, Elissa
LOUISA MAY ALCOTT'S LITTLE MEN
McClure, Maryann T.
FERNGULLY 2: THE MAGICAL RESCUE
McCullum, Victoria
SCOOBY-DOO ON ZOMBIE ISLAND
McGiffert, David
CIVIL ACTION, A
TWILIGHT
McGonigal, Jennifer
STORY OF X, THE
McKernon, Wendy
TEN BENNY
McLeod, Kevin
CRUISE, THE
McNeil, Lesley
SHOOTING FISH
Meier, Kathleen Bambrick
WILD MAN BLUES
Meister, Bob
MIGHTY KONG, THE
Metzler, Jim
GUN, A CAR, AND A BLONDE, A
Miller, Darren
FATAL PURSUIT
Miller, Marilin
DECAMPITATED
Miller, Victor E.
DECAMPITATED
Mills, Adam
SUICIDE KINGS
Mindel, Anthony
ORGAZMO
Monforton, David
LET'S KILL ALL THE LAWYERS
Moody, Michael
STILL BREATHING
Moore, Liza
KISSING A FOOL
Moore, Scott
SAVIOR
Moose, Amanda
OVERNIGHT DELIVERY
Moreu, Rafael
NEXT STEP, THE
Morgan, Mark
RINGMASTER
Morley, Ted
FIRELIGHT
Morris, Wayne
RUSH HOUR
Moszkowicz, Martin
WRONGFULLY ACCUSED
Murphy, Chris
DOUBLE EDGE
Murphy, Richard G.
KNOCK OFF
Nelson, Jessie
STEPMOM
Nelson, Peter
KNOCK OFF
Newman, Ari
NEXT STOP, WONDERLAND
Nichols, Taylor
NEXT STEP, THE
Nimerfro, Scott
TREKKIES
Norris, Guy
BABE: PIG IN THE CITY
Norton, Terry
SIX DAYS, SEVEN NIGHTS
Novick, Susan E.
DENNIS THE MENACE STRIKES AGAIN
O'Neil, Alice
BREAKOUT
Oleschack, Edward
FRENCH EXIT
Oren, Marc
PRINCE, THE
Otterson, Bill
CRACKING UP
Ottman, John
APT PUPIL
Padlog, Judith
WHO THE HELL IS JULIETTE?
Palmer, Sidney
ALMOST PARTNERS
Palmieri, Michael
SIX DAYS, SEVEN NIGHTS
Perry, Sarah
HALLELUJAH!
Pesmen, Paula Dupre
STEPMOM
Peternel, Timothy
BUFFALO '66
Petro, Debra Michael
DANGEROUS BEAUTY
Pinkerson, Daphne
SLAM
Piskura, Tom
SUB DOWN
Poindexter, Larry
WHITE RAVEN, THE
Porchet, Jean-Louis
SWINDLE, THE
Poropat, Yoli
SOUR GRAPES
Porter, Aldric La'Auli
DANCE WITH ME
Poupaud, Chantal
SEVENTH HEAVEN
Poustie, Sandy
SLIDING DOORS
Raugust, Tony
LAST BIG THING, THE
Reade, Ronnie
BAD MANNERS
Reardon, Lisa
PERFECT MURDER, A
Reddin, Keith
ALARMIST, THE
Reed, Tripp
ALONE IN THE WOODS
Rehwaldt, Frank
LANDLADY, THE
Reutlinger, Ilyse
LETHAL WEAPON 4
Reynolds, Kelly Feldsott
MURDER IN MIND
Rich, Ted
RIGHT CONNECTIONS, THE
Risher, Sara
WRONGFULLY ACCUSED
Ritchie, William
REAL HOWARD SPITZ, THE
Robertson, William Preston
JOHNNY SKIDMARKS
Robison, Eric
MEN WITH GUNS
Rocha, Ron
PRINCE OF EGYPT, THE
Rogers, Jean
RUDOLPH THE RED-NOSED REINDEER: THE MOVIE
Rogers, Steven
STEPMOM
Rohovit, Troy
WALKING THUNDER
Rolmensz, Nathan
CASPER MEETS WENDY
Ross, Glenn
MURDER IN MIND
Rotmensz, Nathan
RICHIE RICH'S CHRISTMAS WISH
Rouan, Jean-Francois
POST COITUM, ANIMAL TRISTE
Ruey, Gerard
SWINDLE, THE
Samojlowicz, Jacek
WHITE RAVEN, THE
Sandston, Pat
ARMAGEDDON
Sayles, Doug
MEN WITH GUNS
Schoolnik, Skip
HOLLYWOOD CONFIDENTIAL
Scoles, Paul
BROADWAY DAMAGE
Scott, Jonathan
DECAMPITATED
Sedgwick, Kyra
MONTANA
Segal, Gail
ARGUING THE WORLD
Seid, Lori E.
HIGH ART
Seydelmann, Susi
MILO
Seydoux, Michael
SAME OLD SONG
Shalev, Osnat
SUE
Shapiro, Jay
APT PUPIL
Shareshian, Steven
BELOVED
STOREFRONT HITCHCOCK

Shaw, Michael
SLAMNATION
Shire, Talia
LANDLADY, THE
Siegel, Steven
NOTES FROM UNDERGROUND
Silver, Cary
ALL DOGS CHRISTMAS CAROL, AN
Silverman, Adam
SCARRED CITY
Sloan, Michael
BURN HOLLYWOOD BURN
Sloane, Ari
TWO FOR TEXAS
Slot, Marianne
KINGDOM, PART 2, THE
Smith, Rita
DIRTY WORK
HALF BAKED
WATERBOY, THE
WEDDING SINGER, THE
Smith-Zimmerman, Tamee
FACULTY, THE
Sorlat, Stephane
CHAMBERMAID ON THE TITANIC, THE
Spiotta, Elena
NEIL SIMON'S THE ODD COUPLE II
Stavis, Gene
ALFRED HITCHCOCK: MASTER OF SUSPENSE
Steuer, Robert B.
GUN, A CAR, AND A BLONDE, A
Stevens, Michael
THIN RED LINE, THE
Stevens, Neal
STEPHEN KING'S THE NIGHT FLIER
Stewart, Patrick
STAR TREK: INSURRECTION
Sturm, Robert
SOMEWHERE IN THE CITY
Suckle, Richard
FALLEN
Suhr, Randy
SMOKE SIGNALS
Sutton, Robert
INSIDE/OUT
Suzuki, Toshio
KIKI'S DELIVERY SERVICE
Suzuki, Yuji
GOLGO 13: QUEEN BEE
Tenkhoff, Karen
HORSE WHISPERER, THE
Theimer, Moses
TRUCKS
Thoeren, Carla
HOSTILE WATERS
Thomas, Bradley
DOUBLE EDGE
Thomas, Neris
COUSIN BETTE
Timlake, Farrell
ORGAZMO
Traub, Tom
BAD MANNERS
Tucker, Tom
LET'S KILL ALL THE LAWYERS
Tucker-Davies, Teresa
PERFECT MURDER, A
Tuorto, Larry
TEN BENNY
Turbow, Darren
MEAN GUNS
Turchi, David
EIGHTEENTH ANGEL, THE
Tuttle, Jeffrey S.
DESTINY OF MARTY FINE, THE
Tweed, Shannon
NAKED LIES

Vicari Jr., Clem
WEST NEW YORK
Victor, Daniel J.
NIAGARA NIAGARA
Vilgrain, Bernard
NIGHT AND THE MOMENT, THE
Voeten, P.J.
BABE: PIG IN THE CITY
Waldburger, Ruth
SAME OLD SONG
Waldman, Barry
ARMAGEDDON
Wall, Julia
HANDS ON A HARDBODY
Wang-Lee, Elizabeth
WRONGFULLY ACCUSED
Warren, Andrew
LAND GIRLS, THE
Warren, Linda
U.S. MARSHALS
Wedaa, Jim
BLACK DOG
Weiner, Melanie
JOHNNY MYSTO BOY WIZARD
LITTLE GHOST
MIDAS TOUCH, THE
Wertheim, Allan
DANCE WITH ME
Whitaker, James
PSYCHO
Wiebel, Martin
CHAMBERMAID ON THE TITANIC, THE
Wilder, Scott
SENSELESS
Williams, Yolonda
CAN'T YOU HEAR THE WIND HOWL?: THE LIFE AND MUSIC OF ROBERT JOHNSON
Winant, Ethel
RONIN
Witham, Andrew
MEAN GUNS
Wong, Max
DISTURBING BEHAVIOR
Woodman, Don
WOUNDED
Wu, Barney
DRAGONS FOREVER
Wu, David
BLACKJACK
Yan T. Wong
MAGNIFICENT WARRIORS
Yeskel, Ronnie
MONTANA
Zackson, Carla
TEN BENNY
Zaslow, Harmon
CATHERINE'S GROVE
Zhang Yukang
EAST PALACE, WEST PALACE
Zoller, Stephen
JACK HIGGINS' THUNDER POINT
JACK HIGGINS' THE WINDSOR PROTOCOL
Zuvk, Nick
KID IN ALADDIN'S PALACE, A

CASTING

Abrams, Rachel
BLADE
Abrams, Shirley
NIGHT VISION
Adams, Marie
YOUNG HERCULES
Adler, Laura
SOULER OPPOSITE, THE

Aibel, Douglas
PRICE ABOVE RUBIES, A
Aikins, Stuart
TRICKS
Alderman, Jane
U.S. MARSHALS
Alter, Julie
GIRLS IN PRISON
Ambrose, Lynn
CAN'T YOU HEAR THE WIND HOWL?: THE LIFE AND MUSIC OF ROBERT JOHNSON
Aquila, Deborah
DEAD MAN ON CAMPUS
Arbusto, Nicole
TARZAN AND THE LOST CITY
Armstrong, Maria
BRAM STOKER'S SHADOWBUILDER
Artz, Mary Gail
ALMOST HEROES
EIGHTEENTH ANGEL, THE
MIGHTY, THE
MUSIC FROM ANOTHER ROOM
RUSHMORE
SIMON BIRCH
Ashton-Barson, Julie
CASPER MEETS WENDY
Bacharach, Jean
CARLA'S SONG
Baino, Marilyn
DEAD WATERS
Baker, Georgina
LIKE IT IS
Baker, Roe
REAL THING, THE
Barden, Kerry
54
HIGH ART
LAST DAYS OF DISCO, THE
REACH THE ROCK
SPANISH PRISONER, THE
Barrett, Alison
BABE: PIG IN THE CITY
Barrett, Nikki
BABE: PIG IN THE CITY
Barry, Matthew
RUSH HOUR
Barson, Julie Ashton
RICHIE RICH'S CHRISTMAS WISH
Baumander, Lewis
FALLING FIRE
Bayonas, Datrina
LIVE FLESH
Beach, Lisa
DISTURBING BEHAVIOR
Beardsall, Sarah
SHOOTING FISH
Becket, Daphne
PASSION IN THE DESERT
Bednarski, Andrzej
WHITE RAVEN, THE
Bestrop, Juel
HORTON FOOTE'S ALONE
PRIMARY COLORS
Biehl, Thomas
RAT'S TALE, A
Bird, Sarah
HOSTILE WATERS
WILDE
Black, Marilyn
NEVADA
Blythe, Teri
MEAN GUNS
NEMESIS 4: CRY OF ANGELS
Bowen, Deidre
CUBE

Brace, John
ALWAYS OUTNUMBERED
HOMEGROWN
Bramon Garcia, Risa
PAULIE
Brinkley, Barbara
ONLY THRILL, THE
Brody Tenner Paskal
KISSING A FOOL
Brooksbank, Steve
ESCAPE, THE
NEVADA
Brouse, Susan
ACT OF WAR
DOUBLE EDGE
MISBEGOTTEN
SHATTERED IMAGE
Brown, Deborah
HI-LIFE
Brown, Ross
HALLOWEEN H20: TWENTY YEARS LATER
Brown-Karman, Jaki
REBOUND: THE LEGEND OF EARL "THE GOAT" MANIGAULT
Bucci, Rosina
BLEEDERS
FACE THE EVIL
JACK LONDON'S THE CALL OF THE WILD: DOG OF THE YUKON
Bullington, Perry
CLOCKMAKER
CURSE OF THE PUPPET MASTER
JOHNNY MYSTO BOY WIZARD
KRAA! THE SEA MONSTER
LITTLE GHOST
MIDAS TOUCH, THE
SECRET KINGDOM, THE
SUBSPECIES IV: BLOODSTORM
TALISMAN
Burch, Jackie
I STILL KNOW WHAT YOU DID LAST SUMMER
JANE AUSTEN'S MAFIA!
KRIPPENDORF'S TRIBE
Burks, Hannah
ALONE IN THE WOODS
Campobasso, Craig
OPERATION DELTA FORCE 2
Cannon, Reuben
DOWN IN THE DELTA
JOHN CARPENTER'S VAMPIRES
WHY DO FOOLS FALL IN LOVE?
Capelier, Margot
RONIN
Cassel, Ferne
JOHNNY SKIDMARKS
KISSING A FOOL
Chadwick, Bette
TRUCKS
Chamian, Denise
SAVING PRIVATE RYAN
SMALL SOLDIERS
Charanne, Brian
BRAVE LITTLE TOASTER GOES TO MARS, THE
Charkam, Beth
HUMAN BOMB
Charon, Nathalie
COUSIN BETTE
Chenoweth, Ellen
AFFLICTION
HORSE WHISPERER, THE
LOLITA
SPHERE
Chesley, Marsha
HANGING GARDEN, THE
Chevalet, Paula
POST COITUM, ANIMAL TRISTE
Chinich, Michael
SIX DAYS, SEVEN NIGHTS
Chopin, Kathleen
AFFLICTION
LAST BREATH
PARALLEL SONS
RETURN TO PARADISE
Church, Karen
I LOVE YOU, DON'T TOUCH ME!
I'LL BE HOME FOR CHRISTMAS
Clydesdale, Ross
BLUES BROTHERS 2000
BRIDE OF CHUCKY
Cohen, Abi
LIKE IT IS
TWENTYFOURSEVEN
Cohen, Barbara
ALMOST HEROES
EIGHTEENTH ANGEL, THE
MIGHTY, THE
MUSIC FROM ANOTHER ROOM
RUSHMORE
SIMON BIRCH
Colbert, Joanna
BLUES BROTHERS 2000
BRIDE OF CHUCKY
HALF BAKED
Coley, Aisha
HE GOT GAME
Collins, Annelise
BEST OF THE BEST: WITHOUT WARNING
Colquhoun, Mary
HOSTILE WATERS
SIEGE, THE
SNAKE EYES
Combris, Anne Laure
LOVE IS THE DEVIL: STUDY FOR A PORTRAIT OF FRANCIS BACON
Comerford, Jon
LOVE AND DEATH ON LONG ISLAND
REAL HOWARD SPITZ, THE
TALES FROM A PARALLEL UNIVERSE: EATING PATTERN
TALES FROM A PARALLEL UNIVERSE: GIGA SHADOW
TALES FROM A PARALLEL UNIVERSE: SUPER NOVA
Corrigan, Mitzi
BODY COUNT
Corsalini, Stephanie
I THINK I DO
Cowitt, Allison
LOST IN SPACE
Crittenden, Dianne
BRIGHT SHINING LIE, A
PALMETTO
SHOOTING FISH
THIN RED LINE, THE
Da Mota, Billy
WALKING THUNDER
Davis, Leonora
LES MISERABLES
Davis, Noel
INCOGNITO
MERLIN
Davis, Penny Perry
BRAM STOKER'S SHADOWBUILDER
Day, Kate
LOVE AND DEATH ON LONG ISLAND
de Laubier, Marie
GADJO DILO
Di Stefano, Pat
TERMINAL JUSTICE
Diamant, Illana
KNOCK OFF
Diamond, Josh
SHOPPING FOR FANGS
DiMatteo, Concetta
ALARMIST, THE
Dixon, Pam
MASK OF ZORRO, THE
MY GIANT
Donnellan, Gaye
UGLY, THE
Dordea, Catalin
SUBSPECIES IV: BLOODSTORM
Dougherty, Marion
LETHAL WEAPON 4
Dowd, Kate
ROYAL DECEIT
Dunlop, Eddie
JOHN CARPENTER'S VAMPIRES
Dunsworth, John
HANGING GARDEN, THE
E/Quality Imaging
NAKED ACTS
Edelman, Abra
AIR BUD: GOLDEN RECEIVER
CALL TO REMEMBER, A
FRENCH EXIT
INVADER, THE
OUTSIDE OZONA
TRICKS
WHEN DANGER FOLLOWS YOU HOME
WOUNDED
Eisenstein, Kathryn
APT PUPIL
Elite Casting
JACK HIGGINS' THUNDER POINT
JACK HIGGINS' MIDNIGHT MAN
JACK HIGGINS' THE WINDSOR PROTOCOL
Elite Productions
BLEEDERS
Ettinger, Wendy
CARLA'S SONG
Fay, Maura
JOEY
MR. NICE GUY
UGLY, THE
Feldman, Leslee
ANTZ
Fels, Betsy
MILO
Fennessy, Kevin
ALL THE RAGE
Fenton, Mike
LAND OF THE FREE
LOST IN SPACE
Feuer, Howard
BELOVED
DESPERATE MEASURES
PSYCHO
TRUMAN SHOW, THE
Feyder, Anna
ERNEST IN THE ARMY
Figgis, Susie
AVENGERS, THE
BUTCHER BOY, THE
PHOTOGRAPHING FAIRIES
VELVET GOLDMINE
Filderman, Alan
BROADWAY DAMAGE
Finger, Leonard
STEPHEN KING'S THE NIGHT FLIER
Finn, Mali
HIT ME
YOUR FRIENDS & NEIGHBORS
Finn, Sarah
PAULIE
Fletcher, Jack
KIKI'S DELIVERY SERVICE
Fogel, Alexa L.
LAST BREATH
Forrest, Susan
ELVIS MEETS NIXON
Fox, Celestia
MRS. DALLOWAY

SOLDIER'S DAUGHTER NEVER CRIES, A
TARZAN AND THE LOST CITY
Foy III, Eddie
MIGHTY KONG, THE
Foy, Nancy
BURN HOLLYWOOD BURN
DR. DOLITTLE
PENTAGON WARS, THE
RAT PACK, THE
Frank Sant Cast
MARIE BAIE DES ANGES
Freeman, Lauris
KNOCK OFF
Fronk, Dean E.
LIVING IN PERIL
WHEN TIME EXPIRES
Fronk, Dean
ASYLUM
Fryklund, Renate
JERUSALEM
Fuhrer, Chelsea
HENRY FOOL
Garcia, Risa Bramon
CLAY PIGEONS
HARD RAIN
Gardner, Suzanne
HENRY: PORTRAIT OF A SERIAL KILLER PART 2
Gerussi, Tina
HALF BAKED
IN HIS FATHER'S SHOES
Gervais, Marion
MARIE BAIE DES ANGES
Gilbert, Jo
BRYLCREEM BOYS, THE
Gilburne, Jessica
SCARRED CITY
Glaser, Jan
CLUB VAMPIRE
DETONATOR
MY BROTHER'S WAR
RUNNING WOMAN, THE
SPACEJACKED
STRAY BULLET
WATCHERS REBORN
Gold, Nina
BORROWERS, THE
Goldberg, Mary
DEEP RISING
SIEGE, THE
Goldstein, Libby
GIA
RAGE, THE
Goodman, Elisa
AIR BUD: GOLDEN RECEIVER
CALL TO REMEMBER, A
FRENCH EXIT
INVADER, THE
OUTSIDE OZONA
TRICKS
WHEN DANGER FOLLOWS YOU HOME
WOUNDED
Gorin, Stephanie
BLACK LIGHT
Goulder, Ann
HAPPINESS
Grant, Jacques
FULL SPEED
Green-Keyes, Nancy
RUSH HOUR
Greenberg, Jeff
NIGHT AT THE ROXBURY, A
Greenberg, Jill
GREAT EXPECTATIONS
Griffith, Aaron
CATHERINE'S GROVE
LANDLADY, THE
Groff, Lee Ann
DEE SNIDER'S STRANGELAND
PRINCE VALIANT
Grossman, Iris
GEORGE WALLACE
Guiche, Michelle
SLIDING DOORS
Guillermin, Michelle
LITTLE BOY BLUE
REDLINE
Guish, Michelle
GOVERNESS, THE
MERRY WAR, A
SHAKESPEARE IN LOVE
Hancock, Nancy
WEST NEW YORK
Hardin, Kimberly
PLAYERS CLUB, THE
Harris, Phaedra
BODY COUNT
Havens, Geno
REAL THING, THE
TOP OF THE WORLD
Henderson-Martin, Cathy
IN GOD'S HANDS
LEWIS & CLARK & GEORGE
Henderson/Zuckerman
LAST LIVES
Henry, Noble
ALONE IN THE WOODS
Hicks, Richard
MONTANA
PERMANENT MIDNIGHT
Hidalgo, Mary
BRAVE LITTLE TOASTER GOES TO MARS, THE
BUG'S LIFE, A
Hill, Owens
POLISH WEDDING
Hill/Howard-Field
DENNIS THE MENACE STRIKES AGAIN
Hiller, Randi
CLAY PIGEONS
HARD RAIN
PAULIE
Hopkins, Billy
54
HIGH ART
HUSH
LAST DAYS OF DISCO, THE
REACH THE ROCK
SPANISH PRISONER, THE
Hopkins-Smith-Barden
PECKER
Hubbard, John
BREAK, THE
FIRELIGHT
INFORMANT, THE
KID IN ALADDIN'S PALACE, A
OLIVER TWIST
THEORY OF FLIGHT
WAKING NED DEVINE
Hubbard, Ros
BREAK, THE
FIRELIGHT
INFORMANT, THE
KID IN ALADDIN'S PALACE, A
OLIVER TWIST
THEORY OF FLIGHT
WAKING NED DEVINE
Hughs Moss
SCARRED CITY
Huzzar, Elaine J.
HOLLYWOOD CONFIDENTIAL
PROPOSITION, THE
Hymson-Ayer, Beth
YOUNG HERCULES
Ibsen, Nora
MENDEL
Ireland, Simone
ELIZABETH
GO NOW
HILARY AND JACKIE
INNOCENT SLEEP, THE
SPICE WORLD
UNDER THE SKIN
Isaksen, Eva
JUNK MAIL
Isola, Camilla-Valentine
TALK OF ANGELS
Jacoby, Ellen
LET'S TALK ABOUT SEX
Jaffe, Sheila
BAD MANNERS
MURDER IN MIND
NEXT STOP, WONDERLAND
NIAGARA NIAGARA
SLUMS OF BEVERLY HILLS
TWO GIRLS AND A GUY
Jannetta, Michael
UNDERTAKER'S WEDDING, THE
Jaugey, Florence
CARLA'S SONG
Jay, Jina
GENERAL, THE
Jayawardena, Jina
LEADING MAN, THE
Joffrey, Jennifer
JACK HIGGINS' ON DANGEROUS GROUND
John, Brace
WILD THINGS
John, Priscilla
EVER AFTER
LITTLE VOICE
Johnson, Amanda Mackey
HOLY MAN
OPPOSITE OF SEX, THE
PRACTICAL MAGIC
RONIN
Johnson, Junie Lowry
GIA
SENSELESS
Johnston, Paige
BODY COUNT
Jones, Allison
DEEP IMPACT
Jones, Sue
NIL BY MOUTH
RONIN
Kanner, Ellie
EDEN
ONLY THRILL, THE
Kaufman, Avy
CIVIL ACTION, A
MONUMENT AVE.
REAL BLONDE, THE
ROUNDERS
SAFE MEN
WIDE AWAKE
Kennedy, Lora
DANCE WITH ME
Kent, Rody
CAN'T YOU HEAR THE WIND HOWL?: THE LIFE AND MUSIC OF ROBERT JOHNSON
Kenyon, Andrea
DEAD END
Kes, Risa
BEYOND SILENCE
Kilpatrick, Tracy
LOLITA
SHADRACH
King, Christine
NAPOLEON
Klein, Beth
ELVIS MEETS NIXON
FACE DOWN

MY VERY BEST FRIEND
PRONTO
RIGHT CONNECTIONS, THE
SIN AND REDEMPTION
TRACKED

Klein, Heidi
LOVER GIRL
PASS, THE

Klein, Robin
LOVER GIRL
PASS, THE

Klohn, Thom
ORGAZMO
RUSTY: THE GREAT RESCUE

Klopper, Nancy
MERCURY RISING

Kohler, Allison Gordon
FIRESTORM

Kondratyeva, Ekaterina
DEAD WATERS

Koster, Dorothy
BOYS WILL BE BOYS

Kozak, Sid
SNOWBOUND

Kress, Ronna
BARNEY'S GREAT ADVENTURE—THE MOVIE
LAWN DOGS

Kressel, Lynn
MERLIN
QUICKSILVER HIGHWAY

Kurtzman, Wendy
DANGEROUS BEAUTY
DIGGING TO CHINA
REPLACEMENT KILLERS, THE
SUICIDE KINGS

La Padura, Jason
DEFENDERS: PAYBACK, THE

Lacy, Ross
SIX-STRING SAMURAI

Lafosse, Marie-Christine
DISENCHANTED, THE

Lamb, Irene
DEJA VU
FROM A FAR COUNTRY

Lambert, Ruth
BUG'S LIFE, A

Lande, Ellen
MENDEL

Landsburg, Shana
DESTINY OF MARTY FINE, THE
SNOWBOUND
SOULER OPPOSITE, THE

Lang, Michelle
RETROACTIVE

Le Saint, Claire
POST COITUM, ANIMAL TRISTE

Lecker, Marjorie
HOSTILE INTENT
WHITE RAVEN, THE

Lee, Moonyeen
TARZAN AND THE LOST CITY

Lee, Tony
CAUGHT UP

Leff, Gabriela
RIVER RED

Lennon-Smith, Anna
HEAVEN'S BURNING

Levitt, Heidi
CHINESE BOX, THE
HUSH
WHAT DREAMS MAY COME

Levy, Bruno
ARTEMISIA

Lewis, Ellen
IMPOSTORS, THE
MEET JOE BLACK
PLEASANTVILLE
PRIMARY COLORS
STEPMOM
WHEN PIGS FLY

Liberman, Meg
PLAYING BY HEART

Liberman/Hirschfeld
SOUR GRAPES
X-FILES, THE

Lina Todd Casting
CHARLIE HOBOKEN

Lindsay-Stewart, Karen
MADELINE

Lippens, Amy
MEET THE DEEDLES
STILL BREATHING

Liroff, Marci
JACK FROST

Lockett, Stevie "Black"
I GOT THE HOOK UP

Long, Carolyn
ALARMIST, THE

Lowry, Linda
ALWAYS OUTNUMBERED
HOMEGROWN
WILD THINGS

Lowry-Johnson, Junie
BASEKETBALL
STAR TREK: INSURRECTION

Lyons, John
BIG LEBOWSKI, THE

MacCorkle, Pat
LOVE WALKED IN

MacDonald, Bob
CLOCKMAKER
JOHNNY MYSTO BOY WIZARD
KRAA! THE SEA MONSTER
LITTLE GHOST
MIDAS TOUCH, THE
SECRET KINGDOM, THE

MacDonald, Robert
CURSE OF THE PUPPET MASTER
SUBSPECIES IV: BLOODSTORM
TALISMAN

Machado, Sergio
CENTRAL STATION

Mack Knight, Eileen
RIDE

Mackey, Amanda
MAN IN THE IRON MASK, THE
PERFECT MURDER, A
SPECIES II
U.S. MARSHALS

Maisler, Francine
APT PUPIL
HOW STELLA GOT HER GROOVE BACK
OUT OF SIGHT
YOU'VE GOT MAIL

Malherbe, Annet
DRESS, THE

Maney, Ann
LAST BIG THING, THE

Mann, Gloria
BREAKOUT

Mantscheff, Heta
MENDEL

Manwiller, Debi
DIARY OF A SERIAL KILLER
PHOENIX

Margaret, Mary
COLONY, THE

Margiotta, Karen
COLONY, THE
ELMORE LEONARD'S GOLD COAST
LOUISA MAY ALCOTT'S LITTLE MEN

Margiotta, Mary
COUSIN BETTE
ELMORE LEONARD'S GOLD COAST
LOUISA MAY ALCOTT'S LITTLE MEN

Marin, Mindy
DANGEROUS BEAUTY
SOLDIER
WHEN TRUMPETS FADE

Martinez, Lizzie Curry
MEN WITH GUNS

Marx, Elizabeth
NEXT STEP, THE

Massalas, Valorie
GODS AND MONSTERS

Maura Fay & Associates
TWISTED
UGLY, THE

Mayrs, Coreen
DISTURBING BEHAVIOR
SMOKE SIGNALS

McCaffrey, Valerie
AMERICAN HISTORY X
DARK CITY

McCann, Hank
BOOGIE BOY
HOSTILE INTENT

McCarthy, Anne
CAN'T HARDLY WAIT
FACULTY, THE

McCarthy, Jeanne
CLOCKWATCHERS

McCorkle, Pat
ALMOST PARTNERS

McGann, Hank
BONE DADDY

McGarry, Fiona
I WENT DOWN

McIsaac, Chelsea
CAPTIVE

McSweeney, Tom
ACT OF WAR

Megalarge Casting
I GOT THE HOOK UP

Meyer, Ellen
TRUCKS

Meyers, D. Lynn
CROSSING FIELDS

Mickelson, Pam Dixon
MAJOR LEAGUE: BACK TO THE MINORS
MIGHTY JOE YOUNG

Middleton, Joseph
SLAPPY AND THE STINKERS

Miller, Vera
BLEEDERS
JACK LONDON'S THE CALL OF THE WILD: DOG OF THE YUKON
PEACEKEEPER, THE

Mills, Marion
BLACK LIGHT

Mitchell, Ed
CHILDREN OF THE CORN V: FIELD OF TERROR

Mitchell, Robyn M.
REBOUND: THE LEGEND OF EARL "THE GOAT" MANIGAULT

Moidon, Frederique
SEVENTH HEAVEN

Moiselle, Nuala
SUMMER FLING

Montgomery, Rick
THERE'S SOMETHING ABOUT MARY

Moran, Pat
PECKER
SPECIES II

Morison, Akiko
URBAN SAFARI

Musarra, Penny
ATOMIC DOG
CON, THE
HUNTED, THE

Mussenden, Roger
BIG HIT, THE
DIRTY WORK
I'LL BE HOME FOR CHRISTMAS
SUICIDE KINGS

WATERBOY, THE
WEDDING SINGER, THE
Nadler, Lauren
TEN BENNY
Newberg, Bruce H.
MAKER, THE
Newburg, Bruce H.
LOVELIFE
Nickel, Mr.
STEEL SHARKS
O'Kane, Deirdre
I WENT DOWN
Oberst, Gary
PLUMP FICTION
TRUCKS
Oliver, Dave
CHOSEN ONE: LEGEND OF THE RAVEN, THE
Outcast
RAT'S TALE, A
Pagano, Richard
DIARY OF A SERIAL KILLER
NIGHTWATCH
ONE TRUE THING
PHOENIX
WITHOUT LIMITS
Papsidera, John
ANOTHER DAY IN PARADISE
CHICAGO CAB
URBAN LEGEND
Parasyn, Lisa
BONE DADDY
Pariss, Susie
DAD SAVAGE
Parks, Ellen
TARANTELLA
Paul, Joey
FATAL PURSUIT
INTERLOCKED: THRILLED TO DEATH
3 NINJAS: HIGH NOON AT MEGA MOUNTAIN
Paulsen, Kjersti
JUNK MAIL
Pemrick, Donald Paul
BRYLCREEM BOYS, THE
LIVING IN PERIL
WHEN TIME EXPIRES
Pereira, Vanessa
DARK CITY
ELIZABETH
HILARY AND JACKIE
SPICE WORLD
UNDER THE SKIN
Perry, Penny
BREAST MEN
Peyton, Keri
WITHOUT LIMITS
Phillips, Don
NEWTON BOYS, THE
PHANTOMS
Pianico, Stacey
COURTING COURTNEY
Pietila, Bonita
NOTES FROM UNDERGROUND
Pilu, Lissa
POST COITUM, ANIMAL TRISTE
Prior, Andy
SWEPT FROM THE SEA
Prototype Casting
WELCOME TO WOOP WOOP
Rack, Pamela
FACE THE EVIL
MEN
Ray, Johanna
DISAPPEARANCE OF KEVIN JOHNSON, THE
HOLLYWOOD CONFIDENTIAL
PROPOSITION, THE
Ray, Robyn
CHILDREN OF THE CORN V: FIELD OF TERROR
Rea, Karen
UNCLE SAM
WRONGFULLY ACCUSED
Reed-Humes, Robi
DON KING: ONLY IN AMERICA
WOO
Reich, Llora
COUSIN BETTE
Rene, Keely
LOLIDA 2000
Rennell, Gretchen
HORSE WHISPERER, THE
Rhodes, Shari
SLAPPY AND THE STINKERS
Richmond, Lyn
STEPHEN KING'S THE NIGHT FLIER
Romano, Andrea
BATMAN & MR. FREEZE: SUBZERO
Rona, Nadia
BLEEDERS
JACK LONDON'S THE CALL OF THE WILD: DOG OF THE YUKON
Rose, Patricia
PRINCE, THE
Rosenberg, Alex
NEIL SIMON'S THE ODD COUPLE II
Rosenthal, Laura
CELEBRITY
NO LOOKING BACK
VELVET GOLDMINE
Rubin, David
CITY OF ANGELS
FALLEN
NEGOTIATOR, THE
Rudolph, Elisabeth
BLACK DOG
Sandrich, Cathy
HOLY MAN
MAN IN THE IRON MASK, THE
OPPOSITE OF SEX, THE
PERFECT MURDER, A
PRACTICAL MAGIC
RONIN
SPECIES II
U.S. MARSHALS
Sands, Jill Greenburg
HOME FRIES
Sandvik, Liv
JUNK MAIL
Savenkoff, Elizabeth Carol
ADVENTURES OF MOWGLI
Schiff, Laura
LAST ASSASSINS
Selway, Mary
DANCING AT LUGHNASA
DANGEROUS BEAUTY
LOST IN SPACE
TALK OF ANGELS
Selzer, Julie
TWO FOR TEXAS
Sevleyan, Maya
MARIUS AND JEANNETTE
Shaner, Dan
CON, THE
Shannon-Smith, Jane
NEIL SIMON'S THE ODD COUPLE II
Sheaks, Christine
HALLOWEEN H20: TWENTY YEARS LATER
LOS LOCOS
THURSDAY
Shopmaker, Susan
HURRICANE STREETS
RATCHET
Siciliano, Pat
LOLIDA 2000
Sikes, Mark
LITTLE BIGFOOT 2: THE JOURNEY HOME
Simkin, Margery
FEAR AND LOATHING IN LAS VEGAS
LIVING OUT LOUD
Sinclair, Caroline
SOMEWHERE IN THE CITY
Sinclair, Winsome
BELLY
Skoff, Melissa
BILLBOARD DAD
DREAM FOR AN INSOMNIAC
Slater, Mary Jo
ESCAPE, THE
GINGERBREAD MAN, THE
LET'S TALK ABOUT SEX
MAKER, THE
RUDOLPH THE RED-NOSED REINDEER: THE MOVIE
SPREE, THE
12 ANGRY MEN
Smith, Laurel
DANCER, TEXAS POP. 81
DECEIVER
DOGWATCH
UNDER HEAVEN
Smith, Suzanne
54
HIGH ART
LAST DAYS OF DISCO, THE
REACH THE ROCK
SPANISH PRISONER, THE
Snik, Jeannette
CHARACTER
Speer, Wendell
WHITE RAVEN, THE
Starger, Ilene
PARENT TRAP, THE
SIMPLE PLAN, A
TWILIGHT
Stern, Adrienne
TARANTELLA
WHATEVER
Stevens, Gail
SWEPT FROM THE SEA
Stewart, Karen Lindsay
SUMMER FLING
Stone, Paddy
DAD SAVAGE
Surma, Ron
BASEKETBALL
STAR TREK: INSURRECTION
Swee, Daniel
OBJECT OF MY AFFECTION, THE
Syson, Lucinda
EVER AFTER
Tarzia, James F.
BEST OF THE BEST: WITHOUT WARNING
Taylor, Juliet
CELEBRITY
MEET JOE BLACK
PRIMARY COLORS
Testa, Michael
DANCER, TEXAS POP. 81
Tetzlaff, Carmen
RINGMASTER
Thaler, Todd
MR. JEALOUSY
RESCUERS: STORIES OF COURAGE—TWO COUPLES
RESCUERS: STORIES OF COURAGE—TWO WOMEN
Theimer, Moses
TRUCKS
Thomas, Victoria
ENEMY OF THE STATE
HI-LO COUNTRY, THE
Tillman, Mark
PROPHECY II, THE

Timmerman, Bonnie
ARMAGEDDON
SIX DAYS, SEVEN NIGHTS
Todd, Lina
SUBSTITUTE 2: SCHOOL'S OUT, THE
Tomey, Tricia
SOLDIER'S DAUGHTER NEVER CRIES, A
Trevis, Sarah
REGENERATION
Trumel, Annette
SOLDIER'S DAUGHTER NEVER CRIES, A
Van de Yacht, Bernard
SWAN PRINCESS III: AND THE MYSTERY OF THE ENCHANTED TREASURE, THE
Vernieu, Mary
ABERRATION
CAN'T HARDLY WAIT
FACULTY, THE
SAVIOR
SLAPPY AND THE STINKERS
ZERO EFFECT
Vezina, Myriam
DEAD END
Vogel, Barbara
INHERITORS, THE
Walken & Jaffe Casting
ILLTOWN
Walken, Georgianne
BAD MANNERS
MURDER IN MIND
NEXT STOP, WONDERLAND
NIAGARA NIAGARA
SLUMS OF BEVERLY HILLS
TWO GIRLS AND A GUY
Walker, Heidi
EDEN
Walker, Lindsay
INVADER, THE
Wallin, Katy
ORGAZMO
RUSTY: THE GREAT RESCUE
Webster, April
GODZILLA
Weisberg, Alyssa
ABERRATION
Weitz, Jory
BLADE
Welden, Rosemary
BRAM STOKER'S THE MUMMY
LOVE TO KILL
MISBEGOTTEN
Willett, Susan
HOME BEFORE DARK
Williams, Yolanda
CAN'T YOU HEAR THE WIND HOWL?: THE LIFE AND MUSIC OF ROBERT JOHNSON
Wishingrad, Alysa
PRONTO
Wolifson, Shauna
DARK CITY
Wright, Barbara
RUGRATS MOVIE, THE
Yeskel, Ronnie
HOPE FLOATS
MONTANA
PERMANENT MIDNIGHT
SLAPPY AND THE STINKERS
Yoshikawa, Takefumi
FIREWORKS
Zane, Debra
HOME FRIES
PATCH ADAMS
PLEASANTVILLE
Zimmerman, Jeremy
LAND GIRLS, THE
Zuckerbrod, Gary
RESCUERS: STORIES OF COURAGE—TWO COUPLES
Zuckerman, Dori
IN GOD'S HANDS
LEWIS & CLARK & GEORGE

CHOREOGRAPHERS

Anderson, Lea
VELVET GOLDMINE
Aouni, Walid
DESTINY
Bolger, David
DANCING AT LUGHNASA
Butler, Jean
BRYLCREEM BOYS, THE
Byrd, Donald
NEXT STEP, THE
Clark, Russell
FALLEN
WHY DO FOOLS FALL IN LOVE?
Curtis, Liz
DANCE WITH ME
Daily, Grainne
SPACEJACKED
Eastside, Lori
54
Fabris, Bill
BOYS IN LOVE 2
Garcia, Eddie
RIGHT CONNECTIONS, THE
Gatson Jr., Frank
LIVING OUT LOUD
Gibson, Jane
FIRELIGHT
Glover, Savion
RAT PACK, THE
Kellogg, Mary Ann
NIGHT AT THE ROXBURY, A
Lather, Barry
BLUES BROTHERS 2000
Laughlin, Joe
WHEN DANGER FOLLOWS YOU HOME
Lefton, Sue
ELIZABETH
Matthews, Daryl
DANCE WITH ME
McIntyre, Dianne
BELOVED
O'Brien-Kent, Mairead
WRONGFULLY ACCUSED
Ross, Justin
PLAN B
Sacks, Quinny
SHAKESPEARE IN LOVE
Shankman, Adam
ALMOST HEROES

CINEMATOGRAPHERS

Aaronson, Reuben
PARALYZING FEAR: THE STORY OF POLIO IN AMERICA, A
Ackerman, Thomas E.
EIGHTEENTH ANGEL, THE
Ackroyd, Barry
CARLA'S SONG
UNDER THE SKIN
Acord, Lance
BUFFALO '66
Adefarasin, Remi
ELIZABETH
HUMAN BOMB
SLIDING DOORS
Ahern, Lloyd
CAN'T HARDLY WAIT
Aim, Pierre
MADELINE
Albert, Arthur
DIRTY WORK
Alberti, Maryse
HAPPINESS
VELVET GOLDMINE
Alexandru, Dan
LITTLE GHOST
Anderson, Jamie
NEIL SIMON'S THE ODD COUPLE II
SMALL SOLDIERS
Anderson, John
SLAMNATION
Archambault, Georges
DEAD END
LOUISA MAY ALCOTT'S LITTLE MEN
Arguelles, Fernando
SKIN & BONE
Aronovich, Ricardo
EL CHE: INVESTIGATING A LEGEND
Aronson, John
IN GOD'S HANDS
MURDER IN MIND
Astakhov, Serguei
BROTHER
Astrakhan, Yoram
PLAN B
Atherton, Howard
DEEP RISING
LOLITA
Baca-Asay, Joaquin
RATCHET
Baer, Hanania
DEJA VU
PRINCE, THE
Baffa, Christopher
SUICIDE KINGS
Bailey, John
ALWAYS OUTNUMBERED
LIVING OUT LOUD
Ballhaus, Michael
PRIMARY COLORS
Banks, Larry
SUBSTITUTE 2: SCHOOL'S OUT, THE
Barrett, Michael
SAFE MEN
Barrow, Michael
WHATEVER
Bartkowiak, Andrzej
LETHAL WEAPON 4
U.S. MARSHALS
Bartle, James
TWISTED
Bartley, John S.
DISTURBING BEHAVIOR
TRICKS
Bartoli, Adolfo
SUBSPECIES IV: BLOODSTORM
Basulto, Armando
LENA'S DREAMS
NO ORDINARY LOVE
Baszak, Miroslaw
RESCUERS: STORIES OF COURAGE—TWO COUPLES
RESCUERS: STORIES OF COURAGE—TWO WOMEN
Bava, Mario
RABID DOGS
Bazelli, Bojan
DANGEROUS BEAUTY
Beato, Affonso
INFORMANT, THE
LIVE FLESH
PRONTO
Belcher, Peter
OPERATION DELTA FORCE 2
Benison, Peter
JACK HIGGINS' THUNDER POINT
JACK HIGGINS' THE WINDSOR PROTOCOL

Duba, Martin
FORGOTTEN LIGHT
Dufaux, Guy
POLISH WEDDING
Dunlop, Alan
INNOCENT SLEEP, THE
Dunn, Andrew
EVER AFTER
HUSH
PRACTICAL MAGIC
Dupouey, Pierre
POST COITUM, ANIMAL TRISTE
Eckert, Gary
WALKING THUNDER
Edwards, Eric
ANOTHER DAY IN PARADISE
CLAY PIGEONS
Egger, Edgar
BREAKOUT
UNDERTAKER'S WEDDING, THE
Emerson, Susan
MEN
Escoffier, Jean-Yves
ROUNDERS
Estus, Boyd
ARGUING THE WORLD
Evans, Blake T.
3 NINJAS: HIGH NOON AT MEGA MOUNTAIN
Evans, Kelly
LET'S TALK ABOUT SEX
Evans, Rodney
UNVEILING, THE
Fabre, Jean-Marc
SOLDIER'S DAUGHTER NEVER CRIES, A
Faloona, Christopher
DENNIS THE MENACE STRIKES AGAIN
Farkas, Pedro
OYSTER AND THE WIND, THE
FauntLeRoy, Don E.
ONLY THRILL, THE
Feitshans IV, Buzz
BLACK DOG
Felperlaan, Marc
DRESS, THE
Fenner, John
BORROWERS, THE
Fernberger, Peter B.
ALMOST PARTNERS
Filac, Vilko
CHINESE BOX, THE
Finney, Gavin
DAD SAVAGE
Fiore, Mauro
BILLBOARD DAD
Floquet, Anton
HIJACKING HOLLYWOOD
Flynt, Brendan C.
RUN FOR COVER
Fortunato, Ron
NIL BY MOUTH
ONE TOUGH COP
Foster, John
MY KNEES WERE JUMPING: REMEMBERING THE KINDERTRANSPORTS
Fraisse, Robert
RONIN
Freeman, Jonathan
FALLING FIRE
Fuhrer, Martin
WILDE
Fujimoto, Tak
BELOVED
Fukushima, Toshiyuki
POLTERGEIST REPORT: YUYU HAKUSHO
Fyodorov, Alexei
MOTHER AND SON

Gainer, Steve
CLUB VAMPIRE
Gallo, Christopher
FULL TILT BOOGIE
Garcia, Rodrigo
GIA
Gardiner, Greg
HOMEGROWN
Gaviria, Carlos
GUN, A CAR, AND A BLONDE, A
Geddes, David
CALL TO REMEMBER, A
Georgevich, Dejan
CROSSING FIELDS
Gibson, Sue
MRS. DALLOWAY
Gill, Pierre
LOS LOCOS
Gillham, Dan
NOTES FROM UNDERGROUND
Gilpin, Paul
TARZAN AND THE LOST CITY
Gioseffi, Kenny
ORGAZMO
Gissen, Amy
BOYS IN LOVE 2
Giurato, Blasco
PEREIRA DECLARES
Glennon, James
MY VERY BEST FRIEND
Goi, Michael
FIXER, THE
Goozee, Gerald R.
HOSTILE INTENT
Gordon, Mark J.
HIT ME
Gordon, Melinda Sue
DESTINY OF MARTY FINE, THE
Gravelle, Barry
BLEEDERS
FACE THE EVIL
LOST WORLD, THE
Graver, Gary
INVISIBLE DAD
INVISIBLE MOM
Gray, Mark W.
SAND TRAP
Greatrex, Richard
SHAKESPEARE IN LOVE
Greenberg, Adam
RUSH HOUR
SPHERE
Greenberg, Bryan
STEEL SHARKS
Greenfield-Sanders, Timothy
LOU REED: ROCK AND ROLL HEART
Gruszynski, Alexander
54
Gu Changwei
GINGERBREAD MAN, THE
HURLYBURLY
Guichard, Eric
GADJO DILO
Guilford, Allen
ABERRATION
Hagen, Ron
LITTLE BOY BLUE
Hall, Conrad L.
CIVIL ACTION, A
WITHOUT LIMITS
Hammer, Victor
SOUR GRAPES
Harlow, Mike
LAVENDER LIMELIGHT: LESBIANS IN FILM
Hartowicz, Irek
OUTSIDE OZONA

Heinl, Bernd
JOHNNY SKIDMARKS
SUMMER FLING
Heller, Brian
HOME BEFORE DARK
Helling, Paul
TIMOTHY LEARY'S DEAD
Hennings, David
MEET THE DEEDLES
VERY BAD THINGS
Henriques, Samuel
FARM: ANGOLA, U.S.A., THE
Herrington, David
BLUES BROTHERS 2000
Hobson, Daf
GO NOW
Holender, Adam
PRICE ABOVE RUBIES, A
WIDE AWAKE
Holland, Keith
TRUCKS
Holmes Jr., Chris
TERMINAL JUSTICE
Holosko, John
FACE DOWN
Holzman, Ernest
DOUBLE EDGE
Honisch, Alexander
KILLER CONDOM, THE
Howe, Alex
DEAD WATERS
Howe, Matthew M.
PARALLEL SONS
Hudececk, Robert A.
WHEN DANGER FOLLOWS YOU HOME
Hullard, Keith
NAKED LIES
Hurlbut, Shane
RAT PACK, THE
Hurwitz, Tom
WILD MAN BLUES
Idziak, Slawomir
FROM A FAR COUNTRY
MEN WITH GUNS
Ikegami, Motoaki
DRAGON BALL Z THE MOVIE: DEAD ZONE
DRAGON BALL Z THE MOVIE: THE TREE OF MIGHT
DRAGON BALL Z THE MOVIE: THE WORLD'S STRONGEST
Irwin, Mark
MISBEGOTTEN
THERE'S SOMETHING ABOUT MARY
Isaacks, Levie
NORTH SHORE FISH
Ito, Hiroshi
JUNK FOOD
Ivanov, Stefan
GENEALOGIES OF A CRIME
James, Peter
NEWTON BOYS, THE
Jannelli, Anthony
LOVELIFE
STOREFRONT HITCHCOCK
Jobin, Daniel
HANGING GARDEN, THE
Jodat, Farzad
MIRROR, THE
Johns, William
ENEMY
Johnson, David
HILARY AND JACKIE
Johnson, Frank E.
ALONE IN THE WOODS
Johnson, Jill
MY KNEES WERE JUMPING: REMEMBERING THE KINDERTRANSPORTS

Johnson, Shelly
QUICKSILVER HIGHWAY
Jonze, Spike
FREE TIBET
Jur, Jeffrey
HORTON FOOTE'S ALONE
HOW STELLA GOT HER GROOVE BACK
Jurges, Jurgen
FUNNY GAMES
Kaluta, Vilen
FRIEND OF THE DECEASED, A
Kam, Milton
I THINK I DO
Kaminski, Janusz
SAVING PRIVATE RYAN
Kane, Adam
BOOGIE BOY
Katz, Stephen M.
GODS AND MONSTERS
Kaye, Tony
AMERICAN HISTORY X
Keating, Kevin
MY KNEES WERE JUMPING: REMEMBERING THE KINDERTRANSPORTS
Kelsch, Ken
IMPOSTORS, THE
MONTANA
Kenaston, Nils
DAY AT THE BEACH
Kenichi, Naragawa
HEROES SHED NO TEARS
Kenny, Francis
NIGHT AT THE ROXBURY, A
Keo Kosal, Nara
WESTERN
Kibbe, Gary B.
JOHN CARPENTER'S VAMPIRES
Kimball, Jeffrey L.
WILD THINGS
Kimmel, Adam
ALMOST HEROES
MONUMENT AVE.
King, Lauri
UNVEILING, THE
Kirsch, Aaron
UNVEILING, THE
Kivilo, Alar
REBOUND: THE LEGEND OF EARL "THE GOAT" MANIGAULT
SIMPLE PLAN, A
Klimov, Vladimir
THIEF, THE
Kloss, Thomas
PALMETTO
Kobland, Ken
OFF THE MENU: THE LAST DAYS OF CHASEN'S
Kohnhorst, Michael
HENRY: PORTRAIT OF A SERIAL KILLER PART 2
Komatsubara, Shigeru
EEL, THE
Kosuth, Gabriel
CLOCKMAKER
SECRET KINGDOM, THE
Kovacs, Laszlo
JACK FROST
Kozlov, Sergi
MERLIN
Kress, Eric
KINGDOM, PART 2, THE
Kristiansen, Henning
ROYAL DECEIT
Krizsan, Les
TALES FROM A PARALLEL UNIVERSE: EATING PATTERN
TALES FROM A PARALLEL UNIVERSE: GIGA SHADOW
TALES FROM A PARALLEL UNIVERSE: SUPER NOVA
Kwan Zhe Ching
BEAUTY INVESTIGATOR
Labarthe, Jules
STRAY BULLET
Labiano, Flavio Martinez
DAY OF THE BEAST, THE
Lachman, Edward
WHY DO FOOLS FALL IN LOVE?
Lai Shui-Ming
HONG KONG 1941
Lam, Raymond
MR. NICE GUY
Landerer, Christopher
DIDN'T DO IT FOR LOVE
Landy, Christopher
DETONATOR
Lanser, Roger
PRINCE VALIANT
Lapoirie, Jeanne
FULL SPEED
Lappin, Tom
GODSON, THE
Laskus, Jacek
ELMORE LEONARD'S GOLD COAST
Lau Fung Lam
SHAOLIN TEMPLE, THE
Lau Kwun Wai
PRODIGAL SON, THE
Laustsen, Dan
NIGHTWATCH
Law Wan Shing
MAGNIFICENT WARRIORS
Layton, Vernon
I STILL KNOW WHAT YOU DID LAST SUMMER
Lebaldt, Christian
RICHIE RICH'S CHRISTMAS WISH
Lebo, Henry
EBENEZER
Lebovitz, James
UNCLE SAM
Leguy, Arnaud
POST COITUM, ANIMAL TRISTE
Lehner, Wolfgang
JAMES ELLROY: DEMON DOG OF AMERICAN CRIME FICTION
R.I.P. REST IN PIECES: A PORTRAIT OF JOE COLEMAN
Leiterman, Richard
RIGHT CONNECTIONS, THE
SPREE, THE
Lenar, Piotr
RAT'S TALE, A
Lenoir, Denis
LA SEPARATION
THURSDAY
Lent, Dean
LOVER GIRL
WHEN TIME EXPIRES
Leonetti, Matthew F.
SPECIES II
STAR TREK: INSURRECTION
Lepine, Jean
WOO
Lesnie, Andrew
BABE: PIG IN THE CITY
Letarte, Peter
JANE AUSTEN'S MAFIA!
Leung, Jimmy
DRAGONS FOREVER
Levy, Peter
LOST IN SPACE
Lew, Herman
NAKED ACTS
Lewis, David
ATOMIC DOG
CHAIRMAN OF THE BOARD
CHILDREN OF THE CORN V: FIELD OF TERROR
Libatique, Matthew
PI
Liebler, Todd
WAR ZONE
Lindley, John
PLEASANTVILLE
YOU'VE GOT MAIL
Littlewood, Gregg
REAL THING, THE
Lively, Gerry
BRYLCREEM BOYS, THE
Lohmann, Dietrich
DEEP IMPACT
Longinotto, Kim
DIVORCE IRANIAN STYLE
Lu Gengxin
EMPEROR'S SHADOW, THE
Lubezki, Emmanuel
GREAT EXPECTATIONS
MEET JOE BLACK
Lyster, Russell
RINGMASTER
Ma Chun Wah
MAGNIFICENT WARRIORS
ROYAL WARRIORS
Ma, Jingle
COMRADES, ALMOST A LOVE STORY
MacDonald, William
COURTING COURTNEY
MacMillan, Kenneth
ALMOST HEROES
DANCING AT LUGHNASA
MacPherson, Glen
REAL HOWARD SPITZ, THE
REGENERATION
WRONGFULLY ACCUSED
Mahaffie, John
YOUNG HERCULES
Maibaum, Paul
SLAPPY AND THE STINKERS
Makiura, Chishi
RAZOR: WHO'S GOT THE GOLD?, THE
SLEEPY EYES OF DEATH: FULL CIRCLE KILLING
SLEEPY EYES OF DEATH: SWORD OF ADVENTURE
Maloney, Denis
BAD MANNERS
BODY COUNT
PASS, THE
Maniaci, Teodoro
TARANTELLA
Manley, Chris
RUNNING WOMAN, THE
Manly, Laurence
SPACEJACKED
Mantle, Anthony Dod
CELEBRATION, THE
TRANCEFORMER: A PORTRAIT OF LARS VON TRIER
Marcovich, Carlos
MIDAQ ALLEY
WHO THE HELL IS JULIETTE?
Margulies, Michael
BEST OF THE BEST: WITHOUT WARNING
Mari, Pasquale
STEAM
Maritz, Edward
ELIA KAZAN: A DIRECTOR'S JOURNEY
Markowitz, Barry
TWO GIRLS AND A GUY
Marquinez, Horacio
TEN BENNY
Mason, Steve
BASEKETBALL

Mathieson, John
LOVE IS THE DEVIL: STUDY FOR A PORTRAIT OF FRANCIS BACON
Maxwell, Joe Caramico
KRAA! THE SEA MONSTER
Mayers, Michael
BROADWAY DAMAGE
LEWIS & CLARK & GEORGE
WHATEVER
Mayo, Alfredo
SHAMPOO HORNS
McAlpine, Donald M.
STEPMOM
McCurdy, Sam
KILLING TIME
McElwee, Ross
SIX O'CLOCK NEWS
McKinney, Ashley
DEAR JESSE
Mears, Graeme
FUTURE FEAR
Meheux, Phil
MASK OF ZORRO, THE
Menzies Jr., Peter
HARD RAIN
Mervis, Mark
BILLY'S HOLLYWOOD SCREEN KISS
Messenheimer, Michael
STORY OF X, THE
Metty, Russell
TOUCH OF EVIL: THE DIRECTOR'S CUT
Mickens, Mike
DETONATOR
Mickniewicz, Michael
WATCHERS REBORN
Middleton, Gregory
INVADER, THE
WOUNDED
Miller, Bennett
CRUISE, THE
Millo, Yoram
HEALING BY KILLING
Mills, Charles
BODY COUNT
Milts, Edmund
VIOLET'S VISIT
Mindel, Dan
ENEMY OF THE STATE
Mistretta, Bruno
POST COITUM, ANIMAL TRISTE
Miyagawa, Kazuo
RAZOR: THE SNARE, THE
Molina, William H.
LAST ASSASSINS
Molloy, Mike
WELCOME TO WOOP WOOP
Montgomery, Joseph
RACE TO SAVE 100 YEARS, THE
Mooradian, George
MEAN GUNS
NEMESIS 4: CRY OF ANGELS
RETROACTIVE
Moore, Allen
PARALYZING FEAR: THE STORY OF POLIO IN AMERICA, A
Morgan, Donald
RAGE, THE
Morrill, John A.
ALFRED HITCHCOCK: MASTER OF SUSPENSE
Morris, Nic
FIRELIGHT
Moura, Edgar
TIETA OF AGRESTE
Mullen, M. David
LAST BIG THING, THE

Muller, Jorge
BATTLE OF CHILE: THE STRUGGLE OF AN UNARMED PEOPLE—PART 2: THE COUP D'ETAT, THE
Muller, Robby
SHATTERED IMAGE
WHEN PIGS FLY
Murphy, Fred
DANCE WITH ME
Muska, Susan
BRANDON TEENA STORY, THE
Mutarevic, Sead
INDISCREET
Narita, Hiro
I'LL BE HOME FOR CHRISTMAS
SHADRACH
SUB DOWN
Nasr, Mohsen
DESTINY
Navarro, Guillermo
DREAM FOR AN INSOMNIAC
Nepomniaschy, Alex
ALARMIST, THE
New, Robert
CHOSEN ONE: LEGEND OF THE RAVEN, THE
Newby, John
DEFENDERS: PAYBACK, THE
DIRTY LAUNDRY
DISAPPEARANCE OF KEVIN JOHNSON, THE
Neyman, Yuri
MILO
Ngor, Peter
ARMOUR OF GOD
Nicholson, Rex
PLUMP FICTION
Nickels, Michael
HANDS ON A HARDBODY
Noguchi, Hajime
GOLGO 13: QUEEN BEE
Nowak, Danny
BIG HIT, THE
BONE DADDY
HARD CORE LOGO
Nuttgens, Giles
MERRY WAR, A
Nykvist, Sven
CELEBRITY
KRISTIN LAVRANSDATTER
Okada, Daryn
HALLOWEEN H20: TWENTY YEARS LATER
SENSELESS
Olafsdottir, Greta
BRANDON TEENA STORY, THE
Otzel, Thom
COURTING COURTNEY
Oxman, Joseph
FORMER CHILD STAR
Papamichael, Phedon
PATCH ADAMS
Pau, Peter
BRIDE OF CHUCKY
Pavicevic, Goran
DEE SNIDER'S STRANGELAND
Payvar, Homayon
TASTE OF CHERRY
Pecorini, Nicola
FEAR AND LOATHING IN LAS VEGAS
Pei, Edward J.
OVERNIGHT DELIVERY
Pelletier, David
ACT OF WAR
BRAM STOKER'S SHADOWBUILDER
Pennebaker, D.A.
MOON OVER BROADWAY
Perrin, Bob
FARM: ANGOLA, U.S.A., THE

Persson, Jorgen
DIGGING TO CHINA
JERUSALEM
LES MISERABLES
Peterman, Don
MIGHTY JOE YOUNG
Peterson, Curtis
HUNTED, THE
Petersson, Mark
HOME BEFORE DARK
Petriccione, Italo
NIRVANA
Petrycki, Jacek
KRZYSZTOF KIESLOWSKI: I'M SO-SO
Phelan, Kate
BOYS IN LOVE 2
Pierce-Roberts, Tony
PAULIE
Pittard, Eric
CHILE, OBSTINATE MEMORY
Pivetta, W.S.
LETTER FROM DEATH ROW, A
Pollack, Ekkehart
DIDN'T DO IT FOR LOVE
Pollock, Christophe
MARIE BAIE DES ANGES
Pontecorvo, Marco
TRUCE, THE
Pope, Bill
ZERO EFFECT
Pope, Dick
SWEPT FROM THE SEA
Pratt, Roger
AVENGERS, THE
Prinzi, Frank
NO LOOKING BACK
REAL BLONDE, THE
Psfister, Walter
KID IN ALADDIN'S PALACE, A
Putnam, Mark Allan
I LOVE YOU, DON'T TOUCH ME!
Quinn, Declan
ONE TRUE THING
Raby, Simon
UGLY, THE
Rachini, Pasquale
BEST MAN, THE
Rakoczy, David
ASYLUM
Raschke, Claudia
NO WAY HOME
Reiker, Tami
HIGH ART
Rexer II, William
UNMADE BEDS
Rho, Jonathan
WEST NEW YORK
Ribes, Federico
EL CHE: INVESTIGATING A LEGEND
Richardson, Jeff
DETOUR
Richardson, Robert
HORSE WHISPERER, THE
Richmond, Tom
FIRST LOVE, LAST RITES
SLUMS OF BEVERLY HILLS
Robb, James
ERNEST IN THE ARMY
Robertson, Chris
UNVEILING, THE
Robin, Jean-Francois
LEADING MAN, THE
Rocha, Claudio
UNDER HEAVEN
Rodionov, Alexei
PASSION IN THE DESERT
TALK OF ANGELS

Rodnunsky, Serge
COURTING COURTNEY
Roed, Jan
TRANCEFORMER: A PORTRAIT OF LARS VON TRIER
Rogers, Derek
CUBE
Roll, Gernot
BEYOND SILENCE
Rossotto, Andrea
LOLIDA 2000
Rotunno, Giusepppe
NIGHT AND THE MOMENT, THE
Rowe, Ashley
GOVERNESS, THE
TWENTYFOURSEVEN
Rubin, H. Alex
WHO IS HENRY JAGLOM?
Russell, Ward T.
X-FILES, THE
Saalfield, Catherine Gund
HALLELUJAH!
Sakharov, Alik
AYN RAND: A SENSE OF LIFE
Salvati, Sergio
BEYOND, THE
Samson, Cees
LOU REED: ROCK AND ROLL HEART
Sarin, Vic
URBAN SAFARI
Sarossy, Paul
AFFLICTION
Sasakibara, Yasushi
GONIN
Sayeed, Malik Hassan
BELLY
HE GOT GAME
PLAYERS CLUB, THE
Schliessler, Tobias
ESCAPE, THE
SIN AND REDEMPTION
Schlueter, Stephen
RIVER RED
Schmidt, Eric
MY KNEES WERE JUMPING: REMEMBERING THE KINDERTRANSPORTS
Schmidt, Ronn
JUNGLE BOOK: MOWGLI'S STORY, THE
STAR KID
Schneider, Aaron E.
SIMON BIRCH
Scholz, John P.
DAVID SEARCHING
Schreiber, Eileen
WAR ZONE
Schreiber, Nancy
NEVADA
SILVER SCREEN: COLOR ME LAVENDER, THE
YOUR FRIENDS & NEIGHBORS
Schuler, Fred
12 ANGRY MEN
Schwartzman, John
ARMAGEDDON
Schway, Leonard
BOYS WILL BE BOYS
Seale, John
CITY OF ANGELS
Sebaldt, Christian
CASPER MEETS WENDY
Sekiguchi, Yoshinori
GODZILLA VS. KING GHIDORAH
Sekula, Andrzej
BREAK, THE
COUSIN BETTE
Semb, Helge
MENDEL
Seresin, Michael
MERCURY RISING
Sergovici, Viorel
JOHNNY MYSTO BOY WIZARD
TALISMAN
Serra, Eduardo
SWINDLE, THE
WHAT DREAMS MAY COME
Sharaf, John
STORY OF X, THE
Sharples, David
BARRIERS
Sher, Larry
COURTING COURTNEY
Shiga, Yoichi
ZERO WOMAN
Shimizu, Yoshio
VILLAGE OF DREAMS
Shinoda, Noboru
WHEN I CLOSE MY EYES
Shirai, Hisao
NEW ADVENTURES OF KIMBA THE WHITE LION, THE
Shulman, Daniel
LOVE WALKED IN
Sigel, Newton Thomas
APT PUPIL
FALLEN
Simmons, John
RACE TO SAVE 100 YEARS, THE
Sinkovics, Gerza
FRENCH EXIT
Sinkovics, Geza
LAST SEDUCTION II, THE
Sissel, Sandi
BARNEY'S GREAT ADVENTURE—THE MOVIE
Slovis, Michael
CHARLIE HOBOKEN
SCARRED CITY
WHITE RAVEN, THE
Smith, Chris
BIG ONE, THE
Smith, Keith
DIARY OF A SERIAL KILLER
LOVE TO KILL
Smith, Trey
NIGHT VISION
Smoot, Reed
NOT IN THIS TOWN
Sobocinski, Piotr
TWILIGHT
Sokolsky, Bing
OLIVER TWIST
Soriano, Antonio
BRAM STOKER'S THE MUMMY
Southon, Mike
AIR BUD: GOLDEN RECEIVER
Sova, Peter
PROPOSITION, THE
Spears, Scott
LETTER FROM DEATH ROW, A
Spiller, Michael
HENRY FOOL
NIAGARA NIAGARA
Squires, Buddy
OUT OF THE PAST
Stapleton, Oliver
HI-LO COUNTRY, THE
OBJECT OF MY AFFECTION, THE
Steiger, Ueli
GODZILLA
Stein, Peter
CON, THE
Stevens, Robert
BREAST MEN
PECKER
Stoffers, Rogier
CHARACTER
Storaro, Vittorio
BULWORTH
Storey, Michael
BLACK LIGHT
ELVIS MEETS NIXON
IN HIS FATHER'S SHOES
Strasburg, Ivan
THEORY OF FLIGHT
Stratton, Lon
LET'S KILL ALL THE LAWYERS
Suhrstedt, Tim
MAJOR LEAGUE: BACK TO THE MINORS
WEDDING SINGER, THE
Sunara, Igor
SOMEWHERE IN THE CITY
Sung Woo Lee
RED HAWK: WEAPON OF DEATH
Suschitzky, Peter
MAN IN THE IRON MASK, THE
Suvak, Darko
LANDLADY, THE
STIR
Taczanowski, Hubert
CHICAGO CAB
EDEN
MAKER, THE
OPPOSITE OF SEX, THE
Takahashi, Hirokata
GOLGO 13: QUEEN BEE
Takemura, Yasukazu
SLEEPY EYES OF DEATH: SWORD OF SEDUCTION
Talavera, Ed
SUE
Tattersall, David
SOLDIER
Tau, Bart
CATHERINE'S GROVE
Terendy, John
BULLET ON A WIRE
Thomas, Andrew
BOYS IN LOVE 2
Thomas, John
DEAD MAN ON CAMPUS
HI-LIFE
LAST DAYS OF DISCO, THE
STILL BREATHING
Thomas, Phillip
CAN'T YOU HEAR THE WIND HOWL?: THE LIFE AND MUSIC OF ROBERT JOHNSON
Thompson, Jamie
DECLINE OF WESTERN CIVILIZATION PART III, THE
TRACKED
Thompson, Robert
ARMOUR OF GOD
Thurmann-Andersen, Erling
INSOMNIA
Tickner, Clive
SPICE WORLD
Toll, John
THIN RED LINE, THE
Tougas, Kirk
PLACE CALLED CHIAPAS, A
Tovoli, Luciano
DESPERATE MEASURES
Traver, Mark
CRACKING UP
Tregenza, Rob
INSIDE/OUT
Tsukamoto, Shinya
TOKYO FIST
Unger, Roy
SAND TRAP
Van De Sande, Theo
BLADE

Van Leeuw, Philippe
LIFE OF JESUS, THE
Varriano, Emilio
RABID DOGS
Vasile, Vivi Dragon
MIDAS TOUCH, THE
Vassdal, Kjell
JUNK MAIL
Vendor, Alex
KURT AND COURTNEY
Villalobos, Reynaldo
BURN HOLLYWOOD BURN
HOLLYWOOD CONFIDENTIAL
RETURN TO PARADISE
Visile, Vivi Dragan
SHRUNKEN CITY, THE
Von Haller, Peter
INHERITORS, THE
von Muralt, Felix
ZAKIR AND HIS FRIENDS
Wages, William
DOWN IN THE DELTA
Wakeford, Kent
LAST LIVES
Wan Man Kit
ROYAL WARRIORS
Weathington, Jesse
INTERLOCKED: THRILLED TO DEATH
Westbury, Ken
JACK HIGGINS' ON DANGEROUS GROUND
JACK HIGGINS' MIDNIGHT MAN
Wexler, Howard
CURSE OF THE PUPPET MASTER
RETURN TO SAVAGE BEACH
Widmer, Gretchen
ALL THE RAGE
Wiegand, Lisa
SHOPPING FOR FANGS
Wilson, Chapin John
HANDS ON A HARDBODY
Wilson, Ian
SAVIOR
Winding, Romain
SEVENTH HEAVEN
Windon, Stephen F.
FIRESTORM
Winestine, Zack
NEXT STEP, THE
Woeste, Peter
SNOWBOUND
Wojciechowski, Michael
BLACK THUNDER
Wolski, Dariusz
DARK CITY
PERFECT MURDER, A
Wong, Arthur
ARMOUR OF GOD
KNOCK OFF
Wong, Bill
BLACKJACK
Wood, Oliver
MIGHTY JOE YOUNG
Workman, Jeremy
WHO IS HENRY JAGLOM?
Wussie, Eric
UNVEILING, THE
Yamamoto, Hideo
FIREWORKS
Yanagishima, Katsumi
SONATINE
Yang Shu
FROZEN
Yao-Tang, Lee
ENCOUNTER OF THE SPOOKY KIND
Yates, Paul
MODULATIONS: CINEMA FOR THE EAR
Yazuhata, Takashi
SLAYERS: THE MOTION PICTURE
Yeoman, Robert
DOGWATCH
PENTAGON WARS, THE
PERMANENT MIDNIGHT
RUSHMORE
Zeitlinger, Peter
LITTLE DIETER NEEDS TO FLY
Zhang Jian
EAST PALACE, WEST PALACE
Zhang Li
RED CHERRY
Zielinski, Jerzy
HOME FRIES
Zsigmond, Vilmos
PLAYING BY HEART

CO-PRODUCERS

Albert, Ross
DECLINE OF WESTERN CIVILIZATION PART III, THE
Albrecht, Kurt
BRAVE LITTLE TOASTER GOES TO MARS, THE
PLAYING BY HEART
Aldoo, Blondel
BEST OF THE BEST: WITHOUT WARNING
Alexie, Sherman
SMOKE SIGNALS
Alsobrook, Allen
PLEASANTVILLE
Alvarez, Paco
BREAKOUT
HOT BLOODED
UNDERTAKER'S WEDDING, THE
Ames, Stefani
GUN, A CAR, AND A BLONDE, A
Armbruster, Klaus
ZAKIR AND HIS FRIENDS
Ashburn, Ellie
SIN AND REDEMPTION
Ashley, John
SCARRED CITY
Bahr, Helga
MENDEL
Baker, Richard
COMEDY'S DIRTIEST DOZEN
Baldwin, A. Michael
PHANTASM: OBLIVION
Bales, David
RINGMASTER
Ball, Chris J.
MRS. DALLOWAY
Barnard, Antonia
WELCOME TO WOOP WOOP
Bastian, Rene
SUE
Basulto, Armando
LENA'S DREAMS
Bauman, Ted
ATOMIC DOG
Belmont, Vera
TRUCE, THE
Berg, Eric
AFFLICTION
Berggren, Anders
JUNK MAIL
Berkowitz, Michael
DECAMPITATED
Bernhardt, Kevin
TOP OF THE WORLD
Bernieri, Laura
NEXT STOP, WONDERLAND
Bernstein, Karen
LOU REED: ROCK AND ROLL HEART
Bicker, Christophe
SALTMEN OF TIBET, THE
Bigwood, James
WIDE AWAKE
Block, Bruce A.
PARENT TRAP, THE
Blomquist, Alan C.
WHAT DREAMS MAY COME
Bolt, Jeremy
SOLDIER
Bongirne, Chris
IN GOD'S HANDS
Borg, Laurie
LITTLE VOICE
Bornstein, Joan
ADVENTURES OF MOWGLI
Borowitz, Andy
PLEASANTVILLE
Borowitz, Susan
PLEASANTVILLE
Bouin, Frederic
FRENCH EXIT
Bourne, St. Clair
REBOUND: THE LEGEND OF EARL "THE GOAT" MANIGAULT
Bourne, Timothy M.
EVER AFTER
Bradley, Paul
SOLDIER'S DAUGHTER NEVER CRIES, A
Braga, Sonia
TIETA OF AGRESTE
Brawner, Tina
DANCER, TEXAS POP. 81
Bretschneider, Steve
WEST NEW YORK
Brick, Richard
CELEBRITY
Brilliant Mistake
SHAMPOO HORNS
Brock, Deborah
BUFFALO '66
Brown, Jamie
BRYLCREEM BOYS, THE
Brown, Stephen
U.S. MARSHALS
Bruggeman, Joseph
SAVIOR
Burns, Catherine
ALL THE RAGE
Byard, Eliza Starr
OUT OF THE PAST
Byrne, Gabriel
BRYLCREEM BOYS, THE
Calabrese, James
TARANTELLA
Cameron, John
BIG LEBOWSKI, THE
RUSHMORE
Cantin, Marie
NIGHT AT THE ROXBURY, A
Capra III, Frank
BULWORTH
Carmody, Don
MIGHTY, THE
Carraro, Bill
WOO
Cartlidge, William P.
INCOGNITO
Caruso, Fred
BURN HOLLYWOOD BURN
Casemiro, Eryk
RUGRATS MOVIE, THE
Cathell III, Ed
BAD MANNERS
LEWIS & CLARK & GEORGE
Cathell, M. Cevin
BAD MANNERS

Chaffin, Stokely
RAT PACK, THE
Chasin, Liza
BORROWERS, THE
ELIZABETH
HI-LO COUNTRY, THE
Chiaras, Andrew
SHAMPOO HORNS
Christensen, Mads Egmont
JERUSALEM
Chua Lam
ARMOUR OF GOD
Cohen, Andy
BILLBOARD DAD
Collins, David
BREAK, THE
Cracchiolo, Dan
LETHAL WEAPON 4
Cronyn, Chris
REACH THE ROCK
Cullen, Paddy
UNDER HEAVEN
Cuomo, Alfredo
STEPHEN KING'S THE NIGHT FLIER
Curtis, Bonnie
SAVING PRIVATE RYAN
Curtis, Simon
MRS. DALLOWAY
Daigler, Gary
PENTAGON WARS, THE
Daly, Jed
BEST OF THE BEST: WITHOUT WARNING
Dauterive, Mitchell
PERFECT MURDER, A
David, Lorena
PLUMP FICTION
Davidson, Boaz
MAKER, THE
Deason, Paul
SMALL SOLDIERS
DeSanto, Thomas
APT PUPIL
Despres, Naomi
SAVIOR
ZERO EFFECT
Diegues, Carlos
TIETA OF AGRESTE
DiSalvo, Jody Barr
PRINCE, THE
Divens, Jon
BLADE
Doel, Frances
CLUB VAMPIRE
STRAY BULLET
Doherty, Michael
CAPTIVE
Donnelly, Jesse
RETROACTIVE
Dorr, Chris
CLAY PIGEONS
Downer, Jeffrey
ALWAYS OUTNUMBERED
Dreyfus, Richard
OLIVER TWIST
Driscoll, Tad
BRAM STOKER'S THE MUMMY
Dupont, Rene
MAN IN THE IRON MASK, THE
Dysinger, Elaine
CAUGHT UP
Eisen, Bruce David
TRUCKS
Ergun, Cengiz
STEAM
Eyre, Chris
SMOKE SIGNALS
Falk, Lisanne
SHATTERED IMAGE
Farnsworth, Terri
DOWN IN THE DELTA
Faust, Michael K.
CRACKING UP
Feldcott-Reynolds, Kelley
RETROACTIVE
Felsberg, Ulrich
CARLA'S SONG
Ferrari, Michelle
OUT OF THE PAST
Fischer, Marc S.
MUSIC FROM ANOTHER ROOM
THERE'S SOMETHING ABOUT MARY
Fleming, Bill
TALES FROM A PARALLEL UNIVERSE: EATING PATTERN
TALES FROM A PARALLEL UNIVERSE: GIGA SHADOW
TALES FROM A PARALLEL UNIVERSE: SUPER NOVA
Flom, Jonathn
RUDOLPH THE RED-NOSED REINDEER: THE MOVIE
Fong Xin
FROZEN
Forte, Marlene
LENA'S DREAMS
Frank, Ilana
FACE THE EVIL
Freshman Production Services
CHOSEN ONE: LEGEND OF THE RAVEN, THE
Fung, Raymond
KNOCK OFF
Furukawa, Kazuhiro
FIREWORKS
Garcia, Roger
BIG HIT, THE
Gardner, Erik Scott
DECAMPITATED
Gatien, Jennifer
SHAMPOO HORNS
George, Matt
IN GOD'S HANDS
Gershman, Gerry
BUFFALO '66
Gertner, Jordan
BUFFALO '66
Gertz, John
MASK OF ZORRO, THE
Glasser, David
REAL THING, THE
Goble, Myron
DOWN IN THE DELTA
Goldberg, Amy
RICHIE RICH'S CHRISTMAS WISH
Goldberg, Jason
LOVELIFE
Goldbert, Amy
CASPER MEETS WENDY
Goldfine, Phillip B.
CHAIRMAN OF THE BOARD
TRUCKS
Goodloe, J. Mills
LETHAL WEAPON 4
Goodman, Gregory
POLISH WEDDING
Gordon, Jamie
CHICAGO CAB
Green, Sarah
SPANISH PRISONER, THE
Greene, Justis
I'LL BE HOME FOR CHRISTMAS
Greewald, Nana
PERFECT MURDER, A
Guez, Philippe
COUSIN BETTE
Haines, Richard W.
RUN FOR COVER
Hamill, Mark
WATCHERS REBORN
Hammer, Ross
LOVER GIRL
Hampton, Tim
LOST IN SPACE
Hansen, Kirk Edward
TALISMAN
Harding, Stewart
PEACEKEEPER, THE
Hargett, Hester
BLACK DOG
Harris, Burtt
ILLTOWN
Hawkins, Crawford
BLACK LIGHT
Hayward, Debra
BORROWERS, THE
ELIZABETH
Heath, Hilary
NIL BY MOUTH
Hedien, Jody
MAKER, THE
Hensley, Matthew David
HORTON FOOTE'S ALONE
Herbeck, Bobby
WRONGFULLY ACCUSED
Herrero, Gerardo
CARLA'S SONG
Hess, Jon
AMERICAN HISTORY X
Hewitt, Caroline
LES MISERABLES
Hickey, Barry
CATHERINE'S GROVE
Hickox, S. Bryan
RIDE
Higgins, Billy
SIMON BIRCH
Hildebrand, Frank
JOHNNY SKIDMARKS
Hirtz, Dagmar
MOONDANCE
Hitchcock, Paul
MAN IN THE IRON MASK, THE
Hoehn, Marcel
TRUCE, THE
Hoffman, Todd
EDEN
Holderried, John
I MARRIED A STRANGE PERSON!
Holland, Gill
INSIDE/OUT
Hong, James
CATHERINE'S GROVE
Horne, Andrew J.
BLADE
Horovitz, Rachel
NEXT STOP, WONDERLAND
Imperato, Michelle
PRIMARY COLORS
Irvin, Sam
WHEN TIME EXPIRES
Isaac, Frank K.
AFFLICTION
Ishikawa, Hiroshi
FIREWORKS
Jakoby, Don
JOHN CARPENTER'S VAMPIRES
Jamshidi, Goly
SPACEJACKED
Jansen, Joann Fregalette
PRICE ABOVE RUBIES, A

Jaronecki, Karen
SOMEWHERE IN THE CITY
Jensen, Peter Aalbaek
MENDEL
Johnson, David C.
WOO
Jordan, Kathy
MARS
Joyce, Bernadette
YOUNG HERCULES
Kabuto, Takaaki
WHEN I CLOSE MY EYES
Kahn, Sheldon
SIX DAYS, SEVEN NIGHTS
Kane, Mary
ALMOST HEROES
Keenan, Christopher
I LOVE YOU, DON'T TOUCH ME!
Kelly, Audrey
CLAY PIGEONS
Kelly, John
LAND OF THE FREE
Kerchner, Rob
CASPER MEETS WENDY
RICHIE RICH'S CHRISTMAS WISH
King, Jonathan
ALARMIST, THE
King, Lance
DIARY OF A SERIAL KILLER
King, Sara
LET'S TALK ABOUT SEX
King, Todd
BOOGIE BOY
Koch, Karen
CAN'T HARDLY WAIT
Kolvig, Lars
SUMMER FLING
Koren, Steve
NIGHT AT THE ROXBURY, A
Lafleur, Demerise J.
FUTURE FEAR
Lamal, Andre
PHOENIX
Lancaster, Joanna
DOGWATCH
Lansberg, Cleve
DENNIS THE MENACE STRIKES AGAIN
Lauritson, Peter
STAR TREK: INSURRECTION
LeGresley, Michael J.
BLACK LIGHT
Leonelli, Nadia
HURRICANE STREETS
Leong, Denise
PROPHECY II, THE
Leveen, Robert
PERMANENT MIDNIGHT
Levitt, Heidi
CHINESE BOX, THE
Lew, Scott
ABERRATION
Linson, John
GREAT EXPECTATIONS
Liotta, Ray
PHOENIX
Liu, Jessinta
CHINESE BOX, THE
Lucidi, Paolo
DANGEROUS BEAUTY
Lynn, Edward
PLEASANTVILLE
Lynn, Meredith Scott
BILLY'S HOLLYWOOD SCREEN KISS
MacBride, Demetra
WHEN PIGS FLY
Madsen, Kenneth
ROYAL DECEIT
Magder, Gary
LAST LIVES
Magon, Jymn
ALL DOGS CHRISTMAS CAROL, AN
Makowski, Marc
WEST NEW YORK
Malina, Maggie
DEAD MAN ON CAMPUS
Marck, Nick
JUNGLE BOOK: MOWGLI'S STORY, THE
Martin, Jonathon Komack
KID IN ALADDIN'S PALACE, A
STAR KID
TRUCKS
Martin, Rob
KRAA! THE SEA MONSTER
McAleese, Peter
SPICE WORLD
McBride, Elissa
DEAD END
McDonald, Lawrence
INVADER, THE
McDonnell, Michael
REPLACEMENT KILLERS, THE
McGauley, Victor
BIG HIT, THE
McKenna, David
AMERICAN HISTORY X
McLeod, Eric
LIVING OUT LOUD
McManus, Michael
JANE AUSTEN'S MAFIA!
McMinn, Robert
BREAST MEN
Metzger, Douglas C.
FIRESTORM
Meyer, Constance
CAN'T YOU HEAR THE WIND HOWL?: THE LIFE AND MUSIC OF ROBERT JOHNSON
Meyer-Wiel, Christophe
ARTEMISIA
Miller, Linda
SAND TRAP
Miller, Michael
MY VERY BEST FRIEND
Mitchell, Robert
TEN BENNY
Mobley, Marta M.
CLUB VAMPIRE
DETONATOR
RUNNING WOMAN, THE
Moloney, Alan
SUMMER FLING
Moos-Hankin, Devorah
PATCH ADAMS
Moran, Linda
SUE
Morrow, Carrie
CLAY PIGEONS
Moskowitz, Laura
BRIDE OF CHUCKY
Murphy, Ray
HOLY MAN
Nagy, Gabor
REDLINE
Nathan, Alfred
URBAN SAFARI
Navarro, Bertha
MEN WITH GUNS
Neesan, Paul
DR. DOLITTLE
MERCURY RISING
Norberg, Greg
JANE AUSTEN'S MAFIA!
Noss, Terry L.
SWAN PRINCESS III: AND THE MYSTERY OF THE ENCHANTED TREASURE, THE
Nugent, Ginny
HUSH
Nystedt, Colleen
TRICKS
O'Donnell, Jack
STEPHEN KING'S THE NIGHT FLIER
O'Neill, Martha
SUMMER FLING
O'Sullivan, Morgan
INFORMANT, THE
OLIVER TWIST
Oakes, Chad
EBENEZER
Oedekerk, Steve
PATCH ADAMS
Offenbach, Dana
HAV PLENTY
Papandrea, Bruna
LAST BREATH
Park, Jerry
GENERAL CHAOS: UNCENSORED ANIMATION
Parker, Lansing
LOVER GIRL
Parnell, Cheryl
MY BROTHER'S WAR
Peach, Patrick
SUICIDE KINGS
Peplow, Neil
SHOOTING FISH
WAKING NED DEVINE
Perry, Craig
BIG HIT, THE
Pescarolo, Leo
ARTEMISIA
Peterson, Clark
LANDLADY, THE
Peyrot, Maureen
MERCURY RISING
Pfeiffer, Philip C.
CAN'T YOU HEAR THE WIND HOWL?: THE LIFE AND MUSIC OF ROBERT JOHNSON
Piller, Michael
STAR TREK: INSURRECTION
Pistor, Julia
RUGRATS MOVIE, THE
Polaire, Michael
SIMPLE PLAN, A
Poole, Tom
SLAMNATION
Posner, Joel
LAST BREATH
Prichard, Jennifer
CRACKING UP
Prichard, Robert
CRACKING UP
Proffer, Spencer
RIGHT CONNECTIONS, THE
Quiles, Ignacio
LENA'S DREAMS
Ramsey, Jade
RINGMASTER
Ravich, Rand
MAKER, THE
Reidy, Joseph
HORSE WHISPERER, THE
Reidy, Kevin
EVER AFTER
Reilly, Edward G.
MY BROTHER'S WAR
Remlov, Tom
JUNK MAIL
Reynolds, Raimond
PASS, THE
Rice, Jeff
DANCER, TEXAS POP. 81

Rio Filmes
OYSTER AND THE WIND, THE
Roberts, Mark
PLUMP FICTION
Roch, Edmon
LAST DAYS OF DISCO, THE
Rogers, J.B.
MUSIC FROM ANOTHER ROOM
Rogers, James B.
THERE'S SOMETHING ABOUT MARY
Roque, Cecilia Kate
LAST DAYS OF DISCO, THE
Rosen, Josie
DESPERATE MEASURES
Rosenberg, Scott
DISTURBING BEHAVIOR
Rosenblatt, Elliot Lewis
FEAR AND LOATHING IN LAS VEGAS
Rothschild, Richard Luke
TRUMAN SHOW, THE
Roussel, Jeannine
POCAHONTAS II: JOURNEY TO A NEW WORLD
Rowley, Jim
BARNEY'S GREAT ADVENTURE—THE MOVIE
Rubin, David
LAWN DOGS
Rudd, Rebecca
HOLY MAN
Ruffalo, Mark
DESTINY OF MARTY FINE, THE
Rundell, Steve
BEST OF THE BEST: WITHOUT WARNING
Rutherford, Christopher
FUTURE FEAR
Sanbrell, Aldo
STEAM
Sanders, Ken
LANDLADY, THE
Sassoon, Elan
LOVELIFE
Scanlan, Dana
CLOCKMAKER
SECRET KINGDOM, THE
SHRUNKEN CITY, THE
Schaefer, Art
RUSH HOUR
Schmassmann, Martin
URBAN SAFARI
Scott, Michael
TRUCKS
Sechrist, Steve
KRAA! THE SEA MONSTER
Segal, Douglas
CITY OF ANGELS
Segan, Allison Lyon
SAVING PRIVATE RYAN
Senkowski, Ron
LET'S KILL ALL THE LAWYERS
Severini, Mark D.
TEN BENNY
Shack, Andrew
I GOT THE HOOK UP
Sheaks, Christine
THURSDAY
Shepherd, Bill
MRS. DALLOWAY
Shiffman, Scott
ANOTHER DAY IN PARADISE
Shulman, Marcia
NO WAY HOME
Shuman, Ira
HALF BAKED
WATERBOY, THE
WEDDING SINGER, THE
Slater, Christian
HARD RAIN

Smith-Wait, Kelley
CITY OF ANGELS
Snyder, Fonda
PHOTOGRAPHING FAIRIES
Solares, Adolfo Martinez
NAKED LIES
Solomon, Susan
BLACK DOG
Spencer, Roxy
GO NOW
Spillman, Darin
MY BROTHER'S WAR
RUNNING WOMAN, THE
SPACEJACKED
STRAY BULLET
Spotnitz, Frank
X-FILES, THE
Sprecher, Karen
CLOCKWATCHERS
Spry, Robin
JACK HIGGINS' MIDNIGHT MAN
Stenta, Richard
DIRTY WORK
Stern, Nicolas
IN GOD'S HANDS
Steuer, Philip
YOUR FRIENDS & NEIGHBORS
Stevens, Judy
ONE TOUGH COP
Stewart, Olivia
VELVET GOLDMINE
Strauss, Robert
FRENCH EXIT
Sultan, Susan
WHEN PIGS FLY
Swanson, Ted Adams
INFORMANT, THE
Swicord, Robin
PRACTICAL MAGIC
Swyer, Alan
REBOUND: THE LEGEND OF EARL "THE GOAT" MANIGAULT
Thomas, Allison
PLEASANTVILLE
Thomas, Vickie
BULWORTH
Timmermann, Bonnie
BREAK, THE
Tobin, Thomas J.
SWAN PRINCESS III: AND THE MYSTERY OF THE ENCHANTED TREASURE, THE
Trachta, Jeff
INTERLOCKED: THRILLED TO DEATH
Tso Kin Nam
MR. NICE GUY
Tsui Cheng Aie
BEAUTY INVESTIGATOR
Turner, Irene
BILLY'S HOLLYWOOD SCREEN KISS
Tyrer, William
MRS. DALLOWAY
Van Horn, Kelly
GODZILLA
Veach, Candace
PHOENIX
Vidov, Oleg
ADVENTURES OF MOWGLI
Waite, Hal
RUGRATS MOVIE, THE
Walker, Clark Lee
NEWTON BOYS, THE
Wally, David
MEET JOE BLACK
Walters, Martin
DIRTY WORK
Waterman, Douglas
DOGWATCH

Webb, Gordon
SIX DAYS, SEVEN NIGHTS
Weinberg, Lawrence
PHOTOGRAPHING FAIRIES
Weisler, Michele
PAULIE
SLAPPY AND THE STINKERS
Wells, Llewellyn
GIRLS IN PRISON
White, Patti Obrow
MY VERY BEST FRIEND
Winant, Ethel
GEORGE WALLACE
Winikoff, Cami
STAR KID
Winkler, Knut
SALTMEN OF TIBET, THE
Winston, Don
DECEIVER
Winther, Peter
GODZILLA
Winthrop, Robert
SECRET OF NIMH 2: TIMMY TO THE RESCUE, THE
Wiseman, Kris
LOST IN SPACE
Wolinsky, Judith
DEJA VU
Woodard, Alfre
DOWN IN THE DELTA
Woods, Skip
THURSDAY
Wright, Jeff
BASEKETBALL
Wright, Richard S.
POLISH WEDDING
Zamsky, Meredith
REAL BLONDE, THE
Zanitsch, Noel
LANDLADY, THE
Zhu Bing
FROZEN
Zide, Warren
TOP OF THE WORLD
Zinner, Peter
GUN, A CAR, AND A BLONDE, A
Zuta, Daniel
TRUCE, THE

COSTUMES

Acheson, James
MAN IN THE IRON MASK, THE
Acosta, Nanette
LANDLADY, THE
Adair, Catherine
BASEKETBALL
Albertson, Lisa
CAN'T YOU HEAR THE WIND HOWL?: THE LIFE AND MUSIC OF ROBERT JOHNSON
Alexander, Deborah
JACK HIGGINS' ON DANGEROUS GROUND
JACK HIGGINS' MIDNIGHT MAN
Alexandrova, Natalya
THIEF, THE
Allyson, Dana
DECEIVER
Ambrose, June
BELLY
Anacker, Kristen
ORGAZMO
Ander, Susan
HOME BEFORE DARK
Andre-Guerin, Paul
JACK HIGGINS' THUNDER POINT

Andreatta, Jolie Anna
IN GOD'S HANDS
Anne, Jacqueline Saint
ELMORE LEONARD'S GOLD COAST
Aslin, Jill
TALES FROM A PARALLEL UNIVERSE: EATING PATTERN
TALES FROM A PARALLEL UNIVERSE: GIGA SHADOW
TALES FROM A PARALLEL UNIVERSE: SUPER NOVA
Atwood, Colleen
BELOVED
FALLEN
Aulisi, Joseph G.
STEPMOM
TWILIGHT
Bailey, Annelise
KINGDOM, PART 2, THE
Baker, Maxyne
DOWN IN THE DELTA
FUTURE FEAR
Balaman, S. Betim
SOMEWHERE IN THE CITY
Barbeau, Francois
PEACEKEEPER, THE
Bardon, Terri
HUNTED, THE
Barrett, Kym
ZERO EFFECT
Bartholomew, Julia
BILLY'S HOLLYWOOD SCREEN KISS
Beavan, Jenny
EVER AFTER
Bediri, Anissa
KID IN ALADDIN'S PALACE, A
Bell, Robert
LOST IN SPACE
Benzinger, Suzy
CELEBRITY
Beraldo, Elisabetta
PEREIRA DECLARES
Beraldo, Elizabeth
WHY DO FOOLS FALL IN LOVE?
Bergin, Joan
BRIGHT SHINING LIE, A
DANCING AT LUGHNASA
INFORMANT, THE
Bernay, Lynn
SOULER OPPOSITE, THE
Bertram, Susan
GIRLS IN PRISON
LOVE TO KILL
Bevans, Loren
CHARLIE HOBOKEN
Biel, Timothy
LET'S TALK ABOUT SEX
Bizzarri, Maurizio
DIARY OF A SERIAL KILLER
Blake, Yvonne
WHAT DREAMS MAY COME
Bohn, Jayme
CLUB VAMPIRE
RUNNING WOMAN, THE
WATCHERS REBORN
Boies, Shelly
MEAN GUNS
Borg, Dominique
ARTEMISIA
Borsetto, Marissa
BLACK THUNDER
Bowern, Sarah
LIKE IT IS
Boyce, Marion
JOEY
Boyd, Michael T.
FACULTY, THE
Breslin, Barbara Shulman
ALMOST PARTNERS
Bridges, Mark
CAN'T HARDLY WAIT
LIVING IN PERIL
THURSDAY
Bronson, Tom
JUNGLE BOOK: MOWGLI'S STORY, THE
WATERBOY, THE
Bronson-Howard, Aude
MEET JOE BLACK
Brooks, Anna Marie
BOYS WILL BE BOYS
Brous, Nancy
HURRICANE STREETS
NEXT STEP, THE
Brown-James, Carole
SMALL SOLDIERS
Bruno, Richard
SPECIES II
Bryant, Katherine Jane
BAD MANNERS
MR. JEALOUSY
SCARRED CITY
Bryce, Carol
CRACKING UP
Buarque, Luciana
TIETA OF AGRESTE
Budin, Jackie
SAME OLD SONG
Burnham, Vin
LOST IN SPACE
Burrows, Jami
SLAPPY AND THE STINKERS
Bush, Robin Michel
JOHN CARPENTER'S VAMPIRES
Byrne, Aisling
SPACEJACKED
Byrne, Alexandra
ELIZABETH
Byrne, Ashling
STRAY BULLET
Cabada, Anita
BODY COUNT
PASS, THE
Caines-Floyd, Eydi
RESCUERS: STORIES OF COURAGE—TWO COUPLES
RESCUERS: STORIES OF COURAGE—TWO WOMEN
Caksiran, Boris
SAVIOR
Camargo, Cristina
CENTRAL STATION
Campanale, Ornella
EIGHTEENTH ANGEL, THE
Campbell, Janet
LOUISA MAY ALCOTT'S LITTLE MEN
Canonero, Milena
BULWORTH
Carin, Kate
REGENERATION
SPICE WORLD
Carter, Emily
UGLY, THE
Carter, Ruth E.
HOW STELLA GOT HER GROOVE BACK
Chamberland, Francesca
BARNEY'S GREAT ADVENTURE—THE MOVIE
Chan, Shirley
ARMOUR OF GOD
CHINESE BOX, THE
Chanin, Natalie
REDLINE
Chericoni, Patrizia
NIRVANA
Christl, Lisy
FUNNY GAMES
Chu Sheng Hsi
ENCOUNTER OF THE SPOOKY KIND
Cicek, Selda
STEAM
Clancy, Michael
MADELINE
MONTANA
WOO
Collie, Stephanie
INNOCENT SLEEP, THE
Collin, Dinah
THEORY OF FLIGHT
Corciova, Ioana
CLOCKMAKER
SECRET KINGDOM, THE
Corwin, Kelley Marie
CROSSING FIELDS
Cox, Betsy
SENSELESS
Crabtree, Ane
NO WAY HOME
Crichton, Phillip
TWENTYFOURSEVEN
Cronenberg, Denise
REBOUND: THE LEGEND OF EARL "THE GOAT" MANIGAULT
Cunliffe, Shay
CITY OF ANGELS
CIVIL ACTION, A
Cunningham, Laura
BURN HOLLYWOOD BURN
Curry, Martha
REAL HOWARD SPITZ, THE
Daigle, Suzette
BLACKJACK
DEFENDERS: PAYBACK, THE
Dare, Daphne
CARLA'S SONG
David, Mihaela
TALISMAN
Davis, Sharen
DR. DOLITTLE
RUSH HOUR
Dawson, Thomas S.
LOS LOCOS
De Cossio, Jose M.
LIVE FLESH
de Laval, Susan
SNOWBOUND
de Necker, Yvonne
ERNEST IN THE ARMY
De Vivaise, Caroline
SEVENTH HEAVEN
DeSanto, Susie
HOPE FLOATS
Detoro, Kathleen
DEAD MAN ON CAMPUS
HARD RAIN
OVERNIGHT DELIVERY
Deveau, Marie Sylvie
MIGHTY, THE
Dickson, Ngila
YOUNG HERCULES
Donaldson, Kevin
I THINK I DO
Donati, Danilo
LIFE IS BEAUTIFUL
Donnelly, Maggie
BREAK, THE
Dorleac, Jean-Pierre
ONLY THRILL, THE
Doss, Nikki
NAKED ACTS
Dresbach, Terry
PALMETTO

ROUNDERS
VERY BAD THINGS
Druce, Kim Marie
SUBSTITUTE 2: SCHOOL'S OUT, THE
Dunn, John
LAWN DOGS
OBJECT OF MY AFFECTION, THE
DuPlaga, Marya
WHITE RAVEN, THE
Dwernicki, Sophie
WESTERN
Echerd, Jim
MY VERY BEST FRIEND
Ede, Nic
WILDE
Edwards, Sarah
JACK FROST
LAST DAYS OF DISCO, THE
Elliot, Chris
ABERRATION
Emir, Florence
NIRVANA
POST COITUM, ANIMAL TRISTE
England, Judith
HOSTILE INTENT
Eriksen, Jennifer L.
LENA'S DREAMS
Eshelman, Melinda
BREAST MEN
Eskowitz, Lori
PERMANENT MIDNIGHT
Evans, Cindy
RIVER RED
Everberg, Kirsten
SLUMS OF BEVERLY HILLS
Everton, Deborah
HALLOWEEN H20: TWENTY YEARS LATER
Falcon, Jeffrey
SIX-STRING SAMURAI
Farrell, Victoria
HIGH ART
I THINK I DO
LOVER GIRL
Faur, Brigitte
FULL SPEED
Ferry, April
DON KING: ONLY IN AMERICA
LITTLE BOY BLUE
PLAYING BY HEART
Fiedler, Roseanne
BOOGIE BOY
Fien, Pennie
PROPHECY II, THE
Finlayson, Bruce
FIRESTORM
GODS AND MONSTERS
Fischer, Suzana
DEAD END
Fischnaller, Nicole
INHERITORS, THE
Fleming, Rachael
DAD SAVAGE
GO NOW
LEADING MAN, THE
Fong, Jana Lee
TEN BENNY
Fonne, Runa
INSOMNIA
Foroutan, Dahlia
PLAYERS CLUB, THE
France, Marie
BORROWERS, THE
Frogley, Louise
U.S. MARSHALS
Fung, William
KNOCK OFF
Fyregard, Ann Margret
JERUSALEM
Gadoury, Odette
SNAKE EYES
Galer, Andrea
FIRELIGHT
LOVE AND DEATH ON LONG ISLAND
Garcia, Amber Lynn
LAND OF THE FREE
Gardiner, Lizzy
WELCOME TO WOOP WOOP
Garrison, Stephanie
BREAKOUT
Garvin, Tracie L.
NAKED ACTS
Gautrelet, Sylvie
LA SEPARATION
Gerard-Hirne, Claire
MARIE BAIE DES ANGES
Getman, Julieann
TRUCKS
Giguere, Edi
CLOCKWATCHERS
Gil, Tanya
FRENCH EXIT
Gillesen, Gro
OTHER SIDE OF SUNDAY, THE
Glynn, Gloria
LAST LIVES
Goldsmith, Laura
CLAY PIGEONS
Graef, Vicki
FACE DOWN
HALF BAKED
Graff, Karen
LENA'S DREAMS
Granata, Dona
GINGERBREAD MAN, THE
SHADRACH
Granger, Sevilla
SAND TRAP
Greco, Carolyn
CHICAGO CAB
Greiner, Wendy
I LOVE YOU, DON'T TOUCH ME!
Gresham, Gloria
SIX DAYS, SEVEN NIGHTS
SPHERE
Gretsch, Martha
SHAMPOO HORNS
Guaita, Vittoria
BEST MAN, THE
Guerin, Paul Andre
JACK HIGGINS' THE WINDSOR PROTOCOL
Guerrero, Melissa
STIR
Guidasci, Magali
ARMAGEDDON
Hackett, Rosie
WAKING NED DEVINE
Haernathorn, Duangporn
HEROES SHED NO TEARS
Hall, Douglas
AMERICAN HISTORY X
Hamilton, Cynthia
HOLLYWOOD CONFIDENTIAL
Hannan, Mary Claire
HURLYBURLY
MUSIC FROM ANOTHER ROOM
URBAN LEGEND
Hansen, Joanne
EBENEZER
Hanson, Debra
FALLING FIRE
Hanson, Seth
SUE
Hargreaves, Patricia
AIR BUD: GOLDEN RECEIVER
Harris, Caroline
GOVERNESS, THE
SWEPT FROM THE SEA
Harris, Emily
STEEL SHARKS
Hart, Patricia L.
HENRY: PORTRAIT OF A SERIAL KILLER PART 2
Hartline, Kameron
MEN
Harwood, Shuna
LAND GIRLS, THE
PASSION IN THE DESERT
Hays, Sanja Milkovic
BLADE
STAR TREK: INSURRECTION
Heath, Megan
REAL THING, THE
Hebden, Gilly
LOST IN SPACE
Heimann, Betsy
MERCURY RISING
OUT OF SIGHT
SIMON BIRCH
Hemming, Lindy
LITTLE VOICE
PRINCE VALIANT
Herman, Leslie
CATHERINE'S GROVE
Hernandez, Sandra
HE GOT GAME
Hetland, Carla
FIRESTORM
Hoffman, Anne
HOSTILE WATERS
Hollowood, Ann
MERLIN
Hollywood, Danielle
DIRTY LAUNDRY
Hollywood Raggs
CHILDREN OF THE CORN V: FIELD OF TERROR
Homonnay, Gyorgy
WHEN TRUMPETS FADE
Hoshi, Teruaki
JUNK FOOD
Howie, Frances Susan
OPERATION DELTA FORCE 2
Huber, Sabina
NO ORDINARY LOVE
Huete, Lala
TALK OF ANGELS
Ingerman, Ivan
NEXT STEP, THE
Ingrato, Marika
POST COITUM, ANIMAL TRISTE
Ireland, Druh
WOUNDED
Isaacs, Jhane
I GOT THE HOOK UP
Itoo, Natsu
RAZOR: THE SNARE, THE
RAZOR: WHO'S GOT THE GOLD?, THE
Iturregui, Leonardo
PARALLEL SONS
Iwasaki, Hiroko
TOKYO FIST
Jachymova, Petra
FORGOTTEN LIGHT
Jade, Scarlett
LET'S KILL ALL THE LAWYERS
Jamison-Tanchuk, Francine
NEGOTIATOR, THE
Jensen, Judi
CURSE OF THE PUPPET MASTER
PRINCE, THE

Jensen, Lisa
NEIL SIMON'S THE ODD COUPLE II
Jett, Elizabeth
NEMESIS 4: CRY OF ANGELS
Johnson, Lisa
SUB DOWN
Johnston, Joanna
SAVING PRIVATE RYAN
Jones, Gary
DESPERATE MEASURES
Jorry, Corinne
SWINDLE, THE
UN AIR DE FAMILLE
Joson, Jocelyn
HENRY FOOL
Kaplan, Michael
ARMAGEDDON
Katsaras-Barklem, Jo
TARZAN AND THE LOST CITY
Kaufmann, Susan
KISSING A FOOL
Kavanagh, Alex
UNDERTAKER'S WEDDING, THE
Kay, Shelley
PHANTASM: OBLIVION
Kaye, Elizabeth
EDEN
Keast, James
MERRY WAR, A
Keating, Trish
CALL TO REMEMBER, A
DISTURBING BEHAVIOR
Kelly, Bridget
WIDE AWAKE
Keogh, Liz
DARK CITY
Kidd, Barbara
NIL BY MOUTH
Kilber, Jill
WHATEVER
Kim, Eun-Young
RAT'S TALE, A
King, Danielle
LOVELIFE
Kirk, Freddie
MY BROTHER'S WAR
Kliber, Jill
BROADWAY DAMAGE
Knutzen, Kelly
PLAN B
Komarov, Shelley
NEWTON BOYS, THE
Kreiner, Jillian Ann
DEE SNIDER'S STRANGELAND
Kurland, Jeffrey
LIVING OUT LOUD
Kwan, Ingrid
DRAGONS FOREVER
Kwan, Mable
KNOCK OFF
Laplante, Francois
AFFLICTION
Lapper, Vincent
PLUMP FICTION
Lawson, Merrie
MURDER IN MIND
Leamon, Ron
SMOKE SIGNALS
UNDER HEAVEN
Lecoultre, Francine
SHATTERED IMAGE
Lee, Jenny
BEAUTY INVESTIGATOR
Lentini, Massimo
BEYOND, THE
Lester, Dan
I STILL KNOW WHAT YOU DID LAST SUMMER
Leung, Patrick
HEROES SHED NO TEARS
Lewis-West, Robin
NOT IN THIS TOWN
Line, Mandi
GODSON, THE
Lisle, David
URBAN SAFARI
Litwack, Dana C.
PHANTOMS
Loats, Dana Lynne
LITTLE BIGFOOT 2: THE JOURNEY HOME
Loveniuk, Margaret
MISBEGOTTEN
Lowery, Steve
DECAMPITATED
Luchuck, Sharmon
HOT BLOODED
Lui Fung Shan
MR. NICE GUY
Luk, Ben
KNOCK OFF
Lutter, Ellen
54
PRICE ABOVE RUBIES, A
Lyall, Susan
SPANISH PRISONER, THE
Mackay, Lynne
BRIDE OF CHUCKY
Madden, Betty Pecha
HORTON FOOTE'S ALONE
Maginnis, Molly
MIGHTY JOE YOUNG
Magny, Ginette
SAVIOR
Mah, Gregory
TRICKS
Makovsky, Judianna
GREAT EXPECTATIONS
LOLITA
PLEASANTVILLE
PRACTICAL MAGIC
Malin, Mary
JANE AUSTEN'S MAFIA!
Mani, Maya
I'LL BE HOME FOR CHRISTMAS
Mann, Brigitte
COLONY, THE
Marie, Donna
MARS
Marki, Csilla
TRACKED
Markiegui, Estibaliz
DAY OF THE BEAST, THE
Marshall, Annie
HEAVEN'S BURNING
TWISTED
Martinez, Denise
CON, THE
Marx, Caroline
BRAM STOKER'S THE MUMMY
Maslansky, Stephanie
BREAK, THE
Matheson, Susan
DANCER, TEXAS POP. 81
Matsumoto, Miye
3 NINJAS: HIGH NOON AT MEGA MOUNTAIN
Matthews, Marilyn
TRUMAN SHOW, THE
May, Mona
NIGHT AT THE ROXBURY, A
WEDDING SINGER, THE
Mazon, Graciela
MASK OF ZORRO, THE
McCartney, Malou
CHILDREN OF THE CORN V: FIELD OF TERROR
McDonald, P.J.
ENEMY
McGuire, Debra
SOUR GRAPES
McHugh, Nancy
BRAM STOKER'S SHADOWBUILDER
FACE THE EVIL
McKay, Marcelle
DISAPPEARANCE OF KEVIN JOHNSON, THE
RUSTY: THE GREAT RESCUE
McLeod, Mary E.
MAJOR LEAGUE: BACK TO THE MINORS
McMullen, Gail
RINGMASTER
Meachem, Stewart
SHOOTING FISH
Meltzer, Ileane
STAR KID
Michel, Michele
HIJACKING HOLLYWOOD
Miller, Roxanne
LOLIDA 2000
Mingenbach, Louise
APT PUPIL
NIGHTWATCH
PERMANENT MIDNIGHT
Mirojnick, Ellen
PERFECT MURDER, A
Mitchell, Peter
OPPOSITE OF SEX, THE
Mobley, Kathleen
WHEN PIGS FLY
Mohr, Margaret
BIG HIT, THE
BONE DADDY
Monaghan, Tish
SPREE, THE
Moneva, Natalya
THIEF, THE
Moore, Dan
12 ANGRY MEN
TWO FOR TEXAS
Moore, Wendy May
CUBE
Mor, Tami
CASPER MEETS WENDY
Moricaeu, Norma
BABE: PIG IN THE CITY
Morrison, Kathryn
ANOTHER DAY IN PARADISE
Mossum, Lena
CARLA'S SONG
Mulholland, Vicky
MY VERY BEST FRIEND
Murphy, David
BRYLCREEM BOYS, THE
Murtinho, Rita
OYSTER AND THE WIND, THE
Mussenden, Isis
HI-LIFE
KRIPPENDORF'S TRIBE
Myers, Ruth
DEEP IMPACT
Nadon, Claire
BLEEDERS
JACK LONDON'S THE CALL OF THE WILD: DOG OF THE YUKON
Nadoolman, Deborah
BLUES BROTHERS 2000
Napier, April
YOUR FRIENDS & NEIGHBORS
Napier, Sheena
HUMAN BOMB
MOONDANCE
Nasrallah, Nahed
DESTINY

Neil, Warden
QUICKSILVER HIGHWAY
RETURN TO SAVAGE BEACH
TRUCKS
Nelson, Barbara
WALKING THUNDER
Newhall, Deborah
MONUMENT AVE.
Ng, Dora
COMRADES, ALMOST A LOVE STORY
Nguyen, Ha
LETHAL WEAPON 4
Niehaus, Anja
KILLER CONDOM, THE
Niskanen, Lia
INTERLOCKED: THRILLED TO DEATH
Nixon, Barb
INVADER, THE
Nixon, Kathryn
HAPPINESS
Nolin, Stephanie
WHEN DANGER FOLLOWS YOU HOME
Norris, Patricia
HI-LO COUNTRY, THE
Norton, Rosanna
MAKER, THE
O'Hanneson, Jill
HOME FRIES
Owings, Richard
RIDE
Panova, Alina
NOTES FROM UNDERGROUND
Pasternak, Beth
DIRTY WORK
Pasztor, Beatrix Aruna
BUFFALO '66
PSYCHO
Patch, Karen
DENNIS THE MENACE STRIKES AGAIN
RUSHMORE
Paterson, Maeve
GENERAL, THE
Patterson, Devon
FATAL PURSUIT
Paunescu, Oana
JOHNNY MYSTO BOY WIZARD
LITTLE GHOST
MIDAS TOUCH, THE
SHRUNKEN CITY, THE
SUBSPECIES IV: BLOODSTORM
Pedersen, Anne
MENDEL
Pehrsson, Inger
KRISTIN LAVRANSDATTER
Pelletier, Nicole
CAPTIVE
LOST WORLD, THE
Pepperdine, Judy
MRS. DALLOWAY
Perkins, Kari
LEWIS & CLARK & GEORGE
Pescucci, Gabriella
COUSIN BETTE
DANGEROUS BEAUTY
LES MISERABLES
NIGHT AND THE MOMENT, THE
Pethig, Hazel
PHOTOGRAPHING FAIRIES
Petrova, Antonina
DEAD WATERS
Pfeiffer, Sarah
ALL THE RAGE
Phillips, Arianne
REPLACEMENT KILLERS, THE
Phillips, Erica
SOLDIER
Polak, Leonie
DRESS, THE
Polcsa, Juliet
IMPOSTORS, THE
RETURN TO PARADISE
Porro, Joseph
DEEP RISING
GODZILLA
HOMEGROWN
Powell, Anthony
AVENGERS, THE
Powell, Sandy
BUTCHER BOY, THE
HILARY AND JACKIE
SHAKESPEARE IN LOVE
VELVET GOLDMINE
Preston, Grania
DESTINY OF MARTY FINE, THE
WITHOUT LIMITS
Priest, Heather
KRAA! THE SEA MONSTER
Puisto, Susanna
STILL BREATHING
Raboni, Metella
STEAM
Ralston, Glenn A.
RAGE, THE
Ramon, Rina
CASPER MEETS WENDY
Ramsey, Carol
SOLDIER'S DAUGHTER NEVER CRIES, A
Ransley, Leila
LAST SEDUCTION II, THE
Rao, Wendy Range
NEVADA
Raoul, Nathalie
LIFE OF JESUS, THE
Rhee, Amy
BEST OF THE BEST: WITHOUT WARNING
Robinson, David
MEET JOE BLACK
Robinson, David Carl
LOVE WALKED IN
Rodgers, Aggie Guerard
HOLY MAN
Rogiani, Elisabetta
CHOSEN ONE: LEGEND OF THE RAVEN, THE
Roper, Rhonda
LAST BREATH
Rose, Penny
PARENT TRAP, THE
Rosenblatt, Jana
RATCHET
Roth, Ann
HUSH
PRIMARY COLORS
SIEGE, THE
Routh, May
GEORGE WALLACE
RONIN
Rubeo, Mayes C.
MEN WITH GUNS
Ruskin, Judy
HORSE WHISPERER, THE
PATCH ADAMS
Russell, Rhona
DEJA VU
Rutkiewicz-Luterek, Magda
WHITE RAVEN, THE
Ryack, Rita
MY GIANT
Ryba, Ellen
REACH THE ROCK
Sanchez, Isabelle
LIFE OF JESUS, THE
Sandoval, Lisa Rae
GODSON, THE
Saydah-Dokter, Dalia
TOP OF THE WORLD
Schmidt, Ryck
CASPER MEETS WENDY
RICHIE RICH'S CHRISTMAS WISH
Schreiner, Charmian
ASYLUM
WHEN TIME EXPIRES
Schwarzer, Suzanne
DIRTY LAUNDRY
TARANTELLA
Serdinova, Lyudmila
FRIEND OF THE DECEASED, A
Shannon, Laura Jean
NIAGARA NIAGARA
Shenher, Brenda
BLACK LIGHT
Sheppard, Ania Biedrzycka
FROM A FAR COUNTRY
Sheppard, Anna
OGRE, THE
PROPOSITION, THE
Slotnick, Sara Jane
ILLTOWN
NO LOOKING BACK
Smith, Van
PECKER
Snowe, Darena
TRUCKS
Squarciapino, Franca
CHAMBERMAID ON THE TITANIC, THE
Stamper, Peggy
BLACK DOG
Stanek, Eva
ACT OF WAR
Stauch, Bonnie
ALONE IN THE WOODS
DOGWATCH
INVISIBLE DAD
JOHNNY SKIDMARKS
OUTSIDE OZONA
Stewart, Marlene
ENEMY OF THE STATE
X-FILES, THE
Still, Jane
SIN AND REDEMPTION
Stjernsward, Louise
INCOGNITO
Stofsky, Amy
PENTAGON WARS, THE
Stonestreet, Paula
INSIDE/OUT
Stover, Tami
LAST BIG THING, THE
Strachan, Kathy
I WENT DOWN
Summers, Cynthia
DOUBLE EDGE
RIGHT CONNECTIONS, THE
Surber, Tammy
INDISCREET
Swain, Janet
CAN'T YOU HEAR THE WIND HOWL?: THE LIFE AND MUSIC OF ROBERT JOHNSON
Swartz, Judy B.
BILLBOARD DAD
Symons, Annie
LOVE IS THE DEVIL: STUDY FOR A PORTRAIT OF FRANCIS BACON
Takahashi, Chikae
WHEN I CLOSE MY EYES
Tanalias, Gisele
ROYAL DECEIT
Tavernier, Elizabeth
GENEALOGIES OF A CRIME
Taylor, Jill
SLIDING DOORS
Temime, Jany
CHARACTER

Tempest, Frances
UNDER THE SKIN
Thomas, Bill
TOUCH OF EVIL: THE DIRECTOR'S CUT
Thomas, Cat
SAFE MEN
Thomson, Christine
ATOMIC DOG
Tillen, Jodie
RAT PACK, THE
Tillman, Kimberly A.
WILD THINGS
Tompkins, Joe I.
DANCE WITH ME
Tong Yuet Fung
SHAOLIN TEMPLE, THE
Turturice, Robert
GIA
Tyrrell, Genevieve
SUICIDE KINGS
Ularu, Michaela
GADJO DILO
Venema, Trish
TERMINAL JUSTICE
Verso, Alberto
TRUCE, THE
Versolato, Ocimar
TIETA OF AGRESTE
Von Mayrhauser, Jennifer
REAL BLONDE, THE
Wagner, Karyn
HIT ME
MEET THE DEEDLES
Waknin, Deborah
GUN, A CAR, AND A BLONDE, A
Waller, Liz
TALK OF ANGELS
Waterhouse, Abram
SIMON BIRCH
Weiss, Julie
FEAR AND LOATHING IN LAS VEGAS
SIMPLE PLAN, A
Welker, Alexandra
MEET THE DEEDLES
PHOENIX
RETROACTIVE
Wetherbee, Amy
UNCLE SAM
White, Pauline
BODY COUNT
STEPHEN KING'S THE NIGHT FLIER
White, Tracey
CAUGHT UP
Wilson, Margot
THIN RED LINE, THE
Wingate, Denise
ALARMIST, THE
Winston, Charles E.
DREAM FOR AN INSOMNIAC
Winther-Larsen, Bente
JUNK MAIL
Wolsky, Albert
YOU'VE GOT MAIL
Wong Kwai Ping
SHAOLIN TEMPLE, THE
Wood, Durinda
ALMOST HEROES
Woodman, Jori
WRONGFULLY ACCUSED
Worthen, James A.
HANGING GARDEN, THE
Yano, Kei
ELVIS MEETS NIXON
Yavuz, Gulbin
LAST ASSASSINS
Zakowska, Donna
ONE TRUE THING
POLISH WEDDING
Zophres, Mary
BIG LEBOWSKI, THE
DIGGING TO CHINA
PAULIE
SUMMER FLING
THERE'S SOMETHING ABOUT MARY

DIRECTORS

Abrahams, Jim
JANE AUSTEN'S MAFIA!
Abramson, Neil
RINGMASTER
Addario, Lisa
LOVER GIRL
Adler, Carine
UNDER THE SKIN
Alcorn, Keith
GENERAL CHAOS: UNCENSORED ANIMATION
Allen, Woody
CELEBRITY
Almodovar, Pedro
LIVE FLESH
Altman, Robert
GINGERBREAD MAN, THE
Ames, Stephani
GUN, A CAR, AND A BLONDE, A
Anderson, Brad
NEXT STOP, WONDERLAND
Anderson, Paul
SOLDIER
Anderson, Wes
RUSHMORE
Andreacchio, Mario
NAPOLEON
Angelou, Maya
DOWN IN THE DELTA
Antonijevic, Peter
SAVIOR
Apted, Michael
ALWAYS OUTNUMBERED
Arcadias, Laurence
GENERAL CHAOS: UNCENSORED ANIMATION
Arkush, Allan
ELVIS MEETS NIXON
Arnfred, Morten
KINGDOM, PART 2, THE
Aronofsky, Darren
PI
August, Bille
JERUSALEM
LES MISERABLES
Avati, Pupi
BEST MAN, THE
Aviram, Nitzan
HEALING BY KILLING
Axel, Gabriel
ROYAL DECEIT
Azzopardi, Mario
BONE DADDY
Badham, John
INCOGNITO
Baino, Mariano
DEAD WATERS
Baird, Stuart
U.S. MARSHALS
Balabanov, Alexei
BROTHER
Bancroft, Tony
MULAN
Barker, Marvin
LETTER FROM DEATH ROW, A
Barker, Nicholas
UNMADE BEDS
Barnette, Neema
SIN AND REDEMPTION
Barreto, Bruno
ONE TOUGH COP
Barron, Steve
MERLIN
Barry, Ian
JOEY
Baumander, Lewis
FUTURE FEAR
Baumbach, Noah
MR. JEALOUSY
Bava, Mario
RABID DOGS
Baxter, Alan
BARRIERS
Bay, Michael
ARMAGEDDON
Beatty, Warren
BULWORTH
Becker, Harold
MERCURY RISING
Bender, Jack
CALL TO REMEMBER, A
Benigni, Roberto
LIFE IS BEAUTIFUL
Benjamin, Richard
PENTAGON WARS, THE
Benson, Scott
RACE TO SAVE 100 YEARS, THE
Benton, Robert
TWILIGHT
Berg, Peter
VERY BAD THINGS
Bettman, Gil
NIGHT VISION
Beyer, Troy
LET'S TALK ABOUT SEX
Bienstock, Mark
INDISCREET
Bierman, Robert
MERRY WAR, A
Bill, Tony
OLIVER TWIST
Bindler, S.R.
HANDS ON A HARDBODY
Bindley, William
EIGHTEENTH ANGEL, THE
Bjorkman, Stig
TRANCEFORMER: A PORTRAIT OF LARS VON TRIER
Blanks, Jamie
URBAN LEGEND
Bloom, Jason
OVERNIGHT DELIVERY
Blyth, David
HOT BLOODED
Bogdanovich, Peter
RESCUERS: STORIES OF COURAGE—TWO WOMEN
Boorman, John
GENERAL, THE
Booth, Mike
GENERAL CHAOS: UNCENSORED ANIMATION
Bornedal, Ole
NIGHTWATCH
Bourla, David
WHEN TIME EXPIRES
Bowman, Rob
X-FILES, THE
Boxell, Tim
ABERRATION
Boyum, Steve
MEET THE DEEDLES
Bradshaw, John
BREAKOUT
UNDERTAKER'S WEDDING, THE

Bramer, Monte
PAUL MONETTE: THE BRINK OF SUMMER'S END
Breathnach, Paddy
I WENT DOWN
Brest, Martin
MEET JOE BLACK
Briggs, David
BOYS IN LOVE 2
Brinkerhoff, Joel
GENERAL CHAOS: UNCENSORED ANIMATION
Brolin, James
MY BROTHER'S WAR
Broomfield, Nick
KURT AND COURTNEY
Bross, Eric
TEN BENNY
Bruce, James
LOVE TO KILL
Buechler, John Carl
WATCHERS REBORN
Burns, Edward
NO LOOKING BACK
Burr, Jeff
JOHNNY MYSTO BOY WIZARD
Camacho, Art
LITTLE BIGFOOT 2: THE JOURNEY HOME
Campanella, Juan Jose
LOVE WALKED IN
Campbell, Martin
MASK OF ZORRO, THE
Cannon, Danny
I STILL KNOW WHAT YOU DID LAST SUMMER
PHOENIX
Cardone, J.S.
OUTSIDE OZONA
Carner, Charles Robert
FIXER, THE
Carpenter, John
JOHN CARPENTER'S VAMPIRES
Carroll, Willard
PLAYING BY HEART
Chabrol, Claude
SWINDLE, THE
Chahine, Youssef
DESTINY
Chan, Jackie
ARMOUR OF GOD
Chan, Peter
COMRADES, ALMOST A LOVE STORY
Chang Hsin Yen
SHAOLIN TEMPLE, THE
Chapman, Brenda
PRINCE OF EGYPT, THE
Chappelle, Joe
PHANTOMS
Chechik, Jeremiah
AVENGERS, THE
Chelsom, Peter
MIGHTY, THE
Cherot, Christopher Scott
HAV PLENTY
Cherry, John
ERNEST IN THE ARMY
Cholodenko, Lisa
HIGH ART
Chopra, Joyce
MY VERY BEST FRIEND
Christopher, Mark
54
Chukhrai, Pavel
THIEF, THE
Chung, David
MAGNIFICENT WARRIORS
ROYAL WARRIORS
Clancy, Garrett
DETONATOR
Clark, Larry
ANOTHER DAY IN PARADISE
Clarke-Williams, Zoe
MEN
Clyde, Craig
WALKING THUNDER
Coen, Joel
BIG LEBOWSKI, THE
Cohen, Rob
RAT PACK, THE
Cohn, Alan
DEAD MAN ON CAMPUS
Collins, Vince
GENERAL CHAOS: UNCENSORED ANIMATION
Columbus, Chris
STEPMOM
Condon, Bill
GODS AND MONSTERS
Connelly, Theresa
POLISH WEDDING
Cook, Barry
MULAN
Cooper, Stuart
HUNTED, THE
Coraci, Frank
WATERBOY, THE
WEDDING SINGER, THE
Coscarelli, Don
PHANTASM: OBLIVION
Coto, Manny
STAR KID
Cristofer, Michael
GIA
Cuaron, Alfonso
GREAT EXPECTATIONS
Cullinane, Jeremiah
SPACEJACKED
Cunningham, D. Matt
DECAMPITATED
Currier, Lavinia
PASSION IN THE DESERT
Cybulski, Mary
CHICAGO CAB
D'Or, Daniel
FALLING FIRE
Dahl, John
ROUNDERS
Daniels, Mark
CLASSIFIED X
Dante, Joe
SMALL SOLDIERS
Darby, Jonathan
HUSH
Darnell, Eric
ANTZ
David, Larry
SOUR GRAPES
Davidov, R.
ADVENTURES OF MOWGLI
Davids, Paul
TIMOTHY LEARY'S DEAD
Davis, Andrew
PERFECT MURDER, A
Davis, Bridgett M.
NAKED ACTS
Davis, Julie
I LOVE YOU, DON'T TOUCH ME!
Davis, Tamra
HALF BAKED
de la Iglesia, Alex
DAY OF THE BEAST, THE
De Michiel, Helen
TARANTELLA
de Oliveira, Manoel
VOYAGE TO THE BEGINNING OF THE WORLD
De Palma, Brian
SNAKE EYES
DeBartolo, Tiffanie
DREAM FOR AN INSOMNIAC
DeCoteau, David
CURSE OF THE PUPPET MASTER
TALISMAN
DeLuise, Dom
BOYS WILL BE BOYS
Demme, Jonathan
BELOVED
STOREFRONT HITCHCOCK
Demme, Ted
MONUMENT AVE.
Deutch, Howard
NEIL SIMON'S THE ODD COUPLE II
Devlin, Paul
SLAMNATION
Dezaki, Osamu
GOLGO 13: QUEEN BEE
DiCillo, Tom
REAL BLONDE, THE
Diegues, Carlos
TIETA OF AGRESTE
Dixon, Jamie
BRAM STOKER'S SHADOWBUILDER
Dobkin, David
CLAY PIGEONS
Donar, David
GENERAL CHAOS: UNCENSORED ANIMATION
Done, Harris
SAND TRAP
Donner, Richard
LETHAL WEAPON 4
Dorman, Joseph
ARGUING THE WORLD
Dornheim, Robert
BREAK, THE
Downing, Todd
BOYS IN LOVE 2
Drazan, Anthony
HURLYBURLY
Drilling, Eric
RIVER RED
Driver, Sara
WHEN PIGS FLY
Drury, David
HOSTILE WATERS
Du Chau, Frederik
QUEST FOR CAMELOT
Dugowson, Maurice
EL CHE: INVESTIGATING A LEGEND
Duguay, Christian
SNOWBOUND
Duigan, John
LAWN DOGS
LEADING MAN, THE
Dumont, Bruno
LIFE OF JESUS, THE
Dunne, Griffin
PRACTICAL MAGIC
Dunsky, Evan
ALARMIST, THE
Dupre, Jeff
OUT OF THE PAST
Eberhardt, Thom
FACE DOWN
Elfont, Harry
CAN'T HARDLY WAIT
Eling, Stefan
GENERAL CHAOS: UNCENSORED ANIMATION

Ellery, Tom
POCAHONTAS II: JOURNEY TO A NEW WORLD
Ellin, Doug
KISSING A FOOL
Elliott, Stephan
WELCOME TO WOOP WOOP
Emmerich, Roland
GODZILLA
Enright, Amanda
GENERAL CHAOS: UNCENSORED ANIMATION
Ephron, Nora
YOU'VE GOT MAIL
Eriksen, Gordon
LENA'S DREAMS
Ersgard, Jack
LIVING IN PERIL
Esguerra, George
TALK TO ME
Evans, Betsan Morris
DAD SAVAGE
Evans, Rodney
UNVEILING, THE
Eyre, Chris
SMOKE SIGNALS
Faber, Christian
NEXT STEP, THE
Faenza, Roberto
PEREIRA DECLARES
Farrelly, Bobby
THERE'S SOMETHING ABOUT MARY
Farrelly, Peter
THERE'S SOMETHING ABOUT MARY
Feldman, John Harmon
LOVELIFE
Fink, Kenneth
TRICKS
Fitzgerald, Thom
HANGING GARDEN, THE
Fletcher, Jack
GOLGO 13: QUEEN BEE
Fogel, Eric
GENERAL CHAOS: UNCENSORED ANIMATION
Foley, Maureen
HOME BEFORE DARK
Fons, Jorge
MIDAQ ALLEY
Forestier, Frederic
PEACEKEEPER, THE
Fortenberry, John
NIGHT AT THE ROXBURY, A
Frakes, Jonathan
STAR TREK: INSURRECTION
Franchot, Pascal
MILO
Frankenheimer, John
GEORGE WALLACE
RONIN
Franklin, Carl
ONE TRUE THING
Frears, Stephen
HI-LO COUNTRY, THE
Freeman, Morgan J.
HURRICANE STREETS
Friedkin, William
12 ANGRY MEN
Fujiwara, Ryoji
MOBILE SUIT GUNDAM I
Fulci, Lucio
BEYOND, THE
Fuqua, Antoine
REPLACEMENT KILLERS, THE
Furie, Sidney J.
RAGE, THE
TOP OF THE WORLD
Gallo, Phil
WEST NEW YORK
Gallo, Vincent
BUFFALO '66
Garbus, Liz
FARM: ANGOLA, U.S.A., THE
Garris, Mick
QUICKSILVER HIGHWAY
Gatlif, Tony
GADJO DILO
Geiger, Peter
COLONY, THE
George, Terry
BRIGHT SHINING LIE, A
Gibbons, Rodney
CAPTIVE
LOUISA MAY ALCOTT'S LITTLE MEN
Gilbert, Brian
WILDE
Gilliam, Terry
FEAR AND LOATHING IN LAS VEGAS
Gilliard, Stuart
ESCAPE, THE
Giovinazzo, Buddy
NO WAY HOME
Glatter, Leslie Linka
PROPOSITION, THE
Goldbacher, Sandra
GOVERNESS, THE
Goldberg, Howard
EDEN
Gomer, Steve
BARNEY'S GREAT ADVENTURE—THE MOVIE
Gomez, Nick
ILLTOWN
Gordon-Clark, Lawrence
JACK HIGGINS' ON DANGEROUS GROUND
JACK HIGGINS' MIDNIGHT MAN
Gorris, Marleen
MRS. DALLOWAY
Gosse, Bob
NIAGARA NIAGARA
Gotoh, Daisuke
ZERO WOMAN
Gray, F. Gary
NEGOTIATOR, THE
Greenfield, Matt
SLAYERS: THE MOTION PICTURE
Greenfield-Sanders, Timothy
LOU REED: ROCK AND ROLL HEART
Greengrass, Paul
THEORY OF FLIGHT
Gruber, Markus
MY FIRST NAME IS MACEO
Guediguian, Robert
MARIUS AND JEANNETTE
Guest, Christopher
ALMOST HEROES
Guzman, Patricio
BATTLE OF CHILE: THE STRUGGLE OF AN UNARMED PEOPLE—PART 2: THE COUP D'ETAT, THE
CHILE, OBSTINATE MEMORY
Gyllenhaal, Stephen
HOMEGROWN
Hacker, Melissa
MY KNEES WERE JUMPING: REMEMBERING THE KINDERTRANSPORTS
Hacker, Michael
DESTINY OF MARTY FINE, THE
Hadleigh-West, Maggie
WAR ZONE
Haines, Randa
DANCE WITH ME
Haines, Richard W.
RUN FOR COVER
Hamburg, John
SAFE MEN
Hamm, Nick
TALK OF ANGELS
Hammann, Craig
BOOGIE BOY
Haneke, Michael
FUNNY GAMES
Hanna, William H.
FLINTSTONES: I YABBA-DABBA DOO!, THE
Hardy, Rod
TWO FOR TEXAS
Hartley, Hal
HENRY FOOL
Haynes, Todd
VELVET GOLDMINE
Heap, Jonathan
HOSTILE INTENT
Hedden, Roger
HI-LIFE
Hedegus, Chris
MOON OVER BROADWAY
Hemecker, Ralph
DOUBLE EDGE
Herek, Stephen
HOLY MAN
Herman, Mark
LITTLE VOICE
Herskovitz, Marshall
DANGEROUS BEAUTY
Herzfeld, John
DON KING: ONLY IN AMERICA
Herzog, Werner
LITTLE DIETER NEEDS TO FLY
Hess, Jon
MARS
Hewitt, Peter
BORROWERS, THE
Hickner, Steve
PRINCE OF EGYPT, THE
Hickox, Anthony
PRINCE VALIANT
Higashi, Yoichi
VILLAGE OF DREAMS
Hill, Skip
THURSDAY
Hiller, Arthur
BURN HOLLYWOOD BURN
Hirtz, Dagmar
MOONDANCE
Hoblit, Gregory
FALLEN
Hoge, Bob
GODSON, THE
Holland, Todd
KRIPPENDORF'S TRIBE
Hooks, Kevin
BLACK DOG
Hopkins, Stephen
LOST IN SPACE
Howitt, Peter
SLIDING DOORS
Hung, Sammo
DRAGONS FOREVER
ENCOUNTER OF THE SPOOKY KIND
MR. NICE GUY
PRODIGAL SON, THE
Hunter, Tim
MAKER, THE
RESCUERS: STORIES OF COURAGE—TWO COUPLES
Huse, Michael F.
RAT'S TALE, A
Hutton, Timothy
DIGGING TO CHINA

Hytner, Nicholas
OBJECT OF MY AFFECTION, THE
Ice Cube
PLAYERS CLUB, THE
Iijima, Masakatsu
POLTERGEIST REPORT: YUYU HAKUSHO
Ikehiro, Kazuo
SLEEPY EYES OF DEATH: SWORD OF SEDUCTION
Imamura, Shohei
EEL, THE
Inoue, Yoshio
RAZOR: WHO'S GOT THE GOLD?, THE
Irvin, John
WHEN TRUMPETS FADE
Ishii, Takashi
GONIN
Ivory, James
SOLDIER'S DAUGHTER NEVER CRIES, A
Iwai, Shunji
WHEN I CLOSE MY EYES
Jackson, Doug
DEAD END
Jacobs, Alan
DIARY OF A SERIAL KILLER
Jacobson, Rick
BLACK THUNDER
INTERLOCKED: THRILLED TO DEATH
Jacquot, Benoit
DISENCHANTED, THE
SEVENTH HEAVEN
Jaglom, Henry
DEJA VU
Jameson, Jerry
LAND OF THE FREE
Jean, Vadim
REAL HOWARD SPITZ, THE
Jenkins, Tamara
SLUMS OF BEVERLY HILLS
Johnson, John S.
RATCHET
Johnson, Mark Steven
SIMON BIRCH
Johnson, Tim
ANTZ
Johnston, Heather
LENA'S DREAMS
Jones, Kirk
WAKING NED DEVINE
Jordan, Gregor
TWISTED
Jordan, Neil
BUTCHER BOY, THE
Jubenvill, Ken
EBENEZER
Jud, Reinhard
JAMES ELLROY: DEMON DOG OF AMERICAN CRIME FICTION
Kalmenson, Bill
SOULER OPPOSITE, THE
Kanganis, Charles T.
DENNIS THE MENACE STRIKES AGAIN
Kaplan, Deborah
CAN'T HARDLY WAIT
Kapur, Shekhar
ELIZABETH
Kasdan, Jake
ZERO EFFECT
Kastner, Daphna
FRENCH EXIT
Kaufer, Jonathan
BAD MANNERS
Kaye, Tony
AMERICAN HISTORY X
Keating, David
SUMMER FLING
Keen, Bob
LOST WORLD, THE
Keeter, Worth
LAST LIVES
Keller, Harry
TOUCH OF EVIL: THE DIRECTOR'S CUT
Kellman, Barnet
SLAPPY AND THE STINKERS
Kelly, Sarah
FULL TILT BOOGIE
Kiarostami, Abbas
TASTE OF CHERRY
Kidron, Beeban
SWEPT FROM THE SEA
King, Rick
CATHERINE'S GROVE
TERMINAL JUSTICE
King, Zalman
IN GOD'S HANDS
Kingsberg, Alan
ALMOST PARTNERS
Kirkland, Boyd
BATMAN & MR. FREEZE: SUBZERO
Kirkman, Tim
DEAR JESSE
Kitano, Takeshi
FIREWORKS
SONATINE
Klapisch, Cedric
UN AIR DE FAMILLE
Koch, Ulrike
SALTMEN OF TIBET, THE
Koherr, Bob
PLUMP FICTION
Kollek, Amos
SUE
Kopple, Barbara
WILD MAN BLUES
Kovalyov, Igor
RUGRATS MOVIE, THE
Kowalchuk, William R.
RUDOLPH THE RED-NOSED REINDEER: THE MOVIE
Krishtofovich, Vyacheslav
FRIEND OF THE DECEASED, A
Kwietniowski, Richard
LOVE AND DEATH ON LONG ISLAND
La Salle, Eriq
REBOUND: THE LEGEND OF EARL "THE GOAT" MANIGAULT
LaBute, Neil
YOUR FRIENDS & NEIGHBORS
LaDuca, Rob
LION KING II: SIMBA'S PRIDE, THE
LaGravenese, Richard
LIVING OUT LOUD
Lahiff, Craig
HEAVEN'S BURNING
Lancaster, Quint
RED HAWK: WEAPON OF DEATH
Landis, John
BLUES BROTHERS 2000
Lang, Samantha
TWISTED
Langley, John
DOGWATCH
Lanoff, Lawrence
CHOSEN ONE: LEGEND OF THE RAVEN, THE
Lasseter, John
BUG'S LIFE, A
Lawrence, Mr.
GENERAL CHAOS: UNCENSORED ANIMATION
Lea, Frances
GENERAL CHAOS: UNCENSORED ANIMATION
Leder, Mimi
DEEP IMPACT
Lee, Iara
MODULATIONS: CINEMA FOR THE EAR
Lee Jua Nan
BEAUTY INVESTIGATOR
Lee, Quentin
SHOPPING FOR FANGS
Lee, Robert
ACT OF WAR
Lee, Spike
HE GOT GAME
Lehmann, Michael
MY GIANT
Leitzes, Jennifer
MONTANA
Leland, David
LAND GIRLS, THE
Leong Po-Chih
HONG KONG 1941
Leonhardt, Lutz
ZAKIR AND HIS FRIENDS
Lester, Mark L.
MISBEGOTTEN
Leva, Gary
PLAN B
Levin, Marc
SLAM
Levinson, Barry
SPHERE
Levy, Robert L.
KID IN ALADDIN'S PALACE, A
Levy, Shuki
RUSTY: THE GREAT RESCUE
Lewis, Everett
SKIN & BONE
Lima Jr., Walter
OYSTER AND THE WIND, THE
Lin, Justin
SHOPPING FOR FANGS
Lindsay-Hogg, Michael
HORTON FOOTE'S ALONE
Link, Caroline
BEYOND SILENCE
Linklater, Richard
NEWTON BOYS, THE
Litman, Lynne
RESCUERS: STORIES OF COURAGE—TWO COUPLES
Loach, Ken
CARLA'S SONG
Longinotto, Kim
DIVORCE IRANIAN STYLE
Loo Chun Kok
KILLER ANGELS
Louzil, Eric
FATAL PURSUIT
Luna, Bigas
CHAMBERMAID ON THE TITANIC, THE
Lustig, William
UNCLE SAM
Lynch, Paul
FACE THE EVIL
Lyne, Adrian
LOLITA
MacKinnon, Gillies
REGENERATION
Madden, John
SHAKESPEARE IN LOVE
Main, Stewart
BOYS IN LOVE 2
Malenfant, Rob
LANDLADY, THE
Malick, Terrence
THIN RED LINE, THE
Mamet, David
SPANISH PRISONER, THE
Mandt, Neil
HIJACKING HOLLYWOOD

Pennebaker, D.A.
- MOON OVER BROADWAY

Peretz, Jesse
- FIRST LOVE, LAST RITES

Perry, Pinchas
- PRINCE, THE

Peters, Charlie
- MUSIC FROM ANOTHER ROOM

Pieplow, John
- DEE SNIDER'S STRANGELAND

Pirozek, Sarah
- FREE TIBET

Plympton, Bill
- GENERAL CHAOS: UNCENSORED ANIMATION
- I MARRIED A STRANGE PERSON!

Poirier, Manuel
- WESTERN

Portillo, Ralph
- NAKED LIES

Posner, P.J.
- LAST BREATH

Potamkin, Buzz
- BUSTER & CHAUNCEY'S SILENT NIGHT

Pradal, Manuel
- MARIE BAIE DES ANGES

Proft, Pat
- WRONGFULLY ACCUSED

Proyas, Alex
- DARK CITY

Pulcini, Robert
- OFF THE MENU: THE LAST DAYS OF CHASEN'S

Purvis, Barry
- BOYS IN LOVE 2

Putch, John
- ALONE IN THE WOODS

Pyun, Albert
- MEAN GUNS
- NEMESIS 4: CRY OF ANGELS

Raffo, John
- JOHNNY SKIDMARKS

Raimi, Sam
- SIMPLE PLAN, A

Ramirez, Robert
- BRAVE LITTLE TOASTER GOES TO MARS, THE

Rappaport, Mark
- SILVER SCREEN: COLOR ME LAVENDER, THE

Ratner, Brett
- RUSH HOUR

Ray, Fred Olen
- INVISIBLE DAD
- INVISIBLE MOM

Raymond, Bradley
- POCAHONTAS II: JOURNEY TO A NEW WORLD

Redford, Robert
- HORSE WHISPERER, THE

Reitman, Ivan
- SIX DAYS, SEVEN NIGHTS

Remy, Christopher
- CLOCKMAKER

Resnais, Alain
- SAME OLD SONG

Reynolds, Scott
- UGLY, THE

Rhee, Phillip
- BEST OF THE BEST: WITHOUT WARNING

Rich, Richard
- SWAN PRINCESS III: AND THE MYSTERY OF THE ENCHANTED TREASURE, THE

Richards, Sybil
- LOLIDA 2000

Richman, Meg
- UNDER HEAVEN

Rideau, Wilbert
- FARM: ANGOLA, U.S.A., THE

Roberts, John
- PAULIE

Robin-Collins, Christopher
- TWISTED

Robinson, James F.
- STILL BREATHING

Robinson, Phil
- FERNGULLY 2: THE MAGICAL RESCUE

Rodriguez, Robert
- FACULTY, THE

Rooney, Darrell
- LION KING II: SIMBA'S PRIDE, THE

Roos, Don
- OPPOSITE OF SEX, THE

Rosenow, James
- CROSSING FIELDS

Rosi, Francesco
- TRUCE, THE

Rosler, Alexander
- MENDEL

Rosman, Mark
- INVADER, THE

Rouan, Brigitte
- POST COITUM, ANIMAL TRISTE

Ruben, Andy
- CLUB VAMPIRE

Ruben, Joseph
- RETURN TO PARADISE

Rubin, H. Alex
- WHO IS HENRY JAGLOM?

Ruiz, Raul
- GENEALOGIES OF A CRIME
- SHATTERED IMAGE

Russell, Ken
- TRACKED

Ruzowitzky, Stefan
- INHERITORS, THE

Ryan, Joal
- FORMER CHILD STAR

Ryan, Terence
- BRYLCREEM BOYS, THE

Ryan, William
- REACH THE ROCK

Saalfield, Catherine Gund
- HALLELUJAH!

Sabella, Paul
- ALL DOGS CHRISTMAS CAROL, AN

Saget, Bob
- DIRTY WORK

Salimbeni, Reto
- URBAN SAFARI

Salles, Walter
- CENTRAL STATION

Salomon, Mikael
- HARD RAIN

Salvatores, Gabriele
- NIRVANA

Samuels, Rachel
- RUNNING WOMAN, THE

Sanford, Arlene
- I'LL BE HOME FOR CHRISTMAS

Santucci, Walter
- GENERAL CHAOS: UNCENSORED ANIMATION

Sanzel, Ken
- SCARRED CITY

Sarin, Vic
- IN HIS FATHER'S SHOES

Sayles, John
- MEN WITH GUNS

Schachter, Steven
- CON, THE

Schenkel, Carl
- TARZAN AND THE LOST CITY

Schickel, Richard
- ALFRED HITCHCOCK: MASTER OF SUSPENSE
- ELIA KAZAN: A DIRECTOR'S JOURNEY

Schiff, Brad
- GENERAL CHAOS: UNCENSORED ANIMATION

Schlondorff, Volker
- OGRE, THE
- PALMETTO

Schmoeller, David
- SECRET KINGDOM, THE

Schrader, Paul
- AFFLICTION

Schreiber, Nancy
- STORY OF X, THE

Schroeder, Barbet
- DESPERATE MEASURES

Schwartz, Stefan
- SHOOTING FISH

Scott, Art
- MIGHTY KONG, THE

Scott, Darin
- CAUGHT UP

Scott, T.J.
- YOUNG HERCULES

Scott, Tony
- ENEMY OF THE STATE

Seale, James
- ASYLUM

Seavey, Nina Gilden
- PARALYZING FEAR: THE STORY OF POLIO IN AMERICA, A

Sebast, Dick
- SECRET OF NIMH 2: TIMMY TO THE RESCUE, THE

Semler, Dean
- FIRESTORM

Senkowski, Ron
- LET'S KILL ALL THE LAWYERS

Shadyac, Tom
- PATCH ADAMS

Shainberg, Steven
- HIT ME

Shayne, Linda
- LITTLE GHOST

Shelton, Millicent
- RIDE

Sherwin, Robert
- DIRTY LAUNDRY

Shun Tai Wai
- KICK BOXER'S TEARS

Shyamalan, M. Night
- WIDE AWAKE

Sidaris, Andy
- RETURN TO SAVAGE BEACH

Sigl, Robert
- TALES FROM A PARALLEL UNIVERSE: GIGA SHADOW

Sikora, Jim
- BULLET ON A WIRE

Sikorski, Joseph
- RETURN OF THE KING, THE

Silberling, Brad
- CITY OF ANGELS

Singer, Bryan
- APT PUPIL

Skinner, Emily
- GENERAL CHAOS: UNCENSORED ANIMATION

Skjoldbjaerg, Erik
- INSOMNIA

Skoog, Susan
- WHATEVER

Sletaune, Pal
- JUNK MAIL

Sloan, Brian
- I THINK I DO

Yamazaki, Osamu
WRATH OF THE NINJA: THE YOTODEN MOVIE
Yasuda, Kimiyoshi
SLEEPY EYES OF DEATH: FULL CIRCLE KILLING
Ye Ying
RED CHERRY
Young, John G.
PARALLEL SONS
Yu, Ronny
BRIDE OF CHUCKY
Yuen, Corey
BODYGUARD FROM BEIJING
DRAGONS FOREVER
Zallian, Steven
CIVIL ACTION, A
Zamm, Alex
CHAIRMAN OF THE BOARD
Zanussi, Krzysztof
FROM A FAR COUNTRY
Zhang Yuan
EAST PALACE, WEST PALACE
Zhou Xiaowen
EMPEROR'S SHADOW, THE
Zucker, David
BASEKETBALL
Zuckerman, Steve
NORTH SHORE FISH
Zukovic, Dan
LAST BIG THING, THE
Zwick, Edward
SIEGE, THE

EDITORS

Adair, Dustin
KINGDOM OF SHADOWS
Adair, Sandra
NEWTON BOYS, THE
Adriano, Dexter
TRUCKS
Adrianson, Stephen
LAND OF THE FREE
Albert, Ross
SENSELESS
Albertson, Sean
JOHNNY SKIDMARKS
STILL BREATHING
Allen, India
CHOSEN ONE: LEGEND OF THE RAVEN, THE
Allen, Stan
QUEST FOR CAMELOT
Altschuler, John
ALL THE RAGE
Amundson, Peter
GODZILLA
Anderson, Brad
NEXT STOP, WONDERLAND
Anderson, William
TRUMAN SHOW, THE
Andreson, Judy
SPREE, THE
Anwar, Tariq
COUSIN BETTE
OBJECT OF MY AFFECTION, THE
Appleby, George
SNOWBOUND
Arcidi, Anthony
I MARRIED A STRANGE PERSON!
Aron, Donn
HIT ME
MILO
Atkins, Mark
KURT AND COURTNEY
Audsley, Mick
AVENGERS, THE
Auvray, Dominique
DISENCHANTED, THE
Baino, Mariano
DEAD WATERS
Baker, Marvin
LETTER FROM DEATH ROW, A
Balser, Dean
BONE DADDY
Bank, Mirra
ALFRED HITCHCOCK: MASTER OF SUSPENSE
Barton, Sean
PHOTOGRAPHING FAIRIES
Bartz, Geof
LENNY BRUCE: SWEAR TO TELL THE TRUTH
Basinski, Peter
RESCUERS: STORIES OF COURAGE—TWO COUPLES
Bassett, Craig
ERNEST IN THE ARMY
Baumgarten, Alan
JUNGLE BOOK: MOWGLI'S STORY, THE
Beason, Eric
SIMPLE PLAN, A
Beauman, Nicholas
BRIGHT SHINING LIE, A
Becker, Manfred
PLACE CALLED CHIAPAS, A
Bedford, James Gavin
IN GOD'S HANDS
Beldin, Dale
BLUES BROTHERS 2000
Bensley, Guy
DAD SAVAGE
Berdan, Brian
SMOKE SIGNALS
Berger, Peter E.
STAR TREK: INSURRECTION
Berkowitz, Michael
DECAMPITATED
Berlatsky, David
MISBEGOTTEN
Bessner, Jeff
TERMINAL JUSTICE
Betancourt, Jeff
BILLY'S HOLLYWOOD SCREEN KISS
Bilcock, Jill
ELIZABETH
Billeskov-Jansen, Janus
JERUSALEM
LES MISERABLES
Bindler, S.R.
HANDS ON A HARDBODY
Bini, Joe
LITTLE DIETER NEEDS TO FLY
Binns, Paul
UNMADE BEDS
Binns, T. David
I GOT THE HOOK UP
Blunden, Bill
FROM A FAR COUNTRY
Blunden, Christopher
HUMAN BOMB
Blye, Toni
DAVID SEARCHING
Bock, Larry
GIRLS IN PRISON
Boguski, Barbara
DESTINY OF MARTY FINE, THE
Boisson, Noelle
SOLDIER'S DAUGHTER NEVER CRIES, A
Bonanni, Mauro
STEAM
Bondelli, Roger
EVER AFTER
Bookwalter, J.R.
CURSE OF THE PUPPET MASTER
Bornstein, Charles
CAUGHT UP
Bowers, George
HOW STELLA GOT HER GROOVE BACK
Bradley, Jeff
FATAL PURSUIT
Bradsell, Michael
WILDE
Brandt-Burgoyne, Anita
I'LL BE HOME FOR CHRISTMAS
Breitsenbach, Al
BATMAN & MR. FREEZE: SUBZERO
Brenner, David
LOLITA
WHAT DREAMS MAY COME
Bricker, Randolph K.
BRIDE OF CHUCKY
PHANTOMS
Briggs, David
BOYS IN LOVE 2
Brown, Barry Alexander
COUSIN BETTE
HE GOT GAME
Brown, O. Nicholas
MAJOR LEAGUE: BACK TO THE MINORS
Buckley, Norman
ALARMIST, THE
HORTON FOOTE'S ALONE
MONTANA
NORTH SHORE FISH
Burkert-Nahler, Britta
INHERITORS, THE
Butler, Bill
NOT IN THIS TOWN
Byungtae Chun
RED HAWK: WEAPON OF DEATH
Cambas, Jacqueline
PENTAGON WARS, THE
PROPOSITION, THE
Cannon, Bruce
PAULIE
Capillas, Nacho Ruiz
SHAMPOO HORNS
Carroll, Bryan H.
MAJOR LEAGUE: BACK TO THE MINORS
Cassidy, Jay
REPLACEMENT KILLERS, THE
URBAN LEGEND
Castaldo, Robert J.
NIGHT VISION
Caster, Nicholas
OGRE, THE
Catalena, Mark
BOYS IN LOVE 2
Cavanaugh, Michael
FERNGULLY 2: THE MAGICAL RESCUE
Ceppi, Francois
LA SEPARATION
Chan Ki-hop
COMRADES, ALMOST A LOVE STORY
Chandler, Tammis
DESTINY OF MARTY FINE, THE
Chang Hsin Yen
SHAOLIN TEMPLE, THE
Chang, Joseph
DRAGONS FOREVER
Chang Kwok Kuen
MAGNIFICENT WARRIORS
Chang, William
FALLEN ANGELS
Chang Yao-Chung
ENCOUNTER OF THE SPOOKY KIND
Charfe, Heidi
BOYS WILL BE BOYS
Chaskel, Pedro
BATTLE OF CHILE: THE STRUGGLE OF AN UNARMED PEOPLE—PART 2: THE COUP D'ETAT, THE

Chavance, Pascale
SEVENTH HEAVEN
Cheng Keung
KICK BOXER'S TEARS
Cheong Kwok Kuen
ROYAL WARRIORS
Cherot, Christopher Scott
HAV PLENTY
Chestnut, Scott
MAKER, THE
ROUNDERS
Cheung Keung
KILLER ANGELS
Cheung, Peter
ARMOUR OF GOD
DRAGONS FOREVER
HEROES SHED NO TEARS
MR. NICE GUY
PRODIGAL SON, THE
Chew, Richard
HOPE FLOATS
Chiate, Debra
DEAD MAN ON CAMPUS
Christensen, Pernille Bech
KINGDOM, PART 2, THE
Christiani, Gabriella
DESTINY OF MARTY FINE, THE
Cibelli, Christopher
PROPHECY II, THE
Clayton, Curtiss
BUFFALO '66
POLISH WEDDING
Coates, Anne V.
OUT OF SIGHT
Coburn, Arthur
DANGEROUS BEAUTY
PRICE ABOVE RUBIES, A
SIMPLE PLAN, A
Codron, David
NEXT STEP, THE
OPPOSITE OF SEX, THE
Cody, Alan
MEET THE DEEDLES
Cohen, Steven
DON KING: ONLY IN AMERICA
Coleman, Anthony
FALLING FIRE
Colina, Luis
ANOTHER DAY IN PARADISE
OVERNIGHT DELIVERY
Congdon, Dana
DIGGING TO CHINA
Cook, Wayne
UGLY, THE
Cooke, Tricia
BIG LEBOWSKI, THE
Corrao, Angelo
CROSSING FIELDS
Corriveau, Andre
LOUISA MAY ALCOTT'S LITTLE MEN
Corwin, Hank
HORSE WHISPERER, THE
Cottrell, Belinda
LAST SEDUCTION II, THE
Coughlin, Cari
CON, THE
Crafford, Ian
SAVIOR
WHEN TRUMPETS FADE
Craven, Samuel
LOVELIFE
Cristiani, Gabriella
SAVIOR
Curtis, Tracy
GODSON, THE
Cybulski, Mary
CHICAGO CAB

da Silva, Virgilo
ERNEST IN THE ARMY
Dalesandro, Anthony
RETURN TO SAVAGE BEACH
Dartonne, Monique
GADJO DILO
Das, Poppy
KRAA! THE SEA MONSTER
LOVER GIRL
TALISMAN
Davies Jr., Freeman
HORSE WHISPERER, THE
Davis, Julie
I LOVE YOU, DON'T TOUCH ME!
Davis, Mona
FARM: ANGOLA, U.S.A., THE
Davis, Ron
GENERAL, THE
Day, Mark
THEORY OF FLIGHT
Day, Paul
HOSTILE INTENT
de Luze, Herve
SAME OLD SONG
Dechamps, Yves
LIFE OF JESUS, THE
Dedet, Yann
WESTERN
Deguchi, Keiko
REAL BLONDE, THE
Deimel, Mark
TIMOTHY LEARY'S DEAD
DeKoning, Jessica
CHARACTER
Deseine, Valerie
MARIE BAIE DES ANGES
Devlin, Paul
SLAMNATION
Di Ciaula, Pia
REAL HOWARD SPITZ, THE
REGENERATION
Diver, William
TWENTYFOURSEVEN
Dixon, Humphrey
DANCING AT LUGHNASA
LAWN DOGS
LEADING MAN, THE
Dixon, Paul
MY VERY BEST FRIEND
Dobryanskaya, Marina
THIEF, THE
Doherty, Michael
CAPTIVE
Douglas, Paul
SCOOBY-DOO ON ZOMBIE ISLAND
Downing, Todd
BOYS IN LOVE 2
Dubois, Victor
SIN AND REDEMPTION
Ducsay, Bob
DEEP RISING
STAR KID
Duddleston, Amy
HIGH ART
PSYCHO
Duthie, Michael
SHATTERED IMAGE
Earl, Christopher
AYN RAND: A SENSE OF LIFE
Eckelberry, Stephen
MEN
Edick, Patricia
COMEDY'S DIRTIEST DOZEN
Egeland, Einar
MENDEL
Eliopoulos, Nicholas
WOO

Ellis, Christopher
RIGHT CONNECTIONS, THE
Ellis, Michael
LITTLE VOICE
Ellis, Peter B.
NOTES FROM UNDERGROUND
Elmiger, Suzy
IMPOSTORS, THE
Evans, Rodney
UNVEILING, THE
Fang, Paul
BEAUTY INVESTIGATOR
Fanucci, Agita
COURTING COURTNEY
Fardoulis, Monique
SWINDLE, THE
Farr, Ian
HOSTILE WATERS
Fenn, Suzanne
POLISH WEDDING
Fenton, Kathryn
VIOLET'S VISIT
Ferretti, Robert A.
HUNTED, THE
Fiedler, Milenia
KRZYSZTOF KIESLOWSKI: I'M SO-SO
Finfer, David
KISSING A FOOL
SIMON BIRCH
Finkel, Claudia
FRENCH EXIT
Fiocchi, Massimo
NIRVANA
Fjellvaer, Lillian
OTHER SIDE OF SUNDAY, THE
Flaer, Howard
LITTLE BIGFOOT 2: THE JOURNEY HOME
Flamholc, Leon
TRANCEFORMER: A PORTRAIT OF LARS VON TRIER
Flanagan, Peter Devaney
CHILDREN OF THE CORN V: FIELD OF TERROR
Flaum, Seth
NEIL SIMON'S THE ODD COUPLE II
Fleck, Jane Allison
PLAN B
Fletcher, Nick
PRINCE OF EGYPT, THE
Foley, Pat
FLINTSTONES: I YABBA-DABBA DOO!, THE
Folsey Jr., George
DIRTY WORK
Font, Teresa
DAY OF THE BEAST, THE
Freeman, David
BORROWERS, THE
Freeman, Jeff
ONLY THRILL, THE
Friedkin, Jay
BABE: PIG IN THE CITY
TRICKS
Fries, Tom
DREAM FOR AN INSOMNIAC
Frisa, James
SIX-STRING SAMURAI
STIR
Frisch, Jana
URBAN SAFARI
Frisina, Hibah Sherif
WHEN DANGER FOLLOWS YOU HOME
Fruchtman, Lisa
DANCE WITH ME
Fukumitsu, Shinichi
DRAGON BALL Z THE MOVIE: THE TREE OF MIGHT

DRAGON BALL Z THE MOVIE: THE WORLD'S STRONGEST
Fuller, Brad
NIL BY MOUTH
Gall, Joe
BATMAN/SUPERMAN MOVIE, THE
Gallo, Phil
WEST NEW YORK
Gamble, David
SHAKESPEARE IN LOVE
Gardos, Eva
INFORMANT, THE
Garland, Glenn
BOOGIE BOY
RETROACTIVE
Garvin, Lee
DESTINY OF MARTY FINE, THE
Gaster, Nicolas
PASSION IN THE DESERT
Gazzara, Elizabeth
SOMEWHERE IN THE CITY
SUE
Gengenbach, Pal
JUNK MAIL
Gibbs, Tony
FROM A FAR COUNTRY
GEORGE WALLACE
RONIN
Gibson, J. Kathleen
MR. JEALOUSY
Gilbert, John
ABERRATION
CASPER MEETS WENDY
RICHIE RICH'S CHRISTMAS WISH
Gill, Scott J.
PHANTASM: OBLIVION
Ginsberg, Milton
PRONTO
Girard, Helene
CHILE, OBSTINATE MEMORY
Gleisner, Claudia
ZAKIR AND HIS FRIENDS
Goddard, Bill
IN HIS FATHER'S SHOES
Goddard, Daniel
LOVE IS THE DEVIL: STUDY FOR A PORTRAIT OF FRANCIS BACON
Goenka, Tula
WAR ZONE
Goldblatt, Mark
ARMAGEDDON
Goldenberg, William
PLEASANTVILLE
Goodhill, Dean
ELMORE LEONARD'S GOLD COAST
Gordon, Richard
TARANTELLA
Gottlieb, Mallory
COLONY, THE
Graef, Sue
NO LOOKING BACK
Graham, Carl
FACE DOWN
Granger, Tracy
ILLTOWN
Green, Colin
MERLIN
Greenberg, Gary
AMERICAN HISTORY X
Greenberg, Jerry
REACH THE ROCK
Greenbury, Christopher
THERE'S SOMETHING ABOUT MARY
Greene Bricmont, Wendy
SIX DAYS, SEVEN NIGHTS
Gregory, John
LIVING OUT LOUD
Grieve, Neil
REDLINE
Guidici, Ross
MILO
Gumpel, Emily
WAR ZONE
Guthrie, Sandy
WHATEVER
Gutowski, Joseph
INVADER, THE
Hacker, Melissa
MY KNEES WERE JUMPING: REMEMBERING THE KINDERTRANSPORTS
Hafitz, Andrew
LAST DAYS OF DISCO, THE
Haines, Heidi
BLEEDERS
Haines, Richard W.
RUN FOR COVER
Halsey, Colleen
POCAHONTAS II: JOURNEY TO A NEW WORLD
Halsey, Richard
BARNEY'S GREAT ADVENTURE—THE MOVIE
Hambling, Gerry
TALK OF ANGELS
Hamilton, Steve
HENRY FOOL
Hampton, Janice
PECKER
WOO
Harkema, Reginald
HARD CORE LOGO
Harley, Karen
TIETA OF AGRESTE
Harvey, Marshall
SMALL SOLDIERS
Hasegawa, Keiichi
GONIN
Hayman, Tony
MIGHTY KONG, THE
Hedlund, Brett
WHITE RAVEN, THE
Hegedus, Chris
MOON OVER BROADWAY
Heim, Alan
AMERICAN HISTORY X
Helfrich, Mark
RUSH HOUR
Henry, Bill
LET'S TALK ABOUT SEX
Heredia, Paula
FREE TIBET
MODULATIONS: CINEMA FOR THE EAR
Hess, Augie
12 ANGRY MEN
Hickox, Emma E.
BRYLCREEM BOYS, THE
Higashi, Yoichi
VILLAGE OF DREAMS
Hill, Jim
CHAIRMAN OF THE BOARD
Hindley, Richard
TWISTED
Hines, Suzanne
PLAYERS CLUB, THE
RINGMASTER
Hirakubo, Masahiro
BREAK, THE
HI-LO COUNTRY, THE
Hirsch, Paul
HARD RAIN
MIGHTY JOE YOUNG
Hirtz, Dagmar
MOONDANCE
Hitner, Harry
TARZAN AND THE LOST CITY
Hoenig, Dov
DARK CITY
PERFECT MURDER, A
Hoffman, Sabine
HURRICANE STREETS
Hofstra, Jack
FIRESTORM
Hok, Tom
RUDOLPH THE RED-NOSED REINDEER: THE MOVIE
Holland, Dan
CLUB VAMPIRE
WATCHERS REBORN
Hollyn, Norman
QUICKSILVER HIGHWAY
Honess, Peter
FROM A FAR COUNTRY
MERCURY RISING
Horvitch, Andy
MIDAS TOUCH, THE
Hoy, Maysie
WHAT DREAMS MAY COME
Hoy, William
EIGHTEENTH ANGEL, THE
MAN IN THE IRON MASK, THE
Hubert, Axel
OLIVER TWIST
Hubley, Ray
ONE TOUGH COP
Hunter, Martin
SOLDIER
Hutshing, Joe
MEET JOE BLACK
Ikeda, Michiko
GODZILLA VS. KING GHIDORAH
Iverson, Gil
FLINTSTONES: I YABBA-DABBA DOO!, THE
Iverson, Tim
FLINTSTONES: I YABBA-DABBA DOO!, THE
Iwai, Shunji
WHEN I CLOSE MY EYES
Jablow, Michael
BREAST MEN
CAN'T HARDLY WAIT
HOMEGROWN
Jaglom, Henry
DEJA VU
Jakubowicz, Alain
DIGGING TO CHINA
TOP OF THE WORLD
Jangsoo Kim
RED HAWK: WEAPON OF DEATH
Jaynes, Roderick
BIG LEBOWSKI, THE
Jeffries, Scott
HERCULES AND XENA THE ANIMATED MOVIE: THE BATTLE FOR MOUNT OLYMPUS
Johnson, Stephen L.
WALKING THUNDER
Jones, Janice
CLASSIFIED X
Jones, Leslie
THIN RED LINE, THE
Jones, Robert C.
BULWORTH
Jones, Sherwood
KID IN ALADDIN'S PALACE, A
Jordan, Lawrence
FALLEN
JACK FROST
Juergens, Mark
DAY AT THE BEACH
Kacirkova, Ivana
FORGOTTEN LIGHT

Kahn, Michael
SAVING PRIVATE RYAN
Kahn, Sheldon
SIX DAYS, SEVEN NIGHTS
Kakesu, Syuichi
JUNK FOOD
Kamen, Jay
NIGHT AT THE ROXBURY, A
Karr, Gary
ALMOST PARTNERS
REBOUND: THE LEGEND OF EARL "THE GOAT" MANIGAULT
Katz, Robin
BAD MANNERS
Katz, Virginia
GODS AND MONSTERS
Kawashima, Akimasa
GONIN
Keefe, Tom
HENRY: PORTRAIT OF A SERIAL KILLER PART 2
Keir, Andy
BELOVED
STOREFRONT HITCHCOCK
Keraudren, Francois
I THINK I DO
Kiarostami, Abbas
TASTE OF CHERRY
Kindt, Christa
LET'S KILL ALL THE LAWYERS
Kirk, Neil
PLUMP FICTION
Kirpaul, Amanda
OUTSIDE OZONA
Kitano, Takeshi
FIREWORKS
SONATINE
Klein, Saar
THIN RED LINE, THE
Klier, Simone
KILLER CONDOM, THE
Kling, Elizabeth
PRACTICAL MAGIC
Klingman, Lynzee
CITY OF ANGELS
HUSH
LIVING OUT LOUD
Kloomok, Darren
LOVE WALKED IN
Klotz, Joe
DEAR JESSE
Kobrin, Rob
DANCER, TEXAS POP. 81
Koefoed, Christopher
DIARY OF A SERIAL KILLER
Koford, James D.
SWAN PRINCESS III: AND THE MYSTERY OF THE ENCHANTED TREASURE, THE
Komatsu, Natao
ZERO WOMAN
Korzan, Kelly
WAR ZONE
Kravetz, Carole
ONE TRUE THING
Ku Chi Wai
SHAOLIN TEMPLE, THE
Kucherenko, Natalia
THIEF, THE
Kuge, Michael
BLACK THUNDER
Kuhn, John
KINGDOM OF SHADOWS
Kushner, Jeff
DEE SNIDER'S STRANGELAND
Kwong Chi-leung
COMRADES, ALMOST A LOVE STORY
Lacerda, Felipe
CENTRAL STATION
Ladizinsky, Ian
STRAY BULLET
Ladizinsky, Ivan
INDISCREET
PROPHECY II, THE
Lambert, Robert K.
WITHOUT LIMITS
LaMorte, Steve
RIVER RED
Lange, Bruce
AIR BUD: GOLDEN RECEIVER
TALES FROM A PARALLEL UNIVERSE: GIGA SHADOW
Langford, Jan
LIKE IT IS
Langlois, L. James
BURN HOLLYWOOD BURN
Langlois, Yves
PEACEKEEPER, THE
Lau, Julie
BRAVE LITTLE TOASTER GOES TO MARS, THE
Lauman, Paige
RIVER RED
Lawson, Tony
BUTCHER BOY, THE
Lebental, Dan
DECEIVER
VERY BAD THINGS
Lebenzon, Chris
ARMAGEDDON
ENEMY OF THE STATE
Lecorne, Guy
ARTEMISIA
LIFE OF JESUS, THE
Lee, Quentin
SHOPPING FOR FANGS
LeGrand, Hudson
DISAPPEARANCE OF KEVIN JOHNSON, THE
Leif, Marc
FIXER, THE
Leighton, Robert
HUSH
Leonard, David
BELLY
Leszcylowski, Michal
KRISTIN LAVRANSDATTER
Levesque, Isabelle
LOST WORLD, THE
Levine, Michael
CRUISE, THE
Levy, Vincent
EAST PALACE, WEST PALACE
Lewis, Emir
SLAM
Lewis, Everett
SKIN & BONE
Lewis, Tom
WATERBOY, THE
WEDDING SINGER, THE
Li Yuk Wai
SHAOLIN TEMPLE, THE
Licide, Joseph
EL CHE: INVESTIGATING A LEGEND
Lin, Justin
SHOPPING FOR FANGS
Lind, Ewa J.
UNDER THE SKIN
Linder, Stu
SPHERE
Linson, Phillip
CLOCKMAKER
Lipartiya, Marina
BROTHER
Littler, Rick
DEAD WATERS
Littleton, Carol
BELOVED
TWILIGHT
Livingstone, Russell
DOGWATCH
Lo, Mayin
SUBSTITUTE 2: SCHOOL'S OUT, THE
Loewenthal, Daniel
CATHERINE'S GROVE
Lofstrom, Markus
LAST BIG THING, THE
Loiseleux, Valerie
VOYAGE TO THE BEGINNING OF THE WORLD
Lonsdale, Peter N.
LION KING II: SIMBA'S PRIDE, THE
Lorente, Isabel
GOVERNESS, THE
Lovejoy, Ray
LOST IN SPACE
SUMMER FLING
Lovitt, Bert
BEST OF THE BEST: WITHOUT WARNING
Lowenthal, Daniel
LAST ASSASSINS
Lunger, Jeff
DIDN'T DO IT FOR LOVE
Lusser, Patrick
HALLOWEEN H20: TWENTY YEARS LATER
Lyons, James
FIRST LOVE, LAST RITES
RATCHET
VELVET GOLDMINE
Mabilat, Catherine
CLASSIFIED X
MacArthur, Andrea
MURDER IN MIND
SPICE WORLD
Mackie, Alex
SWEPT FROM THE SEA
Maganini, Elena
WILD THINGS
Mak Chi-Sin
KNOCK OFF
Mandelberg, Neil
ELVIS MEETS NIXON
Manhardt, Mary
FARM: ANGOLA, U.S.A., THE
Manos, Mark
ASYLUM
Manton, Marcus
BURN HOLLYWOOD BURN
Marciano, Eric
DIDN'T DO IT FOR LOVE
Marcovich, Carlos
WHO THE HELL IS JULIETTE?
Mark, Stephen
X-FILES, THE
Marks, Richard
YOU'VE GOT MAIL
Marshall, Neil
KILLING TIME
Martin, Pamela
SLUMS OF BEVERLY HILLS
Martin, Rick
ESCAPE, THE
Marx, Ed
LEWIS & CLARK & GEORGE
Marzullo, Angelo
RABID DOGS
Maslansky, Judd
NEXT STEP, THE
Mastroianni, Ruggero
NIGHT AND THE MOMENT, THE
PEREIRA DECLARES
TRUCE, THE

Matthews, John
BOYS IN LOVE 2
Mayhew, Michael
SAND TRAP
Mazur, Lara
TRUCKS
McArdle, Tom
HI-LIFE
TALK TO ME
McElwee, Ross
SIX O'CLOCK NEWS
McGuinn, Patrick
BOYS IN LOVE 2
McKay, Craig
RETURN TO PARADISE
McKenzie, Bryan
ELIA KAZAN: A DIRECTOR'S JOURNEY
McLeish, Timothy
RAT'S TALE, A
McLeod, David
JACK HIGGINS' THUNDER POINT
JACK HIGGINS' THE WINDSOR PROTOCOL
McQueen-Mason, Edward
NAPOLEON
McTaggart, Kimberlee
TALES FROM A PARALLEL UNIVERSE: EATING PATTERN
Mekler, Sergio
OYSTER AND THE WIND, THE
Melnick, Mark
CALL TO REMEMBER, A
Menke, Salle
NIGHTWATCH
Meyburgh Jr., Felix
OPERATION DELTA FORCE 2
Meyer, Peter W.
CAN'T YOU HEAR THE WIND HOWL?: THE LIFE AND MUSIC OF ROBERT JOHNSON
Meyers, Gary
BRAM STOKER'S THE MUMMY
LOVE TO KILL
Michaels, Bret
LETTER FROM DEATH ROW, A
Mignatti, Victor
BROADWAY DAMAGE
Miller, Michael
ORGAZMO
Miller, Peter
INVISIBLE MOM
Miller, W. Peter
STEEL SHARKS
Mirrione, Steven
CLOCKWATCHERS
Mitler, Matt
CRACKING UP
Molvaer, Skjolg
ENEMY
Mondshein, Andrew
RETURN TO PARADISE
SWEPT FROM THE SEA
WIDE AWAKE
Monroe, Julie
LOLITA
Moore, Nick
LAND GIRLS, THE
Moradian, Vanick
ALONE IN THE WOODS
INVISIBLE DAD
Morgan, Randy Jon
DISTURBING BEHAVIOR
Morita, Seiji
GOLGO 13: QUEEN BEE
Moritz, David
RUSHMORE
Morreale, Andrew
DIRTY LAUNDRY
Morris, Jonathan
CARLA'S SONG
Morrisey, Ken
MEAN GUNS
NEMESIS 4: CRY OF ANGELS
Morriss, Frank
INCOGNITO
Morse, Susan E.
CELEBRITY
Mortimer, Paul
EBENEZER
Murawski, Bob
LAST LIVES
UNCLE SAM
Murch, Walter
TOUCH OF EVIL: THE DIRECTOR'S CUT
Murphy, Paul
SWAN PRINCESS III: AND THE MYSTERY OF THE ENCHANTED TREASURE, THE
Muska, Susan
BRANDON TEENA STORY, THE
Myers, Stephen
ATOMIC DOG
Naudon, Jean Francois
ROYAL DECEIT
Nedd-Friendly, Priscilla
RUSTY: THE GREAT RESCUE
SOUR GRAPES
Neil-Fisher, Debra
BLACK DOG
Nevius, Steve
EDEN
Niami, Ramin
SOMEWHERE IN THE CITY
Nisker, Craig
BRAM STOKER'S SHADOWBUILDER
Noble, Thom
MASK OF ZORRO, THE
Nord, Richard
BODY COUNT
SPECIES II
Nownes, Jim E.
FATAL PURSUIT
Nygard, Roger
TREKKIES
O'Donnell, George
OUT OF THE PAST
O'Meara, Tim
MUSIC FROM ANOTHER ROOM
Oblath, Carol
JOHNNY MYSTO BOY WIZARD
LITTLE GHOST
Okayasu, Hajime
EEL, THE
Olafsdottir, Greta
BRANDON TEENA STORY, THE
Oppenheim, Jonathan
ARGUING THE WORLD
Orland, John
NO ORDINARY LOVE
Ornstein, Michael
TWO FOR TEXAS
Oskarsdottir, Valdis
CELEBRATION, THE
Ostry, David
TALES FROM A PARALLEL UNIVERSE: SUPER NOVA
Ota, Yoshinori
FIREWORKS
Ottman, John
APT PUPIL
Overas, Hakon
INSOMNIA
Oxman, Alan
HAPPINESS
TWO GIRLS AND A GUY
Paggi, Simona
LIFE IS BEAUTIFUL
Palardy, Claude
DEAD END
Pan, Kant
NIGHTWATCH
Panahi, Jafar
MIRROR, THE
Pankow, Bill
SNAKE EYES
Papillon, Denis
JACK LONDON'S THE CALL OF THE WILD: DOG OF THE YUKON
PRINCE VALIANT
Parker, Jed
LOU REED: ROCK AND ROLL HEART
Parker, Trey
ORGAZMO
Patch, Jeffrey
SECRET OF NIMH 2: TIMMY TO THE RESCUE, THE
Pejo, Robert
R.I.P. REST IN PIECES: A PORTRAIT OF JOE COLEMAN
Pellegrino, Rebecca
LOLIDA 2000
Peltier, Kenout
CHAMBERMAID ON THE TITANIC, THE
Pennebaker, D.A.
MOON OVER BROADWAY
Peppe, Chris
LIVING IN PERIL
SUICIDE KINGS
Percy, Lee
DESPERATE MEASURES
54
Peroni, Geraldine
GINGERBREAD MAN, THE
Perry, Mark
TWISTED
Pillsbury, Suzanne
SAFE MEN
Pires, Jay
LAST DAYS OF DISCO, THE
Plisco-Morris, Sabrina
BLACK DOG
Plotch, Joel
YOUR FRIENDS & NEIGHBORS
Polivka, Steve
YOUNG HERCULES
Poll, Jon
KRIPPENDORF'S TRIBE
Polonsky, Sonya
RUNNING WOMAN, THE
Press-Aviram, Naomi
HEALING BY KILLING
Prior, Peck
I STILL KNOW WHAT YOU DID LAST SUMMER
Prochaska, Andreas
FUNNY GAMES
Przygodda, Peter
PALMETTO
Puett, Dallas
LETHAL WEAPON 4
Pulcini, Robert
OFF THE MENU: THE LAST DAYS OF CHASEN'S
Qing Qing
FROZEN
Rabinowitz, Jay
AFFLICTION
WHEN PIGS FLY
Rae, Dan
HUSH
Ransley, David
FUTURE FEAR
Rappaport, Mark
SILVER SCREEN: COLOR ME LAVENDER, THE

Szanto, Annamaria
MEN
3 NINJAS: HIGH NOON AT MEGA MOUNTAIN
Takaki, Troy
SCARRED CITY
Taniguchi, Toshio
RAZOR: THE SNARE, THE
RAZOR: WHO'S GOT THE GOLD?, THE
SLEEPY EYES OF DEATH: SWORD OF SEDUCTION
Tavares, Mair
TIETA OF AGRESTE
Taylor, Barry
SECRET KINGDOM, THE
Taylor, Chris
BULLET ON A WIRE
Taylor, Tobin
LITTLE BOY BLUE
Tellefsen, Christopher
CHINESE BOX, THE
Teltser, Thomas
CHOSEN ONE: LEGEND OF THE RAVEN, THE
Teschner, Peter
DR. DOLITTLE
Thibault, Michael
MY BROTHER'S WAR
Thorson, Sara
WAR ZONE
Tibaldi, Antonio
LITTLE BOY BLUE
Tichenor, Dylan
HURLYBURLY
Timpone, Tara
ZERO EFFECT
Tintori, John
CHICAGO CAB
Tomassi, Vincenzo
BEYOND, THE
Tomaszewicz, Peter
RUGRATS MOVIE, THE
Toniolo, Camilla
REAL BLONDE, THE
Torres, Brunilda
NAKED ACTS
Travis, Neil
STEPMOM
Tregenza, Rob
INSIDE/OUT
Trejo, Paul
THURSDAY
Trigg, Derek
INNOCENT SLEEP, THE
Tronick, Michael
MEET JOE BLACK
Trulove, Ann
DECLINE OF WESTERN CIVILIZATION PART III, THE
Tsukamoto, Shinya
TOKYO FIST
Tulliver, Barbara
SPANISH PRISONER, THE
Tunsil, Aljernon
HALLELUJAH!
Uchida, Kerry
WOUNDED
Unkrich, Lee
BUG'S LIFE, A
Urioste, Frank J.
LETHAL WEAPON 4
Vallee, Jean-Marc
LOS LOCOS
Vandegrift, Randy
MARS
Villena, Fernando
WAR ZONE
Vince, Barrie
DIVORCE IRANIAN STYLE
Virkler, Dennis
PERFECT MURDER, A
Vogel, Virgil
TOUCH OF EVIL: THE DIRECTOR'S CUT
Wagner, Christian Adam
NEGOTIATOR, THE
Wahrman, Wayne
CIVIL ACTION, A
Waite, Trevor
GO NOW
Walker, Leslie
FEAR AND LOATHING IN LAS VEGAS
Walsh, Martin
HILARY AND JACKIE
MIGHTY, THE
WELCOME TO WOOP WOOP
Warden, Rachel
NIAGARA NIAGARA
Warnow, Stan
NO WAY HOME
Warschilka, Edward A.
JOHN CARPENTER'S VAMPIRES
Watson, Earl
RIDE
Webb, Simon
JACK HIGGINS' THE WINDSOR PROTOCOL
Webb, Stan
ANTZ
Webber, Charlie
HIJACKING HOLLYWOOD
Weber, Billy
BULWORTH
THIN RED LINE, THE
Weide, Robert B.
LENNY BRUCE: SWEAR TO TELL THE TRUTH
Weisberg, Steven
GREAT EXPECTATIONS
PERMANENT MIDNIGHT
Wescott, Bruce
WHEN TIME EXPIRES
Whelan, David
ACT OF WAR
Wiegmans, Rene
DRESS, THE
Wiesinger, Folmer
DETONATOR
SPACEJACKED
Wilson, David J.
TIMOTHY LEARY'S DEAD
Wimble, Chris
FIRELIGHT
Wishengrad, Jeff
SLAPPY AND THE STINKERS
Wisman, Ron
BLACKJACK
UNDERTAKER'S WEDDING, THE
Wolf, Jeffrey
MADELINE
MONUMENT AVE.
Wong Ming Lam
FALLEN ANGELS
Wong Ting
SHAOLIN TEMPLE, THE
Workman, Chuck
STORY OF X, THE
Workman, Jeremy
STORY OF X, THE
Wright, Bill
MERRY WAR, A
Wright, John
DEEP RISING
Wu, David
BRIDE OF CHUCKY
Yamaura, Katsumi
GONIN
Yeo, Sean
SHOPPING FOR FANGS
Young, John G.
PARALLEL SONS
Zeitman, Debbie
UNDER HEAVEN
Zennaiter, Nicholas
NAKED LIES
Zhong Furong
EMPEROR'S SHADOW, THE
Zieff, David
LAST BREATH
Zimmerman, Don
HALF BAKED
PATCH ADAMS
Zinner, Peter
GUN, A CAR, AND A BLONDE, A
Zuckerman, Lauren
FULL TILT BOOGIE

EXECUTIVE PRODUCERS

Abell, Keith
HENRY FOOL
Abrams, Peter
BILLBOARD DAD
JANE AUSTEN'S MAFIA!
Abramson, Gary
LOVELIFE
Adelman, Thomas D.
NEVADA
Ader-Brown, Jaimie
MOON OVER BROADWAY
Ah Gui
EMPEROR'S SHADOW, THE
Ainsworth, Susan
LET'S TALK ABOUT SEX
Airoldi, Conchita
ARTEMISIA
Akkad, Moustapha
HALLOWEEN H20: TWENTY YEARS LATER
Ali, Malik B.
HENRY: PORTRAIT OF A SERIAL KILLER PART 2
Ali, Waleed B.
HENRY: PORTRAIT OF A SERIAL KILLER PART 2
Allan, Mark
WHY DO FOOLS FALL IN LOVE?
Allard, Patricia
ARTEMISIA
Almodovar, Agustin
LIVE FLESH
Amin, Mark
CHAIRMAN OF THE BOARD
KID IN ALADDIN'S PALACE, A
STAR KID
TRUCKS
Amritaj, Ashok
INVISIBLE MOM
Anders, Allison
LOVER GIRL
Anderson, Wes
RUSHMORE
Ang, Jerry
LIVING IN PERIL
Arad, Avi
BLADE
Ardi, Dennis
MEN
Arnold, David
RETURN TO PARADISE
Augsberger, Thomas
ALARMIST, THE

Aukin, David
BREAK, THE
Avery, Roger
BOOGIE BOY
Avrutin, Yury
ADVENTURES OF MOWGLI
Backstrom, Tomas
INSOMNIA
Bacon, Kevin
WILD THINGS
Baden-Powell, Sue
DR. DOLITTLE
Badham, John
REBOUND: THE LEGEND OF EARL "THE GOAT" MANIGAULT
Baer, Matthew
JACK FROST
REPLACEMENT KILLERS, THE
Bakalar, Steven
SUBSTITUTE 2: SCHOOL'S OUT, THE
Baker, Todd
GINGERBREAD MAN, THE
Bakshi, Mark
REBOUND: THE LEGEND OF EARL "THE GOAT" MANIGAULT
Baldecchi, John
OLIVER TWIST
SIMON BIRCH
Band, Charles
CURSE OF THE PUPPET MASTER
KRAA! THE SEA MONSTER
SUBSPECIES IV: BLOODSTORM
TALISMAN
Baran, Jack
SHATTERED IMAGE
Barber, Gary
INCOGNITO
MAJOR LEAGUE: BACK TO THE MINORS
Barbera, Joseph
FLINTSTONES: I YABBA-DABBA DOO!, THE
Barbour, Malcom
DOGWATCH
Barclay, Jane
DANCING AT LUGHNASA
Barish, Keith
U.S. MARSHALS
Barker, Clive
GODS AND MONSTERS
Barnett, Bill
DIARY OF A SERIAL KILLER
Barnett, David
LAST BIG THING, THE
Barry, Jeffrey
JACK FROST
Baruc, Robert
BOYS WILL BE BOYS
BRAM STOKER'S THE MUMMY
DEAD END
DIARY OF A SERIAL KILLER
INTERLOCKED: THRILLED TO DEATH
INVISIBLE DAD
Bass, Ron
HOW STELLA GOT HER GROOVE BACK
STEPMOM
WHAT DREAMS MAY COME
Baum, Brent
RINGMASTER
Baum, Carol
ONLY THRILL, THE
Beaucaire, J.E.
CELEBRITY
SPANISH PRISONER, THE
WILD MAN BLUES
Beece, Debby
RUGRATS MOVIE, THE
Beer, Steven C.
HI-LIFE
Behnke, Jim
ZERO EFFECT
Bender, Jack
CALL TO REMEMBER, A
Berg, Barry
SOUR GRAPES
Berg, Dick
SIN AND REDEMPTION
Berger, Albert
SPREE, THE
Bergman Sender, Julie
SIX DAYS, SEVEN NIGHTS
Berman, Bruce
PRACTICAL MAGIC
Bernardi, Barry
DEEP RISING
JUNGLE BOOK: MOWGLI'S STORY, THE
Bernbaum, Paul
RIGHT CONNECTIONS, THE
Berri, Claude
OGRE, THE
Berry, Tom
LOUISA MAY ALCOTT'S LITTLE MEN
Bevan, Tim
BIG LEBOWSKI, THE
Bidegain, Thomas
SHAMPOO HORNS
Bierman, Robert
MERRY WAR, A
Bigel, Daniel
TWO GIRLS AND A GUY
Bigwood, James
BELLY
Birnbaum, Lillian
CENTRAL STATION
Birnbaum, Roger
OVERNIGHT DELIVERY
Blum, Sylvie
DISENCHANTED, THE
Blumenthal, Hank
RATCHET
Bogart, Kevin S.
SAND TRAP
Bonfiglio, Lois
BRIGHT SHINING LIE, A
TWO FOR TEXAS
Borgli, Petter J.
INSOMNIA
Borno, Pascal
MARS
Bozman, Ron
BELOVED
Bradley, Mary M.
DEAD END
Bradshaw, Joan
DEEP IMPACT
Brady, Joe
WALKING THUNDER
Brancato, Paula
SOMEWHERE IN THE CITY
Branco, Paulo
GENEALOGIES OF A CRIME
Brandman, Michael
HORTON FOOTE'S ALONE
Braunstein, Howard
SNOWBOUND
Bressler, Carl
SMOKE SIGNALS
Bronson, Harold
FEAR AND LOATHING IN LAS VEGAS
Brooks, Paul
KILLING TIME
Brown, Bryan
TWISTED
Brown, G. Mac
YOU'VE GOT MAIL
Brown, Jared F.
SWAN PRINCESS III: AND THE MYSTERY OF THE ENCHANTED TREASURE, THE
Brown, Linda
LOVE TO KILL
Brown, Stephen
PERFECT MURDER, A
Brundig, Reinhard
CHINESE BOX, THE
Brunton, Colin
CUBE
Brysh, Michael
TEN BENNY
Buchanan, John
BLEEDERS
JACK LONDON'S THE CALL OF THE WILD: DOG OF THE YUKON
Bullock, Sandra
HOPE FLOATS
PRACTICAL MAGIC
Burg, Mark
GINGERBREAD MAN, THE
Burke, Jim
EIGHTEENTH ANGEL, THE
Burke, Martyn
PENTAGON WARS, THE
Burke, Robyn
JOEY
Burns, Michael
DANCER, TEXAS POP. 81
Bursteen, Alan B.
STEEL SHARKS
WHITE RAVEN, THE
Buzzi, Paolo
STEAM
Byrne, Gabriel
SUMMER FLING
Calamari, Joseph
BLADE
Canter, Ross
KRIPPENDORF'S TRIBE
Caraccilo Jr., Joe
PECKER
Carliner, Mark
GEORGE WALLACE
Carlsen, Esben Hoilund
KRISTIN LAVRANSDATTER
Carmody, Don
54
SENSELESS
Carraro, Bill
AMERICAN HISTORY X
Carroll, Willard
BRAVE LITTLE TOASTER GOES TO MARS, THE
Carson, L.M. Kit
HURRICANE STREETS
Carter, Donald C.
ILLTOWN
Carter, Thomas
DON KING: ONLY IN AMERICA
Cartsonis, Susan
FIRELIGHT
Caruso, D.J.
REBOUND: THE LEGEND OF EARL "THE GOAT" MANIGAULT
Catmull, Edwin
BUG'S LIFE, A
Cavallo, Robert
CITY OF ANGELS
FALLEN
Chaiken, Jennifer
I LOVE YOU, DON'T TOUCH ME!
Chambers, Ernest
DENNIS THE MENACE STRIKES AGAIN
Chan, Peter
COMRADES, ALMOST A LOVE STORY

Chan Pui Wah
ARMOUR OF GOD
Chan Ye-cheng
FALLEN ANGELS
Chang, Martha
SLAPPY AND THE STINKERS
Chang, Terence
BIG HIT, THE
BLACKJACK
REPLACEMENT KILLERS, THE
Chen Mila
EMPEROR'S SHADOW, THE
Chernov, Jeffrey
DESPERATE MEASURES
HOLY MAN
Cherot, S.J.
HAV PLENTY
Chester, Louis B.
HOSTILE INTENT
Chow, Raymond
ARMOUR OF GOD
DRAGONS FOREVER
HEROES SHED NO TEARS
PRODIGAL SON, THE
Chuba, Dan
BRAM STOKER'S SHADOWBUILDER
Chung, Claudie
COMRADES, ALMOST A LOVE STORY
Clapham, Adam
HUMAN BOMB
Clark, Dan
KINGDOM OF SHADOWS
Cohen, Bobby
54
ROUNDERS
Cohen, David
CRUISE, THE
Colichman, Paul
WHEN TIME EXPIRES
Collas, Juan C.
LIVING IN PERIL
Collins, David
I WENT DOWN
Collins, Guy
NO WAY HOME
Colpaert, Carl-Jan
FRENCH EXIT
HURLYBURLY
NEVADA
Coote, Greg
JOEY
TARZAN AND THE LOST CITY
Corley, Al
PALMETTO
Corman, Cis
RESCUERS: STORIES OF COURAGE—TWO COUPLES
RESCUERS: STORIES OF COURAGE—TWO WOMEN
Corman, Roger
CLUB VAMPIRE
DETONATOR
FALLING FIRE
FUTURE FEAR
MY BROTHER'S WAR
SPACEJACKED
STRAY BULLET
WATCHERS REBORN
Corrigan, Kieran
GENERAL, THE
Corsini, Don
RINGMASTER
Cotone, Mario
LIFE IS BEAUTIFUL
Courtney, James A.
LET'S KILL ALL THE LAWYERS
Cowan, Cindy
MONTANA
SAVIOR

Cran, William
HOSTILE WATERS
Creel, Leanna
DANCER, TEXAS POP. 81
Cronyn, Christopher
REACH THE ROCK
Crosby, Denise
TREKKIES
Cusak, John
CHICAGO CAB
Cutler-Rubenstein, Devorah
SUBSTITUTE 2: SCHOOL'S OUT, THE
Dammicco, Pablo
BOYS WILL BE BOYS
INVISIBLE DAD
Dammicco, Stefano
INVISIBLE DAD
Damon, Mark
DECEIVER
ONE TOUGH COP
ORGAZMO
Daniels, Ron
LAWN DOGS
Danton, Steve
OPPOSITE OF SEX, THE
Davidson, Boaz
DOGWATCH
OUTSIDE OZONA
Davis, Andrew
ENEMY OF THE STATE
Davis, Bridget D.
HAV PLENTY
Davis, John
BAD MANNERS
LEWIS & CLARK & GEORGE
De Falco, David
LOLIDA 2000
De Laurentiis, Guido
TRUCE, THE
De Luca, Michael
DARK CITY
LOST IN SPACE
PLEASANTVILLE
de Weers, Hans
MRS. DALLOWAY
Deakin, Michael
HUMAN BOMB
DeFaria, Walt
BORROWERS, THE
Dekrone, Jane
BRANDON TEENA STORY, THE
Del Prete, Deborah
HOSTILE INTENT
Dembitzer, Stephen
PASSION IN THE DESERT
Demme, Johnathan
SHADRACH
Demme, Ted
MONUMENT AVE.
Dershowitz, Elon
FALLEN
DeVito, Danny
PENTAGON WARS, THE
Di Dionisio, Dino
ARTEMISIA
Dietl, Bo
ONE TOUGH COP
DiMartino, Joseph
DEE SNIDER'S STRANGELAND
Dimbort, Danny
DOGWATCH
MAKER, THE
OPERATION DELTA FORCE 2
OUTSIDE OZONA
REDLINE
SCARRED CITY
SHADRACH
TOP OF THE WORLD

DiTocco, Robyn
CATHERINE'S GROVE
Divincentis, D.V.
CHICAGO CAB
Dixon, C. Martin
FATAL PURSUIT
Dizenfeld, David
MY VERY BEST FRIEND
Dizon, Jesse
COURTING COURTNEY
Doerksen, David
BLACK LIGHT
Dominick, Richard
RINGMASTER
Donovan, Paul
TALES FROM A PARALLEL UNIVERSE: EATING PATTERN
TALES FROM A PARALLEL UNIVERSE: SUPER NOVA
Douglas, Diandra
OFF THE MENU: THE LAST DAYS OF CHASEN'S
Dowaliby, James
HUMAN BOMB
Drimmer, Stephen
SUICIDE KINGS
Drysdale, George W.
MIGHTY KONG, THE
Dubrow, Donna
QUICKSILVER HIGHWAY
Dunning, John
BUFFALO '66
JOHNNY SKIDMARKS
Durk, Julie
YOU'VE GOT MAIL
Durkin, Bill
WHATEVER
East, Guy
CLAY PIGEONS
HILARY AND JACKIE
MOONDANCE
PLAYING BY HEART
SLIDING DOORS
Eberle, Oliver
MILO
Eckert, John
BIG HIT, THE
Edmonds, Kenneth "Babyface"
HAV PLENTY
Edmonds, Tracey E.
HAV PLENTY
Ehrhardt, Bo
CELEBRATION, THE
Eichinger, Bernd
PRINCE VALIANT
Ekins, Susan
AVENGERS, THE
SOLDIER
Elbert, Ed
BLEEDERS
Elkins, Hilliard
IN HIS FATHER'S SHOES
Ellenbogen, Eric
RUDOLPH THE RED-NOSED REINDEER: THE MOVIE
Elstein, David
JACK HIGGINS' ON DANGEROUS GROUND
JACK HIGGINS' MIDNIGHT MAN
Emeke, Matthias
ALARMIST, THE
Emerson, Peter C.
CAPTIVE
Emmerich, Roland
GODZILLA
Emmerich, Ute
GODZILLA
Ephron, Delia
YOU'VE GOT MAIL

Hart, Paula
RIGHT CONNECTIONS, THE
Hasegawa, Makoto
WRATH OF THE NINJA: THE YOTODEN MOVIE
Hausman, Michael
TWILIGHT
Havens, Thom
CAN'T YOU HEAR THE WIND HOWL?: THE LIFE AND MUSIC OF ROBERT JOHNSON
Hawley, Richard
SOLDIER'S DAUGHTER NEVER CRIES, A
Hayashida, Fuminori
MILO
Hecht, Albie
RUGRATS MOVIE, THE
Heinlein, Guenter
LAST ASSASSINS
Helfant, Michael
VERY BAD THINGS
Hensleigh, Jonathan
ARMAGEDDON
Hermes, Jorg
WHITE RAVEN, THE
Heuser, H. Michael
HURLYBURLY
LOVELIFE
NEVADA
Heylen, Alexandre
WAKING NED DEVINE
Heyward, Andy
MEET THE DEEDLES
Hibbin, Sally
GOVERNESS, THE
Hillman Sr., Richard
MEN
Hird, Christopher
LIKE IT IS
Ho, Leonard
DRAGONS FOREVER
MR. NICE GUY
Hobson, Howard
WOO
Hofflund, Judy
WHEN TRUMPETS FADE
Holland, Gill
DEAR JESSE
Hornstein, Martin
STAR TREK: INSURRECTION
Howden, Alan
MURDER IN MIND
WILDE
Howell, Jim
JACK HIGGINS' ON DANGEROUS GROUND
JACK HIGGINS' THUNDER POINT
JACK HIGGINS' MIDNIGHT MAN
JACK HIGGINS' THE WINDSOR PROTOCOL
Howsam, Gary
BLEEDERS
CHICAGO CAB
JACK LONDON'S THE CALL OF THE WILD: DOG OF THE YUKON
Hu, Marcus
I THINK I DO
Huggins, Erica
WHAT DREAMS MAY COME
Huggins, Roy
U.S. MARSHALS
Hung, Sammo
HONG KONG 1941
Hyung Dong Ahn
RED HAWK: WEAPON OF DEATH
Ice Cube
PLAYERS CLUB, THE
Inaba, Akinori
CHINESE BOX, THE
Isaac, Margaret French
STEPMOM
Ishige, Eisuke
JUNK FOOD
Ivers, Jeffrey D.
DOUBLE EDGE
RETROACTIVE
Jackson, Ruth
HILARY AND JACKIE
LAND GIRLS, THE
Jacob, Alan
CALL TO REMEMBER, A
Jaffe, Stanley
MADELINE
Jaffe, Steven-Charles
INFORMANT, THE
Jansson, Agneta
JERUSALEM
Jarchow, Stephen P.
GODS AND MONSTERS
WHEN TIME EXPIRES
Jarmusch, Jim
WHEN PIGS FLY
Jaymes, Cathryn
BOOGIE BOY
Jenkel, Brad
OVERNIGHT DELIVERY
Jiang Qitao
RED CHERRY
Jobs, Steven
BUG'S LIFE, A
Jordan, Neil
BUTCHER BOY, THE
Joslin, Burr
PLAN B
Joslin, Elizabeth
PLAN B
Josten, Walter
JACK LONDON'S THE CALL OF THE WILD: DOG OF THE YUKON
Judelewicz, Pascal
MARIE BAIE DES ANGES
Jung, Jo-Ho
DOUBLE EDGE
Kadokawa, Tsuguhiko
SLAYERS: THE MOTION PICTURE
Kappes, David
STEPHEN KING'S THE NIGHT FLIER
Katz, Gail
MIGHTY JOE YOUNG
Katzenberg, Jeffrey
PRINCE OF EGYPT, THE
Kauffman, Gary
RIVER RED
Kazan, Nicholas
FALLEN
Kazui, Kaz
ORGAZMO
Kelmenson, Paul
RONIN
Kessler, Henri M.
SLAM
Kidney, Ric
MERCURY RISING
King, Zalman
IN GOD'S HANDS
Klein, Christa-Maria
RAT'S TALE, A
Kobayashi, Yosuke "James"
NEW ADVENTURES OF KIMBA THE WHITE LION, THE
Koontz, Dean
PHANTOMS
Korris, Jim
NOT IN THIS TOWN
Kozlov, Sergei
THIEF, THE
Kramer, Jon
INVADER, THE
LAST LIVES
TERMINAL JUSTICE
Krane, Jonathan D.
PRIMARY COLORS
Kreditor, Garrett P.
SAND TRAP
Kroopf, Scott
VERY BAD THINGS
WHAT DREAMS MAY COME
Kulzer, Robert
PRINCE VALIANT
WRONGFULLY ACCUSED
Kurdyla, Ted
FALLEN
Kurz, Jeffrey
CHILDREN OF THE CORN V: FIELD OF TERROR
Kushner, Donald
BONE DADDY
CLOCKMAKER
JOHNNY MYSTO BOY WIZARD
LITTLE GHOST
MIDAS TOUCH, THE
RINGMASTER
SECRET KINGDOM, THE
SHRUNKEN CITY, THE
Labadie, Jean
CHINESE BOX, THE
Labaton, Arnold
ARGUING THE WORLD
Lacy, Susan
LOU REED: ROCK AND ROLL HEART
Ladd Jr., Alan
MAN IN THE IRON MASK, THE
Lahiff, Craig
HEAVEN'S BURNING
Lamb, Cindy
EBENEZER
Lance, Peter
BLACKJACK
Landaas, Robert William
EDEN
Lanoff, Lawrence
CHOSEN ONE: LEGEND OF THE RAVEN, THE
Laolagi, Jon
LOVE TO KILL
Lassally, Raul
HOME FRIES
Lau Fong
SHAOLIN TEMPLE, THE
Laubacher, Robert
HOME BEFORE DARK
Leahy, Michael
TREKKIES
Ledford, John
SLAYERS: THE MOTION PICTURE
TEKKEN: THE MOTION PICTURE
Lee, Deborah
GREAT EXPECTATIONS
Lee, Stan
BLADE
Leed, Rick
FIRELIGHT
Leeds, Arthur
3 NINJAS: HIGH NOON AT MEGA MOUNTAIN
Lemchen, Bob
QUICKSILVER HIGHWAY
Leonhardt, Lutz
ZAKIR AND HIS FRIENDS
Lerner, Avi
DOGWATCH
MAKER, THE
OPERATION DELTA FORCE 2
OUTSIDE OZONA

Nemeth, Stephen
DIGGING TO CHINA
PLUMP FICTION
Neufeld, Mace
BLACK DOG
LOST IN SPACE
Nevins, Sheila
LENNY BRUCE: SWEAR TO TELL THE TRUTH
Newell, Mike
PHOTOGRAPHING FAIRIES
Newirth, Charles
CITY OF ANGELS
Newlon, David
INVADER, THE
TERMINAL JUSTICE
Nick, Philip
CAN'T YOU HEAR THE WIND HOWL?: THE LIFE AND MUSIC OF ROBERT JOHNSON
Nicksay, David
NEGOTIATOR, THE
Noble, Kris
TWISTED
Nolte, Nick
AFFLICTION
Norris, Henry E.
NAKED ACTS
Northrop, Keith
SUMMER FLING
Nugent, Ginny
PAULIE
Nunberg, Rebecca
ADVENTURES OF MOWGLI
O'Connor, Robert
ELVIS MEETS NIXON
O'Donnell, John
POLTERGEIST REPORT: YUYU HAKUSHO
WRATH OF THE NINJA: THE YOTODEN MOVIE
Oberauner, Marion
LIVING IN PERIL
Obrow, Jeffrey
BRAM STOKER'S THE MUMMY
Ogden, Jennifer
HOW STELLA GOT HER GROOVE BACK
Okuyama, Kazuyoshi
EEL, THE
GONIN
SONATINE
Oliver, Tony
RUSTY: THE GREAT RESCUE
Oman, Chad
ARMAGEDDON
ENEMY OF THE STATE
Omiya, Koich
JUNK FOOD
Ordesky, Mark
PECKER
Orent, Kerry
ROUNDERS
Ostrow, Randy
WIDE AWAKE
Ouaknine, Jacky
FRIEND OF THE DECEASED, A
Ousey, Ian
ABERRATION
Painter, Paul
JACK HIGGINS' ON DANGEROUS GROUND
JACK HIGGINS' THUNDER POINT
JACK HIGGINS' MIDNIGHT MAN
JACK HIGGINS' THE WINDSOR PROTOCOL
Palau, Julia
LEADING MAN, THE
Paleologos, Nicholas
HURLYBURLY
Pang Ming
FROZEN
Parent, Mary
PLEASANTVILLE
Parkes, Walter F.
DEEP IMPACT
MASK OF ZORRO, THE
SMALL SOLDIERS
Paseornek, Michael
BUFFALO '66
HI-LIFE
Patton, Jody
MEN WITH GUNS
Paul, Hank
BOYS WILL BE BOYS
Peak, Kearie
AMERICAN HISTORY X
Pecht, Wayne M.
FATAL PURSUIT
Pedas, Jim
WHATEVER
Pedas, Ted
WHATEVER
Peipers, David
SLAM
Pelecanos, George P.
WHATEVER
Pepin, Richard
LAND OF THE FREE
Perlmutter, David M.
BONE DADDY
HOSTILE INTENT
Perlmutter, Sam
REDLINE
Perry, Luke
INDISCREET
Perry, Steve
LETHAL WEAPON 4
Pesery, Bruno
SAME OLD SONG
Pevner, Stephen
YOUR FRIENDS & NEIGHBORS
Pfeffer, Rachel
HORSE WHISPERER, THE
Pink, Steve
CHICAGO CAB
Pleshette, Lynn
TRUMAN SHOW, THE
Pojhan, Aladdin
IN GOD'S HANDS
Polone, Gavin
WHEN TRUMPETS FADE
Polyarush, Svetlana
DEAD WATERS
Poon, Dickson
HONG KONG 1941
MAGNIFICENT WARRIORS
ROYAL WARRIORS
Pope, Georgina
HEAVEN'S BURNING
Porter, Pliny
STEPMOM
Poster, Meryl
WIDE AWAKE
Potter, Barr
AFFLICTION
JOHN CARPENTER'S VAMPIRES
Poul, Alan
LOS LOCOS
Powell, Nik
LITTLE VOICE
TWENTYFOURSEVEN
WELCOME TO WOOP WOOP
Power, Ilene Kahn
GIA
Prenn, Kristi
BRYLCREEM BOYS, THE
Pritzker, Gigi
HOSTILE INTENT
Quested, John
NO WAY HOME
Rabins, Sandra
ANTZ
Rabuteau, Veronique
EL CHE: INVESTIGATING A LEGEND
Rachmil, Michael I.
MAJOR LEAGUE: BACK TO THE MINORS
Raffin, Deborah
WILDE
Raimi, Sam
HERCULES AND XENA THE ANIMATED MOVIE: THE BATTLE FOR MOUNT OLYMPUS
YOUNG HERCULES
Randall, Stephen
DANGEROUS BEAUTY
Ranvaud, Donald
CENTRAL STATION
Rashbaum, Buddy
DIRTY LAUNDRY
Redford, Robert
NO LOOKING BACK
SLUMS OF BEVERLY HILLS
Reeve, Tom
SUB DOWN
Rehme, Robert
BLACK DOG
LOST IN SPACE
Remlov, Tom
INSOMNIA
Reo, Ray
DIRTY WORK
Revitte, Joe
PECKER
Rich, Paul
MURDER IN MIND
Ridini, Maryann
FALLING FIRE
FUTURE FEAR
Ripp, Artie
MEET THE DEEDLES
Robbins, Lance H.
CASPER MEETS WENDY
MY BROTHER'S WAR
RICHIE RICH'S CHRISTMAS WISH
Robert, Julia
STEPMOM
Roberts, Lisa
TEN BENNY
Roffer, Steven
BODY COUNT
Rogers, Mimi
TRICKS
Rogow, Stan
DEFENDERS: PAYBACK, THE
Rokisky, Rita J.
DREAM FOR AN INSOMNIAC
Ronson, Rena
MURDER IN MIND
Rose, Hoke M.
CHOSEN ONE: LEGEND OF THE RAVEN, THE
Rosen, Robert L.
WRONGFULLY ACCUSED
Rosenberg, Thomas
HOMEGROWN
Rosenberg, Tom
PHOENIX
Rosenblatt, Bart
PALMETTO
Rosenblum, Paul
MEAN GUNS
NEMESIS 4: CRY OF ANGELS
Rosendahl, Carl
ANTZ

Rosner, Louise
FIRESTORM
Roth, Daryl
I THINK I DO
Rubin, Bob
TRACKED
Rush, Sandra
QUICKSILVER HIGHWAY
Ruskin, Morris
GODSON, THE
Ryan, Lata
PROPOSITION, THE
X-FILES, THE
Ryan, Michael
LEADING MAN, THE
Rywin, Lew
OGRE, THE
Saban, Haim
CASPER MEETS WENDY
RICHIE RICH'S CHRISTMAS WISH
RUSTY: THE GREAT RESCUE
Sacani, Christine A.
SNOWBOUND
Sackman, Jeff
BUFFALO '66
HI-LIFE
JOHNNY SKIDMARKS
MISBEGOTTEN
Sainderichin, Sylvaine
ROYAL DECEIT
Sakaguchi, Kazunao
JUNK FOOD
Sakurai, Darren
DISAPPEARANCE OF KEVIN JOHNSON, THE
Salimbeni, Reto
URBAN SAFARI
Saly, Lilian
ARTEMISIA
Samaha, Elie
MAKER, THE
PEACEKEEPER, THE
SHADRACH
Sams, Alicia
OFF THE MENU: THE LAST DAYS OF CHASEN'S
Sanger, Jonathan
WITHOUT LIMITS
Saperstein, Richard
LOST IN SPACE
Sarandon, Susan
STEPMOM
Saunders, David
IN GOD'S HANDS
Saunders, Ron
NAPOLEON
Saxon, Edward
STOREFRONT HITCHCOCK
Schamus, James
HAPPINESS
Schatz, Chiqui
COURTING COURTNEY
Scheidlinger, Rob
COUSIN BETTE
Scherl, Oscar
VIOLET'S VISIT
Schindler, Peter
MY GIANT
SIEGE, THE
Schlosser, Katrin
MOTHER AND SON
Schonberger, Jane
KIKI'S DELIVERY SERVICE
Schroeder, Romain
JACK HIGGINS' ON DANGEROUS GROUND
JACK HIGGINS' MIDNIGHT MAN
SUB DOWN
Schwartz, Martin
COMEDY'S DIRTIEST DOZEN
Schwary, Ronald L.
MEET JOE BLACK
Schweickert, Joyce
STILL BREATHING
Schwimmer, David
KISSING A FOOL
Scott, Tony
CLAY PIGEONS
Segan, Allison Lyon
HARD RAIN
Seltzer, David
EIGHTEENTH ANGEL, THE
Senkowski, Ron
LET'S KILL ALL THE LAWYERS
Shadyac, Tom
PATCH ADAMS
Shah, Ash R.
BOOGIE BOY
BRAM STOKER'S SHADOWBUILDER
Shah, Eddy
CATHERINE'S GROVE
Shainberg, Steven
HIT ME
Shamberg, Michael
PENTAGON WARS, THE
Shapiro, Susan
NEVADA
Shareshian, Steven
SHADRACH
Sheehy, Michael
ESCAPE, THE
Sheen, Simon
3 NINJAS: HIGH NOON AT MEGA MOUNTAIN
Sher, Stacy
PENTAGON WARS, THE
Shivas, Mark
I WENT DOWN
REGENERATION
Short, Trevor
DOGWATCH
MAKER, THE
OPERATION DELTA FORCE 2
OUTSIDE OZONA
SCARRED CITY
SHADRACH
TOP OF THE WORLD
Shwarzstein, Meyer
LOUISA MAY ALCOTT'S LITTLE MEN
Sidaris, Christian
RETURN TO SAVAGE BEACH
Siefert, Lynn
COUSIN BETTE
Sienega, Corey
BRIDE OF CHUCKY
Sighvatsson, Sigurjon
HOMEGROWN
PHOENIX
POLISH WEDDING
REAL BLONDE, THE
Silberschneider, Kurt
TARZAN AND THE LOST CITY
Silverman, Fred
MY VERY BEST FRIEND
Simandl, Lloyd A.
ACT OF WAR
Simchowitz, Stephan
ALARMIST, THE
Simmons, Rudd
HI-LO COUNTRY, THE
Simon, Randy
PI
Simpson, Peter
RAGE, THE
Sinclair, Nigel
CLAY PIGEONS
HILARY AND JACKIE
PLAYING BY HEART
SLIDING DOORS
Singer, Joseph M.
MERCURY RISING
Singer, Rick
REBOUND: THE LEGEND OF EARL "THE GOAT" MANIGAULT
Singleton, John
WOO
Sinniger, Alfi
SALTMEN OF TIBET, THE
Sirabella, John
ZERO WOMAN
Skinner, David
SMOKE SIGNALS
Skinner, Mary
GODSON, THE
Skotchdopole, James W.
ENEMY OF THE STATE
Slater, Christian
VERY BAD THINGS
Sloss, John
LAST DAYS OF DISCO, THE
MEN WITH GUNS
NEWTON BOYS, THE
Smith, Bradford W.
WOO
Smith, Gary
SHOOTING FISH
Soehnlein, Rainer
MOONDANCE
Soisson, Joel
TREKKIES
Solomon, Frances-Anne
LOVE IS THE DEVIL: STUDY FOR A PORTRAIT OF FRANCIS BACON
Sommers, Stephen
OLIVER TWIST
Sonnenfeld, Barry
OUT OF SIGHT
Spielberg, Steven
DEEP IMPACT
MASK OF ZORRO, THE
Spillman, Darin
DETONATOR
Spry, Robin
JACK HIGGINS' ON DANGEROUS GROUND
JACK HIGGINS' THUNDER POINT
JACK HIGGINS' THE WINDSOR PROTOCOL
Starr, Philip
LAST BIG THING, THE
Steinberg, David A.
FALLING FIRE
FUTURE FEAR
Stern, Jay
RUSH HOUR
Stern, Sandy
VELVET GOLDMINE
Stevens, Andrew
INVISIBLE MOM
Stevens Jr., George
THIN RED LINE, THE
Stillerman, Joel
MONUMENT AVE.
Stipe, Michael
VELVET GOLDMINE
Stipetic, Lucki
LITTLE DIETER NEEDS TO FLY
Stoltz, Eric
MR. JEALOUSY
Stone, Robert
NEGOTIATOR, THE
Stone, Webster
NEGOTIATOR, THE

Yamaji, Hiroshi
ZERO WOMAN
Yamamoto, Mataichiro
GOLGO 13: QUEEN BEE
Yamner, David
CRUISE, THE
Yauch, Adam
FREE TIBET
Ye Ying
RED CHERRY
Yehranian, Yalda
PERMANENT MIDNIGHT
Yerkovich, Anthony
HOLLYWOOD CONFIDENTIAL
Yerxa, Ron
SPREE, THE
Yorn, Julie Silverman
TRICKS
Yoshizaki, Michiyo
BREAK, THE
CHINESE BOX, THE
WILDE
Young, Irwin
WHATEVER
Young, Mark
FLINTSTONES: I YABBA-DABBA DOO!, THE
Young, Sheldon O.
SWAN PRINCESS III: AND THE MYSTERY OF THE ENCHANTED TREASURE, THE
Yusef, Mohammed
BRYLCREEM BOYS, THE
Zachary, Ted
DANCE WITH ME
Zallian, Steven
CIVIL ACTION, A
Ziegler, Peter
TARZAN AND THE LOST CITY
Zollo, Frederick
HURLYBURLY

MAKEUP/FX MAKEUP

Aarons, Marlene
ONE TOUGH COP
Abel, Luisa
SHOOTING FISH
Abrums, Stephen
BLADE
Adams, Sallie
LAST SEDUCTION II, THE
Adams, Susie
SHOOTING FISH
Akhbari, Farnaz Moshir
RAT'S TALE, A
Alan-Dittmar, David
AYN RAND: A SENSE OF LIFE
Alonso, Maite
MARIUS AND JEANNETTE
Alterian Studios Inc.
HUSH
Anderson, David L.
KRIPPENDORF'S TRIBE
Anthony, Art
HENRY: PORTRAIT OF A SERIAL KILLER PART 2
Apone, Allan
SPHERE
Archeneaux, Merc
INDISCREET
Armador, Carlos David
GIRLS IN PRISON
Armstrong, Lynda
INCOGNITO
Arrigoni, Linda
CATHERINE'S GROVE
Artmont, Steve
NEIL SIMON'S THE ODD COUPLE II
Athayde, Pamela
TRUCKS
Baca, Nancy
VERY BAD THINGS
Baker, Rick
MIGHTY JOE YOUNG
Baker, Vivian
HUSH
MAJOR LEAGUE: BACK TO THE MINORS
Banchelli, Gaja
STEAM
Barber, Lynn
BLACK DOG
Barozewska, Elizbieta
BODY COUNT
Bartalos, Gabe
SECRET KINGDOM, THE
Bartels, Annie
TARZAN AND THE LOST CITY
Bartolucci, Christina
PERMANENT MIDNIGHT
Bartram, Jens
HOSTILE WATERS
Bassett, Nancy
3 NINJAS: HIGH NOON AT MEGA MOUNTAIN
Bauman, Rolf
WHEN PIGS FLY
Baylis, Michele
LIKE IT IS
Beck, Kenneth
BOOGIE BOY
Beltramello, Rudy
INVADER, THE
Benevides, Rob
LAST BREATH
NO WAY HOME
Benjamin, Jarmen Janeza
DOUBLE EDGE
INVADER, THE
Benoit, Suzanne
BONE DADDY
REBOUND: THE LEGEND OF EARL "THE GOAT" MANIGAULT
Berger, Howard
FACULTY, THE
JOHN CARPENTER'S VAMPIRES
STEPHEN KING'S THE NIGHT FLIER
Bergeron, Michele
CAPTIVE
Bergman, Bridget
HI-LO COUNTRY, THE
Berkeley, Ron
TRUMAN SHOW, THE
Bigger, Michal
NO LOOKING BACK
STEPMOM
Bihr, Kathryn
SIEGE, THE
Biscoe, Kate Morgan
CLAY PIGEONS
NIAGARA NIAGARA
Black, Jean
BIG LEBOWSKI, THE
Blau, Fred
ARMAGEDDON
BLADE
Blundell, Chris
CARLA'S SONG
Blynder, Karen
PARENT TRAP, THE
Bornia, Cynthia
DIARY OF A SERIAL KILLER
LANDLADY, THE
SMOKE SIGNALS
Bosc, Francoise
WESTERN
Boylan, Debbie
I WENT DOWN
Branche, Stacye
PLAYERS CLUB, THE
Brandy, Adam
CHILDREN OF THE CORN V: FIELD OF TERROR
Braus, Erin M.
CLUB VAMPIRE
PLAN B
WATCHERS REBORN
Brebner, Veronica
GOVERNESS, THE
Broad, Suzan
FIRELIGHT
Broseke, Babette
TALES FROM A PARALLEL UNIVERSE: GIGA SHADOW
Browning, Vanessa Dionne
RINGMASTER
Brownyard, Gail Bailey
SAND TRAP
Bruchon, Catherine
FULL SPEED
Bruns, Ulriko
TALES FROM A PARALLEL UNIVERSE: EATING PATTERN
Buacharern, Shutchai "Tym"
LOLIDA 2000
Buchner, Fern
LAST DAYS OF DISCO, THE
Buechler, John
CASPER MEETS WENDY
Burman, Thomas R.
STAR KID
Burnett, Michael
DEE SNIDER'S STRANGELAND
Burwell, Lois
SAVING PRIVATE RYAN
Busoiu, Dana
JOHNNY MYSTO BOY WIZARD
LITTLE GHOST
MIDAS TOUCH, THE
SUBSPECIES IV: BLOODSTORM
TALISMAN
Cabral, Susan A.
PLEASANTVILLE
Cady, Jill
MAKER, THE
MURDER IN MIND
PHOENIX
Caglione Jr., John
ZERO EFFECT
Caligari Studio
DIRTY WORK
Callaghan, Byron
DEAD END
EBENEZER
Campayno, Joe
HOLY MAN
Cannom, Greg
BLADE
Carroll, Amanda
PHANTOMS
Cate, Russell
CUBE
Chan Kwok Hung
PRODIGAL SON, THE
Chase, Ken
SIX DAYS, SEVEN NIGHTS
Chin, Judy
MONTANA
Christopher, Peter
BOYS WILL BE BOYS
Clarke, Madronica
DAVID SEARCHING
Coker, Gigs
BRIGHT SHINING LIE, A

Considine, Tim
LAST BREATH
Cook, Dewey
CHOSEN ONE: LEGEND OF THE RAVEN, THE
Cooper, Sandy
I'LL BE HOME FOR CHRISTMAS
Coppard, Yvonne
LOST IN SPACE
Cordoba, Charlene
BREAKOUT
HOT BLOODED
UNDERTAKER'S WEDDING, THE
Cossu, Walter
LIFE IS BEAUTIFUL
Crouse, Kathy
PRINCE, THE
Crumloff, Dan
ENEMY
Cunningham, Matt
DECAMPITATED
D'Amore, Hallie
CITY OF ANGELS
PATCH ADAMS
Da Silva, Rosalina
DEEP RISING
Dagenais, Francois
BRAM STOKER'S SHADOWBUILDER
Daly, Grainine
STRAY BULLET
Daly, Grainne
MY BROTHER'S WAR
Damiani, John
CAN'T HARDLY WAIT
Davidson, Debi
UNCLE SAM
Davidson, Debra-Lee
NEVADA
Davison, Diana
MEN
Day, Tarra
GODS AND MONSTERS
MILO
De Rossi, Giannetto
BEYOND, THE
MAN IN THE IRON MASK, THE
Dean, Richard
LOLITA
MEET JOE BLACK
DeHaven, Bonita
I STILL KNOW WHAT YOU DID LAST SUMMER
Del Brocco, Giancarlo
SAVIOR
DeLeon, Eduardo
NAKED LIES
Demers, Lucille
SNAKE EYES
Demers, Nicole
WOUNDED
Denaver, Deborah LaMia
BLADE
Denson, Debra
NIGHTWATCH
SLAPPY AND THE STINKERS
DeWilde, Matthew
BONE DADDY
Diaz, Ken
MASK OF ZORRO, THE
Diaz, Suzanne
FRENCH EXIT
Dinkel, Jeni Lee
CROSSING FIELDS
WILD THINGS
Dion, Michele
PEACEKEEPER, THE
DiPersio, Jane
NO WAY HOME
Direct Effects
LAST BREATH
Dobbie, Jacqueline
BASEKETBALL
RETROACTIVE
Donne, Naomi
OBJECT OF MY AFFECTION, THE
PERFECT MURDER, A
Down, Victoria
CALL TO REMEMBER, A
TRICKS
Dreiband-Burman, Bari
STAR KID
Duprat, Rosa Elisa
MASK OF ZORRO, THE
Dupuis, Stephen
DEEP RISING
WHEN TRUMPETS FADE
Dyer, Tina
LOS LOCOS
Eagan, Lynne
SIMPLE PLAN, A
Earnshaw, Tina
SLIDING DOORS
Eavey III, Rudolph
SHADRACH
Eckholm, Gilbert
DECAMPITATED
Edelman, Debra
TALK TO ME
Elek, Zoltan
REPLACEMENT KILLERS, THE
Elias, Gloria
I GOT THE HOOK UP
Elliott Jr., John M.
DEEP IMPACT
Elsey, Dave
INCOGNITO
Engleman, Leonard
MERCURY RISING
Erbe, Micki
BLACKJACK
Exelby, Sandra
BRYLCREEM BOYS, THE
Farkas, Tibor
HUNTED, THE
Fischer, Denise
FRENCH EXIT
Fontaine, Tyson
TRUCKS
Fording, Chris
BRAM STOKER'S THE MUMMY
Fouche, Debra
OPERATION DELTA FORCE 2
Fowler, Jo Ann
AIR BUD: GOLDEN RECEIVER
Freda, Francesco
TRUCE, THE
French, Callie
HURRICANE STREETS
Friedman, Alan "Doc"
NIGHT AT THE ROXBURY, A
Fry, Elisa beth Deitrich
ANOTHER DAY IN PARADISE
Fukaya, Akira
TOKYO FIST
Fullerton, Carl
BELOVED
STOREFRONT HITCHCOCK
G., Shauna
ALONE IN THE WOODS
Galichet, Dominique
MADELINE
Gallagher, Helen M.
CELEBRITY
Garabedian, Antoine
CENTRAL STATION
Gardner, Betty
DECAMPITATED
Gart, Lily
RUSTY: THE GREAT RESCUE
Gasmi, Beya
MADELINE
George, Tracey
BLACK LIGHT
Gerard, Cedric
GENEALOGIES OF A CRIME
Gibson, Anita
BODY COUNT
HE GOT GAME
Gleason, Kelly
SUBSTITUTE 2: SCHOOL'S OUT, THE
Goodwin, Jeff
PROPOSITION, THE
STEPHEN KING'S THE NIGHT FLIER
Graeser, Erinn
FATAL PURSUIT
Grande, Christina Del
UNDERTAKER'S WEDDING, THE
Gratsky, Heidi
CURSE OF THE PUPPET MASTER
Green, Patricia
BLUES BROTHERS 2000
BRIDE OF CHUCKY
54
Greene, Kimberly
HOME FRIES
PALMETTO
WEDDING SINGER, THE
Grimes, Lee A.
WATERBOY, THE
Gronberg, Kai
MENDEL
Grotsky, Heidi
INVISIBLE MOM
THURSDAY
Guo Junxia
FROZEN
Halston, Yolanda
RICHIE RICH'S CHRISTMAS WISH
Hamel, Dana Michelle
DOUBLE EDGE
INVADER, THE
MISBEGOTTEN
Hamilton, A. Scott
TALES FROM A PARALLEL UNIVERSE: SUPER NOVA
Hammond, Fae
NIL BY MOUTH
Hancock, Mike
HARD RAIN
Haraguchi, Tomoo
FIREWORKS
SONATINE
Harasimiak, Ania
PLUMP FICTION
Harkins, Isabel
CHINESE BOX, THE
Harper, Robert W.
RUSHMORE
Harper, Sally J.
RUSHMORE
Hart, Christine
MIGHTY, THE
Hass, Heidi
TALES FROM A PARALLEL UNIVERSE: SUPER NOVA
Hass, Holdo
TALES FROM A PARALLEL UNIVERSE: EATING PATTERN
Hay, Pat
WILDE
Hegarty, Jennifer
INFORMANT, THE

Helland, J. Roy
PRIMARY COLORS
Henriques III, Edouard F.
ARMAGEDDON
Hernandez, Juan Pedro
LIVE FLESH
Heron, Mary Sue
DEFENDERS: PAYBACK, THE
Hicks, Lori
PRICE ABOVE RUBIES, A
REAL BLONDE, THE
Hill-Patton, Norma
SPREE, THE
Hills, Joan
BORROWERS, THE
MRS. DALLOWAY
Hinks, Jacqueline
RESCUERS: STORIES OF COURAGE—TWO COUPLES
RESCUERS: STORIES OF COURAGE—TWO WOMEN
Hodson, Belinda
EVER AFTER
Holland, Desne
YOUR FRIENDS & NEIGHBORS
Holston, Yolanda
CASPER MEETS WENDY
Homan, Gina
MEET THE DEEDLES
Hoshi, Teruaki
JUNK FOOD
Hughes, Melanie
RUSH HOUR
Hurt, Joseph
WIDE AWAKE
Ilson, Sharon
HARD RAIN
ONE TRUE THING
Inoue, Tadahiro
TOKYO FIST
Irvine, Catherine Davies
BRAM STOKER'S SHADOWBUILDER
FALLING FIRE
FUTURE FEAR
Jackson, John E.
AMERICAN HISTORY X
DON KING: ONLY IN AMERICA
Jacoponi, Enrico
LIFE IS BEAUTIFUL
Jakots, Kati
REDLINE
James, Katherine
OUT OF SIGHT
James, Whitney L.
CIVIL ACTION, A
Jamieson, Dianne
REGENERATION
Jansen, Suzanne
HUMAN BOMB
Jaramillo, Dara
DANCER, TEXAS POP. 81
Jaziri, Fatima
KID IN ALADDIN'S PALACE, A
Jennings, Ken
MOONDANCE
OLIVER TWIST
Johnson, Angela
RIDE
Johnson, Megan
INTERLOCKED: THRILLED TO DEATH
STEEL SHARKS
Johnson, Steve
SPECIES II
Johnston, Graham
LEADING MAN, THE
SPICE WORLD
Jones, Anthony
NAKED ACTS
Jones, Starr
LAST LIVES
Jose-Lopez, Marie
JACK HIGGINS' MIDNIGHT MAN
Jourdan, Saundra
HIJACKING HOLLYWOOD
K.N.B. EFX Group
DESPERATE MEASURES
EIGHTEENTH ANGEL, THE
PHANTOMS
STEPHEN KING'S THE NIGHT FLIER
Kalb, Tali
BREAKOUT
Keil, Jeanet
KINGDOM, PART 2, THE
Kelley, Alexis
LOU REED: ROCK AND ROLL HEART
Keyton, Tonie
RUNNING WOMAN, THE
Khouzam, Henri
BLEEDERS
King, Peter
LITTLE VOICE
TALK OF ANGELS
VELVET GOLDMINE
Klein, Helga
INHERITORS, THE
Knight, Amanda
SWEPT FROM THE SEA
Knyrim, Roy
CHILDREN OF THE CORN V: FIELD OF TERROR
UNCLE SAM
Kolodkina, Nina
THIEF, THE
Koplow, Erin B.
WATERBOY, THE
Kubalskaya, Ludmila
DEAD WATERS
Kuhne, Kathy
CHARACTER
DRESS, THE
Kurtzman, Robert
FACULTY, THE
JOHN CARPENTER'S VAMPIRES
STEPHEN KING'S THE NIGHT FLIER
L'Ecuyer, Rene
NIGHT VISION
Lambe, Clare
DANCING AT LUGHNASA
Lamont-Fisher, Lesley
JACK HIGGINS' ON DANGEROUS GROUND
JACK HIGGINS' MIDNIGHT MAN
Lancaster, Margaux
DIARY OF A SERIAL KILLER
LAST ASSASSINS
Landau, Hariette
SCARRED CITY
Larsen, Deborah
GINGERBREAD MAN, THE
HORTON FOOTE'S ALONE
MIGHTY JOE YOUNG
Lau, Ray W.
SHOPPING FOR FANGS
Law Lai Kuen
DRAGONS FOREVER
Le Marinel, Paul
RONIN
Ledermann, Nicki
HAPPINESS
Levin, Fern
HUNTED, THE
Levon, Jaquetta
LOVE IS THE DEVIL: STUDY FOR A PORTRAIT OF FRANCIS BACON
Levy, Tracey
PAULIE
SLAPPY AND THE STINKERS
Liddiard, Gary
HORSE WHISPERER, THE
LETHAL WEAPON 4
Lindala, Toby
WOUNDED
Linn, Marc
I GOT THE HOOK UP
Lo Shui Lin
CHINESE BOX, THE
Loader, Traci
HOSTILE INTENT
Lober, Petra
ROYAL DECEIT
Lofthouse, Di
ABERRATION
Lopez, Marie Jose
JACK HIGGINS' ON DANGEROUS GROUND
Lopez-Rivera, Sergio
OPPOSITE OF SEX, THE
Love, Lisa
FIRESTORM
Love, Louise
DISTURBING BEHAVIOR
Luddy, Ann Marie
DISAPPEARANCE OF KEVIN JOHNSON, THE
Lulla, Claus
HENRY FOOL
Lyngso, Birthe
KINGDOM, PART 2, THE
Lynne, Rebecca
EDEN
Macaluso, Jerry
CHILDREN OF THE CORN V: FIELD OF TERROR
UNCLE SAM
MacDonald, Marilyn
MERRY WAR, A
Mackintosh, Louise
CUBE
Mackintosh, Ray
CUBE
Macneal, Kelly
BAD MANNERS
Magallon, Al
ATOMIC DOG
Marchenski, Lili
MY VERY BEST FRIEND
RIGHT CONNECTIONS, THE
Markert, Laura
GODSON, THE
Martine, Reala
LITTLE BIGFOOT 2: THE JOURNEY HOME
Martz, Neal
BELOVED
Masters, Todd
JOHNNY SKIDMARKS
Masterson, Ann
STILL BREATHING
Mastrantonio, Vincenzo
SUB DOWN
Matz, Carlan
OUTSIDE OZONA
Maurno, Diane
ELMORE LEONARD'S GOLD COAST
Mayelian, Angela
RETURN TO SAVAGE BEACH
McCann, Robert
LEADING MAN, THE
PRINCE VALIANT
McComas, Tania
HALLOWEEN H20: TWENTY YEARS LATER
McCormack, Lynda
DOWN IN THE DELTA
FACE DOWN

IN HIS FATHER'S SHOES
TRACKED
McCormick, Ryan Marie
WALKING THUNDER
McNulty, Deborah Wolski
CHILDREN OF THE CORN V: FIELD OF TERROR
Medcalf, Cheri
CON, THE
Mejia, Virna
TEN BENNY
Melnik, Alla
FRIEND OF THE DECEASED, A
Mepham, Viv
THIN RED LINE, THE
Mercer, Randy Houston
MEET JOE BLACK
Miller, Christina G.
HAV PLENTY
Minns, Cheri
WHAT DREAMS MAY COME
Miranda
NOTES FROM UNDERGROUND
Mitchell, Leigh
QUICKSILVER HIGHWAY
Miyauchi, Michiyo
FIREWORKS
Mocanu, Leana
GADJO DILO
Monaci, Gina
CLAY PIGEONS
Monsano, Monet
RAGE, THE
TERMINAL JUSTICE
Montagna, Peter
MY GIANT
Montgomery, Jennifer
ASYLUM
WHEN TIME EXPIRES
Moos, Angela
ALMOST HEROES
Morgan, Ashana
LOU REED: ROCK AND ROLL HEART
Morgan, Patricia
LOUISA MAY ALCOTT'S LITTLE MEN
Mowat, Donald J.
BIG HIT, THE
Mowel-Hindley, Aneta
RATCHET
Mucha, Cassandra
RIVER RED
Mungle, Matthew W.
AMERICAN HISTORY X
HOME FRIES
OLIVER TWIST
PSYCHO
Murdock, Judy
WOO
Murphy, Alec
DAY AT THE BEACH
Myers, David
DAD SAVAGE
N'Guyen, Thi-Loan
LA SEPARATION
Napier, Irene
REGENERATION
Nelson, Greg
X-FILES, THE
Nicotero, Gregory
FACULTY, THE
JOHN CARPENTER'S VAMPIRES
STEPHEN KING'S THE NIGHT FLIER
Noe, Douglas
QUICKSILVER HIGHWAY
Nye Jr., Ben
KRIPPENDORF'S TRIBE
O'Connell, Cathy
REAL HOWARD SPITZ, THE
O'Malley, Lois Anne
KRAA! THE SEA MONSTER
O'Reilly, Valli
LIVING OUT LOUD
O'Sullivan, Conor
SAVING PRIVATE RYAN
O'Sullivan, Maire
GENERAL, THE
SUMMER FLING
Oda, Hisashi
SONATINE
Offers, Elaine
PSYCHO
Oldham, Anne
WAKING NED DEVINE
Olson, Don
EBENEZER
Olsson, Kim
KINGDOM, PART 2, THE
Olsson, Lis
KINGDOM, PART 2, THE
Ortman, Evelyn
SUE
Ortmann, Evelyn A.
PARALLEL SONS
Ospina, Ermahn
FACULTY, THE
Ottaviano, Joanne
NEXT STEP, THE
Ottavis, Irene
UN AIR DE FAMILLE
Pala, Ann
DR. DOLITTLE
WEDDING SINGER, THE
Panchenko, Kyra
SAFE MEN
Parker, Connie
I'LL BE HOME FOR CHRISTMAS
SIN AND REDEMPTION
Parker, Daniel
AVENGERS, THE
Pattison, Paul
MR. NICE GUY
TWISTED
Pebbles
NIL BY MOUTH
Pelletier, Dianne
SNOWBOUND
Perez, Jose
MR. NICE GUY
Perticone, Gary
JOHNNY SKIDMARKS
Peterson, Ashlee
BREAST MEN
BURN HOLLYWOOD BURN
Phillips, Pamela
INVISIBLE MOM
THURSDAY
Ponce, Gloria
HOLLYWOOD CONFIDENTIAL
Poon Men Wah
DRAGONS FOREVER
MR. NICE GUY
Powell, Joni Meers
APT PUPIL
Proud, Jojo Meyers
RINGMASTER
Purcell, Julie
HOMEGROWN
Puthe, Werner
ROYAL DECEIT
Quinton, Colleen
JACK HIGGINS' THUNDER POINT
JACK HIGGINS' THE WINDSOR PROTOCOL
Rae, Rhonda
INVISIBLE DAD
Rail, Jason
CLOCKWATCHERS
Rainone, Tom
PHANTOMS
Rappaport, Mark
SHRUNKEN CITY, THE
SUBSPECIES IV: BLOODSTORM
Raschke, Martina
HOSTILE WATERS
Rasizadeh, Bahram
LOU REED: ROCK AND ROLL HEART
Raskin, Carol
CATHERINE'S GROVE
Raymond, Paul
FACE THE EVIL
Rebert, Dan
NEMESIS 4: CRY OF ANGELS
Ree, Veslemoy Fosse
INSOMNIA
Reed, Richard
COURTING COURTNEY
Regan, Patricia Schenkel
LAWN DOGS
Reiner, Susan
LOVER GIRL
Rial, Leah
LEWIS & CLARK & GEORGE
PHANTOMS
Rob, Adela
ACT OF WAR
Roberts, L. Taylor
WRONGFULLY ACCUSED
Roberts, Lisa
WHEN DANGER FOLLOWS YOU HOME
Robertson, Brandi
I LOVE YOU, DON'T TOUCH ME!
Robin, Wendy
DISAPPEARANCE OF KEVIN JOHNSON, THE
Robinett, Melanie
MARS
Rocchetti, Luigi
EIGHTEENTH ANGEL, THE
Rocchetti, Manlio
GREAT EXPECTATIONS
Rodier, Suzanne
JOHNNY SKIDMARKS
Roesler, Tina K.
STAR KID
Roller, Sabine
LAST BREATH
SUBSTITUTE 2: SCHOOL'S OUT, THE
Ross, Anne
URBAN SAFARI
Ross, Morag
BREAK, THE
BUTCHER BOY, THE
LES MISERABLES
Rosse, Sherry
TEN BENNY
Roth, Pamela
GUN, A CAR, AND A BLONDE, A
SUICIDE KINGS
Rott, Julie
DESTINY OF MARTY FINE, THE
Roylance, Bron
TWILIGHT
Rygh, Eva
JUNK MAIL
Sanchez, Carlos
MEN WITH GUNS
Sanchez, Jose Antonio
DAY OF THE BEAST, THE
Sanchez, Mark
WHY DO FOOLS FALL IN LOVE?
Sandoval, Kathleen
BEST OF THE BEST: WITHOUT WARNING

Sasaki, Kaori
TOKYO FIST
Saydah-Dokter, Dalia
COLONY, THE
TOP OF THE WORLD
Scalise, Lizz
MONTANA
Scherer, Karen
LAST BIG THING, THE
Schillinger, Georgie
INHERITORS, THE
Schlenz, Maurine
NEMESIS 4: CRY OF ANGELS
Schreyer, Janeen
DENNIS THE MENACE STRIKES AGAIN
Scott, Ashley
DOGWATCH
Scott, David
BONE DADDY
Scribner, Robert
LETHAL WEAPON 4
Sebert, Leslie
DIRTY WORK
URBAN LEGEND
Seidman, Sara
DECEIVER
Sforza, Fabrizio
DANGEROUS BEAUTY
Sharp, Rick
DANCE WITH ME
DESPERATE MEASURES
12 ANGRY MEN
Sharpe, Jenny
UNDER THE SKIN
Sheen, Edna M.
FALLEN
Sherwood, Marie
RUNNING WOMAN, THE
Shircore, Jenny
COUSIN BETTE
ELIZABETH
LAND GIRLS, THE
Short, Sheri
REAL THING, THE
Shorter, Kate
ALMOST HEROES
Sibblies, Ronnie
LENA'S DREAMS
Sica, Jasen
JANE AUSTEN'S MAFIA!
Single, Annie
YOUNG HERCULES
Sitja, Nuria
WHATEVER
Smarz, Nena
GIA
Smith, Christina
AMERICAN HISTORY X
HOPE FLOATS
PLAYING BY HEART
SMALL SOLDIERS
Smith, Jo-Anne
PENTAGON WARS, THE
SENSELESS
STILL BREATHING
Sobel, Jonathon
CRACKING UP
Solana, Gabriel
MASK OF ZORRO, THE
Soloman, Meribeth
BLACKJACK
Sorel, Perri
SPECIES II
SOTA FX
CHILDREN OF THE CORN V: FIELD OF TERROR
UNCLE SAM
Soupious, Meredith
ALMOST PARTNERS
Spiers, Anne
PASSION IN THE DESERT
Stadlinger, Horst
JERUSALEM
Stanescu, Mihai
CLOCKMAKER
JOHNNY MYSTO BOY WIZARD
LITTLE GHOST
MIDAS TOUCH, THE
Stoenciu, Letita
TALISMAN
Stratton, Rick
ARMAGEDDON
Striepeke, Daniel C.
SAVING PRIVATE RYAN
Subic, Martina
SAVIOR
Tal, Mira
LOVE TO KILL
Taylor, Mike "Boots"
ENEMY
Taylor, Richard
UGLY, THE
Temple, Phyllis
TWO FOR TEXAS
Terry, Marilyn
SIMON BIRCH
Thoen, Mia
HIGH ART
Till, Dominie
UGLY, THE
Tissier, Nathalie
MADELINE
Total Fabrication
I GOT THE HOOK UP
Toyokawa, Kyoko
SONATINE
Trahan, Kelvin
BROADWAY DAMAGE
Trani, Maurizio
BEYOND, THE
Turner, Rebecca
BAD MANNERS
Ulfung, Lotta
JERUSALEM
Van de Donk, Lia
LOU REED: ROCK AND ROLL HEART
Van Phue, Jeanne
LIVING IN PERIL
SENSELESS
Vanderwalt, Lesley
BABE: PIG IN THE CITY
DARK CITY
Verardi, Cecelia M.
GREAT EXPECTATIONS
Vest, Terese
MILO
Voigt, Gabriella
SHAMPOO HORNS
Wald-Cohain, Ariyela
PI
Walters, Brian
DECAMPITATED
Warburton, Amanda
GO NOW
Washam, Chad
BRAM STOKER'S THE MUMMY
Webb, Maggie
MRS. DALLOWAY
Wedge, Stephanie
REGENERATION
Weinberg, Karen
CHARLIE HOBOKEN
Weiss, Jamie
CHICAGO CAB
REACH THE ROCK
Westcott, Lisa
SHAKESPEARE IN LOVE
Westman, Gucci
BUFFALO '66
Westmore, June
U.S. MARSHALS
Westmore, Kandace
RAT PACK, THE
Westmore, Michael
STAR TREK: INSURRECTION
Westmore, Pamela
PRACTICAL MAGIC
Weyhe, Evelyn
LAST BREATH
White, Carla
ROUNDERS
SPANISH PRISONER, THE
Whobrey, Nacoma
PROPHECY II, THE
Wilder, Brad
SOUR GRAPES
TRUMAN SHOW, THE
Wilder, Bradley
PARENT TRAP, THE
Wilkinson, Jacky
URBAN SAFARI
Williams, Cindy Jane
THERE'S SOMETHING ABOUT MARY
Williams, Mark
CURSE OF THE PUPPET MASTER
TALISMAN
Williams, Sandy
BILLBOARD DAD
BRAM STOKER'S THE MUMMY
Wong, Ellen
ENEMY OF THE STATE
Wright, Tory
LOVE AND DEATH ON LONG ISLAND
Wynbrandt, Denise
KISSING A FOOL
XFX
NIGHTWATCH
York, Patty
NEWTON BOYS, THE
Yumoto, Hideo
RAZOR: THE SNARE, THE
RAZOR: WHO'S GOT THE GOLD?, THE
Yurtchuk, Vera
JANE AUSTEN'S MAFIA!
Zaafour, Ferouz
LIFE OF JESUS, THE
Zay, Vera
PASS, THE
Zoltan
GODZILLA
Zornow, Axel
OGRE, THE
Zurlo, Rosemarie
CELEBRITY

MUSIC COMPOSERS

Adkins, Hasil
R.I.P. REST IN PIECES: A PORTRAIT OF JOE COLEMAN
Adler, Mark
ERNEST IN THE ARMY
RAT PACK, THE
Akbar Khan, Ali
ZAKIR AND HIS FRIENDS
Allen, Peter
ACT OF WAR
Altman, John
LITTLE VOICE
PRONTO
TRACKED
Alvarez, Lucia
MIDAQ ALLEY

Anderson, William
MY BROTHER'S WAR
Arem, Keith
CHOSEN ONE: LEGEND OF THE RAVEN, THE
Arnold, David
GODZILLA
Aronson, Leon
JACK HIGGINS' ON DANGEROUS GROUND
JACK HIGGINS' MIDNIGHT MAN
Arriagada, Jorge
DISENCHANTED, THE
EL CHE: INVESTIGATING A LEGEND
GENEALOGIES OF A CRIME
SHATTERED IMAGE
Aserud, Bent
MENDEL
OTHER SIDE OF SUNDAY, THE
Auinger, Sam
JAMES ELLROY: DEMON DOG OF AMERICAN CRIME FICTION
Ayres, Mark
INNOCENT SLEEP, THE
Bacalov, Luis
POLISH WEDDING
TRUCE, THE
Bad Livers
NEWTON BOYS, THE
Baerwald, David
HURLYBURLY
Band, Richard
CURSE OF THE PUPPET MASTER
Barber, Lesley
LOS LOCOS
PRICE ABOVE RUBIES, A
Barnes, Edward D.
NEWTON BOYS, THE
Barry, John
MERCURY RISING
PLAYING BY HEART
SWEPT FROM THE SEA
Bartek, Steve
MEET THE DEEDLES
Beats By Da Pound
I GOT THE HOOK UP
Beck, Christophe
ALARMIST, THE
BONE DADDY
HOSTILE INTENT
Bell, David
SIN AND REDEMPTION
Beller, Marty
CRUISE, THE
Beltrami, Marco
FACULTY, THE
54
Bergeaud, David
KURT AND COURTNEY
PRINCE VALIANT
Berger, Cary
FULL TILT BOOGIE
Bernstein, Charles
WHEN DANGER FOLLOWS YOU HOME
Bernstein, Elmer
TWILIGHT
Bernstein, Peter
ATOMIC DOG
Bilderbeck, Keith
STIR
Bird, Jeff
NIAGARA NIAGARA
Blackstone, Wendy
LOVE WALKED IN
Blanchard, Terence
GIA
Bohren, Geir
MENDEL
OTHER SIDE OF SUNDAY, THE
Bonilla, Marc
CAUGHT UP
HOLLYWOOD CONFIDENTIAL
Boswell, Simon
COUSIN BETTE
DAD SAVAGE
PHOTOGRAPHING FAIRIES
Boutoussov, Viatcheslav
BROTHER
Bramson, Steven
SCOOBY-DOO ON ZOMBIE ISLAND
Branden, Don
LENA'S DREAMS
Breakfast Patties, The
FORMER CHILD STAR
Britting, Jeff
AYN RAND: A SENSE OF LIFE
Brook, Michael
AFFLICTION
Broughton, Bruce
KRIPPENDORF'S TRIBE
LOST IN SPACE
Browman, Michelle
HERCULES AND XENA THE ANIMATED MOVIE: THE BATTLE FOR MOUNT OLYMPUS
Brown, Larry
ELVIS MEETS NIXON
Brown, Shony Alex
DESTINY OF MARTY FINE, THE
Buarque, Chico
OYSTER AND THE WIND, THE
Buckley, Richie
GENERAL, THE
Buckmaster, Paul
MAKER, THE
MURDER IN MIND
Burch, Claire
TIMOTHY LEARY'S DEAD
Burgon, Geoffrey
WHEN TRUMPETS FADE
Burwell, Carter
BIG LEBOWSKI, THE
GODS AND MONSTERS
HI-LO COUNTRY, THE
SPANISH PRISONER, THE
VELVET GOLDMINE
Calamino, Chris
RETURN OF THE KING, THE
Cale, John
SOMEWHERE IN THE CITY
Camillo, Tony
NIGHT VISION
Carpenter, John
HALLOWEEN H20: TWENTY YEARS LATER
JOHN CARPENTER'S VAMPIRES
Carpenter, Michael
LET'S TALK ABOUT SEX
Carter, Kristopher
BOYS WILL BE BOYS
Castellucci, Teddy
WEDDING SINGER, THE
Catherina Early Music Consort
VILLAGE OF DREAMS
Chan, Frankie
FALLEN ANGELS
PRODIGAL SON, THE
Chan, Philip
PRODIGAL SON, THE
Chan Wing Leung
MAGNIFICENT WARRIORS
Chang, Gary
BRIGHT SHINING LIE, A
GEORGE WALLACE
Changkwan Kim
RED HAWK: WEAPON OF DEATH
Charbol, Mathieu
SWINDLE, THE
Chihara, Paul
ALMOST PARTNERS
KIKI'S DELIVERY SERVICE
Chiu Tsang-hei
COMRADES, ALMOST A LOVE STORY
Choi, Edmund
WIDE AWAKE
Christianson, Bob
NO ORDINARY LOVE
Christianson, Paul
PARALYZING FEAR: THE STORY OF POLIO IN AMERICA, A
Chul Shin
RED HAWK: WEAPON OF DEATH
Chung Siu Fung
HEROES SHED NO TEARS
Cipriani, Stelvio
RABID DOGS
Clapton, Eric
LETHAL WEAPON 4
NIL BY MOUTH
Clark, Igor
DEAD WATERS
Clark, Michael
BLACK THUNDER
Clarke, Stanley
DOWN IN THE DELTA
Clausen, Alf
HALF BAKED
Cleary, Siobhan
SPACEJACKED
Clinton, George S.
BLACK DOG
WILD THINGS
Cmiral, Elia
RONIN
Coda, John
DISAPPEARANCE OF KEVIN JOHNSON, THE
3 NINJAS: HIGH NOON AT MEGA MOUNTAIN
Coffing, Barry
LOVE TO KILL
Cohn, Stephen
LAND OF THE FREE
Coleman, Jim
HENRY FOOL
Coleman, Lisa
HAV PLENTY
Colombier, Michel
HOW STELLA GOT HER GROOVE BACK
RIGHT CONNECTIONS, THE
WOO
Conti, Bill
NAPOLEON
WRONGFULLY ACCUSED
Convertino, Michael
DANCE WITH ME
SUMMER FLING
Cooder, Ry
PRIMARY COLORS
Coonce, Cole
LAST BIG THING, THE
Copeland, Stewart
LITTLE BOY BLUE
PECKER
VERY BAD THINGS
WELCOME TO WOOP WOOP
Coster, Toomy
I GOT THE HOOK UP
Cowen, Jeanine
HOME BEFORE DARK
Cox, Rick
BRAM STOKER'S THE MUMMY
Crain, Bill
DETOUR

Crivelli, Carlo
MARIE BAIE DES ANGES
Crooke, John
DEAR JESSE
Cullo, Stephen
BELLY
Cuvillier, Richard
LIFE OF JESUS, THE
D, Chuck
BURN HOLLYWOOD BURN
Dahl, Ken
BROADWAY DAMAGE
Dallwitz, Burkhard
TRUMAN SHOW, THE
Danna, Mychael
REGENERATION
Dante, Carl
KRAA! THE SEA MONSTER
LOLIDA 2000
SECRET KINGDOM, THE
SHRUNKEN CITY, THE
Danza, Joseph Pepe
PLACE CALLED CHIAPAS, A
Daring, Mason
MEN WITH GUNS
OPPOSITE OF SEX, THE
Dashkevich, Vladimir
THIEF, THE
Davey, Shaun
BREAK, THE
WAKING NED DEVINE
Davis, Don
NOT IN THIS TOWN
De Robertis, Federico
NIRVANA
De Scalzi, Aldo
STEAM
De Scalzi, Pivio
STEAM
deAzevedo, Lex
SWAN PRINCESS III: AND THE MYSTERY OF THE ENCHANTED TREASURE, THE
Debney, John
FLINTSTONES: I YABBA-DABBA DOO!, THE
I'LL BE HOME FOR CHRISTMAS
PAULIE
Delia, Joe
NO LOOKING BACK
SUBSTITUTE 2: SCHOOL'S OUT, THE
DeMichele, Gary
IMPOSTORS, THE
Denison-Kimball Trio, The
BULLET ON A WIRE
Di Franco, Paul
DETONATOR
Diaz, Romeo
ROYAL WARRIORS
DiIulio, Ron
RETURN TO SAVAGE BEACH
Dikker, Loek
ESCAPE, THE
DJ Krush
JUNK FOOD
Dobrow, Bill
HENRY FOOL
Dol, Roeland
FROZEN
Doldinger, Klaus
PALMETTO
Donaggio, Pino
RESCUERS: STORIES OF COURAGE—TWO COUPLES
Donaldson, David
ABERRATION
Dorff, Steve
DANCER, TEXAS POP. 81
Doyle, Patrick
GREAT EXPECTATIONS
QUEST FOR CAMELOT
Drotis, David
ENEMY
Dudley, Anne
AMERICAN HISTORY X
Dun, Tan
FALLEN
Dvorak, Michal
FORGOTTEN LIGHT
Edelman, Randy
SIX DAYS, SEVEN NIGHTS
Edmonson, Greg
LAST LIVES
Edwards, Steve
DIARY OF A SERIAL KILLER
Een, Robert
MR. JEALOUSY
Ehrlich, John
PAUL MONETTE: THE BRINK OF SUMMER'S END
Eidel, Philippe
UN AIR DE FAMILLE
Eidelman, Cliff
MONTANA
ONE TRUE THING
El Mougy, Yohia
DESTINY
El Tawil, Kamal
DESTINY
Elfman, Danny
CIVIL ACTION, A
SIMPLE PLAN, A
Eling, Stefan
GENERAL CHAOS: UNCENSORED ANIMATION
Elkis, Boris
GODSON, THE
Elliott, Michael
CLUB VAMPIRE
Ellis, Greg
DESTINY OF MARTY FINE, THE
Endelman, Stephen
PROPOSITION, THE
Eubanks, Kevin
REBOUND: THE LEGEND OF EARL "THE GOAT" MANIGAULT
Fair, Jeff Eden
EIGHTEENTH ANGEL, THE
Fairman, Brad
I GOT THE HOOK UP
Farmer, Jim
REAL BLONDE, THE
Feathers, Charlie
R.I.P. REST IN PIECES: A PORTRAIT OF JOE COLEMAN
Fenton, George
CARLA'S SONG
DANGEROUS BEAUTY
EVER AFTER
LIVING OUT LOUD
OBJECT OF MY AFFECTION, THE
YOU'VE GOT MAIL
Ferguson, David
HOSTILE WATERS
Ferreras, Salvador
PLACE CALLED CHIAPAS, A
Fiedel, Brad
EDEN
Fields, Adam
LOVELIFE
Findlay, Dave
CAPTIVE
Fiorentino, Laurianne
TIMOTHY LEARY'S DEAD
Fitzpatrick, Frank
PLAYERS CLUB, THE
Folk, Robert
JUNGLE BOOK: MOWGLI'S STORY, THE
MAJOR LEAGUE: BACK TO THE MINORS
Fontaine, Bruno
SAME OLD SONG
Ford, Jane
I LOVE YOU, DON'T TOUCH ME!
Forest, Sydney
KIKI'S DELIVERY SERVICE
Forestier, Francois
PEACEKEEPER, THE
Fox, Jim
CLOCKMAKER
Frank, David Michael
BILLBOARD DAD
KID IN ALADDIN'S PALACE, A
PRINCE, THE
Franke, Christopher
TARZAN AND THE LOST CITY
Franti, Michael
ALWAYS OUTNUMBERED
Freeman, Chico
SUE
Freeman, Doug
ELIA KAZAN: A DIRECTOR'S JOURNEY
Frizzell, John
I STILL KNOW WHAT YOU DID LAST SUMMER
Frizzelli, Gianni
JANE AUSTEN'S MAFIA!
Frizzi, Fabio
BEYOND, THE
Fung, Michael
BEAUTY INVESTIGATOR
G-Wiz, Gary
BURN HOLLYWOOD BURN
Gallo, Vincent
BUFFALO '66
Garcia, Roel A.
FALLEN ANGELS
Gatlif, Tony
GADJO DILO
Gavin, Alastair
GO NOW
Gibbs, Richard
DIRTY WORK
DR. DOLITTLE
Gilmore, John R.
MIDAS TOUCH, THE
Giovinazzo, Rick
NO WAY HOME
Glass, Philip
TRUMAN SHOW, THE
Glennie-Smith, Nick
LION KING II: SIMBA'S PRIDE, THE
MAN IN THE IRON MASK, THE
Glinka, Mikhail
MOTHER AND SON
Gohl, Matthias
OUT OF THE PAST
Gold, Daniel
COURTING COURTNEY
Goldenthal, Elliot
BUTCHER BOY, THE
SPHERE
Goldsmith, Jerry
DEEP RISING
MULAN
SMALL SOLDIERS
STAR TREK: INSURRECTION
U.S. MARSHALS
Goldsmith, Joel
DOUBLE EDGE
Golia, Vinny
PASS, THE
Goltont, Jamie
GENERAL CHAOS: UNCENSORED ANIMATION

Goodman, Joel
MY KNEES WERE JUMPING: REMEMBERING THE KINDERTRANSPORTS
Goodwin, Gordon
MY BROTHER'S WAR
Governor, Mark
NOTES FROM UNDERGROUND
UNCLE SAM
Graham, John R.
MY BROTHER'S WAR
Grant, David
BEST OF THE BEST: WITHOUT WARNING
Grassby-Lewis, Richard
LOVE AND DEATH ON LONG ISLAND
Gregson-Williams, Harry
ANTZ
BORROWERS, THE
DECEIVER
ENEMY OF THE STATE
REPLACEMENT KILLERS, THE
Greyboy Allstars, The
ZERO EFFECT
Gronski, Vladimir
FRIEND OF THE DECEASED, A
Gross, Andrew
OVERNIGHT DELIVERY
Grusin, Dave
HOPE FLOATS
Guettel, Adam
ARGUING THE WORLD
Gunning, Christopher
FIRELIGHT
Haden, Charlie
12 ANGRY MEN
Haines, Michael
CAN'T YOU HEAR THE WIND HOWL?: THE LIFE AND MUSIC OF ROBERT JOHNSON
Hajian, Chris
CHAIRMAN OF THE BOARD
TEN BENNY
Halfpenny, Jim
LITTLE BIGFOOT 2: THE JOURNEY HOME
Hamilton, Page
CHICAGO CAB
Hano, Seiji
WRATH OF THE NINJA: THE YOTODEN MOVIE
Hardcastle, Paul
SPICE WORLD
Harpaz, Udi
CASPER MEETS WENDY
Harris, Peter
ELMORE LEONARD'S GOLD COAST
Harrison, Kenneth Richard
BLACK LIGHT
Hart, Mickey
ZAKIR AND HIS FRIENDS
Hartley, Hal
HENRY FOOL
Hartley, Richard
BRYLCREEM BOYS, THE
Hattori, Takayuki
SLAYERS: THE MOTION PICTURE
Hayen, Todd
INVADER, THE
WHEN TIME EXPIRES
Herman, John
BARNEY'S GREAT ADVENTURE—THE MOVIE
Herrmann, Bernard
PSYCHO
Het Paleis van Boem
CHARACTER
Hewerdine, Boo
TWENTYFOURSEVEN
Hhaba, Geoff
SKIN & BONE
Hickman, Johnny
RIVER RED
Hidden Faces
PLAYERS CLUB, THE
Himmelman, Peter
SOULER OPPOSITE, THE
Hirschfelder, David
ELIZABETH
SLIDING DOORS
Hisaishi, Joe
FIREWORKS
KIKI'S DELIVERY SERVICE
SONATINE
Hitchcock, Robyn
STOREFRONT HITCHCOCK
Hladik, Radim
FORGOTTEN LIGHT
Hoenig, Michael
TERMINAL JUSTICE
Hoffman, Jeffrey
BOYS IN LOVE 2
Holbek, Joachim
JUNK MAIL
KINGDOM, PART 2, THE
NIGHTWATCH
Holdridge, Lee
SECRET OF NIMH 2: TIMMY TO THE RESCUE, THE
TWO FOR TEXAS
Holiday, J.J.
TREKKIES
Homma, Yusuke
POLTERGEIST REPORT: YUYU HAKUSHO
Hong, Jong Hwa
BARRIERS
Hopkins, Kenyon
12 ANGRY MEN
Horner, James
DEEP IMPACT
MASK OF ZORRO, THE
MIGHTY JOE YOUNG
Howard, James Newton
PERFECT MURDER, A
Hughes, David
REAL HOWARD SPITZ, THE
Hussain, Zakir
ZAKIR AND HIS FRIENDS
Hvoslef, Ketil
KRISTIN LAVRANSDATTER
Ifukube, Akira
GODZILLA AND MOTHRA: THE BATTLE FOR EARTH
GODZILLA VS. KING GHIDORAH
Iglesias, Alberto
CHAMBERMAID ON THE TITANIC, THE
LIVE FLESH
Ikebe, Shinichiro
EEL, THE
Illarramendi, Angel
SHAMPOO HORNS
Insects, The
GENERAL CHAOS: UNCENSORED ANIMATION
LOVE AND DEATH ON LONG ISLAND
Isham, Mark
BLADE
DEFENDERS: PAYBACK, THE
GINGERBREAD MAN, THE
Ishikawa, Chu
TOKYO FIST
Jackson, Wanda
R.I.P. REST IN PIECES: A PORTRAIT OF JOE COLEMAN
Janko, Alexander
BRAVE LITTLE TOASTER GOES TO MARS, THE
Jenssen, Geir
INSOMNIA
Johnson, Robert
CAN'T YOU HEAR THE WIND HOWL?: THE LIFE AND MUSIC OF ROBERT JOHNSON
Jones, Trevor
DARK CITY
DESPERATE MEASURES
LAWN DOGS
MERLIN
MIGHTY, THE
TALK OF ANGELS
Judson, Tom
DIDN'T DO IT FOR LOVE
Kajanus, Georg
DIDN'T DO IT FOR LOVE
Kam, Peter
MR. NICE GUY
Kamen, Michael
LETHAL WEAPON 4
WHAT DREAMS MAY COME
Kapner, Mark
TIMOTHY LEARY'S DEAD
Kasha, Al
RUDOLPH THE RED-NOSED REINDEER: THE MOVIE
Kassanoff, Neil
HANDS ON A HARDBODY
Kavanagh, Lydia
HENRY FOOL
Keane, Brian
ILLTOWN
STEPHEN KING'S THE NIGHT FLIER
Keenlyside, Tom
ADVENTURES OF MOWGLI
NEW ADVENTURES OF KIMBA THE WHITE LION, THE
Kelly, Dominic
FULL TILT BOOGIE
Kelly, Victoria
UGLY, THE
Kempel, Arthur
STRAY BULLET
Kent, Rolfe
SLUMS OF BEVERLY HILLS
THEORY OF FLIGHT
Kessler, Michael
LAST BREATH
Kikuchi, Shunsuke
DRAGON BALL Z THE MOVIE: DEAD ZONE
DRAGON BALL Z THE MOVIE: THE TREE OF MIGHT
DRAGON BALL Z THE MOVIE: THE WORLD'S STRONGEST
Kilar, Wojciech
FROM A FAR COUNTRY
Kilian, Mark
LOVER GIRL
Kitay, David
CAN'T HARDLY WAIT
NIGHT AT THE ROXBURY, A
Kloser, Harald
BREAK, THE
Koftinoff, Gary
BREAKOUT
Kondor, Robbie
HAPPINESS
Korven, Mark
CUBE
Kosinski, Richard
SUBSPECIES IV: BLOODSTORM
Kymlicka, Milan
DEAD END
LOST WORLD, THE
LOUISA MAY ALCOTT'S LITTLE MEN
Lai, Michael
ARMOUR OF GOD
Lam, Sammy
KILLER ANGELS

Langsbard, Brian
JOHNNY SKIDMARKS
Laraio, John
DREAM FOR AN INSOMNIAC
Larson, Nathan
FIRST LOVE, LAST RITES
Lawrence, David
ALONE IN THE WOODS
HI-LIFE
STEEL SHARKS
Lazar, Alan Ari
BILLY'S HOLLYWOOD SCREEN KISS
Legage, Robert M.
CHILE, OBSTINATE MEMORY
Legg, James
DIRTY LAUNDRY
LeGrand, Michel
MADELINE
Leinheiser, Peter
REAL THING, THE
Leitl, Bruce
EBENEZER
Lena, Battista
DAY OF THE BEAST, THE
Lennertz, Christopher
RUNNING WOMAN, THE
Levin, Cindy
DECAMPITATED
Levy, Krishna
ARTEMISIA
Licht, Daniel
PERMANENT MIDNIGHT
Liebman, Martin
LET'S KILL ALL THE LAWYERS
Lindsey, Steve
HURLYBURLY
Lloyd, Michael
RUDOLPH THE RED-NOSED REINDEER: THE MOVIE
Lock, Brian
LAND GIRLS, THE
LoDuca, Joseph
HERCULES AND XENA THE ANIMATED MOVIE: THE BATTLE FOR MOUNT OLYMPUS
YOUNG HERCULES
Lopez, Peter C.
CHARLIE HOBOKEN
Lovano, Joe
FACE DOWN
Luna
MR. JEALOUSY
THURSDAY
Lundmark, Eric
HIJACKING HOLLYWOOD
LANDLADY, THE
Lundy, Curtis
FARM: ANGOLA, U.S.A., THE
Lurie, John
CLAY PIGEONS
MacColl, Neill
TWENTYFOURSEVEN
Machado, Celso
PLACE CALLED CHIAPAS, A
Machida, Ko
JUNK FOOD
Mader
CLOCKWATCHERS
Mael, Ron
KNOCK OFF
Mael, Russell
KNOCK OFF
Magowan, Shane
INFORMANT, THE
Mahal, Taj
OUTSIDE OZONA
Mainetti, Stefano
SUB DOWN
Mancina, Mark
RETURN TO PARADISE
Mancini, Henry
TOUCH OF EVIL: THE DIRECTOR'S CUT
Manfredini, Harry
CATHERINE'S GROVE
GUN, A CAR, AND A BLONDE, A
Mann, Hummie
GIRLS IN PRISON
RESCUERS: STORIES OF COURAGE—TWO COUPLES
RESCUERS: STORIES OF COURAGE—TWO WOMEN
Mansell, Clint
PI
Manthei, Kevin
MILO
Marcovich, Alejandro
WHO THE HELL IS JULIETTE?
Marinelli, Anthony
DON KING: ONLY IN AMERICA
SCARRED CITY
Marinelli, Dario
I WENT DOWN
Martinez, Cliff
OUT OF SIGHT
Martinez, Dennis
TIMOTHY LEARY'S DEAD
Mason, Roger
JOEY
Master P
I GOT THE HOOK UP
McBroom, Amanda
HERCULES AND XENA THE ANIMATED MOVIE: THE BATTLE FOR MOUNT OLYMPUS
McCarthy, Dennis
BREAST MEN
McCuistion, Michael
BATMAN & MR. FREEZE: SUBZERO
BATMAN/SUPERMAN MOVIE, THE
McElheron, Maureen
I MARRIED A STRANGE PERSON!
McEntire, John
REACH THE ROCK
McGlashan, Don
LIKE IT IS
McLary, David
TALK TO ME
McLaughlin, John
ZAKIR AND HIS FRIENDS
McMathew, Randi
TIMOTHY LEARY'S DEAD
McNaughton, Robert F.
HENRY: PORTRAIT OF A SERIAL KILLER PART 2
McNeely, Joel
AVENGERS, THE
Mellor, Jon
LAST SEDUCTION II, THE
Melnick, Peter Rodgers
ONLY THRILL, THE
Melvoin, Wendy
HAV PLENTY
Menasche, Emile
PARALLEL SONS
Michaels, Bret
LETTER FROM DEATH ROW, A
Miller, Cynthia
DIGGING TO CHINA
LITTLE GHOST
Miller, Paul
SLAM
Miller, Randy
LIVING IN PERIL
WITHOUT LIMITS
Mills, Paul
STILL BREATHING
Mitchell, John
ADVENTURES OF MOWGLI
NEW ADVENTURES OF KIMBA THE WHITE LION, THE
Mo', Keb'
CAN'T YOU HEAR THE WIND HOWL?: THE LIFE AND MUSIC OF ROBERT JOHNSON
Mollerup, Laurence
PLACE CALLED CHIAPAS, A
Moody Blues, The
TIMOTHY LEARY'S DEAD
Moore, Hub
HENRY FOOL
Morales, Mio
NEXT STEP, THE
Morelembaum, Jaques
CENTRAL STATION
Morrell, Steven
PHANTASM: OBLIVION
Morricone, Ennio
BULWORTH
LOLITA
NIGHT AND THE MOMENT, THE
PEREIRA DECLARES
Morrison, Van
MOONDANCE
Mothersbaugh, Bob
MEN
Mothersbaugh, Mark
DEAD MAN ON CAMPUS
MEN
QUICKSILVER HIGHWAY
RUGRATS MOVIE, THE
RUSHMORE
Murayama, Ryuji
ZERO WOMAN
Murphy, John
REAL HOWARD SPITZ, THE
Natale, Lou
SNOWBOUND
Neidhart, Deedee
JAMES ELLROY: DEMON DOG OF AMERICAN CRIME FICTION
Newborn, Ira
BAD MANNERS
BASEKETBALL
Newman, Randy
BUG'S LIFE, A
PLEASANTVILLE
Newman, Thomas
HORSE WHISPERER, THE
MEET JOE BLACK
Niehaus, Lennie
DOGWATCH
FIXER, THE
POCAHONTAS II: JOURNEY TO A NEW WORLD
Nieto, Jose
PASSION IN THE DESERT
Nilsson, Stefan
JERUSALEM
Noll, Norman
TARANTELLA
Norgaard, Per
ROYAL DECEIT
Nussio, Otmar
MOTHER AND SON
Nyman, Michael
OGRE, THE
PRACTICAL MAGIC
Olsen, Marc
UNDER HEAVEN
Ortolani, Riz
BEST MAN, THE
Ottman, John
APT PUPIL

HALLOWEEN H20: TWENTY YEARS LATER
INCOGNITO
Otto, Brian
NEXT STEP, THE
Pagani, Mauro
NIRVANA
Pansy Division
SKIN & BONE
Paradise
IN GOD'S HANDS
Parker, Chris
SLAMNATION
Parks, Van Dyke
BARNEY'S GREAT ADVENTURE—THE MOVIE
OLIVER TWIST
SHADRACH
Parodi, Starr
EIGHTEENTH ANGEL, THE
Pasqua, Alan
WATERBOY, THE
Pearson Jr., Dunn
RIDE
Perry, Robert
NEVADA
Pheloung, Barrington
HILARY AND JACKIE
Pike, Nicholas
STAR KID
Pinto, Antonio
CENTRAL STATION
Piovani, Nicola
LIFE IS BEAUTIFUL
Plakke, David
WAR ZONE
Plan9
ABERRATION
Plowman, Michael Richard
TRUCKS
Plumeri, Terry
WATCHERS REBORN
Pogues, The
INFORMANT, THE
Poledouris, Basil
LES MISERABLES
Portman, Rachel
BELOVED
HOME FRIES
Powell, John
ANTZ
HUMAN BOMB
Pranoto, Steven
SHOPPING FOR FANGS
Preisner, Zbigniew
KRZYSZTOF KIESLOWSKI: I'M SO-SO
Proffer, Spencer
RIGHT CONNECTIONS, THE
Public Enemy
HE GOT GAME
Quan, Donald
FALLING FIRE
FUTURE FEAR
Rabin, Trevor
ARMAGEDDON
ENEMY OF THE STATE
HOMEGROWN
JACK FROST
Rabjohns, Paul
CHILDREN OF THE CORN V: FIELD OF TERROR
COLONY, THE
Ragazzi, Claudio
NEXT STOP, WONDERLAND
Ragland, Robert O.
TOP OF THE WORLD
Ramsey, Kennard
RINGMASTER
Reeves, Alan
BLEEDERS
JACK LONDON'S THE CALL OF THE WILD: DOG OF THE YUKON
Reiser, Niki
BEYOND SILENCE
Remedios
WHEN I CLOSE MY EYES
Revell, Graeme
BIG HIT, THE
BRIDE OF CHUCKY
CHINESE BOX, THE
DENNIS THE MENACE STRIKES AGAIN
NEGOTIATOR, THE
PHOENIX
SIEGE, THE
SUICIDE KINGS
Richman, Jonathan
THERE'S SOMETHING ABOUT MARY
Riparetti, Tony
MEAN GUNS
Robb, Paul
ORGAZMO
Robbins, David
SAVIOR
Robbins, Richard
SOLDIER'S DAUGHTER NEVER CRIES, A
Robinson, J. Peter
FIRESTORM
MR. NICE GUY
Robinson, Peter Manning
CON, THE
HIT ME
SPREE, THE
Roby, John
HANGING GARDEN, THE
Roche, Steve
ABERRATION
Rodby, John L.
FATAL PURSUIT
Roddick, Janet
ABERRATION
Rodgers, Jimmie
TIMOTHY LEARY'S DEAD
Rose, Andrew
PLAN B
Rosen, Arthur
CRACKING UP
Rossner, Jon
DECAMPITATED
Rubenhold, Leon
TIMOTHY LEARY'S DEAD
Ryful
HENRY FOOL
Safan, Craig
SLAPPY AND THE STINKERS
Saito, Ichiro
SLEEPY EYES OF DEATH: SWORD OF ADVENTURE
Saito, Ichiroo
SLEEPY EYES OF DEATH: FULL CIRCLE KILLING
Saitoo, Ichiro
SLEEPY EYES OF DEATH: SWORD OF SEDUCTION
Sakamoto, Ryuichi
LOVE IS THE DEVIL: STUDY FOR A PORTRAIT OF FRANCIS BACON
SNAKE EYES
Sakurai, Hideaki
RAZOR: WHO'S GOT THE GOLD?, THE
Salas-Humara, Walter
WHATEVER
Salvay, Bennet
SAND TRAP
Sanborn, David
LETHAL WEAPON 4
Sandoval, Barnardo
WESTERN
Sanko, Anton
DEE SNIDER'S STRANGELAND
Saracene, Tony
DAY AT THE BEACH
Schell, Johnny Lee
OUTSIDE OZONA
Schifrin, Lalo
RUSH HOUR
Schoen, Gaili
DEJA VU
Schreiner, Gary
RUN FOR COVER
Schuller, Gunther
FACE DOWN
Schwartz, Paul
RATCHET
Scott, John
WALKING THUNDER
Seeber, Eckart
BRAM STOKER'S SHADOWBUILDER
Seibels, David
MIGHTY KONG, THE
Sekacz, Ilona
MRS. DALLOWAY
UNDER THE SKIN
Selby, John
TIMOTHY LEARY'S DEAD
Seymour, Patrick
TRICKS
Shaffer, Paul
BLUES BROTHERS 2000
Shaiman, Marc
MY GIANT
PATCH ADAMS
SIMON BIRCH
Shankar, Ravi
ZAKIR AND HIS FRIENDS
Shapiro, Theodore
HURRICANE STREETS
SAFE MEN
Shearmur, Edward
GOVERNESS, THE
LEADING MAN, THE
SPECIES II
Sherman, Richard M.
MIGHTY KONG, THE
Sherman, Robert B.
MIGHTY KONG, THE
Shire, David
HORTON FOOTE'S ALONE
Shudder To Think
HIGH ART
Silvestri, Alan
HOLY MAN
NEIL SIMON'S THE ODD COUPLE II
PARENT TRAP, THE
Simon, Marty
TALES FROM A PARALLEL UNIVERSE: EATING PATTERN
TALES FROM A PARALLEL UNIVERSE: GIGA SHADOW
TALES FROM A PARALLEL UNIVERSE: SUPER NOVA
Skies, Roni
NEXT STEP, THE
Slaski, Christopher
KILLING TIME
Smith, B.C.
SMOKE SIGNALS
Smith, Cecilia
NAKED ACTS
Smith, Paul Anthony
VIOLET'S VISIT
Snow, Mark
DISTURBING BEHAVIOR
X-FILES, THE
Sobel, Curt
BODY COUNT

Sokolov, Elliot
BROADWAY DAMAGE
Soltoff, Cindy
BROADWAY DAMAGE
Sparks, Richard
SECRET OF NIMH 2: TIMMY TO THE RESCUE, THE
Spencer, Errol G.
TIMOTHY LEARY'S DEAD
Steinman, Paul
WAR ZONE
Stern, Steven M.
INDISCREET
Stirling, Russell
OPERATION DELTA FORCE 2
Stockton, Gerald
GENERAL CHAOS: UNCENSORED ANIMATION
Stolz, Andrew
ENEMY
Stone, Christopher
PHANTASM: OBLIVION
Stringer, Dave
DESTINY OF MARTY FINE, THE
Strummer, Joe
WHEN PIGS FLY
Suchomel, Phil
DECLINE OF WESTERN CIVILIZATION PART III, THE
Sullivan, Billy
TREKKIES
Suozzo, Mark
LAST DAYS OF DISCO, THE
OFF THE MENU: THE LAST DAYS OF CHASEN'S
Sweet, Matthew
CAN'T HARDLY WAIT
Syrewicz, Stanislas
JACK HIGGINS' THUNDER POINT
JACK HIGGINS' THE WINDSOR PROTOCOL
SHOOTING FISH
Talgorn, Frederic
RAT'S TALE, A
Taylor, Stephen James
WHY DO FOOLS FALL IN LOVE?
Tec, Roland
ALL THE RAGE
Thomas, Ray
TIMOTHY LEARY'S DEAD
Thompson, Walter
CROSSING FIELDS
Timmins, Michael
NIAGARA NIAGARA
Tiso, Wagner
OYSTER AND THE WIND, THE
Tomita, Isao
RAZOR: THE SNARE, THE
Toyama, Kazuhiko
TEKKEN: THE MOTION PICTURE
Tozer, Schaun
HARD CORE LOGO
Trecasse, Steve
COMEDY'S DIRTIEST DOZEN
Tregenza, Earekcson Mary
INSIDE/OUT
Trench, Fiancha
MOONDANCE
Truman, Tim
BOOGIE BOY
RETROACTIVE
Turrin, Joseph
KINGDOM OF SHADOWS
Tyler, Brian
SIX-STRING SAMURAI
Tyson-Chew, Nerida
FERNGULLY 2: THE MAGICAL RESCUE
TWISTED
Tzur, Deddy
RICHIE RICH'S CHRISTMAS WISH
Van Eps, John
BUSTER & CHAUNCEY'S SILENT NIGHT
van Rensburg, Wessel
OPERATION DELTA FORCE 2
van Warmerdam, Vincent
DRESS, THE
Vannelli, Ross
WOUNDED
Vanston, Jeffery C.J.
ALMOST HEROES
Varouje
UNDERTAKER'S WEDDING, THE
Vaughn, Ben
LEWIS & CLARK & GEORGE
Veloso, Caetano
TIETA OF AGRESTE
Verdi, Giuseppe
MOTHER AND SON
Vitarelli, Joseph
KISSING A FOOL
PENTAGON WARS, THE
Wall, Cindy
WAR ZONE
Wall, Jack
WAR ZONE
Walton, Jeffrey
INVISIBLE DAD
INVISIBLE MOM
Wang Li Ping
SHAOLIN TEMPLE, THE
Warbeck, Stephen
SHAKESPEARE IN LOVE
Watters, Mark
ALL DOGS CHRISTMAS CAROL, AN
Wedron, Craig
FIRST LOVE, LAST RITES
Weissman, Joe
TIMOTHY LEARY'S DEAD
Weissner, Steve
TIMOTHY LEARY'S DEAD
Welsman, John
IN HIS FATHER'S SHOES
Wenger, Brahm
AIR BUD: GOLDEN RECEIVER
URBAN SAFARI
Werzowa, Walter
TREKKIES
Westlake, Nigel
BABE: PIG IN THE CITY
Whelan, Bill
DANCING AT LUGHNASA
Wilkinson, Alex
DOUBLE EDGE
Williams, Alan
ASYLUM
Williams, David
PHANTOMS
PROPHECY II, THE
Williams, John
SAVING PRIVATE RYAN
STEPMOM
Williams, Joseph
BODY COUNT
JOHNNY MYSTO BOY WIZARD
Williams, Patrick
MY VERY BEST FRIEND
Wiseman, Debbie
WILDE
Wlodarkowicz, Mark Jan
SKIN & BONE
Wong, James
DRAGONS FOREVER
Wood, Jimmy
TREKKIES
World Famous Blue Jays
BIG ONE, THE
Wray, Link
R.I.P. REST IN PIECES: A PORTRAIT OF JOE COLEMAN
Wulff, Frank
SALTMEN OF TIBET, THE
Wulff, Stefan
SALTMEN OF TIBET, THE
Wurman, Alex
FRENCH EXIT
Wurst, David
LAST ASSASSINS
WHITE RAVEN, THE
Wurst, Eric
LAST ASSASSINS
Wurst, Michael
WHITE RAVEN, THE
Xiang Min
EAST PALACE, WEST PALACE
Yared, Gabriel
CITY OF ANGELS
Yasukawa, Goro
GONIN
Yello
SENSELESS
Yoshino, Fujimaru
GOLGO 13: QUEEN BEE
Young, Christopher
HARD RAIN
HUSH
ROUNDERS
URBAN LEGEND
Zara, Paul
MISBEGOTTEN
RAGE, THE
Zaza, Paul J.
FACE THE EVIL
HOT BLOODED
Zehavi, Oded
HEALING BY KILLING
Zelig, Don
INTERLOCKED: THRILLED TO DEATH
Zelkin, Boris
MARS
Zenone, Gabriel
BROADWAY DAMAGE
Zerafa, Guy
REDLINE
Zeretzke, John
SUBSPECIES IV: BLOODSTORM
Zhao Jiping
EMPEROR'S SHADOW, THE
Zimmer, Hans
PRINCE OF EGYPT, THE
THIN RED LINE, THE
Zur, Inon
RUSTY: THE GREAT RESCUE

PRODUCERS

Abe, Suji
WHEN I CLOSE MY EYES
Abrahamsen, Svend
KINGDOM, PART 2, THE
Abrams, Peter
KID IN ALADDIN'S PALACE, A
Aihara, Yoshiaki
WRATH OF THE NINJA: THE YOTODEN MOVIE
Alexander, Beth
IMPOSTORS, THE
Allan, Julie
BLEEDERS
JACK LONDON'S THE CALL OF THE WILD: DOG OF THE YUKON
Allen, India
CHOSEN ONE: LEGEND OF THE RAVEN, THE

Amigo, Angel
EL CHE: INVESTIGATING A LEGEND
Amritraj, Ashok
ALONE IN THE WOODS
BLACK THUNDER
INVISIBLE DAD
STEEL SHARKS
WHITE RAVEN, THE
Anderson, Darla K.
BUG'S LIFE, A
Andreacchio, Mario
NAPOLEON
Anzilotti, Cos
SCOOBY-DOO ON ZOMBIE ISLAND
Arkoff, Lou
GIRLS IN PRISON
Armbruster, Klaus
ZAKIR AND HIS FRIENDS
Arnold, Kathryn
NEVADA
Arnott, Leanne
BLACK LIGHT
Aufiero, Dorothy
HOME BEFORE DARK
Avati, Antonio
BEST MAN, THE
Avellan, Elizabeth
FACULTY, THE
Aviram, Nitzan
HEALING BY KILLING
Aykroyd, Dan
BLUES BROTHERS 2000
Azoff, Irving
JACK FROST
Baba, Daisuke
NEW ADVENTURES OF KIMBA THE WHITE LION, THE
Badalato, Bill
JANE AUSTEN'S MAFIA!
Badish, Kenneth
ERNEST IN THE ARMY
Bain, Barnet
WHAT DREAMS MAY COME
Balabanov, Alexei
BROTHER
Baldecchi, John
DEEP RISING
Ball, David
LAST SEDUCTION II, THE
Balsan, Humbert
DESTINY
POST COITUM, ANIMAL TRISTE
Barnathan, Michael
STEPMOM
Barnett, Bill
BRAM STOKER'S THE MUMMY
LOVE TO KILL
Bartlett, Helen
FIXER, THE
Baskins-Leva, Lulu
PLAN B
Battista, Franco
LOUISA MAY ALCOTT'S LITTLE MEN
Bauer, Hans
MILO
Baumel, Ellin
WHATEVER
Bay, Michael
ARMAGEDDON
Bayly, Stephen
MRS. DALLOWAY
Beasley, William S.
I STILL KNOW WHAT YOU DID LAST SUMMER
Beaton, Jesse
ONE TRUE THING
Beatty, Warren
BULWORTH
Beckman, Chris
NOTES FROM UNDERGROUND
Beddor, Frank
THERE'S SOMETHING ABOUT MARY
Beigel, Herbert
FIRST LOVE, LAST RITES
Belshaw, George
RATCHET
Belzberg, Leslie
BLUES BROTHERS 2000
Ben-Ami, Yoram
3 NINJAS: HIGH NOON AT MEGA MOUNTAIN
Benayoun, Georges
SEVENTH HEAVEN
Bender, Lawrence
PRICE ABOVE RUBIES, A
Benegui, Laurent
FULL SPEED
Berg, Dick
PRONTO
Berman, Rick
STAR TREK: INSURRECTION
Bernart, Maurice
WESTERN
Bernheim, Alain
RETURN TO PARADISE
Bernstein, Armyan
DISTURBING BEHAVIOR
Berquist, Douglas
EBENEZER
Berri, Claude
LA SEPARATION
Berry, Tom
DEAD END
Bertolli, John
MUSIC FROM ANOTHER ROOM
Besman, Michael
OPPOSITE OF SEX, THE
Besson, Luc
NIL BY MOUTH
Beswick, Steve
LAST LIVES
Bettman, Gary M.
GUN, A CAR, AND A BLONDE, A
Bevan, Tim
BORROWERS, THE
ELIZABETH
HI-LO COUNTRY, THE
Bienstock, Mark
INDISCREET
Bill, Tony
FIXER, THE
Bindler, S.R.
HANDS ON A HARDBODY
Binkow, Gary
PLUMP FICTION
Bird, Matthew
HUMAN BOMB
Birnbaum, Roger
HOLY MAN
SIMON BIRCH
SIX DAYS, SEVEN NIGHTS
Bishop, Dennis
TWO FOR TEXAS
Bixler, David
RETROACTIVE
Bleiberg, Ehud
LOVER GIRL
PASS, THE
Blocker, David
DON KING: ONLY IN AMERICA
Blumenthal, Hank
NEXT STEP, THE
Boe, Peter
JUNK MAIL
Boorman, John
GENERAL, THE
Border, W.K.
PROPHECY II, THE
TREKKIES
Bouchareb, Rachid
LIFE OF JESUS, THE
Bourchier, Michael
NAPOLEON
Bradstreet, David
TRUCKS
Braithwaite, Philippa
SLIDING DOORS
Branco, Paulo
VOYAGE TO THE BEGINNING OF THE WORLD
Brandman, Steven
HORTON FOOTE'S ALONE
Braschi, Gianluigi
LIFE IS BEAUTIFUL
Braunstein, George G.
UNCLE SAM
Bregman, Martin
ONE TOUGH COP
Bregman, Michael S.
ONE TOUGH COP
Brehat, Jean
LIFE OF JESUS, THE
Brest, Martin
MEET JOE BLACK
Brezner, Larry
KRIPPENDORF'S TRIBE
Brice, Sandra Saxon
MY VERY BEST FRIEND
Bridges, Beau
DEFENDERS: PAYBACK, THE
Briggs, David
BOYS IN LOVE 2
Brillstein, Bernie
REPLACEMENT KILLERS, THE
Brinbaum, Roger
RUSH HOUR
Bronfman, Ellen
SAFE MEN
Bronson, Harold
WHY DO FOOLS FALL IN LOVE?
Brooks, Paul
REAL HOWARD SPITZ, THE
Bross, Eric
TEN BENNY
Brown, Chris
ABERRATION
Brown, David
DEEP IMPACT
Brown III, L.P.
FATAL PURSUIT
Brown, Jared F.
SWAN PRINCESS III: AND THE MYSTERY OF THE ENCHANTED TREASURE, THE
Brubaker, James D.
GIA
Bruce, Lisa
NO WAY HOME
Bruckheimer, Jerry
ARMAGEDDON
ENEMY OF THE STATE
Brugge, Pieter Jan
BULWORTH
Bryce, Ian
HARD RAIN
SAVING PRIVATE RYAN
Bull-Tuhus, Oddvar
OTHER SIDE OF SUNDAY, THE
Burch, Mary
RIGHT CONNECTIONS, THE
Burg, Mark
BODY COUNT
Burnett, Alan
BATMAN/SUPERMAN MOVIE, THE

DeShazer, Dennis
BARNEY'S GREAT ADVENTURE—THE MOVIE
Desormeaux, Jean
BONE DADDY
Deutchman, Ira
54
Deutsch, Stephen
WHAT DREAMS MAY COME
DeVito, Danny
LIVING OUT LOUD
OUT OF SIGHT
Devlin, Dean
GODZILLA
Devlin, Paul
SLAMNATION
Di Novi, Denise
ALMOST HEROES
Dietrich, Ralph S.
KILLER CONDOM, THE
Dillon, Paul
CHICAGO CAB
DiMilia, Robert E.
DIRTY LAUNDRY
Dini, Paul
BATMAN/SUPERMAN MOVIE, THE
DiNovi, Denise
PRACTICAL MAGIC
DiTocco, Tony
CATHERINE'S GROVE
Dollard, Alicia A.
NOTES FROM UNDERGROUND
Done, Erik
SAND TRAP
Done, Harris
SAND TRAP
Donnelly, Terence A.
12 ANGRY MEN
Donner, Richard
LETHAL WEAPON 4
Donovan, Arlene
TWILIGHT
Donovan, Paul
TALES FROM A PARALLEL UNIVERSE: GIGA SHADOW
TALES FROM A PARALLEL UNIVERSE: SUPER NOVA
Dorman, Joseph
ARGUING THE WORLD
Doumanian, Jean
CELEBRITY
SPANISH PRISONER, THE
WILD MAN BLUES
Dowling, Jonathan
UGLY, THE
Drazan, Anthony
HURLYBURLY
Drilling, Eric
RIVER RED
du Plantier, Daniel Toscan
CHAMBERMAID ON THE TITANIC, THE
Dubovsky, Dana
MISBEGOTTEN
Duncan, Chip
EDEN
Dupre, Jeff
OUT OF THE PAST
Dwyer, Finola
WELCOME TO WOOP WOOP
Earekcson, J.K.
INSIDE/OUT
Eastman, Brian
FIRELIGHT
Eaton, Andrew
GO NOW
Egawa, Shinya
DANCE WITH ME
Eichinger, Bernd
WRONGFULLY ACCUSED
Einbeinder, Scott
OUTSIDE OZONA
Eisenman, Morrie
SUBSTITUTE 2: SCHOOL'S OUT, THE
SUICIDE KINGS
Elliot, James
NAKED LIES
Elliott, Mike
CASPER MEETS WENDY
DETONATOR
RICHIE RICH'S CHRISTMAS WISH
Emilio, Andy
BRAM STOKER'S SHADOWBUILDER
Engelman, Robert
BLADE
Ephron, Nora
YOU'VE GOT MAIL
Epperson, Tom
GUN, A CAR, AND A BLONDE, A
Esguerra, George
TALK TO ME
Estes, Larry
SMOKE SIGNALS
WHEN TIME EXPIRES
Etheridge, Dan
OVERNIGHT DELIVERY
Ettinger, Wendy
MOON OVER BROADWAY
Evans, Rodney
UNVEILING, THE
Falk, Leon
INFORMANT, THE
Fantl, Michele
BOYS IN LOVE 2
Farrell, Mike
PATCH ADAMS
Fatassian, Androush
INTERLOCKED: THRILLED TO DEATH
Feig, Erik
I STILL KNOW WHAT YOU DID LAST SUMMER
Feldman, Edward S.
TRUMAN SHOW, THE
Fellner, Eric
BORROWERS, THE
ELIZABETH
HI-LO COUNTRY, THE
Ferri, Elda
LIFE IS BEAUTIFUL
PEREIRA DECLARES
Fiedler, John
PECKER
Field, Ted
PROPOSITION, THE
Fields, Simon
MIGHTY, THE
Fienberg, Gregg
GODS AND MONSTERS
Fillmore, Bryce
WALKING THUNDER
Finerman, Wendy
STEPMOM
Finnell, Michael
SMALL SOLDIERS
Fischer, Markus
JAMES ELLROY: DEMON DOG OF AMERICAN CRIME FICTION
Fisher, Mary Ann
MY BROTHER'S WAR
SPACEJACKED
STRAY BULLET
Fisher, Sy
DEFENDERS: PAYBACK, THE
Fitzgerald, Thom
HANGING GARDEN, THE
Flint, Kevin
GODSON, THE
Fogel, Alexa L.
LAST BREATH
Foley, Maureen
HOME BEFORE DARK
Font, Teresa
DAY OF THE BEAST, THE
Form, Andrew
KISSING A FOOL
Forte, Kate
BELOVED
Foster, Chase
DANCER, TEXAS POP. 81
Foster, David
MASK OF ZORRO, THE
Foster, Gary
DESPERATE MEASURES
Frankenheimer, John
GEORGE WALLACE
Frankfurt, Peter
BLADE
Freeman, Morgan J.
HURRICANE STREETS
Freeman, Paul
HALLOWEEN H20: TWENTY YEARS LATER
Freilich, Jeff
RESCUERS: STORIES OF COURAGE—TWO COUPLES
RESCUERS: STORIES OF COURAGE—TWO WOMEN
Freixa, Ricardo
LOVE WALKED IN
Friedman, Liz
YOUNG HERCULES
Friendly, David T.
DR. DOLITTLE
Frilseth, Anne
INSOMNIA
Frislev, Michael
EBENEZER
Fruchtmann, Uri
SPICE WORLD
Fry, Carla
LOST IN SPACE
Galin, Mitchell
STEPHEN KING'S THE NIGHT FLIER
Garbus, Liz
FARM: ANGOLA, U.S.A., THE
Gardiner, Tracey
LIKE IT IS
Garfield, Louise
HANGING GARDEN, THE
Garner, Chip
LENA'S DREAMS
Garnett, Tony
HOSTILE WATERS
Garris, Mick
QUICKSILVER HIGHWAY
Garvin, Tom
INSIDE/OUT
Gassot, Charles
UN AIR DE FAMILLE
Geels, Laurens
CHARACTER
Geisler, Robert Michael
THIN RED LINE, THE
Geissler, Dieter
TARZAN AND THE LOST CITY
Gelbart, Arnie
HANGING GARDEN, THE
Geoffray, Jeff
CHILDREN OF THE CORN V: FIELD OF TERROR
George, Loucas
SIN AND REDEMPTION

Getiner, Leman
LAST ASSASSINS
Giarraputo, Jack
WATERBOY, THE
WEDDING SINGER, THE
Gigliotti, Donna
SHAKESPEARE IN LOVE
Giler, David
GIRLS IN PRISON
Gillis, Ann
LETTER FROM DEATH ROW, A
Gilroy, Grace
BRIDE OF CHUCKY
Ginsberg, Yitzhak
LOVER GIRL
PASS, THE
Gladstein, Richard N.
54
HURLYBURLY
Gladstone, Frank
QUEST FOR CAMELOT
Glatzer, Peter
DECEIVER
Glickman, Jonathan
RUSH HOUR
Glickman, Rana Joy
FULL TILT BOOGIE
Glynn, Kathleen
BIG ONE, THE
Goetzman, Gary
BELOVED
Goldberg, Rich
INDISCREET
Goldsman, Akiva
LOST IN SPACE
Goldstein, Gary W.
RINGMASTER
Goldstein, Harel
BRAM STOKER'S THE MUMMY
LOVE TO KILL
Goldstone, John
DEJA VU
Golin, Craig
RUSTY: THE GREAT RESCUE
Golin, Steve
RETURN TO PARADISE
YOUR FRIENDS & NEIGHBORS
Goodman, Gregory
HIT ME
Gordon, Lawrene
HOME FRIES
Gordon, Mark
HARD RAIN
PAULIE
SAVING PRIVATE RYAN
Gori, Rita Cecchi
NIRVANA
Gori, Vittorio Cecchi
NIRVANA
Gorman, James
LES MISERABLES
Graham-Rice, Tracie
PHOENIX
Grant, Julian
HOSTILE INTENT
Grazer, Brian
MERCURY RISING
PSYCHO
Greene, Robyn M.
HAV PLENTY
Greenfield, Matt
SLAYERS: THE MOTION PICTURE
Greenfield-Sanders, Timothy
LOU REED: ROCK AND ROLL HEART
Grey, Brad
REPLACEMENT KILLERS, THE
Grodnik, Dan
RAGE, THE
Gruber, Frank J.
NOTES FROM UNDERGROUND
Gruber, Markus
MY FIRST NAME IS MACEO
Gruendemann, Eric
YOUNG HERCULES
Grunfeld, Gabriel
ONLY THRILL, THE
Guediguian, Robert
MARIUS AND JEANNETTE
Guerin, J.P.
KID IN ALADDIN'S PALACE, A
Gund, George
MODULATIONS: CINEMA FOR THE EAR
Gunning, Barbara
TRICKS
Gunther, Dan
LEWIS & CLARK & GEORGE
Hacker, Melissa
MY KNEES WERE JUMPING: REMEMBERING THE KINDERTRANSPORTS
Hacker, Tamar
LOU REED: ROCK AND ROLL HEART
Hacker, Timothy
LOU REED: ROCK AND ROLL HEART
Haddad, Patrice
ARTEMISIA
Haebler, Christine
HARD CORE LOGO
Hagino, Ken
POLTERGEIST REPORT: YUYU HAKUSHO
Haines, Randa
DANCE WITH ME
Hald, Birgitte
CELEBRATION, THE
Hall, Dolly
54
HIGH ART
Hall, Paul
WHY DO FOOLS FALL IN LOVE?
Hamburger, David S.
HURLYBURLY
Hamed, Shannon
LET'S KILL ALL THE LAWYERS
Hammel, Thomas M.
FIRESTORM
Hamsher, Jane
APT PUPIL
PERMANENT MIDNIGHT
Hanley, Chris
BUFFALO '66
TWO GIRLS AND A GUY
Hannah, David
CROSSING FIELDS
Hansen, Kirk Edward
CURSE OF THE PUPPET MASTER
KRAA! THE SEA MONSTER
SUBSPECIES IV: BLOODSTORM
Hansen, Lisa
BODY COUNT
Harper, Richard
FERNGULLY 2: THE MAGICAL RESCUE
Harris, J. Todd
BAD MANNERS
DIGGING TO CHINA
Harris, Mark R.
GODS AND MONSTERS
Hart, William
EIGHTEENTH ANGEL, THE
Hartley, Hal
HENRY FOOL
Hartley, Ted
MIGHTY JOE YOUNG
Harvey, Rupert
CHAIRMAN OF THE BOARD
Hauptman, Andrew
SAFE MEN
Hayden, Laurette
MY VERY BEST FRIEND
Headley, Mark
JOHNNY MYSTO BOY WIZARD
MIDAS TOUCH, THE
Hebert, James
HOLLYWOOD CONFIDENTIAL
Heckerling, Amy
NIGHT AT THE ROXBURY, A
Heiduschka, Veit
FUNNY GAMES
Helgeland, Axel
MENDEL
Heller, Peter
CAUGHT UP
Henderson, Lyn
MIGHTY KONG, THE
Henson, Lisa
ZERO EFFECT
Herek, Stephen
HOLY MAN
Herskovitz, Marshall
DANGEROUS BEAUTY
Hertzeberg, Paul
BODY COUNT
Herzog, Werner
LITTLE DIETER NEEDS TO FLY
Heuer, Jonathan
I GOT THE HOOK UP
Hibbin, Sally
CARLA'S SONG
Hill, Debra
GIRLS IN PRISON
Hill, Grant
THIN RED LINE, THE
Hiruta, Tomiyo
TEKKEN: THE MOTION PICTURE
Hjort, Karen
KRZYSZTOF KIESLOWSKI: I'M SO-SO
Ho, Leonard
ARMOUR OF GOD
DRAGONS FOREVER
Hoberman, David
I'LL BE HOME FOR CHRISTMAS
NEGOTIATOR, THE
SENSELESS
Hoffman, Peter
SHATTERED IMAGE
Hoffman, Susan
DESPERATE MEASURES
SHATTERED IMAGE
Hoffman, Todd
LOVELIFE
Holland, Gil
HURRICANE STREETS
Holmes, Richard
SHOOTING FISH
WAKING NED DEVINE
Holt, James
ONLY THRILL, THE
Honokideni, Naoharu
POLTERGEIST REPORT: YUYU HAKUSHO
Hope, Ted
HAPPINESS
NO LOOKING BACK
Hopkins, Stephen
LOST IN SPACE
Horberg, William
SLIDING DOORS
Horie, George
ESCAPE, THE
Horiguchi, Juichi
WHEN I CLOSE MY EYES
Hsu, Melinda
BOYS IN LOVE 2
Hu Yuesheng
EMPEROR'S SHADOW, THE

Hubbard, Beth
WOO
Hubbard, Michael
WOO
Hudlin, Reginald
RIDE
Hudlin, Warrington
RIDE
Hughes, John
REACH THE ROCK
Hurd, Gale Anne
ARMAGEDDON
DEAD MAN ON CAMPUS
Iino, Hisa
EEL, THE
Ikeda, Tomoki
WHEN I CLOSE MY EYES
Ilich, Miljan Peter
RUN FOR COVER
Irving, Brian
REDLINE
Isomi, Toshihiro
JUNK FOOD
Jacks, James
SIMPLE PLAN, A
Jackson, G. Philip
FALLING FIRE
FUTURE FEAR
Jackson, George
BODY COUNT
Jacobs, Ronald
LAND OF THE FREE
Jacobson, Tom
MIGHTY JOE YOUNG
Jaffe, Stanley
MADELINE
Janger, Lane
I THINK I DO
Jeanneau, Yves
CHILE, OBSTINATE MEMORY
CLASSIFIED X
Jenkel, Brad
RINGMASTER
Jin Ji-Wu
RED CHERRY
Johns, Richard
KILLING TIME
Johnson, John S.
RATCHET
Johnson, Mark
HOME FRIES
Jones, Robert
DAD SAVAGE
Jones, Steven A.
WILD THINGS
Jonsson, Lars
TRANCEFORMER: A PORTRAIT OF LARS VON TRIER
Joslin, Nancy
PLAN B
Josten, Walter
CHILDREN OF THE CORN V: FIELD OF TERROR
Jung, Christophe
EAST PALACE, WEST PALACE
Kabillio, Eli
NO ORDINARY LOVE
Kacirkova, Ivana
FORGOTTEN LIGHT
Kahan, Jeffrey
FERNGULLY 2: THE MAGICAL RESCUE
Kahn, Harvey
EDEN
Kaiser, Mary Adair
RACE TO SAVE 100 YEARS, THE
Kanesaku, Haruyo
RED HAWK: WEAPON OF DEATH
Kang, James
3 NINJAS: HIGH NOON AT MEGA MOUNTAIN
Kaplan, Alan
BAD MANNERS
Karlsen, Elizabeth
LITTLE VOICE
Karmitz, Marin
SWINDLE, THE
Karnowski, Tom
MEAN GUNS
NEMESIS 4: CRY OF ANGELS
Kasander, Kees
ROYAL DECEIT
WHEN PIGS FLY
Kasdan, Jake
ZERO EFFECT
Kassar, Mario
LOLITA
Kassir, Allan
NORTH SHORE FISH
Katselas Pare, Lisa
MRS. DALLOWAY
Katsu, Shintaro
RAZOR: THE SNARE, THE
RAZOR: WHO'S GOT THE GOLD?, THE
Kawamura, Naonari
NAPOLEON
Kehala, Karen
MERCURY RISING
Kemeny, John
WHEN TRUMPETS FADE
Kemp, Barry
PATCH ADAMS
Kent, Nicholas
HILARY AND JACKIE
Kenworthy, Duncan
LAWN DOGS
Ker, Jonathan
ALWAYS OUTNUMBERED
Kessler, Henri M.
SLAM
Kewvoy, Brad
RETROACTIVE
Key, Don
INTERLOCKED: THRILLED TO DEATH
Khoury, Gabriel
DESTINY
Khoury, Raymond
LITTLE BIGFOOT 2: THE JOURNEY HOME
Kiarostami, Abbas
TASTE OF CHERRY
Kidron, Beeban
SWEPT FROM THE SEA
Kilik, Jon
HE GOT GAME
PLEASANTVILLE
Kindaichi, Ken
TEKKEN: THE MOTION PICTURE
King, Kandice
DIARY OF A SERIAL KILLER
King, Sandy
JOHN CARPENTER'S VAMPIRES
Kirkland, Boyd
BATMAN & MR. FREEZE: SUBZERO
Kirkpatrick, David
OPPOSITE OF SEX, THE
Kirschner, David
BRIDE OF CHUCKY
Kirshbaum, Jeff
MILO
Klainberg, Lesli
PAUL MONETTE: THE BRINK OF SUMMER'S END
Klasky, Arlene
RUGRATS MOVIE, THE
Knell, Catalaine
BODY COUNT
Koch, Mark W.
BLACK DOG
LOST IN SPACE
Kohner, Pancho
MADELINE
Kollek, Amos
SUE
Komaki, Jiro
WHEN I CLOSE MY EYES
Konrad, Cathy
WIDE AWAKE
Kopelson, Anne
PERFECT MURDER, A
U.S. MARSHALS
Kopelson, Arnold
PERFECT MURDER, A
U.S. MARSHALS
Kottenbrook, Carol
OUTSIDE OZONA
Kowalchuk, William R.
BUSTER & CHAUNCEY'S SILENT NIGHT
RUDOLPH THE RED-NOSED REINDEER: THE MOVIE
Krainin, Julian
GEORGE WALLACE
Krausz, Danny
INHERITORS, THE
Krevoy, Brad
DOUBLE EDGE
MUSIC FROM ANOTHER ROOM
OVERNIGHT DELIVERY
Kroonenburg, Pieter
BLEEDERS
JACK LONDON'S THE CALL OF THE WILD: DOG OF THE YUKON
Kroopf, Scott
PROPOSITION, THE
Kufus, Thomas
MOTHER AND SON
Kushner, Donald
BRAVE LITTLE TOASTER GOES TO MARS, THE
Kutner, Willie
GIRLS IN PRISON
Kuzui, Fran Rubel
ORGAZMO
Kyoung Tae Hwang
RED HAWK: WEAPON OF DEATH
La Voo, George
TARANTELLA
Labella, Vincenzo
FROM A FAR COUNTRY
Lake, Michael
JOEY
TARZAN AND THE LOST CITY
Lan, William
BEAUTY INVESTIGATOR
Lancaster, David
TERMINAL JUSTICE
Landis, John
BLUES BROTHERS 2000
Landry, Christopher
CLOCKMAKER
SECRET KINGDOM, THE
Lane, Steve
PHANTOMS
Larsen, Nancy
PARALLEL SONS
Lashbrook, Rick
KISSING A FOOL
Lasky, Richard
ENEMY
Latham, Alan
BRYLCREEM BOYS, THE
Lau, Jeff
FALLEN ANGELS
Lazar, Andrew
MAKER, THE

Le Goff, Christine
CLASSIFIED X
Leach, Sheryl
BARNEY'S GREAT ADVENTURE—THE MOVIE
Leahy, Michael
PHANTOMS
Leake, Helen
HEAVEN'S BURNING
Lee, Quentin
SHOPPING FOR FANGS
Lee, Spike
HE GOT GAME
Leider, Jerry
TRUCKS
Lenkov, Peter M.
CHAIRMAN OF THE BOARD
Lennard, Laurie
SOUR GRAPES
Leonhardt, Lutz
ZAKIR AND HIS FRIENDS
Lerner, Avi
SCARRED CITY
TOP OF THE WORLD
Lerner, Danny
OPERATION DELTA FORCE 2
Lester, Mark L.
MISBEGOTTEN
Leva, Gary
PLAN B
Levin, Marc
SLAM
Levine, Hank
WAR ZONE
Levinsohn, Gary
HARD RAIN
PAULIE
SAVING PRIVATE RYAN
Levinson, Barry
HOME FRIES
SPHERE
Levitt, Zane
MONTANA
Levy, Robert L.
KID IN ALADDIN'S PALACE, A
Levy-Hinte, Jeff
HIGH ART
Lewis, Brad
ANTZ
Lewis, Claudia
SKIN & BONE
Lewnes, Peter
RUN FOR COVER
Li, Jet
BODYGUARD FROM BEIJING
Liber, Rodney
WILD THINGS
Liberman, Meg
PLAYING BY HEART
Liddell, Mickey
UNDER HEAVEN
Lindstrom, Goran
KRISTIN LAVRANSDATTER
Linson, Art
GREAT EXPECTATIONS
Liu Yet Yuen
SHAOLIN TEMPLE, THE
Lloyd, Gwynneth
DAD SAVAGE
Lloyd, Michael
RUDOLPH THE RED-NOSED REINDEER: THE MOVIE
Lo Chia Po
KICK BOXER'S TEARS
Lo Kar Po
KILLER ANGELS
LoCash, Robert
BASEKETBALL

Loeb III, Joseph
FIRESTORM
Lorenz, Carsten
PRINCE VALIANT
Louzil, Eric
FATAL PURSUIT
Lovell, Dyson
MERLIN
Lowery, Ryan
DECAMPITATED
Loyola, Roberto
RABID DOGS
Ludwig, Avram
RIVER RED
Macaulay, Scott
FIRST LOVE, LAST RITES
MacCarley, Kurt
REAL THING, THE
MacGregor-Scott, Peter
PERFECT MURDER, A
Machenko, Mykola
FRIEND OF THE DECEASED, A
MacKay, Anne-Marie
ALWAYS OUTNUMBERED
Madden, David
NEIL SIMON'S THE ODD COUPLE II
Madigan, Paul
BRYLCREEM BOYS, THE
Mancuso Jr., Frank
RONIN
SPECIES II
Mandt, Neil
HIJACKING HOLLYWOOD
Mankiewicz, Christopher
PERFECT MURDER, A
Mann, Mary Beth
DEAR JESSE
Mapp, Vester
FATAL PURSUIT
Marcil, Allan
PRONTO
Marcovich, Carlos
WHO THE HELL IS JULIETTE?
Mark, Laurence
DEEP RISING
OBJECT OF MY AFFECTION, THE
SIMON BIRCH
Marker, Chris
BATTLE OF CHILE: THE STRUGGLE OF AN UNARMED PEOPLE—PART 2: THE COUP D'ETAT, THE
Markey, Patrick
HORSE WHISPERER, THE
Marmion, Yves
CHAMBERMAID ON THE TITANIC, THE
Maseba, Yutaka
RED HAWK: WEAPON OF DEATH
Mason, Andrew
DARK CITY
Masujima, Yumiko
TEKKEN: THE MOTION PICTURE
Matthews, Gina
URBAN LEGEND
Matz, Zachary
FRENCH EXIT
Mauceri, Marc
LAVENDER LIMELIGHT: LESBIANS IN FILM
Maynard, Stephen
CAPTIVE
McDonnell, Michael
URBAN LEGEND
McGauley, Victor
DOWN IN THE DELTA
McGuinn, Patrick
BOYS IN LOVE 2
McHenry, Doug
BODY COUNT

McHugh, Jason
ORGAZMO
Meh, Mehra
CUBE
Meistrich, Larry
BELLY
Meltzer, Howard
PENTAGON WARS, THE
Menage, Chiara
LOVE IS THE DEVIL: STUDY FOR A PORTRAIT OF FRANCIS BACON
Menager, Christophe
EAST PALACE, WEST PALACE
Mendel, Barry
RUSHMORE
Mendelson, Brandon
BOOGIE BOY
Mendillo, Stephen Tag
KISSING A FOOL
Merchant, Ismail
SOLDIER'S DAUGHTER NEVER CRIES, A
Mestres, Ricardo
REACH THE ROCK
Meyer, Peter W.
CAN'T YOU HEAR THE WIND HOWL?: THE LIFE AND MUSIC OF ROBERT JOHNSON
Meyerson, Aaron
MEET THE DEEDLES
Meyner, Stephen
MY FIRST NAME IS MACEO
Michaels, Joel B.
LOLITA
Michaels, Lorne
NIGHT AT THE ROXBURY, A
Michel, Eric
CHILE, OBSTINATE MEMORY
Michell, Scott
INNOCENT SLEEP, THE
Milchan, Arnon
DANGEROUS BEAUTY
NEGOTIATOR, THE
Miller, Bennett
CRUISE, THE
Miller, Bill
BABE: PIG IN THE CITY
Miller, Carolyn
DECAMPITATED
Miller, Donna
WEST NEW YORK
Miller, George
BABE: PIG IN THE CITY
Miller, Jeffery
DESTINY OF MARTY FINE, THE
Miller, R. Paul
MEN WITH GUNS
Mills, Todd Easton
TIMOTHY LEARY'S DEAD
Minoff, Marvin
PATCH ADAMS
Mitchell, Doug
BABE: PIG IN THE CITY
Mitchell, Ron
QUICKSILVER HIGHWAY
Mitler, Matt
CRACKING UP
Mitran, Doru
GADJO DILO
Miura, Kanji
GONIN
Miyato, Tomoyuki
WRATH OF THE NINJA: THE YOTODEN MOVIE
Miyazaki, Hayao
KIKI'S DELIVERY SERVICE
Monks, Gardner
SKIN & BONE

Mori, Masayuki
FIREWORKS
SONATINE
Mori, Yoshimasa
TEKKEN: THE MOTION PICTURE
Morishita, Kozo
DRAGON BALL Z THE MOVIE: DEAD ZONE
DRAGON BALL Z THE MOVIE: THE TREE OF MIGHT
DRAGON BALL Z THE MOVIE: THE WORLD'S STRONGEST
Moritz, Neal H.
I STILL KNOW WHAT YOU DID LAST SUMMER
URBAN LEGEND
Morris, Kevin
HANDS ON A HARDBODY
Morris, Redmond
BUTCHER BOY, THE
Morrissey, John
AMERICAN HISTORY X
Moseley, David
BILLY'S HOLLYWOOD SCREEN KISS
Mossman, Ben
DETOUR
Mossman, Brian
DETOUR
Motoki, Katsuhide
GONIN
Mruvka, Alan
DIGGING TO CHINA
Munch, Axel
LAST ASSASSINS
Muragila, Silvio
SUB DOWN
Murakami, Koichi
WHEN I CLOSE MY EYES
Murillo, R.J.
DOUBLE EDGE
Murphy, Don
APT PUPIL
PERMANENT MIDNIGHT
Murray, Glynis
SHOOTING FISH
WAKING NED DEVINE
Muska, Susan
BRANDON TEENA STORY, THE
Myron, Ben
BURN HOLLYWOOD BURN
Nabatoff, Diane
PROPOSITION, THE
VERY BAD THINGS
Nabeshima, Hisao
SONATINE
Nablusi, Laila
FEAR AND LOATHING IN LAS VEGAS
Nadeau, Michael
RETROACTIVE
Nagasawa, Masahiko
WHEN I CLOSE MY EYES
Nagasawa, Taka
GOLGO 13: QUEEN BEE
Nakamura, Ryohei
NEW ADVENTURES OF KIMBA THE WHITE LION, THE
Naylor, Lynne
HERCULES AND XENA THE ANIMATED MOVIE: THE BATTLE FOR MOUNT OLYMPUS
Neiman, Becky
LAVENDER LIMELIGHT: LESBIANS IN FILM
Nemanska, Alice
FORGOTTEN LIGHT
Nemeth, Stephen
BAD MANNERS
FEAR AND LOATHING IN LAS VEGAS
WHY DO FOOLS FALL IN LOVE?
Nesher, Avi
MARS
Netter, Gil
BASEKETBALL
Nevinny, Victoria
PHOENIX
Newirth, Charles
HOME FRIES
PATCH ADAMS
Newmyer, Bobby
DENNIS THE MENACE STRIKES AGAIN
Ng Ming Toi
BEAUTY INVESTIGATOR
Niami, Ramin
SOMEWHERE IN THE CITY
Niccol, Andrew
TRUMAN SHOW, THE
Nichols, Mike
PRIMARY COLORS
Nicita, Wallis
SIX DAYS, SEVEN NIGHTS
Nickson, Robert
NO WAY HOME
Niederhoffer, Galt
HURRICANE STREETS
Niitsu, Taketo
GONIN
Nikkhah-Azad, V.
MIRROR, THE
Nishioka, Kozen
RAZOR: THE SNARE, THE
RAZOR: WHO'S GOT THE GOLD?, THE
Nordahl, Dag
JUNK MAIL
Norman, Marc
SHAKESPEARE IN LOVE
North, Steve
OLIVER TWIST
Noval, Pierre
NIGHT AND THE MOMENT, THE
Nozik, Michael
NO LOOKING BACK
SLUMS OF BEVERLY HILLS
O'Connor, Matthew
SNOWBOUND
O'Hara, Robin
FIRST LOVE, LAST RITES
Obel, Michael
NIGHTWATCH
Obst, Lynda
HOPE FLOATS
SIEGE, THE
Ogborn, Kate
UNDER THE SKIN
Ohlsson, Bertil
LEADING MAN, THE
Ohnishi, Kuniaki
NEW ADVENTURES OF KIMBA THE WHITE LION, THE
Olafsdottir, Greta
BRANDON TEENA STORY, THE
Oldman, Gary
NIL BY MOUTH
Orr, Betty
CUBE
Ovitz, Mark H.
ATOMIC DOG
JUNGLE BOOK: MOWGLI'S STORY, THE
Owen, Alison
ELIZABETH
Paige, Jeremy
MURDER IN MIND
Palmer, Tim
SUMMER FLING
Panahi, Jafar
MIRROR, THE
Panescu, Vlad
CLOCKMAKER
Parello, Chuck
HENRY: PORTRAIT OF A SERIAL KILLER PART 2
Parfitt, David
SHAKESPEARE IN LOVE
Parker, Maceo
MY FIRST NAME IS MACEO
Pascornek, Michael
JOHNNY SKIDMARKS
Pate, Jonas
DECEIVER
Pate, Joshua
DECEIVER
Paterson, Andrew
HILARY AND JACKIE
Patric, Jason
YOUR FRIENDS & NEIGHBORS
Paul, Steven
BOYS WILL BE BOYS
Paulsen, Daniel
NORTH SHORE FISH
Paunescu, Vlad
JOHNNY MYSTO BOY WIZARD
LITTLE GHOST
MIDAS TOUCH, THE
SECRET KINGDOM, THE
SHRUNKEN CITY, THE
SUBSPECIES IV: BLOODSTORM
TALISMAN
Paxton, Michael
AYN RAND: A SENSE OF LIFE
Pearson, Noel
DANCING AT LUGHNASA
Pennebaker, Frazer
MOON OVER BROADWAY
Penotti, John
PRICE ABOVE RUBIES, A
Perlovich, Vladmir
LAST BIG THING, THE
Perry, Pinchas
PRINCE, THE
Persinger, Marshall
STILL BREATHING
Pescarolo, Leo
TRUCE, THE
Pettijohn, Grace
RUN FOR COVER
Pezzali, Giacomo
FROM A FAR COUNTRY
Pfeffer, Rachel
CIVIL ACTION, A
Piel, Jean-Louis
CHINESE BOX, THE
Pierce, Mark
LOVER GIRL
Pilcher, Lydia Dean
CHINESE BOX, THE
Plympton, Bill
I MARRIED A STRANGE PERSON!
Pollack, Sydney
SLIDING DOORS
Pollock, Dale
MEET THE DEEDLES
Pontamkin, Buzz
BUSTER & CHAUNCEY'S SILENT NIGHT
Portillo, Ralph
NAKED LIES
Posner, P.J.
LAST BREATH
Poul, Alan
THURSDAY
Pressman, Edward R.
TWO GIRLS AND A GUY
Pringle, Robert
PHANTOMS
Proft, Pat
WRONGFULLY ACCUSED

Scott, Ridley
CLAY PIGEONS
Seale, James
ASYLUM
Seavey, Nina Gilden
PARALYZING FEAR: THE STORY OF POLIO IN AMERICA, A
Seeber, Michael
R.I.P. REST IN PIECES: A PORTRAIT OF JOE COLEMAN
Segalla, Kevin
WHATEVER
Segan, Allison Lyon
PAULIE
Serpico, Jim
MONUMENT AVE.
Severin, Karen
JOHNNY SKIDMARKS
Shaffer, Dana
DANCER, TEXAS POP. 81
Shainberg, Steven
HIT ME
Shalofsky, Stephanie
POLTERGEIST REPORT: YUYU HAKUSHO
WRATH OF THE NINJA: THE YOTODEN MOVIE
Sham, John
ROYAL WARRIORS
Shamberg, Michael
LIVING OUT LOUD
Shambert, Michael
OUT OF SIGHT
Shapiro, Stuart S.
COMEDY'S DIRTIEST DOZEN
Shaw, Peter
MERRY WAR, A
Sheinberg, Jon
SLAPPY AND THE STINKERS
Sheinberg, Sid
SLAPPY AND THE STINKERS
Sher, Stacey
LIVING OUT LOUD
OUT OF SIGHT
Sherwin, Robert
DIRTY LAUNDRY
Shestack, Jon
DISTURBING BEHAVIOR
Shi, Nansun
KNOCK OFF
Shigemura, Hajime
WHEN I CLOSE MY EYES
Shimizu, Kenji
DRAGON BALL Z THE MOVIE: THE TREE OF MIGHT
Shliapnikoff, Natasha
STIR
Sho, Koshiro
VILLAGE OF DREAMS
Shostak, Murray
LOST WORLD, THE
Shu Kei
FROZEN
Shuler-Donner, Lauren
BULWORTH
YOU'VE GOT MAIL
Shum, John
HONG KONG 1941
MAGNIFICENT WARRIORS
Shyer, Charles
PARENT TRAP, THE
Siciliano, Pat
LOLIDA 2000
Sidaris, Arlene
RETURN TO SAVAGE BEACH
Sikora, Jim
BULLET ON A WIRE
Silberman, Jack
ADVENTURES OF MOWGLI
Silver, Jeffrey
DENNIS THE MENACE STRIKES AGAIN
Silver, Joel
LETHAL WEAPON 4
Silverman, Lloyd A.
SHATTERED IMAGE
Simandl, Lloyd A.
ACT OF WAR
Simon, Neil
NEIL SIMON'S THE ODD COUPLE II
Simonds, Robert
DIRTY WORK
HALF BAKED
WATERBOY, THE
WEDDING SINGER, THE
Simpson, Holly A.
CAPTIVE
Simpson, Peter R.
FACE THE EVIL
REGENERATION
Singer, Bryan
APT PUPIL
Singer, Joseph M.
DR. DOLITTLE
Singh, Anant
THEORY OF FLIGHT
Skoog, Susan
WHATEVER
Sladek, Daniel
SUB DOWN
Slotnick, Vicki
MURDER IN MIND
Smith, Leslie L.
DAVID SEARCHING
Smith, Russell
MAN IN THE IRON MASK, THE
Snider, Dee
DEE SNIDER'S STRANGELAND
Snipes, Wesley
BIG HIT, THE
BLADE
DOWN IN THE DELTA
Snukal, Robert
RAGE, THE
Soderbergh, Steven
PLEASANTVILLE
Soisson, Joel
PHANTOMS
PROPHECY II, THE
Somers, Eric
FORMER CHILD STAR
Soria, Mireille
EVER AFTER
Southwick, Brad
LIVING IN PERIL
Spellman-Silverman, Erica
HI-LIFE
Spielberg, Steven
SAVING PRIVATE RYAN
Spillman, Darin
CLUB VAMPIRE
WATCHERS REBORN
Spione, James
PARALLEL SONS
Spring, Helena
THEORY OF FLIGHT
Springer, Jerry
RINGMASTER
Stabler, Steven
DOUBLE EDGE
MUSIC FROM ANOTHER ROOM
OVERNIGHT DELIVERY
RETROACTIVE
RINGMASTER
Stack, Jonathan
FARM: ANGOLA, U.S.A., THE
Stampfer, Bernie
BRYLCREEM BOYS, THE
Startz, Jane
MIGHTY, THE
Steel, Charles
SWEPT FROM THE SEA
Steel, Dawn
CITY OF ANGELS
FALLEN
Stefanson, Torin
BLACK LIGHT
Steinberg, Michael
THERE'S SOMETHING ABOUT MARY
Steinberg, Neil
BILLBOARD DAD
Stern, Tom
IN GOD'S HANDS
Steuart, Andrew
VIOLET'S VISIT
Stevens, Andrew
ALONE IN THE WOODS
BLACK THUNDER
INVISIBLE DAD
STEEL SHARKS
WHITE RAVEN, THE
Stewart, Allyn
MADELINE
Stier, Geoff
POLISH WEDDING
Stiliadis, Nicolas
BREAKOUT
HOT BLOODED
UNDERTAKER'S WEDDING, THE
Stillman, Joel
ROUNDERS
Stillman, Whit
LAST DAYS OF DISCO, THE
Stocker, Kurt
INHERITORS, THE
Stone, Dan
ALARMIST, THE
Stone, Matt
ORGAZMO
Stone, Oliver
SAVIOR
Stover, Susan A.
HIGH ART
Stratton, Richard
SLAM
Strauss, Peter E.
BEST OF THE BEST: WITHOUT WARNING
Stroh, Yael
ONLY THRILL, THE
Strohm, Julia
OFF THE MENU: THE LAST DAYS OF CHASEN'S
Stroppiana, Bruno
TIETA OF AGRESTE
Stuckmeyer, John V.
CALL TO REMEMBER, A
Stussak, Heinz
R.I.P. REST IN PIECES: A PORTRAIT OF JOE COLEMAN
Suzuki, Tohru
SLAYERS: THE MOTION PICTURE
Swardstrom, Brian
UNDER HEAVEN
Takamoto, Iwao
FLINTSTONES: I YABBA-DABBA DOO!, THE
Talalay, Rachel
BORROWERS, THE
Tambellini, Flavio R.
OYSTER AND THE WIND, THE
Tan, Jimmy
EMPEROR'S SHADOW, THE
Tannenbaum, Jeremy
GINGERBREAD MAN, THE
Tapson, Polly
SWEPT FROM THE SEA

Tarantino, Paul
COURTING COURTNEY
Tarlov, Mark
PECKER
Taylor, Grazka
TRICKS
Tec, Roland
ALL THE RAGE
Tedesco, Marco
STEAM
Terry, Bridget
SHADRACH
Thomas, Betty
CAN'T HARDLY WAIT
Thomas, Bradley
MUSIC FROM ANOTHER ROOM
THERE'S SOMETHING ABOUT MARY
Thompson, Barnaby
SPICE WORLD
Thompson, David M.
THEORY OF FLIGHT
Thompson, John
SHADRACH
Tichy, Wolfram
TALES FROM A PARALLEL UNIVERSE: GIGA SHADOW
TALES FROM A PARALLEL UNIVERSE: SUPER NOVA
Timm, Bruce W.
BATMAN/SUPERMAN MOVIE, THE
Tolstunov, Igor
THIEF, THE
Tomiyama, Shogo
GODZILLA AND MOTHRA: THE BATTLE FOR EARTH
GODZILLA VS. KING GHIDORAH
Tong Gang
EMPEROR'S SHADOW, THE
Topel, David
BROADWAY DAMAGE
Topping, Jenno
CAN'T HARDLY WAIT
Totti, Maurizio
NIRVANA
Tougas, Kirk
PLACE CALLED CHIAPAS, A
Tremblay, Ray
WALKING THUNDER
Trench, Tracey
EVER AFTER
I'LL BE HOME FOR CHRISTMAS
Tsang, Eric
COMRADES, ALMOST A LOVE STORY
Tsuge, Yasushi
FIREWORKS
Tsukamoto, Hiroe
DRAGON BALL Z THE MOVIE: DEAD ZONE
DRAGON BALL Z THE MOVIE: THE TREE OF MIGHT
DRAGON BALL Z THE MOVIE: THE WORLD'S STRONGEST
Tsukamoto, Shinya
TOKYO FIST
Tucci, Stanley
IMPOSTORS, THE
Tugend, Jennie Lew
STAR KID
Ufland, Harry
ONE TRUE THING
Urbanski, Douglas
NIL BY MOUTH
Ursini, Amadeo
LITTLE BOY BLUE
Vachon, Christine
HAPPINESS
VELVET GOLDMINE
Van Den Brande, Tine
KURT AND COURTNEY

Van Peebles, Mario
LOS LOCOS
Van Sant, Gus
PSYCHO
van Warmerdam, Alex
DRESS, THE
van Warmerdam, Marc
DRESS, THE
Vance, Marilyn
DIGGING TO CHINA
Vaughn, Matthew
INNOCENT SLEEP, THE
Velasquez, James
CHOSEN ONE: LEGEND OF THE RAVEN, THE
Veronis, Nick
DAY AT THE BEACH
Vince, Robert
AIR BUD: GOLDEN RECEIVER
WOUNDED
Vince, William
WOUNDED
Viscidi, Marcus
REAL BLONDE, THE
Visser, Matthias
BOYS IN LOVE 2
Vohlers, John
LOS LOCOS
von Alberti, Irene
DIDN'T DO IT FOR LOVE
Wagner, Paul
PARALYZING FEAR: THE STORY OF POLIO IN AMERICA, A
Wagner, Paula
WITHOUT LIMITS
Wald, Andrew
SPHERE
Waldleitner, Luggi
BEYOND SILENCE
Walker-McBay, Anne
NEWTON BOYS, THE
Wallace, Randall
MAN IN THE IRON MASK, THE
Walpole, Robert
I WENT DOWN
Walters, Brian
DECAMPITATED
Wang, Wayne
CHINESE BOX, THE
Warner, Aron
ANTZ
Watkins, William H.
LAST BREATH
Watson, Eric
PI
Watts, Helen
TWISTED
Wax, Steve
UNMADE BEDS
Weaver, Karen
JOHNNY SKIDMARKS
Webb, William
ASYLUM
Weekly Shonen Jump
DRAGON BALL Z THE MOVIE: THE TREE OF MIGHT
Weide, Robert B.
LENNY BRUCE: SWEAR TO TELL THE TRUTH
Weiner, Gary
ALMOST PARTNERS
Weinstein, Harvey
SHAKESPEARE IN LOVE
Weintraub, Jerry
AVENGERS, THE
SOLDIER
Weisberg, Roni
FACE DOWN

Weisman, Matthew
FIRESTORM
Weissman, Lauren C.
DANCE WITH ME
Wendlandt, Matthias
PALMETTO
Wertheimer, Robert
JACK HIGGINS' THUNDER POINT
JACK HIGGINS' THE WINDSOR PROTOCOL
Wesley, William
TRUCKS
Wessler, Charles
THERE'S SOMETHING ABOUT MARY
West, Imogen
TWENTYFOURSEVEN
White, Jeffery
SUB DOWN
White, Peter
DANCER, TEXAS POP. 81
Whitley, Patrick
IN HIS FATHER'S SHOES
Wick, Douglas
HUSH
Wild, Nettie
PLACE CALLED CHIAPAS, A
Wilder, Scott
DECLINE OF WESTERN CIVILIZATION PART III, THE
Wilhite, Tom
BRAVE LITTLE TOASTER GOES TO MARS, THE
PLAYING BY HEART
Williams, Hype
BELLY
Williams, Michael
HOME BEFORE DARK
Williams, Paul
MEN
Williams, Wade
DETOUR
Williamson, Fred
NIGHT VISION
Williamson, Linda
NIGHT VISION
Wilson, Chapin John
HANDS ON A HARDBODY
Wilson, Colin
SMALL SOLDIERS
Windelov, Vibeke
KINGDOM, PART 2, THE
Windisch, Ingrid
OGRE, THE
Winfrey, Oprah
BELOVED
Wise, Clare
LAST SEDUCTION II, THE
Wlodkowski, Stan
SLUMS OF BEVERLY HILLS
Wobke, Thomas
BEYOND SILENCE
Wodoslawsky, Stefan
DEAD END
Wolf, Scott
DISAPPEARANCE OF KEVIN JOHNSON, THE
Wong Kar-wai
FALLEN ANGELS
Woods, Cary
WIDE AWAKE
Woods, James
ANOTHER DAY IN PARADISE
Woolley, Stephen
BUTCHER BOY, THE
Wooton, Patty
ANTZ
Workman, Chuck
STORY OF X, THE

Wynne, Cordell
ADVENTURES OF MOWGLI
Xu Wei
FROZEN
Yahn, Michelle
WHATEVER
Yamagami, Tetsujiro
VILLAGE OF DREAMS
Yamamoto, Sandy
GOLGO 13: QUEEN BEE
Yamazaki, Shinsuke
ZERO WOMAN
Yang, Janet
SAVIOR
ZERO EFFECT
Yellen, Mark
MONTANA
Yoshida, Takio
FIREWORKS
SONATINE
Yoshimura, Hitoshi
GOLGO 13: QUEEN BEE
Yuen, Corey
DRAGONS FOREVER
Yuval, Peter
LITTLE GHOST
Zahavi, Natan
KID IN ALADDIN'S PALACE, A
Zaizen, Sadoa
SLEEPY EYES OF DEATH: SWORD OF SEDUCTION
Zanuck, Richard D.
DEEP IMPACT
Zarpas, Chris
CLAY PIGEONS
Zaslove, Alan
POCAHONTAS II: JOURNEY TO A NEW WORLD
Zhang Pimin
EMPEROR'S SHADOW, THE
Zhang Yuan
EAST PALACE, WEST PALACE
Zide, Warren
BIG HIT, THE
CAN'T HARDLY WAIT
Zimble, Lisa
ALARMIST, THE
Zimmer, Christopher
LOVE AND DEATH ON LONG ISLAND
REAL HOWARD SPITZ, THE
Zucker, David
BASEKETBALL
Zuev, Victor
DEAD WATERS
Zugsmith, Albert
TOUCH OF EVIL: THE DIRECTOR'S CUT
Zwick, Edward
DANGEROUS BEAUTY
SHAKESPEARE IN LOVE
SIEGE, THE

PRODUCTION DESIGNERS

Abram, Deren P.
BOYS WILL BE BOYS
GODSON, THE
MARS
Acuna, Regina
TRUCKS
Adam, Jori
TALK TO ME
Adamovich, Roman
FRIEND OF THE DECEASED, A
Ahmad, Maher
U.S. MARSHALS
Ako, Yuda
RUSTY: THE GREAT RESCUE
Albin, Lisa
SOMEWHERE IN THE CITY
Allen, Melanie
THEORY OF FLIGHT
Altman, Stephen
GINGERBREAD MAN, THE
Amaral, Roy Allan
ATOMIC DOG
Amarante, Cassio
CENTRAL STATION
Ambrose, Roger
LOLIDA 2000
Amies, Caroline
LAND GIRLS, THE
Ammon, Ruth
MONUMENT AVE.
Ancona, Amy B.
ALARMIST, THE
Armstrong, Charles
SMOKE SIGNALS
Arrat, Patrice
SEVENTH HEAVEN
Ashman, Louis
ALL THE RAGE
Asp, Anna
JERUSALEM
LES MISERABLES
Attaom, Arianna
NIGHT AND THE MOMENT, THE
August, Chris
ERNEST IN THE ARMY
Austin, Shay
PROPHECY II, THE
Bacher, Hans
MULAN
Barchi, Petra
DAY AT THE BEACH
HURRICANE STREETS
Basili, Giancarlo
NIRVANA
Baumane, Signe
I MARRIED A STRANGE PERSON!
Beaudoin, Jocelyn
WHEN PIGS FLY
Bell, John
ANTZ
Benjamin, Al
WOUNDED
Bennett, Elise
NEXT STEP, THE
Benoit-Fresco, Francoise
SWINDLE, THE
Berke, Mayne
DON KING: ONLY IN AMERICA
JACK FROST
WHY DO FOOLS FALL IN LOVE?
Berliner, Roshelle
RIVER RED
Berry, Kelly
BOYS IN LOVE 2
Bickel, Paul
STIR
Bider, Tim
TALES FROM A PARALLEL UNIVERSE: SUPER NOVA
TERMINAL JUSTICE
Bieling, Susann
BEYOND SILENCE
Bishop, Dan
NEIL SIMON'S THE ODD COUPLE II
Blake, Perry Andelin
HALF BAKED
WATERBOY, THE
WEDDING SINGER, THE
Blass, Dave
ASYLUM
RUNNING WOMAN, THE
STRAY BULLET
Blatt, Stuart
WHEN TIME EXPIRES
Blythe, Bernhard
HIGH ART
Bo, Eli
INSOMNIA
Bolles, Susan
ILLTOWN
Bollinger, Frank
MILO
Bolton, Michael
WRONGFULLY ACCUSED
Bomba, David J.
GIA
Bourke, Charlotte
DAY AT THE BEACH
Bourne, Tristan Paris
ORGAZMO
Bowin, Claire Jenora
PALMETTO
Branco, Ze
VOYAGE TO THE BEGINNING OF THE WORLD
Breen, Charles
KISSING A FOOL
MUSIC FROM ANOTHER ROOM
PHOENIX
URBAN LEGEND
YOUR FRIENDS & NEIGHBORS
Bretschneider, Steve
WEST NEW YORK
Brisbin, David
PROPOSITION, THE
Brodie, Bill
BLUES BROTHERS 2000
Bromley, Karen
BLACKJACK
Buckley, Martina
BILLBOARD DAD
LAST BIG THING, THE
OUTSIDE OZONA
Bueno, Clovis
OYSTER AND THE WIND, THE
Bufnoir, Jacques
SOLDIER'S DAUGHTER NEVER CRIES, A
Bunker, Jon
HOSTILE WATERS
Burchiellaro, Giantito
PEREIRA DECLARES
Burke, Charlotte
SUE
Burns, Keith Brian
ALWAYS OUTNUMBERED
Burrough, Tony
GREAT EXPECTATIONS
Butcher, Robert
CATHERINE'S GROVE
Caffe, Carla
CENTRAL STATION
Calinescu, Vali
JOHNNY MYSTO BOY WIZARD
MIDAS TOUCH, THE
Caprara, Gualtro
CHAMBERMAID ON THE TITANIC, THE
Caprara, Walter
CHAMBERMAID ON THE TITANIC, THE
Carbone, Franco-Giacomo
BILLY'S HOLLYWOOD SCREEN KISS
Carlin, Michael
DAD SAVAGE
Carp, Jean-Philippe
FRENCH EXIT
Carruth, Scott
NO ORDINARY LOVE
Caso, Maria
ELMORE LEONARD'S GOLD COAST
Cedar, Phyllis
NO WAY HOME

Cesari, Bruno
CHAMBERMAID ON THE TITANIC, THE
Chalon, Luc
GENEALOGIES OF A CRIME
Chambaret, Clovis
MEN
Chambliss, Scott
KRIPPENDORF'S TRIBE
Chang, William
FALLEN ANGELS
Chapman, David
SIMON BIRCH
Charette, Cynthia
I'LL BE HOME FOR CHRISTMAS
Cherniawsky, Todd
HIJACKING HOLLYWOOD
Childs, Martin
SHAKESPEARE IN LOVE
Chorney, Jo-Ann
DESTINY OF MARTY FINE, THE
Clausen, Michael
OPPOSITE OF SEX, THE
Claytor Sr., James F.
FATAL PURSUIT
Close, Michael
BREAKOUT
HOT BLOODED
UNDERTAKER'S WEDDING, THE
Coates, Nelson
DISTURBING BEHAVIOR
LIVING OUT LOUD
Cochran, Erin
KRAA! THE SEA MONSTER
Cone, William
BUG'S LIFE, A
Connor, Chuck
3 NINJAS: HIGH NOON AT MEGA MOUNTAIN
Conroy, Tom
MOONDANCE
Constable, Gary
NOT IN THIS TOWN
Conway, Frank
SUMMER FLING
Corciova, Radu
CLOCKMAKER
SECRET KINGDOM, THE
SUBSPECIES IV: BLOODSTORM
Corenblith, Michael
MIGHTY JOE YOUNG
Coriciova, Ioana
SHRUNKEN CITY, THE
Cottignoli, Alberto
BEST MAN, THE
Cowley, Anthony
DEFENDERS: PAYBACK, THE
Craig, Stuart
AVENGERS, THE
Crank, David
MAJOR LEAGUE: BACK TO THE MINORS
Creber, William
WITHOUT LIMITS
Cresciman, Vincent J.
PENTAGON WARS, THE
Crisanti, Andrea
TRUCE, THE
Cristante, Ivo
SLAPPY AND THE STINKERS
Cunin, Richard
NIGHT AND THE MOMENT, THE
Danger, Amy
HIT ME
Davis, Dan
YOU'VE GOT MAIL
Davis, Michael
LETTER FROM DEATH ROW, A

de Cotiis, Franco
RESCUERS: STORIES OF COURAGE—TWO COUPLES
RESCUERS: STORIES OF COURAGE—TWO WOMEN
De Vallance, Brendan
MIGHTY KONG, THE
De Vico, Robert
SHATTERED IMAGE
DeGovia, Jack
MY GIANT
Del Rosario, Linda
FIRESTORM
Deprez, Therese
HAPPINESS
NO LOOKING BACK
DeScenna, Linda
PATCH ADAMS
Detweiller, Chad
NEXT STOP, WONDERLAND
DeVico, Robert
DIGGING TO CHINA
Devilla, Debbie
DEE SNIDER'S STRANGELAND
I THINK I DO
RATCHET
Deville, Roland
POST COITUM, ANIMAL TRISTE
Devine, Michael
JACK LONDON'S THE CALL OF THE WILD: DOG OF THE YUKON
Dick, Douglas
BEST OF THE BEST: WITHOUT WARNING
Dilley, Leslie
DEEP IMPACT
Djurkovic, Maria
SLIDING DOORS
WILDE
Dobrowolski, Marek
OVERNIGHT DELIVERY
Donati, Danilo
LIFE IS BEAUTIFUL
Dondertman, John
IN HIS FATHER'S SHOES
Dorman, Laurence
PHOTOGRAPHING FAIRIES
Duffin, Philip
RETROACTIVE
Durand, Patrick
CLASSIFIED X
Ebden, John
WAKING NED DEVINE
Eckel, Tim
BODY COUNT
Edwards, Vaughan
HORTON FOOTE'S ALONE
Elliot, William
DR. DOLITTLE
Elliott, William A.
JANE AUSTEN'S MAFIA!
Estabrook, Dan
FIRST LOVE, LAST RITES
Falcon, Jeffrey
SIX-STRING SAMURAI
Ferguson, David
TRUCKS
Fernandez, Benjamin
ENEMY OF THE STATE
Fernandez Del Paso, Felipe
MEN WITH GUNS
Ferretti, Dante
MEET JOE BLACK
Ferrier, Jim
TWISTED
Fischer, David
SPREE, THE
WHEN DANGER FOLLOWS YOU HOME

Fisk, Jack
THIN RED LINE, THE
Fleming, Jerry
DOGWATCH
JOHNNY SKIDMARKS
PERMANENT MIDNIGHT
Foden, Tom
PSYCHO
Ford, Roger
BABE: PIG IN THE CITY
Foster, Terrence
CAUGHT UP
Frick, John Allen
LITTLE BOY BLUE
ONLY THRILL, THE
Friedberg, Mark
COMEDY'S DIRTIEST DOZEN
Frigerio, Ezio
OGRE, THE
Frutkoff, Gary
OUT OF SIGHT
ZERO EFFECT
Fulton, Larry
HOPE FLOATS
Fung Yuen Chi
HEROES SHED NO TEARS
Galvin, Tim
SPANISH PRISONER, THE
Garner, Pat
SOLDIER'S DAUGHTER NEVER CRIES, A
Garrity, Joseph T.
ALMOST HEROES
DENNIS THE MENACE STRIKES AGAIN
Garwood, Norman
DANGEROUS BEAUTY
LOST IN SPACE
Gasparro, Anthony
SAFE MEN
Gassner, Dennis
TRUMAN SHOW, THE
Geleng, Antonello
ARTEMISIA
Gentry, Cecil
BODY COUNT
Geraghty, Mark
DANCING AT LUGHNASA
INFORMANT, THE
Gillespie, John
HOSTILE INTENT
Gillies, Robert
YOUNG HERCULES
Ginn, Jeff
BONE DADDY
Gogol, Derek
PRINCE OF EGYPT, THE
Goldfield, Daniel
LAST BREATH
Goldman, Dina
BROADWAY DAMAGE
CHARLIE HOBOKEN
WHATEVER
Gorrara, Perri
MY VERY BEST FRIEND
Gorz, Andrzej
KRZYSZTOF KIESLOWSKI: I'M SO-SO
Gottlieb, Max
SHOOTING FISH
Gow, Ronald
KILLING TIME
Greco, Anthony
FACE DOWN
Greco, Dennis
POCAHONTAS II: JOURNEY TO A NEW WORLD
Greenwood, Sarah
GOVERNESS, THE
MERRY WAR, A

Greville-Mason, Marc
IN GOD'S HANDS
Grigorian, Greta
LOS LOCOS
Gringas, Sylvain
LOST WORLD, THE
Groom, Bill
RETURN TO PARADISE
Gropman, David
CIVIL ACTION, A
TWILIGHT
Gross, Holger
DEEP RISING
NEGOTIATOR, THE
Guterres, Candi
COLONY, THE
Hall, C. Daniel
LAST LIVES
Hall, Ian
BRAM STOKER'S SHADOWBUILDER
Hall, Roger
MERLIN
Hall, Tony
JACK HIGGINS' THUNDER POINT
JACK HIGGINS' THE WINDSOR PROTOCOL
Haller, Michael
HURLYBURLY
Hanan, Michael
GEORGE WALLACE
RONIN
Hanania, Caroline
LEADING MAN, THE
MIGHTY, THE
Hanna, Ed
TRACKED
Hardie, Steve
BRYLCREEM BOYS, THE
Harding, Kathleen
CROSSING FIELDS
Hardwicke, Catherine
NEWTON BOYS, THE
Harper, Mark
CLUB VAMPIRE
WATCHERS REBORN
Harris, Andy
REGENERATION
Harris, Rob
FIRELIGHT
Harwell, Helen
INVISIBLE MOM
Heier, Grethe
OTHER SIDE OF SUNDAY, THE
Heinrichs, Rick
BIG LEBOWSKI, THE
Helps, James
JACK HIGGINS' ON DANGEROUS GROUND
JACK HIGGINS' MIDNIGHT MAN
Hemdane, Hamed
DESTINY
Henderson, Lyn
MIGHTY KONG, THE
Herbert, Jacques
PLUMP FICTION
Hermer-Bell, Lindsey
DOWN IN THE DELTA
Heslup, William
SIN AND REDEMPTION
Hetscher, Ingolf
TALES FROM A PARALLEL UNIVERSE: EATING PATTERN
TALES FROM A PARALLEL UNIVERSE: GIGA SHADOW
TALES FROM A PARALLEL UNIVERSE: SUPER NOVA
Higgins, Doug
HUNTED, THE
Hinds-Johnson, Marcia
CAN'T HARDLY WAIT
Hobbs, Christopher
VELVET GOLDMINE
Holland, Simon
SWEPT FROM THE SEA
Holt, Paul
IN GOD'S HANDS
Hoover, Richard
APT PUPIL
NIGHTWATCH
Horner, Grenville
SPICE WORLD
Hosoishi, Terumi
WHEN I CLOSE MY EYES
Howard, Jeffrey
HOLLYWOOD CONFIDENTIAL
Howells, Michael
EVER AFTER
TALK OF ANGELS
Huke, John
LEWIS & CLARK & GEORGE
Hunter, Clark
CLAY PIGEONS
NIAGARA NIAGARA
SUICIDE KINGS
Hutman, Jon
HORSE WHISPERER, THE
LOLITA
Inagaki, Hisao
EEL, THE
Ishiura, Maya
DOUBLE EDGE
Ivanov, Kalina
BREAK, THE
Jackness, Andrew
IMPOSTORS, THE
Jackson, Gemma
BORROWERS, THE
Jackson, Regan
BELLY
Jamison, Peter
SENSELESS
Jefferds, Vincent
BARNEY'S GREAT ADVENTURE—THE MOVIE
Jett, Billy
ALONE IN THE WOODS
MY BROTHER'S WAR
SPACEJACKED
Johnson, Martin
CARLA'S SONG
Johnston, Michael
HUSH
WIDE AWAKE
Jones, Allen
PRINCE, THE
Jones, Bryan
RIDE
Jordan, Steven
BASEKETBALL
NIGHT AT THE ROXBURY, A
Joy, Michael
ESCAPE, THE
SNOWBOUND
Joyal, Paul
MISBEGOTTEN
Juliusson, Karl
KRISTIN LAVRANSDATTER
Junnasch, Emanuel
TALES FROM A PARALLEL UNIVERSE: EATING PATTERN
TALES FROM A PARALLEL UNIVERSE: GIGA SHADOW
Kaczenski, Chester
HOW STELLA GOT HER GROOVE BACK
Kalinowski, Waldemar
DANCE WITH ME
Kanter, Christoph
FUNNY GAMES
Kartakov, Vladimir
BROTHER
Kato, Hitoshi
SLAYERS: THE MOTION PICTURE
Katsioula, Elina
INDISCREET
Keen, Gregory
DIRTY WORK
Kelly, John-Paul
TWENTYFOURSEVEN
UNDER THE SKIN
Kertz, Csaba
CAPTIVE
Keywan, Alicia
BRIDE OF CHUCKY
Kilvert, Lily
CITY OF ANGELS
SIEGE, THE
King, Robb Wilson
RUSH HOUR
Kirkland, Geoffrey
DESPERATE MEASURES
Kljakovic, Miljen Kreka
SPECIES II
Knop, Alexander
TALES FROM A PARALLEL UNIVERSE: SUPER NOVA
Kraner, Doug
I STILL KNOW WHAT YOU DID LAST SUMMER
Kretschmer, John
DECEIVER
Kybartas, Sandra
FACE THE EVIL
Lagola, Charles M.
REBOUND: THE LEGEND OF EARL "THE GOAT" MANIGAULT
Laing, Mark
TALES FROM A PARALLEL UNIVERSE: GIGA SHADOW
Larson, Ken
BRAM STOKER'S THE MUMMY
Lasic, Vladislav
SAVIOR
Lawson, Peta
JOEY
Lederman, Diane
TARANTELLA
Lee, Wing
SUBSTITUTE 2: SCHOOL'S OUT, THE
Leigh, Dan
PRICE ABOVE RUBIES, A
Lentini, Massimo
BEYOND, THE
Leonard, James
INCOGNITO
Leung, James
KNOCK OFF
Liang, Mark
TALES FROM A PARALLEL UNIVERSE: EATING PATTERN
Liddle, George
DARK CITY
Lindstrom, Kara
POLISH WEDDING
Lipton, Dina
PLAYERS CLUB, THE
VERY BAD THINGS
Lo, Dominique
ROYAL WARRIORS
Lomino, Dan
RAGE, THE
Lomofsky, Sharon
BAD MANNERS
HI-LIFE
UNDER HEAVEN

Loquasto, Santo
CELEBRITY
Luczyc-Wyhowski, Hugo
COUSIN BETTE
MADELINE
NIL BY MOUTH
Lui, Bill
KNOCK OFF
Ma, Horace
MR. NICE GUY
MacDonald, Alan
LOVE IS THE DEVIL: STUDY FOR A PORTRAIT OF FRANCIS BACON
MacLeod, Zoe
I WENT DOWN
Major, Grant
ABERRATION
UGLY, THE
Malley, Bill
12 ANGRY MEN
Malmlof, Charlotte
REAL THING, THE
UNCLE SAM
Manoos, Hilda Stark
RAT PACK, THE
Maraffi, Matthew
PI
Marcotte, Pamela
CLOCKWATCHERS
Marsh, Terence
FALLEN
Mavrakis, Eve
INNOCENT SLEEP, THE
Mayhew, Ina
WOO
McAlpine, Andrew
HOLY MAN
McArthur, Amanda
PASSION IN THE DESERT
McAvoy, Edward T.
WILD THINGS
McCullagh, Tom
BREAK, THE
McDowell, Alex
FEAR AND LOATHING IN LAS VEGAS
McHenry, David
LOVE AND DEATH ON LONG ISLAND
Meighen, John
PEACEKEEPER, THE
Miller, Chris Anthony
THURSDAY
Montiel, Cecilia
MASK OF ZORRO, THE
Moore, John J.
PRONTO
Morahan, Ben
MURDER IN MIND
Musky, Jane
OBJECT OF MY AFFECTION, THE
Myhre, John
ELIZABETH
LAWN DOGS
Nava
BLACK THUNDER
CASPER MEETS WENDY
DETONATOR
RICHIE RICH'S CHRISTMAS WISH
Nay, Maria
CHICAGO CAB
Nazarian, Narbeh
LIVING IN PERIL
Nemirsky, Michael
TRICKS
New, Gary
DREAM FOR AN INSOMNIAC
Niculescu, Cristian
LITTLE GHOST
TALISMAN
Niehus, Vicki
HEAVEN'S BURNING
NAPOLEON
Noonan, Donna
LOUISA MAY ALCOTT'S LITTLE MEN
Norlin, Eric
INVADER, THE
Normington, Alice
HILARY AND JACKIE
Norris, Patricia
HI-LO COUNTRY, THE
Nowak, Christopher
REAL BLONDE, THE
X-FILES, THE
Ocztos, Istavan
REDLINE
Ogilvie, Nathan
TRUCKS
Oppewall, Jeannine
PLEASANTVILLE
Ortolani, Stefano Maria
EIGHTEENTH ANGEL, THE
Osborne, Aaron
ANOTHER DAY IN PARADISE
CHAIRMAN OF THE BOARD
LANDLADY, THE
TOP OF THE WORLD
Paino, John
DIRTY LAUNDRY
Paris, Richard
FIRESTORM
Paterson, Owen
WELCOME TO WOOP WOOP
Paul, Rick
HENRY: PORTRAIT OF A SERIAL KILLER PART 2
Paul, Victoria
BLACK DOG
Pearce, Hayden
GO NOW
LAST SEDUCTION II, THE
Pearce, Michael
I GOT THE HOOK UP
Pearson, Rob
ROUNDERS
Peranio, Vincent
PECKER
Perrin, Bryce
NEVADA
Peters, Paul
ONE TRUE THING
Petrov, Victor
THIEF, THE
Petruccelli, Kirk M.
BLADE
Pinter, Herbert
TARZAN AND THE LOST CITY
Pizzini, Denise
STILL BREATHING
Plaxton, James
FALLING FIRE
FUTURE FEAR
Po, Javier
MARIE BAIE DES ANGES
Ponte, Gideon
BUFFALO '66
Pratt, Anthony
BUTCHER BOY, THE
MAN IN THE IRON MASK, THE
Pritchard, Anne
AFFLICTION
SNAKE EYES
Proulx, Michel
BLEEDERS
Raglan, Rex
AIR BUD: GOLDEN RECEIVER
Rajk, Laszlo
WHEN TRUMPETS FADE
Ralph, Steve
STEEL SHARKS
Rawlins, David
LAST LIVES
Raymond, Deborah
CHILDREN OF THE CORN V: FIELD OF TERROR
GIRLS IN PRISON
PHANTOMS
RINGMASTER
Recht, Ray
ALMOST PARTNERS
Rencher, Burton
SHADRACH
STEPHEN KING'S THE NIGHT FLIER
Renha, Lia
TIETA OF AGRESTE
Reynolds, Norman
SPHERE
Richens, David
MRS. DALLOWAY
Riva, J. Michael
HARD RAIN
LETHAL WEAPON 4
SIX DAYS, SEVEN NIGHTS
Rizzo, Michael
NOTES FROM UNDERGROUND
Roberts, Nanci B.
LOVELIFE
Roberts, Rick
EBENEZER
Robillard, Chris
HUMAN BOMB
Robison, Barry
HOME FRIES
Rosen, Charles
SOUR GRAPES
Rosen, Kathleen
HOME BEFORE DARK
Rosenberg, Philip
PERFECT MURDER, A
Rosenzweig, Steve
HENRY FOOL
Ross, Daniel
MONTANA
Roth, Dena
SLUMS OF BEVERLY HILLS
Sallis, Crispian
PRINCE VALIANT
Salvitti, Tom
INTERLOCKED: THRILLED TO DEATH
Sandell, William
SMALL SOLDIERS
Sanders, Tom
SAVING PRIVATE RYAN
Saulnier, Jacques
SAME OLD SONG
Sawyer, Richard T.
CALL TO REMEMBER, A
Schmook, Rando
PASS, THE
Scholl, Oliver
GODZILLA
Scott, Elizabeth A.
LOVER GIRL
Scott, Helen
DEJA VU
Scott, Nigel
TALES FROM A PARALLEL UNIVERSE: EATING PATTERN
TALES FROM A PARALLEL UNIVERSE: GIGA SHADOW
TALES FROM A PARALLEL UNIVERSE: SUPER NOVA
Sfinas, Cindi
PARALLEL SONS
Shankland, Hugh
BLACK LIGHT

SCREENWRITERS

Chermack, Cy
RESCUERS: STORIES OF COURAGE—TWO COUPLES
Cherot, Christopher Scott
HAV PLENTY
Chetwynd, Lionel
HUMAN BOMB
Chin, Stephen
ANOTHER DAY IN PARADISE
Chodorov, Stephen
PARALYZING FEAR: THE STORY OF POLIO IN AMERICA, A
Cholodenko, Lisa
HIGH ART
Christopher, Mark
54
Chukhrai, Pavel
THIEF, THE
Chung Jei Zang
BEAUTY INVESTIGATOR
Clancy, Garrett
DETONATOR
Clark-Williams, Zoe
MEN
Clemens, Monica
LOVE TO KILL
Clyde, Craig
WALKING THUNDER
Coen, Ethan
BIG LEBOWSKI, THE
Coen, Joel
BIG LEBOWSKI, THE
Cohen, Bennett
HUNTED, THE
Cohen, Larry
MISBEGOTTEN
UNCLE SAM
Compton, Jean
CAN'T YOU HEAR THE WIND HOWL?: THE LIFE AND MUSIC OF ROBERT JOHNSON
Conaway, Chuck
FATAL PURSUIT
Condon, Bill
GODS AND MONSTERS
Connelly, Theresa
POLISH WEDDING
Cooney, Michael
MURDER IN MIND
Corica, Gloria
NIRVANA
Corsini, Catherine
FULL SPEED
Coscarelli, Don
PHANTASM: OBLIVION
Costello, Fleur
KILLING TIME
Coto, Manny
HOSTILE INTENT
STAR KID
Cox, Alex
FEAR AND LOATHING IN LAS VEGAS
Craig, Laurie
PAULIE
Creagh, Andrew
VIOLET'S VISIT
Cristofer, Michael
GIA
Croner, Karen
ONE TRUE THING
Cudworth, Tom
TEN BENNY
Cullen, Glen
FUTURE FEAR
Cummings, David
LAST SEDUCTION II, THE
Cunningham, D. Matt
DECAMPITATED
Cunningham, Terry
LAND OF THE FREE
Currier, Lavinia
PASSION IN THE DESERT
D'Or, Daniel
FALLING FIRE
Danielson, Shell
RUSTY: THE GREAT RESCUE
Darby, Jonathan
HUSH
Dash, Sean
WATCHERS REBORN
Dattore, Joseph
ERNEST IN THE ARMY
David, Larry
SOUR GRAPES
Davids, Paul
TIMOTHY LEARY'S DEAD
Davies, Tod
FEAR AND LOATHING IN LAS VEGAS
Davis, Bridgett M.
NAKED ACTS
Davis, Julie
I LOVE YOU, DON'T TOUCH ME!
de la Iglesia, Alex
DAY OF THE BEAST, THE
De Micco, Kirk
QUEST FOR CAMELOT
De Michiel, Helen
TARANTELLA
De Monaco, James
NEGOTIATOR, THE
de Oliveira, Manoel
VOYAGE TO THE BEGINNING OF THE WORLD
De Palma, Brian
SNAKE EYES
De Souza, Steven E.
KNOCK OFF
Dearden, James
LOLITA
DeBartolo, Tiffanie
DREAM FOR AN INSOMNIAC
Decter, Ed
THERE'S SOMETHING ABOUT MARY
DeGroot, John
RACE TO SAVE 100 YEARS, THE
Delorme, Jules
FUTURE FEAR
Desmarais, Alison Rosenfeld
URBAN SAFARI
Desmarais, James J.
URBAN SAFARI
Dettmann, Andrew
YOUNG HERCULES
Devlin, Dean
GODZILLA
Dewhurst, Keith
LAND GIRLS, THE
Diamond, David
BODY COUNT
DiCillo, Tom
REAL BLONDE, THE
Diegues, Carlos
TIETA OF AGRESTE
Dillon, Patrick
SOMEWHERE IN THE CITY
Dini, Paul
BATMAN/SUPERMAN MOVIE, THE
DiTocco, Tony
CATHERINE'S GROVE
Dobbins, Ray
WHEN PIGS FLY
Dobbs, Lem
DARK CITY
Dominy, Jeannine
DANGEROUS BEAUTY
Donaldson, Christopher
ACT OF WAR
Done, Harris
SAND TRAP
Donovan, Paul
TALES FROM A PARALLEL UNIVERSE: EATING PATTERN
TALES FROM A PARALLEL UNIVERSE: GIGA SHADOW
TALES FROM A PARALLEL UNIVERSE: SUPER NOVA
Dorman, Joseph
ARGUING THE WORLD
Douglas, Leroy
I GOT THE HOOK UP
Downing, Todd
BOYS IN LOVE 2
Doyle, Sharon Elizabeth
WHEN DANGER FOLLOWS YOU HOME
Drilling, Eric
RIVER RED
Dubas, Mark
BOYS WILL BE BOYS
Dugowson, Maurice
EL CHE: INVESTIGATING A LEGEND
Duigan, Virginia
LEADING MAN, THE
Duling, Dan
LAST LIVES
Dumont, Bruno
LIFE OF JESUS, THE
Dunsky, Evan
ALARMIST, THE
Dymally, Amentha
PRINCE, THE
Eberhardt, Thom
FACE DOWN
Edmunds, Martin
PASSION IN THE DESERT
Edwards, Michael
NAKED LIES
Eisenberg, Max
CALL TO REMEMBER, A
Elfont, Harry
CAN'T HARDLY WAIT
Ellin, Doug
KISSING A FOOL
Elliott, Ted
MASK OF ZORRO, THE
SMALL SOLDIERS
Emmerich, Roland
GODZILLA
Ephron, Delia
YOU'VE GOT MAIL
Ephron, Nora
YOU'VE GOT MAIL
Epperson, Tom
GUN, A CAR, AND A BLONDE, A
Erb, Greg
SENSELESS
Eriksen, Gordon
LENA'S DREAMS
Ersgard, Jack
LIVING IN PERIL
Ersgard, Jesper
LIVING IN PERIL
Ersgard, Patrick
LIVING IN PERIL
Esguerra, George
TALK TO ME
Eskow, John
MASK OF ZORRO, THE
Estrada, Keith
MIDAS TOUCH, THE
Estrin, Allen
POCAHONTAS II: JOURNEY TO A NEW WORLD

Eszterhas, Joe
BURN HOLLYWOOD BURN
Faenza, Roberto
PEREIRA DECLARES
Falcon, Jeffrey
SIX-STRING SAMURAI
Farrelly, Bobby
THERE'S SOMETHING ABOUT MARY
Farrelly, Peter
THERE'S SOMETHING ABOUT MARY
Fedorenko, Peter
MIDAS TOUCH, THE
Feldman, John Harmon
LOVELIFE
Ferrari, Michelle
OUT OF THE PAST
Ferrell, Will
NIGHT AT THE ROXBURY, A
Fibe Ma
MR. NICE GUY
Fitzgerald, Thom
HANGING GARDEN, THE
Flackett, Jennifer
MADELINE
Fogel, Rich
BATMAN/SUPERMAN MOVIE, THE
FLINTSTONES: I YABBA-DABBA DOO!, THE
Foley, Maureen
HOME BEFORE DARK
Foote, Horton
HORTON FOOTE'S ALONE
Foulkes, Robert
TALK TO ME
Fox, Kevin
NEGOTIATOR, THE
Foyt, Victoria
DEJA VU
Frady, Marshall
GEORGE WALLACE
Franck, Dan
LA SEPARATION
Frank, Scott
OUT OF SIGHT
Franklin, Carl
ONE TRUE THING
Fraser, Paul
TWENTYFOURSEVEN
Freeman, Morgan J.
HURRICANE STREETS
Frey, James
KISSING A FOOL
Friedman, Lewis
BASEKETBALL
Frobenius, Nikolaj
INSOMNIA
Frugoni, Cesare
RABID DOGS
Frumkes, Roy
SUBSTITUTE 2: SCHOOL'S OUT, THE
Frye, E. Max
PALMETTO
Fulci, Lucio
BEYOND, THE
Fuller, Kim
SPICE WORLD
Fuller, Samuel
GIRLS IN PRISON
Furey, Mark
RICHIE RICH'S CHRISTMAS WISH
Gallo, Phil
WEST NEW YORK
Gallo, Vincent
BUFFALO '66
Garris, Mick
QUICKSILVER HIGHWAY
Gatlif, Tony
GADJO DILO
Geels, Laurens
CHARACTER
Geiger, Peter
COLONY, THE
Geller, Lynn
LOVE WALKED IN
Gelt, Gary
IN HIS FATHER'S SHOES
Geoffrion, Robert
PEACEKEEPER, THE
George, Matt
IN GOD'S HANDS
George, Terry
BRIGHT SHINING LIE, A
Gerber, Steve
BATMAN/SUPERMAN MOVIE, THE
Giblets, Hubie
RETURN OF THE KING, THE
Gibson, Channing
LETHAL WEAPON 4
Gigeroff, Lex
TALES FROM A PARALLEL UNIVERSE: EATING PATTERN
TALES FROM A PARALLEL UNIVERSE: GIGA SHADOW
TALES FROM A PARALLEL UNIVERSE: SUPER NOVA
Gilad, Adam
NOT IN THIS TOWN
Gilliam, Terry
FEAR AND LOATHING IN LAS VEGAS
Gilligan, Vince
HOME FRIES
Gilman, David
BAD MANNERS
Giovinazzo, Buddy
NO WAY HOME
Glazer, Mitch
GREAT EXPECTATIONS
Glomm, Lasse
OTHER SIDE OF SUNDAY, THE
Goble, Myron
DOWN IN THE DELTA
Goldbacher, Sandra
GOVERNESS, THE
Goldberg, Harris
I'LL BE HOME FOR CHRISTMAS
Goldberg, Howard
EDEN
Goldman, Bo
MEET JOE BLACK
Goldman, Gina
SUICIDE KINGS
Goldsman, Akiva
LOST IN SPACE
PRACTICAL MAGIC
Golin, Larry
LOVE WALKED IN
REBOUND: THE LEGEND OF EARL "THE GOAT" MANIGAULT
Gomez, Nick
ILLTOWN
Gotoh, Daisuke
ZERO WOMAN
Goyer, David S.
BLADE
DARK CITY
Goyet, Jean-Francois
WESTERN
Graham, Sam
SECRET OF NIMH 2: TIMMY TO THE RESCUE, THE
Grant, Susannah
EVER AFTER
Gray, Robert
LIKE IT IS
Green, Walon
HI-LO COUNTRY, THE
Greenberg, Matt
HALLOWEEN H20: TWENTY YEARS LATER
PROPHECY II, THE
Greenfield, Matt
SLAYERS: THE MOTION PICTURE
Grisoni, Tony
FEAR AND LOATHING IN LAS VEGAS
Gross, Larry
CHINESE BOX, THE
Guedes, Ann
TALK OF ANGELS
Guediguian, Robert
MARIUS AND JEANNETTE
Guerricaechevarria, Jorge
DAY OF THE BEAST, THE
Gyllenhaal, Stephen
HOMEGROWN
Hacker, Michael
DESTINY OF MARTY FINE, THE
Haines, Richard W.
RUN FOR COVER
Halberg, Jonny
JUNK MAIL
Hale, Boyd
ALMOST HEROES
Hamburg, John
SAFE MEN
Hamilton-Wright, Michael
RETROACTIVE
Hammann, Craig
BOOGIE BOY
Haneke, Michael
FUNNY GAMES
Harrald, Chris
PHOTOGRAPHING FAIRIES
Harrison, Lindsay
MY VERY BEST FRIEND
Hartley, Hal
HENRY FOOL
Hartov, Steven
MARS
Hashiba, Chiaki
ZERO WOMAN
Hashimoto, Hiroshi
POLTERGEIST REPORT: YUYU HAKUSHO
Hauser, Stephen
SPHERE
Hawkins, Richard
THEORY OF FLIGHT
Hayes, Al
GINGERBREAD MAN, THE
Haynes, Todd
VELVET GOLDMINE
Healy, Matt
CLAY PIGEONS
Hedden, Roger
HI-LIFE
Hennessy, James
WALKING THUNDER
Hensleigh, Jonathan
ARMAGEDDON
Herlihy, Tim
WATERBOY, THE
WEDDING SINGER, THE
Herman, Mark
LITTLE VOICE
Herzfeld, Jim
JUNGLE BOOK: MOWGLI'S STORY, THE
MEET THE DEEDLES
Hickox, Anthony
PRINCE VALIANT
Higashi, Yoichi
VILLAGE OF DREAMS
Highsmith, Patrick
MARS

Hilaire, Kits
GADJO DILO
Hirschfield, Jerry
TALES FROM A PARALLEL UNIVERSE: EATING PATTERN
TALES FROM A PARALLEL UNIVERSE: GIGA SHADOW
TALES FROM A PARALLEL UNIVERSE: SUPER NOVA
Ho, Ivy
COMRADES, ALMOST A LOVE STORY
Hoblock, Richard
TARANTELLA
Hoeber, Erich
MONTANA
Hoeber, Jon
MONTANA
Hoenger, Simon D.
TWISTED
Hoge, Bob
GODSON, THE
Holmes, Richard
SHOOTING FISH
Hopkins, Karen Leigh
STEPMOM
Horovitz, Israel
NORTH SHORE FISH
Horta, Silvio
URBAN LEGEND
Horton, Peter I.
FALLING FIRE
Hoshikawa, Kiyoshi
SLEEPY EYES OF DEATH: FULL CIRCLE KILLING
Hoshikawa, Seiji
SLEEPY EYES OF DEATH: SWORD OF ADVENTURE
Hoshiyama, Hiroyuki
MOBILE SUIT GUNDAM I
MOBILE SUIT GUNDAM II: SOLDIERS OF SORROW
MOBILE SUIT GUNDAM III: ENCOUNTERS IN SPACE
Hoskikawa, Kiyoshi
SLEEPY EYES OF DEATH: SWORD OF SEDUCTION
Howitt, Peter
SLIDING DOORS
Hsiao, Rita
MULAN
Hubbell, Chris
SECRET OF NIMH 2: TIMMY TO THE RESCUE, THE
Hughes, John
REACH THE ROCK
Hull, Roger
DETOUR
Hung, Sammo
ENCOUNTER OF THE SPOOKY KIND
PRODIGAL SON, THE
Hurst, Michael
ELIZABETH
Iacone, Jeremy
ONE TOUGH COP
Ice Cube
PLAYERS CLUB, THE
Imamura, Shohei
EEL, THE
Irving, Brian
REDLINE
Ishii, Takashi
GONIN
Ives, David
HUNTED, THE
Ivory, James
SOLDIER'S DAUGHTER NEVER CRIES, A
Iwai, Shunji
WHEN I CLOSE MY EYES
Jackson, G. Philip
FALLING FIRE
FUTURE FEAR
Jacquemetton, Maria
BILLBOARD DAD
Jacquot, Benoit
DISENCHANTED, THE
SEVENTH HEAVEN
Jaglom, Henry
DEJA VU
Jakoby, Don
JOHN CARPENTER'S VAMPIRES
James, Maria
LAND OF THE FREE
Janszen, Karen
DIGGING TO CHINA
Jantzen, Naomi
BREAKOUT
Jaoui, Agnes
SAME OLD SONG
UN AIR DE FAMILLE
Jech, Pavel
ACT OF WAR
Jelinek, Milena
FORGOTTEN LIGHT
Jenkins, Tamara
SLUMS OF BEVERLY HILLS
Jhabvala, Ruth Prawer
SOLDIER'S DAUGHTER NEVER CRIES, A
Jiang Qitao
RED CHERRY
Johnson, Bayard
TARZAN AND THE LOST CITY
Johnson, David C.
WOO
Johnson, Denis
HIT ME
Johnson, Jodi Ann
MULAN
Johnson, John S.
RATCHET
Johnson, Mark Steven
JACK FROST
SIMON BIRCH
Johnston, Heather
LENA'S DREAMS
Jones, Kirk
WAKING NED DEVINE
Jordan, Neil
BUTCHER BOY, THE
Ju Wan So
RED HAWK: WEAPON OF DEATH
Jud, Reinhard
JAMES ELLROY: DEMON DOG OF AMERICAN CRIME FICTION
Kaiser, Mary Adair
RACE TO SAVE 100 YEARS, THE
Kalensky, Harry
ADVENTURES OF MOWGLI
Kalfon, Pierre
EL CHE: INVESTIGATING A LEGEND
Kalmenson, Bill
SOULER OPPOSITE, THE
Kamps, John
BORROWERS, THE
Kaplan, Deborah
CAN'T HARDLY WAIT
Kasdan, Jake
ZERO EFFECT
Kastner, Daphna
FRENCH EXIT
Kattan, Chris
NIGHT AT THE ROXBURY, A
Katz, Jordan
INCOGNITO
Kazan, Nicholas
FALLEN
HOMEGROWN
Keating, David
SUMMER FLING
Keenan, William J.
MIGHTY KONG, THE
Kelly, Patrick Smith
PERFECT MURDER, A
Kerchner, Rob
CASPER MEETS WENDY
Kern, Will
CHICAGO CAB
Ketron, Larry
ONLY THRILL, THE
Kiarostami, Abbas
TASTE OF CHERRY
Kijowski, Andrej
FROM A FAR COUNTRY
King, Zalman
IN GOD'S HANDS
Kingsberg, Alan
ALMOST PARTNERS
Kinoy, Ernest
RESCUERS: STORIES OF COURAGE—TWO WOMEN
Kirkland, Boyd
BATMAN & MR. FREEZE: SUBZERO
Kirkman, Tim
DEAR JESSE
Kitano, Takeshi
FIREWORKS
SONATINE
Kjersgaard, Erik
ROYAL DECEIT
Klapisch, Cedric
UN AIR DE FAMILLE
Klass, David
DESPERATE MEASURES
Kletter, Richard
COLONY, THE
Kobler, Flip
LION KING II: SIMBA'S PRIDE, THE
POCAHONTAS II: JOURNEY TO A NEW WORLD
Koch, Ulrike
SALTMEN OF TIBET, THE
Koepp, David
SNAKE EYES
Koherr, Bob
PLUMP FICTION
Kollek, Amos
SUE
Konig, Ralf
KILLER CONDOM, THE
Konner, Lawrence
MERCURY RISING
MIGHTY JOE YOUNG
Koontz, Dean
PHANTOMS
Koppleman, Brian
ROUNDERS
Koren, Steve
NIGHT AT THE ROXBURY, A
Kouf, Jim
RUSH HOUR
Kourkov, Andrei
FRIEND OF THE DECEASED, A
Koyama, Takao
DRAGON BALL Z THE MOVIE: DEAD ZONE
DRAGON BALL Z THE MOVIE: THE TREE OF MIGHT
DRAGON BALL Z THE MOVIE: THE WORLD'S STRONGEST
Kwietniowski, Richard
LOVE AND DEATH ON LONG ISLAND
LaBute, Neil
YOUR FRIENDS & NEIGHBORS
Lafleur, Jean
LOST WORLD, THE

Preston Jr., Richard
LITTLE BIGFOOT 2: THE JOURNEY HOME
Preston, Susana
SIMPLE PLAN, A
Proft, Pat
WRONGFULLY ACCUSED
Proyas, Alex
DARK CITY
Purcell, Daniella
SPACEJACKED
Pyun, Albert
NEMESIS 4: CRY OF ANGELS
Rabe, David
HURLYBURLY
Raffo, John
JOHNNY SKIDMARKS
Ramage, Rick
PROPOSITION, THE
Ramsey, Ben
BIG HIT, THE
Rapp, Jerry
SAND TRAP
Rappaport, Mark
SILVER SCREEN: COLOR ME LAVENDER, THE
Rappaport, Sam
CHOSEN ONE: LEGEND OF THE RAVEN, THE
Ravich, Rand
MAKER, THE
Reece, P.J.
URBAN SAFARI
Reed, Aaron
NEXT STEP, THE
Rehwaldt, Frank
LANDLADY, THE
Reno, Jeff
MEET JOE BLACK
Reynolds, Scott
UGLY, THE
Rhee, Phillip
BEST OF THE BEST: WITHOUT WARNING
Ricciardi, Charles
BARRIERS
Rice, Wayne
SUICIDE KINGS
Richard, Jean-Louis
POST COITUM, ANIMAL TRISTE
Richards, Sybil
LOLIDA 2000
Richey, Eddie
PHOENIX
Richman, Meg
UNDER HEAVEN
Rifkin, Adam
SMALL SOLDIERS
Rintels, Jonathan
SNOWBOUND
Rivera, Jose
JUNGLE BOOK: MOWGLI'S STORY, THE
Roberts, Jonathan
JACK FROST
Robertson, William Preston
JOHNNY SKIDMARKS
Robinson, Bruce
RETURN TO PARADISE
Robinson, James F.
STILL BREATHING
Rodat, Robert
SAVING PRIVATE RYAN
Rogel, Randy
BATMAN & MR. FREEZE: SUBZERO
Rogers, Steven
HOPE FLOATS
STEPMOM
Rolfe, Tim
TWISTED
Roos, Don
OPPOSITE OF SEX, THE
Rose, Reginald
12 ANGRY MEN
Rose, Tokyo
ZERO WOMAN
Rosen, Alan
ELVIS MEETS NIXON
Rosenberg, Scott
DISTURBING BEHAVIOR
Rosenow, James
CROSSING FIELDS
Rosenthal, Mark
MERCURY RISING
MIGHTY JOE YOUNG
Rosi, Francesco
TRUCE, THE
Rosler, Alexander
MENDEL
Rosman, Mark
INVADER, THE
Ross, Gary
PLEASANTVILLE
Rossio, Terry
MASK OF ZORRO, THE
SMALL SOLDIERS
Rossow, Jim
HIJACKING HOLLYWOOD
Roth, Eric
HORSE WHISPERER, THE
Rouan, Brigitte
POST COITUM, ANIMAL TRISTE
Ruben, Andy
CLUB VAMPIRE
Rubin, Bruce Joel
DEEP IMPACT
Rubin, H. Alex
WHO IS HENRY JAGLOM?
Ruffalo, Mark
DESTINY OF MARTY FINE, THE
Ruiz, Raul
GENEALOGIES OF A CRIME
Rukov, Mogens
CELEBRATION, THE
Rulli, Stefano
TRUCE, THE
Rusconi, Jane
HUSH
Russo, Richard
TWILIGHT
Ruvinsky, Morrie
JACK HIGGINS' THUNDER POINT
Ruzowitzky, Stefan
INHERITORS, THE
Ryan, David
FIRST LOVE, LAST RITES
Ryan, Joal
FORMER CHILD STAR
Ryan, Terence
BRYLCREEM BOYS, THE
Sacchetti, Dardano
BEYOND, THE
Salem, Kario
DON KING: ONLY IN AMERICA
RAT PACK, THE
Saltzgaber, Eric
DOUBLE EDGE
Saltzman, Mark
NAPOLEON
Salvatores, Gabriele
NIRVANA
Samuels, Rachel
RUNNING WOMAN, THE
Sandler, Adam
WATERBOY, THE
Sang Wol Ji
RED HAWK: WEAPON OF DEATH
Sanzel, Ken
REPLACEMENT KILLERS, THE
SCARRED CITY
Saunders, George
LANDLADY, THE
Sayles, John
MEN WITH GUNS
Schachter, Steven
CON, THE
Scheerbaum, Peter
RAT'S TALE, A
Schickel, Richard
ALFRED HITCHCOCK: MASTER OF SUSPENSE
ELIA KAZAN: A DIRECTOR'S JOURNEY
Schiff, Stephen
LOLITA
Schiffman, Karl
DEAD END
Schifrin, William
QUEST FOR CAMELOT
Schlondorff, Volker
OGRE, THE
Schrader, Paul
AFFLICTION
Schulman, Tom
HOLY MAN
Schwartz, Mark Evan
LOUISA MAY ALCOTT'S LITTLE MEN
Schwartz, Stefan
SHOOTING FISH
Scott, Allan
REGENERATION
Scott, Darin
CAUGHT UP
Scott, Gavin
BORROWERS, THE
SMALL SOLDIERS
Scott, Mike
SLAPPY AND THE STINKERS
Seale, James
ASYLUM
Seavey, Nina Gilden
PARALYZING FEAR: THE STORY OF POLIO IN AMERICA, A
Sebastiano, Frank
DIRTY WORK
Sedaka, Marc
OVERNIGHT DELIVERY
Seidenberg, Mark
FLINTSTONES: I YABBA-DABBA DOO!, THE
Seltzer, David
EIGHTEENTH ANGEL, THE
MY GIANT
Senkowski, Ron
LET'S KILL ALL THE LAWYERS
Septien, Al
CHAIRMAN OF THE BOARD
Serlin, Beth
BEYOND SILENCE
Shapiro, Peter
MODULATIONS: CINEMA FOR THE EAR
Shaw, Bob
BUG'S LIFE, A
Shelton, Millicent
RIDE
Shepard, Richard
BODY COUNT
Sheppard, John
ARMOUR OF GOD
Shih Hou
SHAOLIN TEMPLE, THE
Shusett, Ronald
BLEEDERS
Shyamalan, N. Night
WIDE AWAKE

Shyer, Charles
PARENT TRAP, THE
Sidaris, Andy
RETURN TO SAVAGE BEACH
Siefert, Lynn
COUSIN BETTE
Sikora, Jim
BULLET ON A WIRE
Simon, Alex
MY BROTHER'S WAR
Simon, Neil
NEIL SIMON'S THE ODD COUPLE II
Simonelli, Rocco
SUBSTITUTE 2: SCHOOL'S OUT, THE
Skjoldbjaerg, Erik
INSOMNIA
Skoog, Susan
WHATEVER
Sletaune, Pal
JUNK MAIL
Sloan, Brian
I THINK I DO
Smith, Leslie L.
DAVID SEARCHING
Smith, Scott B.
SIMPLE PLAN, A
Snider, Dee
DEE SNIDER'S STRANGELAND
Soderbergh, Steven
NIGHTWATCH
Sohn, Sonja
SLAM
Solondz, Todd
HAPPINESS
Sommers, Stephen
DEEP RISING
Sophianopoulos, Al
INTERLOCKED: THRILLED TO DEATH
Soth, Chris
FIRESTORM
Sparling, David
OPERATION DELTA FORCE 2
Spence, Greg
PROPHECY II, THE
Sprecher, Jill
CLOCKWATCHERS
Sprecher, Karen
CLOCKWATCHERS
St. Pierre, Leo
LOST WORLD, THE
Stanleigh, Allan
ADVENTURES OF MOWGLI
Stanley, Justin J.
LAST ASSASSINS
Stanton, Andrew
BUG'S LIFE, A
Stanush, Claude
NEWTON BOYS, THE
Stefano, Joseph
PSYCHO
Stem, J. David
RUGRATS MOVIE, THE
Stevens, Dana
CITY OF ANGELS
Stevens, David
MERLIN
Stewart, James H.
PEACEKEEPER, THE
Stiliadis, Nicolas
HOT BLOODED
Stillman, Whit
LAST DAYS OF DISCO, THE
Stockwell, John
BREAST MEN
Stoker, Bram
BRAM STOKER'S THE MUMMY
Stokes, Michael
BRAM STOKER'S SHADOWBUILDER
Stoppard, Tom
SHAKESPEARE IN LOVE
Stork, Rob
TRACKED
Strandberg, Keith W.
DOUBLE EDGE
Stratton, Richard
SLAM
Strauss, John J.
THERE'S SOMETHING ABOUT MARY
Strauss, Robert
RETROACTIVE
Strick, Wesley
RETURN TO PARADISE
Styron, Susanna
SHADRACH
Swicord, Robin
PRACTICAL MAGIC
Swift, David
PARENT TRAP, THE
Swyer, Alan
REBOUND: THE LEGEND OF EARL "THE GOAT" MANIGAULT
Syracuse, Joe
LOVER GIRL
Szczepanski, Jan Josef
FROM A FAR COUNTRY
Szeto On
KICK BOXER'S TEARS
Szeto, Roy
ARMOUR OF GOD
DRAGONS FOREVER
Szollosi, Tom
BONE DADDY
Tabucchi, Antonio
PEREIRA DECLARES
Taggert, Brian
TRUCKS
Tago, Akihiro
GOLGO 13: QUEEN BEE
Takas, Tibor
REDLINE
Tamasy, Paul
AIR BUD: GOLDEN RECEIVER
Tambellini Jr., Flavio R.
OYSTER AND THE WIND, THE
Tameel, George
BUSTER & CHAUNCEY'S SILENT NIGHT
Tang, Edward
ARMOUR OF GOD
MR. NICE GUY
Tarantino, Paul
COURTING COURTNEY
Tarr, Susan
COUSIN BETTE
Tato, Anna Maria
NIGHT AND THE MOMENT, THE
Taylor, David
TRACKED
Tec, Roland
ALL THE RAGE
Tejada-Flores, Miguel
ATOMIC DOG
Tengen, Daisuke
EEL, THE
Tennant, Andy
EVER AFTER
Terry, Bridget
SHADRACH
Thomas, Michael
WELCOME TO WOOP WOOP
Tieche, Gary
NEVADA
Toback, James
TWO GIRLS AND A GUY
Toledano, Manuel
SHAMPOO HORNS
Tolkin, Michael
DEEP IMPACT
Tomikawa, Motofumi
EEL, THE
Tomita, Sukehiro
POLTERGEIST REPORT: YUYU HAKUSHO
Towne, Robert
WITHOUT LIMITS
Traeger, Michael
DEAD MAN ON CAMPUS
Tregenza, Rob
INSIDE/OUT
Treut, Monika
DIDN'T DO IT FOR LOVE
Trigg, Derek
INNOCENT SLEEP, THE
Truly, Daniel
YOUNG HERCULES
Tsang, John
KICK BOXER'S TEARS
Tsang Kan Cheong
MAGNIFICENT WARRIORS
Tsang, Sammy
ROYAL WARRIORS
Tsukamoto, Shinya
TOKYO FIST
Tucci, Stanley
IMPOSTORS, THE
Tulloch, Richard
FERNGULLY 2: THE MAGICAL RESCUE
Tummolini, Stefano
STEAM
Ubaldo, Joao
TIETA OF AGRESTE
Ui, Takashi
NEW ADVENTURES OF KIMBA THE WHITE LION, THE
Ullmann, Liv
KRISTIN LAVRANSDATTER
van Diem, Mike
CHARACTER
van Megen, Ruud
CHARACTER
Van Peebles, Mario
LOS LOCOS
Van Peebles, Melvin
CLASSIFIED X
van Warmerdam, Alex
DRESS, THE
Vaus, Lyn
NEXT STOP, WONDERLAND
Vecchio, Sergio
PEREIRA DECLARES
Veloz, David
PERMANENT MIDNIGHT
Veronis, Nick
DAY AT THE BEACH
Vicarel, Fred
BEST OF THE BEST: WITHOUT WARNING
Villis, Ray
INNOCENT SLEEP, THE
Vincent, Christian
LA SEPARATION
Vining, Dan
BLACK DOG
Vinson, Chuck
RIGHT CONNECTIONS, THE
Vinterberg, Thomas
CELEBRATION, THE
von Trier, Lars
KINGDOM, PART 2, THE
Vorsel, Niels
KINGDOM, PART 2, THE
Voss, Kurt
PASS, THE

Vought, W.W.
WHEN TRUMPETS FADE
Wade, Kevin
MEET JOE BLACK
Walker, Clark Lee
NEWTON BOYS, THE
Walkow, Gary Alan
NOTES FROM UNDERGROUND
Wallace, Naomi
LAWN DOGS
Wallace, Randall
MAN IN THE IRON MASK, THE
Walters, Brian
DECAMPITATED
Walz, Martin
KILLER CONDOM, THE
Wang Xiaobo
EAST PALACE, WEST PALACE
Warred, John
MAJOR LEAGUE: BACK TO THE MINORS
Wasserstein, Wendy
OBJECT OF MY AFFECTION, THE
Waters, John
PECKER
Watters, Matt
MOONDANCE
Weide, Robert B.
LENNY BRUCE: SWEAR TO TELL THE TRUTH
Weiner, Gary
ALMOST PARTNERS
Weinshanker, Burt
MOONDANCE
Weiss, David N.
RUGRATS MOVIE, THE
Weiss, Matthew
NIAGARA NIAGARA
Weitz, Chris
ANTZ
Weitz, Paul
ANTZ
Welles, Orson
TOUCH OF EVIL: THE DIRECTOR'S CUT
Weston, Ellen
SIN AND REDEMPTION
Whitcomb, Nat
MEAN GUNS
White, Bill Everett
PRINCE, THE
White, Mike
DEAD MAN ON CAMPUS
White, Steven
BARNEY'S GREAT ADVENTURE—THE MOVIE
Wicking, Christopher
JACK HIGGINS' ON DANGEROUS GROUND
Wierzbicki, Krzysztof
KRZYSZTOF KIESLOWSKI: I'M SO-SO
Wild, Nettie
PLACE CALLED CHIAPAS, A
Wiley, Ethan
CHILDREN OF THE CORN V: FIELD OF TERROR
Williams, Hype
BELLY
Williams, Saul
SLAM
Williams, Steve
DAD SAVAGE
Williams, Wade
DETOUR
Williamson, Kevin
FACULTY, THE
Willing, Nick
PHOTOGRAPHING FAIRIES
Willocks, Tim
SWEPT FROM THE SEA
Wilson, Owen
RUSHMORE
Witcher, Theodore
BODY COUNT
Witham, Andrew
MEAN GUNS
Witkins, Doug
NO ORDINARY LOVE
Wolf, Fred
DIRTY WORK
Wolfe, Tom
ALMOST HEROES
Wolff, Jurgen
JACK HIGGINS' MIDNIGHT MAN
REAL HOWARD SPITZ, THE
Wolk, Andy
DEFENDERS: PAYBACK, THE
Wolk, Peter
DEFENDERS: PAYBACK, THE
Wolterstorff, Bob
SLAPPY AND THE STINKERS
Wong, Barry
PRODIGAL SON, THE
Wong Kar-wai
FALLEN ANGELS
Wong Ying
ENCOUNTER OF THE SPOOKY KIND
Woo, John
HEROES SHED NO TEARS
Wood, Bret
KINGDOM OF SHADOWS
Wood, Christopher
STRAY BULLET
Woods, Skip
THURSDAY
Woodward, Meredith Bain
NEW ADVENTURES OF KIMBA THE WHITE LION, THE
Workman, Jeremy
WHO IS HENRY JAGLOM?
Wright, Jeffrey
BASEKETBALL
Wright, Lawrence
SIEGE, THE
Wu Ming
FROZEN
Wynne, Cordell
ADVENTURES OF MOWGLI
Yakin, Boaz
PRICE ABOVE RUBIES, A
Yamamoto, Masaru
MOBILE SUIT GUNDAM II: SOLDIERS OF SORROW
MOBILE SUIT GUNDAM III: ENCOUNTERS IN SPACE
Yamamoto, Masashi
JUNK FOOD
Yamazaki, Kazuo
SLAYERS: THE MOTION PICTURE
Yanagisawa, Ryota
TEKKEN: THE MOTION PICTURE
Yerkovich, Anthony
HOLLYWOOD CONFIDENTIAL
Yglesias, Rafael
LES MISERABLES
Yost, Graham
HARD RAIN
Young, John G.
PARALLEL SONS
Youssef, Khaled
DESTINY
Zallian, Steven
CIVIL ACTION, A
Zamm, Alex
CHAIRMAN OF THE BOARD
Zanussi, Krzysztof
FROM A FAR COUNTRY
Zappia, Robert
HALLOWEEN H20: TWENTY YEARS LATER
Zeik, J.D.
RONIN
Zhang Yuan
EAST PALACE, WEST PALACE
Zilberstein, Guy
POST COITUM, ANIMAL TRISTE
Zoller, Stephen
JACK HIGGINS' THE WINDSOR PROTOCOL
Zucker, David
BASEKETBALL
Zukovic, Dan
LAST BIG THING, THE
Zurla, Martin
DOGWATCH
Zwick, Edward
SIEGE, THE

SET DECORATORS

Alex, Jennifer
SCARRED CITY
Allen, Linda
ALMOST HEROES
Alosinac, Zeljka
RESCUERS: STORIES OF COURAGE—TWO COUPLES
RESCUERS: STORIES OF COURAGE—TWO WOMEN
Alvarez, Miguel Angel
MEN WITH GUNS
Ambroise, Rick
RIDE
Armstrong, Richard
FUTURE FEAR
Austin, John
TOUCH OF EVIL: THE DIRECTOR'S CUT
Baldocchi, Sarah
NEXT STEP, THE
Balous, Ladislav
ACT OF WAR
Barr, Eden
MILO
Barrow, Carlotta
MRS. DALLOWAY
Batre, Perine
UN AIR DE FAMILLE
Beale, Leslie
HUNTED, THE
Beatrice, Steve
LAST BREATH
Becket, Daphne
PASSION IN THE DESERT
Bekmark, Torben
ROYAL DECEIT
Berberian, Betty
JOHNNY SKIDMARKS
Bergstrom, Jan
CAN'T HARDLY WAIT
DEAD MAN ON CAMPUS
I STILL KNOW WHAT YOU DID LAST SUMMER
Berman, Danielle
CASPER MEETS WENDY
Bernstein, Susanna
FRENCH EXIT
Blanchard, Melissa
CLUB VAMPIRE
Bloom, Leslie
MEET JOE BLACK
Boccella, Mia
LOS LOCOS
Bode, Susan
GREAT EXPECTATIONS
OBJECT OF MY AFFECTION, THE

Bodley, Daisy
JACK HIGGINS' ON DANGEROUS GROUND
JACK HIGGINS' MIDNIGHT MAN
Bonetto, Aline
MADELINE
Boston, P.J.
IN GOD'S HANDS
Boswell, Meredith
MIGHTY JOE YOUNG
Bowin, Claire Jenora
PRACTICAL MAGIC
Brandenburg, Rosemary
PSYCHO
SMALL SOLDIERS
Breiding, Christian
CROSSING FIELDS
Bristol, Joe
REACH THE ROCK
Brittan, Ande
LAND OF THE FREE
Brookes, Karen
MERLIN
Brown, Kerrie
BABE: PIG IN THE CITY
TWISTED
Buckley, Martina
PRINCE, THE
Burgee, Pat
PECKER
Bush, John
LITTLE VOICE
Butt Yiu Kwong
DRAGONS FOREVER
Button, Peta
BRYLCREEM BOYS, THE
Camargo, Denise
MASK OF ZORRO, THE
Campana, Enrico
BIG HIT, THE
Carasik, Cheryl
PRIMARY COLORS
Carpenter, Daniel
SNAKE EYES
Carr, Cindy
PLAYING BY HEART
WHAT DREAMS MAY COME
Carr, Jackie
WHY DO FOOLS FALL IN LOVE?
X-FILES, THE
Cartwright, Carolyn
HE GOT GAME
Chalmers, Penny
EBENEZER
Chiasson, David
SPREE, THE
Chien Sum
PRODIGAL SON, THE
Christensen, Ane
MY VERY BEST FRIEND
Christiansen, Ellen
YOU'VE GOT MAIL
Cimino, Bill
WILD THINGS
Claypool, Michael
SLAPPY AND THE STINKERS
Cohen, Natalie
PLAN B
Colohan, Tim
BOOGIE BOY
Conroy, Coldagh
DANCING AT LUGHNASA
Corbett, Ann Marie
DEEP RISING
Costa, Monica
CENTRAL STATION
Courtois, Francesca
WOUNDED
Cowsill, Tiffany
LOVELIFE
Cruey, Brian
CROSSING FIELDS
Cuba, Keith
LAST ASSASSINS
Cummings, Peg
DEEP IMPACT
Davenport, Renee
SOULER OPPOSITE, THE
Davis, Catherine
IMPOSTORS, THE
Davis, Christopher H.
LANDLADY, THE
Desmarias, Chris
RATCHET
DeTitta Jr., George
STEPMOM
Deutsch, Lisa
WEDDING SINGER, THE
Develle, Jeanne
BUFFALO '66
Dick, Jaro
DIRTY WORK
Didul, Claudette
BURN HOLLYWOOD BURN
Donati, Danilo
LIFE IS BEAUTIFUL
Doyle, Tracey A.
CIVIL ACTION, A
PROPOSITION, THE
Dunn, Gilles
GENEALOGIES OF A CRIME
Dwyer, John
STAR TREK: INSURRECTION
Eden, Jill
MR. NICE GUY
Edwards, Trisha
LEADING MAN, THE
Elmblad, Donald
12 ANGRY MEN
Evans, Nick
HAPPINESS
Fallace, Nancy S.
GIRLS IN PRISON
Fann, Valerie
SHADRACH
Farr, Judy
EVER AFTER
Fauquet-Lemaitre, Dominique
FIRESTORM
Fellman, Florence
DANCE WITH ME
Fenney, Jackie
LAST LIVES
Fenton, Andrea
WIDE AWAKE
Ferguson, Piper Renee
UNCLE SAM
Ferrell Jr., James Edward
LAWN DOGS
Ferry, Dawn
SMOKE SIGNALS
Fettis, Gary
PARENT TRAP, THE
Foley, Heather
LAND OF THE FREE
Forrest, Kim
TRUCKS
Fox, K.C.
DR. DOLITTLE
Fraser, Jennifer
I GOT THE HOOK UP
WATCHERS REBORN
French, Andrea
TRICKS
Gaffin, Lauri
LETHAL WEAPON 4
SIX DAYS, SEVEN NIGHTS
Galline, Frank
MAJOR LEAGUE: BACK TO THE MINORS
Gausman, Russel A.
TOUCH OF EVIL: THE DIRECTOR'S CUT
Giger, H.R.
KILLER CONDOM, THE
Gilbert, Rick
HOSTILE INTENT
Giuliani, Chantal
RAT'S TALE, A
Glover, Jon Joseph
GODSON, THE
Goddard, Richard
NEGOTIATOR, THE
Grace, Cheryle
PLAYERS CLUB, THE
Grande, Greg
BLADE
Grass, Sandra
INDISCREET
Greenfield, Robert
SLUMS OF BEVERLY HILLS
Gresti, Karen A.
BEST OF THE BEST: WITHOUT WARNING
Grifo, Alisa
TWO GIRLS AND A GUY
Grigorian, Greta
CLOCKWATCHERS
THURSDAY
Gross, Sam
HORTON FOOTE'S ALONE
Gulko, Heather
LOVER GIRL
Habaschi, Ferid
KID IN ALADDIN'S PALACE, A
Haberecht, Barbara
TWO FOR TEXAS
Haigh, Nancy
FEAR AND LOATHING IN LAS VEGAS
TRUMAN SHOW, THE
Halili, Caroline
I LOVE YOU, DON'T TOUCH ME!
Harris, Mike
BRIDE OF CHUCKY
WOO
Hart, Jay
PLEASANTVILLE
Hartmann, Jeff
CON, THE
Hayashi, China
JUNK FOOD
Heiland, Candis
MR. JEALOUSY
Heinrich, Bernard
HOSTILE WATERS
OGRE, THE
Hertzog, Careen
BORROWERS, THE
Hervieux, Mario
LOUISA MAY ALCOTT'S LITTLE MEN
Herwitt, Jennifer
APT PUPIL
Hitchcock, Darla
DIARY OF A SERIAL KILLER
Holinko, Roberta
MONTANA
WITHOUT LIMITS
Holtshousen, Bryce
NO ORDINARY LOVE
Homann, Bernard
WHEN PIGS FLY
Howitt, Peter
ELIZABETH
Hurpeau, Frederique
FULL SPEED

Isch, Fred
CROSSING FIELDS
Jacobson, Scott
THERE'S SOMETHING ABOUT MARY
Jefferies, John
BASEKETBALL
Johnson, Glen
TWISTED
Johnson, Jane B.
PALMETTO
Jurek, Grid
BRAM STOKER'S SHADOWBUILDER
Karady, Ondine
NO WAY HOME
TARANTELLA
Karges, Chris
UNDER HEAVEN
Kasch, Brian
GINGERBREAD MAN, THE
NIGHTWATCH
Kaufman, Susan
CELEBRITY
Kavanaugh, Lisa Dean
SAVING PRIVATE RYAN
Kaye, Barbara Cole
PHANTOMS
Kelter, Jerie
JANE AUSTEN'S MAFIA!
Kirshbaum, Traci
CLAY PIGEONS
NIAGARA NIAGARA
SUICIDE KINGS
Klompus, Betty
RETURN TO PARADISE
Klopp, Kathe
MY GIANT
Knight, Evette
REPLACEMENT KILLERS, THE
Koschu, Segolen
REAL THING, THE
Kuljian, Anne
SPHERE
Kushnik, Beth
ROUNDERS
Kushon, Jeffrey
PHOENIX
YOUR FRIENDS & NEIGHBORS
Lamman, Patricia
TALES FROM A PARALLEL UNIVERSE: SUPER NOVA
Lamothe, Diane
BARNEY'S GREAT ADVENTURE—THE MOVIE
Lanier, Jessica
SPANISH PRISONER, THE
Larman, Patricia
TALES FROM A PARALLEL UNIVERSE: GIGA SHADOW
Lavoie, Carole
BRIDE OF CHUCKY
LeCorre, Robert
COUSIN BETTE
RONIN
Lederman, Diane
BREAK, THE
NO LOOKING BACK
Lee, Nicole
PLUMP FICTION
Less, Megan
BLACKJACK
DEFENDERS: PAYBACK, THE
DOWN IN THE DELTA
FACE DOWN
ONE TOUGH COP
Letica, Ivana
OUTSIDE OZONA
Levander, Melissa
WHEN TIME EXPIRES
Lewis, Cynthia
CALL TO REMEMBER, A
Lewis, Garrett
ENEMY OF THE STATE
Lohman, Melissa P.
HENRY FOOL
Lombardo, Lance
RUSH HOUR
Lopez, Lisa
STILL BREATHING
Loucks, Cal
MIGHTY, THE
URBAN LEGEND
Loucks, Carolyn A.
SIMON BIRCH
Loughlin, Susan
TALK TO ME
Lowry, Nancy
INTERLOCKED: THRILLED TO DEATH
Lubarskaya, Nadezhda
DEAD WATERS
Lucas, Kathy
VERY BAD THINGS
Luining, Gail
MISBEGOTTEN
Lundin, Beth Ann
ASYLUM
MacAvin, Josie
BUTCHER BOY, THE
MacDonald, Lin
I'LL BE HOME FOR CHRISTMAS
WRONGFULLY ACCUSED
Mak Woo
ENCOUNTER OF THE SPOOKY KIND
Manthey, Karen
KRIPPENDORF'S TRIBE
MAKER, THE
March, Marvin
BULWORTH
Marks, Lydia
DEE SNIDER'S STRANGELAND
Martin, Maggie
OUT OF SIGHT
ZERO EFFECT
Marty, Jack
CAN'T YOU HEAR THE WIND HOWL?: THE LIFE AND MUSIC OF ROBERT JOHNSON
Maybury, Suza
THIN RED LINE, THE
McCulley, Anne D.
BASEKETBALL
SOUR GRAPES
McCullough, Doug
IN HIS FATHER'S SHOES
TRACKED
McElvin, Ric
PATCH ADAMS
McMillan, Stephanie
AVENGERS, THE
McSherry, Rose Marie
DEEP RISING
Medlen, Damon
ELMORE LEONARD'S GOLD COAST
Messina, Kristen Toscano
NEIL SIMON'S THE ODD COUPLE II
Morales, Leslie
HI-LO COUNTRY, THE
HOLLYWOOD CONFIDENTIAL
Mowat, Douglas A.
HOPE FLOATS
Mrsovic, Ljubomir
SAVIOR
Munoz, Michelle
ANOTHER DAY IN PARADISE
Nay, Maria
MERCURY RISING
Nields, Casi
CROSSING FIELDS
Nilsson, Lisa
LAST DAYS OF DISCO, THE
Noreau, Josiane
PEACEKEEPER, THE
O'Connor, Michael
SIN AND REDEMPTION
O'Donnell, Elaine
ONE TRUE THING
O'Hara, Karen
BELOVED
O'Neill, Ruth
HIJACKING HOLLYWOOD
MARS
O'Sullivan, Neil
CHILDREN OF THE CORN V: FIELD OF TERROR
Ogu, Susan
BAD MANNERS
Ozeki, Tatsuo
FIREWORKS
Paizis, Melanie
CAUGHT UP
Pare, Ginette
BLEEDERS
Parenti, Steve
LOLITA
Patsch, Becky
ELIA KAZAN: A DIRECTOR'S JOURNEY
Pearce, Tom
LAST SEDUCTION II, THE
Pearse, Grant
AIR BUD: GOLDEN RECEIVER
DOUBLE EDGE
RIGHT CONNECTIONS, THE
Perkins, Kevin
BREAKOUT
Petersen, Beau
DANCER, TEXAS POP. 81
HALLOWEEN H20: TWENTY YEARS LATER
Peterson, Barbara
WATERBOY, THE
Peterson, Kristen V.
OPPOSITE OF SEX, THE
Peyton, Robin
MEET THE DEEDLES
Philpotts, John
NIGHT AT THE ROXBURY, A
Pilon, Louise
JACK LONDON'S THE CALL OF THE WILD: DOG OF THE YUKON
Pinnock, Anna
LOST IN SPACE
Pizzini, Denise
MUSIC FROM ANOTHER ROOM
PAULIE
Pope, Leslie A.
ONE TRUE THING
Posnansky, Tessa
AMERICAN HISTORY X
Potter, Chuck
DECEIVER
Potter, Kelly
RETROACTIVE
Quertier, Jill
INCOGNITO
SHAKESPEARE IN LOVE
Radomirovic, Jovan
SAVIOR
Rain, Marlene
REAL BLONDE, THE
Rais, Mohsen
KID IN ALADDIN'S PALACE, A
Rau, Gretchen
CITY OF ANGELS

HORSE WHISPERER, THE
SIEGE, THE
Reinschi, Udo
TALES FROM A PARALLEL UNIVERSE: EATING PATTERN
Reiss, Ronald R.
HARD RAIN
JACK FROST
Reynolds-Wasco, Alexandra
RUSHMORE
Richards, Ethel Robins
POLISH WEDDING
Rivera, Irina
STAR KID
Roberts, Nicki
STEEL SHARKS
Roberts, Terry
TERMINAL JUSTICE
Rogers, Dave
HUMAN BOMB
Rollins, Leslie E.
PRICE ABOVE RUBIES, A
Roper, Louise
DISTURBING BEHAVIOR
WHEN DANGER FOLLOWS YOU HOME
Rosemarin, Hilton
HORSE WHISPERER, THE
SIMPLE PLAN, A
Ruben, Neesh
SWEPT FROM THE SEA
Rubino, Beth
TWILIGHT
Samson, James
GODS AND MONSTERS
Scarlata, Maurin
HOMEGROWN
Schedler, Al
URBAN SAFARI
Schiavo, Chris
PARALLEL SONS
Schilling, Lisa
WHATEVER
Schlesinger, David
JOHN CARPENTER'S VAMPIRES
Schneider, Tricia
KISSING A FOOL
Schutt, Debra
LOLITA
PERFECT MURDER, A
Scott, Jeanette
FACULTY, THE
NEWTON BOYS, THE
Seirton, Michael
FALLEN
HUSH
Serdena, Gene
U.S. MARSHALS
Sheets, Suzette
HOME FRIES
SPECIES II
Shewchuk, Steve
BLUES BROTHERS 2000
Shibata, Hirohide
SONATINE
Sibille, Jeff
BODY COUNT
Silverman, Carol
BELLY
Sim, Gordon
HALF BAKED
REAL BLONDE, THE
Simpson, Rick
ARMAGEDDON
Slater, Adam
BRIGHT SHINING LIE, A
Smith, Brendan
BONE DADDY
Smith, Caroline
FIRELIGHT
REAL HOWARD SPITZ, THE
Spellman, Chris
BIG LEBOWSKI, THE
HOLY MAN
Spencer, Katie
GOVERNESS, THE
Spheeris, Linda
RAT PACK, THE
SENSELESS
Stamper, Isabelle
DESTINY OF MARTY FINE, THE
Stepeck, Timothy Smithwick
STEPHEN KING'S THE NIGHT FLIER
Storey, Mary Lou
SNOWBOUND
Stoughton, Diana L.
BLACK DOG
OVERNIGHT DELIVERY
Sullivan, Kate
SOLDIER
Sutton, Linda Lee
LIVING OUT LOUD
Swanepoll, Neil
ERNEST IN THE ARMY
Tanner, Stacey
SUBSTITUTE 2: SCHOOL'S OUT, THE
Taylor, Beck
SUB DOWN
Thomasson, Clive
BLUES BROTHERS 2000
Thomson, Rachel
EDEN
Thune, Vidar
JUNK MAIL
Tokareva, Tanya
DEAD WATERS
Tottleben, Ellen
QUICKSILVER HIGHWAY
Troha, Scott
CHICAGO CAB
Turlure, Philippe
MAN IN THE IRON MASK, THE
Udea, Mayuko
UNDERTAKER'S WEDDING, THE
Usher, Caroline
BRIGHT SHINING LIE, A
Varna, Ica
CLOCKMAKER
JOHNNY MYSTO BOY WIZARD
LITTLE GHOST
MIDAS TOUCH, THE
SECRET KINGDOM, THE
Venturini, Mauro
NIRVANA
Vertigan, Jeanne
MRS. DALLOWAY
Vick, Foster
KRAA! THE SEA MONSTER
Villareal, Gabriella
LITTLE BOY BLUE
Wall, Kim
BLACK LIGHT
Wallace, Jeff
CAN'T YOU HEAR THE WIND HOWL?: THE LIFE AND MUSIC OF ROBERT JOHNSON
Walton, Steve
MY BROTHER'S WAR
SPACEJACKED
Webb, Michael
INVADER, THE
Weinger, Don
ANTZ
Whately, Totty
TALK OF ANGELS
Whittaker, Ian
DANGEROUS BEAUTY
Wiesel, Karin
54
Wigginton, Cynthia
RIDE
Williams, Jennifer
DESPERATE MEASURES
Williams, Linda
ATOMIC DOG
Wilson, Linda
SPICE WORLD
Yaary, Orna
TARANTELLA
Yamin, Mandana
ORGAZMO
Yasuda, Shoichi
VILLAGE OF DREAMS
Zeitler, Yasmin
HOT BLOODED
Zolfo, Victor
GODZILLA

SOUND

Ahern, Ken
FULL TILT BOOGIE
Ailetcher, Jon
BILLBOARD DAD
BRAM STOKER'S THE MUMMY
DOGWATCH
NEVADA
OPPOSITE OF SEX, THE
ORGAZMO
UNCLE SAM
Akerson, Randle
GINGERBREAD MAN, THE
Alexander, Lee
INTERLOCKED: THRILLED TO DEATH
INVISIBLE DAD
Amann, Walter
FUNNY GAMES
Anderson, Coll
SAFE MEN
Anderson, Gord
TRICKS
Anderson Jr., Robert
PLEASANTVILLE
Anderson, Steen K.
TRANCEFORMER: A PORTRAIT OF LARS VON TRIER
Andrew, Felix
SCARRED CITY
Angelella, Rick
PECKER
Archer, Lee
LITTLE BIGFOOT 2: THE JOURNEY HOME
Arnold, Douglas B.
REPLACEMENT KILLERS, THE
Arroyo, Antonio
MODULATIONS: CINEMA FOR THE EAR
SOMEWHERE IN THE CITY
Atzmon, Boaz
TALK TO ME
Auger, Jean-Francois
VOYAGE TO THE BEGINNING OF THE WORLD
Auinger, Sam
JAMES ELLROY: DEMON DOG OF AMERICAN CRIME FICTION
Avery, John
LIKE IT IS
Ayers, Ron
POLISH WEDDING
Bach, David
KID IN ALADDIN'S PALACE, A
Backus, Robert
SIX-STRING SAMURAI

Bailey, Ronald
HUMAN BOMB
Baksht, David
MIDAQ ALLEY
Baldwin, Daniel
TARANTELLA
Balthazuk, Alexandra
MY KNEES WERE JUMPING: REMEMBERING THE KINDERTRANSPORTS
Barosky, Michael
LAWN DOGS
OBJECT OF MY AFFECTION, THE
Bats, Bernard
RONIN
Baumung, Ekkehart
LITTLE DIETER NEEDS TO FLY
Beckett, Ray
CARLA'S SONG
Beentjes, Ray
ABERRATION
Beg, Gerald
INTERLOCKED: THRILLED TO DEATH
Beggs, Richard
GREAT EXPECTATIONS
Behlmer, Anna
THIN RED LINE, THE
Bell, Wayne
DANCER, TEXAS POP. 81
Ben Jacob, Itamar
TWO GIRLS AND A GUY
Benitanai, Kenichi
EEL, THE
Bennett, Jeff
BILLY'S HOLLYWOOD SCREEN KISS
Benoit, Marc
WOUNDED
Bentley, Peter
DECEIVER
MUSIC FROM ANOTHER ROOM
Beres, Nancy
BOYS IN LOVE 2
Bergbom, Brad
UNMADE BEDS
Berkovitz, Glenn
ZERO EFFECT
Bermudez, Jose Antonio
DAY OF THE BEAST, THE
LIVE FLESH
Bernard, Jean-Paul
WESTERN
Berolzheimer, Paul
NIGHTWATCH
Bertrand, Calude
LA SEPARATION
Beville, Dean
PHANTOMS
Bisenz, Bruce
WITHOUT LIMITS
Bock, Richard
SIX O'CLOCK NEWS
Boeddeker, Steve
HORSE WHISPERER, THE
Borcoman, Tiberiu
CLOCKMAKER
LITTLE GHOST
MIDAS TOUCH, THE
SECRET KINGDOM, THE
SHRUNKEN CITY, THE
SUBSPECIES IV: BLOODSTORM
TALISMAN
Borne, Steve
FIRST LOVE, LAST RITES
LAST BREATH
Borrero, Felipe
BURN HOLLYWOOD BURN
HOPE FLOATS
RAT PACK, THE
YOUR FRIENDS & NEIGHBORS
Boullenger, Patrick
JERUSALEM
Bozung, Todd
CHOSEN ONE: LEGEND OF THE RAVEN, THE
Bramonti, Mario
RABID DOGS
Brandau, Thomas
JACK FROST
NOT IN THIS TOWN
Braun, Arnold
PLAN B
STEEL SHARKS
Breindel, Scott
LAST DAYS OF DISCO, THE
Brincat, Paul "Salty"
THIN RED LINE, THE
Brisson, Jean-Claude
CENTRAL STATION
Bross, John
TEN BENNY
Brown, Lance
PERFECT MURDER, A
Bryan, Brad
MARS
Buchanan, Jack
FUTURE FEAR
Burton, Willie
BELOVED
DEAD MAN ON CAMPUS
Butler, William
MY VERY BEST FRIEND
RIGHT CONNECTIONS, THE
Buzaglo, Uri
HEALING BY KILLING
Byer, Allan
BIG LEBOWSKI, THE
HE GOT GAME
ONE TRUE THING
SIEGE, THE
Cabral, Barney
BODY COUNT
Cabral, Kelly
BODY COUNT
Camara, Marcio
OYSTER AND THE WIND, THE
Cameron, Douglas
WALKING THUNDER
Campbell, Veda
WHY DO FOOLS FALL IN LOVE?
Canelos, Damian
HAV PLENTY
Cantamessa, Gene
SIX DAYS, SEVEN NIGHTS
Cantamessa, Steve
SPHERE
Caron, Jo
JACK HIGGINS' THE WINDSOR PROTOCOL
Carrett, G. John
HOME BEFORE DARK
Carter, Craig
NAPOLEON
Carwardine, Bruce
DIRTY WORK
MIGHTY, THE
Casalini, Jean-Christophe
NIRVANA
Castrop, Hans
ZAKIR AND HIS FRIENDS
Catala, Jonathan
WATCHERS REBORN
Caterini, Joe
DEAR JESSE
Causey, Thomas
BULWORTH
STAR TREK: INSURRECTION
Chapman, Greg
BONE DADDY
Chiapeta, Quentin
ARGUING THE WORLD
Choudury, Gautam
CROSSING FIELDS
Christenssen, Kim B.
MEET THE DEEDLES
Clark, Greg
RETURN TO SAVAGE BEACH
Clark, Simon
SHOOTING FISH
Clements, Peter
BREAKOUT
Coburn IV, James H.
RUNNING WOMAN, THE
Cohen, Donald
BARNEY'S GREAT ADVENTURE—THE MOVIE
LOUISA MAY ALCOTT'S LITTLE MEN
Cohen, Harry
PHANTOMS
Colello, Dawn
WAR ZONE
Collins, Ed
FLINTSTONES: I YABBA-DABBA DOO!, THE
Collins, Jake
HENRY: PORTRAIT OF A SERIAL KILLER PART 2
Collins, Jeff O.
SCOOBY-DOO ON ZOMBIE ISLAND
Conlin, Pete
SUBSTITUTE 2: SCHOOL'S OUT, THE
Cooney, Tim
HOLLYWOOD CONFIDENTIAL
LETHAL WEAPON 4
Copestake, Ervin
FACE THE EVIL
Coufal, Don
MY GIANT
Crimmons, Margaret
HALLELUJAH!
Cristianini, Jacqueline
ESCAPE, THE
Crozier, David
HILARY AND JACKIE
INCOGNITO
Currie, James S.
NAPOLEON
Curvelier, Alain
TRUCE, THE
Cusack, Pud
MASK OF ZORRO, THE
Danziger, Neil
HAPPINESS
Davis, Dane A.
PHOENIX
Day, Bryan
ONE TOUGH COP
De Luca, Raffael
BEST MAN, THE
Deasy, Brendan
BUTCHER BOY, THE
GENERAL, THE
Dekker, Viktor
JACK HIGGINS' MIDNIGHT MAN
Delbert, Ken
FARM: ANGOLA, U.S.A., THE
Delpak, M
MIRROR, THE
Demetruis, Pam
NAKED ACTS
Deren, Mark
GIRLS IN PRISON
Desmond, Gary
UNDER THE SKIN

Devlin, Peter
ELMORE LEONARD'S GOLD COAST
HOLY MAN
WILD THINGS
Diego, Antonio
WHO THE HELL IS JULIETTE?
DiSimone, Giovanni
REDLINE
Dog Bark Sound
HALLELUJAH!
Downer, John
WAKING NED DEVINE
Dunnebacke, Elyzabeth
UNVEILING, THE
Dweck, Exra
DECLINE OF WESTERN CIVILIZATION PART III, THE
Eber, Robert
CLAY PIGEONS
Ebner, Heinz
INHERITORS, THE
Edwards, Frederik
DAY AT THE BEACH
Edwards, Harvey
DAY AT THE BEACH
Egorova, Yulia
THIEF, THE
Einarson, Sturla
JUNK MAIL
Ellis, Mary
BLACK DOG
Embry, Henry
BRAM STOKER'S SHADOWBUILDER
Emrich, Brian
PI
Enette, Mark
PI
Enroth, Eric
BOYS WILL BE BOYS
PERMANENT MIDNIGHT
PLUMP FICTION
SUICIDE KINGS
Espantoso, Philippe
CAPTIVE
Everson, Carol
PECKER
Farr, Robert
THEORY OF FLIGHT
Fasal, John Paul
DEEP IMPACT
Faure, Joel
NIGHT AND THE MOMENT, THE
Felce, Christine
DIVORCE IRANIAN STYLE
Fiege, William M.
RUSTY: THE GREAT RESCUE
SAVIOR
Fisher, Robert B.
COURTING COURTNEY
Fontaine, Christian
CHAMBERMAID ON THE TITANIC, THE
WESTERN
Fowler, Michael E.
COLONY, THE
Fraser, Tim
DEJA VU
Frazee, Skip
ONLY THRILL, THE
Freed, Lawrence
HIJACKING HOLLYWOOD
French, Stuart
FACE DOWN
IN HIS FATHER'S SHOES
TRACKED
Frithiof, Berndt
JUNK MAIL
Gaeta, Frank
FIRESTORM
Gagon, Colin
UNVEILING, THE
Ganton, Douglas
BIG HIT, THE
Garcia, Jose Antonio
GODZILLA
Garfield, Hank
BASEKETBALL
JOHN CARPENTER'S VAMPIRES
Garnov, Henrik
SUMMER FLING
Gauthier, Glen
BLUES BROTHERS 2000
SIMON BIRCH
Gegan, Gary
VERY BAD THINGS
Geisinger, Joseph
PAULIE
Gendler, Sandy
BIG HIT, THE
Ghiraldini, Robert
RIVER RED
Ghouti, Steven
TRUCE, THE
Gilad, Chaim
DEFENDERS: PAYBACK, THE
Gilbert, Norbert
CLASSIFIED X
Glossop, Peter
MERLIN
MRS. DALLOWAY
SHAKESPEARE IN LOVE
TALK OF ANGELS
Goen II, George Bruton
OUTSIDE OZONA
Goldman, Josef
DEAD WATERS
Gonzalez, Franklin
CHARLIE HOBOKEN
Goodman, Richard Bryce
MIGHTY JOE YOUNG
PRACTICAL MAGIC
Goosse, Alek
CHARACTER
Gordon, Albee
HOMEGROWN
Gordon, Ted
TIMOTHY LEARY'S DEAD
Goulet, Simon
LOUISA MAY ALCOTT'S LITTLE MEN
Gouvanis, Trisha
MY KNEES WERE JUMPING: REMEMBERING THE KINDERTRANSPORTS
Grass, Barak
DECAMPITATED
Grech, Mark C.
MY GIANT
Greenhorn, Jim
NIL BY MOUTH
WILDE
Grete, Adam
IN GOD'S HANDS
Griffith, Patrick M.
BRAM STOKER'S SHADOWBUILDER
NEMESIS 4: CRY OF ANGELS
NEVADA
Griffiths, Frank
DEEP RISING
Grillo, Marco
STEAM
Gross, Olav
RAT'S TALE, A
Groult, Francois
CENTRAL STATION
Guinta, Carrie
ARGUING THE WORLD
Guthoff, Thomas
ZAKIR AND HIS FRIENDS
Gynn, Clifford
FRENCH EXIT
Halaby, John
CLUB VAMPIRE
KRAA! THE SEA MONSTER
OFF THE MENU: THE LAST DAYS OF CHASEN'S
RUNNING WOMAN, THE
Halaby, John R.F.
WATCHERS REBORN
Halbert, Stephen
DISAPPEARANCE OF KEVIN JOHNSON, THE
NIGHTWATCH
REAL HOWARD SPITZ, THE
Hall, Mike
LAND OF THE FREE
Hambrook, Danny
GOVERNESS, THE
Hamilton, Steve
RATCHET
Hansen, Peter Christian
KINGDOM, PART 2, THE
Hanza, Cameron
THURSDAY
Harlow, Mike
LAVENDER LIMELIGHT: LESBIANS IN FILM
Harper, Peter
HANGING GARDEN, THE
Hasin, Alexander
DEAD WATERS
Haussig, Uve
SALTMEN OF TIBET, THE
Hayashi, Tsuchitaroo
RAZOR: WHO'S GOT THE GOLD?, THE
Hegedus, Chris
MOON OVER BROADWAY
Heissler, Philippe
POST COITUM, ANIMAL TRISTE
Henault, Ludovic
FULL SPEED
SOLDIER'S DAUGHTER NEVER CRIES, A
Herrera, Boris
CHILE, OBSTINATE MEMORY
Hidderley, Tom
DOWN IN THE DELTA
Hines, Tim
CON, THE
Hladik Jr., Radim
FORGOTTEN LIGHT
Hliddal, Petur
LIVING OUT LOUD
Hobbs, Aidan
REAL HOWARD SPITZ, THE
Hoffman, Melisa
REAL THING, THE
Holden, Shawn
GODS AND MONSTERS
RINGMASTER
Holm, Morten
CELEBRATION, THE
Honda, Yasunori
WRATH OF THE NINJA: THE YOTODEN MOVIE
Hong, Jong Hwa
BARRIERS
Hong Yi
EMPEROR'S SHADOW, THE
Hopkins, Mike
ABERRATION
Horgan, Kieran
BUTCHER BOY, THE
DANCING AT LUGHNASA

Horiuchi, Senji
- FIREWORKS
- SONATINE

Howard, Frederick
- AMERICAN HISTORY X

Howell, Lee
- I LOVE YOU, DON'T TOUCH ME!
- LAST BIG THING, THE
- MAKER, THE
- MEAN GUNS
- PASS, THE

Hsu, Paul
- HALLELUJAH!

Husby, David
- FIRESTORM

Hymns, Richard
- SAVING PRIVATE RYAN

Iadarola, Matthew
- VERY BAD THINGS

Inoue, Shuji
- KIKI'S DELIVERY SERVICE

Isais, Carlos
- I GOT THE HOOK UP

Ishii, Ken
- PI

Jacob, Itamar Ben
- STIR

Janiger, Robert
- SOUR GRAPES

John, David
- LES MISERABLES

Johnson, Doug
- RESCUERS: STORIES OF COURAGE—TWO WOMEN

Johnson, Ivan
- POCAHONTAS II: JOURNEY TO A NEW WORLD

Johnson, Tony
- WELCOME TO WOOP WOOP

Johnston, Doug
- TERMINAL JUSTICE

Jones, Alan
- LAST SEDUCTION II, THE

Joseph, Adam
- LOVE TO KILL
- PRINCE, THE

Joseph Productions
- LET'S KILL ALL THE LAWYERS

Judd, Phil
- TWISTED

Judkins, Ronald
- PSYCHO
- SAVING PRIVATE RYAN

Jyrala, Paul
- JERUSALEM

Kaplan, Bill
- ENEMY OF THE STATE

Karp, Judy
- MEN WITH GUNS

Kawashima, Ichiro
- TOKYO FIST

Kaye, Simon
- EVER AFTER
- LOST IN SPACE

Kayne, John
- SLAMNATION

Kelley, Randy
- MAN IN THE IRON MASK, THE

Kelson, David
- MEET THE DEEDLES

Keppler, Joseph
- LOU REED: ROCK AND ROLL HEART

Kharat, Michael
- MADELINE

Khorched, Gasser
- DESTINY

King, Ken
- BREAST MEN
- SMALL SOLDIERS

King, Richard
- GINGERBREAD MAN, THE

Kirby, Godfrey
- PASSION IN THE DESERT

Kirschner, David
- CAN'T HARDLY WAIT
- DR. DOLITTLE

Kitamura, Mineharu
- GONIN

Kitinski, Gabriel
- DEE SNIDER'S STRANGELAND

Kobayashi, Katsuhiko
- SLAYERS: THE MOTION PICTURE

Koppen, Andreas
- SALTMEN OF TIBET, THE

Korda, Susan
- MY KNEES WERE JUMPING: REMEMBERING THE KINDERTRANSPORTS

Koronkeiwicz, Paul
- MY KNEES WERE JUMPING: REMEMBERING THE KINDERTRANSPORTS

Kramer, Louis
- REGENERATION

Kuc, Alex
- RETURN OF THE KING, THE

Kunin, Drew
- CHINESE BOX, THE
- COUSIN BETTE
- HI-LO COUNTRY, THE
- WHEN PIGS FLY

Kusan, James
- DOUBLE EDGE

Kushner, Jeff
- ILLTOWN
- NIAGARA NIAGARA
- PARALLEL SONS

Laabs, Karl-Heinz
- OGRE, THE

Laforce, Jean-Pierre
- ARTEMISIA
- MARIUS AND JEANNETTE
- UN AIR DE FAMILLE

Lafran, Laurent
- MARIUS AND JEANNETTE

Laing, John
- MISBEGOTTEN

Lamberti, Tony
- MAN IN THE IRON MASK, THE

Langballe, Thomas
- TRANCEFORMER: A PORTRAIT OF LARS VON TRIER

Langevin, Owen
- BRIDE OF CHUCKY
- HALF BAKED
- WOO

Larrea, Robert Taz
- HURRICANE STREETS
- I THINK I DO

Larsen, Chris
- BOYS IN LOVE 2

Lawrence, Jonah
- HIGH ART

Lawson, Randy
- FATAL PURSUIT

Lazarowitz, Les
- CELEBRITY

Le Messurier, Nic
- JACK HIGGINS' ON DANGEROUS GROUND

Ledford, Paul
- OUT OF SIGHT

Lee, David
- DARK CITY
- 54

Lee, Ken
- LOVE IS THE DEVIL: STUDY FOR A PORTRAIT OF FRANCIS BACON

Lember, Tovlo
- HEAVEN'S BURNING

Lenoir, Pierre
- SAME OLD SONG

Lenz, Pit
- MY FIRST NAME IS MACEO

Lester, Dominic
- SHAKESPEARE IN LOVE

Leung Chi-tat
- FALLEN ANGELS

Levin, Peter
- WAR ZONE

Lightstone, Richard
- DON KING: ONLY IN AMERICA
- REACH THE ROCK

Lindsay, Peter
- LITTLE VOICE
- VELVET GOLDMINE

Lindvik, Jan
- OTHER SIDE OF SUNDAY, THE

Liu, Jeffrey
- SHOPPING FOR FANGS

Long, Larry
- SHADRACH

Losardo, Tony
- DEAR JESSE

Maayan, Yehuda
- NOTES FROM UNDERGROUND
- RUSTY: THE GREAT RESCUE

Maclane, Rick
- I GOT THE HOOK UP

MacLean, Gael
- TRUCKS

MacMillan, David
- CITY OF ANGELS
- CIVIL ACTION, A

MacRae, Sandy
- FIRELIGHT

Maikoff, Henri
- GENEALOGIES OF A CRIME

Maitland, Tod A.
- BELLY
- HORSE WHISPERER, THE
- STEPMOM

Maltz, Jason
- LOVER GIRL

Marcel, Leonard
- MILO

Marion, Louis
- BLEEDERS
- JACK LONDON'S THE CALL OF THE WILD: DOG OF THE YUKON

Marsh, Vik
- CURSE OF THE PUPPET MASTER

Martin, Paul N.
- IN GOD'S HANDS

Martines, Doug
- GREAT EXPECTATIONS

Mather, Tom
- REAL BLONDE, THE
- URBAN LEGEND

Mathews, Robert "Frog"
- LOLIDA 2000

Mattikow, Curtis
- WHATEVER

Maynes, Charles
- NIGHTWATCH

McCormick, John
- MOON OVER BROADWAY

McGee, Michael
- CALL TO REMEMBER, A

McGill, John
- TALES FROM A PARALLEL UNIVERSE: SUPER NOVA

McGuire, Al
RIDE
McIntosh, Daniel
HENRY FOOL
McKinney, Austin
LAST LIVES
McMillan, David R.B.
TWILIGHT
McMoyler, David
MASK OF ZORRO, THE
McNabb, Mark Hopkins
DEEP IMPACT
SLAPPY AND THE STINKERS
McNamee, Steve
CUBE
Meagher, Jay
FALLEN
FEAR AND LOATHING IN LAS VEGAS
HUSH
STEPHEN KING'S THE NIGHT FLIER
WATERBOY, THE
Megill, John
HOSTILE INTENT
TALES FROM A PARALLEL UNIVERSE: EATING PATTERN
TALES FROM A PARALLEL UNIVERSE: GIGA SHADOW
Meidell, Gunnar
MENDEL
Meiselmann, Peter
BOOGIE BOY
INDISCREET
Menz, Bernardo
BATTLE OF CHILE: THE STRUGGLE OF AN UNARMED PEOPLE—PART 2: THE COUP D'ETAT, THE
LIVE FLESH
Mercado, Richard
NAKED LIES
Metts, Coleman
MILO
Meyers, Randall
INSOMNIA
Micallef, Glenn
PENTAGON WARS, THE
Michael, Danny
MEET JOE BLACK
Midgley, John
SLIDING DOORS
Mikan, Rene
ACT OF WAR
Miksis, Brian
BREAK, THE
BUFFALO '66
TWO GIRLS AND A GUY
WIDE AWAKE
Miller, Peter
WILD MAN BLUES
Mitchell, Patrick
GIA
JOHNNY SKIDMARKS
Mizumoto, Kan
POLTERGEIST REPORT: YUYU HAKUSHO
Moller, Hans
KINGDOM, PART 2, THE
Monahan, Daniel D.
BEST OF THE BEST: WITHOUT WARNING
Montei, Bill
INVISIBLE DAD
Moor, Tom
REAL THING, THE
Moore, Michael M.
AYN RAND: A SENSE OF LIFE
Morales, Beo
ARGUING THE WORLD
Moran, Andrew
NEXT STEP, THE
Morganti, Tullio
LIFE IS BEAUTIFUL
Mrshekari, J.
TASTE OF CHERRY
Mugel, Jean-Paul
CHAMBERMAID ON THE TITANIC, THE
VOYAGE TO THE BEGINNING OF THE WORLD
Munch, Eric
EL CHE: INVESTIGATING A LEGEND
Munch, Jean-Yves
EL CHE: INVESTIGATING A LEGEND
Munroe, Dan
RESCUERS: STORIES OF COURAGE—TWO COUPLES
Murch, Walter
TOUCH OF EVIL: THE DIRECTOR'S CUT
Murphy, Jennifer
HOME FRIES
LITTLE BOY BLUE
Musy, Francois
INSIDE/OUT
Naegelen, Nicolas
GADJO DILO
Nagler, Betsy
WEST NEW YORK
Najafi, Yadollah
MIRROR, THE
Nazarian, Bruce
LIVING IN PERIL
Nelson, Andy
SAVING PRIVATE RYAN
THIN RED LINE, THE
Nelson, Steve
AMERICAN HISTORY X
DESPERATE MEASURES
FACULTY, THE
SPECIES II
Nelson, Tom
GREAT EXPECTATIONS
PERFECT MURDER, A
Newman, Chris
PRIMARY COLORS
YOU'VE GOT MAIL
Nicolay, Matthew
DIARY OF A SERIAL KILLER
GODSON, THE
LAST ASSASSINS
Nicolson, Colin
LEADING MAN, THE
SPICE WORLD
Ninomiya, Kenji
DRAGON BALL Z THE MOVIE: DEAD ZONE
DRAGON BALL Z THE MOVIE: THE TREE OF MIGHT
DRAGON BALL Z THE MOVIE: THE WORLD'S STRONGEST
Norman, Derek
HOSTILE WATERS
Norman, Rick
DESTINY OF MARTY FINE, THE
Novack, David
CRUISE, THE
SUBSTITUTE 2: SCHOOL'S OUT, THE
Novick, Ed
DENNIS THE MENACE STRIKES AGAIN
SIMPLE PLAN, A
Nuccio, Vince
CATHERINE'S GROVE
Nytro, Kari
INSOMNIA
O'Connell, Kevin
ARMAGEDDON
MASK OF ZORRO, THE
O'Connor, Trevor
INFORMANT, THE
O'Donoghue, Robin
SHAKESPEARE IN LOVE
O'Mara, T.J.
PROPOSITION, THE
O'Sullivan, Patrick
SMOKE SIGNALS
Obermeyer, David
KISSING A FOOL
Okumura, Masahiro
SLEEPY EYES OF DEATH: SWORD OF ADVENTURE
Olland, Nigel
TARZAN AND THE LOST CITY
Oosum, Masao
SLEEPY EYES OF DEATH: SWORD OF SEDUCTION
Ooya, Iwao
RAZOR: THE SNARE, THE
SLEEPY EYES OF DEATH: FULL CIRCLE KILLING
Orloff, Lee
BLADE
HARD RAIN
NEIL SIMON'S THE ODD COUPLE II
Ornitz, Kim
MERCURY RISING
RUSH HOUR
WEDDING SINGER, THE
Orsi, Tom
STORY OF X, THE
Ortiz, Anthony
ALARMIST, THE
Osmo, Ben
BABE: PIG IN THE CITY
Paranen, Olli
JERUSALEM
Pardula, Rolf
REBOUND: THE LEGEND OF EARL "THE GOAT" MANIGAULT
TIETA OF AGRESTE
Parker, Ralph
HUNTED, THE
Parsons, Jeffrey
LAST BREATH
Patrick, Ben
BAD MANNERS
MILO
Patrignani, Franco
LOLITA
Patterson, Darryl
ASYLUM
Patterson, Geoffrey
APT PUPIL
X-FILES, THE
Patton, Rick
SNOWBOUND
Paul, Tom
NO WAY HOME
Pearce, Doug
RUDOLPH THE RED-NOSED REINDEER: THE MOVIE
Pearce, Steuart
JOHNNY SKIDMARKS
Perez, Joe
STEEL SHARKS
Persov, Vladimir
MOTHER AND SON
Petersen, Nils
R.I.P. REST IN PIECES: A PORTRAIT OF JOE COLEMAN
Petrucci, Andrea
EIGHTEENTH ANGEL, THE
Phillips, Mark
ERNEST IN THE ARMY
Pietsch-Lindenberg, Andreas
DIDN'T DO IT FOR LOVE
Pilafian, Peter
ALFRED HITCHCOCK: MASTER OF SUSPENSE
Porath, Jonathan
STOREFRONT HITCHCOCK
Porzchen, Josef
RAT'S TALE, A

Pospisil, John
SENSELESS
SIX DAYS, SEVEN NIGHTS
Powell, Daryl
SIN AND REDEMPTION
URBAN SAFARI
Powers, Dave
DIRTY LAUNDRY
Powers, David
SHAMPOO HORNS
WEST NEW YORK
Prentice, Henry
OPERATION DELTA FORCE 2
Prezeau, Gerald
LOU REED: ROCK AND ROLL HEART
Prezeau, Rudolph
LOU REED: ROCK AND ROLL HEART
Price, Matthew
HE GOT GAME
NO LOOKING BACK
Price, Sarah
BIG ONE, THE
Prieto, Juan Carlos
WHO THE HELL IS JULIETTE?
Pritchett, John Patrick
GINGERBREAD MAN, THE
NEWTON BOYS, THE
SPANISH PRISONER, THE
TWO FOR TEXAS
Pullman, Jeff
MR. JEALOUSY
NIAGARA NIAGARA
Quaglio, Laurent
CHAMBERMAID ON THE TITANIC, THE
Quirk, Patrick
MERRY WAR, A
Radka, Theresa
BROADWAY DAMAGE
SUE
Ratajczak, Paul
INVADER, THE
MONTANA
Reade, Dick
UGLY, THE
Reale, Peter
TOUCH OF EVIL: THE DIRECTOR'S CUT
Reed, Barry
BRYLCREEM BOYS, THE
Rejas, Miguel
DAY OF THE BEAST, THE
Ricaud, Marcus
RICHIE RICH'S CHRISTMAS WISH
Richards, George
DAD SAVAGE
SWEPT FROM THE SEA
Rideaux, Patrick
SAND TRAP
Ripper, Velcrow
PLACE CALLED CHIAPAS, A
Ritchie, D.J.
LOVELIFE
MY BROTHER'S WAR
STRAY BULLET
Rizzo, Al
LET'S KILL ALL THE LAWYERS
Robinson, Buck
CLUB VAMPIRE
Rochester, Arthur
ANOTHER DAY IN PARADISE
PLAYING BY HEART
TRUMAN SHOW, THE
Rodgers, Aletha
RUNNING WOMAN, THE
Ronne, David
DANCE WITH ME
DECLINE OF WESTERN CIVILIZATION PART III, THE
I STILL KNOW WHAT YOU DID LAST SUMMER
JANE AUSTEN'S MAFIA!
Rosin, Urmas
HOT BLOODED
Rousseau, Patrick
SNAKE EYES
Rousseaux, Jean-Yves
MARIUS AND JEANNETTE
Rovin, David
I MARRIED A STRANGE PERSON!
Rubin, H. Alex
WHO IS HENRY JAGLOM?
Rudisill, Carl
MAJOR LEAGUE: BACK TO THE MINORS
SHADRACH
Ruschak, Michael
BUSTER & CHAUNCEY'S SILENT NIGHT
Rush, Sean
PARENT TRAP, THE
Russell, Greg P.
ARMAGEDDON
MASK OF ZORRO, THE
Rutledge, Robert R.
CASPER MEETS WENDY
RUSTY: THE GREAT RESCUE
Rydstrom, Gary
BUG'S LIFE, A
HORSE WHISPERER, THE
SAVING PRIVATE RYAN
Sabatier, Thierry
LIFE OF JESUS, THE
Samuels, Alan
LANDLADY, THE
RICHIE RICH'S CHRISTMAS WISH
Samuelson, Ragnar
JUNK MAIL
TRANCEFORMER: A PORTRAIT OF LARS VON TRIER
Sands, Kevin
AIR BUD: GOLDEN RECEIVER
Sanz, Pablo
EL CHE: INVESTIGATING A LEGEND
Sarnat, Zoe
LOU REED: ROCK AND ROLL HEART
Sarokin, William
IMPOSTORS, THE
PRICE ABOVE RUBIES, A
Scharf, Larry
MURDER IN MIND
PHANTOMS
PROPHECY II, THE
TREKKIES
Schexnayder, Richard
QUICKSILVER HIGHWAY
Schiefelbein, John
JOEY
Schmid, Jason
HERCULES AND XENA THE ANIMATED MOVIE: THE BATTLE FOR MOUNT OLYMPUS
Schneider, Peter
LOVE WALKED IN
Schnieder, Peter
TALK TO ME
Schoen, Jan
LOU REED: ROCK AND ROLL HEART
Schroeder, Mark
INVADER, THE
Schulman, Douglas
TOP OF THE WORLD
Scullin, Garrett
SKIN & BONE
Scurry, Tom
SKIN & BONE
Segal, Ken
SLUMS OF BEVERLY HILLS
Sekiya, Yukio
TOKYO FIST
Seretti, Phillip
JUNGLE BOOK: MOWGLI'S STORY, THE
Serveira, Gita
MARIE BAIE DES ANGES
Shatz, Leslie
DEEP RISING
Sheesley, Ernie
ADVENTURES OF MOWGLI
KIKI'S DELIVERY SERVICE
Shen Jianqin
EAST PALACE, WEST PALACE
Sheppard, Bill "Otis"
HARD CORE LOGO
Sherline, Scott
MY GIANT
Sherwin, Dave
DEAR JESSE
Shine, Greg
JACK HIGGINS' THE WINDSOR PROTOCOL
Siegel, Jack
BOYS IN LOVE 2
Sigwalt, Patrick
WESTERN
Simmons, Brian
MRS. DALLOWAY
WHEN TRUMPETS FADE
Sisti, John
POLISH WEDDING
Siwinsky, Todd
DAVID SEARCHING
Skinner, William
SPREE, THE
WHEN DANGER FOLLOWS YOU HOME
Slater, Peter
SPACEJACKED
Slider, Dan
NO ORDINARY LOVE
Smith, J. Byron
STILL BREATHING
Smith, Lee
TRUMAN SHOW, THE
Smith, Scott D.
U.S. MARSHALS
Smith, William
LITTLE GHOST
Snodgrass, Harry
BASEKETBALL
Snyder, Doug
ALL THE RAGE
Somaru, Pratash "Derek"
DAVID SEARCHING
Sorkin, William
RETURN TO PARADISE
Sorlin, Philippe
EL CHE: INVESTIGATING A LEGEND
SOUNDELUX
GODZILLA
Spiers, Annie
PHOTOGRAPHING FAIRIES
Spritz, Neal
MEN
Standel, Felicia
RETURN OF THE KING, THE
Stanomir, Dragos
JOHNNY MYSTO BOY WIZARD
Stearns, Michael
PASSION IN THE DESERT
Stein, Jonathan Earl
RAGE, THE
THERE'S SOMETHING ABOUT MARY
Stephenson, David
BORROWERS, THE
DANGEROUS BEAUTY
ELIZABETH
MAN IN THE IRON MASK, THE
NIGHT AND THE MOMENT, THE

SOURCE AUTHORS

Seidler, Tor
RAT'S TALE, A
Seltzer, David
MY GIANT
Septien, Al
CHAIRMAN OF THE BOARD
Seymour, Gerald
INFORMANT, THE
Sheehan, Neil
BRIGHT SHINING LIE, A
Shibata, Ranzaburoo
SLEEPY EYES OF DEATH: SWORD OF SEDUCTION
Shibata, Renzaburo
SLEEPY EYES OF DEATH: SWORD OF ADVENTURE
Shinohara, Toru
ZERO WOMAN
Sikora, Jim
BULLET ON A WIRE
Simon, Neil
NEIL SIMON'S THE ODD COUPLE II
Smith, Scott B.
SIMPLE PLAN, A
Spice Girls, The
SPICE WORLD
Stahl, Jerry
PERMANENT MIDNIGHT
Stanford, Don
SUICIDE KINGS
Stanush, Claude
NEWTON BOYS, THE
Steakly, John
JOHN CARPENTER'S VAMPIRES
Stoker, Bram
BRAM STOKER'S SHADOWBUILDER
Stokes, Michael
FACE THE EVIL
Strauss, John J.
THERE'S SOMETHING ABOUT MARY
Stuart, Francis
MOONDANCE
Styron, William
SHADRACH
Szilagyi, Steve
PHOTOGRAPHING FAIRIES
Tabucchi, Antonio
PEREIRA DECLARES
Tapert, Robert
YOUNG HERCULES
Tashima, Seizo
VILLAGE OF DREAMS
Tezuka, Osamu
NEW ADVENTURES OF KIMBA THE WHITE LION, THE
Theroux, Paul
CHINESE BOX, THE
Thompson, Hunter S.
FEAR AND LOATHING IN LAS VEGAS
Thompson, Jim
HIT ME
Togashi, Yoshihiro
POLTERGEIST REPORT: YUYU HAKUSHO
Toho Co.
GODZILLA
Toriyama, Akira
DRAGON BALL Z THE MOVIE: DEAD ZONE
DRAGON BALL Z THE MOVIE: THE TREE OF MIGHT
DRAGON BALL Z THE MOVIE: THE WORLD'S STRONGEST
Tournier, Michel
OGRE, THE
Truly, Daniel
YOUNG HERCULES
Tsukamoto, Shinya
TOKYO FIST
Turner, Michael
HARD CORE LOGO
Turner, Richard
VIOLET'S VISIT
Undset, Sigrid
KRISTIN LAVRANSDATTER
Wang, Wayne
CHINESE BOX, THE
Watson, Eric
PI
Wechter, David
FACULTY, THE
Wenders, Wim
CITY OF ANGELS
White, Stephen
BARNEY'S GREAT ADVENTURE—THE MOVIE
Widen, Gregory
PROPHECY II, THE
Wimmer, Kurt
SPHERE
Wolfman, Marv
BLADE
Wong, Barry
ARMOUR OF GOD
Woolf, Virginia
MRS. DALLOWAY
Wright, Lawrence
SIEGE, THE
Wylie, Philip
DEEP IMPACT
Yamazaki, Osamu
WRATH OF THE NINJA: THE YOTODEN MOVIE
Yoshimura, Akira
EEL, THE
Young, Diana
FERNGULLY 2: THE MAGICAL RESCUE
Zeik, J.D.
RONIN
Zurla, Martin
DOGWATCH

SPECIAL EFFECTS

A.B.I. Industries
RIGHT CONNECTIONS, THE
Abades, Reyes
CARLA'S SONG
DAY OF THE BEAST, THE
Allder, Nick
LOST IN SPACE
Almost Human
CLUB VAMPIRE
Alterian Studios, Inc.
SLAPPY AND THE STINKERS
Altrocchi, Alexandra
SMALL SOLDIERS
Andersen, Lars Kolding
KINGDOM, PART 2, THE
Anderson, Larz
TRUMAN SHOW, THE
Arbogast, Roy
WHAT DREAMS MAY COME
Arthur, Colin
PASSION IN THE DESERT
Ashby, Reginald
ONE TOUGH COP
Bajorek, Kim
STILL BREATHING
Balsmeyer, Randall
HE GOT GAME
Barnett, Leslie
SMALL SOLDIERS
Barron, Craig
TRUMAN SHOW, THE
Bauer, Joe
SIMON BIRCH
Baur, Tassilo
BEST OF THE BEST: WITHOUT WARNING
Beauchamp, Wayne
CHILDREN OF THE CORN V: FIELD OF TERROR
HOMEGROWN
LAST ASSASSINS
SAND TRAP
Beier, Thad
BRAM STOKER'S SHADOWBUILDER
Belardinelli, Charles
ALMOST HEROES
Bellisimo/Bejardinelli FX
GIRLS IN PRISON
Bellissimo, Tom
ALMOST HEROES
AMERICAN HISTORY X
Benjamin, Al
INVADER, THE
MISBEGOTTEN
Bentley, Gary
LAST ASSASSINS
TRUCKS
Berg, Russel
CELEBRITY
Berger, Howard
PHANTOMS
Bickerton, Angus
LOST IN SPACE
Bielenberg, Ken
ANTZ
Big Bang Animation
LOST WORLD, THE
Bivins, Ray
DECEIVER
ELMORE LEONARD'S GOLD COAST
MEET THE DEEDLES
Blacklock, Michael
HUNTED, THE
Blank, Herbert
ROYAL DECEIT
Blitstein, David
CITY OF ANGELS
HOME FRIES
PATCH ADAMS
Bochnig, Karl-Heinz
HOSTILE WATERS
RAT'S TALE, A
Boss Film Studios
DESPERATE MEASURES
Bottin, Rob
DEEP RISING
Brennan, Erick
PSYCHO
Bresin, Martin
DENNIS THE MENACE STRIKES AGAIN
Brink, Connie
MEET JOE BLACK
Brink, Jeffrey S.
PERFECT MURDER, A
Brisdon, Stuart
SHAKESPEARE IN LOVE
SPICE WORLD
SWEPT FROM THE SEA
Brooks, Nicholas
WHAT DREAMS MAY COME
Brotherhood, J.C.
BREAK, THE
Brown, Ray
SMOKE SIGNALS
Bryan, Mara
DARK CITY
Buechler, John Carl
WATCHERS REBORN
Buenaflor, Randall D.
BOOGIE BOY
Burton, Tom
RUSTY: THE GREAT RESCUE

Buttgereit, Jorg
KILLER CONDOM, THE
Cabral, Randy
HOME FRIES
Cabrera, Norman
TRUCKS
Camelot Films
MEET THE DEEDLES
Carlucci, Lou
BLADE
CAN'T HARDLY WAIT
PASS, THE
STAR KID
Cavanaugh, Larry
SIX DAYS, SEVEN NIGHTS
Centropolis Effects
GODZILLA
Chamberlayne, Andrew Cotton
WHEN DANGER FOLLOWS YOU HOME
Chiang, Peter
BORROWERS, THE
Chilvers, Colin
BRIDE OF CHUCKY
Chisnall, Kevin
ABERRATION
BRIGHT SHINING LIE, A
Church, Alan
LOVE IS THE DEVIL: STUDY FOR A PORTRAIT OF FRANCIS BACON
Cineffects
CAPTIVE
JACK HIGGINS' THUNDER POINT
LOUISA MAY ALCOTT'S LITTLE MEN
Cinesite
LOST IN SPACE
PRIMARY COLORS
TRUMAN SHOW, THE
Clark, John
EVER AFTER
Clayton, Guy
CIVIL ACTION, A
MERCURY RISING
Cohen, Garry
REGENERATION
Computer Film Company, The
BIG LEBOWSKI, THE
Cooney, Kam
NIGHT AT THE ROXBURY, A
Corbould, Chris
FIRESTORM
Corbould, Neil
SAVING PRIVATE RYAN
Cordero, Laurencio
MASK OF ZORRO, THE
Cosgrove, Ryal
DEAD END
LOUISA MAY ALCOTT'S LITTLE MEN
Courtley, Steve
ARMOUR OF GOD
Cox, Brian
ARMOUR OF GOD
THIN RED LINE, THE
Cox, John
JOEY
Craig, Jordan
WOO
Craig, Louis
SAVIOR
Craig, Ron
FALLING FIRE
FUTURE FEAR
Cramer, Fred
KNOCK OFF
Crawford, John
INVISIBLE DAD
Creature F/X
KRAA! THE SEA MONSTER
Criswell, John
LITTLE BIGFOOT 2: THE JOURNEY HOME
Crosman, Peter
HORSE WHISPERER, THE
Cutler, Rory
SIN AND REDEMPTION
SPREE, THE
TRUCKS
Dagenais, Francois
FACE THE EVIL
Dalton, Burt
DR. DOLITTLE
MERCURY RISING
PRACTICAL MAGIC
Davies, Tom
BABE: PIG IN THE CITY
DARK CITY
Davis, Nick
AVENGERS, THE
Deak, Michael S.
KRAA! THE SEA MONSTER
Demetrau, Georges
RONIN
Desjardin, John "DJ"
FIRESTORM
Digital Armageddon
CURSE OF THE PUPPET MASTER
Digital Filmworks, Inc.
GREAT EXPECTATIONS
Digital Magic Company, The
SPECIES II
Dion, Dennis
RICHIE RICH'S CHRISTMAS WISH
Dodge, Norm
WIDE AWAKE
Donen, Peter
HORSE WHISPERER, THE
U.S. MARSHALS
Donvito, Fabrizio
NIRVANA
Draycott, Kevin
REGENERATION
Dream Quest Images
ARMAGEDDON
DEEP RISING
Drnec, Tim
3 NINJAS: HIGH NOON AT MEGA MOUNTAIN
Drohan II, Eddie
BREAK, THE
Drohan III, Edward A.
WIDE AWAKE
East Coast Effects
HURRICANE STREETS
Ellis, John R.
SUBSPECIES IV: BLOODSTORM
Ellis, Patrick
GODZILLA
Elmendorf, Garry
SNAKE EYES
Engel, Udo
WHEN PIGS FLY
Engel, Volker
GODZILLA
Engelsiepen, Bob
STILL BREATHING
Evolution FX
VELVET GOLDMINE
Farrar, Scott
DEEP IMPACT
Field, Richard
DEAD WATERS
Field, Tim
BORROWERS, THE
Film Factory at VTR, The
COUSIN BETTE
Film Technical Services, Inc.
STAR KID
Finch, Larry
LITTLE BIGFOOT 2: THE JOURNEY HOME
Fioritto, Larry
DOGWATCH
DON KING: ONLY IN AMERICA
PRINCE, THE
REAL THING, THE
TWILIGHT
VERY BAD THINGS
Fisher, James
HUNTED, THE
TRICKS
Foley, Maurice
I WENT DOWN
INFORMANT, THE
Ford, Thomas
LOS LOCOS
NIGHT VISION
Fordham, Joe
QUICKSILVER HIGHWAY
Francis, Jim
BRYLCREEM BOYS, THE
Frazee, Terry
STAR TREK: INSURRECTION
Frazier, John
ARMAGEDDON
HARD RAIN
Fredburg, Jim
FALLEN
Gajdecki, John
ESCAPE, THE
Galich, Steve
FEAR AND LOATHING IN LAS VEGAS
Galimo, Franco
KID IN ALADDIN'S PALACE, A
Gareri, Joe
MY GIANT
Gehr, Rocky
MASK OF ZORRO, THE
Gibbs, George
ELIZABETH
MAN IN THE IRON MASK, THE
Gibson, Jonathan
IN HIS FATHER'S SHOES
Giles, Simon
LOVE IS THE DEVIL: STUDY FOR A PORTRAIT OF FRANCIS BACON
Gittens, Camilla
LOST IN SPACE
Glass, Terry
LES MISERABLES
Godinez, Arturo
NAKED LIES
Gonzalez Jr., Carmen
COLONY, THE
Good, Tim
TRACKED
Gray, John
THURSDAY
Grossberg, Joseph
SPECIES II
Hakian, Joshua
BURN HOLLYWOOD BURN
Hall, Allen
MIGHTY JOE YOUNG
Hall, Lorenzo
BODY COUNT
Hall, Robert
CLUB VAMPIRE
Hamilton, A. Scott
TALES FROM A PARALLEL UNIVERSE: GIGA SHADOW
Hammerhead Productions
BRAM STOKER'S SHADOWBUILDER
Hannigan, Kevin
SUMMER FLING
Hardigan, John
PLAYERS CLUB, THE

Harris, David
INCOGNITO
Harris, Kevin
HOLY MAN
THERE'S SOMETHING ABOUT MARY
WILD THINGS
Harris, Tom
DAD SAVAGE
Hart, Walter
BLUES BROTHERS 2000
Hartigan, John
ASYLUM
HALLOWEEN H20: TWENTY YEARS LATER
HORTON FOOTE'S ALONE
HOW STELLA GOT HER GROOVE BACK
RETROACTIVE
SUICIDE KINGS
UNCLE SAM
Hefzers, Die
TALES FROM A PARALLEL UNIVERSE: EATING PATTERN
Hicks, Enrich Martin
TRUCKS
Hills, Graham
MADELINE
Hodgson, Rob
MAN IN THE IRON MASK, THE
Hollow, Bob
LITTLE VOICE
WILDE
Hollund, Brett
WHITE RAVEN, THE
Holly, Sharon
HOPE FLOATS
Hoover, Richard R.
ARMAGEDDON
Horton, John
MRS. DALLOWAY
Houston, Kent
MAN IN THE IRON MASK, THE
Huitron, Michael
INVADER, THE
Hull, Greg
LAST LIVES
Hunt, Bruce
DARK CITY
Huntley, Leslie
EDEN
Hverven, Pal Morten
JUNK MAIL
Hynek, Joel
WHAT DREAMS MAY COME
Hyper Image
BILLBOARD DAD
Illusion Arts
DANGEROUS BEAUTY
FEAR AND LOATHING IN LAS VEGAS
Image Animation
LOST WORLD, THE
Industrial Light & Magic
DEEP IMPACT
MERCURY RISING
SMALL SOLDIERS
SNAKE EYES
Ingram, Clint
ABERRATION
Ionica, Adriana
CLOCKMAKER
Iordache, Lucian
TALISMAN
Jarvis, Jeff
SPECIES II
Jennings, Brian
SENSELESS
Jim Henson's Creature Shop
LOST IN SPACE
MERLIN

Jiritano, Drew
BELLY
HAPPINESS
LAST BREATH
NO WAY HOME
RATCHET
SUBSTITUTE 2: SCHOOL'S OUT, THE
Jiritano, Greg
RIVER RED
Johns, William
ENEMY
Johnson, Margaret
HOPE FLOATS
Johnson, Steve
SPECIES II
Johnston, Gerry
BREAK, THE
MOONDANCE
Jolliffe, Brock
BREAKOUT
DEFENDERS: PAYBACK, THE
FACE DOWN
HOSTILE INTENT
ONE TOUGH COP
UNDERTAKER'S WEDDING, THE
Jones, Ed
HARD RAIN
Jones, Paul L.
BRAM STOKER'S SHADOWBUILDER
Jones, Richard
EIGHTEENTH ANGEL, THE
Jones, Richard Lee
PALMETTO
K.N.B. EFX Group
PHANTASM: OBLIVION
Kavanagh, Michael
54
MIGHTY, THE
Kawakita, Koichi
GODZILLA AND MOTHRA: THE BATTLE FOR EARTH
GODZILLA VS. KING GHIDORAH
Keen, Bob
PRINCE VALIANT
Kelsey, David
BASEKETBALL
HUSH
PAULIE
Kerby, Kelly
DESPERATE MEASURES
Khan, Rakus
HURRICANE STREETS
King, Dennis
RUSH HOUR
Kirshoff, Steve
GREAT EXPECTATIONS
Kittle, Tom
GINGERBREAD MAN, THE
Knott, Robert L.
NEIL SIMON'S THE ODD COUPLE II
Kobielski, Kaz
BIG HIT, THE
BLUES BROTHERS 2000
Kuehn, Brad
PRIMARY COLORS
Kunz, Peter
LAWN DOGS
NIAGARA NIAGARA
Kurtzman, Robert
PHANTOMS
Lambert, John
PLUMP FICTION
Landerer, Greg
DETONATOR
PLUMP FICTION
Landry, Tim
MEET THE DEEDLES

Lannutti, Albert
RUNNING WOMAN, THE
WATCHERS REBORN
Lantieri, Michael
DEEP IMPACT
Laurie, Anna
REAL HOWARD SPITZ, THE
Lazarowich, Tony
WRONGFULLY ACCUSED
Lester, Dan
CON, THE
RAGE, THE
TOP OF THE WORLD
Linehan, Charles
PAULIE
Ling, Van
JUNGLE BOOK: MOWGLI'S STORY, THE
Lloyd, Steve
BUTCHER BOY, THE
Lockwood, Dean
DISTURBING BEHAVIOR
Lombardi, Joe
WHEN TRUMPETS FADE
Lombardi, Paul
DESPERATE MEASURES
SIEGE, THE
X-FILES, THE
Longhurst, Graham
COUSIN BETTE
MADELINE
Lorimer, Alan
PRIMARY COLORS
Mack, Kevin
WHAT DREAMS MAY COME
Magical Media Industries
WATCHERS REBORN
Magliochetti, Al
JOHNNY MYSTO BOY WIZARD
KRAA! THE SEA MONSTER
MIDAS TOUCH, THE
Maiers, Ralph
SPECIES II
Malivoire, Martin
BLUES BROTHERS 2000
DIRTY WORK
Mark Rappaport Creature Effects
CURSE OF THE PUPPET MASTER
Mason, Andrew
DARK CITY
Matte World
NEWTON BOYS, THE
Mattson, Erik
SMALL SOLDIERS
May, Jim
DEEP RISING
McAlister, Michael J.
TRUMAN SHOW, THE
McAulay, Carol
SAVING PRIVATE RYAN
McCarthy, Kevin
DIARY OF A SERIAL KILLER
LOVE TO KILL
McCarty, Brian
HOME FRIES
McClung, Pat
ARMAGEDDON
McCullough, David
SIX DAYS, SEVEN NIGHTS
McGillivary, Jim
RESCUERS: STORIES OF COURAGE—TWO COUPLES
RESCUERS: STORIES OF COURAGE—TWO WOMEN
McIntyre Jr., Ray
CASPER MEETS WENDY
McLeod, John
FACULTY, THE
NEWTON BOYS, THE

McMurray, Laird
BONE DADDY
TERMINAL JUSTICE
Meagher, Michael "Tony"
PAULIE
Meinardus, Mike
U.S. MARSHALS
Mercurio, Joseph
LOLITA
Mesa, William
QUICKSILVER HIGHWAY
Milinac, John
I STILL KNOW WHAT YOU DID LAST SUMMER
SIMPLE PLAN, A
Mill, The
ENEMY OF THE STATE
Milner, Digby
BORROWERS, THE
Mitchell, Jim
MIGHTY JOE YOUNG
Modern Videofilm
SIMON BIRCH
Molina
LIVE FLESH
Montefusco, Vincent
JOHNNY SKIDMARKS
Montgomery, Amanda
SMALL SOLDIERS
Moore, Randy E.
HOPE FLOATS
Morot, Adrien
BLEEDERS
Morphett, Suzanne
ABERRATION
Mundin, David
DEAD WATERS
Munroe, Bob
TALES FROM A PARALLEL UNIVERSE: SUPER NOVA
Murphy, Paul
BUFFALO '66
Natali, Germano
BEYOND, THE
EIGHTEENTH ANGEL, THE
Neighbour, Trevor
BLACK DOG
Nelson, John
CITY OF ANGELS
Nespoli, Massimo
DANGEROUS BEAUTY
Netter Digital Entertainment Inc.
CHILDREN OF THE CORN V: FIELD OF TERROR
Netter, Jason
CHILDREN OF THE CORN V: FIELD OF TERROR
Newkirk, Dale
COLONY, THE
NIGHTWATCH
STEEL SHARKS
Newquist, Steve
LIVING IN PERIL
Nicholson, Lyn
BORROWERS, THE
Nicholson, Sam
INVADER, THE
JANE AUSTEN'S MAFIA!
Nicotero, Greg
PHANTOMS
O'Neill, Kevin
YOUNG HERCULES
Oda, Takashi
TOKYO FIST
Okun, Jeffrey A.
LOLITA
Orr, William H.
I'LL BE HOME FOR CHRISTMAS
Osmond, Jak
REDLINE
Ottesen, John
BELOVED
PRICE ABOVE RUBIES, A
Owens, Michael
MERCURY RISING
Pacific Title Digital
BULWORTH
MY GIANT
Parry, Julian
TARZAN AND THE LOST CITY
Parsons, Don
HENRY: PORTRAIT OF A SERIAL KILLER PART 2
Paul, Don
PRINCE OF EGYPT, THE
Pelchay, Andre
PEACEKEEPER, THE
Pellegrini, Michael A.
DECAMPITATED
Pepiot, Kenneth
SMALL SOLDIERS
SPHERE
Peristere, Loni
RUSTY: THE GREAT RESCUE
Perry, Daniel
ABERRATION
Philips, Dan
PRINCE OF EGYPT, THE
Pike, Kevin
REACH THE ROCK
Pinny, Clay
SOLDIER
Ponzo, Franco
RABID DOGS
Poolman, Max
ERNEST IN THE ARMY
Pope, Randy
PASSION IN THE DESERT
Port, George
ABERRATION
Pride, Tad
DARK CITY
Prior, D. Kerry
PHANTASM: OBLIVION
Pritchett, Darrell
JOHN CARPENTER'S VAMPIRES
Pritchett, Darryl
ANOTHER DAY IN PARADISE
Rainone, Thomas C.
STAR KID
Ramsey, Joe
REPLACEMENT KILLERS, THE
Rappaport, Mark
INVISIBLE MOM
KRAA! THE SEA MONSTER
Ratliff, Richard
MY GIANT
Ray, Kelley
REPLACEMENT KILLERS, THE
Reedyk, Rae
MY VERY BEST FRIEND
Reeves, Richard
LAST SEDUCTION II, THE
Reynolds, Chris
GOVERNESS, THE
Ricci, Brian
PROPOSITION, THE
Rice, Mark
BRAM STOKER'S SHADOWBUILDER
Riggs, Bob
WITHOUT LIMITS
ZERO EFFECT
Riley, David
ABERRATION
Rivard, Pierre
JACK LONDON'S THE CALL OF THE WILD: DOG OF THE YUKON
Rivas, Rudy
BREAKOUT
Robertson, Jay
BLACK LIGHT
Robertson, Stuart
WHAT DREAMS MAY COME
Rockwell, Oliver
STEPHEN KING'S THE NIGHT FLIER
Rolfshoj, Annette
KINGDOM, PART 2, THE
Ross, Ted
BLUES BROTHERS 2000
Routley, Maurice
EBENEZER
Ryan, Jason
INVISIBLE MOM
Rygiel, Jim
DESPERATE MEASURES
PARENT TRAP, THE
Sagae, Hiroshi
TOKYO FIST
Sander, Jack
HOME FRIES
Saraburi Effects Team
HEROES SHED NO TEARS
Schirmer, Bill
WRONGFULLY ACCUSED
Schmidt, Dan
INVADER, THE
Schultz, Roy
WOUNDED
Schwalm, Jim
HARD RAIN
Scupp, Robert J.
STEPMOM
Senior, Alan
EVER AFTER
Shea, Mike
DEEP RISING
Sheridan, Robert
ATOMIC DOG
Shymkiw, Randy
SNOWBOUND
Silver, Jesse
BASEKETBALL
Simmons, David
PENTAGON WARS, THE
Sirrs, Janek
BIG LEBOWSKI, THE
Smith, Gordon
BREAST MEN
Sony Pictures Imageworks
CITY OF ANGELS
REPLACEMENT KILLERS, THE
Southard, Michael
PLEASANTVILLE
Speed, Ken
SCARRED CITY
SPFX
I GOT THE HOOK UP
Spina, Michele
SMALL SOLDIERS
Staples, Paul
12 ANGRY MEN
Stargate Films, Inc.
INVADER, THE
Stears, John
MASK OF ZORRO, THE
Steinheimer, Bruce
SIX DAYS, SEVEN NIGHTS
Steve Johnson's XFX
PHANTOMS
SPECIES II
Stevens, Randy
RETURN TO SAVAGE BEACH

Stewart, Dean
URBAN LEGEND
Stolba, Jaroslav
LES MISERABLES
Stone, F. Lee
SENSELESS
Streett, J.D.
KRIPPENDORF'S TRIBE
Stromberg, Robert
DANGEROUS BEAUTY
Stubbs, Peter
HEAVEN'S BURNING
MR. NICE GUY
Sturm, Dieter
HI-LO COUNTRY, THE
Stutsman, Richard
ARMAGEDDON
Sweeney, Matt
LETHAL WEAPON 4
Sweeney, Michael
DESPERATE MEASURES
Tarallo, Ken
JOHNNY SKIDMARKS
Tatopoulos, Patrick
GODZILLA
Taylor, Jody
REGENERATION
Team FX
GENERAL, THE
Thompson, Mike
SOUR GRAPES
Thorne, Rich
GREAT EXPECTATIONS
HOPE FLOATS
Tom, Jean S.
SIX DAYS, SEVEN NIGHTS
Total Fabrication
KRAA! THE SEA MONSTER
Traynor, William
MONTANA
Trifunovich, Neil
HORSE WHISPERER, THE
Tristano, Mike
BOOGIE BOY
Trost, Ron
RUSHMORE
Troy, Bill
BOYS WILL BE BOYS
Tunnicliffe, Gary
NEVADA
Turner, Mark
GO NOW
Ultimate Effects
CLAY PIGEONS
GODS AND MONSTERS
MARS
PHOENIX
SLAPPY AND THE STINKERS
SUICIDE KINGS
UNCLE SAM
WHEN TIME EXPIRES
Van Kline, Jor
LITTLE GHOST
Van Zeebroeck, Bruno
GIA
JANE AUSTEN'S MAFIA!
Vasquez, Bob
RIDE
Vazquez, Alex
MEN WITH GUNS
View Studios
STILL BREATHING
VIFX
FIRESTORM
Vogel, Matt
TWO FOR TEXAS
Wagner, David A.
SUBSPECIES IV: BLOODSTORM
TALISMAN
Waine, David
PROPHECY II, THE
SLAPPY AND THE STINKERS
Wald-Cohain, Ariyela
PI
Walsh, Matthew Jason
CURSE OF THE PUPPET MASTER
Ward, Tom
BELOVED
Warren Jr., Gene
EDEN
Watts, Chris
PLEASANTVILLE
Wayne, David
CLAY PIGEONS
Webber, Tim
MERLIN
Weinand, Janine
OPERATION DELTA FORCE 2
Wenger, Carol Lynn
OUT OF SIGHT
Wenger, Cliff
OUT OF SIGHT
PARENT TRAP, THE
West, Kit
BLACK DOG
Weta Ltd.
UGLY, THE
Wibley, Alan
BRYLCREEM BOYS, THE
Wiemketz, Peter
ROYAL DECEIT
Wiessenhaan, Harry
JACK HIGGINS' ON DANGEROUS GROUND
JACK HIGGINS' MIDNIGHT MAN
SUB DOWN
Williams, Joss
AVENGERS, THE
BUTCHER BOY, THE
REGENERATION
Williams, Mark
KRAA! THE SEA MONSTER
Wilson, Lee
WRONGFULLY ACCUSED
Windus, Arthur
DARK CITY
Winston, Stan
PAULIE
SMALL SOLDIERS
Wolfeil, Todd R.
LAST DAYS OF DISCO, THE
STEPMOM
Wynne, Cordell
TALES FROM A PARALLEL UNIVERSE: GIGA SHADOW
Yale, Janet
BIG LEBOWSKI, THE
Yeatman, Hoyt
MIGHTY JOE YOUNG
Yoho, Robert
HURRICANE STREETS
Zarro, Richard M.
SIX DAYS, SEVEN NIGHTS
Ziegler, John
LIVING OUT LOUD

STUNTS

Aguilar, George
MONTANA
OBJECT OF MY AFFECTION, THE
REAL BLONDE, THE
Aiello III, Danny
LOLITA
Akerstream, Marc
DOUBLE EDGE
HUNTED, THE
INVADER, THE
MY VERY BEST FRIEND
WOUNDED
Alon, Roy
GO NOW
Alvarez, Ignacio
I LOVE YOU, DON'T TOUCH ME!
MILO
Anagnos, Bill
SPANISH PRISONER, THE
WIDE AWAKE
Anders, Ed
OUTSIDE OZONA
Armstrong, Vic
BLACK DOG
Arnett, James
DEEP IMPACT
Arnett, Jim
SMALL SOLDIERS
Ashker, John
BASEKETBALL
Ateah, Scott
AIR BUD: GOLDEN RECEIVER
MY VERY BEST FRIEND
REDLINE
Avery, Rick
BLUES BROTHERS 2000
PENTAGON WARS, THE
STAR TREK: INSURRECTION
Banta, Pat
TRUMAN SHOW, THE
Barker, Rick
THERE'S SOMETHING ABOUT MARY
Barrett, David M.
SPECIES II
Barrett, Stan
TWILIGHT
Bates, Kenny
ARMAGEDDON
Baxley, Gary
MAKER, THE
Bernhardt, Chick
WILD THINGS
Bews, Guy
WRONGFULLY ACCUSED
Birman, Matt
URBAN LEGEND
Borden, Chuck
GODS AND MONSTERS
LITTLE BIGFOOT 2: THE JOURNEY HOME
SAND TRAP
Boss, Clay
CAN'T HARDLY WAIT
Boswell, Glenn
DARK CITY
Boue, Richard
BRIGHT SHINING LIE, A
Bovee, Brad
PLUMP FICTION
RUSTY: THE GREAT RESCUE
Boyle, Mark
AVENGERS, THE
INCOGNITO
Brackett, Marc
TEN BENNY
Bradford, Andrew
HUMAN BOMB
Bradley, Dan
PHANTOMS
PLAYING BY HEART
QUICKSILVER HIGHWAY
Bragg, Bobby
INVISIBLE DAD
Bralver, Bob
LOVE TO KILL

Branagan, John
MY GIANT
Brayham, Peter
LEADING MAN, THE
SPICE WORLD
Brazzel, Gregg
PHOENIX
RETROACTIVE
Brewer, Charlie
NEIL SIMON'S THE ODD COUPLE II
Brown, Bobby
FACULTY, THE
NEMESIS 4: CRY OF ANGELS
Brown, Bruce
ABERRATION
Brubaker, Tony
BELOVED
Bryant, Kurt
ASYLUM
INDISCREET
LANDLADY, THE
MURDER IN MIND
Bucossi, Peter
LAST DAYS OF DISCO, THE
LAWN DOGS
NO WAY HOME
SNAKE EYES
Butler, Dick
RAGE, THE
TOP OF THE WORLD
Cadiente, Jeff
SLAPPY AND THE STINKERS
Caldwell, Helen
SLIDING DOORS
Cardwell, Shane
FACE DOWN
54
IN HIS FATHER'S SHOES
PEACEKEEPER, THE
TRUCKS
Carter, Cecil
ERNEST IN THE ARMY
Castle, Danny
HOPE FLOATS
Chan, Billy
PRODIGAL SON, THE
Chan Hui-Ngai
ENCOUNTER OF THE SPOOKY KIND
Chan, Jackie
RUSH HOUR
Chen Yue Sang
HEROES SHED NO TEARS
Chiu Fat
KILLER ANGELS
Cho Wing
MR. NICE GUY
Clark, Roydon
SOUR GRAPES
Clarke, Andy
TWISTED
Coleman, Doug
CITY OF ANGELS
SIX DAYS, SEVEN NIGHTS
Combs, Gary
DEEP RISING
HORSE WHISPERER, THE
Condren, Patrick
BREAK, THE
BUTCHER BOY, THE
INFORMANT, THE
Conna, Edward
CLAY PIGEONS
Cook, Shelly
DEFENDERS: PAYBACK, THE
Copeman, John
LAWN DOGS
SHADRACH
STEPHEN KING'S THE NIGHT FLIER
Cordiero, Tony
HOT BLOODED
UNDERTAKER'S WEDDING, THE
Courtney, Dustin
APT PUPIL
Crane, Simon
SAVING PRIVATE RYAN
Crawford, Jake
GIA
HOMEGROWN
Crosby, Douglas
NO LOOKING BACK
Cross, Garvin
RIGHT CONNECTIONS, THE
Croughwell, Charles
DEEP IMPACT
WHAT DREAMS MAY COME
Crowther, Graeme
EVER AFTER
Cudney, Cliff
NIGHTWATCH
Curtis, Clive
SHOOTING FISH
Dashnaw, Jeffrey J.
PRACTICAL MAGIC
Davis, Gary
U.S. MARSHALS
Davison, Steve
LIVING OUT LOUD
Davison, Tim
X-FILES, THE
De Alessandro, Mark
BURN HOLLYWOOD BURN
Derrien, Yannick
MAN IN THE IRON MASK, THE
Dewer, Thomas
LANDLADY, THE
Dewier, Tom
WHEN TIME EXPIRES
Dimitrescu, Doru
SECRET KINGDOM, THE
SHRUNKEN CITY, THE
Dixon, Shane
SENSELESS
Dowdall, Jim
BORROWERS, THE
Downer, Wayne
DOWN IN THE DELTA
Doyle, Chris
SIMPLE PLAN, A
Drozda, Peter
ACT OF WAR
Dumitrescu, Doru
JOHNNY MYSTO BOY WIZARD
LITTLE GHOST
MIDAS TOUCH, THE
Dunn, Jim
TERMINAL JUSTICE
Dunne, Joe
MERCURY RISING
RONIN
Eastwood, Wade
OPERATION DELTA FORCE 2
Eirickson, Tom
EBENEZER
Elam, Greg
HOME FRIES
Elam, Kiante
HOPE FLOATS
Eliopoulos, Paul
MEAN GUNS
Epstein, Jon
NEMESIS 4: CRY OF ANGELS
NEVADA
Farfel, Roy
DAY AT THE BEACH
Farnsworth, Diamond
ZERO EFFECT
Ferrara, Frank
ALMOST PARTNERS
ONE TOUGH COP
Fierro, Jim
HENRY: PORTRAIT OF A SERIAL KILLER PART 2
File, Randy
JOHNNY SKIDMARKS
Fioramonti, Glory
HUSH
Forrestal, Terry
ELIZABETH
SWEPT FROM THE SEA
Forsayath, Rick
MIGHTY, THE
Fountidakis, Plato
BREAKOUT
Giacomazzi, Mickey
PSYCHO
Gibson, Kinnie
ELMORE LEONARD'S GOLD COAST
Gilbert, Lance
MEET THE DEEDLES
Grace, Martin
DANCING AT LUGHNASA
Graf, Allan
REPLACEMENT KILLERS, THE
WATERBOY, THE
Guegan, Philippe
FULL SPEED
MAN IN THE IRON MASK, THE
Habberstad, Jeff
HARD RAIN
Hessler III, Cort
SCARRED CITY
Hewitt, Jery
ROUNDERS
Hice, Freddie
I STILL KNOW WHAT YOU DID LAST SUMMER
PARENT TRAP, THE
Hobbs, William
DANGEROUS BEAUTY
Hodder, Kane
CHILDREN OF THE CORN V: FIELD OF TERROR
Hooker, Buddy Joe
MEET JOE BLACK
Hospes, Dave
DISTURBING BEHAVIOR
Howell, Chris
GIRLS IN PRISON
RINGMASTER
VERY BAD THINGS
Howell, Norman
TWO FOR TEXAS
Howell, Shawn
HI-LO COUNTRY, THE
Hung, Sammo
PRODIGAL SON, THE
Imada, Jeff
JOHN CARPENTER'S VAMPIRES
Ivanov, Victor
STIR
Ivy, Bob
PHANTASM: OBLIVION
Jackie Chan Stuntmen Club
MR. NICE GUY
Jackie Chan's Stuntmen Club
ARMOUR OF GOD
DRAGONS FOREVER
James, Terrance
GODSON, THE
LOS LOCOS
Jansen, Roly
TARZAN AND THE LOST CITY

Jarrett, Kirk
ATOMIC DOG
BLACK LIGHT
Jensen, Ben
APT PUPIL
Jensen, Gary
APT PUPIL
REAL THING, THE
Jensen, Jeff
DIARY OF A SERIAL KILLER
Johnson, Cal
DECEIVER
MAJOR LEAGUE: BACK TO THE MINORS
RIDE
Jolly, Arthur M.
PARALLEL SONS
Jones, Al
PAULIE
Jones, Brett
3 NINJAS: HIGH NOON AT MEGA MOUNTAIN
Jones, Jamie
REAL BLONDE, THE
Julienne, Remy
MADELINE
Kao, Charlie
3 NINJAS: HIGH NOON AT MEGA MOUNTAIN
Keegan, Donna
HALLOWEEN H20: TWENTY YEARS LATER
Kelley, Terence S.
TRUCKS
Kerns Jr., Hubie
SUICIDE KINGS
Kirten, Kevin Kowboy
LETTER FROM DEATH ROW, A
Kleven, Max
ALMOST HEROES
Koscki, Kim
KRAA! THE SEA MONSTER
Kramer, Joel J.
SIEGE, THE
Kruzel, Michael
TRUCKS
Lai Ying Chau
PRODIGAL SON, THE
Lam Ching-ying
ENCOUNTER OF THE SPOOKY KIND
PRODIGAL SON, THE
Lambert, Steven
ANOTHER DAY IN PARADISE
Lau Chi-Ho
BIG HIT, THE
Lau Kar Wing
ARMOUR OF GOD
Lazarowich, Tony
CALL TO REMEMBER, A
Le Flore, Julius
CAUGHT UP
LeFevour, Rick
REACH THE ROCK
LeFlore, Julius
BELLY
I GOT THE HOOK UP
REAL HOWARD SPITZ, THE
Leonard, Terry
MIGHTY JOE YOUNG
RUSH HOUR
Lerner, Fred
NEWTON BOYS, THE
Leva, Scott
MARS
Lew, James
BOOGIE BOY
Liu, Jason
3 NINJAS: HIGH NOON AT MEGA MOUNTAIN

Loggins, Ben E.
NIGHT VISION
Long, Michael R.
BOYS WILL BE BOYS
Lucescu, Steve
RESCUERS: STORIES OF COURAGE—TWO COUPLES
RESCUERS: STORIES OF COURAGE—TWO WOMEN
Lucy, Tom
SWEPT FROM THE SEA
Ludvigsen, Hans-Peter
KINGDOM, PART 2, THE
Ma Xian Da
SHAOLIN TEMPLE, THE
Magda, Cassimore
CLUB VAMPIRE
Makaro, J.J.
DISTURBING BEHAVIOR
Malesci, Artie
EIGHTEENTH ANGEL, THE
Mang Hoi
ROYAL WARRIORS
Marini, Paul
PROPOSITION, THE
Marks, Glen
LOVE IS THE DEVIL: STUDY FOR A PORTRAIT OF FRANCIS BACON
McBride, Daniel
COLONY, THE
McDancer, Buck
HOLLYWOOD CONFIDENTIAL
McEllroy, Scott
COLONY, THE
McGuire, Darren
BREAKOUT
McKay, Cole
LAND OF THE FREE
McKeown, Dave
BLEEDERS
CAPTIVE
SAVIOR
McLaughlin, John
RIVER RED
McLean, Dwayne
FUTURE FEAR
Michaels, Wayne
SHOOTING FISH
Milne, Gareth
LES MISERABLES
REGENERATION
Munford, Bobby
DIGGING TO CHINA
Mustain, Minor
JACK HIGGINS' THUNDER POINT
JACK HIGGINS' THE WINDSOR PROTOCOL
Neilson, Phil
FALLEN
NIAGARA NIAGARA
STEPMOM
SUBSTITUTE 2: SCHOOL'S OUT, THE
Nielsen, Chris
LAST LIVES
Nomad, Michael
SNAKE EYES
Norman, Michel
MADELINE
Norris, Guy
BABE: PIG IN THE CITY
O'Dell, Phil
FATAL PURSUIT
LAST ASSASSINS
Oliney, Alan
HOLY MAN
Or Sau Leung
ROYAL WARRIORS

Orsatti, Ernie
AMERICAN HISTORY X
DR. DOLITTLE
FALLEN
JANE AUSTEN'S MAFIA!
PLEASANTVILLE
Orsatti, Noon
AMERICAN HISTORY X
Otis, Ron
SMOKE SIGNALS
Palma, Bernabe
NAKED LIES
Palmisano, Conrad E.
LETHAL WEAPON 4
Pan Qing Fu
SHAOLIN TEMPLE, THE
Patrides, Andreas
MRS. DALLOWAY
Paul, Gary
BODY COUNT
GODSON, THE
LAST LIVES
Pearce, Rick
INVADER, THE
Perez, Eddie
BRAM STOKER'S THE MUMMY
PERMANENT MIDNIGHT
Picerni, Charles
DON KING: ONLY IN AMERICA
Picerni Jr., Charles
ENEMY OF THE STATE
Pierce, Denney
AMERICAN HISTORY X
Pistone, Marty
BILLBOARD DAD
Poon Kin-kwun
FALLEN ANGELS
Powell, Greg
LOST IN SPACE
Powell, Nick
GOVERNESS, THE
LAND GIRLS, THE
Quinn, Ian
RAT PACK, THE
Racki, Branko
DIRTY WORK
ONE TOUGH COP
REBOUND: THE LEGEND OF EARL "THE GOAT" MANIGAULT
Ragusa, Angelo
EIGHTEENTH ANGEL, THE
Randall Jr., Glenn
MASK OF ZORRO, THE
Rapivski, Paul
BREAKOUT
Razatos, Sprio
UNCLE SAM
Reid, Alison
FACE THE EVIL
SIMON BIRCH
WOO
Rhee, Phillip
BEST OF THE BEST: WITHOUT WARNING
Riccardi, Mark
CIVIL ACTION, A
PRIMARY COLORS
Ricci, Brian
MONUMENT AVE.
Richmond, B.L.
THURSDAY
Rodgers, Mic
LETHAL WEAPON 4
Romano, Pat
NIGHT AT THE ROXBURY, A
Rondell, R.A.
GODZILLA
Rondell, Ronnie
SPHERE

Runyard, Michael
PERFECT MURDER, A
WEDDING SINGER, THE
Rupp, Jacob
SIN AND REDEMPTION
Sammo Hung's Stuntmen Team
DRAGONS FOREVER
Sanders, David
RUSHMORE
Santiago, Elliot
RIVER RED
Scherer, Michael
LOUISA MAY ALCOTT'S LITTLE MEN
SNAKE EYES
Shanks, Don
WALKING THUNDER
Sheward, Lee
LITTLE VOICE
Short, Paul
AMERICAN HISTORY X
Siverio, Manny
BREAK, THE
HE GOT GAME
Smart, Tony
BRYLCREEM BOYS, THE
FIRELIGHT
Snegoff, Tony
CHOSEN ONE: LEGEND OF THE RAVEN, THE
St. Paul, Stuart
PASSION IN THE DESERT
Stacey, Eddie
INCOGNITO
Statham, Patrick
CASPER MEETS WENDY
INTERLOCKED: THRILLED TO DEATH
Stewart, Bill
URBAN SAFARI
Stofer, Dawn
SPREE, THE
Stoneham Jr., John
BIG HIT, THE
BRAM STOKER'S SHADOWBUILDER
BRIDE OF CHUCKY
CUBE
HOSTILE INTENT
TRACKED
WHITE RAVEN, THE
Strait, Walter
LITTLE BOY BLUE
Stubbs, Melissa
SNOWBOUND
TRICKS
Stuer, Hold
TALES FROM A PARALLEL UNIVERSE: EATING PATTERN
Sui Tak Fu
KICK BOXER'S TEARS
Taylor, Rocky
LAST SEDUCTION II, THE
Tiberghien, Jerome
JACK LONDON'S THE CALL OF THE WILD: DOG OF THE YUKON
Tolbert, R.L.
DOGWATCH
Tomescu, Daniel
CLOCKMAKER
Tough, Neville
MY BROTHER'S WAR
SPACEJACKED
Towery, Russell
CON, THE
STILL BREATHING
Trella, Tim
HI-LO COUNTRY, THE
PALMETTO
Tyukodi, Anton
BONE DADDY
Unger, Bela
WHEN TRUMPETS FADE
Verite, Daniel
MADELINE
Virtue, Danny
ESCAPE, THE
WHEN DANGER FOLLOWS YOU HOME
Vivian, Marc
PI
Walker, Greg
GINGERBREAD MAN, THE
Walstrom, Owen
MISBEGOTTEN
Wang Chang Kai
SHAOLIN TEMPLE, THE
Ward, Jeff
BLADE
HE GOT GAME
Washington, William
PLAYERS CLUB, THE
WHY DO FOOLS FALL IN LOVE?
Wayton, Gary
WATCHERS REBORN
Wedde, Wolfgang
JUNK MAIL
Weston, Gary
OPPOSITE OF SEX, THE
Wiessenhaan, Rick
JACK HIGGINS' ON DANGEROUS GROUND
JACK HIGGINS' MIDNIGHT MAN
Wilder, Glenn
FIRESTORM
Williams, Aaron
BROADWAY DAMAGE
Williams, Sam
UGLY, THE
Woodruff, Rod
LIKE IT IS
LOVE IS THE DEVIL: STUDY FOR A PORTRAIT OF FRANCIS BACON
NIL BY MOUTH
Wu Yue Zhu
BEAUTY INVESTIGATOR
Yansick, Eddie
SNAKE EYES
Yu Hai
SHAOLIN TEMPLE, THE
Yuen Biao
ENCOUNTER OF THE SPOOKY KIND
PRODIGAL SON, THE
Yuen Chun Yeung
ARMOUR OF GOD
Yuen Yan
KILLER ANGELS
Zamperla, Neno
DANGEROUS BEAUTY
Ziker, Dick
U.S. MARSHALS
Zimmerman, John
CATHERINE'S GROVE
Zone, Philippe
I WENT DOWN
MOONDANCE
SUMMER FLING

REVIEW ATTRIBUTION

Films reviewed in this volume are listed below by the author of the review

Black, Art
ARMOUR OF GOD
BODYGUARD FROM BEIJING
CAN'T YOU HEAR THE WIND HOWL?: THE LIFE AND MUSIC OF ROBERT JOHNSON
CHINESE BOX, THE
DRAGONS FOREVER
EAST PALACE, WEST PALACE
FROZEN
GONIN
HEROES SHED NO TEARS
HONG KONG 1941
KINGDOM OF SHADOWS
MAGNIFICENT WARRIORS
MY FIRST NAME IS MACEO
PRODIGAL SON, THE
RED CHERRY
REPLACEMENT KILLERS, THE
ROYAL WARRIORS
SHAOLIN TEMPLE, THE
VILLAGE OF DREAMS

Callahan, David
ALARMIST, THE
ALL THE RAGE
BARRIERS
BROADWAY DAMAGE
BULLET ON A WIRE
CIVIL ACTION, A
CLASSIFIED X
CRACKING UP
CROSSING FIELDS
DAY AT THE BEACH
DESTINY
DIRTY LAUNDRY
DR. DOLITTLE
EDEN
EL CHE: INVESTIGATING A LEGEND
EMPEROR'S SHADOW, THE
FULL SPEED
HALLELUJAH!
INSIDE/OUT
JERUSALEM
KILLING TIME
LET'S TALK ABOUT SEX
LIKE IT IS
MULAN
MY KNEES WERE JUMPING: REMEMBERING THE KINDERTRANSPORTS
NAKED ACTS
OFF THE MENU: THE LAST DAYS OF CHASEN'S
OYSTER AND THE WIND, THE
PARALLEL SONS
PASSION IN THE DESERT
PERMANENT MIDNIGHT
RIDE
RIVER RED
SAFE MEN
SHAKESPEARE IN LOVE
SHOPPING FOR FANGS
SLAM
SOULER OPPOSITE, THE
STEAM
SUE
TALK TO ME
TEN BENNY
THERE'S SOMETHING ABOUT MARY
UNDER THE SKIN
UNVEILING, THE

Camp, Brian
BEAUTY INVESTIGATOR
BIG HIT, THE
COMRADES, ALMOST A LOVE STORY
DRAGON BALL Z THE MOVIE: DEAD ZONE
DRAGON BALL Z THE MOVIE: THE TREE OF MIGHT
DRAGON BALL Z THE MOVIE: THE WORLD'S STRONGEST
EEL, THE
ENCOUNTER OF THE SPOOKY KIND
GENERAL CHAOS: UNCENSORED ANIMATION
GOLGO 13: QUEEN BEE
KICK BOXER'S TEARS
KIKI'S DELIVERY SERVICE
KILLER ANGELS
KNOCK OFF
MIGHTY KONG, THE
MOBILE SUIT GUNDAM I
MOBILE SUIT GUNDAM II: SOLDIERS OF SORROW
MOBILE SUIT GUNDAM III: ENCOUNTERS IN SPACE
NEW ADVENTURES OF KIMBA THE WHITE LION, THE
POLTERGEIST REPORT: YUYU HAKUSHO
RED HAWK: WEAPON OF DEATH
SLAYERS: THE MOTION PICTURE
SOLDIER'S DAUGHTER NEVER CRIES, A
TEKKEN: THE MOTION PICTURE
TOKYO FIST
WRATH OF THE NINJA: THE YOTODEN MOVIE
ZERO WOMAN

Cassady Jr., Charles
ALONE IN THE WOODS
BODY COUNT
BRYLCREEM BOYS, THE
BUSTER & CHAUNCEY'S SILENT NIGHT
CASPER MEETS WENDY
DEAD END
DEJA VU
DESTINY OF MARTY FINE, THE
DOUBLE EDGE
ENEMY
ESCAPE, THE
FORMER CHILD STAR
IN HIS FATHER'S SHOES
INSOMNIA
INVISIBLE DAD
INVISIBLE MOM
JACK LONDON'S THE CALL OF THE WILD: DOG OF THE YUKON
JOHNNY MYSTO BOY WIZARD
LAND OF THE FREE
LITTLE BIGFOOT 2: THE JOURNEY HOME
LITTLE GHOST
MIDAS TOUCH, THE
MODULATIONS: CINEMA FOR THE EAR
NEVADA
NIAGARA NIAGARA
OLIVER TWIST
OUT OF THE PAST
PHOTOGRAPHING FAIRIES
PLAYERS CLUB, THE
PRINCE VALIANT
RAT'S TALE, A
RUSTY: THE GREAT RESCUE
SECRET KINGDOM, THE
SHRUNKEN CITY, THE
SWAN PRINCESS III: AND THE MYSTERY OF THE ENCHANTED TREASURE, THE
TREKKIES
URBAN LEGEND
VOYAGE TO THE BEGINNING OF THE WORLD
WALKING THUNDER
WHITE RAVEN, THE

Chris, Cynthia
HERCULES AND XENA THE ANIMATED MOVIE: THE BATTLE FOR MOUNT OLYMPUS
LOUISA MAY ALCOTT'S LITTLE MEN
MADELINE
NEGOTIATOR, THE
NOT IN THIS TOWN
SMALL SOLDIERS

Diliberto, Joe
DECEIVER
JANE AUSTEN'S MAFIA!
JOHN CARPENTER'S VAMPIRES
MAJOR LEAGUE: BACK TO THE MINORS
MURDER IN MIND
SENSELESS
SIMON BIRCH
STEEL SHARKS
TARZAN AND THE LOST CITY
3 NINJAS: HIGH NOON AT MEGA MOUNTAIN

Faust, M.
AIR BUD: GOLDEN RECEIVER
BEYOND SILENCE
BLACK DOG
BOOGIE BOY

BUFFALO '66
CAUGHT UP
CELEBRATION, THE
CON, THE
CRUISE, THE
DIARY OF A SERIAL KILLER
DOGWATCH
FIRST LOVE, LAST RITES
FROM A FAR COUNTRY
FUTURE FEAR
GADJO DILO
GODZILLA
GODZILLA AND MOTHRA: THE BATTLE FOR EARTH
GODZILLA VS. KING GHIDORAH
HENRY FOOL
HIJACKING HOLLYWOOD
HOSTILE INTENT
IMPOSTORS, THE
KRIPPENDORF'S TRIBE
LAST ASSASSINS
LES MISERABLES
LETHAL WEAPON 4
LEWIS & CLARK & GEORGE
LIVING OUT LOUD
LOU REED: ROCK AND ROLL HEART
MONUMENT AVE.
MOONDANCE
MR. NICE GUY
MUSIC FROM ANOTHER ROOM
PAULIE
PENTAGON WARS, THE
PLAN B
QUICKSILVER HIGHWAY
RETROACTIVE
RUSH HOUR
SAND TRAP
SHATTERED IMAGE
SIX O'CLOCK NEWS
SNOWBOUND
SPREE, THE
SUB DOWN
SUBSTITUTE 2: SCHOOL'S OUT, THE
SUICIDE KINGS
12 ANGRY MEN
SWEPT FROM THE SEA
TIETA OF AGRESTE
TRUCKS
TWO FOR TEXAS
UNDERTAKER'S WEDDING, THE
WAKING NED DEVINE
WHO IS HENRY JAGLOM?

French, Kenneth
BLUES BROTHERS 2000

Galens, David
ALMOST HEROES

Gingold, Michael
ABERRATION
BEYOND, THE
BLEEDERS
BONE DADDY
BRAM STOKER'S SHADOWBUILDER
BRIDE OF CHUCKY
BUTCHER BOY, THE
CHILDREN OF THE CORN V: FIELD OF TERROR
CHOSEN ONE: LEGEND OF THE RAVEN, THE
CLUB VAMPIRE
CUBE
CURSE OF THE PUPPET MASTER
DARK CITY
DAY OF THE BEAST, THE
DEAD WATERS
DECAMPITATED
DEE SNIDER'S STRANGELAND
DEEP RISING
DISTURBING BEHAVIOR
FALLEN
FUNNY GAMES
HALLOWEEN H20: TWENTY YEARS LATER
HENRY: PORTRAIT OF A SERIAL KILLER PART 2
HURRICANE STREETS
I STILL KNOW WHAT YOU DID LAST SUMMER
INVADER, THE
KILLER CONDOM, THE
KRAA! THE SEA MONSTER
LAST BREATH
MEET THE DEEDLES
MILO
NIGHTWATCH
PHANTOMS
SIX-STRING SAMURAI
SLAPPY AND THE STINKERS
SPECIES II
STAR KID
STEPHEN KING'S THE NIGHT FLIER
SUBSPECIES IV: BLOODSTORM
TALISMAN
UGLY, THE
UNCLE SAM
WATCHERS REBORN

Grant, Edmond
CHARLIE HOBOKEN
COMEDY'S DIRTIEST DOZEN
FALLEN ANGELS
FIREWORKS
GINGERBREAD MAN, THE
GIRLS IN PRISON
HOME FRIES
LENNY BRUCE: SWEAR TO TELL THE TRUTH
LIFE IS BEAUTIFUL
MARIE BAIE DES ANGES
PECKER
RAT PACK, THE
RINGMASTER
SAME OLD SONG
SILVER SCREEN: COLOR ME LAVENDER, THE
SONATINE

Kaabe, Michael
KID IN ALADDIN'S PALACE, A

Legare, Patrick
ALMOST PARTNERS
BOYS WILL BE BOYS
BRAM STOKER'S THE MUMMY
BREAST MEN
DON KING: ONLY IN AMERICA
EIGHTEENTH ANGEL, THE
FACE THE EVIL
GIA
INTERLOCKED: THRILLED TO DEATH
LOLIDA 2000
LOS LOCOS
LOVE TO KILL
NEMESIS 4: CRY OF ANGELS
NIGHT VISION
REBOUND: THE LEGEND OF EARL "THE GOAT" MANIGAULT
WHEN TIME EXPIRES

McCarthy, John P.
FRIEND OF THE DECEASED, A
GOVERNESS, THE
SHAMPOO HORNS

Milenski, Aaron
DEAD MAN ON CAMPUS
I'LL BE HOME FOR CHRISTMAS
MR. JEALOUSY
PATCH ADAMS
WHATEVER

Monder, Eric
AFFLICTION
ANOTHER DAY IN PARADISE
ARGUING THE WORLD
ARTEMISIA
AVENGERS, THE
BAD MANNERS
BATTLE OF CHILE: THE STRUGGLE OF AN UNARMED PEOPLE--PART 2: THE COUP D'ETAT, THE
BLACK THUNDER
BRANDON TEENA STORY, THE
BROTHER
CARLA'S SONG
CHILE, OBSTINATE MEMORY
CITY OF ANGELS
CLOCKWATCHERS
DETOUR
DISENCHANTED, THE
DIVORCE IRANIAN STYLE
DOWN IN THE DELTA
FARM: ANGOLA, U.S.A., THE
GODS AND MONSTERS
HALF BAKED
HAPPINESS
HE GOT GAME
HEALING BY KILLING
HOW STELLA GOT HER GROOVE BACK
ILLTOWN
JAMES ELLROY: DEMON DOG OF AMERICAN CRIME FICTION
JUNK FOOD
KINGDOM, PART 2, THE
KRZYSZTOF KIESLOWSKI: I'M SO-SO
LA SEPARATION
LITTLE DIETER NEEDS TO FLY
LIVE FLESH
LOST WORLD, THE
LOVE AND DEATH ON LONG ISLAND
LOVE IS THE DEVIL: STUDY FOR A PORTRAIT OF FRANCIS BACON
LOVE WALKED IN
MEN WITH GUNS

MY BROTHER'S WAR
TARANTELLA

Scheinfeld, Michael
ALFRED HITCHCOCK: MASTER OF SUSPENSE
ALL DOGS CHRISTMAS CAROL, AN
ANTZ
BARNEY'S GREAT ADVENTURE--THE MOVIE
BATMAN & MR. FREEZE: SUBZERO
BATMAN/SUPERMAN MOVIE, THE
BEST MAN, THE
BODY COUNT
BRAVE LITTLE TOASTER GOES TO MARS, THE
BUG'S LIFE, A
BULWORTH
CELEBRITY
CENTRAL STATION
CHAMBERMAID ON THE TITANIC, THE
COUSIN BETTE
DAD SAVAGE
DANGEROUS BEAUTY
DENNIS THE MENACE STRIKES AGAIN
ELIA KAZAN: A DIRECTOR'S JOURNEY
FALLING FIRE
FERNGULLY 2: THE MAGICAL RESCUE
FIRELIGHT
FIRESTORM
FLINTSTONES: I YABBA-DABBA DOO!, THE
GENEALOGIES OF A CRIME
GREAT EXPECTATIONS
HI-LO COUNTRY, THE
HOLY MAN
IN GOD'S HANDS
INCOGNITO
INNOCENT SLEEP, THE
JOEY
JUNGLE BOOK: MOWGLI'S STORY, THE
KISSING A FOOL
LAND GIRLS, THE
LIFE OF JESUS, THE
LION KING II: SIMBA'S PRIDE, THE
LIVING IN PERIL
LOLITA
MAN IN THE IRON MASK, THE
MARIUS AND JEANNETTE
MEET JOE BLACK
MEN
MIGHTY JOE YOUNG
NAPOLEON
NEIL SIMON'S THE ODD COUPLE II
NEXT STEP, THE
NOTES FROM UNDERGROUND
OGRE, THE
ONE TOUGH COP
ONLY THRILL, THE
PARENT TRAP, THE
PASS, THE
PEREIRA DECLARES
PHOENIX
PLAYING BY HEART
POCAHONTAS II: JOURNEY TO A NEW WORLD
PRINCE OF EGYPT, THE
PROPHECY II, THE
QUEST FOR CAMELOT
RABID DOGS
RATCHET
RAZOR: THE SNARE, THE
RAZOR: WHO'S GOT THE GOLD?, THE
REGENERATION
RETURN TO PARADISE
RETURN TO SAVAGE BEACH
RICHIE RICH'S CHRISTMAS WISH
RUDOLPH THE RED-NOSED REINDEER: THE MOVIE
RUGRATS MOVIE, THE
RUNNING WOMAN, THE
SCOOBY-DOO ON ZOMBIE ISLAND
SECRET OF NIMH 2: TIMMY TO THE RESCUE, THE
SHOOTING FISH
SLEEPY EYES OF DEATH: FULL CIRCLE KILLING
SLEEPY EYES OF DEATH: SWORD OF ADVENTURE
SLEEPY EYES OF DEATH: SWORD OF SEDUCTION
SNAKE EYES
SOMEWHERE IN THE CITY
STRAY BULLET
TOUCH OF EVIL: THE DIRECTOR'S CUT
TWILIGHT
TWO GIRLS AND A GUY
U.S. MARSHALS
UN AIR DE FAMILLE
VERY BAD THINGS
WELCOME TO WOOP WOOP
WEST NEW YORK
WESTERN
WHEN I CLOSE MY EYES
WILD MAN BLUES
WILDE
WITHOUT LIMITS
YOUNG HERCULES

Stitzel, Kim
SPICE WORLD
STOREFRONT HITCHCOCK
VELVET GOLDMINE

Thomajan, Dale
BIG LEBOWSKI, THE
BORROWERS, THE
BREAK, THE
CHARACTER
CHICAGO CAB
DANCE WITH ME
DANCING AT LUGHNASA
DIGGING TO CHINA
DRESS, THE
EVER AFTER
GENERAL, THE
GO NOW
HAV PLENTY
HI-LIFE
HIT ME
HURLYBURLY
I MARRIED A STRANGE PERSON!
I WENT DOWN
INHERITORS, THE
JUNK MAIL
LAST DAYS OF DISCO, THE
LITTLE VOICE
MERRY WAR, A
MIRROR, THE
NIL BY MOUTH
OBJECT OF MY AFFECTION, THE
OUTSIDE OZONA
PALMETTO
PRACTICAL MAGIC
PROPOSITION, THE
REACH THE ROCK
REAL BLONDE, THE
ROUNDERS
RUN FOR COVER
RUSHMORE
SHADRACH
SIMPLE PLAN, A
STILL BREATHING
SWINDLE, THE
THIN RED LINE, THE
TWENTYFOURSEVEN
WIDE AWAKE

Trenz, Brandon
ALWAYS OUTNUMBERED
APT PUPIL
BELLY
BIG ONE, THE
BLADE
BURN HOLLYWOOD BURN
DETONATOR
DREAM FOR AN INSOMNIAC
ENEMY OF THE STATE
FACULTY, THE
FIXER, THE
GEORGE WALLACE
HORSE WHISPERER, THE
LAST BIG THING, THE
MASK OF ZORRO, THE
NEWTON BOYS, THE
OUT OF SIGHT
PLEASANTVILLE
POLISH WEDDING
PRICE ABOVE RUBIES, A
PRIMARY COLORS
PRONTO
RONIN
WHEN TRUMPETS FADE
X-FILES, THE

Williams, Karl
AMERICAN HISTORY X
BRIGHT SHINING LIE, A
CHAIRMAN OF THE BOARD
ELVIS MEETS NIXON
LAWN DOGS
LEADING MAN, THE
LET'S KILL ALL THE LAWYERS
MY GIANT
NIGHT AT THE ROXBURY, A
NORTH SHORE FISH
ONE TRUE THING
SMOKE SIGNALS
SOUR GRAPES

Yellin, Todd

AYN RAND: A SENSE OF LIFE
DEAR JESSE
DESPERATE MEASURES
FORGOTTEN LIGHT
FREE TIBET
HILARY AND JACKIE
HOME BEFORE DARK
I GOT THE HOOK UP
I LOVE YOU, DON'T TOUCH ME!
KURT AND COURTNEY
LENA'S DREAMS
MIDAQ ALLEY
SAVING PRIVATE RYAN
THEORY OF FLIGHT
THIEF, THE
TRUCE, THE
WHO THE HELL IS JULIETTE?

OUR CONTRIBUTORS

A.M. Aaron Milenski is assistant director of admissions at Oberlin College. In addition to loving obscure and independent film, he is a guitarist and songwriter for The Palindromes. His wife, Jill, is an artist.

A.B. Art Black has written extensively on Asian and genre films, as well as music from the fringe. He has contributed to countless international periodicals, books, websites, and encyclopediae, and has a regular column in *Psychotronic Video.*

B.C. Brian Camp is the Program Director at CUNY-TV in New York. He has written for *Animation World Magazine, Asian Cult Cinema, Film Comment, Film Library Quarterly, Outre,* and *Sightlines.* He teaches a course on Japanese Animation at the School of Visual Arts in New York.

B.R. Brenda Scott Royce is a freelance entertainment writer and award- winning playwright. She is the author of *Lauren Bacall: A Bio-Bibliography, Hogan's Heroes: A Complete Reference,* and numerous articles.

B.T. Brandon Trenz is a freelance writer based in Detroit, Michigan. He is also a former contributing editor of the reference series *Contemporary Theater, Film and Television,* published by Gale Research.

C.C. Charles Cassady Jr. is a freelance entertainment journalist whose columns appear in *The Cleveland Free Times* and *The Morning Journal,* the daily newspaper of Lorain, Ohio. He has also contributed to the *VideoHound* book series.

C.Ch. Cynthia Chris currently lives in San Diego. Her writing has appeared in *Afterimage, exposure, The Independent,* and *High Performance.* She is working toward a Ph.D. in Communication at the University of California, San Diego.

D.C. David Callahan is the senior film/video librarian for the New York Public Library's Donnell Media Center. He is a regular contributor to *Premiere Taiwan* and has published in *Film History: An International Journal.*

D.G. David Galens is an editor, author, and musician. He edits *Contemporary Authors on CD* and *Drama for Students* at Gale Research. He also plays guitar in the Detroit-based band, the Civilians.

D.O. Donica O'Bradovich is a text writer for the listings department at *TV Guide* and has written freelance movie reviews for *The Village Voice* and *American Film.*

D.T. Dale Thomajan is the author of *From Cyd Charisse to Psycho: A Book of Movie Bests* and the editor of the book *Great Movie Lines.* His articles on film have appeared in *Film Comment, The Village Voice,* and *Spy.*

E.G. Edmond Grant is editor of *The Motion Picture Guide.* He previously served as a staff writer for *TV Guide* and as managing editor of *Movies on TV.* He produces "Media Funhouse," a weekly NYC cable-access television program.

E.M. Eric Monder is the author of *George Sidney* (Greenwood Press, 1994), and has contributed articles to *The New York Times, Film Comment,* and the *Directors Guild of America Magazine.* He lives in Manhattan with his wife, Kathi Patterson, who is also a writer and filmmaker.

J.Di. Joe Diliberto is co-creator of the *Kid Terrific* comic book. He was a film critic for the Prodigy online service, has written for *TV Guide Entertainment Network,* and served as a copy editor for *TV Guide* and *The (Baltimore) Sun.*

J.M. John P. McCarthy has written about film and television for *Daily Variety, Time Out New York, Film Quarterly, Publishers Weekly,* and Cineman Syndicate. He has served as a staff writer at *TV Guide.*

K.Fr. Kenneth French is the author of *Jersey City, 1940-1960: The Dan McNulty Collection,* a book of mid-century urban photography. He is also a librarian specializing in New Jersey history. He lives with his wife and son in Montclair, NJ.

K.S. Kim Stitzel was graduated from the University of Chicago with a degree in Humanities. She is a full-time writer living in New York City.

K.W. Karl Williams is a freelance writer living in northeast New Jersey. His writing and reviews have appeared in *Cinefantastique, Wizard: The Guide to Comics,* and World Wide Web sites including 99 Lives and the Internet Movie Database.

M.F. M. Faust is proprietor of Mondo Video, the coolest video store in Buffalo, NY. He has written about movies for *Video Movie Guide, Movies on TV and Videocassete, The Complete Guide to Videocassette Movies, Video Digest, Video* magazine, *Shock Cinema,* Baseline, and *The Buffalo News.*

M.G. Michael Gingold is the managing editor of *Fangoria* magazine.

M.K Michael Kaabe has written features for the *Asbury Park Press* and other publications. He has served as the theater-arts critic for the *Atlanticville* in Long Branch, NJ, and was the recipient of the 1995 New Jersey Press Association Award for critical writing.

M.S. Michael Scheinfeld is a Senior Movie Writer for *TV GUIDE.* He is also a Contributing Editor for *Leonard Maltin's Movie and Video Guide* and for *Leonard Maltin's Family Film Guide.* In addition, he has programmed film series for Manhattan Cable and worked for AMC and MTV Films.

N.N. Nicholas Nicastro is a filmmaker and critic whose work has appeared in *The New York Times, Film Comment, The New York Observer, Publisher's Weekly,* and *Heterodoxy.* He currently lives in upstate New York.

P.L. Patrick Legare is the Program Guide Editor for HBO in New York and currently contributes to *Cinefantastique, Femme Fatales, CableView* and *PrimeStar magazines.* He served as a Copy Writer for *TV Guide* in New York and an Associate Editor for *CableView Publications* in New Jersey.

P.R. Phil Riley has a degree in philosophy and has done graduate work in film and television criticism. He lives in Austin, Texas.

R.P. Robert Pardi was managing editor and chief film critic of four editions of *Movies on TV.* He is the author of *Movie Blockbusters* and *Who's Who in Cable and TV,* co-wrote *The Complete Guide to Videocassette Movies,* and contributed to *The International Dictionary of Films and Filmmakers.*

S.P. Steven Puchalski is the editor/publisher of *Shock Cinema* magazine. A collection of his cult movie reviews, entitled *Slimetime,* was published in England, and he is a regular contributor to *Fangoria, Sci-Fi Entertainment,* and *Asian Cult Cinema.*

T.Y. Todd S. Yellin, an independent filmmaker, has eluded Chinese soldiers to film Tibetan refugees escaping over the Himalayas and Burmese military intelligence to document human rights violations in Myanmar. He continues to write in the depths of Brooklyn.

Ken Fox is associate editor of the Motion Picture Guide and a movies editor at *TV Guide Online.*

Joe Frazzetta has written for *Films in Review,* and was a movie database researcher at *TV Guide.*

Stephen Pell is an actor, writer, and cofounder of Tweed Theaterworks.